—— Additional Features ——

- Suggested pronunciations for biblical persons and places

- Main entries with Hebrew, Greek, and transliteration fonts

- Summary introductions for long articles

- Helpful outlines for long articles

- Bibliographies

- List of abbreviations

- Index of maps, charts, photos, and illustrations

- Peer reviewed by congregational leaders

- The five-volume set is also available in a fully searchable digital form with color illustrations

THE NEW
INTERPRETER'S®
DICTIONARY
OF THE BIBLE

S-Z
VOLUME 5

EDITORIAL BOARD

THE NEW INTERPRETER'S® DICTIONARY OF THE BIBLE

S-Z

VOLUME 5

ABINGDON PRESS

Nashville

THE NEW INTERPRETER'S® DICTIONARY OF THE BIBLE
S-Z
VOLUME 5

Copyright © 2009 by Abingdon Press

Library of Congress Cataloging-in-Publication Data

The New Interpreter's Dictionary of the Bible.
    p. cm.
  Includes bibliographical references.
  ISBN 0-687-33395-4 (alk. paper)
 1. Bible--Dictionaries. I. Abingdon Press.

  BS440.N445 2006
  220.3--dc22

2006025839

ISBN-13: 978-0-687-33395-0

PUBLICATION STAFF

Project Director: John F. Kutsko
Project Manager: Marianne Blickenstaff
Reference Editor: Heather R. McMurray
Associate Editor: Tim West
Publishing Consultant: Jack A. Keller
Contracts Manager: Lori C. Patton
Production & Design Manager: Ed Wynne
Typesetter: Kevin A. Wilson
Print Procurement: Clara Vaughan
Marketing Manager: Teresa Alspaugh

EXECUTIVE STAFF

President and Publisher: Neil M. Alexander
Editor-in-Chief, Abingdon Press: Mary Catherine Dean

1 2 3 4 5 6 7 8 9 10 – 18 17 16 15 14 13 12 11 10 09

MANUFACTURED IN THE UNITED STATES OF AMERICA

ACKNOWLEDGEMENTS

David Biven/LifeintheHolyLand.com: SAMARIA Fig. 3; SHECHEM, SHECHEMITES Fig. 1

Todd Bolen/BiblePlaces.com: SAMARIA Fig. 1; STABLE Fig. 1; TAANACH Fig. 1; TABOR, MOUNT Fig. 1

British Museum/Art Resource, NY: SETH Fig. 1

DeA Picture Library/Art Resource, NY: ZIGGURAT Fig. 1

Werner Forman/Art Resource, NY: SUMER, SUMERIANS Fig. 1

F. Nigel Hepper: SYCAMORE Fig. 1

Hildi Janzen and Waldemar Janzen: TABERNACLE Fig. 1

Erich Lessing/Art Resource, NY: SALOME Fig. 1; SAMARIA Fig. 2; SEPPHORIS Fig. 1; SHISHAK Fig. 1; SIDON Fig. 1; SINAI, MOUNT Fig.1; STATUES, STATUARY Fig.1, 2; SYNAGOGUE Fig.1; TEMPLE, JERUSALEM Fig. 2; TOMB Fig. 1; UGARIT, HISTORY AND ARCHAEOLOGY Fig. 1; WAR, METHODS, TACTICS, WEAPONS OF (BRONZE AGE THROUGH PERSIAN PERIOD) Fig. 1; WOMEN IN THE ANCIENT NEAR EAST Fig. 1

Madaba Plains Project: TEMPLES, SEMETIC Fig.1; 'UMAYRI, TALL AL Fig. 1, 2

Réunion des Musées Nationaux/Art Resource, NY: SCYTHIANS Fig. 1

Leen Ritmeyer: TEMPLE, JERUSALEM Fig. 3

Rhonda Root: 'UMAYRI, TALL AL Fig. 3

J. Rosenberg: SAMARIA Map

Scala/Art Resource, NY: UR Fig. 1

Vanni/Art Resource, NY: SARDIS Fig. 1; WAR, METHODS, TACTICS, WEAPONS OF (HELLENISTIC THROUGH ROMAN PERIODS) Fig. 1

Bruce Zuckerman and Marilyn Lundberg (Courtesy of Department of Antiquities of Jordan): SEALS AND SCARABS Fig. 1, 2, 3

CONSULTANTS

ARCHAEOLOGY CONSULTANT

JOHN LAUGHLIN
Averett University
Danville, VA

CONSULTING READERS

ERIC ELNES
Scottsdale Congregational United Church of Christ
Scottsdale, AZ

DOTTIE ESCOBEDO-FRANK
CrossRoads United Methodist Church
Phoenix, AZ

RENAE EXTRUM-FERNANDEZ
Walnut Creek First United Methodist Church
Walnut Creek, CA

TYRONE GORDON
St. Luke Community United Methodist Church
Dallas, TX

KEVASS J. HARDING
Dellrose United Methodist Church
Wichita, KS

JAMES A. HARNISH
Hyde Park United Methodist Church
Tampa, FL

JUDI K. HOFFMAN
Edgehill United Methodist Church
Nashville, TN

ROBERT JOHNSON
Windsor Village United Methodist Church
Houston, TX

CHAN-HIE KIM
Upland, CA

SUNGHO LEE
Korean United Methodist Church of Santa Clara Valley
San Jose, CA

MERRY HOPE MELOY
Doylesburg, PA

H. MITCHELL SIMPSON
University Baptist Church
Chapel Hill, NC

EVELENE SOMBRERO NAVARRETE
Holbrook United Methodist Church
Holbrook, AZ

MARIELLEN SAWADA-YOSHINO
San Jose United Methodist Church
San Jose, CA

CONTRIBUTORS

JUDITH Z. ABRAMS
Maqom: A School for Adult Talmud Study
Houston, TX

JOHN AHN
Austin Presbyterian Theological Seminary
Austin, TX

PETER ALTMANN
Princeton Theological Seminary
Princeton, NJ

GARWOOD P. ANDERSON
Nashotah House Theological Seminary
Nashotah, WI

PAUL N. ANDERSON
George Fox University
Newberg, OR

ROBERT T. ANDERSON
Michigan State University
East Lansing, MI

DEBORAH A. APPLER
Moravian Theological Seminary
Bethlehem, PA

BILL T. ARNOLD
Asbury Theological Seminary
Wilmore, KY

PETER ARZT-GRABNER
Salzburg University
Salzburg, Austria

RICHARD S. ASCOUGH
Queen's University at Kingston
Kingston, ON, Canada

JEFFREY R. ASHER
Georgetown College
Georgetown, KY

JAMES P. ASHMORE
Shaw University Divinity School
Raleigh, NC

EMILY ASKEW
Lexington Theological Seminary
Lexington, KY

HAROLD W. ATTRIDGE
Yale Divinity School
New Haven, CT

DAVID E. AUNE
University of Notre Dame
Notre Dame, IN

HECTOR AVALOS
Iowa State University
Ames, IA

RICHARD E. AVERBECK
Trinity Evangelical Divinity School
Deerfield, IL

WILMA ANN BAILEY
Christian Theological Seminary
Indianapolis, IN

WILLIAM R. BAKER
Cincinnati Christian University
Cincinnati, OH

SAMUEL E. BALENTINE
Union Theological Seminary and Presbyterian
School of Christian Education
Richmond, VA

JAMIE A. BANISTER
The Catholic University of America
Washington, DC

JAMES W. BARKER
Vanderbilt University
Nashville, TN

WILLIAM HAMILTON BARNES
North Central University
Minneapolis, MN

JOHN R. BARTLETT
Trinity College (Emeritus)
Dublin, Ireland

DAVID M. BATTLE
Orangeburg, SC

DAVID R. BAUER
Asbury Theological Seminary
Wilmore, KY

KATHERINE BAXTER
Leeds Museums and Galleries
Leeds, United Kingdom

ITZHAQ BEIT-ARIEH
Institute of Archaeology
Tel Aviv University
Tel Aviv, Israel

W. H. BELLINGER, JR.
Baylor University
Waco, TX

ALICE OGDEN BELLIS
Howard University School of Divinity
Washington, DC

DRAYTON C. BENNER
University of Chicago
Chicago, IL

EHUD BEN ZVI
University of Alberta
Edmonton, AB, Canada

MARIAN OSBORNE BERKY
Anderson University
Anderson, IN

SHARON BETSWORTH
Oklahoma City University
Oklahoma City, OK

JULYE M. BIDMEAD
Chapman University
Orange, CA

C. CLIFTON BLACK
Princeton Theological Seminary
Princeton, NJ

J. TED BLAKLEY
St. Mark's Press
Wichita, KS

MARIANNE BLICKENSTAFF
Abingdon Press
Nashville, TN

LINCOLN H. BLUMELL
Tulane University
New Orleans, LA

MARK J. BODA
McMaster Divinity College
McMaster University
Hamilton, ON, Canada

RYAN P. BONFIGLIO
Princeton Theological Seminary
Princeton, NJ

M. EUGENE BORING
Brite Divinity School
Texas Christian University (Emeritus)
Fort Worth, TX

ODED BOROWSKI
Emory University
Atlanta, GA

ALEJANDRO F. BOTTA
Boston University
Boston, MA

MARY PETRINA BOYD
University Temple United Methodist Church
Seattle, WA

SAMUEL BOYD
University of Chicago
Chicago, IL

DONALD L. BRAKE, SR.
Multnomah Biblical Seminary (Emeritus)
Portland, OR

KENT V. BRAMLETT
University of Toronto
Toronto, ON, Canada

ATHALYA BRENNER
University of Amsterdam (Emerita)
Amsterdam, The Netherlands

MARC ZVI BRETTLER
Brandeis University
Waltham, MA

PAMELA BRIGHT
Concordia University
Montreal, QC, Canada

AARON BRODY
Badè Museum
Pacific School of Religion
Berkeley, CA

JOHN DAVID BROLLEY
University of Cincinnati
Cincinnati, OH

DENNIS BROWN
Manchester Grammar School
Manchester, United Kingdom

DEBRA J. BUCHER
Vassar College
Poughkeepsie, NY

SEAN D. BURKE
Luther College
Decorah, IA

TONY BURKE
York University
Toronto, ON, Canada

JOHN BYRON
Ashland Theological Seminary
Ashland, OH

SUSAN CALEF
Creighton University
Omaha, NE

NANCY CALVERT-KOYZIS
McMaster University
Hamilton, ON, Canada

WILLIAM SANGER CAMPBELL
The College of St. Scholastica
Duluth, MN

GREG CAREY
Lancaster Theological Seminary
Lancaster, PA

M. DANIEL CARROLL R. (RODAS)
Denver Seminary
Littleton, CO

PHILIPPA CARTER
McMaster University
Hamilton, ON, Canada

WARREN CARTER
Brite Divinity School
Texas Christian University
Fort Worth, TX

TONY W. CARTLEDGE
Raleigh, NC

JOSEPH R. CATHEY
Dallas Baptist University
Dallas, TX

JAMES H. CHARLESWORTH
Princeton Theological Seminary
Princeton, NJ

ESTHER G. CHAZON
Hebrew University of Jerusalem
Jerusalem, Israel

EMILY R. CHENEY
Spelman College
Atlanta, GA

L. JULIANA CLAASSENS
Wesley Theological Seminary
Washington, DC

RICHARD J. CLIFFORD, SJ
Boston College School of Theology and Ministry
Chestnut Hill, MA

RANGAR CLINE
University of Oklahoma
Norman, OK

TREVOR D. COCHELL
Dallas Christian College
Dallas, TX

CHANNA COHEN STUART
Institute for Geo and BioArchaeology
Vrije Universiteit Amsterdam
Amsterdam, The Netherlands

ADELA YARBRO COLLINS
Yale University
New Haven, CT

JOHN J. COLLINS
Yale University
New Haven, CT

RAYMOND F. COLLINS
Brown University
Providence, RI

R. ANDREW COMPTON
University of California, Los Angeles
Los Angeles, CA

MICHELE A. CONNOLLY, RSJ
Catholic Institute of Sydney
Strathfield, NSW, Australia

EDGAR W. CONRAD
University of Queensland
Brisbane, Australia

MICHAEL D. COOGAN
Stonehill College
Easton, MA

JOAN E. COOK, SC
Georgetown University
Washington, DC

STEVE COOK
Vanderbilt University
Nashville, TN

KATHLYN MARY COONEY
University of California Los Angeles
Los Angeles, CA

ROBERT B. COOTE
San Francisco Theological Seminary
San Anselmo, CA

JEREMY CORLEY
Ushaw College
Durham, United Kingdom

WENDY COTTER, CSJ
Loyola University of Chicago
Chicago, IL

J. R. C. COUSLAND
University of British Columbia
Vancouver, BC, Canada

HARRIET CRAWFORD
University College London
London, United Kingdom

SIDNIE WHITE CRAWFORD
University of Nebraska-Lincoln
Lincoln, NE

TIMOTHY G. CRAWFORD
Bluefield College
Bluefield, VA

JAMES L. CRENSHAW
Duke University (Emeritus)
Durham, NC

STEPHANIE BUCKHANON CROWDER
Belmont University
Nashville, TN

ALAN D. CROWN, AM
University of Sydney (Emeritus)
Sydney, Australia

MARY ROSE D'ANGELO
University of Notre Dame
Notre Dame, IN

CARLY DANIEL-HUGHES
Concordia University
Montreal, QC, Canada

P. M. MICHÈLE DAVIAU
Wilfrid Laurier University
Waterloo, ON, Canada

MAXWELL J. DAVIDSON
Macquarie Park, NSW, Australia

LINDA DAY
Pittsburgh, PA

L. J. DE REGT
United Bible Societies
The Hague, Netherlands

KENDA CREASY DEAN
Princeton Theological Seminary
Princeton, NJ

NANCY DECLAISSÉ-WALFORD
McAfee School of Theology
Mercer University
Atlanta, GA

MARK DELCOGLIANO
Emory University
Atlanta, GA

KATHARINE J. DELL
University of Cambridge
Cambridge, United Kingdom

CAROL J. DEMPSEY, OP
University of Portland
Portland, OR

DAVID A. DESILVA
Ashland Theological Seminary
Ashland, OH

WILLIAM G. DEVER
Montoursville, PA

LAMOINE F. DEVRIES
Missouri State University (Emeritus)
Springfield, MO

MICHAEL B. DICK
Siena College
Loudonville, NY

FRED W. DOBBS-ALLSOPP
Princeton Theological Seminary
Princeton, NJ

TERENCE L. DONALDSON
Wycliffe College
Toronto, ON, Canada

RUDOLPH H. DORNEMANN
American Schools of Oriental Research
Plymouth, MA

CLAUDE DOUMET-SERHAL
British Museum Excavations,
Sidon University College London
London, United Kingdom

F. GERALD DOWNING
Centre for Biblical Studies
University of Manchester
Manchester, United Kingdom

JOEL F. DRINKARD, JR.
Louisville, KY

JEAN DUHAIME
University of Montreal
Montreal, QC, Canada

RUBÉN R. DUPERTUIS
Trinity University
San Antonio, TX

NICOLE WILKINSON DURAN
Trinity United Presbyterian Church
Clifton Heights, PA

PATRICIA DUTCHER-WALLS
Vancouver School of Theology
Vancouver, BC, Canada

JASON C. DYKEHOUSE
Baylor University
Waco, TX

TERRY W. EDDINGER
Carolina Evangelical Divinity School
Greensboro, NC

CARL S. EHRLICH
York University
Toronto, ON, Canada

GÖRAN EIDEVALL
University of Uppsala
Uppsala, Sweden

MARK W. ELLIOTT
University of St. Andrews
St. Andrews, United Kingdom

TAMARA COHN ESKENAZI
Hebrew Union College—Jewish Institute
of Religion
Los Angeles, CA

CRAIG A. EVANS
Acadia Divinity College
Wolfville, NS, Canada

STEPHEN FARRIS
St. Andrew's Hall and Vancouver
School of Theology
Vancouver, BC, Canada

KEN FENTRESS
Montrose Baptist Church
Montrose Christian School
Rockville, MD

STEVEN FINE
Yeshiva University
New York, NY

MICHAEL H. FLOYD
Centro de Estudios Teológicos
Santo Domingo, Dominican Republic

CAROLE R. FONTAINE
Andover Newton Theological School
Newton Centre, MA

MARY F. FOSKETT
Wake Forest University
Winston-Salem, NC

JÖRG FREY
Ludwig Maximilians University
Munich, Germany

STEVEN J. FRIESEN
University of Texas at Austin
Austin, TX

LAWRENCE E. FRIZZELL
Seton Hall University
South Orange, NJ

SERGE FROLOV
Southern Methodist University
Dallas, TX

RUSSELL E. FULLER
University of San Diego
San Diego, CA

DEIRDRE N. FULTON
Pennsylvania State University
University Park, PA

SUSANA DE SOLA FUNSTEN
Claremont Graduate University
Claremont, CA

GARRETT GALVIN, OFM
Franciscan School of Theology
Graduate Theological Union
Berkeley, CA

FRANCISCO GARCIA-TRETO
Trinity University (Emeritus)
San Antonio, TX

HEIDI S. GEIB
Vanderbilt University
Nashville, TN

FRANCES TAYLOR GENCH
Union Theological Seminary
and Presbyterian School
of Christian Education
Richmond, VA

BRUCE W. GENTRY
Southeast Missouri State University
Cape Girardeau, MO

TERRY GILES
Gannon University
Erie, PA

DAVID W. J. GILL
Swansea University
Swansea, United Kingdom

MARK D. GIVEN
Missouri State University
Springfield, MO

GREGORY GLAZOV
Seton Hall University
South Orange, NJ

DEIRDRE GOOD
General Theological Seminary
New York, NY

MARK GOODACRE
Duke University
Durham, NC

FRANK H. GORMAN
Muncie, IN

MICHAEL J. GORMAN
The Ecumenical Institute of Theology
St. Mary's Seminary and University
Baltimore, MD

LESTER L. GRABBE
University of Hull
Hull, United Kingdom

M. PATRICK GRAHAM
Candler School of Theology
Emory University
Atlanta, GA

DEENA GRANT
Barry University
Miami Shores, FL

SANDIE GRAVETT
Appalachian State University
Boone, NC

MARINA GREATREX
Ottawa, ON, Canada

BARBARA GREEN, O.P.
Dominican School of Philosophy and Theology
Graduate Theological Union
Berkeley, CA

JOEL B. GREEN
Fuller Theological Seminary
Pasadena, CA

MARK D. GREEN
Indiana State University
Terre Haute. IN

LEONARD GREENSPOON
Creighton University
Omaha, NE

JAMES P. GRIMSHAW
Carroll University
Waukesha, WI

CAROL GRIZZARD BROWNING
Pikeville College
Pikeville, KY

SUSAN E. HADDOX
Mount Union College
Alliance, OH

GILDAS HAMEL
University of California at Santa Cruz
Santa Cruz, CA

GORDON J. HAMILTON
Huron University College
London, ON, Canada

JEFFRIES M. HAMILTON
Louisville, KY

MARK W. HAMILTON
Abilene Christian University
Abilene, TX

HUMPHREY H. HARDY, II
University of Chicago
Chicago, IL

R. JUSTIN HARKINS
Vanderbilt University
Nashville, TN

WALTER J. HARRELSON
Vanderbilt University (Emeritus)
Nashville, TN

J. ALBERT HARRILL
Indiana University
Bloomington, IN

DANIEL J. HARRINGTON, SJ
Boston College School of Theology and Ministry
Chestnut Hill, MA

TIMOTHY P. HARRISON
University of Toronto
Toronto, ON, Canada

MICHAEL G. HASEL
Institute of Archaeology
Southern Adventist University
Collegedale, TN

JUDITH HAUPTMAN
Jewish Theological Seminary of America
New York, NY

JIONE HAVEA
School of Theology, Charles Sturt University
and United Theological College
North Parramatta, NSW, Australia

RALPH K. HAWKINS
Sack School of Bible and Ministry
Kentucky Christian University
Grayson, KY

WARREN J. HEARD, JR.
St. Charles, IL

CHARLES W. HEDRICK
Missouri State University (Emeritus)
Springfield, MO

F. NIGEL HEPPER
The Herbarium
Royal Botanic Gardens
Kew, United Kingdom

LARRY G. HERR
Canadian University College
Lacombe, AB, Canada

CAROLYN HIGGINBOTHAM
Christian Theological Seminary
Indianapolis, IN

T. R. HOBBS
McMaster University (Emeritus)
Hamilton, ON, Canada

KENNETH G. HOGLUND
Wake Forest University
Winston-Salem, NC

PAUL A. HOLLOWAY
Sewanee: The University of the South
Sewanee, TN

MICHAEL W. HOLMES
Bethel University
St. Paul, MN

MICHAEL M. HOMAN
Xavier University of Louisiana
New Orleans, LA

TERESA J. HORNSBY
Drury University
Springfield, MO

FRED L. HORTON
Wake Forest University
Winston-Salem, NC

BONNIE HOWE
New College Berkeley
Graduate Theological Union
Berkeley, CA

ALICE W. HUNT
Chicago Theological Seminary
Chicago, IL

L. W. HURTADO
University of Edinburgh
Edinburgh, United Kingdom

SUSAN E. HYLEN
Vanderbilt University
Nashville, TN

STUART IRVINE
Louisiana State University
Baton Rouge, LA

MATT JACKSON-MCCABE
Cleveland State University
Cleveland, OH

DAEGYU JANG
Korea Baptist Theological Seminary
Daejeon, Republic of Korea

WALDEMAR JANZEN
Canadian Mennonite University (Emeritus)
Winnipeg, MB, Canada

DAVID JOBLING
St. Andrew's College
Saskatoon, SK, Canada

ANDY JOHNSON
Nazarene Theological Seminary
Kansas City, MO

TODD E. JOHNSON
Fuller Theological Seminary
Oakland, CA

PHILIP S. JOHNSTON
Wycliffe Hall
Oxford, United Kingdom

JUTTA JOKIRANTA
Helsinki Collegium
for Advanced Studies
University of Helsinki
Helsinki, Finland

A. HEATH JONES, III
Nashville, TN

BARRY A. JONES
Campbell University Divinity School
Buies Creek, NC

BRIAN C. JONES
Wartburg College
Waverly, IA

CATHERINE JONES
St. Michael's College
University of Toronto
Toronto, ON, Canada

JUDITH ANNE JONES
Wartburg College
Waverly, IA

MARTHA JOUKOWSKY
Brown University (Emerita)
Providence, RI

LJUBICA JOVANOVIC
Cornell University
Ithaca, NY

NYASHA JUNIOR
University of Dayton
Dayton, OH

ISAAC KALIMI
Northwestern University and
The University of Chicago
Chicago, IL

Eun Hee Kang
Graduate Theological Union
Berkeley, CA

Stephen A. Kaufman
Hebrew Union College—Jewish Institute
of Religion
Cincinnati, OH

Hyun Chul Paul Kim
Methodist Theological School in Ohio
Delaware, OH

Uriah Y. Kim
Hartford Seminary
Hartford, CT

Raz Kletter
University of Helsinki
Helsinki, Finland

Gerald A. Klingbeil
Theological Seminary, Adventist International
Institute of Advanced Studies
Silang, Cavite, Philippines

Todd E. Klutz
University of Manchester
Manchester, United Kingdom

Ernst Axel Knauf
Institute of Biblical Studies
University of Bern
Bern, Switzerland

Michael P. Knowles
McMaster Divinity College
Hamilton, ON, Canada

Jennifer Wright Knust
Boston University
Boston, MA

Yoshitaka Kobayashi
Adventist International Institute
of Advanced Studies
Silang, Cavite, Philippines

John Koenig
General Theological Seminary
New York, NY

Michael Kolarcik, SJ
Regis College
Toronto, ON, Canada

Ingo Kottsieper
Academy of Sciences
Göttingen, Germany

Robert A. Kugler
Lewis & Clark College
Portland, OR

Nathan LaMontagne
The Catholic University of America
Washington, DC

Francis Landy
University of Alberta
Edmonton, AB, Canada

Nathan C. Lane
Palm Beach Atlantic University
West Palm Beach, FL

Peter T. Lanfer
University of California, Los Angeles
Los Angeles, CA

Jacqueline E. Lapsley
Princeton Theological Seminary
Princeton, NJ

John C. H. Laughlin
Averett University
Danville, VA

John I. Lawlor
Grand Rapids Theological Seminary
Grand Rapids, MI

Beatrice J. W. Lawrence
Hebrew Union College—Jewish Institute
of Religion
Los Angeles, CA

Andrew Y. Lee
Institute for the Study of Asian American
Christianity
Staten Island, NY

Joel M. LeMon
Candler School of Theology
Emory University
Atlanta, GA

John R. Levison
Seattle Pacific University
Seattle, WA

GREGORY L. LINTON
Johnson Bible College
Knoxville, TN

KENNETH D. LITWAK
Azusa Pacific University
Azusa, CA

FREDERICK J. LONG
Asbury Theological Seminary
Wilmore, KY

LARRY L. LYKE
Mount Holyoke College
South Hadley, MA

WILLIAM JOHN LYONS
University of Bristol
Bristol, United Kingdom

AREN M. MAEIR
Bar-Ilan University
Ramat Gan, Israel

F. RACHEL MAGDALENE
University of Leipzig
Leipzig, Germany

BRUCE J. MALINA
Creighton University
Omaha, NE

LINDA M. MALONEY
Liturgical Press
Collegeville, MN

ALICE MANDELL
University of California, Los Angeles
Los Angeles, CA

DALE W. MANOR
Harding University
Searcy, AR

CLAUDE F. MARIOTTINI
Northern Baptist Seminary
Lombard, IL

MICHAEL W. MARTIN
Lubbock Christian University
Lubbock, TX

ERIC F. MASON
Judson University
Elgin, IL

STEVEN D. MASON
LeTourneau University
Longview, TX

MICHAEL D. MATLOCK
Asbury Theological Seminary
Wilmore, KY

VICTOR H. MATTHEWS
Missouri State University
Springfield, MO

KATHY R. MAXWELL
Palm Beach Atlantic University
West Palm Beach, FL

NATHAN D. MAXWELL
Palm Beach Atlantic University
West Palm Beach, FL

AMIHAI MAZAR
The Hebrew University of Jerusalem
Jerusalem, Israel

BYRON R. MCCANE
Wofford College
Spartanburg, SC

C. MARK MCCORMICK
Stillman College
Tuscaloosa, AL

LEE MARTIN MCDONALD
Acadia Divinity College (Emeritus)
Wolfville, NS, Canada

THOMAS A. J. MCGINN
Vanderbilt University
Nashville, TN

MICHAEL C. MCKEEVER
Judson University
Elgin, IL

STEVEN L. MCKENZIE
Rhodes College
Memphis, TN

JOHN L. MCLAUGHLIN
University of St. Michael's College
Toronto, ON, Canada

MEGAN M. MCMURTRY
Vanderbilt University
Nashville, TN

James K. Mead
Northwestern College
Orange City, IA

Mark Meehl
Concordia University, Nebraska
Seward, NE

James A. Metzger
Luther College
Decorah, IA

Carol Meyers
Duke University
Durham, NC

J. Ramsey Michaels
Missouri State University (Emeritus)
Springfield, MO

J. Richard Middleton
Roberts Wesleyan College
Rochester, NY

Alan Millard
University of Liverpool (Emeritus)
Liverpool, United Kingdom

Patrick D. Miller
Princeton Theological Seminary (Emeritus)
Princeton, NJ

Milton C. Moreland
Rhodes College
Memphis, TN

Scott N. Morschauser
Rowan University
Glassboro, NJ

James C. Moyer
Missouri State University
Springfield, MO

Hans-Friedrich Mueller
Union College
Schenectady, NY

E. Theodore Mullen, Jr.
Indiana University—Purdue University Indianapolis
Indianapolis, IN

Miles S. Mullin, II
J. Dalton Havard School for Theological Studies
Southwestern Baptist Theological Seminary
Houston, TX

Michele Murray
Bishop's University
Sherbrooke, QC, Canada

Lytton Musselman
Old Dominion University
Norfolk, VA

Susan E. Myers
University of Saint Thomas
St. Paul, MN

Richard D. Nelson
Perkins School of Theology
Southern Methodist University
Dallas, TX

Judith H. Newman
Toronto School of Theology
and the University of Toronto
Toronto, ON, Canada

Carol A. Newsom
Candler School of Theology
Emory University
Atlanta, GA

Paul Niskanen
University of St. Thomas
Saint Paul, MN

Brian Nolan
All Hallows College
Dublin, Ireland

Irene Nowell, OSB
Mount St. Scholastica
Atchison, KS

Ben C. Ollenburger
Associated Mennonite Biblical Seminary
Elkhart, IN

Daniel C. Olson
San Jose, CA

Dennis T. Olson
Princeton Theological Seminary
Princeton, NJ

Sharon Pace
Marquette University
Milwaukee, WI

Alan G. Padgett
Luther Seminary
St. Paul, MN

MICHAEL PASQUARELLO, III
Asbury Theological Seminary
Wilmore, KY

SONG SUZIE PARK
Harvard University
Cambridge, MA

DALE PATRICK
Drake University
Des Moines, IA

DANIEL PATTE
Vanderbilt University
Nashville, TN

KIMBERLY R. PEELER
American Baptist College
Nashville, TN

DAVID L. PETERSEN
Emory University
Atlanta, GA

SUSAN M. PIGOTT
Logsdon School of Theology
Hardin-Simmons University
Abilene, TX

JOHN J. PILCH
Georgetown University
Washington, DC

DANIEL D. PIOSKE
Princeton Theological Seminary
Princeton, NJ

JORGE PIXLEY
Seminario Teologico
Bautista-Managua (retired)
Managua, Nicaragua

ELIZABETH E. PLATT
University of Dubuque
Theological Seminary (Emerita)
Dubuque, IA

PETR POKORNÝ
Charles University in Prague
Prague, Czech Republic

ADAM L. PORTER
Illinois College
Jacksonville, IL

MARK ALLAN POWELL
Trinity Lutheran Seminary
Columbus, OH

EMERSON B. POWERY
Messiah College
Grantham, PA

BRETT S. PROVANCE
Riverside, CA

EYAL REGEV
Bar-Ilan University
Ramat Gan, Israel

STEPHEN BRECK REID
George W. Truett Theological Seminary
Baylor University
Waco, TX

STEFAN C. REIF
St. John's College
University of Cambridge (Emeritus)
Cambridge, United Kingdom

ADELE REINHARTZ
University of Ottawa
Ottawa, ON, Canada

DAVID M. REIS
Bridgewater College
Bridgewater, VA

BENNIE H. REYNOLDS, III
University of North Carolina
at Chapel Hill
Chapel Hill, NC

HENRY W. MORISADA RIETZ
Grinnell College
Grinnell, IA

J. J. M. ROBERTS
Princeton Theological Seminary (Emeritus)
Princeton, NJ

RYAN N. ROBERTS
University of California, Los Angeles
Los Angeles, CA

KEVIN RODRIGUES
University of St. Michael's College
University of Toronto
Toronto, ON, Canada

CALVIN J. ROETZEL
University of Minnesota—Twin Cities
St. Paul, MN

GARY O. ROLLEFSON
Whitman College
Walla Walla, WA

CHRISTOPHER A. ROLLSTON
Emmanuel School of Religion
Johnson City, TN

MARK RONCACE
Wingate University
Wingate, NC

BRIAN D. RUSSELL
Asbury Theological Seminary
Orlando, FL

LEO D. SANDGREN
Silver Springs, FL

DEBORAH F. SAWYER
Lancaster University
Lancaster, United Kingdom

LAWRENCE H. SCHIFFMAN
New York University
New York, NY

BRIAN B. SCHMIDT
The University of Michigan
Ann Arbor, MI

ECKHARD J. SCHNABEL
Trinity Evangelical Divinity School
Deerfield, IL

SANDRA M. SCHNEIDERS, IHM
Jesuit School of Theology
Graduate Theological Union
Berkeley, CA

KARIN SCHÖPFLIN
Georg-August-Universität Göttingen
Göttingen, Germany

ANDREAS SCHUELE
Union Theological Seminary and Presbyterian
School of Christian Education
Richmond, VA

MICHAEL J. SCHUFER
Claremont Graduate University
Claremont, CA

IAN W. SCOTT
Tyndale Seminary
Toronto, ON, Canada

JOSEPH F. SCRIVNER
Samford University
Birmingham, AL

JOANN SCURLOCK
Elmhurst College
Elmhurst, IL

ALAN F. SEGAL
Barnard College
Columbia University
New York, NY

C. L. SEOW
Princeton Theological Seminary
Princeton, NJ

ITZHAQ SHAI
Institute of Archaeology
Bar-Ilan University
Ramat Gan, Israel

DANIEL JENSEN SHEFFIELD
Harvard University
Cambridge, MA

PHILLIP MICHAEL SHERMAN
Knoxville, TN

STEPHEN J. SHOEMAKER
University of Oregon
Eugene, OR

STEPHANIE SKELLEY CHANDLER
Florida State University
Tallahassee, FL

MATTHEW L. SKINNER
Luther Seminary
St. Paul, MN

P. OKTOR SKJAERVØ
Harvard University
Cambridge, MA

THOMAS B. SLATER
McAfee School of Theology
Mercer University
Macon, GA

ABRAHAM SMITH
Perkins School of Theology
Southern Methodist University
Dallas, TX

MARK S. SMITH
New York University
New York, NY

DANIEL L. SMITH-CHRISTOPHER
Loyola Marymount University
Los Angeles, CA

JEREMY D. SMOAK
University of California, Los Angeles
Los Angeles, CA

DANIEL C. SNELL
University Of Oklahoma
Norman, OK

DAUD SOESILO
United Bible Societies
Brisbane, Australia

WILL SOLL
Webster University
St. Louis, MO

F. SCOTT SPENCER
Baptist Theological Seminary at Richmond
Richmond, VA

JOHN STEELE
University of Durham
Durham, United Kingdom

C. MARK STEINACHER
Tyndale Seminary
Toronto, ON, Canada

ERIC C. STEWART
Augustana College
Rock Island, IL

D. MATTHEW STITH
Community Presbyterian Church
West Fargo, ND

JAMES RILEY STRANGE
Samford University
Birmingham, AL

BRENT A. STRAWN
Candler School of Theology
Emory University
Atlanta, GA

JERRY L. SUMNEY
Lexington Theological Seminary
Lexington, KY

MATTHEW J. SURIANO
University of California, Santa Barbara
Santa Barbara, CA

KRISTIN A. SWANSON
Luther College
Decorah, IA

WILLARD M. SWARTLEY
Associated Mennonite Biblical Seminary (Emeritus)
Elkhart, IN

MARVIN A. SWEENEY
Claremont School of Theology
Claremont, CA

BETH LaNEEL TANNER
New Brunswick Theological Seminary
New Brunswick, NJ

RON E. TAPPY
Pittsburgh Theological Seminary
Pittsburgh, PA

JASON R. TATLOCK
Armstrong Atlantic State University
Savannah, GA

EUGENE TeSELLE
Vanderbilt Divinity School (Emeritus)
Nashville, TN

ANTHONY C. THISELTON
University of Nottingham
Nottingham, United Kingdom

CHRISTINE NEAL THOMAS
Harvard University
Cambridge, MA

BONNIE BOWMAN THURSTON
Wheeling, WV

JESSICA TINKLENBERG deVEGA
Morningside College
Sioux City, IA

W. SIBLEY TOWNER
Union Theological Seminary and Presbyterian
School of Christian Education (Emeritus)
Richmond, VA

EMILIE M. TOWNES
Yale Divinity School
New Haven, CT

JOSEPH L. TRAFTON
Western Kentucky University
Bowling Green, KY

ALLISON A. TRITES
Acadia Divinity College (Emeritus)
Wolfville, NS, Canada

PETER TRUDINGER
Flinders University
Adelaide, Australia

JONATHAN N. TUBB
The British Museum
London, United Kingdom

STEVEN SHAWN TUELL
Pittsburgh Theological Seminary
Pittsburgh, PA

PATRICIA K. TULL
Louisville Presbyterian Theological Seminary
Louisville, KY

MAX TURNER
London School of Theology
London, United Kingdom

MICHAEL K. TURNER
Vanderbilt University
Nashville, TN

EUGENE ULRICH
University of Notre Dame
Notre Dame, IN

KATY VALENTINE
Graduate Theological Union
Berkeley, CA

PIETER W. VAN DER HORST
Utrecht University (Emeritus)
Utrecht, The Netherlands

EVELINE J. VAN DER STEEN
Liverpool University
Liverpool, United Kingdom

ROBERT E. VAN VOORST
Western Theological Seminary
Holland, MI

JAMES C. VANDERKAM
University of Notre Dame
Notre Dame, IN

MICHAEL G. VANZANT
Mount Vernon Nazarene University
Mount Vernon, OH

T. DELAYNE VAUGHN
Baylor University
Waco, TX

JOSEPH VERHEYDEN
Catholic University of Louvain
Leuven, Belgium

BURTON L. VISOTZKY
Jewish Theological Seminary
of America
New York, NY

SHELLEY WACHSMANN
Institute of Nautical Archaeology
Texas A&M University
College Station, TX

SZE-KAR WAN
Perkins School of Theology
Southern Methodist University
Dallas, TX

CECILIA WASSÉN
Uppsala University
Uppsala, Sweden

JAMES W. WATTS
Syracuse University
Syracuse, NY

JAMES E. WEST
Quartz Hill School of Theology
Quartz Hill, CA

TRISHA GAMBAIANA WHEELOCK
Gustavus Adolphus College
St. Peter, MN

DEMETRIUS K. WILLIAMS
University of Wisconsin-Milwaukee
Milwaukee, WI

P. J. WILLIAMS
Tyndale House
Cambridge, United Kingdom

TYLER F. WILLIAMS
The King's University College
Edmonton, AB, Canada

JOHN T. WILLIS
Abilene Christian University
Abilene, TX

KELLY M. WILSON
The Catholic University of America
Washington, DC

KEVIN A. WILSON
Merrimack College
North Andover, MA

JOHN D. WINELAND
Kentucky Christian University
Grayson, KY

DEREK E. WITTMAN
Baylor University
Waco, TX

JARED WOLFE
University of California, Los Angeles
Los Angeles, CA

LISA MICHELE WOLFE
Oklahoma City University
Oklahoma City, OK

GORDON C. I. WONG
Trinity Theological College
Singapore, Republic of Singapore

ARCHIE T. WRIGHT
Regent University
Virginia Beach, VA

JACOB WRIGHT
Candler School of Theology
Emory University
Atlanta, GA

ROBERT B. WRIGHT
Temple University (Emeritus)
Philadelphia, PA

JOHN Y. H. YIEH
Virginia Theological Seminary
Alexandria, VA

K. LAWSON YOUNGER, JR.
Trinity Evangelical Divinity School
Deerfield, IL

GENERAL EDITOR'S PREFACE

On behalf of the Editorial Board, I welcome you to the company of users of *The New Interpreter's® Dictionary of the Bible*, a five-volume set offering the best in contemporary biblical scholarship. This new dictionary stands in the continuing tradition of the *Interpreter's®* series, developed for church and synagogue teachers and preachers and with the goal of supporting congregations and all students of the Bible as they seek to learn and grow.

Comprehensive in scope: The dictionary covers all the persons and places mentioned in the Bible. It contains a full range of articles on the cultural, religious, and political contexts of the Bible in the ancient Near East and the Greco-Roman world, and it offers many articles explaining key methods of biblical interpretation. *Theological* in focus: The dictionary includes numerous articles on theological and ethical themes and concepts important to understanding the biblical witness.

The original *Interpreter's Dictionary of the Bible*, published in the 1960s, remained a key reference tool for pastors and teachers for nearly half a century. Yet it was of course a product of its time. Biblical scholarship moved an enormous distance in the intervening years, in knowledge of the literature and culture of the ancient world, and in the development of new approaches that have opened fresh horizons of interpretation, for individual books of the Bible, and for many theological concepts. Study of the Dead Sea Scrolls, of ancient Gnostic documents, and of extra-biblical prophetic texts from the ancient Near East are but a few of the many areas in which scholarship focused on extra-biblical texts has developed new data of great significance for understanding the Bible. Increased attention to gender, ethnicity, and economic class offers new insights into previously neglected aspects of the culture of the biblical world, which in some cases leads to striking new perspectives on biblical texts. Archaeology teams up with a wide range of natural sciences to develop methods that give greater insight into ancient community life in addition to military upheavals. Newly discovered inscriptions and artifacts shed new light on biblical history and on religious beliefs and practices of ancient Israel and early Christianity. Recent progress in the analysis of Hebrew poetry, in understanding of Greek rhetoric, in theories of characterization, as well as new models of social-scientific analysis and cultural studies offer new avenues of inquiry in support of theological reading of the biblical text. To account for these and many other exciting developments, we have produced an entirely new dictionary rather than a revision of the old. While there may not be new information on certain obscure biblical persons or places, the major articles, almost without exception, introduce fresh material and even entirely new topics that were not on the 1960s scholarly horizon.

Of course these many changes in biblical studies have not taken place in a vacuum. The world itself has also changed greatly. As we move through the 21st cent., we face a world grown smaller by speed of communication, yet in many ways politically and economically more fragmented (or at least we are more aware of the fragmentation) than ever before. Ecologically we face a possibly precarious future; factionalism and hostility seems on the increase within and among some religious and racial/ethnic groups, even as signs of reconciliation and search for common ground blossom in unexpected places. While such issues will not be addressed directly on every page, it is the aim of this dictionary to enable wise use of the biblical tradition in theological and ethical approaches to these difficult issues.

As the knowledge of the world surrounding the Bible and also methods for studying the Bible have expanded and changed, so also has the profile of the leaders in biblical scholarship. *The New Interpreter's Dictionary* contributors number approximately 900 women and men in more than 40 different countries from Australia to Africa, from the Americas to Europe, Asia, and the Middle East. Chosen for their scholarly expertise and publication in the areas of their articles, they are identified with Catholic, Orthodox, Jewish, and many different Protestant traditions; they range in personal commitment from conservative to liberal and come from many racial/ethnic and cultural backgrounds. The wide scope of the contributors' contexts reflects the global scope of biblical scholarship of the 21st cent.

The Editorial Board took joint responsibility for nominating the wide range of authors who have contributed to this dictionary. Meetings, followed by numerous conference calls and innumerable rounds of email communication enabled comment and consensus building around the hundreds of nominees. Access to such a global span of contributors was greatly eased by computer and internet technology that could not have been feasible even a decade ago, with a website through which more than 7,100 articles were moved seamlessly and without paper from author to press and then through the various editorial stages. All but the very briefest articles were reviewed for content, balance of perspective, and accessibility by at least one member of the editorial board, and web and email facilitated discussion with authors of any proposed revisions. In addition, experienced pastors were recruited for further review of select longer articles, as an additional check on the readability and theological usefulness of the material for the intended audience.

In guidelines for authors and editors, this project has emphasized openness and generosity to various points of view. In an era when the very notion of one right answer to every question is itself increasingly called into question, we have asked our authors to offer their own perspectives on their topics while still including a clear and charitable presentation of significant alternative scholarly viewpoints. The editors are grateful to the authors for their willingness to write in this style, which will provide a fuller interpretive context for readers who are seeking an introduction to a subject.

As General Editor, it is my joy to express appreciation to the entire Editorial Board for their untiring efforts. The Board itself reflects something of the ecclesial, cultural, and racial/ethnic diversity, as well as the range of scholarly expertise that we have worked to bring to fruition in our contributing authors. Thanks, then, to Samuel Balentine, Brian Blount, Joel Green, Kah-Jin Jeffrey Kuan, Pheme Perkins, and Eileen Schuller for all that each of you has brought to our common work; and thanks to the staff of Abingdon Press, who have shepherded this long process with intelligence, imagination, and love.

KATHARINE DOOB SAKENFELD, GENERAL EDITOR

FEATURES OF
THE NEW INTERPRETER'S® DICTIONARY
OF THE BIBLE

A. The Main Entry

1. Title. Main entries are set in a bold font and highlighted in red. In most instances, where more than one person or place in the Bible shares a name, one article covers all instances of that proper name. For example, the article on JOSHUA will include Joshua, high priest and Joshua, son of Nun. However, in some instances, where the subject material is especially important, we divide articles between experts in various fields, to obtain the best treatments. For example, instead of one article on Abraham, we have ABRAHAM, NT and ABRAHAM, OT.

The articles are listed in alphabetical letter (rather than word) order, with rare exceptions; e.g., when listing all of the entries pertaining to BAAL some minor content sequencing was required.

2. Pronunciation. If the main entry is a person or place in the Bible, it is followed by a preferred pronunciation that is endorsed by the Society of Biblical Literature and derived from the *Bible Pronunciation Guide* (ed. William O. Walker, Toni Craven, and J. Andrew Dearmen Revised edition, 1994). The following pronunciation key is a useful guide to the sounds that are intended by the preferred pronunciation.

a	cat	ihr	ear	ou	how
ah	father	j	joke	p	pat
ahr	lard	k	king	r	run
air	care	kh	ch as in German Buch	s	so
aw	jaw	ks	vex	sh	sure
ay	pay	kw	quill	t	toe
b	bug	l	love	th	thin
ch	chew	m	mat	th	then
d	do	n	not	ts	tsetse
e, eh	pet	ng	sing	tw	twin
ee	seem	o	hot	uh	ago
er	error	oh	go	uhr	her
f	fun	oi	boy	v	vow
g	good	oo	foot	w	weather
h	hot	oo	boot	y	young
hw	whether	oor	poor	z	zone
i	it	or	for	zh	vision
i	sky				

Stress accents are printed after stressed syllables. ´ is a primary stress. ´ is a secondary stress.

3. Biblical Languages. The editors think it important for a dictionary to make the original biblical languages a part of appropiate entries. To satisfy those readers who are trained in Hebrew, Aramaic, and Greek, the key terms are rendered in the original language as part of the main-entry heading. A transliteration is provided in the heading, and also with the first occurrence of any Hebrew or Greek font that is introduced in the body of an article. The transliteration style is based on the "general purpose" guide in the *SBL Handbook of Style*. For some students of the ancient languages, the transliteration style functions as a pronunciation guide, though this dictionary makes no attempt to reconcile English pronunciations with ancient-language transliterations.

4. Outline. Entries with more than 2,000 words ordinarily have an outline to help the reader navigate the information contained in the article.

5. Cross References. In the body of the main entry a reader will encounter words presented in all CAPITALS to signal that this topic exists as a separate entry in the dictionary. It would diffuse the purpose of special emphasis to signal a cross reference through capitalization for every person or place in the Bible. The capitalized cross reference means that information in another article is available to enhance the reader's understanding of a concept or to further explain the meaning of a technical term.

More than 1,300 main entries in the dictionary are linked with cross-references to specific articles that pertain to the person, place, or topic. One of the risks of publishing five volumes over the course of several years is the potential of including "blind" cross references that lead the reader to another cross reference rather than to an article. Great care is taken in our database to prevent this frustration for the reader; if any blind references occur (perhaps if an article failed to appear) we will correct the link upon reprint.

6. Bibliography. This dictionary is not intended as a technical reference tool; therefore, entries do not contain detailed citations within the body of the article, nor footnotes at the end. However, a limited number of technical articles contain parenthetic citations of an author's name, with bibliographic reference at the end of the entry. Bibliographies for articles are necessarily short and select. Works published before the mid-20th cent. generally are avoided in favor of more current works that build on earlier publications.

B. Main Entry List

The definitions included in this dictionary are written in a style that is accessible to students, pastors, and teachers of the Bible. Style decisions are based on the needs, interests, and skills in the primary audience. A group of consulting readers (all pastors of churches) aided us in vetting these articles for comprehension and usefulness in their daily tasks.

We began with the main entries from *The Interpreter's Dictionary of the Bible* (1964, 1975). We subtracted from this list several hundred King James Version spellings of persons, places, and obsolete terms, and replaced these with spellings or terms found in the *New Revised Standard Version* of the Bible. To the list of entries we added terms from other theological handbooks and Bible dictionaries, as well as topics recommended by members of the editorial board and authors. Author input was crucial as we responded to suggestions about dated topics, emerging trends, and more recently published primary sources.

The authors have moved away from the word-study approach that dominated biblical scholarship when the *Interpreter's Dictionary* was published. Scholars have learned that literary context is more important for present day Bible readers than etymology (word origins) or later theological notions of what a word means. A Bible dictionary, like any other dictionary, indexes single words or phrases that label people, places, and subjects. The challenge for the author of a Bible dictionary article is to convey (within the limited word count) the diverse range of meaning that can be represented by major terms.

C. Sources of Style

For English style (e.g., spelling and abbreviations), we relied on a blend of three sources: the *SBL Handbook of Style* (1999), produced by the Society of Biblical Literature, the *Chicago Manual of Style,* 15th Edition, and for issues unique to our project, the *New Interpreter's*® style guide.

When appropriate, we based translation of texts on the *New Revised Standard Version* of the Bible (NRSV), to promote uniformity among articles. Some familiar terms from the King James Version have been omitted, but Volume Three of the dictionary includes an article called KING JAMES VERSION, ARCHAIC TERMS. Readers are also encouraged to read the articles on Bible Translation Theory; Biblical Interpretation, History of; Versions, Authorized; Versions, Bible; and Versions, English for more information.

Other *New Interpreter's*® products consistently use the label "Old Testament" (OT). We decided with this dictionary to maintain the same style. Of course, when discussing the ancient languages more directly, articles refer as necessary to the Hebrew Bible (e.g., the Masoretic Text, with the abbreviation Heb.) or the Septuagint (the Greek text, with the abbreviation LXX).

We use the terms in small caps that are preferred by most scholars for identifying dates: bce, "Before the Common Era" (in place of B.C., "Before Christ") and ce for "Common Era" (instead of A.D. for *Anno Domini* "Year of our Lord").

For further help in navigating the dictionary, please see the list of ABBREVIATIONS at the end of each volume.

S. Symbol representing the Sinaiticus text. *See* SINAITICUS, CODEX.

SABACHTHANI. *See* ELI, ELI, LEMA SABACHTHANI.

SABANNUS [Σάβαννος *Sabannos*]. Father of the Levite Moeth according to the LXX (1 Esd 8:63). The NRSV has "Binnui" here because it is the name that appears in the parallel text (Ezra 8:33). *See* ESDRAS, FIRST BOOK OF.

SABAOTH sab´ay-oth [צְבָאוֹת *tseva'oth*]. In the OT, *Sabaoth* is a common epithet for God, occurring in the phrase "the Lord [God] of Hosts" (yhwh ['elohe] *tseva'oth* יהוה [אֱלֹהֵי] צְבָאוֹת). It is commonly understood as depicting Yahweh as leader of Israel's armies (1 Sam 17:45). Others understand the term as an appositive, hence, "the Lord [God] Almighty." *See* GOD, NAMES OF; HOSTS, HOST OF HEAVEN.

E. THEODORE MULLEN JR.

SABBAIAS. *See* SHEMAIAH.

SABBATH sab´uhth [שַׁבָּת *shabbath*; σάββατον *sabbaton*]. The Hebrew word for "Sabbath" is commonly associated with the verb shavath (שָׁבַת), meaning "to stop" or "to cease." However, it is unlikely that the proper noun *Sabbath* is a derivative of this verb. While the Sabbath eventually became a weekly holiday, characterized as a day of REST, this may not have been its original function. As the Mesopotamian parallel, the Shapattu festival, suggests, the Sabbath day originally marked the celebration of the full MOON, and in many OT texts the word is used to mean the day of the full moon. While certain activities were prohibited on this particular day (in order to avoid provoking the gods' anger), it was not a day of general rest. Also, the Hebrew verb itself does not typically mean "to cease from labor, rest." Rather, shavath can be used in a wide variety of contexts. A famous reference is God's promise to Noah that "seedtime and harvest, cold and heat, summer and winter, day and night, shall not cease" (Gen 8:22). In a number of cases it can also mean "to waste away," "die out," or even "cease to exist" (Josh 5:12; Isa 24:8; Prov 22:10). Thus one is left with the somewhat astonishing picture that neither the original Sabbath nor the verbal root point to what eventually became the seventh day of the week, commemorating both God's rest after the creation of the world (Exod 20:11) and the exodus from Egypt (Deut 5:15). It seems that when the Sabbath took this new role and was associated with the seventh day, this also influenced the semantic spectrum of the verb shavath, which, in connection with Sabbath itself, could now also mean "rest" (Gen 2:2-3). It needs to be mentioned that this development has no precedent in the ANE and hence distinguishes the religion of ancient Israel from its neighboring cultures.

A. Historical Overview
  1. Festival of the full moon
  2. Seventh day of the week
  3. Halakhic discourse
B. The Preexilic Period
  1. General observations
  2. The Holiness Code
C. The Exilic and Postexilic Periods
  1. Jeremiah
  2. Ezekiel
  3. Deuteronomy
  4. Priestly texts
  5. Isaiah
D. Extra-biblical Evidence and the Second Temple Period
  1. Elephantine
  2. Maccabees and the Dead Sea Scrolls
E. The New Testament
  1. Mark
  2. Matthew
  3. Luke
  4. John
  5. Revelation
  6. From Sabbath to Sunday
Bibliography

A. Historical Overview

The historical development of the Sabbath as a weekly holiday and, as such, as the center of the Jewish festival CALENDAR can be divided into three stages.

1. Festival of the full moon

As mentioned above, the Sabbath as the festival of the full moon was originally part of the lunar calendar. While we do not know many specifics about how this particular holiday was celebrated, the texts do not suggest that the Sabbath was a day of general rest. However, the calendar of ancient Israel reflects that, during particular seasons of the year, the seventh day of the week was considered a resting day. Two of the oldest festival calendars in the OT mention such a day in connection with the Passover/Unleavened Bread feast in early spring (Exod 23:12-17; 34:21-24), as well as with the Festival of Booths in the fall. Since these fall into harvesting periods, it is a likely assumption that during the peak seasons of the agricultural year a resting day was observed in order to honor Yahweh as the lord of the land and giver of all goods, as well as to provide a break for the workers.

2. Seventh day of the week

It is debated when exactly the Sabbath changed both its place in the calendar and also its religious function and became the seventh day of the week. According to J. Meinhold's influential theory, this shift occurred around the time of the Babylonian exile. Meinhold regarded the prophet Ezekiel and his followers among the exiles as the creators of the now distinctly Jewish Sabbath that separated the exilic community in Babylon from their cultural and religious environment. While this particular aspect of Meinhold's theory can be contested, there is consensus that the Sabbath as the seventh day of the week marks the single most significant innovation in the religious life of Second Temple Judaism. However, looking at the respective passages of the OT, it does not seem that the Sabbath assumes an equally important role in all the different textual traditions of the postexilic period. The priestly layer of the Pentateuch (especially Gen 2:2-3; Exod 16:22-30; 23:12-17), the Sabbath commandment in both versions of the Decalogue (Exod 20:8-11; Deut 5:12-15), and the book of Nehemiah (9:14; 10:31 [Heb. 10:32]; 13:13-22) are the most explicit witnesses to a new understanding of the Sabbath. The prophetic traditions, on the other hand, show a more ambiguous picture. Deutero-Isaiah (Isa 40–55), as one of the most powerful voices of the exilic and postexilic periods, never mentions the Sabbath; in the book of Jeremiah only one brief passage thematizes it (Jer 17:19-27); and even in Ezekiel, despite numerous references (Ezek 20:12-24; 22:8, 26; 46:1, 4, 12), it is not entirely clear to what extent the Sabbath denotes a weekly holiday or whether it is still considered the full moon festival. Thus it appears that the Sabbath was not an ad hoc innovation that occurred with the end of the exile; rather, its implementation seems to have taken place over an extended period of time and may not have been equally enforced by all the different groups that shaped the religious identity of exilic and postexilic Judaism. Thus it will be especially important to reflect on the social conditions as well as the theological reasoning behind this development. Here it is the Priestly authors of the Pentateuch in particular who offer a fully developed account of the meaning and purpose of the Sabbath, displaying close links to the Passover/Unleavened Bread as the feast commemorating the exodus from Egypt.

3. Halakhic discourse

While the OT references characterize the Sabbath as a day of rest on which no Israelite was supposed to work, the Second Temple period and the NT attest to much more nuanced reflections on what specific kinds of actions were permissible and also on the characteristic protocols for the Sabbath day itself. What one finds in the texts is a "sifting through" all the daily routines to determine if and to what extent they should be altered, suspended, or complemented on the Sabbath. Jesus' controversies with the Pharisees and Sadducees are arguably the richest resource from the pre-rabbinic period about specific ethical questions related to the Sabbath. They attest to the beginnings of the halakhic discourse that come to their full fruition in the Talmud. *See* HALAKHAH.

B. The Preexilic Period

1. General observations

While dating biblical texts is a controversial issue, there are several mentions of the Sabbath in texts that fall most likely into the monarchic period. They share in common that they typically pair the Sabbath with the new moon (khodhesh חֹדֶשׁ), marking the new and the full moon as key dates of the lunar calendar (Hos 2:11 [Heb. 2:13]). No specifics about the Sabbath as a cultic event are known from the biblical texts, although the texts do convey a number of events that were connected with this particular holiday. Amos 8:5 indicates that trading grain (and perhaps any kind of trade) was prohibited on the Sabbath. Second Kings 4:22-23 presupposes that the Sabbath was a day when one would consult mantics and prophets. It also seems to have been the day when the (monthly) work shift for soldiers began or ended (2 Kgs 11:5-7). Isaiah 1:13 suggests that an assembly of the people took place on the Sabbath in the temple area but the details remain unclear (Ps 81:3 [Heb. 81:4] mentions the blowing of the shophar on the day of both the new and full moon). It is also possible that, as the Mesopotamian parallels suggest, the Sabbath in Israel was devoted to worshiping the moon god (this may have been Yahweh himself or a different deity). Several stamp seals with the symbol of the crescent moon have been found that attest to the presence of the moon god in ancient Israel and Judah, but if and to what extent this cult was institutionalized in the festival calendar is uncertain.

2. The Holiness Code

While there is disagreement about whether the Holiness Code antedates or follows the Priestly layer of the Pentateuch, most scholars consider it a collection of legal and cultic materials from the First Temple period. This matches the fact that, with one exception (Lev 23:3), the Sabbath is not yet the seventh day of the week. As a matter of fact, there are several dates in the calendar season that are associated with the term *Sabbath*: the offering of the first fruits (Lev 23:11), the Festival of Weeks (Lev 23:15), and the Day of Atonement (Lev 23:26-32). In most of these cases, the day of a particular festival is determined in relation to its preceding Sabbath, most likely understood as the day of the full moon in the middle of the month. In other words, the Sabbaths of a year provide the framework for Israel's festival calendar. The most notable exception, however, is the Day of Atonement, which is itself called a Sabbath—even a shabbath shabbathon (שַׁבַּת שַׁבָּתוֹן), "a sabbath of complete rest" (Lev 23:32)—although it does not fall on a full moon day. The phrase shabbath shabbathon is revealing, because it suggests that, in the preexilic period, not every Sabbath was necessarily a resting day and, vice versa, not every resting day was also a Sabbath. The festival of trumpets (Lev 23:24), e.g., is called a shabbathon but falls on the first day of the seventh month and, as such, was not a Sabbath. Summarizing this complex picture, there does not seem to be a systematic correlation between Sabbath as a calendric term and the idea of a general resting day. However, the two occasions when these two notions overlap are the DAY OF ATONEMENT and also the PASSOVER AND FEAST OF UNLEAVENED BREAD (Lev 23:5-8). It is a reasonable assumption that in the preexilic period only these two festivals were considered a Sabbath and, at the same time, carried the meaning of a period of rest when no ordinary work was permitted. *See* FEASTS AND FASTS.

This leaves as a question what to make of Lev 23:3, the only reference in the Holiness Code that defines the Sabbath as the seventh day of the week. As the context shows, there are two introductory verses for the following list of festivals, one in 23:2 and another one in 23:4. Thus it seems that, once the Sabbath had been established as the seventh day, it received its own introductory note and was added to the festival calendar that originally began in 23:4.

C. The Exilic and Postexilic Periods

1. Jeremiah

The mention of the Sabbath in Jeremiah is limited to one particular passage of the book, namely Jer 17:19-27. Jeremiah refers to it as the "day of the Sabbath" (yom hashabbath יוֹם הַשַּׁבָּת)—a phrase that, in most cases, is used for the weekly holiday rather than the full moon festival. However, since the Sabbath does not play a role elsewhere in the book of Jeremiah, contextualizing and dating 17:19-27 is difficult. The main issue discussed in this passage is the carrying of burdens and bringing them in through the city gates of Jerusalem. Since it is explicitly the import of goods that is prohibited, it seems safe to assume that what is depicted here are the gates of Jerusalem as the marketplace with people from the Judean countryside trading their merchandise. Jerusalem depended on external food supplies, which were probably brought into the city on a daily basis. The fact that Jeremiah condemns trade on the Sabbath day is an indication that at least parts of

the population did not change their working habits on the Sabbath. This has a close parallel in Neh 13:15: "In those days I saw in Judah people treading wine presses on the sabbath, and bringing in heaps of grain and loading them on donkeys; and also wine, grapes, figs, and all kinds of burdens, which they brought into Jerusalem on the sabbath day; and I warned them at that time against selling food." It remains uncertain whether the Jeremiah text not only addresses the same issue as Neh 13:15 but also dates from the same period. However, from these and related passages, it seems clear that the purpose of the Sabbath—at this relatively early stage of its development into a weekly holiday—was to interrupt any trade-related work as the main occupation of the overall population. The texts of this period suggest that regulations for the Sabbath were quite basic and not anywhere near the sophistication of the sabbatical laws in the rabbinical period. While professional labor and trade were prohibited, other areas of daily life are never mentioned. We do not know, e.g., if and to what extent the Sabbath affected the life of women. Work related to household and family seems to have been below the radar of what was considered a violation of sabbatical laws.

2. Ezekiel

The book of Ezekiel shows a somewhat enigmatic picture regarding the identity of the Sabbath. Looking at the temple vision (Ezek 40–48)—commonly regarded as the most unique expression of Ezekiel's prophecy—the festival calendar of the new era is basically the same as its preexilic antecedents with the Sabbath as the full moon day: "But this shall be the obligation of the prince regarding the burnt offerings, grain offerings, and drink offerings, at the festivals, the new moons, and the sabbaths, all the appointed festivals of the house of Israel" (Ezek 45:17; compare also Ezek 46:3-4). However, a passage that complicates the picture is Ezek 46:1; here it is said that the gate of the inner temple court is to remain closed "on the six working days" but shall be opened on the Sabbath and on the NEW MOON. This seems to suggest that the Sabbath is both the seventh day of the week and also the full moon day. Several explanations have been offered to explain this peculiar double-placement of the Sabbath within one and the same sentence. One could argue that six working days were counted only before the full moon festival but did not yet establish the general weekly schedule. Another, more likely, explanation is that, in Ezekiel, the Sabbath changed its place to the seventh day of week, but continued to mark the full moon day for a certain period of time. This would mean that Ezekiel attests to a transition period in which the Sabbath could take both roles. If one turns to the passages outside the temple vision, the picture is fairly unambiguous: the Sabbath is defined as the holy day that God had ordered the Israelites to observe after their exodus from Egypt as a sign of the covenant (Ezek 20:12, 13, 16, 20, 21, 24). The accusation that Ezekiel puts forth is that Israel forgot or even consciously ignored keeping the Sabbath once they had settled down in the promised land and thus violated God's law and defiled his Temple (Ezek 22:8, 26). One has to read between the lines here in order to understand the particular nuances of the argument: Ezekiel acknowledges that Israel did not observe the Sabbath during the monarchic period. From a historical point of view this confirms the impression that there was no Sabbath prior to the exile. However, Ezekiel goes on to say that the Israelites should have observed the Sabbath regardless, because, in his view, the Sabbath had been given to them at Mount Sinai. Ezekiel thus construes a picture of Israel's past in which the "non-existence" of the Sabbath is not just explained historically but as negligence and failure for which Israel was to be blamed and which was also the reason for Israel's exile. Second Chronicles 36:21 and Lev 26:34-35 seem to presuppose the same view: the years of the exile are a time for Israel to make up for all the Sabbaths that it failed to observe while it still lived on the ground of the promised land. Together with Deuteronomy and the Priestly texts of the Pentateuch, Ezekiel is one of the traditions in the OT that provides a rationale for the Sabbath that, at the same time, serves as a theological argument for why the Sabbath is quintessential for a Jewish identity.

3. Deuteronomy

The core corpus of Deuteronomic law in Deut 7–26, whose earliest layers are typically associated with the reforms of King Josiah in the second half of the 7th cent. BCE, does not include any regulations regarding the Sabbath. Unlike the redacted festival calendar in Lev 23, Deuteronomy does not list the Sabbath as a key festival of the calendar year. However, the Sabbath assumes a prominent role in the Deuteronomic Decalogue. The prologue of Deuteronomy (Deut 1–4) recounts Israel's departure from Mount Horeb, their way through the desert to the brink of the promised land. Here, Moses conveys to the Israelites the "statutes and ordinances" of Yahweh, of which the Decalogue is first piece. The Sabbath commandment emphasizes the intimate connection between the exodus and the observance of Yahweh's law on the ground of the promised land (Deut 5:12-15). As a matter of fact, the Sabbath commandment, in conjunction with Yahweh's self-introduction in Deut 5:6, is the only regulation in the Decalogue with a specific historical reference to Israel's past. Unlike the Priestly version of the Decalogue in Exod 20:8-11, no analogy between God's rest on the seventh day of creation and Israel's rest on the seventh day of the week is intended. Rather, keeping the Sabbath is the expected response to the experience of God's delivering Israel from Egyptian bondage. Looking at the text more closely, Deut 5:13-15 includes two distinct imperatives regarding the Sabbath: to "keep" it (shamar שָׁמַר) and to "remember" it (zakhar זָכַר). While the former requires the Israelites, including their entire households, to refrain from any kind of labor, the latter offers a rationale for this commandment: being able to rest marks the exact opposite of what characterized Israel's existence in Egypt—perpetual labor and being dominated by a foreign ruler. In short, according to Deuteronomy, the Sabbath is a day of remembering Israel's enslavement in the past by enacting its opposite in the present. This also explains another small but significant difference between the Priestly and the Deuteronomic versions of the Decalogue: Exod 20:8-11 determines that from the head of a household to the servants and even the working animals no one shall perform any work on the Sabbath. Deuteronomy 5:14 offers a slightly different wording: "you shall not do any work—you, or your son or your daughter, or your male or female slave, or your ox or your donkey, or any of your livestock, or the resident alien in your towns, so that your male and female slave may rest as well as you." This is not only to say that absolutely no one, not even the stranger, is allowed to perform any labor; rather, the point is that, on the Sabbath, no one must work for any other person. The Sabbath interrupts and temporarily unhinges any kind of servitude and slavery and in that sense commemorates the exodus.

In this perspective, the Sabbath yields a work ethic that acknowledges that any kind of labor is prone to establishing patterns of domination and oppression as well as to exploiting natural resources. While the Sabbath and also the sabbatical year do not abolish these patterns altogether, they suspend them for a period of time, allowing the ground to recover and reminding the Israelites that each member of the covenant has an equal share in it, despite all the factual inequalities among them. *See* LAW IN THE OT.

4. Priestly texts

By far the most elaborate account of the origins and the religious significance of the Sabbath is provided in the Priestly traditions of the Pentateuch. The narrative frame in which the Sabbath is at first anticipated (Gen 2:2-3), then de facto enacted (Exod 16:26-30), and finally commanded (Exod 20:8-11; 31:13-17) has the character of a founding legend for the observance of the seventh day as the Sabbath. As a matter of fact, the Priestly traditions in Genesis and Exodus are the only reference texts in the OT that offer a Sabbath etiology. This should not lead one too quickly to the assumption that the Priestly authors "invented" the Sabbath, but it seems to be the case that it was not before the exilic/postexilic period that an elaborate theology of the Sabbath existed. Furthermore, the motif of the Sabbath in the Priestly stratum of the Pentateuch connects the Primeval History, the exodus, and the Sinai theophany, thus providing a comprehensive nexus between three of the key traditions that shape the overall architecture of the Pentateuch. Only the ancestral narratives show no connection with the implementation of the Sabbath, which may have to do with the fact that they are linked to a different sign of the covenant, namely circumcision.

It has been claimed that Gen 2:2-3 already in itself offers an ETIOLOGY of the Sabbath. However, the text is suggestive rather than explicit about the meaning of the seventh day. All that the text says is that God rested on the seventh day and that he blessed and sanctified it. What kind of impact this should have on the created world remains entirely open at this point. Even one step further, in the exodus narrative, there is no Sabbath commandment yet. God orders the Israelites to collect a ration of manna on six days of the week and a double ration on the sixth day as a supply for the seventh. The reason for this is simple: God does not work on the seventh day and thus does not let any manna grow from the ground. However, there are no instructions about what the Israelites themselves ought to do on the day when God rests. It seems fair to say that up until Exod 20 the significance of the seventh day is a loose end in the narrative flow of the books of Genesis and Exodus, which is tied up eventually in the revelation of God's law on Mount Sinai. Exodus 16:26-30 takes the development beyond Gen 2:2-3 in that the Israelites are told that the seventh day is a Sabbath and that, therefore, they will not find any manna. But there is no explanation of what the Sabbath is and there are also no instructions about how this day ought to be celebrated. However, the story reemphasizes, now on a quite practical level, that the seventh day of the week is a day of rest, not so much because it is prohibited to work on the Sabbath but because there isn't anything that the Israelites could do on that day anyway. It is only in Exod 20:10 and then again in 31:15 that the meaning of the Sabbath and its particular statutes are revealed to the Israelites. It is interesting that, although the seventh day is linked with the exodus events via the Passover (Exod 12:15-16) and the manna story, the Priestly texts do not make this connection the etiological anchor of their Sabbath theology. Unlike in Deuteronomy, it is not the memory of a particular historical event and its reenactment that shapes Israel's ritual and moral actions but the imitation of God's own "rhythms" that are built into the cosmic order itself. The seventh day is a day of rest not because of what happened to the Israelites in Egypt but, on a much grander scale, because of the way the world reflects the ways of the creator.

5. Isaiah

The book of Isaiah displays a somewhat peculiar picture regarding the Sabbath: the Sabbath is mentioned right at the outset in Isa 1:13 in the context of a divine oracle against the temple cult in Jerusalem. More precisely, the prophetic critique here condemns the assemblies held on certain holidays like the Sabbath, which in 1:13 is the day of the full moon. Interestingly, the Sabbath is never mentioned again. However, 1:13 forms an inclusio with the end of the book. Just as much as 1:13 critiques Israel's false worship on the Sabbath, Isa

66:23 envisions a time when all the nations will come to worship God on his holy mountain: "From new moon to new moon, and from sabbath to sabbath, all flesh shall come to worship before me, says the LORD." What makes this inclusio between the beginning and end of Isaiah truly remarkable is the fact that the final form of the book, which most scholars date not before the 4th cent. BCE, connects its vision of true Yahweh worship not, as one would expect, with the Sabbath as the seventh day of the week but (still) as the day of the full moon. While the phrase "new moon to new moon" could be a reference to "monthly," while "Sabbath to Sabbath" could mean "weekly," the poetic language in Isa 66 has its closest parallel in certain Ugaritic texts and *Enuma Elish*, where the rhythm of creation follows the moon phases. Also, no one knows for sure when Israel adopted a luni-solar calendar, which would be necessary to put the Sabbath in the same frame of reference with the new moon.

Given the general silence of the exilic and postexilic prophets about the "new" Sabbath, one is led to the assumption that they did not think that new cultic implementations like the Sabbath were essential for Israel's restoration in the Second Temple period. But there are notable exceptions, especially Trito-Isaiah's (Isa 56–66) understanding of the Sabbath as a way for foreigners and the ritually impure to be included in the covenant. According to Isa 56:2, 6, keeping the Sabbath is defined as doing good deeds, serving Yahweh, and loving his name, which Trito-Isaiah does not consider as exclusively Jewish virtues but as something that every human being is, or ought to be, capable of doing. This inclusion of the stranger seems to have a critical edge against tendencies in the brand of Judaism associated with Ezra and Nehemiah that draw clear-cut demarcation lines between Jews and Gentiles. As a matter of fact, Trito-Isaiah is the only voice in the OT and beyond that defines the Sabbath as a day when all the true believers in Yahweh can worship together, which cuts across national, cultural, and religious divisions.

D. Extra-biblical Evidence and the Second Temple Period

1. Elephantine

Of particular interest among the extra-biblical sources are the papyri from the island of Elephantine, which from the middle of the 7th cent. to the early 4th cent. BCE hosted a Judean/Jewish military colony. Given that this community developed its brand of Judaism in considerable local and cultural distance from its motherland, the question arises as to the significance of the Sabbath in this particular location. While the textual evidence is quite limited—only four inscriptions contain the word *Sabbath*—it is apparent that the Jews from Elephantine in the 5th cent. did observe the Sabbath. However, one cannot say with certainty whether this Sabbath was the full moon festival or the seventh day of the week. The most revealing ostracon inscription reads as follows:

"I am sending you vegetables tomorrow. Meet the boat tomorrow on Sabbath lest they get lost/spoiled. By the life of YHW, if not, I shall take your Life[e]! Do not rely upon Meshullemeth or upon Shemaiah" (*TAD* D7.16:1-9). The concern behind this dispatch seems to be that the sender feared for a delivery of vegetables to go to waste because the Sabbath was underway. This could presuppose that the Sabbath was observed as a day when no professional labor of any kind was permitted. However, since Amos 8:5 gives reason to assume that certain kinds of trade were prohibited on the full moon, this conclusion is not necessarily cogent. Perhaps the stronger argument in favor of the Sabbath as the seventh day is the attestation of the name *Shabbethai* (shabbethay שַׁבְּתַי). In the OT this name is mentioned in Ezra and Nehemiah as a name of Levitical priests (Ezra 10:15; Neh 8:7; 11:16). It is a hypocoristic name that in its full form might have meant "the Sabbath has come/is here." In Elephantine, it seems that this was a name that especially proselytes or even non-Jews who observed the Sabbath gave their children, which is reminiscent of Trito-Isaiah's understanding of the Sabbath as a symbol that integrates even the stranger in the covenant with Yahweh (*see* ELEPHANTINE PAPYRI).

2. Maccabees and the Dead Sea Scrolls

By the time of the Maccabean revolt the Sabbath had become arguably the most distinctive feature of Jewish life, not only because it was a weekly holiday (otherwise unknown in the Greco-Roman world) but especially because of its rigid suspension of any activity that could be identified as physical labor. As such, it was not only the Sabbath as the seventh day of the week but also as a subject of theological reflection and halakhic reasoning that made it the focus of Jewish identity. One of the controversial issues of that time was whether self-defense was allowed on the Sabbath. According to the books of Maccabees, the pagans launched attacks against the Jews preferably on the Sabbath, knowing that they would either not fight back at all or keep their efforts to withstand military force at a minimum (1 Macc 2:32-41). Also, 1 Maccabees mentions that observant Jews were required to worship the heathen gods on the Sabbath so that they would be forced to defile it (1:41-50). Second Maccabees 6:6 summarizes the situation as follows: "People could neither keep the sabbath, nor observe the festivals of their ancestors, nor so much as confess themselves to be Jews." However, more important than the historical information itself is the way in which these documents characterize the Sabbath as the core of Jewish identity, which, at the same time, was its vulnerable spot. Observing the Sabbath was not a private but a public matter, precisely because it meant that, for a certain period of time, Jews would detach themselves from the rhythms and schedules of their cultural environment. Maccabees in particular reflects that being Jewish implied putting oneself at the mercy of external powers whose favorable attitude toward Judaism

was far from certain. The experience of exposure and vulnerability may also be one of the reasons why some texts recommend that Jews separate themselves from Gentiles for the duration of the Sabbath. Apart from its political aspects, the texts from the Second Temple period attest to a number of specific regulations: acts of cleansing and purification on the eve of the Sabbath became an important part of the preparations for the Sabbath day, although it is unclear to what extent those were ritual acts or simply had to do with cleansing oneself before the holiday (2 Macc 12:38; compare CD-A XI, 3–4; 4Q270 6 V). A controversial issue was whether sexual intercourse was permitted on the Sabbath. While later rabbinic Judaism, for the most part, regarded intercourse as an expression of joy that added to the cheerfulness of the Sabbath, the book of *Jubilees* (50:8) and probably also some of the DEAD SEA SCROLLS (4Q270 2 I, 18–19) prohibit sex on the Sabbath for reasons of maintaining a status of purity.

With regard to the sabbatical liturgy the Qumran community seems to have made the recitation of psalms an important part of their worship. While in the biblical edition of the psalter only one psalm is introduced as a "song of the Sabbath" (Ps 92), the psalter in Qumran has fifty-two Sabbath songs, apparently one for each week (although it is not clear whether there was one particular psalm assigned to any given week). Another piece of textual evidence for the Sabbath liturgy is a collection of thirteen *Songs of the Sabbath Sacrifice* (4Q400–407), covering the Sabbath days of the first quarter of the year (*see* SONGS OF THE SABBATH SACRIFICE). Although mostly in fragmentary shape, the content of the songs seems sufficiently clear: they depict the heavenly liturgy around the throne of God, including detailed descriptions of the heavenly sanctuary and the actions of the angelic priests. The idea seems to be that, on the Sabbath, worship on earth participates in the heavenly liturgy. It has been noted that the imagery and language of the songs are reminiscent of Ezekiel's throne-chariot vision (Ezek 1; 10) and that the songs may be regarded as a very early form of MERKAVAH MYSTICISM. A debated question is whether the songs were composed by the Qumran people and, thus, were an expression of their particular piety, or if they were circulated among several different groups (as the copy of the songs found at Masada could suggest), making the mystical experience of the heavenly realm an intrinsic element of Sabbath worship.

E. The New Testament

The NT reveals that on the Sabbath, the congregation assembled in the synagogue to read from the Scriptures, a practice in which Jesus seems to have participated and that also Paul and his associates continued as part of their missionary efforts among Jews (Acts 13:14; 18:4). As a matter of fact, it seems safe to say that prior to the destruction of the Temple in 70 CE, the Sabbath revolved around both the sacrificial worship at the Temple and the study of Scripture in the synagogue. Other details about the halakhic aspects of Sabbath observance include the prohibition against carrying devices such as a mat. While in the OT the emphasis was on the prohibition of carrying merchandise, this regulation appears to have changed its focus in the time of the NT so that the acts of lifting and carrying themselves are inappropriate activities on the Sabbath.

The most characteristic feature of the NT accounts of the Sabbath is Jesus' controversies with the Pharisees about the Sabbath, which one might label pre-rabbinic disputes, especially with regard to the healings that Jesus performed on the Sabbath. Given the number of healings that Jesus performed on the Sabbath, it seems safe to say that he considered the Sabbath as the appropriate day for these healings, while his opponents categorized them as labor and thus judged that they had their proper place on one of the six work days (Luke 13:14). Especially in Matthew and Luke (e.g., Luke 13:18), the healings are linked to the impending nearness of the kingdom of God that was also foreshadowed in the holiness of the Sabbath day.

1. Mark

The individual Gospels show subtle differences with regard to how Jesus' healings on the Sabbath are presented. In Mark, the Sabbath sets the stage for Jesus' teaching and his healing miracles. The two are linked through the notion that Jesus speaks and acts with an authority to which even the demons surrender (Mark 1:21-27). Precisely because of this authority, Jesus, identifying himself as the "Son of Man" (Mark 2:28), claims to be the lord also over the Sabbath as a day that was made for humankind and not the other way round (Mark 2:27). In a nutshell, Mark understands the Sabbath as the day when the Son of Man acts to liberate humankind from demonic powers. This understanding of the Sabbath presupposes the apocalyptic background of Daniel's vision of the Son of Man (Dan 7) coming down from heaven to put an end to the dominion of the monsters that ruled the world before him. This background might also explain why Jesus uses rather dramatic language to explain the true significance of his healings: "Is it lawful to do good or to do harm on the sabbath, to save life or to kill?" (Mark 3:4). For Jesus not to use his powers would in fact equal leaving the world in the hands of the demons that control it now.

2. Matthew

While Mark reports Jesus' healings on the Sabbath right at the outset of his Gospel, it is not before the twelfth chapter that Matthew turns to the Sabbath controversy between Jesus and the Pharisees, and it is only here that the Sabbath surfaces as the stage for Jesus' ministry. Also, Matt 12:12 offers a shortened version of Mark 3:4, leaving out the language of harm and killing. It seems that Matthew deliberately takes some of the controversial edges off the Sabbath debate. For exam-

ple, he mentions that the disciples were hungry when they plucked grain on the Sabbath (Matt 12:1)—a note that is not found in Mark or Luke—because, according to later rabbinic law, hunger constitutes an acceptable reason to break the prohibition to work on the Sabbath. It seems that Matthew is alluding to interpretations of the law that existed in his day, some of which were also included in the Talmud. The claim that the priests break the Sabbath legally by officiating on that particular day (Matt 12:5) seems to refer to a halakhic argument that is not found in the OT itself. Also, Matthew appeals to common sense when he compares Jesus' healings to someone who rescues a sheep that has fallen into a pit (Matt 12:11). There are certain actions that must not be postponed, and, in Jesus' interpretation of the law, healings—understood as a way of saving lives—fall under this rubric (see LAW IN THE NT).

3. Luke

More than the other Gospels, Luke emphasizes the intrinsic connection between Jesus' teaching on the Sabbath in the synagogue and his healings (Luke 4:16, 31; 6:6; 13:10), suggesting that the latter have their proper time and place on the Sabbath rather than on one of the work days, as the Pharisees suggest (Luke 13:14). Luke even adds a healing miracle (the crippled woman in Luke 13:10-17) to the accounts that he found in Mark and Q. This miracle in particular becomes the key to Luke's understanding of the Sabbath. Luke's Jesus points out that everyone would untie an ox or donkey from the stall to give it water even on the Sabbath (v. 15). Interestingly, the issue at stake in this case is the activity of "untying," because this constituted an act of labor, which, however, everyone would do regardless of the day of the week (providing animals or humans with water was permitted on the Sabbath anyway). Luke now interprets Jesus' healings as an act of "untying" or freeing a person from demonic bonds: "And ought not this woman, a daughter of Abraham whom Satan bound for eighteen long years, be set free from this bondage on the sabbath day?" (Luke 13:16).

4. John

While in the Synoptic Gospels Sabbath observance is part of an inner-Jewish controversy between Jesus and the Pharisees, John characterizes Jesus' healings on the Sabbath as a reason for his being persecuted by the Jewish authorities (John 5:16). The narrative pattern is that "the Jews" hear about the healings and then interrogate the ones healed about what had happened (John 5:15; 9:15). Thus there are also no reports in John about Jesus teaching in the synagogue on the Sabbath. It seems to be clear that in John's context the Sabbath was considered a Jewish institution that separated them from the Christians. As such it is also mentioned in connection with circumcision (John 7:23). Another negative association with the Sabbath occurs in the report of the crucifixion. While all the Gospels agree that the crucifixion happened on the day before the Sabbath, John adds as a narrative detail that "the Jews" asked Pilate to expedite the process by having the delinquents' legs broken, so that their bodies could be removed before the beginning of the Sabbath (John 19:31).

5. Revelation

While the Sabbath is never mentioned explicitly in Revelation, there are significant intertextual connections with the creation account in Gen 2:1-3, as well as with Isaiah's prophecy of a new heaven and a new earth (Isa 65–66), indicating that the community behind Revelation reserved an important role for the Sabbath in their assumptions about the end of days. According to John's vision of the new Jerusalem, there will not be a change of day and night anymore, because God's glory will fill the city at all times (22:5). The eschaton is thus imagined as a day without night, which is reminiscent of Gen 2:1-3, where the seventh day is the only day that does not follow the rhythm of evening and morning. While this detail may not be particularly significant for the exegesis of the creation account itself, it gave room for the idea that the history of the entire cosmos was moving toward its final Sabbath as a time of permanent rest from labor, security from danger, and worship of God in the new Jerusalem.

6. From Sabbath to Sunday

While Jewish Christians kept observing the Sabbath as long as they also remained within the synagogal community, it seems that Sunday rather quickly became the day on which the Christians came together to celebrate Christ's resurrection. The significance of what was called the LORD'S DAY is attested already in texts from the 1st cent. CE: "We keep the eighth day with joyfulness, the day also on which Jesus rose again from the dead" (*Barn.* 15:9); Justin Martyr later adds to this argumentation that the eighth day (as the first day of the week) is the day when God created the world (*1 Apol.* 67), which made Sunday also the feast of the new creation. The *Didache*, the oldest community rule of the ancient church, offers the following instructions for celebrating the Lord's Day: "… come together, break bread and hold Eucharist, after confessing your transgressions that your offering may be pure; but let none who has a quarrel with his fellow join in your meeting until they be reconciled, that your sacrifice may not be defiled" (*Did.* 14:1–2).

The role of the Sabbath in the life of the early church surfaces as an issue of controversy in documents from the early 2nd cent. CE onward. The apostolic fathers, especially Ignatius of Antioch and Justin Martyr, mirror a development in which the Lord's Day increasingly replaced the Sabbath, which meant as a consequence that in some areas Christians were not supposed to keep the Sabbath anymore. The effort of Christians to abandon the Sabbath, now understood as a distinctly Jewish holiday, seems to have been motivated by another circumstance: the Sabbath was the day when the Jews circumcised their children. So it seems that, in order to distance themselves from this practice, the Christians increasingly avoided the Sabbath. Tertullian develops this line of argumentation in his "Against the Jews," a document from the early 3rd cent. CE. Tertullian wrote that the Sabbath cannot be salvific, because God did not circumcise Adam, and because God commended Adam's son Abel (see Gen 4:4), even though both men were uncircumcised and did not observe the Sabbath (Tertullian, *Adv. Jud.* 2). However, the fact that the controversy about the Sabbath continued well beyond the ecumenical councils of the 4th and 5th cent. gives reason to assume that the Sabbath remained a holiday in parts of the Christian world even in the early medieval period.

Bibliography: M. Asiedu-Peprah. *Johannine Sabbath Conflicts as Juridical Controversy* (2001); W. A. M. Beuken. "Exodus 16.5, 23: A Rule Regarding the Keeping of the Sabbath." *JSOT* 32 (1985) 3–14; L. Doering. "Purity Regulations Concerning the Sabbath in the Dead Sea Scrolls and Related Literature." *The Dead Sea Scrolls: Fifty Years after Their Discovery.* L. H. Schiffman, E. Tov, and J. VanderKam, eds. (2000) 600–609; D. K. Falk. *Daily, Sabbath, and Festival Prayers in the Dead Sea Scrolls* (1998); G. F. Hasel. "New Moon and Sabbath in Eighth Century Israelite Prophetic Writings (Isa 1:13; Hos 2:13; Amos 8:5)." *Wünschet Jerusalem Frieden.* M. Augustin and K. D. Schunck, eds. (1988) 37–64; I. Knohl. "The Priestly Torah Versus the Holiness School: Sabbath and the Festivals." *HUCA* 58 (1987) 65–117; K. Lake, trans. *Apostolic Fathers,* vol. 1. LCL 24 (1985); R. H. Lowery. *Sabbath and Jubilee* (2000); H. A. McKay. *Sabbath and Synagogue: The Question of Sabbath Worship in Ancient Judaism* (2001); J. Meinhold. *Sabbat und Woche im Alten Testament* (1905); B. Porten. "The Religion of the Jews of Elephantine in Light of the Hermopolis Papyri." *JNES* 28 (1969) 116–21; Y.-E. Yang. *Jesus and the Sabbath in Matthew's Gospel* (1997).

ANDREAS SCHUELE

SABBATH DAY'S JOURNEY [σαββάτου ὁδός sabbatou hodos]. The distance a Jew could travel on the SABBATH according to scribal interpretation. Dating rabbinic materials is difficult, so what this distance was at particular times is hard to establish.

The Torah prohibits travel on the Sabbath: "do not leave your place on the seventh day" (Exod 16:29). Later interpreters argued that "your place" meant "your town" and that a town's boundaries extended a thousand cubits (Num 35:5). Thus, the *Damascus Document* from Qumran (dated to ca. 100 BCE) says that an individual could not travel over 1,000 cubits beyond one's town (CD X, 21). By 200 CE, the rabbis argued that one could travel 2,000 cubits (*m. Eruv.* 4:3), since one could travel 1,000 cubits outside the town and return.

The length of a CUBIT varied over time. During the Hellenistic period it was 18 in.; during the Roman period it was 21 in. Hence, 2,000 Hellenistic cubits were about 3,000 ft. (0.9 km) and 2,000 Roman cubits were 3,600 ft. (1.1 km).

The only author to use this phrase in the Bible is Luke, who says that the distance from Jerusalem to the Mount of Olives was "a sabbath's day journey" (Acts 1:12). Josephus gives two figures for this distance: 6 stadia (3,640 ft. or about 2,000 Roman cubits; *J.W.* 5.70) or 5 stadia (3,034 ft. or about 2,000 Hellenistic cubits; *Ant.* 20.169). Jesus alluded to the limited ability to travel on the Sabbath by suggesting that flight on the Sabbath would be difficult (Matt 24:20).

ADAM L. PORTER

SABBATICAL YEAR sa-bat'i-kuhl. Sabbatical Year is a practice by which the compilers of the Deuteronomic and Holiness Codes sought to regulate slavery and agricultural land management practices for the benefit of the poor and the encouragement of piety. While Deut 15 understands the seventh year primarily as a time of manumitting slaves, Lev 25 develops ancient practices of fallowing land in rotation (see Exod 23:10-11) by connecting them to the Jubilee (*see* JUBILEE, YEAR OF), a utopian scheme for ensuring just distribution of wealth in Israel.

Whether the Sabbatical Year was ever implemented in the Iron Age is unknown, though statewide manumission of slaves, the central feature of the year in Deuteronomy, was a common practice in antiquity, known also in ancient Israel (see Jer 34:8-16). It is difficult to see how the land-fallowing practices envisioned by Leviticus could have been achievable, especially if the Jubilee Year succeeded a Sabbatical Year. Thus the pentateuchal texts on the Sabbatical Year seem to be serious efforts at imagining practices that would remediate injustice rather than descriptions of actual practice. As they developed over time from the earlier (Exodus) to later (Deuteronomy, then Leviticus) stages, the laws surrounding the seventh year attracted further layers of theological reflection and meaning. Tracing this development is important.

A. Antecedent Practices: Crop Rotation and
   Manumission of Slaves
B. Exodus 23:10-11 in Its Ancient Setting
C. Deuteronomy 15:1-11 and the Expanding
   Sabbatical Year
D. Leviticus 25: Sabbatical Year and Jubilee
E. The Sabbatical Year in the Second Temple
   Period
F. Summary
Bibliography

A. Antecedent Practices: Crop Rotation and Manumission of Slaves

Two distinct practices lie behind the developed forms of the Sabbatical law in Leviticus and Deuteronomy, land fallowing and manumission of slaves. First, in ancient Israel, as in all ancient societies, the key agricultural problems were management of land, water, and people. (Modern challenges of technology and finance were not yet decisive issues.) Dry farming dependent on seasonal rains demanded not only collection of drinking water in cisterns but close attention to terracing, crop selection, and village organization. The principal crops, barley, grapes, and olives, as well as secondary crops such as dates and figs and various vegetables, required different techniques. In particular, cereal crops might be rotated on some cycle. Many of the details of ancient Israelite practice remain obscure.

Southern Mesopotamian farmers, whose techniques are better known, used a two-year cycle of planting and fallowing for cereals. Like all fallowing, no-till systems, Sumer's preserved or even enhanced soil nutrition, conserved water, and reduced erosion. Skillful farmers could judge the right amount of surface residue coverage on a fallow field so as to minimize soil-borne pathogens and maximize opportunities for the next crop's growth. Again, details of such management techniques for ancient Israel did not survive, presumably because farmers were mostly illiterate and scribes did not see such details as worth recording.

Second, the freeing of slaves could occur whenever a master desired, but kings sometimes manumitted slaves or forgave other kinds of debts en masse. Exodus 21:1-6 provides for liberation of debt slaves under certain circumstances. Deuteronomy 15 expands this law, connecting it to the Sabbatical Year, while Lev 25 ignores the possibility of enslaving Israelites while connecting manumission (apparently of Gentiles?) to the Jubilee, thus expanding the law in Exodus beyond its original intent to allow for variable length (though limited scope and intensity) of servitude.

B. Exodus 23:10-11 in Its Ancient Setting

The earliest reference in the Bible to a seventh-year fallowing of crops (the precursor to a Sabbatical Year) occurs in Exod 23:10-11, which already embeds an agricultural technique in a theological context. The Covenant Code sets the law between instructions for caring for the needy and vulnerable (Exod 23:1-9) and laws on cultic observances (Exod 23:12-19). In the mind of the Code's compiler, a logical connection existed among these items, with the law on fallowing land bridging two otherwise distinct sets of concerns. The Sabbatical Year would function on a long time scale as the Sabbath did on a short one.

The law of the Sabbatical Year as it stands contains several provisions: "1) For six years you shall sow your land and gather in its yield; 2) but the seventh year you shall let it rest and lie fallow, 3) so that the poor of your people may eat; and 4) what they leave the wild animals may eat. 5) You shall do the same with your vineyard, and with your olive orchard." The loose structure of the law may imply a period of development, much as with the law on negligent care of an ox in Exod 21:28-32. Provision 5 seems an afterthought, indicating that the law, like many others in the Covenant Code, has expanded over time. Provision 4 may also be an afterthought, though this is less clear. Provisions 1-3, however, seem to depend on each other to such an extent that separating them would render the law unintelligible.

The core of the law is vv. 10-11 a. Land should lie fallow one year in seven, with no clear indication that all land should be fallowed simultaneously or that no land could be fallowed more often if needed. Some scholars argue that the word hashevi'ith (הַשְּׁבִיעָה, "the seventh") implies a specific time for all land, and later Jewish law does assume such a standardization of practice. However, Exodus is vague on the point. The clock starts, so to speak, at a different point for each plot of land. The law thus codifies an agricultural practice that must have developed through the experience of farmers in the land of Israel.

The law, however, does not remain purely pragmatic. Rather, it is connected to a humanitarian rationale, the care of the poor and of wild animals (presumably ungulates such as antelope, gazelles, and deer). Under the law's scenario, plants would yield food for the poor, as well as for animals. Unlike other texts envisioning neglect of vineyards as a symbol of disaster (e.g., Ps 80:9-14; Isa 5:5-6), this text views periodic failure to harvest as a resource for rectifying injustice. It is unclear about whether pruning vines would have been permissible during the Sabbatical Year.

C. Deuteronomy 15:1-11 and the Expanding Sabbatical Year

At a later period, the Deuteronomists combined two elements of the Covenant Code, the law of manumitting slaves (Exod 21:1-6) and the law of the Sabbatical Year. The identical time interval in each law may have suggested the combination, which, however, resulted in an innovation: the fixing of the seven-year period for the entire land rather than on a rotational basis. Exegesis of an older text thus allowed for an innovation that dealt with recurring problems in the regulation of slavery and the care of the poor.

Besides identifying several types of theological rationales and even psychological motivations for its expanded law of manumission, Deuteronomy adapts the technical language of the law of the Sabbatical Year. Its sophisticated rhetorical appeal connects the law of debt forgiveness (vv. 1-11) with the law of manumitting slaves. The text distinguishes between obligations to foreigners and those to native Israelites. It also works out a technical vocabulary, drawing in part on Exodus. Thus the noun shemittah (שְׁמִטָּה, "release, manumission") is from the same root (shamat שָׁמַט) as the

verb translated "to lie fallow" in Exod 23:11. A generic term has taken on a technical meaning, expanded even to Deuteronomy's phrase "the seventh year, the year of remission."

By taking the law of freeing slaves out of the realm of family law and making it national in scope (though without involving the monarchy or other civil authorities directly), Deuteronomy frames the act of freeing slaves as a moral obligation enforced by God. The onus falls on the powerful—the potential slave owners—to carry out the law, thus creating a just society.

D. Leviticus 25: Sabbatical Year and Jubilee

The fullest development of the Sabbatical Year law appears in the Holiness Code, which links the seventh-year to the Jubilee. In contrast to Deut 15, Lev 25 does not allow for the enslavement of Israelites at all, thus making rules for manumission superfluous. It also disagrees with Exodus in allowing the aftergrowth of the fallow land to all Israelites, not just the poor.

The law in Lev 25:2-7 contains several provisions: 1) growing food for six years (v. 3); 2) making the seventh year a "sabbath of complete rest" (v. 4); 3) declining to harvest fields or vineyards (v. 5); and 4) extension of the law to all dependents of Israelites (vv. 6-7). Verse 2 prefaces the law by referring both to God's gift of the land to Israel and the ideal of allowing the land to join in Israel's religious commitments as it uses a year for the land to observe a sort of Sabbath. In each case, Leviticus develops the raw materials of the law in Exod 23 toward the theological and political assumptions of the priestly circles. At this point, a number of points deserve special attention.

First, the preface in v. 2 ("when you enter the land that I am giving you, the land shall observe a sabbath for the LORD") and its reiteration in v. 4 ("in the seventh year there shall be a sabbath of complete rest for the land, a sabbath for the LORD") both point to major themes first set forth in connection with the Sabbath in Gen 2:1-4 and expanded in the priestly treatment of the Decalogue (Exod 20:11). In granting the land to Israel as a leasehold, God expects Israel not to exploit the land but to recognize its connection to its creator. Also, whereas Exodus merely speaks of individual plots lying fallow periodically, Leviticus legislates a single period of rest for the entire land. For the priestly circles, the land's integrity as a whole was a major theological concern.

Second, the provision for agriculture in v. 3 quotes Exod 23:10 word-for-word, with two exceptions: it reverses the order of "your land" and "your field" (perhaps simply because the author thought that order sounded better) and adds the phrase "you shall prune your vineyard (kerem כָּרֶם)." The second idea must come from Exod 23:11, the appendix to the original law in Exodus. Leviticus has simply smoothed out a rough spot in its original source, though it does omit the reference to olive culture that appears in Exodus (however, Judg 15:5 may describe an olive grove as a kerem).

Third, Leviticus conceives of the Sabbatical Year, not as a year of "release" as in Deuteronomy, but as a "sabbath of complete rest," a technical phrase from the priestly circles that also describes the Sabbath (Exod 31:15; 35:2; Lev 23:3) and the Day of Atonement (Lev 16:31; 23:32). Violation of the prohibition of labor on the Sabbath was a capital offense, while work on the Day of Atonement, curiously, led only to expulsion from the community (still a serious penalty). Presumably, the Sabbatical Year in Leviticus would involve a prolonged work stoppage. It is difficult to see how such a law could have been implemented without serious economic dislocation.

Fourth, vv. 6-7 attempt to moderate that dislocation by insisting that the rest from agricultural labor extends to the same classes covered by the Sabbath law. The individual farmer is responsible for an extended family and its immediate dependents.

Finally, Leviticus connects the Sabbatical Year to a second annual cycle, the Jubilee. Scholars debate just how realizable the Jubilee was, though there is no evidence for its celebration at any point, even if several biblical texts presuppose a Jubilee-like practice as an unrealized ideal (e.g., Ezek 46:16-17). What is clear is that the compilers of the Holiness Code were not merely fantasizing, but were attempting to reconfigure the economic use of time and relationships to maximize justice and piety. Hence their practical attention to the differences between rural and urban centers (Lev 25:29-31).

E. The Sabbatical Year in the Second Temple Period

Several postexilic texts refer to one or another form of the Sabbatical Year. The Jerusalemites in the 5th cent. BCE swore to fallow the land in the seventh year (Neh 10:31 [Heb. 10:32]). First Maccabees 6:49-53 speaks of the absence of provisions owing to observance of the Sabbatical Year. Josephus (*Ant.* 12.378; 23.234; 14.202–206, 475), Tacitus (*Hist.* 5.4), and Eusebius (*Praep. ev.* 8.7) all speak of Jews observing the Sabbatical Year. How widespread or consistent such observances were is not clear, though the fact that anyone kept the Sabbatical Year at all is remarkable. Belatedly, a practice that began a serious effort of reimagining the relationship between economics and piety became a reality as well as an ideal.

F. Summary

To summarize, what began as two separate practices (freeing slaves and fallowing land) developed into a more ideologically laden set of laws seeking a system of total justice for Israel. Though utopian in some details, the laws of Deuteronomy and especially Leviticus sought a practical outcome, the elimination of systemic injustice through manipulation of common practices. By expanding old traditions and connecting them in new ways, both the Deuteronomic and priestly circles laid the groundwork for much later reflections on social justice, reflections that still survive. *See* BOOTHS, FEAST OR FESTIVAL OF; LAW IN THE OT; SABBATH; SLAVERY.

Bibliography: Jacob S. Bergsma. "Once Again, the Jubilee, every 49 or 50 Years?" *VT* 55 (2005) 121–25; Lee Casperson. "Sabbatical, Jubilee, and the Temple of Solomon." *VT* 53 (2003) 283–96; Calum Carmichael. "The Sabbatical/Jubilee Cycle and the Seven-Year Famine in Egypt." *Bib* 80 (1999) 224–39; Calum Carmichael. "The Three Laws on the Release of Slaves (Ex 21,2-11; Dtn 15,12-18; Lev 25,39-46)." *ZAW* 112 (2000) 509–25; Christopher J. Eyre. "The Agricultural Cycle, Farming, and Water Management in the Ancient Near East." *CANE* 1 (1995) 175–89; J. J. Finkelstein. "Ammisaduqa's Edict and the Babylonian Law Codes." *JCS* 15 (1961) 91–104; Jeffries M. Hamilton. *Social Justice and Deuteronomy: The Case of Deuteronomy 15* (1992); Mignon Jacobs. "Parameters of Justice: Ideological challenges regarding persons and practices in Leviticus 25:25-55." *ExAud* 22 (2006) 133–53; Robert S. Kawashima. "The Jubilee Year and the Return of Cosmic Purity." *CBQ* 65 (2003) 370–89; Moshe Weinfeld. *Social Justice in Ancient Israel and the Ancient Near East* (1995); Rodger C. Young. "Seder Olam and the Sabbaticals Associated with the Two Destructions of Jerusalem, part 2." *JBQ* 34 (2006) 252–59.

MARK W. HAMILTON

SABEANS suh-bee′uhn [סבא seva′]. Saba was a kingdom in South Arabia (present Yemen) from the 7th cent. BCE until the 6th cent. CE. It was situated in the inner, southeastern corner of the Arabian coastal mountain range. Together with their neighbors to the north, the Mineans, to the south, the Qatabanians, and to the southeast, the Hadramis, the Sabeans circled the Sayhad desert, cultivating fields by means of the run-off water from the mountains. The Sabeans organized and controlled the trade in FRANKINCENSE from the 8th through the 5th cent. BCE and thus rose to fame and renown in the Mediterranean world.

A. The Kingdom of Saba and Its History
  1. Language and prehistory
  2. The Kingdom of Saba, 8th through 5th cent. BCE
  3. South Arabia from the 4th cent. BCE to the Islamic conquest
B. Saba and Sabeans in the Bible
  1. Torah
  2. Prophets
  3. Writings
Bibliography

A. The Kingdom of Saba and Its History
  1. Language and prehistory
  Whereas the other languages of ancient South Arabia (Minean, Qatabanian, Hadramitic) belong to the

Southern Semitic branch of Afro-Asiatic (together with the Semitic languages of Ethiopia, and the Modern South Arabian languages still spoken in Hadramaut, Oman, and on the island of Soqotra), Sabaic was a Central Semitic language (like Ugaritic, Aramaic, Hebrew, and Arabic). The script appears in South Arabia at the end of the 2nd millennium BCE, a date that agrees well with its most likely descent from one of the scripts of 2nd-millennium Canaan, a descent betrayed both by the letter order of the South Arabian alphabet and by individual letter forms. Monumental inscriptions in Sabaic set in with the formation of the state in the 8th cent. BCE, and persist until the coming of Islam. A cursive script, used for the transactions of daily life, was also in use (and mostly written on wooden sticks). Geographically, Sabaic looks like an intruder within the territory of the other languages.

One is tempted to conclude that speakers of Semitic languages arrived in South Arabia from the north, and in two waves. A first immigration wave brought the Mineans, Qatabaneans, and Hadramis in the course of the 3rd or early 2nd millennium BCE, and a second wave, the Sabeans in the second half of 2nd millennium BCE. Both migration waves correspond with periods of crisis and breakdown in Syria and Israel: the Intermediate Bronze Age, or Early Bronze/Middle Bronze transition, and the Middle Bronze/Late Bronze transition. The little that is known about the material culture of South Arabia in these millennia leaves a "Chalcolithic" impression. We are dealing with the remnants of a simple tribal (chiefdom) society, based on subsistence agriculture.

2. The Kingdom of Saba, 8th through 5th cent. BCE

Saba originated as a league of sedentary tribes, the head of which bore the title of *Mukarrib* ("Bounder"? "Forwarder"?), whose duties first were predominantly cultic. In the course of the 8th cent., the mukarrib turned into a builder of monumental architecture that was adorned with inscriptions in a highly formalized script, indicative of at least one scribal school and thus, an emerging bureaucracy. In the 7th cent. BCE, the mukarrib Karib'il Watar adopted the title of king and subjected the whole of South Arabia to Sabean rule in a series of bloody campaigns.

State formation in South Arabia was fueled by the emergence of the incense trade. Local trade networks all over the Arabian peninsula were coalescing in the course of the 8th cent., and frankincense (the resin of the incense tree, which only grew, and grows, in Hadramaut and Somalia) became known, and soon highly valued, throughout the Mediterranean, under a name that originated, like the substance, in South Arabia: levonah (לְבֹנָה), libanos (λίβανος), Sabaic *lubân. Saba made use of its central position between the area of production (Hadramaut) and consumption (the Fertile Crescent and the sea beyond) to control the whole business. As a luxury item, small quantities of which represent a huge amount of capital, frankincense was a perfect long-distance trade item in the age of camel transport through a number of unruly tribal areas, all of which—presumably—demanded their share of "protection fees."

Tiglath-pileser III received "tribute" from Saba and other West Arabian tribes and towns as soon as he had conquered Gaza in 734 BCE. Gaza was the Mediterranean outlet of the West Arabian incense route. The speed of the Sabeans' reaction suggests that they had already a permanent trading post at Dedan in North Arabia, if not at Gaza itself, by the time of Tiglath-pileser's visit (a messenger's journey, on camelback, from Gaza to the Sabean capital of Maryab/Mârib, and back, would have consumed at least 60 days).

Assyria's changing ways of addressing the Sabeans attest well to the process of Sabean state formation in contact with the Assyrian/Mediterranean world: "the Sabean"/"the town of Saba" in 734 BCE; "It'amra of Saba-land" in 716 BCE; and "Karib'ilu, king of the land of Saba" ca. 685 BCE.

3. South Arabia from the 4th cent. BCE to the Islamic conquest

The Sabeans kept good relations with the Achaemenid Persians in the 5th cent. BCE, as they had with the Assyrians in the 8th and 7th cent. Unfortunately, Persian domination broke down in Arabia after their loss of Egypt, early in the 4th cent. BCE, and Sabean supremacy over the incense trade was lost to their northern neighbors, the Mineans, for the next 200 years. From the end of the 2nd cent. BCE, the Himyarites re-assembled the Sabaic empire, until South Arabia was reunited again by the 4th cent. CE.

From the 3rd cent. BCE to the 6th cent. CE, incense trade by camel caravans faced sharp competition from incense trade by ship. From the 1st cent. CE onward, the "incense route" lost its international significance. It first disintegrated into local networks; an occasional camel might have carried some Hadrami incense to Mecca, but caravans no longer went all the way from Saba to Syria. The last indigenous rulers of Saba embraced Judaism. In 525 CE, Justinian had Saba conquered by his Christian Abessinian proxy (a kingdom that had its beginning, in the first half of the 1st millennium BCE, in a Sabaic colony on African soil). For the last decennia before Islam, Saba was a colony of Sasanid Persia. The global economy of the 1st millennium BCE had created Saba; the conflict between the two world powers of Late Antiquity destroyed it in the course of the 6th cent. CE.

B. Saba and Sabeans in the Bible
1. Torah

The "list of nations" makes Saba a "son of Cush" (Gen 10:7), i.e., places it within the Egyptian sphere of influence during the reign of the Nineteenth (Ethiopic)

Dynasty (712–664 BCE; *see* CUSH, CUSHITE). The further derivation of Dedan and Sheba from Raamah is based on a simple transformation of a geographic feature: Raamah (Nagran) was a prominent place on the incense route between Dedan in the north and Saba (Maryab) in the south. The variants "Seba" and "Sheba" derive from the correct transcription of the name into Hebrew from Sabaic, Assyrian, or Aramaic (or all of the above), and an equally correct rendering of its Arabic and South Arabian pronounciation. A variant tradition makes Saba a descendant of SHEM via JOKTAN (Gen 10:28). The variant betrays a more detailed knowledge of the people and places of South Arabia than Gen 10:7 and is probably a century or so younger. A third tradition derives SHEBA and DEDAN from Joktan, Abraham and Keturah's son—clearly an attempt not to discriminate against the towns and cities of Arabia vis-à-vis the eponym of the bedouin, Ishmael: if the latter was son of Abraham, how much more so the civilized children of Joktan. There is no trace of the Mineans in the Torah.

2. Prophets

The most prominent Sabean in world literature is, without doubt, the anonymous royal woman who paid SOLOMON a visit (1 Kgs 10:1-13). Because we know nothing about any ruler of Saba in the 10th cent. BCE, we cannot prove that this visit was impossible. It is, however, highly improbable, since none of the prerequisites for this visit—the "touristic infrastructure" presupposed by the narrative, the Sabaic trade-based wealth, or, most important of all, the image of Saba as a paradigmatically wealthy (and therefore skilled, "wise") people in the Mediterranean—emerged before the 8th cent. Given that north Arabian queens visited the Assyrian court in the 8th and 7th cent. (and were appropriately exploited by Assyrian pictorial and textual propaganda), we are most probably dealing with an "Arabian tale" composed to glorify Solomon not earlier than the 7th cent. and no later than the 5th, making use of pieces of "Arabian lore" from various regions and periods. That Solomon fulfilled the queen's every desire (1 Kgs 10:13) gave rise to the Christian Ethiopian tradition that the rule over ETHIOPIA belongs legitimately to the offspring of Solomon and the queen of Sheba (*see* ARAB, ARABIA, ARABIANS; SHEBA, QUEEN OF).

For prophets of the late 7th–6th cent., Saba is not only the source of incense (Jer 6:20) but also of gold (Isa 60:6; Ezek 27:22-3). Whether this gold derives from Arabian mines or came into Sabean hands by way of trade profits is a moot question: for a Jew, as for a Greek of this period, the Sabeans were believed to have it in abundance. Negatively, the merchants of Sheba, Dedan, and Tarshish (i.e., those of the extreme east and west) are represented as all too willingly negotiating Gog's booty (Ezek 38:13).

3. Writings

Concerning Saba, Chronicles does not add to its sources in Genesis and 1 Kings. Seba/Sheba and Tarshish represent the extremes of the earth (Ps 72:10) and its riches (72:15). The reference to the caravans of Sheba trading with Tema (Job 6:19) betrays the book of Job's origins prior to 400 BCE (when Minean caravans would have traded with Dedan). The marauding bands of Chaldeans and Sabeans (Job 1:15), which contribute to the destruction of Job's original wealth, reflect the situation in the Hejaz (northwest Arabia) during Nabonidus' incursion of 553–543 BCE, when the Neo-Babylonian (Chaldean) king tried to wrestle control of the incense trade from the Sabeans—unsuccessfully, as it appears.

Bibliography: P. Crone. *Meccan Trade and the Rise of Islam* (1987); R. G. Hoyland. *Arabia and the Arabs from the Bronze Age to the Coming of Islam* (2001); K. A. Kitchen. "Sheba and Arabia." *The Age of Solomon.* L. K. Handy, ed. (1997) 126–53; E. A. Knauf. "The Migration of the Script, and the Formation of the State in South Arabia." *Proceedings of the Seminar for Arabian Studies* 19 (1989) 78–92; J. B. Pritchard, ed. *Solomon and Sheba* (1974).

ERNST AXEL KNAUF

SABTA. *See* SABTAH.

SABTAH sab´tuh [סַבְתָּא savta', סַבְתָּה savtah]. Ham's descendant and a son of Cush, Sabtah is an unidentified eponym in the Table of Nations (Gen 10:7; 1 Chr 1:9, "Sabta"). Taken geographically, the capital of Hadhramaut, Shabwa, in southern Arabia is its most accepted location. Taken as a person, Sabtah may stand for the first Ethiopian (Cushite) ruler of Egypt, Shabaka.

LJUBICA JOVANOVIC

SABTECA sab´tuh-kuh [סַבְתְּכָא savtekha']. The fifth son of Cush (Gen 10:7; 1 Chr 1:9) who, as with other offspring of Cush, represents a place of unknown location.

SACHAR say´kahr [שָׂכָר sakhar]. 1. The father of Ahiam, one of David's faithful warriors (1 Chr 11:35). Sachar's designation as a HARARITE (perhaps meaning "mountain dweller") may suggest his provenance from the Judean hills. The parallel passage (2 Sam 23:33) preserves a variant form of *Sachar*, SHARAR.

2. The fourth son of Obed-edom. Obed-edom and his sons guard the Temple's south gate and its environs (1 Chr 26:4, 15).

LJUBICA JOVANOVIC

SACHIA suh-ki´uh [שָׂכְיָה sokhyah]. One of the Benjaminite Shaharaim's seven sons, born to his wife Hodesh, according to the genealogy in 1 Chr 8:8-10. According to the generally accepted reading of v. 8, they were born after Shaharaim divorced his other two wives and moved to Moab. The eponymous naming of Hodesh's sons may suggest the eastward expansion of the otherwise small Benjaminite territory. The name *Sachia* means "announcement."

LJUBICA JOVANOVIC

SACKCLOTH [שַׂק saq; σάκκος sakkos]. A rough material made from the hair of a goat or camel, sackcloth has a variety of textile applications, e.g., as the stuff of sails, tents, floor coverings, or clothing. In ancient sources, the term frequently appears (often alongside ASHES) within the context of ANE and biblical rites of MOURNING or as an expression of repentance. As an overt expression of bereavement, sackcloth served as the garb for either an individual or an entire collective, be they human or animal. Such a garment was worn full length with a waist tie holding it in place or as a plain loincloth. In fact, the coarse fabric may have been placed immediately next to the skin without the benefit of an undergarment (compare 2 Macc 3:19; 10:25).

Sackcloth (along with ashes) traditionally represented an expression of mourning (Gen 37:34), a sign of repentance (Dan 9:3; Joel 1:8, 13; Matt 11:21), or the judgment of God (Rev 6:12). When King Ahasuerus ordered all the Jewish people to be killed, Mordecai "tore his clothes and put on sackcloth and ashes ... wailing with a loud and bitter cry" (Esth 4:1). There was "great mourning among the Jews, with fasting and weeping and lamenting, and everybody [author's trans.; NRSV, "most of them"] lay in sackcloth and ashes" (Esth 4:3). The Jews' actions suggest a dual purpose of mourning their impending death and of demonstrating their repentance to God, pleading that God spare them from judgment. When Jonah preached the coming judgment against Nineveh, the Assyrian king and his subjects understood that if the nation would repent from its evil ways, Jonah's god might withhold judgment (compare Jer 18:7-10), so they repented and prayed that Jonah's god would spare them (Jonah 3:5-10).

In Christian tradition, this garment of rough cloth (as was the case with ashes) took on the added role of expressing the mortification of the flesh and aiding the wearer to resist temptations of the flesh. The garment of camel's hair worn by John the Baptist (Matt 3:4; Mark 1:6) is often viewed as a precedent for this custom. Later on, sackcloth was adopted by various religious orders of the Middle Ages in imitation of the early ascetics, and in order to increase the discomfort caused by its use it was sometimes even made of fine wire. *See* CLOTH, CLOTHES; DUST; FAST, FASTING.

BRIAN B. SCHMIDT

SACRAMENTAL THEOLOGY. A fitting place to begin thinking about sacramental theology is John 1:14, in which the mystery of salvation is announced: "And the Word became flesh and lived among us." The meaning of a sacrament for Christians should be understood in light of God incarnate in Jesus Christ, who himself is the fundamental Sacrament, the heart of the mystery of God mediated through creation and God's redemptive purpose for humanity and the world. Any discussion of sacramental theology is inevitably bound up with the central Christian doctrines of TRINITY and INCARNATION, so that *sacrament* will point to and participate in the mystery of God's radical self-engagement with the world and its manifestation as self-giving love (*see* SACRAMENTS).

God's sacramental activity is intensely personal; establishing, sustaining, and perfecting communion with God for which humanity has been created and redeemed. God's active presence is realized in the form and pattern embodied by Jesus; divine grace enabling human freedom and the perfection of human freedom in loving obedience to God. Sacramental theology thus helps to clarify the nature and mission of the church as a visible, human sign of communion between God and the world through the presence of Christ and the empowerment of the Holy Spirit. And if the underlying conviction for a sacramental vision of the church is signaled by John 1, it also encourages a sacramental vision of Scripture as revealing and mediating the activity of God drawing a people through time, transforming them into a sign and witness to God's kingdom on earth.

In this manner, the nature of God's purposes in creation are brought to particular focus in and through sacramental theology. God the Father has sent the Son to assume our humanity, adopting us by grace to be conformed to the divine image by the empowerments and gifts of the Spirit. Within the Triune mystery, the particular rites or "sacraments" of the church can be seen as "appointed means" by which communion between God and humanity is moved toward this final end. BAPTISM and EUCHARIST, the sacraments recognized by most Christian traditions, are thus received and entered into as tangible, sensible signs mediating the wisdom and power of God's ways with humanity through Christ and the Spirit.

Seen from this perspective, baptism is the sacrament of beginning and incorporation into Trinitarian communion, while the eucharist is the sacrament of its nourishment, strengthening, and deepening participation. Because baptism and eucharist are intimately related to the person and work of Christ in the Spirit, he is seen as their primary actor as well as their content, character and consummation. Finally, because Christ is the enfleshment of God's will and purpose, the "dominical" sacraments mediate the life and destiny of the church to be a sign of the life and destiny of all humanity for the life and destiny of the world. This is the mystery or sacrament of GRACE, the rule of God in and through all things.

MICHAEL PASQUARELLO III

SACRAMENTS. The English term *sacrament* comes from the Latin term *sacramentum* (pl. *sacramenta*, meaning "oath," especially one of allegiance by new recruits), a translation of the Greek mystērion (μυστήριον). Contemporary definitions of sacrament, such as an outward sign of an inward grace or a ritual or practice instituted by Christ for his disciples was not the original meaning of this term. What follows is a survey of the foundations for those rites we now describe as sacraments (or "ordinances.")

The term mystērion is found in Wisdom of Solomon, where it is used to speak of "the secret purposes (or plan) of God" (Wis 2:22) and the "knowledge of God" (Wis 8:4). It is most commonly found in the NT in the writings of Paul, where mystērion is God's plan to save humanity through Christ. In Christ the "mystery of God" is embodied (Col 2:2). In deutero-Pauline literature, the MYSTERY is revealed by the Spirit of God (1 Cor 2:10-15) and is now proclaimed by prophets, apostles, and even Gentiles (Eph 3:2-6).

The term mystērion comes into English as "mystery," but in classical antiquity, it did not mean something hidden, perplexing, or puzzling. Instead mystērion was something that spoke to the transcendent quality of human life that connected with the divine. The mystēria (μυστήρια), e.g., were the collection of "MYSTERY RELIGIONS" whose beliefs and practices connected the initiated with the timeless truths of the cosmos and extended salvation from the deities who embodied these eternal verities. Though these groups had an air of secrecy, the central theme of the mystēria was becoming enlightened. For Greek philosophers, the term mystērion described those tangible and visible realities of this world that spoke of eternal truths and symbolically re-presented them. This understanding would have a tremendous influence on the Platonic Christian theologians, especially Augustine.

The Greek Fathers frequently spoke of Christianity as a mystery religion. Clement of Alexandria, e.g., presented Christ as the teacher of eternal mysteries who ushers the initiated into life eternal. Origen—and Cyril of Jerusalem after him—saw the mysteries of God presented paradigmatically in the rites of the church, where one participates personally in the death and resurrection of Christ in baptism (developing Paul's themes of Rom 6).

Although the term mystērion fits most naturally the rite of BAPTISM (as it paralleled the initiation rites of the mystery religions), early Christian apologists Justin, Irenaeus, Clement of Alexandria, and Tertullian also applied this concept to the LORD'S SUPPER because both were seen as ritual expressions of the saving relationship established by Christ in his death and resurrection. According to Paul, we are crucified with Christ in baptism (Rom 6:6-8), and we become the body of Christ in sharing the common loaf (1 Cor 10:17). Other rites could have been seen as mystēria (e.g., footwashing and anointing), but they were rarely referred to as mystēria.

Latin apologists moved the discussion in a decidedly different direction. The term entered the Latin Christian vocabulary through the earliest translations of the Greek Bible into Latin in North Africa, where mystērion was translated as *sacramentum*. *Sacramentum* had a slightly different meaning than mystērion, however. For Romans, *sacramentum* was an oath and/or a pledge of money serving as a guarantee. In both examples the *sacramentum* was an act of self-commitment, a moral obligation within a relationship. This term had obvious parallels to the oaths that one would take in the initiation rites of the mystery religions. Tertullian developed the theological use of this term in reference to the Lord's Supper, but especially in respect to baptism (Tertullian, *Bapt.* 4). This development shifted emphasis away from the gracious act of God's self-revelation of salvation in Christ to the response of the believer to this grace as an act of commitment. It is understandable, therefore, that Tertullian would object to the practice of infant baptism where children could not act on their own volition and make the necessary pledge of faith (*Bapt.* 18).

Augustine brought new clarity and focus to the concept of sacraments, setting the stage for the development of SACRAMENTAL THEOLOGY in the West, in both Catholic and Protestant churches. Though Augustine uses *sacramenta* to describe signs in any religion that signify the sacred without which no religion could exist (*Faust.* 19.11), he understood sacraments within the covenants of Yahweh to convey the presence of Christ (*Faust.* 19.13). Augustine believed that Christ was present in the *sacramenta* of the OT (*Enarrat. Ps.* 74.2; 78.11), such as circumcision (*On Bapt.* 4.24) and the Sabbath (*Serm.* 17.13), in much the same way Paul saw Christ present in the water from the rock (1 Cor 10:4). Augustine also appropriated the term *sacramenta* liberally for a number of Christian rites and events, including the Lord's Prayer (*Serm. dom.* 63), baptism (*Bapt.* 1), laying on of hands (*Parm.* 2.13), and exorcisms (*Enarrat. Ps.* 66.15). Augustine further differentiated those *sacramenta* that come with a promise of Christ's saving presence, specifically baptism (e.g., *Enarrat. Ps.* 3.7), chrismation (*Enarrat.* Ps. 45.17–18), the Lord's Supper (*Enarrat. Ps.* 103.14), marriage (*Enarrat. Ps.* 75.4), orders (*Bon. conj.* 24.32), and penance (*Op. mon.* 21.24).

Augustine's theology of the sacraments comes directly out of his Platonic worldview, where sacraments are visible signs of an invisible reality. In a sacrament, a physical likeness is seen, and the spiritual aspect is grasped through it (*Serm.* 272). Sacraments are visible words; God speaks authoritatively through the liturgical sacraments. Water is just water without the word of God, but with the word of God water cleanses the soul in baptism (*Tract. Ev. Jo.* 80). Augustine's thought is the touchstone for the theology and the debates that would ensue surrounding the sacraments in the West, from the Synod of Rome to the Reformation, to Vatican II, and to the diversity of sacramental understandings in the churches today.

TODD E. JOHNSON

SACRED [קָדוֹשׁ qadhosh; ἅγιος hagios]. In the OT, concepts of sacredness are regularly expressed through the word qadhosh and its cognates, signifying a state of being "set apart," "consecrated," or "dedicated" to God and God's purposes. The concept is widely applied to people, objects, space, time, and actions to signify, especially in the cultic sphere, the essential character of that which is associated with the domain of the sacred over against that of the profane. Despite its infrequency in classical Greek, the LXX almost exclusively renders qadhosh by means of hagios, importing the semantic range of the Hebrew. The NT follows LXX practice, presupposing the conceptual and semantic spectrum of OT meaning as its starting point.

Various disciplines have emphasized a range of features of the concept of the sacred. The psychology of religion has underscored the sacred in terms of the human experience of awe in the encounter with the numinous or the divine. Other disciplines have engaged this pervasive biblical concept through its most systematic and overt expression in the sacred spaces of Sinai, the tabernacle, and the Jerusalem Temple, as well as their attendant personnel and cult. Phenomenology of religion has analyzed these settings in relation to theophany or the incursions of the sacred into profane space. Anthropology has explored the generative role of sacred space's systemic features and signifying systems concerning purity and impurity, especially in the so-called Priestly source (see P, PRIESTLY WRITERS). Moreover, the sociology of religion has underscored this dimension of the sacred's capacity as an organizational metaphor to structure and orient social space in regard to ethnicity, gender, purity, and status.

However, fundamental to biblical expressions of sacredness is God's nature, both as Creator—standing distinct from creation—and in terms of God's moral character and holiness (compare Isa 40:25; 45:18). God's holiness implies a moral responsibility on the part of God's people. Even amid the many injunctions to maintain the inviolable separation between sacred and profane in the holiness code (Lev 17–26), one may infer an ethical character and moral imperative (Lev 19:2; 20:7; compare Ps 15). Indeed, Isaiah's encounter with the sacred in the Temple embraces a number of these themes, encompassing both awe and a sense of moral impurity, as well as a consecration for God's purpose (Isa 6:1-8). Nevertheless, expressions of the sacred do not remain static within the canon. The NT witnesses a movement toward the personalization and spiritualization of sacred space and sacred cult in the service of community identity and moral exhortation. Paul addresses the Christian community as the temple of the Holy Spirit and exhorts them to offer themselves as a holy sacrifice (Rom 12:1-2; 1 Cor 6:19; Eph 2:21). The Gospels and Acts evince

motifs that replace or relativize the Temple as sacred center. Moreover, Revelation, though rigorous in maintaining the Creator/creation divide, nevertheless culminates in a vision of the accessibility and immediacy of God's sacred presence permeating the New Jerusalem, a city proportionate to the Holy of Holies that requires no temple (Rev 21:16, 22). See HOLY, HOLINESS, NT; HOLY, HOLINESS, OT; PROFANE.

MICHAEL C. MCKEEVER

SACRIFICE IN THE NT. See ATONEMENT.

SACRIFICE, HUMAN. From the standpoint of sacrificial theory, no distinction can be made between human and animal sacrifice in terms of the basic functionality of the victim. The Bible's promotion of the potential for animals to serve as substitutes for humans, most notably in Gen 22, supports this claim. Certainly the exact purpose and procedure of a given sacrifice is contextually bound to the circumstances surrounding the killing of the animal or human, yet it is possible to subsume all instances of sacrifice under the general principle that the slayings take place with the fundamental objective of engendering changes at the suprahuman level that will consequently affect living human beings

Human sacrifice in the OT primarily centers on the issue of purity, particularly in regard to the impurity of innocent Israelite heir immolation as well as the need to cleanse the Israelite community or the land of Canaan from the contamination of iniquity. The language utilized by the biblical writers to designate human immolation is varied. The most basic verb for sacrifice in Hebrew, zavakh (זָבַח), or its derivative noun, zevakh (זֶבַח), appears in 2 Kgs 23:20; Ps 106:37-38; Isa 34:1-10; Ezek 16:20-21; 39:17-20; and Hos 13:2. The last is perhaps the most important passage signifying the acceptance of human sacrifice within certain Yahwistic circles. For it is here that one reads in no uncertain terms of the immolation of idolatrous priests upon altars by none other than the exemplar of righteous kingship, Josiah (compare a similar sacrifice in 1 Macc 2:23-26). This incident is part of a series of reforms instituted by the monarch in his attempts to cleanse Judah, which is precisely why the Deuteronomistic writers endorse this form of sacrifice. There are, moreover, several other examples from the Deuteronomistic corpus in which transgressors are sacrificed for the sake of sanctity. The practice of devoting individuals unto Yahweh through destruction, or kherem (חֵרֶם), illustrates this notion precisely, as seen in Deut 20:17-18, which elucidates the necessity of destroying the inhabitants of Canaan lest the Israelite community walk in their abominable ways (compare Deut 7:1-11). That kherem is a type of sacrifice is best illustrated by Isa 34:5-7, wherein Yahweh's judgment upon Edom is specified as both an act of kherem as well as one of zevakh.

Josiah's reforms, explained in part as an attempt to eradicate (bi'er בָּעַר) idolatry from Judah (2 Kgs 23:24), were ultimately unsuccessful because of the sins of Manasseh (2 Kgs 23:26-27), who is categorized as a child immolator (2 Kgs 21:6) and one who inundated Jerusalem with the blood of innocents (2 Kgs 24:3-4). Innocent blood is an important theme in biblical discourse, especially regarding murder. Thus, the sacrifice of innocent children is described in Ps 106:37-38 as resulting in the contamination of the land. The polluting effects of murder can be nullified, literally atoned for (kipper כִּפֶּר) or eradicated (biʿer), by spilling the blood of the killer (Num 35:29-34; Deut 19:13). Given this expressed goal of capital punishment, the execution of murderers should be considered as nothing less than human sacrifice. Both eradication and atonement are found in several other passages that represent capital punishment in a similar light, although innocent blood is not always present (Num 25:10-18; Judg 20:13; 2 Sam 21:1-14). Of greatest importance are the references in Deuteronomy to the eradication of the evil affecting the Israelite community by means of execution (13:5 [Heb. 13:6]; 17:7, 12; 21:21; 22:20-24; 24:7). Remarkably, Israelite children are included in the list of deviants slated for punishment, but this is because they are no longer viewed as innocent victims, having transgressed the laws of Yahweh.

Leviticus 20 likewise emphasizes the need to maintain the sanctity of the Israelite community by slaying those who commit abominations in order that the tribes of Israel would not be in danger of losing the land just as the previous occupants had due to their iniquitous ways. The first apostate singled out for elimination in the passage is the person who sacrifices one of his children to Molech. Here the verb for immolation is literally "to give" (nathan נָתַן), but it should not be misconstrued as indicative of a rite of dedication. While the verb can stand alone as a sacrificial term (Mic 6:7), its pairing with heʿevir (הֶעֱבִיר) in Ezek 16:20-21 to denote the giving of children to a deity by causing them to pass over should be understood in terms of sacrifice, inasmuch as the ritual is specified as an act of slaughter and the verb zavakh is utilized as well. Leviticus 18:21 specifically uses nathan and heʿevir to describe the sacrifice of children to Molech; the appearance of nathan alone in Lev 20 is a shortened form of the compound phrase. Second Kings 23:10 indicates that sacrifices to Molech entailed burning at the TOPHETH in Jerusalem's Hinnom Valley (compare Jer 32:35). In light of Yahweh's association with the Topheth in Isa 30:33, it can be deduced that the sacrifices associated with Molech were at one time accepted by some Yahwists; otherwise, the writers of Jer 7:31; 19:5; and 32:35 would not have perceived of the need to distance Yahweh from the practice. There is even more direct evidence suggesting that Yahweh was at one time the recipient of innocent Israelite heir immolation (see MOLECH, MOLOCH).

While Ezek 23:37-39 merely indicates that people who worshiped Yahweh also performed child immolations and not necessarily to him, a preceding passage (20:25-31) clearly identifies him as the one who had commanded the sacrifice of Israelite firstborn children. Exodus 22:29-30 [Heb. 22:28-29], moreover, is the sole legislative text calling for the sacrifice of all firstborn males that lacks a ransom clause, which when present provides Israelite parents with the opportunity to redeem their children (Exod 13:2, 12-15; 34:18-20; Num 18:14-17). An example of this is found in the NT, when the parents of the infant Jesus dedicate him by offering the traditional sacrifice (thysia θυσία) to redeem a firstborn son (Luke 2:24).

Noteworthy narrative accounts of firstborn Israelite immolation center on foundation immolation and burnt sacrifice (ʿolah עֹלָה). The former is recounted in 1 Kgs 16:34 (compare Josh 6:26) and the latter, especially in Judg 11 and Gen 22. Second Kings 3:27 parallels these texts, but the victim is foreign and the beneficiary is most likely Chemosh. Concerning Jephthah and his unnamed daughter, two points should be emphasized: 1) she is a sacrificial victim, not a woman dedicated to a lifetime of virginity, as indicated by the statement that Jephthah did to her what he had vowed (v. 39); and 2) Yahweh's approval of the promised burnt sacrifice is evinced by his provision of victory, which was the condition upon which Jephthah built his vow.

As for the archetype of Israelite FIRSTBORN sacrifice, it can be inferred from Abraham's immediate acceptance of the divine command to immolate Isaac and God's eventual bestowal of a substitute that the author created the narrative to explain that the sacrifice of innocent Israelite heirs was once accepted without question in Yahwism, but was no longer required (see AKEDAH). Such a move away from innocent heir immolation is reflected throughout the Hebrew texts and seems to have coincided with the end of the Judean monarchy. Hence, the books of Jeremiah and Ezekiel look at the late monarchical era as a period in which Yahwists practiced heir sacrifice, yet they seek to explain that Yahweh does not desire such immolations anymore. The Deuteronomists, too, generally do not endorse innocent Israelite heir sacrifice; instead, they promote the sacrifice of adult and child apostates as well as foreign idolaters for the purpose of maintaining sanctity. In Christianity, the process of animal substitution is reversed and nullified as Jesus, the Lamb of God, is called upon to take away the world's transgressions by means of a cross (John 1:29; Heb 10), which, like the wood for Isaac's sacrifice, is carried by the victim to the place of immolation. An additional departure from earlier traditions is that innocent human blood is spilled through the act of sacrificial capital punishment for the sake of communal purity; indeed, it is Jesus' blamelessness (Matt 27:4; 2 Cor 5:21) that makes the immolation efficacious (Heb 9:11-28). For comparative purposes, 4 Macc 17:17-22 should be noted for its account of the ATONEMENT achieved by the blood of devout humans. Paul describes Jesus as a sacrifice or place of atonement (hilastērion ἱλαστήριον) for all who have faith (Rom 3:21-25). Furthermore, Paul reinterprets the sacrificial system by calling upon the faithful to follow in Christ's footsteps by becoming living sacrifices (thysia Rom 12:1).

Bibliography: John Day. *Molech: A God of Human Sacrifice in the Old Testament* (1989); Karin Finsterbusch, Armin Lange, and K. F. Diethard Römheld, eds. *Human Sacrifice in Jewish and Christian Tradition* (2007); Alberto Green. *The Role of Human Sacrifice in the Ancient Near East* (1975); George Heider. *The Cult of Molek: A Reassessment* (1985); Jon Levenson. *The Death and Resurrection of the Beloved Son* (1993); Paul Mosca. *Child Sacrifice in Canaanite and Israelite Religion* (1975); Ed Noort and Eibert Tigchelaar, eds. *The Sacrifice of Isaac: The Aqedah (Genesis 22) and Its Interpretations* (2002); F. Francesca Stavrakopoulou. *King Manasseh and Child Sacrifice: Biblical Distortions of Historical Realities* (2004); Jason Tatlock. *How in Ancient Times They Sacrificed People* (2006).

JASON R. TATLOCK

SACRIFICES AND OFFERINGS [זֶבַח zevakh, מִנְחָה minkhah, מַתָּנָה mattanah, קָרְבָּן qorban; δόμα doma, δῶρον dōron, θυσία thysia]. The Priestly traditions provide the most detailed instructions concerning the sacrificial offerings, especially Exod 25–40, Leviticus, and Num 5, 15. The primary sacrifices are the burnt offering ('olah עֹלָה), the grain offering (minkhah), the well-being offering (zevakh shelamim זֶבַח שְׁלָמִים), the sin offering (khatta'th חַטָּאת), and the reparation offering ('asham אָשָׁם). The offerer must bring sacrifices and offerings the legitimate altar; a priest must put the blood on the altar (grain offerings are exceptions) and burn the specified parts. Additional offerings include the elevation/dedication offering (tenufah תְּנוּפָה), a gift (offering) (terumah תְּרוּמָה), Passover (pesakh פֶּסַח), the first-fruits (habbikkurim הַבִּכּוּרִים; Lev 23:10b-14; Num 28:26-31), and the secondary harvest (minkhah hadhashah מִנְחָה חֲדָשָׁה; Lev 23:15-21). In the Priestly traditions the Israelites present their sacrifices and offerings to Yahweh who dwells in the tabernacle (mishkan [מִשְׁכָּן]; also the Tent of Meeting ['ohel mo'edh אֹהֶל מוֹעֵד]). Yahweh appointed and consecrated ("made holy" or "set apart") Aaron and his sons to serve as cultic officials in the sanctuary (*see* PRIESTS AND LEVITES).

A. General Introduction

The Yahwist traditions, the Priestly traditions (P and HC), prophetic traditions, Deuteronomic and Deuteronomistic traditions, and the Chronicler's history all speak of Israel's sacrificial rituals. The texts report that key characters offered burnt offerings, e.g., Noah (Gen 8:20), Abraham (Gen 22:13), Gideon (Judg 6:26-28), Manoah (Judg 13:15-20), Samuel (1 Sam 7:9; 10:8), Saul (1 Sam 13:9), David (2 Sam 6:17), Solomon (1 Kgs 3:4; 9:25), and Elijah (1 Kgs 18:38). The Covenant Code (Exod 20:24 [Heb. 20:21]; 32:6), the Deuteronomistic History (Josh 22:26; 1 Sam 1:21; 2 Sam 15:12; 1 Kgs 8:62; 2 Kgs 5:17), and the prophetic traditions (Isa 1:11; Jer 7:22; Hos 3:4) all refer to "sacrifice" (zevakh). A range of traditions refers to the "sacrifices of well-being," e.g., Exod 20:24; 32:6; Judg 20:26; 1 Sam 13:9; 2 Sam 6:17; 1 Kgs 3:15; 2 Kgs 16:13; Ezek 43:27; 45:15, 17; Amos 5:22 uses the singular. Chronicles records the presentation of burnt offerings, well-being sacrifices, and grain offerings, often in association with important cultic days or events associated with the ark and Temple (1 Chr 21:23-26; 2 Chr 5:6, 14).

Narrative texts recognize the existence of multiple sites of sacrifice (e.g., Gen 13:18; 22:9-14; Josh 8:30-31; 1 Sam 1:3; 7:9; 1 Kgs 12:29-33; 2 Kgs 23:7-20), as opposed to a central sanctuary (see Deut 12; Lev 17), and often depict non-priests offering sacrifices (Moses, Lev 8; Saul, 1 Sam 13:8-15; David, 2 Sam 6:12-15, 17-19; Elijah, 1 Kgs 18:20-40; Jeroboam, 1 Kgs 12:32-33). The history of sacrifice in Israel is complex and reflects change and adaptation. The texts suggest that multiple perspectives existed in Israel concerning the reasons for offering sacrifices, the places to offer them, and the role of a cultic specialist, or lack thereof, in presenting them.

The narrative traditions record a variety of situations in which sacrifices were offered. Examples include: demonstrating obedience to Yahweh (Gen 22), in conjunction with petitions to Yahweh (1 Sam 1:3-21), giving thanks for divine blessing (Judg 13:2-23; 1 Sam 22-28) and redemption (Gen 9), providing the Israelites means to engage in conflict with the worshipers of Baal (Judg 6:25-27; 1 Kgs 18:20-40), accompanying inquiries concerning war and its outcome (Judg 6:11-24; Judg 11:29-33; Judg 20:26; 1 Sam 7:7-11), and marking important and joyful occasions associated with both the ark and the Temple (1 Kgs 8:1-13, 62; 2 Sam 6:12-15, 17-19).

The recovery of cultic artifacts and ritual texts in, e.g., Sumer, Assyria, Babylon, Anatolia, Syria, and Egypt demonstrates that Israel practiced sacrificial rituals similar to its neighbors (Malul). Although differences are present, the parallels demonstrate that Israel's cultic practices were not unique. Comparative analysis, however, too often assumes that Israel's rituals were distinct in their conceptual framework and superior to those of their "pagan" neighbors (Kaufmann; Milgrom). Comparison is reduced to a search for evidence that illuminates Israel's cultic practices rather than critical analysis of the larger historical and cultural contexts. Comparison is important, but critical analysis must guard against the imposition of predetermined theological or ideological assumptions and value judgments.

B. The Deuteronomic Code: Deuteronomy 12–26

The Deuteronomic Code (Deut 12–26) addresses a variety of cultic matters relating to sacrifice. Of particular importance, Deut 12 calls for the centralization of worship and the destruction of outlying cultic sites. Clearly, multiple altars and cultic sites existed (see Exod 20:20-26 for an early altar law). The Deuteronomic Code identifies the legitimate place for sacrifice as the place at which Yahweh will cause the divine name to dwell (e.g., Deut 12:5-6, 11; 15:20; 26:2; compare 1 Kgs 8:29, 48). Centralization created a need for a legitimate form of secular slaughter. Deuteronomy 12 identifies the solution: the hunter need only pour the blood of the animal on the ground (vv. 13-16; on the prohibition of blood consumption, see vv. 20-25; compare Lev 17; Gen 9:1-7; Lev 3:17; 7:22-27). The Deuteronomic call for centralization is generally associated either with the reform of Hezekiah (ca. 715 BCE; 2 Kgs 18:1-8) or Josiah (ca. 622 BCE; see 2 Kgs 22–23).

Deuteronomy 12 (compare Exod 20:22-26) specifically recognizes burnt offerings, joyous sacrifices, tithes and contributions, votive and freewill offerings, firstlings of the herd and flock, and the regular feast offerings (vv. 5b-7; compare vv. 8-12; 17-19; compare Exod 20:22-26, an early ruling). When the Israelites enter Canaan they are to set up an altar and present burnt offerings and well-being offerings (27:1-8). The Deuteronomic Code addresses several additional cultic issues: rulings on edible and inedible animals (14:3-21; compare Lev 11:1-47), tithes (14:22-29; 26:12-15; compare Num 18:21-32), economic practices associated with the seventh year (15:1-18; compare Exod 23:10-11; Lev 25:1-7), observance of three annual pilgrimages (Deut 16:1-17; compare Exod 23:14-19; Lev 23; Num 28–29), and a ritual to purge the guilt associated with

innocent blood (a body is found, 21:1-9; compare Num 19). The Deuteronomic Code also addresses social relations. The writers/redactors of the Deuteronomic Code and the Priestly traditions did not view the cult and the practice of just social relations as entirely separate matters; the two are interwoven.

C. The Priestly Traditions

1. Date

The date of the composition of the Priestly cultic traditions remains a disputed issue. Particularly problematic is the failure to achieve a consensus on methodological procedures, the determination of what is used as evidence, and the ways in which such evidence is evaluated. In addition, clear procedures for determining the difference between the time in which a specific cultic act was practiced and the time at which it was included in a written document remains problematic. Efforts to date the Priestly cultic material generally employ the following reference points: the monarchy (ca. 1000–586 BCE; Temple, ca. 922–586 BCE), the Babylonian exile (ca. 586–538 BCE) and return (ca. 538 and after), and the construction of the Second Temple (ca. 520–515 BCE). Since the last quarter of the 19th cent., the writing or redaction of the Priestly traditions was commonly, although not unanimously, located in the exilic or postexilic periods. In recent years, several Jewish scholars have advanced critical arguments for earlier dates of significant portions of the Priestly traditions (e.g., Kaufmann, Milgrom, Knohl). A fairly common view in relation to the Priestly traditions is the recognition that some of the traditions include early material and that the final form of the Priestly traditions reflects a lengthy process of composition and redaction.

The failure to achieve a consensus concerning the date of these traditions creates significant problems for those who employ a critical and historical method and argue that the temporal location of texts is critical for understanding. If, however, the priestly cult was conservative and not open to change, the date of the Priestly traditions might not be as important as generally thought because cultic traditions and practices would have changed little over time. Even if, however, changes have taken place, the interpreter's ability to track these changes remains problematic at best. Recently, in part because of the problems associated with the date of Priestly traditions, attention has focused more on the texts as texts (Gerstenberger; Watts). Two critical questions must be addressed by historical and literary (or some combination of the two) analysis. First, do the depictions of rituals in Priestly traditions provide clear and unobstructed views of rituals as the Israelites concretely enacted them? Second, is critical analysis focused on actual ritual practices or reading practices associated with the literary and textual structures of the texts?

2. The literary and theological context

The Priestly cultic traditions constitute a significant part of Yahweh's instructions to Israel at Mount Sinai (the majority of Exod 24:15–Num 10:10), although the Priestly traditions recognized the observance of SABBATH (Gen 2:1-3), circumcision (e.g., Gen 17:23-27; 21:4), and Passover (Exod 12). Prior to Sinai, Yahweh first provided instructions for sacrifice at Sinai (see PASSOVER AND FEAST OF UNLEAVENED BREAD). The TABERNACLE, the dwelling place of Yahweh, is central to the thinking and theology of the Priestly traditions. Yahweh instructs Moses to collect a gift (terumah) from the Israelites so they may build the tabernacle for Yahweh and Yahweh might dwell in their midst (Exod 25:1-9). Three additional texts emphasize the tabernacle as the dwelling place of Yahweh. First, following the instructions for the daily sacrifices (29:38-42a), Yahweh makes a series of promises concerning the tent: I will meet with you there, I will speak with you there, and I will sanctify it with my glory. I will consecrate the tent and altar and I will consecrate Aaron and his sons to serve as priests. I will dwell in Israel's midst and I will be their God, the one who brought them out of Egypt (Exod 29:42-46). Divine dwelling place, cultic site, and Yahweh's history with Israel are closely interwoven. Second, following the construction of the tabernacle, all of the Israelites see the divine glory fill the tabernacle (Exod 40:34-38). Third, after Aaron presents the sacrifices and offerings for the first time, again, all the people see the glory of Yahweh; fire comes from the tent and consumes the sacrificial offerings on the ALTAR (Lev 9:22-24). The divine fire ignites the altar fire, an indication of divine approval of the tabernacle cult.

D. The Sacrifices and Offerings: Introduction

The Priestly traditions contain three types of sacrificial texts. The first type provides instructions for the five basic types of sacrificial offerings (Lev 1–7) The second identifies lengthier and more complex ritual processes: e.g., the consecration of Aaron and his sons (Lev 8–9), the restoration ritual for one recovered from an unclean skin condition (Lev 13), and the Day of Purification (Lev 16; traditionally the DAY OF ATONEMENT). The third specifies the sacrifices and offerings ordered by Yahweh for the annual observances (e.g., Lev 23; Num 28–29).

1. Introduction: Leviticus 1–7

Leviticus 1–7 contains two separate lists concerning the sacrificial offerings: chaps. 1–5 and chaps. 6–7 (Watts). The instructions are bracketed by an introduction reporting that Yahweh spoke to Moses from the tent (Lev 1:1-2) and a summary statement reporting that Yahweh spoke from Sinai (Lev 7:37-38). The order of the first list is burnt offering, grain offering, well-being offering, sin (purification) offering, and guilt (reparation) offering. The second list follows a different order: instructions for cleaning the altar of burnt offerings, the

grain offering, the special grain offering that Aaron is to offer at the time of his anointing, the sin (purification) offering, the guilt (reparation) offering, and the well-being offering. The first list consists of four Yahweh speeches (1:1; 4:1; 5:14; 6:1), the second of five (6:8, 19, 24; 7:22, 28). A common view suggests that the first list is directed primarily to the people, whereas the second primarily to the priests. Although the second list directs three of the speeches to Aaron and his sons, the final two are addressed to the people. These chapters, however, are not an instructional handbook for the priests; rather, they provide instructions for the people concerning sacrificial offerings.

These five basic types of sacrifices share several common features. First, legitimate sacrifices must be presented at the entrance to the tent of meeting. Second, their enactment reflects a common structure (grain offerings vary somewhat in that they do not include blood manipulation): the one offering the sacrifice brings the animal to the sanctuary, performs the hand-laying act, then slaughters and butchers the animal. The priest puts the blood on the altar, burns the specified animal parts, and disposes of the remains when necessary. Third, acceptable sacrificial animals must be domestic animals, owned by the offerer, and be without physical defect.

Leviticus 1–5 identifies two basic types of sacrificial offerings: voluntary sacrifices (chaps. 1–3) and required expiatory sacrifices (chaps. 4–5). A single Yahweh speech provides instructions for the burnt offering, the grain offering, and the well-being offering (chaps. 1–3). All three are "fire offerings" (or "food offerings") that provide "a pleasing odor" (or "a pleasing fragrance") "for Yahweh" (see 1:9, 13, 17; 2:2, 9, 11, 16 [partial]; 3:5, 11, 16). They identify what to sacrifice and how to sacrifice (i.e., when/if a person brings ... then ...), but not why one makes the sacrifice.

The order of chaps. 1–3 reflects, intentionally or not, the party or parties who consume portions of the sacrifices. The "whole" burnt offering is burned entirely on the altar (the presiding priest receives the hide, 7:8) and belongs to Yahweh. The priest burns a portion of the grain offering on the altar for Yahweh and retains the remainder for himself. Yahweh, the priest, and the offerer all receive a portion of the well-being sacrifice. The order then moves from Yahweh alone, to Yahweh and the priest, to Yahweh, the priest, and the offerer (possibly a reflection of the structure of sacred space in the tabernacle).

Chapters 4:1–6:7 discuss the purification and reparation offerings in three Yahweh speeches: 4:1–5:13 (the sin [purification] offering), and 5:14-19 and 6:1-7 (the guilt [reparation] sacrifice). These are the primary "expiatory" sacrifices and the instructions identify the actions that require their presentation.

2. Voluntary sacrifices: Leviticus 1–3

a. The burnt offering: Leviticus 1. The burnt offering ('olah) is related to the Hebrew verb "to ascend," a reference to the ascending smoke of the sacrifice. The Hiphil sometimes refers specifically to the presentation of a burnt offering (see, e.g., Gen 22:13; Exod 24:5; 32:6; Num 23:2, 4; Deut 12:12, 13). The sacrificial animal must be a male from the herd (Lev 1:3-9), a male from the flock (1:10-13), or birds (turtledoves or pigeons; 1:14-17). The whole animal is burned (see Lev 7:8) and provides a "pleasing odor" ("soothing aroma" or "a pleasant fragrance") for Yahweh. The instructions provide no reasons for why one might offer this sacrifice. The writers may have assumed this information would already be known or they may not have considered this information important for the purposes of this text. Or, the absence may reflect that the burnt offering was considered something of an all-purpose sacrifice (see Lev 22:17-18).

Israel offered burnt offerings very early in its history (see, e.g., Gen 22:2, 7, 8, 13; Exod 10:25; Num 23:15; Judg 6:26; 1 Sam 7:9; 1 Kgs 18:38; 2 Kgs 3:27; 10:24; Job 1:4; 42:8). Milgrom notes the same was true in Canaan, Phoenicia, Anatolia, and Greece (1990). It was offered in conjunction with petition or entreaty (1 Sam 13:12; 2 Sam 24:21-25; Judg 20:26), although Milgrom (1990) suggests that it reflects a wide range of human emotions. If true, it provided a means for ritually concretizing the range of those emotions.

Leviticus 1:4 indicates that the burnt offering was able to accomplish "expiation" (NRSV, "atonement," kipper כִּפֶּר), although this is not typical in the Priestly traditions (but see Levine; Milgrom; Gane). Burnt offerings are generally offered as one in a series of sacrifices in lengthier and more complex ritual processes (e.g., Lev 9:7; 14:20; 16:24) or in conjunction with grain and libation offerings at the divinely mandated annual observances (e.g., Lev 23:12, 18; throughout Num 28–29; note also the morning and evening sacrifices in Exod 28:38-42a; Num 28:3-8). Leviticus 1:4 may reflect a time prior to the priestly incorporation of the sin and reparation offerings as the primary expiatory sacrifices, although it may reflect a different view of expiation than that associated with the sin and reparation offerings. The story of David's census of the people and Yahweh's angry response may provide an example (2 Sam 24). When Yahweh sets a plague on the community, David builds an altar, offers burnt and well-being offerings, and petitions Yahweh to stop the plague (see vv. 18-25). Yahweh responds favorably to David's petition and stops the plague. Although kipper is not used in this text, the notion that the burnt offering turns back the wrath of Yahweh is clearly present. In Num 16–17 the burning of incense plays a similar role. Following the rebellion by and execution of Korah and his cohorts, the people gather against Moses and Aaron and complain about the death of the rebels. Yahweh's wrath moves against the community and unleashes a plague. Moses instructs Aaron to burn incense in his censer and make expiation (kipper) for the people. Aaron takes the smoking censer and stops the plague and, certainly implied, "soothes" the wrath of Yahweh.

These texts demonstrate that the "ascending smoke" of sacrifices and incense turns back or soothe the wrath of Yahweh. Contemporary theological views might consider the notions of divine wrath and "the soothing of Yahweh" to be "ancient" or "primitive," and too anthropomorphic to be used in relation to a contemporary view of God that is thought to be unchanging and unchangeable. Caution must be used in any effort that seeks to impose contemporary theological perspectives and values on ancient texts. The interpreter must maintain a critical distance between the past and the present. The priests report that Yahweh dwelt in a tent in the midst of the community in the wilderness, journeyed with the people, participated in daily meals and sacrificial offerings, and at times was driven to wrath by the people. These statements reflect the views they have passed along in the texts.

b. The grain offering: Leviticus 2. The basic meaning of minkhah is "gift." In non-Priestly traditions, the word refers primarily to political gifts given to demonstrate the power and status of one person in relation to another or to reflect the relationship between two parties (see Milgrom 1990). For example, as Jacob prepares to return to Canaan, he sends "gifts" to Esau in an effort to insure that his brother will welcome him back to the land (Gen 32:3-21). Political expectations associated with the "gifts" allow Ehud to gain access to Eglon and assassinate him (Judg 3:15-22). Several men refuse to give a "gift" to Saul because they view him with contempt rather than respect and honor (1 Sam 10:27). When chased by Saul, David suggests that a "gift" be offered in order "to appease" ("to view favorably") Yahweh (1 Sam 26:17-20). Berodach-baladan of Babylon sends a gift (minkhah) to a sick Hezekiah, an expression of political friendship and concern (2 Kgs 20:12). The Priestly traditions narrows the meaning of "political gift" to "the grain offering" (Anderson).

Leviticus 2 identifies three different types of grain offerings: 1) uncooked flour (wheat), with oil and frankincense added (2:1-3), 2) unleavened dough (without frankincense) cooked either in an oven, on a griddle, or in a pan (2:4-10), and 3) the first ripened grain (both wheat, Num 28:26, and barley, 2 Kgs 4:42, are possible, but the structure of the text suggests the latter; Milgrom). The basic ritual reflects the following structure: the offerer prepares the offering at home and brings it to the priest who turns a representative portion into smoke on the altar. The offering, a food offering, provides a pleasing aroma for Yahweh (Lev 2: 2, 9).

Leviticus 6:14-18 provide additional details concerning the grain offerings. They are most holy and must be eaten in a holy place (v. 16, in the court of the tent). Aaron must present a morning and evening grain offering on the day of the priestly consecration (Lev 6:19-23), perpetual offerings to Yahweh associated with the morning and evening burnt offerings (see Exod 29:38-42a).

In the Priestly traditions, almost three-fourths of the uses of **minkhah** are found in instructional texts (Lev 2: 6-7), formulaic statements specifying the contributions of the tribes to the tabernacle (Num 7), and texts specifying the sacrifices presented at the mandated annual observances (Lev 23; Num 28–29). Numbers 28–29 identify the following grain offerings to be presented on select days of observance: the daily morning and evening burnt offerings, along with the appropriate meal offering and libation (Num 28:3-8); additional morning and evening offerings (burnt, grain, and libation) presented on the Sabbath (28:9-10); special burnt offerings, including grain offerings and libations, on new moons (28:11-15); additional sacrifices and offerings during the Festival of Weeks in conjunction with an offering of new grain (28:26-31).

Three ritual processes, not mentioned above, require grain offerings: the ritual consecration and ordination of the priests (Lev 8), the ritual demanded by a jealous husband (Num 5), and the ritual for the completion of the Nazirite's vow (Num 6). In the priestly ordination ritual, unleavened bread is offered along with the ram of ordination and the burnt offering (Lev 8:22-29). The ritual of a jealous husband requires a "grain offering of jealousy" (Num 5:15) made of barley flour without oil or frankincense. The ritual process for the completion of the Nazirite vow includes a burnt offering, a sin offering, an offering of well-being, a basket of unleavened cakes with oil, unleavened wafers with oil, and additional grain offerings and libations (Num 6:13-15).

Although the grain offering is sometimes viewed as a cheaper form of the burnt offering (Milgrom), this view has several problems. For example, the priest only burns a portion of the grain offering and in many cases a grain offering is offered in conjunction with a burnt offering. The text nowhere indicates that the grain offering is a cheaper form of the burnt offering. Often the grain offering is part of a meal for Yahweh that includes a burnt offering and a libation. The possibility must remain open that some groups in Israel viewed it as a cheaper form of the burnt offering, but this does not account for all of its uses.

c. The well-being offering: Leviticus 3. In the Priestly traditions "the well-being offering" translates zevakh shelamim. Zevakh means "slaughter" (compare mizbeakh [מִזְבֵּחַ], "altar"). Proposals for the meaning of shelamim are numerous: peace offering, fellowship offering, communion sacrifice, a covenant sacrifice, a well-being offering, a gift of greeting, or a legitimate sacrifice. The majority of these views stress that zevakh is an act of sacrificial slaughter, whereas shelamim is understood in terms of its function. The renderings often reflect the interpreter's theological perspectives and commitments and seek a single (limiting) meaning for the sacrifice. The search for a single "functional" meaning will fail to do justice to the complex history of the sacrifice.

The two words were initially separate, but when they were combined and the reasons for their combination remain uncertain. Leviticus 17:5 distinguishes sacrifices offered in the open field (sacrifices) and those that are brought to the entrance of the tent (sacrifices of well-being), although the distinction may reflect the rhetorical concerns of this specific text to distinguish illegitimate from legitimate sacrifices. Several different types of "sacrifices" are identified in the texts: thanksgiving offering (e.g., Lev 7:12; 22:29 [H]; Pss 107:22; 116:17), annual offering (e.g., 1 Sam 1:21; 2:19), clan offering (e.g., 1 Sam 20:29), Passover offering (Exod 12:27; 23:18; 34:25). "Sacrifice" is also used in conjunction with "burnt offering" in various combinations in what are considered early traditions: e.g., Exod 10:25; 18:12; Lev 17:8; Num 15:8; Deut 12:6; 1 Sam 15:22; Jer 7:22; Hos 6:6. This combination may reflect the presentation of a sacrifice burned in its entirety and a sacrifice that provides food.

The texts use three different variations of "the sacrifice of well-being," e.g., Solomon offers "sacrifices" at the dedication of the Temple (1 Kgs 8:62; but compare the sacrifice of well-being in v. 63 and "well-being" in v. 64), "well-being," e.g., the army presents burnt offerings and "sacrifices of well-being" in preparation for war (Judg 20:26; 21:4), and Solomon is said to offer "sacrifices of well-being" three times a year (1 Kgs 9:25), and "offerings of well-being," e.g., the people at Mount Sinai (Exod 24:5; see also Josh 22:23; 1 Sam 10:8, 11:15; 2 Sam 6:17-18; 1 Kgs 8:63). Many of these texts associate well-being sacrifices with critical moments in Israel's history: the covenant at Sinai (Exod 24:5), the installation of Saul as king (1 Sam 11:15), the bringing of the ark to Jerusalem (2 Sam 6:17-18), and the dedication of Solomon's Temple (1 Kgs 8:64). In these cases, the sacrifices are community and/or royal rituals.

The Priestly traditions refers to sacrifice in the same three ways: sacrifice (Lev 17:5, 7, 8; 19:6; 23:37 [H]; Num 15:3, 5, 8), well-being offering (Lev 6:5 (12); 7:14, 33; Num 6:14; 15:8), and sacrifices of well-being (Lev 3:1, 3, 6; Lev 7:21; 17:5 [H]). The instructions in Lev 3 employ the combined form (vv. 1, 3, 6, 9) and indicate that the offering may be a male or female from the herd or a male or female from the flock (no birds are included). Leviticus 7:11-36 provide additional details concerning the presentation and consumption of this offering. Yahweh, the priests, and the one making the offering (along with family and friends) all receive a specified portion. Leviticus 7:11-18 identifies three types of well-being sacrifices: thanksgiving, votive, and freewill. A specific type of situation or experience gives rise to the presentation of these sacrifices; the experiences are enacted in, by, and through the ritual process.

3. Required expiatory sacrifices: Leviticus 4:1–6:7

a. The purification offering: Leviticus 4:1–5:13. "Sin offering" translates khatta'th. The sacrifice is offered in contexts that include sin, but also in contexts that are concerned with ritual impurity (e.g., Lev 12:6-8; 14:19; 15:30). Comparative evidence suggests that "cleansing" or "purging" best state the purpose of this sacrifice. Thus, as Milgrom (1990) has convincingly argued, a translation of "purification sacrifice" is preferred to the traditional "sin offering." Both sinful actions and ritual impurity (see Lev 11–15 for the purity instructions) generate impurity that is attracted to the tent, the dwelling place of Yahweh (Klawans 2006). Milgrom (1990) argues such impurity must be ritually cleansed to maintain the purity of Yahweh's dwelling place. Blood from purification sacrifices is placed on objects, e.g., the tent, the altar, to cleanse them of impurity. At the same time, the person is "forgiven," not for committing the sin, but for generating the impurity. Milgrom's argument constitutes one of the primary contributions to the study of the Priestly traditions in recent years, although questions continue to be raised. A particular concern is the exclusion of the offender and the offender's sin from the effects of the sacrificial process. Would not the sinful act that gives rise to the impurity be as "offensive" and "problematic" as the impurity?

Leviticus 4:1–5:13, a single Yahweh speech, contains two series of statements that identify offenses requiring a purification offering. Leviticus 4:1-35 does this in a general way: "If anyone ... sins unintentionally (bisheghaghah בִּשְׁגָגָה) in doing any one of the things that by the LORD's commandments ought not to be done, and incurs guilt" (vv. 13, 22, 27; the statement does not appear in the case of the high priest). Leviticus 5:1-6 identifies four specific cases that require a purification offering (see below). Numbers 15:22-29 provides another general statement: "If you unintentionally fail to observe all these commandments that the LORD has spoken to Moses" (v. 22). The question of intention obviously plays a significant role in all of these rulings (compare Num 15:29-31 for "high-handed" sin).

b. The purification ritual for sin. The presentation of a purification offering takes place in a larger context. A three-part process is involved: the identification and recognition of the offense, the determination of the proper form of the purification offering, and a statement declaring the positive outcome of the sacrificial process (the ritual enactment).

As noted, Lev 4 is concerned with the unintentional commission of a prohibited act. A central question concerns the nature of "guilt" ('asham) and its relation to the offense (Milgrom 1976; Kiuchi). Four basic positions have been proposed: 1) to incur guilt (juridical in nature); 2) to feel guilt (psychological in nature); 3) to realize guilt (cognitive in nature); 4) to suffer guilt's consequences (experiential in nature). Interpreters generally look for a single explanation that accounts for every

case, although such all-inclusive, systemic consistency is not necessarily operative in the Priestly traditions. Equally problematic is the psychological, cognitive, or experiential analysis of "the guilt" of ancient people based on ancient texts. The fact that the "guilt" in these cases is addressed through a sacrifice indicates a significant difference between their sense of guilt and that of the contemporary interpreter. The precise meanings of words such as "recognize," "know," "realize," or "feel" and the experiences to which they refer are not necessarily equivalent to contemporary understandings or experiences.

The following discussion will demonstrate some of these difficulties. Leviticus 4 addresses the relationship between a sinful act and the guilt associated with it. The anointed priest has sinned and brought guilt on the people; he must offer a bull for a purification offering (4:3). If the whole community has erred and the matter has escaped its notice (has been concealed from the eyes of the community), the community is guilty. When it comes to know (or recognize) its sin, the community must offer a bull (4:13-14). The final two cases address a chief and a common person: if a person sins and realizes (recognizes) the guilt, or the sin becomes known to the person, then the chieftain must offer a male goat and the common person a female goat (4:22-23, 27-28). Numbers 15 requires that the congregation offer a male goat for a purification offering and a bull for a burnt offering, whereas an individual is to offer a female goat (vv. 24, 27; Anderson discusses textual issues).

Leviticus 5:1-13 is often referred to as "the graduated khatta'th" because it takes into consideration the different economic abilities of the Israelites: a female sheep or goat (5:6), two turtledoves or two pigeons (5:7), or a tenth of an ephah of fine flour without oil or frankincense (v. 11). The instructions identify four specific situations that require this sacrifice. First, a person hears a legal call to testify, has relevant information, but does not do so. The offender must bear the guilt associated with the refusal to act (v. 1). Second, a person touches something unclean, the text specifies animal carcasses, but is unaware of the nature of the act (the matter is hidden). That person is "unclean, and ... guilty" (v. 2). Third, a person becomes unclean through contact with human uncleanness (see Lev 11–15), is unaware (of the action or the defiling nature of the action), but then comes to know it and recognizes the guilt associated with it (v. 3). Fourth, a person utters an oath and is unaware of or has forgotten it. The person realizes the failure and is guilty (v. 4). One problem is the difficulty of identifying a single category that encompasses all four cases. In addition, these four cases are not as clearly inadvertent (as required in Lev 4).

Milgrom (1990) seeks to understand these cases in terms of a failure to enact a purification process in a timely fashion. He also argues that "confession" (see v. 5) reduces these cases to inadvertencies that may be addressed by a purification sacrifice as detailed in Lev 4.

His explanations are guided by a desire to demonstrate that all of the Priestly rulings are consistent parts of a larger symbolic system (or a single and consistent system of meaning). Leviticus 5:1-13 may reflect a separate tradition concerning the purification offering, distinct from other Priestly rulings.

Leviticus 4 provides instructions for two forms of the purification offering. If the sacrifice is presented on behalf of the priest or community, the officiating priest takes its blood from the purification sacrifice inside the tent, sprinkles it seven times toward the curtain, places some on the horns of the incense altar, and pours the remainder at the base of the outer altar (vv. 5-7, 16-18). If the sacrifice is presented on behalf of a chieftain or common person, the priest remains outside the tent and puts blood on the horns of the outer altar and pours the remainder at its base (vv. 25, 30). Milgrom (1990) has argued that these rituals correlate social status and sacred space. The high priest and community generate impurity that enters into the tent; the chieftain and the commoner generate impurity that only reaches the outer altar. On the annual day of purification (Lev 16), Aaron takes blood from the purification sacrifices, one presented for himself and his family and one for the people, into the holy of holies, the room that houses the ark. The sins addressed on this day have generated impurity strong enough to enter into the most holy place. He sprinkles some of the blood above the ark and in front of the ark. The text is clear: he does this to purge the holy place from the impurities of the people, because of their transgressions and sins (Lev 16:16; compare v. 21). The precise relationship of the "situational" purification sacrifices offered throughout the year and those offered on the annual day of purification remains unclear (Gammie).

Leviticus 4 states that the purification offerings accomplish two things (the case of the high priest is the exception): purification (**kipper**) and forgiveness (salakh סָלַח). The enactment of the ritual by the priest results in "expiation" (the possibility remains that the ritual may address more than just purification). Many view such "automatic" results to be characteristic of "pagan" rituals (i.e., they employ magic), but not of the Priestly traditions. The texts, however, emphasize the enactment of the ritual and the results, not influences or agents outside the ritual itself (Staal; Bell; Gilders). The second outcome is forgiveness. Milgrom (1990) argues that the forgiveness is directed at the person's generation of impurity, not to the initial sinful act. Leviticus 4, however, states clearly that it is the sinful person who brings the purification sacrifice that is forgiven, but says nothing about forgiveness for causing impurity. If Milgrom is correct, then the priests were more concerned about the impurity generated by sin than the sin itself. The combination of sacrificial slaughter, blood manipulation by the priest, and ritual enactment may accomplish a broad range of results that address sin,

impurity, the offender, and the sacred place (*see* HOLY, HOLINESS, OT).

c. The reparation offering: Leviticus 5:14–6:7. The traditional translation of ʾasham is "guilt offering," but its purpose is to address trespass (maʿal מַעַל) against Yahweh and this requires making reparation. Thus, "reparation offering" is a better translation. The introductory statement reads: "when any of you commit a trespass and sin unintentionally" (Lev 5:15). The Hebrew "trespass" refers to a breaking of faith with a partner in a relationship, in this case, Yahweh. The sin in this case is a misuse or misappropriation of something that belongs to the realm of the holy, e.g., most holy sacrificial remains, animals dedicated to Yahweh, accoutrements of the tabernacle. Leviticus 5:14–6:7 contains two Yahweh speeches. The first speech identifies two cases (5:14-19; see vv. 15-16, 17-19), and the second identifies four ways in which breaking faith with another person through deceit is at the same time breaking faith with Yahweh (6:1-7). Leviticus 7:7-10 gives the instructions for the enactment of the ritual.

The first case (Lev 5:15-16) is concerned with "unknown" trespass on the sacred things of Yahweh. When a person trespasses unintentionally (compare the purification sacrifice in Lev 4) and then comes to realize the trespass, that person must bring a ram for a reparation sacrifice and make full restitution plus an additional twenty percent of the value of that which was misappropriated. The ram must be converted into a monetary payment (the lamb's value is set by the priest and the offender either purchases it from the sanctuary or brings a lamb that is of that value). Like the case of the purification offering, the reparation offering accomplishes expiation (**kipper**) and the offender is forgiven. The critical difference between this case and the purification sacrifice is that this case focuses on "breaking faith."

The second case (5:17-19) is difficult to distinguish from a purification offering: "If any of you sin without knowing it, doing any of the things that by the LORD's commandments ought not to be done" (5:17). The primary difference is in this text's emphasis on the offender "not knowing" that the offense was committed. The offender did the act without knowing it was done, and now begins to suspect that guilt has been incurred and a sacrifice is required. Twice the text states the offender did not know the offense was done (vv. 17, 18) thereby suggesting that this is addressing a suspected trespass (Levine 1989; Milgrom 1990).

The second speech (6:1-7) begins with a general statement: "When any of you sin and commit a trespass against the LORD" and completes the sentence by identifying four types of deceit against another person. The text is clear on one point: deceit of another person constitutes trespass against Yahweh. The offender has deceived another person concerning a pledge or deposit, robbed another person, committed fraud against another person, or found something someone lost and then lied about it. The key is that the person swears falsely concerning these actions. This invokes the sacred realm and implicates Yahweh: it is a misappropriation of the divine name. These cases require restitution plus an additional twenty percent to the person who was wronged and the sacrifice of a ram as a reparation offering or its monetary equivalent. These rulings are concerned that things are set right in relation to the parties that were wronged. Thus, restitution is primary, not punishment.

E. Rituals with Multiple Sacrifices and Offerings

1. Introduction

In Priestly traditions several complex rituals require multiple sacrificial offerings: the consecration of Aaron and his sons (Lev 8–9), the restoration ritual for one recovered from an unclean skin condition (Lev 13), the Day of Purification (Lev 16; traditionally the Day of Atonement), the yearly sacrifices and offerings identified in festival calendars (Lev 23; compare Num 28–29), the ritual demanded by a jealous husband to determine if his wife has been unfaithful (Num 5:11-31), the ritual required if a Nazirite becomes unclean and the ritual for the completion of the Nazirite vow (Num 6:1-21), the installation of the Levites (Num 8:5-22), and the red cow used to purify corpse contamination (Num 19).

These texts clearly state the reasons for the enactment of the ritual. For example, the ritual that consecrates Aaron and his sons is designed to do just that. The ritual to restore a person recovered from an unclean skin condition restores that person to community life. The critical question, however, is not "what" they accomplish, but "how" they accomplish it (Gruenwald; Gilders). Does each separate element of the ritual, e.g., sacrifices, washings, movement between locations, contribute to a specific "outcome" so that the enactment of all the elements in the correct order accomplishes the purposes of the ritual? In this case, the enactment is the key to accomplishment (Smith; Staal; Bell). Or, do the various elements provide specific meanings so that a message is stated in, by, and through the enactment ritual (Douglas; Milgrom)? In this case, determining the "meaning" of the rituals is central to the interpretive process. A final question asks if the instructions in Lev 1–7 are to be used in efforts to understand the lengthier rituals and, in a related fashion, if these lengthier rituals should be used to interpret each other. When the latter two questions guide interpretation, they often include an operating assumption that the Priestly traditions contains a completely consistent symbolic system of meaning.

2. Leviticus 14: analysis

Brief analysis of Lev 14:1-20 will highlight some of the critical elements and interpretive practices employed in contemporary study of Israelite ritual (Gilders; Klingbeil). Often unstated, but essential to interpretation, is the way or ways in which the interpreter understands the nature of ritual. This problem is made more difficult when the concern is a text that depicts a ritual.

Is the interpretation of rituals a hermeneutical search for "meaning" or an effort to understand how the enactment in and of itself accomplishes the purpose for the ritual's enactment (i.e., is it inherently effective)? In addition, the interpreter must be clear on whether interpretation is focused on a ritual or a text that depicts a ritual. This does not, of course, eliminate the possibility that the ritual actions communicate a message; or that (symbolic) "ritual meaning" necessarily excludes the possibility that enactment is itself "meaningful" in terms of outcomes.

Leviticus 14:1-20 depicts an eight-day ritual (temporal category; compare Lev 8–9) that restores a person previously defiled by an unclean skin condition and outside the camp, to community life (locative and spatial categories). On day one (ritual process), the officiating priest has a bird slaughtered over running ("living") water in an earthen container. The text does not identify the slaughter of the bird as a sacrifice in that it takes place outside the camp without access to the altar. The priest takes cedarwood, red yarn, and hyssop (ritual materials) along with a living bird and dips them in the blood of the slaughtered bird (ritual actions), sprinkles the blood seven times on the one being cleansed (manipulation of blood), pronounces him clean (declarative language), and releases the live bird into the open field (ritual gesture; compare the release of the goat on the day of purification, Lev 16). The one being cleansed launders his clothes, shaves his head, beard, and eyebrows (the language reflects the shaving of the beard, although, one assumes, an adapted procedure would have been available to women), bathes, then returns to the camp for a seven-day period of waiting outside his tent. On the seventh day the person again shaves, launders, and bathes (see CLEAN AND UNCLEAN).

On the eighth day the priest gathers the necessary materials for the completion of the ritual and takes them to the entrance of the tent along with the one being cleansed (v. 11; temporal, material, locative). The priest dedicates, through an elevation gesture, a male lamb, to be offered as a guilt offering, and a LOG of oil. After the lamb is slaughtered, the priest puts some of its blood on the right ear, thumb, and big toe of the one being cleansed (compare Lev 8:22-24, the ordination of the priests) and takes the oil, sprinkles it seven times before Yahweh, and puts it on top of the blood already placed on the person's ear, thumb, and toe. The remainder of the oil is poured on the head of the person being cleansed. Following the pouring of the oil, the text states, "And the priest shall accomplish expiation (kipper) on the person's behalf" (v. 18, author's translation; NRSV: "Then the priest shall make atonement on his behalf"). The "and" is generally translated "Then" (suggesting that the following sacrificial acts accomplish the expiation [NRSV]), or "Thus" (suggesting that the preceding acts accomplished expiation [JPS Tanakh]). The priest concludes the ritual with a purification offering, "to expiate," as well as a burnt offering and a grain offering, "to expiate" (vv. 19-20, author's translation; NRSV: "to make atonement").

The text clearly understands this ritual as a cleansing ritual (14:4, 7, 8, 9, 11, 14, 17, 18, 19, 20), a rite of passage that restores the person to community life (a ritual of restoration; Gorman 1991). The relationship of cleansing and expiation in this ritual suggests the purpose of the ritual must be understood in terms of "expiatory purification." The text declares the person clean several times (vv. 8, 9, 20). Cleansing the individual is primary, and the blood of the bird placed on the individual's extremities may function as an agent of purification. The "purification" of the person does not necessarily exclude the "purification." The requirement of a reparation offering is often explained as a response to the possibility that the person has committed a trespass against God, the "skin condition" suggesting divine punishment. This does not explain, however, why its blood is placed on the person's extremities, a clear departure from the typical guilt offering (see Lev 5:14–6:7), and why such blood manipulation also takes place in the ritual of ordination and consecration of the priests.

3. Symbolic interpretation and enactment analysis

The text identifies several key elements of the ritual: e.g., temporal categories, locative and spatial categories, distinct gestures, and multiple ways of manipulating animal blood (Grimes; Bell). Symbolic interpretation seeks to understand ritual as an act of communication and asks how each element of the ritual contributes to the message of the ritual. For example, the ritual discussed above communicates that life overcomes death as the person moves from a place outside of the camp (symbolic death) to a place within the community (symbolic life) and, thus, communicates a message of hope (Milgrom). The freed bird symbolically carries away the "impurity" of the person being purified, the blood of the slaughtered bird linking the person and the bird. The shaving, laundering, and bathing (the cleaning of the body) are symbolic of ritual purification (the cleansing of the impurity; see Olyan). The blood of the reparation offering and the oil placed on the person's extremities symbolize the "death," the symbolic status of impurity outside the camp, and the "life," the symbolic status of restoration in the community. If symbolic meaning is arbitrarily constructed, and if it is only "symbolically" effective (often used to mean, "if it is believed to enact 'real' changes"), the question of enactment becomes pressing: why enact the message when one is able to state it using words?

In recent years attention has begun to shift from the hermeneutical search for meaning to the analysis of enactment in and of itself. This view answers the questions, "Why ritual?" and "Why this specific form of ritual?" with a simple statement: this is the way Yahweh commanded it to be done. To do it otherwise is to disobey Yahweh. Further, failure to enact the ritual in the prescribed way will ensure that the ritual will fail to accomplish its intended purpose.

F. The Prophets and the Temple Cult

Priestly ritual and prophetic justice are often viewed in dichotomous terms. History indicates that Protestant Christianity has been particularly guilty of this, especially in its theological discourse (Klawans 2006). In this case, interpretation may reveal more about the interpreter than the text. The rituals of the priests, this view argues, reflect religious practices based on forms and rules rather than spirit and heart. The dichotomy of exterior practices and inner states has a long history in Christianity, even among those forms that take ritual seriously (Bell). That this distinction was operative among ancient Israelites is doubtful. A very important contribution of ritual studies to the study of the Priestly traditions is the insistence that human existence and experience take place in and through the body and that ritual must be understood as a bodying forth or bodily enactment of human existence and experience (Gorman 1994).

A second set of problems arise from the all too common assumption that "a" single prophetic message existed to which all the prophets adhered, and that "a" single priestly viewpoint existed to which all priests adhered. Prophetic oracles are embedded in specific, concrete, and diverse social contexts and any effort to reduce them to a single message must be viewed as flawed. Prophetic critiques of the cult were spoken in concrete situations and addressed to a specific audience. The critical distance between a specific prophetic oracle and a concrete contemporary social concern is lost in the interpreter's search for contemporary relevance and practice. Recent work on the Priestly traditions demonstrates that these traditions also reflect multiple and diverse views (e.g., P and H; Milgrom 1990; Knohl). Is the contemporary reader to believe that the priests were against social justice because of their commitment to the Temple cult? Were the prophets against Temple worship because of their commitment to social justice?

Even a cursory reading of Leviticus makes clear that the priests were deeply concerned with the integrity of social relations. Leviticus 5 identifies several issues relating to social honesty and integrity; Lev 6 identifies deception, robbery, fraud, and swearing falsely, and indicates that such trespasses against other humans are also trespasses against Yahweh (vv. 1-7). The purification and reparation offerings address specific social relations. The Holiness Code pointedly addresses social issues, but not to the exclusion of cultic matters. Leviticus 17 provides instructions concerning the legitimate altar and acceptable sacrifice. Leviticus 19 emphasizes social issues: e.g., leave some of your harvest for the poor and the stranger (Lev 19:9-10); do not steal or deal deceitfully with each other (v. 11); do not defraud another person (v. 13); do not render an unfair decision and do not profit by the blood of another person (vv. 15-16); and always use an honest balance (v. 36).

The prophets did not relate to the Temple in a single way. Ezekiel, and probably Jeremiah, came from priestly families (Ezek 1:3; Jer 1:1). Isaiah was closely associated with the Temple (see, e.g., the priestly language in Isa 6:1-13). Moses, Samuel, and Elijah offered sacrifices, yet all three are remembered in prophetic terms. Joel (400–350 BCE, but uncertain) called for a cultic renewal that includes the sacrificial cult (e.g., 1:14; 2:1; 2:12-14). Haggai (520 BCE) and Zechariah (520–518 BCE) called for and supported the rebuilding of the Temple after the return from exile. Their primary concern is the failure of the people to compete the task.

The following are the primary passages thought to be of or antagonistic toward the Temple cult: 1 Sam 15:22-23; Isa 1:7-17; 29:13-14; Jer 6:16-21; 7:21-26; Hos 6:6; Amos 5:21-24; Mic 6:6-8 (compare Ps 40:6). Even if additional passages could be added to this list, the number of such oracles remains small in relation to the prophetic corpus. Criticism of the sacrificial cult is not a major theme in the prophets. Are these oracles primarily critiques of the Temple cult? Or do they employ criticisms of the cult as a rhetorical device to criticize the people?

Samuel's prophetic criticism of Saul focuses on Saul's failure to obey Yahweh (1 Sam 15:1-23). Yahweh told Saul to destroy everything of the Amalekites—man, woman, child, infant, ox, sheep, camel, and donkey—after defeating them. Saul and the people, however, spared the best animals and items of value, but destroyed what was despised and worthless (vv. 8-9). Samuel's oracle focuses on Saul's disobedience: "You have rejected the word of the LORD and he has also rejected you from being king" (v. 23). The "critique" of the cult (vv. 22-23) is more pointedly a critique of Saul. To say, "to obey is better than sacrifice," is not the same as saying, "to sacrifice is invalid." Saul's transgression is that he offered sacrifices contrary to Yahweh's instructions, not that he offered sacrifices.

Isaiah (late 8th cent. BCE) creates an image of the land as a waste (1:7-8) and the people laden with iniquity (v. 4) as the context for his critique of the cult (1:10-17). The oracle consists of three primary statements. In the first, Yahweh questions the purpose of sacrifices, incense, and offerings (vv. 10-13a), and in the second, Yahweh declares that Israel's assemblies have become a burden (vv. 13b-14). The turning point of the oracle is the declaration: "your hands are full of blood" (v. 15c). The dual reference is to the blood of sacrifices and the blood of violence. The people must stop doing evil, learn to do good, and practice justice (vv. 16-17). The oracle contrasts a cult that wearies Yahweh and the practice of justice. The bloody hands provide the transitional image. Isaiah exhorts the people to practice justice which is the primary concern of the oracle. Isaiah does not suggest that the Temple cult should be stopped and the Temple closed. The concrete social context of the

oracle (a reference to Jerusalem and Judah when saying, "hear ... you rulers of Sodom ... listen ... you people of Gomorrah"; v. 10) and the probability that Isaiah has employed a rhetorical device to "shock" the people into hearing the call for justice suggests the primary criticism is directed at the people. The cult has become a burden for Yahweh, but that does not necessarily mean that the cult must be destroyed.

Jeremiah's critique of the cult grows out of the people's refusal to obey Yahweh's instructions (Jer 7:8-20; late 7th cent. into early 6th cent. BCE) constructed in historical terms (7:21-26). Yahweh declares: I did not command your ancestors to offer sacrifices when I brought them out of Egypt. I commanded obedience ... yet they did not obey (vv. 22-24). The people of Judah have defiled the Temple by putting their "abominations" in it (7:30). Jeremiah emphasizes that the people are worshiping other gods and, because of that, are not properly observing the Temple cult nor obeying Yahweh. Again, the failure of the people to be obedient is central to the prophet's oracles. This view is supported in that the text does not return to a critique of the Temple cult.

Hosea (mid-8th cent. BCE) tells the people that Yahweh desires steadfast love, not sacrifice, knowledge of God, not burnt offerings (6:6). Amos (8th cent. BCE) announces that Yahweh loathes Israel's festivals, refuses to be appeased by their sacrifices, and pays no attention to their songs. Yahweh wants justice and righteousness (Amos 5:21-25; compare 5:14-15). The critique of the cult is consistently used as part of a rhetorical call for justice and righteousness. Is it also consistently used as a hyperbolic statement designed to highlight the people's failure to enact justice? Micah (late 8th and early 7th cent. BCE) asks what he is to present when he comes before Yahweh. The answer: do justice, love goodness, and walk humbly with God (Mic 6:6-8). In all three cases, the oracles are directed at the actions of the people, their disobedience. This would not, however, necessarily require the dissolution of the sacrificial cult.

The prophetic critique of the cult does not constitute a primary theme in the prophetic corpus. The rhetorical force of the oracles suggests that the people's failure to obey Yahweh is at the heart of the prophetic concern. The prophetic rhetoric is made "shocking" by the hyperbolic critiques of the Temple cult. This does not mean, of course, if given the choice the prophets would choose the cult over obedience to Yahweh. Of course, the priests would argue with just as much passion as the prophets that the sacrificial cult follows the directives of Yahweh and participation in it is a primary means of being obedient to Yahweh. Thus, the priests would make the same choice as the prophets: obedience to Yahweh. Neither the priests nor the prophets, however, present this as a valid, meaningful, or necessary choice. The sacrificial cult in no way necessarily prohibits the people from practicing justice, caring for the poor, or demonstrating concern for the oppressed.

G. The Exile and Second Temple

Babylon's defeat of Jerusalem and the destruction of the Temple brought an end to the regular Temple service. Evidence suggests that people left in the area of Jerusalem continued to offer sacrifices near the ruins of the Temple, especially grain offerings (Berquist; Milgrom 1990). Those taken into exile were faced with a critical problem: how do we worship Yahweh in a foreign land (Ps 137; Isa 40–55)? Although the evidence is limited, the exiles probably began to emphasize prayer as a form of ritualized practice (see Solomon's prayer in 1 Kgs 8:22-53, especially vv. 46-53). In addition, the gathering of Israelites, the reading of and reflection on Torah, and the observance of circumcision, SABBATH and Passover gained in significance in that they provided practices by which the Israelites could maintain their separation from the Babylonians, a separation that contributed to the survival of the people as a religious community (Boccaccini; Cohen; Hayes).

The Babylonian exile was a creative literary and theological time for Israel. Deutero-Isaiah (Isa 40–55) offered hope for a new exodus and return to the land. Ezekiel expressed a certainty that Yahweh had come to dwell with the exiles and he anticipated a future that included a new Temple (Ezek 1; 40–48). The general, but certainly not unanimous, view has located the composition of the Priestly texts in the exilic or post-exilic period. If correct, the priests created a document that emphasized a Priestly sacrificial cult when sacrificial practices were not possible. Why would the priests create such a document (and the "final" document would probably include the redacted Pentateuch) in the exile? Do their traditions address a hoped for future in which the Israelites are again in the land and the Temple is rebuilt? Are these texts designed to provide the necessary information for the enactment of the included rituals? Do these texts attempt to communicate information through the rituals as an effort by the priests to instruct the Israelites? Is it possible that the priests created a document designed for theological reflection when cultic enactment is not possible?

After Cyrus defeated Babylon, he allowed the exiles to return to their own land, if they so desired, and promised to help rebuild the Temple (538 BCE). Progress was slow and both Haggai and Zechariah exhorted the people to finish the project (completed in 515 BCE). Ezra and Nehemiah both played critical roles in Judah's reconstruction, although Ezra was primarily concerned with what he understood to be religious issues. Of particular importance, he staged a public reading of the law, an act that probably became a model for Judaism's regular reading and study of the law. The books of Chronicles indicate that the new Temple, i.e., the Second Temple, continued the practices of the First Temple, but added several new features, e.g., the Levites as singers and musicians and the twenty-four courses of priests who worked in the Temple.

The Jewish faith generated an explosion of creative thinking and writing between ca. 350 BCE and the Roman destruction of the Temple in 70 CE. Discussions concerning the Temple and the sacrificial cult generated a diverse range of perspectives and led to the emergence of diverse groups within Judaism. Hellenization posed problems for many, whereas others embraced it. With the success of the Maccabean rebellion (164 BCE) and the rise of the Hasmonean rule, the people of Judah experienced a period when secular power and religious authority were closely intertwined. The Sadducees, Pharisees, and Essenes came into being in this period and all three held specific, but often divergent, views of the Temple and its ritual practices. A number of the apocryphal books were written in the period between 200 BCE and 100 CE and introduced a number of new and different perspectives, stories, themes, and concerns into Jewish faith. These texts demonstrate that many Jewish writers were involved in a process of change and re-interpretation of the faith. This period also incorporated apocalyptic and eschatological views of history into Jewish faith and thinking. Finally, the Dead Sea Scrolls and the communities associated with them came into being during this period. The size and importance of the *Temple Scroll* indicates that the community was deeply concerned about the Temple, the Temple cult, and the possibility that the future would bring a renewal in Temple worship and practice (Boccaccini; Cohen; Hayes).

The Temple continued to offer an extended number of divinely required sacrifices and offerings. Commentary on the sacrificial offerings developed in conjunction with the study of Torah and the origins of the Mishnah (completed ca. 220 CE) begin to emerge in this period. An ongoing concern and topic for discussion was the status of the Gentiles in relation to Jewish practices and the Temple. In many ways, this discussion was a continuation of the purity and impurity rulings. A Temple tax was collected and paid by persons in and around Jerusalem as well as many in the Diaspora. The tax supported the cost of the regularly required sacrifices (e.g., the morning and evening sacrifices) and helped support the priests and Levites. A "pilgrimage" to Jerusalem became an important religious practice and was almost always undertaken at a time when the traveler would present sacrifices and offerings (*see* TEMPLE, JERUSALEM).

H. Christian Discourse

In terms of the Temple cult, the Jesus traditions are difficult to evaluate because of the many unanswered questions concerning the "historical" Jesus and the Jesus of the Gospels. After cleansing a man of "leprosy," Jesus tells him to go, show himself to the priest, and present his gift as Moses had commanded (Matt 8:1-4; Mark 1:40-45; Luke 5:12-16; compare Lev 13 and 14 for purity rulings on skin impurities). Fredriksen argues that several gospel scenes only make sense if specific ritual requirements are being or have been observed, e.g., Jesus' presence in Jerusalem during the week of purification preceding the Passover (Mark 11:1–14:25) and the assumption of purity for Jesus and the disciples at their final meal together (Mark 14:12-25). Matthew indicates that Jesus paid the Temple tax both for himself and Peter (Matt 17:24-27).

At the same time, Mark reports that Jesus questioned the validity of the food rulings, "thus he declared all foods clean," and shifted the origin of impurity to that which comes from a person's heart: "fornication, theft, murder, adultery, avarice, wickedness, deceit, licentiousness, envy, slander, pride, folly" (Mark 7:1-23; compare Matt 15:1-20). Acts reports that purity issues and observance of the "law" generated issues in the early church, especially in relation to Gentiles (see Acts 15). Jesus disrupts the normal Temple activities and announces its end during his final week in Jerusalem (Mark 11:15-19; 13:1-8; see Fredriksen; Klawans 2006). His actions are not designed to cleanse the Temple, but to shut down its daily operations (a symbolic act pointing to the end of this age?) and declare that it has been turned into a den of robbers. Following Jesus' announcement, Mark notes that the chief priests and scribes continued to look for a way to kill him. In this way Mark suggests that Jesus' prophetic actions in the Temple contributed significantly to his execution. Jesus' statements concerning the destruction of the Temple are clearly part of a larger apocalyptic discourse in Mark's Gospel and may express Jesus' belief that the end was near, not that he was anti-Temple or anti-cult (Fredriksen). An interesting and important absence in the narratives of his final week in Jerusalem is his failure to mention sacrifice. The time he is reported to have spent in the Temple would certainly have given him an excellent opportunity to do so.

The Gospels interpret the Last Supper in covenantal and sacrificial terms. This very likely expresses the efforts of the early church to make sense of Jesus' death. His death did not bring the end; it was a sacrificial death on behalf of the world. Without arguing that the "suffering servant songs" in Deutero-Isaiah are the background for this interpretation of his death, in the years following his death, and probably before that, Judaism certainly thought of suffering in redemptive terms. In light of the prominent role that sin played in the preaching of the early church as expressed in the pre-Gospel letters, the effort to interpret his death in terms of a "sin sacrifice" is understandable.

Paul was comfortable with such a view. As the self-proclaimed apostle to the Gentiles, he certainly recognized the tensions that existed between "Jewish Christianity" and "Gentile Christianity." He frequently addresses the relationship between "law" and "gospel" and emphasizes the death of Jesus in terms of the human experience of God's mercy. In Galatians and Romans Paul employs a variety of analogies to demonstrate that "the law" was, in one way or another, preparatory for God's redemptive work in Christ. Paul's statements concerning sacrifice are for the most part limited to theological or christological interpretations of the death of Christ (e.g., Gal 2:15-21; Rom 3:21-26; 5:18-21; 6:1-11). In Rom 3:24-25 Paul states that God put Christ forward as a sacrifice of atonement (or as the place of atonement) by his blood. God is the one who presents the sacrifice, the sacrifice for atonement (hilastērion ἱλαστήριον), made sacrificially effective (redemptive, apolytrōsis [ἀπολύτρωσις]) by his blood. In this instance, Paul depicts the death in real sacrificial terms— put forward, atonement, blood.

The writer of Hebrews will approach the matter in very different terms. The writer argues that God established a new covenant through the blood and death of Christ. Following his death, Jesus entered into the heavenly sanctuary, contrasted repeatedly with the earthy tent of the wilderness, and sat at the right hand of God (1:3; 6:19-20; 9:1-28). God set up the heavenly sanctuary, of which the earthy one is but a sketch and a shadow (8:2-5). Jesus is both high priest (4:14-5:10; 7:1-28) and makes a sacrifice of atonement for the sins of the people (2:17; 9:26). His sacrifice, unlike the repeated ones of the Israelite priests, was offered once (7:26-28). The writer argues that sacrificial blood was necessary for without the shedding of blood there can be no forgiveness of sin (9:22). The writer draws on a number of practices from the tabernacle cult, especially in relation to the priests and the sacrifices, to demonstrate that the new covenant made in Christ, the high priest and the atoning sacrifice, is better than the former. *See* ATONEMENT.

Bibliography: G. A. Anderson. *Sacrifices and Offerings in Ancient Israel* (1987); C. Bell. *Ritual Theory, Ritual Practice* (1992); C. Bell. *Ritual: Perspectives and Dimensions* (1997); J. L. Berquist. *Judaism in Persia's Shadow* (2003); G. Boccaccini. *Roots of Rabbinic Judaism* (2001); S. J. D. Cohen. *From the Maccabees to the Mishnah.* 2nd ed. (2006); M. Douglas. *Jacob's Tears* (2004); M. Douglas. *Leviticus as Literature* (1997); M. Douglas. *Natural Symbols* (1970); M. Douglas. *Purity and Danger* (1966); R. Firth. *Symbols: Public and Private* (1973); P. Fredriksen. *Jesus of Nazareth* (2000); T. Frymer-Kensky. "Pollution, Purification, and Purgation in Biblical Israel." *The Word of the Lord Shall Go Forth.* C. L. Meyers and M. O'Connor, eds. (1983) 399–414; J. Gammie. *Holiness in Israel* (1989); R. Gane. *Cult and Character: Purification Offerings, Day of Atonement, and Theodicy* (2005); C. Geertz. *The Interpretation of Cultures* (1973); E. S. Gerstenberger. *Leviticus.* OTL (1996); W. K. Gilders. *Blood Ritual in the Hebrew Bible* (2004); F. H. Gorman. *The Ideology of Ritual* (1991); F. H. Gorman. "Priestly Rituals of Founding: Time, Space, and Status." *History and Interpretation: Essays in Honour of John H. Hayes.* M. P. Graham, W. P. Brown, and J. K. Kuan, eds. (1993) 47–64; F. H. Gorman. "Ritual Studies and Biblical Studies:

Assessment of the Past; Prospects for the Future." *Semeia* 67 (1994) 13–36; R. L. Grimes. *Beginnings in Ritual Studies* (1982); I. Gruenwald. *Rituals and Ritual Theory in Ancient Israel* (2003); M. Haran. "The Complex of Ritual Acts Performed inside the Tabernacle." *Scripta Hierosolymitana* 8 (1961) 272–302; C. E. Hayes. *The Emergence of Judaism* (2006); Y. Kaufmann. *The Religion of Israel.* M. Greenberg, trans. (1960); N. Kiuchi. *The Purification Offering in the Priestly Literature* (1988); J. Klawans. *Impurity and Sin in Ancient Judaism* (1997); J. Klawans. *Purity, Sacrifice, and the Temple* (2006); G. A. Klingbeil. *A Comparative Study of the Ritual of Ordination as Found in Leviticus 8 and Emar 369* (1997); G. A. Klingbeil *Bridging the Gap: Ritual and Ritual Texts in the Bible* (2007); I. Knohl. *The Divine Symphony* (1997); I. Knohl. *The Sanctuary of Silence* (1993); B. A. Levine. "The Descriptive Tabernacle Texts of the Pentateuch." *JAOS* 85 (1965) 307–18; B. A. Levine. *In the Presence of the Lord* (1973); B. A. Levine. *Leviticus.* JPS Torah Commentary (1989); H. Maccoby. *Ritual and Morality* (1999); M. Malul. *The Comparative Method in Ancient Near Eastern and Biblical Studies* (1990); J. Milgrom. *Cult and Conoscience: The ASHAM and the Priestly Doctrine of Repentance* (1976); J. Milgrom. *Leviticus 1–16.* AB 3 (1990); J. Milgrom. "Systemic Differences in the Priestly Corpus: Response to Jonathan Klawans." *RB* 112 (2005) 321–29; S. M. Olyan. "What Do Shaving Rites Accomplish and What Do They Signal in Biblical Ritual Contexts." *JBL* 117 (1998) 611–22; J. Z. Smith. *To Take Place: Toward a Theory of Ritual* (1987); F. Staal. "The Meaninglessness of Ritual." *Numen* 26 (1979) 2–22; K. van der Toorn. *Sin and Sanction in Israel and Mesopotamia.* (1983); V. Turner. *The Ritual Process* (1969); J. W. Watts. *Reading Law: The Rhetorical Shaping of the Pentateuch* (1999); J. W. Watts. "The Rhetoric of Ritual Instructions in Leviticus 1–7." *The Book of Leviticus.* R. Rendtorff and R. A. Kugler, eds. (2003) 79–100; J. W. Watts. *Ritual and Rhetoric in Leviticus* (2007); D. P. Wright. *The Disposal of Impurity* (1987).

FRANK H. GORMAN

SACRILEGE. *See* ABOMINATION OF DESOLATION.

SADDLE [כַּר kar]. Shaped saddles designed to provide riders with both comfort and stability do not exist prior to the Roman period. Although bare back cavalry continue through the Macedonian period (4th cent. BCE), Assyrian reliefs from the 8th cent. BCE palace of Sargon II show mounted warriors with tasseled saddle cloths draped over their horses' backs. Saddlecloths also were placed on the backs of DONKEYs (2 Sam 19:26; 1 Kgs 13:13, 27) and camels (Gen 31:34) to ease both animal and rider. Ezekiel 27:20 notes that the northern Arabian city of Dedan profited by trading in SADDLECLOTHS.

VICTOR H. MATTHEWS

SADDLECLOTHS [בֶּגֶד beghedh]. Until the invention of the shaped SADDLE in Roman times, the common practice was to place a blanket or cloth over the back of a DONKEY or HORSE. The decorative saddlecloth provided some comfort for animal and rider and became a marketable item (Ezek 27:20). *See* CLOTH, CLOTHES.

VICTOR H. MATTHEWS

SADDUCEES   sad´joo-see   [צָדוֹק tsadhoq; Σαδδουκαῖος Saddoukaios]. The Sadducees (pl. tsadhoqim צָדוֹקִים) were a religious and social party that played a dominant role in the history of the high priesthood, the Temple, and Jewish law from the Hasmonean period to 70 CE. Josephus mentions them as one of the Jewish "philosophies" that also included the PHARISEES and the ESSENES. He characterizes the Sadducees as rich and aristocratic (*Ant.* 13.298; 18.17). Rabbinic sources (e.g., *m. Eruv* 6:2; *m. Yad* 4:6–7) refer to the Sadducees quite frequently, mostly as the adversaries of the Pharisees or early rabbis in relation to Jewish religious laws (*see* HALAKHAH). The Sadducees are mentioned several times in the NT as among Jesus' adversaries, together with the Pharisees (e.g., Matt 3:7; 16:1, 6, 11)

Although early sources refer to the Sadducees as an active and dominant elite group within Second Temple JUDAISM, they present the Sadducees in a merely polemical fashion, stressing opposition towards the Sadducees without identifying Sadducean individuals, activities, or social status and motivation.

A. Name and Origin
B. Religion and Halakhah
C. History
   1. The Hasmonean period
   2. From Herod to the Great Revolt
Bibliography

A. Name and Origin

Following the designation of the Sadducees as aristocratic and their opposition to the laws of the Pharisees and early rabbis, some scholars regard them as a rich, secular, and Hellenistic group (Sanders). These scholars may have been influenced by later polemical Amoraic references to the Sadducees as non-observant Jews, as well as by much later recensions of the Babylonian Talmud where the Sadducees were designated *minim* (heretics) due to censorship of medieval church authorities. Other scholars, however, noticed Josephus' references to the laws of the Sadducees and the contents of the controversies with the Pharisees in rabbinic sources. Consequently, these scholars acknowledged that the Sadducees had a systematic religion and interpretation of Scripture different (and perhaps more ancient) from those held by the Pharisees and rabbis (Finkelstein).

The name of the Sadducees probably derives from the name of the high priestly house of Zadok. It is uncertain, however, whether any of the Sadducean high priests were of Zadokite descent. The name *Sadducee* is related to the term for righteousness (tsedheq צֶדֶק). Certain scholars tried to trace the origins of the Sadducees (as well as the Pharisees) to the postexilic period and the days of Ezra and Nehemiah. However, only a few of the Sadducees' distinctive characteristics are documented in this period. The only definite conclusion that can be made is that the Sadducees were closer to the Judaism of the earlier Persian period than were the Pharisees.

B. Religion and Halakhah

The Sadducees did not believe in the resurrection of the body or in the persistence of the soul after death (Matt 22:23-28; Mark 12:18-27). Josephus reports that they also denied divine providence and maintained that humans have free choice—that God has nothing to do with human good and evil (*Ant.* 13.173; *J.W.* 2.164–65). In presenting the core of the debate between the Pharisees and Sadducees, Josephus asserted that the Sadducees rejected Pharisaic tradition (ORAL LAW, ORAL TORAH) and considered only the Law of Moses to be valid (*Ant.* 13.297). Josephus also mentioned that the Sadducees were stricter than the Pharisees regarding their penal law (*Ant.* 13.294; 20.199; compare *J.W.* 2.166).

More than twenty halakhic disputes between the Pharisees and Sadducees (including those related to the Boethusians, see below) are mentioned in rabbinic literature (these are indeed later and biased sources, but they have a solid historical basis, which is also supported by partly similar controversies of the Temple Scroll (e.g., 11Q19 XVIII, 9–10; XIX, 17–20; V, 14–15) and the HALAKHIC LETTER. These disputes related to Sabbath laws, calendar, sacrificial cult, purity, and penal laws. For example, the Sadducees disagreed with the Pharisees on which day to harvest the new barley, out of concern for violating the Sabbath (*m. Menah.* 10:3). The Sadducees demanded that the red heifer (whose ashes purify corpse impurity, see Num 19) be burnt by a high priest who is entirely pure at sundown (that is, has immersed in a ritual bath and then has waited for sundown). They opposed the view of the Pharisees, who insisted that the high priest burn the red heifer in a state of incomplete levitical purity (that is, when he had only immersed and did not wait until sundown [*m. Parah* 3:7-8]). The Sadducees said that on the Day of Atonement, the high priest should burn the incense before he enters the Holy of Holies. The Pharisees, on the other hand, insisted that the high priest should first enter the inner sancta and then burn the incense therein (*m. Yoma* 5:1). The Sadducees rebuked the Pharisees for letting the laity touch the Temple menorah (*t. Hag.* 3:35). They also required physical punishment for inflicting injury, evidence that they literally interpreted the command of an "an eye for an eye, a tooth for a tooth" (compare Exod 21:24-27; Lev 24:20; Deut 19:21). The

Pharisees, on the other hand, deduced that these verses allude to monetary compensation equal to the physical damage (Scholion to *Megilat Ta'anit* on 10 Tammuz, Ms. Oxford).

The Sadducees' halakhic positions have several major characteristics: strictness regarding Sabbath prohibitions, purity taboos, and penal law; emphasis on the centrality of the priesthood or the high priest in relation to the laity; commitment to the literal sense of Scripture; rejection of non-scriptural categories; new halakhic definitions; and values that were followed or invented by the Pharisees. Accordingly, it seems that the approach of the Sadducees reflects a conservative and probably more ancient halakhic tradition. These disputes may reside in different perceptions of holiness and how far one should go in defending the sacred from pollution and desecration (*see* HOLY, HOLINESS, OT).

Some Dead Sea Scrolls scholars suggested that the "QUMRAN community" (led by several priests called the "Sons of Zadok") originated from the Sadducees (e.g., 1QS V, 2, 9). However, the historical links between the Sadducees and the Qumranic Zadokites are questionable, since the members of the sect were persecuted by the Sadducees, and since Zadokite priests headed the Qumran sects only at a relatively later stage (*see* ZADOK, ZADOKITES).

There are indeed several laws and legal perceptions common to the Sadducees and the Temple Scroll, the Halakhic Letter and other Qumranic texts: Strictness regarding the purity of burning the red heifer; the view that a liquid poured from a pure vessel into an impure one is defiling (the Pharisees declared that it did not defile the former vessel except in the case of viscous liquids like honey); and the impurity of nonkosher animals bones, which the Pharisees held were pure (*m. Yad* 4:6; 4QMMT B 21–22). In addition, both groups had laws regarding impure menstrual blood that were stricter than the rabbis' (*m. Nid* 4:2; CD V, 6–7). The Temple Scroll and the Sadducees opposed the Pharisaic practice of exhibiting the Temple menorah outside the Temple shrine (*t. Hag.* 3:35). Both the Sadducees and the Temple Scroll rejected the Pharisees' regulation of an annual half-shekel tax and prescribed the annual celebration of the days of ordinances. The Sadducees as well as the authors of the Damascus Document rejected the practice of transforming the courtyard or alley into common property that allows its use on Sabbath.

No less important, however, are the differences between the laws of the Sadducees and the Scrolls. First and foremost, while Qumranic sources followed the 365-day "solar" calendar, there is no sign that the Sadducees did the same. Rabbinic allusions to Sadducean views regarding their count of seven weeks from the sacrifice of the new barley on the altar to the Festival of Weeks imply a lunar-solar calendar similar to that of the rabbis. The Sadducean dates for harvesting the new barley and the Festival of Weeks were different from those in the Scrolls. This was probably the ancient calendar that continued to be practiced at the Temple in the Second Temple period. The Sadducees also disputed the Qumranic law pertaining to cereal offerings of the shelamim (שְׁלָמִים) sacrifice, rejected the Temple Scroll's ideal plan of the Temple, and did not practice the rule in which the payment of half-shekel is raised once-in-a-lifetime. Furthermore, many of the Sadduceen laws—e.g., pertaining to an eye for an eye and the Day of Atonement's incense—are not even mentioned in the Scrolls and were probably not considered by the Qumran movement.

It therefore seems that the Sadducees share with the Temple Scroll, the Halakhic letter and the Qumran sects a basic halakhic heritage that was common in Judaism before the emergence of the Pharisees. Later on, the Sadducees and the pre-Qumranic or Qumranic halakhah developed independently.

C. History

1. The Hasmonean Period

Josephus first mentioned the Sadducees (with the Pharisees and Essenes) in the days of Jonathan the Maccabee who served as a high priest in 152–143 BCE (*Ant.* 13.171–73). During this period, it seems, the Pharisees ruled the Temple. By the last days of the high priest John HYRCANUS (135–104 BCE), Josephus described a rift between Hyrcanus and the Pharisees, when Hyrcanus decided to join the Sadducees, and abrogated the pharisaic regulations (*Ant.* 13:288–99; compare *b. Qidd.* 66a where a similar tale is told about Alexander Jannaeus). *See* HASMONEANS.

The reasons for Hyrcanus' transformation might not have been strictly political. The Pharisees were portrayed as his close colleagues, but one of them, named Eleazar, demanded that Hyrcanus leave the high priesthood and remain a secular governor. This seems to have been an attempt to abolish Hyrcanus' religious authority. Furthermore, all the dealings between the two sides were related to halakhah. Hyrcanus followed the advice of his Sadducean friend Jonathan and suspected that the Pharisees actually agreed with Eleazar. Hyrcanus thus demanded that the Pharisees prove their loyalty to him by decreeing a punishment for Eleazar. However, whereas Hyrcanus expected a death penalty for blaspheming the ruler, the Pharisees prescribed (as Jonathan the Sadducee had already foreseen in his advice), a relatively lenient penalty of stripes and chains; hence Hyrcanus' suspicions came true. This was not surprising since the Pharisees were more lenient than the Sadducees regarding penal laws. In fact, Hyrcanus' annulment of the laws of the Pharisees shows that the core of the conflict was the question of which halakhah should rule.

Alexander Jannaeus faced a civil war with his own Jewish people. Josephus does not say that they were Pharisees, but the manner in which his wife Alexandra later conferred with the Pharisees in order to secure her reign reveals their identity, as well as the description

of this affair in *Pesher Nahum* (4Q169). That means that Jannaeus was a Sadducee, and his religious inclination was probably the reason that the Pharisees rebelled against him. There are indeed hints that the conflict was grounded in the religious tension between Sadducees and Pharisees. Once again, the Pharisees argued that Jannaeus was unqualified for high priesthood. This time people threw citrons at Jannaeus when he stood beside the altar during the Feast of Sukkot. The king reacted by placing a barrier near the altar to isolate the priests from the laity and also killed six thousand of his opponents. A short time later a civil war broke out, in which the people cooperated with the Seleucid king Demetrius Akairos. Finally, Jannaeus won and took revenge on his Jewish enemies by crucifying eight hundred of them and killing others (*J.W.* 1.88–98; *Ant.* 13.372–73, 376-383. For Jannaeus' persecution of the early rabbis, compare *y. Hag.* 2:2, 77d; *b. Ber.* 48a).

According to *Ant.* 13.399–404, in his will to his wife, Jannaeus told Salome Alexandra that the only way she could handle the Pharisees was by giving them a certain amount of power. Alexandra gave the Pharisees full control and let them execute their traditional laws, restoring those that were abolished by Hyrcanus (*J.W.* 1.108, 110–112; *Ant.* 13.408–409). The Pharisees also persecuted Jannaeus' military officers and leading citizens who asked Alexandra for sanctuary in the fortresses (*J.W.* 1.113–14; *Ant.* 13.409–17). Although they are portrayed as Hellenists, these military officers and leading citizens may have been Sadducees. Indeed, the decline of Manasseh's "nobles" and "mighty warriors" is mentioned in *Pesher Nahum* (4Q169 3–4 III, 8–12) between the days of Jannaeus and Pompey's conquest (i.e., the days of Queen Alexandra).

Aristobulus II, the son of Jannaues and Alexandra, who ruled for four years after his mother's death, was probably a Sadducee. In describing the death and exile that Manasseh suffered (probably related to the consequences of Pompey's conquest), *Pesher Nahum* (4Q169 3–4, IV, 3–4) refers to the time when Manasseh's kingship will be weakened, implying Arisobulus' reign as a Sadducean. During Alexandra's reign, Arisobulus defended the persecuted military officers and leading citizens and later won the crown by taking over the fortresses with the cooperation of the Sadducees (*Ant.* 13. 416, 422–27). In the civil war against his brother Hyrcanus II, he enjoyed the support of the priests (*Ant.* 14.20, 25). During Pompey's siege of the Temple Mount, Aristobulus' supporters refrained from any act of warfare during the Sabbath. This was probably the law followed by the Sadducees (compare *Ant.* 14.63–68).

2. From Herod to the Great Revolt

The Sadducees are usually portrayed as men of eminent political power (in the NT) or as confronted and usually defeated by the rabbis. The actual evidence regarding individual Saducean leaders and their social positions is scant. Several sources refer to the

Sadducees as high priests from the time of Herod to the Great Revolt (*see* JEWISH WARS). Ananus son of Ananus was a Sadducee (*Ant.* 20.199). The followers of Joseph Caiaphas were Sadducees (Acts 5:17), hence Caiaphas himself was likely a Sadducee. Ishmael son of Phiabi confronted the early rabbis, wishing to follow the Sadducean halakhah of burning the red heifer in a state of complete purity after sundown (*t. Parah* 3.6). The Boethusians were a group that the rabbis mention interchangeably with the Sadducees and attribute Sadducean laws to them. They should be identified with the high priests of the house of Boethos, first nominated by Herod and regarded as a part of the Sadducean party. There is no historical basis for associating the Boethusinas with the Qumran movement (or the Essenes); the rabbis portray them as aristocratic priests, and the halakhic resemblance between the Boethusinas and the Temple Scroll and the Halakhic Letter is only partial (Regev).

It is probable that the other high priests of the four leading high priestly houses were also Sadducean. These four houses are also mentioned together in a lamentation cited in rabbinic literature (*t. Menah.* 13.21; *b. Pesah.* 57a), which demonstrates that the rabbis regarded them as an opposing and relatively unified class.

The high priestly class appears in Josephus and the NT as secular aristocratic politicians closely related to the Herodian rulers and Roman governors who appointed them. A closer reading, however, reveals that they were in fact concerned with defending the Jewish religion and the Temple's sacredness in particular. They were involved in demanding that the high priest's garments of the Day of Atonement be kept at the Temple instead of in the custody of the Roman governor, and they succeeded in their application to Augustus in that matter (*Ant.* 20.6-14). Ishmael son of Phiabi and others of the high priestly class built a wall to prevent Agrippa II from watching the sacrificial cult from his palace and even went to Rome to get Nero's approval for this screening wall (*Ant.* 20.189-95). Ananus son of Ananus headed the government during the Great Revolt, and called for the defense of the Temple from the violent Zealots (*J.W.* 2.563; 4.318-25, 151, 162-206).

Sadducean high priests led the persecution of Jesus and other early Christian leaders. Joseph CAIAPHAS (who was the governing high priest in ca. 18-36 CE) arrested Jesus. One of the accusations with which Jesus was charged was his threat to destroy the Temple (Matt 26:3, 57; Mark 14:53-65). The Sadducees, including Caiaphas and Ananus the Elder (NRSV, "Annas") reportedly arrested and flogged Peter and the apostles when they preached and healed in the name of Jesus at the Temple Mount (Acts 4:1-22; 5:12-40). According to Acts, after Paul was arrested at the Temple Mount for allowing a Gentile to enter the Temple's sacred precinct, he was brought before the Sanhedrin consisting of Sadducees and Pharisees (who debated the theological problem of resurrection instead of accusing Paul; Acts

22:30–23:10). Ananus son of Ananus the Sadducee and his Sanhedrin judged and stoned James, brother of Jesus, for transgressing the law. The sentence was opposed by other Jerusalemites who strictly observed the law, probably Pharisees (*Ant.* 20:199–201).

Common to all these incidents is the involvement of Jesus, Peter and the apostles, Paul, and James with the Temple. It seems that the main concern of Caiaphas, Ananus, and other Sadducean high priests was the threat, as they viewed it, that the early Christians posed to the Temple, while preaching there for and about Jesus, who personally acted and spoke against the Temple (Mark 11:15-19; 14:57-58; 15:29; Acts 7:13-14; *Gos. Thom.* 71). After all, according to the laws of the Sadducees, defense of the Temple from impurity and desecration was critical, and they were, therefore, probably more sensitive than the Pharisees to what they regarded as subversion of the sacrificial cult or the Temple institutions.

The Sadducees and Pharisees struggled for control of the Temple cult. Each side tried to force the other to follow its laws (*m. Yoma* 1:5; *t. Sukkah* 3:1; *t. Parah* 3.8). Rabbinic literature mentions how the Pharisees defeated the Sadducees, especially in regard to laws pertaining to the Temple cult. Josephus also says that the Sadducees submitted unwillingly to the Pharisees (*Ant.* 18.17). In actuality, however, the Sadducees had the upper hand during most of the Second Temple period. Sadducean high priests held official political authority at the Temple. Furthermore, rabbinic traditions mention Pharisaic laws as being practiced at the Temple only ca. 50 CE, in the days of Gamaliel, Simon son of Gamaliel and Jonathan ben Zakkai (e.g., *t. Sanh.* 2:6; *t. Parah* 3.8). It seems that the Sadducean decline referred to by Josephus and the rabbis occurred during this later period. *See* TEMPLE, JERUSALEM.

Bibliography: A. I. Baumgarten. "The Zadokite Priests at Qumran: A Reconsideration," *DSD* 4.2 (1997) 137–156; J. M. Baumgarten. "The Pharisaic-Sadducean Controversies about Purity and the Qumran Texts," *JJS* 31 (1980) 157–70; R. T. Beckwith. "The Pre-History and Relationship of the Pharisees, Sadducees and Essenes: A Tentative Reconstuction," *RQ* 11 (1982) 3–46; H. K. Bond. *Caiaphas: Friend of Rome and Judge of Jesus?* (2004); F. M. Cross Jr. "The Early History of the Qumran Community." *New Directions in Biblical Archaeology.* D. N. Freedman and J. Greenfield, eds. (1971) 70–89; P. R. Davies. "Sadducees in the Dead Sea Scrolls." *Sects and Scrolls* (1996) 127–38; L. Finkelstein. *The Pharisees: The Sociological Background of Their Faith,* 3rd ed. (1962); M. Goodman. *The Ruling Class of Judaea* (1987); J. S. McLaren. *Power and Politics in Palestine: The Jews and the Governing of Their Land 100BC–AD 70* (1991); J. Painter. *Just James: The Brother of Jesus in History and Tradition* (1998); E. Regev. "The Sadducees, the Pharisees, and the Sacred: Meaning and Ideology in the Halakhic Controversies between the Sadducees and Pharisees." *Review of Rabbinic Judaism* 9 (2006) 126–40; E. Regev. "Were the Priests All the Same? Qumranic Halakhah in Comparison with Sadducean Halakhah." *Dead Sea Discoveries* 12.2 (2005) 158–88; E. Rivkin. "Defining the Pharisees: The Tannaitic Sources." *HUCA* 40–41 (1969–70) 205–49; E. P. Sanders. *Judaism, Practice and Belief, 63 BCE–66 CE* (1992); L. H. Schiffman. "The Temple Scroll and the System of Jewish Law of the Second Temple Period." *Temple Scroll Studies*. G. J. Brooke, ed. (1989) 239–55.; P. Winter. *On the Trial of Jesus*, rev. ed. (1974); Y. Yadin. *The Temple Scroll*. 3 vols. (1977; ET 1983).

EYAL REGEV

SADHE. *See* TSADE.

SAFETY [בֶּטַח betakh, יֵשַׁע yeshaʿ, שָׁלוֹם shalom; διασῴζω diasōzō, σωτηρία sōtēria]. In the OT, "safety" normally refers to physical security or protection from harm, as in discussions of God's care for Israel during the exodus and settlement in Canaan (Deut 12:10; 1 Sam 12:11; Ps 78:53; compare 1 Kgs 4:25) or accounts of warfare (2 Sam 19:24 [Heb. 19:25]; 2 Chr 19:1; Isa 10:31; escape from Jerusalem in Jer 4:6; 6:1; compare the prophecy against Gog in Ezek 38:8, 11). Safety is a sign of God's blessing or deliverance (Deut 33:12, 28; Job 5:11; 11:18; Ps 4:8 [Heb. 4:9]; Prov 11:14-15; compare Ps 12:5 [Heb. 12:6]; Isa 14:30). It frequently is promised in prophetic passages about God's regathering of Israel and Judah (Jer 32:37; 33:16; Ezek 28:26; 34:28; Hos 2:18; compare Zech 8:10; Tob 14:7). In the NRSV, *safety* often translates the noun **betakh** but occasionally renders the nouns **shalom** (1 Sam 20:13; 2 Sam 19:24; 2 Chr 19:1; Zech 8:10) or **yeshaʿ** (Job 5:4, 11; Ps 12:5 [Heb. 12:6]; compare Prov 11:14).

Both uses of *safety* in the NT denote God's deliverance of Paul and his companions from shipwreck. *Safety* is supplied in an idiomatic expression in Acts 27:24, but in Acts 28:1 it reflects the verb diasōzō (compare different translations in Acts 23:24; 27:43-44; 28:4). Phrases including the related noun sōtēria and verb sōzō (σῴζω) account for most NRSV renderings of *safety* in the Apocrypha. Contexts include physical safety in travel (Tob 5:16), warfare (1 Macc 2:44; 5:54; 10:83; compare Jdt 11:3), and even sexual relations (Tob 6:18; 8:4). Note, though, the negative uses in 4 Macc 9:4 and 15:8, where martyrdom is preferred over a renunciation of God that would abate persecution. *See* SALVATION.

ERIC F. MASON

SAFFRON [כַּרְכֹּם karkom]. Saffron (*Crocus sativus*) is only mentioned in a list of ornamental, fragrant shrubs and spices in a pleasure garden (Song 4:14). Like other species of CROCUS, saffron, native to Iran and Kashmir, is grown from bulbs since it is sterile. There is no indication in the biblical text of the use of the very expensive spice produced from its large flowers (150 flowers = 1 g of spice). Most likely it was used as a perfume, its medicinal and culinary uses coming later under the influence of eastern cultures. *See* PLANTS IN THE BIBLE.

VICTOR H. MATTHEWS

SAFI, TELL ES. One of the largest pre-classical sites in the southern Levant (ca. 50 ha.). It is situated in central Israel on the border between the southern coastal plain (Philistia) and the Judean foothills (Shephelah) on the southern bank of the Elah River, approximately halfway between Jerusalem and Ashkelon. The site was settled almost continuously from the Chalcolithic Period to modern times, due to its location on an important crossroads as well as to the rich agricultural land in its vicinity.

Nineteenth-cent. explorers noted the tell's archaeological significance and suggested identifying it with GATH or LIBNAH. In 1899, F. Bliss and R. Macalister undertook a limited excavation of the tell, which was insufficiently published. Analysis of the relevant historical and biblical sources has shown that the identification with Canaanite and Philistine Gath, the city of Achish and Goliath, is to be preferred, and excavations have corroborated this identification.

Recent excavations have uncovered a wealth of archaeological evidence, including Early Bronze and Late Bronze Age levels. Archaeologists have exposed the remains of various stages of Philistine settlement, including a 10th cent. BCE sherd on which two names very similar to the name Goliath are inscribed. A late 9th cent. BCE level shows a siege system surrounding the site, along with extensive evidence of the site's destruction. Hazael of Aram may have undertaken the siege and conquest (compare 2 Kgs 12:18).

Bibliography: Frederick J. Bliss and R. A. Stewart Macalister. *Excavations in Palestine during the Years 1898–1900* (1902); A. M. Maeir. "Zafit, Tel." *The New Encyclopedia of Archaeological Excavations in the Holy Land*. Vol. 5 supp. Ephraim Stern, Ayelet Lewison-Gilboa, and Joseph Aviram, ed. (2008) 2079–81.

ITZHAQ SHAI AND AREN M. MAEIR

SAFIYEH, WADI ES. *See* ZEPHATHAH.

SAFUT, TELL. An ancient city-mound, or tell, located approximately 12 km northwest of present day Amman, Jordan, Tell Safut is situated on a major thoroughfare connecting Rabbath-ammon and central Gilead. The excavations at Tell Safut, which began in 1982 as a joint endeavor between Seton Hall University and the Jordanian Department of Antiquities under the direction of D. Wimmer, show continuous occupation layers with fortifications from the Middle Bronze Age through the end of the Iron II period. Significant archaeological finds from the site include a Late Bronze Age seated tutelary deity with its extended arms wrapped in gold leaf, an Iron I period terracotta clay baboon figurine of Thoth (the Egyptian god of wisdom), an Iron II period inscribed scarab seal, and a military standard from the Iron IIC period. Some scholars have suggested that the site is NOBAH, which Gideon passed by in the process of destroying the army of Zebah and Zalmunna, the kings of Midian (Judg 8:11). It may be connected with biblical Kenath in Gilead (1 Chr 2:23), which the Manassite warrior Nobah conquered and renamed after himself (Num 32:42).

HUMPHREY H. HARDY II

SAGA. A long, prose, traditional narrative, with an episodic structure developed around stereotyped themes or objects. The episodes of the saga present past persons, events, deeds, and virtues that inform or represent the present world and worldview of the narrative. The English term *saga* is derived from German *Sage*, which refers in folklore to a particular type of prose narrative that presents events and persons—whether historical or not—in a historical context in order to represent cultural and national character types, roles, values, and worldview. The German term *Sage* refers specifically to the Icelandic or Nordic works.

Several types of sagas appear in the OT. The Primeval Saga in Gen 1–11 presents a narrative account of the origins of creation that points to ideal expressions of the role of human beings in the world, ritual and ethical behavior, and the temple at the center of creation. The Family Sagas in Gen 12–25 (Abraham) and 25–35 (Jacob) recount the past events of a family unit to illustrate or explain aspects of Judean and Israelite national life and history. The Heroic Saga concerning Moses in the Pentateuch focuses on the life of Israel's leader to explain Israel's national origins, ritual practice, and social values. The People's Saga in Num 1–36 emphasizes the organization of Israel's cultic establishment and its role in defining Israel's relationship with Yahweh.

Bibliography: Rolf P. Knierim and George W. Coats. *Numbers.* FOTL 4 (2005); Robert W. Neff. "Saga." *Narrative Forms in Old Testament Literature* (1985) 17–32.

MARVIN A. SWEENEY

SAGE [חָכָם khakham, חֲכָמָה khakhamah; μάγος magos, νουνέχω nounechō, σοφός sophos, σωφρονέω sōphroneō, φρόνιμος phronimos]. Sage ("wise/wise man/wise woman") appears frequently in the Bible to describe people possessing the traits of wisdom, or as a description of informed, intellectual, reasoned approaches to life or behavior. Eve is attracted to the Tree of Knowledge for its ability to "make one wise" (Gen 3:6); by the time of the NT letters, the wisdom of the sages is embodied in the teachings, person, and resurrection of Jesus of Nazareth. Sage, as a gender-neutral form, is preferred by many modern translations, since it can encompass both male and female activities

(Gen 41; Matt 2:1, 7, 16; Judg 5:29; 2 Sam 14; 20; Jer 9:17-21) and also references the feminine personification of "wisdom."

A. Usage in Nominal Forms
B. History of the Sages
C. Sages in the Biblical Text
D. Teachings of the Sages
E. Sages in the New Testament
F. Usage in Adjectival Forms
Bibliography

A. Usage in Nominal Forms

Along with the classic pair of the priest and the prophet (Jer 18:18), the sages represent one of the three categories of public leaders in charge of the smooth running of government and teaching of the traditions to the young. Ultimately their work overlaps with that of the elders in tribal times (Deut 1:13-15), and with the scribes who prepared, edited, and transmitted the biblical text in monarchic and postexilic times (Ezra 8:16). It is probable that sages composed the books of Job and Ecclesiastes, and that the book of Proverbs represents the literary work of many sages over time. Their theologies are best expressed in Prov 1–9, Eccl 12, and Job 28. Many so-called "wisdom" psalms are also ascribed to the sages (Pss 1; 19; 32; 33; 34; 37; 119, etc.). Other texts are often said to display "wisdom influence" (= typical vocabulary, characters, actions, and themes), and this is sometimes attributed to authorship by an unknown sage or group of sages (Amos 1–3; David's Court History in the books of Samuel [2 Sam 11–1 Kgs 3]; the Song of Songs; Esther; Tobit, etc.).

B. History of the Sages

Sages were familiar, revered figures in the literature and cultures of the peoples surrounding biblical Israel and, later, Roman Judea. In Mesopotamia, primordial sages (**apkallu**) were thought to have existed before the mythic Deluge, and transferred much irreplaceable knowledge to the survivors of the legendary flood. In temple economies that redistributed goods to the surrounding inhabitants, sages were critical for the recording, management, and distribution of material sustenance. Hence, they were always associated with record-keeping, reading, writing, and educational enterprises and the social order such activities create and preserve (*see* PTAH-HOTEP, INSTRUCTION OF; SCRIBE). Sages could be known for other specialties: DREAM interpretation (a main feature of Joseph's work for Pharaoh in Gen 41, and Daniel's service in Babylon), political counsel; (Ahithophel, 2 Sam 16–17), conflict resolution (2 Sam 14; 20), or literary activity (Prov 25:1; Eccl 12). The Bible mentions sages of Egypt (Gen 41:8; Isa 19:11), Edom (Obad 1:8), Tyre (Ezek 28:3-6), Zoan (Isa 19:11), Babylon (Jer 50–51), and Persia (Esth 1:13, "the East"; Matt 2).

While we do not hear much of sages during the ancestral history of Genesis, the figure of Job, the desert chieftain of Uz in Edom, is set in this period. Job presents a detailed, nuanced portrait of how a wise and good sage conducts his life and the benefits his oversight brings to the entire community (Job 29–31). Indeed, rabbinic interpretation portrays Job as one of Pharaoh's wise men, whose torture is a divine ruse to keep the Adversary occupied elsewhere (in Edom) while the baby Moses is rescued from genocide, raised to adulthood, and given his commission to deliver the Israelites from bondage.

In the tribal period (Iron Age I), sages worked primarily in villages where their activities usually overlapped those of elders in the more informal leadership structures of the highland settlements. In these settings, they gave formal and informal guidance to tribal leaders, settled disputes, and probably also were in charge of any educational activities outside of the home. Their authority was rooted in the role of a wise parent teaching children of the household. With the advent of the united monarchy, political sages came into their own as an occupational group. The biblical kingdoms modeled their fledgling state on the bureaucracies of other countries, especially Egypt. Sages served the kings at court and oversaw the management of the kingdoms, while also conducting diplomatic relations with foreign courts (2 Sam 16–17; 1 Kgs 2:9; 5:7; Isa 19:11; 44:25; Jer 8:8-12; Ezek 28:3; Hos 14:10; Pss 49:11; 107:43). During this period, women sages disappear from the biblical texts but no doubt continued their work as informal leaders and resource persons in the time-honored custom of village life.

Once the class of sages, now bureaucrats with the wealth and leisure time needed to master a technical body of writings and duties, were associated with the royal elites and their power struggles, they came under increasing criticism from Hebrew prophets. Too often their counsel was pragmatic and rooted in the class interests of the wealthy, not the plans of God (Isa 5:21; 29:14; 44:25; Jer 8:9–9; 9:11; Obad 1:8). Prophets spoke on behalf of the poor who suffered increasing loss of their tribal lands and livelihoods because of famine, swindling by rich absentee landlords (1 Kgs 21; Mic 2:2), and heavy taxation levied by the crown in order to pay tribute to other conquering nations. In this destruction of the tribal economics based on kinship relationships, the sages seemed all too ready to justify the encroachment of the rich with the standard teachings of the relationship between acts and their consequences. If cosmopolitan elites prevailed over the people of the villages, it must be the result of God's blessing, just as the falling fortunes of farmers had to be the result of punishment for sins, usually unspecified. (The afflictions of the wealthy sage Job are an attempt to address this false ethic of "deserved" suffering.) Further, since the sages were involved in conducting diplomacy and giving counsel for biblical kings (notorious for their short-sighted foreign policies and disregard of their own people's well being), they were often implicated in plots that brought political unrest to the countryside, or the negotiation of tribute and taxes owed to conquering overlords of Israel's enemies. Hence, the prophets were apt to see them as part of the problem—the entrenchment of injustice in the very structures of the monarchy—rather than as a long-established resource for understanding and leading the "good life" as it might be understood outside of the royal court (Jer 8:8-18).

With the collapse of the kingdoms, first Israel in 721 BCE, then Judah in 587 BCE, the sages were among the elites who were exiled to Babylon, with the possibility that some may have fled to become part of the Jewish Diaspora. During the exilic and postexilic periods, biblical sages as an occupational group become more or less indistinguishable from scribes (Ezra 8:16), but reappear in the book of Ecclesiastes, where they are involved in formal teaching (12:9-10).

C. Sages in the Biblical Text

Some biblical sages are known to us directly from the text itself: Joseph is referred to as a sage (wise man) many times in his extended story in Genesis; he is implicitly contrasted in a favorable way with Pharaoh's other advisors and magical experts (Gen 41:8, 33, 39). The Wise Women of Tekoa (unnamed) and Abel in the story of David's court history offer a clear window into the work of women as authorized counselors in public settings (2 Sam 14; 20). In David's court, the political sage Ahithophel gives counsel of such quality as though God were speaking (2 Sam 16:23). When his counsel is ignored, his shame and humiliation, given his reputation, are such that he feels his only course is to take his own life (2 Sam 17:23). The "men" of King Hezekiah edit and compile the proverb collection found in Prov 25:1–29:27, and unnamed sages are mentioned in the invectives of prophets and theologians throughout the days of the kings.

During and after the exile of the 6th cent. BCE, the Bible often finds the sages of other countries to be figures of fun or keepers of inferior traditions that will one day be overturned by the Bible's God (Esther; Jer 50:35; 51:57). The book of Daniel, although written much later in the postexilic period than its 6th-cent. setting, chooses as its main character a wise and pious exile whose wisdom and counsel to the Babylonian king consistently outshines that of the king's own counselors (Dan 2:12-14; 11:35). In the Second Temple period (sometime before 180 BCE), the sage Jesus ben Sira adds his own twist by composing a wisdom book that updates the proverbs of the earlier tradition with his own compositions relevant to the Greco-Roman world in which he lived.

However, the person most associated with the work, patronage, and literary production of the wise is Solomon, the great cosmopolitan king of a so-called "Golden Age" (Prov 1:1; 25:1; 1 Kgs 3:4-28; Sir 47:12-

17; Wisdom of Solomon). Solomon's varied wisdom was legendary throughout the known world (1 Kgs 4:29-34; 10:1-13). He is traditionally held to have authored the Song of Songs during his youth, the book of Proverbs during his middle years, and Ecclesiastes in his old age (Song 1:1; Prov 1:1; 25:1; Eccl 1:1), though modern studies have shown these books were composed well after the time of this great patron of wisdom.

D. Teachings of the Sages

Much of the worldview of this group, especially during the monarchies, seems very alien to the bulk of the Bible's theologies of covenant, election, salvation, and the biblical God's unique action in history. The sages speak of God as Creator and Master Sage, not as historical redeemer with a special task for Israel alone. For the sages, it was not the historical faith that guided them (though they certainly knew and relied upon those traditions). Rather, the observable order found in nature and human interactions spoke to them of a practical morality that anyone could observe and with which they could live in successful accord (Prov 10:12; 13:12; 14:4, 5, 12, 23, 20; 26:27; etc.). Certain acts reliably produced specific consequences: lazy behavior in summer and harvest produced a hungry winter and potential ruin (Prov 6:6-11; 10:5; 12:11; 28:19), gossip produced social discord (Prov 6:12-15; 15:18; 16:28; 22:10; 26:22), and bribery produced blindness in officials and injustice for the poor (Prov 17:8, 23; 21:14). While many of these insights begin as simple (though astute) observations, they clearly press the hearer toward a choice between wise and foolish, responsible choices or stupid, selfish ones. Many of the sayings of the sages are shaped as direct commands or prohibitions, and the "instruction" form binds together the advice of the sages in their roles as parents instructing "children," now transferred to the professional setting of the court.

Based on analysis of their writings, we might call the sages moral philosophers and social scientists. Their reflections show the kind of rational, relational thinking and search for hidden causes that characterizes the scientific method, though they enacted their "experiments" in a literary rather than a laboratory setting. It has been hypothesized that their sophisticated literary musings draw heavily upon the international wisdom movement with its many parallel texts from which the bible's sages drew their inspiration (and sometimes more; compare Prov 22:17–24:22 to the Egyptian Instruction of Amenemope). It may well be that, since their work was done in the postexilic period when king and national theology in support of kingship was no longer as relevant as it had been before the exile, they opted for more universal concepts in which to clothe their theological insights. Still, their most basic confession of faith is the proverbial theory that "fear of the Lord is the beginning of wisdom" (Prov 1:7, 29; 2:5; 3:7; 8:13; etc., Job 28:28; Sir 1:11-30). Unless one

had a proper orientation toward the world grounded in knowledge of and obedience to the biblical Creator who is the wisdom tradition's God, no amount of intellect can make one wise or good. It is easy to see how the biblical traditions of the wise were correlated with the kind of treatises composed or taught by later Hellenistic and Roman philosophers as the OT's canon closed (*see* AMENEMOPE, INSTRUCTION OF).

E. Sages in the New Testament

Several centuries of exposure to the Greek philosophical traditions, and later the social situation of Roman military occupation of Palestine, impacted the concepts and duties of the "wise," now known as the **sophoi** (σοφοί) and associated with the special learning of the classical philosophers. Without their own monarchy to serve, Palestinian sages in a school context (Sir 51:23) focused upon the literary traditions that bound their people together during these times of adversity and cultural uncertainty. The philosophies of the Greeks, the work of Stoic philosophers and others, forced the Torah to "compete" for credibility in a much larger arena of ideas, and the sages were key players in this set of discussions. Jesus ben Sira, writing in the 2nd cent. BCE (and in Jerusalem, compared to Egypt), finds that wisdom is the Torah (24:23) and superior to the philosophy of the Greeks and Romans. This sage then reformulates wisdom theology in terms of what will become known as rabbinic Judaism (Sir 24:8-12, 23-29). The Second Temple book called the Wisdom of Solomon was supposedly written by the great Iron Age king but is actually a Roman-period composition from Egypt (ca. 37–41 CE) displaying a Hellenistic rhetorical style. It addresses the philosophical validity of the Torah, now affirmed as the very method by which God redeemed the Jews. This late sage finds the Jewish tradition to be an excellent equivalent to Hellenistic philosophies and in basic harmony with them. Jewish wisdom continues on in the work of the Jewish philosopher Philo (e.g., *On the Virtues*) and in tractates of the Mishnah and Talmud, especially "THE SAYINGS OF THE FATHERS."

New Testament authors, living in the world of the Roman Empire, reflect a dual view of wisdom. On the one hand, the earliest layer of traditions about Jesus (Q and the *Gospel of Thomas*) clearly presents Jesus as a great and astonishing sage (see Matt 6:19-7:27). This was a natural Jewish framework for understanding the subtle and thought-provoking teachings this rabbi presented in his parables and sayings (Matt 11:25-27), but these early levels of tradition also draw upon the roles of prophet, healer, and exorcist to describe Jesus. The sages of the East attend his wonderful birth and view it as a fulfillment of their own philosophical learning and astrological observations (Matt 2:1, 7, 16; see MAGI). Jesus implicitly names himself as the messenger of mother Wisdom (SOPHIA, in Greek; Luke 11:49), whom we first meet scolding the ignorant and offering life from the heights and market squares of the town in Prov 1. As prophet of Wisdom, he is the child who justifies her teaching (Luke 7:35), and he will give the gift of wisdom to those of his followers who are unjustly accused and tried (Luke 21:15).

Yet the NT letters, for all that they affirm about Jesus as "the Sophia of God" (1 Cor 1:24; see also Eph 3:8-10; 5:15; Col 4:5), nevertheless have their issues with sages and their way of looking at the world. In the context of well known and respected philosophies of their conquerors, the writers of the NT know that their proclamation of the gospel will seem mere "foolishness" (Matt 23:24; Jas 3:13). Paul uses this concept to place his theological arguments before the Corinthians (1 Cor 1:17-25; 2:6-16). Paul said that the things prophesied by the OT have arrived (Isa 29:14): by means of the work and teachings of Jesus, God has frustrated the wisdom of the wise and given true knowledge (belief in the Messiah, the atonement, and resurrection) to infants and those who are weak (1 Cor 1:19-27). Something wonderful, far greater than the wisdom of Solomon, and far beyond the simple calculations of cause and effect, is at work in the world: sages are made into fools, and fools into triumphant followers of the cross (Matt 11:25; Luke 10:21).

F. Usage in Adjectival Forms

When applied as an adjective, "sage" or "wise" refers to the special expertise or "know-how" that a trained person acquires and displays. Often found with the forms of the verbs bin (בִּין), "understand," sakhal (שָׂכַל), "be prudent," or in association with lev (לֵב), "heart/mind," the adjective suggests that being wise is an intellectual activity in which one continually operates. "Skilled" women (literally, "wise of heart") act as mourners within a specific literary tradition; likewise, wise-hearted women use their skills to spin and dye yarns used to fashion the hangings of the desert tabernacle (Jer 9:17-21; Exod 35:25-26). Negatively, some described as "wise" are better thought of as "cunning" or "crafty," knowing the worldly pragmatics necessary to achieve unlawful ends (1 Sam 13:3). Wise speech is especially praised: it is discerning, knowledgeable, and shows a deep understanding of the way the world (or some specialized part of it) works. However, being "wise" in speech, action, or thought is not confined to the sages: slaves can be wise (Prov 17:2; Matt 24:45), along with ordinary Christians (Matt 25:2, 4, 8-9) without regard for social class or gender. The followers of Jesus are advised to be "wise as serpents" (phronimos, Rom 11:25) and "self-disciplined" (1 Tim 1:7), speaking with "sober truth" (sophroneō, Acts 26:25), and answering "wisely" (nounechō, Mark 12:34). *See* COUNSEL, COUNSELOR; UNDERSTAND; WISDOM IN THE ANCIENT NEAR EAST; WISDOM IN THE NT; WISDOM IN THE OT.

Bibliography: Athalya Brenner. *A Feminist Companion to Wisdom Literature* (1995); James L. Crenshaw. *Education in Ancient Israel: Across the Deadening Silence* (1998); John G. Gammie and Leo G. Purdue. *The Sage in Israel and the Ancient Near East* (1990).

CAROLE R. FONTAINE

SAHAB. This major, multi-period site is located 7 mi. southeast of Amman, Jordan, on the edge of the desert. Some identify it with ABEL-KERAMIM of Judg 11:33. Moawiyah Ibrahim conducted excavations there in the 1970s, but the architectural finds are no longer visible due to modern dwellings built over the complete site. The excavations showed that Sahab was occupied from the late Neolithic period to the end of the Iron Age.

The largest settlement was from the late Neolithic and Chalcolithic periods (ca. 5000–3300 BCE) when inhabitants seem to have practiced intensive agriculture and lived in both caves and houses. One of the houses contained a series of rooms around a courtyard, in which were several storage pits lined with stones. After a short hiatus a new settlement began in the Early Bronze Age (ca. 3000–2000 BCE), but excavators found only broken pottery pieces in a deep sounding.

More significant remains came from the Middle Bronze Age (ca. 2000–1550 BCE), which produced a large structure interpreted by Ibrahim as a fort. It was found abutted by a sloping earthen rampart, typical of this period at major sites throughout Israel. At another location excavators discovered a massive city wall. Because the site is so close to the desert, Ibrahim interpreted this settlement as a major element in the defenses against raids from the desert.

Open spaces in the modern town allowed excellent access to remains around the periphery of the Late Bronze Age settlement (ca. 1550–1200 BCE), showing that the shape of the town was a rough oval. Although little of the town's interior was available for excavation, excavators were able to locate a large wall 17 m long with a projecting tower that may have been part of a palace, typical building types in the Late Bronze Age at many sites in Israel. The pottery finds from the town seem to come from all periods of the Late Bronze Age. A large TOMB from the very end of this period was excavated.

Domestic buildings from the Iron I period (ca. 1200–1000 BCE) were uncovered almost everywhere, but no complete houses came to light. Some of the walls reused Late Bronze Age walls, suggesting a continuity of population. In one of the two almost complete houses, a group of collared pithoi (large storage jars; *see* ARCHAEOLOGY §C.2.d) appeared. This was the first discovery of this type of jar in Jordan. This type of pottery was used for storage of surplus food supplies throughout the year. A tomb from this period was also discovered that contained many objects and pottery.

The Iron II town was relatively small, but walled. It produced a significant architectural complex with large rectangular rooms, some with pillars. It was too large to be a house; therefore, Ibrahim suggested a commercial facility. The finds included large quantities of loom weights and grinding stones.

Bibliography: Moawiyah Ibrahim. "Sahab and Its Foreign Relations." *Studies in the History and Archaeology of Jordan* 3 (1987) 73–81.

LARRY G. HERR

SAIDIYEH, TELL ES. Tell es-Saidiyeh, identified as the biblical city of ZARETHAN (Josh 3:16; 1 Kgs 7:45-46), lies at the heart of the central Jordan Valley, on the south side of the Wadi Kufrinjeh. The large mound occupies a key strategic position, commanding the crossroads of two major trade routes, and dominating some of the richest and most fertile agricultural land east of the river Jordan.

The site was first settled in the Chalcolithic period (5th millennium BCE), but the first extensive occupation phase dates to the Early Bronze Age (ca. 3300–2150 BCE). Little has been recovered of the Early Bronze I phase apart from a few traces of a well-constructed city wall, indicating that the settlement was significant and substantial, covering approximately 12 ha. The most extensively excavated phase belongs to the Early Bronze II period. Part of a large palace complex has been uncovered, the function of which seems to have been geared to the industrial-scale production of commodities for export to Egypt. One wing of the complex was devoted to the manufacture of fine textiles, another to the production of wine, but the most fully exposed was found to be responsible for the extraction of olive oil. The palace was destroyed by fire around 2700 BCE.

Following the destruction, the site appears to have been abandoned, and was reinhabited in the Late Bronze Age. During this and subsequent periods, occupation was confined to the eastern side of the mound, giving rise to the existing topography—a high upper tell to the east and a lower bench-like extension to the west.

During the 13th cent. BCE, perhaps in the reign of Ramesses II, the site was taken into Egyptian control, and at this time, the lower tell became used as a cemetery to serve the population inhabiting the upper tell. Tell es-Saidiyeh was further developed by the pharaohs of the Twentieth Dynasty, and during the 12th cent., it became a major trade and taxation center. A remarkable series of public buildings has been uncovered including a palace complex, a large residency, and part of the main eastern gate—all built using Egyptian construction methods—and an Aegean-style water system. The lower tell continued to be used as a cemetery, and a large number of graves has been excavated, many of which show strongly Egyptian characteristics, both in terms of the grave goods and also the burial practices.

Following the withdrawal of the Egyptian Empire in the 12th cent. BCE, the site reverted to local control, but the "Egyptian phase" buildings remained in use until some time in the 11th cent. when they were destroyed by fire. Following this destruction, and a brief abandonment, occupation resumed, but on a much smaller scale. Only in the 9th cent. was the site extensively settled again. Protected by strong fortification walls, a well-planned city was laid out on an intersecting grid of streets and alleyways, and the houses and workshops provide evidence for industrial specialization in the form of weaving and textile preparation. Toward the end of the 8th cent., Tell es-Saidiyeh was again destroyed by fire, this time most probably by the Assyrians. This event effectively put an end to settlement on the site, and although a series of fortresses crowned the highest point of the upper tell throughout the Babylonian, Persian, and Hellenistic periods, no evidence has been found for associated habitation.

Bibliography: J. N. Tubb. *Canaanites*. Rev. ed. (2006).

JONATHAN N. TUBB

SAIL [מִפְרָשׂ mifras, נֵס nes; ἀνάγω anagō]. As a verb, the word denotes the movement across water of a vessel powered by means of a large canvas or cloth sheet exposed to and catching the wind. As a noun, it refers to the large canvas or cloth sheet itself. In the OT, nes is used in Isa 33:23 as the noun *sail*, whereas in other contexts it can mean "ensign," "BANNER," or "STANDARD." More famously, the NT speaks in the Gospels and Acts of various persons "sailing." The Gk. verb means "to lead, bring up." *See* SHIPS AND SAILING IN THE NT; SHIPS AND SAILING IN THE OT.

JAMES E. WEST

SAILOR [אִישׁ אֳנִיּוֹת ʾish ʾoniyoth, מַלָּח mallakh; ναύτης nautēs]. In the OT one of the nouns translated *sailor* comes from the Hebrew word meaning "salty." Hence, a sailor is a "salty" man or a man of the sea. The noun is used in Jonah 1:5 (also in Ezek 27:9, 27, 29, where it is translated *mariner* in the NRSV). The other term for a sailor, ʾish ʾoniyoth, literally means "a man of ships." The Gk. word translated *sailor* in the NT is the etymological origin of the English word *nautical*. It occurs in three places (Acts 27:27, 30; Rev 18:17) and describes those who operate sailing ships or vessels of the sea or lake. *See* SHIPS AND SAILING IN THE NT; SHIPS AND SAILING IN THE OT.

JAMES E. WEST

SAINT [חָסִיד hasidh; ἅγιος hagios]. A common NT designation, better translated "holy one(s)," for the members of the early Christian communities, understood as God's distinctive people in continuity with the people of Israel. Unlike later usage, *saints* in the Bible does not designate a special class of God's people. The Greek adjective hagios (occurring all but once in the plural, hagioi [ἅγιοι]), "holy," used as a noun, is often rendered "saint(s)" in English because English inherited the French word "saint" ("holy"), from the Latin "sanctus."

The word *saint(s)* occurs sixty-six times in the NRSV: once in the psalms, twice in the Wisdom of Solomon, and sixty-three times in the NT, mostly in the Pauline epistles (forty times—twenty-three in the undisputed letters) and Revelation (fifteen). About one-fourth of the NT occurrences are found in epistolary greetings at the beginning or end of letters, where the term is shorthand for "believers" (2 Thess 1:10), disciples of Jesus (1 Cor 1:2), or "brothers and sisters" (Phil 4:21; Col 1:2). The term also served as a generic term to distinguish Christians as a whole from sub-groups such as "widows" (Acts 9:41; 1 Tim 5:10), "leaders" (Heb 13:24), or "apostles" (Rev 18:20). In the NT, in other words, all believers are saints. Nevertheless, it would be a mistake to think that the word was just a name without theological significance.

According to the OT, God has called and "set apart" (the root meaning of "holy," qadhosh [קָדוֹשׁ]), a people to be God's own people, the "holy ones" (qedhoshim קְדֹשִׁים). In some Bibles, the original has been translated "saints" (e.g., KJV; occasionally NIV), though the NRSV and most other modern versions render it as "holy ones" (e.g., Pss 16:3; 34:9; Dan 7:18-27 [Aramaic; possibly meaning "heavenly beings"]). God's saints constitute "a priestly kingdom and a holy nation" (Exod 19:6; see 1 Pet 2:9; Rev 5:10). Because God is holy (separated from humans), God's people are called to be holy, to share in God's differentness (Lev 11:44-45; see 1 Pet 1:15-16). Thus a nearly synonymous term for saints/holy ones is "faithful ones," those marked by faithfulness to the covenant (hasidhim [חֲסִידִים]; e.g., Pss 30:4; 116:15). This Hebrew term is frequently rendered "saints" in the KJV and NIV, and it accounts for the only occurrence of *saint* in the NRSV translation of the OT (Ps 31:23). This all suggests that biblical holiness, or "sainthood," is both gift and task, both "indicative" and "imperative" (to borrow linguistic language).

The term *saint* appears only once in the Gospels (Matt 27:52), referring to the bodily resurrection of "saints who had fallen asleep" that occurs at the moment of Jesus' death. Although the language probably reflects early Christian faith and hope (compare 1 Thess 4:13), the people to whom the Gospel refers must be OT saints.

In Acts the word appears three times in chap. 9 (vv. 13, 32, 41) as a designation for various groups of believers, and once in 26:10, where Paul tells King Agrippa about his persecuting and imprisoning "many of the saints" in Jerusalem. The evident irony of Paul's persecuting holy people, as narrated in that speech, is even more forceful in Acts 9:13, where Ananias voices to the Lord (Jesus) his suspicion of Saul (Paul) because of "how much evil he has done to your [the Lord's] saints"—one of the few NT texts in which the saints are identified explicitly as belonging to the Lord, echoing the OT image of the people as God's own possession (see also Col 1:26; 1 Thess 3:13; and, implicitly, Rev 5:9).

The word *saints* appears in ten of the thirteen Pauline letters, indicating that it was widely used in Paul's communities. Apart from its function as a general designation for believers, it also carries with it special nuances in various contexts. On several occasions the term is used with special reference to believers in need, as if to stress responsibility by an appeal to the solidarity of sainthood. This can be seen in Rom12:13; 15:25, 26, 31; 1 Cor 16:1; and 2 Cor 8:4; 9:1, 12, where the theme appears especially in connection with Paul's call for Christ-like participation in his collection for the poor saints in Jerusalem. (Compare 1 Cor 16:15, 1 Tim 5:10, and the non-Pauline Heb 6:10 regarding service to the saints.)

Occasionally, the OT theology of sainthood as both gift and task comes to the fore. In Rom 1:7 the letter's recipients are said to be "called to be saints," thus stressing God's election of the people to the vocation of holiness, which is spelled out in some detail in chap. 6 and chaps. 12–15 (see references to holiness/sanctification in 1:4; 6:19, 22; 12:1). The same language is used in 1 Cor 1:2, where Paul stresses the close connection between the Corinthians' status as "sanctified," or set apart (gift), and the universal call to all Christians to be saints (task).

The working dimension of sainthood is stressed on a few occasions, in which Paul admonishes his readers to do that which is fitting for those who are saints (Rom 16:2; Eph 5:3). This suggests that even elsewhere the designation *saints* implies a standard of behavior grounded in the fundamentals of early Christian ethics, which embraced virtues such as hospitality, sacrificial love, and sexual purity in defining sainthood or holiness as discipleship to Jesus.

In a number of instances in the Pauline letters, "the saints" is a term associated with eschatological privilege and responsibility, including sharing in Christ's appearance (1 Thess 3:13), worship of him (2 Thess 1:10), and the final judgment (1 Cor 6:1-2). In Colossians and Ephesians, the saints are the recipients of the revelation of God's mystery (Christ) in the present (Col 1:26) and those who will share in a future "inheritance" (Col 1:12; Eph 1:18). Finally, it is significant that in Ephesians, all saints are to be equipped for "the work of ministry" by their pastors and teachers (4:12).

In Hebrews, it is not the cast of heroes (chap. 11) that receives the designation *saints*, but rather all members of the community (6:10; 13:24), as also in Jude (v. 3). In John's Revelation, *saints* is a generic term (22:21) for those ransomed by Christ, the slain lamb of God, "from every tribe and language and people and nation" (5:9). They are depicted as offering prayers (5:8; 8:3-4) and as faithful and righteous, like the prophets and other OT holy ones (11:18; 19:8), in spite of persecution (13:7; 16:6; 17:6; 18:24; 20:9). Yet even saints must be called to faithful endurance in imitation of Christ (13:10; 14:12; compare 1:5, 9).

Saints is more than a common term for "believers." Rooted in the OT, sainthood (or holiness) in the NT comes to mean Christ-likeness in such shared virtues as compassion, service, and faithfulness, because Christ "became for us... sanctification" from God (1 Cor 1:30). Within the Christian tradition, there has sometimes developed both an elitism and a privatism in the use of terms like *saint* and *holiness*. The NT supports neither of these directions. *See* HOLY, HOLINESS, NT; HOLY, HOLINESS, OT.

Bibliography: Stephen C. Barton, ed. *Holiness Past and Present* (2003); Kent E. Brower and Andy Johnson, eds. *Holiness and Ecclesiology in the New Testament* (2007); John Webster. *Holiness* (2003).

MICHAEL J. GORMAN

SAKKUTH AND KAIWAN sak'uhth, ki'wuhn [כִּיּוּן khiyun, סִכּוּת sikkuth]. Sakkuth and Kaiwan are mentioned only in Amos 5:26, which is the high point of the prophet's oracle against the house of Israel. The name *Sakkuth* perfectly matches the consonants of a well-known star deity from RAS SHAMRA and a variety of Mesopotamian locations. The Hebrew vocalization is very similar to shiqquts (שִׁקֻּץ, "detestable thing or abomination," 1 Kgs 11:7), suggesting a possible scornful wordplay by Amos. The prophet's derision continues with the labels "your king" and "star-god." Kaiwan has been identified with the star god Saturn. The pair of names has appeared together in star deity texts. Several commentators have suggested that the appearance of these Assyrian deities indicates textual emendation or a post-Amos editor; however, these names pre-date Amos and were regionally known before the 8th cent. BCE. Amos thus proclaims that those who bear up detestable Assyrian idols in cult processionals will be lifted up and carried into exile.

Bibliography: Shalom M. Paul. *Amos.* Hermeneia (1991); Hans W. Wolff. *Joel and Amos.* Hermeneia (1977).

BRUCE W. GENTRY

SALAMIEL suh-lay'mee-uhl [Σαλαμιήλ Salamiēl]. An ancestor of Judith (Jdt 8:1). The name is a variant spelling of SHELUMIEL in the LXX and Vulg.

SALAMIS sal'uh-mis [Σαλαμίς Salamis]. The largest city on Cyprus, located on the east end of the island. It is sometimes confused with the Greek island near Athens, where the Greeks defeated the Persians in the battle of Salamis in 480 BCE. Salamis was the first stop for Paul and Barnabas when they left Antioch (Acts 13:5). From Salamis, they traveled to the capital of Cyprus, Paphos, on the west end of the island.

Several ancient sources suggest that Salamis had a significant population of Jews. For example, it had several synagogues (Acts 13:5). According to *Acts Barn.*

22–23, a mob of Jews killed Barnabas in Salamis. Finally, during the Jewish uprising in 116/117 CE, Salamis suffered significant destruction. After the Romans quashed the rebellion, Jews were banned from Cyprus.

Archaeologists have found significant remains from the Roman period, including the theater, gymnasium, public baths, the agora, and the harbor. There are also church remains from the Byzantine period.

ADAM L. PORTER

SALECAH sal'uh-kuh [סַלְכָה salekhah]. Narratives concerning the TRANSJORDAN wars (Num 21:21-35; Deut 3:10) note that the Israelites fought with OG, king of BASHAN. Deuteronomy preserves a list of boundary towns, including Salecah, which had previously been under Og's control but were transferred to the half-tribe of Manasseh (Deut 3:13). Salecah bordered Bashan, represented the northeasternmost limit of Og's territory (Josh 12:5; 13:11; 1 Chr 5:11), and was known as Triakome in the Hellenistic-Roman periods. Surface surveys have shown large Greek and Nabatean cultures once flourished at this site.

JOSEPH R. CATHEY

SALEM say'luhm [שָׁלֵם shalem; Σαλήμ Salēm]. The city of King MELCHIZEDEK (Gen 14:18), long associated with JERUSALEM. Genesis 14:17 places the meeting of Abraham and Melchizedek in the "Valley of Shaveh (that is, the King's Valley)," and a "King's Valley" was located near Jerusalem (2 Sam 18:18; *see* SHAVEH, VALLEY OF). Psalm 76:2 [Heb. 76:3] names Salem in parallel with Zion (i.e., Jerusalem) as the home of God in Judah. In the 1st cent. CE, Josephus identified Salem with Jerusalem and the city of David (*Ant.* 7.65–68). Scholarly attempts to disprove the traditional equation have not proved convincing.

Because King Melchizedek of Salem serves as a priest (Gen 14:18-20; compare Ps 110:4), it seems that the author of Gen 14 portrayed Melchizedek as an archetype of the high priest who served in the Temple in Jerusalem. Melchizedek provided blessings and inspired Abraham to respond with a tithe offering.

In the letter to the Hebrews, the priest Melchizedek is seen as a forerunner of Jesus. Just as the author of the letter finds significance in Melchizedek's name ("king of righteousness"), so too does he interpret "king of Salem" as "king of peace" (Heb 7:1-3). Thus, in the NT, Salem is understood as a symbolic name for Jerusalem.

MICHAEL G. VANZANT

SALIM say'lim [Σαλείμ Saleim]. A city that was probably situated west of the Jordan River, 20 to 32 km south of the Sea of Galilee. According to Eusebius' *Onomasticon*, it was approximately 12.4 km south of Scythopolis in northern Samaria. The city is mentioned in John 3:23 in association with AENON, where John the Baptist was baptizing in the Judean countryside (John 3:22). Salim was approximately 0.5 km north of

Aenon. John the Baptist chose Aenon as a locale for baptism because of its proximity to Salim, indicating that Salim was likely situated near springs of the Jordan.

SAMUEL BOYD

SALLAI sal′i [סַלַּי sallay]. Meaning "basketmaker." 1. Eponym of a Benjaminite family who settled in Jerusalem after the return from Babylon (Neh 11:7-9). Another such list is quite different from this one, but it includes a SALLU (1 Chr 9:7).

2. A priest among the Levitical families "in the days of Joiakim" the high priest (Neh 12:20). This Sallai may be connected to Sallu, a priest in the days of Joshua and Zerubbabel (Neh 12:7). The Hebrew spelling of this Sallu (sallu סַלּוּ) is very close to the spelling of Sallai.

CHANNA COHEN STUART

SALLU sal′oo [סַלָּא sallu', סַלּוּא sallu', סַלּוּ sallu]. 1. Sallu and his kinsmen are the first Benjaminites to inhabit postexilic Jerusalem (1 Chr 9:7). For the otherwise unknown Sallu of Benjamin, the parallel list in Neh 11:7 provides an unusually long genealogy that stretches back seven generations.

2. One of the leaders of the priests who returned from exile with Zerubbabel and Jeshua (Neh 12:7). The name probably reappears in Neh 12:20 as SALLAI.

LJUBICA JOVANOVIC

SALMA. *See* SALMON.

SALMON sal′muhn [שַׂלְמָה salmah; Σαλμών Salmōn]. Salmon is mentioned in the genealogies of David and Jesus. According to Ruth 4:20-21, Salmon was the son of Nahshon and the father of BOAZ, the husband of RUTH. Boaz himself was the father of Obed, the grandfather of Jesse, and the great-grandfather of David. This information about Salmon is repeated in Matt 1:4-5 in the genealogy of Jesus. Significantly, Matthew also lists the wives of Salmon and Boaz. Salmon's wife, and the mother of Boaz, was RAHAB, the prostitute from Jericho. Boaz married Ruth, likewise a Gentile. By including the Gentile wives of Salmon and Boaz, Matthew points to the place of Gentiles in God's salvific plan.

KENNETH D. LITWAK

SALMONE sal-moh′nee [Σαλμώνη Salmōnē]. Site of modern Cape Sidero, Salmone was the northeastern portion of Crete and the site of an Athenian temple. When the centurion Julius brought Paul to Rome, the pair boarded an Alexandrian ship in Myra bound for Italy. High winds forced the ship to seek protection by sailing under Crete. As the ship sailed south it passed Salmone (Acts 27:7) and arrived at Fair Havens. The pilot and owner decided to sail for the harbor in Phoenix for the winter, but the ship was blown off course by a storm and sank near Malta.

HEIDI S. GEIB

SALOME suh-loh′mee [Σαλώμη Salōmē]. 1. The name of HERODIAS' daughter according to Josephus (*Ant.* 18.135–36). According to Mark, she instigates John the Baptist's execution under Herodias' orders (6:14-30). Some manuscripts of Mark name the daughter Herodias; but in others she is unnamed (6:22; see NRSV note: "the daughter of Herodias herself"). Whatever her name, Josephus does not mention her in connection with the beheading of John the Baptist (*Ant.* 18.116–19). Christian commentators conflated the Josephan and Markan accounts to produce the Salome of operas, plays, and paintings: seductive, exotic, and deadly; in Mark 6, however, the daughter is comparatively innocent.

Erich Lessing/Art Resource, NY
Figure 1: Salome with the head of Saint John the Baptist, Luini Bernardino (ca. 1475–1532). Kunsthistorisches Museum, Vienna, Austria.

2. Mark lists Salome as the third of the three women who witnessed the crucifixion (15:40) and who came to the empty tomb (16:1). Matthew identifies "the mother of the sons of Zebedee" as the third witness (27:56), leading some commentators to conclude that Salome was this woman's name.

NICOLE WILKINSON DURAN

SALT [מֶלַח melakh; ἅλας halas]. Salt, as a preservative and purifying agent, has both literal and metaphorical functions in the Bible. Salt was often a part of ritual observances. In Exod 30:34-35 it is an ingredient in incense to be used in the Temple (compare Ezra 6:9; 7:21-22; 1 Esd 6:30). Salt must be added to all offerings brought to the sanctuary (Ezek 43:24; Lev 2:13). The understanding of salt as a preservative or cleanser may lie behind the story of Elisha in a town with bad water (2 Kgs 2:19-22) where he used salt to make the water wholesome. Salt is used to preserve fish in Tob 6:6 and is one of "the basic necessities of human life" listed in Sir 39:26. Although salt is often a preservative, it can also destroy or render a place uninhabitable or unusable (compare Ezek 47:11; Jer 17:6). The OT refers to conquerors sowing the land with salt to destroy its fertility (Judg 9:45). God sometimes also treats the land of those who do not worship him with salt (Deut 29:22-28; Ps 107:33-34; Jer 48:9; Zeph 2:9; Sir 39:23).

These senses of *salt* are carried over into its metaphorical uses. Ezekiel 16:4 says infant Israel was not rubbed with salt to emphasize that only God's help allowed Israel to become a people. Numbers 18:19 and 2 Chr 13:5 refer to a "covenant of salt." In Numbers the covenant is between God and Aaron's descendants. In 2 Chronicles God gave David and his descendants the kingship of Israel forever with a covenant of salt. These instances may reflect salt's use as a preservative; it perhaps was understood as making the covenant more permanent and secure (see Lev 2:13). The Synoptic Gospels remember Jesus as referring to his disciples as "the salt of the earth" (Matt 5:13), but warning against the loss of their "saltiness" (compare Mark 9:49-50, where having "salt" in themselves allows them to be at peace with one another; Luke 14:34-35). James refers to the impossibility of salt water producing fresh in exhorting his readers not to let their tongues produce both blessing and cursing (3:12). Similarly, Col 4:6 prescribes Christians' behavior toward "outsiders": "Let your speech always be gracious, seasoned with salt, so that you may know how you ought to answer everyone." See COVENANT, OT AND NT; DEAD SEA; INCENSE; SACRIFICES AND OFFERINGS.

CAROL GRIZZARD BROWNING

SALT SEA sawlt´ see´ [יָם הַמֶּלַח yam hammelakh; θάλασσα τῶν ἁλῶν thalassa tōn halon]. The ancient name for the Dead Sea. Literally the "sea of salt" in all cases where the RSV and KJV translate this phrase as "Salt Sea" (e.g., Gen 14:3; Num 34:3, 12; Josh 12:3); the NRSV uses "DEAD SEA."

SALT, CITY OF. *See* CITY OF SALT.

SALT, PILLAR OF. *See* DEAD SEA; LOT'S WIFE.

SALT, VALLEY OF. *See* VALLEY OF SALT.

SALU say´loo [סַלּוּא salu'; Σαλώμ Salōm]. A Simeonite whose son ZIMRI was killed by PHINEHAS (Num 25:14). Moses ordered the deaths of Zimri and his wife COZBI, a Midianite, for intermarriage and the worship of Midianite deities (Num 25:5-8), an event later cited as a model for the actions of MATTATHIAS against a Jew who sacrificed at the Greek king's command (1 Macc 2:26).

JESSICA TINKLENBERG DEVEGA

SALVATION [יְשׁוּעָה yeshu'ah, יֶשַׁע yesha', תְּשׁוּעָה teshu'ah; σωτηρία sōtēria, σωτήριον sōtērion]. The most fundamental meaning of salvation in Scripture is God's deliverance of those in a situation of need from that which impedes their WELL BEING, resulting in their restoration to wholeness (*see* SHALOM). Wholeness or well-being is God's original intent for creation, and that which impedes wholeness (namely, sin, evil, and death in all their forms) is fundamentally anti-creational. Both the deliverance of the needy and their restoration to well-being in relationship with God, others, and the world are crucial to salvation, and the term may be used for either or for both together.

The primary nouns for salvation (or "rescue, deliverance, help, victory") in the OT are yeshu'ah (seventy-eight times), teshu'ah (thirty-four times) and yesha' (thirty-six times). The noun for savior is moshia' (מוֹשִׁיעַ). The verb related to these nouns is yasha' (יָשַׁע), meaning "to save, help, rescue," although an assortment of other verbs can also be used of God's saving action. The meaning of salvation, however, cannot be contained in such lexical use. Beneath the OT's use of explicit salvation language lies a coherent worldview in which the exodus from Egyptian bondage, followed by entry into the promised land, forms the most important paradigm or model.

In the NT salvation is God's project of rescue and restoration effected through Jesus Christ as the climax of Israel's story and the culmination of creation itself. Salvation is God's gift of life; thus Jesus in John aptly summarizes the NT's message of salvation: "I came that they may have life, and have it abundantly" (John 10:10*b*). Salvation is a comprehensive reality affecting every aspect of existence, and it is both present and future (eschatological, having to do with end times or final things).

The word *salvation* (sōtēria, sōtērion) appears forty times in the NT, including five in the Gospels; the word savior (sōtēr σωτήρ) appears twenty-five times, including four in the Gospels; and forms of the verb *save* (sōzō σώζω, diasōzō διασώζω) appear ninety-seven times—about half of them in the Gospels. (The Greek words for "salvation" and "save" appear a few more times, but are not always translated "salvation" or "save.") Forms of "save" are often in the future tense, referring to final, eschatological salvation. Yet salvation encompasses the past (e.g., "we have been saved"), the present ("we are being saved"), and the future ("we will be saved"). These three dimensions appear, e.g., in Paul: past (Rom 8:24; compare Eph 2:5, 8), present (1 Cor 1:18; 15:2; 2 Cor 2:15), and future (Rom 5:9-10). Thus, salvation cannot be limited to forgiveness of sins or to postmortem existence with God; forgiveness of sins can also be experienced now.

In both OT and NT soteriology (theology of salvation) is eschatology realized, but only partially so in the present; it is inaugurated eschatology (*see* ESCHATOLOGY OF THE NT; ESCHATOLOGY OF THE OT). And because soteriology is eschatology realized, salvation extends beyond Israel to include the Gentiles (that is, all humanity) and beyond the human race to include the entire cosmos. For that reason, soteriology is also protology (theology of origins) renewed and realized. God's intentions for Adam and Eve (humanity) and for the garden (God's good creation within which humanity is to flourish) come to fruition in the salvation accomplished in Christ.

A. The Exodus as Paradigm of Salvation
  1. Impediment to flourishing and well-being
  2. Cry of help from those in need
  3. Yahweh comes into the historical situation of need
  4. The divine king fights for those in need
  5. God often uses creaturely agents
  6. God restores the needy to a situation of flourishing
  7. God comes to dwell with the redeemed
  8. God has a prior relationship with those in need
B. God's Creational Intent for Earthly Flourishing
  1. The human calling as the "image of God"
  2. Humanity as mediators of God's presence
C. Sin and Salvation from Creation to Exodus
  1. God's purpose impeded by human sin
  2. God's call to mediate blessing to the nations
  3. Salvation beyond Israel
D. Wisdom and Torah—The Way of Life
  1. The parallel between wisdom and Torah
  2. The link between exodus and Torah
  3. Wisdom, Torah, and God's creational intent
  4. Prophetic critique of injustice as unfaithfulness to Yahweh
E. Prophetic Visions of Restoration beyond Exile
  1. Return to the land
  2. Restoration and healing of God's people in society
  3. Flourishing of the natural world, including peace among animals
  4. New relationship with the nations, centered in Zion
  5. Forgiveness of sin and new heart
  6. Restoration of righteous leadership for Israel
  7. God's presence among the people in the renewed land
F. The Overall Shape of Salvation in the New Testament
  1. Christocentric
  2. Theocentric and biblical
  3. Narrative soteriology
  4. Corporate salvation
G. Competing Soteriologies
H. Dimensions of Humanity's Salvation in the New Testament
  1. Restoration to wholeness and community
  2. Forgiveness of sins and restoration to covenant relationship

  3. Liberation/redemption from sin and from evil powers
  4. Justification/reconciliation/participation in Christ
  5. Reconciliation with both God and neighbor
  6. Resurrection and eternal life
  7. Escape from future wrath
I. Conclusion: Final Defeat of Sin, Death, Satan, Evil, and Redemption of the Cosmos
Bibliography

A. The Exodus as Paradigm of Salvation

In the OT, the exodus is the paradigm or model of salvation. The experience and memory of this event decisively shaped many other OT salvation texts, and even spills over into the NT. The first thing to notice about the exodus is that it constitutes the sociopolitical deliverance of a community from a real, concrete situation of oppression. The exodus thus resists any "spiritualizing" of salvation, keeping it firmly rooted in life in this world. There are at least eight components of salvation in the exodus that are paradigmatic for salvation in the OT (and in the Bible, generally).

1. Impediment to flourishing and well-being

At the start of the book of Exodus, we find Israel fulfilling the creational mandate to multiply and fill the earth (1:7; compare Gen 1:28). Pharaoh, however, is intent on impeding God's purposes for the flourishing of Israel (and ultimately, as we shall see, for the world's flourishing) by enslaving and oppressing the Israelites (1:10-11). When they continue to flourish despite his efforts (1:12), the Egyptians increase the oppression (1:13-14) and Pharaoh tries to have newly born Israelite males murdered (1:16, 22), thus impeding God's desire for Israel's well-being (1:20).

2. Cry of help from those in need

The Israelites groan in their bondage and cry to God for help. This cry for help is recounted in the exodus narrative (Exod 2:23-25) and is twice mentioned in God's explanation to Moses of why he has come to intervene (3:7, 9; 6:5). Later, Israel's cry of distress from the exodus is recapitulated in the period of the Judges, as various enemies oppress the fledgling nation, and the people's groaning (whereby they echo the exodus cry) is explicitly mentioned as what motivates God to intervene (Judg 2:18). So paradigmatic is this exodus cry for help that Israel's most typical form of prayer is modeled on it. The most common genre of psalm in the OT is the lament, in which the psalmist complains about a concrete situation of need and appeals to God for help. Indeed, a later prophetic text addressing a time of national distress affirms that "everyone who calls on the name of the LORD shall be saved" (Joel 2:32), an affirmation quoted in Acts 2:21 and Rom 10:13 about salvation through Jesus. The NT even portrays the entire created order groaning in its bondage to futility as it awaits God's final redemption (Rom 8:19-23).

3. Yahweh comes into the historical situation of need

Israel's cry for help "rose up to God" (Exod 2:23) and God tells Moses, "I have come down to deliver them from the Egyptians" (3:8). The vertical language reflects the background picture (found in many OT texts) of God's throne in heaven (Pss 2:4; 11:4; 104:1-3; Isa 40:2; 63:15; 66:1-2: Amos 9:6), from which God rules creation (heaven and earth) and from which he comes into human historical experience to deal with all that impedes flourishing. This picture makes an important theological claim about God's transcendence. Precisely because Yahweh rules from heaven, outside the oppressive system of human evil (including Egyptian bondage), this God can be appealed to and realistically expected to care about human suffering (whereas appeals to Pharaoh, who is implicated in the oppressive system, are ineffectual; Exod 5:15-16). Further, as ruler of creation God has the power to transform this situation of oppression. God's transcendence is, therefore, not in contrast to God's involvement; it is precisely the condition of this involvement.

4. The divine king fights for those in need

The Song of the Sea celebrates Yahweh as a warrior (Exod 15:3), and the narrative of the Sea crossing pictures Yahweh fighting on behalf of his people (14:14), overthrowing the forces of evil (in this case, Pharaoh's army). Drawing on the standard Hebrew metaphor of heat for anger, the Song vividly portrays God's wrath consuming his adversaries like stubble (15:7) and blasting a path through the sea with the breath of his nostrils (15:8). Like the sea crossing, the plagues (Exod 7–11) are portrayed as Yahweh's mighty works, the signs and wonders that he brought upon Egypt to force Pharaoh to let the Israelites go (6:1; 7:3-4; 8:19; 9:3). For this reason—because Yahweh has intervened with power to deliver Israel in their time of need—he is celebrated in the Song of the Sea as incomparable among the gods (15:11) and the Song ends with the affirmation that Yahweh "will reign forever and ever" (15:18). The "coming" of Yahweh as king of creation to judge evil is an important motif also in enthronement psalms, and results in celebration among the nations and the nonhuman creation (Ps 96 and 98). Yahweh's coming as judge and savior also becomes a central theme of the OT prophetic tradition (e.g., Mic 1:3-4).

5. God often uses creaturely agents

While Moses tells the people that they are to stand by and watch the salvation that God will work at the sea (Exod 14:13), God tells Moses to participate in the deliverance by stretching out his hand with the staff, thus dividing the waters (14:16), as God did on the second and third days of creation (Gen 1:6-10). That God is the ultimate agent of salvation thus does not conflict with the fact that creational agents are often used in the process of bringing salvation. Not only does Yahweh call Moses to "bring my people, the Israelites, out of Egypt" (Exod 3:10)—using the same verb from the prior statement that God would "bring them out" (3:8)—but the waters of the Red Sea themselves are God's instrument in overthrowing the Egyptian army; and prior to that various forces of the nonhuman creation participate in the ten plagues (Exod 7–12), convincing Pharaoh to let the Israelites go. Later, God will use a series of human agents, such as judges, kings, and prophets, to effect salvation for the chosen people, including even the Persian king Cyrus, who is called God's anointed (Isa 44:28; 45:1, 13), and the suffering servant (Isa 52:13–53:12).

6. God restores the needy to a situation of flourishing

As a consequence of removing the impediment that blocks flourishing, the situation of the needy is transformed as they are restored to the fullness of life. Deliverance is thus never just from that which impedes flourishing; it is goal-oriented, moving the delivered ones toward the restoration of flourishing. Central to this flourishing is the promise of a good land where they can live in safety. Thus Yahweh explains Israel's destination after leaving Egypt: "I have come down ... to bring them up out of that land to a good and broad land, a land flowing with milk and honey" (Exod 3:8). The goal of the exodus is that Israel might flourish in their own land; without this flourishing the exodus would not be complete. This logic explains why the Song of the Sea does not end with Yahweh overcoming the Egyptian army (15:1-12), but goes on to speak of God leading the redeemed people to the promised land, where they can dwell securely (15:13-17)—thus anticipating the narrative arc from Exodus to Joshua. Indeed, in every retelling of the exodus story in the Bible, whether in storytelling psalms (like Pss 78, 105, 106, 136) or in individual prayers or other liturgical restatements (Deut 6:20-25; 26:5-10; Josh 24:1-14; Jer 2:6-7; 32:17-23; Neh 9:6-31), the two linchpins of the story are always the deliverance from bondage and the gift of land.

7. God comes to dwell with the redeemed

Central to the flourishing of the redeemed people is God's presence among them. Thus, in the Song of the Sea, the land toward which Israel is journeying is described as God's "holy abode" (Exod 15:13), and references to "the mountain of your own possession" and God's "sanctuary" (15:17) allude to Zion and the Jerusalem Temple, although it may be that the entire land of Israel is conceived of as the place of God's dwelling. Indeed, God's dwelling with the Israelites is explicitly stated as the purpose of the exodus (Exod 29:45-46). This emphasis on God's presence among the redeemed people makes sense of that significant section of the book of Exodus that describes the tabernacle (chaps. 25–40), the mobile tent whose purpose is to make God's presence available to the people as they journey toward the land of promise. Thus, the narrative of the golden calf (Exod 32–34), which occurs in this section of the book, is an unauthorized attempt to secure the deity's presence. While much postbiblical Christian interpretation of God's dwelling with his people tends to decontextualize the "relationship" (as if the community just holds hands around a fire singing "Kumbaya"), the OT portrays God's presence with the redeemed squarely in the context of their concrete earthly life, first in the wilderness, then in the land.

Even the ancient promise "I will be their God, and they shall be my people," found in Jeremiah's oracle of a new covenant (Jer 31:33; quoted in Heb 8:10) and associated in some texts with God's dwelling with the people (Lev 26:11-12; Ezek 34:30; 37:27; 2 Cor 6:16), is first given to Abraham in connection with the promise of land (Gen 17:7-8). When Yahweh rearticulates this same promise of "relationship" to Moses (Exod 6:7) it is sandwiched between the announcement of deliverance from bondage (6:6) and the gift of land (6:8). It is therefore significant that prophetic restatements of this ancient promise are explicitly linked with God's dwelling with the redeemed people in a safe and bountiful land after the return from exile—since this is what is required for human flourishing (Jer 32:37-41; Ezek 34:25-31; 37:24-28; Zech 8:7-8).

8. God has a prior relationship with those in need

Even before he tells Moses of his plans to deliver the Israelites, and even before he mentions that he has heard their cry, Yahweh identifies himself as "the God of your father, the God of Abraham, the God of Isaac, and the God of Jacob" (Exod 3:6). This identification places the exodus from Egypt firmly in the narrative context of the book of Genesis, recalling God's prior covenant with Israel's ancestors. But not only is Israel's salvation at the exodus rooted in a prior relationship with God, all of God's actions on behalf of human flourishing are rooted ultimately in the relationship of humans to their creator. Thus God can introduce the affirmation of Israel's election with the statement that "the whole earth is mine" (Exod 19:5). Indeed, it is impossible to fully understand the OT portrayal of salvation without beginning with God's original intent for the flourishing of creation. This is because salvation is fundamentally the restoration of the creator's intent from the beginning. Salvation has cosmic roots.

B. God's Creational Intent for Earthly Flourishing

God's affirmation of the validity and goodness of creaturely existence permeates the opening creation account of the Bible. Genesis 1 is peppered with statements of God's evident pleasure in the world he is making. At various stages in the creative process, we are told, "God saw that it was good" (1:4, 10, 12, 18, 21, 25). And when creation is complete, "God saw everything that he had made, and indeed, it was very good" (1:31).

In this opening creation account God also blesses humans and animals with fertility (Gen 1:22, 28) and grants food to both for their sustenance (1:29-30). In Gen 2 God plants a garden for humanity, which provides both aesthetic pleasure and food for nourishment (2:9). God evidently desires the flourishing of creation.

1. The human calling as the "image of God"

While the garden of Eden as the original human environment in Gen 2 is clearly meant to provide for human needs, paradoxically the garden itself needs humans. Genesis 2:4-8 explains that God delayed planting the garden until there was a human to work it. This suggests that the garden is not simply a "natural" phenomenon, but a cultural project that humans are to participate in. Not only are humans made from the ground (Gen 2:7) but they are made for the ground, with a specific task or vocation in mind. Envisioning something beyond a primitive hunter-gatherer society, Gen 2:15 portrays the original human purpose as tilling and keeping the garden; agriculture is the first communal, cultural project of humanity. Indeed, since it is the creator who first planted the garden, it could be said that God initiated the first cultural project, thus setting a pattern for humans—created in the divine image—to follow. Whereas Gen 2 focuses on agriculture, Ps 8 foregrounds animal husbandry as the basic human task in God's world. Humans are crowned with royal dignity and granted authority or dominion over various realms of animal life—on land, air, and water (8:5-8). The domestication of animals is here regarded as a task of great dignity and privilege, in which humans manifest their position of being "little lower than God" (8:5).

Genesis 1:26-28 combines both motifs, in its portrayal of humans as created to rule over the animal kingdom (like Ps 8) and to subdue the earth (similar to tending the garden in Gen 2). And they are to accomplish these tasks as God's representatives, which is the upshot of being made in the "image" and "likeness" of God (Gen 1:26-27). The royal task of exercising power as God's image to transform the earthly environment into a complex sociocultural world that glorifies the creator (the so-called "cultural mandate") is thus a holy task, a sacred calling, in which the human race manifests something of the creator's own lordship over the cosmos.

That humanity is created with an earthly calling or cultural vocation suggests that while the world is "very good" when God has completed the creative process, it is not complete or "perfect" in the sense that it cannot be made better. That is precisely the human task. The pristine world God made is open to improvement by the exercise of human cultural power, a calling granted humans at creation. Thus Gen 4 reports the building of the first city (4:17) and mentions the beginnings of cultural practices, such as forms of worship (4:3-4, 26), nomadic livestock herding, musical instruments, and metal tools (4:20-22). That such cultural practices and products came into being in God's world is due to the human community exercising their cultural power as the image of God (*imago Dei*) to develop the world beyond its primitive beginnings—in accordance with the creator's purpose for earthly flourishing.

The connection of *imago Dei* to the exercise of cultural power is assumed in the book of Proverbs. Just as God constructed the cosmos by wisdom, understanding, and knowledge, so when humans build a house, it requires this very same triad of qualities (Prov 3:19-20; 24:3-4). This adumbration of an *imago Dei* theme makes sense of the portrayal of Bezalel, who is put in charge of constructing the tabernacle in Exod 31. Bezalel is filled with God's Spirit (the same Spirit that hovered over the unformed world in Gen 1:2) and also with wisdom, understanding, and knowledge (Exod 31:2-5; 35:30-35)—the same triad of qualities by which God made the world. By thus imaging/embodying God's wisdom in creation, Bezalel is able to practice good craftsmanship in the building of the tabernacle (a portable earthly shrine for God's presence). The human embodiment of wisdom in earthly construction projects thus reflects the creator's will and recapitulates God's own building of the cosmos, which was also a developmental project, transforming an original unformed and unfilled mass (Gen 1:2) into a complex world, over six days.

2. Humanity as mediators of God's presence

The assumed parallel in the Bezalel account between creation of the world and tabernacle construction (as macrocosmos and microcosmos) suggests the picture of the created order as a cosmic temple, a sacred realm over which God rules, in which all creatures (human and nonhuman) are called to worship their creator. This picture is particularly evident in Ps 148, which calls on a variety of heavenly and earthly creatures (148:1-4, 7-12) to praise their creator (148:5-7, 13-14), as if together they constituted a host of creaturely worshipers in the cosmic sanctuary. According to Isa 66, heaven is Yahweh's throne and the earth is his footstool (66:1a). Therefore the text questions why any human being would bother to build an earthly "house" for God (referring to rebuilding of the Jerusalem Temple after the exile), since God has already created the cosmos as sacred space (66:1b-2).

In this cosmic sanctuary humans are created to be the "image" of God. Just as the cult statue or image in an ANE temple was meant to mediate the deity's presence to the worshipers, so humans—by their cultural power to develop the world—are the divinely designated mediators of the creator's presence from heaven (where Yahweh is enthroned) to earth, thus completing the destiny of the cosmic temple, that God might fully indwell the earthly realm, much as the glory and presence of Yahweh filled the tabernacle (Exod 40:34-35).

One day, "all the earth shall be filled with the glory of the LORD" (Num 14:21).

C. Sin and Salvation from Creation to Exodus

1. God's purpose impeded by human sin

Tragically, human cultural innovation is intertwined in the primeval history (Gen 1–11) with the misuse of power, which impedes God's purposes for the flourishing of earthly life and prevents God's presence from fully permeating creation. This misuse of power begins with the transgression of the first prohibition in the garden (2:17; 3:6), with resultant "curses" (3:14, 17; 5:29). These curses stand in tension with the primordial "blessings" God grants creatures (1:22, 28; 2:3). As a result of the primordial transgression, humans are exiled from the garden and prevented access to the tree of life (2:23-24), work has become painful toil (3:18-19), and childbirth will henceforth yield excessive pain (3:16a). Further, we find the origin of male power over women (3:16b), the first murder (4:9)—which leads explicitly to further "curse" (4:11)—the first case of bigamy (4:19), and revenge killing out of proportion to the injury suffered (4:23-24).

In accordance with the directive of Gen 1:28, humans begin to multiply and fill the earth, but they end up filling the earth with violence (6:11, 13) rather than contributing to the flourishing of God's world or extending the divine presence on earth. Indeed, human violence has so corrupted or ruined the earth (6:11-12) that God is grieved (6:6) and engages in a cleansing operation—the great flood (Gen 6–9). Although Noah, his family, and a remnant of animal life are preserved to allow a new start, the flood does not fundamentally change the direction of the human heart (8:21). Instead, corruption soon permeates human life once again (9:21-27). And the primeval history culminates with the account of the building project of Babel (11:1-9), a parable of the regressive human attempt to guarantee security by settling in one place and constructing a monolithic empire, with a single language, thus resisting God's injunction to the human race to diversify and fill the earth. The project of Babel ends with God's confusing the single language of the builders and scattering the people over the earth, thus defusing human power and restarting the diversified human cultural project.

2. God's call to mediate blessing to the nations

It is in this context of a failed human project that God calls Abraham and his descendants out from all the families and nations of the earth, in order to bring blessing to all families and nations (Gen 12:3; 18:18; 22:18; 26:4; 28:14). The election of Abraham/Israel can thus be seen as a strategic move to counter the destructiveness and violence (with resultant curse) that has pervaded human life, in the ultimate service of the flourishing of the whole world. Initial examples of this blessing in the narrative of Genesis include Abraham's prayer to heal the barrenness of Abimelech's wife and slaves (20:17-18), the blessing Laban experiences due to Jacob (30:27-30), the blessing of Potiphar's household due to Joseph's presence (39:2-6), and Joseph's preservation of the life of the Egyptians (indeed of "all the world") during the famine (41:53-57). These are all concrete examples of salvation.

But this larger macro-purpose of blessing the human family requires first the establishing of Abraham's family as a flourishing people (a microcosm of God's intent for humanity). Hence God promises to bless Abraham with protection from enemies, with many descendants (who will become a great nation), and with a land in which they may live and flourish (Gen 12:2-3, 7; 13:14-17; 22:17; 26:3-4, 24; 28:3-4, 13-15; 35:11-12). Abraham's family is to mediate God's presence and blessing in the world by themselves being an exemplar or model of God's blessing on humanity, which includes their practice of justice and righteousness (18:19).

The subsequent enslavement of the covenant people in Egypt and their deliverance through the mediation of Moses (Exod 1–18) must therefore be understood in two overlapping contexts—God's intent for Israel and for the world. On the one hand, Egyptian bondage is an impediment to God's desire for the flourishing of the covenant people and the exodus is God's act of restoring them to the blessing/flourishing that had been promised to the ancestors. On the other hand, Israel's bondage is an impediment to God's purposes for the flourishing of all humanity and Israel's deliverance is in the service of this larger purpose. The cosmic scope of the exodus is alluded to in numerous statements during the plague cycle and the sea crossing to the effect that not just Israel (Exod 6:7; 7:17; 10:2) but also Pharaoh and all Egypt (7:5; 8:10, 22; 9:14, 29; 10:7; 14:14, 18) would come to know who Yahweh is through these miraculous events. The cosmic scope of the exodus is plainly stated in connection with the seventh plague, when Yahweh affirms that his name will be proclaimed in all the earth (9:14). Indeed, at this point cosmic statements accumulate: Pharaoh will come to know that there is no one like Yahweh in all the earth (9:16) and that the earth belongs to Yahweh (9:29).

After the exodus, when Israel arrives at Sinai, a similar cosmic claim precedes God's reaffirmation of Israel's calling. Although "the whole earth is mine" (Exod 19:5b), says Yahweh, Israel is to be "a priestly kingdom and a holy nation" (19:6), implying a vocation of mediating divine blessing and presence in a world that belongs to God. This universal purpose of Israel's election comes to particular clarity during the Babylonian exile in the so-called servant songs of Isaiah, where God's servant (Israel) is said to constitute God's "covenant" or pledge to the peoples of the world and is called to be a light to the nations (Isa 42:6b; 49:6b), facilitating their release from bondage (42:7).

3. Salvation beyond Israel

It is, however, important to note that blessing/salvation in God's world is not limited to the mediation of Israel. God is at work outside of Israel, bringing blessing and enhancing earthly flourishing for both the chosen people and the rest of humanity. Even when Abraham and Sarah renege on their calling to bring blessing to others by sending Hagar and Ishmael into the arid wilderness, God does not abandon them, but preserves the non-elect from certain death (Gen 16:7-14; 21:15-21). God may even use the non-elect to contribute to the flourishing of the elect, as when both Pharaoh and the Philistine king Abimelech shower Abraham with flocks, servants, and land (Gen 12:6; 20:14-15), or when the Canaanite priest-king Melchizedek blesses Abraham by God Most High (Gen 14:18-20). Later, the Mesopotamian diviner Balaam will bless Israel from a distance, without their even knowing it (Num 22-24). And God is involved in the liberating of nations other than Israel from their bondage (Amos 9:7), although such nations do not thereby become God's elect with a specific vocation to the world.

In the primeval history, prior to Israel, the original human couple brings forth new life (Gen 4:1-2a, 25) in response to the divine command to be fruitful and multiply (1:28), as do their offspring (4:17-22, 26). Despite the primal human transgression and lack of access to the tree of life, the genealogies of Gen 5; 10; and 11:10-32 testify to the continuation, indeed the proliferation, of the human family, and the genealogy of Gen 5 specifically portrays the transmission of the *imago Dei* (5:1-5) as part of this blessing from generation to generation, which endures even after the flood (9:6).

Although outside the garden, Cain and Abel continue the human vocation by fulfilling the divine injunction to subdue the earth and rule the animals (1:28; 4:2b). After Cain's murder of Abel, God ameliorates the ensuing curse and shows compassion for the murderer by placing a mark of protection on him (4:15). And in the midst of the violence that begins to fill the earth, Enoch (5:24) and Noah (6:9) walk with God, and the latter is explicitly described as a righteous man, who—at God's command—is instrumental in the salvation of both humans and animals (6:18–7:5). After the flood, God promises the continuation of the seasons (8:22), rearticulates the primal blessing of fertility for Noah and his family (9:1, 7), inaugurates a law (with sanctions) prohibiting murder (9:6), and enters into a covenant with Noah, his family, all living creatures, and the earth itself (9:9-17), pledging to sustain and protect the created order for their benefit. In the context of this divine commitment to earthly flourishing, the human race proliferates and diversifies—linguistically, culturally, ethnically, geographically, spreading out over the face of the entire earth (Gen 10), until the regressive move of Babel (11:1-9), which God counters with a re-scattering and a diversification of languages. In all these ways, the biblical text testifies to God's intent for the flourishing of earthly life. Hence the psalmist's claim is justified: "You save humans and animals alike, O LORD" (Ps 36:6).

D. Wisdom and Torah—The Way of Life

God's desire for the flourishing of both humanity and the nonhuman world is further clarified by the role of wisdom and TORAH ("law, instruction"). The OT legal and wisdom literature addresses a creation-wide range of topics, including matters of justice, work, money, clothing, housing, food, disease, sex, war, worship, and leadership—there are even laws for the well-being of domestic and wild animals, birds, trees, and the land (*see* WISDOM IN THE OT). That is, the way of wisdom or obedience to Torah is meant to nurture holistic earthly flourishing, restoring the whole of life to what it was meant to be. Thus Israel's obedience to Torah will display their wisdom to the nations (Deut 4:5-8).

1. The parallel between wisdom and Torah

Both wisdom and Torah describe, in strikingly parallel ways, God's norms for life and blessing (that is, the way of salvation or flourishing), and both are contrasted with paths that lead to death. The wisdom literature presents wisdom and folly as the two ways set before each person (Prov 2:20-22). Wisdom is vigorously commended as God's way of righteousness (Prov 2:1-8) that leads to life (Prov 3:13-18), while folly leads to death. Wise living flows from the "fear of Yahweh" or appropriate awe of God (Job 28:28; Ps 111:10; Prov 1:7; 9:10), which is functionally equivalent to allegiance to Yahweh in the Torah.

In the Torah, the fundamental contrast between life and death is linked to the choice between obedience and disobedience to God's laws, commandments, statutes, etc. Obedience is therefore vigorously commended ("choose life") as that which leads to a life of flourishing in the land of promise (Deut 30:15-20), while disobedience results in exile from the land. Obedience is seen as an expression of whole-hearted "love" of Yahweh (Deut 6:4-5). Thus the Decalogue begins with exhorting the people to exclusive allegiance to the one true God (Exod 20:3) and prohibits fashioning idols (20:4-6, 23). This exclusive allegiance to the God of the exodus is meant to ground the communal life of the people (20:7-17) as they seek to live in harmony with the nature of this deliverer God.

2. The link between exodus and Torah

Following upon the exodus from Egypt—on their way to the promised land—Israel arrives at Mount Sinai and receives the Torah, consisting initially of the Decalogue (20:1-17) and an assortment of other laws (21:1–23:19), the so-called "book of the covenant" (24:7) that Yahweh is making with Israel. Yahweh's first words to the people at Sinai explicitly connect deliverance with obedience (19:4-5). The connection between Torah and deliverance is also signaled in the prologue to the Decalogue, which identifies the divine lawgiver as the God of the exodus (20:2). The exodus thus functions as the historical ground for Israel's allegiance to Yahweh and obedience to Yahweh's Torah—both requirements of the covenant God makes with them at Sinai.

While a life of obedience to Torah is clearly an expression of gratitude for the gracious deliverance Yahweh worked in the exodus, such obedience also completes the salvation begun in the exodus. The exodus was only the beginning of the process of Israel's salvation; deliverance from bondage must now be matched by conformity to the creator's will. The Torah thus constitutes God's instructions for holy living, meant to direct the life of the redeemed community toward justice and righteousness, that they might be restored to flourishing.

But there is a more focused way in which the exodus grounds obedience to Torah. There are specific injunctions and exhortations in Exodus, Leviticus, and Deuteronomy, pertaining especially to the treatment of the needy or marginalized, that are linked either: 1) to Israel's experience of suffering in Egypt; or 2) to God's compassion to liberate the oppressed from bondage. With explicit appeals to this twofold motivation, the Torah prohibits Israel from wronging or abusing aliens, widows, or orphans (Exod 22:21-24; 23:9; Lev 19:33-34; Deut 24:17-18) or from taking advantage of anyone in need (Exod 22:25-27; Lev 25:35-38, 39-43), and enjoins the people to release all debt slaves in the year of Jubilee (Lev 25:54-55) and even to "love the alien as yourself" (Lev 19:34; Deut 10:17-19). The exodus thus functions as a lens for understanding the requirements for societal flourishing in a broken world by generating a special focus of concern among the covenant people for the needy or marginalized. The experience of the exodus grounds Israel's insight that human society cannot function properly—that salvation is incomplete—unless the most vulnerable members are protected, provided for, and nourished.

3. Wisdom, Torah, and God's creational intent

Whereas the Torah is linked to the exodus, there is a more fundamental sense in which both Torah and wisdom are expressions of God's will from creation. Proverbs 3:19-20 asserts that God created the world by wisdom/understanding/knowledge and Job 28:25-27 explains that in creating the cosmos God appraised and tested wisdom, thus implying that it is embedded into the very structure of reality. The logic of this claim yields the conclusion that living according to wisdom means going with the grain of the universe, while going against this grain is utmost folly—it destroys life and prevents flourishing.

Jeremiah links creation by wisdom/understanding with creation by the word as parallel ideas (10:12-13). Various psalms identify creation by the word with creation by God's command, statute, or decree (33:6-9; 119:89-96; 148:5-6), the same range of terms used for the Torah that Israel is required to obey. This identification suggests an intimate connection between God's decrees for the entire creation and for Israel. Thus Ps 19 describes in parallel fashion God's revelation in the created order (19:1-6) and in Israel's Torah (19:7-13). Likewise, Ps 147 first portrays God's providence in creation as effected by his word (147:15-18), and then explains that this word was revealed to Israel in the Torah (147:19-20). That God's Torah holds for the entire created order leads Ps 148:8 to describe the wind as obedient to the creator's word and Ps 119:91 can say to Yahweh: "all things are your servants." This is also the basis for Jeremiah's contrast between birds that "observe" the time of their migration (thus doing the will of God) and disobedient humans, who "do not know the ordinance of the LORD" (8:7).

Discerning wisdom and obeying Torah are thus two equivalent ways of speaking of God's creational intent for flourishing. This is why Moses' wise decision-making in settling the people's disputes is described—even prior the giving of the law at Sinai—as his making known to them "the statutes and instructions of God" (Exod 18:15-16). In a similar vein, Isaiah attributes something we might call common sense—namely, the wise plowing and threshing techniques of farmers (28:24-25, 27-28)—to the counsel or instruction of Yahweh (28:26, 29). There is no difference, in principle, between wisely discerning God's will structured into the created order and obeying God's revealed word. Most fundamentally, Torah or wisdom is that which discloses—and thus orients the community to—God's creational intent for flourishing.

4. Prophetic critique of injustice as unfaithfulness to Yahweh

Prophetic critique of Israel's unfaithfulness to Yahweh assumes this understanding of Torah and flourishing. The prophets particularly emphasize that the people's allegiance/submission to Yahweh, the God of the exodus, ought to be manifest in a life that embodies the flourishing God desires (righteousness and justice). The bond between allegiance to Yahweh and practice of justice toward the neighbor is so strong that Jeremiah tells King Jehoiakim that doing justice is equivalent to knowing God (22:16). While the prophets certainly censure idolatry, one significant stream of prophetic critique de-emphasizes correct "worship" activities as relatively unimportant vis-à-vis justice (Isa 1:10-20; 58:1-14; Jer 7:1-15; Amos 5 [especially 4–7, 11–12, 14–15, 21–24]; Mic 6:1-8 [especially 6-8]). Not only is Israel's injustice (the mistreatment of other human beings) subject to critique, their "worship" or cultic activities (such as festivals, feasts, sacrifices) are anathema to Yahweh when such "worship" is substituted for compassion and justice toward others. The logic of the prophetic critique is that whereas "worship" is an explicit claim to allegiance to Yahweh, such a claim must be backed up with justice, which is a concrete demonstration of this allegiance. What God really wants is human flourishing, embodied in the practice of justice and the healing of the social order.

Prophetic texts often utilize an if-then structure, drawing explicitly or implicitly on the covenant sanctions of the Torah. While repentance and new obedience (described especially as right treatment of the neighbor) will result in blessing and shalom (Isa 1:19; 58:6-14; Jer 7:3, 5-7; Amos 5:14-15), persistence in disobedience will result in destruction and even exile from the land (Isa 1:20; Jer 8-9, 14-15; Amos 5:10-12, 16-17, 26-27).

Such covenant sanctions draw on the list of blessings and curses found in Lev 26 and Deut 28. Obedience will lead to blessing in every dimension of life, from fruitfulness of crops and herds, to living without fear, in the city, in the home, to positive international relations (Lev 26:3-13; Deut 28:1-14), while disobedience will lead to being cursed (the opposite of life and flourishing) in equally pervasive ways, resulting ultimately in being ejected from the land of promise (Lev 26:14-45; Deut 28:15-68).

The list of covenantal blessings and curses clearly demonstrates the link between the moral and cosmic orders, so that when the human community is in harmony with God's design their earthly life (including the nonhuman world) flourishes, but when they go against God's intent for flourishing this affects also the earthly environment, to the extent that the land will vomit out its inhabitants (Lev 18:24-28; 20:22). Babylonian exile is the ultimate consequence for unfaithfulness to Yahweh.

E. Prophetic Visions of Restoration beyond Exile

Many prophetic texts promise a renewal of people and land after the judgment of exile. In particular, there are seven promised components of renewal in prophetic texts that together testify to God's purpose for earthly flourishing.

1. Return to the land

First, the return from exile is promised, which involves a resettling of the promised land (Isa 11:10-12, 16; 35:8-10; 42:7; 55:12-13; 60:4; Jer 32:37; Ezek 34:27; 36:8-11; 37:11-14; Amos 9:15; Zeph 3:19-20; Zech 8:7-8). This is the *sine qua non* of all the prophetic promises of restoration. Since the judgment of exile was fundamentally characterized by landlessness and alienation, a return to the land is key to Israel's renewal. This return also fulfills the original state of humanity at creation, where God calls humanity to subdue the earth (Gen 1) or to work the ground from which they are taken (Gen 2). The OT simply cannot conceive of full salvation or flourishing without earthly, landed existence.

2. Restoration and healing of God's people in society

But the promise is not for a bare or marginal existence in the land. Rather, Israel is promised renewal and healing as a people, such that their communal and urban life will be restored to flourishing, fruitfulness, and blessing (Isa 35:5-6*a*, 10; 60:1-2, 18-22; 61:1-4, 7, 9; 62:4-7, 12; 65:18-24; Jer 31:4-6, 11-14; Ezek 34:25-31; 36:33-36; 37:5-6, 12, 14; Amos 9:14; Zeph 3:11-18; Zech 8:1-5, 11-15). Instead of mourning over the corrupt city and bringing judgment on Zion, God will one day "rejoice in Jerusalem" and "delight" in the people (Isa 65:19). This promise reverses Israelite corruption and the destitution and shame of exile, to which they have been subject.

3. Flourishing of the natural world, including peace among animals

Some prophetic visions of restoration depict the flourishing of nature as Israel returns home—both during the return journey from Babylon and when the people resettle the land (Isa 35:1-2, 6*b*-7; 55:12-13; Ezek 34:26-29; 36:8-11, 34-35*a*; 47:1-12; Joel 2:23-24; 3:18; Amos 9:13; Zech 8:12; 14:8). Some texts portray a new harmony with the animal kingdom, such that people and animals will live in peace (Isa 11:6-9; 65:25; Ezek 34:25, 28), while Isa 65:17 even envisions a new cosmos ("new heavens and a new earth") as the context for societal renewal. The salvation of humanity thus has ramifications for the restoration of the nonhuman world.

4. New relationship with the nations, centered in Zion

But it is not only the people's relationship with the natural order and the animal kingdom that will flourish. Since Israel has often been oppressed by other nations (hence the Babylonian exile), the prophets promise a new relationship with the nations, in which enmity is transformed into service, and some texts envision the fulfillment of Israel's vocation of mediating God's blessings to the world as the nations stream to Zion to seek God and his ways (Isa 2:2-4; 60:3; 61:5-6, 9, 11; Jer 3:17; Mic 4:1-4; Zech 2:11; 8:20-23). Isaiah 60 even has the best cultural contributions of the nations being brought to Jerusalem to be transformed and used for Israel's benefit and Yahweh's glory (60:5-16; compare Rev 21:26), while Isa 19 predicts a future parity among Israel, Egypt, and Assyria, when they shall all be Yahweh's people (19:23-25).

5. Forgiveness of sin and new heart

Some prophetic texts also promise inner renewal for the people, in the form of a new covenant, through which God forgives sins, pours out his Spirit, or grants a new heart that will enable the people to keep Torah, to conform to God's requirements (Isa 30:20-21; 59:20-21; Jer 31:31-34; 32:40; 50:20; Ezek 11:19; 36:26; 37:23;

Joel 2:28-29). Given the history of Israel's apostasy and disobedience, it becomes clear that a radical new act of God's grace is required to empower the people to live in righteousness and peace.

6. Restoration of righteous leadership for Israel

Some prophetic texts also promise new, trustworthy leaders for the nation, replacing the corrupt leadership of the past, that the people may be led into righteousness (Isa 11:1-5; 32:1; Jer 3:15; 23:5-6; 30:9; Ezek 34:23-24; 37:22-25; Hos 3:5; Amos 9:11-12; Mic 5:2-4; Zech 9:9-10). These promises are quite disparate, but they become, in the Second Temple Period, the basis of messianic hope, the anticipation that God will raise up someone (from either a royal or priestly line) who will truly lead the nation in fulfilling God's will, thus establishing God's kingdom on earth. Grounded in God's use of creaturely agents in bringing salvation (especially humanity created in the image of God), this theme finds its fulfillment in the NT understanding of Jesus as the Christ, God's chosen one to restore Israel, and indeed the world.

7. God's presence among the people in the renewed land

Tying the above themes together is the promise of God's permanent presence among the redeemed people in the context of the flourishing, bountiful land (Jer 32:37-41; Ezek 34:25-31; 37:24-28; Zech 8:7-8). This is the fulfillment of the ancient and often reiterated claim that it is God's intent to dwell among the redeemed in the context of a divine-human relationship, where he would be their God and they would be his people (Exod 29:45-46; Lev 26:11-12). This intent is rooted, ultimately, in God's purpose from the beginning to manifest his presence on earth through the mediator role of humanity as the authorized image of God in the cosmic temple. Although Israel needed to function as the mediator of God's presence to the nations (because of their sin), the divine presence cannot ultimately be limited to Israel, to the Temple, or to the promised land. Thus, the book of Zechariah envisions God dwelling in the midst of Israel along with the "many nations" who will have joined God's people (2:11) and speaks of the day when Yahweh will become king over all the earth (9:14). Indeed, the prophets predict a day when the earth will finally be filled with the knowledge of God—or of his glory—"as the waters cover the sea" (Isa 11:9; Hab 2:14).

As a prelude to the coming salvation, some prophetic oracles describe a vivid theophany, accompanied by a shaking or melting of the world as the divine Judge approaches (Isa 13:5-10, 13; 14:16, 21; 24:4-13, 17-23; 34:4; 51:6; Jer 4:23-26; Hos 4:3; Joel 2:10, 30-31; 3:15-16; Amos 8:8-9; Mic 1:3-4; Zeph 1:2-3, 18; Hag 2:7; Zech 14:3-5). Such texts draw on visionary aspects of Yahweh's coming to save in the Song of the Sea (Exod 15:1-18) and his subsequent descent upon

Mount Sinai (Exod 19:16-20), utilizing extreme, apocalyptic language. These theophanic visions can depict great destruction, as if the created order itself is coming radically undone. But the coming of the Holy One initiates the destruction not of creation as such, but of sin and evil; as with the flood, the world undergoes a radical cleansing as a prelude to God's presence and to the deliverance and renewal that will ensue (Isa 25:6-9; 26:19; Zech 14:6-8). Thus, the enthronement psalms picture the nonhuman creation rejoicing at Yahweh's coming to judge evil and restore justice on earth (96:10-13; 98:7-9). While judgment is an inescapable reality for those who resist God's will, God's ultimate purpose is to accomplish his original intent for the flourishing of humanity (Israel and the nations), and even the nonhuman world. In the end, the OT anticipates that salvation will be as wide as creation.

F. The Overall Shape of Salvation in the New Testament

One approach to NT soteriology is to analyze the various NT writings and then attempt a synthesis (e.g., Matera and van der Watt). While this approach has merits, we will use a more thematic approach as the framework for discussing some of the common and distinctive aspects of the NT writings. Because NT soteriology is not limited to the occurrences of the "salvation" word-family, we will also consider the kingdom/reign of God, liberation, redemption, reconciliation, and justification. We begin with some preliminary remarks about the overall shape of salvation in the NT.

1. Christocentric

New Testament salvation is thoroughly christocentric. Jesus' claim in John 14:6, "I am the way, and the truth, and the life. No one comes to the Father except through me," is not an exceptional perspective but rather faithfully summarizes the entire NT. Jesus is the one mediator between God and humanity by which God's desire for universal salvation is fulfilled (1 Tim 2:3-6). Peter in Acts also speaks representatively: "There is salvation in no one else, for there is no other name under heaven ... by which we must be saved" (Acts 4:12). The NT thereby claims that the biblical way of salvation—calling on the name (character, power) of the Lord/Yahweh (Joel 2:32)—now means calling on the Lord Jesus (Acts 2:21; 22:16; Rom 10:13; 1 Cor 1:2). Jesus has taken on the divine role of Savior (Luke 2:11; John 4:42; Acts 5:31; Titus 3:6; Phil 3:20; 1 John 4:14). Because NT salvation is christocentric, it is constituted by the narrative of Christ from incarnation and ministry to death and resurrection to parousia. Each part of this narrative has a function in salvation, and different texts focus on different parts of the story. But the most distinctive narrative dynamic of salvation in the NT is that of death and resurrection, both Christ's and ours. Death now (whether literal or metaphorical) means, paradoxically, new life both now and later (John 12:24). This dynamic reaches its apex in Paul's theology of dying and rising with Christ (Rom 6), but it permeates the entire NT. Sacrificial love, service, and suffering will give way to future resurrection, eternal life, and glory (Heb 2:9-10; 1 Pet 1:6-12; 5:1-11; Rev 2:10).

2. Theocentric and biblical

At the same time, however, salvation in the NT is thoroughly theocentric. It is the God of Israel, the one true God, who saves in and through Jesus Christ. The gospel is the "power of God" for salvation because in it God's covenant faithfulness is revealed (Rom 1:16-17). Thus God is also called "Savior" in the NT (Luke 1:47; 1 Tim 1:1; 2:3; 4:10; Titus 1:3; 3:4; Jude 1:25). The confluence of Savior language in Luke for both God (Luke 1:47) and Jesus (2:11) and three times in the Letter to Titus (1:3, 4; 2:10, 13; 3:4, 6) is especially significant and summarizes the NT's perspective: because Jesus is the epiphany of God's grace (Titus 2:11; 3:4), both he and God are rightly and inextricably called Savior. "Salvation belongs to our God who is seated on the throne, and to the Lamb!" (Rev 7:10).

New Testament soteriology is therefore biblical: the NT writers see salvation in Messiah Jesus as the continuation of God's activity in and for Israel both as recounted in the Scriptures and as promised in the Prophets. Throughout the NT, salvation is depicted as new creation, new humanity, new exodus, new covenant, and the like, suggesting both continuity and discontinuity with God's past dealings with Israel. Salvation cannot be understood without knowledge of creation, exodus, and covenant, because what God does in Christ is a reprise of these great acts. Yet there is something so startlingly new in what God does in Christ that the old wineskins cannot contain the new wine (Matt 9:14-17; Mark 2:22; Luke 5:33-39). The biblical ballad continues, but in a new key.

3. Narrative soteriology

New Testament soteriology is thus a narrative soteriology. Not only is it constituted by the story of Christ but the story of Christ is part of a larger narrative from creation to Israel to Christ to church to new creation. To participate in God's salvation offered in Christ is to be "inscribed" (so Matera, Green) into the larger divine narrative. To be saved is to be caught up in a story much bigger than anyone's own personal story of an encounter with the earthly or exalted Jesus, as important as that encounter is. To be saved is to benefit from, and participate dynamically in, God's story, God's metanarrative, God's project—the *missio Dei.*

4. Corporate salvation

Salvation in the NT is therefore inherently a corporate reality. The divine mission is not merely to save individuals but to save a people and indeed humanity itself. In other words, the *missio Dei* is to rescue and restore lost Israel by reconstituting it around Jesus and twelve representative disciples, and to rescue and restore lost humanity by creating one new humanity in Christ, consisting of Jews and Gentiles, males and females, slave and free (John 11:52; Gal 3:28; Eph 2:15).

Finally, NT soteriology is by nature countercultural and even subversive, especially of reigning metanarratives and competing soteriologies. In the 1st cent. there existed numerous beliefs about what salvation meant and how it was accomplished. The NT's claim that true salvation is found only through the actions of Israel's God in Jesus of Nazareth, God's Son and now the Lord of all, leaves no room for other saviors and their respective stories and soteriologies. This is true even of the cosmic perspective on Christ offered in Colossians (see 2:8). Similarly, the NT's soteriology still calls into question soteriologies and metanarratives that offer substitute saviors, whether political or otherwise.

G. Competing Soteriologies

In general, the ancients understood salvation as this-worldly rescue, protection, and benefaction. We will briefly consider two soteriologies that would have been attractive to would-be beneficiaries of the salvation offered in Jesus.

Salvation was commonly thought of as restoration to health, and Asclepius was one of many deities who was called savior. His healing, saving powers were acknowledged and experienced throughout the Roman Empire. Perhaps 300 campus-like shrines to Asclepius dotted the Mediterranean basin. These facilities provided a holistic approach to healing: psychological treatment, hot-spring baths, theatrical entertainment, and (hopefully) night visitations by the god himself. The healing ministries of Jesus and of certain early Christian leaders would have provided an alternative account of healing; an even wider, more holistic view of salvation; and, perhaps most important, an ongoing community of people who were participating in the same salvation together (*see* MEDICINE AND HEALING, GODS OF).

Of perhaps even greater importance was the soteriology of Rome and the emperor, who was seen as son of god and savior (see especially Keesmaat). He represented on earth the savior-god Zeus (*see* EMPEROR WORSHIP). The divinely sanctioned salvation offered by Rome included the imperial "peace and security" (see 1 Thess 5:3) for which Augustus and his successors were famous, but which was possible only by violence and the threat of violence, displayed in the reality of crucifixion. The cross was the symbol of two competing soteriologies: salvation offered by Rome that depended on the crucifixion of many, including "the Lord of glory" himself (1 Cor 2:8), and salvation offered by Israel's God that came about through the crucifixion of one. In each case, the salvation allegedly provided was seen by its adherents and advocates as an expression of power: the power to control or crush opponents versus the power to love and liberate them.

The soteriologies of Asclepius and Rome, with their christocentric alternative, provide an important key to understanding NT soteriology. Salvation is about the gift of life, of wholeness, and about the most unexpected means to receiving that life—death on a cross as the divine means of rescue and restoration.

H. Dimensions of Humanity's Salvation in the New Testament

If salvation is rescue and restoration, it is important to ask, Rescue from what? Restoration to what? The NT's answer is not a univocal one. Rather, it sees salvation as rescue from a multifaceted reality (the fallen human condition), as well as restoration to something that also must be described in a variety of ways. These various perspectives are not ultimately different soteriologies, however; they are explications of different dimensions of the salvation offered through Jesus.

Each dimension of salvation presented in the NT carries with it a perspective on at least the two questions noted above. More generally, the NT answers the question What has God done (or what will God do) to rescue and restore humanity, and what must we do to benefit from that salvation?

New Testament salvation begins with God. It is the faithful yet gracious act of a faithful and merciful God. Paul is of course the NT's premier theologian of grace. He depicts humanity as covenantally dysfunctional (Rom 1:18-32), as weak, ungodly, unrighteous, sinful, enemies of God (Rom 5:6-10), as unable to fix its own problem (Rom 8:3-4). So God, in a fit of sheer grace, intervenes (Rom 3:21-26).

This conviction about grace is hardly unique to Paul, however. Jesus' parables and encounters with individuals include some of the NT's most powerful witnesses to divine grace (Matt 18:21-35; Luke 7:41-50 [note "saved" in v. 50]; 17:4). Especially significant is the collection of parables in Luke 15 that portrays God as the gracious seeker of the lost, who welcomes back any "sinner who repents" (Luke 15:7, 10). Throughout the Gospels Jesus' compassion and initiative in seeking and saving the lost (Luke 19:10) are the channel of divine grace.

Grace—God's initiative in Christ in response to our inability to rescue ourselves—is the starting point for every aspect of salvation. But people who receive God's gracious blessings are expected to respond in appropriate grace-filled ways. This was the ancients' expectation: salvation was like any other form of benefaction—a public dispensation of grace, to which the appropriate response was also a public display of grace as gratitude, expressed in word and deed.

In the NT, then, to be saved is to be rescued and transformed by grace, to be under the sway or power of grace, as Paul puts it (Rom 6:14-15). What does this mean more concretely? The NT texts suggest seven dimensions of salvation.

1. Restoration to wholeness and community

In the Gospel narratives the human condition is presented not as a universally consistent phenomenon but rather on a case-by-case basis: sinners; demoniacs under the power of Satan rather than the reign of God; the physically ill, often said to be oppressed by disease from birth or for many years; the dead, whose departure has caused great grief; those who are both ill and unclean, and thus separated from community; those who practice injustice. We may refer to this cluster of realities as the absence of SHALOM (shalom שָׁלוֹם)—the reality of captivity and brokenness contrary to God's intended wholeness. These portrayals of the human condition indicate how important it is to understand salvation in the NT as more than rescue from sin, wrath, or death; salvation is restoration to wholeness.

The in-breaking of God's kingdom in Jesus addresses all these conditions, but it does so according to the need of the individual. Jesus' ministry, as he describes it in Luke, is "to bring good news to the poor.... to proclaim release to the captives and recovery of sight to the blind, to let the oppressed go free, to proclaim the year of the Lord's favor" (Luke 4:18-19; compare Isa 61:1-2). This proclamation of a Jubilee year (Lev 25) by Jesus will mean that the captives, the blind, and the oppressed—both literally and metaphorically—will experience liberation and restoration to wholeness.

Jesus brings salvation by restoring individuals to wholeness through his powerful words and deeds, especially his exorcisms, healings, and resurrections of the dead. The common element is liberation—the undoing of the reign of death-dealing powers such as Satan, sin, sickness, and death itself. In John, Jesus' deeds (called signs) both convey life and point to Jesus as the source of that life. Jesus liberates from both literal and spiritual blindness (John 9) and death (John 11).

The Synoptic Gospels frequently use the word *save* to describe what has happened to such persons: the woman forgiven at Simon's house (Luke 7:50); the Gerasene demoniac (Luke 8:36); Jairus' daughter (Mark 5:23); the woman with a hemorrhage (Matt 9:18-26; Mark 5:28, 34; Luke 8:40-56); the sick at Gennesaret (Mark 6:56); one of the ten lepers (Luke 17:19); and Bartimaeus/the blind man (Mark 10:52; Luke 18:42). But the NRSV and other translations sometimes render the Greek verb sōzo with "made you well" or "was healed." Luke, consistent with Jesus' program announced in Luke 4:18-19, is especially fond of using sōzo to characterize Jesus' physical healings and exorcisms as deeds of salvation (Luke 8:36, 48; 17:19; 18:42; compare Acts 4:9; 14:9), but only in one case (18:42) does the NRSV translate the text with a form of "save."

While Jesus' deeds do of course make people well, and while these events are sometimes also described with the verb "to heal," failure to translate these texts with forms of the English verb "save" perpetuates the theological error that Jesus' restoration of people to physical wholeness is something other than salvation (*see* HEALING; MIRACLE). As in the OT, however, the Gospel writers do not allow for salvation to be understood in purely "spiritual" terms. Salvation by Jesus is restoration to physical, spiritual, and social wholeness, as illustrated especially by the salvation of the woman with a hemorrhage (Mark 5:25-34).

Another significant dimension of Jesus' salvation, then, is the restoration of individuals to community. This is seen also in the cleansing of a leper (Matt 8:1-4; Mark 1:40-45; Luke 5:12-16), who is restored to relationship with God and will also be reunited with "the people," and in the healing of Peter's mother-in-law, who then serves those around her (Matt 8:16-17; Mark 1:30-31; Luke 4:38-39).

The means of appropriating Jesus' gracious gift is faith—trust that Jesus is the agent of God's kingdom and power. Four times Jesus tells individuals, "Your faith has saved you": the woman forgiven, the woman with a hemorrhage, the leper, and the blind man. Jairus also expresses faith, though it is not explicitly named as such, as do the men who bring the paralytic (Matt 9:1-8; Mark 2:1-12; Luke 5:17-26) as well as others in accounts where restoration to wholeness is narrated but not explicitly described with verbs of saving.

2. Forgiveness of sins and restoration to covenant relationship

Beginning with the Gospels, and throughout the NT, the human condition is often characterized in terms of sins, understood broadly as transgressions of the divine law and particularly as failure to love God and others. Integral to Jesus' mission, and represented by his name ("Yahweh saves"), is what the angel told Joseph: "[Y]ou are to name him Jesus, for he will save his people from their sins" (Matt 1:21). Similarly, Zechariah, father of John the Baptist, prophesies that his son will prepare the way of salvation, which includes first of all FORGIVENESS of the people's sins (Luke 1:77). Throughout Luke and Acts, especially, salvation in the present consists above all in the forgiveness of sins and the corollary experience of the Spirit.

Jesus came to call sinners—the spiritually sick (Mark 2:17)—to seek and save the lost (Luke 19:10). Jesus inaugurates this mission during his ministry, as demonstrated in his reputation for associating with "sinners." The story of the paralytic (Matt 9:1-8; Mark 2:1-12; Luke 5:17-26) demonstrates the close relationship between spiritual and physical salvation. The story of the adulterous woman (John 7:53–8:11) powerfully illustrates Jesus' mission to sinners: not to condemn but to save (John 3:17). Both stories reveal that Jesus' gracious word is sufficient to pardon and restore sinful people.

The ultimate means of forgiveness and restoration in much of the NT is Jesus' death. Paul quotes a common early Christian conviction that "Christ died for our sins in accordance with the scriptures" (1 Cor 15:3; compare Gal 1:4). God's faithfulness and mercy are revealed in Christ's death, which is God's means of redemption and atonement (Rom 3:24-25). Jesus is the one who "gave himself a ransom for all" (1 Tim 2:6). First John calls Jesus the "atoning sacrifice" for our sins and "for the sins of the whole world" (1 John 2:2; compare 4:10). Revelation 1:5 says that Jesus "freed [or perhaps "washed"] us from our sins by his blood."

The Synoptic Gospels and Paul ground this claim in the prior claim of Jesus himself at the Last Supper, during which he spoke about his death as the "new covenant in my blood" (Luke 22:20; 1 Cor 11:25), "poured out for many for the forgiveness of sins" (Matt 26:28). The ministry of forgiveness and restoration announced in Matt 1:21 and Luke 1:77, and practiced by Jesus throughout his ministry, finds both its ultimate basis and its quintessential expression in Jesus' voluntary, self-giving death.

The evangelists note the salvific character of Jesus' death in various ways, both obvious and subtle. In Mark, the centurion recognizes Jesus as the Son of God, and thus the agent of God's kingdom, at his death (Mark 15:39). In John, Caiaphas the high priest, unaware of the significance of his words, announces that Jesus will die for the nation (John 11:50-52; 18:14). Similarly, in Matthew, the words of the people, "His blood be on us and on our children" (Matt 27:25), are an ironic double entendre in which the death of Jesus is unwittingly proclaimed as the means of salvation even by and for those who reject him. Also in Matthew, Jesus' death is followed by the apocalyptic event of the dead being raised to life, indicating that the end-time salvation of God has been inaugurated (Matt 27:51-54). In Luke, Jesus' word of pardon and promise of paradise, uttered from the cross, reveal that his saving death continues his life-giving, saving ministry (Luke 23:32-43).

The covenant-creating character of Jesus' saving death is highlighted particularly in Hebrews. By his death, Jesus is the "mediator of a new covenant" (Heb 12:24; compare Jer 31:31-34; Heb 8:8-12). This new covenant is "better" (Heb 7:22; 8:6-13) than that of Moses because the one-time death of God's Son as our High Priest (in contrast to repeated animal sacrifice: Heb 7:27; 9:12, 26; 10:10) brings about full forgiveness and creates a permanent bond between God and those who acknowledge Jesus' death.

3. Liberation/redemption from sin and from evil powers

Although the NT writers share a common perception of humanity's need for forgiveness from sins (plural) and a corollary need to be empowered to love God and neighbor, they also see humanity in bondage to various powers. The solution to bondage is not forgiveness but liberation (see SIN, SINNERS).

Paul offers a unique contribution to the NT's assessment of the human condition. In Romans, after describing humanity's various sins (Rom 1:18–2:29) and before offering a list of corroborating Scripture texts (Rom 3:10-20), he summarizes his argument in the words "all, both Jews and Greeks, are under the power of sin"—singular (Rom 3:9). This phrase could be translated simply "under sin." Sin is being compared to a slave master, a personified force that controls people like an addictive substance. We should probably indicate the nature of this personified power by naming it "Sin," with an uppercase "S." The power of this reality is palpable to Paul; he retrospectively and representatively describes the human condition outside Christ: "it is no longer I that do it, but sin that dwells within me" (Rom 7:20; compare 7:17).

Paul's attribution of such power to Sin is not meant to excuse human evil but rather to indicate, like a physician's diagnosis, that the symptoms (sins) are evidence of an underlying disease (Sin). Humans need not only forgiveness from transgressions (Rom 3:25-26) but also liberation from Sin—from the power and disease that manifests itself in particular sins; they need redemption (Rom 3:24). They need to be "bought back" from their illicit slave master, and in Christ's death, God has done just that—"bought [us] with a price" (1 Cor 6:20). This redemption liberates people not only from Sin, but also from the self (1 Cor 6:19; compare 2 Cor 5:15) and its misdirected life (compare "futile ways," 1 Pet 1:18), what Paul calls "the flesh" (e.g., Rom 7:5, 14; 8:9-13; 13:14; Gal 5:16-19, 24; 6:8). Believers are not their own but God's—enslaved now to God (Rom 6:22) rather than Sin. The Spirit replaces Sin as the indwelling power (Rom 8:9).

Paul and other NT writers know additional malevolent powers as well, more cosmic in scope than indwelling Sin. In the apocalyptic worldview of Jesus and the NT writers, the coming of the kingdom of God or the arrival of the good news of Christ crucified and resurrected means that humanity can be liberated from these cosmic evil powers.

Apocalyptic thinking divided history into two ages, the present evil age and the age to come. Although Jesus' ministry and death inaugurated the new age, it is not yet here in its fullness. Jesus and the evangelists conceived of his mission as a battle with Satan, and exorcisms as proof of his victory by the power of God's Spirit, proof of the presence of the kingdom (Mark 3:19b-30). This was no small part of Jesus' ministry; demons are mentioned more than fifty times in the Synoptic Gospels. Healing miracles could also be evidence of Satan's defeat (Luke 13:11-17). Paul implies that believers have been freed from the blinding activity of "the god of this world" (2 Cor 4:4), while Hebrews claims that Jesus' death destroyed the devil, who had power over death, liberating believers from fear of death (Heb 2:14-15). Similarly, Paul says that in Christ we are liberated from the reign of death (Rom 5:17, 21), yet death is an enemy we still face (Rom 8:38) that will not be ultimately defeated until the end (1 Cor 15:54-57).

The NT also identifies other "powers" (Rom 8:38; 1 Cor 15:24; Eph 6:12; Col 1:16; 2:15; 1 Pet 3:22) that align themselves against God and humans but that have been defeated by, and are subject to, Christ. Yet evil persists, as apostles and faithful believers repeatedly experience (e.g., 2 Cor 2:11; 1 Thess 2:18; Rev 2:13). Nevertheless, the final defeat of Satan and the powers is certain (Rom 16:20; 1 Cor 15:24), at which time salvation and the kingdom of God will be fully present (Rev 12:7-11).

4. Justification/reconciliation/participation in Christ

If apocalyptic images express one significant dimension of salvation, legal and covenantal images express other dimensions. We have already seen that forgiveness of sins is closely associated with covenant renewal. Especially in Paul, another key component of NT salvation with a close connection to covenant renewal is justification.

The connection of justification to salvation is demonstrated by the way that some of the disputed Pauline letters (Eph 2:8; 2 Tim 1:9; Titus 3:5) refer to salvation by grace and faith, when the undisputed Pauline letters prefer to speak of the same experience as justification (e.g., Rom 3:21-31; 5:1; Gal 2:15-21). Justification language also appears occasionally in the Gospels, where it is used both negatively (self-justification, Luke 10:29; 16:15) and positively (Matt 12:37; Luke 18:14). The latter usage suggests that justification is a relational term. In Jesus' parable, the penitent tax collector, not the self-righteous Pharisee, goes home justified (Luke 18:9-14); he has repented, received mercy, and been restored to relationship with God. His is a story of reconciliation, of covenant renewal (*see* JUSTIFICATION, JUSTIFY).

The meaning of the term *justification* (and related words) in Paul has been hotly debated, some arguing for a narrow judicial, or forensic, understanding of justification simply as unmerited acquittal by the divine judge. Although Paul's justification terminology is partially rooted in such legal images, it draws also on relational, covenantal images (e.g., "reconciliation," "life") and on traditional ethical language (e.g., "justice"). For example, the language of justification and of reconciliation is used interchangeably in Rom 5:1, 9-11, while justification and life are united in Rom 5:18, 21; and Gal 3:11. Moreover, in Gal 2:19-21 justification is paradoxically connected to sharing in Christ's life-giving death.

Reconciliation means forgiveness (2 Cor 5:19), but it also means more. Paul identifies the purpose of Christ's reconciling death: "so that those who live might live no longer for themselves, but for him who died and was raised for them" (2 Cor 5:15; compare Rom 6:11, 22, "alive to God" and "enslaved to God"); "so that in him we might become the righteousness of God" (2 Cor 5:21). The justifying, reconciling act of God in Christ was not a mere judicial pronouncement but an effective act of interchange and transformation—of resurrection

from the dead made possible by Christ's resurrection to life (Rom 4:25; 6:5).

This suggests that a more satisfactory definition of justification in Paul is the restoration of right covenant relations in the present life with certain hope of acquittal and eternal life in the future. This definition holds together both the God-oriented and the others-oriented dimensions of the covenant as well as the present and the future aspects of salvation. Future salvation is the logical extension of present justification. Salvation/justification proceeds from God's grace, but the believing community must "work out" (embody, actualize) "your own salvation" precisely because "God ... is at work in you" (Phil 2:12-13). The essence of salvation in the present is to exist in Christ and with Christ in us, a participation, a mutual indwelling (compare Rom 8:1-17).

This interpretation of justification is solidified by a careful reading of Gal 2:15-21. There Paul explains that justification by virtue of Christ's death (2:21) means receiving a new life "to God" by being crucified with Christ so that the resurrected Christ can live within (2:19-20), even as this all takes place "in Christ" (2:16-17). Furthermore, Paul identifies Christ's death as his act of love for us (2:20) and his act of faith/faithfulness toward God (2:16, 20, taking the NRSV margin as correct: "the faith of Christ/the Son of God"). Paul's interpretation of Christ's death as the quintessential covenant act of faith and love (right relations to God and others) means that those who are justified in Christ and in whom Christ lives—those who are being saved—will demonstrate similar right covenant relations: "faith working through love" (Gal 5:6).

Justification/salvation by faith is thus a comprehensive reality. Faith is more than intellectual assent or even trust. Justification by faith is a death and resurrection experience by which one dies to the old and lives anew. Those brought from death to life have been recreated in Christ for good works (Eph 2:1-10).

5. Reconciliation with both God and neighbor

Salvation is not always understood to have an ethical component, but Jesus and Paul (not to mention James) make it clear that it does. The dual commandment to love God and neighbor appears in various ways throughout the NT. Paul represents the NT's perspective on humanity in need of salvation as those who practice injustice and immorality in their relations with others, coupled with thanklessness and idolatry in their relation to God (Rom 1:18-32). Covenantally dysfunctional human beings need both to be forgiven for their failures and endued with a desire and a power to fulfill the two basic dimensions of the covenant.

The story of Zacchaeus (Luke 19:1-10) illustrates this. Salvation "has come" to Zacchaeus' house because he, once a lost sinner, has agreed to give to the poor and repay those he had defrauded. Zacchaeus' commitment proves that he is truly a child of Abraham (i.e., of the covenant and of God) and demonstrates the inseparability of reconciliation with God and with neighbor. This inseparability is rooted in the unity of the covenant such that there can be no reconciliation with God without reconciliation with neighbor.

Salvation is a holistic and unified reality that does not permit life to be compartmentalized. This suggests also that any distinction between salvation and discipleship is false; discipleship to Jesus fulfills the call to love both God and neighbor (Matt 19:16-30; Mark 10:17-22; Luke 18:18-30). Thus love for others is not a supplement to salvation in the NT but is at its very heart (1 John 3:17).

Participating in the kingdom of God, or living in Christ, means especially inhabiting an ecclesial space for peace (Hauerwas). Those who are both forgiven and forgiving practice together the art of shalom. The centrality of peace and peacemaking to the NT's understanding of salvation is finally receiving the attention it deserves (see Swartley.) An earlier generation's conviction that Jesus came, not as a political savior, but as a "spiritual" one, is giving way to a more biblical understanding of salvation as the establishment of right relations with God and with others, as well as with the world itself—God's garden.

Salvation is the experience of God's shalom. In Matthew, Jesus calls people to love their enemies (5:39-48) and to leave their gifts at the altar to be reconciled to a brother or sister (5:23-24). In Luke, Jesus does not abandon Israel's hope for deliverance from enemies (1:71, 74) but rather offers a nonviolent way to deal with enemies (6:27, 35).

When Paul is "saved" on the Damascus road, he is first of all rescued from his violent persecution of the church and from the assumption that violence is a means of doing God's work. By God's grace, Paul abandons his pursuit of justification through violent zeal, in misguided imitation of Phinehas (Num 25:1-15; Ps 106:28-31). Apprehended by the Messiah of self-giving love, Paul seeks to establish communities guided by the God of peace and the peace of God (Phil 4:7-9). He calls his communities to enemy love (like God's; Rom 5:6-8), nonretaliation, reconciliation, and peace (e.g., Rom 12–15). Other NT writers do the same.

The claim of Colossians that Christ made "peace through the blood of his cross" (1:20) is therefore central to NT soteriology, affirming both the scriptural vision of peace as this-worldly and the paradoxical means by which that peace is established: the reconciling and violence-ending death of Jesus on a Roman cross.

6. Resurrection and eternal life

The NT often compares salvation to resurrection from the dead (see RESURRECTION, NT). The prodigal son "was dead and is alive again" (Luke 15:24). Those dead in their "trespasses and sins" God has made "alive together with Christ" (Eph 2:1, 5); believers have died to sin and become alive to God, walking in "newness of life" (Rom 6:4, 11). Similar is the biblical imagery of

new birth (John 1:12-13; 3:1-10; 1 Pet 1:3, 23; Titus 3:5). Salvation as new, resurrection life happens now.

Yet the ultimate experience of salvation in the NT is future. The only time in the undisputed Pauline letters that Paul uses the verb save in the past tense, he says that "in hope we were saved" (Rom 8:24); salvation has a future orientation. This future salvation occurs on "the day of the Lord" and includes both rescue from wrath (§H.7) and deliverance to eternal life (1 Cor 5:5).

Christ first came to live and die for the sins of the world; he will return to complete his work, "to save those who are eagerly waiting for him" (Heb 9:28). Though no one knows the hour when it will happen (Mark 13:32), this salvation is "ready to be revealed in the last time" (1 Pet 1:5) and is "nearer to us now than when we became believers" (Rom 13:11), but it will nonetheless come when people do not expect it, like a thief in the night (Matt 24:43-44; 1 Thess 5:2, 4; 2 Pet 3:10; Rev 3:3; 16:15).

Whatever else transpires at the PAROUSIA, the gift of eternal life comes to its full realization. The phrase "eternal life" occurs forty-three times in the NT, most frequently in John (seventeen times). It is sometimes said to be something one "inherits" (Matt 19:29; Mark 10:17; Luke 10:25; 18:18) and for which one must somehow be qualified. But even in this image of inheritance (compare Titus 3:7; 1 Pet 3:9), the stress lies on the unmerited gift-character of eternal life. Nonetheless, human activity—such as "reaping to the flesh" or "murder" (Gal 6:8; 1 John 3:15)—can render this grace ineffective. Furthermore, the future gift of eternal life is especially associated with those who are faithful now, whether in exercising love or enduring persecution (Matt 25:31-46; Mark 10:30).

As previously noted, for John eternal life is a present reality (John 6:47) that comes to ultimate expression in the experience of being "raise[d] ... up on the last day" (John 6:40). With a less realized eschatology, Paul speaks of the Spirit as the "first installment" or "pledge" of eternal life (2 Cor 1:22; compare Eph 1:14), its "first fruits" (Rom 8:23).

But what makes eternal life in the future distinct from anything in the present is the transformation that happens to all believers before that future life occurs. In line with the theology of the Pharisees and others, Jesus, Paul, and the rest of the NT writers envision the resurrection of the dead as the commencement of eternal life. This is in contrast to any theology, ancient or modern (e.g., Platonic), that defines eternal life as merely the immortality of the soul or as the survival of the spirit in the memory of others.

According to Acts, some nonbelievers scoffed at the resurrection of the dead (Acts 17:32), and at least in Corinth even some believers did not affirm the future resurrection (1 Cor 15:12). Paul's understanding of believers' resurrection (or, for those alive at the Parousia, their transformation from mortal existence: 1 Cor 15:51) is that they, as embodied selves, will experience both continuity and discontinuity between this present life and eternal life. "We will all be changed" (1 Cor 15:51) means that the body that was "sown" (existed in this life) will be raised and transformed from mortality to immortality (1 Cor 15:42b-44a). The same "it" (embodied self) is both sown and raised. The "spiritual body" is best understood as a new kind of Spirit-enlivened body no longer characterized by mere flesh and blood (1 Cor 15:50) and no longer subject to death, the enemy that will have been defeated (1 Cor 15:54-57). But the human person is still an embodied person; the body has been redeemed by God, not destroyed (compare Rom 8:23). The human future is one of being more "clothed" than ever before (2 Cor 5:4). It is in this mysterious and unimaginably wonderful (1 Cor 2:9) state of being that believers will experience the presence of the Lord forever (Rom 6:8; 2 Cor 5:8-9; Phil 1:23; 1 Thess 4:17).

This future, full eternal experience of salvation can be called glorification—sharing in the radiant presence of God to the fullest extent possible for human beings, something humanity has fallen short of, or lost, since Adam (Rom 3:23). New Testament hope is the hope of sharing in God's glory (Rom 5:2; 8:18; 2 Cor 4:17; Col 1:27; 1 Thess 2:12; 1 Pet 5:1, 4, 10) and in Christ's image and glory (Rom 8:17; Col 3:4; Heb 2:9-10; 1 Pet 1:6-12). For Paul, the process of sharing in Christ's glory begins in the present through transformation into his cruciform likeness (Rom 8:29; 2 Cor 3:18; Phil 3:21). The connection between present and future transformation can be expressed in the word coined by the ancient Eastern Church: theōsis (θέωσις) or deification (compare 2 Pet 1:4)—becoming like God.

The NT sometimes depicts the future experience of salvation as the messianic banquet (Matt 8:11; Luke 22:29-30) or marriage supper (Rev 19:5-9). This image appropriately draws to a conclusion the NT's emphasis on table fellowship and reinforces the meaning of salvation as a communal experience. At the same time, the book of Revelation depicts final salvation as the experience of life in its fullness—symbolized by the "water of life" and the "tree of life" (Rev 22:1-2) in the new heavens and earth. This is, at the very least, a life of worshiping and "seeing" God (Rev 22:3-5) in the company of others from every tribe and nation (Rev 7:9-17), a life of fully knowing God and being known by God (1 Cor 13:12).

7. Escape from future wrath

Throughout Scripture, human sin is met with a response of divine wrath. Though wrath is not the only response—for the biblical message is preeminently a word of transforming grace—it is not something to be dismissed or taken lightly, even in the NT. In the Synoptic Gospels, Jesus warns of "the wrath to come" (Matt 3:7; Luke 3:7). This divine wrath is apocalyptically and graphically depicted in terms of tribulation, earthly and cosmic chaos, and finally punishment (e.g., Mark 13). Similar, of course, is the book of Revelation,

which speaks of the coming wrath of God and the Lamb, a wrath that is so near to hand that it can be said to have already come (Rev 6:17; 11:18). God's wrath in Revelation is particularly directed against the satanically inspired imperial powers that have seduced the world into all kinds of idolatry, immorality, and injustice—and against those who have fallen in line with this "beast" (Rev 14:6-11; 18:1-24). Present and future salvation alike consists in avoiding the lure of this seductive force that has been unleashed in the world by turning in faith and faithfulness to the slaughtered Lamb. He is the redeemer, and together with God the creator, is worthy of worship and obedience.

Paul echoes this theme, claiming both that the WRATH OF GOD is already being revealed in the human folly that comes from disobeying God (Rom 1:18-32; compare Eph 2:3, "children of wrath") and that it will also be revealed in the future, on the day of the Lord—an image taken from the prophetic day of Yahweh as a future time of both judgment and salvation (Rom 2:5, "the day of wrath"; 1 Thess 1:10, "the wrath that is coming"; Col 3:6). Indeed, throughout the NT, the arrival of cosmic distress signals the soon "redemption" of those who belong to Jesus (e.g., Luke 21:28).

For Paul, wrath is implicitly associated with death as the consequence of human sin and rebellion, and rescue from the future wrath of God is the corollary of the gracious gift of eternal life. Indeed, salvation is the very antithesis of wrath (Rom 5:1-11; 1 Thess 5:9). Paul argues that the love of God displayed in Christ's death, which effected justification/reconciliation while we were God's enemies, guarantees deliverance from wrath now that we are God's beloved friends (Rom 5:9-10). There is no condemnation for those in Christ (Rom 8:1), though believers will still be accountable to God and Christ at the final judgment (Rom 14:10; 2 Cor 5:10).

It is especially important to note that Paul says that "we will be saved from the wrath of God ... by his [Jesus'] life" (Rom 5:9-10), that is, by his resurrection. Salvation is dependent on both the cross and the resurrection, because justification now and salvation later are ultimately about sharing in the life of Christ.

In John, wrath is also a constituent part of the antithesis of eternal life, and is therefore associated with condemnation, perishing, and death; those who believe in/obey the Son escape God's condemnation and wrath both now and in the future (John 3:16-18, 36). The means to this salvation is believing in the Son of Man, and in particular in his healing, life-giving death on the cross.

For Jesus, especially according to Matthew, this belief in and knowledge of the Son must translate into active discipleship (Matt 7:15-23); in the parable of the sheep and the goats, eternal life is granted to those who practice compassion toward the needy, and eternal punishment to those who do not (Matt 25:31-46). As noted above, salvation—including now escape from divine wrath and punishment—is inseparable from, and in fact contingent upon, discipleship. Salvation is by grace, but that grace requires and enables faithfulness, as the entire NT declares (e.g., Matt 7:21; 25:31-46; Mark 13:13; 1 Cor 15:2; 2 Cor 13:5; Jas 1:12). It is possible to fall from grace, according to Paul (Gal 5:4) as well as Hebrews (Heb 10:26-39; compare 6:1-8). The book of Revelation calls faithful endurance the guarantor of participation in the marriage feast of the Lamb (e.g., 3:10; 13:10; 14:12).

Insistence on this dynamic does not render the NT writers, or those who take these texts seriously, Pelagian. But for the NT writers, divine grace does not permit any form of what Dietrich Bonhoeffer called cheap grace. Future salvation (or its antithesis) is a natural extension of one's present existence, the logical consequence of one's participation (or not) in the life of God and God's people now.

I. Conclusion: Final Defeat of Sin, Death, Satan, Evil, and Redemption of the Cosmos

The climactic moment of salvation in the NT is still future and involves more than humanity. The NT writers use different images to portray this reality, but the main claim involves the defeat of all evil and the redemption of the cosmos, a "new heaven(s) and a new earth" (2 Pet 3:13; Rev 21:1–22:5; compare Isa 65:17; 66:22).

The apocalyptic, cataclysmic, cosmic events narrated especially in the synoptic Gospels and Revelation are all precursors to what Jesus in Matthew calls "the renewal of all things" (Matt 19:28). Paul writes of "labor pains" that precede the birth of the new creation, which he calls the creation's liberation from its "bondage to decay" (Rom 8:18-25). Similarly, Col 1:20 speaks of the reconciliation of all things to God through Christ's death, a reality working itself out in communities of Christ-believers in anticipation of the end (compare Eph 1:10). Paul says, finally, that God will be "all in all" (1 Cor 15:28).

The vision in Rev 21:1–22:5 speaks most fully and eloquently about this future totality of salvation—of life in abundance. That vision encompasses the glorious presence of God and the Lamb among people; the absence of pain, grief, and death, for God "will wipe every tear" (21:4); the absence of sin; and the "healing of the nations" (Rev 22:2; compare 21:24).

This is a most fitting conclusion to the biblical narrative, of creation restored, humanity flourishing, and God present in the midst of it all—present together with the Lamb whose life, death, and resurrection set in motion this great salvation. In anticipation of the realization of this great divine project, believers now are called to bear witness to it in word and deed.

Bibliography: Dietrich Bonhoeffer. *Discipleship.* Barbara Green, Reinhard Krauss, trans. (2001); John T. Carroll and Joel B. Green, eds. *The Death of Jesus in* *Early Christianity* (1995); Terence E. Fretheim. *God and World in the Old Testament: A Relational Theology of Creation* (2005); Terence E. Fretheim. "Salvation in the Bible vs. Salvation in the Church." *WW* 13 (1993) 363–72; Michael J. Gorman. *Inhabiting the Cruciform God: Kenosis, Justification, and Theosis in Paul's Narrative Soteriology* (2009); Joel B. Green. *Salvation* (2003); Stanley Hauerwas with Mark Scherwindt. "The Reality of the Kingdom: An Ecclesial Space for Peace." *Against the Nations: War and Survival in a Liberal Society* (1992) 107–21; Sylvia Keesmaat. "Crucified Lord or Conquering Saviour: Whose Story of Salvation?" *HBT* 26 (2004) 69–93; Frank J. Matera. *New Testament Theology: Exploring Diversity and Unity* (2007); J. Richard Middleton. *The Liberating Image: The Imago Dei in Genesis 1* (2005); J. Richard Middleton. "A New Heaven and a New Earth: The Case for a Holistic Reading of the Biblical Story of Redemption." *JCTR* 11 (2006) 73–97; Willard M. Swartley. *Covenant of Peace: The Missing Peace in New Testament Theology and Ethics* (2006); Jan G. van der Watt, ed. *Salvation in the New Testament: Perspectives on Soteriology* (2005).

J. RICHARD MIDDLETON AND MICHAEL J. GORMAN

SALVE [κολλούριον *kollourion*]. A medicated ointment to soothe the eyes and used by the Greeks and Romans. The word *collyrium* refers to a variety of solid medicines made into cakes, held together by gum, and dissolved in liquid before being applied to the eyes. Salve functions as a metaphor for cleared spiritual vision by playing on the effect of the salve as a healing agent (Rev 3:18).

VICTOR H. MATTHEWS

SAMARIA suh-mair′ee-uh [שָׁמִיר *shamir*, שֹׁמְרוֹן *shomron*; Σαμάρεια *Samariea*]. The ancient city of Samaria, whose summit rose to a height of 430 m above sea level, lay near the center of the northern kingdom of Israel at approximately 56 km north of Jerusalem, 11 km west of the Ephraimite watershed, and just 17 km east of the main coastal route that connected Egypt and the southern kingdom of Judah with the strategic Jezreel Valley and northern routes to the Phoenician seaports and Damascus (*see* SAMARIA, TERRITORY OF). Its biblical names—"Shamir" (Judg 10:1-2) and later "Samaria" (*shomron*; 1 Kgs 16:24)—mean "watch" or "watchman." The name of the site's first recorded private owner, Shemer (*shemer* שֶׁמֶר), derives from these earlier participial forms (1 Kgs 16:24).

The region of Samaria experienced four successive models of social, economic, and political organization: 1) lineage-controlled villages (such as Shemer's) in the Iron Age I (Josh 16–17; 19:49-50); 2) centrally controlled administrative districts during the united monarchy (1 Kgs 4:7-19); 3) a network of family estates and villas organized around the fortified city of Samaria starting with the rule of Omri during the divided monarchy (2 Kgs 16:23-24); and 4) a foreign-controlled

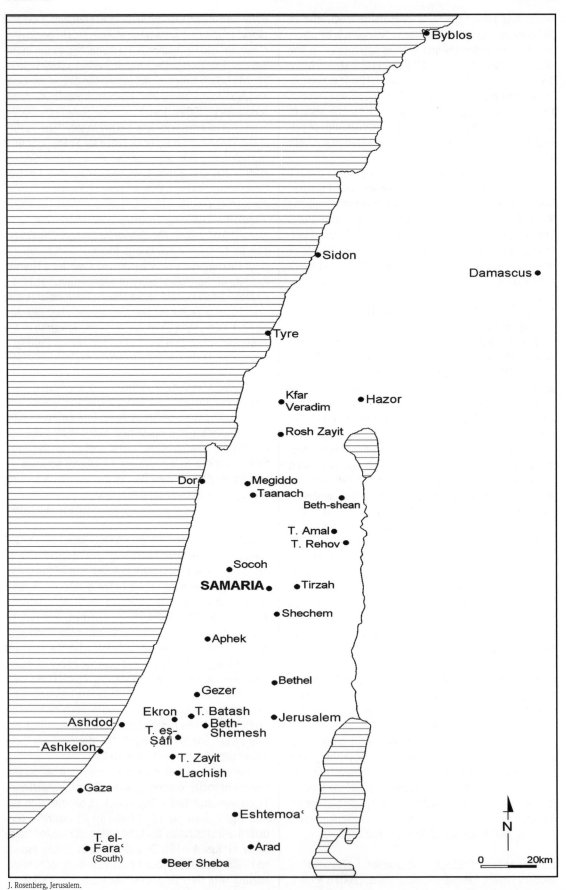

Byblos

Sidon

Damascus

Tyre

Kfar
Veradim

Hazor

Rosh Zayit

Dor

Megiddo

Taanach

Beth-shean

T. Amal

T. Rehov

Socoh

SAMARIA

Tirzah

Shechem

Aphek

Bethel

Gezer

Ekron

T. Batash

Jerusalem

Ashdod

Beth-
Shemesh

T. eş-
Şâfi

Ashkelon

T. Zayit

Lachish

Gaza

Eshtemoa'

N

T. el-
Fara'
(South)

Arad

0   20km

Beer Sheba

imperial province, beginning with Assyrian hegemony in the second half of the 8th cent. BCE (2 Kgs 17:24).

A. Archaeological Exploration and Site History

1. Excavation history

Representing Harvard University, Gottlieb Schumacher directed the first official archaeological exploration of Samaria in 1908. George Andrew Reisner, along with architect Clarence Fisher, succeeded Schumacher in 1909 and 1910. The Harvard excavations focused on the western half of the summit and revealed much of the Israelite royal palace area. A consortium of institutions, mostly from England and Israel, renewed excavations from 1932 to 1935. John Winter Crowfoot directed this "Joint Expedition," while Kathleen M. Kenyon supervised all work in the royal quarter and introduced a new methodology of debris-layer analysis. Kenyon cut a large north-south section across the entire summit east of the earlier excavations by Schumacher and Reisner. Based on the pottery removed from this area, Kenyon attempted to lower the chronology of the stratigraphic history and ceramic traditions at other major Iron II sites in Palestine such as Megiddo and Hazor. Her official report, which did not appear until 1957, offered a new chronological framework against which to understand this period not only at Samaria and in Palestine generally but also at sites in the Aegean world. More recently, the so-called "Low Chronology" for ancient Israel marks a suggested return to certain proposals forwarded earlier by Kenyon (see CHRONOLOGY OF THE OT).

Almost immediately, however, the date of the earliest Iron Age settlement became the subject of considerable controversy. On the basis of 1 Kgs 16:24, Kenyon concluded that no Iron Age occupation occurred at the site prior to Omri's purchase of the hill from Shemer. From there to the 6th–5th cent. BCE, she outlined eight major building phases (Periods I–VIII) and assigned Periods I–VI to the time from Omri to the Assyrian capture of Samaria in 722/21 BCE. Further, she believed that new ceramic traditions accompanied each new building phase.

After comparing the Samaria material with that from Tirzah, Roland de Vaux concluded that the two earliest ceramic phases at Samaria actually predated all Omride building activities and indicated an Iron Age I presence at the site. Later, G. E. Wright and others drew an official distinction between the ceramic and architectural developments at Samaria and dated the earliest Iron Age pottery to a modest, pre-Omride occupation. By the 1990s, L. E. Stager showed that this pre-royal occupation actually reflects the remains of a private, family estate belonging to the clan of Shemer, from whom Omri purchased the property.

2. Pre-Omride settlements

The earliest remains discovered on the summit of Samaria consisted of numerous rock cuttings (cups, pits, etc., hollowed out of the bedrock; see *SS III*, Pl. XI), which the excavators dated to the Early Bronze Age. The fragmentary base of one large vessel included a spout and may have functioned as a separator vat (*SS III*, 92, Fig. C:3). These features seem to indicate the systematic production of olive oil at Samaria in this period. Samaria, therefore, may represent one of the earliest (already by the late 4th millennium BCE) places in Canaan at which this industry occurred.

Recently, however, archaeologists have reinterpreted many of the these cuttings as press platforms, vats, collecting basins, connecting bowls, and mortars dating to the Iron Age I period and reflecting the presence here of a family-owned estate belonging to the lineage of Shemer (or Shomron) from the tribe of Issachar. One strong argument in favor of this new understanding is the sheer quantity of the storage capacity represented by the bell-shaped cisterns, etc., already discovered at Samaria. (Many more such features undoubtedly exist in the unexcavated portions of the site.) These facilities would accommodate the yield from 3,200–4,800 olive trees covering an area of 32–48 ha. on the slopes and in the valleys around the summit. The annual production rate would have supported an overall population of at least 150–200 individuals. Reevaluations of the pottery from Samaria have confirmed this Iron I occupation of the hill and have corrected the excavators' view that an occupational gap existed from the Early Bronze Age to the time of King Omri. In fact, the earliest Iron Age pottery at Samaria dates to the 11th cent. BCE, when the hill belonged to families from the tribe of Issachar. When Tola, a judge who hailed from Issachar, died and was buried at Shamir (Judg 10:1-2), the villa likely passed to his brother Shimron (1 Chr 7:1). Eventually, Shemer inherited the estate and later sold the site to King Omri (1 Kgs 16:24)—another probable kinsman from Issachar and the lineage of Tola (compare 1 Chr 7:1-3 and 27:18).

3. Early royal Israelite occupation (9th cent. BCE)

By the time the population spread west of the Ephraimite watershed in the Iron II period, highland society had become more complex in its political and economic organization. Settlements of a more uniform character (with virtually no ephemeral campsites) appeared on the seaward slopes of the mountains and survived or thrived as part of a much larger network of trade. A new type of dimorphism arose in the symbiosis between capital and countryside. Omri's purchase of the family estate of Shemer and his shift of the region's political center from Tirzah to the hill of Shomron in the early 9th cent. largely accounts for this significant demographic and economic change. Few settlements had previously existed on the western slopes, and they had all remained quite small and very near Shemer's family estate. But the royal shift westward in the 9th cent. BCE created a network of rural villages and at least eleven lateral and local roadways connecting the highlands in the Samaria-Shechem area with the lucrative trade moving along the coastal route. The place names (of at least sixteen separate villages) and clan holdings (representing at least seven separate lineage units) mentioned in the sixty-eight administrative documents known as the SAMARIA OSTRACA indicate that by the early 8th cent. BCE Samaria lay in the center of a tight constellation of towns and family-owned estates. These western-oriented villages facilitated the movement of goods and commodities between the coastal route and various centers situated at higher elevations, including not only the Israelite capital at Samaria but also Tirzah, Tubas, Tappuah, Dothan, and Shechem.

The northern hill country—the "cradle of Israelite culture"—attained its greatest prominence following Omri's rise to power in the early 9th cent. BCE. After leaving Tirzah, Omri and his successors (particularly his son Ahab) transformed this one-time family estate into a relatively small but powerful and cosmopolitan royal city. The topography of the excavated portion of the summit reveals that lateral and longitudinal rock scarps ran along the northern, western, and probably also the southern perimeters of Omri's royal compound. Although portions of these ledges—which often drop as much as 3.5 m in elevation—represent natural formations, it appears that Omri's workers expanded and connected them through extensive quarrying activities. The resultant split-level summit provided a rectilinear dais of solid rock measuring roughly 72 m × 93.5 m (ca. 0.67 ha.). The vertical face of these scarps provided backing for the foundation courses of the city's earliest walls (e.g., Omri's so-called Enclosure Wall 161, north of the courtyard area). This raised, central platform distinguished the central summit from peripheral areas that encircled the royal quarter at least on the northern and western sides. The raised area accommodated only the principal housing (main palace) and activity areas (northern official buildings and main courtyard) of the royal family and attendants. It did not incorporate domestic housing into the royal compound proper.

The palace itself sat near the southwestern corner of the elevated summit, and a series of official buildings lined the northern edge of the area. Two large rock-cut tombs set in the bedrock immediately beneath the northern portion of the palace likely represent the burial chambers for at least some of the Israelite kings who ruled from Samaria (according to biblical traditions, at least Omri, Ahab, Jehu, Jehoahaz, Joash, and perhaps Jeroboam II were interred in the royal center at Samaria; see 1 Kgs 16:28; 22:37; 2 Kgs 10:35; 13:9; 14:16, 29). A series of interconnecting cave-tombs, situated both on the northwestern slopes of the mound nearly 100 m below the royal acropolis (*SS I*, 22–23) and on the nearby hill of Munshara, may have served as burial places for the wealthier occupants of Samaria. A large courtyard extended eastward from the palace and southward from the public buildings. The main city gate lay still farther to the east in a part of the summit that has received less archaeological attention than the palace area. A threshing floor likely existed somewhere just outside the city gate (compare the Micaiah ben Imlah narrative in 1 Kgs 22; in ancient cities, the threshing floor and the city gate sometimes shared a judicial function and, consequently, constituted a word pair in some ancient poetry). Located over 650 m east of the gate area, a trapezoidal-shaped, rock-cut trench (labeled E207; *SS I*, 23–24) apparently represents an Israelite shrine. It remains unknown, however, whether this facility relates in any way to the Asherah or to the temple and altar reportedly built by Ahab and dedicated to Baal as mentioned in 1 Kgs 16:25-33.

In the peripheral zone around and below the central summit platform, various auxiliary rooms occupied the northern part of the compound, while the so-called Ostraca House lay to the west of the palace area. A longitudinal wall (unlabeled on *SS I*, Plan I), located just east of the Ostraca House, ran along the rock scarp immediately behind the palace and defined the western edge of the central summit plateau. Two separate tunnels penetrated the scarp and gave access to the royal tombs mentioned above. Further west, beyond the Ostraca house, the bedrock stepped its way down in regular increments until its more dramatic decline to the valley floor over 150 m below. At least one pool (located near the northwestern corner of the summit) and a drain that led away from the Ostraca House were also set into the rock on the lower level of the summit area. The former feature provides a picture of the berekhath shomron (בְּרֵכַת שֹׁמְרוֹן, "pool of Samaria") where, according to biblical tradition (1 Kgs 22:38), palace servants or soldiers washed the blood from Ahab's chariot following his demise on the battlefield at Ramoth-gilead and where dogs licked up the blood and prostitutes bathed in the crimson water.

The core of this royal city, then, remained considerably smaller than is usually recognized. The compound itself probably could not have accommodated more than 200 individuals. The king and his court, the royal attendants, and the "young men of the governors of the districts" (1 Kgs 20:15) who resided within the city walls alone would have taxed the city's available space. The 7,000 others alluded to in that verse—and certainly

Todd Bolen/BiblePlaces.com

Figure 1: Samaria, ruins of Iron Age acropolis.

the 27,290 "Samarians" that Sargon ultimately claims to have deported from the city—undoubtedly lived in outlying areas around the capital city. The excavator's suggestion that the city itself could have accommodated 30,000–40,000 citizens (*SS I*, 2) remains quite unbelievable.

Throughout its history, Israelite Samaria served only as the seat of royal power; it never became home to large numbers of the king's subjects. Still, the symbolism and status of Samaria grew so impressive that the biblical writers spoke of the city as the undisputed "head of Ephraim" (Isa 7:9), or as Jerusalem's "elder sister" who ruled and influenced numerous "daughters" (outlying villages) of her own (Ezek 16:46, 53, 55, 61; 23:4-5). Bountiful discoveries of ivory fragments and furnishings that likely derive from the time of Ahab into the 8th cent. BCE (though excavators recovered them from much later, secondary deposits dating mostly to the Hellenistic and Roman periods) correlate well with biblical memories of opulent, ivory-appointed houses and royal banquets in the capital (1 Kgs 22:39; Amos 3:15, 6:4; Ps 45:8). That the city ultimately gave its name to the larger region attests to the power that emanated from this new, stately center.

Omri's new economic orientation toward the open markets of the Mediterranean brought the entire region of Samaria into greater contact with foreign cultures. With Ahab's politically motivated marriage to Jezebel, Samaria gained access to Phoenician wealth but also exposure to its religious beliefs and customs. As it became increasingly syncretistic under this influence, the

political leadership incurred the scorn of Elijah (1 Kgs 17–19) and the orthodox religious establishment generally. Ultra-conservative factions with both religious and political aspirations arose. The populist Jehu seized the

Erich Lessing/Art Resource, NY

Figure 2: Carved ivory palm tree plaque, from Samaria, Israel (9th–8th cent. BCE). Israel Museum (IDAM), Jerusalem, Israel.

throne of Samaria in 842 BCE (2 Kgs 9–10)—with backing from the prophetic leadership and, undoubtedly, also conservative social groups and zealous segments of the military—and quickly committed his new government to a pro-Assyrian posture by paying tribute to Shalmaneser III, an act recorded in relief and writing on the Black Obelisk (see OBELISK, BLACK).

While nearly all commentators have assumed that this revolt and the resultant death of the queen and former Sidonian princess (1 Kgs 16:31), Jezebel, may reasonably have jeopardized Samaria's political and commercial ties to Phoenicia, the material remains and depositional history from Samaria do not permit definitive conclusions on this matter. The phasing of levels from the time of Jehu (Kenyon's "Period III") and the following periods ("Periods IV–IVa") received only sparse documentation in the final excavation report and therefore remain somewhat cloudy. In any event, it is clear that even in the late 8th cent. BCE—well over a century after the dramatic takeover by Jehu and his descendants—the Assyrians continued referring to Samaria as the "House [i.e., Dynasty or Kingdom] of Omri" and, like contemporary Hebrew prophets, they often distinguished between the capital city/kingdom of Israel and the countryside of Manasseh/Ephraim, though they also sometimes employed this term for the city.

The rise of the Omride dynasty established the northern power base in the families of Issachar and preserved that tradition for roughly sixty-five of the first eighty-eight years of the nation's overall history. Yet the ruling houses of Issachar controlled the throne in Samaria only for the first four decades of the city's royal history (ca. 885–842 BCE) before yielding to political factions from Transjordan during the violent rise of Jehu.

4. Later royal Israelite occupation (8th cent. BCE)

One of the most prosperous periods of Samaria's history came during the mid-8th cent. reign of Jeroboam II, the son of Joash (ca. 786–746 BCE; 2 Kgs 14:23-29). Though the Deuteronomistic History displays a hint of sympathy for Israel during this reign (2 Kgs 14:26-27), the books of Amos and Hosea, which record prophetic activities in the north at this time, contain harsh criticism of Jeroboam's rule. During this relatively peaceful period, Jeroboam II attempted to expand the borders of his kingdom to the north, east, and south—"from Lebo-hamath as far as the Sea of the Arabah" (2 Kgs 14:25; Lebo-hamath = Lebweh, an important city on the border of the kingdom ruled by Hamath).

Excavations along the lower, western summit, revealed a multi-room storage complex (the Ostraca House) whose floors and subfloor levels contained dozens of laconic shipping dockets. These inscriptions, known as the Samaria Ostraca, record the transfer of various commodities (primarily wine and oil) from outlying villages to the capital city during the reigns of Jehoash and Jeroboam II in the early 8th cent. BCE. By this time, Samaria lay in the center of a tight constella-

tion of towns and family-owned estates that undoubtedly resembled the character of Shomron itself in the pre-royal days of Shemer's family estate. These sites, generally located between five and twelve kilometers from Samaria, served the capital city, while themselves benefiting from interregional trade by offering to passing caravans auxiliary services, such as overnight lodging and animal care. But their close spatial distribution indicates that, despite their small size (100–150 inhabitants/site), not all of these villages represented mere caravan stops; rather, many of them bolstered their own local economies by producing and trading commodities, such as the wine and oil recorded in the Samaria Ostraca, much as the Shemer clan had previously done at their small villa.

While the earliest rulers in the capital at Samaria appear to have hailed from the tribe of Issachar (see above), the violent rise of Jehu—whose ancestral roots may trace to Gilead—succeeded in breaking that tribe's control over the throne at Samaria and in opening the way to greater political influence from areas to the east. Queen Jezebel even linked Zimri's earlier, failed coup against the rulers from Issachar to the designs of Jehu by sarcastically referring to Jehu as "Zimri" (2 Kgs 9:31). From the mid-9th cent. down to the last, Assyrian-appointed ruler, Hoshea (whose birthplace remains unknown), every claimant to the throne of Samaria seems to have come from a transriver area or faction. Ultimately, however, the new seat of power in Transjordan itself proved unstable as competing leaders, such as Shallum, Menahem, his son Pekahiah, and finally Pekah (from roughly 750 to 733 or 731 BCE; 2 Kgs 15:8-31), fell into outright anarchy as they contended for the right to rule from Samaria in the face of an emergent empire in Assyria (all but one man, Pekahiah, seized the throne by murdering the reigning king). Local events during the Syro-Ephraimite War (734–732 BCE) helped place the ultimate fate of Israelite Samaria in Assyrian hands.

5. Assyrian domination

By the late 8th cent. BCE, the Assyrian provinces of Dor, Megiddo, and Gilead (compare Isa 9:1) encompassed the Ephraimite hill country, where Hoshea had risen to power in Samaria around 732 BCE—but only as a puppet of Assyria. His miscalculated rebellion about ten years later naturally brought disastrous consequences to the capital and kingdom. In the late 720s, armies led by Shalmaneser V and then Sargon II penetrated the highlands and focused on the city of Samaria, which they besieged and occupied. The Babylonian Chronicle (1.i.28) states that Shalmaneser "broke [the city of] Samaria." The scribes of Sargon employed a variety of terms to describe his ultimate takeover ca. 720 BCE. According to the Nimrud Prism IV.25–41, which delineates more different types of actions against Samaria than any other single text, Sargon fought against the city, reckoned its people, property, and gods as spoil, formed a chariot corp with Israelite charioteers and equipment, resettled or reorganized Israelite deportees in the Assyrian homeland, increased the population of the city by bringing in peoples conquered elsewhere, appointed a governor over the reorganized city, and counted all the affected individuals as citizens of Assyria.

None of these actions, however, necessarily imply a physical destruction of the city's infrastructure. Although the rooms of the so-called Period V House constituted the last Israelite structures along the northern summit of Samaria, the opinion of the excavators that both these rooms and the Rubbish Pit *i* ended in an "extensive destruction" of the site by Sargon II ca. 720 BCE (*SS III*, 199) has not withstood recent reevaluation, which now demonstrates the lack of a coherent and massive destruction level on the summit of the city at this time. The Assyrians claimed Samaria without destroying it; neither the Assyrian texts nor the archaeological data from Samaria suggest otherwise. During these years, the Assyrians often established a blockade around a region's capital city while their army ravaged the outlying countryside without capturing or destroying the political center itself (compare Sennacherib's different approaches to Lachish and Jerusalem as a possible later parallel), and they may have applied this tactic at Samaria.

Sargon deported large numbers of Israelites and resettled the city primarily with captives from distant Syro-Mesopotamian locations and from southern Arabia (2 Kgs 17:24; compare the Display, Bull, Khorsabad Pavement, and Cylinder inscriptions of SARGON). In this manner, Assyria effectually transformed the Ephraimite hill country into the province of Samerina. Though its southern border remained fixed between Bethel and Mizpah (2 Kgs 17:28), it appears that Samerina eventually subsumed the coastal district of Dor, inasmuch as no governor's name appears for the latter in Assyrian eponym lists and a battle itinerary from Esarhaddon's tenth campaign in 671 BCE records Aphek, in the southern Sharon Plain, as part of the "land of Samerina."

The Assyrian program to resettle foreign populations in Samaria began under Sargon II from 716 BCE on, and the physical refurbishment of selected provincial centers (such as Megiddo) occurred only during the late 8th and 7th cent. BCE, i.e., after the political collapse of the capital itself. Few traces of such a rebuilding effort have appeared at Samaria, however, apparently because of the minimal destruction of the site during the initial conquest. In fact, archaeologists have recovered only a few remains from the entire Assyrian occupation, including a stele fragment (apparently from the time of Sargon II) and appreciable quantities of Palace Ware. But fragments from various cuneiform tablets, some apparently representing a letter to the local governor, suggest that Samaria served as the administrative center of Samerina.

Those who were not deported during the Assyrian and Babylonian exiles came to be known as the Samaritans. This group based its religion strictly on its own interpre-

tation of the Torah (*see* SAMARITAN PENTATEUCH). A small number of Samaritan descendants still reside in Palestine today. They claim an historical connection to the original inhabitants of Samaria who avoided the Assyro-Babylonian deportations, and in *Genesis Rabbah* Sect. 94 Rabbi Meir traces their origin to the old tribe of Issachar. Other Jewish traditions, however, view them as outsiders sent to Samaria by the Assyrians to replace the extracted Israelites. Because these inhabitants did not know or did not keep orthodox Yahwistic traditions, the Assyrians eventually returned to Bethel a priest whom they had deported from Samaria to teach "the fear of Yahweh" (2 Kgs 17:24-28). By the late 4th cent. BCE, a Samaritan temple existed on Mount Gerizim, and a deep schism existed between the Samaritans and the Jews (*see* GERIZIM, MOUNT).

6. Babylonian period

Following the decline of Assyrian influence at home and abroad after 633 BCE and the ultimate fall of Nineveh to the Babylonians in 612, Josiah annexed to Judah at least the southern extent of Samerina, as far as Bethel (2 Kgs 23:4), and perhaps the province in full measure (2 Kgs 23:29-30; 2 Chr 35:20-24). His political and religious reforms led him to desecrate local shrines in the north and to execute their priests (1 Kgs 13:1-2; 2 Kgs 23:15-20), while merely closing the high places of the south and recalling local priests to Jerusalem. But these efforts apparently ended following the death of Josiah in 609 BCE. After the fall of Jerusalem to Nebuchadnezzar in 587/86 BCE, Gedaliah, the Babylonian-appointed governor of Judah, established his administrative center at Mizpah rather than in Jerusalem (Jer 41:1); this decision may belie the south's orientation as much toward Samaria as toward Jerusalem at this time, possibly because those who survived the scourge of Judah needed the stores of grain, honey, and oil that remained available in the region of Samaria (Jer 41:4-8). The view of some scholars, however, that the Babylonians now officially considered the ravaged south a part of Samaria remains uncertain.

While archaeologists have recovered only a few remains from the Babylonian period (Kenyon's Period VIII), Jer 41 alludes to the occupation of the city during this time, even by some remaining Israelites (or Yahwists). Samaria continued as an administrative center under Persian occupation in the late 6th and 5th cent. BCE. A .25 m-thick deposit of fertile brown soil now covered at least a 45 x 50 m area of the former Israelite courtyard and probably represents a garden that surrounded the district governor's house. This feature resembles similar designs found elsewhere in the Babylonian-Persian empires, and the excavators believed the chocolate soil level could not date much later than the 6th cent. BCE. A partially-exposed building, located at the southeastern edge of the garden, included a floor that was built .4 m higher than the rest of the room and two circular vats or plastered pits that were sunk into the lower floor level,

David Bivin/LifeintheHolyLand.com
Figure 3: Hellenistic tower

facts that suggest a possible industrial use for the structure. Between this time and the 1st cent. BCE, remains at Samaria proved extremely fragmentary (*SS I*, 115).

7. Persian period

When Persia conquered Babylon in 539 BCE, Cyrus and his successors retained Samaria (Period IX) as the administrative center in the "Province Beyond the River [Euphrates]" and placed it under the governorship of Sanballat. A 5th cent. Athenian coin, three Sidonian coins from the reign of Abdastart I (370–358 BCE), fourteen Aramaic ostraca, and significant quantities of pottery imported from Aegean centers (e.g., Black- and Red-Figure, White-Ground, and Black-Burnished Wares) attest to the solvency of Samaria's economy, which Persia itself apparently underwrote (Ezra 4:14). It seems likely that the economic dependence of Judah upon Samaria increased during this period (compare Neh 5:1-5). As a result, northern leaders viewed efforts to revitalize Jerusalem as a fortified center of activity late in this period as an act of sedition against Samaria and the Persian empire alike (Ezra 4; Neh 2; 4; 6; 1 Esd 2). The old Israelite defensive/enclosure walls likely remained in use throughout this period. The city of Samaria received mention in the ELEPHANTINE PAPYRI,

a collection of 5th-cent. BCE manuscripts recovered from the Jewish community at Elephantine, in Egypt.

The recovery of only meager remains from the Babylonian and Persian periods suggests that the city of Samaria suffered considerable devastation during the period of Babylonian rule. Nevertheless, when the city reemerged as a political center in the Persian era, tensions escalated between Samaria and Jerusalem, especially around the mid-5th cent. BCE. Correspondence between Sanballat the Horonite (governor of Samaria; Neh 2:10, 19; 13:28), Nehemiah (governor of Jerusalem), and the Persian court epitomizes the strained relations (Ezra 4:10, 17; compare 1 Esd 2:16-30). Sanballat, who maintained an army in Samaria, accused the leaders in Jerusalem not only of preparing to rebuild the walls there—an act that Artaxerxes I (464–423 BCE) had sanctioned (Neh 2:1-8)—but also of planning a rebellion, aspiring to elevate Nehemiah as their king, and restoring a pro-kingship prophetic guild in the south (Neh 4 and 6). While the biblical writers recognize the official status of Nehemiah (and his predecessor Zerubbabel; Hag 1:1) as governor of Judah (Neh 8:9; 10:1; 12:26), they again slight the northern leadership by omitting any acknowledgment of Sanballat's administrative title.

8. Hellenistic period

The local and international economies of the north continued to flourish at Samaria throughout most of the turbulent Hellenistic period, as witnessed in thousands of Rhodian stamped jar fragments recovered from the city in addition to coins from Sidon (ca. 370–358 BCE) as well as from Ptolemy I–II (305–246 BCE) and Antiochus III (222–187 BCE). In the late 4th cent. BCE, when locals assassinated Andromachus, a Greek general whom Alexander the Great had installed as prefect of Syria, Samaria incurred Alexander's full wrath. Citizens who could flee headed eastward with numerous legal and administrative documents written in Aramaic (Samaria Papyri), only to have Alexander's army overtake and execute them in a cave in the precipitous Wadi ed-Daliyeh. As their abandoned city became more fully Greek in character, the center of Samaritan activity shifted to Shechem. A series of beautifully built round towers at Samaria (8.5 m in height; 13 to 14.7 m in diameter)—originally misdated to the Israelite period and the time of Jeroboam II but belonging to the late 4th cent. BCE—and a subsequent massive defense wall (4 m thick) with square towers bear witness to the current political vicissitudes, as the successors of Alexander the Great, the Ptolemies and Seleucids, competed for control over the region. This impressive Greek Fort Wall, from the 2nd cent. BCE, replaced the old Israelite casemate wall system that had remained in use (albeit with some extensive repairs) throughout the early Hellenistic period.

The greatest setback to Samaria, however, emerged more locally. Late in this period (ca. 111–108/107 BCE), the Hasmonean priest John Hyrcanus, who had gained de facto independence in Judea following the death of the Seleucid ruler Antiochus VII in 128 BCE, planned a frontal assault on the region and city of Samaria (Josephus, *Ant.* 13.275–281; *J.W.* 1.64–65). Following the capture of Shechem and the burning of the Samaritan temple on Mount Gerizim, a year-long siege against the city of Samaria destroyed a large section of the Greek Fort Wall and triggered the erosion of massive quantities of soil from inside the city—events that undoubtedly prompted Josephus' claim that Hyrcanus "brought rivulets to [Samaria] to drown it" and "dug such hollows as might allow the water to run under [the city]." In any event, this conquest brought the entire region temporarily under Judean control.

9. Roman period and New Testament

The Roman conquest of Palestine by Pompey in 63 BCE set the stage for the climactic resurgence of Samaria, though the process began rather slowly. The provincial governor Gabinius (57–55 BCE) launched reconstruction projects in Samaria and other cities that had suffered destruction during recent political turmoil (Josephus, *Ant.* 14.86). He secured the city by rebuilding the wall ruined by Hyrcanus and enticed citizens to return to Samaria by creating a new residential area—with houses, courtyards, and shops arranged along narrow streets (all datable by coins sealed beneath the floors of the rooms)—over the north-central slopes of the mound, beginning nearly 30 m outside the line of the earlier Israelite casemate system. It is possible that the earliest phases of the large forum, with an adjacent basilica, might have appeared now on the northeastern slopes of the summit, near the entrance to the city. Prosperity gradually returned to Samaria, and it may well have included an agora and one or more temples, though archaeologists could not reconstruct a detailed layout of the city.

The city and region of Samaria supported Herod the Great in his struggles against Antigonus, the last of the Hasmonean leaders (to whom had belonged John Hyrcanus; Josephus, *Ant.* 14.406–12). Soon after the earthquake in 31 BCE, when Caesar Augustus awarded Samaria to Herod, the Judean ruler quickly renamed the city "Sebaste" (feminine form of Sebastos, "Augustus") in honor of his benefactor. Herod also constructed the Augusteum, an imposing temple (35 x 24 m) and forecourt that covered much of the western summit and destroyed a significant portion of the houses built earlier by Gabinius. A staircase 21 m wide led from the forecourt up 4.4 m to the temple proper. The extension of the forecourt over the northern slopes of the site required the construction of two huge, parallel retaining walls (1.3 and 3 m thick, 15 m high), a large artificial platform extending over the northern slopes and made from massive amounts of fill dirt, and the robbing of both the Israelite Casemate Wall and the Greek Fort Wall to create sufficient space for this towering edifice. Housing for the temple priests lay east of the forecourt.

Herod also expanded the city's fortifications (the perimeter wall stretching for nearly 3 km in circumference and enclosing an area of roughly 160 ac), restocked it with 6,000 new citizens, apportioned territorial properties among his former military allies (including Thracians, Galatians, and Germans), offered all of them special constitutional rights, and reportedly considered Samaria "a fortress for himself...a stronghold against the country," behind only his own palace in Jerusalem and the fortress Antonia which protected the temple there. In short, Samaria became "a monument of his magnificence" (Josephus, *Ant.* 15.292–98; *J.W.* 1.403) and even the site of his wedding to Miriamme (*Ant.* 14.465).

Though the large-scale building campaigns inside Samaria symbolized Herod's sought-after security and grandeur, the writings of Josephus focus only on the city wall—which enclosed a large but irregularly shaped area—and the impressive temple. Excavations have shown that a main entrance gate flanked by two massive round towers stood west of the city. Another round tower was located ca. 50 m north of the gate, but rectangular towers were built into the wall at other points. While other gates likely existed in the northern, eastern, and southern sections of the city wall, excavators were unable to recover substantial remains from these features. The largest building discovered from the Herodian period consists in the Doric stadium, located near the northeastern section of the city wall. The heavy layer of painted plaster, which in this phase covered and concealed rather poor quality masonry, also bore crudely etched figures and a few inscribed names in both Greek and Latin, thus further attesting to the mixed foreign and local population of the city at this time. Ultimately, a certain irony characterized Herod's activities at Samaria, for he sent his mother and other relatives to this city for their protection during his war against Idumea but ultimately had his sons strangled to death there (*Ant.* 14.413; 16.392).

Rebels attacked and burned much of Sebaste during the early stages of the First Jewish Revolt (66–70 CE), and, judging from the relatively paltry remains from that point through the mid-2nd cent. CE, the city endured a long recovery period. It regained considerable status, however, during the reign of Septimus Severus (193–211 CE) and eventually became the colony known as Lucia Septimia Sebaste around 201 CE. Four impressive features belong to this period: the forum colonnades, the basilica, the columned street, and the Corinthian stadium (built over the Doric-style stadium of Herod). The design of the street and stadium alone required more that 760 monolithic columns standing over 4 m in height. The 12.5 m-wide columned street differed from the classic Roman *cardo*, which typically ran straight through a city's central area and between the various public buildings. Instead, this new street angled south of and below the acropolis and eventually approached the summit from the east. A thriving bazaar with shops of all kinds—sporting molded doorjambs and massive masonry—lined this grand walkway, with apsidal rooms on the north side of the street and rectangular, multi-storied rooms on the south. Water arrived at the city from springs located southeast of the mound via an aqueduct of some 4,400 m in length (roughly 2.75 mi). A theater sat on the northeastern slope of the acropolis, and a temple to Kore (related to the Greek goddess Persephone) occupied the area due north of the summit. The West Gate underwent renovation at this time, with a shrine added nearby, while another shrine sat near the paved street. Excavators also identified several well-built tombs in an area southeast of the city.

The Gospels present a mixed view of this group. A SAMARITAN WOMAN expresses suspicion about why Jesus, a Jew, would speak with her (John 4). Others equate being Samaritan with "having a demon" (John 8:48). In Matthew, Jesus instructs the disciples not to go to the Gentiles or enter any town of the Samaritans (Matt 10:5). When Samaritans will not receive Jesus and his disciples, the disciples want to bring fire down on them, but Jesus prevents them (Luke 9:52-55). Jesus uses the unexpected figure of a Samaritan to illustrate true compassion (Luke 10:25-37; *see* SAMARITAN, THE GOOD). Similarly, the unanticipated gratitude of the lone Samaritan leper in Luke 17:11-19 shames the behavior of his Jewish counterparts.

In the midst of increasing architectural grandeur and ethno-cultural diversity during the Roman period, Samaria became a center of celebration, ceremony, and magic (see Acts 8:9). Perhaps for these reasons, Philip, Peter, and John preached to and prayed for the inhabitants of the city, though other followers of Jesus often thought of Samaria as a virtual foreign territory in their early missionary and church-planting efforts (Acts 1:8; 8:1-25; 9:31; 15:3). Owing to the Samaritan-Jewish schism, natives of Judea generally circumnavigated the entire region when traveling to and from Jerusalem (Matt 19:1; Luke 17:11; compare John 4:4-9).

10. Later periods at Samaria

Though Samaria-Sebaste gradually became a "stronghold of paganism" (*SS I*, 37), and even witnessed anti-Christian riots during the reign of Julian (361–363 CE), the conversion of Emperor Constantine brought at least some changes to the city. Beginning with the famous Council at Nicaea in 325 CE, bishops from Sebaste attended no fewer than six councils until 536 CE (including those at Constantinople, Chalcedon, and the Synod of Jerusalem).

Between this time and the Middle Ages, Sebaste remained important in the larger Christian world because of the tradition that it marked the burial site of John the Baptist. In fact, two separate shrines became associated with this martyr—one near the eastern end of the city and another (where Herodias supposedly hid the Baptist's head) higher up on the southern summit area. When compared to earlier periods, the grandeur of Samaria-Sebaste faded during the Late Byzantine period, from which few remains have survived. While some of the Severan houses and streets remained in use, most of the structures formerly associated with paganism were gradually torn down and the areas that accommodated them used as quarries.

B. Historiography and the Biblical View of Samaria

From the rise of the Omride dynasty to the fall of the kingdom between 722 and 720 BCE, fourteen Israelite kings ruled from the city of Samaria. But the regional and even international prominence they brought to the area also presented its capital and religious centers (e.g., Bethel) as the clearest and most dangerous symbols of opposition to the southern kingdom of Judah and its cult at Jerusalem. This deeply rooted north-south schism and the Judahite perspective taken in the final Deuteronomistic History produced a critical treatment of the rulers and activities at Samaria in the Bible, even though some extra-biblical sources (the Mesha Stela; Assyrian annals) often pointed to the capital's political, military, and economic successes, despite periods of severe drought and famine (1 Kgs 17:1, 7; 18:2).

Direct references to Samaria first occur in the historical books, and the books of 1–2 Kings alone account for

62 percent of all such notices in the OT (72 percent including the Chronicler's history). An ominous chord sounds with the very first mention of Samaria (1 Kgs 13:32), which occurs in a context anticipating the ultimate downfall of the capital city and its kingdom. Following this dire pronouncement, the biblical writers focus nearly two-thirds of their references to Samaria on periods of external and internal political turbulence (1 Kgs 16; 20; 22; 2 Kgs 6; 10; 13; 15; 17). A significant percentage of the remaining narratives highlight the perceived social and religious atrocities perpetrated by the city's rulers (1 Kgs 21; 2 Kgs 1) or brought on by periods of economic hardships (1 Kgs 18; 2 Kgs 6). In general, this history draws much more heavily from harshly critical prophetic and popular traditions (Micaiah ben Imlah; Elijah; Elisha) than from available annalistic records. For example, four of the six chapters devoted to King Ahab's reign (1 Kgs 16:29–22:40) rely primarily on narratives involving Elijah (1 Kgs 17–19; 21) or Micaiah ben Imlah (1 Kgs 22). Ahab's fleeting moment of popular acclaim and competent leadership appears only in 1 Kgs 20:1-34. But even this snatch of narrative receives a sudden, severe critique in a vignette drawn from prophetic traditions (1 Kgs 20:35-43).

Neither the historical books nor the OT as a whole show much interest in Samaria after its fall to the Assyrians in the late 8th cent. BCE or the decline of Assryia itself in the late 7th cent. BCE. With the waning of Assyrian influence at home and abroad after 633 BCE, the religious and political reforms of Judah's King Josiah attempted to reannex at least the southern extent of Samerina as far as Bethel (2 Kgs 23:4) and perhaps even the entire province (2 Kgs 23:29-30; 2 Chr 35:20-24; see also 1 Kgs 13:1-2; 2 Kgs 23:15-20). Having already anticipated Samaria's decline in 1 Kgs 13, the DtrH terminates its references to the city with these reports of Josiah's activities.

Subsequent prophetic texts recall the apostasy and just judgment of the Northern Kingdom and its capital city as a didactic warning for Judah and Jerusalem (Jer 23:13; Ezek 16:46, 51; 23:1-10, 33). Only a few other passages provide further historical details about Samaria (see Neh 3:15, 19; Jer 41:1, 4-8). Following the Chronicler's (or some other editor's) comments in the book of Nehemiah, the OT offers no further direct mention of Samaria. Additional details about the city's service as an administrative center during the Persian period, its political vicissitudes during the turbulent Hellenistic period, and its grandeur during the Roman period lie beyond the scope of the OT. Since the few (twelve) direct references to Samaria in the NT also take no notice of these matters, historical reconstruction of these periods depends on archaeology, the Apocrypha (Judith, 1–2 Maccabees, and 1 Esdras), and classical sources (e.g., Josephus). See SAMARITANS.

Bibliography: B. Becking. *The Fall of Samaria: An Historical and Archaeological Summary.* SHANE, vol. 2

(1992); N. Franklin. "The Tombs of the Kings of Israel: Two Recently Identified 9th-Century Tombs from Omride Samaria." *ZDPV* 119 (2003) 1–11; N. Franklin. "Samaria: From the Bedrock to the Omride Palace." *Levant* 36 (2004) 189–202; G. Galil. "The Last Years of the Kingdom of Israel and the Fall of Samaria." *CBQ* 57 (1995) 52–65; G. Galil. *The Chronology of the Kings of Israel and Judah* (1996); J. H. Hayes and J. K. Kuan. "The Final Years of Samaria (730–720 BC)." *Bib* 72 (1991) 153–81; I. T. Kaufman. "The Samaria Ostraca: An Early Witness to Hebrew Writing." *BA* 45 (1982) 229–39; N. Na'aman. "The Historical Background to the Conquest of Samaria (720 BC)." *Bib* 71 (1990) 206–25; A. F. Rainey. "Toward a Precise Date for the Samaria Ostraca." *BASOR* 272 (1988) 69–74; L. E. Stager. "Shemer's Estate." *BASOR* 277/278 (1990) 93–107; R. E. Tappy. *The Archaeology of Israelite Samaria: Vol. 1, Early Iron Age through the Ninth Century* BCE (1992); R. E. Tappy. *The Archaeology of Israelite Samaria: Vol. 2, The Eighth Century* BCE (2001); R. E. Tappy. "The Provenance of the Unpublished Ivories from Samaria." *"I Will Speak the Riddles of Ancient Times" (Ps 78:2b): Archaeological and Historical Studies in Honor of Amihai Mazar on the Occasion of His Sixtieth Birthday.* Aren M. Maeir and Pierre de-Miroschedji, eds. (2006) 637–56; R. E. Tappy. "The Final Years of Israelite Samaria: Toward a Dialogue between Texts and Archaeology." *"Up to the Gates of Ekron": Essays on the Archaeology and History of the Eastern Mediterranean in Honor of Seymour Gitin.* A. Ben-Tor, S. W. Crawford, J. P. Dessel, and A. Mazar, eds. (2007) 258–79; M. C. Tetley. "The Date of Samaria's Fall as a Reason for Rejecting the Hypothesis of Two Conquests." *CBQ* 64 (2002) 59–77; K. L. Younger Jr. "The Fall of Samaria in Light of Recent Research." *CBQ* 61 (1999) 461–82.

RON E. TAPPY

SAMARIA OSTRACA. Over 100 inscribed potsherds (*see* OSTRACA) discovered at SAMARIA. Written in the 8th cent. BCE, probably during the reign of JEROBOAM II (789–748 BCE), they are receipts recording the delivery of wine and oil "to" or "for" certain individuals, expressed by the Hebrew preposition le- (לְ) followed by a personal name. Other names appearing on the ostraca may designate the individuals who transported the goods.

The meaning of the construction le- + personal name has sparked debate. The individuals thus named on the ostraca could have been wealthy landowners living in the city, whose representatives shipped them the goods detailed in the receipts (i.e., the goods were sent "to" the named individual). Alternatively, the ostraca may record tax payments to the king, made to the credit of (or "for") the named individuals.

The ostraca preserve previously unknown geographic names for the region around Samaria. Furthermore, the names preceded by the preposition le- tend to incorporate the divine name Yahweh, while the other names on the ostraca tend to incorporate the divine name BAAL (*see* GOD, NAMES OF). This pattern might suggest a connection between religious practice (at least in naming) and social stratification if the individuals bearing Yahweh-names were wealthy landowners. Finally, the inscriptions indicate that the Hebrew words for "wine" and "year" were pronounced differently in Samaria than in the south (*see* HEBREW LANGUAGE).

PETER ALTMANN

SAMARIA PAPYRI suh-mair'ee-uh puh-pi'ri. The Samaria Papyri were found in 1962 by bedouins who searched a cave in Wadi ed-Daliyeh, situated about 14 km north of Jericho (*see* DALIYEH, WADI ED). Systematic archaeological surveys of the cave added some fragments in 1963/64. Eighteen texts were edited finally by Douglas Gropp together with photographs of the remaining fragments. Though no complete document was found and about 150 small fragments cannot be assigned, the remains of about thirty texts show that they belonged to juridical documents mainly dealing with the sale of slaves (*see* PAPYRUS, PAPYRI). All these deeds seem to have been written at the end of the Persian period between 375 and 335 BCE in the city of SAMARIA, the capital of the Persian province of Samaria. They were written in imperial Aramaic, the official language of the western parts of the Persian Empire, but some fragments show traces of Greek letters.

The contracts are formulated from the viewpoint of the buyer (as in Neo-Babylonian documents) and not of the seller (as in the ELEPHANTINE PAPYRI). They follow a strict form with traditional elements, known especially from the Neo-Babylonian documents, but they also show developments that occur in later Jewish deeds. After writing, the deeds were rolled up, and the scrolls were sealed with the seals of the witnesses, who are mentioned by name in some of the documents. At least some, if not all, contracts were concluded in front of the governor of Samaria. Thus, the documents probably belonged to some wealthy citizens from Samaria who fled to the cave ca. 332 BCE after a revolt against Alexander the Great.

The contracting parties and slaves could be male or female and often bear Yahwistic names. Thus, trading Hebrew slaves appears to have been common in Samaria at the end of the Persian period. There is no indication in these contracts of the legislation concerning the freeing of slaves after seven years or in the year of Jubilee (Exod 21:2; Lev 25:39-42; Deut 15:12); instead, these contracts stipulate that the new ownership of the buyer lasts "forever." *See* SLAVERY.

Bibliography: Douglas M. Gropp. *Wadi Daliyeh II: The Samaria Papyri from Wadi Daliyeh.* DJD 28 (2001);

Mary J. W. Leith. *Wadi Daliyeh I: The Wadi Daliyeh Seal Impressions.* DJD 24 (1997).

INGO KOTTSIEPER

SAMARIA, GATE OF [שַׁעַר שֹׁמְרוֹן sha'ar shomron]. According to two incidents in the lives of AHAB (1 Kgs 22:10; 2 Chr 18:9) and ELISHA (2 Kgs 7:1, 18), the main gate of Iron Age Samaria served as a public gathering space, apparently with a public threshing floor, market, and seats from which kings conducted the business of the court. *See* GATE; SAMARIA.

JAMES RILEY STRANGE

SAMARIA, TERRITORY OF suh-mair'ee-uh [שֹׁמְרוֹן shomron; Σαμάρεια Samareia]. Samaria was a city and region in Israel. Traditionally, the name Samaria derives from a certain Shemer who sold his property to Omri, king of the northern kingdom of Israel (ca. 876–864 BCE) for two talents of silver (1 Kgs 16:24). An alternate explanation holds that because Samaria was first situated on a hill 100 m high, its name signified "watch-mountain" (from the verb **shamar** [שָׁמַר], meaning "to watch" or "to observe"). Once this "watch-mountain" was fortified, Samaria became the new capital city of Israel, replacing Tirzah (Tell el-Fara). Later, the city's name also came to signify the province as a whole.

Initially, the territory of Samaria corresponded to the territories of Ephraim and the western part of Manasseh (Josh 16:5-10; 17:7-13), an area that included the hill country of Ephraim, as well as Mount Ebal and Mount Gerizim. The region was bounded by the Jezreel Valley and lower Galilee to the north, the Beth-shan and Jordan River valleys to the east, the coastal plains of Acco and Sharon to the west, and the valley of Ajalon and Jericho to the south. All told, it encompassed roughly 870 sq. mi. and was roughly 30 mi. long and 27 mi. wide.

Notwithstanding its limited size, Samaria was able to sustain a sizable population. The fertile soil of the valleys and slopes supported wheat, fruit, vines, and olives, while the hills and mountains were well suited for the tending of sheep and goats. Samaria's chief urban centers were the cities of Samaria and Shechem, though both cities were eventually razed by John Hyrcanus about 107 BCE. Samaria was rebuilt and renamed Sebaste in 27 BCE, while the city of Neapolis (modern Nablus) was built in the vicinity of Shechem's ruins by Vespasian in 72 CE.

Samaria's strategic location meant that it could not readily avoid the larger dynastic conflicts of the Levant. Consequently, its boundaries remained in a constant state of flux. When the northern kingdom of Israel was defeated by the Assyrians in 724 BCE, about 30,000 Israelites were deported, with captive Babylonians ("Cutheans") resettled in their place. In 612 BCE, Samaria was made a Babylonian province and, when Jerusalem fell in 586 BCE, the province received the hill country of Judea, and Jerusalem with it. With the Persian conquest of Babylon in 539 BCE, Samaria became a satrapy, though whether Judah remained under the jurisdiction of Samaria during the Neo-Babylonian and Persian periods is still debated. After Samaria's conquest by Alexander in 332 BCE, Samaria and Judea became Hellenic provinces, each of which was divided into nomes or administrative districts (1 Macc 10:30, 38; 11:28, 34; *Ant.* 12.154, 175). The rise of the Hasmoneans, however, eventually culminated in the complete subjugation of Samaria and the destruction of its temple by John Hyrcanus. With the advent of the Romans in 63 BCE, Samaria was eventually ceded to Herod the Great, and upon his death (4 BCE) became part of the ethnarchy ruled by his son Archelaus. When the Romans deposed Archelaus in 6 CE, Samaria was joined with Judea and Idumea to form the Roman province of Judea, except for a brief interlude when it was ruled by Agrippa II (41–44 CE). Despite this political arrangement, Samaria appears to have been popularly regarded as a distinct entity by the Jews of Jesus' day (John 4:9; Acts 8:1-25). Though Jesus and his disciples do visit Samaria once (John 4:4-9; but compare Matt 19:1; Luke 17:11), the disciples are otherwise directed not to enter any town of the SAMARITANS (Matt 10:6), and it is only after Jesus' resurrection that Samaria is evangelized (Acts 1:8; 9:31; 15:3).

J. R. C. COUSLAND

SAMARITAN PENTATEUCH. The Samaritan Pentateuch (SP) is the sacred text honored by the Samaritan community. To this day it serves as guide and ideological center for the faithful. In content, it is quite similar to the PENTATEUCH (first five books) of the Hebrew Bible represented by the Masoretic Text (*see* MT, MASORETIC TEXT), commonly called the Old Testament (similarities and differences will be discussed below).

The precise origin of the Samaritan community is debated, but surely the growing influence of Bethel and Gerizim, and the social conflicts reflected in Ezra-Nehemiah point to the importance of a growing religious sectarianism in Judah/Samaria of the late 6th cent. BCE. Regardless of when the SAMARITANS first coalesced into a recognizable sect, the SP has become a constant companion and cherished treasure of the small but enduring Samaritan community. Today the influence of the SP extends far beyond the bounds of the Samaritan community and has benefited the textual study of the Bible.

The SP preserves a textual tradition that was known in antiquity, evidenced in the QUMRAN scrolls, the Palestinian Talmud (*see* TALMUD, JERUSALEM), and in Christian sources such as the works of ORIGEN (who, while preparing the HEXAPLA, used a Greek translation of the SP called the *Samareitikon*), Eusebius of Caesarea, Epiphanius, Jerome, and others. Decorative amulets and various inscriptions on stone and metal dating as far back as the early 1st millennium use specific

wording also found in the SP, giving evidence of the familiarity and honor accorded the SP tradition.

Although there are no surviving and firmly dated manuscripts of the SP from before the 10th cent. CE, there is manuscript evidence from Qumran, some written in Paleo-Hebrew script and others in the square Hebrew script akin to the Samaritan text type. It is generally concluded now that the textual evidence from Qumran gives evidence of what may have been a proto-Samaritan text type, and that the SP, itself, did not appear until the early centuries of the Common Era.

The Qumran pre-texts are what Qumran scholars call "authentic" texts (as against "reworked" texts, such as the tenth commandment now found in SP Exod 20). These Qumran pre-texts, representing some five percent of the Qumran biblical texts of the Pentateuch, are of the genre that grew into the SP. (Among the more notable surviving manuscripts that belong to this group are 4Q22, 4Q27, and 4Q17).

It is most likely that the SP took shape some time after the Qumran site was deserted for the second time, but certainly before Origen's citation of the *Samareitikon*—in other words, in the period between 135 CE and the early 3rd cent. This places the reformulation of the SP squarely in the period of intensive activity by the Samaritan sages and perhaps during the lifetime of their reforming priest, Baba Rabba. This reconstruction implies that the SP is a late development of the MT in which the greater part of the differences between the MT and the Samaritan text took shape after the turn of the eras (*see* TEXT, HEBREW, HISTORY OF, §G; TEXT CRITICISM, OT, §E).

The SP made a dramatic reappearance in the west during the 17th cent. and immediately assumed an important role in the textual studies of the OT. Often contrasted with the MT and the SEPTUAGINT (LXX), the SP has alternately been said to favor one or the other of these more well-known textual traditions. Since the early 19th cent., many scholars have regarded the Samaritan text as an inferior, corrupt, and harmonizing text, due to the widely publicized and influential pronouncements made upon it by Wilhelm Gesenius (in his classic study published in 1815). Gesenius' conclusions must be revised in light of better textual data now available.

Following Gesenius, it is often reported that there are some 6,000 variants between the SP and the MT. The majority of these are spelling variations appropriate to the different times and places of the scrolls' manufacture and represent no significant variation between the SP and the MT. In fact, this kind of orthographic variation is very common even among different manuscripts within the SP tradition, especially between manuscripts of the 12th and 13th cent. compared to manuscripts of the 14th and 15th cent., and so this kind of variation provides unreliable guidance when attempting a comparison between the SP and the MT. There have been several revisions to Gesenius' analysis, including one by the Samaritan High Priest Jacob ben Aaron, who compiled a listing of significant variations between the SP and the MT (British Library MS Or. 10370). Ben Aaron listed seventy-two variants in Genesis, sixty in Exodus, nine in Leviticus, forty in Numbers, and fifty-eight in Deuteronomy, making a total of 239 variants he deemed significant. This assessment of only 239 significant variants is quite different from the previously observed 6,000 variants and refutes the opinion that the SP is inferior and corrupt.

Although the number is much smaller than previously thought, differences between the MT and the SP do exist. Of these, many relate to Samaritan hermeneutics, ideology, theology, exegesis of the text, and older Samaritan rituals. For example, ideological changes are evident in SP Deut 12:5 and SP Exod 20, both of which assert the priority of Mount Gerizim over Jerusalem in a manner consistent with Samaritan theology (*see* GERIZIM, MOUNT). Some of the variants and rewording are hermeneutical, intended to smooth inconsistencies from the text. Such is the case with SP Exod 7:18, 29; 8:19; 9:5, 19; 10:2; 11:3, etc., where various passages belonging to the same story have been duplicated and inserted into the text. The Samaritan tendency to remove anthropomorphisms in the SP came about under the influence of the fusion of Samaritan and Hellenistic cultures in a style that post dates the LXX.

Major collections of SP manuscripts reside scattered around the world, most notably at Nablus, the John Rylands University Library (University of Manchester), the British Museum, the Bibliotheque Nationale, Michigan State University, and several private collections. It is estimated that there are at least 750 complete SP manuscripts in existence. Of these, fewer than 100 were written prior to the 18th cent., as evidenced by dates on codices and bills of sale frequently incorporated into the scroll. Many of the pre- 18th cent. manuscripts come from the 14th and 15th cent. and originate from one of four different scroll production centers: Damascus, Egypt, Shechem, and Zarephath.

Bibliography: Robert T. Anderson and Terry Giles. *The Keepers: An Introduction to the History and Culture of the Samaritans* (2002); Alan D. Crown, ed. *The Samaritans* (1989); Alan D. Crown, Reinhard Pummer, and Abraham Tal, eds. *Companion to Samaritan Studies* (1993); Alan D. Crown and Lucy Davey, eds. *Essays in Honour of G. D. Sixdenier: New Samaritan Studies of the Societe d'Etudes Samaritaines* (1995); August von Gall. *Der hebraische Pentateuch der Samaritaner.* 5 vols. (1914–18; Repr., 1 vol., 1966); W. Gesenius. *De Pentateuchi Samaritani origine indole et auctoritate commentatio philologico-critica* (1815); Abraham Tal, ed. *The Samaritan Pentateuch* (1994).

ALAN D. CROWN AND TERRY GILES

SAMARITAN WOMAN suh-mair´uh-tuhn [γυνὴ Σαμαρῖτις gynē Samaritis]. A woman of Samaria who

meets Jesus at a well near the city of Sychar, has an extended personal and theological discussion with him, and bears witness to his identity as prophet and Messiah before her townspeople (John 4:1-42). When Jesus initiates the encounter at the well with a request for water, the woman immediately senses the uncomfortable ethnic and gender gap between them: "How is that you, a Jew, ask a drink of me, a woman of Samaria?" (4:9). The narrator's parenthetical aside that "Jews do not share things in common with Samaritans" understates a more deep-seated and volatile ethnic-religious rift (see 2 Kgs 17:24-41; Luke 9:51-56; 10:25-37; 17:11-19; John 4:20-21; 8:48; *Ant.* 11.84–119; 20.118–36). The woman's surprise that Jesus solicits a drink from her is matched by the disciples' astonishment (upon returning from a shopping trip) that "he was speaking with a woman" (John 4:27). However, since this is the only time in the NT where anyone—disciple or opponent—queries Jesus' talking with women, it seems that this scene's potential impropriety pushes beyond the unremarkable fact of male-female conversation. The controversial element of Jesus' dialogue with the Samaritan woman has more to do with its special setting, evocative of familiar biblical marriage deals struck at wells, including this well associated with Jacob (see Gen 24; 29:1-13; Exod 2:15-21).

Marital matters explicitly come into play with Jesus' exposure of the Samaritan woman's relations with five previous husbands and currently a sixth male companion (John 4:16-18). The common interpretation that such a history befits a sexually loose woman, a prostitute even, goes beyond the textual evidence. Other scenarios involving multiple widowhood and/or divorce (for non-adulterous causes) are just as plausible (see Mark 12:18-23). In any case, the story provides no details about the woman's prior marriages, never speaks of her "sin" or deviance, and stresses Jesus' knowledge of her past as a sign of prophetic insight, not incrimination.

John 4:7-26 represents the longest and most evenly balanced dialogue between Jesus and an individual in the canonical Gospels. The Samaritan woman holds her own (speaking roughly as much as Jesus) and proves to be a worthy conversation partner on two matters of theological substance. First, she questions Jesus' offer of "living water" with reference to "deep" scriptural traditions surrounding ancestor Jacob (4:11-12). Second, she initiates discussion about the proper central place for worshiping God, a major dividing point between Samaritans and Jews (4:19-20). Although in both cases Jesus corrects the woman's misunderstanding, she consistently exhibits an open and receptive heart to match her sharp and inquisitive mind.

At the moment when Jesus reveals that he is the Messiah and his disciples return from the city, the Samaritan woman dashes into town, leaving her water pot behind (4:26-28). Although such an abrupt flight initially intensifies the suspense (and suspicion), we soon learn that the woman has rushed home to herald Jesus' messianic character and to invite the townspeople to "come and see" him (4:29). As a result of her "testimony" or "witness" (martyreō μαρτυρέω)—a high vocation in the Fourth Gospel (1:6-9, 15, 19-34, 40-46)—"many Samaritans ... believed in [Christ]," and many others were prompted to hear his "word" (logos λόγος) for themselves and to profess him as "truly the Savior of the world" (4:41-42). *See* SAMARIA; SAMARITANS.

Bibliography: J. Eugene Botha. *Jesus and the Samaritan Woman: A Speech Act Reading of John 4:1-42* (1991); Frances Taylor Gench. *Back to the Well: Women's Encounters with Jesus in the Gospels* (2004); Amy-Jill Levine with Marianne Blickenstaff, eds. *A Feminist Companion to John.* Vol. 1 (2003); Gail R. O'Day. *Revelation in the Fourth Gospel: Narrative Mode and Theological Claim* (1986); Teresa Okure. *The Johannine Approach to Mission: A Contextual Study of John 4:1-42* (1988).

F. SCOTT SPENCER

SAMARITAN, THE GOOD suh-mair´uh-tuhn [Σαμαρίτης Samaritēs]. Jesus gives the parable of the good Samaritan (Luke 10:30-36) in response to a question from a lawyer: "Who is my neighbor?" (Luke 10:29). In the parable, a traveler is attacked by robbers and left for dead. Two representatives of the law, a priest and a Levite, intentionally pass by the injured traveler rather than help him, possibly because of the risk of ceremonial uncleanness. Finally, a Samaritan stops to help the traveler, taking him to an inn and providing financially for his recovery.

The parable would have astonished Jesus' audience because of strong tensions between Jews and Samaritans, tensions that caused the latter group to be looked down upon. More important, as an answer to the lawyer's question, the parable deconstructs the implied exclusivity of the lawyer's words by showing the supposed enemy to be a neighbor. Jesus' answer illustrates that everyone is a neighbor and that we should act neighborly to all who need us. While this parable addresses the command to love one's neighbor (Luke 10:27*b*), the story that follows, Mary and Martha's interaction with Jesus (Luke 10:38-42), teaches how to fulfill the command to love God (Luke 10:27*a*).

The parable of the good Samaritan has shown remarkable generative power in its history of interpretation. Many different groups have identified themselves with the Samaritan and hoped to embody his good qualities.

NATHAN C. LANE

SAMARITANS suh-mair´-uh-tuhn הַשֹּׁמְרֹנִים hashomronim]. Sometimes used to designate all inhabitants of the northern kingdom of Israel or later province of SAMARIA first used in 2 Kgs 17: 29; usually "Samarians" in English. More commonly and for this article the term hashomrim (הַשֹּׁמְרִים), the term used in the Samaritan Chronicles ("Samaritans" in English), refers to a Hebrew sect focused on their Holy Place, Mount Gerizim, and the TORAH, the first five books of the Hebrew Scripture, the source of their doctrines (*see* GERIZIM, MOUNT). They understand their name to refer to themselves as "keepers" (Hebrew meaning of the term hashomrim) of the law, rather than as a geographical designation. Historically they lived primarily in the tribal regions of Ephraim and Manasseh in northern Palestine (Samaria). Today they are mainly located on Mount Gerizim and in Holon, a suburb of Tel Aviv.

A. History
  1. Sources
  2. Historical periods
    a. Assyrian and Babylonian
    b. Persian
    c. Hellenistic
    d. Roman
    e. Byzantine
    f. Muslim
    g. Modern
B. Literature
  1. Samaritan Pentateuch and Targum
  2. Theological works
    a. Tibat/Memar Marqe
    b. Lesser theological works
  3. Chronicles
    a. The Tulida (Genealogy)
    b. The Samaritan book of Joshua
    c. The Kitab at-Ta'rikh of Abu'l Fath
    d. Chronicle II
    e. Chronicle Adler
    f. Al-Asatir
    g. The Salsala
  4. Liturgy
C. Religion
  1. Monotheism
  2. Moses
  3. Torah
  4. Mount Gerizim
  5. Day of Vengeance and Recompense; Taheb; Ra'utah, and Fanutah
  6. Festivals
D. Relation to Other Faiths
  1. Judaism
  2. The Karaites
  3. Christianity
  4. Islam
Bibliography

A. History
  1. Sources
The major explicit sources for Samaritan history are their own chronicles, the Bible, the 1st-cent. Jewish historian, Josephus and several notes added by

scribes in Samaritan documents. Archaeological digs at Elephantine, Qumran, Emmaus, Delos and Thessalonica have produced other texts and inscriptions, and occasional structures have been unearthed, e.g. at Qedumim, approximately 6 mi. west of Nablus, and on Mount Gerizim.

2. Historical periods

a. Assyrian and Babylonian. The best-known account of Samaritan origins is the Jewish account based on 2 Kgs 17 and echoed and expanded by Josephus (*Ant* 9.277–91). According to these sources, the Samaritans are most likely immigrants brought into the region of Samaria by the Assyrians after the defeat of the Northern Kingdom in 722 BCE. They may be products of intermarriage between such immigrants and remnants of the northern tribes (the so-called "lost ten tribes"). If they are a totally foreign population, it is argued, they learned their religion from an Israelite priest commissioned for that purpose by the Assyrian king after the new colonists (called "Cutheans" from Mesopotamia by the Jews) had been attacked by lions. Distorted memories among the Samarian remnant population could have shaped the religion as well.

Samaritan tradition holds that most of their population survived the Assyrian deportation in tact. The Assyrian records of Sargon II (*Annals* 11–17) say 27,290 northerners were deported, a relatively small percentage even of the aristocracy. The real schism occurred, the Samaritan chronicles say, when Eli usurped the high priesthood and established a rival sanctuary at Shiloh.

Jewish sources make no mention of Samaritans being affected by the Babylonian conquest or captivity. Samaritan Chronicles (§B3) are confusing in their story of an exile, sometimes attributing it to the Babylonians and sometimes to the Greeks.

b. Persian. Samaritan tradition does say that it was the Persians who ended the exile and that SANBALLAT, the subsequent political leader of the Samaritans, contested with Zerubbabel, the leader of the Jews, for the support of the Persian King whom the Samaritans identify as "Surdi," presumably Darius spelled backward. Both Jews and Samaritans affirm that the Persian defeat of the Babylonians allowed new freedoms. Jews say that the Persians permitted them to return to Judah and subsidized the rebuilding of the Temple.

According to the Jews (Ezra 4:1-6 and Neh 2:19, 4:2-3, 7-8), Northerners (Samaritans or Samarians) tried to join them in the rebuilding of the city of Jerusalem and the Temple in the time of Ezra and Nehemiah. The Jews rejected them because the northerners were no longer pure. Sanballat's daughter had married the son of the Jewish high priest, and Nehemiah exiled them from Jerusalem (Neh 13:28). Samaritans, as a religious community (hashomrim, "Keepers of the Law") may have been a relatively small proportion of hashomronim ("people of the region of Samaria").

Samaritan traditions say that the Persians favored them and provided funds to build an altar at their sanctuary on Mount Gerizim adjacent to ancient Shechem. Further, according to Samaritan chronicles, the Persians encouraged the Samaritans to impede the building of the Temple at Jerusalem. The Jews aggravated the schism, according to the Samaritans, when Ezra introduced the use of a new Hebrew script. Ezra is further vilified by the Samaritans for his sanction of Jerusalem rather than Mount Gerizim as the Holy Place and the expansion of Scripture beyond the Torah to include the Prophets and the Writings.

That such a schism existed is collaborated by letters from both Jewish and Samaritan priests found among the 5th cent. BCE ELEPHANTINE PAPYRI (CAP, 30). Each side was soliciting support for the building of their respective temples.

There was a political advantage to Persians to keep hostility active between the Samaritans and Jews. Preoccupied with each other, they were unlikely to rebel against Persian rule.

c. Hellenistic. Dating the building of the post-exilic Samaritan sanctuary on Mount Gerizim is difficult. Josephus is the major source for information both on its construction and destruction (*Ant.* 13. 254–56). Since both Jews and Samaritans considered the Persians to be benefactors and the Greeks to be oppressors, both wanted to cite the Persians as sponsors of their temple. The Jews (certainly Josephus) delighted in saying the oppressing Greeks were the sponsors of the Samaritan sanctuary. Josephus is willing to admit that the Persians promised a temple to the Samaritans, and the Samaritans admit that Alexander promised them a temple in the early period when he still had the favor of the Samaritans. Most scholars see Josephus' account of the building of the Samaritan temple as fabricated polemic.

Samaritan Chronicles say that initially Alexander was much impressed by the Samaritans but disturbed them with the request to build a monument to himself on Mount Gerizim. The Samaritans not only declined to do so but rebelled against Alexander while he was in Egypt, thus falling out of favor with the Greeks. Both Samaritans and Jews suffered oppression under Alexander and his successors, in contrast to the beneficence experienced under Persian rule. Josephus argues that the Samaritans colluded with the Greeks so that it was the Greeks rather than the Persians who assisted the building of the sanctuary on Mount Gerizim. During the time of Antiochus IV (175–164), the Samaritan sanctuary was renamed either Zeus Hellenios (willingly by the Samaritans according to Josephus) or, more likely, Zeus Xenios (unwillingly as described in 2 Macc 6:2). The same passage indicates the pro-Syrian bent of the Samaritans.

The building of a Samaritan sanctuary may have been an on-going process. Archaeology has revealed more than one potential temple (in addition to other proposed temples that had been previously excavated). Magen believes that Sanballat, the Horonite, built the earliest Samaritan sanctuary on the Mount in the 5th cent. BCE. Sanballat, a contemporary of Ezra and Nehemiah, was the Persian appointed governor of Samaria. Given the relative lack of political or economic power in the north and of a monarchy that is usually associated with a temple, the Samaritan sanctuary was likely a relatively modest complex.

After Alexander's death, the territory of the Samaritans, like Palestine itself, passed several times between Seleucid (Syrian) and Ptolemaic (Egyptian) control.

Whenever the Samaritan sanctuary was completed, there is general agreement that John Hyrcanus, Jewish governor and High Priest in 128 BCE, destroyed it after the decline of the Seleucids. This was a significant stage in the breach betweens Samaritan and Jews.

Samaritan inscriptions found on the Greek island of Delos witness the presence of a Samaritan diaspora in the Greek islands, who self-identity as Israelites and have their devotion to Mount Gerizim. Subsequent diasporas settled Samaritans in Rome, Thessalonica, Cairo, Damascus and Gaza, among other places.

The few Samaritan literary pieces from the Hellenistic period yield little information about their development. Most significant is a biblical text found at Qumran that reflects an already emerging unique Samaritan reading characterized by expansions that highlight the significance of Mount Gerizim and excludes any biblical books beyond the Torah. James Purvis persuasively argues that this unique reading of the Pentateuch, rather than the building of the sanctuary on Mount Gerizim, is the key to dating the definitive separation between the Jews and the Samaritans.

d. Roman. Herod the Great (r. 40–4 BCE) dominated both Samaria and Judea and assumed jurisdiction over the city of Samaria, which he renamed Sebaste. Josephus agrees that both Jews and Samaritans suffered under Roman rule. Josephus cites the slaughter of 10,000 Samaritans by Trajan on Mount Gerizim, an incident that is related with slight variations in a Samaritan inscription.

From NT comments and stories we can infer the low status that Samaritans had among Jews. "Jews do not share things in common with Samaritans," says John 4:9, and detractors of Jesus denigrate him with the accusation that he is a Samaritan (John 8:48), implying a generally held low opinion of Samaritans. Jesus says that even Samaritans behave better than Jews on occasion, which he illustrates in the stories of the Good Samaritan (Luke 10:25-37) and the grateful Samaritan leper (Luke 17:11-19). He startles his disciples by his openness to discourse with Samaritans (John 4:4-42).

Recent scholarly interest in Galilee not only as the home of Jesus, but also as the possible source of several early Christian documents (Q, Mark and John in particular) put the early Christians in close geographical proximity to Samaria. In the gospels, Jesus is often referred to as a Galilean, emphasizing his cultural connection with the north.

The book of Acts describes Samaria as the earliest major Christian mission field (Acts 8:4-8). Stephen's speech reflects and emphasizes the traditions and heroes of the Samaritan Pentateuch. Substantial arguments have been made that both the Gospel of John and the book of Hebrews had at least some Samaritan audience in mind.

Dissatisfaction with the Jerusalem Temple would have been a common link among Samaritans and Christians, as well as Essenes and other groups. Rabbinic literature reflects a Samaritan status in Jewish thought that ambiguously floats between Israelite and Gentile. They are accepted in some times and circumstances and not in others. Marriage to Samaritans was forbidden. The basic issue of contention is the location of the sacred place, Jerusalem versus Mount Gerizim.

The Samaritans had schisms among themselves during this period, notably between the priestly oriented orthodox and the lay-oriented Dositheans. According to the Samaritan Chronicles, there were eight sects among the Dositheans themselves, and Abu'l Fath offers a brief description of eight different groups in his chronicle. Some traditions say SIMON Magus, who is described in Acts 8:9 as practicing magic that "amazed the people of Samaria," was a Samaritan possibly of a Dosithean orientation (*see* DOSITHEUS, APOCALYPSE OF).

e. Byzantine. Samaritanism reached one of its highest points and one of its lowest during Byzantine times. The 3rd and 4th cent. saw a flourishing of Samaritan synagogues, as evidenced by several surviving Torah inscriptions on marble and descriptions in Samaritan Chronicles. Social structure and polity were dramatically strengthened under the leadership of the charismatic Baba Raba (literally "Great Gate," not an uncommon title for Middle Eastern religious leaders). He revived the council of sages to oversee polity and religion within the Samaritan community and resolved internal sectarian conflict, particularly with the Dositheans.

Complimenting the organizational skills of Baba Raba, Marqe, a theologian, gave a conceptual under girding to the community with his treatise, *Tibat Marqe*, and his hymn writing. These hymns expanded the liturgy and were joined by the works of other hymn writers of the time, particularly the widely imitated Amram Darah and Nanah, respectively father and son of Marqe.

The flourishing Samaritan community became a threat to both Byzantine politics and the growing Christian church, and the Samaritans were increasingly persecuted, sometimes more harshly than the Jews. Samaritans fled to many other areas along the Mediterranean coast. After a revolt in 529, Byzantine forces under Justinian radically weakened the Samaritan community, both numerically and economically.

f. Muslim. Samaritans welcomed and supported the conquest by the Muslims in 636, supplying both troops and guides to the invaders. The political change created a more hospitable atmosphere, and Samaritans found positions in the new government. Nevertheless, there is evidence that the Samaritans were taxed more than other groups, and tensions did increase. Circumstances differed among the urban centers, and Samaritan populations shifted among Nablus, Damascus, Gaza and Cairo as they sought the most hospitable environment.

The Kairaites, an anti-rabbinical sect of Judaism, spread into two of those cities, Cairo and Damascus, and aligned themselves with sects like the Samaritans. In common with the Samaritans they had a complex calendar requiring specialists to identify the feast times. Their practices can be traced back to Zadokite traditions at Qumran and may help establish the development of a particular expression of Judaism.

Muslim rule of Palestine was interrupted for a century or so, from 1099 until 1244, with the arrival of the Crusaders. Although the Crusaders commandeered large amounts of supplies from the Samaritans, Nablus was left unharmed because of the docility of the population and the high percentage of Christians living there.

When the Muslims regained control in 1244, they replaced the church/synagogue on Mount Gerizim with a mosque and increased their oppression of the Samaritans. Arabic became the daily language of the Samaritans and modified the religious use of their own language. Islamic religious language like "There is no God but God" was incorporated into the Samaritan liturgy.

A new renaissance of Samaritanism peaked in the 14th cent., focused on the Abisha scroll, a manuscript of the Torah purported to be written by Moses' great grand nephew. Under the leadership of the High Priest, Pinhas, Abu'l Fath was commissioned to write a Samaritan history, and extensive additions, particularly of hymns, were made to the liturgy. Orthodox (priestly oriented) and Dosithean (laity centered) factions of Samaritanism were reunited, and the community was infused with a new vigor.

g. Modern. A series of natural and political disasters (beginning in the 15th cent. and culminating in the arrival of the Ottoman Turks early in the 16th cent.) began a gradual decline of the size and vitality of the Samaritan community. It reached its nadir in the early 20th cent. when fewer than 200 Samaritans survived in poverty in the environs of Nablus.

Paradoxically as Samaritan fortunes waned, European awareness and interest in the Samaritans came into flower. Early in the 16th cent. a Samaritan grammar made its way to Europe, and Joseph Scaliger, a self-taught linguist, began a correspondence with the Samaritans in an attempt to acquire a Samaritan Pentateuch. One of the issues between post-reformation Protestants and Roman Catholics was the identity of the most authentic OT. Catholics favored the Greek LXX, while Protestants endorsed the Massoretic Hebrew text. Awareness of the Samaritan Pentateuch raised hopes that it would arbitrate the quarrel. Early in the 17th cent. the first Samaritan Pentateuch did arrive in Paris through the agency of the statesman Pietro della Valle. It was studied and published by Jean Morin/Johannes Morinus, who remained at the center of the controversies it engendered. The controversies involved both Protestants and Catholics, each of whom sought and argued that they had found sanction for their translation of the Bible. Scholars from each side became very active in soliciting more pentateuchal manuscripts for comparison. The resulting argument gave birth to modern textual criticism.

The discussion also gave birth to a rather extensive correspondence between European scholars and Samaritans seeking not only Pentateuchs, but also other Samaritan literature and further information about the Samaritan sect. The Samaritans were reluctant to send copies of their sacred Pentateuch to these unknown gentiles, and more than one European scholar pretended to be part of a European Samaritan community as a ruse to solicit manuscripts. Archbishop Usher was interested in collecting Samaritan Pentateuchs as aids to his studies in biblical chronology. As a result, a growing collection of Samaritan documents was gathered in Europe. Today there are significant collections of Samaritan manuscripts in Russia, France, Italy, England and the United States.

Samaritan communities outside Nablus disappeared over the centuries, leaving only a minuscule community in Nablus at the beginning of the 20th cent. Since then the community has enjoyed appreciation and support from individuals and the political states that have governed Nablus. The community has grown to several hundred, who now reside in two major centers, Mount Gerizim and Holon, a suburb of Tel Aviv. They publish a newspaper and facilitate studies of the Samaritan community and religion.

B. Literature

1. Samaritan Pentateuch and Targum

The primary literature of the Samaritans is their Scripture, the first five books of the TANAKH. It is also paraphrased in Aramaic versions (targums) and has been translated into both Arabic and Greek (the latter referred to by Origen in his 3rd cent. CE polyglot *Hexapla*) as the *Samareitikon*, now more of an historical artifact. In many manuscripts translations in Aramaic or Arabic (or both) are in parallel columns beside the Samaritan Hebrew. More than a hundred handwritten pre-18th cent. copies exist, of which the earliest dates from the 9th or 10th cent., comparable in date to the earliest complete Tanakh (the Leningrad codex of the 10th cent.). Notes recording later sales of the manuscript are often written in the vacant space at the end of a biblical book. In addition, several manuscripts have an acrostic running vertically through a section of the Torah, usually

Deuteronomy, using letters from the biblical text that are made to fall into the acrostic channel. These notes provide useful information on the provenance, scribes, date, cost and other data about the manuscript. The manuscripts were produced by scribal families mainly in Nablus, Egypt, and Damascus and reach their peak of production in the 14th and 15th cent.

Apart from spelling and grammatical differences, the SAMARITAN PENTATEUCH also varies from the Tanakh at some points in content. The most notable variation is in the Decalogue, where the Samaritan text adds to Exod 20:17 a commandment affirming Mount Gerizim as the holy site designated by God. Another example of textual difference is Ezra's alleged substitution of Ebal for Gerizim in Deut 27:4. Occasionally verses are "copied" and "pasted" from their original site to a relevant new site. For example, after Gen 30:36, Gen 31:11-13 is added. These interpolations give emphasis to phases of the biblical story, particularly issues important to the Samaritans. The interpolated items also remain in their original place, so the total biblical text has been expanded.

The Samaritans are more reluctant than Jews to refer to God anthropomorphically. When the Masoretic Hebrew text refers to God as a "man of war" in Exod 15:3 (NRSV "warrior"), e.g., the Samaritan Pentateuch refers to God as a "hero." Use of angels to represent the presence of God is often preferred by the Samaritans. In Num 22:20; 23:4, 5 and 16, e.g., the Samaritan Pentateuch uses "angel of God" rather than "God." The Samaritans take any opportunity to enhance the status of Moses. The Samaritan scribes were aware of both the MT and LXX texts, and are somewhat eclectic in their use of both (see MT, MASORETIC TEXT; SEPTUAGINT). A Samaritan type text has been found among the manuscripts at Qumran initiating a new chapter in the history of textual development.

The Aramaic Targum (interpretive paraphrase of the Torah) bears similarities to the Jewish Targum, Onqelos, which may indicate a common oral tradition (see TARGUMS). A Jew, Al-Fayoumi/Joseph Gaon, made the earliest translation of the Torah from Hebrew into Arabic in the 10th cent. The 11th cent. Ab Hasda of Tyre is credited with the first Samaritan Arabic translation of the Pentateuch, although a 13th cent. scribe, Abu Said felt the text was so bad that it was really the work of al Fayoumi. Said then made his own translation including all of the colophons from the text of Ab Hasda.

The most revered artifact of the Samaritan community is the previously mentioned Abisha scroll which tradition attributes to the grandnephew of Moses. Portions of scripture, like Exod 15 and the Ten Commandments, adorned synagogue lintels, amulets and scroll cases and are the subjects of most surviving Samaritan inscriptions.

Several commentaries on the parts of the Pentateuch were written in the 19th and 20th cent.

2. Theological works

a. Tibat/Memar Marqe. During the 4th cent. CE Samaritan renaissance, as Baba Raba gave form to the community with political organization and the building of synagogues, Marqe focused the religious thought of the community with theology and biblical interpretations. His major writing, Tibat Marqe, became so important to the community that subsequent generations interpolated new materials into it while continuing the implied Marqan authorship to affect authority. The Tibat Marqe, written in Aramaic, is divided into six books each with a distinctive emphasis—primarily, the Exodus, biblical ethics, the death of Moses and meditations on the Hebrew letters. It contains many hymns and Midrashim (teachings) on biblical passages.

b. Lesser theological works. There are miscellaneous theological works like the Kafi begun by Joseph of Askar and Tabah by Abu'l Hassan of Tyre, both dating in the 11th cent. Several subsequent brief theological works deal with apologia, liturgy, biblical commentary and critiques of Judaism and the Kairites. Theological observations also appear in Al-Asitir, the book of Joshua, and other chronicles described below.

3. Chronicles

a. The Tulida (Genealogy). The Tulida (Genealogy), or Chronicle Neubauer, is the earliest Samaritan chronicle. Originally compiled in Hebrew in the 12th cent., it has been updated periodically. It lists important Samaritan patriarchs from Adam to Jacob b. Aaron in 1859, with occasional comments on the historical context.

b. The Samaritan book of Joshua. Some time in the 13th cent., this book, distinct from the OT book of Joshua, was compiled. Though the opening section claims that it is a translation from Hebrew, all available texts are written in Arabic. It is a compilation of biblical interpretations, commentary, tales, and history by many hands. The basic story moves from the time of Moses to the renaissance under Baba Raba.

c. The Kitab at-Ta'rikh of Abu'l Fath. This most complete of the Samaritan Chronicles was written in Arabic during the second Samaritan renaissance of the mid-14th cent. It was commissioned by the high priest, Pinhas, to tell the story from the time of Adam to the time of Muhammed. Based on several earlier sources, no Samaritan work provides a richer mirror of Samaritan self-understanding.

d. Chronicle II. The Samaritan story has been periodically updated through the beginning of the 20th cent. by Sepher ha-Yamim, also known as Chronicle II, and the New Chronicle, also known as Chronicle Adler. The original parts of the Sepher ha-Yamim, likely a 14th cent. work, is unique in its extensive use of books from the Tanakh (Joshua, Judges, Samuel, Kings and Psalms) that are outside of the Samaritan Pentateuch and are generally ignored by the Samaritans. The work also is frequently focused on theological issues.

The *Sepher ha-Yamim* contains a passage dated by the copiest in 1616 on the origins of Christianity that is decidedly reconcilatory toward Christians. It blames the Jews for the arrest and crucifixion of Jesus and distances the Samartians from any role: "Now Jesus the Nazarene did not consult the community of the Samaritan Israelites at any time in his life. He did not stand in their way, nor did they stand in his. They did not impose upon him, nor he on them in any way."

e. **Chronicle Adler.** This chronicle, copied in 1900, smoothes many of the apparent inconsistencies in the *Kitab at-Ta'rikh* and focuses more sharply on historical rather than wonder tales.

f. **Al-Asatir.** This work expands on the narratives of the Pentateuch from Adam to Moses with interpretations and anecdotal stories. It also looks at future in anticipation of the coming of the Taheb. It is written in the 10th cent. in an Aramaic that has been heavily influenced by Arabic.

g. **The Salsala.** The Salsala or Chain of the High priests is a brief listing of the high priests to the time of Jacob b. Aaron.

4. Liturgy

The earliest Samaritan liturgical work, compiled between the 4th and 14th cent., is called the Defter. Services were originally focused on biblical texts. Hymns, and later prayers, doxologies and other features were added over the centuries. Amram Dare initiated the golden age of hymn writing in the 3rd cent. His hymn form became a model for many later hymns, and a son, Marqe, the theologian, and grandson, Nonah carried on the hymn writing tradition. A few hymns of Abu'l-hasan/Ab Hasda survive from the 11th–12th cent. a second period of notable activity. Several identifiable hymn writers appear in the third important period that peaked in the 14th cent. Among them was Joseph Ha-rabban, presumably from Damascus where the title, "ha-rabban," was in common usage. Pinhas the son of Joseph, the high priest was the instigator of a religious revival and contributed several hymns, some of which are found in surviving manuscript collections and are in use by the Samaritan community today. Special services for festivals were developed during this period. Pinhas and his two sons, Abisha and Eleazar, contributed to the growing liturgical texts. A CD of contemporary Samaritans singing early hymns is available from the A. B. Institute of Samaritan Studies.

C. Religion

The Samaritan creed is "My faith is in you, Lord; and in Moses, son of Amram, your servant; and in the Holy Law; and In Mount Gerizim Bethel; and in the Day of Vengeance and Recompense."

1. Monotheism

The Samaritans share with Jews and Muslims a rigorous monotheism paralleling both the Jewish Shema, "The Lord your God is One," and the Muslim, "There is no god but God" and emphasizing God's essential nature as "I am Who I am." All anthropomorphisms are avoided. Paradoxically, or in compensation, there are up to eighty-eight attributes given to God, including, Creator, King, Redeemer, Sustainer and the Wise. Great emphasis is put on his "glory." God reveals himself primarily in Creation and the giving of the Torah (*see* GOD, OT VIEW OF).

2. Moses

MOSES, as the bearer of the Torah, is the founder of Samaritanism. He is greatly exalted in hymns, prayers and other parts of the liturgy and theological writings. In some writings he is the incarnate light of the world and a large section of the *Tibat Marqe* describes the departure and final ascent of Moses up the mountain and into the clouds. Some of the Samaritan images of Moses share close similarities with gospel descriptions of Jesus. The prominence given to Moses in the book of Hebrews suggests to some scholars that it was written with a Samaritan audience in mind.

3. Torah

The TORAH is a gift and extension of God offering inspiration, a moral code, liturgical regulations and sanction for the Holy Place. Beautiful hand written copies have been penned on animal skin and paper by families particularly trained as scribes, and these copies have been passed on or sold over generations. Nablus, Damascus and Egypt, particularly in the 14th and 15th cent., were centers of Torah production. Portions of the Torah are inscribed in amulets and synagogue inscriptions. Beautiful inscribed brass and silver scroll cases are made to house the more important copies. The Abisha scroll is the most sacred artifact of the Samaritans.

4. Mount Gerizim

Mount Gerizim is sanctioned as the Holy Place in Deut 5:18 in the Samaritan version of the Decalogue, distinguishing Samaritanism from Judaism with its focus on Jerusalem (*see* GERIZIM, MOUNT). Many of the great events of biblical history are said to have happened here including the setting of the garden of Eden from whose dust Adam was created, the building of the first altar by Abel, the landing of Noah's ark (Samaritans say Gerizim is the world's tallest mountain), and Abraham bringing Isaac to be sacrificed. The Messiah will reign from its peak, and it will be the setting for the Last Judgment. The patriarch, Joseph, inherited the Mount. and he is buried at its foot. Not only did the Samaritans build tabernacles and possibly a temple here, but Hadrian built a temple to Zeus. Churches and mosques were also built on the site. A ring of Samaritan synagogues was built in close proximity to the Mount.

At times occupying forces forbade access to the Mount, and Samaritans had to improvise alternatives for their pilgrimage festivals. In time of oppression,

Samaritans sought refuge on the Mount. In consequence, the Mount sometimes was the site of massacres. In recent times most of the Nablus Samaritan community has relocated to the top of the mountain because of insecurities caused by the Palestinian/Israeli conflict.

5. Day of Vengeance and Recompense; Taheb; Ra'utah, and Fanutah

For the Samaritans, there are three great eras of history, the present era of divine disfavor sandwiched between two periods of divine favor. The original period of divine favor existed when the tabernacle was on Mount Gerizim in the early days of Palestinian settlement, a period of 260 years by Samaritan calculation. The period of divine disfavor (*Fanutah*) began when Eli moved the sanctuary to Shiloh. Samaritans now look forward to the *Ra'utah*, the return of God's favor. A human figure, the Taheb, modeled on the promise of Deut 18:18, will be the harbinger of the new era. During the middle ages the concept of a Second Kingdom, political world dominion was added to the *Ra'utah*. Beyond that a cosmic eschatology has been added.

6. Festivals

Three seasonal festivals, Passover, Pentecost and Booths involve pilgrimages to the top of Mount Gerizim.

The most notable festival today is Passover because it is the only one still carried out with animal sacrifice, the offering of the paschal lambs in accordance with the Deuteronomic regulations. Many travelers have described the drama, a witness to both the significance of the festival and the flexibility of the Samaritans in celebrating it. After weeks of preparatory acts like tending of lambs and personal ablutions, the community makes its way up the Mount, some following the ancient foot path, some taking the modern road, some even hiring taxis. At various points appropriate scriptures are read. Once on the Mount, the women retreat to special shelters, and the men, most dressed in white robes, are led in prayers by the priests as all face to the east. The lambs are brought out, fires are lit and the community prays while the water boils. The lambs are quickly slaughtered, dressed and placed in the ground to roast.

Six days before Passover and Booths is the Day of Simmuth when each Samaritan pays a half shekel and receives the calendar for the coming six months. The DAY OF ATONEMENT (Yom Kippur) is celebrated in the synagogue and is an occasion to display the Abisha scroll. Other festivals are the Feast of Unleavened Bread, the Feast of Weeks, the Feast of the Seventh month and the "eighty days of solemn assembly."

D. Relation to Other Faiths

1. Judaism

Judaism and Samaritanism are rooted in the same historical tradition based on the Pentateuch and, at times, Samaritanism has been considered a sect of JUDAISM.

There are incidents of Jewish influence on Samaritan thought, e.g., the Samaritan list of 613 precepts written by Abraham ha-Qabasi in 1532 embodies statements from the Jewish Spanish exiles also in Damascus at the time. Usually, they have remained distinctive because of their Holy Place, Mount Gerizim, in preference to Jerusalem. Occasionally each has recognized the religious authorities of the other. Samaritans do not celebrate Purim, Hanukkah or the minor Jewish feasts. As an expediency, Samaritan men sometimes marry Jewish women. Jews do not allow Samaritan burials in their cemetery in Tel Aviv.

2. The Karaites

This sect emerged from Judaism in the eighth or 9th cent. CE in Iran and Iraq, and like the Samaritans, survive diminished, but distinct to the present. Among their distinctive differences, shared by the Samaritans, are the lunar calculation festival dates like Pentecost and broad extrapolations of biblical prohibitions to include, e.g., the lighting of fire or allowing it to burn on the Sabbath. The Dead Sea scrolls reveal that some of these practices and thoughts had earlier precedence.

3. Christianity

Christianity and Samaritanism show a long history of interaction. The Samaritans were the first mission field for the Christians. Open hostilities erupted during the Byzantine period. Samaritans exploited Christian sectarian differences in Palestine, sometimes destroying Christian property, and Christians and Samaritans quarreled over access to Jacob's well and Joseph's tomb that were in Samaritan hands. Samaritans rebelled at Byzantine oppression, and the emperor Justinian oppressed and finally decimated the Samaritan community, destroying large populations and their possessions. Many Samaritans fled to other parts of the Mediterranean world. The Samaritans encountered the Christians again when the Crusaders invaded in 1099 and commandeered supplies, and their synagogue was converted into a church. Conceptually, Christ and Moses interchange roles and qualities as the vocabulary of Christians and Samaritans enrich one another.

4. Islam

After the rise of Islam, Arabic became the daily and sometimes the scriptural language of the Samaritans and expressions like "There is no god, but God," became part of a liturgical expression. *See* ISRAEL, HISTORY OF; VERSIONS, ANCIENT.

Bibliography: Robert Anderson and Terry Giles. *The Keepers: An Introduction to the History and Culture of the Samaritans* (2002); Robert Anderson and Terry Giles. *A Tradition Kept: An Introduction to the Sacred and Religious Literature of the Samaritans* (2005); John Bowman. *Samaritan Documents Relating to Their History, Religion and Life* (1977); Alan D. Crown.

A Bibliography of the Samaritans (1993); Alan D. Crown, ed. *The Samaritans* (1989); Alan D.Crown, Reinhard Pummer, and Abraham Tal, eds. *A Companion to Samaritan Studies* (1993); John Macdonald. *The Theology of the Samaritans* (1964); James A. Montgomery. *The Samaritans: The Earliest Jewish Sect* (1968); James Purvis. *The Samaritan Pentateuch and the Origin of the Samaritan Sect* (1965); Edward Robertson. *Catalogue of the Samaritan Manuscripts in the John Rylands Library.* 2 vols. (1938, 1962); Paul Stenhouse. *The Kitab al-Ta'rikh of Abu 'l-Fath: Translated with Notes* (1985).

ROBERT T. ANDERSON

SAMEK [ס s]. The fifteenth letter of the Hebrew alphabet, which derives from the original Semitic word *samk-, though the original meaning is unknown. *See* ALPHABET.

SAMGAR-NEBO   sam´gahr-nee´boh   [סַמְגַּר־נְבוּ samgar-nevu]. One of the four named Babylonian officials who took charge of Jerusalem when the city was captured in 587/586 BCE (Jer 39:3). There are numerous problems associated with the names of all the officials. It is quite possible that Samgar-nebo is the title of NERGAL-SHAREZER instead of a proper name (compare RAB-SARIS; RABMAG). The name *Samgar* is unlike all other known Babylonian names, while *nebo* is the theophoric (divine) element.

MARK RONCACE

SAMLAH sam´luh [שַׂמְלָה samlah]. An early ruler of Edom from MASREKAH. He ruled after Hadad of Avith, son of Bedad, and was succeeded by Shaul of Rehoboth in an apparently nonhereditary type of kingship (Gen 36:36-37; 1 Chr 1:47-48). No extrabiblical historical evidence is known about him.

SAMMUNIYEH, KHIRBET. A site in Galilee north of Megiddo on the edge of the Jezreel Valley. It is generally identified with the biblical city of SHIMRON (Josh 11:1; 19:15). Although the site has not been excavated, archaeological surface surveys have found evidence of occupation from the Early Bronze Age through the Roman period. The connection of Sammuniyeh with Shimron was known already in the time of Josephus, although the Talmud and Mishnah identify Shimron with the site of Simonia. Sammuniyeh's other name, Tell Shimron, makes its identification almost certain. The city fell within the tribal boundaries of Zebulun (*see* ZEBULUN, ZEBULUNITE).

The site is known from Egyptian records beginning in the Middle Bronze Age, as it occurs in some of the Execration Texts. Thutmose III includes Shimron in a list of cities that gathered against him at Megiddo. The AMARNA LETTERS preserve a short letter from Shamu-Adda, the ruler of Shamhuna, which appears to be an Egyptian spelling of Shimron (EA 225). In the

letter, the king assures the pharaoh of his loyalty and his willingness to carry out the pharaoh's orders.

KEVIN A. WILSON

SAMOS say´mos [Σάμος Samos]. Samos is an island in the southeast Aegean Sea 1 mi. west of Asia Minor (modern Turkey), near Ephesos. It is 43 km long and 13 km wide. The most important temple to Hera was built on Samos when the island was an important naval power in the 6th cent. BCE.

Samos appears in the list of cities (1 Macc 15:23) that received a letter from Lucius, the Roman consul, directing their recipients to treat Jews well and to return Judean "scoundrels" seeking refuge to Judea, to be tried by Judean law (1 Macc 15:16-21). On Paul's final journey to Jerusalem, his ship "touched" or spent the night at Samos (Acts 20:15). Some early biblical manuscripts include a variant reading, however, that suggests that Paul may simply have passed near Samos after anchoring at Trogyllium.

ADAM L. PORTER

SAMOTHRACE   sam´uh-thrays   [Σαμοθράκη Samothrakē]. An island located in the north Aegean Sea, approximately 32 km (20 mi.) south of Thrace, on a sea route used by Paul (Acts 16:11).

Samothrace is small (178 km or 69 mi.) and mountainous; its highest mountain, Mount Phengari, rises 1,624 m (1 mi.). In Homer, Poseidon watched the battle for Troy from this peak (*Il.* 13.12–13), which served as a landmark for sailors.

The history of settlement in Samothrace is unclear. Archaeologists have found evidence of limited habitation starting in the Neolithic period. Greeks began to colonize Samothrace during the 8th cent. BCE, perhaps from Samos, Lesbos, or northwest Asia Minor. The Greek colonists integrated themselves into the preexisting Thracian society.

The island was known as a pan-Hellenic religious center, akin in importance to Delphi or Olympia. When the Greeks arrived, they found the inhabitants worshiping deities whom they associated with Greek gods: Axieros/Demeter, Axiokersa/Persephone, Axiokersos/Hades, and Kasmilos/Hermes. These deities were the "great gods," the focus of a mystery cult.

The mystery cult, similar to that of Eleusis, made Samothrace famous. Among the initiates were Lysander, king of Sparta; the parents of Alexander the Great, Philip of Macedonia and Olympias; several Hellenistic kings from the Ptolemaic and Seleucid dynasties; and, later, important Romans, including Julius Caesar's father-in-law and the emperor Hadrian. These famous and wealthy initiates patronized Samothrace lavishly, especially during the 4th cent. BCE.

Archaeologists uncovered evidence of their generosity in the 19th cent. The remains of many buildings from the cult site have been discovered, but the most famous find was the statue known as the *Nike of Samothrace*.

This statue, carved around 200 BCE to commemorate a naval victory, is currently located in the Louvre.

While widely known in the Greek world, Samothrace only appears once in the Bible. Paul departed from Asia, leaving the port of Troas, and sailed to Samothrace. After spending the night, he continued on to Neapolis (16:11) in Macedonia. Although Samothrace lacked a natural harbor, ships could anchor off its north shore and be protected from southern gales. Luke is silent about whether Paul went ashore during his voyage to Macedonia. Luke is also silent about Paul's itinerary on his return voyage from Macedonia to Troas (Acts 20:6), but he may have stopped at Samothrace on this occasion, too. An ancient church, discovered in 1938, may have been built to commemorate Paul's visit. *See* TROAS.

Bibliography: Karl Lehmann. *Samothrace: A Guide to the Excavations and the Museum* (1983).

ADAM L. PORTER

SAMPSAMES samp′suh-meez [Σαμψάμης *Sampsamēs*]. One of the destinations to which the Roman consul LUCIUS sent a letter on behalf of the Jews that they not be harmed (1 Macc 15:23). Sampsames and other names in this list are unknown locations, but perhaps Sampsames was a seaport on the Black Sea, modern Samsun.

EMILY R. CHENEY

SAMRA, KHIRBET ES. Two ancient sites are known by this name, one located west of the Dead Sea and the other located northeast of Amman, Jordan. The Arabic name means "Black Ruin." 1. The site west of the Dead Sea, usually transliterated as "Samrah." This site is one of three fortified villages established in the Buqeiʿa Valley, perhaps during the reign of Hezekiah or Josiah. The Buqeiʿa is a small plain (5 mi. × 2 mi.) located in the Judean wilderness between Qumran and Hyrcania. Most scholars identify it with the Valley of Achor (Josh 7:24-26; 15:7; Hos 2:15). Khirbet es-Samrah, the middle and largest of the three sites, has been identified with Secacah, which is mentioned in Josh 15:61 as one of six towns located in the wilderness district of Judah. The northernmost site, Khirbet abu Tabaq, has been identified with Middin, and the southernmost site, Khirbet el-Maqari, has been identified with Nibshan. An alternative theory identifies Secacah with Qumran and the other two cities with ruins located along the western shore of the Dead Sea.

2. Khirbet es-Samra in Jordan was originally a Nabatean post located on the Via Nova Traiana halfway between Philadelphia (modern Amman) and Bostra. Around 300 CE, the Romans built a fortress measuring 60 m × 60 m. The site has been identified with Hatita, which is mentioned in the Peutinger Table, and with Adtitha, which is mentioned in the Notitia Dignitatum. Seven churches were built in the town during the 6th cent. The site also contains a large cemetery with Greek and Syro-Palestinian inscriptions. Earthquakes and disease caused its abandonment before 800.

Bibliography: Zvi Greenhut. "The City of Salt." *BAR* 19 (1993) 32–43; Jean-Baptiste Humbert and Alain Desreumaux. *Khirbet es-Samra 1* (1998); Lawrence E. Stager. "Farming in the Judean Desert during the Iron Age." *BASOR* 221 (1976) 145–58.

GREGORY L. LINTON

SAMSON sam′suhn [שִׁמְשׁוֹן *shimshon*; Σαμψών *Sampsōn*]. The story of Samson, the last of the major judges (pre-monarchical leaders who have long accounts narrated about them) in the book of Judges, occurs in chaps. 13–16. This is the longest and most colorful account of any of the judges in Judges, and is followed by five chapters recounting two stories in which judges, that is, charismatic military figures raised up by Yahweh, are not present. The interpretation of the Samson material is complex, in part because it may refer to Philistine customs that are not fully clear to us, though we might reconstruct them based on Greek practices, and in part because it is a composite work. It is thus important to ask what each section meant separately, what the entire episode means as a whole, and how it might be interpreted within the larger framework of the book of Judges.

A. Outline and Introduction
B. The Birth Narrative
C. Samson and the Timnite Woman
D. Samson and the Prostitute of Gazah
E. Delilah Leads to Samson's Death
F. The Samson Story as a Whole
G. The Samson Story within the Book of Judges
H. The Afterlife of the Samson Story
Bibliography

A. Outline and Introduction

There is clear internal evidence that the material in chaps. 13–16 is not of one hand. Judges 13:1, "The Israelites again did what was evil in the sight of the LORD, and the LORD gave them into the hand of the Philistines forty years," is formulaic, and is part of the secondary framework of Judges, used to join the stories together. In fact, the next verse is phrased as an introduction, "There was a certain man ..." (13:2), and was once the beginning of the story. Many episodes in Judges end by recounting how long the individual functioned as a judge. This appears twice: in 15:20, the last verse of that chapter, "And he judged Israel in the days of the Philistines twenty years," and 16:31*b*, "He had judged Israel twenty years," suggesting that 15:20 was an earlier ending of the story, and that chap. 16 was added at a later point. Even the stories within 13–15 are not of one hand; they are stylistically different, and assume different origins of Samson's strength. Thus, the material concerning Samson may be divided into sections as follows:

Although each major section has its own logic and tone, some effort has been made by (an) editor(s) to bring the stories closer together, so that the four chapters read reasonably well as a whole. This was facilitated by the fact that the stories in their earlier forms probably shared certain commonalities, such as the focus on Samson's strength and on the role of women in his life.

It is unclear how the various stories about Samson originated, and indeed, if a person named Samson existed in the pre-monarchic period. Many of the stories about Samson, more than other stories in Judges, have folktale elements, and are stories that have parallels in other cultures, including from the Greek world, which influenced the Philistines who originated in the Aegean. Most likely, these stories were appropriated to a traditional hero from the tribe of Dan, and were embellished over time. It is impossible, unfortunately, to trace this process in any detail, and to know when the Samson stories developed.

B. The Birth Narrative

This episode starts with elements of the typical birth narrative and annunciation scene, such as the notice that the mother-to-be is barren, and the appearance of an angel of the LORD announcing the forthcoming birth. A careful look at chap. 13, however, shows that in many ways it fundamentally differs from the typical story. In no other episode does the messenger insist that the child to be born must be a nazirite (though in 1 Sam 1:11, Hannah makes that offer; see NAZIR, NAZIRITE). More significantly, it is likely that this story is suggesting that the messenger himself impregnated Manoah's wife. Judges 13:6, "A man of God came to me," can also be translated as "A man of God had sex with me," and the angel's words in vv. 3-5 are best translated as "Although you are barren, having borne no children, you shall conceive and bear a son ... for you shall conceive and bear a son," suggesting that she has suddenly become pregnant between vv. 3 and 5, while her husband is nowhere to be seen. The sexual interest of this angel in Manoah's wife also explains why when he reappears, the text goes out of its way to state (v. 9)

"she sat in the field; but her husband Manoah was not with her"—elsewhere in the Bible, a "field" is a place for illicit sexual liaisons. Finally, an angelic father offers one explanation of Samson's strength; the background of this story is similar to Gen 6:1-4, where the sons of God take daughters of men, resulting in the birth of the Nephilim, "warriors of renown."

The role of Samson's mother is highlighted in other ways as well in this chapter, prefiguring the role and power that women will have in the entire cycle. Unlike her husband, she realizes that the messenger is angelic; Manoah only understands this after the angel disappears in the flame and does not reappear (vv. 20-21). She convinces her husband that they are not about to die (vv. 22-23). The gender roles in this chapter are expressed well in v. 11: "Manoah got up and followed his wife"—in fact, the name Manoah may mean "the restful one," suggesting the back-seat role he takes to his wife.

Samson is introduced in the last two verses of the chapter: "The woman bore a son, and named him Samson. The boy grew, and the LORD blessed him. The spirit of the LORD began to stir him in Mahaneh-dan, between Zorah and Eshtaol" (vv. 24-25). She, not Manoah, names the child. No etymology is given for the name, though it is most likely a diminutive of the Hebrew shemesh (שֶׁמֶשׁ, "sun"), and some scholars see in this name (a remnant of) a Heracles myth. In the transitional end of this section, Samson's strength is seen as a divine endowment, as "the LORD blessed him. The spirit of the LORD began to stir him," and is not connected to his status or long hair as a nazirite, or to his birth from an angelic father.

C. Samson and the Timnite Woman

In Judg 14:1–15:19, another unnamed woman is introduced, a woman who is selected by Yahweh for Samson (v. 4): "for he was seeking a pretext to act against the Philistines." This brief notice highlights the centrality of theology to this entire episode, where Samson gains strength because "The spirit of the LORD rushed on him" (14:6, 19; 15:14). Samson prays to God so that he may not die of thirst (15:18) and the prayer is heeded. Although Samson prays later in 16:28, none of the other units are as explicitly theological as this one.

Samson uses his God-given strength several times in this unit: he kills a lion (14:6), thirty residents of Ashkelon (14:19), and many Philistines (15:8); he escapes from bonds (15:14); and kills another thousand Philistines (15:15). His main role is to be a thorn in the side of the Philistines, a wild and undisciplined killing machine. This unit depicts much of Samson's killing and destruction as unnatural: slaying a lion with his bare hands (14:6), setting fields afire using three hundred jackals (15:5-6), and killing Philistines with an ass-jaw (15:15-17). There are also many explicit mentions of "going up" and "going down" in this unit, a theme that continues in the next two units as well.

The author of this section is interested in riddles. The first is explicit, when Samson asks the assembled Philistines to decipher (14:14) "Out of the eater came something to eat. Out of the strong came something sweet," meaning in this context that he got honey from a lion's carcass, though some modern scholars believe that this is an old riddle, answered either by vomit or sex. The riddle-style continues as the Timnites answer Samson's original riddle by saying (v. 18), "What is sweeter than honey? What is stronger than a lion?" an allusion to love, or perhaps knowledge, and Samson answers that question with another riddle of sorts (v.18), "If you had not plowed with my heifer, you would not have found out my riddle," where Samson suggests that they had sex with the Timnite woman (= heifer) he was about to marry. This riddling is unique to this unit.

Chapters 14–15 in their current form also hint ahead to Samson's demise, which will come about when Delilah nags him concerning the source of his strength. Judges 14:16-17 prefigure that: "So Samson's wife wept before him, saying, 'You hate me; you do not really love me. You have asked a riddle of my people, but you have not explained it to me.' ... She wept before him the seven days that their feast lasted; and because she nagged him, on the seventh day he told her." In this case, however, the nagging is fatal to the Philistines, but not to Samson. Although these episodes characterize women as nags, they may offer a subtle critique of this view as well, and it is worth recalling the highly positive image of Samson's mother in chap. 13.

The second episode of the story ends with a set of etiologies or stories of origin. In Judg 15:14, Samson comes to Lehi, the word for "jawbone," and the continuation of the story clarifies that the place is named after the jawbone that Samson used to kill a thousand Philistines. Within Lehi, we have an etiology for the place "En-hakkore" (v. 19). Qore' is a homonym in Hebrew, meaning both "partridge" (qore' קֹרֵא) and "caller" (qore' קוֹרֵא). Most likely this place originally meant "the spring of the partridge (qore')," but it is here understood as "the spring of the one who called (or prayed—qore')," connecting the name to the hollow place that was split open in response to Samson's prayer, so he might drink. Thus, this unit is characterized, at least at its end, by significant etiological interest, as it uses tales about Samson to explain the names of certain places.

D. Samson and the Prostitute of Gazah

This is the shortest of the Samson stories, comprised of three verses (Judg 16:1-3). Like the previous story, it is likely etiological, explaining why the gates of Hebron look like they fit the entrance to the distant city of Gaza. But it is etiological in a different sense than the previous section: it explains an odd phenomenon rather than the meaning of a place name. It also picks up on sex and women, a theme of each of the units. Unlike the previous unit, it depicts Samson as naturally strong: he

does not need "the spirit of the LORD [to have] rushed on him" in order to carry these massive city gates so far. It also prefigures the following unit: here Samson merely uproots some city gates, destroying property but harming no one; in the next unit, he will topple temple columns, creating great damage to property and people.

E. Delilah Leads to Samson's Death

These verses (16:4-31a) comprise the fourth, and the best known of the Samson stories, and the only one that names the woman to whom he is connected. Oddly, the text nowhere states her ethnicity, though most readers assume she is Philistine. The name DELILAH is plausibly from the root dll (דלל), which means "hair"; Samson is thus undone by the "hair-lady," to whom he betrays his secret that his strength comes from his hair. This conception that his hair gives him strength is only found in this story. In the first and second stories, "the spirit of the LORD" gives him strength, while in the third, he is naturally strong. In this story, Samson is much like Enkidu in the Epic of Gilgamesh—a wild hairy man, and this episode can be read as the taming of Samson as he is shorn.

Within the Bible, the fourth element of a story is often different or climactic; for example, it is the fourth-born son of Jacob, Judah, who is the most powerful and important. Thus, it is not surprising that this fourth Samson episode is climactic and different from what precedes—Samson will die, but his death will be a great victory: "those he killed at his death were more than those he had killed during his life" (v. 30).

While this final story shares some elements with the previous ones—the power of women over Samson, his lack of tolerance for whining women, sex (see especially v. 19, "She let him fall asleep on her lap," though this may also be read as a birth scene that becomes a death scene; note too that many scholars connect the cutting of Samson's hair as symbolic castration)—it is different from them in a variety of ways. Only here is the fight between Israel and the Philistines viewed as a fight between the deities of the respective nations, a battle that Yahweh wins when he helps Samson topple the temple of Dagon, turning their joy into mourning. Atypically for the Bible as a whole, it uses end-rhyme for emphasis, especially in v. 24: " 'Our god has given Samson our enemy ('oyevenu אֹויְבֵינוּ) into our hand (beyadhenu בְּיָדֵנוּ) ... the ravager of our country ('artsenu אַרְצֵנוּ), who has killed many of us (khalalenu חֲלָלֵינוּ).' " In contrast to the previous units, it uses the three-four pattern: Samson lies to Delilah three times about the source of his strength, and tells her the truth the fourth time. This truth ultimately leads to his heroic death; unlike some later cultures, the Bible does not view suicide as problematic.

F. The Samson Story as a Whole

We cannot know what meaning, if any, was intended by the reactor(s) who joined these stories together, and added some elements to them so that they would read more smoothly as a whole. Certain themes, however, do emerge. One concerns the Philistines, who are depicted as foolish and unable to control their own territory. Thus, these episodes function to justify Judean hegemony over the coastal plain, which the Philistines were also claiming.

Another theme is that Yahweh will save his people from their enemies, and often use unorthodox ways to do so. Humans may be used as pawns to accomplish this: Samson loves Philistine women because God "was seeking a pretext to act against the Philistines" (Judg 14:4). God continues to use Samson in this role even though Samson time after time violates his nazirite vows—he goes to parties at which alcohol was likely served, he comes into contact with corpses that would render him ritually impure, and he tells Delilah the secret of this hair, which she then cuts. Thus, chaps. 14–16 may be seen as an unfolding of continuous violations of the vow (which are narrated in several different forms in chap. 13), for which he is ultimately punished with death. Yet Yahweh saves his people using a grave sinner.

As the rest of the book of Judges, these chapters also disproportionately emphasize women and women's power. A woman is attractive enough that an angelic being has sex with her, and women get Samson into all sorts of trouble, and ultimately lead to his death. The biblical attitudes toward women are complicated, but perhaps these chapters should be connected to Prov 1–9, which also emphasize the power of women, and specifically highlight how the foreign woman (NRSV, "loose woman") can so easily lead astray the Israelite man. Both Prov 1–9 and much of the Samson story emphasize the intersection of xenophobia and misogyny by depicting relationships with foreign women as leading to death.

G. The Samson Story within the Book of Judges

The book of Judges has an introduction and conclusion in which judges, namely tribal leaders, play no role, and a lengthy center that narrates the adventures of various judges whom Yahweh appoints to save Israel. Samson is the last of these judges. The judges form a pattern: as they move from south to north, their behavior is more and more problematic. The initial southern judges, such as the Judean Othniel, are ideal. Samson the Danite is their opposite. Although the Samson stories are depicted as transpiring in the South, before Dan migrated northward (see Judg 17–18), as a Danite, people would have read him as northern. His behavior is quite problematic: he violates all of his nazirite obligations and is involved with Philistine women. Thus, within the larger book of Judges this material prefigures and helps to introduce the following books of Samuel—Kings, which deal with kingship, and stresses that northern kingship, which Samson (among others) foreshadows, is illegitimate.

H. The Afterlife of the Samson Story

The colorful nature of the story, and the gaps (e.g., what was Samson's physical appearance?) and contradictions it contains, have encouraged it to be reinterpreted in both Jewish and Christian tradition. Its most famous retelling is the outstanding poem "Samson Agonistes" by John Milton. Milton was blind when he wrote this masterpiece, and thus it highlights Samson's blindness. It is remarkable that he is not a more popular figure in early post-biblical literature (although in the NT he is listed as one of the faithful Israelite heroes in Heb 11:32). Perhaps the manner in which he is depicted as a very imperfect hero has made later generations somewhat uncomfortable with him.

Bibliography: Marc Zvi Brettler. *The Book of Judges.* Old Testament Readings (2002); Gregory Mobley. *The Empty Men: The Heroic Tradition of Ancient Israel* (2005); Steve Weitzman. "The Samson Story as Border Fiction." *BI* 10 (2002) 158–74.

MARC ZVI BRETTLER

SAMU, ES. Since the mid-19th cent., the site of es-Samu has been identified with biblical ESHTEMOA, a town allotted to the tribe of Judah (Josh 15:50). Approximately 14 km southwest of Hebron, the site lies in the highlands of Judah. Deep ravines to the north and east provided an advantageous defense in ancient times. Es-samu was one of numerous small villages established in the central hill country during the Iron Age II. *See* SYNAGOGUE.

MICHAEL G. VANZANT

SAMUEL sam′yoo-uhl [שְׁמוּאֵל shemu'el; Σαμουήλ Samouēl]. Means "his name is El." Known primarily as a prophet, Samuel is presented in 1 Samuel as a transitional figure embodying the roles of prophet, priest, and judge. Outside of 1 Samuel, he is mentioned in the OT seven times in Chronicles (1 Chr 6:28 [Heb. 6:13], 33; 9:22; 11:3; 26:28; 29:29; 2 Chr 35:18), where he is remembered as the seer from David's reign (drawing on 1 Sam 9:9), and once each in Ps 99:6 and Jer 15:1, both of which invoke Samuel's role as intercessor from 1 Sam 7. In the Apocrypha, Sir 46:13-20 remembers his various roles as prophet, kingmaker, seer, intercessor, and military leader. First Esdras 1:20 and 2 Esd 7:108[38] mention him as a prophet and an intercessor respectively. Three NT texts refer to Samuel in his role as a prophet (Acts 3:24; 13:20; Heb 11:32).

A. Birth (1 Samuel 1)
B. Contrast with Eli (1 Samuel 2–7)
C. King Making (1 Samuel 8–12)
D. King Rejecting (1 Samuel 13; 15)
E. Samuel and David
F. Samuel in Early Jewish Literature and the New Testament
Bibliography

A. Birth (1 Samuel 1)

The narrative of Samuel's birth hints that he is divinely favored, since his mother's pregnancy is an answer to her prayer, in which she vows that he will be a Nazirite ("devoted one") to Yahweh. The story resonates with that of Samson's birth (also a Nazirite, Judg 13). The vow's requirements—avoiding wine and grape products or other intoxicants, not cutting the hair or shaving, and not approaching dead bodies (Num 6)—play a role in the Samson stories but not in Samuel's. Samuel's birth story also alludes to Saul, since the puns on the child's name all involve the verb sha'al (שָׁאַל, the root in Saul's name), "to request," especially in 1:28, where the expression "he is given" could be translated "he is Saul." Historical critics suggest that the story was secondarily adapted for Samuel from an original story about Saul's birth.

B. Contrast with Eli (1 Samuel 2–7)

Following her vow, Hannah leaves Samuel with Eli the priest, who serves as his mentor (1 Sam 2–3), highlighting Samuel's training and preparation for his role as a priest. First Chronicles extends this portrait by injecting Samuel into the genealogy of Kohath, one of the sons of Levi (6:28 [Heb. 6:13]), thereby giving him a Levitical pedigree and legitimating his priestly activities in 1 Samuel, where he is from the tribe of Ephraim, not Levi (1 Sam 1:1). The Samuel narrative has its own agenda, contrasting its namesake with Eli and his sons, thus grooming him as Eli's replacement. The contrast begins before Samuel is born when Eli appears out of touch with the sacred, unable to distinguish Hannah's fervent prayer from drunkenness (1 Sam 1:12-13). Eli's sons are wicked and unsuited to serve as priests (2:12-17), and Eli has lost his moral authority (2:22-25). Samuel, in contradistinction, grows in Yahweh's favor (2:26). Divine revelation is rare under Eli (3:1), and word of the impending fall of his house comes not to him directly but first through a nameless prophet (2:27-36) and then through Samuel (3:11-14). The oracle of the nameless prophet is a Dtr composition anticipating the Ark Narrative in chaps. 4–6 and perhaps explaining the later exclusion of Abiathar's line from the priesthood (1 Kgs 2:27, 35). Samuel's oracle also reflects Dtr retouching or composition. Neither Samuel nor Eli initially recognizes that it is Yahweh who calls (1 Sam 3:2-9), but Samuel is only an initiate, who soon becomes a reliable prophet (3:19–4:1). The end of Eli and his house comes in the Ark Narrative, which is often viewed as an originally independent source in part because Samuel is not mentioned in it. However, this may be the author's way of distancing Samuel from the loss of the ark, which only involves Eli's house. The loss of Eli and his sons marks the decisive point at which Samuel becomes Israel's religious and political leader. The Dtr composition in chap. 7 presents Samuel as the last judge (see Heb. 12:11), who through sacrifice and intercession at Mizpah leads the people in religious reform and invokes God's intervention on their behalf against the Philistines and who then appears as the last of the "circuit judges" (Judg 10:1-5; 12:8-15).

C. King Making (1 Samuel 8–12)

Samuel plays a decisive role in the designation of Israel's first king. Presently, chaps. 8–12 are a Dtr block depicting a three-stage process of king making (9:1–10:16; 10:17-27a; 10:27b–11:15), enclosed within two speeches of Samuel about kingship (chaps. 8; 12). As with Eli, Samuel's sons prove unfit to succeed him, leading the elders of Israel to ask for a king (8:1-5). Yahweh begrudgingly accedes to the request, after having Samuel warn the people about how typical royal policy (the "ways of the king," 8:9) will affect them.

The story of Saul's initial anointing (9:1–10:16) is based on an older folktale about his search for lost donkeys in which he visits a nameless "seer" who consults the deity overnight on his behalf and then forecasts a series of encounters that Saul will have on his way home that will answer his needs, including the whereabouts of the donkeys, and commission him to action against the Philistines. The tale has been transformed, probably by Dtr, into a story of Saul's anointing in private, and the seer has been identified as Samuel. Otherwise, it makes little sense for Saul's servant to speak of Samuel, Israel's national leader, in the larger narrative as an anonymous "man of God" (9:6).

Samuel's role in the story of Saul's public selection by lot (10:17-27a) is similar to that of chaps. 7–8. Both take place in Mizpah, which became Judah's capital after Jerusalem's fall in 586 BCE (2 Kgs 25:23), and Samuel again disapproves of the request for a king (10:19). The use of the lottery elsewhere in the DtrH to discover guilty parties (Josh 7:14-21; 1 Sam 14:36-42) suggests a negative orientation on kingship and Saul here. Hence, this episode is likely a Dtr composition, though perhaps incorporating an older tradition that Saul was chosen because of his height (10:23-24).

The third story relates how Saul proved himself in response to doubters (10:27a). Its original beginning, which was lost from the MT but can be reconstructed from the LXX and Dead Sea Scroll fragments (compare NRSV), attests its original independence as do details in the story that do not presuppose that he is king—especially the fact that the messengers from Jabesh do not go directly to him but that he happens to learn about their plight from the weeping in Gibeah as he returns from the field (11:3-5). The older story presented this victory as the occasion for Saul being made king in the first place (11:15) but has been revised, again probably by Dtr, to refer to renewing the kingship (11:14) in order to fit with the preceding two stories. The addition of Samuel's name (11:7, 12, 14) was part of that revision; he played no part in the original story.

The entire section concludes with Samuel's address to Israel (chap. 12), in which he defends himself of any wrongdoing where the people are concerned and reviews Israel's history in the DtrH, culminating in the ill-advised demand for a king and the reassurance that even with the change in government, Yahweh will not reject Israel as his people so long as they serve him faithfully. This address is sometimes called Samuel's "farewell," an appropriate designation in the sense that, though he does not die for some time (1 Sam 25:1), he recedes from the subsequent narrative in deference to Saul and David.

D. King Rejecting (1 Samuel 13; 15)

As the story in 1 Samuel stands, no sooner is Saul made king than he or his dynasty is rejected by Yahweh—twice, and it is Samuel in each case who delivers the bad news. In chap. 13, Saul offers the burnt offering himself after waiting for Samuel, who then arrives to tell Saul that because he has acted foolishly Yahweh will not establish his kingdom. This is apparently a reference to Saul's dynasty, indicating that his line will not continue to rule, which is effectively what happens in the larger narrative. Chapter 15, though, contains a doublet of sorts. In it, Saul is condemned for failing to carry out Yahweh's order to exterminate the Amalekites, and Yahweh rejects him as king. The latter story is likely a later (post-Dtr) addition, since it, together with 16:1-13, interrupts the continuity between reference to Saul adding valiant warriors to his service in 14:52 and the introduction of David as a warrior in 16:14-23. Also, the Amalekites, purportedly destroyed in chap. 15, resurface later (chap. 30). Samuel appears here in a role that is more or less typical for prophets as the opponent of the king who advocates strict obedience to the word of God over ritual activity. As literary critics especially point out, it is far from clear in both stories exactly what Saul's offense is, and Samuel seems petulant and arbitrary in his judgments. In chap. 13, it was Samuel who was late in arriving at Gilgal after Saul had waited the full seven days as instructed. Besides, it is not clear what was wrong with Saul offering the burnt offering himself. In chap. 15, Saul's retention of the best livestock for sacrifice would seem to satisfy the intent and result of ritual annihilation, and the end of the story suggests that Saul may have been saving King Agag for the ritual execution he ultimately received at Samuel's hand. It is hard to avoid the impression that Yahweh and Samuel simply had it in for Saul, whose role was to be rejected in lieu of David, who was "after [Yahweh's] heart," (see 1 Sam 13:14) that is, favored by him.

E. Samuel and David

Aside from the notice of his death in 25:1, Samuel appears in only three episodes in the David story in 1 Samuel, and all three appear to be late additions. We have already seen that this is the case with 16:1-13. David's depiction as a shepherd in this story employs a common metaphor for a king in the ANE and thus anticipates and symbolizes David's reign. In 16:1-13,

Samuel anoints David after he has been chosen by Yahweh from among his brothers. Samuel's character here seems unstable. He is afraid of Saul (16:2), yet his sudden appearance in Bethlehem elicits fear on the part of its elders (16:4). Most disturbing, he does not share Yahweh's vision and priorities for choosing a king, as he goes by outward appearance rather than inner character (16:6-7).

The secondary nature of 19:18-24 is indicated by two factors. First, it contradicts the statement in 15:35 that Samuel did not see Saul again before he died. Second, Ramah, where this story is set, lay north of Gibeah—the opposite direction from Judah, David's home tribe, where he headed in flight from Saul. It makes little sense historically or logically for David to go to Ramah. The story has an ideological point, adding the prophets to those who side with David against Saul. Indeed, Yahweh here uses prophecy as a weapon against Saul to protect David from him.

In 1 Sam 28, Samuel is summoned from the underworld by the necromancer at Endor whom Saul consults (see ENDOR, MEDIUM OF). He appears as an old man wrapped in a robe, from which Saul recognizes him (28:14). He seems annoyed at having been disturbed and in typical prophetic fashion does not mince words in condemning Saul and announcing his impending death in battle as punishment for his failure to carry out Yahweh's order against the Amalekites (28:16-19). The story therefore presupposes chap. 15 and is secondary. Its function is to make clear that Saul's fate is sealed because of his own disobedience as a counter to any claim that David was responsible for Saul's death.

In sum, analysis of the Samuel materials indicates that there is little about him that goes back to pre-Dtr traditions upon which to base any kind of historical reconstruction. While Samuel may have been known in older tradition, the figure who now stands in the biblical narratives is largely a creation of Dtr and his successors for literary and ideological purposes.

F. Samuel in Early Jewish Literature and the New Testament

Second Temple Jewish literature and the NT remember Samuel as a key prophetic figure in Israel's history. Samuel is one of the Israelite ancestors whom Sirach celebrates (Sir 44–50; compare Heb 11:32-33). Sirach 46:13-20 refers to Samuel as a prophet, judge, and seer. He "anointed rulers" and "judged the congregation," and God responded to his priestly intercession by defeating Israel's enemies (compare 2 Esd 7:108[38]). Sirach notes Samuel's complete blamelessness (v. 19; compare 1 Sam 12:3) as well as his ability to prophesy even after death (v. 20; see §E above), the purpose of which was "to blot out the wickedness of the people."

First Esdras 1:20 (//2 Chr 35:18) emphasizes the importance of the Passover culminating Josiah's reform by noting that there had been no Passover like it "since the times of the prophet Samuel."

In the NT, Peter and John name Samuel as one of the prophets who had predicted "these days"—that is, the suffering and glorification of God's Messiah (Acts 3:24). The apostle Paul's summation of Israel's history in the synagogue in Antioch of Pisidia notes that God gave Israel judges "until the time of the prophet Samuel" (Acts 13:20).

Bibliography: R. W. Klein. *1 Samuel.* WBC 10 (1981); S. L. McKenzie. *King David* (2000); P. K. McCarter Jr. *2 Samuel.* AB 9 (1984); J. Van Seters. *In Search of History* (1983).

STEVEN L. MCKENZIE

SAMUEL THE SEER, WORDS OF. *See* BOOKS REFERRED TO IN THE BIBLE.

SAMUEL, FIRST AND SECOND BOOKS OF [שְׁמוּאֵל ב, א shemu'el a, b; Βασίλειων Α, Β Basileiōn A, B]. The books of Samuel, as this grand historical narrative has traditionally been named, constitute the core of a longer work (Joshua to 2 Kings, with the exception of Ruth) which in the traditional Jewish scriptural nomenclature is known as the Former Prophets, and which contemporary biblical scholarship calls the Deuteronomistic History (DtrH). The latter name, along with variant forms adopted by particular scholars, derives from the insight, mainly associated with the work of Martin Noth, that the Deuteronomistic History, while making use of much earlier materials, and informed by the concerns of the Deuteronomic ideology that had inspired Josiah's reformation in the 7th cent., is a single work that derives from Deuteronomistic circles active during the Babylonian exile, around 550 BCE. The work of Frank Moore Cross has been influential in defining two editions of the Deuteronomistic History, the first, or Dtr[1], actually produced in the historical context of the Josianic Reform, and the second, Dtr[2], exilic. Other scholars have suggested a postexilic origin for the work. While this insight does not obviate the prior (or subsequent) work of critical scholars who have discerned and defined older sources incorporated in the Deuteronomistic History—for example Campbell's "Prophetic Record"—it opens the way for two central elements in the modern study of the books of Samuel. The first is the recognition that the Deuteronomistic History was framed around political and nationalistic, as well as theological/ideological concerns which arose out of the 7th-cent. BCE Josianic reformers' expectations for national and religious renewal, and which had to be recast by the exilic generation in view of the catastrophic demise of the Davidic monarchy, the loss of the Jerusalem Temple and its institutional cult of Yahweh, and the destruction of Jerusalem itself, the "place that [Yahweh] will choose" of Deuteronomic theology, which resulted from the Babylonian invasion of Judah, the siege and destruction of Jerusalem, and the exile of Jerusalem's religious and political elite in the events of 597 and 586 BCE. This means that the classification of these books as history—as in the traditional Christian canons, where they belong in the division called "Historical Books"—or as historiography, as many modern critics have called them, becomes a problem or an impossibility for many today, particularly for those who read them as a literary work composed as late as the postexilic period. This brings us to the second element, which is the recognition that the literary form of the books of Samuel must be given a central role in their interpretation. This is to say that Samuel, whatever kernels of historical fact or ancient poetry or traditional narrative it contains, retains these elements embedded in an integrated literary composition which in many ways anticipates modern works of literary fiction. Having realized this, a careful reader will be constantly aware that literary art and artifice play a central role in the composition of the work. For example, when the "Song of Hannah" in 1 Sam 2 concludes in v. 10 with words which, were they to be read as a flat attempt to present historical facts, would have to be judged simply anachronistic and intrusive at a point when there is still no king in Israel ("The LORD will judge the ends of the earth; he will give strength to his king, and exalt the power of his anointed"), a sensitive reader may detect a proleptic announcement of the central theme of the rise of the chosen king, much as the overture of an opera announces before the fact the melodic themes of the principal arias. The careful reader will also be aware that the characters and the plot elements are intentionally chosen and shaped by the author in the service of the authorial vision of the meaning of narrated events. David in Samuel is the heroic king, admirably bold and chivalrous at times but also, as in the Bathsheba affair and its aftermath, capable of the worst corruption of royal power possible. Conversely, David in Chronicles is consistently and rather tediously pious, Bathsheba is nowhere to be found, and David's adulterous affair with her and the subsequent murder of her husband have no place in the story. For a reader who realizes that the two Davids belong in the two separate literary worlds of two very different authors, each with a very different outlook on the meaning of the Davidic monarchy, even (or in particular) granted the Chronicler's apparent knowledge of Samuel, neither to ask which one is the "real" David nor to attempt to conflate the two into a harmonized single character remains a helpful interpretive procedure.

In recent times, Samuel has been helpfully illuminated by scholars such as David Alter, Robert Polzin, David Gunn, J. P. Fokkelman, and others, whose interpretation centers on viewing this ancient Hebrew book as a great and seminal work of literary art. The story of David, and of David's family and dynasty, is without question the main subject of the books of Samuel. David is "the man after God's own heart" of the story, and his rise to the throne and the subsequent events of his life and reign provide the foundation for the literary reflection on the monarchy that the books of Samuel and Kings carry out. Undoubtedly there were in circulation in ancient Israel many different traditions, stories, popular sayings, literary accounts, poetic compositions, etc., associated with the figure of David, with different formats and provenances. In the books of Samuel many of these are used in ways that sometimes do not resolve contradictions, but on occasion even retain two competing accounts of the same event. The authorial intent of the text that has come down to us is not, after all, academic historiography, but corresponds rather to the artistic meta-genre of what Gunn (1978) would call "serious entertainment." That is to say that the devices and procedures of literary artistry are used to entertain, but in such a way as to engage the readers intellectually and emotionally so that they better understand themselves and others. Cervantes and Shakespeare, and most certainly Dante and Milton, were engaged in producing serious entertainment of this sort. Nevertheless, as David Jobling has concluded, powerful and compelling as the artistry of this meditation on the monarchy of the House of David is, it remains in the end a melancholy tale of loss (1978).

A. Samuel and Eli
B. The Ark
C. Samuel the Last Judge
D. Yahweh's Kingmaker
E. Saul and His Children
F. David and David's House
G. David the Warlord
H. David, King of the South
I. David, King of Israel
Bibliography

A. Samuel and Eli

Although David is the central character in Samuel, the traditional name of the book recognizes the crucial importance of the religious leader who is, after all, the transitional figure who brings the monarchy to birth. Appropriately then, the birth of Samuel is told in a narrative that centers on what Alter has identified as a "type-scene," that is, an episode shaped by audience expectations of a certain sequence of elements in the telling. In this case, the "type scene" (1 Sam 1:9-18) belongs to the class that Alter (1981; 1999) calls the "annunciation ... of the birth of the hero to his barren mother." Unlike the angel who announces the birth of Samson to Manoah's wife in Judg 13 (another example of the type), Eli the priest misunderstands and distorts his own role when he assumes Hannah to be drunk, thus giving the reader a clue that Samuel will be born not only as an answer to Hannah's plight, but to Israel's need for a replacement of the Elide priesthood. The theme of the replacement of inadequate leadership—priestly or royal—as a deliberate and predicted action of Yahweh, which faintly announces itself here and plays out explicitly in the words of the "man of God" (1 Sam

2:27-36) and in young Samuel's dream vision (3:1-18), anticipates the central role this theme takes in the Saul/David story. As has already been suggested above, there are other hints—such as the royal theme which concludes Hannah's song, or perhaps in the all-too-obvious reference to Saul in the "folk etymology" of Samuel's name in 1:20—that lead to the conclusion that a skilled author has arranged these materials to announce and anticipate important themes of the larger story.

Samuel himself is a complex figure, one who recapitulates the main roles of Israel's premonarchic leadership as he functions as a judge in both the military and judicial aspects of that role, but also as a prophet and as a priest. As a result of his mother's vow consecrating him to the service of Yahweh from infancy, Samuel starts out as a young acolyte serving Eli at Shiloh, where the ark represented the presence of Yahweh as the Lord of hosts. There he is not only the vehicle for a dramatic announcement of the end of the Elide priesthood, but its *de facto* successor when it comes to a catastrophic end on the same day that the ark is captured by the Philistines in the battle of Aphek (1 Sam 4). (Of several places by that name, the narrative apparently refers to Aphek of the Sharon plain, located on the banks of the YARKON RIVER, and in relatively close proximity to Ebenezer.)

B. The Ark

An inanimate object rises to the role of a character in 1 Samuel, as the ark rambles through the Philistine cities and returns to the territory of Israel after having caused havoc among the enemy population and defeated their gods. At the beginning of the narrative, the ark—variously called "the ark of God" in 3:3, "the ark of the covenant of the LORD" in 4:3, 5, "the ark of the covenant of God" in 4:4, "the ark of the LORD" in 4:6, and "the ark of the covenant of the LORD of hosts, who is enthroned on the cherubim" in 4:4—is in the care of Eli and his sons Hophni and Phinehas, the priests at Shiloh. The last of these names is associated first with Shiloh, and then, significantly, reappears in the story of David's bringing of the ark to Jerusalem (see 2 Sam 6:2). Ironically, the Philistines, who identify the ark as "the gods who struck the Egyptians with every sort of plague in the wilderness" (1 Sam 4:8), an epithet which the subsequent story will show to be apt, are driven by their fear to strenuous effort, defeat Israel and capture the ark. The results of the battle of Aphek/Ebenezer are immediately disastrous for the Elides, since Hophni and Phinehas are killed in the battle, Eli collapses and dies immediately upon hearing the news, and Phinehas' pregnant wife, forced into labor by the shock of the news, dies in childbirth, but not before she names her newborn son Ichabod ("no glory" or "where is the glory?") because "the glory has departed from Israel, for the ark of God has been captured" (4:22). P. Kyle McCarter Jr. (1980) has pointed out the parallels between the accounts of Eli's reception of the news of the capture of the ark in 1 Sam 4:16-17 and David's reception of the news of Saul's death in 2 Sam 1:3-4, and Polzin convincingly elaborates this and other evidence in the early chapters of 1 Samuel to hear there an intertwining of "the royal voice," "the Davidic voice," and "the Deuteronomist's voice" with the sometimes seemingly naïve story.

Treated as a trophy, the ark is taken to the cities of Philistia, where it begins to show uncanny and dangerous powers. In Ashdod, it causes the image of the god Dagon to fall from its pedestal and its subsequent mutilation. Also in Ashdod, it is the source of a deadly outbreak of a plague of "tumors," and subsequently causes "panic" and "tumors" in Gath and Ekron. This convinces the Philistines to return the ark to Israel, sending along a "guilt offering" of five gold tumors and five gold mice as suggested by their priests and diviners. The return is carried out in a manner that elicits a miraculous (unnatural) response from the two cows hitched to the cart that carries it, who without being driven walk away from their unweaned calves on their way to Beth-shemesh, and ultimately to the small village of Kiriath-jearim, where the ark was to remain until David undertook to move it to Jerusalem (see 2 Sam 6).

C. Samuel the Last Judge

Samuel's career as a judge of Israel is said to center in his residence at Ramah, from where he served a circuit that included Bethel, Gilgal, and Mizpah (1 Sam 7:16).

More than as an embodiment of multiple functions, Samuel's multifarious character derives from his ambiguous relationship to the rise of the monarchy, and to the two first kings of Israel. Nowhere is that ambiguity better expressed than in the confrontation between the elders of Israel and Samuel in chap. 8, where the issue of the desire for a king comes explicitly to the foreground. Much more is clearly at stake than the incompetence of Samuel's sons to replace him—the incident brings forward the central theme of the larger narrative: the role and value of the monarchy in the history of Israel. Samuel acts as a judge, only reluctantly ready to give up his authority (see 8:7-8), but also as a prophet, for whom the monarchy would have to be closely watched for its inherent capacity for abusing its power over the people ("and you shall be his slaves," 8:17). Samuel anticipates the role he is to play in this respect against Saul, as well as Nathan's prophetic criticism of David's abuse of his royal power in the case of Bathsheba and Uriah.

In his involvement in fighting against the Philistines and other enemies of Israel, Samuel appears more as a priestly figure than as a warrior. His function is more to secure Yahweh's intervention by sacrifice and prayer (see for example 1 Sam 7:8-10), than to lead, or even fight, in battle. When, as is the case after the anointing of Saul as king, there is a division of functions, Samuel foreshadows the Deuteronomic claim that the king rules under the constraint of Yahweh's word as expressed by

the prophets. This role will bring Samuel into very significant conflict with Saul twice: first when the latter, impatient to begin battle against the Philistines, takes it upon himself to offer the requisite holocaust at Gilgal in view of Samuel's delayed appearance (13:8-15), and then when Saul disobeys Samuel's injunction to utterly destroy the Amalekites and all their possessions and keeps hapless King Agag alive, presumably as a ransomable hostage whom an angry Samuel "hewed ... in pieces before the LORD in Gilgal" (15:33). Both of these incidents serve to place Saul's monarchy, when it had hardly begun, under Yahweh's judgment of rejection, which Samuel makes explicit in 13:13-15 and in 15:26-29. Ominously, the author lets the reader know, after the second incident, not only that "Samuel did not see Saul again until the day of his death, but Samuel grieved over Saul" (see 19:18-24), but also that "the LORD was sorry that he had made Saul king over Israel" (15:35).

Samuel's last appearance, in chap. 28, is one of the most obviously dramatized scenes in 1 Samuel. As often in the subsequent tradition of Western literature, it is not the long-dead Samuel (28:3) but his ghost that appears, through the ministrations of the "medium," to speak for one last time to Saul at Endor. Saul, who had usurped the place of the prophetic/priestly figure and ignored the divine commands delivered by Samuel, finds himself lost before what is to be his final battle, and desperate enough to violate his own law against necromancy. Samuel's message is a message of doom: not only defeat in battle, but the death of Saul and his sons is in the offing—there will be no Saulide dynasty, but rather "the LORD has torn the kingdom out of your hand, and given it to your neighbor, David" (28:17).

D. Yahweh's Kingmaker

If the books of Samuel are to be read as a literary meditation on kingship in Israel, Samuel the character plays a most important role in exploring its beginnings. Much has been made over the apparent presence of "pro-monarchy" and "anti-monarchy" sources in 1 Sam 8, but the most relevant fact remains that the presence of both "pro-" and "anti-" currents in the narrative stream must be read as an authorial marker for a deep sense of ambiguity about the monarchy. The remarkable words addressed to Samuel by Yahweh in 8:7-9, or Samuel's "Farewell Address" in chap. 12 and other elements of the narrative, express that sense. Samuel will share and express Yahweh's disappointment with Saul, as well as Yahweh's continued yearning for "a man after his own heart" (13:14). And yet, it is Samuel's task to seek out and to anoint both Saul and David, and thus to inaugurate, albeit in a sequence of events marked with ambiguity and disappointment, the monarchy in Israel.

E. Saul and His Children

First Samuel 9 begins Saul's story, in a manner reminiscent of the beginning of Samuel's story in chap. 1, but Kish, unlike Hannah and Elkanah, has a handsome, promising young son, whom he dispatches on an errand—finding his stray donkeys—which will bring Saul to Ramah, Samuel's village. Alter recognizes, in the meeting with some girls of the town "coming out to draw water" (9:11), a hint of the "encounter at the well" type-scene, which in its full form leads to the account of a betrothal (e.g., Abraham's servant and Rebekah, Jacob and Rachel, Moses and Zipporah). In this case, however, the scene veers away from a betrothal, and Samuel sends Saul back the next day secretly anointed as "leader" over Israel (see 9:16; 10:1). Succeeding episodes in chaps. 10 to 12 confirm Saul's election as king to himself and to Israel, but the text always leaves an ambiguous impression. It is not clear, for example, what valuation of Saul's "prophetic frenzy" (10:10-13) is intended, particularly in light of the repeated quotation of the ancient saying, "Is Saul also among the prophets?" in 19:24. The account of Saul's election by lot at Mizpah (10:17-27) not only includes the surprising detail of Saul's hiding among the baggage, so that he could not be found when the lot finally fell on him, but ends on a note of dissension sounded by a hostile faction: "How can this man save us?" Finally, when Saul, acting heroically and much in the manner of a classic judge (*pace* Samuel's speech in 12:1-12), defeats King Nahash of the Ammonites and breaks the siege of Jabesh-gilead, Samuel uses the victory celebration at Gilgal to "renew the kingship" and delivers a classic Deuteronomistic speech, in the course of which he blames the people, not for idolatry, but for having asked for a king to defend them from their enemies, an accusation which the people acknowledge as truth: "we have added to all our sins the evil of demanding a king for ourselves" (12:19).

David Gunn (1980) aptly identifies the specific roots of the tragedy of Saul as twofold—one is a "character flaw (jealousy)" and the other is his rejection, or more specifically, his "knowledge of his rejection." Saul is a king who must struggle with the knowledge that he has already been rejected and replaced by Yahweh, a knowledge that will pervade and impair his rule, and ultimately destroy him and his kingdom. The author of Samuel lets the reader know that Saul, through Samuel's words, knows that Yahweh has rejected him (see for example 13:13-14; 15:28-29), and pairs this with the coming of "an evil spirit from the LORD" to torment Saul (16:14 and others). That spirit will lead to an increasing malaise in the tormented king, which will find its focus in a growing obsessive jealousy towards David, from Saul's annoyance at the popular refrain "Saul has killed his thousands, and David his ten thousands" (18:7), to its expression in foul language and overt aggression against Jonathan, and finally to an all-out murderous pursuit of David which drives David not only out of the court, but into mercenary service with the Philistine forces of Achish of Gath.

Jonathan is not only a witness—and a victim—of his father's mental and moral disintegration, but early on in the story he becomes David's mentor and ally. As the narrative presents him, he is a leader in his own right, capable and brave, and loved by his people, one who could easily have stepped into the role of king. Faced with the obvious unfairness of his father's obsessive, jealous persecution of David, as well as from the outset recognizing David's charisma and talents ("skillful in playing, a man of valor, a warrior ... a man of good presence; and the LORD is with him," as one of the courtiers summarizes David's qualities in 1 Sam 16:18), Jonathan early gave David his allegiance, and "made a covenant with David, because he loved him as his own soul" (18:3; see also 20:12-18). None of this is lost on Saul, who in 20:30-34 explodes in rough (or even obscene) insults against Jonathan, and, transferring his jealous rage to his own son, tries to kill him with his spear as he had once done to David.

Chapter 18 provides two successive accounts of Saul's stratagems to cause the death of David, in which Saul's daughters are offered to his young captain in marriage with the real purpose of placing him in mortal danger at the hands of the Philistines. The first time it is Merab, the eldest, but the offer of marriage is withdrawn as she is summarily given to another. The second time, however, the narrator begins by pointing out that Saul's younger daughter, Michal, loved David, and Saul specifies a bride-price for her which he thinks is sure to lure David to his death: one hundred foreskins of the Philistines. The scheme backfires when David succeeds in the dangerous quest, and marries Michal, leaving Saul to realize "that the LORD was with David, and that [his] daughter Michal loved him," and to become more fearful and jealous of David (18:28, 29). Like her brother Jonathan, Michal chooses to help David escape from Saul (19:11-17), even though she remains in the court, and is later given by her father to another man. Jonathan and two of his brothers are killed by the Philistines at the battle of Gilboa, where Saul takes his own life to prevent being captured alive. The first book of Samuel ends with the report of the pious and daring act of the "valiant men" of Jabesh-gilead, who cross by night into occupied territory to rescue the bodies of Saul and Jonathan, and take them to Jabesh for decent burial.

F. David and David's House

After Samuel travels to Bethlehem to anoint one of Jesse's sons as a replacement for the already-rejected Saul—a scene fraught with irony in which, to the surprise not only of Jesse and his seven grown sons, but also of Samuel, young David, who was left keeping the sheep, turns out to be the chosen of Yahweh (1 Sam 16:1-13)—the story must turn to placing Saul and David together. That these two characters are on divergent trajectories is made clear in many ways, none more explicit than the juxtaposition of 16:13, "the spirit of the LORD came mightily upon David from that day forward" with 16:14, "the spirit of the LORD departed from Saul, and an evil spirit from the LORD tormented him." One answer to the question of how David came to be present in Saul's court is that he was brought in as a personal attendant skilled at playing the lyre, so that "when the evil spirit from God is upon [Saul], he will play it, and [Saul] will feel better" (16:16). When the son of Jesse comes to the court, not only is his playing effective in relieving Saul's melancholia, but such is his personal charisma that "Saul loved him greatly, and he became his armor-bearer" (16:21). Immediately following, the story of David's defeat of Goliath introduces a totally different configuration of the main characters, with David present at the battlefield as a civilian, whose identity is unknown to Saul until the very moment when David leaves to do battle with the Philistine champion. While the two stories are clearly separate traditions, and strictly speaking incompatible (see 2 Sam 21:19), they make sense together if the authorial intention is to stitch together a larger picture in which the effects of the presence of Yahweh's spirit with and in the chosen David are contrasted with the effects of the evil spirit sent by God to torment and ultimately to destroy the rejected Saul. The first story speaks of the gentler gifts by which David at first tames, but eventually angers, the evil spirit that torments Saul: his personal charisma and his musical talent. The second story presents young David as the inspired warrior who challenges and defeats the Philistine "in the name of the LORD of hosts, the God of the armies of Israel, whom you have defied" (17:45). Both stories contribute to the construction of David and Saul as characters shaped and driven by very different kinds of divine spirit—the one charismatic and attractive, well on the way to earning the title of "sweet singer of Israel," but at the same time capable of being a bold and fearsome warrior of the LORD of hosts; the other tortured and isolated by jealousy and suspicion, as well as an ineffective and indecisive military leader before the challenge of Goliath. The vignette in 1 Sam 19:8-10, for example, presents David acting appropriately and successfully in two different venues—he "goes out" to the field to fight the Philistines, and routs them, but in Saul's house he exchanges his weapons for his lyre, and plays music. On the other hand, there is no reference to Saul going out, but inappropriately and ominously, the king "sat in his house with his spear in his hand." Fortunately for David, Saul cannot hit him when he hurls the spear in a botched attempt to "pin him to the wall." His aim is no better in 20:33, where Jonathan is the intended target, and it is clear that the insane (and failed) spear thrust is an authorial means to build the character of Saul as one possessed by the "evil spirit."

David's life in Saul's court is marked by military success against the Philistines, popular acclaim, and the loyalty ("love") of at least two of Saul's children, Jonathan and Michal, who in the end help David to flee from their father's constant plotting against him. David is also protected by Samuel (and "the spirit of God")

in 19:18-24, and tricks Ahimelech, the priest at Nob (21:1-9), into giving him aid. It seems significant that Ahimelech returns Goliath's sword to David at a point in the narrative where David leaves on a path which will eventually make him a mercenary in the service of a Philistine king.

G. David the Warlord

David comes to King Achish of Gath twice in the narrative: the first in the comic episode in 21:10-15, in which David realizes too late, as he reaches the gates of Gath alone in his flight, that his fame has preceded him and puts him in danger in the enemy city. In the classic manner of a trickster, he pretends to be a raving, drooling madman until Achish himself orders his people to throw him out. When one considers the reason for David's flight, the dark humor in this little story becomes apparent. The next time that David comes to Gath, he can offer Achish the services of six hundred seasoned fighting men as a mercenary force, and is readily accepted and given control of Ziklag (27:1-7).

First, however, David builds up his power base in the south of Judah. His parents are sent to Moab for safety, and his brothers and other relatives come to join him at the Cave of Adullam, as well as "everyone who was in distress, and everyone who was in debt, and everyone who was discontented" (22:2). The plot at this point is quite simple: Saul chases David, but is unable to catch him. It is punctuated, however, by incidents that reveal facets of the character of the two major actors: Saul's brutal vindictiveness in ordering the massacre of Ahimelech and the priests of Nob for having helped David, a sacrilege that even his Benjaminite courtiers refuse to carry out, and which falls to Doeg the Edomite, who had informed on the priests, to commit (22:6-19); David, on the other hand, honorably assumes responsibility for the terrible events when Abiathar informs him, because he did not think of the danger in which he placed the priests and their families: "I knew on that day, when Doeg the Edomite was there, that he would surely tell Saul. I am responsible for the lives of all your father's house" (22:22). David also demonstrates his loyalty and respect for the anointed status of Saul by twice sparing his life when he has an opportunity to take it (see chaps. 24 and 26).

David also establishes alliances with prominent clans of Judah, by marriage and by other means. The story of how he came to marry "clever and beautiful" Abigail of Carmel, the wife of Nabal, is a charming one (25:2-42), in which her qualities clearly are a better match for David's than those of her "surly and mean"—and, in light of what happened, none too bright—Calebite husband.

If the Abigail story implies that David was supporting himself and his growing force of warriors by "taxing" the local landowners, it is clear that he was not only taking, but also distributing largesse to the important leaders—the "elders"—of Judah. This is particularly the case when he becomes a "servant" of Achish, and is given Ziklag, a town in the northern Negeb, to garrison with his men. Instead of raiding in Judah, as Achish expected him to do, David and his men put in practice a ruthless plan of attacking "the Geshurites, the Girzites, and the Amalekites" apparently in the territory between southern Philistia and the Sinai. In these raids, David's men would loot cattle and goods, but leave no one alive to tell the tale, and then pretended to Achish that the loot they shared with him came from the Negeb of Judah, of the Jerahmeelites, or of the Kenites. Astutely, David avoided attacking the Judeans, whom he intended to rule, and becoming what he had underhandedly convinced Achish that he already was, "abhorrent to his people Israel" (27:12).

As the Philistine forces mass for the final assault on Saul's army, David is reprieved from having a hand in Saul's defeat and death by the mistrust of the other Philistine lords—the old refrain about "Saul has killed his thousands, and David his ten thousands" appears yet again to haunt David—who force Achish to send him home from the battle field.

As Saul is losing the battle at Gilboa, and ends it all by taking his own life, David is back in Ziklag, rescuing its inhabitants, including his two wives Abigail and Ahinoam, from a raiding party of Amalekites who had availed themselves of the opportunity provided by his absence to take loot and slaves from the territories David defended. Even before the author tells of the deaths of Jonathan, Abinadab and Malchishua, the sons of Saul, and of the rejected and defeated king falling on his sword, the reader learns of David distributing largesse to "his friends, the elders of Judah" (30:26) from the spoils he had captured from the Amalekites, and his political purpose is clear: he knows his time to rule Judah has arrived.

H. David, King of the South

The scene that opens 2 Samuel is a variant of one found with some frequency in the narrative: a messenger brings the news after the battle (for other examples, see 1 Sam 4:10-18 and 2 Sam 18:19-33). In this case, however, the messenger (an Amalekite) not only reports Saul's death, but claims to have been the one who killed him, and brings David Saul's armlet and diadem. Whether the claim is true or not, David has him killed for having said "I have killed the LORD's anointed" (2 Sam 1:16). The narrative shows here, and in a number of other places which deal with the demise of people from Saul's family and camp during David's rise to the throne, the intent to exonerate David from any blame. In fact, this story immediately precedes David's poetic lamentation over the deaths of Saul and Jonathan (1:19-26), which is credited in the introduction to the "Book of Jashar," a long-lost collection of ancient Hebrew poetry. The lamentation is a moving masterpiece expressing David's personal sorrow at the loss of Jonathan, and

at the same time giving voice to Israel's grief at the loss of its first king.

David was anointed king by the people of Judah at Hebron and moved there with his family and retainers (2:1-7). The early period of his reign is marked by a conflict carried on by Abner, Saul's former soldier, in the name of Ishbaal, a surviving son of Saul, and leader of the Benjaminites, and the forces of David, where David's three nephews Joab, Asahel and Abishai, the "sons of Zeruiah," played a leading role. Abner personally killed Asahel early on in the conflict, and Joab, carrying out a personal vendetta, killed Abner after he had come to Hebron to make peace with David and deliver the North to his power. In all of this, as in the immediately following incident of the murder of Ishbaal by two of his soldiers (chap. 4), the narrative takes great care—almost, one might say, at the risk of seeming to "protest too much"—to show David blameless. At the death of Abner, David had him entombed at Hebron, recited a lament (3:33-34) and fasted for a day, something that pleased the people, "just as everything that the king did pleased all the people. So all the people and all Israel understood that day that the king had no part in the killing of Abner son of Ner" (3:36-37). As for the sons of Zeruiah, David confesses that he is powerless to do anything, at least at this point—his deathbed instructions to Solomon in 1 Kgs 2:5-6 will instruct his successor to kill Joab in retribution for the murders of Abner and Amasa (2 Sam 20:8-10). The sons of Zeruiah were David's close kin, and Joab was his indispensable general, qualifications the two soldiers who brought David the head of Ishbaal did not possess. He had them killed and mutilated and their bodies publicly exposed, and reverentially placed Ishbaal's head in Abner's tomb.

I. David, King of Israel

The narrative presents, in quick succession, four crucial events that establish David in the status of king over all Israel: he is anointed by the elders of all the tribes of Israel, who come to Hebron to make a covenant with him; he conquers Jerusalem, a city of the Jebusites, located between the territories of Judah and Benjamin, and makes it his royal residence; and he decisively defeats the Philistines, at Baal-perazim and in the valley of Rephaim. The account of the first battle says that "the Philistines abandoned their idols there, and David and his men carried them away" (5:21), an echo of the fate of the ark which sets up the fourth event: the bringing of the sacred and powerful object to what was to be its resting place in Jerusalem. David sets out (chap. 6) to Baale-judah (Kiriath-jearim) to bring the ark to Jerusalem. After the mishap at the threshing floor of Nacon, in which Uzzah is killed when he takes hold of the ark, David waits for three months, leaving the ark in the care of Obed-edom the Gittite before starting again when it is clear that "the LORD blessed Obed-edom and all his household" (6:11). Running through the seemingly simple stories, with special concentration in these chapters which lead up to the "dynastic oracle" of chap. 7, is a very effective and artful use of the many senses of the word "house" (see Rosenberg) which demonstrates careful and deliberate composition. "House" can be a building—whether the house of cedar that Hiram King of Tyre had built for David, the house of Obed-edom that sheltered the ark or, proleptically but centrally, the Temple that Solomon was to build for it. "House" is also family, household, dynasty, even "house of Israel" (see 6:5) in the sense of "the people of Israel." All of these senses, physical and figurative, are given free play in these chapters, which in telling the story of a family and a dwelling are also engaged in a meditation on a dynasty and a temple.

Michal, called "daughter of Saul" in 6:17, sounds the sour note in the celebration that brings the ark to the city. David had led the ark into the city, dancing and leaping, scantily clad in a linen ephod. There are strong overtones of the identification of fertility as an important component of blessing in all these stories, and in some way, David's dance seems to be related to that, as is his distribution of bread, meat and cakes of raisins—festal food—to "the whole multitude of Israel, both men and women" before they retire to their "homes" (NRSV, the MT reads "houses"). When, his royal duty done, David turns "to bless his household" (NRSV, the MT reads "house") he is met by Michal, who shows nothing but contempt for his behavior, explicitly sexualized in her words in v. 20. David retorts that he had, and would, danced before Yahweh, "who chose me in place of your father and all his household (MT, "house"), to appoint me as prince over Israel, the people of the LORD." The difficult potential issue of the status of a child born of David and Michal, who would have been heir to both "houses" is annulled by the report, at the conclusion of the scene, that "Michal the daughter of Saul had no child to the day of her death" (6:23).

Second Samuel 7 is structured even more tightly around the variety of meanings of "house," and its significance as an important juncture in the narrative, which here provides the dynastic oracle establishing David's succession, as well as the justification for the building of the Solomonic Temple. All of the meanings of "house" are invoked in carefully nuanced language. All three voices heard in the chapter use the word, from the narrator in 7:1 to David, to Yahweh to and through Nathan, and the word structures what they say.

Chapters 8 to 10 pile together a series of reports of David's activity as a king—he is presented variously as a brilliant warrior, ruthless at times against his enemies, capable on the other hand of great magnanimity, as he shows in the case of Mephiboshet, son of Jonathan. The mosaic of examples—the account clearly does not intend to be a complete chronicle of events, nor does it provide a sense of a tight chronology—lets the reader see a young king busy winning the loyalties of his people as a base for the establishment of a fairly extensive hegemonic power over his nation's surrounding peoples. David sets up a court in Jerusalem where, as a king should, he "administered justice and equity to all his people," and organizes the military, bureaucratic, and religious leadership of his kingdom (8:15–18).

All of this takes the reader rapidly from the dynastic oracle and David's answering prayer in chap. 7, which in a way are the ideological zenith of the narrative, to the shocking revelation in chap. 11 of David's abuse of his royal power in the Bathsheba and Uriah affair. Just as the noun "house" dominates chap. 7, so the verb "send" helps to structure 11, from the ironic first verse on: "In the spring of the year, the time when kings go out to battle, David sent Joab with his officers and all Israel with him; they ravaged the Ammonites, and besieged Rabbah. But David remained at Jerusalem." The king did not go to battle, he sent his army, and remained behind. The sense of David's remoteness pervades the narrative—David controls events, but from a distance, by sending for Bathsheba for a casual sexual encounter, or sending Uriah back to the battlefield with the message that will cause him to be killed. Other characters, notably Bathsheba in 11:5 and Joab in 11:18, also "send" David communications at important junctures of the story. Nathan's parable in chap. 12 (and the story made up by the woman of Tekoa in 14:4-20) speak beyond their specific contents to characterize David as a ruler whose courtiers had to address very cautiously when offering reproof, advice, or bad news (see 12:18).

After reporting the death of David's first child with Bathsheba and the birth of Solomon, and the victorious conclusion of the Ammonite war, the narrative turns to relate a tragic chain of events in which David's children play central roles: the rape of Tamar by Amnon, the revenge murder of Amnon by Absalom, and Absalom's revolt against his father, which almost costs David his throne, and costs Absalom his life. Between the "some time passed" that marks the transition to this story in 13:1 and the triumphant return of David to Jerusalem in chap. 20, the narrative is very believably moved by human emotions: pampered Amnon's incestuous lust, Tamar's helpless desolation, Absalom's cold determination for revenge, as well as his parricidal ambition, and all around these characters, the interplay of the machinations of a sordid character like Jonadab, the touching loyalty of Ittai the Gittite, Zadok, Abiathar, and Hushai the Archite, Ahithophel's injured pride, the self-interest of Ziba, the petty vindictiveness of Shimei ben Gera, and others. Joab exerts command with pragmatic ruthlessness, both in the forest of Ephraim and in the gate at Mahanaim, where David realizes too late that Absalom, no matter what he had done or was driven to do, is more dear to him than life itself.

This is not yet the end of David's story—the narrative continues in chap. 19 with David's triumphant return to Jerusalem, marked by acts of royal magnanimity, with Joab's suppression of Sheba ben Bichri's opportunistic revolt (chap. 20), and with a collection including traditional accounts of David's mighty warriors, the poetic

"David's Song of Thanksgiving" and "David's Last words," and the Samuel version of the story of the census, the plague and the purchase of the site of the future Temple, which ends the book. The first two chapters of 1 Kings present us with a bed-ridden, aged David, who dies while the palace intrigue that brought Solomon to the throne swirls about him. *See* DAVID; SAMUEL; SAUL, SON OF KISH.

Bibliography: Robert Alter. *The Art of Biblical Narrative* (1981); Robert Alter. *The David Story: A Translation and Commentary of 1 and 2 Samuel* (1999); Walter Brueggemann. *First and Second Samuel.* Interpretation (1990); Anthony F. Campbell, S.J. *1 Samuel.* FOTL VII (2003); Anthony F. Campbell, S.J. *2 Samuel.* FOTL VIII (2005); Frank Moore Cross. *Canaanite Myth and Hebrew Epic: Essays in the History of the Religion of Israel* (1973); J. P. Fokkelman. *Narrative Art and Poetry in the Books of Samuel: A Full Interpretation Based on Stylistic and Structural Analysis.* 4 vols. (1981, 1986, 1990, 1993); David M. Gunn. *The Fate of King Saul: An Interpretation of a Biblical Story* (1980); David M. Gunn. *The Story of King David: Genre and Interpretation* (1978); David Jobling. *1 Samuel.* Berit Olam (1998); P. Kyle McCarter Jr. *I Samuel.* AB 8 (1980); P. Kyle McCarter Jr. *II Samuel.* AB 9 (1984); Peter D. Miscall. *1 Samuel: A Literary Reading* (1986); Martin Noth. *The Deuteronomistic History* (1991); Robert Polzin. *Samuel and the Deuteronomist* (1989); Joel Rosenberg. *King and Kin: Political Allegory in the Hebrew Bible* (1986).

FRANCISCO GARCÍA-TRETO

SANBALLAT san-bal'at [סַנְבַלַּט *sanballat;* Σαναβαλλάτ *Sanaballat*]. Three governors of SAMARIA during the Persian period bear the name Sanballat. The origin of "Sanballat" is an Akkadian theophoric name: **Sin-uballit,** meaning "Sin (the moon deity) has given life."

1. Sanballat I was governor of Samaria (ca. 445–408 BCE) and one of the bitter opponents of NEHEMIAH. He, together with Tobiah the Ammonite and Geshem the Arabian, opposed Nehemiah's rebuilding of the walls of Jerusalem (445 BCE) and his other activities in Judah (Neh 2:10, 19; 4:1, 7; 6:1-2, 5, 12, 14; 13:28).

Sanballat's designation "the Horonite" (hakhoroni הַחֹרֹנִי) refers to his family's earlier place of residence. Most likely it was in Upper or Lower Beth-horon in Ephraim (Josh 16:3, 5; ca. 10 km north of Jerusalem). However, some suggest that it may refer to Horonaim in south Moab (Isa 15:5; Jer 48:3; if so, then Sanballat was a Moabite, just as Tobiah was an Ammonite). Others change the Hebrew vocalization of **hahoroni** to **haharani** ("the Haranite"), related to the Mesopotamian city Harran—a center for the worship of the moon-god Sin—the theophoric element of the name Sanballat.

Presumably Sanballat was a descendant of the Mesopotamians exiled to Samaria by the Assyrian king Sargon II (721–705 BCE) after the collapse of the Northern Kingdom (720 BCE; 2 Kgs 17:24-41; Ezra 4:2, 10). That Josephus says Sanballat was of the Cuthaean race (*Ant.* 11.302–303) points also in this direction (even though Josephus has mistaken Sanballat III for this Sanballat; see below). However, Sanballat had already adopted Yahweh's worship. He named his sons "Delaiah" and "Shelemiah"—proper theophoric-Yahwistic names, and his daughter married the brother of the high priest in Jerusalem (Neh 13:28).

Sanballat is also mentioned once in a papyrus from Elephantine (Upper Egypt), from the fourteenth year of King Darius II (Ochus) of Persia (ca. 408 BCE; *see* ELEPHANTINE PAPYRI). In their petition for authorization to rebuild the temple of Yaho, the Jews of Elephantine tell Bagoaz, the Persian governor of Judah, that they have written about the matter in a letter to Delaiah and Shelemiah, the sons of Sanballat the governor of Samaria (*ANET,* 492b). The letter testifies that his name and influence were well-known far beyond Samaria and the land of Israel.

The name "Sanballat" appears also on the papyri and on a bulla that were unearthed in a cave of Wadi ed Daliyeh (Jordan Valley, 9 mi. [ca. 14 km] north of Jericho; *see* DALIYEH, WADI ED). The earliest material from the cave is from 375 BCE, while the latest is from 335 BCE. This material indicates that there were two additional governors of Samaria that held the name "Sanballat."

2. Sanballat II presumably was the son of Delaiah and grandson of Sanballat I, who governed in Samaria before 354 BCE.

3. Sanballat III, grandson of Sanballat II and probably the son of Hananiah, was the governor of Samaria at the time of the last Persian Achaemenid king, Darius III (Codomannus; 336–332 BCE), and Alexander the Great. Accordingly, Josephus' story that links "Sanballat" with the erection of the Samaritan temple on Mount Gerizim that was permitted by Alexander the Great (332 BCE; *Ant.* 11.302–11, 321–25, 340–46) refers to Sanballat III (though Josephus confused him with Sanballat I of Neh 13:28).

Bibliography: A. Cowley. *Aramaic Papyri of the Fifth Century B.C.* (1923) 109–10, 113; F. M. Cross. "The Papyri and Their Historical Implications." *Discoveries in the Wadi ed-Daliyeh.* P. W. Lapp and N. L. Lapp, eds. (1974) 17–29; F. M. Cross. "A Reconstruction of the Judean Restoration." *JBL* 94 (1975) 4–18; C. C. Torrey. "Sanballat 'the Horonite'." *JBL* 47 (1928) 380–89; R. Zadok. "Samarian Notes." *BibOr* 42 (1985) 567–72.

ISAAC KALIMI

SANCTIFY, SANCTIFICATION [קָדַשׁ *qadash,* ἁγιάζω *hagiazō,* ἁγιασμός *hagiasmos,* ἁγνίζω *hagnizō*]. The NRSV uses a variety of words to render this word group into English, e.g., sanctify, consecrate, dedicate, set apart, hallow, purify, make sacred/holy, be/become holy, show/display/manifest/maintain holiness, sanctification, consecration, holiness, sanctuary. In general terms, sanctification is the act or process by which persons or objects are cleansed and/or set apart for God's purposes. In its full canonical significance, to be sanctified is to be graciously taken up into, and set apart for active participation in the saving, reconciling purposes of God. For Christians this happens only as they become and remain part of the community of God's people, a people who are corporately and personally being shaped by the Spirit into the image of the crucified Son, and thereby being restored into the image of the holy, life-giving, Triune God.

A. Sanctification and the Divine Mission
B. The Old Testament
  1. Lexical considerations
  2. God's sanctification of Israel
  3. Israel's response: A pattern of
     sanctifying activity
    a. Obedience to ritual demands
    b. Moral/ethical obedience
  4. God's sanctification of his name
     through Israel
  5. Old Testament summary
C. The New Testament
  1. Lexical considerations
  2. The Old Testament and the New Testament
  3. The Synoptic Gospels and Acts
  4. John
  5. Paul and the Pauline tradition
  6. Hebrews
  7. New Testament summary
Bibliography

A. Sanctification and the Divine Mission

At the beginning of the biblical story, the holy God graciously breathes life into humanity (Gen 2:7), creating humanity in God's own image (*see* IMAGE OF GOD) to reflect his gracious rule over creation in a way that would enable all creation to flourish (Gen 1:28; 2:15) and reach its full potential. However, God's purposes are delayed when humankind refuses to live under God's rule and reflect God's gracious rule/image to the rest of creation. Humanity's refusal to engage in this image-bearing pattern of activity makes all of creation susceptible to the forces of death and alienates people from the life-giving God, the created order, and one another, leading to evil, violence, and more death (Gen 4:1-16, 6:5-6, 11-12). Even after the flood (Gen 7–9), humanity is still inclined toward these death-dealing forces (Gen 8:21; 11:1-9). The narrative that runs from Gen 12 to the end of the NT may be read as the overarching story of God's life-giving mission to bring humanity and the rest of creation to its full potential. After Gen 3, this involves saving the created order, including humanity, from the consequences of human rebellion. Sanctification is best

understood within this framework of this "divine mission," sometimes called the *missio Dei*.

B. The Old Testament
1. Lexical considerations

There is no Hebrew noun equivalent to the English noun *sanctification*; the LXX uses the term hagiasmos only eight times, typically in cultic contexts. While the NRSV never uses the word *sanctification* in the OT, forty-eight times in thirty-eight verses it translates the Hebrew verb qadash (used over 680 times in the MT) with some form of the English verb *sanctify*. The LXX regularly uses forms of hagiazō or hagnizō to render qadash into Greek.

2. God's sanctification of Israel

Although these verbs can have either God or human beings as their subjects, holiness other than God's is always derived; that is, people, places, or things become holy only insofar as they are in relation to the Holy One whose character defines holiness. Hence, God's sanctifying activity in initiating and establishing a covenantal relationship with Israel is chronologically and theologically prior to any sanctifying actions of human beings. By electing, delivering, and constituting them as a people, God sets Israel apart from other nations in order that they might be, and become, a holy nation, a priestly kingdom, that is, a publicly distinct people corresponding to his character through which God intends to effect his purposes (Exod 19:3-6; Gen 12:3). Hence, God initially sanctifies Israel by establishing a covenant relationship with them, granting them a holy status, and sustains them as this set-apart people with his ongoing sanctifying activity (e.g., Exod 31:13; Lev 20:8; 21:8; 22:32).

3. Israel's response: A pattern of sanctifying activity

Israel's sanctification is both a gift/indicative and a call/imperative (Lev 20:7-8). Although God's initial and sustaining sanctifying actions frame, enable, and provide the means for them, God's people also engage in sanctifying actions both individually and corporately. Just as priesthood is both a holy status given and a function undertaken, Israel's being/becoming the holy nation God initially makes them is dependent upon the pattern of activity they embody in their life together (Exod 19:5*a*) and toward other nations. Their ongoing sanctification demands exclusive loyalty to Yahweh as their royal sovereign. Such exclusive loyalty is expressed through avoiding idolatry (Exod 20:2-5; Lev 19:4; Deut 5:6-10) and embodying a particular pattern of activity that entails acting in obedience to covenantal demands.

a. Obedience to ritual demands. A rigid distinction between "ritual" and "moral" commandments cannot be maintained. However, in general, impurity in the OT is understood in both ritual (e.g., Lev 11–17) and moral (e.g., Lev 18–20) terms with the latter more associated with sin than the former (*see* CLEAN AND UNCLEAN). The act or process of sanctification takes place within this framework where holiness and impurity are dynamic forces able to transfer their state, with holiness associated with life and impurity with death (*see* HOLY, HOLINESS, OT). In contrast, commonness and purity are inert states that are defined by the absence of holiness and impurity respectively. To be moved from a common to a holy state (i.e., sanctified/consecrated), someone or something must also be/become pure; this is because dangerous consequences follow if forces of holiness and impurity come into contact. Before being sanctified, then, what is impure must be purified. When ritual sanctification is in view, the verb qadash can have various objects. At times, persons (e.g., Israelites, priests, warriors prepared for HOLY WAR), items (e.g., cultic implements), and even space specifically associated with the divine presence (e.g., the sanctuary, the Temple) are set apart by humans and made suitable for an encounter with, or use by, the Holy One. Given the almost unavoidable and contagious nature of ritual impurity in daily life even for priests (*see* CLEAN AND UNCLEAN), the movement into a consecrated/holy state would often have to include a removal of impurity through various God-given means, e.g., cleansing (Exod 19:10-11), sacrificing (Exod 13:15; Lev 16:16-19), or anointing (Exod 30:26-30). Hence, although purification and sanctification are not equivalent, the act/process of sanctification often includes ritual purification.

By engaging in such cultic activity, Israel and/or persons within Israel participate(s) in their own sanctification through God-given means. Israel also avoids particular foods that are sources of impurity (Lev 11, especially vv. 44-45), a practice that distinguishes them from the surrounding nations and reflects the distinct character of their God (Lev 20:24b-26). In addition, in order to maintain their sanctified status, experiencing God's holy presence as life-giving rather than as threatening, they are to avail themselves continuously of the divinely given means of purification from bodily impurities symbolizing the death process—e.g., corpse impurity, scale disease, and the release of blood or semen (Lev 12–14; Num 19).

From a theological perspective, Israel's engagement in ritually sanctifying activity symbolizes 1) Israel's being as distinct from the nations as Yahweh is distinct from other gods (Lev 20:24b-26); 2) Israel's imperative to hold to God's life-giving purposes and reject what is associated with death; 3) Israel's imperative to shape its life together in ways that reflect the character of the holy God it serves. Hence, by engaging in acts of ritual sanctification, Israel is being obedient to Yahweh's command: "You shall be holy, for I the LORD your God am holy" (Lev 19:2). In that process, Israel's identity is being formed as the holy people of God, distinctly set apart from the nations for God's use in achieving God's life-giving mission.

b. Moral/ethical obedience. In Lev 19 a charge for Israel to be holy as Yahweh is holy is followed by a series of (mostly) ethical commandments. They involve avoiding some practices (e.g., idolatry, lying, certain sexual relations, economic injustice) and engaging in others (e.g., respect for parents and the aged, economic generosity, care for aliens, honest business practices). Some of these commandments are oriented toward maintaining Israel's exclusive loyalty to Yahweh and/or underscoring Israel's distinctiveness among the nations (e.g., vv. 26b-28, 31), while others command Israel to mirror Yahweh's character/activity toward them, e.g., integrity (vv. 11-13, 35-36), justice (v. 15), and compassion toward the helpless/marginalized (vv. 9-11, 13b-14, 33-34; compare Exod 22:25-27). Hence, they are the divinely given means of engendering the ongoing sanctification of God's people.

Israel's ritual marking of time has clear moral consequences. Sanctifying/keeping holy (qadash) the SABBATH (Exod 20:8) is in response to, and imitation of, God's own initial sanctifying activity (Gen 2:3; Exod 20:11). Unlike the other nations in which most work to the point of exhaustion, Israel's keeping Sabbath provides revitalizing rest for all within its borders. Conforming their way of marking time to the life-giving patterns of the holy God marks off Israel as distinct, publicly displays the character of God as desiring life for all creation, and gives Israel assurance that God continues to sanctify them (Exod 31:13). Similarly, although probably never carried out, Israel's hallowing/sanctifying (qadash) the fiftieth year (Lev 25:10; *see* JUBILEE, YEAR OF) would have distinguished them from the nations and simultaneously displayed the character of their God as committed to just socioeconomic practices that allow life to flourish. Hence, both these ways of marking time embody Yahweh's thrice-holy nature (Isa 6:3) by displaying Yahweh's righteousness/justice (Isa 5:16) to the nations.

4. God's sanctification of his name through Israel

Yahweh himself would be set apart/sanctified in Israel's midst through their obedience to Torah. Otherwise, his holy name would be profaned (Lev 22:31-33), as Ezekiel maintains it was when the people were exiled because of their disloyalty/disobedience (36:20-23). With the *missio Dei* now delayed, Yahweh's response is: "I will sanctify (qadash) my great name ... and the nations shall know that I am the LORD ... when through you I display my holiness [a passive form of qadash, i.e., 'I am sanctified'] before their eyes" (Ezek 36:23). Yahweh's taking his captive people "out of the nations," giving them "a new heart," and "placing his Spirit in/among" them would enable their obedience to a "new covenant" (36:4-27; 37:6; Jer 31:31-34). Hence, Yahweh promises to shape Israel's future life together into a public display of his own character/holiness before the nations' eyes through the giving of the

Spirit so that ultimately they too would come to know Yahweh (Ezek 36:26; 38:16, 23; 39:7). The Spirit's (re)shaping Israel into the *imago Dei* is inseparable from their participation in the *missio Dei*.

5. Old Testament summary

Although God's sanctifying actions in the OT are always primary (chronologically and theologically), they frame and enable Israel's subordinate/secondary sanctifying actions. The purpose of these latter practices is to sanctify the people's imagination (i.e., their whole self-understanding) by conforming it to the life-giving patterns of the holy God, thereby publicly setting Israel apart from other nations for God's ultimate purposes. Hence, both God's and Israel's sanctifying actions ultimately move toward the corporate formation of a distinct and public people as a set-apart instrument for the *missio Dei*, i.e., God's intent to engender life in all its fullness for Israel, and through Israel, for the nations and creation as a whole.

C. The New Testament

1. Lexical considerations

Whereas the verb **hagnizō** is used six times in the NT, the NRSV uses English cognates of *purify* rather than *sanctify* to render it into English (Acts 21:24, 26; 24:18; Jas 4:8; 1 Pet 1:22; 1 John 3:3). The verb **hagiazō** occurs twenty-eight times, nineteen of which the NRSV renders with a form of the English verb *sanctify*. The noun **hagiasmos** occurs ten times, one of which the NRSV renders verbally ("sanctify"; 1 Pet 1:2), five of which it renders as "sanctification" and four of which it renders as "holiness." *See* HOLY, HOLINESS, NT.

2. The Old Testament and the New Testament

While sanctification in the ritual sense is rarely mentioned in the NT (e.g., Matt 23:17, 19), it does not reject what Israel's engagement in ritually sanctifying activity symbolizes (see §B3.a above). In addition, although the subject of **hagiazō** is almost always God, Christ, or the Spirit in the NT rather than humans (but see 1 Pet 3:15; compare 1 Cor 7:14; 2 Tim 2:21), God's sanctifying activity enables the people of God to engage in a pattern of sanctifying activity.

3. The Synoptic Gospels and Acts

Apart from the LORD'S PRAYER (Matt 6:9//Luke 11:2), **hagiazō** only occurs twice in the Synoptic Gospels (Matt 23:17, 19). The petition for the Father's name to be hallowed/sanctified is parallel to the petition for God's reign/kingdom to come, both of which are exemplified by Jesus' Spirit-empowered activity. With Ezek 36–37 in the background, this is a self-involving prayer when prayed by God's people in/among whom the life-giving Spirit is at work. It is a prayer that God will make their life together a public display of his own character/holiness before the nations so that ultimately they too

will come to know the Lord (i.e., a prayer that corporately they will be an instrument of the *missio Dei*).

The early church in Acts is this sanctified community where members of the nations/Gentiles who switch lordships and receive forgiveness of sins are welcome (Acts 20:32; 26:18). With cleansed hearts accomplished by repentance, baptism, and the reception of the Holy Spirit (Acts 2:38; 15:8-9; compare Ezek 36:25-26) this community is restored and empowered by the same Spirit as was their crucified Lord (Acts 2:36). Inner transformation is assumed here but is not bracketed off from its embodiment in public practices (compare Ezek 36:27). Acting publicly in his name (3:6) in ways that parallel his own actions (compare Acts 3:1-10 to Luke 5:17-26), they thereby embody the character of the Holy One (3:14), displaying a pattern of redemptive activity through which God's mission is being accomplished. They are, therefore, those who have been and remain sanctified by faith/faithfulness in/toward Jesus (26:18).

4. John

In John Jesus is the "the Holy One of God" (6:68-69) in intimate relationship with the Father (10:30, 38). Taking up Israel's mandate as the obedient Son, he is sanctified/set apart by the Father and sent into the world (10:36) to exhibit a pattern of saving activity ("the works of my Father") that expresses the essence of the Father's life-giving, holy character (10:36-38; compare 3:14-17). Echoing this language in 17:17-19, Jesus' prayer for the disciples to be sanctified is a prayer that they, like himself, will be set apart from the world as instruments for the *missio Dei* in that same world. The means for their sanctification is Jesus' imminent self-sanctification/consecration (**hagiazō**, 17:19) which begins when he allows himself to be arrested, effectively setting himself apart as a (living) sacrifice, i.e., the lamb of God who "takes away the sin of the world" (1:29; 19:14-16). This act produces "life" in Johannine terms (3:14-17; 6:47-51; 10:17-18, 27-28). Jesus' cruciform pattern of redemptive activity (compare 13:1-20), then, is meant to effect his disciples' sanctification, aspects of which are evident in 17:20-23. There the disciples' sanctification means their intimately sharing life with the Father, the Son, and one another, all of which is directed toward the world coming to know that the Father has sent the Son. To achieve the latter, the Spirit-enabled (20:22) disciples must engage in what Jesus did when he was sanctified and sent into the world (10:37), "the works of my Father." In John, these are life-giving works of costly love, a pattern of activity that results from, and is enabled by, Jesus' self-sanctification/consecration, the sanctifying effects of which continue in the disciples' life together (17:19*b*).

5. Paul and the Pauline tradition

Although Paul is fully aware that Sin and Death still impact all in "this age," including the people of God, they no longer reign in the church as they do outside it (Rom 5:12-21). The focused presence of the Holy Spirit (God's life-giving power) makes the realm of the church a holy realm in which God's salvation is being worked out (Phil 2:12-13; *see* SALVATION). Hence, the crucified Christ not only reveals the character/holiness of God, those "in Christ" are in the sphere of God's sanctifying activity (1 Cor 1:30) and are "holy ones" (e.g., 1 Cor 1:2 *see* SAINT). Sanctification begins with God's work through the Spirit of establishing and marking out a distinct people (2 Thess 2:13; compare 1 Pet 1:2), cleansing (1 Cor 6:11) and relocating them in, and as, a new space, i.e., the temple of God where the Spirit dwells corporately (1 Cor 3:16-17) and personally (6:11). As such, they are not made unclean by simple contact with those outside the church (1 Cor 5:9-10; 7:12-16) but by engaging in, and/or tolerating, morally impure practices among/by those within the church itself (1 Thess 4:3-8; 1 Cor 5–6). Such activity threatens their holy status and is an impediment to God's will to continue his sanctifying activity among them (1 Thess 4:3-8).The holiness of those "in Christ" is not static but is the consequence of a dynamic relationship in which they are being "perfected" (2 Cor 7:1) so that they can be blameless in holiness at the Parousia (1 Thess 3:13). In 1 Thess 3:12, this occurs by the Lord's enabling them to "increase and abound" in their current practices of self-giving love toward each other and toward those outside the church, (1:3; 3:6; 4:9-10; compare 2:6-12) and through these practices "strengthening" and continuing to transform their character, dispositions, and allegiances (i.e., their hearts) with a view toward their becoming entirely sanctified (1 Thess 5:23). This context favors translating **hagiasmos** in 1 Thess 4:3 and 4:7 as sanctification (a process or its end result) rather than holiness (a state/condition as in 4:4). But if God's own holiness is primarily conceived as a pattern of activity (see above), even if **hagiasmos** refers to a human state/condition here, it is constituted by a particular grace-enabled pattern of human activity (1 Thess 4:4; 1 Tim 2:15) that would not compromise their holy status and impede God's acting to sanctify entirely the whole community (1 Thess 5:23). Hence, as in the case of Israel, persons in the church neither initiate nor complete their sanctification, but are enabled by the Spirit (1 Thess 4:8) to engage in a pattern of activity, taking on some practices and refraining from others (compare 2 Tim 2:21), through which God continues his sanctifying activity. In Romans, God's rectifying, reconciling invasion in Jesus Christ has liberated the audience from the death trap of the chaos/impurity of 1:18-32 and Sin's reign (6:1-14). They are now relocated "in Christ" as "holy ones" (1:7) by participating in his death and resurrection in baptism (6:3-11). Sharing Christ's story of being brought from death to life (6:13), they are counseled by Paul to "join the war" by presenting their members/selves as weapons/slaves of God's rectifying, life-giving, mission (i.e., God's righteousness, 6:13, 18). As they present themselves for God to shape, enable, and use as agents who embody a redemptive/reconciling pattern of activity through which the *missio Dei* continues (compare 2 Cor 5:18-20), God continues their sanctification (hagiasmos, 6:19), the goal of which is the life of the new age (6:22), the final reversal/antonym of death and the impurity/chaos/Sin associated with it. The Spirit who engenders holiness (1:4) enables this allegiance to, reflection of, and participation in, God's rectifying and sanctifying project (8:1-11, especially v. 4 as explicated in 13:8-10). Using cultic imagery in 12:1-2, Paul urges his audience to present their bodies as a singular living corporate sacrifice, holy to God. Their corporate life together as the body of Christ (12:3-8) is the holy locale where the Spirit is active (8:11; 1 Cor 3:16-17) and hence the necessary relational network enabling them to present their members as weapons of God's rectifying/reconciling project in the various cruciform practices of 12:9–15:3 (especially 12:9-21; 15:1-3). In this priestly act of worship in which they, like Christ, are both priests and sacrifice, the effects of being handed over to impurity/chaos (1:24-25) are reversed (compare 12:2 to 1:28). Their sacrifice becomes a part of the sacrificial offering consisting of the Gentiles in 15:16. Arguably then, the goal of Paul's entire mission is that the Gentiles to whom he is sent will become a single sacrificial offering "sanctified by the Holy Spirit" (compare Eph 5:26-27). By establishing and marking out a distinct people and forming in them a cruciform character whereby they practice the kind of costly, self-giving love embodied in the story of Christ (Phil 2:6-11) as agents of God's reconciliation (2 Cor 5:18-20), the Spirit is at work transforming the church and persons within it into the image of the crucified and risen Son (Rom 8:29-30), i.e., into a visible instantiation of the character of the holy God. Such conceptuality stands in tension with the claim made for the emperor that, as head of the imperial body, his is the (divine) likeness into which all should be molded. Hence, sanctification, as a transformative process had (and has) the potential of being politically subversive. God's sanctifying activity culminates at the resurrection when those "in Christ" are raised with "spiritual bodies," "glorious bodies" totally permeated by the "life-giving" Spirit (1 Cor 15:42-49; Phil 3:20-21). Fit for the New Creation, such sanctified bodies are no longer subject to Death and decay's impurity. Patterned after the Lord's risen body, they are embodied displays of God being "all in all" (1 Cor 15:28) and therefore the final result of God's intent to conform a redeemed people to the image of his Son (Rom 8:29; 2 Cor 4:4; Phil 3:21), himself the "image of the invisible God" (Col 1:15). Hence the complete restoration of the *imago Dei* in humanity happens corporately when God, through the Holy Spirit, enables both the bodies of those who share the character/story of Christ and the entire created order to reflect fully Christ's glory (Rom 8:19-22; compare 2 Cor 3:18), itself the visible manifestation of God's holiness.

6. Hebrews

The verb sanctify (hagiazō) occurs more in Hebrews than any other NT document. Assuming the relational framework of covenant and using the imagery of sanctuary ritual and priestly ministry, the writer develops Jesus' death as a one-time sanctifying act initiating a new covenant (8:7-13; 9:15-22; 10:1-18, 29). Depicting Jesus as both faithful priest and sacrifice (2:17; 7:26-28), the writer underscores the efficacy of this one-time offering of Christ's body/blood in sanctifying the audience in the past and continuing to sanctify them in the present (2:11; 10:10; 10:14) as they keep that covenant. Here sanctification is a covenantal reality effected by Jesus' sacrifice of atonement for the people's sins (2:17) resulting in the defeat of "the one who has the power of death" (2:14b-15), the purification of our conscience/consciousness from dead works/sins so that we might serve the living God (9:13-14; 10:2), forgiveness of sins (9:22) and the removal of sin itself (9:26). Ironically, the one who sanctifies, the Son of the living God, does so through the defilement of his own corpse (13:11-13) thereby revealing and conveying life and holiness to the people of the new covenant in order that they may "share [God's] holiness" (Heb 12:10). But, as with Israel, remaining in the sphere of God's sanctifying activity requires remaining in a community that "pursues sanctification" (hagiasmos, 12:14) through a variety of grace-enabled (13:20-21) ecclesial practices (e.g., 12:7, 14-17; 13:1-9, 15-16). It also requires a corporate eschewing of willful sin (10:26-31). Purposely and continually living in unholy ways (10:29), in effect, nullifies the sacrifice for sins that first sanctified the audience (10:26, 29).

7. New Testament summary

Although differences of emphasis exist, NT conceptions of sanctification remain in significant continuity with the OT. Sanctification continues to entail being set apart from those outside the people of God for the sake of God's ultimate life-giving purposes in the *missio Dei*. But both sanctification and the *missio Dei* have been reconfigured in light of the Christ event. Sanctification occurs when persons are forgiven, cleansed, set apart and incorporated into a holy people by means of, and in order to participate in, God's cruciform pattern of redemptive/reconciling activity. The Spirit's enabling of the church to participate in practices of costly, self-giving love is the means by which God continues sanctifying his people, shaping them more fully into the image of the crucified Son, "the Holy One of God." As such, they are being, and will become, fully restored into the image of the life-giving, Triune God, i.e., entirely sanctified. *See* CHURCH, IDEA OF THE; CHURCH, LIFE AND ORGANIZATION OF; FAITH, FAITHFULNESS; HOLY SPIRIT; IMAGE OF GOD; JUSTIFICATION, JUSTIFY.

Bibliography: David Peterson. *Possessed by God: A New Testament Theology of Sanctification and Holiness* (1995); Christopher J. H. Wright. *The Mission of God: Unlocking the Bible's Grand Narrative* (2006).

ANDY JOHNSON

SANCTUARY [קֹדֶשׁ qodesh, מִקְדָּשׁ miqdash; ἅγιος hagios, ναός naos]. Gods and goddesses were never far from the entire range of human affairs in the ancient world. But for people to serve or solicit the deity, these activities often required a particular place. Such places were generically designated with terms based on the notions of sacredness and holiness (e.g., qodesh, hagios) that can be translated as "sanctuary," "temple," or "tabernacle." Sanctuaries took many forms, from locations marked by natural features in the landscape, to a portable tent (*see* TABERNACLE), to the Temple in Jerusalem (*see* TEMPLE, JERUSALEM) and the temples of the Greco-Roman world, and with a diversity of shrines besides (*see* BAMAH; HIGH PLACE). Most sanctuaries shared at least two basic features: the distinctive aura of holiness, which often required preparatory purification, and a hierarchy of degrees of holiness within sections of the sacred precinct.

ROBERT B. COOTE

SAND LIZARD [חֹמֶט khomet]. An animal listed among swarming creatures that transmit uncleanness when dead, both through touching them and touching objects they have touched (Lev 11:30). The particular swarming creatures listed in Lev 11:30 suggest that the khomet is a LIZARD. The similar Aramaic word khumeton (חוּמְטוֹן) is used for a type of skink known as a sand lizard that lives in sandy areas. *See* ANIMALS OF THE BIBLE.

EMILY R. CHENEY

SANDAL THONG. *See* THONG, SANDAL.

SANDALS AND SHOES [נְעָלִים na'alayim; ὑπόδημα hypodēma]. Basic footwear consisted of a sturdy leather sole tied to the foot and/or ankle with thongs (Mark 1:7). More serviceable sandals with leggings were used during construction work or heavy labor, although slaves generally were forced to go barefoot. There are more elaborate types of shoes depicted on Assyrian monumental inscriptions like the Black Obelisk of Shalmaneser III (*see* OBELISK, BLACK) or the Lachish reliefs from the royal palace in Nineveh, but it is possible these were foreign styles familiar to the Assyrian artists and not the actual sandals regularly worn by Israelites. In any case, the well-dressed individual was one who had quality sandals (Song 7:1 [HEB. 7:2]; Ezek 16:10). However, since sandals protected the feet and trod through the debris associated with the secular world, they were to be removed when one wished to enter sacred space (Exod 3:5; Josh 5:15; Acts 7:33). Aside from their utilitarian function as foot protection, sandals also served as culturally recognized symbols. For example, preparation for a journey characteristically includes tying one's clothing up with a belt, putting on sandals, and taking up a walking staff (Exod 12:11; Ezek 24:17; Matt 10:10). The pairing of belt and sandals also provides a metaphor for a man's violent character, as in David's accusation against Joab that he had put "the blood of war on the belt around his waist, and on the sandals on his feet" (1 Kgs 2:5). Personal well-being is also tied to the condition of one's footwear. Thus the Gibeonites are able to disguise themselves as pilgrims by donning dusty, worn-out clothes and patched sandals (Josh 9:5), while the strength and vibrancy of the enemy nation employed by Yahweh to punish the unfaithful Israelites is shown by the fact that none have even a single broken sandal thong (Isa 5:27).

Persons in mourning or those who wished to graphically display their penitence, could wear sackcloth and walk barefoot like David, who trudges up the Mount of Olives as he flees from Jerusalem in the face of his son Absalom's revolt (2 Sam 15:30). Playing on this theme of lost status, the prophet Isaiah enacted his prophecy of an approaching and potentially devastating catastrophe for Judah by walking about practically naked and barefoot (Isa 20:2-4). In this case, the prophet is mimicking the fate of prisoners of war, who are forced to walk into captivity after being stripped of their identity through the removal of their garments and sandals. This picture of a person without resources is transformed in the NT injunction to the seventy disciples to begin their mission with "no purse, no bag, no sandals" and thus rely for their daily needs and shelter on those whose hospitality shares in the paired disciples' expression of "peace" (Luke 10:4-5; note Mark 6:9 does allow the Twelve to wear sandals (sandalia σανδάλια) during their mission of evangelism). When someone was received with favor by a patron, the evidence of their new prosperity included the receipt of clothing and footwear. Thus the prodigal son is restored to his place within his father's household when he is clothed in a robe and given a ring and sandals (Luke 15:22). In much the same way, the redeemed foundling in Ezek 16:8-13 is not only given her life by the divine adoptive parent, but is officially welcomed into the household after being cleansed with water and oil by the gifting of clothing, jewelry, and "sandals of fine leather" (16:10).

The legal symbolism attached to footwear in ancient Israel is made clear in several ways. For instance, when a person wished to confirm a land transaction, either through redeeming or exchange, then it was the custom to remove one's sandal and hand it to the person who would now have legal title to the property (Ruth 4:7-8). Also drawing upon the range of symbolic cultural meanings attached to the sandal, the act of taking possession of a plot of land, as King Ahab does of Naboth's vineyard, is accomplished by walking off its boundaries (1 Kgs 21:16-17). In a similar manner, God instructs Abram to "walk through the length and the breadth of the land" that had been promised to his household (Gen 13:17; retold in Josh 24:3).

Since common sandals were inexpensive, they functioned quite well as figurative examples in oaths such as Abram's solemn vow not to accept any of the spoil taken in his defeat of Chedorlaomer, not even "a sandal-thong" (Gen 14:22-23). Amos uses the insignificant price of sandals as part of his condemnation of the corrupt judges in Israel, who "sell the righteous for silver [bribery], and the needy for a pair of sandals [into debt slavery]" (2:6). In a like manner, John the Baptist denigrates his own role by comparing his unworthiness to one for whom he is not "worthy to carry" sandals (Matt 3:11; variations include "untie the thong" of sandals in Acts 13:25 and "stoop down and untie" in Mark 1:7).

There are also negative connotations associated with sandals. According to the legal narrative in Deut 25:5-10, when a widow's levir refuses to carry out his obligation to his relative's household by impregnating the widow, she publicly removes his sandal and spits in his face. This serves as a sign of contempt and of his loss of honor within his community. The contempt one has for an enemy also involves the use of a shoe. In Pss 60:8[10] and 108:9[10] the restored Israel will take revenge on its enemy neighbors, shouting in triumph and even casting a shoe at Edom. *See* CLOTH, CLOTHES; THONG, SANDAL.

VICTOR H. MATTHEWS

SANHEDRIN san-hee′druhn [συνέδριον synedrion]. In the NT often a designation for the supreme Jewish council in Jerusalem in the Second Temple period (henceforth Council). The term can also be used to describe the local council governing the affairs of cities and towns.

  A. Terminology
  B. Historical Uncertainties
  C. Origin and History
  D. Jesus and the Sanhedrin
  E. The Apostles and the Sanhedrin
  Bibliography

A. Terminology

The Greek term synedrion (from syn- [σύν], "together," and hedra [ἕδρα], "seat") is used in literary and documentary sources with four different but related meanings: 1) a governing board, e.g., a local council of a town; 2) an official session of a council, a council meeting; 3) the meeting room of the council; 4) the council of the Jews in Jerusalem. A council is not simply a court of law, nor necessarily a legislative assembly, but an assembly of notables who are responsible for the affairs of a town or city or, as is the case with regard to the Sanhedrin in Jerusalem, of a provincial assembly, or of private associations or boards of trade. Details of membership, function, jurisdiction, and procedures depend on the historical, political, cultural, and geographical context. In later Hellenistic Greek, synedrion is used for law courts.

Josephus uses synedrion for the council in Jerusalem (*Ant.* 14.167–180; *Vita* 62), as well as for the councils of the five districts created by Gabinius (*Ant.* 14.89–91). These councils were regional assemblies of traditional leaders whose main responsibility was tax collection and the maintenance of civil order in their districts. Josephus also uses the term synedrion for the numerous "councils" of family, friends, and officials that Herod I summoned to settle disputes at his court (*J.W.* 1.537), and for other ad hoc meetings of advisers, such as the sessions in which Josephus discussed military strategy with his friends in Galilee (*Vita* 368), and Titus' meeting with his generals during the siege of Jerusalem (*J.W.* 6.243). Josephus uses the same term as designation for the venerable Senate in the city of Rome (*J.W.* 2.25).

In the NT the term is most often used for the highest Jewish council in Jerusalem (Matt 26:59; Mark 14:55; 15:1; John 11:47; Acts 5:27, 34; 6:12; 22:30; 23:1, 15, 28; 24:20). In Luke-Acts, synedrion probably refers to the assembly room in which the Council meets (Luke 22:66; Acts 4:15; 5:41; 6:15; 23:6, 20) or to a session of the Council (Acts 5:34). In Matt 5:22; 10:17; Mark 13:9 local councils with judicial jurisdiction are in view.

Another term is gerousia (γερουσία from gerōn [γέρων], "old man"), which means "Council of Elders" or "Senate" and is used for various councils, especially at Sparta, but also in other cities (Aristotle, *Pol.* 2.6.15). This was apparently the term for the Jerusalem Council during the Persian period (Jdt 4:8; 1 Macc 12:6; 2 Macc 1:10; Josephus, *Ant.* 13.166). Luke uses the term gerousia together with synedrion in Acts 5:21: "they called together the council (synedrion) and the whole body of the elders (gerousia) of Israel." If the word *and* (kai καί) is understood here in an explicative sense, Luke is explaining (for his non-Jewish readers) that the term synedrion means "the Council of the Elders" (Dionysius Halicarnassus, *Ant. rom.* 2.12 and the inscription *CIG* 2.3417 use both terms for the same body).

In Luke 22:66 and Acts 22:5, the term presbyterion (πρεσβυτέριον), translated as "council of elders," refers to the highest Jewish council in Jerusalem, and is used here as a synonym for synedrion. Another likely synonym is boulē (βουλή), "council." Josephus of Arimathea is described in Mark 15:43; Luke 23:50 as a bouleutēs (βουλευτής), i.e., as a "member of the boulē," evidently referring to the Sanhedrin (Mark 15:1; Luke 22:66). In Greek texts, the term boulē is the standard term for city councils, particularly the ruling council of a polis (πόλις), the independent city, which meets in the bouleutērion (βουλευτήριον, "council chamber" or "senate house"). The members of the Greek boulē were elected by the eligible voters. Josephus uses the term boulē for the Senate in Rome (*J.W.* 1.284; *Ant.* 13.164; often in *Ant.* 18–19), for local

Roman city councils (*Ant.* 14.230), the council of the city of Tiberias (*Vita* 64; *J.W.* 2.639–41), the city council of Antioch (*J.W.* 7.107), the supreme council of the Samaritans (*Ant.* 18.88), and for the Council in Jerusalem (*Vita* 204; *J.W.* 5.532; in 5.144 the term bouleutērion is used for the meeting place of the Council).

B. Historical Uncertainties

The discussions about the Sanhedrin raise the question of the structure and the leadership of Jewish society in the Second Temple period. Neither the terms used for leadership groups, nor the Greek political terminology that we find in Jewish texts written in Greek, are used with precision. Jewish society in Judea underwent many political changes in the 400 years from 300 BCE to 100 CE, dominated in turn by the Ptolemaic kings, the Seleucid kings, the Hasmonean rulers, the Herodian dynasty, and Roman governors. The available primary sources do not allow us to trace in detail the organizational changes that were either forced on the Jewish commonwealth or initiated by the Jewish leadership in response to the shifts in the changing balance of power. It is a fair assumption that the membership, the leadership, the powers, and the functions of the Jerusalem Sanhedrin and other regional assemblies varied according to the political circumstances. Strong Jewish leaders such as Alexander Jannaeus and Herod I created a different political climate, which affected all political and legal institutions, than weak Roman governors who nevertheless imposed external control in certain areas. This means that all Jewish institutions were bound to experience change, even transformation, including the Sanhedrin. While its members surely represented the Jewish people in some fashion, it should not be confused with a democratic House of Representatives, as found in the United States, who deliberate political, legal, economic, and cultural/religious matters.

To illustrate the difficulty of interpreting the available evidence, we can look at several texts in Josephus that speak of a synedrion in Jerusalem. In *Ant.* 14.167–68, the synedrion in Jerusalem, headed by the high priest Hyrcanus II, puts Herod on trial; in *Ant.* 15.173 Herod shows incriminating letters to the synedrion with the result that Hyrcanus is executed; in *Ant.* 20.216–17 King Agrippa II convenes a synedrion on the request of the Levites that was to grant them permission to wear linen robes like those of the priests; in *Vita* 62, Josephus relates that he wrote to the synedrion in Jerusalem for instructions on how to proceed in Galilee during the initial stages of the war against Rome. In the first two texts the Greek text uses the definite article (to synedrion τό συνέδριον), "the Sanhedrin," suggesting a known deliberative body. The other two texts, as in most other texts that use the term synedrion, formulate without an article ("a Sanhedrin"), which may suggest that ad hoc gatherings for specific purposes are in view, especially plausible in the context of the conduct of military operations. What complicates matters is the fact that

Josephus occasionally speaks of a boulē in Jerusalem in various formulations: the chief priests and the boulē (*J.W.* 2.331), the priests, the powerful citizens, and the boulē (*J.W.* 2.336), and leaders, boulē, and people of Jerusalem (addressed in a letter by Claudius, *Ant.* 20.11). As the boulē is usually mentioned alongside the leading citizens including the chief priests, the term appears to describe an institution that comprises more members than the leading citizens, having some sort of advisory role. Josephus clearly is not consistent in his terminology; he never defines these terms nor does he relate the boulē to the synedrion. Generally, Josephus uses the terms gerousia (senate) or boulē (council) for the standing deliberative body in Jerusalem. We should note that there is no clear evidence that Jerusalem was a Greek polis in the formal sense: civic institutions such as the gymnasium (gymnasion γυμνάσιον) and fixed times and places for national assemblies are missing; and we can assume that elections in Jerusalem would have left some traces in the extant sources.

The MISHNAH, a rabbinic document redacted ca. 200 CE, states that there were two courts in Jerusalem: the "greater Sanhedrin" (or, more frequently, "House of Justice" or "tribunal") consisting of seventy-one judges, and the "lesser Sanhedrin" consisting of twenty-three judges (*m. Sanh.* 1:6). Some scholars assumed that this text also describes the situation in Judea before 70 CE and argued that there was a political body (boulē), a college of priests (synedrion), and the Great Sanhedrin, which regulated the religious life of the Jews. A similar reconstruction assumed a political Sanhedrin, a priestly Sanhedrin, and a scribal Sanhedrin, the latter identical with the Great Sanhedrin. It is open to question, however, whether the Mishnah can be used to reconstruct institutions in Judea before the destruction of Jerusalem in 70 CE.

The available sources suggest that there was a permanent council in Jerusalem, sometimes called synedrion (Sanhedrin), but also known as gerousia (senate) and boulē (council), consisting of the chief priests and the leading citizens (of Jerusalem), that had power (or, depending on the political situation, influence) over Judea and the rest of Palestine. The Sanhedrin was not a representative parliament. Despite the fact that the permanent council in Jerusalem was called boulē, it is unlikely that the members of the Council were elected, since Jerusalem was not a Greek polis.

C. Origin and History

During the postexilic period, the chief priests and the heads of the leading families governed whatever decision-making power the Persians and then the Ptolemies and Seleucids granted their Jewish vassal-state (Neh 5:17; Josephus, *Ant.* 12.138, 142). When the Seleucid kings sought to exert more direct control over Judea, they frequently exchanged the high priest; the "Council of the Elders" (gerousia) continued to play an important role (1 Macc 12:6; 2 Macc 1:10;

11:27). When the Hasmoneans restored the hereditary high priesthood, and when some Hasmonean rulers assumed the title "king," the "Elders of the Jews" continued to be an influential body (Josephus, *Ant.* 13.408–9, 428). Under Queen Salome Alexandra (76–67 BCE), the PHARISEES became perhaps the most influential voice in the Sanhedrin (*Ant.* 13.408–9). Apart from this short period, the Sanhedrin was dominated by the chief priests and other priests (the SADDUCEES), and wealthy nobles or elders; while many of the priests must have had scribal training, many of the scribes who belonged to the Sanhedrin would have been Pharisees.

After Pompey brought Judea into the orbit of Roman rule in 63 BCE, terminating the royal dimension of Hasmonean rule (he prohibited the high priest Hyrcanus to wear a diadem), the chief priests were permitted "to have the leadership [prostasia προστασία] of the nation" (*Ant.* 20.244). Josephus mentions the term synedrion (Sanhedrin) for the first time in connection with Gabinius, the Roman governor of Syria, who divided Palestine in 57 BCE into five synedria (συνέδρια, plural of synedrion), one of them in Jerusalem (*Ant.* 14.91). In 47 BCE Julius Caesar came to Syria and confirmed Hyrcanus II as high priest and ethnarch of the Jews, while Antipater was nominated procurator of Judea (*Ant.* 14.137, 194–200); Hyrcanus was explicitly given jurisdiction in internal Jewish affairs (*Ant.* 14.195). It appears that during this period (47–40 BCE) the synedrion in Jerusalem, under the leadership of Hyrcanus, assumed jurisdiction for all Palestine, including Galilee, with the power to indict Herod, Antipater's younger son, who had been given control of Galilee, for murder (*Ant.* 14.168–80). The speech of Semaias, one of the Council members, implies that the Jerusalem Sanhedrin regularly heard criminal cases (*Ant.* 14.172).

When Herod I became king, he purged the Sanhedrin of his opponents, making sure that it made only such decisions as were favorable to himself and his court. According to Josephus, the Sanhedrin continued to function as a body with the power to execute (*Ant.* 15.173), but Herod was perfectly willing to execute any person who seemed to get in his way, with or without the approval of the Sanhedrin. Some have suggested that during Herod's long reign (40/37–4 BCE), the Sanhedrin dealt mainly with religious matters. Once Herod had become king, Josephus uses the term synedrion of the ad hoc meetings that Herod convened (*Ant.* 16.357–67; 17.46).

The picture that emerges from the NT and Josephus concerning the Sanhedrin in the 1st cent. CE is in basic agreement. The control of national affairs is in the hands of the chief priests, the traditional Jewish aristocracy. They controlled the temple service, they promulgated the laws, they tried cases. They constituted the highest Jewish authority in the land when there was no Jewish king such as Herod Archelaus (4 BCE–6 CE), Herod Agrippa I (41–44 CE) or Agrippa II (50–92 CE).

The priestly aristocracy generally ruled by means of a council (synedrion, gerousia, boulē), chaired by the incumbent high priest. The majority of its members, in the 1st cent., seem to have come from the ruling priestly families (the Sadducees), with other members of the Jewish elites, and SCRIBEs, sitting on the Council as well. When the high priest Ananus engineered the execution of James, the brother of Jesus, in 62 CE, Pharisees protested before Agrippa II and before the Roman governor Albinus—successfully, as they achieved the replacement of Ananus (Ant. 20.200–203). This indicates that even though some members of the Sanhedrin may have been Pharisees, they did not control its proceedings at this particular time. Moreover, this incident indicates that even though the Sanhedrin was led by the high priest, he did not have the power to convene it without the consent of the Roman governor (Ant. 20.202).

Recent efforts to depreciate (or even deny) the existence of the Sanhedrin as a formal supreme court with a fixed and known membership are unconvincing: the unity of civil and religious law in the Torah makes it impossible for any Jewish ruler to govern without an institution whose members include priests and other Torah experts (scribes). The scarcity of references to the Sanhedrin in Josephus is an argument from silence that does not convince: when Josephus recounts that during the reign of Queen Salome the Pharisees condemned people to death and executed them (J.W. 1.113), that they possessed other juridical competence (Ant. 13.409), and that Salome ordered the Jewish people to obey the Pharisees when she reintroduced legal decisions of the Pharisees that had been rescinded by John Hyrcanus I (Ant. 13.408), it goes without saying that all of these scenarios require a council in which relevant decisions are made. Political power and political rule require legislative and executive bodies, especially if the basis for legal decisions is the Torah and the tradition of the elders. Even the capricious King Herod was not able to govern without the help of the Sanhedrin.

The Sanhedrin was a permanent council with legislative and executive functions, evidently covering whatever was important to Jewish society, including judicial and civil matters, and, of course, the affairs of the Temple. The sources suggest that the Council, particularly in the person of the high priest, represented the Jewish people to foreign rulers. The tradition of seventy-one members—seventy council members plus the presiding high priest—that is found in early rabbinic sources (m. Sanh. 1:6) may be correct, but early sources do not confirm this information. As mentioned above, when we regard the Sanhedrin as a permanent council with legislative and executive functions, we must not rule out the likelihood that the composition of this Council changed repeatedly depending on the political circumstances, and that either the Jewish king, or the high priest, or the leading priestly families manipulated the Council and put its members under pressure or made decisions without consulting this institution.

The Sanhedrin convened in or near the temple precinct. The reference in Mark 14:53-55 to the courtyard of the high priest's residence seems to refer to a preliminary hearing, not to a full meeting of the Sanhedrin. According to Josephus, J.W. 5.144, the boulē met in the area where the first city wall coming from the Xystus met the west wall of the Temple, i.e., in or above the Tyropoeon Valley outside the Temple. According to rabbinic tradition, the Sanhedrin met in the Lishkat ha-Gazit (lishkath haggazith לִשְׁכַּת הַגָּזִית), the Chamber of Hewn Stone (m. Mid. 5:3-4), which in m. Sanh. 11:2 is located in the inner courts of the Temple proper. However, as the term gazithis translated in the LXX as xystos (ξυστός, "polished," see 1 Chr 22:2; Amos 5:11), the designation Lishkat ha-Gazit can be understood as "the Hall beside the Xystus." A bridge connected the Xystus to the Temple Mount (J.W. 2.344). The localization inside the Temple forecourts is hardly reliable, as it is unlikely that a room in the inner forecourt would have been used for anything but priestly purposes. According to another rabbinic tradition, the Sanhedrin moved forty years before the destruction of the city (in 70 CE) from its previous location in the Lishkat ha-Gazit to the Khanut (khanuth [חָנוּת], "shops"; b. Shabb. 15a), perhaps a reference to the Royal Portico at the southern end of the Temple Mount. Those who assume besides the Sanhedrin as "supreme court" also a "city council" (boulē) locate this civic body in the area of the Huldah Gates (compare t. Hag. 2:9; t. Sanh. 7:1). After the destruction of Jerusalem and the Temple in 70 CE, the Sanhedrin was moved to Jamnia (m. Sotah 9:11; m. Sanh. 11:4), and in 118 CE it was moved to Galilee.

The Sanhedrin, presumably under the supervision of the chief priests, had security or police forces at their disposal (compare Luke 22:52). They tried cases and, at times, performed executions. Despite their authority, the chief priests had to take into account popular sentiment, which was frequently linked with the position of the Pharisees (Ant. 13.288, 298, 400–402; 18.15, 17).

D. Jesus and the Sanhedrin

According to John 11:47-53, the chief priests and the Pharisees react to Jesus' raising of Lazarus by convening the Sanhedrin, chaired by the high priest Caiaphas, which deliberates about the removal of Jesus. In the Jewish trial of Jesus, the Gospels mention the Sanhedrin consisting of the chief priests, scribes, and elders who call witnesses, who pass a sentence, and insist before Pilate, the Roman governor, that Jesus should be executed (Matt 26:59; Mark 14:55; 15:1; Luke 22:66; 23:50; John 11:47).

It continues to be disputed whether the Sanhedrin had the jurisdiction for capital cases and the right to execute offenders, a question that is significant for a historical evaluation of Jesus' trial (compare John 18:31; Josephus, J.W. 6.126; see also y. Sanh. 18a; 24b: forty years before the destruction of the Temple the power to pass death sentences was removed by the Romans). As Roman governors kept capital cases under their own jurisdiction, most scholars assume that when Judea was under direct Roman rule, the Sanhedrin could pass death sentences only in exceptional cases: when Gentiles contravened the ban, inscribed on the wall that divided the Court of the Gentiles from the Temple courts, not to trespass beyond the gates leading into the Temple, and perhaps for other clearly religious offenses (compare *m. Sanh.* 7:2: the stoning of a priest's daughter for adultery; compare John 7:53–8:11).

E. The Apostles and the Sanhedrin

Luke reports several encounters between leading representatives of the followers of Jesus with the Sanhedrin. Peter and John appear before the Sanhedrin (consisting of chief priests, rulers, elders, and scribes) on account of their preaching about the risen Jesus (Acts 4:5–6:15). In Acts 5:21, 34 the high priest "and those with him" convene the Sanhedrin (here also called **gerousia**), which included Pharisees such as Gamaliel, who successfully counsels against killing Peter and the apostles. In Acts 6:12-14 the elders and the scribes bring Stephen before the Sanhedrin for his inflammatory statements about the Temple and the law of Moses; Stephen is allowed to speak, but he is eventually executed (Acts 7:54-58).

If Luke gives a historically accurate account, when Paul is arrested in the Temple after his presence caused disturbances, a Roman centurion manages to convene the chief priests and the entire Sanhedrin in order to establish the accusations of Paul's Jewish opponents (Acts 22:30). In this meeting of the Council, both Pharisees and Sadducees are present and discuss matters pertaining to the law, including the resurrection from the dead (Acts 23:6-9, 28-29). After Paul has been taken to Caesarea, the high priest Ananias and several elders (members of the Sanhedrin), together with a lawyer with rhetorical training, present their accusations against Paul before the Roman governor (Acts 24:1).

Josephus recounts that the Sadducean high priest Ananus II convened "the judges of the Sanhedrin" to indict James, the brother of Jesus, for transgressing the law and to execute him (*Ant.* 20.200), an event that took place in the year 62 CE (compare Acts 12:2). *See* JERUSALEM; PRIESTS AND LEVITES TRIAL OF JESUS.

Bibliography: Raymond E. Brown. *The Death of the Messiah* (1994); David Goodblatt. *The Monarchic Principle: Studies in Jewish Self-Government in Antiquity* (1994); Martin Goodman. *The Ruling Class of Judaea: The Origins of the Jewish Revolt Against Rome A.D. 66–70* (1987); Martin Hengel. *Judaica et Hellenistica I.* (1996); Sidney B. Hoenig. *The Great Sanhedrin: A Study of the Origin, Development, Composition, and Functions of the Bet Din ha-Gadol during the Second Jewish Commonwealth* (1953); Howard C. Kee. "Central Authority in Second-Temple Judaism

and Subsequently: From Synedrion to Sanhedrin." *Annual of Rabbinic Judaism* 2 (1999) 51–63; Lee I. Levine. *Jerusalem: Portrait of the City in the Second Temple Period (538 B.C.E–70 C.E.)* (2002); Hugo D. Mantel. *Studies in the History of the Sanhedrin* (1965); Steve Mason. "Chief Priests, Sadducees, Pharisees and Sanhedrin in Acts." *The Book of Acts in Its Palestinian Setting.* R. Bauckham, ed. (1995) 115–77; James S. McLaren. *Power and Politics in Palestine: The Jews and the Governing of Their Land, 100 BC–AD 70* (1991); Shmuel Safrai. "Jewish Self-Government." *The Jewish People in the First Century.* S. Safrai and M. Stern, eds. (1974) 377–419; E. P. Sanders. *Judaism: Practice and Belief 63 BCE–66 CE* (1992); Emil Schürer. *The History of the Jewish People in the Age of Christ (175 B.C.–A.D. 135).* Rev. ed. (1973–87); Victor Tcherikover. "Was Jerusalem a 'Polis'?" *IEJ* 14 (1964) 61–78.

ECKHARD J. SCHNABEL

SANSANNAH san-san′uh [סַנְסַנָּה *sansannah*]. A town listed in the territory of Judah near the border with Edom (Josh 15:31). Its name, which means "date palm branch," suggests a fertile grove in the parched plains of the Negev region. Its probable location is present-day Khirbet esh-Shamsaniyat, near the hills of Hebron. Sansannah may also appear in the descriptions of the territory of Simeon under the names HAZAR-SUSAH (Josh 19:5) and Hazar-susim (1 Chr 4:31).

LJUBICA JOVANOVIC

SANT, WADI ES. The Arabic name means "valley of the acacia." The Wadi es-Sant is located about 15 mi. west by southwest of Bethlehem. It is identified with the biblical valley of Elah (literally, "valley of the terebinth") where David slew Goliath (1 Sam 17:2, 19; 21:9). *See* ELAH, VALLEY OF.

JEFFRIES M. HAMILTON

SAPH saf [סַף *saf*]. Saph fought for the Philistines against David and was killed at Gob (2 Sam 21:18). The parallel passage in 1 Chr 20:4 renders Saph as Sippai (sippay סִפַּי) and the unknown location of Gob as Gezer. The NRSV calls Saph "one of the descendants of the giants"; the Hebrew text identifies him as a descendant of the Raphah (harafah הָרָפָה), leading scholars to associate him and his fellows with the REPHAIM (2 Sam 21:22).

LJUBICA JOVANOVIC

SAPPHIRA suh-fi′ruh [Σάπφιρα *Sapphira*]. In Acts 5:1-11, Sapphira and her husband ANANIAS sell a piece of property but turn over to the apostles only a portion of the proceeds, for which they are miraculously killed. While the nature of their sin and the severity of their punishment are difficult to understand, the narrative contrasts their behavior to that of BARNABAS, who turned over the full proceeds from the sale of his property to the apostles (Acts 4:36-37).

RUBÉN R. DUPERTUIS

SAPPHIRE [סַפִּיר sappir; σάπφιρος sapphiros, ὑάκινθινος hyakinthinos]. Listed as the fifth stone in the high priest's breastpiece (Exod 28:18, 39:11); used in association with theophanies (Exod 24:10; Ezek 1:26, 10:1); as adornment for the king of Tyre (Ezek 28:13); in comparison to wisdom (Job 28:6, 16); as a metaphor for beauty (Lam 4:7; Song 5:14); in the foundation walls of the New Jerusalem (Isa 54:11; Rev 21:19); and in the gates of Jerusalem (Tob 13:16). Whereas the NRSV uses sapphire as a component of the apocalyptic horse riders' breastplates (Rev 9:17; huakinthinos), other English translations use JACINTH. The Hebrew sappir is probably one of the few words from the OT related to its English equivalent: sapphire. Sapphire has been mistakenly associated with LAPIS LAZULI because of its deep blue color, so the NRSV uses either term when translating the same Hebrew word.

Sapphire, a true gemstone, is the same mineral as ruby, corundum, but has a blue color originating from iron and titanium. Sapphires were used more for beads and rings than for engravings, and they were prevalent in the Roman period (presumably because of increased trade with central Asia).

ELIZABETH E. PLATT

SARAH sair′uh [שָׂרָה sarah ; Σάρρα Sarra]. 1. Sarah (Gen 11:29–13:1; 16:1–18:15; 20:2–21:12; 23:1-2, 19; 24:36; 25:10, 12; 49:31; Isa 51:2; Rom 4:19; Gal 4:21-31; Heb 11:11; 1 Pet 3:6) is the first matriarch in the Hebrew line. Her original name Sarai (saray שָׂרַי) is an earlier form of Sarah, both meaning "princess." She is renamed at the time that the birth of her son, Isaac, is announced (Gen 17:15). Her husband is Abram (renamed Abraham in Gen 17:5), one of the three sons of Terah. Her parentage is unclear. When Abram passes Sarai off as his sister to King Abimelech of Gerar, Abram claims that she is his half-sister, the daughter of his father, but not of his mother. However, when Gen 11 says that Abram and his brother Nahor married Sarai and Milcah, respectively, it states that Milcah is the daughter of Haran, one of Terah's sons, but it does not indicate Sarai's father.

Sarai travels with Abram from Ur of the Chaldees in southern Mesopotamia via Haran in northern Mesopotamia to Canaan in response to God's promise of land and descendants (Gen 11). Having arrived in Canaan, famine forces them to flee to Egypt where the promise of offspring is immediately threatened (Gen 12). Abram passes Sarai off as his sister because he is afraid that he will be killed because of Sarai's great beauty. Sarai is taken into Pharaoh's house as a wife, and Abram is given much livestock and servants. God, however, is not pleased and sends plagues upon Pharaoh. Pharaoh sends them away with all their possessions. The narrator does not pass any explicit moral judgment on Abram's behavior, but focuses rather on God's saving the vulnerable Sarai. The incident foreshadows the future bondage of the Hebrews in Egypt and God's rescue of the oppressed people.

A similar incident occurs later when the couple (now named Abraham and Sarah) is in Gerar (Gen 20). This time, however, God warns Abimelech, the king of Gerar, in a dream. The narrator states that Abimelech has not yet touched Sarah. Again, Abraham is enriched, but the reader wonders whether Abraham is a slow learner or whether perhaps one incident has turned into two after centuries of storytelling.

Sarah is the first of the line of Hebrew matriarchs who has difficulty bearing a child (see BARREN, BARRENNESS). She decides to do something about the problem and gives HAGAR, variously described as her handmaid and her slave, to Abraham to bear a child for her, a custom known from Mesopotamian sources. Some commentators criticize Sarah for taking matters into her own hands and view her giving of Hagar to Abraham as a sign of her lack of faith in God's promises. Others note that the text does not report that Sarah had heard the promises made to Abraham. Still others believe that she is a model of human involvement in God's promises, even though it turns out that she is able to bear her own child and the family tensions created by the surrogate motherhood are terrible. Surrogate motherhood did not always involve these kinds of challenges, as is clear from the stories of Rachel and Leah and their handmaids, who also served as surrogate mothers. Rachel and Leah had issues with each other, but not with the surrogate mothers.

The plan does not turn out as Sarah apparently intends. Once Hagar is pregnant she becomes contemptuous of Sarah. Sarah blames Abraham, who gives her free rein to deal with Hagar. Sarah abuses Hagar, though in precisely what manner is not described. Hagar runs away, and the angel of the Lord instructs her to return, but not before promising her a son to be named Ishmael who will be a "wild ass of a man" (Gen 16:12). Hagar returns, bears a son, and Abram (soon renamed Abraham) rather than Sarah (as in the other cases of vicarious motherhood in the Bible) names the child Ishmael.

When the ninety-nine-year old Abraham is told by God that he and the ninety-year-old Sarah will have a son, Abraham laughs; God gently but firmly reaffirms the promise (Gen 17). Later, when three men come to visit Abraham and they are eating the meal that Abraham and Sarah have prepared, the Lord (one of the men/angels?) asks Sarah's whereabouts. When told, the Lord again announces the birth of a son in the spring. Sarah, who can hear the conversation outside her tent, laughs, and the Lord asks Abraham why, pointing out her lack of faith in God's ability to do anything. Sarah denies her laughter out of fear (Gen 18). While the couple may have been older, their extremely advanced age may not be literal, as the OT sometimes attributes long years to show respect (see AGING).

After Isaac's birth, Sarah sees Ishmael playing with Isaac (Gen 21:9). The word "playing" comes from the same root as Isaac's name in Hebrew. Some interpreters have seen sexual abuse in this incident, but even if Ishmael's behavior is innocent, the name Isaac (yitskhaq יִצְחָק) from the same root as the word tsakhaq (צָחַק, "laugh" or "play") implies that Ishmael was doing what Isaac was intended to do, thus usurping his role. Sarah implores Abraham to send Hagar and Ishmael away. Abraham is reluctant, but God tells Abraham to obey Sarah because the divine promise to Abraham will be fulfilled through Isaac, and that Ishmael will also become a nation. Some commentators have viewed this expulsion as cruel; others have understood it as emancipation.

In the rivalry between Sarah and Hagar, modern interpreters have sometimes seen resonance with modern racial tensions; in this reading Sarah becomes the wealthy, white wife and Hagar the poor black African slave (see SLAVERY). However, scholars cannot be sure how the skin color of the two women compared, and they may have been more similar in complexion than contemporary readers imagine. In addition, the oddity of a Hebrew woman having an Egyptian handmaid/servant/slave should be noted. Generally, the Egyptians were in a higher social position than were the Hebrews in ancient times, and here the story may prefigure (in reverse) the Hebrews' subsequent slavery to the Egyptians.

Modern readers often see Sarah as cruel. Some commentators explain that Sarah was part of a social system that put pressure on her to produce a male heir who would be her caretaker and financial support in old age. Sarah dies before Abraham, but if the reverse had been true, and if Ishmael had been Abraham's primary heir, Sarah and Isaac would have been the ones wandering in the wilderness, trying to eke out a precarious existence. Womanist and feminist commentaries discuss the implications of Hagar's status as a slave and her oppression, regardless of skin color.

After assuring that Isaac is Abraham's primary heir, Sarah largely disappears from the narrative. She plays no role in the near sacrifice of Isaac. She dies in Hebron, and Abraham buries her in Canaan in the cave of Machpelah. In Isa 51:2 she is described as the mother of the Hebrew people.

In the NT Sarah is mentioned along with Abraham as an exemplar of faith. In Rom 4:19 Abraham's faith in spite of his age and Sarah's barrenness is highlighted. In Rom 9:9 the focus is on the children of promise rather than of flesh; (Gen 18:10). In the allegory in Gal 4:21-31, Sarah (referred to simply as the "free" woman) represents the new covenant; she is the one whose children will be considered the true inheritors, whereas, ironically, Hagar represents the old covenant.

In Heb 11 various OT characters are praised for their faith. Sarah is among them, but several variants in the Greek manuscripts and in grammatical construction re-

sult in lack of clarity. The RSV renders 11:11: "By faith Sarah herself received power to conceive, even when she was past the age, since she considered him faithful who had promised." However, the NRSV translates, "By faith he [Abraham] received power of procreation, even though he was too old—and Sarah herself was barren—because he considered him faithful who had promised." Thus, it is not clear whether Sarah is herself lifted up as a model of faith or whether she is merely a footnote to Abraham's faith.

In 1 Pet 3:6 Sarah is presented quite differently. Here she is a model for wives' obedience to husbands. *See* ABRAHAM, OT; HAGAR; ISAAC; ISHMAEL, ISHMAELITES.

2. Sarah, the daughter of Raguel, is exorcised of the demon Asmodeus and marries Tobias, the son of Tobit, through the intervention of the angel Raphael (see, e.g., Tob 3:17; *see* TOBIT, BOOK OF).

Bibliography: Alice Ogden Bellis. *Helpmates, Harlots, and Heroes: Women's Stories in the Hebrew Bible* (1994).

ALICE OGDEN BELLIS

SARAPH sair´uhf [שָׂרָף saraf]. Means "burning, fiery." A descendant of Judah's son Shelah. According to the ambiguous passage 1 Chr 4:22-23, Saraph and his kinsmen were royal potters who either ruled over Moab or married Moabite women ("married into Moab"). It is possible that they returned to Lehem.

SARASADAI sair´uh-sad´i [Σαρασαδαί Sarasadai]. Ancestor of Judith (Jdt 8:1) listed as "son of Israel." A variant of ZURISHADDAI.

SARDIS sahr´dis [Σάρδεις Sardeis]. Sardis, located in the Roman province of Asia (present-day Turkey), was about 60 mi. from Smyrna and Ephesus. It was the capital of the Lydian Empire (late 7th cent. to mid-6th cent. BCE) and the home of the legendary King Croesus. Croesus ruled from ca. 560 to ca. 550 BCE. Throughout ancient history, it remained an important city for succeeding empires, serving as a key city for the Persian, Seleucid, and Roman administrators. Revelation 1:11 and 3:1-6 mention the city (*see* REVELATION, BOOK OF), and Obad 20 refers to Sardis as "Sepharad." Gyges was the first king of Sardis known to the Assyrians. The Assyrians called Gyges "Gugu." The name Gugu became "Gog" in Ezek 38–39 (see also Rev 20:8).

Hemer argued that Jews lived in Sardis in the 4th cent. BCE. They came for commercial reasons. Josephus writes that Antiochus III resettled 2,000 Jewish families there (*Ant.* 12.149). Jewish persons became integral members of society politically and financially. They built a large synagogue as well as a GYMNASIUM for the education of their sons. An unusual feature of the synagogue is the presence of Lydian religious reliefs. This type of assimilation of religious traditions, as well as the

Vanni/Art Resource, NY

Figure 1: The temple of Artemis in Sardis. This Hellenistic ionic temple (ca. 300 BCE) was enlarged in 175–170 BCE and in ca. 150 CE.

Greek-style education of their sons, indicates a level of accommodation by some Jews with their surrounding community.

The major deity was Artemis/Cybele, who resembled the Greek goddess Demeter. Coins bore her image/symbols and a large temple was built in her honor. Artemis/Cybele was the protector of the city of Sardis. Her customary attributes were ears and stalks of corn, poppy flowers, two flaming torches, and a coiled serpent. She was often depicted in a vehicle drawn by two winged serpents. The major male deities were Zeus Lydios, whose symbols were an eagle and a scepter. Other male gods included Heracles and Dionysus. Most male deities were to some degree consorts of Artemis/Cybele.

There was a strong interest in Sardis in life after death and Rev 3:1c ("you have a name of being alive, but you are dead") might reflect this tradition. A prime example is the Croesus legend that was made widespread (if not created) by Herodotus (*Hist.* 1). This version had extensive influence in antiquity. Croesus wanted to guard against Cyrus' advance. Sending messengers to various oracles, he received the answer he thought he wanted from the oracle at Delphi: that if he crossed the Halys, the frontier of the Lydian Empire, he would bring down a kingdom. Disregarding other alternatives, he fabricated reasons for a military campaign and captured Pteria. When Cyrus and his army arrived on the scene, Croesus and Cyrus fought an inconclusive battle.

Croesus withdrew to Sardis where he felt he would be safe for the winter, sending home his military allies from Egypt, Babylon, and Sparta until the spring. Cyrus, on the other hand, had no intention of waiting for spring to resume the battle. Unbeknownst to Croesus, Cyrus had quietly followed him. Cyrus laid siege to the city and Sardis fell in fourteen days. Cyrus took Croesus alive and placed him on a pyre to be burned alive. Croesus remembered the warnings of the sage Solon of Athens and cried his name. Learning of this, Cyrus changed his mind and decided to allow Croesus to live. However, the fire could not be extinguished. At this time, Apollo sent a rainstorm to save Croesus. Croesus then became an advisor to Cyrus. The kingdom that Croesus brought down was his own. Hemer sees pure legend here because the Persians considered fire sacred and would not desecrate it by associating it with death. Moreover, Croesus and Solon lived in different periods.

It could have been that Croesus mounted the pyre himself in order to avoid becoming a slave to Cyrus. Hemer has argued that such self-sacrifice would ensure immortality as one purified one's mortality by fire. Thus, this form of death might be a type of apotheosis for persons from that region in antiquity. Several examples would support this argument.

A major example is the Attis-Cybele cult, an excellent example of the indigenous Anatolian religion. It has been argued that the 6th-cent. BCE Minotaur relief discovered in Sardis is a Hellenized version of the *taurobolium*.

The *taurobolium* was a rite that reinvigorates the devotee with the life-blood of a slain bull. The devotee bathes in the blood.

The cult of Attis also reflected the seasons of the year: winter represented death; spring, rebirth. Attis and Cybele were also the guardians of the grave and the afterlife. Serpents were often associated with Cybele because they were reborn when they lost their skins. Along with the Croesus legend and the Attis-Cybele cult, other examples included Heracles' fiery death, the myth of Tylus and Masnes, and Pelops, a Lydian hero. Hemer sees parallels with these indigenous traditions and Rev 19:17–20:15. A resurrection faith such as Christianity would have been intelligible within such a context.

Sardis also sought the designation nēōkoros (νηωκόρος), an official site of the Roman imperial cult. In the eastern Roman provinces, the bestowing of divine honors upon the ruler had a long history. Many cultures believed their ruler was the son or adopted son of their national deity. When Alexander the Great conquered these lands, a new politico-religious reality faced the many peoples of his vast new empire. The people turned to traditional ways of relating to their rulers in order to relate to Alexander. While it was not unheard of to refer to a Greek ruler as an offspring of a god, non-Greeks took this affirmation much more seriously and reverently than did the Greeks. Alexander's Seleucid and Ptolemaic successors received similar honors. In turn, when Caesar Augustus became the sole ruler of the Roman Empire, he received similar forms of adoration. Price argues persuasively that the neokorate enabled these cities to relate to their rulers in meaningful, traditional ways. On the pragmatic side, it established positive commercial and political relationships between the *princeps* and the local municipality. On the one hand, it affirmed the loyalty of the municipality to the ruling power, often expressed in religious terms, while, on the other hand, it sought to bring imperial benefactions to the city.

Roman citizens in Asia were required to worship the divine Julius Caesar and the goddess Roma, while provincials were required to worship Augustus and the goddess Roma. Augustus' sister Octavia was worshiped in the 1st cent. BCE and Claudius' grandmother received divine honors in the 1st cent. CE. Sardis was one of several cities in Roman Asia that competed for and received the designation nēōkoros in the 1st and 2nd cent. CE. Persons who did not participate in this longstanding religio-political tradition would have been hard-pressed, if not outright harassed, to explain themselves. *See* ANGELS OF THE SEVEN CHURCHES; SEVEN CHURCHES.

Bibliography: C. J. Hemer. *The Letters to the Seven Churches of Asia in Their Local Setting* (2001); Simon

R. F. Price. *Rituals and Power: The Roman Imperial Cult in Asia Minor* (1984).

THOMAS B. SLATER

SAREA sair′ee-uh. One of five scribes, trained to write quickly, who recorded the Scriptures to be restored as God conveyed them to Ezra (2 Esd 14:24).

SARGON sahr′gon סַרְגוֹן sarghon]. Sargon II (Akk. Sharru-kin, "the king is legitimate") was king of Assyria (722–705 BCE). While Sargon is explicitly mentioned only once in the OT (Isa 20:1), his impact is reflected in numerous passages throughout the first part of the book of Isaiah, as well as in 2 Kgs 17:1-6, 24, 29-31 and 18:9-12.

Sargon's accession to the Assyrian throne is shrouded in darkness. First, he never mentions his father in his inscriptions, with the exception of a circular inscription on a tile pommel in which he declares himself to be the "son of Tiglath-pileser." More noteworthy is a fragmentary letter from an official to Sargon written in Neo-Babylonian script in which the official identifies TIGLATH-PILESER III as "your (Sargon's) father." This indicates that Tiglath-pileser III was the father of Sargon II, though it does not explain the lack of recognition of this filiation. Second, it is uncertain whether Yaba, the royal consort of Tiglath-pileser III, known from inscribed objects from a tomb recently discovered at Kalhu (Nimrud), was Sargon's mother or not. Found in the same sarcophagus with her skeleton is the skeleton of Atalia, the royal consort of Sargon, identifiable by inscribed objects in her name (*see* SENNACHERIB).

While recent scholarship has demonstrated that SHALMANESER V (727–722 BCE), who preceded Sargon II as king, died of natural causes, the ensuing internal struggles seem to point to a less than legitimate power seizure by Sargon. In one text, Sargon states that he pardoned 6,300 Assyrians that were "guilty" of rebellion, i.e., who were part of the opposition to him. Nevertheless, he deported them to Hamath. According to another text, Shalmaneser V had imposed grievous tax and corvée on Assur and Harran, which were traditionally free cities. As a result, the god Illil became angry and overthrew him and promoted Sargon. With these internal struggles, Sargon was unable to conduct a foreign campaign until his second year.

In that year (720 BCE), Sargon attempted the recovery of Babylonia, which was lost at his accession when Marduk-apla-iddina II (biblical MERODACH-BALADAN), the wily leader of the Chaldean tribe of Bit Yakin, seized the Babylonian throne. The ensuing battle of Der is recorded in three versions. Sargon claimed victory in his inscriptions, Marduk-apla-iddina did the same in his cylinder inscription, and the Babylonian Chronicle recorded that Marduk-apla-iddina's ally, the Elamites, defeated the Assyrians before Marduk-apla-iddina even arrived on the battlefield. Whatever happened tactically, the battle was a strategic lost since Marduk-apla-iddina ruled unchallenged until 710.

Also in 720, likely encouraged by the battle of Der, Iau-bi'di, the ruler of Hamath, organized a coalition against Sargon that included the states of Arpad, Simirra, Damascus, Hatarikka, and SAMARIA (Samaria is always listed last). Sargon defeated this coalition at the battle of Qarqar (where Shalmaneser III had fought a western alliance in 853 BCE). Iau-bi'di's public flaying while he was still alive is depicted in realistic detail on one of Sargon's reliefs.

Soon after this battle Sargon captured Samaria. The kingdom of Israel had become vassal to Assyria during the reign of Tiglath-pileser III (745–727 BCE), with all but the rump state of Samaria being annexed by Assyria in 732. Hoshea, the last monarch of this greatly reduced state, rebelled. In response, Shalmaneser V besieged Samaria, conquering the city in 722 (Babylonian Chronicle I i.27-32; 2 Kgs 17).

There are different views about the fall of Samaria. A number of scholars have interpreted the evidence as referring to a singular event. Thus, a few see the conquest as solely the work of Sargon II. Several think that Shalmaneser V initiated the siege, but Sargon II brought it to an end. And some believe that Sargon II simply usurped Shalmaneser V's accomplishment. But it is preferable to understand the evidence relating to two separate events: one to Shalmaneser's action in 722, and the other to Sargon's Levantine activities in 720. Sargon asserts in eight different inscriptions that he conquered Samaria (COS 2:293-297); and in every instance, this is tied to his 720 campaign. Thus Shalmaneser's and Sargon's actions were separate (the Mesopotamian sources do not conflate the two different events). On the other hand, the biblical narrative (2 Kgs 17) telescopes many years into its presentation, covering the entire Sargonid period (Sargon, Sennacherib, Esarhaddon and Assurbanipal). Sargon II was the king primarily responsible for the deportations from Samaria, as well as many of the deportations to Samaria.

After this reconquest of Samaria, Sargon subdued Judah (Isa 10:27-32 may possibly relate to this event). He captured Gibbethon and Ekron, and defeated an Egyptian army, destroying the Egyptian border city of Raphia (deporting 9,033 captives). He also reconquered Gaza (capturing its king Hanunu and deporting him).

In 716/715 BCE, Sargon was again in Philistia. This campaign was more commercial than military, and Shilkanni (Osorkon IV), the king of Egypt, sent Sargon twelve magnificent horses as a gift. (Isaiah 19:23 may refer to this expedition.)

In 714, Sargon unleashed a mighty campaign against his northern neighbor Urartu. This was one of the most significant achievements of Sargon's career, and it is recorded in a unique text known as "Sargon's Letter to the God."

In 712/711, ASHDOD rebelled, removing its pro-Assyrian king and replacing him with a commoner named

Yamani. Sargon dispatched his commander-in-chief who besieged and conquered Ashdod, Gath, and Ashdod-Yam. Isaiah 20:1 refers to this campaign. Although Yamani escaped to Egypt, a new inscription records his delivery into Assyrian hands (COS 2:299–300).

In 710, Sargon launched a major offensive against Marduk-apla-iddina to reassert Assyrian control over Babylonia. This campaign was a success and Marduk-apla-iddina had to seek refuge in Elam. Sargon actually ruled from Babylon until 707. In 706, Sargon completed his new capital, Dur-Sharruken ("Fort Sargon," modern Khorsabad). An Assyrian letter records that Israelite deportees were involved in the city's construction.

Only a year later in 705, Sargon was unexpectedly killed on the battlefield in Anatolia, and his body was not recovered (preventing an important traditional royal burial). Sargon was the first and only Assyrian king killed on the battlefield. The result was the abandonment of Sargon's new capital and immediate revolts throughout the empire.

Some scholars think that the song of Isa 14:4b-21 (applied secondarily to a king of Babylon) was describing Sargon's death, asserting that Sargon's fall was heard in the very depths of Sheol, rousing the Rephaim into sarcastic rejoicing. Thus Sargon II greatly impacted the southern Levant, both in his life and death, in politics as well as in literature. See ASSYRIA AND BABYLONIA.

Bibliography: B. Becking. *The Fall of Samaria: An Historical and Archaeological Study* (1992); M. Dietrich. *The Babylonian Correspondence of Sargon and Sennacherib* (2003); W. R. Gallagher. "On the Identity of Helel ben Shahar of Isa. 14:12-15." *UF* 26 (1994) 131–46; J. D. Hawkins. "The New Sargon Stele from Hama." *From the Upper Sea to the Lower Sea: Studies on the History of Assyria and Babylonia in Honour of A. K. Grayson.* G. Frame, ed. (2004) 151–64; G. W. Vera Chamaza. "Sargon II's Ascent to the Throne: The Political Situation." *SAAB* 6 (1992) 21–33; K. L. Younger Jr. "The Deportations of the Israelites." *JBL* 117 (1998) 201–27; K. L. Younger Jr. "The Fall of Samaria in Light of Recent Research." *CBQ* 61 (1999) 461–82; K. L. Younger Jr. "Recent Study on the Inscriptions of Sargon II: Implications for Biblical Studies." *Mesopotamia and the Bible: Comparative Explorations.* M. W. Chavalas and K. L. Younger, eds. (2002) 288–329.

K. LAWSON YOUNGER JR.

SARID sair'id [שָׂרִיד *saridh*]. A town on the southern border of Zebulon (Josh 19:10, 12), located in a region that prospered from the time of Israel's settlement down to the 1st cent. CE. Sarid was the closest town to Megiddo in northern Israel and thus was near the site of the battle between the Israelites and Canaanites described in Judg 4–5. The site has been identified with Tel Shadud, 5 mi. southwest of Nazareth. Excavations at nearby EN-SHADUD in the valley of Jezreel revealed a thriving community in the Early Bronze I Period.

LJUBICA JOVANOVIC

SAROTHIE suh-roh'thee [Σαρωθιέ Sarōthie]. One of Solomon's servants. First Esdras 5:34 mentions his descendants among those returning from the Babylonian exile with Zerubbabel. The analogous lists in Ezra 2:55-57 and Neh 7:57-59 do not record them.

SARSECHIM sahr'suh-kim [שַׂר־סְכִים sar-sekhim]. Personal name, partial name, or title of one of the royal Babylonian officials who took control of Jerusalem from ZEDEKIAH (Jer 39:3, 13). It is possible that scribes were confused by the list of foreign words in this verse, leading to errors in transcription; in the LXX Sarsechim is called Nabousachar (Nabousachar Ναβουσαχάρ). Sarsechim's title is RAB-SARIS, "chief of the eunuchs" (Jer 39:13).

LJUBICA JOVANOVIC

SASH [אַבְנֵט 'avnet, חֲגוֹרָה khaghorah, מוּסָר musar, קִשֻּׁרִים kishurim; ζώνη zōnē]. A girdle or belt, which may be richly decorated, worn around an inner or outer garment (e.g., Exod 28:39-40; Lev 8:7, 13; Isa 3:20, 24). The sash may be a symbol of authority (Isa 22:21; Rev 1:13). See CLOTH, CLOTHES.

SATAN say'tuhn [שָׂטָן satan; Σατανᾶς Satanas]. In the OT satan is a Hebrew noun meaning "adversary" or "accuser." When used to refer to one of the divine beings in the heavenly council of the Lord, it is transliterated and capitalized (Satan) in most English translations as if it were a proper name. In the NT Satan becomes more particularized as an opponent of God's intentions for humankind.

A. Satan in the Old Testament
    1. Human adversary
    2. Divine beings acting as a satan or adversary
      a. Numbers 22
      b. Job 1–2
      c. Zechariah 3
      d. 1 Chronicles 21:1
    3. Summary and overview
B. Satan in Second Temple Literature
C. Satan in the New Testament
    1. Satan in the Gospels and Acts
    2. Satan in the letters of Paul and in 1 Timothy
    3. Satan in Revelation
D. Concluding Overview
Bibliography

A. Satan in the Old Testament
   "Satan," an adversary who opposes or obstructs another, can be either a human or divine being.

1. Human adversary
   The Philistine chiefs were concerned that David might become their adversary ("satan") if he were allowed to accompany them in battle (1 Sam 29:4; see 2 Sam 19:22). Solomon in his message to Hiram King of Tyre says that he, unlike his father, who was surrounded by enemies, can build the Temple because God has given him rest with "neither adversary nor misfortune" (1 Kgs 5:4). Later, however, it is reported that the Lord raised up adversaries against Solomon, Hadad the Edomite (1 Kgs 11:14), and Rezon son of Eliada (1 Kgs 11:23, 25). The psalmists also refer to their human opponents as accusers ("satans") (Pss 71:13; 109:6, 20, 29).

2. Divine beings acting as a satan or adversary
   a. Numbers 22. The book of Numbers contains the story of Balaam, who encountered an angel of the Lord as an adversary ("satan"). Balaam was summoned from his home along the Euphrates by Balak, king of Moab, to travel to Moab in order to curse the Israelites, who had come from Egypt and settled next to him. Balak was frightened by the Israelites' presence; they were spreading over the whole area. Balaam's services were sought because he had a reputation that whoever he blessed would be blessed and whoever he cursed would be cursed. On two different occasions when messengers of Balak call upon Balaam requesting that he come to Moab, Balaam seeks the Lord's advice. The story makes it clear that the Lord is less than enthusiastic about Balaam traveling with the messengers to Moab and wants to ensure that Balaam will do only what the Lord tells him. When Balaam sets out on his journey riding on his donkey, the Lord becomes angry with him "and the angel of the LORD took his stand in the road as his adversary [satan]" (22:22). While the angel appears on three separate occasions, only the donkey is able to see him. Two times the donkey turns off the road, only to be beaten by Balaam. After the third appearance the way is so narrow that, to avoid the angel, the donkey lies down in the road. Again he is struck by Balaam, who threatens to kill him. At this point the donkey speaks, asking why Balaam is striking him. In the ensuing conversation with the donkey Balaam agrees that the donkey has not acted this way before. Then the Lord opens Balaam's eyes "and he saw the angel of the LORD standing in the road, with his drawn sword in his hand; and he bowed down, falling on his face. The angel of the LORD said to him, 'Why have you struck your donkey these three times? I have come out as an adversary (a satan), because your way is perverse before me'" (22:31-32). Because of the donkey's actions, Balaam's life is spared. It is clear from this text that the angel is performing the role of "a satan" at the behest of the Lord to obstruct Balaam's journey. The action of the adversarial angel is not malevolent. He is acting on behalf of the Lord to prevent Balaam from going to Moab without the presence of the Lord to ensure he does nothing without the Lord's approval.

b. Job 1–2. The story about the upright and blameless Job in the first two chapters of the book presents a heavenly being as "the satan." Although "the satan" is rendered in most English translations as "Satan," it should not be understood as a proper name. Proper names in Hebrew are not preceded by a definite article. Rather "the satan" refers to the role enacted by one of the heavenly beings (literally sons of God). When the sons of God, including the satan, present themselves before the Lord (1:6), the satan's task becomes clearer in his conversation with the Lord. The Lord asks: "Have you considered my servant Job? There is no one like him on the earth, a blameless and upright man who fears God and turns away from evil" (1:8). The Lord is pointing to an individual about whose behavior the satan is to gather information. The satan does this not in opposition to the Lord but as a functioning member of the heavenly entourage. When the satan proposes to test Job by taking away his riches, the Lord agrees, giving the satan power over everything Job possesses. However, the satan is not to harm Job himself. Chapter 2 of the book concerns a second encounter when the sons of God come to present themselves before the Lord, who again asks the satan, "Have you considered my servant Job?" The satan responds that Job has passed the test and his integrity remains. However, the satan proposes to the Lord that Job's integrity will not be sustained if he endures bodily inflictions. Again, the Lord puts Job in the satan's hands, indicating that the satan can do with Job as he pleases but that the satan is not to take Job's life. According to the narrative that closes the book (the satan is not mentioned), we are told that Job endures even these trials in which Job's body is covered with "loathsome sores." His integrity and loyalty to the Lord remain unaffected by the trials set by the satan, and the Lord restores Job's fortunes to twice as much as he had had before (42:10).

It is important to note here that the satan carries out the trials and tribulations he inflicts on Job only on the Lord's approval. However, unlike the satan who appears to Balaam, apparently only as the result of the Lord's initiative to protect Balaam, the Lord casts some blame on the satan for Job's afflictions. He says to the satan, "You incited me against him, to destroy him for no reason" (2:3).

c. Zechariah 3. The satan (Satan in most English translations) also appears in a scene depicted in Zechariah. The incident needs to be understood against the backdrop of the divisions in the community when the exiles are returning to Jerusalem. The setting resembles that of a trial in which Joshua the high priest is standing beside "the angel of the LORD" with the satan "standing at his right hand to accuse him" (3:1). Here the role of the satan appears to be like that of the satan in Job who gathers intelligence about the behavior of people to be used in a kind of legal adversarial role. However, the Lord himself, who appears abruptly in the scene, cuts short the proceedings, rebuking the satan for

his accusations (3:2). The angel orders the filthy clothes of Joshua to be removed and for Joshua to be dressed in rich apparel with a clean turban on his head. The story seems to suggest cleansing of any filthy conduct in which Joshua may have been involved so that he can be granted the normal privileges of a high priest. The satan appears to be rebuked because he is continuing to accuse Joshua when his guilt has been pardoned.

d. 1 Chronicles 21:1. A final reference is made to a satan in 1 Chr 21:1 where it is mentioned that he "incited David to count the people of Israel." This action angers the Lord, who punishes David. The reference to satan in this passage is ambiguous and offers several possible explanations: 1) Some understand its use here as a proper name, Satan, since the word does not have a definite article as it does in Job and Zechariah. However, this would be the only such reference in the OT. 2) Others interpret this satan to be like one of the heavenly beings in Job and Zechariah, who carries out the role of an adversary or accuser. Significantly, the Lord still holds David, not Satan, responsible for his actions. In 2 Sam 24:1, a passage that recounts the same episode, it is God's anger that incites David to carry out the census. David's culpability and the alternative passage in which God's anger provokes the action suggest that in the Chronicles passage satan may be operating not as a rival to God's power but as a member of the heavenly entourage. 3) Finally, some understand "a satan" who incited David to take the census to be a human adversary or enemy.

3. Summary and overview

Since the OT provides only limited glimpses of the divine beings surrounding the Lord and of angels who act as his messengers, the function of these "supernatural" satans is sketchy. It is clear that they carry out the role of a satan only with the Lord's approval. While there are indications in Job and Zechariah that the Lord rebukes the heavenly satan for being perhaps too zealous, there is no suggestion that a divine satan embodies evil opposing God's intentions for humankind. Indeed, in the OT God's power is without rival. Notions of Satan as the personification of evil opposing God's rule as his adversary or enemy are ideas about Satan's identity not found in the OT.

B. Satan in Second Temple Literature

Satan as a personal enemy opposed to God's reign over creation does appear in later tradition, but the lines of development are obscure. Some have argued that, when Persia came to power, Jewish thought was influenced by Zoroastrianism with its dualistic notion of a good god, Ahura Mazda, and an evil god, Angra Mainyu or Ahriman. But how this influence might have been brought to bear is unknown. The notion of an all powerful God responsible for both the good and bad experienced by his people, depending on their rightful actions (the prevailing view in the OT), may have become more difficult to sustain after the experiences of foreign rule. For example, the Seleucid king Antiochus Epiphanes, in the 2nd cent. BCE, outlawed both circumcision and the study of Torah and also rededicated the Temple to the Greek god Olympian Zeus. Incidents such as these would have been difficult to attribute to God's punishment for disobedience.

Both *Jub.* 7 and *1 En.* 6–7 relate the story of angels called the Watchers. They fail in their responsibility of supervising the earth and fall from heaven when they have sexual relations with the daughters of men whom they find to be desirable (see Gen 6:1-4). This union gives birth to the Nephilim, the giants, who increased lawlessness in the earth so that the thoughts of humankind were evil continually. The notion of angels watching over the earth calls to mind the satan in Job who seems to be carrying out a similar action when he walks to and fro in the earth. However, the leader of these fallen angels is not Satan but Semjaza in *1 Enoch* (6:3) and Mastema in *Jubilees* (10:8). In *1 Enoch* a story is told of another fallen angel, Azazel, who brought corruption and godlessness to the earth by introducing the arts of metallurgy.

In *Jubilees* Mastema provokes God to test Abraham's faith by commanding him to sacrifice his son Isaac (17:16-18)—an action similar to that of the satan in Job who incites God to test Job's faith. However, Mastema was put to shame for this request, and he fell from the heavenly realm. Although Mastema has some affinities with the satan of Job, Satan is also mentioned in *Jubilees.* At the close of the book, it is envisioned that at the end Israel will be cleansed "and there shall be no more a Satan or any evil one, and the land shall be clean from that time for evermore" (50:4; see 10:12). It is not clear if Mastema and Satan in these verses are the same, if Mastema is the evil one, or if the "evil one" is identified with neither of these.

Another satanic figure, Belial, appears in the *War Scroll* from Qumran (1QM), where he is described as leading the sons of darkness in the war against the sons of light. Belial is identified in the *War Scroll* as an angel of hostility whose purpose is to bring about wickedness and guilt. According to the *War Scroll,* in the final confrontation God will defeat Belial and his forces (1QM I, 14–15). Belial is mentioned by Paul although with the alternative spelling Beliar (2 Cor 6:15).

This short survey indicates that Jewish literature not found in the OT but influencing later Christian thought portrays different satanic figures. There are interesting parallels between these figures—but also differences. These complexities make it impossible to provide a well honed argument positing a clearly defined linear history of Satan's emergence as personified evil and the archenemy of God, the character he becomes in later Christian thought.

C. Satan in the New Testament

Satan becomes more identifiable as a personified figure in the NT, but once again only fleeting glimpses are given of his identity. *Satan* occurs thirty-three times in the NT. However, other names are used often interchangeably in the same literary context. These other names include: the Devil (ho diabolos [ὁ διάβολος], the usual LXX translation of the Hebrew word for Satan, occurs thirty-six times); Beelzebul (Matt 10:25; 12:24, 27; Mark 3:22; Luke 11:15, 18, 19); and Beliar (2 Cor 6:15). He is also designated as the tempter (Matt 4:3; 1 Thess 3:5), the evil one (Matt 13:19; 1 John 5:18), the accuser (Rev 12:10), the ruler of the demons (Matt 9:34; 12:24; Mark 3:22; Luke 11:15), the ruler of this world (John 12:31; 16:11), and the ruler of the power of the air (Eph 2:2).

1. Satan in the Gospels and Acts

Mark 1:12-13 is a short account of how the Spirit drove Jesus into the desert for forty days where he was tempted by Satan. Wild beasts surrounded Jesus, who was waited upon by angels. In a longer account in Matthew (4:1-11), the Devil, "the tempter," tries to entice Jesus to show himself as the Son of God. He suggests that Jesus turn stone into bread. He urges Jesus to jump off the parapet of the Temple since it is written that he would be supported by the angels. He urges Jesus to accept power over all the kingdoms of the earth if Jesus would fall down and worship Satan. Jesus refuses each time, and the last time he responds, "Away with you, Satan! for it is written, 'Worship the Lord your God, and serve only him'" (4:10). The devil departs and the angels wait on Jesus. A similar account occurs in Luke 4:1-13. Here Satan, who is performing the role of testing faith, appears to have some connection to "the satan" who tests Job and to Mastema who encourages God to test Abraham in *Jubilees.* The texts are not explicit, however, about whether God condones Satan's role or whether Satan is acting independently. That the text states that the "Spirit" leads Jesus into the desert leaves open the possibility that God was complicit in this testing. Satan is also understood in the parable in Mark 4:15 as taking away the word as soon as it is sown in individuals. In a preceding verse (4:12) Jesus quotes from Isa 6:9 in which God instructs the prophet to prevent the people from hearing the word. It is also possible here that God is condoning Satan's actions.

At the end of Matthew and Mark, when Jesus tells his disciples that he is the Messiah and that he must go to Jerusalem to endure suffering, Peter attempts to persuade Jesus not to go. His response to Peter is "Get behind me, Satan! You are a stumbling-block to me; for you are setting your mind not on divine things but on human things" (Matt 16:23; see also Mark 8:33). Here Peter's actions attempting to lead Jesus astray are likened to those of Satan who tempted him in the wilderness.

Satan also enters into individuals such as Judas Iscariot, who schemes to have Jesus turned over to the authorities (Luke 22:3 and John 13:27), and into Ananias who lies to the Holy Spirit about the sale of a piece of property (Acts 5:3). The passage in Luke 22:31, in which Jesus says to Simon Peter, "Satan has demanded to sift all of you like wheat," suggests that Satan may be acting here with the tacit approval of God.

While it is possible to draw lines of connection between these references in the Gospels to the heavenly being in the OT who acts as God's adversary (satan), other passages suggest relationships with the fallen angels noted in the Second Temple literature. In these stories the demons enter the world when the angels engage in sexual activity with the "daughters of man."

Satan is also associated with the demons who are presented in the Gospels as causing physical and psychological disabilities. Jesus frees the crippled woman whom Satan had bound for eighteen years (Luke 13:16). When Jesus heals the blind and dumb demoniac, he is accused by the Pharisees of casting out demons only by the power of Beelzebub, the prince of demons (Matt 12:24; Mark 3:22; and Luke 11:15). Jesus responds that he is not Satan, responsible for demonic possession. This is a nonsense since if he were Satan he would be casting out Satan, whose kingdom would fail (Matt 12:26; Mark 3:23; Luke 11:18).

Luke 10 speaks about the seventy who return to Jesus after he sent them out to prepare the way for him. They had been curing the sick, announcing that the "Kingdom of God has come near." When they return they say, "Lord, in your name even the demons submit to us!" (10:17). Jesus responds by saying that he observed Satan falling "from heaven like a flash of lightning" (10:18). This echoes notions of the Watchers who fall from heaven in *Jubilees* and *1 Enoch*. Paul's reference to Satan in Acts 26:18 when he speaks of opening the eyes of the Gentiles so that they may "turn from darkness to light and from the power of Satan to God" suggests what could be interpreted as a dualistic concept. Here Satan is reminiscent of Belial who leads the army of darkness, and this reference resonates with 2 Cor 6:15 where the contrast between the believer and unbeliever is paralleled by the distinction between Christ and Beliar.

2. Satan in the letters of Paul and in 1 Timothy

In Paul's letters Satan appears as an adversary. Paul says in 1 Thess 2:18 that he and his associates wanted to return to Thessalonica on many occasions "but Satan blocked our way." Paul exhorts the Corinthians not to be "outwitted by Satan; for we are not ignorant of his designs" (2 Cor 2:11). Sexual immorality is understood to be surrendering to the temptations of Satan (1 Cor 7:5), and Paul instructs that a man who is living with his father's wife should be given "over to Satan for the destruction of the flesh, so that his spirit may be saved on the day of the Lord" (1 Cor 5:5; see 1 Tim 1:20; 5:15). Paul also says that "a thorn was given me in the flesh, a messenger of Satan to torment me, to keep me from being too elated" (2 Cor 12:7). Whether this is a physical illness or an opponent is not clear.

In some ways the role of Satan in the passages just cited links with that of the satan, the adversary, in the OT. However, other passages depict Satan as like a fallen angel. In 2 Cor 11:14, Paul says that "Satan disguises himself as an angel of light," recalling the figure of Belial. Paul also speaks of "the lawless one" in 2 Thess 2:9 as delaying the coming of the day of the Lord. The "lawless one" is described as being "apparent in the working of Satan, who uses all power, signs, lying wonders" (2 Thess 2:9). The lawless one "opposes and exalts himself above every so-called god or object of worship, so that he takes his seat in the temple of God, declaring himself to be God" (2:4). His identity is not known, but it is conjectured that he may be the Roman emperor, some other supernatural being, or perhaps Satan himself.

At the end of his letter to the Romans Paul says, "The God of peace will shortly crush Satan under your feet. The grace of our Lord Jesus Christ be with you" (16:20). Traditionally, this verse has been associated with God's curse on the serpent in Gen 3:15. However, this association, which may seem unproblematic when read uncritically in light of subsequent theological thought, is not straightforward. In the Genesis passage the curse involves continual enmity between the offspring of the woman and the offspring of the serpent. The passage in Paul also has parallels with Jesus' words in Luke 10:18-19. After seeing Satan fall from heaven like a flash of lightning, Jesus gives his followers the "authority to tread on snakes and scorpions, and over all the power of the enemy."

3. Satan in Revelation

In the beginning chapters of Revelation, "Satan" is used when John writes to the angels in the seven churches. Here the phrase "synagogue of Satan" is used twice (2:9 and 3:9) for those who are slandering the members of the churches. The slanderers are falsely laying claim to being Jews. These references to the synagogue of Satan appear to be associated with Satan (2:10) as one who is testing the people in the role of an adversary. "Satan's throne" and the place "where Satan lives" (2:13) apparently refer to the specific location of a particular individual who is testing the faith of the church members. "The deep things of Satan" (2:24) appear to be heretical teachings that test the faith.

Although the idea of Satan as an adversary who tests faith is possible, images in the book of Revelation also emphasize the dualistic struggle between the good God and Satan as the embodiment of evil. The devil who is also called Satan is identified with the dragon that was thrown down along with the angels (12:9). This throwing down with the angels resonates with the stories of the Watchers who were thrown out of heaven. The dragon is an allusion to the monster that inhabited the chaotic waters when God created the world. In Ps 74:13-14 the Lord is praised because he "broke the heads of the dragons in the waters" and "crushed the heads of Leviathan" (see also Ps 89:10).

At the end of Revelation the angel will come down and bind Satan (the devil, the dragon) and throw him into the abyss for a thousand years before he is released for a short time (20:2, 7). The binding of Satan is evocative of the account of angels in the book of *Jubilees* who bound Mastema to prevent him from accusing the children of Israel when they crossed the Red Sea (48:15).

D. Concluding Overview

In the Bible, Satan is not a well-defined figure. There are some differences between the notion of Satan in the OT and the NT, and nowhere is there a definitive description of Satan. As a number of recent publications have pointed out, Satan is a character who continued to develop post-canonically in different directions in Christian history. *See* BEELZEBUL; COSMOGONY, COSMOLOGY; LUCIFER.

Bibliography: Henry Ansgar Kelly. *Satan: A Biography* (2006); Elaine Pagels. *The Origin of Satan* (1995); T. J. Wray and Gregory Mobley. *The Birth of Satan: Tracing the Devil's Biblical Roots* (2005).

EDGAR W. CONRAD

SATED. *See* ABUNDANCE; CONTENTMENT; FULL, TO BE OR TO FILL; PROSPERITY.

SATHRABUZANES sath´ruh-byoo´zuh-neez [Σαθραβουζάνης Sathrabouzanēs]. Official in 1 Esd 6–7 who is called SHETHAR-BOZENAI in Ezra 5–6.

SATIRE. *See* IRONY AND SATIRE.

SATIRE ON THE TRADES. *See* DUA-KHETY, INSTRUCTION OF.

SATISFACTION [שָׂבַע sava‘; εὐάρεστος euarestos]. The fulfillment of a want, need, or appetite. In Prov 18:20, the term denotes the satisfaction that comes from productive speech.

The fourth Servant Song (Isa 52:13–53:12) states that the Servant of the Lord will somehow experience satisfaction following his own suffering and death (Isa 53:7-9). The Servant was "cut off from the land of the living" (Isa 53:8), and yet Second Isaiah asserts that "out of his anguish he shall see light; he shall find satisfaction through his knowledge" (Isa 53:11). The second line of v. 11, in developmental parallelism with the first, explains that the Servant's satisfaction will result from his having seen "light," which apparently means that in the end he will recognize that what he has done has not been in vain.

In Titus 2:9, Paul instructs slaves to be "submissive to their masters" and to give them "satisfaction in every respect," apparently with a view toward the transformation of oppressive relationships (compare Eph 6:5).

RALPH K. HAWKINS

SATRAP, SATRAPY say´trap, say´truh-pee [אֲחַשְׁדַּרְפְּנִים ’akhashdarpenim; אֲחַשְׁדַּרְפְּנַיָּא ’akhashdarpenayya’; σατραπεία satrapeia, σατράπης satrapēs]. The title of a governmental official who ruled over a large portion of the Persian Empire. This term seems to have originated during the reign of Darius I (521–486 BCE) and continued until the time of Alexander the Great. The Persian term means "protector of power or kingdom." It appears on the Behistun inscription to describe two of Darius I's representatives. Herodotus (*Hist.* 3.89–94) records that Darius I created twenty satrapies and placed a satrap to rule each, although the number of satrapies varies in Herodotus. Syro-Palestine was a part of the Fifth Satrapy, which was known as the "Province beyond the River." In the Bible, *satrap* appears almost exclusively in the plural (Ezra 8:36; Esth 3:12; 8:9; 9:3; Dan 3:2, 3, 27; 6:1-7; 1 Esd 3:2, 14, 21; 4:47, 49). Daniel 6:1 mentions 120 satraps, but this number probably includes governors (compare Esth 1:1). The satrap had great powers, which included absolute authority in his satrapy, and he answered only to the great king. The Persian kings, in order to keep satraps under control, retained the appointment of the satrap's secretary and chief financial officer. The king also sent messengers to monitor the satraps' activities.

JOHN D. WINELAND

SAUL. *See* PAUL, THE APOSTLE; SAUL, SON OF KISH; SHAUL.

SAUL OF TARSUS. *See* PAUL, THE APOSTLE.

SAUL, SON OF KISH sawl [שָׁאוּל sha’ul; Σαούλ Saoul, Σαῦλος Saulos]. Means "one requested, asked for," likely a shortened form of a name meaning "requested of Yahweh" and comparable to Shealtiel, "I requested [him] of God." The name is attested in Assyrian spelling (sa-u-li), and a similar name occurs in a 3rd-cent. CE Aramaic honorary inscription from Palmyra (sh’yl’). Saul was the first king of Israel according to the book of Samuel.

A. Family
B. Biblical Narratives: Literary Craft and Creativity
  1. Birth (1 Samuel 1)
  2. Designation as king (1 Samuel 9–11)
  3. Rejections (1 Samuel 13–15)
  4. Rivalry with David (1 Samuel 16–2 Samuel 1)
C. Saul in Historical Perspective
  1. Political role

2. Nature of Saul's kingdom
   a. Length of reign
   b. Capital
   c. Military achievement
   d. Administration
   e. Extent of domain
Bibliography
D. Saul in Second Temple Judaism and the New Testament

A. Family

The Bible contains contradictory information about Saul's family. The introduction to him in 1 Sam 9:1 calls him the son of a wealthy or prominent Benjaminite and traces his ancestry back five generations, thus: Saul < KISH < Abiel < Zeror < Becorath < Aphiah. But the last three of these names are not found in other Benjaminite genealogies in the Bible. Similarly, 1 Sam 10:21 refers to Saul as a Benjaminite of the otherwise unknown clan of the Matrites. Elsewhere, 1 Chr 8:29-34; 9:35-40 place Saul in the line of the Gibeonites, who are subsumed under the Benjaminites (8:40), and they name NER, rather than ABIEL, as Saul's grandfather (8:33; 9:39). The only other mention of Abiel in the Bible (1 Sam 14:50-51) has him as the father of Ner, presumably Saul's uncle, but does not relate him to Kish, Saul's own father. The description "Saul's uncle" could also refer to ABNER rather than to Ner.

Saul had a wife, AHINOAM (1 Sam 14:50), and a concubine, RIZPAH (2 Sam 21:8). As was the case with his forebears, the various references to Saul's children do not agree. Three sons (JONATHAN, Ishvi, and Malchishua) and two daughters (MERAB and MICHAL) are attributed to him in 1 Sam 14:49. But then 1 Sam 31:2 (//1 Chr 10:2) names Jonathan, Abinadab, and Malchishua as the three sons killed with Saul on Mount Gilboa. Saul's successor is ISHBOSHETH (NRSV, Ishbaal; 2 Sam 2:8), which probably reflects a pious scribal substitution of bosheth (בֹּשֶׁת, "abomination") for the divine name ba'al (בַּעַל). Eshbaal is found in some early Greek versions (Eisbaal Εἰσβάαλ) and in Chronicles (1 Chr 8:33; 9:39). The unanticipated appearance of Ishbaal leads Van Seters to suggest that the material about him is a post-Dtr addition to Samuel. The Chronicles verses just cited harmonize the lists in Samuel and identify Ishvi with Eshbaal. This identification requires the interchange of the first letters of the names (ALEF [ʾ א] and YOD [y י]) or the loss of the alef in the full orthography of Ishbaal. Additionally, it requires the assumption that Ishvi (yishwi יִשְׁוִי) was a misspelling of Ishyo (yishyo [יִשְׁיוֹ], transposing WAW and yod) with –yo being an abbreviation for the name Yahweh, which might be replaced by the epithet baal (lord). Also problematic for this identification is that Ishvi is listed as Saul's second son in 1 Sam 14:49, while Ishbosheth/Ishbaal seems to be his youngest. Saul's two sons by Rizpah were executed by David, as were five of his grandsons through Merab (2 Sam 21:8-9). The im-plication is that only Jonathan's son MEPHIBOSHETH, perhaps originally MERIB-BAAL (1 Chr 8:34; 9:40) was left to Saul's line, and it is through his son Micah that the line is traced for nine more generations (1 Chr 8:35-38; 9:41-44).

B. Biblical Narratives: Literary Craft and Creativity

The narratives about Saul in the OT are effectively limited to the book of 1 Samuel, plus 2 Sam 1 and 1 Chr 10 (//1 Sam 31). Otherwise, there are scattered references to him in 2 Samuel and Chronicles, and in the headings of a handful of psalms (18; 52; 54; 57; 59), and Isa 10:29.

1. Birth (1 Samuel 1)

The Bible has no account of Saul's birth. However, the story of SAMUEL's birth (1 Sam 1) appears to derive, at least in part, from an original story about Saul. This assertion is based on the puns it contains, all of which relate to Saul's name, not Samuel's. Thus, the verb "ask, request" (sha'al שָׁאַל) occurs repeatedly in 1:20, 27, 28. Verse 20 specifically relates the newborn son's name to this verb with a formula typically employed in etiologies. Yet the son's name is not Saul, as the pun leads the reader to expect, but Samuel. Then, v. 28 even uses the passive form sha'ul, identical to Saul's name, to designate the boy. These puns indicate that a narrative originally about Saul's birth has been secondarily used for Samuel.

2. Designation as king (1 Samuel 9–11)

Some scholars have perceived a three-fold ritual pattern in the story of Saul's rise to kingship, perhaps historically based and consisting of anointment, testing, and confirmation. However, close consideration of the three episodes in 1 Sam 9:1–10:16; 10:17-27a; 10:27b–11:15 indicates that once independent tales have been skillfully edited together in order to present a unique portrait of Saul becoming king in three stages—private anointing, public designation, and as a result of military victory. The updating of the term seer in 9:9 shows editing of the story in 9:1–10:16. The initial reference to the seer simply as "a man of God" (9:6) suggests that his identification as Samuel, who at this point in the overall narrative is Israel's national leader, is secondary. Samuel's revelation of the whereabouts of the donkeys (v. 20) immediately after his statement that he would reveal to Saul "all that is on your mind" the next morning (v. 19) indicates that a tale about Saul's search for lost animals has been editorially refocused into a story of his anointing as king. In the original tale, the nameless "man of God" required the intervening night to inquire of Yahweh and receive a revelation about the donkeys' whereabouts. Thus, those elements of the present story that name Samuel and assume advance knowledge of his arrival and special status (e.g., vv. 22-24) are editorial. The original tale continued with Saul's overnight visit and dismissal the next morning (9:25-

26). The man of God informed Saul that his inquiry about the donkeys and need for food (see 9:7) would be met in a series of subsequent encounters (10:2-4). The editor, probably the Deuteronomistic historian (Dtr), added the account of Saul's anointing (9:27–10:1) and emphasized its private nature in the account of Saul's interview with his uncle (10:14-16), which in turn prepared for the subsequent story of his public election as king (10:17-27a).

Some scholars have posited two traditions behind this second story—one in which Saul was present and selected by lot (10:20-21a) and another in which he was chosen because of his height or by prophetic oracle (10:21b-24). While there may be older elements, the present account is probably Dtr's composition. The account's setting in Mizpah, the religious and administrative capital of Judah after Jerusalem's destruction in 586 BCE, indicates its later composition. Also, the use of a lottery, found elsewhere in the Bible for ferreting out law- and vow-breakers, hints at Dtr's negative orientation toward Saul. The doubt about Saul's ability to save Israel at the end of the story (10:27) provides a segue into the story of Saul's victory in 10:27b-11:15.

The story of Saul's rescue of Jabesh-Gilead has its proper beginning in the paragraph in 10:27b (NRSV) that was lost from the MT but can be restored on the basis of the LXX and the Dead Sea Scroll fragments (4Q51). The paragraph accounts for Nahash's aggression against Jabesh, which otherwise lay outside of the area of territorial dispute between Ammonites and Israelites. It also shows the once independent nature of the story it introduces. This independence is signaled by other features as well. The fact that the messengers from Jabesh do not deliberately go to Gibeah or to Saul, who only happens to find out about the crisis when he hears the people weeping (11:3-5), shows that he is not yet recognized as king. In the older version of the story, Saul was "made king" only after his victory (11:15). The reference to renewing the kingship (11:14) reflects editorial revision in order to fit this story into the sequence established by the previous two stories. The refusal of Saul (and Samuel) to execute those who doubted Saul's capability (11:12-13) is an obvious editorial link to the ending of the story of Saul's election by lot (10:27a). As in 9:1–10:16, the references to Samuel in this third story are part of the (Dtr) editorial revision.

In sum, two of the three stories about Saul's rise in 1 Sam 9–11 were originally independent tales that were revised to depict a three-stage process involving private and public designations followed by a military proving. Most, if not all, of this revision was effected by the Dtr, whose composition of 10:17-27a and the speeches in chaps. 8 and 12 alluded to problems with Saul's kingship.

3. Rejections (1 Samuel 13–15)
The original tale behind 9:1–10:16 appears to have continued with an account of Saul's defeat of the Philistine garrison at Gibeah/Geba and seizure of the Michmash pass underlying chaps. 13–14 (see especially 13:4) in compliance with the order in 10:5-7 to go there and "do whatever your hand finds to do" (an idiom for military activity; NRSV, "see fit to do"). Saul's victory has largely been attributed to Jonathan or replaced by one in which Jonathan is the hero. The perspective on Saul in chaps. 13–15 is now quite negative, as first his kingdom (13:14) and then his kingship (15:23, 26) are rejected. Saul's foolish vow detracts from the victory in between (chap. 14), which is largely attributed to Jonathan anyway.

Moreover, in the two stories about Saul's rejection, the nature of his offenses is far from clear. In 13:13, Samuel accuses Saul of not keeping Yahweh's commandment. But Saul waited the seven days specified by Samuel, who was late (13:8). Besides, Saul does not appear to be the only king who offered sacrifices himself. David's sons are called priests (2 Sam 8:18), and David himself donned the ephod and sacrificed (2 Sam 6:13-14). In the second story, probably a Dtr composition, Saul is accused of disobedience through failing to "utterly destroy" the Amalekites (1 Sam 15:14-23). This utter destruction (kherem חֵרֶם) was not unique to Israel and represented the ritual devotion of an enemy to the national god. Saul's claim to be saving the best of the animals for sacrifice, therefore, seems tantamount to the same thing—devotion to Yahweh but in a cultic setting rather than on the battlefield. As for AGAG, the Amalekite king, the fact that Saul kept him alive at the time does not necessarily mean that he had pardoned him. The issue is complicated by textual problems in 15:32. However, if Agag came before Samuel "in bonds," as is the most likely reading (NRSV, "haltingly"), fearing that "the bitterness of death" had arrived, then perhaps Saul had reserved him for ritual execution of the sort that he received from Samuel's hand (15:33).

The stories about Saul in 1 Sam 13–15, then, depict a tragic figure who cannot do anything right where Yahweh and Samuel are concerned because he is destined to fail or at least to be rejected in preference to the man after Yahweh's own heart, i.e., the man whom Yahweh favors (13:14). That man, of course, is David.

4. Rivalry with David (1 Samuel 16–2 Samuel 1)
The contrast between Saul and David is set up in 16:13-14, where Yahweh's spirit comes on David and abandons Saul. At first, their relationship is very close (16:21), and Saul relies on David to gain relief from the evil spirit (16:23)—an irony considering that David is, in a way, the cause of Saul's agitation. Following David's victory over Goliath, against whom Saul is impotent (1 Sam 17), the praise lauded on David evokes Saul's jealous suspicion (18:6-9) and leads him to undertake a series of subtle moves against David. The subtlety of these moves has been obscured by expansions in the MT that are recognizable by their absence from the LXX in

addition to their nature as doublets (18:1-5, 10-11, 17-19, 29b-30). In the remaining story, Saul first removes David from his presence by making him the commander of 1,000, perhaps hoping that David will fall in battle. The strategy backfires when David's military successes increase his popularity (18:12-16). Saul next offers his daughter Michal to David for a bride price of Philistine "foreskins" (likely a euphemism), in the hope that the Philistines will kill him. David's success wins him status and legitimacy as the king's son-in-law. Still, Saul attempts to arrest David the next morning, assuming that 19:11-17 describes the wedding night and was originally the direct sequel to 18:20-29a. The episode further shows how even Saul's own children favor David over their father, and this is also the point of the notice of Jonathan's restoration of David to Saul (19:1-7), which likely followed David's flight after his wedding night in an older stage of the material, particularly since Saul's overt attempt on David's life (19:8-10) seems to represent a decisive break between the two. Jonathan's further attempt to reason with his father on David's behalf elicits a comparable attack, confirming Saul's murderous intent (20:26-34). In all of these episodes, Saul is portrayed as insanely jealous and malicious toward David, whose innocence and beneficial leadership for Israel are evident in everyone else's devotion to him.

Saul's instability reaches its nadir in his slaughter of the priests of NOB (1 Sam 22:6-19). The use of prophetic frenzy to protect David (19:18-24) showed divine favor of David at Saul's expense. In attacking the priests, Saul tries to carry out the destruction he should have completed against the Amalekite enemies of Yahweh in chap. 15 and thus effectively wages war against God. As a result, Yahweh guides David away from Saul in the wilderness and protects him when Saul gets too close (chap. 23). Yahweh saves David from himself, when David becomes outraged (chap. 25) and gives David opportunities to kill Saul, which David piously declines (chaps. 24; 26). In both cases, Saul acknowledges that David is in the right and at least hints that he will be king. The two stories make clear that David had nothing to do with Saul's eventual death at the hands of the Philistines (1 Sam 31; 2 Sam 1). Saul's fate is sealed beforehand (1 Sam 28), and David is far away when it comes (1 Sam 27; 29). It is obvious that a pro-David, anti-Saul agenda infuses this material and has helped to shape it.

C. Saul in Historical Perspective

Absent any artifactual or inscriptional evidence, the Bible is the only source of historical information about Saul.

1. Political role

Saul in the Bible is clearly a transitional figure who moves Israel from charismatic leadership of the judges to monarchy. Scholars have proposed different models to explain this process. Older views regarded monarchy as a Canaanite political system borrowed by Israel in agreement with the cry of the people in 1 Sam 8:5 to be like "other nations." More recent scholarship, in contrast, sees it as the result of a continuous, natural process toward statehood, but the models differ. Alt understood the judges as charismatic figures whose intertribal leadership was temporary because it dealt with immediate external threats. Saul followed in the tradition of the judges in that his authority was military. But his leadership was permanent, albeit not hereditary—intended to last his lifetime in the face of the continuing threat from the Philistines. Miller and Hayes considered Saul more in continuity with figures like Jephthah, Abimelech, and (subsequently) David, rather than charismatic judges, as a self-styled military leader with a private army who imposed "protection" on local people in exchange for "gifts" of support. Eventually, Saul succeeded where Jephthah and Abimelech had failed in being proclaimed king. A third model, especially prevalent in the 1980s, adopted social-scientific approaches to suggest that Saul was properly a chieftain rather than a full-fledged king and that the period of his leadership was one of change in Israel from a segmented, egalitarian society to a monarchic state. Edelman, in contrast, argues that Saul was a full-fledged king and the founder of the Israelite state. She defines Saul's Israel as a territorial- (i.e., noncentralized) rather than a nation- or city-state, and eschews the use of comparative models taken from primary state formation, contending that Israel's development must be understood as a secondary state formation in the wake of the collapse of the empire system in Late Bronze Age Levant.

2. Nature of Saul's kingdom

The theories of Saul's political role have arisen in an effort to account for various features of Saul's reign that differ from those of his successors.

a. Length of reign. The regnal formula for Saul in 1 Sam 13:1 (MT) states that he was a year old when he began to reign and that he reigned two years. Assuming that the second figure, like the first, is incomplete, it seems likely that the original number was either twelve or twenty-two years. In either case, the formula is part of the chronological frame adopted by Dtr for the monarchy and as such may be artificial and historically unreliable. In the first story of his anointing (1 Sam 9:1–10:16) Saul seems to be a young man, unmarried and still living in his father's house. But in the continuation of that story in chap. 13, as it now stands, Saul is an older man with a grown son, Jonathan. While the stories set in Saul's reign could easily be placed within a period of just a few years, his military successes and the authority he develops over Israel in these stories imply a period of at least a couple of decades. Still, any estimate about the length of Saul's reign must remain speculative in view of the Bible's incomplete and inconsistent information.

b. Capital. Saul is widely associated in the Samuel narratives and even beyond (1 Sam 11:4; Isa 10:29) with GIBEAH, which appears to have served as his capital (1 Sam 22:6). However, the fact that his family tomb was in ZELA (2 Sam 21:14, probably Khirbet es-Salah between Jerusalem and el-Jib) strongly indicates that it, rather than Gibeah, was his home, and ZELZAH, where Saul was to meet the two men who informed him of the status of the lost donkeys (1 Sam 10:2) may be a misspelling of Zela. The identification of Gibeah is disputed. Often identified as Tel el-Ful, there is reason to believe that Gibeah and GEBA in 1 Sam 13–14 are identical and are both to be identified as Jaba' opposite Michmash on the other side of the pass, perhaps with Gibeah (meaning "hill") being the more general term for the elevation and Geba indicating the village proper. Control of the Michmash pass would have been strategically important for the access it afforded to the east–west route from the Jordan valley to the coastal plain and resulting control of the Benjaminite hinterland. A few scholars hold that Saul's home and capital was actually Gibeon (1 Chr 8:29-40; 9:35-44; *see* GIBEON, GIBEONITES), where Israel's first national sanctuary stood, but that Dtr suppressed this detail in favor of Gibeah out of bias toward Jerusalem. In either case, Saul's "capital" appears to have been much more rustic and unsophisticated than those of his successors as it lacked a palace and other accoutrements of typical Near Eastern kings.

c. Military achievement. In an unusually positive comment, 1 Sam 14:47-48 credits Saul with victories over Moab, Ammon, Edom, Zobah, the Philistines, and the Amalekites. The positive nature of the comment has led most scholars to consider it historically reliable. Some caution is in order, as the list is, with the exception of Lebanon, a register of the countries around Israel. There are narratives about Saul's battles with the Ammonites (1 Sam 11), Philistines (1 Sam 13–14; 17) and Amalekites (1 Sam 15), but none about battles with Moab, Edom, or Aram-Zobah. Nonetheless, the narratives, despite their generally negative perspective on Saul, agree about his military success, which would have been a significant factor in his inauguration of the monarchy and perhaps the state of Israel.

d. Administration. Saul's rule seems to have been primarily military in nature. This is suggested by the statement in 1 Sam 14:52 that there was hard fighting all of Saul's days. In the same passage, Saul's uncle, Abner, is the only named member of Saul's cabinet (14:50). As with his capital, Saul's administration was not as sophisticated as those of his successors. There are allusions to other offices—especially commanders of hundreds and of thousands (1 Sam 22:7) and the more general "servants" (1 Sam 18:5, 30)—all of which seem to describe military roles. This may be true as well of the enigmatic "chief of Saul's shepherds" (1 Sam 21:7 [Heb. 21:8]), who is later called the one in charge of (nitsav נִצָּב) Saul's servants (22:9). While the exact role of these different officials remains unclear, they suggest that Saul developed a standing army that may have been supported by the spoils of battle and "gifts" secured through intimidation.

e. Extent of domain. The places through which Saul and his servant passed in their search for the lost donkeys (1 Sam 9:4) hint at the scope of his initial kingdom, encompassing Benjamin and the highlands of Ephraim. Certainly, this area remained the heartland of Saul's domain. After his death, 2 Sam 2:9 reports the territories to which Ishbaal laid claim, namely Gilead, the Ashurites, Jezreel, Ephraim, Benjamin, and all Israel. The claim is clearly idealized, considering that Ishbaal at the time is ensconced in Mahanaim east of the Jordan where he had been forced to flee from the Philistines. It is also not clear what precise area may be intended by each of the names in the list. For instance, "Gilead" may simply refer to the region around Mahanaim, rather than the entire hill country later identified as Gilead, and "Jezreel" may not have included the entire length of the Valley; Saul's death on Mount Gilboa ceded at least the eastern end of the Jezreel to the Philistines. The identity of "Ashur" is disputed, some associating it with the southwestern Ephraimite highlands, others taking it as a mistake for "Geshur," located in the Golan Heights. In all cases, there were no firm borders as with modern states. Territorial claims were based on temporary military forays, highlighting again the military focus of Saul's rule, followed by provisional loyalty on the part of the targets of the foray, and at best a loosely organized system of administrative outposts. The point may be illustrated by a potentially significant shift of prepositions in 2 Sam 2:9—Ishbaal was made king *to* ('el אֶל) Gilead, Ashur, and Jezreel, but *over* ('al עַל) Ephraim, Benjamin, and all Israel, whatever may have been intended by this final term.

Bibliography: A. Alt. "The Formation of the Israelite State in Palestine." *Essays on Old Testament History and Religion* (1989) 171–237; G. A. Cooke. *A Text-Book of North-Semitic Inscriptions* (1903); D. V. Edelman. *King Saul in the Historiography of Judah* (1991); C. S. Ehrlich, ed. *Saul in Story and Tradition* (2006); J. W. Flanagan. *David's Social Drama* (1988); F. S. Frick. *The Formation of the State in Ancient Israel* (1985); D. M. Gunn. *The Fate of King Saul* (1980); B. Halpern. *The Constitution of the Monarchy in Israel* (1981); W. L. Humphreys. "From Tragic Hero to Villain: A Study of the Figure of Saul and the Development of I Samuel." *JSOT* 22 (1982) 95–117; V. P. Long. *The Reign and Rejection of King Saul* (1989); P. K. McCarter Jr. *1 Samuel.* AB 8 (1980); J. M. Miller and J. H. Hayes. *A History of Ancient Israel and Judah* (2006); K. L. Tallqvist. *Assyrian Personal Names* (1914); J. Van Seters. *In Search of History* (2006).

STEVEN L. MCKENZIE

D. Saul in Second Temple Judaism and the New Testament

Two of the longest retellings of King Saul's story in Second Temple period texts appear in Josephus (*Ant.* 6.45–378) and PSEUDO-PHILO (*L.A.B.* 54; 56–65). In both cases, Saul's story is expanded and reinterpreted. The events at Nob and Endor become a focus of debate regarding which of Saul's actions led to the downfall of Israel's first king.

Pseudo-Philo, highlighting Saul's negative characterization, places the story of the slaughter of the priests of NOB immediately before the story of Saul's consultation with the necromancer at Endor (1 Sam 22; 28; *L.A.B.* 63–64; *see* ENDOR, MEDIUM OF). According to *L.A.B.* 63:2, it is Saul who kills Ahimelech along with the other priests, not Doeg (compare the MT, LXX, and Josephus). Thus Pseudo-Philo makes Saul directly responsible for the slaughter of innocent men. The result of the Endor scene according to Pseudo-Philo is that Saul willingly goes out to die in battle, and so will receive redemption for the murder of the priests and his persecution of David. This is clear from Saul's reaction to Samuel's prophecy, "Behold, I am going to die with my sons; perhaps my destruction will be an atonement for my wickedness" (64:9; *OTP* 2:377).

Although 1 Chr 10:13-14 lists the encounter of Endor as one of the primary causes of Saul's downfall, Josephus, in contradistinction, makes Endor the turning point in Saul's life. Like Pseudo-Philo, Josephus places part of the blame for Saul's demise on his order to kill the priests of Nob (*Ant.* 6.378). According to Josephus, when Saul learns that he will die, he willingly goes out to battle, thus becoming a tragic hero (*Ant.* 6.336; 343–49). Both Josephus and Pseudo-Philo offer redemption to Israel's first king by making his sacrifice at Gilboa an atonement for his sins against God's chosen agents, David and the priests of Nob.

Although direct reference to Saul only appears in Acts 13 in the NT, where Luke stops referring Paul as Saul, there are many parallels between Paul and his Benjaminite forebearer. In a speech similar to Stephen's that recounted Israel's history, Paul says, "Then they asked for a king; and God gave them Saul son of Kish, a man of the tribe of Benjamin, who reigned for forty years. When he had removed him, he made David their king" (Acts 13:21-22). By placing this proclamation of the replacement of King Saul with David on the lips of the Benjaminite Paul himself, Luke gives us notice that Saul of Tarsus is now Paul the apostle. Saul, the former persecutor of Jesus' followers—a Benjaminite like Saul who persecuted David, Jesus' ancestor—is officially the champion of the church as it further takes hold in the Gentile world.

HEATHER R. MCMURRAY

SAVE. *See* SALVATION.

SAVIOR. *See* SALVATION.

SAVIOR, DIALOGUE OF THE. This text has survived in a single exemplar of twenty-eight quite fragmentary papyrus pages written in the Coptic Sahidic dialect. The author is anonymous. The final compilation of the text took place no later than the 4th cent. CE, at which time the Nag Hammadi Codices were buried. The Coptic is a translation of an earlier Greek original, composed perhaps in the early decades of the 2nd cent. CE. (Sources employed in its composition may go back to the late 1st cent., however.) Its fragmentary condition makes literary analysis problematic. The text does not appear to be a unified composition. In structure it takes the form of a dialogue between the Savior (neither the name *Jesus* nor the title *Christ* appears) and his disciples (*Dial. Sav.* 124:23–127:19; 128:23–129:16; 131:19–133:21 [?]; 137:3–146:20). Judas, Matthew, and Mary are the named dialogue partners of the Savior (sometimes called *Lord*), but other unnamed members of the twelve disciples are also present and join in the dialogue as a group (compare *Dial. Sav.* 142:24-25). Other materials are inserted into this early dialogue source as the savior responds to questions posed by the disciples: parts of a creation myth, based on Gen 1–2 (*Dial. Sav.* 127:19–128:23; 129:16–131:18); a list of cosmological wisdom teaching (*Dial. Sav.* 133:21[?]–134:24); and an apocalyptic vision (*Dial. Sav.* 134:24–137:3). This composite "dialogue" was then provided an opening address by the Savior to introduce the dialogue (*Dial. Sav.* 120:2–124:22), and a final section of the Savior's ethical instructions concludes it (*Dial. Sav.* 146:20–147:22).

Parallels to the sayings of Jesus known from Matthew, Luke, John, and especially the *Gospel of Thomas*, echo in the Savior's responses, but there is no apparent literary relationship between the *Dialogue of the Savior* and these texts. The author does not directly refer to the canonical tradition. Similarities also exist between the language of the *Dialogue of the Savior* and language used in the Deutero-Pauline letters, Hebrews, and the Catholic letters, but again there is no direct literary dependence. In its present form the text is best described as Gnostic-Christian. It draws on the Christian tradition for its ornamental features (i.e., the Savior, the Twelve, and certain named disciples from the orthodox tradition), but in substance the ideas belong to a developed Gnostic tradition. The conceptual matrix of the *Dialogue of the Savior* is not the world of Palestinian Judaism but the highly speculative world of Gnosticism. The Savior in this text is a mystagogue initiating orthodox disciples into arcane gnosis. *See* GNOSTICISM; NAG HAMMADI TEXTS; THOMAS, GOSPEL.

Bibliography: Stephen Emmel, ed. *Nag Hammadi Codex 5: The Dialogue of the Savior* (1984); Marvin Meyer, ed. *The Nag Hammadi Scriptures* (2007) 297–311.

CHARLES W. HEDRICK

SAVIOR, GOSPEL OF THE. The modern title given to a vestigial collection of parchment fragments acquired by the Berlin Egyptian Museum in 1967 (P. Berol. inventory number 22220). Its character as an early Christian gospel was not recognized until 1996 during the early stages of its preparation for publication. The entire collection of three fragmentary sheets (twelve pages), plus two fragmentary leaves (four pages) and twenty-nine smaller fragments represents an original text of some thirty pages roughly 20 × 29 cm, to judge from the extant pages.

The vellum manuscript dates to the 5th/6th cent. The text is written in the Coptic Sahidic dialect but was originally composed in Greek no later than the latter half of the 2nd cent. The *Gospel of the Savior* was composed during a time when the oral Christian tradition still competed with the written tradition and the canonical Gospels had not yet achieved the prominence of position in early Christian orthodoxy that they later came to enjoy.

The text consists of a series of brief discourses by the Savior made in the context of dialogues between the Savior (the names *Jesus* and *Christ* do not occur) and his disciples. Only three disciples are named in the text: Andrew, John, and either Jude or Judas. Numerous parallels exist between the *Gospel of the Savior* and the NT Gospels; the closest parallels are with the Gospels of Matthew and John, which has led to the conclusion that the *Gospel of the Savior* knew these texts in some form. There are also close parallels to the Strausbourg Coptic Papyrus.

The *Gospel of the Savior* contains a saying attributed to the 2nd-/3rd-cent. theologian Origen that also appears in the *Gospel of Thomas* as Saying #82: "Who is near me is near the fire; who is far from me is far from the kingdom." The *Gospel of the Savior*, however, concludes the final line of the couplet with "far from life."

Bibliography: Stephen Emmel. "The Recently Published *Gospel of the Savior* ("Unbekanntes Berliner Evangelium"): Righting the Order of Pages and Events." *HTR* 95 (2002) 45–72; Charles W. Hedrick. "Caveats to a 'Righted Order' of the *Gospel of the Savior.*" *HTR* 96 (2003) 229–38; Charles W. Hedrick and Paul A. Mirecki. *Gospel of the Savior: A New Ancient Gospel* (1999).

CHARLES W. HEDRICK

SAW [מְגֵרָה megherah, מַשּׂוֹר mashor; πρίζω prizō]. Saws were used to cut both stone and wood. Stonecutters used a saw with a single-handled blade whose teeth faced in opposite directions (megherah; 1 Kgs 7:9); they dusted the cut with stone dust as an abrasive to speed the process. Fortifications could also be dismantled with picks, saws, and iron chisels to prevent them from being used again (2 Sam 12:31). Carpenters cut wood using a saw whose teeth were set in only one direction and could only be dragged (mashor; Isa 10:15). An appalling use of the saw was to execute prisoners (Heb 11:37). *See* TOOLS.

VICTOR H. MATTHEWS

SAY, SPEAK [אָמַר ʾamar, דָּבַר davar; λέγω legō, λαλέω laleō]. This word group refers to the learned human ability to communicate with words enabled by complex physiological, rational, psychological, and sociological components. It is a powerful trait that signifies the difference of humans from all other living creatures. Only human beings talk like God (Gen 2:18, 23). Of all creation, human beings alone talk to God, and outside of speaking the world into existence (Gen 1:1-24) and self-communication (Gen 1:26), God talks only to people. Harnessing the mysterious force of speech for good is a moral concern throughout the Bible.

When God speaks, it is with unmatched authority, whether to nature (Gen 1–2), to people (e.g., Noah [Gen 6–8], Abraham [Gen 12:1-5; 15:1-5], Moses [Exod 3:1-23]), or through spokespersons (e.g., Moses, David, or the prophets). God's silence can cause someone like Job to accuse God of injustice against humanity (Job 3–37), yet God's speaking can also silence such railings (Job 38–42). God can speak through a donkey (Num 22:28-30), a bush (Exod 3:4), or angels (Gen 18:1-8), but more often speaks through dreams (Gen 37:1-11; Ezek 37:1-14; Acts 10:9-16; Rev 4–22) and predominantly through prophets. God's speaking may invoke judgment or blessing. "Thus says the Lord" in the prophets is a harbinger of doom (Jer 47:2; Ezek 25:3; Amos 1:3) or equally a preamble for restoration (Isa 44:2; Jer 30:2; Ezek 36:33).

Jesus speaks both to God (Matt 26:32) and for God (John 7:16-17). He speaks in radical parables, enigmatic sayings, and scriptural interpretation (e.g., Matt 5–7). He speaks with authority to the wind (Mark 4:39), illness (Matt 8:3), and demons (Luke 8:32), and also to his enemies (Matt 26:64). He and they quote written Scripture as God's authoritative voice (e.g., Luke 4:1-13).

Also, the speech of ordinary people is powerful, having "the power of life and death" (Prov 18:21). The hurtful things that people say can be devastating to others, whether gossip, slander, mockery, flattery, deceit, or lies. God desires human speech to be gracious, uplifting, and honest (Prov 10:11; 16:24; 25:11; Eph 4:29; Col 3:16; 4:6; 1 Pet 3:15; Jas 5:12).

Some suggest that the biblical world considered some words magical, having an irreversible life of their own once they leave the mouth of their human source, especially curses and blessings invoked in the name of God. Yet the Ephraimite woman's curse against the thief is reversed by her blessing when she discovers it is her son (Judg 17:1-4). Saul's curse on anyone in his army who eats during battle does not fall on his son Jonathan who unknowingly eats honey (1 Sam 14:28). Undeserved curses are ineffective: "Like a sparrow in its flitting, like a swallow in its flying, an undeserved curse goes nowhere" (Prov 26:2). As invoked, God supervises human blessings and curses; they are not unrestricted agents. *See* BLESSINGS AND CURSINGS; CREATION; MOUTH; TONGUE.

Bibliography: William R. Baker. *Sticks & Stones: The Discipleship of Our Speech* (1996); Anthony C. Thiselton. "The Supposed Power of Words in Biblical Writings." *JTS* 24 (1974) 283–99.

WILLIAM R. BAKER

SAYINGS OF JESUS. *See* JESUS, SAYINGS OF; OXYRHYNCHUS PAPYRI; Q, QUELLE.

SAYINGS OF THE FATHERS. A tractate of the MISHNAH known in Hebrew as *Pirqe 'Avot*, literally "chapters of the Fathers." In manuscripts, *'Avot* appears in different positions, indicating that it was either a later addition to or a closing tractate of the Mishnah. *'Avot* differs from the remainder of Mishnah, which is HALAKHAH, while *'Avot* is primarily HAGGADAH. *'Avot* consists of five chapters, the first two made up of a chain-of-tradition that traces rabbinic authority from Moses at Sinai to Rabbi Yochanan ben Zakkai and his disciples following the destruction of the Jerusalem Temple in 70 CE. Such chains of authority were common among the philosophical schools of the Hellenistic world. In significant measure, the wisdom of *'Avot* conforms to common Stoic doctrine of the era. There is a block of material from the Gamalielite dynasty interpolated into this chain-of-tradition, indicating a later necessity for this family to justify their right to rule the rabbinic community as patriarchs.

Maxims, ethical sayings, and wisdom literature are the mainstay of this tractate, which quotes early rabbinic and even proto-rabbinic figures such as Hillel and Simeon the Righteous. The fifth chapter of *'Avot* is organized around the mnemonic of numbers, such as "by ten speech-acts God created the world" or "there are four qualities among students." A pseudepigraphic sixth chapter was appended to *'Avot* in the Middle Ages, so that the tractate might be studied devotionally, one chapter per week, during the six Sabbaths between Passover and Shavuot. Because of this practice, the Sayings of the Fathers is among the most ubiquitous works of rabbinic literature, found not only in the Mishnah but also in the rabbinic prayer-book or Siddur.

Bibliography: Herman L. Strack and Gunter Stemberger. *Introduction to the Talmud and Midrash* (1992).

BURTON L. VISOTZKY

SCAB [יַלֶּפֶת yallefeth, שָׂפָּח sippakh]. A crust of dried secretions (e.g., blood) that forms over a wound. Scabs disqualify people from presenting offerings to Yahweh (Lev 21:20), and they disqualify animals from use in sacrifice (Lev 22:22). Yahweh promises to put scabs on the heads of the "haughty" daughters of Zion (Isa 3:16-17).

JOHN J. PILCH

SCABBARD [תַּעַר ta'ar]. Holster or covering for a sword (Jer 47:6). Elsewhere translated "SHEATH."

SCALES [מֹאזְנַיִם mo'znayim; ζυγός zygos]. Scales, or BALANCES, usually have two dishes. On one side is placed a precious metal or money (Jer 32:10) or some item being purchased (Isa 46:6; compare Rev 6:5), while the other side holds a weight. The Bible urges the need for just scales (Job 31:6) and condemns false scales that benefit their owner (Amos 8:5; Mic 6:11). *See* WEIGHTS AND MEASURES.

KENNETH D. LITWAK

SCALES, FISH [קַשְׂקֶשֶׂת qasqeseth; λεπίς lepis]. The OT states that fish with fins and scales can be consumed, but fish without scales are an abomination (Lev 11:9-12; see also Deut 14:9-10). "Scales" constitute a type of armor in 1 Sam 17:5. LEVIATHAN's scales are like a shield (Job 41:15). Something like scales falls from Paul's blinded eyes (Acts 9:18). *See* DISEASE; FISH.

ODED BOROWSKI

SCAPEGOAT. *See* AZAZEL.

SCARAB. *See* SEALS AND SCARABS.

SCARECROW [תֹּמֶר tomer]. Jeremiah 10:5 compares idols to scarecrows in a field of cucumbers (as in Ep Jer 70). **Tomer** also appears in Judg 4:5 as the place where Deborah sat to judge the Israelites. In this instance, however, the NRSV renders it as "palm (tree)," as does the LXX. Because Jer 10:5 likens idols to wooden objects made from a palm tree and placed in a cucumber field, "scarecrow" is a logical translation.

Bibliography: Jack Lundbom. *Jeremiah 1–20.* AB 21A (1999).

JASON R. TATLOCK

SCARF. *See* HEAD COVERING.

SCARLET [שָׁנִי shani; κόκκινος kokkinos]. A shade of RED produced by an expensive, highly prized dye. The female shield louse (*Kermococcus vermilio*), which is found on the kermes oak, is the source of scarlet dye. A single pound of dye requires the bodies of 70,000 insects. Scarlet dye was used particularly in luxury items and items associated with the cult (*see* CRIMSON).

The dye is colorfast and does not fade. Thus, scarlet is a metaphor for sin in Isa 1:18. Yahweh promises that Israel can be purified of its sins, even though they are like the permanent red stain of scarlet. Scarlet wool was used in purification rituals (Heb 9:19; compare Lev 14).

Scarlet was used on expensive clothing, like the robe the soldiers used when mocking Jesus (Matt 27:28), and the clothing of the woman who symbolizes Babylon/Rome (Rev 17:4). Merchants mourn when they hear that Babylon is destroyed, for they have lost the market for their luxury items, including scarlet cloth (Rev 18:11-17). *See* COLORS.

Bibliography: Elizabeth J. W. Barber. *Prehistoric Tex-tiles: The Development of Cloth in the Neolithic and Bronze Ages with Special Reference to the Aegean* (1991); Stuart Robinson. *A History of Dyed Textiles* (1969).

MARY PETRINA BOYD

SCENTED WOOD [θύινος thuinos]. Timber from the sanderac tree (*Tetraclinis articulata*), which is an evergreen conifer like a cypress, with small four-part cones. The tree is native to northwest Africa and its timber was esteemed by Greek and Roman woodworkers for fine cabinets and tables. "Scented wood" is included in a list of exotic imports in Rev 18:12. Confusingly, sanderac wood is sometimes known as "citrus wood," although it has no connection with oranges and lemons. Today it is sometimes planted as an ornamental tree or as hedging in the Mediterranean area. *See* PLANTS OF THE BIBLE.

F. NIGEL HEPPER

SCEPTER [מַטֶּה matteh, שֵׁבֶט shevet, שַׁרְבִיט sharvit; ῥάβδος rhabdos]. A scepter is a royal STAFF or ROD. With the exception of the book of Esther (4:11; 5:2; 8:4), which uses the late Hebrew word sharvit in reference to the king only, the word for rod or staff is translated by the NRSV as "scepter" when it appears in a royal context. Thus, in the difficult Gen 49:10, shevet (an earlier Hebrew form of the word sharvit) is translated as "scepter" on the assumption that the reference is to Judean kingship. As king, God possesses a scepter (e.g., Ps 110:2). The scepter represents royal power (Num 24:17), so Zechariah can say, "the scepter of Egypt shall depart," meaning it will become weak (Zech 10:11; compare Ps 89:44 [Heb. 89:45]; Isa 14:5).

The scepter is a well-known ANE symbol for kingship, and many ANE reliefs and statues show kings with a scepter. For example, the relief atop Hammurabi's laws shows the god Shamash giving Hammurabi a scepter. In some cases, the depiction of the scepter in art is highly decorated and clearly royal, but in other cases, it is little different from a walking stick or staff that a commoner would have used.

In the NT, scepter occurs only in Heb 1:8-9 (quoting Ps 45:6-7 [Heb. 45:7-8]) in a string of quotations that apply to Christ, therefore associating him with the divine throne. The meaning in Ps 45 is debated, since it is the only passage in the OT to suggest explicitly that the Davidic king was viewed as divine, noting in reference to him, "Your throne, O God, endures forever and ever. Your royal scepter is a scepter of equity" (Ps 45:6 [Heb. 45:7]). Compare shevet in Isa 11:4, which says in reference to the future ideal Davidic king, "he shall strike the earth with the shevet [NRSV, "rod"] of his mouth."

MARC ZVI BRETTLER

SCEVA see´vuh [Σκευᾶς Skeuas]. Itinerant Jewish exorcists identified as the "seven sons of a Jewish high priest named Sceva" were active in Ephesus (Acts 19:14). Acts explains that God was performing miracles through Paul: handkerchiefs or aprons that had touched his skin were being used to heal the sick and drive out evil spirits (Acts 19:11-12). The sons of Sceva sought to imitate Paul by invoking the name of Jesus to cure a possessed man. Roving exorcists were common in the 1st cent. CE (see Josephus, *Ant.* 8.42–48), and the formula used by Sceva's sons resembles those found in magical papyri (e.g., Paris Magical Papyrus no. 574). But the evil spirit possessing the man refused to obey Sceva's sons, and the man attacked them (Acts 19:13-16). The account in Acts establishes a distinction between the effective miracles performed through Paul and the ineffective use of magic. Indeed, many in Ephesus gave up the practice of magic after hearing of the defeat of Sceva's sons (Acts 19:17-19).

The identification of Sceva as a "high priest" (archiereus ἀρχιερεύς) is problematic. The term may refer to the Jewish high priest himself (e.g., the LXX of Lev 4:3) or to a chief priest, i.e., a male member of any high priestly family in the late Second Temple period. There is no record of a Jewish high priest or chief priest named Sceva. Alternatively, Sceva may have adopted the title "high priest" or "chief priest" to legitimate himself as an exorcist; priests were knowledgeable in the divine names used by exorcists. Perhaps he was a high priest in the imperial cult or some other cult and not of a Jewish priestly family at all, since his name is apparently Latin and not Hebrew. One manuscript of Acts (Codex Bezae) calls Sceva simply a "priest." This text is unlikely to be original, however, since it is difficult to explain why "priest" would have been altered to "high priest."

Bibliography: Ben Witherington III. *The Acts of the Apostles: A Socio-Rhetorical Commentary* (1998).

KENNETH D. LITWAK

SCHISM siz´uhm. In the earliest years of the Jesus-movement, the followers of Jesus were not separate from Judaism. They all were law-observant Jews. Scholars of Christian origins long have addressed the question of why a separate religion called CHRISTIANITY eventually emerged from this sect of Judaism that believed that Jesus was the promised messiah (*see* MESSIAH, JEWISH). In the past, these scholars searched for one precise historical event in antiquity that irreversibly affected Jewish-Christian relations and prompted the "schism" or "parting of the ways." Recent scholarship, however, has recognized that the notion of an early, sharply defined Christian identity caused by a single historical act is at odds with the complicated, nuanced relationship that existed between Jews who believed Jesus was the messiah and those who did not. Rather, the schism between Judaism and Christianity is best understood as an incremental process that developed as the result of several different events and decisions, beginning in the 1st cent. CE and continuing for several centuries thereafter.

One of the earliest steps in this lengthy process of separation was the decision of Paul, a Jewish apostle of Jesus, to accept as converts to the Jesus-movement Gentiles who did not first convert to Judaism. In his letter to the Galatian churches, Paul argued that Gentile Christians were not obligated to follow the Mosaic law, and that JUDAIZING (promoting the observance of Jewish law by Gentile Christians) in any fashion undermined both Gentile Christian faith in Jesus as well as the unity of early Pauline Christian communities (Gal 3–5). Although in his own day Paul's perspective was a minority view that was vigorously opposed by other Jewish Christians (Gal 2; Acts 15), his opinion eventually came to dominate as Christianity spread throughout the Roman Empire (see JEWISH CHRISTIANITY).

The First Jewish Revolt against Rome (66–73 CE), which resulted in the destruction of the Jewish Temple in Jerusalem in 70 CE, is acknowledged as one event among many that contributed to Christianity's growing apart from Judaism (in contrast to the outdated argument that 70 CE marked the ultimate separation between the two traditions). The Bar Kochba revolt in 132–135 CE, with its strong messianic overtones, probably had a more significant effect on Jewish-Christian relations than did the earlier revolt. Because Christians of both Jewish and Gentile origin had placed their faith in Jesus as messiah, they did not join fellow Jews in support of Simon Bar Kochba's claim to this title, and they experienced Jewish persecution as a result (Justin, *1 Apol.* 31.5–6). When Emperor Hadrian banned Jews from living in Jerusalem in the aftermath of the failed revolt, the effect on the Jerusalem church was considerable: Jewish Christians—who had up until this point led the church—were replaced by Gentile Christians (Eusebius, *Hist. eccl.* 4.5). In the 2nd cent. CE, Gentile Christianity began to gain ascendancy, while Jewish Christianity became increasingly marginalized.

While certain NT documents reflect hostility toward Jews and Judaism, the nature of the hostility is collegial or fraternal. Jewish leadership in this period was quite diverse, and Jesus was among the Jewish teachers who debated how to be faithful to TORAH (see JUDAISM §D.3). In the earliest layers of the NT Gospel texts, no hostility towards Judaism is observable. The texts that picture Jesus debating issues of Jewish law with the Pharisees reflect Jesus' own Jewish piety, not something radically different; these debates are not evidence that Jesus was "against" the Law. (Indeed, the Gospel of Matthew states just the opposite: "Do not think I have come to abolish the law or the prophets; I have come not to abolish but to fulfill" [Matt 5:17]).

The authors of all four NT Gospels, sharply aware that Jesus' death by crucifixion—a humiliating Roman punishment—could be, at the very least, a liability in their attempt to present their movement as respectable in Roman eyes, shifted the blame for the death of Jesus from the Roman authorities to the Jews (see DEATH OF CHRIST). As the tradition developed, the Jews were progressively inculpated and Pilate exculpated; Pilate emerges, in the latest of the four Gospels (John), as a sensitive and sympathetic figure.

The Gospel of John contains several negative references to Jesus' adversaries as "the Jews" (most scholars today understand "the Jews" to refer to a particular group of adversaries to the Johannine community). In support of this interpretation, the Fourth Gospel (chaps. 5–9) includes a description of Jewish believers in Jesus being fearful of facing expulsion from the SYNAGOGUE because of their faith (see TWELFTH BENEDICTION).

In some non-canonical early Christian documents, the enmity takes on more of an "us-versus-them" tone, with Jews being portrayed as the "other." The author of the late 1st cent. CE *Epistle of Barnabas* asserts that the covenant with God belongs to the Christians alone (4:11; 13:1; 14:1-2), while Justin Martyr, in his *Dialogue with Trypho* of the 2nd cent. CE, pronounces Christians—and not Jews—to be the "true Israel" (*Dial.* 111–142). Melito of Sardis, in a sermon written in the late 2nd cent. CE, declares that Judaism is defunct and superseded by Christianity (*Homily*, lines 224–44, 255–79, 280–300). In the first extant charge of deicide, he states that the Jews alone are responsible for the death of Jesus, and consequently, the death of God (*Homily*, lines 562–608, 693–716). Yet even in these writings, an underlying complexity to Jewish-Christian relations is evidenced, for the authors' anti-Jewish statements seem to derive in large part from their concern about the strong attraction Judaism held for some of their Christian congregants. Meanwhile, from the Jewish perspective, as the church became progressively more Gentile and non-Torah observant, Jews increasingly came to see Christians as "other" rather than as Jews who had gone astray.

In the 4th cent. CE, Emperor Constantine translated Christian bias against Jews into legal rulings, e.g., forbidding Jews to own Christian slaves and making conversion to Judaism a criminal offense. Local and ecumenical councils sought further to separate the two religious groups by enacting canons that restricted Christian participation in Jewish ceremonies (e.g., the synods of Elvira in 306; Nicea in 325; Antioch in 341). By the end of the 4th cent., certainly among ecclesiastical leaders, Christianity was deemed fully distinct and separate from Judaism. Nevertheless, the existence of continuing interaction between Jews and Christians at a popular level can be surmised from ongoing anti-Jewish legislation and from the writings of certain Christian leaders, such as John Chrysostom of Antioch in 386–87. See ANTI-JUDAISM; ANTI-SEMITISM; CHRISTIAN-JEWISH RELATIONS.

Bibliography: James D. G. Dunn. *The Parting of the Ways Between Christianity and Judaism.* 2ⁿᵈ ed. (2006); Walter Harrelson and Randall M. Falk. *Jews and Christians: A Troubled Family* (1990); Amy-Jill Levine. *The Misunderstood Jew: The Church and the Scandal of the Jewish Jesus* (2007); Jack T. Sanders. *Schismatics, Sectarians, Dissidents, Deviants: The First One Hundred Years of Jewish-Christian Relations* (1993); Alan Segal. *Two Powers in Heaven: Early Rabbinic Reports about Christianity and Gnosticism* (1977); S. Wilson. *Related Strangers: Jewish-Christian Relations 70–170* (1995).

MICHELE MURRAY

SCIENCE AND THE BIBLE. The extent to which biblical authors convey accurate scientific information about their world has been a topic of discussion from the first encounters between Greco-Roman authors and their Jewish and Christian counterparts. This article concentrates on: 1) the attitudes toward empirical observation and logical reasoning used by biblical authors in constructing their worldview in an ANE context; and 2) the role of the Bible in discussions about science from antiquity to the present.

- A. Defining Science
- B. Science in the Ancient Near East
- C. Attitudes toward Empirical Investigations in Israel
- D. Cosmology
- E. Medicine
- F. Weight and Measures
- G. The Bible and the History of Science
- H. Conclusion
- Bibliography

A. Defining Science

The definition of *science* remains hotly contested. As used by modern scientists, *science* describes the systematic attempt to understand the universe through evidence derived from one or more of the five natural senses and/or logic. Methodological naturalism, which refers to the assumption that only natural causes should be used in explaining natural phenomena, also is an essential part of modern science.

Under this view, all supernatural phenomena, including miracles, are undetectable through scientific methods. In particular, two general definitions of miracles have been at issue. One is that miracles constitute violations of natural law. Objections to this position center on the fact that the existence of universal natural laws is itself an untestable claim. Other scholars define a miracle as an event effected by the direct agency of a supernatural entity. Under such a definition, miracles become irrelevant for scientific explanations because supernatural agency cannot be detected scientifically (*see* MIRACLE).

Although biblical authors assume that all phenomena were ultimately controlled or caused by Yahweh, they also recognize that some events were beyond routine human experience. Seas did not part every day, and time-keeping devices did not normally reverse course (2 Kgs 20:10). Such extraordinary events often were described with variants of the Hebrew root pl᾿ (פלא) in the OT (e.g., plagues on Egypt in Exod 3:20). The Greek words teras (τέρας), dynamis (δύναμις), and sēmeion (σημεῖον) are used similarly in the NT (e.g., Matt 7:22; Acts 2:22). Insofar as such events were viewed as special acts of a deity, the word *miracle* represents an adequate translation.

Given these preliminary remarks, the presence of science in the Bible is not an all-or-nothing scenario, but rather one of proportion. Biblical authors have a predominantly non-scientific view of the cosmos and its components. However, we can still detect attitudes and explanations that use empirical observation and reasoning to understand the world.

B. Science in the Ancient Near East

In the predominant historical view, Greece is the birthplace of scientific thinking. By the 6ᵗʰ cent. BCE, Thales of Miletos attempted to explain the origin of the world through purely natural phenomena. Aristotle (4ᵗʰ cent. BCE) argued that true knowledge derives from inductive conclusions about the world through experience. These conclusions can then be used to make deductions and predictions about new experiences. Some of the works attributed to Hippocrates (5ᵗʰ–4ᵗʰ cent. BCE), "the father of medicine," explicitly argued against supernatural causation.

However, many Assyriologists contend that Mesopotamia offers the first indications of scientific thinking, particularly in the form of divinatory texts, which predict events on the basis of observations of liver anatomy or a variety of other events (e.g., a dog crossing one's path). Such omens were often expressed in the form "If X is the case, Y will occur," which can be found in genres ranging from law codes to medical texts. Regardless of its accuracy, divination attempts to draw causational links between observations and events. Consequently, recordings of astronomical phenomena became more precise, and such recordings led to genuine predictive abilities for eclipses, among other events.

Many Egyptologists argue that Egypt generated the earliest scientific achievements. According to James Henry Breasted (1865–1935), the eminent American Egyptologist, the Edwin Smith Surgical Papyrus (approximately 1550 BCE) is the earliest known scientific document. This medical manual lists physical conditions based on observation, presents diagnoses devoid of supernaturalistic language, and recommends purely naturalistic therapy.

C. Attitudes toward Empirical Investigations in Israel

Whether Greece, Egypt, or Mesopotamia is the birthplace of scientific thinking, one perennial issue centers on why ancient Israel did not develop science even as far as those neighboring cultures. At least two answers have been proposed. The first is that the Bible is not concerned primarily with the physical world, but rather with ethics and Israel's historical relationship with Yahweh. Sometimes "scientific" knowledge is presupposed, but not explained in certain stories. For example, the story of Bathsheba demonstrates that the relationship of the menstrual cycle to pregnancy was understood. Briefly, in that story the narrator emphasizes that David had sexual relations with Bathsheba after her menstrual cycle (2 Sam 11:4), leaving no uncertainty about David's responsibility for Bathsheba's pregnancy.

Another view centers on the antipathy of some biblical authors toward the natural senses in making conclusions about the world. For example, the Deuteronomistic History exhibits an "audiocentric" strand that prefers hearing over seeing, as illustrated by Deut 4:12: "Then the LORD spoke to you out of the fire. You heard the sound of words but saw no form; there was only a voice." The denial that the Israelites saw any form of Yahweh is directly linked to a warning not to make any visual representations of Yahweh or anything else in the world (vv. 16-19). Furthermore, this passage affirms that hearing was sufficient for Israelites to receive correct information about Yahweh's will.

But the antipathy toward sight was not restricted to divine beings. In 1 Sam 16:6, Samuel relies on his vision, and mistakenly concludes that Eliab, the oldest brother of David, was chosen by Yahweh as Saul's replacement. Yahweh responds, "Do not look on his appearance or on the height of his stature, because I have rejected him; for the LORD does not see as mortals see; they look on the outward appearance, but the LORD looks on the heart" (1 Sam 16:7).

This aversion to the use of vision, and the concomitant recommendation to rely on "seeing with the heart," may have deterred the systematic use of empirical observation. However, such a theory must be balanced by the fact that many Greek authors also devalued sight as the most certain means to gather information. Moreover, not all biblical authors preferred hearing over seeing (e.g., Job 42:5).

By the time we reach Second Temple literature, we find reference to the classic five senses (and more) as a proper means to acquire information (e.g., Sir 17:5-7; T. Reu. 2:4-6). Yet an anti-empirical stance may have continued into early Christianity. For example, the author of the Gospel of John may be distinguishing his view of Christian epistemology from Hellenistic empirico-rationalism in Jesus' response to the skeptical Thomas, "Blessed are those who have not seen and yet have come to believe" (John 20:29; compare 1 Cor 1:22-23).

D. Cosmology

Although biblical authors do not undertake systematic empirico-rationalist investigations, their view of the world was typical in the Near East. The Bible has a pre-scientific and telic (purposive) understanding of the origins of the earth as a place meant for human beings (Gen 1:26-27; Isa 45:18). While no one systematic picture of the cosmos is presented, a tripartite structure, consisting of sky, earth, and sea, is presumed in Gen 1 (see also Deut 5:8). Each domain is associated with particular creatures (e.g., flying creatures with the sky).

A tripartite view of the universe also can be found in the Greek *Iliad* (15.187–93), which states that "all things are divided into three domains" to which a god is assigned: heaven (Zeus), seas (Poseidon), and the underworld (Hades). The earth constitutes a fourth zone where all beings are equally welcome. The allotment of different portions of the earth to different gods is attested in the Bible (Deut 32:8-9).

However, the Bible evinces no clear evidence of the planet's true shape. The earth apparently was conceived as a flat disk surrounded by water, and with a metallic dome for a sky (raqiaʿ [רָקִיעַ]; Gen 1:7). The sky was supported by pillars (Job 9:6). Water is stored above this dome. The "circle of the earth" in Isa 40:22 is probably a reference to the circle traced by the horizon rather than a reference to any spherical shape of the earth. Such views are duplicated in Mesopotamia and other neighboring cultures.

Genesis 1 provides the most familiar biblical cosmogony, which begins with a chaotic mass of water stirred by a divine wind. God shaped that mass by division and differentiation, and added, through the divine spoken word, many of the entities that populate it. A watery beginning also is posited by some Greek cosmologists (Thales) and by *Enuma Elish* ("When high above"), the Babylonian creation epic (early 1st millennium BCE). Differentiation, consisting principally of polar opposites (light/dark; male/female; hot/cold), is central to many Near Eastern cosmogonies, including the one in *De rerum natura* (*On the Nature of Things*; 1st cent. BCE) by Lucretius, perhaps the most systematic expositor of anti-supernaturalism in the ancient world.

By the 5th cent. BCE in Greece, we find explicit recognition that the earth is spherical and that it might be suspended in space. By the 3rd cent. BCE, Eratosthenes, an astronomer at Alexandria, had calculated the circumference of the earth with relative accuracy. Aristarchus of Samos (3rd cent. BCE) proposed a heliocentric universe long before Copernicus. In contrast, biblical authors seem to assume that the sun moved (Josh 10:12) over an immovable earth (Ps 93:1).

Although biblical authors acknowledged the initial creation of all types of living things, they recognized that the generation of new organisms required certain pre-existing conditions. For example, one must plant seeds and water fields in order to harvest crops (2 Sam 23:4; Luke 20:9; 1 Cor 3:6). Biblical authors recognized that certain environments could support only a finite amount of herding (Gen 13:5-6).

The need for increased precision in scheduling agricultural, military (2 Sam 11:1), and building activities was a major factor in the emergence of systematic observations of the heavens (see Gen 1:14-18). The origin of the seven-day week is uncertain, but many link it to knowledge of seven planets, although identification of specific stars or constellations is debated (e.g., Orion and the Pleiades in Job 9:9). By the time the Bible was penned, the lunar cycle of 29½ days was common knowledge. The fact that the lunar cycle and solar year were not in synchrony was a well-known fact, and contrasts between lunar and solar calendars became a significant issue reflected in the Dead Sea Scrolls, among other Jewish writings of the Second Temple period. The non-canonical book of *Jubilees* (ca. 3rd cent. BCE) prefers a solar calendar in opposition to the lunar calendar that became normative in Judaism.

There seems to be no recognition of the celestial mechanics behind the phases of the moon or eclipses, which were portentous events in the ANE. Some Greek astronomers, in contrast, clearly understood the mechanics of both lunar and solar eclipses. The recent extended decipherment of the famed Antikythera mechanism (ca. 1st cent. BCE) reveals that highly sophisticated celestial timepieces could be manufactured in ancient Greece.

In the Bible, the ability to predict future events was, as it is in modern science, a sign of the reliability of a person's understanding of the world. In contrast to modern science, biblical prediction was principally based on a prophet's special access to Yahweh. However, discussions about how to recognize true prophecy (Deut 18:20-21) reflect that genuine epistemological issues were recognized with the use of prediction. For example, Jer 28:8-9 notes that war is so common that it is not as useful a sign of true prediction as is peace.

Closely tied to cosmology are meteorological phenomena. Yahweh's character as a storm god is illustrated in, among other passages, Exod 15:8, where he is described as blowing wind through his nose and mouth. Yahweh was associated with earthquakes and volcanic activity (Exod 19). Rain is controlled by God (1 Kgs 17:1; Job 5:10). But observation also was used to conclude that north winds signal rain (Prov 25:23) and to identify general rainy seasons (Jer 5:24). *See* COSMOGONY, COSMOLOGY.

E. Medicine

Medicine, in the sense of a naturalistic approach to the explanation for, and healing of, illnesses, did not exist in the Bible. However, such was the case in almost every other neighboring culture. Approaches to illness were intimately related to how biblical authors viewed the origin and nature of human-divine relations. According to Gen 2:7, humanity was formed from clay, a fragile material (Job 4:19). Divine breath is needed to bring the clay to life. Wind and breath were viewed as related phenomena insofar as both involved movement of air. Thus, biblical authors understood that air flow, or what we could call "respiration," was essential to human life (see 2 Kgs 8:15). Life was also thought to reside in the blood (Gen 9:4).

Yahweh was ultimately responsible for healing and illnesses, including injuries that had a visible cause (e.g., an arrow in 1 Kgs 22:34). Because of the biblical emphasis on monolatry, Yahweh's responsibility for both illness and healing (see Job 5:18) contrasts with that found in polytheistic cultures where the deity who sent the disease may not be the same as the one who cures it. In the NT, much as in polytheistic cultures, demons are held responsible for illnesses (Mark 5:1-13).

Nevertheless, there are instances where biblical authors concluded, perhaps on the basis of empirical trial and error, that certain natural substances had curative properties. These include balm for healing wounds (Jer 8:22; 46:11) and figs for curing certain skin conditions (2 Kgs 20:7). The recommendation that a little wine was good for the stomach (1 Tim 5:23) may be based on empirical trial and error.

Although some scholars have claimed that the Israelites recognized the contagious nature of some illnesses, the evidence is weak. The expulsion from the community of those afflicted with the illness often mistranslated as LEPROSY (tsaraʿath צָרַעַת) is sometimes cited as evidence (see Lev 13:44-46). That illness probably encompasses a number of skin ailments that were not were contagious (e.g., psoriasis, vitiligo). Equally debated is the idea that health concerns were the reasons for recommending circumcision or the prohibition of pork. Health reasons are certainly not the stated motives in the biblical texts (Gen 17:11; Lev 11:7-8). *See* DISEASE; HEALING; HEALTH CARE.

F. Weight and Measures

The rise of commerce and bureaucracies is intimately related to the development of metrology, the science of weights and measures. Measures of weight and capacity are useful in transporting and selling foodstuffs. Dimensional measurements are used in activities ranging from building to property exchanges. Israel's metrology was largely adapted from its neighbors. For example, the cubit (approximately 18 in. long), the basic unit of linear measurement, apparently derives from Egypt. The longest measures mentioned usually were reserved for long-distance journeys (Jonah 3:3).

But the types of mathematics used in biblical metrology never reach beyond commercial, military, and proprietary concerns. This contrasts with Greece, where, by the 3rd cent. BCE, Eratosthenes of Alexandria reportedly measured, by means of parallax, the distance to the moon. On the other hand, even Lucretius thought that the sun and stars were only as large as we see them (compare Rev 6:13). *See* WEIGHTS AND MEASURES.

G. The Bible and the History of Science

While "religion" and "science" may be largely modern constructs, the difference between natural and supernatural explanations was clearly made in ancient Greece and Rome (Hippocrates; Lucretius). Accordingly, there are two basic historical positions concerning the relationship between science and the Bible: incompatibilism and compatibilism.

Incompatibilism argues that the biblical view of the world is incompatible with conclusions drawn from scientific investigation. Compatibilism argues that the Bible (or religion) and science are harmonious, and disharmony arises from misunderstanding of the Bible or from the improper application of science. Thus, the church father Tertullian (ca. 160–220 CE) pioneered the idea that nature and Scripture are two complementary revelations of God's workings.

Second Temple Judaism exhibits the first attempts to defend biblical authors against the charge that the Bible had faulty science or that biblical authors did not develop the advanced sciences in Greco-Roman cultures. Josephus (*Ant.* 1.164), the famed Jewish historian of the 1st cent., responded that it was actually Abraham who had taught Egyptians astronomy and mathematics. For Josephus, the transmission of scientific knowledge could be schematized as follows: Mesopotamia (Abraham, the Chaldean) > Egypt > Greece. Thus, Josephus anticipated modern debates about whether Egypt, Mesopotamia, or Greece had priority in the development of science.

Similarly, Christian compatibilists developed their arguments in encounters with non-Christian authors who ridiculed many of the stories found in the Bible. Origen (185–254 CE), the early Christian apologist, defended the biblical account of Noah's flood in light of the objections of his famed opponent, Celsus, who used empirical observations to conclude that the ark was too small to support the number of species known to exist.

In light of such problems with the biblical record, Augustine (354–430), the influential church theologian, developed an "accommodationist" view in which God's revelation was tailored to the simpler understanding of human beings. Not everything in the Bible should be interpreted literally. Yet Augustine also proposed divine miracles to explain scriptural statements (e.g., angels ferrying animals to Noah's ark from distant islands). Accommodationism became one solution through the medieval period, where theology was regarded as the highest of the sciences by Thomas Aquinas, among other major theologians. Nevertheless, the idea that biblical authority superseded natural observation dominated.

The Renaissance and Enlightenment periods saw the first clear expressions of incompatibilism in Western cultures, especially because new instruments (e.g., the telescope by 1610) brought results that were incompatible with biblical cosmology. In particular, Galileo Galilei (1564–1642) sought to confirm the theory, developed by the Polish astronomer Nicolaus Copernicus (1473–1543) in his *De Revolutionibus Orbium Coelestium* (1543; *On the Revolutions of the Celestial Spheres*), that the sun was the center of the universe. Based on Ps 93:1, among other passages, the Catholic Church argued for a geocentric universe. But even Galileo still thought that the Bible needed to be reinterpreted, not rejected, as a scientific authority.

Further steps toward incompatibilism were taken by the Protestants Johannes Kepler (1571–1630) and Francis Bacon (1561–1626). In his *Novum organum* (1.65), Bacon explicitly rejects the use of the Bible, reinterpreted or not. For Bacon, the Bible was a source for moral guidance and higher truths, and not an authority on science. With Kepler and Bacon we see a clear dichotomy between the realm of science and the realm of biblical theology.

More complete rejections of the Bible came with geologists such as Charles Lyell (1797–1875), who shifted from viewing the Bible as irrelevant to science to viewing the Bible as an obstacle to science. A more developed "warfare" attitude has been attributed to Andrew Dickson White, the president of Cornell and author of *History of the Warfare of Science with Theology in Christendom* (1896), which is actually a plea for understanding "true" religion in light of science. Today, the main representative of the view that religion is completely incompatible with, and hostile to, science is biochemist Richard Dawkins, the author of *The God Delusion* (2006).

Gaining ground is the complexity thesis proposed by John H. Brooke, who argues that religious ideas sometimes led to pathbreaking scientific investigations. Isaac Newton (1643–1727), one of the greatest scientists in history, was motivated by religious agendas and yet made discoveries that required no religious premises. At other times, reliance on the Bible hindered scientific understanding. Repeated surveys, for instance, find that the overwhelming majority of Americans reject evolution in large part because they believe it contradicts religious or biblical beliefs.

"Creationism" is particularly prominent in current conflicts between science and the Bible. Modern creationism is a response to the rise of evolutionary theory, initially expounded in *Origin of Species* (1859) by Charles Darwin. Moreover, the 20th-cent. development of "Big Bang" cosmology, which posits that our entire universe derives from the expansion of an infinitesimally small and dense entity some 13–15 billion years ago, also seemed to contradict the Bible.

Eventually, two major creationist positions developed: 1) old-earth creationism; and 2) young earth creationism. The former adheres to a twenty-four-hour-day creation. The latter admits that modern scientific measurements of the age of the universe are accurate, and "days" in Gen 1 have been reinterpreted to mean longer periods. A third option, theistic evolution, is chosen by most theologians and believing scientists.

One hallmark of modernity, particularly in America, is the use of the legal system to define the role of the Bible in science. One famous example is the John Scopes Trial (1925), wherein a Tennessee schoolteacher was prosecuted for teaching evolution. Supreme Court decisions urging a stronger separation of church and state, particularly in the 1960s, led to the development of "scientific creationism," which claimed an ability to show, without any recourse to biblical statements, that the universe was created. In the landmark case of *Edwards v. Aguillard* (1987), the U.S. Supreme Court ruled that "scientific creationism" was not science because it ultimately presented a biblical view of the universe.

The Edwards decision generated a movement known as Intelligent Design (ID), which has been even more reluctant to appeal to the Bible to make its arguments that the universe is designed. Instead, concepts such as "fine-tuning" or the "anthropic principle" center on the large number of pre-existing conditions that had to be "right" for life to exist on earth. For example, if the charge of the electron or proton were different, then life would not be possible. Likewise, if the earth were not positioned where it is in our solar system, then it might be either too cold or too hot for life to exist. The large number of improbable conditions that need to be present for life to exist is what leads proponents of ID to argue, without the use of biblical texts, that the earth was created for life.

Opponents of ID argue that it expresses another version of the teleological argument found already in William Paley's *Natural Theology* (1805), which defends, through purely natural observation, biblical views about the purpose for the earth (compare Isa 45:18). Opponents also note that all the improbable preconditions needed for human life are also necessary for the existence of undesirable phenomena (e.g., the AIDS virus, infantile disabilities), but few ID advocates argue that these undesirable entities were designed. As in the case of "scientific creationism," a federal court ruled (*Kitzmiller v. Dover*, 2005) that Intelligent Design was not science, but rather another form of biblical creationism.

H. Conclusion

The history of the Bible and science is one of reversals. Prior to the Enlightenment, nature was primarily interpreted in light of the Bible. After the Enlightenment, the Bible was primarily interpreted in light of nature. As even the Intelligent Design movement illustrates, the ability to demonstrate biblical claims without appeal to the Bible is the dominant approach among believing scientists and theologians. Yet biblical interpretation still affects scientific research on, among other areas, stem cell research and AIDS. Moreover, some scholars have opted for postmodernist approaches that question the objectivity of science, or that argue that science is ultimately as much a faith system as religion. But most modern Jewish and Christian scholars and scientists remain accommodationists, who adjust biblical interpretation to the findings of science. *See* CREATION; NATURE, NATURAL PHENOMENA.

Bibliography: Hector Avalos. "Heavenly Conflicts: The Bible and Astronomy." *Mercury: The Journal of the Astronomical Society of the Pacific* 27 (1998) 20–24; Hector Avalos. "Introducing Sensory Criticism in Biblical Studies: Audiocentricity and Visiocentricity." *This Abled Body: Rethinking Disabilities in Biblical Studies.* Hector Avalos, Sarah Melcher, and Jeremy Schipper, eds. (2007); Richard J. Blackwell. *Galileo, Bellarmine, and the Bible* (1991); John H. Brooke. *Science and Religion: Some Historical Perspectives* (1991); Gary Ferngren, ed. *Science and Religion: A Historical Introduction* (2002); Robert T. Pennock, ed. *Intelligent Design Creationism and Its Critics: Philosophical, Theological, and Scientific Perspectives* (2001); John C. Polkinghorne. *Exploring Reality: The Intertwining of Science and Religion* (2007).

HECTOR AVALOS

SCIENCE, EGYPT. The concept of "science," understood in the sense of comprehending the world through observation, testing, and the formulation of axioms, is demonstrated in pharaonic EGYPT in different ways, the combination of which bears witness to this nation's well-earned reputation for ingenuity in antiquity. On an immediate level, the Egyptians' practice of science can be gleaned from physical evidence retrieved by archaeologists. Artifacts attest to their ability to solve the complexities involved in areas such as metallurgy, demonstrated by the casting of copper, gold, and the creation of alloys. The process of mummification, whereby preservatives were developed to prevent the decaying of bodies, likewise indicates knowledge of chemistry, as does the creation of cosmetics, paints, dyes, and sundry drugs. The Egyptians' familiarity with physics and engineering is vividly seen from the monumental remains at places like Giza, which show their skill in overcoming problems surrounding the movement of stone. While most of the written sources concerning the theory behind such technology have disappeared, pictorial evidence has survived, portraying stupendous feats as workers pulling a colossus in the Twelfth Dynasty, and the conveying of a gigantic obelisk by ship from Aswan to Thebes during the reign of Hatshepsut (Eighteenth Dynasty).

Fortunately, a few texts indicate that Egyptian scribes did devote thought to the mechanics involved in these endeavors. For example, a limestone flake of the Old Kingdom refers to the construction of an arc at the base of Snefru's pyramid. A so-called "Satirical Papyrus" (P. Anastasi I) of the Nineteenth Dynasty contains "examination" questions, which variously deal with the erection of obelisks, the creation of ramps for raising heavy blocks into place, and the logistical requirements for labor forces. In terms of the mathematical prowess for these endeavors, papyri attest to the use of a detailed numerical system, including fractions for calculating distances, weights, and measures. Most pertinent is the Papyrus Rhind from the Second Intermediate (Hyksos) Period, which addresses issues of geometry, such as figuring the area of a trapezoidal-shaped field, as well as problems of addition, subtraction, multiplication, and division.

Similar concerns are demonstrated by the use of "Nilometers": gauges for marking the height of the annual inundation. An annalistic text of the Old Kingdom known as the "Palermo Stone" contains recordings of this seasonal event, and actual Nilometers have been found, showing that the Egyptians well understood a connection between the Nile flood and crop yields (see NILE RIVER). In like fashion, a Middle Kingdom papyrus commemorates priests' monitoring the rising of the star Sirius, a yearly event marking the arrival of the inundation. Egyptian mortuary literature and decoration concerning the travels of the deceased also contained detailed charts of the heavens, in which constellations are portrayed, along with their movements during the night. Such observation of the cosmos led to the development of solar and lunar calendars, even as time was divided on a daily basis, exemplified by horological devices like the water clock. Moreover, royal inscriptions demonstrate that unusual astronomical phenomena were observed, including a falling star during the reign of Thutmose III (Eighteenth Dynasty), and an eclipse in the Twenty-second Dynasty.

Nevertheless, it is in the realm of medicine that one can best glean evidence of genuine science within ancient Egypt. Medical texts include diagnostic procedures accompanied by terminology referring to anatomy and pathology. There is an impressive array of pharmacological recipes, associated with specific ailments, including borrowings from Semitic and Helladic sources. Other prescriptions are glossed by the endorsement, "I have seen it (work) with my own eyes," or "very effective," indicating a linkage between treatment and cure verified by observation. Although Egyptian texts and Hellenistic writers attribute the origins of medicine to the First Dynasty, no primary documentation remains from this period. But there are references to physicians—including specialists, such as oculists and dentists—from Old Kingdom tomb inscriptions, with an allusion to medical personnel citing their "books," in treating a Fifth Dynasty courtier who was stricken while watching a procession. The oldest surviving medical treatise thus far comes from a Middle Kingdom papyrus (P. Kahun) dealing with gynecology—whose practitioners were sought out by kings of the Near East for their courts—as well as veterinary concerns. The most celebrated texts, however, are copies that date to the Second Intermediate Period and the beginning of the New Kingdom. The best preserved are the so-called Papyrus Ebers, and the Edwin Smith Papyrus, both of which contain citations from older sources.

Papyrus Ebers is a compendium of prescriptions for a wide range of illnesses, cosmetic and hygienic concerns, and even pest control, but its most intriguing feature is its discussion of the heart and description of a kind of circulatory system. Papyrus Ebers notes that "there are vessels from the heart to every limb," whose "movements" can be felt when placing the "fingers to the temple, back of the head, upon the hand, the chest, the arms, or the legs." This is a clear recognition of the pulse, which is further depicted as the heart "speaking through the vessels of every limb," and whose assessment was made through counting. While it is doubtful that the Egyptians fully understood that the heart itself pumped blood, medical texts observe that connective structures carried air, blood, and other material throughout the body. Likewise, there are references to noxious agents—designated as wekhedu, "traveling corruption"—that provided the foundation for a broad theory of disease.

The principle that direct examination was essential for treatment is most evident in the Edwin Smith Papyrus. This document preserves forty-eight cases that deal with wounds, breaks, contusions, and dislocations. It is remarkable for its systematic treatment of the body, beginning with injuries to the skull and proceeding downwards to the spinal column. Had it been complete, it likely would have included trauma to the abdomen and lower extremities. Each case is organized into a prescription for a wound, which is typified by character (e.g., "smash," "split," "penetrating") and injury (e.g., simple or compound fracture, perforation). This is followed by an examination (literally, "a measuring"), specified as the "palpation" of the affected area. A diagnosis concluded with one of three verdicts based upon the severity of the affliction: "an illness which I will treat;" "an illness with which I will contend;" "an illness not to be treated." Pointing to triage, the declarations might also have had implications concerning professional liability, though changes in condition could lead to a reassessment. Yet even in cases where it is plain that the patient would not survive, the attendant is counseled to keep the individual comfortable "until his time of crisis has passed." Noteworthy for its humane qualities, the Edwin Smith Papyrus is also exemplified by its detached tone, whereby symptoms are rigorously noted by feel, sight, and—in cases of infection—smell. Strikingly, observations concerning the emotional status of the patient attribute "abnormalities" in behavior to physical injury rather than supernatural influences, whose reference is largely missing from the treatise. Like Papyrus Ebers, Edwin Smith contains a section on the heart, and other anatomical structures are identified. Most extraordinary is its description of the brain— the earliest reference in medical literature. In a treatment for skull-fracture, this organ is said to look "like those convolutions which form on molten copper," at whose touch, there is "throbbing and fluttering under the examiner's fingers." Additionally, the papyrus notes a relation between head injury and paralysis to other regions of the body.

The sophistication of these documents has led some scholars to regard Egyptian medicine as a secular discipline, to be distinguished from more "superstitious" concerns. This division is artificial: along with physicians, functionaries of the plague goddess Sekhmet are designated as "users" of the Edwin Smith Papyrus, and other medical texts refer to "priests" and "magicians," just as "spells" and "incantations" are a normal part of cures. Further passages point to the training of medical personnel in religious centers, although an institution called "the House of Life" is also mentioned. Sometimes equated with a medical school, a more general archive or library might be indicated by the term. But shrines did serve as hospitals, with birth "clinics" and healing cults—most especially, that of the Old Kingdom "wise man" Imhotep (later equated with ASCLEPIUS)—being situated within temples. Nevertheless, even when religious language occurs in medical texts, scientific thinking is in evidence, particularly in the employment of mythic analogies. Stories, whereby a deity had been healed of some misfortune (e.g., snake or scorpion bite), offered a reassuring precedent for the now-suffering client. These models demonstrate that for the Egyptians, psychology was an important factor in health. In fact, in *Ramesside omina*, there is categorization by "personality": dreams are taken as signs as to whether one was a "man of Horus"—e.g. law-abiding—or a "person of Seth", e.g., anti-social; prefiguring the "Apollonian/Dionysian" archetypes derived from Hellenistic literature.

Notwithstanding their technological inventions, it has been questioned as to whether the ancient Egyptians were concerned with "science" in the abstract. One can certainly cite attempts to comprehend the cosmos on an intellectual level. The so-called "sun temples" of the Fifth Dynasty, containing reliefs of the world in its seasonal rhythms, testify to the orderliness of creation under the concept of maʿat. Maʿat, which literally means "that which is presented (by the god Re to the world), and that which is to be given back (by mortals to the gods)," has the quality of natural law, which bound and kept the universe in balance. Accordingly, adherence to, or violation of, these orders of creation had discernible consequences in physical events. This principle of reciprocity lent itself to speculation regarding ontological causality, reflected in wisdom precepts, legal ordinances, and cosmological narratives.

By the time of the New Kingdom, during Egypt's imperial age, it is evident that the wider workings of the world beyond the Nile Valley had come under scrutiny. Exotic fauna and flora were brought back by kings on campaign, with Thutmosis III creating a zoo and botanical garden for his trophies. Likewise, texts contain pungent comments on the habits, character, and linguistic traits of foreign groups and their environs, providing a basic ethnography, even as, ironically, spe-

cialists from the Hurrians and Hittites were imported for their expertise in horse raising and chariotry. Yet the most extraordinary demonstration of Egyptian scientific interest is evidenced by a group of writings from the Ramesside and Third Intermediate periods that are simply titled scribal instructions. Likely regarded as a sub-genre of sapiential literature, modern Egyptologists have preferred to call them "onomastica." The *incipit* of one of these documents stipulates that its teaching is for "the instruction of the ignorant and for learning all that exists, (namely) what Ptah created, what Thoth copied down: heaven with its matters, the earth (and) its contents, what the mountains belch forth, the watering of the Flood, along with all the things which Re illumines, (and) all that springs from the surface of the earth." There follows comprehensive groupings of the sun, moon, and stars, and terrestrial phenomena; divisions of ranks and occupations; towns and cities; foreign lands and inhabitants; architectural features; foodstuffs; and body-parts. Admittedly dry in character, these lists classify the world into natural and social hierarchies, creating a veritable catalogue of the universe. Alan Gardiner has observed that these writings' attempts to name the variety of objects in the world are the first steps toward the creation of an encyclopedia.

Bibliography: Marshall Clagett. *Ancient Egyptian Science.* 2 vols. (1995); Alan H. Gardiner. *Ancient Egyptian Onomastica.* 2 vols. (1947); John F. Nunn. *Ancient Egyptian Medicine* (1996); Anthony Spalinger, ed. *Revolutions in Time: Studies in Ancient Egyptian Calendrics* (1994); Edward Wente. *Letters from Ancient Egypt* (1990).

SCOTT MORSCHAUSER

SCIENCE, MESOPOTAMIA. The development of writing in Mesopotamia was intimately connected with the needs of administrative record keeping and, in particular, keeping track of numbers of animals, grain, and other kinds of produce. In the earliest preserved written texts on clay, dating from the 4th millennium BCE, we find several different metrological systems for denoting the numbers of individual kinds of objects. By the end of the 3rd millennium BCE a common numerical notational system emerged: the sexagesimal place value system. A place value system describes a number system where the value of a digit depends upon its position in writing of the number. For example, in our decimal system, the digit 3 can mean 3 units, 3 tens, 3 hundreds, etc., or 3 tenths, 3 hundredths, etc., depending upon how many places it is before or after a decimal point. In Mesopotamia, the standard number system used 60 as its base (i.e., each digit can be a value from 0 to 59, and the value of each place is sixty times greater or smaller than its neighbor). Conventionally, modern scholars separate sexagesimal digits with commas and indicate the transition from integers to fractions using a semicolon. Thus 2,13;20,10 means 2 sixties (= 120) plus 13 units (= 13) plus 20 sixtieths (= 20/60) plus 10 three-thousand-six-hundredths (= 10/3600), which, written decimally, equals 133.3361 .... In cuneiform texts there is generally no indication of where the separation between integers and fractions occurs and so the absolute value of a number is usually only apparent from the context.

A large number of mathematical cuneiform tablets are known today. Most of the preserved tablets come from either the early part of the 2nd millennium BCE or the second half of the 1st millennium BCE. The bulk of the tablets can be divided into either problem texts, containing one or more mathematical problem and its solution, or table texts listing sequences of numbers. Both types of texts are found in the context of scribal education as well as in temple and private scholarly archives.

Many of the problems in mathematical texts are framed in terms of practical examples of construction or administration, but it is apparent that the problems are set out in this way only to provide a context for teaching or practicing more general mathematical techniques. Analysis of the language used in mathematical texts has shown that underlying many of these techniques is a form of cut-and-paste geometry. Among the table texts we find many lists of reciprocals, squares, cubes, and multiplications. Often these lists include numbers with many sexagesimal places and can have had no practical application in the context of building work or determining inheritances.

Astronomy played an important role in Mesopotamian society. The calendar used throughout Mesopotamia used lunar months, which began on the evening of the first sighting of the new moon crescent. Since twelve lunar months only equal about 355 days, an intercalary thirteenth month was added in certain years. By the 5th cent. BCE a cycle of nineteen years containing twelve normal years and seven intercalary years had been adopted in Babylonia. This cycle is identical with the Metonic cycle known from ancient Greece.

References to astronomical phenomena appear in omen texts from the early 2nd millennium BCE. However, the practice of recording night-by-night astronomical observations appears to have begun in Babylon in the middle of the 8th cent. BCE and continued until the 1st cent. CE. The tablets on which the Babylonians recorded their astronomical observations are known today as "Astronomical Diaries." The earliest preserved Diary dates to 652 BCE, but we have tablets containing collections of reports of lunar eclipses including observations from the middle of the 8th cent. BCE which appear to have been compiled from the observations in the Diaries, and so it seems that the tradition of writing Astronomical Diaries started around this earlier date.

The Astronomical Diaries are divided into monthly sections. Each section contains astronomical data including: the length of the previous month (i.e., whether the new moon's crescent was first seen on the twenty-ninth or the thirtieth evening of the previous month);

the time interval, measured in US ("time degrees" = 1/360 day = 4 minutes), between sunset and moonset; the lengths of the five similar time intervals between the sun and moon crossing the horizon during the month (four around the middle of the month and one towards the end of the month on the day of last lunar visibility); the date of the moon's passage by one of the so-called "Normal Stars" used as reference points in the sky, together with the distance of the moon away from the star measured in cubits and fingers (1 cubit = 24 fingers = ca. 2.2 degrees); dates of any first and last visibilities of the planets; dates of any stationary points of the planets; the date of a visible planet's passage by one of the Normal Stars together with the distance in cubits and fingers above or below the star; dates and descriptions of any observed or predicted eclipses of the sun or moon; the dates of solstices, equinoxes and first and last visibilities of Sirius. In later Diaries the date on which a planet passes from one zodiacal sign to another is also recorded. At the end of each monthly section we find some non-astronomical data: the height of the river Euphrates; the prices of six staple commodities (barley, dates, mustard or cuscuta, cress or cardamom, sesame and wool); and any important historical events that took place during the month.

In addition to describing astronomical observations, some predictions of astronomical phenomena are also recorded in the Diaries, frequently when bad weather prevented observations being made. Astronomical phenomena that could be predicted include solar and lunar eclipses, the dates of the first and last visibilities and stationary points of the planets, and the six time intervals connected to the moon's crossing the horizon around sunset and sunrise. It is very likely that the planetary predictions were made using the Babylonians' identification of characteristic periods after which planetary phenomena repeat on more or less the same day in the Babylonian calendar and at roughly the same position in the sky. These periods, dubbed by modern scholars "Goal-Year Periods," are forty-six years for Mercury, eight years for Venus, seventy-nine and forty-seven years for Mars, seventy-one and eighty-three years for Jupiter, and fifty-nine years for Saturn. Texts known today as "Goal-Year Texts" contain collections of planetary visibility and station dates and passages by Normal Stars where the planetary data is taken from 1 period before the Goal-Year. A Goal-Year Text for year 100 of the Seleucid Era would therefore contain Mercury data from year 54 of the Seleucid Era, Venus data from year 92, Mars from years 53 and 21, Jupiter from years 17 and 29, and Saturn from year 41. The repetition of planetary phenomena after these periods meant that by simply combining and rearranging the planetary data chronologically, texts known today as "Normal Star Almanacs" and "Almanacs" containing predicted planetary phenomena for a coming year could be produced (in practice the Babylonians made small corrections to the dates during this process in order to improve the accuracy of their predictions).

In the 4th cent. BCE Babylonian astronomers developed new mathematical methods for predicting astronomical phenomena which existed alongside the simpler Goal-Year methods. These new methods applied mathematical models to the calculation of the date and position of the moon at syzygy and the planets at first visibility, stationary points, acronychal rising, and last visibility. An essential tool in the development of these theories was the invention of the zodiac as an abstract division of the sky into twelve equal length segments, each of which was divided into 30 US "degrees". The twelve signs of the zodiac are first attested in Babylon is the 5th cent. BCE, but were abstracted from constellations in the path of the moon that were known much earlier.

Underlying all of Babylonian theoretical astronomy is the concept of the period relation, similar to the approach found in Goal-Year astronomy. For example, in one of the Jupiter theories, it is assumed that 391 occurrences of a particular phenomenon of Jupiter (e.g., Jupiter's first visibility) take place in exactly 427 years, and that during those 427 years Jupiter has made thirty-six complete passages through the zodiac. If these phenomena were distributed evenly, this would imply that the synodic arc (the difference in celestial longitude between two consecutive occurrences of a phenomenon) would be equal to $36 \times 360 \div 391 = 33.1457 \ldots$ degrees. Written sexagesimally this is $33;8,44,48 \ldots$ degrees. However, as Jupiter and the Sun do not move with constant speed, the synodic arc will at times be greater than or less than this value. Two methods were developed by the Babylonians for dealing with this problem. In models referred to by modern scholars as "System A" the synodic arc is functionally dependent upon the position of the planet in the zodiac. For example, in the simplest System A model for Jupiter, the synodic arc is equal to 30 degrees when Jupiter is situated between 0 degrees of Sagittarius and 25 degrees of Gemini, and equal to 36 degrees when Jupiter is between 25 degrees of Gemini and 0 degrees of Sagittarius. In the alternate approach, referred to as "System B," the synodic arc is functionally dependent upon the previous value of the synodic arc, and follows a zig-zag function, increasing and decreasing by a fixed amount. In both cases the average synodic arc calculated over time equals that given by the underlying period relation. Babylonian lunar theory uses the same step-functions and zig-zag functions as the planetary models, but in much more subtle ways in order to calculate the time and position of the moon at each conjunction and opposition of the sun. Calculating the time of each syzygy required separating the variable contributions to the length of the month from the changing lunar and solar velocities, and is a remarkable achievement of ancient science.

All Babylonian astronomical theories are arithmetical rather than geometrical or physical as we find in the epi-cyclic models of ancient Greek astronomy. Nevertheless, we have extensive evidence for the transmission of Babylonian astronomy to Greece and India. For example, Greek papyri excavated from Oxyrhynchus in Roman Egypt show that Babylonian planetary theories were frequently used in the Greco-Roman world. Many astronomical parameters, such as the canonical value of the mean synodic month found in ancient and medieval astronomy (29;31,50,8,20 days), are of Babylonian origin.

Cuneiform texts relating to medicine are known from all periods of ancient Mesopotamian history. They largely fall into two categories: diagnostic texts and therapeutic texts. Diagnostic texts contain omens which generally predict whether the patient will live or die on the basis of the symptoms of his illness. Therapeutic texts, however, describe treatments for particular illnesses. Most of these treatments involve the prescription by the physician (asû) of remedies made from plants or animal parts. Sometimes the treatment would have a magical or cultic aspect, for example by exposing the remedy to the light of a certain star or planet, or by applying it at a particular time of day. Diseases frequently treated in Mesopotamian medicine included skin complaints, digestive ailments, strokes, rectal and renal problems, and complaints of the eyes and ears.

Bibliography: Jens Høyrup. *Lengths, Widths, Surfaces: A Portrait of Old Babylonian Algebra and Its Kin* (2002); Hermann Hunger and David Pingree. *Astral Sciences in Mesopotamia* (1999); Otto Neugebauer. *Astronomical Cuneiform Texts* (1955); Eleanor Robson. "Mesopotamian Mathematics." *The Mathematics of Egypt, Mesopotamia, China, India, and Islam: A Sourcebook.* Victor J. Katz, ed. (2007) 58–186; Francesca Rochberg. *The Heavenly Writing: Divination, Horoscopy, and Astronomy in Mesopotamian Culture* (2004); Abraham J. Sachs and Hermann Hunger. *Astronomical Diaries and Related Texts from Babylonia* (1988–); JoAnn Scurlock and Burton R. Anderson. *Diagnoses in Assyrian and Babylonian Medicine: Ancient Sources, Translations, and Modern Medical Analyses* (2005); John M. Steele. "Celestial Measurement in Babylonian Astronomy." *Annals of Science* 64 (2007) 293–325; John M. Steele. *A Brief Introduction to Astronomy in the Middle East* (2008); Marten Stol. "Diagnosis and Therapy in Babylonian Medicine." *JEOL* 32 (1991–92) 42–55.

JOHN STEELE

SCIPIO AEMILIANUS. Son of Lucius Aemilius Paullus and grandson through adoption of SCIPIO AFRICANUS. Known for using popular support to advance his political aspirations, he was elected as a Roman consul at a very young age without the regular civic credentials. After a two-year siege, he led the Roman army to destroy Carthage (146 BCE) during the Third Punic War.

He also put an end to the struggle against Numantia in 134 BCE after several failed Roman campaigns.

KATHY R. MAXWELL

SCIPIO AFRICANUS. This Roman consul's given name was Publius Cornelius Scipio, and he is perhaps best known for defeating the Carthaginian hero Hannibal during the Second Punic War (262–241 BCE). After his North African success, Scipio added "Africanus" to his other names. He acquired a number of political enemies and eventually withdrew from public life. In Cicero's *Dream of Scipio* (51 BCE), Scipio Africanus addresses the younger SCIPIO AEMILIANUS, who would defeat Carthage in 146 BCE.

KATHY R. MAXWELL

SCOFFER [לֵץ lets; καταφρονητής kataphronētēs, ἐμπαίκτης empaiktēs]. Contempt for others, worldly cynicism, and inflated self-esteem are the marks of a scoffer, a stock character in the OT, appearing once in Psalms, twelve times in Proverbs, and twice in Isaiah (Ps 1:1; Prov 1:22; 9:7-8; 13:1; 14:6; 15:12; 19:25, 29; 21:11, 24; 22:10; 24:9; 29:8; Isa 28:14; 29:20). The sages and prophets warn youngsters not to emulate the scoffer, who uses language to deride the views of others but shows little ability to profit from their speech (rebukes) in return. God scorns such people, for they speak only to tear down what others present or propose. A scoffer, then, obstructs the wise and misleads the ignorant, and should be ignored and avoided at all costs. In Isaiah, scoffers are associated with government leaders and warring nobles at the royal court: they scorn the laws of the Lord, make unlawful treaties instead of trusting God, and do not fear the dire future laid out for them because of their actions (Isa 28:14; 29:20). At the time of salvation, they will be absent from the land, and the meek whom they have sought to trap and for whom they attempt to deny justice will prevail at last. In Acts 13:41, and allusion to the LXX of Hab 1:41, Paul warns the synagogue attendees not to reject forgiveness of sins through Jesus. Scoffers will deny that Christ will return (2 Pet 3:3) and will reject God's authority (Jude 18). *See* BYWORD; REPROACH; TAUNT.

CAROLE R. FONTAINE

SCOLD [רָגַן raghan, שָׁסַע shasaʿ; ἐμβριμάομαι embrimaomai]. When David had an opportunity to kill Saul, David's men encouraged him to do so. But David was horrified and "scolded (shasaʿ) his men severely and did not permit them to attack Saul" (1 Sam 24:7). The verb raghan (Deut 1:27; Ps 106:25; Prov 16:28; 18:8; 26:20; Isa 29:24), normally translated "grumble" or "complain," also carries the connotation of the English word *scold*. The same is true of embrimaomai (Dan 11:30 [LXX]; Mark 1:43; 14:5), where it means "censure," "snort," "scold," or "rebuke." "Snorting in contempt" is the basic idea of the word. Of interest to readers of the Gospel of Mark is the fact that the verb

occurs at the beginning of the Gospel (Mark 1:43) to describe Jesus' abrupt order to the leper and toward the Gospel's end (Mark 14:5), indicating the disciple's disdain for the woman who had anointed Jesus.

JAMES E. WEST

SCOPUS. Mount Scopus is part of a ring of hills surrounding Jerusalem, including Mount Scopus to the north and the Mount of Olives to the east. Because it was outside the city walls, in the Second Temple period Mount Scopus was used for burials, several of which have been excavated. When besieging Jerusalem in 70 CE, the Romans encamped on Mount Scopus, since it is higher than Jerusalem. *See* ANTIOCHUS; PTOLEMY.

ADAM L. PORTER

SCORPION [עַקְרָב ʿaqrav; σκορπίος skorpios]. Eight-legged arthropods that belong to the *arachnid* class and are known for their claws, a curved tail, and a stinger that (among certain species) delivers neurotoxin venom unsurpassed by few other toxins. The dangerously poisonous varieties of scorpions (there are many non-threatening varieties) belong to the biological family Buthidae. The species *A. crassicauda* and *Leiurus quinquestriatus* are among the toxic varieties known in Israel. From the time the Babylonians named the constellation Scorpio, these small arthropods have captured the human imagination. The Romans viewed scorpions as agents of the devil, and they were depicted on representations to Mithras. The Ebers papyrus contains medical advice for the Egyptians including how to rid the house of scorpions and how to treat bites. In the NRSV, the term occurs mostly in the plural. Scorpions, along with poisonous snakes, symbolize the potential danger of wilderness (Deut 8:15), through which Yahweh guides the Israelites. Likewise, Jesus pronounced that his disciples had authority to tread on snakes and scorpions (Luke 10:19; *see* SERPENT). The term can also be symbolic of one's opponents as those of the rebellious house of Israel who reacted against Ezekiel's message (Ezek 2:6) or a symbol of judgment against the ungodly (Sir 39:30). King Rehoboam spurned the request of lighter labor (than his father Solomon) from the northern Israelites and threatened them instead with the discipline of scorpions (1 Kgs 12:11). Rehoboam's refusal resulted in the split of the kingdom of Israel. Jesus pointed out the absurdity of a loving parent granting a child a scorpion instead of food (Luke 11:12). In the Apocalypse, locusts with tails and stingers like scorpions ascend from the bottomless pit and are granted authority like that of scorpions (Rev 9:3, 10).

Bibliography: Gary A. Polis, ed. *The Biology of Scorpions* (1990).

BRUCE W. GENTRY

SCOURGE [μαστιγόω mastigoō, φραγελλόω phragelloō]. As a prelude to his crucifixion, Jesus is scourged (phragelloō from the Latin loan word *phragello*, Matt 27:26; Mark 15:15; mastigoō, Luke 18:33; Matt 20:19; Mark 10:34; John 19:1).

Scourging was apparently standard pre-crucifixion procedure in Roman times (Josephus, *J.W.* 2.306). It was done with a whip made of several leather straps to which were attached sharp, abrasive items such as nails, glass, or rocks. Scourging resulted in severe laceration of the skin and damage to the flesh beneath. Josephus tells of one Jesus son of Ananias (ca. 62 CE), whose prophecies of Jerusalem's doom resulted in his being brought before the Roman governor, although in the end the man was not executed as the ruling priests wished (*J.W.* 6.304). Jesus of Nazareth warned his followers that they too face the danger of scourging (Matt 10:17; 23:34).

Paul is threatened with beating (Acts 16:22; 22:24-25; compare 2 Cor 11:25). Rabbinic law in late antiquity laid down rules regarding scourging (*m. Sanh.* 1:2; *b. Sanh.* 10a). Scourging could be meted out in the local synagogue (*m. Mak.* 3:10; Epiphanius, *Pan.* 30.11; Eusebius, *Hist. eccl.* 5.16.12, where Christian converts are beaten in the synagogue).

In the LXX, mastigoō is found in reference to persons who are punished with floggings (Deut 25:2-3; compare Josephus, *Ant.* 4.238). The word is sometimes used metaphorically in reference to discipline: "for the LORD reproves the one he loves, as a father the son in whom he delights" (Prov 3:12; compare 19:25; 27:22). It is also a metaphor for punishment as well: "O LORD, do your eyes not look for truth? You have struck them, but they felt no anguish; you have consumed them, but they refused to take correction" (Jer 5:3). *See* CROWN OF THORNS; CRUCIFIXION.

CRAIG A. EVANS

SCREECH OWL. *See* OWL.

SCREEN [מָסָךְ masakh, פָּרֹכֶת parokheth]. A decorated cloth suspended on gilded poles. Screens marked the three entrances in the TABERNACLE complex.

The first screen (masakh) rested at the entrance of the tabernacle courtyard (Exod 27:16). This screen was composed of fine linen and colorfully embroidered with a cherubim design. The second screen (masakh), of similar construction, hung at the entrance to the tabernacle (Exod 26:36). The lampstand, the bread of the Presence, and the altar of incense all stood behind this screen, and the area was only accessible to certain Levites (Num 8).

The third screen (parokheth) was erected inside the tabernacle toward the back (Exod 35:12), dividing the most holy place and the ark of the covenant from the rest of the tent. Like the other screens, it was composed of fine linen, though this screen's colorful cherubim design appears to have been woven into the cloth. Only the high priest could go behind this screen, and that was only allowed on the DAY OF ATONEMENT (Lev 16).

This innermost "screen" (author's trans.; NRSV, "curtain") also appears in Solomon's temple (2 Chr 3:14). *See* VEIL OF THE TEMPLE.

Bibliography: Michael M. Homan. *To Your Tents, O Israel! The Terminology, Function, Form, and Symbolism of Tents in the Hebrew Bible and the Ancient Near East* (2002).

MICHAEL M. HOMAN

SCRIBAL ERROR. *See* DITTOGRAPHY; HAPLOGRAPHY; HARMONIZATION; HOMOIOTELEUTON; ITACISM; QERE-KETHIBH; TEXT CRITICISM, NT; TEXT CRITICISM, OT; TEXTUAL VARIANT; TRANSPOSITION.

SCRIBE [סֹפֵר sofer; γραμματεύς grammateus]. A scribe was a member of a trained class of professionals who filled a variety of functions related to reading and writing within the governmental and religious administrations of ANE societies. In the early Jewish and NT eras, a scribe was an elite scholar who specialized in the teaching and interpretation of religious texts, particularly Torah.

Comparative data from Syria, Mesopotamia, and Egypt greatly aids our understanding of scribes before the Babylonian exile of 586 BCE. The earliest evidence for scribal training comes from Sumerian sources, which describe schools where apprentice scribes were called "sons of the tablet house." Mesopotamian sources from the Old Babylonian period depict scribes as a highly educated caste of professionals who operated across broad social circles. For instance, in Mesopotamian culture scribes formed an integral part of the royal court, especially as part of international diplomatic affairs. Scribes also operated as independent professionals who could be hired for their craft by various people within the community.

Scribes are also known from the earliest periods of Egyptian history. During the Old Kingdom, scribes became a necessary part of the administrative apparatus of the royal court, particularly for purposes of economic record keeping. The rise of scribal training in ancient Egypt appears to have been closely associated with the education and training of princes within the royal court. The Egyptian sources also depict scribes as intimately involved in the operations of priest at various temples, particularly during the New Kingdom period.

A particularly rich body of evidence exists for the activity of scribes in the Late Bronze Age Levant (1550—1200 BCE). The collection of letters written by Canaanite scribes discovered at Tell el-Amarna, Egypt provides important testimony to the training and role of scribes during this time (*see* AMARNA LETTERS). These letters demonstrate that scribes were multilingual professionals who formed an essential part of local ruler's international diplomatic administration. The Akkadian sources discovered at Ugarit also contain important glimpses of scribes during this period. These sources depict scribes working in close connection with temple rather than the governmental circles. One particularly important scribe named Ilimilku, e.g., is described in one text as the apprentice of the high priest. There is evidence that the scribes at Ugarit were responsible for translating Akkadian, and possibly Hurrian, texts into Ugaritic. This translation activity attests to the scope of scribal education already in the Late Bronze Age.

References to scribes appear in numerous places in OT literature. Most of the references occur in the books Samuel–Kings, suggesting a close association between scribes and the rise of the monarchy in ancient Israel. There are also a relatively large number of references to scribes in the book of Jeremiah and in the books of Chronicles. Other allusions to scribes are found in Isaiah, Ezekiel, Esther, Ezra, Nehemiah, and Psalms. Interestingly, there are no explicit references to scribes in the Pentateuch. This is particularly surprising for the book of Deuteronomy, which shows interest in and reflection of scribal activity.

The various allusions to scribes in Samuel–Kings indicate that they held a prominent place in the administration of the royal courts of Israel and Judah (2 Sam 8:17; 20:25; 1 Kgs 4:3; 2 Kgs 22). Most notably, scribes appear in the lists of officials included in the government bureaucracies of David and Solomon (2 Sam 8:16-18; 1 Kgs 4:1-6). A well-known illustration of how a scribe functioned within the royal court occurs in the description of King Josiah's reforms in 2 Kgs 22. According to this text, a scribe is called to read the newly discovered "book of the Law" before Josiah to initiate the king's religious reforms. Other descriptions of scribes in Samuel–Kings suggest that they functioned as international emissaries. For instance, 2 Kings depicts scribes as some of the emissaries that Hezekiah sent to the Assyrian king Sennacherib during his campaign to Judah (18:18, 37).

The descriptions of two scribes in the OT warrant special mention. First, the most complete description of a scribe in the OT is that of the prophet Jeremiah's scribe BARUCH. Baruch pens Jeremiah's words (Jer 36:10) and holds a prominent position within the Judean government (36:32). Baruch is also depicted as the king's personal secretary responsible for overseeing the fulfillment of the king's orders at different levels of the royal court (36:20). He had a personal chamber within the palace complex (36:12) and oversaw legal documents, such as the sale of land (32:12-15).

Second, the priest Ezra stands out in postexilic biblical literature as the paradigmatic scribe-scholar for early Judaism. According to the Aramaic text of Ezra 7, Ezra is both a "scribe skilled in the law of Moses" (v. 6) and "scribe of the law of the God of heaven" (v. 12). Moreover, Ezra 7:10 also describe the priest-scribe as someone who "had set his heart to study the law of the Lord…and to teach the statutes and ordinances in Israel" (v. 10). These passages depict Ezra as the quint-essential Torah scholar who functioned not only as a copyist for the royal court, but also as a learned religious interpreter and teacher. Similar descriptions of Ezra as a student of the Torah also occur in the book of Nehemiah (8:1-8, 13). The descriptions of Ezra in these passages anticipate the role and function of rabbis as interpreters of Torah in later Jewish society.

An important source of information about the work of scribes comes from the various scribal notations, annotative glosses, and other textual clarifications found in the OT texts (Fishbane). For instance, one finds numerous examples where scribes have inserted a small explanatory note within a particular text for purposes of clarification. One classic example of this activity occurs in Ps 68:8 [Heb. 68:9], which contains the gloss "this is Sinai" (zeh sinay זֶה סִינַי) as an explanatory note to the previous line of the verse. These scribal notes attest to a rich exegetical activity that existed as part of the scribal enterprise in ancient Israel and early Judaism. It also points to the work of scribes as creative and dynamic participants in the development or religious tradition during these periods.

Jewish texts from the Second Temple period demonstrate that the model of Ezra as scribe-scholar persisted well beyond the Persian period. For instance, Sirach describes a scribe as a person who "devotes himself to the study of the law of the Most High" (39:1) and is able to "reveal instruction in his teaching, and will glory in the law of the Lord's covenant" (39:9). Later Second Temple Judaism saw the full development of scribes into TORAH scholars involved in the interpretation and teaching of scripture. The importance of the Torah scholars to Judaism is most vividly illustrated in *m. Abot* 1:1, which states that after Moses received the Torah on Sinai, he passed it on to Joshua, who passed it on to the elders, who passed it on to the prophets, who passed it on to "the Men of the Great Assembly." Since Jewish tradition recognized Ezra as the leader of the Great Assembly, this text established the scribe-scholars as the one who was responsible for preserving and interpreting the Torah.

That scribes formed an important part of the governmental apparatus of Jerusalem during the Hellenistic era is illustrated in Josephus' record of Antiochus' letter to Ptolemy (ca. 200 BCE). "Scribes of the temple" are listed along with priests and temple singers as being exempt from paying various taxes (*Ant.* 12.3.3). The most complete picture of a scribe during the Second Temple period occurs in the 2nd-cent. text Sirach (38:34–39:11). This text equates scribes with wisdom and wisdom traditions: a scribe is one "who seeks out the wisdom of all the ancients, and is concerned with prophecies" (39:1) and "the hidden meanings of proverbs" (39:3). Sirach also vividly presents a scribe as someone who receives divine guidance for the interpretation of Scripture: "If the great Lord is willing, he will be filled with the spirit of understanding; he will pour forth words of wisdom of his own and give thanks to the Lord in prayer. The Lord will direct his counsel and knowledge, as he meditates on his mysteries" (39:6-7).

There are numerous references to scribes in the NT. The Synoptic Gospels also depict scribes as those professionals engaged in the interpretation and teaching of Torah. The Gospels frequently pair scribes with PHARISEES, especially in Jesus' indictment: "Woe to you scribes and Pharisees, hypocrites!" (Matt 23:13-33; Luke 11:39-52). It is possible that the pairing of these groups in the Gospels derives from similarities in their theological beliefs, such as belief in resurrection. Several other NT passages present scribes as questioning Jesus' actions and authority (Mark 2:13-17; 11:27-28). The frequent references to scribes in these indictments no doubt reflect the Gospel writer's efforts to depict Jesus as deeply divided against the scribes in the interpretation of the Torah. These depictions, which are particularly prominent in Matthew, should be understood as having a specific location within the early church's rivalry with rabbinic Judaism.

Several NT texts give us glimpses of the social status held by scribes during the Second Temple period. For instance, Mark 12:30-40 describes scribes as those who walk around in long robes expecting to be greeted in marketplaces and given good seats in synagogues and banquets (see also Matt 23:5-7). The description of scribes in this passage suggests that scribes held a high social status within Jewish society. The high social status of scribes can also be inferred from their position within the SANHEDRIN, the main governing body of Judaism during the Second Temple period (Acts 4:6).

Bibliography: Y. Avishur and M. Heltzer. *Studies on the Royal Administration in Ancient Israel in Light of Epigraphic Sources* (1996); James L. Crenshaw. *Education in Ancient Israel: Across the Deadening Silence* (1998); Michael Fishbane. *Biblical Interpretation in Ancient Israel* (1985); N. S. Fox. *In the Service of the King: Officialdom in Ancient Israel and Judah* (2000); B. Landsberger. "Scribal Concepts of Education." *The City Invincible.* Carl H. Kraeling and Robert Adams, eds. (1960) 94–102; T. D. Mettinger. *Solomonic State Officials* (1971); A. Millard. *Reading and Writing in the Time of Jesus* (2001); A. J. Saldarini. *Pharisees, Scribes and Sadducees in Palestinian Society: A Sociological Analysis* (1988); C. Schams. *Jewish Scribes in the Second-Temple Period* (1998); W. M. Schniedewind. *How the Bible Became a Book: The Textualization of Ancient Israel* (2004); R. J. Williams. "Scribal Training in Ancient Egpyt." *JAOS* 92 (1972) 214–21.

JEREMY D. SMOAK

SCRIPTURE, AUTHORITY OF. *See* AUTHORITY OF SCRIPTURE.

SCROLL [מְגִלָּה meghillah, סֵפֶר sefer; βιβλίον biblion, χαρτίον chartion]. A long, rolled piece of papyrus, leather, parchment, or metal (such as copper),

inscribed with literary material in vertical columns. The Hebrew and Greek terms for scrolls are often anachronously translated "BOOK" in the NRSV and NIV. *See* PAPYRUS, PAPYRI; ROLL; WRITING AND WRITING MATERIALS.

JOEL M. LEMON

SCROLLS, DEAD SEA. *See* DEAD SEA SCROLLS; QUMRAN.

SCULPTURE. *See* ARTS; CARVING; SCULPTURED STONE; STATUES, STATUARY.

SCULPTURED STONE [פָּסִיל pasil]. The story of Ehud mentions "sculptured stones" as a landmark near GILGAL (Judg 3:19, 26). Some suggest that these "sculptured stones" are the stones that Joshua erected near Gilgal after the Israelites crossed the Jordan (Josh 4:20-24). But the Hebrew word pasil is usually translated "IDOL" (e.g., Deut 7:5) or "IMAGE" (e.g., Isa 21:9) and can refer to "carved images" (2 Kgs 17:41) cut in wood or stone. These forbidden images are to be burned (Deut 7:5) or broken into pieces (Isa 21:9). Since the stones set up by Joshua are nowhere considered as illicit worship objects, it would seem these sculptured stones are not the same as Joshua's. The sculptured stones of Judges were probably carved images, similar to images of Baal found at Ugarit or images of the Assyrian storm deity astride a bull.

JOEL F. DRINKARD JR.

SCURVY [גָּרָב garav]. Scurvy is an ailment caused by vitamin C deficiency, whose symptoms can include a rash on the legs. It occurs in a list of punishments from God in Deut 28:27. The term garav indicates some sort of skin disease but not necessarily scurvy (compare Lev 21:20; 22:22). A cognate word in Arabic means "eczema."

KEVIN A. WILSON

SCYTHE [δρεπανηφόρος drepanēphoros]. A long-handled, long-bladed tool for mowing and reaping grain or crops, consisting of a long wooden shaft with a perpendicular handle at one end, another in the middle, and a long curved blade attached to the other end. The scythe was not introduced in Israel until after the biblical period, during which time the SICKLE remained the basic harvest tool. The Egyptians and the Persians attached scythes to war chariots. The scythed CHARIOT is listed among the military equipment utilized by Antiochus V Eupator and Lysias in their conflicts with Judas Maccabeus (2 Macc 13:2). *See* WAR, METHODS, TACTICS, WEAPONS OF (BRONZE AGE THROUGH PERSIAN PERIOD); WAR, METHODS, TACTICS, WEAPONS OF (HELLENISTIC THROUGH ROMAN PERIODS).

RALPH K. HAWKINS

SCYTHIANS sith′ee-uhnz [Σκύθης Skythēs]. Semi-nomadic tribes of horse-riding warriors who originally inhabited the steppes north and east of the Black Sea. By the 8th cent. BCE they invaded Urartu (modern day eastern Turkey) and northwestern Iran. Assyrian records note that Sargon II (722–705 BCE) stopped their advance and that they were defeated by Esharhaddon in 676 BCE. Herodotus indicates that they controlled the Near East for twenty-eight years (653–625 BCE; *Hist.* 1.116; 4.1). They allied with the Assyrians in the late 7th cent. BCE and may have served as mercenaries for the Babylonians during their attack on Jerusalem in 586 BCE. The Scythians were capable archers on horseback (Herodotus, *Hist.* 4.46). They used distinctive three-bladed bronze arrowheads, which have been found during excavations in Jerusalem. Scythian settlement in the area of Beth-Shan may explain this city later being called SCYTHOPOLIS, meaning "city of the Scythians" (see LXX Judg 1:27).

Réunion des Musées Nationaux/Art Resource, NY

Figure 1: Scythian archer, red figure amphora, 510–500 BCE (height: 24.4 cm; diameter: 28.3 cm). Euphronius. Louvre, Paris, France.

The ASHKENAZ (Gen 10:3; 1 Chr 1:6; Jer 51:27) are usually identified with the Scythians because of the close relationship of this word with the Ishkuza, the Akkadian word for Scythian. A minority of scholars identify the Scythians with the unnamed "people coming from the north" mentioned in Jeremiah (1:14; 4:29; 5:15-17; 6:22-26; 50:41-42) rather than the more likely Babylonians.

The barbaric nature and cruelty of the Scythians is well known in the ancient world (see 2 Macc 4:47;

3 Macc 7:5; 4 Macc 10:7). Herodotus gives the most vivid examples of Scythian behavior, claiming that they drank alcohol in excess (*Hist.* 4.84), used hemp (4.74–75), drank the blood of their enemies (4.64), scalped victims, and used their skulls as drinking bowls (4.65). The Scythians as barbarians, and their potential for change, is the thrust of Paul's argument for the unifying nature of the gospel of Christ (Col 3:11).

JOHN D. WINELAND

SCYTHOPOLIS sith-op′uh-lis [Σκυθῶν πόλις Skythōn polis, Σκυθοπολῖται Skythopolitai]. Capital of the DECAPOLIS and Greek name for BETH-SHAN. Holofernes camped between Geba and this city (Jdt 3:10), located about 75 mi. from Jerusalem (2 Macc 12:29-30).

SEA [יָם yam; θάλασσα thalassa]. In the Bible, *sea* is used for any large body of water, including the Mediterranean Sea, called the "Great Sea" (Num 34:6) and the "Western Sea" (Deut 34:2); the DEAD SEA, called the "the Sea of Salt" (Num 34:3, author's trans.; NRSV, "Dead Sea") and the "sea of the Arabah" (Deut 3:17); and the "Sea of Reeds" (Exod 13:18, author's trans.; NRSV, "Red Sea"). It is also used of the fresh-water Sea of Chinnereth (Josh 13:27), later also called the "Sea of Galilee" and the "Sea of Tiberias" (John 6:1); Luke calls the same body of water "the lake of Gennesaret" (Luke 5:1).

Because there were no natural harbors on the parts of the Mediterranean coast that the Israelites controlled, for most of their history they were not actively engaged in maritime commerce, unlike their northern neighbors the Phoenicians. Only during the reigns of Solomon (1 Kgs 9:26-28; 2 Chr 8:17-18) and Jehoshaphat (1 Kgs 22:49) is sea trading attributed to them. As a result, "the way of a ship on the high seas" (Prov 30:19) was considered mysterious.

As in the ANE more generally, in the Bible *sea* can also have a mythological meaning, and it is one of the terms used for the primeval watery adversary of the storm god. In the Babylonian myth *Enuma elish*, this adversary is Tiamat, and in Ugaritic it is Prince Sea (in parallel with Judge River), the dragon, and Leviathan. In the Bible, along with "deep" (tehom [תְּהוֹם]; linguistically related to Tiamat), the adversary is called Leviathan and the serpent (Isa 27:1), Rahab (Job 26:12; Ps 89:10 [Heb. 89:11]; Isa 51:9), the rivers (Nah 1:4), and the mighty waters (Hab 3:15). At the appearance of Yahweh, the sea retreats (Ps 114:3), and Yahweh defeats the sea (Job 26:12-14; Isa 51:9-10), treading on it as a victor would trample his enemies (Job 9:8). Having defeated the sea, like Marduk in *Enuma elish*, Yahweh then creates the world (Pss 74:13-17; 89:9-12 [Heb. 89:10-13]). The primeval waters of chaos were symbolically represented in the Temple by the enormous "molten sea" (1 Kgs 7:23-26) in the Temple courtyard.

The same mythological background continues in the NT, where it is Jesus who walks on the sea (Mark 6:48) and whom the sea obeys (Mark 4:41). At the end time, after the final victory of the forces of good over the forces of evil, the sea will be no more (Rev 21:1). *See* CREATION; RED SEA, REED SEA; RIVER; SEA OF GLASS, GLASSY SEA; SEA, GREAT; TRADE AND COMMERCE.

MICHAEL D. COOGAN

SEA GULL [שַׁחַף shakhaf]. Mentioned only in the biblical lists of unclean birds (Lev 11:16; Deut 14:15), the shakhaf is often identified as the sea gull, a tradition going back to the LXX (laros [λάρος]; Vulg. *larus*, the species name for gulls). G. R. Driver has argued that this bird's position within the list indicates that it is an OWL. If shakhaf really denotes a gull, the black-headed gull (*Larus ridibundus*) is a likely candidate. Whereas other gulls are frequent along the coast, this species is spread throughout the country. *See* BIRDS OF THE BIBLE.

Bibliography: G. R. Driver. "Birds in the Old Testament: I. Birds in Law." *PEQ* 87 (1955) 5–20.

GÖRAN EIDEVALL

SEA MONSTER [תַּנִּין tannin; κῆτος kētos]. A large, terrifying water creature. *See* DRAGON; LEVIATHAN; RAHAB.

SEA OF CHINNERETH. *See* GALILEE, SEA OF.

SEA OF GALILEE. *See* GALILEE, SEA OF.

SEA OF GLASS, GLASSY SEA [θάλασσα ὑαλίνη thalassa hyalinē]. "Something like a sea of glass, like crystal" appears in John's vision of the heavenly throne room in Rev 4:6. Like many images in Rev 4, the sea of glass alludes to Ezekiel's prior vision of heaven (Ezek 1). Ezekiel saw "something like a dome, shining like crystal" over the heads of the four living creatures (Ezek 1:22). The understanding of a sea or waters in heaven is common in the OT (i.e., Pss 104:3; 148:4) and may be related to Gen 1:6-8, which describes the sky as a dome that God created to separate the upper and lower waters. Because the SEA was often understood as a chaotic force, the stillness of the sea of glass represents God's dominion over such powers (compare Job 9:8; Pss 74:13-14; 89:9 [Heb. 89:10]). In Rev 15:2, John sees a "sea of glass mixed with fire." The fire here may be a reflection of the flashes of lightning that emerge from the throne (Rev 4:5). It may also evoke the image of a heavenly "stream of fire" seen in other apocalyptic works (e.g., Dan 7:10). The fire may symbolize God's judgment (compare Isa 66:15-16; Mal 3:2).

SUSAN E. HYLEN

SEA OF REEDS. *See* RED SEA, REED SEA.

SEA OF SODOM. *See* SODOM, SEA OF.

SEA OF THE ARABAH. *See* ARABAH; ARABAH, WADI; DEAD SEA.

SEA OF TIBERIAS. *See* GALILEE, SEA OF.

SEA PEOPLES. *See* PHILISTINES; PHOENICIA.

SEA, GREAT [הַיָּם הַגָּדוֹל hayyam haggadhol, יַמָּא רַבָּא yamma' rabba'; ἡ θάλασσα ἡ μεγάλη hē thalassa hē megalē]. The Great Sea is the Mediterranean Sea, which when referenced in the Bible is usually identified as the ideal western boundary of the land of Israel (e.g., Num 34:6; Josh 15:12). In actuality, for most of its history Israel had no control of cities along the Mediterranean coast, and references to seagoing activity by Israel's tribes are both rare and obscure (Gen 49:13; Judg 5:17). For the most part, the coast was occupied by the PHILISTINES in the south and the Phoenicians in the north. It was not until the Maccabean era that the Jews gained control of the port city of JOPPA (1 Macc 10:76). In the 1st cent. BCE, Herod the Great constructed CAESAREA MARITIMA, the first all-weather harbor on Israel's Mediterranean coastline.

The Great Sea, also known as the "WESTERN SEA" (e.g., Deut 11:24) or simply "the SEA" (e.g., Josh 16:8), was distinguished from the SALT SEA on Israel's eastern border not only by its greater size but also in that it was teeming with life (Ezek 47:8-10). It was also noted as the home of great sea monsters (Gen 1:21) and a place of violent and dangerous storms (Jonah 1:4). The vast collection of salt waters that was the Great Sea remained an ongoing symbol of the forces of death-dealing CHAOS (Dan 7:2). The Hebrew term for "deep" (tehom תְּהוֹם) is a poetic synonym for the sea, especially under this threatening aspect (e.g., Isa 51:10; Jonah 2:5; *see* DEEP, THE).

PAUL NISKANEN

SEA, MOLTEN [הַיָּם hayyam, הַיָּם מוּצָק hayyam mutsaq, יָם הַנְּחֹשֶׁת yam hannekhosheth]. A large circular water container made of BRONZE and with the external shape of a LOTUS flower (1 Kgs 7:26 NRSV, "lily"), which stood in the southeast corner of the Temple courtyard (1 Kgs 7:39).

The Sea was built by HIRAM from Tyre (1 Kgs 7:13-14) during the reign of Solomon. It was supported by twelve bulls arranged in four groups of three, each facing one of the cardinal points. The bull represents the fertility and rain god Baal, which might suggest that the basin was used to collect rain water as part of its symbolic use. First Kings 7:23 describes it as 10 cubits in diameter, 5 cubits high, 30 cubits in perimeter, and having a capacity of 2,000 baths (2 Chr 4:2 = 3,000 baths). Josephus makes it a hemisphere with a capacity of 3,000 baths. There is disagreement about how to convert its precise measures and capacity into modern units (*see* WEIGHTS AND MEASURES §C.3.b.).

Water basins in Assyrian and Egyptian temples had an important role in the cult, as they also did in Canaan and Phoenicia. There was an artificial lake by the temple of Marduk (Babylon); and Lucian reports (*Syr. d.* 45a) that a sacred lake was built adjacent to the Hierapolis temple in Siria (in Mabbugh).

The Sea might have served as an iconic representation of the primordial waters. The Temple as the link between heaven and earth has its roots in the primeval SEA. For example, water plays an important role in Ezekiel's vision of the Temple (Ezek 47:1-12). The lotus shape reflects a common Canaanite motif as exemplified in the Ahiram sarcophagus from Byblos (ca. 1000 BCE) and the mural decorations of Kuntillet ʿAjrud in northern Sinai (9th cent. BCE).

Chronicles (2 Chr 4:6) demythologizes its symbolic-cultic use and suggests that it provided the water for the priests' ablutions, a very difficult task when the Sea was standing over 7 ft. high.

Ahaz (736–739 BCE) "removed the sea from the bronze oxen that were under it, and put it on a pediment of stone" (2 Kgs 16:17). When the Temple was destroyed in 587–586 BCE the Babylonians broke the Sea in pieces and carried them to Babylon (2 Kgs 25:13; Jer 52:17). *See* TEMPLE, JERUSALEM.

Bibliography: John Byl. "On the Capacity of Solomon's Molten Sea." *VT* 48 (1998) 309–14; Kjell Hognesius. "The Capacity of the Molten Sea in 2 Chronicles IV 5: A Suggestion." *VT* 44 (1994) 349–58; G. M. Hollenback. "The Dimension and Capacity of the 'Molten Sea' in 1 Kgs 7, 23.26." *Bib* 81 (2000) 391–92; Martin J. Mulder. *1 Kings. Volume 1: 1 Kings 1–11* (1998).

ALEJANDRO F. BOTTA

SEACOAST [חֶבֶל הַיָּם khevel hayyam, חוֹף הַיָּם khof hayyam; παραλία paralia, παραθαλάσσιος parathalassios]. The rich, densely populated Mediterranean coastland on the western edge of the biblical lands (Deut 1:7; Jdt 1:7; 2 Macc 8:11). The PHILISTINES inhabited its southern maritime plain, while Phoenicians lived in its northern coastal cities. The region is the object of God's wrath in Ezek 25:15-17 and Zeph 2:5-7. *See* CANAAN, CANAANITES; PHOENICIA.

LJUBICA JOVANOVIC

SEAFARER. *See* SAILOR; SHIPS AND SAILING IN THE NT; SHIPS AND SAILING IN THE OT.

SEAH see'uh [סְאָה seʾah]. A dry measure of capacity used for flour and cereals, mentioned in the NRSV's footnote at Gen 18:6. *See* WEIGHTS AND MEASURES.

SEAL, TO [חתם khatham; σφραγίζω sphragizō]. Sealing was used primarily to secure and verify official documents. A deed, such as Jeremiah's (Jer 32:6-15), would have been folded, tied, and sealed with clay bullae impressed with the witnesses' seals or signet rings. When Jeremiah purchased the field in Anathoth, he made two copies of the deed: a sealed copy with the terms and conditions and an open copy. Jeremiah and witnesses signed the deed, then sealed it, and both copies were preserved in an earthenware jar. Should any question arise in the future, the original witnesses or their descendants would verify their seals. An intact seal shows that no one has tampered with the original document.

Letters carried the authority of the seal's owner, regardless of the writer or sender. In 1 Kgs 21:8, Jezebel wrote letters in the name of King Ahab, sealed them with his seal, and sent them to Naboth's town; the elders and nobles then acted on the assumption that they were following the king's command. In Esth 3, Haman sent instructions under the seal of the king to all the provinces of Persia concerning the Jews (compare Esth 8; Dan 6:17).

In a general—and sometimes metaphorical—sense, sealing refers to closing or securing (Job 14:17; 41:15; Song 4:12; Matt 27:66; Rev 20:3). Symbolically, people are sealed by God or the Spirit to mark God's authority over them (2 Cor 1:22; Eph 1:13; Rev 7). Prophetic messages or visions are to be sealed until the proper time (Isa 8:16; 29:11; Dan 8:26; 9:24; 12:4, 9; Rev 5:1; 10:4; 22:10). *See* SEALS AND SCARABS.

JOEL F. DRINKARD JR.

SEALS AND SCARABS [חוֹתָם khotham; σφραγίς sphragis]. Seals were often used in the ANE in legal, economic, and political contexts. There were two major types of seals in the ANE: cylinder seals and stamp seals. Cylinder seals were very common in Mesopotamia and Syria during various periods. Cylinder seals would often be rolled onto the soft clay of a completed cuneiform tablet or on an envelope containing a cuneiform tablet. Cylinder seals were normally very small, often just 2–3 cm in length. Some cylinder seals have both writing and iconography, but some have just iconography. Stamp seals (sometimes also called scarab seals) were normally made of precious stones (e.g., carnelian, agate, dolerite) and were very common during the Iron Age in the southern Levant (e.g., Israel, Ammon, Moab). The book of Ben Sira refers to "precious stones engraved like seals" (Sir 45:11), a fitting statement because of the materials out of which seals were made. It should be noted in this connection that seal-makers are sometimes mentioned in biblical literature (e.g., Exod 28:11) and they seem to be accorded some status. However, at least at times, they were not considered to be elite members of society but rather as artisans (Sir 38:27). Because stamp seals are the most relevant for the study of the Bible, this article will focus predominantly on them, although there will be some reference to cylinder seals as well.

Stamp seals were often drilled so that a cord could be threaded through them. Some were drilled so that a small metal ring could be attached to them. Although rare, some excavated stamp seals have been discovered with the ring still attached (see below). Stamp seals are often divided by lines etched into the seal itself, with the segmented components referred to as "registers." Stamp seals are very small, rarely as large as a thumb nail. There were two different types: anepigraphic (i.e., seals with iconography but no writing) and epigraphic (seals with writing). In this connection, note that some epigraphic stamp seals do not have iconography (these are referred to as aniconic), but some epigraphic seals do have iconography. Furthermore, in terms of the technology, it should be stated that epigraphic seals are inscribed in reverse (mirror image) so that the orientation and direction of the writing will be correct in the impressed clay. Using a stamp seal required that the holder impress it into soft clay, with the result that the clay was impressed with the image of the seal. There is a beautiful text in the book of Job that captures this process superbly: "It is changed like clay under the seal" (Job 38:14). Sometimes the clay that was impressed was a small lump, and the resulting impressed clay is referred to as a bulla (pl. bullae) or a seal impression. Sometimes, however, the soft clay that was impressed was a jar (especially the handles) and the resulting impression is called a jar impression.

A. Format, Function, and Usage of Seals
B. Sealed Papyri and Impressed Jar Handles
C. The Scripts of Seals
D. The Iconography of Seals
E. Seals and the Antiquities Market
F. Literary and Metaphorical Usage
Bibliography

A. Format, Function, and Usage of Seals

Seals functioned as a means of identification and also to demonstrate ownership. For this reason, epigraphic seals normally consist of a personal name, that is, the name of the owner of the seal. Almost always, the personal name is preceded by a prepositional LAMED (1 ל, which can be translated "belonging to") that signifies ownership. For example, a Hebrew seal from Megiddo (WSSS #85) contains the following inscription: lʾsp (לאסף, "belonging to Asaph"). Often, however, seals will also include a patronymic, that is, a reference to the name of the father of the seal owner. There are multiple reasons for this practice, but the most important was to indicate with more precision the identity of the owner. After all, certain names were very common in certain regions at certain times. For example, an Old Hebrew seal from Arad (WSSS #70) contains the following inscription: "Belonging to Elyashib son of Ishyahu." An Old Hebrew bulla from the City of David (WSSS #515) reads "Belonging to Yadayahu son of Meshullam." Rarely, a seal will contain two patronymics, as is the

case with a Hebrew seal from Beth Shemesh that reads "Belonging to Ahab, son of Baadiel, son of Adael" (WSSS #52). Note that because the word son was so common on seals, it was sometimes (albeit rarely) omitted, as in the case of a Hebrew seal from Iron Age Jerusalem that reads "Belonging to Mattanyahu Azaryahu" (WSSS #261). Of course, the fact that seals functioned as mechanisms for identification is reflected in the biblical narrative. That is, Tamar (disguised as a prostitute) requested from Judah his seal (NRSV, "signet"), cord, and staff (Gen 38:18) as surety for compensation. The fact that the seal was sufficient subsequently to incriminate Judah is predictable, as it arguably contained his name.

Sometimes a title is present in an ancient seal, and this often served as a means of conveying not simply the identity of the owner but also something about the authority of the owner (or user) of the seal. This was especially the case when the owner of the seal was associated with a figure of high political office. For example, an Iron Age Hebrew seal from Megiddo contains the following inscription: "Belonging to Shema the servant of Jeroboam" (WSSS #2). Note that the term servant is often associated with the royal palace (hence, a "servant" is actually a high official). Thus, because this seal contains a political title, was found at the strategic northern Israelite city of Megiddo, contains the name JEROBOAM (the personal name of an 8th cent. Israelite king), and the script can be reliably dated to the 8th cent., it is normally argued that this seal belonged to an official who was part of the administration of the northern Israelite king Jeroboam. Because this seal was that of a high official of Jeroboam, documents sealed with it were of greater import and significance. After all, they reflected the power and authority of the throne. An Iron Age Ammonite bulla from Tell el-Umayri contains the following inscription: "Belonging to Milkomur the servant of Baalyasha" (WSSS #860). Because this seal is Ammonite, can be dated to the early 6th cent., and contains the title "servant," the Baalyasha of this bulla is often identified with biblical King Baalis of Ammon (Jer 40:14). The documents upon which it was used would have been considered particularly important. A fragmentary 4th-cent. bulla from the site of Wadi Daliyeh (near Samaria) is inscribed with the words "Sanballat governor of Samaria" (WSSS #419), a figure often considered to be the grandson of SANBALLAT I (mentioned in Neh 6:1-14). With regard to titles on seals as a means of conveying authority, the narrative about Jezebel's plot against Naboth is especially apropos. Because she was able to use Ahab's seal (and thus his royal authority), she was able to orchestrate the death of Naboth (1 Kgs 21:8). For a similar demonstration of the authority sometimes associated with the holder of a seal, note the text in the book of Revelation that refers to the binding dictates uttered by an angel that had "the seal of the living God" (Rev 7:1-2). Of course, some titles are not political and the owner of the seal was not connected with the throne. For example, an Iron Age

Hebrew seal from the City of David contains reference to "[Tobshillem] son of Zakar, the physician" (WSSS #420). Nevertheless, the majority of the titles preserved on provenanced seals are political in nature.

B. Sealed Papyri and Impressed Jar Handles

Papyrus was used widely in the ancient Levant as a medium for writing documents, especially those that were intended to be permanent. Thus, contracts, deeds of purchase, marriage licenses, divorce certificates, and literature were often written on papyrus. A text in the book of Tobit provides a nice example of the sealing of a marriage document. It refers to the fact that after Tobias confidently states that he wishes to marry Sarah, "writing material" was brought out to produce a "marriage contact," and after it was written the document was "sealed" (Tob 7:13-14; LXX Vaticanus and Alexandrinus). Note that ancient papyrus documents were often rolled after being written. A string was then wrapped around the rolled papyrus scroll so as to secure it (and keep it from unrolling), and then a small, rounded lump of soft clay would be placed on the string (the impressions from the strings are consistently visible on the reverse side of bullae). Then the seal of those that were part of the agreement would be pressed into the wet clay. To be sure, some documents had just a single seal (i.e., bulla); however, because multiple people would often be part of a legal agreement, multiple seals are sometimes present. In such cases, each person could take a small lump of moist clay and press it onto a wrapping string and impress it with their seal (each lump of clay could be put on a separate string). Obviously, the more seals on a document, the more important the document normally was (as more people were party to the agreement written on the papyrus document).

The sealed documents would then be stored in some fashion (e.g., in a personal archive, temple archive, etc.). Of course, these documents would often remain sealed forever. Indeed, the fact that opening a sealed document was a relatively rare (and serious) venture is implied in Isaiah. The text states that "the vision of all this has become for you like the words of a sealed document. If it is given to those who can read, with the command, 'Read this,' they say, 'We cannot, for it is sealed'" (Isa 29:11). In this connection, it should be noted that on the rarest of occasions, papyri will actually be discovered with the clay sealing(s) still in place. For example, some of the ELEPHANTINE PAPYRI and some of the SAMARIA PAPYRI have been discovered still sealed. Normally, however, sealed papyrus documents have not survived the ravages of time, though they were never opened in antiquity. Naturally, however, the bullae used to seal the papyrus documents have sometimes survived. One of the most striking caches of bullae was in Jerusalem's City of David excavations. At this site, more than fifty bullae were discovered. The papyri documents they had once sealed were destroyed in a conflagration, but some of the bullae survived (in part, because they were literally "fired" in the conflagration). Nevertheless, in antiquity, there were times when a sealed document would need to be opened (e.g., when there was a legal dispute, at which time the documents would be opened in the presence of a judicial figure). Indeed, at the city of Lachish a number of bullae were discovered all together in a small jug; thus the papyrus documents they had once sealed had been opened for some reason (ostensibly a legal reason). Striking, however, is the fact that after these documents were opened someone decided (for some reason) to deposit the bullae in a jug for storage. Again, most sealed documents would have never been opened.

The book of Jeremiah contains a wonderful synopsis of the process of signing and sealing legal documents (Jer 32:9-15). Within this pericope, there is reference to the fact that Jeremiah signed the deed of purchase with its terms and conditions, paid the agreed sum, and sealed the document. Significantly, this pericope mentions not just the "sealed deed" but also an "open copy." Naturally, the production of two copies, one sealed and one open, would have been useful. The sealed copy would be the one consulted in a legal case (as the seals were proof that there had been no tampering with the document). The open copy, however, could have been used for easy reference (e.g., in non-judicial contexts). Significantly, there are multiple references in the book of Revelation to the opening of sealed documents; among the most important is the reference to the scroll sealed with seven seals (Rev 6:1-17; 8:1-2). Because the opening of a sealed document often constituted a "judicial day of reckoning" for litigants, the occurrence of the "opening" in the Apocalypse is envisioned as a momentous occasion, something that is reflected in dramatic form in the verbiage (e.g., Rev 6:16). Note also that within the book of Revelation (e.g., Rev 6) the seals (i.e., bullae) are removed one by one, something occasioned by the fact that each bulla was attached to a separate string (as in the case of the Samaria Papyri).

Although seals are often associated with papyrus documents (and the sealing of those documents), seals were also impressed into clay jars at times. During the late 8th cent., large storage jars associated with the Judean crown in some fashion were impressed with LMLK SEALS, that is, seals that contained the words "belonging to the king." These inscriptions would routinely have a place-name on them as well. Of some consequence is the fact that during the middle of the 20th cent., scholars often dated the "Lamelech Jar Handles" to the late 7th and early 6th cent. However, since the final decades of the 20th cent., a strong consensus has developed that these jar handles are to be dated to the late 8th and early 7th cent. Indeed, the "Lamelech Jar Inscriptions" are often associated with the reign of the Judean king Hezekiah (r. ca. 715–687 BCE). To date, there are more than 1,000 of these "Lamelech Jar Handles" with Old Hebrew inscriptions from this period.

C. The Scripts of Seals

The scripts of seals are important for two major reasons. First and foremost, the script can assist in assigning the seal to a particular series. For example, there are distinctive features of the Old Hebrew script, distinctive features of the Phoenician script, and distinctive features of the Aramaic script. Understanding the national features of script series permits the paleographer to assign a seal to a particular national group. Second, diachronic development is present in scripts. This can be analyzed, and diagnostic features can be discerned. Therefore, a seal can often be dated paleographically. There is, however, a caveat that must be articulated: most seals (but not all) are written in a semi-formal cursive script. Because of the conservative nature of the semi-formal seal-script, the plus and minus range (of possible absolute dates) must be greater than for a cursive script (e.g., of ostraca). One standard *modus operandi* for dating seals is to subject each letter to a paleographic analysis, but to put substantial emphasis on the latest (i.e., most typologically advanced) paleographic features. That is, the latest paleographic features will often be the most indicative of the chronological horizon during which a seal was manufactured.

It should be noted in this connection that the epigraphic stamp seals that have so far been found in the southern Levant (e.g., Israel, Ammon, Moab, and even Phoenicia) date to the 8th cent. (or late 9th cent.) and subsequent chronological horizons. Scores of anepigraphic seals and bullae (i.e., seals and bullae without writing) have been found that are to be dated to chronological horizons of the 10th and 9th cent., but no epigraphic seals dating to these horizons have been discovered to date.

D. The Iconography of Seals

Cylinder seals and stamp seals often have a fair amount of iconography, sometimes reflecting certain religious motifs (some of which shed light on biblical texts and references). Note, e.g., that a seal from Megiddo has some beautiful iconography, including an ambulating winged creature with the body of a lion and the head of an eagle, that is, a griffin (*WSSS*, #160). Creatures such as this are often referred to as "composite" because they participate in various realms (e.g., the king of the beasts and the king of the air). Within ANE art and iconography, these sorts of mythological creatures are often protectors of the divine (e.g., sacred space such as temples) and also protectors of the representative of the divine (e.g., the divinely appointed monarch). The biblical descriptions of cherubim and seraphim are drawn heavily from ANE art and thus the iconography of seals can often shed light on biblical imagery such as this (*see* CHERUB, CHERUBIM; SERAPH, SERAPHS).

Nevertheless, the iconographic material is much deeper than this. Thus, the solar disk and lunar disk are also very common on seals. An Ammonite bulla found at Umayri, Jordan, in 1989 mentions a certain Milkomur

and contains these iconographic features (Herr 1989). Moreover, a stunning Hebrew seal from Lachish is replete with some majestic iconography, including a four-winged beetle, two ankhs, and sun disks (*WSSS* #59). Falcons are also well-attested on seals. For example, a Hebrew seal from Cadiz contains two falcons (*WSSS* #267). Similarly, another Ammonite seal found in 1989 at Tell Umayri contains some stunning iconography, including a falcon (Herr 1997). During excavations at Lachish, a beautiful Old Hebrew seal was found (*WSSS* #385). Incised into this seal is a two-winged uraeus (snake) in the top register facing an ankh. It is often the case that a rose or lotus will be present. Such is the case with numerous seals, including a rather crude one from the excavations at Ketef Hinnom, Jerusalem (*WSSS* #326). The fact of the matter is that seals constitute a substantial reservoir of iconographic data. *See* ʿUMAYRI, TALL AL.

E. Seals and the Antiquities Market

It should be emphasized that the majority of the seals and bullae that are often discussed within the field of epigraphy are not from excavations. Rather, they surfaced on the antiquities market. Some of these are modern forgeries. Among the most famous such forgeries is the seal that contains the inscription "Belonging to Baruch the son of Neriah, the scribe" (*WSSS* #417). Those attempting to work with seals, bullae, and scarabs should use the utmost caution (Rollston).

F. Literary and Metaphorical Usage

Because seals were such important aspects of the daily lives of the ancients, some language that can be considered "figurative" is used of seals. For example, sealing a document (with one's own seal) was an act that demonstrated that the person believed the document to be authentic. For this reason, the author of the Gospel of John could state that "whoever has accepted his testimony has sealed [NRSV, "certified"] this, that God is true" (John 3:33). Similarly, seals signified possession, ownership, and authority. For this reason, the writer of the Apocalypse considered the term *seal* to be an acceptable means of conveying the fact that certain people were God's people: they have the "seal of God on their foreheads" and are demonstrably his; therefore, they are to be spared from the divine punishment meted out to the wicked of the earth (Rev 9:4). Similarly, the book of Haggai can refer to Zerubbabel and state that Yahweh has declared him to be "like a signet ring" because Yahweh has "chosen" him (Hag 2:23; compare Sir 49:11). Along these same lines, the author of 2 Timothy can state that "God's firm foundation stands, bearing this seal [NRSV, "inscription"]: 'The Lord knows those who are his'" (2 Tim 2:19). In the Song of Songs the bride tells her groom to "set me as a seal upon your heart, as a seal upon your arm; for love is strong as death, passion fierce as the grave" (Song 8:6); the seal is a symbol of affection and a strong bond that both desire. In the NT, the term *seal* is often associated with the gift of the Holy Spirit. For this reason, Paul can state that the Christians at Ephesus "were marked with the seal of the promised Holy Spirit" (Eph 1:13). Similarly, Paul can state that Christians "were marked with a seal for the day of redemption" (Eph 4:30). He also refers to God as "putting his seal on us and giving us his Spirit in our hearts" (2 Cor 1:22). Furthermore, because a sealed document was considered (at one level) to be "concealed," the author of the Apocalypse was told to "seal up what the seven thunders have said, and do not write it down" (Rev 10:4), that is, to conceal it so that it could not be read. Sometimes the seal served as proof of something. For example, Paul refers to the sign of circumcision as a "seal of the righteousness" that Abraham had (Rom 4:11). He also refers to the Corinthians as the "seal of my apostleship in the Lord" (1 Cor 9:2). Finally, the term *seal* could also be used of the sealing of a tomb (Matt 27:66) or the door of a building (e.g., Bel 14-15). *See* INSCRIPTIONS; JEWELRY; JEWELS AND PRECIOUS STONES.

was found are securely dated (based on the archaeological materials found in them) to the 8th through mid-6th cent. Based on the script of this seal, this seal dates to the 8th or early 7th cent.

Photo by Bruce Zuckerman and Marilyn Lundberg. Courtesy of the Department of Antiquities of Jordan.

Figure 2: ʿUmayri Seal (J16685) [Reversed with Photoshop].

This seal is from the Tell al-ʿUmayri Excavation in Jordan. It is inscribed on two sides, and both sides have some iconography, the obverse with a bird and the reverse with a ram (Herr). The inscription on the obverse reads "Belonging to Il-Amuts, son of Tamik-il." The inscription on the reverse reads simply "belonging to Il-Amuts." It is important to note that although many seals are inscribed on just one side, some are inscribed on both. Note that the name "Il-Amuts" means essentially "Il is strong," and Tamak-il means essentially "Il sustains." This seal has been dated to the 7th cent. The script is, of course, Ammonite.

Photo by Bruce Zuckerman and Marilyn Lundberg. Courtesy of the Department of Antiquities of Jordan.

Figure 1: Umm Udeinah Seal (J14653) [Reversed with Photoshop].

This beautiful seal (J14653) was found replete with the ring. Of course, seals normally have holes in them for rings (or strings), but it is rare actually to find the ring. This one, however, comes from a tomb (hence, the fine preservation of the seal and ring). Some astrological iconography adorns the top of this seal. Two clear personal names are inscribed on the seal, namely, "Palatiy, ben Maas." Significantly, a title (presumably of Palatiy) is given as well, namely, mzkr (מזכר), a title also attested in biblical literature, and often rendered "the herald" (e.g., 1 Kgs 4:3). The tombs where this seal

Photo by Bruce Zuckerman and Marilyn Lundberg. Courtesy of the Department of Antiquities of Jordan.

Figure 3: ʿUmayri Seal (J19332) [Reversed with Photoshop].

This seal consists of two clear registers. It has been drilled. The top register reads lʾzn bn and the bottom register reads brkʾil ("belonging to ʾOzen ben Barak-il").

This seal demonstrates the fact that although iconography is common, some seals do not have any iconography.

Bibliography: Larry G. Herr. "The Inscribed Seal Impression." *Madaba Plains Project: The 1984 Season at Tell el-'Umeiri and Vicinity and Subsequent Studies* (1989) 369–74; Larry G. Herr. "Epigraphic Finds from Tall al-'Umayri during the 1989 Season." *Madaba Plains Project: The 1989 Season at Tell el-'Umeiri and Vicinity and Subsequent Studies* (1997) 323–30; Christopher A. Rollston. "Non-Provenanced Epigraphs II: the Status of Non-Provenanced Epigraphs within the Broader Corpus of Northwest Semitic." *Maarav* 11 (2004) 57–79; William A.Ward. "Beetles in Stone: The Egyptian Scarab." *BA* 57 (1994) 186–202.

CHRISTOPHER A. ROLLSTON

SEASONS [מוֹעֵד moʿedh, עֵת ʿeth; καιρός kairos]. Annual calendrical periods, each about three months, typically revolving around the agricultural cycle (e.g., 1 Kgs 5:13-14; Amos 7–8) and defined by the position of the heavenly luminaries (Gen 1:14). More generally, *season* refers to the appropriate time or period for something to happen (Eccl 3:1; compare Prov 15:23). The rains should come in their season, that is, at the right time (Lev 26:4; Deut 11:14; Jer 5:24; Ezek 34:26), and one harvests the crops in the appropriate period (Num 13:20; Job 5:26; Ps 1:3; Hos 2:9; Matt 21:34, 41; Gal 6:9).

The Bible mentions at least four seasons by name (Gen 8:22; Amos 3:15; Zech 14:8; Ps 74:17). The reckoning of the YEAR usually begins in the spring, when plants and animals bear new life and rain is appropriate (Zech 10:1). Summer is the season of heat (Ps 32:4) and a stage in the agricultural cycle (Prov 10:5; Jer 8:20; compare Dan 2:35; Sir 50:8; Matt 24:32; Mark 13:28; Luke 21:30). There is no clear name for the autumn, which is the time for harvesting the late crops (*see* HARVEST) and for several holidays, including the Festival of Tabernacles. Winter is the season for cold and inclement weather (Ezra 10:9, 13; Matt 24:20; Mark 13:18; Acts 27:12; 28:11; compare 2 Tim 4:21) and includes the festival of Hanukkah (1 Macc 4:52-59; 2 Macc 10:8; John 10:22-23). Later Jewish texts are more explicit about the seasons and their length (*1 En.* 72–82; *b. Eruv.* 56a; 1QS X, 5–8; 4Q211 1 II, 4; *Jub.* 6:23, 28-29; Philo, *Spec. Laws* 4.235). *See* CALENDAR; SUMMER AND WINTER.

JAMES C. VANDERKAM

SEAT [כִּסֵּא kisseʾ, כַּפֹּרֶת kapporeth, מוֹשָׁב moshav, שֶׁבֶת sheveth; βῆμα bēma, καθέδρα kathedra]. Several words in the OT and NT are translated as "seat." These terms, in their context of usage, offer a range of nuances. In most uses, *seat* implies more than merely an object for physical repose; in many texts status is inherent to the usage.

Four Hebrew terms create the rhetorical range of meaning for the word *seat* in the OT. Kapporeth refers to the MERCY SEAT (LXX hilastērion [ἱλαστήριον]; see Heb 9:5), the covering of the ark of the covenant.

In Num 21:15 reference is made to the "wadis that extend to the seat (sheveth) of Ar," an expression that seems best understood as a reference to the location (i.e., the "geographical sitting place" of Ar). In Prov 31:23, the husband of the virtuous woman "takes his seat among the elders of the land," a description that seems to carry both literal as well as metaphorical implications (see also 1 Kgs 10:19, the description of the Queen of Sheba's throne prepared by Solomon).

Moshav is used as a term of location in several senses. First Samuel 20:18, 25 speaks of David's and Saul's "seats/places" at a table for eating. Job "took his seat" in the city square (Job 29:7); this seems somewhat similar to Prov 31:23. The intent of the Ps 1:1 reference to the "seat of scoffers" seems a bit more elusive. Ezekiel 8:3 speaks of the "seat of the image of jealously" and 28:2 refers to the "seat of the gods."

Kisseʾ is translated "throne" or "seat" in the NRSV. It is used four times in the Samuel-Eli narrative. Hannah's prayer includes a reference (1 Sam 2:8) to Yahweh's raising the poor and needy "to make them sit with princes and inherit a seat of honor." Lady Wisdom sits "at the door of her house, on a seat at the high places of the town" (Prov 9:14).

Two words are at the core of the discussion in the NT, kathedra and bema. Two uses of kathedra are rather picturesque. In Matt 23:2 Jesus links the scribes and Pharisees' "sitting on Moses' seat" with teaching. Is this to be understood merely metaphorically (i.e., the Pharisees were carrying out the Mosaic role of teaching); or was there also a very physical aspect to it as well (i.e., a seat in the synagogue in which an authoritative teacher sat)? Perhaps this is the background of Jesus' indictment of the Pharisees as recorded in Luke 11:43: "you love to have the seat of honor (prōtokathedrian πρωτοκαθεδρίαν) in the synagogue." Three texts in Acts describe Herod (12:21) and Festus (25:6, 17) as taking their seats on the tribunal (bēma, "seat of judgment"). Matthew 27:19 places Pilate on "the judgment seat" in the context of Jesus' trial; Rom 14:10 and 2 Cor 5:10 reference the "judgment seat of God" and "of Christ," respectively. Hebrews 12:2 emphasizes Jesus' divine status by noting that he has "taken his seat at the right hand of the throne of God" (compare Matt 19:28; 26:64; Eph 1:20; Col 3:1). James 2:3 chastises its readers for according status in their assemblies to the rich by saying, "Have a seat here, please," while to the poor they say, "Stand there" or "Sit at my feet." In James' view, such distinctions make them "judges with evil thoughts" (v. 4).

JOHN I. LAWLOR

SEAT, MOSES' [Μωϋσέως καθέδρα Mōyseōs kathedra]. An expression that describes legitimate teaching authority. Moses provided Israel with the law, but after that time it was necessary for other teachers to expound and apply this law, and those who did so with authority were said to sit on Moses' seat. In Matt 23:2 Jesus speaks of the scribes and Pharisees as sitting on the seat of Moses. In the immediate context, Jesus advises his disciples to adhere to the words that the scribes and Pharisees speak when they sit on the seat of Moses, that is, when they expound the words of TORAH.

CATHERINE JONES

SEBA see´buh [סְבָא sevaʾ]. Cush's firstborn (Gen 10:7; 1 Chr 1:9) and the eponymous ancestor of a people or place (Ps 72:10; Isa 43:3). *See* CUSH, CUSHITE; SABEANS.

SEBA, TEL ES. Tel es-Seba (ca. 1.1 ha), also known as Tell BEER-SHEBA, is located in the Beer-Sheba–Arad Valley in southern Israel. Its earliest settlements were villages (12th–10th cent. BCE, Str. 9–6). In the 9th cent. BCE, during the Iron Age IIB Period, a city was founded at the site (Str. 5). The city was fortified with a solid wall measuring up to 4 m in width, and its plan included a four-room gate structure, dwelling quarters, public buildings, a sophisticated underground water system, and a network of radial and bisecting streets. The city was destroyed and rebuilt at the end of the 9th cent. BCE (Str. 4); it was destroyed again at the beginning of the 8th cent. BCE.

A new city (Str. 3 and 2) probably served as the administrative center of the Judean Negev district in the 8th cent. BCE. This city preserved the plan of the 9th-cent. city (Str. 5 and 4), but introduced many significant changes. A casemate wall now defended the city, large storehouses were built, and the tunnel of the water system was widened. A temple at the site was probably destroyed during the reform of King Hezekiah at the end of the 8th cent. BCE (Str. 2). The city was destroyed by the Assyrian king Sennacherib in the year 701 BCE.

During the Persian Period (5th–4th cent. BCE), a small settlement was founded on the tel. In the Hellenistic Period (3rd cent. BCE), a fort and temple were constructed. In the Early Roman Period (1st cent. CE), a governor's residence stood there, and in the Late Roman Period (2nd–3rd cent. CE), a Roman fort was erected. In the Early Islamic Period, the site functioned as a way station.

ITZHAQ BEIT-ARIEH

SEBAM. *See* SIBMAH.

SECACAH si-kay´kuh [סְכָכָה sekhakhah]. The name means "protection" or "cover." Located within the wilderness of Judah in the region between JERICHO and EN-GEDI (Josh 15:61), Secacah shared a developed system of fortifications with MIDDIN and NIBSHAN. Scholarship has generally identified Secacah with Khirbet es-Samrah, around 7 km southwest of Khirbet

Qumran. Iron Age antiquities present at the site suggest occupation around the 7th cent. BCE.

Bibliography: Maurice Baillet, J. T. Milik, and Roland de Vaux. *Discoveries in the Judaean Desert of Jordan III* (1962); Aharon Kempinski and Ronny Reich. *The Architecture of Ancient Israel* (1992).

JOSEPH R. CATHEY

SECOND ADAM [ὁ ἔσχατος Ἀδάμ ho eschatos Adam]. Paul calls Jesus the "last Adam" in 1 Cor 15:45. He contrasts the first Adam, created as a living being (Gen 2:7), with the last Adam, who became a "life-giving spirit." Paul states that in the first Adam all die, while in Christ "all will be made alive" (1 Cor 15:22). For Paul, Adam is a type of Christ (Rom 5:14), and in Rom 5:12-21 Paul argues that Jesus overcomes and corrects what the first Adam did. Adam's transgression brought death. But through Jesus, God's grace was made available to many, which demonstrates that Christ is greater than Adam.

KENNETH D. LITWAK

SECOND COMING [παρουσία parousia]. A belief held by many Christians that at the conclusion of history Jesus will return bodily and inaugurate a new kingdom of God on a newly constituted earth. The most explicit NT sources for this belief are 1 Thess 4:16 and Rev 1:7. *See* PAROUSIA.

SECOND QUARTER [מִשְׁנֶה mishneh]. An area of the city of Jerusalem mentioned as the home of HULDAH the prophetess (2 Kgs 22:14; 2 Chr 34:22). The location was likely to the southwest of the First Temple. The place is also mentioned as a site of wailing (Zeph 1:10).

Bibliography: Lawrence Stager. "The Archaeology of the East Slope of Jerusalem and the Terraces of the Kidron." *JNES* 41 (1982) 111–21.

JESSICA TINKLENBERG DEVEGA

SECOND TEMPLE PERIOD. The period (ca. 515 BCE–70 CE) after the Babylonian exile, when the rebuilding of the Jerusalem Temple began under Zerubbabel, the governor of Judah, and Jeshua, the high priest. The Temple would have a number of transformations during this period, ultimately becoming a massive precinct under Herod the Great, until it was destroyed again (by the Romans) in 70 CE. Judah was under the control of a series of foreign powers—Persian, Hellenistic (Ptolemaic and Seluecid), Hasmonean, and Roman—during this time. This period is defined by DIASPORA Jews living under foreign control, the development of SYNAGOGUE worship, and the process of establishing a CANON OF THE OLD TESTAMENT (§E).

GARRETT GALVIN, OFM

SECOND TEMPLE PERIOD JEWISH LIFE. Second Temple Judaism is often associated with the major sects and parties—Pharisees, Sadducees, Essenes, and Zealots. The substantial differences in the practices, beliefs, and social organizations of these groups, however, should not obscure the common core shared not only with one another but also with the unaffiliated "common people" and that would have been recognized as "Jewish" by Jews and Gentiles alike, in Palestine and in the DIASPORA.

The Second Temple era covers the period between the latter part of the 6th cent. BCE, which saw the return of Jewish exiles to Jerusalem and the beginning of the lengthy rebuilding of the Temple, and the year 70 CE, when the Temple was destroyed again during the course of the failed first Jewish Revolt against Rome. Except for 145–63 BCE, Judea was a vassal and often contested territory within the Persian (Achaemenid) Empire (550–330 BCE) and Alexander the Great's Hellenic Macedonian Empire (ca. 330 BCE), the satrapies of the Seleucid Empire and Ptolemaic Egypt, and, from 63 BCE onward, the Roman Empire. Throughout this period, Jews in Palestine and the Diaspora were strongly influenced by Hellenism. At the same time, distinctive Jewish practices and beliefs continued to develop, along with a growing sense of communal identity and identification with Jewish history that did not, however, preclude political religious and social rivalry and disharmony. Diaspora Jews paid the temple tax and, when possible, made pilgrimage to Jerusalem. Similarly, Jews in both Palestine and the Diaspora were alarmed at the threat of the Roman emperor Gaius Caligula to have his statue erected in the Temple in 41 CE.

A. Sources
B. Everyday Life
C. Beliefs
D. Practices
   1. Sabbath, holy days, and pilgrimage festivals
   2. Sacrifice and prayer
   3. Circumcision, purity, and dietary laws
   4. Charity and deeds of loving-kindness
Bibliography

A. Sources

The most detailed literary sources for Second Temple period Jewish life in Palestine are Josephus' *The Antiquities of the Jews* and *The Jewish War*. Also important are the NT, the Dead Sea Scrolls, and numerous archaeological remains. For the Diaspora, the writings of Philo are the most illuminating. Information can also be gleaned from the OT apocrypha, including the books of the Maccabees and the apocryphal novels Susanna, Greek Esther, Judith and Tobit, and the comments by Greek and Latin authors, which often corroborate beliefs and practices described in Jewish sources. Rabbinic sources, notably the Mishnah, the Babylonian Talmud, and the Jerusalem Talmud, must be used with care.

Although these sources may include traditions that date back to the Second Temple period, they were compiled in the centuries after the Temple's destruction, that is, from the 3rd to the 6th cent. In all cases, the date, purpose, target audience, and social-historical situation of the author(s) must be kept in mind.

Archaeological and material remains for this period are also abundant, if incomplete. Inscriptions and papyri provide insights into the aspects of Jewish life, including the role of women and the participation of Gentiles, while archaeological remains of synagogues, homes, ritual baths and other structures help us to visualize the everyday life as well as the role of public institutions.

B. Everyday Life

As in our own day, ordinary people spent most of their time on work. Residents of cities such as Jerusalem would have been engaged in a broad range of occupations, such as the manufacturing of stone vessels and linens for priestly robes, and the tourist trade, which in Jerusalem would have peaked during the three annual pilgrimage festivals. Throughout Palestine and the Diaspora, many people would have been involved with agriculture, including viticulture and the cultivation of olives. Men likely were responsible for planting, plowing, and harvesting; women were engaged with food preparation, such as grinding the grain, baking, and cooking. Essential to the diet were foods such as wheat, milk, and oil. At least half of the daily caloric intake would have been in the form of grain. Also important were legumes, olive oil, and fruit, such as dried figs. Other important foods included grapes and grape products such as wine, dairy products made from the milk of goats and sheep, honey, dates, eggs, onion and garlic. While poultry and fish, where available, would have been consumed regularly, red meat would be served on rare occasions, perhaps only on festivals.

Textiles were also an important part of the economy (*see* CLOTH, CLOTHES). Men sheared the sheep and carded the wool, as well as the plowing and harvesting of wool. Women likely were most closely involved with the production and care of clothing, including spinning, weaving, sewing, washing, though some tasks, such as wool dyeing, would have been done by professionals. Men and women wore knee-length tunics, over which they wrapped a long mantle. Archaeological evidence points to the abundant use of red and blue dyes.

C. Beliefs

Jewish religious life and everyday life were intertwined; both were grounded in two primary articles of faith: the belief in and worship of the God of Israel, and the belief in the Scriptures as the revealed word of God. Faith included the belief that the God of Israel was the one who created the physical universe and controls history and the fate of humankind, that God exercises justice and mercy in the life of the individual and community, and that God elected the people Israel as God's partner in covenantal relationship.

D. Practices

The belief in Scripture as divine revelation undergirded a commitment to observe Jewish law as decreed in Scripture and amplified through authoritative interpretation. This commitment, however, did not include the expectation that the law could and would be fulfilled to perfection. Rather, human imperfection and the vagaries of life guaranteed the inevitability of transgression. Except for major sins such as idolatry, adultery, and homicide, repentance and atonement for transgression were built into the liturgical calendar and into regular life, by means that included prayer, sacrifices, and the annual Day of Atonement.

Practice focused on three physical locales—the Jerusalem Temple, the synagogue or local community gathering-place, and the home—and included Sabbath and holy days, worship of God through prayer and sacrifice, ritual and family purity laws, circumcision, dietary laws, charity, and deeds of loving-kindness.

1. Sabbath, holy days, and pilgrimage festivals

Jews and non-Jews alike considered the SABBATH to be the most unusual aspect of standard Jewish practice. The weekly Sabbath began at the sundown marking the end of the sixth day of the week and the beginning of the seventh, and required the cessation of everyday activities. Sabbath was a day of rest devoted to worship, reading and studying the Torah, spending time with family and friends, and resting. Special sacrifices were offered in the Temple.

The most solemn days of the year included the period from the New Year through the Day of Atonement, during which the people individually and as a community repented and atoned for transgressions. By contrast, the three pilgrimage festivals—Tabernacles, which occurred five days after the Day of Atonement, Passover in the spring, and the Feast of Weeks seven weeks later—were not only religious but also festive occasions marked not only by sacrifices but also by feasting with family and friends. While it is extremely difficult to estimate the size of the holiday crowds, Jerusalem would have been filled to capacity. Although all Jewish males were commanded to make pilgrimage, it was impractical for Jews of ordinary means, especially those who lived at some distance from Jerusalem, to undertake pilgrimage on a regular basis (see FEASTS AND FASTS).

2. Sacrifice and prayer

The sacrifices, whether individual or communal, were performed in the Temple for the purposes of worship, glorification of God, thanksgiving, purification, atonement for sins, and feasting. The sacrifice, which included not only animals (sheep, goats, cattle) but also grains, wine, and birds (doves or pigeons), was either burned or eaten by the priests, or, on occasions such as

the Passover, by the community (see SACRIFICES AND OFFERINGS).

Although private prayer is well-attested, it is unclear whether and to what extent there was a liturgy with fixed prayers at the time of the Second Temple, and whether these were performed in the Temple, synagogue, the home, or all three. The Shema (Deut 6:4—"Hear, O Israel: The LORD is our God, the LORD alone" [NRSV]) was written on parchment and placed inside the mezuzah (small container placed on the doorframes) and tefillin (phylacteries, boxes strapped onto the arm and forehead for morning prayers). It is likely that Jews, both in Palestine and in the Diaspora, gathered together, often in special buildings (SYNAGOGUEs) on the Sabbath, for the purposes of reading and studying Scripture.

3. Circumcision, purity, and dietary laws

The commandment to circumcise male children on the eighth day of life, recorded in Gen 17:10-14, was widely observed. Although this practice was not unique to the Jews, it was closely associated with them. In theory it was incumbent upon the father to circumcise his son, though in practice it was often a trained professional who did the actual removal of the foreskin.

Purity, not to be confused with cleanliness or hygiene, was expressed in ritual, moral, and family life. In ritual life, it pertained to the state in which one would be permitted to enter the Temple and participate in the sacrificial rituals. Ritual purity was morally neutral and pertained to states of being that were normal and often desirable aspects of life. For example, contact with a corpse imparted ritual impurity, yet it was important to take care of the dead and prepare them carefully and properly for burial. Similarly, seminal emissions, menstruation, and childbirth are all natural occurrences necessary for the fulfillment of the commandment to be fruitful and multiply, yet they too imparted temporary ritual impurity. Moral impurity was contracted through negative behavior such as sexual immorality and idolatry. These could be alleviated only through repentance and atonement, with the accompanying sacrifices. Family purity laws required that the married couple refrain from intercourse at the time of the woman's menses, and, in some interpretations, several days thereafter (see CLEAN AND UNCLEAN).

Purification rituals most often involved immersion, either in a natural body of water or in a ritual bath, known as a mikveh. The typical bath was approximately 7 ft. deep and held 3,800 U.S. gallons. It often had two sets of stairs, separated by a barrier. One set was used in order to descend into the pool and the other for ascent after immersion. It is unlikely that purification was needed in order to enter the synagogue in the Second Temple period, but ritual paths were often located nearby as a matter of convenience.

Kashruth, or the dietary system, was based on biblical injunctions that designated certain animals, such as pigs and crustaceans, as unclean and therefore not permissible for consumption. Also forbidden are the main fatty parts of an animal and its blood; special slaughtering methods were required. Certain combinations of foods were not permitted. For example, the biblical text forbids the cooking of a goat in its mother's milk (Exod 23:19, 34-37; Deut 14:21), a restriction that was later extended to all milk and meat products. To guard against the possibility of eating food that had been used in idol worship, it was customary for Jews to avoid wine, oil, and bread made by Gentiles (*see* DIETARY LAWS).

4. Charity and deeds of loving-kindness

Charity and good deeds were both expressions of communal responsibility but also enshrined in law. The laws of tithing supported Levites and priests and also the poor; other laws required farmers to leave some of their harvest for the poor.

Our sources provide vivid glimpses into Second Temple Jewish life both in Palestine and in the Diaspora. While much is known, for example, about the sacrificial system, the practices associated with the synagogue and the home are less clear. Ongoing textual and archaeological investigation may help to clarify these and other aspects of Second Temple Jewish life.

Bibliography: Lester L. Grabbe. *Judaic Religion in the Second Temple Period: Belief and Practice from the Exile to Yavneh* (2000); Aharon Oppenheimer. *The 'Am Ha-Aretz: A Study in the Social History of the Jewish People in the Hellenistic-Roman Period* (1977); E. P. Sanders. *Judaism: Practice and Belief 63 BCE–66 CE* (1992).

ADELE REINHARTZ

SECRET [מִסְתָּר mistar, סוֹד sodh, סָתוּם sathum, סֵתֶר sether, תַּעֲלֻמָה ta'alumah; κρυπτός kryptos, λάθρα lathra, μυστήριον mystērion]. In the OT, a secret is typically an item of human knowledge kept hidden by people from other people (Prov 11:13; Tob 12:7), and this meaning continues in typical NT usage (Matt 6:4, 6, 18). In OT prophecy, in apocalyptic at the end of the OT period, in Second Temple Judaism, and often in the NT, the term can also denote something kept hidden by God, but in due time revealed by God as a part of the revelation of God's plan and will (e.g., Ezek 28:3; Amos 3:7; 2 Esd 10:38; Mark 4:11; Rom 16:25; 1 Cor 2:7). This revelation becomes transformative for the people of God, as they can better locate themselves in the cosmic sweep of God's plan for the universe. *See* MYSTERY; SECRET, MESSIANIC.

ROBERT E. VAN VOORST

SECRET BOOK OF JOHN. *See* JOHN, APOCRYPHON OF OR SECRET BOOK OF.

SECRET GOSPEL OF MARK. *See* MARK, SECRET GOSPEL OF.

SECRET, MESSIANIC. "Messianic secret" refers to the motif, chiefly in the Gospel of Mark, in which Jesus is presented as suppressing knowledge of his identity. In Mark, Jesus silences demons who proclaim his divine identity (1:25, 34; 3:11-12) and commands persons for whom he has performed miracles not to discuss their experiences (a leper, 1:43-44; Jairus' daughter, 5:43; a deaf and mute man, 7:36; compare a blind man ordered to go home rather than to his village, 8:26). The striking exception is the account of the Gerasene demoniac (5:1-20), who wishes to accompany Jesus on his travels but instead is instructed by Jesus to tell his (presumably Gentile) neighbors about his encounter with Jesus. When Peter confesses Jesus as the Messiah at Caesarea Philippi, Jesus orders the disciples not to tell others (8:30), and the disciples present with Jesus at his transfiguration are instructed to say nothing about the event until after the Son of Man has risen from the dead (9:9). Similarly, Jesus often is said to teach privately and avoid crowds (even in the Gentile area near Tyre, 9:24), and his disciples characteristically do not understand his message.

The classic discussion of the motif is William Wrede, *Des Messiasgeheimnis in den Evangelien* (1901; translated into English as *The Messianic Secret*, 1971). Wrede reacted against contemporary interpretations of Mark's Gospel that understood Jesus as beginning his ministry as Messiah at his baptism but concealing this identity. Likewise, Jesus' predictions of his forthcoming death and resurrection after Peter's confession (which indicated the disciples' gradual enlightenment to his identity) were viewed as intended to disabuse the disciples of traditional Jewish notions of the Messiah so they instead could understand him in light of the cross (*see* MESSIAH, JEWISH). Wrede rejected these claims, arguing that an intentional secrecy motif is foreign to the author of Mark, whose own intentions must be sought; the folly of such external theories was evidenced by internal factors in the Gospel such as Jesus' use of the messianic title "Son of Man" both before and after Peter's confession, the public nature of most of his miracles, and parables in which Jesus strongly hints at his messianic identity (bridegroom, 2:19-20; strongman, 3:23-27). Instead, Wrede argued that the historical Jesus never claimed to be the Messiah, but the post-resurrection conviction in early Christianity of Jesus' divinity and messianic identity caused the church to rework genuine reminiscences of Jesus to express this theology.

Wrede's theory has spawned numerous adaptations and rebuttals, but his abiding contribution is his emphasis on Mark as a theological text rather than a straightforward historical account. Whereas Wrede credited the secrecy motif to the early church that provided Mark's sources, recent interpreters tend to highlight the literary skills of the evangelist, especially his emphasis that Jesus cannot be understood apart from the cross. *See* CHRIST; MARK, GOSPEL OF.

Bibliography: Christopher Tuckett, ed. *The Messianic Secret.* IRT 1 (1983); William Wrede. *The Messianic Secret.* J. C. Greig, trans. (1971).

ERIC F. MASON

SECRETARY. *See* SCRIBE.

SECRETS OF ENOCH. *See* ENOCH, SECOND BOOK OF.

SECTS, SECTARIANS. The topic of sects and sectarians can be approached 1) as something with which people in antiquity conceptualized their reality, or 2) as a concept that modern scholars of antiquity find useful.

In antiquity, the Jewish historian Josephus used the Greek term hairesis (αἵρεσις, "choice") in his description of three philosophical schools, those of Pharisees, Sadducees, and Essenes (*Ant.* 13.171; 18.11; *J.W.* 2.119); he also utilized this term for the Fourth Philosophy (*Ant.* 18.23), and for the group of Judas the Galilean (*J.W.* 2.118). In the NT, hairesis is used of Pharisees, Sadducees, and Nazarenes (Christians), indicating that these were considered as distinct schools, groups, or teachings in Judaism (e.g., Acts 5:17; 15:5; 24:5). The term is also used for schisms and heresies among Christians (1 Cor 11:19; Gal 5:20; 2 Pet 2:1). The meaning varies between "school of opinion" (in a positive or negative sense, i.e., right or wrong opinions) and "adherents to particular opinions/customs; distinct group." The translation of this word as "sect" is not unproblematic. The Latin translation is hairesis or *secta* ("following," deriving from *sequor,* "to follow," not from *seco,* "to cut, to separate"). The use of hairesis has a negative tone in NT letters whereas Josephus thinks highly of these Jewish circles, the Essenes especially. Only a minority of Jews belonged to the Essenes, but Josephus regards them as representative of Jewish thought and practice. He introduces them as a superior philosophy (their manliness, endurance, and piety, their views on the soul and fate).

Many investigators take *sect* in a non-technical sense and consider it suitable for describing the diversity and particularism of Judaism in the Second Temple period, without any value judgments or assessment of the sociological stances. This is close to the neutral use of hairesis. Sects were variations of Judaism. The Sadducees were an elitist, priestly party, into which members were born; whereas the Pharisees, the Qumranites, and the Essenes had, to some extent, voluntary membership, and can be compared to other voluntary associations in the Greco-Roman world. There were also followers of individual leaders (Judas the Galilean; Bannus; John the Baptist; Jesus of Nazareth) as well as politically colored parties (Hellenizers; Hasidim; Zealots) in Second Temple Judaism—in addition to the majority who did not belong to any of these. The flourishing of sects is traced back to differing reactions towards the Maccabean success and the subsequent Hasmonean state. The social setting for the rise of sectarianism included urbanization, increased literacy, and an unstable political situation. The relations with and attitudes towards the Temple played a major role along with other legal opinions and practices. Divergent views on the afterlife, eschatology, or the origin of evil were probably more easily tolerated.

It must be noted that mapping Jewish groups is not the same as mapping Jewish thoughts and ideas. Apocalyptic ideas, e.g., gained ground in several groups in Second Temple Judaism. Recent research has proposed that there was a distinct movement, "Enochic Judaism"; other scholars prefer to speak of a distinct "discourse" since we lack clear evidence of the social reality behind Enochic texts and ideologies. Sometimes we can be confident of the existence of groups but not sure of their exact relationships. The case of the communities related to the Qumran documents and the Essenes as described in Josephus, Philo, and Pliny is a classic example. If a connection is seen between the two, it is suggested that either 1) the Essenes were the parent movement of the later Qumranites; 2) both were virtually the same (there were two kinds of members among the Qumran/Essene movement, those who married and those who did not); or 3) the Essenes were a later development of what we know from the much earlier sources of the Qumran movement (dated between the 2nd cent. BCE and the 1st cent. CE).

In a sociological framework two understandings of *sect* have been prominent in biblical studies, both arising from different research questions. The first seeks to explore the dividing moments between religious traditions. This interpretation is connected to the church-sect distinction: a sect deviates from and eventually leaves the parent body (church), and the two stand in opposition to each other. Just as the concept of heresy requires the existence of an official and orthodox doctrine, a sect must depart from a monolithic establishment. Even though no normative and unified religion existed in the ancient Judeo-Christian context, many scholars maintain that sects were schismatic and define the parent body as centralized authorities. At a certain point, a deviant group was either forced outside the parent body—e.g., the Samaritans, since they had their own temple on Mount Gerizim—or a group made itself an outsider by replacing the central institutions of the parent body and by stepping outside normal boundaries—e.g., Pauline congregations that accepted Gentiles into their eucharistic table-fellowship. The point is reached where joint membership in the sect and the parent body becomes impossible. In this sense, Josephus's philosophical schools were not sectarian, and the Jesus movement was not yet a sect. Pauline congregations also began on the basis of the Jewish household, attempting to preserve ties to Judaism. Nevertheless, the NT was largely written at the time when the "parting of the ways" was underway or had already taken place, and legitimation of the split was needed. Protest against social exploitation shifted to protest against "unbelievers." The NT is "sectarian" literature.

Another approach in modern research seeks to compare various sectarian groups with one another or to place them in a broader setting. The traditional church-sect distinction was overtly Christian and thus problematic; rather than deviant groups against the parent body, sects are studied in a broad socio-cultural setting. According to one definition, "religious institutions" adapt to societal change whereas "religious movements" (sects, cults) wish to cause or prevent social change, thus standing in high tension with their environment. Sects vary in their degree of tension, and the stance of the sect can change if the counterpart changes; thus sectarianism is dependent on societal context. According to this line of interpretation, the Pharisees and the Sadducees were not strongly sectarian but rather represented the powerful elite or circles that defined the norms for the masses. The Qumran movement was in high tension with its socio-cultural environment, shown by group members' deviant norms (in matters of calendar and Sabbath observance, ritual purity, food laws, and Temple sacrifices), their claim to unique legitimacy (dualistic beliefs, exclusive membership), and separation (restriction of social relations mainly to insiders and avoidance of contacts with the outsiders, e.g., in marriage). The Essenes of Josephus showed similar sectarian tension. Palestinian followers of Jesus faced conflict with the Jewish authorities, and confrontation and tension marked their existence. Many early Christian groups in urban settings were characterized by: 1) their deviant belief in Jesus as the resurrected Messiah, but also by their crossing over traditional ethnic and social boundaries; 2) deviations from Mosaic Law; e.g., circumcision, table-fellowship, female roles; 3) admission and solidarity rituals, i.e., baptism and Eucharist; and 4) creation of household communities and ethical codes that partly insulated them from the world. Outsiders first labeled them Christianoi (Χριστιανοί), "Christ-sympathizers." Sectarian outlook is of a "virtuoso" type, of persons who seek higher holiness and qualification. These groups are sometimes called "cults," if cults are understood as deviant religious groups that have novel beliefs within their area.

In this type of research, high-tension sects can be analytically distinguished according to their responses to the experienced evil. Thus, the Qumran movement is seen to display introverted (the world must be abandoned) and revolutionist (the world will be overturned by God) responses. Several early Christian groups attest to a conversionist response (God will change the world by changing us). Many groups in antiquity held thaumaturgical beliefs (God will work specific miracles in the world). Other analytical responses are manipulatory (the world can be manipulated with extraordinary means), utopian (humans will reconstruct the world), and reformist (the world can be amended). According to sociological understanding, each response emerges in specific cultural conditions.

From the 2nd cent. onward, early Christianity moved towards a non-sectarian stance. Nevertheless, several Christian movements or teachers can be identified that later came to be regarded as heretical. Most notably, Gnostic teachers (Cerinthus, Basilides) and movements (Sethians, Valentinians) have distinct and successful ideologies and practices. Marcion's church, with its denial of the OT, for centuries presented a challenge to the emerging Catholic Church. Several groups continued to observe Jewish customs (Jewish-Christian groups, e.g., Ebionites, Nazarenes) or were characterized by prophetic activity (Montanism). Often the evidence for these movements is drawn indirectly from quotations in patristic writings and other secondary sources. See CHURCH, LIFE AND ORGANIZATION OF; DEAD SEA SCROLLS; ENOCH; ESSENES; GNOSTICISM; HALAKHAH; HELLENISM; JUDAISM; MESSIANIC MOVEMENTS; PHARISEES; SADDUCEES; SAMARITANS; ZEALOT.

Bibliography: A. I. Baumgarten. *The Flourishing of Jewish Sects in the Maccabean Era: An Interpretation* (1997); David J. Chalcraft, ed. *Sectarianism in Early Judaism: Sociological Advances* (2007); John H. Elliott. "The Jewish Messianic Movement: From Faction to Sect." *Modelling Early Christianity: Social-Scientific Studies of the New Testament in Its Context,* ed. Philip F. Esler (1995) 75–95; Philip F. Esler. *The First Christians in Their Social Worlds: Social-Scientific Approaches to New Testament Interpretation* (1994); Gunnar Haaland. "What Difference Does Philosophy Make? The Three Schools as a Rhetorical Device in Josephus." *Making History: Josephus and Historical Method*, ed. Zuleika Rodgers (2007) 262–88; Bengt Holmberg. *Sociology and the New Testament: An Appraisal* (1990); Antti Marjanen and Petri Luomanen, eds. *A Companion to Second-Century Christian "Heretics"* (2005); George Nickelsburg. *Ancient Judaism and Christian Origins: Diversity, Continuity, and Transformation* (2003); Rodney Stark and William Sims Bainbridge. *A Theory of Religion* (1987); Ernst Troeltsch. *The Social Teaching of the Christian Churches* (1931); Bryan R. Wilson. *The Social Dimension of Sectarianism: Sects and New Religious Movements in Contemporary Society* (1990).

JUTTA JOKIRANTA

SECU see'kyoo [שֶׂכוּ sekhu]. Saul's pursuit of David found Saul at Secu, on the route between Gibeah and Ramah, seeking information from the inhabitants concerning David's whereabouts (1 Sam 19:22). The location of Secu is unknown, bringing into question the type of settlement and occupation that existed at Secu. Some Latin and Greek manuscripts describe the site as on a bare hilltop or even a threshing floor on a hilltop. Whether a village or merely a "great well" (NRSV) on a hilltop where workers gathered, it was here that

Saul received report of David and Samuel's presence in Naioth in Ramah.

MICHAEL G. VANZANT

SECULAR. The English word *secular* is derived from the Late Latin *saecularis*, meaning "of the present world," and as an English adjective it means "worldly" or "not specifically religious." The idea of the secular is a relatively modern concept. We see its development in the 19th cent., with industrialization and scientific advancement leading to an increased faith in science, rather than religion, as the appropriate realm for the discovery of truth. Accompanying this adjusted world-view came the division of life into religious and secular realms. This division of reality was not characteristic of ancient peoples, including ancient Israelites, for whom every aspect of the created order formed the stage for God's activity among them. For these people, no area of life was outside of the purview of religion. The notions of SACRED and PROFANE more accurately convey the distinctions that we see in the OT and the NT.

MARIAN OSBORNE BERKY

SECUNDUS si-koon'duhs [Σεκοῦνδος Sekoundos]. One of Paul's companions on the journey from Macedonia to Jerusalem (Acts 20:4). Secundus and Aristarchus were Gentile Christians from Thessalonica, possibly delegates bearing money for Paul's collection for the Jerusalem church (Acts 24:17; 2 Cor 8:1-6). It is uncertain whether Secundus and the rest of the group traveled ahead of Paul and met him in Troas or traveled with Paul to Philippi and Troas after celebrating the Festival of Unleavened Bread (Acts 20:5-6).

HEIDI S. GEIB

SECURE. *Secure* generally means to "cause to inherit," "establish," "make safe," or "live protected," and, as an adjective, "protected," "strong," "steadfast," or "free from peril." The NRSV translates the Hebrew roots ʾmn (אמן), ʾmts (אמץ), ʾrz (ארז), byt (בית), btkh (בתח), ytsq (יצק), yshb (ישב), kwn (כון), lwn (לון), nkhl (נחל), ʿmd (עמד), tswr (צור), sgb (שׂגב), shlw (שׁלו), shmr (שׁמר) and the Greek asphalizō (ἀσφαλίζω) and sōzō (σῴζω) as "secure."

Sometimes possessing or acquiring the ability to be secure is prompted by God's warning. During the exodus, both Israelites and Egyptians brought their charges into a "secure place" upon God's warning, lest they be struck by hail in the plague (Exod 9:19-20). God tells Moses to empower Joshua to "secure" the land of Canaan (Deut 1:38; 3:28). Being secure is more than simply being safe from physical danger; it suggests inner peace. The one who trusts in the Lord can proclaim, "my heart is glad, and my soul rejoices; my body also rests secure" (Ps 16:9). Indeed, the experience of dwelling secure may belie one's circumstances since it comes from the relationship one has with God. Those who obey God's commandments are secure even when en-

countering "evil tidings" (Ps 112:7) and are shielded from "dread of disaster" (Prov 1:33). The saving God rescues the threatened, allowing them to be as the sure-footed deer, "set secure on the heights," even after encountering the enemy or upon facing evil, suffering, and death (Ps 18:33).

At other times, however, security may be illusory. The OT shows that security can only be fleeting when it rests upon principles that are an affront to God. Both Assyria and Babylon, for example, do not recognize that that their victories are due to the power of the God of Israel who creates destinies for nations in order to pursue justice. Complacent in their false security, living as though there were no consequences for arrogance and cruelty, they soon discover that although they "lived secure" (Zeph 2:15) they will become a desolation (Isa 47:10-11). This indictment against illusory complacency is not brought against foreign nations alone. The prophet Amos, for example, proclaims that "those who are at ease in Zion" and "those who feel secure on Mount Samaria" will soon be judged by God (Amos 6:1).

The security to which the righteous aspire and which is granted to the kings who truly act as God's servants anticipates a future where goodness triumphs over evil and where the world ultimately becomes a dwelling place for God. The psalmist can proclaim that God's servant David is rewarded with "an everlasting covenant, ordered in all things and secure" (2 Sam 23:5).

In the NT, Pilate insists on securing Jesus' tomb (Matt 27:64-66). Jesus speaks of the future unreadiness of people at the time of the second coming when those who wish to secure their lives will be lost (Luke 17:33). *See* CONTENTMENT; PROSPERITY; SHALOM; WELL BEING.

SHARON PACE

SEDER [סֵדֶר sedher]. The Seder ("Order") is a liturgical celebration of Passover (pesakh פֶּסַח) that commemorates a foundational event for Jewish faith and identity: God's deliverance of the Israelites from slavery in Egypt (Exod 12:1-51). The Seder meal is held in homes the first (and sometimes second) night of Passover week (beginning the fifteenth of Nisan, which falls in March–April; *see* PASSOVER AND FEAST OF UNLEAVENED BREAD). Many Seder traditions are based on the story of the first Passover in Exod 12 and on rabbinic teachings in tractate *Pesahim* of the MISHNAH. The liturgy is called the *Seder Haggadah Shel Pesach* (sedher haggadhah shel pesakh סֵדֶר הַגָּדָה שֶׁל פֶּסַח), "the order of the story/narrative belonging to Passover."

In preparation for the Seder meal, the house is first cleared of all leaven, and symbolic foods are prepared. UNLEAVENED BREAD or *matzah* (matsah מַצָּה) signifies the haste with which the slaves had to leave; a roasted shank bone represents the paschal LAMB; a roasted egg symbolizes sacrifice; BITTER HERBS signify the bitterness of slavery; salt water is a reminder of the slaves' tears; a mixture of apples, nuts, and wine called *haroset* (kharoseth חֲרוֹסֶת) symbolizes the mortar the slaves were forced to use in Pharaoh's building projects; and a green vegetable represents new life. In memory of their origins among the dispossessed, families are encouraged to invite strangers and the poor to share the meal.

During the meal, the youngest child asks, "Why is this night different from all other nights?" (*m. Pesah.* 10:1–7). The head of the household tells the story of the exodus so that celebrants can share in their ancestors' experience of redemption and celebrate their freedom from slavery. Four cups of WINE are consumed (*m. Pesah.* 10:1), each cup symbolizing one of God's four promises of deliverance (Exod 6:6-7): "I will free you," "I will deliver you," "I will redeem you," and "I will take you as my people." A cup is poured for the prophet Elijah, who is expected to return during Passover to announce the day of the Lord (Mal 4:5). Traditional songs, prayers, and blessings (that vary from community to community) accompany the meal. Customarily, a piece of matsah called the *afikomen* ('afiqoman אֲפִיקוֹמָן) is hidden at the beginning of the Seder for the children to find and share with the group as the last item to be eaten at the meal. *See* HAGGADAH.

Bibliography: Baruch M. Bokser. *The Origins of the Seder* (1984); Pamela B. Schaff. *Family Haggadah: A Seder for All Generations* (1998); Scherkan Zlotowitz. *Family Haggadah: Haggadah Shel Pesach* (1981).

MARIANNE BLICKENSTAFF

SEDHEQ se´dek [צֶדֶק tsedheq]. A West Semitic god mentioned in a deity list from Ugarit (*KTU* 1.123.14), briefly in Damascius' *Vita Isidori*, and most extensively in the *Phoenician History* of Philo of Byblos. The word tsedheq means "rightness," "righteousness," "what is legitimate," or "loyalty," and it is likely that this meaning reflects the god Sedheq's function within the West Semitic pantheon.

Sedheq is often associated with Misor ("justice"). According to Philo of Byblos, Sedheq and Misor were brothers who discovered how to use salt. Together, the gods Sedheq and Misor were probably the West Semitic counterparts to the gods Kittu ("right," "truth") and Misharu ("justice," "uprightness") in the Babylonian pantheon, both of whom were sons of the Babylonian sun god Shamash and served as attendant deities at Shamash's right hand.

The term "Sedheq" does not appear as the name of a deity in the Bible; however, the personification of the noun tsedheq as an efficacious hypostasis of Yahweh is not unusual in the OT. In Ps 85:11 [Heb. 85:12], tsedheq looks down from heaven. Tsedheq is placed in a parallel position with Yahweh in Isa 51:11. In Ps 89:14 [Heb. 89:15] tsedheq and mishpat (מִשְׁפָּט, "justice") are said to be the foundation of Yahweh's throne, while in Ps 85:13 [Heb. 85:14] tsedheq goes before Yahweh to "make a path for his steps." Isaiah 41:10 de-

scribes Yahweh supporting Israel with "the right hand of my tsedheq," while Ps 48:10 [Heb. 48:11] describes tsedheq as filling Yahweh's right hand; the imagery could be viewed as similar to Kittu serving as an attendant deity at Shamash's right hand. The personification of tsedheq is also found in the Qumran texts (e.g., 1QM XVII, 8).

There are some biblical names that contain the root tsdq (צדק). Most often, the inclusion of the root can be interpreted as being based on its general meaning. However, there are a few names that probably refer to the god Sedheq instead: MELCHIZEDEK ("my king is Sedheq"; Gen 14:18; Ps 110:4; Heb 5–7), ADONI-ZEDEK ("my lord is Sedheq"; Josh 10:1, 3), and perhaps Zadok (2 Sam 15–19; 1 Kg 1–2). All three names have connections with JERUSALEM: Melchizedek and Adoni-zedek as pre-Israelite kings of Salem/Jerusalem, and Zadok as a priest at Jerusalem (*see* ZADOK, ZADOKITES). There are a few passages that might also support the connection of Sedheq with Jerusalem, if tsedheq is understood as containing a reference to the deity (Isa 1:21, 26; Jer 31:23).

JAMIE A. BANISTER

SEDUCTION. Several different Hebrew words describe enticing or coercive activity that can be translated or interpreted as "seduction." The verbal root pth (פתה) in the Piel form provides the most frequently occurring example. Most often, it refers to persuasive or beguiling speech. For example, pth is used when the Philistines threaten Samson's first wife and command her to "entice" (NRSV, "coax") Samson to explain his riddle (Judg 14:15). Later, they command Delilah to "entice" (NRSV, "coax") Samson in order to find the source of his strength (Judg 16:5). Job proclaims that he has not been "enticed" by a woman (Job 31:9).

In Hos 2:14 (Heb. 2:16), Yahweh, as an aggrieved husband, will "entice" (NRSV, "allure") his wife, Israel, after punishing her for her infidelity. Other texts claim that Yahweh "entices" various prophets (Jer 20:7-8; Ezek 14:9 [NRSV, "deceive"]). In addition, pth is used to describe "being seduced into turning away" from proper worship of Yahweh (Deut 11:16).

In the Covenant Code, the man who "seduces" a woman who is not engaged to be married and has sex with her must pay a bride-price and marry her (Exod 22:16 [Heb. 22:15]; compare Deut 22:23-27). If her father refuses to give her to him, the man must still pay the bride-price (v. 17).

The verbal root t'h (תעה) means "to wander" in the Qal stem, but in the Hiphil stem it means "to lead astray" both physically and morally. For instance, during the reign of Manasseh, he "misled" (RSV, "seduced") the people of Judah (2 Kgs 21:9; 2 Chr 33:9).

The verbal root khnp (חנף) is translated "to be polluted" in the Qal stem, but it can mean "to make profane" in the Hiphil. In Dan 11:32, the verb may be taken to mean that the ruler will seduce those who violate the covenant. In the apocryphal book of Judith, Holofernes intends to "seduce" Judith (Jdt 12:12 [epispaō ἐπισπάω], 16 [apataō ἀπατάω]).

Some biblical characters, particularly women, have been associated with seduction due to centuries of literary and artistic interpretations of their actions. For example, some interpreters treat Eve as a seducer because she gave fruit from the tree of the knowledge of good and evil to Adam (Gen 3:6; compare 1 Tim 2:13-14). Also, the wife of Potiphar is regarded as attempting to seduce Joseph (Gen 39:7, 12), although she commands him to lie with her in these verses. Furthermore, some interpreters regard Bathsheba's bathing on her roof as a provocative action designed to gain David's attention (2 Sam 11:2-5). A number of feminist biblical scholars have countered these traditional treatments of female characters by pointing out that the biblical text does not attribute any particular motivations to the actions of these characters.

Bibliography: Alice Bach. *Women, Seduction, and Betrayal in Biblical Narrative* (1997); D. J. A. Clines and D. M. Gunn. "'You Tried to Persuade Me' and 'Violence! Outrage!' in Jeremiah XX 7-8." *VT* 28 (1978) 20–27.

NYASHA JUNIOR

SEED, SEEDTIME [זֶרַע zeraʿ, פְּרֻדוֹת perudhoth; κόκκος kokkos, σπέρμα sperma, σπορά spora]. Dependent on the fertility of their fields and the rain (Deut 11:10-11), the farmers of ancient Israel planted their seed in the proper season (Gen 8:22) with great care in hope that it would yield a bountiful harvest (Isa 30:23; Matt 13:24). Drought, invading armies, and God's wrath meant that this hope was not always rewarded (Joel 1:17; Hag 1:6), but each new planting season had fresh expectations, as the metaphor in Zech 8:12 indicates. *See* AGRICULTURE; SEASONS.

VICTOR H. MATTHEWS

SEEING [רָאָה raʾah; חָזָה khazah; βλέπω blepō, ὁράω horaō]. The physical sensory ability to perceive with the EYEs appears in biblical literature (Gen 16:13; Exod 2:12; Acts 9:40). Yet, the ability to see denotes more than visual perception, implying the notions of inspecting, witnessing, or experiencing (Gen 8:8; 2 Chr 9:5-6; Ps 34:8 [Heb. 34:9]; Acts 1:9-11) as well as knowing or understanding (Deut 4:35; Isa 5:19; compare Gen 3:5). Furthermore, biblical concepts of seeing highlight human limitations in only seeing the outward appearance rather than the inner HEART (1 Sam 16:6-7; Pss 17:2; 139:24; Wis 4:15), the visible rather than the invisible (Sir 16:21; 1 Cor 13:12), and the believable rather than the unbelievable (John 6:62; 20:25-29). To the contrary, God's seeing encompasses both the goodness of God's creation (Gen 1:4, 31) and the obduracy of humanity (Gen 11:5; Jer 5:21; Sir 23:19; Matt 13:13-17). God's seeing also connotes a gracious regard with favor upon

frail human beings (Gen 9:16; Ps 10:14; compare Num 6:25-26; Matt 6:4, 6, 18). Therefore, God is the one who opens human eyes (Gen 21:19; 2 Kgs 6:17, 20; Tob 3:17), even to see the presence or glory of God (Exod 3:2-6; 16:7; 24:9-11; Isa 6:5; Job 42:5; Matt 5:8). *See* PROPHET, PROPHECY; VISION.

HYUN CHUL PAUL KIM

SEEK [בָּקַשׁ baqash, דָּרַשׁ darash; ζητέω zēteō]. The language of seeking is ubiquitous in biblical literature. The English word in various forms appears 374 times in the NRSV (and even more frequently in the more literal KJV). Although *seek* translates primarily two different Hebrew words (baqash and darash) and a set of Greek cognates (zēteō, ekzēteō [ἐκζητέω], epizēteō [ἐπιζητέω]), the terms are virtually synonymous in use. The meaning of *seek* in any instance is tied to what is being sought and who is doing the seeking.

In its mundane sense, seeking refers simply to the pursuit and possible acquisition of an object of interest to the seeker, and a majority of biblical references have no further significance than this. Not infrequently, *seek* merely contributes a conative force along with a verbal complement (e.g., "seek to destroy").

As an ethical-religious motif, however, greater significance is attached to the object of seeking. So, e.g., those of Judah exiled in Babylon are urged to "seek the welfare of the city where I have sent you into exile, and pray to the LORD on its behalf, for in its welfare you will find your welfare" (Jer 29:7). Here, as often, it is clear that seeking involves not so much a quest to find as the active promotion of the thing sought, whether peace, justice, or the good (e.g., Neh 2:10; Pss 34:14 [compare 1 Pet 3:11]; 119:155; Isa 1:17; 16:5; Amos 5:14; Zeph 2:3). It is perhaps in this context that Jesus' programmatic words "But strive [zēteō] first for the kingdom of God and his righteousness" make best sense (Matt 6:33; compare Luke 12:31).

In a common biblical idiom (at least a fourth of the uses), humans are urged to seek God (e.g., Ps 24:6; Isa 51:1; Lam 3:25; Wis 1:1; Heb 11:6) or his benefits (e.g., Pss 17:7; 31:1). God is thus presented as the supreme focus of human attention and fealty, and the call to seek evokes a wide range of appropriate correlative responses: prayer, worship, contrition, consultation, trust, and obedience. Whereas a failure to seek God is often cited as the explicit basis of Israel's reproach (e.g., Isa 9:13; 31:1; Jer 10:21), "seeking the LORD" epitomizes repentance from idolatry and independence, a return to the true source of guidance and to the one uniquely worthy of allegiance (e.g., Deut 4:29-30; Isa 55:6-7; Jer 29:12-14; Hos 3:5; Amos 5:4-6).

Strikingly, not only humans, but God also is a seeker. Yahweh is the shepherd who seeks wayward sheep (Ezek 34:6-16); the Father seeks worshipers (John 4:23). Indeed, Luke's Jesus summarizes his mission in just these terms: "For the Son of Man came to seek out and to save the lost" (19:10), a theme given its most poignant and memorable expression in a trio of parables earlier in the Gospel (15:1-32). *See* KNOWLEDGE; PEACE IN THE NT; PEACE IN THE OT; PRAYER; PROSPERITY; REPENTANCE IN THE NT; REPENTANCE IN THE OT; SALVATION; WEALTH; WORSHIP, NT CHRISTIAN; WORSHIP, OT.

GARWOOD P. ANDERSON

SEEK REFUGE. *See* CITY OF REFUGE; REFUGE; SAFETY.

SEER. *See* PROPHET, PROPHECY.

SEFIRE. In the 1930s, local people uncovered parts of two inscribed basalt stelae and a rectangular slab at Sefire, 15 mi. southeast of Aleppo. Assyrian records indicate a date for the inscriptions prior to the fall of ARPAD in 740 BCE. The Aramaic texts preserve treaties, including the curses imposed by the gods on those who violate the treaty stipulations.

They are significant for OT studies as examples of treaty stones (Deut 27:4, 8; Josh 8:32), 1st-millennium treaty forms, and curses. *See* COVENANT, OT AND NT; CURSE; INSCRIPTIONS.

Bibliography: Joseph A. Fitzmyer. *The Aramaic Inscriptions of Sefire.* 3rd ed. (1995); Delbert R. Hillers. *Treaty Curses and Old Testament Prophets* (1964).

ALAN MILLARD

SEFUNIM CAVES. The Sefunim sites consist of a large cave (ca. 22 m wide and 50 m deep) and a nearby shallow rock shelter located on the western slope of Mount Carmel 10 km south of Haifa, Israel, and about 8.5 km east of the modern Mediterranean shoreline (*see* CARMEL, MOUNT). Occupations occurred inside the cave and rock shelter as well as on broad terraces outside. Although the rock shelter contains evidence of habitation only during the later Middle Paleolithic and early Neolithic periods, the cave has a long cultural succession. The sequence begins with a butchering station ascribed to the latest Levantine Mousterian (Middle Paleolithic) period, just as cultural development was verging on the Upper Paleolithic. Radiocarbon dates indicate that the Upper Paleolithic in the cave is represented by a very late Levantine Aurignacian, which is then followed by either an Epipaleolithic or an early Neolithic layer. Later, a Pre-Pottery Neolithic B occupation is relatively substantial, as is a Chalcolithic use of the cave. Finally, there is subsequent sporadic use of the cave during the Early Bronze Age, the Iron II period, Roman–Byzantine times, and Islamic times.

Bibliography: Avraham Ronen, ed. *Sefunim Prehistoric Sites, Mount Carmel, Israel* (1984).

GARY O. ROLLEFSON

SEGUB see′guhb [שְׂגוּב seghuv]. A proper name, likely a shortened form of ′elseghuv (אֶלְשָׂגוּב, "El has shown himself exalted"). 1. The name first appears in conjunction with the rebuilding of JERICHO (1 Kgs 16:34). The narrator indicates that HIEL built the city at the cost of the lives of his two sons, Segub and ABIRAM. While it may simply be that the death of his sons was the fulfillment of the curse in Josh 6:26, it is also possible that Hiel sacrificed his infant sons to ensure the success of the city's foundation, a practice known from other sources in the ANE.

2. The father of Jair, son of HEZRON, and great-grandson of Judah (1 Chr 2:21-22; *see* JAIR, JAIRITE).

Bibliography: Mordechai Cogan. *1 Kings.* AB 10 (1988).

JOSEPH R. CATHEY

SEILUN, KHIRBET. *See* SHILOH, SHILONITE.

SEINE [מִכְמֶרֶת mikhmereth]. In order to increase their catch, fishermen used a dragnet to trap their prey. Nets may have been classified according to the size of their mesh or their materials. Since life at times depended upon the success of the hooks, nets, and seine (dragnet) used, it is not surprising that their owner would give thanks for their effective properties and consider them of great value (Hab 1:15-16). *See* NET; TOOLS.

VICTOR H. MATTHEWS

SEIR see′uhr [שֵׂעִיר se′ir]. 1. Genesis 36:20-30 refers to a man named Seir, from which the region supposedly took its name. His descendants lived in Seir before the coming of Esau, who settled in Seir and became the ancestor of the Edomites (Gen 36:8-14; Deut 2:12).

2. The region east of the Arabah where Edom was located, although some texts suggest that it also included areas west of the Arabah (Deut 1:44). It is also possible that originally Edom signified the northern section of the hill country east of the Arabah, while Seir represented the south. The area is often referred to as the hill country of Seir (Gen 14:6; Josh 24:4) or Mount Seir (2 Chr 20:10; Ezek 35:3), which may also refer to a particular mountain within the region. An intriguing reference in Judg 5:4 designates Seir as the place from which Yahweh marched forth to battle. Deuteronomy 33:2 likewise connects Yahweh with Seir, in parallel with Mount Sinai. This suggests that Mount Sinai was located in the same region as Seir, perhaps in the Hejaz southeast of the Gulf of Aqaba. *See* EDOM, EDOMITES; IDUMEA; SEIR, MOUNT.

KEVIN A. WILSON

SEIR, MOUNT see′uhr [הַר־שֵׂעִיר har-se′ir]. Means "hairy." A mountain located at Judah's northern border (Josh 15:10), possibly Shoresh Beth-Meir, located ca. 14.5 km west of Jerusalem. The mountain probably derived its name from its having been heavily wooded in antiquity, because of its location on the western slopes of the Judean range. When the Israelites attempted to invade the hill country from the south, this Seir appears to have been the northernmost point, which they reached before being repelled by the Amorites (Deut 1:44). This or another Mount Seir is mentioned in the AMARNA LETTERS (EA 288, line 26).

RALPH K. HAWKINS

SEIRAH see´uh-ruh [שְׂעִירָה se´irah]. Meaning "forested mountain range" or "goat mountain," this word occurs only once in the Bible (Judg 3:26), making its identification tentative. As early as Eusebius, Seirah has been debated as either a topographical feature or geographical proper noun. If topographical, the narrator most likely was seeking to note a densely forested mountain range. Uniquely shaped stone structures (i.e., quarries) near Ghor by the Jordan River may support the topographical reading. Geographically, Seirah has often been located a few kilometers northwest of Nablus.

Bibliography: Loren R. Fisher. *Ras-Shamra Parallels.* Vol. 2 (1972); J. Simons. *The Geographical and Topographical Texts of the Old Testament* (1958).

JOSEPH R. CATHEY

SELA see´luh [סֶלַע sela´]. 1. A city of uncertain location mentioned in Judg 1:36, which, along with the ascent of Akrabbim, defines some part of "the border of the Amorites." The ascent of Akrabbim lies about 20 mi. southwest of the Dead Sea, but its relationship to Sela is unclear (*see* AKRABBIM, AKRABBIN).

2. An Edomite stronghold once conquered and renamed "JOKTHE-EL" by the Judean king Amaziah (2 Kgs 14:7; 2 Chr 25:12). The city lies near the VALLEY OF SALT where Amaziah "killed ten thousand Edomites" (2 Kgs 14:7) before storming the city. Assuming that the Valley of Salt denotes the wide valley stretching south from the Dead Sea, one naturally seeks Sela east of the valley among the rocky crags inhabited by the Edomites. Modern es-Sela´, lying some 20 mi. south of the Dead Sea and 2.5 mi. northwest of Buseira (biblical Bozrah), is the likeliest candidate. Not only does the coincidence of the ancient and modern names recommend this identification but archaeologists have found at es-Sela´ evidence of continuous and significant occupation long before and after the 8th cent. BCE. The previously popular identification of Sela with UMM AL-BIYARA or el-Habis in the Petra region is now deemed unlikely, due to a lack of evidence for occupation before the 7th cent. BCE. A place called Sela, associated with the Edomite tribe of Kedar, is mentioned in Isa 42:11; it is unclear whether this is the Sela of 2 Kgs 14:7 and 2 Chr 25:12.

Because the name *Sela* and the common Hebrew noun meaning "rock" or "crag" share the same spelling, it is not always clear whether sela´ should be understood as a proper name or as a common noun. In two oracles directed toward Edom (Jer 49:16; Obad 3), the Edomites are addressed as people who "live in the clefts of the rock." For these two verses, footnotes in the NRSV offer the alternate reading "Sela" in place of "the rock."

3. A city mentioned in Isa 16:1. Moabite refugees fleeing south are urged to send a gift of lambs from this location to "the ruler of the land" in Jerusalem. The city has not been identified.

Bibliography: Manfred Lindner. "Edom Outside the Famous Excavations: Evidence from Surveys in the Greater Petra Area." *Early Edom and Moab.* Piotr Bienkowski, ed. (1992) 143–66.

BRIAN C. JONES

SELAH. *See* MUSIC.

SELED see´lid [סֶלֶד seledh]. Mentioned only as the son of Nadab and brother of Appiam, Seled is a descendant of Jerahmeel in Judah's genealogical list (1 Chr 2:30). Significantly, Seled is said to have died without leaving any children, which likely means without any male children (*see* BARREN, BARRENNESS).

SELEMIA sel´uh-mi´uh. One of five scribes, trained to write quickly, who recorded the Scriptures to be restored as God conveyed to Ezra (2 Esd 14:24).

SELEUCIA si-loo´shuh [Σελεύκεια Seleukeia]. The name given to a number of Greek cities founded in the Near East in the early Hellenistic period, most or all ostensibly named for the founder of the Seleucid dynasty (*see* SELEUCUS). According to the Roman writer Appian (*Hist. rom.* 9.57), Seleucus founded more than thirty cities, nine of them named Seleucia. A number of important cities were referred to as Seleucia at some time during their history, including Gaza, Gadara, and Abila. Five cities called by this name are of importance. 1. Seleucia-in-Pieria, which is also known as Seleucia-on-the-Sea (1 Macc 11:8; Acts 13:4; *see* SELEUCIA IN SYRIA).

2. Seleucia-on-the-Bay-of-Issus has been identified with Seleucia-in-Pieria, but the two are probably different.

3. Seleucia-on-the-Tigris was a strategic foundation, apparently meant as the capital of Seleucus' empire. Identified with the current site of Tell Umar, only a small portion has been excavated. Burials and other finds suggest a significant non-Greek population, but it is a good example of early Hellenization in Mesopotamia. It was apparently an extensive city, exceeding even Antioch on the Orontes. Pliny the Elder (*Nat.* 6.30) alleged that it was meant to receive the population of Babylon and to replace it as a major city, but recent study suggests that Babylon continued not only to survive but even to thrive. Seleucia was taken over by the Parthians about 141 BCE.

4. Seleucia-Zeugma (Seleucia the Bridge) was the major crossing point on the Euphrates, supposedly going back to Alexander, who had a bridge constructed on the spot so that his army could cross the river. Antiochus III confirmed its importance by being married there in 221 BCE.

5. Seleucia was the name given to Tralles for about a century and a half (Pliny the Elder, *Nat.* 5.108), probably by Antiochus I (281–261 BCE), while it was under Seleucid rule. When the city came under control of the Attalid dynasty of Pergamum (mid-2nd cent. BCE), it reverted to the name Tralles.

LESTER L. GRABBE

SELEUCIA IN SYRIA   si-loo´shuh [Σελεύκεια Seleukeia]. Also known as Seleucia Pieria, modern Suweydiyah [Turkey], near the mouth of the Orontes River, 25 km southwest of Antioch-on-the-Orontes (*see* ANTIOCH, SYRIAN). The old name of the town in pre-Seleucid times was Hydatos Potamoi ("Rivers of Water"; Strabo, *Geogr.* 16.2.8). The city was founded ca. 300 CE by Seleucus I Nicator after his victory over Antigonus in the battle of Ipsus as a port city at the foothills of Mount Koryphaios, the south ridge of Mount Pieria, which belongs to the range of the Amanos Mountains. Together with Antioch, Apameia, and Laodicea, Seleucia belonged to the Syrian Tetrapolis of cities founded by Seleucus I in northern Syria. According to Strabo, the Orontes River was navigable; the journey from Seleucia up the Orontes to Antioch could be completed in one day. Before the 2nd cent., a canal was cut that allowed travelers to bypass a shallow section of the river, allowing larger vessels to reach Antioch.

Seleucus I established Seleucia as the new capital of Syria. The first colonists were Greeks settlers of Antigonia in Greece, as well as Jews. The city was surrounded by a wall 12 km in length, extending as far as the acropolis that was situated on Mount Pieria. According to Polybius, in 219 BCE ca. 6,000 free (adult male) citizens lived in the city (*Hist.* 5.61.1), indicating a total population of ca. 30,000 people; this number would have been higher in later periods. Polybius (*Hist.* 5.58–61) describes suburbs, the commercial center, temples, and public buildings. The terraced cliffs above the lower city supported the residential area. The acropolis served as a military citadel and as the location of the monumental public buildings of the city. A large Doric temple (37 × 19 m) dominated the city.

Seleucus established a mint in the city. His burial place in Seleucia was marked by a temple that was called Nikatoreion ("Belonging to the Nicator [Conqueror]"; Appian, *Hist. rom.* 10.63), honoring the king in a cult of uncertain character. The institutions of the Greek city, including magistrates, priests, and a governor, are attested by inscriptions, and the Gurob papyrus (P. Petrie II 45; III 144; Fragmente der griechischen Historiker [FGrH] 160) describes the welcome given to the Egyptian ruler Ptolemy III who captured the city in 246 BCE (some scholars suggest that Dan 11:7-9 refers to Seleucia's capitulation to the Egyptian army). The Seleucid king Antiochus III regained the city in 219 BCE; by this time the capital of the Seleucid Empire had been moved to Antioch. Seleucia was captured again by the Ptolemaic rulers of Egypt; King Ptolemy VI took the city in 146 BCE (1 Macc 11:8), before entering Antioch where he had himself proclaimed king of the Seleucid Empire. In 138 BCE, the Seleucid ruler Antiochus VII conquered Seleucia and there was proclaimed king. In 108 BCE Seleucia received autonomy in 108 BCE.

Seleucia was the naval base of the Seleucid kings, a city of strategic military and economic importance, rivaling Alexandria as the most important seaport of the Ptolemaic kings. The seaport consisted of an artificial inner and an outer harbor, which was in danger of silting up, which prompted the Roman emperor Vespasian (r. 69–79 CE) to dig a tunnel of 1,300 m (1420 yds.) through a mountain spur in order to divert a seasonal stream away from the harbor.

Pompey, the Roman consul and general who reorganized the eastern provinces, confirmed Seleucia's autonomy (ca. 63 BCE), honoring the city's resistance against the kings of Armenia and Pontus who had invaded Syria and Palestine challenging the hegemony of Rome by invading Syria-Palestine. The city remained an important naval base for the imperial fleet.

In processions honoring Zeus Keraunios (Zeus of the Thunderbolt), two elected keraunophoros (κεραυνοφόρος, bearers of the thunderbolt) carried the symbol of the god, a thunderbolt, which supposedly indicated the site at which Seleucus I founded the city. Coins minted in Seleucia portray a large stone within a four-pillared temple, with the legend "Zeus Kasios"; the stone perhaps represents Mount Kasios, located south of the city and visible from there, which may mean that there was no cult-statue of this local version of Zeus in the sanctuary.

Seleucia is mentioned in the NT as the seaport from which Paul, Barnabas, and John Mark sailed to Cyprus on their missionary journey that eventually took them to southern Galatia, probably in 45 CE (Acts 13:4: "they went down to Seleucia; and from there they sailed to Cyprus"). The statement in Acts 14:26 that Paul and Barnabas "sailed back to Antioch" probably means that they sailed past Seleucia up the Orontes to Antioch; some scholars assume that the reference implies that the missionaries disembarked at Seleucia and traveled by land to Antioch. The disagreement between Paul and Barnabas on account of the suitability of John Mark as a missionary (Acts 15:39-41) on the eve of the mission that was planned for cities in the province of Asia, which eventually took Paul to Macedonia and Achaia, probably took place at Antioch, although Seleucia is a possibility as well (Acts 15:39: "Barnabas took Mark with him and sailed away to Cyprus").

At the beginning of the 4th cent., Roman soldiers who worked on dredging the harbor mutinied. The Roman authorities blamed the Christians for inciting the rebellion (Eusebius, *Hist. eccl.* 8.6.8), evidently an excuse for the persecution of the Christians. Later in the 4th cent. Bishop Zenobios was active in Seleucia; he attended the Council of Nicea in 325. One of the earliest church buildings in Seleucia was a tetraconch church, with the large central space capped by a dome. In the 6th cent. the *Notitia episcopatuum* of Antioch lists Seleucia Pieria as an "autocephalous archbishopric," suffragan of Antioch; the diocese existed until the 10th cent. In the 6th cent., Simeon the Younger lived on a column (as a "stylite") between Seleucia and Antioch, establishing a monastery nearby on the Miraculous Mountain (Mount Simeon). During the Crusades, the seaport of Seleucia was known as Saint Symeon. *See* ANTIOCHUS; SELEUCIA; SYRIA.

Bibliography: Kevin Butcher. *Roman Syria and the Near East* (2003); John D. Grainger. *The Cities of Seleukid Syria* (1990); A. Hugh Martin Jones. *The Cities of the Eastern Roman Provinces* (1937, 2004); Fergus Millar. *The Roman Near East, 31 BC–AD 337* (1993).

ECKHARD J. SCHNABEL

SELEUCID EMPIRE si-loo´sid. After the death of Alexander the Great in 323 BCE his generals (known as the Diadochi or "Successors") fought for control of his empire for the next forty years. One of the players was the commander of Alexander's elite guard named Seleucus (*see* SELEUCUS). Within a couple of years Seleucus was recognized as having responsibility for Babylon, though he lost this in subsequent fighting. In 312 BCE, with the help of Ptolemy in Egypt, Seleucus was able to retake Babylonia (inaugurating the "Seleucid era"), and later treaties allotted him the huge territory stretching from northern Syria to the borders of Egypt, including Asia Minor. His descendants ruled over this diverse empire for the next two and a half cent.

The Seleucid Empire was a huge and ramshackle structure that included many Greek cities, with Greek settlers, but the bulk of the population was made up of the original ANE inhabitants whose cultures continued to flourish. All this made governance and administration difficult; furthermore, the capital was moved from its natural center of Babylon to Antioch on its western border. This removed the heart of the empire even further from the eastern sector, and ca. 250 BCE the Parthians successfully revolted in the northeast. This began the loss of the eastern provinces, eventually leaving the Seleucids in control mainly of Asia Minor and Syria (though periodically a Seleucid ruler would march east to try to take back some of the old territory).

Through the 3rd cent. BCE the Seleucids unsuccessfully fought four "Syrian Wars" against the Ptolemies over the area of southern Syria and Palestine, to which they claimed legal title. It was in the Fifth Syrian War in 200 BCE that ANTIOCHUS III finally took this territory for the Seleucid Empire; however, the Romans intervened to stop Antiochus III's expansion of his realm and did the same when Antiochus IV tried to bring Egypt under his rule in 168 BCE. After this, the Seleucid Empire gradually declined as Roman power increased. About 150 BCE a rival dynasty arose, and by 95 BCE a multiplicity of individuals were claiming the Seleucid throne. The last ruler (Antiochus XIII) was a puppet king enthroned by the Romans, but they removed him in 65 BCE, bringing the Seleucid Empire formally to an end.

It was under the Seleucids that Judah became an independent kingdom for a time. This was achieved partly because the Seleucid ruler generally had more important matters claiming his attention and partly because the Hasmonean rulers (*see* HASMONEANS) were able to exploit the rival claimants to the Seleucid throne. The history of the Maccabean kingdom was entwined with that of the declining Seleucid kingdom. Although independence was declared under SIMON Maccabee about 142 BCE, several Seleucid rulers continued to assert their rule over Judah. Even as late as 88 BCE the Seleucid claimant Demetrius III (*see* DEMETRIUS) marched against Alexander Janneus. By this time, however, the Seleucid realm was only a shadow of its former self.

LESTER L. GRABBE

SELEUCUS si-loo´kuhs [Σελεύκος *Seleukos*]. Six kings of the Seleucid dynasty (*see* SELEUCID EMPIRE) had the name Seleucus, including the founder of the Seleucid dynasty. Of these, four can be considered significant.
1. Seleucus I Nicator (312–281 BCE) was one of the Diadochi ("Successors") who divided up Alexander's empire after his death. During the wars of the Diadochi, he received Babylonia as his portion; however, he was driven from Babylon by Antigonus Monophthalmus (another one of the Diadochi) in 316 BCE, but with the help of Ptolemy I (*see* PTOLEMY) he returned to retake Babylon in 312 BCE (the "Seleucid era," widely used as a dating system in antiquity, counts from this year). The peace treaty of 301 assigned Palestine and southern Syria to Seleucus; however, Ptolemy seized the territory and refused to turn it over, but Seleucus I's successors pursued it in a series of "Syrian Wars."

2. Seleucus II Callinicus (246–226 BCE) was son of Antiochus II (261–246 BCE). Ptolemy III began the Third Syrian or Laodicean War (246–241 BCE) shortly after Seleucus II was crowned, but a famine in Egypt forced the Ptolemaic army home. Seleucus' younger brother Antiochus Hierax (*see* ANTIOCHUS) was given authority in Asia Minor, where he established an independent kingdom. Seleucus could not tolerate this. In the "War of the Brothers" (ca. 240–237 BCE) that followed, Seleucus was defeated, but then Hierax was himself vanquished in a succession of fights with Attalus I of Pergamum. The rise of the Arsacid dynasty in Persia began the erosion of the eastern part of Seleucus' empire.

3. The elder son of Seleucus II became Seleucus III Ceraunus (226–223 BCE). He tried to bring Attalus I of

Pergamum to heel, but the attempt failed. Losing confidence in Seleucus, some of his officers brought his short reign to an end. An uncle of Seleucus restored discipline, and his younger brother was crowned to become Antiochus III.

4. The one individual to appear in Jewish sources is Seleucus IV Philopator (187–175 BCE; 1 Macc 7:1; 2 Macc 3:3; 4:7; 5:18; 14:1; 4 Macc 3:20; 4:3, 4, 13, 15). According to 2 Macc 3, Seleucus sent his officer Heliodorus to confiscate the treasure of the Jerusalem Temple, but the latter did not succeed (an angel reportedly fought him off). The precise event behind this story is unclear, though Seleucus may have regarded the current high priest as disloyal since he was holding funds for the Ptolemaic supporter Hyrcanus Tobiad (2 Macc 3:11). Seleucus was assassinated by Heliodorus not long after the Jerusalem incident.

LESTER L. GRABBE

SELF-CONTROL [מַעְצָר לְרוּחוֹ ma'tsar lerukho; ἀκρασία akrasia, ἐγκράτεια enkrateia, ἐγκρατεύομαι enkrateuomai, παθοκρατεία pathokrateia, σωφρονέω sōphroneo, σωφροσύνη sōphrosynē]. Both the OT and NT expect God's redeemed, holy people to exercise self-control, the virtue of restraining destructive desires and passions forbidden by God's command/Torah. In the NT, self-control is also characterized by a Spirit-enabled, stable pattern of thinking and acting that conforms to the power of God made strong in human weakness.

Generally referring to moderation or restraint, sōphrosyne was one of the cardinal virtues. It could also have the sense of self-control. Closely related to sōphrosyne, enkrateia is the virtue of self-mastery. Its opposite is akrasia, lack of self-mastery. Because of his willingness to remain faithful to his teachings to the point of death rather than succumb to his desires for survival, Socrates was the prime model for self-control. In Aristotle, to be fully virtuous, persons' minds must be characterized by a settled and stable disposition so that they always and only perform the good, not having a mind divided between desiring and not desiring to do what is right. Conflicting desires indicate the absence of full virtue. Therefore, neither the "weak-willed" person who at times displays a lack of self-control (akrasia) nor the "strong-willed" person who, in the face of conflicting desires, always displays self-control (enkrateia) is fully virtuous. For the Stoics, however, fully virtuous persons have already eliminated ordinary emotions and desires (resulting in apatheia) that generate false beliefs and set their minds in conformity with the divine logos (or rationality) of nature itself. Hence, self-control connotes a stable and settled state of mind in fully virtuous persons without the constant struggles with conflicting desires.

The word groups discussed here are relatively rare in the Bible. The LXX uses a cognate of enkrateia only twice (enkrateuomai in Gen 43:31; 1 Sam 13:12) and the only place in the OT where the NRSV uses the

English term *self-control* is in its rendering of ma'tsar lerukho (restraint of one's spirit) in Prov 25:28. Self-restraint is praiseworthy but not automatic in the OT (e.g., Joseph's self-restraint with the mirror opposite of Potiphar's wife in Gen 39:6-18; compare Prov 7). However, self-control consists not of autonomously determining the good from nature and setting one's mind on it but of heeding the good located in God's command/Torah (e.g., Gen 3; Mic 6:8).

Self-control is the primary focus of 4 Maccabees where sōphrosynē gives reason mastery over all desires (1:31; 2:4). However, unlike Stoicism where all ordinary desires and passions are to be extirpated, 4 Maccabees represents a "Jewish philosophical" position where reason tames desires forbidden in Torah (e.g., forbidden foods [1:33-34], desiring another's wife [2:2-5]). Hence, Torah teaches self-control (5:23; as does personified Wisdom [Wis 8:7]) and provides the standards for its exercise (1:34; 5:34; 15:10).

In the NT, other than Matt 23:25, where Jesus accuses the Pharisees of greed and akrasia, explicit language of self-control is absent from the Gospels. However, within the larger framework of its saving significance, early gospel audiences may have understood Jesus' faithfulness to God to the point of death as a paradigmatic example of self-control (like Socrates). In Acts 24:24-25 Paul connects justice and self-control with each other (as was typical in the Greco-Roman world) and connects both to "the coming judgment." In 2 Pet 1:6, self-control appears in a chain of virtues in which the audience is to make every effort to progress. Such moral progress (paralleled in Stoicism) is based here on God's call and gifting that ultimately equips the audience to share in the divine nature (*see* SANCTIFY, SANCTIFICATION).

All other NRSV references to self-control in the NT appear in Pauline and deutero-Pauline literature. In 1 Cor 7:1-7, Paul concedes that married couples, by mutual agreement, may temporarily abstain from normal sexual relations if they resume them later lest Satan tempt them because of their "lack of self-control" (1 Cor 7:5). Such akrasia that could result in porneia (πορνεία; 7:2) is clearly a danger for some in this community who are acting like "weak-willed" persons by engaging in what is decidedly not "normal" Christian behavior (1 Cor 5; 6:12-20). In 7:8-9 Paul advises unmarried men and widows to abstain from marriage if possible (like him) but not if they are unable to control their sexual passions. Such advice is not grounded in a Stoic-like opposition to expressing sexual passion within marriage (either here or in 1 Thess 4:3-6b), but is eschatologically driven (7:17, 24, 31). Hence, even though the time is short, for any in this particular audience prone to akrasia in sexual matters, Paul encourages mutual sexual satisfaction within marriage to ward off porneia. In 1 Cor 9:25, Paul portrays his own self-discipline in 9:1-22 as the kind of strenuous self-control practiced by an athlete. Hence, unlike the Stoics, self-control for Paul may include mental struggle with contrasting desires (compare the Spirit-empowered Christ of Mark 14:36). It is, however, characterized by a stable pattern of thinking and acting in line with Paul's understanding of God's power made manifest in the crucifixion, i.e., when God's power is revealed in human weakness, so that the weak shame the strong of 1 Cor 1:18–2:5.

As a "fruit of the Spirit" (Gal 5:22) such self-control is completely dependent on being "led/guided by the Spirit" (Gal 5:18, 25). It is the Spirit-given ability for those who belong to Christ to crucify the passions and excessive and destructive desires of the flesh exemplified in 5:19-20, i.e., those who do not seek God's power through weakness. Hence, as most recent scholarship recognizes, Paul is not depicting the kind of akrasia portrayed in Rom 7:14-25 as his own current experience and certainly not as the norm for those in Christ.

In Titus, God's salvific grace is the basis for self-control (2:11-12), which is a qualification for overseers/bishops (1:8) and is urged for young wives (2:5) and young men (2:6). *See* FRUIT OF THE SPIRIT; HOLY, HOLINESS, NT; LUST; MACCABEES, FOURTH BOOK OF.

Bibliography: David A. deSilva. *4 Maccabees: Introduction and Commentary on the Greek Text in Codex Sinaiticus.* Septuagint Commentary Series (2006); David A. deSilva. "Paul and the Stoa: A Comparison." *JETS* 38 (1995) 549–64; Troels Engberg-Pedersen. "Paul, Virtues, and Vices." *Paul in the Greco-Roman World: A Handbook.* J. Paul Sampley, ed. (2003) 608–34; Stanley K. Stowers. "Paul and Self-Mastery." *Paul in the Greco-Roman World: A Handbook.* J. Paul Sampley, ed. (2003) 524–50.

ANDY JOHNSON

SELF-DENIAL. *See* ASCETICISM; GNOSTICISM; SELFISHNESS.

SELFISHNESS [ἀκρασία akrasia, ἐριθεία eritheia, πλεονεξία pleonexia]. An attitude of self-interest that exceeds appropriate bounds; an excessive concern for oneself or for one's own group. In biblical texts, this attitude is expressed in at least three interrelated ways: "selfish gains," selfish ambition, and self-indulgence. First, selfish gains or greedy pursuits are achievements that are not informed by God's decrees (Ps 119:36). In general, self-seeking gain (sometimes also described as dishonest gain or greed) is condemned in the OT (Exod 18:21; 1 Sam 8:3; Pss 10:3; 119:36; Prov 1:19; Jer 6:13; 8:10) and in the NT (Mark 7:22; Rom 1:29; 1 Cor 5:10, 11; 6:10; 2 Cor 9:5; 1 Thess 2:5; 4:6; Eph 4:19; 5:3, 5; Col 3:5; 2 Pet 2:3, 14). Likewise, covetousness or covetous persons are condemned (Exod 20:17; Deut 5:21; 7:25; Mic 2:2; Acts 20:33; Rom 7:7, 8; 13:9). Still, gain or possession of wealth in itself is not unworthy but gain or wealth that is not requisite with God's instructions or with a concern for others is

rejected. Luke, for example, critiques this excessive self-seeking attitude in the parable of the Rich Fool (Luke 12:15-21; *see* ABUNDANCE; also compare the parable of the Rich Man and Lazarus, Luke 16:19-31). Luke's perspective on the proper attitude toward and use of possessions is further illustrated in Acts with a stark contrast. On the one hand, Luke draws BARNABAS as an ideal figure whose proceeds on the sale of a field were wholly given to the early community of believers in Christ. On the one hand, Luke depicts ANANIAS and SAPPHIRA as a deceiving married couple who secretly kept a part of the proceeds on the sale of some of their own property while pretending to have given the whole amount to the early believers (Acts 4:32–5:11). All of the SYNOPTIC GOSPELS writers address the problem of excessive concern for possessions, moreover, in the story of a would-be-follower of Jesus, a man unwilling to part with his "many possessions" (Mark 10:17-31; compare Matt 19:16-30; Luke 18:18-30).

Second, while a healthy concern for the self is appropriate, selfish ambition is not, and this problem is repeatedly addressed by Paul (Phil 1:17; 2:3; 2 Cor 12:20; Rom 2:8) and others (compare Jas 3:14, 16) to help their audiences negotiate the highly competitive climate of the Mediterranean world. In their own way, the Synoptic Gospels also address this climate, as Jesus seeks to steer his disciples away from the desire to be the greatest (Mark 9:33-37; compare Matt 18:1-5; Luke 22:23-27) or the desire to sit in seats of privilege over others (Mark 10:35-45; compare Matt 20:20-28; Luke 22:23-27). Thus, ends should not be achieved at the neglect or expense of all others.

Third, biblical texts also frown on the quest for unlimited pleasure for oneself or self-indulgence (Matt 23:25; Gal 5:13; Col 2:23; compare Eph 2:3), which was also critiqued in the larger society through discourses on self-mastery (compare Xenophon, *Mem.* 2.1.1–7; Diogenes Laertius, *Vit. Phil.* 2.75; 4 Macc 5:34; Josephus, *J.W.* 1.34; Philo, *Spec. Laws* 2.195; Epictetus, *Diatr.* 3.7.28; Plutarch, *Lib. ed.* 7F).

ABRAHAM SMITH

SEMACHIAH sem′uh-ki′uh [סְמַכְיָהוּ semakhyahu]. The sixth son of SHEMAIAH and a Korahite gatekeeper at the Jerusalem Temple (1 Chr 26:7). The list of Obed-Edom's sons in vv. 4-8 appears to be an addition, as OBED-EDOM was not a Levite.

SEMANTICS. Semantics and pragmatics are branches of modern linguistics that study meaning, whether of words, sentences, paragraphs, or whole texts. The disciplines overlap considerably, and pragmatics was historically a sub-discipline of semantics (and is still arguably such). When contrasted crudely, semantics asks, "What does this word, phrase or sentence (taken, perhaps, in isolation, written on a class chalkboard) mean?" Pragmatics asks, "What is a person conveying and doing with the sentence(s) just uttered (whether in speech, or in a letter, etc.)?" In a sentence such as "Orange is great," semantics might contrast the meaning-possibilities of the word "orange" (color? fruit? juice?) and "great" (size? estimation? desirability?), and thus the range of natural sentence-meanings. Pragmatics notes the way contextual and presuppositional factors define sentence-meaning in any one uttered instance. If the waiter points to a display of different fruit juices and signals (perhaps non-verbally, with a shrug and open arms), "Which do you want?" the reply "Orange is great!" counts not as some general declarative about oranges, but as the request, "Give me orange juice, please!" (a non-natural meaning of the sentence). Uttered in another context, the sentence might be simply emotive (= "I love [team] Orange [I hope they win!]"), etc. Understanding at both semantic and pragmatic levels is essential to biblical interpretation (indeed to all communication).

A. Semantics and Biblical Interpretation
   1. Lexical semantics
   2. Distinctions of sense, denotation, and
      reference
   3. Discourse analysis and text-linguistics
B. Pragmatics and Biblical Interpretation
   1. Contextual contribution to
      utterance meaning
   2. Presupposition-pool contribution to
      utterance meaning
   3. Conventional contributions to
      utterance meaning
   4. More global perspectives
Bibliography

A. Semantics and Biblical Interpretation

Barr was first to signal the colossal semantic confusions regularly perpetrated in even some of the most prestigious biblical scholarship—and the problems continue. Semantics has clarified some cardinal points of relevance:

1. Lexical semantics

What does a word, like *boy* mean? Semantics distinguishes, in a notional triangle, the English lexical form *boy* (the letters here printed, and at the left base of the triangle) from the sense of the English word (*boy* = human, male, non adult, at the apex), then again from the denotation of *boy, garçon, Junge*, etc. (at the right base), which is the class of all entities in the world to which the lexeme applies. We must not confuse a cultural conception of boys (as, say, rude, untidy, and querulous) with the sense of *boy*. Some of the major biblical dictionaries before Barr confused the sense/concept distinction (and did so on a grand scale).

The "sense" of a word can be defined in two related dimensions: conceptual and intra-linguistic. One may define *chair* conceptually, and minimally, by describing the properties of a prototypical chair (=a seat for one, with four legs and a back). Or one can define it in

relationship to other words in the same semantic domain of furniture one sits on. "*Chair*" differs from *sofa* (=soft seat for several), *bench* (=hard seat for several, without back), *stool, chaise-longue*, etc. One word-form usually has several quite distinct senses (a lexeme is defined as the combination of one word-form + one single sense). *Chair* can denote an item of furniture (chair$_1$), or head of a committee (chair$_2$), or "university professor" (chair$_3$; contrast "senior lecturer," *reader*), or the mechanical link between the rail track and the sleeper (chair$_4$): so four separate lexemes. Competent users do not confuse or blur the senses of these lexemes. Appeal to etymology/word-formation (plausible for *blackbird*, but more problematic for *ladybird* or *butterfly*) or some "basic meaning" for a word, is generally flawed. There is no "basic/communal" sense to the multitude of lexemes with the word-form *running*: as in "She is running a marathon" (competing in it? Organizing it?), "She is running guns," "Her nose is running," "The colors are running," "The story is running," "The lease is running for three years," etc. The explanatory model is rather one of evolution of different species. A word like charisma (χάρισμα), in the NT, must be defined in terms of both 1) its word-formation as a result of the verb charizomai (χαρίζομαι=to give freely as a favor): so "a gracious gift" (not as charis [χάρις]+ -ma [μα], "an event of divine grace"), and 2) its relations to other words for "gift," such as appear in parallel in Rom 5:15-21 (charis, dōrea [δωρεά], and dōrēma [δώρημα]; and elsewhere doma [δόμα], dosis [δόσις], etc.), where, incidentally, it is clear that charisma does not mean the oft-assumed short "event" of gifting (like a single expression of tongues or other ministry), but actually refers to eternal life (compare Rom 6:23).

A cardinal test of lexical sense is whether native language users regard proposed sentences as linguistically anomalous. "It is a bicycle, but it has two wheels" would be recognized as a denial of the very sense of the word "bicycle." Conversely, the oft-suggested sense of Greek agapē (ἀγάπη) as "selfless, self-giving, love" (in contrast to eros [ἔρως=sexual love], philē [φίλη=friendly liking/warmth], etc.) is demonstrably falsified by such statements as "And people loved (from agapaō [ἀγαπάω]) darkness [=evil] rather than light" (John 3:19; compare John 12:43; 1 John 2:15, etc.)

2. Distinctions of sense, denotation, and reference

This takes us to the border of semantics and pragmatics. "Reference" is the speaker's intended relation of words and sentences, in any particular utterance, to specific "things" (objects, events, or whatever) in the world. The word *referent* is used to designate some particular "thing" in question. Sentences, such as "Washington is in a mess," do not have any reference (because Washington could be the name of a city, a boat, a cat, or whatever) unless they are uttered (in speech or writing) in a particular and defining context.

Not all utterances are referential. I may utter "Ugh!" or "The fool will be servant to the wise " (Prov 11:29), but neither is referential, unless in the latter case it is contextually clear I am speaking of some particular fool or wise person. Sentences may have sense, and the words in them may have general denotation, but only utterances (spoken or written) can be referential. Confusions abound here. For example, the Greek word kephalē (κεφαλή, "head") has distinct senses: 1) anatomical head (literal or metaphorical); 2) superior rank ("head" of family, clan, etc.); and 3) extremity, point (in Greek, the "head" of the screw is the pointy bit, not our flat one), and "end." In (rare) occasional utterances, kephalē refers to the source of a river (one of its extremities, ends). Some exegetes, shy of allowing Paul (in 1 Cor 11; compare Eph 5) to say men are "head" of women in sense #2, have argued that *head* can have the sense "source." But this confuses sense, denotation, and reference. In the only relevant utterances, *head* refers to either end of a river (whether "source" or "mouth"), not specifically to its "source." So the word *head* (on such occasions) just has the sense (and denotes) "end" (not "source"). It is illegitimate to confuse co-referentiality with sense. If I exclaim, "the nasty contraption has let me down again!" referring to my bicycle, that does not mean I consider that part of the linguistic sense of "contraption" is "two-wheeled, pedal-driven vehicle" (the minimal "sense" of *bicycle*).

3. Discourse analysis and text-linguistics

These sub-disciplines mainly analyze texts and utterances well beyond the simple sentence level. They typically explore the formal characteristics of a passage, such as Eph 1:3-14, in terms of how its structure and components relate to provide meaning: in this case suggesting that the three participles "blessing" [us] (1:3), "foreordaining" [us] in 1:5, and "making known" [to us] in 1:9, linguistically dominate (as providing more semantic information) the flow of meaning. Repetitive prepositional clauses confirm a structure of six strophes: 1:3-4, 5-6, 7-8, 9-10, 11-12, and 13-14, achieving a semantic climax in vv.9-10, with God as the semantic agent, and thence descending to clauses with "you/us" as the semantic agent.

B. Pragmatics and Biblical Interpretation

Pragmatics is the study of how utterances convey meaning and are used. It began with the works of Austin and Searle, analyzing "performative utterances," i.e., ones that actually do something, and may change the world, like the declarative "I take you to be my lawfully wedded wife." They analyzed these and other utterances, which they took to be speech-acts, as representatives (statements of the speaker's belief about a state of affairs), such as "God raised him [=Christ] above all other powers"; expressives, conveying the speaker's psychological/emotional experience, such as "I am very sorry!" spoken as an apology; directives, such as

"Prepare a guest room for me" (Phlm 22); and commissives such as the promise "I will repay it" (Phlm 19). But the enquiry soon opened out to broader aspects of "utterance" meaning. We may mention some interrelated cardinal points:

1. Contextual contribution to utterance meaning

An often-analyzed sentence, such as "The shooting of the hunters she heard, but to pity it moved her not" is, as reader-response critics rightly declare, ambiguous. But it is not at all ambiguous if uttered about a specific woman hearing, say, some hunters being shot. Context may unequivocally define utterance-meaning. In normal discourse, both external and internal factors define "context." We know what Churchill's utterance "Never in the field of human conflict has so much been owed by so many to so few" means, because we know he said that in a speech, on August 20, 1940, about the Royal Air Force's role in "the battle of Britain." By contrast, we know what Paul's utterance of the letter to Philemon means (as we have no external information) only by deducing from the letter itself what the context was (The return of a runaway slave? Of a slave trying to find Paul as a mediator with his master? Of a slave sent to Paul by Philemon, but delayed in return?).

Pragmatics identifies the usual internal markers of context especially in terms of deixis: the use of words that take their meaning from a situation—pronouns such as "I"/"you," "this/that"; nouns or adverbials such as "now," "today," "yesterday," etc.

2. Presuppostion-pool contribution to utterance meaning

Most utterances convey meaning that is not specifically stated. It would be laborious, time-wasting, and pedantic to say it all. When Paul says "I am appealing to you for my child, Onesimus, whose father I have become during my imprisonment" (Phlm 10), he does not need explain his metaphor. He can assume a pool of common presuppositions about how people are brought to faith by one who may thereby be "father" to the other. When John has the risen Lord address the Laodiceans, "You are neither cold nor hot. Because you are lukewarm ... I am about to spit you out of my mouth" (Rev 3:15-16), he assumes a presuppositional pool that includes the Laodicean understanding that nearby Colossae is famed for its cold refreshing water, and Hierapolis for its hot healing waters, while Laodicea is infamous for its lukewarm sludgy water. So his utterance counts as the rebuke: "Your works bring neither healing nor refreshment, and so (unless you repent) I reject you."

3. Conventional contributions to utterance meaning

How does the hearer decode a simple utterance, such as "It's cold in here, James!" said by the master to his butler, to mean "Please shut the window (with the mild rebuke "why had you not?")?" Grice famously argued that we understand on four cardinal, communal, and essentially co-operative assumptions: those of Quality, Quantity, Relevance, and Manner. Specifically, speakers respectively will 1) be truthful, with adequate evidence; 2) contribute no more and no less than they expect the exact information required; 3) be totally contextually relevant; and 4) be perspicuous (avoiding ambiguity, being brief and orderly, etc.). On Grice's principles my son recognizes my utterance "Oh! I do like the look of your back!" as an ironic request for him to move away so that I can watch the TV, from which his insertion is blocking my vision. Post-Gricean analysis has moved to Relevance Theory as a more neurological explanation of how we link unspecified information into cognition, but, as yet, the different theories seem to be complementary.

4. More global perspectives

Against merely formalistic, open-ended, and reader-response interpretations of biblical texts, pragmatics strongly suggests that "meaning" is located in the author's intentional-and-contextual communication—especially in the speech-act the author makes. The eulogy in Eph 1:3-14 is not foremost a bland statement of beliefs, nor merely Paul's own thanksgiving, but an active invitation to the corporate blessing of God for his manifold salvific initiatives in which the readers participate. And, more importantly, we need to read Philemon not first as an "open text" with endless multiple meanings, but as Paul's specific contextually defined communication to Philemon, and to his "church," and as what he intends the letter to do: to invite, even perform, some act of deep reconciliation, the precise boundaries of which are a little fuzzy. Then, again, if one regards the letter as part of Scripture, one is invited to read it as God's speech-act to Philemon's church, and, more significantly, part of God's whole speech-act to the people of God, consisting primarily in the canon.

Bibliography: J. L. Austin. *How to Do Things with Words* (1976); J. Barr. *The Semantics of Biblical Language* (1961); G. Brown and G. Yule. *Discourse Analysis* (1983); P. Cotterell and M. Turner. *Linguistics and Biblical Interpretation* (1989); David A. Cruse. *Lexical Semantics* (1986); P. Grice. *Studies in the Way of Words* (1989); Y. Huang. *Pragmatics* (2007); J. Lyons. *Linguistic Semantics: An Introduction* (1995); J. Searle. *Speech Acts: An Essay in the Philosophy of Language* (1970); K. J. Vanhoozer. *The Drama of Doctrine: A Canonical-Linguistic Approach to Christian Theology* (2005).

MAX TURNER

SEMEIN sem´ee-uhn [Σεμεΐν Semein]. The father of Mattathias and the son of Josech in the Lukan genealogy (Luke 3:26). A similar name, SHIMEI, appears in the genealogy of 1 Chr 3:19.

SEMEN [זֶרַע zeraʿ]. Fluid secreted by the penis, containing sperm. The Hebrew word zeraʿ also means "seed," which suggests that ancient Israelites assumed that the procreative material was male (compare Gen 38:9). Indeed, one Hebrew phrase for "sexual relations" (Lev 19:20) or "intercourse" (Num 5:13) is literally "a laying of seed" (shikhevath-zeraʿ שִׁכְבַת־זֶרַע). That phrase, translated as "an emission of semen," also appears in descriptions of semen as impure. Any man, woman, or material that was exposed to an emission of semen required washing in water and remained unclean "until evening" (Lev 15:16-18, 32). Similarly, seminal emission rendered a priest unfit to eat the holy offering (Lev 22:4). The power of that impurity was understood to be communicable, a common view throughout the ancient world. Debate persists as to the explanation for semen's impurity; perhaps it was due to apprehension over losing a life-giving substance, suspicion of the penis as carrier of both seed and waste, or a stance of awe before the mystery of procreation. *See* BARREN, BARRENNESS; CLEAN AND UNCLEAN; KINSHIP; LEVIRATE LAW; MARRIAGE, OT.

Bibliography: Jacob Milgrom. *Leviticus 1–16.* AB 3 (1991); Richard Whitekettle. "Leviticus 15:18 Reconsidered: Chiasm, Spatial Structure and the Body." *JSOT* 49 (1991) 31–45.

LISA MICHELE WOLFE

SEMIOTICS sem´ee-ot´ik. Derived from the Greek word sēmeiōtikos (σημειωτικός), meaning an interpreter of symptoms and signs, semiotics is the study of sign-communication and signification (the production of meaning), and provides theoretical models for biblical exegesis and hermeneutics.

Communication through signs and the signs' relationship to the world were already the concern of Plato and Aristotle. Augustine viewed the sign (Lat. *signum*) as the universal means of communication, examined the relationship between natural signs and human-made signs, and pondered symbol systems and sacraments ("sacred signs") as ritual acts involving material signs (e.g., water, bread, wine). For Augustine a sign appears as one thing to the senses but as something else to the mind (*Dial.* 5). This triadic view of sign, a framework for semiotic reflections in theology and biblical interpretation through the centuries, is reflected in Charles Sanders Pierce's triadic hermeneutical model (logic, pragmatism, and communication) and Ferdinand de Saussure's linguistic semiotic model; a sign is the arbitrary relation of a signifier (e.g., the four letters "tree") and a signified (the mental concept of "tree"), with connotations resulting from the interrelations of signs in a system (e.g., a natural language).

Since a sign is always a sign of something to some mind, Saussure's followers, including Umberto Eco and A. J. Greimas, developed analytical models to account for the ways readers produce meaning with a given text (a semiotic system) by relating the text to other semiotic systems (in their culture) through the text's narrative (or didactic) features, through its semantic and symbolic features, or through its discursive and rhetorical features. Semiotic theory provides a powerful tool for understanding the multiplication of critical methods and the multiplicity of biblical interpretations. *See* BIBLICAL CRITICISM; BIBLICAL INTERPRETATION, HISTORY OF.

Bibliography: Umberto Eco. *A Theory of Semiotics* (1979); Algirdas Julien Greimas and Joseph Courtés. *Semiotics and Language* (1982); Daniel Patte. *Religious Dimensions of Biblical Texts: Greimas's Structural Semiotics and Biblical Exegesis* (1990); Charles Sanders Pierce. *Collected Papers.* Vol. 2 (1932); Ferdinand de Saussure. *Course in General Linguistics* (1916).

DANIEL PATTE

SEMITE sem´it. *Semite* is used with three very different senses—genealogical, linguistic, and cultural—in contemporary literature. *Semite* refers to a descendant of the eldest of Noah's sons, SHEM, as reckoned by several genealogies in the Bible (Gen 5:32 [P]; 10:21-31 [largely J]; 11:10-26 [P]; 1 Chr 1–8, particularly 1:17-27; Luke 3:23-38). Some notable Semites named in these genealogies include the eponymous ancestor of the Hebrews, EBER (Gen 10:21, 24; 11:14-16); the first person portrayed as being called by God, Abraham (Gen 11:10-26; 12:1-3); the principal leaders in the wilderness, MOSES, Aaron, and MIRIAM (1 Chr 6:1-3 [Heb. 5:27-29]); the second king of Judah and Israel, DAVID (1 Chr 2:1-15); and Jesus (according to the universalizing genealogy of Luke 3:23-38). *See* AARON, AARONITE; ABRAHAM, OT; GENEALOGY, CHRIST; HEBREW PEOPLE.

Semite also refers to a speaker or writer of one of the Semitic family of languages. This modern linguistic sense of *Semite* is similar to another criterion used to organize some of the ancient biblical genealogies, "by their languages" (Gen 10:5, 20, 31). The Semitic family of languages belongs to a super-family termed the Afro-Asiatic languages (whose other members are Egyptian, Berber, Cushitic, Omotic, and Chadic). The Semitic family can be divided into two major branches, East Semitic and West Semitic, each with subdivisions. Shared, distinctive linguistic features delineate those branches and their subdivisions.

East Semitic is generally termed Akkadian. Early in the 2nd millennium BCE its southern dialect is called Babylonian and its northern, Assyrian (each with an extensive history thereafter). East Semitic languages were almost always written in a logographic-syllabic cuneiform script adapted from a non-Semitic scribal tradition, Sumerian. *See* AKKADIAN; ASSYRIA AND BABYLONIA; EBLA TEXTS; LANGUAGES OF THE ANCIENT NEAR EAST; SUMER, SUMERIANS.

West Semitic encompasses a wide range of languages. It has two major subdivisions, South Semitic and Central Semitic. South Semitic includes the languages of Ethiopia (e.g., Ge'ez, Amharic, Tigrinya) and probably Epigraphic (or Old) South Arabian. Central Semitic comprises Arabic (Classical and Modern) and a grouping termed Northwest Semitic. Before 1000 BCE, Northwest Semitic is witnessed by 1) the earliest consonantal alphabetic inscriptions from Egypt, the western Sinai and Canaan (only partially deciphered); 2) over 6,000 Amorite personal names from Mesopotamia and some names from Egypt's Second Intermediate Period; 3) Canaanite glosses, grammatical features, and names in the Amarna correspondence; and 4) over 1,200 texts written in alphabetic cuneiform script found at or near Ugarit (although the classification of the latter continues to be debated). After 1000 BCE, Northwest Semitic further divided into two linguistically distinct subgroups: Canaanite (including Phoenician, Hebrew [biblical and epigraphic], Ammonite, Moabite, Edomite, and Punic) and various forms of Aramaic (which became the lingua franca of the late Neo-Assyrian, Neo-Babylonian, and Persian Empires). Although ancient Hebrew and Aramaic were closely related linguistically, they appear to have become mutually incomprehensible without previous study (2 Kgs 18:26). *See* ALPHABET; HEBREW LANGUAGE; UGARIT, TEXTS AND LITERATURE.

The OT is written almost entirely in one Semitic language, Hebrew, or, much less frequently, in another, Aramaic. On occasion some NT authors transcribed Aramaic expressions into Greek (e.g., Mark 5:41; 11:9-10; 15:34; Rom 8:15; 1 Cor 16:22) or appear to have some of their Greek phrasings influenced by Aramaic. *See* ARAMAIC, ARAMAISM; GREEK LANGUAGE; HEBREW BIBLE.

A Semite is a bearer of features of Semitic culture, including religious beliefs. *Semitic* is sometimes used to denote elements common to all Semites (e.g., the earliest Semitic pantheon [Roberts]). Cultural features are occasionally assigned specifically to either the East or West Semitic branches (e.g., the origins of the West Semitic alphabet [Hamilton]; enduring institutions from either the West or the East Semitic cultural spheres [Hallo]). Whether referring to Semites as a whole or in part, such generalizations can have the merit of setting larger cultural or religious issues in starker relief (e.g., "El, Creator of Earth" was a common belief among West Semites documented from both inside and outside the Bible; *see* GOD, NAMES OF).

Note that contemporary studies rarely use *Semite* simply as a designation for biological descendants of Shem, since parts of the biblical genealogies run counter to linguistic and cultural senses of that word. Three examples may illustrate where an ancient genealogical sense collides with a modern linguistic and/or cultural one: Shem's firstborn son, Elam (Gen 10:22; 1 Chr 1:17), is the eponymous ancestor of a nation whose language and culture are not classified as Semitic; another son of Shem, Arpachshad (Gen 10:22; 11:10), very likely bears a non-Semitic name; and the language of Canaan was Semitic, although its eponymous ancestor is depicted as being a descendant of Ham, not of Shem (Gen 9:18-27; 10:6). *See* ARPACHSHAD; CANAAN, CANAANITES; ELAM, ELAMITES. The biblical genealogies express the closeness of social, cultural and political relationships from the perspectives of later writers (see especially Borowski on the Table of Nations in Gen 10). Not infrequently they also seek to interpret those relationships theologically, rather than record historically verifiable or even consistent lines of descent (e.g., contrast the different lineages given for Jesus in Matt 1:1-16 and Luke 3:23-38). *See* ANTI-SEMITISM.

Bibliography: Oded Borowski. "The Table of Nations (Genesis 10): A Socio-Cultural Approach." *ZAW* 98 (1986) 14–31; William W. Hallo. *The Ancient Near Eastern Background of Some Modern Western Institutions* (1996); Gordon J. Hamilton. *The Origins of the West Semitic Alphabet in Egyptian Scripts* (2006); Robert Hetzron, ed. *The Semitic Languages* (1998); John Huehnergard. "Features of Central Semitic." *Biblical and Oriental Essays in Memory of William L. Moran.* Augustinus Gianto, ed. (2005) 155–203; John Kaltner and Steven L. McKenzie, eds. *Beyond Babel: A Handbook for Biblical Hebrew and Related Languages* (2003); J. J. M. Roberts. *The Earliest Semitic Pantheon: A Study of the Semitic Deities Attested in Mesopotamia before Ur III* (1972).

GORDON J. HAMILTON

SENAAH suh-nay'uh [סְנָאָה *senaʾah*; Σαναάς *Sanaas*]. Meaning "thorny." The inhabitants or descendants of Senaah returned with Zerubbabel to Jerusalem. Depending on the report, Senaah had 3,630 (or 3,930 or 3,330) descendants (Ezra 2:35; Neh 7:38; 1 Esd 5:23). The family of Senaah ("sons of Hassenaah") worked on the construction of the Jerusalem walls, and are mentioned as the ones that built the FISH GATE (Neh 3:3).

CHANNA COHEN STUART

SENATE [γερουσία *gerousia*]. A senate is a council of elders. However, it can refer specifically to the Roman senatorial institution (1 Macc 8:19; 12:3). In biblical contexts, it is clear that the senate is an authoritative body that had a role in significant political exchanges (e.g., 2 Macc 11:27, where King Antiochus addresses the "senate of the Jews"). This authoritative council forms a part of the SANHEDRIN (Acts 5:21).

KEVIN RODRIGUES

SENATOR [βουλευόμενος *bouleuomenos*, γέρων *gerōn*]. Referring originally to members of the Roman Senate, *senator* (from Lat. *senex*, "old man, elder") is used in modern scholarship for a member of any of the councils of elders in the ancient world, including the

gerousia (γερουσία, "council of elders," from gerōn, "old man, elder, senator") known from a variety of contexts, such as Sparta and Carthage. It is not clear whether 2 Macc 6:1 refers to an "Athenian senator" (NRSV; geronta Athēnaion [γέροντα Ἀθηναῖον], perhaps a member of the Athenian council), to an "elderly Athenian," or to "an Athenian named Geron." First Maccabees 8:15 uses a synonym (bouleuomenos, literally, "counselor") to refer to "senators" in Rome.

LESTER L. GRABBE

SEND [חלשׁ *shalakh*; ἀποστέλλω *apostellō*, πέμπω *pempō*]. In the OT one can send another person somewhere (e.g., Gen 28:5). One can be sent by God in call narratives (e.g., Exod 3:10; *see* CALL, CALLING, CALL STORIES). *Send* possibly could be understood as a catchword for the commissioning of a prophet. God's sending is still analogous to human sending in that, just as a man may send another person somewhere (e.g., Gen 28:5), God is also portrayed as sending persons as his emissaries or spokespersons (e.g., Isa 6:8). In conflicts between true and false prophecy, whether someone has been sent by God plays a decisive role in the veracity of the person's words (e.g., Jer 14:14-15).

In the NT, the words apostellō and pempō are both used for sending. Josephus used these words as synonyms, but the NT writers seem to use them with subtle shades of difference. In the NT, pempō contains the thought of authorization, such as in the case of a special envoy. The Gospel of John frequently uses pempō to emphasize God's intimate participation in his work through the act of sending Jesus (4:34; 5:23, 24, 30, 37; 6:38; et al). The most common term for sending in the NT is apostellō, which seems to be preferred when the emphasis is on the commission itself. A derivative of this is the term apostolos, meaning "messenger" or "apostle." Apostolos is used specifically for the "twelve apostles" (Matt 10:2) sent out by Jesus (e.g., Matt 10:2), and more broadly for the first Christian missionaries (e.g., Acts 14:4; Gal 1:19; Rom 16:7; 1 Cor 15:7). *See* APOSTLE.

RALPH K. HAWKINS

SENECA sen'uh-kuh. Lucius Annaeus Seneca (ca. 4 BCE–65 CE), the son of the Roman rhetorician Seneca the Elder, was a Stoic, a Roman philosopher trained in rhetoric. Seneca was exiled from Rome by Emperor Claudius in 41 CE but returned later to tutor a young NERO. Seneca became wealthy in late life, but was accused of conspiracy by Nero and was forced to commit suicide.

Seneca is perhaps best known for his tragic plays, reconstructions of plays by Euripides, which include *Phaedra* and *Medea*. Some of the main differences between Euripides and Seneca lie in Seneca's emphasis on moralizing and rhetoric. Seneca also wrote moral dialogues, other works of prose, and epistles. The epistles are helpful in the study of early Christianity; Jerome and Augustine both refer to a correspondence between Seneca and Paul. A document containing this correspondence exists, but it is widely considered to be a forgery. The Christian attraction to Seneca could stem from his Stoic emphasis on morality and virtue. Tertullian adopted Seneca as a Christian, and some medieval Christians believed that Seneca was converted by Paul. However, all evidence indicates that Seneca remained a Stoic. *See* RHETORIC AND ORATORY; STOICS, STOICISM.

KEVIN RODRIGUES

SENEH see´nuh [סְנֶה senneh]. One of two sharp crags flanking the pass of Michmash; the other is Bozez (1 Sam 14:4). The area is located approximately 11 km northeast of Jerusalem. In 1 Sam 14, Seneh is mentioned in the detailed description of Jonathan's approach to the camp of the Philistines at Michmash. The etymology of the name is uncertain: some derive it from the word for "tooth," referring to the shape of the crag; others suggest that it means "thorny" and refers to the surrounding flora.

Bibliography: Michael Avi-Yonah and Anson F. Rainey. *The Holy Land: A Historical Geography from the Persian to the Arab Conquest* (2006); Anson F. Rainey and R. Steven Notley. *The Sacred Bridge: Carta's Atlas of the Biblical World* (2006).

JOSEPH R. CATHEY

SENIR see´nuhr [שְׂנִיר senir]. Following the recollection in Deut 3:1-8 of how the Israelites had taken from the Amorites the land between the Wadi Arnon and Mount Hermon, Deut 3:9 notes that Senir is the Amorite name for Mount Hermon. Both 1 Chr 5:23 and Song 4:8, however, appear to make a distinction between Senir and Hermon. Ezekiel 27:5 identifies Senir as a source of fir trees. *See* HERMON, MOUNT.

TREVOR D. COCHELL

SENNACHERIB suh-nak´uh-rib [סַנְחֵרִיב sankheriv; Σενναχηρείμ Sennachēreim]. Sennacherib ("the god Sin has replaced the brother") was the king of Assyria (704–681 BCE) who invaded Judah during the reign of HEZEKIAH. He was the son of SARGON II, king of Assyria (721–705 BCE). Although Sennacherib never mentions Sargon's name as a patronym in his royal inscriptions, the father-son relationship between the two is clear from other inscriptions.

Sennacherib's accession to the Assyrian throne was anything but normal. Sargon II was killed on the battlefield in Tabal, and his body was not recovered. Hence, Sennacherib could not perform his traditional duty of burying his deceased predecessor in the city of Assur. In a text (perhaps written at the time of his son ESARHADDON), Sennacherib attempted to ascertain the nature of Sargon's alleged sin that caused this inauspicious death. Upon his accession, Sennacherib moved the capital to Nineveh, motivated at least in part

by the fear that Sargon's ghost might still be present at Dur-Sharruken (the new capital that Sargon had completed building in 706).

Thus, while Sennacherib inherited a vast empire from his father, Sargon's death precipitated significant revolts, particularly in Babylonia and the Levant. It took Sennacherib until 700 BCE to put down these revolts, with the bulk of his attention given to Babylonia, where Marduk-apla-iddina II led the resistance (the same enemy faced by Sargon). Known as MERODACH-BALADAN in 2 Kgs 20:12-15, this ruler sent envoys to Hezekiah possibly to coordinate the resistance to Assyria. This passage in 2 Kings is ordered literarily, not chronologically.

Throughout 704–702, Sennacherib campaigned to crush the rebellion in the south. The campaign began with the conquest of the city of Cutha and then the defeat of Marduk-apla-iddina and his Aramean, Elamite, and Arabian allies at Kish, though Marduk-apla-iddina escaped (see *COS* 2:300–302). The deportation from Cutha that followed this initial success, as well as other mass deportations from Babylonia, is very likely referred to in 2 Kgs 17:24, 30. In the city of Babylon, Sennacherib installed Bel-ibni, a local aristocrat, as a puppet king. While the pursuit of Marduk-apla-iddina proved fruitless, a campaign in 702 in the Zagros region reasserted Assyrian rule in the east.

In 701, Sennacherib campaigned against the rebellious states in the west. Labeled as his "third" campaign, it is certainly the best known and most discussed military operation undertaken by Sennacherib for two reasons: it is the most detailed description of an Assyrian campaign to the west in the cuneiform sources, and it is the most well-attested event in all of the Bible, famous for Sennacherib's attack on Jerusalem.

In the Assyrian sources, the campaign is attested in Sennacherib's annals (seven textual exemplars, the earliest being the Rassam Cylinder, dated to 700 BCE; see *COS* 2:302–303), in the Bull inscriptions (composite Bull 2/3 and Bull 4), and possibly in the so-called "Azekah" Inscription (*COS* 2:304–305), though there is debate whether this text belongs to Sennacherib or to Sargon II. In addition, there are Assyrian reliefs from the South-West Palace at Nineveh that illustrate the capture of the Judahite city of LACHISH, clearly identified by an epigraph. The biblical texts that refer to the campaign are: 2 Kgs 18:13–19:37 (usually divided into an A source: 2 Kgs 18:13-16; and a B source: 2 Kgs 18:17–19:37); Isa 36:1–37:38; 2 Chr 32:1-23. There are also allusions to the campaign (e.g., throughout Isa 1–35 and in Mic 1). Moreover, there are Greek accounts in Herodotus (*Hist.* 2.141) and Josephus, quoting Menander (*Ant.* 9.283–87). There is much archaeological evidence of the campaign, most notably at sites like Lachish (destruction layer in Level III and evidence of a siege ramp), BETH-SHEMESH, and Timnah (*see* TIMNAH, TIMNITE). It appears that Hezekiah had been making preparations for the revolt: rebuilding the walls of Jerusalem, strengthening and reorganizing his military (2 Chr 32:5-6), building storehouses for food and stalls for animals (vv. 28-29), and constructing the Siloam tunnel (*COS* 2:145–46) to transport water from the Gihon spring inside the city walls (2 Kgs 20:20; 2 Chr 32:30). The lmlk (למלך) jar handles appear to date to the reign of Hezekiah and indicate his preparations for the invasion (*see* LMLK SEALS).

Noting some of the differences between Sennacherib's account of his third campaign and the biblical materials, several scholars have suggested that Sennacherib undertook a second campaign against Judah after 689, but there is no conclusive evidence for this idea.

Both the biblical and Assyrian accounts of this campaign have sophisticated literary, ideological, and religious features, complicating the process of historical reconstruction of the campaign. While both follow an overall chronology, neither account follows a strict chronological order (some events are clearly out of order). In the Assyrian narration, the presentation starts with the easiest victories and climaxes with the most difficult, demonstrating the Assyrian king's invincibility. The biblical text gives a summary (2 Kgs 18:13-16) followed by a backtracking and overlapping narrative (2 Kgs 18:17–19:37) that gives a detailed narration of the Assyrian king's actions and hubris and Yahweh's intervention (compare Sir 48:17-21; 2 Macc 8:19; 15:22; 3 Macc 6:5). Sennacherib's name is possibly employed in a wordplay in 2 Kgs 19:16-17, 24 (= Isa 37:17-18, 25) with the Hebrew roots for "shame" (khrp חרף) and "destroy" (khrb חרב). Neither account is free from the biases imposed by its own ideological agenda, but together they can produce a reasonable reconstruction.

The campaign can be divided into two phases: the Phoenician phase and the Southern Levantine phase. In the first phase, Lulli, king of Sidon, being overwhelmed with fear, fled from Sennacherib's force to Cyprus; Tuba'alu was installed in his place, and eight kings of the region submitted with payment of tribute. In the second phase, the Assyrian army captured some of the cities of Ashkelon; Sidqa, its king, was captured and deported along with his family, and Sharru-lu-darri was installed in his place. The citizens of Ekron had handed over their king Padi, a pro-Assyrian monarch, to Hezekiah. They petitioned Egypt and Nubia for aid, but the coalition was defeated by Sennacherib at Eltekeh. Ekron was captured and its citizens tortured. The Assyrian attack on the land of Judah is the last episode of the campaign. Forty-six Judahite cities were conquered (including Lachish), and Jerusalem was placed under siege. Although failing to take the city, the Assyrians forced Hezekiah to release Padi, who was reinstalled at Ekron. Hezekiah was forced to pay a heavy tribute to the Assyrian king.

Finally, Sennacherib campaigned in 700 in Babylonia where the rule of Bel-ibni had been unstable because of the ongoing machinations of Marduk-apla-iddina and another Chaldean, Mushezib-Marduk. Sennacherib devastated the rebel territories, and Marduk-apla-iddina and Mushezib-Marduk fled to Elam. Sennacherib installed his eldest son, Ashur-nadin-shumi, on the Babylonian throne, an arrangement that finally ended Sennacherib's initial problems in Babylonia, ensuring Assyrian control for the next six years.

However, renewed warfare occurred in Babylonia in 694–689, with the chief enemy being the Elamites and the Chaldean Mushezib-Marduk (Marduk-apla-iddina having died in 700). After a lengthy siege, Babylon was captured in 689. The city was totally destroyed, a drastic measure that had far-reaching consequences (*COS* 2:305).

The relative peace of 689–681 enabled Sennacherib to turn his attention to numerous building projects. Compared to Sennacherib, there is no other Mesopotamian king who left such a vast amount of inscriptions regarding his building activities. He not only moved the Assyrian capital to Nineveh but also converted it into a metropolis. He boasted of having personally introduced a number of metallurgical and horticultural innovations.

While there were no major foreign threats after 689, the domestic situation deteriorated, primarily because of the struggle for succession. It is not entirely clear who was Sennacherib's first crown prince. It may have been his eldest son, Ashur-nadin-shumi; there is some evidence, however, that it was Urdu-Mullissu, or at least this man expected to be his father's successor. Whatever the case, in 683 Sennacherib chose to designate a younger son, perhaps even his youngest son, as crown prince: Esarhaddon, a child of his wife Naqi'a. Sennacherib forced everyone, including Urdu-Mullissu, to swear a loyalty oath in favor of Esarhaddon. Nevertheless, conspiracy soon developed against Esarhaddon, and he was forced into exile.

In 681, Sennacherib was assassinated by Urdu-Mullissu and his accomplices, who may have stabbed him to death between the bull colossi of a temple at Nineveh. The biblical accounts (2 Kgs 19:37; 2 Chr 32:21; Isa 37:38) link Sennacherib's violent death, allegedly accomplished in the temple of Nisroch, with his campaign against Judah. They also mention another son, Sharezer, as being involved. The murderers fled, seeking refuge in the kingdom of Urartu as Esarhaddon ascended the throne (compare Tob 1:15-22). *See* ASSYRIA AND BABYLONIA; TIRHAKAH.

Bibliography: M. Cogan. "Sennacherib's Siege of Jerusalem: Once or Twice?" *BAR* 27 (2001) 40–45, 69; S. Dalley. "Yabâ, Atalya and the Foreign Policy of Late Assyrian Kings." *SAAB* 12 (1998) 83–98; W. R. Gallagher. *Sennacherib's Campaign to Judah: New Studies* (1999); M. Garsiel. *Biblical Names: A Literary Study of Midrashic Derivations and Puns* (1991); S. C. Melville. "Neo-Assyrian Royal Women and Male Identity: Status as a Social Tool." *JAOS* 124 (2004) 37–57; S. C. Melville. *The Role of Naqia/Zakutu in Sargonid*

Politics (1999); J. M. Russell. *The Writing on the Wall: Studies in the Architectural Context of Late Assyrian Palace Inscriptions* (1999); D. Ussishkin. *The Renewed Archaeological Excavations at Lachish (1973–1994)* (2004); K. L. Younger Jr. "Assyrian Involvement in the Southern Levant at the End of the Eighth Century BCE." *Jerusalem in Bible and Archaeology: The First Temple Period.* A. G. Vaughan and A. E. Killebrew, eds. (2003) 235–63; K. L. Younger Jr. "The Repopulation of Samaria (2 Kings 17:24, 27-31) in Light of Recent Study." *The Future of Biblical Archaeology.* J. K. Hoffmeier and A. R. Millard, eds. (2004) 242–68; K. L. Younger Jr. "Yahweh at Ashkelon and Calah? Yahwistic Names in Neo-Assyrian." *VT* 52 (2002) 207–18.

K. LAWSON YOUNGER JR.

SENTINEL, SENTRY [צֹפֶה tsofeh, שֹׁמֵר shomer; σκοπός skopos, φύλαξ phylax]. Various terms are used for a sentinel or sentry. Tsofeh, from the root tsafah (צָפָה), meaning "to spy, look out, look out for," is used in 2 Sam 18:24-27. Shomer, from shamar (שָׁמַר), denoting the concept of watching or guarding, appears other places (e.g., Ps 127:1; Isa 21:11-12). In the NT, the Gk. word meaning "sentinel" or "sentry" (e.g., Acts 5:25; 12:6, 19) is related to the verb phylasso (φυλάσσω), normally translated "watch," "GUARD," "defend," or "imprison." Sentries, then, have the responsibility of watching out for, or over, something or someone to ensure their safety. In the OT in particular (e.g., Ezek 3; 33) the failure of the "watchmen" (the prophets and princes) to warn the people of impending judgment for their sin brings about serious condemnation by God. *See* WATCHTOWER.

JAMES E. WEST

SEORIM see-or'im [שְׂעֹרִים seʿorim]. The fourth priest of twenty-four Aaronides assigned duties in the Temple on King David's initiative. Seorim, possibly the descendant of Ithamar, is mentioned once in the Bible (1 Chr 24:8) and also in 4Q320 1 I, 12. *See* PRIESTS AND LEVITES.

SEPHAR see'fuhr [סְפָר sefar]. Meaning "number or numbering." Mentioned only once in the Bible: the sons of Joktan inhabited the area that lies between MESHA and Sephar (Gen 10:30). Believed to be identical to the city of Zephar or Zaphar on the Indian Ocean, between the Persian Gulf and the Red Sea, the ancient site of Zaphar was the capital of the Himyartic Kingdom and lies some 130 km south-southwest of Sanaa, in modern Yemen. The Himyarites ruled over much of Southern Arabia between 115 BCE and 525 CE. Sephar or Zaphar was the most prosperous city of this kingdom.

CHANNA COHEN STUART

SEPHARAD sef'uh-rad [סְפָרַד sefaradh]. A place to which some Jewish residents of Jerusalem were exiled (Obad 20). The biblical text does not identify the exact location. Three suggestions have been offered: 1) Sefarad, located in modern Spain; 2) a city in Media; 3) the most common identification, Sardis in Asia Minor (modern Turkey), the capital city of Lydia. Sardis was incorporated in the Persian Empire after it was conquered by Cyrus in 546 BCE. Located near the modern village of Sart, Sardis was an important trade center along the Royal Road of Persia which tied it to the Persian capital of Susa. An Aramaic-Lydian inscription discovered at Sardis preserves the Aramaic name of the city with the same four consonants, sprd (סְפָרד), as the text of Obad 20. The ancient ruins have been extensively excavated and have uncovered a large 2nd cent. CE synagogue, which attests to a significant Jewish population.

JOHN D. WINELAND

SEPHARVAIM sef'uhr-vay'im [סְפַרְוַיִם sefarwayim]. A city in Mesopotamia, located somewhere along the Euphrates River; its precise location is unknown. It was conquered by the Assyrians sometime in the 8th cent. BCE. After the Assyrians conquered Samaria in 722 BCE and deported the Israelites to cities in the eastern part of the Assyrian Empire, they resettled peoples from other conquered cities in the towns of Samaria. The new settlers included Sepharvites (2 Kgs 17:24, 31). The Deuteronomistic Historian states that although the Sepharvites worshiped Yahweh, they continued to worship their deities Adrammelech and Anammelech and practiced child sacrifice (2 Kgs 17:31-33). It is probable that both ADRAMMELECH and ANAMMELECH were manifestations of the deity Molech (*see* MOLECH, MOLOCH). The deity Adrammelech should not be confused with Adrammelech, son of Sennacherib, who collaborated in the murder of his father (2 Kgs 19:37; Isa 37:38).

Some twenty years later, in 701 BCE, the Assyrian king Sennacherib besieged Jerusalem. He sent an embassy to King Hezekiah to induce him to surrender. Sennacherib's representative, the Rabshakeh, noted that the gods of many cities, including Sepharvaim, had failed to save their cities from the Assyrian army, and he argued that Yahweh would likewise be unable to save Jerusalem (2 Kgs 18:34; 19:13; Isa 36:19; 37:13). Thus, the fall of Sepharvaim served as a symbol of Assyrian might. The Assyrians failed to capture Jerusalem, however, and for the Deuteronomistic Historian, the deliverance of Jerusalem from the Assyrians is proof that Yahweh is superior to the gods of cities like Sepharvaim.

JOSEPH R. CATHEY

SEPPHORIS sef'uh-ris. Also known as Diocaesarea, Zippori, and Saffuriyeh. Located on the southern ridge of the Bet Netofa valley in Lower Galilee, Sepphoris was a commercial and political center from the 2nd cent. BCE to the 6th cent. CE.

Sepphoris is never mentioned in the Bible, but appears frequently in other sources. Josephus notes that Alexander Jannaeus defeated Ptolemy Lathyrus there in

Figure 1: The "Mona Lisa" of the Galilee, detail from the mosaic floor. Sepphoris, Israel.

103 BCE (*Ant.* 13.337). When the Romans invaded in 63 BCE, they limited the power of the Hasmoneans by assigning select major cities to government by local assemblies including Sepphoris (*Ant.* 14.91). Herod the Great used the city as a command center in suppressing Hasmonean loyalists (*Ant.* 14.414) and Herod's son, Herod Antipas, declared it "Autocratoris" (an uncertain designation, possibly reflecting local governance) and turned it into "the Ornament of all Galilee" (*Ant.* 18.27). Sepphoris, 5 km north of Nazareth, would have influenced the smaller villages of the Lower Galilee.

During the First Jewish Revolt, Josephus presents an inconsistent picture of the city, which suggests a divided attitude toward the revolt. In one place, Josephus claims it refrained from conflict with Rome (*J.W.* 3.30–31). Coins minted at Sepphoris in 67/68 CE proclaim it "Eirenopolis" or "City of Peace."

Within rabbinic literature, Sepphoris is the seat of an influential rabbinic academy. Rabbi Judah Ha-Nasi moved from Beth Shearim to Sepphoris near the end of the 2nd cent. CE and according to tradition assembled the MISHNAH there. Several major rabbinic authorities came from Sepphoris, and its weights and measures were regarded as standards for all Galilee.

It is not known when Christianity arrived at the city. An early account by the Pilgrim of Piacenza (ca. 570 CE) remarks that Sepphoris was the hometown of the parents of Mary, Anna, and Joachim. Much later, the Crusaders maintained a garrison at the city and built a large church in honor of Saint Anne, much of which remains intact. Following the Arabic conquest, Saffuriyeh (the Arabic form of Sepphoris) became one of the leading Palestinian cities in the Galilee.

Archaeological investigation began in the 1930s when the amphitheater was first discovered. Sustained excavation of the city since the early 1980s has exposed a number of remarkable features. A Roman villa near the amphitheater was richly decorated with mosaics, including a stunning portrait of a young woman, known as the "Mona Lisa of the Galilee."

In the same area, excavations encountered a series of deeply seated column foundations, apparently all that remains of a large Byzantine church. On the outskirts of the city, an extensive water system has been revealed, with large plastered cisterns built into natural crevasses in the native limestone, and aqueducts channeling water into the city. Within the city an elaborate cardo bears a mosaic inscription crediting repairs to "Bishop Eutropius" indicating a growth in prominence of the Christian community in the Byzantine period. On one end of the cardo is a building with well-preserved mosaics depicting the Nile and mythological scenes, and on the other end a possible synagogue was encountered, with a zodiac mosaic.

Bibliography: Rebecca Martin Nagy, Carol L. Meyers, Eric M. Meyers, and Zeev Weiss, eds. *Sepphoris in Galilee: Crosscurrents of Culture* (1996).
                                                    KENNETH G. HOGLUND

SEPTUAGINT sep'*too*-uh-jint. The Septuagint (LXX) is the Greek translation of the Hebrew Scripture, known as the "Old Testament" (OT) among Protestant Christians.

A. The *Letter of Aristeas*

No accounts by any LXX translator have been preserved, if indeed any ever existed. Nor are there any records contemporary with the translators to provide timely documentation. What we do have is the *Letter of Aristeas*, about which there is considerable disagreement on all but two points: It is not a letter and it was not written, as purported, by an eye-witness to the events it describes (*see* ARISTEAS, LETTER OF).

The *Letter of Aristeas*, begins with a conversation between the royal librarian Demetrius and Ptolemy II Philadelphus, the second ruler of his dynasty and the patron/founder of the greatest intellectual institution of antiquity. Demetrius alerts Ptolemy to a gap in his massive and otherwise rather complete collection: the Laws of the Jews in a "proper" (that is, "Greek") version. In order to remedy this circumstance, Ptolemy sends an envoy to Jerusalem, to entreat the High Priest to send him seventy-two elders (six from each of the twelve tribes) to prepare such a text. The High Priest readily agrees and selects the requisite number of men, each characterized by exceptional piety in the Jewish tradition as well as skill in the Greek language. Ptolemy holds a series of lavish banquets, with learned disquisitions serving as the main entertainment.

Thereafter, the Jewish elders are sequestered on an island in palatial splendor, working in committees and sub-committees to arrive at an agreed-upon Greek rendering of the five books that make up the TORAH. This text is read out loud, winning royal appropriation and, of at least equal importance, the approval of the Jewish community. So serious is the latter taken that a curse is put upon anyone who would add or omit or in another way alter this apparently now sacred text.

Although the preparation of this Greek version takes up only a relatively small percentage of the *Letter of Aristeas* as a whole, it is nonetheless clear that this is the main subject of the letter. Thus it is significant that the Alexandrian Jewish community's acceptance of this Greek version is reminiscent—in fact, undoubtedly modeled on—the acceptance by the Israelites of the Law in Exod 34 and elsewhere in the Hebrew Scripture

(OT). In short, the Greek translation, as well as the Hebrew original, is Scripture (*see* HELLENISM).

There is no way to determine to what degree the *Letter of Aristeas'* high regard for the Greek Pentateuch approximates (if at all) whatever view the earliest translators and their patron(s) had. Certainly an extended period of time, probably a century or more, separates the *Letter of Aristeas* from the time period it purports to describe with eyewitness accuracy. It is, in fact, certain historical inaccuracies—prominent among them being Demetrius' role as librarian during the reign of Ptolemy II—that have led scholars since the Renaissance to doubt the accuracy of this account. It would be fair to say that most Septuagint scholars today are very skeptical of the claims made by the *Letter of Aristeas*. While skepticism is wholly in order in this case, it would be equally unfortunate if this stance were carried too far.

Among the issues most in doubt is the contention that the impetus for the Greek version came from outside the community, and especially at the behest of the royal court. However, although this specific commission is not documented elsewhere, such literary patronage is chronicled elsewhere for Ptolemy II. Moreover, it is difficult to understand why someone writing for Jews, as the author of the *Letter of Aristeas* was, would create a fictional role for Ptolemy that simply raises more questions than it could possibly answer.

In general, the modern critic seeks origins for the Septuagint within the Alexandrian Jewish community itself, whose members were becoming more and more at home in this cosmopolitan capital where speaking Greek was the norm. In such a circumstance, it is asked, would not the community's leadership itself have initiated this process? Rather than viewing this as an either/or proposition, I believe that it makes more sense—and is closer to the historical reality—to see in the origins of the LXX an example (of which there are many, even within the relatively limited scope of the history of Bible translation) of both/and; that is, the confluence of interests that brings about a desirable result on the part of several parties. It is impossible to know whether a copy of the Greek Pentateuch was ever deposited in the Library, but there is ample documentary evidence to demonstrate that the Jewish law in this form became known up and down the Nile in the decades and centuries that followed. If there is, as we believe to be the case, an historical basis or kernel for the letter's account, then the activities it narrates would have taken place ca. 275 BCE. There is some internal evidence for placing the Greek Pentateuch in this period: much of the vocabulary (and related phenomena) it displays can be found in Greek papyri securely dated to this time. And, it should be noted, there are features that distinctively link these five books, when compared to other material that makes up the LXX. At the same time, careful study demonstrates conclusively that there were at least five different translators responsible for the Pentateuch (one for each book), and probably a sixth for the last part of the book of Exodus. Thus it is that in this instance, as in many others in connection with the *Letter of Aristeas*, neither wholesale rejection nor uncritical acceptance is in order.

B. Revisors and Revisions vs. "The" Original

The letter's concluding section, as described above, has about it a certain tone of urgency, as if its author, independent of whatever feelings the original translators may have had, was deeply concerned about guarding what he (and, most likely, at least some within his community) saw as the LXX's sacred status against even the slightest alteration. Such urgency most likely reflects the times and circumstances of the letter's author, whose Greek-speaking Jewish community was faced with one or more revisions of a text upon which tradition had bestowed the immutable status of Scripture. On the basis of known revisers active at least a century after the *Letter of Aristeas*, which can be broadly dated to the mid-2nd cent. BCE, we can suggest that earlier, unknown revisers were likewise concerned with differences between the established Greek text and the recognized Hebrew text of various biblical books.

Even though the translators responsible for the Greek Pentateuch followed a reasonably literal rendering of the Hebrew text that lay before them (sometimes called their *Vorlage*), there were instances where the Hebrew and Greek differed. Such differences could be quantitative—that is, one text was shorter than the other [or longer, depending on one's perspective] or material was in a different order—or qualitative, where the texts were roughly equal in length, but exhibited all sorts of other variations. For the ancient reviser, the Hebrew was the standard to which any Greek text should be "revised." For the author of the *Letter of Aristeas*, the Greek text—as passed down to this community—needed no changes of any sort.

This observation leads to additional questions, all of which are of considerable importance in the study and evaluation of the LXX. The first might be phrased in this manner: Was the *Letter of Aristeas*, or rather its author, successful in establishing his community's Greek Bible as uniquely authoritative? The proliferation of revisers or new translators after his time is indicative of a decidedly negative response to this query. In addition to the individuals traditionally named THEODOTION, Aquila, and SYMMACHUS (*see* AQUILA'S VERSION), there are other anonymous Greek manuscripts exhibiting biblical texts. Hitherto unknown Greek readings were also uncovered at Qumran and in neighboring sites. Moreover, close analysis of "Scriptural" citations and allusions by NT writers points to their occasional reliance on Greek versions that would otherwise be entirely lost to us. "Septuagint" references in the church fathers and other early Christian sources reveal numerous textual deviations. Although many such instances seem to be the result of authorial intervention or even faulty memory, all such differences can be accounted for in that way.

Clearly, many individuals, and the communities for/in which they worked, were not the least bit deterred by the anathema threatened in the *Letter of Aristeas* (if they were indeed familiar with it).

But this issue is not so easily resolved. In particular, it cannot be ascertained whether those citing a Greek biblical text had any idea that they were dealing with a revised, re-worked, or in any sense updated version of the original. Their reliance on "what was written" as proof text or authoritative probably depended on an understanding of its being reliably the Word of God.

This is especially the case within the developing Christian world, where the relatively sober account of the letter was embellished over and over again, so as to add to the miraculous quality of what had increasingly become Scripture. The case of Justin, who lived in the 2nd cent. CE, is instructive in this regard. In his writings, he strongly maintained the authority and integrity of the LXX against any and all later Greek translations or revisions. Ironically, the Greek text he quoted was not done by the earliest translators. Of course, from Justin's perspective, all of these readings were an old Greek translation—but certainly not always the Old Greek or first rendering..

The great codices containing the LXX exhibited a text that was far from uniform. In the case of the book of Daniel, e.g., they all have, in place of the earlier text (known elsewhere from a single papyrus fragment and two other sources), the revision identified with Theodotion. For Song of Songs, a literal version, similar to Aquila's, is found in all witnesses, including the codices. For the books of Samuel and Kings (collectively known as "Reigns" in the tradition of the LXX), parts of the text look old, but in other parts a revision has supplanted the more ancient wording. Although the motivation of those who collated this material is not known (e.g., if they made a conscious choice or simply incorporated what was available), it is likely they would have asserted that their compilation, however uneven it might appear, was a secure representation of what the inspired translators initially wrote down.

Even the Jewish philosopher Philo, himself a resident of Alexandria in the 1st cent. CE, exhibited this tendency, expressing a reverential attitude towards the work of translators (whom he termed prophets), thereby allotting to the LXX's unique features the same authority possessed by the Hebrew. So it is that the concept championed by the *Letter of Aristeas* was maintained, even as the reality of such a text (if it ever existed) faded further and further into the past.

C. The Greek Translators

So far as we can determine, one of the factors that motivated revisers was the perceived need to "correct" an earlier Greek version of the Hebrew text in use within their community. The assumption underlying such efforts at "correcting" is clear: The Hebrew was the standard against which any other rendering needed to be compared. Variations from this standard were mistakes caused by translators whose faults or flaws ran from incompetence to indolence to the introduction of material they might actually have considered improvement (though, from this perspective, they were badly mistaken). Is there validity to this ancient viewpoint?

This is the very issue that has divided—and, to an extent, continues to divide—LXX specialists. Prior to the Second World War, it was widely asserted that the MT, at least its consonants, represented throughout antiquity (as it does today) the standard against which all transcribers and translators would regularly check their work (see MT, MASORETIC TEXT). It was this text that, by and large, the LXX translators had before them. Thus, deviations from the MT are the fault of scribes, whose minds were muddled or distracted. The "original" LXX, in this reconstruction, can be located in those manuscripts that are closest to the MT (see MASORA; MASORETES).

Not all scholars, even during the first half of the 20th cent., were comfortable with this formulation. Surely, it can be agreed, a consonantal text very much like our MT was available to some LXX translators whose abilities and attention to details varied. Nonetheless, is it not also possible that the Hebrew that lay before LXX translators sometimes differed extensively from the MT? It was the discovery and publication of biblical scrolls from Qumran that provided primary data to support both of these views (see DEAD SEA SCROLLS).

Some of the biblical scrolls present a consonantal text that is indeed, to all extent and purposes, identical to our MT. In many cases, all that separates these texts is greater use of the letters YOD and WAW to indicate pronunciation in the Dead Sea scroll. This indicates the MT represents an ancient and authentic textual tradition.

At the same time, there are Qumran scrolls that bear witness to a Hebrew text that is close to what the LXX translators may have had in front of them. This is true for portions of the books of Samuel and Jeremiah in particular. Thus it is likely that the LXX translators would frequently follow the Hebrew whether or not it happened to be consistent with what we term the MT.

The biblical scrolls from Qumran give no support for those who would argue that the MT presented a "better" or more widely accepted version. As it happens, there are multiple copies of many of the biblical books that apparently circulated at the same time at Qumran—and with seemingly equal weight and authority. This provides firsthand evidence for what is often spoken of as textual fluidity in the period prior to the destruction of the Jerusalem Temple by the Romans in 70 CE. It becomes apparent that even where there was a consensus of what constituted sacred Scripture, this applied only to books as a whole and not to the particulars or details of wording. Thus, there is no good reason to assert that the LXX, where it follows its Hebrew Vorlage ("pattern"), presents an aberrant or secondary tradition.

No matter what the Hebrew wording, isn't it also possible that an ancient translator, much like his modern counterpart, might stray from that Hebrew for any number of reasons: to make theological or stylistic "improvements" for the sake of consistency, to update references that would be obscure for his intended audience, to reshape even more radically whole sections for purposes of clarity, relevance, etc.? This, of course, is what the revisers did; however, it makes little sense to limit such "freedom" to the revisers. The evidence, including Greek scrolls from Qumran and nearby sites, reveals a varied and variegated history that is old as the oldest Greek Bible (see BIBLE TRANSLATION THEORY).

What of changes made by translators themselves? In such cases (which are apparent in all translated Greek of the LXX, to a greater or lesser extent), it is helpful to distinguish between those the translator subconsciously or accidentally made, and those that were made as a result of conscious efforts on a translator's part. As for the former, they consist primarily of omissions—caused by similar wording at the beginning or end of words or phrases, or by other easily confused graphic elements. The net result of such "accidents" is to shorten the text in comparison with the Hebrew that is being rendered. This accords with the observation that to some extent the work of a translator (as of a scribe) involved the drudgery of facing long passages to be worked on; the eye was constantly moving forward or downward on the page and often skipped similar wording (see TEXT CRITICISM, OT).

Conscious or deliberate intervention by translators tends to lengthen the text, as the translator seeks to clarify, smooth out, explain, update, or otherwise "improve upon" the Hebrew text these alterations may be referred to as quantitative changes. On occasion, substituted wording does not result in any substantive change in the text's length; these are referred to as qualitative changes. Of course, there is considerable scholarly difference of opinion, especially in this area, as to whether the LXX is indeed the result of activity on the part of the translator or rather is an accurate representation of the Hebrew Vorlage, which in these instances differs from the MT.

Increasingly over the past half-century or so, LXX specialists have minutely analyzed the Greek text to ascertain what translation technique(s) each book or block of material exhibits. For no matter what determination is made in a specific instance, there is complete agreement that each book or block of material must be studied on its own in order to determine such characteristics. This is not to say that scholars of one LXX book cannot learn from specialists in another—indeed they can and do. For example, it is clear that the individual responsible for LXX Joshua had access to the earlier Greek renderings of the books of the Pentateuch.

Scholars must resist the temptation to apply globally what is the case for a given book. In the past, lack of such restraint has led to the positing of a strong anti-anthropomorphic tendency throughout the LXX or an equally widespread promotion of certain messianic ideas. Neither of these assertions has stood the careful scrutiny of later researchers.

D. The Translators of the Pentateuch

When all is said and done on this crucial issue, we are largely dependent on the interpretations offered by the most respected and seasoned researchers. Thus a book like Proverbs is widely understood as containing a number of passages reflective of the translators themselves rather than their Hebrew text. In other cases, such as the Greek Pentateuch, we can appropriately speak of the five (or six) individuals responsible for this material as reasonably literal in their renderings, without concluding that every difference vis-à-vis the MT is due to a divergent *Vorlage.*

It is interesting to observe that scholars continue the quest for models, within Jewish culture or more broadly Ptolemaic-Hellenistic ALEXANDRIA, of which these translators may have availed themselves (*see* DIASPORA). To a large extent, the individuals responsible for the Greek Pentateuch were setting rather than following precedent. In general, Greek speakers did not see much reason to translate significant or sacred texts from other languages into Greek, secure as they were in the illusion that they had much to offer but very little to learn from others. Given their role as pioneers, these earliest LXX translators might be thought to have hit upon an essentially literal approach as the safest way— and also the least painful—to render their Hebrew.

We cannot imagine that anyone with the talents and desire to participate in this project would have lived in total isolation from trends, movements, and other activities in their community at large. For Jews in Alexandria, this would have meant some exposure to the political, civic, and intellectual life of this cosmopolitan center— and this would be true whether or not we give any credence to the *Letter of Aristeas'* claim of royal patronage. Thus, parallels can be adduced between the LXX translators and the office or position of dragoman, whose primary responsibilities involved translating governmental and business texts. In such circumstances, it was natural to follow a literal approach parallel to that found in many portions of the Greek Pentateuch.

There are other portions of the Greek biblical text that reflect a heightened interest in literary and other stylistic features of the Hebrew—and such interest does not always reflect the type of Hebrew being rendered. It is clear that many passages of the Greek Pentateuch are very difficult to fathom without access to the underlying Hebrew. A number of recent discussions have posited an interlinear model for the LXX of the Pentateuch and certain other books. It is not necessary, according to this approach, to insist that the Greek was literally placed the Hebrew in a line by line format (although that eed have been the case); only that the Greek was ded—at least in its earliest usage, as envisioned

by the translators themselves—to stand as an independent document apart from the Hebrew. The location for such translational activity was not the synagogue but the school. At the moment, there is lively scholarly debate but no consensus. Above, the results of the efforts that led to the Greek Pentateuch were characterized as "responsibly literal." At the same time, almost all descriptions of this Greek speak of passages that are unintelligible. Of course, a judgment such as this could be simply the result of a modern perspective of what the LXX's original audience would have been able to understand, but it is not realistic to think that we can dismissively eliminate all such difficulties in this manner.

E. The Greek Book of Isaiah

Given the historical and theological significance of the Pentateuch and its rendering, it is not entirely surprising that it continues to be the object of strenuous analysis and debate. The book of Isaiah in the Septuagint is an example of the shifting of scholarly consensus. For over fifty years, scholars held the view that the "translator" of Isaiah engaged in wholesale updating of the Hebrew prophets' words, such that they now applied specifically to the Alexandria contemporary with the translator.

Recently, and only by careful reexamination of individual passages plus an effort to place this translator within the broader intellectual context of Hellenistic Alexandria (especially its museum), scholars are rethinking how this individual worked.

F. The Terms "Septuagint" (or "LXX") and "Canon"

Throughout this article, the term "Septuagint" or "LXX" has been used as if its contents or extent was self-evident. This is not the case in contemporary scholarly literature, nor was it the case in antiquity. In ancient times, the term "LXX" had more than one meaning, sometimes in one and the same author, often in one and the same tradition. It is almost universally asserted that the term "LXX" or "Septuagint" referred initially only to the translation of the Pentateuch. In even a brief review of these matters, it is worth noting that the above statement is not accurate.

The evidence shows the following: where the earliest Greek translation was limited to the Pentateuch, the term LXX was not used; where the term was used, it was generally not limited to the Pentateuch. It is possible to discern as many as six different uses for the term LXX in antiquity: the earliest Greek translation of the Pentateuch (Jerome was virtually alone among early church leaders in insisting on this limitation for the term), the earliest Greek translation of the entire OT, the fifth column of Origen's Hexapla (with all of the signs indicating quantitative changes to be made and also including numerous unmarked qualitative changes), any authoritative Greek text recognized as scriptural (but not viewed as part of the NT), and the entire

Greek tradition (including revisions, recensions, various fresh translations, etc.).

Three 3rd to 4th-cent. CE Greek codices written in UNCIAL script form the earliest manuscript evidence for the LXX (see CODEX). The number of books that make up the LXX, their order, their contents, and their wording differ in each of these three codices. Although one scribe was primarily responsible for each manuscript, the biblical material each contains is quite varied: some of it appears to be a rather literal, straightforward Greek version of the traditional or Masoretic Hebrew text. Other books, or parts of books, seem to present an equally literal or straightforward rendering of a Hebrew text, but not the traditional one. Still other sections exhibit characteristics that we would associate with literature composed in Greek rather than translated into Greek. Finally, there are large blocks of Greek that have the appearance of a revision rather than a fresh translation or original composition. These codices present a window into the major issues we confront in any attempt to provide a coherent account of the origins, development, and nature of the LXX. The 4th cent. CE manuscript "Codex Vaticanus" contains all of the books of the Hebrew Scripture or Protestant OT, and the following material that is today classified as deuterocanonical: 1 Esdras, 2 Esdras, Psalm 151, the Wisdom of Solomon, Ecclesiasticus or Ben Sirach, the additions to Esther (several of which were originally composed in a Semitic language; others of which are original Greek compositions), Judith, Tobit, Baruch, the Letter of Jeremiah, and the additions to Daniel (Azariah and the Three Jews, Susanna, and Bel and the Dragon). The 5th cent. Codex Alexandrinus contains all of this and, in addition, 1–4 Maccabees, and the Odes of Solomon. Codex Sinaiticus is the third manuscript, but it is impossible to ascertain the complete contents, given the nature of its modern state of preservation). Other manuscripts and traditions include further works or omit material contained in these uncial codices (see ALEXANDRINUS, CODEX; SINAITICUS, CODEX; VATICANUS, CODEX).

Modern scholars generally regard as authoritative the ordering and contents of the text in the critical edition of the Septuagint (Septuaginta) edited by Alfred Rahlfs, an early 20th-cent. Septuagint scholar: Genesis, Exodus, Leviticus, Numbers, Deuteronomy, Joshua, Judges, Ruth, 1–4 Reigns (=1–2 Samuel and 1–2 Kings), 1–2 Chronicles, 1 Esdras, 2 Esdras, Esther (including additions now found only in Greek), Judith, Tobit, 1–4 Maccabees, Psalms (including Ps 151), Odes, Proverbs, Ecclesiastes, Song of Songs, Job, Wisdom of Solomon, Ben Sirach, Psalms of Solomon, the Twelve Minor Prophets, Isaiah, Jeremiah, Baruch, Lamentations, the Letter of Jeremiah, Ezekiel, and Daniel (with additions).

We might ask about the origins of the view that certain books and additions to books were somehow sacred, especially as it concerns material that is not part of the Hebrew Scripture (or Protestant OT). This relates to the very thorny question of canon: its meaning, development, extent, etc. As noted earlier, there is wide acceptance of the view that books were given special status considerably earlier than the text of those books.

That said, we are still left wondering why, for example, Tobit, Judith, Ben Sirach, 1 and 2 Maccabees, among others, did not make it into the canon of rabbinic Judaism, but were accepted by other Jews and later by the Christians. No fully satisfactory explanation for the process of canonization has been offered. Within religious communities, propositions are propounded as to inclusion or exclusion, but without any sure textual or historical basis. We cannot be sure whether there was ever a Jewish community that held as sacred the books listed in the great codices or collected in the work of Rahlfs. Unfortunately, but in accordance with the best evidence available, this gives to the term Septuagint a degree of uncertainty or ambiguity that is difficult to ignore.

Beyond the circle of specialists, the term Septuagint is often applied or misapplied to almost any Greek "biblical" text outside of the NT. Although such imprecision can, as suggested above, be traced back to ancient usage itself, it is not conducive to clear thinking or argumentation. In part to provide further clarity, LXX scholars often use the term "Old Greek" (OG) to designate the earliest rendering into Greek of a given book or body of material to the extent that it is recoverable.

G. The Septuagint in Early Christianity and Rabbinic Judaism

It is in connection with the NT that great strides have been made with respect to terminology. It was common practice throughout most of the 20th cent. to characterize "OT" citations in the NT as Septuagintal, probably because they—like the LXX—have been transmitted in Greek. In recent decades, scholars harkening back to some of the fine work of late 19th-cent. researchers, have been far more careful and discriminating in their designation of such material. There are some passages that replicate (or, nearly so) wording preserved in our best manuscripts of the LXX. In many cases this is not so. We need to take into account a number of possibilities: the NT author was working with a known revision of the earlier Greek, the author was working with an otherwise unknown revision of the earlier Greek, the author consciously re-shaped an earlier Greek version to accord with the literary or theological context into which it was being placed, the author (mis-)quoted from memory, and/or the author provided a fresh translation of the Hebrew on his own. Only when we consider all of these possibilities and their myriad permutations have we done justice to the manifold ways in which the early Christian community adopted and adapted "Scripture."

In connection with other Jews of the first centuries CE—that is, those who remained with their ancestral faith)—it is often asserted that Jews abandoned the LXX when (or very soon after) it was adopted by early Christians. Although it is certainly the case that the LXX was ultimately pushed to the sidelines (with the exception of Greek-speaking Jewish communities, where a developing form of Aquila's version was still being used well into the Byzantine period) and never appears to have achieved the relatively lofty status that the Targums, or Aramaic versions, enjoyed, the term "abandon" and the relatively short timeline suggested seem extreme. First, we note once again that at least some parts of the version attributed to Theodotion and that of Aquila (and possibly also Symmachus) reflect a revision of the earlier Greek. A revision, which (unlike a fresh translation) includes substantial portions of an earlier text in the target language, reflects the judgment of the reviser that the earlier text has substantial value and is valid, except where changes are required. Additionally, the 1st-cent. Jewish philosopher Philo, himself a resident of Alexandria, apparently knew "Scripture" only from Greek texts. This is surely far short of total abandonment.

Moreover, the rabbinic sources, as recorded and preserved in the Talmud, are multi-, not uni-vocal. Alongside condemnations of a Greek version of the Torah (as, e.g., *Sof.* 1.7), there are positive statements (as in *b. Meg.* 9a) about biblical versions in languages other than Hebrew; such statements are often specifically directed toward the Greek text. It is not easy to place such statements into historical, geographical, or even theological contexts or categories; at the least, they are evidence of a lively and far-flung discussion among the leaders of rabbinic Judaism about the place of the LXX within their communities.

H. The Septuagint in Later Judaism and Christianity

Regrettably, the openness of at least some rabbis to the study and appreciation of the LXX was short-lived. It was not until the early part of the 19th cent. that Jewish scholars began once again to look seriously at it as a valuable part of their heritage from the distant past. In so doing, they uncovered many places where interpretative material in the LXX reflected concerns found in rabbinic discussions and instances of what might be termed rabbinic-like midrash.

It has been primarily among Christians that the texts of the LXX have been passed down, interpreted, and analyzed throughout most of the centuries that separate us from its initial formulations. The great codices are products of their Christian communities, as are almost all of the remainder of the papyri and parchment evidence we have, in cursive as well as uncial script. It might be surmised that Christian scribes would have regularly manipulated the text they were copying or passing down in order to bring it into more explicit agreement with and support for distinctively Christian concepts. Careful analysis of myriad manuscripts has resulted in the uncovering of surprisingly little conscious manipulation of this sort.

Perhaps the paucity of such changes is due to strong interpretive traditions that had already thoroughly Christianized the understanding of these originally Jewish texts. But another factor may have played a significant role: the growing sense that what was being passed down was indeed the divine word. For the most part, early Christian leaders drew their "OT" from the LXX (where this term is understood very broadly), and not from the Hebrew. Jerome was one of the few who had direct access to the Hebrew, which he learned from rabbis. It was the Hebrew that stood as the basis for the Latin translation (in large part intended as a revision of earlier, unsatisfactory renderings) that came to be known as the Vulgate.

Be that as it may, there was, over the millennium that followed Jerome, very little impetus for the Christians of Europe to engage in deep study of the Greek or the Hebrew once the Latin text had been vouchsafed priority and pride of place. In the East, where Greek continued in use, the LXX was the OT portion of the Bible. It was regularly quoted, cited, and alluded to—but there was little, if any effort made to engage in what we might term scientific investigation into the type of text or family affiliation of the particular manuscript used in a given community.

Western Christians rediscovered the LXX as part of the re-birth of interest in antiquity that characterized the Renaissance. When utilized in this context, it was the source or resource for ascertaining the true Word of God during a period when this was a very much contested issue. Not only the Greek but also the Hebrew was re-discovered and carefully analyzed during this time. These efforts culminated in about a century of unmatched activity on the Septuagint that lasted from the end of the 19th through the early part of the 20th cent.

I. The Modern Study of the Septuagint

As the 20th cent. ended and the new millennium commenced, the LXX has returned to center stage (or as close to center stage as it is likely ever to occupy) through a number of projects that involve the translation of the LXX into modern languages, along with commentaries on the versions that result.

From a chronological point of view, the first of these projects is La Bible d'Alexandrie. The project originated in 1981 under the leadership of Marguerite Harl, professor of Post Classical Greek at the Sorbonne in Paris. Assisting her have been Professors Gilles Dorival and Olivier Munnich. A number of volumes have been published by Editions du Cerf, each featuring a French-language translation of a portion of the LXX, along with an extensive introduction and copious notes. The primary emphasis of this series is on what we might term the reception history of the LXX in Jewish and later in Christian communities during the early centuries of its existence. Relatively little attention is paid to the goals of the translators and their technique; priority of analysis is given to its use in varied settings and cultures.

The second project began about a decade later. Titled the New English Translation of the Septuagint (NETS), this enterprise is an undertaking of the International Organization for Septuagint and Cognate Studies. As its title makes clear, these renderings are intended to replace earlier editions of the LXX in English, most notably the bold but dated work of Lancelot Brenton. The first volume to appear was the Psalms, prepared by Albert Pietersma. Along with Benjamin Wright, Pietersma served as editor of the project, which appeared in publication in 2007 under the aegis of Oxford University Press. The primary goal of NETS translators is to ascertain and present in English the oldest recoverable wording of the Greek for each book of the LXX. The primary focus is on the work of the translators and their interaction with the Hebrew that they were rendering. It is in this context that the interlinear model was developed and tried out. The translation volume itself contains an introduction for each book and some text notes. Full commentaries are planned.

While one group of scholars worked on NETS, another English translation and commentary series began. Published by Brill, it bears the title Septuagint Commentary Series. Unlike NETS, which bases itself on the eclectic Greek texts (where available) prepared by those associated with The Septuaginta Unternehmen (Septuagint Institute) in Göttingen, those responsible for volumes in this series work with the text of one of the great codices. The first fruits of this series appeared in 2005 with an edition of the book of Joshua.

The Septuaginta Deutsch (German Septuagint), under the leadership of Wolfgang Kraus and Martin Karrer, is also well underway. As reported by project leaders, this translation is intended for both academic and more general audiences of German speakers. Translators aim to reproduce lexical and other features of the Greek as closely as possible in the German language.

Through the internet and a variety of specialized computer software programs, modern scholars have access to a wide array of ancient Greek texts as well as to translations of the Greek into languages such as Armenian, Coptic, and Ethiopic. Concordances and other aids allow for instantaneous searches either unimagined or impossibly time-consuming by researchers in earlier generations.

Bibliography: A. Graeme Auld. *Joshua: Jesus Son of Naue in Codex Vaticanus.* Septuagint Commentary Series (2005); Jennifer M. Dines. *The Septuagint* (2004); Natalio Fernández Marcos. *The Septuagint in Context* (2000); L. Greenspoon. "Hebrew into Greek: Interpretation In; By; and Of the Septuagint." *History of Biblical Interpretation.* Vol. 1. Alan J. Hauser and Duane F. Watson (2003) 80–113; Martin Hengel. *The Septuagint as Christian Scripture: Its Prehistory and the Problem of Its Canon* (2002); Sylvie Honigman. *The Septuagint and Homeric Scholarship in Alexandria: A Study of the Narrative of the Letter of Aristeas* (2003); Karen H. Jobes and Moisés Silva. *Invitation to the Septuagint* (2000); Wolfgang Kraus and R. Glenn Wooden, eds. *Septuagint Research: Issues and Challenges in the Study of the Greek Jewish Scriptures* (2006); Alberts Pietersma and Benjamin Wright, eds. *A New English Translation of the Septuagint and Other Greek Translations Traditionally under That Title* (2007); Alfred Rahlfs, ed. *Septuaginta* (1935, 1979); Emanuel Tov. *The Text-Critical Use of the Septuagint in Biblical Research*, 2nd ed. (1997); Ronald L. Troxel. *LXX–Isaiah as Translation and Interpretation: The Strategies of the Translator of the Septuagint of Isaiah* (2007); John W. Wevers. "The Interpretative Character and Significance of the Septuagint Version." *Hebrew Scripture/Old Testament: The History of Its Interpretation.* Magne Saebo, ed. (1996) 84–107.

LEONARD GREENSPOON

SEPULCHRE. *See* HOLY SEPULCHRE; TOMB.

SEPULCHRE, HOLY. *See* HOLY SEPULCHRE.

SERA, TEL. Located northwest of Beer-Sheba along the Nahal Gerar (Wadi esh-Sharia) and situated between Tell Haror and Tell Halif. Tel Sera (Tell esh-Sharia) was an important locale in this quadrant of the Negev. Several suggested identifications of the site, such as Hormah, Gerar, and Gath, have been proposed, but its association with biblical ZIKLAG has received wide recognition. Excavations have revealed occupational levels from the Chalcolithic, Early to Late Bronze, Iron, Persian, Hellenistic, Roman, Byzantine, early Islamic, and Mamluk eras. In addition to the possible connections of the site with Ziklag, Tel Sera is worthy of consideration for its apparent role as an Egyptian administrative center in the 12th cent. and as an Assyrian fortress in the 7th cent.

Bibliography: Eliezer Oren. "Ziglag–A Biblical City on the Edge of the Negev." *BA* 45 (1982) 155–66.

JASON R. TATLOCK

SERABIT EL-QADEM. *See* ALPHABET; INSCRIPTIONS.

SERAH sihr′uh [שֶׂרַח *serakh*]. Serah, the daughter of Asher, is mentioned only three times in the Bible and without any accompanying details. In Gen 46:17 she is listed as one of Jacob's descendants who went down to Egypt. The list, which is organized by Jacob's wives (compare 46:15, 18, 22, 25), identifies Serah as one of Zilpah's grandchildren. Both here and in 1 Chr 7:30, Serah is described as the sister of Imnah, Ishvah, Ishvi, and Beriah, sons of Asher. Numbers 26:46, which reports the census of the new generation of Israel, states parenthetically that Asher had a daughter named Serah. The meaning of her name and the significance of her inclusion in Asher's genealogies remain unclear. *See* ASHER, ASHERITES.

SUSAN M. PIGOTT

SERAIAH si-ray´yuh [שְׂרָיָה serayah; Σαραία Saraia, Σαραίας Saraias, Ζαραίας Zaraias]. 1. A scribe or secretary of David (2 Sam 8:17); the name, however, is questionable because in the same list elsewhere he is called SHEVA (2 Sam 20:25), SHAVSHA (1 Chr 18:16), and Shisha (1 Kgs 4:3).

2. Son of Kenaz and father of Joab in the tribe of Judah (1 Chr 4:13-14).

3. Son of Asiel and father of Joshibiah in the tribe of Simeon (1 Chr 4:35).

4. One of the leaders of the returning Babylonian exiles (Ezra 2:2; 1 Esd 5:8) whose grandson, JESHUA, was an important high priest after the return (1 Esd 5:5).

5. The first official in a list of twenty-one priests who signed Nehemiah's covenant (Neh 10:2 [Heb. 10:3]).

6. A priest in Jerusalem after the exile (Neh 11:11); he is called an "officer of the house of God." Some suggest emending the text based on a similar list in 1 Chr 9:11 where Seraiah does not appear.

7. A priest who returned from exile with Zerubbabel (Neh 12:1, 12).

8. Son of Azriel, deployed by King Jehoiakim to arrest Jeremiah and Baruch; the Lord foiled their attempt (Jer 36:26).

9. Son of Tanhumeth who joined Gedaliah at Mizpah after the destruction of Jerusalem (2 Kgs 25:23; Jer 40:8).

10. Ezra 7:1 (1 Esd 8:1) identifies Ezra as the son of Seraiah, son of Azariah; this cannot be the same Seraiah of 1 Chr 6:14, although both have an Azariah as their father. (See #11 below.)

11. Chief priest who was arrested and executed by the Babylonians after the fall of Jerusalem (2 Kgs 25:18-21; Jer 52:24-27). It is likely that the Seraiah of 1 Chr 6:14 is the same Seraiah as here; if so, he is the son of Azariah and father of Jehozadak. Alternatively, he may be identified as the Seraiah of Jer 36:26 (see #9 above).

12. Son of Neriah, and brother of Baruch the scribe (compare Jer 32:12), Seraiah was the "quartermaster" who journeyed with King Zedekiah to Babylon in 593 BCE (Jer 51:59-64). Jeremiah took the opportunity to send with Seraiah a word of doom against the city of Babylon, presumably meant to cheer the exiles (from 598 BCE).

MARK RONCACE

SERAPH, SERAPHS ser´uf [שָׂרָף saraf, שְׂרָפִים serafim; σεραφείμ serapheim]. Heavenly creatures, often called "seraphim," with six wings and human voices serving as divine attendants in Isaiah's throne room vision (Isa 6:2, 6, 7). Elsewhere the Hebrew word designates a ERPENT (Num 21:8; Isa 14:29), thus suggesting serine bodies for the seraphim in Isaiah. *See* ANGEL.

STEPHANIE SKELLEY-CHANDLER

SERAPIS si-rah´pis. A Hellenized version of an Egyptian deity, popularized by the Ptolemies, the Greek kings who ruled Egypt from 323–31 BCE. The Egyptians had previously associated Osiris and Apis (*Serapis* is a contracted form of "Osiris-Apis"), but Ptolemy I brought the cult to Alexandria and patronized it lavishly. He changed the iconography of both Serapis and his consort, Isis, to resemble Greek deities.

The cult of the Egyptian gods became very popular in the Roman world. Their distinctive cultic sanctuaries have been found in a number of cities. Unlike typical Greco-Roman temples, they include assembly halls to accommodate crowds of people, as did synagogues and, later, churches.

ADAM L. PORTER

SERED sihr´id [סֶרֶד seredh]. A descendant of Zebulun. In Gen 46:14, Sered is listed among "the names of the Israelites, Jacob and his offspring" who immigrate to Egypt. Numbers 26:26 identifies Sered as progenitor of the Seredites.

SERENITY. *See* CONTENTMENT; PROSPERITY; SHALOM; WELL BEING.

SERGIUS PAULUS. *See* PAULUS, SERGIUS.

SERMON ON THE MOUNT. The "Sermon on the Mount" is the traditional designation for a section of Matthew's Gospel (chaps. 5–7) that presents the teaching of Jesus on matters of discipleship.

The name "Sermon on the Mount" derives from Matt 5:1, which indicates that Jesus delivered this teaching to his disciples on a mountain. It has been called this at least since the time of Augustine (354–430 CE) who wrote what is believed to be the first commentary on the Sermon on the Mount around 392–394 CE. About half of the material in the Sermon on the Mount finds parallel in a section of Luke's Gospel in which Jesus instructs a multitude of people "on a level place" (Luke 6:17); this portion of Luke's Gospel is accordingly called the Sermon on the Plain (Luke 6:20-49).

The Sermon on the Mount contains material that has been extremely influential on the Christian religion and on secular civilization in areas where Christianity has flourished. It is here that one finds the BEATITUDES (Matt 5:3-12), the Golden Rule (Matt 7:12; *see* GOLDEN RULE, THE), and the LORD'S PRAYER (Matt 6:9-13). Here Jesus speaks of the meek inheriting the earth (Matt 5:5) and identifies his followers as "the salt of the earth" (Matt 5:13). He urges people to "turn the other cheek" and to "go the second mile" (Matt 5:39, 41). He refers to "wolves in sheep's clothing" (Matt 7:15), "serving two masters" (Matt 6:24), storing up "treasure in heaven" (Matt 6:20), and "casting pearls before swine" (Matt 7:6). These and other expressions from the Sermon on the Mount have achieved notoriety in secular contexts. Indeed, a survey conducted by *Reader's Digest* magazine at the beginning of the millennium revealed their readers to be familiar with more material from Matt 5–7 than with any other portion of the NT. Thomas Jefferson identified the Sermon on the Mount along with the Ten Commandments as expressive of the moral principles on which the United States of America should be founded.

As presented in Matthew's Gospel, the overall theme of the Sermon on the Mount is discipleship or response to the call of Jesus. The sermon follows Jesus' announcement that "the kingdom of heaven has come near" (Matt 4:17) and explains the implications of this announcement for those who repent and follow Jesus. It also provides a compendium of the commands of Jesus that missionaries will teach to their converts when they seek to fulfill the Great Commission given at the end of Matthew's Gospel (Matt 28:19-20).

The Sermon on the Mount begins with the Beatitudes, which indicate for whom the advent of the kingdom will be a blessing, and then proceeds to describe the "greater righteousness" that is to mark followers of Jesus. These expectations are detailed with explicit contrast to traditional ethical teachings, including those that this Gospel attributes to the scribes and Pharisees. The sermon then turns to private religious duties (almsgiving, prayer, and fasting) and describes the proper attitude toward wealth and material things that characterizes those who seek God's kingdom above all else. It continues with exhortations commending self-critical humility and trust in God, and with multiple warnings regarding laxity, false prophets, and evildoers. It concludes with a parable likening obedient and disobedient disciples to wise and foolish builders whose homes are built on rock or sand.

A. Sources

Jesus is not likely to have preached the material found in Matt 5–7 as a single sermon in the form that we now have it; rather, sayings of Jesus that Christians remembered or attributed to him were gathered and compiled in the format of a sermon. John Calvin called the Sermon on the Mount a "summary of the doctrine of Christ … collected out of his many and varied discourses" (*Harmony of the Gospels* 1.168). The organizing principle of a single sermon was useful for mnemonic and teaching purposes, and it brought diverse material together in a way that imparted greater theological consistency.

Since Matthew's Gospel was composed about fifty years after the time of Jesus' Galilean ministry, it is thought that the material underwent a process of redaction: Aramaic sayings of Jesus were translated into Greek and amended in ways that would serve the developing needs of the church. Scholars disagree in their estimates of how extensive this editing may have been.

Most scholars attribute the final composition of the Sermon on the Mount (as we now have it) to the author of Matthew's Gospel, but many believe this evangelist already possessed a similar though less-developed sermon in the pre-Gospel material that is commonly called "the Q source." A number of scholars also think that the author of Luke's Gospel had access to this source and, so, those parts of Matthew's Sermon on the Mount that parallel Luke's "Sermon on the Plain" are believed to represent material that both evangelists derived from Q. Following this logic, Q appears to have contained a sermon by Jesus that began with beatitudes and concluded with the parable of the two builders. Other scholars, however, think that the author the Gospel of Luke made use of Matthew's Gospel, and other options are championed as well (*see* SYNOPTIC PROBLEM). In any case, we find that this material occurs in the same sequence in both Matthew and Luke's version of Jesus' sermon:

Sermon Material Shared by Matthew and Luke		
	Matthew	Luke
Beatitudes	5:3-12	6:20-23
Love of enemies	5:38-47	6:27-36
Judge not	7:1-2	6:37-38
Speck and log	7:3-5	6:41-42
Tree and its fruit	7:16-20	6:43-45
Lord, Lord	7:21	6:46
Parable of builders	7:24-27	6:47-49

The Golden Rule (Matt 7:12//Luke 6:31) also occurs in both the Sermon on the Mount and the Sermon on the Plain, although its placement is slightly out of sequence. A common theory holds that Matthew constructed his Sermon on the Mount by inserting a lengthy central section (including all of Matt 6) into the sermon that he found already formed in Q.

The matter is complicated by the fact that other parts of the Sermon on the Mount have parallels to material found elsewhere in Luke, including:

Sermon Parallels Elsewhere in Luke	
Matt 5:13-16	Luke 14:34-35
Matt 5:25-26	Luke 12:57-59
Matt 6:9-13	Luke 11:2-4
Matt 6:19-21	Luke 12:33-34
Matt 6:22-23	Luke 11:34-36
Matt 6:24	Luke 16:13
Matt 6:25-34	Luke 12:22-31
Matt 7:7-11	Luke 11:9-13
Matt 7:13-14	Luke 13:23-24
Matt 7:22-23	Luke 13:26-27

Such passages are generally thought to derive from the Q source, though not necessarily from a single or coherent sermon of Jesus presented in Q.

All told, 62 of the 106 verses that make up the Sermon on the Mount have close parallels to material in Luke's Gospel. A few more verses have parallels in Mark's Gospel (Matt 5:31-32//Mark 10:11-12; Matt 6:14-15//Mark 11:25-26): these could have come from Q (and represent points at which Q and Mark overlapped) or they could be items that Matthew took from Mark and integrated into the sermon material from Q. The rest of the Sermon on the Mount consists of material not found in the other Gospels (Matt 5:17-24, 27-30, 33-37, 48; 6:1-8, 16-18; 7:6, 15); this could be material derived from Q that Luke did not use, or it could be material that Matthew composed himself or took from sources unknown to us.

Some attention must also be paid to parallels between passages in the Sermon on the Mount and NT epistolary literature. The following comparisons are especially noteworthy:

Comparison of Sermon on the Mount to Epistles	
Matthew	Epistles
5:10	1 Pet 3:14
5:11-12	1 Pet 4:13-14
5:16	1 Pet 2:12
5:31-32	1 Cor 7:10-11
5:34-37	Jas 5:12
5:39	Rom 12:17; 1 Thess 5:15; 1 Pet 3:9
5:44	Rom 12:14; 1 Cor 4:12
5:48	1 Pet 1:15
6:19-20	Jas 5:1-3
6:25	Phil 4:6
7:1-2	Rom 2:1-3; 14:10
7:7	Jas 1:5; 1 John 5:14-15
7:16b	Jas 3:12
7:21-27	Rom 2:13; Jas 1:22

Such parallels are striking because the authors of these epistles are not thought to have had access to either Matthew's Gospel or the Q source (see Q, QUELLE). The common suggestion, therefore, is that such sayings were attributed to Jesus via oral tradition in various sectors of the church.

This data allows for a spectrum of opinions regarding the composition of the Sermon on the Mount. On the one hand, virtually all of the material can be attributed to Q or to comparable pre-Gospel sources; in this case the contribution of the Matthean author may be regarded as modest, limited primarily to structural organization and the provision of a theological framework for primitive material that had been passed on to him. On the other hand, over a third of the Sermon on the Mount can be attributed to the evangelist himself or to late sources; in this case, the contribution of the Matthean author may be deemed considerable.

B. Structure

A number of proposals have been offered with regard to the structure of the Sermon on the Mount. It has been suggested that the Beatitudes found in Matt 5:3-10 not only introduce the sermon but offer a reverse outline for its interpretation (Matt 5:11-16 comments on 5:10; Matt 5:21-26 comments on 5:9; Matt 5:27-37 comments on 5:8; Matt 5:38–6:4 comments on 5:7; Matt 6:5-18 comments on 5:6; Matt 6:19-34 comments on 5:5; Matt 7:1-6 comments on 5:4; and Matt 7:7-12 comments on 5:3).

Various chiastic outlines for the Sermon have also been proposed, usually (but not always) with the Lord's Prayer at the center. Luz (2007) suggests the following: 5:1-2 (situation) corresponds to 7:28–8:1a (reaction of audience); 5:3-16 (introduction) corresponds to 7:13-27 (conclusion), with emphasis on the kingdom of heaven (5:3, 10; 7:21); 5:17-20 (introit) corresponds to 7:12 (conclusion of main section), with emphasis on law and prophets; 5:21-48 (antitheses) corresponds to 6:19–7:11 (possessions, judging, and prayer), as two main sections of equal length; 6:1-6 corresponds to 6:16-18, with dual emphasis on righteousness before God; and 6:7-15 (Lord's Prayer, with frame) is at the center of the concentric arrangement.

Less elaborate thematic outlines have seemed more persuasive to the majority of scholars. Most interpreters, though, do identify the introduction to the sermon as Matt 5:3-16 and the conclusion as Matt 7:13-27. These two sections complement each other insofar as the former promises blessings and the latter warns of judgment; together, they present a duality of grace and demand that is typical of Matthean theology.

Two more sections of the sermon also exhibit fairly tight and obvious construction. Matthew 5:17-47 deals with the theme of the greater righteousness, which is introduced in 5:17-20 and then elaborated with a series of six antitheses in 5:21-47. Likewise, Matt 6:1-18 deals with the topic of private piety in a manner that would show remarkable symmetry were it not interrupted by the presentation of the Lord's Prayer in 6:9-15. It is sometimes said that these two well-constructed sections of the Sermon are meant to be read as presenting instruction on the believer's relationship with the neighbor (5:17-47) and with God (6:1-18).

The most problematic section from a structural standpoint is Matt 6:19–7:12. One suggestion holds that the section can be read as commentary on the Lord's Prayer: 6:19-24 expounds upon 6:9-10; 6:25-34 addresses 6:11; 7:1-5 is an exposition of 6:12; and 7:6 reflects on 6:13. This has not carried the day: most interpreters find some of the presumed connections tenuous or forced. Still, few have proffered alternative proposals for this structurally troublesome section. Often, Matt 6:19–7:12 is thought to present miscellaneous injunctions and exhortations in a way that lacks any discernible logic or order.

The Sermon on the Mount also displays a penchant for triads: three practices of piety (almsgiving, prayer, fasting) are addressed in Matt 6:1-18; a three-fold injunction to ask, seek, and knock is found in Matt 7:7-8; the six antitheses (Matt 5:21-47) and the six petitions of the Lord's Prayer (Matt 6:9-13) both divide easily into two sets of three. Seizing on this, Davies and Allison (1988) propose that the entire sermon is constructed of triadic groupings from beginning to end. The resulting outline sometimes seems forced. A more natural arrangement also recognizes a fondness for doublets: twin sayings about salt and light (Matt 5:13-14); twin proverbs regarding waste (Matt 7:6); twin examples of birds and lilies (Matt 6:25-30) and of bread and fish (Matt 7:9-10); dualistic sayings (Matt 5:45); and discussions intended to force a choice between two masters (Matt 6:24-25), two ways (Matt 7:13-14), or two builders (Matt 7:24-27).

Both the potential and the difficulty of imposing a triad model on the entire Sermon may be illustrated with regard to a key text, the beatitudes. Matthew 5:3-10 presents eight "indirect discourse" beatitudes worded in the third-person. Matthew 5:11 presents a single "direct discourse" beatitude worded in the second person. If these nine beatitudes are grouped together, they may be read as a series of three (a triad of triads). The more natural arrangement, however, may be to take the first eight as a separate entity, which actually divides very nicely into two stanzas, each of which concludes with a reference to righteousness (5:6, 10). This is the approach taken by most interpreters.

C. Contexts for Interpretation

The Sermon on the Mount is understood in light of three interpretative contexts: the time and place of Jesus' ministry, the developing era of the early church, and the literary composition of Matthew's Gospel.

1. Historical Jesus

Interpreters seek to determine the meaning that individual passages would have had for Jewish peasants in Galilee around 30 CE. They also compare the passages to other sayings of Jesus and try to relate the meaning of particular texts to what appear to have been prominent concerns articulated by Jesus. Such investigation usually involves consideration of whether the passage has undergone redactional development and, if so, whether a reasonable reconstruction of the original content can be sustained. A high degree of confidence has attended much of the Sermon on the Mount material in this regard, making it a focal point for study of the historical Jesus and his earliest followers. Such studies typically interpret the Sermon on the Mount within the context of Palestinian Judaism, reading it more as a Jewish document than as a Christian one.

2. Early church

Interpreters seek to determine what various passages would have meant to followers of Jesus in the years between Easter and the composition of the Gospels. Betz (1995) has argued that the entire Sermon on the Mount existed as a completed unit prior to its incorporation into Matthew's Gospel. Betz's proposal is that the Sermon was compiled and used by Christians in Jerusalem thirty years before Matthew's Gospel was written and therefore offers a valuable resource for understanding the Christian faith at that critical stage of development. Scholars who are not convinced of this may nevertheless focus their study on the source materials that appear to stand behind the Sermon on the Mount (especially Q) and conclude—like Betz, but on different grounds—that the Sermon on the Mount grants access to pre-Gospel material that would have circulated in the developing church around the same time as the letters of Paul. Such studies often compare and contrast the views of Paul and the Sermon on the Mount in order to delineate the points of diversity and continuity between two early expressions of what would become the Christian religion.

3. The Gospel of Matthew

The most prominent approach to the Sermon on the Mount in modern scholarship has sought to interpret the material as a constitutive part of Matthew's Gospel. Scholars emphasize connections between the Sermon on the Mount and other portions of Matthew's Gospel and they interpret the Sermon on the Mount in light of what appear to have been the theological priorities of this particular evangelist. They recognize that much of the material in the Sermon may have a pre-Matthean origin, but they ask what the various passages would have meant to the author of this Gospel and to the community for which the Gospel was written. The usual view is that Matthew's Gospel was composed by a Jewish-Christian in an urban Roman setting (possibly Antioch) around 85 CE. The Matthean church struggled to define itself over against the varieties of synagogue-based Jewish religion that were emerging in the days following the destruction of the Temple in 70 CE. The author of Matthew's Gospel considered his church to represent a true expression of Israel's faith; indeed, he believed that the Christians in his church were followers of the Messiah and, thus, more faithful to the traditions of Israel than any other Jewish group. This position, however, had become increasingly hard to maintain given 1) the unusually large influx of Gentile converts that was shifting the ethnic balance within the community, and 2) the bare fact that virtually all other Jewish groups viewed the Christian movement as an aberration. In addition, Matthew's church needed to come to grips with its status within the Roman Empire: it had to define what allegiance to Jesus meant within a secular, urban environment that despised and persecuted those whose commitments and conduct did not agree with the imperial program.

Within the literary context of Matthew's Gospel, the Sermon on the Mount is typically seen as one of five major discourses delivered by Jesus in this Gospel, which are sometimes thought to mirror the "five books of Moses" that compose the Torah. The other addresses are the "Missionary Discourse" found in Matt 10, the "Parables Discourse" in Matt 13, the "Community Discourse" in Matt 18, and the "Eschatological Discourse" in Matt 24–25. Each of the five speeches concludes with a reference to the final judgment (Matt 7:21-27; 10:40-42; 13:47-50; 18:35; 25:46) and is followed by a formulaic statement (e.g., "When Jesus had finished saying these things") that serves to mark off the unit from what follows (Matt 7:28; 11:1; 13:53; 19:1; 26:1). The effect of these five speeches on the structure of the Gospel as a whole is to establish an alternating pattern in which narrative material is periodically interrupted by extended discourse material. In Matthean studies, the Sermon on the Mount is often compared to the other four blocks of discourse material and is specifically identified as addressing the theme of "Discipleship."

The Sermon on the Mount is strategically placed in Matthew's Gospel following Jesus' announcement that the kingdom of heaven is near (Matt 4:17) and his initial calling of disciples to follow him and "fish for people" (Matt 4:18-22). Matthew had earlier established the credentials of Jesus as the Messiah of Israel (Matt 1:1, 16) and Son of God (Matt 2:15; 3:17). Born of a virgin, Jesus embodies the presence of God among God's people (Matt 1:23) and is destined to save his people from their sins (Matt 1:21). As the one in whom God is well-pleased (Matt 3:17), he triumphs over the devil's temptations (Matt 4:1-11), and embarks on a public ministry of preaching, teaching, and healing (Matt 4:23) that fulfills the prophecies of scripture (Matt 4:14-16) and brings him the acclaim of multitudes (Matt 4:25). In short, the material in Matthew's Gospel prior to the Sermon on the Mount focuses heavily on the identity and authority of Jesus; the effect of locating the Sermon on the Mount after such material is to accentuate the claim that these are the words of one who possesses divine authority surpassing what might be attributed to any other human being (Matt 7:28-29). Matthew's reader is expected to hear and obey the words of Jesus presented in the Sermon on the Mount not simply because they are inherently sensible but because they are spoken by Jesus the Messiah, the Son of God.

D. Setting and Audience

Matthew's Gospel specifies the setting for the Sermon on the Mount as "the mountain" and the primary audience for these words as Jesus' disciples (Matt 5:1).

The reference to an unnamed mountain is ambiguous and the precise geographical location that Matthew might have intended cannot be determined. It is likely, however, that readers are expected to regard this mountain as the same one to which the risen Jesus summons his disciples at the end of the Gospel to give what is called the Great Commission (Matt 28:16-20). Further, the location of his teaching on a mountain recalls the giving of the law to Moses in Exod 19–31. Just as God gave the law to Moses, who then became the great teacher of Israel, so here Jesus gives divine commandments to his disciples who will teach them to a church composed of people from all nations (Matt 16:18; 28:19-20).

The designation of Jesus' disciples as the intended audience for the Sermon on the Mount indicates that the author of this Gospel understands the words that follow as primarily Christian teaching rather than as an exposition of moral behavior to be expected of or imposed upon the world at large. Baptized persons who want to be "made disciples" (Matt 28:19-20) will obey these commandments of Jesus, which call for a greater righteousness than is exhibited by people in general (Matt 5:20). At the conclusion of the sermon, however, the reader suddenly learns that the words have also been overheard by the crowds, who were astounded at Jesus' teaching, since he taught "as one having authority, and not as their scribes" (Matt 7:28-29). The point of the crowds' astonishment is not simply that Jesus taught in an authoritative style, but that his teaching revealed him to be a person authorized to speak for God in a way that other religious teachers were not (compare Matt 8:5-13; 9:8; 10:1; 21:23-27; 28:18). In this way, Matthew seems to acknowledge that the Sermon on the Mount possesses an inherent wisdom capable of impressing or challenging those for whom it was not primarily intended. For Matthew's community, "the crowds" may represent the unbelieving world in which their church is situated, those who have not experienced Jesus' call, but who have heard snippets of his message. Although they do not know what to make of Jesus or his message, such people may be astonished at the authority evident in his words. Thus Matthew's Gospel presents the Sermon on the Mount as teaching that is explicitly intended for the church, but it does so with an awareness that people outside the church might find these words stimulating as well.

E. Content of the Sermon

1. The Beatitudes (Matt 5:3-12)

The Sermon begins with a poetic prelude that presents Jesus' vision for what will happen when the rule of heaven becomes established (compare Luke 6:17, 20-23). A two-stanza poem (5:3-10) is followed by direct commentary offered to the disciples themselves (5:11-12). The poem, consisting of eight beatitudes worded in the third-person, has been read in two different ways, which differ mainly with regard to how the first four blessings are to be understood.

One view takes 5:3-6 as promising rewards to persons who exhibit various virtues: for example, the poor in spirit may be linked with the unpretentious, those who mourn with the penitent, the meek with the humble, and those who hunger for righteousness with those who earnestly desire to do what is right. Proponents of this first view usually maintain that Matthew has spiritualized the beatitudes that were found in the Q source, which are preserved more faithfully in Luke's account. An alternative reading takes 5:3-6 as promising reversals to those who live in unfortunate circumstances: the poor in spirit are the despondent, people with no reason for hope; those who mourn are the miserable, who have no cause for joy; the meek are dispossessed people who have been deprived of their share of the earth's resources; and those who hunger for righteousness are victims of injustice who long to see God's righteousness prevail. On this reading, Matt 5:6 does not speak of those who yearn to be righteous people (to do "what is right") but, rather, of those who yearn to be treated with righteousness (to have "what is right" done to them). This view sees the first four Matthean Beatitudes as basically consistent with the Lukan Beatitudes, which explicitly promise reversals for the unfortunate rather than rewards for the virtuous.

In any case, the second stanza (5:7-10) promises rewards for people who are godly in their attitude and conduct, exhibiting mercy and integrity, actively working for peace, and displaying a willingness to suffer so that God's will might be done. Since these four beatitudes cannot reasonably be read as promises of reversal, the first view of 5:3-6 described above seems to have the advantage of internal consistency within the Matthean poem, which may then be read as offering eight blessings of eight virtues. But proponents of the second view find consistency of a different sort: the virtues praised in 5:7-10 are specifically ones enacted on behalf of the unfortunate persons described in 5:3-6, thus the advent of God's kingdom will be a blessing both to those who are suffering and to those who join God in alleviating suffering. In either case, Jesus promises that the rule of God will come and that the things for which the faithful strive (peace, righteousness, mercy) will be realized:

the coming of God's rule will itself provide the ultimate blessing for those who seek it.

Jesus appends to the Beatitudes a strong word of warning, addressed directly to his disciples: any who join God in working for justice and righteousness will themselves become oppressed and persecuted. Still, it is to these that the establishment of God's rule will be a blessing. So, elsewhere in Matthew, Jesus declares that when God's will is done, "many who are first will be last, and the last will be first" (Matt 19:30; 20:16).

2. Sayings on salt and light (Matt 5:13-16)

Jesus uses two metaphors to describe the relationship his disciples are to bear to the world: they are to be its salt and its light (compare Mark 4:21; Luke 11:33). The original sense of the sayings may have applied to Israel and to its role among the nations, but for Matthew that role appears to have been assumed by the messianic community (i.e., the church). Exactly what is meant by the symbol of salt is hard to identify since salt was used for a variety of purposes: as seasoning, as a preservative, and in religious ceremonies involving sacrifices or covenants (compare Mark 9:49-50; Luke 14:34-35). The light imagery is more familiar from OT contexts, and turns up in variant forms elsewhere in the synoptic tradition (Mark 4:21; Luke 11:33). Notably, in the Gospel of John, Jesus himself is identified as the "light of the world" (John 8:12; compare 1:3-5, 9; 3:19; 12:35, 46). By applying an acclamation that Christians probably used for God and for Christ (compare Matt 4:12-16) to the followers of Jesus, Matthew's Gospel exhibits a high evaluation of Christian potential. This is in keeping with Matthew's view that Jesus' disciples embody the presence of Jesus and of God in the world (Matt 10:40). Some precedent for such a move may be found in the writings of Isaiah, where an image traditionally used for God (e.g., Ps 27:1) is applied to the community of the new age that will draw the nations to God (Isa 2:1-5; 42:6; 49:6; 60:1-3, 14, 19-20).

The point of the sayings for Matthew is that Jesus' followers are not to withdraw from the world that persecutes them (Matt 5:11-12) but are to engage that world in ways that have a beneficial effect upon it. They are to do this through the performance of good works (5:16) which, in context, must be assumed to include acts of mercy and peacemaking performed from a pure heart and for the sake of righteousness (5:7-10).

3. The greater righteousness (Matt 5:17-20)

Jesus declares that he has come to fulfill the law and the prophets, which will remain valid as long as heaven and earth endure (also Luke 16:17; but compare Matt 24:35). This is the first of four explicit "statements of purpose" in Matthew (compare 9:13, 10:34, 20:28). The whole of Matthew's Gospel reveals Jesus as one who does indeed fulfill the law and prophets. He is often said to fulfill the prophets when details from his life match quotations from these revered writings (Matt 1:22-23;

2:5-6, 15, 17-18, 23; 4:14-16; 8:17; 12:17-21; 13:14-15, 35; 21:4-5; 27:9-10). He fulfills the law by living in a way that is perfectly consistent with the will of God and by authoritatively interpreting the law through his own teaching. In a broader sense, the phrase "law and prophets" may be taken as a shorthand designation for "the scriptures"; in that case, Jesus would be presented here as the one who fulfills all that Israel's scriptures promise or portend.

Jesus' endorsement of the entire law (Matt 5:18) has been considered problematic because it seems to contradict the more dismissive or relaxed attitude toward portions of Jewish law that would become typical of Christianity and that seems to find support elsewhere in the NT canon (e.g., Mark 7:20; Rom 10:4). Did the Matthean community continue to practice circumcision and various dietary requirements? Scholars within some religious traditions have sought to resolve this problem by suggesting that the phrases "until all is accomplished" and "until heaven and earth pass away" in Matt 5:18 refer to the death and resurrection of Christ, which inaugurates a new law-free age. More likely, Matthew's community accepted every detail of the law itself as valid while also allowing for a fairly generous program of "binding and loosing" the law (compare Matt 16:19; 18:18); thus, commandments may be recognized as eternally valid but also as paradoxically inapplicable for a given context.

While demanding full compliance with the law, Jesus grants that those who fail to meet his best expectations may still find some acceptance among those who are "least in the kingdom." There is a minimal level of righteousness that must be met, however, and the scribes and Pharisees exemplify those who fail to come up to this level. For the latter point to make sense, the "scribes and Pharisees" must not be identified with the historical persons who confronted Jesus in Galilee or with their counterparts who may have been hostile to the Christian community in Matthew's own day, since all evidence indicates that those persons would have been exemplary with regard to many behavioral matters important to Matthew. Rather, the exemplars of righteousness unbefitting the kingdom of heaven are the scribes and Pharisees who serve as characters in Matthew's story, literary figures who are presented in the narrative as an irredeemably evil "brood of vipers" (Matt 12:34; 23:33; compare 9:4; 16:4), as plants that the heavenly father did not plant (Matt 15:13; compare 13:24-25), and as implacable opponents of God (Matt 23:34-36).

4. The antitheses (Matt 5:21-48)

Jesus illustrates what he means by his summons to a greater righteousness (Matt 5:17-20) with six concrete examples of the moral behavior expected of his followers. These examples are traditionally called "antitheses" because in each case the expectation of Jesus contrasts with a more moderate or contradictory expectation

indicative of what conventional wisdom may have regarded as scriptural teaching. In some instances, Jesus introduces his teaching with an actual quote from scripture that he thinks is sometimes interpreted or applied in ways deserving of comment (e.g., 5:38); in other instances, he introduces his teaching with a paraphrase of an idea that was probably regarded by many as scriptural even though it is not found in scripture as such (e.g., 5:43). In either case, Jesus' operating principle is that the goal of moral instruction should be nothing less than perfection: his followers should strive for the sort of righteousness exhibited by God (5:48).

Jesus expands upon the commandment prohibiting murder to indicate that harboring vicious thoughts against another person also violates the will of God (Matt 5:21-26). Jesus' followers are not to insult each other. Reconciliation must be a first priority in the family of God's people, or else the worshiping community will be no different from the world at large, where festering pride and resentment lead people to drag each other into court and throw each other into prison (compare Luke 12:57-59).

Jesus likewise expands upon the prohibition against adultery by insisting that lustful thoughts and glances are unacceptable (Matt 5:27-30). He punctuates this with extreme statements about plucking out one's eye or cutting off one's hand to insure righteousness (compare Matt 18:8-9; Mark 9:43-48). Such hyperbole is intended to emphasize the necessity of forestalling temptation and of dealing with potential problems before they become actual ones.

Jesus goes on to liken divorce and remarriage to a form of legalized adultery (Matt 5:31-32; compare 19:3-9; Mark 10:11-12; Luke 16:18). He seems to grant that scripture allows for such a practice but wants to maintain a distinction between what is merely allowed and what is truly pleasing to God. Jesus does, however, recognize one exception to his ruling: remarriage is not to be considered adulterous when the divorce is enacted because of porneias (πορνείας, translated "unchastity" in the NRSV). Just what is envisioned by this exception clause has been a matter of discussion: some interpreters think it applies to a marriage in which one of the partners has been unfaithful; others believe the reference is to a marriage that involves incestuous union or some other arrangement that may have been condemned within Jewish circles but practiced among Gentiles.

Jesus radicalizes the traditional view regarding the swearing of oaths (Matt 5:33-37; compare 23:16-22). Conventional wisdom taught that one must always carry out a vow; Jesus insists that it is wrong to offer vows in the first place. His reason is that the ability to fulfill the vow may depend on factors beyond one's control. People should not promise what they might not be able to deliver.

Finally, Jesus repudiates vengeance and insists on a practice of nonretaliation (Matt 5:38-48; compare Luke

6:27-36). The justification for vengeance lies in a scriptural provision intended to limit the scope of retaliation (Exod 21:24-25), but (as with divorce) Jesus says that his followers should forego their right to claim what the scriptures allow. The preferred way is revealed in the nature of God, who shows kindness to good and bad alike. So, followers of Jesus should be known as those who "turn the other cheek" and "go the second mile." They will love their enemies and pray for their persecutors. Why? Because God does this, and they want to be godly.

When all six antitheses are considered together, Matthew's reader is presented with a consistent portrayal of the attitude and behavior that Jesus expects of his followers. The greater righteousness of which he spoke previously (Matt 5:20) goes beyond superficial obedience to legal requirements; his followers will conform themselves inwardly to the will of God and will seek what would be ideal rather than settling for what is acceptable. They will not simply ask about what is required or what is allowed but will always seek that which would be most pleasing to God.

5. Practicing piety (Matt 6:1-18)

Jesus declares that his followers are not to practice piety in ways that will call attention to themselves. If they do so, he says, that attention itself constitutes all the reward they will ever receive for their pious actions, for such is the way of hypocrites (6:2, 5, 16). Hypocrisy is a key theme in Matthew (see 7:5; 15:7; 22:18; 23:13-29; 24:51). The connection here seems to be that those who practice piety to win attention for themselves are only pretending to be pious; in reality, they are more concerned with gaining honor for themselves than for God. The theme of heavenly reward is also present elsewhere in Matthew (10:41-42; 19:27-29) and is more prominent in this Gospel than in the others.

Three instances of piety are mentioned: almsgiving (Matt 6:2-4) involved charitable contributions above and beyond the stipulated tithes and offerings that everyone was expected to make; prayer (Matt 6:7-15) included the recitation of certain memorized or liturgical prayers at key times of the day (according to some authorities, the Shema was to be said twice and the Tefilla, three times); and fasting (Matt 6:16-18) meant going without food or, at least, restricting one's diet in penitence for sin, in observance of a holiday, as an expression of mourning, or simply as a way of strengthening one's communion with God. Jesus assumes that his followers will do all these things but encourages them to practice such duties in a manner that does not call attention to themselves (Matt 6:4, 6, 18).

6. The Lord's Prayer (Matt 6:9-13)

The teaching on prayer in Matt 6:5-15 is interrupted by Jesus' presentation of a model prayer that has come to be called "the Lord's Prayer" or the "Our Father" (compare Luke 11:2-4); it is not only preserved in the Gospels of Matthew and Luke but is also found in an early nonbiblical writing called the *Didache*. The prayer is exceptionally Jewish in form and content. Indeed, in Matthew, Jesus presents it in explicit contrast to the type of prayers said by Gentiles (Matt 6:7).

The metaphorical identification of God as "Father" is typical for Matthew, occurring ten times in Matt 6:1-18 alone (see also Matt 5:16, 45, 48; 6:26, 32; 7:11, 21; 10:32, 33; 12:50; 16:17; 18:10, 14, 19, 35; 20:23; 25:34; 26:29, 42, 53; 28:19). For Matthew, this image presents God as both a caring parent and an authority figure, as the one whose unilateral decisions are to be respected by the whole family of believers (compare Matt 23:9). By encouraging his followers to call God "Father," Jesus urges them both to respect God's authority and to trust in God's generosity and providential wisdom.

The prayers for God's name to be hallowed, for God's kingdom to come, and for God's will to be done are parallel petitions that state the same basic request three times in slightly different words. For Matthew, the essential request is for God to bring to fulfillment what has begun with Jesus. The kingdom has already drawn near (Matt 4:17), Jesus and his followers are bringing God's will to accomplishment (4:17), and God's name is being glorified on account of them (Matt 5:16). Jesus' followers are to pray for the work of Christ to continue.

Three more petitions make simple requests of God, ones that Jesus deems appropriate for people to make at any time. The request for "daily bread" flows from an assumption that all followers of Jesus will embrace a simple lifestyle. Bread serves as a metaphor for life's necessities; Jesus' followers are to ask that God provide them with what they need, no more, but also no less.

The request for forgiveness of sins (literally, debts) is traditional for Judaism. Jesus attaches to it a reminder that those who seek such forgiveness ought also to forgive others. To emphasize the point, Matthew quotes another saying of Jesus on this subject (Matt 6:14-15) and, elsewhere, records a parable Jesus told to illustrate the lesson (Matt 18:23-35). Within the Sermon on the Mount, this need to forgive others becomes the only facet of Jesus' moral teaching deemed so important that his followers are to remind themselves of it every time they pray.

The next petition is easily misunderstood when translated, "Lead us not into temptation," since neither Matthew nor Jesus would have wanted to imply the possibility that God might tempt people to sin. Rather, the request is for God to guide Jesus' followers in such a way that they will not experience trials that could test their faith (compare Matt 26:41). According to the parable of the Sower (Matt 13:2-9, 18-23) such trials might take the form of hardship ("trouble or persecution") or distraction ("the cares of the world and the lure of wealth"). Elsewhere, Matthew indicates that some trials are inevitable (Matt 18:7; 24:9-13). Thus, the petition continues with the plea, "deliver us from evil" (or "the evil one"). Jesus' followers are to ask that they be spared trials whenever possible and—when this is not possible—that they be protected from the potentially destructive consequences of such experiences (compare Jas 1:2-4; 1 Pet 1:6-7).

A well-known conclusion to the Lord's Prayer ("Thine is the kingdom and the power and the glory forever and ever, Amen") was not originally in the Bible. It was written by early Christians when the prayer came to be used in liturgical worship. Later, some copies of the NT began adding the conclusion to the text with the result that it is found today in a few English translations (including KJV).

7. Seven sayings on discipleship (Matt 6:19–7:11)

The structure of the Sermon becomes somewhat looser after the segment on the practice of piety (Matt 6:1-18), but many scholars believe that there are seven distinct units of material here, which lead up to a concluding affirmation that has come to be called the Golden Rule (Matt 7:12).

The first four units or groups of sayings all seem to address a theme of undivided allegiance to God. First, a saying on storing up treasures in heaven (Matt 6:19-21; compare Luke 12:33-34) indicates that Jesus' followers are to value the things of God over the things of the earth. This is followed by an obscure group of sayings about a "healthy eye" (Matt 6:22-23; compare Luke 11:34-36); the precise meaning of these verses is difficult to determine, but the basic point may be that those whose allegiance to God is undivided have clarity of vision, while those with divided loyalties have blurred vision. This leads to a third bit of advice, the parabolic affirmation that no slave can serve two masters (Matt 6:24; compare Luke 16:13). Then, Jesus launches into an extended address on the subject of anxiety. He warns that concern for such things as food and clothing may distract one from seeking what truly counts: God's kingdom and righteousness (Matt 6:25-34; compare Luke 12:22-31). According to Jesus, anxiety is a sign of "little faith" (Matt 6:30; compare 8:26; 14:31; 16:8; 17:20), since God is generous and can be trusted to provide for those whose loyalties are undivided.

Three more units of material take up miscellaneous topics in what appears to be a random order. In a section on judging (Matt 7:1-5; compare Luke 6:37-38, 41-42), Jesus warns his followers not to let their concern for righteousness set them on a crusade to correct the faults of others while ignoring their own failings. Matthew makes clear elsewhere that he would not want these words of Jesus to discourage church members from holding each other accountable for their sins (Matt 18:15-18), but they are to make self-improvement their first priority and they are to be merciful in their assessment of others. In this sense, judging might be regarded

as the opposite of forgiving (compare Matt 6:14-15; 18:21-35).

The next set of sayings offers twin proverbs regarding waste (Matt 7:6). Just as one does not throw pearls into a pig pen or take sanctified food from an altar and toss it out in the street as scraps for dogs, so Jesus' followers ought not waste what God has given them. These proverbs could have numerous applications and no specific reference point is provided within the Sermon itself. Later in Matthew's narrative, Jesus will urge his followers to show discernment in their proclamation of the gospel: they should seek new audiences rather than wasting their efforts on the stubbornly unperceptive (Matt 10:5, 14, 23). This may be the sense in which Matthew wanted the proverbs on waste in the Sermon on the Mount to be understood.

Finally, a group of sayings urge Jesus' followers to be confident in prayer (Matt 7:7-11; compare Luke 11:9-13). Jesus encourages his followers to seek "good things" from God and to believe that God will grant their requests. Notably the two examples he uses for God's gifts are bread and fish. Later in the Gospel story, Jesus will demonstrate quite literally how God provides these items (Matt 14:15-21; 15:32-39). Jesus says that prayer for such necessities is to be offered in the trust that God is like a father who has both the means and the desire to provide for them; this is consistent with the language of the model prayer he offered his disciples in Matt 6:8-13.

8. The Golden Rule (Matt 7:12)

Jesus offers his followers an ethical maxim that he says encapsulates "the law and the prophets" (compare Matt 5:17). He indicates that if people treat others the way they want to be treated themselves, their behavior will be consistent with the will of God (compare Luke 6:31). Matthew's Gospel is filled with stories in which religious leaders get things wrong because they ignore this principle (Matt 12:1-8, 9-14; 15:3-6). Elsewhere, Jesus restates this rule as the "law of love" (Matt 22:34-40). Statements similar to the Golden Rule are found in many other religious writings, including the book of Tobit (4:15), the *Didache* (1:2), and the letters of Paul (Rom 13:10). The closest parallel may be the so-called negative version of the rule attributed to Rabbi Hillel in the Babylonian Talmud, a 6th cent. commentary on the Jewish Mishnah. Hillel, who lived a few years before Jesus, is asked by a potential convert, "Teach me the Torah, that is, teach me all of your traditions, your values, your practices, and your theology while standing on one foot." Hillel responds, "What is hateful to you, do not do to your fellows. Go and learn" (*Sabbath* 31a). Ethicists have compared the negative formulation of the rule offered by Hillel to the positive formulation offered by Jesus with mixed results. On the one hand, the positive formulation is credited with being proactive while the negative version can lead to passivity. On the other hand, the positive formulation is criticized (often, but not exclusively, by Jewish scholars) as being egocentric, failing to discern that the wants and needs of the neighbor may be different from one's own.

9. The Two Ways (Matt 7:13-27)

Jesus concludes the Sermon by contrasting the way that leads to life with that which leads to destruction. First, he indicates that the way to life is like "a narrow way" or a rough road and that there are few who find it (Matt 7:13-14; compare Luke 13:23-24). The imagery that Jesus uses here is conventional (compare Ps 1:6; Jer 21:8; Sir 21:10; *4 Ezra* 7:1-19) and could be used in a secular sense to indicate that the most popular course of action is not always the wisest one. Here, however, Jesus applies this generic observation to ultimate participation in the kingdom of heaven—the "life" to which Jesus refers is to be found in a blessed paradise after death. The point, then, is that eventual participation in this future life makes the enactment of self-discipline and the bearing of present hardship and persecution worthwhile (Matt 18:8-9; 24:6-13).

Accordingly, Jesus says more about those who will not enter the kingdom and he warns his followers that false prophets will come among them to lead people astray (Matt 7:15-23; compare Luke 6:43-45). Such persons are "evildoers" (Matt 7:23, literally, "lawless ones"), and like wolves "in sheep's clothing" (Matt 7:15), they may bear a superficial resemblance to true followers of God. They may use Jesus' name, call him their Lord, and even work miracles or drive out evil spirits in spectacular ways (Matt 7:22; compare 24:24). Still, if one knows what to look for, the false prophets can be detected as surely as a tree may be identified by its fruit: they will be people who do not live in accord with the will of God (i.e., with the will of God as explicated by Jesus in this sermon).

The two ways described by Jesus are further elucidated by his brief parable of two builders (Matt 7:24-27; compare Luke 6:47-49). Those who act on his words (live in accord with what is presented in this sermon) will have a sure foundation for life, while those who do not will see the collapse of all they hoped to accomplish. Notably, the two houses in the parable suffer the same tribulations, but only the house on rock survives. Thus, Jesus does not indicate that his faithful followers will be spared adversity, but rather maintains that they will endure such trials and ultimately be saved (compare Matt 24:13).

F. Theological Interpretation

In the Ante-Nicene period, the Sermon on the Mount was used apologetically to combat Marcionism and, polemically, to promote the superiority of Christianity over Judaism. The notion of Jesus fulfilling the law and the prophets (Matt 5:17) seemed to split the difference between two extremes that the church wanted to avoid: an utter rejection of the Jewish matrix for Christianity on the one hand, and a wholesale embrace of what was regarded as Jewish legalism on the other. In a similar vein, orthodox interpretation of the Sermon served to refute teachings of the Manichaeans, who used the Sermon to support ideas the church would deem heretical. In all of these venues, however, the Sermon was consistently read as an ethical document: Augustine and others assumed that its teaching was applicable to all Christians and that it provided believers with normative expectations for Christian behavior. It was not until the medieval period and, especially, the time of the Protestant Reformation that reading the Sermon in this manner would come to be regarded as problematic.

The primary difficulties that arise from considering the Sermon on the Mount as a compendium of Christian ethics are twofold. The first and foremost is found in the relentlessly challenging character of the Sermon's demands. Its commandments have struck many interpreters as impractical or, indeed, impossible, particularly in light of what the NT says elsewhere about human weakness and the inevitability of sin (including Matt 26:41 *b*). The second and related problem is that obedience to these demands appears to be closely linked to the attainment of eschatological salvation (Matt 5:20, 22, 29-30; 6:15; 7:2, 14, 19, 21-23); thus, the sermon appears to present a theology of works-righteousness that conflicts with the Christian doctrine of grace. The history of interpretation from the Middle Ages to the present reveals multiple attempts at dealing with these concerns.

1. Does the Sermon present an impossible ethic?

Thomas Aquinas was one of the first to call attention to these difficulties and also to attempt a resolution. Aquinas suggested that the ethic of the sermon includes not only mandates for all Christians but also optional counsels for those who would strive for perfection (such as clergy and others who pursue religious vocations). Though influential in Roman Catholic thought, this view has been largely rejected by Protestants; it has been critiqued in Catholic circles as well. Protestant polemic has tended to exaggerate Aquinas' view, such that it is often said that "the Catholic interpretation" of the Sermon on the Mount does not view its demands as applicable to the ordinary Christian. In actual fact, the two-level principle of interpretation has been applied selectively and sparingly in Catholic interpretation, usually with limited reference to individual passages (e.g., those that would be interpreted as commending absolute poverty or chastity).

Martin Luther stressed a distinction between enactment of the Sermon's demands in personal and religious life as opposed to application within the social, secular sphere. Thus, the Christian might practice nonretaliation in his or her personal relationships, but if he or she is a soldier or law officer, the active resistance to evil that is dictated by common sense must be allowed to prevail. Some consideration of the distinction between personal and social ethics would become standard for most interpretations of the Sermon on the Mount from the Protestant Reformation to the present day. Numerous critics, however, have noted problems with this approach: such a distinction can negate the Sermon's ability to address individuals who excuse unethical behavior as a necessity of political life or, indeed, impede its effectiveness at challenging social systems designed to promote values at variance with those the Sermon encourages. Exegetical interpreters question whether Matthew intended to present Jesus' teaching as personal ethics rather than as the ethic of the community (compare Matt 18:15-18, which emphasizes personal subscription to a community ethic); theologians also question on philosophical grounds whether any individual action is ever without social consequence.

John Calvin sought to resolve the issue of the Sermon's impractical demands by an appeal to canon. In keeping with a hermeneutical method he called *analogia fidei*, Calvin insisted that many dictates that seem absolute within the Sermon itself may be recognized as situational or relative when considered within the broad context of scripture. Thus, the Sermon on the Mount appears to prohibit all oaths (5:34) but this is mitigated by Heb 6:16 and by Paul's habit of calling upon God as witness to ensure the truth of what he says (Rom 1:9; 2 Cor 1:23; Gal 1:20; Phil 1:8; 1 Thess 2:4). Calvin's general principle of "interpreting scripture in light of scripture" has been widely adopted in most confessional traditions, but, again many interpreters find its application problematic when it serves to dismiss the relevance of what the Matthean author (if not the historical Jesus) considered to be imperative concerns.

Radical Anabaptists rejected all attempts to domesticate the Sermon's demands and insisted on literal obedience, even if that meant nonparticipation in a world that compromises Christ's ethic: a Christian can not be a soldier (see Matt 5:39) or a judge (see Matt 7:1) or any official required to swear oaths of office (see Matt 5:34). While this view would always remain a minority position, it has had such prominent advocates as Leo Tolstoy, the Russian novelist, and Leonhard Ragaz, the father of Christian socialism. In the late 19th cent., Tolstoy summarized the Sermon's demands in a popular fashion as consisting of five key rules: Be not angry, commit no adultery, swear not, go not to law, war not.

Another of the Reformers, Huldrich Zwingli, proposed a distinction between external and internal realms of application and emphasized that the Sermon's main purpose was to form the "inner person." This idea did not attract significant support in the 16th cent., but it was revived with considerable success three centuries later within the 19th-cent. movement called "Protestant liberalism." Adolf von Harnack, Wilhelm Herrmann, and others spoke of the kingdom of God as a present and inner reality and, so, read the Sermon on the Mount as more concerned with inculcating a certain disposition within believers than with prescribing literal behavior.

Indeed, literal application of the Sermon's demands would be impossible and undesirable, but when read as a non-legalistic "ethic of disposition" (to use Hermann's term), the Sermon bore witness to the transformed mental and spiritual orientation that marks people of godly character. This understanding was critiqued by Johannes Weiss as losing contact with the apocalyptic perspective of Jesus. Still, it would influence Rudolf Bultmann and other existentialist critics and continues to be expressed in modified or chastened terms to the present day.

Albert Schweitzer followed Weiss' lead and came to question the relevance of the Sermon altogether. Schweitzer maintained that the radical demands of the Sermon were supposed to have represented an "interim ethic": the Sermon presupposes an imminent expectation of the end-times and becomes impractical in contexts that have lost that sense of urgency. Martin Dibelius also couched the problem of interpretation in these terms and yet thought the Sermon could continue to provide some sort of eschatological stimulus for Christian ethics: even those whose vision of the future is not apocalyptic may be affected by knowledge of what a complete transformation of the world in accord with God's righteousness would bring.

In the latter half of the 20th cent., the notion that the Sermon on the Mount was predicated in its entirety on imminent eschatology would be questioned and all but discarded by theologians who considered the attribution of an exclusively future outlook to Jesus unsustainable. Rather, Jesus proclaimed the kingdom of God as both still to come (perhaps, but not necessarily in the near future) and as already present (in mysterious but readily identifiable ways). This modified understanding of Jesus' eschatology would yield a stance toward the Sermon's ethic that continues to draw significant support among modern interpreters: the Sermon presents the ethic of God's kingdom and Christians seek God's kingdom (and its righteousness) by striving to live in compliance with the Sermon's demands (Matt 6:33). To the extent that the kingdom is already present, they will find some success—sufficient to be salt for the earth and light for the world. Their failures serve as reminders that the kingdom is not yet fully present and that God's rule over their own lives remains incomplete. Thus, the Sermon presents an ethic that Christians are to live by, striving to live in the present as they are destined to live for eternity.

2. Does the Sermon's legalism conflict with a doctrine of grace?

Martin Luther was particularly bothered by the Sermon's tendency toward "works righteousness" and he sought to interpret the moral expectations of the Sermon as manifestations of grace: one does not behave as the Sermon indicates in order to earn God's favor; rather, the Christian who has been put right with God by sheer grace will show the fruit of God's salvation in a life marked by good works, such as those that the Sermon describes. This understanding, dependent on Augustine, would become fairly standard for interpretations of the Sermon in most confessional traditions.

The movement known as Protestant Scholasticism (post-Reformation followers of Luther and Calvin) radicalized the tendency to interpret the Sermon in this light. In both popular and scholarly treatments, the Sermon was made to serve the evangelical function of preparing people for the gospel by making them aware of their need for grace: since no human can keep the Sermon's demands, those who try will be brought to despair and left to trust in nothing but the mercy of Christ. This manner of reading the Sermon remained prominent in many Protestant circles for hundreds of years (20th cent. advocates included Carl Strange, Gerhard Kittel, and Helmut Thieleke), but it was sharply critiqued exegetically by Joachim Jeremias (1963) and theologically by Dietrich Bonhoeffer (in his 1940 work *The Cost of Discipleship*).

In the modern era, all attempts to read the Sermon on the Mount in a manner that would be compatible with a Pauline doctrine of justification have fallen on hard times. The critical era of biblical studies has allowed for more theological diversity within the canon and many interpreters today would simply grant that the Sermon on the Mount assumes a soteriology that would not be acceptable from a Pauline perspective. This view has been bolstered by the work of numerous Jewish interpreters. The theological recommendation of Christian scholars is sometimes to value the Sermon for its ethical teaching while regarding its understanding of soteriology as inadequate. To force any reading of the text from the perspective of what ultimately became orthodox Christian theology does not do justice to the theology of Matthew or the intentions of the historical Jesus.

Bibliography: Clarence Bauman. *The Sermon on the Mount: The Modern Quest for Its Meaning* (1985); Hans Dieter Betz. *The Sermon on the Mount* (1995); Warren Carter. *What Are They Saying about Matthew's Sermon on the Mount?* (1994); W. D. Davies. *The Setting of the Sermon on the Mount* (1964); W. D. Davies and Dale C. Allison. *The Gospel according to St. Matthew, Vol. 1* (1988); Terence Donaldson. *Jesus on the Mountain: A Study in Matthean Theology* (1985); Robert A. Guelich. *The Sermon on the Mount: A Foundation for Understanding* (1982); Herman Hendrickx. *The Sermon on the Mount* (1984); Joachim Jeremias. *The Sermon on the Mount* (1963); Warren S. Kissinger. *The Sermon on the Mount: A History of Interpretation and Bibliography* (1975); Jan Lambrecht. *The Sermon on the Mount: Proclamation and Exhortation* (1985); Pinchas Lapide. *The Sermon on the Mount* (1986); Ulrich Luz. *Matthew 1–7.* 2nd ed. (2007); John Meier. *The Vision of Matthew: Christ, Church, and Morality in the First Gospel* (1979); Georg

Strecker. *The Sermon on the Mount* (1988); Charles H. Talbert. *Reading the Sermon on the Mount* (2004).

MARK ALLAN POWELL

SERMON ON THE PLAIN. The "Sermon on the Plain" is the traditional designation given to a section of Luke's Gospel (Luke 6:20-49) that parallels the better known SERMON ON THE MOUNT found in the Gospel of Matthew (Matt 5–7). The name derives from Luke 6:17, which indicates that Jesus spoke to his disciples and a great crowd of people "on a level place" (compare Matt 5:1, which indicates that similar teaching was presented to the disciples on a mountain). Material found in the Sermon on the Plain deals with discipleship and is presented in four broad sections: 1) proclamation of eschatological blessings and woes (6:20-26); 2) ethical instruction regarding relationships between believers and people outside the faith community (6:27-38); 3) ethical instruction regarding relationships among believers within the faith community (6:39-45); 4) exhortation to act on Jesus' words (6:46-49).

Luke's Sermon on the Plain is often compared to Matthew's Sermon on the Mount. Both begin with BEATITUDES (Luke 6:20-23; Matt 5:3-12) and end with the Parable of Two Builders (Luke 6:47-49; Matt 7:24-27), and both present the Golden Rule as the summary of Christian ethics (Luke 6:31; Matt 7:12). Still, the Sermon on the Plain is distinctive in a few notable ways.

First, the Sermon on the Plain is much shorter than the Sermon on the Mount and is more tightly focused on behavior that deals with human relationships. By comparison, the Sermon on the Mount contains much material that deals with prayer and devotion to God (e.g., Matt 6:9-13, 24; 7:7-11). In Luke, material of that sort is found elsewhere in the Gospel (Luke 11:2-4, 9-13; 16:13), not as a part of the inaugural sermon on discipleship.

Second, the Sermon on the Plain has been edited to address Gentile believers in the Greco-Roman world. For example, whereas Matthew cites "tax-collectors" or "Gentiles" as examples of typically unfaithful people (Matt 5:46-47), Luke refers simply to "sinners" (Luke 6:42-43). Luke's version of the sermon lacks material related to the continuing validity of the Jewish law (e.g., Matt. 5:17-20) but retains all material encouraging congruity of word and deed (e.g., Luke 6:43-49), a theme that would resonate with Greco-Roman philosophy and one that is stressed elsewhere in material unique to Luke's Gospel (e.g., 8:21; 11:28).

Third, the Sermon on the Plain includes "woes" alongside beatitudes (Luke 6:20-26; compare Matt 5:3-10). This is consistent with Luke's emphasis on presenting the effects of God's judgment as a great reversal of fortune and status (1:46-55; 16:19-31; 18:14).

Finally, the unique comment in the Sermon on the Plain that "everyone who is fully qualified will be like the teacher" (Luke 6:40) fits well with Luke's high estimate of human potential. In the book of Acts, some of the disciples who heard Jesus deliver the Sermon on the Plain will be portrayed by Luke as fully qualified church leaders, people whose insights and conduct are fully in line with the example set by Jesus in the Gospel. Peter, for instance, interprets Scripture (Acts 2:14-21), heals the sick (Acts 3:6-7), raises the dead (Acts 9:40), challenges the leaders of Israel (Acts 4:8-12), interacts with angels (Acts 12:1-9), and declares God's authoritative judgment (Acts 5:1-11) in ways that recall the activity of Jesus in the Gospel (Luke 4:19-21; 5:17-26; 7:11-17; 11:37-52; 22:43; 23:28-31). *See* LUKE, GOSPEL OF.

MARK ALLAN POWELL

SERON sihr'on [Σήρων Sērōn]. A commander of the Syrian army (1 Macc 3:13, 23). When Seron heard of Judas' success in raising an army against the Syrian kings, he gathered a large company at Beth-horon to fight against them, hoping to win fame for himself (1 Macc 3:14). While Judas' army was much smaller, it defeated Seron's army, further spreading Judas' fame among the Gentile population (1 Macc 3:26).

JESSICA TINKLENBERG DEVEGA

SERPENT. There are a variety of terms used to denote snakes within the OT. These are: nakhash (נָחָשׁ, translated as "serpent" or "snake" in the NRSV); tannin (תַּנִּין, "sea monster," "snake," "serpent," or "dragon"); saraf (שָׂרָף, "poisonous serpent," "fiery serpent," "serpent," or simply transliterated as "seraph" or as "poisonous") or pethen (פֶּתֶן, "asp" or "adder"); tsefaʿ/tsifʿoni (צֶפַע/צִפְעוֹנִי, "adder"); ʾefʿeh (אֶפְעֶה, "viper"). The terms nakhash, tannin, and saraf occur in narrative and poetic contexts; the remainder of the terms denoting snakes occur only in poetic passages.

Although late 19th and early 20th cent. natural histories of the Levant cataloged several varieties of snakes, and attempts have been made to match these snakes to the various terms used within the Bible, definitive identifications are not altogether clear. Since most of these terms are used in poetic contexts in parallel with other terminology for snakes, the emphasis seems to be on qualities and characteristics of snakes in general as opposed to specific snakes.

Snakes that appear in narrative contexts have magical or mythological characteristics. In Gen 3, the snake is introduced at the beginning of the chapter as the most clever (ʿarum עָרוּם; also meaning "shrewd" or "sensible") of all the creatures that the Lord God had made. This term appears to be a play on words with ʿarom (עָרוֹם, "naked") from the previous verse (Gen 2:25). The snake exhibits its cleverness by seeing through the apparent untruth that the Lord God had told the humans in Gen 2:17, namely, that the humans would die if they ate from the tree of the knowledge of good and evil. The serpent points out to the woman that they will not die, and indeed this turns out to be true; they eat and do not die, but instead attain knowledge. The end

of the chapter indicates that the humans would have died whether or not they ate from the tree; the Lord God banishes them from the garden, not for disobedience, but in fear that the humans might now eat from the tree of life and attain immortality.

Magical snakes appear in the exodus narrative. In Exod 4:3 (part of Moses' call narrative), God turns Moses' staff into a nakhash as a reassuring sign that God will be with him. This staff is alluded to again in Exod 7:15. In other references in chap. 7, Aaron's staff changes to a snake (here tannin) in competition with the magicians of Egypt. Aaron's staff/snake wins the competition by swallowing those of the Egyptians. The term tannin also seems to indicate snakes in Deut 32:33 and Ps 91:13; in each of these verses, tannin is used in a parallel construction with pethen (translated as "asp" in Deut 32 and "adder" in Ps 91).

In the Ugaritic literature, the noun tunnanu is found in a vocabulary list implying the meaning "serpent." In Ugaritic mythological texts, the tunnanu is listed with other mythological creatures as inhabiting the sea and also as the enemy of the storm god Baal. Certain biblical passages in which tannin occurs also seem to imply a mythological sea snake or monster. Genesis 1:21, Ps 74:13, and Isa 27:1 describe it as inhabiting the waters or seas; Job 7:12 and Ps 148:7 use the term in conjunction with the sea/deep; and Isa 27:1 and 51:9 use the term in parallel with Leviathan and Rahab, respectively, terms that refer to mythological sea monsters that represent the forces of chaos that God is able to subdue through creation. In Isa 27:1, Leviathan is described as "the fleeing serpent" and "the twisting serpent," terms that are used to describe ltn (compare with Leviathan) in the Ugaritic literature.

Numbers 21:4-9 describes an episode in the wilderness when the Israelites complain about the food, and the Lord responds by sending poisonous snakes that bite and kill the people. Here, saraf is used as an adjective ("poisonous") to describe the serpents (nakhash). The Israelites appeal to Moses for help, and he prays on their behalf. The Lord then instructs Moses to make a snake (saraf) and place it on a pole. Moses makes a bronze serpent (nakhash) that cures snakebite when a bitten person looks at it. This episode is typical of the "murmuring motif" found in Numbers: the Israelites complain and sometimes long for the old days in Egypt, God punishes them, and Moses is caught in the middle trying to appease both parties. The function of the saraf in this narrative suggests that it may be an Egyptian uraeus cobra; the serpent that is placed on a pole has an apotropaic function, that is, it is a human made object used to avert the ill effects of its real-life counterpart. Some Egyptian amulets, including those in the shape of snakes, had this function. The use of the term saraf in Isa 6 also suggests that this term may indicate the uraeus cobra. In Isa 6:1-7 (the narrative of Isaiah's call), serafim (שְׂרָפִים) are described as "standing" in attendance on each side of the Lord's throne. They have wings, and they may also spit fire; after they call to each other, the temple is filled with smoke. This image of an upright, winged snake in a protective type of posture is typical of the uraeus cobra that was understood to protect the pharaoh, the sun god Re, and other deities. One of its means of protection was by spitting fire that consumed the enemy. The bronze serpent of Num 21 is alluded to in 2 Kgs 18:4; here it is reported that King Hezekiah of Judah destroyed the bronze serpent that Moses had made (see SERPENT, BRONZE).

Serpent language is used in the prophetic literature to describe God's judgment. In these instances, serpents are always depicted as dangerous or malevolent. Serpents are used to illustrate God's punishment through military threats or potential invaders. Isaiah 14:29 combines imagery of snakes and trees to warn the Philistines not to rejoice at the downfall of their enemy, for "from the root of the snake will come forth an adder, and its fruit will be a flying fiery serpent"; in other words, the enemy will return. Jeremiah 8:17, an announcement of judgment against Judah, describes the invaders as biting snakes let loose among the people. Snakes are also used to illustrate God's judgment against those who are complacent and pervert justice. In Isa 59:5, these hatch adders' eggs, which then hatch out a viper. Amos 5:19 condemns those who oppress the poor, yet are awaiting the day of the Lord as if it will be a day of reward for them; rather, the day of the Lord will be like being bitten by a snake unexpectedly. Jeremiah 46:22 describes Egypt as a snake slithering away from conquering enemies. In a judgment against Israel, God is described as commanding a sea snake to find people trying to hide at the bottom of the sea (Amos 9:30).

Serpent language is also used in descriptions of hope and restoration. In these cases, serpents are still viewed as dangerous animals. In Isa 11:8 (a description of a peaceful reign under the Davidic monarch) and Isa 65:25 (a vision of a new creation), snakes, among other dangerous creatures such as wolves, leopards, lions, and bears, will live in harmony and will not be harmful to humans. Micah 7:17 describes Judah's enemies as snakes that will be in dread of God and the people of Judah.

In the wisdom literature and Psalms, serpent imagery is used for comparative purposes. Enemies and evildoers are compared to snakes: in Ps 58:4 (Heb. 58:5), the wicked are described as venomous snakes that cannot be charmed, and in Ps 140:3 (Heb. 140:4), evildoers have tongues like snakes with venom under their lips. In the same vein, Job 20:14 and 16 use serpent imagery to describe the consequences of the wicked. In Proverbs and Ecclesiastes, serpent imagery appears in observations of nature, human and otherwise, and its ironies.

In the NT, four terms are used to denote serpents: ophis (ὄφις, "snake" or "serpent"); drakōn (δράκων, "dragon"); echidna (ἔχιδνα, "viper"); and aspis (ἀσπίς, "viper").

The serpent (ophis) is described as wise; this is reminiscent of Gen 3:1, where the serpent is described as clever or sensible. Every other reference to snakes within the Synoptic Gospels carries the connotation that snakes are dangerous or evil: giving a snake to a child instead of a fish is an unthinkable act (Matt 7:10//Luke 11:11); Jesus gives authority to tread on snakes (Luke 10:19). John 3:14 and 1 Cor 10:9 each make reference to the episode in the wilderness in Num 21, and in 2 Cor 11:3, Paul says the people will be led astray just as the serpent deceived the woman in the garden in Gen 3.

In Revelation, the terms ophis and drakōn are used interchangeably to refer to "that ancient serpent, who is called the Devil and Satan" (Rev 12:9; 20:2), one of the symbols representing evil in this text.

Jesus is portrayed as condemning the Pharisees and their religious practices as hypocritical with the phrase "you brood of vipers" (Matt 3:7; 12:34; 23:33; Luke 3:7). Writing well after the destruction of the temple in 70 CE, when Pharisaism had emerged as the dominant surviving form of Judaism, and at a time when Jewish Christians and Pharisaic Jews were each asserting their positions as the legitimate form of Judaism, the author of the Gospel puts in the mouth of Jesus the polemic that Jewish Christians of the evangelist's own era employed against their opponents.

In Rom 3:13, Paul quotes Ps 140:3 (Heb. 140:4) about the venom of vipers to illustrate his point that no one is righteous; all people are under the power of sin. See ANIMALS OF THE BIBLE; FIERY SERPENT OR POISONOUS SNAKE.

Bibliography: Karen Randolph Joines. *Serpent Symbolism in the Old Testament* (1974).

KRISTIN A. SWANSON

SERPENT, BRONZE [נְחַשׁ נְחֹשֶׁת nekhash nekhosheth]. As the Israelites neared Canaan at the end of the wilderness period, they once again complained bitterly about conditions in the wilderness. God sent snakes that bit and killed many people. Moses interceded on their behalf, and, after receiving instructions from God, Moses made a bronze serpent and placed it on a pole; when the people looked at it, they lived (Num 21:4-9). In this context, the bronze serpent has an apotropaic function; i.e., the image serves to avert the evil of its real-life counterpart.

According to 2 Kgs 18:4, the bronze serpent that Moses made, here called Nehushtan, was an object of worship destroyed by King Hezekiah of Judah during his religious reforms. Given the function of the serpent as a type of amulet in Num 21, and Hezekiah's use of Egyptian royal symbolism on the lmlk jar handle impressions, it may be possible to understand the serpent of 2 Kgs 18:4 as an Egyptian royal symbol, the *Uraeus* cobra. See FIERY SERPENT OR POISONOUS SNAKE.

In the NT, Jesus compares himself to "the serpent" that Moses "lifted up" in the wilderness (John 3:14). Whereas Moses' serpent brought healing, Jesus himself will bring eternal life.

KRISTIN A. SWANSON

SERUG sihr'uhg [שְׂרוּג serugh; Σερούχ Serouch]. Meaning "branch." A descendant of Noah, the son of Reu, and the father of Nahor, as well as the great-grand-father of Abraham (Gen 11:20-23; 1 Chr 1:26; Luke 3:35). Serug fathered Nahor when he was thirty, after which he continued to live another 200 years, and he had more sons and daughters not mentioned in the list of descendants of Shem.

CHANNA COHEN STUART

SERVANT [נַעַר na'ar, נָתִין nathin, עֶבֶד 'evedh; διάκονος diakonos, δοῦλος doulos, παῖς pais]. Servants are persons under a superior for whom they perform tasks. They clearly are not chattel slaves. While a number of biblical terms may be translated as servant, there is not always a clear distinction between who is a servant and who is a slave. The terminology covers a broad semantic domain and a translation of either servant or slave depends on the specific context.

In the OT, servants look after the affairs of individuals (Gen 24:2; Exod 24:13; Judg 7:10; 1 Kgs 19:21; 2 Kgs 4:12), are part of extensive households (Judg 19:3; 1 Sam 9:3), oversee laborers (Exod 5:15-16; Ruth 2:6; 1 Kgs 11:26; 2 Chr 13:6), serve in the military (1 Sam 22:6-10; 2 Sam 2:12-17; Isa 36:9), advise the king (1 Sam 16:15; 1 Kgs 1:2; Esth 6:3-5), and assist in the temple (1 Chr 9:2; Ezra 2:43; Neh 7:46). Conquered peoples are sometimes designated as servants of the king (2 Sam 8:2, 6, 14). The role of servants varies widely but it is clear that these individuals are not in a restricted, permanent form of slavery. Indeed, many of them have the respect of the people they serve.

In a religious context, prominent individuals, kings, and prophets are designated as servants of God, a title that describes their humility, piety, and/or obedient performance of tasks given to them by God. Included among these are: Abraham (Gen 26:24; Ps 105:6), Moses (Exod 14:31; Num 11:11; Ps 105:26), Joshua (Judg 2:8), David (2 Sam 3:18; Ps 144:10), Hezekiah (2 Chr 32:16), Isaiah (Isa 20:3), Nebuchadnezzar (Jer 25:9), and Daniel (Dan 6:20).

The theme finds its most significant theological expression in the Servant Songs of Second Isaiah (Isa 40–55). Scholarship debates whether the servant is to be understood as a corporate or individual figure. While a number of the references clearly designate the nation of Israel as the servant, others are ambiguous and some portray the servant as an individual who will suffer on behalf of Israel (Isa 53). Both Judaism and Christianity adopted the Servant Songs as a paradigm for under-standing the vicarious suffering of righteous ones as having redemptive power.

In the NT, individuals continue to understand themselves as God's servants (Luke 1:38; Jas 1:1; Titus 1:1), and with the advent of Christianity, servants of Christ (Rom 1:1; Gal 1:10; Phil 1:1). Again, a translation of either servant or slave depends on the context.

A more specific term for servant in the NT is diakonos, which in ancient Greek denotes a table server, messenger, or minister. The earliest, most ample evidence for the term in early Christianity is found in Paul. Although commonly associated with the office of deacon (1 Tim 3:8-13), the majority of occurrences are less specific. Paul refers to himself and others as servants of the gospel, God, and Christ (1 Cor 3:5; 2 Cor 11:23; 1 Thess 3:2), a designation also found in the disputed epistles (Eph 3:7; 6:21; Col 1:7, 23, 25; 4:7; 1 Tim 4:6). As servants of God, these emissaries are entrusted with the gospel (2 Cor 3:5) and have earned the right to be heard (2 Cor 6:4). On the other hand, some are the servants of Satan who oppose the servants of righteousness (2 Cor 11:14-15). Apart from individuals Paul calls Christ the servant of the circumcision (Rom 15:8), but not of sin (Gal 2:17). Government is also the servant of God (Rom 13:4). There is early evidence that diakonos became a more specific title for a local church office during Paul's lifetime (Rom 16:1; Phil 1:1), but the exact role of this position is unclear.

Diakonos is used sparingly in the Gospels: Herod's attendants (Matt 22:13), table waiters (John 2:5, 9), followers of Jesus (John 12:26), and Jesus' teachings on becoming the servant of all (Matt 20:26; 23:11; Mark 9:35; 10:43). More significant than terminology is the Gospel writers' identification of Jesus with the Servant of God in Isa 40–55 (Matt 8:17; 12:18-21; John 12:38; compare Acts 3:13, 26; 4:27, 30; 8:32-35). The most illustrative depiction of Jesus as servant is the foot-washing scene in John 13:1-11. Jesus' servile actions, followed by the servant sayings (13:13-17), provide a highly developed, theological understanding of Jesus as the ultimate expression of what it means to be the Servant of God and servant of all. *See* DEACON; DEACONESS; SERVANT OF THE LORD; SLAVERY.

Bibliography: John Byron. *Slavery Metaphors in Early Judaism and Pauline Christianity* (2003); John N. Collins. *Diakonia: Re-interpreting the Ancient Sources* (1990).

JOHN BYRON

SERVANT OF THE LORD, THE [עֶבֶד־יְהוָה 'evedh-yhwh; ὁ δοῦλος κυρίου ho doulos kyriou, ὁ παῖς τοῦ θεοῦ ho pais tou theou]. Several individuals and some groups are identified as servants of the Lord in the Bible.

    A. Nomenclature
    B. Deutero-Isaiah
       1. First servant passage (Isa 42:1-4)
       2. Second servant passage (Isa 49:1-6)

3. Third servant passage (Isa 50:4-9)
4. Fourth servant passage (Isa 52:13–53:12)
C. Major Questions
1. Identity of the servant
2. Vicarious suffering
3. Death of the servant
D. Christian Use of the Deutero-Isaian Passages
Bibliography

A. Nomenclature

Typically, the individuals identified as servants of the Lord in the OT are not so identified in titular fashion but by means of pronominal suffixes meaning "my," "his," and "your." The prophets of Israel are identified as servants of the Lord (e.g., Amos 3:7, 2 Kgs 9:7; 10:10; Ezra 9:11) and by implication in 2 Kgs 9:7, although the epithet also appears to describe worshipers of Yahweh other than the prophets (see Pss 134:1; 135:1). The biblical use of "servants of the Lord" to designate the worshipers of Yahweh is akin to ANE usage that describes the worshipers of any deity as servants of that God (see 2 Kgs 10:23).

The individuals most often identified as servants of the Lord in the OT are Moses (e.g., Exod 14:31; compare Rev 15:3) and David (e.g., 2 Sam 3:18). Moses is described as a "servant of the Lord" (ʿevedh-yhwh) in Josh 14:7 and 2 Kgs 18:12 (compare Neh 10:29), as is Joshua in Josh 24:29 and Judg 2:8. Abraham (Gen 26:24), Isaac (Gen 24:14), and Jacob (Ezek 28:25) are identified as the Lord's servants, as are Caleb (Num 14:24), Hezekiah (2 Chr 32:16), Zerubbabel (Hag 2:23), and the prophets Ahijah (1 Kgs 14:18), Elijah (2 Kgs 9:36), Jonah (2 Kgs 14:25), Isaiah of Jerusalem (Isa 20:3), and the enigmatic Job (Job 1:8).

The Hebrew ʿevedh and its Greek equivalent, doulos (occasionally pais), mean "slave" and imply a total subservience of these individuals to the will of the Lord. Accordingly, Nebuchadrezzar is identified as a "servant of the Lord" because he carried out the will of the Lord (Jer 25:9; 27:6; 43:10).

With some modification, "servant of the Lord" appears in the NT. The book of Revelation identifies Moses as a "servant of God" (doulos tou theou [δοῦλος τοῦ θεοῦ], Rev 15:3) and speaks of the idealized people of Israel as the "servants of our God" (Rev 7:3). James is called "a servant of God and of the Lord Jesus Christ" (Jas 1:1). "Slaves of God" as well as "servants" are used in reference to evangelists (Acts 16:17), Christian leaders (2 Tim 2:24), and all Christians (1 Pet 2:16).

Writing about civil authority instituted by God, Paul uses "servant of God" (theou diakonos θεοῦ διάκονος) to describe public officials (Rom 13:4, twice). The apostle identifies himself and his co-workers as "servants of God" (theou diakonoi θεοῦ διάκονοι) in 2 Cor 6:4, while Epaphras is called a servant of Christ (diakonos Christou διάκονος Χριστοῦ) in Col 1:7 (see DEACON).

B. Deutero-Isaiah

Another servant figure appears in four seemingly related passages of Deutero-Isaiah (Isa 42:1-4; 49:1-6; 50:4-9; 52:13–53:12). Deutero-Isaiah's servant of the Lord is not identified with the title "Servant of the Lord."

The four passages, collectively known as the Servant Songs, were isolated by Bernhard Duhm in the late 19th cent. Duhm considered them to have been independent compositions later interpolated into the text of Deutero-Isaiah. Despite Hubert Irsigler's late 20th cent. support of Duhm's thesis, the majority of contemporary biblical scholars hold that the correlation between the songs and their immediate contexts warrants their being considered part of the original text of Deutero-Isaiah.

1. First servant passage (Isa 42:1-4)

Yahweh presents the servant as one whom he has chosen and to whom he gives his spirit, but the servant is not otherwise identified. His task is to bring justice to the nations who await his teaching (Torah). He is to pursue his task in a manner, which eschews oracular prophecy. The text briefly alludes to the hardships that the servant endures but affirms that the servant will not fail until he has accomplished his task.

2. Second servant passage (Isa 49:1-6)

The servant speaks to foreign nations, rehearsing his prophetic call (compare Jer 1) and recalling that Yahweh has designated him as his servant and provided him with strength. The images of v. 2 portray Yahweh's preparation of the servant and the protection that he will give him. The servant acknowledges a period of failure but affirms that God has given him a double mission to be God's agent in the restoration of Israel and in the salvation of the nations, for whom he is a light (compare Isa 42:6).

3. Third servant passage (Isa 50:4-9)

The passage does not include any use of the term ʿevedh (compare Isa 52:10). It develops the theme of suffering (compare Isa 42:4; 49:4). In a kind of monologue, the servant speaks of Yahweh Adonai ("the Lord God"), who is mentioned four times in the space of a few verses (50:4, 5, 7, 9; compare Isa 40:10; 51:22; 52:4). The Lord God has given the servant a disciple's tongue so that he may comfort the disheartened Israelites in exile. The Lord God has spoken to him so that he learns to experience suffering (at the hands of Israelites) from which he does not flinch. The Lord God sustains him, steeling him in his suffering and preserving him from humiliation. Confident of his vindication, the servant defiantly proclaims, "Who will contend with me?" "Who are my adversaries?" Reaffirming that the Lord God helps him, the servant utters another defiant taunt, "Who will declare me guilty?" and affirms that his oppressors will receive their due.

4. Fourth servant passage (Isa 52:13–53:12)

The longest of the four servant passages is framed by two oracles (Isa 52:13-15; 53:11b-12) in which Yahweh speaks about the one whom he calls "my servant" (Isa 52:13; 53:11b). The first oracle is a solemn presentation of the exalted servant. While the multitude (a group of Israelites) are appalled at or mourn because of his appearance, the nations are dumbfounded because of what they will see and hear. The body of the text begins with Israel's confession (Isa 53:1-2) and a description of the servant who is unattractive as a desert weed, his appearance such that he was avoided much as a leper would have been (compare Pss 22:6-7; 88:8). Israel recognizes that the sufferings that God inflicted on him were those that their sins deserved. Verses 7 and 8 depict the servant's willing submission to this suffering that may go beyond what justice demanded. His sufferings were such that even his burial was prepared. It was not to be an honorable burial, for his grave would be with those of the wicked and rich. The body of the passage concludes with a clear affirmation that the servant's sufferings resulted from God's will and a prayerful expression of hope that God will accept what the servant endured as a means for the justification of Israel. The concluding oracle proclaims the vindication of the servant, God's righteous one. Because of the servant's suffering, Israel will be made righteous. He will be ranked among the great ones, sharing spoils like a conqueror. Restored and transformed, he will be vindicated because of his fidelity to the will of Yahweh.

C. Major Questions

The so-called "servant songs" are embedded within the narrative flow of Isa 40–55, without which they cannot be adequately interpreted. Three major and interrelated questions emerge from the general discussion: the identity of the servant, the idea of vicarious suffering, and the death of the servant.

1. Identity of the servant

The term "servant" first appears in Deutero-Isaiah in Isa 41:8-9: "But you, Israel, my servant, Jacob, whom I have chosen ... You are my servant, I have chosen you and not cast you off"; this language is echoed in Isa 42:1. Despite the contention of Duhm and others who have followed him that "Israel" is a later interpolation into the text of Isa 49:3, the verse supports the identification of the servant as Jacob/Israel: "You are my servant, Israel, in whom I will be glorified" (see also Isa 44:1-2, 21; 45:4; 48:20). The servant's sufferings become a metaphorical description of the hardships of exile.

On the other hand, the role of the servant in the restoration of Israel (Isa 49:1-6), the physical nature of the servant's sufferings (Isa 50:4-9; 52:12–53:12), his oppression at the hands of Israelites, and the preparation for his burial (Isa 53:9) seem to indicate that the servant is an anonymous historical individual. On any reading

of the texts, the servant is inseparable from Israel; he is the bearer of individual and national traits. The title and mission of Israel are attributed to him. Thus Childs takes "Israel" in Isa 49:3 as a predicate, reading "You are my servant, you are Israel."

An issue related to the identity of the servant is whether, given the diverse application of the servant title in the OT, the servant is cast as a royal or as a prophetic figure. On balance, the servant appears to be a prophetic figure albeit exercising his task by example rather than by uttering prophetic oracles.

2. Vicarious suffering

Later Christian use of Isa 53:4-6, 8, 11 has led to a reading of these verses through the prism of a sophisticated doctrine of vicarious atonement. They should, however, be read in the light of the text itself and by way of analogy with other prophetic suffering in the exilic era (compare Jer 16:1-4; Ezek 12:17-20).

3. Death of the servant

Isaiah 53:8 states that the servant was cut off from the land of the living. Many commentators take these words (compare Jer 11:19) along with the reference to the preparation of a burial place (Isa 53:9) to mean that the servant had died. Others, however, see in "the land of the living" a reference to the land of Israel or the Temple and note that, although his grave was prepared, there is no reference to his burial. Should there be no clear reference to the servant's death, it follows that there can be no reference to his resurrection.

D. Christian Use of the Deutero-Isaian Passages

From the time of Justin (*1 Apol.* 50; *Dial.* 13) Christian interpreters have taken the servant passages, particularly Isa 52:13–53:12, as referring to Jesus, seeing in them a kind of messianic prophecy (see MESSIAH, JEWISH). However, the Deutero-Isaian texts do not foretell the ministry of Jesus by way of predictive prophecy. They are to be understood primarily within the literary context of the OT. The authors of the NT have, however, made use of these passages in their scripturally formulated reflections on Jesus. For example, material from the servant passages appears in two fulfillment citations in the Gospel of Matthew (12:18-21): Jesus miraculously cures the sick (Isa 53:4) and is realized in the role of the idealized nation (42:1-4).

Some scholars hold that the formulation of the Markan passion predictions (Mark 8:31; 9:31; 10:33-34), reprised by Matthew (16:21-28; 20:17-28) and Luke (9:22-27; 18:31-34), has been influenced by Isa 53. Isaiah 50:6 may have influenced the Synoptics' portrayal of Jesus being spat upon (Mark 10:34; 15:19; Matt 27:30). Others find in the fourth servant passage the background for the formula "in accordance with the Scriptures" of 1 Cor 15:3-4 and the christological hymn of Phil 2:6-11 (see KENOSIS). Just prior to the passion narrative, the Johannine author cites Isa 53:1 in a portrayal of the people's lack of belief in Jesus (John 12:38). Some interpreters find in the Johannine "lifting up" motif (John 3:14; 8:28; 12:32-34) an allusion to the vindication of the servant (Isa 52:13). In a striking scene, Luke describes an Ethiopian eunuch reading Isaiah and asking Philip to interpret Isa 53:7-8. Philip responds by effectively identifying Jesus with the Deutero-Isaian servant (Acts 8:26-40).

In a departure from the NT's use of the Deutero-Isaian servant passages to flesh out a portrayal of Jesus, Paul exploits Isa 49:1-6 in a self-portrayal as having been called from the womb (Gal 1:15; Isa 49:1). He worries he might have labored in vain (Gal 2:2; 4:11; Phil 2:16; 1 Thess 3:5; compare 1 Cor 15:58; Isa 49:4). He uses the fourth servant passage to speak about the proclamation of the gospel (Rom 1:1-9; compare Isa 52:13–53:12), and in Rom 10:16 Paul cites Isa 53:1 in a reflection on the non-reception of the gospel. In Rom 15:21 he cites Isa 52:15 to explain his determination not to preach the gospel where it had previously been proclaimed. Luke places on Paul's lips Isa 49:6 as a scriptural warrant for the apostolic mission to the Gentiles (Acts 13:47).

First Peter 2:21-25 interpolates the fourth servant passage into a paraenetic section of a household code urging slaves to be obedient to their masters (Isa 53:4, 5, 6, 9, 12). The author portrays a suffering Christ as an example for slaves who are treated unjustly. *See* ISAIAH, BOOK OF; SERVANT; SLAVERY.

Bibliography: M. L. Barré. "Textual and Rhetorical-critical Observations on the Last Servant Song." *CBQ* 62 (2000) 1–27; R. E. Brown. *The Death of the Messiah: From Gethsemane to the Grave* (1994); A. R. Ceresko. "The Rhetorical Strategy of the Fourth Servant Song." *CBQ* 46 (1994) 42–55; B. S. Childs. *Isaiah*. OTL (2001); B. Duhm. *Das Buch Jesaia: übersetzt und erklärt*. 4th ed. (1922); M. Gignilliat. *Paul and Isaiah's Servants: Paul's Theological Reading of Isaiah 40–66 in 2 Corinthians 5.14–6.10* (2007); H. L. Ginsberg. "The Oldest Interpretation of the Suffering Servant." *VT* 3 (1953) 400–404; J. Goldingay and D. Payne. *A Critical and Exegetical Commentary on Isaiah 40–55*. ICC (2006); M. D. Hooker. *Jesus and the Servant: The Influence of the Servant Concept of Deutero-Isaiah in the New Testament* (1959); L. A. Huizenga. "The Incarnation of the Servant: The 'Suffering Servant' and Matthean Christology." *HBT* 27 (2005) 25–58; H. Irsigler. *Ein Weg aus der Gewalt? Gottesknecht kontra Kyros im Deuerojesajabuch* (1998); C. R. North. *The Suffering Servant in Deutero-Isaiah*. 2nd ed. (1956); C. Westermann. *Isaiah 40–66*. OTL (1969).

RAYMOND F. COLLINS

SERVE, TO [עָבַד 'avadh; διακονια diakonia, διάκονεω diakoneō, δούλευω douleuō, λατρεύω latreuō]. There are a number of terms in the Bible translated as "to serve" or "service." *Service* has a broad range of meanings including: slavery, working for another, and participation in religious activities. In the LXX the most common translation of 'avadh is douleuō, but slavery type service is not always in view. Context is important for determining the type of service, as with the rendering of latreuō as "worship" (NRSV) in a religious context (Judg 2:11; 2 Sam 15:8; 2 Kgs 17:12, 16, 33, 35). In general, *service* expresses various forms of a relationship based on loyalty and/or obligation that can be legal, social, political, or religious.

Examples of service in the OT include: Esau serving Jacob (Gen 25:23), Jacob serving Laban (Gen 29:15, 30), Israel serving Egypt (Exod 1:14; 14:12), Israel serving God (Josh 22:5), Levites serving the cult (Num 8:25; Ezra 6:18), advisors serving the king (2 Sam 16:19), and children serving a parent (Mal 3:17). Even animals can serve (Job 39:9).

The connection between service and worship is a central theme of the OT. Worshiping "other gods" is the antithesis of serving Yahweh, is prohibited for the first time in the Decalogue ("You shall not bow down to them or serve them" Exod 20:5; Deut 5:9), and is repeatedly stated in Deuteronomy (4:19; 8:19; 11:16; 17:3; 29:25 [26]; 30:17). This antithesis is highlighted by the numerous instances of Israel abandoning service to Yahweh for service to "other gods" resulting in their subsequent oppression by and service to foreign conquers (Deut 28:48; Judg 2:7; 3:8; 9:28, 38; 10:6, 13; 1 Kgs 9:9; 2 Chr 12:8; Jer 5:19). Israel is restored when they return to serving/worshiping Yahweh exclusively (Judg 10:16; 1 Sam 7:3; Jer 30:8-9).

In the NT, the theme of serving includes both slave- and non-slave-type service. Paul refers to various forms of service using douleuō (Rom 12:11; 14:18; 16:18; Phil 2:22; 1 Thess 1:9). More often he uses diakoneō/diakonia to describe service in the community of the believers (Rom 12:7; 15:25; 1 Cor 12:5), caring for one another (2 Cor 9:1, 2-13), and his personal ministry (Rom 11:13; 2 Cor 4:1). Paul places an emphasis on a type of service that consists of preaching/teaching in the church accompanied by charity to others. This is illustrated by Stephanas' example of discharging service in love (1 Cor 16:15) and Paul's extended discussions about the offering he is collecting for the Jerusalem church (2 Cor 8:4, 20; 9:1-2).

Similar understandings of serving/service are found elsewhere in the NT (1 Pet 4:10-12; Heb 1:14). Love, faith, and patient endurance are qualities associated with service (Heb 6:10-11; Rev 2:19). Serving can simply mean discharging the office of a deacon (1 Tim 3:10, 13) or the act of caring for those in prison (1 Tim 1:18).

In the Gospels and Acts, service/serving often carries the idea of table service (Matt 8:15; Luke 10:40; Acts 6:2), but a distinction between douleuō and diakoneō/diakonia is not always strictly maintained (compare Matt 20:25-27; Mark 10:42-45). The OT connection between worship and service is restated ("Worship the Lord your God, and serve only him,"

Matt 4:10; Luke 4:8), and the prohibition against serving "other gods" finds new application in the two masters saying ("No one can serve two masters.... You cannot serve God and wealth" Matt 6:24; Luke 16:13).

Service characterizes the essence of Jesus' ministry, which is based on the OT command of love of neighbor. This is illustrated in the Son of Man saying, "For the Son of Man came not to be served but to serve, and to give his life a ransom for many" (Mark 10:45), which defines service by the act of self-sacrifice. The parallel sayings in Luke 22:26-27 and Matt 20:24-28 emphasize the requirement of giving one's self in service to others rather than seeking greatness. In Matt 25:42-44, service (diakoneō) is defined by Jesus as including activities such as feeding the hungry, clothing the naked, providing shelter to strangers, and visiting the sick and the imprisoned. These acts of service delineate the service of a true disciple and exhibit the Christian obligation to love one's neighbor. In John, service is linked to following Jesus, which results in being honored by the father (John 12:26). *See* DEACON; DEACONESS; SERVANT.

Bibliography: John Byron. *Slavery Metaphors in Early Judaism and Pauline Christianity* (2003); Philippa Carter. *The Servant Ethic in the New Testament* (1997); John N. Collins. *Diakonia: Re-interpreting the Ancient Sources* (1990).

JOHN BYRON

SESOSTRIS. Three PHARAOHs by this name (also transcribed "Senwosret") ruled Egypt during the Twelfth Dynasty (ca. 1990–1785 BCE). None of them are mentioned in the Bible. 1. Sesostris I was the second king of the Twelfth Dynasty. His forty-five-year reign was responsible for establishing the might of Middle Kingdom Egypt, consolidating much of the power of local rulers. He is the pharaoh who comes to power in the *Tale of Sinuhe*, the Middle Kingdom story of a man who flees to Israel after the assassination of Amenemhet I.

2. Sesostris II, the fourth king of the Twelfth Dynasty, ruled for fewer than ten years.

3. Sesostris III, the fifth king of the Twelfth Dynasty, ruled at least twenty and possibly as long as forty years. He was responsible for extending Egyptian power into Nubia through four campaigns into that area and continued to bring local power into the hands of the king.

KEVIN A. WILSON

SESTHEL ses'thuhl [Σεσθήλ Sesthēl]. One of Addi's descendants who dismissed his foreign wife and their children (1 Esd 9:31). The name is BEZALEL in the parallel passage (Ezra 10:30).

SETH seth [שֵׁת sheth; Σήθ Sēth]. 1. Third son of Adam and Eve, who was born after Cain, the firstborn, murdered his brother Abel. Seth's name is explained in Gen 4:25 when Eve says, "God has appointed (shath

שָׁת) for me another child instead of Abel, because Cain killed him."

Seth's birth immediately follows the genealogy of Cain, inviting comparison between the two. First, people began calling on the name of the LORD in conjunction with Seth's descendant Enosh (4:26). In contrast, Cain's lineage is distinguished by technological and musical skills (4:17-22). Second, Adam's genealogy is transmitted through Seth, not Cain, implying that Seth has been given the role of firstborn (compare 1 Chr 1:1). Thus, as is common elsewhere in Genesis, the older brother is supplanted by his younger brother. Third, just as humanity was created in the image and likeness of God (Gen 1:26), Seth is born in the likeness and image of his father (5:3). Seth did not just replace Abel; he also superseded Cain as the progenitor of Adam's family. Sirach 49:16 holds Seth in high honor, along with Shem and Enosh, but reserves the highest esteem for Adam. Luke traces Jesus' genealogy back to Adam through Seth (3:38).

SUSAN M. PIGOTT

Figure 1: Egyptian limestone stela of Aapehty with the god Seth on the left (later Nineteenth Dynasty, ca. 1200 BCE). British Museum, London, Great Britain.

2. In Egyptian mythology, Seth is one of four siblings (Osiris, Isis, Seth, and Nephthys) born to Geb and Nut. Seth is often associated with confusion and disorder: within his family, he brings death into the world by murdering Osiris and further embodies strife in his fight

with his nephew Horus. Nevertheless, Seth retains a prominent place in Egyptian civilization. Pharaohs, for example, represent Horus reconciled to Seth. In the Ramesside period (1295–1069 BCE), Seth becomes a god of state as demonstrated by several royal names (Sety I and II and Sethnakht). *See* GODS, GODDESSES.

STEVE COOK

SETHUR see´thuhr [סְתוּר sethur]. The son of Michael and representative from the tribe of Asher who, with representatives from the other eleven tribes, was charged by Moses with the task of scouting the land of Canaan to determine its fruitfulness and the strength of its inhabitants (Num 13:13).

SEVEN. *See* NUMBERS, NUMBERING.

SEVEN CHURCHES [αἱ ἑπτὰ ἐκκλησίαι hai hepta ekklēsiai]. The book of Revelation is addressed to "the seven churches" in Ephesus, Smyrna, Pergamum, Thyatira, Sardis, Philadelphia, and Laodicea, in the Roman province of Asia (Rev 1:4, 11), depicted as seven golden lampstands and associated with angels described as seven stars (Rev 1:16, 20). The stars are held in Christ's right hand as he stands among the lampstands (Rev 1:13), indicating that the churches enjoy his protection in their conflict with evil. While the letters of Rev 2–3 address individual churches, the whole "book" is an open letter for public reading. In each of the seven letters, the Christ of Rev 1:12-20 addresses each church's angel with a commendation, a rebuke, and a promise.

The seven churches are representative: each letter ends with the exhortation to "listen to what the Spirit is saying to the churches" (Rev 2:7, 11, 17, 29; 3:6, 13, 22). Other churches in Asia included Colossae, Troas, Magnesia, Hierapolis, and Tralles. Perhaps the seven were chosen because couriers could travel in a circuit from Ephesus north and then southeast, with other churches easily reached from these seven. Alternatively, since "seven" in Revelation typically indicates perfection, the churches may be indicated by the choice of seven. *See* ANGELS OF THE SEVEN CHURCHES; REVELATION, BOOK OF.

Bibliography: Colin J. Hemer. *The Letters to the Seven Churches of Asia in Their Local Setting* (1986); Roland H. Worth. *The Seven Cities of the Apocalypse and Greco-Asian Culture* (1999).

MAXWELL J. DAVIDSON

SEVEN WORDS FROM THE CROSS. Also sometimes called the "seven last words" of Jesus, this is a traditional set of seven sayings created by conflating the four canonical accounts of the CRUCIFIXION. None of the sayings appears in all four Gospels, and most occur only in one. No single account contains all seven sayings.

According to the traditional order, the seven words are: 1) Jesus' prayer for those who are crucifying him: "Father, forgive them; for they do not know what they are doing" (Luke 23:34). This prayer is absent from several important manuscripts and may be a later addition. It is, however, consistent with Luke's theology. In Acts 3:17 Peter echoes Jesus' words when he tells his Jewish audience that they and their rulers acted in ignorance when they crucified Jesus. Similarly, Stephen prays as he is being stoned, "Lord, do not hold this sin against them" (Acts 7:60). 2) Jesus' promise to the repentant criminal who is being crucified beside him: "Truly I tell you, today you will be with me in Paradise" (Luke 23:43). 3) Jesus' words to his mother Mary and to the beloved disciple: "Woman, here is your son.... Here is your mother" (John 19:26-27). 4) Jesus' cry of abandonment, cited in Hebrew (Matt 27:46) or Aramaic (Mark 15:34) and translated by the evangelists: "My God, my God, why have you forsaken me?" The cry mirrors the opening words of Ps 22 (v. 1 [Heb. 22:2]), a fact that has given rise to much debate over whether Jesus spoke the words in despair or in hope. 5) "I am thirsty" (John 19:28). 6) "It is finished" (John 19:30; compare John 17:4). 7) "Father, into your hands I commend my spirit" (Luke 23:46). This final phrase is a quotation from a psalm expressing trust in God's deliverance (Ps 31:5 [Heb. 31:6]).

JUDITH ANNE JONES

SEVEN, SEVENTH, SEVENTY [שֶׁבַע shevaʿ; ἑπτά hepta]. The number seven, with its combinations and multiples, is found throughout the ANE and the Hellenistic world as a significant or sacred number. Israel, Judaism, and early Christianity were influenced by this tradition, which they developed in characteristic ways.

As sacral associations of twelve were related to the lunar cycle and 360 with the solar cycle, the special position of seven was almost certainly due to observation of the four phases of the moon, in seven-day periods. Seven was an important sacred number in Greece long before the number of planets was fixed at seven, and some cultures regarded seven as a sacred number without having a fixed number of planets. In the Hellenistic world seven and the seven-day cycle were sometimes connected with astronomical, astrological, and mystical associations, but these were secondary interpretations unrelated to the origins of the number's significance.

In Mesopotamia, the number seven appeared with extreme frequency in important and sacred enumerations. For example, Ishtar had seven sacred names, the god Enlil manifested himself in seven stars, the ziggurats in Borsippa and Babylon each had seven stories, seven was often found in incantations and rituals, and ritual acts were often repeated seven times. In the Gilgamesh epic, the flood ends after seven days, purification and burial rites are often prescribed for seven-day periods, and the underworld is guarded by seven walls, through which one enters by seven or fourteen gates. Similar lists could be given for Ugarit, Egypt, and the later Hellenistic world.

The meaning of this "sevenness" of things, not always conscious or explicit, seems in all ancient cultures to have been associated with the idea of fullness or completeness. The seven-day cycle fulfills and completes a period, then begins anew. In Hellenistic times, a book called *Hebdomades* ("Sevens," now lost) by M. Terentius Varro (116–27 BCE) expressed a widespread view that human life and the universe itself was structured on the principle of sevens. Varro was probably the originator of the idea that the world capital was located on seven hills (there are actually more, and the precise list of which seven the "City of Seven Hills" includes has varied over the centuries). Likewise, although the lists varied, there were precisely seven wonders of the ancient world, and more than one author spoke of the "seven ages of man." When biblical authors in Israel, Judaism, and early Christianity incorporated seven into their patterns of religious thought, it often had this connotation of wholeness. A full life is seventy years (Ps 90:10). Lamech lived as fully as possible, 777 years (Gen 5:31). The seven nations dispossessed so that Israel could receive the promised land (Deut 7:1; Josh 3:10; 24:11; Acts 13:19) represent God's complete gift of the land; the seventy Gentile nations represent the whole world (*1 En.* 89:59-60, developed from the "table of nations" in Gen 10); in Luke 9 Jesus sends out the Twelve to Israel, and in Luke 10 he sends out seventy as a prolepsis of the Gentile mission; the LXX or the SEPTUAGINT (so named because it was said to have been the product of seventy-two scholars) represents the translation of the OT into the language of the Gentiles, i.e., all the nations of the earth; the seven generations of Gen 4:17-18 points to the designated period of time as a self-enclosed totality; the sevenfold vengeance promised Cain is total and comprehensive (Gen 4:15); the seven churches of Rev 1–3 represent not merely seven particular congregations, but the church in its totality; the seven CATHOLIC EPISTLES are directed not to individuals or individual congregations but to the church as a whole.

The number seven is the most common sacral number in the Bible. Seven (sheva῾, hepta) and its compounds occur 739 times in the OT, sixty-six times in the Apocrypha/Deuterocanonicals, and 108 times in the NT. Not all these have a particularly sacred or symbolic meaning, of course, though the majority have at least this overtone. By no means are all the instances of seven made explicit. There are, e.g., seven epithets of Zion in Ps 48; seven attributes of the coming king in Isa 11; a sevenfold voice of Yahweh in Ps 29; seven woes in Matt 23; seven petitions in Solomon's prayer (1 Kgs 8:29-53) and the Lord's Prayer (Matt 6:9-13); and seven beatitudes in Revelation (1:3; 14:13; 16:15; 19:9; 20:6; 22:7, 14). The ubiquitous seven is beneath the surface in numerous other ways not obvious to the reader of the English Bible, for example in the untranslated names Shiba, Beer-sheba, and Bathsheba, in the Festival of Weeks (festival of sevens, there being seven weeks of seven days between Passover and Pentecost), and in the use of oaths (*swear* is a verbal form of *seven*; *oath* is a cognate form of *seven*). *See* WEEKS, FEAST OF.

The Israelite cult is saturated with sevens, which structured sacred calendar, sacred space, and ritual acts. Passover and Booths are seven-day festivals. The seventh month is especially sacred, encompassing the New Year, Yom Kippur, and Booths (*see* FEASTS AND FASTS). The SABBATH, the seventh day, is supremely sacred, grounded in both creation (Gen 2:2; Exod 20:8-11) and salvation history (Deut 5:12-15). The seven-branched menorah (Exod 25:31-37) is only one of a multitude of examples of the hebdomadal pattern found in the furnishings and decorations of the Temple (e.g., 1 Kgs 7:17; Ezek 40:22, 26). From its very beginning, apocalyptic thought was fond of seven and its multiples (e.g., Dan 4:16, 23, 25, 32; 9:2, 24, 25).

Matthew 1:17 makes explicit that the author has structured the genealogy of Jesus in terms of sevens, i.e., three sets of fourteen generations each from Abraham to Jesus, omitting some generations in order to achieve the desired result (even though he actually mentions only forty-one names). Though the author does not call attention to it, the genealogy in Luke 3:23-38 is likewise configured with seven as the structuring principle, with fifty-six generations from Abraham to Jesus and the whole of human history from Adam to Jesus divided into seventy-seven generations. In the differing versions of the Markan feeding stories (the 5000, Mark 6:30-44; the 4000, 8:1-10; compare 8:15-21), the differing numbers may have symbolic overtones, the seven baskets of abundant fragments representing Gentiles, corresponding to the Jewish connotations of the twelve baskets; so also in Acts 6 the seven Hellenist leaders may be the Gentile counterpart of the twelve Jewish apostles.

The book of Revelation uses the number seven, and its multiples and cognates, more frequently than any other NT book (sixty times), surpassed in the OT only by Numbers (eighty times), Genesis (sixty-seven times) and Leviticus (eighty times). In relative frequency, Revelation has almost twice as many sevens as Numbers, its nearest competitor (4.53 instances per thousand words; Numbers 2.32 per thousand). There are numerous explicit sevens, e.g., seven stars, lampstands, and churches (1:20); seven spirit/angels (1:4; 4:5; 5:6); the Lamb with seven horns and eyes (5:6), imitated by the beast with seven heads (12:3); seven thunders (10:3); seven plagues (15:1); seven kings and seven mountains (17:9). The book is explicitly structured by the series of seven seals (5:1, 5; 6:1–8:1); seven trumpets (8:2–11:15); and seven bowls (15:7–16:17). The seventh represents the last, the fullness of time, the eschatological fulfillment of God's saving plan (*see*

ESCHATOLOGY IN EARLY JUDAISM; ESCHATOLOGY OF THE NT; ESCHATOLOGY OF THE OT; NUMBERS, NUMBERING; SYMBOLISM).

Bibliography: A. Y. Collins. "Numerical Symbolism in Jewish and Early Christian Apocalyptic Literature." *ANRW* II, 21/1 (1984) 1221–87; D. Varley. *Seven: The Number of Creation* (1976).

M. EUGENE BORING

SEVEN, THE [οἱ ἑπτά hoi hepta]. The designation in Acts 21:8 for the seven men selected to address complaints by Hellenists regarding the distribution of the community's resources (Acts 6:1-7). The passage in Acts 6 presents a number of difficulties, including the exact nature of the men's task, which is apparently to alleviate the Hellenists' concerns and allow the Twelve apostles to devote more time to prayer and preaching. The first two men listed in Acts 6:5, Stephen and Philip, appear later in the narrative where they are attributed activities that are seemingly at odds with the task for which the seven were selected (6:8–7:50; 8:26-40; Philip is referred to as an EVANGELIST; 21:8). The remaining five are Prochorus, Nicanor, Timon, Parmenas, and Nicolaus. The latter is identified as a "proselyte of Antioch," which can suggest that the men were Greek-speaking Jews from Palestine. Although all seven names are Greek, it is unclear whether the men are members of the Hellenists. In its context, this passage illustrates the community's ability to successfully address internal conflict in an orderly way. Later tradition understands the seven as the first men appointed to the office of DEACON, but this is not indicated in Acts.

RUBÉN R. DUPERTUIS

SEVENTEEN. *See* NUMBERS, NUMBERING.

SEVENTY. *See* NUMBERS, NUMBERING.

SEVENTY, THE. Translation of the Latin *septuaginta*, referring to the Greek translation of the Torah undertaken (according to tradition) by seventy-two Jewish elders (*see* SEPTUAGINT). Among Christians, the term came to encompass the Greek translation of the entire Hebrew Bible, plus other works (generally designated as apocryphal) that were either translated into Greek from a Semitic original or initially composed in Greek.

LEONARD GREENSPOON

In Luke 10:1, Jesus sends out seventy (hebdomēkonta ἑβδομήκοντα) more disciples (in addition to the twelve [9:1-6]), on a second mission to proclaim the kingdom and heal the sick (*see* TWELVE, THE). Some households and towns will welcome them, and others will reject them (10:2-16). Even so, the seventy report that in Jesus's name even the demons submit to them (10:17). Some manuscripts have "seventy-two," the number of

NATIONS enumerated in LXX Gen 10, an indication that Luke is introducing the world-wide mission featured in Acts.

MARIANNE BLICKENSTAFF

SEWING [תָּפַר tafar; ἐπιβάλλω epiballō, ἐπιράπτω epiraptō]. Sewing is the act of using a NEEDLE and thread or strips of leather to stitch a piece of cloth or leather. Sewing can be piecing, gathering, or reinforcing, or hemming edges of fabric together. Sewing can be embroidering a pattern, mending fabric, or attaching one piece of fabric on top of another. Sewn items and tools used for sewing have been found in archaeological excavations.

Sewing is mentioned as part of several biblical stories (e.g., Gen 3:7; Job 16:15; Eccl 3:7). Ezekiel condemned those sewing magical amulets (Ezek 13:18). Jesus used the metaphor of sewing unshrunk new fabric to old fabric to explain why he and his disciples were doing things in a new way incompatible with older traditions (Matt 9:16; Mark 2:21; Luke 5:36). *See* CLOTH, CLOTHES; EMBROIDERY AND NEEDLEWORK.

Bibliography: Avigail Sheffer. "Needlework and Sewing in Israel from Prehistoric Times to the Roman Period." *Fortunate the Eyes That See.* A. B. Beck, A. H. Bartelt, P. R. Raabe, and C. A. Franke, eds. (1996) 527–59.

MARY PETRINA BOYD

SEX, SEXUALITY. The term *sex,* as opposed to GENDER, refers to the physical characteristics that are used to define human beings within the biological categories of male and female. *Sexuality* refers to physical behavior related to the sexual parts of the body, and emotions and sensations associated with this behavior. In modern times *sexuality* often refers to sexual orientation and has become a key indicator of identity (*see* GENDER STUDIES). In the ancient world an individual's identity was not understood primarily or essentially in terms of sexuality, that is, through the categories of homosexual, heterosexual, or bisexual. Sexual acts, however, could be defined within these categories.

An overarching factor characterizing the biblical treatment of sex is the impetus to regulate its practice. It is this factor that reveals that for the biblical authors sex was a very dangerous aspect of human existence. It was dangerous because biblical religion is based on common identity passed on through the family of Abraham. To ensure this genealogy was not compromised, the correct paternity was vital, and sex must not stray outside the marriage bed. Sexual desire was a force that had to be contained, "For love is strong as death, passion fierce as the grave" (Song 8:6).

    A. The Old Testament
        1. Genesis: the creation of sex
        2. Ritual purity
        3. Marriage and virginity

A. The Old Testament

1. Genesis: the creation of sex

The concept of two biologically distinct sexes is defined and described in the opening chapters of Genesis. In Gen 1:27-28 the creation of male and female is announced, and in Gen 2:4*b*–3:24 this creation is explained in detail in terms of relationships and roles. By intertwining biological make-up with gender roles the Genesis account presents us with an essentialist form of gender construction. Male and female together make up humanity, created in the divine image (Gen 1:27). This binary ensures the main concern of Genesis, the creation of the people of God, is at the heart of God's creative intent. Once their creation has been announced, God tells them to "be fruitful and multiply" (Gen 1:28). In Jewish tradition this is understood as the first commandment (mitswah מִצְוָה) of the TORAH, making procreation obligatory for all Jews. This presentation also provides the biblical basis of heterosexuality (*see* §A.5.d below).

In Gen 1:26-28 both male and female are called to procreate, subdue the earth, and be the stewards of the natural world created for them. However, when we look at the account of the first couple in Gen 2 we see a sexual hierarchy emerging from the narrative. God creates Adam first, and on declaring that "It is not good that the man should be alone; I will make him a helper as his partner" (Gen 2:18), God parades every living creature in front of him. Adam gives names to them all, but does not recognize any creature as a helper, as his partner. And so Eve is created out of Adam's rib. These verses have been at the heart of debates on male and female roles and sexual hierarchy for centuries, and contemporary scholarship continues the arguments. While some scholars argue that the relationship between Adam and Eve is characterized by complementarity, others argue that the text is clear that procreation is the primary purpose for Eve's creation, and whereas Adam was created for God's purpose, Eve was created in a secondary role, so that Adam might have descendants. The text explains that "a man leaves his father and his mother and clings to his wife and they become one flesh" (2:24). "Become one flesh" expresses their sexual union and also implies fidelity, signaling the im-

portance of ensuring the paternal line for the people of God, who will emerge as the nation of Israel in the larger biblical narrative. The context of this Genesis account influences other biblical narratives and legal texts on sexual matters such as masturbation, homosexuality, virginity, sex inside and outside of marriage, polygamy, and extra-marital relationships.

Eve is to experience pain in childbirth, yet her desire will be for her husband, who will rule over her (Gen 3:16). Eve will have sexual desire for her husband, but within that relationship, she will not be an equal partner. In the garden the first couple are naked but not ashamed; however, their first act, once they have gained knowledge of good and evil from the forbidden fruit, is to try to make clothes. Lost innocence is marked by the need to cover the sexual organs, and this distinguishes humanity in the created world. This text implies that human sexuality must be hidden, even from or especially from the presence of God (3:10-11).

2. Ritual purity

In the OT great care is taken to ensure that there is no mixing of the sexual and the sacred, or, more precisely, the sexual and the holy, as represented by the cult and, essentially, by the divine presence. One factor in vouchsafing ritual purity is sexual abstinence, illustrated by Moses commanding the Israelite men not to approach a woman for three days in preparation for the arrival of the divine presence on Sinai (Exod 19:15), and also by David's assurance to Abimelech that his men have not been with women for three days and can, therefore, eat the hallowed bread (1 Sam 21:5). The outward signs of sexuality, the menstrual cycle (Lev 15:19-30), giving birth (Lev 12), and the flow of semen (Lev 15:1-18), are markers of uncleanness that demand processes of purification. There is no moral judgment intended in these definitions and processes, only the intent to maintain the separation between the holy and the profane. Israel has to be distinct from its neighbors whose practices, according to the biblical writers, include sexual perversions that were unacceptable in the sight of the God of Israel (Lev 18:24-30). The aspiration of ritual purity for Israel reflects their identity as God's chosen people and explains the separation between sex (the profane) and purity (the sacred). Procreation is a sign of their humanity; holiness is a sign of their chosenness (*see* CLEAN AND UNCLEAN; HOLY, HOLINESS, OT).

3. Marriage and virginity

The most important function of marriage was the production of children to carry on the father's name. Biblical parameters to sexual behavior stem from preoccupation with identifying and maintaining the patrilineal character of Israel. This is achieved by males in the family controlling the female members (evidenced by the way in which a father is entitled to sell his daughter into slavery, Exod 21:7). Fathers exercise control over their daughters and husbands over their wives.

Severe punishments are dealt out when these boundaries are breached, either by premarital sex or adultery. Instructions regarding the treatment of unlawful sex with a woman who is betrothed to another illustrate how her sexual state, her virginity, is a guarded possession of her father (see VIRGIN). Both the man and the woman should be stoned to death if there is evidence that the woman was a willing party, that is, if no witnesses heard her scream out in protest. If there are no witnesses present or if the act occurred in an isolated place, the woman's life is spared (Deut 22:23-27). If a man rapes a virgin he is required to give fifty shekels of silver to the young woman's father and then take her as his wife (Deut 22:28-29). See RAPE.

A narrative that illustrates this prescription is the story of Dinah (Gen 34). Shechem, an uncircumcised Hivite, rapes Dinah, who, as the unmarried daughter of Jacob, is still part of her father's household. An alliance is struck between the two families for Shechem and Dinah's marriage (as well as other marriages between the two groups) on the condition that Hamor's people agree to be circumcised. While Hamor's men are still recovering from the circumcisions, two of Dinah's brothers attack Hamor's city, kill all the males, and take Dinah back to their father's house. The text is open to multiple interpretations: were Shechem and Dinah secretly in love and by having sexual relations forced their fathers' hands in allowing their union? Or was Dinah forced into the marriage because she was raped? In either case, Dinah had little control over her destiny.

A father who gives a daughter in marriage must be able to prove that she is a virgin, and if a man wanted to rescind the marriage on the grounds that his bride was not a virgin, the marriage bed sheet has to be inspected (Deut 22:17). The males' control over female sexuality ensures the paternity of any offspring. Once a woman is within the husband's household, the responsibility for her sexual behavior transfers to him. See MARRIAGE, OT.

4. Prohibited sex

Both Leviticus and Deuteronomy list practices that are to'evah (תּוֹעֵבָה, Deut 14:3; 17:1; Lev 18:26-30), a term traditionally translated "abomination." The practitioner is also "abhorrent" (to'evah) to the deity (Deut 22:5; see ABOMINATION). Contemporary scholarship rejects the idea that to'evah has the moralistic overtone that is often conveyed in translation and, therefore, removes it to a more neutral socioreligious frame to mean the "transgression of borders." The practices described in this way are extremely wide-ranging and include dealings with unclean animals (Deut 14:3), defective sacrifices (Deut 17:1), cross-dressing (Deut 22:5), as well as certain sexual acts (Lev 18:22). In Proverbs the term can refer to those who are responsible for the miscarriage of justice (Prov 28:9).

One passage in particular from Leviticus characterizes the ancient Israelite attitudes toward sexuality. The so-called "forbidden degrees" express in a concise form unacceptable sexual behavior (Lev 18:6-20). The passage is framed by an introduction (vv. 1-5) and conclusion (vv. 24-30) that make it clear that sexual restraint is one of the distinguishing features of the people of Israel, something that will make them identifiable as God's people among their Near Eastern neighbors. They will not behave like the Egyptians or the Canaanites, who presumably practice some of the prohibited things (Lev 18:3).

a. Incest. The "forbidden degrees" list inappropriate sexual partners for Israelite men and has attracted myriad theories as to its origin and meaning from anthropologists, sociologists, and psychoanalysts, as well as from theologians and biblical scholars. This list comprises prohibitions against incestuous practices, but also prohibits certain sexual unions that do not involve blood relatives. Many of the "forbidden degrees" are concerned with the preservation of family boundaries, or, more explicitly, the boundaries of any one patriarch's realm. Any sexual coupling that blurs these boundaries is forbidden. This includes, for example, relations between stepbrothers and sisters, whether or not they share a blood link. These individuals are part of one patriarch's family, and their primary identity would become confused if they associated with another patriarch, or with someone who will become patriarch of his own FAMILY group.

Gen 19:30-38 and Gen 38 are two narratives that stand in stark contradiction to the biblical proscriptions on incest. Both, however, present a context where the family name could become extinct unless incest takes place. In both cases the male participant is tricked, and the female partners instigate the incestuous liaisons. LOT'S DAUGHTERS scheme to acquire children by making their father so drunk that he is unaware that he is impregnating them (Gen 19:30-38). The narrative does not praise or condemn the daughters (19:37-38).

In contrast, even though incest is involved, TAMAR is deemed more righteous than her father-in-law Judah (Gen 38:26) for instigating a sexual union with him to procure a child. The Tamar and Judah narrative (Gen 38:1-26) raises a number of issues that illustrate biblical attitudes to sexual matters: the issue of levirate marriage, "onanism" (subsequently adopted as a euphemism for masturbation), prostitution, as well as incest. When Tamar's husband, Judah's firstborn son, dies without children, Judah follows the LEVIRATE LAW and gives his second son, Onan, to Tamar so that so that she can bear a child to carry on the line of her dead husband. But Onan spills his semen on the ground, and for this act he is struck down by God (Gen 38:9-10). When Judah sends Tamar away without offering her his third son, she takes on the disguise of a prostitute and engineers a sexual meeting with Judah, who does not recognize her as his own daughter-in-law. Thus, Tamar is not impregnated by her dead husband's brother, as the law requires, but by his father. Ironically, it is not by fulfilling the levirate law that Tamar's redemptive pregnancy comes about (she bears twin sons, one of whom, Perez, is the ancestor of David), but instead, by Judah's breaking the law of incest, "You shall not uncover the nakedness of your daughter-in-law: she is your son's wife; you shall not uncover her nakedness" (Lev 18:15). The double standard between men and women's sexual behavior is illustrated in the Tamar and Judah story when the narrative does not question Judah's liaison with a prostitute but describes the condemnation of his pregnant daughter-in-law: "Bring her out, and let her be burnt" (Gen 38:24; see also Deut 22:20-21; Lev 21:9).

b. Adultery. ADULTERY is listed in the Decalogue alongside murder, stealing, bearing false witness, and coveting a neighbor's possessions (Exod 20:13-17) because, like these other trespasses, it is a socially destabilizing phenomenon. The legislation on adultery is defined only from the male perspective, as a sin against the husband; thus sex between a married man and an unmarried woman does not come within this prescription. If, however, the woman is still living in her father's house as a daughter (rather than a slave, for example), then the married man has committed an offense against her father. The penalty for adultery is severe: death for both parties (Lev 20:10; although compare John 8:3-11). Even the case of a suspected adulteress, that is, a woman whose behavior has somehow aroused jealousy in her husband (even if he has no proof of adultery), is discussed within the law codes (Num 5:11-31), and a ritual is prescribed to ascertain whether the husband's suspicions are justified (see TRIAL BY ORDEAL).

c. Prostitution. Genesis 38 includes both of the common biblical terms for prostitute, zonah (זוֹנָה; 38:15) and qedeshah (קְדֵשָׁה; 38:21). Zonah is derived from a verb that refers to sex practiced by an unmarried woman, punishable by death for any woman outside of the class of prostitute. The term qedeshah literally means a holy or consecrated person, and its sexual connotation is derived from biblical contexts. The existence of cultic prostitutes in Canaanite religion, apart from references to this in polemical biblical passages, is increasingly questioned. The imagery of prostitution to depict Israel's lack of fidelity to God and promiscuous adherence to foreign cults is a common biblical motif (Hos 1:2; 2:2-13; also Lev 20:5; Judg 2:17; Jer 3:1).

Cultic prostitution may be mentioned in other biblical texts (e.g. 1 Kgs 14:24, although scholars increasingly view such texts as referring to ordinary prostitutes; compare JPS translation). To the extent that the OT writers may have imagined that surrounding cultures were characterized by sexual practices unacceptable to Israel, they wanted to draw a clear contrast between such practices and the ideal behavior set out for God's holy nation. The picture of a lascivious world of cultic prostitution, painted with particular confidence by earlier biblical scholars, was heavily dependent upon one source, Herodotus' *Histories,* to form a stark contrast between God's holy nation and its pagan neighbors (see FERTILITY CULT). This use of the evidence has been viewed with increasing suspicion by contemporary classical and biblical scholars. The backdrop of rampant, universally practiced, cultic prostitution against which biblical moral imperatives were set is no longer widely regarded as a credible scenario. See PROSTITUTION.

d. Sex between men. Among the "forbidden degrees" is the verse that has been used down the centuries in western and colonial worlds to legislate against and ostracize from society those who practice homosexual acts: "You shall not lie with a male as with a woman; it is an abomination" (Lev 18:22). The restriction on homosexual intercourse and the restriction on bestiality that immediately follows in the text (18:23) can be read as boundary markers. The first demarcates maleness and the other humanness. It follows then that in the case of bestiality the prohibition applies to both men and women. These distinctions take us back to the opening chapters of Genesis, but here the legislation spells out more clearly the primary distinctions between male/female, human/animal. When the animals were paraded in front of Adam he recognized no "partner." The centrality of reproduction as the key to Eve's role is an even more convincing explanation if we look at Gen 2 in the light of Lev 18. Sexual acts between two men compromise male power, because the male who is penetrated is emasculated; he is likened to a woman. Likewise inappropriate touching of male genitalia by a woman, although expedient, attracts extreme retribution that can be understood in terms of avoiding confusion regarding gender identity, "If men get into a fight with one another, and the wife of one intervenes to rescue her husband from the grip of his opponent by reaching out and seizing his genitals, you shall cut off her hand; show no pity" (Deut 25:11-10). In this instance the woman could appear to be taking the initiative in sexual matters and, in doing so, taking on a male role.

Deuteronomy contains another prohibition against behavior that more explicitly confuses gender identity, "A woman shall not wear a man's apparel, nor shall a man put on a woman's garment; for whoever does such things is abhorrent to the LORD your God" (22:5). Earlier scholars interpreted this verse, like the Leviticus verses prohibiting homosexual practices and bestiality, as a reactionary response to foreign cultic practice in the ANE.

Alongside "forbidden degrees" mentioned above, purity laws provide another key to these sexual prohibitions, and recent scholarship has identified the concept of "mixing" as key to understanding the prohibition against the act of male anal sex, because this act can involve the mixing of two defiling emissions—semen and excrement. Although homosexual acts might have had negative associations with "foreign" cults, in biblical terms impermissible sexual acts are judged to be infringements of familial/social boundaries. This can be illustrated by the narrative accounts of Lot and his daughters in Gen 19 and the Levite and his concubine in Judg 19. In these stories the most extreme anti-social behavior is manifested in attempted homosexual gang rape, and this behavior is set in sharp contrast to the obligation to offer hospitality to those who are alien to your homeland. Indeed it is the antithesis of the injunction to "love the alien as yourself" (Lev 19:34). In both stories, in Genesis and in Judges, there is the good host, in both stories there are violent local men, and in both stories women are proffered as a means of diverting the worst atrocity imaginable in that culture: the rape of men by men.

5. Sexual pleasure

Running counter to the restrictions on sexual practices is the biblical theme of sexual pleasure, and the Bible contains many tales of love and passion. Most famous of all is the Song of Songs. This extended love poem probably retained its place in Jewish and Christian canons only by virtue of its allegorical interpretations. Along with its enduring popularity, however, and despite its secular rather than religious content, its language stands in the text as testimony to the passion that animated the relationships of ancient Israelites. The power, even danger, of sexual love, as well as its pleasure, is articulated in Song 8:6 and reflected in the perceived need to regulate sexual desire in the law codes. The relationship between the man and the woman described in this text is one of mutual love and interdependency, in physical and emotional terms. As such it contrasts to biblical literature that describes, and prescribes for, relationships from an Israelite male perspective. The anarchic nature of unbridled passion is well attested in, for example, the story of Joseph and Pharaoh's wife (Gen 39:6-20), Samson and Delilah (Judg 16:4-31), David and Bathsheba (2 Sam 11–12:23); and accounts such as these lend support for Israel's legislation in such personal relationships. The love story of David and Jonathan provides an intimate insight into the emotional dimension of same sex relationships, but this too ends in tragedy (2 Sam 1:26). The biblical ideal for the enjoyment of sexual pleasure is within marriage, "... rejoice in the wife of your youth ... may you be intoxicated always by her love" (Prov 5:18-19). This early passion is encouraged in order to cement the marriage and is recognized in legislation that exempts the newly wedded husband from military service so that he may be "free at home one year, to be happy with his wife" (Deut 24:5).

6. Eunuchs

In biblical accounts of ancient Israel we encounter eunuchs, men who have been castrated and are therefore sexually impotent and incapable of procreation. The Hebrew noun saris (סָרִיס) is used to refer to a court official, and this is its primary meaning in the contexts where we find it in the OT. Saris became associated with the concept of the eunuch because of the type of officers who officiated in the vicinity of the

harem situated within the king's court. Eunuchs were men who could be trusted in the presence of the royal women. Mention of these court officials is common in biblical accounts of Israel's neighbors: Egypt (Gen 40:2), Babylon (Dan 1:3), and Persia (Esth 1:10). The Torah's regulations for priests do not allow anyone who has crushed testicles and is, in effect, a eunuch (Lev 21:20, also Deut 23:1), to hold priestly office. This regulation does not seem to have extended beyond the cult since eunuchs were evident in the royal courts of Israel as well as those of its neighbors, although all of them mentioned may have been foreigners (see e.g., 1 Kgs 22:9; 2 Kgs 8:6; 9:32; 1 Chr 28:1; Jer 38:7).

A passage from Isaiah provides a textual thread between the references to eunuchs in the OT, either as unfortunate males who have had the testicles crushed or as castrated foreign officials and the attitude to sexuality promoted in certain NT texts. As part of a universal eschatological vision of the end time, God promises the righteous eunuchs that they will receive, "a monument and a name better than sons and daughters; I will give them an everlasting name that shall not be cut off" (Isa 56:5).

7. Euphemisms

The use of euphemistic language is the preferred style for biblical writers to represent sexual matters. There is a clear avoidance of words that are considered offensive, and in their place we find words that convey meaning on two levels: the literal and, for those who know the code, the sexual. By disguising the sexual dimension of the texts in this way, at least in the process of articulating the text, if not of receiving it, the sacred and the profane are kept apart. The verbs "to know," and "to uncover" are used to refer to sexual intercourse, and "nakedness" and "feet" indicate sexual organs. Explicit sexual language is avoided primarily in order to maintain purity within the text and its reception rather than for strictly moral purposes. Human emissions associated with sexual practice and stimulated by the imagination were ritually unclean. Key examples of this euphemistic language include, the use of the phrase "to uncover the nakedness" in Lev18–20; the seraphim covering their "feet" in Isaiah 6:2; the first biblical account of human sexual intercourse when "the man knew his wife Eve" in Gen 4:1 (for more examples, see EUPHEMISM).

B. The New Testament
1. Jewish values in Greek and Roman contexts

The attitudes and regulations regarding sex and sexual practices largely remain in place as the framework for Judaism in the Second Temple Period. Within the context of the Greco-Roman world, Judaism is distinctive as a religious tradition that is concerned with sexual matters, and, furthermore, presumes to regulate for individuals' lives in this respect. The NT provides importance evidence, not only for emergent Christianity in the 1st cent. but also for Judaism of this time. The apostle Paul reflects the pietism of his Jewish background in his horrified reaction to the news of forbidden sexual liaisons in the Corinthian community: "It is actually reported that there is sexual immorality among you, and of a kind that is not found even among pagans; for a man is living with his father's wife" (1 Cor 5:1). The urban Pauline communities consisted of both Jews and Gentiles, making more evident the differing cultural and religious attitudes to sexual behavior. Paul comments adversely on lesbian as well as and male homosexual practices, although the former acts are not mentioned in the Torah (Rom 1:26-27). Also, men as well as women are culpable in the act of fornication (1 Cor 6:9). Paul's version of what should be considered forbidden acts reflects the permissive urban contexts of the Roman Empire that extend far beyond what could have been imagined from agrarian Israelite society.

2. Imminent eschatology, celibacy, and household codes

Early Christian attitudes to sex that negated central social values, namely marriage and procreation—alien attitudes to both Jewish and pagan cultures—have to be understood within an eschatological context. Thus, in addition to Jewish standards for sexual behavior, imminent eschatology also had a significant influence on earliest Christianity's perspectives on sexual practice. In the light of the expected PAROUSIA, earliest Christianity called on its adherents to abrogate former family ties and actively discouraged them from creating their own families. The apocalyptic language that describes the horror and devastation of the last days, for families as well as nations, makes aspiring to family life anomalous (Mark 13:12). Jesus is recorded as redefining family in terms of common faith rather than blood-ties (Mark 3:32-35). Paul advises the unmarried members of Corinthian community against marriage, unless they are unable to control their sexual appetites and, thereby, be led into immoral acts: "to the unmarried and the widows I say it is well for them to remain unmarried as I am. But if they are not practicing self-control, they should marry. For it is better to marry than to be aflame with passion" (1 Cor 7:8-9). Paul is most anxious for his communities to avoid sexual immorality (porneia πορνεία) (1 Cor 7:2), and there is little evidence to suggest that he offers an alternative "pure" form of sexual passion in its place, the sexual pleasure expressed within marriage and idealized in the OT. Paul's call for CELIBACY is made in light of the imminent return of Christ and the dawn of the new age, "... the appointed time has grown short; from now on, let those who even have wives be as though they had none ..." (1 Cor 7:29). He views sexual appetite as a distraction from the urgent need to further the gospel. For brothers and sisters in Christ within the family of God, procreation was unnecessary; new siblings were born of the Spirit, not the flesh. In early Christianity the procreative purpose of marriage, together with sexual

relations, so clearly articulated in the OT's narrative and law is redundant in such an eschatological climate.

In the NT, the righteous faithful who choose furtherance of the gospel over sexual pleasure and the procreation of children will be raised up, like Christ (Rom 6:4), at the end time, "for the present form of this world is passing away" (1 Cor 7:31, also Rom 13:11-14). In a similar vein a passage in Matthew's Gospel expresses the concept of being called by faith to be a eunuch, a way of inferring celibacy, "For there are eunuchs who have been so from birth, and there are eunuchs who have been made eunuchs by others, and there are eunuchs who have made themselves eunuchs for the sake of the kingdom of heaven. Let anyone accept this who can" (Matt 19:12). Interestingly, the Ethiopian eunuch mentioned in Acts was reading from Isaiah, albeit Isa 53:7-8, when Philip approached him and encouraged him to be baptized. The description of this individual matches the role of eunuchs described in the royal courts of the ANE, as an official of the queen's court.

In contrast to Roman legislation and ideals for family life, which were quite similar to those of the OT and were intended to strengthen the power of the empire from its foundations upward, the early Christian attitude that rejects marriage and family was regarded in terms of political action against the state, as well as "anti-social." This challenge to the very foundation of the empire deepens our understanding of the external perception of Christianity in the first centuries. A political threat is posed by the practices emerging in early Christian communities when they are seen from the Roman perspective.

While communities existed that nurtured an imminent eschatological worldview, and continued with these beliefs into the second century with movements such as Montanism, alongside them within the empire were communities adapting more to the challenges of existing in the present than anticipating a cataclysmic event in the near future. This pluralism characterized earliest Christianity; indeed, it is more accurate to discuss early "Christianities" rather than try to create an artificial monolithic picture of belief and practice during these early years. Evidence from the NT reveals clear divergence in attitudes to marriage and celibacy between communities, especially those in receipt of Pauline pastoral letters termed "deutero-Pauline" (e.g., Colossians, Ephesians) and those regarded as recipients of authentic letters from the Apostle. While the former reflect a community aspiring to an internal structure in line with social organization across the empire, the latter suggest communities eagerly looking forward to the culmination of God's messianic plan to overturn that status quo. These divergent worldviews had direct impact on how members of the communities lived their lives. Within the millenarian groups marriage, sexual relation, and procreation were subordinated to the urgency to preach the gospel (1 Cor 7), whereas, within other groups, marriage was invested with divine purpose. In a context where persecution was a lived reality, the urge to conform and therefore present a harmless face to the wider world would have been strong (Titus 3:1). To avoid a situation where women community members scandalized society by rejecting relationships and marriage in place of missionary work, some communities developed a theology for Christian marriage that ensured women conformed to the norms of life in Greco-Roman society. The "HOUSEHOLD CODES" (Eph 5:21-6:9; Col 3:18-4:1; 1 Pet 3:1-7) bear a striking resemblance to Aristotelian ideas on natural order (*Politics* 1.1260a) with the added ingredient of divine sanction and blessing. The Christian family, and the hierarchical relationships within it, becomes the microcosm for the relationship between Christ and the church. An air of permanence rather than imminence pervades these communities. The church, like the family, must mirror social order, with a model of male leadership clearly in place (1 Tim 3:1-7) and female members carrying out their natural duty. In complete contrast to Paul's churches, where women were leaders and were encouraged to remain unmarried and celibate, a particular interpretation of the Eden narrative provided the theological underpinning not only for Christian marriage but also for procreation as the purpose for and salvation of women. Adam was formed before Eve, but she became the first transgressor (1 Tim 2:13-14; compare Gen 1–2). However a woman "will be saved through child bearing," so long as she has faith, love, and holiness characterized by modesty (1 Tim 2:15). *See* MARRIAGE, NT.

Bibliography: A. Bach, ed. *Women in the OT* (1999); M. Bal. *Lethal Love: Feminist Biblical Readings of Biblical Love Stories.* (1987); M. Beard, J. North, and S. Price. *Religions of Rome.* Vol.1: *A History* (1998); S. Bigger. "The Family Laws of Leviticus 18 in Their Setting," *JBL* 98 (1979) 187–203; P. Bird. "The Harlot as Heroine: Narrative Art and Social Presupposition in Three Old Testament Texts," *Semeia* 46 (1989) 119–39; D. Boyarin. "Are There Any Jews in 'The History of Sexuality'?" *Journal of the History of Sexuality* 3 (1995) 333–55; M. Brett. *Genesis: Procreation and the Politics of Identity* (2000); B. J. Brooten. *Love Between Women: Early Christian Responses to Female Homoeroticism* (1996); V. Burrus. *Begotten, Not Made: Conceiving Manhood in Late Antiquity* (2000); C. Carmichael. *The Laws of Deuteronomy* (1974); A. Clark. *Desire: A History of European Sexuality* (2008); E. A. Clark. *Reading Renunciation: Asceticism and Scripture in Early Christianity* (1999); D. J. A. Clines. *What Does Eve Do to Help? And Other Readerly Questions to the Old Testament* (1990); M. Douglas. *Leviticus as Literature* (1999); H. Eilberg-Schwartz, ed. *People of the Body: Jews and Judaism from an Embodied Perspective* (1992); E. Fantham et al. *Women in the Classical World* (1994); L. Foxhall and J. Salmon, eds. *When Men Were Men: Masculinity, Power and Identity in Classical Antiquity* (1998); D. B. Martin. *The Corinthian Body* (1995); D. B. Martin. *Sex and the Single Savior* (2006); H. Moxnes, ed. *Constructing Early Christian Families: Family as Social Reality and Metaphor* (1997); S. M. Olyan. "'And with a Male You Shall Not Lie the Lying Down of a Woman': On the Meaning and Significance of Leviticus 18.22 and 20.13." *Journal of the History of Sexuality* 5.2 (1994) 179–206; I. N. Rashkow. *Taboo or not Taboo: Sexuality and Family in the Hebrew Bible* (2000); D. F. Sawyer. *God, Gender and the Bible* (2002); D. F. Sawyer. *Women and Religion in the First Christian Centuries* (1996); K. Stone. *Sex, Honor and Power in the Deuteronomistic History* (1996); G. C. Streete. *The Strange Woman: Power and Sex in the Bible* (1997); P. Trible. *God and the Rhetoric of Sexuality* (1978); M. Wyke, ed. *Gender and the Body in the Ancient Mediterranean* (1998).

DEBORAH F. SAWYER

SEXUAL ABUSE. Stories about and laws concerning sexual abuse certainly appear in the Bible. Although the NT contains scattered references to such activity, the majority of the relevant material occurs in the OT. From the brutal violation of the Levite's concubine in Judg 19:22-26, to Amnon's forced intercourse with his half-sister TAMAR in 2 Sam 13:1-22, to reports of women's treatment following battle (see, e.g., Judg 5:30; Isa 13:16; Zech 14:2), women's susceptibility to sexual violation comes across clearly. Men also faced danger. Both Gen 19 and Judg 19, for instance, depict males as targets of sexual aggression. Additionally, texts on appropriate and inappropriate sexual contact (see Lev 18; 20 or Deut 22:13-21) outline legal approaches to these issues.

Ancient understandings of sex and sexual violence, however, differ markedly from modern ideas. While forcible sexual intercourse certainly happened in the cultures that produced these texts, such acts most often receive definition as property infringement. Deuteronomy 22 offers two examples—one for engaged and one for unengaged virgins.

In the first instance, an engaged virgin has sexual intercourse (shakhav שָׁכַב) with a man other than her fiancé within the city limits. Unless she cries out for help, the law stipulates stoning for both parties (Deut 22:23-24). She dies for failing to seek assistance, while he stands condemned for violating or humiliating ('anah עָנָה) another man's wife. In short, they commit a crime equated to adultery. Note how vv. 25-27 offer a variant. If the offense occurs in the open country, the man alone dies because no one could hear the presumed cries of the woman and rescue her. The text lacks the term for humiliation ('anah), instead absolving the woman of any blame or consequence and likening the man's action to murder.

Deuteronomy 22:28-29 describes a man who meets, seizes (tafas תָּפַשׂ), and sleeps with (shakhav) an unengaged virgin. Caught in the act, neither receives death.

The law here stipulates that the man pays the woman's father fifty shekels of silver and must marry her and remain married to her. The money functions as a bride price and alleviates the humiliation ('anah) of the woman by compensating the financially and socially wounded party—her father. A nonvirginal, unwed daughter loses her exchange value; no longer suitable for marriage with another family, she brings shame upon her own kin unless the perpetrator takes and keeps her as his wife.

When these texts label a woman as violated or humiliated, they most often refer to compromised social status. Marriage can resolve the issue for the unwed woman, as seen above. Once wed, she becomes a viable part of the social system again. But the violation of a wife or an engaged woman raises concerns about the production of an unquestioned familial line. Unless forced to commit the sexual act, she becomes an adulteress and, by law, deserves death. In this cultural setting, women sexually active outside of marriage—and thus apart from the accepted family structure—get labeled as whores. Few options existed for women in such circumstances.

The perspective of women rarely receives mention in these laws or in texts that depict what contemporary readers often interpret as sexual abuse. Only the narrative concerning David's daughter TAMAR gives voice to a woman's refusal to a sexual encounter. When approached by her half-brother Amnon requesting sex (shakhav; 2 Sam 13:11), Tamar begs him not to humiliate her ('anah; v. 12; NRSV, "forced"). He, however, uses his superior strength to attack her ("But he would not listen to her; and being stronger than she, he forced her ['anah] and lay [shakhav] with her"; v. 14). By contrast, the Levite's concubine in Judg 19 never speaks. She is portrayed as simply enduring the assault and struggling unsuccessfully for access back into the home of her host (v. 27).

The lack of interest in the woman's point of view makes Gen 34—the story of Jacob's daughter DINAH—particularly difficult to read. Her interaction with Shechem indicates in v. 2 that he took her (laqakh לְקַח), slept with her (shakhav), and thus humiliated her ('anah). Subsequently, he negotiates with her family for a marriage (vv. 8-12), but the writers indicate Dinah's status as ritually unclean (vv. 5, 27) and present her brothers' claim that Shechem treats their sister as a whore (v. 31). Dinah lives in Shechem's household throughout the story, but the text records nothing of her reaction to the situation. Whether Shechem seized her and forced her into sex—acting on his prerogative as a prince in the land—or if she consented to the encounter without the benefit of marriage remains unknown.

These stories and others highlight the sexual vulnerability of women. David's initial encounter with BATHSHEBA comes after he spies her performing a ritual bath and orders her brought to him (2 Sam 11:2-4). Even though he knows of her marriage, he sleeps with and impregnates her. Could she refuse the king? Absalom, during his coup d'état against his father, sleeps with all of his father's concubines (2 Sam 16:22) to demonstrate his fitness to serve as king.

Women gain status through their relationship with men and the children they produce. No consideration of their needs or desires appears; their concerns center solely on place in the household. In fact, the narrators present Tamar's objection to Amnon as prompted only by his suggestion of sex outside of marriage. They underplay the physical assault and emphasize instead her diminished social status (see 2 Sam 13:20b, "So Tamar remained, a desolate woman, in her brother Absalom's house"). Activities associated with war heightened the danger for women. Judges 5 describes "a girl or two for every man" (v. 30a) as part of the spoils for the victors. Zechariah 14:2 describes the rape of women (shaghel שָׁגֵל) as part of the fall of Jerusalem, as does Lam 5:11 ('anah). Metaphorical assaults also occur on cities, countries, and peoples imagined as women (see Jer 13:22; Ezek 16:37; 23:10, for examples). Deuteronomy 20:14 affirms the right of the men of Israel to take women as booty, although Deut 21:10-14 says that if such a woman becomes a wife, she can never be sold as a slave.

Although not nearly as prevalent, several biblical texts also mention potential sexual abuse of men. Genesis 19 and Judg 19 present situations where men of a town seek to assault male guests in their cities—even though no such crime occurs in either case. The language in the Samson saga describes him as humiliated ('anah, Judg 16:19) by Delilah's actions. His punishment at the hands of the Philistines—"he ground at the mill in the prison" (Judg 16:21)—might indicate sexual violation (compare Job 31:9-10; Lam 5:13). A few passages depict God as attacking men in words suggesting sexual abuse. Most famously in Jer 20:7 the prophet complains that God seduces and overpowers him. Likewise, in Job 30:11 the main character contends God looses his bowstring and humiliates ('anah) him. The feminization of these men brings shame upon them, not because of any sexual act, but because of their loss of social status.

Unlike contemporary understandings, sexual abuse in the biblical material most often violates not the person, but their standing in the community. Although associated with shame and humiliation, the crime frequently rests in the assault on the property of a man with status. Women and men of lesser stature possessed no legal recourse since they held no standing from which to press a case. No word for "RAPE," then, exists in biblical Hebrew. The writers of the OT simply impressed a variety of verbal roots into service to describe violent, nonconsensual sexual acts. Modern readers must, therefore, consider both ancient understandings of the cultural and social conditions defining sexual abuse in balance with modern concerns when exploring the biblical material.

Bibliography: Alice Bach, ed. *Women in the Hebrew Bible: A Reader* (1999); Tikva Frymer-Kensky. "Virginity in the Bible." *Gender and the Law in the Hebrew Bible and the Ancient Near East.* Victor H. Matthews, Bernard M. Levinson, and Tikva Frymer-Kensky, eds. (1998) 79–86; Sandie Gravett. "Reading Rape in the Hebrew Bible: A Consideration of Language." JSOT 38 (2004) 279–99; James E. Miller. "Sexual Offences in Genesis." JSOT 90 (2000) 41–53; Gail Corrington Streete. *The Strange Woman: Power and Sex in the Bible* (1997); Edward Ullendorff. *The Bawdy Bible* (1978); Harold C. Washington. "Lest He Die in Battle and Another Man Take Her: Violence and the Construction of Gender Laws in Deuteronomy 20–22." *Gender and the Law in the Hebrew Bible and the Ancient Near East.* Victor H. Matthews, Bernard M. Levinson, and Tikva Frymer-Kensky, eds. (1998) 185–213; Renita Weems. *Battered Love: Marriage, Sex, and Violence in the Hebrew Prophets* (1995); E. J. van Wolde. "Does 'innâ Mean Rape? A Semantic Analysis of a Controversial Word." VT 52 (2002) 528–44.

SANDIE GRAVETT

SHAALABBIN. *See* SHAALBIM.

SHAALBIM shay-al'bim [שַׁעַלְבִים *shaʿalvim*]. A town in the allotment of Dan. It is called "Shaalabbin" (shaʿalabbin [שַׁעֲלַבִּין]) in the account of Dan's territory in Josh 19:42. Judges 1:35 explains that the Danites were unable to capture Shaalbim from the Amorites. Solomon's second administrative district (1 Kgs 4:9) included Shaalbim and three other towns. *See* SHAALBON.

Shaalbim has been variously identified with Salaba (within the borders of Sabaste), Selbi, and Salbit in the northwestern Aijalon valley. N. Avigad and E. Sukenik excavated at Salbit, uncovering a striking number of mosaics in a structure dated to the 4th cent. CE. On the basis of an inscription in the mosaics and their iconography, scholars assume that the building was once a Samaritan synagogue.

Bibliography: A. F. Rainey and R. S. Notley. *The Sacred Bridge: Carta's Atlas of the Biblical World* (2000); J. E. Taylor, ed. *The Onomasticon by Eusebius of Caesarea* (2003).

JOSEPH R. CATHEY

SHAALBON shay-al'bon [שַׁעַלְבֹנִי *shaʿalvoni*]. Literally, "Shaalbonite," the residence of Eliahba, one of David's Thirty (2 Sam 23:32; 1 Chr 11:33). It may be the same as the city called Shaalbim. *See* DAVID'S CHAMPIONS.

SHAALIM shay'uh-lim [שַׁעֲלִים *shaʿalim*]. A young Saul, searching for his father's lost donkeys, passed through the land of Shaalim (1 Sam 9:4). The text seems to locate Shaalim in the territory of Benjamin, although the

exact location is unknown. While not supported by textual evidence, it is possible that SHAALBIM is meant.

MICHAEL G. VANZANT

SHAAPH shay'af [שַׁעַף *shaʿaf*]. 1. The youngest son of Jahdai (1 Chr 2:47). Though the sons of Jahdai are listed among the descendants of Caleb, the text does not make clear the genealogical connection between Jahdai and Caleb, rendering the ancestry of Shaaph ambiguous as well.

2. A son of Caleb, born to his concubine Maacah (1 Chr 2:49); father of Madmannah.

T. DELAYNE VAUGHN

SHAARAIM shay'uh-ray'im [שַׁעֲרַיִם *shaʿarayim*]. A town in Judah (Josh 15:36), probably located along the Wadi es-Sant, near Socoh and Azekah. After defeating the Philistines, the Israelites pursued them from Shaaraim to Gath and Ekron (1 Sam 17:52). The town was inhabited by Simeonites, according to 1 Chr 4:31; perhaps it is the "Sharuhen" of Josh 19:6.

Bibliography: Zechariah Kallai. *Historical Geography of the Bible* (1986); Anson F. Rainey and R. Steven Notley. *The Sacred Bridge: Carta's Atlas of the Biblical World* (2006).

JOSEPH R. CATHEY

SHAASHGAZ shay-ash'gaz [שַׁעֲשְׁגַז *shaʿashghaz*]. The eunuch responsible for the second harem where King Ahasuerus' concubines reside (Esth 2:14). The LXX identifies both Hegai, the overseer of the harem of virgins, and Shaashgaz as Gai (Add Esth 2:8, 14).

SHABBETHAI shab'uh-thi [שַׁבְּתַי *shabbethay*; Σαββαταῖος *Sabbataios*]. The name derives from the noun "Sabbath" and may mean "one who belongs to the Sabbath," e.g., a priest. Shabbethai was a leader of the Levites (Neh 11:16) who assisted Ezra in prosecuting Israelites who had taken foreign wives (Ezra 10:15; 1 Esd 9:14). He also served as an interpreter when Ezra read the law (Neh 8:7; 1 Esd 9:48).

JOSEPH R. CATHEY

SHADDAI. *See* ALMIGHTY; EL SHADDAI; GOD, NAMES OF.

SHADE. *See* SHADOW.

SHADES [רְפָאִים *refaʾim*]. In the ANE, shades, or spirits of the dead, were believed to have some power to cause harm to the living. This kind of power is minimal or nonexistent in the OT. In fact, the OT is not very interested in the underworld or its inhabitants (*see* DEATH, OT; SHEOL). *Shades* is often used in parallel to death or the dead, and the term appears only in exilic or postexilic contexts. *Shades* does not occur in the Apocrypha or the NT.

The biblical shades are neither named nor associated with any founder or patron. They simply exist as lifeless, nebulous, shadowy creatures in the underworld and never have any contact with the living. They are not consulted in necromancy, nor invited to feasts. They tremble before Yahweh (Job 26:5), but they are unable to praise him (Ps 88:10 [Heb. 88:11]). They are so lethargic that they must be roused when a newcomer arrives in Sheol (Isa 14:9-10). Connections have been drawn between biblical shades and the Ugaritic rpum (see REPHAIM), but this is uncertain.

Sometimes biblical writers associate a moral aspect with shades. A proverb warns that "whoever wanders from the way of understanding will rest in the assembly of the shades" (Prov 21:16, author's trans.; NRSV, "the dead"). The ways of the "loose woman" or adulteress lead to the shades (Prov 2:18), while the guests of the "foolish woman" of Prov 9:18 are "shades" (alternative translation of "the dead"; see NRSV footnote). The shades include oppressive rulers or enemy kings destroyed by Yahweh (Isa 26:14). Yet, both wicked and righteous seem to be included in the promise of Isa 26:19: "Your dead shall live, their corpses shall rise. O dwellers in the dust, awake and sing for joy ... the earth will give birth to the shades" (alternative translation of "to those long dead"; see NRSV footnote). See IMMORTALITY.

Bibliography: Philip S. Johnston. *Shades of Sheol* (2002).

JAMES C. MOYER

SHADOW [צֵל tsel; ἀποσκίασμα aposkiasma, σκιά skia]. The word *shadow* is used figuratively to refer to something protective (e.g., the king's [Lam 4:20] and especially God's protection [Ps 91:1-2], including over the poor and needy [Isa 25:4]). Yahweh is depicted as a large bird whose wings protect (Pss 17:8; 36:7). Yahweh's hand also provides protection (Isa 49:2).

As a shadow moves and eventually disappears, so too the transitory nature of human life (Job 14:1-2; Ps 144:4; Eccl 6:12). The days of life are like an evening shadow (Ps 102:11), and those in poor health compare themselves to waning shadows (Ps 109:23). See DEATH, OT.

Shadow (skia) occurs seven times in the NT. In Matt 4:16, "shadow of death" is influenced by Isa 9:2 [Heb. 9:1], as is perhaps Zechariah's prophecy in Luke 1:79, "to give light to those who sit in darkness and in the shadow of death." The idea that the law is the "shadow of what is to come" (Col 2:17; Heb 10:1) originates in Hellenistic religion where a contrast is drawn between the body and the reality. Similarly in Heb 8:5 the Jewish earthly Temple is only a copy and a shadow of the heavenly temple.

Some ancient people, such as the Egyptians, assumed that the shadow of a deity, or one sent by the deity, could have a powerful positive effect upon another person. In Luke 1:35 the angel told Mary that the Most High would overshadow her, and she would become pregnant and bear a child. Slightly different is Acts 5:15 where the Jerusalemites carried the sick out into the street hoping that Peter's shadow would fall on them when he passed with the result that they would be healed. In Jas 1:17, "no ... shadow (aposkiasma) due to change" refers to the consistency of God. *See* LIGHT AND DARKNESS.

JAMES C. MOYER

SHADRACH, MESHACH, ABEDNEGO shad´rak, mee´shak, uh-bed´ni-goh [שַׁדְרַךְ shadhrakh, מֵישַׁךְ meshakh, עֲבֵד נְגוֹ ʿavedh negho]. Shadrach, Meshach, and Abednego were, according to Dan 1:3-7, companions of Daniel, who, along with him, are taken into the court of the Babylonian king Nebuchadnezzar during the time of the Israelite exile in Babylon. They are described as being "of the royal family"; v. 6 states they are of the tribe of Judah and of the nobility, "young men without physical defect and handsome, versed in every branch of wisdom, endowed with knowledge and insight, and competent to serve in the king's palace" (Dan 1:3-4). These four, apparently along with many other young men (Dan 1:10, 13), were to be taught the literature and language of the "Chaldeans" for three years in preparation for positions within the king's court (Dan 1:4-5).

Nebuchadnezzar's chief eunuch, Ashpenaz, changes their Hebrew names to Babylonian names as part of the grooming process. Daniel, whose Hebrew name means "God judges," becomes Belteshazzar, an Akkadian word meaning "protect his life" or "protect the life of the king"; Hananiah, "God is gracious," becomes Shadrach, meaning "command of Aku" (a Mesopotamian lunar deity); Mishael, "who is that which God is," is called Meshach, meaning "who is that which Aku is"; and Azariah, whose Hebrew name means "God is my help," becomes Abednego, which means "servant of Nabu" (Nebuchadnezzar's personal deity).

The adventures of the four companions are recorded in Dan 1–3. Even though given a daily ration of rich food and wine, they strive to remain faithful to their religious traditions and dietary laws. They challenge their palace guard to give them only vegetables to eat and water to drink for ten days and then to compare their appearances with those of the young men who ate the royal rations. And at the end of the ten days, the four "appeared better and fatter than all the young men who had been eating the royal rations" (Dan 1:15). When the four are brought before Nebuchadnezzar, no others compare with them and the king stations them within his court. Eventually Daniel is made the ruler over the whole province of Babylon while the other three are made administrators in the kingdom (Dan 2:48-49).

In Dan 3, Nebuchadnezzar decrees that all people must bow down and worship a golden image that he had crafted. Disobedience would result in being thrown into "a furnace of blazing fire." When word came to the king that Shadrach, Meshach, and Abednego refuse to worship the image, he commands that they be thrown into the fire, but they are saved by a figure in the fire, described in Dan 3:25 as having "the appearance of a god." Nebuchadnezzar decrees protection for the God of Shadrach, Meshach, and Abednego, saying "there is no other god who is able to deliver in this way" (Dan 3:29), and promotes the three to higher positions within Babylon. In the Greek additions to the book of Daniel, the Prayer of Azariah and the Song of the Three Young Men adds the words spoken by the three while they are in the fiery furnace.

First Maccabees 2:59 lists Azariah, Hananiah, and Mishael among those who are faithful to God. *See* AZARIAH, PRAYER OF; DANIEL, ADDITIONS TO; DANIEL, BOOK OF; NEBUCHADNEZZAR, NEBU-CHADREZZAR; SONG OF THE THREE JEWS.

NANCY DECLAISSÉ-WALFORD

SHAGEE shay´gee [שָׁגֵה shagheh]. In the MT, 1 Chr 11:34 lists Shagee the Hararite as the father of Jonathan, one of the "Thirty" among DAVID'S CHAMPIONS. The LXX gives his name as Sola. In 2 Sam 23:11, 32-33 Jonathan's father is named Shammah in the LXX, and the MT omits "son of," listing both Jonathan and Shammah among David's warriors but not designating Shammah as Jonathan's father.

JOAN E. COOK, SC

SHAHARAIM shay´huh-ray´im [שַׁחֲרַיִם shakharayim]. One of the descendants of Benjamin, although the relationship is not specified (1 Chr 8:8). Shaharaim's descendants were said to have inhabited Moab.

SHAHAZUMAH shay´huh-zoo´muh [שַׁחֲצִימָה shakhatsimah, שַׁחֲצוּמָה shakhatsumah]. One of the border towns and villages mentioned as delimiting the allotment of Issachar (Josh 19:22). As described, the territory of Issachar stretched to Shahazumah, Tabor, along the Jordan, and down to Beth-shemesh, among the sixteen villages or unwalled hamlets listed in Issachar's territory. The ancient site has not been identified and, from the description in Joshua, must be located along the region of the Jordan.

CHANNA COHEN STUART

SHAKE [מוֹט mot, נוּד nudh, נוּט nut, נוּעַ nuaʿ, רָחַף rakhaf, רָעַד raʿadh, רָעַשׁ raʿash; ἐκτινάσσω ektinassō, κινέω kineō, σαλεύω saleuō, σείω seiō]. The concept of shaking is represented by a rather significant number of terms in the OT and NT, and consequently there is a variety of textual settings and scenarios of which shaking is a part. Cataclysmic shaking is represented by the Hebrew root rʿsh (רעשׁ): the earth (2 Sam 22:8; Ps 18:7), the foundations of the earth (Isa 24:18), the heavens (Joel 2:10), the heavens and earth (Joel 3:16), the mountains (Jer 4:24), and the coastlands (Ezek 26:15). Exodus 20:18 uses nwʿ (נוע) to describe Israel's response to the giving of the Decalogue and Yahweh's shaking the nation as with a sieve (Amos 9:9). Human bones shake (Job's, Job 4:14; Jeremiah's, Jer 23:9). Heads shake in derision in Lam 2:15 and metaphorically in Jer 48:27.

Common LXX and NT terms include seiō of earth and heaven (Heb 12:26), ektinassō of dust from the foot (Matt 10:14; Mark 6:11; Luke 9:5), kineō of the head in derision (Matt 27:39; Mark 15:29), and saleuō of the powers of heaven (Matt 24:29; Mark 13:25; Luke 21:26).

JOHN I. LAWLOR

SHALEM [שָׁלֵם shalem; Σαλήμ Salēm]. A Canaanite god often paired with the god Shahar (shakhar [שַׁחַר], "dawn") in Ugaritic texts. While Shahar represents the dawn, Shalem represents the dusk (or perhaps Venus as the evening star). According to *KTU* 1.23.51-52, Shahar and Shalem were the offspring of the god El, supreme deity of the Ugaritic pantheon.

"Shalem" does not appear as a reference to a deity in the Bible. However, it is likely that Shalem was the patron god from which JERUSALEM received its name ("city of Shalem"; urusalim in the Amarna tablets).

"Shalem" is used as a place name in the MEL-CHIZEDEK narrative of Gen 14:18 (compare Heb 7:1-2); Melchizedek is listed as the king of Salem [shalem in Hebrew, possibly a shortened form of "Jerusalem," and as a priest of El-Elyon ("God Most High"). The identification with Jerusalem is also supported by the occurrence of the place name Shalem in a parallel position with Zion in Ps 76:2 [Heb. 76:3]. Some suggest that shalem in Gen 33:18 should be read as the place name instead of the adverb "safely" (as translated in the NRSV). Also, a "valley of Salem" (based on the Greek spelling) is mentioned in Jdt 4:4.

Etymologically, the Semitic root shlm (שׁלם) means "be completed," "come to an end," "keep peace," "remain healthy." *See* SHALOM.

JAMIE A. BANISTER

SHALISHAH shuh-li´shuh [שָׁלִשָׁה shalishah]. Saul's search for his father's lost donkeys led him from Gibeah through the hill country of Ephraim, the "land of Shalishah," on through the land of Shaalim, the land of Benjamin, and finally to Zuph (1 Sam 9:4-5). These geographic notations seem to place Shalishah north of Ephraim on a circuitous journey leading back south to Benjamin, although the itinerary is vague. Approximately 30 km northeast of Jaffe, possibly near Khirbet Kefr Thilth, the city of BAAL-SHALISHAH (2 Kgs 4:42) may provide the location of a Baal cultic site in the land of Shalishah.

MICHAEL G. VANZANT

SHALLECHETH, GATE OF shal´uh-kith [שַׁעַר שַׁלֶּכֶת shaʿar shallekheth]. Hosah's family (compare 1 Chr 26:10; "Shuppim" is an error) was made gatekeepers for the western wall of the temple precincts, "at the gate of Shallecheth on the ascending road" (1 Chr 26:16). This may be the same as the "SUR GATE" (2 Kgs 11:6) and/ or the "GATE OF THE FOUNDATION" (2 Chr 23:5).

JAMES RILEY STRANGE

SHALLUM shal'uhm [שַׁלּוּם shallum; Σαλημος Salēmos]. The name of several persons, most of them associated with the Levitical priesthood. 1. The youngest son of Naphtali, the son of Jacob and Bilhah (1 Chr 7:13). His name appears as Shillem in Gen 46:24 and Num 26:49.

2. A descendant of Simeon and the father of Mibsam (1 Chr 4:25).

3. A Judahite, he was the son of Sismai and the father of Jekamiah (1 Chr 2:40-41).

4. The son of Zadok and the father of Hilkiah, the high priest (1 Chr 6:12-13 [Heb. 5:38-39]; 9:11). He was one of the ancestors of Ezra (Ezra 7:2; 1 Esd 8:1; 2 Esd 1:1; Bar 1:7). His name appears as Meshullam in 1 Chr 9:11 and Neh 11:11; 12:13.

5. The son of Jabesh, he was the sixteenth king of the northern kingdom of Israel (745 BCE). He killed Zechariah, king of Israel, the son of Jeroboam II, and assumed the throne but he reigned in Samaria only one month (2 Kgs 15:10-15). He was killed and succeeded by Menahem.

6. The father of Jehizkiah, one of the leaders of the tribe of Ephraim (2 Chr 28:12) in the days of Ahaz, king of Judah.

7. The son of Tikvah, he was the husband of the prophetess Huldah (2 Kgs 22:14) and a temple official in charge of the ritual vestment used in the Temple by the priests and Levites. Shallum appears as the son of Tokhath in 2 Chr 34:22.

8. The youngest son of Josiah (1 Chr 3:15), he became king of Judah after the death of his father in 609 BCE (Jer 22:11). Known also as Jehoahaz, his mother was Hamutal, the daughter of Jeremiah of Libnah (2 Kgs 23:30-31). It is possible that Shallum was his given name and that Jehoahaz, a name containing the divine name, was his throne name. Shallum reigned three months in Judah, whereupon Pharaoh Neco of Egypt deposed him and took him to Egypt where he died (2 Kgs 23:30-34).

9. The father of Hanamel and an uncle of the prophet Jeremiah (Jer 32:7). During the siege of Jerusalem by the Babylonians, Hanamel asked his cousin Jeremiah to buy his property in their hometown of Anathoth.

10. The father of Maaseiah, a Levitical priest in the days of Jeremiah (Jer 35:4). Maaseiah was "the keeper of the threshold," one who kept watch over the entrance to the Temple.

11. A Levite and a descendant of Kore, he was one of the gatekeepers in the Temple (1 Chr 9:17). He seems to be identical with the Shallum mentioned in 1 Chr 9:19, 31. Shallum probably was the head of a family of gatekeepers, mentioned in Ezra 2:42; Neh 7:45; and

1 Esd 5:28, whose descendants returned from the exile in Babylon. He is called Shelemiah in 1 Chr 26:14; Meshullam in Neh 12:25; and Meshelemiah in 1 Chr 9:21. He probably was the Levite and gatekeeper of the Temple who married a foreign wife and was forced to divorce her (Ezra 10:24).

12. A Levite and a descendant of Binnui who had married a foreign wife and sent her away in the days of Ezra (Ezra 10:42).

13. The son of Hallohesh and a "ruler of half the district of Jerusalem," he and his daughters helped repair the walls of Jerusalem (Neh 3:12).

14. The son of Col-hozeh, he was the administrator of the district of Mizpah during the days of Nehemiah. His name is spelled as Shallun (in Hebrew), possibly a variant of Shallum. He rebuilt the Fountain Gate and repaired the wall of the Pool of Shelah located in the king's garden, as far as the stairs that go down from the City of David (Neh 3:15).

CLAUDE F. MARIOTTINI

SHALMAI shal'mi [שַׁלְמָי shalmay, שַׂמְלַי shamlay]. The sons of Shalmai are recognized in Neh 7:48 and Ezra 2:46 (where the name is Shamlai shamlay) as one of the families who returned to Judah from the Babylonian exile together with Zerubbabel in the Persian period and who participated in Israelite religious life as cultic functionaries called the NETHINIM (NRSV, "temple servants"), a class of individuals given over to assist the Levites (Ezra 8:20).

JASON R. TATLOCK

SHALMAN shal'muhn [שַׁלְמָן shalman]. Name of a king whose destruction of BETH-ARBEL is compared to the coming destruction of Israel: "as Shalman destroyed Beth-arbel" (Hos 10:14). The king and location of battle, apparently known to Hosea's audience, is otherwise unattested. Most scholars locate Beth-arbel at the site of Irbid in Gilead, but the identity of Shalman is more debatable. Some scholars believe Shalman is a variant or corruption of SHALMANESER, because Shalmaneser V campaigned against Samaria (726–722 BCE) and could have destroyed Beth-arbel along the way. This view, however, makes the text too late for Hosea's prophecies. Others have proposed that it was Shalmaneser III, whose destruction of Damascus (841 BCE) Hosea invoked as a picture of judgment. Finally, other scholars point to Salamanu, a Moabite king found in a tribute list of Tiglath-pileser III. This suggestion is supported by Moabite military activity further south in the Transjordan (Amos 2:1-3) as well as Moabite raids into Israel (2 Kgs 13:20).

RYAN N. ROBERTS

SHALMANESER shal'muh-nee'zuhr [שַׁלְמַנְאֶסֶר shalman'eser; Ενεμεσσαρος Enemessaros]. Five Assyrian kings go by the name Shalmaneser (Akk. Shulmanu-asaredu: "the god Shulman is preeminent"), the first reigning from 1273–1244 BCE and the last from 726–722 BCE. Of these five, two are particularly important for Israelite history—Shalmaneser III and Shalmaneser V—but only the latter is referred to by name in the OT (2 Kgs 17:3; 18:9). 1. Shalmaneser III, the son and successor of Ashurnasirpal II, ruled Assyria from 858–824 BCE. No other king left more inscriptions and annals than he; and he was apparently the first Assyrian king to summarize his military campaigns by order of his regnal year—a common practice among later monarchs. His father bequeathed a large and powerful kingdom to Shalmaneser III, but upon assuming power, he faced growing unrest. As a result, he was forced to campaign almost every year with a total of thirty-four campaigns recorded, many to the west. It was there that Shalmaneser faced a north Syrian coalition under the leadership of Bit Adini. After finally defeating this group and annexing Bit Adini to his empire, Shalmaneser faced another coalition, this one under the leadership of Hadadezer of Damascus, Irhuleni of Hamath, and, notably, AHAB of Israel. According to the Kurkh Monolith, which records this event and is the earliest mention of the northern kingdom of Israel and its king, Ahab is credited with 2,000 chariots and 10,000 soldiers, by far the largest chariot brigade in the coalition, equal to that of Assyria itself. The battle between these forces took place at Qarqar in 853 BCE, Shalmaneser's sixth regnal year. Shalmaneser's records claim the victory, saying he killed some 25,000 people, but scholars have questioned the accuracy of this statement largely because the king did not push further west at this time and because later records indicate he faced the same group again three more times in subsequent years. But, despite its prowess, this coalition eventually broke—finally and definitively in 841, when Shalmaneser was able to achieve a decisive victory over them, thereafter receiving tribute from the coalition's constituent groups. This tribute reception is described and depicted in several of the twenty panels on the Black Obelisk (completed ca. 828/27 BCE, see OBELISK, BLACK), where the king of Israel (probably Jehu) is among those shown bringing gifts and doing obeisance to the Assyrian monarch (see *ANEP*, figs. 351–55). This famous depiction remains the only contemporaneous representation of an Israelite king known from antiquity.

2. Shalmaneser V was the son and successor of TIGLATH-PILESER III. Outside the Bible and his role in the destruction of Samaria recorded therein (see 2 Kgs 17:1-41; 18:1-12; compare Tob 1:2; 2 Esd 13:40), little is known of this king and his brief reign. Second Kings 17 recounts that king HOSHEA of Israel became a vassal to Shalmaneser (v. 3) but subsequently rebelled, appealing to help from "King So" (Osorkon IV? or "king of Sais"?) of Egypt and withholding tribute (v. 4). The Assyrian army subsequently besieged Samaria, and, after a three-year siege, the city fell (vv. 5-6a). After Samaria was taken, many of its inhabitants were de-

ported to locales in Assyria and peoples from elsewhere were imported into the Northern Kingdom (vv. 6b, 24; 18:11). Outside the biblical texts, the sack of Samaria is (probably) only mentioned in the Babylonian Chronicle, which indicates it to be the only significant occurrence in Shalmaneser V's rule. Other records, however, indicate that it was SARGON II (721–705 BCE) who took Samaria and deported its inhabitants. While the exact details remain unclear, many scholars synthesize the evidence by suggesting that the city fell in 722, the year of Shalmaneser V's death and Sargon II's ascension, with the former responsible for the city's destruction and the latter the deportation of its inhabitants. More recently, however, scholars have allowed for the possibility that the Babylonian Chronicle is referring to a capture of Samaria prior to 722 BCE and/or that Sargon II's actions against Samaria belong to a later campaign. Whatever the precise case, the chronology seems to demonstrate that later biblical sources that remember Shalmaneser as the deporter of the northern tribes (Tob 1:2; 2 Esd 13:40) or that recount the life of northern exiles "in the days of Shalmaneser" (Tob 1:16; compare v. 13) are mistaken or simply fictive. *See* ISRAEL, HISTORY OF; MESOPOTAMIA.

Bibliography: Bob Becking. *The Fall of Samaria: An Historical and Archaeological Study* (1992); A. Kirk Grayson. *Assyrian and Babylonian Chronicles* (1975); A. Kirk Grayson. *Assyrian Rulers of the Early First Millennium BC II (858–745 B.C.)* (1996); Amélie Kuhrt. *The Ancient Near East* (1995); Gwendolyn Leick. *Who's Who in the Ancient Near East* (1999); Shigeo Yamada. *The Construction of the Assyrian Empire: A Historical Study of the Inscriptions of Shalmanesar III (859–824 B.C.) Relating to His Campaigns to the West* (2000); K. Lawson Younger Jr. "The Fall of Samaria in Light of Recent Research." *CBQ* 61 (1999) 461–82; K. Lawson Younger Jr. "Sargon II (2.118)." *COS* 2 (2000) 293–300; K. Lawson Younger Jr. "Shalmaneser III (2.113)." *COS* 2 (2000) 261–72.

BRENT A. STRAWN

SHALOM shah-lohm´ [שָׁלוֹם shalom]. The root shlm (שׁלם) has many meanings ranging from the basic conceptual notion of well-being, safety, and contentment to the more traditional understanding of shlm as a status absent of warfare and violence.

People go or travel in safety (Gen 26:29) and can die in peace (Gen 15:15). Shalom expresses greeting and personal blessing (Gen 29:6; 37:14; Num 6:26; 1 Sam 1:17; 25:6; 2 Sam 11:7), victory in warfare (2 Sam 8:10; e.g., after offering "peace" to a city, Deut 20), or "surrender" (1 Kgs 4:24).

The term comes to be used as "safety" in many contexts, suggesting freedom from animal predators or human intruders (e.g., Pss 4:8; 29:11; 85:8; 122:7; Isa 9:7; 32:18; 54:13; Jer 12:12; Nah 1:15). When used in connection with treaty-making, however, it is clear that a more political meaning of peace is intended (Deut 2:26; 1 Sam 7:14) and related to the practice of justice (Zech 8:16). **Shlm** is explicitly used in distinction to war in wisdom and prophetic literature (Eccl 3:8; Jer 12:12; Mic 3:5). The root **shlm** is used increasingly as part of personal names in the postexilic period (1 Chr 2:40; 4:25; Neh 3:12).

DANIEL L. SMITH-CHRISTOPHER

SHAMA shay′muh [שָׁמָע shama‛]. One of David's mighty men (1 Chr 11:44), listed in what appears to be an expansion of the original list in 11:11-41a and 2 Sam 23:8-39. Many of the sixteen named in the expanded list were from Transjordan. *See* DAVID'S CHAMPIONS.

SHAME [בֹּשֶׁת bosheth; κατησχύνοντο katēschynonto, ἐντροπὴν entropēn]. Shame constitutes the flip side of the pivotal Mediterranean value, HONOR, significantly contrasting with modern Northwestern concept of "guilt" (Plevnik). Women are specifically vulnerable to shame—their own and their menfolks'. Men will do everything to avoid shame, the loss of honor, or its increase (a gain being open to men only). The founders of this "Mediterranean" analysis themselves insisted that shame seems to be universal, and guilt is simply internalized shame (Peristiany). In the Bible, fathers and mothers are to be honored, as is the "good wife" (Prov 31:10-31), as are all Christians by one another (Rom 12:10). Being shamed does matter (2 Sam 13:12; Ps 35:26; Isa 61:7; Luke 14:9; 1 Cor 11:6, 14) but not above all other considerations. Thus, with little regard for shame a patriarch may surrender his wife to safeguard his life (Gen 12:13; 20:2; 26:7), and David plays the imbecile (1 Sam 21:13). Jesus' followers are expected to welcome shameful treatment (Luke 6:22), just as Jesus himself disregarded shame (Heb 12:2). It was in fact entirely possible to be "shameless," unconcerned for honor or dishonor, as CYNICS claimed to be, and in which Paul joined them (1 Cor 4:10; 2 Cor 6:8). *See* SEXUAL ABUSE; RAPE.

Bibliography: J. G. Peristiany and J. Pitt-Rivers. *Honor and Grace in Anthropology.* (1992); J. Plevnik. "Honor/ Shame." *Biblical Social Values and their Meaning.* J. J. Pilch and B. J. Malina, eds. (1993) 95–104; M. Sawicki. *Crossing Galilee* (2000).

F. GERALD DOWNING

SHAMGAR sham′gahr [שַׁמְגַּר shamgar]. One of Israel's lesser known judges mentioned in only two verses (Judg 3:31; 5:6). The scantiness of references and the lack of a narrative suggest that there are many speculations about him. Was he a foreigner? Did he campaign on behalf of Israel? Did Israel borrow his deeds for their cause?

Both references to Shamgar identify him as the "son of Anath," but it is not clear who or what Anath was. Was it a person, the Canaanite goddess Anath, or a

town (e.g., the Canaanite town in Galilee named after the goddess Anath or the town near Jaffa in southern Palestine; compare Judg 11:1 where "Gilead" is father to Jephthah)? The ambiguity concerning Anath masks the identity of Shamgar, whose name may be traced to Hittite, Hurrian, Canaanite, or a combination of Hebrew and Egyptian words.

The first reference to Shamgar (Judg 3:31) comes at the end of the narratives of Othniel (Judg 3:5-11) and Ehud (Judg 3:15-30), and before the narrative and song of Deborah (Judg 4–5), which contains the second reference (Judg 5:6). The first reference interrupts the flow of the narrative from Judg 3:30 to Judg 4:1, from the narrative of Ehud to the narrative of Deborah, and sits uneasily among the narratives of Israel's judges.

The introduction of Shamgar does not contain the expected Deuteronomistic template: Israel offends Yahweh; Yahweh hands them over to foreign enemies; Israel cries to Yahweh; Yahweh raises up a judge who delivers Israel (compare Judg 3:7-10). Nonetheless, like other Israelite judges, Shamgar fought against non-Israelite powers. Whereas Othniel delivered Israel from King Cushan-rishathaim of Aram-naharaim and Ehud delivered Israel from King Eglon of Moab, Shamgar is not linked to a foreign king. Judges 3:31 simply reports that he slew six hundred Philistines with an ox-goad, and that he was a champion of Israel. Did he fight on behalf of Israel? Did he deliver Israel from the Philistines?

The second reference to Shamgar links him to Jael (Judg 5:6), who hammered a tent peg through the head of Sisera, thus contributing to the overthrow of King Jabin of Canaan (Judg 4:17-24). Associating Shamgar with Jael implies that both were non-Israelites, but the victory of Jael is remembered with more details in the story of Deborah, an Israelite prophetess (Judg 4). The association of Shamgar with Jael and Deborah unsettles the reference to his slaying of Philistines, because they did not become enemies to Israel until later (compare 1 Sam 4). Did Shamgar really slay 600 Philistines? Did he prevent the Philistines from becoming a national enemy of Israel? Was he more of a resistance fighter than a national leader?

Yahweh may not have raised Shamgar up in response to the cry of Israel against a foreign enemy, but he is most likely a non-Israelite, like Rahab (Josh 2) and Jael (Judg 4), who is remembered in the rise of Israel in Canaan. He would be remembered differently, if at all, in Philistine circles.

Bibliography: Eva Danelius. "Shamgar Ben ‛Anath." *JNES* 22 (1963) 191–93; Nili Shupak. "New Light on Shamgar ben ‛Anath." *Bib* 70 (1989) 517–25; S. D. Snyman. "Shamgar ben Anath: A Farming Warrior or a Farmer at War?" *VT* 55 (2005) 125–29; Adrianus van Selms. "Judge Shamgar." *VT* 14 (1964) 294–309.

JIONE HAVEA

SHAMHUTH sham´huhth [שַׁמְהוּת shamhuth]. Shamhuth, an Izrahite (descendant of Zerah) appears in 1 Chr 27:8 as the fifth of David's twelve commanders whose 24,000-member divisions rotated duties throughout a twelve-month cycle. Shamhuth is the only one of the twelve commanders whose name does not appear elsewhere.

SHAMIR shay´muhr [שָׁמִיר shamir]. 1. One in a list of cities in the southwestern hill country of Judah (Josh 15:48). The name survives in modern Khirbet Somera, a site some 20 km southwest of Hebron.

2. A city in the hill country of Ephriam and the home of Tola son of Puah (Judg 10:1-2). This site is to be identified with Khirbet es-Sumara, some 11 km south of Balatah.

3. The Chronicler lists Shamir son of Micah as one of the Levites appointed by David to serve in the house of the Lord (1 Chr 24:24).

JOSEPH R. CATHEY

SHAMLAI sham´l*i* [שַׁמְלַי shamlay]. Kethibh and variant in Ezra 2:46 for SHALMAI, a temple servant whose descendants returned to Jerusalem after the exile.

SHAMMA sham´uh [שַׁמָּא shamma²]. The eighth of eleven sons of Zophah, warriors and heads of households among the descendants of Asher (1 Chr 7:37).

SHAMMAH sham´uh [שַׁמָּה shammah, שִׁמְעָה shim²ah, שִׁמְעָא shim²a², שַׁמָּא shamma²]. Variations of this name include Shimeah, Shemiah, Shimei, and Shimea. The difference in spelling is unexplained, but the name could be derived from a theophoric name having the verb shama² (שָׁמַע) "to hear." Several individuals bear this name. 1. Third son of Reuel and grandson of Esau (Gen 36:13, 17; 1 Chr 1:37).

2. The third son of Jesse (1 Chr 2:13-16) who was passed over for kingship (1 Sam 16:9). He later went to battle against the Philistines (1 Sam 17:13). He is also identified as the father of Jonadab and Jonathan (perhaps the same person) whose actions carry both positive (2 Sam 13:32-33; 2 Sam 21:21//1 Chr 20:7) and negative consequences (2 Sam 13:3).

3. One of the three MIGHTY MEN of David known for holding his ground against the Philistines in a field of lentils (2 Sam 23:11). There is some confusion if Shammah the Harodite (2 Sam 23:25) is the same as Shamma the Hararite (2 Sam 23:33), but most scholars view them as the same person and locate Harod near Bethlehem.

RYAN N. ROBERTS

SHAMMAI THE ELDER. Shammai, who is designated by the pre-rabbinic title "Elder," lived in the early 1st cent. CE and was a forebear of the rabbinic movement. Along with Hillel (*see* HILLEL THE ELDER, HOUSE OF HILLEL), Shammai is listed in the SAYINGS OF THE FATHERS as the last of the "pairs" who led Judaism before the Roman destruction of Jerusalem.

Bibliography: Jacob Neusner. *The Rabbinic Traditions about the Pharisees before 70.* 3 vols. (1971).

BURTON L. VISOTZKY

SHAMMOTH sham´oth [שַׁמּוֹת shammoth]. Shammoth of Harod (MT, "Haror") is listed among DAVID'S CHAMPIONS in 1 Chr 11:27. In 2 Sam 23:25 his name is given as SHAMMAH of Harod. In another list, SHAMHUTH the Izrahite (1 Chr 27:8) might be a conflation of the other two names, or it might also be the earlier form.

JOAN E. COOK, SC

SHAMMUA sha-myoo´uh [שַׁמּוּעַ shammua²]. The name of several individuals in the OT, *Shammua* comes from the Hebrew root shm² (שׁמע), meaning "renown" or "the one who is heard." 1. Son of Zaccur, who represented the Reubenite tribe as one of the spies Moses sent to examine the land of Canaan (Num 13:4). Shammua disagreed with the report of Joshua and Caleb.

2. One of the sons of David born in Jerusalem to Bathsheba/Bath-Shua (2 Sam 5:14; 1 Chr 14:4). Called SHIMEA in 1 Chr 3:5. Brother to Solomon, Shobab, and Nathan.

3. Numbered among the Levites who lived in Jerusalem after the exile (Neh 11:17). Grandson of Jeduthun, son of Galal, father of Abda. Called Shemaiah in 1 Chr 9:16 (where Abda is called Obadiah).

4. Head of the priestly house of Bilgah in the time of the high priest Joiakim (Neh 12:18).

PETER T. LANFER

SHAMSHERAI sham´shuh-r*i* [שַׁמְשְׁרַי shamsheray]. The first of Jeroham's six sons, descendants of Benjamin, living in Jerusalem, and heads of households (1 Chr 8:26).

SHAPHAM shay´fuhm [שָׁפָם shafam]. A leader, second in command in the tribe of Gad and a resident of Bashan (1 Chr 5:11-12).

SHAPHAN shay´fuhn [שָׁפָן shafan]. Meaning a "rock badger," "hyrax," or "dassie." 1. In the Judean kingdom, Shaphan served under King Josiah as an official state scribe (2 Kgs 22:3-14; 2 Chr 34:8-20), a position similar to a modern Secretary of State. Likewise, scholars have argued that he would have been a natural to head up the scribal school in Jerusalem. It is clear from the context in both Kings and Jeremiah that Shaphan was friendly to Josiah and Jeremiah (Jer 36; 39–41). He, along with his son Ahikam, took the "book of the law" to Huldah the prophetess at the behest of Josiah (2 Kgs 22:14). It was Shaphan and his sons who intervened during the days of Jehoiakim and saved Jeremiah from a mob (Jer 26:24).

2. In Ezek 8:11, Ezekiel's visions reveal Jaazaniah the son of Shaphan as an inciter of popular idolatry among the exiles.

Bibliography: Jack R. Lundbom. *Jeremiah 21-36.* AB (2004); William McKane. *Jeremiah.* ICC (1996).

JOSEPH R. CATHEY

SHAPHAT shay′fat [שָׁפָט shafat; Σαφάτ Saphat]. 1. A Simeonite, one of the spies sent by Moses to reconnoiter Canaan (Num 13:5).

2. Father of the prophet Elisha (1 Kgs 19:16, 19; 2 Kgs 3:11; 6:31), from Abel-meholah.

3. Youngest of the six sons of Shemaiah, and a descendant of David and Zerubbabel (1 Chr 3:22).

4. A Gadite (1 Chr 5:12).

5. Son of Adlai, a herdsman in charge of David's animals (1 Chr 27:29).

6. One of the servants of Solomon who returned with Zerubbabel (1 Esd 5:34).

JOSEPH R. CATHEY

SHAPHIR shay′fuhr [שָׁפִיר shafir]. Meaning "beautiful/fairview." Shaphir occurs only in Mic 1:11 functioning as a paronomasia (*see* WORDPLAY IN THE OT) where Micah laments the destruction of cities in the Shephelah that should have provided the bulk of Jerusalem's defense. Scholars have suggested sites such as Es-Suwafir, Tel 'Eitun, or Khirbet el-Kôm. Others (e.g., Eusebius) have argued SHAMIR (Josh 15:48) and Shaphir were the same place but due to textual corruption have different spellings. At present it is best to understand Shaphir as still unidentified.

Bibliography: Yohanan Aharoni. *The Land of the Bible* (1967); Yoel Elitzur. *Ancient Place Names in the Holy Land* (2004); Zecharia Kallai. *Historical Geography of the Bible* (1986).

JOSEPH R. CATHEY

SHARAI shair′i [שָׁרַי sharay]. One of the returnees from Babylon who gave up their foreign wives (Ezra 10:40). His name does not appear in the parallel list (1 Esd 9:34).

SHARAR shair′ahr [שָׁרָר sharar]. Sharar the HARARITE was the father of Ahiam, listed in 2 Sam 23:33 as one of DAVID'S CHAMPIONS called "the Thirty."

SHAREZER shuh-ree′zuhr [שַׁר־אֶצֶר sar-ʾetser, שַׂרְאֶצֶר sarʾetser]. 1. Son of Sennacherib, king of Assyria. Sharezer conspired with his brother to murder their father (2 Kgs 19:37; Isa 37:38).

2. One of two ment sent from Bethel to Jerusalem to ask if the people should continue to mourn on the anniversary of the fall of Jerusalem (Zech 7:2). *See* BETHEL-SHAREZER.

TREVOR D. COCHELL

SHARON, SHARONITE shair′uhn, shair′uh-n*it* [שָׁרוֹן sharon, שָׁרוֹנִי sharoni; Σαρῶν Sarōn]. 1. Based on the geographical depiction of the region, the roots yshr (יָשַׁר), meaning "straight" or simply "plain," and shyr (שִׁיר), meaning "to sing" (because the region was so lush and beautiful), have been suggested as the etymology of Sharon.

The coastal plain of Sharon has three sets of parallel corridors stretching from the south (Joppa) or Yarkon River to the north (Mount Carmel) or Tanninim (Crocodiles) River. The natural landscape of this central plain is composed of sand dunes, Samaria foothills, kurkar ridges, red loam hills, seasonal pools, and alluvium soils. Five major rivers carry the waters from the western slopes of the mountain to the Mediterranean. Controlling the flow and drainage of water, depending on which socio-political power was in control, determined whether the region was to be a major economic contributor or merely a fringe zone for pastoral groups and other marginalized persons. But even as a fringe zone, the area was productive for animal husbandry.

The historical reconstruction of this region during the Late Bronze III and Iron Age I is based on ancient Egyptian and Hebrew literary sources. The Harris papyrus, annals of Amenhotep II, AMARNA LETTERS, and the books of Joshua (12:1-24; 17:1-13) and Judges (1:27–28) are all central in showing the Egyptian and subsequently the Philistine influence and its eventual domination of the region. An important trade route and cities (Aphek, Socho, Yaham, and Eg Migdalen) led to Syria. During the divided monarchy, the northern kingdom of Israel controlled Sharon from the central highlands with Dor as its main port. However, the southern kingdom of Judah controlled the port city of Joppa. From the Assyrian period down to Hellenistic times, the administrative center shifted to the province of Dor. During the Roman era, major changes and expansions took place. Herod the Great transformed the entire region by building the artificial port city of Caesarea. This promulgated an entire system of network and infrastructure development with paved roads, causeways, and bridges. It was during this time that the region was divided into four districts: Antipatris, Apollonia, Caesarea, and Dora.

The OT and the NT record the following references to Sharon: 1 Chr 5:16; Song 2:1; Isa 33:9; 35:2; 65:10; and Acts 9:35. According to 1 Chr 5:16, Sharon is not the central coastal plain, but a region east of the Jordan River, with pasture lands associated with Bashan and Gilead. Because of this geographical variance, some scholars have suggested that this reference in Chronicles be emended to "Sirion" (LXX), another name for Mount Hermon, or even "tableland," a southern territory of Gad (Josh 13:9, 17, 21) with tangential support from the Mesha Inscription. With the careful observation of the verse "the pasture lands of Sharon to their limits" providing important clues, conjectural emendation is no longer acceptable. The region was indeed representative of the choicest quality pasture land (1 Chr 27:29; Isa 65:10). In the same way that the author of Chronicles expanded Israel's border to include the Nile to the Euphrates, this reference may in fact be describing the expansion of good pasture stretching from the western coastal plains to the far stretches of the eastern side of the Jordan. Thus, the verse does indeed indicate a locale outside the coastal plain, but the description and the phrase "to their limits" fit cohesively within the overall theological outlook of the authors of Chronicles.

In Song 2:1, the beloved describes herself as "a rose (crocus) of Sharon" (*Hibiscus syriacus*). This deciduous flower shrub in the *Malvaceae* family is native to Asia and the Middle East.

While the oracle of doom in Isa 33:9 describes the nature of the region's volatility, vitality, and verdant beauty being transformed into withering waste, the message of salvation in 35:2 describes it as bursting into majestic bloom. It should reemphasized that the inland Via Maris (The Way of the Sea) connected all the major trade cities through this coastal plain from Egypt to Syria in addition to all the important maritime ports from Egypt, Israel, Cyrus, and Lebanon to the greater Mediterranean basin.

In Acts 9:35, the healing of Aeneas the paralytic, who had been bedridden for eight years, is said to have taken place in Lydda in the region of Sharon. Likewise, Dorcas (Tabitha), who lived in Joppa near Lydda is brought back to life (vv. 36-43). These stories are set in the most fertile and beautiful area of Israel's past where renewal, restoration, and resurrection from the dead have literal meaning.

Bibliography: I. Finkelstein. *Living on the Fringe: The Archaeology and History of the Negev, Sinai and Neighbouring Regions in the Bronze and Iron Ages* (1995); Y. Gadot. "Aphek in the Sharon and the Philistine Northern Frontier." *BASOR* 341 (2006) 21–36; R. Gophna and J. Portugali. "Demographic Processes in Israel's Coastal Plain from the Chalcolithic to the Middle Bronze Age." *BASOR* 269 (1988) 11–28; Y. Karmon. "Geographical Influences on the Historical Routes in the Sharon Plain." *PEQ* 93 (1961) 43–60; N. Liphschitz, S. Lev-Yadun, and R. Gopha. "The Dominance of Quercus Calliprinos (Kermes Oak) in the Central Coastal Plain in Antiquity." *IEJ* 37 (1987) 43–50; P. Machinist. "Biblical Traditions: The Philistines and Israelite History." *The Sea Peoples and Their World: A Reassessment.* E. D. Oren, ed. (2000) 53–83; I. Singer. "Mernephtah's Campaign to Canaan and the Egyptian Occupation of the Southern Coastal Plain of Palestine in the Ramesside Period." *BASOR* 269 (1988) 1–10; D. W. Roller. "The Northern Plain of Sharon in the Hellenistic Period." *BASOR* 247 (1982) 43–52.

JOHN AHN

2. A resident of SHARON, used of Shitrai, a shepherd in the pastures of Sharon (1 Chr 27:29).

A. HEATH JONES III

SHARUHEN shuh-roo′huhn [שָׁרוּחֶן *sharukhen*]. A town in Simeon's allotment (Josh 19:6), located in the Negev of the Cherethites on the Besor Brook. The three principal sites that have been tentatively identified with Sharuhen are Tell el-Far'a (south), Tell el-Ajjul, and Tel Haror. Egyptian records mention a Hyksos town known as S'rahuna. It is to Sharuhen that the Hyksos retreated after their defeat at the hand of Ahmose and the loss of their capital at Avaris.

Bibliography: Eliezer D. Oren. "The 'Kingdom of Sharuhen' and the Hyksos Kingdom." *The Hyksos: New Historical and Archaeological Perspectives.* Eliezer D. Oren, ed. (1997); Anson F. Rainey and R. Steven Notley. *The Sacred Bridge: Carta's Atlas of the Biblical World* (2006).

JOSEPH R. CATHEY

SHASHAI shay′shi [שָׁשַׁי *shashay*; Σεσεὶς *Seseis*]. A descendant of Binnui, one of the lay families who returned from Babylon with Zerubbabel and who agreed to divorce their foreign wives at Ezra's urging (Ezra 10:40; 1 Esd 9:34). According to Neh 7:15 Binnui's returning descendants numbered 648; Ezra 2:10 refers to them as Bani's descendants and counts them at 642, the differences in names and numbers perhaps the result of combining different lists.

JOAN E. COOK, SC

SHASHAK shay′shak [שָׁשָׁק *shashaq*]. The seventh of eight sons of Elpaal, Jerusalem Benjaminites who were heads of households (1 Chr 8:14). Shashak was the father of eleven sons (1 Chr 8:25).

SHASU. The Shasu (or Shosu) are a group of bedouin-like people known from Egyptian texts of the Eighteenth and Nineteenth Dynasties (16th–12th cent. BCE) where they are described as pastoralists who lived in tent camps and harassed Egyptian forces moving through Canaan. Their semi-nomadic lifestyle has fostered the supposition that early Israelites originated from a Shasu background. Such an opinion corresponds to a peaceful-infiltration or symbiosis type theory on Israelite settlement, given the supposition that the Israelites (or proto-Israelites) migrated to the central hills of Palestine in the early Iron Age and took up residence at the periphery of urbanized society. Over time they transitioned into permanently settled agriculturalists and developed into Israel and Judah. Beyond the similarities in lifestyle, there are more substantive reasons for deducing some form of connection between the two groups: Yahweh is often associated with southern Canaan, such as Edom, in the biblical texts (compare Judg 5:4-5), which is where the Shasu were know to have lived; and a

14th-cent. BCE text of Amenhotep III identifies a yhw among the Shasu. The Shasu, then, might have brought Yahwism to the central hills. *See* EDOM, EDOMITES; HABIRU, HAPIRU; ISRAEL, ORIGINS OF; PASTORAL NOMADS.

Bibliography: Beth Alpert Nakhai. "Israel on the Horizon: The Iron I Settlement of the Galilee." *The Near East in the Southwest.* B. A. Nakhai, ed. (2003) 131–51; Anson Rainey. "Rainey's Challenge." *BAR* 17 (1991) 56–60, 93; Frank Yurco. "3,200-Year-Old Picture of Israelites Found in Egypt." *BAR* 16 (1990) 20–38; Frank Yurco. "Yurco's Response." *BAR* 17 (1991) 61.

JASON R. TATLOCK

SHAUL shawl [שָׁאוּל sha'ul]. Means "one asked for" (*see* also SAUL, SON OF KISH). 1. The seventh Edomite king, who hailed from the region of REHOBOTH. He reigned before there were kings in Israel (Gen 36:37-38; 1Chr 1:48-49).

2. The child of Simeon whose mother was a Canaanite. This Shaul was the progenitor of the Shaulite clan (Gen 46:10; Exod 6:15; Num 26:13).

3. The descendant of Levi and one of the sons of Kohath (1 Chr 6:24).

CHRISTINE D. JONES

SHAVEH, VALLEY OF shay'vuh [עֵמֶק שָׁוֵה 'emeq shaweh]. The place where Abram encountered the king of Sodom and Melchizedek after Abram routed King Chedorlaomer and his allies and reclaimed Lot (Gen 14:17; compare v. 5). In Gen 14:17, this place name is updated as 'emeq hammelekh (עֵמֶק הַמֶּלֶךְ), "King's Valley" (compare 2 Sam 18:18). Josephus indicates that Absalom's pillar in the "King's Valley" (2 Sam 18:18) would be situated where the Kidron Valley is positioned (*Ant.* 7.243). Corroboration from other ancient sources suggests this site lies in the juncture of the valleys of Kidron, Hinnom, and Tyropoeon. *See* KIDRON VALLEY.

MICHAEL D. MATLOCK

SHAVEH-KIRIATHAIM shay'vuh-kihr-ee-uh-thay'im [שָׁוֵה קִרְיָתָיִם shaweh qiryathayim]. Mentioned as the location where Chedorlaomer, the king of Elam, defeated the Emim (Gen 14:5). Because shaweh means "plains" or level ground, Shaveh-kiriathaim might be the plains of Kiriathaim in Moab (Jer 48:1). The modern site is probably El Qareiyat, about 7 km to the north of Dibon in Moab. The city Kiriathaim was allotted to Reuben, who fortified the city (Num 32:37; Josh 13:19).

CHANNA COHEN STUART

SHAVING [גָּזַז gazaz, גָּלַח galakh; ξυράω xyraō]. Israelite men usually wore beards, and shaving was limited to special circumstances. Levites prepared for their consecration by shaving their whole bodies (Num 8:7). At the completion of their vows, Nazirites shaved their heads and burned the hair (Num 6:13-20). During a vis-

it to Jerusalem, Paul sought to show his respect for the law of Moses by making a Nazirite vow, which included shaving his head (Acts 21:23-24; compare 18:18). Shaving was employed in the diagnosis of "leprosy" (Lev 13:32-33) and in subsequent purification (e.g., Lev 14:8-9). Forcefully shaving another's beard was a means of humiliation carried out on enemies, prisoners, or slaves (e.g., 2 Sam 10:4; Isa 7:20; Jer 48:37; compare 1 Cor 11:5-6).

Shaving or tearing hair from one's beard and head was associated with mourning for the dead, practiced by Israel's neighbors (*ANET* 88, 139) and by some Israelites (Isa 15:2; Jer 16:6; 41:5; 47:5; 48:37; Ezek 7:18; 27:31; Mic 1:16). Such rites were forbidden to priests (Lev 21:5) and to all Israelites (Lev 19:27-28; Deut 14:1). Occasionally, however, Yahweh commanded shaving as a sign of mourning over sinfulness (Isa 22:12; Amos 8:10). *See* BALDNESS; BEARD; HAIR, HAIRS; LEPROSY; MOURNING; NAZIR, NAZIRITE; RAZOR.

RALPH K. HAWKINS

SHAVSHA shav'shuh [שַׁוְשָׁא shawsha']. Shavsha was David's court secretary according to 1 Chr 18:16. Similar Deuteronomistic lists give his name as Seraiah (2 Sam 8:17) and Sheva (2 Sam 20:25). He is probably also the "Shisha" whose two sons are named as secretaries in Solomon's court (1 Kgs 4:3). The mention of a royal secretary near the top of a short list of officials underscores the importance of his role. He may have been responsible for keeping statistics related to taxation and conscription: his Hebrew title, sofer (סוֹפֵר; *see* SCRIBE), literally means "one who counts."

TONY W. CARTLEDGE

SHAVU'OT. *See* WEEKS, FEAST OF.

SHEAF [אֲלֻמָּה 'alummah, עָמִיר amir, עֹמֶר omer, קָצִיר qatsir; δράγμα dragma]. After reaping, cereal crops are bundled into sheaves (Jdt 8:3). For the benefit of the socially vulnerable, Deut 24:19 prescribes abandoning forgotten sheaves in the field. The people of Israel brought the sheaf of their FIRST FRUITS to the priest to raise before the Lord (Lev 23:9-14). Joseph dreams of sheaves bowing down, a vision of his superiority over his family (Gen 37:6-8). *See* AGRICULTURE.

DRAYTON C. BENNER

SHEAL shee'uhl [שְׁאָל she'al; Ἀσάηλος Asaēlos]. Descendant of Bani, who returned to Jerusalem after the Exile and among those whom Ezra instructed to send away their foreign wives and children in accordance with God's commandments, an attempt to cleanse the land of their polluting effect (Ezra 10:29). In the parallel text (1 Esd 9:30) the name rendered "Sheal" in the NRSV is Asaēlos.

EMILY R. CHENEY

SHEALTIEL shee-al′tee-uhl [שְׁאַלְתִּיאֵל she'alti'el; שַׁלְתִּיאֵל shalti'el; Σαλαθιήλ Salathiēl]. In testamental and apocryphal references (1 Chr 3:17; Ezra 3:2, 8; 5:2; Neh 12:1; Hag 1:1,12, 14; 2:2, 23; 1 Esd 5:5, 48, 56 [LXX 5:47, 54]; 6:2; Luke 3:27; compare Matt 1:12), Shealtiel is primarily recognized in his role as the father of Zerubbabel; hence, a descendant of David and forefather of Jesus. The NRSV follows MT 1 Chr 3:19 by listing the father as Pedaiah, but LXX preserves the standard paternity. Shealtiel, like Saul, is derivative of sha'al (שָׁאַל), indicating that the child resulted from entreaty (compare 1 Sam 1:27).

JASON R. TATLOCK

SHEARIAH shee′uh-ri′uh [שְׁעַרְיָה she'aryah]. The fourth of Azel's six sons and a descendant of Benjamin (1 Chr 8:38; 9:44) and therefore also of King Saul.

SHEAR-JASHUB shee′uhr-jay′shuhb [שְׁאָר יָשׁוּב she'ar yashuv]. Isaiah's son (Isa 7:3). In Isa 10:20-21, she'ar yashuv is a prophetic statement ("a remnant will return"), not a name. In Hebrew the subject-verb order emphasizes she'ar ("remnant"). Isaiah 10:20 implies the certainty of a remnant's return: "surely a remnant will return" (compare the NRSV trans.). A different emphasis occurs in Isa 10:22 where "only a remnant will return" (out of a countless number of Israelites). In Isa 7:3, the nature of the emphasis is disputed. Is it a threat ("only a remnant will survive," and is Judah or Syria-Ephraim threatened?) or reassurance ("surely a remnant will return")? Is it a physical (safe) return of troops or a spiritual return toward God? See ISAIAH, BOOK OF; REMNANT.

GORDON C. WONG

SHEATH [תַּעַר ta'ar, נָדָן nadhan; θήκη thēkē]. A case or holder for a sword, normally attached to the belt. Sheaths were not generally employed in early Israelite warfare, as most warriors carried a curved sword over the shoulder. Goliath, Joab, and an angel of the LORD in the OT (1 Sam 17:51; 2 Sam 20:8; 1 Chr 21:27) and Peter in the NT (John 18:11) are equipped with sheaths. Ezekiel uses the removal of a sword from its sheath as a metaphor for the unleashing of God's wrath (e.g., 21:3 [Heb. 21:8]).

T. DELAYNE VAUGHN

SHEBA shee′buh [שְׁבָע sheva']. 1. The Table of Nations (Gen 10:7) gives evidence of a descendant of HAM, CUSH, and RAAMAH known as Sheba, mentioned again in the Adam to Abraham genealogy in 1 Chr 1:9. A close reading of the narratives supports either a person or a tribe located in mountainous southwestern parts of Arabia.

2. Geographically the descendants of Sheba (known tentatively as SABEANS) were located in a lush region of the Arabian Peninsula that facilitated their trade. Sabeans were known to trade in precious stones, gold,

and frankincense. The book of Job records that Sabeans also were slave traders (Job 1:15; 6:19). Men from Sheba are portrayed as "tall of stature" (Isa 45:14). In the OT text Sheba often occurs in the context with Egypt and Cush (both African countries). Both Herodotus and Josephus speak of Sheba being located in North Africa, specifically Meroë. Yet others have suggested based on Josh 19:2 and 15:28 that Sheba is not a geographical entity but rather a corruption based upon Beer-sheba. This supposition has not been well received. See SHEBA, QUEEN OF.

3. Sheba son of Bichri led the northern tribes of Israel against David (2 Sam 20). Joab catches up with Sheba at Abel of Beh-maachah and beseiges the city. A woman of the city agrees to hand over Sheba's head in order to save the town.

4. A Gadite (1 Chr 5:13).

Bibliography: Michael David Coogan. *West Semitic Personal Names in the Nurašû Documents* (1976); Dennis Pardee. "Letters from Tel Arad." *UF* 10 (1978) 289–336; Fred V. Winnett. "The Arabian Genealogies in the Book of Genesis." H. T. Frank and W. L. Reed, eds. *Translating and Understanding the Old Testament* (1970) 171–96.

JOSEPH R. CATHEY

SHEBA, QUEEN OF shee′buh [מַלְכַּת־שְׁבָא malkath-sheva']. The visit of an unnamed dignitary from SHEBA, identified by title only, to the court of King SOLOMON bolsters the biblical perspective that the monarch oversaw a prosperous empire, which he ruled as a just king, renowned for his sagacity (1 Kgs 10:1-13; 2 Chr 9:1-12). The queen's acknowledgment of the God of Israel as the source of Solomon's affluence corresponds to the motif of the foreign proselyte, a concept reiterated in the NT, where she is referred to as the QUEEN OF THE SOUTH (Matt 12:42; Luke 11:31). The Islamic traditions (Qur'an 27:16-44) depict her in a similar light, as one who, in making the journey from southern Arabia, arrives at a spiritual destination. The identification of ancient Yemen with Sheba is confirmed by 8th-cent. BCE inscriptional evidence from the area, which provides the royal designation "mukarrib [i.e., federator] of Saba'." Yemen, too, is known as the area of the south (literally, "right hand," from the viewpoint of one facing east); hence the NT phrase "queen of the South."

Bibliography: St. John Simpson, ed. *Queen of Sheba: Treasures from Ancient Yemen* (2002).

JASON R. TATLOCK

SHEBANIAH sheb′uh-ni′uh [שְׁבַנְיָה shevanyah, שְׁבַנְיָהוּ shevanyahu]. 1. A priest who served with others as a trumpeter in the presence of the ark of the covenant during the Davidic monarchy (1 Chr 15:24).

2. A name associated with several individuals, mainly identified as Levites, in the era of Nehemiah's gover-

norship (Neh 9:4, 5; 10:4, 10,12 [Heb. 10:5, 11,13]; see 12:14). Because other names appear redundantly in Neh 10, perhaps only a single Levite named Shebaniah existed at that time. To further complicate the matter, several Greek and Syriac versions of Nehemiah list SHECANIAH for Shebaniah.

JASON R. TATLOCK

SHEBARIM sheb´uh-rim [שְׁבָרִים shevarim]. The Shebarim, or "quarries," were the site of battle and defeat of the Israelites by the men of Ai (Josh 7:5). The word does not appear in the LXX, and the place cannot be identified today.

SHEBAT shee´bat [שְׁבָט shevat; Σαβάτ Sabat]. Name of the eleventh month in the Hebrew calendar and equivalent to January–February. Shebat was the month when Zechariah received a vision (Zech 1:7) and Ptolemy and his men murdered Simon, his two sons, and his servants (1 Macc 16:14). See CALENDAR.

EMILY R. CHENEY

SHEBER shee´buhr [שֶׁבֶר shever]. Sheber was the first son of Caleb and his concubine Maacah (1 Chr 2:48) in the second genealogical list of Calebites in 1 Chr 2. The first list is in 1 Chr 2:18-24.

SHEBNA sheb´nuh [שֶׁבְנָא shevna', שֶׁבְנָה shevnah]. Shortened form of Shebaniah (Neh 9:4): "Return now, O Yahweh"; also spelled "Shebnah." *Shebna* appears on Iron Age II seals from Lachish and other sites. Shebna himself was an official during the reign of Hezekiah who held the title "master of the household" (Isa 22:15-25). He was second in command under the king and supervised affairs in the capital as well as the kingdom. Yahweh announced that he would replace Shebna with Eliakim, who would bear "on his shoulder the key of the house of David" (v. 22), because Shebna constructed an extravagant tomb for himself and rode in splendid chariots. It is uncertain whether a tomb discovered on the slopes of Silwan is Shebna's.

Shebna/Shebnah, now occupying the office of "secretary," supervisor of state annals and royal correspondence, accompanied Eliakim, who was "in charge of the palace," and Joah the recorder as representatives of Hezekiah when Sennacherib sent the Rabshakeh to demand the surrender of Jerusalem (2 Kgs 18:18-26, 37//Isa 36:1-12, 22). Hezekiah's officials asked the Rabshakeh to speak in Aramaic so that the besieged citizens would not understand his threats. Later, Hezekiah sent Eliakim, Shebna, and senior priests to ask Isaiah to pray for Jerusalem's remnant (2 Kgs 19:1-7//Isa 37:1-7). The prophet assured them that Yahweh would eliminate Assyria's threat.

JOHN T. WILLIS

SHEBNAH. *See* SHEBNA.

SHEBUEL shi-byoo´uhl [שְׁבוּאֵל shevu'el; Σουβαήλ Soubaēl]. 1. Son of Gershom and grandson of Moses (1 Chr 23:16). He is the "chief officer in charge of the treasuries" (1 Chr 26:24). It appears that the Shubael of 1 Chr 24:20 is the same person as Shebuel of 23:16 and 26:24. The LXX reads Shubael in all three places, suggesting it is the proper reading.

2. One of the sons of Heman appointed by David to prophesy with musical instruments (1 Chr 25:4). Again, Shubael is a variant (1 Chr 25:20).

MARK RONCACE

SHECANIAH shek´uh-ni´uh [שְׁכַנְיָה shekhanyah, שְׁכַנְיָהוּ shekhanyahu]. The name, meaning "Yahweh has dwelled," is confused with SHEBANIAH in certain Latin, Greek, and Syriac manuscripts of Nehemiah (see 9:4, 5; 10:5, 11, 13; 12:3, 14). Nevertheless, at least six individuals bearing the name can be identified. 1. A priest living in the days of Hezekiah (2 Chr 31:15).

2. A priest who accompanied Zerubbabel in his return from exile (Neh 12:3) and whose name served to designate a priestly household (LXX Neh 12:14; see 1 Chr 24:11; Ezra 8:3; 1 Esd 8:29).

3. A descendant of Zattu and son of Jahaziel, who accompanied Ezra on his journey to Jerusalem (Ezra 8:5; 1 Esd 8:32).

4. A descendant of Elam and son of Jehiel, known from the days of Ezra (Ezra 10:2).

5. The father of Shemaiah and a member of the postexilic royal family (Neh 3:29; 1 Chr 3:21-22).

6. The father-in-law of Tobiah, an adversary of Nehemiah (Neh 6:18).

JASON R. TATLOCK

SHECHEM, SHECHEMITES shek´uhm, shek´uh-mit [שְׁכֶם shekhem, שִׁכְמִי shikhemi]. 1. The son of Hamor and prince of the region in Canaan that Jacob enters with his family (Gen 33:18-19). Shechem rapes Jacob's daughter DINAH, and then demands to marry her (Gen 34:2-4). When Jacob and his sons learn of the rape, they deceitfully agree to the marriage, on the condition that Shechem and all the men of the city be circumcised (Gen 34:11-18). Dinah's brothers take advantage of the subsequent incapacitation of the men, killing Shechem and his father (Gen 34:26).

2. A male descendant of Manassseh, son of Joseph (Josh 17:2).

3. A son of Shemida, also from the family of Manasseh, but described as part of a subsequent generation from the man listed in Josh 17 (1 Chr 7:19).

JESSICA TINKLENBERG DEVEGA

4. Shechem ("shoulder") was one of the most prominent biblical sites. It is to be identified with the 6-ac. mound of Tell Balatah, ca. 40 mi. north of Jerusalem. Shechem is strategically situated in Mount Ephraim in the pass between Mount Ebal and Mount Gerizim near modern Nablus. The site was excavated by the

German archaeologist E. Sellin in 1913–14 and again (with G. Welter) in 1926–34. American excavations were sponsored by Drew and McCormick seminaries, with Harvard University, in 1957–68, directed by G. Ernest Wright. Brief final campaigns were directed by R. Boling in 1968; J. D. Seger in 1969; and W. G. Dever in 1972–73.

Strata XXIV–XXIII (ca. 4500–3300 BCE) represent a small pre-historical agricultural village in the valley near the spring, characterized by circular huts and crudely made pottery. Then the site was abandoned throughout the Early Bronze period.

Strata XXII–XXI remains indicate that massive imported fill created a mound for a major strategic site in the pass, contemporary with Egyptian Twelfth Dynasty references to a campaign against a local prince there (in the "Execration Texts"). The only monumental remains, however, consist of a large building interpreted by Wright as a "Courtyard Temple" associated with the settlement of the biblical patriarchs in Canaan (Gen 12:6; 34:1–35:4). Others, however, dispute the sacred character of this structure. Elsewhere there are a few private houses. The wheel-made pottery during this occupation level is excellent, with clear Syrian connections.

Strata XX–XVII (ca. 1750–1650 BCE) reveal the origins of a large, prosperous, heavily fortified urban site of the so-called HYKSOS period. Massive stone and mudbrick walls enclosed the "Courtyard" area (Wall 900), buttressed by a sloping earthen rampart.

The "Courtyard" area in Field VI continued in use for several strata, with many elaborations, probably as an administrative complex. Several burials signify the activities of elites.

There is evidence in Strata XVI–XV (ca. 1650–1500 BCE) that Shechem became a major urban site with a series of fortifications that surpass those of nearly every other Middle Bronze III (Albright's Middle Bronze II C) site in the country. Both an outer city wall (Wall A) and an inner wall (Wall B) encircled the mound, accompanied by a massive earthen GLACIS between them. Finally a casemate or double wall was built atop the complex. Wall A along the northwest quadrant had a stone socle that stood at least 30 ft. high. There were two city gates: a typical three-entryway gate on the northwest (Field VI); and a rarer two-entryway gate to the east (Field III).

In Field V, just inside the northwest gate, there was a large complex that consisted not only of the gate and all three wall systems, but also a multi-room barracks adjoining the gate to the north (Building 7200; Field IV), a small two-story colonnaded tripartite "royal chapel" to the south (Temple 7300), and a nearby monumental fortress-temple (Field V). The latter, with stone walls nearly 17 ft. thick, two or three stories high, is nearly identical to a Middle Bronze III temple found at Megiddo (attributed to Str. VIII). In Field XIII a large structure, an elite residence, contained numerous luxury items.

David Bivin/LifeintheHolyLand.com
Figure 1: Shechem temple of Baal-berith

Three separate destructions were distinguished during this 150-year period. The last destruction was a fiery conflagration that left the northwest city gate, temple, and barracks covered with heaps of burned mudbrick debris that are still visible on the surface today. This destruction has been convincingly attributed to the Egyptian Eighteenth Dynasty campaigns that accompanied the expulsion of the Hyksos, or Asiatic rulers, from the Delta, between ca. 1530 and 1470 BCE. The presence of transitional Middle Bronze III/Late Bronze I A ceramic forms—such as Chocolate Ware, Cypriot Base Ring I, and White Slip I wares—suggest that the final destruction of Shechem was fairly late in this period. It was perhaps due to the Nineteenth Dynasty Egyptian Pharaoh Thutmosis III, whose Asiatic campaign of ca. 1468 BCE is well documented. In any case, Shechem was deserted throughout the rest of Late Bronze IA.

Stratum XIV shows that Shechem gradually recovered from the Egyptian destruction, and it eventually became one of the key city-states governed by the Egyptian New Kingdom Empire in Canaan. Parts of the city walls and the East Gate were rebuilt, as was the Field V fortress-temple. The domestic area excavated in Field XIII revealed a large complex of well constructed houses, some of them probably elite residences.

The zenith of Late Bronze Age occupation (Str. XIII; ca. 1400–1300 BCE) at Shechem came during the Amarna Age. The Amarna archives (*see* AMARNA LETTERS), found in Egypt, consisted of cuneiform letters written by local Canaanite rulers, mostly to Pharaoh AKHENATEN (Amenhotep IV) in Egypt, reporting to their overlords on local conditions. One of the Shechemite petty-princes, Lab'ayu, is notorious for his rapacious actions toward his rivals, as well as his cunning mastery of political intrigue. But Lab'ayu's city was violently destroyed, probably by the Egyptians.

Stratum XII (ca. 1300–1200 BCE) represents a partial rebuild, but the site was in marked decline during that period. Some scholars have tried to relate the biblical accounts of the rape of Dinah and the plundering of Shechem by Simeon and Levi (Gen 34) to this era, but there is no direct evidence to corroborate these stories. In any case, neither an Israelite destruction nor any evidence of Israelite occupation is to be found in the late 13th cent. BCE. Shechem is not mentioned in the list of conquered cities in Josh 12:7-24.

The Late Bronze Age Canaanite city continued without interruption well into the 12th cent. BCE, and in Str. XI, including the Field V migdal temple. The latter was rebuilt as a slightly smaller temple, but the stone altar and a large standing stone in the forecourt went out of use. The temple was then violently destroyed and later converted apparently into a granary.

Wright related these changes first to the story of Joshua's covenant-making and the erection of a standing stone at Shechem (Josh 24). Wright then related Str. XI to the story of Abimelech's rebellion and the destruction of the Temple (Judg 9), seeing a further parallel.

This interpretation is debatable; some scholars disagree with interpreting the archaeological evidence of the destruction of the temple area and the East Gate ca. 1100 through the lens of the Bible (*see* ARCHAEOLOGY). A gap in occupation of some 150 years followed.

After its reoccupation (Str. X–IX; ca. 975–810 BCE), Shechem became an important site of the united and divided monarchies. Upon the death of Solomon, Rehoboam went to Shechem to attempt to claim the throne (1 Kgs 12:1). Jeroboam I is said to have refortified the site (1 Kgs 12:25). A casemate wall probably belongs to this general period. The slope down to the old East Gate area has several private houses that attest to improved economic conditions. Stratum X was destroyed in the late 10th cent. BCE, undoubtedly in the raid of the Egyptian pharaoh Sheshonq (SHISHAK), ca. 918 BCE (see 2 Chr 12:1-12).

Shechem revived and most likely continued as an administrative center in Mount Ephraim (Str. VIII–VII; ca. 810–724 BCE). One of the SAMARIA OSTRACA mentions taxes from there paid in wine. Several fine private houses are known, especially a typical example of an Israelite "pillar-courtyard" house in Field VII on the acropolis. It was found completely burnt and collapsed, destroyed in the well attested Neo-Assyrian campaigns of ca. 734–721 BCE. Other nearby buildings were similarly destroyed.

Stratum VI dates to ca. 724–586 BCE. After a very poor attempt at reconstruction under Assyrian dominance, Iron Age Shechem declined by ca. 600 BCE. This may have been related to the Babylonian destruction of Judah (586 BCE) and the final fall of the Southern Kingdom.

The Neo-Babylonian and early Persian periods (Str. V; ca. 600–475 BCE) saw Shechem nearly abandoned, especially after the mid-5th cent. BCE.

After the conquest of Alexander the Great in the east, Shechem revived as a small Hellenistic city (Str. IV–I; ca. 331–107 BCE). Following the break with the Jewish community, Shechem became the center of a Samaritan enclave (still existing at nearby Nablus). The fortifications were partially rebuilt, and several fine houses were constructed in Str. IV. This occupation continued in Str. III, dated by Ptolemaic coins to the late 3rd cent. BCE. The destruction of Str. III may have been due to the wars between the Ptolemies of Egypt and the Seleucids of Damascus, which ended with the triumph of Antiochus III in 198 BCE.

Stratum I ends with the destruction by the Hasmonean king John Hyrcanus (ca. 107 BCE), who completely obliterated the remains. The old traditions of the area continued, however, when the Roman emperor Flavius built Neapolis approximately 1 mi. west of the mound at the other end of the pass (modern Nablus). Remains recently investigated by Israeli archaeologists include a large hippodrome, a theater, and a Samaritan synagogue. The fabled Samaritan temple on the heights of Mount Gerizim has also been brought to light by Israeli archaeologists led by Y. Magen since 1984. The fortified city of Mount Gerizim, some 100 ac. in size, includes many residential and service dwellings, as well as an elaborate sacred complex. It dates to the time of Antiochus III (223–187 BCE) and was destroyed by John Hyrcanus between 114 and 111 BCE, when nearby Shechem was devastated.

Bibliography: Robert Boling. "Bronze Age Buildings at the Shechem High Place: ASOR Excavations at Tananir." *BA* 32 (1969) 81–103; E. F. Campbell and G. R. H. Wright, eds. *Shechem III: The Stratigraphy and Architecture of Shechem/Tell Balatah: Texts and Illustrations* (2002); D. P. Cole. *Shechem I: The Middle Bronze IIB Pottery* (1984); W. G. Dever. "The MB IIC Stratification in the Northwest Gate Area of Shechem." *BASOR* 216 (1974) 341–52; J. P. Seger. "Shechem Field SIII, 1969." *BASOR* 205 (1972) 20–35; J. P. Seger. "The MB II Fortifications at Shechem and Gezer: A Hyksos Retrospective." *EI* 12 (1975) 34–35; L. E. Toombs. "Temple or Palace: A Reconsideration of the Shechem Courtyard Temple." *Put Your Future in Ruins.* H. O. Thompson, ed. (1985) 42–58; G. E. Wright. *Shechem: Biography of a Biblical City* (1965).

WILLIAM G. DEVER

SHECHEM, TOWER OF shek'uhm [מִגְדַּל־שְׁכֶם mighdal-shekhem]. A fortified TOWER in the city of Shechem that, along with its stronghold (tseriakh צְרִיחַ), was known as "the house of El-berith" or "the temple of El-berith" (beth ʾel berith בֵּית אֵל בְּרִית). The book of Judges describes the destruction of this site by Abimelech (Judg 9:46-49).

The Judges narrative presents some difficulties for identifying the Tower of Shechem. The final destruction of the city of Shechem seems to occur in 9:45, but only afterward does the gathering in the Tower of Shechem occur (v. 46). This has led some commentators to conclude that the Tower must have been located apart from the city of Shechem. It seems more likely that the report of the complete destruction of Shechem by Abimelech (9:42-45) refers to the destruction of the lower part of the city, whereas the temple fortress, situated atop the acropolis, had not yet fallen to him (9:46-49). *See* SHECHEM, SHECHEMITES.

Bibliography: Lawrence Stager. "The Fortress-Temple at Shechem and the 'House of El, Lord of the Covenant'." *Realia Dei: Essays in Archaeology and Biblical Interpretation in Honor of Edward F. Campbell Jr., at His Retirement.* Prescott H. Williams Jr. and Theodore Hiebert, eds. (1999) 228–49.

RALPH K. HAWKINS

SHEDEUR shed'ee-uhr [שְׁדֵיאוּר shedheʾur]. Shedeur's name appears five times in Numbers as a member of the tribe of Reuben and as father of ELIZUR (e.g., Num 2:10; 7:30, 35). Elizur was the Reubenite representa-

tive among those who conducted Moses' first census (Num 1:5, 20-21); the members of his clan numbered 46,500. The Reubenites, descendants of Jacob's firstborn son, were the first tribe to leave Mount Sinai, immediately behind the tabernacle (Num 10:18). *See* REUBEN, REUBENITES.

JOAN E. COOK, SC

SHEEP GATE [שַׁעַר הַצֹּאן shaʿar hatsoʾn; ἡ πύλη ἡ προβατική hē pylē hē probatikē]. One of the gates in the city wall of Jerusalem, probably located in the northeast section of the city, near the Temple platform. It was rebuilt in the time of Nehemiah (Neh 3:1, 32; 12:39). The gate may also have been known as the BENJAMIN GATE. The gate is mentioned in John 5:2, where it is associated with the Pool of Beth-zatha.

JAMES RILEY STRANGE

SHEEP, SHEEPFOLD [כֶּשֶׂב kesev, כֶּבֶשׂ keves, צֹאן tsoʾn, שֶׂה seh; ἀμνός amnos, ἀρνός arnos, πρόβατον probaton]. All of these Hebrew and Greek terms are translated "sheep" in the NRSV, although at times they are translated "LAMB," "FLOCK," or "RAM" as well. Additionally, a number of other Greek and Hebrew terms are sometimes rendered "sheep."

Sheep were as important as GOATS for Israelite economy, culture, and religion and were kept in herds, or folds, the size of which depended on available space and resources such as water and grazing land. Sheepherders resided in villages and towns and were not semi-nomadic like goat-herders because, unlike goats, sheep cannot stand semi-arid or arid conditions.

Large numbers of sheep were often among the indicators of wealth (Gen 12:16; 1 Kgs 1:25; 4:22-23; 8:5; Neh 5:18; Job 1:3; Ps 144:13) or significant gifts (Gen 20:14; 21:27). In conquests sheep sometimes became BOOTY (Num 31:32; Josh 7:24; Judg 6:4; 1 Sam 14:32). But at times, under the rules of the DEVOTED things, sheep belonging to conquered enemies were destroyed (*see* DESTROY, UTTERLY) (Josh 6:12; 7:24; Judg 6:4; 1 Sam 15:3-15).

Sheep were raised for their milk, meat, DUNG (for fuel) and WOOL. Although the quality of wool in biblical times was not likely as good as today's, wool was used for weaving fabrics and making clothes (Lev 13:47; Ezek 34:3; Prov 31:13). Dyed wool and wool garments were prized by the Assyrians and taken as booty. Large numbers of objects related to WEAVING found in archaeological excavations provide evidence of its wide usage.

Shearing sheep was done once a year in April–May before the summer heat. When water was available, the sheep were washed beforehand (metaphorically in Song 4:2; 6:6), but otherwise, the wool was sold by the fleece and not by weight, since it was likely dirty and heavy. Before the invention of scissors around 1000 BCE, the wool was pulled rather than shorn. Shearing required a number of people to control and shear the animals and occasioned great celebration and feasting (1 Sam 25), offering opportunity for ABSALOM to assassinate AMON (2 Sam 13:23-28), for REBEKAH to steal LABAN's household gods (Gen 31:19), and for TAMAR to trick her father-in-law JUDAH into impregnating her (Gen 38:13). Shearing a firstborn sheep was prohibited (Deut 15:19), and the first shorn wool was devoted to God (Deut 18:4).

Because sheep were valuable commodities and essential for survival, they were also a focus of Israelite LAW (Exod 22:1, 4, 9-10; Deut 14:4; 17:1; 22:1) and of the system of SACRIFICES AND OFFERINGS (Exod 22:30; 34:19; Lev 1:10; 4:32, 35; 22:27; Num 18:17; 31:37; Deut 14:4; 1 Kgs 1:9).

Since sheep were common in the ANE, sheep, SHEPHERD, and fold metaphors abound in biblical texts (Num 27:17; 2 Sam 24:17; 2 Chr 8:16; Pss 44:11, 22; 49:14; 95:7; 100:3; Isa 40:11; 53:6-7; Jer 23:1; Ezek 34; Mic 2:12; Zech 10:2; Matt 9:36; 10:16; 25:32-33; Mark 6:34; John 21:15-17; Heb 13:20; 1 Pet 2:25), and they are often the subjects of parables, especially where Jesus or God is compared to a shepherd, or where the sheep have gone astray (Matt 12:11-12; 18:12-13; Luke 15:4-6; John 10:2-27).

Bibliography: Oded Borowski. *Every Living Thing: Daily Use of Animals in Ancient Israel* (1998).

ODED BOROWSKI

SHEEPFOLD. *See* SHEEP, SHEEPFOLD.

SHEEPSHEARING, SHEEP SKIN. *See* SHEEP, SHEEP-FOLD.

SHEERAH shee´uh-ruh [שֶׁאֱרָה she'erah]. The daughter of Ephraim, Sheerah built Lower and Upper Beth-Horon and Uzzen-sheerah (1 Chr 7:24). The OT often offers names that can be both personal and place, and Myers suggests Sheerah may have been a central encampment of western Ephraimite clans.

Bibliography: J. Myers. *1 Chronicles.* AB 12 (1965).

JOAN E. COOK, SC

SHEHARIAH shee´huh-ri´uh [שְׁחַרְיָה shekharyah]. The second of Jeroham's six sons, Benjaminites who lived in Jerusalem and were heads of households (1 Chr 8:26).

SHEKEL shek´uhl [שֶׁקֶל sheqel; σίκλος siklos]. The basic unit of weight in the Bible; only in postexilic periods did it mean a coin. Three types of shekel can be distinguished: 1) the "shekel of the sanctuary," mentioned in the Pentateuch and Ezekiel, containing 20 gerahs (Exod 30:13); 2) the royal shekel or "stone of the king" (author's trans.; NRSV, "by the king's weight"; 2 Sam 14:26); and 3) the regular or common shekel, containing 24 gerahs. Inscribed stone weights from Iron Age Judah

indicate that one common shekel weighed 11.33 g. *See* MONEY, COINS; WEIGHTS AND MEASURES.

RAZ KLETTER

SHEKINAH shuh-ki´nuh. In post-biblical Jewish literature, the term Shekinah ("dwelling, resting") refers to God's numinous presence in the world. The term is not found in the Bible; biblical analogues are Spirit or Holy Spirit, God's creative Word, and Woman Wisdom (*see* SOPHIA). The Bible's presentation of the divine glory resident in the wilderness tabernacle and in the Temple of Solomon, provides much of the ground for the later understanding of the divine presence in the form of the Shekinah. The Shekinah is sometimes an alternative term for God. Its feminine characteristics are strongly represented in Jewish mystical literature.

The Shekinah is also understood to be a special endowment granted to particular places or resting upon particular groups or individuals. The biblical counterparts are, of course, the Spirit of God in the book of Judges and elsewhere, the Word of God disclosed to prophets, and—in the NT—the Holy Spirit. See in particular the angel Gabriel's visit to Mary (Luke 1:26-38). The Gospel of John presents Jesus the Messiah in terms akin to the rabbinic view of the Shekinah. Both the divine Word and the Shekinah are connected with light, with glory and radiance. The Shekinah resides in the wilderness tabernacle, just as the divine Word "tabernacles" or dwells among human beings (John 1:14). The promise of the PARACLETE in John 14 may also reflect a similar understanding.

The Shekinah is one of the prominent ways by which post-biblical Judaism explained how the Creator of heaven and earth related to the people of the covenant and to individuals. The Shekinah had a special relationship to Israel. She was not to be found among the nations. But she was also utterly free to be present where she saw fit to be present, just as the Spirit "blows where it chooses" (John 3:8). Jewish thought makes clear, however, that the Shekinah is not another deity or a reality that in any way compromises God's unity. In place of the emphasis on God's Glory, present in tabernacle and Temple, this line of thought insists that "you heard the sound of words but saw no form" (Deut 4:12) at the revelation on Mount Sinai. Holding fast to the unity of God and careful to avoid all dualisms and every form of idolatry, Jewish circles developed the picture of the Shekinah, a feminine reality, sharing the life of God with the faithful, resting upon particular individuals, but present also in the very structure of the universe. Christian counterparts include Woman Wisdom, the church as Christ's bride, Mary the mother of Jesus, and the Holy Spirit. *See* DIVINE PRESENCE; GLORY, GLORIFY; NAME OF GOD; SPIRIT; SPIRIT, HOLY.

WALTER HARRELSON

SHELAH shee´luh [שֵׁלָה shelah, שֶׁלַח, shelakh; Σαλά, Sala]. 1. Son of Arpachshad and father of Eber (Gen 10:234; 11:12-15; 1 Chr 1:18, 24; Luke 3:35).

2. Youngest of the three sons of Judah and the daughter of Shua the Canaanite (Gen 38:5; 46:12; Num 26:20; 1 Chr 2:3; 4:21). Judah promised Shelah as a husband for Tamar, who had previously been married to his older brothers, Er and Onan, both killed by the LORD (Gen 38:7-11). But Judah hid Shelah from Tamar, fearing that he might also be killed (Gen 38:11, 14, 26). Tamar then tricked Judah into having offspring with her (Gen 38:18).

JESSICA TINKLENBERG DEVEGA

SHELAH, POOL OF shee´luh [בְּרֵכַת הַשֶּׁלַח berekhath hashelakh]. A body of water located in close proximity to the king's garden and the Fountain Gate in Jerusalem (Neh 3:15). Its wall is said to have been rebuilt by Shallum, who also rebuilt the Fountain Gate. The spring of Gihon would have functioned as its source of water. There is debate over whether it or the artificial pool mentioned in Neh 3:16 is to be identified with the King's Pool (Neh 2:14). It may also be related to the pool of Siloam (John 9:7; compare "waters of Shiloah" Isa 8:6). *See* GIHON, SPRING; WATERS OF SHILOAH.

DEREK E. WITTMAN

SHELEMIAH shel´uh-mi´uh [שֶׁלֶמְיָה shelemyah, שֶׁלֶמְיָהוּ shelemyahu; Σελεμίας Selemias]. Several individuals with this name appear in the OT, especially in conjunction with the late monarchical and early exilic periods. 1. The father of Zechariah, appointed by David to watch over the eastern gate of the Jerusalem sanctuary (1 Chr 26:14).

2. The grandfather of Jehudi (Jer 36:14).
3. The son of Abdeel (Jer 36:26).
4. The father of Jehucal/Jucal (Jer 37:3; 38:1).
5. The father of Irijah (Jer 37:13).
6–7. The two individuals identified in the era of Ezra as having been illicitly married to foreign women (Ezra 10:39, 41; 1 Esd 9:34).
8. The father of one who rebuilt a portion of the Jerusalem wall (Neh 3:30). 2
9. The priest commissioned by Nehemiah to help oversee the redistribution of the priestly allotment (Neh 13:13).

JASON R. TATLOCK

SHELEPH shee´lif [שֶׁלֶף shelef]. The so-called "Table of Nations" (Gen 10) represents the Israelite perspective on the origins of the people groups who inhabited their world. The ancestors of these nations were the three sons of Noah: Shem, Ham, and Japheth. Sheleph is one of several primogenitors in the Semitic line, being one of the thirteen sons born to Joktan, son of Eber, great grandson of Shem (Gen 10:26; 1 Chr 1:20).

JASON R. TATLOCK

SHELESH shee´lish [שֶׁלֶשׁ shelesh]. An Asherite, the third of four sons of Helem who were both heads of households and warriors (1 Chr 7:35).

SHELOMI shi-loh´mi [שְׁלֹמִי shelomi]. One "leader" (nasiʾ נָשִׂיא) was selected from each of the tribes for the apportionment of the land in accordance with God's directions, and Shelomi is listed as the father of Ahihud, the leader from the Asher tribe (Num 34:27).

SHELOMITH shi-loh´mith [שְׁלֹמִית shelomith]. Meaning "peaceful," this plural (sing. Shelomi) feminine name form was sometimes confused with the masculine SHELOMOTH (see 1 Chr 23:9; 24:22; 26:25-28). 1. A daughter of Dibri of the tribe of Dan who married an Egyptian and gave birth to a son. This unnamed son traveled with the Israelites in the wilderness as a sojourner. In a conflict with an Israelite, he blasphemed the Name in a curse. His punishment was death by stoning according to the edict of Moses (Lev 24:10-23).

2. A daughter or son of Rehoboam by his wife Maacaah (2 Chr 11:20).
3. The daughter of Zerubbabel (1 Chr 3:19).
4. A Levite who was chief of the sons of Izhar (1 Chr 23:18; compare 24:22, where the name is Shelomoth).
5. Son of Josiphiah who led a household of Bani and returned with Ezra from Babylon (Ezra 8:10; 1 Esd 8:36).

MICHAEL G. VANZANT

SHELOMOTH shi-loh´moth [שְׁלֹמוֹת shelomoth]. A masculine plural form meaning "peaceful," Shelomoth was sometimes confused with the feminine SHELOMITH (see 1 Chr 23:18; 24:22). 1. The son of Izhar the Levite (1 Chr 24:22).

2. A Gershonite Levite; one of Shimei's sons and head of a clan (1 Chr 23:9).
3. A descendant of Moses through Eliezer and one of the temple officials of David (1 Chr 23–26). He and others were placed in charge of all the riches gathered through the wars of Samuel, Saul, Abner, Joab, and David that were dedicated to God (1 Chr 26:25-26).

MICHAEL G. VANZANT

SHELTER [חָסוּת khasuth, מַחֲסֶה makhseh, מְלוּנָה melunah, סֹךְ sokh, סֻכָּה sukkah, סֵתֶר sether, צֵל tsel; σκηνόω skēnoō]. Something that provides cover or protection, as from the elements or other dangers (Job 24:8; Isa 25:4). A HOUSE provides shelter (Gen 19:8 [tsel, literally, "shadow"]; Exod 9:19), as does a tent (Ps 27:5) or a hut (melunah; Isa 1:8; author's trans.; NRSV, "shelter"). The act of taking shelter is often used figuratively for putting confidence in someone or something, such as in falsehood (Isa 28:15) or in Egypt (Isa 30:2-3). Positively, Wisdom is said to have been a shelter to the Israelites during the period of wilderness wandering following the exodus (Wis 10:17). Ultimately, Yahweh is the only sure shelter (e.g., Pss 27:5; 31:20 [Heb. 31:21]; 61:4 [Heb. 61:5]; 91:1; Isa 4:5-6; Sir 34:19), and those who have no trust in the Lord "will have no shelter" (Sir 2:13). In Rev 7:14-15, God will shelter (skēnoō, literally "spread a tent over") those who "have come out of the great ordeal."

RALPH K. HAWKINS

SHELUMIEL shi-loo′mee-uhl [שְׁלֻמִיאֵל shelumiʾel]. "God is my peace." The son of Zurishaddai and leader of the tribe of Simeon (Num 1:6). He assisted Moses at Mount Sinai in conducting a census of men able to go to war. He was the leader of the Simeonite army and directed the tribe to its camp position south of the tabernacle (Num 2:12) and to its marching position (Num 10:19). He presented the tribe's offering at the dedication of the altar (Num 7:36-41) on the fifth day of a twelve-day celebration. *See* PRINCE; SALAMIEL.

TERRY W. EDDINGER

SHEM shem [שֵׁם shem; Σήμ Sēm]. The oldest son of Noah and the brother of Ham and Japheth. He lives through the flood, along with Noah, his brothers, and their wives. After the flood, God blesses Shem and his brothers and creates a covenant with them (Gen 9:1, 17). Shem also plays a part in the story of Noah's drunkenness, when Ham sees his father's nakedness and goes and tells his brothers. Placing a garment on their shoulders, Shem and Japheth walk backwards into Noah's tent and cover him up (9:23). As a result of these actions, Ham's son Canaan is cursed, while Shem and Japheth are blessed (Gen 9:26-27).

The Bible divides the world's inhabitants into three lines descended from the three sons of Noah, who repopulated the world after the flood. In the genealogical lists of Noah's sons, known as the "Table of Nations" (Gen 10), Shem is listed last (vv. 21-31). His descendants inhabit areas that are mostly found to the east of Canaan. Shem's descendants include Eber, whose name is the source of the term *Hebrew*. In Gen 11:10-26, a second genealogy of Shem traces the line of his descendants down to Abram. In 1 Chronicles, the author closely follows the Genesis lists to compile his own genealogies in 1:17-27.

In the Apocrypha, Shem is mentioned once in Sir 49:16, which states, "Shem and Seth and Enosh were honored, but above every other created living being was Adam." In the NT, Shem appears in the genealogy of Jesus in Luke 3:36, which is a linear genealogy from Jesus to God. This genealogy serves to place Jesus in the broader historical context of biblical history.

Bibliography: Marshall D. Johnson. *The Purpose of the Biblical Genealogies.* 2nd ed. (1988); Gary N. Knoppers. *1 Chronicles 1–9.* AB 12 (2003); E. A. Speiser. *Genesis.* 3rd ed. AB 1 (1981).

DEIRDRE N. FULTON

SHEMA shee′muh [שְׁמָע shemaʿ; Σαμμοῦς Sammous]. Meaning "sound." 1. A town in southern Judah near Hebron (Josh 15:26).

2. A Judahite, son of Hebron, father of Raham, and descendant of Caleb (1 Chr 2:43-44).

3. A Reubenite, son of Joel from Aroer, father of Azaz (1 Chr 5:8), and perhaps the same as Shemaiah in v. 4.

4. A Benjaminite, son of Elpaal who, along with his brother Beriah, was the father of a household in Aijalon and ran out the people of Gath (1 Chr 8:13). He is called Shimei in 1 Chr 8:21.

5. One of six men standing on Ezra's right side when Ezra conducted a public reading of the Law (Neh 8:4; 1 Esd 9:43).

TERRY W. EDDINGER

SHEMA, KHIRBET. An ancient village located south of Meiron and west of Safed in the Upper Galilee, northwest of the Sea of Galilee. Excavations in 1970–72 directed by E. M. Meyers produced two important discoveries: 1) Middle/Late Roman family tombs (180–306 CE); and 2) a Late Roman/Early Byzantine synagogue (284–419 CE).

The tombs at Khirbet Shema were typical (though roughly hewn) underground chambers, each one large enough to hold the remains of a family group. Loculi, i.e., deep narrow niches for the deposition of one body, were carved into the walls of the tombs. Secondary burial was the normal practice: excavators found bones gathered both in the loculi and in small pits within the loculi. *See* BURIAL.

The SYNAGOGUE was a broadhouse, i.e., a rectangular building oriented toward a long wall, in this case the southern wall. Thus the Khirbet Shema synagogue was oriented toward Jerusalem. A bema, i.e., a platform for reading the Torah, was situated in the middle of this wall; during the Byzantine period, a Torah shrine was installed here as well. Two rows of interior columns supported the roof. A small room for the storage of scrolls (a genizah) adjoined the synagogue, as did a room with low benches around the walls, probably a "house of study."

The Late Roman synagogue at nearby Meiron was a basilica, not a broadhouse, and the close proximity of two synagogues of different orientation in the same period exemplifies the rich diversity of early synagogue architecture.

BYRON R. MCCANE

SHEMA, THE shuh-mah′ [שְׁמַע shemaʿ]. The Shema is a prayer (Deut 6:4-9; 11:13-21; Num 15:37-41) that states the core beliefs of Judaism, primarily monotheistic faith: "Hear (shemaʿ), O Israel: the LORD is our God, the LORD alone." The first paragraph declares God is the only supreme force; the second introduces reward and punishment; and the third recalls the exodus. These three themes underlie the obligation to obey God's commandments. The exhortation to

"Recite [these words] ... when you lie down and when you rise" (Deut 6:7) was understood by tannaitic tradition as a command to recite the Shema morning and night. In later tradition the Shema was recited on one's deathbed or on the verge of martyrdom. The Dead Sea Scrolls allude to the recitation of the Shema twice daily (1QS X, 10), which is also the first topic of discussion in the Mishnah. The Shema articulates several core commandments of Judaism: to love God and serve God with all of one's resources; to teach this to children; to recite the Shema; to wear PHYLACTERIES and affix a MEZUZAH to each doorpost; not to worship other gods. The mezuzah and phylacteries (written on small scrolls, rolled or folded into their respective cases) feature in the first two paragraphs of the Shema. The third paragraph commands to attach fringes to four-cornered garments in order to protect people from temptation and sin so that they will be holy. God then recalls that it is he who accomplished the exodus "to be your God" (Num 15:41).

The Nash Papyrus (ca. 150 BCE) contains Deut 6:4-5 as well as the TEN COMMANDMENTS. The tefillin and mezuzot found at Qumran also contain the first two paragraphs of the Shema, although inclusion of additional passages distinguishes them from modern tefillin.

In the NT (Mark 12:28-31), Jesus is asked, "Which commandment is the first?" He recites the Shema (Deut 6:4-5) and adds a second commandment, "You shall love your neighbor as yourself" (Lev 19:18). In the Matthean parallel (22:36), Jesus begins the quotation with Deut 6:4b, "You shall love the Lord your God ...," connecting the love of God and love of neighbor, and emphasizing the primacy of these two principles, upon which "hang all the law and the prophets" (Matt 22:40). Jesus' quotations confirm the significance of the Shema in the Jewish practice of his time. *See* GOD, OT VIEW OF.

LAWRENCE H. SCHIFFMAN

SHEMAAH shi-may′uh [שְׁמָעָה shema‛ah]. A Benjaminite from Gibeah and the father of Joash and Ahiezer. He was one of David's mighty warriors, archers and ambidextrous stone-slingers, at Ziklag (1 Chr 12:3).

SHEMAIAH shi-may′yuh [שְׁמַעְיָה shema‛yah, שְׁמַעְיָהוּ shema‛yahu, שַׁמּוּעַ shammua‛; Σαμαίας Samaias]. A theophoric personal name that means "Yahweh has heard." 1. The prophet who instructs Rehoboam (1 Kgs 12:22-24//2 Chr 11:2-4) against trying to crush the rebellion of the northern tribes led by Jeroboam because the events were sanctioned by God (1 Kgs 12:15). In the LXX's insertion after 1 Kgs 12:24 it is Shemaiah instead of Ahijah who gives ten pieces of his garment to Jeroboam as a sign of his future reign over the ten northern tribes. The prophet Shemaiah appears again in the Chronicles expansion of 1 Kgs 14:25-28 (2 Chr 12:1-8) addressing the king and officials of Jerusalem

when Pharaoh Shishak invades Judah. Shemaiah's exhortation led to their repentance and subsequent sparing of the city. The Chronicler mentions "the acts of Shemaiah the prophet and Iddo the seer" as one of its sources (2 Chr 12:15).

2. Son of Shecaiah, father of five, and a descendant of David (1 Chr 3:22).

3. A descendant of Simeon (1 Chr 4:37) perhaps to be identified with Shimei (1 Chr 4:27).

4. Son of Joel, from the tribe of Reuben (1 Chr 5:4).

5. Son of Hasshub, a Levite representing the branch of Merari (1 Chr 9:14//Neh 11:15), one of those "in charge of the work outside the house of God" (Neh 11:16).

6. Son of Galal and father of Obadiah and a descendant of Jeduthun, he is a prominent leader of a singer guild (1 Chr 9:16//Neh 11:17b).

7. A chief and one of the descendants of Kohath (1 Chr 15:8, 11), one of the three main Levitical families ordered by David to bring the ark of the Lord from the house of Obed-edom (13:14) to Jerusalem (16:1).

8. A scribe, son of Nethanel, a Levite, who registered the distribution of priestly duties of the families of Eleazar and Ithamar (1 Chr 24:6).

9. A member of the Korahite lineage (1 Chr 26:4, 6-7), firstborn of Obed-edom and father of "men who exercised authority in their ancestral houses for they were men of great ability" (26:6).

10. One of the Levites that composed the group of eight Levites and two priests sent by King Jehoshaphat to the cities of Judah to teach the people the law of the Lord (2 Chr 17:8).

11. A son of Jeduthun (2 Chr 29:14), one of the fourteen Levites representing seven Levitical families who followed King Hezekiah's command to cleanse the house of the Lord (29:15).

12. One of the six Levites that, following the order of King Hezekiah, distributed the gifts from the clergy collected in Jerusalem (2 Chr 31:15).

13. One of the six chiefs of the Levites and brother of Nethanel and Conaniah, who contributes for the Passover's offering established by King Josiah (2 Chr 35:9//1 Esd 1:9).

14. A descendant of Adonikam who came with Ezra from Babylon to Jerusalem (Ezra 8:13//1 Esd 8:39).

15. One of the leading men sent by Ezra to Casiphia to request Levites to serve in Jerusalem (Ezra 8:16//1 Esd 8:44).

16. A descendant of Harim (Ezra 10:21; 1 Esd 9:21 conflates the descendants of Harim with the decendants of Immer) who was among the priests who had married foreign women, and afterward sent them away with their children (Ezra 10:18, 44).

17. A descendant of Harim (Ezra 10:31; mentioned as Sabbaias 1 Esd 9:32), he is counted among "Israel" (i.e., non-clergy) in the list of those who married foreign women and sent them away afterwards. (The name **Samatos** [Σάματος], one of the sons of Ezora,

who married foreign wives and sent them away afterward, mentioned in 1 Esd 9:34 is too vaguely related to Shemaiah.)

18. Son of Shecaniah (Neh 3:29), keeper of the east gate of Jerusalem who helped repair a section of the walls of the city under the direction of Nehemiah (Neh 2:17-20).

19. The son of Delaiah (Neh 6:10) hired by Tobiah and Sanballat to intimidate Nehemiah, prophesying that Nehemiah should hide in the Temple to save his life (Neh 6:10-14).

20. One of the priests and head of a priestly family who came from Babylon with Zerubbabel that signed Nehemiah's pledge to adhere to the law of God (Neh 10:8; 12:6, 18).

21. One of the priests participating in the procession led by Ezra to dedicate the walls of Jerusalem (Neh 12:34).

22. Grandfather of Zechariah and a descendant of Asaph (Neh 12:35).

23. One of the Levite musicians that followed Ezra in the dedicatory procession of the walls of Jerusalem (Neh 12:36).

24. One of the Levite musicians that followed Nehemiah in the dedicatory procession of the walls of Jerusalem (Neh 12:42).

25. Father of Uriah, who prophesied during the times of Jeremiah (Jer 26:20).

26. A false prophet from Nehelam who prophesied in Babylon to the priest Zephaniah to induce him to rebuke the prophet Jeremiah. For this rebellious act, God instructed Jeremiah to prophesy punishment on Shemaiah and his descendants (Jer 29:24-32).

27. Father of Delaiah, one of the officials present when the scroll of Jeremiah was read (Jer 36:12).

28. Father of Ananias and Nathan/Jathan, relatives of Tobias (Tob 5:14; NRSV gives Shemaiah as an alternative for Shemeliah).

Bibliography: J. Blenkinsopp. *Ezra–Nehemiah*. OTL (1988); S. Japhet. *1 and 2 Chronicles*. OTL (1993); R. W. Klein. *1 Chronicles*. AB 12 (2006); Z. Talshir. *1 Esdras: A Text Critical Commentary* (2001).

ALEJANDRO F. BOTTA

SHEMAIAH THE PROPHET, WORDS OF. *See* BOOKS REFERRED TO IN THE BIBLE.

SHEMARIAH shem′uh-ri′uh [שְׁמַרְיָה *shemaryah*, שְׁמַרְיָהוּ *shemaryahu*]. Meaning "preserved" or "Yahweh has preserved." 1. A Benjaminite warrior who joined David at Ziklag as one of David's mighty men (1 Chr 12:5 [Heb. 12:6]).

2. A son of Rehoboam born to Mahalath (2 Chr 11:19).

3. A son of Harim and one of the Israelites who dismissed their foreign wives after returning from the

Babylonian exile according to Ezra's instructions (Ezra 10:32).

4. A son of Binnui who, like the Shemariah above, put away his foreign wife after the exile (Ezra 10:41).

MICHAEL G. VANZANT

SHEMEBER shem-ee′buhr [שְׁמְאֵבֶר *shem'ever*]. A king of Zeboiim, listed among the kings defeated by a rival coalition of five kings in the Valley of Siddim (Gen 14:2). The account of this battle is situated within the Abraham narrative. Though there is no extrabiblical corroboration of these events, the name of this king is reminiscent of West Semitic names occurring from the early 2nd millennium BCE.

R. JUSTIN HARKINS

SHEMED shee′mid [שֶׁמֶד *shemedh*]. Shemed, "who built Ono and Lod with its towns," is listed with Eber and Misham as sons of Elpaal (1 Chr 8:12) in a genealogy of descendants of Benjamin, which is difficult to reconcile with other genealogies (e.g., 1 Chr 7:6-11). Shemed appears only here.

SHEMER shee′muhr [שֶׁמֶר *shemer*]. 1. The owner (either an individual or a clan) of the hill that the Israelite king Omri bought to build his capital city, which was then named Samaria after Shemer (1 Kgs 16:24).

2. A Levite of the Merari lineage, who was an ancestor of Ethan, a cult singer appointed by David (1 Chr 6:46 [Heb. 6:31]).

3. A member of the tribe of Asher listed in 1 Chr 7:34, usually understood as Heber's son Shomer (7:32).

SUSAN E. HADDOX

SHEMIDA shi-mi′duh [שְׁמִידָע *shemidha'*]. Meaning "God (literally, "the Name") knows." A son of Gilead and head of the clan of the Shemidaites (Num 26:32). His clan belonged to the tribe of Manasseh, along with the clans of Abiezer, Helek, Asriel, Shechem, and Hepher (Josh 17:2). Their tribal allotment lay west of the Jordan. In 1 Chr 7:19, Shemida and his four sons (Ahian, Shechem, Likhi, and Aniam) are listed in the genealogical section on Manasseh. Data from the 8th-cent. BCE Samaria Ostraca, along with modern Arab site toponyms, confirm that the Shemidaites held land west of Samaria. Shemida's nephew, Zelophehad, died without a male heir (*see* ZELOPHEHAD).

ANDREW Y. LEE

SHEMINTH. *See* MUSIC.

SHEMIRAMOTH shi-mihr′uh-moth [שְׁמִירָמוֹת *shemiramoth*]. 1. A harpist from the second rank of Levitical musicians, appointed to accompany the ark's procession from the house of Obed-edom into Jerusalem and to play before the ark after its installation in the tent that David constructed (1 Chr 15:18, 20; 16:5).

2. Jehoshaphat assigned another Levite by the same name to be one among several officials who would

teach throughout Judah from the book of the law (2 Chr 17:8).

JOEL M. LEMON

SHEMUEL shem´yoo-uhl [שְׁמוּאֵל shemuʾel]. Shemuel is also an alternate English spelling for Samuel. 1. The representative of the tribe of Simeon designated to assist in apportioning the land to the twelve tribes (Num 34:20).

2. One of the sons of Tola, a descendant of Issachar (1 Chr 7:2).

SHENAZZAR shi-naz´uhr [שֶׁנְאַצַּר shenʾatsar]. The fourth of King Jehoiachin's (Jeconiah's) seven sons (1 Chr 3:18). Second Kings 24:12-15 does not mention his sons among the members of Jehoiachin's family and household who were deported with him to Babylon by Nebuchadnezzar in the First Deportation in 597 BCE, leaving open the possibility that they were born in Babylon.

JOAN E. COOK, SC

SHEOL shee´ohl [שְׁאוֹל sheʾol, שְׁאֹל sheʾol; ᾅδης hades]. The underworld according to Israelite religion was named sheʾol. This term occurs sixty-six times (e.g., Gen 37:35; Num 16:30; Deut 32:22; 1 Sam 2:6; Job 7:9; Ps 6:5; Isa 5:14). Much ANE literature was concerned with the dead and their abode, as reflected, for instance, in the Egyptian *Book of the Dead* (among many other texts), and in Mesopotamia in the Gilgamesh epic, *The Descent of Ishtar*, and *Nergal and Ereshkigal*. The OT, by contrast, shows little interest in the underworld abode of the dead, with infrequent mention and minimal description. This suggests that it did not fascinate or intrigue the biblical writers as it did others, though it remains debated how authentically this lack of reference reflects Israelite religion.

Death is a frequent OT theme, with the root **mwth** (מות; **muth** [מות], "die"; **maweth** [מָוֶת], "dead, death") occurring 1,000 times. However, while precision is difficult, there are only some 100 references to the underworld, a strikingly small number. Underworld references occur mostly in psalmodic, reflective, or prophetic literature. Thus it is a concept that involves some emotional engagement. There is minimal description of underworld conditions, though occasional glimpses suggest flaccid, somnolent existence (Isa 14:9-10) or a vast, subdivided burial chamber (Ezek 32:21-28). The underworld is sometimes mentioned as a cosmological extremity, in contrast to the heavens above, but mostly to indicate a human destiny that the wicked merit and the righteous seek to avoid. Since no alternative destiny is proposed, except tentatively in a few psalmic and proverbial expressions of hope.

The underworld's inhabitants are sometimes called SHADES (refaʾim רְפָאִים). This term also occurs of a reputed ancient people (Deut 2:11), of Philistine giants (1 Chr 20:4), and of a valley near Jerusalem (Josh 15:8). The similar Ugaritic term **rpum** also apparently indicates both the living and the dead. The parallel is intriguing, but the complex relationship between the two meanings remains unclear. Further, the dead Israelite REPHAIM are never thought to interact with the living, unlike their Ugaritic counterparts. The dead are also twice called ʾelohim (אֱלֹהִים), "gods" (1 Sam 28:13; Isa 8:19), though in contexts of illicit consultation. The general paucity of such references shows official disapproval and/or disinterest.

The LXX normally translated sheʾol as hades. The concept of compartmentalization within Hades was developed (notably *1 En.* 22), with the wicked consigned to GEHENNA. The term hades occurs in the NT with various connotations: as a place where the unrepentant will go at the judgment (Matt 11:23; Luke 10:15), as an opposing force to heaven (Matt 16:18), as a place of torment (Luke 16:23), and as a metaphor for death (Rev 1:18; 6:8). *See* ANCESTOR WORSHIP; DEAD, ABODE OF THE; DEATH, NT; DEATH, OT; NECROMANCY.

Bibliography: P. S. Johnston. *Shades of Sheol* (2002).

PHILIP S. JOHNSTON

SHEPHAM shee´fuhm [שְׁפָם shefam]. Town marking the northeastern boundary of the land of Canaan that Yahweh had promised to Moses (Num 34:10-13). Shepham's precise location is unknown.

SHEPHATIAH shef´uh-ti´uh [שְׁפַטְיָה shefatyah, שְׁפַטְיָהוּ shefatyahu]. 1. The fifth son of David of those born to him at Hebron (2 Sam 3:2-5; 1 Chr 3:1-3).

2. A Benjamite warrior who joined David's army at Ziklag (1 Chr 12:5) while David was hiding from Saul.

3. Son of Maacah, the leader of the tribe of Simeon during the reign of David (1 Chr 27:16).

4. A son of King Jehoshaphat of Judah (2 Chr 21:2), later killed by his brother Jehoram (21:3-4).

5. A son of Mattan (Jer 38:1) and prince in King Zedekiah's (597–586 BCE) court (Jer 38:4). During the Babylonian siege of Jerusalem, Shephatiah and other officials alleged that Jeremiah's prophecies were traitorous and undermining morale, and they convinced Zedekiah to kill the prophet by casting him into an empty cistern (38:6).

6. The ancestor of a family that returned to Judah following the exile; 372 returned with Zerubbabel (Ezra 2:4; Neh 7:9) and 81 with Ezra (Ezra 8:8).

7. A descendant of Solomon's servants who returned from the exile with Zerubbabel (Ezra 2:57; Neh 7:59).

8. The eponymous ancestor of the family of Meshullam, Benjamites who returned to Jerusalem after the exile (1 Chr 9:8).

9. A descendant of Perez and the eponymous ancestor of a Judahite family that lived in Jerusalem during the time of Nehemiah (Neh 11:4).

RALPH K. HAWKINS

SHEPHELAH shi-fee′luh [שְׁפֵלָה shefelah; Σεφηλά Sephēla]. From a Hebrew root word meaning "to make low" or "to humble," Shephelah is used twenty-one times in the OT. It is translated "Shephelah" thirteen times, "lowland" seven times, and used once in Isa 32:19 to emphasize the complete destruction (i.e., laying low) of a city. Shephelah is used once as a proper noun (**Sephēla**) in the Greek Apocrypha (LXX 1 Macc 12:38). The term is used to designate the southern two-thirds of a 50-mi.-long region of gently sloped limestone hills and fertile valleys separating the Judean hill country from the western coastal plain. Approximately 10 mi. wide, the region extends northward from Beer-sheba to Yehem. The Shephelah is located within the boundaries of the land originally given to Dan and Judah. Rainfall on the western slopes of the hill country (elevations up to 3,982 ft.) drain onto the lower Shephelah (elevations between 500 and 800 ft.) and flow through its valleys as it makes its way to the Mediterranean Sea. Because of its strategic location, the region functioned as both buffer zone and battleground in ancient Israel. For this reason, ancient Israel placed defensive cities along the strategic Shephelah Valley roadways to defend its hill country from the incursion of western coastal people and tribes. Today, orchards and crops grow on the Shephelah's gentle slopes and valley floors; herds of sheep and goats graze on its steeper regions.

Among the ancient valley roads that crossed the Shephelah, four were strategically important. 1) The Aijalon Valley was the easiest and northernmost of the valley transportation routes. Guarded by the double-walled city of Gezer, the valley was the site of frequent battles beginning during Joshua's leadership (Josh 10:12), continuing into the period of the Maccabees (1 Macc 3:16-24), and extending into the time of the Crusades. 2) The valley of Sorek crossed the Shephelah south of Gezer. Samson traveled down this valley when he killed the lion (Judg 14:5-6) and later when he tied the tails of 300 foxes together (Judg 15:4). It was along this valley that Israel watched the return of the ark of the covenant to Beth-shemesh (1 Sam 6). The 19th cent.-Jaffa-Jerusalem railway was constructed along this valley. 3) The valley of Elah runs eastward from Gath (home of Goliath, 1 Sam 17:4) to Socoh before ending in the uplands west of Bethlehem. The Philistines conducted several invasions through this valley in their attempt to seize control of the Judean hill country. The valley was the stage for the famous battle between David and Goliath (1 Sam 17). 4) The Lachish Valley was the southernmost strategic route across the Shephelah. Its guardian city of the same name was second only to Jerusalem in importance during the 8th cent. BCE. When the city of Lachish was captured by the Assyrian king Sennacherib in 701 BCE, he commissioned a relief depicting the city's inhabitants impaled and skinned alive to adorn the walls of his palace in Nineveh.

MARK D. GREEN

SHEPHER, MOUNT shee′fuhr [הַר־שֶׁפֶר har-shefer]. A campsite (location unknown) between Kehelathah and Haradah where the Israelites stopped as they journeyed from Egypt to Canaan (Num 33:23-24).

SHEPHERD [רֹעֶה ro'eh; ποιμήν poimēn]. Biblical references to shepherding reflect the agricultural environment of the ANE, in which sheep and goats (domesticated from 7000 BCE or earlier) were a primary source of food, wool, and hides. Accordingly, livestock constituted a significant component of familial wealth (so Gen 26:12-14; 1 Sam 25:2; Job 42:12; Ps 144:13; etc.).

In Scripture, the antiquity of shepherding is evident from the fact that Abel is a "keeper of sheep" whose sacrificial offering pleases God (Gen 4:2-4), and that Abraham, Isaac, and especially Jacob (Gen 30:37-43) share this role. When blessing Joseph, the aged Jacob declares, "God...has been my shepherd all my life to this day" (Gen 48:15 compare 49:24; Ps 80:1). Moses was tending sheep when confronted by the burning bush (Exod 3:1-2), just as the Israelites were obliged to become "shepherds in the wilderness" during their forty-year sojourn between Egypt and the promised land (Num 14:33). But the biblical portrait of the shepherd is indebted above all to DAVID, who in youth cared for the family flock (1 Sam 16:11; 17:34); hence the terms of God's commission: "It is you who shall be shepherd of my people Israel, you who shall be ruler over Israel" (2 Sam 5:2; compare Ps 78:70-71). Likewise the Davidic psalms characterize the life of faith in pastoral imagery: "The LORD is my shepherd; I shall not want" (Ps 23:1; compare 28:9; 68:10). Such metaphors are a staple feature of Israel's worship: "For he is our God," declares Ps 95:7, "We are the people of his pasture, and the sheep of his hand" (similarly Pss 79:13; 100:3; 119:176).

Later prophets frequently denounce national leaders as unfaithful shepherds who abuse the flocks in their care (Isa 56:11; Jer 12:10; 23:1-2; 50:6; Ezek 34:2-10; Zech 10:2-3). Ironically, God threatens through the prophet Zechariah to punish his people by raising up worthless shepherds who will bring them to ruin (Zech 11:15-17). Yet the prophets also promise that God will raise up faithful shepherds for his people (Jer 3:15; 23:4). Indeed they foretell a day when God himself will once more shepherd the nation, as in the memorable wording of Isa 40:11: "He will feed his flock like a shepherd; he will gather the lambs in his arms, and carry them in his bosom." These themes are most fully expounded in Ezek 34, which promises the return of a shepherd like David: "I will set up over them one shepherd, my servant David, and he shall feed them ... And I, the LORD, will be their God" (Ezek 34:23-24).

This passage in particular forms the background for Jesus' bold announcement, "I am the good shepherd. The good shepherd lays down his life for the sheep" (John 10:11; compare 10:14). His words run counter to the apparently low reputation of shepherds in his day (Philo, *Agriculture* 61; *m. Qidd.* 4:14; *m. B. Qam.*10:8-9)—which also accounts for the unusual choice of shepherds as the first to learn of Jesus' birth (Luke 2:8-20). In his teaching Jesus reiterates prophetic language by characterizing previous leaders as "thieves and robbers" (John 10:8) and God's people as lost sheep (Mark 6:34; Luke 15:4-7), with himself as their true shepherd (Matt 15:24, 25:32; Mark 14:27; compare Matt 2:6). According to John 10:16, this ministry also embraces those outside ethnic Israel: "I have other sheep that do not belong to this fold. I must bring them also, and they will listen to my voice. So there will be one flock, one shepherd."

In similar terms, Jesus commissions Peter to care for his followers ("Feed my lambs ... tend my sheep," John 21:15-17), and the early church continues to use shepherding language both for Jesus (Heb 13:20; 1 Pet 2:25) and for those who pastor in his name (Acts 20:28; 1 Pet 5:2-4). Scripture's last word on this theme, however, points back to Jesus and the eternal destiny of the saints: "For the Lamb at the center of the throne will be their shepherd, and he will guide them to springs of the water of life, and God will wipe away every tear from their eyes" (Rev 7:17). *See* SHEEP, SHEEPFOLD.

MICHAEL P. KNOWLES

SHEPHERD OF HERMAS. *See* HERMAS, SHEPHERD OF.

SHEPHI shee´fi [שְׁפִי shefi]. Son of Shobal (1 Chr 1:40), named SHEPHO in Gen 36:23.

SHEPHO shee´foh [שְׁפוֹ shefo]. The fourth of five sons of Shobal (Gen 36:23), whose clan belongs among the Horites in Edom. The same list in 1 Chr 1:40 has SHEPHI (shefi שְׁפִי), a variant or a misspelling, confusing w (ו)and y (י).

SHEPHUPHAM shi-fyoo´fuhm [שְׁפוּפָם shefufam]. In Num 26:39, Shephupham is listed as the fourth of five children in Benjamin's genealogy. This genealogy was recorded during the second census by Moses and Eleazar of the Israelites who came out of the land of Egypt (Num 26:1). Possible variants of this name are seen in Gen 46:21 (Muppim); 1 Chr 7:12, 15 (Shuppim). The genealogies of Benjamin, as recorded in Gen 46:21; 1 Chr 7:6-12; and 1 Chr 8:1-40, present varying lists of his descendants. There is no scholarly consensus on how the variants in Benjamin's genealogies or the variants in the name of Benjamin's fourth child arose.

KELLY WILSON

SHEPHUPHAN. *See* SHEPHUPHAM.

SHERD. *See* POTSHERD; POTTERY.

SHEREBIAH sher´uh-bi´uh [שֵׁרֵבְיָה sherevyah; Σαραβιά Sarabia, Σαραβίας Sarabias]. 1. A Levite who returned from exile in the days of Zerubbabel (Neh 12:8).

2. A Levite who accompanied EZRA in his return from exile. Ezra was pleased to receive from Casiphia this "man of discretion" (Ezra 8:18), together with his immediate relatives and additional Levites. Sherebiah would subsequently play a significant role as a priestly leader in Jerusalem (Ezra 8: 24; Neh 8:7; 9:4, 5; 10:12 [Heb. 10:13]; 12:24; 1 Esd 8:47, 54; 9:48). He is particularly recognized for his assistance in the covenant renewal process instigated by Ezra, through which the people repented in response to the reinstitution of Mosaic law (*see* LEVI, LEVITES).

JASON R. TATLOCK

SHERESH shihr´ish [שֶׁרֶשׁ sheresh]. One of the sons of Machir and his wife Maacah (1 Chr 7:16) in the list of the descendants of Manasseh.

SHESHAI shee´shi [שֵׁשַׁי sheshay]. One of the three sons of Anak (Num 13:22; Josh 15:14; Judg 1:10), who were giants living in the vicinity of Hebron when the Israelites invaded Canaan. Scholars are divided over the meaning of this personal name, but it is probably Hurrian in origin.

JOSEPH R. CATHEY

SHESHAN shee´shan [שֵׁשָׁן sheshan]. A descendant of Jerahmeel of the line of Judah; he is the son of Ishi and father of Ahlai (1 Chr 2:31). Oddly, however, 1 Chr 2:34-35 indicates that Sheshan had only daughters (no sons) and that he gave one of his daughters in marriage to his Egyptian slave JARHA. This discrepancy has evoked a variety of solutions: textual emendations (switching names), AHLAI as the name given to Jarha, Sheshan had no sons alive at his death, Ahlai is a daughter, or evidence of different sources in the genealogy. Verse 34 has been cited in discussion of Israelite adoption practices.

MARK RONCACE

SHESHBAZZAR shesh-baz´uhr [שֵׁשְׁבַּצַּר sheshbatsar; Σαναβάσσαρος Sanabassaros]. A person mentioned four times in Ezra (1:8, 11; 5:14, 16; wanting a patronym) and four times in 1 Esdras (2:12, 15; 6:18, 20), but not even once in any other biblical or extra-biblical sources. According to Ezra 1:7-11, he was the leader of the Jews who retuned from Babylonia to Judah (538 BCE). The meaning of Sheshbazzar's name, his ethnic origin, and personal identification, as well as his historical activity and exact role in the restoration period is quite controversial among scholars.

Some derive Sheshbazzar from the Akkadian theophoric name Shamash-apla-usur, i.e., "(the sun god) Shamash protects the son." Possibly, Sheshbazzar is a variation of the name Shenazzar, the fourth son of

Jehoiachin king of Judah (1 Chr 3:18), and the two names represent the same person. The name comes from the common Neo-Babylonian name Sin-ab-usur, which means "(the moon god) Sin, protect the father." If Sheshbazzar indeed is identical with Shenazzar, the son of Jehoiachin, it means that he was a descendant of the house of David, just as was Zerubbabel ("seed of Babylon"), the governor of Judah (Hag 1:14; 2:2, 21, 23). This itself provides a good reason for the appointment of Sheshbazzar as the head of the Judean restoration from the Babylonian exiles to Jerusalem, following the royal decree of Cyrus the Great, king of Persia (538 BCE; Ezra 1:1-4//2 Chr 36:21-23). The treasurer Mithredath counted out to Sheshbazzar "the vessels of the house of the Lord," which Nebuchadnezzar II had carried away from Jerusalem in 587/6 BCE (Ezra 1:7-11; 5:13-15; see also Isa 52:11-12).

According to Ezra 1:8, Sheshbazzar holds the title "the head of Judah" (NRSV, "prince"). The term *Judah* in the current context probably includes also the smaller tribal elements of Benjamin and Levi that accompanied the main group of Judahites (see Ezra 1:5; 4:1; 10:9; Neh 11:4, 7 etc.). The term nasiʾ (נָשִׂיא) here definitely does not mean melekh (מֶלֶךְ, "king") as it appears in Ezek 34:24 concerning David. Possibly it is roughly equivalent to the Aramaic title of Sheshbazzar— pekhah (פֶּחָה, "governor")—that appears in Ezra 5:14. Yet Judah did not have the status of an independent province in the Persian Empire at the very beginning of the restoration. Accordingly, none of the terms reflect Sheshbazzar's official title but rather point out his general status in the Babylonian Jewish community as the recognized leader, and were anachronistically attached to him by the biblical author.

As maintained by Ezra 5:14, 16, Sheshbazzar built the foundation for the renewed house of the Lord in Jerusalem. This information, however, is contradicted by Ezra 3:8, which attributes that action to Zerubbabel: "And in the second year of their coming to the House of God at Jerusalem, in the second month, began Zerubbabel the son of Shealtiel, and Joshua the son of Jozadak, and the rest of their brothers the priests and the Levites, and all those who came back from exile to Jerusalem ... to supervise the work of the House of the Lord" (compare Hag 1:1–2:9; Zech 4:8-10a: "the hands of Zerubbabel have laid the foundation of this house"). Moreover, since there is no information in the biblical literature about the end of Sheshbazzar, and similarly nothing about the starting point of Zerubbabel's activity, some scholars assume that in fact the two names represent just one person (e.g., Josephus, *Ant.* 11.13–14; Rabbi Abraham ibn Ezra on Ezra 1:8): Sheshbazzar was another—or official—name of Zerubbabel. Accordingly, Shenazzar, who is mentioned in 1 Chr 3:18, was the uncle of Zerubbabel/Sheshbazzar rather Sheshbazzar himself. But if this assumption is indeed correct, one would expect that the biblical writer clearly identify the names, as commonly occurs in many other places (e.g.,

"Hadasah that is Esther," Esth 2:7). The contradiction concerning the foundation of the Temple can be explained by the fact that although Sheshbazzar laid the foundation for the Temple, due to several financial, administrative, and social difficulties the work was stopped soon after, and restarted by Zerubbabel thereafter, with the enthusiastic encouragement of the prophet Haggai, and continued until its successful establishment.

According to 1 Esdr 6:18, the vessels of the Jerusalem Temple stored in Babylon were "delivered to Zerubbabel and Sheshbazzar (**Sanabassaros**)." In other words, Sheshbazzar and Zerubbabel were two figures that served in Judah at the same time, and Zerubbabel played an important part as a major Jewish leader, from the very beginning of the restoration, alongside Sheshbazzar. However, the biblical sources mention Sheshbazzar always during the time of Cyrus II, and Zerubbabel in the time of Darius I. Thus, seemingly the name "Zerubbabel" in the text under review is a later addition in order to enhance his reputation as one who was also in charge of the Temple's vessels. In any case, this source reflects that Sheshbazzar and Zerubbabel were not considered as one and the same person.

The parallel lists of Ezra 2:2//Neh 7:7 register the names of the returnees who came from Babylon, and mention the name of Zerubbabel, but not that of Sheshbazzar. The disappearance of Sheshbazzar from the Judean leadership is commonly attributed to the late age of his appointment, the short duration of his leadership, or even the quality of his leadership.

Bibliography: W. F. Albright. "The Date and Personality of the Chronicler." *JBL* 40 (1921) 104—24; S. Japhet. "Sheshbazzar and Zerubbabel against the Background of the Historical and Religious Tendencies of Ezra-Nehemiah." *From the Rivers of Babylon to the Highlands of Judah: Collected Studies on the Restoration Period* (2006) 53–95; I. Kalimi. "'So Let Him Go [to Jerusalem]': A Historical and Theological Observation on Cyrus's Decree in Chronicles." *An Ancient Israelite Historian* (2005) 143–57; I. Kalimi. "The Twilight of Jerusalem: King Jehoiachin and the Temple Vessels in the Deuteronomistic and Chronistic History." *An Ancient Israelite Historian* (2005) 115–23; T. C. Mitchell. "The Babylonian Exile and the Restoration of the Jews in Palestine." *The Cambridge Ancient History.* J. Boardman et al., eds. 2nd ed. (1991) 3:410–60.

ISAAC KALIMI

SHETH, SHETHITE sheth [שֵׁת *sheth*]. In one of Balaam's oracles the sons of Sheth ("Shethites," NRSV) are synonymous with Moabites, to be crushed by an Israelite ruler who would conquer areas of Transjordan (Num 24:17). The reference alludes to Adam's son SETH, who lived in Transjordan.

JOAN E. COOK, SC

SHETHAR shee'thahr [שֵׁתָר shethar]. One of the seven officials of King Ahasuerus's court, who collectively possessed the highest rank in the kingdom and had personal access to the king (Esth 1:14). As one of the seven ministers, Shethar advised the king to depose VASHTI. He is mentioned only once in Esther.

TRISHA GAMBAIANA WHEELOCK

SHETHAR-BOZENAI shee'thahr-boz'uh-n*i* [שְׁתַר בּוֹזְנַי shethar bozenay]. Persian official who, along with Tattenai, sent a letter to Darius regarding the building of the Temple in Jerusalem under Zerubbabel (Ezra 5:3, 6). It is unclear what position Shethar-bozenai held. He is listed second after Tattenai, suggesting he was an assistant or scribe. It would have been their responsibility to report the building activity to the king, especially given the political unrest during Darius's reign (521–486 BCE). The letter, contra a number of commentators, was not threatening or antagonistic. In response, Darius instructed them to help with the rebuilding; they obeyed (Ezra 6:6-13). Some have suggested that Shethar-bozenai is better understood as a title of Tattenai, not a proper name of another individual.

MARK RONCACE

SHEVA shee'vuh [שְׁוָא shewa']. 1. David's court secretary (2 Sam 20:2). The same official is identified as Seraiah in 2 Sam 8:17 and Shavsha in 1 Chr 18:16. Two sons of "Shisha," possibly the same person as Sheva, are named as secretaries in Solomon's court (1 Kgs 4:3). The royal secretary, or "counter," probably had responsibility for overseeing the collection of taxes and determining military or labor levies.

2. The Chronicler's genealogy lists Sheva as a son of Caleb's concubine Maacah, and as the father of Machbenah and Gibea (1 Chr 2:48-49). He is otherwise unknown.

TONY W. CARTLEDGE

SHIBAH shi'buh [שִׁבְעָה shiv'ah]. The name Isaac gave to a well his servants dug (Gen 26:33). The name is provided as an etiology for BEER-SHEBA (compare Gen 21:31-33 where Abraham names the well "Well of Seven" [see NRSV note]). The story with Isaac is, perhaps, an alternate etiology for the place, or simply an account describing Isaac's rediscovery (and renaming) of the well dug by Abraham. In either case, shiv'ah is a play on the verb shava' (שָׁבַע, "swear an oath") in the previous v. 31. Shibah, therefore, becomes Beer-sheba, the "Well of the Oath."

SUSAN M. PIGOTT

SHIBBOLETH shib'uh-lith [שִׁבֹּלֶת shibboleth]. In Judg 12:1-6, after the Gileadite warrior Jephthah achieves victory over the Ammonites and sacrifices his daughter, the Ephraimites cross the Jordan eastward into Gileadite territory and a battle ensues in which Jephthah's Gileadite forces defeat the Ephraimites. The Gileadites hold the fords of the Jordan against the retreating Ephraimites; if an Ephraimite comes and denies his tribal identity, the Gileadites ask him to pronounce the word shibboleth, which means both "ear of corn" and "river." The Ephraimites apparently cannot pronounce the phoneme "sh" and say "SIBBOLETH" instead. As a result, 42,000 Ephraimites are killed. Idiomatically, shibboleth refers to any expression that serves to distinguish one set of people from another.

There has been extensive discussion of this pronunciation test in the context of the development of early West Semitic phonology, in which sibilants were both varied and mobile. Woodhouse reviews previous scholarship, and suggests, on the basis of late Egyptian transcriptions, that the determining factor may have been the neighboring high vowel /i/, which, in Gileadite ears, turned the Ephraimite /sh/ into an /s/.

The historicity of the book of Judges is a highly contentious issue. Some scholars ascribe extremely little facticity to the accounts of Judges, while others regard them as evidence for actual events and processes in pre-monarchic Israel. This narrative, like others in Judges, suggests tension between Cisjordanian and Transjordanian groups, as well as dialectic variation. The story may reflect anti-Ephraimite polemic, as do other texts in Judges (Amit).

Judges 12, like Judges in general, has been well-served by a variety of methodological perspectives. This article will focus on three contributions. The first is the structuralist analysis of David Jobling. Jobling contends that Judg 12 is the last of a series of five stories, each of which raises the problem of the Jordan as the divinely ordained boundary of Israel and the ambiguous status of the Transjordanian tribes. With Judg 12, the breach between east and west is complete, and the series is exhausted. Jobling suggests that Cisjordan (Ephraim) and Transjordan (Gilead) are symbolically coded as male and female respectively; the Gileadites are consequently marginal, neither inside nor outside the sacred and patriarchal polity of Israel.

Second, Mieke Bal adopts a feminist and political perspective, which argues for counter-coherence to the dominant male heroic narrative. The shibboleth incident exemplifies the fatality of language in the book, in which the sword and the word are conflated. For Bal, it is a microcosm of the Jephthah story as a whole. Jephthah, the master of language, is destroyed by language, notably in the vow that condemns his daughter. Shibboleth signifies the life-giving potential of Israel; "ear of corn" and "river" complement each other as masculine and feminine sources of fertility. By reducing the word to its materiality, its sound, the Gileadites enact the failure of meaning in Judges.

Third, Frank Yamada, following a powerful 1986 essay by Jacques Derrida, has recently contributed a deconstructive reading of the narrative. For Yamada, like Derrida, shibboleth is a "pass-not-word," a violent index of alliance and exclusion. For him it exemplifies all the problems of identity and culture in the narrative as well as the rest of the book of Judges. Jephthah is a figure whose identity—as Gileadite, as warrior and diplomat—is always in doubt; similarly, the Ephraimites claim that the Gileadites are fugitive Ephraimites, and wish to reincorporate them into the body politic. Cultural identification is the product of violent differentiation; fords and crossing-points, however, offer the possibility of transition, hybridity, and hope.

Bibliography: Yairah Amit. *Hidden Polemics in Biblical Narrative* (2000); Mieke Bal. *Death and Dissymmetry: The Politics of Coherence in Biblical Narrative* (1988); Jacques Derrida. "Shibboleth." *Midrash and Literature.* Geoffrey Hartman and Sanford Budick, eds. (1986) 307–47; David Jobling. *The Sense of Biblical Narrative: Structuralist Analyses in the Hebrew Bible Vol. II* (1986); David Jobling. "Structuralist Criticism." *Judges and Method.* Gale Yee, ed. (1995) 91–118; Robert Woodhouse. "The Biblical Shibboleth Story in the Light of Late Egyptian Perceptions of Semitic Sibilants: Reconciling Divergent Views." *JASOR* 123 (2003) 271–89; Frank M. Yamada. "Shibboleth and the Ma(r)king of Culture." *Derrida's Bible.* Yvonne Sherwood, ed. (2004) 119–34.

FRANCIS LANDY

SHIELD. *See* WAR, METHODS, TACTICS, WEAPONS OF (BRONZE AGE THROUGH PERSIAN PERIOD); WAR, METHODS, TACTICS, WEAPONS OF (HELLENISTIC THROUGH ROMAN PERIODS).

SHIELD OF ABRAHAM [מָגֵן אַבְרָהָם maghen ʾavraham]. Attested only in the Hebrew text of Sir 51:12, this divine epithet is likely a reflection of the characterization of God as Abram's shield/defender in Gen 15:1. *See* GOD, NAMES OF.

SHIELD-BEARER [נֹשֵׂא הַצִּנָּה nose ʾ hatsinnah]. Used only in reference to an assistant who carried the shield of the Philistine warrior Goliath (1 Sam 17:7, 41). *See* ARMOR-BEARER.

SHIGGAION. *See* PSALMS, BOOK OF.

SHIHOR shi´hor [שִׁיחוֹר shikhor]. Although it is clear that the Shihor is a river, its precise identification is uncertain. Jeremiah chides the people for going to Egypt to drink the waters of Shihor, which are in parallel with Assyria and the waters of the Euphrates (Jer 2:18). As the Euphrates is the main river in Assyria, this would suggest that the Shihor is the Nile. Isaiah 23:3 strengthens this association, placing the Shihor and the Nile in parallel with one another. Joshua 13:3, however, states that the Shihor is in the east of Egypt, which might suggest it is the Pelusaic branch of the Nile, the eastern most branch in the delta. This would match the evidence in 1 Chr 13:5, where the Shihor is seen as

the idealized western boundary of Israel. The name is probably a form of the Egyptian p3 š-ḥr, "the waters of Horus."

KEVIN A. WILSON

SHIHOR-LIBNATH shi´horlib´nath [שִׁיחוֹר לִבְנָת shikhor livnath]. Possibly a river, Shihor-libnath formed part of the western boundary of the territory allotted to Asher (Josh 19:26) in the vicinity of modern Haifa. The MT lists it as a single place while the LXX indicates two places, Zion and Libnath.

JOAN E. COOK, SC

SHIKKERON shik´uh-ron [שִׁכְּרוֹן shikkeron]. A place located on the northwestern border of the territory allotted to the tribe of Judah (Josh 15:11). It is located approximately 25 mi. west of Jerusalem, near the territory of Philistia and the Mediterranean Sea.

SHILHI shil´hi [שִׁלְחִי shilkhi]. Maternal grandfather of Jehoshaphat. No other information is given about him in either 1 Kgs 22:42 or 2 Chr 20:31.

SHILHIM shil´him [שִׁלְחִים shilkhim]. One of the twenty-nine towns allotted to the tribe of Judah (Josh 15:32). The town of Shaaraim, assigned to Judah in Josh 15:36 (see also 1 Sam 17:52), and Sharuhen, allotted to Simeon in Josh 19:6, are possibly the same place.

JOAN E. COOK, SC

SHILLEM shil´uhm [שִׁלֵּם shillem]. In the list of those who migrated with Jacob to Egypt, Gen 46:24 lists Shillem as the youngest son of Naphtali, who was the son of Jacob and Bilhah, Rachel's maid. In another list of Naphtali's offspring, the name appears as SHALLUM (1 Chr 7:13). In the results of Moses' second census Shillem appears as the ancestral head of the Shillemites (Num 26:49).

JOAN E. COOK, SC

SHILOAH, WATERS OF shi´loh´uh [מֵי הַשִּׁלֹחַ me hashiloakh; ὕδωρ τοῦ Σιλωάμ hydōr tou Silōam]. A canal along the eastern slope of Jerusalem (Isa 8:6), likely the same as the pool of SILOAM (John 9:7).

SHILOH, SHILONITE shi´loh, shi´luh-nit [שִׁלֹה shiloh, שִׁילֹה shiloh, שִׁלֹו shilo, שִׁילֹו shilo, שִׁילוֹנִי shiloni]. 1. A town mentioned in the Former Prophets, Jeremiah, and Psalms. Since E. Robinson's visit to the site in 1838, Shiloh has been commonly identified with Khirbet Seilun, located about 31 km (19 mi.) north of Jerusalem and roughly halfway between Ramallah and Nablus (*see* SHECHEM, SHECHEMITES), just east of the main road connecting them. This identification, supported by Jerome, Eusebius, and the MADABA MAP, is based (apart from the assumption that the modern Arabic name stems from the ancient Hebrew toponym) on Judg 21:19, which places Shiloh "north of Bethel, on the east of the highway that goes up from Bethel to

Shechem, and south of Lebonah." An attempt to claim that variant spellings of the toponym in both Hebrew and Greek suggest the existence of two different locations named Shiloh, one at Khirbet Seilun and another at Khirbet Beit Sila southwest of Ramallah, has found little support.

In the book of Joshua, Shiloh functions as a pan-Israelite sanctuary, repeatedly housing pan-Israelite gatherings. In Shiloh, Joshua completes the division of the promised land among the tribes (18:1; 19:51), sets aside cities for the Levites (21:1-3), and announces to the Transjordanian tribes that they have fulfilled their military obligations and may return to their allotments (22:1-9). When these tribes erect their own altar, "the whole assembly of the Israelites gathered at Shiloh, to make war against them" (22:12). Shiloh housed the TABERNACLE (Josh 18:1; 1951); in Shiloh, Joshua "cast lots ... before the LORD" to determine distribution of tribal territories (18:8, 10); the presence of ELEAZAR (19:51) and PHINEHAS (22:13), respectively, the son and grandson of Aaron, confirm Shiloh's status as a sanctuary site. However, the allotments of several tribes, including such important ones as Judah, Ephraim, and Manasseh, are apparently apportioned in GILGAL rather than Shiloh (14:6), and shortly before his death Joshua summons the people to present themselves "before God" in Shechem (24:1; compare 24:25). Although Judg 18:31 mentions "the house of God" in Shiloh, elsewhere in Judges it is a minor and obscure locale. Israelite leaders not only casually sanction an act of unprovoked violence against it, advising the men of Benjamin to restore their recently decimated tribe by abducting young women of Shiloh (21:19-22), but also have to provide uniquely detailed directions to the town (v. 19). The ritual occasion that made the abduction possible—the "yearly festival of the Lord," during which young women danced in the vineyards (vv. 19-21)—is not attested elsewhere in the OT and should be viewed therefore as a local tradition (perhaps related to Canaanite fertility rites) that does not indicate Shiloh's lasting significance. Given that Bethel and Mizpah function in the same narrative as pan-Israelite shrines and political centers (Judg 20:1, 18, 26-28; 21:1-2; note especially the mention of the ARK OF THE COVENANT and Phinehas in 20:27), this change in Shiloh's fortunes fits in with the overall trajectory of the Israelite worship according to the Deuteronomistic writer. This writer presumes that before the construction of the Jerusalem Temple, Yahweh's sanctuary remained itinerant and no location was particularly favored by the deity (2 Sam 7:6-7; 1 Kgs 8:16; 9:3). If so, Shiloh derived its importance solely from the presence of the tabernacle and the ark in it and sank back into obscurity as soon as the sacred objects were removed.

A different notion of Shiloh as a cultic site is operative in Jer 7:12 ("Go now to my place that was in Shiloh, where I made my name dwell at first, and see what I did to it for the wickedness of my people Israel")

and Ps 78:60 ("[God] abandoned his dwelling at Shiloh, the tent where he dwelt among mortals"). In both fragments, the location is initially favored by Yahweh and abandoned not because the itinerant shrine simply moved on, but as a punishment for the people's transgressions (see especially Ps 78:56-58). A similar concept appears to underlie 1 Sam 1–4, where Shiloh, to which HANNAH and her family make annual pilgrimages (1:3, 21) and eventually dedicate her son SAMUEL (1:24-28), re-emerges as a pan-Israelite cultic center (note references in 2:14, 22, 28, 29 to "all Israel" making sacrifices there). This time, however, Shiloh not only houses the itinerant shrine, complete with the tabernacle (2:22) and the ark (3:3; 4:3) but also boasts a permanent structure referred to as the "temple (hekhal הֵיכָל) of the Lord" (1:9; 3:3; note also the references to a doorpost in 1:9 and a door in 3:15). The chapters thus implicitly characterize Shiloh as a counterpart not of the temporary cultic sites mentioned in Joshua and Judges, but of the Jerusalem Temple—the only other "hekhal of the Lord" in the OT (e.g., 2 Kgs 18:16; Jer 24:1; Ezek 8:16), which also combined the ark and the tabernacle with a permanent temple structure (see especially 1 Kgs 8:3-8). Jeremiah makes the link between Shiloh and Jerusalem explicit by repeatedly warning the latter that it will suffer the destruction that befell the former (7:14; 26:6, 9).

The concept of Shiloan priesthood in 1 Sam 1–4 is likewise idiosyncratic: the personal, hereditary, and irrevocable commission of ELI and his sons HOPHNI AND PHINEHAS, who are in charge of the sanctuary (1:3), is traced back not to the election of Aaron (Exod 28:1-3) but to a revelation received by an unnamed ancestor in Egypt (1 Sam 2:27, 30). This configuration links the concept in question to Deut 18:5 that sets the tenet of eternal hereditary priesthood without specifying its Aaronide ancestry (note also the verbal parallels between Deut 18:3-5 and 1 Sam 2:13, 29). Since Deuteronomy also requires concentration of all worship in a single location (see especially Deut 12:1-28), Shiloh is characterized in 1 Sam 1–4 as a sanctuary that fully conforms to the Deuteronomic ideal of cultic organization. The result is blatant abuse of power (according to 1 Sam 2:12-17, Hophni and Phinehas embezzled sacrificial meat) that leads to a military defeat (4:1-10), the loss of the ark to the Philistines (4:11), and the apparent demise of Shiloh as a cultic site (in 1 Sam 7:5-9, Israelites assemble and make sacrifices in Mizpah). In sum, 1 Sam 1–4 not only stands in considerable tension to the Deuteronomistic trajectory of the Israelite cult, but also exposes the Deuteronomic principles of cultic organization as impracticable.

Khirbet Seilun was excavated by the National Museum of Denmark in 1926, 1929, and 1932, with a brief follow-up expedition in 1963, and by Bar-Ilan University (Israel) in 1981–84. These excavations showed that the site, strategically situated near a major north-south trade route and overlooking a highly fertile valley, was first settled during the Middle Bronze age, in the 18th cent. BCE, and was heavily fortified about a hundred years later. Since the settlement's size remained small and no residential quarters of the period were found, it probably served mostly as a fortress as well as an administrative and cultic center. During the Late Bronze age (16th–13th cent. BCE), the site was largely abandoned, although there are some indications that the local sanctuary continued to function for at least a part of the period. The settlement flourished again from the late 12th through mid-11th cent. BCE (Iron Age I); relatively sophisticated pillared structures dating from this time have been identified as the only known Iron Age I public buildings in the hill country of Canaan. Absence of living quarters suggests that at this period Shiloh again served mainly as an administrative and cultic center. Destroyed by a massive conflagration in the mid-11th cent. BCE, it re-emerged as a small village only toward the end of Iron Age II (8th–7th cent. BCE). Gradually abandoned, the site remained unoccupied or sparsely occupied until the late Hellenistic to early Roman period (1st cent. BCE–1st cent. CE).

Archeological findings outlined above confirm the contention of 1 Sam 1–4 that in the period immediately preceding the establishment of kingship in ancient Israel, Shiloh was a location of primary, perhaps exclusive, importance; its destruction, clearly attested in the archeological record, could be the direct result of the Israelites' defeat by the Philistines reported in 1 Sam 4:10. However, the references to Shiloh's devastation in Jeremiah and Psalms (see above) never clearly allude to these chapters, and 1 Kgs 14:2, 4, where Shiloh is mentioned as the residence of the prophet AHIJAH, presupposes that in the late 10th cent. BCE the town was still populated. With this in mind, it is possible that the references in question assume that Shiloh was destroyed in 721 BCE, when Assyrians overran the Northern Kingdom (2 Kgs 17:5-6). The mention of pilgrims from Shiloh in Jer 41:5 confirms that the site was settled in the early 6th cent. BCE.

Although there are multiple circumstantial indications of cultic activity at Khirbet Seilun, no buildings or enclosures identifiable as sanctuaries have been found at the site. The OT thus remains the only available source of information concerning the nature of worship at Shiloh and its significance as a cultic center; given that the testimony of the biblical authors is heavily colored by their presuppositions and agendas, reliability of this information cannot be evaluated with any degree of certainty. In particular, the parallels between Shiloh and Jerusalem in 1 Sam 1–4 (see above) may in principle indicate that the cultic tradition of the latter, symbolized above all by the ark, were inherited from the former. But it is also possible that Shiloh in these chapters is mostly, if not exclusively, a polemical construct designed to subvert the Deuteronomic/Deuteronomistic ideal of cultic centralization, embodied by the Jerusalem Temple. Significantly, in Judg 18:30-31, Shiloh is genetically linked not to Jerusalem, but to Dan, and a rival shrine founded by JEROBOAM I as a cultic center of the Northern Kingdom (1 Kgs 12:29-30).

2. Gentilic of Shiloh, used of the prophet Ahijah in 1 Kgs 11:29; 12:15; 15:29; 2 Chr 9:29; 10:15. In 1 Chr 9:5 and Neh 11:5, the term most likely refers to descendants of SHELAH the son of Judah and should therefore be rendered "Shelahide."

Bibliography: Marie-Louise Buhl and Svend Holm-Nielsen. *Shiloh: The Danish Excavations at Tall Sailun, Palestine in 1926, 1929, 1932 and 1963. The Pre-Hellenistic Remains* (1969); Israel Finkelstein. *The Archaeology of the Israelite Settlement* (1988) 205–34; Israel Finkelstein, Shlomo Bunimovitz, and Zvi Lederman. *Shiloh: The Archaeology of a Biblical Site* (1993); Serge Frolov. "'Days of Shiloh' in the Kingdom of Israel." *Bib* 76 (1995) 210–18; Serge Frolov. *The Turn of the Cycle: 1 Samuel 1–8 in Synchronic and Diachronic Perspectives* (2004); Menahem Haran. *Temples and Temple-Service in Ancient Israel: An Inquiry into the Character of Cult Phenomena and the Historical Setting of the Priestly School* (1978); Jon Lindblom. "The Political Background of the Shiloh Oracle." *Congress Volume: Copenhagen 1953* (1953) 78–87; A. T. Richardson. "The Site of Shiloh." *PEQ* 59 (1927) 85–88; Donald G. Schley. *Shiloh: A Biblical City in Tradition and History* (1989).

SERGE FROLOV

SHILSHAH shil´shuh [שִׁלְשָׁה *shilshah*]. The ninth of Zophah's eleven sons, descendants of Asher who were both warriors and heads of households (1 Chr 7:37).

SHIMEA shim´ee-uh [שִׁמְעָא *shimʿaʾ*]. 1. Third son of Jesse (1 Chr 2:13) and older brother of David. Called SHAMMAH in 1 Sam 16:9. Father of Jonathan who slew a giant from Gath who had twelve fingers and toes (1 Chr 20:7). Called SHIMEI in 1 Sam 21:21. Father of Jonadab who schemed with Amnon to rape his sister Tamar (2 Sam 13:3, 32; here he is called SHIMEAH).

2. Son of David born to Bath-Shua/Bathsheba in Jerusalem (1 Chr 3:5). Brother to Solomon, Shobab, and Nathan. Called SHAMMUA in 2 Sam 5:14 and 1 Chr 14:4.

3. Descendant of Merari, son of Levi (1 Chr 6:30 [Heb. 6:15]).

4. Ancestor of Asaph (1 Chr 6:39 [Heb. 6:24]) one of the temple singers.

PETER T. LANFER

SHIMEAH. See SHIMEA.

SHIMEATH shim´ee-ath [שִׁמְעָת *shimʿath*]. Father of one of the assassins of King Joash of Judah (2 Kgs 12:21; 2 Chr 24:26). There is some confusion of names in the two accounts. See SHIMRITH; SHOMER.

SHIMEATHITES shim´ee-uh-th*it* [שִׁמְעָתִים *shim'athim*]. Part of the Calebite family of Hur (1 Chr 2:55). They are one of three groups or families of scribes that lived at Jabez, a location that is unknown. The verse is difficult. It is unclear if the scribal name indicates a function or a family. The Vulgate (Latin) renders the term "Shimeathites" as *resonantes*, meaning "those who make melodies." The Targum of 1 Chronicles understands it to refer to scribes who were to proclaim the tradition of Torah. The Shimeathites are related to the KENITES, who are associated with the Rechabites (compare Jer 35). *See* CALEB, CALEBITES; RECHAB, RECHABITES.

MARK RONCACE

SHIMEI shim´ee-*i* [שִׁמְעִי *shim'i*; Σεμεΐς *Semeis*]. *Shimei* is an abbreviated form of Shemaiah, "Yahweh hears." 1. A Benjaminite, the son of Gera of Saul's family, who cursed David and threw stones at him as he fled from Absalom (2 Sam 16:5, 13). Shimei's accusation that David was guilty of murder and "all the blood of the house of Saul" (16:8) suggests that David may have been complicit in the deaths of Saul and Jonathan (1 Sam 31–2 Sam 1), Abner (2 Sam 3), and Ishbaal (2 Sam 4) or at least that he was suspected of complicity, and also hints that David's motive in the subsequent execution of Saul's heirs (2 Sam 21:1-9) may have been political. David refused to have Shimei killed (2 Sam 16:9-12), and when David returned victorious, Shimei once more came to meet him and to beg his pardon (2 Sam 19:16-20). David again refused to have him executed (19:21-23), perhaps in part because of the 1,000 Benjaminites accompanying Shimei (v. 17). Shimei was executed by Solomon, following David's death-bed request (1 Kgs 2:8, 36-46). Solomon's motives were also likely political—to consolidate his hold on power in the face of the Benjaminite family of the former king, Saul, and in the face of his older brother, Adonijah, and his supporters. David's death-bed order was probably a fiction providing an apologetic legitimation for Solomon's actions (*see* BENJAMIN, BENJAMINITES).

2. The grandson of Levi and son of Gershon and hence a Levitical clan (Exod 6:17; Num 3:18, 21; 1 Chr 6:17 [Heb. 6:2]; 23:7, 10; Zech 12:13). In 1 Chr 23:9 *Shimei* is probably an error for one of the sons of his brother Ladan/Libni in v. 8, since four sons are listed for Shimei in vv. 10-11: Jahath, Zina/Zizah, Jeush, and Beriah. The notice that the last two were enrolled together because of their size suggests the merger of the two subclans. In 1 Chr 6:42-43 (Heb. 6:27-28), Shimei and Jahath have apparently been inverted.

3. David's brother (2 Sam 21:21), elsewhere called SHIMEA (2 Sam 13:3, 32; 1 Chr 2:13; 20:7) or Shammah (1 Sam 16:9; 17:13).

4. An official in David's court who did not support Adonijah's bid to become king (1 Kgs 1:8).

5. The son of Ela, who served as the official in charge of the province of Benjamin in Solomon's redistricted

kingdom (1 Kgs 4:18). He may be identical with #3, in which case his office was likely a reward for his support of Solomon.

6. The brother of Zerubbabel (1 Chr 3:19).

7. The son of Libni and great grandson of Merari (1 Chr 6:29 [Heb. 6:14]). Perhaps an error, since Shimei #2 is Libni's brother.

8. An individual or clan of Simeon (1 Chr 4:26-27). It is not clear whether this genealogy is linear and each name represents a generation or segmented so that Shallum, Mibsam, and Mishma are Shaul's sons and Hammuel, Zaccur, and Shimei all Mishma's. *Shimei* and *Mishma* pun on *Simeon*, as all three are from the same Hebrew root (*see* SIMEON, SIMEONITES).

9. An individual or clan within Reuben (1 Chr 5:4); the son of Gog, the grandson of Joel, whose connection with Reuben is not clear (*see* REUBEN, REUBENITES).

10. One of five heads of Benjaminite families (1 Chr 8:21), called SHEMA in 8:13.

11. One of the individuals or families of Levitical singers in the line of JEDUTHUN (1 Chr 25:17, and restored in v. 3). The rotation of the singers in 25:9-31 reflects regular alternation and indicates the artificiality of the claim that it resulted from lottery.

12. An official from Ramah who was in charge of David's vineyards (1 Chr 27:27).

13. A Levite of the line of Heman who helped implement Hezekiah's directive to cleanse the Temple (2 Chr 29:14).

14. A Levite, the brother of CONANIAH, who was second in charge of the contributions to the Temple under Hezekiah (2 Chr 31:12-13). Perhaps the same as #13.

15. A Levite forced to divorce his foreign wife (Ezra 10:23; 1 Esd 9:23).

16. A son or descendant of Hashum, who was forced to divorce his foreign wife (Ezra 10:33; 1 Esd 9:33).

17. A son of Bani or, more likely, Binnui, based on the Greek reading (Ezra 10:38; compare 1 Esd 9:34), who was forced to divorce his foreign wife.

18. A Benjaminite ancestor of Mordecai and descendant of Kish (Esth 2:5). Possibly the same as #1.

STEVEN L. MCKENZIE

SHIMEON shim´ee-uhn [שִׁמְעוֹן *shime'on*; Σεμεών *Semeon*]. Variant spelling of Simeon (*see* SIMEON, SIMEONITES). A son of Harim numbered in the census taken by Ezra (Ezra 10:31), Shimeon and his brothers Eliezer, Isshijah, Malchijah, and Shemaiah are listed among the returned exiles who married foreign women. Possibly called SIMON Chosamaeus, a descendant of Annan, in the parallel passage 1 Esd 9:32.

PETER T. LANFER

SHIMON shi´muhn [שִׁימוֹן *shimon*]. Head of a clan in the tribe of Judah and father of four sons (1 Chr 4:20).

SHIMRATH shim′rath [שִׁמְרָת shimrath]. The genealogical list in 1 Chr 8:21 includes Shimrath, a son of Shimei, among the descendants of Benjamin. His name, along with most of the names in the list, differs from other Benjaminite lists in 1 Chr 7:6-12, Gen 46:21, and Num 26:38-40.

SHIMRI shim′ri [שִׁמְרִי shimri]. 1. Son of Shemaiah and ancestor of Ziza who was a family leader of the tribe of Simeon (1 Chr 4:37).

2. Father of Jediael and Joha, who were two of David's warriors (1 Chr 11:45).

3. Son of Hosah of the sons of Merari. The Chronicler draws attention to the fact that he was appointed chief even though he was not the firstborn (1 Chr 26:10).

4. Son of Elizaphan and brother of Jeuel. One of the Levites commanded by Hezekiah to cleanse the house of the Lord (2 Chr 29:13).

R. ANDREW COMPTON

SHIMRITH shim′rith [שִׁמְרִית shimrith]. According to 2 Chr 24:26, Shimrith, a Moabitess, was the mother of Jehozabad, one of the conspirators who assassinated the Judean monarch Joash to avenge the wrongful death of Zechariah. In 2 Kgs 12:21, the name appears in the shortened, masculine form SHOMER. *See* SHIMEATH.

JASON R. TATLOCK

SHIMRON shim′ron [שִׁמְרוֹן shimron]. 1. A son of Issachar and the ancestral tribal head of the Shimronites (Gen 46:13; Num 26:24; 1 Chr 7:1).

2. A Canaanite city during the conquest. The king of Shimron joined Jabin to oppose Joshua and was defeated by Israel (Josh 11:1; 19:15). Geographically, Shimron is located ca. 11 km west of Nazareth. Many have noted the similarity between Shimron and Tell Semuniya although scholarship is not unanimous on this identification. *See* SHIMRON-MERON.

Bibliography: Yoel Elitzur. *Ancient Place Names in the Holy Land* (2004); Anson F. Rainey and R. Steven Notley. *Cartas Atlas of the Biblical World: The Sacred Bridge* (2006).

JOSEPH R. CATHEY

SHIMRON-MERON shim′ron-mee′ron [שִׁמְרוֹן מְראֹון shimron mer’on]. A Canaanite city whose king is listed among those whom Joshua defeated (Josh 12:20). Achshaph's association with SHIMRON in Josh 11:1 and with Shimron-meron in Josh 12:20 suggests Shimron-meron may be the city's full name.

EMILY R. CHENEY

SHIMSHAI shim′shi [שִׁמְשַׁי shimshay; Σαμσαί Samsai, Σαμέλλιος Samellios]. Persian official in the province "Beyond the River," which included Jerusalem. Rehum and his adjutant, Shimshai the scribe, wrote to Artaxerxes from their base in Samaria, asking that the Jews be barred from rebuilding Jerusalem (Ezra 4:8-24; 1 Esd 2:16-30). This letter is one of the few OT passages composed in Aramaic, the official language of the Persian court. Artaxerxes acquiesced, and Rehum and his associates stopped the Jews by force.

R. JUSTIN HARKINS

SHINAB shi′nab [שִׁנְאָב shin’av]. Shinab, king of Admah (Gen 14:2), was one of five kings, including the kings of Sodom and Gomorrah, who rebelled against and were defeated by CHEDORLAOMER and his three allies in the Valley of Siddim along the coast of the Dead Sea.

JOAN E. COOK, SC

SHINAR shi′nahr [שִׁנְעָר shin‘ar]. The general area of southern Mesopotamia (modern south Iraq), known in ancient times as Babylonia. The association of Shinar with Babylon is confirmed by the frequent translation of *Shinar* in the LXX as "Babylon" (Isa 11:11; Zech 5:11; Dan 1:2). According to Gen 10:8-10, Nimrod's kingdom first included cites in Shinar and later extended north into Assyria, and Shinar was the location of the tower of Babel (Gen 11:2). The mention of Shinar in both contexts is the exegetical basis for the association of Nimrod with the building of the tower in later Jewish interpretive texts (e.g., Josephus, *Ant.* 1.113–15). King Amraphel of Shinar was a member of a coalition that fought to subdue five rebelling kings near the Dead Sea (Gen 14:1-3).

PHILLIP MICHAEL SHERMAN

SHION shi′uhn [שִׁיאֹן shi’on]. A place in the promised land that was divided by Joshua (Josh 18–19). Shion was one of the sixteen cities that fell to the lot of the tribe of Issachar (Josh 19:19). Some have proposed that the original city existed near Mount Tabor, but a positive identification has not yet been made. *See* ISSACHAR, ISSACHARITES.

NATHAN P. LAMONTAGNE

SHIPHI shi′fi [שִׁפְעִי shif‘i]. Father of Zita and son of Allon in a genealogy of Simeon's descendants (1 Chr 4:37).

SHIPHMITE shif′mit [שִׁפְמִי shifmi]. Appellation given to Zabdi, overseer of the produce in David's vineyards, indicating he came perhaps from SHEPHAM or SIPHMOTH (1 Chr 27:27).

SHIPHRAH shif′ruh [שִׁפְרָה shifrah]. A MIDWIFE (Exod 1:15-21). She and her fellow midwife, PUAH, were commanded by Pharaoh to kill any boys born to the Hebrew mothers they tended. The two refused and, when confronted by Pharaoh, suggested that the Hebrew mothers were delivering before the midwives could arrive. Their protective act of deception was rewarded by the Lord, who gave them families of their own.

JESSICA TINKLENBERG DEVEGA

SHIPHTAN shif'tan [שִׁפְטָן shiftan]. To apportion the inheritance, the conquered land, God instructed Moses to select one leader from each of the twelve tribes, among whom KEMUEL, the son of Shiphtan, was selected from the tribe of Ephraim (Num 34:24).

SHIPMASTER [κυβερνήτης kybernētēs]. Commander of a ship, who steered the ship and so controlled its helm, and who might also be its owner, but not always: Acts 27:11 clearly indicates that this ship's pilot (kybernētēs) and the owner are two different people. Since the livelihood of shipmasters depended on transporting merchants' cargo, it is understandable that they would lament the burning of Rome, for few would be purchasing the merchants' goods or providing them goods to transport (Rev 18:17-18). **Kybernētēs** is often translated "PILOT" (LXX Ezek 27:8, 27-29; 4 Macc 7:1; Acts 27:11). See BOAT; OAR; SHIPS AND SAILING IN THE NT; SHIPS AND SAILING IN THE OT.

EMILY R. CHENEY

SHIPS AND SAILING IN THE NT. Boats on the Sea of Galilee form the setting for Jesus' ministry. The first disciples were fishermen (Matt 4:19; Mark 1:17; Luke 5:10). Jesus preached from boats to the masses on the shore (Matt 13:1-3; Mark 3:9; 4:1). Several miracles concern fishing (Matt 17:24-27; Luke 5:1-11). Insight into this milieu is crucial to understanding the ministry of Jesus.

The Sea of Galilee served several vital purposes. It abounded with fish, which resulted in the development of a local fishing industry. The lake also served as a vital transportation hub between the Galilee, the Golan Heights, and the Jordan Valley (see GALILEE, SEA OF). In the 1st cent. CE the lake was ringed by more than a dozen small fishermen's harbors. The harbors consisted of breakwaters that created enclosed areas protected from the prominent local winds. A shore-side promenade permitted land access.

A hull discovered during a 1986 drought added to our understanding of seafaring in the Gospels. Known as the Kinneret Boat, the Galilee Boat, or less accurately as the "Jesus Boat," it comes from the western shore of the lake, just north of the ancient site of Migdal. The BOAT is now exhibited at the Yigal Allon Museum in Kibbutz Ginosar, adjacent to its discovery site. The vessel has been dated to the first centuries BCE–CE based on analysis of the techniques used in its construction, on pottery, and on radiocarbon dates. The boat was preserved to a length of 8.2 m, a maximum breadth of 2.3 m, and reached a height of 1.2 m (26.9 × 7.5 × 3.9 ft.). After laying the keel, stem, and sternposts, the vessel's builders raised the sides of the hull by edge-joining the planks (strakes) to the keel and then to one another with pegged mortise-and-tenon joinery. Once the hull had been raised the builder(s) inserted frames, attaching them to the hull with iron nails. While most of the planks were made from Lebanese cedar and the

frames of oak, a total of twelve wood types have been identified. The multiplicity of wood types and the use of recycled timber indicate that either wood was difficult to come by or that the boat's owner was impoverished. A vessel this size was probably used primarily for FISHING with a large seine NET (Matt 13:47-48). It could also have served as an all-purpose vessel to transport people and commodities around the lake.

The boat could have moved under OAR or SAIL. A mosaic from Migdal dating to the 1st cent. CE probably depicts a model of this type of vessel. It has a cutwater bow and a recurving stern and is shown under oar with a reefed square sail. At least two types of watercraft existed on the lake in the 1st cent. CE: the Kinneret Boat is an example of the larger type. The Migdal Boat Mosaic depicts two oars and a quarter rudder on its port side: with complementary oars on the starboard side, this would require a crew of five—four rowers and a helmsman/captain. Thus, it is possible to determine the crew sizes of the boats owned by Zebedee and Simon Peter. Mark 1:20 relates that when Jesus called James and John to him, they were in the boat with Zebedee and the hired men: they would have made a crew of five or more. Similarly, when Simon Peter went fishing, he took with him six disciples, making a crew of seven (John 21:2-3); when fishing, more men would have been required. In assembling his sham fleet at Migdal to attack a recalcitrant Tiberias, Josephus assigned four-man crews and a captain to each of his boats (J.W. 2.635, 641; Life 163). Thus, the boat, the mosaic, and the descriptions in the Gospels and by Josephus all represent the same type of boat.

The existence of a smaller boat type in use on the lake is hinted at in the story of Josephus' hasty escape from a hostile crowd in Tiberias (J.W. 2.619; Life 96). His rapid exit would seem to preclude the use of a boat of the larger size in this case.

The Kinneret Boat may explain some NT passages related to seafaring. For example, Jesus is described in the Synoptic Gospels as sleeping during a voyage when a storm arose on the lake (Matt 8:24; Mark 4:38; Luke 8:23). Mark includes additional details: Jesus was "in the stern, asleep on the pillow." A practical reason for choosing to sleep in the stern relates to the influence of the seine net. This net required a large deck at the stern for preparing and spreading. The crawl space created beneath this deck would have been the most sheltered location on the boat. The "pillow" may have been a sandbag used to ballast the vessel. Normally these were used to keep the vessel on an even trim, but when not in use they could be stored away beneath the stern deck.

Mediterranean seafaring played an important role in the spread of early Christianity. Paul and other leaders of the early church often traveled on ships (Paul's first missionary journey: Acts 13:4-5, 13; 14:24; second missionary journey: Acts 16:11; 17:14-15; 18:18, 21-22;

third missionary journey: Acts 20:2-6, 13-16, 38; 21:1-3, 6, 7[?]).

Shipwreck was a constant peril (1 Tim 1:19-20; compare Wis 14:1-5). Paul reports having been wrecked three times (2 Cor 11:25). The best known and only detailed description of these experiences is the wreck of a ship on which he was being transported to trial in Rome, described in detail in Acts 27. The first leg of Paul's voyage, along with other prisoners, was on a ship from Adramyttium (Acts 27:2). The ship sailed to Sidon and from there continued "under the lee"— that is, along the southern coast—of Cyprus because of contrary winds (Acts 27:4). After passing the island the ship headed north arriving at Myra, a port on the Lycian coast.

At Myra the prisoners transferred to a ship plying the Alexandria to Rome route. These large vessels were built specifically to supply Rome with Egyptian grain. Apart from its main cargo, it also carried passengers: Luke mentions 276 persons on board (Acts 27:37). This number need not surprise us: Josephus survived shipwreck during a trip to Rome and recounts some 600 persons on board his ship (*Life* 15).

Paul's ship continued westward to Cnidos but then, due to headwinds again, changed course and sailed south reaching Salmone in eastern Crete and sailing along the island's southern coast, arriving at Fair Havens, a harbor on Crete's southern coast (Acts 27:7-8).

Sailing the Mediterranean in antiquity was a seasonal activity: the sailing season lasted from spring to fall. By now Paul's ship found itself very late in the sailing season. The captain, against Paul's advice, made a run for a more suitable winter anchorage at Phoenix in southwestern Crete, but a northeasterly blew the ship off course (Acts 27:14-16).

In dealing with the storm the crew carried out specific activities. All the crew's actions are in accordance with efforts carried out in severe weather when ships were in danger of sinking. They hauled the ship's boat on board, "undergirded" the ship, set out a sea anchor, threw the cargo overboard (compare Jonah 1:5), and eventually even cut away the rigging (Acts 27:16-19). When soundings indicated that the ship was approaching land the sailors laid out four anchors from the stern (Acts 27:27-29). The term used for "undergirding" is one normally used in connection with long and narrow warships, which required additional longitudinal support. These undergirdings appear in lists of Athenian trireme equipment in the 5th cent. BCE: their appearance and exact use remains illusive. This is the only reference to the undergirding of a merchant ship. Lines of amphoras (two-handled wine jars) have been discovered in deep water at Skerkie Bank off Sicily: these represent the archaeological evidence for lightening a ship by throwing the cargo overboard.

The ship's crew coped with the situation during the storm, only trying to escape from the ship when they sounded and found that the vessel was approaching land: the sailors then lowered the ship's boat and tried to escape in it, an action prevented by Paul (Acts 27:27-32). The ship ultimately ran aground on a reef. Paul and the other prisoners reached shore by clinging to pieces of the disintegrating ship (Acts 27:41-44).

Ships and their equipment also are used allegorically in the NT (Rev 8:9; 18:11-13, 17-19). In Heb 6:19, the author describes the "hope set before us" as "a sure and steadfast anchor of the soul." James 3:4-5 compares the

S. Wachsmann

Figure 1: The Kinneret Boat in its exhibition hall at the Yigal Allon Museum, Kibbutz Ginosar, Israel.

tongue to the rudder of a ship: just as large ships are "guided by a very small rudder wherever the will of the pilot directs," so the tongue, though small, "boasts of great exploits." In Revelation, those who lament over the fall of "Babylon" (i.e., Rome) include the "merchants of the earth" because no one buys their cargo (18:11-13). In 18:17-19, "all shipmasters and seafarers, sailors and all whose trade is on the sea," cry out and put dust on their heads as they lament the loss of wealth represented by the city's fall (compare 8:9, where the blowing of the second trumpet results in the destruction of "a third of the ships"; Wis 5:8-10, where the unrighteous lament that their arrogance and boasted wealth has vanished like a ship that leaves no tracks in the water). *See* TRADE AND COMMERCE; TRAVEL AND COMMUNICATION IN THE NT.

Bibliography: M. Fitzgerald. "The Ship of Saint Paul: Comparative Archaeology." *BA* 53 (1990) 31–39; N. Hirschfield. "The Ship of Saint Paul: Historical Background." *BA* 53 (1990) 25–30; A. F. Rainey and R. S. Notley. *The Sacred Bridge: Carta's Atlas of the Biblical World* (2006); M. Nun. *Ancient Stone Anchors and Net Sinkers from the Sea of Galilee* (1993); M. Nun. "Cast Your Net upon the Waters: Fish and Fishermen in Jesus' Time." *BAR* 19 (1993) 46–56, 70; M. Nun. *The Sea of Galilee and Its Fishermen in the New Testament* (1989); M. Nun. *Sea of Galilee: Newly Discovered Harbours from New Testament Days.* 3rd rev. ed. (1992); P. Throckmorton. "Shipwrecks and St. Paul." *History from the Sea* (1987) 78–80; S. Wachsmann. *The Sea of Galilee Boat: A 2000 Year Old Discovery from the Sea of Legends* (2000); E. Werker. "Identification of the Wood in the Ancient Boat from the Sea of Galilee." *Atiqot* 50 (2005) 233–36.

SHELLEY WACHSMANN

SHIPS AND SAILING IN THE OT [אֳנִי 'oni, אֳנִיָּה 'oniyah, סְפִינָה sefinah, צִי tsi]. Various terms were used for ships and boats in the OT. 'Oniyah, "ship," and 'oni, a collective term typically translated "ships" or "fleet," appear most frequently. In general the ancient Israelites were an agrarian and pastoral people whose focused settlement was in the hill country of the southern Levant, distant from any sea. Ships and sailing are thus rare topics in the OT. Neighboring cultures to the west, such as the Canaanites and their descendants the Phoenicians, lived in territories along the Mediterranean littoral and were maritime societies par excellence.

There are longstanding misconceptions that the coastline of the region had few good natural ports, and so harbors were not considered a major component of the historic geography of the southern Levant. This idea has been overthrown recently by archaeological surveys, the excavation of sites in the coastal plains, and underwater archaeology in shallow and deep waters that demonstrate that the Mediterranean Sea played a vital role in ancient settlements, lifeways, economy,

and commerce of the southern Levant (Stieglitz 2001). This is especially significant when the region is viewed not only as a land-bridge between Syro-Mesopotamia and Egypt but also as the hub of maritime connections between these two dominant cultural spheres of the ANE. Geomorphological work has demonstrated that the modern terrain surrounding coastal settlements may have been greatly altered since ancient times by the silting of rivers, lagoons, and bays; by changes in sea level; and by tectonic forces. Thus the most likely areas to harbor ships are often drastically different from their ancient appearance, size, and even location. Shipwreck archaeology has also demonstrated that ancient vessels tended to be modestly sized, with a shallow draft that would allow for anchorage in small, natural or human-constructed ports.

People have sailed the Mediterranean and settled its islands from prehistoric times (*see* SEA, GREAT). International maritime commerce along the Levantine littoral is attested from the Early Bronze Age; grew in scope to include Cyprus, Crete, and the Aegean in the Middle Bronze Age; and peaked in the Late Bronze Age. The earliest attestation of ships in the OT is found in poetic sources portraying the tribal world of premonarchic Israel (Gen 49:13; Judg 5:17). Three northern tribes have maritime or seafaring links: Zebulon, Asher, and Dan. Zebulon and Asher have tribal claims in the Akko plain and economic links to harbor cities in the region (Gen 49:13; Deut 33:18-19; Judg 1:31-32; 5:17). The passage describing Dan dwelling in ships is usually associated with the early settlement of the tribe in the southern coastal plain (Judg 5:17). However, a good overland route links the more northerly region of Dan, above the Sea of Galilee, to the coast around TYRE. Therefore, this poetic passage may describe Danites residing and working on Tyrian ships after the tribe's move to the north. While greatly diminished from the voluminous maritime trade of the Late Bronze II period, archaeology demonstrates that overseas commerce between southern Lebanon, northern Israel, and Cyprus continued in the Iron I period, which is traditionally associated with the premonarchic period of the judges. Seafaring and ships of this same period are also found in the Egyptian tale of Wenamun, that details a commercial sea voyage from Egypt along the Levantine coast, which is blown off course to Cyprus on its return trip (*see* WENAMUN, JOURNEY OF).

During the period of the united monarchy, the OT documents cooperative maritime ventures on the Red Sea between the kingdom of Israel and the Phoenician city-state of Tyre (1 Kgs 9:26-28; 10:11, 22; 2 Chr 8:18; 9:21). Solomon's control over Elath and the port of Ezion-geber gave Israel unprecedented access to direct sea routes to the southern region of the Arabian peninsula and the far-off land of OPHIR. However the fledgling kingdom lacked the maritime know-how and resources to construct, crew, and pilot the ships needed for such an important, royally sponsored economic venture. This explains the crucial partnership with King Hiram of Tyre, who supplied his own fleet, or at minimum the crew for the Israelite ships, for the ventures to Ophir. It is probable that the components for building the ships in the Red Sea fleet were sailed down from Lebanon to a harbor on the Mediterranean under Solomon's control, and then hauled overland to Ezion-geber. The region around Elath lacks the natural resources for shipbuilding, and the only alternative for getting ships to Ezion-geber involves circumnavigating Africa. Archaeologically the Iron IIA period, traditionally equated with the time of the united monarchy, shows increased contact with Cyprus and limited commerce between the Levant and Eubeoa in northeastern Greece. Thus maritime links with the Aegean are reestablished after a hiatus since the end of the Late Bronze Age. This contact with Greece marks the beginning of westerly exploration and trade in the Mediterranean by the Phoenicians (*see* PHOENICIA).

From the period of the divided monarchy there is even less information regarding maritime expeditions down the Red Sea, perhaps because of the loss of control over the region around Elath to the Edomites. One failed incident is reported during the reign of King Jehoshaphat of Judah (1 Kgs 22:48-49 [Heb. 22:49-50]; 2 Chr 20:36-37). The royal ships are wrecked before they have even left for Ophir, in port at Ezion-geber. Whether or not this was a joint venture with King Ahaziah of northern Israel is not clear because of variations between the accounts in Kings and Chronicles. The archaeology of this period, the Iron IIB–IIC, shows an increase in Mediterranean commerce, with maritime trade coming to the coasts of the southern Levant from Lebanon, Syria, Cyprus, Egypt, Asia Minor, Greece, and in rare instances Italy. During this period the Phoenicians and Greeks establish overseas settlements and trade stations throughout the coasts and islands of the Mediterranean.

Two 8th-cent. BCE Phoenician shipwrecks in deep waters off of the coast of Ashkelon give us a wealth of direct evidence for the size of Iron II merchant vessels, the makeup and capacity of their cargoes, and lifeways of their crews (Stager). The handful of excavated shipwrecks from before the Hellenistic period demonstrate that merchant ships were typically 10–18 m in length, their width was approximately one-third their length, they were constructed hull-first with interior ribbing added second, and had multi-ton carrying capacities. Rare Iron II representations of ships on seals and on a tomb wall from the southern Levant (Stieglitz 2001) suggest that these commercial ships had rounded hulls and were powered by a single sail, like their Bronze Age predecessors. It is likely that these vessels were steered by dual rudders near the stern of the ship. Pilots navigated using visible land formations, buildings in harbor, and landmarks on promontories; followed winds, waves, currents, cloud patterns, and the flight of birds; and used the stars and constellations as guides at night,

practicing an art passed down through generations of experience.

Given this Iron II nautical evidence, the increased awareness of Mediterranean cultures and ships found in contemporary and later prophetic literature, especially First Isaiah, Ezekiel, and Jonah, is not surprising (Isa 2:16; 18:1-2; 23:1-14; 33:21, 23*a*; Ezek 27; Jonah 1). The merchant vessels, often referred to as ships of TARSHISH after a distant Phoenician port that supplied silver and other precious goods, were used as prophetic symbols of negative pride and arrogance. Ships were some of the most complex and grand constructions of the ancient world, and maritime trade brought in untold wealth; therefore the use of the ship as a negative metaphor by prophets advocating social justice is apt.

Ezekiel 27 is a particularly poignant commentary against Tyre, and the wealth gained by this city-state through its prowess in shipping and maritime commerce. The Phoenician city is compared metaphorically to a ship, and we are given rare information on various components of a vessel and its crew (Stager; Stieglitz 1971). The notoriously difficult text describes the different types of wood used in constructing portions of the ship, the source of the wood used for each component, and parts of the ship itself; such as, hull planks, mast, oars, and a pilot's or deck cabin (27:5-6). A decorated SAIL, made from Egyptian linen, and an awning, colored with purple dyes from the coast of Cyprus, are also detailed (27:7). Rowers, oarsmen, sailors, merchants, pilots, and repairmen from various Phoenician cities are detailed crewing the ship (27:8-9, 26-29). Ezekiel gives a convincing description of a Phoenician merchant galley of the late Iron Age, known primarily through depictions on Assyrian palace reliefs. The prophet also details the complex network of international commerce and goods coming through Tyre in the early 6th cent. BCE, both overland and overseas (27:12-25).

Jonah 1:3-16 provides numerous nautical details. As a passenger, the prophet pays a fare to sail from Joppa to far-off Tarshish. The ship may have been fully or partially decked, as Jonah is hidden in the hold, asleep when a storm threatens the vessel. The captain and crew respond to the storm in both a profane and religious manner: they throw items overboard to lighten the ship's load to better ride out the storm and pray to their gods for divine assistance or intervention. The sailors cast lots to determine divine will, throw Jonah overboard to appease Yahweh and calm the tempest, and offer a sacrifice and make vows to God in thanks for calming the storm and saving their lives. This is all evidence for the specialized religious practices and beliefs of seafarers, not shared by their terrestrial counterparts (Brody). The Persian period Ma'agan Mikhael shipwreck, excavated off of the Carmel coast of Israel (Linder and Kahanov), gives us direct evidence of a merchant vessel from the period in which the book of Jonah was written.

Storms, shipwrecks, and sea monsters are detailed in Pss 48:7 (Heb. 48:8); 74:13-14; 104:25-26; 107:23-

30; and Job 41:1-8 (Heb. 40:25-32). These passages show that the "vast and wide" sea (Ps 104:25), and sailing on it, was to be feared; the ship itself, Yahweh, and other deities provided protection against its depths and dangers. When a vessel sank, mariners left their ships for dry land to pay tribute to their fellow sailors lost at sea (Ezek 27:27-29). This may indicate taboos against mourning the dead while aboard ship. The dangers and fears of seafaring, however, were outweighed by the commercial efficiency of shipping and profit brought by maritime trade. This made ships and sailing critical to the peoples and economies of the southern Levant from prehistoric times to the present. *See* SAILOR; TRADE AND COMMERCE; TRAVEL AND COMMUNICATION IN THE OT.

Bibliography: Aaron J. Brody. *"Each Man Cried Out to His God:" The Specialized Religion of Canaanite and Phoenician Seafarers* (1998); Elisha Linder and Yaakov Kahanov. *The Ma'agan Mikhael Ship: The Recovery of a 2400-Year-Old Merchantman, Final Report Vol. 1* (2003); Raphael Patai. *The Children of Noah: Jewish Seafaring in Ancient Times* (1998); Lawrence E. Stager. "Phoenician Shipwrecks and the Ship Tyre (Ezekiel 27)." *Terra Marique: Studies in Art History and Marine*

Archaeology in Honor of Anna Marguerite McCann. John Pollini, ed. (2005) 238–54; Robert R. Stieglitz. *Maritime Activity in Ancient Israel* (1971); Robert R. Stieglitz. "Hebrew Seafaring in the Biblical Period." *Seafaring and the Jews.* Nadav Kashtan, ed. (2001) 5–15.

AARON BRODY

SHISHA. *See* SHAVSHA.

SHISHAK shi´shak [שִׁישַׁק shishaq, שׁוּשַׁק shushaq]. The Egyptian king Shishak plays a pivotal role in the biblical accounts of the division of the kingdom after the death of King SOLOMON, by harboring the fugitive rebel JEROBOAM (1 Kgs 11:40) and attacking Judah (1 Kgs 14:25-26; 2 Chr 12:2-9). The biblical Shishak was Sheshonq I (or Shoshenq I), the first king of the Twenty-second Dynasty who ruled EGYPT 931–910 BCE or 945–924 BCE.

Shishak, from a prominent Libyan family in the western delta, commanded the army under Psusennes II, last king of the Twenty-first Dynasty. Among his familial connections was the marriage of his oldest son Osorkon to Princess Merikare. When Psusennes II died without a direct male heir, Shishak claimed the throne.

Figure 1: Shishsak (Sheshonq I) holding Semitic prisoners by their long hair. Temple of Amon Hall, Karnak, Thebes, Egypt.

He secured his rule by placing his sons in high posts and constructed major monuments at THEBES, MEMPHIS, and el-Hiba. A statue bearing the names of both Shishak and Abibaal, king of Byblos, attests to relations between Egypt and PHOENICIA.

According to the biblical accounts, Shishak allied himself with Jeroboam in opposition to the Davidic monarchy. When Jeroboam's rebellion against Solomon failed, he fled to Egypt and found refuge at the court of Shishak (1 Kgs 11:40). After Solomon's death, Jeroboam returned and led the rebellion of the northern tribes against Solomon's successor, REHOBOAM. In Rehoboam's fifth year, Shishak mounted a military campaign against Jerusalem and plundered the royal and temple treasuries (1 Kgs 14:25-26; 2 Chr 12:2-9). Although the 1 Kings account does not mention battles, the Chronicler notes the capture of Judean fortified cities prior to the assault on Jerusalem (2 Chr 12:4). The LXX adds that Jeroboam wed an Egyptian princess during his stay at court (4 Kgdms 12:24), paralleling the story of Solomon (1 Kgs 3:1).

Only two contemporary Egyptian inscriptions provide evidence for Shishak's relationship with Israel and Judah, a stele fragment found at MEGIDDO and Shishak's triumphal relief in the Karnak temple at Thebes. The stele was found in a disturbed context and is quite broken. Enough can be read of the names and epithets of the king to ensure that he is Shishak I, but no other historical information is preserved. The triumphal relief comprises a text celebrating the king's conquest of all Egypt's enemies thanks to the god Amun; a stylized scene of the king smiting his captive foes, identified in the caption as both Nubians and Asiatics; and a list of toponyms with a superscription identifying them as northern and southern lands captured during his first campaign of victory. Some of the toponyms do not appear elsewhere and have yet to be identified, and several have been partially or completely destroyed. Those that can be read are located in the Negev, the Shephelah, the Ephraimite hills or Gilead. Conspicuously missing are sites in the Judean hills, the area where the Bible locates Shishak's campaign.

Typically scholars have given priority to the Egyptian evidence, arguing that Jerusalem or other Judean sites might appear in the badly damaged sections of the toponym list and that the 1 Kings report simply ignored the continuation of the campaign into Israel. Recently Kevin Wilson has argued that Shishak's toponym list was not intended to record an itinerary but functioned with the rest of the triumphal relief as a kind of execration text, magically protecting Egypt from all its enemies.

The biblical account of a campaign by Shishak against Judah, resulting in the submission of Rehoboam and the payment of tribute, is plausible, though not independently substantiated. The erection of a stele at Megiddo establishes that Israel was subordinate to Egypt, but need not indicate a military engagement. If the evidence of the toponym lists is discounted, there is little basis for determining whether Shishak would have continued his tour north to impress upon Jeroboam the might of the Egyptian army and to receive his submission and tribute, or returned directly to Egypt and more pressing concerns.

The biblical account of Shishak's relationship with Jeroboam accords well with the Egyptian practice of fomenting unrest among Syro-Palestinian polities. When these polities were at war with each other, or resisting the sovereignty of their Assyrian or Babylonian lords, they posed less of a threat to Egypt itself. The division of the Solomonic kingdom served Egyptian interests, especially with Jeroboam beholden to Egypt. *See* PHARAOH.

Bibliography: Kenneth A. Kitchen. *The Third Intermediate Period in Egypt (110–650 B.C.).* 2nd ed. with supp. (1986); Kevin A. Wilson. *The Campaign of Pharaoh Shoshenq I into Palestine.*

CAROLYN HIGGINBOTHAM

SHITRAI shit´rī [שִׁטְרַי shitray]. King David put Shitrai "the Sharonite" in charge of his cattle that were pastured in Sharon (1 Chr 27:29).

SHITTIM shi´tim [שִׁטִּים shittim]. Means "acacia trees." Located approximately 14 km northeast of the JORDAN RIVER's mouth, and 13 km west-northwest of HESHBON, on the Wadi el-Kafrein—a system that drains the region southwest of Amman (OT "Rabbath-Ammon") into the Jordan River. The site is generally associated with the as-of-yet unexcavated Tel el-Hammam. Numbers 25:1 has Israel staying at Shittim at the end of their forty years of wandering and prior to their entrance into the land of Canaan. The same text further indicates that while camped there the Israelite men began to have sexual liaisons with the daughters of Moab; this initiates the disastrous covenant-violation incident of BAAL-PEOR. Numbers 33:49 describes Israel as camped "from Beth-jeshimoth (7 km southwest of Shittim, approximately 4 km northeast of the northeast shoulder of the Dead Sea) as far as Abel-shittim"—a distance of 7 km. Joshua 2:1 indicates that the two-man spy mission into Canaan, in advance of and in preparation for Israel's crossing, was initiated by Joshua from this location. Joshua 3:1 records Israel's departure from Shittim and camping overnight at the Jordan River prior to their crossing.

Later, in the period of the divided monarchy in the context of a covenant disputation text, Yahwah calls upon the nation to remember "what happened from Shittim to Gilgal"—apparently a reference to the Jordan crossing—as a way of knowing "the saving acts of the LORD" (Mic 6:5; the LXX reads "from the reeds to Gilgal").

JOHN I. LAWLOR

SHITTIM, WADI [נַחַל הַשִּׁטִּים nakhal hashittim]. The ACACIA (shittah) tree is a hardwood noted for its durability and ability to grow in arid places. The Wadi Shittim (literally, "wadi of the acacias," rendered Valley of Shittim in some translations) is a dry or seasonal riverbed where only the acacias can grow due to inconsistent moisture. In Joel 3:18 (Heb. 4:18) the imagery of the Wadi Shittim illustrates the renewal of Israel as the dry and arid valley is replenished through a flow of water from the Lord's house in Jerusalem. The southern desert areas of Israel in the Negev and into the Sinai still produce the tough trees.

MICHAEL G. VANZANT

SHIZA shi′zuh [שִׁיזָא shiza᾽]. The father of the warrior Adina, a descendant of Reuben who led thirty Reubenites in David's army (1 Chr 11:42).

SHOA shoh′uh [שׁוֹעַ shoaʿ]. In Ezekiel's oracle against OHOLAH AND OHOLIBAH, Shoa is an unknown group of people listed with the Babylonians, Chaldeans, Pekod, Koa, and Assyrians prophesied to conquer Jerusalem (Ezek 23:23).

SHOBAB shoh′bab [שׁוֹבָב shovav]. 1. Son of Caleb and his wife AZUBAH, although the role of JERIOTH is not clear (1 Chr 2:18).

2. Child born to David and BATHSHEBA in Jerusalem (2 Sam 5:14; 1 Chr 3:5; 14:4).

SHOBACH shoh′bak [שׁוֹבָךְ shovakh]. Commander of the Aramean forces under King Hadadezer, when David fought a decisive battle against them at Helam in Transjordan, which saw the Arameans routed and Shobach killed (2 Sam 10:15-19). Shobach, known as "Shophach" in the parallel account in 1 Chr 19:16-19, led an expanded Aramean response to Israelite victory over the Ammonites in Transjordan. The Ammonites had allied themselves with kings from emerging Aramean states in Syria, such as Damascus, Hamath, and Zobah. The Aramean alliance under Shobach illustrates how the southernmost Arameans were sensitive to expanding Israelite power; their desire to contain that threat led to conflicts between Jerusalem and the Aramean polities that, nevertheless, resulted in David's establishing hegemony over parts of Syria.

KENT V. BRAMLETT

SHOBAI shoh′bi [שֹׁבָי shovay; Σωβαί Sōbai]. The head of a family of gatekeepers (and the name of that family) whose descendants returned to Jerusalem with Zerubbabel after the exile (Ezra 2:42; Neh 7:45; 1 Esd 5:28).

SHOBAL shoh′buhl [שׁוֹבָל shoval]. The name of several individuals in the OT. The occurrence of the name in several genealogies reflects the complex, interconnected literary and historical relationships among persons, tribes, geographical locations, and changing political structures found in the biblical text. 1. Son of Seir the Horite, tribal chief in the land of Edom (Gen 36:20, 23, 29; 1 Chr 1:38, 40).

2. Son of Hur, descendant of Caleb (1 Chr 2:50, 52).

3. Son of Judah and, according to the typical pattern of genealogies in Chronicles, brother of Hur (1 Chr 4:1-2).

NATHAN D. MAXWELL

SHOBEK shoh′bek [שׁוֹבֵק shoveq]. One of the postexilic "leaders of the people" (Neh 10:24) who, along with Nehemiah, signed a covenant of confession and obedience (Neh 9–10).

SHOBI shoh′bi [שֹׁבִי shovi]. One of three men who provided food and shelter for David and his party when they fled Jerusalem after Absalom seized power (2 Sam 17:27). Shobi and the others met David in Mahanaim, east of the Jordan River.

Shobi is described as the son of Nahash, an Ammonite king who apparently had congenial relations with David. Some scholars presume that David appointed Shobi to rule Ammon after crushing a revolt led by Shobi's brother Hanun, who had succeeded Nahash (2 Sam 12:26-31). Others argue that the chronology is confused, that Nahash was still alive during Absalom's revolt, and that Shobi had come as Nahash's representative. Ammon would have benefited by supporting David's minority position, encouraging further political instability in Israel.

TONY W. CARTLEDGE

SHOES. See SANDALS AND SHOES.

SHOFAR CHESTS shoh′fahr [שֹׁפָרֹת shofaroth]. Thirteen ram's horn-shaped chests for collections in the Second Temple and in the provinces. In the Second Temple, these thirteen chests were inscribed with the names of these funds: New Shekel-Dues, Past Shekel-Dues, Bird Offerings, Young Birds for Burnt Offerings, Wood, Frankincense, Gold for the Holy Ark Cover; and on six chests, For Voluntary Offerings (m. Sheq. 5:1). Each adult Jew was obligated to contribute a half-shekel to the sanctuary so that he or she would have a part in the communal daily offerings (Exod 30:11-16). This practice is still commemorated with the reading of this passage from TORAH on a SABBATH in the spring called Shabbat Shekalim. These are the chests referred to in Mark 12:41-44, where Jesus notes the relative size of each person's gift compared to that person's net worth. See JOSEPHUS, FLAVIUS; TEMPLE, JERUSALEM; TREASURE, TREASURER, TREASURY.

JUDITH Z. ABRAMS

SHOMER shoh′muhr [שׁוֹמֵר shomer]. 1. The father of Jehozabad, one of the two servants who assassinated

King Joash of Judah (2 Kgs 12:21). In 2 Chr 24:26 the name is given as SHIMRITH, a feminine form, indicating, perhaps, the mother of Jehozabad. *See* SHIMEATH.

2. A son of Heber of the tribe of Asher (1 Chr 7:32).

JOAN E. COOK, SC

SHOPHACH. *See* SHOBACH.

SHOPHAR. *See* MUSICAL INSTRUMENTS; NEW YEAR.

SHOSHANNIM, SHOSHANNIM EDUTH. *See* MUSIC.

SHOULDER [עַרֹזְ zeroaʿ, כָּתֵף kathef, שְׁכֶם shekhem; ὦμος ōmos]. The shoulder is the upper part of the foreleg of a sacrificial animal, which part is to be given to the priest (Num 6:19; Deut 18:3; Josh 4:5). *Shoulder* also commonly refers to the human body part as it is used to carry heavy objects (Gen 21:14; 24:15; Luke 15:5; 1 Esd 1:4), and it is often used metaphorically (Gen 49:15; Neh 9:29; Job 31:36; Isa 22:22; Zech 7:11; Matt 23:4; Sir 6:25).

JOAN E. COOK, SC

SHOVEL [יָעַ yaʿ, רַחַת rakhath]. Cultic utensils employed in the tabernacle (Exod 27:3; 38:3) or the Temple (e.g., 1 Kgs 7:40, 45; 2 Chr 4:11; Jer 52:18). In reference to the tabernacle, shovels are associated with the bronze altar for burnt offerings, and listed along with pots for the ashes, basins, forks, and firepans. All these utensils, including the shovels, were made of bronze and were used for cleaning the altar after the burnt offering was completed. Shovels made of burnished bronze were used in the Temple. Shovels were also used as winnowing tools (Isa 30:24). In excavations at Tell Dan, three iron shovels were discovered in one of the rooms adjacent to the sanctuary precincts. These shovels, each about 54 cm long, were apparently used to clean the altar.

Bibliography: Avraham Biran. *Biblical Dan* (1994).

JOEL F. DRINKARD JR.

SHOW HOSTILITY. *See* ANGER.

SHOWBREAD. *See* BREAD OF PRESENCE.

SHRINE [בֵּית אֱלֹהִים beth ʾelohim, בָּמָה bamah; ἐσώτερον esōteron, σηκός sēkos]. A structure used as a place of worship. In premonarchic Israel, the Israelites established shrines throughout the land. Though there is considerable scholarly debate on their exact nature, they were likely open-air raised platforms used for offerings and sacrifices (*see* HIGH PLACE). First Samuel 9:12-25 describes a sacrificial meal at such a shrine. Shrines contained other cultic paraphernalia, such as

the ephod and teraphim in Judg 17:5. After the monarchy and the centralization of worship at the Jerusalem Temple, all other shrines were outlawed. The reforms of Hezekiah and Josiah (2 Kgs 18:1-7; 23:4-25) included destruction of the high places, reflecting the widespread, albeit unorthodox, continued popularity of local shrines throughout ancient Israel. In the NT, *shrine* describes an altar behind a curtain (Heb 6:19) as well as replicas of the shrine of Artemis (Acts 19:24; compare 17:24).

JULYE M. BIDMEAD

SHROUD [לֹוט lot, עֲרָפֶל ʿarafel]. A cloth wrapper prepared for a corpse (*see* BURIAL; LINEN). Isaiah 25:7 states that the pall worn for the dead will be removed when the people join in the divine feast provided by God on his holy mountain. When Yahweh appeared at Horeb, the top of the mountain was "shrouded in dark clouds" (Deut 4:11).

VICTOR H. MATTHEWS

SHUA shoo'uh [שׁוּעַ shuaʿ, שׁוּעָא shuʿaʾ]. 1. A Canaanite man, whose daughter married Judah (Gen 38:2). Shua had three grandsons (Er, Onan, and Shelah) through his daughter and Judah. Both Er and Onan died at the Lord's hand (Gen 38:7-10; compare 1 Chr 2:3), and Shua's own daughter later died (Gen 38:12). *See* BATH-SHUA.

2. An Asherite, the daughter of Heber (1 Chr 7:32).

JESSICA TINKLENBERG DEVEGA

SHUAH, SHUHITE shoo'uh, shoo'hit [שׁוּחַ shuakh, שׁוּחִי shukhi]. 1. Shuah was one of six sons born to Abraham by KETURAH, his concubine (Gen 25:2; 1 Chr 1:32).

2. BILDAD the Shuhite, i.e., a descendant of Shuah, is referenced in several passages from the book of Job (2:11; 8:1; 18:1; 25:1; 42:9). He, together with Job's other friends, Eliphaz the Temanite and Zophar the Naamathite, attempts to commiserate with Job and to enlighten him as to the reason for his suffering. Their central message is that purity yields prosperity, iniquity bears punishment, and repentance results in restitution.

JASON R. TATLOCK

SHUAL shoo'uhl [שׁוּעָל shuʿal]. 1. According to 1 Sam 13:17, the "land of Shual," near Ophrah, was the object of one of three Philistine raids designed to provoke King Saul. The area, otherwise unknown, would have been in the northern part of the Benjaminite hill country.

2. A descendant of Asher (1 Chr 7:36).

TONY W. CARTLEDGE

SHUBAEL. *See* SHEBUEL.

SHUHAH shoo'huh [שׁוּחָה shukhah]. First Chronicles 4:11 lists "CHELUB the brother of Shuhah" as a descendant of Perez of the tribe of Judah, part of a list thought to be a collection of fragments inserted there to preserve the names. The LXX reads "Caleb the father of Ascha" instead.

SHUHAM shoo'ham [שׁוּחָם shukham]. Apparently the only son of Dan and head of the single clan called Shuhamites within the tribe of Dan (Num 26:42). In a parallel genealogy, the name provided is HUSHIM (Gen 46:23; NRSV, "HASHUM"). *See* DAN, DANITES.

SHULAMMITE shoo'luh-mit [שׁוּלַמִּית shulammith]. This title is used twice for the dancing woman in the SONG OF SONGS (6:13 [Heb. 7:1]). Grammatically, it is not a personal name but an adjective, and could be translated "Shulammite woman" or "maid of Shulem"; nevertheless, its first occurrence in Song 6:13 is most often understood and reproduced in translation as a proper name: "O Shulammite."

In Hebrew the title is phonetically similar to the name of King Solomon (**shelomoh** שְׁלֹמֹה), to whom the Song is attributed by title and tradition; hence, some interpreters think that the title identifies the woman as Solomon's consort or lover. Others derive the word from a place name, such as Shulem/Shunem, near Jerusalem, the birthplace of Abishag the Shunammite, concubine of King David (1 Kgs 1:3). Most interpreters of the Song read it as a continuous poem with the same two young lovers, a woman and a man, as its protagonists. Therefore, it has become customary to name the Song's female protagonist "the Shulammite" or "Shulammit."

Bibliography: J. Cheryl Exum. *The Song of Songs.* OTL (2005); Marvin H. Pope. *The Song of Songs.* AB 7C (1995).

ATHALYA BRENNER

SHUMATHITE shoo'muh-thit [שָׁמָתִי shumathi]. Member of a Judahite family dwelling in Kiriath-jearim (1 Chr 2:53). The Shumathites were descended from Perez the son of Judah and his daughter-in-law Tamar (1 Chr 2:4).

SHUNA (NORTH), TELL ESH. This long, narrow site (700–1000 m long by 100–150 m wide) is located within the boundaries of a modern town in the northern Jordan Valley south of the Wadi el-Yarmuk. The most extensive remains comprise wall fragments, beaten-earth floors, pits, and infrequent small finds dating to the Chalcolithic to Early Bronze I periods (ca. the 4th millennium BCE). A few potsherds may go back as early as the very end of the Neolithic period (the late 5th millennium BCE). The Early Bronze I remains are very significant and seem to represent continuous occupation for the complete period.

Unfortunately, the function and dates of a very large building with five thick parallel walls (each over 2 m thick) were not determined. The possible dates for the

building range from Early Bronze I to Hellenistic. Other fragmentary Hellenistic structures and graves were also found. Pottery from other periods including the Iron Age (1st millennium BCE) and the Roman and Byzantine periods (1st millennium CE) was also found.

LARRY G. HERR

SHUNEM, SHUNAMMITE shoo'nuhm, shoo'nuhmit [שׁוּנֵם shunem, שׁוּנַמִּית shunammith]. The town of Shunem was located in the territory of Issachar (Josh 19:18) at the foot of the hill of Moreh, opposite Mount Gilboa. It has been identified with the modern village of Solem. Shunem appears in Egyptian records as a royal Canaanite city in the Late Bronze Age. The town is mentioned in the list of cities conquered by Thutmosis III (1490–1436 BCE), and in the list of cities captured by SHISHAK, pharaoh of Egypt (935–914 BCE). Shunem is also mentioned in the El Amarna letters as being destroyed by Labayu, king of Shechem, and rebuilt by Biridiya, the ruler of Megiddo in the 14th cent. BCE (EA 250). In the final battle between the Philistines and Israelites in the days of Saul, king of Israel, the Philistine army gathered at Shunem, across from the Israelite army, which was camped on Mount Gilboa (1 Sam 28:4).

Shunem was the birthplace of Abishag, the maiden brought to the elderly King David to keep him warm and to nurse him (1 Kgs 1:3); hence she is called "the Shunammite." She has been erroneously identified with the Shulammite of the Song of Songs (6:13 [Heb. 7:1]). Shunem was the home of the wealthy woman who prepared a room in her house for the prophet Elisha. The Shunammite woman received from the prophet the promise of the birth of a son; after the child died, the prophet miraculously revived him (2 Kgs 4:8-37).

CLAUDE F. MARIOTTINI

SHUNI, SHUNITES shoo'ni, shoo'nit [שׁוּנִי shuni]. Shuni was one of the seven sons of Gad (Gen 46:16), and the eponymous ancestor of the Shunites (Num 26:15).

SHUPHUPHAN. *See* SHEPHUPHAM.

SHUPPIM shuh'pim [שֻׁפִּים shuppim]. 1. Brother of Huppim, from the tribe of Benjamin (1 Chr 7:12). Shuppim and Huppim also appear in Manasseh's genealogy (1 Chr 7:15), while variants of *Shuppim* occur in Benjaminite genealogies in Gen 46:21 ("Muppim" and "Huppim"), Num 26:39 ("SHEPHUPHAM"), and 1 Chr 8:5 ("Shephuphan"). This variety may result from textual corruption.

2. A Levite gatekeeper stationed on the western side of the Temple in the time of David (1 Chr 26:16).

EUNHEE KANG

SHUQBA CAVE. A cave in the Wadi en-Natuf, northwest of Jerusalem, containing animal bones (mainly gazelle, but also domesticated canine), flint tools, and human remains from the prehistoric Natufian culture. This culture, centered in Galilee and Carmel, witnessed humanity's transition to agriculturally based subsistence near the start of the Neolithic era.

Bibliography: O. Bar-Yosef and F. Valla. "The Natufian Culture and the Origin of the Neolithic in the Levant." *Current Anthropology* 31 (1990) 433–36; Brian Boyd and Zoë Crossland. "New Fieldwork at Shuqba Cave and in Wadi en-Natuf Western Judea." *Antiquity* 74 (2000) 755–56.

JASON R. TATLOCK

SHUR, WILDERNESS OF shoor [מִדְבַּר־שׁוּר midhbar-shur]. The WILDERNESS crossed by the Israelites after the exodus from Egypt (Exod 15:22). Its exact location is unknown, but could have been along Canaan's southern border with Egypt. The etymology of shur, which means "wall" (Gen 49:22; 2 Sam 22:30; Ps 18:30; Ezra 4:12-13, 16), has led to speculation that Shur was a string of Egyptian fortifications constructed along Egypt's eastern border.

The Israelites suffered for three days without water due to the arid climate of this region (Exod 15:22). Moses averts a crises by transforming bitter water into potable water at MARAH (Exod 15:23-27). Numbers 33:8, however, identifies the wilderness of ETHAM as the site of this event.

In the patriarchal accounts, Hagar flees to a well between Kadesh and Shur (Gen 16:7). Here, "the way to Shur" could be a reference to a trade route named Darb el-Shur—a caravan route running from Hebron to Egypt. Abraham dwelt between Kadesh and Shur (Gen 20:1). Ishmael's descendants inhabited the region from Havilah to Shur, described as being opposite Egypt, in the direction of Assyria (Gen 25:18). Saul (1 Sam 15:7) and David (1 Sam 27:8) each pursue the Amalekites "as far as Shur, to the land of Egypt," which pinpoints Shur along the Egyptian border.

ALICE MANDELL

SHURUPPAK, INSTRUCTIONS OF. A collection of proverbs purportedly communicated to a certain Ziusudra (known from other legends) by his father, Shuruppak son of Ubar-tutu. Composed in Sumerian, the collection was translated into other Mesopotamian languages, attesting the popularity of proverbs in wisdom literature throughout the region. Shuruppak was probably not a historical personage, although the name does appear in a list of Sumerian kings. *See* SUMER, SUMERIANS; SUMERIAN TEXTS; WISDOM IN THE ANCIENT NEAR EAST.

R. JUSTIN HARKINS

SHUSHAN EDUTH. *See* MUSIC.

SHUTHELAH shoo'thuh-luh [שׁוּתֶלַח shuthelakh]. In Num 26:35, Shuthelah is listed as the first of three sons in Ephraim's genealogy. Shuthelah is the only son to have his descendant, Eran, recorded in the genealogy (Num 26:36). In 1 Chr 7:20, Shuthelah is listed as the first of many descendants of Ephraim, some of which are duplicates (Tahath and Shuthelah are both listed twice). There is no scholarly consensus on the presence of duplicates in Ephraim's genealogy in 1 Chr 7:20 or on the discrepancies between the two records of the genealogy.

KELLY WILSON

SHUTTLE [אֶרֶג ʾeregh]. A tool that holds the weft thread in weaving. It is thrown through the open sheds of warp threads. Job reflects on the speed at which the shuttle carries the thread, comparing the transitory nature of his existence to the swiftness of the shuttle moving across the LOOM (Job 7:6).

Bibliography: E. J. W. Barber. *Prehistoric Textiles: The Development of Cloth in the Neolithic and Bronze Ages with Special Reference to the Aegean* (1991).

MARY PETRINA BOYD

SIA si'uh [סִיעָא siʿaʾ]. Ancestor of a family of temple servants who returned to Judah from the Babylonian exile (Neh 7:47). In the parallel passage in Ezra 2:44, the name is spelled "Siaha."

SIBBECAI sib'uh-ki [סִבְּכַי sibbekhay]. Sibbecai "the Hushathite" is credited with the heroic killing of a Philistine named Saph, identified as "one of the descendants of the giants" (2 Sam 21:18). Sibbecai the Hushathite is named as one of DAVID'S CHAMPIONS in 1 Chr 11:29, though the parallel text in 2 Sam 23:27 has the name "Mebunnai the Hushathite," which is probably an error.

Sibbecai the Hushathite, "of the Zerahites," is also named by the Chronicler as the commander of 24,000 troops, who are listed eighth among the twelve divisions of David's army (1 Chr 27:11).

TONY W. CARTLEDGE

SIBBOLETH sib'uh-lith [סִבֹּלֶת sibboleth]. The Ephraimite pronunciation of the word SHIBBOLETH, "ear of wheat" or "river," which resulted in their extermination by the Gileadites (Judg 12:6).

SIBMAH sib'muh [שְׂבָם sevam, שְׂבְמָה sivmah]. A town originally allotted to Reuben (Num 32:38; Josh 13:19) but later incorporated into Moab. A variant form of the name, Sebam, appears in Num 32:3. Sibmah was located in the vicinity of Heshbon on the plateau of Moab. Although its exact location is unknown, scholars have proposed identifying it with Khirbet Qarn al-Qibsh, approximately 5 km southwest of Heshbon. The prophetic oracles of Isaiah (16:8-9) and Jeremiah (48:32-33) make clear its economic importance to Moab, in a region known for grape and wine production.

KENT V. BRAMLETT

SIBRAIM sib'ray-im [סִבְרַיִם sivrayim]. A place between Damascus and Hamath on the northern boundary of the restored Israel in the vision of Ezekiel (47:16); its exact location is uncertain.

SIBYLLINE ORACLES sib'uh-leen or'uh-kuhl. The Sibyl was a legendary prophetess in Greek lore. She was associated with shrines in Asia Minor and at Cumae in Italy. The Cumaean Sibyl was immortalized by Virgil (*Aeneid* 6.63–173). An official collection of Sibylline oracles in Rome was consulted by the Senate in times of crisis. Only a few pagan Sibylline oracles survive. These oracles were written in epic hexameters in archaic Homeric Greek. Beginning in the 2nd cent. BCE, Jews appropriated the genre in order to suggest that the Sibyl was praising Judaism. Later, Christians appropriated the genre. The Jewish and Christian oracles are longer and more coherent than the extant pagan ones. Use of the genre continued into the Middle Ages.

The standard collection of Sibylline oracles is a combination of two collections, one of which contains books 1–8, the other books 9–14. Since books 9 and 10 repeat material from the first collection, they are omitted from modern printed editions. The Prologue to the collection is dated about 500 CE. There are many citations of the *Sibylline Oracles* in writing of the church fathers prior to that date (e.g., Lactantius; see below).

The oldest Jewish Sibylline oracles are found in book 3 and date to the 2nd cent. BCE (*Sib. Or.* 3:97–294; 545–808). Several passages in that book (vv. 193, 318, 608-609) predict a great change in the reign of "the seventh king of Egypt from the line of the Greeks," suggesting a date in the middle of the 2nd cent. BCE. The Sibyl praises the Jews for refraining from idolatry, homosexuality, and abortion and urges the Greeks to send gifts to the Jewish Temple. These oracles are supplemented in book 3 by others of diverse provenance. The most striking of these is a denunciation of Rome from the 1st cent. BCE in vv. 350–800, which predicts the vengeance of Asia on Rome.

Sibylline Oracles 4 and 5 contain Jewish oracles from the 1st and early 2nd cent. CE. The fourth book is structured by a sequence of four kingdoms, Assyrians, Medes, Persians, and Macedonians. Then follows the rise of Rome, which is not assigned a number in the sequence. It would seem that this passage was inserted to update an older oracle, which was originally written to predict the downfall of the Greek Empire. The oracle in its present form predicts the eruption of Vesuvius and the return of Nero, and so should be dated after 79 CE. It ends with a call to repentance and a prediction of conflagration and the resurrection of the dead.

The fifth book also presupposes the destruction of Jerusalem and is bitterly anti-Roman. This book also predicts the return of Nero as a virtual antichrist, but also the coming of a savior figure from heaven (*Sib. Or.* 5:108, 256, 414). It ends, however, with a conflagration that leaves the sky starless. At least parts of this book seem to presuppose the revolt against Rome in the Jewish Diaspora in 115–17 CE.

There is also considerable Jewish material in *Sib. Or.* 1–2. These books originally constituted a unified oracle, structured by a prediction of ten kingdoms. The first seven generations are preserved in *Sib. Or.* 1:1–323. There is no mention of eighth or ninth generations. Instead we find a passage on the incarnation and career of Christ, followed by the climactic tenth generation. In its present form, this oracle is Christian, probably from the 2nd cent. CE. The underlying Jewish oracle may date to the 1st cent. CE. It is thought to derive from Phrygia, which is said to be the first land to emerge after the flood. Further Christian oracles are found in books 6, 7, and 8. Book 8 falls into two quite different sections. Verses 1–216 are mainly concerned with political prophecies and may well be Jewish. Verses 217–500 are largely taken up with christology. The first part seems to derive from the reign of Marcus Aurelius (d. 180 CE). The latest possible date for the second part of the book is supplied by Lactantius, who cites it extensively, around 300 CE (*Inst.* 1.6). Books 11–14 have no evident Christian material and are of little theological interest. They are concerned with political prophecies. The latest of these oracles presuppose the Arab conquest of Egypt and are no earlier than 700 CE. *See* PSEUDEPIGRAPHA.

Bibliography: John J. Collins. "Sibylline Oracles." *OTP* 1(1983) 317–472.

JOHN J. COLLINS

SICARII si-kahr'ee-*i* [σικάριος sikarios]. A sikarios is a bandit or outlaw. The plural "sicarii" (sikarii σικάριι) often refers to insurrectionist Judeans in the 1st cent. CE that used guerilla and terrorist tactics in their determination to free their land from Roman domination. Josephus distinguishes these politically motivated "sicarii" from common bandits (lēstēs [λῃστής], robbers or highwaymen [*J.W.* 2.57]); the sicarii, he says, are "bandits of a different sort" (heteron eidos lēstōn ἕτερον εἶδος λῃστῶν) who first appear while Marcus Antonius Felix is procurator of the province of Judea (52–60 CE). Josephus describes how these assassins hid a small dagger (sikarion [σικάριον], from Latin *sica*) in their clothing, with which they swiftly and expertly stabbed Roman sympathizers, always in broad daylight and in crowded places, then joined the crowd with feigned anguish and shock at the attack. According to Josephus, the high priest Jonathan was the first person these "daggermen" targeted (*J.W.* 2.253–60; see also *Ant.* 20.186).

Scholars debate whether the sicarii were an organized political group, or whether these revolutionaries worked somewhat independently and were labeled "sicarii" along with other outlaws. Another uncertainty is whether they were affiliated with the Zealots (see ZEALOT). Josephus claims that the sicarii represent a "fourth philosophy," a belief that none but God can rule over the Jews (*Ant.* 18.11–24; compare *J.W.* 7.323, 410; the first three "philosophies" are the Pharisees, Sadducees, and Essenes).

The sicarii are mentioned only once in the Bible, when a Roman tribune mistakes the apostle Paul for a certain rebel who led a number of "assassins" (andras tōn sikariōn ἄνδρας τῶν σικαρίων, literally, "men of the sicarii") in a revolt (Acts 21:38; see Josephus, *J.W.* 2.264–65). Though the sicarii occur only one time in the NT, their beliefs and actions historically are an important aspect of the complicated political and religious context of Jewish life under Roman occupation that constitutes the back-story of the NT (e.g., though Jesus was not a sikarios, he was arrested and crucified for insurrection).

During the Jewish War (66–70 CE), the sicarii captured MASADA, Herod's fortified residence built high on a cliff near the Dead Sea. Josephus' account (in which the sicarii resemble brigands more than revolutionaries or assassins) details how they raided the town of En-gedi for supplies and killed its residents (*J.W.* 4.398–405). Josephus describes the sicarii's last stand at Masada, which took place ca. 73 CE, about three years after Jerusalem fell to the Romans. A group of over 900 rebels (including women and children) withstood months of a siege, but when the Romans eventually broke through the fortress walls, they found only dead bodies. The rebels had chosen to die rather than surrender (*J.W.* 7.280–406). Archaeological evidence of an assault ramp and Roman encampments corroborate part of Josephus' story; however, there is no evidence of hundreds of deaths, which suggests the rebels were taken into captivity. Josephus' purpose in writing about the heroic deaths may have been apologetic, to convince Roman readers that these Jews died honorably.

Bibliography: Mark Andrew Brighton. *The Sicarii in Josephus's Judean War: Rhetorical Analysis and Historical Observations* (2009).

MARIANNE BLICKENSTAFF

SICK, SICKNESS. *See* DISEASE.

SICKLE [חֶרְמֵשׁ khermesh, מַגָּל maggal; δρέπανον drepanon]. A cutting tool used for harvesting grain and other agricultural produce (Deut 16:9; 23:25 [Heb. 23:26]; 1 Sam 13:20). "Harvest" is a frequent metaphor for God's judgment in the Bible, and the sickle may symbolize judgment (Joel 3:13), especially in the dramatic imagery of Rev 14:14-19 (compare Jer 50:16; Mark 4:29).

EUNHEE KANG

SICYON sish´ee-uhn [Σικυών Sikyōn]. A city on the south shore of the Gulf of Corinth, 25 km west of Corinth. Sicyon appears in the list of cities (1 Macc 15:23) that received a letter from Lucius, the Roman consul, requesting kindly treatment of Jews and the return of Judean "scoundrels" to Judea. Although the city declined during the Roman Empire, archaeologists have found remains of two Christian churches from that period. In the Byzantine period, it became the seat of a bishop.

ADAM L. PORTER

SIDDIM, VALLEY OF sid´im [עֵמֶק הַשִּׂדִּים ʿemeq hasiddim]. Prior to the destruction of Sodom and Gomorrah (Gen 19), the area now covered by the DEAD SEA was once dry land, known as the Valley of Siddim (Gen 14:3, 8; compare Gen 13:10). In the days of Abraham, the king of Elam and his allies came to the Valley of Siddim to suppress a revolt led by the kings of five nearby cities: Sodom, Gomorrah, Admah, Zeboiim, and Bela (or Zoar). When the local kings fled, some fell into BITUMEN pits in the valley (Gen 14:10). Some scholars suggest that the late 3rd millennium BCE settlements at Bab adh-Dhraʾ, Numayra, and elsewhere along the southeastern shore of the Dead Sea may be reflected in biblical accounts of cities near the Dead Sea.

KENT V. BRAMLETT

SIDE (IN PAMPHYLIA) si´dee [Σίδη Sidē]. A port in Pamphylia, in southern Asia Minor, now known as Selimiye. During the 1st cent. BCE, pirates used Side as a port. Side appears in the list of cities (1 Macc 15:23) that received a letter from Lucius, the Roman consul, in 142 BCE requesting kindly treatment of Jews and the return of Judean "scoundrels" to Judea (1 Macc 15:21). Archaeological remains show that the city flourished during the Hellenistic and early Roman periods, but began to decline in the 3rd cent. CE.

ADAM L. PORTER

SIDON si´duhn [צִידוֹן tsidhon; Σιδών Sidōn]. Sidon and TYRE, the twin Phoenician cities (Jer 25:22; 27:3; 47:4; 1 Chr 22:4; Matt 11:21, 22; 15:21; Mark 3:8; 7:24, 31; Luke 6:17; 10:13, 14; Acts 12:20; Jdt 2:28; 1 Macc 5:15; 2 Esd 1:11) 35 and 40 km south of Beirut, were for many centuries independent of each other. Sidon was considered from the classical period onward to be the most ancient and the most prominent of the Canaanite/Phoenician coastal cities. Sidon is mentioned in the OT as "the firstborn of Canaan" (Gen 10:15; 1 Chr 1:13). The terms *Sidon* and *Sidonians* were not only used in a narrow sense of the city itself and its inhabitants but also included at times the whole of PHOENICIA (Judg 10:12; 18:7; 1 Kgs 5:6; 11:1, 5; 16:31; 2 Kgs 23:13; Ezek 32:30). Early use of the names in this wider sense indicates a period in antiquity during which Sidon was powerful enough to impose her rule and her name upon large areas outside the city. *Sidonian* and *Phoenician* were at times synonymous.

The ancient city of Sidon is situated on the northwest slope of a rocky promontory and has a natural harbor sheltered from the prevailing winds by a rock that is geologically part an offshore reef. Genesis 10:19 puts Sidon at the border of Canaan. An inscribed clay prism of the Assyrian king SENNACHERIB (704–681 BCE) provides a list of seven satellite towns (including Sarepta, also mentioned in the NT [Luke 4:26, "Zarephath"]) under Sidon's control.

Until recently, most of the archaeological discoveries come from the suburbs of Sidon or "Greater Sidon" (Josh 11:8; 19:28), "Sidon Sadé." The main source of information is based on the large 19th-cent. necropoli located on the outskirts of the city, which yielded numerous sarcophagi including those of the Sidonian kings Eshmunazar and Tabnit and the famous "Alexander" sarcophagus. Another important site within Sidonian territory is the temple complex known as Bostan esh-Sheikh where a number of temples dedicated to Eshmun the Phoenician god of healing, later identified with Asclepios, were found.

Erich Lessing/Art Resource, NY

Figure 1: Anthropoid sarcophagus of King Eshmunazar II of Sidon (489–475 BCE). From the royal necropolis of Maqharas, Sidon, Lebanon.

The major obstacle to excavation in the heart of the ancient city, the so-called "port-city," also called "little Sidon" in Assyrian Annals and "land by the sea" in Phoenician inscriptions, was modern Sidon, which, like many other cities in the Near East, covers what lies below. In 1998 the British Museum began excavations on the ancient mound of Sidon. These excavations have provided evidence for the city's development from the end of the 4th or beginning of the 3rd millennium through to the 1st millennium BCE. The ancient city, with its ramparts and two castles, today looks very similar to the one described by 19th-cent. travelers. The land castle built on a tell overlooking the city is known as the castle of Saint Louis. The sea castle was built by the Crusaders during the winter of 1227–28 on an offshore rock linked to the mainland by a bridge. An artificial mound outside the ramparts is known as *Murex* hill and was probably where ancient dye manufacture took place, a craft for which the Phoenicians were renowned.

Six levels of occupation for the 3rd millennium BCE have been found, suggesting a continuous development and a gradual uninterrupted evolution from around 3000 BCE to around 2300 BCE. Mesopotamian fallow deer, wild boar, aurochs and hippopotamus, and large carnivores such as lion and bear were all hunted at Sidon (see the "wild beasts of Lebanon"; 1 Kgs 4:33; 2 Kgs 14:9; 2 Chr 25:18).

Immediately above the 3rd-millennium levels there was a layer of sand that had been brought to the site from the nearby seashore. This represented a change of function rather than a gap in occupation. So far sixty burials of the 2nd millennium BCE have been excavated (some of which were in this sandy layer), including constructed graves of warriors buried with their bronze weapons, and jar burials of children. The site was reinhabited around 1750 BCE. An important building (Middle/Late Bronze Age period) more then 45 m long was used at the end of the Middle Bronze Age for cultic activity with pottery vessels designed for the consumption of food and beverages. Also excavated, from the Late Bronze Age, is a building of which only one underground room, the cella or "holies of holies," was found. This building is comparable to Syrian temples of the period; it was built at ground level with the "holy of holies" below-ground and was probably entered via a door placed high up in a wall and reached via an internal wooden staircase. The building was destroyed by a fierce conflagration. Nevertheless the wooden arbutus beams from the roof, which were lying on the floor, survived in a relatively good state having been carbonized. According to calibrated ^{14}C dating, the trees from which these beams were made were grown around 1390–1120 BCE.

Another major discovery was part of a cuneiform tablet, the first to have been found in Sidon, dating to about 1400 BCE. The tablet is an inventory of objects made of wood. Given Lebanon's importance as a source of wood, it is probable that the listed luxury goods were destined for export. It appears that cuneiform writing was used in daily commerce, a consideration hardly imaginable in Lebanese sites before this discovery. Evidence of strong direct links with Egypt during the Late Bronze Age was also found: a faience vessel, an Egyptian import, decorated in black with a frieze of lotus petals was another important find; it bears within "cartouches" the throne- and birth-names of Queen Tawosret. This vessel can be dated with great precision to around 1190 BCE, with the margin of error not exceeding ten years. This is important evidence that Egypt still maintained good relations with Sidon during a time of massive disruption elsewhere in the Levant, possibly caused by the incursions of the "Sea Peoples" in the early 12th cent. Sidon's dominant position among the Phoenician coastal cities during this period seems clear. In biblical accounts (Deut 3:9; Josh 13:6; Judg 3:3; 10:12; 18:7) it is Sidon, not Tyre, which appears as a powerful city. An inscription of the Assyrian king Tiglath-pileser I (1114–1076 BCE) establishes the preeminence of Sidon. We learn from the report of an Egyptian envoy, Wen-Amun, that around 1080 BCE the city's harbor held fifty commercial vessels. Sidon was conquered by the Assyrian king Sennacherib and again in the 7th cent. by his successor ESARHADDON (680–669 BCE). Little is written about Sidon in Babylonian historical texts. The prophet Jeremiah mentions Sidon in the fourth year of the reign of Jehoiakim, king of Judah (Jer 25:22; 27:1-3), at the beginning of Zedekiah's reign and again in a prophecy against the Philistines (Jer 47:4). Sidon recovered from Esarhaddon's destruction but did not regain its preeminence over Tyre until the Achaemenid period in the 5th/4th cent. BCE. The Persians had a garrison in the city and a pleasure garden mentioned by Diodorus of Sicily.

The Sidonians were master shipbuilders and the Persian fleet used ships built at Sidon for its battles against the Greeks. Sidon is also mentioned by Pliny the Elder as the place where "glass was made." The city was also famous according to Homer for its bronze industry.

CLAUDE DOUMET-SERHAL

SIEGE. *See* WAR, METHODS, TACTICS, WEAPONS OF (BRONZE AGE THROUGH PERSIAN PERIOD); WAR, METHODS, TACTICS, WEAPONS OF (HELLENISTIC THROUGH ROMAN PERIODS).

SIEVE [כְּבָרָה kevarah, נָפָה nafah; κόσκινον koskinon]. An agricultural tool used to WINNOW grain, thus separating grain from chaff or refuse (Sir 27:4). Sieving grain is a metaphor for separating the wicked from the righteous in Isa 30:28 and Amos 9:9.

SIFRA, SIFRE [סְפְרָא sifra', סְפְרֵי sifre]. Literally, "the book" or "books," these works are the earliest rabbinic (Tannaitic) commentaries on the TORAH. The Sifra,

a close reading of Leviticus, is attributed to the "school" of Rabbi Akiva (*see* AKIVA, RABBI). Yet it contains materials from the "school" of Rabbi Ishmael, such as the introduction, which enumerates Rabbi Ishmael's thirteen hermeneutic rules for interpretation of HALAKHAH from passages of Scripture. The Sifre are early rabbinic (Tannaitic) interpretative works on the biblical books of Numbers and Deuteronomy, which stem from both "schools" mentioned above. These Tannaitic midrashim (*see* MIDRASH), also called Midrash Halakhah, were redacted shortly after the MISHNAH, in early 3rd-cent. CE Palestine. These works share traditions also found in the Mishnah, yet present them in exegetical fashion, linking them to verses of the Torah; while the Mishnah presents the same traditions based on the apodictic authority: "Rabbi So-and-so says." It is likely that the midrashic traditions preserved in these works are among the oldest rabbinic materials extant.

Bibliography: David Halivni. *Midrash, Mishnah, and Gemara: The Jewish Predilection for Justified Law* (1986); H. L. Strack and G. Stemberger. *Introduction to the Talmud and Midrash* (1992).

BURTON L. VISOTZKY

SIGMA [σ s, ς s, Σ S]. The nineteenth letter of the Greek alphabet, from the Phoenician *shin or *shan, which gave its form and position in the alphabet to sigma but its name to san; the source of the name sigma is uncertain, but some have derived it from Phoenician *samk [*simk ?]. *See* ALPHABET.

P. KYLE MCCARTER

SIGN. *See* MARK, GOAL, SIGN; SIGNS IN THE NT; SIGNS IN THE OT; SIGNS AND WONDERS.

SIGNAL [נֵס nes; πρόσκλησις prosklēsis, σάλπιγξ salpinx]. A military term describing a BANNER or flag that served as a rallying point for attack or retreat. The term often connotes judgment, as in the nations rallying against Israel (Isa 5:26; also the Babylonians against Jerusalem [Jer 6:1] or the Medes against the nobles of Babylon [Isa 13:2]). Isaiah provides the stark image of total defeat as a signal on a hill (30:17). The term can also signify hope for the returning exiles (Isa 11:10, 12; Zech 10:8). More generally, *signal* may indicate a sign to begin a particular action or event (1 Macc 4:40; 2 Macc 4:14). *See* STANDARD.

BRUCE W. GENTRY

SIGNATURE [תָו taw]. *Signature* (literally, "mark") only occurs in the NRSV in Job 31:35. The term is important to the book because Job is challenging the Almighty as though in a court of law. Job wishes for a signed response (indictment) from God (Job's adversary) instead of the silence from the heavens he has so far received. Job boasts that he would use the words of the Almighty to justify his innocence (31:36-37). The term taw also occurs in Ezek 9:4, 6 (NRSV, "mark"), where it refers to a mark on the forehead of the innocent, which exempts them from judgment (*see* MARK, GOAL, SIGN).

BRUCE W. GENTRY

SIGNET RING. *See* JEWELRY; JEWELS AND PRECIOUS STONES.

SIGNS AND WONDERS אוֹתֹת וּמוֹפְתִים 'othoth umofethim; σημεῖα καὶ τέρατα sēmeia kai terata]. This word pair occurs first in Exod 7:3. It then recurs across the biblical canon. For the majority of the occurrences the phrase refers to the power that God first unleashed against Egypt in the deliverance of Israel and later released to usher in the new era of salvation through Jesus Christ. This tradition is used by different authors to make a variety of theological claims. The OT usages cluster in the book of Deuternomy (nine of eighteen). In the NT, occurrences in the book of Acts dominate (nine of sixteen).

In Hebrew, pala' (פָּלָא) and pele' (פֶּלֶא) are in the same semantic range as 'othoth umofethim. In Greek, dynamis (δύναμις) covers a similar field as sēmeia kai terata. Dynamis occurs in the same context as "signs and wonders" in Acts 2:22 and 6:8; Rom 15:19; 2 Cor 12:12; 2 Thess 2:9; and Heb 2:4.

The OT deployment of "signs and wonders" focuses broadly on the revelation of God. God's saving actions in delivering Israel from Egypt served as the locus for God's self-revelation.

The initial occurrence of "signs and wonders" is in Exod 7:3—"But I will harden Pharaoh's heart, and I will multiply my signs and wonders in the land of Egypt." This verse is proleptic for the coming struggle between God and Pharaoh. The wider context demonstrates that the "signs and wonders" served a revelatory function. As a result of God's unleashing of "signs and wonders" against Egypt, the "Egyptians shall know that I am the LORD" (Exod 7:5). Thus, God's mighty actions in Egypt served to establish God's reputation not only before Israel, but also among the nations. Knowledge of God was a primary goal and effect of the deliverance of God's people from Egypt.

Deuteronomy contains the majority of occurrences in the OT. The phrase "signs and wonders" becomes part of a living tradition within Israel. Seven of the ten occurrences in Deuteronomy cite explicitly the exodus tradition of God's mighty actions. God's actions in the exodus however were not merely past historical events; they had profound implications for the present and future of Israel's faith. Deuteronomy establishes four key categories for understanding "signs and wonders" around the rubric of revelation.

First, "signs and wonders" performed against Egypt served to make a theological claim about God (Deut 4:34-35). Deuteronomy 4:35 draws out the expected response of Israel to God's actions: "To you it was shown so that you would acknowledge that the LORD is God; there is no other besides him." In other words, "signs and wonders" revealed enough of God to establish a relationship between Israel and God and to assert God's uniqueness vis-à-vis the "gods."

Second, "signs and wonders" are offered as the basis for Israel's ongoing relationship of faithful obedience to God (Deut 6:22; 26:8; and 29:3 [Heb. 29:2]). The recitation of God's mighty acts grounds Israel's present life firmly on a foundation of grace. God acts—Israel responds with faithful obedience. Moreover, the "signs and wonders" of the exodus secure Israel's future (Deut 7:19). Israel need not fear encounters with future enemies because the same God who delivered the exodus generation guarantees Israel's future. Deuteronomy 28:46 interprets the curses that result from disobedience to God's Torah as "signs and wonders." In the same way that the "signs and wonders" of the exodus serve as the basis for faithful obedience, the curses stand as a witness to the dangers of disobedience.

Third, the language of "signs and wonders" is deployed in a context that gives a stern warning against apostasy initiated by a false prophet (Deut 13:1-2 [Heb. 13:2-3]) who performs a "sign or wonder." It should be noted that these occurrences are in the singular, i.e., "a sign or wonder." Even a "sign or wonder" cannot serve as the grounds for an exhortation to worship or follow other gods. God's revelation with Israel was grounded in the "signs and wonders" of the exodus. Subsequent claims of new revelation are subservient to previously received revelation from God. See below discussion of this phenomenon in the NT data.

Last, "signs and wonders" are used to buttress the authority of Moses (Deut 34:11). Moses' authority as preeminent prophet in Israel is authenticated by the "signs and wonders" that God worked through him in the events of the exodus.

Subsequent OT occurrences of "signs and wonders" are mostly derivative of the pentateuchal core surveyed above. In the psalms, "signs and wonders" are used as a short-hand for recounting God's salvation of Israel from Egypt (Pss 78:43; 105:27; and 135:9). God's actions in the exodus are the basis for Israel's praise in these psalms. In his prayer of confession, Nehemiah praises God for the "signs and wonders" of the exodus (Neh 9:10). On the basis of these acts, Nehemiah prays, "You made a name for yourself which remains to this day." This again emphasizes the role of "signs and wonders" in the exodus as a means of revelation to Israel and the nations about the character of God. Moreover, in the context of Nehemiah's prayer the implication is that the same God remains available for the present generation. Jeremiah 32:20-21 recount God's "signs and wonders" against Egypt and which have continued "to this very day." God's actions established God's name in Israel and all humankind. This revelation stood as a witness against the apostasy of Israel. In Isa 8:18, Isaiah proclaims himself and his children to be "signs and wonders" from God in the midst of an apostate generation.

These "signs and wonders" announce a new work of God in the midst of Israel.

Only the occurrence in Isa 20:3 does not fit neatly into the above categories. Isaiah goes around Israel naked and barefoot as a "sign and wonder." This physical sign served as a foretelling or portent of the ill fate that awaited Egypt and Cush at the hands of Assyria.

The NT use assumes the OT tradition of signs and wonders as revelation of God, but it pushes the motif forward to focus primarily on the authorization of God's agents in the new era of salvation announced and initiated through the life, death, and resurrection of Jesus Christ.

The book of Acts contains nine of the sixteen occurrences of "signs and wonders" in the NT. Acts draws upon the motif of "signs and wonders" from the OT. In Acts 2:19, Peter alludes to Exod 7:3 and Joel 3:20 to explain the manifestation of "signs and wonders" occurring in the presence of the gathered worshipers at Pentecost. Peter's sermon deploys "signs and wonders" two additional times (2:22, 43). The force of these usages is that God's eschatological work of salvation has begun, first in Jesus of Nazareth and now in Jesus' apostles. Thus, "signs and wonders" attest to the authority and authenticity of the apostles as persons through whom God is unleashing a new age of salvation (compare 4:30; 5:12; 6:8; and 7:36). Moreover, in these contexts, there is a link between miraculous act and the proclamation of the gospel. The "signs and wonders" are not left uninterpreted. In the remaining two occurrences within Acts, the authenticity and authorization of the Gentile mission is at stake. Acts 14:3 and 15:12 mark Paul and Barnabas as persons who performed "signs and wonders." These actions serve to demonstrate the presence and blessing of God on their work in the Gentile world.

There are seven additional occurrences in the remainder of the NT. These may be examined in three groups. First, "signs and wonders" are used to authenticate persons as legitimate agents of God (Rom 15:19; 2 Cor 12:12; and Heb 2:4). Second, "signs and wonders" will be performed by counterfeit messiahs (Matt 24:24//Mark 13:22 and 2 Thess 2:9). In these contexts, the faithful will not be deceived because of their prior commitment to the truth of the gospel. "Signs and wonders" can demonstrate a new work from God only if they can be linked to prior revelation (see above on Deut 13:1-2). Last, John 4:48 records Jesus saying, "Unless you see signs and wonders you will not believe." On the surface this text reads like a rebuke, but a closer reading suggests a more nuanced response by Jesus. Jesus acts to heal a man's son (vv. 49-50). Jesus' point seems to be this: those watching for "signs and wonders" may miss God's work of salvation that Jesus has indeed come to do. *See* AUTHORITY; GOD, OT VIEW OF; MIRACLE; PLAGUES IN EGYPT; SIGNS IN THE NT; SIGNS IN THE OT.

Bibliography: C. K. Barrett. *Acts 1–14: A Critical and Exegetical Commentary on the Acts of the Apostles.* ICC (1992); Lyle Eslinger. "Freedom or Knowledge? Perspective and Purpose in the Exodus Narrative (Exodus 1–15)." *JSOT* 52 (1991) 43–60; John Goldingay. *Old Testament Theology Volume One: Israel's Gospel* (2003); S. V. McCasland. "Signs and Wonders." *JBL* 76 (1957) 149–52.

BRIAN D. RUSSELL

SIGNS IN THE NT [σημεῖον sēmeion, σημεῖα sēmeia]. With some exceptions, where it means simply "symbol" or "mark," a sign is an apparent indication of supernatural or divine presence and activity. There has been some debate as to whether the term takes on an explicitly Christian connotation in the NT literature to differentiate it from terms such as dynameis (δυνάμεις, "miracles"; NRSV, "deeds of power"). Signs often speak to the legitimacy of a divine agent even when that legitimacy is questioned or disavowed by witnesses.

The term *sign* bears the greatest theological, indeed christological, weight in the Gospel of John where certain works of Jesus in the first part of the Gospel are explicitly identified as signs. These include: water into wine (2:1-11); the healing of the royal official's son (4:46-54); the healing of the paralytic at Bethsaida (5:1-15); the multiplication of loaves (6:1-14); the curing of a blind man (9:1-17); and the raising of Lazarus (11:38-48). Some would also include Jesus walking on the Sea of Galilee (6:16-21) in this category although it is not described as a sign, and the miraculous catch of fish (John 21:1-14) seems to be a post-resurrection sign in all but name. Because of the Gospel's repeated use of *sign*, scholars have proposed that the evangelist used a "signs source" that has been redacted and developed in light of the Gospel's particular christological perspective.

Although the signs performed by Jesus in the Gospel of John are related to his divine identity, a degree of ambivalence emerges in the relationship between signs confirming Jesus as the son of God and the faith of those who encounter him and witness his works. It is almost as if only those who already acknowledge him as the one who is one with the Father (e.g., 14:10-13) have the capacity to recognize the true meaning of the signs and how they relate to Jesus' identity. This does not necessarily come about by reflecting on the nature of the miraculous acts that Jesus performs but because the observer has already been born anew—of above (John 3:2-3) or of God (John 1:12-13). It is possible, even typical, to witness Jesus performing a sign and still be ignorant or at least uncertain of his origins and of his identity (e.g., John 7:31; 9:16). The social circumstances in which the Gospel was written and redacted reflect a perspective made explicit in Jesus' Farewell Discourse (chaps. 14–17): it is only after he has returned to the Father and the Paraclete has come that the truth of what Jesus has said and done can be fully understood (e.g., 2:22). This privileges the reader over against those who encounter Jesus in the Gospel. Despite the signs they do not always know who he is, whereas the Gospel and its signs are written so that the reader may believe (John 20:30-31).

The term sēmeia is not used as frequently in the Synoptic Gospels and is subordinated to the more general term dynameis when a reference is made to Jesus' acts of prophetic and divine power. Indeed, unlike its use in the Gospel of John, the term is never used directly for a miracle of Jesus in the Synoptic Gospels. The phrase "signs and wonders" is used repeatedly and often in an eschatological context. So in Matthew and Mark Jesus warns that false prophets will produce great signs and omens (sēmeia kai terata σημεῖα καὶ τέρατα) in order to lead people astray as the last days approach (Matt 24:24; Mark 13:22). As in John (e.g., 4:48) the synoptic Jesus is depicted as impatient about requests for signs. Despite the many healings, exorcisms, and other miracles he performs in the Synoptic Gospels, he insists that the only sign that will be given to this evil generation—whose wickedness is evident in the very request for a sign—is the sign of Jonah (Matt 12:38-39; 16:1-4; Luke 11:29-32; see also Luke 11:16). Mark does not refer to the sign of Jonah but the Second Gospel also depicts Jesus as lamenting "this generation's" desire for a sign since none will be forthcoming (Mark 8:11-12). Of particular interest is the note in the longer ending of Mark that dramatic signs will confirm the identity of believers as they proclaim the gospel (Mark 16:14-20).

Although Luke does not use the term in several passages that parallel Matthew and/or Mark's explicit reference to "sign," Luke does use the term in some of his special material and in a way that tends to be more positive. The angel's announcement to the shepherds assures them that the Messiah has been born and the sign of his identity is that he is "wrapped in bands of cloth and lying in a manger" (Luke 2:12). More dramatic is Luke's note, omitted by both Matthew and Mark, that dreadful portents and great signs from heaven will herald the end of the age (Luke 21:11). Again, while Matthew and Mark do not use the term, in Luke Jesus assures his disciples that "there will be signs in the sun, the moon and the stars" (Luke 21:25). Matthew does note that the sign of the Son of Man will appear in heaven (Matt 24:30); Mark and Luke do not in their parallel verses (Mark 13:26; Luke 21:27 [quoting Dan 7:13]). Luke also does not refer to Judas' kiss as a sign (Luke 22:47-48), again contrary to the parallel verses in Matthew and Mark (Matt 26:47-49; Mark 14:43-48). It is only Luke, however, that speaks of Herod Antipas' desire to see Jesus perform a sign (Luke 23:8). Luke's tendency to reserve the use of the term to refer to divine portents to a much greater extent than either Matthew or Mark is continued in Acts (assuming, with most scholars, that Luke and Acts come from the same author).

References to signs in Acts are plentiful and seem most heavily dependent on the usage of the terms ʾothoth (אוֹתֹת, "signs") and mofethim (מוֹפְתִים, "wonders") in the OT, especially as a demonstration of divine power and deliverance. The phrase "signs and wonders," or a variant thereof, is found throughout the first part of Acts (2:19-22, 43; 4:30; 5:12; 6:8; 7:36 [referring to Moses]; 8:6, 13; 14:3; 15:12), where the apostles' divine agency by implication corresponds to that of Moses. The phrase and the term are not found after chap. 15, which coincides with the greater role that Paul plays in the narrative, even though there are several events that could accurately be described as signs in that they manifest the power of God. This may relate to the sources used in Acts. *See* SIGNS AND WONDERS.

The term is found several times in the Pauline epistles and is again marked by ambivalence because of the connection of signs to faith. Paul notes that "the Jews demand signs and the Greeks desire wisdom" (1 Cor 1:22) but it is faith in "God's foolishness" that is paramount. Paul's reluctance to see signs as necessary for faith is encapsulated in his observation that Abraham "received the sign of circumcision as a seal of the righteousness he had by faith while he was still uncircumcised" (Rom 4:11). This reference to Abraham, as well as reflecting Paul's views on circumcision, captures both the straightforward meaning of the sign of circumcision as a mark or distinguishing feature and as symbolic of the reality of God's action on behalf of the people that exists independently of any manifestation. Nevertheless, Paul's own identity as an apostle is marked by his capacity to perform signs, and he is frustrated at the Corinthian Christians inability to respond appropriately (2 Cor 12:12). This echoes Paul's note in Romans concerning his efforts to "win obedience from the Gentiles, by word and deed, by the power of signs and wonders ... I have fully proclaimed the good news of Christ" (15:18-19). Paul describes speaking in tongues, unlike prophecy, as a sign for unbelievers (1 Cor 14:22). The Pauline epistles also show awareness of the possibility of signs being used deceptively (2 Thess 2:8-9) and the insistence that it is Paul who writes the letter as proven by the sign of the handwritten greeting (2 Thess 3:17) although here sēmeion is translated as "mark" in the NRSV.

The biblical phrase "signs and wonders" is found once in Hebrews where it is extended to include "miracles" as part of God's testimony to the truth of the message of salvation (2:4). Revelation uses the term in warnings about the forces opposed to God that have the capacity to perform supernatural signs as the apocalyptic scenario unfolds (13:13-14; 16:14; 19:20). *See* MIRACLE; SIGNS IN THE OT.

Bibliography: Jeffrey Gibson. "Jesus' Refusal to Produce a 'Sign' (Mark 8:11-13)." *JSNT* 38 (1990) 37–66; J. Louis Martyn. *History and Theology in the Fourth Gospel.* 2nd ed. (1979); Harold Remus. "Does

Terminology Distinguish Early Christian from Pagan Miracles?" *JBL* 101 (1982) 531–51.

PHILIPPA A. CARTER

SIGNS IN THE OT [אוֹת 'oth; σημεῖον semēion]. A sign is an action, event, ritual, or object used to stand for something else. It may be a physical emblem representing a family or nation (Num 2:2; Ps 74:4, 9). When Rahab of Jericho hides two Israelite spies in Joshua, she asks for a sign (2:12) that they will spare her family, and she is given a crimson cord to tie on her window. However, in biblical usage a sign usually indicates a divine pledge or warning, such as Cain's sign warning others against killing him (Gen 4:15).

Two divine covenants in Genesis are sealed by signs: a rainbow signifies God's PROMISE never again to destroy all flesh with a flood (Gen 9:12, 17), and CIRCUMCISION signifies God's pledge to give Abraham offspring and land (17:11). The first is a divine action; the second a command for human action. In the remainder of the Pentateuch and beyond, these two kinds of signs prevail—signs carried out by God and those commanded of humans, both signaling divine intent. Blood of Passover lambs on the doorposts of Israelite houses is commanded as a sign protecting families from the plague against Egypt (Exod 12:13; *see* PASSOVER AND FEAST OF UNLEAVENED BREAD). Worship at Mount Horeb (Exod 3:12), Passover (13:9), the offering or redemption of the firstborn (13:16), and the Sabbath (31:13, 17, see also Ezek 20:12, 20) are all commanded as reminders of God's distinctive relationship with the Israelites. In Num 16:38, bronze censers of Levites who die challenging Moses' leadership are hammered into an altar covering as a reminder that only Aaronic priests may offer incense. Likewise, Aaron's staff, which unlike others bears blossoms and almonds, becomes a sign warning rebels (17:10). In Deut 6:8 and 11:18, Israelites are told to bind God's command as a sign upon their hand (*see* PHYLACTERIES). In Josh 4:5-7, twelve stones remind Israelites of the Jordan River crossing, and in Isa 19:20 an altar and pillar in Egypt will signify God's deliverance of Egyptian worshipers.

A motif introduced in Exodus and repeated widely is God's deliverance of Israel from Egyptian slavery by means of "signs" or "SIGNS AND WONDERS." Moses is first given three miraculous signs to demonstrate God's intent (Exod 4:8-30). Subsequently God pledges to "multiply my signs and wonders" in the land of Egypt (7:3, see also 8:23, 10:1-2) to force Pharaoh to free the slaves. This phrase, repeated frequently in Deuteronomy, and in Nehemiah, Psalms, and Jeremiah, summarizes deliverance from Egypt.

Although "signs and wonders" usually signify the events surrounding the exodus, other uses of this phrase also appear, often translated differently. The Israelites are warned against signs or wonders presented by other prophets or diviners who lead astray (Deut 13:1-3; see also Isa 44:25). The curses that will come upon disobedient Israelites—pestilence, drought, military defeat, deprivation, and exile—will be signs and wonders warning against rebellion (Deut 28:46, see also Ezek 14:8). The prophet Isaiah, his children, and his symbolic actions are said to be signs and wonders for Israel (Isa 8:18, 20:3). Kings Nebuchadnezzar and Darius proclaim signs and wonders wrought through Daniel (Dan 4:2-3; 6:27).

In Judges, Samuel, Kings, and the narratives of Isaiah, signs are given as pledges of divine action. When Gideon seeks a sign that it is God who commissions him to defeat the Midianite invaders (Judg 6:17), his food offering is consumed by fire. The death of Eli's two sons on the same day signifies God's rejection of his family (1 Sam 2:34). When Samuel anoints Saul king he offers several signs of God's participation (1 Sam 10:1 [LXX, 7-9]). Jonathan proposes to his armor-bearer a sign that God will defeat the Philistines through them (1 Sam 14:10). Isaiah directs King Ahaz of Judah to request a sign of Israel's and Syria's defeat. When Ahaz refuses, Isaiah says God will give him the sign of Immanuel: the two enemy nations will disappear before an unborn child reaches the age of accountability (Isa 7:11-16). Isaiah likewise offers Hezekiah signs of Assyrian defeat (2 Kgs 19:29; Isa 37:30) and of his own healing (2 Kgs 20:8-9; Isa 38:7, 22). Jeremiah's prediction of Pharaoh's defeat (Jer 44:29) and Ezekiel's sign-act concerning Jerusalem (Ezek 4:1-3) convey warnings of the future. Finally, a few texts portray heavenly bodies as signs (Gen 1:14, Ps 65:8; Jer 10:2). *See* SIGNS IN THE NT.

PATRICIA K. TULL

SIHON si′hon [סִיחוֹן sikhon]. The Amorite king who, when approached by Israelite emissaries, refused Israel peaceful passage through his territory, resulting in his defeat (Num 21:21-32; Josh 12:2, 5). The capital of his kingdom, which reached from the Jabbok to the Arnon rivers (Josh 12:2, 5) was located at HESHBON (Num 21:26-28). This conquered territory subsequently became the tribal inheritance of Reuben (Num 32:33; Josh 13:10, 21, 27). The Solomonic official Geber, son of Uri, was situated in Gilead, identified in 1 Kgs 4:19 as the (former) land of Sihon.

That this divinely provided defeat of Sihon was a pivotal event in Israel's history is evidenced by the prominent place it was given in the nation's literary tradition. Deuteronomy alone contains eleven references to the event (1:4; 2:24, 26, 30, 31, 32; 3:2, 6; 4:46; 29:7; 31:4). Twice, in the record of Israel's conquest of Canaan, Israel hears from Canaanite residents that the word of the defeat of Sihon had reached Canaan. In the case of Jericho, the news, according to Rahab, had caused great fear (Josh 2:8-10); the Gibeonites deceptively cited the event as attracting them to Canaan in order to make league with the Israelites (Josh 9:1-11). In the context of the Jephthah narrative, Jephthah, unconvincingly, cites Yahweh's provision of the victory over Sihon in his negotiation with the Ammonites over land rights to the eastern plateau (Judg 11:19-21). Along with reference to striking down the firstborn of Egypt, Ps 135 cites the defeat of Sihon as evidence that Yahweh does what he pleases (135:8-12; compare 136:19). Ezra's postexilic reform was accompanied by a review of Yahweh's dealings with the nation; among the many divine accomplishments in behalf of the nation is a rehearsal of the victory over Sihon (Neh 9:22).

JOHN I. LAWLOR

SILAS si′luhs [Σιλᾶς Silas]. Latinized as *Silvanus*, both names refer to the same person. Acts retains the Jerusalem community's designation (Silas) while Paul and 1 Peter retain the name used in Greco-Roman communities (Silvanus). Silas is first mentioned in Acts wherein he is sent as a delegate (with Paul, Barnabas, and Judas Barsabbas) from the Jerusalem church to report to the church at Antioch the results of the Jerusalem conference (Acts 15:22-35). Judas and Silas, named as "prophets," are said to have encouraged and strengthened the believers there (v. 32) before departing, leaving Paul and Barnabas in Antioch (see, however, the NRSV note taking account of one ancient variant asserting that Silas remained as well). After Paul's split with Barnabas, Silas becomes one of Paul's missionary companions (Acts 15:40–18:5). He is imprisoned with Paul in Philippi for exorcising a slave girl; while praying and singing in prison, their bonds are loosened by an earthquake (16:16-28), and they are released after Paul identifies them as Roman citizens (v. 37; compare 1 Thess 2:1-2). Silas accompanies Paul to Thessalonica, where Paul's preaching creates an uproar; they then travel to Beroea, where Silas stays behind with Timothy when Paul departs (17:1-15). Silas and Timothy rejoin Paul in Corinth (Acts 18:5) for an extended sojourn (2 Cor 1:19). After Paul's departure from Corinth, Silas remains behind and this apparently brings to an end their missionary work together. Before departing Paul's company, Silas coauthors with Paul and Timothy 1 and 2 Thessalonians (1 Thess 1:1; 2 Thess 1:1). First Peter also mentions Silvanus as perhaps the secretary (AMANUENSIS) of the letter (5:12). Some have used this to argue for Petrine authorship, but the proposal remains doubtful. *See* PAUL, AUTHORSHIP; PAUL, THE APOSTLE; PETER, FIRST LETTER OF; PETER, THE APOSTLE.

DEMETRIUS K. WILLIAMS

SILENCE [דָּמַם damam, חָס khas, חָרַשׁ kharesh, חָשָׁה khashah; σιγή sigē, σιωπάω siōpaō]. Silence in the biblical literature is expressed through a variety of Hebrew and Greek terms. Silence is imaged both positively and negatively; human and divine silence are addressed, and some texts represent it as imposed. Three of the eight uses of the interjection khas ("be silent!/hush!") represent response to the presence of Yahweh (Hab 2:20; Zeph 1:7; Zech 2:13).

Fools appear to be wise by their silence (Prov 17:28) and an intelligent person keeps silence (Prov 11:12). Using the same root four times, Num 30:4, 7, 11, 14 describe the silence of a father or husband in a vow-making context. In striking contrast to the congregational response of Lev 9:24, Aaron was silent (Lev 10:3). Concern over the possibility of divine silence is expressed in the Psalms (28:1; 35:22; 39:12; 83:1; 109:1).

Silence is imposed on Zechariah prior to the birth of his son (Luke 1:20). In contrast to the sounds associated with each of the first six seals, a dramatic silence is the response to the opening of the seventh seal (Rev 8:1). Noteworthy also are the narrated silences of Elihu (Job 32:4) and Jesus (Luke 23:9).

JOHN I. LAWLOR

SILK [σιρικός sirikos]. Developed in ancient China, silk is a luxury fiber made from the cocoons of a moth. Unlike wool and cotton, silk was little known in the biblical world. Only in Rev 18:12 is there a clear reference to silk, where it appears in a list of luxury items. The NRSV notes *silk* as a variant reading for "linen" in Ep Jer 6:72.

MARY PETRINA BOYD

SILLA sil′uh [סִלָּא silla᾽]. Mentioned only at 2 Kgs 12:20 [Heb. 12:21] as a place relative to the MILLO. Its precise location, as well as its significance, is unknown. Silla may have been a landmark or district located east-southeast down the slope of the city of David in the Kidron Valley.

KENT V. BRAMLETT

SILOAM si-loh′uhm [שִׁלֹחַ shiloakh, שֶׁלַח shelakh; Σιλωάμ Silōam]. A water reservoir or pool in the southeast corner of ancient Jerusalem that is fed by the Gihon ("Gushing") Spring, later known as the Virgin's Fountain (*see* GIHON, SPRING). The name seems to be derived from a Hebrew term meaning "aqueduct" or "(water) channel."

Its earliest appearance in the OT is in Isa 8:6, a passage relating to the Syro-Ephraimite War (ca. 735–732 BCE), in which the prophet castigates the people for "refus[ing] the waters of Shiloah that flow gently"—presumably an allegorical reference to life-sustaining divine aid in a time of war. Although both the LXX and English translations treat shiloakh in this case as a proper noun ("Siloam"), the placement of the prefixed definite article in the Hebrew indicates that it is probably functioning as a common noun, in which case the text should more properly be understood as "the waters of the aqueduct that flow gently." This impression is strengthened when one looks at the only other possible OT reference to this geographical feature. Nehemiah 3:15 refers to the building of "the wall of the Pool of Shelah of the king's garden" (*see* SHELAH, POOL OF). Deriving from the same Hebrew root, the only difference between the two passages is in their vowel pointing, which—albeit a late addition to the Hebrew text—is supported in both instances by the LXX transcriptions. Here, as in the Isaiah passage, the word in question is preceded by the definite article and appears as the second element in a nominal construct chain. Nonetheless, in spite of NRSV's translation of the Hebrew shelakh in Neh 3:15 as "Pool of Shelah," most other translations interpret it as a common noun and translate the phrase along the lines of "irrigation pool."

In the writings of Josephus (e.g., *J.W.* 5.140), the Pool of Siloam is referred to as a "fountain." He locates it in the southern TYROPOEON VALLEY, which is where the modern Pool of Siloam is located. By this time the probable original meaning of the term had been forgotten, and the "Pool of Siloam" became the name of a well-known site in Jerusalem. In Byzantine times a church was built at the pool, upon the site of which a mosque, which still stands, was later erected. Siloam lives on in the name of Silwan, the village hugging the eastern slope of the KIDRON VALLEY.

It may have been in this large pool that Jesus told a blind man to immerse himself in order to effect a cure of his malady (John 9:7, 11). Luke 13:4 refers to an otherwise unknown incident in which eighteen people "were killed when the tower of Siloam fell on them." It is reasonable to consider this tower as an architectural feature associated with the pool. The Pool of Siloam was the source of the water used in a ritual that the Talmud claims was observed on the Festival of Booths (*see* BOOTHS, FEAST OR FESTIVAL OF) during the time of the Second Temple (*b. Sukkah* 4.9). A number of additional texts in the OT that do not refer to Siloam by name have also been brought into the discussion. These focus on the measures that King HEZEKIAH of Judah is supposed to have undertaken in the years 705–701 BCE in anticipation of an Assyrian attack. These measures include various types of fortification, among which the securing of Jerusalem's water supply seems to have played a central role. In its summary of the reign of Hezekiah, 2 Kgs 20:20 refers to "how he made the pool and the conduit and brought water into the city." The pool in question is generally identified as the original Pool of Siloam, while the conduit is identified as the youngest and longest of the three major water systems associated with Jerusalem in the Iron Age II. Other texts make reference to additional pools in ancient Jerusalem, but their exact identification—including the question of which one is to be identified with the Siloam Pool—is open to interpretation (compare "the upper pool," Isa 7:3; 2 Kgs 18:17//Isa 36:2; "the lower pool," Isa 22:9; "a reservoir between the two walls" and "the old pool," Isa 22:11; "the King's Pool," Neh 2:14; "the artificial pool," Neh 3:16). Second Chronicles 32 relates additional details about Hezekiah's efforts, although one must be cautious in evaluating any information related in Chronicles and not attested in other sources. The Chronicler states that Hezekiah had the sources of water stopped up and redirected (2 Chr 32:4), and specifically

relates how he had this done to the Gihon Spring (2 Chr 32:30). Sirach 48:17, an even later source, implies that Hezekiah built more than one water cistern.

Archaeologists have discovered and cleared three underground water systems associated with Iron Age Jerusalem. The oldest is what is known as "Warren's Shaft," after the British explorer who first identified it in 1867. It is a natural karstic formation that allowed residents of Jerusalem to lower buckets down to the waters of the Gihon Spring from inside the city.

The second aqueduct is a 400 m channel carved into the rock on the eastern slope of the City of David that served to irrigate the Kidron Valley by means of a series of outlets hewn out of the rock. Since it is probably the aqueduct referenced in Isa 8:6, it is often referred to as the "Siloam Tunnel/Channel." Its major weakness from a military perspective was that it lay outside the perimeter of the city's defensive walls.

The nomenclature gets confusing once the third water system is considered. This is most probably the water channel that was hewn during the reign of Hezekiah. One of the great engineering feats of the ancient world, this tunnel currently stretches for 533 circuitous meters—although it may have been slightly longer in ancient times—and empties into the Siloam Pool. Often referred to as Hezekiah's Tunnel, it also bears the designation of Siloam Tunnel, and is confused with the aforementioned Siloam Tunnel. After withholding tribute to Assyria following the death of SARGON II (705 BCE), Hezekiah apparently enclosed many of the extramural dwellings of Jerusalem with a massive wall and redirected the Gihon waters into the more centrally located Siloam Pool by means of this tunnel, hewn through the bedrock underneath the City of David. The tunnel's winding path has engendered much speculation regarding its reasons, ranging from the following of karstic faults in the rock to the primitive methods of communication between the engineers of the project on the surface and those doing the actual work underground. Near the center of the tunnel one can find evidence of the last few imperfect attempts of the two crews of workers, one hewing from the north and the other from the south, to meet up. Nonetheless, when the tunnel was finally completed, the differential in height between its beginning in the northeast and end in the southwest of the southeastern spur upon which the City of David is located was just 32 cm, which allowed for a steady yet controlled flow of water.

Some 6 m from the southern end of the tunnel an inscription associated with the completion of the work was found. This so called Siloam Tunnel Inscription is the longest Hebrew inscription thus far found from the Iron Age and was—perhaps unexpectedly—not written in praise of the king who ordered the work. Instead it details the last stages of work on the tunnel and the excitement of the workers as their labors were brought to a successful completion.

In the early 21st cent., archaeologists found another pool about 50 m to the east of the traditional Pool of Siloam. The excavators argue that this new discovery is the actual Pool of Siloam mentioned in the Bible but have yet to persuade the majority of scholars. The two pools are sometimes called the "New Pool" and the "Byzantine Pool" to differentiate them.

Bibliography: Amos Frumkin and Aryeh Shimron. "Tunnel Engineering in the Iron Age: Geoarchaeology of the Siloam Tunnel, Jerusalem." *Journal of Archaeological Science* 33 (2006) 227–37; Dan Gill. "The Geology of the City of David and Its Ancient Subterranean Waterworks." *City of David Excavations Final Report IV* (1996) 1–28; Stig Norin. "The Age of the Siloam Inscription and Hezekiah's Tunnel." *VT* 48 (1998) 37–48; K. Lawson Younger Jr. "The Siloam Tunnel Inscription: An Integrated Reading." *UF* 26 (1994) 543–56.

CARL S. EHRLICH

SILVANUS. *See* SILAS.

SILVANUS, TEACHINGS OF sil·vay′nuhs. A 3rd-cent. CE non-gnostic exhortation to asceticism representative of early Christian wisdom literature. The text possibly originated in Alexandria.

Bibliography: J. Zandee. *The Teachings of Silvanus (Nag Hammadi Codex VII.4). Text, Translation and Commentary* (1991).

SILVER [כֶּסֶף kesef; ἀργύριον argyrion]. *Silver* appears in the Bible in two basic meanings: as a precious metal and as currency. As a precious metal it ranks in value just below gold: GOLD and silver (and sometimes BRONZE) are usually mentioned together to denominate wealth, both in a literal sense (Abraham was rich in silver and gold; Gen 13:12; 24:35) and metaphorically to symbolize wealth (e.g., 2 Sam 2:14; Hag 1:8). The wealth of Solomon was so great that he did not even use silver for his tableware, but all his vessels were made of gold (1 Kgs 10:21). In general, however, silver was used for the vessels in the temple and in the palaces of the kings. Joseph's precious drinking cup, when he was viceroy in Egypt, was made of silver (Gen 44:2). The furnishings of the tabernacle in the desert were also mostly made of silver, as were the furnishings of the temple in Jerusalem.

Gods and idols were often made of silver and gold, or at least plated with it (Exod 20:23; Isa 2:20; 40:19). Refining of silver with lead was a common metaphor for spiritual purification in the OT (Jer 6:29-30; *see* METALLURGY).

The most common use of silver was probably for JEWELRY. Silver jewelry is regularly mentioned in the Bible. It was worn by both men and women, but it seems to have been more common for women as earrings, rings, bracelets, armlets, pendants, and beads. Silver jewelry is regularly found in archaeological excavations.

Silver was also the most common currency in the biblical period. The Bible contains numerous references expressing the value of various items in weight units of silver. Common units are the gerah (.416 grams), the shekel (20 gerahs), the mana (50 shekels), and the talent (3,000 shekels). Abraham bought the field with the cave of Mahpelah for 400 shekels of silver. The hill of Samaria, on which Omri built his capital, was bought for two talents of silver; in the days of Solomon an Egyptian chariot cost 600 shekels of silver, and a horse 150.

In the Persian period coins became more common as a means of payment. These were also weight units, and the names did not change: a shekel of silver would weigh the same in silver scrap, or in coinage. Silver coins have been found bearing the name of various cities, such as Ashdod, Samaria, Gaza, and Juda, showing that these cities minted their own coins. In Dor three silver-plated copper coins were found dated to the Persian period.

Silver coins from the Hellenistic and Roman periods are common all over Palestine. As forgery was as common then as it is in any period, methods were developed to test whether a coin consisted of solid silver. It would be nicked with the point of a sword, a chisel, or a specially developed tool that left a recognizable mark, which could at the same time serve as a mark of ownership. Thus, all the silver tetradrachms in a hoard found in Dor, dated to the Hellenistic period, have one or more punch marks (*see* also MONEY, COINS).

Silver hoards have been found in Megiddo, Gezer, Shechem, Eshtemoa, and elsewhere. They have sometimes been interpreted as scrap that was meant for remelting, but in light of the fact that silver was the standard metal used for currency, it is more likely that the material was actually "money." The largest hoard was found in Eshtemoa, dated to the 9th cent. BCE, and consisted of five pottery jars, with a total weight of 62 lbs. of silver. Much of the scrap in the jars consisted of silver jewelry, but there was also a large amount of silver in small blocks, broken off from so-called "chocolate-bar ingots." These ingots were shaped like segmented chocolate bars, so that pieces of equal size and weight could easily be broken off, suggesting that they were meant as currency from the beginning. The hoard has been interpreted as part of the administrative tax collection.

The use of silver as jewelry, display of wealth, and as currency is illustrated in bedouin societies in the ANE. Women wore head ornaments, bracelets, earrings, and necklaces made of silver coins. This jewelry not only served as ornaments but also, being the personal property of the woman, as insurance against poverty in case of divorce (compare Luke 15:8-9).

EVELINE J. VAN DER STEEN

SILVERSMITH צוֹרֵף tsoref; ἀργυροκόπος argyrokopos]. A craftsman working in precious metals. The Hebrew word tsoref is usually rendered "GOLD-SMITH"; in Judg 17:4, it refers to a craftsman who makes a statue out of silver, and is thus translated "silversmith." Silver statues or idols were often made of silver and covered with gold leaf.

The speech of Demetrius the silversmith (Acts 19:24-27) refers to the cult shrines used in house cults, an integral part of Greek society. The construction of such shrines provided a fair number of silversmiths with a good living. The techniques used by the silversmith were largely the same as those used for gold objects and included casting, chasing, and embossing. *See* CRAFTS; JEWELRY; METALLURGY; SILVER.

EVELINE J. VAN DER STEEN

SIMEON BEN ELEAZAR BEN SIRA. The author of SIRACH as named in the early Hebrew manuscripts, although the NRSV, following the Greek, names the author "Jesus son of Eleazar son of Sirach" (Sir 50:27).

SIMEON, SIMEONITES sim´ee-uhn, sim´ee-uh-n*i*t [שִׁמְעוֹן shim'on; בְּנֵי שִׁמְעוֹן bene shim'on; Συμεών Symeōn]. Simeon is a personal name of uncertain etymology that occurs in both the OT and NT. The most common explanation of the name is based on Gen 29:33, which derives the name from the Hebrew word for "to hear" (shama' שָׁמַע). The -on ending is generally explained as a common Hebrew diminutive ending. By this explanation, the name would mean "(the deity) has heard." A second explanation is that the root should be related to an Arabic word for hyena, yielding the meaning "little hyena." 1. The most common usage of the name in the OT is to designate the tribe of Simeon. According to Gen 29:33, Simeon is the second son born to JACOB and LEAH. Genesis 29:31-35 lists the birth of Jacob's and Leah's first four sons: Reuben, Simeon, Levi, and Judah. The births of two additional sons, Issachar and Zebulun, and one daughter, Dinah, are recorded in Gen 30:16-21 (see also Gen 35:23). Each of the six sons became the eponymous ancestor of one of the tribes of Israel. Members of the tribe of Simeon were thus considered Simeonites.

Simeon, in conjunction with his older brother Reuben, is next mentioned in Gen 34, which presents the events associated with the rape of their sister Dinah by Shechem son of Hamor, the chief of the area. If the name *Shechem* is taken as suggesting a relationship to the city by that name, mentioned previously in Gen 33:18-20, then this story takes place in central Palestine. Shechem, desiring to make Dinah his wife, accompanies his father to meet with Jacob and his sons to request the marriage. Jacob's sons deceive Hamor and Shechem by agreeing to the marriage on the condition that all of the men of the settlement be circumcised (Gen 34:13-17), a condition that they, as well as the men of the city, accept. Three days after the men of the town are circumcised—and while they are still in pain (34:25)—Simeon and Levi attack the city, slaughtering all of the males, including Hamor and Shechem, taking Dinah with them. The remaining sons of Jacob then plunder the city, taking everything that remains. As a result, Simeon and Levi receive a weak reproach from their father for their brutal deed (Gen 34:30; compare 49:7, quoted in 4 Macc 2:19, which refers to Simeon and Levi's actions as "irrational slaughter," arguing for the superiority of reason over the emotions). Interestingly, the other sons who completely plundered the city receive no such expression of disapproval. Many commentators connect this event, or something similar to it, with the condemnation of Simeon and Levi for their violent natures in the blessing of Jacob (Gen 49:5-7), proclaiming that these two tribes would be scattered through Israel.

Simeon also plays a role in the Joseph story, being the brother whom Joseph holds hostage to ensure that his other brothers will do his bidding (Gen 42:24, 36; 43:23). Exodus 6:15 provides a list of the offspring of Simeon, while the census accounts in Numbers list the clans and their total size for the wilderness period (1:22-23; 26:12). Simeon is also named as one of the six tribes who are to stand on Mount Gerizim for the blessing of the people once they enter the promised land (Deut 27:12; Josh 8:33).

In the accounts of the conquest, however, Simeon's status as a full-fledged tribe seems to have diminished. As is the case with Dan, no boundary list is given for Simeon. Instead, Simeon seems to have been incorporated into the tribe of Judah at some point early in the history of the monarchy. Joshua 19:1-9 provides a list of cities, all in the northern Negeb in the vicinity of Beersheba, which were controlled by the Simeonites. This list is closely related to the list of cities allotted to Judah in Josh 15:26-32 and to a later list found in 1 Chr 4:28-32. The latter list makes reference to the expansion of the Simeonites into Philistine territory (4:34-43). This southern location is reinforced by the account in Judg 1:1-17, which describes how Judah, along with other smaller groups, like Simeon, takes possession of the southern portion of Judah's allotment, noting explicitly the conquest of Zephath/Hormah (v. 17).

In the book of Judith, "Uzziah son of Micah, of the tribe of Simeon" is one of the magistrates of Bethulia who hears Achior's testimony concerning Holofernes' plans to destroy the Israelites. In Jdt 9:2, Judith prays to the "Lord God of my ancestor Simeon" for help in defeating Holofernes and the Assyrians, recalling Simeon and Levi's revenge for the rape of Dinah.

2. Ezra 10:31 refers to a man named Simeon son of Harim in a list of inhabitants of Jerusalem who had taken foreign wives.

3. Luke 2:25-35 contains the account of an otherwise unknown man named Simeon, described as a "righteous and devout" man who was expecting the "consolation of Israel." The NUNC DIMITTIS (2:29-32)

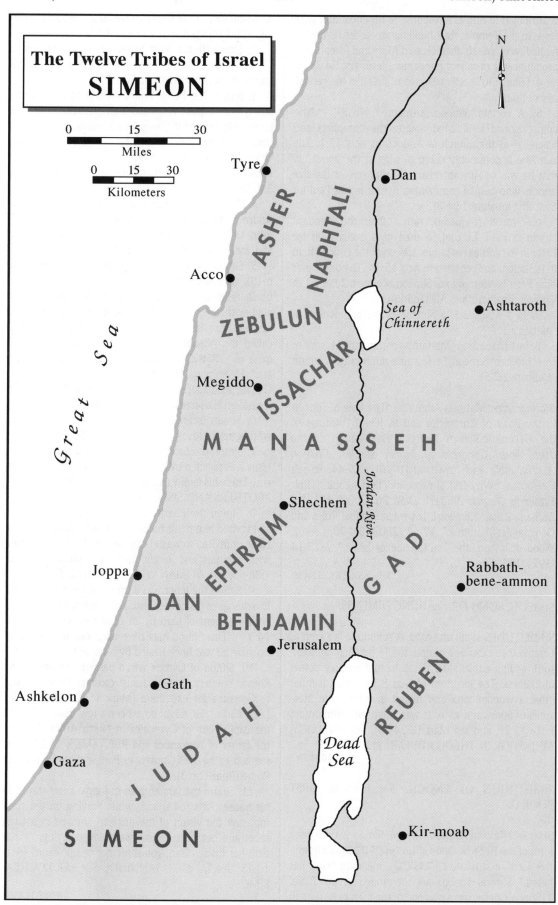

The Twelve Tribes of Israel
SIMEON

0   15   30
Miles

0   15   30
Kilometers

N

Great Sea

ASHER

NAPHTALI

ZEBULUN

ISSACHAR

MANASSEH

EPHRAIM

DAN

BENJAMIN

GAD

JUDAH

REUBEN

SIMEON

Tyre ●

● Dan

Acco ●

● Ashtaroth

Sea of Chinnereth

Megiddo ●

● Shechem

Jordan River

Joppa ●

Rabbath-bene-ammon ●

Jerusalem ●

● Gath

Ashkelon ●

Dead Sea

● Gaza

● Kir-moab

is attributed to him as a response to his encounter with Jesus in the Temple, thus fulfilling an earlier revelation he had received. He then blessed Mary and Joseph, and pronounced a prophecy concerning Jesus (vv. 34-35).

4. Luke 3:30 lists Simeon son of Judah in the genealogy of Jesus.

5. A certain Simeon, surnamed NIGER ("dark-complexioned"), is listed among the "prophets and teachers" in the church at Antioch in Acts 13:1. The surname is commonly taken to suggest the possibility that he was of African origin. He was one of the five leaders who helped commission Barnabas and Paul for their first mission (13:1-3).

6. Simeon (Symeōn), rather than the standard Simon (Simōn Σίμων), is used as a designation for Peter in the context of James' speech at the council held in Jerusalem and reported in Acts 15:14. The only other time Peter is referred to as Simeon occurs in 2 Pet 1:1 in Codices Sinaiticus and Alexandrinus.

7. In 1 Macc 2:1, a Simeon is the grandfather of Mattathias.

8. In 1 Macc 2:65, Mattathias commends his sons to their brother "Simeon," elsewhere referred to as Simon (compare 2:2-5).

Bibliography: Matthias Augustin. "The Role of Simeon in the Book of Chronicles and in Jewish Writings of the Hellenistic-Roman Period." *Proceedings of the 10th World Congress of Jewish Studies. Division A: The Bible and Its World* (1990) 137-44; Joseph Fleishman. "Why Did Simeon and Levi Rebuke Their Father in Genesis 34:31?" *JNSL* 26 (2000) 101-16; Zecharia Kallai. "Simeon's Town List: Scribal Rules and Geographical Patterns." *VT* 53 (2003) 81-96; Leon J. Wood. "Simeon, the Tenth Tribe of Israel." *JETS* 14 (1971) 221-25.

E. THEODORE MULLEN JR.

SIMEON, SONG OF. *See* NUNC DIMITTIS.

SIMILITUDES si-mil′uh-ty*oo*d. A similitude is a kind of parable that extends a simple simile (explicit comparison), adding explanatory detail to indicate key points of likeness. The kingdom of God is like yeast (simile) "that a woman took and mixed in with three measures of flour until all of it was leavened" (similitude; Luke 13:21, and see Matt 13:24-50). *See* ANALOGY; METAPHOR IN THEOLOGY; PARABLE.

BONNIE HOWE

SIMILITUDES OF ENOCH. *See* ENOCH, FIRST BOOK OF.

SIMON si′muhn [Σίμων Simōn]. Simon is the Greek form of the Hebrew name shim'on (שִׁמְעוֹן), a diminutive form of shime'e'l (שְׁמָעֵאל), meaning "God has heard." Several Simons are mentioned in the Bible.

1. Simon Chosamaeus was one of the men in Jerusalem who sent away their foreign wives and children in keeping with Ezra's purity law (1 Esd 9:32).

2. Simon II the high priest (d. 198 BCE), son of ONIAS II, was remembered for repairing the Temple and restoring its service (Sir 50:1-21).

3. Simon the Benjaminite, captain of the Temple, falsely accused Onias III, the high priest, of embezzlement; this resulted in a surprise inspection of the temple treasury by HELIODORUS, who was stopped only by a vision of a gold armored rider on a caparisoned horse with two strong young men fighting by his side (2 Macc 3:4-40).

4. Simon Peter, son of Jonah (or John) and brother of Andrew, was a fisherman from Bethsaida (Matt 16:17; John 1:40-44) who became a leading disciple of Jesus and was named "Peter" (*see* PETER, THE APOSTLE).

5. Simon the Zealot, another disciple of Jesus (Luke 6:15), was so called either because he was enthusiastic in religious piety or because he was once associated with the resistant forces against the Roman rule in Palestine. In Mark 3:18 and Matt 10:4 he was called the "Cananaean," a transliteration of Aramaic qana'na' (קַנְאָנָא), meaning "ZEALOT" or "enthusiast." Hegesippus identified him with Simeon, son of Clopas, who succeeded James as head of the church in Jerusalem (Eusebius, *Hist. eccl.* 3.11, 32).

6. Simon Iscariot was father of Judas, the disciple who betrayed Jesus (John 6:71; 13:2, 26).

7. Simon the brother of Jesus was mentioned when Jesus was rejected by his hometown people in Nazareth who knew his family (Mark 6:3; Matt 13:55; *see* JESUS, BROTHERS AND SISTERS OF).

8. Simon the Pharisee regarded Jesus as a prophet and invited him to his house for dinner, where a woman came uninvited to wash Jesus' feet with tears, dry them with her hair, and anoint them with ointment (Luke 7:36-50; *see* WOMAN WHO ANOINTED JESUS).

9. Simon the leper was a friend of Jesus in Bethany. In a dinner in his house, Jesus was anointed on the head with ointment of nard by an unnamed woman (Mark 14:3-9). This Simon may have been called "the leper" because he was once healed by Jesus of his LEPROSY.

10. Simon of Cyrene was a passerby compelled by Roman soldiers to carry Jesus' cross as he was taken to Golgotha for execution (Mark 15:21; Matt 27:32; Luke 23:26). He might have been a Jew from CYRENE, the capital city of Cyrenaica in North Africa. He was the father of Alexander and Rufus (Mark 15:21) who seemed to be well known to Paul and the church in Rome (Rom 16:13).

11. Simon the tanner lived in Joppa. Peter stayed in his house (Acts 9:43) and, while praying on the rooftop, saw the vision of the unclean animals in a large sheet and heard the voice from heaven saying, "What God has made clean, you must not call profane" (Acts 10:15; *see* TANNER, TANNING). *See* BAR KOCHBA, SIMON.

JOHN Y. H. YIEH

12. Simon the Maccabee was the last of the Maccabee brothers (see HASMONEANS; MACCABEES, FIRST BOOK OF) to lead Judah during its struggle for independence in the 2nd cent. BCE. He acted as general and second in command under his brother Jonathan (see JONATHAN). When Jonathan was taken captive and executed by Tryphon ca. 143 BCE, Simon took over leadership; he was now the third of the Maccabean brothers to become leader of the Hasmonean movement.

By this time the majority of the Palestinian Jews seem to have accepted the Maccabees as leaders. With this popular backing and a temporary calm, Simon could continue the efforts of his brothers to effect independence (1 Macc 13:33). He negotiated with Demetrius II (see DEMETRIUS) who still sought to regain the throne. Demetrius made a variety of far-reaching concessions in a letter to Simon, even including permission to mint his own coinage (though no such coins have been discovered), and the author of 1 Maccabees could write that in Simon's first year in power—the 170th year of the Seleucid era (143–142 BCE)—"the yoke of the Gentiles was removed from Israel" (13:41-42). Judea was now an independent state.

There is no doubt that this was a significant event since Judah had been a vassal state of one sort or another for ca. 600 years. Subsequent events were to show that this state of "liberation" was short-lived. Nevertheless, for a time the Judeans dated their contracts and legal documents from Simon's first year (see the summary of his reign in 1 Macc 14:4-15). In Simon's third year, a stela was erected that recounted his and his brothers' deeds and confirmed him in the office of high priest (1 Macc 14:27-47). Simon is credited with a variety of accomplishments: perhaps the most important of these was at last taking the Jerusalem Akra in 142 BCE, which removed the last formal symbol of Seleucid rule (1 Macc 13:49-52). He also renewed the treaties with Rome and Sparta (1 Macc 14:16-24; 15:15-24), made Joppa into a Jewish port, and took Gazara (OT Gezer).

After Demetrius II had made concessions to Simon to enlist his friendship, he marched east and was replaced by Antiochus VII Sidetes (138–129 BCE; see ANTIOCHUS). When besieging Tryphon in Dor, Antiochus received aid from Simon. With Tryphon out of the way, however, Antiochus turned on Simon with demands, which showed that he considered Judea still a Seleucid vassal. Simon was now too aged to take to the field, but his sons John and Judah assumed command and were able to defeat Antiochus' force.

After a rule of eight years, Simon was invited to a banquet in Jericho by his son-in-law, the Jewish general Ptolemy. Ptolemy used the occasion to assassinate Simon and imprison Simon's wife and two other sons, but the third son John Hyrcanus was forewarned and escaped. Thus, the last of the Maccabean brothers met his end by violence. Nevertheless, Simon's achievement was considerable and his reign an important watershed in Jewish history. See JUDAS; MACCABEES, MACCABEAN REVOLT; MATTATHIAS.

LESTER L. GRABBE

13. Simon Magus (Simōn Magos Σίμων Μάγος) was a popular practitioner of magical arts in SAMARIA encountered by Philip the evangelist and the apostle Peter in Acts 8; and he was the villainous progenitor of gnostic heresy denounced by certain early church fathers.

Within the NT, Simon Magus appears only in Acts 8, first in the context of PHILIP the evangelist's gospel-preaching and miracle-working mission in the city of Samaria (8:5-13). Before Philip's arrival, Simon had enjoyed widespread fame among the Samaritans for his dynamic magical works (mageia μαγεία) and personal claims. We are not told what types of "magic" Simon performed, but as with other reputed wonder workers in antiquity, he likely dabbled in various dramatic forms of pain relief, healing therapy, and demon expulsion, as well as more frivolous stunts and exhibitions (see MAGIC, MAGICIAN). In any case, his magical repertoire was impressive enough to elicit "all" the people's ("from the least to the greatest") amazement "for a long time." As for his message, Simon audaciously announced himself to be "someone great (megan μέγαν)," which probably amounted to a claim to deity, to being a "divine man"—the exalted "Great One." Accordingly, the charismatic Simon captured the Samaritans' close attention ("All of them ... listened to him eagerly") and rapt devotion, as they hailed him "the power of God that is called Great" incarnate.

Against this historical backdrop, Philip's thriving messianic mission in Samaria is effectively cast as displacing Simon's influence or breaking his control (spell) over the "nation." On the one hand, Philip beats Simon at his own game, performing such astounding "signs and great miracles (dynameis megalas δυνάμεις μεγάλας)," including dramatic exorcisms and healings, that Simon himself becomes amazed along with the crowds (8:6-8, 13). On the other hand, however, Philip takes a very different tack, promoting not himself, but Jesus the Messiah as God's true revealer and humanity's true redeemer—in other words, the genuine "Power of God"—worthy of faith and adherence (8:5-6). Philip's (or rather, Christ's) supplanting of Simon is sealed by the Samaritans'—including Simon's—belief and baptism "in the name of Jesus Christ" (8:12-13).

But Simon's story is not so neatly settled. Soon serious questions arise about the sincerity of his conversion. When Peter and John arrive from Jerusalem and impart the Holy Spirit to the Samaritan believers through the laying on of hands, Simon offers to purchase this marvelous Spirit trick, as he perceives it, from the apostles (8:14-19). His implied motivation remains courting popular favor and exploiting financial opportunity (magicians were notorious in the ancient world for their money-grubbing schemes). Likely, Simon seeks to buy the ability to transmit the Spirit so he can charge people for this "magical" service. But Peter sees through Simon's chicanery and blasts his blasphemy against the Spirit, as it were: "May your silver perish with you, because you thought you could obtain God's gift with money! You have no part or share in this, for your heart is not right before God" (8:20-21). As God's freely bestowed gift, the Spirit cannot be manipulated by human hands for selfish ends.

Simon's only hope is to "repent" of his terrible "wickedness" and pray for forgiveness (8:22-23). The narrative leaves open his ultimate fate: whereas a fearful Simon petitions Peter's intercession, we do not know whether Simon or Peter ever plead for God's mercy on Simon's behalf (8:24). Overall, the Simon Magus story fits with other incidents in Acts warning against the pitfalls and perfidies of self-promoting "magical" practices (compare 13:6-12; 16:16-18; 19:11-20) and avaricious profiteering within as well as outside the Christian community (compare Acts 1:16-20; 5:1-11; Luke 8:14; 22:3-6).

Whereas the canonical Acts leaves the future of Simon Magus hanging in the balance, early patristic and apocryphal writings continue plotting his saga in various directions. Although stressing different aspects of his character and influence, these materials cohere in regarding Simon as a persisting, diabolical threat to authentic (orthodox) Christianity, evidenced in the sprouting and spread of various "Simonian" sects and movements into the 2nd and 3rd cent. Although many scholars agree that Simon was a popular, charismatic religious figure in 1st-cent. Samaria (along the broad lines of Acts' portrait), the sharply polemic nature of post-NT depictions (Simon is consistently cast as an inveterate villain and/or heretic) and the dearth of direct, comparative material from "Simonian" sources make it difficult to assess the validity of Simon's image and legacy, to separate history from legend.

Himself a native of Samaria, the 2nd-cent. Christian apologist JUSTIN MARTYR tracked the origins of Simon Magus to the Samaritan village of Gitta; eventually, however, Simon took his "demon"-inspired magic act to Rome during the reign of Claudius (41–54 CE). Justin reports that Simon attracted many followers who worshiped him as "first god"; among these adherents was a notable woman named Helena who became Simon's chief consort and prime emanation of his redemptive "first thought" (Justin, 1 Apol. 1.26). IRENAEUS further associated Simon Magus with the heterodox philosophical-religious system of GNOSTICISM that flourished toward the end of the 2nd cent. Indeed, Irenaeus dubbed Simon the founding "father of all heresies," especially those of a gnostic stripe that rejected the Jewish Scriptures, promoted the salvific value of esoteric knowledge, and engaged in licentious behavior. Simon sought to supplant Christ's true apostles and establish his own diabolical succession. Moreover, he claimed to be the incarnate God himself, empowered

to liberate enslaved human souls, starting with Helen's. Eventually, "Simonian" devotees known to Irenaeus began to worship Simon and HELENA in the images of Zeus and Minerva (Irenaeus, Haer. 1.23). In the early 3rd cent. Hippolytus further developed Simon's profile: shifting Simon's nefarious magic-working in Rome to the period of Nero (54–68 CE) rather than Claudius; reporting Simon's death as the result of his ill-fated scheme to be buried alive and rise (à la Christ) three days hence; and exposing Simon's heretical teaching in a document (of disputed origins) called the "Great Revelation" (Apophasis Megalē Ἀποφάσις Μεγάλη), where he allegedly claims to be the eschatological "Standing One" ("the one who stood, stands, and will stand"), and his followers tout him as the manifestation of the suffering Son in Judea, the powerful Father in Samaria, and the Holy Spirit throughout the world (Hippolytus, Haer. 6.9–20; compare Epiphanius, Pan. 21.1–7).

Although these depictions of Simon build on Acts' foundational portrait of a megalomaniacal Samaritan magician, they move considerably beyond the canonical image, especially in elaborating Simon's teaching, relationship with Helen, and gnostic orientation. Attempts by some scholars to read an anti-gnostic polemic back into Acts 8 (e.g., suggesting that Peter's reproof of Simon's wicked "intent [epinoia ἐπίνοια] of heart" [8:22] is a veiled reference to Simon's "first thought [ennoia ἔννοια]" embodied in Helen) remain highly speculative and anachronistic.

Less concerned with Simon's gnostic bent, certain apocryphal writings focus upon Simon's wonder-working competition with the apostle Peter (Philip drops from the picture). The Pseudo-Clementine literature fills in Simon's background, attributing his extensive knowledge of the "magical arts" to a period of study in Egypt and associating him with an elite circle of thirty disciples of John the Baptist, including another Samaritan magician named Dositheus, who became Simon's chief rival. After John's death, Simon bested Dositheus in a magic-wielding duel (Dositheus' Moses-like rod passed right through Simon like smoke, leaving him unharmed) and proved himself the true "Standing One" and "Prophet-like-Moses" (Ps.-Clem. Homily 2.22–24; Recognitions 2:8–11). However, Simon later engages in an extended disputation with Peter that demonstrates the fraudulence of Simon's powers and pretensions. Whereas huckster magicians like Simon perform their tricks to "astonish and deceive," genuine apostles like Peter work true miracles in Christ's name to "convert and save" (Ps.-Clem. Homily 2.33).

The Acts of Peter recounts in fantastic fashion Peter's calling out Simon to a public duel in the Roman forum. Peter issues his challenge through the voice of a "great dog" that stands upright on its hind legs and loudly denounces Simon as "you most wicked deceiver of simple souls" (Acts Pet. 9). Through a series of extraordinary beneficent miracles, the apostle Peter thoroughly defeats Simon Magus. In a last-ditch effort to vindicate himself, Simon takes to the air, flying around the temples and hills of Rome in the sight of Peter and amazed crowds. Peter promptly beseeches Christ to bring down this presumptuous aerial acrobat, causing him to be maimed (his leg broken in three places) but not killed. However, when Simon crash-lands just as Peter had prayed, the people stone the charlatan magician and "believe in Peter." Though he was taken up by some of his diehard supporters and underwent surgery, "Simon, the angel of the devil" soon dies, broken and humiliated (*Acts Pet.* 32).

Bibliography: A. Ferreiro. *Simon Magus in Patristic, Medieval and Early Modern Traditions* (2005); S. Haar. *Simon Magus: The First Gnostic?* (2003); E. Hennecke and W. Schneemelcher. *New Testament Apocrypha*, vol. 2 (1992); G. Lüdemann. "The Acts of the Apostles and the Beginnings of Simonian Gnosis." *NTS* 33 (1987) 420–26; C. R. Matthews. "The Acts of Peter and Luke's Intertextual Heritage." *Semeia* 80 (1997) 207–22; W. A. Meeks. "Simon Magus in Recent Research." *RelSRev* 3 (1977) 137–42; K. Rudolph. *Gnosis: The Nature and History of Gnosticism* (1983); F. S. Spencer. *The Portrait of Philip in Acts: A Study of Roles and Relations* (1992).

F. SCOTT SPENCER

SIMON BEN ELEAZAR. A sage from the period 170–200 CE and probably a student of Rabbi Meir, the rabbi likely lived in Tiberius, Israel. He was a contemporary of Rabbi Yehudah Hanasi, the editor of the MISHNAH, with whom he was apparently often in controversy. Perhaps as a consequence, very few of his teachings are found in the Mishnah, although they are cited in later rabbinic works. Once, after insulting an ugly man, he was publicly shamed and thereafter preached that "a man should always be gentle like a reed, not unyielding as a cedar" (*b. Taan.* 20a). *See* RABBI, RABBONI.

JUDITH Z. ABRAMS

SIMON PETER. *See* PETER, THE APOSTLE.

SIN OFFERING. *See* SACRIFICES AND OFFERINGS; SIN, SINNERS.

SIN, SHIN sin, shin [שׂ s, שׁ sh]. The twenty-first letter of the Hebrew alphabet, derived from the Semitic word **tann-*, "composite bow." *See* ALPHABET.

SIN, SINNERS [חַטָּאת khatta'th; ἁμαρτία hamartia]. Israel's prophets, poets, priests, story-tellers, wisdom teachers, and lawgivers reflected on sin in a variety of ways. Early Christian heirs of Israel continued that reflection on sin in the light of their experience of God's action in Christ.

A. Old Testament
B. Prophets
C. Covenant Code
D. Leviticus
E. Holiness Code
F. Pentateuchal Narratives
G. Deuteronomy and the Deuteronomic History
H. The Psalms
I. The Sapiential Perspective
J. Apocalyptic Traditions
K. New Testament
Bibliography

A. Old Testament

The OT uses a variety of terms to label harmful or rejected behavior, and to refer to those who engage in it. It also offers an array of means for dealing with the problems caused by such behavior. It may be possible to offer a simple definition of sin as behavior that offends God and impairs relationship with the divine. Yet such a heuristic definition may oversimplify the complex range of understandings of evildoing, its effects and how it is to be dealt with.

The vocabulary used for problematic behavior within the OT indicates some of the complexity. The most common terms for such behavior are "sin" (khatta'th), or "missing the mark," "transgression" (pasha‘ פֶּשַׁע), "iniquity" (‘awon עָוֺן), or rebellion (meri מְרִי); or simply "evil" (ra‘ רַע). Some terms used to describe sinful behavior indicate why it is problematic. Sin is often described as an abomination (to‘evah תּוֹעֵבָה) to God, behavior that he hates and that arouses his ire. Particularly in the priestly tradition, some of the ways in which sin is treated suggest that it has an objective quality. Like impurity, which is not per se sinful, sin functions as a miasma that must be cleansed from people, sacred spaces, or the land. Priestly traditions offer cultic remedies for such cleansing or for propitiation of the offended deity. Yet intra-human restitution usually accompanies such cultic remedies. Prophetic voices, echoed in the psalms, insist on the importance of repentance, confession of guilt, and the effort to reform behavior. The prophets often criticize reliance on cult as a way of dealing with sin. Wisdom teachers focus on the practical results of improper behavior, although they recognize the importance of "fear of the Lord" in maintaining social norms. They also cast a skeptical eye on some of the theological constructs about sin and its consequences developed in prophetic and priestly traditions.

Problematic human behavior, actions that breech societal norms or offend other people can be described apart from the category of "sin," although in the canonical compositions such traditions or strata are usually subsumed under one or another of the categories for sin, construed as an offense against God.

B. Prophets

Prophetic literature displays two broad strands of denunciation of wrongdoing. Many focus on social and economic evils, denouncing the oppression of the poor. A second major focus of attention is fidelity to Israel's God. The prophets also call for repentance and, while threatening divine judgment, hold out hope for restoration.

Although Amos denounces sins of sexual deviation ("father and son go in to the same girl") and idolatry (Amos 2:7-8; 5:25-26), he reserves his most stinging condemnations for social injustice, which will be a continuing focal point for reflection on sin in the prophetic tradition. After a series of oracles against the nations, he lashes out at the transgressions (pasha', Amos 2:4, 6) of Judah and Israel, who do not follow the law (torah תּוֹרָה) and statutes (khoq חֹק) of Yahweh. The specific accusations against them include "sell[ing] the righteous for silver, and the needy for pair of sandals," for trampling the poor and rejecting the needy (2:6-7; 8:4). The "cows of Bashan" sin precisely in oppressing the poor and crushing the needy (4:1). The epitome of Israel's sin is to take a bribe and push aside the needy (5:12).

Hosea focuses on Israel's infidelity to its God. He builds his message of judgment and hope using marriage as a metaphor for Israel's relationship to Yahweh and adultery as a metaphor for Israel's sin, an image that will long influence the prophetic tradition (e.g., Ezek 16; 23; Rev 17). Specific religious practices are in view: "My people consult a piece of wood, and their divining rod gives them oracles ... they sacrifice on the tops of the mountains, and make offerings upon the hills" (Hos 4:12-13); "men themselves go aside with whores, and sacrifice with temple prostitutes" (4:14); they "keep on sinning (yosifu lakhato' יוֹסִפוּ לַחֲטֹא) and make a cast image for themselves, idols of silver made according to their understanding" (13:2). In addition to worship of strange deities and other cultic practices, Israel's infidelity comprises other actions: "swearing, lying, and murder, and stealing and adultery break out; bloodshed follows bloodshed" (4:2). In some cases, the connection is more direct: "Ephraim is joined to idols—let him alone. When their drinking is ended, they indulge in sexual orgies; they love lewdness more than their glory" (4:17-18).

Hosea promises certain divine judgment. Israel has "broken my covenant, and transgressed my law" (Hos 8:1). It has therefore "sow[ed] the wind, and they shall reap the whirlwind" (8:7). Oppressed under foreign rule, they will "writhe under the burden of kings and princes" (8:10), for "the days of punishment have come, the days of recompense have come" (9:7).

Like other prophets, Hosea sharply criticizes attempts to deal with sin through the cult. "When Ephraim multiplied altars to expiate sin, they became to him altars for sinning.... Though they offer choice sacrifices, though they eat flesh, the LORD does not accept them" (Hos 8:11-13). In a sentiment often echoed, Yahweh declares, "I desire steadfast love and not sacrifice, the knowledge of God rather than burnt offerings" (6:6).

Hosea also holds out hope for restoration. Repentance is possible, if the people will say, "Come let us return to the LORD; for it is he who has torn, and he will heal us.... After two days he will revive us; on the third day he will raise us up" (Hos 6:1-2). He proclaims, "But as for you, return to your God, hold fast to love and justice, and wait continually for your God" (12:6). Familial imagery expresses the prophet's hope, when he portrays Yahweh as a loving father who called his son out of Egypt (11:1) and fed his people in the wilderness (13:6). That loving God will finally say "I will not execute my fierce anger; I will not again destroy Ephraim; for I am God and no mortal, the Holy One in your midst, and I will not come in wrath" (11:9), and again: "I will heal their disloyalty; I will love them freely" (14:4).

Micah denounces the transgression (pasha') and sins (khatta'th) of Jacob and Israel (Mic 1:5), which consist primarily of their cultic places, images, and idols (Mic 1:6-7). Religious practices are also included in the realm of transgression and sin when Micah sketches his hope for a restored Israel without sorceries or soothsayers, images, pillars, or sacred poles (5:12-14). The prophet's primary focus remains, as in Amos, on social sin. Evil deeds consist of social and economic actions, coveting and seizing property (2:2). The wealthy, with their "treasures of wickedness," engage in fraud, using "dishonest weights" as well as violence and lies (Mic 6:10-12; compare Lev 19:35; Deut 25:13-16). The ruling classes "abhor justice and pervert equity," judges take bribes, priests teach for a price, prophets give oracles for pay (Mic 3:9,11; bribery: 7:4). Graphic imagery describes such oppression: the rulers of Jacob and Israel act like cannibals, flaying the oppressed and treating their bodies like the ingredients of a stew (3:2-3).

Habakkuk denounces the powerful of his day, the proud and the arrogant wealthy, whose greed mimics the wide throat of Sheol (Hab 2:4-5). They "build a town by bloodshed, and found a city on iniquity" (2:12). Their luxurious living involves drink and sex (2:15), and they trust in dumb idols (2:18-19).

Nahum portrays evildoers as enemies, plotting against Yahweh (Nah 1:8-9). Concerned with idolatry, Zephaniah denounces those who "bow down on the roofs to the host of the heavens" and "swear by Milcom" (Zeph 1:5), but the leading sinners are, as so often, the ruling classes. The officials and judges are like savage beasts; the faithless prophets and profane priests do violence to Torah (3:3-4).

Covenant fidelity frames Malachi's discussion of wrongdoing. He first focuses on the failings of priests. Invoking God's covenant with Levi, the prophet upholds an ideal of priestly integrity and uprightness, one not matched by his contemporaries. They instead have "turned aside from the way" and have "caused many to stumble" by their instruction (Mal 2:8). Malachi indicts Judah as a whole for being "faithless to one another, profaning the covenant of our ancestors" (Mal 2:10). Two areas display this infidelity, the Temple and the home. The prophet first denounces the "abomination" that has been committed by the profanation of the sanctuary with "the daughter of a foreign god," probably a cultic image, whom Judah "has married" (2:11). He then decries marital infidelity to the wife of one's youth, one's "companion and...wife by covenant" (2:14). The divine displeasure is made clear by a word of Yahweh, who desires "godly offspring" and "hate[s] divorce" (2:15-16). Malachi does not ignore other types of "arrogant and...evildoers" (Mal 4:1), but threatens judgment against sorcerers, adulterers, those who swear falsely, who oppress the hired workers in their wages, who oppress the widow and the orphan, who thrust aside the alien and do not fear God (3:5).

Isaiah 1–39, sometimes called Proto-Isaiah, castigates (Isa 1:4) a "sinful nation" (goy khoteʾ גּוֹי חֹטֵא), a "people laden with iniquity (kevedh ʿawon כְּבֶד עָוֹן)." Sin consists of murder (1:21), theft and bribery (1:23; 5:23), and despoliation of the poor (3:14-15). Criticism of the wealthy becomes more specific when the prophet singles out real estate dealings, the adding of "house to house...field to field" (5:8) as objectionable. Rulers "make iniquitous decrees...write oppressive statutes, to turn aside the needy from justice and to rob the poor" (10:1-2). Sin also is manifest in attitudes of haughtiness and pride (2:17; 5:15), provocative sexual behavior (3:16), luxurious display (3:18-23), and indulgence in drink and festivity (5:11-12, 22; 28:7), all activities of the "nobility of Jerusalem" (5:14). Such a corrupt ruling class has made "a covenant with death," with lies as their refuge and falsehood their shelter (28:15). The author of Isa 56–66, sometimes called Trito-Isaiah, echoes many of these sentiments in his denunciation of "iniquities" (ʿawon) that have been a barrier between Israel and God (59:1): hands stained with blood, lying lips, unjust lawsuits (59:3-4). Using a wide-ranging vocabulary for sin, the prophet, on behalf of the people, confesses "transgressions" (pashaʿ), "sins" (khattaʾth), and "iniquities" (ʿawon), talking of "oppression" (ʿosheq עֹשֶׁק) and "revolt" (sarah סָרָה) (59:12-13). With lying words (divre-shaqer דִּבְרֵי־שָׁקֶר), justice stumbles (v. 14).

Isaiah also denounces the "house of Jacob" for infidelity to Yahweh (2:5). Their land is full of "diviners from the east and ... soothsayers like the Philistines" (Isa 2:6) and "their land is filled with idols; they bow down to the work of their hands" (2:8). The denunciation of idolatry looms even larger in Isa 40–55, or Deutero-Isaiah, with its dismissive question, What is an idol? (40:18-20) and its graphic depictions of how idols are made (44:9-20) and worshiped in vain (46:6-7). Trito-Isaiah (Isa 57:1-13) continues the tradition, with a denunciation of Israel's idolatry that evokes many prophetic themes, including the image of adultery (57:5, 8), worship under every green tree and on every lofty mountain (57:5, 7), and worship of Molech (57:9).

Like his prophetic predecessors, Isaiah has harsh words for a blind reliance on cult. In God's name he says "I have had enough of burnt offerings of rams and the fat of fed beasts" (Isa 1:11). God will not listen to hands stained with blood (1:15). The people may draw near with their mouths, but their heart is distant (29:13). Instead of such superficial piety, Isaiah calls on Israel to "cease to do evil, learn to do good; seek justice, rescue the oppressed, defend the orphan, plead for the widow" (1:16b-17). Trito-Isaiah continues the theme, with a denunciation of fasting (58:1-9), which, in the face of "rebellion" (pashaʿ) and "sins" (khattaʾth) (58:1), is of no avail. Instead Israel is summoned "to loose the bonds of injustice, to undo the thongs of the yoke, to let the oppressed go free, and to break every yoke" (58:6).

Isaiah warns that sin is subject to divine judgment. Since everyone was "godless and an evildoer," the divine "anger has not turned away; his hand is stretched out still" (Isa 9:12, 17, 21). Sin will be punished: "The light of Israel will become a fire, and his Holy One a flame; and it will burn and devour his thorns and briers in one day" (10:17). The Lord God of hosts has a "day of tumult and trampling and confusion" (22:5) in which the Lord will "lay waste the earth and make it desolate" (24:1), because of the weight of its transgression (24:20).

The prophet's denunciation of sin aims to elicit repentance (Isa 1:27) and he couples predictions of judgment with hope for a "remnant" (10:21; 11:16) and a realm presided over by a righteous ruler (11:1-9; 32:1-5). Other powerful images of restoration include the portrait of a feast for all nations on God's holy mountain (25:6), when death will be destroyed and all tears will be wiped away (25:7-8; compare Rev 21:4). Equally powerful is the image of Zion restored, cleansed of its idols (30:32) with Yahweh as its majestic ruler (33:20-22). Isaiah's hopeful words are echoed in the messages of comfort of Deutero-Isaiah (40:1-5) and in the vision of ultimate restoration of Trito-Isaiah (60:1-7), when God will be the light of a restored Zion (60:19-20; compare Rev 22:5).

A remarkable passage on sin and its effects appears in the "servant song" of Isa 52:13–53:12. Whether the servant is a particular prophetic figure or the people of Israel as a whole, the poem depicts one who has suffered because of the sins of others: "wounded for our transgressions, crushed for our iniquities; upon him was the punishment that made us whole, and by his bruises we are healed ... the LORD has laid on him the iniquity of us all" (53:5-6). The text may depict the suffering of this righteous one as a sacrifice, although the reading of 53:10, "When you make his life an offering for sin (ʾasham אָשָׁם), he shall see his offspring," is not certain. It is clear that by the servant's suffering and death he "bore the sin of many, and made intercession for the transgressors" (53:12). This image of vicarious suffering, though used sparingly in the NT (compare Acts 8:32-33; 1 Pet 2:21-25), undergirds later

Christian theologies of the atonement effected by the death of Jesus.

Jeremiah forcefully continues the condemnation of idolatry as Israel's major sin. Echoing Hosea, he complains that Israel has long since been rebellious and acted like an unfaithful partner: "For long ago you broke your yoke and burst your bonds, and you said, 'I will not serve!' On every high hill and under every green tree you sprawled and played the whore" (Jer 2:20; compare 3:1, 6-9, 13; 13:27; 17:2). People have made offerings to Baal and gone after other gods (7:9; 9:14), they make cakes to the queen of heaven and pour out libations to other gods (7:18). The people of Judah have done evil, setting their "abominations" (shiqquts שִׁקּוּץ) in the Lord's house. They build a high place of Topheth and burn their sons and daughters in the valley of the son of Hinnom (7:30-31). Idols sprout up "like scarecrows in a cucumber field" (10:4-5). Israel "burn[s] offerings to a delusion" (18:15). Even after the destruction of Jerusalem, Israelites living in Egypt continued to make offerings to the queen of heaven (44:17-19).

Jeremiah also denounces other misdeeds, in familiar prophetic language: "Everyone is greedy for unjust gain" (Jer 6:13). Aliens, orphans, and widows are oppressed and innocent blood is shed (7:6; 22:17). People steal, murder, commit adultery, and swear falsely (7:9). Deceit and oppression prevail (9:5-6). Defrauding workers of their wages is to build a house by unrighteousness (22:13). For all of these reasons, Israel has broken the covenant and is subject to its curses (11:3; compare Deut 27:15-26).

Divine punishment for sin, a form of pollution, is sure. Yahweh promises that he "will doubly repay their iniquity and their sin, because they have polluted my land with the carcasses of their detestable idols, and have filled my inheritance with their abominations" (Jer 16:18; 32:34-35). Idolatry and injustice will make the valley of the son of Hinnom a valley of Slaughter (19:4-6). The Lord's anger, like a whirling tempest, will wreak its devastation (23:19; 25:32; 30:23; 32:30), all because Israel's "guilt is great," her "sins are so numerous" (30:15). Most concretely, disobedience will result in seventy years of exile (25:8-12).

Repentance is always a possibility, and it comes to expression sporadically. "Although our iniquities ('awon) testify against us, act, O Lord, for your name's sake; our apostasies (meshuvah מְשׁוּבָה) indeed are many, and we have sinned (khata' חָטָא) against you" (Jer 14:7; compare 14:20). The prophet is sent to call on the king of Judah to act justly, defending the widow and the orphan (22:3-4). Priests he calls to "amend your ways ... and obey the voice of the Lord" (26:13). With repentance, as usual, comes a hope of restoration (23:3; 30:17-22; 31:1-14), overseen by a "righteous Branch" from the house of David (23:5; 33:15). Restoration will be internal as well as external and will involve a new covenant written on the human heart (31:33; 32:40). Within that covenant relationship, sin will be overcome, for God

promises to "forgive their iniquity, and remember their sin no more" (31:34; compare Heb 8:12; 10:16-17).

Ezekiel's rhetoric can be even more intense than that of Jeremiah, although it lacks some of the familiar prophetic vocabulary for sin. He denounces the ways of Jerusalem, which has "rebelled against my ordinances and my statutes, becoming more wicked than the nations" (Ezek 5:6). Idolatry again is at the core of the people's malfeasance. Their "abominations" (to'evah)—a favorite word of Ezekiel, parallel to "sins" (khatta'th) at 16:51—and "detestable things" (shiqquts) pollute the sacred Temple (5:9, 11). Such "abominations" include idols and incense stands (6:6), and images portrayed on the wall of a chamber in the Temple, images of "all kinds of creeping things, and loathsome animals, and all the idols of the house of Israel" (8:10). Worship of false gods also involves practices such as passing children through the fire (20:31). The familiar trope equating idolatry and sexual immorality reappears in the allegory of the sisters Oholah and Oholibah (chap. 23).

The greatest sinners are Israel's leaders, the elders (Ezek 8:11, 12) and the named officials who "devise iniquity and who give wicked counsel in this city" (11:2). Ezekiel uses vivid imagery to criticize this leadership. Princes are like "a roaring lion tearing the prey" (22:25). Priests have violated divine teaching and profaned what is holy (22:26). Other officials are like "wolves tearing the prey, shedding blood, destroying lives to get dishonest gain" (22:27). Ezekiel also castigates false prophets, who have uttered "falsehood and lying divination" (13:6; 22:28). All Israel's leaders are false shepherds who will be duly punished for the neglect of God's flock (34:1-10).

Ezekiel's notion of sinful "abomination" extends beyond idolatry, as is evident in his argument that the individual sinner, not his descendants, bears the burden of guilt. He decries the sinner who is "violent, a shedder of blood ... who eats upon the mountains, defiles his neighbor's wife, oppresses the poor and needy, commits robbery, does not restore the pledge, lifts up his eyes to the idols, commits abomination; takes advance or accrued interest" (Ezek 18:10-13; compare 18:15-17; 22:3-4, 10-12, 29). Rebellion against God involves rejecting divine commands and statutes. Among these, profaning the Sabbath receives special attention (20:13, 16, 21; 22:8; 23:38; compare also Jer 17:19-27).

Judgment is swift and sure; God's sword is drawn (Ezek 21:3, 9; 33:2). God will even punish the righteous, if they transgress (pasha'), commit sin (khata'), or engage in iniquity ('awel [עָוֶל], 33:12-13). Cleansing accompanies punishment; God will "purge [the] filthiness (tum'ah טֻמְאָה)" from Israel by scattering them to the nations (22:15). Babylonian siege works are like a boiling pot that will purge Israel's filth (24:3-13).

Nonetheless, repentance, individual as well as collective, will preserve sinners from utter calamity (18:21-32). The prophet stands as a sentinel, calling the wicked to repent (33:7-9). Balancing the warning to the righteous is an assurance to sinners that repentance from their wickedness (resha' רֶשַׁע), combined with restitution and reform, will lead to life (33:14-16). Ezekiel finally holds out hope for restoration for a sinful nation in a covenant of peace (34:25). He envisions an Israel cleansed and renewed with a new heart and spirit (chap. 36; compare Jer 31:31-34; Ezek 39:21-29), returned as if from the grave (37:1-14), with a new Temple in a restored land (chaps. 40–48). The specific manifestations of sin will be no more. Only Zadokite priests who have not committed idolatry will serve in the Temple (44:15), and the rules of the people will eschew violence and oppression, not evict the poor, and will use proper weights and measures (45:9-12).

C. Covenant Code

One of the earliest strata of the Pentateuch's legal material, the Covenant Code of Exod 20:22–23:9, consists largely of case law with a strong focus on social relations. Within the code itself, the actions condemned are not explicitly labeled with one of the many words for sin and the category is not an organizing principle of this compilation. Insofar as there are remedies for sin in the Covenant Code, they are also part of the ruptured social realm. Remedies include restitution or compensation (Exod 21:19, 22, 30-32; 22:1-14) and punishment (20:20), including capital punishment (21:15-17; 22:18-20). The framing story of the divine revelation on Mount Sinai implicitly describes infractions of the code as sin, since the purpose of the revelation is to instill in Israel a fear of committing sin (khata'; 20:20). That frame, with the Decalogue (Exod 20:2-17; compare Deut 5:1-22), provides the categories that will define the general contours of sin for Jewish and Christian traditions: idolatry, profanation of the divine name, infringement of the Sabbath (a capital offense: Exod 31:14; 35:2; Num 15:32-36), disobedience to parents, murder, adultery, theft, false witnessing, and covetousness.

D. Leviticus

The Priestly tradition devotes elaborate attention to sin and what may be done about it through the mechanism of cult. There are tensions in the regulations, and the cultic system certainly developed over time. Leviticus highlights two major types of sacrifice: the sacrifice for sin (khatta'th) and the guilt sacrifice ('asham). The regulations for the former specify that it is offered to affect atonement (kofer כִּפֶּר) for unintentional inadvertent sins of priests, rulers, or people in general (a similar restriction on the limits of cultic atonement appears at Num 15:22-31). The examples of sins given in Lev 5:1-4 include both matters of ritual purity and behavior. Uncleanness arising from touching a corpse (v. 2), or touching some human substance (semen, menstrual blood are probably in view, v. 3; compare Lev 15) are easily understood as inadvertent infringements of purity codes. Failing to testify when there has been a public adjuration to do so (v. 1), or uttering aloud a rash oath (v. 4) involve behavioral matters. In all such cases, confession of the sin accompanies the offering of an appropriate sacrifice, depending on one's means (sheep, goat, v. 6; two turtle doves, v. 7; one-tenth of an ephah of flour, v. 11).

Leviticus does not specify the frequency of the sin offering. Numbers 28–29 indicates when sacrifices are to be offered and specifically designates a goat as a sin offering on a monthly basis (Num 28:15), at Passover (v. 22), at the feast of weeks (v. 30), the "Festival of Trumpets," later to be known as the New Year's Festival or Rosh Hashanah (29:5); the Festival of Booths or Sukkoth (29:16, 19, 22, 25, 28, 31, 34, 38).

Treatment of uncleanness derived from contact with a corpse involves another set of procedures using the "waters of purification," prepared with the ashes of a red heifer (Num 19). The treatment of the issue of corpse uncleanness does not apply the category of sin to the uncleanness itself, but stipulates that entry to the sanctuary without treating the condition is punishable by being cut off from the assembly (19:20).

Another, and less restrictive, approach to the cultic treatment of sin appears in Lev 6:1-7 (Heb. 5:20-26). The examples of sins for which atoning sacrifices can be made here include deliberate acts. The introduction to the section speaks of "sinning and committing a trespass" against Yahweh. The sins consist of deception in the matter of a deposit, robbery, fraud, lying about the recovery of a lost object, and perjury. The list does not extend to capital offenses but focuses on deliberate crimes against the neighbor's economic well-being. In all such cases, the sinner, whose behavior toward a neighbor has offended God, must deal with both parties, by making restitution to the neighbor and a guilt offering ('asham) to God. The rules for this type of sacrifice are the same as that of the sin offering, as Lev 7:7 explicitly stipulates. A similar process appears in Num 5:5-10, where the remedy for "breaking faith" is confession, full restitution, plus a one-fifth penalty to the one wronged (or the priest if the wronged party is unavailable), and a sacrifice of a "ram of atonement."

A singular priestly mechanism for dealing with sin and its effects is the ritual of Yom Kippur, the Day of Atonement. On that day, Aaron and his successors, the high priests, offered a young bull as a sin offering (Lev 16:3, 11; compare the offering at the consecration of the Levites, Num 8:12), for himself and his house (Lev 16:6), and then took two goats, one of which is another sin offering; the other is to be sent into the wilderness "to Azazel" (16:10). (Another version of the sacrifices for the day appears at Num 29:7-11, which mentions the one goat as a sin offering, "in addition to the sin offering of atonement," presumably the bull.) The priest then sprinkles the blood of the bull on the "mercy seat," where the tablets of the covenant reside (16:14). The same action follows with the blood of the sacrificed goat. All of this aims to "make atonement for the sanctuary, because of the uncleanness of the people of Israel, and because of their transgressions (pasha‵), all their sins (khatta᾽th)" (16:16). The priest then sprinkles some of the blood on the altar "and cleanse it and hallow it from the uncleannesses of the people of Israel" (16:19). The implication of these rituals is clearly that sin is defiling and that defilement can be removed only with the most potent of cleansers, blood. The notion reappears in the ritual for dealing with the situation of an unknown homicide (Deut 21:1-9).

Cleansing the altar and the sanctuary is only a part of the treatment for sin. The scapegoat sent to the desert bears with him the "all the iniquities of the people of Israel, and all their transgressions, all their sins" (Lev 16:21). Sin then is imaged not simply as a stain or blot, but as a tangible substance, a lingering presence or miasma that must be removed from the presence of the people and its sacred places.

E. Holiness Code

An important part of the Priestly tradition highlights the value of holiness, which is characteristic of God and to which God's people is called. This section of Leviticus (18–22) offers a vision of the holy people, equally attentive to matters of ritual purity and social responsibility.

The heart of this priestly admonition to holiness, and perhaps its earliest stratum, is Lev 19, in which Yahweh calls the people to be holy as is Yahweh. The admonition contains both positive demands, to honor father and mother (Lev 19:3), to eat a sacrifice when it is made (vv. 5-8), to leave the edges of a harvested field for the poor (vv. 9-10), to reverence Sabbath and sanctuary (vv. 3, 29-30), and to respect the elderly (v. 32). The text also enumerates a series of prohibitions, many of which parallel those of the Decalogue. Thus the congregation of Israel is enjoined not to steal, lie, or swear falsely (vv. 11-12); to defraud a neighbor, steal, withhold wages overnight (v. 13), revile the deaf or impede the blind (v. 14); not to render unjust judgment, show partiality, or slander (v. 16). More generally, the code prohibits hatred or bearing a grudge (vv. 17-18). It also contains some case law: what to do if a man has sexual relations with a slave (vv. 20-22), and limitations on harvesting from newly planted fruit trees (vv. 23-25). The code prohibits a father prostituting his daughter (v. 29), consultation with mediums and wizards (v. 31, famously infringed by Saul, 1 Sam 28: 3-25; 1 Chr 10:13), oppressing a resident alien (vv. 33-34), or cheating in weights and measures (v. 35).

Like the covenant code of Exodus, the traditional material in this compilation, with the exception of Lev 19:7, lacks an overarching category to describe the actions condemned. That verse, which links with the framing material in Lev 18 and 20, declares the delayed eating of sacrificial meat an "abomination" (piggul פִּגֻּל). The framing chapters contain a larger theoretical framework.

After a proem declaring that the code consists of Yahweh's "ordinances" and "statutes" which will separate Israel from the Canaanites (Lev 18:2-5), the discourse begins in chap. 18 with sexual matters, prohibiting relations ("uncovering the nakedness") of various relations and in-laws (vv. 6-18). It then prohibits specific types of intercourse: sex with a menstruant woman, adultery, lying with a male as with a woman, sex with animals (vv. 19-23). In the midst of this roster of sexual sins, Leviticus prohibits offering children to Molech (v. 21). All of these acts are considered "abominations" (to‵evah) that "defile" (tum᾽ah; vv. 22, 24), and will cause the land to "vomit out" those who commit them (v. 25). Sin therefore in this priestly world is a matter of defilement.

The framing material continues in Lev 20, with a repetition of the same concerns expressed in chap. 18 and in the central portion of the code. Thus sacrifices to Molech (vv. 2-5), resort to mediums and wizards (vv. 6-9), adultery, same sex relations, bestiality (vv. 10-16), sex with near relatives (vv. 17-21) are all condemned, some as "depravity" (zimmah [זִמָּה], v. 14). All of the rejected practices, which run counter to Yahweh's "statutes" and "ordinances" (v. 22), are practices of the nation driven out from the promised land. Yahweh expects Israel to be separated from that nation and from the practices that he "abhorred" (vv. 23-24). Here the social function of the priestly definition of sin is clear. The holiness of the people, like the holiness of the priests, demands separation from the profane. As priests are made ritually unclean by corpses (Lev 21:2-3) and various bodily discharges render any Israelite unclean (Lev 15) and at least temporarily unfit to participate in the cult, the practices described in the holiness code render the people unfit to participate in the holiness of the promised land.

F. Pentateuchal Narratives

The narratives of the origins of humankind in the opening chapters of Genesis, like many other stories of origin, offer explanations of natural and social phenomena. Thus snakes lack limbs because of their role in deceiving the first human beings (Gen 3:14); women suffer birth-pangs because of their role in the first act of disobedience (3:16). Such etiological legends offer a broader explanation for the human condition by painting the originators of the species as curious but disobedient creatures of God. Thus, though the story of the "fall" of the first humans in the Garden of Eden in Gen 3 does not use the category of sin, it defines in narrative form what that category means.

The next stage of the tale of human origins becomes more explicit in the story of the first murder. A striking personification of sin appears at Gen 4:7, in God's remarks to Cain: "If you do well, will you not be accepted? And if you do not do well, sin (khatta᾽th) is lurking at the door; its desire is for you, but you must master it." Sin here appears as a demon (so REB), or perhaps as a seductress, waiting perhaps to ravish the sinner. In addition to describing the first fratricide, the story explicitly depicts the ever-present reality of a disposition to do evil.

The story of the flood continues the development of the theme. Once people began to multiply upon the earth, Yahweh saw that there was nothing but wickedness (ra'; Gen 6:5) and people thought constantly about nothing but evil. The divine attempt to obliterate evil from the face of the earth is, of course, unsuccessful, something that Yahweh recognizes as soon as Noah, again on dry land, sacrifices to him (8:20). Either pleased by the sacrifice, or resigned to what humans are, God promises never to curse the earth again "because of humankind, for the inclination (yetser יֵצֶר) of the human heart is evil (ra') from youth" (8:21).

Although wickedness had long abounded, the first explicitly named sinners in the story come on stage after Abram and Lot separate, when Lot settles among the people of Sodom, who "were wicked, great sinners against the LORD" (Gen 13:13), although what their sins were is not initially specified. Their sinful character emerges later. Despite Abraham's efforts to bargain with Yahweh for their survival, they prove themselves sinners by the attempt to molest two angelic visitors to Lot (19:5). As a result, Yahweh rains down sulfur and fire on Sodom, Gomorrah, and all the plain (19:24). The precise nature of the sins of Sodom is not specified; it is no doubt obvious within the cultural world assumed by the text. Despite the name they have given to a type of sexual behavior, the major failing of the Sodomites seems to be their utter disregard for any norms of hospitality, much like the Benjaminites who in Judg 19 rape the concubine of a guest.

That sin (khatta'th) involves an offense against God is clearly the presupposition of the story of Abraham's deceptive behavior regarding Sarah, his wife. After Abraham has told Abimelech, king of Gerar, that Sarah is his sister, the king's dream warns him against taking Sarah as his wife (Gen 20:3). Abimelech protests his innocence; he had acted in ignorance (20:5). God responds, assuring him that he had acted with integrity and that God himself had sent the dream in order to prevent Abimelech from sinning against him (20:6).

Abimelech's subsequent address to Abraham reveals another dimension of sin. The king asks Abraham how he had sinned against the patriarch so that Abraham should have brought such guilt on him and his people, adding "You have done things to me that ought not be done" (Gen 20:9). It is suggestive of the social mechanism for treating the results of sin that Abimelech provides compensation to Abraham and Sarah: sheep, oxen, slaves and a thousand pieces of silver (20:14-16), despite his acknowledged innocence of any wrongdoing in trying to take Abraham's wife from him.

Genesis describes various actions that might be considered sinful, but the category does not appear in connection with them. The rape of Dinah was an "outrage"

(nevalah [נְבָלָה]; Gen 34:7), but was not explicitly labeled an offense against God. Upon returning to Bethel, Jacob requires his family to put away their foreign gods and purify themselves (Gen 35:2), implying that keeping those foreign deities was a source of impurity, but that is not made explicit. Onan "spilled his semen" (Gen 38:9), an act that would later provide a name for masturbation. Onan's offense, which "was displeasing in the sight of the LORD" (38:10), was shirking his fraternal responsibility to raise children for his deceased brother Er, who had been slain by Yahweh for his wickedness (38:7). The attempt of Potiphar's wife to seduce Joseph is assumed to be problematic. Joseph's brothers in retrospect use the language of "doing wrong" (42:22) for what they did to Joseph.

The idolatry of the golden calf (Exod 32:2-14) is explicitly categorized as "a great sin" (32:30), for which Moses seeks to make atonement. Yahweh's response is a chilling "Whoever has sinned against me I will blot out of my book...I will punish them for their sin" (32:33-34). Despite the subsequent plague (32:35), the next episode shows a more compassionate side to Yahweh, who graciously grants the Israelites a second chance with new tablets of the Law. Resonant poetry celebrates that event, praising God who is "slow to anger, and abounding in steadfast love and faithfulness," who balances mercy and justice, as one "forgiving iniquity and transgression and sin, yet by no means clearing the guilty, but visiting the iniquity of the parents upon the children" (34:6-7). Moses responds with a humble act of contrition, requesting that God "pardon our iniquity and our sin, and take us for your inheritance" (34:9).

A similar picture of divine mercy and justice is drawn at other times during the wandering in the desert when the people rebel. In Num 14:1-35, the people complain loudly about their trials and tribulations (vv. 1-2). The refrain celebrating Yahweh's compassionate mercy reappears (v. 18) before God both forgives (v. 20) and punishes by preventing Israelites who left Egypt from entering the promised land (vv. 22-23). Numbers 20:2-13 tells of the episode at Meribah, where Moses' failure to trust Yahweh's promise of water from the rock prevents his entry to the land (v. 12; compare Num 27:14, where Moses' action is labeled one of "rebellion"). Numbers 21:4-9 records the episode of the bronze serpent, a device that Yahweh graciously provides to deal with the serpents sent to punish complaining Israelites (v. 6), but only when they have repented and confessed their sin (v. 7). The desert rebellion will become a paradigm case of collective sin in the homiletic tradition (compare 1 Cor 10; Heb 3–4). Divine compassion is less evident when the people worship the Baal of Peor (Num 25:2). The act does not need to be named as sin, since it provokes divine wrath (v. 3) as much as intermarriage with Midianites provokes the zealous vigilantism of Phinehas (v. 8).

Sin plays a cameo role in the etiological legend for the origins of the priestly hierarchy in Num 16–18.

The revolt of the Levites, Korah, Dathan, and Abiram protesting the arrogation of priestly authority to Aaron (Num 16:3) is a sin (16:22) that elicits Yahweh's fiery retribution (vv. 31-35), which in turn leads to a plague on the whole congregation (v. 47). Aaron, standing between the living and the dead, makes atonement for the people and the plague ceases. The result of the episode is a division of labor between the Aaronid priests responsible for dealing with offences (18:1), and the Levites who do more menial services (18:4).

Balaam, summoned by Balak to curse Israel, has to confess to the angel who stands in his way that he has sinned (Num 22:34), not knowing that the angel was there, despite the efforts of his wise ass to tell him. Here "sin" appears in its most primitive form, not an offense against the deity, but as "missing the mark." The peccadillo is quickly forgiven and Balaam goes on his mission to bless Israel.

Two kinds of moral evil receive special treatment in the collection of legal material interspersed in the narrative of Numbers, although neither is prominently labeled as sin. In the case of marital infidelity, the burden falls on a woman suspected of adultery (Num 5:11-30). The man who suspects adultery is to bring a "grain offering," which "brings iniquity ('awon) to remembrance." The major burden of the process falls on the suspect wife, who is forced to drink water mixed with ashes from the altar, which will curse her to infertility if she is guilty but prove harmless if she is innocent.

Murder is generally to be punished with death, usually at the hands of an "avenger of blood" (Num 35:19, 27), but for unintentional homicide a refuge is available in the six "cities of refuge" (compare also Deut 4:42-43; 19:1-13) to which the killer may flee or be sent after trial (Num 35:22-25) and in which he must stay until the death of the high priest (v. 28). Otherwise, the one who commits murder must die, for the blood of the victim pollutes the land and can only be cleaned by the blood of the perpetrator (v. 33). In the context of this specific regulation, the evil of homicide and the shedding of blood is a treated as a natural process, with no reference to the deity.

G. Deuteronomy and the Deuteronomic History

The last book of the Pentateuch retells the story of Israel's covenant relationship with Yahweh as Israel prepares to enter the promised land. In the process it highlights the centrality of fidelity to the Lord alone (Deut 6:4) in what would become the confessional prayer of the Jewish tradition. The alternative to such fidelity is disobedient rebellion, a theme highlighted in the introductory chapters that offer a reprise of the rebellious experience of Israel in the desert (1:26; compare 9:8-29).

The major form of infidelity is idolatry and the worship of other gods, and Deuteronomy repeatedly insists that this is the greatest transgression imaginable. Moses introduces his reiteration of the Sinai revelation with a description of the way in which God spoke to the people out of the fire at Horeb. His imageless presence to Israel instructed the people to "not act corruptly (shakhath שָׁחַת) by making an idol for yourselves, in the form of any figure--the likeness of male or female, the likeness of any animal that is on the earth," etc. (Deut 4:15-18; compare 5:8-10; 6:13; 7:4-6; 11:16-17; 12:29-31; 16:21). Scattered prohibitions of alien practices are gathered and given special force. So passing a son or daughter through fire, presumably a ritual enacting or imitating child sacrifice, is certainly forbidden, as are divination or casting spells, all of which are "abhorrent" (to'evah) to the Lord (18:9-14).

To fail and act corruptly by way of idolatry will provoke God to anger and cause the people to be destroyed from their God-given land (Deut 4:25-27). They will be scattered abroad and forced to serve other gods, made with human hands (4:28), until they repent and return. Their sin will thus merit a deserved punishment, but will not abrogate divine fidelity. The threat and the promise of Deut 4:31 constitute a theology of history, repeated at 5:33 (compare 6:18, 25; 7:12-16), "You must follow exactly the path that the LORD your God has commanded you, so that you may live, and that it may go well with you, and that you may live long in the land that you are to possess." The major sin of idolatrous infidelity to the God of the covenant caused Israel's maltreatment at the hand of its enemies and ultimately resulted in its exile in the 6th cent. Yet Yahweh who punished will also be faithful to his covenant promises.

As part of its theology of history, Deuteronomy reflects on the conditions that might produce infidelity. To forget the Lord in the midst of prosperity can lead to failure to keep his commandments, ordinances, and statutes (Deut 8:11). "Forgetting" Yahweh will lead to the worship of other gods and the consequent penalty upon the people (8:19). Because it is perceived to be such a serious threat to the very existence of Israel, idolatry or the temptation to it coming from prophets or even kin is punishable by death (13:1-18; 17:2-7).

Deuteronomy also offers an institutional framework for dealing with the social consequences of legal disputes, appeal to the "levitical priests" at the cultic center, which Deuteronomy assiduously promotes ("the place that the LORD your God will choose," Deut 17:8-13). The decision of these authorities is final and one who is disobedient is liable to death, a remedy that will purge evil from the land (v. 12).

Despite the general focus of Deuteronomy on the sin of idolatry, there are scattered references to other sinful behaviors, such as the prohibition on the moving of boundary markers (Deut 19:14), or bearing false witness (19:15-20). Such behavior is also worthy of capital punishment and elicits the principle "Show no pity: life for life, eye for eye, tooth for tooth, hand for hand, foot for foot" (19:21). Equally to be dreaded is the fate of the rebellious son (21:18-21). Cross-dressing is prohibited for both sexes (22:5), as are various kinds of mixing (22:9-11).

The treatment of sexual matters covers some of the same territory as Lev 18 and Num 5, but with a different accent. Suspicions about a bride's virginity are dealt with not by trial, but on the basis of evidence (Deut 22:13-19), but if the evidence does not support her, she is to be stoned (22:21), because she committed a "disgraceful act" (**nevalah**) and the evil (**ra**') needs to be "purged" from Israel. The purgation of evil caused by sexual transgression runs as a refrain through cases of adultery (22:22); seduction of a betrothed women "in the town" (22:23-24), or in the country (22:25-27), though in that case only the man may be punished. Rape of a woman not betrothed elicits a lesser penalty (22:28-29). The refrain of purgation recurs in cases of other crimes, such as kidnapping (24:7).

Economic and social relations are subject to regulation and certain specific behaviors are forbidden, although they are seldom described with such heavily laden terms as those used for idolatry and serious capital crimes. Thus one may not take a millstone in pledge (24:6); collateral for loans cannot be taken by force (24:10-13); a widow's garment may not be taken in pledge (24:17); wages of the poor must not be withheld (24:14-15). The latter action is one that would incur "guilt" (**khete**' [חֵטְא]; 24:15). Those who use dishonest weights and measures are "abhorrent" (to'evah) to Yahweh (25:13-16).

Deuteronomy's concluding scenes reinforce the book's theme that fidelity to God's law produces blessings and infidelity produces curses. After offering firstfruits, the people of Israel are to proclaim that "I have neither transgressed nor forgotten any of your commandments" (Deut 26:13). When Israel passes into the land, it is to set up twelve stones inscribed with the Law, while they listen to the Levites curse those who make idols, dishonor parents, move boundaries, mislead the blind, deprive aliens, orphans or widows, lie with an animal, commit incest, strike down a neighbor, take a bribe or otherwise fail to observe the Law (Deut 27:15-26). Blessings are obtained by those who observe the Law (28:3-14), but the rhetorical emphasis lies on the curses and the punishments that Israel will suffer for disobedience (28:15-68). Against those dire predictions, Deuteronomy still holds out the hope of repentance and restoration after the affliction of exile (30:1-5).

The strict connection between sin and suffering continues in the historical works written under the influence of Deuteronomy's theology. The people of Israel and its leaders who commit sin regularly suffer. Conversely, unsuccessful rulers or the people when they have suffered defeat are clearly men who have committed sin.

Sinners appear throughout the pages of Israelite history. Shortly after Joshua has assumed leadership and taken the town of Jericho, he meets defeat at Ai because Achan took some of the spoils of war which should have been reserved for Yahweh. The Lord tells Joshua that defeat has come because "Israel has sinned (khatta'th); they have transgressed ('aver עָבַר) my covenant" (Josh 7:11). After Joshua's death, Israel abandon's Yahweh and worships Baal and Astarte, kindling the Lord's wrath (Judg 2:11-15). The behavior of the Israelites at that point establishes a pattern that is an explicit plot of the book of Judges, a pattern of continual transgression ('aver) of the covenant (2:18-20). Judges will come and go, but Israel's rebelliousness remains. So Midianite oppression, occasioned by failure to abide by the covenant (6:10) occasions the rise of Gideon, who liberates Israel, but in turn sets up an idol, with which Israel, in the familiar prophetic image, soon "prostitutes" herself (8:27), leading to further prostitution with the Baals (8:33). Israel worships the Baals and Astartes, the gods of Aram, Sidon, and Moab (10:6), and are oppressed by the Philistines and Ammonites until they confess their sin (10:10, 15).

One theme of Judges, tangentially related to estimation of Israel's sin, is the claim that before the establishment of the monarchy, everyone "did what was right in their own eyes" (Judg 21:25), a notion graphically exemplified by the book's final episode, the rape of a Levite's concubine (chap. 19) and the subsequent reprisals on the tribe of Benjamin, which was barely saved from extinction (chaps. 20-21). The deed can be described as a "crime" or something evil (ra'; 20:12), though not a "sin" like the worship of false deities.

The account of Israel's history in the books of Samuel and Kings continues the theological perspective governing Joshua and Judges. Sinners include the sons of Eli, whose great sin (khatta'th) was to treat offerings to Yahweh with contempt (1 Sam 2:17). Their blaspheming (**meqallim** מְקַלְלִים), an "iniquity" ('awon) known to Eli (3:13), led to their destruction and the loss of the ark of the covenant to the Philistines (4:10-11). Samuel's sons are no better; they accept bribes and pervert justice (8:3), leading to a demand for a king.

In agreeing to the people's demand, Samuel reminds them of their history of sinful infidelity to Yahweh and the consequent punishment (1 Sam 12:10). Samuel tells them that it is not a monarchy that will keep them save, but "fear [of] the Lord" (vv. 14, 24). The historian's ambivalence to the monarchy surfaces in the report that the people recognize that by their very demand for a king they have sinned (v. 19).

Saul begins the long history of monarchical sinning. In sparing some of the spoils of war with Amalekites, he disobeys the divine command that all such spoils should be dedicated to Yahweh (15:3; compare 28:18). His action elicits Samuel's poetic judgment "rebellion (**meri**) is no less a sin than divination" (15:23). Saul confesses his sin (15:24), but too late to save his throne.

Despite the overall theology governing the history, a divine promise guarantees the position of David and his house. God will be a father to him; his iniquities will be punished, but his throne will be forever (2 Sam 7:14-16; compare 1 Kgs 2:2-4). The episode of Bathsheba dramatically illustrates the principle. Neither adultery nor the arranged death of her husband, Uriah (2 Sam 11), suffices to unseat David. Brought to his senses by the prophet Nathan's parable of the poor man's ewe lamb (12:1-6), the king recognizes that he has sinned (12:13). Bathsheba's child dies (12:15) and dynastic troubles are promised (12:11), but David himself remains secure, despite committing a further sin of conducting a census (24:10).

Sin in the form of infidelity to Yahweh continues to plague the monarchy. Despite the glory of Solomon's reign, his devotion to his numerous foreign wives led him astray to worship Astarte, Milcom, the "abomination of the Ammonites," and various other deities (1 Kgs 11:4-8). Hence the monarchy is divided, leading to further idolatry. The first northern king, Jereboam, establishes golden calves in Bethel and Dan, and "this thing became a sin" (khatta'th; 1 Kgs 12:30). The sins of Jereboam (13:34; 14:16; 15:30) lead to disaster for his son, Nadab (15:28). The subsequent dynasties of Baasha, Zimri, and Omri do no better (15:34; 16:13, 19, 25, 30). Ahab, son of Omri, receives special attention. With his wife Jezebel, daughter of the king of Sidon, he worships Baal and sets up an Asherah (or sacred pole) (16:1-33). Ahab's program meets resistance in the form of the prophet Elijah, who successfully confronts the priests of Baal on Mount Carmel (18:20-40) and those who had "forsaken [the] covenant" with Yahweh (19:10, 14). Elijah, like the writing prophets, was concerned not only with idolatry, but also with Ahab and Jezebel's abuse of power in their murderous seizure of Naboth's vineyard. Doing "what is evil in the sight of the LORD" (21:20) sealed Ahab's fate. Though Jezebel dies with Ahab, her memory lived on in early Christian polemics (Rev 2:20). Ahab's son Azariah, who follows in his father's evil ways (1 Kgs 22:52), elicits Elijah's criticism, and divine punishment, for consulting Baal-zebub, the god of Ekron (2 Kgs 1:2-4). The roster of northern kings, with the refrain that they did "what was evil in the sight of the LORD," continues with Jehoram (2 Kgs 3:2-3; 9:22). Jehu, who despite eliminating Ahab and persecuting Baal-worshipers, kept the old golden calves in Bethel and Dan, thus continuing the "sins of Jeroboam" (10:29-31). The same judgment falls on Jehoahaz (13:2, 6); Jehoash (13:11); Jeroboam II (14:24); Zechariah (15:9); Menahem (15:18); Pekahiah (15:24); Pekah (15:28), and Hoshea (17:2). In his reign the Assyrian captivity took place "because the people of Israel had sinned against the LORD their God" (17:7). The historian summarizes all that was wrong with Israel. It had sinned by despising his covenant and worshiping idols, serving the host of heaven and Baal, passing their sons and daughters through fire, using divination and augury (17:8-18; compare 34-40).

Meanwhile Solomon's successors in the kingdom of Judah also follow a checkered path. Rehoboam builds high places, pillars, and sacred poles "on every high hill and under every green tree," as Jeremiah would say (1 Kgs 14:23). His descendants follow in his footsteps,

with varying degrees of fidelity to Yahweh. Kings lax on issues of idolatry receive negative judgments, including Abijam (1 Kgs 15:3); Jehoram, who married a daughter of Ahab (2 Kgs 8:18); Ahaziah (8:27); and Ahaz, who even "made his son pass through the fire" and sacrificed on high places (16:2-4). The more rigorous kings receive kinder treatment, including Asa (1 Kgs 15:11-14); Jehoshaphat (1 Kgs 22:43-46); Jehoash (2 Kgs 12:3); Amaziah (14:3-4); Azariah (15:3-4); and Jotham (15:34-35), although none of these eliminate the "high places" where people continue to sacrifice. The righteous Hezekiah does eliminate high places and idols, including the old bronze serpent of Moses (18:3-5), but his son Manasseh reverses the cultic cleansing and did all the evils that the historian so disliked (21:2-9), paralleling the sins of the kings of Israel (compare 17:34-40). His "abominations" (to'evah, 21:11) were worse than those of the Amorites. In addition to Manasseh's idolatry he had shed much innocent blood and caused Judah to sin (21:16). His son Amon followed Manasseh's ways (21:21). Josiah did things right (22:1–23:25), but his reforms did not suffice to thwart Yahweh's wrath (23:26-27). Jehoiakim (23:37), Jehoiachin (24:9), and Zedekiah (24:19) return to negative form, leading to the Babylonian exile.

The Chronicler retells the history of the kingdom of Judah, with slightly different accents. Saul died because he "was unfaithful" (ma'al מָעַל) in not keeping Yahweh's command and by consulting a medium (1 Chr 10:13). David and Solomon are idealized and their sins ignored. The focal point of Solomon's reign is the establishment of the Temple, which has its appointed role in obtaining forgiveness for the sins of the people, a function highlighted in the king's dedicatory prayer (2 Chr 6:22, 24, 26-27, 30, 36-39; 7:14). He also receives a direct warning from God that he and his house should be faithful (7:19-22), a warning recalled at the invasion of the Egyptian pharaoh Shishak (12:5). The subsequent history of Judah's monarchs mirrors that of 2 Kings, with significant differences of detail. Thus, for example, Asa was eager to remove idols (14:3-5; 15:16), as was Jehoshaphat (20:32), although they left the high places intact. Jehoram "led...the inhabitants of Jerusalem into unfaithfulness (wayyezen [וַיֶּזֶן], from znh [זנה], "commit adultery"), earning a written rebuke from Elijah (21:11-15). Joash, by contrast, served the sacred poles and idols (24:18), and Uzziah (= Azariah) "was false (ma'al) to the LORD" (26:16), which explains his leprosy (26:19; compare 2 Kgs 15:5). The Chronicler records Manasseh's "abominations"(33:3-6), but, after a brief Babylonian captivity, he repents and is restored (33:10-13), events unknown to 2 Kings. Manasseh's story foreshadows the finale of Chronicles, which records the fulfillment of Jeremiah's prophecy and the decree of Cyrus releasing Judah's exiles (36:22-23).

The historical books of Ezra and Nehemiah, continuing the work of the Chronicler, report the "faithlessness" (ma'al) of the returned exiles, particularly in their intermarriage with foreign women (Ezra 9:4). Ezra's penitential prayer confesses iniquities (ʿawon), acknowledges guilt (ʾasham אָשֵׁם), admits forsaking God's commandments, by accepting the pollutions (niddah נִדָּה) and abominations (toʿevah) of other nations (9:6-15). Confronted with the scribe's charge that they have trespassed (maʿal) they too repent in order to avert God's fierce wrath (10:12-14). As Nehemiah describes the scene, they confessed their sins (khattaʾth) and the iniquities (ʿawon) of their ancestors (Neh 9:2). The prayer of Ezra in this context rehearses the history of Israel, highlighting the ways in which the people "were disobedient and rebelled" against God (Neh 9:26).

H. The Psalms

The psalms offer eloquent expression to the attempts to wrestle with sin, and echo the calls for confession and repentance found in the prophets and historians. The best known of the penitential psalms, Ps 51, offers a comprehensive review of sin and its impact. The psalm, whose inscription attributes it to David after the Bathsheba episode, calls on God's mercy and steadfast love (Ps 51:1; compare Exod 34:6-7) to blot out his transgressions (pashaʿ), wash away his iniquity (ʿawon), and cleanse his sins (khattaʾth), with the implication that sin is a form of uncleanness. The psalm also insists on how sin, or doing "what is evil in your sight," has affected the sinner's relationship with God (v. 4). The sinner abjectly confesses that he was "born guilty," a sinner from his very conception (v. 5), hyperbolic words that will later support a doctrine of original sin. Recalling prophetic themes, the psalmist asks for interior renewal (v. 10-12; compare Jer 31:31-34; Ezek 36), and disparages the cult as the way to deal with sin (vv. 16-17).

Other psalms mention specific and mostly familiar sins: idolatry (31:6; 82:8; 106:19, 36); atheism or disbelief in God's providence (10:4; 14:1; 78:32; 94:7); lack of trust in God (78:22; 106:24); deceit (5:5; 7:14; 10:7; 12:2; 31:17-18; 32:2; 50:19; 62:4); violence and thirst for blood (7:16; 10:8; 11:5; 55:23; 64:4-6; 94:5; 140:4); theft and extortion (50:18; 62:10); duplicity (28:3); and adultery (50:18). The wicked offend God by persecuting the poor (10:2; 12:5; 37:14, 35) and lending at interest and taking bribes (15:5). In the face of such pervasive sin, the psalmists occasionally despair (12:1; 14:4).

I. The Sapiential Perspective

Although hardly speaking with one voice, the prophets, the Deuteronomistic historians, and the priestly legalists all forge a connection between sin, often conceived of as infidelity to God and God's covenant, and punishment. Wisdom literature presents an alternative perspective on the understanding of sin and a critique of simplistic views about divine retribution.

The most traditional wisdom texts, the book of Proverbs, worries not so much about sin but about folly (Prov 10:8, 14, passim), and the vocabulary for "sin" familiar from the Torah and Prophets is rare. Thus "sin (khattaʾth) is a reproach to any people" (14:34; compare 20:9) and anyone who "loves transgression" (pashaʿ) loves strife (17:19). Proverbs does, however, regularly condemn "evil" (raʿ; 2:14) or the behavior of the "wicked" (rashaʿ רָשָׁע, 14:11). Avoidance of such behavior plays a major role in forming a wise person. The sinners who try to entice the "child" from the path of virtue plot violence against the innocent that will secure their wealth (1:10-12; 3:31). The depiction of sinners is conventional, as is the generic description of the evil life from which prudence will preserve the wise. The way of evil (raʿ) involves perverse speech, walking in the way of darkness, and rejoicing in evil (2:12-14); the way of the wicked is like "deep darkness" (4:19). What Yahweh hates are "haughty eyes, a lying tongue, hands that shed innocent blood, a heart that devises wicked plans ... a lying witness ... and one who sows discord" (6:16-19; compare 8:13). Wicked behavior is in general the sport of the foolish (10:23). The proverbialist frequently becomes more concrete, defining as foolish or wicked those who bribe or accept bribes (17:8, 23), who are partial to the guilty (18:5; 24:23-24; 28:21), who use diverse weights and measures (20:10, 23), who oppress the poor (22:16, 22; 29:13-16), or who remove ancient landmarks (22:28; 23:10). Proverbs pays special attention to what people say, since "death and life are in the power of the tongue" (18:21). It condemns those who use "lying lips" (10:18; 12:22; 26:28) and dissembling speech (26:24-26), bear false witness (19:5, 9), utter slander (10:18), gossip (11:13; 20:19; 26:22), or whisper (24:28), mock the poor (17:5), engage in backbiting (25:23) or flattery (29:5).

One particular evil stands out with greater definition in the world of Proverbs, adultery. The way of the "loose woman" who entices the budding sage to adultery leads to death (Prov 2:16-19). Her lips drip with honey, but what she delivers is wormwood (5:3-4). The sage delights in detailed descriptions of those honeyed lips and the seductive words they speak (7:10-20; 9:13-17), from which wisdom will preserve her pupil (6:24; 7:5). The considerations advanced by Proverbs for avoiding adultery reveal much about the kind of wisdom it inculcates. It is not the defiling character of the act but the consequences of being caught that inspire chaste prudence. The man who touches his neighbor's wife "will [not] go unpunished" (6:29). He will get "wounds and dishonor" and will be ruined by a jealous husband (6:32-35). Hence the adulterer "has no sense" (6:32).

Some images of sinners evoke their condition, without specifying their sinful deeds. Thus the wicked lie sleepless unless they have done wrong and made someone stumble (Prov 4:16). The "scoundrel and ... villain" (ʾadham beliyaʿal ʾish ʿawen אָדָם בְּלִיַּעַל אִישׁ אָוֶן], literally, "a man of wickedness, a man of iniquity"; *see* BELIAL) uses crooked speech, winking eyes, and shuffling feet as he sows discord (6:12-15). Along with the images of the wicked and foolish, Proverbs catalogues the dispositions leading to wickedness, including being arrogant (16:5, 18; 21:4; 29:23), cruel (11:17; 12:10), covetous (12:12), greedy (15:27; 28:25), rash (12:18; 14:29), hot-tempered (15:18; 29:11, 22), lazy (6:6; 12:24, 27; 15:19; 19:15, 24; 20:4; 24:30-31; 26:15), insolent (13:10), fond of wine (23:20-21, 30-35, a vivid portrait of a drunkard; 26:10; 31:4-6), lacking self-control (25:28), quarrelsome (26:21), or jealous (27:4).

In contrast to, and often in antithetical parallelism with, the depiction of the sinner, Proverbs limns the outlines of a person of virtue. The characteristics or virtues of the wise man enable him to avoid the specific acts of sinful folly. Thus he is restrained in speech (Prov 10:19; 25:11-15), humble (11:2), diligent (12:24; 13:4; 14:23), loyal (16:6; 19:22), slow to anger (16:32), discrete (25:7-10), "walks in integrity" (28:18), and knows the rules of etiquette (23:1-3; 25:6-7).

Such wisdom can be given a veneer that renders it compatible with the perspective of the prophets and the legal traditions of Israel. Thus all wisdom is designed to instill "fear of the LORD" (Prov 1:7; 2:5; 8:13; 9:10; 10:27; 14:2, 27). Yahweh's eyes are ever present (15:3); keeping the commandments leads to life (19:16) and wisdom leads away from Sheol (15:24). One characteristic of wisdom is respect for traditional piety: the wise person will delight in prayer (15:8) and will not mock a traditional sacrifice (14:9). Observing the law (TORAH) is characteristic of the wise and those who forsake it praise the wicked (28:4-9; 29:18). Yet wisdom is above all eminently practical. To pursue wisdom guarantees a life of wealth and prosperity (Prov 8:18-21; 13:21); "the LORD does not let the righteous go hungry" (Prov 10:3), but "a babbling fool will come to ruin" (10:8).

The stark contrasts between the wise and the fool, the righteous and the wicked, leaves little room for the possibility of repentance, which plays such a significant role in the prophets and is part of the priestly Torah. Yet Proverbs at least gives a nod in that direction, noting that "no one who conceals transgressions will prosper, but one who confesses and forsakes them will obtain mercy" (Prov 28:13).

Beneath the surface of piety a serene and sometimes smug rationalism pervades Proverbs. Other texts have a more critical edge. Job in particular tackles the orthodoxies of priest and prophet. Through its portrait of the undeserving sufferer confronting his conventional friends, Job challenges traditional theories of the relationship between sin and suffering.

Job's friends continually assault his innocence, known to the reader from the framework that introduced Job as "blameless and upright" (Job 1:1). They know he must have sinned to suffer so and their speeches are replete with traditional theologies of sin and its effects. Eliphaz begins by asking, "Who that was innocent ever perished?" (4:7). Bildad picks up where Eliphaz left off and insists on God's righteousness, which implies that Job and his children must have sinned (khatta'th) and

committed transgression (pasha') (8:1-4). Zophar too insists that Job's claims of innocence are unbelievable (11:3-4) and calls on him to repent (11:13).

Job regularly responds by lamenting his fate and asks how he has done wrong (6:24-27). He is blameless (9:21) and will defend his ways to God's face (13:15). He begs to know his iniquities, sins, and transgressions (13:23). As the increasingly acrimonious dialogue continues, Eliphaz accuses Job of further sin by his resistance to their arguments. He is "doing away with the fear of God" (15:4). Eliphaz cites as ancestral wisdom the claim that "the wicked writhe in pain all their days" (15:20). Job does not waver in maintaining his innocence, stubbornly names God, not his own guilt, as the source of all his woes (19:8-15), but also declares his hope that "his redeemer lives" (19:25). To Zophar's repeated affirmation that sinners suffer justly (chap. 20), Job responds with the facts of experience, that the "the wicked live on, reach old age, and grow mighty in power" and that their families continue to thrive (21:7-8).

Through the first stages of the dialogue, sin, wickedness, and transgression are formal categories. They must be involved, claim Job's friends, to explain Job's suffering. As the dialogue progresses, Job and his friends explore the concrete realities of sin. Eliphaz pointedly challenges Job by identifying his wickedness, echoing the prophets' criticism of the abusive ruling classes of Israel and Judah. Job has been, says Eliphaz, exacting pledges from his family without reason and stripping the naked of their clothing, giving the weary no water and withholding bread from the hungry (22:6-7). Job's response continues to call on observed reality of prosperous sinners, again citing specifics of experience: "The wicked remove landmarks; they seize flocks and pasture them. They drive away the donkey of the orphan; they take the widow's ox for a pledge" (24:2-3); "The murderer rises at dusk to kill the poor and needy, and in the night is like a thief. The eye of the adulterer also waits for the twilight" (24:14-15). Yet God prolongs their life and gives them security (24:22-23).

Bildad's final intervention affirms the universal reality of sin: "How then can a mortal be righteous before God? How can one born of woman be pure?" (Job 25:4). Job responds by both affirming the mysterious sovereignty of God (26:1-14) and solemnly defending his innocence: "until I die I will not put away my integrity from me. I hold fast my righteousness, and will not let it go" (27:5-6). In his final defense, Job catalogues sins of which he is not guilty. He has not been "enticed by a woman," or "lain in wait at my neighbor's door" (31:9); he has not rejected the cause of his slaves (31:13); he has not "withheld anything that the poor desired" nor "caused the eyes of the widow to fail" (31:16); he has not failed to clothe the naked nor has he oppressed the orphan (31:19-21). His trust was not in wealth (31:24-28); he did not rejoice in the ruin of his enemies (31:29), nor commit sin by cursing (31:30).

Neither was he a hypocrite, concealing transgressions or iniquities (31:33).

Despite Elihu's defense of divine justice (Job 34:24), by the end of the book, Job's "integrity" (27:5) remains intact. God finally responds to Job's challenge to convict him of sin, but refuses to do so. Speaking from the whirlwind, God can only bring Job to submission by evoking the mystery of his cosmic power (Job 38:1–41:34). Yet God also declares to the friends that Job was right (42:7), dramatically affirming the radical critique of traditional theology enshrined in Job's responses. Whatever one makes of the mysterious ways of God, sin and suffering cannot be simply defined as cause and effect.

The sapiential tradition's skeptical strand also dominates Ecclesiastes, which is less concerned with specific moral advice or developing a taxonomy of sin than with understanding how to live in a world where sin is not subject to divine retribution. The preacher observes the fact that the righteous and the wicked both have their place under the sun. After consoling himself with the thoughts that God will judge, that in the meantime God is testing them, a darker thought comes to dominate his mind. Both righteous and wicked both are dust and to dust will return (Eccl 3:16-20). Divine providence is absent: "There are righteous people who perish in their righteousness, and there are wicked (rasha`) people who prolong their life in their evildoing" (7:15). The expected outcomes for the righteous and the wicked are often reversed (8:14), and the same fate awaits the pious and the impious (9:2). The "race is not to the swift, nor the battle to the strong" (9:11). Such a situation is a part of the "vanity" that marks human existence (1:2, 14; 8:14; 9:1-2; 12:8).

Despite what seems to be a counsel of despair, the preacher admonishes the pursuit of righteousness and avoidance of wickedness; with a hint of irony he advises his reader not to be "too wicked" or foolish (Eccl 7:17-18). Despite the success of sinners, the preacher knows that it will be well with those who fear God (8:12-13), though well-being is to be found in the pursuit of meaningful work, with enjoyment of food, drink, and companionship (8:15; 9:7-10).

What counts as wickedness and sin in the preacher's eyes is familiar from the proverbial and prophetic traditions: "oppression of the poor and the violation of justice and right" (Eccl 5:8); bribery that corrupts the heart (7:7); acting in anger (7:9); swearing falsely (9:2). Like the proverbialist, he is distrustful of a woman who could be a seductive trap (7:26). The preacher does not dwell on the particularities of sin, but is content, like Bildad in Job, to note its general presence among humankind: "Surely there is no one on earth so righteous as to do good without ever sinning (khata')" (7:20).

J. Apocalyptic Traditions

In the post-exilic period, first under Persian and then under Greek rule, Israel's sages explored the issue of sin in new ways. What would become an influential view about the origins of human sinfulness appears first in a portion of the non-canonical book of *Enoch*, which probably dates to the 3rd cent. BCE. In developing a tradition encountered in Gen 6, it tells of the heavenly "watchers" whose intercourse with human women led to moral decay.

The major canonical witness to apocalyptic expectations, the book of Daniel, spends little time reflecting on sin, although it dramatically depicts acts assumed to be sinful, which its heroes avoid, such as eating improper food (1:8-17) or the worship of images (3:1-18). One new dimension appears in the suggestion that the transgressions have a divinely ordained limit (8:23), which when reached will trigger decisive divine intervention.

More traditional ideas of sin as breach of covenant fidelity are found in the additions to Daniel, especially in the confessional Prayer of Azariah in the fiery furnace, who confesses that "we have sinned and broken your law ... we have not obeyed your commandments" (Pr Azar 6-7). As had the psalmist, the youth prays for deliverance, asking God to accept a contrite heart in place of sacrifice (Pr Azar 16-17).

K. New Testament

The NT has a more restricted vocabulary for sin. The primary term is hamartia, which has a semantic range similar to that of the Hebrew khatta'th. Other important terms are "wickedness" (kakia κακία) and "lawlessness" (anomia ἀνομία).

The traditions about the teachings of Jesus found in the Synoptic Gospels display traditional understandings of sin. The accounts of John the Baptist suggest the ethos of the revival movement out of which Jesus emerged. In view of impending divine judgment, John called for repentance and baptism, understood to be for the "forgiveness of sins" (Mark 1:4; Luke 3:3; compare Mark 1:5; Matt 3:6). While he reportedly preached honesty (Luke 3:7-14), John denounced the sinful character of the religious leaders of his generation, a "brood of vipers" (Matt 3:7; Luke 3:7). A major focus of his critique was the tetrarch, Herod Antipas, and his marriage to his brother's wife, which led to his arrest and execution (Matt 14:1-12; Mark 6:14-29; Luke 9:7-9; compare Mal 2:15-16).

The ministry of Jesus is understood by the evangelists to involve salvation from sin (Matt 1:21; John 1:29). As the "Son of Man" he claimed have power to forgive sin a claim contested by his adversaries as blasphemous (Matt 2-5, 6; Mark 2:1-12; Luke 5:17-26). Jesus himself seems to have welcomed people conventionally considered to be sinners and developed a reputation as their friend (Matt 9:10-13; 11:19; Mark 2:13-17; Luke 5:27-32; 7:34). He is portrayed as admonishing those whom he heals not to sin again (John 5:14).

While the stories about Jesus and his engagement with sin may reflect the concerns of early Christian communities, there are teachings attributed to Jesus that probably reflect important emphases of his preaching. The need to be forgiving of one another's sins, enshrined in the Golden Rule and the Lord's prayer (Matt 7:12; Luke 11:4) and in the injunction to forgive "seventy-seven times" (Matt 18:21-22), probably capture the authentic voice of Jesus. Following in the footsteps of John the Baptist, Jesus probably warned about the dangers of sin and some of the hyperbolic admonitions to remove the scandalous members suggest a concern to prevent the possibility of sin (Matt 18:8-9), a concern that shapes Matthew's presentation of the "antithetical" teachings of Jesus (Matt 5:21-48). Specific warnings against sin include the notion of an unforgivable sin against the Holy Spirit (Matt 12:32; Mark 3:29; Luke 12:10).

The sins for which Jesus reserved his harshest critique were the failings of the seemingly righteous, particularly the religious authorities (Matt 23:1-36; Mark 12:38-40; Luke 11:37-52). He also seems to have been concerned about the administration of the Temple, although the focus of his concern was interpreted differently by accounts of his prophetic "cleansing." If he thought that the priestly leadership had made the house of God a den of thieves (Matt 21:13; Mark 11:17; Luke 19:46), he may have objected to the speculation and greed of the ruling class, as had Israel's classic prophets.

While there is no probing theological exploration of sin in the Gospels, there is evidence of debates about the subject, which are entirely comprehensible within a 1st-cent. context. Thus Jesus questions an assumed linkage between suffering and sin when he asks whether the eighteen on whom a tower fell were "worse offenders" than all the other inhabitants of Jerusalem (Luke 13:4). The healing of a blind man prompts the question of whose sin caused the disease, that of the man or his parents, which Jesus undercuts with his claim that the condition was an occasion to display God's glory (John 9:2).

Although the Gospels preserve teachings of Jesus, they also reflect the concerns of the evangelists. Luke's account highlights the theme of repentance and focuses on the forgiveness available to sinners through Christ. The poignant parable of the prodigal son (15:11-32) may teach other lessons, but it certainly offers in the character of the father an image of one who is able to forgive with abundant generosity. That figure recalls another specifically Lukan character, the good shepherd (15:3-7), whose rejoicing over the lost sheep mirrors heaven's rejoicing at the repentance of a sinner.

Images of repentant sinners abound in Luke: the sinful woman, later erroneously identified with Mary Magdalene, whose tears wash Jesus' feet and whose hair dries them (Luke 7:36-50); the toll collector Zacchaeus, who repents of his extortions and promises restitution (19:1-10); the good thief crucified beside Jesus, whose implicit repentance elicits a promise of eternal bliss (23:39-43). The ultimate example of forgiveness to which the Gospel calls all its readers is Jesus

himself, one of whose final prayers on the cross is that God forgive those who have crucified him (23:34, not in all manuscripts).

Three of the most probing theologians of the NT explore the theme of sin and its remedies. Paul offers the most complex treatment of sin, its pervasive reality, and its effects. Not all of his writing is on that level of reflection. He can at times reproduce simple lists of vices and sinful behavior from which his converts have been liberated (Rom 1:29-31), or from which he warns them (Rom 13:13; 1 Cor 5:2-11; 6:9-10; 2 Cor 12:20-21; Gal 5:19-21). Such lists, mirroring concerns of Hellenistic moralists, focus more on personal moral behavior than on prophetic denunciations of social sin. The Galatians list, for example, notes that "works of the flesh are obvious: fornication, impurity, licentiousness, idolatry, sorcery, enmities, strife, jealousy, anger, quarrels, dissensions, factions, envy, drunkenness, carousing, and things like these."

Paul's most reflective letter, Romans, offers the most elaborate treatment of sin. The letter's overarching goal is to explain to the Roman community Paul's understanding of the Law and Israel in God's plan for humankind. His first move is to insist on the universal reality of sin (Rom 1–3), which God's action in the sacrifice of Christ was designed to counter (Rom 3:25-26). In developing this theme, Paul uses the testimony of the psalms (Pss 14:1-3; 53:1-3 at Rom 3:10-18), as well as imaginative personification and lively dialogue. In the process, following in the footsteps of the prophetic tradition, and Hellenistic Jewish literature such as Wis 13–15, he identifies the fundamental sin as idolatry, from which all other sins flow. Among these Paul features prominently the sin of same-sex intercourse, echoing the taboos of Leviticus (Rom 1:26-27; compare Lev 18:22; 20:13). Of even greater prominence in the diatribe is the act of hypocritical judgment (Rom 2:17–3:8) by those who would share the basic perspective of Paul's analysis. Whatever the particulars of individual sins, Paul, citing texts from the psalms (Rom 3:9-18, including Pss 5:9; 10:7; 14:1-3; 53:1-3; 140:3), summarizes his sketch of the unredeemed human condition as one in which sin is universal and all, Jew and Gentile alike, "fall short of the glory of God" (3:23).

Against that universal reality of sin, Paul, probably drawing on a traditional formula, suggests that God has provided relief through Christ, whose death is imaged as a sacrificial offering that expiates or atones for sin. In describing that offering, Paul uses the language of hilastērion (ἱλαστήριον) or "mercy seat" (Rom 3:25), the term for the cover of the ark where blood was sprinkled on the Day of Atonement. Whether that is the precise focus of Paul's allusive language is debated, but the thrust of his argument is clear. He does not explain the logic of the action, but takes it as a given on which he builds his argument.

Paul alludes elsewhere to the Christ event in terms of its effects on sin, although in each case without fully developing the theme. Thus, in 2 Corinthians, while celebrating his ministry as a continuation of God's work in Christ, he describes the process of reconciliation: "For our sake he made him to be sin who knew no sin, so that in him we might become the righteousness of God" (2 Cor 5:21). Paul may have in mind the notion of the scapegoat of Lev 16, or a simple identification of the death of Christ as a "sacrifice for sin" (Lev 5), but the point is the same. God has effectively dealt with the reality of sin in order to liberate and empower those who are now "in Christ."

Paul in Romans continues his reflection on sin and its power through a meditation on the sin of the first human being. In a passage influential for Christian notions of original sin, Paul notes that as Adam sinned, so, by imitation, did all who have descended from Adam (Rom 6:12). Paul's Greek expression, en ho (ἐν ᾧ), "inasmuch as," or "because" (NRSV) all sinned, was later translated into Latin in a literal way, as "in whom" all sinned. That translation provided a scriptural basis for a conception of original sin automatically transmitted to all Adam's descendants. Although Paul does not articulate such a theory, he is committed to the claim that sin's power is universal and pervasive.

Examination of sin's universal power reaches its climax in Paul's attempt in Rom 7 to explain how he can recognize the Law as holy and good and, at the same time, claim that it does not provide a vehicle for a saving relationship with God. The answer, he argues, is in the fundamental character of human nature, "the flesh," which is beset by the force of passionate desire that overcomes the rational recognition of what is right. Paul's argument moves through two stages. In the first, using a fictive "I" to describe the experience, he evokes the scriptural command not to covet (7:7). Paul's adopted persona may be that of the primordial pair, Adam and Eve, whose response to the divine prohibition Paul evokes. Using that persona, Paul suggests a psychological insight, that prohibitions, far from preventing negative behavior, can actually stimulate it.

The second stage of Paul's argument probably owes much to Greco-Roman discussions of weakness of the will (akrasia ἀκρασία) and artistic portrayals of passions run amok (akolasia ἀκολασία). In language echoing poetic archetypes, Paul describes a self divided between the good that the mind acknowledges and the evil that the will pursues (Rom 7:16-20). Paul's persona resembles the mythic figure Medea, who before slaying her children as an act of vengeance against Theseus, could say, "I see the better and approve of it, but I pursue what is worse" (Ovid, *Metam.* 7.20–21). Paul too frames the human condition as one of bondage to overwhelming passion. Against such a force, he claims, the Torah is powerless.

Paul's answer to this predicament is the result of Christ's death and resurrection, a new life mediated through baptism, in which the believer becomes identified with Christ (compare Rom 6:1-11). That identifi-

cation makes possible life "in the spirit," which transforms the self, making it "dead to sin" (6:11; 8:10), and enables the appropriate alignment of mind and heart, spirit and will. All of this may be inspired by the hopes for interior transformation expressed by Jeremiah and Ezekiel. Paul celebrates that eschatological transformation in the following chapter (8:1-17), while recognizing that it is still a work in progress (8:18-30). The condition of sinful humanity has not been obliterated by the life of the spirit, which lives within believers and "groans" (8:22) with the faithful in expectation of the completion of the process of renewal.

The Johannine corpus offers a fundamental reinterpretation of the category of sin. The theme first appears when John the Baptist identifies Jesus as the Lamb of God who takes away the sins of the world (John 1:29). The proclamation foreshadows the crucifixion, particularly John 19:36, where a scriptural citation, Exod 12:46, identifies Jesus as the paschal lamb. The identification already presumes a development in the understanding of the function of the sacrifice of Passover, which initially was simply an apotropaic symbol to ward off the angel of death. The requirement that blood be smeared on the lintels and doorposts of Israelite residences perhaps absorbed connotations of cleansing from rituals such as that of Yom Kippur (Lev 16:16, 19), and popular tradition may have assimilated the Passover sacrifice to sacrifices for sin. Such traditions, as well as the interpretation of the death of Jesus as a Passover sacrifice, attested in 1 Cor 5:7, was certainly a Christian tradition before the composition of the Fourth Gospel.

As it does with other traditions, the Fourth Gospel probes the affirmation for its deeper meaning, although sin generally plays a limited role in John. It is an issue in the interpolated pericope of the adulteress (John 8:1-12), in some polemical remarks about Jesus and sin (8:21, 34, 45), in discussion of the status of the man born blind (9:2, 34, 41) or the sinfulness of his opponents (15:22, 24), and in the prediction that the Paraclete, the Holy Spirit, would come to convict the world of sin (16:8-9). The last remark is significant for the way in which the Gospel ultimately treats the issue of sin.

The treatment of sin is a corollary of the interpretation of the death of Jesus as a liberating and revelatory event. Much of the Gospel's narrative and discourse material points ahead to the "hour" of the death and resurrection of Jesus. Thus, for example, the Son of Man sayings in John 1:51 and 3:14 anticipate the death of Jesus, when he becomes, like Jacob's ladder (Gen 28:12, alluded to in 1:51), a means of access to heaven, or like the serpent in the desert (Num 21:9, alluded to in 3:14), something that heals when seen with the eyes of faith. What is thus "seen" is the "truth" that liberates (8:32), which is also "way" and "life" (14:6). The similitude of the good shepherd hints at the content of that truth, a willingness to give up one's own life for the good of the sheep (10:15). The ultimate content of the revelation disclosed at the final "hour" is encapsulated in the last discourses in the form of a command and a proverb, the command to love as Jesus loved (13:34) and the proverb that "No one has greater love than this, to lay down one's life for one's friends" (15:13).

The connection of this "revelation" with sin is made explicit in the scene of the appearance of Jesus to his disciples on the night of his resurrection, when he breathes the spirit into them and commissions them to forgive (20:22-23). Thus the Lamb who takes away the sin of the world does so by creating a community of friends empowered by the spirit to love and forgive as he did. Against the strength of that community, sin has no force.

The third major theological reflection on sin in the pages of the NT appears in the Epistle to the Hebrews, which exhibits structural similarities and thematic differences from Paul and John. In the process of exhorting to renewed fidelity a community in danger of slipping away from commitment to Christ (Heb 2:1), this anonymous author offers a bold reinterpretation of the significance of Christ's death. That reinterpretation builds on the kind of cultic understanding of that death evident in the traditional formula found in Rom 3:25-26. Here, however, there is no doubt about the derivation of the interpretive framework. The author of Hebrews portrays the death of Christ as the ultimate Yom Kippur sacrifice, designed to affect lasting and effective atonement for sin (Heb 8–10). The development of the theme exhibits a polemical edge, in its rhetorical contrast of between the "old" and the "new." The Yom Kippur sacrifice of the Tabernacle involved the "blood of goats and bulls" (9:13), and could only effect a superficial cleansing and not the elimination of sin. Lurking behind this critique may be both prophetic charges against the superficiality of cultic sacrifice and contemporary rationalistic critiques of religious practice. In any case, the "true," sacrifice of Christ, consummated in the "heavenly tent" not with animal blood but with his spirit (9:14), has the effect of cleansing "consciences" from sin, and thereby making the faithful "perfect" or fit to enter into the divine presence (10:14). Sin, therefore, is implicitly understood to be what weighs on the conscience, a category then receiving significant attention among Hellenistic moralists.

The author of Hebrews does not probe how that cleansing takes place. He does not, as do Paul and John, appeal explicitly to the presence of the Spirit in the lives of followers of Christ as the agent transforming sinful humanity. Instead, he uses another traditional biblical image, covenant, to define the new reality that he had experienced. Jeremiah's promise of a "new" covenant, one written on hearts and minds (Jer 31:31-34, cited at Heb 8:8-12; 10:16-17), forms the basis for this interpretive move. This "writing" takes place through the example provided by Jesus of fidelity to God in the face even of death. As such a faithful person, he is the "pioneer and perfecter" of the community's faith (12:2).

Within that community, the faithful can be assured that the effects of sin no longer prevail. Through Jesus they can have access to the presence of God, to the heavenly throne where God's son sits to intercede for them and dispense mercy (4:16). The author does not address the question of how sin is removed from human consciences. He only needs the words of Jeremiah's prophecy of a new covenant, words put on the lips of God, who promises to "remember ... no more" the sins of the people (8:12; 10:17).

From the position that sin had been "forgotten" for members of the community of the new covenant, the author of Hebrews seems to have drawn an inference that would continue to trouble Christians into the 2nd cent. Although Hebrews does not baldly claim that Christian do not sin, the author does issue a dramatic warning against the sin of apostasy (6:4-6). He threatens that for those who have "tasted the heavenly gift" and then fallen away, there is no possibility of repentance. Although more rhetorical gesture than dogmatic proposition, the passage seems to express the sense that serious sin seems to be incompatible with Christian life. More significantly, the passage, as well as similar stern warnings (2:1-4; 6:4-6) suggest that apostasy from the new covenant community has taken the place for Hebrews of what had been the archetypal sin in the biblical tradition, idolatry.

Authors influenced by Paul and John continue elements of their reflection on sin. The deutero-Pauline epistles, often focused on creating a framework for moral order in Christian communities, occasionally reflect on the theological significance of sin (Eph 1:1-4), but more frequently focus on the virtues to be pursued and vices to be avoided (Eph 4:17-21; 5:3-4). The Epistle of James warns against the temptation of desire (Jas 1:12-13), condemns the "sin" of partiality (Jas 2:9, citing Lev 19:18), and urges care of the tongue, a source of potent iniquity (Jas 3:6; compare Prov 18:21). Second Peter, among the latest writings of the NT, vehemently denounces false prophets and their "licentious ways" (2 Pet 2:1-22).

In Johannine circles, the first epistle of John is particularly concerned with sin. That concern may, in part, be a reaction against elements in the reinterpretation of sin found in the Fourth Gospel. One might, that is, infer from the reality of the love revealed on the cross, that sin is no more, and that members of the Johannine community need not worry about its presence in their midst. They may have shared some of the optimism that informs Hebrews warnings about post-baptismal sin. Against that overly optimistic stance, the author of First John declares that the blood of Christ cleanses from sin, that he who claims to be without sin is a liar (1 John 1:7-8, 10), and that confession of sin will lead to forgiveness (1:9). While reinforcing the reality of sin and the need for both Christ's atoning sacrifice (2:2; 3:5) and the believers' response, the author continues to use language that might have generated the problem in the first place. Sin, defined as "lawlessness" (3:4), is incompatible with life as a follower of Jesus (3:6). To commit sin is to be a child of the devil (3:8; compare John 8:44). Part of the writer's apparent inconsistency may rest on his distinction between "mortal" sin, or "sin unto death" and ordinary sin (5:16). When brethren commit the latter they can be admonished. What counts as the more serious sin is not specified.

The concerns of First John also surface in the pericope of the adulteress (John 8:1-12), probably added to the Gospel some time in the 2nd cent., but still absent from many late antique manuscripts. The account of Jesus turning aside the murderous wrath of those who would stone the adulteress reinforces the forgiveness that was available through him, particularly in the kind of case that troubled the church in the 2nd cent. Against the rigorist position implied by Hebrews and resisted by First John, the *Shepherd of Hermas* had declared a new revelation, that forgiveness for post-baptismal sin, including adultery, was possible, at least once (*Herm. Vis.*, 5:7; *Herm. Mand.* 4.3.16). Such a position was viewed as dangerous laxity by teachers such as Tertullian, who called Hermas the "Shepherd of the adulterers" (*Pud.* 20).

A much different approach to sin appears in the book of Revelation, which has loose ties to the tradition of the Fourth Gospel and the Johannine Epistles. Language of "sin" is absent from the book, although there are numerous examples of sinful behavior. The initial messages to the churches of Asia Minor note what is most problematic for the seer: they "eat food sacrificed to idols and practice fornication" (Rev 2:14, 20). Communities that too readily cross the boundary with the world and participate in the rituals of their environment are in grave danger. The identification of "fornication" as the archetypical sin evokes the use of sexual imagery by prophets such as Hosea and Jeremiah for the idolatry they condemned. The inimical powers of evil, the great dragon, the beast from the sea, and the beast from the land, whose relationships are sketched in chaps. 12–13, are incarnate in political forces, of the Roman Empire (13:1-10) and its local aristocratic supporters in Asia Minor (13:11-18), who enforce "worship ... of the beast." Sexual imagery finally defines this power in the depiction of the whore of Babylon (17:3-6), a transparent symbol of Rome. Sin is ultimately to participate willingly in the realm dominated by this whore.

Revelation envisions a realm where the Beast's idolatrous power does not hold sway. It is at present the heavenly realm to which the seer has access (1:10; 4:1). That realm will be a future reality, when death is finally overcome (20:14). In the interim, the follower of Jesus can participate in the victory already won (11:15; 12:10) by exercising faithful endurance (13:9-10). The reality of God's victory over sinful powers may be experienced in the New Jerusalem that is already coming to earth, the "city" founded on the names of the apostles

(21:14). In that present and future sacral reality, where God and his Christ are present without the mediation of a temple (21:22), sinners are not allowed, neither "the cowardly, the faithless, the polluted, the murderers, the fornicators, the sorcerers, the idolaters, and all liars" (Rev 21:8). Through its vivid images, the book of Revelation forcefully expresses its version of the conviction that sin is incompatible with the Messianic community.

Bibliography: Gary A. Anderson and Saul M. Olyan, eds. *Priesthood and Cult in Ancient Israel* (1991); Mark E. Biddle. *Missing the Mark: Sin and Its Consequences in Biblical Theology* (2005); Timothy L. Carter. *Paul and the Power of Sin: Redefining "Beyond the Pale."* (2002); Tikva Frymer-Kensky. "Pollution, Purification, and Purgation in Biblical Israel." *The Word of the Lord Shall Go Forth: Essays in Honor of David Noel Freedman in Celebration of His Sixtieth Birthday.* Carol L. Meyers and M. O'Connor, eds. (1983) 399–414; Jonathan Klawans. *Impurity and Sin in Ancient Judaism* (2000); Patrick D. Miller Jr. *Sin and Judgment in the Prophets: A Stylistic and Theological Analysis* (1982); Jay Sklar. *Sin, Impurity, Sacrifice, Atonement: The Priestly Conceptions* (2005); K. van der Toorn. *Sin and Sanction in Israel and Mesopotamia: A Comparative Study* (1985); David P. Wright. *The Disposal of Impurity* (1987).

HAROLD W. ATTRIDGE

SIN, WILDERNESS OF sin [מִדְבַּר־סִין midhbar-sin]. The wilderness of Sin (not to be confused with the wilderness of Zin; *see* ZIN, WILDERNESS OF) is mentioned four times as part of the exodus itinerary (Exod 16:1; 17:1; Num 33:11, 12). The Israelites' complaints about food shortages result in the appearance of manna and quail in the WILDERNESS. Some scholars posit that the wilderness of Sin is on the southwestern edge of the Sinai plateau, in the vicinity of Debbet ar-Ramleh or the plain of el-Markha. Those who argue for a northern location for Mount Sinai, however, situate the wilderness of Sin in the general vicinity of mountains located in the Sinai peninsula, the Negev, and the land of Midian (*see* EXODUS, ROUTE OF; NEGEB, NEGEV; SINAI, MOUNT).

ALICE MANDELL

SINAI PENINSULA *si'ni.* The Sinai Peninsula is a large triangular desert region that lay east of ancient Egypt and south of Canaan. The Mediterranean coastal plain in the northern part of the peninsula formed a land bridge that connected northern Africa with southwest Asia, providing a major trade route between Egypt and other nations of the ANE.

The peninsula contains the six wilderness regions that are mentioned in the Israelites' journey through the wilderness from Egypt to Canaan: Shur (Exod 15:22), Etham (Exod 13:20; Num 33:6-8), Sin (Exod 16:1;

17:1; Num 33:11-12), Sinai (Exod 19:1; Num 10:12; 33:15), Paran (Num 10:12; 12:16; 13:3, 26), and Zin (Num 20:1; 33:36). Although the precise location of "the mountain of God" known as Mount Sinai or Horeb (Exod 3:1-2; 19:11, 18, 20) is disputed, some traditions point to its location in the mountainous southern region of the Sinai Peninsula. *See* SINAI, MOUNT.

Bibliography: G. I. Davies. "The Wilderness Itineraries and Recent Archaeological Research." *Studies in the Pentateuch.* J. A. Emerton, ed. (1990) 161–76.

DENNIS T. OLSON

SINAI, MOUNT si'ni [הַר סִינַי *har sinay*; ὄρος Σινᾶ *oros Sina*]. Mount Sinai is the mountain in the wilderness at which God appeared to the Israelites and gave them laws and a covenant on their way from Egypt to the promised land of Canaan in the books of Exodus, Leviticus, and Numbers.

A. The Names of "the Mountain"
B. Sinai, Horeb, and Their Diverse Traditions
C. Geographical Location of Sinai/Horeb
D. The Theological Meanings of Sinai/Horeb
Bibliography

A. The Names of "the Mountain"

Diverse biblical traditions within the Pentateuch refer to this one sacred mountain with various designations: "Mount Sinai" (sixteen times in Exodus–Numbers), "Sinai" (Deut 33:2, 16); "the mountain of God" (Exod 3:1; 4:27; 18:5; 24:13), "the mount of the LORD" (Num 10:33), "Mount Horeb" (har horev [הַר הֹורֵב]; Exod 33:6), "Horeb" (Exod 3:1; 17:6; 33:6; Deut 1:2, 6, 19; 4:10, 15; 5:2; 9:8; 18:16; 29:1), "Mount Paran" and "Seir" in poetic parallelism with "Sinai" (Deut 33:2), and most often simply "the mountain" (Exod 19:2, 3; 20:18; 24:4, 12; 32:1, 15; 34:3; etc.).

Outside the Pentateuch, the mountain is remembered as "Sinai" (Judg 5:5; Ps 68:8, 17; Jdt 5:14; Sir 48:7), "Mount Sinai" (Neh 9:13; 2 Esd 3:17; 14:4; Acts 7:30, 38; Gal 4:24, 25), and "Horeb" (1 Kgs 8:9//2 Chr 5:10; 1 Kgs 19:8; Ps 106:19; Mal 4:4).

B. Sinai, Horeb and Their Diverse Traditions

The Bible uses two different names, Sinai and Horeb, for the same "mountain of God," and there has been much debate about the reasons for the two names. Early interpreters suggested that perhaps the two names designated two different mountains within the same mountain range. Others surmised that one of the names was the name of a broader region while the other name was a specific mountain peak within that region. Others suggested that the two names were simply interchangeable for the same mountain.

Later, advocates of the so-called Documentary Hypothesis (JEDP) of the Pentateuch argued that the alternation between Sinai and Horeb is the result of dif-

ferent traditions that have been edited and combined in the present form of the Pentateuch. Thus, the so-called J (Yahwistic) and P (Priestly) traditions in Exodus–Numbers consistently prefer the name "Sinai." The E (Elohist) source in Exodus and the D (Deuteronomic) source in the book of Deuteronomy tend to use the name "Horeb."

More recently, some scholars have questioned whether a separate E (Elohist) source existed at all in the Pentateuch, proposing instead that places in the book of Exodus where the use of "Horeb" and other distinctive markers of what were once thought to be the Elohist tradition may instead be intrusions of a later D or Deuteronomic editor into the combined J and P version of the book of Exodus. Still others have argued that the sprinkling of references to "Horeb" in the book of Exodus was not done by a Deuteronomic editor. Rather, one or more late post-Priestly editors (a comprehensive Pentateuch editor in the postexilic period) sought to integrate the originally separate book of Deuteronomy (which used "Horeb" for the mountain of God's revelation) into the narrative structure of Exodus–Leviticus (which used "Sinai" for the mountain of God). This editorial integration was done by introducing the name "Horeb" at certain key junctures in Exodus alongside references to "Sinai," thereby helping to merge the identities of Sinai and Horeb.

C. Geographical Location of Sinai/Horeb

The precise location of Mount Sinai or Horeb has been a matter of considerable debate from ancient times to the present. At least twelve different mountains have been nominated as the location for Mount Sinai. Two main options have been suggested.

One proposal connects Mount Sinai with the region of "Midian" (Madian [Μαδιάν]; see Aquila, Symmachus, and Theodotion; Greek versions of the OT; or Madiam [Μαδιάμ]; Exod 18:1), a region or city located in northwest Arabia. This location lies east of the Sinai Peninsula, south and east of the land of Israel or Canaan. Madian/Madiam is an ancient city near a large set of mountains in northwest Arabia, so a number of early Jewish and Christian sources associated the biblical Mount Sinai in Midian with a tall mountain in that area of Arabia. The NT apostle Paul seems to reflect this tradition of identifying Sinai with Arabia (Gal 4:24-25). In the book of Exodus, Midian is the homeland of Jethro, Moses' father-in-law. Midian is the region where Moses was tending sheep when he encountered the burning bush at "Horeb, the mountain of God." Two other biblical texts in Judg 5:4-5 and Deut 33:2 connect Mount "Sinai" with the regions of Edom, Seir, and Mount Paran, which lie south and east of Canaan, also in northwest Arabia (modern-day southern Jordan and northern Saudi Arabia).

A second proposal is that Mount Sinai is located in the southern end of the relatively barren Sinai

Erich Lessing/Art Resource, NY
Figure 1: Saint Catherine's Monastery. Byzantine, 15th cent. CE. Mount Sinai, Sinai Desert, Egypt.

Peninsula, which lies just east of Egypt. This part of the peninsula contains the highest mountains of the region. This suggestion assumes that the Israelites took a southern route on the wilderness trek through the "wilderness of Sinai." Already in the 4th cent. CE, a number of Christian interpreters argued for this location. The early Christian monastery of Saint Catherine (first built around 530 CE) was established at the foot of a specific mountain called Jebel Musa (Arabic for "mountain of Moses"), which Christian monks and pilgrims identified as Mount Sinai; the monastery remains there to this day.

Certain biblical texts may support this location of Sinai/Horeb in the Sinai Peninsula rather than in Arabia. In Exod 3:18, Moses asks Pharaoh to let the Israelites go from Egypt on "a three days' journey into the wilderness" to sacrifice to God. Presumably the sacrifice was to occur at "Horeb, the mountain of God" where Moses first encountered God in the burning bush (Exod 3:1-2). A three days' journey from Egypt would land them only in the Sinai Peninsula, not as far east as Arabia. Deuteronomy 1:2 observes that it was an eleven-day journey from "Horeb" to the final wilderness campsite of Kadesh-barnea "by way of Mount Seir." This observation seems to assume that Mount Sinai/Horeb and Mount Seir (located in northwest Arabia and Edom) are not identical but are rather far apart from one another, supporting the more southern Sinai Peninsula as the proper location for the "mountain of God."

D. The Theological Meanings of Sinai/Horeb

In the ANE, mountains were often considered the special dwelling places of the gods. Their height and proximity to "the heavens," massive size and grandeur, enduring presence, and association with clouds, storms, and volcanoes symbolized the majesty, power, awe, and transcendence associated with the divine in the ancient world. Several different mountains appear throughout the Bible as special places of divine revelation or activity: Abraham's near-sacrifice of Isaac on Mount Moriah (Gen 22), God and Moses on Mount Nebo (Deut 34), the prophet Elijah's contest with the Baal prophets on Mount Carmel (1 Kgs 18:9-40), Jesus and his Sermon on the Mount (Matt 5–7), and the Mount of Transfiguration (Matt 17:1-13; Mark 9:2-8; Luke 9:28-36). However, the two most significant mountains related to God's relationship with Israel in the OT are 1) Mount Sinai (or Horeb), associated with Israel's wilderness wandering and receiving God's law and covenant, located outside the land of Israel, and 2) Mount Zion, located inside the land of Israel in Jerusalem and associated with God's election of the royal dynasty of King David and God's presence in the Temple (1 Kgs 8:1, 20-21; Pss 48:1-2; 74:2; 78:68; Isa 2:2-3; 40:9; 66:20; Dan 9:16; Joel 3:17; Mic 4:1). These two great sacred mountains of the Bible—Sinai and Zion—represent the complex interplay of law and promise in the theological imagination of biblical writers and post-biblical interpreters.

The mountain of Sinai/Horeb evokes several key themes in the biblical story of God, God's people, and

God's leaders. Exodus 3 and 1 Kgs 19 focus on Mount Horeb as assuring presence. The "mountain of God" makes its first biblical appearance as the place where God encounters Moses in a burning bush at the foot of Mount Horeb (Exod 3:1). There God calls Moses to lead the Israelites out of their slavery in Egypt. The majesty, holiness, and power of "the mountain of God" are paired in this encounter with the more intimate, nearer, and more accessible burning bush. Holy power (mountain) and divine intimacy (burning bush) combine to reassure Moses that God's power as well as God's close presence would support him on his mission.

In the last major biblical appearance of Horeb in 1 Kgs 19, the mountain again plays a role in balancing the demonstration of God's power and God's intimacy. A frightened prophet Elijah arrives at Mount Horeb and witnesses great signs of power in a mountain-splitting wind, an earthquake, and a fire. God, however, is not present in any of these displays of power. Instead, God passes by as the "sound of sheer silence," quietly reassuring Elijah to go back and resume his prophetic work in Israel.

The theme of Mount Sinai/Horeb as a foundational source of divine revelation is the focus of Exod 19–24 and Deut 4–5. Even though God "comes down" out of heaven to dwell "upon" Mount Sinai (Exod 19:11), God also maintains a distinction or boundary between God and the people. Only certain people can "come up" to God on the mountain. Some texts permit only Moses to "come up" (Exod 24:12). Another allows Moses and the high priest Aaron (Exod 19:24). Another tradition allows Moses, Aaron, Aaron's two sons, and seventy elders to go up (24:1). One verse permits all the people (not just the leaders) to "go up to the mountain" (Exod 19:13b). The dominant tradition, however, is that Moses alone speaks and interacts with God in a special relationship (Exod 33:17; Num 12:6-8; Deut 34:10-12). Moses must repeatedly (eight times in the book of Exodus) "go up" or "come up" the mountain (e.g., Exod 19:23; 24:1, 12; 32:30; 34:2).

Sinai is portrayed as the definitive place of God's revelation to Israel at the foundation of its life as a people. God's powerful but veiled presence on the mountain is marked by dazzling visual signs (thunder and lightning, black clouds, smoke, a volcanic shaking—Exod 19:16-19). Other traditions within Exod 19–24 focus less on these visual elements and more on the verbal speaking of God from the mountain, either speaking directly to the people in the Ten Commandments (Exod 20:1-21) or speaking through the mediation of Moses in the book of the covenant (Exod 20:22–23:33). In Deuteronomy, God remains "in heaven" rather than coming down on Mount Horeb. Instead, God is linked to the mountain by a column of divine "fire" leading from heaven to Mount Horeb, conducting God's heavenly word through Moses who stands between God and the Israelites (Deut 4:12, 15, 36; 5:5).

In Exod 20–31, the book of Leviticus, Num 1–10, and Deut 5–26, Sinai/Horeb appears as the single unifying source of ancient Israel's diverse law codes. Scholars agree that the Pentateuch contains a number of different legal collections that emerged from different groups in ancient Israel with their own histories, emphases, and theologies. These include the Ten Commandments (Exod 20:1-17; Deut 5:1-21), the book of the covenant (Exod 20:22–23:33), the tabernacle instructions (Exod 25:1–31:18), the cultic code (Exod 34:10-26), the Priestly Code regarding sacrifices, worship, and purity (Lev 1:1–18:30), the Holiness Code (Lev 19:1–26:46), the levitical code (Num 2:1–10:10), and the Deuteronomic Code (Deut 6:1–26:19). Yet this diverse legal material in Exodus–Numbers is presented as if given all at one and the same time by God to Moses at Mount Sinai.

At the same time, this definitive collection of Sinai legislation remains fluid and in need of supplements and interpretation. Additional laws continue to be revealed once Israel leaves Mount Sinai and embarks on its journey to the promised land (Num 15; 18:1–19:22; 27:1-11; 28:1–30:16; 35:1–36:13). As Israel's wilderness journey continues after leaving Sinai, the ark of the tabernacle and the tent of meeting replace the fixed mountain of Sinai as mobile vehicles of God's presence and sources for ongoing revelation and legal interpretation (Num 10:33-36; 27:2).

Exodus 32–34 views Mount Sinai as place of intercession and restoration of God's covenant with Israel. While Moses is with God on top of Mount Sinai, the Israelites construct a golden calf at the foot of the mountain and worship it in violation of the commandments against apostasy and idolatry. In response, God tells Moses that God intends to destroy Israel for their sin. However, Moses intercedes and convinces God to forgive them (Exod 32:1-24). Moses also convinces God to continue to dwell in the midst of the sinful Israelites as they travel from Sinai to the promised land (Exod 33:12–34:9). As a sign of the restored relationship between God and Israel, a new covenant is proclaimed and new stone tablets are written (Exod 34:10-28).

Bibliography: Th. Booij. "Mountain and Theophany in the Sinai Narrative." *Bib* 65 (1984) 1–26; G. I. Davies. *The Way of the Wilderness: A Geographical Study of the Wilderness Itineraries in the Old Testament* (1979); Allen Kerkeslager. "Mt. Sinai—in Arabia?" *BRev* 16 (2000) 32–39, 50; Jon Levenson. *Sinai and Zion: An Entry into the Jewish Bible* (1985); Baruch Schwartz. "What Really Happened at Mount Sinai?" *BRev* 13 (1997) 20–30, 46.

DENNIS T. OLSON

SINAITICUS, CODEX koh´deks sin´i-it´uh-kuhs. Codex Sinaiticus (designated by ℵ or S) was discovered in the 19th cent. by Constantine von Tischendorf at St. Catherine's Monastery in the Sinai peninsula (hence its

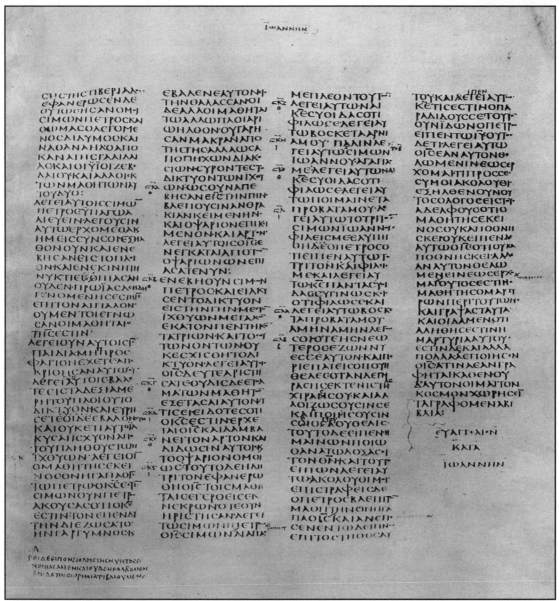

Figure 1: End of John 21:1-25, mid-4th cent CE. British Library, London, Great Britain.

name) and is one of the oldest copies of the Christian Bible in Greek. The codex was recovered by Tischendorf over a series of visits to St. Catherine's between 1844 and 1859. He published a facsimile edition in 1862.

The codex is made of vellum (sheepskin and goatskin) with pages measuring ca. 15 × 13.5 in. It has four columns per page (two in poetic books) with forty-eight lines per column and no spaces between words, accents, or breathing marks. The original manuscript consisted of ca. 730 leaves likely containing the entire Bible with Apocrypha, as well as the *Epistle of Barnabas* and the *Shepherd of Hermas*. There are ca. 405 leaves extant in four locations. 1) The British Museum has 347 leaves, 199 containing 1 Chr 9:27–11:22; Tob 2:2–14:15 (end); Jdt 1:1–11:13; 13:9–16:25 (end); 1 Maccabees; 4 Maccabees; Isaiah; Jer 1:1–10:25; Joel;

Obadiah; Jonah; Nahum; Habakkuk; Zephaniah; Haggai; Zechariah; Malachi; Psalms; Proverbs; Ecclesiastes; Song of Songs; Wisdom of Solomon; Sirach; Job; and 148 with the complete NT as well as *Barnabas* and *Hermas* (to *Mand.* 4.2.3). 2) The University Library at Leipzig has (as Codex Friderico-Augustanus) forty-three leaves containing 1 Chr 11:22–19:17; 2 Esd 9:9–23:31 [end]; Esther; Tob 1:1–2:2; Jer 10:25–52:34 [end]; Lam 1:1–2:20. 3) St. Catherine's Monastery reportedly has twelve leaves and fourteen fragments containing undisclosed portions of the Pentateuch. 4) Fragments of three leaves containing verses from Gen 23–24; Num 5–7; Jdt 11:13–13:9; and *Herm. Mand.* 2.7–3.2; 4.3.4–6 remain at the National Library in St. Petersburg.

The script is written in an iron compound ink with an unornamented uncial hand; recent scholarship has identified the work of three scribes and up to nine correctors. The majority of scholars date it to the mid-4th cent. CE on paleographical grounds. Three different locations have been posited for its origin: Rome, Alexandria, and Caesarea.

The character of the text, with its many corrections, is uneven. The extant portions of the OT tend to agree with Codex Vaticanus (*see* VATICANUS, CODEX), and are judged to contain superior readings in some books (e.g., 1 Chronicles, 2 Esdras, Isaiah). Similarly, the NT is of a high quality (with the exception of Revelation) and tends to agree with Vaticanus (especially the Gospels and Acts).

In 2006 the Institute for Textual Scholarship and Electronic Editing at the University of Birmingham, in cooperation with the British Library and the three other holding libraries, began a project to produce a new facsimile of the entire codex, as well as an online edition and other tools. *See* SEPTUAGINT; TEXT, NT; VERSIONS, ANCIENT.

Bibliography: James Bentley. *Secrets of Mount Sinai* (1986); Helen and Kirsopp Lake. *Codex Sinaiticus Petropolitanus* (1911–22); Bruce Metzger. *Manuscripts of the Greek Bible* (1981); J. M. Milne and T. C. Skeat. *Scribes and Correctors of the Codex Sinaiticus* (1938); J. M. Milne and T. C. Skeat. *The Codex Sinaiticus and the Codex Alexandrinus* (1955); T. C. Skeat. *The Collected Biblical Writings of T.C. Skeat* (2004).

TYLER F. WILLIAMS

SINCERITY [תָּמִים tamim; ἀληθής alēthēs, ἀνυπόκριτος anypokritos, εἰλικρίνεια eilikrineia]. The quality or condition of being genuine, pure, or true (Wis 7:25; 1 Cor 5:8; 2 Cor 1:12; 2 Pet 3:1). Etymologically the word means "tested by the light of the sun," a fascinating image to consider when reading 2 Cor 2:17 *b*, where Paul insists that he and his coworkers "speak as persons of sincerity, as persons sent from God and standing in his presence." The ensuing discussion asserts that the old covenant that derived from God's presence has been completely surpassed by the new (3:1–4:6). However, Paul's underlying concern is still the defense of his own godly sincerity introduced in 1:12, arguably the thesis of the letter. Philippians 1:17 reflects a related concern that Christ might not be proclaimed sincerely (ἀγνῶς hagnōs).

Sincerity and its cognates are also sometimes used to translate various other Hebrew and Greek terms pertaining to being "genuine" (Josh 24:14; 3 Macc 3:19, 23; 2 Cor 8:8; Phil 2:20; 1 Tim 1:5; 2 Tim 1:5; 1 Pet 2:1), "pure" (Job 33:3; Wis 1:1), and "true" (Tob 8:7; 14:7; Wis 6:17; Matt 22:16; Mark 12:14; 2 Cor 11:3). *See* HONESTY.

MARK D. GIVEN

SINEW [גִּיד gidh; νεῦρον neuron]. The connective tissue in the body joining muscle to bone (4 Macc 7:13; 9:28).

In Job 10:11 and Ezek 37:6-8, the addition of sinews is envisioned as a stage in the fashioning of a human body. In a variation on the metaphor of a stubborn person as "stiff-necked" (e.g., Exod 32:9), Isaiah states that the hard-hearted Israelites have an "iron sinew" in their neck (48:4). It has been suggested that *sinew* is a euphemism for the genitalia in the description of Behemoth (Job 40:17).

Colossians 2:19 admonishes against "not holding fast to the head," Christ, "from whom the whole body, nourished and held together by its ligaments and sinews, grows with a growth that is from God."

ANDREW Y. LEE

SINGERS, SINGING, SONG. *See* MUSIC; WORSHIP, EARLY JEWISH.

SINITES sin'īt [סִינִי sini; Ἀσενναῖον Asennaion]. Designation for a people group and a geographic region. This term appears in extra-biblical texts in Ugaritic (syn) and in Neo-Assyrian (sianum), which situate this region in modern-day Syria. The Sinites are mentioned in the Table of Nations (Gen 10:17; 1 Chr 1:15) among the eleven peoples descending from Canaan—all are situated in Asia Minor, the northern Levant, and the southern Levant.

The "land of the Sinites" is mentioned in Isa 49:12 (NRSV, "Syene"; NRSV gives the Hebrew "Sinim" in a note), which narrates the return of the exiles, though by this time its whereabouts are ambiguous, being either north or on the coast of Israel. The land of the Sinites may have been equated with SYENE in Ezek 29:10 and 30:6 (compare Syēnēs [Συήνης] in LXX Ezek 30:6), modern-day Aswan, the site of the Jewish settlement at Elephantine during the 6th–5th cent. BCE. The LXX, however, understands the land of the Sinites to be in the east and substitutes "Sinites" in Isa 49:12 with "the land of the Persians."

ALICE MANDELL

SINNER. *See* SIN, SINNERS.

SIPHMOTH sif'moth [שִׁפְמוֹת sifmoth]. A village in Judah where David sent some of the spoils taken during his Amalekite campaigns (1 Sam 30:28; see "Shiphmite" in 1 Chr 27:27). The location is unknown.

SIPPAI. *See* SAPH.

SIPPOR, TEL. A small archaeological site 3 km northwest of the Philistine site of Gath. Three seasons of excavations at the site in the mid-1960s revealed occupation in the Middle and Late Bronze ages, as well as Iron Age I. By the beginning of the 10th cent. BCE, the site had been abandoned. The excavations also yielded figurines from the Persian period and a cache of coins from the Hellenistic period. The Iron I layers contained a good amount of Philistine pottery, although a few Israelite cultural remains were found alongside Philistine elements in the latest layer. Tel Sippor has not been identified with any of the towns mentioned in the Bible. The excavators have characterized the site as a small cult center or gathering place.

KEVIN A. WILSON

SIRACH sí′ruhk [Σιράχ *Sirach*]. This long wisdom writing (sometimes called Ecclesiasticus) was composed in Hebrew in Jerusalem by a scribe named Ben Sira in the early 2nd cent. BCE. Because it was included in the SEPTUAGINT but excluded from the rabbinic canon (*see* CANON OF THE OLD TESTAMENT), it is classed as one of the Apocrypha (or deuterocanonical books; *see* APOCRYPHA, DEUTEROCANONICAL). The work combines theological and practical teaching on many topics, ranging from the fear of God and divine retribution, to friendship and conduct at banquets.

    A. Name of the Book
    B. Structure and Outline
    C. Background
       1. Context of the author
       2. Literary influences
    D. Textual Transmission
    E. Religious Significance
       1. Theological thought
       2. Social ethics
       3. Place in the wisdom tradition
       4. Links with the New Testament
       5. Usage in Judaism and Christianity
       6. Religious value for modern readers
    Bibliography

A. Name of the Book

The name of this work is confusing for beginners. While the original Hebrew title is uncertain, the book is generally called the Wisdom of Ben Sira. The short Greek name for the work is Sirach, and the Latin designation is Ecclesiasticus (not to be confused with the briefer canonical wisdom book named Ecclesiastes or Qoheleth). The author's Hebrew name is usually thought to be Jeshua Ben (son of) Sira, which in the Greek translation became Jesus son of Sirach (50:27). For convenience, this article will employ the name Ben Sira for the author and Sirach for the book.

B. Structure and Outline

The structure of Sirach is provided by eight poems focusing on finding wisdom (1:1-10; 4:11-19; 6:18-37; 14:20–15:10; 24:1-34; 32:14–33:18; 38:24–39:11; 44:1-15). These poems are often seen as introducing the eight major sections of 1:1–50:24. The book ends with postscripts (50:25-29) and appendices (51:1-30). The grandson's prologue explains his reasons for translating the book from Hebrew to Greek, probably in Alexandria.

After the prologue, Part 1 (1:1–4:10) concerns "Understanding Wisdom." All wisdom is a gift from the Lord, available to his friends (1:1-10). The fear of the Lord (involving the devout following of your conscience) is the beginning and fullness of wisdom (1:11-30). God's servants must be prepared for testing, but can hope for a merciful deliverance (2:1-18). Honoring parents may involve caring for them if they lose their faculties, but such action atones for your sins (3:1-16). Do not seek things beyond you (perhaps the cosmological speculations of Greek philosophy or the apocalyptic traditions about Enoch), but attend to what has been revealed, namely, the Torah (3:17-29). Proper social responsibility includes care of the widow and orphan (3:30–4:10).

Part 2 (4:11–6:17) deals with "Applying Wisdom Personally." Pursuing wisdom will produce rewards, but only after the student has been tested (4:11-19). Be ashamed of sinful deeds, but not of speaking the truth (4:20-31). Do not delay to turn away from sin, because both grace and wrath can come from God (5:1-8). Be careful of your words, because the tongue can bring either honor or dishonor (5:9–6:4). Be cautious in choosing friends, but value a faithful friend (6:5-17).

Part 3 (6:18–14:19) considers "Applying Wisdom Socially." The search for wisdom involves hard work, but will produce a great harvest (6:18-37). Be humble in your dealings with others (7:1-17). Social responsibilities apply to friends and family members, but also to the temple priests and the poor (7:18-36). Be careful in your dealings with the authorities and with difficult people (8:1-19). Beware of loose women (9:1-9). Choose wise and God-fearing friends (9:10-16). Adopt a humble attitude, since God overturns the proud (9:17–10:18). True honor consists in fearing God who can raise up the wise and humble (10:19–11:6). Trust in the providence of God, who can enrich the poor but also punish on the day of death (11:7-28). Beware of befriending a slanderer, who can disrupt your household (11:29-34). Do good deeds for a good person, but not for a sinner (12:1-7). A false friend will pretend to be benevolent but will end up mocking you (12:8-18). The rich can use their power to mistreat and exploit the poor, so real friendship between rich and poor is impossible (13:1-23). Earthly wealth does not last, so make the most of it by treating yourself well (13:24–14:19).

Part 4 (14:20–23:27) concerns "Applying Wisdom to Speech and Thought." The student (presumably male) who courts wisdom assiduously will encounter her as a bride and a mother (14:20–15:10). Human beings, endowed with free will, are invited to make the right choices (15:11-20). Do not rejoice in a large number of children unless they fear the Lord (16:1-4). God is able to punish sinners, as has happened during Israel's history (16:5-23). The Creator of the world decreed tasks for all his works (16:24-30). God created human beings to praise him, and gives them a limited lifespan on earth (17:1-14). The Lord recompenses human conduct and welcomes back the repentant (17:15-24). Glorify God while on earth, because those in the netherworld can no longer offer praise (17:25-32). Being far greater than human beings, the Creator is merciful to them (18:1-14). Be wise, humble, and generous (18:15-29). Control your bodily appetites (18:30–19:3). Instead of repeating an accusation, question a friend to see if it is true (19:4-17). Proper wisdom involves keeping the Torah, whereas the cleverness of the wicked is not real wisdom (19:20-30). The sensible person stays quiet till it is time to speak (20:1-8). Some people mistakenly expect to be rewarded for their generosity (20:9-17). Avoid saying false things, but do not hide wisdom (20:18-31). Flee from sin as from a poisonous snake (21:1-10). The words of the wise bring life, but a fool's chatter is burdensome (21:11-22). It is a waste of time speaking to a fool, who will not heed wisdom (22:1-18). Instead of betraying a friend, remain faithful (22:19-26). Avoid guilt by keeping control over your tongue and your passions (22:27–23:27).

Part 5 (24:1–32:13) deals with "Applying Wisdom to Household Life." The wisdom pervading the cosmos came to dwell in Zion, and is expressed in the book of the Torah (24:1-34). Among the ten good things in life, the greatest is the fear of the Lord, more important even than wisdom (25:1-11). While a good wife benefits her husband, an evil wife causes him all kinds of distress (25:13–26:27). Whereas the righteous speak wisely, the conversation of fools is offensive (26:28–27:15). Betraying secrets brings friendship to an end (27:16-21). Harm rebounds on the one who practices it (27:22-29). Forgive your neighbor, so that God will forgive you (27:30–28:7). Beware of the quarrelsome, who stir up trouble like a fire (28:8-26). It is a kindness to help your neighbor by loans, charitable gifts, or serving as guarantor, but be aware that you may not recover your money (29:1-20). Be content with a moderate lifestyle (29:21-28). Treat a child with firm discipline rather than overindulgence (30:1-13). Health is important and can be helped by a cheerful attitude (30:14-25). Wealth can be an obstacle for the rich (31:1-11). Enjoy food and wine at banquets, but show good manners and a humble attitude (31:12–32:13).

Part 6 (32:14–38:23) considers "Using Wisdom to Make Good Decisions." True guidance comes from God, whose providence raises some people and brings down others (32:14–33:18). Keep control of your property, and be strict with your servants (33:19-33). Whereas dreams and divination are untrustworthy, experience is more reliable, but most beneficial is fear of the Lord (34:1-20). Religious actions like sacrifice are unacceptable if the rights of the poor are trampled upon (34:21-31). A generous sacrifice shows gratitude for God's kindness (35:1-13). The God of justice will intervene like a warrior to break the power of the wicked (35:14-26). Ben Sira prays for God to deliver the tribes of Jacob and to destroy their enemies (36:1-22). Discernment is needed in choosing food, a wife, friends, and advisors

(36:23–37:15). One who uses wisdom to serve his people wins everlasting honor (37:16-26). Avoid ill-health by moderation in eating (37:27-31). Accept the help of a medical doctor when sick, but also pray for healing (38:1-15). When mourning for the dead, do so moderately (38:16-23).

Part 7 (38:24–43:33) concerns "Demonstrating the Results of Wisdom." While society needs skilled manual workers, the scribe can with God's help achieve everlasting fame by his wisdom (38:24–39:11). God's good creation helps the virtuous but turns evil for the wicked (39:12-35). Human life has its share of miseries, but righteousness endures forever (40:1-17). The fear of God is better than other things that make life pleasant (40:18-27). Begging is worse than death (40:28-30). Although death is not wanted by the healthy, it can be welcomed by the very ill (41:1-4). Whereas sinners leave a bad reputation, a good name lasts forever (41:5-15). Some forms of conduct deserve shame, but there is no disgrace in following the Torah (41:16–42:8). A father is worried about his unmarried daughter (42:9-14). God deserves praise for his marvelous works in creation, such as sun and moon, stars and rainbow, storms and snow (42:15–43:33).

Part 8 (44:1–50:24), the "Praise of the Ancestors," is a single extended poem that celebrates devout leaders from Israel's history. The introduction states that this poem will praise various ancestors who gained lasting glory by their wise conduct (44:1-15). According to the Greek text, Enoch was taken up to heaven as an example of repentance (44:16). Righteous Noah was granted the covenantal promise that God would never send another great flood (44:17-19). Because of his fidelity under testing, Abraham received a covenant from God to give him many descendants, including Isaac and Jacob (44:20-23). Moses was the recipient of the life-giving Torah (45:1-5). Aaron received the glorious office of the priesthood, which he passed to his descendants (45:6-22). Aaron's grandson Phinehas was granted the eternal covenant to maintain the sanctuary (45:23-26). Joshua and Caleb led the Israelites into the promised land (46:1-10). Those judges who were faithful have left an eternal name (46:11-12). The prophet Samuel called for help from God, who answered him (46:13-20). King David defended his people and devoted himself to the worship of God (47:1-11). Although King Solomon was famed for his wisdom and temple building, he blotted his honor by his liaisons with women and thereby caused the division of the kingdom in the days of his son (47:12-25). The prophet Elijah burned with zeal for God, and was taken up into heaven (48:1-11). Elisha the prophet worked twice as many miracles as Elijah (48:12-16). King Hezekiah and the prophet Isaiah obeyed God, and in their day Jerusalem was delivered from the Assyrian attack (48:17-25). Whereas King Josiah followed God wholeheartedly, the sins of other kings led to the fall of Jerusalem, as the prophet Jeremiah had warned (49:1-7). Ezekiel, Job, and the Twelve Prophets are briefly mentioned (49:8-10). Praiseworthy were Zerubbabel, Jeshua, and Nehemiah for their reconstruction after the exile (49:11-13). Notable among the early patriarchs were Enoch and Joseph, but most important was Adam (49:14-16). At the climax of the extended poem, the recently deceased high priest Simeon the Just is praised as the glory of his people, especially when celebrating the temple liturgy (50:1-24).

Sirach concludes with postscripts and appendices (50:25–51:30). There is an unflattering postscript on Judah's neighbors (50:25-26) and an indication of the book's authorship (50:27-29). The work ends with Ben Sira's thanksgiving psalm for personal deliverance (51:1-12) and an alphabetic poem on his search for wisdom (51:13-30). Between these last two poems the medieval Hebrew text adds a litany of uncertain authorship, patterned after Ps 136 (51:12*i-xvi*).

C. Background

1. Context of the author

Because the poem praising Simeon II (50:1-24) uses phrases such as "in his days" (50:3), it was probably written after the death of this high priest around 196 BCE, so this is the book's earliest possible date. On the other hand, the lack of reference to the religious turmoil (1 Macc 1:10-64) that followed the accession of the Seleucid king Antiochus IV Epiphanes (175–164) suggests 175 BCE as the latest possible date for the book. A date between 195–175 BCE also fits the grandson's statement in the prologue to his Greek translation: "I came to Egypt in the thirty-eighth year of the reign of Euergetes [= 132 BCE] and stayed for some time."

Almost certainly, Jerusalem was the place where Ben Sira composed his Hebrew work, since the city plays a major role in his book, and the Greek text of 50:27 calls him "the Jerusalemite." The praise of the high priest Simeon II describes repairs to the Temple and city walls (50:1-4) and gives a detailed account of the temple service (50:5-21). Ben Sira also prays for God to save the holy city of Jerusalem (36:18-19) with the words: "Have mercy upon us" (36:1). Furthermore, the wisdom that he celebrates in 24:1-29 comes to dwell in Jerusalem (24:10-11).

The society in which Ben Sira lived had felt the influence of Greek culture ever since Alexander the Great's conquest of Palestine from the Persian Empire in 332 BCE. In the 3rd and early 2nd cent. BCE the land of Israel was under the control of Hellenistic rulers, first the Ptolemies of Egypt (301–200 BCE) and thereafter the Seleucids of Syria. King Antiochus III conquered Palestine for the Seleucid Empire at the Battle of Panium around 200 BCE. At first, the people of Jerusalem welcomed Antiochus III, who issued a decree reducing taxation on the city, but after the Peace of Apamea (188 BCE) the Seleucid overlords levied further taxes. Since Greek culture predominated in civil life, those Jews who wished to gain advancement were tempted to abandon their ancestral faith (Sir 41:8) and follow the ways of the pagan ruling power, particularly after 175 BCE (1 Macc 1:11-15).

Chronological Table
332: Alexander the Great's conquest of Palestine
301: Egyptian Ptolemies take control of Palestine
ca. 245: Ben Sira's birth
219–196: High priesthood of Simeon II
217: Ptolemy IV's victory over Seleucid Antiochus III at battle of Raphia
200–198: Syrian Seleucids conquer Palestine
ca. 198: Decree of victorious Seleucid king Antiochus III
196–174: High priesthood of Onias III
ca. 195–175: Completion of Ben Sira's book and death of Ben Sira
175: Accession of Seleucid king Antiochus IV Epiphanes
167–164: Maccabean revolt against Antiochus Epiphanes
132: Arrival of Ben Sira's grandson in Egypt
ca. 117–100: Grandson's publication of Greek translation

Ben Sira evidently ran an educational establishment in Jerusalem ("house of instruction" in 51:23), and we can view the description of the scribe in 39:1-11 as a self-portrait of the author. Perhaps he belonged to the "scribes of the temple" mentioned by Josephus (*Ant.* 12.3.3 §142). Although the book includes long passages on priestly figures (Aaron, Phinehas, Simeon II), it is uncertain if Ben Sira himself was a priest. His widespread traveling (34:9-13) may indicate that on occasions he was a diplomat or court advisor (38:33; 39:4). Although in 24:33 he sees his ministry as prophetic, elsewhere he regards himself not as one of the earlier biblical prophets, but rather as a gleaner gathering fruits left behind by previous harvesters (33:16-17).

The sage directs his words to young men (9:1-9; 36:26-31; 42:9-14) whom he often addresses individually as "my child" (e.g., Sir 3:12, 17; 4:1), following a tradition among wisdom teachers (e.g., Prov 1:10; 2:1; 3:1). His purpose was to educate these students to become leaders of Israelite society. While some were doubtless training to be temple scribes (38:34), others were probably aspiring to be civil servants (8:8; 39:4). The sage presumes that a student could soon have servants and livestock, as well as a wife and children (7:19-26). He points out that a wise civil servant can come to serve before kings (11:1; 39:4). He also expects some of his students to travel, perhaps as diplomats, as he himself had traveled (34:12; 39:4). Although his students were probably from the upper class, he warns them against the unbridled pursuit of wealth (31:5-7) and urges them to care for the poor (4:1-10).

2. Literary influences

Sirach's ideas and language show familiarity with earlier biblical writings. Indeed, the first part of the Praise of the Ancestors alludes to passages from the five books of the Torah (44:17–45:26). The following section (46:1–49:10) refers in the order of the Hebrew Bible canon to passages from the eight books of the Former and Latter Prophets, up to the Twelve Prophets in Sir 49:10.

Sirach's Use of Torah and Prophets
Sir 44:17-23: Genesis
Sir 45:1-13: Exodus
Sir 45:14-17: Leviticus
Sir 45:18-20: Numbers
Sir 45:21-22: Deuteronomy
Sir 46:1-10: Joshua
Sir 46:11-12: Judges
Sir 46:13–47:11: 1–2 Samuel
Sir 47:12–48:16: 1–2 Kings
Sir 48:17-25: Isaiah
Sir 49:5-7: Jeremiah
Sir 49:8: Ezekiel
Sir 49:10: Twelve Prophets

Since the final part of the Hebrew biblical canon (the Writings) was still unfinished in Ben Sira's time, his references to it are incomplete. Nevertheless, he mentions Job (49:9) and refers to David's provision of psalms for divine worship (47:9-10; compare 1 Chr 16:4). The sage speaks of the postexilic figures of Zerubbabel, Jeshua, and Nehemiah (Sir 49:11-13), but surprisingly makes no reference to Ezra. While his work shows similar concerns to Qoheleth, some of his clearest biblical allusions are to the book of Proverbs, as we see from a comparison of Sir 24 with Prov 8 (both poems of 36 lines).

Sirach 24 Parallels with Proverbs 8
Wisdom revealed to humankind (Sir 24:1-2; Prov 8:1-3)
Wisdom's first-person speech (Sir 24:3-22; Prov 8:4-36)
Wisdom existing from creation (Sir 24:3-6; Prov 8:22-31)
Wisdom above and below earth (Sir 24:5; Prov 8:27)
Wisdom formed before all else (Sir 24:9; Prov 8:22)
Warning to heed wisdom (Sir 24:22; Prov 8:36)

The beginning and ending of Sirach show some affinities to the book of Proverbs. The theological poems in Sir 1–2 have a general similarity to Prov 1–2. Thus, Sir 1:14 recalls Prov 1:7: "The fear of the LORD is the beginning of knowledge" (compare Prov 9:10). Moreover, the poem on the fear of the Lord in Sir 1:11-30 (including 1:21) follows the 22-line pattern of Prov 2:1-22, which mentions the fear of God (Prov 2:5). The conclusion of Sirach is also reminiscent of the end of the book of Proverbs, since both works close with an

alphabetic acrostic poem (twenty-two lines in Prov 31:10-31; twenty-three lines in Sir 51:13-30). While Prov 31:10-31 praises the "capable wife" or "valiant woman," Ben Sira celebrates the female figure of Wisdom as (by implication) the truly "capable wife" whom his young male students should seek.

Sirach also reflects some ideas found in Greek literature. While opposing Greek polytheism (1:8), Ben Sira shows the influence of Hellenistic culture in his valuing of friendship, banquets, and travel. His doctrine of a balance of paired opposites echoes the teaching of the Stoic philosopher Chrysippus, while there is a Stoic ring to his dictum about God: "He is the all" (43:27). The need for leisure to acquire wisdom (38:24) matches the view of Aristotle (*Metaph.* I.i.18 §981b), while Ben Sira's contrast between friendship for utility and friendship based on virtue (6:5-17; 9:10-16) is also reminiscent of the teaching of Aristotle (*Eth. nic.* 8–9). The importance of the Logos or word in human society (Sir 37:16-18) is highlighted in Isocrates' praise of the Logos (*Antid.* 253–57; *Nic.* 5–9). Although some of Ben Sira's sayings are reminiscent of Greek authors (e.g., Euripides, Xenophon, Hesiod, and Isocrates), a literary dependence is hard to prove, and some of these parallels may have arisen simply because the sage inhabited a Hellenized cultural world. While it is uncertain how he could have become acquainted with various foreign writings, the Egyptian city of Alexandria, with its huge library of Greek texts, was not too distant for him to have visited on his travels (34:9-13). Ben Sira is content to use any wise insights, regardless of whether they derive from Israel's Scriptures or whether they were first uttered by a Greek.

The closest parallels are with the elegiac verse of the 6th-cent. BCE Greek poet Theognis. Such parallels concern social dealings: caution in friendship (Sir 6:5-17; Theognis 61–82 and 115–28); forgiveness (Sir 10:6; Theognis 323–26); discrimination in social relations (Sir 12:1-18; Theognis 93–114); and proper behavior at banquets and sensible wine drinking (Sir 31:12–32:13; Theognis 467–510). Some theological resemblances occur, such as the belief in the divine determination of fortune (Sir 11:10-19; Theognis 165–72; 585–90) and the call to take earthly enjoyment (Sir 14:16; Theognis 1070 A–B).

It is likely that Ben Sira is also influenced, directly or indirectly, by some Egyptian writings. Most clearly, 38:24–39:11 draws on the ancient Egyptian Satire on the Trades, praising the scribal profession in comparison with manual occupations. In addition, Ben Sira's work has some echoes of other Egyptian instructions (Ptahhotep, Amenemope, and Ankhsheshonq). Further passages are reminiscent of a demotic Egyptian wisdom writing known as Papyrus Insinger. For instance, among a list of things where "small is beautiful," the Egyptian text mentions the bee: "The little bee brings the honey" (Papyrus Insinger 25.2), which is reminiscent of Sir 11:3: "The bee is small among flying creatures, but what it produces is the best of sweet things." The Egyptian writing also warns: "He who does harm for harm, his old age will be harmed" (Papyrus Insinger 33.20), which offers the same message as Sir 7:1: "Do no evil, and evil will never overtake you." Other parallel thoughts include the value of using medicine (Sir 38:4; Papyrus Insinger 24.2; 32.12) and the pointlessness of being miserly (Sir 14:3-10; Papyrus Insinger 17.4-8).

D. Textual Transmission

For many centuries, the Hebrew text of Sirach was unknown, except for a few rabbinic quotations. The original Hebrew had been lost because the rabbinic canon had excluded the book, although some rabbis continued to refer to it. The grandson's Greek translation, however, passed into Christian usage because of its presence in the Septuagint. The Cairo Genizah manuscripts, copied in the 10th–12th cent. CE, survived because they were the work of a non-rabbinic Jewish grouping (the Karaites). Worn-out Hebrew manuscripts were placed in the storeroom (Genizah) of the synagogue at Old Cairo, where they were rediscovered in 1896. As a result, we now have six Genizah manuscripts covering about two-thirds of Sirach, though they contain many textual corruptions. However, the Hebrew text is missing for 1:1–3:5 and most of 16:27–30:10.

Half a century after the first Cairo Genizah discoveries, much older texts of Sirach were found at Qumran among the Dead Sea Scrolls. In 1952, excavators in Cave 2 discovered small late 1st-cent. BCE fragments of Sir 6. Then in 1956, discoveries in Cave 11 included the great Psalms scroll (early 1st cent. CE), a liturgical collection containing half of Ben Sira's concluding poem on wisdom (51:13-20). Most significantly, however, a scroll was found at Masada in 1964 containing parts of six chapters of Sirach (39:27–44:17). This manuscript dates from the early 1st cent. BCE, barely a hundred years after the original composition.

Before 1896, the book was mainly known from the grandson's Greek version, preserved in important LXX manuscripts, though the text was also transmitted in Latin and Syriac translations. The Latin version, predating Jerome (d. 420 CE), was used for ethical instruction of Christian converts (hence the name Ecclesiasticus or "Church Book"), but originally it lacked chaps. 44–50. The Syriac version, translated from Hebrew but including a few Christian alterations, was included in the Syriac Bible. While the ancient translations convey Ben Sira's general message, we now know that each version makes some changes and additions to the original Hebrew work. For example, the Hebrew text of 41:11 says: "The human body is a fleeting thing, but a virtuous name will never be blotted out." By contrast, the Greek version has: "People grieve over the death of the body, but the bad name of sinners will be blotted out." This change may have been motivated by the Greek translator's belief in the afterlife, a belief not shared by Ben Sira himself.

Accordingly, a major problem faced by students of Sirach is the question of the text. Because the work was not considered canonical by rabbinic Jews, it was not preserved with the care accorded to the MT of the Hebrew Bible. From a careful use of published editions, the researcher needs to establish whether a particular form of the text of Sirach derives from the original Hebrew author, or from the grandson's Greek translation, or from a subsequent addition. For example, Sir 1:1-10 consists of eight verses in the NRSV, which omits vv. 5 and 7 from the main text because they are not in the earliest manuscripts (see NRSV footnotes there). The Greek version serves as the basis of the NRSV translation because it covers all fifty-one chapters, whereas only two-thirds of the Hebrew text has survived. However, all Greek manuscripts of Sirach disrupt the sense by exchanging 30:25–33:16a with 33:16b–36:13, so the NRSV restores the correct order found in the Hebrew (hence the verse numbers 36:14-15 do not represent any actual text).

In the course of time, scribes copying the Hebrew and Greek manuscripts added extra lines, which sometimes came to be included in the verse numbering. These later Jewish or Christian scribal additions were made to update Ben Sira's teaching, such as by inserting references to life after death. For instance, the Hebrew original of Sirach has no clear expectation of an afterlife (Sir 10:11; 14:16; 17:27-28), and its text of 7:17 (NRSV footnote) speaks of the decay of a human corpse buried in the ground after death: "The expectation of mortals is worms." But to supply a reference to punishment after death, the Greek version reads: "The punishment of the ungodly is fire and worms" (compare Jdt 16:17; Mark 9:48). Thus, the grandson's Greek translation, like other Septuagintal books (Wis 3:1-9; 2 Macc 7:9-23), follows Dan 12:1-3 in expressing belief in an afterlife.

E. Religious Significance
1. Theological thought

In comparison with earlier writings, Ben Sira's work makes several theological advances. It is the first book to integrate the Jewish theologies of law, wisdom, creation, history, and prophecy. Whereas Israel's legal and sapiential traditions had previously been somewhat apart, Ben Sira draws them together, equating wisdom with the Torah (24:23; compare Bar 3:36–4:1), or perhaps more accurately, seeing the Torah as the embodiment of divine wisdom (compare Deut 4:6). Similarly, while Israel's previous creation theology had sometimes been separate from its understanding of history, Ben Sira follows Ps 136 and Neh 9:6-37 in referring to the creation and then God's mighty deeds in Israel's history, since he places his poem on God's marvels in creation (42:15–43:33) immediately before his praise of the Israelite ancestors from Noah to the high priest Simeon II (44:1–50:24). Whereas earlier Jewish wisdom literature (Job, Proverbs, Qoheleth) built on its international heritage by having few references to Israel's history (apart from Solomon, mentioned in Prov 1:1 and implied in Qoh 1:1), Ben Sira deliberately includes a long section celebrating heroes from the nation's past. In addition, his teaching also incorporates elements of the prophetic tradition, such as calls to repentance (17:25-26) and pleas for social justice (34:21-31). Underlying his wide-ranging vision is his belief that "all wisdom is from the Lord" (1:1). Furthermore, Ben Sira does not separate secular and religious activities, since his book treats both banquets (31:12–32:13) and the law of God (32:14-24).

As heir to Israel's wisdom tradition, Ben Sira offers teaching on how to understand the world and make progress in life. However, in his view real wisdom is not separate from showing true respect to God or obeying the commandments: "The whole of wisdom is fear of the Lord, and in all wisdom there is the fulfillment of the law" (19:20). Thus, cleverness without virtue is not really wisdom at all (19:24). Rather, the fear of God, wisdom, and the Law together provide guidance for right living and a happy life (1:26-27; 9:14-16; 21:11). Fear of God is not to be regarded as the opposite of love of God, but rather they are parallel qualities (Sir 2:15-16, echoing Deut 10:12-13). Hence the sage draws on the earlier scriptures to assert that wisdom begins with fearing the Lord (Sir 1:14; Prov 1:7; 9:10; Ps 111:10). By means of the biblical theme of the fear of God, Ben Sira brings various aspects of social ethics, dealing with matters of everyday life (6:16; 25:11; 27:3), into the realm of Israelite religion.

According to Ben Sira, God is Maker of the world (16:26-30; 42:15–43:33) as well as Creator of human beings (17:1-14). The sage speaks of God's choice of the people of Israel (24:12; 37:25) and his placing of wisdom in Jerusalem (24:10-11). The Praise of the Ancestors celebrates seven pentateuchal patriarchs with whom God made or renewed a covenant (44:17–45:26), then a series of Israelite leaders from Joshua to Nehemiah (46:1–49:13), and finally a contemporary high priest, Simeon the Just (50:1-24). As in Israel's earlier traditions (Exod 34:6-7), God is capable of both mercy and anger (5:6; 16:11). Ben Sira follows the Deuteronomic system of retribution (Deut 30:15-18), whereby good conduct is rewarded and bad behavior is punished (Sir 15:11-20; 17:20-24), though God is merciful to those who repent (17:29).

Ben Sira gives special attention to questions of THEODICY (16:1-23; 33:7-15; 39:12-35). Among Israel's wisdom writers, his particular contribution is his doctrine of balanced opposing pairs: "Good is the opposite of evil, and life the opposite of death; so the sinner is the opposite of the godly. Look at all the works of the Most High; they come in pairs, one the opposite of the other" (Sir 33:14-15; compare 42:24-25). Here Ben Sira reflects the teaching of a contemporary Stoic philosopher, Chrysippus (d. ca. 207 BCE), who wrote that good and evil were necessary

opposites (*On Providence* 4). This solution to the problem of theodicy makes God the source of evil as well as good (Isa 45:7). Elsewhere the sage refines his thought: "From the beginning good things were created for the good, but for sinners good things and bad. The basic necessities of human life ... are good for the godly, but for sinners they turn into evils" (Sir 39:25-27). If that explanation fails to satisfy some people, Ben Sira ultimately invokes the mystery of God: "No one can say, 'What is this?' or 'Why is that?'—for everything has been created for its own purpose" (39:21).

As an explanation for human suffering, Adam's sin plays a minor role in Ben Sira's theology, though an echo of Gen 3:1-5 may be implied in Sir 21:2. While human beings are mortal (17:1; 40:1; 41:3-4), death is portrayed as "the Lord's decree for all flesh" (41:4), perhaps an allusion to Adam's punishment (Gen 2:17 and 3:19). However, Sir 25:24 refers to the sin of Eve, depicted as the equivalent of the Greek figure of Pandora (Hesiod, *Op.* 42–105).

Several passages in the Hebrew text of Ben Sira suggest that the sage followed earlier biblical tradition (Job 14:7-12; Qoh 3:19-21; Ps 115:17) in having no belief in an afterlife, beyond a shadowy existence in Sheol. In his view the netherworld offers no possibility either of enjoyment or of praising God (14:16; 17:27-28; 38:21; 41:4). In this matter he does not anticipate the expectation of life after death found in some pre-Christian Jewish writings (Dan 12:1-3; Wis 3:1-9; 2 Macc 7:22-23; *see* RESURRECTION, EARLY JEWISH), an expectation perhaps connected with the killing of the Maccabean martyrs who died resisting the persecution unleashed by Antiochus Epiphanes (2 Macc 7:3-5).

Rather than having the afterlife as an explanation for the injustices of this earthly life, Ben Sira believes that God brings justice during a person's time on earth. In his view, the wicked are punished during their own lifetime, even at their last breath (9:11-12; 11:26-28), while the virtuous will be rewarded on this earth, even if they must sometimes experience suffering and testing (2:1-11; 44:20). Whereas evildoers will be punished by having a bad name and a lack of offspring (40:15-16; 41:6), the righteous will be rewarded with a good reputation and many descendants (3:5; 41:12-13). Thus, for Ben Sira there are two ways in which a person can survive death: through having descendants (16:4; 30:4; 40:19; 44:11-12) and through being remembered well (37:26; 39:11; 41:11-13; 44:14).

Although Ben Sira may have had some hope for the fulfilment of the promises to David (2 Sam 7:13-16; Ps 89:29-37), he offers no picture of an expected Messiah, and a careful reading of Sir 45:25 may suggest that he saw these promises being fulfilled in his day through the high priest. However, Sir 48:10 refers to the future return of the prophet Elijah, promised in Mal 4:5-6 (and later applied to John the Baptist in Luke 1:17). Ben Sira offers a rather eschatological description of Isaiah's role: "He revealed what was to occur to the end of time, and the hidden things before they happened" (Sir 48:25;

compare Isa 42:9). Yet the sage opposes the speculations of Enochic apocalypticism, generally rejecting revelations in dreams as deceptive unless sent by God (Sir 34:1-8), and he warns against delving into mysteries beyond human understanding (3:17-24).

2. Social ethics

As in other ancient Mediterranean cultures, honor and shame were strong social forces in Ben Sira's society. While earlier Israelite texts testify to the value of winning honor and avoiding shame (e.g., Ps 25:2-3; Prov 10:5; 28:7), the influence of Greek social values (Theognis 409–10) led Ben Sira to place greater emphasis on acquiring prestige and keeping away from disgrace (4:20-21; 41:16–42:8).

For the sage, a fear of dishonor pervades the whole of life. He warns that shame can be caused by the male student's undisciplined conduct (Sir 6:2-4; 18:30–19:3), as well as by the breach of social norms by one's wife or children (Sir 26:8; 41:8-9; 42:9-14). According to the patriarchal system, it is shameful for a wife to support her husband (Sir 25:22; Tob 2:11–3:6), just as it is a disgrace for a man to resort to begging (Sir 40:28-30; Luke 16:3; compare Papyrus Insinger 27.3; Theognis 181–82).

Elsewhere, however, Sirach redefines honor, not in terms of military glory or favor from the Greek-speaking rulers, but in terms of obedience to God (Sir 10:19). Hence, in 41:16–42:8 the sage distinguishes between actions that deserve shame (e.g., betraying a friend's confidence) and forms of conduct that carry no dishonor (e.g., following the Torah).

Because of his fear of disgrace, the sage's teaching on behavior in society advocates extreme caution (e.g., 7:4-7; 8:14-19; 13:9-11; 32:19-23; 33:20-22). Indeed, caution is even necessary in friendship, since it is wise to test a potential friend (6:7), be wary of one's friends (6:13), and realize that not every self-proclaimed friend actually is one (37:1). Above all, the sage stresses the need to gain a good reputation, since this benefit will last for ever (41:13).

In keeping with other sages, Ben Sira considers control of speech an important part of wise social behavior. Because dishonor can easily come from the tongue (5:13), the sage prays for control of what he says (22:27–23:6). A wise person knows the right time to speak and the right time to be silent (20:5-8), and so the sage advises careful listening before answering (5:11; 11:8). Moreover, 27:16-21 teaches that the betrayal of confidences spells the end of friendship.

In accordance with previous biblical teaching (Exod 22:22-24; Isa 1:17; Prov 22:22-23), Ben Sira insists on the need for social justice (3:30–4:10). This aspect is prominent in 13:15-23, which graphically describes the mistreatment of the impoverished by the wealthy. Moreover, in 34:21–35:22 the denunciation of injustice toward the poor takes on a sharp prophetic tone: "To take away a neighbor's living is to commit murder; to deprive an employee of wages is to shed blood" (34:26-27).

However, Sirach exhibits a regrettable prejudice against women (Sir 25:13-26; 42:14). Some ancient Greek writings were also misogynistic, such as the work of the 6th-cent. BCE author Semonides of Amorgos, *On Women*, which refers to women as the worst plague made by Zeus. Similarly, a character in Euripides' play *Phoenician Women* (line 805) calls women the "wildest evil." Such a misogynistic attitude, abhorrent to modern readers, was not uncommon in his time. Ben Sira lived in a patriarchal society, where male dominance was strengthened by Greek restrictions on female roles (Aristotle, *Pol.* 1260a), and he may also have been influenced by his proximity to the Jerusalem Temple, whose priests were male.

Like earlier sages (Prov 31:10-31), Ben Sira praises a good wife, though her goodness is measured by her benefit to her husband (Sir 26:1-4; compare Prov 31:11-12; Papyrus Insinger 8.5). More extensively, Ben Sira speaks of the dangers of a bad wife (Sir 25:16-26) or a loose woman (9:3-6). In his warnings against an evil wife he alludes to Eve, viewed as a kind of Pandora: "From a woman sin had its beginning, and because of her we all die" (Sir 25:24; compare 1 Tim 2:14). The sage is especially concerned to preserve a daughter's chastity by restricting her to her parental home (Sir 42:9-14), following common Greek practice in the Hellenistic era (e.g., 2 Macc 3:19; 4 Macc 18:7; Philo, *Spec. Laws* 3.169). A similar instruction appears in the work of a 1st-cent. BCE Jewish teacher known as Pseudo-Phocylides, who advises not letting young women out of the house until their wedding day (lines 215–16).

Because his students were young men (7:26; 9:1), Ben Sira employs gendered language for the search for wisdom. Indeed, he portrays wisdom as a female figure (51:13-22), embodying features of a bride and a mother (15:2). In personifying wisdom as female, as well as in warning against loose women, Ben Sira follows the opening chapters of Proverbs (Prov 5:1-14; 7:6-27; 9:16).

3. Place in the wisdom tradition

Although Sirach belongs to Hebrew wisdom literature, its composition during the time of Hellenistic rule over Palestine means that it is written partly in response to various aspects of Greek philosophy (*see* HELLENISM). Unlike Prov 10:1–22:16, Sirach is generally made up of focused passages on a particular theme, whether theological or practical, and thus more like Prov 1–9. Apart from King Solomon, Ben Sira is the earliest Jewish wisdom author whose name and date is known. Although most of Sirach consists of didactic poems, the book includes some prayers (22:27–23:6; 36:1-22) and hymnic passages (18:1-7; 39:16-35; 42:15–43:33; 51:1-12), as well as a long encomium (the Praise of the Ancestors in 44:1–50:24).

Sirach has similarities with various Qumran wisdom texts. For instance, 4Q525 contains several beatitudes (perhaps originally eight) on the model of Sir 14:20-27 (compare Matt 5:3-10). The Qumran text says: "Blessed is the one who attains wisdom, and walks in the law of the Most High, and directs his heart to her ways" (4Q525 2 II, 3–4), with echoes of phrases in Sirach (6:18; 14:20-21; 42:2). Pursuit of wisdom also leads to promotion: "With kings she shall make him sit" (4Q525 2 II, 9), as in Sir 11:1. Another sapiential text, 4Q420, says: "One should not answer before one has listened.... With patience one should give a reply" (4Q420 1 II, 1–2). This admonition is almost identical to Sir 11:8 ("Do not answer before you listen") and the Hebrew text of Sir 5:11 ("With patience give a reply"). The long Qumran sapiential work, 4Q416, also resembles Sirach in some teachings, such as respect for parents (Sir 3:1-16; 4Q416 2 III, 15–19), while a parallel to Sir 6:25 appears in its admonition, "Bring your shoulder under all instruction" (4Q416 2 III, 13). In addition, 4Q300 employs the phrase "root of wisdom" (4Q300 1 II, 3), also found in Sir 1:6.

In the 2nd and 1st cent. BCE a body of apocalyptic tradition developed around the patriarch Enoch (Gen 5:18-24), who is mentioned in Sir 44:16 (not in the Masada text) and 49:14. While Sirach is sapiential and the Enoch literature is mainly apocalyptic, connections may be made between the two literary traditions. For instance, *1 En.* 92:1 calls Enoch "wisest of men," and the theme of wisdom is important in the Enochic writings (compare *1 En.* 32:3, 6; 82:2-3; 99:10). Both works claim to be the result of divine revelation, albeit received in different ways. Sirach acknowledges that "all wisdom is from the Lord" (Sir 1:1), and wisdom is gained through experience and study (34:9-13; 39:1-11), whereas the apocalyptic work regards Enoch as the revealer of heavenly mysteries given by the angelic Watchers (*1 En.* 1:2). Ben Sira's poem glorifying God for astronomical and meteorological marvels (42:15–43:33) deals with similar phenomena to the Astronomical Book (*1 En.* 72–82), although in a very different style. An intriguing contrast exists between the descent of heavenly Wisdom to earth so as to lodge in Israel (Sir 24:3-12), and the unsuccessful descent of Wisdom which returned to heaven (*1 En.* 42:1-2), but this passage was probably composed after Sirach.

4. Links with the New Testament

The sharp contrast between Ben Sira's favorable attitudes to scribes (39:1-11) and the Synoptic Gospels' hostility to them (especially Matt 23) might suggest a huge gulf between Sirach and early Christianity. Indeed, unlike the Talmud, the NT has no explicit quotations of Sirach. Nevertheless, NT passages on several topics are close to Ben Sira's thought, especially where he is developing traditional Jewish ethical teaching.

While it is hard to prove that Jesus had read Sirach, some of his parables deal with similar themes. Thus, the parable of the unforgiving debtor (Matt 18:21-35) uses a story to present the message of Sir 28:3-4: "Does anyone harbor anger against another, and expect healing from the Lord? If one has no mercy toward another like himself, can he then seek pardon for his own sins?" Moreover, the parable of the rich fool (Luke 12:16-21) amplifies Ben Sira's observation on the wealthy man: "When he says, 'I have found rest, and now I shall feast on my goods!' he does not know how long it will be until he leaves them to others and dies" (Sir 11:19). In addition, the parable of the widow who persists in seeking justice (Luke 18:1-8) echoes Sir 35:15-17: "The Lord is the judge, and with him there is no partiality.... He will not ignore the supplication of the orphan, or the widow when she pours out her complaint."

Jesus' appeal for a humble attitude toward God and neighbor also reflects Ben Sira's teaching. The call for humility in Matt 18:4 is like Sir 3:18: "The greater you are, the more you must humble yourself; so you will find favor in the sight of the Lord." While the instruction on taking the lowest place at a banquet (Luke 14:7-11) echoes Prov 25:6-7, a similar theme appears in Sir 32:1-2. A humble stance also implies being docile to the God-given yoke. While Jesus' declaration, "I am gentle and humble in heart" (Matt 11:29), recalls the humility of Moses (Num 12:3), his invitation, "Take my yoke upon you ... and you will find rest for your souls" (Matt 11:29), is reminiscent of the sage's appeal to carry wisdom's yoke: "Bend your shoulders and carry her.... For at last you will find the rest she gives" (Sir 6:25-28). This theme recurs in the sage's final poem: "Put your neck under her yoke.... See with your own eyes that I have labored but little and found for myself much serenity" (Sir 51:26-27).

Gospel references to the Torah also include some echoes of Sirach. For instance, in his dialogue with the rich young man, Jesus' recitation of several of the Ten Commandments adds the prohibition, "Do not defraud" (Mark 10:19), which is not in Exod 20 but appears in Sir 4:1 (NRSV, "Do not cheat"). Moreover, the Torah's admonition on fraternal correction (Lev 19:17) inspired not only the teaching of Sir 19:13-17 but also the guidance for the early church (Matt 18:15-17) and for the Qumran community (1QS V, 24–VI, 1).

In addition, the prologue of John's Gospel recalls themes in Sir 24. Just as the Gospel speaks of the Word as the divine utterance (John 1:1), Wisdom declares: "I came forth from the mouth of the Most High" (Sir 24:3). Later in Ben Sira's poem, Wisdom's search for a home is resolved by settling in Israel (as in a tent): "My Creator chose the place for my tent. He said, 'Make your dwelling in Jacob'" (Sir 24:8). In the Gospel the divine Word (similar to Wisdom) settled in human flesh: "The Word became flesh and lived [or "pitched his tent"] among us" (John 1:14).

Finally, the Letter of James treats topics that already occur in Sirach. Just as Ben Sira warns his students: "When you come to serve the Lord, prepare yourself for testing" (Sir 2:1), the Letter of James commends anyone who endures temptation or testing (Jas 1:12-15). The sage's repeated emphasis on control of the tongue

(Sir 5:9-13; 23:7-15; 28:10-12) finds an echo in the Letter of James (Jas 3:1-12), and the appeal to hear more readily than to speak (Jas 1:19) echoes Sir 5:11: "Be quick to hear, but deliberate in answering." *See* WISDOM IN THE NT.

5. Usage in Judaism and Christianity

While early Jewish respect for Sirach is evident from the Hebrew copies that have survived from the Dead Sea area, the work dropped out of favor in rabbinic Judaism, perhaps because the Greek version of the book was widely used in the Christian church. According to the Talmud (*y. Sanh.* 10:1), its religious use was banned by Rabbi Akiba (d. ca. 132 CE). Nevertheless, the Mishnah tractate *Pirke Aboth* (the Sayings of the Fathers) has echoes of Sirach; for instance, *m. Abot* 4:4 cites Sir 7:17 as a saying of Rabbi Levitas. Later, Sirach is several times quoted in the Talmud, sometimes with the phrase "it is written" (e.g., Sir 3:21-22 in *b. Hag.* 13a; Sir 38:1 in *y. Taan.* 3:6). The longest Talmudic quotation (*b. Sanh.* 100b) refers to various Sirach passages (6:6; 9:8-9; 11:29, 32; 25:26; 26:1, 3; 30:23; 42:9-10).

Sirach was included in the LXX, which became the OT for the Greek-speaking church, and was later translated into Latin. Ben Sira is quoted (often as Scripture) in many patristic writings. For instance, Sir 4:31 appears in several early Christian texts (*Did.* 4:5; *Barn.* 19:9; *Apos. Con.* 7.12.1), while Sir 12:1 is echoed in *Did.* 1:6. Several times Origen's homilies quote Ben Sira as scriptural (on Gen 12:5; Josh 15:6; Jer 16:6). While Jerome mentions seeing a Hebrew text of Ben Sira (PL 29:427-28), he does not regard the work as canonical (PL 28:600-603, 1242), yet he also cites the book with the phrase "scripture says" (PL 24:67D). Around the same time in North Africa, the Council of Carthage (397 CE) accepted the book as canonical, and Augustine (d. 430 CE) preached sermons on passages from Sirach. The earliest surviving Latin commentary is the 9th-cent. writing by Rabanus Maurus. In the early 16th cent. (around 1514), the Spanish priest Bartolomé de Las Casas was struck by a vivid realization of the evils of the mistreatment of the Native American population in the Caribbean when he reflected on Sir 34:21-27 (*History of the Indies* 3.79).

The book's canonicity for Roman Catholics was defined at the Council of Trent (1546), whereas many Protestant Reformers followed Jerome and the rabbinic tradition in rejecting it from the biblical canon (e.g., the Westminster Confession of 1647). Yet despite the view of Sirach as apocryphal among the more radical Reformers, the work continued to be read after the Reformation. It was included in an appendix to the Luther Bible of 1534 and the King James Bible of 1611. Martin Rinckart's famous Reformation hymn, "Now thank we all our God" (*Nun danket alle Gott*), was based on the Greek text of Sir 50:22-24. Among Shakespeare's quotations from the book, we find Sir 13:1: "They that touch pitch will be defiled" (*Much Ado About Nothing* III.iii.61).

He also echoes Sir 38:16-18: "Moderate lamentation is the right of the dead; excessive grief the enemy to the living" (*All's Well That Ends Well* I.i.65-66). Many First World War memorials in British villages have the inscription "Their name liveth for evermore" (Sir 44:14 KJV), and commemoration services for the dead (e.g., among Episcopalians) sometimes read from 44:1-15 (KJV: "Now let us praise famous men"). In recent years, older disputes about canonicity have largely given way to the recognition of the value of Sirach as an important witness to Jewish wisdom thinking two centuries before Jesus.

6. Religious value for modern readers

Ben Sira recognizes that the search for wisdom is essentially religious (1:1) and reverence for God is the way to find true understanding (1:26-27). While the quest for wisdom will involve trials and tribulations (2:1-6; 4:17; 6:20-25), the seeker will eventually reap its rewards (4:18; 6:28-31). God's wisdom comes in many ways: through the Bible (24:23); through creation (42:15–43:33); in the lives of the devout predecessors (44:1–50:24); and through experience and travel (34:9-11).

The sage's spirituality is immersed in many ordinary realities of everyday life: human relationships, social responsibility, careful speech, the use of money, political conduct, and other aspects of living in the world. Thus, his wisdom is grounded, not just in Israel's faith, but also in human experience. He also shows a deep appreciation of creation. In a beautiful poem he praises God for the sun, moon, stars, meteorological phenomena, and sea-creatures (42:15–43:33). His aphorisms are full of analogies from nature (e.g., 3:30; 22:19-20; 27:9-10; 28:10-12), as are his poetic descriptions (e.g., 24:13-17; 50:6-10). Such an appreciation of the natural world may serve as a fruitful source for creation spirituality.

In modern society, where friendship is becoming increasingly important, Ben Sira's reflections on the topic offer insights. He sees friendship as essentially something good (25:1, 9), although less important than marriage (40:23). Admittedly, there is a need for caution in friendship, since "some friends are friends only in name" (37:1). Because a supposed friend may desert you later (6:8-10), it is wise to test potential friends (6:7) to see if their actions match their fine words. However, it is important to show fidelity in friendship (27:17), as a faithful friend is more valuable than wealth (6:15). Finally, reverence for God is the way both to find friends and to be a true friend (6:16-17).

Modern concern for social justice can draw inspiration from Ben Sira's prophetic denunciations of injustice: "Like one who kills a son before his father's eyes is the person who offers a sacrifice from the property of the poor" (34:24). Indeed, his whole indictment of the way the wealthy treat the needy (34:21-31) resounds as forcefully as when it was first written. In response to social inequities, Ben Sira advocates justice and humility in rulers (10:1-6; 40:12) and generous giving from others (3:30–4:10).

Despite its valuable insights, Sirach is liable to criticism, particularly for its patriarchal attitude. The sage's diatribes on the evils of women (25:13-26) seem irredeemably misogynistic for modern readers. Like many scriptural texts, Ben Sira does not question the institution of slavery. Indeed, like Prov 26:3, he urges harsh treatment for the stubborn slave, though he advocates kindness to the loyal servant (33:25-33). Moreover, in urging beating for the disobedient son (30:12), Ben Sira may be following older traditions (Prov 13:24; 23:13-14), but physical punishment of children has been repudiated in many modern societies.

Christian readers will wish to modify some of Ben Sira's statements in light of Jesus' teaching. Besides reservations about the sage's lack of belief in the afterlife, another problem for Christians is his restriction of charity to good persons: "Give to the devout, but do not help the sinner. Do good to the humble, but do not give to the ungodly" (Sir 12:4-5; compare Theognis 105–108; 955–56; 1162; 1QS I, 10). This teaching conflicts with Jesus' call to do good to wicked and good people alike (Matt 5:43-47). To a large extent, Ben Sira was a child of his time. Nevertheless, his book offers many valuable insights for the people of today. *See* WISDOM IN THE OT.

Bibliography: R. A. Argall. *1 Enoch and Sirach: A Comparative and Conceptual Analysis of the Themes of Revelation, Creation and Judgment* (1995); P. C. Beentjes, ed. *The Book of Ben Sira in Modern Research* (1997); P. C. Beentjes. *"Happy the One Who Meditates on Wisdom" (Sir. 14,20): Collected Essays on the Book of Ben Sira* (2006); D. Bergant. *Israel's Wisdom Literature* (1997); R. J. Coggins. *Sirach* (1998); J. J. Collins. *Jewish Wisdom in the Hellenistic Age* (1997); J. Corley. *Ben Sira's Teaching on Friendship* (2002); J. Corley and V. Skemp. *Intertextual Studies in Ben Sira and Tobit* (2005); J. L. Crenshaw. *The Book of Sirach. NIB* 5 (1997); J. L. Crenshaw. *Old Testament Wisdom* (1998); D. A. deSilva. *Introducing the Apocrypha* (2002); R. Egger-Wenzel, ed. *Ben Sira's God* (2002); D. J. Harrington. *Jesus Ben Sira of Jerusalem* (2005); D. J. Harrington. *Wisdom Texts from Qumran* (1996); J. D. Harvey. "Toward a Degree of Order in Ben Sira's Book." *ZAW* 105 (1993) 52–62; T. R. Lee. *Studies in the Form of Sirach 44–50* (1986); B. L. Mack. *Wisdom and the Hebrew Epic* (1985); R. A. F. MacKenzie. *Sirach* (1983); O. Mulder. *Simon the High Priest in Sirach 50* (2003); R. E. Murphy. *The Tree of Life* (2002); E. D. Reymond. *Innovations in Hebrew Poetry: Parallelism and the Poems of Sirach* (2004); J. T. Sanders. *Ben Sira and Demotic Wisdom* (1983); P. W. Skehan and A. A. Di Lella. *The Wisdom of Ben Sira* (1987); W. C. Trenchard. *Ben Sira's View of Women* (1982).

JEREMY CORLEY

SIRAH, CISTERN OF si'ruh [בּוֹר הַסִּרָה bor hassirah]. The cistern of Sirah was a well that Josephus locates north of Hebron (*Ant.* 7.34). ABNER went there when David dismissed him after a raid, and the messengers of JOAB retrieved Abner at the cistern and took him back to Hebron, where Joab killed him (2 Sam 3:26).

JOAN E. COOK, SC

SIRION sihr'ee-uhn [שִׂרְיֹן siryon]. The Sidonian (i.e., Phoenician) name for Mount Hermon (Deut 3:9). Located at the southern tip of the Anti-Lebanon Range, it is the highest peak in the Levant (compare Arabic Jebel esh-Sheikh, "chief mountain"). An alternate form, si'on (שִׂיאֹן), also refers to Mount Hermon (Deut 4:48). Sirion appears in poetic parallelism with Lebanon in Ps 29:6, supporting the theory that Ps 29 was originally a Phoenician hymn to Baal later reworked to reflect Yahwistic piety. In the corrupt Hebrew text of Jer 18:14a, the NRSV reconstructs: "Does the snow of Lebanon leave the crags of Sirion (Heb. sadhay שָׂדַי, "field")?" *See* HERMON, MOUNT; SENIR.

JOEL M. LEMON

SIROCCO. *See* ISRAEL, CLIMATE OF.

SISERA sis'uh-ruh [סִיסְרָא sisera']. Sisera, the general of the Canaanite king Jabin's army, appears in Judg 4 and 5. Judges 4 offers a narrative account of the same events recorded in Judg 5 in poetic form. According to Judg 4:3, Sisera had cruelly oppressed the Israelites for twenty years before he met his match in JAEL, the wife of Heber the Kenite. The prophet Deborah directs Barak to lead the Israelite forces into battle against Sisera and his army. Apparently anxious about the chances of success, Barak says he will go only on the condition that Deborah accompany him into battle. She assents, but reveals that there will be no glory for Barak in this campaign; rather, "the LORD will sell Sisera into the hand of a woman" (4:9). Yet in the heat of battle, Deborah urges Barak on with a somewhat different exhortation: "Up! For this is the day on which the LORD has given Sisera into your hand" (4:14). With this assurance, Barak goes into battle and the LORD throws Sisera's army into disarray before Barak and the Israelite forces. Fleeing the chaos on foot, Sisera stumbles upon Jael's tent, who invites him in, offers him food, drink, and a place to lie down before driving a tent peg through his temple, killing him. Thus through Jael's efforts, "God subdued King Jabin of Canaan before the Israelites" (4:23). In the poetic account, Sisera's mother is depicted gazing through her window, awaiting the return of her son from battle, a return that will never come.

The text presents Sisera as a detested enemy whose death at the hands of Jael releases Israel from the oppression of the Canaanites. It may be that the narrative casts his death in an ignominious light (at the hands of a woman, while he is sleeping), though some commentators see Jael's actions as a violation of hospitality, thus rendering Sisera something of a victim. Many readers are troubled by the way that Jael tricks Sisera into trusting her, a trust that leads to his death. Yet she bears many similarities to Rahab (Josh 2 and 6), another non-Israelite woman whose deceitfulness leads to the defeat of Israel's enemies, and who is thus celebrated in Israel's traditions. How are the actions of such women to be assessed? Some feminist scholars focus on the ways in which the entire text seems permeated with the patriarchal values of war and militarism, while others ask how we might understand Sisera's mother, who seems to condone the rape and kidnapping of Israelite women (5:28-30), though due to Sisera's defeat it is ironically her and her fellow Canaanite women whom the text casts in that role. Does the text thereby condone rape and kidnapping as long as the victims are non-Israelite?

Bibliography: Mieke Bal. *Murder and Difference: Gender, Genre, and Scholarship on Sisera's Death* (1988); Dennis Olson. *Judges. NIB* 2 (1994) 721–888; Katharine D. Sakenfeld. "Deborah, Jael, and Sisera's Mother: Reading the Scriptures in Cross-Cultural Context." *Women, Gender, and Christian Community.* J. D. Douglass and J. F. Kay, eds. (1997) 13–22.

JACQUELINE E. LAPSLEY

SISINNES si-sin´es [Σισίννης *Sisinnēs*]. Governor of Coele-Syria and Phoenicia (1 Esd 7:1) who objected to Darius about the Jews' rebuilding of the Temple (1 Esd 6:3, 7). When a search of the royal archives yielded the decree from Cyrus, Darius ordered Sisinnes to comply and reconstruction resumed (1 Esd 6:27).

SISMAI sis´mi [סִסְמָי *sismay*]. Of the tribe of Judah, he was son of Eleasah and father of Shallum (1 Chr 2:40). *See* SHESHAN.

SISTER [אָחוֹת ʼakhoth; ἀδελφή *adelphē*]. *Sister* appears less frequently than *brother* in the Bible, in part because women in general receive less attention than men, and in part because both the Hebrew and Greek words for *sister* are feminine forms from the same root as *brother*, and the masculine form often includes the feminine (especially in the plural). In most cases, the NRSV has chosen to translate the masculine with a non-gendered term (e.g., "kindred" Deut 1:16, 28; 2:4) or to make this inclusion explicit by adding "sister" (e.g., Rom 1:13; 7:1; 8:12).

In the OT, *sister*, like *brother*, may refer to a full or half sibling (Gen 4:22; Lev 18:9, 11), to extended kin (Gen 24:60), or to a companion, or may express honor or love (Song 4:9-12; 5:1). Miriam is identified as the natural sister of Moses and Aaron in Num 26:59 and Exod 6:20 [LXX], but in Exod 15:20, where she is described as "the prophet, the sister of Aaron," the reference may be to her status as a leader in Israel, like Aaron. Personifications of Israel and Judah, Samaria, Sodom, and Jerusalem as sisters seem to combine the

ideas of companion or equivalent and kin (Jer 3:7-10; Ezek 16:45-52).

These patterns combined with a similar range of meaning for the Greek words to form early Christian use of *sister*. Sister might mean a full or half sibling (John 19:25; Acts 23:16), or a more distant female relative, though the Greek words for cousins and extended kin are also used in the NT (Luke 1:36, 58, 44; Rom 9:3; 16:7, 11, 21). The "sisters of Jesus" mentioned in the company of his mother and brothers are probably siblings (Matt 12:50; 13:56; Mark 3:32; 6:3). Like *brother*, *sister* became a way of addressing or referring to members of the community (Mark 3:35; 1 Cor 7:15; 1 Tim 5:2; Jas 2:15); in some cases *brother* and *sister* seem to have been distinguished missionary partners or coworkers. Thus 1 Corinthians is signed by "Paul the apostle and Sosthenes the brother" (1:1; compare 2 Cor 1:1; Phlm 1), and Paul inquires of them whether or not he has the right to be accompanied by a "sister, a woman/wife" (1 Cor 9:5; NRSV, "a believing wife"). When Paul greets "Apphia the sister" does he address Philemon's sibling, his wife, or a missionary worker? The same questions arise when Paul greets "Nereus and his sister" (Rom 16:15). Phoebe, commended by Paul in Rom 16:1 as "our sister," is clearly both believer and coworker. When the author of 2 John addresses an "elect lady" and sends greetings from "the children of her elect sister," do "sister" and "children" designate a woman church worker and the assembly in her house? Personified churches? Woman prophet and her followers (compare Rev 2:20-23)? The case of Martha and Mary is particularly intriguing. Two very different stories of these women are told in Luke 10:38-42 and John 11:1–12:10, each involving hospitality and home. These disparate stories preserve their memory as a missionary couple: Martha the diakonos (διάκονος; compare Rom 16:1) and Mary the sister, who preside together over a house church.

MARY ROSE D'ANGELO

SIT, DWELL [יָשַׁב *yashav*; κάθημαι *kathēmai*, καθίζω *kathizō*, κατοικέω *katoikeō*]. The Hebrew root yshb (ישׁב), the basic meaning of which is "to sit, dwell, remain," is used 1,088 times in the OT. The term is used in a variety of contexts and with a variety of nuances throughout the OT. Perhaps the most obvious nuance, but not necessarily the most commonly employed, is that of literally "sitting," perhaps on a seat of some kind, designated or undesignated: in Exod 2:15 Moses "sat down by a well"; in Exod 17:12 he sat on a stone; in Ezra 10:16 selected Judeans sat down to examine a matter.

Often, where sitting does or does not occur, and for what reason, is to be noted: 1) in the city gate: Lot, Gen 19:1; Babylonian officials, Jer 39:3; Boaz, Ruth 4:1, 2, 4; 2) prophets sitting before Elisha, 2 Kgs 4:38; 3) "sitting outside" to relieve oneself, Deut 23:13; 4) not sitting in the seat of scoffers, Ps 1:1; not sitting with "men of emptiness," Ps 26:4 (NRSV, "the worthless").

Yahweh sits in the heavens ("enthroned," Ps 123:1). In a double use of the root in Ps 29:10, Yahweh "sits enthroned over the flood" and he "sits enthroned as king forever." Yahweh of Hosts sits—is enthroned—on cherubim (1 Sam 4:4). According to Ps 9:4, Yahweh "sat on the throne giving righteous judgment." While in some texts, "sitting on a throne" is to be understood quite literally (1 Kgs 22:10), more often "sitting on a throne" is to be taken as a metaphor for "reigning" (Solomon in 1 Kgs 1:46; 2:12; anticipation of a restored Davidic throne in Jer 22:2).

Non-royal metaphorical uses include 1) military encampment (1 Sam 13:16, the Philistines at Michmash; 1 Kgs 11:16, Joab and the Israelite army in Edom); 2) ambush—human and animal (Judg 16:9, men lying in wait; Ps 10:8, wicked sit in ambush; Ps 17:12, a young lion lurking); 3) metaphorical "sitting on the ground" (Isa 3:26, Jerusalem; Isa 47:1, virgin daughter Babylon); 4) remaining at home (2 Kgs 14:10, Jehoash to Amaziah: "stay at home," i.e., "be content with your victory over Edom"); 5) "living" under various conditions (Isa 9:2, living in a land of deep darkness; Jer 10:17, living under siege).

Kathēmai and kathizō seem to be the most commonly used NT terms representing the English word "sit," while katoikeō tends to be rendered by the English term "dwell." New Testament uses also include both literal ("sit and beg," John 9:8; Acts 3:10; sit in a chariot, Acts 8:31) and metaphorical nuances ("sit in darkness," Luke 1:79; "sit to calculate cost," Luke 14:28, 31; expressing a position of honor, Matt 19:28; 20:21, 23; 25:31).

JOHN I. LAWLOR

SITES, SACRED. From antiquity to the present, in religious traditions around the world, places are set apart as holy spaces where the divine and the human spheres are believed to meet. These may be private, such as a domestic shrine; local, such as a temple, synagogue, church, or mosque; and larger—a city, such as Jerusalem, Mecca, or Benares; and even a land—a holy land (see Zech 2:12). At such places, both private and public rituals take place, and these rituals are often linked with the histories of specific, and often successive, traditions. Many such sacred sites are known from the Bible, and from archaeological discoveries in the biblical lands.

Some of these sacred sites are imposing geographical phenomena, such as mountains, which have an intrinsically numinous quality. In biblical tradition, these include Mount Carmel, Mount Sinai, Mount Tabor, Mount Hermon, and Mount Zion. All are identified as places where rituals of various sorts were performed and where theophanies occurred. The name of Mount Hermon indicates its sacred character: it is the mountain "set apart" (from the root kharam [חָרַם], which can

be translated "devote") for the deity, who may be Baal (Judg 3:3; see BAAL-HERMON) or Yahweh (Ps 89:13). Like Tabor, Hermon is also identified as the unnamed mountain that was the site of Jesus' transfiguration, his theophanic appearance with Moses and Elijah (Matt 17:1-8//Mark 9:2-8//Luke 9:28-36). The sacredness of Hermon, whose elevation of over 9,000 ft. above sea level makes it the highest mountain in the region, is further indicated by the many shrines and temples on its peaks and at its base (see HERMON, MOUNT). Other sacred sites are associated with distinctive features of the landscape, such as rivers and trees.

Some sacred sites are the locations of tombs of revered leaders or ancestors. Thus, Hebron is the location of the family tomb where Abraham and Sarah (Gen 23:19; 25:9-10), Isaac and Rebekah, and Jacob and Leah (Gen 49:29-31) were buried, and the traditional site of that tomb remains a holy place for both Jews and Muslims to the present. Other important burial sites that become places of pilgrimage or at least are remembered are those of Rachel (Gen 35:19-20), Joseph (Josh 24:32), and Elisha (2 Kgs 13:20-21). In Christian tradition, the site identified as the tomb of Jesus, whether correctly or not, also became sacred, as did the tomb of Mary, the mother of Jesus, in Orthodox Christian tradition.

Other sacred sites are specifically connected with events described in the Bible. Although in many cases, such as Mount Sinai and locations associated with the life of Jesus, the actual sites cannot be identified, over the ages communities of faith selected specific places for pilgrimage and worship because of their presumed connections with biblical geography.

The site of Shechem illustrates many of these features. Strategically situated at the eastern end of the narrow pass between Mount Ebal and Mount Gerizim, it had a succession of temples uncovered by archaeologists, like other urban centers of the 2nd millennium BCE. Biblical tradition mentions a temple or temples of the Canaanite deities El and Baal (Judg 9:4, 46) at Shechem, and also a large oak or terebinth tree that was located there (Gen 12:6; 35:4; Deut 11:30; Josh 24:26; Judg 9:6). As a preexisting place of worship, the sacred area of Shechem became central to developing Israelite tradition. Joshua is reported to have built an altar on Mount Ebal (Josh 8:30), and both Deuteronomy (11:29; 27:12-13) and the book of Joshua (8:33; 24:1) describe it as the place for covenant renewal. As such, its significance was retrojected into earlier times: Abraham too is said to have built an altar there, near the oak (Gen 12:6-7), as is Jacob (Gen 33:20), and the tomb of Joseph is nearby (Josh 24:2). In the Hellenistic period a temple was constructed there by the Samaritans to rival that in Jerusalem.

The Temple Mount in Jerusalem is another case in point. From at least the 10th cent. BCE, this has been a sacred site, the holiest place within the "holy city"

(Isa 52:1; Matt 4:5; etc.). According to 2 Sam 24:18, David built an altar on the threshing floor of Araunah the Jebusite, and according to 2 Chr 3:1, this was the site of the Temple built by Solomon. It is possible that David's altar was on an already existing Jebusite sacred site, which then became a place for the worship of Yahweh. In any case, the site of the Temple, frequently called Mount Zion, and by extension all of Jerusalem, becomes the central sacred site of ancient Israel and of Judaism subsequently. Like sacred sites elsewhere, it is understood as the "center of the earth" (Ezek 38:12; compare Judg 9:37), the "center of the nations" (Ezek 5:5), where heaven and earth meet. Because of its centrality, it is linked with earlier events; in late biblical tradition, the site of Solomon's Temple is identified as Mount Moriah, the place where Abraham was to sacrifice Isaac (Gen 22:2; 2 Chr 3:1). The last Jewish Temple was destroyed by the Romans in 70 CE, but since the Middle Ages the western retaining wall of the platform on which the Temple had been built (the "Western Wall" or the "Wailing Wall") has been a place of pilgrimage and prayer for Jews. After the destruction of the Temple, a temple to Zeus was built on its site by the Roman emperor Hadrian in the early 2nd cent. CE, to be followed by the Muslim sanctuary of the Dome of the Rock in the late 7th cent., which was briefly converted into a Christian church during the Crusader period. The status of Jerusalem as "holy city" thus extends over at least three millennia, and it remains such for Jews, Christians, and Muslims, illustrating the continuity of sacred sites, even though the religious communities who regard them as such have changed. *See* CARMEL, MOUNT; SHECHEM, SHECHEMITES; TABOR, MOUNT; TEMPLE, JERUSALEM; THEOPHANY IN THE OT; ZION.

MICHAEL D. COOGAN

SITHRI sith´ri [סִתְרִי sithri]. The genealogy in Exod 6:14-25 lists Sithri as a great-grandson of Levi and grandson of Kohath (v. 22). His father, Uzziel, was the brother of Amram, the father of Moses, Aaron, and Miriam, and thus Sithri was their cousin. The genealogy follows immediately after the divine commission to Moses, establishing the Levitical lineage of the family.

JOAN E. COOK, SC

SITNAH sit´nuh [שִׂטְנָה sitnah]. Second of three wells dug by Isaac's servants in the valley of Gerar (Gen 26:21). The herders of Gerar feuded with Isaac's herders over the water rights, so the well was named Sitnah ("enmity"). Its location is unknown.

SIVAN si´van [סִיוָן siwan; Σιουάν Siouan]. Name of the third month in the Hebrew calendar (Esth 8:9; Bar 1:8), equivalent to today's May–June. *See* CALENDAR.

SIX. *See* NUMBERS, NUMBERING.

SIX HUNDRED AND SIXTY-SIX [ἑξακόσιοι ἑξήκοντα ἕξ hexakosioi hexēkonta hex]. The number of the beast (Rev 13:18). Over the centuries popular interpreters have identified countless persons and institutions with this eschatological mystery, but two lines of interpretation have won endorsements from critical interpreters. A symbolic interpretation posits that 666 conveys an emphatic sense of imperfection. In Revelation seven frequently indicates perfection, so the repetition of "six" could imply absolute corruption; however, the only other occurrence of "six" reveals the number of wings on the four living creatures (Rev 4:8; compare Isa 6:2), hardly suggesting imperfection.

A second line of interpretation emphasizes 666 as the number of a person, as Revelation dares its audience to "calculate" the riddle. One theory identifies this person as the emperor Nero. In Hebrew gematria (numerical symbolism), the value of the name qsr nrwn (קסר נרון) is 666. This interpretation is extremely complicated, suggesting that Revelation takes the less common Hebrew form of a Latin name, calculates its value, then presents the riddle in Greek. Two factors support the identification of Nero as Revelation's beast. First, some ancient manuscripts render the number instead as 616. The Hebrew n carries a value of fifty; when it represents a word's final consonant, it often drops away. Thus, manuscripts with 616 suggest that ancient Christian opinion linked the number to Nero. Second, one of the beast's heads has a mortal wound that has been healed (Rev 13:3, 12, 14; 17:11). This detail may represent the tradition that Nero would return from his death to persecute the saints (see *Ascen. Isa.* 4; *Sib. Or.* 8:140–59).

GREG CAREY

SIXTEEN. *See* NUMBERS, NUMBERING.

SIXTY. *See* NUMBERS, NUMBERING.

SKEPTICISM, POPULAR. Skepticism is an attitude of doubt or a systematic method of questioning that any knowledge is "true." Examples of skepticism range from simple reactions of incredulity toward events or persons to the philosophical schools of the Cynics and Epicureans.

The biblical material includes examples of people questioning God. Job demonstrates skepticism of God's goodness (24:1-12; *see* THEODICY). Qohelet writes that the ways of God are inscrutable (Eccl 8:17). An attitude of skepticism could be construed in narratives such as the book of Ruth, the account of succession (2 Sam 9–1 Kgs 2), the book of Esther, or 1 Maccabees, where overt divine intervention is unexpected. Biblical characters regularly express skepticism: Sarah laughs when she hears that she will bear a son (Gen 18:9-15); Moses protests that he cannot be a spokesman (Exod 4:1, 8). Zechariah and Mary are skeptical about the news they will have children (Luke 1:18-20, 34). Even Jesus' miracles were met with skepticism by those closest to him. For example, the disciples regularly doubt or fear the things Jesus says and does (e.g., Matt 14:22-27), and while some apparently believed immediately in the miracle of Jesus' resurrection, there were some who remained skeptical. Most notably, Thomas doubted the resurrection until he could see physical proof (John 20:25), and some of the eleven disciples doubted when they saw the resurrected Jesus (Matt 28:17).

Biblical writers favored reliance on Yahweh rather than on magic. The magicians of Pharaoh were bested by Moses' miracles (Exod 7), and Saul consulted with a medium at Endor only when Yahweh did not answer him (1 Sam 28:8-19; *see* ENDOR, MEDIUM OF). Only prophets who worked miracles by the power of God receive positive characterizations (e.g., Moses, Elijah, and Elisha; *see* PROPHET, PROPHECY).

With the exception of Jesus of Nazareth, we know of few magicians or miracle workers from the early Common Era (*see* MAGIC, MAGICIAN; MIRACLE). Magicians include the MAGI (Matt 2:1-12) and SIMON Magus (Acts 8:9-12). Miracle workers include the 1st-cent. HANINAH BEN DOSA and HONI, and the 2nd-cent. Apollonius of Tyana (*see* PHILOSTRATUS, FLAVIUS), who performed miracles very similar to those of Jesus.

While the abilities of physicians were trusted, people were more skeptical of magic and miracles. Philo (*Sacrifices* 70) agreed with Plutarch (*Mor.* 920B) that people were more likely to call for a physician than to pray. One of the most thorough exposures of fraudulent claims is HIPPOLYTUS' *Refutation of All Heresies*.

The "New Academy" that began with Carnades (213–129 BCE) accepted critical empiricism that suspended judgment. The Epicureans believed in deities completely detached and uninvolved (*see* EPICURUS, EPICUREANISM). The Cynics publicly ridiculed any ideas of special providence or foreknowledge (*see* CYNICS, CYNICISM). Skepticism is featured in Sextus Empiricus' *Outlines of Pyrrhonism* and *Against the Mathematicians* (160–210 CE).

Bibliography: T. Klutz, ed. *Magic in the Biblical World* (2003); P. Veyne. *Did the Greeks Believe Their Myths?* (1988).

SKIFF [אֳנִיַּת אֵבֶה 'oniyath 'eveh]. A light, fast boat made of lashed sedge stems, appearing once in the plural in Job 9:26 (literally, "ships of reed"). It occurs with the images of a runner and a swooping eagle to describe the swiftness of Job's life. *See* SHIPS AND SAILING IN THE OT.

JOEL M. LEMON

SKIN [עוֹר 'or; αἴγειος aigeios, βυρσεύς byrseus, δέρμα derma, χρώς chrōs]. The term 'or is the most commonly used term in the OT when referencing human or animal skin. Frequently 'or refers to human skin in the extended discussion of skin disorders in Lev 13, where the term is used forty-five times. In Leviticus *skin* also refers to animal skins in the context of sacrifice (4:11; 7:8; 8:17; 9:11; 16:27), and in reference to clothing (11:32; 15:17). It can also refer to a container for keeping wine (1 Sam 10:3; 16:20; Matt 9:17).

Descriptive contexts of the term's use in reference to animal skin include the Edenic covering (Gen 3:21), Jacob's deceit of Isaac (Gen 27:16), use in the construction of the tent of meeting (Exod 25:5; 26:14; 29:14; 35:7, 23; 36:19; 39:34), the tent of meeting service of the Kohathites (Num 4:6, 8, 10-12, 14; NRSV, "covering of fine leather"), sacrifice (Num 19:5; red heifer), the Midianite scenario (Num 31:20), Elijah's belt (2 Kgs 1:8), and the taming of Leviathan (Job 41:7). The LXX consistently uses derma to translate 'or.

Items that touched Paul's skin could heal the sick (chrōs, Acts 19:12). Hebrews mentions those who lived by faith who wore sheep and goat skins (aigeios, 11:37).

JOHN I. LAWLOR

SKIRT [כָּנָף kanaf, סָבַב savav, שׁוּל shul]. The hem, fringe, or loose corner of a larger garment (Jer 2:34; Ezek 5:3). Job uses *skirts* metaphorically for the edges of the earth (38:13). More frequently, however, *skirts* is employed metaphorically to refer to the shaming of the people by God, who says that he will expose their nakedness ("lift up your skirts") as a punishment for their iniquities (Jer 13:22, 26; Nah 3:5; compare Lam 1:9). Footnotes in the NRSV explain that a man who has "violated his father's rights" by marrying or having intercourse with his own mother has literally "uncovered his father's skirt" (Deut 22:30 [Heb. 23:1]; 27:20). As a verb, *skirt* means "to travel around" (Deut 2:1, 3). *See* HEM; TRAIN.

JESSICA TINKLENBERG DEVEGA

SKULL, PLACE OF THE. *See* GOLGOTHA.

SKY. *See* HEAVEN.

SLANDER [דִּבָּה dibbah, רָגַל raghal, רָכִיל rakhil; δυσφημέω dysphēmeō, καταλαλιά katalalia]. Slander is a false statement that defames someone. The Mosaic law forbids slandering (Lev 19:16), especially slandering a woman by claiming she is not a virgin (Deut 22:14). Those who walk blamelessly do not slander (Ps 15:3), while those who reject the true God speak slander (Jer 6:28; Ezek 22:9; Rom 1:30). God will destroy those who secretly slander a neighbor (Ps 101:5). Those who utter slander are fools (Prov 10:18).

Slander, or BLASPHEMY, is an evil thing that comes from the heart (Matt 15:19). Paul complains that he is slandered regarding his apostolic mission (1 Cor 4:13). Paul tells believers to put away slander (Eph 4:31; Col 3:8), as does Peter (1 Pet 2:1). Paul says that women must not be slanderers (1 Tim 3:11; Titus 2:3).

False teachers produce slander (1 Tim 6:4; 2 Pet 2:10-12; Jude 8-10).

KENNETH D. LITWAK

SLAVE GIRL AT PHILIPPI. When a slave girl follows Paul and Silas around PHILIPPI while crying out that they are "slaves of the Most High God" who proclaim salvation, Paul becomes annoyed and exorcises her spirit of DIVINATION, thus removing a lucrative source of income for her owners, who have Paul and Silas flogged and imprisoned (Acts 16:16-23; see 1 Thess 2:2). The story does not say what happened to the girl; some interpreters imagine that through her encounter with Paul she, too, became a "slave of the Most High God" and a follower of Jesus, like Lydia (Acts 16:14-15) and the slave Onesimus (Phlm 10-16). *See* SLAVERY.

Bibliography: F. Scott Spencer. *Dancing Girls, Loose Ladies, and Women of the Cloth: The Women in Jesus's Life* (2004).

MARIANNE BLICKENSTAFF

SLAVERY [עֶבֶד 'evedh; δοῦλος doulos, παῖς pais]. Previous scholars relied on law exclusively for their understanding of ancient slavery. This methodological mistake mistreats the ancient evidence. A better approach defines the phenomenon comparatively, on the level of personal relations, and without exclusive reference to property ownership. Slavery is not simply owning a human being as property (chattel), the equivalent of forced labor, the denial of civil rights, or the loss of freedom. Its distinctiveness lies in the permanent and violent domination of persons alienated from birth who live in a general state of dishonor (Patterson). This preliminary definition from historical sociology offers a useful model of slavery as "social death."

Hebrew for slave is 'evedh. Greek terms include doulos and pais ("child"). While pais means "child" or "youth," when referring to a slave, it describes an infantilized adult (and so does not refer to a slave's age). Each term covers a wide semantic range to express all kinds of dependent people in addition to actual chattel slaves. Even high-ranking freeborns were called (and called themselves) "slaves" in a metaphorical sense, such as before a monarch or deity. Because 'evedh, doulos, and pais can also be translated "servant," the modern translation "servant" or "slave" depends on the specific context. However, overuse of the translation "servant" can mask the absolute domination, harshness, and social death that the original language describes.

A. Old Testament
   1. Slaves in the Ancient Near East
   2. Slavery and the exodus
   3. Hebrew slave laws
   4. Early Judaism

B. New Testament
   1. Slavery in the Roman Empire
   2. Gospels and Acts
   3. Pauline letters
C. The Legacy of Slavery and the Bible
Bibliography

A. Old Testament
1. Slaves in the Ancient Near East

The Bronze and Iron Age civilizations of Mesopotamia, Anatolia, Syro-Palestine, Egypt, and the Aegean all had slaves, but none should be named a genuine slave society. The importance of the designation lies not with slave totals, which are rarely known, but with slave position in the ancient economy and society. Slaves were not found, as a general rule, in every occupation and all economic levels. These conditions apply exclusively to the later, and only, genuine slave societies of antiquity: classical Athens and imperial Rome.

The economies of Mesopotamia and much of the ANE concentrated slave ownership in the huge agricultural and commercial complexes of the major temples. Individual holdings were very small (two or three slaves per aristocratic home) and kept mainly for domestic work, performing arts, and as family retainers. Neo-Babylonian and late Assyrian sources begin to mention slaves working in all kinds of trades (weavers, leather-workers, gem-cutters, dyers, fullers, fowlers, bakers), and some slaves carried their own cylinder and stamp seals to conduct business in their own signature. But few slaves had access to expensive materials, education, or time away for the apprenticeship that a trade required. The economic and social status of slaves could vary, even if their juridical status did not; elite slaves could even own slaves themselves. As a group, therefore, slaves did not constitute a "class" in the modern sociological sense. At no time did slavery compete with free labor.

The various law collections from Mesopotamia and Asia Minor, most notably the Babylonian *Code of Hammurabi* (ca. 1750 BCE), prescribe a number of rules for the lives and deaths of slaves (*see* HAMMURABI, CODE OF). There are paragraphs regulating slave sale, slave marriage, and the movement of slaves within and outside the city walls. Kidnapping nationals as slaves is prohibited, and the debt bondage of distressed freeborn people is limited. The slave's mark (special tonsure) receives particular note. The "slaves of the palace" (royal slaves) have distinctive roles.

There is, however, a large methodological question about the use of legal evidence in historical inquiry. Our access to the law of the ANE is dependent largely on the discoveries of archaeology. The synthetic and prescriptive nature of the extant documentary legal sources should caution against their uncritical use as social description or in reconstructing history. To describe ancient society from legal sources is methodologically questionable because legal codes provide inexact knowledge about social practice and can present a highly misleading model of slavery. Monolithic claims about "the law" are highly problematic.

The OT describes owners acquiring slaves as prisoners of war (Deut 20:11-14; 21:10-14; Joel 3:6-8) and from debt bondage. Itinerant traders offered slaves as part of other wares (Gen 37:27-28; Ezek 27:13), but supply and demand were not high or stable enough to create a specialized profession of "slave traders" until the Hellenistic period (2 Macc 3:41). Other sources included infant exposure (Exod 2:3-4) and the sale of minors by their families. Slaves could eventually be adopted as heirs (Gen 15:1-3). Slave revolts or rebellions are not attested in the Bible or the ANE, but individual slaves did flee their masters and sought asylum—a possibility that biblical law recognizes (Deut 23:15-16; compare 1 Kgs 2:39-40). In light of the extensive concern for the capture and return of runaways in other Near Eastern law codes (*Code of Hammurabi* §§15–20), the OT prohibition of fugitive slave extradition is unusual and possibly inspired by the formation of the exodus story.

Personal slave ownership in ancient Israelite society is represented in texts as having occurred in the time of the patriarchs, often mentioned together with the possession of domesticated animals—oxen, sheep, camels, and donkeys. When Abram (Abraham) moves to Egypt as a resident alien, he finds favor from Pharaoh who rewards him with "male and female slaves" and other livestock (Gen 12:16). After his covenant with the Lord, Abraham circumcises "all the [male] slaves born in his house or bought with his money" (Gen 17:23) along with other males of the household. Abraham's son Isaac grows up to become a large slaveholder in his own right and puts his slaves to backbreaking manual labor, such as digging wells (Gen 26:25). Isaac's own son and heir, Jacob, in turn becomes "exceedingly rich" and has "large flocks, and male and female slaves, and camels and donkeys" (Gen 30:43). Another OT hero, the slaveholder Job, points to a master's fairness—personal attention to every complaint of one's slaves—to challenge God's severity with him (Job 31:13-15).

The OT acknowledges the sexual vulnerability of slaves under their masters, but without protest. Sarah, presented as a slaveholder in her own right, gives Abraham her maid HAGAR to use as a secondary wife, to produce an heir, regardless of the slave's wishes (Gen 16). As an adolescent, Joseph was sold into slavery by his own brothers (Gen 39–41), which the psalmist saw as a divine test of his character (Ps 105:17-19). The youth discovers from the wife of Potiphar, his Egyptian master, the daily threat of RAPE that even male slaves faced (Gen 39:1-23). The episode in the Joseph cycle condemns the specific victimization of a wrongfully enslaved Israelite, not of all slaves by their masters.

According to the author of 1 Kings, Israelite state slavery began with the corvée (unpaid labor given to a ruler) by Solomon for his massive building projects in Jerusalem, Lebanon, and throughout his dominion.

To establish a national shrine, strengthen his monarchy, and supply the military, Solomon conscripted slave labor to build the Jerusalem Temple, his royal palace, and numerous "storage cities" (army bases). Two texts give contradictory versions of the labor force. First Kings 5:13-18 speaks of a corvée from all Israel, but 1 Kgs 9:15-22 claims that only aliens (most likely vanquished Canaanites) were conscripted. The apologetic claims of the latter text are doubtful: it is an ETIOLOGY justifying the existence of slavery in the time of the author ("to this day"; 2 Chr 8:3-10). A different biblical writer places the origin of Israelite state slavery to the time of Joshua's conquest (Josh 9:22-27).

Yet another etiology appears in Noah's curse of Canaan for the sin of Ham (Gen 9:18-27). The curse functioned in ancient Israelite society to justify the enslavement of Canaanites forever as a consequence of their ancestors, Canaan and his father Ham. However, the text of Genesis makes no mention of skin color, in particular blackness, as part of the curse. The so-called "Curse of Ham," a racist etiology for the enslavement of BLACK Africans, originates not with the OT or ancient Judaism but rather from the link between black skin color and slavery that occurred in 7th cent. CE Arabia, after the Islamic conquest of Africa (Goldenberg). The exegetical innovation appeared in Muslim adaptations of the biblical story of Ham (which does not appear in the Qur'an) and subsequently entered medieval and early modern Christian and Jewish biblical interpretation (*see* ETHNICITY; RACISM).

The Bible applies the moral principles of slavery to Israel's relationship with God. If Israel misbehaves, God is prepared to hand over even the chosen people to its enemies for enslavement (Jer 34:8-22). Jeremiah proclaims slavery to be a sign of God's punishment and applies the theology in the same way and with the same rigor to every disobedient group of people universally, without distinction.

This context makes OT stories about God's punishment intelligible (although we may still reject the ancient morality). For example, some stories assert God's right to enslave—and to sell—Israel as chattel. The violation of covenant prompts Yahweh to hand over Israel to a foreign lord (Judg 6:1-13). The metaphor, if we can call it that, is of a master selling off his recalcitrant slave and so connects to the ancient social practice. The story of Elisha and his slave GEHAZI offers another illustration of how the metaphor of slavery connects directly to the institution of slavery (2 Kgs 4:8–5:27). Gehazi is the "bad slave," a stock type, paired with its moral polarity of the "good slave," represented by the prophet ELISHA and the Syrian commander NAAMAN who unselfishly serve the Lord. These types function together as a literary device to teach readers a lesson about the importance of absolute loyalty to God. Elisha's punishment of the wicked slave Gehazi by permanently scarring his body conforms to common practice in the ANE. It also reveals the morality tale's deep implication in ancient practices and ideologies of slavery.

Further OT stories use the ideology of slavery to construct a theology of kingship. The Lord is king, even when Israel desires a human monarch (see KING, GOD AS; KING, KINGSHIP). Samuel warns the Israelites that all kings require slaves—from the population's children, its current slave holdings, and the bodies of the subjects themselves (1 Sam 8:4-19). The narrative of Saul's kingship, and God's subsequent abandonment of Saul, depends on the language of slavery; even David pledges himself as a loyal slave of the doomed king (1 Sam 17:4-9, 31-37). The story of King Rehoboam associates the clear imagery of slavery, especially the WHIP, to make intertextual echoes of the exodus. Rehoboam acts like second pharaoh, against the sage advice of his elder Solomonic advisors (1 Kgs 12:1-28). In these and many other ways, the authors of the OT make the metaphor of slavery "real" by explicit connection to the actualities of the social institution.

The reality of the theological slave metaphor depended on the actuality of the social institution. Inscriptions attest that the title "slave (ʿevedh) of the king" was apparently an office of high rank and status in the ANE. The Hebrew word for worship is ʿavodhah (עֲבֹדָה, "servitude," "service"), which also describes the manual labor of a slave (Exod 5:11); in other words, to "serve" ("be a slave to") God had specific cultic connotations (Josh 22:27). Like Abraham, Isaac, and Jacob before him, Moses is called a "slave of God," in a personal relationship to no other deity as an extension of the Lord's will and so the authorized leader of Israel (Deut 9:27; Ps 105:6, 26, 42). The metaphorical usage of slavery in the OT points, therefore, to the condition of absolute dependency on, control by, and service to another Lord ("master").

2. Slavery and the exodus

In New Kingdom EGYPT (Dynasties 18-20; 1550–1069 BCE), individuals bought and sold slaves, but the majority of slaves were the property of temples or the king. New Kingdom pharaohs undoubtedly used large amounts of unfree labor in major royal building projects, such as the temples at Karnak and Luxor, but slaves would have worked alongside otherwise free individuals conscripted through a corvée system or those who worked voluntarily in the agricultural off-season. The majority of slaves in Egypt were foreigners, and large groups of Asiatic, Libyan, and Nubian slaves worked in a kind of state serfdom. These were more akin to helots than actual slaves. The helots were not chattel slaves but tied to particular estates as a whole population subjugated collectively under a dominant nation. They are familiar from the history of the later, Greek Peloponnesian states of Sparta and Messenia.

As resident aliens, the Hebrews are described in Exodus as being forced into manual labor without straw for making bricks and worked to death by rod-wielding taskmasters (Exod 1–5). Although conditions described in the exodus story are not precisely mirrored in the Egyptian evidence, it is clear that the exodus tradition draws on these varying definitions of slavery present in Egypt at multiple times down through the 1st millennium BCE. The historian would best describe them as helots. Unlike chattel slaves they have an identity and religious life independent of the master (PHARAOH), retain their own language and family structures, and are not bought and sold. This classification is important because the story of Exodus itself recognizes this difference. The fifth and tenth plagues (diseased livestock and death of the firstborn) kill not only Egyptians but also their non-Hebrew slaves, privately owned chattels (Exod 9:20-21 and 11:5), in contrast to the Hebrew "communal slaves" of Pharaoh. Classifying the Hebrews as helots rather than chattel slaves does not diminish the horror of their experience, however. The story begins with Pharaoh ordering the death of all male Israelites (Exod 1:22), an act of extermination against which the Hebrews mount a helot revolt and obtain liberation from the bondage of Pharaoh (see EXODUS, BOOK OF).

This liberation is described as "redemption," the "purchase back" of slaves by the original owner from a foreign master. The Sinai covenant with Moses thus obligates the redeemed Israelites and their descendants to "serve [literally, "be a slave to"] Yahweh (Exod 13:3-10; 20:2; Deut 6:20-25; Lev 25:42; Josh 24:16-19; Judg 6:7-10; 1 Kgs 9:9). The bond that the covenant creates is one paradigm among many for the divine-human relationship (father-son, husband-wife, teacher-disciple, king-subject). The covenant is also voluntary, clearly modeled on the ANE suzerain-vassal treaty, and obligates God to Israel just as it obligates Israel to God. A vassal, however, is not exactly a slave. The text thus mixes the language of vassalage and slavery in its description of Israel's relationship to Yahweh (see COVENANT, OT AND NT).

Celebration of the exodus becomes an annual ritual that combines the Jewish agricultural festivals of Unleavened Bread and of Passover (see PASSOVER AND FEAST OF UNLEAVENED BREAD). The Lord redeeming Israel from the bondage of another power recurs as a leitmotiv in the liturgical calendar and the biblical canon itself. It has special prominence in connection to the Persian restoration of the Judeans from the Babylonian exile, described as a repeat of the exodus (2 Chr 36:16-21; Isa 45:1-25; Lam 5:1-22; Ezra 6:19-22; 9:8-9).

But the exodus did not inspire a call for the abolition of slavery in ancient Israelite society. At least five of the Ten Commandments support slavery and presuppose an audience of male Israelite masters. The Fourth (or Third) Commandment requires Israelite landowners to make their slaves, and livestock, rest on the Sabbath (Exod 20:10 = Deut 5:14). Rather than investing the slave with intrinsic worth as a human being, as 19th cent. abolitionist interpreters later claimed (and followed by many 20th cent. biblical scholars), the commandment assimilates slaves and livestock; such "animalization" of the slave is familiar from the wider ANE and Mediterranean world. The main concern is to reform the master, not the slave. The law anticipates that masters might try to forgo the Sabbath requirement by having their slaves do their work for them (*see* REST; SABBATH).

The Six (or Fifth) Commandment, on murder, mainly concerns the homicide of the freeborn Israelite within a legally recognized KINSHIP and household structure (Exod 20:13 = Deut 5:17); the subsequent discussion gives different casuistic formulations on the killing of a slave (Exod 21:12-17, 28-32; *see* FAMILY; HOUSEHOLD, HOUSEHOLDER). The Eighth (or Seventh) Commandment forbids not robbery in general (which, after all, is the subject of a different commandment, the Tenth) but more likely the abduction of freeborn Israelites for sale into slavery (Exod 20:15 = Deut 5:19; see 24:7; compare Gen 40:15). The focus remains the protection of the freeborn Israelite, not the slave.

Property rights protection goes hand in glove with ancient ideologies of slavery. The prohibition of adultery in the Seventh (or Sixth) Commandment on adultery does not forbid a married Israelite man from having sex with his own household slaves (Exod 20:14 = Deut 5:18) against their will (what we would call rape). Such an admonition treats slaves as legitimate sexual victims of their masters. The Tenth (or Ninth and Tenth) Commandment reads: "You shall not covet your neighbor's house; you shall not covet your neighbor's wife, or male or female slave, ox, or donkey, or anything that belongs to your neighbor" (Exod 20:17 = Deut 5:21). The abridgement "You shall not covet," all too typical in Decalogue postings today, conceals how the commandment authorizes a master to covet his own slave, even sexually. Explicit statements like Deut 15:15 and Exod 22:20-23 do suggest that the exodus, or the memory of the exodus, did prompt preaching about reform in the treatment of vulnerable and marginalized Israelites.

3. Hebrew slave laws

The OT laws about the Hebrew slave appear in three discrete collections that share a literary relationship: the so-called Book of the Covenant (Exod 20:22–23:33), which is older than the Decalogue; the Deuteronomic Code (Deut 12–26), associated with the reforms of the Judahite King Josiah in 621 BCE; and the Holiness Code (Lev 17–26). Yet one must avoid harmonizing the various laws of slavery in the Pentateuch as if they constituted some monolithic Mosaic "code." The laws are different from each other and result from a complex historical and literary development. They are also specific to ancient Israelite society, not universal admonitions for the world or even the ANE (*see* COVENANT, BOOK OF THE).

The law in Exod 21 envisages the wealthy Israelite landowner acquiring male Hebrews from previous owners (Exod 21:2-6). It also presupposes that female slaves are acquired from fellow Israelites selling their daughters as wives (Exod 21:7-11). The acquisition of female slaves may reflect a wider Mesopotamian type of adoption-marriage contract familiar from the provincial town of Nuzi, in the small Hurrian kingdom of Arrapha, and from the OT itself (Gen 31:14-16; compare Hos 3:2). Male or female, the Hebrew slave receives protection in law, to be sure. But there is no evidence that this law was observed at any time in Israelite history.

Changes to the law in Lev 25 suggest the ineffectiveness of the original version. The redactor sharpens the law of Exod 21 by distinguishing between Hebrew and non-Hebrew slaves (Lev 25:39-55). The term "Hebrew" refers specifically to a client or family retainer (Lev 25:35, 39) understood to be male (Lev 25:44). Hebrews are "dependent on you" and impoverished so as to "sell themselves to you." They may not "serve as slaves," be bought or sold "as slaves are sold," or be mastered "with harshness." Rather, "they shall remain with you as hired or bound laborers." In the fiftieth year (the Jubilee) they must be freed, along with their children, to "go back to their own family and return to their ancestral property." The Jubilee year of manumission gives the law greater importance by its echo of Mesopotamian proclamations of liberty in the land by the monarch to show his justice on the occasion of his coronation (*see* JUBILEE, YEAR OF).

But foreign-born slaves enjoy no such Jubilee manumission or protection from harsh treatment, the Holiness Code asserts (*see* H, HOLINESS CODE). Foreign (Canaanite) slaves are chattels, capable of being bought and sold, and socially dead. The male Israelite landowner (the intended audience) may acquire this kind of real slave from the surrounding nations, and/or from the resident aliens and their families tied in serfdom to the master's land as dependents. "They may be your property," the Priestly author decrees, "a possession for your children ... to inherit as property" (*see* P, PRIESTLY WRITERS). "These you may treat as slaves." By the explicit contrast with the Hebrew slave, the meaning is clear. The Canaanite slave properly receives "harsh" treatment (Lev 25:44-46). The detailed provision on the redemption of distressed Hebrews owned by foreigners continues this contrast of the Hebrew and the Canaanite slave (Lev 25:47-55). The redacted law in Lev 25 proposes to lower the debt bondage of distressed Hebrews by increasing the enslavement of Canaanites in ancient Israelite society.

Deuteronomy 15:12-18 also revises the legislation in Exod 21, providing further evidence of non-compliance in ancient Israelite society. The redactor makes it more straightforward. The set of admonitions follows directly from a discussion of the nationwide sabbatical year of remission (Deut 15:1-11). It also concerns only distressed Hebrews fallen into debt indenture and favors the release of those Hebrews from servitude in a seventh year of debt remission, more frequently than what Leviticus had proposed. The meaning of the term "Hebrew" clearly denotes any Israelite, regardless of client status or gender (Deut 15:12). Curses enforce the legal penalties of covenant violation (Deut 27:26). The national memory of the exodus is the sole warrant for the admonitions (Deut 15:15; see also Deut 5:15; compare Exod 20:8-11). This warrant also motivates the additional stipulation not to release the distressed Hebrew "empty-handed" (Deut 15:13-14). The law addresses a single issue—Israelite landowners indenturing free Israelites—and does not consider problems that may arise from the purchase of (possibly, Hebrew) slaves from other owners.

Each of the laws in Exod 21 and Deut 15 imagines the Hebrew slave to be so fully integrated into the Israelite household as to develop "love" for his master. A persona of the Hebrew slave actually declines the master's offer of manumission out of personal ties of affection and general good life: the passage prescribes a ritual procedure of piercing his ear and thus transforming him into a permanent chattel slave (Exod 21:5-6; Deut 15:16-17). Piercing the ear with an awl through the doorpost marks the slave body as a permanent possession of the landowner. The line between the Canaanite chattel slave and the Hebrew indentured servant has begun to blur.

The *Code of Hammurabi* has a paragraph (§117) that restricts the time of debt bondage of distressed Babylonians to three years. Because the tenure of service is half what the parallel passages in Exodus and Deuteronomy recommend, the cuneiform source does not seem "less humane" than the biblical one, as commonly asserted. To be sure, there are differences between the two sets of laws. The laws of Hammurabi say nothing about the head of household selling himself into slavery and contain no suggestion that the indenture could be made permanent, as Exodus and Deuteronomy do. The OT laws do give the enslaved Israelite more protection and divine favor than other Near Eastern law codes for their own enslaved or indentured nationals.

An additional parallel from the comparative history of ancient slavery is also helpful. In response to a widespread indebtedness crisis at Athens, the Athenian democratic lawmaker SOLON (ca. 600 BCE) outlawed debt bondage for citizens altogether. By enacting the measure, Solon formally defined the Athenian citizen body and forced landholders to turn to outsiders for dependent labor. The Solonic debt reforms thus enabled classical ATHENS to emerge as a genuine slave society, which established an economic basis for democracy. The Hebrew slave law does not reform Israel to the extent that Solonic law does Athens.

In fact, the commercial slave traffic and debt-bondage of fellow Hebrews continued throughout the biblical period (2 Kgs 4:1; Amos 2:6; 8:6; Mic 2:9). King

Zedekiah of Judah proclaimed his large-scale manumission legislation to curry favor with the Lord so as to avert the Babylonian siege of Jerusalem, but without success. The king manumitted all Hebrew debt slaves in the same year and without regard to tenure of service, introducing a modification to Hebrew slave laws even as he asserted to uphold their unchanging divine sovereignty. But as soon as the siege seemed to let up, the people re-enslaved the very Hebrews they had manumitted, which prompted Jeremiah's oracle against Jerusalem (Jer 34:8-22). After the Babylonian exile, the debt bondage of citizens was so widespread that Nehemiah moved to outlaw it completely (Neh 5:1-13), a legislative action resembling that of Solon.

All this evidence shows why we must avoid harmonizing the various Hebrew slave laws into some single, comprehensive system of social welfare legislation. They did not offset the rise of debt bondage or reduce the commercial traffic of chattel slaves. Israelites "may buy male and female slaves from among the nations around them" and these "may be your property" (Lev 25:45). If a master strikes his chattel slave "with a rod and the slave dies," the master is to be punished, unless the slave survives "a day or two" because "the slave is his money" (Exod 21:20-21). The foreign ("Canaanite") slave was a permanently dishonored person, an object whose worth before God was nothing more than its monetary value (*see* DEBT, DEBTOR; POOR; POVERTY; PROPERTY).

4. Early Judaism
The late prophetic book of Malachi has God ask why the deity fails to get the respect that a master gets from his slave, or a father from his son (Mal 1:1-6). Thus the slave emerges as an undifferentiated "thing," a theological and moral topos, for authors to "think with." In this way, early Jewish sources modify the Torah's slave legislation.

One major change is harmonizing the various Hebrew slave laws to neutralize the possibility that the Bible could contradict itself. For example, the Septuagint version changes the passage of Exod 21:16 (LXX Exod 21:17) to conform to the wording in Deut 24:27, which limits the prohibition of kidnapping to only the abduction of the "sons of Israel" (fellow Jews). Philo of Alexandria harmonizes the Torah's slave legislation to Hellenistic discussion on household management following the tradition of Aristotle's *Politics* (as does another Hellenistic Jewish author, Pseudo-Phocylides). Philo interprets the Hebrew slave laws also through the Stoic philosophical principle of justice—reciprocity in the duties of masters and slaves—and so argues that masters must manage their anger and other passions in order to be good masters of their slaves (*Decalogue* 167; *Spec. Laws* 2.90–92). Making the Jewish law intelligible in a Hellenistic worldview, Philo explains that sometimes a slave turns out to be the "real" free person in terms of philosophical liberty (*Good Person*

19). Similarly, Ben Sira praises the value of a "clever slave," a figure more learned than his master (Sir 7:20-21; 10:25; 33:25-33; see Prov 29:19-21). Conventional tropes of Greek "New Comedy" emerge more clearly in the didactic fiction of the book of Judith, which has the title character play a slave in order to pursue her cause (Jdt 11:5-19). Impersonating the slave allows Judith to get away with otherwise morally questionable behavior. All these Jewish authors offer practical guides for their fellow Jewish masters in a Hellenistic world.

Furthermore, instructions for slaveholders appear in the Dead Sea Scrolls. The *Damascus Document* of the Qumran community prohibits a master from "provoking" (or "urging") his male or female slave to work on the Sabbath (CD XI, 12) or to sell his circumcised slave to a gentile (CD XII, 10–11). In contrast, both Flavius Josephus (*Ant.* 18.21) and Philo of Alexandria (*Good Person* 79) claim that the Essenes did not practice slavery. These claims attempt to make the Jewish group intelligible to a gentile (pagan) audience by conflation with the ancient Cynics, a Greco-Roman philosophical school famous for its adherence to natural living. Philo describes another community of "philosophers" (possibly imaginary) in similar stock language, the so-called Therapeutae in the Egyptian desert (*Contempl. Life* 70). The Therapeutae and Essenes live philosophically (naturally), without normal cultural institutions like slavery, marriage, private ownership, and commerce. Early Jewish writers imagine, therefore, that the abolition of slavery is tantamount to the wholesale rejection of all human culture and civilization, a view consistent with other thinkers in the ancient Mediterranean world.

B. New Testament
1. Slavery in the Roman Empire

Imperial Roman society is the particular historical context for understanding slavery in the NT (*see* ROMAN EMPIRE). Although evidence from classical Greece (5th- and 4th-cent. BCE Athens) can usually illuminate the history of the development of Hellenistic practices in the east, slavery in classical Athens has in fact little direct relevance to early Christianity. The same problem of anachronism, which plagues the other "biblical theology" approach, applies to any attempt to use the OT as evidence for slavery in the NT. Slavery had fundamental importance in the structure of urban life during the central period of Roman history (from roughly 200 BCE to 200 CE). Slaves were at all levels of the economy and society, at least in Italy, Sicily, and a few other urbanized provinces—a genuine slave society. The main sources of slaves included the professional slave trade, kidnapping (banditry), infant exposure, children born from slave mothers, and the punishment of criminals. Above all else, warfare remained the greatest supplier of slaves. In his campaigns in Gaul alone (58–51 BCE), Julius Caesar is reported to have shipped back to Rome nearly one million enslaved prisoners of war. Slaves by the tens of thousands poured into the markets of Sicily and peninsular Italy as early as the First Punic War (264–241 BCE), a direct result of the annual pattern of military expansion of Rome's borders during the late Republic. Even after the late republican wars of expansion, battles continued to be an important source of slaves; Rome's enormous slave population did not reproduce enough to replace itself.

Race was not a factor. The Romans acquired their slaves from all over the Mediterranean world: Britain, Scythia, Greece, Palestine, Ethiopia, Spain. An anecdote about the Roman Senate best illustrates the inconspicuous ubiquity of slaves in urban society. The political body once debated a bill to distinguish slaves from free people by their dress, but it defeated the measure soundly upon realizing the danger of making apparent to slaves their number (Seneca, *On Mercy* 1.24.1).

The fact that slaves came from all the ethnicities and nationalities made most Romans doubt Aristotle's theory of "natural slaves." Aristotle had claimed that some humans by virtue of their very bodies were naturally designed for slavery (*Politics* 1.1–7; *Nicomachean Ethics* 8.11). Romans favored a Stoic philosophy about a common humanity between slave and free, which argued for arbitrary fate as the creator of slaves and masters (reversible for all people at any time) and not nature (Seneca, *Letters* 47).

Likewise, in Roman law, slavery is an institution of the Law of Nations by which, contrary to nature, one person is subjected to the power of another (Justinian, *Institutes* 1.3.2; *Digesta* 1.5.4.1). Remarkably, this case is the only one in the entire extant corpus of Roman law in which the Law of Nations and the Law of Nature are in conflict. This particularly Roman definition of slavery is but one reason why we must keep Athenian and Roman evidence separate.

Another reason is the particular ideology of mastery that the Romans called *auctoritas* ("mastery"), influential on much early Christian thinking about slavery. The Romans thought of the ideal slave not as a mere "living ['breathing'] tool" (as does Aristotle) but as an independent agent with recognized subjectivity. Mastery (*auctoritas*) was achieved in a series of specific, concrete events in which the slave expressed acceptance of the master's point of view so fully as to anticipate the master's wishes. Rather than merely following orders in mechanical fashion, like an automaton, the "good slave" competed and developed what the master had only suggested or even unconsciously desired—a task that in practice encouraged the actual slave to develop moral intuition. This personalized power (influence) over the slave was a central tenet in the Roman discourse of authority. Authors from the period discussed the hard work and constant maintenance that such mastery over a subjective self required. The value was also deeply moral, belonging to Rome's fundamentally hierarchical society. It envisaged slavery as merely the absolute in a continuum of domination and subordination that every person (except perhaps the emperor) experienced.

In Roman society, slaves were found in every occupation and not segregated from free people in work or types of job performed. Some slaves held positions of considerable power, one important example of which were the slaves and freedmen of the Roman emperor ("slaves of Caesar") who held posts in imperial administration. Owners prized a literate and educated slave. Slaves were physicians, architects, business managers, artists, teachers, poets, professional philosophers, as well as in primary production (agriculture, mining, manufacture). But most slaves were of quite modest means and worked as ordinary laborers. Because slaves could be found at all economic levels of society—a few slaves even accumulated considerable wealth in their *peculium* (personal funds)—they had no cohesion as a group and lacked anything akin to class-consciousness.

Slavery went far down the socio-economic scale, with even clients and the free poor owning slaves. In such poorer households, slaves had to be jacks-of-all-trades. At the other end of the scale, the households of the aristocratic elite, dozens and even hundreds of household slaves (in both urban and rural estates) were conventionally assigned to very precise duties (e.g., fuller, glazier, saddler, midwife, chamberlain, furniture polisher). This extraordinary specialization reflected not only the Roman cultural habit of categorization and hierarchy but also the particularly Roman understanding of *auctoritas*. Masters were aware of the need for slaves to be motivated to increase labor efficiency: a position (rank) in a "servile hierarchy" in the household gave an individual slave motivation to work industriously, because only he or she would be held accountable for the work performed. Most slaves were supervised by elite slave managers (overseers) known in Latin as *vilici*.

In such aristocratic urban households, manumission was a highly conventional practice, but it was not automatic after a certain term of service. Only a fraction of slaves were actually freed in Roman society, but the possibility, nonetheless, proved to be a powerful incentive for slave obedience. An unusual feature of Roman slavery, compared with the institution in classical Athens or the Hellenistic east, was that a slave legally manumitted by a Roman citizen owner using formal procedures became also a Roman citizen. Even so, the freedman or freedwoman still owed the former master, now patron, a specific number of work days (*operae*) and formal deference (*obsequium*), including forfeiture of the right to sue. Manumission was conventionally practiced because it suited the masters' interests, reinforcing the institution and ideology of slavery.

All slaves were answerable by their bodies: brutal punishment, TORTURE, and abuse were daily realities of slavery. Slave owners weary of the effort could hire the services of professional torturers. Inscriptions attest the services of professional floggers and domestic executioners for a flat fee. Outright slave rebellion was rare, two in ancient Sicily (136–132 BCE and 104–101 BCE) and the one led by the gladiator Spartacus in an-

cient Italy (73–71 BCE), none of which received the support of rural poor or urban slaves. Yet these revolts occurred in a very limited time span in the context of massive military expansion and political upheaval under the late Republic, and they coincided with relaxation—not tightening—of control over the slave population. Although there were some opportunities for high status, resistance, and liberation for a select group of the most resourceful and fortunate slaves, most slaves lived and died under a brutal system that never questioned the morality of enslavement and had no abolitionist movement.

2. Gospels and Acts

No extant saying of Jesus or any apostle condemns the institution or ideology of slavery as intrinsically evil or sinful. Indeed, there are many references to and anecdotes about slaves and slavery in the Gospels and book of Acts. One finds individuals like the centurion's slave (Luke 7:1-10; Matt 8:5-13), the temple slave of the Jewish high priest (Mark 14:47; Matt 26:51; Luke 22:50-51; John 18:10, 26), the ETHIOPIAN EUNUCH (Acts 8:27-40), the running maid RHODA (Acts 12:13-15), and the prophesying SLAVE GIRL AT PHILIPPI whom Paul shuts up and so reduces her market value to her owners (Act 16:16-24).

Importantly, the synoptic Jesus tells a number of parables whose plots revolve around slave characters or servile types: the Parable of the Unforgiving Slave (Matt 18:23-35) and the Parable of the Dishonest Manager (Luke 16:1-13). The explicit fiction of these texts offered early Christian authors opportunities for literary imagination about the character portrayal of slaves and the morality of *auctoritas*.

In the Parable of the Talents (Matt 25:14-30; see Luke 19:12-27), a man leaving on a journey summons three of his household slaves and entrusts talents (a unit of money) to each "according to his [each slave's] ability." The narrative's introduction makes explicit the inherent difference in moral worth among the three slaves. The one having the least ability is entrusted only with a single talent. Although that slave complies with the literal commands of the master, he is said to be "useless" because he has not internalized the master's influence (*auctoritas*) fully enough to anticipate and complete the master's will. Paralysis from fear of merciless punishment—the master is called a "harsh man"—causes the slave to act as an automaton and hide the money in the ground. His more worthy fellow slaves go out and trade the talents to make more. The master, in Matthew's reckoning, rightly rewards the entrepreneurial "good slaves," who subsequently receive greater household responsibilities and "enter into the joy of their master" and rightly punishes the "bad slave." The master yells at the terrified piece of chattel, calling him a "wicked and lazy slave" and throws him "into the outer darkness, where there will be weeping and gnashing of teeth" (25:26-30), perhaps in reference to the beating of his life, employing domestic torturers used regularly for such purpose. In the parable, the author of Matthew portrays a bland moralistic polarity of "bad slave" and "good slave," a tale of *apsente ero* (when the master's away) familiar from Roman comedy, and communicates the moral value of *auctoritas* recast as Christian theology about responsibility in the interim period (before Christ's return) to his audience.

The literary theme recurs in the Parable of the Faithful and the Unfaithful Slave (Matt 24:45-51; see Luke 12:42-48 and Mark 13:33-37). A master leaves home, placing an elite slave in charge of the other slaves in a servile hierarchy (typical for a Roman household situation). In this tale of *apsente ero*, the slave manager (evoking the well-known *vilicus* figure in Roman literary imagination, the bailiff or elite slave overseer) takes advantage of his master's prolonged absence by abusing his fellow slaves and by gluttonous living, perhaps an author's vision of slave psychology—that the weak and abused will invariably become a sadistic abuser when given power and authority. The parable ends with an eschatological warning about torture: the master will return, on a day not expected, and he "will cut him [that bad slave] to pieces ["cut him off"]" and put him where there will be weeping and gnashing of teeth (Matt 24:51). The Lukan version advances *auctoritas* even more explicitly: "That slave who knew what his master wanted, but did not prepare himself or do what was wanted, will receive a severe beating" (Luke 12:47). Instructing the faithful by making examples of others who are unfaithful, the parable teaches a theological point about delayed eschatology and the judgment of God. God will be like a very harsh slave master. Christians, in the opinion of the synoptic Jesus, will be held accountable for their internalization and anticipation of God's will as a slave must internalize and anticipate the master's will even when the master delays in returning.

The theological message of such slave parables reinforced and depended upon the social hierarchy of master and slave. The goal was not to teach ancient audiences the behavior of actual slaves and masters, which they presumably already recognized and saw quite well in the stories, but to communicate early Christian ethics through the slavery allegory. Warnings of beatings "light" to "severe," especially dismemberment and other torture, for "bad slaves" in the Gospel admonitions about watchfulness served not to inform readers about the actual treatment of slaves but about the eschatological judgment of God. This allegorical use of slavery expressed not social description but religious beliefs. Bible readers today who try to use such texts as direct evidence of the practice of slavery in early Christianity must do so only with great caution and methodological control.

These parables and other NT narratives reveal how slavery shaped the thinking of the early Christians. To borrow the famous formation of the anthropologist Claude Lévi-Strauss, early Christians apparently found slaves "good to think with." Indeed, the dramatic persona of "the slave" served both Christians and non-Christians as a literary device for thinking about community, social categorization, hierarchy, and the proper relationship to the divine. The choice to promote such stories (stock moral exempla) thus had great missionary value because of their universal appeal in classical culture.

3. Pauline letters

The greatest missionary in the NT is the apostle Paul, whose authentic letters use the metaphor of slavery in key passages. He calls himself a "slave of Christ," an apostolic designation (Rom 1:1; Phil 1:1; Gal 1:10; see 1 Cor 9:16-18), and the "slave of all," a commonplace trope of servant leadership (1 Cor 3:5; 9:19-23; 2 Cor 4:5). Paul urges congregations to accept this good slavery for themselves (Rom 12:11; 13:4; 14:4, 18; 1 Cor 7:22-23; Gal 5:13) and to avoid the bad slavery to sin (Rom 7:14) and desire (loss of self control) (Rom 16:18; 1 Cor 9:27; compare Titus 2:3; 3:3; Eph 2:3). The apostle invokes favorably the triumph scene of war captives paraded as new slaves (2 Cor 2:14; compare Col 2:15), the slave market and slave trading (1 Cor 6:19-20; 7:23; compare 1 Tim 1:10), the indignity that actual slaves suffer (2 Cor 11:20), and much manumission (redemption) language (Rom 3:24; 6:6-23; 8:12-23; Gal 3:13-14; 4:1–5:1). An early ritual song (hymn) about Christ taking the "form of a slave" by crucifixion (a slave's punishment) also appears in a prominent epistolary place (Phil 2:6-11; compare 2 Cor 11:7). Clearly, the metaphor of slavery shaped Pauline theology (*see* KENOSIS).

Paul addresses actual slaves only in three principal passages: the Letter to Philemon, 1 Cor 7:20-24, and Gal 3:28 (see parallel in 1 Cor 12:13; compare Col 3:11). The first text is a letter of reference for the slave ONESIMUS, whom Paul met and converted while in prison, to the householder (master) Philemon. The letter appeals to the "partnership" between Paul and Philemon to urge a new future for Onesimus, namely, to be of service to Paul in the gospel (Phlm 13). Paul tactfully tries to create a bond of obligation by evoking the language of a future oral agreement, perhaps aiming for Philemon to hand over Onesimus to Paul as an apprentice. Whether Paul also wants Philemon to manumit his slave is curiously unclear in the letter; also uncertain is how Onesimus came to Paul in prison. Speculation about the letter's occasion has led to many stories about Onesimus, each of which recent scholarship has brought into serious doubt—especially the hypothesis that Onesimus originally came to Paul as a runaway slave. Because Paul's diction is unusually deferential and circumspect, many exegetical issues remain open questions (*see* PHILEMON, LETTER TO).

First Corinthians 7:20-24 deals explicitly with the question of manumission, but its exegesis is no less contested than Philemon. The debate centers on verse

21, a sentence ambiguous in the original Greek and difficult to translate because of an ellipsis: "Were you a slave when called [baptized]? Don't worry about it. But if you can become free, rather use ...." But use what? Does Paul say, "make use of your present condition [of slavery] more than ever" (NRSV), or "avail yourself of the opportunity [for freedom]" (RSV)? Paul's failure to complete his sentence creates the possibility of contradictory, opposing readings of the verse.

There may be a possible solution. First, the passage's grammar, syntax, and distinctive diatribe formula favor the "use freedom" interpretation. Second, the history of slavery in ancient Corinth confirms a Roman social context: Corinth was rebuilt as a Roman colony, founded by Italian freedmen and clients of Julius Caesar. Such a Roman city would witness the conventional practice of manumission as part of the institution of slavery. From this evidence, Paul arguably accepts and even encourages the manumission of (urban) slaves. The apostle's acceptance of manumission is not a cry for abolitionism, however. By incorporating the Roman institutionalized practice of manumission into his theology, Paul speaks in ways similar to other Greco-Romans connected to slave-ownership. Social conservatism (and support of slavery) in the Greco-Roman world did not include the restriction of manumission.

Because 1 Cor 7:21 fails to criticize slavery, readers often turn to Gal 3:28 as the clear text breaking down the categories of free and slave. And indeed Paul does say this. But the specific context is the ritual language of baptism, which articulates a new creation "in Christ" (not in society or the world). The words are formulaic and draw on certain aspects of the Adam legends of human unity—neither male nor female, neither Jew nor Greek, neither slave nor free—when all were one (Gen 1:26-27). Other Greco-Roman writers invoked a world without such social distinctions, but usually to highlight its utopian, unattainable nature. Although such utopian language had undeniable appeal in a society as hierarchical as classical antiquity, it is doubtful that any ancient person, even Paul, could image the ritual language in Gal 3:28 as a feasible basis for actual practice or social reform, as indeed his puzzling and tentative statements on fixed gender roles for women indicate (1 Cor 11:3-16; see also 14:33-36).

In any case, the later writers of the Pauline circle make clear that slaves must accept their slavery by including Aristotelian household (domestic) codes, which form a discrete set of parallel texts (Eph 6:5-9; Col 3:22–4:1; 1 Tim 6:1-2; Titus 2:9-10; 1 Pet 2:18-25; compare 1 Tim 3:4-5, 12; *Did.* 4.10–11; *Barn.* 19.7). These texts function as early Christian self-definition (clarifying roles in the household) and apologetics, defending Pauline churches against charges of subversion to Greco-Roman patriarchy and family values (*see* HOUSEHOLD CODES). The domestic codes command slaves "to obey your earthly masters with fear and trembling, in singleness of heart" (Eph 6:5; Col 3:22). A few

passages also exhort masters to remember their subordination to another lord ("master"), an echo of the *vilicus* (bailiff, elite slave overseer) motif familiar from Greco-Roman agricultural handbooks.

C. The Legacy of Slavery and the Bible

In the 19th-cent. conflict over the Bible and slavery, American abolitionists, many of whom were Christian evangelicals, ransacked Scripture for texts condemning slavery, but found few. As a consequence, they developed new hermeneutical strategies to read the Bible to counter the "plain sense" (literalist) reading of proslavery theology.

The most significant hermeneutics developed was that of moral intuition. The hermeneutics of moral intuition combined an emphasis on personal emotion (individual, experiential religious truth) and the moral philosophy of Common Sense Realism with its notion of conscience. With evangelical religion and moral philosophy combined, the "plain sense" of the Bible became what one's personal experience intuited it to be. Such new exegesis constituted an early form of biblical criticism, which promoted more critical readings of the biblical text. The moral imperative of antislavery forced many evangelical Christians away from biblicism into a less literal reading of Scripture.

The political imperative of proslavery fostered a strong move back to literalism. Most embarrassing for today's readers of the Bible, the proslavery clergymen were holding the more defensible position from the perspective of historical criticism. The passages in the Bible about slavery signal the acceptance of an ancient model of civilization for which patriarchy and subjugation were not merely desirable but also essential.

The opposing values of literalism and moral intuition remain at odds in American religious culture. Nineteenth-century debates over whether the Bible condemns slavery carry over today in hermeneutically similar debates over race relations, military conflict, capital punishment, poverty, abortion, full emancipation of women (including ordination as church pastors), and lesbian, gay, and transgender rights. The study of slavery in the Bible teaches theology that biblical criticism is seldom able to settle Christian moral debate, but Christian moral debate can and does shape broad and influential trends in biblical criticism. *See* AFROCENTRIC INTERPRETATION; IDEOLOGICAL CRITICISM; LIBERATION; LIBERATION THEOLOGY; SOCIAL SCIENTIFIC CRITICISM, NT; SOCIAL SCIENTIFIC CRITICISM, OT; WOMANIST INTERPRETATION.

Bibliography: Gregory C. Chirichigno. *Debt-Slavery in Israel and the Ancient Near East* (1993); Moses I. Finley. *Ancient Slavery and Modern Ideology.* Brent D. Shaw, ed. Exp. ed. (1998); Jennifer A. Glancy. *Slavery in Early Christianity* (2002); David M. Goldenberg. *The Curse of Ham: Race and Slavery in Early Judaism, Christianity, and Islam* (2003); Albert J. Harrill.

The Manumission of Slaves in Early Christianity (1995); Albert J. Harrill. *Slaves in the New Testament: Literary, Social, and Moral Dimensions* (2006); Catherine Hezser. *Jewish Slavery in Antiquity* (2005); Dale B. Martin. *Slavery as Salvation: The Metaphor of Slavery in Pauline Christianity* (1990); Orlando Patterson. *Slavery and Social Death: A Comparative Study* (1982).

J. ALBERT HARRILL

SLAVONIC ENOCH. *See* ENOCH, SECOND BOOK OF.

SLEDGE, THRESHING [חָרוּץ kharuts; מוֹרַג moragh]. A machine pulled by animals over grain many times until the grain was separated from the stalks. It consisted of wooden planks into which sharp stones or metal had been inserted into holes underneath to facilitate the separating process (2 Sam 24:22; Job 41:30; Isa 28:27; 41:15; Amos 1:3). *See* THRESHING.

EMILY R. CHENEY

SLEEP. *See* AWAKE.

SLIME [תֶּמֶס temes]. The mucus secretion of an animal, such as a snail. In Ps 58:8 [Heb. 58:9], the psalmist, imagining that snails "dissolve" into slime, uses the image to express the hope that the wicked will perish. *See* SNAILS.

SLING [מַרְגֵּמָה margemah, קֶלַע qela'; σφενδόνη sphendonē]. Although it does not appear frequently, the primary Heb. word for "sling" in the OT is qela'; the term margemah in Prov 26:8, translated "sling" by the NRSV, may be etymologically related to the Arabic rujm ("heap of stones"). The characteristic LXX term is sphendonē. The sling is not attested in the NT.

Among the many ANE implements of warfare, the sling was considered one of the most important "long-range" weapons, second only to the bow and arrow. The sling was composed of two thongs, usually leather, and the "hand" (kaf כַּף), the "hollow" in which the projectile was placed (1 Sam 25:29). The sling was used primarily for military purposes, but also for hunting. The sling is well attested both in biblical and extra-biblical literature.

In the biblical literature, as early as the period of the judges, the 700 left-handed Benjaminites were renowned for their accuracy with the sling—"they could sling a stone at a hair, and not miss" (Judg 20:16). This acknowledgment of such skill is included in the narrative of the Benjaminite war. David's engagement of the Philistine giant Goliath perhaps best portrays the sling's effectiveness in warfare (1 Sam 17:40, 49-50; see also Sir 47:4). In the days of the divided monarchy (early to mid-8th cent. BCE) Uzziah is credited with organizing an army that included slingers (2 Chr 26:11-15). In a vivid preexilic judgment oracle that employs the metaphor of a slinger, Jeremiah declares that Yahweh

will "sling" the inhabitants of Judah from their land (Jer 10:18). In an engaging postexilic eschatological salvation oracle laden with military terminology, Zechariah records Yahweh's declaration of Israel's superiority over Javan—a confrontation in which the metaphorical bow (Judah) and arrow (Ephraim) are imaged as superior to "stones of the sling" (Zech 9:11-15).

In the ANE and the classical world the sling is documented in various ways. Linen slings were recovered from the tomb of Tutankhamen (mid-14th cent. BCE). Reliefs from Sennacherib's palace in Nineveh (late 8th to early 7th cent. BCE) depict slingers, with slings in hand, participating with archers in the Assyrian siege of Lachish. Herodotus (5th cent. BCE) makes reference to the involvement of slingers in Greek military engagement (*Hist.* 7.158), and Roman armies were known to hire foreign mercenaries as slingers.

JOHN I. LAWLOR

SLOTH. *See* IDLENESS.

SMELL. *See* ODOR.

SMELT [צָרַף tsaraf]. To purify a metal (Job 28:1-2). Synonymous with "refine," it symbolizes God's purifying action (Isa 1:25; compare Ezek 22:18-22). The Hebrew is also translated as "tried" (Ps 66:10). *See* METALLURGY; REFINING.

SMITH [חָרָשׁ kharash; χαλκεύς chalkeus]. Three smiths are mentioned by name in the Bible: TUBAL-CAIN, the instructor of metal workers (Gen 4:22), HIRAM of Tyre, who cast the copper or bronze implements of Solomon's Temple (1 Kgs 7:13-20), and Alexander, who strongly opposed Paul (2 Tim 4:14; *see* ALEXANDER, FALSE TEACHER, COPPERSMITH). Other biblical texts such as 1 Sam 13:19; Prov 25:4; Isa 54:16; 2 Kgs 24:14, 16; and Jer 24:1; 29:2 indicate the importance and roles of smiths in ancient societies. Sirach 38:28 contains a visceral description of the smith at the anvil; although praising the smith's work (vv. 31-32a), Sirach contrasts the smith with the scribe, whose contemplation of the law is regarded as a nobler vocation (38:32b–39:11).

The KENITES were a tribe of smiths who lived south of the Dead Sea in the desert region. This professional specialization is reflected in the tribal society of the 19th cent. BCE in the same region where specialists could live with the tribes they worked for but could not intermarry with them or change their tribal affiliation.

EVELINE J. VAN DER STEEN

SMOKE [עָשָׁן 'ashan, קְטֹרֶת qetoreth, קִיטוֹר qitor; ἀτμίς atmis, καπνός kapnos]. A phenomenon often accompanying theophany (Exod 19:18; 2 Sam 22:9; Isa 6:4; Rev 15:8) or conveying the WRATH OF GOD (e.g., Deut 29:20; Ps 18:8). Smoke is also a sign of destruction (e.g., Gen 19:28; Josh 8:21; Isa 34:10; Rev 18:9) and a portent of God's judgment (Joel 2:30; compare Rev 9:2). In ritual contexts, smoke rising from INCENSE and SACRIFICES AND OFFERINGS pleases God with its aroma (e.g., Exod 29:18; Lev 1:9; compare Rev 8:4). Several texts describe something transitory by comparison with smoke (e.g., Ps 37:20; Isa 51:6; Hos 13:3). *See* FIRE; THEOPHANY IN THE NT; THEOPHANY IN THE OT.

JOEL M. LEMON

SMYRNA smuhr´nuh [Σμύρνα Smyrna]. Smyrna, the modern city of Izmir, Turkey, was at the foot of Mount Pagros at the mouth of the Melas River on the southern shore of the Gulf of Izmir. It is mentioned in Rev 1:11 and 2:8-11. It was an Greek community from the 10th cent. BCE to the early 20th cent. CE. After conquering the indigenous population, the Aeolians initially settled the northern shore of the gulf. They controlled it until the 8th cent. BCE. At that time, the Ionians came and settled on the southern shore of the gulf. The Lydians, centered in SARDIS, captured Smyrna ca. 600 BCE. They deported the residents throughout the region; however, the deportees' sense of identity was so strong that they continued to refer to themselves as "Smyrnaeans."

Alexander the Great located Smyrna on its present site. Lysimachus established it as a city after the battle of Ipsus in 301 BCE and Smyrna grew politically, economically, and culturally in the next century. Smyrna retained a significant degree of influence even when it came under the dominion of the Seleucids in 281 BCE. Thus, it felt strong enough to align itself with the Romans early in the 2nd cent. BCE against the Seleucids. Indeed, it appealed to Rome for military assistance against Antiochus III in 197 BCE, according to Tacitus (*Ann.* 4.56). As a sign of loyalty and appreciation, Smyrna built a temple to the goddess Roma, the cult-deity of the Roman state, in 195 BCE.

Smyrna remained an independent and powerful city under Roman rule. However, it made an unfortunate alliance with Mithridates VI against the Romans. The Romans defeated Mithridates and punished Smyrna for its disloyalty and reduced its status in 85 BCE. For the next half-century, the history of the entire region was replete with one military campaign after another. It culminated in the defeat of Mark Antony by Caesar Augustus in 30 BCE. Ultimately, Smyrna became one of four cities of provincial assembly with Ephesus, Sardis, and Pergamum, four of the cities addressed in Rev 1:11 and Rev 2–3.

Smyrna was governed by a town council that supervised the work of city magistrates/administrators. There was also a council of elders, as well as an additional representative body with little power. Smyrna was also a center of the provincial cult and had three temples built by Tiberius, Hadrian, and Caracalla. Smyrna had a very liberal policy of granting citizenship to immigrants. This raises the possibility that the Christian community there might have been multicultural.

Smyrna was also designated neōkoros (νεωκόρος), an official center of the imperial cult (late 1st/early 2nd cent. CE). The neokorate established strong ties between the imperial family and the local municipality. It also brought economic, political, and cultural benefactions to a given city. Moreover, it reinforced the traditional, centuries-old ways in which persons in the eastern Mediterranean regions related to their rulers as representatives of their god in some way. Frequently, the ruler was referred to as an offspring of one's god. Politics and religion reinforced one another and established a worldview that connected heaven and earth. A development of the people themselves, it reflected their attempt to make sense of their place in the world. The neōkoros expressed political reality as religious obeisance to the emperor.

Smyrna had very strong local traditions. It claimed to be the birthplace of Homer and the home of noted historian Hermogenes, the orator Aelius Aristides, and the biographer Philostratus. Evidence of this strong local pride can be seen by the fact that 7th-cent. BCE deportees from Smyrna continued to refer to themselves as "Smyrnaeans." Two aspects of communal identity stood out for people of ancient Smyrna: suffering and beauty.

In antiquity, many believed that the name "Smyrna" derived from myrrh (myron μύρον), a fragrance used in preparing bodies for burial. Ovid, Homer, Pausanias, and Theodoret, to name a few, made this connection or a similar one to connote Smyrna as a city of suffering. This connotation was very influential in antiquity. However, others have provided a more prudent assessment. For example, it has been argued that the name is an adaptation of a Semitic word (perhaps myrra). There is indeed a local legend that the city was founded by an unnamed Amazon. This legend reflects a time when an actual Hittite outpost existed in the area. The Semitic presence has been supported by rock-reliefs in the area and also numismatic evidence.

Smyrna was also known as a very beautiful city. The city itself proclaimed as much on its coins. It is also a regular theme in Aelius Aristides and Philostratus' biography of Apollonius of Tyana. It was not the natural beauty that was celebrated, but the architectural beauty of Smyrna that gained the city this renown. For example, Aelius Aristides frequently likened Smyrna to a flower or to a well-sculptured statue. Ramsay also argued that a crown was a major metaphor employed to convey the beauty of the city (e.g., Philostratus, *Vit. Apoll.* 4.7). Hemer concurred and noted the crown image on pre-imperial coins from Smyrna. The crown could connote various things in Smyrna: athletic triumph, municipal festivities, distinguished and/or praiseworthy public service, or a royal visit. It is within such a context that "I will give to you the crown of life" (Rev 2:10) must be understood, evidence that John possessed specific local knowledge of Smyrna. Thus, while the seven messages collectively spoke to the entire Christian community (see Rev 2:7, 11, 17, 29; 3:6, 13, 22), each message contains specific references that spoke solely to the community to which the individual message was addressed. *See* REVELATION, BOOK OF.

Bibliography: C. J. Hemer. *The Letters to the Seven Churches of Asia in Their Local Setting* (1986, 2001).

THOMAS B. SLATER

SMYRNEANS, EPISTLE TO THE. *See* IGNATIUS, EPISTLES OF.

SNAILS [שַׁבְּלוּל shabbelul]. The Hebrew word translated "snail" is related to a word meaning "fluid." The name may refer to the creature's high moisture content, the wet trail it leaves behind, and its propensity to melt away. In Ps 58:8, the psalmist wishes that her or his enemies would disappear "like the snail that dissolves into slime." This context seems to describe the gastropod mollusk we call "snail" but could perhaps indicate a slug or worm. Snail shells were widely used in the ANE as a source of purple dye.

LISA MICHELE WOLFE

SNAKE. *See* FIERY SERPENT OR POISONOUS SNAKE; SERPENT; SNAKE CHARMING.

SNAKE CHARMING [לַחַשׁ lakhash; ψιθυρισμός psithyrismos]. Placating a SERPENT by, literally, whispering to it (Eccl 10:11; Sir 12:13). The serpent's painful and even lethal bite encouraged comparison with a dangerous person (e.g., Gen 49:17; Ps 140:3 [Heb. 140:4]). In Ps 58:4-5 [Heb. 58:5-6], the wicked are likened to the deaf adder, which cannot be charmed because of its stopped ear. Similarly, Jeremiah describes the "foe from the north" as adders that cannot be charmed (Jer 8:17).

JOEL MARCUS LEMON

SNARE. *See* HUNTING; TRAPS AND SNARES.

SNOW [שֶׁלֶג shelegh; תְּלַג telagh; χιών chiōn]. With the exception of Mount Hermon in the north, modern-day Israel does not experience snow on an annual basis. Occasionally, however, snow does fall on other mountainous regions, including the hills of Jerusalem. Psalm 147:16 acknowledges its presence in the environs of Jerusalem as one of the provisions of Yahweh. Elsewhere, snow epitomizes spiritual purity and exemplifies the color white. Thus, Isa 1:18 and Ps 51:7 utilize snow to illustrate the state of cleanness that results from the removal of sin's stain; the paleness of a severe skin disease, LEPROSY (tsara'ath), is compared to the look of snow (Exod 4:6; Num 12:10; 2 Kgs 5:27); and the brilliance of white snow serves to describe the appearance of heavenly beings (Dan 7:9; Matt 28:3; Rev 1:14). *See* ISRAEL, CLIMATE OF; SUMMER AND WINTER.

Bibliography: Yair Goldreich. *The Climate of Israel: Observation, Research and Application* (2003).

JASON R. TATLOCK

SNUFFERS [מֶלְקָחַיִם melqakhayim, מְזַמְּרֶת mezammereth]. Instruments used to snuff out lamps (*see* LAMP, OT) and trim wicks. The melqakhayim used to extinguish the lamps of the lampstand (Exod 25:38; 37:23; Num 4:9) were made of pure gold. Melqakhayim is also translated as "tongs" (1 Kgs 7:49), which were used to lift and carry hot coals (Isa 6:6) and were likewise made of pure gold (2 Chr 4:21). The mezammereth (2 Kgs 12:13 [Heb. 12:14]; 25:14; Jer 52:18; 2 Chr 4:22) is probably better understood as a knife used to trim wicks; it was also made of pure gold (1 Kgs 7:50).

JOEL F. DRINKARD JR.

SO soh [סוֹא so']. The pharaoh whom King Hosea of Israel asked for assistance against Shalmaneser of Assyria a few years before the destruction of Israel in 721 BCE (2 Kgs 17:4). King So is likely Pharaoh Osorkon IV, the last king of the Twenty-third Dynasty, who ruled Egypt until 724 BCE. Others have suggested that the name derives from the Egyptian for "the one of Sais" (*p3-n-s3w*), a city in the delta. Those that follow this suggestion often claim Tefnakht is the king to whom Hosea appealed. Tefnakht was the first king of the short-lived Twenty-fourth Dynasty. He came to the throne in 724 BCE, establishing his capital at Sais.

KEVIN A. WILSON

SOAP [בֹּרִית borith, מֵי־שֶׁלֶג me-shelegh; πόα poa]. A cleansing agent, usually symbolizing moral or spiritual purification. For example, Mal 3:2 describes the refinement of the Levites by God's messenger, who is compared to the soap of fullers. Jeremiah portrays Judah's iniquities as unable to be cleansed with soap (Jer 2:22). In both texts, NRSV translates "soap" for a Hebrew term (borith) meaning "lye" or "alkali." In both cases, the LXX has another purifying agent in view, namely, herbs (poa). In Job 9:30, the NRSV also renders me-shelegh (literally "waters of snow") as "soap" (compare Ps 51:7 [Heb. 51:9]).

JOEL MARCUS LEMON

SOBATA. Located in the west-central Negev (*see* NEGEB, NEGEV), 40 km southwest of Beer-sheba, this large site was situated on a route linking the Nabatean towns of Oboda, Sobata, and Nessana. Founded in the Nabatean period during the reign of the Nabatean king Obodas III (30 BCE–9/8 BCE) or Aretas IV (9/8 BCE–40 CE), Sobata flourished under the last Nabatean king, Rabbel II (70–106 CE), with an economy based on desert agriculture and horse breeding. In the interval before the Byzantine period, the town was eclipsed, but by the mid-4th cent. it became a monastic center, a site for Christian pilgrims, and an agricultural settlement. The splendid South Church, with its cruciform baptismal font, and the North Church were constructed during this period. After the Arab conquest, the site continued for another 200 years until the 8th–9th cent. and perhaps later.

Sobata is important because of its Byzantine town plan, which covers an area of 430 m (north-south) by 330 m (east-west). It is situated on a gradual slope leading to the town center, with three city squares. Emerging from the city squares are nine wide meandering streets with gates enclosing large plots of courtyard houses and cisterns. Water was carried down streets and Nabatean channels to two large Nabatean reservoirs in the town center.

E. H. Palmer first described Sobata in 1870, and A. Musil drew a plan of the site in 1901. A dedicatory inscription to Dushara, dated to the reign of Aretas IV, was found in 1906. In 1958–60 the town plan was defined, and A. Negev, A. Segal, S. Margalit, and J. Shershevski, representing various institutions, have continued to work in various sectors. In the 1960s, the ancient terraces and water channels were restored as part of an environmental campaign under the direction of Michael Even-Ari.

MARTHA JOUKOWSKY

SOCIAL SCIENTIFIC CRITICISM, NT. The models and methods of the social sciences have been fruitfully incorporated into the study of early Christian origins and early Christian texts, usually as a complement to historical-critical examination. This interdisciplinary enterprise has taken two principal directions.

The first investigates the social world of the early Christian movement and the particular communities represented by the texts that are our primary artifacts. This avenue seeks to discover what can be known about the social and economic level of early Christian communities, the social networks and institutions of which early Christians were a part or with which they were competing, the process of group formation, rituals, organization and authority within the group, cultural values (honor, purity, and pollution), and "scripts" (e.g., patronage relationships, the ethos of family) that provided the context for communication and relationships, the preindustrial economy, and the like (*see* COMMUNITY; FAMILY; RITUAL).

The second direction concerns the interpretation of early Christian texts as documents shaped by particular factors in the social setting of the author and audience, and seeking to have particular effects upon the social group they address in relation to that social setting. Drawing on the findings of the first kind of investigation, this avenue examines how a particular text reinforces or challenges group boundaries, constructs or legitimates authority within the group, seeks to mobilize resources, and shapes interaction with other distinct groups and relations with the larger society. Investigators explore the economic, behavioral, and theological tensions in the social setting and their interrelationship, the rela-

tionship between symbolic language in the text and behaviors/values embraced by (or promoted to) the group, and the ways in which the text is crafted to advance the interests of its author(s).

These two mutually informing modes of analysis have greatly enriched our understanding of the complexities of the real-life settings of early Christian churches and the ways in which setting and Scripture were mutually formative. Practitioners have been cautioned about excessive dependence on social scientific models, particularly where these are used to supply what is not found in the texts or where they become a deterministic grid, and about the danger of reducing religious phenomena to social forces. Nevertheless, the proper attention to social scientific questions guards against another kind of reductionism, namely an interest merely in the theological and ethical "ideas" communicated by the text without the flesh-and-blood context in which those are given expression. *See* BIBLICAL CRITICISM.

Bibliography: David A. deSilva. "Embodying the Word: Social-Scientific Interpretation of the New Testament." *The Face of New Testament Studies: A Survey of Recent Research.* Scot McKnight and Grant R. Osborne, eds. (2004) 118–29; David A. deSilva. *Honor, Patronage, Kinship, and Purity: Unlocking New Testament Culture* (2000); John H. Elliott. *What Is Social-Scientific Criticism?* (1993); Bengt Holmberg. *Sociology and the New Testament: An Appraisal* (1990); David G. Horrell. *Social-Scientific Approaches to New Testament Interpretation* (1999); Jerome H. Neyrey, ed. *The Social World of Luke–Acts: Models for Interpretation* (1991); Gerd Theissen. *Social Reality and the Early Christians* (1992).

DAVID A. DESILVA

SOCIAL SCIENTIFIC CRITICISM, OT. Social scientific criticism is an interpretive method that uses heuristic models from the social sciences to understand the social context of ancient Israel and to interpret texts created within that context. In current practice, social scientific criticism draws widely from anthropology and sociology to provide interpretive frameworks, which are constructs designed to: 1) comprehend and order social data; 2) identify patterns and regularities in social observations; 3) provide models for cross-cultural, comparative, and systemic analysis; and 4) suggest questions that can be asked to open up social categories for interpretation. These frameworks or models are applied intentionally and heuristically, helping interpreters understand social phenomena embedded in texts by, e.g., seeing previously unnoticed social relationships, setting isolated data into social patterns, or allowing reconstructions of social organizations and structures. Also, these frameworks drawn from the social sciences are suggestive, not determinative or normative; the social scientific scholar allows the model to interpret data and equally allows the data to refine the model. Social scientific criticism is often combined with other methods, particularly the study of ancient Israelite and Near Eastern history and archaeology, in order to increase the data available for analysis.

While rooted in the early developments of sociology as a discipline in the 19th cent., recent social scientific criticism in biblical studies has flourished from the 1960s onward. In the first decades of this period, studies used anthropological and sociological analysis to examine such varied social phenomena in the OT as ritual pollution, myths, tribes, prophetic behavior, and peasantry. Since the 1980s, scholars have used a wide range of social scientific approaches, including cultural and political anthropology, ethnography, macro-sociology, social psychology, and the sociology of knowledge. Equally varied have been the topics and social phenomena studied. Social scientific models have been used to describe, analyze, and contextualize social realities, such as social groups (e.g., family, clan, tribe, elite classes); cultural relationships (e.g., honor/shame, marriage, debt servitude); patterns of behavior (e.g., sacrifice, prophecy, gender); political structures (e.g., monarchy, empire); political, economic, and social change (e.g., emergence of states, changes in social stratification); historical eras (e.g., early Israel, Judah under Persian rule); and socially constructed realities (e.g., ethnicity, language and rhetoric, symbolism). When practiced with postmodern and ideological criticisms, social scientific criticism also identifies the social context of the interpreter and its influence on the construction and use of models and interpretation of data. *See* BIBLICAL CRITICISM; BIBLICAL INTERPRETATION, HISTORY OF.

PATRICIA DUTCHER-WALLS

SOCKET [פֹת poth, אֶדֶן 'edhen]. A stone or piece of metal with an opening that served as a holder for pivots on which doors and gates swung (1 Kgs 7:50). Excavations have found many of these devices. *See* ARCHITECTURE, OT; DOOR; GATE.

SOCO, SOCOH soh′koh [שׂוֹכוֹ sokho, שׂוֹכֹה sokhoh].
1. A descendant of Judah (1 Chr 4:18), perhaps the person for whom the town of Socoh located in the Shephelah was named.
2. A town in the Shephelah of Judah, according to Josh 15:35, where it is listed with Jarmuth, Adullam, and Azekah, in the second district. During the battle between David and Goliath, the Philistine army was camped between Azekah and Socoh on one mountainside with Israel on the opposite mountainside and the Valley of Elah between them (1 Sam 17:1-3). Socoh was one of the strategic fortified cities guarding one of the main access points into the heart of Judah and Jerusalem. For this reason it was probably later fortified by Rehoboam (2 Chr 11:17) along with the other cities on the border zone between Philistia and Judah. During the time of Ahaz, the city appears to have been

taken for a short time by the Philistines (2 Chr 28:18). It is widely identified with Khirbet 'Abbad and adjacent Khirbet Shuweikah located at the southern part of the Elah valley. Archaeological surveys indicate an occupation during the Iron II, Hellenistic, and Persian periods. Three-fourths of lmlk (meaning "for the king") royal jar handles bearing the name Socoh have been found in the Shephelah and may be related to this site or the nearby valley. Others have argued for the hill-country location (*see* LMLK SEALS).

3. A town by the same name mentioned in Josh 15:48 is located in the fifth district of Judah together with the sites Shamir, Jattir, and Dannah and identified with Khirbet Shuweikah southwest of Hebron.

4. A town in the central hill-country cited as the center of Solomon's third district (1 Kgs 4:10) is generally identified with Shuweiket er-Ras near the pass leading to Shechem.

MICHAEL G. HASEL

SOCRATES. Born in 469 BCE, Socrates was tried and executed in Athens in 399 BCE on charges of impiety and corrupting the youth with his teachings. As he left no writings of his own, the information we have comes from other writers, notably Plato and Xenophon, in whose dialogues Socrates is a protagonist (e.g., both wrote works titled *Apology of Socrates*). As these sources differ, it is unclear what should be attributed to Socrates and what comes from the later writers. A public figure in Athens for much of his adult life, Socrates spent many hours engaging others in conversation and questioning assumptions and traditionally held views. In the Hellenistic and Roman periods, Socrates became a symbol of the philosophical ideal and was claimed by a number of different philosophical schools. His enormous influence is in part the result of the prominence of Plato and Xenophon's writings in Greco-Roman education and rhetorical training. Some scholars think that traditions about Socrates' trial and death may have influenced the portrayal of the trial and death of Jesus in Luke 22:47–23:56 and the rhetoric of the apostles (e.g., Acts 17:16-34).

RUBÉN R. DUPERTUIS

SODI soh′dī [סוֹדִי sodi]. From the tribe of Zebulun, the father of Gaddiel, whom Moses charged with the task of scouting Canaan to determine its fruitfulness and the strength of its inhabitants (Num 13:10).

SODOM, SEA OF sod′uhm [Lat. *mare Sodomitum*]. A Latin term referring to the DEAD SEA (NRSV; "SALT SEA" in the MT and LXX [e.g., Gen 14:3]). The name derives from its supposed proximity to the legendary city of Sodom (Gen 19:1-29). An apocalyptic vision in 2 Esd 5:7 describes a dissolution of order in which the Sea of Sodom casts up fish—an utter impossibility, since no aquatic life can survive its high salinity.

JOEL M. LEMON

SODOM, SODOMITE sod´uhm, sod´uh-mīt [סְדֹם sedhom; Σόδομα Sodoma]. 1.Sodom is first mentioned in the list of nations in Gen 10:1-32. It appears in a geographical description of Canaan (10:19) and as the land of the cursed descendants of Noah's son, Ham, the Canaanites (9:22-27). One boundary extends to the southeast in the direction of "Lasha," as far as, but not including, "Sodom, Gomorrah, Admah, and Zeboiim" (10:19; compare Gen 13:10, 12-13; 14:2, 8). These four cities, with a fifth, "Bela," later called "Zoar" (13:10; 14:2, 8; 19:22-23, 30), form a region known collectively as the "cities of the Plain" (Gen 13:12; 19:29).

These cities play an important role in the Abraham cycle in Genesis, effectively offering the patriarch an alternative mode of existence to that which he is to bequeath to his descendants. They are notable for their attractiveness (to LOT and to later Israelites), their proverbial wickedness (as homes to every sin), and their deserved destruction (an ever-present threat to a "wicked" people of God). In subsequent texts, the cities (in different combinations) will reappear as exemplars to be shunned whenever these themes are invoked by later writers (see below).

When Abraham (Abram until Gen 17:5) receives Yahweh's contingent promise of relationship, descendants, and the land of Canaan in Gen 12:1-7, he departs Haran (having previously left Ur), taking along his barren wife, Sarah, and his nephew and heir, Lot (Gen 12:4; compare 11:27-30). A brief sojourn in Egypt (Gen 12:10-20) leaves the two men so wealthy that, on their return to Canaan, their men fight each other (13:1-7). As a resolution, Abraham offers Lot half of Canaan—the north or the south. On seeing the lush lands to the east, however, Lot rejects the land, his place as heir, and the divine promise (13:8-9; compare 15:2), choosing instead the cities of the plain (13:12). Narratorial asides about their wickedness (13:13) and eventual destruction (13:10) underscore his poor choice.

Lot reappears, however. Genesis 14 describes how the five kings of the cities of the plain rebel against Chedorlaomer, the king of Elam (14:1-4). Following their defeat, the people and goods of Sodom and GOMORRAH—including Lot—are carried off (14:8-11). When Abraham hears this, he pursues the victors and defeats them (14:13-15). He returns with those captured and all of the goods (14:16), offers a tenth to the priestly Melchizedek, king of Salem, after receiving his blessing (14:18-20), and rejects the king of Sodom's offer of the goods so as to avoid any later claim that the king had enriched him (14:22-24). Now free, Lot returns to Sodom. By Gen 19:1, he will have lived outside the promise for twenty years or so (compare 15:2; 16:16–17:1).

In Gen 18:1-8 the deity, in the guise of three visitors, is offered hospitality by Abraham. As the patriarch escorts them on their way, Yahweh wonders if Abraham should be told about the forthcoming divine investigation of the outcry against Sodom and Gomorrah (18:17-19). Knowing the meaning of these events will, the deity concludes, allow the patriarch to teach his descendants, Israel, how nations—themselves included (compare, e.g., Exod 32:10; Num 14:12)—that choose violence over righteousness will be judged (Gen 18:19). The destruction of the Northern Kingdom in 721 BCE and the Babylonian conquest of Jerusalem in the 6th cent. BCE provide local examples of destruction/defeat that would inevitably resonate with the ideas embodied in Gen 18–19 and indeed may have contributed to the development of the text's final form.

On hearing of the investigation, Abraham, told to be a blessing to the nations in 12:1-3, intervenes, seeking justice from the "Judge of all the earth" (18:25). His intention is difficult to discern, however, because his premise—that judging the righteous and the wicked without distinction would be profane—is seemingly contradicted by his argument that the presence of the righteous within the cities should save the wicked. It has been suggested that Abraham is arguing for a vicarious function for the righteous (Brueggemann), or that he wishes to invoke a collective argument in order to save the city (von Rad), or that Yahweh is limited in capability (Ben Zvi). Lot's presence in Sodom also gives Abraham a further, perhaps more concrete, factor to consider, however. The deity responds positively to a series of questions by which the number of the righteous required is reduced by Abraham to just ten. At that number, Yahweh departs.

When the two men, now described as "angels," arrive in Sodom at nightfall (the third presumably being detained by Abraham), they find Lot sitting in the gate of the city, a signifier of his place within Sodom's economy. No hospitality is forthcoming from Sodom, so Lot takes it upon himself to offer it to the men before him (19:3-4). Later, when the city's occupants, or rather, its menfolk—the description of the populace as "the men of the city, the men of Sodom, both young and old, all the people to the last man" clearly indicates the original text's patriarchal assumptions—arrive outside his house, wishing to molest his guests (19:4-5), Lot goes outside and tries to deflect them from this wicked act. Instead he offers them his two virginal and betrothed daughters to do with as they please. Though this has been viewed as the act of a righteous host defending his guests (Matthews), the movement of Lot's characterization from a relatively righteous insider (with Abraham) to an increasingly unrighteous outsider (with the men of Sodom) suggests otherwise. Unplaced, the mob is blinded by the visitors (19:11) before judgment is pronounced upon their city (19:13), a decision that effectively takes the attempted assault in Sodom as proof of the wickedness of the five cities and their inhabitants, whether man, woman, or child. The righteous ten are clearly absent.

The two men effectively drag the dithering Lot and his family out of the doomed city (19:16), cautioning him not to look back (19:17). Finally, and only when outside Sodom, he recognizes Yahweh for himself (19:18). At his own request, Lot goes first to Zoar, a city that, ironically, is saved by his intervention even as Sodom is being destroyed despite the attempted intervention of Abraham (19;18-23), before he flees to the hills with his daughters (19:30), his wife having turned to salt as she looked back (19:26). According to 19:29, Lot is saved for the remembrance of Abraham, a salvation best understood as a personal favor rather than as a direct consequence of either Abraham's argument or Lot's own righteousness. Finally, the incestuous origins of Israel's neighbors, Moab and Ammon, are recounted, as Lot's daughters lie in turn with their drunken father (19:30-38).

The story of Sodom proved highly popular in subsequent biblical texts (compare Deut 29:23 [Heb. 29:22]; 32:32; Ps 11:6; Isa 1:9-10; 3:9; 13:19; Jer 23:14; 49:18; 50:40; Lam 4:6; Ezek 16:46-56; Amos 4:11; Zeph 2:9; Matt 10:15; 11:23-24; Luke 10:12; 17:28-32; Rom 9:29; 1 Tim 1:10; 2 Pet 2:6; Jude 7; Rev 11:8) and in artistic representations (e.g., Abraham with angels [Chagall], pleading for Sodom [Guisto], Lot with angels [Blake], the Sodomites [Rembrandt], Lot fleeing [Raphael], Sodom's destruction [Turner], Lot's wife [Maître], and Lot's "seduction" by his daughters [Velázquez]; a 1963 Robert Aldrich epic, *Sodom and Gomorrah*, starred Stewart Granger, and the Marquis de Sade's libertine and scatological *120 Days of Sodom* was filmed by Pasolini in 1976).

Central to its afterlife was speculation about the sin—or sins—of Sodom, whether sexual (e.g., lust [Philo, *Abraham* 134-45], fornication [*Jub.* 16:5-6], sex with prostitutes [*T. Levi* 14:6], unnatural sex [*T. Naph.* 3:4], sex between males [Augustine, *Civ.* 16:30], and licentiousness [2 Pet 2:7]) or not (e.g., arrogance [Sir 16:8], xenophobia [Josephus. *Ant.* 1.194-95], greed [*b. Sanh.* 109a; *m. Ab.* 5:10], and either a failure [Matt 10:14-15] or a refusal to be hospitable [Wis 19:14]). Sodom is most commonly connected in the Christian tradition with the designation *sodomite* and the practice of sodomy, a term invented by the medieval writer Peter Damien and intended by him to encompass all forms of male same-sex desire (Carden). It remains the case, however, that, in collective terms, those who reflected on Sodom and its afterlife usually understood, if only implicitly, that it formed an "anti-type" of the contemporary people of God, whether Israel or the church. It was a place of such general wickedness—home to virtually every sin—that no single sin could ever have predominated there.

Bibliography: Ehud Ben Zvi. "The Dialogue Between Abraham and Yahweh in Gen 18:23-32: A Historical-Critical Analysis." JSOT 53 (1992) 27–46; W. Brueggemann. *Genesis*. Interpretation (1982); M. Carden. *Sodomy: A History of a Christian Biblical Myth* (2004); W. W. Fields. *Sodom and Gomorrah:* *History and Motif in Biblical Narrative* (1997); W. J. Lyons. *Canon and Exegesis: Canonical Praxis and the Sodom Narrative* (2002); V. H. Matthews. "Hospitality and Hostility in Genesis 19 and Judges 19." *BTB* 22 (1992) 3–11; E. Noort and E. J. C. Tichelaar, eds. *Sodom's Sin: Genesis 18-19 and Its Interpretations* 2004); G. von Rad. *Genesis.* OTL (1961).

WILLIAM JOHN LYONS

2. A man who engages in sexual relations with other men. Sodomites (arsenokoitēs ἀρσενοκοίτης) are listed among the "wrongdoers" in 1 Cor 6:9-10 and among the "lawless" in 1 Tim 1:8-10. The English term derives from the interpretative tradition that the city of Sodom was destroyed because its citizens practiced homosexuality (Gen 19:1-26; compare Jude 7). However, many scholars have suggested that the people of Sodom were punished for their violation of hospitality rules (compare Ezek 16:49). *See* HOMOSEXUALITY; PROSTITUTION; SEX, SEXUALITY.

JESSICA TINKLENBERG DEVEGA

SODOM, VINE OF sod'uhm [גֶּפֶן סְדֹם gefen sedhom]. "Vinestock of Sodom" (Deut 32:32) is a metaphor used to describe an enemy that wrongfully attributes its success over Israel to its own power, rather than to God. Its poisonous fruit awaits God's recompense, just as the Lord's people await divine vindication (Deut 32:35-36).

Josephus reports that by the Dead Sea, near the traditional site of Sodom and Gomorrah, grew plants whose beautiful fruit dissolves into "smoke and ashes" when picked (*J.W.* 4.484–85). Tradition identifies the "vine of Sodom" (apple of Sodom, Ein Gedi apple; *see* APPLE) with various wild plants, including *Calotropis procera* and *Solanum linnaeanum*.

SHARON PACE

SOJOURNER [גֵּר ger; πάροικος paroikos, προσήλυτος prosēlytos]. The meaning of ger, traditionally translated "sojourner," varies through the OT. Some uses suggest persons living in a place not their own, even a foreign country, but ger should probably be defined in class rather than ethnic terms. Landlessness seems fundamental to the meaning.

There are about ninety occurrences of ger, and a like number of its cognates: the verb gur (גּוּר) or the derived noun maghor (מָגוֹר). Over two-thirds of the instances of ger are in law codes in Exodus to Deuteronomy, and many others directly refer to these codes (e.g., Jer 7:6, alluding to the legal prohibition on oppressing the ger). Only about a dozen instances of ger are independent of legal discourse. By contrast, only a quarter of the occurrences of the cognates are in legal discourse, usually linked with ger itself in the expression "the ger who resides (gur) among you" (e.g., Exod 12:49). Many others denote "to live" or "(place of) habitation" in a general sense (e.g., Job 18:19). Hence the cognates cannot safely be used to broaden the understanding of ger unless the context clearly implies features specific to ger itself. Ger is sometimes linked with another noun, toshav (תּוֹשָׁב; from yashav [יָשַׁב], "to dwell"; e.g., Num 35:15). This seems simply a hendiadys, though perhaps it underlines the long duration of ger status.

NRSV translates ger normally as "alien" or "resident alien," but occasionally as "stranger." In references to Israel's ancestors living in Canaan it typically uses "live as an alien," but elsewhere translates the cognates in various ways. Ger (pl. gerim [גֵּרִים]) is not translated here; for the cognates, "sojourn," "sojourning," etc., are used.

A. Possible Early Uses
B. Deuteronomic Law
C. P and Chronicles
D. Extended Meanings
Bibliography

A. Possible Early Uses

Outside of law codes, scattered occurrences may attest to an early usage of ger for individuals living in territory not their own: Abraham in Canaan (Gen 23:4), Moses in Midian (Exod 2:22), an Amalekite in Israel (2 Sam 1:13). There is likely an etymological connection with Arabic jar, a term known from Bedouin life for an outsider who seeks protection from a local chief. The verb "sojourn" occurs often in similar situations: in addition to the ancestors in Genesis, Ruth's Judahite in-laws "sojourn" in Moab (1:1), Elijah in Sidon (1 Kgs 17:20), an Israelite woman in Philistia (2 Kgs 8:1-2). These stories sometimes suggest reasons for an extended stay in a place not one's own, most often famine but also threat of vengeance (Jacob) or legal reprisal (Moses). Such individuals may prosper, but more often they are in distress. There is some expectation that they will provide labor for people who protect them (Jacob, Moses). Perhaps the most adequate English word is "refugee."

A recurring theme in Genesis is that Israel will one day possess the land of Canaan where their ancestors "sojourned" (also Ps 105:23; Heb 11:9). "Sojourn" can be used of Israel in exile (Ezek 20:38; Ezra 1:4). There might be no change of country. In Judg 19:16, an Ephraimite "sojourns" in another part of Israel, while in 2 Sam 4:3 an entire kin-group does so. Presumably less distant displacements were the rule rather than the exception; people in distress would choose the nearest place of survival and safety. Another kind of instance of Israelites "sojourning" in Israel is provided by the Levites of Judg 17:7-9; 19:1. Levites "sojourn" where they can find a place (17:8).

The ger to whom Job shows hospitality (31:32) seems a transient visitor, but this is unusual. The status of ger is normally of long duration or permanent, passing even to the descendants of gerim.

B. Deuteronomic Law

Deuteronomic law (including the early stage of this tradition found in Exod 20–23) places considerable stress on equality for the ger before the law. According to the Decalogue (Exod 20:10; Deut 5:14), gerim must keep Sabbath, and they are to be full participants in festivals (Deut 26:11). In Deuteronomic law, ger is not (as it is in priestly law) contrasted with some opposite status. Nonetheless, gerim are separated rhetorically from Israel in that they are not part of the "you" to whom the law is addressed; they are referred to as a separate group in the third person.

Gerim must not be deprived of justice (Deut 24:17, compare the curse in 27:19), nor must their wages be withheld (24:14). In such legislation, they are often associated with widows and orphans. There is a fundamental assumption that gerim will be needy or even destitute, objects of charity. Gerim, widows, and orphans are sometimes associated also with Levites (14:29; 16:11; 26:12-13).

God is the protector of gerim, "providing them food and clothing" (Deut 10:18); but an even greater motive for not oppressing them, frequently reiterated, is that "you were gerim" in Egypt (Exod 22:21 [Heb. 22:20]; Deut 10:19; 23:7 [Heb. 23:8]). Gerim are not to be treated as the Egyptians treated Israel.

However, it is accepted that gerim are a source of menial labor (Deut 29:11), and if gerim prosper more than the Israelites to whom Deuteronomy is addressed, this is an indication of divine curse, a reversal of normal order (Deut 28:43). Thus, despite the powerful pro-ger theological rhetoric, there are limits to Deuteronomic championing of the ger.

Gerim in Deuteronomic law have traditionally been regarded as non-Israelites who, for whatever reason, reside in Israel. But many now think of them in class rather than ethnic terms, as a legally disadvantaged class. The groups with which they are constantly associated, widows, orphans, and Levites, are certainly Israelites. Hebrew has other terms for foreignness as such (especially nokhri [נָכְרִי]); a passage like Deut 14:21 clearly distinguishes gerim from foreigners. Israel's being "gerim in Egypt" may refer to sociopolitical status rather than foreignness. When Deut 23:8 [Heb. 23:9] mentions the possible admission into Israel's assembly of the offspring of certain foreigners, these are not called gerim.

We should not entirely deny a connotation of alienness to ger in Deuteronomy. Perhaps the existence of the class of gerim was rationalized, with whatever degree of truth, in terms of their having originated elsewhere than where they live. Perhaps ger was an available legal category for people who continued to arrive as refugees. But the simple definition of ger as "resident alien" is not viable. Probably the defining characteristic of ger is landlessness—not having an "inheritance" within a traditional system of land tenure. This is how Levites are always defined (e.g., Deut 14:29).

Succoring gerim fits well into the Deuteronomic ideology of social justice and equality, likely inherited from Israel's premonarchic mode of production. However, Deuteronomic law in its present form is the product of centuries of life under monarchy, and there is much evidence that the Deuteronomists had to compromise with this new, dominant mode of production. In this framework, a convincing case has been made that, through the laws covering gerim, widows, and orphans, the Deuteronomists have become complicit with the state in keeping disadvantaged groups in their place, as objects of charity, rather than furthering their aspirations.

C. P and Chronicles

In P, the affirmation of a single law for the ger and the mainstream Israelite is almost absolute. Ger is frequently juxtaposed to ʾezrakh (אֶזְרָח), translated "citizen" or "native." Leviticus 24:22 generalizes many particular statements: "You shall have one law for the ger and for the ʾezrakh." The ger is here rhetorically included in the "you" to whom the law is addressed. The ger is an equal as regards participation in the assembly (Num 15:15-16). If ʾezrakh were correctly translated "native," then ger must imply alien origin. But ʾezrakh occurs much less frequently than ger, and is virtually always paired with it, so there is no independent evidence of what ʾezrakh means, other than non-ger.

The ger is mentioned in many more priestly laws than Deuteronomic ones, especially laws concerning sacrifices and purity issues. In direct negation of Deut 14:21, the ger is aligned with the ʾezrakh rather than with the foreigner, in not being allowed to eat of animals that die naturally (Lev 17:15). P does, however, seem to know and occasionally use Deuteronomy. Leviticus 19:33-34 prohibits oppressing the ger, with the motive "for you were gerim in the land of Egypt." "The poor and the ger" have the same sort of gleaning rights in Lev 19:10; 23:22 as in Deut 24:19-21. These references create some distance between the ger and the ʾezrakh, at least economically. This distance is at its greatest in Lev 25: vv. 44-46 suggest that a ger, unlike a kinsperson ("brother"), may be enslaved (the word ger is not actually used—the ones who may be enslaved are home-born children of a toshav "sojourning" in Israel—but there seems to be no distinction in this case). Conversely, an Israelite falling into debt-slavery to a ger has greater rights than if the master is a fellow Israelite (Lev 25:47).

Dynamics within postexilic Judaism probably account best for the priestly treatment of the ger. It is likely that the dominant Jews, those returning from exile with Persian sponsorship, borrowed the old term ger as a designation for "the people of the land" who had remained in Palestine and whose spokespersons the Deuteronomists were, and at the same time coined the term ʾezrakh for themselves. This distinction satisfied their sense of being the only authentic Jews and justified their economic privilege. However, their community was small and needed to be built up by the orderly admission of the people of the land, so they had to compromise theologically with the Deuteronomic position. This explains the prevalent affirmation that ʾezrakh and ger are to be one in respect of sacred law. Ezekiel, a book edited by the priestly party, envisages granting the children of gerim an inheritance—incorporating them into the land tenure system (47:22-23).

It is possible that, later in the postexilic period, ger came to be understood as covering also genuine outsiders who sought conversion to Judaism. This is suggested by the fact that LXX translates ger in the Pentateuch as prosēlytos (proselyte), unless the context makes this implausible (e.g., Deut 23:7 [Heb. 23:8]).

The books of Chronicles, with a postexilic point of view related but not identical to the priestly, mention gerim several times in their idealized picture of the kingdom of Judah. Gerim are liable to be conscripted for public works projects (1 Chr 22:2; 2 Chr 2:17-18). The latter reference suggests strata in ger society, in that minorities are to be "overseers" rather than menials. The number of gerim in this census (over 150,000) is probably exaggerated.

Chronicles' attitude to the divided kingdoms of monarchical times is important. In 2 Chr 15:9, deserters from the north are said to "sojourn" in the south. However, when the kingdoms are reunited in Hezekiah's Passover, the northerners are specifically distinguished from gerim (30:25). This reunion, in which "authentic" Jews readmit renegade ones, is theologically analogous to the postexilic joining of returned exiles with "people of the land." Chronicles stresses the unity of the communities even more than P does.

D. Extended Meanings

Ger undergoes metaphorical or theological extensions. Being a ger before God is an expression of human existence as such (1 Chr 29:15; Ps 39:12 [Heb. 39:13]; compare life as "sojourn" in Gen 47:9 and see also 1 Pet 1:17)—the point seems to be the transitory, more than alien, nature of existence. Israelites are gerim with Yahweh in a more specific sense, since God is the sole owner of the land (Lev 25:23); this links with the theme of landlessness. Psalmists speak of "sojourning" in God's presence at the Temple (15:1; 61:4 [Heb. 61:5]); but evil cannot "sojourn" with God (Ps 5:4 [Heb. 5:5]). Along a different line, God acts like a ger toward Israel in Jer 14:8, that is, as a passing visitor rather than a permanent resident. See FOREIGN, FOREIGNER; STRANGER.

Bibliography: Harold V. Bennett. *Injustice Made Legal: Deuteronomic Law and the Plight of Widows, Strangers, and Orphans in Ancient Israel* (2002); Christiana van Houten. *The Alien in Israelite Law* (1991).

DAVID JOBLING

SOLDERING [דֶּבֶק deveq]. In its broadest sense, the joining of two pieces of metal by any of several means, including nailing, riveting, hammering, or the use of fusible alloys as in Isa 41:7, where it is a method for making idols. Despite the technological skill exhibited in the creation of these idols, the prophet judges them useless against the advancing Cyrus of Persia, Yahweh's agent of judgment (i.e., the "victor from the east"; Isa 41:2). *See* METALLURGY.

JOEL M.S LEMON

SOLDIER. *See* ARMY; WAR, METHODS, TACTICS, WEAPONS OF (BRONZE AGE THROUGH PERSIAN PERIOD); WAR, METHODS, TACTICS, WEAPONS OF (HELLENISTIC THROUGH ROMAN PERIODS).

SOLEM. Modern Solem (or Sulam) is located along the periphery of the Jezreel Valley at the southwestern base of Mount Moreh, directly across from Mount Gilboa. Despite the thick alluvial deposits covering a great deal of the material remains, surveys and limited excavations have revealed a long occupational history that stretches back from modernity to the Neolithic period. In antiquity, the site was inhabited throughout the Bronze and Iron Ages as well as the Persian, Roman, and Byzantine eras. Scholars have recognized the village's ancient name, biblical Shunem, since the middle of the 19th cent., but it was already called Sulam by at least the Byzantine era. *See* SHUNEM, SHUNAMMITE.

Bibliography: Karen Covello-Paran. "Tel Shunem." *Journal Hadashot Arkheologiyot—Excavations and Surveys in Israel* 118 (2006); Zvi Gal. *Map of Har Tavor (41)*; *Map of 'En Dor (45)*. Archaeological Survey of Israel (1998).

JASON R. TATLOCK

SOLEMN ASSEMBLY [מִקְרָא־קֹדֶשׁ miqra'-qodhesh, עֲצָרָה 'atsarah]. Two different Hebrew expressions have been rendered by the English "solemn assembly" in the NRSV: 'atsarah and miqra'-qodhesh. Both are used together in Lev 23:36. The more common translation of the latter is "holy convocation." In describing the seven-day Succoth observance, Lev 23:34-36 identifies the first day as a miqra'-qodhesh observed with seven days of offerings. The eighth day is a "solemn assembly" ('atsarah). Three additional texts, Num 29:35; 2 Chr 7:9; and Neh 8:18, all of which describe Succoth, call for an eighth-day "solemn assembly." Curiously, Deut 16:8 presents the seventh day of Passover as an 'atsarah, while Exod 12:16 refers to the first and seventh days as miqra'-qodhesh. Isaiah 1:13 and Amos 5:21 employ expressions of divine displeasure over the nation's solemn assemblies when accompanied by iniquity or absent of justice. Using repetitive language, Joel 1:14 and 2:15 call for an 'atsarah in the context of seeking a reversal of a locust plague. The Jer 9:2 use of 'atsarah is striking

because it is apparently the only non-cultic use of the term; it perhaps represents a double entendre.

JOHN I. LAWLOR

SOLITARINESS [אֵין שֵׁנִי 'en sheni]. The state of being alone ('en sheni, literally, "not/without a second one"), a topic taken up in the discourses of Qoheleth (Eccl 4:7-12). Qoheleth reckons solitariness as "VANITY and an unhappy business" (Eccl 4:8). Without family (NRSV, "sons or brothers"), the solitary individual works only for himself or herself. Never satisfied with accumulated riches, work never ceases, and the solitary individual has no pleasure. Qoheleth concludes that two are better than one, for they can work for each other, help each other up, keep each other warm, and join forces in their common defense. *See* ECCLESIASTES, BOOK OF; LONELY.

JOEL M. LEMON

SOLOMON sol'uh-muhn [שְׁלֹמֹה shelomoh; Σαλωμών Salōmōn]. The third monarch of Israel and son of David, Solomon reigned, according to the Bible, in the mid-10th cent. BCE. The biblical stories about Solomon emphasize his connections with the building of the Jerusalem Temple, and his efforts at centralizing political power in the monarchy. While the historicity of some of the stories about him is debatable, it seems clear that his reign marked a transition in the development of Israelite political life.

Solomon's reputation survives because of the extended reports of his life in 1 Kings and 2 Chronicles. The task of modern scholars is, first, to understand how those reports came to be and how they correlate with other types of historical evidence, and, second, to consider those reports as the works of high literary and theological artistry that they are. These two goals exist in some tension, particularly in the case of Solomon, for a purely historical interest in his reign ends up somewhat skeptical of what we can know for sure about him, while a purely literary approach will ignore historical problems as it, rightly, recognizes the intricacy of the literary presentations in the Bible. Keeping both approaches in mind simultaneously is the goal. The skepticism toward assured results inevitable in sound historical analysis—some things we simply do not know—should not blind the reader to the achievements of the Deuteronomists (and their successors) as skilled literary historians and as insightful theologians.

A. Sources for Reconstructing the Reign of Solomon
  1. Archaeological issues
  2. Textual evidence
B. The Literary Presentations of Solomon's Reign
  1. Solomon in 1 Kings
    a. Solomon's ascent to the throne
      (1 Kgs 1:1–2:46)

b. Solomon's political savvy
   (1 Kgs 3:1–5:12)
c. Solomon's building projects
   (1 Kgs 5:13–9:22)
d. Solomonic miscellanies (1 Kgs 9:23-28)
e. The visit of the queen of Sheba
   (1 Kgs 10:1-13)
f. Tribute lists (1 Kgs 10:14-29)
g. Solomon's amours and downfall
   (1 Kgs 11:1-43)
h. A major theme: Solomon and the
   dynastic promise
2. Solomon in 2 Chronicles
   a. David's final charge (1 Chr 28:1–29:30)
   b. Solomon's early reign (2 Chr 1:1–2:18)
   c. The Temple and other artifacts of rule
      (2 Chr 3:1–8:18)
   d. The later reign of Solomon (2 Chr 9:1-28)
   e. The conclusion of Solomon's reign
      (2 Chr 9:29-31)
C. The Developing Solomonic Tradition in the
   Bible and Second Temple Judaism
Bibliography

A. Sources for Reconstructing the Reign of Solomon

Unlike the case with David, no inscriptions mentioning Solomon exist, either in Syria-Palestine or in Egypt or Mesopotamia. The latter gap is unsurprising, since both traditional imperial centers were in decline during the 10th cent. BCE. However, the absence of direct evidence from the land of Israel itself poses problems, which are compounded by the fact that the dating of large monuments that might be Solomon's is controversial. Thus the only direct evidence for his reign comes from the Deuteronomistic and Chronistic traditions, both of which date much later than the 10th cent. BCE, at least in their current forms. Sorting through the archaeological evidence will aid historical reconstruction by setting limits to possible interpretations of texts.

1. Archaeological issues

Earlier scholars excavating the monumental gatehouses, palaces, and "stables" (better: storage galleries) of Megiddo, Gezer, and Hazor attributed them to Solomon on the basis of 1 Kgs 9:15-19, which describes those cities and others as major centers. Even grander possibilities for Solomon's rule appear in 1 Kgs 5:4 (MT; NSRV, 4:24), "For he dominated all of 'Across the River,'" from Tiphsah to Gaza," i.e., all the kings of 'Across the River,' indicating political sovereignty of some sort over the entire region west of the Euphrates. According to the reconstruction that takes such statements at face value, Solomon was the true founder of the Israelite state's taxation system and bureaucracy, and the builder of impressive state-run compounds (most notably the Jerusalem Temple). Similarly, copper smelting facilities near the eastern arm of the Red Sea at Tell el-Kheleifeh were attributed to Solomon on the basis of the report in 1 Kgs 9:26 that he built ships in this region. In short, scholars up through the 1970s or so believed that Solomon's reign was well attested in the archaeological record, confirming the literary critics' picture of a Solomonic renaissance, a time of high cultural achievement.

This reconstruction has come under fire from several directions over the past three decades. Some objections are more serious than others. Among other issues, first of all, Israel Finkelstein and others have questioned the dating of relevant architectural strata to the 10th cent. He argues that Str VA-IVB at Megiddo dates to the 9th cent. BCE, the period of the Omride dynasty, and that the same would be true of the similar architecture at Gezer and Hazor. He claims parallels between these sites and Jezreel, which is clearly Omride. If correct, such a dating would imply that the biblical texts retrojected later developments to an earlier period, perhaps in order to minimize the considerable achievements of the Northern Kingdom rulers Omri and Ahab.

Second, the copper smelting works at Tell el-Kheleifeh seem best to fit the 8th cent. BCE, even though the pottery is difficult to link directly with Transjordanian sites from either the time of Solomon or that of Hezekiah. The anomalous material culture seems most like that of the later period. Thus when 1 Kgs 9:26 reports Solomon's shipbuilding activities at Ezion-geber on the Gulf of Aqaba, it is either retrojecting later events to his reign or referring to a location not yet discovered (which seems less likely).

Third, a number of scholars have argued for wholesale anachronism in the biblical material about Solomon, arguing for example that the House of the Forest of the Lebanon, part of Solomon's palace compound in Jerusalem (1 Kgs 7:2-5), mirrors Persian palatial architecture, with the great Audience Hall of Persepolis being the most obvious example. The references to "Across the River" (NRSV, "the region west of the Euphrates") might also date to the Persian period, when that was a title of a satrapy in the Persian Empire. This line of reasoning reckons the literary accounts of Solomon's reign to be later fictions created by the Deuteronomists or even later redactors of the text.

Some of these arguments are more convincing than others. To take them in reverse order, the extent of anachronism in the biblical text is highly debatable. The absence of Persian loanwords or explicit references to Persian practices in 1 Kings places the burden of proof on anyone dating the literary evidence too late. Moreover, the House of the Forest of the Lebanon is only slightly larger than known examples of the combined porticoes and courtyards onto which Late Bronze Age Syro-Palestinian palaces (as at Tel Brak, Tel Hammam, Alalakh, and Qatna) opened. "Across the River" also appears as the name of the region in Neo-Assyrian texts, two centuries before the Persian period, during the period of the Deuteronomists' major activity. While accounts of Solomon's wisdom and wealth are probably hyperbolical, as indicated by the frequent reference to his superiority to "all kings of the earth," hyperbole does not necessarily indicate lateness. Ancient propaganda often drew on literary tropes from epic literature and elsewhere to aggrandize kings, even during their lifetimes. Exaggeration does not equal fabrication.

The most serious problems arise with the dating of what earlier scholars called Solomon's Stables in Megiddo, Hazor, and Gezer. Even the most recent excavators of Megiddo (Finkelstein and Ussishkin) disagree as to whether the city was inhabited throughout the 10th cent. BCE, in which case Solomon is a candidate for their builder, or whether there was a gap in settlement in the 10th cent., in which case the large-scale architecture must be Omride. At least Megiddo's six-chambered gate must post-date Solomon because of its relationship to the fortifications around it (which are earlier). However, the palaces and fortifications may be from the 10th cent. BCE. Nor is it clear that Jezreel is sufficiently well preserved to serve as a control for evaluating state-sponsored architecture at other sites. Thus the archaeological evidence is unclear, prompting a heated discussion among experts. It seems likely that an intermediate position on the united monarchy (and thus the reign of Solomon) will prove most tenable: while Israel was not a major regional empire during the 10th cent. BCE, or at least not for long, as earlier scholars thought, it was an incipient state that briefly dominated its neighbors and saw more than modest construction projects as well as the beginnings of bureaucratic life.

The uncertainty extends most fully to the site at which the Bible locates Solomon's most impressive construction works, Jerusalem. The fact that the Dome of the Rock sits atop the Temple Mount means that no possibility exists of finding Iron Age remains of the Temple of Yahweh. Recently found large buildings south of the Temple Mount in the City of David may be connected to David or Solomon, though the evidence is still unclear. Most extant fortifications in Jerusalem date either to the Middle Bronze Age or to the 8th cent. BCE, but not to the age of Solomon. The so-called "stepped structure" in the City of David underwent repeated repairs, and so its history and purpose remain unclear. Though it may date to the Late Bronze Age, it is not clear whether the royal palace lay near it (though it may have), or whether David and Solomon had anything to do with it. The absence of monumental architecture from the 10th cent. and the small size of settlements in Judah during this period make it unlikely that Jerusalem was a major capital or that the grandeur of the biblical Temple was attributable to Solomon, though it does not follow that his reign was insignificant. "Major" is a relative term, and allowance for exaggeration in the biblical tradition does not rule out the possibility of a significant historical kernel to its portrayal of Solomon.

2. Textual evidence

A challenge, then, is to discern historically authentic material within 1 Kings and 1–2 Chronicles that might reflect on Solomon's reign. To ferret out such information, it is important to understand what sorts of material the compilers of these texts had available, and the sorts of topics they might discuss. An even more significant challenge and one that promises more impressive results, lies in recovering the literary and historiographic techniques that made such extraordinary portrayals of Solomon survive in 1 Kings and 2 Chronicles. One might expect an ancient author, particularly one recounting past events, to use any available source materials, including oral traditions, royal archives (including contracts, letters, and receipts), annals, and inscriptions. In the absence of such sources, an ancient historian might compose fresh stories about a known character from the past. Thus ancient authors, like modern ones, worked creatively with their source material, sometimes conservatively incorporating extensive passages whose viewpoints diverged from the author's own, and other times freely adapting or even inventing material. In reading the biblical stories about Solomon, it is important to exercise critical judgment and ask whether the events recounted seem plausible given what we know about the ancient world. Often it is impossible to be certain.

However, a fair assessment of 1 Kings would suggest that its author was familiar enough with the scribal conventions of ANE courts to incorporate material much like that from surrounding cultures. This is not to say that 1 Kings definitely used actual archival sources from the Jerusalem chancery, but such usage seems probable. This material includes lists of officials (1 Kgs 4:2-19), ration lists (1 Kgs 4:22-24 [Heb. 5:2-4]), reports of construction projects (1 Kgs 9:15-19) and of arms trades (1 Kgs 10:26-29). Even more to the point, at least some of the material now in 1 Kings uses the sort of high-blown rhetoric common to ancient inscriptions aggrandizing monarchs, particularly in the Neo-Assyrian Empire. Thus a statement such as "Judah and Israel were as numerous as the sand by the sea; they ate and drank and were happy" (1 Kgs 4:20), while clearly influenced by Deuteronomistic language, is not far removed from the claim of Tiglath-pileser III (ca. 745–727 BCE): "I annexed lands larger than the territory of Assyria ... I kept on pasturing them in verdant meadows" (Iran Stele, IIB.15'-17'). The sophisticated, yet conventionalized, language of the royal courts appears above all in the flowery summaries of Solomon's achievements (see 1 Kgs 4:20-21, 29-34 [Heb. 4:20–5:1; 5:9-14]), indicating that the biblical text is not isolated from the ideas of the Jerusalem court, which must have been in touch with neighboring chanceries. It is not possible to date 1 Kgs 1–11 with certainty, much less to attribute the bulk of it to the 10th cent. BCE, but good reasons exist for dating most of it to the Iron Age, rather than the Persian or Hellenistic periods. Insofar as 2 Chronicles draws on 1 Kings, the same is true for it, although the

Chronicler does include later material, including his own free compositions.

Reflecting their cosmopolitan origins, both the Deuteronomistic and Chronistic works (the latter of which depends heavily on the former) also use other literary forms widely employed in the ANE, such as dream reports (1 Kgs 3:3-14; 9:1-9) and prayers (1 Kgs 8:22-66). Much of this material comes from the Deuteronomistic editors and presumably was not intended by its authors to report Solomon's words. Such free composition of speeches for historical figures was commonplace in ancient historiography.

While the ancient editors of Kings and Chronicles had access to still older sources, they would have felt compelled to portray Solomon, or any king, in a limited number of possible ways following the literary and political conventions of the times. Kings could not convincingly play an infinite number of roles, and there were many ways to misplay even these, leading to criticism even after their lifetimes (as, for example, in the many scathing legends about Naram-Sin and Shulgi, 3rd-millennium rulers of southern Mesopotamia who were vilified for centuries after their deaths). In the ANE, monarchs portrayed themselves as builders, conquerors, wise men, sponsors of cults, and progenitors of dynasties. Above all, they represented the gods (or in Israel, Yahweh), casting every innovation as obedience to a new divine directive and every attempt at continuity as a return to the divinely appointed cosmic order.

The stories about Solomon pick up many such themes, revealing Iron Age conventions of kingship that an ancient audience would expect of any successful ruler. However, both 1 Kings and 1–2 Chronicles downplay the major theme of monarch as conqueror. In sharp contrast to the Neo-Assyrian monarchs, who highlighted their numerous victories, or even the 8th-cent. petty rulers of Zençirli/Sam'al or Suḫu, who celebrated far fewer, the Solomonic tradition records no major campaigns. Notions of a Solomonic empire come from 1 Kgs 4:21, which reports that "Solomon was ruler in all the kingdoms from the River of the Land of the Philistines (that is, the border of Egypt)." The LXX lacks a text at this point, but 3 Kgdms 2:46k and 10:26a offer a version of the text that describes his realm as stretching "from the River [that is, the Euphrates] until the Land of the foreigners, namely the boundary of Egypt." The difference between the MT and the Hebrew source of the LXX would have been only a couple of letters. (English translations such as the NRSV render a text that did not, strictly speaking, exist in antiquity, though the sense of it may well be correct.) In any case, the notion of a Solomonic empire hangs by the thinnest thread and should be given up. As the Chronicler took pains to emphasize (see below), Solomon was a man of peace, not a warrior.

B. The Literary Presentations of Solomon's Reign

The Deuteronomistic and Chronistic presentations of the reign of Solomon differ in important respects, even though the latter clearly uses the former as a primary source. The basic outlines of the reign are similar, but the Chronicler has systematically removed most of the criticisms of Solomon, preferring to blame the secession of the Northern Kingdom on Rehoboam and Jeroboam. A further complication arises from the fact that the LXX of 1 Kings differs significantly from the MT, indicating a further level of revision of that text. A chart of the parallel accounts illustrates where the Chronicler either followed, or deviated from, his source.

The two most glaring changes in 2 Chronicles are its omission of the story of Solomon's brutal ascent to the throne (apparently a coup d'état) and the idolatrous tendencies of his harem and resulting punishments. Most of the other alterations are more subtle, though tending in a similar direction, namely, the rehabilitation of Solomon's reputation. It will be useful to consider the separate presentations of his reign at this point.

1. Solomon in 1 Kings

First Kings weaves together several sources for the reign of Solomon. Much of the material seems to be pre-Deuteronomistic, though the redactors of the work in the late pre-exilic period and even later played a role in the composition. It is no longer possible to be certain as to which text comes from which layer of redaction. However, the highly nuanced picture of the king as a ruler capable of cruelty and mercy, of wisdom and folly, of piety and idolatry does not result from accidental literary accretions, but from an intentional editorial process. The Deuteronomists, who were primarily responsible for the shape of 1 Kings (though later hands may also play a role), deliberately used the figure of Solomon as a test case for the temptations and opportunities of kingship. Consider each episode in the story.

a. Solomon's ascent to the throne (1 Kgs 1:1–2:46). In the ANE, as in many monarchies, succession to the throne may pose serious problems, especially when the dying king has numerous wives and sons with rival power bases, or when he has lost his grip on power. Solomon's ascent to the throne apparently prompted discussion about his legitimacy. A legacy of the discussion appears in 2 Sam 12:24-25, which relates an apologetic story of Solomon's birth; he was conceived only after the death of his older brother and not as the direct result of David's adultery with Bathsheba. The story forestalls charges that Solomon's origins were too sordid to allow him to be king.

First Kings 1:1-53, meanwhile, picks up the thread by reporting that Solomon gained the support of his dying father and his major supporters despite the fact that his brother Adonijah had already completed a coronation ceremony. The story offers an apology for Solomon's ascent to the throne, since he was one of David's youngest sons and not connected through his mother to a major Israelite family. The author of the story gives a clue to the author's rhetorical aim by having Bathsheba argue that, "But you, my lord the king—the eyes of all

Reign of Solomon	
1 Kings	**1–2 Chronicles**
	David's final charge (1 Chr 28:1–29:30)
Solomon's ascent to the throne (1:1–2:46)	
Alliance with Egypt (3:1-2)	
Solomon's wisdom (3:3-28)	Solomon's wisdom (2 Chr 1:1-11)
Solomon's government (4:1-28 [Heb. 4:1–5:8])	Solomon's wealth (1:12-17)
Solomon's wisdom (part 2) (4:29-34 [Heb. 5:9-14])	
Alliance with Tyre (5:1-12 [Heb. 5:15-26])	Alliance with Tyre (2:1-15)
Corvee labor battalions (5:13-18 [Heb. 5:27-32])	Corvee labor battalions (2:17-18 [Heb. 2:16-17])
Temple-building (6:1-38)	Temple-building (3:1–5:1)
Palace-building (7:1-12)	
Temple-building (7:13-51)	
Dedication of the Temple (8:1-66)	Dedication of the Temple (5:2–7:10)
The dynastic promise renewed (9:1-9)	The dynastic promise (7:11-22)
Settling with Hiram (9:10-14)	Settling with Huram (8:1-2)
Corvee labor battalions (9:15-22)	
Solomonic miscellanies (9:23-28)	Solomonic miscellanies (8:3-18)
The visit of the queen of Sheba (10:1-13)	The visit of the queen of Sheba (9:1-12)
Tribute lists (10:14-29)	Tribute list (9:13-28)
Solomon's amours (11:1-8)	
The dynastic promise qualified (11:9-13)	
Revolts (11:14-40)	
Deuteronomistic regnal summary (11:41-43)	Chronistic regnal summary (9:29-31)

Israel are on you to tell them who shall sit on the throne of my lord the king after him. Otherwise, it will come to pass, when my lord the king sleeps with his ancestors, that my son Solomon and I will be counted offenders [literally, sinners]" (1 Kgs 1:20-21). Bathsheba's subtle argument leaves unstated both her expectations concerning David's decision in her son's favor (thus making the choice appear to be David's alone) and the fact that Solomon faced opposition because of David's own action, and thus the only way to redeem David's reputation was through legitimizing his son born after adultery. The polite court language ("my lord the king" rather than "you") reflects the author's desire for veri-

similitude in portraying Bathsheba's ability to address a political problem without seeming to.

Like other rulers felt by some of their subjects to be usurpers (for example, Darius the Great in the Bisitun Inscription), Solomon (at least according to 1 Kgs 1) must have employed rhetorical strategies for defending his legitimacy. It does not follow, of course, that 1 Kgs 1 dates to the time of Solomon or accurately records the events surrounding his rise to power, but the story must come from someone who felt a need to defend Solomon from charges of usurpation. It is difficult to imagine that such an issue would have remained live much later than Solomon's own reign, at least not for many persons.

In any case, 1 Kgs 2 continues the story by having Solomon eliminate his potential political rivals, especially members of the upper echelons of his father's government, albeit on David's instructions. The characters in the story, if not necessarily the storyteller, justify the apparent pitilessness of the coup on the grounds that the victims of Solomon's purge were themselves brutal murderers. More to the point, 1 Kgs 2, when combined with 1 Kgs 1 at some point in the evolution of the story (probably very early), created a complex picture of Solomon as a decisive, if ruthless, ruler who follows his father's instructions faithfully.

b. Solomon's political savvy (1 Kgs 3:1–5:12). This section opens and closes with stories of alliances (though the LXX omits the opening reference to Pharaoh's daughter), framing the discussion of Solomon's initial achievements. Arguably, the reference to worship at the high places in 1 Kgs 3:2 may be a criticism of Solomon, though the absence of a central Temple in Jerusalem made such a practice less culpable than it would be later, as a comparison with 1 Kgs 11 makes clear.

The key to the section lies in the emphasis on Solomon's wisdom. The theme first appears in the vision at Gibeon, in which Solomon foregoes wealth and military power for wisdom. The story does not deny the importance of Yahweh's gift to him of "riches and honor" beyond all other kings (3:13), but insists that such successes result from the superior gift of wisdom. In connecting political power, wealth, and wisdom, the narrative is following ANE convention. For example, the coronation hymn of the Assyrian monarch Assurbanipal (ca. 668–627 BCE) asks the gods to "Grant to Assurbanipal, king of Assyria, our lord, long days, many years, a strong weapon, a long reign, years of abundance, a good name, and reputation, contentment, happiness, good repute, and first rank among kings" (translated by Foster). The same ruler boasted of his ability to "read inscriptions from before the Flood," meaning that he was highly skilled at deciphering cuneiform. Similarly, Solomon is said to have acquired wisdom greater than famous (Canaanite and Egyptian) sages (4:30-31) and to have composed numerous proverbs and songs (4:32-33), all now lost unless perhaps the book of Proverbs contains a few of them. It was apparently important for the Deuteronomists' sources, if not for the final editors of the book, to boast of Solomon's achievements, and in particular to compare him favorably with famous foreigners. Again, we are dealing here neither with solid history nor with late legends, but with the sort of over-the-top language of the royal court (probably from Judah in the late monarchy) that would have celebrated the achievements of a monarch, especially a famous ancestor of a lesser present-day king.

c. Solomon's building projects (1 Kgs 5:13–9:22). In any case, the main section of 1 Kings' depiction of Solomon centers on his building projects. Ancient rulers often celebrated their work reconstructing ancient temples and building new cities or palaces. Such efforts brought glory to the gods, employment to the populace, and dignity to the king. Solomon's building projects fit the normal pattern of the region.

The section begins and ends with references to forced labor battalions, a new reality in ancient Israel, though common throughout the Near East. As so often in the Bible, the narrator does not comment on the appropriateness of such a shift in labor practices, neither defending nor condoning what would have been a socially disruptive practice. The small size of the labor units as compared to the overall Israelite population may indicate that Solomon's innovations seemed modest to the author of the text, at least relative to what it might have been.

The focus of the text, however, lies on the construction of the Temple itself, which is described in some detail. The building's basic three-part floor plan (vestibule, Holy Place, Most Holy Place) corresponds to contemporary temples at ʿAin Daraʿ and Tel Taʿyinat in Syria. Although any remains of the Iron Age Jerusalem Temple are long lost and may be unrecoverable (probably lying under the Haram es-Sharif), the fact that Israelite texts attributed its construction to Solomon is telling. Surely a fictional account would have assigned it to David, the more famous king of the dynasty. Moreover, the descriptions of the artistic patterns in 1 Kgs 7 have good parallels in Iron Age artifacts. Solomon built some sort of temple, if not necessarily the grand structure of 1 Kgs 7.

However, 1 Kings in its current state also includes a substantial Deuteronomistic element in the prayer of dedication in chap. 8. In fact, the prayer probably includes at least two editorial layers. The references to exile and return in 1 Kgs 8:46-53 (compare Deut 30:1-5) probably date to the Babylonian exile, when the hope for national restoration would have prompted close attention to the ancient stories of royal grandeur. (Alternatively, the text may have in mind earlier deportations of northern Israelites, using their history as a source of warning and hope.) Such attention does not evoke narrow nationalism because 1 Kings contains extensive and sophisticated critiques of past rulers, including Solomon. Moreover, the prayer allows for the incorporation of foreigners into the religious life of Israel (8:41-43), an extraordinary concession for victims of Babylonian invasion. In short, the text's sophisticated reflections on political power, tied up always with religious practice, allowed for a nuanced view of the known past and of possible futures. In the literary plot of Deuteronomy–Kings, Solomon, like Moses and Joshua, thus becomes the spokesman for the Deuteronomic viewpoint at a critical transition in Israel's life.

The cosmopolitan viewpoint of chap. 8 also appears in the description of the Temple itself in chap. 7. While 1 Kings apparently knew a great deal about the Iron Age Temple (if not necessarily that of the historical Solomon), the text emphasizes elements of its iconography and furniture that employed what might be called the international style of the time, the style of Phoenicia. Moreover, the text reports that the chief artificer of the Temple was half-Phoenician (7:13-14), again demonstrating that narrow national interest did not conflict with a notion of national election or divine favor, either in the minds of the Deuteronomists or in their sources.

Although the oldest recension of the LXX lacks 1 Kgs 9:15-25, both the MT and LXX of 2 Chr 8:3-10 show that the Chronicler knew some version of the MT text of 1 Kgs 9. The MT ending preserves information about Solomon's activities in major cities in the land of Israel as well as his subjugation of remaining Canaanites. Whatever the historicity of these notices, they serve as a framing device for 1 King's account of Solomon's major activities. His successes depended on reorganizing Israel's work force for state service. Of all possible building projects, he proved his loyalty to Yahweh and thus worthiness for the throne by building a great sanctuary in Jerusalem.

d. Solomonic miscellanies (1 Kgs 9:23-28). The following brief section serves as sidebar to what precedes it. The editor has thrown together stray notices, largely repeating earlier statements, in order to give a sense of Solomon's varied activities. Perhaps the most interesting is 1 Kgs 9:25, which reads, "Three times a year Solomon used to offer up burnt offerings and sacrifices of well-being on the altar that he built for the LORD offering incense before the LORD. So he completed the house [i.e., the Temple]." The Hebrew text is not entirely clear in other respects, but it undoubtedly refers to the three pilgrimage festivals of Exod 23:14-19. Thus the notice predates the priestly calendars of Lev 23 and Num 28–29, and probably reflects the practices of the monarchs of Judah, and perhaps even Solomon himself. The text takes pains to establish the role of the monarch in the Temple's ongoing activity, even if chap. 11 will insist that, ultimately, he was an idolater.

e. The visit of the queen of Sheba (1 Kgs 10:1-13). The legend of the visit of the queen of Sheba illustrates the statement in 1 Kgs 4:34 (Heb. 5:14): "People came from all the nations to hear the wisdom of Solomon; they came from all the kings of the earth who had heard of his wisdom." In some sense, then, this and the following section resume the earlier themes set forth in 1 Kgs 3:1–5:12 (Heb. 3:1–5:26). Since wisdom in the ancient world was international in scope, with similar subjects, literary genres, and social practices appearing in many Near Eastern cultures, it is not surprising that stories about Solomon would have portrayed him as a sage. Nor is it surprising that a story about a visitor would pick a point of origin as exotic as Sheba, or Saba. That kingdom in the southwest corner of the Arabian peninsula was a major regional power during the first half of the 1st millennium BCE, owing to its control of the spice trade. Thus the story of a visit for a fantastically rich Sabaean queen would have seemed plausible

to ancient readers. It is no longer possible to ascertain the historical basis, if any, of the story.

However, it is not difficult to understand why 1 Kings tells the story. Not only does it point to the extraordinary success of Solomon, it also foreshadows the source of his ultimate downfall, as the Deuteronomists see it, namely, his marriage of foreign women and adoption of their religious practices.

f. Tribute lists (1 Kgs 10:14-29). This section returns to a theme addressed several times, the wealth of Solomon based on tribute and trade. The list of exotic items such as sandalwood, peacocks, and apes impresses the reader with the extraordinary wealth of Solomon as well as his sense of taste. As a connoisseur of all things elegant, he set the tone for his world. A later author would have emphasized his splendid court as an antidote to any insecurity felt by the contrast with the great Assyrian monarchs.

Allowing for the hyperbole of such descriptions of Solomon's wealth as "Nothing like it was ever made in any kingdom" (1 Kgs 10:20) or "Thus King Solomon excelled all the kings of the earth" (1 Kgs 10:23), the description of his throne (1 Kgs 10:18-20) makes it sound much like royal furniture of the Iron Age, if in an unusually grand style, while the list of luxury goods for his court is much like what Assyrian inscriptions (e.g., the Black Obelisk) portray. Visual art translates into literary art as 1 Kings depicts a parade of the world's most colorful things. In other words, while 1 Kings may exaggerate Solomon's splendor, it does not fabricate it out of thin air. Rather, the text attributes to him what the great emperors of the Near East would actually have experienced.

Moreover, the text gives some interesting evidence for prices of military equipment, confirming what many Mesopotamian texts reveal, that the international arms trade drew heavily on national resources off and on for centuries. It is difficult to know what conclusions to draw from the claim that Solomon hoarded gold (1 Kgs 10:14-21) while exporting silver (1 Kgs 10:29): "The king made silver as common in Jerusalem as stones" (1 Kgs 10:27). The text describes a condition that would have led to a significant rise in commodity prices (except precious metals), the opposite of the ideal for which many monarchs strove (see for example the inscription of Kilamuwa of Sam'al a century or so after Solomon or, again, the coronation hymn of Assurbanipal). However, the author seems to see such an event as a positive thing, reflecting an ancient understanding of economics focusing on precious metals. Again, it is difficult to know how to interpret this evidence.

g. Solomon's amours and downfall (1 Kgs 11:1-43). Such a difficulty does not arise in the final section of 1 Kings' life of Solomon. Just as 2 Sam 11–18 makes national turmoil the due retribution for royal misbehavior, so 1 Kgs 11 opens with a litany of Solomon's sins and ends with stories of insurrections. While modern scholars are tempted to connect the revolts to the centralizing tendencies of Solomon's taxation policies, the Deuteronomists connect them to idolatry and, arguably, excessive displays of sexual prowess.

In some respects, 1 Kgs 11 marks an anticlimactic end to Solomon's reign, almost a surprise given the extraordinary achievements of his earlier years. Still, much of the previous narrative has set up this conclusion. While it seems unlikely that the early chapters of 1 Kings were intended to be satirical, contrary to the view of a few contemporary scholars, much in those stories raise the possibility that Solomon's alliances offered temptations that would prove his undoing. Certainly someone conditioned by the suspicion of monarchy seen in 1 Sam 8 or Deut 17:14-20 (possibly a later text) would have found the amassing of gold and purchase of horses and chariots as a dangerous trend. The Deuteronomists' final reflections on the reign of Solomon tried to strike a balance between his successes and his failure, offering no final judgment, but rather almost a regretful sigh that his early promise did not lead to a hoped-for utopia.

h. A major theme: Solomon and the dynastic promise. Second Samuel 7 reports a conversation in which Yahweh promises David a dynasty with all its attendant privileges. Although such a story probably originated in the propaganda machinery of the monarchy of Judah, serving to validate the hold of David's family on the throne for four centuries, the Bible contains numerous reflections on the limits and challenges of this promise (see Ps 89; Zech 10–14). First Kings 1–11, in particular, reflects on the promise in several ways. First, Solomon's twin dreams (3:1-9; 9:1-9), which bracket the accounts of his successes, refer directly to the promise, stating conditions under which Yahweh would punish the dynasty and the nation or, alternatively, reward them. Second, Solomon's temple dedication speech in 1 Kgs 8:17-21 connects three major theological themes (exodus, Davidic dynasty, and Temple) and probably a fourth (creation) to offer hints at a multidimensional theology of Israelite existence in the cosmos. Third, and most revealingly of Deuteronomistic reflections on Solomon's reign and perhaps kingship in general, 1 Kgs 11:31-39 has the prophet Ahijah reflect on the dynastic promise, dealing with the problem of Solomon's obedience in an innovative way. Rather than terminating the Davidic dynasty or confirming it in its power, Yahweh will separate the northern Israelite tribes from Judah. In other words, the text uses the dynastic promise and its execution as an etiology for the existence of two Israelite kingdoms, while also developing a nuanced understanding of how Yahweh keeps promises, in spite of human complications. Politics, theology, and history intersect, and the reign of Solomon epitomizes the history of the dual Israelite monarchies as a whole. His early successes gave way to ultimate failure and division, or so the Deuteronomistic History argues.

2. Solomon in 2 Chronicles

The Chronicler sees things otherwise. As a historian drawing heavily on 1–2 Samuel and 1–2 Kings, the Chronicler adapted his sources in several ways, ranging from copying it straight out to replacing problematic stories (from his point of view) with more acceptable ones. The newer work rectified literary inconsistencies or gaps, chronological contradictions, theological infelicities, and other sorts of perceived blemishes in its sources. The Chronicler's version of the story of Solomon is no exception to the rule. By creating new characters and eliminating old ones, by recasting troubling behaviors, and by adding clearer statements about divine judgment on actions, he presented a view of the reigns of David and Solomon that removed their most signal blemishes while highlighting their sponsorship of the Temple and skill at governance. The life of Solomon in 2 Chr 1–9 thus does not so much contradict the picture in 1 Kings as simply omit the most damning aspects of his reign, as a review of each episode will demonstrate.

a. David's final charge (1 Chr 28:1–29:30). Very differently from 1 Kgs 1–2, 1 Chronicles ends with a national assembly in which David designates Solomon his heir, praying for divine aid and enlisting the leaders of Israel under the new king's banner. The story emphasizes David's own nobility of character, important role in preparing for the Temple's construction, and complete self-control, all in sharp contrast with the account in 1 Kings. The Chronicler thus argues for a seamless transfer of power and a model of kingship commendable to a Persian-era audience longing for past glories.

b. Solomon's early reign (2 Chr 1:1–2:18). The opening of 2 Chronicles follows the basic outline of 1 Kings but compresses speeches and summarizes similar material from several parts of 1 Kings to form a more straightforward picture. He spells the name of the king of Tyre as Huram, a minor variation. *Inclusio* is a favorite literary technique for demarcating units of material. The Chronicler also omits the story of the prostitutes in 1 Kgs 3:16-28, which might have seemed an overly tawdry and trivial example of royal wisdom. Moreover, he makes some theological revisions. For example, whereas 1 Kgs 3:4 explains the location of Solomon's dream at Gibeon by saying that it "was the principal high place," 2 Chr 1:3 reads "for God's tent of meeting, which Moses the servant of the LORD had made in the wilderness, was there." By harmonizing the pentateuchal and Kings traditions, the Chronicler presents Solomon as a thoroughly orthodox ruler. He and his readers were worried about their past in ways that the Deuteronomists were not.

c. The Temple and other artifacts of rule (2 Chr 3:1–8:18). Still following the basic plot of 1 Kings, the Chronicler's account of the building of the Temple takes up more space than any other part of Solomon's life, and it lifts material from the Deuteronomistic account in a wholesale fashion. Although all aspects of his kingdom are portrayed at the apex of glory, whether geographic extent, world reputation, governmental organization, or economic and military might, the Chronicler's version of the story centers on the magnificent Temple for which David prepared. On the whole, the Chronicler felt comfortable with his source's portrayal of Solomon's Temple-building, making it the centerpiece of his presentation of the king's reign. Modifications are mostly minor, though they do offer a tantalizing look at early scribal exegetical practices in Israel.

The Chronicler's primary literary technique is compression. He often omits irrelevant or problematic details. He also eliminates some of the repetition so common in 1 Kings, attempting to produce a more straightforward text. He also adds material to harmonize 1 Kings with postexilic practice, as when he mentions Temple choirs in 2 Chr 5:12-13 or specifies festival rituals in 2 Chr 8:13-16, providing material absent from his source. He also expands Solomon's realm by having him build "Tadmor" (Palmyra) in 2 Chr 8:4 (rather than the "Tamar" of 1 Kgs 9:18).

A good illustration of 2 Chronicles' alteration of its source appears in the introduction and conclusion of Solomon's prayer dedicating the Temple (2 Chr 6:13, 40-42), both of which add new material to the Kings source, which the Chronicler otherwise follows fairly closely. The introduction describes a sacred space, a platform on which Solomon stood while praying; the addition underscores the grandeur of his Temple. It also separates him from the altar (in contrast to 1 Kgs 8:22), thus underscoring his theological notion that the king should not offer sacrifices (see 2 Chr 26:16-21).

Even more important, the conclusion offers a modified version of Ps 132:8-9: "Rise up, O LORD, and go to your resting place, you and the ark of your might. Let your priests be clothed in righteousness, and let your faithful shout for joy." Thus Solomon is portrayed as knowing a favorite hymn (whatever its time of origin) and participating properly in the temple cult as a singer rather than one offering sacrifices. The account in 2 Chr 6 also harmonizes the ark tradition, mentioned in Ps 132, with the Zion tradition, thus carrying on an unspoken but significant exegetical dialogue with the psalm itself. For the Chronicler, the Temple is not merely the house of prayer for all Israel as 1 Kings has it, but is also a proper residence for Yahweh on earth. In other words, with a simple addition, the Chronicler expands the theological significance of the Temple. This expansion would have validated the centrality of the Temple for an audience for whom the glories of the monarchy were a thing of the distant past.

d. The later reign of Solomon (2 Chr 9:1-28). This section follows 1 Kings with few exceptions. The Chronicler believed it to provide a fitting summary of Solomon's achievements, making him a monarch comparable to any foreign ruler, including the Persian rulers of his own time.

e. The conclusion of Solomon's reign (2 Chr 9:29-31). The author's desire to rehabilitate Solomon's reputation from the more mixed review in his source led him to remove all the material about his idolatry and the subsequent revolts that closed his reign (see 1 Kgs 11:1-40). He does retain the Deuteronomistic concluding regnal summary (see 1 Kgs 11:41-43) but modifies it by referring to prophets, each of whom he thought should record the history of his own era: "And as for the rest of the deeds of Solomon, from first to last, are they not written about in the words of Nathan the prophet, and in the prophecy of Ahijah the Shilonite, and in the visions of Iddo the seer concerning Jeroboam the son of Nebat?" (2 Chr 9:29).

To what sources does the Chronicler refer? Assuming that he has not simply invented the sources (possible but unlikely), two possibilities present themselves: 1) he cites sources that he expected his reader to know but that are now lost, or 2) he referred to the beginning and end of the life of Solomon in 1 Kgs 1–2 and 11. The first possibility probably enjoys more support among scholars, though it is of course impossible to prove the use of sources that no longer exist. The second option has the merit of referring to known material, which, moreover, refers to two the prophets in question and must have been known to the Chronicler. It has the disadvantage of making the Chronicler cite sources that he obviously sought to downplay because they undermined his rosy portrayal of his hero, Solomon. Solving this problem would demand a thorough discussion of the Chronicler's relationship to his sources and whether he sought to preserve them through epitome or to replace them altogether. Perhaps the problem is not solvable with the current state of knowledge.

C. The Developing Solomonic Tradition in the Bible and Second Temple Judaism

During the Second Temple period, Solomon's reputation for wisdom grew, overshadowing all negative aspects of his reign. While early postexilic books like Proverbs (which contained much preexilic material) already saw him as a patron of wisdom, later texts such as Qoheleth, Wisdom of Solomon, and the *Psalms of Solomon* used his reputation to validate much later views. Song of Songs used him as a foil to the idealized male lover of the book, taking kingship as both threat and promise. Later still, in Late Antiquity and the early Middle Ages, some circles came see him as an adept at magic and secret lore. Thus the historical man lay buried beneath legends serving purposes foreign to either Solomon or the earliest surviving traditions about him. Yet the interest that these generations of Bible readers paid to him laid the groundwork for our own.

Whatever one says about the historical Solomon, the literary character has led a charmed life. It has survived the trenchant critique of the Deuteronomists, who used Solomon as a test case for the limits and opportunities of monarchy. With the help of the Chronicler, Solomon became an exemplary ruler and thus a touchstone for later, less glorious, kings. To some extent, he remains so even today. *See* BATHSHEBA; DAVID; HIRAM; JERUSALEM; KING, KINGSHIP; SHEBA, QUEEN OF; SHEBA; TEMPLE OF SOLOMON; TIGLATH-PILESER III; TYRE.

Bibliography: Paul S. Ash. "Solomon's District List." *JSOT* 67 (1995) 67–86; Ehud Ben Zvi. *History, Literature and Theology in the Book of Chronicles* (2006); Jeffrey Blakely. "Reconciling Two Maps: Archaeological Evidence for the Kingdoms of David and Solomon." *BASOR* 327 (2002) 49–54; Fernand Braudel. *The Wheels of Commerce.* Siân Reynolds, trans. (1982); Antony Campbell and Mark O'Brien. *Unfolding the Deuteronomistic History* (2000); Mordechai Cogan. *I Kings.* AB (2000); William Dever. *What Did the Biblical Writers Know and When Did They Know It?* (2001); Israel Finkelstein and David Ussishkin. *Megiddo III: The 1992–1996 Seasons* (2000); Benjamin R. Foster. *Before the Muses: An Anthology of Akkadian Literature.* 3rd ed. (2005); M. Patrick Graham, Kenneth G. Hoglund, and Steven L. McKenzie, eds. *The Chronicler as Historian* (1997); Mark W. Hamilton. *The Body Royal: The Social Poetics of Kingship in Ancient Israel* (2005); Georgina Herrmann, ed. *The Furniture of Western Asia: Ancient and Traditional* (1996); Sara Japhet. *I and II Chronicles: A Commentary.* OTL (1993); Sara Japhet. *From the Rivers of Babylon to the Highlands of Judah: Collected Studies in the Restoration Period* (2006); Isaac Kalimi. "Jerusalem–The Divine City: The Representation of Jerusalem in Chronicles Compared with Earlier and Later Jewish Compositions." *The Chronicler as Theologian.* M. Patrick Graham, Steven L. McKenzie, and Gary Knoppers, eds. (2003); Isaac Kalimi. *The Reshaping of Ancient Israelite History in Chronicles* (2005); Philip J. King and Lawrence E. Stager. *Life in Biblical Israel* (2001); Gary Knoppers. "The Vanishing Solomon: The Disappearance of the United Monarchy from Recent Histories of Ancient Israel." *JBL* 116 (1997) 19–44; Dale Launderville. *Piety and Politics: The Dynamics of Royal Authority in Homeric Greece, Biblical Israel, and Old Babylonian Mesopotamia* (2003); Mario Liverani. *Israel's History and the History of Israel* (2005); Peter Machinist. "Kingship and Divinity in Imperial Assyria." *Text, Artifact, and Image: Revealing Ancient Israelite Religion.* Gary Beckman and Theodore J. Lewis, eds. (2006) 152–88; John W. Olley. "Pharaoh's Daughter, Solomon's Palace, and the Temple: Another Look at the Structure of 1 Kings 1–11." *JSOT* 27 (2003) 355–69; Thomas Römer. *The So-Called Deuteronomistic History: A Sociological, Historical and Literary Introduction* (2007); Marvin Sweeney. *I and II Kings.* OTL (2007); Hayim Tadmor. *The Inscriptions of Tiglath-pileser III King of Assyria* (1994); Andrew Vaughn and Ann E. Killebrew, eds. *Jerusalem in Bible and Archaeology: The First Temple Period* (2003); Ziony Zevit. "Israel's Royal Cult in the Ancient Near Eastern *Kulturkreis.*" *Text, Artifact, and Image: Revealing Ancient Israelite Religion.* Gary Beckman and Theodore J. Lewis, eds. (2006) 189–200.

MARK W. HAMILTON

SOLOMON, BOOK OF THE ACTS OF. *See* BOOKS REFERRED TO IN THE BIBLE.

SOLOMON, ODES OF. The *Odes of Solomon* have attracted the interest of Jewish scholars and specialists in such diverse fields as the NT, Jewish Christianity, Gnosticism, and patristics. These odes (or psalms or hymns) are attractive because of their poetic language and thought. The dominant theme is joy in experiencing acceptance and love at the appearance of the Messiah: "My joy is the Lord" (7:2). Numerous aspects of Jesus' life appear in the *Odes*, including his birth (*Ode* 19), his baptism (*Ode* 24), his walking on the water (*Ode* 39), his elevation on a cross (*Odes* 27, 42), his resurrection (*passim*), and his descent into hell (*Ode* 42). Note the beautiful thought in this excerpt:

> Who can interpret the wonders of the Lord?
> Though he who interprets should perish,
> yet that which was interpreted will remain.
> (*Ode* 26:11; *OTP* 2:759)

Forty-two odes were composed and attributed to Solomon, who according to ancient lore composed 1,005 songs (1 Kgs 4:32). Two Syriac manuscripts preserve portions of these odes. Codex Harris of the 15th cent. CE contains *Odes* 3:1*b* to 42:20 (the end). Codex Nitriensis of the 10th cent. CE preserves only *Odes* 17:7*b* to 42:20. The Greek of *Ode* 11, with more verses than in any other manuscript, appears in the 3rd-cent. Bodmer Papyrus XI. Five odes are quoted in Coptic in the 4th-cent. manuscript of the *Pistis Sophia* (Codex Askewianus). The first ode seems to be preserved in this manuscript with the caption "Solomon in his nineteenth Ode," and that would be the number of *Ode* 1 if the *Psalms* and *Odes of Solomon* were numbered in that order and consecutively (in the two Syriac manuscripts they are numbered consecutively but in each the *Psalms of Solomon* follow the *Odes of Solomon*). In the 4th cent., Lactantius quoted *Ode* 19:6-7 in Latin (*Epit.* 4.12.3).

Some scholars think that the *Odes* were originally composed in Greek. Other scholars conclude that they were composed in Syriac or a form of Aramaic-Syriac. The Greek copy is full of Semitisms, is inferior linguistically to the Syriac, and the latter preserves many features usually typical of an original language (e.g., paronomasia, alliteration, assonance, metrical scheme, parallelism, rhythm).

The date of the *Odes* has been a focus of debate since 1909 when J. Rendel Harris identified the *Odes* in a Syriac manuscript on his shelf. Most scholars now conclude that the *Odes* received their present form about 125 CE. Since a collection of "hymns" or poems would probably not have been written in one year, we should imagine some decades for the composition of these forty-two *Odes*. If the original language is Syriac, then the most likely place of origin is Antioch, Edessa, or western Syria (which might include Galilee).

The character of the *Odes* has been debated widely, probably more than any other ancient document. A. Harnack contended that the *Odes* were composed by a Jew and redacted by a Christian. The *Odes* have been judged to be gnostic, Jewish-Christian, Jewish, perhaps Essene, or patristic. These terms or categories have been defined in diverse, usually mutually exclusive ways. In the last twenty-five years, scholars have concurred that Gnosticism was preceded by a worldwide philosophy or religion defined as gnosis (seeking salvation through knowledge), that Jewish thought influenced some forms of gnostic thought, and that Jewish Christianity is an amorphous category. There is wide agreement today that the *Odes* should not be branded as gnostic. Most scholars are reticent to label some documents that predate 135/6 (the defeat of Bar Kokhba) as "Jewish" or "Christian," because there are insufficient criteria to distinguish between these two interrelated categories. Even though the forty-two *Odes* seem to originate with one person, this person most likely was a Jew who became a follower of Jesus Christ. Hence, some *Odes* could be Jewish, with others influenced by gnosis or earliest forms of Gnosticism (as in the *Hymn of the Pearl*, the *Gospel of Thomas*, and the *Gospel of Truth*), or reflecting the type of thought known from the Gospel of John.

The complex relationship with the Qumranic *Thanksgiving Hymns* (the Hodayoth formula "I thank you, Lord," found in the Psalter only in 118:21, appears in *Ode* 5:1) and the *Rule of the Community* (compare 1QS III, 19 and *Ode* 18:6) has indicated to some experts that the author, before he became a "Christian," was an Essene or was close to that Jewish sect. Attempts to prove that the *Odes* are dependent on the Gospel of John have not been convincing to most scholars, although these two documents share numerous terms, ideas, and a conceptual worldview. R. Bultmann imagined that the author of the Gospel of John was influenced by the type of thought found in the *Odes*, but it is unlikely that the *Odes* directly influenced this Gospel. Most scholars who have focused research on the *Odes of Solomon* and the Gospel of John conclude that these poems and John come from the same area, community, or even school. Challenging are such thoughts as these:

> The Son is the cup,
> and the Father is he who was milked;
> and the Holy Spirit is she who milked him.
> (*Ode* 19:2; OTP 2:752)

Bibliography: J. H. Charlesworth. *Critical Reflections on the Odes of Solomon* (1998); J. H. Charlesworth.

"The Dead Sea Scrolls and the Gospel according to John." *Exploring the Gospel of John*. R. A. Culpepper and C. C. Black, eds. (1991) 43–64; J. H. Charlesworth with A. Culpepper. "The Odes of Solomon and the Gospel of John." *CBQ* 35 (1981) 298–322; J. A. Emerton. "Some Problems of Text and Language in the Odes of Solomon." *JTS* 18 (1967) 372–406; M. Lattke. *Die Oden Salomos in ihrer Bedeutung für Neues Testament und Gnosis.* 4 vols. (1979–1986).

JAMES H. CHARLESWORTH

SOLOMON, PSALMS OF. The *Psalms of Solomon*, the most important ancient Jewish psalmody after the biblical Psalter, is a collection of eighteen psalms of lament, wisdom, prayer, and thanksgiving.

A. Introduction
B. The Textual Evidence and the Languages of Transmission
C. Authorship
D. Location and Setting
E. The Messiah in the *Psalms of Solomon*
F. The Return from the Diaspora and Ideas of Resurrection
G. The *Psalms of Solomon* and the New Testament Bibliography

A. Introduction

The *Psalms of Solomon* apparently are an eyewitness account of the first Roman invasion of Jerusalem by the general Pompey in 63 BCE and the incursions of Herod the Great and the Roman general Sosius during their siege of Jerusalem in 37 BCE: "Gentile foreigners went up to your place of sacrifice; they arrogantly trampled (it) with their sandals" (*Pss. Sol.* 2:2; *OTP* 2:652).

The *Psalms of Solomon* also contain the most detailed description of the expected Jewish Messiah before the NT. This "Son of David" will expel the Romans invaders, purify the Temple, restore the proper cult, and establish a righteous kingdom: "See, Lord, and raise up for them their king, the son of David ... their king shall be the Lord Messiah" (*Pss. Sol.* 17:21, 32; *OTP* 2:667).

Furthermore, these poems clearly articulate the Jewish belief in resurrection just before the beginning of the Christian movement: "This is the share of sinners forever, but those who fear the Lord shall rise up to eternal life, and their life shall be in the Lord's light, and it shall never end" (*Pss. Sol.* 3:12; *OTP* 2:655).

Pompey is able to breach the Temple walls, and his army can tread the altar because the Jews themselves have already defiled the sanctuary and the cult in their misconduct of its services (*Pss. Sol.* 8:11-13, 22). For the author the conquest is God's righteous judgment.

What distinguishes these psalms from the biblical Psalter is their didactic character. The author does more than report the invasion; he explains how this suffering serves as discipline for the righteous of his own people but also punishment for the Gentiles and for the sinners in the nation. God's role here is Judge.

Jerusalem and the Temple have been attacked and desecrated, but not destroyed, suggesting that the psalms reached their final form before 70 CE. The last half of the 1st cent. BCE appears to be the most suitable time for the composition and editing of the *Psalms of Solomon*.

B. The Textual Evidence and the Languages of Transmission

The earliest direct historical evidence we have of the text of the *Psalms of Solomon* is from the early 5th cent. CE when the "18 Psalms of Solomon" were included in the catalogue of the Codex Alexandrinus, following the Septuagint, the NT, and the two Clementine Epistles. However, the leaves at the end of the codex that would have contained the *Psalms of Solomon* are missing. Only the title remains. The *Psalms of Solomon* are included in several canon lists from the 6th to the 13th cent., but are usually accorded a status less than fully canonical.

The *Psalms of Solomon* were composed in Hebrew, perhaps by the turn of the Common Era, and translated into Greek, and sometime later into Syriac. The Syriac has usually been seen as a translation from the Greek text. New philological research now strongly suggests that the Syriac is indeed a direct translation from an early Hebrew text, perhaps with some reference to the Greek. There are no surviving Hebrew manuscripts, and the extant twelve Greek and four fragmentary Syriac manuscripts date from the 10th to the 16th cent. CE.

C. Authorship

The *Psalms of Solomon* are ascribed to Solomon, although there is no reference to him within the poems themselves. He was likely identified as the author of the *Psalms of Solomon* based on the phrase "son of David" in *Pss. Sol.* 17:21. Next to David, Solomon enjoyed a reputation as a poet (1 Kgs 4:32-34). It is unknown whether this attribution to Solomon was in the Hebrew text, or if it was added to the Greek translation.

The authorship of the *Psalms of Solomon* has most often been attributed to the Pharisees, but that identification can no longer be maintained. The *Psalms of Solomon* have been credited variously to the Hasidim, to the Essenes, to the Sadducees, or even to the Christians, or to another unknown group with an eschatological orientation. While few would locate Qumran as the source of the *Psalms of Solomon*, there are many similarities to various DEAD SEA SCROLLS.

A group of pious Jews who were horrified by the corruption in the Temple and in the government that brought on the military intrusion into the holy city, the authors vent their rage in *Pss. Sol.* 1, 2, 8, and 17, the so-called "historical psalms." The remainder of the psalms are more conventional, describing common themes such as evil and good, sin and salvation, and

threat and rescue, very much like the biblical Psalter and the Qumran *Hymn Scroll* (1QH^a).

The writers call themselves "the pious" and the *Psalms of Solomon* contain the most occurrences of the term in an ancient Jewish text. Even more frequent is the use of the term *righteous* in these psalms. These two words are the chief self-designations of the authors of these poems. However, the use of "the pious" in these and other texts appears to be generic, and does not necessarily indicate that the authors belong to a formally organized group who also took that name, known to us as "the Hasidim."

D. Location and Setting

Because of its unusual prominence, there is little doubt that Jerusalem is the venue of the *Psalms of Solomon*. Jerusalem's Temple is desecrated (*Pss. Sol.* 1; 8). The corruption of the Jerusalem leadership (*Pss. Sol.* 4) and the anticipation of God's blessings on the holy city (*Pss. Sol.* 11) support this suggestion. Jerusalem is attacked (*Pss. Sol.* 1; 8), is addressed (*Pss. Sol.* 11), speaks (*Pss. Sol.* 1), and is the seat of the Sanhedrin (*Pss. Sol.* 4:1).

There are some indications that the *Psalms of Solomon* emerged from a SYNAGOGUE setting. They call their gatherings "the assemblies of the pious" (*Pss. Sol.* 8:34; 10:6; 17:16). The community apparently worshiped apart from the Temple, without sacrifices. Piety had become a substitute for sacrifice, so that sins were now cleansed through confession and penance in the "synagogues of the devout" (*Pss. Sol.* 17:16; 10:7), where they give thanks to God (*Pss. Sol.* 10:5, 6).

The appearance of several rubrics for musical settings that echo the biblical Psalter gives further evidence that these hymns were used in synagogue services or simply in emulation of the biblical psalms. The *Psalms of Solomon* were later appended to the Christian collection of hymns known as the *Odes of Solomon* (see SOLOMON, ODES OF). This suggests that the *Psalms of Solomon* were used in the liturgy of the Syriac church.

Most seditious writings, such as Daniel and Revelation, veil themselves in cryptic vocabulary innocuous to the eyes of outsiders. However, the *Psalms of Solomon* is an open call for rebellion against both internal corruption and foreign domination. Unless these psalms were kept in a strictly controlled circulation, the community was either very careless or were emboldened by their belief in an imminent divine intervention.

E. The Messiah in the *Psalms of Solomon*

In post-biblical Jewish literature, there was an expectation of a coming Messiah who would be a military deliverer from earthly oppression and persecution. This type of expectation longed for a reestablishment of the Davidic monarchy with its immediate aim of a political and military overthrow of the occupying power. The *Psalms of Solomon* present images of this Son of David, this "Lord Messiah," who would lead the pious in a rebellion and establish an independent and holy Jewish theocratic state. Those in the Diaspora would return to their lands and foreign nations would be subordinate to this Messiah and to his God (see MESSIAH, JEWISH).

"Son of David" as a title for the Messiah occurs only in *Psalms of Solomon* (17:21) and was a clear rebuke to the non-Davidic Hasmonean dictatorial rule. During Jesus' ministry "Son of David" and "Messiah" apparently had become synonyms. Targums describe the Messiah as the SON OF DAVID who was expected to be a warrior king, who would rule with supreme authority.

The expectation of this Davidic redeemer in the *Psalms of Solomon* is based firmly on their readings from the OT, specifically in the promise to David: "Lord, you chose David to be king over Israel, and swore to him about his descendants forever, that his kingdom should not fail before you" (*Pss. Sol.* 17:4; *OTP* 2:665). This Lord Messiah is not a supernatural being. However, he will be sinless and have a "holy people" whom he will "lead in righteousness." The Messiah will bring the "salvation of the Lord" upon Israel forever (*Pss. Sol.* 12:6).

The description of the rule of this Davidic leader continues (*Pss. Sol.* 17:22-43), showing how he will "purge Jerusalem from gentiles who trample her to destruction" (v. 22) and will "gather a holy people whom he will lead in righteousness; and he will judge the tribes of the people" (v. 26). Verse 32 adds, "And he will be a righteous king over them, taught by God. There will be no unrighteousness among them in his days, for all shall be holy, and their king shall be the Lord Messiah" (*OTP* 2:667).

F. The Return from the Diaspora and Ideas of Resurrection

The authors of the *Psalms of Solomon* pray, "Bring together the dispersed of Israel with mercy and goodness" (*Pss. Sol.* 8:28). "Announce in Jerusalem the voice of one bringing good news" (*Pss. Sol.* 11:1-2). Indeed, the Lord Messiah "will distribute them [the Jewish people] upon the land according to their tribes" (*Pss. Sol.* 17:28). The author of the *Psalms of Solomon* is elated by the thought:

Stand on a high place, Jerusalem, and look at your children,
    from the east and the west assembled together
      by the Lord.
From the north they come in the joy of their God;
    from far distant islands God has assembled
      them."
          (*Pss. Sol.* 11:2-3; *OTP* 2:662)

However, there is some ambiguity about the fate of the Gentiles. In many of the prophets the Gentiles will join Israel in the worship of God (Zech 8:20-23;

Isa 49:6; Jer 3:17). The *Psalms of Solomon* echo this: "[God will have] nations to come from the ends of the earth to see his glory" (17:31). But most often in the *Psalms of Solomon*, the fate of the Gentiles was unqualified destruction at which Israel would rejoice. *Psalms of Solomon* 3:11 promises, "The destruction of the sinner is forever." Sinners shall "perish forever" (15:12, 13). In fact, the Messiah was expected to purge Jerusalem and the Temple of all Gentiles, aliens, and foreigners (*Pss. Sol.* 17:22-30). "Sinners shall be taken away to destruction, and no memory of them will ever be found" (*Pss. Sol.* 13:11).

This last psalm also indicates the possibility of resurrection, but it is resurrection for the righteous alone (compare *Pss. Sol.* 2:31; 3:12): [*Pss. Sol.* 3:12].

For the Lord will spare his devout,
    and he will wipe away their mistakes with
      discipline.
For the life of the righteous (goes on) forever,
    but sinners shall be taken away to destruction,
      and no memory of them will ever be found.
         (*Pss. Sol.* 13:10–11; *OTP* 2:663)

G. The *Psalms of Solomon* and the New Testament

Expectations of a Davidic Messiah, much as articulated in the *Psalms of Solomon*, were pervasive in Jesus' world. However, Jesus does not clear the Temple of Gentiles, but for them: "My house shall be called a house of prayer for all the nations" (Mark 11:17; compare Isa 56:7). The passage that Jesus quotes in his visit to the Temple, in other words, includes the very people that the Messiah, according to *Pss. Sol.* 17, would exclude.

With the title "Lord Messiah," these psalms link for the first time the concepts of "Messiah" and "Lordship" into a new construct available in the contemporary religious environment for Luke to use as a title for Jesus (Luke 2:11), and which the NT develops into the image of "Christ the Lord," a theme central in the development of NT christology.

One frequent element in the Gospels does not appear in the *Psalms of Solomon*: the forgiveness of sins. The classic description of the Messiah in *Pss. Sol.* 17–18 speaks of his overcoming demons, ushering in a righteous government, judging the godless, and of his righteousness and even sinlessness (17:36), but not of his ability to forgive sins.

The author of the *Psalms of Solomon*, who describes a triumphant and politically successful king, never would have been satisfied with Jesus, who neither purged Jerusalem nor placed the Gentiles "under his yoke" (*Pss. Sol.* 17:30). See PSEUDEPIGRAPHA.

Bibliography: Kenneth Atkinson. "Herod the Great, Sosius, and the Siege of Jerusalem (37 BCE) in Psalm of Solomon 17." *NovT* 38 (1996) 313–22; Robert Hann. *The Manuscript History of the Psalms of Solomon*

(1982); R. B. Wright. *The Psalms of Solomon: A Critical Edition of the Greek Text* (2007); R. B. Wright. "Psalms of Solomon." *OTP* (1985) 2:639–70.

ROBERT B. WRIGHT

SOLOMON, TESTAMENT OF [Διαθήκη Σολομῶντος Diathēkē Solomōntos]. The *Testament of Solomon* is a Late Roman pseudepigraphon in which a supramundane ring plays an instrumental role in the rise and fall of King Solomon, son of David. The ring is given to Solomon by God, through the agency of the archangel Michael, in response to prayer for authority over a demon who has been afflicting a young acquaintance of the king's (1:2-7). In accordance with Michael's instructions Solomon uses the ring to subdue the evil spirit, coerce several demons into assisting in the construction of the Jerusalem Temple, and acquire knowledge about the demons and magico-medical healing (1:8–18:42). However, after using the ring successfully for those and related purposes, Solomon entangles himself in a web of religious and moral error that undermines his honor and demonstrates his inferiority to one who will come later and "be crucified by the Jews on a cross" (*T. Sol.* 22:20).

As *Testament of Solomon's* main narrator, Solomon presents the achievements of his earlier years as less important than the failures of his final days. Those two periods in *Testament of Solomon's* life of Solomon correspond closely to the main sections of the text's structure: namely, the demonological handbook in the first eighteen chapters, and the rewriting in *T. Sol.* 19–26 of the biblical account of Solomon's decline (1 Kgs 10:1–11:40). Those two sections, moreover, differ in several noteworthy ways: *T. Sol.* 1–18, for instance, evinces a positive perspective concerning Solomon and shows strong interest in both astrology and folk healing, whereas *T. Sol.* 19–26 offers a subtle critique of the king and shows almost no interest in either astrology or healing.

The *Testament of Solomon* is attested in eighteen Greek manuscripts. None of the copies of its long form is earlier than the 15th cent. However, the authors of the *Dialogue of Timothy and Aquila* (ca. 6th cent. CE) already seem to know the long form of the *Testament of Solomon*.

The iconographic tradition of Solomon as horseman—a popular form of Syro-Palestinian art attested by a number of apotropaic amulets some of which have been dated to the 3rd cent. CE—may shed valuable light on the question of date; the depiction in that tradition of Solomon on horseback triumphing over a demonic figure helps to create a context in which *Testament of Solomon's* portrayal of the demon Ephippas ("on horseback") as facilitating the fall of Solomon would amount to a strong rhetorical riposte.

Interest in diminishing the honor of Solomon is collocated in *Testament of Solomon* with various demonic testimonies to the supremacy of Christ (e.g.,

T. Sol. 22:20). That particular combination of features is well suited to a context of debate between early Jews and Christians over the respective merits of Solomon and Jesus. It also suggests that at least some Christians, such as the final editor(s) of *Testament of Solomon*, perceived the popularity of the Solomonic tradition of magico-medical practice to be a threat to the uniqueness of Jesus as a source of cosmic power against the demons of illness. Thus, by shaming Solomon, the editor(s) of *Testament of Solomon* probably intended to put the legendary king's bequest of magico-religious healing outside the boundaries of legitimate Christian health care, and thereby to safeguard the uniqueness of Jesus vis-à-vis other cosmic powers in the same religious economy. *See* DEMON; MAGIC, MAGICIAN; PSEUDEPIGRAPHA; SOLOMON.

Bibliography: Todd E. Klutz. *Rewriting the Testament of Solomon: Tradition, Conflict, and Identity in a Late Antique Pseudepigraphon* (2005); C. C. McCown. *The Testament of Solomon* (1922).

TODD E. KLUTZ

SOLOMON, WISDOM OF [σοφία Σαλωμῶνος sophia Salōmōnos]. The work of this unknown author, composed during the early Roman period of Egypt, is known as the Wisdom of Solomon according to the LXX or as the book of Wisdom according to the Vulgate. A few Greek manuscripts add an adjective to characterize the quality of this particular wisdom as "all virtuous" (hē panaretos sophia [ἡ πανάρετος σοφία], "all virtuous wisdom"), and there are multiple variations in the Old Latin manuscripts including *liber sapientiae* (the book of Wisdom) and *liber sapientiae salomonis* (the book of the Wisdom of Solomon). The Greek Fathers commonly refer to the book as the Wisdom of Solomon, and it is likely they who provided the impetus for this title to appear in the Greek manuscripts.

The author exhibits a distinct reliance on biblical tradition but also displays familiarity with several key features of Greek thought. The biblical traditions appearing throughout the book are: Genesis, Exodus, Davidic kingship, Isaiah, and the sapiential texts of Proverbs and Sirach. Familiarity with Greek rhetoric and with Platonic and Stoic philosophical discourse occurs throughout the author's argumentation. Such integration of Greek thought with Hebrew tradition is found in no other biblical text. The Wisdom of Solomon represents an extraordinary enculturation of the Jewish community in the Greek world.

Political unrest in Egypt and Palestine under Roman rule tested the very limits of Jewish enculturation. The Wisdom of Solomon shares this struggle for identity in the midst of cultural turbulence. The author is clearly familiar with apocalyptic works that abounded in Palestine and the Jewish diaspora alike. Yet the author prefers the sapiential tradition as the prime context for developing arguments to exhort the contemporary

Jewish community. The work can best be understood as a poetic apologetic for the Jewish faith in trying times when tensions within and without the Jewish community were straining the boundaries of Jewish identity. The end result is an aesthetic work in the sapiential tradition that displays unusual breadth of argumentation to probe the very origins of faith and to unmask the flight to unbelief.

A. Literary Structures
    1. Exhortation to justice (1:1–6:21)
    2. Solomon desires wisdom (7:1–8:21)
       a. Solomon prays for wisdom (9:1-18)
       b. Wisdom accompanies the righteous
          (10:1–11:1)
    3. The exodus from Egypt: reflections
       (11:2–19:22)
B. Canon
C. Author
D. Date and Place of Composition
E. Genre
F. Wisdom and Apocalyptic Literature
Bibliography

A. Literary Structures

1. Exhortation to justice (1:1–6:21)

All three major parts of the book display literary patterns through which the author maintains a specific argument. The first part, Wis 1:1–6:21, an exhortation to justice, is conveyed through an intricate concentric structure that highlights the major building blocks of the author's argument for justice and immortality.

A 1:1-15	Exhortation to justice Warning against death
B 1:16–2:24	Speech of the wicked Their defense of injustice through power and might
C 3:1–4:20	Three diptychs contrast the just with the wicked The defense of injustice by the wicked is dismantled
B´ 5:1-23	Speech of the wicked Their confession of error; the final judgment
A´ 6:1-21	Exhortation to wisdom Warning against injustice

The exhortation to justice takes on significant urgency through the introduction of the figure of death. With the menacing presence of death, the exhortation is quickly transformed into dissuasion from taking on death by the practice of injustice. Through wisdom humans find the path of virtue that leads to immortality.

2. Solomon desires wisdom (7:1–8:21)

The second part of the book moves rather smoothly from the conflict between justice and injustice, death and immortality, to the efficacious qualities of wisdom. Two concentric structures of this section give shape to the author's praise of wisdom.

A 7:1-6	Solomon is mortal and limited
B 7:7-12	Wisdom is superior to all goods
C 7:13-22a	God is the guide of wisdom God gives knowledge and wealth
D 7:22b–8:1	Eulogy of wisdom Twenty-one attributes of wisdom
C´ 8:2-9	Solomon desires to have wisdom as a bride Wisdom knows all things and is a source of wealth
B´ 8:10-16	Wisdom grants success and fame
A´ 8:17-21	As a child Solomon was gifted but still needs God's wisdom

a. Solomon prays for wisdom (9:1-18)

A 9:1-3	God has formed humanity through wisdom
B 9:4	Solomon asks for the wisdom that sits by God's throne
C 9:5-6	For Solomon is weak and limited
D 9:7-8	Yet called to be king and judge over God's people
E 9:9	Wisdom knows what is pleasing to God
F 9:10ab	Prayer for God to send wisdom
E´ 9:10c-11	So that Solomon may learn what is pleasing to God
D´ 9:12	He will judge God's people justly
C´ 9:13-17a	For human beings are weak and burdened
B´ 9:17b	unless God's wisdom and spirit come from on high
A´ 9:18	and through wisdom humanity is saved

The very last comment in Solomon's prayer for wisdom declares wisdom to be the savior of humanity. This declaration moves the text to a midrashic reflection on key personages from Genesis and Exodus, starting with Adam and ending with Moses.

b. Wisdom accompanies the righteous (10:1–11:1). In seven short diptychs the author shows how it was wisdom who came to the aid of the righteous while the unrighteous floundered in failure: 1) 10:1-3, Adam is contrasted with Cain; 2) 10:4, Noah is contrasted with those who perished in the flood; 3) 10:5, Abraham is contrasted with the nations of Babel; 4) 10:6-8, Lot is contrasted with those who perished in the cities of the plain and with his wife; 5) 10:6-12, Jacob is contrasted with Esau and with his personal opponents; 6) 10:13-14, Joseph is contrasted with his brothers and with Potiphar's wife; 7) 10:15-21, and finally the Israelites and Moses are contrasted with their oppressors, the Egyptians.

3. The exodus from Egypt: reflections (11:2–19:22)

The final section of the Wisdom of Solomon proceeds smoothly into the midrashic treatment of the entire exodus narrative. The author returns to the study of the way of the righteous and the way of the wicked through contrasts and comparisons similar to the first part of the book. One major difference is that whereas the first part looked to a future judgment or "visitation by God" to resolve the disparity between justice and injustice, the last part understands this visitation by God to have occurred in Israel's past, namely in the great saving events of the exodus. A series of diptychs and reflections give shape to the author's argument. Another significant difference

between chap. 10 and the midrashic treatment of the exodus is the disappearance of the figure of wisdom. In chap. 10 it was Lady Wisdom who is understood to have protected the righteous in all their trials. In the last part of the work, Lady Wisdom disappears, and instead it is God who becomes the protagonist in coming to the aid of the righteous with all the forces of creation.

B. Canon

The first unambiguous reference to the Wisdom of Solomon stems from the 2nd cent. CE in the writings of Irenaeus (ca. 140–202). Two references are made to Wis 2:24 and 12:10: "Everyone follows the desires of his depraved heart, nurturing a wicked jealousy through which death entered the world" (*Haer.* 3.4.); "from generation to generation the Lord gives an opportunity to repent to all those who desire to return" (*Haer.* 7.5.). The book of Wisdom is cited among the list of books held to be canonical by the church in the Muratorian Canon (ca. 180–190 CE). Interestingly, in the Muratorian Canon, the Wisdom of Solomon is located among the books of the NT.

Although Origen (ca. 185–255 CE) cites the Wisdom of Solomon among his writings and commentaries on Scripture, he shares the uncertainty of its canonical status with others. Jerome follows Origen's hesitancy and accepts as canonical the twenty-two books of the Hebrew canon (according to a certain combination of books), the number of which corresponds to the twenty-

Five Diptychs and Seven Antitheses in the Wisdom of Solomon (11–19)		
Causal relationship 11:16	Antithetical relationship 11:5, 13	
Sins	Plagues	Blessings
1) 11:6-14, killing of infants	1) 11:6-14, undrinkable water	water in the desert
2) 11:15–16:14, animals adored	2) 16:1-4, animals suppress the appetite	delicious animals (quails)
1st reflection, 11:17–12:27	— God's power and mercy to save and to punish	
2nd reflection, 13–15	— the origins of false worship and critique	
Minor reflection, 16:5-14	— the brazen serpent, God has power over life and death	
	3) 16:5-14 animals that kill	the saving brazen serpent
3) 16:15-29 refusal to recognize the true God	4) 16:15-29 rain, hail; creation destroys by fire; lack of food	creation saves; the manna resists burning by fire
4) 17:1–18:4 enslaving Hebrews	5) 17:1–18:4 captivity by darkness	pillar of fire in the darkness
5) 18:5–19:21 killing of infants in the river	6) 18:5-25 death of the firstborn	Aaron stops the destroyer
Minor reflection, 18:20-25 *Aaron stops death*		
Minor reflection, 19:6-21 *Creation*	7) 19:1-9 drowning in the sea	Israel passes through the Red Sea

two letters of the Hebrew alphabet. The greatest impetus for the formal inclusion of the Wisdom of Solomon in the canon of Scripture came from Augustine (354–430 CE). For Augustine, the long and venerable reading of the Wisdom of Solomon in the liturgy by all Christians revealed its veritable canonical status (Augustine, PL 44.979–80). However, it was very clear to early Christian writers like Origen and Augustine that the Solomonic authorship of the book was practically impossible. Although many candidates had been proposed (from the nephew of Ben Sira to Philo of Alexandria), there was no consensus regarding the authorship of this fascinating work.

C. Author

The great affinity between many phrases in the Wisdom of Solomon and in the writings of Philo (ca. 20 BCE–50 CE) has brought attention to their relationship. Although they share a common set of concerns and many phraseological affinities, there are no clear citations between them. It would be tempting to see in the Wisdom of Solomon the result of Philo's personal attempt to write a more religious and poetic work over and above the philosophical, apologetical, and allegorical works for which he is famous. The greatest stumbling block to identifying Philo as the author of the Wisdom of Solomon is his penchant for allegorical interpretation and its absence in Wisdom. Similarly, although Wisdom's personification of wisdom bears similarities to the Logos theology of Philo, the former does not employ platonic philosophical categories as Philo does. Still, the affinities between the two testify to the distinct likelihood that they shared a common cultural background and could not have been far apart in time.

D. Date and Place of Composition

According to Philo, the Jewish population in Egypt reached one million (Philo, *Flaccus* 43), and much of it lived in Alexandria. Although that number may be an exaggeration, there is no doubt that the Jewish community was a major force in the economic and cultural fabric of the city. The Jews formed their own politeuma (πολίτευμα), an organization with economic and educational rights. Such Jewish literary figures as Aristobulos (180–145 BCE) and Philo show how far the Jewish community had integrated many aspects of Hellenism into its own tradition. Whether they gained access to the gymnasium or established their own educational centers in synagogues parallel to those of the Greeks is difficult to establish. What is certain is that their leading figures were thoroughly conversant with Hellenism.

The tension among various groups in Alexandria reached tragic proportions in 38 CE when the Jews were attacked in a pogrom-like manner. Synagogues were destroyed or desecrated with portraits of Caligula bearing divine titles. The following year, Philo himself led the Jewish delegation to Emperor Caligula to argue for the rights that had originally been granted them by Augustus. But no positive results were forthcoming. With the assassination of Caligula in 41 CE, the Jews revolted in Alexandria. This led the new emperor Claudius to settle the dispute once and for all with his forceful letter to the Alexandrians in 41 CE. The letter of Claudius essentially maintained the status quo.

This combination of a thorough familiarity with and respect for the best in Hellenism that the Jewish community manifested, as well as the tension between the Greeks and the Jewish community, makes Alexandria the likely site for the composition of the Wisdom of Solomon.

The question as to whether the NT writers were familiar with the Wisdom of Solomon is difficult to resolve. There are special affinities between Paul and John and the Wisdom of Solomon. But the common phraseology and ideas are general enough to suggest that they arise from common concerns and values rather than from literary dependency.

E. Genre

The Wisdom of Solomon in its entirety does not fit into any particular genre. The work is the result of a creative and imaginative writer who has produced a rather unique piece of literature. Two forms of discourse that stem from Aristotelian rhetoric have been proposed: protreptic discourse, which is governed by exhortation and persuasion, and the epideictic discourse of the encomium, which praises a figure and entertains throughout a sustained argument (Aristotle, *Rhet.* 3.14.10–15.9). Both genres, however, include exhortation and praise. The question is, which is at the service of the other? Since we lack extant sources and examples of these forms of literature from the time of the book of Wisdom, it is not an issue that can be easily decided.

The author makes use of several forms of writing. There is diatribe, especially noticeable in the first part, where the author sets up speakers in order to critique their arguments. There are literary diptychs, which make use of the comparing and contrasting features of synkrisis (σύγκρισις). These are especially noticeable in the first part of the book, where the lives of the just are contrasted with the lives of the wicked, and in the later part of the book, where the Egyptians are contrasted with the Israelites. The second part of the work makes use of eulogy in order to sustain the contemplation of the beauty and attractiveness of wisdom. Finally, though it is difficult to call the style of writing known as MIDRASH a genre because of its loose structure, it is clear that the author makes use of this general style of interpretation when treating biblical texts. In the first part of the book, the author employs a series of images from Isaiah in a manner that has been called midrashic or homiletic. In commenting on the events of the exodus in the last part of the book, the author is clearly following the events as recounted in Exodus and Numbers and attempting to give them a specific interpretation from a unique point of view. This is typical of midrashic writing. All of these styles have been combined by a skilled writer who was able to make use of devices and forms according to the movement of the argument.

F. Wisdom and Apocalyptic Literature

Although the Wisdom of Solomon is clearly based on the biblical sapiential tradition, traits of apocalyptic values surface in various portions of the work. There is reference to the "hidden mysteries of God" in Wis 2:22, and the cosmic judgment of God in Wis 5:15-23. The midrashic treatment of the exodus events are presented as a cosmic judgment. However, in all cases where the author borrows a motif from apocalyptic literature, the particular theme is encased within the sapiential didactic concern to convince the reader through argumentation of the value of justice for immortality.

The attribution of the work to a Solomonic figure, as the sapiential works of Proverbs and Qoheleth, testifies to a deliberate intention on the part of the author to formulate the work according to the values and perspectives of the sapiential tradition (see WISDOM IN THE OT). The theme of divine judgment in the first and third parts of the book is inspired by Isaiah and the book of Exodus. However, the divine judgment is portrayed with the positive perspective of creation that is so central to the wisdom tradition. The many forces of the cosmos are involved in overthrowing lawlessness, and the foundations of creation are understood as passing away or being transformed for the benefit of the righteous. Both the Wisdom of Solomon and apocalyptic writings portray a divine judgment that is inspired by the prophetic "visitation of the Lord." However, the Wisdom of Solomon portrays the cosmos as working alongside the Lord for justice precisely because God has created it through wisdom.

The foundational difference between the Wisdom of Solomon and apocalyptic writing (such as *1 Enoch*) is the source of authority through which the writing exhorts its audience. The Wisdom of Solomon aims to convince the reader through arguments based on a reflection on human experience, often with an aesthetic sense of beauty and order. Apocalypticism tries to convince the reader through arguments based on special divine revelation modeled on the manner of the prophet, most notably through the mediation of "visions" or personal divine revelation. Apocalyptic writing is especially suited to polemic elaboration in times of political upheaval and unrest. Given the Wisdom of Solomon's late date, it would be surprising for apocalyptic features not to appear in the work. What is more surprising is the extent to which the author grounds the apocalyptic features of the work, namely divine judgment and cosmic transformation, in a positive perspective on creation and the cosmos, which is a main characteristic of wisdom literature. See APOCALYPSE; APOCALYPTICISM; PSEUDEPIGRAPHA.

Bibliography: Samuel Cheon. *The Exodus Story in the Wisdom of Solomon* (1997); John J. Collins. *Jewish Wisdom in the Hellenistic Age* (1997); Michael Kolarcik. *The Ambiguity of Death in the Book of Wisdom (1–6)* (1991); Michael Kolarcik. "The Book of Wisdom: Introduction, Commentary, and Reflections." *NIB* 5 (1997) 433–600; George W. E. Nickelsburg. *Jewish Literature between the Bible and the Mishnah.* 2nd ed. (2005); David Winston. *The Wisdom of Solomon.* AB 43 (1979).

MICHAEL KOLARCIK, SJ

SOLOMON'S PORTICO [ἡ στοὰ τοῦ Σολομῶνος hē stoa tou Solomōnos]. The court of Herod's Temple was surrounded by colonnaded porches or porticoes. Tradition attributed the eastern portico to Solomon (Josephus, *Ant.* 20.221). While the line of the eastern portico may follow that of Solomon's Temple Mount and some of its foundations may date back to Nehemiah, Herod the Great probably built the portico.

Jesus identified himself as the Messiah while walking in Solomon's Portico (John 10:22-29). The early followers of Jesus worshiped in the Temple (Luke 24:52), and according to Luke the apostles met regularly in Solomon's Portico in executive council (Acts 3:11, 5:12). See JERUSALEM; TEMPLE, JERUSALEM; TEMPLES, HEROD'S.

ADAM L. PORTER

SOLOMON'S SERVANTS [עַבְדֵי שְׁלֹמֹה ʿavdhe shelomoh; παῖδες Σαλωμών paides Salōmōn, δοῦλοι Σαλωμών douloi Salōmōn]. An expression denoting members of Solomon's state bureaucracy (1 Kgs 9:27), his household, and his state slaves (1 Kgs 9:20-21), some of whom some were assigned to the Temple. The "descendants of Solomon's servants" (Ezra 2:55; Neh 11:3) are among the returnees led by ZERUBBABEL, and together with the NETHINIM numbered 392 (Ezra 2:58; Neh 7:60; the number is 372 in 1 Esd 5:35). They are listed among the temple personnel and were exempt from taxation (Ezra 7:24). See SLAVERY.

ALEJANDRO F. BOTTA

SOLOMON'S TEMPLE. See TEMPLE OF SOLOMON; TEMPLE, JERUSALEM.

SOLON [Σόλων Solōn]. Athenian poet, lawgiver, and statesman who lived from ca. 639 BCE to ca. 559 BCE. He was instrumental in spurring the Athenians to retake the island of Salamis from neighboring Megara (ca. 600). Elected chief archon in 594/3, he instituted numerous legal, political, and economic reforms. Solon revised the law code of Draco so that it was more humane. He divided the population into four classes in order to dilute the power of the ruling nobles. He created the Council of Four Hundred to prepare business for the assembly, he opened the assembly to all freemen, and he enhanced the role of the Areopagus. His reforms laid the foundations for democracy in Athens and later civilizations. For ten years following his reforms, he traveled to Egypt, Cyprus, and possibly Lydia.

GREGORY L. LINTON

SON [בֵּן ben; בַּר bar; υἱός huios]. *Son* is one of the most common words in the OT, both literally and idiomatically. In the biological sense, *son* refers to immediate offspring (e.g., Gen 4:1) and more distant descendants (e.g., Gen 31:28). In the plural it may denote both male and female children or descendants, especially when used with reference to a nation (e.g., "sons of Israel" means the Israelites). The high value placed upon children in general, and sons in particular, as a blessing from God is evidenced throughout the Bible (e.g., Gen 15:2-5; Isa 56:5; Ps 127:3-5). The special importance of male children relates to their role in continuing the family's name and ancestral heritage within the tribal structure of Israel (Deut 25:6).

Idiomatically, *son* frequently occurs in construct with another term ("son of…") and signifies one belonging to a specified group (e.g., "the SONS OF PROPHETS," 2 Kgs 2:7) or bearing specified characteristics (e.g., "sons of strength," Judg 18:2 [NRSV, "valiant men"]). *Son* may also be used in a figurative form of address, expressing intimacy or, as in wisdom literature, to refer to a student (e.g., Eccl 12:12; NRSV, "child"). It also denotes subordination to the parent, teacher, or other authority (e.g., 2 Kgs 16:7).

In the NT, *son* is used especially to refer to Jesus as "the SON OF MAN" (e.g., Matt 8:20), the "SON OF GOD" (e.g., Matt 27:54), the "SON OF DAVID" (e.g., Matt 21:9), or simply "the Son" (e.g., Matt 24:36). Paul uses *son* as a term of affection for churches and individual Christians whom he has brought to faith in Christ (e.g., 1 Cor 4:14, 17; NRSV, "child," "children"). Paul also refers to Christians as sons of God by adoption who share in the sonship of Christ (e.g., Rom 8:14-17; Gal 4:4-7). *See* CHILD, CHILDREN; FAMILY; FIRSTBORN; GOD, SONS OF; INHERITANCE IN THE NT; INHERITANCE IN THE OT.

PAUL NISKANEN

SON OF DAVID day'vid [בֶּן־דָּוִיד ben-dawidh; υἱός Δαυίδ huios Dauid]. In the OT, the phrase primarily refers to SOLOMON (2 Chr 1:1; 13:6; 35:3; Prov 1:1; compare Eccl 1:1) or a descendant of DAVID (2 Chr 11:18; compare Matt 1:20; Luke 3:31). It subsequently became a title referring to the royal Messiah, stemming from the promise God made to David regarding the eternal reign of David's offspring (2 Sam 7:12-16; *see* MESSIAH, JEWISH).

In the NT, the title is applied to Jesus, exclusively in the Synoptic Gospels (e.g., Matt 1:1; 9:27; 12:23; 20:30-31; see also Luke 1:32; John 7:42; Rom 1:3). Jesus never explicitly claimed to be the Son of David, perhaps because of the nationalistic and militaristic overtones. The title refers to Jesus' earthly life and is

subordinated to other christological titles, especially "CHRIST" and "SON OF GOD."

DAVID R. BAUER

SON OF GOD [בְּנִי beni; בַּר־אֱלָהִין bar ʾelahin; ὁ υἱὸς τοῦ θεοῦ ho huios tou theou]. Biblical authors use "son of God" or its equivalents (e.g., "my son," "son of the Most High") with reference to a variety of persons or groups. Most famously, "son of God" appears in the NT as a title or appellation for Jesus, and was subsequently taken up into the later christological and trinitarian debates from which it emerged as a primary component of creedal orthodoxy ("the only Son of God, eternally begotten of the Father, of one being with the Father"). Although this later development has its roots in the NT, the later use of the term should not simply be read back into the NT in disregard of the intervening stages of development. Awareness of the non-christological uses of the term—in the OT, the Apocrypha, other Jewish writings, and the NT—will help to bring the earliest christological uses of the term into clearer perspective.

    A. Old Testament
        1. Heavenly beings
        2. The king
        3. Israel
    B. Apocrypha and Other Jewish Writings
        1. Heavenly beings
        2. Israel
        3. Individuals
        4. Philo's usage
    C. New Testament
        1. Referring to persons other than Jesus
        2. Referring to Jesus
            a. Mark
            b. Matthew
            c. Luke–Acts
            d. Johannine literature
            e. Pauline literature
            f. Hebrews
            g. Other
        3. Origin and development of "Son of God" as a
           christological term
    Bibliography

A. Old Testament

Although *son* is used most commonly in the OT to denote physical descent and genealogical status, any discussion of "son of God" needs to recognize that *son* is also used more broadly as a term of relationship, characterization, or classification (*see* SON). Thus we encounter "sons of Zion" (Israelites; Ps 149:2), or "sons of the troop" (soldiers; 2 Chr 25:13), or a "son of strength" (mighty man; 1 Sam 14:52), or even "sons of [the] quiver" (arrows; Lam 3:13). A "son of God," then, is a person or group that stands in some particular relationship with God.

1. Heavenly beings

The OT contains several references to a company of heavenly beings who form part of a divine council: "the assembly of God" (Ps 82:1); "the congregation" or "council of the holy ones" (Ps 89:5, 7 [Heb. 89:6, 8]). On several occasions these heavenly beings are referred to as "sons" of God or of the gods. The idea of a council that participates with God in the administration of the world is to the fore in Job, where Satan makes his proposal to test Job's faithfulness on a day when the "sons of God came to present themselves before the LORD" and to report on their activities (Job 1:6; also 2:1; 38:7). Divine administration is also present in Deut 32:8, where, according to the most probable reading, the Most High is said to have "fixed the boundaries of the peoples according to the number of the sons of God" (NRSV, "... number of the gods"). The idea of a heavenly council is probably of Canaanite origin, but Israel's modification of the idea is exemplified in two other sets of passages. A concern to emphasize the Lord's superiority over the "sons of the gods" is found in Ps 29:1 and 89:6. In a second set of passages God's sovereignty over "the sons of God" (Gen 6:4) or "of the Most High" (Ps 82:6; also called "gods" [vv. 1, 6]) is also present, but in the sense that the "sons of God" are rebelling against divine sovereignty or are fostering the spread of evil in the world. The only appearance of the singular form is Dan 3:25, where Nebuchadnezzar sees a fourth figure in the fire whose appearance is like "a son of God" (also called an "angel" [v. 28]).

2. The king

The king is described as God's "son" in several passages. God is the speaker in each of them, which means that "son of God" is not used explicitly. Still, the concept is present. Second Samuel 7:11-16 contains the Lord's promise to David, conveyed through the prophet Nathan, to raise up one of David's sons as king and to "establish the throne of his kingdom forever" (v. 13). The promise continues: "I will be a father to him, and he shall be a son to me" (v. 14). In 1 Chronicles, this promise appears three times: once in a repetition of the whole scene (17:13) and then in speeches by David himself, first to Solomon (22:10) and subsequently to the leaders of Israel (28:6). Even though David's immediate successor is in view in each case, the repeated reference to an everlasting kingdom (also 1 Chr 17:14; 22:10; 28:7) suggests that the father-son relationship is to characterize the dynasty as a whole. Such a dynastic or generalized use of the term is present in Ps 2, which seems to reflect a royal ritual. In vv. 6-7 the Lord first speaks ("in his fury") to the hostile nations: "I have set my king on Zion, my holy mountain"; then he declares to the king himself, "You are my son, today I have begotten you." Similar themes, though without explicit use of "son," are also present in Ps 89. Here the king speaks first: "You are my Father, my God and the rock of my salvation"; then God replies: "I will make him the firstborn, the highest of the kings of the earth" (vv. 26-27 [Heb. 27-28]). Throughout these passages the father-son relationship is one in which, on one side, God has chosen the king and promised him protection, steadfast love and, when necessary, discipline; and, on the other side, the king is expected to remain loyal to God and to lead the people in accordance with God's ways.

Divine sonship ideas were essential components of royal ideologies in the ANE, and there is little doubt that Israel was dependent on its neighbors for some of the components of its own. The closer parallels are to be found, however, in those traditions where the enthronement of the king was seen as a divine adoption (e.g., Assyria), rather than those in which the king was a divine being in himself (e.g., Egypt).

3. Israel

Old Testament writers also apply sonship language to Israel as a corporate entity, a usage that sets Israel apart from its neighbors. As with the previous category, the most important references are found in divine speech. In Exod 4:22-23, the Lord instructs Moses to say to Pharaoh: "Thus says the LORD: Israel is my firstborn son.... Let my son go so that he may worship me." The exodus is also in view in Hos 11:1 ("out of Egypt I called my son"), though the passage is primarily a prophetic admonition of the "son" for his subsequent waywardness. In Jer 31:20, a passage dealing with the anticipated reunion of Israel and Judah, the Lord asks, "Is Ephraim a dear son to me?" an affirmative answer being implied by the context. It is not clear whether Ephraim represents all of Rachel's sons, lost in exile, or just the Northern Kingdom. But in either case, "son" has a corporate sense. In Deuteronomy, a father-son relationship forms part of a simile on two occasions: "as a man carries" (Deut 1:31) or "disciplines" (Deut 8:5) "his son," so "the LORD your God" has done for Israel. In addition, Israelites collectively are referred to as "sons" of God (Deut 14:1; Isa 43:6; Jer 3:19; Hos 1:10). That there is no fundamental tension between the singular and plural form is apparent in Jer 3:19, where the plural ("I thought how I would set you among my sons") stands in parallel with the singular ("I thought you would call me 'My father'"). The plural form seems to open up the possibility that an individual Israelite could be a "son of God," but such a singular usage does not appear in the OT. The father-son relationship in these passages is similar to that found in royal sonship ideas: election, protection, steadfast love, and discipline on one side; faithfulness, obedience, and trust on the other.

B. Apocrypha and Other Jewish Writings

In the Apocrypha sonship conceptions are not widespread, appearing only in Wisdom of Solomon, Sirach, Judith, and LXX Esther, and only with reference to righteous individuals or Israel as a whole. In Wis 2:12-20, the "righteous man," who is oppressed and abused by the wicked but who eventually is vindicated by God, is described by his tormentors as one who is known as "God's son" (2:18; compare 2:13) and "boasts that God is his father" (2:16).

Beginning with chap. 3, the singular gives way to the plural ("the righteous ones"; 3:1), and we encounter several subsequent references to Israelites as "sons" of God (5:5; 12:19, 21; 16:26; "sons and daughters" in 9:7). The final occurrence, however, is singular: after "their firstborn were destroyed," the Egyptians recognized Israel to be "God's son" (18:13). It is unclear, then, whether the righteous man/son of God of chap. 2 is to be seen as an ideal Israelite (one of the righteous ones) or as a personification of Israel itself. Perhaps both readings are appropriate. In Sir 4:10 the singular is used (albeit in a simile) of a righteous individual: "Be a father to orphans ...; you will then be like a son of the Most High." The plural appears with reference to faithful Israelites in Jdt 9:4 ("your beloved sons who burned with zeal for you") and LXX Esth 16:16 ("sons of the living God"). In Sir 36:17 Israel is referred to as God's "firstborn," though without any explicit use of "son."

Since no sharp line of demarcation can be drawn between the Apocrypha and other Jewish literature of the later Second Temple period, it is appropriate to provide a brief survey of this material as well, especially since some of it has a bearing on NT developments.

1. Heavenly beings

Although the LXX renders "son(s) of God" as "angel(s)" in some cases (LXX Deut 32:8; LXX Job 1:6; 2:1; 38:7; OG Dan 3:92 [3:25]), "son(s)" is retained elsewhere (LXX Gen 6:4; LXX Ps 28:1 [29:1]; 88:6 [89:6]; "son" in Theod. Dan 3:92 [3:25]). In *1 Enoch* the angelic Watchers are referred to as the "sons of heaven" (13:8), and Lamech describes his infant son Noah ("a strange child") as being like "the sons of the angels of heaven" (106:5).

Given the presence of royal sonship ideas in the OT, it is natural to expect that, as messianic expectations developed, "son of God" would come to be associated with a royal messiah. Until the discovery of the Dead Sea Scrolls, however, solid evidence of such usage was lacking. To be sure, "my son" is used with reference to the "Messiah" in *4 Ezra* (7:28-29; 13:32, 37, 52; 14:9), but the Latin *filius meus* is almost certainly a rendering of "my servant" (in a Greek source and ultimately in a Semitic original). Likewise, "I and my son" in *1 En.* 105:2 is more probably a reference to Enoch and Methuselah than to God and the Messiah (*Sib. Or.* 3:776 is undoubtedly a Christian interpolation). Three fragments from Qumran, however, have provided more conclusive evidence that "son of God" was being used in a royal messianic sense by the 1st cent. CE. Citing the promise to David in 2 Sam 7:14 ("he shall be a son to me"), *4QFlorilegium* (4Q174) connects this to the "branch of David" who will appear "in the last days" "to save Israel" (1 I, 10–13). Also from Cave 4, an Aramaic apocalypse speaks of a coming "eternal kingdom" associated with one who "will be called son of God, and they will call him son of the Most High" (4Q246 II, 1). Finally, the *Rule of the Congregation* (1Q28a) speaks of a time when someone (God, perhaps; there is a lacuna in the text) "will beget the Messiah" (II, 11–12).

2. Israel

Israel continues to be described in sonship terms through this period. *4QWords of the Luminaries* (4Q504) combines the straightforward ascription of Exod 4:22 ("For you called Israel 'my son, my firstborn'") with the comparative language of Deut 8:5 ("and have corrected us as one corrects his son"), linking both with a plural formulation ("you have established us as your sons"; 1–2 III, 5–7). A similar echo of Deut 8:5 is present in *Pss. Sol.* 18:4, while *4 Ezra* 6:58, echoing Exod 4:22, describes Israel as God's "first-born, only begotten." Israelites collectively are referred to as God's "sons" on a number of occasions (*Sib. Or.* 3:702; *T. Jud.* 24:3; *T. Mos.* 10:3; *Jub.* 1:24-25; *L.A.B.* 32.10).

3. Individuals

In addition to the messianic references, several other individuals are described as God's "son." *Psalms of Solomon* 13:9 simply applies the language of Deut 8:5 to a generic individual: "he will admonish the righteous (person) as a beloved son." In *Joseph and Aseneth*, however, when Joseph appears in all his heavenly brilliance ("the sun from heaven has come to us on its chariot"; 6:2), Aseneth recognizes him as a "son of God" (6:3, 5; also 13:13; 21:4) and not, as she formerly thought, simply "the shepherd's son from the land of Canaan" (6:2). Upon her marriage to Joseph, Aseneth herself becomes "a daughter of the Most High" (21:4). In a different vein, sonship language is applied to two Jewish miracle workers in later rabbinic tradition: Honi "the circle drawer" (1st cent. BCE) prays to God "like a son who importunes his father" (*m. Taan.* 3.8), and his prayers are heard; Haninah ben Dosa (1st cent. CE), whose prayers were "more effective than those of the High Priest on the Day of Atonement," was referred to by a heavenly voice as "Haninah my son" (*b. Taan.* 24b).

4. Philo's usage

Philo cites Deut 14:1 as evidence that "those who live in the knowledge of the One are rightly called 'sons of God,'" though for him such sonship is modeled by "God's first-born, the Word" (*Confusion* 145–146). The Logos is also called God's "firstborn" in *Dreams* 1.215, a passage in which the Logos is further described as the High Priest of God's primary temple, the cosmos. The cosmos itself is called God's "son" in *Spec. Laws* 1.96, though elsewhere a distinction is made between the cosmos that is perceived through the senses ("the younger son of God") and the cosmos approached only through the mind ("the elder") (*Unchangeable* 31).

C. New Testament

1. Referring to persons other than Jesus

Although "son of God" appears in the NT most frequently and characteristically with reference to Jesus, sonship language is also used of believers, usually in the plural but occasionally in the singular. Believers collectively are called sons "of God" (Matt 5:9; Luke 20:36; Rom 8:14, 19; Gal 3:26), "of your Father who is in heaven" (Matt 5:45), and "of the Most High" (Luke 6:35; compare John 12:36; see GOD, SONS OF). Additionally, believers are simply called "sons" in contexts where divine sonship is implied (Matt 17:26; Gal 4:5, 6; Heb 2:10; 12:5-8; compare Matt 7:11// Luke 11:13); in one instance we find "sons and daughters" (2 Cor 6:18). In a related formulation, believers are said to have received adoption (Rom 8:15, 23; 9:4; Gal 4:5; Eph 1:5; see ADOPTION). In both Paul and Hebrews, the sonship of believers and of Christ are intimately linked, so that the former are said to be Christ's "brothers" (Rom 8:29; Heb 2:10, 17). In Luke 20:36 those who experience resurrection in the coming age are said to be "sons of God" in the sense that they are "like angels." The singular form appears, albeit in a generalizing sense, in Rev 21:7 with reference to the one "who overcomes" ("I will be his God and he will be my son"), in Gal 4:7, and in Heb 12:5. In addition, Adam is described as "[son] of God" in Luke's genealogy (Luke 3:38; huios understood from v. 23).

2. Referring to Jesus

a. Mark. The identity of Jesus is a central theme in Mark's Gospel and "Son of God" plays an important part in his development of the theme. A certain duality is apparent. On one hand, it is not until the centurion's confession in 15:39 ("Truly, this man was God's son") that any human character in the narrative recognizes Jesus as "son of God." The only other use of the term by a human character (other than Jesus) appears in the question of the high priest: "Are you the Messiah, the Son of the Blessed One?" (14:61). On the other hand, Jesus' divine sonship is declared by God (at the baptism [1:11] and transfiguration [9:7]), recognized by demons (3:11; 5:7), and referred to by Jesus himself. The clearest instance of the latter comes in Jesus' reply to the high priest's question—"I am [i.e., the Son of the Blessed One]" (14:62)—though he immediately goes on to refer to himself as the heavenly SON OF MAN. Given the earlier references to Jesus' sonship, his statement that the time of the end is known not by "the angels in heaven nor the Son, but only [by] the Father" (13:32) undoubtedly is to be read as a reference to himself. Another possible instance is the reference to the "beloved son" in the parable of the tenants (12:6).

The centurion's confession thus serves to tie together two Markan strands. One is Mark's redefinition of messiahship in terms of the suffering Son of Man. The first half of Mark's Gospel reaches its climax with Peter's confession of Jesus as Messiah (8:29). Immediately and for the first time Jesus begins to speak of the necessity "that the Son of Man must undergo great suffering" (8:31), a necessity that dominates the narrative from this point forward. Jesus' role as a suffering figure is recognized and affirmed by the centurion in his own confession of Jesus' identity. Because he identifies Jesus precisely as "Son of God," however, the centurion's confession also serves to link Jesus' suffering to the more exalted, transcendent figure of the Son of God found earlier in the narrative. Whether this linkage is signaled already in the title of the Gospel (1:1) depends on an answer to the vexed question of whether huiou theou (υἱοῦ θεοῦ) was part of the original text or not.

What can be said about Mark's usage with reference to the larger context? The probable allusion in 1:11 to Ps 2:7 serves to connect the term to the tradition of royal sonship, a connection that is perhaps also implied in 1:1, if "Son of God" is original. Still, it cannot be said that Mark emphasizes the messianic aspects of the term. Likewise, while Jesus' statement in 13:32 places "the Son" in a category akin to that of the angels, there is no indication that the term itself is aligned with heavenly council traditions. Mark's "Son of God" may draw on some already existing traditions, but its profile—a transcendent figure who is also a suffering and vindicated messiah—is a more characteristically Christian creation. In this connection, however, while we need to take full account of the transcendent element, Mark's presentation of Jesus' sonship contains no explicit indication of preexistence.

b. Matthew. Matthew takes over almost every instance of the term in Mark (compare Mark 1:1; 3:11), which means that much of what was said of Mark is true of Matthew as well. Nevertheless, Matthew develops the theme in his own way. Some of the added material simply extends elements already present in Mark. The figure of the king's "son" in the parable of the wedding banquet (22:2) is similar to that of the vineyard owner's son in Mark 12:6. The use of "the Son" in parallel with "the Father," found in the limited-knowledge saying of Mark 13:32 (also in Matt 24:36), appears also in Matt 11:27 ("no one knows the Son except the Father ...") and in the triadic formula of the Great Commission (28:19). In Matthew's version of the episode in which Jesus challenges the identification of the messiah as the "son of David" (Matt 22:41-45; compare Mark 12:35-37), his addition of the question "Whose son is he?" presumably invites the answer "the Son of God" (rather than of David). While Matthew extends the cosmic significance of the Son (e.g., 28:18-20) and adds an account of Jesus' miraculous birth (where Jesus is "a son" borne by Mary; 1:21, 23, 25), indications of preexistence are just as lacking in his Gospel as they are in Mark.

One way in which Matthew differs from Mark, however, has to do with human recognition of Jesus' divine sonship. Matthew takes over (and embellishes) the account of the centurion's confession (27:54), but the centurion is not the first to acclaim Jesus as Son of God. In Matthew's account, Peter confesses Jesus not only as "the Messiah" but also as "the Son of the living God" (16:16), a confession which Jesus commends unequivocally (16:17-19). And even before this, when the disciples witness Jesus' walking on the sea, they "worshiped him, saying, 'Truly you are the Son of God'" (14:33; compare Mark 6:51-52). Jesus' identity as Son in Matthew is something that can be fully understood even before the cross and resurrection.

The other significant Matthean development is rooted in Israel typology. An explicit connection between Jesus and Israel as God's "son" is found in Matt 2:15, where Matthew declares the return of Jesus and his family from Egypt to be a fulfillment of scripture: "Out of Egypt have I called my son" (Hos 11:1). Although this citation has sometimes been seen simply as prooftexting, the presence of similar typology in the temptation narrative (4:1-11) suggests that Matthew has picked up and elaborated something already present in his sources. In the temptation narrative, the scriptural passages that Jesus cites in response to the Tempter are all drawn from Deut 6 and 8, (8:3; 6:16, 13), a passage in which Moses is reminding Israel of the lessons they should have learned in their forty years of wilderness wanderings (compare Jesus' forty days and nights in the wilderness) and in which their relationship with God is compared to that between a father and a son (Deut 8:5). The implication is that in his calling as God's Son (e.g., 3:17) Jesus' task is to recapitulate Israel's experience and to bring Israel's calling as God's son to fulfillment. In the temptation narrative, the Tempter tries to deflect Jesus from this path of humble obedient sonship by holding out another model of sonship, one based on royal power and privilege. The Tempter's role is reprised later in the Gospel by Peter (16:21-23) and the mockers at the cross (27:38-44). In Matthew's version of the story, it is precisely because Jesus remains faithful to his calling, following the path of obedient sonship to its end, that he is vindicated by God and, as a result, is elevated to a position in which he as Son exercises universal sovereignty (28:18-20).

c. Luke–Acts. Even though Luke's use of sonship language overlaps considerably with Mark and Matthew, several unique features of the Gospel are to be noted. First, two instances of the term in Mark are not taken up in Luke: Jesus' statement about the Son's limited knowledge (Mark 13:32), which Luke simply omits, though he takes over the rest of the passage (Luke 21:29-33; compare Mark 13:28-32); and the centurion's confession, which in Luke (23:47) becomes "Certainly this man was innocent." Second, Luke links the term with messianic expectations at two points: in Gabriel's annunciation to Mary, where "Son of the Most High" stands in parallel with "the throne of his ancestor David" (1:32); and in 4:41, where Luke interprets the cry of the demons ("You are the Son of God") as an indication of their knowledge "that he was the Messiah."

Third, in the annunciation scene Gabriel links Jesus' identity as "Son of God" with the virginal conception (1:35).

The term appears only twice in Acts, both times with messianic connections. In Acts 9 Paul's proclamation of Jesus as "the Son of God" (9:20) is, for Luke, equivalent to the message that Jesus "was the Messiah" (9:22). A little later (13:33), also in Pauline preaching, the resurrection of Jesus is presented as a fulfillment of Ps 2:7. (See also the Western interpolation at 8:37.)

d. Johannine literature. With sonship language as with so many other things, the Fourth Gospel presents us with a perplexing combination of Synoptic overlap and Johannine uniqueness. As with the Synoptics, "Son of God" is a title attributed to Jesus by others in a quasi-confessional way (1:34, 49; 11:27). Likewise, the title is treated as the equivalent of (or at least is placed in parallel with) "Messiah" (11:27; 20:31) or "King of Israel" (1:49). Indeed, the evangelist declares that his purpose is to confirm his readers in the belief "that Jesus is the Messiah, the Son of God" (20:31).

Several other aspects have Synoptic parallels but are much more prevalent in John. "The Son" as an unqualified term used in association with "the Father" appears in only two separate Synoptic traditions (a total of four appearances) but some twelve times in John (3:35, 36; 5:19, 20, 21, 22, 23, 26; 6:40; 8:36; 14:13; 17:1; compare 3:17). Likewise, while Jesus uses the term of himself (or accepts such usage) in a small handful of Synoptic passages, such usage is widespread and unrestrained in John, appearing some twenty-two times.

Turning to the unique aspects of John, we first note that some Synoptic features are absent. There are no exorcisms in John and thus no instance where Jesus' sonship is recognized by demons. Nor is there any instance where God identifies Jesus as "my Son"; John contains no account of Jesus' baptism (but compare 1:34) or transfiguration, and elsewhere God speaks only once (12:28). The latter point becomes virtually insignificant, however, in the context of the most striking feature of John's christology—the almost complete equality between the Son and the Father: "whatever [the Father] does, the Son does likewise" (5:19); "I and the Father are one" (10:30); "if you know me, you will know my Father also" (14:7). While there may be a hint of subordination—what the Son possesses has been "granted" by the Father—the result is virtual equality: "For just as the Father has life in himself, so he has granted the Son also to have life in himself" (5:26; compare 5:22). Closely related to the theme of equality are two other christological elements: the uniqueness (monogenēs μονογενής) of the Son (3:16; 18; compare 1:14, 18) and his preexistence (e.g., "so now, Father, glorify me in your own presence with the glory that I had in your presence before the world existed"; 17:5; also 8:58; 16:28; etc.)

Similar patterns of usage are present in the epistles, though without explicit statements of equality with

God and preexistence. "Son of God" appears as a confessional term (1 John 4:15; 5:5, 10, 13; compare 3:8; 5:12, 20); "the Son" and "the Father" are paired (1 John 2:22, 23, 24; 2 John 9); the Son is monogenēs (1 John 4:9). Unique features in the epistles are the formulations "his Son" (1 John 1:3, 7; 3:23; 4:10; 5:9, 10, 11, 20) and "the Son of the Father" (2 John 3).

e. Pauline literature. Sonship language appears in Pauline literature much less frequently than other christological terms (e.g., Lord, Christ), being found only fifteen times in the undisputed epistles and once each in Ephesians (4:13) and Colossians (1:13). The most frequent formulation is "his Son" (twelve times, including Col 1:13); "Son of God" appears four times (including Eph 4:13) and "the Son" once (1 Cor 15:28).

Romans 1:3-4 is of particular interest in that it is generally understood to contain pre-Pauline tradition. These verses both link Jesus' sonship with Davidic descent and identify the resurrection at the point in which he was designated as "Son of God." Elsewhere sonship language is used with respect to Jesus' salvific death (Rom 5:10; 8:32; Gal 2:20), to believers' union or participation with Christ (Rom 8:29; 1 Cor 1:9; Gal 2:20; 4:6-7; Eph 4:13), and to the Parousia and eschatological consummation (1 Cor 15:28; 1 Thess 1:10; compare Col 1:13). On several occasions Paul also speaks of God's "Son" as the content of his gospel (Rom 1:9) or of his preaching (2 Cor 1:19), which is closely connected to Gal 1:16 where he describes his Damascus experience as the event in which God "was pleased to reveal his Son to me, so that I might preach him among the Gentiles" (Gal 1:16). Given that Paul seems to conceive of Christ's preexistence (1 Cor 8:6; Phil 2:6-8), statements that the Son was "sent" by God (Rom 8:3; Gal 4:4) may well have similar overtones (unlike the Synoptics). In Colossians, the hymn in praise of "the firstborn of all creation" (1:15-20) is predicated of God's "beloved Son" (1:13).

f. Hebrews. Jesus' identity as God's Son plays an important part in the distinctive christology of Hebrews. The treatise begins with an elegant period (1:1-4) in which the Son is identified as the agent of creation, the heir of all things and the one through whom God has spoken definitively "in these last days." This leads into a section in which the Son's superiority to the angels is established by means of a catena of scriptural citations, including two royal sonship passages (Ps 2:7; 2 Sam 7:14). The theme of the Son's superiority is picked up later in the work as well: in 3:6, the author declares Jesus to be superior to Moses as a son is superior to a household servant; in 7:28, the Son, a high priest "who has been made perfect forever," is contrasted to human high priests, "who are subject to weakness." The latter passage is part of an extended discourse on Jesus as the "great high priest," the most distinctive christological feature of the work. Sonship comes into this discourse in several ways. In 5:5, the author cites Ps 2:7 with reference to Christ's high priestly appointment, a striking priestly adaptation of a royal psalm. In 7:3, Melchizedek is said to resemble the Son of God in that he has "neither beginning of days nor end of life" and thus "remains a priest forever." Further, since a high priest needs to be able to identify with his people, Jesus as Son is able "to sympathize with our weaknesses" (4:14-15), has even "learned obedience through what he suffered" (5:8) and thus is able to call those whom he sanctifies his "brothers" (2:11), which means that they can also be called "sons" (2:10; compare 12:5-6).

g. Other. Elsewhere Jesus' divine sonship appears in 2 Peter, in a retrospective account of the transfiguration (1:17), and in Revelation, where the letter to the church in Thyatira conveys "the words of the Son of God" (2:18). Also in Revelation, the messianic "son, a male child, who is to rule all the nations with a rod of iron" (Rev 12:5; compare Ps 2:8-9) and who is borne by "a woman clothed with the sun" (12:1), is to be identified with Jesus.

3. Origin and development of "Son of God" as a christological term

How are we to describe and account for the process by which "Son of God" came to function as an expression of the kind of elevated christology found in the Johannine literature (and to a lesser extent in Hebrews)? To keep the question manageable, we might ask more specifically whether this development can be explained by something in the term itself as it was used in various contexts and traditions in the Judaic or Greco-Roman worlds, or whether the term simply functioned as a convenient vehicle for a christological development that was driven by other factors.

There has been no shortage of attempts to argue the former. To be sure, the lack of NT interest in the term as used with reference to angels or the divine council means that this aspect of biblical usage has attracted little attention. The same can be said of Jewish tradition more generally, except as it has been influenced by its wider environment. But with respect to the Greco-Roman environment, extensive effort has been devoted to various attempts to derive elevated Son of God christology from the mystery religions, divine man traditions, gnostic redeemer myths, royal and imperial cults, and the like. It is not to be doubted that such conceptions helped to shape the environment in which early christology was first formulated and then was heard and assessed. But the absence of precise terminological similarities and the difficulty in establishing material connections make it unlikely that we can account for the emergence of elevated Son of God Christology on the basis of the term itself. We are on safer ground to say that the term readily lent itself as a way of expressing elevated conceptions that were driven by other factors in early Christian experience and reflection (*see* CHRISTOLOGY; RESURRECTION, NT; WORSHIP, NT CHRISTIAN).

If John's presentation of Jesus as the human incarnation of the preexistent divine Son of God represents both the latest and the most elevated form of NT christology, what can be said of earlier forms and stages? Even on the most stringent assessment of the Jesus tradition, it is evident that sonship themes go back to the time of Jesus' earthly ministry. On one hand we have Jesus' use of *Abba* as a term of address for God, which at least could have been understood as implying a father-son relationship of some special sort. On the other hand, while Jesus himself seems to have been chary of messianic titles, his activity evoked enough messianic speculation to draw royal and messianic sonship themes into the mix. As with other aspects of early Christian theology, however, it was most probably the resurrection experiences (however they are to be understood) that provided the catalyst and impetus for further development. The pre-Pauline tradition reflected in Rom 1:3-4 indicates that at an early point sonship was associated in a special way with Jesus' resurrection. While one might speculate as to whether there was an even earlier form in which Jesus was viewed simply as messiah designate (compare Acts 3:19-21), so that his sonship was an identity to be assumed in the eschatological future, it is certainly the case that Jesus' identity as Son of God was linked with the Parousia (1 Cor 15:28; 1 Thess 1:10). In the Gospels Jesus' divine sonship is connected with various events in his earthly life: crucifixion (e.g., Mark 15:39); transfiguration; baptism; birth (Matt 2:15); virginal conception (Luke 1:35); preexistence (John). It is tempting to link these in a process of development in which Jesus' identity as Son is progressively pushed back from his resurrection, or even his Parousia, to his preexistence. Although aspects of the evidence lend themselves to such a reconstruction, however, it is probable that christological development was by no means a linear process, and that it developed in different ways and in different directions within various strands of the early Christian movement.

Bibliography: Wilhelm Bousset. *Kyrios Christos* (1970 [1921]); Oscar Cullmann. *The Christology of the New Testament* (1963); James D. G. Dunn. *Christology in the Making* (1989); Simon J. Gathercole. *The Pre-Existent Son: Recovering the Christologies of Matthew, Mark, and Luke* (2006); Ferdinand Hahn. *The Titles of Jesus in Christology* (1969); Martin Hengel. *The Son of God* (1976); Larry W. Hurtado. *Lord Jesus Christ: Devotion to Jesus in Earliest Christianity* (2003); Geza Vermes. *Jesus the Jew* (1973).

TERENCE L. DONALDSON

SON OF MAN [בֶּן־אָדָם ben-ʾadham, בֶּן־אֱנוֹשׁ ben-ʾenosh; בַּר אֱנָשׁ bar ʾenash; υἱὸς ἀνθρώπου huios anthrōpou, ὁ υἱὸς τοῦ ἀνθρώπου ho huios tou anthrōpou]. In Hebrew and Aramaic, an idiom that means simply the generic "man" or refers indefinitely to "a man," used primarily in poetic contexts in the OT.

Neither the indefinite nor the definite Greek phrase is idiomatic Greek, but reproduces the Semitic idiom. The definite form is used when a particular man or man-like figure is meant. The NRSV's emphasis on gender-neutral language means that these terms are often rendered with "human being/humanity," "mortal," "people," "one/anyone," and so forth.

A. In the Old Testament
   1. In the Pentateuch and historical books
   2. In the prophets
   3. In Psalms, Proverbs, and Job
   4. In Daniel
B. In the Dead Sea Scrolls
   1. The Hebrew documents
   2. The Aramaic documents
C. In the Similitudes of Enoch
D. In *4 Ezra*
E. In the Teaching of the Historical Jesus
F. In the New Testament
   1. In Mark
   2. In Matthew
   3. In Luke–Acts
   4. In the Gospel of John
   5. In the book of Revelation
Bibliography

A. In the Old Testament

1. In the Pentateuch and historical books

In Num 23:19, in the poetic context of Balaam's oracle, the seer tells Balak that God is not a man (ʾish אִישׁ; NRSV, "human being") that he should lie, nor a son of man (ben-ʾadham; NRSV, "mortal") that he should change his mind. In Deut 32:8, in the poetic context of the song of Moses, reference is made to God dividing the sons of man (bene ʾadham בְּנֵי אָדָם), that is, all humanity, into various peoples. In 2 Sam 7:14, in the context of an oracle from God received by the prophet Nathan, God says that he will make the offspring of David God's son and that if he does wrong, God will punish him with blows like those the sons of man (bene ʾadham), that is, human beings or men, give to their children when they err.

2. In the prophets

In Isa 52:14, in the context of the last of the servant poems, his form is said to be beyond the sons of man (bene ʾadham), that is, beyond human likeness. In Isa 56:2, in the poetic context of a prophetic oracle in general and in a beatitude in particular, the phrase "son of man" (ben-ʾadham) occurs parallel to "man" (ʾenosh אֱנוֹשׁ): "Happy is the man (NRSV, "mortal") who does this, the son of man (NRSV, "one") who holds it fast."

In Jer 32:19, in the context of a prayer, Jeremiah praises God by saying, "(your) eyes are open to all the ways of the sons of man (bene ʾadham)," that is, to the ways of human beings. In a judgment oracle, the Lord declares that Edom shall be desolate like Sodom and Gomorrah: "no man (ʾish) shall live there, and no son of man (ben-ʾadham) shall settle in it" (49:18). The same declaration with the same terms occurs in Jer 49:33 in an oracle against Hazor and in 50:40 in an oracle against Babylon. A similar declaration occurs in another oracle against Babylon: "a land in which no man (ʾish) lives, and through which no son of man (ben-ʾadham) passes" (51:43).

In the book of Ezekiel, God addresses the prophet ninety-three times as "son of man" or "you son of man" (beginning with 2:1). The phrase "son of man" (ben-ʾadham) here is an address that avoids both the personal name of the prophet, as well as his office, but focuses on him as part of the created order and suggests a contrast between the human and the divine, the master and the servant.

In Joel 1:12, in the poetic context of a lament over the ruin of the country, it is said that "joy withers away among the sons of man (bene ʾadham)," that is, from among the people of the land. In a poetic passage in Micah (5:7) concerning the future role of the remnant of Israel, it is said that they will not depend on any man (ʾish) or wait on the sons of man (bene ʾadham).

3. In Psalms, Proverbs, and Job

Psalm 8 is a (poetic) hymn that praises God for exalting humanity. In v. 4, the question is raised, "what is man (ʾenosh) that you are mindful of him, and a son of man (ben-ʾadham) that you care for him?" This verse, and the next two, which speak about the exaltation and glorification of "man" (NRSV, "human beings," "mortals"), is cited (from the Septuagint) and applied to Jesus in Heb 2:6-8. In the LXX, the terms are anthrōpos (ἄνθρωπος) and huios anthrōpou (υἱὸς ἀνθρώπου).

In a number of psalms, the phrase "sons of man" (bene ʾadham) is used to refer to human beings in general (Pss 11:4; 12:1, 8; 14:2 and many more). In at least one psalm, the phrase "son of man" (ben-ʾadham) is used to refer to a human being in the sense of any human being or humankind (146:3).

Psalm 45 is a song for a royal wedding. In v. 2, the king is praised as "the most handsome among the sons of man (bene ʾadham)," that is, among men. Psalm 49 is a poetic instruction, opening with a summons to all the peoples, to all the inhabitants of the world, to listen. This call is elaborated in v. 2, which the NRSV translates "both low and high, rich and poor together." A more literal translation is "Both sons of man (bene ʾadham) and sons of man (bene-ʾish בְּנֵי־אִישׁ), wealthy and poor together." A similar construction is found in Ps 62, which is a song of trust in God alone. The NRSV translates v. 9a as "Those of low estate are but a breath, those of high estate are a delusion." A more literal translation is "sons of man (bene ʾadham) are breath, delusion are the sons of man (bene-ʾish)."

Psalm 80:17 is an interesting case. The psalm is a poetic prayer for Israel's restoration. Verse 17 petitions the Lord, "But let your hand be upon (the) man (ʾish) of your right hand, upon (the) son of man (ben-ʾadham) whom you have made strong for yourself." Although both nouns lack the article, "man" and "son of man" refer here to the king.

Psalm 144 is a prayer for national deliverance and security. Verse 3, similar in meaning to Ps 8:4 (see discussion above), asks, "O LORD, what is man (ʾadham) that you regard him, or a son of man (ben-ʾenosh) that you think of him?"

In the context of a poetic personification of Wisdom, she is portrayed as calling out, "To you, O men (ʾishim אִישִׁים), I call, and my cry is to sons of man (bene ʾadham)" (Prov 8:4). It is not clear whether these terms are inclusive of both men and women or whether, due to social assumptions and practices, only men are expected to pursue wisdom. In Prov 8:31 Wisdom says that, at the time of creation, she was "rejoicing in (the Lord's) inhabited world and delighting in the sons of man (bene ʾadham)." The context makes clear that, as in many of the psalms, "sons of man" here refers to humankind (so also 15:11).

In one of Job's poetic speeches (16:21), the phrase "son of man" (ben-ʾadham) is used indefinitely to mean "a man" or "a human being." In a poetic speech of Bildad (25:6), the same meaning is expressed with two parallel phrases, "a man" (ʾenosh) and "a son of man" (ben-ʾadham).

4. In Daniel

In chap. 8, Daniel has a vision involving a ram and a goat. As he was trying to understand it, Gabriel appeared to explain it to him. When Daniel saw Gabriel, he became frightened and fell on his face. Gabriel then addressed him (8:17) as "son of man" (ben-ʾadham), in a way similar to God's address of Ezekiel (see the section on the prophets above). In chap. 10, on the bank of the Tigris River, Daniel sees a vision of a being that is clearly an angel, probably Gabriel. When the angel speaks to him, Daniel turns his face to the ground and becomes speechless. The next verse (10:16) states that then "one like the likeness of human beings (kidhmuth bene ʾadham כִּדְמוּת בְּנֵי אָדָם) touched my lips," that is, a heavenly being in human form touched his lips. In 10:18, the same idea is expressed with the phrase "one who had the appearance of a man" (kemarʾeh ʾadham כְּמַרְאֵה אָדָם).

The most influential passage in the Son of Man tradition is of course Dan 7, which is in Aramaic. That chapter contains a report of a vision and its interpretation. The first part of the vision involves four beasts rising from the sea. These beasts signify four kingdoms. In contrast to these symbolic animals, the second part of the vision involves two figures with a human appearance. One is the Ancient of Days (7:9), and the other (7:13) is described as "one like a son of man" (kevar ʾenash כְּבַר אֱנָשׁ). Apart from the preposition signifying "like" (ke כְּ), this Aramaic expression is equivalent to the Hebrew phrase "son of man" (ben-ʾadham).

Although different Hebrew expressions are used in 10:16 and 18, it is likely that the figure with a human appearance in 7:13 is a heavenly being, probably an angel, like those described in chap. 10. Since the angel of 7:13 is associated with the kingdom of the people of the holy ones of the Most High (7:27), it is likely that this angel is Michael (compare 10:13; 12:1). Later the "one like a son of man" in 7:13 was interpreted as the Messiah of Israel (see the discussion of the Similitudes of Enoch and *4 Ezra* below).

B. In the Dead Sea Scrolls

1. The Hebrew documents

In the *Community Rule*, the Hebrew phrase "sons of man" (bene ʾadham) is used to mean humankind (1QS XI, 15; so also in 1QHᵃ XII, 32; XIII, 11, 15; XIV, 11; XIX, 6). In the *Community Rule*, the phrase "son of man" (ben-ʾadham) was used to refer to the generic human being, that is, to all humankind (1QS XI, 20). Later, a scribe added the definite article before "man" making the phrase definite (ben haʾadham בֶּן הָאָדָם). This change may change the meaning slightly, from "son of man" to "son of Adam." In a passage in the *Thanksgiving Hymns*, 1QHᵃ IX, 27, the original scribe wrote the phrase "sons of Adam" (bene haʾadham) in order to refer to all human beings. In the same work, in X, 24–25, the equivalent indefinite phrase is used, bene ʾadham, which may be translated "sons of man." Since the definite phrase, "sons of Adam," occurred shortly before this point in the work, the indefinite phrase may also have that sense here. Quite a bit further on, in 1QHᵃ XII, 30, the singular, generic form "a son of man" (ben-ʾadham) is used, parallel to "man" (ʾenosh). Here again, the phrase signifies the generic human being, humankind in general.

2. The Aramaic documents

The *Genesis Apocryphon* is an Aramaic paraphrase of some of the narratives about the patriarchs in Genesis (stories about Noah and Abraham survive). In this work, the phrase "son of man" (bar ʾenosh) is used in a speech of God addressed to Abram, in which God promises to multiply Abram's descendants like the dust of the earth, which "no son of man," that is "no one" can count (1Qap Genᵃʳ XXI, 13).

The TARGUMS are translations of biblical books from Hebrew to Aramaic. A fragmentary targum of Job was discovered at Qumran. As noted above, in one of Bildad's speeches, in the Hebrew text (25:6) the phrase "a man" (ʾenosh) is used in a way parallel to the phrase "a son of man" (ben-ʾadham). The second phrase is translated in the targum with (bar ʾenosh) (11Q10 IX, 9). The Aramaic phrase is the same as the one that appears in Dan 7:13 (apart from the comparative preposition ke, "like"). The phrase is used here to contrast human beings with God. Similarly, in Job 35:8*b*, one of Job's friends, Elihu, makes the point that a human being's righteousness adds nothing to God but only affects

other human beings. In the Hebrew text, the phrase "a son of man" (ben-ʾadham) is used in the sense of the generic human being. In the targum this phrase is translated with "son of man" (bar ʾenosh), as in the translation of Job 25:6. Here the generic singular has the sense of human beings in distinction from God.

C. In the Similitudes of Enoch

The Similitudes of Enoch or the Parables of Enoch is a title given by modern scholars to a portion of a composite work preserved in Ethiopic, *1 Enoch*, as chaps. 37–71 of that work. All the other, apparently once independent, parts of the work have been found, at least in fragmentary form, among the Dead Sea Scrolls. Another Enochic work, the Book of the Giants, has been found at Qumran, but it is not part of the current composite work. Because of its absence from the Dead Sea Scrolls, some have argued that the Similitudes of Enoch is much later than the Gospels. Most specialists, however, continue to date the work to the 1ˢᵗ cent. CE.

In this work, a heavenly being is portrayed who is referred to with a variety of terms: righteous one, anointed one (messiah), chosen one, and son of man (three different Ethiopic phrases are used to express this idea). This heavenly messianic figure is referred to as "son of man" in chaps. 46–48 and 62:2-71. The Ethiopic phrase meaning "son of man" used most frequently is the one also used in the Ethiopic Bible to translate "one like a son of man" in Dan 7:13 and the Son of Man sayings in the NT. In the context of the final judgment, the hiddenness of the son of man is discussed, as well as his revelation to the chosen (62:7). It is clear that the term "son of man" comes from Dan 7, especially in chaps. 46–48.

The data suggests that the author of the Similitudes interpreted the "one like a son of man" in Dan 7:13-14 as the Messiah and understood him to be a pre-existent, heavenly being. He sits on a throne of glory, equivalent to the throne of God, and will be God's agent, acting as judge in the final judgment. Salvation for the chosen involves being with the son of man (presumably in heaven) in the new age.

D. In *4 Ezra*

This work is a Jewish apocalypse preserved in the deuterocanonical work known as 2 Esdras. It comprises chaps. 3–14. Chapters 1–2 and 15–16 are two independent Christian supplements. The Jewish work is made up primarily of dialogues between Ezra and the angel Uriel and of visions seen by Ezra. In one of the dialogues, in response to a question from Ezra, Uriel tells Ezra that, at some point in the future, the Messiah will be revealed (7:28-29). Later, Ezra has a vision of an eagle and a lion (11:1–12:39). The angel explains that the lion is the Messiah, a descendant of David, who will set free the remnant of the people of Israel (12:32-34). Soon thereafter Ezra has a vision in which the wind stirs up the sea. Then the wind causes "something like the figure of a man [to] come up out of the heart of the sea." This man "flew with the clouds of heaven," and everything trembled under his gaze and his voice made those who heard it melt like fire (13:1-4). He will defeat the nations, who will assemble against him, and gather the people of Israel, including the lost ten tribes. He will save the survivors in the holy land and show them wonders (13:5-50).

The references to him as a "something like the figure of a man" and his flying with the clouds of heaven indicate that this messianic figure is modeled, in part, on Dan 7. The fact that this figure seems to be the same one referred to as the Messiah in chap. 7 and as the Davidic Messiah in chap. 12 suggests that the author interpreted Dan 7:13-14 as a reference to the Messiah. Like the Similitudes of Enoch, *4 Ezra* presents the Messiah as a pre-existent being who will be "revealed" at the end of this age.

E. In the Teaching of the Historical Jesus

In the Synoptic Gospels, "Son of Man" is a title used to characterize Jesus, even though it most often occurs in his own speech. Commentators generally divide the Son of Man sayings in the Synoptic Gospels into three groups: sayings that speak of the Son of Man 1) as coming, 2) as suffering death and rising again, and 3) as now at work.

There are two main theories about the origin of all these sayings. One is that all the Son of Man sayings derive from the use by Jesus of a Semitic idiom in which "son of man" means "a man" (the indefinite use of the idiom) or "man" in general (the generic use). More likely is the theory that the oldest Son of Man sayings are the ones that allude to Dan 7 and the other types derive from these.

The first theory is problematic for several reasons. The Aramaic sources used to support it are much later than the time of Jesus. Furthermore, the alleged usage of the idiom that could best explain some of the sayings of Jesus is not clearly supported even by those late sources. Finally, the clear and early usages of the Aramaic idiom do not fit any of the sayings attributed to Jesus very well. For example, it is unlikely that the saying "the Son of Man has authority on earth to forgive sins" (Mark 2:10) meant, at any stage of the tradition, that human beings in general have such authority.

The most persuasive reconstruction of the teaching and deeds of Jesus is the view that he was a prophet of Jewish restoration eschatology or an apocalyptic prophet. Given that general context, it is likely that the apocalyptic Son of Man sayings are the oldest, that is, sayings that refer to the Son of Man coming on the clouds or being revealed. The other sayings derived from these.

The fact that the Son of Man sayings in the synoptic tradition are definite ("the" Son of Man in a titular sense) can be explained in two ways. One is to argue that Jesus himself referred to Dan 7 in his teaching about the kingdom of God and spoke about "the" son

of man (that is, the one in Dan 7) as about to come to inaugurate the kingdom of God on earth. The other is that the phrase "one like a son of man" in Dan 7:13 was transformed into a title for Jesus after his death by his followers who identified the risen and exalted Jesus with the figure of Dan 7.

F. In the New Testament

1. In Mark

In Mark, the Son of Man sayings are closely bound up with the theme of the identity of Jesus and the secrecy about it. The author of Mark takes Dan 7:13 as prophecy and seems to see its fulfillment in Jesus in two stages. During his public activity, he is the Son of Man who has authority to forgive sins and to interpret the commands of God concerning the Sabbath (2:10, 28). "Son of Man" and "Messiah" are equivalent in Mark (8:29-31; 14:61-62). So in the sayings about the Son of Man as now at work, Mark implies that Jesus has authority on earth as the Messiah, since he was appointed to this office by God at the time of his baptism (1:9-11).

Yet the messiahship of Jesus is hidden from the human characters in the narrative until the acclamation of Peter. In the depiction of Jesus as the authoritative Son of Man in chap. 2, there is no obvious allusion to Daniel. The audience of the narrative, having been instructed, can appreciate "the Son of Man" as a title for Jesus. But the characters are not enlightened about its significance. Although they do not object or question Jesus, there is no indication that they understand what the phrase means. The scribes, e.g., are silenced by the miraculous healing of the paralyzed man.

In the middle section of Mark, the title Son of Man is used in the three passion predictions. The disciples are the only characters within the narrative to hear these predictions. Both the disciples and the audience seem to accept the equivalence of "Messiah" and "Son of Man." The messianic use of the title "Son of Man" seems to presuppose a messianic interpretation of Dan 7:13. When Dan 7:13 is evoked in association with the passion predictions, a shocking paradox emerges. The one like a son of man is a glorious, heavenly figure who is given eternal kingship. Yet Mark portrays this Son of Man, identified with the earthly Jesus, as undergoing great suffering, rejection, and death. The tension of this paradox was too great to maintain for long. Many later interpreters have taken "Son of Man" as representing the humanity of Jesus and "Son of God" as expressing his divinity.

The second stage of the fulfillment of Dan 7:13 according to Mark will take place in the future. The sayings about the Son of Man "coming," or more broadly, the apocalyptic Son of Man sayings, express the expectation of this second fulfillment. The first such saying in Mark also occurs in the middle section: "Those who are ashamed of me and of my words in this adulterous and sinful generation, of them the Son of Man will also be ashamed when he comes in the glory of his Father with the holy angels" (8:38). This saying is closely related to the depiction of the coming of the Son of Man in the apocalyptic discourse of chap. 13. The significance of the saying about the Son of Man being ashamed when he comes is that he will not gather those who were ashamed of him. They will lose their place among the elect who are gathered by the angels to be with the Son of Man.

The final Son of Man saying in Mark occurs in the trial before the Sanhedrin, or more accurately, the Judean council (14:62). When the high priest asks Jesus, "Are you the Messiah, the Son of the Blessed One?" he responds, "I am; and 'you will see the Son of Man seated at the right hand of the Power,' and 'coming with the clouds of heaven.'" In one way, this saying is a turning point in the theme of Jesus' identity in Mark. He reveals openly that he is the Messiah and will be the heavenly, coming Son of Man. In another way, this trial and the rest of the account of Jesus' rejection, suffering, and death still portray him as the hidden Son of Man. This is so because the high priest and all the others in authority do not recognize him as Messiah and Son of Man. Further, no revelation of the glory and power of Jesus takes place to convince them otherwise. For the audience, however, the saying makes clear that Jesus will exercise his messianic office when he comes as Son of Man.

The saying of Jesus before the high priest conflates allusions to Ps 110:1 and to Dan 7:13. Psalm 110 is used to depict the exaltation of Jesus after death, and Dan 7 to portray his coming in glory. The introduction to the saying "you will see" makes clear that the emphasis in relation to the narrative context is on the public vindication of Jesus as Son of Man.

2. In Matthew

Two distinctive features of the Son of Man sayings in Matthew are the emphasis on the Son of Man as eschatological judge and the notion that the Son of Man has a kingdom. The portrayal of the Son of Man as judge is clearest in the response of Jesus to Peter's question, "Look, we have left everything and followed you. What then will we have?" Jesus replies, "Truly I tell you, at the renewal of all things, when the Son of Man is seated on the throne of his glory, you who have followed me will also sit on twelve thrones, judging the twelve tribes of Israel" (Matt 19:27-28). As noted above, the phrase "the throne of his glory" also occurs in the Similitudes of Enoch with reference to the throne of "that Son of Man," that is, the figure of Dan 7, whom the Similitudes portray as a pre-existent, heavenly Messiah.

In the parable of the weeds, which is unique to Matthew, the man who sowed good seed in his field is interpreted as the Son of Man (Matt 13:24, 37). The enemy who sowed weeds among the grain is interpreted as the devil (13:25, 39). The harvest is the end of the age (13:30, 39). The interpretation of the parable is no-

table for its explicit teaching that the Son of Man has a kingdom (13:41). Since the field is interpreted as "the world" (13:38), the kingdom of the Son of Man is also the whole world. This portrayal is similar to 1 Cor 15, in which the risen "Christ" also has a kingdom (1 Cor 15:24).

The Son of Man of Matthew's parable "will send his angels, and they will collect out of his kingdom all causes of sin and all evildoers, and they will throw them into the furnace of fire, where there will be weeping and gnashing of teeth. Then the righteous will shine like the sun in the kingdom of their Father" (13:41-43a). This passage depicts the Son of Man as judge, as well as king. The reference to "the kingdom of his Father" shows that he is God's agent in exercising judgment. Similarly, Paul argued that, after he had conquered all the enemies, Christ would hand the kingdom over to his Father (1 Cor 15:24). The portrayal of the Son of Man as judge is also found in the Similitudes of Enoch (1 En. 46:4-8; 69:29).

As noted earlier, Mark has a saying about the Son of Man being ashamed of those who are ashamed of him. Matthew rewrites that saying to introduce once again the notion of the Son of Man as judge: "For the Son of Man is to come with his angels in the glory of his Father, and then he will repay everyone for what has been done" (Matt 16:27). Immediately following the saying about the Son of Man being ashamed of those who are ashamed of him, the Markan Jesus states: "Truly I tell you, there are some standing here who will not taste death until they see that the kingdom of God has come with power" (Mark 9:1). Matthew rewrites this saying to introduce the idea that the Son of Man has a kingdom: "Truly I tell you, there are some standing here who will not taste death before they see the Son of Man coming in his kingdom" (Matt 16:28). This change is related to the theme of the Son of Man having a kingdom in the parable of the weeds. Both passages are probably dependent on Dan 7:13-14.

The Son of Man also appears in the description of the final judgment that closes the apocalyptic discourse of Jesus in Matthew. The scene is introduced with the statement: "When the Son of Man comes in his glory, and all the angels with him, then he will sit on the throne of his glory" (Matt 25:31). The narrative that follows combines an explicitly judicial setting with the dispensation of rewards and punishments. As in the Similitudes of Enoch, the Son of Man here acts as God's agent in judging the just and the wicked.

Finally, the title "Son of Man" is so strongly associated with Jesus in Matthew that it is equivalent to the first-person pronoun and is interchangeable with it. This feature is clear in the opening of the scene in which Peter acclaims Jesus as Messiah and son of God: "When Jesus came into the district of Caesarea Philippi, he asked his disciples, 'Who do people say that the Son of Man is?' And they said, 'Some say John the Baptist, but others Elijah, and still others Jeremiah or one of the prophets.' He said to them, 'But who do you say that I am?'" (Matt 16:13-15).

3. In Luke–Acts

The Gospel of Luke seems to present Jesus, the Son of Man, as both the advocate of his faithful followers in the heavenly court and as the eschatological judge. He appears as advocate in the following saying: "And I tell you, everyone who acknowledges me before others, the Son of Man also will acknowledge before the angels of God; but whoever denies me before others will be denied before the angels of God" (Luke 12:8-9). This saying envisages a scene in the heavenly court in which Jesus as Son of Man plays the role of advocate of those who have acknowledged him in public on earth. The second half of the saying may imply that he will act as the accuser of those who have denied him. This passage shares with Dan 7 the characteristics of the heavenly scene, the judicial setting, and the presence of the Son of Man. It is likely that Dan 7 had an influence in the creation of this saying.

The role of the Son of Man as eschatological judge is not as clear in Luke as in Matthew. It seems to be implied, however, in several sayings. At the end of the Lukan version of the apocalyptic discourse, the audience is exhorted to watch and pray so that they may "stand before the Son of Man" (Luke 21:36). The language seems to portray defendants standing before a seated judge and thus evokes the tradition of the final judgment. In this case, as in Matthew, this judge is Jesus, the Son of Man.

In another context, the Lukan Jesus says that, as Jonah became a sign to the people of Nineveh, so the Son of Man will be to this generation: "The queen of the South will rise at the judgment with the people of this generation and condemn them, because she came from the ends of the earth to listen to the wisdom of Solomon, and see, something greater than Solomon is here" (11:30-31). The point is that the general resurrection and final judgment will reveal that Jesus is the Son of Man and thus confound those of "this generation" who rejected him. Not only will the wicked see that Jesus has been vindicated by God, they will discover that he has an exalted role as the agent of God in the eschatological judgment. Although it is not explicit, it is likely that the implied role is that of judge. The queen of the South and the people of Nineveh will play the role of witnesses at the judgment.

In Acts, when Stephen is stoned, he gazes into heaven and sees Jesus standing at the right hand of God. He says, "I see the heavens opened and the Son of Man standing at the right hand of God" (Acts 7:56). This is one of the very few times that the title "Son of Man" occurs on the lips of someone other than Jesus. Like Mark 14:62, this saying combines the idea of Jesus being exalted to the right hand of God (Ps 110:1) with the identification of the risen Jesus with the "one like a son of man" in Dan 7:13.

4. In the Gospel of John

Like the Similitudes of Enoch, Matthew, and Luke, the Gospel of John portrays the Son of Man as the eschatological judge. The Johannine Jesus says to the Judeans (or Jews), "The Father judges no one but has given all judgment to the Son" (5:22). A little further on he says, "and he has given him authority to execute judgment, because he is the Son of Man (huios anthrōpou)" (5:27). Several features of this text indicate that it is an allusion to Dan 7:13-14. One is the fact that it is indefinite, as is the phrase "one like a son of man" in Daniel. Both the Old Greek and the Greek translation of Daniel attributed to Theodotion translate the phrase bar ʾenash with huios anthrōpou, the same phrase used in John 5:27. Another indication of dependence on Daniel is the link of the phrase "son of man" with the remark that the Father has given him authority. In the Old Greek, immediately following the description of the "one like a son of man," it is stated that "authority was given to him." The use of the passive voice here implies that God (the Ancient of Days) gave him authority. The contexts of two other Son of Man sayings in John suggest that the role of the Son of Man as judge is one of the connotations of the name (compare 8:28 with 8:15-16, 26; and 9:35 with 9:39).

The Son of Man is described as being "lifted up" in the Gospel of John (3:14; 8:28; 12:34; compare 12:32). This description is typically Johannine ironic language. The verb "lift up" (hypsoō ὑψόω) has two usages: to lift up (physically) and to exalt. In these sayings, both meanings are intended. Jesus will be lifted up on the cross, and this event is his exaltation. These sayings are the Johannine equivalents of the Markan passion predictions, according to which the Son of Man must suffer, die, and rise from the dead. Two other sayings also speak paradoxically about the passion of Jesus as the glorification of the Son of Man (12:23; 13:31). It is probably in light of these "passion" sayings that the first Son of Man saying in John should be understood (1:51). When Nathanael recognizes Jesus as the son of God and the king of Israel (as Peter recognizes Jesus in Mark 8:29), Jesus says to him and the others present, "Very truly, I tell you, you will see heaven opened and the angels of God ascending and descending upon the Son of Man." The death and resurrection of Jesus is probably implied here as one of the "greater things" that Nathanael will see (compare 1:50 with 14:12). When Jesus "has gone to the Father," he will become the mediator between heaven and earth. The image of angels descending and ascending on the Son of Man is both an interpretation of Jesus' death and an allusion to the ladder that Jacob dreamed about (Gen 28:12).

Another saying that alludes to the death of the Son of Man occurs in the discourse about bread in chap. 6. Jesus instructs the crowd to work for the food that does not perish, which the Son of Man will give them, rather than for the food that perishes (6:27; referring to the multiplication of the loaves in 6:1-15). Later, Jesus defines the food that does not perish as the flesh and blood of the Son of Man (6:51). This saying is analogous to the saying in Mark 10:45, which speaks about the Son of Man giving his life as a ransom for many.

The most distinctive Son of Man sayings in John are those in which the evangelist portrays the Son of Man as pre-existent. As noted above, the same idea is expressed in the Similitudes of Enoch. This idea appears in John 3:13 and 6:62. The first saying occurs in the monologue of Jesus that follows his dialogue with Nicodemus. Jesus chides him for not believing earthly things and asks how he will believe the heavenly things that Jesus will reveal (3:12). He then goes on to say, "No one has ascended into heaven except the one who descended from heaven, the Son of Man" (3:13). This saying is analogous to the statement that "the Word became flesh and lived among us" (1:14). Daniel 7, however, may have played a role in the formation of this saying also. If the composer of this saying held the view that the "one like a son of man" in Dan 7:13 was preexistent, as the authors of the Similitudes of Enoch and *4 Ezra* did, the descent of that heavenly being may have been identified with the incarnation of the Logos.

The second saying occurs in the discourse on the bread of life in chap. 6. When many of the disciples have difficulty accepting the teaching about eating and drinking the flesh of the Son of Man, Jesus says, "Does this offend you? Then what if you were to see the Son of Man ascending to where he was before?" (6:61-62). The ascent referred to here is the same event described in other Son of Man sayings as the "lifting up" and the "glorification" of the Son of Man, that is, the crucifixion of Jesus. This saying has a further element, however, one that it shares with the saying in 3:13, namely, the idea that the Son of Man is pre-existent and has come down from heaven. If the name "Son of Man" in the saying alludes to Dan 7:13, the ascent spoken of may have been identified with the depiction of the "one like a son of man" "coming" in order to be presented to the Ancient of Days.

5. In the book of Revelation

Revelation opens with a preface (1:1-3) followed by the opening elements of a letter (1:4-6). The epistolary opening is followed by two prophetic sayings. The first reads, "Look! He is coming with the clouds; every eye will see him, even those who pierced him; and on his account all the tribes of the earth will wail" (1:7). This saying alludes to both Dan 7:13 and Zech 12:10-14; the same two texts are conflated in Matt 24:30. Whereas the Matthean passage explicitly mentions "the Son of Man," the corresponding saying in Revelation does not. In the context of the work as a whole, however, it is clear that Rev 1:7 refers to the coming of Jesus and interprets that event as fulfilling the prophecy of Daniel in 7:13.

Revelation 1:9–3:22 is an account of an appearance of the risen Jesus to John, including the messages that Jesus dictated to John for the seven churches. The risen Jesus is described as "like a son of man" (homoion huion anthrōpou ὅμοιον υἱὸν ἀνθρώπου) in 1:13. The Greek word homoion ("like") does not appear in any known manuscript of Dan 7:13. It is likely that the author of Revelation (John the prophet) used it here and in 14:14 to translate the particle ke ("like") in the Aramaic text of Dan 7:13 known to him.

Like the angel who appeared to Daniel (10:5), the one "like a son of man" is girded with a golden belt (Rev 1:13). Both the risen Jesus and the angel have eyes like flaming fire (Rev 1:14; Dan 10:6). The feet of the risen Jesus are like burnished bronze (Rev 1:15), as are the arms and legs of the angel (Dan 10:6). Finally, the portrayal of the face of the risen Jesus as shining like the sun (Rev 1:16) is analogous to that of the angel's face as like lightning (Dan 10:6). The similarities between Rev 1:13-16 and Dan 10:5-6 imply that the risen Jesus is an angel or like an angel. Perhaps John's understanding was that the risen Jesus was equivalent to the principal angel described in some extra-canonical Jewish texts, e.g., the *Apocalypse of Abraham*. That text says that the highest angel, Iaoel, had a head of hair like snow (11:2).

The one like a son of man is also depicted as having hair that is "white as white wool, white as snow" (Rev 1:14). This characteristic seems to identify the "one like a son of man" with the "Ancient of Days," who, according to Dan 7:9, has a garment "white as snow" and hair "like pure wool." The analogy with Iaoel suggests that the principal angel or fully authorized agent of God appears like God because this being takes the place of God in relation to human beings, e.g., as judge.

Revelation 14:14-20 is a vision of a symbolic harvest and vintage carried out by one "like a son of man" (homoion huion anthrōpou, 14:14) and three (other) angels. Alluding to Joel 3:13, the images of harvest and vintage signify divine judgment on the nations on the Day of the Lord (compare Joel 3:12, 14). Note how the imagery of vintage shifts into battle imagery in Rev 14:20 (compare *1 En.* 100:3).

The title "Son of Man" (ho huios tou anthrōpou) does not occur in Revelation. The reason is probably that the author knew Hebrew and Aramaic as well as Greek. He recognized that the phrase "one like a son of man" in Dan 7:13 is a Semitic idiom meaning "one with a human appearance." Another reason may be that John was unaware of, or at least unaffected by, the transformation of the phrase into a title for Jesus in the synoptic tradition.

Bibliography: Delbert Burkett. *The Son of Man Debate: A History and Evaluation* (1999); Adela Yarbro Collins. "The Origin of the Designation of Jesus as 'Son of Man.'" *HTR* 80 (1987) 391–407; Adela Yarbro Collins. "The Apocalyptic Son of Man Sayings." *The Future of Early Christianity: Essays in Honor of Helmut Koester.* Birger A. Pearson, ed. (1991) 220–28; John J. Collins.

"The Son of Man in First Century Judaism." *NTS* 38 (1992) 448–66; John R. Donahue. "Recent Studies on the Origin of 'Son of Man' in the Gospels." *A Wise and Discerning Heart: Studies Presented to Joseph A. Fitzmyer. CBQ* 48 (1986) 485–98; Joseph A. Fitzmyer. "The New Testament Title 'Son of Man' Philologically Considered." *A Wandering Aramaean* (1979); Paul Owen and David Shepherd. "Speaking Up for Qumran, Dalman, and the Son of Man: Was Bar Enasha a Common Term for 'Man' in the Time of Jesus?" *JSNT* 81 (2001) 81–122; Norman Perrin. *A Modern Pilgrimage in New Testament Christology* (1974); Heinz Eduard Tödt. *The Son of Man in the Synoptic Tradition* (1965); James C. VanderKam. "Righteous One, Messiah, Chosen One, and Son of Man in *1 Enoch* 37–71." *The Messiah: Developments in Earliest Judaism and Christianity.* James H. Charlesworth, ed. (1992) 169–91.

ADELA YARBRO COLLINS

SONG OF DEBORAH. *See* DEBORAH, SONG OF.

SONG OF SOLOMON. *See* SONG OF SONGS.

SONG OF SONGS [שִׁיר הַשִּׁירִים shir hashirim; Ἆσμα Asma]. From the opening poetic fragment (1:2-4) in the sequence of love poems known as the Song of Songs (a superlative construction in Hebrew, i.e., "the most sublime of songs"; compare "king of kings," Dan 2:37), we are plunged head-first into the dizzying depths of erotic desire. "Let him kiss me with the kisses of his mouth" (1:2) runs the first line, stating the speaker's want plainly and openly, though not un-playfully. Verb and object ("kiss from kisses") share the same Hebrew root (nshq נשׁק), which allows for some pleasant alliterating and redoubles, to good effect, the depth of the want named. The addition of the last word in the line, "his mouth," signals the hyperbolic register in which much of the poetry that follows is enacted—first love and young love by its nature must be over the top, the very definition of hyperbole. It also elicits a play in the Hebrew between the verbs for kissing (nshq) and drinking (shqh שׁקה)—especially obvious when these verbs' respective imperfective forms are used (compare 8:1-2). The longing here is not for a familial (Gen 27:26) or ceremonial (1 Sam 10:1) kiss, but the deep-throated kiss of lovers that can only be gulped greedily for fear that the thirst (for love) will be too quickly quenched. And, in fact, the second line of the couplet cinches the play as the best, finest wine is used as the standard of comparison: "for better is your love than wine." This fine wine kind of "love" is above all a physical, sexual love (e.g., Ezek 16:8; 23:17; Prov 7:18). It is a love that is to be tasted, smelled, felt, and ultimately praised and reveled in. And it is with a pleasurable muscularity that we should hear the girl's—and that the speaker is female becomes clear from the feminine adjectives ("black and beautiful") in 1:5—favorite pet name for the boy (occurring twenty-six times in the Song), "my love" or "my

lover" (but not the too quaint "my beloved" by which the term is usually rendered in the Song).

The switch from third to second person in this line ("his mouth"/"your love") is startling. The reader hardly has the opportunity to grasp that there is a "him" and a "me"—who are they?—before a "you" is added—is this (masculine) "you" the same as the just mentioned "him"? Apparently so. This mild disorientation turns severe over the next eight lines, as first person singular and plural, second person masculine singular, and third person singular and plural pronominal and verbal forms are intermingled in ways that all but defy logic. No names. Just *mes*, *hes*, *wes*, *yous*, and *theys*. The dizzying blur of these first lines of love chasten the over-controlling reader, taming the temptation to master, and thus preparing her or him to enjoy the feast of love that is to come—to taste, feel, smell the delights that this garden of verse places on offer: "Eat, friends, drink, and be drunk with love" (5:1; compare Prov 5:19; 7:18).

    A. Authorship, Date, Reading
    B. Poetry of Love
    C. Love of Two—Among Others
    D. A Closing Reading
    Bibliography

A. Authorship, Date, Reading

The Song of Songs is the original love poem in the Western literary tradition, enacting a poetic fiction that Dante, Petrarch, Sidney, Shakespeare, and every poet of love down through the ages has emulated, translated, or obliterated. Love poetry was also a common staple of the ANE literary tradition, with fine exemplars from Mesopotamia (Leick) and Egypt (Fox) in particular. And though commonly thought unique to the Bible, even there the Song is not quite the anomaly it is so often made out to be. Isaiah of Jerusalem in the middle of the 8th cent. uses a love poem as the basis for his so-called "Song of the Vineyard" (Isa 5:1-7)—in fact, a small bit of that song (vv. 1-2) strongly resembles a number of lines in Song 8 (v. 11). And the much later editor(s) of the Psalter responsible for the various psalmic superscriptions still know(s) about love songs (Ps 45:1; compare Ezek 33:32). The dating of the Song itself remains debated. The only truly tractable datum is the language of these poems, and on present evidence it appears to be a variety of late biblical Hebrew, most likely originating sometime between the late 4th and early 2nd cent. BCE (Dobbs-Allsopp 2005). But like much biblical literature the Song comes down to us mostly decontextualized, so certain issues and modes of inquiry will be of only limited productivity. The question of date is a case in point; authorship is another one. In antiquity, actual authors (as moderns think of the person responsible for composing a literary work) were not always (or even regularly) explicitly credited. Instead, a common practice was to attribute authorship to some well-known figure. Thus many of the psalms, for example, are attributed to David (e.g., Pss 3:1; 4:1) and Proverbs to Solomon (Prov 1:1), and the translators of the Septuagint identify Jeremiah as composing Lamentations. The initial line (or *incipit*) of the Song is most often construed as assigning authorship to Solomon—"the Song of Songs, which is Solomon's." If so (the syntax of the Hebrew may be interpreted in other ways as well) it is of this latter kind of attribution, since the late date of the language alone makes genuine Solomonic authorship unlikely—neither is Solomon a speaker, subject, or center of interest in any of these poems. In fact, most assume that the line is an editorial superscription, presumably added to an otherwise already complete composition. The ascription to Solomon is not, however, totally unmotivated. He is mentioned (possibly) a half-dozen other times in the Song (1:5; 3:7, 9, 11; 8:11, 12), mostly figuratively or by way of example as a part of a larger royal thread that wends its way through these poems; and he was renowned as both lover and poet (1 Kgs 5:12; 11:3).

Owing to the authenticity of the female voice in the Song, the possibility of female authorship has been considered (Goitein; compare Exum). However, authorial gender is not really deducible from linguistic and literary cues alone, nothing else exists for readers to judge by, and historically and culturally the likelihood is that the author was male. Still, the thesis is of heuristic value, for the gender of an author will often impact how readers interpret specific phrases and passages. Besides, the earliest recorded named author is in fact a woman, Enheduanna, daughter of Sargon of Akkad (ca. 2300 BCE) and priestess of the moon god at Ur.

If 1:1 is a superscription, it may well be, as M. Fox suggests, the first step in a readerly tradition of assimilating the Song, in this case, to one of early Israel's most fabled royal personages. Later Jewish and Christian interpreters would appropriate the Song for more explicitly religious purposes by way of allegory, explaining the relationship between the two lovers as if it referred to the relationship between God and Israel or Christ and the church (or the individual believer). Ironically, such revoicings bring the Song closer, in certain ways, to how the poetry of love in Mesopotamia was most commonly staged, through the voices of gods and goddesses or the king and divine consort. Several things may be noted about the allegorical tradition of reading the Song. First and foremost, it is entirely a readerly strategy imposed on the text from without. That is, there is nothing within the Song itself or within the tradition of love poetry from the ancient Mediterranean world more broadly that requires (or authorizes) such a strategy of reading. The Song, like much of the preserved Egyptian love poetry, is what it appears to be, a celebration of the love of two flesh-and-blood people, a girl and a boy, with no mention whatsoever of the God of Israel. In fact, the garden of love so prominently on display in these poems (e.g., 1:6; 2:8-17; 4:12-15; 5:1; 6:11; 7:12; 8:12) is a garden meant specifically for human habitation (however idyllic), and thus the direct antithesis of Eden

(compare Song 7:12), which was always God's garden home (compare Gen 13:10; Ezek 28:13-16), not fit for humans. Second, such allegorical sifting makes startlingly obvious precisely how metaphorical is all language about the gods when conceptualized through the category of being. Finally, the trenchant persistence of this manner of interpreting the Song, even today still prominent in many circles, underscores in striking fashion just how readerly dependent is the entire hermeneutical enterprise of textual interpretation. Ultimately, the reader is everything; he or she is responsible for the readings that are enacted and constructed. How to read is, finally, a highly moral undertaking. Reading the Song is no different. To choose to read with empathy and interest the fiction actually wrought by the Song's ancient poet is a moral act, albeit one that may also prove to be salvific and even fun, as these poems open onto a host of issues with contemporary resonance (e.g., otherness, gender relations, sexuality, eroticism, aesthetics, play, and pleasure).

B. Poetry of Love

The love story that is the Song is, in point of fact, not a story at all, or at least it is not told as a story—though that story, the story of the love between an unnamed boy and a girl who only belatedly gets called "the Shulammite" (6:13 [Heb. 7:1]), most assuredly lies in the background of the poems that make up the Song. But the poems themselves are lyric poems, where things like plot, story, narrative development, and character are not really of prime interest, and if they occur at all are deployed, ultimately, to specifically lyric ends. The poems of the Song literally sing about love and its "many splendored" affects, good and not so good, in a non-narrative kind of verse that poets East and West have been composing for millennia. Without the cohering effects of plot, character, and the like, lyric verse is dependent almost exclusively on language to carry out its fiction. Plays, puns, and euphony pervade the Song. Song 1:6 offers a paradigm example. The girlfriends (literally, "the daughters of Jerusalem," 1:5) are implored not to "gaze at" the girl's black skin that has been "gazed" upon by the sun. The Shulammite explains her exposure to the hot Mediterranean sun as a consequence of her brothers' anger that prompted them to set her as a "guard" in the vineyards. The phrase "they were angry with me" may also be read as "they burned against me," playing on the scorching look of the sun that burns the skin. And the verse ends by playing on the literal and figurative meanings of "vineyard" in the Song. The vineyard, garden, or field is the conventional locale of lovemaking in the Song (and throughout ANE love poetry). In the Song, however, the vineyard (or garden) is also used as a figure for the girl herself (especially 4:12–5:1; 6:2). It is the latter on which the final line in 1:6 turns: if she was set to "guard" the family's literal "vineyards," her own more figurative "vineyard" she has not "guarded"—this last bit said, no doubt, as a happy boast, which also suggests that the exclamation in 1:5 ("I am black and beautiful!") is in no way demurring.

Other non-literal features are integral to the Song and its lyric mode of discourse. Two additional examples may be offered by way of illustration. Metaphor, which epitomizes the tropologically dense discourse of lyric verse (Kinzie), is at the heart of the Song's poetry of love. Love is like the finest wine, only better (1:2, 4; 4:10); like a wonderful if debilitating sickness (2:5; 5:8); like spring (2:8-17); a garden of delights (4:12–5:1; 7:12-13); beyond all wealth (8:7, 11-12); indomitable, unassailable even by the very powers of chaos (8:7). Perhaps the most famous metaphor used for love in the Song is death: "love is strong as death" (8:6). One might well infer that love, or at least this particular love, is to be imagined as locked in mortal combat with Death personified (e.g., Exum)—all love inevitably comes to an end, even if only through the actual death of (one of) the lovers. But there is a meaningful surplus that accompanies the play of metaphors and resists an exact accounting, that even (necessarily) affronts our semantic sensibilities. In this case, love's strength cannot be disentangled from the dark gloom and violence of its conceptualization in terms of death. And, in fact, the Song is laced throughout with an awareness of the dark side of love that is always at risk of being unleashed—the Shulammite is beaten by the night guard for love (5:7), becomes sick (2:5; 5:8), and warns her girlfriends three times over not to arouse love prematurely (2:7; 3:5; 8:4); her lover is assaulted by her very glances (4:9; 6:5) and not infrequently imagines her through a militaristic lens.

A second trope emblematic of the Song's lyric means for making sense (love) is iteration. The Song is replete with repetition at every level, from the morpheme to images and whole poems. Often the repetition is local and (mostly) exact, as in the twice repeated "your love than wine" and "they love you" in 1:2-4. The repetitions are not always exact. For example, the Shulammite's oath repeats verbatim on the first two voicings (2:7; 3:5), and then it varies some in the last two (5:8; 8:4). The effects are multifaceted and not predictable ahead of time. The redoubling in the couplet in 8:6 ("Set me as a seal upon your heart, as a seal upon your arm") may be taken to mime the actual putting on of the stamp seal, fastening and tightening it to ensure that it does not fall off. In the following triplet, the threefold figuration derived from the underworld (Death, Sheol ["the grave"], and the flaming arrows, which presumably are to be associated with the somewhat obscure though clearly chthonic Canaanite deity Reshep), troubles any reading that attempts to ignore or rush too quickly past the dark and monstrous side of love's power.

Not only words are repeated, but images (e.g., the garden in its many inflections) too, and even whole poems. The short poem in 3:1-5 and its echo in 5:2-8 showcase the workings of iteration at almost every

level, and, despite the obvious narrative quality that infuses these runs of verses (Linafelt, Exum), their informing lyricism, especially with regard to the trope of iteration, is never in doubt. Song 3:1-5 comes first in the sequence, and this is crucial to how 5:2-8 is heard. The poem's base storyline may be simply stated. The Shulammite, desiring her absent lover, searches the city for him, and eventually finds him, though not before she herself is found by the night watch. She seizes him and brings him to her mother's house, at which point the story breaks off and the poem concludes with an adjuration to the Shulammite's girlfriends. The transition from the first ("Upon my bed at night") to the second line ("I sought him whom my soul loves") is all important, as it disturbs from the outset any straightforward narrative construal. Is she dreaming or thinking to herself, longing for her lover? Does she actually leave her bed to search for her lover? Or is it all imagined? None of these questions can be answered definitively, and thus should serve as the reader's initial cue that something more than a charming story is afoot.

The so-called companion piece in 5:2-8 is in many respects quite different. It comes as a section of a larger poem; repetition is not the governing trope that it is in 3:1-5; and the language, with but a few, albeit critical, exceptions, is almost entirely different. Still, similarities persist. This poem is also set at night (we may infer), when the girl is sleeping (or on the verge thereof, v. 2), features another search for her lover (v. 6), exhibits clear narrative qualities, and closes with an adjuration to the "daughters of Jerusalem" (v. 8). Therefore, in encountering 5:2-8 after 3:1-5 we cannot help but read with that earlier poem in mind. In fact, 5:2-8 invites this retrospective reading strategy rather explicitly at several points, chiefly through repeated key words (e.g., *seek* and *find*) and images in vv. 6-8. Contrary to 3:1-5, the focus here is on the narrative action that happens prior to the search itself (vv. 2-6). Separation, not absence, is the poem's initial preoccupation. The boy comes to the door, knocks, and begs to be let in out of the heavy nighttime dew (v. 2). The girl, who has already gone to bed, is somewhere (in the sleeping room) on the other side of the door. She dithers (playfully) and by the time she opens the door, her lover has fled (v. 6). The telling to this point is deliberate, the pace very slow. Readers are allowed to sense how very close to a union our lovers come—the boy even managing to reach through the ancient Egyptian-styled lock, the very lock the girl manipulates to open the door (vv. 4-5)—whatever allusions to sexual intercourse that this sequence may conjure remain but allusions and are left to the reader's imagination. The pace picks up and we begin to encounter vocabulary familiar from the earlier poem—seek, find, and the guards making their rounds of the city. The Shulammite's "soul" literally goes forth (v. 6) in search of her lover, or in the language of 3:1-5, "him whom my soul loves." She seeks but does not find, and, again as in 3:3, the night watch finds her instead. The reader takes all in stride, as this is familiar territory, we have quite literally been down this road before. And then comes the hammer—or the club, as the case may be. The guards beat, batter, and (literally) disrobe the Shulammite. End of story, but the poem continues. The reader, reeling from the naked violence, the girl's brutal violation, hardly is able to take in the closing adjuration, which either asks rhetorically about what the girlfriends will tell the Shulammite's lover, namely, that she is love-sick, or swears them not to tell him this. In either case, the chief result of the story is not narrative but lyrical in nature, to make concrete the pain and hurt that the sickness that is love (compare 2:5) can cause, a sensibility felt all the more sharply at the unexpectedness induced through the trope of iteration.

The question of whether the Song is one poem or many remains debated among scholars (e.g., Exum). Without going into detail, two considerations in particular make the thesis that the Song is comprised of many poems especially attractive (how many exactly—fourteen, thirty-one, forty-two—is a disputed matter). First, most commentators admit that even without meta-discursive indications (of the type, a "psalm of David" or "thus says the LORD") a number of discrete poems are discernible (e.g., 2:8-17; 3:1-5; 5:2–6:3). Second, the issue of scale is consequential. A certain smallness of scale is generally associated with the lyric. Such brevity results from the lyric's routine eschewal of narrative devices that would enable more encompassing discourse; and, as a practical matter, it means that lyric poems will be limited in the scope of their subject matter. Nonetheless, lyric poems extend their reach and scope through a number of strategies. Form, such as the alphabetic acrostic in Ps 119, which serves to help auditors navigate the expanded discourse space (176 verses), offers one such technique. Another common strategy for increasing the lyric's typically confining amplitude is to successively link a number of individual lyric poems and mold them into a greater, organic whole. What gets enacted in such a process, then, is a sequence or collection of lyric poems whose nature and dynamic, holistically considered, is essentially that of a lyric poem writ large. The latter offers a most apt characterization of the Song, especially as the alternative theory most frequently pressed, namely, that the Song is one long, lyric poem, is difficult to imagine outside of the most literate of cultures (where, in fact, the long poem has thrived).

There are, however, strong centripetal forces (e.g., consistency of language, style, and voice, the same kinds of imagery used, the recurrent topics entertained, the prominence of iteration itself) in the Song that give the whole a distinct sense of cohesiveness—a quality that seems to be a (the) chief motivation in the single poem theory of the Song. Sometimes continuity in the speaking voice (e.g., the girl speaks at the end of 1:9-17 and the beginning of 2:1-7) or a shared setting and imagery (e.g., the mountains in 4:1-7 and 4:8–5:1) help

to ease the transition between poems in the Song. But more often readers simply need to accommodate and negotiate the junctures and disjunctions that erupt between (and disrupt) contiguous poems. Such aggregation creates the dialectic dynamic typical of sequences and collections wherein each individual poem's "inside meaning"—the meaning comprised of a poem's own internal character—plays off of, into, and against the aggregate's "outside meaning"—the meaning that is created when the individual poems are structured as parts of a more inclusive order; the whole is always giving way to the individual poems and vice versa. The play between 5:2-8 and 3:1-5, briefly examined above, exemplifies this dynamic. In the Song, the amalgamation that constitutes its underlying means of discourse suggests the heterogeneity of the love experience itself. The need, that is, for love to be taken one moment at a time, from day to day, and, quite literally, from poem to poem. Structurally, the Song as a whole—the accumulation of its several and varied poems and bits of poems at one time and in one place (namely in a manuscript) remains stubbornly loose, open, unprogrammed, and idiosyncratic.

C. Love of Two—Among Others

The love that is sung, explored, celebrated, and worried over is a love of two—a girl and a boy—rendered in dialogue. The two are given roughly the same number of lines, with the girl, the Shulammite (not insignificantly) actually having just a bit more. It is the girl's voice that both opens and closes the sequence as a whole and that readers habitually find the most compelling. She betokens a vibrant, knowing agency. The Shulammite throughout the Song is someone who knows her own mind and acts on it. Infused with intention, initiative, self-assurance, and energy, she takes charge from the outset. It is her own desire that the Shulammite seeks to slake. She shows no hesitation in doing what is necessary to realize her desire—whether it means pursuing her beloved into the noontime pasture lands (1:7-8), searching the city streets at night for him (3:1-5; 5:1-8), or seeking him in his garden (6:1-2). She is confident and comfortable in her own countercultural, sun-darkened skin (1:5) and will determine where and when to give her love (7:12). And while there is no question that she is most specifically gendered—her evocativeness, passion, innocence, and interest in interior feelings and relationships may be described, historically and culturally, as feminine (compare Leick)—these characteristics and actions are not those most commonly associated with other female characters in the Bible. She is more whole, even more real(istic). Why this is so is not obvious. Some transgressive intentions are apparent: the several references to mothers and especially the "mother's house" (instead of the otherwise ubiquitous designation of the family household as "the house of the father"; see 1:6; 3:4, 11; 6:9; 8:1, 2, 5), the lack of interest paid to the topics of marriage and children, and the Shulammite's frequent figuration through militaristic metaphors (e.g., 4:4; 6:5; 8:10; compare Meyers 1986). But the fuller portrayal of the Shulammite may also come, at least in part, from the Song's being staged chiefly in what we might call the domain of domesticity, a domain not otherwise prominently on display in biblical texts. And it is precisely in this domain where women—mothers!—exercised real power, formal and informal alike (Meyers 1988). In any case, the attention paid to the Shulammite in the Song, her characterization, and the depth of her psychological development are each unique in the Bible.

The boy's voice, by comparison, appears a little less spectacular and special. This is partly a consequence of his fewer lines and of readers' lack of access to his inner thoughts and feelings (compare Exum). His desire for (e.g., 2:14; 7:9; 8:13) and love of (e.g., 2:4; 4:10; 8:11-12) the Shulammite are clearly indicated, and that he finds her utterly attractive is also patent (e.g., 1:9-11, 15; 4:1-7). But only occasionally do we glimpse anything else of his inner life, such as his being undone by the girl's merest glance (4:9; 6:5). And yet there is substance, complexity, and even surprise to the boy's figuring. For example, in some respects, his masculinity is in keeping with cultural norms—one connotation of the royal tableau against which the boy is frequently imagined (e.g., 1:2, 12; 3:6-11; 6:12; 7:5) is to bathe him in the light of his culture's paradigm of masculinity, the king (Ps 45); he is the literal "image" of what the Shulammite and her girlfriends clearly find attractive and desirable (5:9–6:3). But there are transgressive aspects to this version of masculinity, too. Marriage and progeny are never specifically in the foreground; there is no evidence of the casual attitude toward sex otherwise so typical of ANE constructs of masculine sexuality (compare Cooper); and the boy, like the girl, is able, when appropriate, to give way to the other, that is, to exhibit a generous passivity that opens onto another's agency—to be led away (3:4; 8:2) or held captive (7:6) or possessed (6:3) by the other lover.

Perhaps our deepest impressions about the boy and the girl accumulate over the course of the sequence and arise from the dialogic shape of their discourse. We encounter two individuals by turns speaking and listening to each other. This is neither insignificant nor a given. The extant Egyptian love poetry, for example, is almost all monologic in nature (Fox), as is much of the love poetry in the Western literary canon. In the dialogic conceit of the Song, we are treated to at least two different takes on love, which from the outset explodes all attempts to see love as just one thing or another. And through the Song's capacity to be re-uttered, so typical of lyric verse (Dobbs-Allsopp 2006), the subjectivity of the speakers (and listeners) is made available to readers (and hearers) such that they may entertain the lovers' statements, poses, and feelings, try them on, and re-experience them from the inside, as it were. Inevitably and happily, in this instance of lyrical impersonation,

the giving over of our readerly selves to these other speaking voices entails (among other things) imaginative engagements with sexualities and gender positions not our own. Moreover, dialogue itself is the mode *par excellence* of ethical discourse, a linguistic gesture through which life, respect, and otherness is imputed to another, difference is acknowledged, and the possibility for real exchange is created (compare Dobbs-Allsopp 2004). Beyond all that gets said, then, it is the way of love's *saying* in the Song that matters and says so much. We hear, not uncommonly for the Bible, a male speaking and a female being spoken to; but we also hear a girl who, in rather spectacular fashion, seizes the occasion to speak ("I am black and beautiful," 1:5) and a boy who yearns to listen ("Let me hear your voice," 2:14).

Though the Song is the duet performed by the girl and the boy, the Shulammite and her lover, others are present as well, and they sometimes speak. The girl's companions, her girlfriends, are addressed and speak throughout (e.g., 1:5; 2:7; 5:9); her brothers appear briefly in the beginning (1:6) and are perhaps also to be heard in the unidentified "we" of 8:8-9; her mother is briefly ventriloquized by the boy (6:9). Still others in varied capacities and incarnations populate the margins of the Song without voice, e.g., the "they" of 1:3-4, the night watch (3:3; 5:7), figurative kings and shepherds (e.g., 1:4, 7-8, 12), Solomon (e.g., 3:6-11), gazelles, dove, jackals, and all manner of flora and fauna (e.g., 2:8-17). These all are instantiations of what E. Levinas calls the "third party," the Song's knowing nod to the other's other, the recognition that love between a self and an other must finally be embedded in and embrace and flourish among a community of others, in a world teeming with life beyond the human. These are but openings onto the political path. The Song itself never travels very far down these paths toward which it constantly points. But the openings are enough to inscribe a powerful awareness of the Song's perennial need for supplementation. The Song sings a particular and most partial song about two (young) people in love. Its contentions and commendations are self-consciously limited (e.g., culturally, literarily, linguistically, and topically).

D. A Closing Reading

There is more to say, of course, about the Song and its song of love, as ever will be the case, for reading, too, is an unending task. Even at its most capacious and comprehensive, there is always room in reading for another reading, a fuller reading, a different reading. The main tack taken above has been to sample the Song and its feast of love, to read closely and lovingly some of its parts and poems and alluring tropes, in the hope of winning other readers for the Song, inspiring other readings. To end, then, one last reading of one final (but not the final) poem may be offered.

Song 7:6-13 is typical of the Song's component poems. It is shaped as an asymmetrical dialogue. The boy begins. His part turns out to be the shorter of the two sections, consisting of only seven lines (7:6-9)—two couplets and a closing triplet. The girl is addressed throughout as a "you"—the second person feminine suffix is repeated five times ("your stature," "your breasts" [twice], "your nose," "your mouth"). The girl's intimidating inaccessibility is once again figured (compare 2:14). She is imagined as a beautiful, stately palm, one of the oldest cultivated fruit trees in the ancient world and rich in cultural symbolism (compare Keel). The girl's cluster-like breasts are high and out of reach. And though the boy is determined to scale the scary height (the date palm grows to be between eighty and a hundred feet tall) and to lay hold of the desired fruit, the shaping of the couplets in the unbalanced limp of the qinah meter (long line followed by short line) tellingly figures—laments!—his discouragement, his doubts about accomplishing such a feat. That is, the qinah-shaped assertion comes off as a mumbled complaint: —sure "I say I will climb the palm tree and lay hold of its branches" but.... And thus readers are not surprised to find the boy's closing triplet pitched more as a wish (NRSV, "Oh, may your breasts ..."") and the image shifted ever so slightly but crucially. Would that the girl's breasts were more like clusters of grapes on the vine, down low and quite reachable, than the date clusters of the tall palm. The accessibility implied in the vine image appears to energize the boy's imagination and the lines move quickly forward and by an associative logic at several levels, i.e., anatomy (breasts, nose, mouth; compare 4:1-7), smells and tastes of the vine and its product (compare 4:10), the sensorial effectuation of proximity. Here the boy's desire is phrased in language that echoes the girl's opening ejaculation (1:2-3), thus symbolizing (yet again) the lovers' harmonious commensurability.

The next line enacts another of the Song's high moments. The image of wine continues, literally "going down ... smoothly" (7:9; compare Prov 23:31). But the movement is directed specifically "to my lover," the girl's pet name for the boy. Apparently, we must infer she now is the speaker, interrupting and completing the boy's speech. That lovers come to know what each other will say and can complete the other's thoughts is a common enough experience. But what is so very delectable is just how the poet musters language to figure a kiss, linguistic intercourse both literal and figural. Here is as close as the Song comes to actually showing the lovers joining together, satisfying their own and the other's want. And yet, of course, the joining is not itself represented or narrated. All that is said is that the fine wine to which the girl's mouth is likened goes down smoothly.

The interruption and slight disorientation allows the image to linger. The girl's final rendition of her declaration of mutuality (2:16; 6:3) effectively extends this pause, stating (and thus redoubling), in essence, one aspect of what has just been figured. Moreover, the torquing achieved in the second line of v. 10 ("and his desire is for me") names what the reader has just witnessed, eliciting our consenting nod, while at the same time alluding to the Eden story (Gen 2–3) and reversing the curse there placed upon Eve (Gen 3:16; 4:7). Desire in the Song's re-visioning of the garden story is mutual and attentive to the other's singularity. And if it may be properly said of the Song that it constitutes (in a manner of speaking) the first telling of paradise regained, what is in fact (re)gained is a paradise of a different sort altogether, cultivated by and for human beings. The staging of love (whether of lover, mother, or other), like the garden paradise that is love's setting in the Song or the poetry in which the Song's garden and the love that it harbors and betokens is rendered, is as much a thing made as found, a cultural work dependent on human cultivation and imagination, if it is to flourish, however momentarily.

From v. 11 the poetry again quickens its pace. The second and longer half of the poem (vv. 10-13) is rendered in the girl's voice—the interrupted speech in v. 9 holding the two parts of the poem together. The lines are mostly short and choppy, set with but one exception (the last part of v. 12) as couplets. The repetition of "my lover" in the first and last lines (vv. 10, 13; see also v. 11) frames this section of the poem. The body of the section (vv. 11-13) is given over to the girl's invitation to her lover to join her in the garden. The language reprises and replays the boy's earlier invitation to the girl (2:10-13), and thus the gesture of respect and mutuality effected in the boy's rewording of the girl's language at the poem's outset (especially v. 10) is returned in kind here by her own rewording. The desire for the garden is shared by two: "let us go forth ... let us see ...." The lusciousness of the garden imagery here matches in tone and tenor the fruit-full imagery in the first part of the poem, adding yet another layer of cohesion to bind the poem together as a whole.

The one triplet in this section of the poem comes at the end of v. 12. It stands out like a bump in the section's otherwise uniform surface of couplets. The Shulammite is in the midst of urging her lover to rise early in the morning and accompany her to the garden, both a favorite place for the couple's trysts and an emblem of the girl herself and her budding sexuality (especially 4:12-15; compare 1:6; 2:1; 4:16; 5:1). The final line breaks off the invitation and description of the garden to announce, with some emphasis: "There I will give you my love." "My love(making)" here plays on (quite obviously) the fourfold repetition of "my love(er)," the first person imperfective form ("I will give") echoing the alliterative use of the same forms ("I will climb .... I will take hold") in the boy's earlier assertion of intent. Desire matches desire. Here, then, is one last rendition of the give and take idiom that plays throughout the Song but is especially prominent in this poem.

Not all in this poem is easily readable—whether due to the rarity of terms, textual problems, or lack of clarity of reference. These resistant disruptions of reading quite literally defeat our attempts to comprehend the other of the text, to read it fully, once and for all, and in the process remind us (with a wink and a nod to the Song's allegorical tradition of interpretation) that reading with love and fidelity, like any relationship that merits the name of love, like the relationship between the Shulammite and the boy in the Song of Songs, is to be undertaken with an openness to the unknown and to the un-thought, to the hither side of "the mountains of spices."

Bibliography: Y. Amichai. *Open Closed Open* (2000); J. S. Cooper. "Enki's Member: Eros and Irrigation in Sumerian Literature." *Dumu-ez-Dub-Ba-A: Studies in Honor of Ake J. Sjöberg* (1989) 87–89; F. W. Dobbs-Allsopp. "Late Linguistic Features in the Song of Songs." *Perspectives on the Song of Songs* (2005) 27–77; F. W. Dobbs-Allsopp. "Psalms and Lyric Verse." *The Evolution of Rationality: Interdisciplinary Essays in Honor of J. Wentzel van Huyssteen* (2006) 346–79; F. W. Dobbs-Allsopp. "R(az/ais)ing Zion in Lamentations 2." *David and Zion: Biblical Studies in Honor of J. J. M. Roberts* (2004) 21–68; J. C. Exum. *Song of Songs.* OTL (2005); M. Fox. *The Song of Songs and the Ancient Egyptian Love Songs* (1985); S. D. Goitein. "Women as Creators of Biblical Genres." *Proof* 8 (1988) 1–33; R. Greene. *Post-Petrarchism* (1991); D. Grossberg. *Centripetal and Centrifugal Structures in Biblical Poetry* (1989); M. Kinzie. *A Poet's Guide to Poetry* (1999); G. Leick. *Sex and Eroticism in Mesopotamian Literature* (1994); E. Levinas. *Entre nous: On Thinking-of-the-Other* (1998); T. Linafelt. "Arithmetic of Eros." *Int* 59 (2005) 244–58; C. Meyers. *Discovering Eve: Ancient Israelite Women in Context* (1988); C. Meyers. "Gender Imagery in the Song of Songs." *HAR* 10 (1986) 209–23; S. Moore. *God's Beauty Parlor* (2001); R. Murphy. *Song of Songs.* Hermeneia (1990); M. Pope. *Song of Songs.* AB 7C (1977); N. Walls. *Desire, Discord and Death: Approaches to Ancient Near Eastern Myth* (2001) 9–92.

FRED W. DOBBS-ALLSOPP

SONG OF THE SEA. A poem found in Exod 15:1-19 often called the "Song of MIRIAM" because of vv. 20-21 and the association of women with victory songs (e.g., 1 Sam 18:7). The song celebrates God's victory over the Egyptians and the deliverance of Israel. Most scholars date the poem to the late-12th/early-11th cent. BCE and consider it much older than the prose account of crossing the sea (Exod 14). Those that believe in the antiquity of the song consider it to be one of the two oldest texts in the Bible alongside the Song of Deborah (Judg 5), which they date to the same period.

KEVIN A. WILSON

SONG OF THE THREE JEWS. The Greek translation of Dan 3 inserts two prayers into the mouths of the three young men during their ordeal in the furnace (be-tween 3:23 and 3:24): the Prayer of Azariah and the Song of the Three Jews (or Song of the Three Young Men). In the latter, the three youths praise God directly (Dan 3:52-56 [LXX]) and then invite all creatures to offer a blessing (thanks and praise) to the creator. Drawing heavily upon Pss 103; 148; and 150, the text seems to be liturgical, perhaps translated from Hebrew (*see* SONGS OF THE SABBATH SACRIFICE). The six-day structure of Gen 1:1–2:1 may be background for Dan 3:74-82 [LXX], with human beings represented in history by the descendants of Israel (Dan 3:83-87 [LXX]). Hananiah, Azariah, and Mishael exhort themselves to celebrate God's intervention to deliver them from death (Dan 3:88 [LXX]). The goodness and mercy of God are manifest (see the refrain of Ps 136 in Dan 3:89 [LXX]); God deserves the praise of all true worshipers (Dan 3:90 [LXX]).

The relation between creation and history is stressed in the phrase "God of our Fathers" (Dan 3:52 [LXX], author's trans.; NRSV, "God of our ancestors") and in the rescue of the heroes. The chosen people, constituted by the divine promise to the patriarchs (Dan 3:83 [LXX]), are represented by priests and Levites ("servants of the Lord," Dan 3:85 [LXX]) and exemplified by righteousness ("holy and humble in heart," Dan 3:87 [LXX]) like that of the three youths of the tribe of Judah (Dan 1:6). They believed that God the creator can place the forces of nature at the service of the righteous (see Wis 19:6, 20-21). The conclusion (Dan 3:88-90 [LXX]), drawing on a litany response of temple worship (Pss 106:1; 136), links the hymn to the dilemma of the youths.

Early Christians under persecution found inspiration in the hymn and expanded upon its ending. By the late 4th cent CE, it was sung throughout the church; then it became the canticle of Sunday Lauds, celebrating the divine work of creation and the Christian doctrines of the Trinity and the resurrection of Jesus. Although the Jewish liturgy does not use these prayers preserved in Greek Daniel, many of the themes of the hymn are developed in *Pereq Shirah*. See AZARIAH, PRAYER OF; DANIEL, ADDITIONS TO; DANIEL, BOOK OF.

LAWRENCE FRIZZELL

SONG, SONGS [שִׁיר shir, שִׁירָה shirah; ψαλμός psalmos, ὕμνος hymnos, ᾠδή ōdē]. Many songs in the OT share characteristics of what is commonly called "lyric verse," although biblical Hebrew does not have a term that is equivalent to the Greek-derived notion of "lyric." Instead, reference is made to what appear to be genre designations, such as mizmor (מִזְמוֹר, "psalm"), mashal (מָשָׁל, "proverb"), and qinah (קִינָה, "dirge, lament"). The most widely used word of this type in the OT is shir. It designates a diverse set of forms, including celebratory songs (e.g., Exod 15:1; Judg 5:1; 2 Sam 22:1; compare 1 Sam 18:6), love songs (e.g., Song 1:1; Ezek 33:32), prophetic oracles of various kinds (e.g., Isa 5:1; 23:15-16; 42:10), and psalms (e.g., Pss 30; 45; 46; 48; 83; 96; 120).

In the NT, psalmos, hymnos, and ōdē are used in reference to songs of praise (1 Cor 14:26; Jas 5:13; Rev 5:9; 14:3; 15:3). All three are mentioned together in Eph 5:19 and Col 3:16, making it difficult to distinguish the precise nuances of each term. The term psalmos is also used to refer to the book of Psalms (Luke 20:42; Acts 1:20). *See* DEBORAH, SONG OF; HANNAH, SONG OF; HYMNS, NT; HYMNS, OT; MAGNIFICAT; MUSIC; NUNC DIMITTIS; PSALMS, BOOK OF; SONG OF THE SEA; THANKSGIVING.

FRED W. DOBBS-ALLSOPP

SONGS OF ASCENT [שִׁיר הַמַּעֲלוֹת shir hammaʿaloth]. The superscriptions of Pss 120–134 identify each of them as "A Song of Ascents." The frequent references to Jerusalem and Zion in these psalms (Pss 122:2, 6; 125:1-2; 126:1; 128:5; 129:5; 132:13; 133:3; 134:3) most likely account for their ascriptions. Since Jerusalem sits on a hill, one always "goes up" to Jerusalem.

Pilgrims traveling to Jerusalem may have sung the Songs of Ascent, which—with the exception of Ps 132—are brief and thus easy to memorize. Although these psalms likely come from a variety of times and places in ancient Israel, the message of the collection is that Jerusalem is the place for the coming together of God's people for celebrations and commemorations and for acknowledging the goodness and help of their God. The Songs of Ascent are traditionally recited at the Feast of Booths, which commemorates God's care during the wilderness wanderings, reinforcing the pilgrimage theme of these psalms (*see* BOOTHS, FEAST OR FESTIVAL OF).

Bibliography: Loren D. Crow. *The Songs of Ascents (Psalms 120–134): Their Place in Israelite History and Religion* (1996).

NANCY DECLAISSÉ-WALFORD

SONGS OF THE SABBATH SACRIFICE. The *Songs of the Sabbath Sacrifice* is a liturgical cycle of songs for the first thirteen Sabbaths of the year. It follows the fixed 364-day solar calendar and, therefore, could have been repeated quarterly. Each song has a title (e.g., "For the Instructor. Song of the sacrifice of the seventh Sabbath on the sixteenth of the month") and then opens with invitations to the holy angels to praise God. In a self-deprecating comparison with the angels ("[What] is the offering of our mortal tongue compared with the knowledge of the g[ods/angels]?" 4Q400 2 7–11) the human worshipers identify themselves as the speakers reciting this liturgy. The body of the *Songs of the Sabbath Sacrifice* consists of elaborate descriptions of the ranks of the highest angels and their praise in the heavenly Temple. The structures of the heavenly Temple are also said to praise God, and multiple sanctuaries and chariot thrones are mentioned. The liturgical cycle begins in Song 1 with the establishment of the angelic priesthood, reaches the psalms and blessings of the seven

angelic chief princes in the sixth song, with a mid-cycle climax of hypnotic sevenfold praises in the seventh song followed by the praises of the seven angelic priesthoods and the seven deputy princes in the eighth song, and builds to a grand finale with the radiant cherubim (see Ezek 1; 3; 10) singing as they accompany the divine merkabah chariot throne (Song 12), with the angelic high priests bedecked in their splendid vestments offering sacrifices in the heavenly Temple (Song 13).

This sublime content, the numinous style particularly of the seventh song, and the impressive parallels with the later mystical *Hekhalot* literature led some scholars to propose that the *Songs of the Sabbath Sacrifice* functioned as a vehicle for a quasi-mystical experience of communing with the angels in the heavenly Temple (Newsom) or, further, as a mystical praxis attaining a communal ascent and union with the angels (Alexander). Others scholars see the *Songs of the Sabbath Sacrifice* as falling short of a mystical praxis (Wolfson) or view their function in the earthly arena as a substitute for the Sabbath sacrifice, assuming the *Songs of the Sabbath Sacrifice* are sectarian in origin (Maier), or, more recently, as liturgical accompaniment in the Jerusalem Temple, assuming a non-sectarian provenance (Regev). While the question of the *Songs of the Sabbath Sacrifice*'s origin is still under debate, the nine manuscripts from QUMRAN (4Q400–407; 11Q17; a single manuscript was found at Masada) leave little doubt as to this liturgy's significant role in the spiritual life and religious practice of the Qumran community. Irrespective of their origin, at Qumran the *Songs of the Sabbath Sacrifice* could have served simultaneously as a substitute for the Sabbath sacrifice in the Jerusalem Temple and as a means of linking the community's praise with that of the angels and attaining some sense of the angelic worship in the heavenly Temple. *See* DEAD SEA SCROLLS.

Bibliography: Philip Alexander. *The Mystical Texts: Songs of the Sabbath Sacrifice and Related Manuscripts* (2006); Jonathan Maier. "Shire ʿOlat hash-Shabbat. Some Observations on Their Calendric Implications and Style." *The Madrid Qumran Congress: Proceedings of the International Congress on the Dead Sea Scrolls* (1992) 543–60; Carol Newsom. *Songs of the Sabbath Sacrifice: A Critical Edition* (1985); Eyal Regev. "Temple Prayer as the Origin of Fixed Prayer (On the Evolution of Prayer during the Period of the Second Temple." *Zion* 70 (2005) 5–29; Elliott Wolfson. "Mysticism and the Poetic-Liturgical Compositions from Qumran: A Response to Bilhah Nitzan." *JQR* 85 (1004) 185–202.

ESTHER G. CHAZON

SONS OF GOD. *See* GOD, SONS OF.

SONS OF PROPHETS [בְּנֵי הַנְּבִיאִים bene hannevi'im]. A professional guild or "company of prophets." In the time of Elisha, such groups lived in Bethel (2 Kgs 2:3) and Jericho (2:5, 15). They had no independent income but received assistance from Elisha (2 Kgs 4:1, 38; 6:1) and Naaman (2 Kgs 5:22). Elisha commissioned one of them to anoint Jehu king of Israel (2 Kgs 9:1-3).

JOAN E. COOK, SC

SONS OF THUNDER. *See* BOANERGES.

SOOTHSAYER [מְעוֹנֵן meʿonen]. One who tells fortunes by various means (Deut 18:10; Isa 2:6; Jer 27:9; Mic 5:12). Soothsayers were associated with diviners and others who claimed to mediate supernatural knowledge (*see* DIVINATION). Israelites were prohibited from consulting soothsayers, either foreign (Deut 18:14, Canaanites; Isa 2:6, Philistines) or domestic (a mark of King Manasseh's wickedness; 2 Kgs 21:6; 2 Chr 33:6).

F. SCOTT SPENCER

SOPATER soh´puh-tuhr [Σώπατρος Sōpatros]. Sopater, the son of PYRRHUS, was a companion of Paul, mentioned in Acts 20:4 as traveling with Paul from Greece back to MACEDONIA. His name—meaning "savior of his father"—indicates that Sopater introduced his father to Christianity. Sopater may be the same as SOSIPATER (Rom 16:21).

STEPHANIE BUCKHANON CROWDER

SOPHERETH sof´uh-rith [סֹפֶרֶת sofereth, הַסֹּפֶרֶת hassofereth; Ἀσσαφειώθ Hassapheiōth]. Means "scribe." Head of a family of temple servants (*see* SOLOMON'S SERVANTS) who returned from the Babylonian exile with Zerubbabel and Jeshua (Ezra 2:55; Neh 7:57; 1 Esd 5:33).

SOPHERIM. *See* EMENDATIONS OF THE SCRIBES; SCRIBE.

SOPHIA soh-fee´uh [חָכְמָה khokhmah; σοφία sophia]. Wisdom, personified as a woman, is an important, if somewhat puzzling, construct in the OT. There, "Wisdom" (or khokhmah) is grammatically feminine in gender, as are most abstract concepts in the Hebrew language (e.g., "torah," "understanding"). One must distinguish whether the text is referring to Woman Wisdom, the character and patron of the sages, or the overall concept of knowledge, learning, and skill. Within Proverbs and elsewhere, both uses are found: at times, Woman Wisdom is speaking to those who scorn her, love her, or might be advised to seek her (Prov 1:20-33; 3:19; 8:1-36; 9:1-6); in other places, the skill of the specially trained is meant (Exod 28:3; 31:3; 35:31; 1 Kgs 2:6; 4:29-34 [Heb. 5:9-14]; Prov 14:8; Isa 29:14).

Skilled workers, artisans, authors, leaders, and teachers are said to possess the wisdom of their trades. In Exodus, all those "wise of heart," that is, trained, use their special gifts to build and decorate the desert tabernacle (Exod 28:3; 31:3; 35:31). In Deuteronomy, the most discerning of the elders are chosen to lead the peo-

ple (Deut 1:13-15; 34:9); and leaders of foreign nations as well as Israel and Judah are referred to as using the skills of statecraft to secure their success (e.g., 2 Sam 14:20; 1 Kgs 2:6; 3; 4:29-34 [Heb. 5:9-14]; Prov 24:3; Eccl 1:16; Isa 10:13; Ezek 28; Dan 1:4-20). Both males and females can display such skill (Judg 5:29; 2 Sam 20; Prov 31:26; Jer 9:17-21 [Heb. 9:16-20]); children, slaves, and foreigners are all potential possessors of wisdom (Prov 14:35; 17:2; Sir 7:21; 10:25).

The prologue (chaps. 1–9) to the book of Proverbs features the literary figure of personified Wisdom. As a female figure of much public power and authority, it is perplexing to find her in the midst of writings that strongly reflect the gender ideologies of antiquity. While regular women were expected to occupy themselves with the world of the home and its management, Woman Wisdom can be found in public places where male leaders like prophets exhort the populace. She speaks authoritatively based on her "cosmic portfolio": she existed before creation, was a "model" for it, and was beside God during these acts, delighting in the created world, especially humanity (Prov 8). She uses harsh language and vows to laugh at all those who disregard her advice when the results of their own stupidity come to fruition. She eagerly invites young men to her side, to walk in her ways and dine at her table. Her language is often an exact duplicate of that of her social and theological "evil twin," Woman Folly, who can be either adulteress or foreigner (Prov 9:1-9 versus 9:13-18). Wisdom demonstrates the admirable traits found in the Good Woman (NRSV, "capable wife" of Prov 31:10-31), but is comfortable and recognized in arenas normally inhabited by only one sex, serving, in effect, as a reliable mediator between them. In sum, she offers "the good life" and makes the sort of claims one usually finds attributed to Israel's (male) God.

Research into the roles of female figures within the biblical text and in the ANE world has helped to contextualize this remarkable character. She has been seen as the personification of the female attributes sages admired in real or legendary women and linked to the roles of elite women in the Persian period. In both Egypt and Mesopotamia, the scribal guilds had goddesses of Wisdom for their professional patron (Maʿat; Nisaba), and aspects of the goddess complex, Inanna-Ishtar, have been transferred onto Woman Folly in the biblical poems about her. The indigenous Canaanite tree (mother) goddess ASHERAH may be the origin of the statement that Wisdom is a Tree of Life (Prov 3:18; this popular motif may be found on pottery and jewelry throughout most periods of biblical Syro-Palestine). In later Second Temple texts, Woman Wisdom is identified with the Torah and redemption of the Jews in history (Sir 24:8-12, 23-29; Wis 10:15). She is often found associated with "glory" or "spirit," "discerning comprehension" (see e.g., Wis 1:6; 9:6-16; Sir 1), concepts that later link female Wisdom to the "Logos" prologue to the Gospel of John and to trinitarian theology.

One of the earliest ways communities understood Jesus of Nazareth was in the role of sage. His use of proverbs, parables, and shrewd observations of life all marked him as a master teacher. Luke speaks of Jesus quoting a proverb that suggests he is one of the messengers Woman Wisdom has sent (Luke 11:49; NRSV, "Wisdom of God"), only to be rejected. By his teachings as a child of Wisdom, he justifies the validity of her teachings (Luke 7:35). Paul goes even further in 1 Corinthians; he makes the claim that Jesus is the Sophia of God (1 Cor 1:24; see also Eph 3:8-10; Col 4:5, Eph 5:15).

Yet, in Corinthians and elsewhere (e.g., Jas 3:13-15), we find the concept of two wisdoms, a heavenly one that is mysterious and secret but known to believers (1 Cor 2:13; 3:19; 2 Cor 1:12; Eph 1:8, 17) and a wisdom of the world that is calculating, cunning, and dismissive of the spiritual realities of redemption. Some posit a "wisdom mythology," based on gnostic writings behind these ideas, of a motherly female figure whose teachings are rejected by the world when she descends from heaven to earth, and with whom Jesus particularly associates himself. Woman Wisdom's chagrin at being rejected in Proverbs, however, also presents a biblical pattern for these wisdom motifs, and the NT writers' views had already been expressed in the prophetic denunciations of the cunning calculations of the wealthy sages of earlier times. In both the OT and the NT the inclusion of a powerful, cosmic female figure to explain the work of God in the world may have been a self-conscious theological adaptation of nourishing aspects of female imagery from neighboring cultures. *See* COUNSEL, COUNSELOR; PROVERBS, BOOK OF; SAGE; SCRIBE; UNDERSTAND; WISDOM IN THE ANCIENT NEAR EAST; WISDOM IN THE NT; WISDOM IN THE OT.

CAROLE R. FONTAINE

SOPHIA OF JESUS CHRIST. *See* JESUS CHRIST, SOPHIA OF; NAG HAMMADI TEXTS.

SOPHOCLES [Σοφοκλέης Sophoklees]. Along with Aeschylus and EURIPIDES, one of the three major Athenian playwrights of the 5th cent. BCE. Born ca. 496 BCE, Sophocles appears to have won his first major theatrical prize in 468 BCE, thereafter becoming a mainstay of the two major Athenian dramatic competitions—winning over twenty victories and numerous second prizes—until his death in 406 BCE. He is said to have written over 120 plays; however, only seven complete plays survive. The most famous of his plays are *Antigone*, *Oedipus the King*, and *Oedipus at Colonnus*. Unlike Aeschylus' trilogies, these three plays, known later as the Theban cycle, were written years apart and were never performed together. Sophocles' plays exerted significant influence on the later Greek and Western literary tradition, in part because later writers such as Aristotle and Quintillian held up his plays as paradigms

of their genre and as models to be imitated in education. *See* GREEK RELIGION AND PHILOSOPHY.

RUBÉN R. DUPERTUIS

SORCERY. *See* MAGIC, MAGICIAN.

SOREK, VALLEY OF sor'ik [נַחַל שֹׂרֵק nakhal soreq]. The sole biblical reference to this valley comes in the description of Samson's love for Delilah, who resided there (Judg 16:4). "Sorek" primarily refers to a relatively broad valley in the SHEPHELAH approximately 13 mi. west of Jerusalem, principally running between the towns of Zorah and Timnah. Since Samson was born in Zorah, he too is from this Sorek area (Judg 13). More broadly, "Sorek" also signifies the periodic river and drainage system linked to the Chesalon and Rephaim valleys, functioning as a 10-mi. section of the watershed west of Jerusalem. In the lower section of the valley, in the Shephelah region, the alluvial soil provides a rich, fertile valley. Thus, the Philistines were persistently determined to occupy this valley, an area adjacent to the Philistine plain. The tribe of Dan migrated out of the Sorek Valley to Laish (Judg 18).

MICHAEL D. MATLOCK

SORES [חַבּוּרָה khabburah, שְׁחִין shekhin; ἕλκος helkos]. Strictly speaking, these Hebrew and Greek words signify a localized skin condition of humans (and animals; see Exod 9:9-10; NRSV, "boils") characterized by swelling, most likely resulting from an inflammation. Modern medicine would call these furuncles, boils, or—if ruptured—ulcers. Job (2:7) and Lazarus (Luke 16:20-21) suffered from them. Revelation 16:2, 11 identifies them as divine punishment inflicted upon unrepentant idolaters by angels. *See* DISEASE; LEPROSY.

JOHN J. PILCH

SORREL. *See* COLORS.

SORROW [יָגוֹן yaghon, תּוּגָה tughah; λύπη lypē]. *Sorrow* refers to grief or sadness. The Hebrew word *yagon* is fairly consistently translated "sorrow." Other Hebrew words that are associated with pain or anguish are occasionally translated "sorrow."

Yaghon appears only fourteen times in the books of Genesis, Psalms, Isaiah, Jeremiah, Ezekiel, and Esther. Sorrow is typically associated with death, exile, being attacked by an enemy (existentially or potentially), or loss. Sorrow is the opposite of happiness (Esth 9:22). Typically sorrow is thought to be something that others, either human or divine (Jer 45:3), impose upon a person or group. Sorrow can be a punishment imposed by God (Ezek 23:33). Life can be lived in sorrow (Jer 20:18). Sorrow can be experienced empathically because of how others are treated (Jer 8:18). Death can be experienced in sorrow though this is undesirable and not necessary (Gen 42:38; 44:31). Sorrow can be remedied. Returning to Zion results in a fleeing away of sorrow (Isa 35:10; 51:11). God can turn sorrow into happiness (Jer 31:13). In the psalms appeals are made to God to deliver people from sorrow (Ps 31:9-10 [Heb. 31:11]), because it is believed that God can and wills to do so. Also in the psalms, sorrow is a characteristic result of suffering. Sorrow is experienced when one is suffering knowing that God can bring relief but does not (Ps 13:2 [Heb. 13:3]).

A second word translated "sorrow" is tughah. Tughah occurs four times in Proverbs and Psalms. Proverbs 14:13 in its literary context declares that for the wicked "following happiness is sorrow" (NRSV, "the end of joy is grief"). The two states are paired rather than presented as opposites. A cause of sorrow (NRSV, "grief," "no joy"), according to both Prov 10:1 and 17:21, is having offspring who are fools. Psalm 119:28 presents another remedy for sorrow. It is the "word" (meaning the Torah).

Words for pain or anguish are sometimes translated "sorrow," though it is not clear in the context why that is a better choice than the more usual translations of those words. The well known "man of sorrows" phrase from Isa 53:3 uses the Hebrew word makh'ovoth (מַכְאֹבוֹת), often translated "pains."

The Greek word lypē is sometimes translated "sorrow" in the NT. John 16:6 and Rom 9:2 provide the location of sorrow, which is given as the heart. In John 16:6, Jesus causes sorrow in the hearts of his followers by telling them that they will suffer in the future. In Romans, Paul speaks about the sorrow in his own heart. Another place where *sorrow* is used in some translations is 2 Cor 2:7, where forgiveness is mandated so that an erring person is not overwhelmed by sorrow. Sorrow (NRSV, "pain") in the NT can also be transformed into joy according to John 16:22. The joy is caused by the return of Jesus. *See* EMOTIONS; MOURNING; PEACE IN THE NT; PEACE IN THE OT; SUFFERING AND EVIL.

WILMA ANN BAILEY

SOSIPATER soh'sip'uh-tuhr [Σωσίπατρος Sōsipatros]. 1. A general under Judas Maccabeus in his battle against Timothy's army (2 Macc 12:19, 24).

2. One of the persons from whom Paul sends greetings to the Christians in Rome. Paul describes Sosipater as his relative or compatriot, along with Lucius and Jason (Rom 16:21). He is often considered to be the same person as SOPATER in Acts 20:4.

SHARON BETSWORTH

SOSTHENES sos'thuh-neez [Σωσθένης Sōsthenēs]. 1. The ruler of the synagogue in Acts 18:12-17 who initiated charges against Paul.

2. In 1 Cor 1:1, Sosthenes is included in Paul's greeting as co-sender of the letter. Paul frequently mentions co-senders (2 Cor 1:1), but it is rare in letters of the day to mention a co-sender. This underlines the collaborative nature of Paul's ministry with coworkers. Some

argue that Sosthenes was Paul's scribe. We cannot be certain whether this co-sender is the same Sosthenes as the Sosthenes of Acts. Sosthenes was a common name but many suggest his dramatic conversion.

ANTHONY C. THISELTON

SOSTRATUS sos'truh-tuhs [Σώστρατος Sōstratos]. Seleucid governor of the citadel in Jerusalem during the reign of ANTIOCHUS IV. He was responsible for collection of revenue and requested payment from MENELAUS of money he promised the king in exchange for appointment as high priest. Menelaus did not pay, and he and Sostratus were summoned by the king (2 Macc 4:28-29). *See* SELEUCID EMPIRE.

SEAN D. BURKE

SOTAH [סוֹטָה sotah]. The fifth tractate of the third order (*Nashim*) of the MISHNAH. The tractate primarily covers the laws governing treatment of a suspected adulteress (sotah), including the trial of the "water of bitterness" (Num 5:11-31).

SOTAI soh'ti [סוֹטַי sotay]. Head of a family of SOLOMON'S SERVANTS, who returned from the exile to Jerusalem with Zerubbabel (Ezra 2:55; Neh 7:57).

SOTERIOLOGY soh-tihr'ee-ol'uh-jee. Soteriology envisages the relationship between God and human beings restored to full harmony. Old Testament narratives such as Exodus portray God's salvation in history, while the prophets look to union with God either in the present or in a final, cataclysmic DAY OF THE LORD. In the NT, salvation is rescue from sin and its effects. The Christian is saved by entering through baptism into the life, death, and resurrection of Jesus Christ. *See* SALVATION.

MICHELE A. CONNOLLY, RSJ

SOUL [נֶפֶשׁ nefesh; ψυχή psychē]. In ancient Greek sources, psychē refers to the principle of life or movement or the basis of perception (Aristotle, *De an.* I 405a–407b). Plato reflects a Pythagorean and Orphic tradition in which the soul is divine, inherently immortal and separable from its prison the body (*Phaed.* 62b). In other contexts the soul has a tripartite structure, the source of appetites, the spirited part of the soul, and the rational or intellectual faculties (Plato, *Respecially* IX, 580d-581a; *Phaed.* 246a-b, 253c-255b; *Tim.* 69d-72d). For much of the Christian tradition, *soul* has referred to the spiritual part of a human distinct from the physical or as an ontologically separate entity constitutive of the human person. In his *Treatise on the Soul*, Tertullian (ca. 160–225 CE) represented the theological tendency to assert the immortality of the soul, the superiority of the soul over the body, and the related view that the person is detachable from his or her body, which then requires discipline in order to function as the soul's instrument. Questions about that traditional body-soul dualism have arisen especially on two fronts. The first is biblical studies, which since the early 20th cent. almost unanimously supported a unitary account of the human person. The second is neuroscience, which since its 17th-cent. origins has demonstrated again and again the close mutual interrelations of physical and psychological occurrences, documenting the neural correlates of the various attributes traditionally allocated to the soul.

Biblical scholars have underscored the witness of Gen 1–2 that the human person does not possess a "soul" but is a soul; noted that the same is also true of animals, who are "souls" or, better, "living beings" (nefesh, compare Gen 1:30; 2:7); and more generally argued that the OT is generally uninterested in speculation about human essences, instead presenting the human person in profoundly relational terms. Throughout the OT, nefesh is used with reference to the whole person as the seat of desire and emotion, not to the "inner self" as though this were something separate from one's being. **Nefesh** can be translated in many places as "person," or even by the personal pronoun (e.g., Lev 2:1; 4:2; 7:20). Within the OT, **nefesh** typically refers to life and vitality—not life in general, but as instantiated in human persons and animals; not a thing to have but a way to be. To speak of loving God with all of one's "soul" (Deut 6:5), then, is to elevate the intensity of involvement of the entirety of one's being. From time to time, the Hebrew term **basar** (בָּשָׂר, "flesh, body") stands in parallel with but not in contrast to **nefesh**—the one referring to the external being of the person, the other to the internal (e.g., Ps 84:2; Isa 10:18). Although **basar** frequently refers to the fleshly aspect of a person (e.g., Gen 40:19), it can also refer to humankind (e.g., Gen 6:12), including humanity in terms of its frailty (in contrast to God; e.g., Ps 78:39). **Basar** and **nefesh** might thus refer to different aspects of personal existence, but not to discrete parts of the human person. The OT employs other terminology, too, to speak of humans from the perspective of their varying functions—e.g., lev (לֵב), with reference to human existence, sometimes in its totality (e.g., Gen 18:5; Ezek 13:22), sometimes with reference to the center of human affect (e.g., Prov 14:30) or perception (Prov 16:9); and **ruakh** (רוּחַ), used with reference to humans from the perspective of their being imbued with life (e.g., Gen 2:7; Job 12:10; Isa 42:5). In short, the OT provides no particularly "scriptural" vocabulary for anthropological analysis, but rather draws on the common terminology of the ANE in order to depict the human person as an integrated whole.

The background on which the NT writers drew was heavily influenced by Israel's Scriptures, but also by Greco-Roman thought. Greco-Roman perspectives on body and soul were more varied than usually represented, however. Although belief in a form of body-soul duality was widespread in some philosophical circles, for example, most of these regarded the soul as composed of "stuff," some combination of atoms and spirit, for example (Lucretius, *De rerum natura* 3.231–257). Moreover, ancient medical writers emphasized the in-

separability of the body's internal processes ("psychology") and its external aspects ("physiology"); this is because any differentiation between inner and outer was fluid and permeable. Read against the backdrop of the OT and within its own cultural milieu, then, the NT continues the holistic anthropology of the OT.

Thus, for example, Matt 10:28 ("Do not fear those who kill the body but cannot kill the soul; rather fear him who can destroy both soul and body in hell") may echo the martyr-theology of such texts as Wis 16:13-14 and 2 Macc 6:30. These Hellenistic Jewish texts maintained that persecutors have access only to the body, but only God has power over the whole person. Nevertheless, the parallel in Luke 12:4 suggests no more than that those who are persecuted should take comfort in knowing that martyrdom is the end only of one's existence in this world and not the end of one's life. Accordingly, **psychē** would refer not to "soul" but to "vitality." To cite another example, nor does Paul's benediction in 1 Thess 5:23 provide testimony to a tripartite understanding of human nature (spirit, soul, and body). The parallelism of the two phrases—"May the God of peace himself sanctify you completely//and may your spirit and soul and body be preserved in entirety, free from blame…"—signifies that Paul uses these three terms to repeat and expand on the idea of "completely." This is not a list of "parts," then, but a reference to "your whole being."

Taken as a whole, the biblical witness affirms the human being as a biopsychospiritual unity and provides no support for the later substance dualism of Descartes. Accordingly, the term *soul* would refer to embodied human life and especially to present, embodied human capacities for personal relatedness vis-a-vis the cosmos, the human family, and God. *See* AFTERLIFE; BODY; HEART; SPIRIT.

Bibliography: Klaus Berger. *Identity and Experience in the New Testament* (2003); Robert A. Di Vito. "Old Testament Anthropology and the Construction of Personal Identity." *CBQ* 61 (1999) 217–38; Christopher Gill. *The Structured Self in Hellenistic and Roman Thought* (2006); Joel B. Green. *Body, Soul, and Human Life: The Nature of Humanity in the Bible* (2008); Joel B. Green, ed. *What about the Soul? Neuroscience and Christian Anthropology* (2004); John P. Wright and Paul Potter, eds. *Psyche and Soma: Physicians and Metaphysicians on the Mind-Body Problem from Antiquity to Enlightenment* (2000).

JOEL B. GREEN

SOURCE CRITICISM. 1. The phrase "source criticism" refers to the hypothesis that biblical authors and/or editors used sources when writing and/or compiling OT literature. Many biblical books contain citations to such sources: "Wherefore it is said in the Book of the Wars of the LORD …" (Num 21:14); "These are other proverbs of Solomon that the officials of King Hezekiah of Judah copied" (Prov 25:1). Moreover, there are references to sources even if they are not quoted, e.g., "the Book of the Annals of the Kings of Judah" (2 Kgs 23:28). In addition, there is strong evidence that biblical authors used other comparable sources, e.g., a collection of psalms of ascent (Pss 120–134), even if these sources bore no formal titles. Nonetheless, "source criticism," for most biblical scholars, reflects theories regarding the formation of particular bodies of literature, e.g., that the books of Samuel are made of up separate narrative sources, one of which is the so-called ark narrative (1 Sam 4:1–7:2). Of such theories, that addressing the formation of the PENTATEUCH has pride of place. The DOCUMENTARY HYPOTHESIS involves the claim that the first five books of the OT represent the combination of four distinct sources or "documents." In its classic form, these sources were known as "J," the Yahwistic source ("J" for the German spelling of Yahweh)—e.g., Gen 2:4b–3:24; "E," the Elohistic source—e.g., Gen 20; "D," the Deuteronomic source—the book of Deuteronomy; and "P," the Priestly source—e.g., Gen 1:1–2:4a. This hypothesis holds that the TETRATEUCH represents an interweaving of JEP and that D is present in Deuteronomy. Though many scholars continue to defend this hypothesis, others have offered alternatives, e.g., that the Pentateuch grew from an early narrative with a series of supplements or that, like Samuel, the Pentateuch is made up originally of a series of collections that were combined during the Persian period. Regardless of the fate of the Documentary Hypothesis, few scholars would deny that the creators of the OT used sources. As a result, some form of "source criticism" will remain important in biblical studies. *See* BIBLICAL CRITICISM; BIBLICAL INTERPRETATION, HISTORY OF; BOOKS REFERRED TO IN THE BIBLE; D, DEUTERONOMIC, DEUTERONOMISTIC; E, ELOHIST; J, YAHWIST; P, PRIESTLY WRITERS; REDACTION CRITICISM, NT; REDACTION CRITICISM, OT.

DAVID L. PETERSEN

2. In NT studies, source criticism analyzes NT texts in the attempt to discover the materials used by their authors. The process aspires to gain historical, literary, and theological insights into the early Christian authors, their texts, and their communities. Source Criticism focuses especially on Matthew, Mark, and Luke, which are known as the "Synoptic Gospels" because they can be read side by side in a "synopsis." The synopsis shows major agreements in wording and order among the Synoptic Gospels, and the "SYNOPTIC PROBLEM" is the study of this evidence.

The basis of the Synoptic Problem is that there is some kind of literary relationship between the Synoptic Gospels. There are four major types of material, triple tradition (common to all three Synoptics), double tradition (common to Matthew and Luke alone), Special Matthew and Special Luke. In the triple tradition material, Mark is usually the "middle term," which means

that the agreements between Matthew and Luke are mediated through Mark. The most common explanation for this phenomenon is called "Markan Priority" or the "Priority of Mark," the idea that Mark was the primary source for Matthew and Luke. If Matthew and Luke used Mark independently of one another, the double tradition material necessitates the postulation of a hypothetical source "Q" (*see* Q, QUELLE). This is the "Two Source Theory," that Matthew and Luke used two sources, Mark and Q; it is currently the dominant view in the guild. An alternative view is the "Farrer Theory," which accepts Marcan Priority but dispenses with Q by suggesting that Luke knew Matthew. The "Griesbach theory" proposes that Matthew was written first and that Luke used Matthew and Mark used all three.

Source criticism of John's Gospel is focused on two major questions: 1) Was John familiar with any of the Synoptic Gospels? and 2) Did John have a "signs source" for the passages in his Gospel that narrate Jesus' signs? Scholars remain divided on these issues.

MARK GOODACRE

SOURON. *See* HIRAM.

SOUTH. *See* ORIENTATION.

SOUTH ARABIA. *See* ARAB, ARABIAN, ARABIA.

SOUTH, THE. *See* NEGEB, NEGEV.

SOUTHERN KINGDOM. *See* ISRAEL, HISTORY OF.

SOW, SOWER [זרוע zeroaʿ; σπείρω speirō]. In an agrarian economy, the planting of crops is central to the survival of society. Since ancient Israel was an agrarian society, it is not surprising that the role of the sower and the act of sowing are an important part of biblical imagery.

In the OT, sowing is not merely the planting of crops. Sowing defines the parameters of Israel's covenant relationship with God. As a result, the law lists several restrictions about the sowing of seed including: when, what kind, and how often (Exod 23:10; Lev 19:19; 25:11, 22; Deut 22:9). The connection between God and farming is emphasized by the number of times that the sowing of seed is either blessed or cursed depending on Israel's faithfulness to God (Ps 107:37; Isa 30:23; 55:10; Mic 6:15; compare Isa 19:7; Jer 50:16).

Because the process of sowing and reaping was reflective of much of life, it easily lent itself to the realm of metaphor. God is described as a sower who plants Israel and Judah in the land (Jer 31:27; Hos 2:23; Ezek 36:9), and sows peace in Zion and righteousness among the nations (Isa 61:11; Zech 8:12). Acts of repentance are described with agrarian imagery in which righteousness is a crop that is sown (Jer 4:3; Hos 10:12). The imagery is used to warn against sowing trouble (Job 4:8), discord (Prov 6:19), and injustice (Prov 22:8) since people will reap what they have sown (compare Jer 12:13). Conversely, those who sow tears will reap joy (Ps 126:5-6).

In the NT, the imagery is used either metaphorically or as part of a parable. Paul reiterates the OT aphorism that a person reaps what was sown (Gal 6:7-8). Sometimes he describes his ministry through the imagery of sowing (1 Cor 3:6-8; 9:11). More significant, however, is Paul's adaptation of sowing imagery to describe the resurrection. The picture of sowing a seed is correlated with the death and burial of the human body. Just as a seed is buried and brings forth a crop greater than the original seed, so too the resurrected body will be greater than the former (1 Cor 15:36-44; compare John 12:24). Paul uses sowing imagery when encouraging the Corinthians to give generously towards the Jerusalem offering. Although they are not under compulsion, Paul reminds them that God loves a generous giver and will reward them according to the amount they have sown (2 Cor 9:6-10).

In the Gospels, all references to sowing are contained in Jesus' parables. Jesus uses the imagery of sowing to describe the expansion of the kingdom of God (Matt 13:31; Luke 13:19), and how both evil and good are sown into the world (Matt 13:24-30; 36-43). The most significant of these parables is that of the sower in the Synoptic Gospels (Matt 13:3-23; Mark 4:3-20; Luke 8:5-15). It is clear that, as with God in the OT, Jesus is the sower and his message is the seed that is sown into the various types of soil. *See* AGRICULTURE; PARABLE.

JOHN BYRON

SPAIN spayn [Σπανία Spania]. The Romans called the Iberian peninsula, located between the Mediterranean Sea and Atlantic Ocean, Hispania (Hispania Ἰσπανία). Today, Portugal and Spain share the peninsula.

Spain has been occupied since the Paleolithic period. By around 1500 BCE, its inhabitants fell into two major groups. Celtic tribes occupied the central and northwestern quadrant of the peninsula. The southern and eastern portions of the peninsula were occupied by non-Indo-Europeans known as Iberians, perhaps from north Africa or the eastern Mediterranean.

By around 1100 BCE, Phoenicians began to establish colonies along the southern coast. The Greeks did likewise during the 7th cent. BCE. While these settlements had land to grow grain, they were primarily trading posts. They did not exert military or political control over the hinterland. This changed after the first Punic war (264–241 BCE).

In the first Punic war, Rome defeated Carthage (initially a Phoenician colony) and captured Sardinia. This prompted Carthage to begin to conquer the Iberian peninsula. After the second Punic war (218–202 BCE), Rome assumed control of Spain and gradually conquered its natives and Romanized them, building roads, aqueducts and irrigation systems, and many

towns and colonies (compare 1 Macc 8:1-4). The inhabitants resisted fiercely, and the peninsula was not pacified until the reign of Augustus (27 BCE–14 CE). The Roman colonies in Spain produced several emperors (Trajan, Hadrian, Maximus, and Theodosius) and also literary figures (Seneca the Elder, Seneca the Younger, and others).

Spain does not feature prominently in the Bible. It may have been the destination of Jonah, since Tarshish (Jonah 1:3) may possibly be Tartessus. Paul desired to travel to Spain (Rom 15:24, 28), but whether he did so is unclear. Luke says that Paul spent two years in Rome, where he was allowed to teach "without hindrance" (Acts 28:30). Perhaps during this time he traveled to Spain. Around 96 CE, Clement wrote that Paul traveled to "the farthest bounds of the West" (*1 Clem.* 5:7), presumably Spain. The 2nd-cent. *Acts of Peter* mentions Paul's departure from Rome's harbor (chap. 3). And the Muratorian Canon, compiled around 170 CE, also mentions Paul's Spanish mission (lines 38–39). But if Paul made such a trip, why would Luke not mention it? Perhaps the mission failed; no Spanish church claimed to have been founded by Paul. Alternately, Paul did not go to Spain: this was the opinion of the 5th-cent. pope Gelasius and most modern scholars.

The first clear evidence of Christianity in Spain comes from a mid-3rd cent. debate about whether two Spanish bishops should retain their positions after having sacrificed to pagan deities during the persecution of Decius in 250. A Spanish church council at the beginning of the 4th cent. shows that there were at least thirty-seven Christian congregations by the 3rd cent. But the origin and early history of the church in Spain is unclear.

Bibliography: O. F. A. Meinardus. "Paul's Missionary Journey to Spain: Tradition and Folklore." *BA* 41 (1978) 61–63; J. S. Richardson. *The Romans in Spain* (1998); M. Williams. *The Story of Spain* (2000).

ADAM L. PORTER

SPAN [זֶרֶת zereth, רֹחַב rokhav; ἡλικία hēlikia]. A unit of length, roughly the distance between the tip of the thumb and the tip of the little finger of an outstretched hand (Exod 28:16; 39:9; 1 Sam 17:4, etc.). Ezekiel (43:13) identifies it as half a cubit (25 cm). It is also used to refer to a length of time (Ps 90:10; Sir 30:22; Matt 6:27; Luke 12:25). *See* WEIGHTS AND MEASURES.

RAZ KLETTER

SPARROW [צִפּוֹר tsippor; στρουθίον strouthion]. The apparently onomatopoeic tsippor can be regarded as a generic term for all passerine birds (*see* BIRDS OF THE BIBLE). In some OT passages, it is used in that wide, generic sense, where the most appropriate translation is "bird" (Gen 7:14; Deut 4:17; 14:11; 22:6; Pss 8:8 [Heb. 8:9]; 11:1; Prov 7:23; Ezek 17:23; 39:4; Amos

3:5). In other cases, when tsippor is mentioned in conjunction with another word designating a specific bird, it is better to translate "sparrow," as with the sparrow and the swallow, seemingly a conventional pair (Ps 84:3 [Heb. 84:4]; Prov 26:2). In these cases, the reference is probably to the house sparrow (*Passer domesticus*), a common sight in all cities and villages, rather than the marsh sparrow (*Passer hispaniolensis*). Huge colonies of the latter can be found in the Jordan Valley. In the NT period, sparrows were sold in great amounts and at very low prices in the market places. The saying in Matt 10:29-31 and Luke 12:6-7, where Jesus underlines God's care for each sparrow, should be understood against that background.

GÖRAN EIDEVALL

SPARTA spahr′tuh [Σπάρτη Spartē]. A city in southern Greece, also known as Lacedaemon. Sparta became the most powerful Greek city after defeating Athens in the Peloponnesian War (431–401 BCE).

Sparta is mentioned several times in 1–2 Maccabees. According to 2 Macc 5:9, Jason fled to Sparta (author's trans.; NRSV, "to the Lacedaemonians") because of "kinship." This may suggest that a colony of Jews had settled in Sparta, or it may allude to common Abrahamic ancestry (1 Macc 12:20). The Hasmoneans sought allies against the Seleucids, including Sparta (1 Macc 12:1-2; 14:20-23). Also, Sparta appears in the list of cities (1 Macc 15:23), which received a letter from the Roman consul Lucius in 142 BCE, requesting kindly treatment of Jews and the return of Judean "scoundrels" to Judea.

ADAM L. PORTER

SPEAR. *See* WAR, METHODS, TACTICS, WEAPONS OF (BRONZE AGE THROUGH PERSIAN PERIOD); WAR, METHODS, TACTICS, WEAPONS OF (HELLENISTIC THROUGH ROMAN PERIODS).

SPECK [κάρφος karphos]. A small piece of material used metaphorically to refer to something very small by comparison to something else. In Wis 11:22 the world to a speck contrasted with God's power. In Matt 7:3-5 (//Luke 6:41-42) with regard to judging others, Jesus reminds us of the subjectivity of our perspectives. We magnify others' small transgressions, while overlooking our own.

EMILY ASKEW

SPECKLED. *See* COLORS.

SPELT [כֻּסֶּמֶת kussemeth]. A hard-grained variety of WHEAT cultivated in the ANE (*Triticum aestivum var. spelta*). It is possible that the biblical *spelt* is actually emmer (*Triticum dicoccum*), although it has a tougher husk. Sown in the fall, spelt can be grown in poorly drained, sandy, low-fertility soil and comes to harvest later than barley (Exod 9:32; note that spelt was not native to Egypt). Ground into flour with other grains for bread (Ezek 4:9), spelt has a sweet, nutty flavor. It may have had lesser value to farmers since it is placed on the field's border in the agricultural metaphor in Isa 28:25, rather than in rows like wheat (*Triticum durum*). *See* GRAIN.

VICTOR H. MATTHEWS

SPICE [בֹּשֶׂם bosem; ἄμωμον amōmon, ἄρωμα arōma]. Given the pungent odors that permeated human dwellings and cities, it is not surprising that the ancient world put a high premium on fragrant spices that could mask the smells associated with both life and death. Some of these products (BALM, CUMIN, DILL, MINT) could be obtained in Israel, but the more exotic formed a lucrative portion of the caravan trade throughout the ANE (ALOES from southwest Arabia, CALAMUS from Asia, CINNAMON from Sri Lanka). For example, when the Queen of Sheba visited Solomon, her camels were laden with valuable presents including an unheard of quantity of spices (1 Kgs 10:2, 10). Trading networks are mentioned in the lament for Babylon in Rev 18:13, which describes vast commercial interests that trafficked in cinnamon, spices, and incense as well as ivory, grain, and slaves (compare the lament for Tyre's trading network in Ezek 27:22). The high value attached to spices is demonstrated by Hezekiah's boasting display of his storehouses for the envoy sent by the Babylonian king Merodach-baladan, which featured among his most precious possessions a large quantity of spices (2 Kgs 20:13).

Within the realm of religious practice, spices functioned as a means of defining sacred space and enhancing ritual performance. Thus, the spice offerings required of the people as part of their service to the tabernacle (Exod 25:6) were used to create a distinctive fragrance in the lamp oil that marked this place as holy (Exod 35:28). In addition, spices were incorporated into the recipe for the anointing oil used by the priests (Exod 30:23). Their use in sacred ritual is solemnized by the assignment of a group of priests to the task of mixing spices for ceremonies in the Temple in Jerusalem (1 Chr 9:30).

On a more mundane level, spices served as condiments adding flavor to food and drinks (see the comparison between manna and CORIANDER SEED; Exod 16:31). Most often, however, spices such as calamus, SAFFRON, and NARD are mentioned in relation to the manufacture of PERFUME (see especially the metaphorical use of spiced fragrances in Song 5:1, 13 and the reference to spices and aromatic plants in the pleasure garden in Song 4:12-15). Various spices, such as CASSIA, were mixed with myrrh and cinnamon to perfume robes (Ps 45:8 [Heb. 45:9]) and to freshen bed linens (Prov 7:17). To honor the dead and to mask or delay the smells associated with the decaying of the body, spices were mixed to anoint the corpse (see the preparations made for Jesus' body; Mark 16:1; Luke 23:56), and were sprinkled into the folds of the linen winding cloth (John 19:40). For state funerals, such as that for King Asa of Judah, huge quantities of spices were mixed by professional perfumers and mingled with the wood of his bier. When burned, the resulting fragrance would have marked him as a powerful man (2 Chr 16:14). *See* PLANTS OF THE BIBLE.

VICTOR H. MATTHEWS

SPIDER [עַכָּבִישׁ ʿakkavish]. An arachnid. Biblical poets use its delicately built dwellings as a metaphor for that which is transitory. In Isa 59:5-6, the inadequate works of sinners and the unjust are compared to clothing made of spider webs. Bildad asserts that the "trust" of the godless is a "spider's house" (Job 8:14). In a footnote to Prov 30:28, the NRSV offers the reading "spider" for "lizard." Also, in a footnote to Wis 5:14, the NRSV offers the reading "spider's web" as an alternative for "light frost." *See* INSECTS OF THE BIBLE.

LISA MICHELE WOLFE

SPIES [חָפַר khafar, רָגַל raghal, תּוּר tur; ἐγκάθετος enkathetos, κατασκοπέω kataskopeō, κατάσκοπος kataskopos]. The Bible primarily describes spies in an official, military context where they are sent out to reconnoiter enemy towns prior to a military encounter (Gen 42:9 [Joseph accuses his brothers of being spies]; Josh 2:1 [spies sent into Jericho]) and to track enemy movements (1 Sam 26:4 [David's spies track Saul]; 1 Macc 12:26 [Jonathan's spies watch Demetrius's forces]). Of note are the spy narratives in Num 13:1–14:45 and Josh 2:1-24 (compare Heb 11:31).

Spies are sent by the scribes and chief priests to trap Jesus concerning paying taxes in an effort to hand him over to the civil authorities (Luke 20:20). One should be careful choosing friends because the proud can be like spies (Sir 11:30). Paul calls those who insist on circumcision for Gentile Christians "spies" (Gal 2:4).

R. ANDREW COMPTON

SPIN, SPINNING. *See* CLOTH, CLOTHES; DISTAFF.

SPINDLE. *See* DISTAFF.

SPIRIT. *See* HOLY SPIRIT; SPIRITUAL GIFTS; SPIRITUALITY.

SPIRIT, HOLY. *See* HOLY SPIRIT.

SPIRITS IN PRISON [τὰ ἐν φυλακῇ πνεύματα ta en phylakē pneumata]. This enigmatic phrase in 1 Pet 3:19 has been understood to refer to the souls of dead humans (1 Pet 4:6 speaks of the gospel being preached to the dead). The NT, however, never uses *spirits* (pneumata) to refer to the dead. The NT and other Christian and Jewish literature use *spirits* to refer to malevolent angelic beings, often associated with the "sons of God" who mated with human women (Gen 6:1-4), and their demonic offspring. The "prison" is not the abode of

the dead, but the place evil powers are restrained, as in 2 Pet 2:4; Jude 6; Rev 20:7. So, Christ confirms the condemnation of these evil beings when he proclaims his victory to them.

JERRY L. SUMNEY

SPIRITS, DISCERNMENT OR TESTING OF [διάκρισις πνευμάτων diakrisis pneumatōn]. Paul mentions the "discernment of spirits" as a spiritual gift (1 Cor 12:10). This gift probably had two dimensions. First, discernment meant determining whether a spirit came from God or from another source. In 1 John 4:1, the advice to "test the spirits to see whether they are from God" implies that a person could be inspired by some being other than God. Second, discernment meant evaluating messages from those known to possess the gift of prophecy (1 Cor 14:29; 1 Thess 5:20-22) in order to determine whether a particular prophetic utterance fitted the congregation's needs and represented God's word to them at that moment. Since prophecy in the early church was the gift of proclaiming the specific word from God that fitted a specific community's needs, the whole church also participated in determining whether the message was from God. *See* PROPHET IN THE NT AND EARLY CHURCH.

JERRY L. SUMNEY

SPIRITUAL BODY [σῶμα πνευματικόν sōma pneumatikon]. In opposition to some at Corinth who envisioned the afterlife as an immortal soul communing with God without the encumbrance of a body, in 1 Cor 15:35-58 Paul describes human existence in the resurrection as a spiritual body (v. 44). This resurrection body is patterned after the body of the resurrected Christ and participates in the new life initiated by Christ's resurrection. For Paul, "spiritual" does not mean "nonmaterial." Ancient writers thought different types of matter existed in different realms. The spiritual body partakes of a finer, eternal matter. It is related to—and continuous with—the present body, but radically transformed, composed of elements of a higher order. So though not "flesh and blood," it is still a material body. Only as bodily beings can those resurrected have fully human existence. The concept of a spiritual body affirms the goodness of embodied existence. *See* ANTHROPOLOGY, NT THEOLOGICAL; RESURRECTION, NT.

Bibliography: Dale Martin. *The Corinthian Body* (1995).

JERRY L. SUMNEY

SPIRITUAL FRUIT. *See* FRUIT OF THE SPIRIT.

SPIRITUAL GIFTS [χαρίσματα charismata]. Spiritual gifts are a characteristic feature of the apostle Paul's theology. Best known in the context of the ministry of early congregations, spiritual gifts are formulated in controversy with certain members of the Corinthian church called "Pneumatics" (pneumatikoi πνευματικοί), who regard their newfound powers, especially glossolalia, as a spiritual endowment (see TONGUES, GIFT OF). They boast in their extraordinary abilities by designating them "spiritual things" (pneumatika πνευματικά), because they feel empowered and endowed by the Spirit. In response, in 1 Cor 12–14 Paul redefines these abilities as "gifts" (charismata), without denying the presence of the eschatological Spirit in their midst. Thus, while conceding the spiritual nature of these extravagant abilities, Paul insists that they are free gifts given by God the giver, so that the Corinthians have no ground to boast, and the status differentials engendered thereby must be brought under scrutiny (see HOLY SPIRIT). In the NT, the term charisma (χάρισμα, "gift") occurs only in Paul's letters, in writings influenced by him (1 Tim 4:14; 2 Tim 1:6), and in 1 Pet 4:10.

What prompts Paul's elaborate discussion of charismata in 1 Cor 12–14 is glossolalia. This is clear from the movement of these chapters towards the climactic discussion of this issue in chap. 14. Paul does not question the legitimacy of speaking in tongues, since he lists it among the gifts (12:10, 28, 30). He even admits to speaking in tongues himself, in fact, more than anyone else (14:18). But he does question the Pneumatics' penchant for using it to enhance their status in the community. Glossolalia, like many theological issues in Corinth, divided the community along social lines. "Esoteric speech" was regarded as the language of gods and spirits (compare Paul's "tongues of angels" of 13:1); anyone with such ability was thought to be capable of communicating with higher beings and could therefore claim high status in the community.

Elitism has deleterious effects on the community, for conflicts along social lines are inimical to the egalitarian vision of the early Jesus-movement. As an immediate response to glossolalic elitism, Paul places glossolalia at the bottom of his list of gifts (12:28) and couples it with the ability of interpretation (12:10, 30; 14:4, 13, 26). Here as well as throughout 1 Corinthians, Paul exhorts the Pneumatics who have achieved high status to forego their personal privileges for the sake of those who have yet to reach these lofty heights. If "all things are permissible" (so claim the Pneumatics), Paul answers that they must also ask if what they do is also beneficial to the whole community (1 Cor 6:12; 10:23). That is why Paul elevates interpretation of tongues over the gift of tongues, for while the latter benefits only the speaker, interpretation translates esoteric language into intelligible words that would benefit all people and thus build up the community (14:5, 13-18, 27-28; compare also v. 12).

To lay the groundwork for his pointed answers to the Corinthians' obsession with tongues, Paul in 1 Cor 12 contextualizes this extraordinary power in a larger theological vision of the community as "body" and individual spiritual powers as "gifts." That Paul begins the discussion with his typical introductory formula,

"Concerning the spiritual gifts ... I do not want you to be ignorant" (12:1; compare 1 Thess 4:9, 13; 5:1; etc.), strongly suggests this is a topic the Corinthians themselves raised with Paul. It is also likely that they are the ones who designate their extraordinary abilities, especially glossolalia, as "spirit-endowed things." The Pneumatics place the emphasis on the power itself and the person endowed with such power. Paul does not deny the spiritual origins of these abilities, which is why he returns to and stays with the Corinthians' terminology in chap. 14, where he takes up glossolalia head on. He even concedes in 14:12 that it is perfectly legitimate to pursue such "spiritual things." In 12:4, however, he switches from "spiritual things" to "gifts" because he wants to accentuate the active agency of the divine Spirit.

The active agency of the Spirit is already mapped out in the enigmatic 12:2-3, where Paul sets up the premise for his ensuing argument. Verse 2 emphatically reminds the Corinthians that during their pagan days, when they were dealing with mute idols, they were little more than passive pawns being led from place to place. If so, how much more true would it be with the Holy Spirit? The transition from v. 2 to v. 3 is based on analogy (Bassler): if the Corinthians are empowered to say "Jesus is Lord"—and they are, so that is not the point of controversy—then that is proof enough that the Spirit is free and active. This point Paul in fact makes explicit in 12:11: "All these are activated by one and the same Spirit, who allots to each one individually just as the Spirit chooses." The determinative freedom of the Spirit is further strengthened by the liberal use of divine passive "is given" in 12:7-8 and implied in 12:9-10. A few verses later, Paul similarly reminds the Corinthians of God's freedom in choosing to endow the body with individual members (12:18). Accordingly, it would seem to suit Paul's argument better to read 12:4 as "there are allotments of gifts, but the same Spirit."

If the same Spirit stands behind all forms of power, then these are nothing more than manifestation of the one Spirit. As such, they are designed to fulfill the purpose intended by the Spirit—"for the benefit of the community" (NRSV, "for the common good," 12:7; compare use of the same expression in 6:12; 7:35; 10:23, 33). At issue is the egalitarian vision of the community being threatened by the Pneumatics' inflated sense of self-aggrandizement. Without this egalitarianism, schism would take place (12:25). In response, Paul contends that everyone has gifts (compare 7:7 and Rom 12:6), even if not everyone has the same gift (12:14-21). In 12:4, 7-10, the repetition of "Spirit" indicates that Paul is willing to grant the Pneumatics the connection between charisma and the Spirit, but the insistent refrain "the same Spirit" strikes a counter-note of equality, which is a foundation for unity (12:12-26). This Paul elaborates using the metaphor of the body: "For just as the body is one and has many members, and all the members of the body, though many, are one body, so it is with Christ" (12:12; compare Rom 12:4-5).

First Corinthians 12–14 makes use of terminology and imagery that are part and parcel of Hellenistic political discourse of Paul's days (Mitchell). The body as a political metaphor in that context is a hierarchical construct (Martin), but Paul questions it by giving disproportionate significance to the weak, the dishonorable, shameful members of the body (possible euphemisms for the genitals), for these are in fact clothed with greater honor and respect than other parts of the body, according to him (12:22-25). Thus, in a reversal of Hellenistic logic, these lower functions have received higher status in Paul's imagery (Martin). The reason is that their protection and elevation in status serves the greater good of the whole body, whose well-being transcends the concerns for status of individual members. That is why the greatest spiritual gift of all, when the body principle is applied, is love (13:1-13). It is clear that this argument, alongside the consistent effort of listing speaking in tongues last in the list of spiritual gifts or subordinating it under interpretation of tongues, is part and parcel of Paul's overall strategy to combat glossolalic elitism (so John Chrysostom, *Hom. 2 Cor.* 32.2).

There can be no denying that "first apostles, second prophets, third teachers; then ..." (12:28) represents some form of ranking. *Apostle* is a contested title for Paul, for it carries the authority of being commissioned by the risen Lord. Given how eager he claims the title for himself and how slighted he feels whenever the title is denied him, it is not surprising that he would rank it high on the list. A prophet is one who proclaims a revelation in a worship setting, as many scholars have noted and as Paul himself makes clear in chap. 14. A prophet is different from a teacher not so much because one is spontaneous and the other is not; rather, a prophet announces, proclaims, and judges, whereas a teacher transmits, communicates, explains, and interprets (Thiselton). Nevertheless, in spite of a seeming reinstatement of hierarchy in the body, it should be remembered that Paul's list of spiritual gifts in 1 Cor 12 is neither systematic nor exhaustive but occasional—for the purpose of resisting elevating glossolalia above all else. The controlling pattern of thought is one of spiritual gifts all working together for the greater good of the body. That the list of spiritual gifts in Rom 12:6-8 is different in content and in order should counsel against absolutizing any form of ranking.

But the inclusion of functions of ministry among the charismata does start a development of vesting offices with the power of the Spirit, which reaches its full form in the Pastorals. According to the author of 1 Timothy, the gift is now the property of leaders of the emerging church, which can be passed on from generation to generation. Thus, Timothy the minister receives this gift "through prophecy with the laying on of hands by the council of elders" (1 Tim 4:14), as well as "the laying on of my hands" by the literary Paul himself (2 Tim 1:6). While this gift is characterized not by "a spirit of cowardice, but rather a spirit of power and of love and of self-discipline" (2 Tim 1:7), the exclusive nature of the conferral indicates that this gift is coterminous with the apostolic authority vested in the office Timothy now occupies. The use of **charisma** in 1 Pet 4:10, on the other hand, does not reflect the Pastorals' proprietary understanding of gifts. In connecting it explicitly to grace but still grounding it in ministry, "Like good stewards of the manifold grace of God, serve one another with whatever gift each of you has received," it rather echoes Paul's usage in Rom 12:6.

Bibliography: Jouette Bassler. "1 Cor 12:3—Curse and Confession in Context." *JBL* 101 (1982) 415–21; E. Earle Ellis. "'Spiritual' Gifts in the Pauline Community." *Prophecy and Hermeneutic in Early Christianity* (1978) 23–44; Gordon D. Fee. *God's Empowering Presence: The Holy Spirit in the Letters of Paul* (1994); Ernst Käsemann. "Ministry and Community in the New Testament." *Essays on New Testament Themes* (1964) 63–94; John Koenig. *Charismata: God's Gifts for God's People* (1978); Dale Martin. "Tongues of Angels and Other Status Indicators." *JAAR* 59 (1991) 547–89; Ralph Martin. *The Spirit and the Congregation: Studies in 1 Corinthians 12–15* (1984); Margaret Mitchell. *Paul and the Rhetoric of Reconciliation: An Exegetical Investigation of the Language and Composition of 1 Corinthians* (1991); Anthony Thiselton. "The 'Interpretation' of Tongues: A New Suggestion in the Light of Greek Usage in Philo and Josephus." *JTS* 30 (1979) 15–36; Anthony Thiselton. *The First Epistle to the Corinthians.* NIGTC (2000).

SZE-KAR WAN

SPIRITUALITY. *Spirituality* is a term whose meaning has changed radically in the past fifty years, and no one definition is generally accepted either by practitioners of the spiritual life or by scholars who study the subject. The term is actually a substantive derived from the adjective "spiritual," which Paul coined to refer primarily to that which is under the influence of the/a "spirit," usually the Spirit of God. For example, gifts (Rom 1:11; 1 Cor 12:1), law (Rom 7:14), persons (1 Cor 2:15), food and drink (1 Cor 10:3-4), and hymns (Eph 5:19; Col 3:16) could all be qualified as spiritual. Today the term *spirituality* is not necessarily religious in meaning, much less Christian, and often has little or nothing to do with the divine Spirit. Most often its referent is the experience of the human spirit or whatever is considered most central to the human person. Consequently, it is necessary to specify the term carefully for the purposes of this article. We will proceed from the most general meaning of the term, to its specificity in Christian tradition, to one dimension of Christian spirituality, namely, the biblical.

A. What Is Spirituality?

Spirituality in contemporary discourse can have an anthropological or an experiential referent. All humans, no matter their age, gender, race, religion or lack thereof, life circumstances, etc., are constitutively "spiritual," i.e., they have the capacity for personal self-transcendence through relationship with whatever they perceive as ultimate. This capacity is an anthropological constant, a feature of the *humanum* as such. However, the term *spirituality* is usually reserved for actual, i.e., experiential, relationship rather than merely the capacity for such. Furthermore, actual spirituality is not simply any particular relationship but the relation of the whole of the self to the whole of reality. It is a global self-situation within the horizon of whatever is considered ultimately real, valuable, meaningful, e.g., humanity (which might give rise to a humanistic spirituality), a value such as love (which might ground a spirituality of non-violence), or God (as in Christian or Jewish spirituality). Paul also talks about "spiritual forces of evil" (Eph 6:12) but in this case he is distinguishing these powers from material or inner-worldly forces. One would usually not speak of an essentially evil orientation to reality, e.g., alcoholism or Nazism, as a spirituality, even though they can have global and life-organizing power.

Spirituality in this experiential sense can be defined as the lived experience of conscious involvement in the project of life integration through self-transcendence toward the ultimate value one perceives. This working definition, which deliberately prescinds from specification by religion itself or religious tradition, captures several salient features of spirituality as it is understood today among scholars in the field. First, spirituality is not a set of beliefs or practices or even a series of mystical or transcendent episodes, however powerful. It is a conscious, ongoing life project that orients the whole person to the whole of reality as that person perceives it. Second, this project is progressively self and life-integrating. It gradually brings together thought, feeling, relationships, commitments, beliefs, hopes, loves, and practices into a coherent subjectivity. The person as a whole, inner and outer, material and spiritual, physical and emotional, intellectual, individual and social, personal and political

is the subject of spirituality. Not all people achieve a mature spirituality any more than all develop integrated personalities. But the less fragmented the person's orientation toward and relation with reality as a whole the more we recognize in her or him an authentic spirituality. Third, spirituality is integrating precisely because it is a process of self-transcendence that draws persons out of self-absorption, dispersion, and fragmentation by orienting them toward reality as a whole. And that orientation toward the whole is defined for the person by a horizon of ultimate concern, a perception of value that relativizes and orders the person in relation to everything other than the self.

B. Christian Spirituality: One or Many?

For the religious person the horizon of ultimate concern is God, however that term is understood or named. For the Christian, this ultimate reality is the triune God revealed in Jesus Christ and communicated to the believer by the Holy Spirit. Thus, Christian spirituality is the lived experience of progressive life-integration through participation in the paschal mystery of Jesus Christ, which involves participation in the ecclesial community, service in and to the world, ongoing and ever-deepening relationship with God through personal and corporate prayer, profession of a particular articulation of the faith, moral responsibility, and so on. But what makes this a spirituality, rather than simply membership in a religious organization, is that it is a personal, experiential, ongoing life project, which, under the action of the Spirit, progressively transforms the person into Christ according to her or his own personal constitution and life situation. Spirituality, in short, is personally appropriated and consciously lived experience of one's faith.

The previous paragraph suggests that certain common features characterize all Christian spirituality (e.g., monotheistic, trinitarian, and incarnational faith, ecclesial belonging, moral commitment, mission to the world, etc.). But, because spirituality is essentially experiential, it will be, like personality, also unique and diverse. The principles of division by which scholars in this field try to organize this diversity are numerous, overlapping, and not parallel or adequately distinct. For example, Christian spiritualities can be distinguished by denomination (e.g., Lutheran or Catholic) or tendencies (evangelical or liberal); by central traits (sacramental or scriptural) or devotions (Marian or liturgical); by charisms (Franciscan or Calvinist) or states of life (lay or clerical or monastic); by sensibility (nature-affirming or ascetical) or ecclesiastical organization (congregational or hierarchical) and so on. Even within such spiritualities, groups and/or individuals will manifest unique spiritualities. Again, analogous to the way we speak of personality as an anthropological constant that might be expressed in introverted or extroverted personalities, and of Mary's particular introverted personality, we speak of spirituality as an anthropological constant, of

Christian or ecological spiritualities, and of the spirituality of Teresa of Avila or Martin Luther.

C. What Is Biblical Spirituality?

1. All authentic Christian spirituality is biblical

The Bible understood as sacred Scripture, i.e., as canonical and revelatory, is central to Christianity because Scripture, and especially the NT, is the normative witness to Jesus Christ who is, for Christians, the locus of the revelation of God (*see* AUTHORITY OF SCRIPTURE; INSPIRATION AND REVELATION). Therefore, any authentic Christian spirituality must be biblical in the sense that it flows from, incarnates, is normed by, and rests upon the authority of Scripture for its claim to be a genuine response to the initiative of God in revelation.

2. Differences in the biblical character of Christian spiritualities

However, just as all Christian spiritualities share certain common features and yet are distinctive and manifest differences that are sometimes striking, so the biblical character that all authentic Christian spiritualities share can be diversely expressed. Protestantism, for example, was much more characterized by its devotion to the word of Scripture (and thus to preaching-based liturgy) during the post-Reformation period than was Catholicism, which was more sacramental (although the sacraments were biblically informed). Among religious/monastic orders there are spiritualities that are pervasively biblical, like Benedictinism, which is organized around the divine office primarily made up of readings from both testaments and *lectio divina* or prolonged meditation on biblical texts. But there are also ministerial orders in which service to the neighbor through the works of mercy limits the amount of time and energy devoted expressly to engagement with Scripture. Among individual Christians one finds those whose spirituality is almost exclusively biblical and others whose spirituality involves a variety of kinds of devotion, service, and practice that is not always explicitly scriptural. In short, there can be no authentic Christian spirituality that is not ultimately based on and expressive of the biblical revelation that inspires and norms the faith of the church. How individual believers, various groups, and different denominations, incorporate Scripture into their prayers and practice differs in extent and explicitness.

3. Specific meanings of biblical spirituality

Both the general term (Christian) *spirituality* and the more specialized term "biblical spirituality" can be used not only for the lived experience of faith (which has been the subject of this article up to this point) but also for the academic discipline that studies that experience. We have just been examining the former referent of biblical spirituality, namely, that engagement with the Bible as Scripture that characterizes in some way all lived experience of Christian faith. The following sections will be more concerned with biblical spirituality as an academic discipline in which the term is currently used in a variety of ways that can be grouped under three headings.

a. Spirituality in the Bible as a whole and in its parts. The student of the Bible who is interested in spirituality may have as a project to discern, describe, analyze, clarify, or present the spirituality of the Bible as a whole (e.g., as the covenant life of God and the people) or, more likely, the spirituality of some segment of Scripture (e.g., Deuteronomistic or Johannine spirituality), of some figure (e.g., Moses or Paul), of some type of texts (e.g., the psalms or the parables), or some theme (e.g., Exodus or discipleship). The project is to understand the experience of God that comes to expression characteristically in the texts under consideration. Old Testament scholars like Walter Brueggemann explicating the contrary orientations of monarchy and prophecy toward the relation of Yahweh to Israel, Abraham Heschel on the engagement of the prophets with God and the people, Roland Murphy on sapiential spirituality, John Endres on the psalms, Barbara Green on the spirituality of figures like Saul and Jonah, or the scholars who have worked on covenant spirituality, the theme of liberation, or Anawim spirituality demonstrate well this type of study. In the NT field scholars like Raymond Brown, Mary Coloe, Walter Wink, Marcus Borg, Luke Timothy Johnson, John R. Donahue, a number of feminist scholars investigating the faith and roles of women, and others who have worked on ecclesial spirituality, discipleship, indwelling, faith, conversion, prayer, and social justice in the NT also demonstrate this concern even when they would not (or at least not yet) use the term *spirituality* to describe their focus. What all of these scholars and their work have in common is the project of discerning and explicating the spirituality, i.e., the lived experience of relationship with God, which comes to expression in the biblical text.

b. Influence of the Bible as Scripture on readers. A second type of scholarship that might be called biblical spirituality comprises studies of the presence and role of biblical influence in the spirituality of particular individuals or groups. For example, Colin Thompson has published a remarkable study of the role of Scripture in the life and writings of John of the Cross. One could study the role of the Sermon on the Mount in the pacifist spirituality of Ghandi or Dorothy Day, or the influence of Exodus motifs in the rhetoric and practice of Martin Luther King, Jr. Critical studies of the biblical adequacy of certain presumably Christian spiritualities, of cults or new religious movements, or of the theology and practice of certain individuals are needed. In this case, what is being studied is not the spirituality that comes to expression in the Bible but the biblical character (or lack thereof) of the spiritualities of certain Christian groups or individuals. The purpose of such studies is usually analysis, explication, and criticism leading to deeper understanding of how Scripture can and should (and should not) function in Christian life.

c. Transformative engagement with the biblical text through interpretation. A third meaning of biblical spirituality as an academic discipline refers to the work on the text of the scholar, i.e., to a particular way of engaging the biblical text as a focus of study. Until relatively recently there was consensus among biblical scholars that the primary purpose of biblical study was to discern the intention of the biblical author(s) through historical-critical exegesis (*see* EXEGESIS; HISTORICAL CRITICISM). That consensus has imploded in the last few decades as a multiplicity of purposes for biblical study has generated a wide variety of approaches and methods (*see* BIBLICAL INTERPRETATION, HISTORY OF). Those seeking to change societal structures, to energize liberation movements, to resource new theological projects, to appreciate the narrative dynamics and rhetorical effectiveness of biblical texts as literature, to establish what can be known of the "historical Jesus," to exploit biblical resources for psychological understanding and growth, and so on have realized that their objectives could not be achieved by traditional methods (*see* FEMINIST INTERPRETATION; HISTORICAL JESUS; LIBERATION THEOLOGY; LITERATURE, THE BIBLE AS; PSYCHOLOGY AND BIBLICAL STUDIES).

Biblical spirituality as a way of dealing with the text belongs to this hermeneutical and critical development. Scholars whose approach to the text is that of biblical spirituality are interested in studying the biblical text, not in order to ascertain either the historical realities to which it refers or the intention of the author but, more like readers of great literature in general, in order to enter into the religious and spiritual world generated by the text in order to expand their own existential reality, to become different, through engagement with the word of God in the biblical text.

This transformative objective is not unlike that of the patristic and medieval commentators who approached Scripture as the word of God inherently capable of facilitating their spiritual quest for relationship with God (*see* PATRISTIC BIBLICAL INTERPRETATION). However, the approach and methods of these scholars differ significantly from those of their pre-Enlightment forebears in that they take completely seriously the advances in scholarship that produced the historical-critical method and its successors. The goal of personal transformation through interpretation and the explication of the text in such a way as to make its transformative potential accessible for both colleagues and non-professional readers is the same. But its hermeneutical and methodological sophistication makes it a modern and even postmodern project. Scholars who take a biblical spirituality approach to their work see the biblical text as Scripture and study it accordingly. But they also see themselves as scholars and their work as a contribution to the academic field of biblical study and proceed accordingly. Scholar and biblical text come together in the act of interpretation motivated by the quest for meaning that is genuinely transformative not only of the one studying but also of those who will be enlightened by the interpretation, and even eventually of the church and world for whom the Word became flesh and is now encountered in the biblical text.

Bibliography: M. Borg. *Meeting Jesus Again for the First Time* (1995); W. Brueggemann. *The Prophetic Imagination* (1978); J. Endres. "Psalms and Spirituality in the 21st Century." *Int* 56 (2002) 143– 54; R. E. Brown. *A Retreat with John the Evangelist: That You May Have Life* (1998); M. Coloe. *Dwelling in the House of God: Johannine Ecclesiology and Spirituality* (2007); J.R. Donahue and R. E. Brown. *Life in Abundance: Studies of John's Gospel* (2005); B. Green. *Jonah's Journeys* (2005); A. J. Heschel. *The Prophets* (1962); A. Holder, ed. *The Blackwell Companion to Christian Spirituality* (2005); L.T. Johnson. *Living Jesus: Learning the Heart of the Gospel* (2000); Roland Murphy. *The Psalms are Yours* (1993); Roland Murphy. *The Tree of Life: An Exploration of Biblical Wisdom Literature* (2002); P. Ricoeur. *Interpretation Theory: Discourse and the Surplus of Meaning* (1976); S. M. Schneiders. "Spirituality in the Academy." *TS* 50 (1989) 676–97; C. Thompson. *St. John of the Cross: Songs in the Night* (2002); B. Thurston. *Spiritual Life in the Early Church: The Witness of Acts and Ephesians* (1993); W. Wink. *The Powers that Be: Theology for a New Millenium* (1999); R. D. Witherup. *Conversion in the New Testament* (1994).

SANDRA M. SCHNEIDERS, IHM

SPIT [יָרַק yaraq, רָקַק raqaq; ἐμπτύω emptyō, πτύσμα ptysma, πτύω ptyō]. Spitting signifies derision and shame, as well illustrated in Isa 50:6 and Num 12:14. Deuteronomic legislation specifies that a widow must spit in the face of a brother-in-law who refuses the levirate responsibility (Deut 25:9). Spitting at an individual expressed the community's disdain for that person, as in the case of Job (30:10). Jesus had predicted that he would be spit at (Mark 10:34; Luke 18:32) amid his final suffering (Matt 26:67; 27:30; Mark 15:19). Spitting was also a means of transferring uncleanness (Lev 15:8). In contrast, spittle or saliva was considered a healing agent in the Greco-Roman period. Thus Jesus occasionally used his own saliva along with touch in his healings (Mark 8:23; John 9:6). *See* BLINDNESS; HEALING; MIRACLE.

LISA MICHELE WOLFE

SPLENDOR [הָדָר hadhar, הוֹד hodh; δόξα doxa]. Primarily associated with deity and/or royalty—although not exclusively—splendor is expressed by a variety of OT and NT terms; chief among them in the OT are hodh ("splendor, majesty") and hadhar ("splendor, ornament"). Striking are the eight uses of hodh and hadhar together (1 Chr 16:27; Job 40:10; Pss 21:5 [Heb. 21:6];

45:3 [Heb. 45:4]; 96:6; 104:1; 111:3; 145:5]. With the exception of the Job text, all are descriptive of deity or royalty. According to 1 Chr 16:29; 2 Chr 20:21; and Pss 29:2; 96:9, Yahweh was to be worshiped/praised in "holy splendor." The splendor (hodh) of deity and royalty also merges in texts such as 1 Chr 29:11; Ps 8:1 [Heb. 8:2]; and Zech 6:13. Using hadhar, Isa 2:10, 19, and 21 convey the same pairing. Human royal splendor is imaged in 1 Chr 29:25 (hodh), while Ps 8:5 [Heb. 8:6] indicates that all humanity has been "crowned ... with glory and honor (hadhar)." Cities (Jerusalem) and regions (Carmel, Sharon) are characterized by hadhar in Ezek 16:14 and Isa 35:2, respectively. Doxa is the leading LXX counterpart of hodh and hadhar, among many. Of the more than 160 NT uses of doxa, the NRSV translates it as "splendor" only twice (Matt 4:8; Rev 18:1).

JOHN I. LAWLOR

SPOIL. *See* SPOILS OF WAR.

SPOILS OF WAR [שָׁלָל shalal]. "Spoils of war" or "BOOTY" are the valuables that are confiscated by an invading army after a military victory, including captives (2 Kgs 24:15-16; Jer 21:9; 38:2; Dan 1:3-4), precious metals (Josh 7:21; 22:8) and jewelry (Judg 8:24), weapons (1 Sam 21:9), clothing (Josh 7:21; Judg 5:30; 2 Chr 20:25), livestock and cattle (Deut 2:35; 3:7; Josh 8:2; 11:14; 1 Sam 14:32; 30:20; 2 Chr 15:11; Ezek 38:13), and agricultural harvest (Judg 6:3-5). In a poetic celebration of the defeat of Sisera, captain of the Canaanites, the Israelites triumphantly imagine Sisera's mother speculating about why he is delayed: "Are they not finding and dividing the spoil? A girl or two for every man ... pieces of dyed work embroidered for my neck as spoil?" (Judg 5:28-30).

The laws of warfare in Deut 20:10-15 that governed the conquest of Canaan allowed women, children, livestock, and other spoils to be taken from a city located outside the allotted territory of Canaan, but within the promised land it was forbidden to leave anything alive that breathed (Deut 20:16-18). The "ban" (kherem חֵרֶם) allowed the confiscation of livestock and spoils (Josh 8:27; 11:14) but required the utter destruction of the inhabitants "so that they may not teach you to do all the abhorrent things that they do for their gods" (Deut 20:18; *see* DESTROY, UTTERLY). In some situations, when a war was carried out at the will of God, the Israelites were not allowed to take any spoils for themselves; e.g., after the defeat of Jericho, Israel was warned "not to take any of the DEVOTED things" (Josh 6:18). David presented spoils he retrieved from the Amalekites to the elders of Judah (1 Sam 30), and after the defeat of Hadadezer, David dedicates the spoils of gold, silver, bronze, and gold shields to the Lord (2 Sam 8:3-12).

A common practice in the ANE and Egypt was to present spoils to the gods in gratitude for their protection and victory. Human captives could be renamed to reflect the triumph of one god over other gods: e.g., the Babylonians renamed Daniel "Belteshazzar," Hananiah "Shadrach," Mishael "Meshach," and Azariah "Abednego" (Dan 1:6-7). Nebuchadnezzar placed the treasures of the Jerusalem Temple and palace in the temple of his god in Babylon (2 Kgs 24:13-14; Dan 1:1-3). In Egyptian campaign reliefs, the final narrative scenes after the return of the king depict the presentation of captives and spoils to Amun or the Theban triad. For example, SHISHAK (Sheshonq I) of Egypt looted the treasures of the Temple and the palace, taking as spoil the gold shields that Solomon had hanging in his palace to Egypt (1 Kgs 14:25-26; 2 Chr 12:9; *see* MEGIDDO). The Philistines captured the ark of the covenant and placed it in the temple of Dagon in Ashdod (1 Sam 5:1-4), while the armor of Saul was placed in the temple of Ashtoreth (1 Sam 31:9-10). The Israelites placed the sword of the Philistine Goliath in the sanctuary at Nob (1 Sam 21:9). While the NT does not record the taking of spoils, the late 1st cent. Arch of Titus in Rome depicts the Romans' plunder of the Temple after the defeat of Jerusalem in 70 CE. *See* WAR, METHODS, TACTICS, WEAPONS OF (BRONZE AGE THROUGH PERSIAN PERIOD); WAR, METHODS, TACTICS, WEAPONS OF (HELLENISTIC THROUGH ROMAN PERIODS).

MICHAEL G. HASEL

SPONGE [σπόγγος spongos]. A sponge was placed at the end of a stick to transfer sour wine from the ground to the dying Jesus' lips (Matt 27:48; Mark 15:36; John 19:29). This ties Jesus' death to a psalm for help during persecution, where the sufferer is given vinegar to drink by the persecutors (Ps 69:21).

EMILY ASKEW

SPORT IN THE BIBLE. *See* GAMES, NT; GAMES, OT; RACE, SPORT.

SPRING [עַיִן ʿayin, מַעְיָן maʿyan; πηγή pēgē]. In arid lands, springs of water issuing from within the ground were vital (Gen 16:7; 24:16, 45; 1 Sam 29:1). Symbolically, springs represented prosperity or eternal life (Deut 8:7; Ps 84:6 [Heb. 84:7]; John 4:14; Rev 7:17; 21:6). *See* FOUNTAIN; SEASONS; WATER; WELL OR FOUNTAIN OF LIVING WATER, LIFE.

EMILY R. CHENEY

SPRING RAIN. *See* EARLY AND LATE RAINS.

SPROUT [פָּרַח parakh, צָמַח tsamakh; ἐκβλαστάνω ekblastanō, προβάλλω proballō]. The new growth of a plant or the verb describing the coming out of new growth, as in the sprouting of Aaron's staff (Num 17:5) or Jesus' sign of new fig leaves (Luke 21:30). *Sprout* can convey the hope of renewal as a new sprout from a cut tree (as opposed to the death of humans who will never sprout again [Job 14:7-10]), the gift of righteousness from the heavens (Isa 45:8), or the prosperity of the wicked (Ps 92:7). Ezekiel tells the parable of a vine transplanted by an eagle whose sprout will not prosper, symbolizing the futile hopes of Israel (Ezek 17:1-10). The sprouting of the horn of David, which signified a powerful, prosperous leader for Israel, was celebrated as a gift from God (Ps 132:17).

BRUCE W. GENTRY

SQUAD [τετράδιον tetradion]. A group of four Roman soldiers. Herod Agrippa I seized James the son of Zebedee and had him beheaded. Seeing that this pleased the Jews, he also seized the apostle Peter and assigned four squads of Roman soldiers to guard him (Acts 12:4). In the case of Peter, this probably meant two soldiers with him in the cell (12:6) and two guards outside of the cell. Roman procedure was to assign four squads, sixteen soldiers in all, each squad covering one of the four watches of the night. Acts 12:6-19 recounts Peter's miraculous escape from prison. When Peter could not be found by the guards, Herod had them executed. The *Code of Justinian* (9.4.4) stipulates that a soldier who allows a prisoner to escape faces the same penalty the prisoner faced, in this case death.

KENNETH D. LITWAK

SQUARE, PUBLIC [רְחֹב rekhov]. Translated "square" or "public square," rekhov literally means "broad place," sometimes "main street." Excavations of Israelite cities have uncovered open areas just inside the city gates that may have served for public assemblies (e.g., Deut 13:16; Judg 19:15; 2 Chr 32:6; Neh 8:1; Isa 15:3). Since city gates were commonly the locale for legal proceedings (Ruth 4:1-12), public deliberations would likely have been held close by. *See* CITY; GATE.

DANIEL C. OLSON

Todd Bolen/BiblePlaces.com

Figure 1: Megiddo stables with manger and tethering posts

STABLE. Although the word *stable* does not appear in the NRSV, archaeological evidence for such a facility is found throughout Palestine. Archaeologists have uncovered many tripartite buildings that seem to have served as a place to hold animals while providing food and water for them. Present on some of the columns in these buildings are holes that may have been used to tether the animal. Stone mangers were also found lo-

cated beneath the holes. In the NT, Luke's infancy narrative reports that Jesus was laid in a manger, indicating that Mary and Joseph found accommodations in a stable (Luke 2:7).

KELLY WILSON

STACHYS stay'kis [Στάχυς Stachys]. A Christian whom Paul greets in Rom 16:9 as "my beloved." The uncommon personal name means "oat" or "grain."

STACTE stak'tee [נָטָף nataf]. Among the ingredients listed in the recipe for the sacred INCENSE to be burned only within the tabernacle is stacte, also translated as "gum resin" (Exod 30:34). The word comes from the Hebrew for "to drip" (Job 36:27), indicating its gummy appearance when the plant is cut. It may be opobalsamum (*Commiphora gileadensis*), a wild scrub native to southern Arabia and also cultivated in the semi-tropical conditions around Jericho and En-gedi, where equipment for processing balsam oil has been found in excavations. Others suggest the storax tree (*Styrax officinale*), which produces a sweet, flowery, balsam-like fragrance. *See* SPICE.

VICTOR H. MATTHEWS

STADIA. *See* WEIGHTS AND MEASURES.

STAFF [מַטֶּה matteh, מִשְׁעֶנֶת mish'eneth; ῥάβδος rhabdos]. A variety of Hebrew and Greek words with a variety of functions are reflected in the NRSV "staff." In some cases (e.g., Zech 8:4; Heb 11:21), a staff is used by the elderly like a cane. Often, however, staffs function as walking sticks (e.g., 1 Sam 14:43; Matt 10:10). The "staff of bread" (Ps 105:16) is therefore food that sustains individuals so they may stand. Shepherds used staffs (Mic 7:14) to negotiate difficult terrain, count their sheep (Lev 27:32), and hit their flock to guide them (compare Num 22:27). This image is inverted in Ps 23:4, where Yahweh's staff "comfort[s]" the individual. Staffs could be highly individualized and recognizable as belonging to a particular person (Gen 38:25).

As an everyday object, the staff could be used to perform miracles, as in the case of Moses and Aaron. Moses' staff turned into a snake (Exod 4:1-5), initiated plagues against Egypt, split the Reed Sea (Exod 14:16), and brought forth water from the rock (Num 20:2-13). As such, it is twice called "the staff of God" (Exod 4:20; 17:9). This suggests that a prophet's staff had magical powers and explains why Gehazi tried to use his master Elisha's staff to revive a dead child (2 Kgs 4:29-31). Staffs were typically made of dead wood from sturdy trees—hence the miraculous flowering staff of Aaron (Num 17:1-11 [Heb. 17:16-26]; *see* AARON'S STAFF), and the image of Egypt compared to a "broken reed of a staff," which is both weak and sharp (e.g., 2 Kgs 18:21). *See* ROD.

MARC ZVI BRETTLER

STAG [אַיָל ʾayyal]. A male deer, a ruminant mammal that ranges primarily in forested areas. Unlike other ruminants, the stag features antlers instead of horns and is considered one of the swiftest (2 Sam 22:34; NRSV, "deer") and most agile (Isa 35:6; NRSV, "deer") of the animals. Love poetry compares the vitality of the male lover to a stag (Song 2:9, 17; 8:14). However, the gullible man who is enthralled by the seductive speech of the "loose woman" (Prov 7:5) is compared to the stag who can easily be trapped in a snare (Prov 7:21-23). *See* ANIMALS OF THE BIBLE.

VICTOR H. MATTHEWS

STAIRS [לוּלִים lullim, מַעֲלֶה maʿaleh]. Stairs have been discovered in archaeological excavations as early as the 9th–8th millennium BCE. At Jericho, a circular stone tower with internal stairs was found preserved to a height of 7.75 m. Stairs of stone or wood have been found in both domestic and monumental or royal structures. In the OT, stairs or steps (maʿaleh) are mentioned in reference to the altar of burnt offering (Exod 20:26; NRSV, "steps"), the Temple (1 Kgs 6:8; 2 Chr 9:11; NRSV, "steps"), the gates of the Temple of Ezekiel's vision (Ezek 40:22, 26; NRSV, "steps"), a throne (1 Kgs 10:19; NRSV, "steps"), and the STAIRS OF THE CITY OF DAVID (Neh 3:15; 12:37). *See* ARCHITECTURE, OT; HOUSE; LADDER.

JOEL F. DRINKARD JR.

STAIRS OF THE CITY OF DAVID [מַעֲלוֹת עִיר דָּוִיד maʿaloth ʿir dawidh]. A staircase hewn into a rocky scarp on the south end of the City of David, measuring 1.5 m wide and 11 m long. These stairs are located in the Tyropoeon Valley about 75 m southeast of the pool of Siloam and descend from the City of David to the Fountain Gate. Nehemiah mentions them in a description of the restoration of the walls of Jerusalem (Neh 3:15) and as part of the path Ezra and the elders of Judah took during a celebratory procession for the completion of the wall's restoration (Neh 12:37).

TERRY W. EDDINGER

STALL [אֻרְיָה ʾuryah; מַרְבֵּק marbeq, רֶפֶת refeth, φάτνη phatnē]. Domestic animals are kept and cared for in stalls. **Marbeq**, meaning "a tying-place," is mentioned in reference to "fattened calves" (Jer 46:21; Amos 6:4; Mal 4:2 [Heb. 3:20]). **Refeth** is used only in the plural in Hab 3:17 in connection with large cattle, while **ʾuryah** is used for horses and large cattle (1 Kgs 4:26; 2 Chr 9:25; 2 Chr 32:28). Stalls appear on Mesopotamian cylinder seals and bas-reliefs as sheds where milking and milk processing took place (Borowski, 1998). Although some tend to interpret the Iron Age II tripartite buildings (e.g. in Megiddo) as stables, others argue that these buildings were basically store-houses (Borowski 2002). *See* ASS; HORSE; MULE.

Bibliography: O. Borowski. *Agriculture in Iron Age Israel* (2002); O. Borowski. *Every Living Thing: Daily Use of Animals in Ancient Israel* (1998).

ODED BOROWSKI

STAND FIRM [יָצַב yatsav; στήκω stēkō]. To stand firm means to have courage, strong resolve, and faith in God: "If you do not stand firm in faith, you shall not stand at all" (Isa 7:9). Moses tells the people to stand firm, because God would deliver them from the advancing Egyptian army (Exod 14:13). Those who are loyal to God stand firm and take action (Dan 11:32). Phinehas is remembered as having been particularly zealous for God and for standing firm when others turned away (Sir 45:23; see Num 25:11-13). The apostle Paul uses "stand firm" to urge resolve against the external influences that characterize Paul's polemical adversaries (e.g., Gal 5:1). Paul uses "standing firm" in parallel with "resolve" (1 Cor 7:37) and "striving" (Phil 1:27) to indicate ongoing commitment, and he praises those who have stood firm in faith (2 Cor 1:24). Paul reinforces his readers' commitment when he directs them to stand firm "in the Lord" (Phil 4:1; 1 Thess 3:8), "in faith" (1 Cor 16:13), and "in unity of spirit" (Phil 1:27). *See* BOLDNESS, CONFIDENCE IN FAITH; COURAGE; FAITH, FAITHFULNESS; ZEAL, ZEALOUS.

KEVIN RODRIGUES

STAND UP [יָצַב yatsav, עָמַד ʿamadh, קוּם qum; ἀνακύπτω anakyptō, ἐγείρω egeirō]. This English phrase is used to translate a variety of Hebrew and Greek words in the Bible. The OT often uses the phrase with respect to one's posture towards God or within an assembly of God's people (e.g., Josh 7:10; Neh 9:5; Job 30:28; Isa 49:7; Ezek 2:1). In the NT the phrase appears in Jesus' healing of paralytics (Matt 9:5-6; Mark 2:11; Luke 5:23-24; John 5:8).

STEVEN D. MASON

STANDARD [דֶּגֶל deghel, נֵס nes]. Object or BANNER atop a pole calling a group to action, especially battle, or identifying or locating a group/tribe (Num 2; 10; Isa 31:9; symbolically Jer 4:6, 21; 51:12, 27).

STAR OF BETHLEHEM. If one sticks to the narrative of Matt 2:1-12, the so-called Star of Bethlehem might better be named the Star of the "King of the Judeans" (NRSV, "Jews"; ["his star" in Matt 2:2]) or the Star of the Messiah (Matt 2:4). The name "Jews" (see Matt 2:2; 27:11, 29, 37: "King of the Judeans") was the non-Israelite name for the house of Israel (Matt 10:6; 15:24). Israelites called their people and region "Israel" (so Matt 27:42). Magi, Zoroastrian priests, observed this star "at its rising" (Matt 2:2b). To relate a newly rising star to a king in Israel, the star would have to appear in the constellation governing the "land of Israel" (Matt 2:20-21), that is, the Roman province of Syro-Palestine. This constellation was Aries, the springtime constellation, the first-created, celestial Lamb of God. Further, spring marked the onset of the dry season, offering the possibility of night travel.

In antiquity, only royalty and entire peoples had relevant horoscopes. Earth, sea, and sky formed a single social environment. Astronomers/astrologers could read the sky, understood to be analogous to reading books. Their readings did not so much foretell the future as "forthtell" (announce) what was occurring among people in the regions over which the celestial entities had their impact.

The passage speaks of an astēr (ἀστήρ, "star," "comet," or even "planet"). Traditionally, exegetes interpreted this star as a portentous sign. For modern astronomers and their computer simulations, this star was either a nova or a conjunction of planets (usually Jupiter, Saturn, Mars, 6 BCE) or a comet (5 BCE). The magi in the story followed a star that moved and stopped and moved (acting like the pillar and cloud in Num 9:17). Such motion befits comets and planets when occulted (hidden for a time behind the moon or sun). Comets often (but not always) were interpreted to mean political disturbance, notably for kings and people in the regions over which they appeared. The appearance of a comet over Judea would mean trouble or regime change for the local king, in this case, Herod (Matt 2:3). The most famous comet of the period, much celebrated and depicted on countless Roman coins, was the star of Julius Caesar (*sidus Iulium*, 44 BCE) that announced that the recently deceased Caesar had become a god, and his son Augustus, a son of a god.

In Matt 1–2 people learn of God's will through dreams, angels, stars, and Israel's Scriptures. Only Herod, informed by Israel's Scriptures, disobeys. *See* ASTRONOMY, ASTROLOGY; BETHLEHEM; MAGI; SIGNS IN THE NT.

Bibliography: Raymond E. Brown. *The Birth of the Messiah* (1977); Colin J. Humphreys. "The Star of Bethlehem—a Comet in 5 B.C.—and the Date of the Birth of Christ." *Quarterly Journal of the Royal Astronomical Society* 32 (1991) 389–402; Mark Kidger. *Astronomical Enigmas: Life on Mars, the Star of Bethlehem, and Other Milky Way Mysteries* (2005); Mary Frances Williams. "The *Sidus Iulium*, the Divinity of Men, and the Golden Age in Virgil's *Aeneid*." *Leeds International Classical Studies* 2 (2003) 1–29.

BRUCE J. MALINA

STARS. *See* ASTRONOMY, ASTROLOGY; NATURE, NATURAL PHENOMENA; SCIENCE AND THE BIBLE; SCIENCE, MESOPOTAMIA; STAR OF BETHLEHEM.

STATUES, STATUARY אֶבֶן 'even, אֱלֹהִים 'elohim, אֵפֹד 'efodh, אֲשֵׁרָה 'asherah, סֶמֶל semel, פֶּסֶל pesel, צֶלֶם tselem, תְּרָפִים terafim; εἴδωλον eidōlon, εἰκών eikōn]. Statues are sculptures or images of humans, deities, or other subject matter cast in metal, carved from wood or stone, or molded in clay. Archaeologists have discovered many examples of statuary from a variety of ancient cultures.

Statues were sometimes called ELOHIM, "gods" (Gen 31:20; 35:4; Exod 20:23; Deut 4:28; 28:36, 64; 29:17 [Heb. 29:16]; Josh 24:3; 2 Kgs 19:18). Polemical texts against idols indicate they were made of stone, as in Deut 4:28; 28:36; Hab 2:19; 2 Kgs 19:18. A cult statue was sometimes called an EPHOD (Judg 17:5; 18:14-17). Another term for small idols or statues was TERAPHIM, which is always plural even when it refers to a single object (1 Sam 19:13). In Gen 31:19-20, Rachel steals her father's "household gods," which probably were statues of departed ancestors, family gods, or household authority figures; many examples have been found at NUZI. When Saul threatens to kill David, Michal helps David escape, then dresses an idol with a goat's-hair wig and clothing to deceive Sau's messengers into thinking the statue is David lying sick in bed (1 Sam 19:11-17). That these statues also were used in NECROMANCY supports the theory that they might have symbolized departed ancestors (Ezek 21:21; Zech 10:2; 2 Kgs 23:24).

A. Old Testament
    1. Prohibitions against cult images
    2. Archaeological evidence for cult images in Israel
    3. A statue of Yahweh?
B. Apocrypha
C. New Testament
Bibliography

A. Old Testament
1. Prohibitions against cult images

In Gen 1:26-28, the human being is created in the IMAGE OF GOD. However, in the rest of the OT, human beings are prohibited from creating images of any heavenly and earthly thing (Exod 20:4-5; Deut 5:8-9). Hand-crafted images made by the Canaanites should be destroyed (Num 33:52), as was a statue of BAAL (2 Kgs 11:18//1 Chr 23:17). In the book of Daniel, Jews refuse to worship the statue that Nebuchadnezzar set up (Dan 3:1). There are expressed prohibitions against cult images not only in the Ten Commandments but also in the Covenant Code (Exod 20:23-24; 34:13), the Holiness Code (Lev 19:4; 26:1); and Deut 4:16-18; 30 (*see* IDOL; IDOLATRY).

Many modern scholars believe that these formulations of a programmatic eradication of iconography are late, none earlier than the mid-6th cent. BCE (Dick 1999; Mettinger 1995), although there already was rhetoric against idolatry in Hosea, Isaiah, and Deuteronomy. Whereas Exod 19:21 had stated that the people did not gaze at Yahweh during the Sinai theophany, Deut 4:12 says Yahweh had no temunah "form/representation" whatsoever to look at. Therefore, the people should not make any temunah "form/representation" of God

(Deut 4:15-18). The actual biblical legal strictures were probably subsequent to Josiah's reforms in the late 7th cent. and were intertwined with the emergence of expressed monotheism.

Parodies against making statues can be found in Isa 40:19-20; 41:1-14; 44:6-22; Jer 10:1-6. There are polemics in Pss 115:3-8; 135:15-18; Ezek 5:11; 20:7-8; 23:3-4; Hos 8:4-6; 13:2-3; Mic 5:12-13; Hab 2:18-19. Most of these are late. However, Mettinger (1995) cites 1 Sam 5:1-5, where the broken statue of DAGON lies prostate before the ark of the covenant, as evidence that programmatic aniconism (prohibition of idols) may be older than the Deuteronomist.

2. Archaeological evidence for cult images in Israel

There is a continuous stream of cult figures in Palestine from Neolithic times until the Hellenistic period (5000–63 BCE), which clearly shows that in everyday life, Israel was not as opposed to the cultic statue, as many (late) biblical texts would suggest. However, there are many difficulties in interpreting which statues or statue fragments are deities and which are human (see Lewis). If a statue bears clear indications that it is a deity, then which deity? Not all seated figures are El, nor are all standing smiting deities Baal. Female figurines are especially problematic. The emblems of the three main goddesses Anat, Asherah, and Astarte frequently overlap. The same is true of images such as the bull, which could represent El, Baal, Yahweh, or the moon god. Second, many statues are not found in clearly datable strata; several have been reused at later times (perhaps as heirlooms). Third, the archaeological context is also essential: Was the figure found in a cultic context?

Many bronze figurines were supposedly found in the Iron Age I–II A (1200–900 BCE) strata of such cities as BETH-SHAN; BETH-SHEMESH; HAZOR; MEGIDDO; SAMARIA, and Shechem (see SHECHEM, SHECHEMITES). The Hazor bronze figurine can serve as an example of the problems involved. G. Ahlström called the bronze seated figurine found in area B in Stratum XI of Hazor (beneath the floor of locus 3283) "an Israelite god figurine," presumably Yahweh, portrayed after the model of the seated Canaanite El.

Erich Lessing/Art Resource, NY

Figure 1: Seated god from Hazor. Israel Museum (IDAM), Jerusalem, Israel.

Erich Lessing/Art Resource, NY

Figure 2: Smiting god from Megiddo. Israel Museum (IDAM), Jerusalem, Israel.

However, a closer examination points to its being part of an earlier Late Bronze Age metal hoard, and therefore pre-Israelite. The actual center of cult focus in room 3283 was probably on a banana-shaped stone on a raised ledge. Most of the figurines found above were probably leftovers from the Late Bronze Age and say little about the emerging Israelite religion. The most evocative item was a bronze fist found in Jerusalem that might have belonged to a bronze statue of a smiting god (40 cm in height). The fist was found in a 10th-cent. fill and had been reused in the 10th cent. as an amulet. Bronze statues from Iron Age II B (900–700) have also been found at Tell Abu el-Kharaz (Jordan Valley), Gezer, Tel Zeror (northern Plain of Sharon), Tell el-Oreimeh (ancient Kinneret), Dan, and Kfar Kanna (north of Nazareth). Fragments of an almost life-size terracotta male statue were found in a 9th-cent. temenos wall at Dan; it is impossible to determine if the statue is of a god or king.

Bronze bull statues in a cultic context have been found in Palestine from the Middle Bronze to Iron Age I A (2000–1150 BCE).The latest was a bronze bull found near an Iron Age I A open-air sanctuary east of DOTHAN. In general the bull is difficult to interpret, but many scholars argue that it could represent Yahweh, who is undoubtedly called the "bull of Jacob" in Ps 132:2 (also see Num 23:22; 24:8). It could also be the pedestal for Yahweh. Bull figurines were the statues erected by Jeroboam in Dan and Bethel. These figures were no longer tolerated by the 8th-cent. prophet Hosea. After Iron Age II A (900 BCE) they are less common, however they continued to be represented on seals until the appearance of Apis bull figurines in the 7th cent. The Bronze Serpent removed by King Hezekiah (2 Kgs 18:4) was clearly perceived as a cult figure said to have been made by Moses himself (Num 21:4-9). Although the serpent is the emblem of several deities, this cult figure might have been an atropaic figurine against snake bite (*see* SERPENT, BRONZE). Copper snakes were found in the Aravah at TIMNA in a shrine and at the Late Bronze II A temple at Tel Mevorakh near DOR. The serpent is also found on several terracotta cult stands.

Manasseh sets up an "image of ASHERAH" in the house of the Lord (2 Kgs 21:7; 2 Chr 33:7-15), perhaps to the Canaanite goddess Asherah, the consort of El. Despite the (ambiguous) new inscriptions from Tel Miqne (biblical EKRON), scholars do not agree on whether Asherah continued to be worshiped in the Iron Age (1200–586 BCE). However, she is possibly found in 1 Kgs 15:13 and 18:19. The term asherah, especially in the plural ('asherim אֲשֵׁרִים), refers to a cult symbol, probably wooden, which at some time represented the goddess. These are imagined as cultic poles, set alongside altars, which could be cut down and burned. We may have the remnants of such an asherah in the excavations of Lachish, Stratum V (period of the united monarchy?), locus 81, which is a cult place with a pillar. The round circle of olive-wood ash facing the stand-

ing pillar may well be the remains of a burnt asherah. Originally, such cult objects may have been humanoid, as in a seal from Mari where the goddess has both arboreal and humanoid features. Some asherim might also have had human features, like a statue. An asherah is probably portrayed on the two Taanach cult stands found by Sellin and Lapp (950–800 BCE).

In Israel the asherah's use may have been influenced by the importance of sacred trees (Gen 35:4, 8; Josh 24:26-7). The asherim could be made, cut down, burned, set up, built, or planted. In Exod 34:13; Deut 7:5; 12:3 these cult symbols are related to the religious practices of the Canaanites. The term is frequent in the DEUTERONOMISTIC HISTORY (1 Kgs 16:32-3; 2 Kgs 17:16; 23:15) and in Chronicles. The asherim often accompany altars and sacred pillars and seem to have been a consistent feature of monarchic Israelite and Judahite religion.

The controversial inscriptions from KUNTILLET ʿAJRUD in the southern Negev and from Khirbet el-Qom suggest that by around 800 BCE the asherah had lost its linkage with the goddess and was now reduced to an attribute of Yahweh. The inscription on pithos A from Kuntillet ʿAjrud reads "I bless you by Yahweh of Samaria and by his asherah." The vast majority of statuary from Iron Age Israel is terracotta. Over 3,000 female terracotta figurines of a woman have been found in Israel. An increasing number of male clay figurines representing deities have been found, most from Iron II B–C. We have several hundred figurines of a man riding a horse from Iron Age II C, 119 in Jerusalem alone. Their identity remains controversial, however some relate them to the "horses of the sun" (2 Kgs 23:11). Models with a sun disk between the horse's ears and in the scarab from Iron Age II C were discovered at Beth-shan.

Figurines with divine symbols were more prevalent in the Late Bronze Age. Pillar figurines were particularly popular in Judah. Many of the types, such as a woman holding her breasts might have served as a talisman to promote lactation; another type, of a woman holding a disk, probably represents a cultic musician with either a small drum or cymbals.

3. A statue of Yahweh?

An increasing number of scholars claim that prior to the emergence of the Yahweh-Alone Movement and the Deuteronomist, there were cult statues of Yahweh in Judah: the cherubim chair was not empty. (Such an image, if it existed in the Solomonic Temple, would probably have been destroyed either in 597 or 586 BCE.) Niehr argues that the phrase "seeing the face of [Yahweh]" (Pss 17:15; 42:3; 63:3) would imply looking upon Yahweh's cult statue, as it would in Mesopotamian religions. Also, passages like Ps 68:25-26 describe the procession of Yahweh's cult image into the sanctuary, also a common practice in Mesopotamia. Niehr also claims that the preexilic prophetic visions such as 1 Kgs

22:19 and Isa 6 cannot be reconciled with the notion of an empty cherubim throne. Postexilic prophetic visions (after the supposed destruction of the cult image of Yahweh) were no longer of a figure but of symbols (Ezek 1; 10; Zech 4:14). Uehlinger claims that a terracotta object said to come from Tel Beit Mirsim (late 8th and early 7th cent. BCE) could represent Yahweh and his Asherah. It would appear that a bearded male and a female are depicted on the throne; they are flanked by animals tentatively identified as lions or sphinxes. The position of the two figures with the female seated slightly behind the male suggests a male and his consort. Uehlinger tentatively identified these as Yahweh and his Asherah, and the presence of sphinxes would reinforce this. Edelman argues that the male figure on a Persian era Yehud (Judah) coin portrays Yahweh seated on a winged throne, perhaps based on (the memories) of a cult statue. The coin was probably minted during the reign of Governor Bagohi (380–360 BCE). In sum, these claims are intriguing and should not be immediately dismissed, but they are hardly probative. Scholars should leave open the possibility that the programmatic aniconism movement only gradually asserted its dominance over a religion that had been quite comfortable with divine statuary. A pillar probably represented Yahweh at a temple such as Arad, however, this would not preclude that there might have been a statue of Yahweh in the Jerusalem Temple; we know that in many cases there was a main cult statue (e.g., Marduk in Babylon), but elsewhere the deity was represented by symbols or emblems.

B. Apocrypha

The Apocrypha contain several developed attacks on idolatry: Bel and the Dragon, the Epistle of Jeremiah, and Wis 13–14. The prolonged excursus in the WISDOM OF SOLOMON has been influenced by both Hellenistic Greek philosophy and the OT. Wisdom 14:12-31 contains two theories of the origins of idolatry modeled after the philosophy of the Greek writer Euhemerus, who was to have strong influence on patristic writers. In 1 Macc 3:48 the Torah served the role that statues do outside of Judaism.

Specific examples of forbidden statuary are 2 Macc 1:54, where the author refers to the "desolating sacrilege" also mentioned in Dan 11:31 (see Matt 24:15; Mark 13:14), a reference to the desecration of the Temple by Antiochus Epiphanes. Wisdom 14:11 refers to "heathen idols," and Wis 14:17 to a "graven image."

C. New Testament

In Rom 2:22, Paul seems to refer to the OT Decalogue in mentioning the prohibition against idols. Acts 7:41 refers to the golden calf of Exod 32 (see CALF, GOLDEN). One of the issues facing the early Christians was eating meat sacrificed to idols; since most meat available for eating came from temple sacrifices, this placed a burden on the small community of Christians to decide whether or not its consumption indicated they were tacitly worshiping the idol (1 Cor 10:14-22). Here Paul also considers idolatry as an offering to demons, a concept based on the LXX (Deut 32:17; Ps 96:5 [LXX 95:5]; Isa 65:3) and the Apocrypha (e.g., Bar 4:7). In many NT passages, the worship of idols becomes a metonym for any deviant worship (Col 3:5; 1 John 5:21; Rev 22:15) and no longer refers specifically to cult statues. Revelation refers to an eikōn to mean a cult statue (Rev 13:14-15; 14:9, 11; 15:2; 16:2; 19:20; 20:4). However, in most cases eikōn refers to Christ as "the image of God" (eikōn tou theou εἰκὼν τοῦ θεοῦ; compare Gen 1:26).

Bibliography: M. B. Dick. "The Mesopotamian Cult Statue: A Sacramental Encounter with Divinity." *Cult Image and Divine Representation in the Ancient Near East* (2005) 43–67; M. B. Dick. "Prophetic Parodies of Making the Cult Image." *Born in Heaven, Made on Earth: The Making of the Cult Image in the Ancient Near East* (1999) 1–53; D. V. Edelman. "Tracking Observance of the Aniconic Tradition through Numismatics." *The Triumph of Elohim: From Yahwisms to Judaisms* (1995) 185–225; J. M. Hadley. *The Cult of Asherah in Ancient Israel and Judah: Evidence for a Hebrew Goddess* (2000); R. S. Hendel. "Aniconism and Anthropomorphism in Ancient Israel." *The Image and the Book: Iconic Cults, Aniconism, and the Rise of Book Religion in Israel and the Ancient Near East* (1997) 205–28; O. Keel and C. Uehlinger. *Gods, Goddesses, and Images of God in Ancient Israel* (1997); E. C. Larocca-Pitts. *"Of Wood and Stone": The Significance of Israelite Cultic Items in the Bible and Its Early Interpreters* (2001); T. J. Lewis. "Syro-Palestinian Iconography and Divine Images." *Cult Image and Divine Representation in the Ancient Near East* (2005) 69–107; T. N. D. Mettinger. *No Graven Image? Israelite Aniconism in Its Ancient Near Eastern Context* (1995); H. Niehr. "In Search of YHWH's Cult Statue in the First Temple." *The Image and the Book: Iconic Cults, Aniconism, and the Rise of Book Religion in Israel and the Ancient Near East* (1997) 73–95; C. Uehlinger. "Anthropomorphic Cult Statuary in Iron Age Palestine and the Search for Yahweh's Cult Images." *The Image and the Book: Iconic Cults, Aniconism, and the Rise of Book Religion in Israel and the Ancient Near East* (1997) 97–155.

MICHAEL B. DICK

STATUTE. *See* ORDINANCE.

STEADFAST LOVE. *See* KHESED; LOVE IN THE OT.

STEADFASTNESS [כּוּן kun, לְעוֹלָם le'olam; μακρωθυμία makrōthymia, προσκαρτερέω proskartereō, ὑπομένω hypomenō, ὑπομονή hypomonē]. One of several terms that describe active, abiding commitment to and nurture of the relationship between God and humans, or relationships among the people of God. Other English terms include "ENDURANCE," "patient endurance," "PATIENCE," and "perseverance," translating a variety of Hebrew idioms or Greek words that express a range of nuances.

Frequently, *steadfastness* refers to maintaining loyalty to God in the face of adverse circumstances or doubts. In the OT, people are steadfast if they remain firmly grounded in worship of God, particularly when threatened by unrighteous people or unfortunate events (Pss 57:7 [Heb. 57:8]; 78:37). In the NT, persistence (hypomonē) in faith and deeds in difficult circumstances is encouraged (Matt 10:22; Rom 8:25; 1 Cor 13:7; Heb 10:36; Rev 1:9; 2:2) and is a defining Christian characteristic (Rom 5:3-4; 2 Pet 1:6).

Another use is its reference to devotion or perseverance in regular prayer, study, or worship. In the OT, this may circumvent threats (Josh 1:7; 23:6). In the NT, it is part of the ideal lifestyle (proskartereō; Acts 2:42, 46; Rom 12:12). It can also refer to persistence in a relationship, despite the shortcomings of the other party. A primary characteristic of God in the OT is "steadfast love" (khesedh [חֶסֶד]; *see* KHESED), an unfailing commitment to humans (e.g., Ps 136). God holds off on acting in anger (Rom 2:4; 9:22). Christians should be patient (makrōthymia) with others (1 Cor 13:4; Eph 4:2; 1 Thess 5:14). A final usage refers to continuing or eternal existence. Things associated with God "endure forever" (idiomatically often le'olam, "forever," without a verb; Pss 45:6 [Heb. 45:7]; 136; Eccl 3:14).

PETER TRUDINGER

STEALING. *See* CRIMES AND PUNISHMENT, OT AND NT.

STEED [אַבִּיר 'abbir, אָמֹץ 'amots, פָּרָשׁ parash, קַל qal, רֶכֶשׁ rekhesh]. A strong, swift horse (1 Kgs 4:28 [Heb. 5:8]; Esth 8:10, 14; Isa 30:16; Jer 46:4; Mic 1:13; Zech 6:7). This term often has military connotations (e.g., Judg 5:22).

STEER [פַּר par]. Elsewhere translated "young bull" or "calf," in Isa 34:7 par is rendered "young steers" (NRSV) to contrast with "mighty bulls." *See* BULL; CALF.

STELE stee'lee. A stele (pl. stelae) is an upright stone or wood block carved, incised, or decorated on one face. A stele contrasts with a MASSEBAH, which may not be worked on a face. Stelae were often used as boundary markers; they also often served as burial markers in Egypt and Greece. In Mesopotamia and Syria-Palestine, stelae were more frequently used for memorial or commemorative purposes. The Merneptah stele (13th cent. BCE) commemorated Merneptah's victory over numerous entities in Lybia and as far as Syria-Palestine, including Israel. Similarly, the Mesha stele (*see* MOABITE STONE) describes the accomplishments of King Mesha

of Moab (9th cent. BCE), including his defeat of Israel and his building projects. Although no Hebrew word is translated as *stele* in the NRSV, the sense of the word may be captured by Hebrew yadh (יָד, literally "hand") in its specialized sense of "monument" (1 Sam 15:12; 2 Sam 8:3; 18:18), as well as by Hebrew tsiyun (צִיּוּן), also translated "monument" (2 Kgs 23:17). Both words refer to monuments set up by a royal figure in precisely the manner one finds stelae used in the ANE. *See* INSCRIPTIONS; OBELISK.

JOEL F. DRINKARD JR.

STEPHANAS stef'uh-nuhs [Στεφανᾶς Stephanas]. Mentioned only in 1 Cor 1:16 and 16:15-18, Paul remembers baptizing Stephanas' household in CORINTH but does not recall whether he baptized anyone else there (1 Cor 1:16). While Paul's ministry was not to baptize but to proclaim good news (1 Cor 1:17), the apostle points proudly to Stephanas' household as the "first-fruits" of his work in Achaia, commending their service to the Corinthian Christians (1 Cor 16:15). According to 1 Cor 16:17, Stephanas, FORTUNATUS, and ACHAICUS had recently visited Paul in Ephesus. *See* CORINTHIANS, FIRST LETTER TO THE.

FRED L. HORTON

STEPHEN stee'vuhn [Στέφανος Stephanos]. One of the seven HELLENISTS (Greek-speaking Jews) and the first martyr (Acts 7:60) in Luke's depiction of the early Jesus movement in Jerusalem. Acts does not associate Stephen and the other Hellenists with the origin of the "deacon's" office in the PASTORAL LETTERS, as some commentators have assumed when they link the verbal form diakonein (διακονεῖν, "to serve," Acts 6:2 author's trans.; NRSV, "to wait on tables") to the nominal form diakonos (διάκονος, "deacon," 1 Tim 3:8, 12; 4:6). Instead, as one of the seven (Acts 6:3), Stephen is initially appointed to resolve an internal problem (the neglect of Greek-speaking Jewish widows in the daily distribution of food, 6:1). His work extends, however, beyond "table service" and includes the performance of "great wonders and signs" (6:8), a feat evoking both the work of the apostles in the earlier part of Acts' narrative (2:43; 5:12; compare 4:30) and ultimately that of MOSES (Deut 7:19; 11:3; 28:46; 29:2; compare Stephen's speech, 7:36). Though the narrative does not indicate the reception of Stephen's deeds, the powerful force of his words (6:10) leads to an external problem, because members of the Freedmen's synagogue, with whom Stephen had disputed (6:9), bring him before the provincial council (6:12) on the false charge of blasphemy against Moses and God (6:11), i.e., speaking words against "this place" (the Temple, 6:13, 14), the law (6:13), and the customs of Moses (6:14). Thereafter, and repeatedly, his words (including a long speech) are met with outright rejection (7:54, 57), with the result that he is stoned to death (7:58), the Levitical punishment for blasphemy (Lev 24:16; *see* STONING), and buried by devout men (8:2). A fuller accounting of Stephen's narrative role in Luke's depiction of the internal and external problems of the early Jesus movement, though, requires an overview of the larger narrative development of Acts, the architecture of the first third of that larger development, and the strategic placement of Stephen.

A. The Larger Narrative Development of Acts
B. The Architectonic Development of
   Acts 1:12–8:1a, the First Narrative Movement
C. Strategic Placement of Stephen in the Narrative
   of Acts
Bibliography

A. The Larger Narrative Development of Acts

In Acts, leading characters (Stephen, Peter, and Paul) are strategically cast as mediating authorities who herald the Jewish God's claim to be the universal benefactor. Repeatedly stylized in the OT pattern of suffering and rejected prophets or of philosophers who speak with boldness even in the presence of provincial and imperial elites (2:29; 4:13, 29, 31; 9:28; 13:46; 14:3; 19:8; 26:26; 28:31), the leading characters journey everywhere, from Jerusalem to the imperial center, to demonstrate the cosmic influence of their God over every level of the society (Edwards, 1989).

Accordingly, after a brief introduction (Acts 1:1-11), the narrative develops in three movements as the witnesses extend their geographical reach, and as they encounter pivotal scenes of suffering (i.e., death or near-death escapes). The first movement (limited to Jerusalem, 1:12–8:1a), both demonstrates God's influence in the powerful oratory and deeds of the twelve and the seven and stylizes the opposition to the witnesses as attempts to control the witnesses' influence among the people. Thus, after a series of increasingly more hostile arrests the movement ends with the death of Stephen.

In the second narrative movement (in and around Judea and Samaria, 8:1b–12:25), persecution abounds from beginning (on the very day Stephen is stoned) to end, but notice is given of God's ability to affect persons and places at all levels of society from all parts of the world (8:1b–11:26). Climactically, this narrative movement virtually ends with the daring angelic rescue of Peter near the Passover season and the equally angelic destruction of AGRIPPA I—a stark contrast between God's response to the humility and supplication of some and to the hubris and self-aggrandizement of another (12:1-23).

Finally, in the third narrative movement (ending with Rome, the imperial center, 13:1–28:31) Saul (Paul) fully dominates the narrative stage. Envious opponents pursuing his steps throughout parts of modern-day Turkey and Europe cause him to suffer in ways similar to Stephen and the other witnesses, and in the closing scenes that take Paul from Jerusalem to Rome, the hand of God leads Paul from one adventure after another—imprisonment, trials, and even a storm and shipwreck.

B. The Architectonic Development of Acts 1:12–8:1a, the First Narrative Movement

Given this overall narrative development, Stephen is introduced in the first narrative movement (1:12–8:1a). In this initial movement, Luke strategically treats the virtually idyllic political community's resolution of internal and external problems in Jerusalem. The internal ones include: the selection of a replacement witness for the ministry once assigned to Judas (1:12-26); the need to address the deceptive patronage of ANANIAS and SAPPHIRA (in contrast to the exemplary patronage of BARNABAS, 4:32-5:11); and the selection of the seven to address the neglect of the Greek-speaking Jewish widows (6:1-7). The external ones include: several conflict scenes (4:1-31) that follow Luke's depiction of the origin and initial mediation of God's beneficence to others (2:1–3:26); a more intensive set of conflict scenes that follow the idealized community's subsequent extension of God's beneficence (5:12-42); and the arrest, unjust trial, and stoning of Stephen who himself had mediated God's beneficence to the people through signs and wonders (6:8–8:1a). Concomitant with the positive portrait of the idealized community's ability to resolve the external problems, moreover, is the use of stylized invective to portray the opposition to the witnesses (Penner 2004).

C. Strategic Placement of Stephen in the Narrative of Acts

Given the staging of the first narrative movement within the whole narrative development, the scenes about Stephen appear to have three strategic goals. First, Stephen is linked to Luke's presentation of Jesus as a prophet with philosophical bearing. Parallels between them include: the influence of the Spirit; the OT's prophetic suffering/rejection motif; an unjust trial; wisdom, and self-mastery. Just as Jesus was filled with the Holy Spirit (Luke 4:1), Stephen was selected as one of seven men "full of the Spirit" (Acts 6:3; compare 6:5, 8, 10; 7:55). Stephen's entire speech (the longest speech in Acts) is saturated with references to the OT, with most of it cast in the language of rejection of the route or person God selects to fulfill God's promise to Abraham (7:17; compare 7:5), from the rejection of Joseph by his brothers to the rejection of Moses (the subject of the largest portion of the speech) to the killing of the prophets and the Just One (Johnson 1977; Kilgallen). Moreover, like other speeches in Acts (or like the parables of Jesus in Luke's Gospel), Stephen's speech reveals Luke's ideology, i.e., the speech is a commentary on the larger narrative. Stephen's speech, then, is not intended only or even primarily to respond to the charges leveled against him. Rather, the speech structurally sets up a typological paradigm (between good leaders and those who oppose them) as the very prism through which

Stephen's own rejection is to be understood (Penner 2004). Both Jesus and Stephen also suffer unjust trials: the charges for both are trumped-up and rushed, with a mob-like environment in sway. Like Jesus, who was also full of wisdom (Luke 2:40; compare 2:52), Stephen also possesses wisdom (Acts 6:3, 10). Like Jesus whom Luke constructs as calm, innocent and paradigmatic in the face of death (Sterling), moreover, Stephen also displays self-mastery (Smith; D'Angelo) in contrast to his stylized opponents who display fury (compare 7:54) and obstinacy (7:57; compare 7:51).

Second, Stephen is drawn as a Hellenist, but not to establish a Gentile Christian vs. Jewish Christian contrast, for all of the believers in the first narrative movement are Jewish, whether they are Palestinian Jews or diaspora Jews. As a tightly woven narrative heavily drawing on stylized character portraits, Acts should not be read as the re-articulation of an earlier tradition that had cast Stephen and the Hellenists as Jews with a more favorable disposition to the inclusion of the Gentiles than the Hebrews (Aramaic-speaking Jews, 6:1). Instead, Stephen is drawn as a Hellenist to reiterate a theme and to provide a transition in the narrative. Just as the idealized community, virtually from its Spirit-filled inception, embraced a diversity of Jews (Palestinian Jews and diaspora Jews, 2:5; compare 2:41), Luke reiterates that theme with scenes about the Hellenist Stephen whose endowment of the Spirit, mediation of beneficence, and courage in the face of the provincial elites are as paradigmatic as that of the Twelve (Penner, 2004). As a Hellenist, moreover, and in accordance with Jesus' programmatic prediction (1:8), Stephen's death prepares Luke's auditors for the idealized community's transition away from Jerusalem (Balch; see 11:19), as does PHILIP, the other well-known Hellenist who proclaims God's good news to the SAMARITANS, to a traveling ETHIOPIAN EUNUCH, and to persons in several towns on his way to CAESAREA MARITIMA (8:5-40; compare 21:8). The persecution of believers that follows in the wake of Stephen's death highlights that transition by indicating the larger geographical reach of the idealized community as it offers God's beneficence to others: "all except the apostles were scattered throughout the countryside of Judea and SAMARIA" (8:1) and "those who were scattered because of the persecution that took place over Stephen traveled as far as PHOENICIA, CYPRUS, and Antioch" (11:19).

Third, Stephen is linked to (Saul) Paul. Luke places Saul on the scene at the stoning of Stephen (7:58). Saul's presence and approval of the killing of Stephen (8:1; compare 22:20) thus prepares Luke's auditors for Saul's role as a provincial representative "breathing threats" against Jesus' disciples in areas outside of Jerusalem (9:1; compare 22:4-5; 26:10) as had the provincial elites made "threats" against the apostles in Jerusalem (4:21; compare 4:29). In part, though, the link is ironic. That is, Paul, who is present at the violent end of the first narrative movement (1:12–8:1a) and who becomes a violent persecutor of the witnesses within the second narrative development (8:3; 9:1) will eventually face violence himself and become the most ardent defender of the idealized community at the end of the third narrative movement (21:17–28:15). As well, the one at first approving Stephen's killing will later confirm Stephen as one of God's witnesses (22:20).

Bibliography: David Balch. "The Genre of Luke–Acts: Individual Biography, Adventure Novel, or Political History." *SwJT* 33 (1990) 5–19; Rose D'Angelo. "Knowing How to Preside over His Own Household: Imperial Masculinity and Christian Asceticism in the Pastorals, Hermas, and Luke–Acts." *New Testament Masculinities.* Stephen D. Moore and Janice Capel Anderson, eds. (2003) 265–95; Douglas Edwards. "Acts of the Apostles and the Graeco-Roman World: Narrative Communication in Social Context." *SBLSP* (1989) 362–77; Luke Timothy Johnson. *The Acts of the Apostles.* SP 5 (1992); Luke Timothy Johnson. *The Literary Function of Possessions in Luke–Acts* (1977); John Kilgallen. "The Function of Stephen's Speech (Acts 7:2-53)," *Bib* 70 (1989) 173–93; Todd Penner. "Early Christian Heroes and Lukan Narratives: Stephen and the Hellenists in Ancient Historiographical Perspective." *Rhetoric and Reality in Early Christianities.* Willi Braun, ed. (2005) 75–97; Todd Penner. *In Praise of Christian Origins: Stephen and the Hellenists in Lukan Apologetic Historiography* (2004); Earl Richard. *Acts 6:1–8:4: The Author's Method of Composition* (1978); Abraham Smith. "'Full of Spirit and Wisdom': Luke's Portrait of Stephen (Acts 6:1–8:1a) as a Man of Self-Mastery." *Asceticism and the New Testament.* Leif E. Vaage and Vincent L. Wimbush, eds. (1999) 97–114; Gregory Sterling. "Mors Philosophi: The Death of Jesus in Luke," *HTR* 94 (2001) 383–402; Robert Tannehill. *The Narrative Unity of Luke-Acts: Vol 2 (The Acts of the Apostles)* (1990).

ABRAHAM SMITH

STEPHEN, REVELATION OF. The *Revelation of Stephen*, known only in a Slavonic version, details the final days before Stephen's martyrdom, recounted in Acts 6:1–8:1. The narrative, set two years after Jesus' death, purports to describe Stephen's contest with the crowds in Jerusalem over the significance of Jesus. After three days, the crowd sends for Saul of Tarsus, who condemns Stephen as an apostate and sentences him and his supporters (including Nicodemus and Gamaliel) to death. Pilate, who buries Stephen, visits his tomb but finds it empty. The following night, however, Stephen appears to the procurator and instructs him to build a shrine for the martyrs and to institute a festival commemorating their deaths. The romance was likely a source for the 5th-cent. writer Lucian, whose own story detailed the discovery of the martyrs' bodies. The Gelasian Decree, attributed to Pope Gelasius in 494, included it among its list of apocryphal works. *See* APOCRYPHA, NT.

DAVID M. REIS

STEPPE [מִדְבָּר midhbar, עֲרָבָה ʿaravah]. *Steppe* is sometimes used instead of the more common terms *wilderness* and *desert* to translate midhbar and ʿaravah in referring to a flat, wide belt of land running along the eastern boundary of Palestine, bridging arable and non-arable lands (1 Chr 6:78 [Heb. 6:63]; Job 39:6). The steppe supports some grass and scrub but no trees, and it can be used for grazing animals. Symbolically, it represents a region hostile to human habitation.

DANIEL C. OLSON

STEWARD, STEWARDSHIP [עַל־בַּיִת ʿal-bayith; ἐπίτροπος epitropos, οἰκονομία oikonomia, οἰκονόμος oikonomos]. A steward manages the affairs of a large household. In the OT, a steward is described as being "over the house" (ʿal-bayith) responsible for service at the master's table (Gen 43:16), the oversight of other servants (Isa 22:15), and general household duties (Gen 43:19; 44:1, 4; 2 Kgs 10:5).

In the NT, two terms are used to designate a steward. One term (epitropos) denotes a guardian (Gal 4:2) or a manager (Matt 20:8; Luke 8:3). Managers (oikonomos) are likewise described in two of Jesus' parables (Luke 12:42-44; 16:1-2). The title can also refer to a municipal officer (Rom 16:23).

Paul figuratively refers to himself as a steward (oikonomos, 1 Cor 4:1), entrusted by God with spiritual authority. Paul characterizes his ministry as a commission (oikonomia) relegated to him by God to proclaim the blessings of the gospel (1 Cor 9:17; Col 1:25). Stewardship involves the dispensation of time, talents, possessions, and self (Eph 3:2; Titus 1:7; 1 Pet 4:10). *See* ALMS, ALMSGIVING.

CATHERINE JONES

STIFF-NECKED [קְשֵׁה־עֹרֶף qesheh-ʿoref]. An expression that denotes obstinate or rebellious behavior, especially IDOL worship or rebellion against Yahweh, which eventually leads to rejection by Yahweh (e.g., Exod 34:9; Deut 9:6, 13; 2 Kgs 17:14). The phrase occurs first in the Golden Calf episode (Exod 32:9; 33:3, 5) with reference to both the Israelites' worship of a false idol and their constant bickering in the wilderness. Subsequent uses refer to this initial wilderness period or analogize contemporary Israelite behavior to it. In Sirach (16:11) and Baruch (2:30), as well as in the NT book of Acts (7:51), the term is used in the author's recounting of Israelite history. *See* CALF, GOLDEN; COVENANT, OT AND NT.

JARED WOLFE

STOCKS [מַהְפֶּכֶת mahpekheth; ξύλον xylon]. Instruments of imprisonment, punishment, and possibly public humiliation. Stocks were often reserved for the prophets of Yahweh in an attempt to harness their message. King Asa of Judah imprisoned in stocks the seer who criticized him for trusting in the armies of Aram rather than the Lord (2 Chr 16:1-10). Jeremiah was placed overnight in stocks located in the upper Benjamin Gate in the Jerusalem Temple because he proclaimed the coming destruction of the city (Jer 20:2-3; compare 29:26). Twice, Job complained that God had placed his feet in stocks and watched all his paths (Job 13:27; 33:11). In Philippi, Paul and Silas were placed in stocks in the innermost part of the prison after being charged with disturbing the peace for casting the spirit out of a servant girl who was making money for her owners (Acts 16:16-24).

BRUCE W. GENTRY

STOICS, STOICISM stoh´iks, stoh´i-siz´uhm [Στοϊκός Stoikos]. From the Greek stoa (στοά), referring to the porch or colonnade where the Athenian school met. The founder of Stoicism was Zeno of Citium (ca. 334–262 BCE). The school laid claim to a Socratic lineage through a succession of teachers from Zeno to the Cynics Crates and Diogenes, Antisthenes, and ultimately Socrates himself (compare Philodemus, *On the Stoics*, cols. 12-13).

Historians have traditionally divided Stoicism into three phases. Early Stoicism refers to the successive leadership of the school by Zeno, Cleanthes, and Chrysippus in the 3rd cent. BCE. Because it was Chrysippus who systematically worked out the basic positions taken by Zeno, his writings above all came to be considered definitive of Stoic orthodoxy. Middle Stoicism refers to a period from the mid-2nd to the mid-1st cent. BCE, and especially to the apparently modified form of Stoicism brought to Rome by Panaetius (ca. 185–110 BCE) and his student Posidonius (ca. 135–50 BCE). Late Stoicism refers to the shape the philosophy took in the period of the Roman Empire.

Stoicism was a self-consciously systematic philosophy, presented in three interdependent divisions: logic, physics, and ethics. The present summary will focus only on physics and ethics, the latter of which was the Stoics' own primary concern.

The Stoics envisioned the universe as a unified material being, a continuum with active and passive aspects. Passive matter is informed by an immanent, active structuring principle called logos that gives shape to any given instance of matter. The four elements are likewise either active (fire, air) or passive (water, earth). Fire was said to be the preeminent element inasmuch as it is ultimately constitutive of the others, and alone cannot be resolved into something else. It was associated closely with both logos (λόγος) and, particularly after Chrysippus, pneuma (πνεῦμα) or "breath."

The Stoics identified God variously as that active principle, whether logos or fire, that gives structure and purpose to the universe, or as Nature or the world itself, pictured (rather like the human being) as a living body governed by reason. Humans were thought to have a special kinship with God as a result of their own rational nature. The world was envisioned as a Great City whose law was the divine logos, and whose citizens were the gods and humans who lived by that law (Cicero, *Leg.* 1.23). The whole world, in fact, was providentially created for the benefit and use of those endowed with reason (e.g., Cicero, *Nat. d.* 2.133).

The Stoic assumption regarding divine providence led them to the view that all aspects of the world were divinely predetermined so as to conform to the best, most rational world-order possible. What is more, since that order could not possibly be improved upon, the same sequence of events that constitutes the present world are continually replayed on a never-ending loop from conflagration to conflagration.

While this determinism might seem to preclude human moral responsibility or what subsequent philosophers would call free will, the Stoics insisted this was not the case. As rational beings, what humans are free to do at any given moment is to accept or resist the will of God as it plays out in the world—much as a dog, tied to a moving cart, can choose whether to walk along willingly or be dragged.

The Stoics accepted the traditional Greek philosophical identification of the basic goal of life as happiness. In Stoicism, though, "happiness" means specifically bringing one's own will into conformity with the will of God, one's own reason into harmony with the "right reason" that providentially governs the world as divine law. The basic aim of Stoic ethics, then, was "living harmoniously" with the providential world-order as it unfolds, or, put another way, living in accord with nature.

Nature itself is said to help lead humans to this end by providing them (as indeed all animals) with an innate tendency to distinguish things that are beneficial to themselves from things that are injurious. Every action on the part of an animal, including the human, is said to originate in an impulse prompted by a sensory impression of something that inspires such a subjective evaluation. In the case of the rational animal, however, logos becomes the "craftsman of impulse" (Diogenes Laertius, *Vit. Phil.* 7.85–86), so that human action depends not merely upon instinct (e.g., to eat in response to a presentation of food) but upon assent to the propositions that the logos supplies regarding such presentations (e.g., "it is good for me to eat this food"). As the mature human being becomes increasingly aware that his or her nature is defined fundamentally by reason, (s)he can (ideally) come to realize what is truly good for that nature: not things like wealth or status, or even health and life itself—which, all things being equal, are admittedly preferable—but simply the alignment of one's own reason with the reason that orders the universe, and thus of one's own impulses with what is in any case the preordained will of God.

The Stoics identified virtue as the consistent and unshakeable disposition of the soul characterized by right reason. Vice, conversely, represented the alternative: a soul characterized not by right reason but "passion," which they defined as "excessive impulse," i.e., an impulse to achieve or avoid some end that goes beyond what right reason dictates.

The fundamental goal of Stoicism, in short, was "the natural perfection of a rational being as rational being" (Diogenes Laertius, *Vit. Phil.* 7.94). While conceding that the actual accomplishment of this end was as rare as the mythical phoenix, the Stoics nonetheless emphasized its real possibility.

The Stoics are explicitly mentioned only once in the Bible, in an incident of dubious historicity. Acts 17:16-34 places Paul in the Athenian agora, engaged in a stereotypically Athenian activity of philosophical debate with, among others, Epicureans and Stoics (17:18). As is typical of the literary portrayal of audiences in Acts, this one too is said to be split between those who are potentially receptive to Christian teaching and those who are not (17:32; compare 2:12-13; 14:4; 23:6-9; 28:24). The key stumbling block in this case is said to be Paul's teaching about resurrection of the dead, a notion generally alien to Greek philosophy, which typically envisioned afterlife, if at all, in terms of an immortal soul rather than a revivified body. That being said, it is noteworthy that Chrysippus and subsequent Stoics taught that after death humans would regain their same "shape" after a period of time. Whether Luke intends to imply a perceived resonance between the two ideas on the part of some of the Stoics in the audience (compare 17:32) is by no means clear. The Stoic view was in any event radically different from the one we are to assume Luke's Paul has been teaching the Athenians. The latter idea comes from Jewish apocalypticism, which assumes a linear construction of time. As can be seen in their doctrine of the cosmic cycle, however, the Stoics understood time to be circular. What Chrysippus had in mind, then, was essentially an everlasting repetition of one's current life. Indeed, from the Stoic point of view one's present life, insofar as it has been preceded by others in the everlasting cycle, is itself already an example of such existence after death.

The significance of Stoicism for the Bible extends well beyond this singular reference in Acts 17. The portrayal of the cosmic figure of Wisdom in the Wisdom of Solomon, for example, owes much to the Stoic notion that the cosmos is pervaded and fashioned by a rational pneuma (e.g., Wis 1:7; 7:22, 24; 8:1, 4-6)—a notion that also stands rather clearly in the background of the Johannine logos hymn (see especially John 1:1-4). The Stoic identification of logos as a divinely given law, on the other hand, is clearly at work in the discourse on law found in both 4 Maccabees (e.g., 1:15-17; compare 5:22-26) and the Letter of James (especially 1:21-25), and perhaps also in Paul's notion that Gentiles can do the law "by nature" (Rom 2:14). *See* GREEK RELIGION AND PHILOSOPHY.

Bibliography: Keimpe Algra et al. *The Cambridge History of Hellenistic Philosophy* (1999); John J. Collins. *Jewish Wisdom in the Hellenistic Age* (1997); Troels Engberg-Pedersen. *Paul and the Stoics* (2000); Brad Inwood. *Ethics and Human Action in Early Stoicism* (1985); Brad Inwood, ed. *The Cambridge Companion to the Stoics* (2003); Matt A. Jackson-McCabe. *Logos and Law in the Letter of James: The Law of Nature, the Law of Moses, and the Law of Freedom* (2001); Michelle V. Lee. *Paul, the Stoics, and the Body of Christ* (2006); Anthony A. Long and David N. Sedley. *The Hellenistic Philosophers.* 2 vols. (1987); Anthony A. Long. *Epictetus: A Stoic and Socratic Guide to Life* (2002).

MATT JACKSON-MCCABE

STOMACH [בֶּטֶן beten, חֹמֶשׁ khomesh, מֵעֶה me'eh, קֵבָה qevah; κοιλία koilia, στόμαχος stomachos]. The internal organ for digestion (Sir 36:23). In animal offerings, it was designated for the priests (Deut 18:3, qevah). Twice in 2 Samuel, the area of the stomach was the site of a fatal wound (2:23; 3:27, khomesh). Hunger (Ezek 7:19, me'eh) and satisfaction (Prov 18:20, beten) reside there. It exemplifies bodily functions generally (Phil 3:19, koilia; NRSV, "belly"), and digestion of food specifically (1 Tim 5:23, stomachos; Matt 15:17; Mark 7:19; 1 Cor 6:13; Rev 10:9, all koilia). *See* HEART; SACRIFICES AND OFFERINGS.

LISA MICHELE WOLFE

STONECUTTER [חֹצֵב khotsev]. A worker who prepares stone for its use in construction, both by quarrying rough blocks of stone and by squaring them (1 Kgs 5:15 [Heb. 5:29]). Solomon employed Israelite, Tyrian, and Gebalite stonecutters (1 Kgs 5:18 [Heb. 5:32]) when building the Temple (compare 1 Chr 22:2, 15; 2 Chr 2:2, 18 [Heb. 2:1, 17]). Jehoash also hired stonecutters and masons to repair the Temple (2 Kgs 12:12 [Heb. 12:13]).

EUNHEE KANG

STONES [אֶבֶן 'even]. Stone was one of the natural building materials in the ANE, along with wood and mudbrick.

Most of the arable land of ancient Syria-Palestine is strewn with stones. When new ground is being prepared the field stones have to be cleared (Isa 5:2) and are often piled on the perimeter of the field. Stones or rock are also the raw material from which important metals and gemstones are extracted (Job 28:1-6).

The fieldstones found in many regions were used in many of the cruder forms of construction. These stones would simply be gathered and stacked, often with no mortar, for fences, walls, and even houses. Similar size stones could be used to produce rather uniform layers; smaller stones could be used to fill in spaces between larger ones. Such fieldstones were termed *unhewn* (Josh 8:31, literally "complete, whole") and were com-

manded for use in specific instances as altars (Deut 27:6). Although any fieldstone could be used in simpler structures, the most common stones used for more significant construction projects in ancient Syria-Palestine were limestone and basalt.

Any available stone of the size to fit in the hand might be used as a weapon, to throw with intent to injure (2 Sam 16:6, 13), or to strike to kill (Num 35:17), or for stoning ones (Lev 20:2). Stones shaped more spherical by wind and water were used as slingstones (2 Sam 17:40). Many of the ancient houses excavated in Syria-Palestine also have spherical stones. These would have served as multipurpose tools. They could be a hammer to pound a nail or shell a nut, or a grindstone to grind grain into meal or flour.

Ore deposits are also called stone, such as deposits that include iron and copper ore (Deut 8:9). Job 28:1-2 speaks of silver and gold, iron and copper, and of the smelting and refining necessary to extract the metal from its ore. In addition to ore deposits, gems and semiprecious stones are also called stones (Gen 2:12; Job 28:3-6), although most of the references are probably to gemstones that have been cut and polished (Exod 28:9, 11).

Worked stones make up the primary architectural usage of stones in larger construction projects, especially in monumental structures, and in many utensils. The terms used to describe these stones often reflects the degree of shaping or working involved. The stones may be rough-hewn or semi-hewn. They are either fieldstones that have been shaped into rough rectangular blocks or quarried stones with a rough rectangular shape. Hewn stones are more finely shaped. Amos implies that the wealthy oppressors in Israel built houses of hewn stone (Amos 5:11).

Ashlar masonry is the finest shaping of stones. The corners would have true 90° angles. At least one surface, visible to viewers, would have a very smooth finish or a raised boss. Such bosses may have served a decorative purpose as well as making movement from quarry to building site easier. The surfaces of ashlars are so carefully shaped that no mortar is needed between courses. Good examples of Israelite ashlar masonry include royal construction projects at Hazor, Megiddo, Samaria, Ramat Rahel, and Dan. However, one of the finest examples is the later Herodian use of ashlars in the Temple platform in Jerusalem. Ashlars could be hewn or sawed, the finest quality being sawn. Although no archaeological evidence has been recovered, the dressed stones of the foundation of Solomon's Temple (1 Kgs 5:17) were undoubtedly ashlars as were the hewn stones in his palace (1 Kgs 7:9-11). Cornerstones would also probably have been ashlars (compare Isa 28:16; Ps 118:22).

In addition to the use of stone blocks in structures, other worked stones served as structural pillars or columns to support upper stories or roofs. Such pillars or columns could be free-standing (as in the Iron Age pillared buildings) or could be incorporated in walls as the major load-bearing member. The remainder of such walls would be made of fieldstones; this technique is called pier and rubble construction.

Stones were often shaped into vessels, tools, and weapons. Stone tools are a mark of the modern human species. Although metal came to replace many of these tools, flint tools and stone vessels continued to be used. Examples of common utensils include mortars and pestles (Prov 27:22), grindstones, millstones (Isa 47:2), roof rollers, and storage vessels. Because stone vessels were not considered susceptible to uncleanness, they were used to store water for ritual purposes (John 2:6). Flint knives were used for circumcision (Exod 4:24-26; Josh 5:2-3). Special purpose stones could be either fieldstones or worked stones. They are noteworthy due to the special functions they served.

Blocking stones were used to close the entrance of caves (Josh 10:18, 25), wells (Gen 29:2-3), and tombs. Family tombs in the Iron Age often were cut into hillsides and included multiple chambers. At a family member's death, the body would be placed in one chamber and it would be sealed with a single blocking stone or multiple smaller ones. The other chambers were still available for use. Stones also served as stoppers or covers for pottery vessels.

Stones were used throughout the ANE as boundary markers or landmarks. Such markers could be large single stones or piles of smaller stones. The legal codes prohibited moving or removing these landmarks (Deut 27:17). In Babylonia, incised stones recording land grants were placed in temples as evidence of property rights.

Stones were commonly used for monuments and memorials. Absalom had no son to carry on his name, so he set up a stone monument during his lifetime to ensure he would be remembered (2 Sam 18:18). Kings frequently set up victory stelae describing their successful campaigns. The Mesha Stele is an example of a stone memorial recounting King Mesha's accomplishments throughout his reign (see 2 Kgs 3:4). One particular type of memorial is the tomb marker. Dolmens and menhirs are examples of prehistoric stone burial makers. Jacob set up a stone pillar as a tomb marker for Rachel after her death (Gen 35:20).

Some stones had a particular cultic usage. The cultic aspect typically was not dependent on whether the stone was worked or not, but in some cases unhewn stones were specified. Stone altars have been found in a number of archaeological excavations including Arad, Beersheba, Lachish, Megiddo, and Dan. The altar at Arad was made of unhewn fieldstone just as biblical law prescribed (Exod 20:25). The hewn stones of a large horned altar were discovered at Beersheba in secondary use in a later wall. Many examples of smaller incense altars were carved from a single stone. During the Early Bronze Age, Megiddo had a large circular altar constructed of fieldstones that was 26 feet in diameter, 5 feet high, and reached by seven steps.

Stones were often erected as standing stones to commemorate a religious encounter. After Jacob had his dream at Bethel, he set up the stone that had served as his pillow as a pillar (Gen 28:11-19). Joshua set up two sets of twelve stones, one in the midst of the Jordan River where the Israelites crossed (Josh 4:9) and one at Gilgal where they encamped after the crossing (Josh 4:2-8, 19-20, compare Deut 27:2-6). Not all standing stones were considered legitimate objects of reverence. The Israelites were forbidden to set up stones with carved figures, idols, images, and pillars (Lev 26:1).

Standing stones have been discovered in cultic contexts at numerous excavations including Hazor, Shechem, Dan, Bethsaida, and Arad. An example of the idols referred to as "gods of wood and stone" (Deut 4:28; 28:36, 64) is a recently discovered stele from Bethsaida depicting a horned, bull-headed deity, probably El. See ARCHITECTURE, NT; ARCHITECTURE, OT; BOHAN, STONE OF; CITY; CORNERSTONE; FIGURED STONE; HOUSE; INSCRIPTIONS; ISRAEL, GEOLOGY OF; HEAP OF STONES; JEWELS AND PRECIOUS STONES; MEMORIAL, MEMORY; ROAD MARKER; SCULPTURED STONE; STONECUTTER; STONING; TOMB; WAR, METHODS, TACTICS, WEAPONS OF (BRONZE AGE THROUGH PERSIAN PERIOD); WAR, METHODS, TACTICS, WEAPONS OF (HELLENISTIC THROUGH ROMAN PERIODS); ZOHELETH.

Bibliography: Uzi Avner. "Sacred Stones in the Desert." *BAR* 27(2001) 30–41; Doron Ben-Ami. "Mysterious Standing Stones—What Do These Ubiquitous Things Mean?" *BAR* 32 (2006) 38–45; Carl F. Graesser. "Standing Stones in Ancient Palestine." *BA* 35 (1972) 34–63; Larry Herr. "Tripartite Pillared Buildings and the Market Place in Iron Age Palestine." *BASOR* 272 (1988) 47–67; Aharon Kempinski and Ronny Reich. *The Architecture of Ancient Israel* (1992); G. R. H. Wright. *Ancient Building in South Syria and Palestine* (1997).

JOEL F. DRINKARD JR.

STONES, PRECIOUS. *See* JEWELS AND PRECIOUS STONES.

STONING [סָקַל *saqal*, רָגַם *ragham*; λιθάζω *lithazō*, λιθοβολέω *lithoboleō*]. A type of capital EXECUTION via pelting of stones. It typically involved transport of a person outside of the camp or the city (Lev 24:14; Deut 17:5), where the person was stoned initially by witnesses of the offense and, if death did not ensue, by onlookers (Deut 17:7). In biblical times, it was one of three types of judicial punishments, the others being burning and hanging. Stoning was exacted as the punishment for several infractions, including idolatry or seduction of others to idolatry (Lev 20:2; Deut 13:6-10), BLASPHEMY (Lev 24:14), and breaking the Sabbath (Num 15:32-36). Both Stephen (Acts 7:58) and Paul (Acts 14:19) were stoned, the former with a fatal end. A woman also escaped a possible stoning by virtue of Jesus' challenges to her accusers (John 8:7). In the Talmud, stoning is listed (with strangling, death by sword [including beheading], and burning) as an appropriate form of capital punishment (e.g., *y. Sanh.* 22d; 23b–c). Stoning was also prominent among the Persians and the Greeks. *See* CRIMES AND PUNISHMENT, OT AND NT.

ABRAHAM SMITH

STORE-CITIES, STOREHOUSES [אָסֹף ʾasof, בֵּית אֹסֵף beth ʾotsar, מִסְכְּנוֹת עִיר miskenoth ʿir; ταμεῖον tameion]. Cities (2 Chr 16:4) or buildings (2 Kgs 20:13; Neh 13:12-13) used for the storage of government supplies. Solomon (1 Kgs 9:19, author's trans.; NRSV, "storage cities"), Jehoshaphat (2 Chr 17:12), and Hezekiah (2 Chr 32:28), built store-cities or storehouses. Storehouses were usually long, rectangular buildings with double walls and deep foundations. This design helped insulate against moisture and prevent mold. Storehouses at Beer-sheba were built against the city walls and gate. Goods such as flour, oil, and wine were stored in large ceramic jars. Excavations at Dothan revealed jars stacked on top of one another. The Temple also had a storehouse (Mal 3:10) and some storehouses were privately owned. *See* TRADE AND COMMERCE.

Storehouse is used metaphorically to describe the places where God "stores" atmospheric phenomena such as rain, snow, hail, and wind (e.g., Deut 28:12; Job 38:22; Ps 33:7; Jer 10:13; 51:16; Sir 43:14). Empty storehouses indicate economic misfortune (Joel 1:17; 2 Esd 6:22).

Bibliography: Oded Borowski. *Agriculture in Iron Age Israel* (1987).

TERRY W. EDDINGER

STORK [חֲסִידָה khasidhah]. A bird called khasidah, a name apparently meaning "the faithful one," is included in the lists of ritually unclean birds (Lev 11:19; Deut 14:18). It is assumed by several modern translations (e.g., NRSV) that the stork, famous for its conjugal loyalty, is intended. From the few and fragmentary OT references to the khasidah, this bird is a migrant (Jer 8:7), andnests in tree tops (Ps 104:17), and has large wings (Zec 5:9). This description applies to the white stork (*Ciconia alba*), but also to the common HERON (*Ardea cinerea*). In some instances (e.g., Ps 104:17), the LXX renders khasidah with erōdios (ἐρωδιός) "heron." As suggested by Driver, the Hebrew term may have been an inclusive designation, covering both the stork and the heron. *See* BIRDS OF THE BIBLE.

Bibliography: G. R. Driver. "Birds in the Old Testament: I. Birds in Law." *PEQ* 87 (1955) 5–20.

GÖRAN EIDEVALL

STORM [סוּפָה sufah; λαῖλαψ lailaps]. The general region of ancient Canaan is located in one of the earth's sub-tropical zones, though the more discrete area of the Jordan Valley has been characterized as a tropical zone. As such, the region undergoes two major seasons: a dry one spanning June to September, and a wet season lasting from October to April with May being a transitional period. Biblical writers divided the wet season into two parts, the early rain and the late rain. Seventy to seventy-five percent of the rainfall occurs between November and February. The overall precipitation levels and climatic conditions of Canaan have not undergone significant deviation for the past 10,000 years. One can reasonably conclude that the Late Bronze to the Roman periods—the time span that roughly corresponds to what is often referred to as "biblical times"—was not much different from that of today.

Storms possess a beneficent, life-supporting aspect because they provide the rains, as well as an ominous chaotic aspect owing to their destructive potential. The peoples of the ANE held that storms—most often seen on mountain tops in the region encompassing ancient Canaan—were expressions of divine self revelation. The wind or the lightning and thunder that often accompanied storms were viewed as the manifestation of the divine voice. The deity's power as revealed in the storm was thought to display the deity's majesty as giver of the rains and fertilizer of the land. Associations such as these explain why the cult of the storm god was so prominent among sedentary populations in the region of ancient Canaan where rain-fed agriculture was widely practiced. Yet, this same god could also express divine anger in the storm, aimed at his wayward people or at their enemies as a form of judgment or curse. The resultant, seemingly dual character of the god elicited one of two responses on the part of humanity, either trust or fear.

Similar associations between storm and god are preserved in biblical characterizations of Yahweh. According to Judg 5:4-5, the earth trembles, clouds release water, and mountains quake at Yahweh's appearance. When Yahweh is described as rescuing his beloved, he is surrounded in darkness (and) thick clouds full with water constitute his canopy (Ps 18:11 [Heb. 18:12]). When Yahweh lifts up his voice, the thunder resounds (Ps 18:13 [Heb. 18:14]) and elsewhere Yahweh's voice is described as originating from within a thunderstorm (Exod 9:28). Other traits that have been identified as evidence for Yahweh's character as storm god include several shared with (or "appropriated from"?) Yahweh's nemesis and rival Balu, another well-known and widely attested storm god. These include the portrayal as "god of the hills" (1 Kgs 20:23) and the identity of Yahweh's hilltop abode as mount Zaphon (Ps 48:2), the inherited baalistic epithet, "rider of the clouds" (Ps 68:4 [Heb. 48:5]), and Yahweh's victory over Yam or "Sea." It has even been suggested that the etymology of the name *Yahweh* is indicative of storm god status, that is, if the form yhwh means "he blows (the winds)" or "he causes to fall (rain or lightning)."

BRIAN B. SCHMIDT

STOVE. *See* OVEN.

STRABO stray'boh. Greek historian and geographer (63 BCE–21 CE) from Amaseia in Pontius. Born into a wealthy family, Strabo received a Greek education completed in Rome under the tutelage of Peripatetics and was an adherent of Stoicism (*see* STOICS, STOICISM). He traveled extensively until 7 BCE, when he returned home and remained there until his death. His *Historical Sketches* in forty-seven books is lost; but his *Geographia* in seventeen books survives. This work, completed by 7 BCE, is an invaluable source for information on geographical knowledge, politics, and history of the regions in the Roman Empire during the Augustan Age.

MICHAEL J. SCHUFER

STRAIGHT, RIGHT. *See* RIGHTEOUSNESS IN EARLY JEWISH LITERATURE; RIGHTEOUSNESS IN THE NT; RIGHTEOUSNESS IN THE OT.

STRANGE [זָר zar, לַעַז la'az; μέγας megas, ξενίζω xenizō, ξένος xenos, παράδοξος paradoxos]. *Strange* almost exclusively refers to strange gods (Deut 32:16), languages (Ps 114:1), or practices, denoting something that is outside the experience of the speaker (Luke 5:26). It describes things that are either incomprehensible or inexplicable. *See* FOREIGN, FOREIGNER.

NATHAN P. LAMONTAGNE

STRANGER [גֵּר ger, זָר zar, נָכְרִי nokhri; ἀλλογενής allogenēs, ἀλλότριος allotrios, ξένος xenos, πάροικος paroikos, προσήλυτος prosēlytos, χωρίζω chōrizō]. Conceptions of *stranger* in the Bible relate to the differing cultural, socio-political, and, to some extent, socio-religious classes among people. The term may also refer to the manner in which a person exists, lives, or resides (e.g., in a city). Other connotations of *stranger* pertain to the avoidance or limitation of association with someone or the lack of kinship relations with another person.

A. Selected Biblical Passages Illustrating the Uses of *Stranger*
  1. Old Testament
  2. Apocrypha
  3. New Testament
B. Major Theological Concerns
Bibliography

A. Selected Biblical Passages Illustrating the Uses of *Stranger*
1. Old Testament
A stranger (zar) is 1) someone from a socio-political group or class of persons not native to a dominant group or land; and 2) someone or something illegitimate, unauthorized, or foreign in terms of kinship or moral behavior. Thus, a stranger (zar or exō anēr [ἔξω ἀνήρ, "outside man"]) is an illegitimate or unauthorized person who cannot be married to an Israelite woman in the levirate marriage (Deut 25:5). Similarly, zarim (זָרִים) are employed as metaphors for strange gods that the Israelites have idolized (Jer 2:25; 3:13). Often, the insider group regards the alterity of zar with latent or overt hostility, thus viewing the zar as an ENEMY. Zarim are depicted as creditors who seize another's possessions (Ps 109:11; Prov 11:15; 14:10; 20:16). Some biblical texts represent the zar as a stranger who is an enemy of the nation (Jer 5:19; 30:8; Ezek 7:21; Joel 3:17 [Heb. 4:17]; Obad 11).

A stranger (ger) is most typically a person of a different geographical or cultural group than the dominant cultural group and whose right of landed property, marriage, and participation in jurisdiction, cult, and war has been restricted; the most appropriate translation for most occurrences is "immigrant" or "resident alien." In some contexts the more general connotation "stranger" is appropriate. As strangers in foreign lands, Israel's ancestors constituted the quintessential gerim (גֵּרִים, Gen 23:4; 1 Chr 16:19; Ps 105:12). The gerim surface in the well-known Deuteronomic passage that treats the essence of torah for Yahweh's covenant people: God is a God who "executes justice for the orphan and the widow, and who loves the strangers, providing them food and clothing. You shall also love the stranger, for you were strangers in the land of Egypt" (Deut 10:18-19). The Israelites are exhorted to parallel Yahweh's just treatment of the gerim. The gerim are often mentioned alongside other disenfranchised or powerless persons, such as the poor, slaves, widows, and orphans and are in more need than the primary groups to whom the Deuteronomic torah is addressed (Deut 10:18; 16:11, 14; compare Pss 94:6; 146:9). In Job 31:32, ger is a "traveler"; a traveling stranger in ANE cultures was in need of a good host to provide safe lodging and nourishment.

"Stranger" (nokhri) also denotes a "foreigner," someone who is not in the same clan, land area, or religion as the speaker and thus not in close association or limited association with the designated speaker. For example, Joseph treats his brothers who visit him in Egypt in need of food as nokhri, as strangers from a foreign land (Gen 42:7). Job complains that, whereas he should be intimately known and accepted in his own household, he has now become an alien and a stranger, implying he has become unknown and unrecognizable to those closest to him (Job 19:15).

2. Apocrypha
A xenos is a person belonging to a socio-political group other than the dominant cultural or socio-political group. Often the primary distinction is situated between geographical alterity and lack of previous knowledge

and/or familiarity. Wisdom 19:13-15 recounts how the Egyptians mistreated the Israelite slaves as "strangers," in a violation of the hospitality code. The Egyptians hated these dissimilar socio-political "strangers" (xenos), refused to receive the "strangers" (misoxenia μισοξενία), and treated the "strangers" (allotrios) with hostility (compare 2 Esd 16:46). Allotrios denotes, in many cases, an outsider—a person or group of people who do not belong to another group because of relative alterity (1 Macc 1:38; Sir 8:18).

In wisdom sayings with respect to the difficulties of being a stranger or guest, paroikos indicates a person who lives for a period of time in a place not his normal residence and who is, as a consequence, in an undesirable state of dependence (Sir 29:26-27).

In the moral tale of Judith, Judith prays, acknowledging God's power in Simeon to avenge Shechem's rape of Dinah, his sister (Jdt 9:2; compare Gen 34:25-31). In her prayer, Shechem and his people, the Hivites, who are a different and, in this case, hostile socio-political group having different kinship from Jacob's clan, are referred to as "strangers" (allogenēs). Third Maccabees 2:25 excoriates Ptolemy IV Philopator and his comrades, who are "strangers (chōrizō) to everything just."

3. New Testament

In the NT, *stranger* (xenos) frequently implies the status of a suppliant who should be treated as a guest (Matt 25:35, 38, 43-44; compare 3 John 5, in which the guests are Christians). Cleopas' question to the resurrected Jesus, "Are you the only stranger (paroikos) in Jerusalem who does not know the things that have taken place there in these days?" presumes that Jesus has not lived in Jerusalem because of his apparent lack of knowledge of Jesus' arrest and crucifixion (Luke 24:18). In John 10:5, the "sheep" will not follow a "stranger" (allotrios) whose voice they do not know, i.e., someone like a thief or bandit who is unrecognized by their social group.

B. Major Theological Concerns

One should appraise the theological importance of the "stranger" in that portion of Scripture summarizing all the positive Deuteronomic formulations of the acceptable human response to the Lord (Deut 10:18-19). God's people, the Israelites, originated as a diverse group, but each had in common their stranger or immigrant status and their commitment to Yahweh. Yahweh is described as having a unique concern for an assortment of human problems including those who have fewer rights than the dominant group. Frank Spina conjectures that this may have been the first time in human history in which the divine supported the side of the stranger, the disenfranchised, and other marginalized groups.

Also, a consideration of "stranger" in Jer 14:8 reminds us that exile changes God's children's recognition of and relationship to the Lord. When the people of God are exiled from God, the Lord becomes a stranger to the people of God, a shadowy figure who seems distant from them.

In the NT, representing strangeness or otherness becomes an issue of rhetoric primarily linked to language and politics. In formulating someone or something as "other," a biblical text participates in a program of self-definition with forceful cultural and political implications. We find certain NT texts either maintaining or disowning stranger status for Christians.

Hebrews 11:13 claims this "stranger" status for Christian identity to underscore the distinctiveness of Christian identity and to justify the existence of Christians as a clearly defined group. The stranger topos became an adaptable rhetorical resource that early Christians could employ for the purposes of identity formation—promoting internal self-definition and the external situating of Christian identity within the vast range of social, philosophical, and cultic identities and practices that burgeoned in the Roman world.

Jesus identifies himself as a stranger (xenos): "for I was hungry and you gave me food, I was thirsty and you gave me something to drink, I was a stranger and you welcomed me, I was naked and you gave me clothing, I was sick and you took care of me, I was in prison and you visited me" (Matt 25:35; see also 25:38, 43-44). This Matthean eschatological teaching about righteousness comes from Deut 10:18-19, where Yahweh loves disenfranchised and marginalized groups and provides for their basic physical needs (see §A1). In Matt 25:31-46, God's people are exhorted to love strangers because in so doing they love Jesus, whose identity is wrapped into the stranger.

Passages such as Eph 2:11-22 indicate that Christians themselves were once strangers, as Gentiles. These Gentile Christians are no longer strangers (xenos) and aliens (paroikos) but citizens and members of the household of God (Eph 2:19; compare Gal 3:26). In Pauline theology, the Gentiles have become Abraham's offspring; Paul claims that in Christ there is no distinction between the Jew and Gentile (Gal 3:28-29). For Paul, there are no strangers among those who are in Christ. *See* SOJOURNER.

Bibliography: Benjamin Dunning. *Aliens and Sojourners: Self as Other in Early Christianity* (2009); José Ramírez Kidd. *Alterity and Identity in Israel* (1999); Frank Spina. "Israelites as gerim, 'Sojourners' in Social and Historical Context." *The Word of the Lord Shall Go Forth.* Carol Meyers and Michael O'Connor, eds. (1983) 321–35.

MICHAEL D. MATLOCK AND BILL T. ARNOLD

STRANGLING [מַחֲנָק makhanaq; πνικτός pniktos]. With reference to human beings, a method of execution (Job 7:15; Tob 2:3; 3:8, with NRSV footnote); with reference to animals, a type of slaughter. Strangling was never prescribed in the OT as a form of capital punishment, but is listed as a method in the Talmud. Since Mosaic codes (Lev 3:17; Deut 12:23-25) prohibited the eating of animals whose carcasses were not properly drained of blood, *strangling* was used to refer to other methods of slaughter. As a concession to their Jewish brethren, the Gentile converts of Antioch, Syria, and Cilicia (Acts 15:20; compare 15:29; 21:25) were asked, among other things, to refrain from "whatever has been strangled," though not all MSS include this dietary concession, as the NRSV indicates in footnotes. *See* CRIMES AND PUNISHMENT, OT AND NT.

ABRAHAM SMITH

STRATON'S TOWER [Στράτωνος πύργος *Stratōnos pyrgos*]. A 4th-cent. BCE Hellenistic city on the coast of Palestine, probably named for Straton I of TYRE. Herod the Great began building his capital city of Caesarea on the ruins of Straton's Tower in 22 BCE. *See* CAESAREA MARITIMA.

STRAW [מַתְבֵּן *mathben*, קַשׁ *qash*, תֶּבֶן *teven*; καλάμη *kalamē*]. The stems of any number of grain plants such as barley or wheat grown in the ANE. The biblical usage of this term admits of two primary uses. First, it was commonly used as food for animals (e.g., Judg 19:19). In this capacity the straw was sometimes mixed with the grain proper (1 Kgs 4:28 [Heb. 5:8]). Second, straw was used as a building material. Exodus 5:10-19 depicts the use of straw in brick making, and the one occurrence of straw in the NT (1 Cor 3:12) also refers metaphorically to a building material.

T. DELAYNE VAUGHN

STREAM [נָהָר *nahar*, נַחַל *nakhal*]. As a noun, *stream* refers to a body of running water. For example, Jacob, his family, and his goods crossed the stream to enter the land of Canaan (Gen 32:23). When Moses ground up the image of the calf, he tossed the dust into the stream that flowed down from the mountain (Deut 9:21). Streams can also represent abundance or provision (Deut 8:7; Ps 46:4 [Heb. 46:5]; Song 4:15; Ezek 31:4; Joel 3:18) or a source of satisfaction and nourishment (Pss 1:3; 42:1 [Heb. 42:2]; Isa 35:6; Jer 17:8). Metaphorically, Isaiah speaks of the stream of the wealth of the nations that the Lord will bring to Zion (Isa 66:12), and Amos calls for justice to roll down like a stream (Amos 5:24). Daniel saw a "stream of fire" flow from the Ancient One (Dan 7:10). As a verb, *stream* refers to the type of motion produced by running water. In Isa 2:2 the prophet foresees a day when the nations will stream to the mountain of Zion (Mic 4:1; compare Jer 51:44). In the NRSV, *stream* does not occur in the NT. *See* BROOK; RIVER.

JORGE PIXLEY

STREET. *See* BROAD PLACE; CITY; SQUARE, PUBLIC.

STRENGTH [חֹזֶק *khozeq*; ἰσχυρός *ischyros*]. *Strong* or *strength* generally refers to a quality of God's nature that both emboldens and protects the faithful. Because strength in both the OT and NT is considered a quality of God's, the individual's strength or the strength of a people is not derived from their own human capacities. To have fortitude and courage as an individual or as a people comes from being accompanied by God, reminded of God's nature, or gifted by God with these qualities. Thus, in the OT Moses exhorts both Israel and Joshua to be strong and bold as they cross to the promised land, because God accompanies them (Deut 30:6-7). In Ps 140 the petitioner reminds the listener that God is not just the deliverer but the strong deliverer who protects against the violent enemies. Note that a distinction is made between "strong" and "violent." God is strong, and the enemies of God are violent. God's strength protects against violence but is not itself violent; God's strength is a marker of God's righteousness.

God's gift of strength to individuals in both the OT and NT is also paradoxical, for God chooses as God's emissaries those whom the world would consider weak. Moses, who is "slow of speech and slow of tongue," is chosen to lead God's people (Exod 4:10). With God's aid, David, the physically weaker contestant, overpowers the mighty Philistine, Goliath (1 Sam 17). In the NT, a young, unwed woman is chosen as the bearer of God's Son (Luke 1:26-38). In the Lukan version, the birth of Jesus takes place in the lowliest of places, a stable (Luke 2:6-7), from which comes one whose power is greater even than death. At his crucifixion, Jesus appears to be weak to non-Christian witnesses by not resisting his own death (Matt 27:38-43). Theologically, Jesus' strength is often attributed to his faith, manifest as not fighting against his crucifixion. Because he accepts this death, he fulfills the will of God. This interpretation has challengers, however. Feminist and womanist theologians see this interpretation of passivity in the face of brutality as as theological support for tolerating physical, spiritual, and emotional abuse in the present life with remediation in the next life.

The paradox of NT strength is supported by the letters of Paul. In 1 Cor 1:27 Paul reminds the church at Corinth: "God chose what is weak in the world to shame the strong." Thus God's emboldening of the weak serves to "take down" the power of the socially and politically strong. Here it is the strength of faith and not the strength of might that serves God's aims. When one proclaims one's strength, Paul continues, one proclaims the strength given by God and not mortal strength. In 2 Cor 12:9 Paul reports God telling him, "My grace is sufficient for you, for power is made perfect in weakness." *See* POWER, POWERFUL; STRONG AND WEAK; WEAKNESS.

EMILY ASKEW

STRINGED INSTRUMENTS. *See* MUSICAL INSTRU-MENTS.

STRIPES. *See* SCOURGE; WHIP.

STRONG. *See* MIGHTY MEN.

STRONG AND WEAK [אַבִּיר *'abbir*, אָמַל *'amal*, דַּל *dal*; ἀσθενής *asthenēs*, ἰσχυρός *ischyros*]. Both Testaments give voice to the weak more often than to the strong. Often under the heel of oppressors and acutely conscious of its vulnerability, weak Israel found strength to endure in the surpassing might of God (Isa 40:10; Exod 13:9; Ps 89:8) and hope for a divine reversal that would expose the fragility of earthly power (Dan 11–12), which would empower the weak to say, "I am a warrior" (Joel 3:10). In the painful memory of oppression and brutalizing slavery, Israel later found an ethical imperative to care for the weak (Deut 5:15; Isa 35:3; Job 4:3), the POOR (Amos), and enslaved (Deut 5:15, "remember, you were a slave in the land of Egypt.").

Steeped in the traditions of his people, Paul more than any NT writer (but see Matt 26:41//Mark 14:38) offered variations on these themes, and in one case in defense of his apostolic legitimacy reflected at some length on the nature of true power. Note, for example, his admonition to the Thessalonians to "help the weak" (1 Thess 5:14; Gal 4:9), to be sensitive to the vulnerable, to attend to the weak of conscience (1 Cor 8:7–9:22; 8:7, 10, 12; Rom 14:1–15:13), and to affirm the surpassing might of God's power (1 Cor 1:25: "God's weakness [asthenēs] is stronger than human strength." In the death and resurrection of Christ, Paul found evidence that God was intervening to vindicate the weak (1 Cor 15:43; 2 Cor 13:4) and demonstrate divine power.

It was an assault on his apostolic legitimacy and fitness for ministry, however, that inspired some of Paul's most creative thinking about power and weakness (see 2 Cor 1–13:10). An invasion of itinerant apostles triggered a brutal public fight between Paul and the partisans of these "super apostles" that sent him limping away in shameful retreat to craft a defense. The slanderous charges of these agents of Satan (2 Cor 11:14-15) and their acolytes inflicted festering wounds that provoked a scalding response from Paul.

A discourse of the body pervades 2 Corinthians. Against Paul's feeble frame, a "clay jar" in which a treasure is hidden (3:7-12), stood the confident, charismatic, eloquent, radiant, visionary, miracle-working persona of the antagonists (3:1-18). They scorned him as weak; they mocked the bravado of "his weighty and strong" letters (10:10); they ridiculed his bodily presence as weak (asthenēs); they demeaned his incompetent speech (10:10) and fake bravery. Their taunts provoked Paul's bitterly sarcastic retort: "I who am humble (tapeinos ταπεινός) when face to face with you, but bold toward you when I am away" (10:1*b*).

Adopting the persona of the fool—a stock character who entertained, amused, criticized, and unmasked pretensions to power—Paul initiated a farcical boasting contest. Rejecting scars on the chest as cultural markers of a brave warrior, he sarcastically led a directed reading of the scars on his back that were signifiers of servility, shame, degradation and weakness. Etched on his back by whip, rod, and stone, these scars, Paul noted, told a story, not of valor but of weakness or womanishness. In a flash of brilliance, he connected them to the scars cut on the kneeling back of Jesus as a prelude to his crucifixion. He owned the epithet "weakness," hurled at him as a slur, and turned it into a badge of strength. "Who is weak," he offered, "and am I not weak?... If I must boast, I will boast in the things that show my weakness" (2 Cor 11:26-30). On the lips of his critics, "weakness" rendered him unfit for apostolic ministry. An inventory of Paul's use of the word "weakness" is instructive. After the single occurrence in 2 Cor 10:10 on the lips of his adversaries, in response Paul bundles six adjectival forms in 11:30; 12:5, 9, 10; and 13:4; three verb forms in 11:21, 29; 12:10, and inserts two examples of his weakness in 10:30-33 (a cowardly escape from Damascus under the cover of darkness), and 12:7-8 (a bodily nemesis, or "thorn in the flesh"). His earnest, thrice-repeated petition for relief (12:7-8) elicits only a poignant refusal of his request: "'My grace is sufficient for you, for [my] power (dynamis δύναμις) is made perfect in weakness (asthenēs).' So I will boast all the more gladly of my weaknesses ... insults, hardships, persecutions, and calamities for the sake of Christ; for whenever I am weak (asthenō ἀσθενῶ), then I am strong (dynatos δυνατός)" (12:9-10). Thus the epithet hung on him as a signifier of shame and unfitness for ministry, he recast as an imitation of Christ (12:10). This radical ideology of power in weakness radically subverted the "dominant male discourse of the body" and through the elevation of weakness into a symbol of power suggested that in Christ one was able to win by losing. *See* CORINTHIANS, FIRST LETTER TO THE; IDOL; LORD'S SUPPER; MEAT; POWER, POWERFUL; STRENGTH; WEAKNESS.

Bibliography: J. A. Glancy. "Boasting of Beatings (2 Corinthians 11:23-25)." *JBL* 123 (2004) 99–135; Calvin J. Roetzel. "The Language of War (2 Cor. 10:1-6) and the Language of Weakness (2 Cor. 11:21*b*—13:10)." *BibInt* 17 (2009) 77–99; Brent Shaw. "Body/Power/Identity: Passions of the Martyrs." *JECS* 4 (1996) 269–312.

CALVIN J. ROETZEL

STRONG DRINK [שֵׁכָר *shekhar*; σίκερα *sikera*]. The term may originally have referred to barley beer but eventually signified any type of alcoholic beverage. Strong drink, like WINE, had a place in celebration: Deut 14:26 presumes that the consumption of both was a recognized part of celebrations. But excessive use of strong drink and DRUNKENNESS were regarded as a vice (Isa 5:11-13, 22-24; compare 1 Sam 1:13-15; Mic 2:11). Strong drink formed the drink offering of the morning and evening sacrifices at the tabernacle (Num 28:7-8). However, priests were forbidden to drink wine or strong drink before entering the sanctuary (Lev 10:9), and Nazirites had to abstain from strong drink for the duration of their vow (Num 6:3; compare Judg 13:4, 7, 14; 1 Sam 1:11; Luke 1:15).

TRISHA GAMBAIANA WHEELOCK

STRONGHOLD [אַרְמוֹן 'armon, בִּצָּרוֹן bitsaron, מִבְצָר mivtsar, מִסְגֶּרֶת misgereth, מָעוֹז ma'oz, מֵצַד metsadh, מְצוּדָה metsudhah, מִשְׂגָּב misgav, עֹז 'oz, צְרִיחַ tseriakh; ὀχύρωμα ochyrōma]. Any of several types of structures promising protection: e.g., a vault (Judg 9:46), a citadel (Isa 34:13), or a fortified city (2 Sam 5:9). In a figurative sense, the term can refer to Yahweh as well (e.g., 2 Sam 22:3; Ps 27:1). See CITADEL; FORTRESS; TOWER.

JOEL M. LEMON

STRUCTURALISM AND DECONSTRUCTION. Structuralism and deconstruction belong to the movement of POSTMODERN BIBLICAL INTERPRETATION, which embraces a plurality of methods. Structuralism originated in 1930s Europe, among members of the Prague linguistic school (R. Jakobson, V. Mathesius), and later developed in the school of Copenhagen (J. Hjelmslev).

Structuralism includes philosophies and methods that consider the structure of a phenomenon as autonomous in relation to its individual parts. Structuralism thus provides an alternative to positivism's inductive method of interpreting the world. Methodologically, the analysis of structure becomes the starting point in the interpretation of any text. Structuralism's priority is synchronic analysis, i.e., interpreting a text as a whole without regard to its history, including sources and redaction. But structuralist interpretation does not prohibit diachronic analysis, i.e., interpreting a text as it developed over time.

Structuralism maintains that content cannot be deciphered apart from the structures that contain it. For example, the holistic method of structuralism stresses that individual sayings of Jesus should be interpreted in relation to the story of Jesus as represented in the narrative frame of a particular Gospel. The "structures" studied by structuralism include a range of linguistic systems that generate meaning, such as grammar and genre. These structures are pervasive and make communication possible; thus, they constitute the human world and are not to be disregarded as mere "forms." In its present application, structuralism often underscores the referential function of biblical language (i.e., revelation understood through contingent events of history). Jan Mukařovský, an heir of the Prague school, has drawn attention to the social dimension of any literary structure.

Deconstruction, pioneered by the French philosopher J. Derrida, emerged as a methodological challenge to structuralism's hermeneutical claims. A deconstructive hermeneutic emphasizes that meaning can be evasive, and that the study of structure does not unlock all of a text's significance. See BIBLICAL CRITICISM; BIBLICAL INTERPRETATION, HISTORY OF; EUROPEAN INTERPRETATION; LITERATURE, THE BIBLE AS.

PETR POKORNY

STUBBLE [קַשׁ qash; καλάμη kalamē]. The short remnants of HAY or GRAIN after harvesting. The pharaoh forced the Israelites to make bricks from stubble rather than STRAW (Exod 5:12). Stubble is easily blown away or ignited, so it is often used symbolically (e.g., Isa 40:24; 47:14). The image of stubble consumed by fire represents brevity, such as the power of those who oppose Yahweh (Exod 15:7; Joel 2:5) and those who reject his counsel (Isa 5:24). Stubble also depicts the result of divine judgment (Isa 33:11; Obad 18; Mal 4:1 [Heb. 3:19]). The strength of the righteous is compared to sparks running through stubble (Wis 3:7). See CHAFF; THRESHING.

BRUCE W. GENTRY

STUBBORN [סוֹרֵר sorer, קָשֶׁה qasheh, שְׁרִירוּת sheriruth; σκληρός sklēros]. Stubborn often describes human resistance to God (Ps 78:8; Jer 5:23), including APOSTASY (Jer 9:14), UNBELIEF (2 Kgs 17:14; Mark 16:14), and refusing to heed God's call (Neh 9:29; Acts 19:9). Wisdom literature warns against stubbornness in general (Prov 29:1; Sir 3:26-27; 30:8, 12; see WISDOM IN THE OT). See HARDEN THE HEART; STIFF-NECKED.

A. HEATH JONES III

STUFF [צֶבַע tseva']. Stuff, in the specialized sense of a finished textile, suitable for making clothing, occurs only in the phrase "dyed stuffs" (Judg 5:30). "Dyed stuffs" are mentioned in parallel with "dyed work embroidered for my neck," underscoring their value as luxury items among the spoils of battle. Elsewhere, stuff occurs only at Gen 25:30, when Esau asks his brother Jacob for some lentil stew, which he refers to casually as "that red stuff." See COLORS; DYE; SCARLET.

CAROL GRIZZARD BROWNING

STUMBLING BLOCK [מִכְשׁוֹל mikhshol; σκάνδαλον skandalon]. A "stumbling block" can refer literally to an obstacle in one's path, as in the command not to put a stumbling block in front of the blind (Lev 19:14). More commonly, it is used metaphorically. Money, idols, or other people can be spiritual stumbling blocks (Ezek 7:19; 14:3-4; Matt 18:6; Rev 2:14). Paul instructs believers to avoid putting stumbling blocks before each other (Rom 14:13; 1 Cor 8:9). A stumbling block might be an obstacle to faith (1 Cor 1:23) or to obeying God, such as when Peter says Jesus should not suffer (Matt 16:21-23). Jesus is often referred to as a rock that causes stumbling (e.g., Luke 20:17-18, citing Ps 118:22-23, and 1 Pet 2:8, quoting Isa 8:14).

KENNETH D. LITWAK

SUAH soo'uh [סוּחַ suakh]. The first son of ZOPHAH in the lineage of Asher. The name is found only in the military census (1 Chr 7:36).

SUBAS soo'buhs [Σουβάς Soubas]. Head of a family descended from SOLOMON'S SERVANTS that returned to Jerusalem with Zerubbabel (1 Esd 5:34). He is absent from the parallels in Ezra 2:57 and Neh 7:59.

SUCATHITES soo'kuh-thit [שׂוּכָתִים sukhathim]. One of three families of scribes, along with the Tirathites and the Shimeathites, who resided in Jabez in Judah (1 Chr 2:55). They were descendants of Caleb and included Kenites and Rechabites in their lineage.

SUCCEED [מָלַךְ תַּחַת malakh takhath, צָלֵחַ tsaleakh; εὐοδόω euodoō, λαμβάνω διάδοχος lambanō diadochos]. To succeed means to follow in sequence, usually referring to a change of leadership (e.g., Gen 36:31-39; 1 Kgs 1:13-30; Acts 24:27).

To succeed also refers to successfully carrying out what one intends to accomplish. In a sense, one can effect one's own success by depending on God and seeking to adhere to the law (Num 14:41; Josh 18:1; 1 Chr 22:13; 2 Chr 24:20; Ps 1:3). But success can also be in opposition to God (2 Chr 13:12; 24:20; Ps 1:4; Prov 28:13; Jer 12:1; 22:30; Ezek 17:15), leading to questions about God's benevolence: "Why does the way of the guilty prosper?" (Jer 12:1). The theme of THEODICY affirms that, while those who are opposed to God may appear to prosper for a time (Dan 8:12, 24), their success will be short-lived because God is preparing their judgment (Dan 11:36). In the end, those who persist in transgression against the Lord "will not succeed" (Num 14:41). True success, on the other hand, whether in a military campaign (e.g., 1 Kgs 22:12, 15), a construction project (1 Chr 22:11), or one's activity in general (e.g., Ps 1:3; Rom 1:10), is predicated on God's assistance or presence.

RALPH K. HAWKINS

SUCCOTH suhk'uhth [סֻכֹּת sukkoth]. The name of two cities in the OT. The Hebrew name means "booths," although this would not apply to the Egyptian city of Succoth. 1. A city in the Transjordan near the Jabbok River. It is identified with Tell Deir ʿAlla (see DEIR ʿALLA, TELL). Excavations at Deir ʿAlla revealed fragments of a text mentioning BALAAM, the prophet known from Num 22–24. It should be noted, however, that H. Franken, the excavator of Deir ʿAlla, does not identify it with Succoth. It has also been suggested that

Succoth occurs in the topographical list of Shoshenq I, although this reading is highly problematic.

Succoth lies on the "way of the Plain" (2 Sam 18:23), a north–south road on the east side of the Jordan River. Jacob lived in Succoth after meeting his brother Esau. The text provides an etiology for the name of the place, noting that Jacob built booths there for his cattle (Gen 33:17). Succoth fell within the territory given to the Gadites after the conquest (Josh 13:27). When Gideon was pursuing the Midianites, he requested supplies from Succoth but was turned down (Judg 8:4-9).

2. A city or region in the eastern delta of the Nile. Succoth was the first place the Israelites reached during the exodus after they had left the cities of PITHOM and Rameses (see RAAMSES) where they worked (Exod 12:37; Num 33:5). Succoth is often identified with Tell el-Maskhuta in the Wadi Tumilat. The name *Succoth* appears to be a Hebraizing of Egyptian ṯkw, and a number of inscriptions from Tell el-Maskuta bear the name ṯkw. Tell el-Maskhuta was not occupied before the 7th cent. BCE, however. Prior to that time, the main fortress in the area was located at Tell er-Retabeh, 13 km to the west of Maskhuta. This site is known as the "fortress of Merneptah-Content-with-Truth, which is in ṯkw" in Papyrus Anastasi VI from the late 13th cent. BCE. This text preserves a report of an official at a border fortress, who notes that he has allowed a group of Shasu Bedouin from Edom to pass the fortress in order to pasture their flocks at the pools in ṯkw. This text suggests that ṯkw is a region instead of a city, and it is probably to be identified with the area of the Wadi Tumilat.

Bibliography: H. Franken. "The Identity of Tell Deir ʿAlla, Jordan." *Akkadica* 14 (1979) 11–15; James K. Hoffmeier. *Israel in Egypt* (1997).

KEVIN A. WILSON

SUCCOTH-BENOTH suhk'uhth-bee'noth [סֻכֹּות בְּנוֹת sukkoth benoth]. A deity worshiped by Babylonian colonists in Samaria after Assyria's resettlement of the territory (2 Kgs 17:30). Mentioned only once in the OT and not attested in any cuneiform sources, the identity of this deity remains uncertain. Literally, the name means "tents of daughters/girls," which some argue indicates a place of prostitution. Others suggest the name is a corruption of the Babylonian goddess Zarpanitu, a consort of MARDUK. Most likely, the term means "aspect/image of Banitu," with Banitu being a popular epithet of the mother goddess or "creatress." See GODS, GODDESSES.

JOEL M. LEMON

SUD suhd [Σούδ Soud]. A river in Babylon mentioned only in Bar 1:4. It probably is not the river Euphrates, which bisects the city, but may refer to a canal. Many of the exiles from Jerusalem settled near the river and gathered with King Jeconiah and his sons to hear Baruch read his book. After this they fasted and sent money to the priests in Jerusalem, so that they might offer sacrifices for their sins.

SUSAN E. HADDOX

SUDIAS soo′dee-uhs [Σουδίας Soudias]. A Levite (1 Esd 5:26), possibly the same as HODAVIAH (Ezra 2:40; 3:9).

SUETONIUS swi-toh′nee-uhs. Born to an equestrian family, Gaius Suetonius Tranquillus (ca. 70–130 CE) held administrative duties under the emperors Trajan and Hadrian. He published widely on a variety of subjects. His most influential contribution is in the genre of biography. In antiquity his works *De Viris Illustribus* and *De Vita Caesarum* helped determine the form of this genre and became models for later biographies written by both non-Christian and Christian authors.

MICHAEL J. SCHUFER

SUFFERING AND EVIL. The words *suffering* and *evil* belong to a universal grammar of life. No dictionary, ancient or modern, can omit these words or their semantic equivalents, if it is to provide a complete register of the human discourse about the reality of the world in which we live. The commonality of such vocabulary, however, will necessarily be shaped by cultural, social, political, and religious conceptions that provide particularized contexts for either affirming or challenging regnant definitions. What constitutes acceptable experiences of suffering in one culture may be defined as extraordinary and excessive in another. What is equated with *misfortune* in one society may require the words *heinous* or *evil* in another. The lexical registers of *suffering* and *evil* are generally distinct. There is no necessary connection between them: suffering is not evil; evil is neither the cause nor the inevitable consequence of suffering.

Absent a religious worldview, neither suffering nor evil necessarily calls the meaningfulness of life into question; both are essentially part of the givenness of human existence, experiences to be endured and overcome more than problems to be solved. From its opening words—"In the beginning God" (Gen 1:1)—to its final revelation from the One who speaks with full knowledge about both "the beginning and the end" (Rev 22:13), the Bible locates the vocabulary of life within the grammar of faith. Inside this distinctively religious worldview, both Jewish and Christian scriptures affirm that any description of suffering and evil, however lexically discreet the terms may be, must factor God into the definition. Because God defines the beginning and the end of all the Bible has to say about suffering and evil, the conjunction *and*, as the assigned title of this entry hints, becomes acutely important.

A. Suffering in the Old Testament
  1. Finding the words
  2. Constructing a story: sin-suffering-divine punishment
  3. Rumblings of discontent: innocent suffering
  4. Suffering and evil and God
B. Suffering in the New Testament
  1. The abiding witness of the Old Testament
  2. The suffering of Christ
  3. The suffering of Christ's followers
Bibliography

A. Suffering in the Old Testament

At a base level, suffering has no voice (Scarry). What the human body feels and the brain translates is a physical and psychic sensation of pain that initially resists speech. The first audible response may be a wordless sigh, a cry, wailing—instinctive reactions that have linguistic analogues in the whimpering of infants or the bleating of animals. Elemental noises may be accompanied by physical gestures, external registers of internal feelings: fists clinch, eyes flutter, the face wrinkles and winces, the body curls into fetal position. Suffering ultimately finds a voice by drawing upon the various grammars available in a given culture. Physicians examine symptoms and locate them within a medical lexicon that provides definition and context. Artists, poets, sculptors, and musicians give aesthetic shape and form to brokenness and loss, opening the sufferer's imagination to the correspondence between personal experience and public discourse. To these and other available resources, religious communities add authoritative scriptures that invite the suffering to locate their experiences within the context of faith.

1. Finding the words

The OT has a large registry of words that express diverse aspects of suffering. Those who suffer personal loss, economic poverty, physical distress, imprisonment, or other forms of oppression are counted among the "poor" (dal [דָּל], e.g., Gen 41:9; Amos 4:1), the "weak and needy" (ʿani weʾevyon [עָנִי וְאֶבְיוֹן], Deut 15:11; Ps 35:10), the "faint," "sorrowful," and "wearied" (ʿayef [עָיֵף], yageaʿ [יָגֵעַ], e.g., Deut 25:18), the "crushed" and "broken" (dakh [דַּךְ], shavar [שָׁבַר], e.g., Jer 23:9; Job 20:19), and the "shamed"/"humiliated"/"disgraced" (boshah [בּוֹשָׁה], kherpah [חֶרְפָּה], e.g., Jer 15:9; Lam 2:1). Verbal expressions include "to grieve, suffer" (yaghah [יָגָה]) or "to be in pain, to grieve, hurt" (khaʾav [כָּאַב], e.g., Job 14:22), "to be bowed down, oppressed" (qadhadh [קָדַד], kharaʿ [כָּרַע]), "to become dark, gloomy" (qadhar [קָדַר]), and "to be devastated, frightened, troubled/in difficulty" (paʿam [פָּעַם], qashah [קָשָׁה] e.g., Gen 41:8; Jos 10:2; 1 Sam 1:15). Some verbs express instinctive human reactions to pain, such as "sigh, groan" (ʾanaqah [אֲנָקָה], e.g., Ezek 9:4), "weep" (bakhah [בָּכָה]) and "mourn" (ʾaval

[אֵבֶל], e.g., Gen 23:2; 1 Sam 30:4; 2 Sam 3:3). Others express primal sounds normally associated with animals, e.g., "howl" (Isa 52:5) "roar" (Isa 5:29), , and "growl" (Isa 59:11). The OT records many instances of people who, in their anguish, "cry out" (e.g., Exod 2:23; Job 35:12), "cry aloud" (e.g., Pss 3:4; 27:7), and "call for help" (e.g., Job 35:9).

The psalms include a high density of expressions for pain and suffering, especially in individual laments (often replicated elsewhere, e.g., Isaiah, Jeremiah, Habakkuk, Lamentations, Job), where somatic terms convey imagistic representations of woundedness, diminishment, and incapacitation (Cottrill). Suffering causes the body to "weaken," (Jdg 16:19), "fail" (Isa 17:32), "twist" (4 Macc 9:17), and "waste away" (Ezek 4:16; 33:10). Suffering is described as bones shaking (Job 4:14), burning (Job 3:30; Ps 31:10), becoming "scattered" (Ezek 6:5) and separated (Ps 22:14). Eyes "grow dim" with grief (Job 17:7; Ps 88:9). The heart "melts" (Jos 14:8; Ps 22:14; Isa 13:7), "breaks" (Ps 69:20), "throbs" (Ps 38:10; Isa 16:11), becomes "hot" (Ps 39), "weighed down" (Prov 12:25), "faint" (Job 19:27), "withered" (Ps 102:4) and "pierced" (109:22). The psalmists associate the physical diminishment that accompanies pain and suffering with alienation from friends and loved ones, who stand "far away" (e.g., Ps 38:11), and from God, who appears to have joined them (e.g., Ps 38:21; compare Pss10:1; 22:11; 35:22).

Biblical writers were generally aware of the distinctions we moderns make between human and nonhuman forms of communication, but their relationship with the world was in many ways necessarily more personal and intimate. In the book of Job, for example, Job invites his friends to "ask the animals" what wisdom they have to impart about human suffering (Job 12:7-9), a strategy that God also seems to embrace when responding to Job himself at the end of the book (Job 38:1–42:6). Multiple texts personify the land as a sensate creature who "mourns" (e.g., Isa 24:4; Jer 4:28; Hos 4:3; compare Hayes, Davis) its afflictions and is sickened to the point of "vomiting" (Lev 18:25, 28; 20:22) when it ingests what is not healthy. The trajectory of such imagery extends to the NT, nowhere more evocatively than in Paul's description of creation "groaning" (Rom 8:22) in travail, like a woman in labor, until its present sufferings come to an end.

Experiences of suffering measure values and vulnerabilities of various forms. Illness, death, loss of possessions, military defeat, estrangement and rejection, fear of failure—all such experiences equate suffering with the diminishment of what is dear in life. The grammar of suffering is therefore both a window into what people in any given time and place care about deeply and a means of constructing a comprehensible narrative about how to live when reality exacts its inevitable purchase on what we love (Nussbaum).

2. Constructing a story: sin-suffering-divine punishment

Old Testament writers construct a story that weaves suffering's palpable presence into Scripture's truth about God, world, and humankind. The canonical form of the story is a complex amalgamation of different perspectives, each conditioned by and responsive to the shifting cultural, social, and political realities that shaped ancient Israel. The separate parts of this composite story require and invite critical scrutiny, but a dominant story line, which locates suffering within a strategic nexus of sin-suffering-divine judgment, emerges early on.

The first mention of suffering occurs in Gen 3. As a result of the first couple's disobedience (3:1-6), God announces that "pangs"/"toil" (3:16, 17) will now be part of God's "very good" world (Gen1:31). From this point forward, the causal link between disobedience (named "sin" for the first time in Gen 4:7), suffering, and divine punishment leaves its footprint on virtually every chapter of the ensuing story. The "pangs" suffered by the first man and woman extend to their claims to the ground, which brings forth "thorns and thistles" (3:18), and to successive generations, who bring forth such "wickedness" and "evil" (Gen 6:5) that God, even in judgment, is ensnared in a reciprocating divine "grief" (6:6).

The moral coherence of this sin-suffering-judgment etiology rests on Israel's covenantal theology, which interprets suffering as the just and expected consequence of disobedience to God's commandments (compare Exod 19–24). Texts from each major section of the OT—Torah, Prophets, and Writings—appeal in different ways to the reliability of this calculus. Perhaps the most dominant cross-sectional appeal is to a retribution theology that subsumes experiences of suffering under the affirmation that God repays (Latin: *re* ["back"] + *tribuere* ["to pay"]) sin with punishment, which includes suffering in all its physical and psychic manifestations. Reduced to its essence, this appeal typically responds to questions about why "the LORD has done such a thing" by answering, "Because they have forsaken the LORD ... therefore the LORD has brought this disaster [literally, "evil"] upon them" (1 Kgs 9:8-9; compare Deut 30:15-20; Judg 2:11-16; 2 Kgs 17:7-18; Ps 1; Prov 8:32-36; 10:23-32; Job 4:7-11; 8:8-19; 11:13-20; Jer 9:12-16; 16:10-13; Amos 4:1-3; Mic 3:9-12). Within this retributive model, the key to enduring the experience of suffering and to finding meaning within it is to confess, repent, and trust God to forgive.

A variation on the retribution model is the idea that God uses suffering not only to punish wrong behavior but also to discipline and teach persons right behavior (e.g., Deut 8:5-6; 11:1-2; Pss 6:1; 38:1; 39:11; Isa 26:16; Jer 6:19; 7:28; 31:18; Hos 7:12, 15; Sanders). Israel's sages employ a parenting metaphor, now deeply rooted in proverbial wisdom—"Spare the rod and spoil the child" (compare Prov 13:24)—to describe God's correcting discipline that, even when severely applied, should be welcomed more as an assurance of God's love than an indication of God's anger (e.g., Prov 1:7-8; 3:11; 15:5; 19:18; 22:15; 29:15, 17). Even extreme suffering, when interpreted in this way, can be a reminder of the depths of God's commitment to the relationship and consequently an invitation to rejoice, counter-intuitive as it may seem to those on the receiving end, for God only disciplines those whom God loves (e.g., Prov 3:12; 13:24; 23:13-14; Job 5:17-18; Sir 30:1-2, 13). God speaks in multiple ways, Job's friend Elihu says, including "chastening with pain," but the ultimate purpose is always to save those whom God loves from a course of certain destruction (Job 33:19-22, 29-30; compare Prov 6:23; 10:17; 12:1; 23:13-14).

Three additional interpretive strategies exemplify how the OT moves to contain suffering within a sin-suffering-divine judgment model that remains comprehensible, even when harsh realities threaten its capacity to persuade. A collection of "Suffering Servant" poems embedded within Isa 40–55 (Isa 42:1-4; 49:1-6; 50:4-11; 52:13–53:12) address a demoralized community in Babylonian exile. Although the identity of the "servant" is (perhaps intentionally) ambiguous, multiple references scattered throughout the texts (42:2, 4; 49:4; 50:6) make it clear that obedient suffering unto death, even if "by a perversion of justice" (53:8), is an integral part of the servant's mission to the world. Other texts locate the meaning of suffering not in this world but in the world to come. At a time and place of God's choosing, the "very good" world of God's primordial hopes and expectations will be fully realized. An Edenic peace and harmony among all creatures will claim the final victory over suffering, and the full meaning of God's covenant commitment will be revealed (e.g., Isa 2:2-4; 11:6-9; 65:25; Ezek 34:25-31; Hos 2:18). "In that day," according to the well-known lines from Isa 25:8, "[the Lord] will swallow up death forever ... [and] wipe away the tears from all faces" (compare Isa 35:10; 51:11; 65:19; Rev 21:4). A third approach is to lodge the meaning of suffering in the mystery of God. An anonymous prophet delivering God's words to the exiles summarizes the thrust of this approach: "My thoughts are not your thoughts, nor are your ways my ways, says the LORD" (Isa 55:8; compare Prov 16:9; 19:21; 21:30-31). The truly wise learn to be at home with the "riddles" of life in relation to God (compare Sir 39:3), trusting that they will be safe in God's inscrutable providence (e.g., Prov 14:26; 16:3, 20; 18:10; 28:25; 29:25).

3. Rumblings of discontent: innocent suffering

Suffering seldom respects the explanations that try to limit its assault on meaning. When it presses its claim on the body and mind, settled theories about sin-suffering-divine judgment convulse under the weight of dissenting questions. "All this has come upon us," the psalmist says, "yet we have not forgotten you, or been false to your covenant ... Why do you hide your face? Why do you forget our affliction and oppression?" (Ps 44:18, 24). Such questions about God's inequitable

administration of justice raise the issue scholars call THEODICY. They emerge throughout the OT, for example, in the vexed questions posed by Abraham (Gen 18:25), Moses (Exod 32:11-12; Num 11:11-15; 14:13-16), Joshua (Josh 7:6-9), Jeremiah (Jer 12:1-4; 15:18; 17:15-18; 20:18), Habakkuk (Hab 1:1-4, 12-17), and the psalmists (Pss 10:1; 13:1-4; 22:1-2; 44:17-26; 74:1, 10-11; 79:5; 88:13-14; 89:46-49). Even when sin is acknowledged, the sufferer may protest that it in no way justifies the punishment God has delivered (compare Lam 1:5, 9, 14, 18, 20, 22 with Lam 1:12; 2:20; 5:20-22; see also Job 7:20-21).

The most acute questions and the most sustained assault on God's covenantal faithfulness is found in Job (see JOB, BOOK OF), where innocent suffering presses Israel's sages to construct meaningful sentences about divine justice that include the words EVIL and "for no reason." The Prologue (Job 1–2) sets the table for all that follows by introducing Job as a "blameless" and "upright" man who, by God's admission, always "turned away from evil" (1:1, 8; 2:3; compare 2:9). In spite of (or because of) Job's innocence, "evil" (2:11; NRSV, "troubles") comes into his world, leaving in its wake the loss of his property, health, and, most grievous of all, the deaths of seven sons and three daughters, all of this, again by God's admission, "for no reason" (Job 2:3). The SATAN poses the question that draws Job, his friends, God, and all readers of the book into faith's most exacting challenge. If God is complicit in suffering that happens "for no reason," then will Job "fear (or reverence) God for no reason" (Job 1:9)?

4. Suffering and evil and God

The OT's lexicon of suffering, as noted above, is extensive, its various expressions a reflection of the many different ways suffering leaves its mark on life in this world. The grammar of "evil," by contrast, is constructed from basically one Hebrew root ra'a' (רָעַע) and its derivatives, which occur almost 800 times in the OT. The elasticity of this root is indicated by the different ways it is used with respect to human beings and God. When humans experience or actively effect something that is ra'a', the net result ranges from misfortune, to disaster/calamity, to evil, depending on how one evaluates it on the scale of things that are conventionally labeled either "good" or "bad." Biblical writers employ roughly the same calculus when using the word ra'a' with respect to God, although here one can sense a tension in both Hebrew and in English. When God effects ra'a', that is, when God "does," "plans," "declares"/"threatens," or "brings" ra'a', the context typically involves a punitive response to human disobedience that has meaning within a covenantal understanding of divine justice. On those rare occasions when a covenantal context must make room for the confession that God is the originator of both "prosperity" and "disaster" (Isa 45:7, NIV; NRSV, "woe"; compare Isa 32:1), the accent is typically on God's predisposition towards unmerited grace, not undeserved punishment (e.g., Hos 11:8-9), even if the decision causes God pain or "regret," or to "repent" (Exod 32:12, 14; 2 Sam 24:16 [= 1 Chr 21:15]; compare Jer 18:8; 26:3, 13, 19; 42:10; Joel 2:13; Jonah 3:10; 4:2; Amos 7:3, 6; Fretheim, Schlimm).

Twelve texts describe God as the subject of the verb ra'a' (Exod 5:22; Num 11:11; Josh 24:20; Ruth 1:21; Ps 44:2; Jer 25:6, 29; 31:28; Mic 4:6; Zeph 1:12; Zech 8:14). The majority of these cases locate God's decision "to cause suffering" within the context of a justified punishment for disobedience. When the suffering God causes is not or cannot be explicitly connected to sin, the protesting interrogative "Why?" once again inches its way into the vocabulary of pained faith (Exod 5:22; Num 11:11; compare Ruth 1:21). Such questions strike at the heart of embraced understandings about the nature and character of God. If God causes suffering "for no reason," as the narrator of the Joban Prologue concedes (Job 2:3; see above), then the difference between God and those who "wantonly ambush the innocent" is disconcertingly negligible. As Israel's sages advise, the wise should not follow this path in life; those who do "run to evil" (Prov1:11, 15-16; compare Prov 3:30; 24:28; 26:2).

B. Suffering in the New Testament
1. The abiding witness of the Old Testament
New Testament writers draw upon the deep deposits of Hebrew Scripture for both the basic vocabulary of suffering and the general framework for understanding it within the context of faith. Catalogues of afflictions call upon stock vocabulary, now shaped by the particular constraints of life in a Greco-Roman world, for example, toil, hardship, hunger, thirst, homelessness, persecution, beatings, imprisonment, slander, and destruction (compare 1 Cor 4:10-13; 2 Cor 4:8-9; 6:4-10; 11:23-27). Confronted with such obstacles to faith, people "grieve"/"mourn" (pentheō πενθέω), "suffer" (paschō πάσχω, pathētos παθητός), "become sad" (lypeō λυπέω) and "troubled" (thlibō θλίβω), and "cry out" for help (boaō βοάω, klaiō κλαίω, krazo κράζω). As in the OT, the NT's registries of words for suffering and "evil" (ponēros πονηρός, ponēria πονηρία, kakos κακός, kakia κακία) are generally distinct. Semantic overlaps may be conveyed with phrases like "suffer evil/hardship" (kakopatheō κακοπαθέω) and "suffer evil/hardship with someone" (synkakopatheō συνκακοπαθέω), but for the most part the connections between suffering and evil are qualitative. Physical affliction, trouble and misfortune, and abusive human behavior may be evil, but such descriptions do not necessarily convey moral evaluations. When moral agency is implied, that is, when evils suffered are attributable to active and malicious intent, the NT assigns culpability either to the evil intentions of the human heart (e.g., Matt 12:34-35; 15:18-19; Mark 7:21-23; 1 Tim 6:4; Heb 3:12), which is set in opposition to God, or more specifically to the devil or Satan, "the evil one"

(ho ponēros [ὁ πονηρός]; Matt 13:19; compare Mark 4:15; Luke 8:12), whose power to lead humans into evil is real but vincible, supremely so in Christ's ultimate triumph over the devil and his reign (compare Heb 2:14-15; Rev 20:2-3, 10). In essence, the NT deals with the OT's Joban problem, the struggle to construct a grammar of faith that includes the words *suffering*, *evil*, and *God* in the same sentence, by creating space for a distinctively different line of thinking. God is not "tempted by evil," and God does not use evil to tempt or test anyone (Jas 1:13).

New Testament writers locate the meaning of suffering within basically the same nexus of explanations offered in the OT: God's just punishment of sin, the burden and blessing of God's discipline, the eschatological promise of vindication and justice, and the assurance that God works in and through suffering to effect redemption. To buttress these common interpretive moves, the NT looks to the OT for examples of faithful suffering: Jesus cites Israel's prophets in support of his summons "to rejoice and be glad" when those who follow him suffer similar persecution (Matt 5:11-12// Luke 6:22-23; compare Matt 23:37); Stephen appeals to the witness of Israel's ancestors—Abraham, Isaac, and Jacob—to defend himself against those who bring false charges against him (Acts 7:1-53); James cites the "endurance of Job" when exhorting his contemporaries to discern God's compassion and mercy (Jas 5:11); Heb 11 appeals to the heroes and heroines of Israel, those whom God "is not ashamed to be called their God" (v. 16), to define the true meaning of faith.

2. The suffering of Christ
Building upon all these connections with the OT, the NT plots a story line about suffering that distinctively shapes and transforms Christian faith. According to the Gospel of Matthew, which introduces the final form of this story, Jesus is born into a world of innocent suffering and death (Matt 2:17-18). The beginning of the story, as all the Gospels confirm, anticipates its ending. The child born into a world of innocent suffering will himself die as innocent sufferer, and in the miracle of his resurrection, he will transform the meaning of suffering for all those who will follow his way of embodying the hopes and expectations of God.

Of the Gospel writers, it is Luke who accents Jesus' compassion for those robbed of life by illness and affliction, those whom society treats as outcasts on the assumption that all suffering is punishment for sin. Luke reports that Jesus begins his ministry in Nazareth by embracing Isaiah's ethical imperative to release persons from all forms of bondage—spiritual, economic, political, and physical (4:18-19; compare Isa 58:6; 61:1-2). He exegetes scripture's mandate with acts of indiscriminate healing, demonstrating that because pain and suffering are no respecters of persons, neither must be the compassion and comfort his disciples extend to them (e.g., 4:31-44; 7:1-17; 8:2656; 13:10-17; 17:11-19). He tells a parable about a "good Samaritan" whose compassion for the afflicted models the behavior Jesus expects (10:29-37), and another that explains that those who are welcomed at his table are "the poor, the crippled, the lame, and the blind" (14:7-14). After his death and resurrection, Jesus appears to his disciples, once again breaking bread at table with them, now with a poignant invitation that they not only "look" and "see" but also "touch" his wounded hands and feet (24:36-43). Tactile proximity to those who are bruised and broken, being close enough to touch and feel the pain they experience, Jesus indicates, is the prerequisite for understanding Scripture's truth about suffering in God's redemptive plans for the world: "Thus it is written, that the Messiah is to suffer (pathein παθεῖν) and to rise from the dead on the third day, and that repentance and forgiveness of sins is to be proclaimed in his name to all nations" (24:46-47).

Jesus' last words in Luke underscore the importance the Synoptic Gospels, along with Acts, Hebrews, and 1 Peter, attach to Jesus' suffering. In the Synoptics and Acts, Jesus always uses the word pathein (the aorist infinitive of paschō) to describe his own sufferings, both the "great suffering" that precedes his crucifixion (Matt 16:21//Mark 8:31; Matt 17:12//Mark 9:12; Luke 9:22; 17:25) and the suffering that is his death (Luke 22:15; 24:26, 46; Acts 1:3; 3:18; 17:3; compare Heb 2:9; 13:12; 1 Pet 2:21, 23; 4:1). The exclusive use of this word with respect to Jesus accents the NT's assertion that his suffering, eventuating in his death and resurrection, is unique. He suffers not because he is too weak to resist an alien experience, but because it is part of God's design (Matt 16:21; Luke 13:33; 17:25; 24:26; Acts 17:3); not because he does not know what it means to question God's presence when "deeply grieved, even to death," but because he trusts in God's abiding presence during even the darkest moments of his life (compare Matt 26:37 and 27:46; Mark 14:34 and 15:34; Luke 22:40-46 and 23:46); not because innocent suffering is a perversion of life, but because, as Israel's prophets declared, the suffering of God's righteous servant has the capacity to redeem the lives of others (compare the citations of Isa 52:13–53:12 in Matt 8:17 and 1 Pet 2:22, 24). In all these ways, Jesus is able to "sympathize with our weaknesses," because he has been "tested as we are, yet without sin" (Heb 4:15). He is therefore the "example" of how his followers are to cope with suffering (1 Pet 2:21).

3. The suffering of Christ's followers

Jesus calls disciples to take up their own crosses and follow him (e.g., Matt 16:24-28//Mark 8:34–9:1//Luke 9:23-27), but when he speaks of the sufferings they will endure, he never uses the word pathein. Paul uses pathein to speak of his own sufferings (e.g., Col 1:24; 2 Tim 1:12) and those of his readers who are "partners in suffering" (2 Cor 1:7), and he stresses that suffering "on behalf of Christ" is a "privilege," a gift of participating in the kingdom of God (Phil 1:29; compare 2 Thess 1:5). Paul also speaks of "suffering (sympaschō συμπάσχω) with him [Christ]" (Rom 8:17), but the accent here, as in all of these Pauline uses of pathein, does not collapse the important distinction Jesus makes between his own suffering, which has salvific purposes, and the suffering of Christians, which is part of the missional activity of the church. This distinction is clear in 1 Peter, which contains the highest number of occurrences of pathein outside the Gospels. Following Christ may mean "suffering unjustly" (1 Pet 2:19), being publicly "maligned" for doing good (1 Pet 3:14, 16; compare 1 Pet 2:12; 3:17), and being punished by the courts as common criminals (1 Pet 4:15). When persons suffer because they are "aware of God" (1 Pet 2:19) and living "in accordance with God's will" (1 Pet 4:16, 19), they are living out their true "calling" (1 Pet 2:21). The adversities Christians endure "for a little while" (1 Pet 5:10; compare 1:6) will pale in comparison to the reward of their "eternal glory in Christ" (1 Pet 5:10; compare 1:7; 4:13-14).

Bibliography: S. E. Balentine. "For No Reason." *Int* 57 (2003) 349–69; S. E. Balentine. *Job.* Smith & Helwys Bible Commentary (2006); J. Christian Becker. *Suffering and Hope* (1987); A. Cottrill. *Language, Power, and Identity in the Lament Psalms of the Individual* (2008); J. Crenshaw. *Defending God: Biblical Responses to the Problem of Evil* (2005); E. Davis. *Remembering the Land: Reading the Bible through Agrarian Eyes* (2008); T. Fretheim. *The Suffering God: An Old Testament Perspective* (1984); E. S. Gerstenberger and W. S. Schrage. *Suffering* (1977); N. Habel and P. Trudinger, eds. *Exploring Ecological Hermeneutics* (2008); D. J. Hall. *God and Human Suffering: An Exercise in the Theology of the Cross* (1986); K. Hayes. *"The Earth Mourns": Prophetic Metaphor and Oral Aesthetic* (2002); O. Leaman. *Evil and Suffering in Jewish Philosophy* (1995); F. Lindström. *Suffering and Sin: Interpretations of Illness in the Individual Complaint Psalms* (1994); J. Marcus. *Jesus and the Holocaust: Reflections on Suffering and Hope* (1997); W. McWilliams. *Where Is the God of Justice? Biblical Perspectives on Suffering* (2005); J. Neusner, ed. *Evil and Suffering* (1998); M. Nussbaum. *Upheavals of Thought: The Intelligence of Emotions* (2001); J. Sanders. *Suffering as Divine Discipline in the Old Testament and Post-Biblical Judaism* (1955); E. Scarry. *The Body in Pain: The Making and Unmaking of the World* (1985); M. Schlimm. "Different Perspectives on Divine Pathos: An Examination of Hermeneutics in Biblical Theology." *CBQ* 69 (2007) 673–94; D. Simundson. *Faith Under Fire: Biblical Interpretations of Suffering* (1980); D. Soelle. *Suffering* (1975); A. Tambasco, ed. *The Bible and Suffering: Social and Political Implications* (2001).

SAMUEL E. BALENTINE

SUFFERING SERVANT. *See* SERVANT OF THE LORD, THE.

SUICIDE. Although the biblical text does not explicitly prohibit suicide, several references suggest that suicide is against God's will and purpose for one's life. The OT prohibits killing in general (Exod 20:13; Deut 5:17), and in the NT Paul teaches that it is wrong to destroy one's body, which is a temple of the Holy Spirit (1 Cor 3:17; 6:19). In addition, Jer 29:11 indicates that God plans a future filled with hope for each person.

Nevertheless, several biblical figures do kill themselves: Samson (Judg 16:30), Saul and his armor bearer (1 Sam 31:4-5), Ahithophel (2 Sam 17:23), Zimri (1 Kgs 16:18), and Judas (Matt 27:3-5; compare Acts 1:18). The mortally wounded Abimelech requests his armor bearer to kill him (Judg 9:54). Paul convinces his desperate jailer not to kill himself (Acts 16:27-28).

Also, several figures wish for death as a release from suffering, most notably Job (6:8-13; 14:13). The prophets Moses (Num 11:15), Elijah (1 Kgs 19:4), and Jonah (Jon 4:3, 8) also express a wish to die. Paul longs for death, not to evade suffering but in order to be with Christ (Phil 1:20-26). Finally, according to Revelation, in the trials of the last days "people will seek death but will not find it" (9:6).

ARCHIE T. WRIGHT

SUKKIIM suhk'ee-im [סֻכִּיִּים sukkiyim]. A group reported to have accompanied Shoshenq I on his campaign against Jerusalem in the 10th cent. BCE (2 Chr 12:3; *see* SHISHAK). Although they are identified with the tktn known from Egyptian sources, their origin is unclear. Papyrus Anastasi IV mentions them serving at the oases of Dakhleh and Khargah in the western desert of Egypt.

KEVIN A. WILSON

SUKKOT. *See* BOOTHS, FEAST OR FESTIVAL OF.

SULFUR [גָּפְרִית gaferith; θεῖον theion, θειώδης theiōdēs]. Translated as "brimstone" in many older translations. An easily combustible element that is mentioned in the Bible in contexts of judgment, accompanied by images of fire and heat (e.g., Gen 19:24; Ps 11:6; Rev 19:20; 20:10).

GREG CAREY

SULLA, CORNELIUS. A plebeian branch of the Roman patrician family Cornelii whose other branches included the Scipiones, Rufini, and Lentuli. The Sullae branch became prominent through Lucius Cornelius Sulla Felix (ca. 138–78 BCE) when he became dictator. His son Faustus Cornelius Sulla aligned himself with POMPEY and participated in the military tribune that subdued JERUSALEM and captured the Temple Mount in 63 BCE.

MICHAEL J. SCHUFER

SUMER, SUMERIANS soo'muhr, soo-maihr'ee-uhn. The silty plain that makes up the extreme south of Iraq, ancient Mesopotamia, was known in the 3rd millennium BCE as Sumer. Scholars have identified the region as part of the land of Shinar, which is described in the OT as lying east of Israel with major cities at Babel (Babylon), Erech (Uruk), and Akkad. There is also a strong folk tradition that the area was the site of the Garden of Eden. By 2100 BCE the Sumerians had founded a technologically advanced, sophisticated, and bureaucratic state in this part of Iraq.

A. Who Were the Sumerians?
  1. The Sumerian language
  2. Sumerian script and its uses
  3. Sumerian religion
  4. Sumerian mythology
B. The World of the Sumerians
  1. The physical setting
  2. The cities of the Mesopotamian plain
  3. The city of Ur
  4. The *Temenos*
C. Everyday Life
  1. Town and country
  2. The organization of society
D. The Sumerians in Context
  1. Neighboring states
  2. Trade and diplomacy
E. Conclusion
Bibliography

A. Who Were the Sumerians?

The origin of the Sumerians was a major topic of research in the early to mid-20th cent. as many scholars of the time were preoccupied with questions of race. The evidence they used has now been shown to be flawed. Initially, for example, it was thought that a study of the shapes of skulls could indicate race, but this methodology has now been totally discredited.

In addition, such acceptable evidence as we have is contradictory. There are elements of continuity in the archaeological record, most strikingly in religious architecture, which point to the presence of Sumerians in south Mesopotamia from as early as the mid-5th millennium BCE. On the other hand, many new archaeological features appear in the middle of the 4th millennium such as the first cylinder seals and the first attempts at a writing system. These innovations suggest the possibility that new people moved in to the plain at about this time, although an indigenous development cannot be ruled out. The contemporary written evidence, clay tablets with impressed symbols on them, is also inconclusive because the symbols consist mainly of pictographic signs, rather than of syllables or letters, and such symbols can be read in any languages the reader chooses. By the time the first syllables appear in these pictographic texts, ca. 3000 BCE, the language is Sumerian, and the obvious continuity in the shape of the signs and the sequences in which they occur make it probable that the earliest tablets were written in this language as well, but this cannot be proved beyond doubt.

Modern scholarship now regards the origin of the Sumerians as an insoluble and largely irrelevant problem. It has become irrelevant partly as a result of the poor quality of the evidence and its ambiguity, but more especially because it is now clear that south Mesopotamia was peacefully infiltrated over millennia by new peoples from the Levant, from Syria, from Iran, and from Arabia. The civilization that we know as Sumerian was in fact an amalgam and the result of the fertile mixing of peoples of many different origins. By the time of the first comprehensible written documents about 3000 BCE, the majority of these people apparently spoke and wrote the Sumerian language, but their origins were almost certainly many and varied. By the middle of the millennium the balance of the population had shifted in favor of the people speaking Semitic Akkadian, probably as a result of the constant, overwhelmingly peaceful flow of immigrants from the margins of Sumer into the center. By 2000 BCE the Sumerians had effectively disappeared.

For convenience, what is loosely known as the Sumerian period is divided into sections based on the archaeological evidence and is known as the Jemdat Nasr (ca. 3000–2800 BCE), Early Dynastic (ca. 2800–2300 BCE), and Ur III periods (ca. 2100–2000 BCE). The Early Dynastic and Ur III periods are separated by a phase known as the Agade (ca. 2300–2100 BCE) when Semitic rulers from north of Sumer united the Sumerian city states under their control for little more than a century.

1. The Sumerian language

The Sumerian language has no modern relatives and does not fit into either the Semitic or the Indo-European language groups. It has many loan words from Semitic Akkadian, which is better understood than Sumerian, as Akkadian is related to modern languages such as Arabic and Hebrew. At the moment Sumerian stands alone. By the end of the 3rd millennium BCE Sumerian ceased to be a spoken language and was used only as a liturgical and literary language that continued into the Christian era. It was superseded as a spoken language by first Akkadian and then Babylonian and other West Semitic dialects such as that spoken by the Amorites.

2. Sumerian script and its uses

The cuneiform script seems to have been invented to record the Sumerian language, but in its early stages the script is very hard to understand as it is little more than a mnemonic system. Some of the signs represent single sounds or syllables, but most are ideograms and numbers. The cuneiform script was used to write both Sumerian and, a little later, Akkadian. It appears to have been developed in the first instance as an administrative tool (see below). The script is found mainly on clay and gypsum tablets, but later was also inscribed on many different materials and artefacts ranging in size from tiny seals made of semi-precious stone to monumental stelae. On the earliest clay tablets, the symbols were drawn with a pointed instrument whose blunt end could be used to make circular impressions representing numbers. Later, a stylus with a straight-edged or triangular head was impressed into the clay to create each sign using varying numbers of wedges. Initially the symbols were pictographic and stood for commodities and quantities but became gradually more abstract. Each symbol could represent an ideogram, a syllable, or a sound, which allowed it to be used for writing proper names and for other languages. By the middle of the 2nd millennium BCE, it was used from Anatolia to Iran and is found in the Levant and Egypt as well. In Sumer itself the script was being used for many purposes by the mid-3rd millennium. In addition to its administrative role it was also used for the writing of hymns, prayers, myths, proverbs, poems, and royal inscriptions. These early royal inscriptions help us to reconstruct a history of the period; the myths, hymns, and prayers tell us something of the religious beliefs of the Sumerians; the poems and proverbs provide a glimpse into their daily life.

3. Sumerian religion

The Sumerian picture of the cosmos was of a floating disk of land that rested on the primordial waters from which it had emerged. Above was a second disk that formed the heavens, the abode of the gods, and the two were separated by the air. The location of the underworld is still debated by scholars. It may have been in the mountains to the north and east rather than below the earth. Human beings were created by the great gods from clay as servants to undertake the menial work that had previously been done by the lesser gods themselves.

Sumerian religion was polytheistic and the pantheon was somewhat flexible, allowing gods to take on new responsibilities and new gods to be incorporated as new territories were conquered. The gods were irascible and unpredictable, and their society, headed by the sky god and father of humankind Anu, was as highly stratified as that of the human world. The divine hierarchy could be modified to reflect the changing political realities on the ground. For example, as Babylon became of major political importance in the post-Sumerian period, its patron god, Marduk, rose up the celestial ranks. The gods were represented in the iconography in human form wearing a distinctive horned crown, and each had symbols and animals associated with them that reflected their main areas of responsibility and made them easily identifiable. The major gods reflected the forces of nature: Shamash the sun god and the god of justice, Sin the moon god, Ea/Enki the god of sweet waters and friend of mankind, and Enlil, god of air and the patron god of Sumer itself. Fertility was embodied in the mother goddess Ninhursag, while other important figures included Inanna the goddess of physical love and of war. Each god had one city that was seen as a chief abode and whose prosperity the god was expected to protect. If the city offended in some way it was doomed. The prime duty of the ruler of such a city was to make sure that the god was worshiped with due respect, placated with offerings, and that the deity's commands were obeyed. In this manner the goodwill of the deity was retained and the people assured of health and prosperity.

In addition to the major gods, a new concept emerged during the second half of the 3rd millennium. Men and women were thought to have personal gods who were somewhat comparable to the guardian angel of Christian times. They were minor deities whose duty was to look after the interests of their protégées and to intercede on their behalf with the great gods if this should become necessary. A Sumerian proverb says, "A man's personal god is a shepherd who finds a grazing ground for him. Let him lead him like a sheep to the grass he can eat." These personal gods are depicted on many cylinder seals dating to the last century of the 3rd millennium, standing with raised hands in an attitude of supplication behind the owner of the seal and presenting him or her to one of the great gods.

The concept of the just ruler, the shepherd of his people who obeyed the commands of his city's god, was established by the end of the Sumerian period. Obedience to the gods was the key to happiness and success in this life and the next. There was a belief in the afterlife, but the underworld was pictured as a grey and miserable place where comfort could be ensured only by presents to the relevant deities, a well-appointed grave, and a large number of sons who would make the appropriate offerings of food and drink to alleviate the suffering of the deceased. Personal morality did not apparently bring these rewards; status, wealth and a large family, together with obedience, were more likely to achieve a reasonable standard of living in the hereafter.

Something of this belief can probably be seen in the famous tombs of the so-called Royal Cemetery at Ur dating to the middle of the 3rd millennium in the Early Dynastic period. The tombs were richly furnished with goods that include items of precious metals, magnificent jewelry, weapons, furniture, and musical instruments as well as food and drink. Most spectacularly, in sixteen of the graves there is evidence for human sacrifice on a large scale. More than seventy bodies, apparently those of guards and servants, were found in one grave. There is also some slight evidence for offerings being made after the tombs were sealed. It is still unclear if these luxuries were meant as presents for the gods of the underworld or to keep the main occupants of the tombs in the style to which they were accustomed. There is some slightly later literary evidence that suggests that the former was the case. In a poem lamenting the death of Ur-Nammu, the first king of the Ur III dynasty, he was said to have given luxurious gifts to all the major figures in the underworld and was rewarded with a throne and an appointment as a judge. It is also worth noting that the graves of the kings of the Ur III dynasty were designed as grand dwellings or even small palaces.

Werner Forman/Art Resource, NY

Figure 1: Hair ornaments, earrings, and necklaces mounted on a model. Jewelry of this kind was worn by many of the woman attendants of Queen Pu-Abi (ca. 2500 BCE). British Museum, London, Great Britain.

4. Sumerian mythology

Many of the surviving myths relate the doings of the gods, and some of the themes found in these stories are later echoed in the books of the OT. The parallels between the OT and Sumerian myth are especially close in the flood story that survives in a Sumerian, and a better preserved, probably approximately contemporary, Babylonian version as part of the so-called Epic of Gilgamesh (see GILGAMESH, EPIC OF). In both versions the gods decide to send a flood to wipe out mankind and in both a righteous man, a king in the Sumerian version, is warned of the impending disaster by Ea/Enki the water god, who tells him to build a boat into which he loads his family and many animals. The storm breaks out, and the world is devastated. After seven days and seven nights the flood abates; in the Babylonian version Utnapishtim, the Babylonian Noah, sends out a series of birds until at last one does not return. Land emerges from beneath the water and in both the Sumerian and the Babylonian versions Utnapishtim (and his Sumerian predecessor Ziusudra) leave the boat and makes offerings of oxen and sheep to placate the gods. The gods reward him and his wife with everlasting life.

Other themes, too, occur in Sumerian literature and mythology that can be matched in greater or lesser detail to themes in the OT. The tensions between farmers and the herders exemplified in the story of Cain and Abel are to be found, particularly in a description of the nomadic Amorites as a ravaging people with the instincts of beasts that have no houses and are not buried when they die. The story of the righteous sufferer, with the theological problems that story poses, is also found in Sumerian literature. Although the earliest extant version comes from the early 2nd millennium, it is thought that it had its origins in the Sumerian period. Whole genres known in the Bible, such as proverbs, are also found from the late 3rd millennium across much of the ancient world, so it is difficult to know where they originated.

B. The World of the Sumerians

1. The physical setting

The Sumerian heartland, the southern plain of Iraq, is a low-lying, silty region bounded on the west by the Euphrates and on the east by the Tigris rivers. The climate is harsh with summer temperatures reaching over 100 degrees (Fahrenheit), while storms and floods are a regular hazard. The land is potentially extremely fertile, but as it lies outside the area where rain-fed agriculture is possible it is necessary to divert river water to the fields by a canal system. The economy of the region, until the discovery of oil, has always rested on the twin pillars of irrigation agriculture and herding, while hunting and fishing also provided valuable protein. These resources together provided sustenance for the inhabitants and a surplus that could be turned into manufactured goods like textiles. These were traded in exchange for the raw materials that were lacking on the plain such as metals, hard woods, and high-quality stone.

2. The cities of the Mesopotamian plain

Sumerian civilization was essentially an urban one, and in this it presents a sharp contrast to the contemporary world in the Levant. By about 3000 BCE the Mesopotamian plain was home to a number of urban centers, some of very considerable size and each surrounded by an area of cultivated land lying along the rivers and canals. The uncultivated region between the towns and cities provided seasonal grazing for huge flocks of sheep and goats, often belonging to the major public institutions, and to nomadic herdsmen who played an important role in supplying additional animal and dairy products to the settled people and in disseminating goods and information across a series of informal networks. The towns soon began to group together into small city-states, which fought amongst each other for temporary domination, but by the late 3rd millennium they were briefly united into what have been described as the first empires. The first ruler to achieve this was

the Semitic Sargon of Agade whose power base lay to the north of the Sumerian plain, soon followed by Ur-Nammu, the first king of the so-called Ur III dynasty, whose home city was Ur/Urim, known in the Bible as Ur of the Chaldeans (e.g., Gen 11:28, 31).

Ur-Nammu founded a state that comprised the whole of the southern plain and an area to the east of the Tigris. It was to last about one hundred years and had its capital at Ur, which was under the patronage and protection of the moon god Nannar/Sin. It was here at Ur that, according to one tradition, Abraham is supposed to have been born, though other cities also claim him, and from here that he set out on his long journey with his family first to Haran and then to Canaan.

3. The city of Ur

Thanks to the painstaking work of the renowned British archaeologist Sir Leonard Woolley, who excavated at Ur from 1922 to 1934, it is possible to paint a reasonably detailed picture of the city at the height of the Ur III "empire," between ca. 2100 and 2000 BCE (see UR). In outline, this picture is also true for the Early Dynastic period, although the scale may have been different. All the cities of the plain stood on waterways and Ur stood on two, the Euphrates and a large canal. They not only brought water to the city itself and to the surrounding agricultural land but were also major arteries of communication and transport of bulk goods. The heart of the city stood on a high mound, or tell, partly composed of the remains of earlier settlements, which was protected by a revetment of mud brick on top of which was the actual city wall built of baked brick. Both the revetment and the wall served to defend the city from enemies and also from flooding, a perennial problem. The walled area formed an irregular oval approximately 1200 x 800 m in size enclosing about 90 ha., beyond which lay the suburbs, close to the foot of the mound. Inside the wall the city was divided into a number of quarters by roads and small canals, all dominated by the massive *temenos* or religious enclave rising above the rest of the buildings at its center.

4. The *Temenos*

This religious enclave was composed of a number of different public buildings clustered round the staged tower, or ziggurat. From at least the middle of the 3rd millennium, and perhaps earlier, each city had such a tower dedicated to its patron deity. The 1st-millennium ziggurat described by Herodotus at Babylon is generally thought to have been the origin of the biblical story of the tower of Babel. The ziggurat at Ur was probably founded in the early 3rd millennium, but our picture of it is clearest at the time of Ur-Nammu, the founder of the Ur III dynasty. It stood in an inner courtyard that was connected by steps to a lower court that in turn gave access to the town. Each court was surrounded by rooms which seem to have been used for storage, and was equipped with various amenities such as altars and offering places. The upper court also had a well and a secondary temple, now badly destroyed.

The great rectangular ziggurat originally had three stages, like a giant wedding cake, but is now badly eroded and only the lowest tier is well preserved. Because of the erosion it is impossible to establish with certainty what stood on the top of the structure, but Herodotus tells us that a small shrine was located at the top of the ziggurat at Babylon. He states that some form of sacred marriage took place in this shrine and it is possible that this was also the case at Ur, although it must be remembered that Herodotus is describing something that took place about 1,500 years later.

The lowest stage of the ziggurat measured 30m × 50m and stood 11 m high. It was built of mud brick with a skin of burnt brick to protect it from the elements. The walls sloped slightly inward and were decorated with buttresses and recesses, while weeper holes in the façade allowed the mass of unbaked bricks within to "breathe" slightly. The first stage rose 11 m above the terrace on which it stood and was approached by a massive triple stair, one stair at right angles to the platform the other two running up its face on either side of the first. All three met below the level of the platform to form a single ceremonial access.

The second tier of the "wedding cake" rose a further 5 m or so above the first, while the fragmentary remains of the third level seem to have been just less than 3 m higher, giving a total elevation above the platform of about 19 or 20 m. Later levelling and rebuilding combined with erosion have made it impossible to be sure of the exact measurements. The shrine, if one was present, must have been quite small, as the area of the third stage was only 20m × 11.3m. The only other structure for which we have archaeological evidence was a small building lying against the southeast face of the second stage of the ziggurat whose floor was covered in small copper amulets, or charms, in the shape of crescents, flies, and boats, suggesting it may have been a storage facility for offerings. Crescents were certainly one of the symbols of Nannar/Sin, the moon god to whom the ziggurat was dedicated.

The ziggurat courtyards were surrounded by other religious buildings as well as what may be the remains of a royal palace, an important grave complex, and a monumental gateway that, it is thought, was the place where justice was dispensed. There was a treasury to house the wealth of the god and an impressive building that combined the functions of temple and home to the high priestess of the moon god, who from the end of the Early Dynastic period was often the daughter of the king. She seems to have been "married" to the god in the same way that diplomatic alliances were formed by marrying off her siblings to other royal houses in neighboring areas. The temple and its priestess controlled large amounts of land and livestock as well as very considerable resources in terms of imports, raw materials, and personnel so that such a marriage was economically

as well as religiously advantageous. We are fortunate in that one priestess, Enheduanna of Agade, daughter of Sargon, was a poetess whose work has survived; her hymns and poems, together with a unique relief carving on a limestone disk showing her supervising libations to the god, give us a rare glimpse of a woman who lived more than 4,000 years ago.

The home of the priestesses was known as the Giparu and contained living quarters and a private chapel as well as a large kitchen where it seems likely that her staff were fed. A weaver's pit reminds us of the temple's obligation to keep the god equipped with clothing and all the other necessities of life. There was also a special quarter where it seems that the high priestesses were buried, but the rooms are badly destroyed by later activities on the site and little remains. The larger half of the building is taken up by an impressive temple approached through a fine courtyard across which the statue of the god, standing in its niche at the back of the cella, would have been visible to passers-by clad, no doubt, in all its finery. The plan of this temple marks a departure from the plans of earlier examples where the inner sanctum, the scene of many of the most important ceremonies, was normally hidden from public view so that the ceremonies that took place there were seen by only a few initiates. The change in the planning of the temples that included a far wider audience in the rituals may, perhaps, reflect some deeper theological change that saw the gods becoming more accessible to humanity.

Fragmentary remains of another building within the sacred enclosure were interpreted by the excavator as a palace. Many questions remain about both the plan and the function of this building, but it is not improbable that the rulers of Ur had a palace here. It was planned around a series of courtyards and presumably had domestic, administrative, and formal sectors as did other contemporary and better-preserved palaces. What is clear is that a royal grave complex lay on the edge of the *temenos* not far away. The tombs themselves, which had been thoroughly robbed soon after their construction, lay below elaborate funerary chapels that had originally been lavishly decorated with gold and semiprecious stones such as lapis lazuli and carnelian. Here offerings were made to the deceased, and the inscriptions of these kings tell us that they were seen as divine during their lifetimes and were worshiped after their deaths. The concept of the divine king begins to emerge at the end of the Early Dynastic period, when rulers start to claim that they had been fathered by a god or that they had been suckled by goddesses. It was a fairly short step from here to the assumption of divinity itself by Naram-Sin, perhaps the most successful king of the Agade dynasty around 2300 BCE. His immediate successors continued the practice, and it was also adopted by the second ruler of the succeeding Ur III dynasty and his heirs. These are the kings thought to have been buried in the grave complex close to the palace of the same date.

C. Everyday Life

1. Town and country

There is a striking paradox at the heart of life in Sumer in the second half of the 3rd millennium. The majority of the population lived in towns, although villages also existed, but most of these urban dwellers made their living by working the land. Each town was surrounded by intensively farmed gardens where date palms, fruit trees, and vegetable crops were grown along the banks of the water courses; then came the arable fields, which could be easily reached from the town and where barley was the most common crop. Barley was a staple food and was also the main ingredient of the beer, which was the drink of choice. Barley had other advantages, too, as it was resistant to the salinization of the land, a constant threat to its fertility and the result of intensive irrigation in a land where drainage was a perennial problem. In addition to the arable crops, large numbers of sheep and goats grazed the land further from the water, while cattle provided milk, meat, and hides, and together with donkeys ploughed the fields and pulled carts.

The texts tell us that much of the land and the stock were owned by the temples and the palaces, but some were rented out to tenant farmers, and private land ownership became more widespread during the course of the Sumerian period. Many of the laborers who worked the land were tied in some way that is not fully understood to the royal and religious bureaucracies and worked in exchange for food and clothing. Some also had the use of small plots of land themselves. Those who did not work on the land often worked in industrial units producing textiles and many other goods for the benefit of the temples and the palaces.

Some of the earliest documents we have list the different professions present in Sumerian society, each with its own internal hierarchy. They include what might be called white-collar workers such as priests, merchants, and scribes as well craftsmen specializing, among other things, in metalwork, jewelry making, seal cutting, and leather working. There were also soldiers, fishermen, hunters, and many others. Professions seem to have been handed down from father to son, while wives and daughters were sometimes involved in the family business as well. Slaves were present but do not seem to have made up a significant proportion of the labor force. Some were foreign captives, and some were debt slaves who could be redeemed when the debt was paid off.

The great conurbations like Ur seem to have been divided into districts, each inhabited by one group of people who were linked not only by their professions but also by family ties. Excavations at Ur revealed a unique picture of one such quarter and allow us to recreate the society in surprising detail. The main roads were large and often paved with sherds, while small alleys gave access to nearby private houses. These ranged from the large, well-planned units housing the more prosperous to tiny crooked rooms squashed into vacant lots; there were also chapels, shops, and schools for the children of the well-to-do. All were built of mud brick, and the standard house faced inward with blank walls onto the street and was built around one or more courtyards, which provided light and air. There was usually one room larger than the rest that was used as a guest room and the main living area, while at the back of the building the more prosperous houses had a chapel in which some members of the family were buried and where the family archives might be stored. The size of some houses suggests that they were inhabited by extended families, while others seem to have been used by smaller nuclear units. There is no evidence that women were secluded or that they were excluded from public life. Indeed, women from the higher strata of society often had important religious and economic responsibilities.

The neighborhood chapels are small versions of the great temples in the *temenos* area, with a small shrine in which stood a statue of the deity, visible across a courtyard from the street. There was also simple living accommodation for the priest. The schools are identified by the number of tablets containing exercises of increasing complexity as the student progressed through the education system, although the plans of the buildings are similar to those of the domestic units, suggesting that the teachers, too, lived on the job. Small shops and a bakery were also identified in this particular quarter.

We know far less about the villages that undoubtedly also existed as they are difficult to find and are seldom excavated. We may suggest that they were similar to the typical traditional village in the south of Iraq today, with mud brick buildings grouped into compounds behind walls or fences of brushwood. Each compound contains a guest room, living rooms for the patriarch and a number of married sons, as well as cooking facilities, storage, and accommodation for animals. Another group that is also underrepresented in the archaeological record is the nomadic people who lived on the fringes of the agricultural land. They had few material goods, and those that they had were of perishable materials leaving little trace in the archaeological record. Nomadic relations with the villagers and townspeople were sometimes hostile, but at other times friendly enough for nomads to serve in the army, and exchanges of goods, services, and news were a regular part of life. The relationship was fundamentally a symbiotic one, and each group needed the other.

2. The organization of society

It will be seen from the above brief account that Sumerian society was a complex one that required a sophisticated administrative system to allow it to function. This administrative system was in the hands of a highly professional cadre of civil servants who were trained in literacy and numeracy in the scribal schools. They might also learn special skills like singing or medicine. These skills were learned by rote; examples of school tablets have survived showing the initial attempts of the young scribes to copy first, single cuneiform signs drawn out for them by their teachers, and then more complex words and lists. The scribe's badge of office was his cylinder seal, which by the Ur III period was often inscribed with his name and his job description.

Like other professions, that of scribe ran in families, and although the majority of scribes were male there are records of some females as well, especially in the households of queens and princesses. The scribes undertook a wide variety of tasks from surveying fields and issuing agricultural tools to overseeing industrial production in the temple and palace workshops. They were also responsible for assessing taxes and for royal and diplomatic correspondence. Letters between rulers and their officials, or other local kings, usually begin with the phrase "Say to my lord …" as the rulers themselves were frequently illiterate. The position of royal secretary was an extremely influential one.

In addition to the central organization, there is also evidence for local "councils" in the various districts of each city, probably composed of adult males, who were in charge of day-to-day administration, including the hearing of some legal disputes and the handing down of verdicts. There has been much debate about the presence or absence of central assemblies or parliaments and about their powers. The evidence is mounting to show that these were present and that they may have had some influence over major decisions of state, such as that to go to war. It is clear that the priests, too, had considerable power, which rested on their "hotline" to the gods and especially, perhaps, on their interpretation of the omens that the ruler took before making decisions. Even when the ruler had assumed divinity and so was often personally privy to the commands of the gods, he was far from being an absolute monarch.

The final years of the 3rd millennium saw centralization and standardization of weights and measures and of calendars across the land ruled by the kings of the Ur III dynasty, more evidence of the increasing power of the king and of the complexity of the bureaucracy. Previously each city had its own system, making administration and trade extremely complicated. There was of course no coinage as such, but barley or copper were used as a standards, and other goods were valued against them; such values were also laid down centrally as were prices and even in some cases, wages.

The same period also sees the compiling of the first so-called law codes, though they seem rather to have been in part records of executive decisions on prices and wages and in part records of specific cases, possibly those tried by the king in his capacity of chief justice, which could be used for reference. Cases were normally heard initially by local courts and could be referred up to a higher court and finally to the king himself. Statements were taken from witnesses, and ordeals were sometimes ordered when witness statements were contradictory. These could involve being thrown into the river, for instance, or the taking of oaths. The best preserved of the Sumerian codes is that attributed to Ur-Nammu, the first ruler of the Ur III dynasty, but almost certainly compiled under his successor. It is fragmentary, but enough survives to demonstrate that monetary penalties were the norm for crimes of violence, although murder carried the death penalty, and that the *lex talionis* that we see in the OT was introduced in the early years of the 2nd millennium by Amorite rulers such as Hammurabi of Babylon. There was no provision for imprisonment under the Sumerian system.

D. The Sumerians in Context

1. Neighboring states

The world of the Sumerians was bounded by the Mediterranean to the northwest, by the Arabian Gulf to the south, by desert to the south and southwest, and by mountains to the north and east. None of these boundaries was impermeable, but they serve as a frame within which we can place the Sumerians of the 3rd millennium. Within this swath of the ancient world there were other significant civilizations. In northern Syria and northern Iraq the 3rd millennium saw the apparently independent emergence of urban settlements such as Mozan, Hamoukar, and Beydar in the central area, Chuera and Ebla to the west (*see* EBLA TEXTS), and Leilan and Brak to the northeast. These settlements were smaller than those of the southern plain of Sumer and were laid out rather differently, but they boasted monumental buildings, powerful rulers, advanced technologies, and sophisticated administrative systems. In some cases it seems that their writing systems and the style of their cylinder seals were borrowed directly from Sumer. Indeed, it has been suggested that scribes from Ebla had actually been trained at Kish, just north of Sumer. These northern towns frequently lay on trade routes that linked north and south or east and west and formed a network of small polities that do not seem to have combined into larger political units until the very end of the period.

One exception to this may have been the much larger centre at Brak, a site that may have been urban from as far back as the early 5th millennium and that seems to have stood in a rather different relationship with Sumer than the other towns mentioned. From time to time Brak seems to have been actually under the control of rulers in the southern plain. For example the Agade king Naram-Sin built a great fortified storehouse there where we may suggest that goods were stored on their way southward. At other times it was the center of a city state that probably also included the site of Mozan, ancient Urkesh.

The last of the Early Dynastic kings, Lugalzagesi, claims to have reached the Mediterranean, as does his successor Sargon of Agade, but these were probably lightning raids rather than more permanent conquests. There is little archaeological evidence for contact with western Syria or the Levant, and there is no evidence for interaction with Old Kingdom Egypt.

Iran was home to urban centers that were arguably as old and as developed as those of Sumer. The most significant of these during the 3rd millennium was SUSA in the southwest, but other important centers are known on the plateau such as Anshan, and the mythical city of Aratta, known from a famous Sumerian myth called *Enmerkar and the Lord of Aratta*, which recounts the relationship between Aratta and the city of Kish to the north of the Sumerian plain.

Interactions with Arabia seem to have been confined to the east coast and the offshore islands, most significantly with the Bahrain islands and, slightly later, with Failaka, which lies off the coast of Kuwait. This region was known as Dilmun, which by the end of the 3rd millennium was one of Sumer's most important trading partners. Dilmun had its capital first on the Arabian mainland, then at the site known as the Bahrain fort, and finally on Failaka. Dilmun was a vital entrepot and linked Sumer with areas as far away as the Indus Valley civilization of Pakistan.

2. Trade and diplomacy

Relations between Sumer and its neighbors took many different forms from conquest to diplomatic alliances cemented by royal marriages, but underlying all of them was trade. Trade was imperative for the survival of Sumerian society. The region was lacking in many raw materials; in order to supply essentials such as metal tools and weapons, as well as the luxury goods that an ever more prosperous society demanded, regular exchanges with areas rich in raw materials were essential. Imports of manufactured goods were relatively rare, but a steady supply of manufactured goods was necessary to provide the exports required to keep the wheels of commerce turning.

Many of these goods were supplied by the workshops of the temples and the palaces of Sumer, but private investment became more significant towards the end of the period. Textiles, usually of high quality, were probably the most common exports, but the texts mention many other commodities such as cereals, leather goods, and aromatic oils. Lighter, high-value goods had many advantages, as land transport was still difficult with no roads and only pack animals or solid-wheeled carts to transport them. Bulk goods could really only be transported by water either along the Euphrates or the Arabian Gulf, and it was these waterways that carried the copper and other base metals that were crucial to the functioning of the state. High-quality stone for royal statues and great timbers for public buildings also traveled this way, while luxuries such as lapis lazuli and other decorative stones, together with gold and silver, may have come overland. Trade was closely linked to diplomacy and merchants were frequently also envoys.

E. Conclusion

Sumer was not unique; it was one of a number of urban civilizations that developed in the region during the 4th and 3rd millennia. If it has a claim to primacy it lies in the development of cuneiform and in the literary and mathematical skills of its scribes, traces of which can still be found in our world today. The twenty-four-hour clock and the number of degrees in a circle, for instance, both relate back to the sexagesimal system of counting invented by the Sumerians. More controversially, it can be suggested that Sumer also saw some of the earliest experiments with democracy in the shape of the town and neighborhood councils. *See* ASSYRIA AND BABYLONIA.

Bibliography: J. Black, G. Cunningham, E. Robson, and G. Zolyomi, eds. *The Literature of Ancient Sumer* (2004); Harriet Crawford. *Sumer and the Sumerians.* 2nd rev. ed. (2003); W. W. Hallo and W. K. Simpson. *The Ancient Near East: A History.* 2nd ed. (1998); W. W. Hallo, ed. *The Context of Scripture: Archival Documents from the Biblical World.* 3 vols. (2003); A. Kuhrt. *The Ancient Near East.* 2 vols. (1995); J. N. Postgate. *Early Mesopotamia: Society and Economy at the Dawn of History* (1992); J. Sasson. *Civilisations of the Ancient near East.* 4 vols. (1995).

HARRIET CRAWFORD

SUMERIAN TEXTS *soo*-maihr´ee-uhn. The earliest Sumerian texts are arguably the oldest texts written in the oldest script ("cuneiform" = "wedge-shaped" writing on clay tablets, prisms, cones, etc.), and in the oldest written language in the history of the world, Sumerian. The origin of the CUNEIFORM writing system is, to some extent, lost in the prehistory from which it emerged sometime during the latter half of the 4th millennium BCE, at Uruk in southern Mesopotamia. It seems to have developed out of combining a pre-existing accounting notation system (clay tokens representing commodities, people, etc., and numerals for counting them) with the creative genius necessary to write signs and texts that represent fully human language: sentences rather than just lists of items counted.

About ninety percent of the earliest tablets are economic and administrative in their content, and the writing is pictographic in character. This means that they can be read in any language that has a word for what is pictured. Since it is difficult to discern the pronunciation of the texts, the language in which they are written is obscure. Recent scholarship, however, has left little doubt that the language of these earliest texts was Sumerian from the start.

Archives consisting largely of economic and administrative texts (bureaucratic records, legal transactions, etc.) written in Sumerian have been discovered from the end of the 4th millennium (Uruk) to the end of the 3rd millennium (e.g., the Ur III empire, 2112–2004 BCE), when Sumerian ceased to be a common spoken language, although it continued as a literary and religious language for 2,000 years after that. The Ur III empire was highly bureaucratic and left behind thousands of these kinds of texts. Multitudes of such texts also from Lagash and Umma, for example, are found all over the world in various library and museum collections.

The other 10 percent of these earliest texts are what we call lexical lists. These are especially important for several reasons: 1) they have the longest history of any genre of Sumerian texts, extending for about three millennia; 2) they are the native dictionaries that were used in the training of scribes and, therefore, essential to our modern understanding of the Sumerian language; and 3) they were the Sumerian form of science, serving as inventories of their knowledge of the world from their own cultural point of view. The last of these had the effect of transmitting Mesopotamian culture across the entire ANE through cuneiform scribal training down through the millennia.

The earliest of these lexical texts are just lists of signs in one language (probably meant to be read in Sumerian, but readable also in Semitic), but later bilingual lists developed (Sumerian and Akkadian), some with syllabic writings to indicate the pronunciation of the Sumerian signs. Some are arranged by signs in ordered sign sequence with the translations into (Semitic) Akkadian, and others according to themes such as trees and objects made of wood, then stones and objects made of stone, etc. Later on lists appear in multiple languages, not just Sumerian and Akkadian but also Hittite or Hurrian or Ugaritic or some combination of these.

The category of texts we call "literary" is hard to define and delimit. For our purposes here, whatever texts are not economic, administrative, or lexical are considered literary. There may be just a few literary tablets found among the early Uruk and archaic Ur texts, but we cannot be sure because we cannot read them with any certainty in our current state of knowledge. Literary texts begin to appear around the middle of the 3rd millennium (ca. 2600 BCE) at Fara (ancient Shuruppak) and Abu Salabikh, with a few from other sites. Here we have what appear to be early fragmentary exemplars of later more fully developed literary compositions known from the Old Babylonian period; for example, the Instructions of Shuruppak, the Temple Hymn Collection, the Kesh Temple Hymn, and some stories about Lugalbanda, a legendary king of Uruk. We also have texts written in an orthography that has yet to be fully deciphered called UD.GAL.NUN (the sequence of signs for the name of the god "Enlil" in this peculiar system). Some have speculated that there may be some connection between this special orthography and the EME.SAL (literlly, "thin tongue") dialect known first in the Old Babylonian period (18th cent. BCE). It was used especially in certain kinds of lamentations and sometimes in speeches between goddesses.

A substantial number of royal and private dedicatory inscriptions in Sumerian have been discovered mainly from Lagash in the Presargonic period, written on clay tablets and cones as well as stone slabs and statues, etc., some of them in multiple copies and with various versions (ca. 2500–2334 BCE; the Akkadian Sargonic period begins with Sargon the Great, ca. 2334 BCE). Other sites include Adab, Kish, MARI, Nippur, Umma, Ur, and Uruk. These are the earliest examples of historiographic literature available to us. They are important, therefore, for the study of history-writing in the ANE. Some of these texts recount several generations of previous history leading up to the time of the inscription. One of them (The Reforms of Urukagina) is the first social and religious reform text in history.

Semitic Akkadian became the official literary language during the (Old Akkadian) Sargonic period (ca. 2334–2154 BCE). The Sumerian literary tradition, however, regards the daughter of Sargon, Enheduanna, to be the author of several very important Sumerian compositions during this period. These include, for example, "The Exaltation of Inanna" and "The Collection of Sumerian Temple Hymns" in its later canonical version.

After the Sargonic period came a flowering of Sumerian literature down to the end of the 3rd millennium, sometimes called the classical period. Perhaps the greatest extant Sumerian literary composition is the temple building hymn composed in eloquent poetic style and inscribed on the "Gudea Cylinders" (two clay barrels, each about 2 ft. high and over a foot in diameter). Gudea was the ruler of Lagash around the time of the beginning of the Ur III kingdom (2112–2004 BCE) or perhaps a little earlier. He also dedicated almost thirty inscribed statues of himself to various deities, commemorating his pious deeds on their behalf.

The Ur III ("Neo-Sumerian") kings developed one of the great bureaucracies of ancient days. Urnammu (or perhaps Shulgi) promulgated the first law code. They left behind inscriptions dedicating temples and other pious deeds to the gods. They also lauded their own wondrous kingly qualities (sometimes reflecting their own deification) in a genre known as "royal hymns" (see especially the many Shulgi hymns). Although composed on the basis of earlier oral tradition, some scholars believe that most of the Sumerian literary compositions extant in only (or largely) Old Babylonian copies or from later times (2nd and 1st millennium) were first put into writing in the Ur III period. These include: 1) narrative myths about the gods Enki, Enlil, Inanna, Ninurta (Ningirsu), etc.; 2) hymns to deities; 3) royal praises or prayers to deities, the latter sometimes in letter form; 4) laments over the destruction of various cities and their temples; 5) love poems, some of which may be related to the celebration of sacred marriage rites; 6) epic tales about supposed early rulers, especially Gilgamesh, Lugalbanda, and Enmerkar; 7) proverbial instructions for life, a farmer's almanac, and a sort of Sumerian Job called "Man and His God"; 8) literary debates between elements of nature or implements (summer and winter, tree and reed, hoe and plow, etc.); 9) literary texts about school activities, life as a scribe, laments over the death of the scribe's parents, and dialogues between students; 10) various tales and fables about men and animals; 11) incantations against evil spirits; and 12) liturgical songs, mostly laments for rituals concerning temples that have been destroyed and need reconstruction. *See* GILGAMESH, EPIC OF.

Bibliography: Jeremy Black, et al. *The Literature of Ancient Sumer* (2004); Jean-Jacques Glassner. *The Invention of Cuneiform: Writing in Sumer* (2003); M. W. Green. "The Construction and Implementation of the Cuneiform Writing System." *Visible Language* 15 (1981) 345–72; William W. Hallo, ed. *The Context of Scripture.* 3 vols. (1997, 2000, 2002) 1.509–99, 2.385–438, 3.293–318; John L. Hayes. *A Manual of Sumerian Grammar and Texts.* 2nd rev. and exp. ed. (2000) 385–95; Thorkild Jacobsen. *The Harps That Once … Sumerian Poetry in Translation* (1987); Piotr Michalowski. "Sumerian Literature: An Overview." *CANE* 4 (1995) 2279–91.

RICHARD E. AVERBECK

SUMMER AND WINTER. The weather patterns and SEASONS in Israel are divided between cool, wet winters and hot, dry summers. The spring and fall seasons are relatively short and are not mentioned in the Bible. The biblical authors appear to have thought of the seasons in two agricultural cycles: "seedtime and harvest, cold and heat, summer and winter" (Gen 8:22; see also Ps 74:17; Zech 14:8). Summer days are characterized by dry, hot air (80°–90° F), with cool winds off the Mediterranean Sea in the late afternoons. Rain is extremely rare in the summer. Winter, the rainy season, brings a variety of weather patterns. The central hills, Galilee, and the mountains to the north (Hermon) receive frost and snow, especially in the high elevations. Along the coast and in the rift valley the temperature is mild. A strong, dry wind from the east is common in the spring (April-May) and fall (October-November). *See* ISRAEL, CLIMATE OF.

MILTON C. MORELAND

SUN [שֶׁמֶשׁ *shemesh*, חֶרֶס *kheres*; ἥλιος *hēlios*]. The earth's light source, considered a deity in the ancient world. Kheres appears only twice (Judg 14:18; Job 9:7), and khammah (חַמָּה, "the hot one"; Isa 24:23; 30:26; Job 30:26; Song 6:10) and 'or (אוֹר, "light"; Gen 1:14-18; Job 31:26; etc.) are sometimes substituted.

Most biblical references are to the physical object. In Gen 1 the "greater light" is fixed into the firmament with the moon and stars to distinguish between night and day. Together they serve "for signs and for seasons and for days and for years" (Gen 1:14). The sun's annual changing warmth helped determine the agricultural seasons and thus the passing of the year itself, requiring regular adjustments to the lunar calendar. As the source of light and heat, the sun was considered beneficial, such that to "see the sun" (Eccl 7:11; 11:7; contrast Ps 58:9; Eccl 6:5; compare Jer 15:9; Mic 3:6) connoted

being alive. Nonetheless, its intense heat could have negative effects (Isa 49:10; Jonah 4:8; Ps 121:6 [compare 91:6]; Jdt 8:3; Matt 13:6; Jas 1:11).

The sun was less significant in the Israelite cultus than the MOON. Its rising and setting determined the timing of the morning and evening sacrifice (Exod 29:38-39; Num 28:2-4), and sunset marked the end of purification from inadvertent uncleanness (Lev 22:7; Deut 23:11) and the time of the Passover sacrifice (Deut 16:6). The passing of seven days established the Sabbath, starting with sunset at the end of the sixth day.

The sun's reappearance each day confirmed the divinely established cosmic order (Pss 72:5; 89:36) and was a metaphor for Yahweh's relationship with Israel (Jer 31:35-36). Thus, a darkened sun signified eschatological judgment (Isa 13:10; Ezek 32:7; Joel 2:10; 2:31; 3:15; Amos 8:9; Matt 24:29//Mark 13:24; Acts 2:20; Rev 6:12; 8:12). But when Jerusalem is restored the sun's light will increase sevenfold (Isa 30:26), while in Isa 60:19-20 and Rev 21:23 God's presence will replace the sun's light (compare Zech 14:7).

A 364-day calendar appears in *1 En.* 72–82 and the book of *Jubilees.* Their importance at Qumran, alongside the *Temple Scroll* and other sectarian literature, indicates the solar calendar was followed there rather than the older lunar calendar.

All ancient cultures had a sun-god. In Egypt, Re was the chief god of Egypt, and other deities were sometimes syncretized with him (e.g., Amon-Re). The 14th-cent. BCE pharaoh Akhenaten replaced the Egyptian pantheon with the sole worship of Aten, the sun disk, but his efforts did not long survive his death, and direct links to later Israelite monotheism cannot be demonstrated. The sun god was usually male, but Shapash at Ugarit and Samash in Old South Arabic were female (this is reflected in the Hebrew noun, which can be either gender).

Because the sun passed over the earth daily, the sun god was an all-seeing judge characterized by justice, especially for the weak. Shamash gave Hammurabi his law code partly to limit the power of the rich. Passing through the underworld at night, the Semitic sun god ruled the underworld deities (e.g., *CTU* 1.6.VI.45–49) and was an intermediary with the dead (e.g., Shapash aids in Baal's retrieval from Mot/Death [*CTU* 1.6.I.8–15; IV.1–24]).

Place names indicate that a sun cult existed in Canaan before the Israelite period. Four towns are called Beth-Shemesh ("House [Temple] of the sun"), one each in Judah (Josh 15:10; 19:22; etc.), Naphtali (Josh 19:38), and Issachar (Josh 19:22), plus one in Egypt (Jer 43:13); Ir-Shemesh ("CITY OF THE SUN"; Josh 19:41) probably refers to the first of these. Other geographic names with "sun" as a divine name include En-Shemesh ("the Spring of the Sun"; Josh 15:7; 18:17) on the border of Judah and Benjamin; Timnath-heres ("portion of the sun; Judg 2:9; Timnath-serah in Josh 19:50; 24:30) in Ephraim; Har-heres ("Mountain of the

Sun"; Judg 1:35) in the Aijalon Valley; and Ascent of the Sun (Judg 8:13) east of the Jordan.

Sun worship is forbidden (Deut 4:19; 17:3), and Job denies doing so (Job 31:26); all three texts imply it was occurring. In 2 Kgs 17:16; 21:3, 5; Jer 19:13; and Zeph 1:5 people worship the "host of heaven" (the sun is enumerated as one of them in Deut 4:19; 17:3; 2 Kgs 23:5; Jer 8:2). Manasseh built altars to the sun in the Temple (2 Kgs 21:5), Josiah removed horses dedicated to the sun from the Temple entrance and burned the "chariots of the sun" (2 Kgs 23:11), and men prayed bowing towards the sun in the Temple's inner court (Ezek 8:16). Even the Deuteronomists considered the sun to be a real deity, given to other nations by Yahweh (Deut 4:19). This is supported by Isa 24:23, where the sun is shamed as part of Yahweh's punishment of the host of heaven (v. 21); vv. 21-23 point to more than a physical object. Similarly, the sun striking the psalmist in Ps 121:6 may have referred to the sun god's power (compare Ps 91:6).

Israelite sun-worship has been attributed to Assyrian hegemony, but the place names listed above show that solar worship in Canaan predates Assyrian influence. Consequently, some argue that solar worship was an accepted part of early Yahwism, and even that Yahweh and the sun were equated. Some claims cannot be supported (e.g., that the sun shone into the Holy of Holies at the equinoxes) but there is evidence of a solar Yahwism. The names Samson (Judg 14–16) and Shimshai (Ezra 4:8-9, 17, 23) are derived from shemesh, and other biblical names link Yahweh with possible solar activity: Uriah/Uriyahu ("Yahweh is my light"; 2 Sam 11:3; 2 Kgs 16:11; etc.), Sheariah ("Yahweh is the dawn"; 1 Chr 8:26), Zerahiah ("Yahweh has shone forth"; 1 Chr 5:32; 6:36; Ezra 7:4; 8:4), and Izrahiah ("Yahweh will shine forth"; 1 Chr 7:3; Neh 12:42). Similarly, Yahweh (or the divine glory) rises (Isa 2:21; 60:1-2), shines forth (Deut 33:2; Ps 50:1-2; Ezek 43:2; compare Isa 58:8; 60:1-3), and dawns (Deut 33:2). "Yahweh is my sun" in Ps 84:11 is inconclusive, since shemesh can also mean "rampart" (Isa 54:12), but Hab 3:4, where Yahweh's "brightness was like the sun; rays came forth from his hand," is striking. Hoping to see God in the morning (Pss 17; 27; 63) has also been linked to the rising sun (compare God's wings in Pss 17:8; 63:7 and the winged sun disks common in ancient iconography). While some of these texts may be metaphorical, the frequent solar connection in many contexts is suggestive.

The presence of both altars and the horses and chariot of the sun in Yahweh's Temple (2 Kgs 23:11) indicates some, if not many, considered them acceptable. The sun traversing the sky in a chariot was a common motif in the ANE and is reflected in two 10th-cent. Israelite artifacts: the Taanach cult stand with a horse and sun disk on the top level and a terra cotta horse head with a sun disk from Hazor. Elijah's fiery horse-drawn chariot (2 Kgs 2:11) is probably the sun's, and Yahweh drives horses and chariots (linked to solar language in v. 4) in Hab 3:8. Ezekiel encounters Yahweh on his chariot in Ezek 1 (note the light imagery in v. 27) and in Ezek 43:2, 4, God's glory rides this same chariot from the east. Combined with the divine glory "rising" in Isa 60:1-2 and "shining forth" in Ezek 43:2, this suggests that the sun was a manifestation of Yahweh's glory, which the men in Ezek 8:16 worshiped.

As monotheism developed, the sun's divinity was downplayed. The heavenly host are subordinate members of Yahweh's retinue in 1 Kgs 22:19, and in Ps 148:3 the sun praises Yahweh. Genesis 1 and many other texts insist that the sun is simply a created object. Nonetheless, solar imagery for Yahweh continued throughout the late Second Temple period. Sirach 42:16 parallels the rising sun with Yahweh's glory, 1QH[a] VII, 25 calls God "an eternal luminary," 2 En. 39A:4 says God's eyes are "like the rays of the sun," and the Odes of Solomon call God "my sun" (15:2) and "like a sun upon the earth" (11:13). A 4th-cent.-BCE Judean coin (ANEP 226) with a deity enthroned on a winged wheel depicts Yahweh's sun chariot, which is also reflected in MERKAVAH MYSTICISM (chariot mysticism).

By the NT period, the sun's divine associations were mostly forgotten but not completely lost. The eschatological texts noted above echo God's defeat of the sun (god), while Jesus shines like the sun at the transfiguration (Matt 17:2). This is echoed in Paul's encounter with Jesus on the road to Damascus as a light brighter than the sun (Acts 26:13), and eventually in Jesus proceeding from God as "light from light" in the Nicene Creed. See DIAL; HOSTS, HOST OF HEAVEN.

Bibliography: John Day. *Yahweh and the Gods and Goddesses of Canaan* (2000); J. Glen Taylor. *Yahweh and the Sun: Biblical and Archaeological Evidence for Sun Worship in Ancient Israel* (1993).

JOHN L. MCLAUGHLIN

SUN, CITY OF THE [עִיר הַחֶרֶס *'ir hakheres*]. According to Isaiah's prophecy, this is one of five Egyptian cities whose people—speaking the Canaanite language—would express allegiance to God (Isa 19:18). Also promised to its inhabitants is a savior who would deliver them from their oppressors and bring them healing. The textual reading "City of Destruction" (*'ir haheres* עִיר הַהֶרֶס) in the KJV has divided support among modern translations. The NIV and NASB concur with the KJV; but the RSV, NRSV, REB, NAB, and JB accept the variant reading. "City of the Sun." Texts offering modern translations' support for accepting the variant as the better reading include some copies of the MT, the Qumran scroll 1Q Isa[a], some medieval Hebrew manuscripts, Symmachus' Greek version, the Targum, and the Vulgate. In addition, the textual reading is rejected since it does not fit the positive emphasis of Isa 19:18-22. This City of the Sun is probably the same as HELIOPOLIS, mentioned in Jer 43:13.

EMILY R. CHENEY

SUN, HORSES OF THE. *See* SUN.

SUPH soof [סוּף suf]. An area (possibly a city) east of the Jordan River, mentioned only in relation to the location of the Israelites at the time of the last speech of Moses (Deut 1:1). The precise location of Suph is unknown.

SUPHAH soo′fuh [סוּפָה sufah]. An oasis east of Jordan and southeast of the Dead Sea, mentioned in a quotation of archaic lines of poetry (Num 21:14). The area described is on the border of Moab, near the Arnon River and its valley. Perhaps the same as SUPH (Deut 1:1).

EMILY R. CHENEY

SUPPER. *See* MEALS.

SUPPER, LAST. *See* LAST SUPPER, THE.

SUPPER, THE LORD'S. *See* LORD'S SUPPER.

SUPPLIANT, SUPPLICANT [עָתָר ʿathar; ἱκέτης hiketēs]. Someone who prays to or makes a request from another, whether from God or anyone else. The verb ʿathar (עָתַר) means "to pray," but the noun can also have the sense of "worshiper." In one sense, a suppliant is a beggar who seeks the goodwill of others; in another sense, anyone who comes before God is a suppliant, even if he or she comes to bring an offering rather than to make a request. It is worth noting that in the Bible the suppliant is always received and welcomed by the one he or she approaches. Therefore, just as it is the privilege of the believer to make supplication before God (Zeph 3:10), both with prayer and with offerings of thanksgiving, so also it is the obligation of believers not to turn away those suppliants who come to them (Sir 4:4). *See* PRAYER.

NATHAN P. LAMONTAGNE

SUPPORT. *See* ORPHAN; WIDOW.

SUR soor [סוּר sur; Σούρ Sour]. 1. A temple gate at which some of the king's guards stood watch (2 Kgs 11:6). This particular gate is mentioned only in this passage; the parallel in 2 Chr 23:5 names the GATE OF THE FOUNDATION.

2. A town mentioned in Jdt 2:28, apparently located on or near the Mediterranean coast. It is otherwise unknown.

JESSICA TINKLENBERG DEVEGA

SUR GATE soor [שַׁעַר סוּר shaʿar sur]. Meaning "gate of departure" (LXX, "gate of the ways"). Second Kings 11:6 suggests a location in the north or northwest section of an enclosure around the temple courts and the adjacent palace. The later parallel passage in 2 Chr 23:5 calls it the "GATE OF THE FOUNDATION"

(LXX, "middle gate"; compare Jer 39:3). *See* GUARD, GATE OF THE; MUSTER GATE.

JAMES RILEY STRANGE

SURETY [חָבַל khaval, עָרַב ʿarav, תָּקַע taqaʿ; ἐγγύη engyē]. A PLEDGE given as a guarantee for the fulfillment of some act. A person can act as surety, such as when Judah pledges himself in exchange for Benjamin, obtaining Jacob's permission to take Benjamin to Egypt (Gen 43:9; 44:32). Job asks for a pledge but wonders who would put himself forward as surety (Job 17:3). Proverbs declares that it is senseless to give oneself as surety (Prov 17:18; compare Prov 22:26). Pledging a surety is seen as both positive and negative. Proverbs counsels to take the pledge given as surety for foreigners (Prov 20:16; 27:13), but Sirach reflects mixed perspectives: a good person will give surety for a neighbor (Sir 29:14), yet doing so has ruined many (Sir 29:18 [LXX 29:17-18]).

KENNETH D. LITWAK

SURGERY. *See* HEALING; HEALTH CARE.

SURNAME. Surnames in the sense of family names such as Smith do not occur in the Bible, but in a number of cases people are surnamed by receiving an additional name. In Isa 45:1-4, e.g., God surnames Cyrus, saying, "For the sake of my servant Jacob, and Israel my chosen, I call you by your name, I surname you, though you do not know me." The surname is not specified, although it may be "my anointed." From the context, it appears that God is giving Cyrus a throne name. The priest Mattathias had a son John, surnamed Gaddi (1 Macc 2:2).

Jesus surnames some of his disciples. He gives Simon the name Peter (Mark 3:16; *see* PETER, THE APOSTLE), and he gives James and John the name Boanerges, which Mark translates as "Sons of Thunder" (Mark 3:17). In Acts, the apostles give a Levite named Joseph the surname Barnabas, which means "son of encouragement" (4:36).

JUDITH ANNE JONES

SUSA soo′suh [שׁוּשַׁן shushan; Σοῦσα Sousa, Σουσίς Sousis]. Susa was one of the most prominent cities in the ancient region of Elam (modern Khuzistan, in southwest Iran). Susa was occupied continuously from the beginning of the 4th millennium BCE until the Mongol invasion in the 13th cent. CE. Excavations at Susa have uncovered tablets inscribed in the undeciphered Proto-Elamite script dating to 3100–2900 BCE. Susa is first mentioned in Old Akkadian (2500–1900 BCE) records, which reveal conflict between Mesopotamia and Elam. Despite constant war, the city thrived, and there is extensive evidence for trade with the Persian Gulf and Central Asia. Elamite civilization reached its apex in the Middle Elamite period (1300–1100 BCE), when Shutruk-Nahhunte (ca. 1200 BCE) plundered the Code of Hammurapi (excavated at Susa) from Babylonia, along with the statue of the god Marduk. King Nebuchadnezzar I (1146–1123 BCE) drove the Elamites out of Babylonia. Susa resurged in the 8th cent., but the city was sacked by Ashurbanipal in 640 BCE.

After the rise of the Achaemenid Empire under Cyrus (559–530 BCE), Susa became the winter capital of Darius I and his successors. During this period, Susa was a cosmopolitan city, located on the Royal Road, connecting it to the west as well as to the other capitals of Ecbatana and Persepolis. Darius I began building new palaces, and the construction of the residential palace is well documented in inscriptions found during excavation. These inscriptions reveal that the labor and materials used to build the palace came from all over the empire. Again demonstrating the cosmopolitan nature of the capital, a statue of King Darius was excavated at Susa, bearing Egyptian hieroglyphs as well as trilingual cuneiform inscriptions. These building projects were completed by Darius' son, Xerxes, including the palace gatehouse (compare Esth 2:19, 21; 5:9, 13; 6:10; the plot of Esther centers on "the citadel of Susa"; see, e.g., Esth 1:2, 5; 2:3, 5, 8; 3:15; 4:8, 16; 8:14, 15; 9:6-18; and corresponding verses in the Additions to Esther plus 11:3; 16:18). The archaeological data regarding Xerxes' palace corresponds with the description given in Esther, demonstrating the author's awareness of the palace architecture. Susa is mentioned in the books of Ezra (4:9), Nehemiah (1:1), and Daniel (8:2), as well as in the book of *Jubilees* (8:21; 9:2). The city was captured by Alexander the Great in 331 BCE. In the later Sasanian period, Susa, which had a large Christian population, was destroyed by the army of Shapur II (309–379 CE) after a rebellion. In the 9th cent. CE, the Arab historian al-Tabari described a shrine in Susa that allegedly contains the tomb of the prophet Daniel, and today it is a major site of pilgrimage for Iran's Shiite Muslims and its Jewish population. *See* DARIUS; ELAM, ELAMITES; ESTHER; ESTHER, BOOK OF; PERSIA, HISTORY AND RELIGION OF; XERXES.

Bibliography: Rémy Boucharlat. "Susa under Achaemenid Rule." *Mesopotamia and Iran in the Persian Period.* John Curtis, ed. (1997) 54–67; Pierre Briant. *From Cyrus to Alexander: A History of the Persian Empire* (2002); Prudence Harper, Joan Aruz, and Francoise Tallon, eds. *The Royal City of Susa* (1992); Carey Moore. "Archaeology and the Book of Esther." *BA* 38 (1975) 62–79; Daniel Potts. *The Archaeology of Elam* (1999); Edwin Yamauchi. *Persia and the Bible* (1990).

DANIEL JENSEN SHEFFIELD

SUSANNA   *soo*-zan´uh [Σουσάννα Sousanna]. 1. Susanna is one of three additions to Daniel found in Greek versions of the Bible, namely, the LXX, where it appears as the thirteenth chapter of Daniel and, in somewhat different form, in THEODOTION's version,

where it opens Daniel. Although set in Babylonia, the book was probably written in the Hellenistic Diaspora. Its latest possible date is ca. 100 BCE, when the LXX translation of Daniel was likely completed. Susanna is part of the Roman Catholic canon, but not of the Jewish or Protestant canons. The text is found only in Greek, though some scholars have argued that there must have been an original Hebrew version. Susanna reflects the concerns of a secure and wealthy Diaspora Jewish community that, while not threatened by outside powers, is anxious to inculcate piety and sexual morality in its members.

Susanna, a beautiful and God-fearing Jewish woman, is married to Joakim, a wealthy and honored Jew of the Babylonian Diaspora. Among the frequent visitors to Joakim's home are two unscrupulous judges. These two elders are overcome with passion for the beautiful Susanna and spy on her daily as she takes the air in her husband's garden. One day, no longer able to control themselves, they lie in wait for her in the garden. When she is alone, they confront her with a wicked ultimatum: either she sleeps with them or they accuse her publicly of committing adultery with a young man. Susanna cries out but refuses to give in to them. The next day she is tried and, on testimony from the elders, sentenced to death for adultery. Her voluble prayer for help is answered by a young man, Daniel, who demands a retrial. He cross-examines the two elders, separately this time, and catches them in their lies. The crowd swiftly condemns them to death for bearing false witness.

Susanna must be read as a story rather than history. Indeed, alongside apocryphal stories such as Judith, Tobit, and Greek Esther, Susanna has been referred to as an ancient Jewish novel, and is perhaps best described as a courtroom drama. When read in context in the book of Daniel, Susanna testifies to the young prophet's wisdom as well as his role as God's agent and the answer to Susanna's heartfelt prayer. Like Esther and Judith, this female protagonist represents the Diaspora Jewish community and in doing so provides a model for Jewish behavior grounded in a piety that values sexual fidelity above life itself.

From a literary perspective, the story contrasts Susanna and the elders with regard to piety, honesty, and integrity. But a more subtle contrast is evident as well, between Susanna's husband, Joakim, and her young savior, Daniel. Unlike Joakim, who stands by quietly and passively as his wife is sentenced to death, Daniel shouts for justice to be done. Daniel defends Susanna's piety and chastity as her husband should have done, and he is utterly convinced of her innocence, as her husband should have been. Daniel takes on the role of judge and arbiter that Joakim should have claimed as the most honored man in the community. Daniel is quite literally the answer to Susanna's prayers (42-45).

Susanna has inspired numerous works of art (e.g., paintings by Rembrandt and Artemisia Gentileschi), music (e.g., Handel's oratorio *Susanna*), and literature (e.g., Wallace Stevens's poem "Peter Quince at the Clavier").

2. Susanna was one of the women among those who accompanied Jesus and supported his ministry financially in Luke 8:3.

Bibliography: Carey A. Moore. *Daniel, Esther, and Jeremiah: The Additions.* AB 44 (1977); Lawrence M. Wills. *The Jewish Novel in the Ancient World* (1995).
ADELE REINHARTZ

SUSI *soo'si* [סוּסִי susi]. The father of Gaddi, who represented the tribe of Joseph (i.e., Manasseh) in the mission to spy out the land of Canaan (Num 13:11).

SUSIYA, KHIRBET. A village in the area south of Hebron that was inhabited by a substantial Jewish population during the 2nd–7th cent. CE. Located in the area known as the Darom, the site contains the remains of an important SYNAGOGUE building with beautiful mosaic floors. Khirbet Susiya was not the ancient village name; it is an Arabic name that does not correspond to any known ancient town in this region. It is likely that the inhabitants of the town were once connected to the nearby town of Carmel (Khirbit Kurmul) that lies approximately 1 mi. to the northeast. In the Roman and Byzantine periods, Khirbet Susiya was essentially "South Carmel."

The area of the Darom extends east in a 10–15 mi. wide belt from Lachish through mountainous terrain to the Dead Sea town of En-Gedi. Eusebius reports in his catalog of biblical sites, the *Onomasticon* (4th cent. CE), that there were seven Jewish villages in this region, in addition to two Christian communities (see Magness). Beginning in the 2nd cent. CE, the Darom was rich with the remains of Jewish synagogues and other artifacts. Khirbet Susiya and other towns in this region (Maʿon, Eshtemoa, Rimmon, Horvat ʿAnim, Horvat Kishor) gained in popularity in the Middle Roman period as Jews moved south away from the destruction in the area of Jerusalem that resulted from the Bar Kochba Revolt (135 CE). In the 4th to the 7th cent. Christianity became more popular in the area as is seen in the building of Byzantine churches throughout the Darom.

Khirbet Susiya is on and around a horseshoe-shaped hill, with open access from the north. The occupants lived on the western slope and around the semi-circular hilltop. The slope of the eastern arm of the hill is covered with burial caves. Terraced agricultural fields are found within the horseshoe and in the surrounding hills around the site. With roots in the 1st cent. CE, the town was an agricultural center with wine and olive oil production. Many cisterns, wine-making installations, and olive presses have been located in and around the site. A large cave at the site is thought to have been used for the storage and fermentation of wine; thus it has been named the Wine-Cellar Cave. A fortified tower and defensive building have also been excavated at the site.

The synagogue at Khirbet Susiya adds to our knowledge of the Jewish community in the Byzantine period. The synagogue was located on an adjoining hill, just west of the town. It was used by the Jewish community from the late 4th cent. through at least the 7th cent. CE. The nearby Menorah Cave (named for the menorah that is carved in the lintel design above the cave entrance) may have originally been functionally connected to the synagogue building. The synagogue is oriented east-west and is comprised of a large prayer hall with three rows of stepped benches, an open courtyard, an exedra, and a second hall south of the prayer hall. The building underwent several phases of repair while it was used as a synagogue. During its second phase, a new bema was installed and the floor was paved with a color mosaic. Besides several important Hebrew inscriptions and depictions of the torah ark and menorahs, the mosaic floors contained a zodiac, which occupied the central panel in the prayer room. In the Early Islamic period (during the 9th cent.), a mosque was built in the courtyard, and parts of the synagogue building were incorporated into this new building phase. Following the victories of Saladin in the 12th cent., the site was abandoned.

Bibliography: Jodi Magness. *The Archaeology of the Early Islamic Settlement in Palestine* (2003).
MILTON C. MORELAND

SWADDLING [חֲתֻלָּה khatullah; σπάργανον sparganon]. In biblical times, newborns were customarily bathed in water, rubbed with salt, and swaddled by having their limbs and torsos securely wrapped in bands of cloth to ensure that they would grow straight and strong (Ezek 16:4; compare Pliny, *Nat.* 7.2–3; Plato, *Leg.* 7). Job 38:9 depicts God swaddling the newborn sea in clouds and thick darkness. Mary wraps the newborn Jesus in bands of cloth (compare Wis 7:4, "I was nursed with care in swaddling cloths"), and the child thus wrapped is the angels' sign to the shepherds (Luke 2:7, 12). *See* BIRTH.
JUDITH ANNE JONES

SWALLOW [דְּרוֹר deror, סוּס sus; χελιδών chelidōn]. The swallow is used as an image only infrequently in the Bible. It represents a constituent part of wildlife, as well as the settings and instincts that wild animals recall. For instance, the swallow can elicit images of home making (Ps 84:3 [Heb. 84:4]) or be an example of animals knowing their proper place and role in creation (Jer 8:7). The swallow is also known for its agility and restlessness, so that it can be used as an image for things that do not or cannot come to rest (Prov 26:2; Isa 38:14). Since swallows only live in uninhabited areas, it is also used to describe the temples of pagan idols (Ep Jer 22). *See* BIRDS OF THE BIBLE.

NATHAN P. LAMONTAGNE

SWAMP [בִּצָּה bitsah]. A wetland partly or seasonally covered with water and consisting of much woody vegetation (Isa 35:7), as near the Dead Sea (Ezek 47:11). *See* MARSH.

SWAN [κύκνειος kykneios]. Rare visitors in Palestine, swans are not mentioned in the biblical bird lists (despite the KJV in Lev 11:18; Deut 14:16). However, in 4 Macc 15:21, a moving comparison is made between voices of children and the songs of sirens and swans, clearly the whooper swan (*Cygnus musicus*). *See* BIRDS OF THE BIBLE.

GÖRAN EIDEVALL

SWARMING CREATURES. *See* CRAWLING AND CREEPING THINGS.

SWEARING. *See* OATH.

SWEAT [זֵעָה zeʿah, יְזַע yezah; ἱδρώς hidrōs]. Perspiration as the result of work (2 Macc 2:26) or stress and suffering (4 Macc 6:11). The curse upon Adam and Eve states that they must labor to produce food, which they will eat "by the sweat of [their] face" (Gen 3:19). Ezekiel states that priests should not wear garments that cause them to sweat (44:18). In Gethsemane, Jesus prays so fervently that his sweat "became like great drops of blood" (Luke 22:44). The martyred Eleazar is praised as an example of one who is willing to die rather than eat impure foods and thus shields the law of Moses with his "blood and noble sweat" (4 Macc 7:8).

KENNETH D. LITWAK

SWINE [חֲזִיר khazir; χοῖρος choiros, ὗς hys]. The domesticated pig, a descendant of the wild boar, is probably the only animal domesticated solely for consumption. Remains of domesticated pigs were found at several Chalcolithic, Early, Middle and Late Bronze age sites in Israel. Pigs were raised in two ways: as herds roaming the forests (Ps 80:13 [Heb. 80:14]) under the watchful eye of a swine herder or as individuals in the house or sty. The pig's two main activities are eating and sleeping, but unlike other animals the pig can feed continuously for hours and then sleep for many hours. Pigs scavenge and feed on foods on which dogs and humans can live, which makes the pig easy to raise and an efficient meat producer.

In biblical tradition, the pig is singled out as an unclean animal with special prohibitions against eating its meat and touching its carcass (Lev 11:7; Deut 14:8; *see* CLEAN AND UNCLEAN). The date of origin of this prohibition is hard to determine, but the negative attitude also expressed in Isaiah (65:4; 66:3, 17) suggests that in the postexilic Jewish community the pig was consid-

ered unclean. This attitude underlies Prov 11:22: "Like a gold ring in a pig's snout is a beautiful woman without good sense." It continues in the NT in such instances as the admonition not to throw pearls before swine (Matt 7:6), Jesus' exorcism of the Gerasene demoniac when he sent the unclean spirits into a herd of swine (Mark 5:1-13), and the prodigal son who found himself so desperate that he took a job feeding pigs (Luke 15:15-16). *See* ANIMALS OF THE BIBLE; HOLY, HOLINESS, OT.

Bibliography: Oded Borowski. *Every Living Thing: Daily Use of Animals in Ancient Israel* (1998).

ODED BOROWSKI

SWORD [חֶרֶב kherev; μάχαιρα machaira, ῥομφαία rhomphaia]. In the Early Bronze Age, the sword was short and straight, a dagger. In the Middle Bronze Age the sword became broader and longer. Half of the uses of *kherev* occur in the prophets Isaiah, Jeremiah, and Ezekiel to announce God's imminent judgment on Israel/Judah or the nations (e.g., Jer 25:27-31; Ezek 23:25, 47). Another fourth occur in Joshua–Kings and Chronicles, mostly with literal connotation, a weapon to injure and kill. *Sword* may also connote "guarding" (Gen 3:24) or be used figuratively to describe violence generally (Gen 27:40; 49:5). The twenty uses in Psalms occur in outcries to God to save from the sword (22:20), to deliver from (17:13) or destroy the wicked by the sword (7:12). The wicked that live by the sword will die by the sword (Ps 37:14-15). Since military imagery for God is metaphorical and human use of the sword is descriptive, Scripture's violent imagery does not endorse human use of the sword or violence. While God's defeat of Egypt may be viewed as a triumph of war (Exod 15:3), it was achieved not by the sword (Ps 44:3-6). The weapons of war Yahweh uses to overthrow his enemies or punish Israel include catastrophes in the natural order. This frequent use of military analogies for God's judgment precipitated dangerous perceptions of God as violent and wrathful (McDonald). Nonetheless, character descriptions of God's steadfast love and faithfulness abound (*see* KHESED).

The most ethically significant sword texts in the OT are Isa 2:1-4//Mic 4:1-5 and Joel 3:10 [Heb. 4:10]. Isaiah's and Micah's call to "beat swords into plowshares" echoes numerous psalms in which Yahweh destroys the weapons of war (Pss 20:7; 33:16; 44:3-6; 46:6-9; 76:3; 147:10). Similar emphases anticipating the messianic reign of peace permeate the prophetic oracles (Isa 9:4-7; 11:4; 31:1-3; Hos 14:3; Zech 9:9-10). Faith reflections upon Israel's conquest depreciate the "sword" but magnify Yahweh's miraculous deliverance (Exod 14:14; Josh 24:12; Judg 7; 1 Sam 17). Joel, however, appears to reverse Isaiah and Micah: "Beat your plowshares into swords, and your pruning hooks into spears" (3:10). Wolff rightly notes that the larger context, however, indicates that the call to arms is sarcastic, for Yahweh will shatter military might, thus executing judgment (vv. 11-12). Pannenberg argues, contra Wolff, that Isa 2:1-4//Mic 4:1-5 are eschatological while Joel 3:10 [Heb. 4:10] speaks to present history, for peace can come only as the law of the Lord goes forth to the nations and peoples seek to live by the law, acknowledging justice as the framework for politically negotiating peace. Only then can the eschatological vision of messianic peace be realized. But Pannenberg overlooks that Joel addresses the oracle to Tyre and Sidon and the regions of Philistia (v. 4). The sarcastic call to arms is aimed at the nations round about, which will be judged so that Judah's fortunes can be restored (3:1-3, 16-21). The text, in fact, accords with the prophetic mainstream call for humans to trust in Yahweh for defense (Isa 7:3-9; 30:15). The sword is regarded negatively in all three texts.

In Eph 6:17 *sword* is used metaphorically to describe the believers' spiritual armor to withstand evil. Echoing God's armor in the OT (Isa 7:9*b*; 11:4, 5; 49:2; 52:7; 59:17), believers are to put on the belt of truth, breastplate of righteousness, shoes to proclaim the gospel of peace, shield of faith, helmet of salvation, and sword of the Spirit, which is the word of God. The single Gospel use of *sword* outside the Passion Narrative is Matt 10:34: "I have not come to bring peace, but a sword." Luke clarifies by substituting *division* for sword, indicating that Jesus' statement does not mean military war. Some commentators contend that the saying anticipates the end-time apocalyptic persecution (as does Luke 22:35-36), but that is debatable since the context (vv. 35-39) clearly specifies divisions within families. Mauser explicates the text in tandem with Luke 10:17-20; 11:21-22; Matt 11:12, where violence marks the coming of God's kingdom. Mauser rightly holds that these texts, together with Matt 10:34, describe the warfare between the kingdom of God inaugurated by Jesus and the backlash of Satan. Since Jesus' coming fulfills apocalyptic hope, "division within families" is the concrete expression of the eschaton's arrival. *See* WAR, METHODS, TACTICS, WEAPONS OF (BRONZE AGE THROUGH PERSIAN PERIOD); WAR, METHODS, TACTICS, WEAPONS OF (HELLENISTIC THROUGH ROMAN PERIODS).

Bibliography: Hubert Frankemölle. "Peace and Sword in the New Testament." *The Meaning of Peace* (2001) 191–210; I. Howard Marshall. "New Testament Perspectives on War." *EvQ* 57 (1985) 115–132; Ulrich Mauser. *The Gospel of Peace: A Scriptural Message for Today's World* (1992); Patricia M. McDonald. *God and Violence: Resources for Living in a Small World* (2004); Wolfhart Pannenberg. "Response to Hans Walter Wolff." *The Meaning of Peace* (2001) 229–34; Willard M. Swartley. *Covenant of Peace: The Missing Peace in New Testament Theology and Ethics* (2006); Hans Walter Wolff. "Swords into Plowshares: Misuse of a Word of Prophecy?" *The Meaning of Peace* (2001) 211–28; Perry B. Yoder and Willard M. Swartley, eds. *The Meaning of Peace: Biblical Studies* (2001).

WILLARD M. SWARTLEY

SYCAMORE [שִׁקְמָה shiqmah; συκομορέα sykomorea]. The sycamore (or sycomore) fig (*Ficus sycomorus*). Old sycamore trees have massive trunks with clusters of small fig fruits growing through the bark of the trunk and branches. They are edible but not as delicious as the common fig. The young fruits are pollinated by certain wasps, some of which die inside and pollute the ripe fruit, so an ancient technique of cutting the young fruits was used to hasten their ripening and purity. As a "dresser of sycamore trees," Amos performed this work (7:14). Luke 19:3-4 narrates how Zacchaeus, the short tax collector, climbed up a sycamore to see Jesus; the tree's low branches made it easy to climb. Sycamore timber is soft and white, unlike harder and reddish cedar wood, but was appreciated in Palestine where wood was in short supply (1 Kgs 10:27; Isa 9:10). In ancient Egypt the timber was important for sarcophagi but the frosting of sycamore fruits was a calamity (Ps 78:47). *See* FIG TREE, FIGS; FRUIT; PLANTS OF THE BIBLE.

F. NIGEL HEPPER

F. Nigel Hepper

Figure 1: Sycamore (*Ficus sycomorus*)

SYCHAR si´kahr [Συχάρ Sychar]. A city in Samaria that is "near the plot of ground that Jacob had given to his son Joseph" (John 4:5; see Gen 33:18-20; 48:22). The unknown site is thought to be located either at the village of Khirbet Askar (Iskar) or Shechem. The story indicates that the location was on the road north from Jerusalem at the point where the route passes between Mounts Ebal and Gerizim. In the Gospel of John this is the setting for the extended story of the Samaritan woman who came to believe in Jesus, along with "many Samaritans from that city" (4:39). The story reports that Jesus rested here, near JACOB'S WELL, and this became the setting for his statements about "living water" (4:10).

The location of Jacob's well has been associated with a pilgrimage site east of the Roman city of Nablus (Neapolis, founded in 72 CE) near Tel Balatah (ancient Shechem). Although this area is rich with natural water resources—a detail that is relevant to John's story—the location of ancient Sychar is problematic. Since Shechem was destroyed in 107 BCE, it is difficult to directly associate Sychar with a city in ruins in the 1st cent. CE. The city of Neapolis, built near the end of the 1st cent. CE, is not a viable candidate either. Since the mid-19th cent., Khirbet Askar has been considered a likely location for Sychar because of its location a half mile from the well, but no archaeological evidence supports this identification.

MILTON C. MORELAND

SYENE s*i*-ee'nee [סְוֵנֵה seweneh]. Egyptian town found on the east bank of the first cataract of the Nile, opposite Elephantine, now known as modern Aswan. Mentioned three times in the Bible (Isa 49:12; Ezek 29:10; 30:6), Syene represents the far south of EGYPT.

Isaiah mentions the Egyptian town in relation to the people's return to Zion. Only two places south of Israel have a similar name: an Egyptian border city called Sin (sin [סִין]; Ezek 30:15; NRSV, "Pelusium") and the desert between Elim and Sinai (Exod 16:1; *see* SIN, WILDERNESS OF). Hence, ancient versions struggled with this form and translated largely based on context. The LXX translates "the land of the Persians," and the Targum reads "from the land of the south." Ezekiel's references to Syene are part of the oracles against Egypt, in which he declares that the land will be an utter waste from "Migdol to Syene." The Masoretic vocalization for Syene, however, is ambiguous (Ezek 29:10; 30:6). As Migdol (mighdal מִגְדֹּל) is not only a proper name but a noun that means "tower," it could refer to a generic fortification; however, Jeremiah's reference to Judeans living in Migdol (Jer 44:1) strengthens the case that Migdol is a town at the northernmost part of Egypt. Thus, Ezekiel indicates the extent of the Egyptian destruction, geographically, from the north to the south, calling the destruction a divine act.

RYAN N. ROBERTS

SYMBOLISM. The Bible is replete with symbolism. For readers and hearers who, through the centuries and today, have perceived these books as religious, and eventually as Scripture, symbolism is one of the most significant features of biblical texts. This symbolism fascinates them all the more that it calls for interpretation. Believers enter this interpretive process by pondering biblical symbolism in their devotional readings, in communal worship services and liturgies, in preparation for sermons. Drawn into this symbolism they bring their lives into it, even as it becomes alive for them. From early centuries, such readings of the biblical symbolism have given rise to midrashic, targumic, pesher-like, typological, allegorical, and mystical interpretations.

Critical biblical scholars are, of course, suspicious of these religious and devotional interpretations. But as they strive to account for biblical symbolism, they find that this dimension of biblical texts is elusive and presents a special challenge for them.

A. Defining Symbolism
B. The Symbolism of Biblical Texts
    1. The biblical figurative language and its intertexts behind the text
    2. The biblical figurative language as inscribed in the text
    3. The biblical figurative language of the text as symbolism for the readers
Bibliography

A. Defining Symbolism

The etymology of "symbol" (from **symballō** [συμβάλλω], "to throw together, connect") points to its function. Symbols represent the connections between individuals and communities with a mysterious reality. A blindfolded woman holding balanced scales, a national flag, a cross as symbols respectively represent and make present the connections between individuals and communities with justice, the spirit of a nation, and Christianity as mysterious realities. Theologians from Augustine to Paul Ricoeur and David Tracy underscore that religious texts use symbols and symbolic systems, including figurative language, to represent the connections between humans and ultimate reality. However this mysterious dimension of life might be envisioned—e.g., as a presence of the holy, the sacred, the divine, the Other, the kingdom, the communion of saints—humans do experience this reality, be it in "religious" and "spiritual" experiences or as a "secular" face-to-face loving encounter of the mystery of an Other. Yet one cannot directly speak of, refer to, or present this mysterious reality. By definition, a mystery is beyond whatever one can say about it, as apophatic theologians argue; words (signs) as signifiers that "refer to" (denote) specific signifieds (*see* SEMIOTICS) are inadequate. The only possibility is to express indirectly how this mysterious reality is "connected" to individuals and communities, namely through symbols and systems of symbols.

Since symbols are unlike signs that refer to something (as the linguist Louis Hjelmslev showed), the study of symbolism cannot be performed with those procedures of biblical studies designed to elucidate what a text "refers to." Symbolism cannot be studied with historical critical methods, including the social-scientific methods (and in the case of fictions, certain narrative approaches) designed to elucidate the historical (or fictive) life-situation to which the text "refers." It cannot be studied with the procedures aimed at elucidating the theological views of the author to which the text "refers"—e.g., philological methods ultimately aimed at discerning the theological argument of a didactic text or those of the redaction critical approaches aimed at elucidating the theological views of the redactor. These approaches— the vast majority of the approaches used in critical biblical studies—are inappropriate for the study of symbolism, because symbols do not "refer to" anything.

Symbols represent a connection that can be perceived and apprehended only when one enters the system of symbols and participates into it, and thus when one abandons the critical distance that, since the Enlightenment, biblical scholars thought they needed to maintain so as to develop a truly critical interpretation. Yet, in a postmodern perspective attentive to communication theories and to the ways readers/hearers produce meaning with a text or discourse (semiotics), the critical study of symbolism can be envisioned.

It is enough to allude to a pure system of symbols—a musical score—to understand that it is only when one enters the system of symbols and participates in it that one "makes sense of" (produces meaning with) this system of symbols. Paraphrasing Umberto Eco's example, for a pianist or a trumpet player, a musical notation such as "note C" in the middle register does not refer to anything except to a position in the system of notes that will be maintained despite various transpositions. For the musician, "note C" makes sense only insofar as she hears it in relation to other notes on a musical score (a particular system of symbols). Actually, it is only as the pianist fully enters the musical score and its relational network, as she connects with the mystery of the music, as she is inhabited by the music and embodies it, as she experiences it in and through her entire body (a proprioceptive or thymic experience, in psychological vocabulary), as she loses herself in the music, submerges herself in and submits to the music (a heteronomous experience), that she produces the music that envelops the hearers who, in turn, are lost in it. Then, because the particular piece of music is embodied by different pianists (or the same pianist bringing to it different situations or moods), each of its performances is unique—a dynamic rendering that the composer hoped for (as contemporary composers commonly express). Furthermore the performances of that same piece of music may be radically different—as, without a sound, a modern ballet ensemble (such as the Limón Dance Company) interprets, e.g., Bach's *A Musical Offering,* by fully entering and embodying the rhythm of the music, representing the connections between individuals with the mysterious world of this piece of music.

One can describe and analyze the score, and with the proper scientific instruments (oscillographs, spectrographs) determine the mathematical values of the sound events it represents. But this is missing the music. So it is with the symbolism of a biblical text. It can be described. But a detached description of the biblical symbolic score is missing the symbolism. It is only when we account for the way in which this symbolism is performed that we can recognize how this text connects its readers (or hearers) to an ultimate reality. Yet, before

this, we need to identify the biblical symbolic score— the symbolism of a biblical text.

B. The Symbolism of Biblical Texts

The symbolism of a text includes its relatively few pure symbols—e.g., Jacob's dream of the ladder with angels ascending and descending on it (Gen 28:12), which is interpreted by words of the Lord (Gen 28:13-15) as representing the connection between Jacob and God's presence; the "the desolating sacrilege set up where it ought not to be" (Mark 13:14) as marked by the comment "let the reader understand"; the description of the curtain of the Temple being torn in two when Jesus died (Mark 15:38); the star of "the king of the Jews" (Matt 2:2, 9-10). But the symbolism of a text is primarily formed by the symbolic dimension of the overall text, its figurative language—a network of figures, including but broader than its symbolic markers, such as metaphors, similes, synecdoches, metonymies, parables—and by the necessary extensions of this symbolic system beyond the text.

The figurative language of biblical texts is a good place to start, because it often has a very clear referential function in addition to its symbolic function. A first example clarifies what difference it makes to read a figure as a part of a symbolic system, and how this symbolic system extends beyond the text.

The figure of Jesus-preaching-the-Sermon-on-the-Mount (Matt 5–7)—Jesus as Moses-like, and thus as more than Moses, teaching with an authority greater than that of the scribes—has several possible referential functions. It refers to Matthew's theological view (when studied, along side other Matthean figures, through redaction criticism); it refers to the sociopolitical situation of Matthew's church addressed by this authoritative teaching of Jesus (when studied using a socio-political/religious approach); it even refers to the historical Jesus (when, with the use of form criticism and philological approaches, one elucidates the sayings of the Sermon on the Mount that can be ascribed to the historical Jesus). But beyond such referential functions, Jesus-on-the-Mount is a figure, i.e., a part of the symbolism of Matthew (as a symbolic system) that, together with other figures, represents for readers the connections between humans and ultimate reality, i.e., a system of convictions (self-evident truths), a semantic universe, or a mythical world, in which believers can live in the presence of the divine.

This figure of Jesus, inscribed in the text of Matthew (5–7; the entire Gospel), necessarily also extends behind and in front of the text, because any figure presupposes: a) an intertext behind the text; b) a symbolic system within the text (to which the figure belongs); and c) an intertext in front of the text (that of the readers as they enter and embody the symbolic system).

1. The biblical figurative language and its intertexts behind the text

Commonly, one first apprehends a figure, in this case Jesus-on-the-Mount, by recognizing that it summons other texts and traditions—intertexts. This is readily recognizable when one seeks to name this figure. If we say that the figure of Jesus-on-the-Mount conveys that "Jesus is Moses-like," we say that this figure makes sense if, and only if, one recognizes that this presentation of Jesus calls forth the image of Moses on Mount Sinai (or Horeb) in other biblical texts and traditions. Note that the figure of Jesus-on-the-Mount varies with the intertext that one chooses to make sense of this figure. Jesus can be Moses-like in that he proclaims from the Mount a) the revelation of a (new) covenant between God and God's people, when one envisions Jesus in terms of Exod 19; or b) the revelation of God's will as expressed in commandments and their (re-)interpretations, when one envisions Jesus in terms of Exod 20; or c) the revelation of the (new) Torah, when one envisions Jesus in terms of Jewish traditions common in Mathew's time that Moses received the Torah on Mount Sinai (*Sifra* on Lev 26:46; see also *Pirke Abot* 1:1); and so on.

This is enough to recognize that the figure Jesus-on-the-Mount extends behind the text to earlier intertexts and that the interpretation varies according to which of these intertexts is chosen as primary. The study of such figures requires adopting a comparative mode that characterizes the "history of religion" methodology and certain philological studies, in a quest for the possible intertexts for each figure—and in each case there are many. For instance, as one takes into account the ways in which the figure Jesus-on-the-Mount is presented in Matthew, one of its key features, the symbolic mountain, calls forth many intertexts regarding mountains as places of revelation, thus representing a connection between humans and the divine. Of course, as scholars show, intertexts could be found in early Babylonian, Assyrian, Mandaean, Greek, and Palestinian traditions. But they have often ambivalent connotations (mountains as source of both blessings and dangers; their association with "false gods") make them unlikely intertexts for Matthew and his community. The appropriate intertexts are, of course, in the OT and early Jewish texts and traditions—as Matthew signals by repeatedly quoting Scripture. Thus commentators on Matthew, such as W. D. Davies and Dale Allison, point to OT texts that emphasize the superior power of God by presenting mountains as symbols of power (enduring forever, Gen 49:26; Ps 125:1) although they are no match for God's power; thus mountains tremble before God (e.g., Nah 1:5; Jer 4:24; 51:25) or melt before God (Mic 1:4; Isa 64:1 [63:19]; Ps 97:5; Jer 51:25); consequently, mountains carry connotations related to judgment. Mountains are also associated with a sense of the nearness of God (from where God's blessings and curses are called upon people; e.g., Deut 11:29) and as sites for theophanies (especially Mount Sinai and Mount Zion) and thus called the "mountain of God" (e.g., Horeb in Exod 3:1; 4:27). Thus, as Davies and Allison note, for many early Jewish texts, such as *Jub.* 1:2-4; *T. Levi* 2; *T. Naph.* 5:1; Bar 13:1, mountains are symbolic places of divine revelation.

These and many similar texts and traditions (listed by the many commentators who affirmed that Matthew recalls Mount Sinai and presents Jesus as a new Moses) are "potential" intertexts behind Matthew's text. But, and this is a characteristic of symbolic language, the particular intertext is not specified. There is no formula quotation (such as "this is to fulfill what is written in Exod 19–20"). Thus, for instance, the figure Jesus-on-the-mount makes a great deal of sense when read as alluding to texts and traditions about Mount Zion (as Donaldson does). In sum, the readers are called upon to make the connection, or more exactly to participate in the symbolic texts and to conceive of their connections to the mysterious revelatory presence of God that this figurative language invites them to make. A symbolic text does not dictate which intertext behind the text should be chosen.

Continuing with our example, other aspects of the figure of Jesus-on-the-Mount multiply the range of potential intertext. For instance, Matthew's presentation of Jesus as sitting down in the midst of his disciples opens up the possibility of relating this figure with traditions regarding rabbis and scribes who, likewise, were teaching their disciples while sitting down. And so it is with all the figurative language that participates in the symbolism of religious texts. The more one studies the potential intertexts behind a religious text through the comparative approaches of the history of religion and philological studies, the broader the range of potential intertexts, and the clearer it becomes that one cannot and should not try to formulate its "symbolic meaning" into some kind of propositional formula. The symbolic meaning of the text is not some content of the text. It is an invitation to enter the text and to perform this text whatever might be the instruments or the mode of performance (a piano, an orchestra, a ballet company) we choose. Nevertheless, despite the many possible performances of this symbolism, there are constraints posited by the text. In each instance, one should be able to recognize that this is indeed a performance of the symbolism of a particular text. Whatever might be the transposition, the performance needs to represent the inter-connections inscribed in the text (as score) among all the features of the symbolic system, so that the symbolic interpretation might be recognizable as a performance of Matthew (and not of Mark or Exodus).

2. The biblical figurative language as inscribed in the text

The symbolic system of a biblical text as a score to be performed is made up of recurrent themes (recurring figures) that are supported by the melody.

Recurring figures in a text invite readers to interpret them together. To continue with the preceding example, the figure of Jesus-on-a-Mount is recurring throughout Matthew. Jesus is on a Mount being tempted by the devil (Matt 4:8); teaching the Sermon (5:1); praying (14:23); healing the sick and feeding a crowd (15:29); being transfigured and talking with Moses and Elijah (17:1); on the Mount of Olives from where he will enter Jerusalem (21:1), where he gives the apocalyptic discourse (24:3), and where he is with his disciples before being arrested (26:30). Finally Jesus is on the mount appearing to his disciples as the resurrected Christ with "all authority in heaven and on earth" and "commissioning" them (28:16-18)—a scene which in turn is connected with (indeed the fulfillment of) 26:64 where Jesus prophecies he will come back with power (quoting Dan 7:13), and consequently with the figure of the "coming of the Son of Man in his glory," also mentioned in Matt 24:27 and 25:31-46, where he functions as the eschatological judge. Thus, through its variations from pericope to pericope, the figure of Jesus-on-a-Mount alludes to additional potential intertexts and unfolds throughout Matthew in ever more complex ways. The figure of Jesus-on-a-Mount is further modulated by Matthew's uses of the mountain-figures in Jesus' teaching—a city on a mount cannot be hidden (5:14); a mountain can be moved through prayer (17:20; 21:21); a mountain as the place where the 99 sheep are left by the shepherd who is searching for the lost sheep (18:12); and as a place of refuge in the end of time (24:16). Matthew's symbolic system inter-connects all these figures of Jesus-on-a-Mount in a thematic way that also relates it to other figures in this Gospel. The performance of the symbolism by readers (see below) needs to represent the contrasting or supporting thematic interconnections among all these figures.

Yet these themes "make sense" (connect the readers to an ultimate reality; become live symbolism) only in so far as they are perceived as an integral part of the melody that frames them. The Matthean figures and the entire figurative system they form together do not make sense if they are disconnected from the narrative semantic universe that frames them through its literary devices. (The same could be said about a didactic discourse, its figures, semantic universe, and rhetorical devices.)

A most common literary device in biblical books is the inclusio, where the beginning and end of a section are similar, thus "including" the intervening material as if between bookends. As a triadic literary device, the inclusio highlights both 1) the relationship between the bookends—which have parallel features (that signal them as forming an inclusio) but also differences (thus an inclusio can be viewed as underscoring the "inverted parallelism" between its bookends)—and 2) the center of the inclusio, in which case it is viewed as a "chiasm" (often involving progressive concentric inclusios).

Continuing the above example, commentators (e.g., Davies and Allison, Luz) who pay close attention to the symbolism of Matthew readily identify inclusios as well as triads (or triadic groupings, which in effect form inclusios). For instance, in the Sermon on the Mount, both the introduction (Matt 4:23–5:2) and the conclusion (7:8–8:1) features Jesus' interaction with the crowds and the mountain—ascending or descending it (a first signal of inverted parallelism). Next, progressively going into the Sermon, the three triads of beatitudes (5:3-12) find counterpoints in the three warnings about the prospect of eschatological judgment (the two ways, beware of false prophets, the two builders; 7:13-27). Between the bookends of an introductory statement about the law and the prophets (5:17) and the golden rule as the law and the prophets (7:12), the body of the Sermon on the Mount includes three parts: Jesus and the Torah (5:17-48); the Christian cult (6:1-18); and social issues (6:19–7:12). At the center of the chiastic structure of the Sermon on the Mount, the section on the Christian cult is itself centered on the Lord's Prayer (6:9-13).

The identification of such symbolic structures inscribed in a biblical text (as revealed through a detailed analysis of its literary devices) complements the interpretation of the figurative language in terms of intertexts (discussed above). It elucidates the basic connotations that clarify the significance of the figures and suggests ways in which these figures can be and should be performed by the readers in order to enter the connection between humans and ultimate reality represented by the symbolism of the text.

To continue our example, Luz (and Davies and Allison) sees the Lord's Prayer, the center of the chiasm, as the key to interpret the entire Sermon on the Mount, and ultimately the figure of Jesus-on-the-Mount. From this perspective, entering the symbolic world of the Sermon is participating in a certain kind of worship—a prayer which sets the believers/readers in a particular kind of connection with the divine as "our Father in heaven" in an eschatological and apocalyptic mode, "Your kingdom come." This prayer is thoroughly Jewish, as its symbolism and its intertexts show. Thus, the figure of a Moses-like Jesus-on-the-Mount is to be viewed as underscoring continuity with Jewish worship—rather than a discontinuity that would emphasize the newness in Jesus and his teaching (also potentially present, since saying that Jesus is like-Moses is also saying that he is somewhat unlike-Moses, as Ricoeur emphasizes about metaphors).

Alternatively, one can emphasize the significance of the inverted parallelisms by noting the semantic differences between the "bookends" and how these semantic oppositions are mediated by the intervening material. Such a systematic analysis is called "structural," because, following Lévi-Strauss, it seeks to elucidate the "mythical structure" or system of convictions that frames a religious text and its symbolism. To continue our example, one investigates the significance of the striking similarities and contrasts between the beginning and end of the Sermon on the Mount (see Patte's structural commentary on Matthew). The emphasis is on the contrast between Jesus' authority as the new Moses and that of the scribes (7:29), an authority based on a counter-cultural discernment of those who are blessed (not the rich, satisfied, successful, dominant, but the depressed [poor in spirit], those who mourn, the meek, those who struggle for justice, etc. 5:3-12) and of those who are cursed (those who chose the easy way, false prophets, those who build on the sand, 7:13-27). The emphasis on the eschatological judgment in Matt 7:23-27 leads to a strong emphasis on the eschatological dimensions of the figure of Jesus-on-the-mount—associated with "new" revelation, theophany, and judgment. The distinctiveness of the figure of Jesus, by contrast with the scribes, is still perceived in a Jewish perspective (thus continuity), but underscores the eschatological and even apocalyptic character of Jesus. Entering the Matthean symbolism means entering an eschatological/apocalyptic world where prophecies and the law are fulfilled and thus reinterpreted in a radical way.

This brief illustration suggests that the study of the symbolism of a biblical text should not be limited to the study of the intertexts behind it by means of history of religion and philological approaches—necessary as these are. One also needs to account for the ways in which this symbolism is inscribed into the text. It is the symbolism as both enriched by intertexts and as inscribed into the text that readers are invited to perform, so that this symbolism might indeed function as symbolism by establishing a connection between the readers and ultimate reality.

3. The biblical figurative language of the text as symbolism for the readers

Studying the musical score is necessary, yet performing it brings to life the music. The symbolism of a biblical text is live-symbolism when readers enter it and perform it. As long as critical biblical studies does not account for the place of the readers in the symbolism it actually fails to account for the symbolism.

The importance of reader-response approaches in critical biblical studies has been repeatedly shown. When dealing with symbolism the role of the readers becomes even more essential. Symbolism is a process through which meaning is multiplied, broadening the readers' perspective. Symbolism connects readers to ultimate reality, but only insofar as it functions as live-symbolism when, with their own symbolic world, readers enter the symbolic world of the text. In the resulting "fusion of horizons," the readers' symbolic world (an intertext in front of the text) is transformed.

In order to understand the process of "making sense with" the symbolism of a religious text, and the way in which one experiences the connection with the ultimate to which the text invites its readers, it is useful

to come back to Gen 28:12-22. Jacob's dream of the ladder with angels ascending and descending, including its interpretation by words of the Lord (Gen 28:12-15), is for Mircea Eliade an instance of "hierophany," "an irruption of the sacred in the profane world." This hierophanic dream is the equivalent of a symbolic text. A symbolic system is a dream-like vision. The author provides an interpretation of this vision by presenting the story as symbolic. Thus, for readers, entering into this connection with the sacred means interpreting the symbolism of the biblical text as one interprets hierophanic dreams—most dreams in the biblical tradition—namely by seeking to discern into their daily life the place of the sacred as manifested in the dream. As Lou H. Silberman has shown regarding the Pesher from the Dead Sea Scrolls, this is exactly how the members of Qumran community interpreted prophetic texts (e.g., Habakkuk). They discerned how the features of the prophecies were connected to their profane, concrete world (including Roman legions, Jewish authorities in Jerusalem, the Temple, their community) and in the process gained a vision of where in their context the sacred is manifested or can be expected. This is following the pattern of Joseph's interpretation of dreams (Gen 31–41), or that of Jacob in Gen 28. When Jacob woke up, connecting his dream-vision to his life-context, he envisioned the place of the sacred in his profane world, and marked it by creating a sacred space: building an altar and calling that place Bethel (Gen 28:18-19). He used elements of his life-context—the stone he used as a pillow and oil—to represent his connection with the sacred. He played the musical score with whatever instrument was at hand, and in the process made the necessary transpositions.

The symbolism of a text "makes sense"—is a live symbolism, rather than a bunch of dead symbols—only insofar as it is connected to the life-context of the readers, confirming, refining, or challenging their previous experiences of the presence of the mysterious in their life. Thus, biblical scholars who study the symbolism of a biblical text—as they should if they want to account for this central aspect of any religious text—must include in their critical study an examination of the ways in which present-day and historical readers/believers related this symbolism to their particular life-contexts and their previous religious experiences. Among these interpretations of biblical symbolism, one can discern three main approaches.

A first approach involves creating sacred spaces and times structured by the biblical symbolism so that believers might enter it. This is the type of hermeneutics of the symbolism found, for instance, in haggadic Midrash. The participants in the Passover Seder say "we went out of Egypt" (not "they," the Israelites of old) and in the process gain an identity that they continue to have in their daily life. Then Scripture and its symbolism functions as a "family album" (or "book of the covenant"), providing an overall framework for life in particular contexts.

A second approach involves recognizing with the help of the biblical symbolism the manifestations of the sacred in one's daily life. For instance, this is the type of hermeneutics found in the Pesher of Qumran and also in most typological interpretations found in NT texts. Looking at one's life context through the corrective lens of the biblical symbolism, one can recognize the manifestations and presence of the sacred in one's life-context; profane life is viewed as the locus of the sacred.

A third approach involves fusing the symbolic horizon of the text with one's own, so much so that entering the symbolism of biblical texts is an integral part of one's mystical experience of the holy through which believers are "sanctified," that is, intimately connected with the Holy. This is the type of hermeneutics found in mystical interpretations of biblical texts as Holy Scripture that emphasize the allegorical character of the symbolism, and also in iconic interpretations of Scripture.

Far from being aberrant readings of biblical texts that "enlightened" critical biblical scholars should exclude, such readings account for a most significant dimension of these religious texts, namely their symbolism. Not accounting for the way this symbolism is performed by readers amounts to killing this symbolism and to reducing it to a set of propositional statements of theological or ethical arguments, or reducing symbols to signs that refer to some historical contexts. The description of a score cannot replace its performance, without which there is no experience of the music. The identification of the symbols and their behind-the-text intertexts, as well as the description of the ways in which the symbolism is inscribed in the text, are necessary. But all these scholarly efforts would be for nothing if one does not examine how this symbolism functions as symbolism by observing how individuals and communities read it as connecting them and their lives to ultimate reality. *See* COLORS; IMAGE; METAPHOR IN THEOLOGY; NUMBERS, NUMBERING; SIGNS IN THE NT; SIGNS IN THE OT.

Bibliography: Augustine. *On Christian Doctrine.* D.W. Robertson, trans. (1958); W. D. Davies and Dale C. Allison. *The Gospel According to Matthew.* ICC (1988–1997); Terence L. Donaldson. *Jesus on the Mountain: A Study of Matthean Theology* (1985); Umberto Eco. *A Theory of Semiotics* (1976); Mircea Eliade. *The Sacred and the Profane: The Nature of Religion* (1959); Mary Gerhart and Allan Melvin Russell. *Metaphoric Process: The Creation of Scientific and Religious Understanding* (1985); Cristina Grenholm and Daniel Patte. "Overture: Receptions, Critical Interpretations, and Scriptural Criticism." *Reading Israel in Romans* (2000) 1–54; Louis Hjelmslev. *Prolegomena to a Theory of Language* (1943; 1961); Claude Lévi-Strauss. *Structural Anthropology* (1957); Ulrich Luz. *Matthew.* Hermeneia 1 (2007); Daniel Patte. *The Gospel ac-cording to Matthew: A Structural Commentary on Matthew's Faith* (1985); Paul Ricoeur. *Interpretation Theory* (1976); Paul Ricoeur. *The Rule of Metaphor: Multi-disciplinary Studies of the Creation of Meaning in Language* (1977); Paul Ricoeur. *Figuring the Sacred: Religion, Narrative, and Imagination* (1995); Lou H. Silberman. "Unriddling the Riddle: A Study in the Language of the Habakkuk Pesher." *RevQ* 3 (1961) 224–64; David Tracy. *Plurality and Ambiguity* (1987); John Welch, ed. *Chiasmus in Antiquity* (1981).

DANIEL PATTE

SYMEON sim´ee-uhn [Συμεών Symeōn]. The Greek form of the name "Simeon." The NRSV offers this reading in footnotes (Luke 2:25, 34). *See* MINISTRY, CHRISTIAN; PROPHET IN THE NT AND EARLY CHURCH.

SYMMACHUS sim´uh-kuhs. Author of one of the three Greek versions Origen used to construct his HEXAPLA (the other two are Theodotion and Aquila). He appears to have been active in the late 2nd or early 3rd cent. CE; the majority of scholars today hold that he was Jewish. His version, which is characterized by good Greek style and distinctive Jewish exegesis, was probably at least in part a fresh translation rather than a revision of an existing Greek text. Jerome made use of Symmachus' work in the preparation of his VULGATE. *See* SEPTUAGINT.

LEONARD GREENSPOON

SYNAGOGUE sin´uh-gog [συναγωγή synagōgē]. *Synagogue*, from the Greek synagōgē (literally, "bringing together," or "meeting place"), generally refers to a Jewish community, a gathering of people, the area or edifice in which the people gather, or all three. It parallels the Hebrew beth-keneseth (בֵּית־כְּנֶסֶת, "house of meeting") and the Aramaic kenishta᾽ (כְּנִשְׁתָּא). In particular, the synagogue was (and is) an assembly drawn together for purposes of religious worship and study, with distinct emphasis on the public reading and explication of Scripture. This article examines the origins of the Jewish synagogue, surveys its development during the Greco-Roman period, and explores significant aspects of synagogue art and architecture.

A. Synagogue Origins
B. Second Temple Period Palestinian Synagogues
C. Late Antiquity: The Late Roman and Byzantine Periods
D. Diaspora Synagogues, 4th–6th Centuries Bibliography
E. Synagogues in the New Testament

A. Synagogue Origins

Theories of synagogue origins are numerous. The earliest recorded opinion regarding the origin of the synagogue is that of Philo of Alexandria (ca. 20 BCE–50 CE); it is clear that he views the proseuchē (προσευχή), "place of prayer," attended by members of Rome's Jewish population, to have originated with Moses himself (*Moses* 2.215–16; *Creation* 128; compare Acts 16:13). Flavius Josephus (ca. 37–sometime after 100 CE) also offers testimony in which he explicitly ascribes to Moses the practice of weekly Sabbath gatherings dedicated to religious worship and education (*Ag. Ap.* 2.175).

The comments of Philo and Josephus are notable in that neither author presents an argument supporting Mosaic origins of synagogues. Nor does either of them attempt to produce biblical passages to bolster the proposition—in fact, Josephus invokes Apion's alleged statement connecting Moses with this weekly gathering (*Ag. Ap.* 2.10–11) but does not invoke Scripture. It is improbable that Philo and Josephus independently happened upon an innovative explanation of the synagogue's beginnings; their views were apparently familiar to the point of being common knowledge among Roman-period Jews.

This attitude regarding a Mosaic origin of the synagogue fits well with the OT's focus upon Moses as primary transmitter of the TORAH. Both Philo's and Josephus' accounts include observations that the Jews of 1st-cent. CE Palestine, Rome, and Alexandria—if not 1st-cent. Jews in general—assemble to hear the law and to study it. Even had Josephus not explicitly credited Moses with ordaining this weekly ritual, Moses' biblical profile as the/an original articulator of divine law, his identification with such events as the consecration of the priesthood and the establishment of the Tabernacle, and the OT's portrayal of him as Israel's deliverer from Egyptian slavery make him a natural candidate as inventor of an institution that many 1st-cent. Jews associated with Torah study, community, and worship.

The Mosaic attribution of synagogue origins proved powerful and durable. In Acts 15:21 Stephen exclaims: "For in every city, for generations past, Moses has had those who proclaim him, for he has been read aloud every sabbath in the synagogues." Rabbinic sources credit Moses as having instigated weekly study of Torah (e.g., *y. Meg.* 4:1, 75a).

The view that the synagogue originated during the Babylonian exile does not appear in published form until 1583, when Renaissance humanist scholar Carolus Sigonius proposed that the institution of the synagogue was a direct response to the destruction of the Temple and Jerusalem and the subsequent exile of Judeans throughout the Babylonian Empire. Thus, the notion of the synagogue as an organic phenomenon of DIASPORA life not only proved attractive to Renaissance and Enlightenment thinkers for whom the synagogue was an object of study, but made its way into modern scholarship, where it fuels many modern theories regarding synagogue origins.

The Babylonian exile theory, or group of theories, reflects at least two distinct approaches. Some scholars of the Bible and the ANE point to both scriptural and ex-tra-biblical witnesses as indicators of a concerted effort among Diaspora Judeans to establish houses of study and worship in the wake of the First Temple's destruction in 586 BCE. Jeremiah 39:8 is often cited as evidence that exilic and post-exilic leaders were conscious of this vacuum and the religious destitution that accompanied it: "The Chaldeans burned the king's house and the houses of the people (beth-ha'am בֵּית־הָעָם)and broke down the walls of Jerusalem." Some modern translations, following David KIMCHI's medieval commentary (d. 1235), choose to render the term beth-ha'am as a collective, "houses of the people." The passage then simply becomes testimony to the physical devastation and cultural disorientation of the exile in general. However, many scholars prefer the literal reading, "house of the people," suggesting that it reflects the existence of religious meeting places beyond the Temple even in pre-exilic times.

Some view Ezek 11:16 as evidence that a movement existed to establish local meeting houses for purposes of worship and study in the absence of a functioning Temple, and that the prophet himself was familiar with, or perhaps even engaged in, that process: "Say then: Thus said the Lord GOD: I have indeed removed them far among the nations and have scattered them among the countries, and I have become to them a diminished sanctity (miqdash me'at מִקְדָּשׁ מְעַט) in the countries whither they have gone" (JPS; NRSV, "Therefore say: Thus says the Lord GOD: Though I removed them far away among the nations, and though I scattered them among the countries, yet I have been a sanctuary to them for a little while in the countries where they have gone"). It is doubtful that the term miqdash me'at (translated "diminished" or perhaps "lesser" sanctity) refers to a specific alternative to Temple culture and activity. Ezekiel's position as the only biblical prophet whose entire prophetic activity is bound by the exile has led some scholars to connect him with attempts to launch some form of proto-synagogue as a means of dealing with the presumed breakdowns of religion and government brought about by the exile. Other scholars disagree, pointing to Ezekiel's priestly status as well as his exhortations in chaps. 40–48 regarding restoration of the Temple itself and reinstatement of its rituals and personnel.

Theories placing the synagogue's origins within the Babylonian exile also rest upon textual evidence that many Judeans chose not to return to Jerusalem/Palestine during the Persian restoration period, even though Cyrus explicitly decreed permission for such a return in 538 BCE. Moreover, documents discovered in the Archive of the Murashû family of merchants contain several dozen names of Jewish origin, some of which involve theophoric formulae incorporating the divine name, so members of the Jewish community in restoration-era Nippur had apparently managed to maintain at least a semblance of their religious identity. Some scholars view Cyrus' edict (Ezra 1:1-4) and the

Murashû documents as proof that Judeans throughout the Persian diaspora had developed institutional means of addressing the religious, political, and social requirements once addressed primarily (if not solely) by the Temple (*see* MURASHÛ, ARCHIVES OF). However, no written or archaeological witness has been found testifying to the synagogue's physical existence or cultural role during that period.

As most modern scholars are now willing to suggest, the theory of Babylonian origins has no archaeological support, and its textual support involves extensive credulity and expansive interpretation. Theories placing the synagogue's origins in the Babylonian exile ultimately boil down to one fundamental proposition: the destruction of the Temple in Jerusalem constituted a radical decentralization of worship and study. Judaism in general and Diaspora Jews in particular responded to this religious and sociopolitical deficit by developing local centers for worship and study that avoided transgressing Jewish law by refusing to engage in such Temple-related cultic rituals as animal sacrifice.

More recent theories place the origins of the synagogue in 3rd cent. BCE Egypt, asserting that Jewish "prayer places" (proseuchē) described in inscriptions were in fact the earliest synagogues, or elsewhere in the western Diaspora. These approaches assert the priority of exile and hence distance from the Jerusalem Temple as a determining factor in the formation of the synagogue. In recent years the origins of the synagogue in biblical Israel have been asserted. According to this theory, the Second Temple period synagogue was the descendant of the "city gate" as in Ruth 4:11. The OT contains many references to a particular gate that presumably served as a main entrance to whatever city is being discussed in a given passage. The significance of this gate was its role as a gathering place for a town's or city's leaders, elders, and movers and shakers. Biblical passages such as Gen 19:1; Deut 25:7; Ruth 4:1-12; 2 Sam 15:2; 19:8; and 2 Kgs 7:1 indicate that this area was not only used as a place to discuss current events, but also to gather and address public audiences, and even render publicly witnessed official decisions regarding property rights and other legal matters. None of these approaches is supported by sufficient data, and at some level participate in what the historian Marc Bloch called the "idolatry of origins."

The origins of the synagogue are obscure and will probably never be known. This is in part because the synagogue developed in a non-revolutionary manner, its significance recognized only once it was a well-established institution of Jewish life. A hint of the original function of this institution may be found in its most prominent Greek and Hebrew names used in antiquity, synagōgē and beth-keneseth. Both refer to an assembly or house of assembly. An approach that is more clearly supported by the available evidence suggests that the synagogue as a place for religious ritual was a development of the later Second Temple period. This

approach begins with the fact that institutions known as "synagogues" are clearly evidenced in literary and archaeological sources from the 1st cent. CE and cautiously assumes a development that occurred before synagogues were mentioned in literary texts without asserting a specific moment when the first synagogue appeared. The general trend toward smaller religious and communal associations, standing side-by-side with the major cults of each city, was adopted by Jews in Palestine and in Diaspora settings. This phenomenon may be evidenced in Egypt as early as the 3rd cent. BCE, if the "prayer places" (proseuchē) known from epigraphy were in any way similar to "prayer places" known from the writings of the 1st-cent. Egyptian scholar Philo of Alexandria (*Moses* 2.216; *Flaccus* 7.44). A Jewish "prayer place" from the 2nd cent. BCE was discovered on the Greek island of Delos. We have no idea what kinds of "prayer" took place in these early "prayer places." By the 1st cent. (and undoubtedly much earlier) the increasing significance of Scripture and its interpretation in Second Temple period Judaism set the liturgical frame for these synagogues. This focus on Scripture and scriptural interpretation is expressed early on in the public ceremony of reading and interpreting the Pentateuch described in Neh 8, a Persian-period text that exercised a profound influence upon later synagogue practice.

B. Second Temple Period Palestinian Synagogues

Archaeological and literary evidence for Jewish synagogues begins to appear in Palestine from the last third of the 1st cent. BCE onward. The least equivocal evidence for synagogues during the 1st cent. is a monumental inscription found in a cistern just south of the Temple Mount in the so-called "City of David" in Jerusalem by R. Weill in 1913–14. This Greek inscription translates:

Theodotos, son of Vettenos the priest and synagogue leader, son of a synagogue leader (archisynogōgos ἀρχισυνάγωγος) and grandson of a synagogue leader, built the synagogue for the reading of the Torah and studying of the commandments, and as a hostel with chambers and water installations to provide for the needs of itinerants from abroad, which his fathers, the elders (sing. presbyteros [πρεσβύτερος]) and Simonides founded. (Reich)

The *terminus ad quem* for the inscription is the destruction of Jerusalem by the Romans in 70 CE. It provides evidence of three generations of priestly synagogue leaders. The liturgical focal point for this, and for every other Second Temple period text that has been recovered, is scriptural study. This is clearly the element that distinguished synagogue liturgy, both for Jews and non-Jews. Unfortunately, the area where Weill discovered the inscription has yet to be excavated, and the origins of the inscription are thus obscure. The proximity of this synagogue to the Temple is significant. An early rabbinic text reflects on how easily a Second Temple period Jew could move from Temple to synagogue and back again. This text describes the festival of Sukkoth (Tabernacles), when the ceremony of the Water Drawing was performed at the Temple:

> Said Rabbi Joshua son of Hananiah: "All the days of the celebration of the Water Drawing we never saw a moment of sleep. We would arise in time for the morning daily whole-offering [in the Temple]. From there we would go to the synagogue. From there to the additional offering [in the Temple]. From there to eating and drinking. From there to the study house. From there to the Temple for the whole sacrifice at dusk. From there to the celebration of the Water Drawing."
>
> (*t. Sukkah* 4:4; trans. Fine)

Philo of Alexandria (*Good Person* 81–82) provides a description of Sabbath liturgy in a synagogue of the Essenes that, like the Theodotus inscription, makes no mention of synagogue prayer:

> For that day has been set apart to be kept holy and on it they abstain from all work and proceed to sacred places that they call synagogues. There, arranged in rows according to their ages, the younger below the elder, they sit decorously as befits the occasion with attentive ears. Then one takes the books and reads aloud and another of especial proficiency comes forward and expounds what is not understood.

Like Philo and the Theodotus inscription, Luke 4:16-30 and Acts 13:15-16 provide additional early illustrations of public Scripture reading and explication in synagogues. It is unknown whether other liturgical acts were performed in synagogues at this time. Ezra Fleisher and Lee Levine have argued from silence that the fact that prayer is not mentioned as a synagogue function proves that synagogue prayer did not exist at this early date. While this may be true, it is just as possible that communal prayer, a common practice within Greco-Roman associations, goes unmentioned because it was not sufficiently distinctive as a Jewish cultural marker to warrant mention. Ample numbers of later Second Temple period Jewish prayer texts are extant from Masada and Qumran as well as from within the NT, Apocrypha/Pseudepigrapha, and early strata of rabbinic literature. It seems likely that the extant evidence focuses upon the uniquely Jewish element of synagogue liturgy, and not upon communal prayer—a rather ubiquitous feature of Greco-Roman fellowship groups.

It is likely that the earliest synagogue buildings—like many after them—were simply rooms within domestic structures with no special renovations, and hence are unidentifiable archaeologically. Five purpose-built or purpose-renovated buildings that might be identified as later Second Temple period synagogues have been excavated in Israel. These were uncovered at Masada, Gamla, Herodian, Kiryat Sefer, and Modiʾin. Other supposed synagogues, at Magdala, Capernaum, and Jericho, are far less likely. The Gamla synagogue was the most impressive of all known Second Temple period synagogues. This large public building was built on the eastern side of Gamla, next to the city wall. The synagogue was built of local basalt. It was a rectangular structure (25.5 × 17 m) situated on a northeast-southeast axis. The main entrance was on the west, with an exedra and an open court in front of it. A ritual bath was discovered to the right of the court (*see* MIQVAH, MIQVEH). The center of the hall (13.4 × 9.3 m) was surrounded by stepped benches and unpaved. A small basin that the excavator believes was used for hand washing was uncovered. The lintels were decorated with the image of a rosette flanked by palm trees, and the capitals were also decorated. The synagogue at Masada is a 10 m^2 room that was converted by the Jewish rebels who inhabited this desert fortress between 66 and 74 CE. The rebels added banks of benches on each wall, and a small room on the northwestern wall within which were found fragments of the books of Deuteronomy and Ezekiel. The construction of this room on the northwest corner of the synagogue may suggest alignment toward Jerusalem, if this principle was already in effect at this early date. No liturgical furniture from 1st-cent. synagogues is extant, though it is likely that they were furnished with tables and perhaps storage boxes for scrolls. All of the manuscripts discovered on Masada were found within 30 m of the synagogue, suggesting that these texts, which include liturgical texts, originated there. The literary definition of the 1st-cent. synagogue as a house of assembly where Scripture was studied is uniquely paralleled in this structure. At Herodian a room was converted by Jewish rebels with the addition of benches that were similar to those at Masada. Discovered in 1995, the synagogue at Kiryat Sefer (a Jewish village in the Judean hills, approximately 32 km northwest of Jerusalem) was a free-standing structure, measuring 9.6 × 9.6 m. The façade was constructed with large ashlars, dressed with framing rims reminiscent of Herodian masonry. Benches line three walls of the hall, and the roof was supported by columns sporting Doric capitals. The principal phase of the synagogue near modern Modiʾin (Umm el-ʿUmdan), discovered in 2000/01, measures 12 × 10 m; two rows of columns supported the roof, and benches lined all walls. Fragments of white, red, and yellow painted plaster were found within this hall. A smaller room, measuring 11 × 6.5 m, existed in the first phase of this building, which some identify as a Hasmonean-period synagogue. It seems likely that these communal buildings served as synagogues as well, though there is no epigraphic evidence to support this identification.

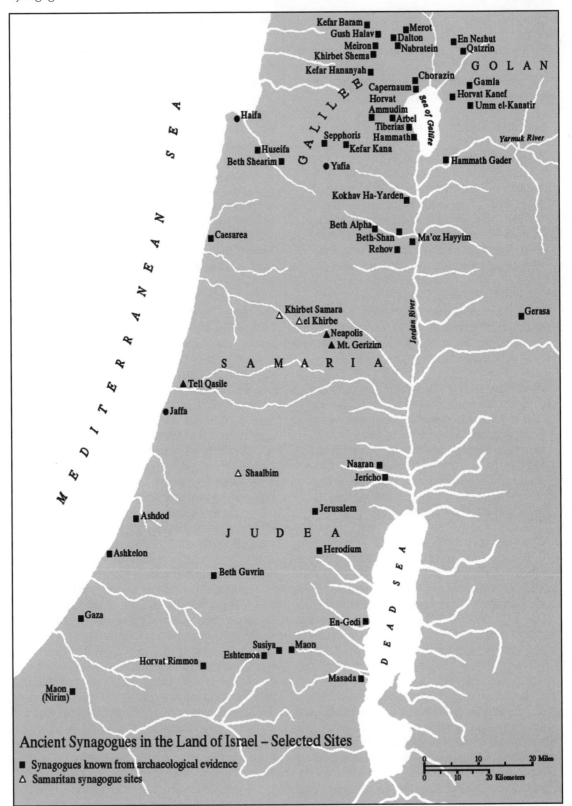

Ancient Synagogues in the Land of Israel – Selected Sites

■ Synagogues known from archaeological evidence
△ Samaritan synagogue sites

C. Late Antiquity: The Late Roman and Byzantine Periods

Archaeological evidence for Jewish synagogues during the late 1st through the 4th cent. CE is rare. A recent discovery in the Judean lowlands suggests real continuity with synagogues of the Second Temple period. The apparent synagogue of Horvat Ethri in the Judean Shephelah was built after the First Jewish Revolt, and apparently destroyed as a result of the Bar Kokhba Revolt (132–135 CE). The synagogue is a rectangular structure, with an entrance at the center of its broad wall. The roof was supported by three columns, topped with Doric-like capitals. A larger and a smaller ritual bath were discovered in close proximity. The excavators of the Nabratein synagogue, in the upper Galilee, report a 2nd-cent. synagogue in the first phase of the synagogue (Meyers). The building had four columns, and evidence of a "reader's lectern" may be imprinted in the plaster floor. The building is aligned toward the south, apparently toward Jerusalem.

The synagogue discovered at DURA EUROPOS, a border city in the Syrian desert, is the most impressive preserved structure of the period before Constantine. Excavated in 1932, the Dura synagogue was a renovated private dwelling. Sometime before 244/45, and perhaps as early as the latter 2nd cent. CE, this dwelling was converted as a synagogue. The largest room (13.65 × 7.68 m) was renovated for this purpose, with a large Torah shrine built on the western (Jerusalem-aligned) wall and benches around the walls. The façade of the Torah shrine was decorated with the image of the Jerusalem Temple, flanked on the right by the Binding of Isaac (which according to 2 Chr 3:1 took place on "Mount Moriah," the Temple Mount in Jerusalem) and on the left by a seven-branched menorah, a palm frond, and citron. There was some other painting, lost in a massive renovation of the synagogue that took place in 244/5 CE. At that time the walls were completely covered with paintings drawn from the OT, and read through the prism of Jewish biblical interpretation (see MIDRASH). Sixty percent of the paintings have been preserved. Themes are generally heroic, reflecting such events as the discovery of Moses by the daughter of Pharoah, the crossing of the Red Sea, the tribes encamped around the tabernacle, Ezekiel's vision of the dry bones, and Esther before King Ahasuerus. The paintings show profound parallels with traditions preserved in rabbinic literature, as do Aramaic and Persian inscriptions on the paintings. A parchment fragment bearing a Hebrew liturgical text was found in close proximity to the synagogue. This text has many parallels with rabbinic prayer of this period, and is close to the rabbinic grace after meals in many details. The Dura synagogue has often been interpreted as a forerunner of Christian art and as evidence for a supposed late antique "non-rabbinic Judaism." The evidence is actually much closer to rabbinic tradition than some recent scholars have suggested.

Considerable evidence for Jewish synagogues during the 2nd through the 4th cent. is preserved in literary sources. Rabbinic literature from Palestine and from Sassanian Babylonia (modern Iraq) present synagogues as regular features of the Jewish communal landscape. Early rabbinic (Tannaitic) literature mentions a broad range of activities that took place within synagogues. These included the recitation of Aramaic translations of the Torah reading (m. Meg. 4:6, 10), Torah blessings (t. Kippurim 3:18), sounding of the ram's horn on the new year (m. Rosh. Hash. 3:7), use of the palm frond, myrtle, willow, and citron on the feast of Tabernacles (m. Sukkah 3:13; t. Sukkah 2:10), recitation of the book of Esther reading on the Feast of Esther (Purim), possibly even by women (m. Meg. 2:4), recitation of the Hallel psalms (t. Pesah. 10:8), eulogies (t. Meg. 2:18), public oaths (m. Shevu. 4:10), local charity collection (t. Shabb. 16:22; t. Tem. 1:10; t. B. Bat. 8:4; Matt 6:2), communal meals (m. Zabim 3:2; Bek. 5:5). By the 3rd cent. they were also used as elementary schools (y. Meg. 3:4, 73a). Rabbinic literature suggests the development of an increasingly standardized public liturgical tradition, important elements of which were enacted within synagogues (e.g., m. Ber. 7:3). Rabbinic public prayer (the "public" defined as a quorum of at least ten men) took place in formal thrice-daily sessions as well as in the context of communal meals. In antiquity there was considerable variation in custom dependent on locality and scholar, modern scholars differing on the balance between variation and standardization. Rabbinic liturgy was built around the recitation of the "Shema (Deut 6:4-9; 11:13-21; Num 15:37-40) and its blessings" together with the Eighteen Benedictions (also known as the "standing prayer," the Amidah) morning and evening, and the Eighteen Benedictions with accompanying liturgy in afternoon prayers. Prayer times, though not the content of these rituals, were associated with the times of the Temple sacrifices. By the 3rd cent., public prayer was described homiletically as being equivalent in efficacy to sacrifices in the Temple, though the notion of the rebuilding of the Jerusalem Temple was never questioned in liturgical terms until the advent of modern Reform Judaism. In rabbinic times synagogue prayer and the pre-existing public reading of Scripture melded into a single liturgical structure. The Torah was publicly read, with attendant blessings, in the morning and afternoon services on the Sabbath and festivals and on Monday and Thursday mornings. A reading from the Prophets accompanied the Sabbath morning and festival Torah reading. Scripture reading was simultaneously translated into Aramaic (later concretized in Targum texts such as Targum Neofiti and Targum Onqelos), a tradition that was popular into the early Middle Ages and is still followed by Yemenite Jews (see TARGUMS). Various cycles for reading Torah existed in antiquity. Palestinians generally completed the entire Pentateuch in something more than three years, while Babylonians read on a yearly cycle. The Babylonian custom is followed in all traditional communities today.

The increase in synagogue functions was paralleled by the developing notion that synagogues were in some way holy. M. Megillah 3:1-3 describes the centrality of Scripture within the synagogue, as well as the transient holiness ascribed to this institution by the early rabbis. At the focal point of the synagogue, this text suggests, was the Torah scroll that stood at the top of a hierarchy:

The people of a town who sold their town square, they must buy a synagogue with its proceeds. If they sell a synagogue, they must acquire a (scroll) chest. If they sell a (scroll) chest, they must acquire cloths (to wrap sacred scrolls). If they sell cloths, they must acquire books (of the Prophets and Writings). If they sell books, they must acquire a Pentateuch (scroll). But, if they sell a Pentateuch, they may not acquire books (of the Prophets and Writings). And if they sell books, they may not acquire cloths. And if they sell cloths, they may not acquire a chest. And if they sell a chest, they may not acquire a synagogue. And if they sell a synagogue, they may not acquire town square. (trans. Fine)

Tosefta Sukkah 4:6 projects a 2nd-cent. Palestinian reality onto a great synagogue in Alexandria. This text focuses attention on a large podium upon which the biblical texts were read, with no mention of a Torah shrine:

Said Rabbi Judah: "Whosoever has never seen the double colonnade of Alexandria of Egypt has never seen the great glory of Israel in his entire life. It was a kind of large basilica, one colonnade within another. Sometimes twice as many (people) as those who went out of Egypt were within it. There were seventy-one thrones there, one for each of the seventy-one elders, each one made of twenty-five talents, with a wooden platform in the center. The leader of the assembly stands upon it at its horn, with flags in his hand. When one begins to read, the other would wave flags so (the people) would answer 'amen' for each and every blessing. Then that one would wave the flags and they would answer 'amen.' They did not sit in a jumble, but the goldsmiths sit by themselves, the silversmiths by themselves, the common weavers by themselves, the Tarsian (that is, fine) weavers by themselves, and the blacksmiths by themselves." (trans. Fine)

An ideal synagogue is described in *t. Meg.* 21–23, which establishes categories that set the parameters of Jewish legal discussions of synagogue architecture for the next two millennia. At the same time it suggests a second focal point within synagogues: orientation toward Jerusalem.

The Community leader arises to read, someone stands until the time when he reads. How do the elders sit? Facing the people, their backs to the qodhesh (קוֹדֶשׁ). When they set down the (Scroll) chest—its front is toward the people, its back to the qodhesh. The Community leader faces the qodhesh. All the people face the qodhesh. For it is said: "and the congregation was assembled at the door of the tent of meeting" (Lev 8:4). The doors of the synagogue are built on the eastern side, for thus we find in the Tabernacle, for it is said: "Before the Tabernacle toward the east, before the tent of meeting eastward" (Num 3:38). It is only built at the highest point of the town, for it is written: "Above the bustling (streets) she (wisdom, i.e., Torah) calls out" (Prov 1:21). (trans. Fine)

The location of the synagogue and some of its internal arrangement are articulated through reference to the biblical tabernacle and the Temple of Jerusalem. Alignment toward Jerusalem as focused through a Torah cabinet became basic to synagogue architecture, as did the notion that the ideal synagogue should be higher than the surrounding structures (which was generally kept in the breach). The identification of the synagogue with the Temple was a developing concept throughout antiquity and the medieval period. By the 3rd cent. the cabinet (tevah תֵּבָה) was being called ʾaronaʾ (אֲרוֹנָא, cabinet, reminiscent of the ark of the covenant), and its curtain parokhathaʾ (פְּרוֹכְתָא), reminiscent of the Temple curtain. There is no evidence for the physical separation of men and women in ancient synagogues, though a social distinction existed. Physical separation is known beginning during the early Middle Ages, when it was seen as an expression of the holiness of the synagogue due to its conceptual relationship with the Temple (where gender separation occasionally seems to have occurred). The dual foci—the scrolls as local cult object, along with a more subtle physical alignment in the direction of Jerusalem—became ideologically significant features of almost all synagogues until modern times.

Archaeological evidence for purpose-built late antique Palestinian synagogues expands toward the late 4th cent., becoming common between the 5th and 9th cent. Synagogues conforming to three main architectural types were constructed by Jews in late antique Palestine: the broadhouse, the "Galilean-type" basilica, and longhouse basilicas, which from the latter 5th or 6th cent. onward often had apses at their focal points. The basilica form was used by both Jews and Christians beginning around the turn of the 4th cent. CE. The basilica was uniquely suited to both the church and synagogue, providing a large, open meeting place for the "community of God."

The interior space of most of these synagogues was aligned toward a permanent Torah shrine, which usually stood on the Jerusalem-oriented side of the synagogue. Alignment of the Torah shrine toward Jerusalem was not absolute during this period and a number of synagogues had their shrines on walls other than the one aligned with Jerusalem. Interior alignment became more pronounced as the period progressed. Archaeological evidence for the existence of permanent Torah shrines in late antique Palestinian synagogues exists from the

4th cent. onward. The Torah shrine, the area around it, and alignment toward Jerusalem became the major elements in the sanctification of synagogue buildings during late antiquity. These issues were worked out in somewhat different ways in each of the three major architectural types.

"Broadhouse-type" synagogues have been discovered at Khirbet Shema in the Upper Galilee and at Horvat Rimmon 1, Eshtemoa, Maon, and Khirbet Susiya in Judea. Benches were built around the interior walls of these synagogues, focusing attention upon the center of the room. Aligned toward the south, the walls of the synagogue at Khirbet Shema (latter 4th cent.) were lined with benches. A Torah shrine on a stone platform that rose nearly 70 cm was built sometime after the synagogue's initial construction on the southern (Jerusalem) wall, partially covering the bench.

The broadhouses from the Hebron hills form a regional type. The entrances of these halls were aligned toward the east. The eastward alignment is perhaps modeled upon the Temple, and parallels *t. Meg.* 3:23. The interior of the synagogue hall was aligned toward the Torah shrine, which stood on the Jerusalem-aligned wall. The result is a rather awkward double alignment: the facade toward the east, the shrine toward Jerusalem to the north. At Eshtemoa the Torah niche was flanked by two smaller niches. In the third phase at Khirbet Susiya a larger and a smaller platform were constructed on the broad wall. The major bema is surrounded by a screen, decorated with images of the menorah, the Torah shrine, and floral motifs. A narrative is illustrated

on one panel of the Khirbet Susiya partition, of which little is left. Remains of wall decorations that framed the Torah niche flanked by two smaller niches further emphasized the shrine from Khirbet Susiya. In the floor mosaic, before the smaller bema, we find the image of an enclosed Torah shrine flanked by two menorahs. The interior arrangement of broadhouses created a less monumental and more intimate environment than that of basilicas.

Galilean-type synagogues are so called because they were all constructed in Galilee. This group includes Horvat Ha-Ammudim, Arbel Capernaum, Chorazin, Meiron, and Nabratein Kefar. Galilean-type synagogues are architecturally related to the narrow gable churches of nearby Syria. Like these churches most Galilean-type synagogues were entered through three portals. It is unlikely that the use of triple entrances in synagogues had any specific symbolic function, but rather provided immediate access to the nave and two side aisles. A unique feature of these buildings is the arrangement of the interior columns. Columns were constructed on the northern, eastern, and western sides of the hall, creating a KHET (kh ח) shaped arrangement. This focused attention on the interior of the southern, Jerusalem wall with its three portals. Scholars have posited that Torah shrines were constructed between the doors on the Jerusalem wall at Capernaum, Chorazin, and Meiron. Such an arrangement was discovered in the Meroth and Gush Halav synagogues. At Chorazin a chair was discovered upon which a prominent member of the community apparently sat.

Figure 2: The synagogue of Capernaum, 4th cent. CE. Capernaum, Israel.

Synagogues were constructed in the form of basilicas throughout the land of Israel beginning with the late 4th or early 5th cent. synagogue at Hammath Tiberias B. In "basilica type" synagogues the visitor might traverse the atrium, sometimes a narthex, and the nave to reach the Jerusalem-aligned wall. At the center of this wall was the building's focal point, the Torah shrine, which often stood upon a raised platform. From the late 5th cent. onward, the basilical synagogue often included an apse on the Jerusalem wall that housed the Torah shrine. This feature was borrowed from contemporary churches. The apse both accommodated and promoted the enlargement of the Torah shrine and its compound.

A screen, called a "chancel screen" in Christian contexts, sometimes separated the apse from the bema. Remains of stone screens were discovered at Hamath Gader, Rehov, Ma'oz Hayyim 3, Beth Alpha, Gaza, Ashkelon, and elsewhere. Remnants of a wooden screen were discovered at Ein Gedi. A synagogue screen seems to be described in the Cairo Genizah version of a text known as *Pereq Mashiah* (Fine 1999). It is likely that the description of "reed mats made as a partition for the bema" in this text refers to synagogue screens:

R. Eliezer son of Jacob says: The great study house of the Holy One, Blessed be He, in the future will be eighteen thousand myriad parsangs (in size), for it is written: "Its circumference (will be) 18,000" (Ezra 48:35). The Holy One, Blessed be He, sits on the chair among them, and David sits before him, for it is said: "His chair is like the sun before me" (Ps 89:37). All the placid women who teach and pay so that their sons may be taught Torah, Scripture and Mishnah, manners, pious sincerity and honesty stand by (or, within) reed mats made as a partition for the bema and listen to the voice of Zerubabel son of Shaltiel when he stands as translator. (trans. Fine)

The ornamentation of stone screens often includes images of menorahs. The screens from Khirbet Susiya, the most elaborate exemplar preserved, contain images of the Torah shrine, a MENORAH, floral patterns, and a narrative scene in which the hand of God apparently reaches down from a cloud holding a scroll. The Beth Alpha mosaic shows curtains tied back to reveal the shrine complex. The curtains would have effectively closed off the shrine from sight. The development of the shrine area at Ma'oz Hayyim is representative of the general expansion of shrine compounds in basilica-type synagogues: a Torah shrine on the Jerusalem wall in the first phase was replaced by a shrine set within an apse in the second phase. A raised platform enclosed by a screen appeared in the third phase.

Archaeological sources provide limited evidence for ways that Torah shrines were constructed in late antique synagogues. The significance of the Torah shrine is reflected in two lapidary inscriptions. An inscription discovered at Naveh in modern Syria commemorates the donation of a Torah shrine:

(... son of) Yudan
(and ...)yh son of his brother
(donated) the house of the ark. May (they) be remembered (for good).

An inscription from Dalton in the Upper Galilee calls the Torah shrine the "Receptacle of the Merciful (One)," which suggests reverence toward the shrine as seat of God's revelation, the Torah.

As we might suspect from literary sources, the "ark" did not have the appearance of the ark of the covenant, but rather of a contemporaneous cabinet or small shrine. Our clearest image of how Palestinian Torah shrines might have looked emerged from illustrations within mosaic panels discovered at Hammath Tiberias B, Sepphoris, Beth Shean A, Beth Alpha, Na'aran, and Khirbet Susiya and in stone carvings from Chorazin, Capernaum, and other sites. The discovery in 1981 of the pediment of an aedicula from Nabratein, with rampart lions on each side, a conch below, and a hole to suspend a lamp at the apex of the conch, provided a three-dimensional structure that is strikingly similar to that illustrated in the Beth Alpha mosaic. Stone Torah shrines and raised platforms are identifiable at numerous sites. Aediculae were commonly used to house the cult objects of religious communities during late antiquity.

The lions resting on top of the gable of the Nabratein aedicula, like the birds of the Beth Alpha pavement, add a sense of majesty to the Torah shrine. Three-dimensional lions that may have flanked Torah shrines (as represented in the shrine panel from Beth Alpha) convey a similar sense to the entire ark compound. At Khirbet Susiya a large frame that enclosed the main Torah niche and its flanking niches is partially preserved.

Most images of Torah shrines in ancient Jewish art are flanked by menorahs, or are in close proximity to menorahs. It is likely that Torah shrines stood in synagogues, flanked by seven-branched menorahs, as is represented in numerous contexts. Seven-branched menorahs have been discovered at a number of synagogues from the 5th cent. onward, though they are described in earlier literature. The lamps from the Judean hills region, from Eshtemoa, Maon, and Khirbet Susiya, are quite similar in conception and execution, and may represent a regional type. The "bulb and calyx" motif that articulates the branches of many of these menorahs hearkens back to the biblical description of the menorah of the tabernacle. The practice of flanking the shrine with two menorahs maintained the symmetry of the ark area. This placement of menorahs beside the "ark" is only vaguely reminiscent of the Temple arrangement. In the Temple one menorah stood to the left of the parokheth (פָּרֶכֶת).

Lamps were sometimes suspended from the branches of the menorahs, providing additional light. Lamps suspended from the menorahs appear on the screen from Khirbet Susiya, at Khirbet Kishor, on a tomb door from Kefar Yasif, and in the mosaics at Beth Shean B and Na'aran. Within churches, lamps were sometimes suspended from large crosses in a similar manner. A single translucent glass lamp was sometimes suspended immediately before the shrine, which provided a singular focal point for the shrine area and thus for the entire meeting room. In contemporaneous churches the altar that was the focal point of the apse was also brightly literally The effect would have been a brightly lit focal area within the church or synagogue (*see* LAMP, OT; LAMPSTAND).

The art of Palestinian Jewish synagogues, particularly decorated mosaics, is an integral part of the late Roman and Byzantine artistic tradition. The synagogue at Beth Alpha contains the most completely preserved Byzantine period mosaic, and well exemplifies this tradition. It builds on iconography well known from the Hammath Tiberias B, 2a mosaic, with its images of the zodiac and a panel containing a Torah shrine flanked by two menorahs. The Beth Alpha mosaic is divided into three panels. As at Hammath Tiberias, closest to the Torah shrine of the synagogue is a panel containing the image of a shrine flanked by lighted menorahs. In the center is a zodiac wheel, personifications of the seasons in the corners, and unique to this building, closest to the entrance to the synagogue, the image of the binding of Isaac (Gen 22).

Zodiacs and some other images are often labeled in Hebrew, the language of Scripture and most liturgy, even as dedicatory inscriptions appear in Aramaic and Greek. At Beth Alpha the narrative of the scene is glossed with biblical citations in Hebrew. Biblical themes in other synagogues include David (Gaza), Daniel in the lion's den (Na'aran, Susiya?), and Noah's ark, labeled in Greek (Gerasa). Sepphoris contains the angelic visitation to Abraham (Gen 18), the binding of Isaac, Aaron before the tabernacle, and other cultic imagery. A synagogue mosaic discovered in 2007 at Khirbet Wadi Hamam near the northwest corner of the Sea of Galilee contains images of artisans and laborers with a saw and a chisel, and others with various-sized hammers building what may be the tabernacle or Solomonic Temple. Jews continued to use images of the zodiac long after Christians abandoned this imagery, owing to the significance of the heavens and constructions of time in Jewish thought and liturgy.

Archaeological remains of late antique Jewish synagogues show important parallels to contemporaneous liturgical and rabbinic texts. This is particularly evident in inscriptions, where formulae show clear relationships with literary sources. A very significant example is the Rehov inscription, discovered in the narthex of a 6th-cent. synagogue. This 29-line inscription, which deals with local agricultural law, is the earliest extant physical evidence of a rabbinic text. Increased decoration of the physical environment of Palestinan synagogues paralleled the development of increasingly complex liturgical texts. Professional poets composed prayers for each Sabbath and festival according to the local reading cycles. These texts were often quite complex. Named poets appear from the 4th cent. onward, beginning with Yosse ben Yosse, Yannai, Eleazar son of Rabbi Qallir, Yehuda and Yohanan the Priest. These strongly homiletical texts parallel public homilies and traditions in Targumic literature. There is no theme in synagogue art that does not find important parallels in these literatures.

D. Diaspora Synagogues, 4th–6th Centuries

At least 150 Diaspora synagogues are known from literary and archaeological sources. Known Diaspora synagogues during this period conform to local architectural norms. What unifies them are the presence of a large Torah shrine and often images of menorahs. Other than Dura, the most impressive extant Diaspora synagogues were uncovered in Ostia Antica, the ancient port of Rome, and in Sardis in Asia Minor. Synagogue buildings were also uncovered at Illici in Spain, Bova Marina in Italy, Hamman Lif (Naro) in North Africa, Saradana in Albania, Stobi in Macedonia, Plovdiv in Bulgaria, Priene in Asia Minor, and Apamea in Syria. The Ostia synagogue building was first constructed toward the end of the 1st cent. CE, though it is not known whether it served as a synagogue at this point. The use of the building as a synagogue went through two stages. It was enlarged during the 2nd and 3rd cent., and was enlarged further and partly rebuilt at the beginning of the 4th cent. The triple entrances in the facade of the 2nd-3rd cent. basilica are aligned toward the east-southeast, perhaps in the direction of Jerusalem. A stepped podium stood on the wall opposite the main entrance. A Latin and Greek inscription from this phase makes mention of a shrine for the Torah:

> For the well-being of the emperor!
> Mindus Faustus established and built
> (it) and set up the ark
> of the Holy Torah … (trans. Fine)

During the 4th cent. the southernmost entrance portal on the eastern wall of the synagogue was sealed and replaced with a large freestanding Torah shrine. This Torah shrine is structurally contiguous with images of shrines in wall paintings and gold glasses discovered in the Jewish catacombs of Rome and with images on oil lamps discovered in Ostia.

The SARDIS synagogue is the largest and the grandest synagogue yet uncovered, its main hall measuring 54 × 18 m. It has been estimated that the synagogue could accommodate 1,000 people. This impressive building, the largest synagogue known before the modern period, was part of the municipal center of Sardis and taken

Ancient Synagogues in the Diaspora – Selected Sites

○ Synagogues known from literary sources
■ Synagogues known from archeological evidence

over by the Jewish community and remodeled as a synagogue during the 4th cent. It formed the southern side of the civic center of Sardis. The remodeling included the installation of two aediculae on stepped podia on the eastern wall of the synagogue and the construction of a podium in the center of the hall. The significance of these aediculae is made clear both by their prominence and by an inscription found near them that reads, "Find, open, read, observe." Another Greek inscription refers to the Torah shrine as the nomophylakion (νομοφυλάκιον), "the place that protects the Torah." A molding from the synagogue contains both an inscribed menorah and the image of a Torah shrine with its doors open to show scrolls stacked horizontally within it.

We know little of the liturgies of Jews in the western Diaspora. John Chrysostom describes synagogue customs in 4th-cent. Antioch as part of his polemic *Against the Jews*, aimed against Judaizers within his community. These include blowing the ram's horn on Rosh ha-Shanah, walking barefooted and fasting on Yom Kippur (known from rabbinic literature), and incubation in synagogues. He also knows that Jews and non-Jews considered synagogues to be holy places, the sanctity of the place being construed as deriving from the presence of biblical scrolls. Chrysostom suggests that reading of Psalms was important to synagogue liturgy. Inscriptions, most notably a Greek rendition of Ps 135:25 discovered in ancient Nicaea (today Iznik in Turkey), support this. These characteristics (other than incubation) were also prevalent in synagogues in Palestine and in Sassanian Iraq that are described in the Babylonian Talmud. The great significance of Torah shrines and images of shrines full of scrolls suggests the centrality of Scripture within Diaspora communities, as it was for communities in the land of Israel.

Jewish synagogues in both Palestine and in Roman Diaspora communities fared far better than polythe-

istic cult centers during the government-sponsored Christianization of the Roman Empire that began during the late 4th cent. Roman legal traditions preserved in the *Codex Theodosianius* suggest that beginning during the late 4th cent., Jewish synagogues were afforded some imperial protection against local Christian destruction and appropriation, though this protection slowly gave way. Thus we see in a law promulgated by Honorus with Theodosius in 423:

It seems right that in the future none of the synagogues of the Jews shall either be indiscriminately seized or put on fire. If there are some synagogues that were seized or vindicated to churches or indeed consecrated to the venerable mysteries in a recent undertaking and after the law was passed, they shall be given in exchange new places, on which they could build, that is, to the measure of the synagogues taken.... No synagogue shall be constructed from now on, and the old ones shall remain in their state.

(*Codex Theodosianus* 16:8:25, trans. A. Linder)

Patristic sources describe and ritualize the rededication of synagogues as churches. At Gerasa in Transjordan a synagogue was destroyed and replaced with a church, and at Illici in Spain a synagogue was consecrated a church. Elements of synagogue buildings were reused for Christian purposes; examples include the marble architectural member bearing a large menorah and citation from Ps 136:25 that was reused in a baptismal pool in Nicaea (Fine and Rutgers), a marble plaque with a carved menorah discovered in what seems to be secondary use in the large church at Priene, and most evocative of all, a column recently discovered at Laodicea upon which an inscribed cross was superimposed on a menorah (Fine 2009).

Bibliography: Marc Bloch. *The Historian's Craft* (1992); James D. G. Dunn. *The Parting of the Ways: Between Christianity and Judaism.* 2nd ed. (2006); I. Elbogen. *Jewish Liturgy: A Comprehensive History* (1993); Steven Fine. *Art and Judaism in the Greco-Roman World: Toward a New Jewish Archaeology.* 2nd rev. ed. (2009); S. Fine. "'Chancel' Screens in Late Antique Palestinian Synagogues: A Source from the Cairo Genizah." *Religious and Ethnic Communities in Later Roman Palestine.* H. Lapin, ed. (1999) 67–85; Steven Fine. *Jews, Christians, and Polytheists in the Ancient Synagogue: Cultural Interaction during the Greco-Roman Period* (1999); Steven Fine, ed. *Sacred Realm: The Emergence of the Synagogue in the Ancient World* (1996); Steven Fine. *This Holy Place: On the Sanctity of Synagogues during the Greco-Roman Period* (1998); Steven Fine and Leonard V. Rutgers. "New Light on Judaism in Asia Minor During Late Antiquity: Two Recently Identified Inscribed Menorahs." *Jewish Studies Review* 3 (1996) 1–23; Ezra Fleischer. "On the Beginnings of Obligatory Hebrew Prayer." *Tarbiz* 59 (1990) 397–441; Phillip Harland. *Associations, Synagogues, and Congregations: Claiming a Place in Ancient Mediterranean Society* (2003); Lee I. Levine, ed. *Ancient Synagogues Revealed* (1981); Lee I. Levine. *The Ancient Synagogue: The First Thousand Years* (2000); Amnon Linder, ed. *The Jews in Roman Imperial Legislation* (1987); Eric M. Meyers, James F. Strange, and Carol L. Meyers. "The Ark of Nabratein: A First Glance." *BA* 44 (1981) 237–43; James Parkes. *The Conflict of the Church and the Synagogue: A Study in the Origins of Antisemitism* (1961); R. Reich and H. Shanks, trans. *The City of David: Revisiting Early Excavations: English Translations and Reports by Raymond Weill and L.-H. Vincent* (2004) 86–89; A. Runesson. *The Origins of the Synagogue* (2001); Dan Urman and Paul V. M. Flesher, eds. *Ancient Synagogues: Historical Analysis and Archaeological Discovery* (1995).

STEVEN FINE AND JOHN DAVID BROLLEY

E. Synagogues in the New Testament

All four of the canonical Gospels report that Jesus taught in synagogues (Matt 4:23; 13:54; Mark 1:21-22; Luke 4:16; 6:6; John 6:59; 18:20) and that he also healed there (Matt 4:23; Mark 1:23-27). The Gospel of Luke introduces Jesus's ministry with the pronouncement—in the synagogue in Nazareth—that he had come to fulfill the prophet Isaiah (Luke 4:16-21).

According to the Acts of the Apostles, Paul went to the synagogues in all the towns he visited to try to persuade Jews (and Gentile converts to Judaism) to follow Jesus as the Messiah (e.g., Acts 9:20; 13:5, 14-16; 14:1; 17:1-2, 10, 17; 18:4, 7-8, 19, 26; 19:8; in 16:13, he goes to a "place of prayer," proseuchē). Even though Paul's own letters do not confirm this practice (indeed, Paul says he went to the Gentiles, not Jews), Acts provides literary evidence of the many synagogues throughout the Mediterranean area in the 1st cent., their function as a central gathering place for Jews (including sojourners like Paul), and the attendance of Gentile seekers.

In the 1st–2nd cent. CE, the growing tension between Jews who believed Jesus was the Messiah and those who did not sometimes took place in the context of the synagogue (*see* SCHISM). For example, while one leader of the synagogue (archisynagōgos ἀρχισυνάγωγος) was receptive to Jesus (Mark 5:22-24, 35-42; compare Matt 9:18-19, 23-25), another questioned his authority (Luke 13:10-14). The book of Acts describes both positive and negative responses to the gospel message preached in synagogues (Acts 13:42-50; 14:1-2; 17:1-9; 19:8-10).

By the time the Gospel of John was written (late 1st cent.), evidence of a rift within the synagogues becomes greater, as John refers to adversaries of Jesus collectively as "the Jews" and reports that those who proclaim Jesus to be the Messiah risk being expelled from the synagogue (John 9:22; 12:42; 16:2; *see* TWELFTH BENEDICTION). In the book of Revelation (also late 1st cent.), the author bitterly claims that the people "who say they are Jews and are not" are a "synagogue of Satan" (2:9; 3:9). These conflicts within and around the synagogue need to be understood as disagreements among 1st-cent. Jews who were grappling with great complexity of belief and not as a condemnation of Jews or Judaism. *See* ANTI-SEMITISM; CHRISTIAN-JEWISH RELATIONS; JOHN, GOSPEL OF.

MARIANNE BLICKENSTAFF

SYNAGOGUE, THE GREAT. Rabbinic literature uses the expression "Men of the Great Assembly" or "Men of the Great Synagogue" to designate the individuals who transmitted the Torah while Israel was under Persian rule. Thus, the Great Synagogue was an important link in the chain of tradition from Moses to the rabbis themselves (*m. Avot* 1:1). Members included Ezra and Nehemiah (compare Neh 8–10) as well as the prophets Haggai and Zechariah; the last member was Simon the Just. The Great Synagogue's enactments, foundational for rabbinic law, treated liturgy, the biblical canon, the festival of Purim, and the tripartite classification of Oral Torah as midrash, halakhah, and haggadah.

STEVEN FINE

SYNCRETISM sin′kruh-tiz′uhm. Syncretism refers to the clustering of religious ideas and observances from distinct cultural contexts. Most non-Jews considered worship of all manifestations of divine power to be wise and prudent, so that even the skeptical participated in religious activities at times.

Israelite religion moved from monolatry, devotion to a single god among many gods, to monotheism, the belief that only one God exists. Influences from religions of the surrounding peoples played a role in shaping OT traditions.

Many peoples believed that their tribe was governed by a deity who protected and guided them. In the sagas of Genesis, Abraham, Isaac, and Jacob have separate cycles of stories, and we notice that Isaac's clan worship centers on "The Fear of Isaac" (Gen 31:42, 53) while Jacob's clan has "The Mighty One of Jacob" (Gen 49:24). Later when these cycles are united, the patriarchal deity will be attested as one and the same.

Canaanite influences are evident in formulae concerning the "El" (god), who rules a geographical area. Genesis notes the shrines of "El Elyon" (God Most High) at Salem (Gen 17:1), "El Shaddai" (God Almighty) at Hebron (Gen 17:1), and "El Olam" (God Everlasting) at Beer-sheba (Gen 21:33)—all places where Abraham worships. The shrine to "El Roi" (God of Seeing) at Beer-lahai-roi (Gen 16:14; 24:62) is connected to Isaac, and the shrine to "El Bethel" (God of Bethel) to Jacob (Gen 35:6-7). The cult at these shrines focuses on times of thanksgiving for harvests. Jewish writers will use the sum of these, in the plural, "Elohim," to stand as the name for their one and only "Lord."

Exodus introduces a warrior God, Yahweh, who raises up Moses to lead the Israelites. Although this God identifies himself as "The God of your father, the God of Abraham, the God of Isaac, and the God of Jacob" (Exod 3:6), he is like a soldier who defeats Pharaoh's whole army (Exod 14–15), guides his people in the wilderness, and mandates a holy war on the people of Canaan (Josh 1–12). His worship needs no special site; the Tent of Meeting (Exod 33:7-11) and the ark of the covenant (Exod 25:10-22) are portable.

When God chooses the king and adopts him as a Son, the Davidic monarchy adopts religious traditions associated with monarchies. The Jebusite shrine to "El," the one Lord of the cosmos, was converted to a shrine to Yahweh. The ark's presence made Jerusalem the "holy city," and the king God's anointed (see Pss 24; 47; 48; 76; 78; 98; 137).

The global reach of the Roman Empire during the NT period provided a common cultural base for the syncretistic influences on the presentation of Jesus' person and message.

The concept of a woman impregnated by a god who takes human form was familiar in non-Jewish myths, notably among the Greeks. Heracles, the most famous of the heroes, son of Zeus and Alcmene, and Asclepius, the beloved divine doctor, son of Apollo and Coronis, were perhaps the best known. Alexander the Great claimed himself a son of God, alleging that his real father was Zeus. Julius Caesar tied his family to Venus. Jews considered such ideas blasphemous. Infancy narratives in Matthew (Matt 1:18-23) and Luke (Luke 1:26-38) claim that Jesus is Son of God, due to divine paternity. Yet it is made clear that the Virgin Mary conceives in her womb only by the power of God's Holy Spirit (see VIRGIN BIRTH).

Mystery cults, such as the Eleusinian mysteries, as well as those linked to the Great Mother, Isis, and Mithras, featured the death of a loved one followed by a mysterious return to life. These deities welcomed devotees from every stratum of society. Secret rites involved a ritual in which the devotees heard the sacred story, suffered with the god/goddess, rejoiced in the return of life, and saw, tasted, and touched sacred objects revealed by the priests. Initiates emerged feeling a new intimacy with the deity, a surety of the god's protection and care. Christian meetings were not secretive, and had certain parallels in the recitation of Jesus' death and resurrection (Gal 3:1-5), the ritual meal for members where one shared the body and blood of the Lord (and unworthy reception brought death, the penalty for offense to a deity [1 Cor 11:30]), a new identity as brothers and sisters of Jesus, and the promise of a like resurrection.

Apotheosis refers to the transformation of a human into a divinity. The most important model was the Romans' founder, Romulus, who disappeared into heaven and was given a new name, Quirinius. Appearing to a knight, Julius Proclus, he sent him to the Roman people with a message of encouragement and a promise of his protection. The Romans massively promulgated the state-approved apotheosis of Augustus and other popular emperors such as Claudius, Vespasian, and Titus because it declared a divine approval of this emperor whose decisions were clearly united to the will of heaven. This public sign of God's approval explains Philo's treatment of an apotheosis for Moses (*Moses* 2.290–92; *On the Virtues* 73–76), when Deut 34:6 stated he had been buried. Apotheosis indicated immortal life and divine approbation. Thus the post-resurrection appearances of Jesus (Matt 28:1-10, 16-20; Luke 24:13-35, 36-49, 50-53; John 20:1-18, 19-23, 24-28; 21:1-23) fit very well the model of apotheosis. The claim would have been universally understood as a divine vindication of Jesus and a holy authorization by God for his eternal Lordship. *See* CROSS-CULTURAL INTERPRETATION; CULTURAL STUDIES; EXCLUSION.

Bibliography: Amy-Jill Levine, Dale C. Allison Jr., and John Dominic Crossan eds. *The Historical Jesus in Context* (2006); Mark S. Smith. *The Memoirs of God* (2004); Robert Turcan. *The Gods of Ancient Rome* (2001).

WENDY COTTER, CSJ

SYNOPTIC GOSPELS sin-op′tik. "Synoptic Gospels" refers to the first three canonical Gospels, Matthew, Mark, and Luke, which are universally recognized as having some kind of interdependent literary relationship (*see* SYNOPTIC PROBLEM). The adjective *synoptic* itself is based on the Greek term **synopsis** (συνόψις), meaning "seeing all together." The term *synoptic* was first applied to the first three canonical Gospels by Johann Jakob Griesbach (1745–1812), who entitled the first part of his edition of the Greek NT *Synopsis Evangeliorum Matthaei Marci et Lucae* ("Synopsis of the Gospels Matthew, Mark, and Luke"), published in 1774.

DAVID E. AUNE

SYNOPTIC PROBLEM sin-op'tik. The term *synoptic* refers to the first three canonical Gospels—Matthew, Mark, and Luke. This word originated with J. J. Griesbach in the late 18th cent. and refers to the way in which these Gospels "view" (-optic) the story of Jesus "together" (syn-), or in similar ways (*see* SYNOPTIC GOSPELS).

The "Synoptic Problem" is the nature of the exact literary relationship among these three Gospels. Rarely do two Gospels record an event with exactly the same words. Frequently, the differences in the details are minor (e.g., John the Baptist's preaching of repentance in Matt 3:7-10//Luke 3:7-9). In many cases, however, they are significant. For example, was Jesus unwilling (Matt 13:58) or unable (Mark 6:5) to perform miracles in his hometown synagogue? In fact, it is not unusual for even Jesus' words to be recorded differently from one Gospel to the next, though it is clearly the same occasion being described (e.g., Jesus' interpretation of the parable of the Sower in Matt 13:18-23; Mark 4:13-20; and Luke 8:11-15). This is a problem, especially if one's primary question is "What did Jesus actually say or do in any particular event?"

A. Explanation of the Synoptic Problem
  1. Agreement in wording
  2. Agreement in narrative order
  3. Summary of relationship
    a. Triple tradition
    b. Matthew and Luke follow Mark's order
    c. Mark contained in Matthew and Luke
    d. Matthew and Luke rarely agree against Mark
    e. Agreements follow Mark's order
    f. Mark the middle term
    g. Double tradition
    h. Double tradition order differs
B. History of the Problem: Which Gospel Is First?
  1. Augustinian theory
    a. Fragmentary hypothesis
    b. Primitive gospel hypothesis
  2. Griesbach hypothesis
  3. The Two-source hypothesis
  4. The Four-source hypothesis
  5. Farrer hypothesis
C. The Priority of the Gospel of Mark
  1. Length
  2. Grammar
  3. Difficult expressions
  4. Verbal agreement and order
  5. Argument from redaction
  6. More primitive theology
  7. Summary
D. Introduction to "Q"
  1. Arguments for the existence of "Q"
    a. Evidence for shared material
    b. Narrative sequence
    c. Independent use
    d. Best argument
  2. Two main problems for postulating "Q"
    a. Minor agreements in wording
    b. Major agreements in order
E. Summary
Bibliography

A. Explanation of the Synoptic Problem

1. Agreement in wording

There are many similarities among the three Synoptic Gospels. Matthew, Mark, and Luke share much of the same wording. The similarity varies from passage to passage. But there are similar general features of importance. There are numerous verbatim agreements throughout individual pericopes. This agreement in wording occurs, of course, in the Greek, a language which was not Jesus' language of choice (if he knew it and used it at all). His primary language was Aramaic. Occasionally, the Gospel authors preserve remnants of Jesus' Aramaic words (e.g., Mark 5:41; 15:34). This is significant. The occurrence of this agreement in the Greek wording makes it probable that there is some type of literary interrelatedness among the Gospels.

2. Agreement in narrative order

Also, the Gospel stories share much of the same narrative order. Review an index in the back of any synopsis (a volume that places the first three canonical Gospels in parallel columns). One would expect some of the material to be in the same sequence in all three Gospels. For example, the birth narrative would not make as much sense following Jesus' baptism by John. Jesus' death and resurrection should come, as expected, at the end of the story. Other accounts of shared chronology are best understood as pointing to some level of literary dependence. There is chronological logic in the narrative order. This is not, however, always the case. There are stories, such as the "call of the disciples," that appear in different chronological sequences in each of the Gospels. In the Gospel of Mark, it is Jesus' first public activity, following his announcement of God's reign (Mark 1:16-20). In the Gospel of Luke, Jesus summons close followers slightly later in his mission (Luke 5:1-11). In the Gospel of Mark, Jesus curses the fig tree before his symbolic temple "cleansing" (Mark 11:12-19), but in Matthew, he curses the fig tree after this event (Matt 21:12-22). Theories responding to the synoptic problem must offer explanations that best account for similarities and differences among the respective Gospels.

3. Summary of relationship

Many of the similarities and the differences may be explained in a variety of ways. The list, summarized here, provided by E. P. Sanders and Margaret Davies, is useful. The following eight statements account for how the Gospels are related to one another. Granted, the authors of these eight "summary statements" are proponents of the priority of Mark, which may seem to skew their statements. But the sixth statement (§A.3.f) indicates that Markan priority is not the only option to draw from the prior statements. Furthermore, they are not advocates of the hypothetic sayings source called "Q," despite the propositions mentioned here that support this viewpoint (see §D). All viable theories must account for all of these individual statements in some manner.

a. **Triple tradition.** When the same passages appear in all three Synoptic Gospels, this is called "triple tradition."

b. **Matthew and Luke follow Mark's order.** Frequently in the triple tradition, Matthew, Mark, and Luke agree in the order of stories. When they do not agree, either Matthew or Luke will follow Mark's arrangement.

c. **Mark contained in Matthew and Luke.** Ninety percent of the Gospel of Mark is found within the Gospel of Matthew. More than 50 percent of the Gospel of Mark is found within the Gospel of Luke.

d. **Matthew and Luke rarely agree against Mark.** When either Matthew or Luke disagrees with Mark, the other agrees. Within the triple tradition, besides verbatim agreements among all three, there are substantial agreements between Matthew and Mark against Luke, and between Mark and Luke against Matthew, but relatively few agreements between Matthew and Luke against Mark.

e. **Agreements follow Mark's order.** Agreement between Matthew and Luke begins where Mark begins and ends where Mark ends. For example, the Gospel of Mark begins with John the Baptist. The Gospels of Matthew and Luke begin before the appearance of John, with birth narratives, but the birth narratives are not in the same order in each Gospel. Matthew and Luke begin to agree with each other when they start to tell about John the Baptist, which the Gospel of Mark also records.

f. **Mark the middle term.** Because of these phenomena (§§A.3.b–e) in the triple tradition, it is best to recognize that Mark is the middle term (the Gospel of Mark always stands in the middle of the other two Gospels). The Gospel of Mark is closer to Matthew and Luke than they are to each other. All solutions to the synoptic problem must explain this fact. Many argue that the Gospel of Mark was the first Gospel written; others argue that it was third.

g. **Double tradition.** Matthew and Luke share approximately 200 verses that are not found within the Gospel of Mark. Virtually all of these verses are sayings of Jesus. These shared verses are called the "double tradition."

h. **Double tradition order differs.** The double tradition material is not arranged the same way in the Gospels of Matthew and Luke.

B. History of the Problem: Which Gospel Is First?

In the history of this discussion, various ways have been offered to account for the arrangement of the Gospels. The synoptic "problem" is almost as old as Christianity itself. In the 2nd cent. CE, a Syrian Christian named Tatian developed a volume called the Diatessaron (from the Gk. dia [διά], "through," and tessarōn [τέσσαρων], "the four," referring to the four Gospels) in order to combine the four canonical Gospels into one account, removing duplications, contradictions, etc. This was one type of response to the problem. An engagement with this issue in Synoptic Gospel interpretation, however, has intensified over the last 200 years.

From the early history of Christianity until the 19th cent., the Gospel of Matthew has held pride of place as the first written Gospel. Over the last 200 years, the Gospel of Mark has become accepted as the first Gospel and the one on which the other two depend. Let us survey several prominent theories on the origins of the Gospels throughout this history.

1. Augustinian theory

Saint Augustine, the Bishop of Hippo in North Africa, advocated a view that the canonical order was the chronological order. The Gospel of Matthew was written first (in Hebrew, he surmised) and the author of the Gospel of Mark wrote (in Greek), fully aware of the first Gospel. According to Augustine, Mark seems to have followed closely in Matthew's footsteps, abbreviating his work as he went along (*Cons.* 1.4). When the author of the Gospel of Luke wrote, he knew only the Gospel of Mark. What the author of Luke knew about the Gospel of Matthew, he knew only through Mark. This view has more recently been defended by B.C. Butler. This theory has received a very small but influential following in contemporary circles.

a. **Fragmentary hypothesis.** Throughout the centuries since Augustine, there were various responses to this traditional view of the order of the Gospels by influential thinkers. Toward the end of the 18th cent. and the beginning of the 19th cent., the discussion had reached a new level. Friedrich D.E. Schleiermacher (1768–1834), one of the most influential German theologians of this period, developed a theory known as the "fragmentary hypothesis." There are several features to this theory. 1) The Gospels arose out of short stories (or memorabilia) of Jesus' life and teaching; 2) the stories were written down by the apostles; they did not derive from larger sources; 3) these stories were collected together under (now technically called) "form-critical" categories, such as nature miracles, parables, exorcisms, etc. (*see* FORM CRITICISM, NT). The fragmentary hypothesis is inadequate because it fails to account for the large agreement in order among the Gospels.

b. Primitive gospel hypothesis. The names of G. E. Lessing (1729–81) and J. G. Eichhorn (1752–1827) are associated with another such proposal, the "primitive gospel hypothesis." Another name for this theory is the "Ur-gospel theory" (*Ur* is German for "original"). There are two basic elements: 1) This proto-gospel was originally written in Aramaic and then translated into Greek; this makes sense, historically, in light of our knowledge of Jesus' primary, original language; 2) each synoptic writer used a different version of this Ur-gospel, which accounts for the similarities and the differences of each Gospel. The Ur-gospel theory is inadequate because of the lack of historical evidence for the existence of such a document in Aramaic.

2. Griesbach hypothesis

The 18th-cent. scholar J. J. Griesbach maintained the traditional view of the priority of Matthew; he called into question, however, the chronological order of the second and third Gospels.

This hypothesis, also known as the "Griesbach hypothesis," maintains the historical priority of the first canonical Gospel, the Gospel of Matthew. The author of the third canonical Gospel (Luke) was fully aware of the first Gospel when he wrote. When the author of the Gospel of Mark wrote, he was fully aware of both Gospels (Matthew and Luke).

J. J. Griesbach also developed the first major synopsis, which became a crucial tool for his theory. D. F. Strauss' famous critical biography of Jesus was based on Griesbach's view of the order of the Gospels. More recently this position has received an influential proponent in William R. Farmer, who explored the significance of Matthean priority on theological issues, such as the faithful witness of women in the Gospels and God's special commitment to the poor (1994).

3. The two-source hypothesis

The two-source hypothesis represents the most popular theory among contemporary scholars. The Gospel of Mark replaces the Gospel of Matthew as the first narrative of Jesus produced. Both Matthew and Luke wrote their respective Gospels fully aware of the second canonical Gospel. Equally important, in this solution, is that Matthew and Luke utilized the Gospel of Mark independent of each other. That is, neither one was aware of the content of the other's narrative.

In light of this independence, another source is assumed, called "Q" (*see* Q, QUELLE), as part of this solution in order to account for the "double tradition," the verses shared between the Gospel of Matthew and the Gospel of Luke (see §A.3.g; §D). This solution is often associated with Heinrich Holtzmann (1863) in Germany. Others held this view prior to Holtzmann, but most scholars have advocated the two-source hypothesis since Holtzmann.

4. The four-source hypothesis

B. H. Streeter developed a four-source hypothesis out of the popular two-source theory above. In this hypothesis, in addition to Mark and "Q," Matthew and Luke each had access to another independent written source. These sources—"M" (Matthew's special material) and "L" (Luke's special material)—represent passages unique to each individual Gospel, which are not derived from either Mark or "Q."

5. Farrer hypothesis

The most recent theory in this discussion was initiated by A. M. Farrer, is also known as the "Mark without 'Q' theory." Markan priority is maintained; the author of the Gospel of Matthew wrote his book fully aware of the Gospel of Mark. When the author of the third Gospel wrote, he knew both the Gospels of Mark and Matthew. The contemporary advocates of this position include Michael Goulder, E. P. Sanders, and Mark Goodacre. In response to the most dominant solution (i.e., the two-source hypothesis), this theory 1) challenges the independent use of the Gospel of Mark by the other Gospel authors; and, 2) argues for Luke's knowledge and use of the Gospel of Matthew (compare Griesbach hypothesis, §B2).

C. The Priority of the Gospel of Mark

One of the most important conclusions of the last 200 years in gospel research is that the Gospel of Mark should be considered the "middle term." As noted above, this phenomenon implies that the Gospel of Mark may be first or third in order. Below are the main arguments in favor of Markan priority, a crucial element in the most dominant theory in the synoptic relationship today.

1. Length

The Gospel of Mark's overall narrative is shorter than the others. Both the Gospel of Matthew and the Gospel of Luke contain a large body of material not present in Mark. Yet, within individual passages, the Gospel of Mark tends to be longer. If Mark is not first, one has to explain why the author would omit so much material from the other Gospels (e.g., the Sermon on the Mount, birth narratives). Perhaps the author of the Gospel of Mark desired to provide a condensed version of the Gospel for use in the church (this was Augustine's position). It is difficult to imagine Mark as an abbreviated version overall (in the larger narrative), while it maintains numerous longer individual pericopes.

2. Grammar

The assumption of Markan priority allows interpreters to explain more accurately Matthew's and Luke's grammatical improvements to the Greek of the second Gospel (this is difficult to see in English translations). In addition to specific grammatical changes, Matthew and Luke also make other language-oriented alterations to improve the flow of the depictions, including the omission of Aramaic words (e.g., compare Mark 7:34 and Matt 15:30) and the omission of redundancy (view a synopsis at Mark 1:32; 2:18).

3. Difficult expressions

At times, the Gospel of Mark appears to offer "harder" readings (difficult to understand) that are softened or omitted in Matthew or in Luke. For example, in Jesus' hometown synagogue, the author of the Gospel of Matthew alters Jesus' inability ("he could do no deed of power" in Mark 6:5) to Jesus' unwillingness ("he did not do many deeds of power" in Matt 13:58).

Moreover, both Matthew and Luke omit Mark's references to Jesus' family thinking of him as insane (see Mark 3:21). The description of Jesus in the Gospel of Mark is a more difficult theological image to acknowledge. Many have suggested that the author of the Gospel of Matthew must have changed the other's description, because imagining the opposite is challenging.

4. Verbal agreement and order

In both cases (wording and order), the lack (or insignificant number) of agreements between the Gospel of Matthew and the Gospel of Luke against the Gospel of Mark, as compared to Mark–Matthew against Luke, and Mark–Luke against Matthew, can be best explained by the priority of Mark. This argument, of course, only proves that Mark is the "middle term."

5. Argument from redaction

Redaction criticism is the study of the way authors of the Gospels "edited" the tradition(s) they received (see REDACTION CRITICISM, NT). If redactional features of each Gospel can be identified and located within other Gospels, then positive steps can be made toward ascertaining the order of these sources. For example, the term *immediately* is a (literary) redactional element of the Gospel of Mark; it occurs more than forty times in Mark, almost twice as many times as in the Gospels of Matthew and Luke combined. Since the other authors use this term in their descriptions less frequently, it is striking when they do. More likely, they are dependent on a source, like the Gospel of Mark, for its usage.

6. More primitive theology

If the tendency of the early theological tradition can be determined, then tracing this tradition through the Gospel narratives could be accomplished. For example, scholars generally assume that the overall early Christian tradition moved from a lower CHRISTOLOGY (more human Jesus) to a higher christology (less human Jesus). In Mark 1:40-45, the author describes Jesus' emotions: Jesus was both "moved with pity" (1:41) and "stern" (1:43). Neither the author of the Gospel of Matthew nor of Luke describes Jesus in these ways. Such emotional descriptions show the more human side of Jesus, which is often (not always) avoided in the Gospels of Matthew and Luke.

7. Summary

The difficulty of the last two observations is that both are determined a priori. One way to determine the tendencies (redactional features) of the third Gospel, e.g., is to look at the way that author shaped his tradition. To determine these tendencies, the Gospel of Mark must be assumed as the tradition standing behind the others. The last two arguments are weaker than the others. They are more speculative. The other four arguments, however, are significant in themselves. All solutions to the problem of the Synoptic Gospels must deal with them. It is the cumulative weight (Stein) of these six observations that provides support for the position of the priority of the Gospel of Mark. In each of these arguments, the key is to recognize that the reverse (that the author of the Gospel of Mark knew the Gospel of Matthew and/or the Gospel of Luke) does not allow us to account for these observations as well as the priority of the Gospel of Mark.

D. Introduction to "Q"

In addition to the priority of the Gospel of Mark, the other important component of the two-source hypothesis is the proposal for a hypothetical source known as "Q."

This hypothesis suggests that authors of the Gospels of Matthew and of Luke each were aware of the Gospel of Mark and were aware of the hypothetical source "Q" when composing their respective Gospels.

What is "Q"? It stands for the German word *Quelle*, which means "source." This term represents a source that includes passages that the Gospels of Matthew and Luke share that do not appear in the Gospel of Mark. The authors of Matthew and Luke derive these 200 verses or so, many of which are the words of Jesus, from "Q." Here are a few examples of these passages: 1) Temptation of Jesus (Matt 4:1-11; Luke 4:1-13); 2) Beatitudes (Matt 5:3-12; Luke 6:20-23); 3) Love for Enemies (Matt 5:39-48; Luke 6:27-36); 4) John the Baptist Questions Jesus (Matt 11:2-19; Luke 7:18-35); 5) The Lord's Prayer (Matt 6:9-13; Luke 11:2-4); 6) The Sign of Jonah (Matt 12:38-42; Luke 11:29-32); 7) Parable of the Talents (Matt 25:14-30; Luke 19:11-27). For centuries, many scholars have thought that every story, event, or saying that was written down within a Gospel narrative must have derived from an earlier written source. This assumption is basically the foundation of source criticism (see SOURCE CRITICISM).

1. Arguments for the existence of "Q"

It would be helpful to trace briefly the arguments for the existence of this hypothetical source. Let me do so by offering the three most important literary arguments.

a. Evidence for shared material. The Gospel of Luke in the triple tradition lacks Matthean additions (or "M," material unique to the first Gospel). Since the Gospel of Luke generally follows the Gospel of Matthew in all suggested solutions in the history of the discussion, then one might expect more "M" material to be present within the Gospel of Luke. Since this is not the case, the possibility of a source—from which the authors of Matthew and Luke derive their shared material—increases.

b. Narrative sequence. The "Q" material appears in a different order in the narrative sequences of each Gospel. (If the "double tradition" material—synonymous with "Q"—was in the same order, one might suspect a relationship between Matthew and Luke.) Matthew and Luke both follow the basic order of Mark. If following the Markan order is indicative of the way Matthew and Luke regularly treat their source material, a similar usage of their other "source" (i.e., "Q") should be expected.

c. Independent use. The Gospel of Matthew does not always contain the most primitive form of the double tradition ("Q"); in fact, the more primitive form usually appears in the Gospel of Luke. It is rarely, if ever, suggested that the Gospel of Luke preceded the Gospel of Matthew; the reverse is always attested. If the author of Luke knew the Gospel of Matthew, which is more likely than the reverse, then the third Gospel's more primitive form of the double tradition material can only mean that their respective authors utilized this source independently of one another. Therefore, it raises the historical possibility of a source like "Q."

d. Best argument. Of these three, the second argument is considered by many scholars to be the strongest support for the hypothesis of the existence of "Q" and, in turn, for the two-source hypothesis. As E. P. Sanders and Margaret Davies observe: that the authors of Matthew and Luke disagree in the way they place Q material in the structure of Mark shows that both of them began with Mark as an outline and inserted other material. This also shows that they did so independently. If Matthew or Luke had known the work of the other, this knowledge would have influenced the placement of the material.

Because of this argument, combined with the others, the two-source hypothesis has dominated the field of biblical studies for 150 years. This hypothesis has become the starting point for most scholarship on the Gospel narratives over the last two centuries and into the 21st cent. as well.

2. Two main problems for postulating "Q"

Not all scholars assume the hypothetical source "Q" to be essential to the resolution of the synoptic problem. Two primary, literary concerns are discussed from this perspective.

a. Minor agreements in wording. In the triple tradition, there are minor agreements in wording between the Gospels of Matthew and Luke, against the Gospel of Mark, in virtually every pericope. There are two types of minor agreements: positive agreements (words that Matthew and Luke share) and agreements of omission (words within the Gospel of Mark but absent from the other two Gospels). Any proponents of the dominant theory (i.e., the two-source hypothesis) have to explain each agreement, both the positive agreements and the agreements of omission in order to maintain the Gospel of Matthew's and Luke's independence of each other. Common explanations from the "two-source" proponents include the following: occasionally, the authors of Matthew and Luke agreed coincidentally; omissions reduce Mark's wordiness; or, occasionally it is their different perspective on Jesus that accounts for the agreements. Many proponents of the dominant two-source hypothesis, especially Frans Neirynck, have worked diligently to respond to each of these "agreements." Many scholars have been convinced by their efforts.

b. Major agreements in order. There are major agreements in the order of the double tradition.

The Gospels of Matthew and Luke share the order of some of the double tradition (i.e., "Q"). This argument is a direct challenge to the best argument for the existence of "Q" as stated above, that passages within the double tradition occur in different narrative sequences within the Gospels of Matthew and Luke. Eventually, these passages become labeled "Mark–Q overlaps," because such passages are occasionally found within the Gospel of Mark as well as in the same order within the double tradition. John's preaching of repentance (Matt 3:7-10; Luke 3:7-9) and the temptation of Jesus (Matt 4:1-11; Luke 4:1-13) are two examples of these passages. Proponents of the two-source hypothesis respond that the Gospel of Mark and "Q" simply overlapped in these few cases. In an environment in which oral traditions and written traditions about Jesus were simultaneously in circulation, this should not be surprising (*see* TRADITION, ORAL). For example, proponents explain that the authors of Matthew and Luke had more material on John the Baptist than was available from the Gospel of Mark, and they placed it in its logical position. As the number of Mark-Q overlaps increases, so does the potential for some relationship between the Gospel of Mark and this other source. If the author of Mark knows "Q," then the dominant theory is in jeopardy. The author's awareness of "Q" could be another way of supporting J. J. Griesbach's hypothesis, that is, the Markan author's knowledge of the Gospels of Matthew and Luke.

E. Summary

Scholars are confident that the oral environment of the 1st cent. was more complicated than any theory for which the order of the Gospels can account. But the dominant theory of the two-source hypothesis remains convincing as a general working theory. And, the priority of Mark is most commonly held by a clear majority of scholars. Indeed, it is rare to find a scholarly introduction on the NT, an academic commentary on either the Gospel of Matthew or the Gospel of Mark, or a critical historical work on Jesus that does not accept Markan priority.

Why does the order of the Gospels matter? For students of early Christianity, it is a fundamental question of importance. For scholars interested in the historical reconstruction of Jesus, determining the value and order of the sources for this question is essential. For historians of 1st-cent. religious movements, staking a claim on this issue is essential for assessing the elements of various historical developments. Did the earliest Christians hold "high" christological views? Or does "Q" represent another stream within primitive Christianity less cross-centered than Paul?

However scholars may view the chronological sequence of these narratives, it is certain that these various documents represent a vibrant religious movement with varying degrees of distinctions within their attempts to hand on faithful traditions for the following generations. At best, they provide future generations with a potential 1st-cent. dialogue that was fundamental to Christian life in the small villages and communities they have come to represent.

Bibliography: Kurt Aland. *Synopsis Quattuor Evangeliorum.* 15th ed. (1996, 1997); B. C. Butler. *The Originality of Saint Matthew: A Critique of the Two-Document Hypothesis* (1951); David L. Dungan. *A History of the Synoptic Problem: The Canon, the Text, the Composition and the Interpretation of the Gospels* (1999); Johann Gottfried Eichhorn. "Uber die drey ersten Evangelien." *Allgemeine Bibliothek der biblischen Literatur* 5 (1794) 759–996; William R. Farmer. *The Gospel of Jesus: The Pastoral Relevance of the Synoptic Problem* (1994); William R. Farmer. *The Synoptic Problem: A Critical Analysis.* 2nd ed. (1976); A. M. Farrer. "On Dispensing with Q." *Studies in the Gospels.* D. E. Nineham, ed. (1955) 57–88; Mark Goodacre. *The Synoptic Problem: A Way through the Maze* (2001); Michael D. Goulder. *Luke: A New Paradigm* (1989); J. J. Griesbach. *Synopsis Evangeliorum Matthaei, Marci, et Lucae* (1776); Heinrich Julius Holtzmann. *Die Synoptischen Evangelien: Ihr Ursprung und ihr geschichtlicher Charakter* (1863); Karl Lachmann. "De ordine narrationum in evangeliis synopticis." *TSK* 8 (1835) 570–90; Gotthold Ephraim Lessing. "New Hypothesis Concerning the Evangelists Regarded as Merely Human Historians." *Lessing's Theological Writings.* Henry Chadwick, trans. (1956) 65–81; Frans Neirynck, Theo Hanson, and Frans Van Segbroeck. *The Minor Agreements of Matthew and Luke Against Mark with a Cumulative List* (1974); Pheme Perkins. *Introduction to the Synoptic Gospels* (2007); E. P. Sanders and Margaret Davies. *Studying the Synoptic Gospels* (1989); Friedrich Schleiermacher. *Luke: A Critical Study.* C. Thirlwall, trans. (1993); Albert Schweitzer. *The Quest of the Historical Jesus: A Critical Study of Its Progress from Reimarus to Wrede* (1906); Robert Stein. *The Synoptic Problem: An Introduction* (1987); D. F. Strauss. *The Life of Jesus* (1835); B. H. Streeter. *The Four Gospels* (1924); Christopher M. Tuckett. *Q and the History of Early Christianity: Studies on Q* (1996).

EMERSON B. POWERY

SYNTYCHE sin'ti-kee [Συντύχη Syntychē]. A female leader in the Philippian community who may have presided over a house church and who probably also evangelized non-believers (Phil 4:2-3). Paul encourages her to "be of the same mind" with her co-worker Euodia (Phil 4:2).

Bibliography: Ross Shepard Kraemer and Mary Rose D'Angelo. *Women and Christian Origins* (1999); Carolyn Osiek, Margaret Y. MacDonald, and Janet H. Tulloch. *A Woman's Place: House Churches in Earliest Christianity* (2006).

NANCY CALVERT-KOYZIS

SYRACUSE sihr'uh-kyooz [Συράκουσαι Syrakousai]. The city of Syracuse (modern Siracusa) is located in the southeast corner of Sicily on one of the largest natural harbors in the Mediterranean. It was founded—traditionally in 733 BCE—as a Greek settlement by colonists from Corinth. The original settlement was on the island of Ortygia. The monumental 5th-cent. BCE temple of Athena can still be seen built into the walls of the cathedral. Syracuse was the focus of the major Athenian attack (and defeat) on Sicily in 415–413 BCE recorded by Thucydides in his *Peloponnesian War.*

Sicily became a Roman province after the First Punic War (264–241 BCE), though Syracuse technically retained its independence as an ally of Rome. The city unwisely sided with Carthage and, after a long siege, Syracuse was captured by Rome in 211 BCE and became the center for Roman administration. One of the most infamous governors in the time of the Republic was Verres, notorious for his theft of the island's treasures. A Roman colony was established at Syracuse by the emperor Augustus in 21 BCE.

The ship taking Paul from Malta to Italy stopped at Syracuse for three days (Acts 28:12). From Sicily he sailed for Rhegium (Reggio di Calabria) on the Straits of Messina, and from there to Puteoli.

Bibliography: Bonna D. Wescoat and Maxwell L. Anderson. *Syracuse, the Fairest Greek City: Ancient Art from the Museo archeologico regionale 'Paolo Orsi'* (1989); Roger J. A. Wilson. *Sicily Under the Roman Empire: The Archaeology of a Roman Province* (1990).

DAVID W. J. GILL

SYRIA sihr´ee-uh [Συρία Syria]. The geographical area of the present-day state of Syria covers an area from the Mediterranean coast and the mountains that border it: the Amanus in the north, the Jebel Ansariyah through most of its length, and the Lebanon Mountains and Anti-Lebanon in the south. The chain is broken by a plain north of Latakia and the Akkar plain on the border with modern Lebanon. Moving inland, the Orontes Valley winds generally northward through valleys and plateaus from the Homs gap, with Jebel Zawiyeh, the Aleppo plateau, and the plateau of the Syrian desert to the east. The Euphrates River borders the plateau of the Jezireh on the west. The Khabur, Balikh, and their tributaries stretch north from the Euphrates with the Tigris River and the Assyrian heartland on the Iraq border at the northeast. In the south the Oasis of Damascus fed by the Barada and the Ghouta springs is the major center north of the Yarmouk River, with the basaltic Hawran stretching to the desert in the east. Syria can be divided basically into three climatic zones: a temperate zone along the Mediterranean littoral; a semiarid intermediate zone east of the coastal mountain ranges from the Jezireh in the north to the Aleppo Plateau down to the Damascus Oases; and a desert-like steppe to the southeast. The geographical extent of early Syrian state entities varied through time.

Historically this area at times is occupied by one or more political states or many independent cities with dependent areas that form very much of a border area culturally and politically between the major powers in the east, north, and south, at least from the Bronze Age through the Islamic period. Archaeologically, the long prehistoric sequence culminates in the Geometric Keberan and the Natufian at the end of the Epipaleolithic. Many of the essential features present in Neolithic settlements develop gradually when the balance between hunting wild animals and gathering wild grains is shifting to a landscape populated by an increasing number of habitation sites. At this time hunters and gatherers are starting to turn to domestication of certain species of animals, primarily sheep and goats, and plants, particularly wheat and barley, to provide their subsistence.

A. Earliest Periods: From Hunter-Gatherers to Early Villages to Earliest Cities
B. Beginning of the Bronze Age: Expanding Urbanism
C. Early Bronze Age III and IV: From City-States to Early Empires
D. Middle Bronze Age: Retrenchment to Struggles between Super-States
E. Late Bronze Age: Growing and Competing Empires
F. Iron Age I: New State Beginnings from the Collapse of Late Bronze Age Systems
G. Iron Age II: From Growing States to Ever Larger Empires

H. Persian Period: Last Major Empire before Alexander the Great's Conquests
Bibliography

A. Earliest Periods: From Hunter-Gatherers to Early Villages to Earliest Cities

As the Neolithic shifts from aceramic to ceramic phases, many cultural changes are regional and uneven in their spread and development. Architecture tends generally from rounded dwellings to rectilinear architecture. The use of gypsum and lime plasters is one of many features that demonstrate increasing technological capability. Plaster is used for architectural purposes but also for a time, and possibly in specific locations, for containers, when a shift is made from primarily perishable baskets and wooden vessels to common use of pottery vessels. Pottery was used already in the Neolithic for animal and human figurines. Different traditions using ceramic containers develop early with dark-face burnished wares common in the west and elaborate Halaf-painted wares in the north. By the end of the 6th millennium BCE, elaborate forms and decorations are distinctive features of the ceramic assemblages. Distinctive burial practices, evidenced also in the south, include the custom of separate burial of the skull from the rest of the body and the decoration of the skull with plaster and sometimes paint and other materials. Distinctive flint and bone tools and polished stone vessels show exceptional competence in production techniques at the end of a long tradition before it seems to atrophy and almost vanish, possibly as metal tools come into use.

Development through the next phase, the Chalcolithic, is also uneven, with limited documentation. The "Halaf" tradition, with its distinctive polychrome painted pottery and "tholos" structures, covers a broad geographical area from north Syria, southeast Anatolia, northern Iraq, and northeastern Iran, eventually extending to the west and gradually giving way to an equally wide-spread "Ubaid" culture. Significant steps in the development of urban societies are demonstrated at this time by differentiation in architecture between domestic and apparently "monumental" structures.

The end of the period, the 4th millennium BCE, shows significant advances in urbanism, either stimulated by or in reaction to influences from southern Mesopotamia. Questions concerning the founding, flourishing, and declining of "Uruk colonies" at various locations along the middle Euphrates is much discussed. The new urban development in northern Syria is particularly well documented in the Euphrates Valley, and also radiates out from the Euphrates and follows the river north into Turkey. Excavations conducted at Habuba Kabire/Tell Kanas reveal a town with an organized pattern of streets with drainage systems, separate areas for monumental buildings, and an elaborate fortification system with gateways set in a triple line of walls. At nearby Jebel Arudah, a series of temples surrounded by a crenellated wall and separated from well-built domestic structures was excavated. Characteristic "Uruk" pottery is found at both sites, including the typical beveled-rim bowl and a specific reserved slip decoration on jars.

At Jebel Arudah tablets and bullae with cylinder-seal impressions and tablets with the earliest written notation demonstrate that the Euphrates sites are as sophisticated as the type site of Uruk. Other sites have yielded limited information on this period so far, but have provided a basic cultural sequence and points of reference. One of the notable features is the use of quite sophisticated copper technology. As a result, it is possible to assess the role of foreign influences as opposed to local traditions and local innovations. The cultures of many areas of the Near East attained a remarkable stage of crystallization by the middle of the 4th millennium BCE. Administrative structures were created to exploit and facilitate exchange of commodities, supervise agriculture and animal husbandry systems, control technological and other modes of production, and often make their influence felt over considerable distances.

B. Beginning of the Bronze Age:
Expanding Urbanism

Even less well documented are the beginning phases of the Early Bronze Age, around 3000 BCE. It would seem unlikely that the developments in urbanism at the end of the 4th millennium BCE did not continue from the late phase of the Chalcolithic through to the exceptionally well documented Early Bronze Age III and IV, all over Syria. Few extensive archaeological exposures exist so far but enough is available to give us a basic idea of the assemblages involved. Two distinctive traditions develop in the eastern and western areas of Syria. "Ninnivite" sequences in the northeast of Syria were characterized by simple temple structures and rounded storage buildings, by distinctive cup and jar forms, and by painted, incised, and "excised" decoration. Many sites in the northwest and in the middle Euphrates provide characteristic ceramics, namely the beginning of plain-simple wares, a distinctive variety of reserved slip wares, and red-black burnished wares. Cups and bowls with cyma-recta profiles and diminutive, low bases are the hallmark of Early Bronze II.

C. Early Bronze Age III and IV: From City-States to
Early Empires

By the middle of the 3rd millennium BCE, Early Bronze Age civilization flourished at many sites throughout the country. Many of the cultural features characteristic of the second half of the 3rd millennium BCE may be traced back for centuries, possibly even to the beginning of the millennium, as excavations continue but currently there is a disconnect for lack of information. It is difficult to summarize briefly the extensive body of information available from the middle of the 3rd millennium to the beginning of the 2nd. In the past three decades excavations on many tells have added to our knowledge. Extremely revealing is the presence of many Early Bronze Age sites like Rawda documented in surveys on the desert fringe from near Salamiya south to Mishrife. Few sites have been excavated in the Homs, Damascus, or Hauran areas to demonstrate the distinctive cultural features of these areas.

Not only are regional cultural assemblages present in extensive detail, but larger exposures provide a better understanding of the planning and organization of sites, many tombs have been found, and a new dimension is present, an extensive collection of written documentation from Mari, Ebla, and Nabadu. The material culture seems to maintain the earlier dichotomy between east and west. In addition, the Euphrates River Valley from Hariri to the Turkish border is united by distinctive features with clear parallels to southern Mesopotamian traditions. A disparity in wealth is evident between palatial and temple buildings and simple domestic structures. Sculptured statues and stelae, seal impressions, inlayed plaques and furniture, metal tools, and weapons, in particular, trace a sequence parallel to the late Early Dynastic, Sargonid, and Ur III periods in Mesopotamia. Stone vessels of Egyptian manufacture, some of which carried the royal names of Chephren, Pepi I, and Pepi II, rulers of the Fourth and Sixth Egyptian Dynasties, were found in Palace G at Ebla. Plain simple, buff, or tan wares are common throughout with specific wares and forms providing regional or temporal indicators. Also present are grey-ware jars, bowls and cups, red-banded jars, corrugated cups, corrugated jars with cylinder-seal impressions on the rim, band painted and incised goblets, and metallic wares of many varieties.

A new historical geography is emerging for the Bronze Age in the Khabur area with excavations at Mozan, identified with Urkish, and Braq, probably to be identified with Nawar. Hurrian ethnic features are documented starting in the Sargonid period in the northern Khabur. Semitic populations continue to be documented consistently throughout the remaining area. The texts from Mari and Ebla indicate a fierce rivalry between two major powers that controlled large portions of Syria (*see* EBLA TEXTS; MARI TEXTS, LETTERS). Tablets provide insights into political situations from the end of the Early Dynastic through the Ur III periods. Particularly intriguing are the indications of control of a broad area under the Mesopotamian Sargonid dynasty and a lasting effect on the area when that control weakened. Mesopotamian texts indicate an early empire created particularly under the rulers Sargon and Naram Sin. Everyday commercial transactions are documented in the texts, as are mentions of the major centers on trade routes, records of farm production and industrial manufacture of essential goods, and many other details.

The end of the period seems to show limited occupation in the coastal areas and increased occupation on the desert fringes. Each area seems to have its own peculiarities at the end of the Early Bronze Age. In some places like the Orontes Valley, at Qarqur, probably Asharna, and in the Amuq, the Early Bronze Age traditions seem to continue into the 2nd millennium and possibly overlap with the beginning of the Middle Bronze Age elsewhere. The same may be true in the Euphrates Valley but it is hard to distinguish in the ceramics. Like Qarqur, Hadidi, Hariri, Mardikh, and other sites seem to show continuous occupation from the 21st to the 18th cent. BCE. The period of the Shakkinaku at Mari continues into the 2nd millennium. A similar continuation seems to be true at Bi'a and possibly farther along the Euphrates at Hadidi and elsewhere. By the time the Middle Bronze Age tradition is well established in the 18th cent. BCE, ceramics, settlement patterns and material culture have changed dramatically.

D. Middle Bronze Age: Retrenchment to Struggles between Super-States

Ceramic materials are again the basic cultural evidence to block out the beginning of the Middle Bronze Age. In the Amuq, Cilician, and Khabur areas, distinctive painted decoration styles became characteristic features of local ceramic assemblages. Along the Euphrates, painted decoration, as was the case earlier, is extremely rare. The ceramic sequence is defined by specific rim profiles and vessel forms and comb-incised decoration. The art style reflected on cylinder seals and sculpture carry on conventions that go back to Mesopotamian Early Dynastic glyptic. A decline in occupation in the Jezireh continues through most of the millennium. Selenkahiye and Sweihat in the Euphrates Valley were abandoned and at Hadidi and Munbaqat there are significant reductions in the sizes of the sites. The same is true at Judaideh and Chatal Hüyük in the Amuq, while the major site of Ta'yinat is abandoned and settlement shifted 2 km south to Atchana (Alalakh). At Hama and Qarqur in the Orontes Valley basic ceramic assemblages are documented but little is known about the size and organization of the sites. Important archaeological sequences were excavated at Hadidi, Halawa, Habuba, and Qanas in the Tabqa dam salvage area of the Euphrates. Major palace structures were erected over large buildings of the Early Bronze Age at Hariri at the beginning of the 2nd millennium but the overall size of the site is unclear. At this time a large urban settlement including temples, palaces and tombs, was surrounded by a massive defense system at Mardikh.

The major collections of written materials found in the palace archives at Mari are a rich source of information on the interaction of city-states from the Khabur area, Assyria, and Iran to the northeast, Mesopotamia to the southeast, the Aleppo area to the west, and possibly sites farther south and as far as the Mediterranean littoral. Also, an important relationship with a significant component of non-urban populations was illustrated. A "middle" chronology has commonly been used to organize the cultural sequences of the Middle and Late Bronze Ages and provides a basis for the relative chronology of the previous periods. Recent arguments to shift the Mesopotamian dates almost a century later, by adjusting the date of Hammurabi from1792–1750 BCE in the middle chronology to 1696–1654 BCE for the low chronology, may provide a better fit for the Syrian sequence.

Mari tablets show that the ruler Yahdun Lim (1825–1810 vs. 1729–1714 BCE) was followed by his son Zimri Lim as king of Mari (1782–1759 vs. 1686–1663 BCE) after a period of external domination of Mari under Yasmah Adad who had been installed there by his father Shamshi Adad (1815–1782 vs. 1719–1688 BCE) the ruler of Assyria. Zimri-Lim's rule was brought to an end by Hammurabi of Babylon in the thirty-third year of Hammurabi's reign. Excavation at Leilan, identified as Shamshi Adad's capital city of Shubat Enlil, and the tablets from Mari demonstrate the vitality of the Assyrian state at this time. With the fall of Mari, political power shifted north along the Euphrates to Ashara (Khana), documented by recent excavations. Contemporary records have been excavated in western Syria in the level VII palace at Tell Atchana (Alalakh).

A rich material culture has also been brought to light at Hariri, Mardikh, and Atchana. The material represented on cylinder-seals, plaques, sculpture, and murals documents a distinctive style for the period. International influences are clearly evident in the incorporation of Mesopotamian, Egyptian, or Anatolian motifs. The destruction of Babylon by the Hittite ruler Mursilis I put an end to the Old Babylonian period in Mesopotamia around 1600 (vs. 1499) BCE. It followed a victorious campaign through Syria and down along the Euphrates, in effect bringing the Middle Bronze Age to an end.

E. Late Bronze Age: Growing and Competing Empires

International interaction with Syria was more intense during the Late Bronze Age than in any earlier period. Egyptian temple reliefs, particularly some attributed to Thutmoses I and Thutmose III, refer to campaigns into north Syria, with Hadidi (Azu) and Munbaqat (Ekalte) among the cities mentioned along the Euphrates. Cuneiform tablets and other documentation for this period come from a greater number of sites and paint a vivid, though still frustratingly laconic picture. Egyptian (Amarna), Hittite (Bohazkoi), and Mesopotamian sources also provide significant information. In a series of increasingly larger empires in the west, Hurrian domination gives way to Hittite control and then competition between Egypt and Hatti. A Middle Assyrian Empire expanded in the east at the expense of the Hittites and Hurrians. Atchana, Hadidi, and Munbaqat provide information for the end of the Mitannian period. Portions of Mitannian palace and/or temple buildings have been excavated at Braq, al Hamadiya, and Bi'a. Domestic occupation and monumental buildings have also been excavated at numerous sites.

Archives from the beginning of the Late Bronze Age provide stratified seal impressions and insights into Hurrian cultural practices, as well as a wealth of personal names peculiar to each region. The polished glyptic style of the previous centuries was modified and a class of common cylinder seals, often faience or frit, was produced with abstracted, simplified renderings that became very common over a wide area from Egypt and Palestine to Iran and Turkey. Distinctive fine "Nuzi" and "Atchana" luxury ceramic wares are also hallmarks of the Mitannian period. The art style of the beginning of the period is represented by a few pieces of sculpture like the statue of Idrimi at Atchana, a crude seated statue in a palace at Braq, and very crude basalt human figures at Hadidi, Atchana, Hama, and elsewhere.

The newly found archives at Mishrife (Qatna) provide a local perspective on the confrontation between Hatti and Egypt in central Syria at the end of the 15th and the 14th cent. BCE. The Egyptian view is documented in the archives from Amarna in Egypt and from Egyptian temple inscriptions. Some records from Ugarit and Ras Ibn Hani overlap this period as well, and others are tied into the final chapter of the Hittite Empire. The use of multi-storied buildings demonstrates the existence of a compacted urban settlement at Ugarit, which probably was the case in other urban centers at the time. Certainly the art and architectural styles were lively, inventive, and flourishing, but the flowering was short-lived and the old traditions continued on as underlying constants. The dual temples at Emar, the continuation of the use of the temples at Munbaqat, and the variation of temple types in the long sequence of temples at Atchana (with the dominance in the traditional local axial types) are excellent examples of such continuity. Some architecture shows marked Hittite influence in several of the temples at Atchana, in fortification, gate, and tomb construction at Ras Shamra, and in domestic buildings at Meskene.

A wealth of fine arts and other materials were found at Ugarit and its dependencies, Ras Ibn Hani and Minet el Beidha, in addition to the tablet collections. As a major commercial center on the coast, Ugarit's international contacts were extensive. Egyptian influence made a strong impression on the art style of Ugarit, clearly evident in palatial ivories and cylinder seal impressions. Hittite motifs were common in the last centuries of the Late Bronze Age, but Mesopotamian traditions and motifs maintained primary importance. Imported pottery from Cyprus and the Aegean area is common at Ugarit and its dependencies, and occurs at many other north Syrian sites. Despite these influences, the hand of the local artist is clear in the selection and shaping of foreign ideas and the choice of themes of their products. Beautifully carved seated statues flanking the entrance of a rich royal tomb at Mishrife (Qatna) are rare large-size art objects. Very common, on the other hand, are examples of minor arts: copper, bronze, gold and silver objects, and clay figurines, mold impressed plaques,

carved ivories, faience vessels, beads, and amulets. Middle Assyrian glyptic is well represented at Sheikh Hamad, Fakhariya, and other sites. Hittite seals with their typical motifs and hieroglyphic inscription are found at a number of sites in northern Syria.

Religious texts from a temple area at Ugarit have provided important comparative material for the study of biblical texts by revealing temple rituals, a complicated pantheon of deities, and a rich collection of important mythological texts in an Ugaritic language with many similarities to archaic Hebrew. Though the major international language remained Akkadian, a new, basically alphabetic cuneiform script was used for most religious texts and for many regional administrative documents. The script marks a significant stage in the development of writing.

Texts from Ugarit, Emar, and elsewhere document the end of the Late Bronze Age and the dramatic diplomatic and military activities at the end of the Hittite Empire. A major disruption is documented archaeologically with devastation and destruction common at many sites in Syria. The extent of the destruction caused by Aegean peoples to sites along the coast and the extent to which they founded their own new settlements there is unclear. Thirteenth and 12th cent. BCE archives at the Assyrian city of Sheikh Hamad on the lower Khabur mention Shalmaneser I, and archives at Chuera in the Khabur triangle and Khirbet esh-Shenef on the Balikh mention Tukulti Ninurta I. They show the strength and influence of the Assyrian rulers in confrontation and eventual political domination of the Hittites at the end of the period.

F. Iron Age I: New State Beginnings from the Collapse of Late Bronze Age Systems

The beginning of the Iron Age has often been called a "dark age." Recent excavations give us a better understanding of the period, so the use of that term is now difficult to justify in many regions. Clearly many Bronze Age cities were destroyed and new Aegean elements become an integral part of Iron I culture. How much of a break with the past occurred is very much a question, since Iron I sequences spanning the period have now been excavated at numerous sites. There are clear indications that several Late Bronze Age states continued in the west, particularly at Carchemish and Aleppo/Amuq. The site of 'Ain Dara in the Afrin Valley west of Aleppo was occupied at the end of the Bronze Age and apparently continued through much of the Iron Age. Recent excavations on the Aleppo citadel have uncovered the venerated temple of the storm god with astounding, large decorated orthostats on its exterior walls. One inscription on the reliefs mentions an apparent 12th-cent. ruler of Aleppo whose kingdom extended into the Amuq. Middle Assyrian kingdom continues for some time in the 12th and 11th cent. BCE in the east and the Assyrians used the term Hattina to refer to the area it confronted in the west. With the gradual dissipation of foreign state domination starting at the end of the 13th cent. BCE, the 12th cent. BCE was clearly a period of instability and reorganization on many levels. There seems to be a general shift from territorial states to smaller regional entities.

Ceramic production at sites near the coast showed a major change with monochrome decoration and specific cup and jar forms reflecting Aegean models of the 12th cent. BCE and earlier. This pottery has been excavated on the coast and farther south in Philistine cities. Further inland, there was a drastic reduction in the number of inhabited sites and at the few sites that exist painted pottery is rare. Relatively few Iron I sites have been identified in other areas of Syria so far.

G. Iron Age II: From Growing States to Ever Larger Empires

Regional state structures were rebuilt, reformatting essentially preexisting social, linguistic, and artistic elements and incorporating new features. Many independent city-states seem to have developed across Syria by the end of the 11th cent. BCE. The Bronze Age pattern of struggle between rival cities and coalitions resumed. In periods of strength, states extended their control over their neighbors or formed alliances with them to meet a growing threat from a developing and expanding Neo-Assyrian state. New social and political configurations, like the influence of Aramean elites and royalty, became entrenched and gradually played a leading role in Syrian culture. Aramaic gained in importance as a spoken and written language, and gradually played a significant role throughout the Assyrian and subsequent empires. The city-states of northwest Syria were included in a broader culture area with cities in Cilicia and southeastern Anatolia reaching as far as Malatya and Arslantepe, and also extending south to Damascus. Features of Hittite tradition, like Leuwian hieroglyphic inscriptions or Hittite artistic conventions in sculpture, continue at Carchemish, 'Ain Dara, Aleppo, Hama, and elsewhere. The term "Neo-Hittite" is often used to designate political and cultural features of northwest Syria at this time. As the economies of the area flourished, the local rulers expended some of their wealth on new buildings and artistic endeavors.

Major Iron Age centers were established at Ahmar (Til Barsib), Jerablus (Carchemish), and Aleppo in the west. The spectacular temple at 'Ain Dara was reused over a period of centuries with elaborate sculptural decoration, including files of animals and dignitaries on the temple walls and surrounding platform, and rows of monstrous lions and sphinxes guarding both the entrances to the temple and the holy of holies. A range of styles is evident, from those with earlier Hittite features, to local art styles to those with Assyrian influenced features. The direct access floor plan continues the long-standing Syrian tradition, while the meter-long footprints on the door sills are a unique feature. Through almost four centuries of the Iron Age several

long stretches of walls were decorated with sculptured orthostats at Carchemish. Reliefs also decorated the "hilani" complex and royal citadel at Halaf. Many of the Halaf sculptures are notable for their awkward proportions and remarkable combination of stylistic features. Many other sites have also yielded isolated sculptures of the 10th and early 9th cent. BCE. The Syrian artistic development, as part of a regional manifestation, progressed through a series of phases influenced by the incorporation of styles that became more and more subsumed into a new fabric created under Assyrian domination.

Neo-Assyrian rulers encounter and eventually absorb several opposing coalitions of cities in northwest Syria in the 10th and 9th cent. BCE, generally moving from east to west and then south. Major opposition to the Assyrian advance was organized by various states over a period of time. Some sites show long habitation sequences and some exhibit monumental architecture. In many cases precision is lacking on the length of use for specific phases and establishing the contemporaneity of individual building phases is often not possible, even when inscriptions mentioning Assyrian rulers are present. The situation is complicated when monumental sculpture is reused, and early reports and excavation techniques make it difficult to place artifacts clearly in their original context.

Written materials are limited and a preponderance of these are royal inscriptions. It is still difficult to place this information clearly in the context of the written evidence available from Egypt, Greece, Assyria, Babylonia, Palestine, and the biblical record. The statue of Adad-it'i/Hadad-yis'i found at Fakhariyah (probably dating to the middle of the 9th cent. BCE) shows considerable Assyrian influence but the awkwardness of the earlier sculptures is also obvious. The bilingual inscription on the statue in Aramaic and Assyrian seems intended to address different audiences. On current evidence, the area of Fakhariyah (Sikan)/Halaf (Gozan) does not maintain the tradition of using Luwian hieroglyphic script as is the case at Carchemish, Ta'yinat, Malatya, and Hama. The monuments of Kilamuwa of Zinjirli (Samal) demonstrate the characteristic art style common in the region.

The political situation in north Syria changed after Shalmaneser III's confrontation at Qarqar with the Aramean, Israelite, Ammonite, etc., coalition in 853 BCE and subsequently. Portions of citadel complexes have been excavated at Hama, Ta'yinat, Zinjirli, and Sakjegözü at this time with many featuring distinctive "hilani" buildings characterized by pillared entrance porticos and main rooms at right angles to the axis of the porticos, and also temple buildings. Strong Assyrian influence is clear and the associated monumental inscriptions of the local rulers indicate that they were allowed a degree of freedom to maintain their local traditions and independent status. A stronger reliance on Assyrian artistic tradition to the east at Ajaja on the Khabur is clearly demonstrated in the decoration of the gateway with flanking lions in a style characteristic of late 9th/early 8th cent. Assyria. By the end of the 8th cent. BCE, Assyria had founded its administration of northwest Syria at Ahmar on the Euphrates. That site is well known archaeologically for its palace decorated with elaborate Assyrian style murals, mirroring in polychrome the Assyrian palace reliefs of the time. Before the city's decline, merchant and elite residences in the lower town were decorated with black and white pebble mosaics and were furnished with a full representation of Assyrian ceramic wares and decorative arts of the 7th cent. BCE.

The long cultural development is shown in other art factual evidence in addition to artistic production and architecture. Red-slip decoration on a range of vessel forms, particularly bowls, platters, and jugs, is a ceramic hallmark of the period. Painted, often polychrome decoration replaces the characteristic monochrome painted pottery of the earliest centuries of the Iron Age. International contacts increase as the Iron Age continues. Trade and exchange increases with clear competition between Phoenicians, Greeks, and Cypriots. Imports from Cyprus and the Aegean become more frequent through the 8th and 7th cent. BCE. So far, there is little evidence that Greek imports reached very far inland in quantity from places like Al Mina on the coast.

Most remarkable for the end of the Assyrian period is the material excavated at the site of Sheikh Hamad on the Khabur. Palatial buildings with impressive sculptures and painted wall decorations were used for administrative and residential purposes in the 7th and 6th cent. BCE. Tablets with correspondence and administrative documentation of the last days of the Assyrian Empire were excavated in these buildings. New buildings over this destruction contained tablets of the Neo-Babylonian period.

The Assyrian Empire fell to a coalition of Medes and Babylonians. The Neo-Babylonian Empire quickly consolidated its victories with apparent continuation of earlier administrative structures and boundaries to the full extent of the earlier empire, down into Egypt. The shift to Persian control was also swift and complete with the empire spreading to gain a strong grip on Egypt, Anatolia, and Iran.

H. Persian Period: Last Major Empire before Alexander the Great's Conquests

The Persian period is becoming better defined throughout Syria but it is still not very well attested. The assemblages and sequences, where they exist, are still enigmatic and considerable refinement is necessary to differentiate Late Assyrian, Neo-Babylonian, and Persian ceramics; similarly, it is difficult to distinguish the end of the Persian period from the Hellenistic. The few administrative and official residential buildings reused fortifications and contemporary records indicate efficient, seemingly unobtrusive administration. Arwad-Amrit, like the Phoenician cities to the south, represents a major commercial and industrial complex. The urban area of the city stretched for miles along the seacoast. Transitional aspects of the Persian period are typified by the minting of some of the earliest coinage along the Phoenician cities; the production of many sculptures in a style heavily influenced by archaic Greek and Cypriote models; the common appearance of distinctive horse and rider, and also "astarte" figurines; and the remains of an early hippodrome. The Persian kings relied heavily on shipping through all of the Phoenician ports and the navies of these cities for military purposes. Wide-ranging international trade, diplomacy, and warfare welded a poorly appreciated empire that was absorbed into Alexander's empire in the late 4th cent. BCE. *See* ARAM, ARAMEANS.

Bibliography: P. M. M. G. Akkermann and G. Schwartz. *The Archaeology of Syria: From Complex Hunter-Gatherers to Early Urban Societies (ca 16,000–399 BC)* (2003); G. Bunnens, ed. *Essays on Syria in the Iron Age* (2000); E. Lipinski. *The Aramaeans: Their Ancient History, Culture, Religion* (2000); P. Paolo Matthiae, M. van Loon, and H. Weiss, eds. *Resurrecting the Past: A Joint Tribute to Adnan Bounni* (1990).

RUDOLPH H. DORNEMANN

SYRIAC APOCRYPHAL PSALMS. *See* PSALMS, NON-CANONICAL.

SYRIAC BARUCH. *See* BARUCH, SECOND BOOK OF.

SYRIAC LANGUAGE. *See* ARAMAIC, ARAMAISM.

SYRIAC MENANDER. *See* MENANDER.

SYRIAC VERSIONS. *See* VERSIONS, SYRIAC.

SYRO-PALESTINIAN ARCHAEOLOGY. *See* ARCHAEOLOGY.

SYROPHOENICIAN WOMAN si´roh-fi-nish´uhn [Συροφοινίκισσα Syrophoinikissa]. In Mark 7:24-30, Jesus goes away "to the region of Tyre," where he is met by a woman of "Syrophoenician origin" (**Syrophoinikissa**). Phoenicia was a region north of Galilee with major cities named Tyre and Sidon. Tyre was a bitter enemy of the Jews (Josephus, *Ag. Ap.* 1.70; *J.W.* 2.478), so that "the region of Tyre" (7:24) is a potentially hostile territory for Jesus. In Matthew's version (Matt 15:21-28), the woman is identified as a "Canaanite," a people associated with Sidon (Gen 10:19); with this anachronistic designation, Matthew may be alluding to even older conflicts (e.g., Exod 33:2; Josh 3:10; Judg 1:1) between the Israelites and Canaanites.

The Syrophoenician woman bows at Jesus' feet to beg him to cast out a demon from her daughter, but quite abruptly and unexpectedly, Jesus dismisses her: "Let the children be fed first, for it is not fair to take the children's food and throw it to the dogs" (Mark 7:27// Matt 15:26). Jesus' response is disturbing, even shocking to readers; nowhere else does he speak in such a demeaning way to someone who needs help (e.g., contrast Mark 5:1-20). Moreover, Jesus calls the woman and her people DOGs. Dogs are unclean scavengers that eat filth and lick up blood (Exod 22:31; 1 Kgs 21:19, 23, 24; Prov 26:11; Matt 7:6); therefore, *dog* is a term of insult (1 Sam 17:43; 2 Sam 9:8; 2 Kgs 8:13; Phil 3:2; Rev 22:15).

Interpreters have suggested various reasons for Jesus' uncharacteristically harsh response. Perhaps he objects to a woman approaching him—but Mark cites other examples of women who approach, speak to, and even touch Jesus (e.g., the hemorrhaging woman [Mark 5:27//Luke 8:46] and the anointing woman [Mark 14:3-9//Luke 7:37-38]). Perhaps, then, Jesus is testing her. Maybe, because he is in hostile territory, he is reacting to her people's oppressive treatment of the Jews (Ringe). Perhaps he is upset by the news of John the Baptist's execution (6:17-29), or perhaps he is simply exasperated, because he "did not want anyone to know he was there" (7:24).

However, for the purposes of this story, Jesus' reference to "children" and "dogs" suggests that he rejects the woman's request because she is a Gentile. This fact is so important that Mark indicates her identity three times: Jesus is in non-Jewish territory (7:24), the woman is a "Gentile" (7:26) and "of Syrophoenician origin" (7:26). Jews regarded Gentiles as outsiders because they worshiped idols and did not observe the Law (*see* NATIONS). That Jesus refers to "the children's food" is no accident; the Jews did not eat with Gentiles because the Gentiles did not keep Jewish DIETARY LAWS.

Undaunted by Jesus' rejection, the Syrophoenician woman replies, "Sir, even the dogs under the table eat the children's crumbs" (7:28). The story does not indicate the manner in which the woman says these words, although there have been many suggestions—humbly, imploringly, dialogically, cleverly, boldly, or angrily— but the result is that Jesus changes his mind: "For saying that you may go. The demon has left your daughter" (7:29; compare Matt 15:28, where Jesus heals the daughter because of the woman's great faith).

A disturbing aspect of the story for many readers is that Jesus seems to imply that Gentiles are not welcome at God's table. To the contrary, according to Jewish tradition, the Gentiles will be included at a great banquet that God hosts (Isa 25:6-8; see also Isa 2:2-4; Jer 3:17; 4:2; Mic 4:1-4; Zech 2:11; 8:20-23; Matt 8:11). This story may reflect a later development in Jewish-Gentile relations in the early church, because TABLE FELLOWSHIP was a hotly contested issue (e.g., Gal 2:11-14). The Gospel of Mark, written some thirty or forty years after Jesus' ministry, perhaps includes this story at this point in the Gospel to indicate a turning point, when the Jewish messiah decides it is time to include the Gentiles, in fulfillment of the prophets' visions of the messianic age when the nations will come to the banquet (i.e., even if the Jews are fed first, the Gentiles still will be fed). In support of this theory, it is significant that just before his encounter with the Syrophoenician woman, Jesus discusses eating with "unclean hands" (Mark 7:1-23) and tells the Jewish leaders that nothing from "outside" can defile a person (thus, he declares all foods clean; Mark 7:19; compare Acts 10:9-16). This boundary-breaking statement sets the stage for the "outsider" (the Syrophoenician woman) to challenge Jesus. As a result, Jesus, who eats with outsiders such as tax collectors and sinners (Mark 2:13-20) now welcomes Gentiles to the table. Mark reinforces this development a few verses later when Jesus enters "the region of the Decapolis" (Mark 7:31)—Gentile territory—and miraculously feeds 4,000 people (Matt 15:32-39//Mark 8:1-9).

Bibliography: John Donahue and Daniel Harrington. *The Gospel of Mark.* SP 2 (2002); Joel Marcus. *Mark 1–8.* AB 27 (2000); Sharon H. Ringe. "A Gentile Woman's Story, Revisited: Rereading Mark 7.24-31." *A Feminist Companion to Mark.* Amy-Jill Levine and Marianne Blickenstaff, eds. (2004) 79–100.

MARIANNE BLICKENSTAFF

SYRTIS suhr'tuhs [Σύρτις Syrtis]. The Greek name for two gulfs off the northern coast of Africa between Cyrene and Carthage: the Greater Syrtis, now called the Gulf of Sidra; and the Lesser Syrtis, now called the Gulf of Gabes. Ancient sailors feared these treacherous shallow waters. Acts 27:17 states that while Paul was being taken to Rome, a storm struck the ship near Crete, and the sailors feared running aground in these gulfs.

SEAN D. BURKE

SYSTEMATIC THEOLOGY. Systematic theology seeks to discover and expound a coherent vision of biblical and traditional doctrine in the context of contemporary culture. The term "systematic theology" is typically used by Christian scholars to denote a branch of theology that seeks to organize, clarify, and plumb the meaning of central biblical and traditional doctrines, offering helpful revisions where necessary. Like the word *science*, *theology* can designate both a set of doctrines and the process by which these doctrines are received, examined, and expounded. We can think of theology as a discipline seeking to know God in conceptual, spiritual, and practical ways. There is no reason that scholars from other religions could not use the designation "systematic theology" (e.g., Jewish or Muslim theologians). Here for the sake of simplicity we assume a Christian approach.

Systematic theology differs from biblical studies and biblical theology, but it is essentially related to them (*see* BIBLICAL THEOLOGY). Christian theology is a response to the word of God, and thus rooted and grounded in the witness of Holy Scripture. There can be no proper systematic theology without careful biblical exegesis and biblical theology. While systematic theology draws upon biblical studies and biblical theology it must also go beyond them, developing the core teachings of Christian faith in conceptual, practical, and spiritual dimensions for women and men today.

The impulse to develop biblical faith in an organized and thematic way is a very old one in Christianity. Early on in Christian witness, worship, education (catechism), preaching, and apologetics, pastor-theologians began to develop summaries of Christian teaching. Some of these were quite brief (like those baptismal summaries that eventually became the Apostles' Creed; *see* CREED). Others were longer summaries for the learned. Examples of early work in systematic theology include Origen, *On First Principles* (3rd cent. CE); Irenaeus, *Against Heresies* (2nd cent. CE); Augustine, *The City of God* (5th cent. CE); Gregory of Nyssa, *Great Catechetical Oration* (4th cent. CE); and John of Damascus, *The Orthodox Faith* (8th cent. CE). The practice continued and developed, and later classic texts of systematic theology include Thomas Aquinas, *Summa Theologiae* (13th cent.); John Calvin, *Institutes of the Christian Religion* (16th cent.); F. D. E. Schleiermacher, *The Christian Faith* (19th cent.); and Karl Barth, *Church Dogmatics* (20th cent.). What these works have in common is an attempt to give a thematic overview of Christian teachings in dialog with the issues of the day, often sparked by practical needs such as the correction of heresies, the education of Christian leaders, the presentation of Christian faith over against alternative worldviews (e.g., pagan, Muslim, or scientific-materialist), and the general need of Christian preachers and leaders for a faithful summary of Christian doctrine.

The term *systema* (Latin) was not used for theology until the early modern period and was simply one way among others of speaking of a summary, compendium, handbook, elements, or institutes of the Christian faith. This variety of terms indicates a desire to provide an organized and thematic expression of biblical, traditional Christian doctrines. Among classic Christian authors the goal was always to develop biblical faith and explore its meaning and structure, not to impose a constructed system upon biblical religion. Yet in seeking to bring biblical, traditional doctrines into conversation with contemporary thought, systematic theology has always drawn upon other disciplines including philosophy, politics, and literature. Aquinas is an excellent example of the use of philosophy in developing a systematic theology that does not neglect the biblical witness. These other disciplines provide a conversation partner for the theologian in her calling to engage contemporary culture with the gospel in a reasonable manner. As systematic theology developed over the centuries some authors journeyed rather far from biblical theology, drawing more fully upon philosophy, science, and contemporary thought. Paul Tillich's *Systematic Theology* (mid-20th cent.) is a recent example of this trend.

As a general rule, however, systematic theologians seek to discover—not simply impose or construct—the inner coherence of biblical faith. There are broadly three types of coherence in systematic theology, which we can illustrate from theology's most difficult problem: evil and suffering. The first type is logical coherence. This type allows for a very loose order, since sentences are logically coherent just in cases where they do not contradict each other. Theology is a truth-seeking discipline of the mind. No Christian theologian wants a theology that is incoherent since nothing incoherent can be true. But mere lack of incoherence does not provide much order. An example of logical coherence is the free will defense in responding to the problem of evil. This is a defense rather than a theodicy just because it merely shows that the existence of evil is not logically incompatible with classical theism. A second and more organizing type is narrative coherence. The doctrines of the faith are organized like a story, in a historical form. A great example of this is Augustine's *The City of God* with its overall theme of the triumph of God over the evil and suffering that are so typical of the earthly city. The third broad type of coherence is thematic fit and topical order. This type of fit or order seeks to discover a conceptual fit or congruence among doctrines. Thematic unity is not, strictly speaking, logical so much as aesthetic: it seeks a beautiful and harmonious arrangement in our practical, spiritual, and conceptual knowledge of God and of all other things as they relate to God. In responding to the problem of evil, a specific theology of suffering (including the suffering of God) would be an example of this third type of coherence.

Systematic theology seeks not only coherence among the doctrines of the faith, but the contemporary meaning and import of that faith for the broader culture of our times. Theology has an important role in service to the worship and mission of the church. For this reason, systematic theologians are not content to simply organize the teachings of the past. Rather, they very often propose revised notions of traditional and biblical doctrines, grounded in the larger witness of Scripture and the classical Christian tradition, but also creating new understandings of these doctrines in the light of modern-day reason and experience.

ALAN G. PADGETT

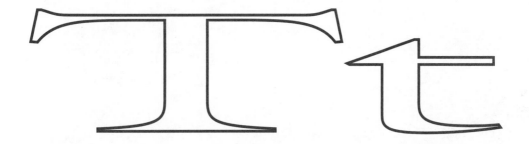

TAANACH tay´uh-nak [תַּעֲנַךְ taʿnakh]. Tell Taʿannek occupies a commanding position on the last line of ridges of the central hill country along the Esdraelon Plain's south edge. The triangular summit of the tell encompasses 11 ac. and sharply rises 70 m above the Esdraelon Plain. The site is easily defensible, with the Early and Middle Bronze Age fortifications enhancing the naturally steep slopes of the tell. The modern village occupies the shoulder on the southeast side of the mound, where the center of population has been located since the Roman period. The tell's modern name (Tell Taʿannek or Tiʿinnek) preserves the ancient one (Taanach), allowing scholars to connect events to this site with a high degree of certainty.

Tell Taʿannek commands three major travel and communication routes. The site overlooks the main route to the Esdraelon Plain from the coast, which runs through Wadi ʿAruna to Megiddo, then past Tell Taʿannek to Jenin and south to Jerusalem. A second road from the coastal plain to the Esdraelon—strategically important but less frequently used—leads to Tell Taʿannek through the hills southwest of the site. A third significant road passes to the northeast of Tell Taʿannek through the Harod Valley to Beth-shan, connecting with the major international trade route in the Jordan Valley.

Three excavations have revealed a succession of ancient towns on Tell Taʿannek dating back to the Early Bronze Age. The first of the major expeditions, led by Ernst Sellin, excavated several large areas and numerous probes atop the tell between 1902 and 1904. The second expedition, led by Paul Lapp, conducted excavations in 1963, 1966, and 1968, providing the essential material for dating and reconstructing the ancient occupations. A third team, from Birzeit University, excavated a portion of the Ottoman town among the buildings of the modern village.

Significant remains from the Early Bronze Age II–III and Middle Bronze Age III–Late Bronze Age I strata indicate the site's importance during these periods. Massive fortification systems protected the site while well-constructed buildings occupied the summit. In the first campaign of his twenty-third regnal year, THUTMOSE III led a punitive expedition into Syria-Palestine and subdued a coalition of rebellious rulers who had assembled in the Esdraelon Plain. The Egyptian king, stubbornly discounting the advice of his generals who counseled taking the secondary road that passed Taanach, marched boldly up the main road through the Wadi ʿAruna and defeated the rebels. On this expedition in the late 15th cent. BCE, Thutmose destroyed Middle Bronze Age III–Late Bronze Age I Canaanite Taanach.

Excavated material and literary sources indicate the site was occupied throughout the remainder of the Late Bronze Age. Although Taanach was only sparsely resettled after the city was destroyed by Thutmose III, this later Late Bronze Age I occupation produced thirteen Akkadian cuneiform tablets. Sellin found seven complete tablets and parts of five others, and Lapp's team found one, all of which date to the mid-15th cent. BCE. One of the AMARNA LETTERS may refer to the Late Bronze Age IIA occupation of Tell Taʿannek. Yashdata wrote letter EA 248 to the Egyptian monarch, describing the loss of all his possessions to men from a town whose name may be restored as Taanach (uru ta-ah-n[a-k]a). This reference, if the reconstructed reading of line 18 is correct, points to an Amarna-period occupation at Tell Taʿannek. The remains of the initial Iron Age occupation (periods IA and IB, ca. late 13th to late 12th cent. BCE) reveal that early Iron Age I Taanach was an unfortified town occupied primarily by farmers. Excavated material remains, including a grain shipment invoice written on a tablet in a variant form of the Ugaritic alphabet, suggest that period I Taanach continued to have close ties to the Canaanite population to the north as it had in the Middle and Late Bronze ages.

Biblical sources confirm that in the early Iron Age Taanach remained a Canaanite town connected with the Canaanite urban centers in the Esdraelon Plain. Traditions in the books of Joshua and Judges indicate that early Iron Age Taanach was a Canaanite center worthy to be listed among the cities against which the Israelites fought. According to the writers of Joshua, the Israelites defeated Taanach's king and those of the nearby Canaanite centers Megiddo and Jokneam (Josh 12:7-24). Taanach and several neighboring cities (Beth-shan, Ibleam, and Megiddo) were included in the tribal territory of Manasseh but remained Canaanite strongholds that the Israelites were not able to control until the time of David (Josh 17:7-13; Judg 1:27-28; 1 Chr 7:29).

The early Iron Age Song of Deborah (Judg 5:19, 21) refers to Taanach and the nearby KISHON River, locating the battle between the Israelites under Barak and Deborah and the army of the northern Canaanite kings led by Sisera there. As the Israelite forces approached the Canaanite army, they may have taken the route that emerged into the Esdraelon Plain at Tell Taʿannek (the same route favored by Thutmose's advisors), accounting for the reference to Taanach.

When Israel grew more powerful under David, Taanach and the Esdraelon Plain towns were brought under Israelite control. Solomon organized Taanach, Jokmeam (Tell el-Mazar), Beth-shan, and Megiddo into an administrative district under Baana son of Ahilud (1 Kgs 4:12). The period IIA occupation of Taanach (ca. late 11th to mid-10th cent. BCE) was the town David took over and ruled. After partial destruction, the period IIA town was leveled and rebuilt by Solomon as the smaller, more specialized administrative center of the Israelite nation-state of period IIB (ca. the mid- to late 10th cent.). After Israel controlled the region, Taanach and Gath-rimmon, a second Manassite city, were allotted to the Kohathite families of the Levites (Josh 21:25). The period IIB occupants built a cult structure and used ornate incense burners or offering stands that exhibit Canaanite religious motifs. One of the most famous cult stands ever discovered in Israel was found here (Beck).

Todd Bolen/BiblePlaces.com
Figure 1: Incense altar

Egyptian and biblical records contain one final episode involving Taanach. SHISHAK, the first king of Egypt's Twenty-second Dynasty, led a military expedition against Jerusalem in the late 10th cent. (1 Kgs 14:25-26). The Babastite Portal inscription shows the god Amun handing Shishak the towns of Megiddo, Taanach, Beth-shean, and Rehov. The Babastite Portal is a common type of relief that depicts the king as one who protects the land of Egypt from chaos but does not record battles or campaigns; thus, it does not indicate that Shishak destroyed these towns (archaeological evidence is mixed: some show signs of destruction, and others do not).

Taanach never regained the prominence it had enjoyed during the united monarchy. Fortified and rebuilt by Israel in the 9th cent. (period III), Taanach eventually came under Assyrian control in the late 8th cent. (period IV). When Judah's influence expanded into the region in the 7th cent. under Josiah (2 Kgs 23:19-20; 2 Chr 34:6-7), Taanach was rebuilt as an unfortified town (period V), only to be destroyed by the Babylonians. The Persians reoccupied and fortified part of the tell in the 5th cent. (period VI), then abandoned Taanach around 400 BCE.

Bibliography: Pirhiya Beck. "The Cult-Stands from Taanach: Aspects of the Iconographic Tradition of the Early Iron Age Cult Objects in Palestine." *From Nomadism to Monarchy: Archaeological and Historical Aspects of Early Israel.* Israel Finkelstein and Nadav Na'aman, eds. (1994) 352–81; Albert E. Glock. "A New Ta'annek Tablet." *BASOR* 204 (1971) 17–30; Delbert R. Hillers. "An Alphabetic Cuneiform Tablet from Taanach (TT433)." *BASOR* 173 (1964) 45–50; Paul W. Lapp. "The 1968 Excavations at Tell Ta'annek." *BASOR* 195 (1969) 2–49; Paul W. Lapp. "The 1966 Excavations at Tell Ta'annek." *BASOR* 185 (1967) 2–39; Paul W. Lapp. "The 1963 Excavation at Ta'annek." *BASOR* 173 (1964) 4–44; Kevin A. Wilson. *The Campaign of Pharaoh Shoshenq I into Palestine* (2005).

MARK MEEHL

TAANATH-SHILOH tay'uh-nath-sh*i*'loh [תַּאֲנַת שִׁלֹה ta'anath shiloh]. A town marking the northeast border of the territory allotted to the tribe of Ephraim (Josh 16:6). It is located in the hill country between Michmethath and Janoah, approximately 7 mi. southeast of Shechem. The town is most commonly identified with the modern site of Khirbet Ta'na el-Foqa, where the remains of a hill fort have been found. The name may mean "approach to Shiloh."

SUSAN E. HADDOX

TABBAOTH tab'ay-oth [טַבָּעוֹת tabba'oth; Ταβαώθ Tabaōth]. A temple servant (*see* NETHINIM) whose descendants returned to Judah with Zerubbabel following the Babylonian exile (Ezra 2:43; Neh 7:46; 1 Esd 5:29). The name means "signet rings."

TABBATH tab'uhht [טַבָּת tabbath]. A location in Transjordan that served as a landmark for the extent of the flight of the Midianites following Gideon's attack (Judg 7:22). Its location remains unclear, since it depends on the locations of Beth-shittah, Zererah, Abel-meholah (Judg 7:22), and Succoth (Judg 8:4-8), all of which remain unknown. Ras Abu Tabat has been suggested as a possible location.

Gideon returned to Israel by way of the Ascent of Heres (*see* HERES, ASCENT OF). The location of this place is also unknown, though some manuscript evidence suggests that the original reading may have been "from upon the mountains." If this is the case, it may refer generally to the Transjordanian highlands, the approximate area in which Tabbath would likely be located.

RALPH K. HAWKINS

TABEEL tab´ee-uhl [טָבְאַל *taveʾal,* טָבְאֵל *taveʾel;* Ταβέλλιος *Tabellios*]. 1. An Aramean official in Samaria who, along with his colleagues Bishlam and Mithredath, coauthored a letter to Artaxerxes I in a successful attempt to halt Jewish reconstruction of the walls of Jerusalem (Ezra 4:7; 1 Esd 2:16 [LXX 2:12]).

2. The father of an unnamed individual whom kings Pekah and Rezin hoped to place on the Judean throne as a puppet king, in place of Ahaz, during the Syro-Ephraimite war (ca. 735–734 BCE; Isa 7:6). The vocalization taveʾal may be a Hebrew wordplay meaning "no-good," intended to ridicule the would-be puppet king of the Syro-Ephraimite coalition. The original form of the name may have been taveʾel ("God is good"; compare Ezra 4:7).

RALPH K. HAWKINS

TABERAH tab´uh-ruh [תַּבְעֵרָה *tavʿerah*]. Means "burning." Site where the Israelites first camped after Sinai (Num 11:3; Deut 9:22). Angered by the people's complaints, God burned the outlying parts of the camp.

TABERNACLE tab´uhr-nak´uhl [מִשְׁכָּן *mishkan*]. The portable tent sanctuary constructed by the people of Israel in the Wilderness of Sinai according to instructions given by God to Moses on Mount Sinai after God's conclusion of a covenant with Israel. Together with its cultic personnel and its rituals, the tabernacle constitutes the archetype of OT worship. In complex interrelationship with the Temple in Jerusalem, it has exerted a shaping influence on the worship of Judaism and Christianity.

A. The Old Testament

1. Terminology and occurrences

Tabernacle (from Lat. *tabernaculum,* "hut," "tent") is the traditional English term for Israel's desert shrine, referred to in the OT by three designations.

a. Tabernacle. Mishkan is usually translated "tabernacle," with very few exceptions (e.g., "dwelling"; Lev 26:11; Ps 78:60). It means "a place where one lives" and is related to the verb shakhan (שָׁכַן, "to dwell" for shorter or longer times in houses or tents). Its structure and its Sinai and wilderness wandering context define the tabernacle as a tent. Although used also in other contexts, mishkan refers to the Sinai sanctuary over 100 times out of a total of 139 occurrences (fifty-eight of these in the "tabernacle texts," Exod 25–31; 35–40).

b. Tent of meeting. The phrase ʾohel moʿedh (אֹהֶל מוֹעֵד) combines two nouns: ʾohel ("tent") and moʿedh, ("appointed time" and/or "place"), which is related to the verb yaʿadh (יָעַד, "to appoint," "designate," "meet by appointment"). Of the 133 occurrences of ʾohel moʿedh, thirty-two are found in the tabernacle texts, but most of the rest also refer to the tabernacle; only a small number may derive from a separate (older?) tradition about a tent of revelation outside the camp (Exod 33:7-11; Num 11:16-29; 12:1-15; and possibly Deut 31:14-15).

c. Sanctuary. The word miqdash (מִקְדָּשׁ, "what is hallowed/sanctified," "holy place") is derived from the root qdsh (קָדַשׁ, "holy"). It designates sacred places generally and frequently the Temple in Jerusalem, but about fourteen of seventy-five occurrences refer to Israel's desert sanctuary and are then virtually synonymous with mishkan and ʾohel moʿedh.

d. Occurrences. When used in reference to Israel's desert sanctuary, these three terms are virtually synonymous (see all three in Num 3:38). Some nuancing in emphasis between "tabernacle" and "tent of meeting" may exist, "tabernacle" highlighting God's dwelling in Israel's midst (e.g., Exod 25:8; 29:45) and "tent of meeting" stressing the encounter between God and God's people or their representatives. Such nuancing may explain the choice of "tabernacle" in Exod 25–27, where the dwelling is described, and "tent of meeting" in Exod 28–31, where concern with the priesthood predominates. Virtual identity of meaning is emphasized by combinations such as "tabernacle of the tent of meeting" (Exod 39:32; 40:2, 6, 29; 1 Chr 6:32 [Heb. 6:17]), by their parallel use in several texts (e.g., Exod 40:35; Num 3:7), and by the parallel construction of phrases "tabernacle of the covenant" (e.g., Exod 38:21; Num 1:53) and "tent of the covenant" (e.g., Num 9:15; 18:2).

The LXX generally translates both mishkan and 'ohel mo'edh with skēnē (σκηνή, "tent") and sometimes with skēnōma (σκήνωμα, "tent"), thus largely obliterating any nuancing between the Hebrew terms. The LXX's choice of skēnē may be influenced by the similarity of consonants with mishkan.

2. The tabernacle texts, Exod 25–31; 35–40

a. **Overview of the narrative.** Readers of the pentateuchal narrative (Genesis–Deuteronomy) first encounter the tabernacle in Exod 25–31 and Exod 35–40, separated from each other by the story of the golden calf and its sequels (Exod 32–34). After the covenant conclusion at Mount Sinai (Exod 19–24), Moses ascends the mountain in order to receive further Instruction (24:12-18). There the Lord tells him in detail how Israel is to construct a sanctuary—the tabernacle with all its accessories (Exod 25–27; additions in Exod 30), followed by instructions concerning the special clothes for the priests, "Aaron and his sons," and directives for their consecration (Exod 28–29). Two divinely equipped master craftsmen, BEZALEL and OHOLIAB, shall take charge of the work (31:1-11). Further, Israel is to keep the Sabbath as a sign of the covenant (31:12-17). Finally, Moses receives "the two tablets of the covenant" ('edhuth עֵדוּת) and descends from the mountain (31:18). Meanwhile, the people below, aided by Aaron, enact their self-devised form of worship centering on the image of the so-called golden calf, accompanied by revelry (32:1-6).

Seeing this grave breach of covenant, Moses breaks the two stone tablets in anger, calls Aaron and the people to account, and wrestles, as it were, with God. Upon the intercession of Moses, however, God's grace prevails (32:7-33:23). In a new theophany to Moses, God renews the covenant. Moses writes the "Ten Words" (Commandments) onto new tablets and descends from the mountain, his face shining in reflection of the Lord's glory (Exod 34).

Moses then assembles the people and conveys to them God's earlier instructions, beginning with the Sabbath (35:1-3). A chastened Israel is ready now to contribute materials and labor for the work. Moses emphasizes repeatedly that participation should be voluntary, but the response is so generous that he has to put a halt to the flow of offerings (35:4–36:7). The work, under the oversight of Bezalel and Oholiab (35:30–36:1), begins with the construction of the tabernacle itself (36:8–38:31). The making of priestly attire follows (39:1-31). When Moses inspects the finished work, he finds that it was done "just as the LORD had commanded" (39:32-43). A brief recapitulation of God's tabernacle instructions (40:1-16) and their implementation (40:17-33) follows. The Implementation, and with it the book of Exodus, reaches its culmination as the glory of the Lord fills the tabernacle (40:34-38).

b. **Literary structure and characteristics.** As instruction and implementation, Exod 25–31 and Exod 35–40 are linked stylistically and logically in a way that invites continuous narrative reading, the chapters separating them (Exod 32–34) notwithstanding. These tabernacle texts, traditionally classified as Priestly (see §5.b below), show a preoccupation with sacred space and time, sacred personnel, and prescriptions for ritual, expressed in a style marked by characteristic vocabulary, technical terminology, meticulous attention to detail, and repetitious phrasing.

Readers who can overcome the widespread negative attitude towards the supposedly "legalistic requirements" and "empty rituals" may well be caught up in the energetic momentum of divine communication; the rhythm and delight in the listing of materials, patterns, and colors; the parade of items of exquisite aesthetic design and crafting; the evocative and at times tantalizing symbolism; the frequent and skillful use of parallelism and chiasm; the sustained reminders of central concerns through recurrent formulas; and the sparsely interspersed explicit theological explanations. Above all, such modern readers may recapture some of the beauty and grandeur of holiness that pervades the encounter when the transcendent God deigns to dwell in the midst of a people with a special calling.

The Instruction (Exod 25–31) is a long address by God, with Moses as the silent listener. The Implementation, by contrast, is a narrative telling how Moses directs the people in constructing the tabernacle and making the priestly vestments. There is much (sometimes verbatim) repetition of content, but the logic (divine instruction followed by human implementation) is a literary device to emphasize the central concern of obedience in tabernacle theology.

3. God instructs Moses to build a tabernacle

The Instruction begins with the Lord's request to Moses to take an offering of building materials from those Israelites "whose hearts prompt them" (25:1-2), in order to "make [God] a sanctuary (miqdash), so that I may dwell (weshakhanti וְשָׁכַנְתִּי) among them" (25:8). Readers are not presented with a static, blueprint-like account, but with a master's—God's—lively flow of instructions, detailing for his subordinate—Moses—step-by-step what is to be done: "You [sing.] shall make ... you shall make ... you shall make" is reminiscent of the creation story: "And God said ... made ... called." Such verbal cadence can be varied by second- and third-person plural instructions (e.g., 25:9-10), for while Moses alone receives God's orders, all (willing) Israelites are the true builders. God shows Moses, possibly in a vision, a plan or pattern (tavnith [תַּבְנִית]; 25:9, 40), probably not of a heavenly prototype or even God's heavenly dwelling, as tavnith is often interpreted, but of the tabernacle yet to be built (see the close analogies in 2 Kgs 16:10; 1 Chr 28:11-19). The meticulous instructions in the following chapters provide a verbal flowchart of procedures. Construction shall follow a theological order, proceeding from the most holy center to the less holy outer parts. The ARK OF THE COVENANT is to be made first, a box 2.5 × 1.5 × 1.5 cubits in length, breadth, and width (1 cubit = ca. 17.5" = ca. 45 cm). On it rests the MERCY SEAT or cover (kapporeth כַּפֹּרֶת), flanked by two cherubim facing each other with outspread wings, thus embracing the space over the mercy seat. Into the ark shall be placed "the covenant (ʿedhuth) that I [God] shall give you" (25:21). According to Exod 16:31-34, a jar of manna was also to be placed into the ark. The ark and mercy seat are the only items to be placed into the most holy place, but later Aaron's staff will be added (Num 17:10-11 [Heb. 17:25-26]). The ark and mercy seat are to be overlaid with and decorated in gold, as are all their accessories. All furnishings of the tabernacle are to be made portable by poles inserted into attached rings.

The tabernacle itself (not including the court) is to be a tent-structure of four layers of curtains draped one on top of the other over supporting frames (qerashim קְרָשִׁים) of ACACIA wood (Exod 26:1-30). The innermost layer, visible from inside the tent, is to be made of "fine twisted linen, and blue, purple, and crimson yarns ... with cherubim skillfully worked into [the curtains]" (26:1). This refined layer shall be covered with a protecting layer of goats' hair called the "tent over the tabernacle" (26:7). This is followed by a layer of "tanned rams' skins" (NIV, "ram skins dyed red") and a final layer of "fine leather" (ʿoroth tekhashim [עֹרֹת תְּחָשִׁים]; 26:14; NIV, "hides of sea cows"; NJPS, "dolphin skins").

The frames, 10 cubits tall and 1.5 cubits wide, shall be lined up to form a rectangle: 20 frames each for the north and south side and 6 for the rear, or west side, with two frames for the corners, whose arrangement is unclear. The frames shall be held together by five horizontal bars on the north, south, and west side, but since neither the structure or thickness of the frames nor their relation to each other is indicated, the shape and proportions of the tabernacle defy precise reconstruction. The front, or east side, is left open for access, shielded by a screen supported by five pillars. Various structural features (clasps, loops, rings, poles, pegs, bases, and utensils) are also described in some detail. Metals, fabrics, and workmanship are always listed in the same order from the inside outward, the most precious materials and the most skilled workmanship found closest to the holiest place, and the others following in descending order (e.g., fine gold, gold, silver, bronze).

Within the tent, a special curtain (parokheth פָּרֹכֶת) akin to the inner tent covering in workmanship and cherubim decoration (26:31) shall be draped on four pillars so as to separate the holy from the most holy place. A table for the BREAD OF PRESENCE and utensils for INCENSE and drink offerings, as well as an exquisitely

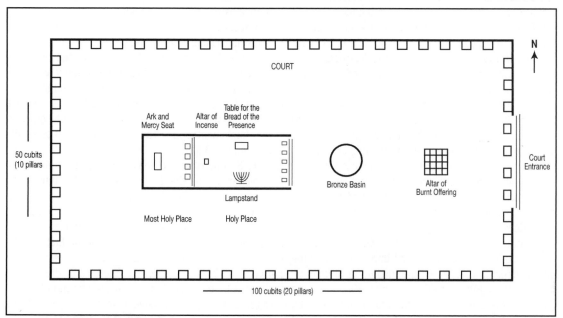

Hildi Janzen and Waldemar Janzen

Figure 1: Traditional conception of the tabernacle

wrought six-armed LAMPSTAND with seven lamps, one on each branch and one atop the stem, together with an altar of incense (introduced in 30:1-10) and its accessories are to make up the furnishings of the holy place.

A rectangular court shall surround the tabernacle, enclosed by a wall of hangings of twisted linen 5 cubits high—too high for even a tall person to look in—held up by a total of 60 pillars placed at intervals of 5 cubits. The court's dimensions shall be 100 × 50 cubits, with a gate 20 cubits long centered in the east side and shielded by a screen of "blue, purple, and crimson yarns, and of fine twisted linen, embroidered with needlework" (27:16). The eastward orientation of the tabernacle is nowhere explained or theologically developed. Into the court shall be placed the bronze altar and a bronze washing basin for the priests (not introduced until 30:17-21). That the tribes of Israel are encamped around the tabernacle is not explicitly stated here, but is implied by God's intention to dwell among them (25:8; 29:45; compare Num 2).

4. Israel builds the tabernacle

a. Relationship between instruction and implementation. Readers encounter a considerable duplication of content, often with identical wording, as they move from Instruction to Implementation. The order of presentation is almost reversed in the Implementation, however, as in mirror images or in a loosely constructed chiasm pointing to the Sabbath at the center. Theologically, the Instruction starts with the most holy items (ark and mercy seat; ephod and breastpiece) and moves further away from this center, while the Implementation follows the building logic of providing shelter first (the tent structure), to be equipped next with its furnishings. The altar of incense and the bronze basin now appear in the expected places in several lists (e.g., in 37:17-24; 40:4-5). A tendency toward clarification and simplification is also evident in the Implementation (compare 25:11 and 37:2). Different authorship and time of origin for the Instruction and the Implementation have been suggested, generally with the assumption that the Implementation originated later, but there is no consensus.

Some further differences also follow logically: God speaks and Moses listens in the Instruction; Moses gives orders to individuals and groups in the Implementation while God is silent (except in the summary of instructions in 40:1-15). Israel, under the direction—and at points, active participation—of Moses, and headed by the master craftsmen Bezalel and Oholiab, carries out the various tasks.

A further difference between the two sections is the omission of several items from the Implementation: the oil for the lamp (27:20-21); the institution of daily offerings (29:38-46); the half-shekel levy (30:11-16); and above all, the consecration of the priesthood (29:1-37; except in the summaries in 40:12-15, 30-32, texts that anticipate Lev 8). Installing the priesthood would have been premature before the settling of the glory of the Lord on the tabernacle (40:34-38). The installation will be performed in Lev 8-9 and the census in Num 1.

b. Preparations and building. Before the work begins, Moses announces that strict Sabbath observance must govern the building project (35:1-3). Then he proclaims the Lord's order to raise an offering of materials for the sanctuary from everyone who "is generous of heart" (vv. 4-9), followed by a call to "all who are skillful" to "make all that the LORD has commanded" (vv. 10-19). The people withdraw, and those whose "heart was stirred" and "whose spirit was willing" (v. 21), "both men and women" (v. 22), return and bring all the materials—from gold and precious stones to goat's hair and bronze—and provide the various skills required (vv. 20-29).

The master craftsmen Bezalel and Oholiab are now presented again as "filled ... with divine spirit, with skill, intelligence, and knowledge in every kind of craft" (35:31). They shall build the sanctuary, together with "everyone skillful to whom the LORD has given skill and understanding" (36:1). The offerings keep flowing in such overabundance that Moses has to order a halt. The work can begin. Certain emphases dominate the narrative: the potential involvement of the whole people— men and women, rich and poor, and of different kinds and levels of skill—restricted, however, by the condition of joyful and voluntary giving and participation. Thus a self-selected core of the faithful forms, ready to do the will of the Lord as mediated through Moses. Yet since the skills are divinely inspired, the reader senses that the Lord is instrumental in the last instance in bringing the project to completion.

A beehive of activity sets in as the various items are produced in this order: tent, ark, mercy seat, table, lampstand, altar of incense, altar of burnt offering, bronze basin, and court; all with their component parts and accessories (36:8-38:20). An account of the precious metals and money used, including the sanctuary shekel, is introjected (38:21-31) before the project is completed with the making of the priestly garments (39:1-32). Then Moses inspects the work and finds it to be "just as the LORD had commanded" (v. 43; a phrase occurring with slight variations over twenty times in the Implementation). Thereupon Moses blesses the people (39:33-43).

c. Summary and climax. For the first time in the Implementation, the Lord appears again, introduced by the formula "The LORD spoke to Moses" (40:1; as in 25:1 and six more times in the Instruction). God orders Moses in a terse sequence of commands to set up the tabernacle "on the first day of the first month" (40:2; v. 17 completes "in the second year"). This closes the bracket opened in Exod 12:2, the time of the first Passover celebration, in the first month of the first year, signifying that Israel is about to experience the completion of what had begun then: God's liberation of Israel from Egypt. (For Israel's arrival at Sinai, see 19:1.)

Moses is to set up the tabernacle with its furnishings in the order of their construction (36:8–38:20; the mercy seat, not mentioned in 40:1-15, was included, according to v. 20). In a series of priest-like functions, Moses shall anoint the tabernacle and consecrate it with everything in it, "so that it shall become holy" (v. 9). He shall anoint and consecrate the altar of burnt offering as most holy, and then anoint and consecrate the basin. Further, he shall wash, anoint, robe, and consecrate Aaron and his sons, and therewith admit them to a "perpetual priesthood" (v. 15; for the full ceremony, see Lev 8).

Exodus 40:17-33 summarize tersely Moses' implementation of the above orders. How he can do all this in one day single-handedly is not explained. In a further priest-like function, Moses offers the burnt offering and the grain offering on the altar (v. 29). "So Moses finished the work" (v. 33).

The last five verses of the tabernacle texts, and therewith of the book of Exodus, bring the tabernacle work to its climax when "the cloud covered the tent of meeting and the glory of the LORD filled the tabernacle" (v. 34). Even Moses cannot enter when the cloud rests upon the tent. It signifies the Lord's presence among the people (25:8; compare 17:7), and therewith the fulfillment of the purpose for which the tabernacle has been built (25:8; 29:42b-46). The Lord will henceforth dwell with the people, meet their consecrated representatives above the mercy seat in the tabernacle, and guide the setting out and halting on their journey.

5. Tabernacle theology in the Pentateuch: diachronic (source-historical) perspective

a. The sources. A diachronic study of the tabernacle texts must primarily concern itself with the youngest Priestly source (P) of the Pentateuch (*see* DOCUMENTARY HYPOTHESIS; PENTATEUCH). Many scholars regard P as an originally discrete source, redactorially combined eventually with the older sources J and E. Others consider P to be the final major redactional level of the TETRATEUCH (Genesis–Numbers), incorporating older sources (whether conceived as J and E or otherwise), into its own structural framework and theological concerns. In this view, advocated here, the final P-redaction comes close to the canonical Tetrateuch, although an even later slight Deuteronomistic editing is likely. P's basic theological frame—presupposing and embracing the older sources—consists of a fourfold historical periodization marked off by three covenants instituted by God: with Noah (Gen 9:1-17), with Abraham (Gen 17), and with Israel at Mount Sinai, under the divine names Elohim, El Shadday, and Yahweh, respectively (*see* GOD, NAMES OF). The third and last covenant is the theme of the long Sinai pericope (Exod 19:1–Num 10:10), framed by the wilderness wandering sections (Exod 15:22–18:27 and Num 10:11–36:13). This pericope reaches its apex in the Implementation, Exod 35–40, when the glory of the Lord descends to

take up residence in the tabernacle in the midst of Israel (Exod 40:34-38).

b. Contextualizing Priestly theology. The exilic or early postexilic period (before Ezra) is the likely time of the last pentateuchal redaction. It is therefore widely regarded as the proper extra-textual (historical) interpretive context of the tabernacle texts and used to address questions such as these: Was the tabernacle and its worship intended: 1) As a temporary solution for continuing worship after the loss of the Jerusalem Temple? 2) As a critical alternative to the Temple, now destroyed by God's judgment? 3) As the center of a gathered religious community after a return from exile, a community that could exist under Persian overlordship? 4) As the program of an Aaronide priestly group, suppressed during the monarchy, but revived in exile? or 5) As a vision for a sanctuary in an unidentified (eschatological?) future? To many scholars, the tabernacle program seems to address these and other questions faced by the exilic or postexilic Jewish community.

Preexilic historical contexts for interpreting tabernacle theology are also maintained by prominent scholars, however. These understand tabernacle theology in a variety of ways: 1) As the archaic form of worship maintained as an ideal over the years, perhaps by a continuing anti-Temple group; and 2) As a critical counter-proposal to the Temple in later monarchic times, surfacing during the reforms of Hezekiah or Josiah, and advocating cult reform and centralization. As such it would share elements with the prophetic and Deuteronomic critique of the Temple (e.g., Jer 7; 26; Ezek 8). 3) Some scholars propose two levels of context: an earlier one during the time of monarchy and a later one in the time of exile or restoration.

Not to be overlooked are serious attempts to uphold the historical context claimed in the pentateuchal sources themselves, i.e., the context of a historical ancient exodus of Israel from Egypt, in which the tabernacle in some form was central to Israel's original covenant-based worship mediated by Moses. This view need not imply that there was no reworking of the ancient tradition to adapt it to later contexts.

It is clear that tabernacle theology will have held powerful messages for Israel in the historical context in which it originated—whenever that was—as well as in multiple later contexts. It is important also to remember that all the contextualizing interpretations except the last-mentioned—whether they are taken as historical or as retrojections of an ideal—are painstakingly avoided in the tabernacle texts and their pentateuchal continuation in Leviticus–Numbers. The canonical text tirelessly invites its implied readers to transcend any fixed contextuality of its origin and to keep a God–Israel relationship "for all your generations" in view.

All source-critically achieved dating of the tabernacle texts (or of more extensive literary layers, like P) and the interpretive proposals—historical, sociological, or theological—dependent on such dating remain of necessity hypothetical in nature and are challenged in almost every respect by significant alternative hypotheses. This, together with changes in the mental climate of our time, has led to an increasing adoption of synchronic methods.

6. Tabernacle theology in the Pentateuch: synchronic (literary-canonical) perspective

Synchronic interpretation of the canonical pentateuchal text itself does not in principle eschew locating that text in an extra-textual historical setting, but it privileges the final text over its hypothetically reconstructed antecedent forms as the basis for discerning the appropriate historical context. Such an approach is also cautious not to override the literary-theological world of the text itself as interpretive context for the implied reader by adducing extra-textual data, especially where the latter are apparently deliberately withheld by the author(s) or redactor(s).

The tabernacle texts (Exod 25–31; 35–40) lead the reader from God's command to construct a sanctuary to its finished state. They are both foundational in content and sufficiently coherent as a self-contained narrative unit to commend themselves as the starting point and core for synchronic interpretation of tabernacle theology, followed by consideration of the widening macrostructures in which they are now embedded: Exodus, Leviticus–Numbers, and Genesis–Deuteronomy.

a. The tabernacle texts, Exod 25–31; 35–40. A few brief and explicit theological statements capture the core of tabernacle theology: Exod 25:8, 22; 29:42*b*-46; 40:34-38. God instructs Moses: "Have [the Israelites] make me a sanctuary, so that I may dwell among them" (25:8). God, not a human patron like a king (e.g., Solomon in 1 Kgs 5:2-6 [Heb. 5:16-21]), commissions the construction of a sanctuary. God chooses a people, Israel on the move, in order to live "among them." The ancient traditional axis God–place is replaced by the axis God–people. This mobility of God's presence finds concrete expression in the portability of the tabernacle.

The nature of God's presence is expressed by the name of the sanctuary: "tabernacle," "dwelling" (mishkan), and its related verb "to dwell" (shakhan). The tabernacle's other frequently used name, "tent of meeting," although occurring also in four instances of intermittent divine appearances to Moses outside the camp (Exod 33:7-11; Num 11:16-30; 12:1-15; and possibly Deut 31:14-15), should not be used to posit a theology of God's intermittent appearance in the tabernacle. God's ongoing presence and reliable accessibility is central to tabernacle theology, without jeopardizing God's transcendence. Within the tabernacle, the divine–human encounter occurs in the most holy place, above the mercy seat (e.g., Exod 25:22; Lev 16:1-2; Num 7:89). The Lord's verbal communication is directed to Moses/Aaron, but the ultimate addressees are the people of Israel.

The content of the divine speaking is specified as delivering "all my commands" (Exod 25:22; literally, "everything that I will command you [sing.; i.e., Moses]).'' The location of God's speaking above the ark suggests its association with the ark's content, the "covenant or testimony" (usually ʿedhuth, sometimes berith [בְּרִית]; e.g., Num 10:33), i.e., minimally the tablets with the Ten Commandments. Exodus 16:31-34 adds a jar of manna as testimony to God's gracious provision. The future tense of the verb, as well as the formulation "everything that I will command you" (25:22; author's trans.; NRSV, "all my commands"), point also—beyond the witness function of these covenant documents— to an ongoing verbal revelation (see also Lev 1:1-2; 24:10-23; Num 7:89; 9:6-14; 27:1-11; 36:1-13), possibly related to the oracular function of the URIM AND THUMMIM.

The central significance of the covenant in the divine–human encounter embraces both its responsibilities and its blessings (law and promise). Israel's propitiatory sacrifices, culminating in the atonement ritual performed by the high priest in the most holy place once a year on the DAY OF ATONEMENT (yom hakkippurim [יוֹם הַכִּפֻּרִים]; Lev 16:1-2, 13-17; 23:27-28; 25:9), are directed to the mercy seat (kapporeth, literally "atonement"). Further, the high priest is to carry the names of the twelve sons of Israel inscribed on the stones of remembrance on his shoulder pieces and on the breastpiece of judgment on the ephod (Exod 28:12) "when he goes into the holy place, for a continual remembrance before the LORD" (28:29-30). Apparently, the Lord, invisibly present over the mercy seat, is to be reminded— in a strongly anthropomorphic gesture—of the covenant relationship. The inscription on the high priest's rosette of the turban, "Holy to the LORD"—another bold but divinely ordered anthropomorphism—presumably serves the same function, "in order that they might find favor before the LORD" (28:36-38). Possibly Israel also "reminds" God of their meritorious role in building the tabernacle. These inscriptions represent the only verbal expressions brought to the divine–human encounter from the human side. The priesthood's silent (and barefoot) service can be interpreted as deference to the holiness of God, as total subjection to God's will, and perhaps as eschewing every temptation to the magical employment of words. Only the little bells on the fringe of the high priest's robe, "so that he may not die," draw the attention of God through sound—another daring anthropomorphism (28:35).

The absence of speech (and song) is also a reminder that the divine–human encounter is at its heart a numinous theophanic experience, thus only partially containable in words and concepts like law, grace, judgment, propitiation, etc., even when expressed in prayer and praise. (Compare the combination of theophany [Exod 19] and verbal expression of God's will [Exod 20–23] in God's revelation at Mount Sinai.)

By contrast, the area "at the entrance of the tent of meeting before the LORD" (29:42b, i.e., the eastern part of the court), is visualized as the busy center of priestly activity, accessible for common people on personal and public occasions: sacrifices (see Lev 1–7), priestly verdicts in matters of uncleanness (e.g., Lev 14:11, 23), and many others. It is the place where God's numinous presence becomes real or "meets" the people (Exod 29:42b-43). At high points, this may take the form of the appearance of the glory (kavodh כָּבוֹד) of the Lord, the intermittent visible theophany, to be distinguished from the ongoing invisible presence and the enveloping cloud, both for assurance (Exod 40:34-35; Lev 9:23; Num 14:10) and for judgment (Num 16:19, 42 [Heb. 17:7]).

Two explicitly theological texts commanding Sabbath observance close the Instruction (Exod 31:12-17) and open the Implementation (35:1-3), placing the preparation of sacred space into a context of sacred time. With explicit reference to Gen 1:1–2:3, Israel's work on the tabernacle is to proceed within God's time frame for work and rest embedded in creation and modeled by God (31:17).

Above all, exact compliance with the worship pattern mandated by God, emphasized by the precise following of God's own Instruction narrated in the Implementation, marks proper service in tabernacle theology. This compliance is underscored by the numerous occurrences of the formula "as the LORD had commanded Moses" (over twenty times, with slight variations). Such theology of service and worship, however, does by no means consist of slavish obedience and "empty" ritual but embraces a rich interplay of theophanic and covenantal-ethical elements.

Canonical interpretation calls for caution in drawing theological conclusions from silence, such as the absence of polemic against idols or other sanctuaries; of reference to monarchy, including even explicitly royal references pertaining to God; of stated attitudes to the Temple; and of an historical or eschatological future. A canonical approach is also hesitant, though not in principle opposed, to supply extra-textually what the author(s)—apparently deliberately—withheld. Such caution includes the adducing of comparative religio-historical data. (For explicit textual links to creation, see §A.6.d below.)

b. Exodus. The tabernacle texts are now firmly bound into the story of the book of Exodus, constituting its end and goal: "I will dwell among the Israelites, and I will be their God. And they shall know that I am the LORD their God, who brought them out of the land of Egypt that I might dwell among them; I am the LORD their God" (Exod 29:45-46). When the glory of the Lord fills the tabernacle (40:34), this goal has been achieved.

The Exodus context enriches and nuances the theology of the tabernacle texts through a number of clearly intentional features: 1) The golden calf incident and its sequels (Exod 32–34), separating the instruction and implementation, are now firmly linked with them by Exod 31:18 and 34:29-32. This aligns Exod 25–31, 32–34, and 35–40 into a covenant–covenant-breaking–covenant renewal sequence. 2) The same linking relates tabernacle building and golden calf construction to each other as antitypes: Israel's rebellious, self-designed form of God's perceived presence to lead them on the way is set in contrast to God's own chosen form of presence and leading (compare 32:1 and 25:8; 40:34-38). 3) Idolatrous image worship (32:1-6) is warningly set in profile by the aniconic encounter with God in a context of holiness in the tabernacle. 4) The Sinai covenant conclusion (24:1-11), preceded by the theophany (Exod 19) and instruction (Exod 20–23), is joined to the tabernacle chapters by 24:12-18, so that the location of God's revelation is transferred from Mount Sinai to the mobile tabernacle, a "Sinai on the move," as it were. 5) The association of the tabernacle with Sinai embeds it in the exodus narrative, linking it to the revelation of the divine name "the LORD" to Moses in the burning bush at the "mountain of God" (3:1-6, 13-15; 6:2-8). This in turn evokes the Abrahamic promise/covenant theme that propels the exodus forward (Exod 2:23-25; 3:16-17; 6:2-8; see also §A.6.d below). 6) Finally, the tabernacle texts function in Exodus as the conclusion of God's victory over Pharaoh. In the beginning of Exodus, a dispirited Israel was doing slave labor in the building projects of a ruthless tyrant claiming ultimate power, apparently in the absence of God (but see 2:23-25). At the end of Exodus, the reader sees a liberated people dedicating their offerings and their labor freely to the construction of a proper habitation for the only true sovereign of the universe, so that the Lord might "dwell" among them. In this perspective, the tabernacle gains the image of a royal palace occupied by a victorious king; language eschewed in the tabernacle texts themselves.

c. Leviticus–Numbers. The books of Leviticus and Numbers continue the story of the tabernacle, which now succeeds Mount Sinai as the place of further divine revelation (Lev 1:1; Num 7:89). While the style on the whole continues to be "Priestly," some repetition and unevenness together with the inclusion of a large amount of ritual and legal material evidence complex redactional activity. The duality of the names "tabernacle" and "tent of meeting" also continues. Nevertheless, the narrative of Israel's wilderness wandering towards the promised land moves forward in a generally coherent story line. The location continues to be the Wilderness of Sinai until the cloud rises, the tabernacle is disassembled, and Israel moves on to the Wilderness of Paran (Num 10:11-12) and eventually to the Plains of Moab (Num 22:1). Further divine commands in these books express or assume the determinative fact of God's dwelling among Israel in the tabernacle and report intermittent appearances of the Lord's glory (Lev 9:23; Num 14:10; 16:19, 42 [Heb. 17:7]; 20:6).

The focus in Leviticus and Numbers, however, shifts from the building of the tabernacle in Exodus to the functioning of the tabernacle-centered cultus (*see* WORSHIP, OT). Leviticus 8 loops back, as it were, to report the consecration of Aaron and his sons, commanded in Exod 29:1-27, but not carried out in the Implementation. In Lev 9, Aaron brings his first offerings and then blesses his people, "and the glory of the LORD appeared to all the people" (Lev 9:22-23).

The central theological concerns with respect to the tabernacle in Leviticus and Numbers are twofold: 1) Israel's ongoing maintenance or restoration of holiness and ritual purity in view of God's tabernacle in their midst (Lev 15:31); 2) The obedience of Israel to the Lord's will as laid down in the covenant or subsequently revealed through Moses, and then also Aaron and his successors. (Leviticus 10:10-11 summarizes both concerns.)

Sacrifices and rituals at the tabernacle are available to atone for both the loss of holiness and for acts of disobedience. Thus the Lord's dwelling in the tabernacle in the midst of Israel is a gracious gift of God's covenant faithfulness and blessing (Lev 26:11-13). Atonement culminates on the special Day of Atonement (Lev 16). At the same time, the Lord's presence can manifest itself as consuming wrath in cases of negligence or willful disobedience (e.g., Lev 10:1-7; Num 16).

d. Genesis–Deuteronomy. The most comprehensive macrostructure (or literarily coherent interpretive context) for the tabernacle texts is the Pentateuch as a whole, extending from creation to the border of the promised land. Textual linking between tabernacle and creation is evident in the association of Israel's Sabbath observance in Exod 31:12-17 (as a covenant sign) and Exod 35:1-3 with God's own Sabbath observance after creation (Gen 2:1-3). Israel's construction of the tabernacle is aligned with God's intention for the world. (Note also the similar description of God's completion of creation and Israel's completion of the tabernacle: Gen 1:31; 2:1, 3; and Exod 39:32, 43; 40:33.)

On the other hand, identifying the seven sections in the tabernacle Instruction introduced by "The LORD said to Moses" (Exod 25:1; 30:11, 17, 22, 34; 31:1, 12) with the seven days of creation (Gen 1:1–2:3) seems textually unwarranted. Caution is also called for in pursuing the creation–tabernacle association into structural and decorative tabernacle details, or in the close identification of master builder Bezalel's equipment through the divine spirit (Exod 31:3; 35:31) with God's own creating spirit hovering over primordial chaos (Gen 1:2).

Further, a synchronic reading must refrain from interpreting the creation–tabernacle nexus by means of the ANE mythological combat myth, in which the god, after victory over the chaos powers, is enthroned in his palace (e.g., the Babylonian cosmogonic myth *Enuma Elish*). Traces suggestive of this and other ANE mythology, though recognizable, have been absorbed by P-theology—embracing also the older pentateuchal sources—into the pentateuchal narrative propelled forward by the two intertwined themes of promise and covenant: God's promise of descendants and land to Abraham (Gen 12:1-3 and further), and God's covenants with Noah (Gen 9), Abraham (Gen 17), and Israel at Sinai.

Within this framework, however, recent scholarship has rightly highlighted the thematic parallelism between the primeval history (Gen 1–11) and the Sinai story (Exod 19–40). In each narrative, the gracious gift of God (creation/Sinai covenant) is jeopardized by threat of annihilation (great flood/sequels to golden calf worship), but restored through God's use of one person (Noah/Moses) to mediate God's grace (covenant with Noah and humanity/covenant renewal and God's dwelling among Israel).

Tabernacle does not occur in Deuteronomy, while "tent of meeting" is found only in Deut 31:14-15, where a one-time appearance of God seems to be meant (as in Exod 33:7-11); but in view of the tent's association in that context with the ark carried by the Levites (Deut 31:24-25), the text has the tabernacle in mind. By contrast, Deuteronomy generally conceives the presence of God among Israel as God's name dwelling at the place that the Lord will choose (e.g., Deut 14:23; 16:6, 11). Although clearly distinguished from the pentateuchal narratives by its theological emphases, its structure, and its distinctive style, Deuteronomy takes up the pentateuchal story and offers a commentary on it in the form of sermons by Moses in the Plains of Moab, concluding with Moses' death. At the brink of Israel's entry into the promised land, Moses exhorts the new generation to a faithful life in the land ahead. This orientation toward the future adds to the futuristic and idealizing thrust of the Pentateuch evidenced earlier (as in the repeated phrase "throughout all your generations" in the tabernacle texts).

Although older pentateuchal literary strata may well have included the occupation of the land promised to Abraham and his descendants, the final canonical shaping concluded the Torah/Pentateuch at the death of Moses, with the land still ahead as the promised and awaited goal. For future generations of believers, therefore, the two aspects of the dual goal of the Abrahamic promise and the exodus from Egypt—God's presence and the promised land—was defined: Israel's identity as Abraham's descendants would be determined by their living and worshiping obediently the God who had deigned to dwell in their midst, even while the land still lay in the future.

7. The tabernacle in the rest of the Old Testament (with Apocrypha)

a. The canonical texts. Beyond the Pentateuch, scattered references trace the story of the tabernacle (under both the names "tabernacle" and "tent of meeting") from Joshua to the Solomonic Temple. According to the DtrH, Israel sets up the tent of meeting at Shiloh (Josh 18:1), where the land is distributed (19:51). The land can now be called "the LORD's land, where the tabernacle stands" (22:19, 29). At Shiloh, Eli and Samuel serve at the tent of meeting (1 Sam 2–3)—a sanctuary repeatedly designated, however, as a "house" (= temple; e.g., Judg 18:31; 1 Sam 1:7, 24; 3:15)—until the ark is captured by the Philistines (1 Sam 4) and the sanctuary is destroyed (Ps 78:60; Jer 7:12-14; 26:6-9). The ark is eventually retrieved and housed by David in an apparently newly provided tent in the City of David (2 Sam 6). God, through the prophet Nathan, forbids David to build a "house" (= temple), since "I [the LORD] have been moving about in a tent and a tabernacle" (2 Sam 7:6; 1 Chr 17:5). This enigmatic wording minimally characterizes Israel's pre-monarchic central sanctuary as a mobile tent-shrine. Once Solomon's Temple is built, the ark, the tent of meeting (but compare 2 Chr 1:3), and all the holy vessels are transferred to the Temple, and the ark is set up under the wings of the cherubim in the most holy place; nothing is said about the placement or storage of the tent of meeting. Then the glory of the Lord fills the house of the Lord (1 Kgs 8:1-11; compare Exod 40:34-35).

According to the books of Chronicles, David provides for service by Levites before the ark, in the tent he had pitched for it in Zion (1 Chr 16:1-6, 37; 2 Chr 1:4), while Zadokite priests minister before the tabernacle (tent of meeting) with the altar of burnt offering set up at the high place of Gibeon (1 Chr 16:37-40; 21:29; 2 Chr 1:1-13). Solomon brings the ark, the tent of meeting, and all the holy vessels into the new Temple, placing the ark under the cherubim in the most holy place (2 Chr 5:1-14; as in 1 Kgs 8:1-11). It is not clear how the tabernacle is accommodated in this move.

Both in the DtrH and in Chronicles, the reader senses the full confidence that the transition from the desert tabernacle to the Solomonic Temple, beset with many moves and external difficulties, is a theologically smooth one, except in the confrontation between David and Nathan (2 Sam 7:1-16//1 Chr 17:1-14). That this encounter leads to a postponement of Temple building, in view of a long pre-history of worship "in a tent and tabernacle" (be'ohel uvmishkan [בְּאֹהֶל וּבְמִשְׁכָּן]; 2 Sam 7:6), does suggest a politico-religious resistance from a traditional (prophetic?) group to the notion of a royal sanctuary where the Lord dwells in a house (= temple). According to the canonical text, however, God accommodates, as it were, even at this juncture to a gradual transition from tabernacle to Temple, but on God's own terms.

That the worship of God in tabernacle and Temple came to be seen as theologically continuous is further indicated by a conflation such as "the tabernacle of the house of God" (1 Chr 6:48 [Heb. 6:33]) and by repeated references to the Temple as "tabernacle" or "tent of meeting," under various designations: Pss 26:8 (NRSV, "where your glory abides"); 43:3 (pl.; NRSV,

"dwelling"); 46:4 [Heb. 46:5] (pl.; NRSV, "habitation"); 74:7-8 (NRSV, "your sanctuary//dwelling-place of your name//meeting places of God [pl.; TNK, 'God's tabernacles']"); 84:1 ([Heb. 84:2], pl; NRSV, "dwelling place"); 132:5, 7 (pl.; NRSV, "dwelling-place"); Lam 2:6 (['ohel] mo'edh, lit., "[tent of] meeting"; NRSV, "tabernacle"); Ezek 37:27 (NRSV, "dwelling place"). Ezra 7:15 also calls the Temple in Jerusalem God's "dwelling."

These instances of tabernacle terminology are widely considered to be poetic or figurative references to the Temple, but R. E. Friedman (1980) has argued that the historical tabernacle was indeed stored in the most holy place of the Solomonic Temple, under the cherubim, a space fitting his postulated dimensions for the tabernacle (20×8 cubits). Minimally, these passages testify to an ongoing tabernacle theology that laid claim to the Temple as succeeding and embodying the tabernacle, and probably as being validated thereby.

b. The Apocrypha. The few references to the tabernacle in diverse texts of the Apocrypha render it as "tent" (skēnē and skēnōma), as do references in other (non-canonical) Jewish writings of similar date (ca. 200 BCE–150 CE; not treated here). These texts witness to the ongoing life of the Exodus-based tent sanctuary tradition, although the use made of that tradition shows various nuances. In some texts, *tabernacle* appears in parallelism to the Jerusalem Temple or in clear reference to it. Tobit encourages the exiles among the nations to repent and to pray in anticipation "that [God's] tent may be rebuilt in you in joy" (Tob 13:10 [LXX 13:11]). Ben Sira has Wisdom tell how God ordered her: "Make your dwelling (kataskēnoō [κατασκηνόω], literally, 'encamp') in Jacob" (Sir 24:8). There she ministered before God in the "holy tent" and became established in Zion (v. 10), where she spread a pleasant odor "like the odor of incense in the tent" (v. 15). Judith, in a story placed in the time of Nebuchadnezzar, prays to God to break the strength of the "Assyrians" who "intend to defile your sanctuary (hagios ἅγιος), and to pollute the tabernacle (skēnōma)" (Jdt 9:8). King Solomon, in a prayer for wisdom, recalls how God has commanded him to build the Temple, "a copy of the holy tent that you prepared from the beginning" (Wis 9:8). Finally, there is the story that Jeremiah, after the departure of the exiles and upon receiving an oracle, hid the tent, the ark, and the altar of incense in a cave on Mount Nebo and then sealed it (2 Macc 2:4-8). He rebuked certain people who had followed him, telling them that the place should be unknown until God would gather his people again, show his mercy, and reveal the place of hiding. Then "the glory of the Lord and the cloud will appear, as they were shown in the case of Moses, and as Solomon asked that the place should be specially consecrated" (2:8).

8. Historical aspects

Age-old questions as to how a group of escaped slaves from Egypt could have erected an elaborate and costly sanctuary in the Sinai wilderness seemed to have found their answer in J. Wellhausen's dismissive characterization of the tabernacle concept as a fictitious, postexilic, priestly agenda retrojecting its own ideal of worship into the Sinai context to provide Mosaic authorization for it. The tabernacle, rather than being the model for the Solomonic Temple, was its copy, reduced to half its proportions. The inadequacy of this interpretation was pointed out forcefully by F. M. Cross in 1947 and later. Cross has argued convincingly that the 2nd millennium BCE tent of El, the highest god in Canaanite mythology, shows many features suggestive of the Priestly tabernacle, including details of structure, terminology, and iconography, like qeresh/qarshu (qerashim, the tabernacle frames), har moʿedh (הַר מוֹעֵד; mount of meeting [of the assembly of gods]), and El's cherubim throne. These and other resemblances suggest that the tabernacle texts have adapted very ancient tent-sanctuary traditions, some not shared by the Solomonic Temple.

Pre-Temple existence of an ancient Israelite tent-centered worship has also been upheld by other interpreters on various grounds. Many consider the Mosaic tent of meeting outside the camp (Exod 33:7-11; Num 11:16-30; 12:1-15; and possibly Deut 31:14-15) to reflect a small desert sanctuary on the assumption—challenged by some—that it belongs to the older pentateuchal sources, a shrine akin to small Bedouin tent shrines known from much later times. The assumption, however, that large and elaborate tents could not have been known in Israel's early history has been put in question by an Akkadian text from Mari featuring a portable large public tent at Mari, supported by frames (qersu; again the qerashim of the tabernacle, appearing as qrsh in El's tent already), and apparently carried by forty-three men (see D. E. Fleming). While this proves nothing regarding the existence and nature of an early Israelite tent-sanctuary, it cautions against assuming a certain primitivism in Israel's early worship. Egyptian features and terminology in the tabernacle reports have also been discovered (see Hoffmeier).

The sanctuary at Shiloh, though called a "house" (e.g., Judg 18:31; 1 Sam 1:7, 24; 3:15), is elsewhere referred to as "tent of meeting" (Josh 18:1; 19:51; 1 Sam 2:22; Ps 78:60) and may well have been the tabernacle (M. Haran) or possibly housed it. Cross suggests that the tent David provided for the ark (2 Sam 6:17), probably incorporating earlier traditions, could have been sufficiently elaborate to have provided a model for the Priestly tabernacle. The witness to a pre-monarchic mobile tent/tabernacle worship in 2 Sam 7:6//1 Chr 17:5 should also not be discounted, especially since David's quick surrender of his Temple building plans suggests strong opposition from an influential tent-sanctuary tradition.

While tabernacle and Temple share certain widespread and common features of ancient temple building, especially in their inner space allocation (see V. Hurowitz), they now appear as less identical than has traditionally been assumed. R. E. Friedman's proposal (see §A.7.a), although problematic in some aspects, demonstrates how imprecise our knowledge of the tabernacle's construction and measurements is, and how much the pattern of the Temple has influenced scholars' interpretations of the tabernacle as a half-scale Temple imitation. While Friedman's arguments for the continued physical presence of the tabernacle in the Solomonic Temple may not be fully convincing, they should not be dismissed lightly, either. The repeated extra-pentateuchal references to the Temple by way of tabernacle terminology add further to the cumulative indications that a significant mobile sanctuary tradition accompanied Israel's worship from earliest times to the postexilic era.

However congruent the canonical accounts of the tabernacle may be with ancient historical realities that we can know or postulate with some confidence, the tabernacle texts almost certainly received significant final shaping in the exilic or postexilic period, a process inevitably influenced by the Temple. How consciously or unconsciously the old mobile tent tradition was adjusted to Temple realities in affirmation of the Temple, or was accentuated in critique of it, will probably never be known to us. It is important to recognize in the intertwined history of tabernacle and Temple the canonical OT's profound response to the basic human question: "Is the LORD among us or not?" (Exod 17:7).

B. The New Testament

The NT uses the following tabernacle-related terms: skēnē twenty times (NRSV, "dwelling[s]" five times, "tent[s]" thirteen times, "dwelling place" one time, "home" one time, suggesting "tabernacle" in the margin as an alternative translation ten times [all except one in Hebrews]); skēnōma three times (NRSV, "dwelling place," "body," and "death [i.e., putting off of the tent of the body]," one time each); skēnos (σκῆνος) two times (NRSV, "tent [of the body]"); and the verb skēnoō (σκηνόω) five times (NRSV, "live" one time, "shelter" [i.e., God tents over them as a sheltering presence] one time, "dwell" three times).

Of these thirty occurrences, the following eleven show no or very indirect—or enigmatic, as in the three synoptic passages—connection to the tabernacle, understood as the sanctuary of God: skēnē, Matt 17:4; Mark 9:5; Luke 9:33; 16:9; Acts 7:44; 15:16; Heb 11:9; skēnōma, 2 Pet 1:13-14; skēnos, 2 Cor 5:1, 4.

The remaining nineteen occurrences are more or less closely associated historically and theologically with the Sinai tabernacle; they occur in four texts or text groups:

1) In his retrospective speech Stephen recalls, "Our ancestors had the tent of testimony in the wilderness, as God directed." They brought it into the land under Joshua, where it was until the time of David. Solomon built a house for God, but "the Most High does not dwell in houses made with human hands" (Acts 7:44-

48). A critique of the human-initiated Temple, in contrast to the obediently constructed tabernacle, must have been sensed by the hearers, for they became enraged as Stephen developed this theme, and they proceeded to kill him.

2) The letter to the Hebrews contains the NT's fullest theological reflection on the tabernacle, with eight explicit references to it (Heb 8–9). The writer offers a reverent and relatively comprehensive description of the Mosaic tabernacle, detailing its main furnishings and features, as well as its priesthood's ministry, headed by the high priest (9:1-10). This earthly sanctuary was the "first tent" (9:8), "a symbol of the present time" (9:9), merely "a sketch and shadow of the heavenly one" (8:5). It is associated with the first covenant, marked by sacrifices, a covenant bound to be replaced by the new covenant (with extensive reference to Jer 31:31-34). Now, however, Jesus Christ has come, the true high priest, "a minister in the sanctuary and the true tent that the Lord, and not any mortal, has set up" (8:1-2), to exercise "a more excellent ministry" in the context of a "better covenant" (8:6) and a "greater and perfect tent" (9:11), where he entered "once for all into the Holy Place, not with the blood of goats and calves, but with his own blood, thus obtaining eternal redemption" (9:12). In Hebrews, Jesus' relation to the tabernacle is central to the author's christology, and its development represents a major hermeneutic of relating the Testaments to each other, a hermeneutic that does not—as sometimes held—exhaust itself in an allegorical relationship between the heavenly and the earthly but finds its framework in the eschatological movement from the old covenant to the new.

3) John 1:14, when read with attention to tabernacle motifs, belongs here: "And the word became flesh and lived (eskēnōsen ἐσκήνωσεν) among us, and we have seen his glory, a glory as of the father's only son, full of grace and truth" (compare Exod 25:8; 40:34-35; Lev 9:23; see also Sir 24:8; Col 1:19). As in Hebrews, Jesus Christ assumes here the function of the tabernacle in a fuller way, by incarnating the answer to the question, "Is the LORD in our midst or not?" (Exod 17:7). Tabernacling language may also connote the temporary nature of God's incarnation in Jesus on this earth. Christians throughout church history have rightly observed the typological connection between the tabernacle and Jesus, although this has often led to overly fanciful allegorizing.

4) In Revelation, three texts transfer the tabernacle to the heavenly realm. According to Rev 13:6, God's dwelling (skēnē) is now "those who dwell (skēnountas σκηνοῦντας) in heaven." In Rev 15:5, the seer has a vision of "the temple of the tent of witness [LXX rendering of "tent of meeting"] in heaven." And, almost like an echo of Exod 29:45-46, we read: "See the home (skēnē) of God is among mortals [in the heavenly Jerusalem]. He will dwell (skēnōsei σκηνώσει) with them as their

God; they will be his peoples, and God himself will be with them" (Rev 21:3).

Though infrequent, the invocation of the tabernacle in the NT functions in all four contexts cited to make central Christian affirmations about the presence of God among God's people. Stephen's critique of the Temple, however, is not sufficient evidence for positing an anti-Temple employment of tabernacle theology in the NT, as the combination of Temple and tent of testimony in Rev 15:5-6 shows most clearly. Similarly, God will "shelter" (skēnōsei, i.e., tent over them as a sheltering presence) those worshiping in the Temple day and night (Rev 7:15). Certain uses of *Temple* come close to those of "tent" or "tabernacle" (e.g., compare Col 1:19 and John 1:14; Rev 15:5-6 and 16:1, 17). In spite of some tensions, the NT tabernacle references, like most of the extra-pentateuchal OT ones, suggest a theological continuity between the two great OT paradigms of worship—tabernacle and Temple—but not a complete melding that would rob the tabernacle of its ongoing and distinctive theological voice. *See* DIVINE PRESENCE; GLORY, GLORIFY; TEMPLE, JERUSALEM.

Bibliography: Walter Brueggemann. "The Book of Exodus." *NIB* 1 (1994) 677–981; Brevard S. Childs. *The Book of Exodus: A Critical Theological Commentary.* OTL (1974); Richard J. Clifford. "The Tent of El and the Israelite Tent of Meeting." *CBQ* 33 (1971) 221–27; Frank Moore Cross. *Canaanite Myth and Hebrew Epic: Essays in the History of the Religion of Israel* (1973); Frank Moore Cross. *From Epic to Canon: History and Literature in Ancient Israel* (1998); Frank Moore Cross. "The Tabernacle: A Study from an Archaeological and Historical Approach." *BA* 10 (1947) 45–68; John I. Durham. *Exodus.* WBC 3 (1987); Daniel E. Fleming. "Mari's Large Public Tent and the Priestly Tent Sanctuary." *VT 50* (2000) 485–98; Terence E. Fretheim. *Exodus.* IBC (1991); Terence E. Fretheim. "The Priestly Document: Anti-Temple?" *VT 18* (1968) 313–29; Richard Elliott Friedman. *The Exile and Biblical Narrative* (1981); Richard Elliott Friedman. "The Tabernacle in the Temple." *BA 43* (1980) 241–48; Menahem Haran. *Temples and Temple Service in Ancient Israel: An Inquiry into Biblical Cult Phenomena and the Historical Setting of the Priestly School* (1985); Martin Ravndal Hauge. *The Descent from the Mountain: Narrative Patterns in Exodus 19–40* (2001); James K. Hoffmeier. *Ancient Israel in Sinai: The Evidence for the Authenticity of the Wilderness Tradition* (2005); Cornelis Houtman. *Exodus.* Vol. 3. Historical Commentary on the Old Testament (2000); Victor (Avigdor) Hurowitz. *I Have Built You an Exalted House: Temple Building in the Bible in Light of Mesopotamian and Northwest Semitic Writings* (1992); Victor (Avigdor) Hurowitz. "The Priestly Account of Building the Tabernacle." *JAOS* 105 (1985) 21–30; Waldemar Janzen. *Exodus.* Believers Church Bible Commentary (2000); Craig R. Koester. *The Dwelling of God: The*

Tabernacle in the Old Testament, Intertestamental Jewish Literature, and the New Testament (1989); Jon D. Levenson. *Creation and the Persistence of Evil: The Jewish Drama of Divine Omnipotence* (1988); William C. Propp. *Exodus 19–40: A New Translation with Introduction and Commentary.* AB 2A (2006); Rolf Rendtorff. *Canon and Theology* (1993); Benjamin D. Sommer. "Conflicting Constructions of Divine Presence in the Priestly Tabernacle." *BibInt* 9 (2001) 41–63; Julius Wellhausen. *Prolegomena to the History of Ancient Israel* (1878).

WALDEMAR JANZEN

TABERNACLES, FEAST OF. *See* BOOTHS, FEAST OR FESTIVAL OF; FEASTS AND FASTS.

TABGHA. Beginning in the 4th cent. CE, Christian pilgrims venerated the miracle of the multiplication of loaves and fishes (Mark 6) at this site on the northwest side of the Sea of Galilee. The area has also been associated with the post-resurrection appearance story of Jesus feeding the disciples breakfast (John 21) and with the Sermon on the Mount. Egeria's late 4th-cent. pilgrimage narrative provides the first literary reference to Christian veneration at the site (*CCSL* 175.99). The Arabic name Tabgha derives from the site's Greek name Heptapegon ("seven springs").

The remains of ancient churches were uncovered in the early 20th cent. A 4th-cent. chapel lies beneath a late 5th-cent., three-nave church adorned with elaborate mosaics depicting water flora and fauna. A damaged mosaic inscription in this Byzantine church refers to the "memory and repose" of the building's sponsor, Patriarch Martyrios of Jerusalem (served 478–86 CE). A stone found beneath the ancient altar may have been venerated as the rock of the multiplication. A bread and fish mosaic is located near the altar. The Byzantine church was destroyed in the early 7th cent. A modern church was first built on the site in 1933. The present Church of the Multiplication of Loaves and Fishes was completed in 1982 and contains part of the foundations and the restored mosaics of the earlier period.

Nearby on the seashore, the Church of the Primacy of Peter was built in 1933 on the ruins of a 4th-cent. church that is still partially visible beneath the present structure. The church encompasses a large rock in front of the altar, which has been venerated as the place where Jesus made the disciples' breakfast. A third Byzantine chapel commemorating the Sermon on the Mount stood on the hill overlooking Heptapegon. The current Church of the Beatitudes was built in 1938.

MILTON C. MORELAND

TABITHA. *See* DORCAS.

TABLE FELLOWSHIP. The term "table fellowship" does not occur as such in the Bible, but the theme merits close attention because references to eating and drinking in the presence of God or Christ or angels are so numerous. The account in Gen 18:1-15 of Abraham's serving a lavish meal to three strangers becomes an archetype for communion with the divine both in postbiblical Judaism (*Testament of Abraham*) and in the NT (Luke 16:22; Heb 13:2). According to Exod 24:9-11, the giving of Torah includes an ascent by Israel's elders to Mount Sinai, where they behold God and eat and drink. Psalm 23:5 portrays God as Israel's host, preparing a table in the presence of its enemies. This image may derive from the foundational tradition of God's feeding Israel with MANNA, a food termed "the bread of angels" in Ps 78:25. In 1st-cent. Judaism both the Sabbath eve dinner and the yearly Passover seder assumed God's saving presence as a reality. For some Jews, the Passover seder had acquired a strongly eschatological character (Mark 14:25).

Jesus associated hope for the fullness of God's reign with several types of meals. Known as a guest at the tables of marginal people (often referred to as "tax collectors and sinners"; Luke 7:33-35), he celebrated their joyful participation in the kingdom of God that he proclaimed (Mark 2:13-20). Many narratives, sayings, and parables show Jesus using the meals he attends to challenge popular understandings of purity, honor, uprightness, and repentance (e.g., Matt 22:1-14; Luke 7:36-50; 14:1-24; 15:11-23; 19:1-10). Jesus' expectation of a great banquet marking the full establishment of the kingdom (Matt 8:11) is probably based on a vision in Isa 25:6-8 of a feast that God will host on Mount Zion for "all nations." Jesus' meal practice seems to be a sign and foretaste of this inclusive event. At a last supper with his disciples on the evening of his arrest, he links the future kingdom meal with his impending death (Mark 14:25).

New Testament resurrection accounts are sometimes pictured as reunions with Jesus at a meal (Luke 24:13-42; John 21:1-23; Acts 1:3-4; 10:41). From such experiences, plus those of the Last Supper and the Spirit-filled KOINONIA meals at Pentecost (Acts 2:42-47), there soon evolved ritual dinners in the NT churches (the "breaking of the bread" and "Lord's supper"). Paul highlights the communion between believers and the crucified and risen Christ that occurs at these dinners (1 Cor 10–11). He also sees them as optimal occasions for receiving and sharing charismatic gifts (1 Cor 12–14). Thus the koinonia of the Spirit (2 Cor 13:13) is often realized at table. *See* MEALS.

Bibliography: Bruce Chilton. *Pure Kingdom: Jesus' Vision of God* (1996); John Koenig. *The Feast of the World's Redemption: Eucharistic Origins and Christian Mission* (2000).

JOHN KOENIG

TABLE, TABLES [שֻׁלְחָן *shulkhan*; τράπεζα *trapeza*]. "Table" is the most frequent translation of **shulkhan** and **trapeza** in the English versions of the Bible. *Table* often refers simply to a place to dine or to a piece of furniture (e.g., 1 Kgs 13:20; 2 Kgs 4:10). Ben Sirach makes references to the dining table and appropriate manners there (Sir 14:10; 29:26; 31:12).

Tables are associated with temple sacrifice. Ezekiel 40:38-43 describes eight tables at the vestibule of the Temple's north gate for the slaughtering of sacrifices and four additional tables for sacred utensils and butchered meat (but see 1 Chr 28:16). Solomon made ten tables for the Temple according to 2 Chr 4:8, and the Mishnah increases the number to thirteen (*m. Sheq.* 6:4), including two for the showbread. The large table in front of the idealized sanctuary in Ezek 41:21-22 is of uncertain function. The unusual syntax of these verses suggests that the table in question had the appearance of an altar but was, instead, made of wood. Perhaps Ezek 44:16 refers to the same table. Malachi 1:7, 12 may employ this tradition by setting "altar" (1:7) in parallel with "the Lord's table" (1:12).

According to Exod 25:23-30, the table of showbread was of gold-plated acacia wood (*see* BREAD OF PRESENCE). Constructed for rapid mobility, this table had a frame with two gold rings on each side into which Aaron and his sons would insert two poles of gold-plated acacia so that the Kohathites (Num 3:27-32) could carry it (Num 4:8, 15*b*). Solomon furnished his Temple with a new golden table of showbread (1 Kgs 7:48) but Hezekiah had to cleanse it in the wake of King Ahaz's apostasy (2 Chr 29:18). This table was the model for the golden table in Lev 24:7-8, where Aaron is instructed to set out twelve cakes weekly in two rows on a golden table with sticks of incense interspersed between the rows (see also 2 Chr 13:11). Antiochus IV (r. 175–164 BCE) stole the table of showbread from the Second Temple (1 Macc 1:22). So, following the Maccabean reconquest of the Temple Mount, the priests built a new table of showbread (1 Macc 4:49). The table of showbread from Herod's Temple is pictured on the Arch of Titus in Rome as part of the loot taken from Jerusalem.

There is mention of a table for food offerings for the god Bel (Bel 18, 21). In Isa 65:11 there is reference to a table for the god Fortune. For a description of the kinds of tables, used by money-changers, that Jesus overturned (Matt 21:12; Mark 11:15; John 2:15), see *b. B. Metz.* 26b. *See* also MONEY-CHANGER.

Metaphorical and metonymical uses of *table* occur throughout the Bible. Tables of kings signify the king's power (Judg 1:7), largesse (1 Sam 20:29; 34; 2 Sam 9:7; 1 Kgs 2:7), or prosperity (1 Kgs 10:5; 2 Chr 9:4). Eating at the king's table is a metonym of personal status and is used in that sense in 2 Sam 9:7, 10, 11, 13; 19:28; 1 Kgs 2:7; 4:27; 10:5; 18:19; 2 Chr 9:4. The psalmist expresses God's goodness by declaring that God has prepared a table for him in the presence of his enemies (Ps 23:5). The rehabilitation of Jehoiachin is signified by the fact that he dined regularly at the table of the Babylonian king (2 Kgs 25:29//Jer 52:33). The figure is not, however, limited to kings. Nehemiah regularly

served 150 at his spacious table during the rebuilding of Jerusalem's walls (Neh 5:17), and in Job 36:16 a table represents Job's restored wealth and power.

In 1 Cor 10:21, Paul explicitly uses "cup of the Lord" and "table of the Lord" as a figure of the eucharistic meal and, by extension, the fellowship of those who partake, contrasting this cup and table with the "cup of demons" and the "table of demons." *See* TABLE FELLOWSHIP.

FRED L. HORTON

TABLELAND [מִישׁוֹר mishor]. A number of biblical translations, including the NRSV, understand this term to designate the plain of Moab. The Wadi Arnon forms its southern boundary. Important cities to the north include DIBON (Josh 13:17), MEDEBA (Josh 13:16), and HESHBON (Josh 13:21). Above these cities lies the Iron Age state of Ammon. Archaeologists have found a number of important Moabite ruins in this region, including the Iron Age Mesha Stele. *See* ISRAEL, GEOGRAPHY OF; MESHA; MOAB, MOABITES; MOABITE STONE; PLAIN.

GARRETT GALVIN, OFM

TABLES OF DUTIES. *See* LISTS, ETHICAL.

TABLET [לוּחַ luakh; δέλτος deltos, πινακίδιον pinakidion, πλάξ plax]. In the Bible, *tablet* usually refers to the two hewn stone tablets (Exod 34:1; Deut 10:1) that Moses received at Mount Sinai (e.g., Exod 24:12; 31:18; Deut 4:13). A vibrant biblical tradition affirms that these tablets were placed in the ark of the covenant (Deut 10:5; 1 Kgs 8:9; 2 Chr 5:10; Heb 9:4). Inscribing in stone would normally require the use of a hammer and chisel. Sometimes *tablet* arguably refers to a papyrus (or vellum) roll (e.g., Isa 8:1). There are also times when the term *tablet* is used in a generic sense to refer to writing surfaces in general: letters in ink on pottery, letters incised in pottery, or even letters in ink on a clay tablet (see Isa 8:1; 30:8; Hab 2:2). In 1 Macc 8:22; 14:18 (compare 14:27, 48) a treaty is inscribed on bronze tablets. Zechariah requests a "writing tablet" to write the name he wished for his son to be given (Luke 1:63; compare 2 Esd 14:24); this tablet was probably an example of the reusable WRITING BOARDS attested throughout much of the ANE and the Mediterranean world. The OT uses *tablet* as a metaphor for the human heart: "write them on the tablet of your heart" (e.g., Prov 3:3; 7:3; compare Jer 17:1). This usage persists in Paul's writings (2 Cor 3:3; compare 2 Cor 3:7).

Clay tablets were the most common medium for writing CUNEIFORM texts. A writing stylus was used to impress the clay. Tablets could vary in both size and shape. Tablets needed to be moist at the time of writing; afterward, they were dried in an oven, or more commonly dried in the sun. The earliest clay tablets date to the late 4th millennium BCE. *See* INSCRIPTIONS; WRITING AND WRITING MATERIALS.

Todd Bolen/BiblePlaces.com
Figure 1: Mount Tabor aerial view from northwest

Bibliography: Jean-Jacques Glassner. *The Invention of Cuneiform: Writing in Sumer* (2003); Ernst Posner. *Archives in the Ancient World* (1972).

CHRISTOPHER A. ROLLSTON

TABOR tay′buhr [תָּבוֹר *tavor*]. A Levitical city in Zebulun (1 Chr 6:77 [Heb. 6:62]). *See* TABOR, MOUNT; ZEBULUN, ZEBULUNITE.

TABOR, MOUNT tay′buhr [הַר תָּבוֹר *har tavor*]. Mount Tabor is a dome-shaped outcropping in lower Galilee rising to approximately 1,850 ft., lying about 11 mi. southwest of Tiberias and overlooking the Jezreel Valley at the intersection of the tribal territories of Zebulon, Issachar, and Naphtali. Also known by its Arabic name Jebel et-Tur, in postbiblical times the mountain became associated with Jesus' transfiguration.

The word *Tabor* occurs twelve times in the OT, with half of these instances referring to place names other than the mountain: towns in tribal boundary lists that were near the mountain (Josh 19:12, 22, 34); a Levitical city in Zebulon (1 Chr 6:77); a Transjordanian site (Judg 8:18); and an oak near Bethel (1 Sam 10:3; *see* TABOR, OAK OF). Mount Tabor itself figures prominently in the narrative of Deborah's victory over Sisera (Judg 4:6, 12, 14). The remaining three references are in poetic (Ps 89:12 [Heb. 89:13]) and prophetic (Jer 46:18; Hos 5:1) texts. The etymology of *Tabor* as a proper name is not completely certain, but some scholars suggest a possible Phoenician derivation from the name of a Semitic god, who is known in Greek as Zeus Atabyros (Manns).

Mount Tabor derived its strategic military importance from its location overlooking the Jezreel Valley and the main road linking Egypt with the Beqa Valley in the north (Dorsey). Deborah's army, under the command of Barak, used the mountain as a staging ground for their assault on Sisera's troops, whose chariots were limited to less rugged places. Josephus testifies to the fortifications on Mount Tabor during the Roman campaign of 67 CE, which led to his capture (*Life* 188).

Mount Tabor functions as a literary metaphor, in parallel with Mount Carmel, of the approaching might of King Nebuchadnezzar's army (Jer 46:18). The mountain also serves as a natural source of praise to God, used in parallel to Mount Hermon (Ps 89:12 [Heb. 89:13]). Deuteronomy 33:18-19, alluding to the worship offered by Zebulon and Issachar, may suggest that Mount Tabor is the mountain where those tribes "offer the right sacrifices" (see Hos 5:1).

The NT does not mention Mount Tabor, but according to rabbinic tradition revelation was given on this mountan (e.g., *Gen. Rab.* 99:1), and Jesus' transfiguration was tied to Mount Tabor possibly as early as Origen (ca. 185–254 CE; *Hom. Jer.* 15.10), although the synoptic Gospels seem to place Jesus in the vicinity of Caesarea Philippi when the transfiguration occurs, lending support to Mount Hermon as the location (e.g., Mark 8:27). Nevertheless, Mount Tabor continues to be revered as a holy place, with Franciscan and Greek Orthodox churches currently occupying its summit.

Bibliography: David A. Dorsey. *The Roads and Highways of Ancient Israel* (1991); Rivka Gonen. *Biblical Holy Places* (2000); Frédéric Manns. "Mount Tabor." *Jesus and Archaeology.* James H. Charlesworth, ed. (2006) 167–77; Anson F. Rainey and R. Steven Notley. *The Sacred Bridge* (2006).

JAMES K. MEAD

TABOR, OAK OF tay'buhr [אֵלוֹן תָּבוֹר *'elon tavor*]. Site where, according to Samuel, Saul was to receive the second sign that he would be king (1 Sam 10:3); its exact location is uncertain.

TABRIMMON tab-rim'uhn [טַבְרִמֹּן *tavrimmon*]. The compound name means "Rimmon is good." Tabrimmon was son of Hezion and father of Ben-hadad, the king of Aram in Damascus (1 Kgs 15:18). Tabrimmon reigned as king of Damascus and enjoyed good treaty relations with Abijah (Abijam), king of Judah (compare 2 Chr 16:3). On the basis of this treaty their sons Ben-Hadad and Asa, king of Judah, entered into an alliance against Baasha, king of Israel (1 Kgs 15:16-22; compare 2 Chr 16:1-10) during the early 9th cent. BCE.

KEN FENTRESS

TACKLE [σκευή *skeuē*]. Fishing techniques and tackle are rarely noted in the Bible. The term *tackle* itself occurs in the NRSV only in Acts 27:19. The majority of interest is found in the Gospel stories about several of Jesus' disciples being fishers (Mark 1:16-20). Archaeological investigations and ancient literary sources reveal that several different fishing techniques were popular in ancient Israel. Various sizes and types of nets were used to catch fish. A small casting NET with weights on the end could be cast from a boat or from the shore (Matt 4:18). In Hab 1:14-15 there is a reference to a HOOK and a SEINE net. Large nets are also used in trammel fishing, which is usually done at night. This technique employs a series of three layered nets of different mesh sizes that are tied together with corked rope on top and weighted rope on the bottom. Matthew 17:27 refers to using a hook to catch a fish; angling with a rod, linen line, and FISHHOOK was common. Ancient fishing techniques also involved traps and harpoons. In 1998 off the Mediterranean coast at Dor, an assemblage of fishing tackle objects was discovered during the underwater excavation of a 7th-cent. CE shipwreck. A floating fire basket for use in night fishing was discovered, along with the iron head of a harpoon, and lead weights for casting nets. Hooks, weights, and a fishing boat have also been discovered in and around the Sea of Galilee.

Bibliography: Mendel Nun. "Cast Your Net upon the Waters: Fish and Fishermen in Jesus' Time." *BAR* 19.6 (1993) 46–56, 70.

MILTON C. MORELAND

TADMOR tad'mor [תַּדְמֹר *tadhmor*]. An important caravanserai about 150 mi. northeast of Damascus on the trade route between that city and Mesopotamia. In Hellenistic and Roman times, the site was known as Palmyra.

According to 2 Chr 8:4, Solomon "built Tadmor in the wilderness"; in the MT 1 Kgs 9:18 reads "Tamar in the wilderness," but the Masoretic tradition prefers that the text be read "Tadmor" (*see* MASORETES; QERE-KETHIBH). The site of Tadmor presumably lay within territory that Solomon's father David had brought under Israelite control (2 Sam 8; 1 Chr 18). Taking territory this far to the north and east allowed Israel to control the entire length of the King's Highway, the major trade route through the Transjordan. Israel enjoyed enviable wealth as a result of its control of the King's Highway as well as the Via Maris, the major trade route along the Mediterranean coast. However, this control did not outlast the reign of Solomon.

TIMOTHY G. CRAWFORD

TAHAN tay'han [תַּחַן *takhan*]. A son of Ephraim and clan leader (Num 26:35). First Chronicles 7:25 apparently refers to a later descendant of Ephraim, Tahan son of Telah, who was also an ancestor of Joshua son of Nun.

TAHASH tay'hash [תַּחַשׁ *takhash*]. One of the children born to Reumah, the concubine of Abraham's brother Nahor (Gen 22:24).

TAHATH tay'hath [תַּחַת *takhath*]. 1. A place (location unknown) where the Israelites camped during their wilderness wanderings (Num 33:26-27).

2. A son of Assir and descendant of Kohath (1 Chr 6:24 [Heb. 6:9], 37 [Heb. 6:22]), who was a descendant of Levi (Gen 46:11).

3. Son of Bered, of the tribe of Ephraim (1 Chr 7:20).

4. Son of Eleadah, and grandson of Tahath son of Bered, of the tribe of Ephraim (1 Chr 7:20).

KEN FENTRESS

TAHCHEMONITE tah-kee'muh-n*i*t [תַּחְכְּמֹנִי *takhkemoni*]. A gentilic in 2 Sam 23:8 identifying one of David's mighty men, Josheb-basshebeth. Regarded as a textual corruption of "HACHMONI" (*khakkmoni* חַכְמוֹנִי) in 1 Chr 11:11. *See* JASHOBEAM.

TAHPANHES tah'puhn-heez [תַּחְפַּנְחֵס *takhpankhes*, תְּחַפְנְחֵס *tekhafnekhes*]. Egyptian city located in the northeastern Nile Delta region, about 18 mi. east by southeast of Tanis and about 20 mi. west of the probable site of Migdol (Exod 14:2; Num 33:7; Jer 44:1). Tahpanhes guarded the northeast frontier of Egypt. In Hellenistic times it was known as Daphnae (modern Tell Defenneh).

Jeremiah names Tahpanhes and Memphis as symbols of Egyptian power (2:16). In Ezek 30, God proposes to devastate Egypt by sending Nebuchadnezzar II of Babylon against its cities, including Tahpanhes (v. 18, variant spelling "Tehaphnehes"). Likewise, in Jer 46:13-26, the prophet delivers an oracle promising a Babylonian invasion of Egypt, and Tahpanhes is mentioned alongside Memphis and Migdol (v. 14).

After the Babylonians captured Judah in 587 BCE, they appointed Gedaliah as leader of the territory (Jer 40:5). A renegade member of the royal family of Judah murdered Gedaliah and the Babylonian officials with him (Jer 41). Fearing a Babylonian reprisal and rejecting the advice of Jeremiah, the Judeans decided to take refuge in Egypt (Jer 42:1–43:7). One of the places to which the Jews fled was Tahpanhes (43:7), where Jeremiah performed a prophetic sign, burying large stones in the soft pavement in front of the government building. These stones were meant to serve as a support for the throne of Nebuchadnezzar when he invaded the land (43:8-13). Jeremiah 44 contains an oracle directed against the Judean refugees in the land and their Egyptian host cities, including Tahpanhes, Migdol, and Memphis, as well as against Upper Egypt in general ("Land of Pathros," 44:1). Epigraphical evidence of a substantial Jewish colony in Upper Egypt in the 5th cent. BCE survives in the ELEPHANTINE PAPYRI; perhaps this colony was founded by Judean refugees in the early 6th cent.

Bibliography: Peter C. Craigie, Page H. Kelley, and Joel F. Drinkard, Jr. *Jeremiah 1–25*. WBC 26 (1991); Gerald L. Keown, Pamela J. Scalise, and Thomas G. Smothers. *Jeremiah 26–52*. WBC 27 (1995).

TIMOTHY G. CRAWFORD

TAHPENES tah′puh-neez [תַּחְפְּנֵיס takhpenes]. Personal name or title of an Egyptian queen, the wife of a pharaoh who ruled during the Twenty-first Dynasty of Egypt. According to 1 Kgs 11:19-20, Tahpenes was the wife of the pharaoh who sheltered Hadad the Edomite, the only member of Edom's royal family who survived the campaign led by David and Joab. Hadad and some of his father's royal officials fled to Egypt. The king of Egypt gave them asylum (1 Kgs 11:14-18). He also gave Hadad a wife, the sister of Tahpenes. Hadad and his wife had a son, Genubath, whom Tahpenes raised in her household.

Although the NRSV takes the word as a proper name, it is possible that *Tahpenes* is the queen's title, i.e., the Hebrew transliteration of the Egyptian word t3-hmt-p3-nsw ("the wife of the king"). Tahpenes is also called the "queen mother" or the "great lady" (gevirah גְּבִירָה; NRSV, "Queen," 1 Kgs 11:19). Her title indicates the important position she occupied in the king's palace.

CLAUDE F. MARIOTTINI

TAHREA. *See* TAREA.

TALE OF THE ELOQUENT PEASANT. *See* PEASANT, PROTESTS OF THE ELOQUENT.

TALENTS tal′uhnt [כִּכָּר kikkar; τάλαντον talanton]. In the OT, a measure of weight approximating seventy-five lbs.; in the NT, a monetary unit roughly equal to 6,000 drachmas (greater than sixteen years' wages for a laborer). *See* WEIGHTS AND MEASURES.

TALITHA CUMI tal′uh-thuh-koo′mi [ταλιθα κουμι talitha koumi]. Greek transliteration of the Aramaic sentence "Little girl, get up!" (talitha′ qumi טְלִיתָא קוּמִי). In Mark 5:41, Jesus speaks in Aramaic, commanding a young girl (talitha) who appears to have died, to "get up" or "rise" (Greek koumi). The best Greek texts, however, read talitha koum (ταλιθα κουμ, transliterating Aramaic talitha′ qum [טַל יתָא קֻם]) here, not talitha koumi, and the addition of -i in some texts was probably an effort to make the Aramaic imperative qum, which appears to be masculine singular, agree with the feminine singular talitha′.

Over time, however, the Aramaic feminine singular imperative lost the ending -i. In the Talmud (*b. Shabb.* 110ab), Aramaic qum is a feminine singular imperative within a healing command to a woman with venereal disease. This loss of -i is a feature not only of Eastern Aramaic, like Talmudic Aramaic or Syriac, as was once thought; the form also appears in Galilean Aramaic. There is, however, no evidence for the change as early as the 1st cent. CE.

Mark 5:41 is not the only place in Mark where the Aramaic grammar of Jesus' healing commands comes into question. In Mark 7:34 Jesus addresses the ears of a deaf man by using the masculine singular Aramaic command ephphatha (ἐφφαθά), "Be opened!" (*see* EPHPHATHA). The *ears* are feminine dual in Aramaic, and in no historical instance of the Aramaic language would this formulation have been grammatical. Most likely, the best text of Mark 5:41 (talitha koum) is, like ephphatha in Mark 7:34, a wooden and ungrammatical use of the masculine singular imperative by someone not well acquainted with Aramaic. It is difficult to understand how this Aramaic formulation could reflect a memory of the language of Jesus, as some have held.

Bibliography: Fred L. Horton Jr. "Nochmals ἐφφαθά in Mk 7:34." *ZNW* 77 (1986) 101–108; E. Y. Kutscher. *Studies in Galilean Aramaic* (1976).

FRED L. HORTON

TALL. *See* TEL, TELL.

TALL AL-ʿUMAYRI. *See* ʿUMAYRI, TALL AL-.

TALMAI tal′mi [תַּלְמַי talmay]. 1. One of the Anakites, who were giants living in the area of Hebron (Num

13:22). The name may be Hurrian in origin; *Talmai* means "great" in Hurrian. According to Josh 15:14, Caleb defeated Talmai, whereas Judg 1:10 states that the Judahites defeated him.

2. Son of Ammihud and ruler of Geshur, a small kingdom east of the Sea of Galilee. David married Talmai's daughter Maacah, apparently as part of a treaty arrangement, and she became the mother of Absalom (2 Sam 2:3; 1 Chr 3:2). After Absalom arranged the murder of his half-brother Amnon, he sought refuge with Talmai in Geshur (2 Sam 13:37).

Bibliography: Baruch Levine. *Numbers 1–20.* AB 4 (1993).

TIMOTHY G. CRAWFORD

TALMON tal′muhn [טַלְמֹן talmon; Τολμάν Tolman]. A returnee from exile and head of a house of Levitical gatekeepers (1 Chr 9:17; Ezra 2:42; Neh 7:45; 1 Esd 5:28).

TALMUD tal′mood [תַּלְמוּד talmudh]. The Babylonian Talmud or Bavli is one of the enduring accomplishments of Jewish religious literature. It has captured the imagination and energy of centuries of Jewish scholars on a level of respect otherwise only accorded to the Bible. Generations of students have studied Talmud as both an intellectual endeavor and a spiritual exercise from the era of its redaction to the present.

A. Rabbinic Judaism in Babylonia
B. Tannaitic Literature and Amoraic Activities (ca. 70–500 CE)
C. Stam (Anonymous Editorial Activity)/Saboraic Redactorial Activities (ca. 500–600 CE)
D. Review of Tractates of Talmud
E. Sample Selections
F. Gaonic Commentary and Responsa (ca. 600–1000 CE)
G. "Extra-Canonical" Tractates
H. Medieval Commentators (ca. 1000–1500 CE)
I. Responsa and Codes
J. Modern Study of the Talmud (1500 CE–present)
Bibliography

A. Rabbinic Judaism in Babylonia

From the time of the Babylonian exile in 587/86 BCE, a Jewish community flourished in Babylonia (roughly congruent with modern Iraq). Unfortunately, from the close of the biblical period until the 3rd cent. CE little is known about the status and welfare of the Jewish community there. By the mid-3rd cent., under the Sassanian, Zoroastrian rule of Shapur I, the Jewish community of Babylonia emerged as a rabbinic community. With the initial rabbinic leadership of a student of Rabbi Judah the Patriarch, the editor of the Mishnah, disciple circles dedicated to the study of that document were established. This student and rabbinic leader was called

by his title *Rav* (the Babylonian form of *rabbi*), or by the name Abba Arikhah (which might also be a title). Later tradition credits Rav with establishing the "school" of Sura, while his Babylonian colleague Samuel is credited with establishing the "school" of Pumbeditha. These two schools remained centers for the study of rabbinic literature up to the demise of the Gaonate in 1040 CE.

B. Tannaitic Literature and Amoraic Activities (ca. 70–500 CE)

Intensive study of the MISHNAH was the basic curriculum of these schools. The rabbis and their students compared Mishnah to Tosefta and to the corpora of other Tannaitic dicta they had memorized (*see* TOSEPHTA, TOSEPTA, TOSEFTA). These statements were most often harmonized with one another so that the earlier Tannaitic (*see* TANNA, TANNAIM) materials were made to appear monolithic and in general agreement with the Mishnah, even where they in fact contradicted, overturned, or expanded its purview. The later rabbis, who came to be called Amoraim (sing. Amora), also undertook to provide biblical justification for many of the apodictic pronouncements of the Mishnah (*see* AMORA, AMORAIM). This activity of proof-texting continued even in the immediate post-Talmudic era. The hallmark of Babylonian Amoraic activity was dialectical argument about virtually every aspect of the Mishnah. These arguments were a form of intellectual exercise that taught students a mode of dialectical thinking that remains the *sine qua non* of Talmudic activity. The hermeneutic of this dialectic allowed for inferences from silence, consideration of the implications of applying the law under discussion to parallel circumstances, analogical reasoning, and exhaustive iterations of the various permutations of arguments. A given unit of thought brought to its conclusion was then transmitted for subsequent generations to study. Such a pericope was called a sugheya' (סוּגְיָא) in Aramaic.

The arguments about rabbinic HALAKHAH were provided with narrative relief and illustration through the inclusion of Greco-Roman style CHREIA about the Palestinian Tannas. As time went on, the Babylonian sages also reworked stories about their Palestinian Amoraic counterparts, often retelling these tales with a Babylonian ideological cast. The Babylonian rabbis also related didactic narratives about their own colleagues. This corpus of HAGGADAH complemented the halakhic materials that were transmitted in Babylonian disciple circles. Over time, the disciple circles became actual academies, and the narrative material came to include folklore, folk medicine, natural science, "history," exegeses of the Bible (*see* MIDRASH), and the like. By the redaction of the Talmud, roughly one-third of its content was haggadic. The other two-thirds were made up of Mishnaic materials and halakhic.

C. Stam (Anonymous Editorial Activity)/Saboraic Redactorial Activities (ca. 500–600 CE)

Babylonian rabbis are reckoned by generations of teachers and their disciples. Thus, Rav and Samuel are among the very first generation of Babylonian Amoraim, and it is customary to count as many as seven generations of these rabbis. The period of the Babylonian Amoraim extends from ca. 220 CE through the end of the 5ᵗʰ cent. Ravina and Rav Ashi were the leaders of the sixth generation who flourished in the early 6ᵗʰ cent. They traditionally are considered to mark the formal end of Talmudic activity. Following their generation, redaction of the Talmud was undertaken by an anonymous editor or series of editors, called the Stam (from setam [סְתָם] pl. Stammaim), or Stam GEMARA.

Current scholarship attributes a great deal of the dialectic of the Talmud to the editorial art of the Stam, who arranged the generations of received Amoraic traditions into argumentation. Other scholars hold the Stam responsible for the reworking of haggadic narratives about Palestinian rabbis to conform to a Babylonian rabbinic worldview. In any case, editorial activity continued on a lesser level well into the Middle Ages, as the text of the Talmud remained somewhat fluid in both oral and even written recensions. The generations after the formal close of the Talmud are called the era of Saboraim, and this group of transmitters and redactors also added biblical proof-texting to Tannaitic materials and to halakhic sugheyoth (סוּגְיוֹת).

D. Review of Tractates of Talmud

Despite the thoroughness of Talmudic dialectic in considering the details of Mishnaic pronouncements, not all of the sixty-three tractates of Mishnah are, in fact, commented upon by the Babylonian Talmud (or, for that matter, by the Talmud Yerushalmi; *see* TALMUD, JERUSALEM; and *see* MISHNAH for a complete listing of tractates). All told, only thirty-seven tractates of Mishnah are discussed by the Babylonian Talmud, and of these, some considerations are partial. These tractates of Talmud are listed as follows, in the order in which they appear in standard printed editions: 1) Agriculture (*Zeraim*)—*Berakhot* (Since the laws of agriculture only apply in the land of Israel, the Babylonian academies did not study these tractates and therefore only tractate *Berakhot* is considered for this order.); 2) Calendar/ Holidays (*Moed*)—*Shabbat, Eruvin, Pesahim, Rosh HaShannah, Yoma, Sukkah, Betzah, Megillah, Taanit, Moed Qatan, Hagigah, Sheqalim* (there is no Bavli for this tractate. Printed editions have *Yerushalmi Sheqalim* in its place); 3) Women (*Nashim*)—*Yevamot, Ketubbot, Nedarim, Nazir, Sotah, Gittin, Qiddushin*; 4) Torts (*Neziqin*)—*Bava Qamma, Bava Metzia, Bava Batra, Avodah Zarah, Sanhedrin, Shevuot, Makkot, Horayot*; 5) Sacred Things (*Qodashim*): *Zevahim, Menahot, Bekhorot, Hullin, Arakhin, Temurah, Keritot, Meilah, Tamid* (Gemara only to chaps. 1; 2; 4); 6) Purities

(*Teharot*): *Niddah* (there is Gemara for this tractate only).

E. Sample Selections

No amount of explanation or exposition can capture the give and take of a Talmudic argument. The halakhic selection below, from *Mo'ed Qatan* 13b–14a, is a reasonably typical example. We begin with the Mishnah and follow with the Talmudic discussion on who may cut their hair and do laundry during the intermediate days of the biblical pilgrimage festivals of Sukkot and Passover. The discussion considers the question in particular, but the general issue is to what degree these intermediate days are like the festivals regarding prohibitions, and to what degree are these day like the mundane work days of the non-festival calendar. In the author's translation that follows, words in brackets are added explanatory material.

> MISHNAH 3:1. And these may cut their hair on the [intermediate days of a biblical pilgrimage] festival: one who arrives from the maritime provinces, or from captivity, or one coming out of prison, or one who was banned whom the sages absolved, and also one [who had taken a vow] and had asked a sage [for release from that vow] and been released, and the nazarite and the leper [ascending] from his [state of ritual] impurity to his purity. And these may do laundry on [the intermediate days of] the festival: one who arrives from the maritime provinces, or from captivity, or one coming out of prison, [14a] or one who was banned whom the sages absolved, and also one [who had taken a vow] and had asked a sage [for release from that vow] and been released. Handtowels, and barbers' towels, and bath-towels, men and women with a [genital, venereal] flow, menstruants, and women who have given birth, and all who are ascending from [a state of ritual] impurity to [ritual] purity, behold these are permitted; and all other persons are prohibited.

> GEMARA. "And all other persons" what is the reason they "are prohibited?" As was recited to us [in a Mishnah from *Taanit* 2:7 regarding service in the Jerusalem Temple]: "Men on Watch [viz., local priests during their turn of service in Jerusalem] and men on Post [viz., the group from that locale who were supporting their priests during their turn] are prohibited to cut their hair or do laundry. But on Thursday they are permitted because of the honor of the Sabbath."

> And Rabbah b. Bar-Hana quoted R. Elazar: 'What is the reason [they are forbidden to barber and launder during their turn of service]? So that they should not begin their Watch when they are disheveled.' Here, too, [they are forbidden to bar-

ber and launder during the intermediate days of the festival] so that they do not begin the festival [itself] when they are disheveled.

R. Zera asked, 'If a person had lost an object on the eve of the festival, would he then be permitted [to barber and launder on the intermediate days] since he was unavoidably prevented [from doing those things beforehand due to searching for what he had lost]? Or, since the matter [of his lost item and being unavoidably prevented] was not obvious to all, he would not [be permitted to barber and launder on the intermediate days of the festival]?'

Abaye said, 'Shall we then say "All loaves are prohibited, but the loaves of Boethius are permitted?"' [Abaye invokes a principle from Babylonian Talmud *Pesahim* 37a, regarding loaves baked in a mold for Passover. This principle prohibits making exceptions to the rule, even if the Boethius loaves were "kosher for Passover," since it would not be obvious to the casual onlooker].

But given your reasoning, what of the statement of Rabbi Assi who quoted Rabbi Johanan, "Anyone who has only one garment may launder it on the intermediate days of the festival." There, too, shouldn't one say, "All loaves are prohibited, but the loaves of Boethius are permitted?" This statement arises [in response]: Mar son of Rav Ashi said, 'His undergarment is proof for him [that he has no alternative but to launder it, since if he had a second garment, he'd be wearing it and not doing his laundry with his undergarments showing].'

Rav Ashi taught [the tradition somewhat differently, as follows]: Rabbi Zera asked, "If an artisan lost an object on the eve of a festival, what is the [rule]? Is it the case that since he is an artisan [and people would be frequenting his shop in preparation for the festival, therefore] the matter would be obvious [that he was unavoidably prevented from barbering and laundering before the festival and therefore he is permitted to do so]? Or perhaps [even so] the matter is not obvious to all, like these others [mentioned in the Mishnah] and therefore he is not [permitted to barber and launder during the intermediate days of the festival]? *Teku* [lit., "the matter stands," which is to say: unresolved].

A second Talmudic passage, from *Shabbat* 31a, recounts a haggadah about Hillel (*see* HILLEL THE ELDER, HOUSE OF HILLEL) in which he is credited with reciting a negative formulation

of the Golden Rule (compare Matt 7:12; Luke 6:31). This tale is told in the style of the Greco-Roman CHREIA, in which the sage pronounces a memorable apothegm. Note that Hillel's principle is rendered in Aramaic, a common literary convention for reporting dialogue. The brief Hebrew phrase that is interjected may be a gloss added by the anonymous narrator.

A further story [is related by the rabbis] regarding a gentile who came to Shammai and said to him, "Convert me on the condition that you teach me the entire Torah while I stand on one foot." He pushed him away with the building cubit which was in his hand. He came to Hillel, who converted him. He told him [in Aramaic], "What is hateful to you, do not to your colleague. [Hebrew:] This is the entire Torah. [Aramaic:] The rest is commentary, go study."

F. Gaonic Commentary and Responsa (ca. 600–1000 CE)

With the Talmud text reaching substantial closure in the 6th cent., the scholars of the Babylonian academies turned from editorial work to commentary. It should be emphasized that even in this stage of Talmudic history much of the transmission of the text took place orally. The vast majority of the curriculum of the Gaonic academies was devoted to the study of the Talmud and its application within the Jewish community through Gaonic law courts. Most of the literature that survives is either commentary on the Talmud or legal responsa (see below and RABBINIC LITERATURE).

Part of the extreme focus on the Talmud stemmed from a challenge to rabbinic authority within the Jewish community from a group who claimed allegiance to only biblical authority: the Karaites. As the Karaite movement engaged in study of the Bible, the rabbis emphasized the study of the Mishnah and Talmud. Rav Sherira Gaon of Pumbeditha wrote a responsum (987 CE) to his North African colleague Rabbenu Yaakov ibn Shaheen of Kairawan, tracing the rabbinic movement from its earliest days through the time of the Talmud, in an attempt to buttress rabbinic authority. Sherira's epistle was the first work to offer a history of the Talmud text, the various generations of rabbis, and the composition of the work. It remains a resource for Talmudic historians even now.

G. "Extra-Canonical" Tractates

During the period immediately following the close of the Talmud, a number of tractates were composed that were not commentary on the Mishnah but dealt with matters of Jewish law. The one exception to this generalization is *Avot of Rabbi Nathan,* a Tosefta-style expansion on Mishnah *Pirqe Avot* (*see* SAYINGS OF THE FATHERS). In keeping with the content of that tractate, *Avot of Rabbi Nathan* recounts didactic legends of the rabbinic sages. It serves, as it were, as a rabbinic "Lives of the Saints." This so-called minor tractate exists in two separate recensions. The date of its redaction is debated by current scholarship.

Other extra-canonical tractates unrelated to the Mishnah include tractates *Soferim* (scribal and liturgical practices), *Semahot* (or *Evel Rabbati*, on mourning), *Kallah* (obligations to a bride), and *Derekh Eretz* (ethics). Additional minor tractates of the Gaonic period include: *Pereq Hashalom* (on the virtues of peace), *Sefer Torah* (on the writing of the pentateuchal scroll), *Mezuzah* (on the parchment placed on doorposts in keeping with Deut 6:9), *Tefillin* (on phylacteries, see Deut 6:8), *Tzitzit* (on ritual fringes, see Num 15:38-40), *Avadim* (the laws relating to slavery), *Gerim* (on proselytes) and *Kutim* (relating to Samaritans). These small works resemble the Mishnah, in that they are in Hebrew and are organized into chapters and sub-sections. Many of the "extra-canonical" tractates may be found in printed editions of the Talmud, usually following the order *Neziqin* (Torts).

H. Medieval Commentators (ca. 1000–1500 CE)

With the shifting of the rabbinic Jewish community to population centers in North Africa and Europe during the first half of the 2nd millennium, study of the Talmud and commentary upon it followed. The first commentary is that of Rabbenu Hananel ben Hushiel (Kairawan, now in Tunisia; ca. 990–1050). Rabbenu Hananel wrote a terse commentary on the Babylonian Talmud that was distinguished by his quotation of relevant passages from the Talmud Yerushalmi. His colleague in Kairawan, Rabbenu Nissim ben Yaakov ibn Shaheen, also wrote reference work *qua* commentary on a number of Talmudic tractates, cross-referencing passages therein. Shortly thereafter, Rabbi Nathan ben Yehiel of Rome (1035–1110) wrote a lexicon of rabbinic Hebrew, including citations, etymologies, and definitions.

A few decades earlier in Germany, Rabbenu Gershom of Mainz (ca. 960–1028) composed explanatory lectures on various tractates, which his students subsequently published. Thereafter, Rabbi Solomon ben Isaac, or Rashi (Troyes, France, d. 1105), wrote extensive commentary on most tractates of the Talmud (*see* RASHI). His commentary explains difficult words (often translating them into his local French vernacular), concepts, and legal questions. Rashi's magisterial commentary has accompanied every printed edition of Talmud. Rashi's sons-in-law and grandsons also wrote Talmud commentaries that focused on reconciling disparate contradictory passages. These are often published together with some other 12th- and 13th-cent. commentators under the rubric *Tosafot* (lit., "supplemental" commentaries).

In late 13th-cent. Provence, Rabbi Menaham ben Solomon, who was called Meiri (or in Provençal: Don Vidal Solomon), published a commentary on the Talmud called *Bet Habehirah*. Like Rashi, the Meiri sought to explicate difficult passages and often summarized the various legal viewpoints of his fellow commentators and legalists. His halakhic commentary remains a particularly lucid exposition that, like that of Rashi, is still a much-studied guide to the Talmud. In nearby Barcelona, Rabbi Solomon ben Aderet (1235–1310) wrote novella on the Talmud, as did his younger colleague from Sevilla, Rabbi Yom Tov ben Avraham (1250–1320). These commentators also continue to be studied. Finally, their German contemporary (1250–1327) Rabbi Asher ben Yehiel wrote Talmud commentaries even as he fled persecutions of the Jews in Germany and settled in Sefardic lands, ultimately accepting a post as rabbi of Toledo. His works were later edited by his son (see below) and became a prominent digest of rabbinic law.

We close this section on medieval Talmud commentary by noting an epitome of the haggadic passages found in the Babylonian Talmud by Rabbi Jacob ben Solomon ibn Habib (ca. 1445–1515). This work, called *Ein Yaakov*, also included passages from the Talmud Yerushalmi. Ibn Habib also wrote his own commentary, which quoted Rashi and other medieval commentators. The first part of this work was published in ibn Habib's hometown of Salonika in the last year of his life, with the remainder published by his son following his death.

I. Responsa and Codes

As the sample passage above indicates, the Talmud was fascinated with dialectic and did not always reach halakhic conclusions. From the Gaonic era onward, however, the assertion of rabbinic authority in local communities necessitated attention to legal conclusions. This is clearly the case with the previously discussed Gaonic responsa. The tendency toward clear legal decision making continued among the medieval rabbis who, in addition to writing their just-mentioned commentaries, also wrote responsa for their communities in North Africa and Europe.

A form of hybrid legal writing was the Talmud commentary, which also served as a legal code. In these quasi-codes, the law is organized according to the Talmud text, yet a clear decision of law is rendered. Two famous Gaonic works of this nature are the *Halakhot Gedolot* (Greater Laws), attributed to Simon Qayarra in the early 8th cent., and the *Halakhot Pesuqot* (Adjudicated Laws), attributed to Yehudai Gaon in the mid-8th cent.

Following this method, Rabbi Isaac al-Fasi (of Fez, 1013–1103 CE) extracted each halakhic sugya of the Talmud, leaving behind a version of legal writing entirely stripped of haggadah, which rendered a clear decision on each issue. Al-Fasi's work *Hilkhot Harif* (the acronym for Rabbi Isaac al-Fasi), continues to appear in printed editions of the Talmud. Moses Maimonides (North Africa and Andalusia, 12th cent.) went even further. He organized Jewish law into fourteen books, according to a system of Muslim law, and rendered his decisions without quoting the Talmudic precedents. His

Mishneh Torah became a legal work of towering authority in the Sefardic Jewish world. A century later, in Ashkenaz, Rabbi Eliezer ben Joel Halevi collected his halakhic decisions, Talmudic novellas, and responsa into a volume called *Sefer Raviah* (following the acronym for his name).

Also in 13th-cent. Ashkenaz, Rabbi Asher ben Yehiel composed a Talmud commentary on the work of al-Fasi, which also incorporates the code of Maimonides as well as the responsa and commentaries of the Ashkenazic Tosafot. Because Rabbi Asher began his life in Ashkenaz and ended up in Toledo, and because he incorporates the decisions of both Ashkenazic and Sefardic authorities, his commentary became a standard work throughout the entire rabbinic Jewish world. The prestige of his work was enhanced when his son, Rabbi Jacob ben Asher, published an epitome of his father's legal decisions. Rabbi Jacob went on to organize his own legal code, called *Arbaah Turim* (The Four Pillars), which organized the talmudic material in four broad subject areas. This work soon eclipsed that of his father, and joined with Maimonides' Code as a monument of Jewish legal authority.

We conclude this section with acknowledgment of the great 16th-cent. legalist Joseph Karo. He began by writing commentary on Rabbi Jacob ben Asher's *Arbaah Turim,* in which he included his own commentaries on the Talmud and on Gaonic literature. His discussions consider the works of al-Fasi, Maimonides, and Rabbi Asher, and show his clear preference for the Sefardic authorities of his own community. Between the years 1550–75, Karo reworked his commentary into his own independent work called the *Shulkhan Arukh* (Set Table). This work also used Rabbi Jacob's four broad content categories of organization. It almost immediately became, and still remains, the authoritative work of Talmudic law (for the above, *see* RABBINIC LITERATURE).

J. Modern Study of the Talmud (1500 CE–present)

The study of and commentary upon the Talmud continued unabated. It must suffice to mention the work of the 18th-cent. Eastern European rabbi Elijah Gaon of Vilna. Rabbi Elijah was not technically a Gaon, of course (that title belonging to the heads of Babylonian academies before the year 1040 CE), but the title was accorded to him as a mark of respect for his keen insight into the Talmudic text and his leadership of the intellectual faction of the rabbinic Jewish community.

In 19th-cent. Germany, the study of Talmud and rabbinic literature moved into the university world through the enlightenment intellectual movement called *die Wissenschaft des Judenthums* (lit., "science of Judaism"). Once in the academy, Jewish and Gentile scholars (each with their own biases) who studied the Talmud classified the literature and attended to textual criticism (much as was being done for the classics and the NT). Nevertheless, it was recognized that fixing the text was a daunting task, given the oral transmission history that preceded the writing down of the Talmud text. Even now there is scholarly debate about the location of Talmudic literature within oral or written culture, or some hybrid thereof. Current scholarship has embraced oral performance theory as a means of dealing with this crux.

A history of the written transmission of the Talmud text can be accomplished by working backwards from printed texts to manuscripts and fragments. In the 19th cent., R. Rabbinovicz published a multi-volume work called *Diqduqe Soferim*, which noted readings of the Talmud at variance with the standard printed editions of the Talmud. The printed Talmud text was first published in Venice from 1520–23 by a non-Jew named Daniel Bomberg. His pagination and layout has remained standard up to the present. There were earlier, partial printings of the Talmud in Spain, Portugal, and Italy in the 15th and 16th cent., as well. These have survived in fragmentary form.

Manuscripts of the Talmud are extant in great number, but all are fragmentary save for Codex Munich (Hebr. #95). Part of the reason for the paucity of complete manuscripts is due to Christian censorship and burning of Talmud texts during the Inquisition. A treasure trove of manuscript fragments was found in the "worn-out book-depository" (Geniza) of the medieval synagogue of Old Cairo. The Cairo Geniza has yielded tens of thousands of manuscript fragments from the medieval world, a significant portion of which are Babylonian Talmud texts. In recent years, these and other Talmud text variants have been collated on a CD-ROM published as the *Lieberman Data Base* by the Jewish Theological Seminary. This complements a CD-ROM of virtually all standard editions of rabbinic literature published in Israel by the Bar Ilan University Responsa Project. To date, many translations have been made of the Talmud: in German, a number in English, and even one in modern Israeli Hebrew, with a commentary by Rabbi Adin Steinsaltz.

Modern scholarly approaches under *Wissenschaft des Judenthums* were historical-critical, and included philology, positivist historiography, and even biography of rabbinic personalities. Form criticism was also applied in an attempt to find a synagogal "situation in life" for many Talmudic traditions. Source and redaction criticism were and continue to be employed as a means of reconstructing earlier traditions, isolating the layers of Talmudic redaction, and evaluating the editorial work of the Stam.

Recently, in keeping with a general shift in the academic world and under the particular leadership of Jacob Neusner and his students, there has been a turn away from the historical-critical approach. Their research has proven the futility of attempting to write rabbinic biography and history from works of religious, didactic literature. Instead, more recent scholarship on the Talmud has tended toward writing intellectual history and appreciating how the rhetoric of the Talmud attempted to influence the Jewish community of its day. Both of these latter approaches avoid the pitfall of determining the reliability of factual reportage within the Talmudic narrative and also within the legal sections. Instead, even fictional verisimilitude may be appreciated as testimony to the stages of intellectual development or rhetorical attempts at persuasion. The most current scholarship is focused on literary approaches to the Talmud text. Some attempts at synthesis of the historic and literary methods have been attempted under the rubric of "new historicism." It remains to be seen whether this latter approach will bear fruit.

Throughout its long history, the Babylonian Talmud has been a monument of rabbinic Jewish thought. The variety of current academic approaches and the breadth of its study in both university and Jewish religious settings insure that the Talmud will remain an enduring accomplishment of intellectual and religious life in this millennium.

Bibliography: Robert Brody. *The Geonim of Babylonia and the Shaping of Medieval Jewish Culture* (1998); Isaiah Gafni. *The Jews of Babylonia in the Talmudic Era: A Social and Cultural History* (2006); David Kraemer. *The Mind of the Talmud: An Intellectual History of the Bavli* (1990); Jeffrey Rubenstein. *The Culture of the Babylonian Talmud* (2003); Adin Steinsaltz. *The Essential Talmud: Thirtieth Anniversary Edition* (2006); Hermann L. Strack and Günter Stemberger. *Introduction to the Talmud and Midrash* (1992).

BURTON L. VISOTZKY

TALMUD, JERUSALEM tal'mood, ji-roo'sah-luhm. Compiled in the first half of the 5th cent. CE in the Jewish Galilee of Roman (Christian) Palestine, the Talmud Yerushalmi (Jerusalem Talmud) ostensibly serves as a commentary on the Mishnah (*see* MISHNAH). The rabbis quoted in the Yerushalmi sought to harmonize the Mishnah with other Tannaitic works, such as the Tosefta (a 3rd-cent. companion work to the entirety of the Mishnah; *see* TOSEPHTA, TOSEPTA, TOSEFTA). Unlike the Tosefta, however, the redacted Yerushalmi neglects substantial portions of the Mishnah, lacking commentaries on any tractates of order *Qodashim* (Sacred Things), and ignoring all but three chapters of tractate *Niddah* of the entire order of *Teharot* (Ritual Fitness). In addition, the Yerushalmi refrains from commenting on tractates *Eduyyot, Pirqe Avot,* and the first two chapters of *Makkot* in the order *Neziqin* (Torts). There is also no Yerushalmi commentary on the final four chapters of tractate *Shabbat* in the order *Mo'ed* (Calendar). The Jerusalem Talmud actually only offers commentary on thirty-nine of the sixty-three tractates of the Mishnah, and some of these are partial.

As part of its program of harmonizing the Tannaitic teachings so that these rabbinic works of the first two centuries CE appear to be monolithic, the Talmud

Yerushalmi presents Tannaitic teachings not in the Mishnah (*see* BARAITA), thus preserving this otherwise unedited material. The Yerushalmi sporadically offers biblical proof texts for the apodictic Mishnaic laws, attempting to justify or buttress the early rabbinic authorities. Throughout, the Yerushalmi quotes five generations of rabbis (*see* AMORA, AMORAIM) from the 3rd and 4th cent. who are engaged in commentary and arguments regarding Mishnaic laws (*see* GEMARA). These rabbis also are presented adjudicating case law in the villages of the Galilee. The reliability of the opinions attributed to these rabbis has been questioned by scholars in recent decades, as has the historicity of many of the events reported in the Yerushalmi.

A significant amount of narrative material (*see* HAGGADAH) is preserved in the Talmud Yerushalmi. This includes fanciful and/or theologically based retellings of biblical stories, as well as stories about the rabbinic sages and their disciples. These narratives are often woven into legal discussions or serve as relief from the intricacies of the dialectic. Segments of both the legal (*see* HALAKHAH) and the narrative materials are repeated in varying tractates of the Talmud Yerushalmi. These duplications, along with the roughly hewn argumentation, make the Yerushalmi appear to be crudely edited. Further, because of the economic and political strength of the Babylonian Jewish community (*see* BABYLONIAN JUDAISM), in subsequent centuries the Babylonian Talmud (*see* TALMUD) took preeminence. This precluded later generations of rabbinic scholars from refining the edited text of the Yerushalmi. In the last century, the study of the Talmud Yerushalmi has experienced a renaissance in academic circles.

Bibliography: H. L. Strack and G. Stemberger. *Introduction to the Talmud and Midrash* (1992); Burton L. Visotzky. "The Literature of the Rabbis." *From Mesopotamia to Modernity: Ten Introductions to Jewish History and Literature.* Burton L. Visotzky and David Fishman, eds. (1999) 71–102.

BURTON L. VISOTZKY

TAMAR tay'mahr [תָּמָר *tamar;* Θαμάρ *Thamar*]. Means "palm tree." 1. Genesis 38 depicts Tamar as a woman who takes the law into her own hands when fate and the "system," represented by her father-in-law Judah, place her in limbo and in jeopardy. She is the wife of Judah's firstborn son ER, whom God kills on account of his wickedness (v. 6). Judah gives Tamar to Er's brother, ONAN, in accordance with expected custom, the LEVIRATE LAW, in which a deceased man's brother is responsible for impregnating the deceased's childless widow and, presumably, taking care of her economically as well (v. 8). When Onan abuses the situation by copulating with Tamar but not impregnating her, God strikes him dead as well (vv. 9-10). Understandably, Judah is afraid to give Tamar to his youngest surviving son, SHELAH, and sends her to languish at her father's home with the subterfuge that the last son is still too young (v. 11). But Tamar takes matters into her own hands when she sees that Judah has no intention of fulfilling his promise and obligation to her. Refusing the role of a victim who remains on the margins of society (and story), she begins to act independently. After Judah loses his wife, Tamar removes her widow's garment and sits, veiled, at a location on Judah's path (vv. 13-14). The name of this location, pethakh ʿenayim (פֶּתַח עֵינַיִם, "opening of the eyes"; Gen 38:14; NRSV, "entrance to ENAIM"), symbolizes the ensuing transformation. Ironically blind to Tamar's identity, Judah's encounter with her in this place will eventually open his eyes to the injustice he perpetrated. Thinking that Tamar is a prostitute, Judah negotiates for her services and consents to her demand that he surrender to her his cord, staff, and signet ring (v. 18). These items constitute the hallmarks of a person's identity, equivalent to a modern person's driver's license and major credit cards. Only then does Tamar agree to have sex with him and, as a result, becomes pregnant (without Judah's awareness of the fact).

The friend Judah sends to retrieve the signet ring, cord, and staff refers to the mysterious woman as a holy woman (qedheshah קְדֵשָׁה), a term often translated "temple prostitute," as in the NRSV of 38:21 (but see below), during his unsuccessful search for her. When Tamar's pregnancy is later reported to Judah, Judah— still blind to what has transpired—condemns her to death for harlotry. She sends him his property, remarking that she is pregnant by the man to whom these belong. Then Judah's eyes open; he not only realizes what happened but also affirms Tamar's superior righteousness and justified action: "She is more in the right than I, since I did not give her to my son Shelah" (v. 26).

Tamar soon gives birth to twin sons, a sign of divine blessing in the Bible. Through this, as well as Judah's words, the narrative tacitly supports Tamar's breaking of taboos to achieve, through subterfuge, righteous goals. Tamar represents one of several tricksters in Genesis who are powerless to secure justice for themselves through official means. But the "opening of the eyes" that she affects seems to transform Judah as well: he grows in stature after this episode, able to take responsibility—as his later actions on behalf of Benjamin, his half brother, demonstrate (Gen 42–44).

Readers sometimes suppose that Tamar masquerades as a prostitute to deceive Judah deliberately. The text, however, is ambiguous. While Judah mistakes her for a prostitute, it is not self-evident that this was her intention. In a story so filled with ironies, the reader may be expected to see Judah's response as yet another error (unable to recognize his daughter-in-law when she wears a veil). The reference to her as a qedheshah may be an attempt to mask Judah's indiscretion and give his liaison with the unknown woman a more genteel public face. Although earlier interpreters understood qedheshah to be a cult official involved in sexual activi-

ties, this understanding of the term no longer holds (see PROSTITUTION, §B).

Tamar is later invoked as a blessing in the book of Ruth (Ruth 4:12) and is one of only four women mentioned in Matthew's genealogy of Jesus (Matt 1:3).

2. Second Samuel 13 describes the RAPE of Tamar, King David's beautiful daughter, by her half-brother AMNON. Amnon, who falls in love with her, desires her so strongly that he gets sick (v. 2). His friend advises him to ask King David to send Tamar to feed him. At David's request (v. 7) Tamar innocently comes to Amnon's chamber to prepare his food, but after sending all the attendants out, Amnon expresses his true intentions. The narrator presents Tamar as wise and courageous when trying to deflect Amnon's passion. She first asks for compassion and, when this fails, exhorts him instead to ask the king for permission to marry her, adding that the king would not refuse him; but nothing she says stops him, and rape ensues (vv. 11-14). Moreover, he then throws her out, his great "love" having turned into great hate (v. 15). Tearing her clothes in mourning, Tamar goes away screaming over this deed. Her brother ABSALOM immediately grasps what has happened and tells her to keep the incident to herself for the time being (v. 20). King David, although angered, does nothing to Amnon. The LXX (followed by the NRSV) adds that David does not punish Amnon because he loves Amnon (13:21). Two years later, Absalom avenges the rape of Tamar by killing Amnon (vv. 23-29). Tamar herself remains desolate in Absalom's house. Although interpreters often emphasize Absalom's gallant treatment of his sister, some criticize him for silencing her and for using her tragedy as an opportunity to eliminate the man who stands between him and David's throne.

3. The daughter of Absalom (2 Sam 14:27), most likely named after her aunt Tamar of 2 Sam 13. Like her aunt, this Tamar is also "a beautiful woman." Nothing further is told about her.

TAMARA COHN ESKENAZI

4. Town located on Israel's southern border (Ezek 47:19, 48:28). Second Chronicles 20:2 identifies Hazazon-Tamar with En-gedi, and Roman sources have understood Tamar as Tamar Mesad.

EMILY R. CHENEY

TAMARISK tam′uh-risk [אֶשֶׁל ʾeshel, חָצִיר khatsir]. A tall, shady tree with deep roots, particularly suitable to the sandy soil of the Sinai, Negev, Dead Sea, Israel, and Jordan. Various natural explanations for MANNA (Exod 16:14) have been connected with species of tamarisk, the closest of which may be a honey-like substance excreted from the tamarisk bush that is called "manna" by Bedouin.

After Abraham and Abimelech made a covenant, the patriarch planted a tamarisk tree in Beersheba, where he called on the name of the Lord (Gen 21:33). The tree may have marked the site as sacred (e.g., 12:6-7;

13:18) or may have been linked to the act of worship. Prior to his slaughter of the priests of Nob, Saul sat at Gibeah "under the tamarisk tree on the height" (1 Sam 22:6). It is not clear whether this is intended to be a neutral, positive, or negative statement of Saul's whereabouts. In a more positive context, after Saul's body is recovered from the walls of Beth-shean, it is honored by being buried "under the tamarisk tree" (1 Sam 31:13; compare 1 Chr 10:12). Isaiah uses the tree as a symbol of new life, describing Israel, withered by the hardships of exile, producing offspring that will "spring up like a green tamarisk" (Isa 44:4).

RALPH K. HAWKINS

TAMBOURINE. *See* MUSICAL INSTRUMENTS.

TAMMUZ tam'uhz [תַּמּוּז *tammuz*]. The Hebrew name for the Sumerian deity Dumuzi, the lover of Inanna or ISHTAR, goddess of sex and war. Sumerian texts describe the relationship between Dumuzi and Inanna, on which two important religious institutions were based: 1) In the sacred marriage, practiced mainly during the Third Dynasty of Ur and the Isin period, Sumerian kings served as the symbolic counterpart of Dumuzi in a ritual marriage to Inanna, intended to guarantee the fertility of vegetation, animals, and humans; 2) The festival of Dumuzi included ritual weeping for the death of Tammuz, who was consigned to the underworld as a substitute for Inanna after she was trapped there.

The custom of weeping for Tammuz was apparently imported into Judah from Mesopotamia. In Ezek 8:14, women are said to be "weeping for Tammuz" in the entrance of the north gate of the Temple. In this, the only occurrence in the OT, a definite article is attached to Tammuz, reducing it from a proper noun to a common noun, with the effect that the women are weeping for "the tammuz" (hattammuz הַתַּמּוּז), a thing rather than a deity. This is a simple but common device biblical authors used to deny the existence of deities other than Yahweh (e.g., Judg 10:6, "the Baals").

RALPH K. HAWKINS

TANAKH tahn'ahk. Hebrew acronym (tanakh תַּנַ"ךְ) denoting Jewish Scriptures. An acronym of three Hebrew words representing the three parts of the Hebrew Scriptures: 1) Torah (torah תּוֹרָה) includes Genesis, Exodus, Leviticus, Numbers, and Deuteronomy; 2) Nevi'im (nevi'im נְבִיאִים), the Prophets, the second major part of the Hebrew Canon, consists of these books in this order: Joshua, Judges, 1 and 2 Samuel, 1 and 2 Kings, Isaiah, Jeremiah, Ezekiel, Hosea, Joel, Amos, Obadiah, Jonah, Micah, Nahum, Habakkuk, Zephaniah, Haggai, Zechariah, and Malachi; 3) Ketuvim (kethuvim כְּתוּבִים), the Writings, the third major section of the Scriptures, includes these books in this order: Psalms, Proverbs, Job, Song of Songs, Ruth, Lamentations, Ecclesiastes, Esther, Daniel, Ezra, Nehemiah, and

1 and 2 Chronicles. *See* AUTHORITY OF SCRIPTURE; CANON OF THE OLD TESTAMENT.

JUDITH Z. ABRAMS

TANHUMETH tan-hyoo'mith [תַּנְחֻמֶת *tankhumeth*]. Means "consolation." Tanhumeth, a Netophathite, was the father of SERAIAH, who was a captain when Babylonia conquered Jerusalem (2 Kgs 25:23; Jer 40:8).

TANIS tan'is [Τάνις *Tanis*]. Greek name (Jdt 1:10) for the Egyptian city ZOAN.

TANNA, TANNAIM [תַּנָּא *tanna'*, תַּנָּאִים *tanna'im*]. The Hebrew term for a rabbi (*see* RABBI, RABBONI) living in the Mishnaic era (*see* MISHNAH), ca. 70–200 CE. These rabbis interpreted Scripture (*see* MIDRASH) and made legal pronouncements, helping Judaism survive the destruction of the Jerusalem Temple as an academic, Hellenized, and religious movement. Their dicta are collected in the Mishnah, in other works of that era such as the Tosefta, and, later, in the Talmuds. The term *Tanna'* also refers to the memory expert who transmitted rabbinic teachings.

Bibliography: H. L. Strack and Günter Stemberger. *Introduction to the Talmud and Midrash* (1992).

BURTON L. VISOTZKY

TANNER, TANNING [אָדָם *'adham;* βυρσεύς *byrseus*]. Tanning is the complex process by which animal skins are made usable for garments, tents, parchment, and other items. The tanning process includes curing the skin, removing the hair, and then actually tanning the skin using liquids known as tannins, generally made from vegetable matter. Under the Mosaic law, touching a dead thing made one unclean. Therefore, a tanner would have been almost perpetually unclean. The Mishnah (*m. Ketub.* 7:10) and the Talmud (*b. Pesah.* 65a; *Qidd.* 82b) viewed tanners as despised because of their uncleanness and the foul smell of their work.

While the act of tanning is not mentioned in the OT, Exodus specifies that tanned ram skins were to be used in the construction of the tabernacle (Exod 25:5; 26:14; 35:7, 23; 36:19; 39:34), along with LEATHER. According to Acts 9:43, Peter stayed with a tanner named Simon in Joppa. Peter was staying with Simon (19:6, 32) when he had the vision of the sheet full of clean and unclean animals (10:9-16).

KENNETH D. LITWAK

TAPHATH tay'fath [טָפַת *tafath*]. BEN-ABINADAB's wife, who was Solomon's daughter (1 Kgs 4:11).

TAPPUAH tap'yoo-uh [תַּפּוּחַ *tappuakh*]. 1. A place name, meaning "quince," that occurs six times in the Bible: Josh 12:17; 15:34; 16:8; 17:8 (twice); 1 Chr 2:43. (*See* BETH-TAPPUAH and EN-TAPPUAH.) In

Josh 12:17 its king appears in a list of kings defeated by the Israelites. In Josh 16:8 it appears as one of the boundaries of the territory of the tribe of Ephraim. In Josh 17:8 the land around the town was assigned to the tribe of Manasseh while the town itself was given to Ephraim. The site is Tell Sheikh Abu Zarad about 8 mi. southwest of modern Nablus and 5 mi. northwest of biblical Shiloh. Joshua 15:34 apparently refers to a different place by this name since it is among the lowland towns allocated to the tribe of Judah. The Judean town may be identified with Beit Nettif 3 mi. southeast of Azeqah.

Bibliography: R. Boling and G. E. Wright. *Joshua.* AB 6 (1982).

TIMOTHY G. CRAWFORD

2. The second of four sons of Hebron among Judah's descendants (1 Chr 2:43).

EMILY R. CHENEY

TARALAH tair′uh-luh [תַּרְעֲלָה *tar'alah*]. One of the fourteen towns in the western portion of the land allotted to the tribe of Benjamin (Josh 18:27).

TAREA tair′ee-uh [תַּאְרֵעַ *ta'area'*, תַּחְרֵעַ *takharea'*]. A Benjaminite, son of Micah (1 Chr 8:35; spelled "Tahrea" in 9:41).

TARGET [מַטָּרָה *mattarah*, מִפְגָּע *mifga'*; σκοπός *skopos*]. A mark at which arrows are shot (Wis 5:12, 21). Job complains that God is using him as a target (Job 7:20; 16:12).

TARGUMS tahr′guhm [תַּרְגּוּם *targum*, תַּרְגּוּמִים *targumim*]. The Jewish Aramaic versions of Scripture (from the Hebrew/Aramaic verb tirgem (תִּרְגֵּם, "to translate, read aloud").

A. Origins
B. The Texts
  1. Pentateuch
    a. Onqelos
    b. Pseudo-Jonathan
    c. Palestinian
  2. Prophets
  3. Hagiographa
C. Translation Techniques and Principles
  1. The treatment of divine anthropomorphisms
    a. The word for ear in the Old Testament
    b. Genesis 49:10
  2. Function
  3. Themes
Bibliography

A. Origins

Jewish tradition generally traces the origin of the oldest Targums back to the time of Ezra, based on the bibli-

cal passage describing his reading of the Law meforash (מְפֹרָשׁ, i.e., "with explanation," in Neh 8:8). At the same time the most authoritative Targum of the Torah, *Targum Onqelos*, is ascribed to a figure explicitly dated to the mid-2nd cent. CE. Scholarly consensus and rabbinic tradition may thus be said to be largely in agreement, then, that the Targums, at least those of the Torah and Prophets, began in oral Aramaic renditions in late Second Temple times and achieved written status and a level of canonicity only in the Mishnaic period. Manuscripts are known only from medieval and later times, however (*see* RABBINIC LITERATURE §C3).

At Qumran, a complete Aramaic translation of the book of Job is attested, but no other certain Targums (e.g., the fragmentary Aramaic text 4Q156, corresponding somewhat to the Day of Atonement ritual described in Lev 16, is not a targum, per se.) Since Job was long known from rabbinic tradition to have received special treatment in this regard, the absence of Aramaic versions of the other biblical books is to be seen as definitive evidence that other Targums, if they already existed, remained in oral form during that period.

B. The Texts
1. Pentateuch

We know of three distinct text traditions of Jewish Aramaic renderings of the Torah: *Targum Onqelos* (also *Onqelos*), *Targum Pseudo-Jonathan*, and the Palestinian targumic tradition. The dialects, content, and textual evidence for each of these are distinctive.

a. Onqelos. *Targum Onqelos*, the most authoritative of Targums, is undoubtedly the oldest as well. It is composed in a literary Aramaic dialect that is rather similar to that used in the Aramaic texts from Qumran that is usually now referred to as "Jewish Literary Aramaic." Within the general constraints of targumic translation techniques (see below) it is a relatively straightforward and literal rendering of the text of the Torah. On halakhic matters (*see* HALAKHAH), it reflects the opinion of the community of 2nd cent. CE Pharisaic Judaism and should not necessarily be associated with the rulings of any particular school, although modern scholars have often attempted to do so. Early on, it became a regular part of the liturgy, the text of the Torah being read twice, and that of *Onqelos* once; and it was thus accepted as authoritative in the Babylonian talmudic academies. In the Babylonian Talmud it is referred to as "our targum" (*see* TALMUD). In rabbinic Bibles it is printed immediately next to the Hebrew text.

b. Pseudo-Jonathan. The title *Targum Jonathan* properly belongs to the *Targum of the Prophets*, but due to a confusion between the Hebrew abbreviations for "Yonatan" and "Yerushalmi," it is known by scholars as *Targum Pseudo-Jonathan.* "Yerushalmi," i.e., "Palestinian," is the additional complete Targum to the Torah printed in the Second Bomberg rabbinic Bible and its subsequent derivatives. ("Jonathan" and "Onqelos" are the names of famous 2nd-cent. Scripture translators but are almost certainly properly to be ascribed to the Greek versions of "Aquila" and "Theodotion.") This is a late composition, with some material as late as the 9th cent. CE, incorporating material from *Onqelos*, the early Palestinian tradition, and extensive additional midrashic sources. Recent research has determined that the original material in this Targum, along with other late Targums to the Hagiographa (see below) is written in a definite dialect, which has been termed by this writer "Late Jewish Literary Aramaic." It is known from only one manuscript (in the British Library), which probably served as the proximate source for the Bomberg version. Scholars have often pointed out substantial contextual links between *Pseudo-Jonathan* and the late midrashic compilation *Pirke Rabbi Eliezer* (see MIDRASH).

c. **Palestinian.** Scattered throughout the *Pseudo-Jonathan* targumic text in some rabbinic Bible editions are fragmentary quotations of yet another targumic tradition. These are considered to be remnants of an authentic Palestinian targumic tradition that continued to be used in the land of Israel while *Onqelos* served liturgical and exegetical purposes in Babylonia. Manuscripts of such excerpts have also been found; together they are referred to as the "fragment targum." When the Cairo GENIZAH material was analyzed around the turn of the 20th cent. it was also found to contain targumic manuscripts from this tradition, but extended pieces of text rather than excerpts. (Some of these Genizah manuscripts also contain additional poetic material of Byzantine and perhaps later times incorporated into the targumic material.) It was thus clear that there had been a Palestinian targumic tradition for the Torah separate from that of *Onqelos*; but no complete version of that Palestinian tradition was known until a manuscript was discovered in the Vatican Library, known now as *Targum Neofiti* (after its original manuscript identification). There are some rather substantial recensional differences among these versions, but the ultimate origin of all of these texts in a single version cannot be doubted. Characteristic of this version in particular are extensive midrashic expansions (many of which made their way into the *Pseudo-Jonathan* Targum, which is often, though erroneously, thus referred to as a Palestinian text) and an authentic, albeit literary, Palestinian Aramaic dialect.

In sum, then, the targumic traditions of the Torah may be said to have developed as follows: 1) A literary Aramaic tradition, similar to the Aramaic texts found among the Dead Sea Scrolls developed in the land of Israel during the 1st cent. CE. That tradition, further developed and having become semi-canonical among the Babylonian Jews, is *Targum Onqelos*. 2) Meanwhile, in the land of Israel the tradition of translation and exegesis of the Torah text in a liturgical context continued to develop and expand, with the addition of substantial midrashic expansions and "Palestinizing" of the literary language well into the Byzantine period. This is the Palestinian Targum in its various guises. 3) In

post-talmudic times, the by-now canonical *Onqelos* was artfully combined with substantive interpretive expansions from the Palestinian tradition along with other rabbinic sources to create the text known now as *Pseudo-Jonathan*.

2. Prophets

The Targum to the prophetic books (both Former and Latter) is primarily attested in a single targumic tradition known as *Targum Jonathan*. In general the language and style of this material is very much like that of *Onqelos*, although minor differences with *Onqelos* and among the Targums of the several books have been identified. In the difficult poetic chapters of the writing prophets (as is also the case in *Onqelos* in such poetic chapters as Gen 49; Num 22–24; and Deut 32) the Aramaic version is highly exegetical rather than literal, but it is not expansive in the manner of the Palestinian Targum. Given its close relationship to the *Onqelos* tradition, a dating and origin not significantly different from that of *Onqelos* is generally assumed.

There are extensive additional targumic materials to selected chapters of both the Former and Latter Prophets, stemming from various traditions and generally in mixed dialects, known as targumic tosefta.

3. Hagiographa

The Targums to the Hagiographa constitute a mixed bag of materials in terms of origin and language, but in general, they are all highly midrashic in content. The Targums to Job and Psalms are closely related in language and probably in origin to the Pseudo-Jonathan Targum, while those to Lamentations, Ecclesiastes, Ruth, and Chronicles seem to stem from a Palestinian source but are strongly influenced by the *Onqelos* traditions. Song of Songs and Esther have only late and very expansive targumic traditions. Unfortunately, though, the manuscript tradition to all of this material is not very reliable.

C. Translation Techniques and Principles

1. The treatment of divine anthropomorphisms

One of the well-known features of the ancient versions is the avoidance of anthropomorphic language in the description of God. Targumic practice is somewhat irregular in this regard (both among the various Targums and comparing the Targums to the Greek) and questions have been raised as to whether such practices are due to stylistic rather than theological principles. A particularly distinctive and important feature here is the strong tendency of the Palestinian Targum traditions to substitute expressions such as "the speaking facility of the Lord," for the divine name when divine speech is mentioned. This use of the Aramaic term **memar** (מֵימַר) has justifiably been associated with the Greek logos (λόγος) traditions (see WORD, THE), but no definitive explanation for the connection has yet appeared.

It is important to realize that these texts, albeit in several different dialects and from several different periods, constitute—unlike Midrash—the true rabbinic biblical philological commentary tradition during the 1st millennium CE; indeed they were the primary repository of the exegetical traditions of scripture for the communities of Aramaic-speaking Jews in that millennium. Their "translations" were careful and precise where precision was necessary, and interpretive and expansive where such was the need. A study of some examples should make this clearer as well as provide evidence of the kind of interrelationship obtained among the various Targums.

a. The word for ear in the Old Testament. The Hebrew word ʾozen (אֹזֶן, literally "ear") occurs thirty-one times in the Torah, but it is used in two quite different contexts. In fourteen occurrences, it has its literal meaning a physical ear. In such cases *Onqelos*, *Pseudo-Jonathan*, and *Neofiti* all render the Hebrew with the cognate Aramaic term ʾdn (אֻדְן). Most of the time, however, the word is used in the context of "hearing" or "listening"—for example at Gen 20:8: "he spoke all these words beʾoznehem (בְּאָזְנֵיהֶם, 'in their ears')." In these instances *Onqelos* renders instead "he spoke these words before them," while *Neofiti* uses the more detailed, "in the hearing of." (*Targum Jonathan* and the Hagiographic Targums all follow the *Onqelos* tradition here.)

b. Genesis 49:10. Where the Hebrew text is highly poetic and/or obscure, even *Onqelos* becomes expansive in its explanation. For example, the famous crux at Gen 49:10 (ʿadh ki-yavoʾ shiloh עַד כִּי־יָבֹא שִׁילֹה), variously translated "until tribute comes to him," or "until Shiloh comes" (KJV), or "until he comes to whom it belongs" (RSV), is rendered as follows by the attested targumic sources (author's trans.): 1) *Onqelos*: "until the Messiah comes, to whom belongs the kingship"; 2) *Pseudo-Jonathan*: "until the time when Messiah comes, the smallest of his sons, into whose (the nations shall disappear)"; 3) *Neofiti*: "until the time when the Messiah comes, to whom belongs the kingship"; 4) *FragTarg P* "until the time when the Messiah comes who shall arise from the house of Judah"; 5) *FragTarg V* "until the time when the Messiah comes, to whom belongs the kingship."

2. Function
The Targums began as a purely practical matter, providing interpretation of Scripture in a liturgical context for those who could no longer follow the original Hebrew; but, undoubtedly, they early on acquired other functions, and there can be little doubt that the latest strands of targumic materials were strictly literary creations. The proximate origin of the *Fragmentary Targum* manuscript tradition remains in dispute.

3. Themes
The Targums incorporate all of the basic themes of rabbinic Judaism into their interpretive strands, such as messiah, angels, afterlife, resurrection, and the like, but simply as allusions, not as prescriptions. There is no systematic theology in the Targums; knowledge of rabbinic lore is just assumed, as in the above-cited passage from Gen 49:10 where the coming of the Messiah is a given but is not described.

Bibliography: Bernard Grossfeld, ed. *A Bibliography of Targum Literature.* 3 vols. (1972–90); Martin McNamara, ed. *Aramaic Bible: The Targums.* 22 vols. (1987–).

STEPHEN A. KAUFMAN

TARSHISH tahrʹshish [תַּרְשִׁישׁ tarshish]. A term that is used three ways in the OT, as a proper name, a location, and a precious stone (often rendered BERYL). 1. An eponymous reference to the coastland settlements in the Table of Nations (Gen 10:4-5; 1 Chr 1:7) as those descended from Jephthah through Javan (see KITTIM).

2. One of Benjamin's descendants (1 Chr 7:10).

3. The name of one of the seven counselors of Ahasuerus in Esther (1:14).

4. A geographic reference to an ancient site whose location is uncertain. While there is no intrinsic reason to assume only one site in the ancient world was known as Tarshish, its identity is now lost. Jonah's flight from God's mission to Nineveh began as a journey to Tarshish (Jonah 1:3; 4:2). Given Jonah's embarkation for Tarshish at Joppa on the Levantine coast (Jonah 1:3), it would appear that Tarshish was somewhere in the Mediterranean basin. *See* JONAH, BOOK OF.

The region was well known for its trade in silver and other metals and as a trading broker in general (Jer 10:9; Ezek 27:12; 38:13). The list of metals identified with Tarshish in Ezek 27:12—silver, iron, tin, and lead—has led some scholars to identify the region with southern Spain, which Strabo notes had plentiful resources of gold, silver, copper, and iron (*Geogr.* 3.2.8). Both Strabo (*Geogr.* 3.2.11) and Herodotus (*Hist.* 1.163; 4.152) refer to southern Spain as "Tartessus."

Instead of reading Tarshish in Isa 23:10, the LXX reads "Carthage" (Karchēdonos Καρχηδόνος), with which some have identified Tarshish. This notation may refer to the Carthage on the northern coast of Africa near Tunis. However, Strabo refers to a New Carthage in southern Spain (*Geogr.* 3.2.10) to which the LXX may have referred instead.

The ships of Tarshish were so well known that people sought either to employ them as their transport vessels (1 Kgs 10:22; 2 Chr 9:21) or replicate them for their own fleets (1 Kgs 22:48 [Heb. 22:40]). References to ships sailing to Tarshish from Ezion-geber (1 Kgs 9:26-28; 10:22; 2 Chr 9:21) near Eloth imply that Tarshish was accessible from the Red Sea. Herodotus (*Hist.* 4.42) notes a three-year-long seafaring journey initiated by

Pharaoh Neco that circumnavigated the African continent beginning at the Red Sea and ending in Egypt in the Mediterranean. Perhaps these trips from Eziongeber skirted the African coast, gathering goods along the way, and dropped anchor at Tarshish in southern Spain.

DALE W. MANOR

TARSUS tahr´suhs [Ταρσός Tarsos]. A major port city on the river Cydnus near the Mediterranean Sea, directly north of the eastern tip of Cyprus. The city's history is inevitably tied to the biography of Paul in important ways (Acts 9:11, 30; 11:25; 21:39; 22:3).

A. Location
B. History of "an important city" (Acts 21:39)
C. Paul in Tarsus
D. Paul's Greek Bible, the Septuagint
Bibliography

A. Location

Tarsus stands at the intersection of the fertile plain of East CILICIA and the Taurus Mountains to the north that extend to the sea. Its strategic location at a crossroads between north and south, east and west, and on a harbor miles from the sea made Tarsus safe from pirates and storms, promoted trade and commerce, and encouraged vigorous cultural exchanges. The road to the north ran through a rugged mountain pass, the Cilician Gates, linking it to Syria at the top of the Fertile Crescent and offering a place where Hellenistic and Semitic cultures could meet and enjoy a vital reciprocity. Moreover, vigorous cultural and commercial exchanges took place over the sea-lanes to Alexandria, Egypt, in the south and to Rome and Greece to the west. It still stands on the site in modern Turkey that it has occupied for over 5,000 years.

B. History of "an important city" (Acts 21:39)

Beginning in the 3rd millennium BCE, Tarsus was continuously inhabited until its destruction by the Assyrian king SENNACHERIB in 696 BCE. Occupied by the Hittites (18th–14th cent. BCE), the Sea Peoples (13th cent. BCE), the Assyrians (7th cent. BCE), the Persians (5th–4th cent. BCE), the Greeks (4th–1st cent. BCE), and the Romans (1st cent. BCE–7th cent. CE), Tarsus enjoyed—or suffered—a checkered history. After the battle of Ipsus in 301 BCE, the Greek Seleucids and later the Romans offered Tarsus a degree of autonomy and favored status that nourished a cultural achievement that others could only envy (although apparently Tarsus did revolt on occasion [2 Macc 4:30]). Strabo, a Greek geographer and historian of the 1st cent. BCE, named Tarsus one of the three most important cities of the Mediterranean world along with Alexandria and Athens (Geogr. 14.5.12–15). Under Roman rule its good fortunes increased, and to honor Julius Caesar it renamed itself Iuliopolis. Under Mark Antony it gained

free city (i.e., tax-free) status with some degree of autonomy. The legendary rendezvous of Mark Antony with Cleopatra on her ship anchored in the Tarsus harbor would nudge history on a tragic course that neither of them anticipated. Under the shadow of this tryst, the "Sea Gate" in time became "Cleopatra's Gate." Antony's divorce of Octavia, Octavian's sister, to marry Cleopatra set Mark Antony on a collision course with Octavian that would end in the defeat of Mark Antony and Cleopatra at Actium in 31 BCE and be followed by their suicide back in Alexandria in 30 BCE.

Now under the control of Octavian (anointed Augustus by the Senate), the privileges Mark Antony had bestowed on Tarsus were renewed. Moreover, Julius Caesar's earlier decree that guaranteed the Jews the right to practice their ancestral religion was extended by Octavian and his successors. As a recipient of the imperial largesse, the Tarsus Paul knew flourished, and the Jewish community in which he was schooled and nurtured thrived. Under Roman rule, such a Jewish community was often granted limited autonomy over its own affairs, could arrest miscreants, collect and remit the half-shekel tax to Jerusalem, and might dispatch embassies to the emperor. Normally it would also be exempt from certain taxes (e.g., the poll tax) and would have enjoyed an intermediate status somewhere between citizens and indigents (metics). Many authors now believe Paul's citizenship was of such a colony of Jews known as a *politeuma* rather than a citizen of Rome (see Roetzel). *See* PAUL, THE APOSTLE.

Even under Roman control, however, Tarsus was more Greek and Semitic than Latin. While eastern influence was formative, long before Paul's day the later Greek or Hellenistic presence established Tarsus as a center of learning. Strabo was impressed by the high intellectual achievement of Tarsus and claimed that their schools of philosophy and rhetoric surpassed those of Athens and Alexandria (Geogr. 13.5.13). Strabo names Stoic philosophers (Antipater, Archedemus, Nestor, and two Athenodoruses), grammarians (Artemidorus and Diodorus), and esteemed poets like Dionysides among the intellectual elite in Tarsus (Geogr. 14.5.14–15).

As glorious as it was, however, Tarsus did have a mixed reputation. Apollonius of Tyana studied there as a young man and found the atmosphere was not conducive to philosophic life, given the luxury he found in the city (Philostratus, *Vit. Apoll.* 1.7). Dio Chrysostom, a 1st-cent. Greek orator and philosopher, heaped ridicule on the pretentious claims of Tarsus to a divine ancestry (*1 Tars.* 33). In spite of these attempts to smear the reputation of the city of Paul's youth, this center of learning and commerce was no worse than Alexandria, Athens, or Corinth, with which it is favorably compared.

Clearly this rich cultural environment shaped Paul's thinking. There Greek became his first language; there he studied the SEPTUAGINT (LXX), the Greek translation/interpretation of the OT; there he learned to copy the form of Hellenistic letters; there he inherited Stoic and Cynic influences; there he came to know himself by the Greco-Roman name *Paul* (Paulos Παῦλος), in addition to his Hebrew name *Saul* (sha'ul [שָׁאוּל]; see Acts 13:9). Interestingly, the name *Saul* appears nowhere in Paul's own letters. Thus, as a young man his feet were firmly planted in two different worlds: the Hellenistic world with its rich cultural heritage, and the world of the people Israel with its Scriptures, traditions, and law. So firmly comfortable in both was he that he was an ideal person for translating a gospel that was fundamentally Jewish for the Hellenistic environment of his converts.

C. Paul in Tarsus

How and when Paul's family came to live in Tarsus is unknown. Jerome's 4th-cent. claim that a Roman occupier enslaved and relocated the family in Tarsus has enjoyed little support (*Comm. Phlm.* 23). Given that nine out of ten Jews of Paul's day lived in the Diaspora, and given the prominence and prosperity of Tarsus, a forced repatriation is hardly necessary to explain the presence there of Paul's family. While the letters nowhere mention Tarsus, the speech put on his lips in Acts that fixes Tarsus as Paul's birthplace is credible (Acts 22:3). It carries no ideological bias to place it under suspicion, and it best accounts for the blend of cultures we find in Paul's speech.

But did he live there long enough to be shaped by its culturally rich Hellenistic environment? Acts suggests that he did not but at a young age (Acts 26:4) was sent to Jerusalem to be "brought up ... at the feet of Gamaliel" (22:3). But against this claim stand his nigh exclusive use of the LXX, his preference for Greek as his first language, and the Stoic influence on his letters (e.g., the virtue and vice lists), his catalogs of suffering, and his use of the diatribe form of argumentation. Moreover, the absence of a single reference in the letters to studying with the learned Pharisee Gamaliel II in Jerusalem, even when it would have been to his advantage to do so (Phil 3:5), argues against Paul's spending his formative years in Jerusalem. Also, the symbolic value of Jerusalem as the *axis mundi* in Luke–Acts raises questions about the historicity of the claim that Paul studied in Jerusalem at the feet of Gamaliel. If this should be the case, then we must read the letters in a wholly different way.

But would it have been possible for Paul to be a strict Pharisee (Acts 26:5) had he been raised and educated in Tarsus? While evidence for Pharisees in the Diaspora is weak, given the paucity of evidence caution is needed. Paul and Josephus are our only 1st-cent. authors with secure Pharisaic ties. Both prefer the Pharisaic interpretation of the law (Gal 1:14; Phil 3:4-6; Josephus, *Life* 9–12), but there is no hard evidence that either spent many years in a school devoted exclusively to the study of that one approach. Moreover, there was more diversity in 1st-cent. Judaism than is usually acknowledged. While we cannot know if Paul's parents or his commu-

nity was the source of his Pharisaic tendencies, we can recognize them in his letters: e.g., his broad view of what was scriptural; his view of the resurrection and afterlife; his tendency to spiritualize the Temple (1 Cor 3:16-17; 6:19), the sacrificial rites (Rom 12:1-2), circumcision (Rom 15:8; Phil 3:3), and leaven (1 Cor 5:7); and his emphasis on the holy, as in "holy ones" in the salutation of most of his letters (e.g., 1 Cor 1:2; author's trans.; NRSV, "saints"). In the end the complex mingling of Hellenistic and Jewish traditions in Paul's letters argues for an education and youth in a pious Jewish home in a Jewish Diaspora community that was open to surprises from the Hellenistic world and was fiercely committed to its ancestral religion.

D. Paul's Greek Bible, the Septuagint

The LXX was in Paul's blood. His citations of biblical texts come almost exclusively from the LXX. As the work of many hands over at least two centuries in Alexandria, Egypt, the LXX rendered the Hebrew biblical texts into the Greek vernacular of the day and became popular in Greek-speaking Jewish communities rimming the Mediterranean. While the translation of the Torah was fairly literal, other translations (e.g., Isaiah) bordered on being paraphrases.

All of the translations, however, were inevitably interpretations. For example, although the monotheism advocated in the Scriptures, both Hebrew and Greek, pushes against the ecumenical tendencies of Hellenism, the translators cleverly avoided renderings that would unnecessarily alienate the Jewish minority from the dominant Hellenistic culture. Except in times of persecution, the majority of Jews were willing to engage the Hellenistic culture and to be open to its surprises. Even while locating himself within the traditions of Israel, this same engagement is evident Paul's openness to Gentiles. Paul's messianism, combined with certain ecumenical tendencies of his LXX text, informed his Gentile gospel in powerful ways.

In spite of this accommodation, tension between Jews and Greeks was a part of the daily experience of Tarsus. Jews there were isolated, vulnerable, and very conscious of their minority status. Acutely aware of this tension, Paul warned the church in Rome of the dangers of conformity (Rom 12:1-2); he recalled how the converts in Thessalonica turned from the worship of "idols" to the "living and true God" (1 Thess 1:9); he reminded the church in Philippi that its "citizenship" was in heaven (Phil 3:20). Nevertheless, Paul did not advocate withdrawal from the world. In the Jewish community of his youth he had learned to mediate the conflicts that inevitably arose between the conflicted expressions of inclusion and exclusion in this community (Furnish).

In summary, Paul's theologizing, his rhetorical strategies, his sense of his own identity, his understanding of his mission, and his ability to negotiate two worlds all point to him spending his formative years in a vibrant, committed, pious, Diaspora Jewish community in Tarsus. When he became an apostle of Christ, he was often called to negotiate the perilous conflicts between Jewish and Gentile believers (Rom 14), and between his own Gentile gospel and that of other Jewish apostles of Christ (2 Cor 11:5, 22-24; Gal 1:1–2:21). Spending his early years in Tarsus in a setting of both clashes with and accommodations to the majority culture well equipped Paul for this challenge.

Bibliography: Victor Paul Furnish. "Inside Looking Out: Some Pauline Views of the Unbelieving Public." *Pauline Conversations in Context.* J. C. Anderson, P. Sellew, and C. Setzer, eds. (2002) 104–24; Hetty Goldman. *Excavations at Gözlü, Tarsus: The Hellenistic and Roman Periods.* 5 vols. (1950–63); J. Andrew Overman. "Kata Nomon Pharisaios: A Short History of Paul's Pharisaism." *Pauline Conversations in Context.* J. C. Anderson, P. Sellew, and C. Setzer, eds. (2002) 180–93; W. M. Ramsey. *The Cities of St. Paul: Their Influence on His Life and Thought* (1960); Calvin J. Roetzel. *Paul: The Man and the Myth* (1999); Anthony J. Saldarini. *Pharisees, Scribes and Sadducees in Palestinian Society: A Sociological Approach* (1988).

CALVIN J. ROETZEL

TARTAK tahr'tak [תַּרְתָּק tartaq]. Tartak and NIBHAZ were deities of the Avvites, one of the peoples whom the Assyrians settled in Samaria sometime after the fall of the Northern Kingdom (2 Kgs 17:24, 31). Because they worshiped these and other deities, Yahweh sent lions among the people who were settled in Samaria (17:25). No ancient sources apart from the Bible mention the deity Tartak or a people called the Avvites.

TREVOR D. COCHELL

TARTAN tahr'tan [תַּרְתָּן tartan]. The second ranking officer (Akk. tartannu, turtanu) after the king in the Assyrian army as of the Middle Assyrian period. As such, he gave his name to a year. Shalmanesar III stationed a turtanu at Til-Barsip (Tel Ahmar), which he rebuilt and renamed Kar-Shalmanesar. Henceforth the turtanu job was to govern the province centered around Til-Barsip and to coordinate the activities of the western tier of Assyrian provinces to meet military emergencies in this region. It was as military viceroy of the west that a turtanu appears in 2 Kgs 18:17 as leader of Sennacherib's campaign against Jerusalem and in Isa 20:1 as leader of Sargon's campaign against Ashdod. Sargon II created a second tier of administration, centered in Kummuhu (Commagene) and led by a new official called the turtanu of the left wing, to coordinate the provinces of northern Syria and southwestern Anatolia.

JOANN SCURLOCK

TASKMASTER [נֹגֵשׂ noghes]. One who imposes heavy work demands. The term is a participle of the verb naghas (נָגַשׂ), which connotes oppressive pressure for either labor or payment. The cruelty of taskmasters is reflected throughout the Exodus narrative (Exod 3:7; 5:6-14). David and Solomon employed taskmasters to superintend labor gangs (e.g., 2 Sam 20:24). Solomon had so many laborers that it required the oversight of 3,850 supervisors (1 Kgs 5:15-16; 9:23; 2 Chr 2:17-18; 8:10). The burden of forced labor and taxation was so heavy under Rehoboam that it led to an uprising (1 Kgs 12:16). When Rehoboam sent Adoram, the chief over forced labor (2 Sam 20:24), to cope with the rebellion, "all Israel stoned him to death" (1 Kgs 12:18). Although the term rarely has positive overtones, one of Third Isaiah's oracles promising redemption to Jerusalem states that Yahweh "will appoint Peace as your overseer and Righteousness as your taskmaster" (Isa 60:17).

RALPH K. HAWKINS

TASSELS [גְּדִלִים gedhilim; צִיצִת tsitsith]. The FRINGE or twisted threads on a garment's corners, usually called tsitsith, are referred to as *tassels* in Deut 22:12. Gedhilim also refers to decorations on the capitals of pillars in Solomon's Temple (1 Kgs 7:17). *See* CLOTH, CLOTHES.

TATIAN. *See* DIATESSARON; VERSIONS, ANCIENT.

TATTENAI tat'uh-ni [תַּתְּנַי tattenay]. Governor of the western half of the Persian province or satrapy, Beyond the River during the time of Haggai and Zechariah (Ezra 5:3, 6; 6:6, 13).

TATTOO [קַעֲקַע qa'aqa']. Words, numbers, or signs of ink written into skin by puncturing it. Leviticus 19:28 prohibits tattoos. Since the Holocaust, when Jews were forcibly tattooed with numbers, this prohibition is particularly strongly felt.

TAU tou [τ t, Τ t]. The twentieth letter of the Greek alphabet, based on the Phoenician *taww. See* ALPHABET.

TAUNT [חָרַף kharaf, חֶרְפָּה kherpah; ὀνειδίζω oneidizō, ὀνειδισμός oneidismos]. A taunt is a reproach in the form of insult or ridicule (e.g., Ps 102:8; Ezek 5:15). The NRSV consistently translates the same Hebrew and Greek words as "taunt." Although *taunt* does not appear in its rendition of the Apocrypha, the terms oneidizō and oneidismos often do. But these, like their Hebrew counterparts, can be translated variously (e.g., "reproach," 1 Macc 1:39; Sir 8:5). The quintessence of biblical taunting is embodied by the two occurrences of the word in the NT where Jesus is ridiculed in a public setting (Matt 27:44; Mark 15:32). *See* REPROACH; SCOFFER.

JASON R. TATLOCK

TAV [ת t]. The final letter of the Hebrew alphabet. The original meaning of the letter was arguably "sign, mark" (compare Job 31:35, "signature"). The shape and name of the Greek letter TAU derive from tav.

TAVERNER'S BIBLE. A Bible version edited by Richard Taverner and published in 1539. It was a revision of the MATTHEW BIBLE that took the original Greek into account. It had limited influence on subsequent English translations. *See* VERSIONS, ENGLISH.

TAVERNS, THREE. *See* THREE TAVERNS.

TAW. *See* TAV.

TAX BOOTH [τελώνιον telōnion]. A tax collector's place of business and, according to the Synoptic Gospels, Levi's/Matthew's location when Jesus called him (Matt 9:9; Mark 2:14; Luke 5:27). *See* TAX COLLECTOR; TAXES, TAXATION.

TAX COLLECTOR [τελώνης telōnēs]. A "tax" or (preferably) "toll" collector was usually stationed at a "toll booth" (telōnion τελώνιον) and was responsible for collecting the toll, tariff, or customs duty (telos τέλος) on transported goods.

In the Greco-Roman world, toll collectors collected tariffs for the variety of goods transported into the territory. At various times, a group of *publicani* (Lat. for "tax collectors") would have also been contracted to secure the necessary levies on farm production (telōnēs can also be translated "farmer"), although the intricacies of how they accomplished their task is complex. Generally, many people hated and despised toll collectors since they were able to exploit the toll collection system to their own advantage. This negative attitude is present in the Gospels. Fabian Udoh argues that it was the fact of Roman toll at all and not the (high) rate of tariff that remained troubling for many Jews. On the other hand, there are positive stories of toll collectors in Jewish communities as well (e.g., "John, the tax collector" in Josephus' *J.W.* 2.287). Indeed, the payment of tolls itself is not always viewed negatively (compare Rom 13:6-7).

The appearance of the toll collector is common within the Synoptic Gospel tradition and the popular sentiment about such a person appears within these descriptions (Matt 5:46; 9:10, 11; 10:3; 11:19; 18:17; 21:31, 32; Mark 2:15, 16 [2x]; Luke 3:12; 5:27, 29, 30; 7:29, 34; 15:1; 18:10, 11, 13). The term never occurs in the Fourth Gospel.

In Mark, the term occurs in one story (Mark 2:13-17), combining two scenes. Jesus invites Levi—who was stationed at a toll booth (telōnion)—to join his group; then, immediately after this summons, Jesus ate at Levi's house, in which there was a challenge to Jesus' table-fellowship practices; a number of scribes associated with the Pharisees question Jesus' disciples, "Why does he eat with tax collectors and sinners?"

The bias in the Markan narrative is clear. 1) Toll collectors are associated with "sinners" (i.e., transgressors of the Jewish law). The phrase is repeated three times in Mark, twice in the narrator's description of the scene, and once in the words expressed by the pharisaic scribes. The association of toll collectors with sinners—without any explanation or apology—supports the general assessment that many Jews would have been troubled by the professional activity of these collecting agents; 2) Toll collectors may, however, become followers of Jesus. Levi is the specific example in this account. But other toll collectors ("tax collectors," NRSV) are said "to follow" him as well (2:15).

Before Matthew's account of the meal with toll collectors, Jesus expresses his own bias against this group in his opening sermon: "for if you love those who love you, what reward do you have? Do not even the tax collectors do the same?" (Matt 5:46)

Jesus' dinner with "tax collectors and sinners" in Matthew's account is similar to Mark's, with one change in Jesus' response. His final response includes the additional words, "Go and learn what this means, 'I desire mercy, and not sacrifice'" (9:13). Jesus' table-fellowship practices will become cause for critique later in Matthew's story, in which Jesus is charged to be a "friend of tax collectors and sinners" (11:19). Despite Jesus' inclusive actions, the more common refrain throughout the narrative is disassociation from the toll collector (compare 18:17; 21:31-32). The cultural bias against toll collectors rings true in this account as well.

In the Lukan narrative, a group of toll collectors seeks association with John the Baptist (3:12-13), an account that prefigures the "call of Levi" (5:27-32). Apparently, a few succeed since it is reported later in the narrative that a group of toll collectors had received the baptism of John (7:29). In Jesus' meal with toll collectors, only Luke describes that Levi "left everything" to follow Jesus (5:28), a clear sign of full commitment. Jesus' response to his table-fellowship practices includes language of "repentance" (5:32), a common Lukan theme (compare 3:3, 8; 15:7; 24:47) and a term absent from the other two Gospel accounts.

Only in Luke is Jesus' rationale provided, albeit in parables, for his association with toll collectors (Luke 15). These stories highlight Jesus' views on the larger community—and the toll collectors' original connection to it—and his views on their wandering from the community, whether as lost "sheep" or "coins" or "children." It is clear from these parables that Jesus shares the general assessment that toll collectors are classified as "sinners" (i.e., breakers of the law) who have committed error against the larger community of Israel in some way. But he also thinks it is important to invite them back into the larger community, albeit after "repentance" of their wrongdoing. What is not clear is whether their "straying" (i.e., misconduct) is inherent to their role as toll collectors or whether it is the manner in which they carried out their task (compare Luke

3:12-13). The story of Zacchaeus, the "chief collector" (architelōnēs ἀρχιτελώνης) in Jericho, is another example of Luke's (19:1-10). Jesus considers Zacchaeus "a son of Abraham" and announces "salvation" over his house when this toll collector notes that he gives half of his possessions to the poor and repays fourfold to anyone he has defrauded (19:8-9).

One other parable (only in Luke) provides Jesus' further thoughts. It poses a "tax collector" against a righteous "Pharisee" (18:9-14). The humility of the toll collector's prayer attracts God's mercy (18:13-14). This striking comparison would not go unnoticed in 1st-cent. Palestine.

Bibliography: E. Badian. *Publicans and Sinners: Private Enterprise in the Service of the Roman Republic* (1983); Fabian E. Udoh. *To Caesar What Is Caesar's: Tribute Taxes, and Imperial Administration in Early Roman Palestine (63 B.C.E.–70 C.E.)* (2005).

EMERSON B. POWERY

TAXES, TAXATION [מַשְׂאֵת maseth; κῆνσος kēnsos, φόρος phoros]. The biblical traditions constantly engage and reflect the structures and daily realities of aristocratic-controlled empires. Empires employ a proprietary theory whereby ruling elites claim a material share of all things: land, production, traded goods, and labor. The payment (often in kind) of taxes, tributes, rents, and forced labor by peasants to local and foreign elites ensures a continual source of wealth. Peasants who usually seek to supply their own needs locally are thereby forced to produce a "surplus." Taxation does not benefit the common good. Rather, it supports the privileged lifestyle of elites. Taxation exerts control over land, its production, and those who work it, maintaining a hierarchical societal structure benefiting a few at the expense of most.

The biblical documents refer to varying forms of taxation. Claiming control of land (Gen 41:41), the Egyptian pharaoh exacted 20 percent of the crop to offset famine among his own residents (Gen 41:33-36) and nations (Gen 41:57). Subsequently, Egypt imposed another form of taxation on Israelites, that of forced labor. Israelites were forced to work "in mortar and brick" and in the fields (Exod 1:12-14). During Israel's monarchy, Assyria took tribute from Israel (2 Kgs 15:20) and from Judah after Assyria invaded Judah in 701 BCE (2 Kgs 18:13-16). A century later, Egypt exacted tribute from Judah, forcing Jehoiakim to tax the land to meet Pharaoh Neco's demands (2 Kgs 23:28-35). Babylon exacted tribute after taking Jerusalem in 597–587 BCE (2 Kgs 24:13).

Israel and Judah not only paid taxes to empires, they themselves exacted forced labor from conquered Canaanites (Deut 20:11; Josh 16:10; 17:12-13; Judg 1:28-35). King Solomon taxed the people. He established twelve districts to sustain the king for a month each by taxation (1 Kgs 4:7-19, 22-28). Solomon also conscripted labor from Israel (1 Kgs 5:13), taxed merchants and trade (1 Kgs 10:15), and received tribute from nations (1 Kgs 4:21; 10:15b). When the people protested the harshness of such demands, his son and successor, Rehoboam, increased taxes, causing Jeroboam to lead a revolt. The division of the kingdoms resulted (1 Kgs 12). Previously, when the people had demanded a king, Samuel had warned that harsh taxation was inevitable (1 Sam 8:11-17).

Under Persian rule, taxation and the means of collection were extended. King Ahasuerus, the Persian emperor (486–465 BCE), taxed "the land and ... the islands" (Esth 10:1). His successor, King Artaxerxes, levied "tribute, custom, or toll" as direct sources of royal revenue (Ezra 4:13), exempting, though, Jerusalem temple personnel (Ezra 7:24). Under Nehemiah, governor of Judah from 445–433 BCE, these taxes, along with forced labor to rebuild Jerusalem's walls, were harsh, requiring some to mortgage fields and vineyards (Neh 5:1-5; 9:36-37). Moreover, Persian-appointed governors of the province of Judah collected another level of taxes comprising food, wine, and money for themselves, though Nehemiah declares he did not do so (Neh 5:14-19).

Under the Ptolemies and Seleucids, tax collecting took a different form. Instead of the king's officials collecting taxes, they were contracted to local elites for collection (Josephus, *Ant.* 12.154–55). This system profited rulers in guaranteeing levels of payment, as well as elites who collected and pocketed a surplus. Taxes included tribute, and salt, crown, and crop taxes (1 Macc 10:29-31; 11:34-35).

Initially, the same system continued when Rome established power post-63 BCE. By the 1st cent. CE, the system seems to have been modified. Some taxes, probably land and head taxes, were paid directly to officials employed by governors or to local councils. Tolls on transit and distribution collected at city-gates and seaports were contracted to TAX COLLECTORs. Zacchaeus is described by the unusual term "chief tax collector," suggesting that he perhaps owned collection rights on transportation tolls around Jericho, and supervised local collectors (Luke 19:1).

The Roman historian Tacitus attests the central role of taxation in the Roman Empire. He narrates unrest about taxation during the emperor Nero's reign (54–68 CE). Nero considers the abolition of indirect taxes on transportation of goods. His advisers "praise his magnanimity" but point out "that the dissolution of the empire was certain if the revenues on which the state subsisted were to be curtailed" (Tacitus, *Ann.* 13.50).

In addition to Roman taxes, there were other layers. King Herod (39–4 BCE) taxed agrarian production (Josephus, *Ant.* 15.303) and purchases and sales (Josephus, *Ant.* 17.205). Herod Antipas (4 BCE–39 CE) collected similar taxes and tolls in Galilee. The Jerusalem Temple required the "first fruits" tithe paid in kind (Neh 10:32-39), and a tax of a half-shekel paid by males twenty years and older, including Jews in the Diaspora (Exod 30:11-16; Josephus, *Ant.* 18.312). It is difficult to predict exact levels of taxation. Estimates range between ca. 20–50 percent of peasant and artisan production was removed through taxes, a significant and damaging amount for those living near subsistence levels.

"Tax collectors" appear often in the Synoptic Gospels, though not in John's Gospel. The criterion of multiple attestation indicates Jesus' association with them (Mark 2:15-16; Q: Matt 11:19 and Luke 7:34; L: Luke 15:1-2). In Galilee tax collectors worked on behalf of Herod Antipas, not directly for Rome. Several features mark their presentation in the Gospels. Tax collectors are frequently associated with excessive collection. John the Baptist instructs repentant toll collectors not to collect excess (Luke 3:12-13). The wealthy Zacchaeus recognizes that he has defrauded or exploited people (Luke 19:8). Further, tax collectors were socially despised and regarded as "sinners." This unspecified term seems, in part, to express unacceptability of a group (Matt 9:10; 11:19; Mark 2:15; Luke 5:30-31; 7:34; 15:2). Matthew links tax collectors with "Gentiles," suggesting social distance (Matt 5:46; 18:17). The term *sinner* also indicates morally unacceptable behavior. A Pharisee associates tax collectors with "thieves, rogues, adulterers" (Luke 18:11). Matthew's Jesus links them with prostitutes (Matt 21:31). The crowd grumbles when Jesus goes to the home of Zacchaeus, "a sinner" (Luke 19:7). Yet tax collectors are often responsive to Jesus' ministry. Levi abandons his toll-collection booth to follow Jesus (Matt 9:9; Luke 5:27-28). A tax collector cries out for God's mercy (Luke 18:13). Zacchaeus receives salvation by receiving Jesus and making fourfold restitution to the poor (Luke 19:8-9).

Jesus' followers had to cooperate with Rome's tax requirements. Rome regarded refusal to pay as a denial of its sovereignty. Josephus has Agrippa declare that Jewish nonpayment of tribute to the governor Florus in 66 CE is an "act of war," whereas its payment would clear them of the "charge of insurrection" (*J.W.* 2.403–404). Refusal to pay often brought a military response (Tacitus, *Ann.* 3.40–41; 6.41). New Testament writers do not endorse violent resistance. As often happens with powerless groups, they mix cooperation with disguised and self-protective protest.

In the difficult passage Rom 13:1-7, Paul declares God's sanction of ruling authority and the requirement of obedience. Yet he had previously described the world as corrupt (Rom 1:18-32) and under God's judgment (Rom 8:18-25; compare 1 Cor 2:6-8), an emphasis he repeats in Rom 13:11-12. In the previous chapter, he instructed Jesus' believers not to conform to this world (Rom 12:1-2). Paul's instruction to pay taxes (Rom 13:6) seems to be a matter of pragmatic survival while recognizing elsewhere God's purposes that would deny to tax payment the claim of Rome's ultimate sovereignty. Sovereignty belongs to God. Perhaps contextualized by

unrest in the 50s because of Nero's taxes (Tacitus, *Ann.* 13.50–51), Paul protectively warns believers to cooperate and pay. A refusal might provoke reprisals against Rome's Jewish community, including Jewish believers, already vulnerable to anti-Jewish sentiments.

Similar ambivalence involving cooperation yet disguised as critique is evident in Jesus' instruction about taxes: "give to the emperor the things that are the emperor's, and to God the things that are God's" (Mark 12:13-17). Jesus' instruction cleverly combines apparent deference to Rome with a subversive agenda. He employs ambiguous, coded, and self-protective speech to uphold paying a coin bearing the emperor's image (contrary to the Decalogue), while also asserting overriding loyalty to God. "The things of God" embrace everything since "the earth is the LORD's and all that is in it" (Ps 24:1). The "hidden transcript" says the earth does not belong to Caesar despite Rome's claims of ownership (the "public transcript") that the tax represented.

But instead of prohibiting payment, Jesus orders payment of Caesar's things to Caesar. The verb *give* or *render* literally means "give back." Disciples are to "give back" to Caesar a blasphemous coin that, contrary to God's will, bears Caesar's image. Paying the tax literally removes this illicit coin and its illegitimate claim from Judea. As much as Rome sees, the tax is paid; compliance is expressed. But Jesus' instruction reframes the act. "Giving back" to Caesar becomes a disguised, dignity-restoring act of resistance that recognizes God's all-encompassing claim.

Jesus gives another instruction about taxes that also hides yet expresses resistance. Jesus instructs Peter to pay the half-shekel tax with a coin found in a fish's mouth (Matt 17:24-27). The tax under discussion was paid, prior to 70 CE, to the Jerusalem Temple. But after Jerusalem's defeat in 70, the emperor Vespasian co-opted it as a punitive tax on Jews paid to Rome (Josephus, *J.W.* 7.218; Dio Cassius, *Rom.* 65.7.2). He used it, insultingly, to rebuild and maintain the temple of Jupiter Capitolinus in Rome, thereby reminding Jews not only of Rome's superior power but also of Jupiter's superiority to the God of Israel. Jesus' conversation with Peter in Matthew's Gospel, written post-70 CE, concerns this tax. Matthew's Jesus reframes an action intended to humiliate by attributing to it a different significance that dignifies the dominated and attests God's sovereignty, not Rome's.

Jesus reminds Peter in Matt 17:25-26 of the well-known taxing ways of kings and emperors. Everyone pays taxes except the rulers' children. Not paying the tax is not an option because it will bring reprisals (Matt 17:27*a*). Instead Jesus instructs Peter to catch a fish and find there the coin to pay the tax.

The key to understanding Jesus' instruction lies in the Gospel's previous scenes involving fish. Twice, in Matt 14 and 15, Jesus has exerted God's sovereignty over fish, multiplying small fish to feed crowds. Contrary to

Rome's claims that the emperor rules the sea and owns its creatures, expressed by taxing the fishing industry, the Gospel asserts that the sea and its creatures belong to God. They are subject to God's sovereignty. God supplies the fish with the coin in its mouth. Disciples are to pay the tax. It appears to Rome that they are submissive and compliant, but for disciples the tax coin has a special significance. Supplied by God, it testifies to God's sovereignty. The tax that is supposed to enact and acknowledge Rome's control is reframed to witness to God's reign. Paying the tax is an ambiguous act, an expression of hidden protest.

Bibliography: Warren Carter. "Paying the Tax to Rome as Subversive Praxis: Matthew 17:24-27." *Matthew and Empire: Initial Explorations* (2001) 130–44; John Donahue. "Tax-Collectors and Sinners: An Attempt at Identification." *CBQ* 33 (1971) 39–61; K. C. Hanson and Douglas Oakman. *Palestine in the Time of Jesus* (1998); James Scott. *Domination and the Arts of Resistance* (1990).

WARREN CARTER

TAYINAT, TELL. A large Early Bronze and Iron Age mound, located on the southern edge of the Amuq Plain in southeastern Turkey; it is identified as ancient Kunulua, capital of the Neo-Hittite/Aramean kingdom of Patina/Unqi. Excavations uncovered several large palatial complexes (or **bit-hilani**), a megaron-style temple fronted by gracefully carved lion column bases, numerous carved stone reliefs and sculptures, and stelae inscribed with Luwian (Neo-Hittite) hieroglyphic inscriptions. The monumental remains (9th–8th cent. BCE) share architectural features with the Solomonic Temple and palace described in 1 Kgs 6–7.

TIMOTHY P. HARRISON

TEACHER [מֵבִין mevin, מְלַמֵּד melammedh, מוֹרֶה moreh; διδάσκαλος didaskalos, ῥαββι rhabbi]. The term *teacher* is used to translate mevin, "one who discerns," suggesting that the teacher helps others to be able to distinguish ideas (1 Chr 25:8); moreh "one who throws," indicating that a teacher is one who pours out knowledge to others (Hab 2:18); and melammedh, "one who teaches," the most common word used for learning and instruction (Ps 119:99).

God is the foremost teacher. The TORAH is frequently translated "law," but it also means "teaching" or "instruction." Isaiah 40:14 challenges the hearer to ponder just who "taught" God, the creator of the heavens and the earth, "the path of justice" and "the way of understanding," indicating that God is the only ultimate "teacher" of the ways of the world. Isaiah 48:17 states, "I am the LORD your God, who teaches you for your own good." The psalmists call on God to "teach" them (Pss 25:4, 5; 119:12, 26, 108; 143:20); celebrate God as "teacher" (Pss 71:17; 94:10, 12; 119:171; 132:12); and invite others to listen to their teachings (Pss 34:11;

51:13). Various figures in the OT are designated "teachers." Moses acts as teacher of torah to the Israelites in Deut 4:1, 5, 14; 5:31. Parents are admonished to "teach" their children the words of God (Deut 11:19). God instructs Moses and Aaron to be teachers of the story-song of their history (Deut 3:19).

"Teacher" is sometimes the translation of Qohelet (qoheleth קֹהֶלֶת), the Hebrew name of the book commonly known as Ecclesiastes. Qoheleth comes from the verb qahal (קָהַל), which means to "gather" or "assemble," so that the translation "teacher" indicates someone who gathers and assembles knowledge.

The evidence for schools in ancient Israel is limited and debated; the greatest evidence comes from the books of Proverbs and Ben Sirach. The sociological evidence from other cultures in the ANE suggests that scribal schools may have existed in Israel as early as the beginning of the monarchy. Within such schools, religious, administrative, and sagacious traditions would have been transmitted, copied, and preserved for future generations. Thus we may surmise that the role of teacher was an important part of Jewish culture in the period preceding and leading up to the time of Jesus (*see* EDUCATION, OT). In the NT "teacher" is used to translate a number of Greek words. *Rabbi* (rhabbi, from the Aramaic rav [רַב], meaning "great") is used once in reference to John the Baptist (John 3:26) and once in a derogatory manner in reference to the scribes and Pharisees (Matt 23:7-8). In the remainder of its occurrences, *rabbi* refers to Jesus (*see* RABBI, RABBONI). *Teacher* is also used some thirty times in the NT to translate didaskalos, from the verb didaskō (διδάσκω, "teach"), which conveys the idea of teaching someone, not just something. Jesus is frequently portrayed teaching (e.g., Matt 11:1; Mark 4:1-2; Luke 4:15; John 7:14), as are the apostles (e.g., Acts 5:21-28). Paul teaches (e.g., 1 Cor 3:16) and counts teaching as a gift of the spirit (1 Cor 12:28-29). A "false teacher" (pseudodidaskalos [ψευδοδιδάσκαλος]; 2 Pet 2:1) or "false apostle" (pseudapostolos [ψευδαπόστολος]; 2 Cor 11:13) is someone with a different or "unorthodox" doctrine. *See* EDUCATION, NT.

Bibliography: Bruce Chilton. *Rabbi Paul: An Intellectual Biography* (2005); James L. Crenshaw. *Education in Ancient Israel: Across the Deadening Silence* (1998); A. R. Millard. *Reading and Writing in the Time of Jesus* (2000); Karel van der Toorn. *Scribal Culture and the Making of the Hebrew Bible* (2007); Brad H. Young. *Meet the Rabbis: Rabbinic Thought and the Teachings of Jesus* (2007).

NANCY DECLAISSÉ-WALFORD

TEACHER OF RIGHTEOUSNESS [מורה הצדק mwrh htsdq]. In the DEAD SEA SCROLLS, the Teacher of Righteousness (mwrh htsdq, "correct teacher" or "legitimate teacher") was the leader of the Qumran sect who arose after the sect was founded and immediately before or after it settled in the area of Qumran. Variant forms of this name are mwrh tsdq (מורה צדק, CD I, 11; XX, 32) and mrh htsdqh (מורה הצדקה, 1QpHab II, 2). This term may derive from Joel 2:23 where the expression moreh litsedhaqah (מוֹרֶה לִצְדָקָה) means "early rain for your vindication." The Scrolls seem to have translated moreh, "early rain," as "teacher." This respected leader, a descendant of a priestly family, is also called mwrh hykhyd (מורה היחיד), "the unique teacher" (CD XX, 1, 14), which some have proposed emending to mwrh hykhd (מורה היחד), "the teacher of the community." He may also be identical with dwrsh htwrh (דורש התורה), "the interpreter of the law" (CD VI, 7) and mlyts d't (מליץ דעת), "the interpreter of knowledge" (4Q171 I, 27). The Teacher of Righteousness was credited with the correct interpretation of the Scriptures, especially the secret lore discovered by divine inspiration. This lore includes the nistar (נסתר), hidden law known only to the Qumran sect, and the pesher (פֵּשֶׁר), contemporizing exegesis of biblical passages.

It was originally thought that 4Q394–99 (4QMMT), the HALAKHIC LETTER, was written by the Teacher of Righteousness to his opponents in Jerusalem, but the sect's official history in the *Damascus Document* makes it most likely that the *Halakhic Letter* was composed some twenty years before the Teacher of Righteousness arose as leader of the sect. At that time a group or movement had formed, but it had not yet coalesced or developed its characteristic teachings. The Teacher of Righteousness provided not only leadership but also definitive rulings on the interpretation of Torah. While his rulings allowed the sect to gain adherents, they were also a source of controversy with other Jews and perhaps also within the sect. The Teacher of Righteousness also might have had a hand in the sectarians' decision to establish a center at Qumran. He led the sect into its intensely apocalyptic, sectarian mentality and the adoption of practices that were originally based on Sadducean law but eventually became unique to the sect. According to CD I, 11, the Teacher of Righteousness was sent by God to the sect to lead the faithful and to be a legislator and interpreter of the law. In its interpretation of Ps 37:23, "The steps of a man are prepared by the Lord" (NJPS), 4Q171 III, 15–16 writes: "Its interpretation refers to the priest, the Teacher of [Righteousness, whom] God [pr]omised would arise, fo[r] he (God) prepared [i.e., predestined him (the Teacher)] to build for him a congregation" (author's trans.).

The Teacher of Righteousness was an expert in the mysteries of the prophets (1QpHab VII, 3–5), and some scholars have maintained that he composed the Rule of the Congregation and certain Thanksgiving Hymns, known among scholars as the "Teacher Hymns." While both of these documents provide a basic theological sketch of the sect, there is no direct evidence as to who authored them. In the case of the *Hymns*, the first-person character of these compositions has led to

the suggestion that the Teacher composed them. If the Teacher of Righteousness authored them, they reveal his inner spiritual contemplations but, unfortunately, no biographical facts that can be used definitively to ascertain his identity.

Some speculate that the Teacher of Righteousness was not one person but an office, filled by successive administrators. But the evidence of the Scrolls seems to argue strongly for his having been one person, who, after his death, would be replaced by a variety of sectarian officials. While his teachings were meant to instruct the sect for the period until the imminent coming of the messiah, the Teacher of Righteousness himself was not a messianic figure, nor did he live until the messianic era. CD XIX, 35–XX, 1 records his death, and his functions were apparently performed thereafter by various officers.

During his career, the Teacher of Righteousness was challenged by the "treacherous ones" and the "Man of Lies" (1QpHab II, 1–2) who rejected his teachings; these are probably designations for the Pharisees, although it is possible that "treacherous ones" referred to a group within the sect who rebelled against his rule or, perhaps, who left the group. 1QpHab V, 9–12 describes a dispute between the Teacher of Righteousness and an opposing group known as the "Men of Lies" and states that some group stood by silently and allowed it to happen. The "liar" of *Pesher Habakkuk* and *Pesher to Psalms* and/or "the scoffer" of the *Damascus Document* led rival groups whose arguments with the Teacher of Righteousness were based on his interpretations of Jewish law.

One of the early Hasmonean rulers, known in 1QpHab as the Wicked Priest, also mistreated the Teacher of Righteousness, perhaps because he was a rival priest (*see* PRIEST, WICKED). Some scholars have argued that the Teacher of Righteousness might have actually been the high priest between 159 BCE and 152 BCE when Jonathan the Hasmonean was appointed, but there is no evidence for this claim. 1QpHab VIII, 8–13 records that at first Qumran sectarians considered the Wicked Priest to be a good ruler. But then "his heart became haughty and he abandoned God, and he rebelled against the laws for the sake of wealth," and he defiled the Temple. This adversary later became ill and suffered at the hands of his enemies, and, according to the sect, his suffering was God's punishment for what he had done to the Teacher of Righteousness (1QpHab IX, 9–12). Since these events took place in the early Hasmonean period, some time after 152 BCE, the Wicked Priest might be identified with either Jonathan (160–143 BCE) or Simon (142–134 BCE), the first two rulers of the Hasmonean dynasty. Either of them could have been contemporaries of the Teacher of Righteousness. In any case, throughout the Scrolls there is antipathy toward the Hasmoneans.

The most dramatic of these confrontations is related in 1QpHab XI, 4–8 when the Wicked Priest came in "wrathful anger" to "the place of exile" (presumably Qumran) on the Day of Atonement. "He (the Wicked Priest) appeared before them, to swallow them up and to make them stumble on the day of the fast of their abstention from work." The gravity of this action was apparent for its having taken place on the holiest day of the year. In addition, this text provides confirmation of an interesting detail: since the Wicked Priest traveled to confront the Teacher of Righteousness on the Day of Atonement, it becomes apparent that while the Teacher of Righteousness was celebrating the fast, it was not the Day of Atonement according to the Wicked Priest. This fact demonstrates that the sectarians had a variant calendar from that observed in Jerusalem.

All these confrontations of the Teacher of Righteousness with the Pharisees and the Jerusalem establishment show that there was much friction and even animosity between the Qumran sect and their opponents. On a more symbolic plane, the Teacher of Righteousness and the Wicked Priest represented the forces of good and evil in the pre-messianic age. In the eschatological battle at the end of days, the Sons of Light would battle the Sons of Darkness. After the dawn of the messianic age and the ultimate triumph of good, a messianic figure like the Teacher of Righteousness, perhaps the one termed in the Scrolls as the messiah of Aaron, would once again interpret the law.

Early in the study of the Dead Sea Scrolls, speculation centered on the possibility that the Teacher of Righteousness might be Jesus. This is, of course, impossible as is proved by ^{14}C dating of the *Pesher Habakkuk* to the second half of the 2nd cent. BCE. However, certain aspects of the Teacher's career and role in the formation of his community can properly be compared with the career of Jesus. The role of the Teacher of Righteousness as a teacher and expounder of biblical interpretation and law shares certain features in common with that of the Pharisaic-rabbinic sages.

Bibliography: J. J. Collins. "The Origin of the Qumran Community: A Review of the Evidence." *To Touch the Text: Biblical and Related Studies in Honor of Joseph A. Fitzmyer, S.J.* M. P. Horgan and P. J. Kobelski, eds. (1989) 159–78; F. García Martínez and A. S. van der Woude. "A 'Groningen' Hypothesis of Qumran Origins and Early History." *RevQ* 14 (1990) 521–41; M. A. Knibb. "The Teacher of Righteousness—A Messianic Title?" *A Tribute to Geza Vermes: Essays on Jewish and Christian Literature and History.* P. R. Davies and R. T. White, eds. (1990) 51–65; L. H. Schiffman. *Reclaiming the Dead Sea Scrolls: The History of Judaism, the Background of Christianity, the Lost Library of Qumran* (1994) 117–21.

LAWRENCE H. SCHIFFMAN

TEACHING IN THE EARLY CHURCH. Teaching was an individual spiritual gift used for the edification of the whole church (Rom 12:7), distinct from preaching (Acts 4:2; 1 Tim 5:17). *See* CHURCH, LIFE AND ORGANIZATION OF; PREACHING.

TEACHING OF JESUS. As the followers of Jesus were called "Christians" from earliest times (Acts 11:26; 26:28; 1 Pet 4:16), their loyalty was recognized as being connected with their convictions concerning the person of Jesus as the messianic Son of God, sharing in divine glory, whose death and resurrection reconcile both the world and the sinners who inhabit the world with God the Father (John 1:1-18; Phil 2:6-11; Col 1:15-20; *see* CHRISTOLOGY). For Luke, followers of Jesus were people who adhered to and who proclaimed the teaching of Jesus (Luke 1:1-4; Acts 1:1). The early Christian missionaries were committed to teaching the new converts, both Jews and Gentiles, to obey everything that Jesus commanded (Matt 28:20). The foundational significance of the teaching of Jesus can also be seen in the fact that by the 2nd cent., many Christians were committed to the four canonical Gospels of Matthew, Mark, Luke, and John that were placed, not by accident, at the beginning of the CANON OF THE NEW TESTAMENT.

A. Sources and Scholars
B. The Context of Jesus' Teaching
 1. Jesus and Jewish society
 2. Jesus and Jewish politics
C. The Forms of Jesus' Teaching
 1. Sermons
 2. Parables
 3. Sayings
 4. Pronouncements
 5. Prophecies
 6. Miracles and exorcisms
D. The Coming of the Kingdom of God
 1. Israel's unfinished story
 2. Jesus' proclamation of the kingdom of God
E. The Messianic Son of Man
 1. Son of Man
 2. Messiah
 3. The death and vindication of the Son of Man
F. The Call to Repentance and Faith
 1. Repentance and judgment
 2. Faith and the good news
 3. The welcome of sinners
G. The New Community
 1. The Twelve and discipleship
 2. Righteousness and the will of God
 3. Sabbath and food
 4. The Temple and the conversion of the nations
Bibliography

A. Sources and Scholars

The available sources for the description of the teaching of Jesus are without exception Christian documents: the Gospel of Mark, perhaps the first of the four canonical Gospels, presumably written some time between 60–70 CE, the Gospel of Matthew, the Gospel of Luke, as well as the Gospel of John. The latter has often been excluded from consideration for a historical description of the life and teaching of Jesus. This seems to be changing, as biblical scholars are increasingly willing to include the Fourth Gospel among the historical sources for the study of Jesus and his teaching. Scholars who accept one of the many scholarly reconstructions of the source—essentially the material that Matthew and Luke have in common but which is not found in Mark, about 200 verses consisting of sayings of Jesus—regard this document as the earliest written source for the teaching of Jesus, perhaps written around 50 CE. Many scholars regard the apocryphal *Gospel of Thomas* as another source for a description of Jesus' teaching—a collection of 114 sayings of Jesus, written some time between the end of the 1st and the end of the 2nd cent. (the earliest Greek fragment is P. Oxy. 1; only the Coptic version provides the entire work). Other early Christian documents both within the NT and outside of the NT canon reflect Jesus' teaching, but the primary sources are these Gospels.

Any description of the teaching of Jesus depends on the decisions regarding the authenticity, or nonauthenticity, of the material in the Gospels. Some critics have been rather skeptical concerning the reliability of the Gospels, claiming that they are expressions of faith that make it nearly impossible to retrieve reliable information concerning the historical Jesus. Some have argued that the Christian faith does not depend on scholarly reconstructions of the life and the teaching of Jesus, but on an existential, or dogmatic, or traditional commitment that is independent of history. It has become increasingly obvious that this bifurcation of personal convictions and historical reliability is unwarranted, unless scholars are willing to concede that we know next to nothing about any person or event in ancient history; all sources, whether literary or documentary, have an agenda. Thus a historical description of Jesus' teaching remains important, whether a consensus about larger issues or details of interpretation can be achieved or not. The following description of Jesus' teaching follows what could be described as a canonical approach.

B. The Context of Jesus' Teaching

Jesus was recognized by his contemporaries as a prophet (Mark 6:14-16; 8:27-30) who was teaching the people of Israel (Mark 5:35; 9:17; 10:17; John 3:2). The message of teachers and prophets is always connected with the political, historical, and cultural circumstances of their time.

1. Jesus and Jewish society

Jesus was a Jewish teacher and a Jewish prophet. This explains, among other things, why Jesus' teaching was, at least at the surface, not about himself but about God, the almighty Creator (Mark 10:6; 13:19), the God of Abraham, Isaac, and Jacob (Matt 8:11; 22:32; Mark 12:26; Luke 16:22-24). Jesus taught Jews (Matt 10:5; 15:24); very rarely did he speak with Gentiles (Matt 8:5-13; Mark 7:26-29). There is a fundamental continuity between Jesus' teaching and the central elements of the OT and of Jewish faith and practice: he affirmed the validity of the Law and the Prophets (Matt 5:17-19), he taught about the fulfillment of the prophecies of the OT prophets (Matt 5:17; Mark 1:15; 4:4-9; Luke 4:16-30; 7:22; etc.), he preached about God's future judgment (Mark 13), and he spoke positively about the righteousness of the Law experts and the Pharisees (Matt 5:20; 23:2-3).

Many interpret Jesus' teaching as aiming at the renewal of Judaism. The calling of twelve disciples (Mark 3:14-19) symbolizes the restoration of Israel as God's covenant people that the prophets envisioned for the last days and that many Jews expected in connection with the appearance of the Messiah. This means that the conflict between Jesus and the leaders of the Jewish people was an internal Jewish dispute, comparable to the tensions between Jeremiah and his fellow Jews in the 6th cent. BCE. This also means that Jesus' emphasis on compassion for the people who did not care about the law, or who were powerless, or who were sick, or who lived on the fringes of society (Mark 6:34; 8:2; Luke 15:20) was much more than a virtue of heroic individuals or a radicalized form of personal ethics. Rather, Jesus teaches compassion for sinners, for the poor, and for the sick as a core value for the people of God in the days of the arrival of God's kingdom (see §D). The inclusiveness of Jesus' teaching and practice—he had twelve male disciples, but there were also women who followed him (Mark 15:41; Luke 8:1-3); his disciples included a politically suspect tax collector (Matt 10:3); he ate with "tax collectors and sinners" (Matt 9:10-11; 11:19; Mark 2:15-16; Luke 15:1); he spoke about prostitutes entering the kingdom of God (Matt 21:31); he touched and healed lepers (Mark 1:41)—represents a model of the kind of people Israel should be.

2. Jesus and Jewish politics

Jesus criticized the ruling political and religious elites. He spoke against the rich and the greedy (Mark 10:25; 12:38-40; Luke 6:24-26; 12:13-21). He referenced the non-Jewish rulers as negative examples of how not to behave (Mark 10:42-43). He charged the religious leadership of Jerusalem with having turned the Temple into a "den of robbers" (Mark 11:17). He accused them in a parable of murdering God's prophets (Mark 12:1-9).

At the same time, Jesus accepted invitations of leading Pharisees who had a house large enough to give a banquet (Luke 14:1-14). He pronounced salvation for the family of a rich tax collector (Luke 19:1-10). When asked about his position concerning the payment of taxes, he asserted that one should pay the taxes that the governors of the Roman Empire demand (Mark 12:14-17). Jesus did not teach political revolution. But Jesus prepared his followers for persecution by Jewish and pagan authorities (Mark 13:9-13), which implied the knowledge that the message of the arrival of the kingdom of God and of the consequences of this new reality for personal and corporate behavior would be regarded as a political menace. And, of course, eventually Jesus himself was regarded as a threat both by leading members of the Jewish elite and by the Roman governor, resulting in his arrest and in his execution (Mark 14:43–15:37). Jesus' teaching was certainly not harmless: it was potentially dangerous as it required a thoroughgoing transformation of corporate and personal values and modes of behavior.

C. The Forms of Jesus' Teaching

1. Sermons

Jesus taught in Galilean synagogues (Mark 1:21; Luke 4:16-22; 6:6), in the open air (Mark 2:13; Luke 5:3), and in the Temple in Jerusalem (Mark 11:17; John 7:14). Examples of his sermons include material concerning the kingdom of God (Mark 4), missionary work (Matt 10:7-16; Mark 6:10-11; Luke 9:3-5; 10:1-16), the last days (Matt 24; Mark 13; Luke 17:20–18:14; 21:5-38), and the scribes and Pharisees (Matt 13). Also note the material collected in the Sermon on the Mount (Matt 5–7) and in the Sermon on the Plain (Luke 6).

2. Parables

The most characteristic form of Jesus' teaching are his PARABLEs. Depending on one's definition and classification, the Synoptic Gospels contain some forty parables. Parables are metaphors, i.e., figures of speech in which a comparison is made between the kingdom of God, or actions and expectations of God, and human (or more particularly Jewish) ways of thinking, acting, or expecting. Jesus' parables have been compared with the rabbinic parables, which are often triadic, comparing the good behavior of the wise with the wicked behavior of the foolish, both kinds of behavior evaluated by a figure representing God. Jesus' parables do not simply illustrate some theological or moral truth. Rather, they invite the listeners to see themselves, or their world, in the light of Jesus' message of the arrival of God's kingdom.

3. Sayings

Short, memorable sayings that crystallize insight (logia [λογία], "aphorisms") constitute another characteristic form of Jesus' teaching. We find sentences about professions (on slaves, Matt 10:24); on students, Luke 6:40); on prophets (Luke 4:24); about human beings in general (Matt 16:26; Mark 8:36; Luke 9:25); about the consequences of actions (Matt 25:29; Luke 18:14); about the future (Mark 4:22; Luke 12:2); wisdom sayings (Matt 8:20); legal sayings (Mark 7:6-8; note the so-called "sentences of holy law," e.g., Matt 18:15-17); sentences involving argumentation (*a minore ad maius*, "from the lesser to the greater"; Luke 16:10; 23:31); rules of thumb (Mark 9:40; John 2:10); and independent "I-sayings" (Matt 9:13; 12:7; Luke 11:23). The frequency of such sayings prompted some scholars to interpret Jesus as a teacher of wisdom.

4. Pronouncements

As Jesus interacted with his contemporaries, fascinating sympathizers and provoking opponents, he made pronouncements that are sometimes called apophthegms ("statements") or chreiai (χρεῖαι; from chreia [χρεία], "usage," i.e., a statement that can be "used" in life; *see* CREIA). They are different from sayings (logia) as they emphasize the connection between a statement of Jesus and the person of Jesus. His teaching includes pronouncements about his family and his hometown (Mark 3:20-21, 31-35; 6:1-6; Luke 11:27-28), about his relationship with John the Baptist (Matt 11:2-15; Mark 11:27-33), about the calling and sending of his disciples (Mark 1:16-20; 10:17-27), about his relationship with disciples (Mark 10:28-31), about female followers (Mark 14:3-9; Luke 7:36-50; 8:1-3; 10:38-42), about Peter's messianic confession (Mark 8:27-33), and about the relationship with his opponents (Pharisees: Matt 23; Mark 2:23–3:6; 7:1-23; 10:2-12; 12:13-17; Sadducees: Mark 12:18-27; scribes: Mark 12:28-40; Herodians: Mark 3:4-6; 12:13-17). Scholars who focus on this material describe Jesus as a charismatic leader.

5. Prophecies

Jesus teaches not only about Israel's past and about the present conditions of Jewish society, but also about the future. Scholars who interpret Jesus' teaching about the coming of the kingdom of God exclusively in terms of an event in the future understand Jesus as an apocalyptic prophet who announced the (imminent) transformation of the present world. Scholars who see Jesus much more, or even primarily, concerned with addressing his audience about pressing concerns of contemporary Jewish society still generally acknowledge a strong prophetic element of his teaching referring to future events. Jesus' contemporaries certainly saw him as a prophet (Mark 6:14-16; 8:27-30).

Jesus' teaching about the kingdom of God (see §D2) has a strong focus on the future. The Lord's Prayer includes a petition for the coming of the kingdom of God (Matt 6:10; Luke 11:2). Jesus repeatedly speaks about the future rule of God (Mark 14:25; Luke 11:2; 14:15; compare *Gos. Thom.* 51). The Beatitudes on the poor, the hungry, the sorrowing, and the persecuted are linked with assertions concerning the future (Matt 5:3-4, 6; Luke 6:20-21). Jesus takes up the OT expectation of the future pilgrimage of the nations to Zion (Matt 8:11; Luke 13:28-29). Jesus speaks about the date of the arrival of the kingdom in power (Mark 9:1). Jesus also teaches about the signs that indicate the future destruction of Jerusalem and the end of the present world order (Matt 24–25; Mark 13; Luke 24). Scholars who focus on this aspect of Jesus' teaching describe him as a prophet.

6. Miracles and exorcisms

Jesus' MIRACLEs are not mere charitable actions intended to alleviate the suffering of the people. They are an integral part of this teaching, as Jesus' answer to the question of John's disciples (Matt 11:2-6; Luke 7:18-23), his answer to the question concerning the source of his authority to exorcise demons (Mark 3:22-30), as his provocative healings on the Sabbath (Mark 1:21-28; 3:1-6) indicate. Jesus' miracles raise the question of what kind of teacher he really is (John 3:2), as Israel's teachers generally did not perform miracles. Jesus' teaching about the significance of his miracles is linked with his proclamation of the arrival of the kingdom of God (see §D.2). Scholars who focus on this aspect of Jesus' ministry describe him as a miracle worker or exorcist.

D. The Coming of the Kingdom of God

The authors of the Synoptic Gospels summarize Jesus' teaching with reference to his proclamation of the coming of the kingdom of God (Matt 4:23; 9:35; Mark 1:14-15; Luke 4:43; 8:1; compare Matt 10:7; Luke 9:1-2). The frequency of references to the kingdom of God in the Gospels, together with the relative infrequency of this phrase in the literature of Second Temple Judaism, suggests that Jesus' teaching was focused on the realization of God's transforming presence.

1. Israel's unfinished story

Mark's summary of Jesus' teaching begins with the assertion that "the time is fulfilled" (Mark 1:15). Some scholars claim that Mark 1:15 is formulated from a post-Easter perspective; others argue that Mark's statement is indeed an authentic summary of Jesus' teaching. Jews were very much aware of the fact that the last chapter of Israel's history had not yet been written: many if not most Jews waited for the fulfillment of various predictions of the prophets, such as the arrival of the Day of the Lord, the establishment of God's universal rule focused on the Temple and on Israel, deliverance from foreign oppressors, the divine judgment of the nations, and the conversion of the nations who come to Zion. Jesus repeatedly spoke about the fulfillment of the prophecies of the OT prophets (see §B1), suggesting that the last chapter of Israel's unfinished story is about to be written or is in the process of being written. Jesus made this claim in his synagogue sermons (Luke 4:16-30), in his response both to sympathetic inquirers (Matt 11:2-6; Luke 7:18-23) and hostile critics (Mark 3:22-30), as well as in parables (note, e.g., the parable of the Wicked Tenants, Mark 12:1-12). Fulfillment sayings include Jesus' Beatitude on eyewitnesses (Mark 13:16-17; Luke 10:23-24), the saying about fasting in the present (Mark 2:18-22), and the sayings about his preaching concerning wisdom and repentance surpassing the wisdom of Solomon and the preaching of Jonah (Matt 12:41-42).

2. Jesus' proclamation of the kingdom of God

Most scholars today acknowledge that Jesus' teaching about the kingdom of God (basileia tou theou βασιλεία τοῦ θεοῦ) contains assertions both about the present reality of the kingdom and about the future realization of the kingdom. The claim that "the kingdom of God has come near" (Mark 1:15) must be understood in the context of the immediately preceeding claim that "the time is fulfilled." Jesus teaches that the arrival of the kingdom or rule of God, predicted by the prophets, is happening in the present. With his teaching concerning the arrival of the kingdom of God, Jesus went beyond the fundamental Jewish convictions about the present rule of God who is King over creation and the Ruler of the world. Jesus asserted that the transformation of the state of affairs in Israel and in the world, which the prophets expected for the last days when God would establish his rule against all enemies and against evil, was happening in the present.

Apart from the fulfillment sayings (see §§B.1 and D.1), the saying about the kingdom of God taken by storm (Matt 11:12-13; Luke 16:16) asserts that according to Jesus' teaching, the kingdom of God is a present entity since the days of John the Baptist; this is particularly significant since John himself is described as being "more than a prophet" (Matt 11:9). Jesus teaches that "the kingdom of God is among you" (Luke 17:21; compare *Gos. Thom.* 3; 113), a statement which is often understood in a spatial sense: the kingdom of God is present in the person of Jesus; a dynamic interpretation sees the kingdom of God "in the sphere of experience" of those who observe Jesus' ministry. In the parables of growth Jesus teaches that the decisive event, the sowing, has already taken place—Israel's expectations concerning the arrival of God's rule are presently fulfilled in terms of a small beginning, which will grow into something great without fail (Mark 4:26-32; Luke 13:18-19). The parable of the Sower teaches not only that the realization of God's rule has a small beginning (seeds are sown) but also that God's rule is ignored and rejected by many (Matt 13:1-9; Mark 4:1-9; Luke 8:4-15).

Jesus teaches that the reality of demons being driven out demonstrates that the rule of God has indeed arrived (Matt 12:28; Luke 11:20). Jesus' reference to the "finger of God" (Luke 11:20) is an allusion to Moses' miracles before the exodus from Egypt (Exod 8:15), which suggests, on the one hand, that the present coming of the kingdom of God represents the new exodus and the new covenant that some of the prophets predicted; and it suggests, on the other hand, that the present coming of God's rule means judgment for those who reject it. In the Beelzebul debate (Matt 12:22-32; Mark 3:19-30; Luke 11:14-23) Jesus teaches that Satan has been conquered as otherwise his exorcisms would not be possible. This discussion about the source of his authority, as well as his statement about unclean spirits and "this evil generation" (Matt 12:43-45; compare Luke 11:24-26), indicates that Jesus teaches that Israel's real enemy is not Rome but Satan, and that the final "house cleaning" is taking place in connection with his ministry.

Jesus' teaching about the arrival of God's rule in the present does not imply an "overrealized" eschatology that claims that everything is happening now, with nothing left for the future. Jesus teaches that there will be a future coming of the kingdom of God, a consummation of God's rule that is not yet happening in the present. He taught his disciples to pray for the coming of the kingdom of God (Matt 6:10; Luke 11:2); he spoke about a future coming of the kingdom in power (Mark 9:1), about the kingdom as a future banquet (Mark 14:25), and about a future entry into the kingdom (Matt 7:21-23). Jesus' teaching about admission formulates conditions for both the present and the future entry into the kingdom of God (Matt 5:20; 7:21; 18:3; Mark 9:43-48; 10:15, 23-25; Luke 18:17, 24-25; John 3:5).

Jesus teaches that the arrival of the kingdom of God is a mystery (Matt 13:11-17; Mark 4:10-12). This mystery can be understood in two ways. The present fulfillment of the prophets and of Israel's expectations is an initial fulfillment with the full consummation of God's rule still in the future. The present arrival of the kingdom of God is a mystery because it cannot be grasped, or accepted, without God's help, effectively communicated by God himself. The parable of the Sower (Matt 13:1-23; Mark 4:1-9) teaches that many in Israel will ignore and reject the arrival of God's rule, while only those whom God has given eyes to see and ears to hear enter into the reality of God's kingdom.

E. The Messianic Son of Man

Jesus' regular self-designation as SON OF MAN, which appears only on the lips of Jesus, links his teaching about God and the arrival of God's rule with his own person. Of particular interest are statements of Jesus in which he comments on his authority.

1. Son of Man

Jesus teaches that as Son of Man he has the authority to forgive sins (Matt 9:6-8; Mark 2:10-12; Luke 5:24-26), that he is the lord of the SABBATH (Matt 12:8; Mark 2:27-28; Luke 6:5), that his mission is so manifestly of God that the attribution of his exorcisms to Satan is blasphemy (Matt 12:31-32; Mark 3:28-29; Luke 12:10), that acknowledgment of himself in the present guarantees acceptance by God on the day of judgment (Matt 10:32-33; Luke 12:8-9), that the Son of Man will come to earth with divine power and glory (Matt 16:27//Mark 8:38//Luke 9:26; Matt 24:29-31//Mark 13:24-27//Luke 21:25-28; Matt 26:63-66//Mark 14:61-64//Luke 22:67-71). Scholars do not agree whether all or only some of these sayings are authentic, but there is little doubt that Jesus referred to himself as Son of Man with both implicit and explicit allusions to Dan 7:13. Since the phrase "Son of Man" does not seem to have been an established messianic ti-

tle at the time of Jesus' ministry, allowing ambiguities of understanding among his listeners, these self-references of Jesus were understood by his followers as describing his status (note the awkwardness of the Greek phrase ho huios tou anthrōpou [ὁ υἱὸς τοῦ ἀνθρώπου]). In the context of references to his authority and to God's judgment, the allusion to Dan 7:13 links Jesus' teaching about the nature of his mission and about his own role and identity with the claim that he represents God's people and indeed that he represents God.

2. Messiah

Jesus' announcement of the arrival of God's kingly rule, of God's Spirit, and of the fulfillment of God's promises in the present, his calling of twelve disciples, and his modification of the Law (see §§G.3-4) were bound to have raised the question of whether he was the Messiah. On account of the fact that messianic ideas were mostly connected with political expectations (2 Sam 7:12-13, 16; Isa 11:1-2; 4Q174 1 10-12; *Pss. Sol.* 17-18; *Shemoneh Esreh* ["Eighteen Benedictions"] 14), it is not surprising that Jesus' ministry was regarded by contemporary observers, at least initially, as prophetic (Mark 6:14-16//Luke 9:7-9; Matt 16:13-20//Mark 8:27-30//Luke 9:18-20) rather than as messianic.

It seems, however, that Jesus' healings gave rise to popular speculations about whether he was the messianic "Son of David" (Matt 20:29-34//Mark 10:46-52//Luke 18:35-43). This may be the background for the Zebedee brothers' petition for seats on the right and left of Jesus in his kingdom (Matt 20:20-21//Mark 10:35-37). As Jesus' opponents succeeded in charging Jesus before the Roman governor who executed him for claiming to be "King of the Jews" (Matt 27:37//Mark 15:26//Luke 23:37-38//John 19:19-21), it is beyond doubt that members of the Jewish elites regarded Jesus as a political threat. Potential political claims are probably implied in the question of whether one should pay tribute to Caesar (Matt 22:15-22//Mark 12:13-17//Luke 20:20-26). Jesus' demonstrative entry into Jerusalem (Matt 21:1-11//Mark 11:1-11//Luke 19:28-40//John 12:12-19) and his statements concerning the destruction of the Temple (Matt 24:2//Mark 13:2//Luke 21:6; note Mark 11:17 in the context of Jer 7) had messianic connotations.

At one point Jesus raised the question of his identity with his disciples; Peter affirmed that he believed Jesus to be the Messiah (Matt 16:13-20//Mark 8:27-30//Luke 9:18-20). Jesus' reaction is instructive: he ordered his disciples to keep silent (Matt 16:20//Mark 8:30//Luke 9:21), and then announced that the Son of Man "must undergo great suffering, and be rejected by the elders, the chief priests, and the scribes, and be killed, and after three days rise again" (Matt 16:21//Mark 8:31//Luke 9:22), an assertion that Peter and the disciples cannot understand. Jesus accepts the "identification" with the Messiah, but he redefines traditional understandings of messiahship in terms of suffering, death, and vindication by God. Jesus' response to Caiaphas' question in the trial of Jesus of whether he is "the Messiah, the Son of the Blessed One" (Matt 26:63//Mark 14:61-62// Luke 22:67-70) should be understood similarly: Jesus is Messiah in terms of the mission of the Son of Man who is (about) to suffer and die.

3. The death and vindication of the Son of Man

Jesus repeatedly spoke about his death: he is the bridegroom who will be removed (Matt 9:15//Mark 2:20//Luke 5:35). He is the Son of Man who will suffer as Elijah suffered (Matt 17:12//Mark 9:12). He is one of the prophets who tends to perish in Jerusalem (Luke 13:33). He is the suffering Son of Man who is rejected by "this generation" (Luke 17:25). He is the Son of Man who has come not to be served but to serve and to give his life as a ransom for many (Matt 20:28; Mark 10:45). He is the rejected son in the parable of the Tenants (Matt 21:33-46//Mark 12:1-12//Luke 20:9-19), anointed by a woman as a preparation for his burial (Matt 26:6-13//Mark 14:8//John 12:1-8). As these statements are remarkably free of the atonement theology of the early church (including Paul), there is no reason to dispute the authenticity of Jesus' predictions of his suffering and death in Matt 16:21//Mark 8:31// Luke 9:22; Matt 17:22-23//Mark 9:31//Luke 9:44; Matt 20:17-19//Mark 10:33-34//Luke 18:31-34.

Jesus evidently taught his disciples on several occasions that his death and vindication is an integral part of the effective coming of the kingdom of God. Several OT texts as well as some Jewish traditions already connected God's promise to redeem his people, to forgive sins, and to renew his covenant with the suffering of Israel and with the suffering of righteous individuals, sometimes involving death (Isa 40–55, in particular 52:13–53:12; Ezek 4:1-6; Dan 11:31-35; 12:1-10; Zech 12:10; 13:1-7; Wis 2:12-20; 2 Macc 7:36-38; 4 Macc 6:27-29; *Tg. Isa.* 53). Jesus' words at the Last Supper (Matt 26:26-28; Mark 14:22-24; Luke 22:15-20) can thus be understood as a focused summary of his teaching about the present coming of the kingdom of God: God saves Israel as Jesus suffers God's judgment and dies, accomplishing the forgiveness of sins and the promised renewal of the covenant as the messianic Son of Man is vindicated by God.

F. The Call to Repentance and Faith

1. Repentance and judgment

Jesus' teaching concerning the present coming of the kingdom of God in and through his own ministry, inaugurating the promised time of salvation, is aimed at leading people to accept the new reality of God's rule. Jesus' call to repentance (Mark 1:15) is the challenge to his Jewish contemporaries to abandon the old ways of seeking to please God, as a righteousness is required for entering the kingdom of God that exceeds the righteousness described and practiced by the law experts and the Pharisees (Matt 5:20). Jesus challenges

his listeners to enter through the "narrow gate" (Matt 7:13-14), to acknowledge him and to do the will of God whose rule Jesus proclaims (Matt 7:21-23; Luke 6:46; 13:26-27). People who ignore or reject the presence of the kingdom of God will suffer God's judgment. In the parable of the Marriage Feast, those who are first invited exclude themselves from the kingdom of God (Matt 22:1-14//Luke 14:16-24). As several Galilean cities refused to repent and accept the presence of God's rule in Jesus' miracles, they face divine judgment (Matt 11:20-24//Luke 10:13-15). When Jesus compares himself to the prophet Jonah (Matt 12:41-42) whose message of judgment prompted the conversion of the people of Nineveh, he clarifies that the present is a time of decision, a time in which the people on whom judgment is pronounced can still repent and be saved.

Judgment is pronounced on, and thus repentance required of, "this generation" (Matt 23:35-36//Luke 11:49-51), the leaders of Israel (Matt 23), and members of individual families (Matt 24:40-41; Luke 17:34). Jesus portrays God's judgment as a formal legal process (Matt 18:23-25; note in Matt 12:41-42 the appearance of witnesses), punitive military action (Matt 22:7), a reckoning (Matt 25:14-30//Luke 16:1-2; 19:15-24), harvest (Matt 13:30, 41-42), unexpected catastrophes (Matt 7:24-27//Luke 6:47-49; Matt 24:37-39//Luke 17:26-27), and exclusion from the eschatological banquet (Matt 8:11-12; Matt 22:1-14//Luke 14:16-24; Matt 25:1-13). The judgment happens both now (on Satan, Luke 10:18; Matt 12:28//Mark 3:26//Luke 11:18; Matt 12:22-32//Mark 3:22-27//Luke 11:14-23) and in the future: on the day of judgment, the intercession of the Son of Man is dependent on the people's present confession of Jesus (Matt 10:32-33; Mark 8:38; see also Matt 24:45-51; 25:31-46).

2. Faith and the good news

As Jesus proclaims the good news of the arrival of God's kingdom as fulfillment of God's promises, he calls people to "believe in the good news" as the required response to the arrival of God who brings salvation (Mark 1:15). The imperative of Jesus' call to faith is the "indicative" of the reality of the presence of God's kingdom. The faith that Jesus demands is trust in God's gracious rule and trust in Jesus as mediator of God's kingdom (Mark 8:35; 13:10; 14:9). Jesus asserts that his followers comply with the demand of faith when their trust in him is an expression of their willingness to "take up their cross" and to "follow me" (Mark 8:27-38). Authentic followers of Jesus renounce self-determination and even life and accept the leadership of Jesus who will enable them to a way of life that complies with the inaugurated kingdom of God.

Jesus' call to faith corresponds to the entrance requirements for the kingdom of God (Matt 19:13-30// Mark 10:14-15, 17-25//Luke 18:15-30). The arrival of God's gracious rule must be accepted as a child accepts gifts: with joyous gladness and with unreserved trust.

Those who gain entrance into God's kingdom have to become so "small" that they could pass through the eye of a needle, i.e., they have to recognize their own spiritual and religious impotence and acknowledge God's new initiative in granting salvation.

Faith that leads to a miracle is faith in God (Matt 17:14-21//Mark 9:14-29//Luke 9:37-43; compare Matt 21:20-22//Mark 11:20-25): as only God who has created "everything" can do "everything," the faith that Jesus both demands and makes possible is unreserved trust in the sovereign power of God revealed in Jesus' person, message, and ministry.

3. The welcome of sinners

Jesus teaches that he came "to call not the righteous but sinners" (Matt 9:13//Mark 2:17//Luke 5:32). Jesus does not deny that people such as the Pharisees are righteous according to the traditional understanding of righteousness in the law, as he does not deny that some people are healthy (Mark 2:17a). Nor does Jesus dispute that there are people who are sinners or people who are sick. The point of Jesus' teaching here is, on the one hand, that Jesus voices criticism of those who dismiss others as sinners on the basis of their own understanding of the Law and their own definitions of what constitutes God's will. On the other hand, the parable of the Prodigal Son (Luke 15:11-32) demonstrates that there are indeed "real" sinners who violate the will of God (e.g., by breaking the commandment to honor father and mother, or by dissolute living), and, equally important, that the righteous who have never left the father's house are called upon to acknowledge and accept the father's extraordinary forgiveness and generosity; if they refuse to join the father who forgives the sinner, they will in turn become "lost sons." Jesus' teaching and his association with sinners (in Luke compare 5:8; 7:34, 37, 39; 15:1-2, 7, 10; 18:13; 19:7) affirms that God's kingdom was open to them too.

G. The New Community

Jesus did not organize the thousands of followers who sympathized with his message into local communities, with the exception of the circle of the Twelve (Mark 3:14-19) and a larger circle that included women (Mark 15:41; Luke 8:1-3). As no hard distinction can be made between these circles of disciples and other followers of Jesus (compare Matt 10:40-42//Mark 9:38-41//Luke 9:49-50), Jesus' teaching for his more immediate disciples is of concern to his followers more generally.

1. The Twelve and discipleship

Disciples are people who respond to Jesus' call to be with him (Mark 3:14) and to learn from him, who are willing to be sent out to proclaim the news of the presence of the kingdom of God (Mark 3:14c), who are recruiting others for the kingdom of God as "fishers of people" (Mark 1:17; compare Matt 10:40), who deny themselves and take up their cross (Matt 10:38; Mark 8:34), who are willing to obey Jesus even when he asks for the sale of one's possessions (Mark 10:21). Disciples are people who are willing to serve (Mark 10:41-45), people who pray as Jesus prayed (Luke 11:1-4), who suffer as Jesus suffered (Matt 5:11-12; 10:24-25; Mark 8:34-37). As Jesus trusts in the father, so his disciples have childlike trust in God (Matt 6:25-33//Luke 12:22-31).

2. Righteousness and the will of God

When Jesus teaches his followers to pray, their first priority is the holiness of God's name, the coming of God's kingdom, and the doing of God's will (Matt 6:9-11; Luke 11:2). This is a prayer that God would make his gracious rule, which the prophets had promised an effective reality in the present and in the future, a reality in which his name would no longer be desecrated by the way in which people conduct themselves in their everyday lives. In the fourth Beatitude Jesus teaches his followers that those are blessed "who hunger and thirst for righteousness" (Matt 5:6). This righteousness is understood as a "gift" ("they will be filled [by God]"), as a reality that represents the fulfillment of the promised new covenant (compare Jer 31:25).

The blessing on those "who are persecuted for righteousness' sake" (Matt 5:10) affirms that righteousness is not a quantitatively superior fulfillment of the Law by Jesus' followers (for which they would not be persecuted): the disciples are persecuted because they proclaim the arrival of the kingdom of God in Jesus' person and ministry (Matt 5:11-12). Even though word and deed must not be separated, it is the disciples' message that is central, a message that focuses on the righteousness of God that cannot be separated from Jesus.

As righteousness is described and defined for Jesus' contemporaries in the Law as the revelation of the will of God, Jesus' teaching regarding the Law becomes an issue. According to Matt 5:17-20, Jesus teaches that the Law remains valid in the way in which he teaches the Law, controlled by the presence of the kingdom of God, by the gift of righteousness that the prophets anticipated for the new covenant, which qualifies for entrance into God's kingdom, and by his own interpretation of the Law.

As God's righteousness involves the free and gracious forgiveness of sins, Jesus teaches in the parable of the Unforgiving Servant (Matt 18:23-35) that the salvation graciously granted by God should cause his followers to also show compassion toward sinners.

Jesus' teaching on marriage and divorce emphasizes, against contemporary debates about legitimate grounds for divorce, that it is God's will that the union of his creations—man and woman—be a permanent union that people must not destroy (Matt 5:32; 19:3-9; Mark 10:2-12; Luke 16:18).

3. Sabbath and food

Jesus had a high regard for the Sabbath as a gift from God (Mark 2:27). His provocative healings on the Sabbath and his teaching that the Son of Man is "lord ... of the Sabbath" (Matt 12:8//Mark 2:28//Luke 6:5) show that he refused to treat the observance of the Sabbath as a criterion for covenant righteousness. Over against concerns about details of Sabbath observance, Jesus emphasizes fundamental first principles such as doing good and saving life (Matt 12:9-14//Mark 3:1-6//Luke 6:6-11).

Regarding food, whose acquisition, storage, and consumption were controlled by the purity laws of the Torah, Jesus teaches that people are defiled not by what they eat but by what is in their hearts (Matt 7:14-23; Mark 7:14-23). Jesus' teaching could be heard as emphasizing the priority of the purity of motives and intentions, or as an outright antithesis implying that Israel's purity laws no longer apply to his followers.

4. The Temple and the conversion of the nations

In the discussion about which commandment is the greatest (Matt 22:34-40//Mark 12:28-34//Luke 10:25-28), Jesus implies that his kingdom's agenda, understood in the context of the OT's focus on the love of Yahweh and of one's neighbor, replaces the sacrificial system of the Temple.

Jesus teaches, evidently toward the end of his ministry, that the Temple no longer has a central role in the kingdom of God. His action in the Temple during the last week of his life (Matt 21:12-17//Mark 11:15-17//Luke 19:45-48//John 2:13-22) did not aim at cleansing the Temple of corrupting practices. Jesus' teaching on this occasion focuses on the quotation of Isa 56:7 LXX and the allusion to Jer 7:11 LXX: Jesus announces the possibility of universal worship of Israel's God by all people, including the unclean and the Gentiles, and he prophesies the destruction of the present Temple (the subject of Jer 7).

When the disciples marvel at the Temple's structure, Jesus more explicitly announces the destruction of the Temple (Mark 13:2 par.). According to Jesus' teaching, the Temple is no longer necessary for the life of the people of God. This implies that holiness, the forgiveness of sins, and the cleansing from defilement are provided in a manner that is independent of Israel's procedures of dealing with sin—a way into the presence of God that is mediated through Jesus' authority via the mission of Jesus' disciples who are sent to make disciples of all nations, instructing them to follow Jesus and his teaching (Matt 28:18-20). *See* AGRAPHA; APOCALYPTICISM; CHURCH, IDEA OF THE; DISCIPLE, DISCIPLESHIP; FORM CRITICISM, NT; JESUS CHRIST; JOHN, GOSPEL OF; KINGDOM OF GOD, KINGDOM OF HEAVEN; LAW IN THE NT; LOVE IN THE NT; LUKE, GOSPEL OF; MARK, GOSPEL OF; MASTER, TITLE OF JESUS; MATTHEW, GOSPEL OF; MESSIAH, JEWISH; POETRY IN THE NT; RESURRECTION, NT; SERMON ON THE MOUNT; TEACHER; TEMPTATION OF JESUS.

Bibliography: Richard Bauckham. *Jesus and the Eyewitnesses* (2006); Markus N. A. Bockmuehl, ed. *The Cambridge Companion to Jesus* (2001); Marcus J. Borg. *Jesus* (2006); Bruce Chilton and Craig A. Evans. *The Proclamation of Jesus* (1997); John Dominic Crossan. *The Historical Jesus* (1991); James D. G. Dunn. *Jesus Remembered* (2003); Craig A. Evans and Bruce Chilton, eds. *Authenticating the Words of Jesus* (1998); Arland J. Hultgren. *The Parables of Jesus* (2000); Scot McKnight. *Jesus and His Death* (2005); John P. Meier. *A Marginal Jew* (1991–2001); E. P. Sanders. *Jesus and Judaism* (1985); Wolfgang Schrage. *The Ethics of the New Testament* (1988); Gerd Theissen and Annette Merz. *The Historical Jesus* (1998); Geza Vermès. *Jesus in His Jewish Context* (2003); Ben Witherington. *Jesus the Sage* (1994); N. T. Wright. *Jesus and the Victory of God* (1996).

ECKHARD J. SCHNABEL

TEACHING OF THE APOSTLES [διδαχή τῶν ἀποστόλων didache tōn apostolōn]. The phrase appears in a summary description of the life of the early Christian community in Jerusalem, in which believers are described as devoted to the apostles' teaching, community, breaking of bread, and prayers (Acts 2:42). While the content of the teaching is not specified, in the context of Acts it should probably be understood in the light of the various speeches attributed to the apostles throughout the narrative. A later, possibly 2nd-cent. CE text titled *The Teaching of the Twelve Apostles* (Didache tōn dōdeka apostolon Διδαχὴ τῶν δώδεκα ἀποστόλων) includes what is thought to be a baptismal catechesis plus instructions on baptism, the eucharist, and church order. *See* DIDACHE.

RUBÉN R. DUPERTUIS

TEARS. *See* MOURNING.

TEBAH tee'buh [טֶבַח tevakh]. First son of Reumah, Nahor's concubine (Gen 22:24). Probably an etiological reference to Syrian Tubihi, mentioned in the AMARNA LETTERS; perhaps identical to BETAH in 2 Sam 8:8 and TIBHATH in 1 Chr 18:8.

TEBALIAH teb'uh-li'uh [טְבַלְיָהוּ tevalyahu]. Third son of Hosah and one of the temple gatekeepers in David's time (1 Chr 26:11).

TEBETH tee'bith [טֵבֵת teveth]. Tenth month of the year, November–December in the Gregorian calendar. Esther was presented to King Ahasuerus in the month of Tebeth (2:16). *See* CALENDAR.

TEETH. *See* TOOTH.

TEHAPHNEHES. *See* TAHPANHES.

TEHINNAH tuh-hin´uh [תְּחִנָּה *tekhinnah*]. Descendant of Judah and father/founder of IR-NAHASH (1 Chr 4:12).

TEKEL. *See* MENE, MENE, TEKEL, AND PARSIN.

TEKOA tuh-koh´uh [תְּקוֹעַ *teqoaʿ*; Θεκῶε *Thekōe*]. 1. A town on the edge of the Judean desert, which today is identified with Khirbet Tequ´a. It is located about 10 km southeast of Bethlehem and 16 km south of Jerusalem. To the east the land slopes down toward the Dead Sea in a series of desolate hills called the Wilderness of Tekoa (2 Chr 20:20; 1 Macc 9:33). Seasonal sheep grazing is possible in this area, whereas to the west enough moisture falls during the rainy season to sustain some agriculture. The Talmud identifies Tekoa as renowned for its olive trees and oil (*b. B. Bat.* 145b; *b. Menah.* 85b). In ancient times the town lay on one of the two north–south routes from Hebron to Bethlehem, and a road descended eastward from Tekoa to En-gedi on the western shore of the Dead Sea.

In Josh 15:59 (LXX; not found in MT), Tekoa appears in the list of towns assigned to the tribe of Judah. Eusebius also places Tekoa in Judah in his *Onomasticon* (98:17; see also 86:13). Nevertheless, there have been occasional defenders of a northern location. The rabbinic commentator David KIMCHI situated it within the territory of Asher. Some scholars have located the town in the Galilee as well. The principal reason for suggesting an alternative site is that the prophet Amos, whose hometown was Tekoa, is said to have been a DRESSER OF SYCAMORE TREES (Amos 1:1; 7:14). These trees were known primarily for producing strong beams and secondarily for their fruit, the fig. They do not grow, however, in the drier climate or at the elevation of the customary location for Tekoa. The sycamore could grow in the Shephelah (1 Kgs 10:27; 2 Chr 1:15; 9:27; compare *Tg. Amos* 7:14; *b. Ned.* 38a) and in the Jericho Valley. This fact has no bearing, however, on the location of Tekoa. Whatever Amos' relationship to these trees (owner or caretaker), there would have been no obstacle to his traveling to the low-lying hills to the west or towards the Jordan River to attend to them.

Tekoa is not mentioned often in the OT. In order to spur David to be reconciled with his son Absalom, Joab sent for a WISE WOMAN OF TEKOA (2 Sam 14:2). The fact that this woman was from Tekoa has been utilized to argue that the area in general was known for its wisdom and that accordingly the basic theological framework of the prophet Amos was clan wisdom (Wolff). The mention of one such person from this town is not sufficient evidence, however, to make such a sweeping claim. Ira, one of David's Mighty Men and a commander of one of his army divisions, also was a native of Tekoa (2 Sam 23:26; 1 Chr 27:9). After the return from exile, men from there helped rebuild sections of the walls of Jerusalem, working close to the Fish Gate and along the wall of Ophel. The noblemen of Tekoa, though, did not participate (Neh 3:5, 27). Their refusal may point to some conflict between the returnees and the leadership of those who had remained in the land.

The strategic position of Tekoa at a crossroads and at the boundary between the steppe land and the Judean hill country led to its periodic fortification over the centuries. In the last quarter of the 10th cent. BCE, Rehoboam, Solomon's son, strengthened the defenses of fifteen towns, including Tekoa, in order to protect the southern and western approaches to Jerusalem (2 Chr 11:5-12). Scholars disagree whether this was done in anticipation of or in response to the invasion of the Egyptian pharaoh SHISHAK, also known as Shoshenq I (1 Kgs 14:25-28; 2 Chr 12:1-12). Several decades later, during the reign of Jehoshaphat, a coalition of Moabites and Ammonites attempted to invade Judah by way of En-gedi but were miraculously defeated in the Wilderness of Tekoa (2 Chr 20:1-30). Apparently, Tekoa continued to serve as an important Judean military outpost up until the fall of Jerusalem at the hands of the Babylonians. The prophet Jeremiah calls for the warning trumpet blast to be blown from there to signal the impending attack (Jer 6:1). During the Maccabean revolt against the Seleucid Empire (ca. 160 BCE), Simon and Jonathan retreated to the Wilderness of Tekoa after the death of Judas. After engaging the two brothers in battle by the Jordan River, the Seleucid general Bacchides, like others before him, fortified the town as part of a defense system to guard Jerusalem (1 Macc 9:28-53; Josephus, *Ant.* 13.1–17). One Simon of Gerasa, a rebel leader during the First Jewish Revolt against Rome (66–73 CE) camped there in his efforts to take the Idumean fortress at Herodium (Josephus, *J.W.* 4.514–28). After the destruction of Jerusalem by Titus, Josephus checked the viability of Tekoa with the Roman commander Cerealius as a possible place to post a garrison (*Life* 420).

That a Jewish presence continued at Tekoa is evident by the existence for a time of a rabbinic school there (*b. Menah.* 72a). In the first centuries of the Christian era it was a famous pilgrimage site. The prophet Amos was said to have been buried in a cave there, and a Byzantine church called the "Propheteum of Amos" was constructed as a memorial. Two convents (or lauras) were built in the area. The first one was established by the Monophysite monk Romanus in 454–58 after his expulsion from his order for his unorthodox beliefs, but the community did not last long. In 508, a group of followers of St. Sabas founded another monastery in the vicinity. It became a center of Origenism, which was condemned by the Second Council of Constantinople (553). Shortly thereafter, Eustochius, patriarch of Jerusalem, went personally to the laura and expelled its monks; he replaced them with others who were in agreement with official doctrine. Tekoa continued as a town with a significant Christian presence until the Crusades. It was given to the Order of the Holy Sepulchre of Jerusalem, a Catholic chivalric order, in 1132. Tekoa was overrun, however, by Turks in 1138.

Ruins of the church, a fortress, and an impressive baptismal font have been noted by visitors over the centuries. Travelers to Palestine in the 19th and early 20th cent.—such as Karl Ritter, William Thomson, and Harry Emerson Fosdick—give detailed and picturesque accounts of the travails of their travel to Tekoa, their impressions of these ruins, and the view in all directions from the hill. Although a few surveys and brief explorations have been carried out, to date there have been no extensive excavations of the site. Near the ancient town lie the Arab village of Taqqu᾿ and the modern Israeli village of Tekoa.

2. A descendant of Judah through the lineage of Hezron. His father, Ashhur, was born after his grandfather died (1 Chr 2:24). The genealogy relating to Tekoa in Chronicles is somewhat confusing. While 1 Chr 4:5 mentions that his father Ashhur had two wives, Helah and Naarah, the subsequent listing of the sons of the wives does not include Tekoa.

Bibliography: Yohanan Aharoni. *The Land of the Bible: A Historical Geography.* Rev. ed. (1979); Harry Emerson Fosdick. *A Pilgrimage to Palestine* (1933); Gerhard F. Hasel. *Understanding the Book of Amos: Basic Issues in Current Interpretations* (1991); Martin H. Heicken. "Tekoa: Historical and Cultural Profile." *JETS* 13 (1970) 81–89; Anson F. Rainey and R. Steven Notley. *The Sacred Bridge: Carta's Atlas of the Biblical World* (2006); Karl Ritter. *The Comparative Geography of Palestine and the Sinaitic Peninsula* (1865); Stanley N. Rosenbaum. *Amos of Israel: A New Interpretation* (1990); Richard C. Steiner. *Stockmen from Tekoa, Sycamores from Sheba* (2003); P. D. F. Strijdom. "What Tekoa Did to Amos." *OTE* 9 (1996) 273–93; William Thomson. *The Land and the Book* (1880); Hans W. Wolff. *Amos the Prophet: The Man and His Background* (1973); Hans W. Wolff. *Amos.* Hermeneia (1977).

M. DANIEL CARROLL R. (RODAS)

TEL DAN INSCRIPTION. *See* INSCRIPTION, TELL DAN.

TEL EL-MAZAR. *See* MAZAR, TELL EL.

TEL EL-MILH. *See* MALHATA, TEL.

TEL MALHATA. *See* MALHATA, TEL.

TEL, TELL tel [תֵּל tel]. Also known in Arabic as a *tall.* A tell is an artificial mound containing the material remains of its past human inhabitants

Translated in the Bible as "ruin" or "heap of ruins" (Deut 13:16 [Heb. 13:17]; Josh 8:28), tells are a distinctive characteristic feature of Near Eastern archaeological sites. Their formation is a complex process involving the activity of humans (especially war), erosion, earthquake, and burrowing animals. It is not unusual for tells to have been occupied for many thousands of years and to contain many strata or layers of debris. In Israel, tells vary in size, with few reaching more than 10–20 ac.

Much information about the cultures whose remains lay buried in tells was missed by early excavators. Today it is appreciated that everything in a tell can have significance for understanding and interpreting the past. As archaeological methods and interpretive models continue to increase in sophistication, hopefully "the tale of the tell" will be heard with greater clarity by future excavators.

Bibliography: William G. Dever. "The Tell: Microcosm of the Cultural Process." *Retrieving the Past: Essays on Archaeological Research and Methodology.* Joe D. Seger, ed. (1996) 37–45.

JOHN C. H. LAUGHLIN

TEL-ABIB. *See* ABIB, TEL.

TELAH tee᾿luh [תֶּלַח telakh]. A descendant of Ephraim and an ancestor of JOSHUA (1 Chr 7:25).

TELAIM tuh-lay᾿im [טְלָאִים tela᾿im]. Meaning "lambs." Perhaps the same as Telem (Josh 15:24), Telaim was situated in the southern part of Judean territory in the Negev. Its location is not known for certain, but suggestions include Khirbet Umm es-Salafe and Khirbet ez-Zeifeh. At Telaim, Saul mustered his forces for the attack on the Amalekites (1 Sam 15:4). Samuel had instructed Saul to utterly destroy the Amalekites in retribution for their attacks on Israel during Israel's wilderness travels.

Bibliography: Robert G. Boling and G. Ernest Wright. *Joshua.* AB 6 (1982); P. Kyle McCarter Jr. *1 Samuel.* AB 8 (1980).

TIMOTHY G. CRAWFORD

TELASSAR tel-as᾿ahr [תְּלַאשָּׂר tela᾿ssar]. According to RABSHAKEH of Assyria under the reign of SENNACHERIB, Telassar was the geographical area where the "people of Eden" dwelled (2 Kgs 19:12; Isa 37:12). The descendants of Eden (or Adini; *ANEP* 362) formed "the kingdom of Eden" (**bit adini** in the Assyrian records). Amos calls Damascus "Beth-Eden" (House of Eden) in the metaphorical sense of "the kingdom of Bliss" (Amos 1:5), which is not directly related to **bit adini** of the Aramean region in Mesopotamia. Telassar may be identified with Til-Ashuri ("hill of Ashur") that Tiglath-pileser III mentions (*AR* I, 278, 291). It may well have been a place commemorating the name of the Asshur (Gen 10:22), the ancestor of the later Assyrians. The specific location of Telassar is unknown.

YOSHITAKA KOBAYASHI

TEL-AVIV. *See* ABIB, TEL.

TELEILÂT EL-GHASSÛL. *See* GHASSÛL, TELEILÂT EL.

TELEM tee′lim [טֶלֶם telem; Τέλημ Telēm]. 1. Variant for TELAIM (Josh 15:24).

2. A gatekeeper who dismissed his foreign wife (Ezra 10:24; 1 Esd 9:25).

TEL-HARSHA. *See* HARSHA, TEL.

TELL. *See* TEL, TELL.

TELL AL-JUDAIDAH. *See* JUDAIDAH, TELL AL.

TELL DEIR ʿALLA. *See* DEIR ʿALLA, TELL.

TELL EL-FAʿRA. *See* FARA (SOUTH), TELL EL; TIRZAH.

TELL EL-KHELEIFEH. *See* KHELEIFEH, TELL EL.

TELL EL-MASKHUTA. *See* MASKHUTA, TELL EL.

TELL EL-QEDAH. *See* HAZOR.

TELL EL-UMEIRI. *See* ʿUMAYRI, TALL AL.

TELL EN-NASBEH. *See* MIZPAH, MIZPEH.

TELL ESH-SHUNA (NORTH). *See* SHUNA (NORTH), TELL ESH.

TELL ES-SAIDIYEH. *See* SAIDIYEH, TELL ES.

TELL ES-SEBA. *See* SEBA, TEL ES.

TELL JEZER. *See* GEZER, GEZERITES.

TELL JUDEIDEH. *See* JUDEIDEH, TELL.

TELL TAYINAT. *See* TAYINAT, TELL.

TEMA tee′muh [תֵּימָא temaʾ]. 1. Ninth of the twelve sons of Ishmael (Gen 25:15; 1 Chr 1:30; *see* ISHMAEL, ISHMAELITES).

2. A city known for its trading caravans (Job 6:19) and associated with DEDAN (modern el-ʿUla; see Isa 21:13-14; Jer 25:23) and the Sabeans (Job 6:19; *see* SHEBA), Tema has been firmly identified with Taymaʾ in northern Arabia. The root of the name may signify "slave," "servant," or "to swear an oath," the last of these perhaps suggesting that Taymaʾ was a tribal center. Occupation of Taymaʾ is evidenced archaeologically for the late 2nd millennium BCE and for the Neo-Assyrian, Babylonian, and Persian periods; it is mentioned in the Assyrian Tiglath-pileser III's records (ca. 733 BCE).

Tema flourished under the Babylonian Nabonidus, who occupied it for debated motives (political, economic, religious?), ca. 552–542 BCE.

The biblical references to Tema appear to date from the 6th cent. BCE. Jeremiah lists the city, along with Dedan and Buz "and all who have shaven temples," among those nations who are to drink the cup of the wine of God's wrath (25:15-29; see v. 23). In a short oracle (Isa 21:13-15), the inhabitants of Tema are commanded to bring water and bread to fugitives (possibly the "caravans of Dedanites," v. 13) from battle (vv. 14-15), the enemy perhaps being Edom (*see* EDOM, EDOMITES). Some scholars propose to redivide these lines, interpreting the oracle as urging the Dedanite caravans to bring water, and the inhabitants of Tema to provide bread, for unspecified fugitives. The events reflected in Isa 21:13-15 remain historically obscure.

Though numbered in the prophetic tradition among the nations upon whom God's wrath will come (Jer 25:15-29), Tema is charged with no specific crime, and in another tradition her people belong to the Abrahamic family, since Tema is identified as a son of Ishmael (Gen 25:15; 1 Chr 1:30). In Wisdom literature, Job, disappointed in his search for understanding from his friends, compares himself to "caravans of Tema" and "travelers of Sheba" (Job 6:19) who cannot find water in the desert. *See* TEMANITE.

JOHN R. BARTLETT

TEMAH tee′muh [תֶּמַח temakh; Θόμει Thomei]. An ancestor of temple servants among the exiles who returned from Babylon (Ezra 2:53; Neh 7:55; 1 Esd 5:32).

TEMAN tee′muhn [תֵּימָן teman; Θαιμάν Thaiman]. 1. One of the descendants of Esau and father of an Edomite tribe (Gen 36:9-11).

2. The name Teman is sometimes used as a synonym for Edom (Jer 49:7, 20; Obad 9; *see* EDOM, EDOMITES), but other texts seem to depict Teman as a region within Edom (Ezek 25:13). The name *Teman* means "south," which is consistent with Edom's location relative to Israel and the rest of the ANE. In Amos 1:12, Teman is set in par. with BOZRAH, a city in Edom. Some have read this to mean Teman is a region in the northern part of Edom with its capital at Bozrah. It is in this area that the Edomite state first began to form.

An inscription from Kuntillet ʿAjrud in Sinai refers to "Yahweh of Teman." This may par. Hab 3:3, which pictures God as marching forth from Teman. This has strengthened the position of those who argue that Yahwism originated in the area of Edom or Midian.

KEVIN A. WILSON

3. An inhabitant of Teman, in Edom near Petra; and a descendant of Esau. Job's countryman ELIPHAZ was a Temanite (Job 2:11; 4:1; 15:1; 22:1; 42:7, 9). *See* TEMA.

JOAN E. COOK, SC

TEMENI tem´uh-n*i* [תֵּימְנִי temeni]. Judahite son of Ashhur and his wife Naarah (1 Chr 4:6).

TEMPLE OF SOLOMON.

King SOLOMON built the first permanent Temple for Yahweh in Jerusalem in the mid-10th cent. BCE, thus completing his father David's program of turning Jerusalem into the religious as well as political capital of the united kingdom of Israel and Judah. David began this process when he appointed two high priests in Jerusalem from rival priestly families from the different halves of his kingdom, and he furthered it when he brought into his new capital the ark of the covenant, the most revered cultic object of the earlier Israelite league. David sought divine permission to build a permanent temple to house the ark, the symbol of Yahweh's presence, which would have completed his transformation of Jerusalem into the permanent religious center of his kingdom, but his plan was temporarily thwarted by Nathan's negative oracle (2 Sam 7). Though David was not allowed to build the Temple, he may have begun collecting material for its construction, as the Chronicler claimed (1 Chr 22; 28–29). It was Solomon, however, who actually built the Temple, beginning its construction in the second month of his fourth year and completing it in the eighth month of his eleventh year (1 Kgs 6:1, 37-38). *See* TEMPLE, JERUSALEM.

J. J. M. ROBERTS

TEMPLE SCROLL.

The Temple Scroll was discovered in Cave 11 at Qumran in 1956 among the DEAD SEA SCROLLS. As its name suggests, the Temple Scroll's main concern is with the Temple and its cult, its ritual purity, and the purity of those who live in the land surrounding the Temple.

The Temple Scroll (11Q19) is the longest complete scroll found at Qumran, being 7.94 m long in its present condition. It consists of nineteen sheets of leather preserving sixty-seven columns; two different scribes wrote the scroll in Hebrew. Its paleographical date is the late 1st cent. BCE. In addition to the large scroll from Cave 11, one or possibly two other copies were found in Cave 11 (11Q20, 11Q21?), and one copy in Cave 4 (4Q524). The Cave 4 copy is the oldest, dating to ca. 150 BCE. In addition, a set of fragments labeled 4Q365a overlaps with portions of the Temple Scroll and may be part of its source material.

The Temple Scroll presents itself as a direct revelation from God (speaking in the first person) to Moses. That Moses is the recipient is clear from the reference in col. XLIV to "your brother Aaron" (line 5). The text is a collection of laws, which come from several sources and can be divided as follows:

Col. II	Introduction; the covenant relationship
Cols. III–XII	Temple building and related structures
Cols. XIII–XXIX	Festival calendar
Cols. XXX–XLIV	Temple courts and related structures
Cols. XLV–XLVII	Sanctity of the holy city
Cols. XLVIII–LI, 10	Purity regulations
Cols. LI, 11–LVI	Deuteronomic paraphrase
Cols. LVII–LIX	Law of the King
Cols. LX–LXVII	Deuteronomic paraphrase continued

The material of the scroll is heavily dependent on Exodus, Leviticus, and especially Deuteronomy, of which it quotes whole sections. However, the Temple Scroll is a "rewritten Scripture" text; that is, it takes the scriptural material relevant to the topic at hand and weaves it into a unified whole. Therefore, in many cases the Temple Scroll presents a thoroughgoing rewriting of large passages of the Pentateuch, often with additions to make its legal position clear. That position is exceedingly strict, particularly in the laws regarding the purity of the Temple.

Many of the Temple Scroll's provisions are unusual. The architectural plan the scroll outlines for the Temple differs from any other known account of Jewish temple architecture. The festival calendar includes a number of festivals not found in the Torah or rabbinic literature, e.g., the festivals of New Wine and New Oil. The Law of the King contains several unique provisions, including the prohibition of royal polygamy and the subordination of the king to the high priest in matters of war.

The question of the authoritative stature of the Temple Scroll is difficult to resolve. While it makes a clear claim to authority as a direct revelation from God, we lack definitive evidence that the Qumran community accepted that claim. The Temple Scroll contains no overtly sectarian language as found in other Qumran documents; however, the scroll does have clear affinities with a group of texts that were important works for the community: *1 Enoch*, *Jubilees*, *Aramaic Levi*, and the *Damascus Document*. Like these works, it espouses a solar calendar and a strict interpretation of the Torah. In addition, several smaller details of the Temple Scroll show affinity with other Qumran documents. Therefore, it seems likely that the Temple Scroll is part of an older body of material inherited and preserved by the Qumran community.

Bibliography: S. W. Crawford. *The Temple Scroll and Related Texts* (2000); F. García Martínez, E. Tigchelaar, and A. S. van der Woude. *Qumran Cave 11, II, 11Q2–18, 11Q20–31: Discoveries in the Judaean Desert XXIII* (1998); E. Puech. *Qumrân Grotte 4, XVIII; Textes Hébreux (4Q521–4Q528, 4Q576–4Q579)* (1998); Y. Yadin. *The Temple Scroll.* Rev. Eng. ed.; 3 vols. (1983).

SIDNIE WHITE CRAWFORD

TEMPLE SERVANT. *See* NETHINIM.

TEMPLE TAX [δίδραχμον didrachmon]. Israelite males were required to pay a half-shekel annually to support the Jerusalem Temple (Matt 17:24). After the Temple's destruction, Vespasian required that Israelite males pay this tax to the temple of Jupiter Capitolinus in Rome (Josephus, *J.W.* 7.218). *See* COINS; TAXES, TAXATION.

TEMPLE, JERUSALEM [בַּיִת bayith, הֵיכָל hekhal, מִקְדָּשׁ miqdash; ἅγιον hagion, ἱερόν hieron, ναός naos, οἶκος oikos]. In its long history Israel built numerous sanctuaries and temples for its God, Yahweh, but of these, the historically most important were the three chronologically successive temples built on the same site in Jerusalem. The first was built by Solomon in the mid-10th cent. BCE. This Temple continued with minor and major repairs and alterations until it was looted in 598 BCE, and then utterly destroyed in 587 BCE. The Second Temple was built by Zerubbabel, the Persian appointed governor of Judea, on the site of the ruins of the First Temple between 520 and 516 BCE. This Temple endured various vicissitudes during its almost 500 year history, but it remained standing until Herod the Great tore it down ca. 20 BCE in order to make way for his new Temple. Herod rebuilt the Temple proper in only a year and six months, but his work on the larger temple precincts, which he massively enlarged and adorned with elaborate structures, lasted some eight and a half years (Josephus, *Ant.* 15.380, 420–21). His work was so significant that the Jerusalem Temple of the 1st cent. CE is usually referred to as Herod's Temple. Nonetheless, work actually continued on the complex well after Herod's reign, until ca. 63 CE, during the reign of Herod Agrippa II and the procuratorship of Albinus. Herod's Temple was destroyed in 70 CE when the Romans sacked Jerusalem at the end of the Jewish War. Whether any Jewish temple structure worthy of the name was built during Bar Kokba's brief occupation of Jerusalem during the Second Jewish Revolt against Rome in 132 CE remains a subject of debate.

A. Terminology
B. Israelite Temples
C. Sources

D. Solomon's Temple
  1. Location
  2. Structure
  3. Contents
    a. The shrine
    b. The central hall
    c. The vestibule
    d. The courtyards
  4. Changes
  5. Theology
E. Second Temple
  1. Location
  2. Structure
  3. Contents
  4. Changes
F. Herod's Temple
  1. Courtyards and porticoes
  2. The Temple
  3. Theology
G. The New Testament
Bibliography

A. Terminology

Because there are many terms for temple in the Bible, these designations are discussed here in a separate section. The most common Hebrew terms the OT uses for temple are bayith (oikos, "house") and hekhal (naos), a loanword derived ultimately from Sumerian (e₂-gal, literally, "big house") but usually rendered as "temple" or "palace." Both terms for temple indicate the underlying understanding of the temple as the house or mansion where the deity lived. On occasion, however, both terms could be used to designate a particular part of the temple. Another common term for the temple is miqdash (hagion [ἅγιον, LXX], hagiasma [ἁγίασμα, LXX], hagiastērion [ἁγιαστήριον, LXX]) "sanctuary, holy place, sacred areas," a designation emphasizing the sacred nature of the divine abode. The cognate term qodhesh (קֹדֶשׁ; hagion, LXX, "holiness"), is also sometimes used as a designation for "the holy place." The term mishkan (מִשְׁכָּן; LXX skēnē [σκηνή], skēnōma [σκήνωμα], kataskēnōsis [κατασκήνωσις]) is the common designation for the TABERNACLE of the wilderness period, but it is also used to refer to the Temple as God's "dwelling place." The parallel term ʾohel (אֹהֶל), "tent," while normally used to refer to the wilderness tent of meeting or to David's tent sanctuary in Jerusalem, occasionally in Psalms must refer to Solomon's Temple. Less common designations for the Temple include naweh (נָוֶה, "pasture, dwelling place"), maʿon (מָעוֹן; katoikētērion [κατοικητήριον], "dwelling place"), sokh (סֹךְ; LXX topos [τόπος], "den, shelter, dwelling place"), and birah (בִּירָה; LXX oikodomē [οἰκοδομή]; oikos), "fortress," a term that points to the Second Temple's secondary role as a citadel.

The NT uses two Greek words for the Temple and its precincts. **Hieron,** translated "temple," refers to the Temple with its surrounding courtyard spaces. **Naos** generally refers to the sanctuary itself; thus it is sometimes translated "Temple" (e.g., Matt 26:61; Mark 14:58), but also may be translated as "sanctuary" (e.g., Luke 1:9, 21, 22) or "shrine" (Acts 17:24; 19:24).

B. Israelite Temples

The Temple in Jerusalem was neither the first nor the last temple built by the Israelites for the worship of their God, Yahweh. According to the earliest epic sources, even in the pre-conquest period of wilderness wandering, Israel had a moveable tent sanctuary. It was used to house the ARK OF THE COVENANT, which, as the primary symbol of the divine presence, represented Israel's cultural equivalent of the divine image in the surrounding cultures. The description of this tent sanctuary, or tabernacle, in Exod 25–31; 35–40, portrays a moveable sanctuary far too elaborate, heavy, and richly adorned to fit the primitive conditions in the Sinai wilderness prior to Israel's occupation of Canaan. For that reason, this description is sometimes dismissed as a fictional and anachronistic retrojection of aspects of Solomon's Temple back into the pre-settlement period. It seems more likely, however, that the detailed description of the tabernacle is based on an actual tent sanctuary, but a tent sanctuary that was enriched by the largess of a grateful king with abundant booty to lavish on the dwelling place for his God. That would most likely be the tent sanctuary King David set up in Jerusalem to house the ark of the covenant when he brought it up from Kiriath-jearim to his new capital in Jerusalem (2 Sam 6:17).

Before elaborating this point, it might be helpful to trace the housing of the ark from the period of the occupation until the time that David co-opted it for his own purposes. Even after the settlement in Canaan, the ark of the covenant continued to be housed in a tent sanctuary that for much of this period seems to have had no permanent location. It moved with the Israelite camp from Gilgal (Josh 5:1-12), to Jericho (Josh 6:6-7), and from there to Shechem (Josh 8:33), and somewhat later it is mentioned as being in Bethel for a time (Judg 20:26-27). Toward the end of the pre-monarchic period the ark appears to have acquired a more permanent home in Shiloh. The sanctuary there is sometimes referred to as "the house of Yahweh" (1 Sam 1:7; NRSV LORD) or "the Temple of Yahweh" (1 Sam 1:9; NRSV LORD), which has led some scholars to suggest that this was a permanent building of some kind, not a tent sanctuary, though other texts refer to it as a tent (Ps 78:60). Whatever the nature of this particular structure, it appears to have been destroyed by the Philistines following the battle of Aphek (1 Sam 4; Ps 78:60; Jer 7:12-14), when the Philistines captured the ark of the covenant. The ark remained in Philistine hands for a period of time, but it was eventually restored to Israel and remained in Kiriath-jearim for a number of years in the house of a certain Abinadab, whose son Eleazar was consecrated to care for the ark (1 Sam 7:1-2). It would appear that the house of Abinadab was a sanctuary of some kind, though of only local importance. The ark remained there until David brought it up first to the house of Obed-edom near Jerusalem, and then from there into Jerusalem, his new royal capital (2 Sam 6:1-19).

The tent sanctuary that housed the ark was not the only sanctuary in pre-monarchial Israel, however. There was a sanctuary in Shechem that appears to have been a permanent temple (Josh 24:25-26; Judg 9:6, 46). Gideon also established a sanctuary in Ophrah (Judg 8:27), and the Danites set up an early sanctuary at Dan (Judg 18:27-31) that eventually, along with Bethel, became one of the royal temples of the breakaway northern kingdom (1 Kgs 12:27-33; Amos 7:13). The origin of the temple at Bethel dates long before the monarchy, much less the division of the monarchy, since its founding legend associates it with the dream of the patriarch Jacob (Gen 28:10-22). Other early sanctuaries that continued to be frequented by northerners after the split of the kingdom existed at Gilgal and Beersheba (Amos 4:4; 5:5; 8:14), and Samaria, after it became the capital of the northern kingdom, also seems to have acquired a royal sanctuary (Hos 8:5-6). The survivors of the Shiloh priesthood apparently established a new sanctuary at Nob, just north of Jerusalem, that was an important cult site until Saul butchered the priestly families there for supporting David (1 Sam 21:1-9 [Heb. 21:2-10]; 22:6-19). Earlier, during Samuel's lifetime, there were important centers of worship at the high places in Ramah, Bethel, Gilgal, Mizpah, and Gibeah (1 Sam 7:16-17; 9:11-14; 10:3-5). During David's reign there was probably also a sanctuary at Hebron, in the south, since Absalom pretended to go there to fulfill some vows he had made to Yahweh (2 Sam 15:7-9). The excavators of Arad, even further in the south, claim to have found a temple in Arad as well. Moreover, early in Solomon's reign, before he built the Temple in Jerusalem, the most important place of sacrificial worship in the area appears to have been at the great high place in Gibeon, not in David's tent sanctuary in Jerusalem (1 Kgs 3:4), perhaps because the tent sanctuary was too small to accommodate the massive number of Solomon's offerings. In the later exilic and post-exilic period, after the destruction of Solomon's Temple, there was a temple of Yahweh in Elephantine in Egypt, and even later, in the Hellenistic period, in the time of Ptolemy and Cleopatra, Onias, a high priest from Jerusalem, built a temple to Yahweh in Leontopolis, Egypt, modeled on but smaller and poorer than the Temple in Jerusalem (Josephus, *Ant.* 13.62–73).

Nonetheless, David's modest tent sanctuary in Jerusalem represented the wave of the future. The other cultic sites in the south were destroyed by Hezekiah ca. 715 BCE during the course of his early Deuteronomistic reform that focused on centralizing worship in the Temple in Jerusalem (2 Kgs 18:4, 22; compare 2 Chr 29:3-21). A century later, during the far more thorough Deuteronomistic reform of Josiah, Josiah not only destroyed rival cult sites in the south that had reappeared under Manasseh (2 Kgs 23:1-14); he also moved north and desecrated such northern sanctuaries as the temple at Bethel and the high places in the cities of Samaria (2 Kgs 23:15-20). Any long-term restoration of these destroyed cult sites was prevented by Nebuchadnezzar's total destruction of Judah. With the return of the exiles from Babylon, there was a strong desire to rebuild the Temple in Jerusalem, but the continuity of worship at these other early cultic sites had been broken for too long, and they were not reestablished by the returning exiles. The temple at Elephantine was a stopgap measure, apparently intended to provide the Judean exiles at this Egyptian site far from Jerusalem with a local replacement for the Jerusalem Temple, and the Elephantine temple was soon destroyed by hostile Egyptians. The later temple at Leontopolis was even more dependent on the influence of the Jerusalem Temple, and it made no more long-term impact on the world than the ephemeral temple at Elephantine (*see* TEMPLES, LEONTOPOLIS AND ELEPHANTINE).

To return to the theological development of Solomon's Temple in Jerusalem, David, Solomon's father and the founder of the Judean dynasty, had begun as a soldier in the service of the preceding Israelite king, Saul. In the course of his service with Saul and then as a suspected rebel and fugitive from Saul, David had obviously seen first hand how Saul's conflict with Samuel and the priestly representatives of the old order in Israel had contributed to the instability of Saul's royal rule. Once David had seized the throne of Israel as well as that of Judah after a long but eventually successful civil war against Saul's successors, David made several clever moves to prevent a similar problem from arising to weaken his own dynasty. He tried to cement his ties to the northern tribes by moving his royal capital from Hebron in Judah to Jerusalem, a neutral city lying between Judah and Israel that had no ancient ties to either Judah or Israel. He also brought the ark of the covenant, the most sacred object of the northern tribes, into his new capital in Jerusalem, and to service his sanctuary in Jerusalem, he brought in two high priests from different priestly families. Abiathar, the sole survivor of the priests of Nob, was a representative of the old Israelite priesthood of Shiloh, and Zadok, his other high priest, was probably from the Judean priesthood of Hebron.

David's successful imperial wars meant that David had great wealth to lavish on Yahweh's sanctuary (2 Sam 8:1-12), so the massive amount of precious metal and expensive fabrics associated with the description of the tabernacle in Exod 25-31, 35-40, would be within reason were this actually a description of David's tent shrine. Moreover, David wanted to build a permanent temple for Yahweh, just as he had built a permanent palace for himself, and it is likely that the tent sanctuary, built according to the plan that God had shown to Moses on the Mount (Exod 25:9, 40) provided something of a model for the much larger temple structure

that replaced it, a structure that the Chronicler says was based on a divine plan that David passed on to Solomon (1 Chr 28:11-12, 18-19). Nonetheless, David could not get oracular approval for the construction of the permanent temple that he wanted. According to Nathan's oracle, Yahweh much preferred living in a tent (2 Sam 7:4-7). David may have made some preliminary preparation for the building of the Temple (1 Chr 21:28-22:19), but it was not until the fourth year of his successor Solomon that actual work on the Temple in Jerusalem began (1 Kgs 6:1).

C. Sources

The primary source for the appearance of Solomon's Temple is the account of the temple building in 1 Kgs 5:1–8:13 [Heb. 5:15–8:13]. This account probably goes back to an early written source or sources, so it can be trusted to give a fairly reliable picture of the Solomon's Temple. The major difficulty with the account is the abundance of technical vocabulary that raises a number of problems of translation and understanding. The later account in 2 Chr 2:1–6:11 [Heb. 1:18–6:11] is clearly dependent in significant part on the account in Kings, but where it differs with the Kings account it is more problematic, since the Chronicler's description may have been influenced by the appearance of the Second Temple contemporary with the writer. Finally, while it must be used with caution as a visionary description of a future Temple, Ezekiel's temple vision (Ezek 40–47) is probably rooted in realities of the first Jerusalem Temple toward the end of its existence. It may be particularly useful for suggesting the width of the various walls and doorways in the structure. No extensive description of Zerubbabel's Temple exists, though there is some brief material in the late 2nd cent. BCE *Letter of Aristeas* (*Let. Aris.* 83–88). More extensive material on Herod's Temple may be found in Josephus and in the tractate *Middoth* of the Mishna.

D. Solomon's Temple

1. Location

Solomon constructed his temple complex north of the old city of David, on the site of a threshing floor where David had set up an ALTAR to appease the anger of Yahweh (2 Sam 24:18-25; 2 Chr 3:1). The successful reconciliation with the deity through this sacrificial action provided cultic legitimation for building the temple complex here, but the site was further legitimated by identifying it with Mount Moriah, the mountain where Abraham had attempted to sacrifice Isaac (Gen 22:1-14; 2 Chr 3:1). There is general agreement that Solomon's Temple complex stood within the area now occupied by the Muslim sacred precincts that houses the Dome of the Rock in the southeastern corner of the present walled city of Jerusalem, but the precise location of the central hall of the Temple within this larger area remains disputed. Solomon also built his new palace in this general area, and it seems clear that the Temple was easily accessible from the royal palace, presumably sharing a common courtyard. In the time of Ahaz there was a covered walkway from the palace to the Temple for the king's use on the Sabbath and a special royal entrance into the temple complex, but Tiglath-pileser III apparently demanded that Ahaz remove these as a sign of his vassal status (2 Kgs 16:18). How long these remained closed remains uncertain. Ezekiel complains that the king's doorway was too close to the Temple's doorway, that there was only a wall between the temple complex and the palace (Ezek 43:8), so the special royal access to the Temple may have been restored sometime after Ahaz.

2. Structure

The main structure of the original Jerusalem Temple belongs to a temple type well attested in 10th cent. BCE Syria-Palestine. The closest parallels are the north Syrian temple at Tell Tainat near the bend in the Orontes River toward the plain of Antioch and especially the remarkably similar contemporary temple at Ain Dara northwest of Aleppo. The central feature of the Jerusalem Temple was a long central hall some 60 cubits long, 20 cubits wide, and 30 cubits high, probably constructed on an elevated platform. There were two different cubit measures; the smaller equaled approximately 18 in., the larger cubit was slightly longer, so these figures would give a building approximately 90 ft. long by 30 ft. wide by 30 ft. high in its internal measurements. One entered this building from the east through a 10 cubit deep VESTIBULE of the same width and height as the main building. The back or western end of the central hall was separated from the rest of the central hall by a wooden wall that created an enclosed shrine or cella some 20 cubits deep, 20 cubits wide, and 20 cubits high. The 10 cubits difference in height between the cella and the rest of the central hall or nave suggests, based on parallels with the contemporary north Syrian temple of Ain Dara, that the floor of the cella was elevated 10 cubits above the floor of the nave, and thus must have been reached by steps or a ramp, though the biblical accounts mention neither. The other, less likely, alternative is to assume that the shrine had a false roof and that there was a 10 cubit dead space between the roof of the shrine and the ceiling of the nave. The cella or shrine is variously designated as haddevir (הַדְּבִיר, the term is of uncertain meaning—perhaps "the back room"), qodhesh haqqodhashim (קֹדֶשׁ הַקֳּדָשִׁים; Hagia Hagiōn [Ἅγια Ἁγίων], "the holy of holies"; see MOST HOLY PLACE), and habbayith happenimi (הַבַּיִת הַפְּנִימִי, "the innermost house/room"). The rest of the central hall, the great hall or nave, is designated as bayith ("house/room"), hekhal ("temple, nave"), or haqqodhesh (הַקֹּדֶשׁ, "the holy place").

In Solomon's Temple both the entrance from the vestibule into the central hall and the entrance from the central hall into the shrine was through wooden double doors, though some scholars think there may have been a cloth veil behind the door into the shrine. In the later temples of Zerubbabel and Herod the wooden doors into the shrine appear to have been replaced by a veil, though the passageway from the portico into the nave appear to have had doors as well as a veil behind the doors. In Solomon's Temple the doors into the shrine were of olive wood, covered with carvings of cherubim, palm trees, and open flowers, and overlaid with gold. The pilasters that framed the doorway and protected the turning doorposts did not have a flat surface, but were recessed toward the opening in five levels. The pilasters that framed the doorway into the nave from the vestibule were made of olivewood, and they were also recessed toward the opening, but with only four levels. The doors themselves were made of cypress wood, and like the doors to the shrine, they were covered with carved cherubim, palm trees, and open flowers, and overlaid with gold. These double doors were apparently much wider and taller than the doors into the inner shrine, however, and they appear to have been fitted with a smaller double door that could provide access to the nave without opening the whole massive doorway.

The inside walls of the nave were lined with boards of cedar from the floor to the rafters of the ceiling, and the floor of the building was covered with boards of cypress. The shrine was apparently lined entirely of cedar, however. Moreover, the cedar planking had carvings of gourds and open flowers, and the wooden lining of the house was so complete that no stone was visible within the house. Then the wooden lining of both the shrine and the nave was overlaid with pure gold. There were also golden chains drawn across the front of the doors leading into the shrine from the nave.

Built around three sides of the main structure on the north, west, and south was a secondary three-story structure whose bracing rested on abutments in the outside walls of the main structure, but did not penetrate into the interior of the main structure. The bottom floor of this secondary structure was 5 cubits wide and 5 cubits high, but the upper floors, while the same height, became progressively wider—6 and 7 cubits respectively—since the outside wall of the main structure decreased in thickness as it grew higher. Access to these secondary rooms was through doorways on the southeast and perhaps the northeast ends. The entrance to the middle and third story was by way of a winding staircase on the south side (1 Kgs 6:8), but the location of the entrance to the first floor is not indicated. The rooms on these three floors were probably used as temple storerooms and for the use of the priests. Similar external storerooms are attested on three sides of the temple building at Ain Dara.

There may have been decorated, fake windows on the exterior walls of the temple similar to those at Ain Dara. This may be the meaning of the troublesome technical expression rendered in the NRSV as "windows with recessed frames," but which seems more literally to mean "closed, framed windows" (1 Kgs 6:4).

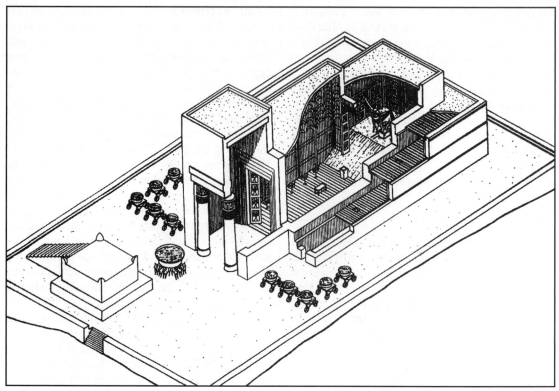

Figure 1: Solomon's Temple

Some who adopt this understanding suggest there were probably also genuine windows to provide some light into the central shrine. Otherwise with only the open eastern doorway as a source of natural light, the building would have been very dark, particularly in the shrine at the greatest distance from the doorway. On the other hand, the archaic poetic fragment in 1 Kgs 8:12-13 suggests that the deity wished to live in thick darkness. Whether or not there were actual windows as a source of natural light, it is clear that oil lamps were necessary in the central shrine to provide enough light for the exercise of priestly tasks in the building.

The dimensions assigned to the Temple in this account seem to indicate the internal dimensions of the rooms, i.e., the height from floor to ceiling, not the height from outside pavement to top of the roof, the width from internal wall to internal wall, not the width from one edge of the outside wall to the other edge, the internal length from entrance to inside back wall, not the external measurement from the outside front of the Temple to the outside of the back or western wall. If one were describing the appearance of the Temple from the outside, the measurements would be much larger. For such a description the width of the external walls and the height of any foundation platform and roof structure would have to be taken into account, information that is not given in the account in Kings. Some significant variation in the figures given in other accounts may reflect such a difference in what is being measured rather than any actual difference in the size of the structures.

Thus if one may use the width of the walls as given by Ezekiel, the external length of the house from the back wall of the external three-story structure to the front wall of the vestibule would include the thickness of the wall of the external structure (5 cubits), internal space of bottom floor (5 cubits), thickness of the back wall of the shrine (6 cubits), internal space of the shrine (20 cubits), thickness of the partition wall between the shrine and the nave (2 cubits?), internal space of the nave (40 cubits), thickness of the wall between the nave and the vestibule (6 cubits), internal space of the vestibule (10 cubits), and the thickness of the front wall of the vestibule (6 cubits), for a total length of 100 cubits. The total external width of the Temple from outside wall of the external structure on the south to the outside wall of the external structure on the north would include the thickness of the wall of the external structure (5 cubits × 2), the internal width of the external structure (5 cubits × 2), the width of the outside wall of the central hall (6 cubits × 2), and the internal width of the hall (20 cubits), for a total width of ca. 52 cubits. It is not entirely clear whether the exterior walls of Solomon's vestibule extended beyond the exterior walls of the main hall to provide a facade for the front of the three-story exterior structure as well, but in Herod's Temple it did, and it actually had shoulders that may have extended beyond the exterior structure, since the front facade of Herod's Temple was 100 cubits long. *See* SOLOMON'S TEMPLE.

3. Contents

a. The shrine. The elevated shrine, a 20-cubit cube, contained two giant cherubim, human-headed, lion-bodied, eagle-winged sphinxes, protective deities often associated with thrones in the art of Syria-Palestine. These creatures were made of olive wood, plated with gold, and each stood 10 cubits high with their wings outstretched. They stood side by side facing the doorway into the central hall, and their outer wings touched the sidewalls of the shrine, while their inner wings touched one another. Thus the outstretched wings of the cherubim formed a continuous platform across the whole breadth of the shrine at a height of about 10 cubits, roughly 15 feet or one and a half times the height of a modern basketball goal (10 ft.). This platform provided the seat, or the base for the invisible seat of Yahweh, one of whose principal epithets is Yahweh who sits enthroned on the cherubim (e.g., Ps 99:1). Below and between the cherubim was placed the ark of the covenant, with its long carrying poles extending toward the two side walls of the shrine. A curtain blocked a direct view of the cherubim and the ark from the shrine's open doorway, but gaps between the curtain and the doorway from that vantage point allowed one to see the ends of the carrying poles. The ark beneath the cherubim was considered the footstool on which the feet of the invisibly enthroned Yahweh rested (1 Chr 28:2; Pss 99:1, 5; 132:7). No mention is made of them in 1 Kgs 6, but Isaiah's inaugural vision (Isa 6:1-2) suggests that, at least in the time of Ahaz, there were two pole-mounted winged-cobras, or seraphim, rising above and behind the throne formed by the cherubim. Iconographic representation of such pole-mounted seraphim from Palestine are found embossed on bronze bowls taken as booty by Tiglath-pileser III in 733–732 BCE. Seraphim are also widely represented on Judean stamp seals from the 8th cent. BCE, but they disappear from Judean iconography shortly thereafter. Some twenty-three years after Isaiah's vision during Hezekiah's religious reform of 715 BCE, Hezekiah removed at least one such pole-mounted serpent from the Temple, even though tradition had attributed its creation to Moses and the wilderness period (2 Kgs 18:4).

b. The central hall. The nave or central hall contained a golden altar for INCENSE, a golden table for laying out the daily bread offering, and ten golden LAMPSTANDs, along with all the utensils that serviced each of these objects. Five of the lampstands were to be placed along the south wall and five along the north wall, but the location of the altar and the table are not specified. Nonetheless, the altar probably stood in front of the door into the shrine, and the table along the northern wall of the central hall, judging from the location of these objects in the tabernacle (Exod 40:22-26).

c. The vestibule. The vestibule apparently had two load-bearing pillars that were topped with capitals of lily-work some four cubits high. In addition to these structural pillars, there were two free-standing bronze pillars in front of the doorway into the vestibule that had a circumference of 12 cubits and a height of 18 cubits. These were topped by highly decorated capitals 5 cubits high. The free-standing pillar on the north was named Boaz, the one on the south Jachin. The names are obviously symbolic, but their meaning and what they symbolized is still debated. One suggestion analyzes the name Boaz as the preposition b (ב) "in" + ʿoz (עֹז) "strength," and interprets it as an abbreviated sentence name: "in the strength of Yahweh the king rejoices." The name Jachin is obviously built off a verbal form of the root kun (כּוּן), "to establish, make firm," and probably expresses some thought to the effect that Yahweh or God "firmly establishes" the world (see Ps 24:2). *See* JACHIN AND BOAZ.

d. The courtyards. The inner courtyard in front of the Temple contained a number of objects. Unless the account in Kings is textually defective, Solomon apparently placed the relatively small (5 cubits long, 5 cubits wide, and three cubits high; Exod 25:1-8) bronze altar for burnt sacrifices that had been in David's tabernacle there, though since it was not large enough to accommodate all the sacrifices at the dedication of the Temple, Solomon consecrated the whole middle of this courtyard as a temporary place of sacrifice (1 Kgs 8:64). About two hundred years later in 732 BCE, Ahaz had a new altar for burnt offerings built, modeled on one he saw in Damascus. He placed this new altar in the courtyard in front of the Temple to serve as the regular place of sacrifice, but the older bronze altar was not destroyed. He moved it to the north of the new altar and reserved it for those occasions when he wanted to inquire of Yahweh, apparently believing that the traditional altar provided better access to the God of Israel (2 Kgs 16:10-16). In contrast with the account in 1 Kings, the Chronicler has Solomon build a bronze altar 20 cubits long, 20 cubits wide, and 10 cubits high (2 Chr 4:1). In Ezekiel's vision the altar had a base 1 cubit high and 1 cubit wide, then from the base to the lower ledge 2 cubits with a width of 1 cubit, from the lower ledge to the higher ledge 4 cubits with a width of 1 cubit, and then 4 more cubits to the top of the altar hearth, which was a 12 cubit square surrounded by a 14 cubit square ledge, with steps on the east side leading up to the top of the altar (Ezek 43:13-17). When these figures are added together it would give a stepped altar whose ground measurements equal a 20 cubit square. This suggests that the Chronicler and Ezekiel may have been visualizing the same altar, but whether its origin was Solomonic remains doubtful; it may owe more to Ahaz's innovation.

There was also a huge round bronze water basin, 10 cubits across, 30 cubits in circumference, and 5 cubits high, holding approximately 23,000 gallons of water. The basin rested on 12 bronze bulls, three facing each of the four directions, with their hindquarters to the inside (1 Kgs 7:23-26). This object, known as the "molten sea," obviously had symbolic significance, probably symbolizing the deity's conquest and ordering of the primeval sea. It stood in the courtyard at the southeast corner of the Temple (1 Kgs 7:39). There were also 10 moveable stands of bronze decorated with cherubim, lions, and palm trees, holding smaller bronze water basins of approximately 475 gallons. These were stationed 5 on the south side of the house, and 5 on the north side (1 Kgs 7:27-39). They were clearly to provide water for cleansing during the messy sacrificial work of the priests. Most of this bronze work disappeared under Ahaz's reign, sent as tribute to Assyria. The bronze bulls were replaced with a stone base, and the bulls, the panels of the moveable stands, and their bronze basins all disappeared from the temple courtyard (2 Kgs 16:17).

Judging from the account in Ezek 40–46, there was also an outer courtyard with a wall separating the whole sacred enclosure from the surrounding area. There also appear to have been various structures between the outer and inner courtyards, but it is difficult to be more specific about these.

4. Changes

Ahaz's alterations were not the only changes that befell the temple complex between its construction by Solomon in the 10th cent. and its destruction by Nebuchadnezzar in the 6th. Rehoboam, Solomon's immediate successor, had to take some of the treasures from the Temple to pay off Shishak of Egypt in the late 10th cent. (1 Kgs 14:26). Asa (early 9th cent. BCE) used what was left in the temple treasury to buy a treaty with the Aramean Ben-Hadad against Baasha of Israel (1 Kgs 15:18-19). Late in Jehoash's reign (late 9th/early 8th cent. BCE), major structural repairs were apparently needed and finally made to the Temple through special contributions (2 Kgs 12:4-15 [Heb. 12:5-16]). During Amaziah's reign, Jehoash of Israel (early 8th cent. BCE) captured Jerusalem and plundered gold and silver and all the precious vessels that were in the Temple (2 Kgs 14:13-14). Jotham built or perhaps rebuilt what is called the upper gate of the Temple, probably a gate leading into one of the courtyards of the Temple (2 Kgs 15:35). Hezekiah removed the bronze serpent from the Temple early in his reign (ca. 715 BCE, 2 Kgs 18:4), but in response to Sennacherib's campaign against Jerusalem in 701 BCE, Hezekiah had to empty the temple treasury and even strip the gold from the doors and doorposts of the Temple (2 Kgs 18:13-16) in order to pay the enormous tribute that the Assyrians assessed. Manasseh apparently set up a carved image of Asherah in the Temple and built altars in the courtyards for the host of heaven (2 Kgs 21:4-7). Josiah did major repair work on the Temple during which time the book of the law was discovered (2 Kgs 22:3-10), and in the reform that followed he removed from the Temple all the vessels made for Baal, Asherah, or the host of heaven, as well as the image of Asherah. He also destroyed various structures in the temple precincts that were used for male prostitution or the worship of Asherah (2 Kgs 23:4, 6-7). He also

removed the horses that the kings of Judah had dedicated to the sun from the entrance to the Temple, burned their chariots, and destroyed the altars that Manasseh had built for the host of heaven in the two courtyards of the Temple (2 Kgs 23:11-12). Then in 597 BCE, when Nebuchadnezzar captured Jerusalem the first time, he looted the treasures and gold from the Temple (2 Kgs 24:13). When the city fell to Nebuchadnezzar the second time in 587/586 BCE, the Temple was burned and its remaining precious objects were looted (2 Kgs 25:9, 13-17). It is apparent from even a cursory reading of these texts that the contents and even aspects of the physical structure of the temple complex changed over time.

5. Theology

The reason people began to build houses for their gods was because they perceived that the presence of the gods in their midst provided them with a continuing source of prosperity and blessing. It was hoped that a permanent, luxuriously appointed house with attending servants (priests) meeting the god's needs for food, music, and other concerns would secure the enduring presence of the deity and the blessings associated with that presence. One should note that David brought the ark of the covenant, the symbol of Yahweh's presence, into his capital city Jerusalem only after he observed that its presence in the house of Obed-edom had resulted in obvious blessings on Obed-edom and his whole household (2 Sam 6:11-12). To please the deity and keep the deity in residence, it was important to build the temple according to the deity's specifications. Thus from very early times one encounters the motif of the deity providing his human patron with the divine blueprint for the temple to be built. One sees this already in the late 3rd millennium BCE in the account of the Sumerian king GUDEA's temple building, and it is visually represented in the diorite statue of Gudea that shows him seated on his throne with the divine blueprint for his Temple spread out over his lap. This concern to build according to divine specifications is so strong that when one rebuilt decaying or ruined temples, it was important to build them precisely on their earlier foundation lines. Late Neo-Babylonian kings boasted of the care with which they did this, and the Assyrian king Sennacherib attempted to totally destroy the foundation trenches of the Babylonian temples as a way of preventing the Babylonian temples from ever being rebuilt. Thus it is not surprising that the biblical tradition records the motif that Solomon's temple (1 Chr 28:19), like the preceding tabernacle (Exod 25:9, 40), was built according to the plan that God had revealed to his human servant.

Yahweh was not just a city god, however, and Jerusalem was not just a local high place. Yahweh was the national god of Israel, and Jerusalem was the royal capital of a kingdom that under David and Solomon acquired imperial status. Thus the theology associated with the Temple in Jerusalem takes on imperial qualities.

In ANE mythology imperial deities acquire their kingship over the other gods by their conquest over the powers of chaos, and in both the Ugaritic Baal cycle and *Enuma Elish*, the Babylonian creation epic, this triumph over chaos is followed by the construction of a palace for the victorious divine king. In Israel this triumph over chaos is attributed to Yahweh, and like Marduk in the *Enuma Elish*, Yahweh follows this triumph over chaos with the creation of the stable world on the carcass of the primeval seas (Pss 24:1-2; 74:12-17; 93:1-4; 95:3-5), and like both Baal and Marduk, Yahweh returns in triumph from his victory over his enemies to ascend his throne in his new palace in the royal capital (Pss 24:7-10; 47:1-9 [Heb. 47:2-10]; 68:17-20, 24-35 [Heb. 68:18-21, 25-36]). According to Israelite imperial theology, Yahweh chose Jerusalem as his permanent dwelling place (Pss 68:16-17 [Heb. 68:17-18]; 132:13-14), and because Yahweh lives within it, the city is protected from its enemies (Pss 46; 48; 76) and is blessed with abundance (Ps 132:15-16). As the abode of the imperial God, the city acquires the mythological topography appropriate for the dwelling place of the king of the gods. The relatively modest Mount Zion, the temple mount, overshadowed even by the neighboring MOUNT OF OLIVES, which is significantly higher, is nonetheless identified with Baal's Mount Zaphon (Ps 48:1-2 [Heb. 48:2-3]: "His holy mountain, beautiful in elevation, is the joy of the whole earth; Mount Zion is the heights of Zaphon (author's trans.; NRSV, "in the far north"), the city of the great King," the mountain where the divine assembly meets (Isa 14:13), and Mount Zion is envisioned in this mythological topography as the tallest mountain of the world (Isa 2:2; Mic 4:1; Zech 14:4-5). As the abode of the imperial god, Jerusalem is also identified as a reincarnation of the primeval Garden of Eden, and in its mythological topography, the city is assigned a life-giving river (Ps 46:4 [Heb. 46:5]; Isa 33:21-24; Ezek 47:1-12; Zech 14:8), perhaps identified with the modest stream fed by the Gihon spring where Solomon was anointed king (1 Kgs 1:38-48). Note that one of the rivers of Paradise is named Gihon (Gen 2:13). This imperial glorification of the royal capital of the Davidic dynasty and its imperial god Yahweh would also include the motif of the pilgrimage of the foreign nations, Israel's vassals, to Jerusalem to pay their tribute and have their disputes arbitrated at the imperial court (Ps 68:29 [Heb. 68:30]; Isa 2:3-4; Mic 4:2-3). In line with general Near Eastern practice, such foreign dignitaries must have been present at the great seven-day celebration Solomon hosted for all Israel to dedicate his new Temple (1 Kgs 8:62-66).

This imperial theology of Yahweh's kingship, his rule over the powers of chaos, and his glorification as the source of life, abundance, and world order, is clearly reflected in the iconography of the Temple. The giant cherub throne in the inner shrine where God sat enthroned as king (Isa 6:1-5) gave visual representation to the notion of Yahweh's royal rule over the world.

The rest of the iconography that filled the Temple from its very beginning—the carvings of cherubim, palm trees, and open flowers in the inner shrine, the central hall, and on the doors leading into both rooms, the lily work, the lattice work, and the pomegranates on the bronze pillars, the bronze oxen under the molten sea, and the cherubim, lions, palm trees, oxen, and wreaths on the moveable basin frames, and at some point the pole-mounted seraphim—all had a symbolic significance, though it is difficult to articulate the full range of what these images meant to the Israelite and Judean worshipers in the Temple. Tyrian craftsmen were responsible for much of the work on the temple complex (1 Kgs 7:13-46), and this has led some to suggest that the iconography that filled this structure was essentially pagan and non-Israelite, but that judgment seems highly dubious. The evidence rather suggests that Israel shared much of the same symbolic world with their Canaanite, Phoenician, and Syrian neighbors. The structural similarity between Solomon's Temple and those of north Syria like Ain Dara and Tell Tainat points in this direction. So does the similarity between the Temple's cherubim throne and the rather common cherubim thrones of Syria-Palestine from the 11th cent. down into Hellenistic times. The same may be said for the iconography of late 8th cent. Judean stamp seals with their protective cobras and for the mythological symbols embossed on many of the bronze bowls from Israel carried away as booty by Tiglath-pileser III in 732 BCE.

The pomegranates, lilies, wreaths, and palm trees suggest great fertility, and they probably imply that the source of such fertility was the presence of the deity. The later vision of Ezekiel in which living waters arose from the threshold of the Temple (Ezek 47) is not a late theological development, but simply a restatement of a very ancient view that the earthly abode of the deity was a reimbodiment of the primeval garden of eden (compare Ps 46:4 [Heb. 46:5]). The cherubim throne with the ark as its footstool pointed to Yahweh as the divine king, imperial ruler of the world. The cherubim and seraphim were protective spirits that gave expression to the awesomeness, power, and terror-inspiring quality of the deity (compare Isa 6:2-5), and the bulls, whatever their precise symbolic significance as the base for the molten sea, were ancient symbols of the power of Yahweh (Num 23:22; 24:8), one of whose most ancient epithets was ʾavir yaʿaqov (אֲבִיר יַעֲקֹב, Gen 49:24; Ps 132:2; Isa 49:26; 60:16) or ʾavir yisraʾel (אֲבִיר יִשְׂרָאֵל, Isa 1:24), which should be rendered "the bull of Jacob" and "the bull of Israel." The bull iconography of the golden calf (Exod 32:1-4) and of Jeroboam I's rival northern cult centers (1 Kgs 12:28-29) was not a late innovation. The molten sea probably alluded to the primeval sea, and its presence in Yahweh's temple complex suggested the deity's conquest of the sea and his ordering of the cosmos as a consequence of that primeval victory. The meaning of the two bronze pillars is still disputed, but they most likely point to the strength of the deity and the stability of the ordered world that rested upon that strength.

In the earliest material the belief that God had taken up his abode in his new Temple in Jerusalem does not appear to have created any theological problems. One spoke of Yahweh living in the Temple in the same way that one spoke of the human king living in his palace, using the verb yashav (יָשַׁב, 1 Kgs 8:12-13), the normal verb one used for living in a house. Moreover, no distinction seems to have been drawn between God's heavenly dwelling and his abode in the earthly Temple. Like Marduk's temple in Babylon, Yahweh's Temple in Jerusalem marked the meeting place between heaven and earth and, as it were, participated in both worlds. The conception is most clearly expressed in the cult legend for the sanctuary at Bethel (Gen 28:12-17), where the house of God (beth-ʾel בֵּית־אֵל) is identified as the "gate of heaven." In Babylonian religious thought, the city of Babylon (bab-ili in Akkadian, ka₂.dingir.ak in Sumerian) is similarly etymologized as "the gate of the god." In these early Israelite texts, one could speak of Yahweh sending help from the sanctuary in Zion (Ps 20:3 [Heb. 20:4]) and of God's helping his anointed and answering him "from his holy heaven" (Ps 20:6 [Heb. 20:8]) in the same psalm without any apparent difference in meaning (see also Ps 18:7, 10 [Heb. 18:8, 11]). In the course of time, however, Israelite theologians were increasingly bothered by the problem of explaining the apparent conflict between divine immanence and divine transcendence. How could the deity who had created the whole world live in a mere house built by human hands (1 Kgs 8:27; Isa 66:1)? In response to this difficulty new formulations arose in different theological attempts to resolve these problems. In the Deuteronomistic theology, explicitly elaborated in the prayer attributed to Solomon at the dedication of the Temple (1 Kgs 8:27-53), the heavenly and earthly spheres were split apart. The earthly Temple no longer shared a common identity with the heavenly dwelling place of the deity. The heavenly deity could not actually live in a mere earthly house built by human hands; the real abode of the deity was in heaven, and it was only the "name" of the deity, a hypostatic presence of the deity, that resided in the earthly Temple. If one prayed toward the Temple, the "name," somewhat like a microphone, would pick up the prayer and transmit it to heaven, the real dwelling place of God, and God in heaven would hear the prayer and respond from heaven. In the priestly theology, one spoke rather of God's glory (kavodh כָּבוֹד), another hypostatic representation of the presence of the deity, that took up temporary residence, a kind of "tenting" (shakhan שָׁכַן), in the earthly Temple. The choice of "tenting" (shakhan) rather than "dwelling" (yashav יָשַׁב) was to emphasize the deity's freedom of movement, and for the Priestly theologians it was important, because, whatever the origins of their theology, its final formulation took shape during the time of the Babylonian exile, when

the Temple lay in ruins, and no permanent house for Yahweh existed anywhere. Thus they needed a theology that spoke of Yahweh's presence among his people even in the absence of a permanent house. Despite the different formulations, the later theologies indicate a dissatisfaction and reticence toward the earlier naiveté with which one could speak of God's living in a Temple. Nevertheless, the older language of God's dwelling in the Temple never completely dies out.

Finally, the divine presence in the Temple, whether conceived of realistically or in a more sophisticated fashion as a mere hypostatic representation of the deity, gave the Temple a quality of holiness that set it apart and made it far more dangerous than ordinary space. Though it is not as explicitly stated with regard to the Temple in the earliest sources, the conception seems to have been that like the tabernacle there were radiating gradients of sanctity or holiness. The inner shrine was the holiest of holies, a dangerous place to approach, because there Yahweh sat enthroned upon his cherubim throne. Nonetheless, the rigid restrictions of access to the holy of holies reflected in Lev 16, which appears to limit access to the high priest on one day of the year, the DAY OF ATONEMENT, certainly were not in effect during the monarchical period. Kings obviously had access to the inner shrine, as Hezekiah spread out the letter from Sennacherib before the Lord, apparently as he stood in the entrance to the inner shrine in front of the cherubim (2 Kgs 19:14), and certain prophets also seemed to have had access. Isaiah's inaugural vision is best explained as reflecting a visual familiarity with the contents of the inner shrine (Isa 6:1-5). Chronicles reports that king Uzziah was struck with leprosy because he attempted to make an offering on the altar of incense despite the opposition of the priests (2 Chr 26:16-21), but the historicity of this account is suspect. Uzziah was probably barred from the Temple because of the ritual uncleanness associated with his leprosy (2 Kgs 15:5), but whether a conflict between the king and the priests over the king's Temple prerogatives preceded this sickness is far less certain.

The central hall as the place of daily priestly activity was slightly less charged with sanctity, though dangerous enough to be off limits to most except the king and perhaps other high royal officials, priestly functionaries, and prophets. The vestibule and particularly the courtyard were less dangerous and open to the worshiping public, but nonetheless it was important that those who entered the courts of Yahweh reflect on the kind of people the deity accepted in his presence (Pss 15; 24:3-6).

E. Second Temple

After Solomon's original Temple was totally destroyed by the Babylonians in 587/6 BCE, the Temple remained in ruins for almost seventy years. There may have been a feeble attempt at rebuilding it soon after the first exiles from Babylon returned to Judah in 539/8 BCE, but the attempt fizzled. It was not until 520 BCE, under the vigorous urging of the prophets Haggai and Zechariah, that Zerubbabel, the Persian-appointed Judean governor of the province of Judah, began work on the Temple in earnest, and the work was not completed until 516 BCE (Ezra 6:13-15).

1. Location

There is little in the way of description of this Second Temple in our sources, but given the ANE temple theology which placed a premium on rebuilding ruined temples precisely on the foundation lines of the earlier temple, it is likely that the location and general shape of the Temple, particularly of the inner shrine and central hall, would have been identical to that of the First Temple.

2. Structure

Ezra 6:3 gives no figure for the length of the Temple, but it offers 60 cubits as both the height and width of the building. It is unclear, however, precisely what is being measured. If the text is correct, these figures probably represent the outside measurements of the Second Temple rather than the inside measurements. Interpreting these figures as internal measurements would suggest a square structure in contrast to the rectangular structure of Solomon's Temple, and that would create serious theological problems of continuity. Moreover, Josephus describes the central hall of Herod's Temple, the replacement of the Second Temple, as 60 cubits long and 20 cubits wide (Josephus, *J.W.* 5.215), though he does agree with Ezra that it was 60 cubits high. Even if the height were an internal dimension, such an increase in height would have no bearing on the foundation lines and suggests that in this regard Herod's Temple, and perhaps even the Second Temple, was actually larger than the first. Haggai 2:3-9 implies that contemporaries of Zerubbabel who were old enough to remember the First Temple saw the Second Temple as insignificant by comparison, but this response seems to have had less to do with the size of the Second Temple, and far more to do with its lack of gold and silver ornamentation.

It is also possible that the height of the vestibule was expanded in the Second Temple. That might be suggested by the Chronicler's notice that the vestibule was 120 cubits high (2 Chr 3:4) and the odd note that the pillars in front of the vestibule were 35 cubits high, with a capital of 5 cubits on top of that (2 Chr 3:15). But if the Chronicler raised the height of the vestibule and the pillars from the figures in Kings, he left the 20 cubit length of the vestibule, just enough to stretch across the width of the nave, untouched (2 Chr 3:4).

3. Contents

There is no evidence that the giant cherubim throne or the ark of the covenant that occupied the Holy of Holies in Solomon's Temple were ever recovered or replaced by new models after the destruction of the First Temple. Apparently the sanctity of these objects was so great that no such replacement without the miraculous intervention of the deity to authorize it seemed viable. Since such intervention did not take place, these objects remained absent in the Second Temple. Josephus says that the inner shrine was totally empty (*J. W.* 5.219). In sharp contrast, the incense altar, the table of showbread, and the lampstands of the central shrine were reconstituted and took their place in the Second Temple (Josephus, *J.W.* 5.216–18).

4. Changes

Between the completion of the Second Temple in 516 BCE and its replacement by Herod the Great in 20 BCE, many repairs and changes must have taken place, but we have little information on these developments. Some indication of the number of changes that may have taken place during this extended time is provided by several rather random references. Ben Sira praises the high priest Simon II, son of Onias (ca. 218–215 BCE), as one who repaired the house, fortified the Temple, founded the height of the courtyard, built a high retaining structure for the temple enclosure, and quarried out a large cistern of water for the temple precincts (Sir 50:1-3). Some years later (ca. 168 BCE) the Syrian king Antiochus Epiphanes desecrated the temple complex, sacrificing a pig on the altar of burnt offerings, and plundering the golden altar, the lampstand, the table of presentation, and all the precious vessels of the Temple (1 Macc 1:20-54). When Judas Maccabeus recaptured the temple complex some three and a half years later, the temple courtyards were described as grown up with plants, the doors burned, and the altar desecrated. Judas removed the stones of the old altar of burnt offerings for safe keeping until a prophet should arise to give instructions what to do with them, and he had a new altar of burnt offering constructed. He also had a new golden altar, lampstand, table of presentation, and other sacred vessels constructed to replace those removed by Antiochus. He also replaced the veils, rebuilt the priests' quarters, restored doors, cleared the courtyards, and refortified the sacred precincts (1 Macc 4:38-59). In the pseudepigraphal *Letter of Aristeas* (ca. 130 BCE), Aristeas gives a brief description of the temple mount, the altar of burnt offering, the water supply for the Temple, and a rather poetic description of the veil between the vestibule and the nave constantly billowing in the wind when the door into the nave was open (*Let. Aris.* 83–88). This purports to be a description of the Temple from the time of the high priest Eleazar (ca. 260–245 BCE), but while it does appear to reflect the impressions of a writer who had actually seen the Second Temple, it probably reflects the appearance of the Temple in the late 2nd cent. BCE, probably even after the Maccabean cleansing of the sanctuary.

F. Herod's Temple

In the eighteenth year of the reign of Herod the Great, Herod decided to undertake a massive rebuilding and beautification of the temple complex. Such a project had potentially negative repercussions, however. Rebuilding the Temple would require the deconstruction of the previous Temple, and any such destruction of the existing Temple, even for purposes of improvement, runs the risk of offending the God of the Temple. No one likes to live in a house under construction. To cite a very ancient parallel, Naram-Sin of Akkad did major reconstructive work on the temple of Enlil in Nippur. According to Naram-Sin's own inscriptions, this was an act of piety on the part of the king, but later Sumerian traditions treated Naram-Sin's necessary preliminary destructive work on the temple of Enlil as a sign of great impiety and the basis for the ultimate punishment of Naram-Sin and Akkad. Moreover, if the time gap between the destruction of the old temple and the reconstruction of the new temple extended too long, the hiatus in important cultic activity that required the temple would become a threat to the well-being of the cultic community. To allay such fears, Herod promised his subjects that he would not tear down the old Temple until everything was prepared for the rapid construction of the new Temple, and according to Josephus, Herod kept that promise (*Ant.* 15.389). The main temple building was rebuilt in only a year and six months, while the elaborate temple enclosures with their magnificent porticoes took eight years to complete (*Ant.* 15.420–21). Nonetheless, this represents only the initial reconstruction of the temple complex. Work either of beautification or repair continued for many years, extending well beyond the reign of Herod the Great. According to John 2:20-21, at the time of Jesus' ministry this work on the Temple had already been going on for forty-six years. It continued long beyond the death of Jesus, into the reign of Herod Agrippa II and the procuratorship of Albinus, ending only around 63 CE (Josephus, *Ant.* 15.390), just a few years before the outbreak of the Jewish revolt.

1. Courtyards and porticoes

One of Herod's major innovations was to enlarge and level out the whole area of the sacred enclosure. The outer enclosure constituted approximately a square with each side about a stadion (ca. 200 m) in length. Along the outer border of this enclosure on the west, north, and east double porticoes were built supported by rows of magnificent columns. Along the southern border broad triple porticoes were built, again supported by rows of magnificent columns, with the middle portico much higher than the other two. This was known as the royal portico. There were four gates in the wall on the west side, one to the king's palace, two to the upper city, and one to the lower city. For some reason, Josephus does not provide as much information about the gates in the northern, eastern, and southern walls.

Since the temple enclosure was protected on the west, south, and east by deep valleys and very steep inclines in addition to the enclosure walls, any assault on the temple area was most likely to come from the north. Thus additional fortifications were located in that area. On the northwest corner, just beyond the temple enclosure stood the massively fortified tower of Antonia. This fortification provided protection for the temple complex, but it also provided Herod the means of controlling the temple complex, should problems break out in the sacred areas. Herod had a secret tunnel built between the tower of Antonia and the eastern gate of the inner courtyard just in front of the Temple, where Herod had a tower, so that he could intervene in the temple complex if the need arose. It was the capture of the tower of Antonia by the Romans in the Jewish War of 70 CE that marked the beginning of the end for the Temple. Once the tower of Antonia fell, the battle spread to the adjoining northern portico of the outer court, part of which the Jews set aflame in a defensive maneuver. Eventually almost all of the porticoes of both the outer and inner courtyards were burned in the course of the fierce battle for control of the temple mount.

Inside the first enclosure there was another square enclosure, this one surrounded by a stone partition three cubits high. Upon this wall at regular intervals stood pillars with inscriptions, some in Latin, some in Greek, warning foreigners not to enter into the second enclosure on pain of death. This second courtyard was elevated above the first courtyard, and was accessed from the first by means of fourteen steps. At the top of the steps there was a level area 10 cubits wide, then another set of steps leading up 5 more cubits to the gates. There were four gates on the north and four gates on the south side, and two gates on the east. One of the eastern gates led into the partitioned Court of Women, where Jewish women could worship. There was access to this partitioned area on the north and south side as well, but the women were not allowed to continue beyond this restricted area. There were no gates on the western side of the second enclosure.

The inside wall between the gates consisted of pillared porticoes similar to the porticoes of the outer enclosure. The gates themselves were huge. Each had two doors, 30 cubits high and 15 cubits wide. There were large spaces within of 30 cubits, and on each side they had side rooms 40 cubits in height supported by massive pillars. Nine of the ten gates were the same size, but the eastern gate directly in front of the Temple itself was much larger. It was 50 cubits high, its doors 40 cubits, and it was more richly adorned than the other gates.

Within this inner courtyard there was another area marked off by a wall of partition about one cubit in height. This partition surrounded the altar and the Temple and restricted this inmost area of the inner courtyard to the priests alone. The altar of burnt offering stood in this restricted area in front of the Temple.

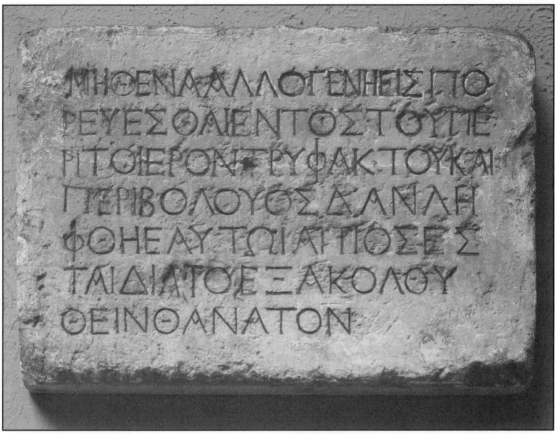

Erich Lessing/Art Resource, NY

Figure 2: Interdiction for non-Jews to enter the inner sanctum of the Jerusalem Temple. Greek inscription from the outer wall of the Temple. Plaster cast (3rd cent. BCE–1st cent. CE). Museo della Civilta Romana, Rome, Italy.

The altar was 15 cubits high and 50 cubits square. Access to the top was by a very gradually sloping ramp, not steps.

2. The Temple

Finally, deeper in the inmost area of the inner courtyard, west of the altar, stood the Temple itself. When Herod began his work on the Temple, he removed the old foundations and laid new ones. The external length of the house was 100 cubits, and its external height was about 120 cubits at its highest point in the center (Josephus, *Ant.* 15.391), though the auxiliary structures on either side of the long hall were not as high. Apparently some of this height was lost in the course of time due to the sinking of the foundations, and repair work was undertaken during the reign of Nero to restore this lost height. The Temple was built of huge white ashlars, 25 cubits long, 8 cubits high, and 12 cubits wide.

According to Josephus, the front of the Temple was 100 cubits high and 100 cubits in length, i.e., it stretched across the whole 20 cubit width of the main hall, and had shoulders that extended 20 cubits beyond the main hall on either side (*J.W.* 5.207). That does not quite calculate, because it gives a total of only 60 cubits, but Josephus fails to mention the three-story external

structure that ran around three sides of the main hall. If one adds this structure of uncertain dimensions, perhaps larger than in Solomon's Temple, along with the width of the walls, then the 100 cubit length of the vestibule makes sense. The stairways leading into the different stories of the external structure were probably enclosed in these shoulders at either end of the vestibule. There were windows into the rooms of this external structure, located high enough on the wall to require a person to be lifted up by another person in order to reach them, and it was through one of these windows on the north side that a Roman soldier threw a burning firebrand that resulted in the burning down of the Temple (Josephus, *J.W.* 6.252).

One approached the vestibule by twelve steps, indicating that the whole structure rested on a larger elevated platform, and at the top of the steps there was a huge doorway opening some 70 cubits tall and 25 cubits wide. There were no doors to this entranceway. The inside dimensions of the open part of the vestibule, not counting space occupied by the stairways at the two ends, appear to have been 90 cubits high, 20 cubits wide, and 50 cubits long. The vestibule was decorated with gold, and it had golden vines above it from which clusters of grapes hung as tall as a man's height. The outward front of the house was covered with plates of

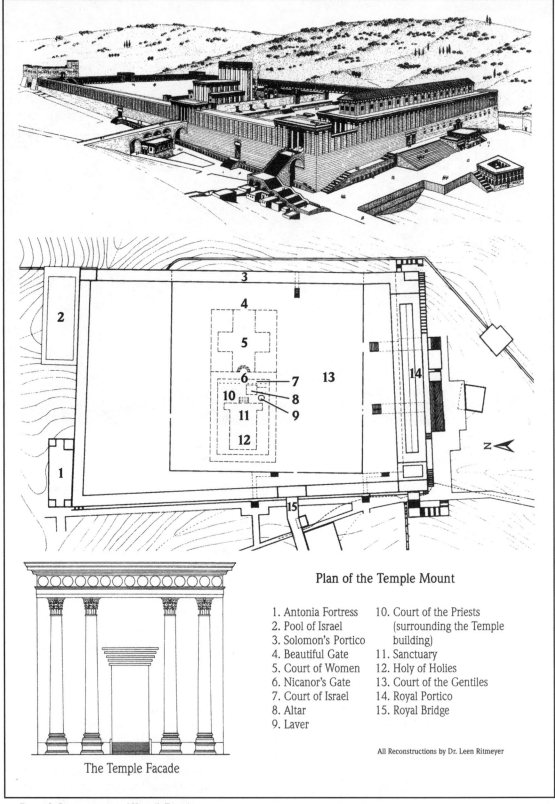

Plan of the Temple Mount

1. Antonia Fortress
2. Pool of Israel
3. Solomon's Portico
4. Beautiful Gate
5. Court of Women
6. Nicanor's Gate
7. Court of Israel
8. Altar
9. Laver

10. Court of the Priests
   (surrounding the Temple
   building)
11. Sanctuary
12. Holy of Holies
13. Court of the Gentiles
14. Royal Portico
15. Royal Bridge

All Reconstructions by Dr. Leen Ritmeyer

The Temple Facade

Figure 3: Reconstruction of Herod's Temple

gold of great weight, and at sunrise it reflected back a fiery splendor. At a distance the house looked like a mountain covered with snow, because those parts of it that were not covered in gold were very white. The very top of the house along the center roofline was covered with metal spikes with sharp points in an attempt to prevent birds from nesting on the roof and so polluting the Temple with their droppings. Apparently the top of the front facade of the vestibule was flat for a breadth of 8 cubits, which allowed a large number of priestly defenders of the Temple to mass there in the final stages of the battle for the Temple in 70 CE. Josephus reports that the priests pulled up the metal roof spikes and their lead bases from the temple roof to throw down at the Romans (*J.W.* 6.278). He also reports an incident of a young priest coming down from the roof to get water from the Romans, then to the Romans' chagrin, fleeing back to his comrades on the roof with the extra water he had acquired (*J.W.* 6.318–20). Apparently he came down via one of the stairways at the two ends of the vestibule.

Between the vestibule and the central hall there was another doorway, this one only 55 cubits high and 16 cubits wide, and this doorway had both golden doors and a large veil or curtain the same size as the doorway. The first room of the central hall, the nave, was 40 cubits long, 20 cubits wide, and 60 cubits high. It contained the golden altar of incense, the golden lampstand, and the golden table for the bread of the presence. Finally, the innermost room of the central hall, the Holy of Holies, was 20 cubits long, 20 cubits wide, and apparently the same height as the nave, or 60 cubits high. It was separated from the rest of the central hall by a veil (Josephus, *J.W.* 5.219). According to Josephus there was absolutely nothing in this inner shrine.

It is obvious from a comparison of these dimensions that at least in height, particularly in the internal height of both the vestibule and the central hall, Herod's Temple was much taller than the Temple of Solomon. It was probably also taller than the Second Temple, though this is hard to demonstrate given the lack of firm evidence about the size of the Second Temple.

3. Theology

Despite some changes in the outward appearance of the Temple from the Temple of Solomon's day to that of Herod's time, the underlying theology remained much the same. The existence of the Temple symbolized God's presence among his people, so in some sense God, or some hypostatic aspect of God, was still thought of as residing in the Temple. One also retained and perhaps gave even more weight to the conception of the radiating degrees of holiness, with holiness most concentrated in the inner shrine and then gradually decreasing as one moved through the nave to the vestibule, then into the inner courtyard of the priests, from there into the inner courtyard of Jewish men, then into the courtyard of the women, from there into the outer courtyard area open to Gentiles, finally outside the temple precincts into the holy city Jerusalem, and ultimately outside the city into the land of Israel. Nonetheless, if one may judge from Josephus' statements, the older sacred symbolism embedded in traditions of Syria-Palestinian-Phoenician iconography was gradually being replaced under the influence of later Hellenistic iconographic traditions. Josephus says that the lack of doors at the entrance

of the vestibule represented the universal visibility of heaven that cannot be excluded from any place (*J.W.* 5.208). The veil that separated the vestibule from the nave was a Babylonian curtain embroidered with blue, fine linen, scarlet, and purple, and these, according to Josephus, represented an image of the universe—scarlet signified fire, fine linen the earth, blue the air, and purple the sea. The veil was also covered with all sorts of mystical figures with the exception of the signs of the Zodiac (Josephus, *J.W.* 5.212–14). The seven lamps of the golden lampstand in the nave represented the seven planets, the twelve loaves on the table of presentation represented the circle of the Zodiac and the year, and the altar of incense with its thirteen different kinds of spices signified that God was the possessor of all things in both the inhabited and uninhabited parts of the world and that all are to be dedicated to him (Josephus, *J.W.* 5.217).

One of the most interesting passages in Josephus is his account of the signs and omens that, correctly understood, foreshadowed the fall of Jerusalem (*J.W.* 6.289–315). Among these omens was the mysterious opening of the large eastern gate of the inner court on its own accord, which Josephus interprets as a sign that God planned to open the gates of his Temple to the Roman enemy (*J.W.* 6.293–95). In many respects, this omen and its interpretation is analogous to Ezekiel's much earlier vision of Yahweh's abandoning his Temple prior to its destruction by the Babylonians (Ezek 10:1–11:23). Another omen involved a certain Jesus, son of Ananus, a commoner who for four years prior to the fall of Jerusalem went about pronouncing woe upon Jerusalem and the Temple, and who, despite harsh punishment by the authorities, continued his lament until he was killed by a large stone shot into the city during the siege of Jerusalem (*J.W.* 6.300–309). His pronouncement of woe upon Jerusalem cannot help but remind one of Jesus of Nazareth's much earlier lament over the city of Jerusalem (Matt 23:37-39).

G. The New Testament

Though Jesus was offended by the commercial activity that took place in the courtyards of the Temple and once created a disturbance by overturning the tables of the money changers (Matt 21:12; Mark 11:15-17; Luke 19:45; John 2:14-17), Jesus visited the Temple, taught in its porticoes, and apparently participated in temple worship in the same way that other Jews of his time did (e.g., Luke 2:41-49). His followers continued this practice long after Jesus' death, apparently seeing no conflict between their participation in the sacrificial worship of the Temple and their devotion to Jesus as Christ and Lord. Even Paul, the Hellenistic Jewish Christian whose devotion to the law and the ancient traditions of the Jews became suspect, continued to visit the Temple and (if the account in Acts is historically accurate) apparently paid for the sacrifices of four Jewish Christians for the completion of vows they had made

(Acts 21:17-26). Unfortunately Paul had been seen in the city earlier in the company of Gentiles, and some of the crowd of worshipers thought he had brought Gentiles into the restricted area of the Temple, so a riot broke out in response to this transgression against the holiness of the temple area (Acts 21:27-36). Even after Paul's arrest, however, Jewish Christians appear to have continued frequenting the Temple almost to the time of the Jewish revolt.

Nonetheless, Jesus did make certain statements that, in the long run, contributed to the denigration of the theological importance of the Temple for his followers. He apparently predicted the destruction of the Temple (Matt 24:1-2; Mark 13:1-2; Luke 19:41-44), and in a widely reported and confusing claim in which Jesus said, "Destroy this temple, and I will rebuild it in three days," Jesus, at least in the understanding of his followers, seemed to suggest the replacement of the Jerusalem Temple by his own person (Matt 26:61; 27:40; Mark 14:58; 15:29; John 2:19-21). Such disparagement of the earthly Temple perhaps reflects both the early awareness that the infinite God could not be limited to houses built by human hands (Acts 7:47-50; 17:24; compare Isa 66:1-2) and the theological need to postulate a heavenly Temple as an abode for God and repository for such long lost sacred objects as the ark of the covenant (Rev 11:19), a need that arose in those periods when the earthly Temple no longer existed, but continued even in those periods after the reconstruction of the Temple (Rev 14:17; 15:5).

In Paul's predominantly Gentile churches there was a growing tendency to replace the Jerusalem Temple as the dwelling place of God with the Christian community as the real Temple, the real dwelling place of God (1 Cor 3:16-17; 6:19; 2 Cor 6:16; Eph 2:21), a tendency that is probably rooted in Paul's identification of the church as the body of Christ. Even in the Petrine churches, the identification of the church as the spiritual temple was made (1 Pet 2:4-5), and in the Johannine literature the identification of the person of Jesus as the manner in which God became flesh, manifested God's glory (doxa δόξα) and "tented" (skēnoō σκηνόω) among us (John 1:14), underscores the extent to which Jesus replaced the Jerusalem Temple for the Johannine churches as the symbol of divine presence among humankind. This tendency to favor the person of Jesus and the community of his followers may have been accelerated by a growing alienation between the Jewish Christian community and the Temple authorities that may have eventually led to an exclusion of the Christian community from the sacrificial worship of the Temple (Heb 13:10-16).

Indications of this shift in perspective are embedded in the Gospel accounts of the omens that accompanied the death of Jesus on the cross. All three Synoptic Gospels report that at the moment of Jesus' death the VEIL OF THE TEMPLE was split from top to bottom (Matt 27:51; Mark 15:38; Luke 23:45). None of these accounts make clear whether this was the veil between the vestibule and the nave or the veil between the nave and the inner shrine, but the author of Hebrews appears to interpret the tradition as referring to the veil leading into the inner shrine. Jesus as the new high priest has opened the way into the inner shrine and thus into the presence of God for his followers (Heb 6:19-20; 10:19-20), and this change, for the author of Hebrews, clearly marks the replacement of the old Temple, the old altar, and the old priesthood for the followers of Jesus, who are to join their leader outside the present Jerusalem and its earthly Temple (Heb 13:10-16). In a similar fashion the author of Ephesians devalues the Jerusalem Temple. According to this writer, the old partition wall in the Jerusalem Temple that separated Gentile and Jewish worshipers and prevented the Gentiles from going farther into the temple complex with their Jewish brothers has been broken down by the death of Jesus Christ (Eph 2:14-22). In the person of Jesus Christ a new Temple is in the process of being formed in which the old hostility between Jew and Gentile has been forever dissolved, and the two are becoming one holy people as the new dwelling place for God.

In some ways this development is best captured in John's reworking of Ezek 40–47, in his marvelous vision of the New Jerusalem in Rev 21–22. The vision is obviously based on the vision of Ezekiel, from which John borrows extensively, particularly in the description of the river of the water of life, which flows from the throne of God and the lamb (Rev 22:1-2; compare Ezek 47:1-12). Nonetheless, in contrast to Ezekiel's vision, in John's vision of the New Jerusalem there is no Temple (Rev 21:22). There is no Temple, because the Temple is a way of symbolizing God's presence among his people, and in this New Jerusalem such a symbol is replaced by the real presence of God and the Lamb. Jesus the human incarnation of God will be there ruling in the midst of God's people as their king. In the presence of the real, all mere hypostatic representations or symbolizations of God's presence—name, glory, Temple, whatever—will have lost their relevance.

Bibliography: Menahem Haran. *Temples and Temple Service in Ancient Israel* (1985); Victor (Avigdor) Hurowitz. *I Have Built You an Exalted House: Temple Building in the Bible in Light of Mesopotamian and Northwest Semitic Writings* (1992); Benjamin Mazar. *The Mountain of the Lord* (1975); John Michael Monson. "The New 'Ain Dara Temple, Closest Solomonic Parallel." *BAR* 26 (1999) 20–35, 67; J. J. M. Roberts. "The Theological Significance of the Visual Elements in Isaiah's Vision in Isaiah 6." *From Babel to Babylon: Essays on Biblical History and Literature in Honour of Brian Peckam.* Joyce Rilett Wood, John E. Harvey, and Mark Leuchter, eds. (2006) 197–213; J. J. M. Roberts. "Yahweh's Foundation in Zion (Isa 28:16)." *JBL* 106 (1987) 27–45; J. Simons. *Jerusalem in the Old Testament: Researches and Theories* (1952);

L. E. Stager. "Jerusalem and the Garden of Eden." *ErIsr* 26 (1999) 183–194.

J. J. M. ROBERTS

TEMPLES, HEROD'S. Herod the Great (ca. 73 BCE–4 BCE) built many temples throughout the eastern Mediterranean. In some cases, these were rebuilds of old temples as at Rhodes where he reconstructed the fire-damaged temple to Pythian Apollo. Sometimes Herod contributed to the completion of an ongoing temple project such as in the case of the temple to the Olympian Zeus in Athens. The temples he constructed at Tyre and Berytus were part of a larger rebuilding of those cities in the Roman style (Josephus, *J.W.* 1.422).

Since Octavian had presented Herod with the city of Samaria after the battle of Actium, Herod seized the occasion of the Senate's conferral of the title "Augustus" to Octavian in 27 BCE to dedicate a rebuilt Samaria to his patron. By 22 BCE, the new city, now called Sebaste (Greek for *Augustus*), was complete. In addition to a stadium, a forum, and a wall around the city, Herod had provided its citizens with a new temple to Augustus, a temple built in the elevated Italian style and integrated with a peristyle court on a large artificial platform. Many of these same ideas would reappear in Herod's reconstruction of the temples in Jerusalem and Caesarea.

In gratitude for Augustus' trip to Syria (20 BCE), Herod built another temple to Augustus at either Banias or the nearby site of Horbat Omrit, where monumental architectural remains from the 1st cent. have been discovered. This temple served as an entrance to the venerable grotto of Pan and was constructed of white stone (imported marble; Josephus, *J.W.* 1.404–406; *Ant.* 15.363–64). A coin of Herod's son Philipp, dating to 8/9 CE, bears on its reverse side the representation of a tetrastyle shrine that may be Herod's temple to Augustus.

Although Herod had no qualms about building temples to Apollo, Roma, and Augustus, he considered himself a Jew and reserved his grandest effort for his temple in Jerusalem. Little remains of this construction now except for retaining walls around the enlarged temple platform and associated structures. A visitor can still see vestiges of a double and triple gate on the south face of this wall, springers for an arch on the southwest corner (Robinson's Arch), and Wilson's Arch, some 200 m north of Robinson's Arch on the western retaining wall. Excavations next to the southwestern and southern wall faces have revealed a monumental staircase of thirty steps leading up to the gates on the southern wall. An ancient worshiper would enter these gates into underground vaulted walkways that ascended through the Huldah Gates to the large temple plaza where one could see the porticos surrounding the esplanade and view the sanctuary itself. The sanctuary rose above walls that delineated the courts of the temple plaza allotted to Gentiles, to (Jewish) women, and to (Jewish) men. In front of the sanctuary stood the altar where the daily sacrifices burned. Excavations in the Tyropoeon Valley have revealed broken decorations and architectural fragments that continue to allow scholarly reconstruction of Herod's Jerusalem temple. *See* TEMPLE, JERUSALEM.

Arguably, Herod's last temple was the temple to Roma and Augustus in his own capital city of CAESAREA MARITIMA, dedicated 10/9 BCE. The Combined Caesarea Expeditions under the direction of K. G. Holum have succeeded in finding the massive foundation of this temple on an artificial platform above the harbor. In many ways, this temple was like the first temple to Augustus in Samaria. Constructed of local stone on an artificial platform, the facade that faced the sea was some 30 m in length, while its depth was twice that. A monumental staircase descended to the harbor just as its sister structure at Samaria had featured a similar monumental staircase. Although none of the columns are still in place at Caesarea, excavation and chance finds have brought to light column drums and capitals of local kurkar stone. According to Josephus, the structure towered so high that sailors could see it and the giant statues of Roma and Caesar within it "a great way out" on their way into the port (*Ant.* 15.339). *See* CAESAREA PHILIPPI; HEROD, FAMILY; RHODES; SAMARIA.

Bibliography: Lisa C. Kahn. "King Herod's Temple of Roma and Augustus at Caesarea Maritima." *Caesarea Maritima: A Retrospective after Two Millennia.* Avner Raban and Kenneth G. Holum, eds. (1996) 130–45; Peter Richardson. *Herod: King of the Jews and Friend of the Romans* (1996); Duane W. Roller. *The Building Program of Herod the Great* (1998).

FRED L. HORTON

TEMPLES, LEONTOPOLIS AND ELEPHANTINE. Deuteronomy 12:13-28 says there is to be only one Temple, in Jerusalem. But during the Second Temple period (538 BCE–70 CE), there were two Jewish temples in Egypt. The older, located at the southern border of Egypt (near modern-day Aswan), was on the island of Elephantine. The other, located in the eastern portion of the Nile delta, was in the region of Heliopolis, perhaps in Leontopolis.

The history of the Elephantine military colony is known from papyri documents and archaeological excavations (*see* ELEPHANTINE PAPYRI). When Jews first settled in Elephantine is unclear, but many Judeans fled the Babylonian army (around 586 BCE), escaping to Egypt (2 Kgs 25:26; Jer 42–43); some of these may have gone to Elephantine. The papyri suggest that the Jewish soldiers built a temple by 525 BCE.

Archaeologists have discovered what they believe to be the Elephantine Jewish temple, but because the Nile eroded the western portions of the island, its exact length is uncertain. The 6 m by 16 m(?) temple was located off-center in a 23 m by 40 m(?) courtyard. An altar for burnt offerings stood west of the temple, but its exact location is unknown. The temple probably had two chambers. It was not built in imitation of the Jerusalem Temple as described by 1 Kgs 6 and 2 Chr 3. Rather, it more closely resembled the description of the TABERNACLE in Exod 25–27. The walls of the temple and its courtyard were constructed of mud-brick with stone doorways. The temple's roof was made of cedar beams, covered with reeds and a layer of mud-plaster.

In 410, the temple was destroyed by the priests of the Egyptian god Khnum, who bribed a Persian official. The reason for the destruction is unclear, but two possibilities have been suggested: 1) since Jews slaughtered rams, they may have offended the Egyptians, since rams were sacred to Khnum; 2) the Khnum sanctuary expanded at this time, requiring moving the courtyard wall of the Jewish sanctuary. During the demolition, the priests and soldiers opportunistically looted and burned the Jewish temple.

The Elephantine Jews wrote to the high priest in Jerusalem, asking for his help. Receiving no response, they then wrote to the governors of Judea and Samaria, who gave them permission to rebuild their temple. Interestingly, the governors did not give them permission to resume animal sacrifice, either for fear of offending the Egyptians or perhaps because they thought that, while incense and meal offerings could be made elsewhere (Mal 1:11), animal sacrifice was limited to Jerusalem. The temple was rebuilt before 402.

The last document from Elephantine is dated to 399 BCE. What happened to the community after this period is unknown. At some point, the temple was turned into a stable, since archaeologists found its tiled floor covered in animal dung, possibly a deliberate desecration.

The temple in Heliopolis is known from the Jewish historian Josephus, but the accounts he provides in *Jewish War* and *Jewish Antiquities* differ substantially. Where the temple was located precisely is unknown, but traditionally scholars said it was in Leontopolis. The temple was built by Onias IV, the nephew of the high priest Jason mentioned in 2 Macc 3–5, sometime between 163 and 145 BCE. Ptolemy VI Philometor gave Onias land in Heliopolis because the region already had a significant Jewish population and may have been a military colony.

The appearance of the temple is uncertain. Sometimes Josephus says the temple was modeled on the Jerusalem Temple (*J.W.* 1.33; *Ant.* 12.388; 13:63, 67, 285; 20.20.236), but in other places, he describes it as a tower of large stones different from the Temple in Jerusalem (*J.W.* 7.427) as well as being smaller and poorer (*Ant.* 13.72). Hence, its appearance is unclear.

The temple continued to function until Vespasian ordered it to be closed in 73 CE. Interestingly, its importance seems limited: it is not mentioned by Philo of Alexandria or other Jewish literature from Egypt. Egyptian Jews made pilgrimages to Jerusalem and worshiped locally in synagogues, known as "prayer-houses." Thus, Egyptian Jews do not seem to have revered Onias' temple.

Bibliography: G. Bohak. *Joseph and Aseneth and the Jewish Temple in Heliopolis* (1996); J. Jörg Frey. "Temple and Rival Temple–The Cases of Elephantine, Mt. Gerizim, and Leontopolis." *Gemeinde Ohne Temel, Community Without Temple.* B. Ego, A. Lange, and P. Pilhofer, eds. (1999) 171–203; S. G. Rosenberg. "The Jewish Temple at Elephantine." *NEA* 67 (2004) 4–13.

ADAM L. PORTER

TEMPLES, SEMITIC. This article is concerned with the temples of the ANE that relate to the Jerusalem Temple of Solomon. There is some mention of the desert TABERNACLE and the postexilic temple of Zerubbabel.

A. Definitions
B. Sacred Space
C. The Architecture of the Ancient Temples
D. Architectural Parallels
E. Architectural Typology of Temples
F. Temple Furnishings
Bibliography

A. Definitions

The following definitions reflect the usage of archaeologists and students of the Bible for several words associated with temple and religious worship in ancient Israel. There is no precise agreement on some of the meanings and the definitions below are approximations of common usage.

The term *temple* (Hebrew **hekhal** [הֵיכָל], or **beth** [בֵּית]) is usually used for a large, public building, often located in a high, prominent position in the settlement. The size of the structure can depend on the status of the deity or deities. Major temples are often in prominent locations and may be situated within enclosures. Sometimes they include exterior altars of sacrifice; large altars (at least 7 ft. [2 m] on a side) could accommodate the burning of complete animals, while smaller altars (usually around 3 ft. [1 m] on a side) would be used for animal parts or fruit and grain offerings (first fruits). Sometimes there was also a small pit or basin for libations. Some altars were not intended for sacrifices, but were meant to hold offerings in kind to be presented to the god, thus a "presentation altar." Or a temple could contain a podium for an iconic representation of the deity with nearby benches for votive gifts. Examples include the single stone presentation altar from the Iron I period at Tall al-ʿUmayri in Jordan; it was found about 60 cm in front of a standing stone that probably symbolized a deity; because it was from the time of the judges, it is reminiscent of the story of Micah in Judg 17. Benches around the inner room of a temple were found at the Iron II Arad temple; they lined the sides of the room beside the cultic niche that contained two standing stones.

The Hebrew word **bamah** (בָּמָה), usually translated "high place," refers to informal enclosures where sacrifices were offered. They were very frequent during the time of the judges and such esteemed men of God as Samuel were considered essential at such places of worship (see 1 Sam 9, for instance). Solomon received his wisdom vision at the high place of Gibeon (1 Kgs 3:4-5). Later on, high places were condemned by the Deuteronomistic Historians and were apparently destroyed as part of the centralizing reforms of Hezekiah and Josiah.

The word *sanctuary* is used in a more general way to refer to any type of sacred building or enclosure. Some authors use the word to refer to small structures that seem to carry some temple functions, but are not monumental enough to be termed "temples." Among students of the Bible, the term is often used for the desert "tabernacle" or sacred tent. Neither term, however, carries sufficiently precise architectural meanings to be used in archaeological discussions. The term *cult* is often used with other terms, such as "cultic niche," "cultic enclosure," "cultic corner," or "cultic features," to refer to informal objects or architectural spaces that seem to have religious significance. The term does not carry the modern connotation of strange, non-establishment religious groups.

The term *shrine* is used for small spaces within other buildings or small areas within a settlement dedicated to religious purposes. There is usually some focal point dedicated to a deity or deities and sufficient space for a worshiper to perform informal rituals and, perhaps, leave a small offering. Archaeological excavations often find them in city gates, such as the gates of Dan, Bethsaida, and Tirzeh (Tell el-Far'ah).

B. Sacred Space

In the OT the Temple is called the "house of Yahweh" (beth yhwh בֵּית יהוה), as in 1 Kgs 6:37. Other words often associated with God in his temple include *dwelling*, *place*, and "house of God," among others. The Temple is thus understood to be God's house on earth. But, although the Deuteronomistic Historian approved centralizing reforms by Hezekiah and Josiah that destroyed all places of worship except the Jerusalem Temple, in the early periods God was not limited to just one house. After Jacob saw his vision of the angels ascending and descending the ladder, he named the place Bethel ("house of El" or "house of God"), reflecting the biblical understanding that where God is present on earth, there is his house (Gen 28). There was also an Iron I temple in Shechem during the time of one of Gideon's sons, Abimelech (Judg 9:46). There were also many high places frequented by Samuel (1 Sam 9, for instance).

As a microcosm of God's heavenly abode, the Temple and its rituals mirror the function of God's activities in heaven. Moreover, in 1 Sam 7, the account of the establishment of the Davidic covenant, David and Nathan

Madaba Plains Project
Figure 1: A standing stone, suggesting a religious function for at least part of the house in Field A, Tall al-'Umayri, Jordan.

assume that God wants to dwell in houses similar to those of his people. Whereas God dwelt in a tent during the early days of Israel's wilderness experience and the time of the judges, now that the monarchy was established and the king (and his people) lived in stone houses, they assumed God would want a new dwelling made of stone and cedar.

Because the "glory" of God was too great for many humans to bear directly, walls were necessary to separate the "holy" from the profane. In the OT there was a strong awareness that finding oneself too close to God could be risky (Gen 32:33, for instance). Thus Israelites were enjoined to "fear God." Yes, God brought blessings, but he was also the bringer of evil (judgment) in hundreds of texts. For this reason, his earthly abode hid his overwhelming glory from view. Only the high priest was allowed into his personal space once a year on the Day of Atonement. Even then, there was an element of risk (Exod 28:34-35).

The Temple was thus not a place where normal worshipers entered. It was God's space. Temple services were conducted outside in the courtyard, primarily at the altar or in other, related spaces where small-group or private rituals could be conducted. The sounds and smells of animals dying, burning fat, oil, and grain would have accompanied prayers and songs sung in groups here and there. Large-scale communal worship probably did not occur every day and, even then, was concerned more with sacrificial rituals than with communal readings.

These aspects of Israelite cult and practice were probably more or less true for the other people groups surrounding them. These nations, too, established sacred space, offered sacrifices, brought offerings, prayed, and sang to their gods in similar ways as ancient Israel (see the MESHA Inscription and the religious texts from Ugarit). Throughout the ANE, once a place was made holy by the presence of a divinity, it often remained so throughout centuries, even when people groups and deities changed. The biblical Israelite temple compound is now a major Islamic holy area, the Haram esh-Sharif.

C. The Architecture of the Ancient Temples

The description of the Jerusalem Temple in 1 Kgs 6 and 7 is the fullest description of sacred architecture in any ancient literary source. The architectural similarities with other contemporary temples can be related to this description. The plan of the Jerusalem Temple was a basic two-room plan with a porch. The Temple was actually part of Solomon's palace complex. Worshipers had to pass through the palace compound before entering the temple area. Such a relationship was a constant reminder to the people that the Davidic king was the anointed representative of God on earth.

Any discussion of temple architecture must take into account the use of Phoenician architects and craftsmen (1 Kgs 5) who worked on the Temple and its associated features. Israelites had never worked at this level of architecture and decoration before. It is fair, therefore, to assume that some element of Phoenician style was present in the final product. See TEMPLE, JERUSALEM for a full description of the Temple.

D. Architectural Parallels

The closest parallel to the architectural plan of the Temple was discovered at Tell Tayinat in Syria. It, too, was annexed to a palace complex (for a plan, see King and Stager 2001). Like the description of the Jerusalem Temple in the Bible, this temple was a long building with three rooms in proportions similar to the Jerusalem Temple. The portico contained two pillars at the entrance, the outer room was longer than it was wide, but the inner room was not a square (the remains do not extend high enough to tell us about its height). It was also somewhat smaller than the Jerusalem Temple (about 25 m or 80 ft. long).

A second parallel is the temple at 'Ain Dara', especially noted here for its decorative parallels (King and Stager 2001). Although the room proportions were not similar to the Jerusalem Temple and the inner room was separated from the outer room only by a raised portion of the floor, there was a portico with two pillars and two ritual rooms. A stairway ascended to the portico; narrow storerooms surrounded the building on its sides and back; the storerooms contained a method of

supporting multiple stories; cherubs lined the lower portions of the walls; door frames and false windows are recessed; from huge footprints on the thresholds it seems that the deity was conceptualized to be very large (Ezek 40); and, based on the orientation of the footprints, the deity entered the building from the east, similar to God in Ezek 40:43.

Within a fortress at Arad in the northern Negev east of Beer-sheba, archaeologists discovered a small temple that seems to have been dedicated to Yahweh. At least, it was Judean as the names and script on over a hundred ostraca testify. But its plan is nothing like that of the Jerusalem Temple. The courtyard was very small; the altar was large enough only to burn small sacrifices; there was no stairway approaching the entrance; there was no portico and no Jachin and Boaz; the outer room was broad instead of long; the inner room was an elevated niche; and instead of two cherubs in the inner room, there were two standing stones. This was obviously a much more informal building for religious rituals than the Jerusalem Temple. It may have been dedicated to a more popular level of Israel's religion venerating both Yahweh and Asherah as the two standing stones seem to suggest (see Zevit 2001; Dever 2005).

A second structure at Dan may have supported a small temple. Indeed, it may have contained the young golden bull set up by Jeroboam I mentioned in 1 Kgs 12:28-29. It was a small platform approached by a monumental stairway, but the traces of walls on the top of the platform were not clear enough to suggest a plan for the building. It probably was a temple because there were signs of an altar in front of the platform near the bottom of the stairway, and rooms along the side of the courtyard contained cultic objects and small altars (see King and Stager 2001 for an artist's rendering). One of the sources of the Jordan rises near the structure and many ancient temples and shrines are located at heads of rivers. Excavations have not gone below the Iron II period here, but earlier holy precincts may have existed at such a site.

A third temple has recently been discovered east of the Dead Sea at Ataruz in the Israelite territory conquered by MESHA, according to the Mesha Inscription (personal communication from Chang-Ho Ji). Although as yet unpublished, the excavator (Ji) has shown this author a long room oriented east to west with a platform at the western side. The platform contains a standing stone and perhaps room for a second one. A few cultic furnishings were found on the floor. The excavator suggests the pottery found in the room dates to the 9th cent. BCE.

E. Architectural Typology of Temples

Like anything connected with human beings, architectural styles of temples developed over time. In this section we will look at how Semitic temples changed through time, noting how the desert tabernacle and the Jerusalem Temple fit into this continuum. In order for the symbolism of temple architecture and decoration to be meaningful to the ancient Israelite, it was necessary for these structures to correspond to other religious buildings and symbols in recognizable ways. Put simply, in order to call a building a temple, people had to recognize it as a temple.

The following is a quick summary of temple structures and plans through time as archaeologists have discovered them in the Holy Land.

Because temples were considered to be houses of the gods, the earliest examples looked like houses, but, as they developed, this similarity disappeared. The earliest probable examples of temples are two pre-pottery Neolithic buildings at ʿAin Ghazal dating to around 6000 BCE. Both were broad rooms (that is, upon entering the room one would perceive a wide room) with a platform opposite the door and a stone-lined pit, possibly for libations. The large temple complex at En Gedi from the Chalcolithic period (ca. 4500–3200 BCE) was a very long broad room with benches along the walls for offerings. Similar buildings were found at Ghassul and Gilat, though they were not as well preserved.

The house-like feature continued into the early stages of the Early Bronze Age (ca. 3200–2000), but began to develop more monumental aspects part way through. The long broad room of the Chalcolithic temples gradually shrank to a narrower broad room during Early Bronze I–III (ca. 3200–2300 BCE) at sites like Megiddo Stratum 19, Hartuv, Ai, the White Building at Yarmut, and the twin temples at Arad. A single line of pillars often supported the roof. During Early Bronze II–III some structures became more monumental still, narrowing the broad room even more and sometimes adding a portico in front, such as Megiddo Stratum 15 temples 4040, 5192, and 5269, all grouped together into a triad. Two very similar temples were also discovered at Zayraqun near Irbid in Jordan. In fact, both temple complexes, dated to Early Bronze III, also contained large circular stone sacrificial altars. Thus, during the Early Bronze Age, the breadth of the broad rooms was narrowing and, near the end of the period, porticos could be added at the front. In all of them, platforms, probably to hold symbols or icons of the god, generally occurred opposite the doorway.

During the Middle Bronze Age (ca. 2000–1550 BCE), the portico occurred more often, even developing into a second anteroom toward the end of the period, such as the Area H temple at Hazor, the Area F double temple at Hazor, possibly Haror, Shechem "Temple 7300" (though access may have been limited from an adjacent "palace"), Givʿat Sharett, Kitan, and possibly the gate sanctuary at Ashkelon complete with its ceramic shrine and bronze bull. The development was, however, not uniform during this stage. Early examples could contain pillared broad rooms with no porch, such as at Nahariya. A brand-new type of temple with very thick walls (called a **mighdal** [מִגְדָּל] or "fortress" temple because of the massive walls) began at several sites during

this period. Excavations have discovered them on the upper city of Hazor, Hayyat, Shechem, and Kitan.

Several of the Middle Bronze temples continued into the Late Bronze Age (ca. 1550–1200 BCE) with little or no change. However, by this time the two-room plan had become standard, such as the Lachish Acropolis temple, the Stratum 7 temple at Beth-shan, possibly the Area F double temple at Hazor, the Area H temple at Hazor, possibly Abu Hawam, Kitan, and possibly ʿUmayri. It is interesting that the desert tabernacle, which Bible writers dated to this period, was also a two-room structure. Sometime toward the end of the period, a third room was added, this time with two columns flanking the entrance as in the Area H temple at Hazor. Fortress temples also continued to exist at Hazor and Shechem, while new ones were built at Megiddo temple 2048 and Pella. Different types of temples were built, perhaps representing the international communities moving to Canaan at this time (Egyptians, Hittites, possibly Hurrians, etc.), such as the Fosse temple at Lachish, the Stratum R3 temple at Beth-shan, Mevorakh, Deir ʿAlla, and Timnaʿ. The Amman Airport structure, called a "temple" by early discoverers, was most likely not a temple. It was a square building probably dedicated to funerary rites.

The numbers of temples dropped off significantly during the early Iron Age (ca. 1200–1000 BCE). Although already beginning at the end of the Late Bronze Age, two-room temples now often added a portico or entrance room at the front (sometimes with two pillars at the entrance), such as Beth-shan Strata 6 and 5 and possibly Jaffa. Fortress temples also continued into the Iron I period at Megiddo, Shechem, and Pella. A different type of temple, probably connected with Philistine worship, seems to have been dedicated to three deities at Miqne. Another Philistine temple was at Qasile. We should note that the plan of the Jerusalem Temple was very similar to those dated to the end of the Late Bronze Age and the Iron I period—two rooms with a portico flanked by two columns. This plan was fundamentally different than that of the desert tabernacle, but represented developments in temple plan that had occurred between their respective constructions. Thus the Jerusalem Temple tended to conform (loosely) to reasonably recent developments and should be considered part of the continuum of temple architecture.

We have already mentioned the two Iron II temples at Arad (Judah) and Dan (Israel). Another possible example, though so far not clearly established, was at Qedesh in the Jezreel Valley. Other temples from this period were probably not Israelite, and they could take on different plans. A Philistine temple was uncovered at Miqne (King and Stager 2001) in the 1990s, while a Moabite (or Israelite according to the excavator) example has very recently been discovered at Ataruz south of Madaba. All these temples were fundamentally single long-room structures with a platform at one end. The two other temples were both Edomite.

One, at Busayra, the capital city of the Edomites, seems to have been influenced by Assyrian forms, while the other, at Qitmit, was in western Edom and was probably dedicated to three deities. We should also mention two single room shrines found recently, one in Moab at Mudayna Thamad and another in Edom at Hazeva in the Arabah, but these were not "temples."

The only Persian temple known so far outside Jerusalem was the "Solar Shrine" at Lachish. It seems to have continued into the Hellenistic period.

F. Temple Furnishings

Until recently, artists and biblical students who have tried to reconstruct the design of the Temple and its furnishings based their ideas on the verbal descriptions in 1 Kgs 6–8, using also a healthy dose of imagination. But archaeological finds and heightened linguistic insights over the past eighty years (and especially the last fifty) have given us a much better starting point for our reproductions. For instance, now that scores of cherubs have been found in paintings and sculptures from the ancient world, we know that they are composite beings, as described above, not the usual post-medieval human forms with wings depicted in so many artistic renderings.

In the courtyard, the altar of sacrifice was the focal point (1 Kgs 8:22). It is not described in 1 Kings, but it is mentioned in several stories of the Bible and seems to have been changed from time to time (2 Kgs 16:10). The pre-Solomonic altar, which seems to have been reused in the early stages of the Jerusalem Temple, apparently had horns at the corners similar to the altar found at Beer-sheba. First Kings 1:51 and 2:28 describe Adonijah and Joab respectively grasping the horns of the altar claiming protection. From 1 Kgs 8:65 we learn that it was made of bronze and that it was too small to offer complete animals as sacrifices. A small altar like this was found in the temple at Arad. Undoubtedly, a larger one to handle whole sacrifices was soon constructed, perhaps mentioned in 1 Kgs 9:25 where it says Solomon built it. This large altar probably had stairs leading to the top so the fires could be built and the animals brought to the top.

Also in the courtyard was the huge bronze sea, the work of Hiram the Phoenician. It was 10 cubits (5 m or 15 ft.) in diameter, was decorated with gourds, and stood upon twelve bronze oxen, three together on a side. Unfortunately, we have no parallels or artistic renditions of this item. Because multiple sacrifices could be taking place at the same time, there were ten bronze, wheeled mobile stands with lavers to bring water from the "sea" to the location of any sacrifice. The stand was decorated with cherubs, lions, and oxen (1 Kgs 7:29). At Larnaca in Cyprus, an almost identical bronze, wheeled stand decorated with cherubs was found (Keel 1997). Spoked wheels, most likely from a similar stand, were found at Miqne (King and Stager 2001). The water would have been used to clean up the blood at the location of the sacrifices and, if hot, to help remove the wool from the dead animal.

Many other items were used for the sacrificial ceremonies. Shovels were used to carry burning coals from a central fire to the incense altars. Once the coals were in place ground frankincense or myrrh could be sprinkled on top to give off the smoke. Coals could also be carried to light the sacrificial fires. Shovels have been found in several locations. Three were found in a side room of the Dan temple (King and Stager 2001). A long handle of about 40 cm (ca. 15 in.) was attached to a rectangular bowl about 7–10 cm long (ca. 3–4 in.). Bronze bowls, some more highly decorated than others, have been found at many sites. The bowls could have been used with the water and sacrifices, or to hold food offerings to God, or to contain food eaten by worshipers at feasts similar to the marzeakh (מַרְזֵחַ) described in Amos 6:7 and Jer 16:5, and possibly the feast in Judg 9:27.

Sacrifices were not the only activities that went on in the courtyard. It was a general meeting place, as well, where people heard speeches and proclamations. Forms of divination undoubtedly occurred, though they could occur elsewhere, too. But where God was close was an ideal place to discover his will. The Bible often speaks of "casting lots" or "consulting the Lord." There were many different ways to do this in the ancient world, from consulting sheep livers to consulting the URIM AND THUMMIM on the high priest's breastplate. Almost every site has produced astragali (slightly altered knuckle bones of sheep or goats) that could be used like dice today, either in games or divination. Several dice, looking much like modern ones, were found at Dan.

When we leave the courtyard, we proceed from the world of people into the "private" space of God. The portico, flanked by the massive, highly decorated columns and capitals of Jachin and Boaz, each a total of about 23 cubits high (ca. 11.5 m or 35 ft.) and almost 4 cubits in diameter (ca. 2 m or 6 ft.), was a transitional zone to the outer room, or the Holy Place. Here were the items, which only the priests attended in their service of Yahweh. Although other ANE temples were seen as places where the gods were fed, Yahweh never seems to consume his sacrifices or offerings as food (though he does describe some of them as a "sweet smelling savor").

Inside the Holy Place was the gilded furniture of Yahweh's house: an altar probably for incense, a table for bread, and ten lampstands. Incense altars from the ancient world came in three basic shapes. One was a solid rectangular stone standing on end with a shallow bowl and often with horns at the corners. Two of these types stood before the inner niche in the temple of Arad. Scores of these altars were found at Miqne in industrial settings. They were thus not limited to temples in the Philistine world. A second type was a simple or decorated bowl placed on top of a ceramic stand, sometimes decorated. The third type was a bowl perched atop a long, narrow stone column-like stand, sometimes turned on a lathe. An example of this kind was found at a shrine in Moab at Mudayna Thamad. Coals were put in the bowl and ground frankincense and/or myrrh were sprinkled on top to give off smoke. Tongs and shovels would have been used to work the coals. Like the incense altars at Arad, these may have been placed near the entrance into the Most Holy Place.

Tables must have been common features in ancient houses, but, because they were normally made of wood, are not usually preserved archaeologically. Artistic depictions show them as rather small, often simple slabs balanced atop a single stand. A low table was found in a Middle Bronze Age tomb at Jericho that had three legs so it could rest on uneven ground without rocking or tipping. The bread itself was probably flat bread, something like modern pita. It could be baked quickly, using little fuel, but it also dried out quickly. Stacks of flat bread standing on end are depicted on small tables in Egyptian tombs of the Old Kingdom. The table in the Temple may have symbolized feasting and hospitality, as it would have done in most Israelite houses. The ancient values of hospitality were very strong (Gen 19; Judg 19–20) and the metaphor of God as an enthusiastic host follows the metaphor of God as the loving shepherd in Ps 23, in whose house, the psalmist concludes, he wants to dwell all the days of his life.

Potters made ancient lamps as bowls and then, when the clay was leather-hard, one side of it was squeezed into a nozzle. When the bowl was filled with oil a flax wick was laid into the oil and into the nozzle. The resulting flame was similar to that of a modern candle. Several ancient lamps with multiple nozzles have been found. At Tel Dan, the excavator found seven wick oil lamps in cultic contexts (Areas A and T) dating to Iron Age II.

On the other hand, the type of menorah we usually see in modern times is patterned after the lampstand carved into the decorations on the Arch of Titus in Rome, commemorating that general's conquest of Jerusalem in 70 CE. However, forms such as this were not known in the Iron Age. Instead, notes Carol Meyers (1976), the lamp was probably a single lamp with seven nozzles. According to Meyers, this single lamp probably sat on top of the central pole of the lampstand. It obviously symbolized the fullness of light with its seven flames.

But the lampstand also symbolized life with its six tree branches radiating off the central pole, the seventh "branch." Images of the tree of life abound in the ANE world like no other iconographic motif. It seems to have been a symbol of Asherah, one of the goddesses of fertility, as she feeds animals (often symbolized by goats), but was not limited to her. The images of light and life are thus combined in the symbolism of this piece of furniture.

In the inner room, the Most Holy Place, were two large gilded cherubs with their wings touching the walls of the room. As mentioned above, cherubs were ubiquitous in ancient art and statuary, usually in groups of two. They were seen as guardian beings flanking access to the object being guarded. Indeed, that was their primary function in the Bible, as well, where one pair guarded the entrance to the Garden of Eden after the God removed Adam and Eve and, in the Temple, they guarded the approach to God's Most Holy Place. In the ANE they often appear flanking doorways into temples and palaces or at the sides of royal thrones.

It is clear that these large cherubs stood guard over the ark of God, located between the cherubs. The construction of the "ark," which means "box" in Hebrew, is described in Exod 25. It was the box that held the law of God and was seen as the focal point of his presence and power, symbolizing theologically the human relationship with God through the law. More than simply guardians, cherubs seem to have been an iconographic symbol of Yahweh, as well. They are a ubiquitous artistic motif in the temple, and they may be associated with Yahweh on a highly decorated incense stand found at Taanach (the second tier from the bottom).

The ark also appears to have been visualized as the seat or throne of God. But we should not make too much of some translations that connect a "mercy seat" with the ark. The Hebrew word unfortunately translated "mercy seat" really means simply "covering"; that is, it is the lid of the box. However, God seems to rule and direct his power from the ark, much like a king rules from his throne. In the psalms, God is often described as "enthroned" (Ps 29:10, for instance). It is probably in this aspect that the cherubs were placed on the lid of the ark. A small sculpture found in Cyprus at Ayia Irini may suggest a correction from popular modern depictions of just how the ark looked. A king sits upon a throne with his feet upon a footstool (compare this with Yahweh's footstool in Isa 66:1). Two cherubs flank the throne, each having a pair of wings, though in this example they are somewhat fragmentary. The inner wings of both cherubs curve up and behind the king forming the back of the throne. The only way in which this cherub-throne differs from the ark as described in Exod 25 is that the faces of the cherubs do not face each other. It may very well be, then, that the heads of the cherubs on the ark were simply turned to face each other. *See* ARTEMIS; BETHEL, SHRINE; CORINTH; GIBEON, GIBEONITES; GILGAL; HIGH PLACE; MAMRE; OLYMPIAN ZEUS, TEMPLE OF; PILLAR; SAMARITANS; SHILOH, SHILOHNITE; ZEUS.

Bibliography: Avraham Biran, ed. *Temples and High Places in Biblical Times* (1981); J. Andrew Dearman. *Religion and Culture in Ancient Israel* (1992); William G. Dever. *Did God Have a Wife? Archaeology and Folk Religion in Ancient Israel* (2005); Barry M. Gittlen. *Sacred Time, Sacred Place: Archaeology and the Religion of Israel* (2002); Othmar Keel. *The Symbolism of the Biblical World* (1997); Philip J. King and Lawrence E. Stager. *Life in Biblical Israel* (2001); Carol Meyers. *The Tabernacle Menorah: A Synthetic Study of a Symbol from a Biblical Cult* (1976); Patrick D. Miller, Paul D. Hanson, and S. Dean McBride, eds. *Ancient Israelite Religion* (1987); Beth Alpert Nakhai. *Archaeology and the Religions of Canaan and Israel* (2001); Ziony Zevit. *The Religions of Ancient Israel: A Synthesis of Parallactic Approaches* (2001).

LARRY G. HERR

TEMPT, TEMPTATION [πειράζω peirazō, πειρασμός peirasmos]. Though the verb *tempt* (peirazō) and noun *temptation* (peirasmos) appear over 100 times in the biblical tradition, current English versions translate them most often with "test" not "tempt/ temptation." Of the fifty-plus uses in the NT, the NRSV translates just over ten as "tempt/temptation," several of which concern Jesus' temptation (*see* TEMPTATION OF JESUS).

The NT presents temptation as being enticed to sin, to be unfaithful to God's purposes. Believers can be enticed by their own desires (Jas 1:14), by the devil (1 Cor 7:5; 1 Thess 3:5), and by unspecified sources (Gal 6:1). James insists that God is not drawn to evil and "tempts no one" (1:13). Perhaps this dictum, along with context clues, influences the translation of the remaining references as "test" or "trial" (compare Matt 6:13, "do not bring us to the time of trial"). Here the emphasis is on discerning quality of commitment. God tests Abraham (Gen 22:1; Jdt 8:25-26; Heb 11:17), finding him faithful (1 Macc 2:52; Sir 44:20; Wis 3:5). God tests Israel in the wilderness (Wis 11:9-10) "to know what was in your heart whether or not you would keep his commandment" (Deut 8:2; compare Judg 2:22; 3:1, 4; 2 Chr 32:31), "whether you indeed love the Lord" (Deut 13:3; compare Exod 15:25-26; compare 16:4; 20:20; Heb 3:8-9). The psalmist prays for God to test his faithful living (Ps 26:2-3; compare Sir 2:1).

While God's testing of people is presented positively, the people's testing of God is generally negative. This testing is forbidden (Isa 7:12; Sir 18:23). Testing God in the wilderness (Exod 17:2, 7; Deut 33:8; Ps 95:9) disobeyed (Num 14:22) and "provoked" God, "rebelled against him" and "did not observe his decrees" (Ps 78:41, 56). They "put God to the proof though they had seen my work" (Ps 95:9; compare Jdt 8:12-13).

People test to discern themselves (Sir 37:27) and others. The queen of Sheba tests Solomon's knowledge (1 Kgs 10:1), the wicked test the righteous (Wis 2:17, 19), the influential test the lowly (Sir 13:11), wealth tests a person (Sir 31:10), tyrants test the faithful (4 Macc 9:7). One gains friends through testing (Sir 6:7) and tests people through conversation (Sir 27:5, 7).

In the Synoptic Gospels, Jesus' conflicts with Jewish leaders are identified as "tests" that pressure Jesus' faithfulness to God's will (Matt 16:1; 19:3; 22:18, 35; Mark 8:11; 10:2; 12:15; Luke 11:16). John lacks this motif but has Jesus testing Peter (John 6:6). Jesus warns

disciples about times of testing (Matt 6:13; 26:41; Mark 14:38; Luke 11:4; 22:40, 46). Other writings continue the negative references to testing the Spirit (Ananias and Sapphira, Acts 5:9), God (Acts 15:10), and Christ (1 Cor 10:9). Testing or discerning faithfulness remains a given for Christian existence (Jas 1:2; 1 Pet 1:6; 4:12; Rev 3:10). One tests oneself (2 Cor 13:5), Paul tests the Galatians (Gal 4:14), opponents test Paul (Acts 20:19), congregations test leaders (Rev 2:2), the devil tests believers (Rev 2:10). Some fall away in testing (Luke 8:13). Paul assures believers that God will not let them be tested beyond their strength but will empower them to endure (1 Cor 10:13). *See* LORD'S PRAYER.

WARREN CARTER

TEMPTATION OF JESUS. Accounts of Jesus' temptation or "testing" (*see* TEMPT, TEMPTATION) appear only in the three Synoptic Gospels (Matt 4:1-11; Mark 1:12-13; Luke 4:1-13). Though the devil instructs Jesus to do things Jesus accomplishes in his ministry (supply food, Matt 14:13-21; rule the world, Matt 28:18; Luke 1:33), Jesus refuses the devil's orders. The scenes follow God's identification of Jesus as God's son in the baptism (Matt 3:13-17//Mark 1:9-11//Luke 3:21-22). Jesus' refusal and the location of the scenes in the Gospel narratives highlight that this scene is not so much concerned with what Jesus does but with whether he will remain faithful to God's will. Will God or Satan authorize and determine his ministry? The scenes establish cosmic opposition to Jesus' ministry and present him as the reliable and faithful agent of God who carries out his God-given ministry in Rome's sociopolitical world, which is under the devil's control (Matt 4:8-9; Luke 2:1-3; 4:5-7).

Similarities in the Gospel accounts include duration (forty days [and nights, Matthew]), a wilderness location, the Spirit's leading of Jesus, and cosmic opposition from the devil. Mark's scene comprises only two verses (1:12-13), significantly shorter than in Matthew (4:1-11) and Luke (4:1-13).

While Mark refers to the adversary only as "Satan" and Luke only as "the devil," Matthew employs "devil," "tempter," and "Satan." Matthew and Luke include a threefold exchange of Scriptures between Jesus (citing Deut 6:13, 16; 8:3) and the adversary (citing Ps 91) that is absent from Mark. Yet Matthew (bread-Temple-empires) and Luke (bread-empires-Temple) present the elements in different order.

One detail unique to Mark—Jesus with the "wild beasts" (1:12)—echoes the temptation of Adam. Jesus the new Adam resists the devil and regains paradise by successfully remaining faithful to God, dwelling peaceably with the animals, and being served by angels.

Not absent from Mark, but more pronounced in Matthew and Luke, are echoes of Israel's testing in the wilderness. The previous baptismal scene recalls the parting of the sea (Exod 14). Both Jesus and Israel are divinely led in the wilderness for forty days/nights/

years (compare Deut 8:2, 4). The number forty recalls Moses' absence for forty days and nights on Mount Sinai to receive the commandments, the measure of Israel's faithfulness to God's will (Exod 24:18; 34:28). Both Jesus and Israel are identified as God's son (Exod 4:22-23; Jesus in the previous baptismal scene). Both encounter the Spirit (compare Isa 63:10). Jesus appeals to the wilderness experience—hunger (Deut 8:3), worship of God alone (Deut 6:4-15), not testing God's fidelity (Deut 6:16)—to reject the adversary's commands. In this context of similarities a significant difference emerges. Though the scenes recall Israel's wilderness experience, Jesus demonstrates faithfulness to God's purposes at the outset of his public activity.

While the Gospels focus on Jesus' faithfulness to God, Hebrews, the only other NT writing to reference Jesus' testing, twice presents it in solidarity with and as the basis for assistance to followers who are being tested (2:18; 4:15). *See* CHIEF, HIGH PRIEST; HOLY ONE; LAMB; LORD; MASTER, TITLE OF JESUS; RABBI, RABBONI; SATAN; SERVANT; SON OF DAVID; SON OF GOD; SON OF MAN.

WARREN CARTER

TEN. *See* NUMBERS, NUMBERING.

TEN COMMANDMENTS [עֲשֶׂרֶת הַדְּבָרִים 'asereth haddevarim]. Literally "the ten words" (Exod 34:28; Deut 4:13; 10:4), which is the source of the alternative designation "Decalogue." A body of divine instruction in the form of eight prohibitions and two positive commandments preceded by a brief self-presentation formula on the part of the deity: "I am the LORD your God, who brought you out of the land of Egypt, out of the house of slavery" (Exod 20:2; Deut 5:6).

The Ten Commandments appear in two versions, Exod 20:1-17, where they are the Lord's direct address to all the people of Israel at Mount Sinai after they have escaped from Egypt, and Deut 5:6-21, where the commandments are repeated, though not precisely in the same form as in Exod 20, this time by Moses on the plains of Moab prior to Israel's entering the land of Canaan. They are part of Moses' recollection and recapitulation of the journey through the wilderness from Sinai (known as Horeb in Deuteronomy) to the present moment.

A. Relation to Context
B. Order and Numeration
C. Literary and Redactional Features
D. Contents
  1. The Prologue (Exod 20:2//Deut 5:6)
  2. The First Commandment (Exod 20:3// Deut 5:7)
  3. The Second Commandment (Exod 20:4-6// Deut 5:8-10)
  4. The Third Commandment (Exod 20:7// Deut 5:11)
  5. The Fourth Commandment (Exod 20:8-11// Deut 5:12-15)
  6. The Fifth Commandment (Exod 20:12// Deut 5:16)
  7. The Sixth Commandment (Exod 20:13// Deut 5:17)
  8. The Seventh Commandment (Exod 20:14// Deut 5:18)
  9. The Eighth Commandment (Exod 20:15// Deut 5:19)
  10. The Ninth Commandment (Exod 20:16// Deut 5:20)
  11. The Tenth Commandment (Exod 20:17// Deut 5:21)
Bibliography

A. Relation to Context

In both instances the Commandments are identified as the direct address of God to the whole community, followed by but separated from further divine instruction mediated through Moses (Exod 20:21–Num 10:10; Deut 12–26). The reason for the shift to mediated divine communication is said to be the fear of the people that if they encounter the Lord face to face any further, they will surely die (Exod 20:18-20; Deut 5:22-33). The priority and foundational character of the Commandments relative to all the other divine instruction in the statutes and ordinances of Exod 20:22–Deut 26:19 is indicated by several features: 1) The Commandments are the only clearly explicit direct address of God to the people of Israel in the entire legal corpus; the rest of the law is presented as Moses' mediation of the Lord's teaching (Deut 4:13-14). 2) The Decalogue, unlike any other body of divine instruction, is repeated in two different biblical books. 3) In both versions the Commandments are placed prior to and separated from the rest of the law. 4) The Decalogue is described as having been written on stone tablets—thus permanent—by the finger of God—and so by divine authorship (Exod 31:18; 32:15-16; Deut 4:13; 9:10; 10:1-4). 5) The Commandments are equated with the covenant between God and Israel (Exod 31:18; 34:28-29; Deut 4:13-14; 9:11, 15). The rest of the law, therefore, is not simply further or additional law but a development of the basic guidelines in the Decalogue. The statutes and cases that follow in the rest of the TORAH or PENTATEUCH serve to explain, specify, and illustrate the meaning and effects of these guidelines.

The connection of the Commandments with the rest of the legal instruction is best seen in Deuteronomy. There a distinction is made between the "ten words" or "covenant," which the Lord "declared to you" and "charged you to observe," and the "statutes and ordinances," which "the LORD charged me (i.e., Moses) to teach you" (Deut 4:13-14; compare Exod 20:22; 34:32). The Mosaic teaching happens through Moses' sermonic instruction in chaps. 6–11 and in the teaching embodied in the Deuteronomic Code (chaps. 12–26), a collection of statutes and ordinances that seems to be organized thematically according to the sequence of the commandments (Braulik, Kaufman, Olson). After Moses' presentation of the law, that is, the Deuteronomic Code in chaps. 12–26, he instructs the Levites to place "this book (i.e., scroll) of the law" beside the ark of the covenant (Deut 31:24-26), in which the two stone tablets on which the Commandments were written were to be kept (Deut 10:1-5; compare Exod 25:16, 21; 1 Kgs 8:9). The Ten Commandments are called "the words of the covenant" (Exod 34:28), "the covenant" (Deut 4:13), and "the tablets of the covenant" (Deut 9:11, 15), providing at least one rationale for the title "ark of the covenant." This association of the Commandments with the covenant has received some further confirmation from extra-biblical data, as the Commandments in their context have been seen to have some analogy to and possibly a precedent in the suzerainty treaties of the ANE, especially of the Hittites (Mendenhall).

The Commandments are thus distinguished from but still closely associated with the statutes and ordinances found in the Book of the Covenant (Exod 20:22–23:33) and the Deuteronomic Code (Deut 12–26). In addition to the form of presentation and reception—direct divine address versus Mosaic mediation—the distinction is evident in particular features of the two sets of teaching. The form of the Commandments is direct address ("You shall not ..."), while the statutes and ordinances are a mix of direct address and third person reference (e.g., "If someone steals a sheep ..." Exod 22:1 [Heb. 21:37]). The prohibitive form of the Commandments, sometimes called apodictic law, is thus different from the case law that dominates the statutes and ordinances. The Commandments are a form of absolute law, without designation of circumstance or punishment, though some of the statutes and ordinances that seem to reflect the Commandments in fairly direct and simple fashion point to the absolute character of the Commandments by prescribing capital punishment as the penalty (e.g., Exod 21:12, 15, 16, 17; compare 31:14-15; 35:2; compare Deut 27:15-26). The association of the Commandments with the statutes and ordinances is reflected especially in the way the latter take up matters set forth under fairly simple prohibitions in the Commandments and develop them relative to particular circumstances and cases. While this is most noticeable in the book of Deuteronomy in the connection between the Decalogue (chap. 5) and the Deuteronomic Code (chaps. 12–26), it is also present in the book of Exodus in the way that many of the statutes and ordinances of the Book of the Covenant develop and spell out dimensions of the Commandments. So also in the Holiness Code of Leviticus (chaps. 17–26) the Decalogue is reflected, sometimes directly, as in chap. 19, and at other times in the more detailed specifying—in both direct address and case law—of matters that grow out of the simple directives of the Decalogue.

B. Order and Numeration

On the basis of the tradition that the Commandments were written on two tablets (Exod 34:29; Deut 9:9; 10:3), they are commonly understood to be comprised of two tables or parts, the first describing obligations to the Lord and the second obligations to one's neighbor. Generally, this is understood to mean that the first table goes through the Sabbath commandment though it is possible to include the obligation to honor parents because such "honor" is analogous to honoring or revering God. In any event, that commandment serves as a bridge, moving from those belonging to the proper worship of God to the neighbor obligations by beginning with those members of the community to which one is most closely related—one's parents.

There are considerable differences among various Christian traditions and Jews about how to number the Commandments, since features of the text permit or tend toward different numberings. For example, what some traditions call the Prologue is seen as the First Commandment in the Jewish tradition. That seems less strange when one realizes that the actual title for the Commandments is "the ten words," and the first word God speaks is "I am the LORD your God." Such a numeration serves to place greater weight on the opening sentence as the foundation of what follows.

In some numberings, no separation is made between not worshiping other gods and not making or worshiping idols, since the plural "them" in the sentence "You shall not bow down to them ..." syntactically can refer back only to the "other gods" of the First Commandment. Elsewhere the reference to bowing down and worshiping regularly refers to "other gods" not images (see below).

If the prohibitions against having other gods and making and worshiping images are construed as a single commandment, a count of ten is usually accomplished by dividing the coveting command. In the Deuteronomic version, the conjunction "and" or "neither," which is used to separate each of the commandments of the second table, occurs between the two prohibitions against coveting (Deut 5:21a and 21b), suggesting that these may be regarded as two separate commandments.

There are textual references to the Decalogue that suggest variations in the order of the Commandments, at least for the second table, and especially the three commandments prohibiting murder, ADULTERY, and theft. They occur in several different orders, e.g., adultery, murder, and theft in some of the LXX manuscript versions of the Decalogue, as well as Philo, the Nash Papyrus, and some quotations of the Commandments in the NT (e.g., Luke 18:20; Rom 13:9). Still other variations can be found in prophetic citations, such as Jer 7:9 and Hos 4:2 as well as other NT texts. There are enough differences in the sources to suggest some freedom and variability in the history of the formation of the Decalogue.

C. Literary and Redactional Features

The Deuteronomic form of the Decalogue shows signs of a redactional arrangement or editing of the Commandments to center them on the Sabbath commandment. This is accomplished in part by catchword association. The commandment reaches back to the beginning of the Decalogue with its reference to God's bringing Israel out of Egyptian slavery. It also reaches forward to the last commandment by including the ox and ass among the animals to receive rest, unlike the Exodus form of the Sabbath commandment, which makes no reference to ox and ass. As Norbert Lohfink has observed, the Deuteronomic structure centers on the Sabbath commandment further by its chiastic arrangement of the Commandments into the following groupings: long (Prologue and commandments against other gods and making and worshiping images), short (the name of God), center (Sabbath), short (honoring parents), and long (killing, adultery, stealing, false witness, and coveting—all held together by the Hebrew conjunction waw, reflected in the English "neither" in the translation of Deuteronomy in the NRSV and other translations).

It is not possible to determine the age of the Commandments, at least in their earliest stage. In its present form, Deut 5 is to be associated with the main form of Deuteronomy and so probably late 7th–early 6th cent. BCE, though it could be later. The commandment to honor parents, for example, includes characteristic Deuteronomic language with its additions to the Exodus form: "as the LORD your God commanded you" (compare the end of the Sabbath commandment, Deut 5:15) and "that it may go well with you." The Exodus version seems, therefore, to be antecedent to Deuteronomy. It is difficult to determine, however, if the present Exodus form reflects the later hand of the Priestly stratum or represents a tradition on which the Priestly tradition drew in elaborating the place of the Sabbath in creation (so Childs). The identification of the Sabbath as a "sign" between Israel and the Lord and as an "eternal covenant," a formulation that seems to belong to the Priestly theology (Exod 31:12-17), is not present in the Exod 20 version of the Sabbath commandment.

The presence of both positive and negative formulations in the Commandments indicates the possibility of placing such fundamental directives in either mode. This has led to interpretation of the Commandments that identifies both positive and negative aspects and implications. As noted above, the address of the Commandments is direct and singular ("you"). The content indicates that the addressees were the free male heads of household and property owners in the community (e.g., Clines), as reflected in the masculine verbal forms and the references to "your son/daughter," "you/your neighbor's ox/donkey," "your neighbor's wife/house," "you/your neighbor's male or female slave," etc. Such form of address is to be expected in a largely patriarchal society if the Commandments were to be comprehensive and all encompassing. At the same time, the redaction has created some tension and opened the address up more broadly. In the narrative context the addressees are the whole community of Israel gathered at Sinai (e.g., Exod 19:8, 10-12; 14-17 [but compare v. 15b]; Deut 5:1-5, 22). The presence of women and children, as well as strangers, in the assembly that covenants with the Lord and keeps the commandments and the statutes is indicated more than once (Deut 29:10-13 [Heb. 29:9-12]; 31:12-13; Josh 8:34-35). Further indication that the Commandments have been articulated in ways that encompass the women as well as the men is evident in the use of the verb na'af (נאף), "to commit adultery," which requires no object and is used with reference to women who disobey the commandment as well as men (e.g., Lev 20:10), instead of the more common idiom, "lie with (+ object)," which would require the female or male object. The text is more open. It has been suggested that the wife may be addressed implicitly in the Sabbath commandment—where she is not listed or mentioned—by the use of a non-gendered infinitive absolute for the initial imperative in both versions of that commandment (Schmidt)

D. Contents

1. The Prologue (Exod 20:2//Deut 5:6)

The opening sentence of the Decalogue—"I am the LORD your God, who brought you out of the land of Egypt, out of the house of slavery"—is not a commandment, either positive or negative, though it is counted as the first of the ten words in the Jewish tradition (see above). While there is no commandment here, its importance for the Decalogue is clear and recognized by the Jewish numbering. That is, the first word is foundational in the most literal sense of the term. It grounds the specific commandments that follow. An implicit "therefore" stands between the Prologue and the first actual commandment, for the Prologue provides the basis for the claim on Israel's obedience. In this respect, whether or not the Prologue is derived from the suzerainty treaty model, it is analogous to it: the good deed of the suzerain, in this instance the deity Yahweh, is the rationale for expecting the subjects created by his beneficent work to live in proper relationship with the king/deity and one another. Because specific emphasis is placed upon Israel's deliverance from slavery, the Commandments that follow are to be understood as marking the way to live as a freed people.

2. The First Commandment (Exod 20:3// Deut 5:7)

The heart of the matter is a prohibition against "having" other gods. Israel may not claim any attachment to or exercise devotion toward any deity other than the one who brought them out of Egyptian slavery and addresses them in the Commandments. More specifically, however, the Commandment goes on to say, "You shall not have any gods (that is, put any gods) before me ('al-panay עַל־פָּנָי)." In the Hebrew, this last phrase is ambiguous in the true sense of the term, capable of multiple meanings in a single context. The prepositional phrase can mean "in front of me" or "before me" indicating that no deity may be given place prior to or ahead of Yahweh in Israel's worship and obedience. It can mean "in addition to me," that is, no deity beside or alongside Yahweh, as well as "in preference to me," or "in place of me," that is, no deity besides Yahweh. Finally, the phrase can also mean "over against me," that is, in hostile encounter or conflict with Yahweh. Various arguments are made in behalf of each of these readings as conveying most accurately what is meant in the Commandment, but it is difficult to say that one of these meanings is to be chosen in place of all the others. In some sense, all of these possible relations to other deities are ruled out, though at any particular time in Israel's history one nuance may have carried more weight than another.

3. The Second Commandment (Exod 20:4-6// Deut 5:8-10)

As indicated above, these verses may be and are read both as a separate commandment and as a part of the First Commandment, elaborating and spelling it out. The interpretation of the commandment as a separate word from the prohibition of other gods rests on the first sentence of the text proscribing making idols, a command that is interpreted in several ways, first of all by understanding the commandment to say that no one is to make a physical image of anything in all the world, that is, no artistic representation because any such representation might become an object of worship. The second verse of the commandment underscores this danger as the true point of concern. No human-made physical representation is ever to serve as an object of worship and adoration. Here, however, is where connection to the First Commandment comes in. The language of bowing down to and worshiping or serving is fairly common in the OT, but it is used exclusively with reference to bowing down and worshiping "other gods" or things like the sun and moon, which can be regarded as deities (e.g., Deut 4:19; 30:17; Josh 23:16). Idols may be included in the range of objects, as is surely the case here, but understanding of the object as idols is not inherent in the expression and is not found in its use elsewhere. Also the plural antecedent of the objective pronoun "them" can only be "other gods" in the preceding verse (see above). The sentence thus ties these verses to the preceding ones, serving both to elaborate the First Commandment—no worship of other gods—and to make a further point: no making and/or worship of physical representations of other gods.

A further ambiguity concerns whether the reference to image or idol has in mind images of other gods or images of Yahweh. The usual interpretation is the former, precisely because of the sequencing of the sentences:

"You shall not make ..." and "You shall not bow down to them...." At the same time, one cannot rule out images of Israel's own deity as what is intended, not only because of the inclusiveness of the prohibition but also because in Deut 4, which seems to be a kind of Mosaic sermon on this commandment, the language about making an idol follows a strong emphasis on the fact that Israel saw no form when the Lord spoke at Sinai/ Horeb: "Since you saw no form when the LORD spoke to you at Horeb out of the fire, take care and watch yourselves closely, so that you do not act corruptly by making an idol for yourselves in the form of any figure ... the likeness of any animal that is on the earth ..." (vv. 15-18; compare v. 12). The prohibited image here seems to be an image of the Lord.

4. The Third Commandment (Exod 20:7// Deut 5:11)

The primary interpretive question is the force of the final word, lashow' (לַשָּׁוְא), customarily translated "in vain." The basic force of the expression is "emptily," "to no good purpose." The term appears again, however, in the Deuteronomic version of the Ninth Commandment against false witness, where the same word, show' (שָׁוְא), is used to describe the "false" character of the testimony. Because the parallel term in the Exodus version of the Ninth Commandment is clearly a word for lying or falsity, and because that commandment is directed at telling lies against the neighbor, especially and primarily in the court, the Third Commandment has come to be understood as prohibiting swearing falsely, that is, taking an oath that invokes God and not keeping it, or lying under an oath taken in the name of the Lord. Thus the New JPS translation reads, "You shall not swear falsely by the name of the LORD your God ..." (contrast NRSV, "You shall not make wrongful use ..."). Such an interpretation is central to the force of this commandment and is echoed elsewhere in the Bible (e.g., Deut 6:13; Jer 5:2). At the same time, the very use of the term show' opens the commandment to a somewhat broader meaning, suggesting that God's name is not to be used in empty and insubstantial ways.

5. The Fourth Commandment (Exod 20:8-11// Deut 5:12-15)

There are two closely related dimensions to the Sabbath commandment. One is the sanctification of a day to the service and worship of the Lord; the other is taking a day regularly to rest from one's labors. They are the same day, however, and the two aspects are held even more tightly together by the way in which the Exodus version of the commandment roots its observance in an imitation of the Lord's rest from the creation on the seventh day. What has been hallowed by the Lord shall be hallowed by the people. The rest that came at the end of the Lord's work of creation signals the need—and opportunity—for the people's rest from their work. As the motivation clauses in the two versions suggest, the Sabbath is both God's command (Deut 5:12*b*, 15*b*) and God's gift (Exod 20:11*b*).

The Deuteronomic version differs from Exodus in its motivational sentences. Rather than connecting the Sabbath to the Lord's rest after creation, it understands the Sabbath as a day of rest from labor so that Israel will be led to remember how the Lord delivered them from unceasing hard labor in Egypt (Deut 5:15). Consistent with this, a second purpose is given for taking a regular day of rest: ensuring that those who are in some form of slavery or indenture—as Israel was in Egypt—are given a break (Deut 5:14*b*).

The Sabbath commandment is one of two that are positive in form ("Remember/Observe the Sabbath day …"), but it also includes the more common prohibitive form ("you shall not do any work"), suggesting that the commandments were from the start capable of positive and negative formulations. It is not likely, however, that the sentence "Six days shall you labor" is meant to be a command. Rather it is delimitation, restricting the hard work—something unavoidable in that culture—to only six days at a time.

6. The Fifth Commandment (Exod 20:12// Deut 5:16)

A second positive command is given in the Fifth Commandment. Honoring parents is an obligation analogous to honoring God, for the same language is used for both kinds of acts. The commandment is to be understood as addressed to adults and having to do with how grown children respond to and treat their older parents (compare Deut 21:18-21), though learning to act in the proper way presumably begins when the children are young. As noted above, children were a part of the assembly that received this divine instruction.

The motivation clause indicates there is a connection between a long and good life and keeping this commandment. That is probably to be understood as having to do with each generation learning how to care for its older folk so that each new generation can count on a long and good life as it is honored by the next generation. It is to be presumed that the parents are worthy of the children's honor. That is, the commandment is not meant to imply obedience to parents who are abusive and harmful to their children. In the NT, the commandment becomes explicitly reciprocal (Eph 6:1-4; Col 3:20-21). A further, less obvious, implication of the commandment, reflected in the statutes of Deuteronomy connected to the Fifth Commandment, is that the people are to honor those in authority over them, such as prophets, priests, elders, and judges, that is those in religious, political, and judicial authority (compare Deut 16:18–18:22).

7. The Sixth Commandment (Exod 20:13// Deut 5:17)

The central interpretive issue of the Sixth Commandment is how extensive is its prohibition against taking life. Some translations follow the traditional interpretation, "You shall not kill," while others translate, "You shall not murder." The latter has become more common, for example, in the NRSV and the New JPS translations. It reflects awareness that the verb of the commandment, ratsakh (רָצַח), is not one of the more general words for killing of any sort. It is generally confined to instances of high-handed killing, that is, homicide in the form of murder. The verb, however, is also used for manslaughter, and its explication in the statutes has much to do with that as well as with murder (Num 35:22-28). The term is also used in at least one instance for capital punishment (Num 35:30), so it is capable of more extended reference than simply murder. The basic point is clear: you shall not take the life of your neighbor. Its positive form is found in whatever it takes to protect the life of one's neighbor. Many interpreters have inferred from that the responsibility to keep one's neighbor from any harm and ensure the neighbor's good.

8. The Seventh Commandment (Exod 20:14// Deut 5:18)

The prohibition against committing adultery is intended, as is true of the rest of the commandments in the second table of the Decalogue, to ensure against harming one's neighbor or, in the familiar positive form, to show love of neighbor. In this instance love of neighbor is with respect to protection of the neighbor's marriage. In so doing, one's own marriage will be protected by the reciprocality inherent in the commandments. At the same time the family is protected and enhanced both in maintaining the bond between husband and wife and ensuring that progeny are indeed those of the husband and wife.

9. The Eighth Commandment (Exod 20:15// Deut 5:19)

The original force of this commandment may have been the protection of the freedom of the individual Israelite. That is, it may have originally prohibited stealing a person (compare Exod 21:16; Deut 24:7). Such an act usually would have had some economic intent, as, for example, in the case of Joseph's brothers kidnapping him and selling him for profit rather than killing him, as was first proposed (Gen 37:26-28). As the commandment stands, however, there is no object to the verb "steal," and, in the statutes that elaborate the force of the commandment, it is clear that the commandment is meant to safeguard any of the property and possessions of one's neighbor.

10. The Ninth Commandment (Exod 20:16// Deut 5:20)

The connections between this commandment and the Third Commandment have already been identified. Swearing falsely is now seen to be a matter of neighbor relation as well as one's relation to God.

The prohibition against false testimony is aimed primarily at safeguarding the judicial process so that it may not be used to harm one's neighbor. In Israel as elsewhere, the courts were the place of last resort for the administration of justice. The commandment reflects what was and is the case; that everything in the court depends upon testimony. False testimony can lead to all sorts of consequences. The story of Ahab's theft of Naboth's vineyard is a classic example of the use of false witnesses to steal the property of another and, in the process, to murder the owner of the property. The most vulnerable at this point were the poor, as some of the statutes indicate (e.g., Exod 23:1-3, 6-9). The potential for violence in giving false testimony is evident in the various references to a "malicious witness," literally, "a witness of violence" (Exod 23:1; Deut 19:16; Ps 35:11). The concern for truthful testimony and awareness of the dangers of false testimony led to various statutes requiring multiple witnesses for conviction and severe punishment of those who gave false witness (e.g., Deut 17:6-7; 19:15).

The focus of the commandment on the judicial process did not rule out its applicability on a broader basis. That is, its intention is to prohibit lying about a neighbor to the detriment of the neighbor. That may happen in gossip and slander as well, and in some of the statutes, this kind of lying against the neighbor is also prohibited (e.g., Lev 19:11, 16; compare Exod 23:1).

11. The Tenth Commandment (Exod 20:17// Deut 5:21)

The last of the commandments seeks to place some restraint on inordinate desire. It recognizes that desire and avarice can lead to breaches of other commandments and violation of the neighbor's rights and goods. One of the central interpretive issues is whether the commandment addresses only action or also is meant to speak about attitude and emotion, even if not acted upon. In a number of instances, the verb khamadh (חָמַד) occurs in a situation where someone desires or covets something and takes it (e.g., Deut 7:25; Josh 7:21; Mic 2:2). Thus the commandment clearly has in mind unrestrained desire, something evident even where the word is not used, as, e.g., in the royal appropriation of Naboth's vineyard by King Ahab. The force of the commandment cannot be confined to action, however. It is a final word to call for restraint on desire in itself, as is indicated by the use of a different second verb (hith'awwah (הִתְאַוָּה)) in Deuteronomy, which may refer only to the desire itself, whether or not acted upon.

This last commandment forms a bridge from the Decalogue and the OT into the NT, where the Commandments are presumed and referred to by Jesus (e.g., Matt 5:21-37; 19:16-22//Mark 10:17-22//Luke 18:18-25), Paul (e.g., Rom 2:21-22; 13:8-10), and others (Jas 2:11). The second table is commonly what is in view, and those commandments are equated with the love of neighbor. Control of urges and desire is lifted up and underscored in the Sermon on the Mount, where, in reiterating the commandments against murder and adultery, Jesus warns against anger and lust as incipient modes of those actions. The heart and mind as well as individual actions are placed under control in obeying the Commandments. Careful observance of the whole was understood to manifest the true worship of the Lord and ensure both the well-being of the neighbor and the common good. *See* COVENANT, OT AND NT; IDOLATRY; LAW IN THE OT.

Bibliography: Georg Braulik. "The Sequence of the Laws in Deuteronomy 12–26 and in the Decalogue." *A Song of Power and the Power of* Song. Duane L. Christensen, ed. (1993) 313–35; Brevard Childs. *The Book of Exodus.* OTL (1974); David J. A. Clines. "The Ten Commandments, Reading from Left to Right." *Interested Parties: The Ideology of Writers and Readers of the Hebrew Bible* (1995) 26–45; Walter Harrelson. *The Ten Commandments and Human Rights* (1980); Stephen A. Kaufman. "The Structure of the Deuteronomic Law." *Maarav* 1–2 (1978–79) 105–58; Paul Lehmann. *The Decalogue and a Human Future* (1995); Norbert Lohfink. *Theology of the Pentateuch* (1994); George Mendenhall. *Law and Covenant in Israel and the Ancient Near East* (1959); Ernest Nicholson. "The Decalogue as Direct Address of God." *VT* 27 (1977) 422–33; Eduard Nielsen. *The Ten Commandments in New Perspective* (1968); Dennis Olson. *Deuteronomy and the Death of Moses* (1994); A. Phillips. *Ancient Israel's Criminal Law* (1978); Werner Schmidt, with Holger Delkurt and Axel Grouper. *Die Zehn Gebote im Rahmen Alttestamentlicher Ethik* (1993); Ben-Zion Segal, ed. *The Ten Commandments in History and Tradition* (1985); J. J. Stamm and M. E. Andrew. *The Ten Commandments in Recent Research* (1967).

PATRICK D. MILLER

TENT [אֹהֶל 'ohel; σκηνή skēnē]. Portable dwelling used by nomads, shepherds, and armies. The structure consisted of poles held upright and connected with cords stretched between them and grounded with wood pegs hammered into the ground using a wooden mallet. Hand-woven goat's hair, animal skins, or other materials served as covering for the roof and sides (Judg 4:21; Song 1:5; Isa 40:22; 54:2; Jer 10:20). Tents would usually be pitched near shade and a water supply (well, river, lake, etc.; Gen 18:1, 4). Less well-to-do families shared a tent, with a divider separating men's quarters from that of the women (Judg 15:1). Wealthier families had separate tents for wives, children, and servants (Gen 31:33). Furnishings were generally sparse, with coarse straw mats, goat's hair, or wool rugs sometimes used to cover the ground, and straw mats used for beds and chairs (Judg 4:18-21). A piece of leather spread on the floor served as the table (Ps 23:5; Isa 21:5). Cooking was done on stoves and ovens often consisting of nothing more than a few stones placed at the entrance of the tent or simply a hole in the ground. The head of the family sat in the entrance to guard his family and belongings as well as to watch for travelers (Gen 18:1; Exod 33:8; Judg 4:20).

The OT identifies Israel's ancestors (Gen 12:8; 13:3; 18:6; 24:67; 25:27; 31:25, 33) as well as other groups from the surrounding territories (Gen 4:20; 9:27; 13:5; Judg 4:17-20; 6:5; 2 Kgs 7:7; 1 Chr 5:10; Isa 13:20) as tent dwellers. Likewise, the OT recalls that the Israelites lived in tents during the exodus journey (Exod 33:8; Num 24:2; 33:5-49 [khanah חָנָה]). After settling in Canaan, the Israelites generally lived in houses, although soldiers camped (khanah) in tents during military expeditions (1 Sam 29:1). *Tent* sometimes was used to refer to the more permanent "home" (1 Kgs 8:66). Prior to the construction of the Jerusalem Temple, the Israelites utilized a movable sanctuary called the "tent of meeting" ('ohel mo'edh אֹהֶל מוֹעֵד) or simply the "tent" (Exod 33:7-11; compare 2 Macc 2:4-5) or TABERNACLE.

In the NT, *tent* often has this OT concept of tent/tabernacle in view. Hebrews 8–9, in which approximately half of the occurrences of the term are located, e.g., compares the earthly tent/tabernacle constructed by Moses and the true or heavenly tent/tabernacle (see also Acts 7:43-44). The NT also speaks of tents as the portable dwellings of the ancestors Abraham, Isaac, and Jacob (Heb 11:9) and metaphorically as the "fallen tent" or house/kingdom of David (Acts 15:16; compare Amos 9:11 [LXX]). In addition, the transfiguration scenes in the synoptic Gospels all have Peter asking about putting up tents (NRSV, "dwellings") for Jesus, Moses, and Elijah, a reference to movable shelters as well as an allusion to the Jewish Feast of Booths (Matt 17:4; Mark 9:5; Luke 9:33). In 2 Cor 5:1-5 the apostle Paul contrasts the metaphorical "earthly tent" that the Corinthians live in now with the "heavenly dwelling" with which God will clothe them, and for which the Spirit was sent as a guarantee. *See* BOOTH; BOOTHS, FEAST OR FESTIVAL OF.

WILLIAM SANGER CAMPBELL

TENT OF MEETING אֹהֶל מוֹעֵד 'ohel mo'edh]. Place of God's communication with Moses. *See* TABERNACLE.

TENTMAKER [σκηνοποιός skēnopoios]. The occupation of Paul, Aquila, and Priscilla (Acts 18:3). Paul never uses the term, but his references to working with his hands (1 Cor 4:12; compare Acts 20:34-35; 1 Cor 9:6; 2 Cor 11:27; 1 Thess 2:9; 2 Thess 3:8) imply some type of handicraft. Thus, Luke's report is plausible. Tents could be made from cloth woven from goat hair—typically a product of Cilicia—or from leather. Thus, Paul was either a weaver or a leatherworker. His work need

not have been restricted to the manufacture of tents, especially if he was a leatherworker. *See* OCCUPATIONS; PAUL, THE APOSTLE.

ABRAHAM SMITH

TENUPHA. *See* ELEVATION OFFERING.

TEPHON tee'fon [Τεφών Tephōn]. One of several Judean towns around which BACCHIDES built walls with gates (1 Macc 9:50) in order to keep Judea in his possession. Josephus (*Ant.* 13.15) indicates the town might be TEKOA, but Tephon is more likely TAPPUAH, located near Hebron (Josh 17:7), or BETH-TAPPUAH (Josh 15:53).

TERAH ter'uh [תֶּרַח terakh; Θάρα Thara]. 1. The father of Abram/Abraham, Nahor, and Haran (Gen 11:24-28, 31-32; Josh 24:2; 1 Chr 1:26). He is mentioned in Luke's genealogy of Jesus (3:34). The meaning of the name is uncertain. It may be related to the name of a place northeast of Haran, the city to which Terah moved with his sons (Gen 11:31); or it may be related to the Akk. word meaning "mountain goat" or "ibex." *See* PATRIARCHS.

2. The name of a place on the Israelites' exodus journey (Num 33:27-28).

TIMOTHY G. CRAWFORD

TERAPHIM ter'uh-fim [תְּרָפִים terafim]. An object of worship or devotion, often in the form of a figurine. The term *teraphim* is frequently associated with shrines (Gen 31:19-35; Judg 17:5; Ezek 21:21), but it would be incorrect to assume that all teraphim were divine figures. It is as likely that they were ancestor figures or emblems of authority for the household. Teraphim were also associated with divination. The king of Babylon is portrayed using teraphim to lead the country to war (Ezek 21:26). Hosea notes the paucity of leadership in Israel, stating that they "shall remain many days … without ephod or teraphim" (Hos 3:4; compare Zech 10:2). The teraphim created by Micah are a substitute for leadership in the days "when there was no king in Israel" (Judg 17:1-6).

JESSICA TINKLENBERG DEVEGA

TEREBINTH ter'uh-binth [אֵלָה 'elah; τερέμινθος tereminthos]. The NRSV translates *'elah* as "terebinth" twice in the Prophets (Isa 6:13; Hos 4:13) and *tereminthos* once in the Apocrypha (Sir 24:16), as a positive portrait of Wisdom. In Hos 4:13, the term refers to fertility worship, and *terebinth* is used in par. to hills, OAK, and poplar (see Ezek 6:13, where *'elah* is translated "oak"). Isaiah described the remnant of Israel as what would survive after the burning of terebinth or oak (6:13). Some scholars have associated the term with the turpentine tree (*Pistacia terebenthus*), but others would translate the term in a more nonspecific way. *'Elah* is translated as "oak" in other places, such as the oak where an angel of Yahweh sat before Gideon (Judg 6:11, 19), the oak that caught the head of Absalom (2 Sam 18:9), and the oak under which sat the nameless prophet whom Jeroboam approached (1 Kgs 13:14). The term is also used in geographical references such as the oak near Shechem where Jacob hid his gods (Gen 35:4), the Valley of Elah (1 Sam 17:2, 19) where the Israelites confronted the Philistines, and the oak of Jabesh, the burial place of King Saul (1 Chr 10:12).

BRUCE W. GENTRY

TERESH tihr´esh [תֶּרֶשׁ teresh]. A guardian of the king's threshold who, along with BIGTHAN, became angry with King Ahasuerus and plotted to assassinate him (Esth 2:21; 6:2). Mordecai discovered the scheme and reported it to Esther, who reported it to the king. Teresh and Bigthan were impaled on stakes, and Mordecai was rewarded for his loyalty. *See* ESTHER, BOOK OF.

TRISHA GAMBAIANA WHEELOCK

TERMINOLOGY, ISRAEL AND PALESTINIAN TERRITORIES. *See* PALESTINE AND ISRAEL, TERMINOLOGY FOR.

TERMINOLOGY, NAMES FOR ISRAEL AND PALESTINE. *See* PALESTINE AND ISRAEL, TERMINOLOGY FOR.

TERROR. *See* FEAR.

TERRORISM. The Assyrians were notorious for employing terror as a means of coercion and psychological warfare. Their reputation for burned cities, corpses piled high, and bodily mutilation served to dissuade future resistance and encourage surrender. The speech of the RABSHAKEH in 2 Kgs 18:19-35, intended to be overheard by the citizenry of Jerusalem, invokes Assyria's brutal record (18:33-35; compare 19:11-13) and the horrors of siege warfare (18:27; compare Deut 28:52-57; 2 Kgs 6:28-29) in order to discourage resistance. Nahum 2:1–3:3 reverses the images of military terror for which Assyria was notorious so that they are wreaked upon hated Nineveh itself.

Ancient warfare could be pitiless. The OT abounds with examples of rape (Isa 13:16; Lam 5:11; Zech 14:2), gouged-out eyes (1 Sam 10:27; 11:2; 2 Kgs 25:7; compare amputated thumbs and toes in Judg 1:6-7), desecration of corpses (1 Sam 31:10; 2 Sam 4:12), devastation of the infrastructure (Josh 6:24; 8:28; Judg 9:45; 2 Kgs 3:19, 25; Jer 6:6), and slaughtered prisoners of war (2 Sam 8:2). Deuteronomic law attempted to constrain some of these abuses (Deut 20:10-11, 19-20; 21:10-14). The massacre of defeated populations could be a matter of expediency (Judg 21:10-12; 1 Sam 27:9-11; 1 Kgs 11:16) or done in obedience to the dictates of religion (Deut 7:1-2; 20:16-17; Josh 6:21; 8:24-26; 11:11; Judg 20:48; 1 Sam 15:3; *see* HOLY WAR). Analogous

to the modern notion of war crimes, collective moral judgment condemned certain vicious military practices directed against civilians, particularly ripping open pregnant women and battering infants to death (2 Kgs 8:12; 15:16; Isa 13:16; Hos 10:14; 13:16; Amos 1:13; Nah 3:10; Jdt 16:4).

The contemporary concept of terrorism features violence against innocent civilians in the furtherance of political aims by nongovernmental clandestine groups with religious or nationalistic motivations. As such, it rests upon modern ideals and notions not explicitly present in ancient culture. Perhaps the closest parallel in the biblical world would be the Sicarii of the 1st cent. CE, who knifed their political opponents under the cover of Jerusalem crowds (Josephus, *J.W.* 2.254–57; *Ant.* 20.165, 186–87). Josephus calls these assassins, along with other insurrectionists against Roman rule, lēstēs (ληστής, "bandits"). The NT uses this term for Barabbas (John 18:40) and the two men crucified with Jesus (Matt 27:38; Mark 15:27).

Bibliography: Susan Niditch. *War in the Hebrew Bible: A Study in the Ethics of Violence* (1993); John A. Wood. *Perspectives on War in the Bible* (1998).

RICHARD D. NELSON

TERTIUS tuhr´shee-uhs [Τέρτιος Tertios]. In Rom 16:22, the only passage in which his name appears, Tertius identifies himself as the one who wrote Romans—meaning that, as Paul's AMANUENSIS or secretary, he wrote it down. Paul's reliance on secretaries is implied by 1 Cor 16:21 and Gal 6:11. Although some Greco-Roman authors expected their secretaries to draft letters from a summary of ideas, the consistency in style and theology among Paul's undisputed letters indicates that his secretaries took dictation in longhand. Tertius adds his own greeting, which suggests that the Roman Christians knew him.

JUDITH ANNE JONES

TERTULLIAN tuhr´tuhl´ee-uhn. A late 2nd- and 3rd-cent. CE early church writer from Carthage whose Latin works on the Trinity, creation, incarnation, and resurrection are largely extant. His treatise *Against Marcion*, a defense of the OT and God's role as creator written in response to Marcion, offers a striking example of Tertullian's often polemical apologetic approach. Recent scholarship has called into question the details of his biography. EUSEBIUS remembers Tertullian as a legal mind (*Hist. eccl.* 2.2.4). Some scholars suggest that he is the Roman jurist by the same name, but others dispute this claim. JEROME states that Tertullian was a priest (*Vir. ill.* 3.53), though Tertullian does not reveal himself as such. Tertullian was invested in the 2nd-cent. charismatic movement "the New Prophecy," identified by later Christian writers as Montanism. In ensuing centuries, this affiliation earned him the title of heretic and had a damaging impact on the survival of his writings. See APOLOGETICS; MARCION, MARCIONISM; MONTANUS, MONTANISM.

CARLY DANIEL-HUGHES

TERTULLUS tuhr-tuhl′uhs [Τέρτυλλος Tertyllos]. The spokesman or attorney (rhētōr ῥήτωρ) representing Jewish leaders from Jerusalem as they bring charges against Paul before the governor Felix (Acts 24:1-9). Tertullus charges Paul with sedition and profaning the Temple. Following good classical style, the author of Acts gives Tertullus a speech that, however brief, conforms to rhetorical convention. The relationship between Tertullus, whose name is Roman, and the Jewish leaders is debated, in part because the Western Text of Acts (see BEZAE, CODEX) contains additional material (24:6b-8a; the NRSV offers this reading in a footnote) that suggests that Tertullus has a Jewish background. See ACTS OF THE APOSTLES.

RUBÉN R. DUPERTUIS

TERUMA. See ELEVATION OFFERING.

TEST. See TEMPT, TEMPTATION.

TEST OR DISCERNMENT OF SPIRITS. See SPIRITS, DISCERNMENT OR TESTING OF.

TESTAMENT tes′tuh-muhnt [διαθήκη diathēkē]. The word testament does not occur in the NRSV, except in the notes to Lev 16:13 and 24:3, which offer it as an alternative translation for covenant (ʿedhuth עֵדוּת). See COVENANT, OT AND NT.

In its traditional Greek usage, the term testament refers to a will or testament whereby a person arranges for the disposition of his or her property after death. This is the sense in which testament is used to refer to a literary genre that emerged, and continued to be used, in the Second Temple period. The OT contains several farewell discourses delivered by exalted figures before they die, such as Jacob (Gen 49), Moses (Deut 33), and Joshua (Josh 23–24); in the Apocrypha, Mattathias, father of Judas the Maccabee, delivers such a discourse (1 Macc 2:49-68), as does Tobit (Tob 14:3-11). Such speeches usually contain blessings and directions for future behavior. Testaments as independent literary works include, e.g., the Testaments of the Twelve Patriarchs, the Testament of Job, and the Testament of Moses. The genre often contains blessings, ethical teaching, and predictions of the future. See ABRAHAM, TESTAMENT OF; JOB, TESTAMENT OF; MOSES, ASSUMPTION OF; PATRIARCHS, TESTAMENTS OF THE TWELVE.

CECILIA WASSÉN

TESTAMENT OF ABRAHAM. See ABRAHAM, TESTAMENT OF.

TESTAMENT OF BENJAMIN. See PATRIARCHS, TESTAMENTS OF THE TWELVE.

TESTAMENT OF DAN. See PATRIARCHS, TESTAMENTS OF THE TWELVE.

TESTAMENT OF ISSACHAR. See PATRIARCHS, TESTAMENTS OF THE TWELVE.

TESTAMENT OF JOB. See JOB, TESTAMENT OF.

TESTAMENT OF JOSEPH. See PATRIARCHS, TESTAMENTS OF THE TWELVE.

TESTAMENT OF JUDAH. See PATRIARCHS, TESTAMENTS OF THE TWELVE.

TESTAMENT OF LEVI. See PATRIARCHS, TESTAMENTS OF THE TWELVE.

TESTAMENT OF MOSES. See MOSES, ASSUMPTION OF.

TESTAMENT OF NAPHTALI. See PATRIARCHS, TESTAMENTS OF THE TWELVE.

TESTAMENT OF REUBEN. See PATRIARCHS, TESTAMENTS OF THE TWELVE.

TESTAMENT OF SIMEON. See PATRIARCHS, TESTAMENTS OF THE TWELVE.

TESTAMENT OF SOLOMON. See SOLOMON, TESTAMENT OF.

TESTAMENTS OF THE TWELVE PATRIARCHS. See PATRIARCHS, TESTAMENTS OF THE TWELVE.

TESTIMONIA TEXT. Discovered in Cave 4 at Qumran (see DEAD SEA SCROLLS) and only one column long, Testimonia (4Q175) is a collection of excerpts with eschatological significance. Quotations from Numbers and Deuteronomy (in the sequence Deut 5:28-29; 18:18-19; Num 24:15-17; Deut 33:8-11), listed without any accompanying interpretations, provide the scriptural basis for the expectation of three eschatological figures: a future prophet, a royal messiah, and a priestly messiah (these are mentioned together in 1QS IX, 11). The last quotation is from a sectarian text, the Apocryphon of Joshua (4Q378–79), which elaborates upon Joshua's curse against anyone who rebuilds Jericho (Josh 6:26). This section may be a polemical allusion to a Hasmonean ruler, possibly John Hyrcanus I, who developed Jericho. Dated to about 100 BCE, Testimonia supports a theory that the early Christians might have composed collections of proof texts concerning the identification of Jesus as the Messiah.

CECILIA WASSÉN

TESTIMONY [עֵד ʿedh, עֵדָה ʿedhah, עֵדוּת ʿedhuth; μαρτυρία martyria, μαρτύριον martyrion, μάρτυς martys]. Throughout the Bible the idea of testimony is prominent. Terms like *testimony* and *witness* occur often in religious settings and have special meaning there, culminating in the development of the Greek martys (witness) into the English *martyr*. The NRSV regularly translates the Hebrew ʿedhuth as "decrees" rather than the traditional rendering "testimonies," except in 1 Kgs 2:3 (Deut 4:45; 6:17, 20; 2 Kgs 23:3; 1 Chr 29:19; 2 Chr 34:31; Pss 25:10; 78:56; 99:7), though it renders the term as "warnings" in Neh 9:34. One of the principal uses of testimony or witness is in a forensic context, and this proves to be of considerable importance in both Testaments.

A. The Old Testament
B. The Principle of Multiple Witnesses
C. The Apocrypha
D. The Talmud
E. The New Testament
Bibliography

A. The Old Testament

Israel believed that God had revealed the divine will in the law that Moses set before the children of Israel: "These are the decrees (ʿeduth, "testimonies") and the statues and ordinances that Moses spoke to the Israelites when they had come out of Egypt" (Deut 4:45). The Israelites were instructed to keep the divine commandments and testimonies (Deut 6:17), and explain the law to their children (Deut 6:20-25). A copy of these divine instructions was placed in the "ark of the testimony" (Exod 30:6, 26; 31:7; 39:35; 40:3, 5, 21; NRSV, "ark of the covenant," "testimony" in footnotes) and called "The Testimony" (Exod 16:34; 25:21; NRSV, "covenant"). The "ark of the testimony" was located beyond the veil in the Most Holy Place in the tabernacle. There upon the mercy seat above the ark, surrounded by the two angelic cherubim, God promised to meet with the covenant people (Exod 25:22; 30:6; Num 7:89). At the end of Moses' divine encounter God gave him a physical reminder of the Ten Commandments, described as "the two tablets of the testimony [covenant] ... written with the finger of God" (Exod 31:18; compare 32:15; 34:29). The Levites were charged with the care of "the tabernacle of the testimony," sometimes translated as "the tabernacle of the covenant" (Num 1:50, 53 NRSV).

In the occupation of the Holy Land under Joshua, the priests were commanded to bear the sacred "ark of the covenant" (or "testimony") out of the Jordan River (Josh 4:16). David charged Solomon to keep God's "testimonies" (1 Kgs 2:3; compare 1 Chr 29:19). King Josiah agreed to observe God's "testimonies" wholeheartedly (2 Kgs 23:3). Thus the Israelites recognized God's "testimonies" (often translated as "decrees"), which they understood were to be respected and obeyed (Pss 19:7; 25:10; 78:56; 93:5; 99:7; 119 [22 times; e.g., vv. 2, 14, 22, 24, 36]; Jer 44:23).

In ancient Israel testimony was frequently given in juridical situations. Thus witnesses were called upon to attest important legal agreements. For example, Boaz acquired Ruth as his wife and redeemed the family property before witnesses (Ruth 4:9-11). In similar fashion Jeremiah bought a field at Anathoth from his cousin Hanamel and had the transaction duly attested by witnesses (Jer 32:10, 12, 25, 44; compare Isa 8:1-2). Sometimes animals or even inanimate objects such as an altar or a pile of stones could serve as objective testimony that an agreement had been concluded (Gen 21:30; 31:48, 52; Josh 22:27; 24:27). On some occasions God was called upon as a witness in an oath to confirm an agreement or solemn affirmation (1 Sam 12:5-6; 20:23; compare Matt 26:63, 72, 74; Rom 1:9; Phil 1:8; Heb 6:13-18).

B. The Principle of Multiple Witnesses

The testimony of two or three witnesses was necessary to establish a case, and this was insisted upon in cases involving a death sentence (Deut 17:6; 19:15; Num 35:30). Witnesses were expected to take the lead in carrying out the sentence (Deut 17:7; compare 13:9; 1 Kgs 21:13; Acts 7:58). False testimony was strictly prohibited by the Decalogue (Exod 20:16; Deut 5:20), but was clearly not unknown (Exod 23:1-2; compare Ps 35:11; Prov 6:19). If convicted as a malicious witness, a person guilty of false testimony would be subject to the same punishment he meant to inflict (Deut 19:16-19; compare Prov 19:5, 9). Despite the prohibitions, false testimony was common in both the OT and the NT (Ps 27:12; Prov 12:17; 24:28; Matt 26:60; Mark 14:55-59; Acts 6:13; compare 21:27-28).

C. The Apocrypha

The striking case of Susanna reveals the crucial importance of reliable testimony. Under Daniel's probing cross-examination the testimony of the accusing witnesses against Susanna collapses, and Daniel convicts them of bearing false witness (Sus 54, 58, 61). They are put to death in accordance with the law of malicious witness (Sus 62). God is cited as a "witness" in Wis 1:6—a use that is later found in the writings of Paul (Rom 1:9; 2 Cor 1:23; 1 Thess 2:5, 10; Phil 1:8).

D. The Talmud

The Jewish Talmud maintained the traditional requirement of several witnesses to establish any charge. In fact, it was viewed as sinful for a single person to lay a charge against someone (*Pesah*. 113b; compare *Sanh*. 9b). On the other hand, one who refused to come forward as a witness when solemnly charged to do so was considered sinful (Lev 5:1). In Jewish courts some people could not serve as witnesses including minors, women, close relatives, tax collectors, and slaves (*Sanh*. 3:3, 4; *B. Qam*. 88a; compare Josephus, Ant. 4.219; *m. Rosh Hash*. 1:8).

E. The New Testament

Here again the principle of multiple witnesses is frequently mentioned (Matt 18:16; John 8:17; 2 Cor 13:1; Heb 10:28; Rev 11:3). The Christian message is attested by a plurality of witnesses (Mark 3:14-19; 9:2; Luke 9:1-6; 24:48; John 15:26-27; Acts 1:22; 10:38-43; 1 Pet 5:1; 2 Pet 1:16; 1 John 1:1-3), and their testimony is important in establishing the credibility of the claims advanced for Christ (Luke 1:1-4).

Much of John's Gospel takes the form of a lawsuit over the claims of Christ as Messiah and Son of God; truth is, in effect, on trial (John 18:37-38; 20:31; Trites 2004; Lincoln). A number of witnesses are introduced to make the case. John the Baptist serves as a witness "to testify to the light," and his testimony is given a prominent place (1:6-8, 15, 19-34; 5:33-36; 10:41-42). Other witnesses include the Samaritan woman (4:39), the Scriptures (5:39), the works of Christ (10:25), the Father (5:37; 8:18), and Jesus himself (8:18), who speaks to "bear witness to the truth" (18:37). The apostles also are witnesses (15:27), and so is the Holy Spirit, who gives powerful testimony to the claims of Christ (15:26; compare 1 John 5:6-12, where the testimony theme is also prominent). The Spirit acts as the Advocate (paraklētos [παράκλητος], 14:16, 26; 15:26; 16:7; compare 1 John 2:1), convincing or convicting the world "concerning sin, righteousness and judgment" (16:8-11). The testimony of these witnesses is vigorously debated in John's Gospel, particularly in chaps. 1–12. The trustworthiness of the Gospel itself hinges on the author's testimony (19:35; 21:24). Here, as elsewhere in Greco-Roman antiquity, "testimony" often includes the notion of "advocacy" and not the sort of "objectivity" frequently associated with the term today (Marincola).

The testimony theme is also important in the book of Acts. The apostles give their crucial, indispensable eyewitness testimony to the life, death, and resurrection of Jesus (Acts 1:8, 21-22; 2:32; 3:14-15; 10:39-43; compare Luke 1:2; 24:46-48; 1 Pet 5:1). They particularly highlight the fact of Jesus' resurrection (Acts 1:22; 2:24, 32; 3:15; 4:33; 10:41; compare 1 Cor 15:5-8 and the Gospel accounts of the resurrection). They are joined by other Christian leaders such as Stephen (7:2-60), Philip (8:4-40), and Apollos (18:24-28), who speak boldly, giving testimony for their Lord. The Holy Spirit (5:32) and the Scriptures (13:32-41; 28:23) also provide testimony to Jesus. Paul is a major figure in this outward expanding movement, as his missionary efforts show (13:1–28:31). A helpful summary of his testimony is found in his defense before the Ephesian elders at Miletus, where he describes his ministry in terms of testifying "to both Jews and Greeks about repentance toward God and faith toward our Lord Jesus" (20:21). Here he is plainly an advocate of his Lord, acting boldly "to testify to the good news of God's grace" (20:24). The book of Acts closes with Paul continuing to offer this Christocentric testimony—"proclaiming the kingdom of God and teaching about the Lord Jesus Christ with all boldness and without hindrance" (28:31).

The Pauline epistles occasionally speak of testimony. The apostle Paul rejoiced in writing to the Corinthians "the testimony (martyrion) of Christ has been strengthened among you" (1 Cor 1:6). He declared, "this is our boast, the testimony of our conscience: we have behaved in the world with frankness and godly sincerity" (2 Cor 1:12). Paul insisted that God supported his integrity as well as the people who knew him (1 Thess 2:10; compare v. 5; Rom 1:9; Phil 1:8). Later in the Pastorals, Timothy is reminded that he had made "the good confession" of his faith, giving public testimony, possibly at his baptism or ordination, "before many witnesses" (1 Tim 6:12). He also is instructed not to "accept any accusation against an elder except on the evidence of two or three witnesses" (1 Tim 5:19; compare Deut 19:15).

In the book of Revelation, Jesus, "the Lamb that was slain" (Rev 5:6), but who conquered death and became "the firstborn of the dead" (1:5), provides the key testimony and is rightly called "the faithful and true witness" (1:5). He suffered and died in utter faithfulness to God, and those who follow him might expect to face similar suffering and persecution (1:9). For that reason they are repeatedly counseled to be spiritually prepared and obedient: "Let anyone who has an ear listen to what the Spirit is saying to the churches" (2:7, 11, 17, 29; 3:6, 13, 22). Wonderful encouragement for Christians giving their testimony in hostile times came from the risen Christ: "Do not be afraid; I am the first and the last, and the living one. I was dead, and see, I am alive ... ; and I have the keys of Death and of Hades" (1:18). Already Antipas had experienced martyrdom (2:13); thus the churches were to be ready for hard times (2:10), where patient endurance (hypomonē ὑπομονή) was called for (1:9; 2:2, 3, 19; 3:10; 14:12). The seer in prophetic vision "saw the souls of those who had been beheaded for their testimony to Jesus and for the word of God" (20:4). Since they had refused to be part of the idolatry and false worship around them, they were promised ultimate victory if they remained faithful, and the prospect of reigning with Christ (20:6). Thus the book prepares the way for the later technical meaning of *martyr* (compare Acts 22:20, where similar mention is made of the fact that "the blood of your witness Stephen was shed" [Trites 1973]). The apocalypse closes with words of encouragement from the victorious Jesus, who has sent his messenger "with this testimony for the churches" (Rev 22:16), and his assurance, "Surely I am coming soon" (22:20).

Testimony is offered in a strictly legal sense in the Synoptic accounts of the trial of Jesus (Matt 26:59-60; Mark 14:55-56; Luke 22:71), where the enemies of Jesus "testify against" him (katamartyreō [καταμαρτυρέω], Matt 26:62; 27:13; Mark 14:60). Their evidence is described as "false testimony" (pseudomartyria [ψευδομαρτυρία], Matt 26:59; compare 15:19).

False witness is mentioned in several other passages as something prohibited (Matt 19:18; Mark 10:19; Luke 18:20). In Matthew's Gospel testimony is cited as a rule of order in the local faith community (Matt 18:16; compare Deut 19:15). In Luke the testimony of "eyewitnesses" (1:2) is recognized and used by the author in establishing the historical truth of the Christian message (compare 2 Pet 1:16). *See* ARK OF THE COVENANT; HOLY SPIRIT; JESUS CHRIST; MARTYR; PAUL, THE APOSTLE; WITNESS.

Bibliography: J. M. Boice. *Witness and Revelation in the Gospel of John* (1970); L. E. Keck. *Mandate to Witness—Studies in the Book of Acts* (1964); Andrew Lincoln. *Truth on Trial: The Lawsuit Motif in the Fourth Gospel* (2000); John Marincola. *Authority and Tradition in Ancient Historiography* (1997); Allison A. Trites. "*Martyrs* and Martyrdom in the Apocalypse: A Semantic Study." *NovT* 15 (1973) 72–80; Allison A. Trites. *New Testament Witness in Today's World* (1983); Allison A. Trites. "The Idea of Witness in the Synoptic Gospels—Some Juridical Considerations." *Them* 5 (1968) 18–26; Allison A. Trites. *The New Testament Concept of Witness* (1977; 2004); Allison A. Trites. "Two Witness Motifs in Acts 1:8 and the Book of Acts." *Them* 7 (1970) 17–22; H. van Vliet. *No Single Testimony: A Study in the Adoption of the Law of Deut. 19:15 par. into the New Testament* (1958).

ALLISON A. TRITES

TET [ט t]. The ninth letter of the Hebrew alphabet, which derives from the original Semitic word *tayt-* or *tit-*, though the meaning is unknown. *See* ALPHABET.

TETRAGRAMMATON tet´ruh-gram´uh-ton. *Tetragrammaton* (tetragrammatos τετραγράμματος) literally means "having four letters" (tetra = four; gramma = letter). It is the technical term for the covenantal name of God, in the OT. The name appears written with four consonants: **YHWH** (יהוה). Scholarship has customarily linked the Tetragrammaton with the verb hayah (הָיָה, "to be"), so that the NRSV, e.g., renders the name "I am who I am" or "I am" (Exod 3:14-15), but etymological connections are problematic. The Masoretic Text of the OT (*see* MASORA) follows a reverent Jewish tradition designed to avoid pronouncing the name of God. Using a system called QERE-KETHIBH, the vowels from 'adhonay (אֲדֹנָי, "my Lord") are incorporated with the consonants of the Tetragrammaton to remind the reader to say aloud or read 'adhonay in place of the holy name. However, Christians sometimes pronounce the Tetragrammaton as "Yahweh" (or mistakenly as JEHOVAH). Commonly rendered "LORD" in English translations, the Tetragrammaton occurs 6,828 times in the OT. *See* GOD, NAMES OF; LORD.

MICHAEL D. MATLOCK

TETRARCH, TETRARCHY tet´rahrk [τετράρχης tetrarchēs, τετραρχία tetrarchia]. *Tetrarch* originally meant "one of four rulers," but it came to describe a ruler with less autonomy or status than a king. This specialized hierarchy of royal titles is evident among the successors of Herod the Great (*see* HEROD, FAMILY). Herod held the title of king, but after his death his kingdom was divided among three of his sons. One son, Archelaus, received the core of his realm—Judea and Samaria—and was given the title ETHNARCH. Two other sons, however, were named tetrarchs and ruled smaller territories (ANTIPAS over Galilee and Perea, and PHILIP over the area east and northeast of the Sea of Galilee). Some texts use the terms with less precision than other texts. For example, while Mark 6:14 calls Herod Antipas a "king" (basileus βασιλεύς), the par. texts in Matt 14:1 and Luke 9:7 use the more precise term *tetrarch* (tetrarchēs; NRSV, "ruler," with "tetrarch" in footnote). Luke–Acts maintains the technical term for Antipas (Luke 3:19; Acts 13:1; NRSV, "ruler") and cites three tetrarchies to provide a date for the activities of John the Baptist (Antipas, Philip, and LYSANIAS of Abilene in Luke 3:1; NRSV, "ruler"). *See* GOVERNOR.

STEVEN J. FRIESEN

TETRATEUCH tet´truh-tyook. The term *Tetrateuch* comes from the Greek tetras (τετράς, "four") and teuchos (τεῦχος, "tool, implement"), yielding "four (book) implement." It designates the first four books of the CANON OF THE OLD TESTAMENT—Genesis, Exodus, Leviticus, and Numbers. In antiquity the Torah, or PENTATEUCH, came to be regarded as the foundational unit of the OT. However, the rise of critical scholarship led to abandonment of Mosaic authorship of the Torah and to separation of the five books into various sources (*see* SOURCE CRITICISM). After various propositions of a HEXATEUCH (Genesis–Joshua), Deuteronomy generally became separated from the first four books because of its idiosyncratic style. Scholars from the 19th and early 20th cent. saw Deuteronomy as having more affinities with the subsequent books of Joshua–2 Kings, leading to the almost universally accepted theory of a DEUTERONOMISTIC HISTORY binding the books from Deuteronomy to 2 Kings (minus Ruth) together. With Deuteronomy gone, scholars generally saw the other sources (J, E, and P; *see* DOCUMENTARY HYPOTHESIS) running throughout the tetrateuchal books. The basic notion of the Tetrateuch continued in spite of ensuing scholarly doubt surrounding the sources of J (Yahwist) and E (Elohist).

The tetrateuchal corpus covers the narratives of creation, the ancestors and ancestresses, captivity and exodus from Egypt, Sinai, the forty-year wilderness wandering, and conquest of the Transjordanian kingdoms of Sihon and Og. The narrative ends in the plains of Moab (see Num 35:1) without any significant denouement. In addition to the narratives, the Tetrateuch contained various legal material such as the Covenant Code in

Exod 20–23, the Holiness Code in Lev 17–26, the Priestly ordinances and directives for building the tabernacle in Exod 25–Lev 16, and assorted laws throughout the book of Numbers. Some subjects are addressed multiple times, such as the festival ordinances in Exod 23:14-19; 34:22-26; Lev 23:1-44; and Num 28–29. Further genres include songs, such as the SONG OF THE SEA in Exod 15, and various genealogies throughout Genesis and especially Numbers.

An alternate model to the Tetrateuch-plus-DtrH model has been proposed in recent German-speaking scholarship. This model postulates that the first version of the whole block of material from Exodus–2 Kings was joined together before the addition of Genesis. This model necessarily questions the idea of a Tetrateuch, because Exodus through Numbers becomes detached from Genesis.

PETER ALTMANN

TEXT CRITICISM, NT. New Testament textual criticism—traditionally defined as the science and art of recovering, on the basis of the surviving copies and citations of a document, its original text—is increasingly viewed as having two goals: 1) identifying the earliest recoverable form of a document; and 2) investigating textual variants for the light they shed on the history of the early church and its controversies. The differences between these two ways of viewing textual criticism are the primary focus of contemporary discussion within the discipline.

This essay will focus on text-critical methodology; the synergistic relationship between methodology and a textual critic's view of the history of textual transmission; and current discussion of the goals of textual criticism. For a survey of the rich material resources with which NT textual criticism works—manuscripts, versions, and citations—see TEXT, NT.

A. Methodology
B. Methodology and the History of Transmission
C. Goals and Objectives
Bibliography

A. Methodology

New Testament textual criticism works with two sorts of evidence, external (that provided by the manuscripts and other witnesses themselves) and internal (having to do with authorial style and vocabulary and scribal habits and practice). External evidence includes the relative age of the available witnesses (relative, because a late manuscript may be a direct or near-direct copy of a much older ancestor), their geographic distribution and variety, and the relative weight of the witnesses supporting competing readings. Internal evidence consists of two categories, transcriptional (which assesses the impact of scribal habits, practices, and mistakes on the transmission of a document) and intrinsic (which considers authorial style and characteristics).

Seeking to do justice to both sorts of evidence, nearly all contemporary textual critics utilize a methodological approach known as "reasoned eclecticism." This approach focuses on a fundamental guideline that governs all other considerations: the variant most likely to be original is the one that best accounts for the existence of the others. For example, when confronted by two or more variant readings in a text, reasoned eclecticism seeks to determine which one (if any) best explains, in terms of both external and internal considerations, the origin of the competing readings, and therefore should be considered to be the earliest recoverable form of the text. In this context it is important to stress that "best accounts for" must be understood as encompassing both internal and external considerations. It is precisely on this point of encompassing "all the evidence" that competing approaches such as "rigorous eclecticism" (which privileges internal evidence almost exclusively) and a "Majority text" approach (which emphasizes selected elements of external evidence virtually exclusively) fall short, in that each argues for the originality of variants on the basis of only part of the total available evidence or considerations.

Reasoned eclecticism is required by the nature of the NT manuscript tradition. The classical genealogical approach that seeks to determine the earliest recoverable form of a manuscript tradition by developing a "family tree" of relationships (and thereby trace a line back to the earliest surviving source or ancestor) is inapplicable to NT textual criticism because of the universal presence of "mixture" ("cross-pollination" or "contamination") in the manuscript tradition. That is, instead of being copied from a single exemplar, NT manuscripts (or their ancestors) reflect the results of having been copied from or corrected against multiple exemplars (models). The practical consequence of this "cross pollination" is that any given point, any manuscript or group of manuscripts, may preserve the reading that is the source of all other variants (or, vice versa, may preserve a secondary reading). Thus it is necessary to evaluate every instance of variation on its own terms, applying all external and internal considerations in combination and evaluating the character of the variants in light of the manuscript evidence (and vice versa) in an effort to determine which variant (if any) best explains the others, and thus should be considered as the earliest recoverable form of the text.

B. Methodology and the History of Transmission

Agreement regarding methodology, however, has not produced agreement regarding results. Opinions about the quality of the most widely used Greek text—the United Bible Societies/Nestle-Aland Greek testament—vary widely. To some extent, this is a consequence of differing judgments about how much weight to give various kinds of evidence—e.g., whether to weight more heavily one strand of external evidence than another, or to rely more on transcriptional than intrinsic considerations. To a larger and more important extent, however, differences in how the dominant method is applied reflect differing reconstructions of the history of the transmission of the text. Westcott and Hort, e.g., viewed the Byzantine textual tradition as a synthesis of two chronologically earlier traditions, the Neutral/Alexandrian and the Western, and thus incapable of independently preserving an authentic reading (a view largely shared by the editorial committee responsible for the UBS/Nestle-Aland text). Some, however, consider the Byzantine textual tradition as the sole direct representative of the earliest tradition, and the Western and Alexandrian traditions as later offshoots of it (and thus incapable of independently preserving authentic readings). In contrast, Zuntz argues that all the roots of all three traditions reach back to the earliest stages of the transmission of the NT text, and therefore any one of the three alone may preserve authentic readings no longer found in the others.

In short, the assessment of particular instances of variation is fundamentally influenced by one's perception of the history of the text as a whole (which is, of course, in turn shaped by one's assessment of individual readings). Methodology does not operate in a vacuum; there is a synergistic relationship between methodology and history, and one's view of the history of the text is no less important than one's basic approach to methodology. Despite this importance, one shortcoming of recent discussion is a relative lack of attention to the history of the transmission of the text as a whole.

C. Goals and Objectives

Traditionally NT textual criticism has had a single goal: recovering the original text, to the extent permitted by the evidence. Contemporary discussion increasingly conceptualizes the discipline in terms of two (closely related) goals: 1) identifying the "earliest recoverable form" (*Ausgangstext*) of a document's textual tradition; and 2) exploring the place and role of textual variation in the history and culture of the early church for the light it sheds on the theological, hermeneutical, liturgical, and social contexts of the individuals and communities that transmitted (and sometimes deliberately altered) the NT texts.

With regard to the first goal, the change in terminology from "original text" to "earliest recoverable form" of the history of transmission of a text (a change reflecting, in a sense, differences between Enlightenment and postmodern perspectives) arises out of 1) a growing realization of the problematic nature of the concept of "original text," and 2) increasing awareness of the possibility of intervening stages between the "original text" and its "earliest recoverable form." To put the first point in its simplest form, does "original text" mean the "autograph," or the specific source text (which may or may not be the autograph) from which all surviving copies descend? If it is the latter, that raises the possibility that all surviving copies descend from an imperfect copy of

the document (for it is virtually impossible for any hand-written copy perfectly to match its model) and would share its mistakes.

For example, what is the source of all surviving copies of Philippians: 1) the letter that Paul sent to Philippi; or 2) the copy he almost certainly kept for his own archives (which would be a close but not perfect copy of the sent letter); or 3) some later copy of either one that became part of the collected edition (*corpus Paulinum*) of the Pauline letters that some scholars (for good reasons) think is the source of all known copies? If the answer is #1, then the gap between the "earliest recoverable form" of Philippians and the letter Paul sent would be minimal; but if the answer is #3, then it is possible for there to be a three- or four-generation gap between the "earliest recoverable form" of Philippians and the letter Paul sent. For these and other reasons (including the possibility of multiple editions, especially in the case of Acts, for example), it is increasingly common for the goal of textual criticism to be defined not in terms of reconstructing the "original text" but rather of determining the "earliest recoverable form" of the text possible on the basis of the surviving evidence. Furthermore, the sharp separation between literary and textual criticism previously maintained is now increasingly recognized as artificial; both must be pursued in tandem, and the results of each can influence the other.

With regard to the second point, the study of the history of the transmission of the text has always been an important aspect of textual criticism, because a fundamental prerequisite to reaching a judgment between competing variant readings is the reconstruction of their history. What is different in current discussion is a greater focus on the study of the history of the variants as a source of insight in their own right. That is, whereas previously secondary readings were viewed largely as chaff, to be discarded once they were determined to be secondary, it is now evident that some secondary readings (especially those intentionally created), while clearly not original, nonetheless can shed significant light on the theological, hermeneutical, liturgical, and social contexts of the individuals and communities that created and/or transmitted them. This fruitful emphasis represents the flourishing, since ca. 1990, of a perspective first articulated in the early and mid-20th cent.

Although in some quarters this recent emphasis might appear to replace the traditional goal of recovering the text (however that goal is defined), in fact it presupposes it (one cannot identify and analyze the effect of intentional variation without a baseline text as a starting point). Indeed, there is a synergistic relationship between the two goals: an understanding of the history of the transmission of the text is prerequisite to identifying its earliest recoverable stage, which in turn makes possible the identification and investigation of secondary readings for the light they have to contribute.

Bibliography: Kurt Aland and Barbara Aland. *The Text of the New Testament: An Introduction to the Critical Editions and to the Theory and Practice of Modern Textual Criticism.* 2nd ed. (1989); Bart D. Ehrman. *The Orthodox Corruption of Scripture: The Effect of Early Christological Controversies on the Text of the New Testament* (1993); Bart D. Ehrman. *Studies in the Textual Criticism of the New Testament* (2006); Bart D. Ehrman and Michael W. Holmes. *The Text of the New Testament in Contemporary Research: Essays on the* Status Quaestionis (1995); Eldon Jay Epp. *Perspectives on New Testament Textual Criticism: Collected Essays*, 1962–2004 (2005); Eldon Jay Epp. "It's All about Variants: A Variant-Conscious Approach to New Testament Textual Criticism." *HTR* 100 (2007) 275–308; Eldon Jay Epp and Gordon D. Fee. *Studies in the Theory and Method of New Testament Textual Criticism* (1993); Michael W. Holmes. "Textual Criticism." *Interpreting the New Testament: Essays on Methods and Issues.* David Alan Black and David S. Dockery, eds. (2001) 46–73; Michael W. Holmes. "The Case for Reasoned Eclecticism." *Rethinking New Testament Textual Criticism.* David A. Black, ed. (2002) 77–100; Michael W. Holmes. "The Text of the Epistles Sixty Years After: An Assessment of Günther Zuntz's Contribution to Text-Critical Methodology and History." *Transmission and Reception: New Testament Text-Critical and Exegetical Studies.* Jeffrey Childers and D. C. Parker, eds. (2006) 89–113; Bruce M. Metzger and Bart D. Ehrman. *The Text of the New Testament: Its Transmission, Corruption, and Restoration.* 4th ed. (2005); David Parker. "Textual Criticism and Theology." *ExpTim* 118 (2007) 583–89; David Parker. *An Introduction to the New Testament Manuscripts and Their Texts* (2008); David C. Parker. *The Living Text of the Gospels* (1997); Maurice A. Robinson. "The Case for Byzantine Priority." *Rethinking New Testament Textual Criticism.* David A. Black, ed. (2002) 125–39; B. F. Westcott and F. J. A. Hort. *The Greek New Testament* (2007); Günther Zuntz. *The Text of the Epistles: A Disquisition upon the* Corpus Paulinum (1953).

MICHAEL W. HOLMES

TEXT CRITICISM, OT. In the study of Greek and Roman literature, textual criticism has been traditionally defined as "the science of discovering error in texts and the art of removing it" (Housman). While the discovery and removal of error in the text of the OT is certainly part of the task of textual criticism, it does not exhaust it. The situation of the textual criticism of the OT is unusual in that witnesses to the text vary greatly in date and exist in numerous languages. Some of the witnesses to the text in Hebrew and Greek may even preserve evidence of editions or versions of biblical compositions more ancient than those that later became canonical in Judaism or Christianity. This is especially true of the biblical manuscripts among the DEAD SEA SCROLLS.

Because of this complex situation the textual criticism of the OT may also necessarily include the study and clarification of the end stages in the literary production of biblical compositions, not simply their transmission. The relationships among the various versions of a composition are likely to require clarification.

A. The Form of the Text
B. Critical Editions of the Old Testament
C. How Does the Text Change?
D. Procedures and Rules
E. Textual Witnesses
Bibliography

A. The Form of the Text

What form of the text should be the focus of the textual critic's activity? Should he or she focus only on the canonical composition based on the text of the MT or should the textual critic cast a broader net and attempt to reconstruct earlier forms of the text so that the history of the development of the composition is revealed?

Presently in the field of the textual criticism of the OT there are proponents of each of these two approaches. One position is that the proper task of the textual criticism of the OT is establishing the "final" form of the text based on the MT (Sanders). In this understanding of the task, parallel or earlier forms of the text are not relevant. The textual critic focuses on the form of the Hebrew text that became normative in Judaism even if the textual evidence allows the recovery of earlier forms of the text (Tov). The textual critic determines the best readings in the final, canonical form of the text.

The other position is that the task of the textual criticism of the OT requires the textual critic to recover the earliest form of the text that the evidence allows. This understanding of textual criticism aims to recover the archetype of the biblical composition (Ulrich). In delving into the history of the text, some early witnesses provide evidence of earlier forms of the text. If these forms are recoverable, the textual critic working with this approach would attempt to reconstruct those earlier or parallel forms.

B. Critical Editions of the Old Testament

Textual critics of both persuasions agree that one of the important tasks of textual criticism is the creation of a critical edition of the text of the OT using all of the available textual evidence. But there agreement ends. There are two models or philosophies concerning the creation of critical editions of the OT. The first model has been the norm in the field for over two centuries. In this model, scholars present the text of one manuscript as accurately as possible. This diplomatic edition of the manuscript is accompanied by apparatuses that present the readings of other textual witnesses that offer variants or other readings of interest. The text of the manuscript that serves as the basis for the edition may be corrected where there are obvious scribal errors. Otherwise, variants and other corrections are presented in the apparatuses. The *Biblia Hebraica*, which began with Rudolf Kittel at the beginning of the 20th cent. and continues with the *Biblia Hebraica Quinta*, follows the model of the diplomatic critical edition. That project has used the St. Petersburg Codex (Firkowitz B 19A) since the third edition of 1937. Another diplomatic edition of this manuscript is found in *Biblia Hebraica Leningradensis* prepared by Aron Dotan. Regrettably, this edition does not include critical apparatuses. The Hebrew University Bible also follows this model, but uses the Aleppo Codex as the base text where it is extant. Both of these editions present extensive additional readings from other textual witnesses in critical apparatuses.

In the second model of creating a critical edition of the Hebrew text, no single manuscript is used as the base text; rather the editor(s) reconstruct the text based on an evaluation and analysis of all the manuscript evidence. This sort of edition is called an eclectic critical edition. Examples of this type of critical edition are the UBS Greek New Testament and the Göttingen Septuagint. Currently the only attempt to create an eclectic critical edition of the text of the OT is the Oxford Hebrew Bible, edited by R. Hendel. This project is still in its early stages and no sections of it have appeared in print as of 2009. The Oxford Hebrew Bible will use the St. Petersburg Codex as a copy text and insert corrected readings where in the editors' judgment the manuscript evidence warrants it.

Although these two approaches to the textual criticism of the OT seem to be at loggerheads with each other, in reality there is a great deal of cooperation and cross-pollination between the various critical edition projects.

C. How Does the Text Change?

The textual criticism of the OT is necessary because over time scribal errors and intentional changes have crept into the text. Errors enter the textual tradition primarily through mistakes made when the texts are copied. Scribes make certain types of mistakes that have to do with the copying process. We make the same sorts of mistakes today even though we may use very different technology. Unintentional scribal mistakes occur primarily either because of the skip of the scribe's eye to the wrong point in the text being copied or through mishearing a text being read aloud to be copied.

Some scribal mistakes make the text longer. Expansions include both unintentional and intentional expansions. Unintentional expansions include: 1) dittography, literally "double writing," where the scribe unintentionally repeats a letter, word, or series of words; and 2) unintended expansions, which might be words that clarify the meaning of a text that the scribe added without conscious reflection. Also in this category are the addition of epithets, titles, or formulae that were familiar to the scribe.

Intentional expansions could include: 1) Modernization, which occurs when scribes change the text to make it more understandable, especially by replacing archaic or rare forms with contemporary forms. Some of the biblical manuscripts from the Judean desert preserve readings where the scribes changed the text to bring it into line with contemporary usage. 2) Glosses are words or expressions added to clarify rare or unusual terms. Glossing could be understood as a type of modernizing. 3) Explications are additions that function to make explicit something that is unexpressed or only implied in the text. Explications or explicating glosses function similarly to glosses and could be either intended or unintended. 4) Conflation involves the combination of variant readings that may have originally been synonymous. Variants that are preserved in a single witness may be described as conflated readings. Conflated readings may also result when a scribe compares different copies of a text and combines readings from those witnesses into a third text. This process of conflating readings from different witnesses is called contamination. The scholar should be suspicious of expansions since texts that are frequently copied tend to accrete readings over time.

Some scribal errors make the text shorter. Haplography, or literally "single writing," is the unintentional writing of a letter or word or series of words once when they should have been written more than once. Haplography is a frequent type of scribal error, which is caused by the scribe's eye skipping to the wrong place in the text while copying. Haplographies may be described as the result of parablepsis, literally "to see wrong" or "overlook"; they result in the loss of text and so create shorter readings. The scholar must be wary of shorter readings, which may result from scribal error. Parablepsis may be further refined by the whether the scribe's eye skipped from the beginning of a word or from the end of a word (compare HOMOIOTELEUTON).

Some errors do not affect the length of the text. A good example is graphic confusion. In the handwriting of many of the scribes of the 3rd through 1st cent. BCE some letters have such similar shapes that they were easily confused by copyists or translators. The confusion of letters may lead to the creation of a reading that makes sense in the context, which makes the error difficult to discern, or to a reading that does not make good sense in the context.

D. Procedures and Rules

The most important rule in the textual criticism of the OT is the rule of reason. Reason and logic should be applied to each and every textual problem encountered. There is no rule of greater importance. The rule of reason is simply the application of common sense and good judgment. It finds expression in the following two traditional forms. 1) *Difficilior lectio potior*, meaning "the more difficult reading is preferable." The sense of *difficilior* in this statement is perhaps better given as "complex." It is seldom the simplest reading that is preferable, but rather the more complex reading. Scribes have a tendency to simplify the text, to make the text more understandable. 2) *Utrum in alterum abiturum erat?* means, roughly, "Which would have been more likely to give rise to the other?" Given a variety of readings among witnesses, this general guideline can be very helpful to keep in mind.

These traditional rules should be understood more as guidelines to which any textual problem may be an exception. Each textual problem must be examined individually in the light of all available evidence. The evidence of a given witness must be evaluated in the context of that witness. That is to say, the reading must be understood in the broad context of the witness before it can be properly applied to a textual problem in the OT.

E. Textual Witnesses

For the textual criticism of the OT, of foremost importance are those witnesses to the text in the Hebrew or Aramaic languages. The most valuable of these witnesses are the biblical manuscripts from the Judean desert, including the Dead Sea Scrolls and the Masoretic codices, such as the St. Petersburg Codex (Firkovich I B19A) and the ALEPPO CODEX. For the text of the Pentateuch the SAMARITAN PENTATEUCH is also essential. The medieval Hebrew manuscripts are not considered to be of great importance by most scholars except where they agree with more ancient witnesses, since for the most part they preserve only minor orthographic variations from the Masoretic codices.

The biblical manuscripts from the Judean desert have revolutionized our understanding of the history of the text of the OT and our knowledge of scribal practices. Some of these manuscripts attest forms of biblical compositions that predate the form that ultimately became canonical in Judaism and Christianity. In these cases scholars are able, at least in part, to trace the final stages in the composition of biblical books. As is well known, the biblical manuscripts among the Dead Sea Scrolls and other biblical manuscripts from the Judean desert in Hebrew are the oldest biblical manuscripts in existence. They range in date from ca. 275 BCE to 68 CE. One of the results of the study of these manuscripts and comparison with the MT and the LXX is the realization that the text of the OT for many of the biblical compositions was still fluid in the period from ca. 300 BCE to ca. 100 CE. Because of the great increase in the number of early Hebrew biblical manuscripts as well as citations of biblical texts in early Hebrew exegetical literature, Hebrew witnesses have become the most important resources for the textual criticism of the OT.

Although the witnesses to the text in Hebrew are of primary importance, the ancient translations of the Hebrew text cannot be ignored and are also of great importance for textual criticism. The textual critic must know the ancient translations exceedingly well to make use of them for the textual criticism of the OT. Apparent differences between the MT and the ancient translations may be the result of translation techniques, exegesis, or scribal error rather than a reflection of an actual Hebrew variant. Nevertheless, the ancient translations remain an important resource and potential source of variant readings. The Hebrew sources for the ancient translations must first be reconstructed in order to make use of them for the textual criticism of the OT. Even when the ancient translation do not preserve Hebrew variants, they are important resources for the study of early biblical exegesis in Judaism and Christianity.

Foremost among the ancient translations is the ancient Greek translation commonly known as the SEPTUAGINT. The nature of the Greek translation varies from book to book, from the literal to the paraphrastic. The textual critic must know the work of the various translators, their techniques and favorite word choices, very well in order to make use of the Greek text. The LXX and other Greek versions can provide important data for individual readings as well as for the history of the final stages in the literary development of the biblical compositions and the transmission of the text.

The PESHITTA preserves some variants from the MT that may reflect actual Hebrew variants, but for the most part the Peshitta closely follows the MT. The same is true of the various TARGUMS and the VULGATE. For the most part, when not exegetical in nature, these textual traditions reflect the MT. The Greek and other ancient translations must be used with great care. They must first be understood in their own right as coherent versions of the biblical text before they can be utilized for the textual criticism of the OT. *See* TEXT, HEBREW, HISTORY OF.

Bibliography: Ellis R. Brotzman. *Old Testament Textual Criticism: A Practical Introduction* (1994); A. E. Housman. "The Application of Thought to Textual Criticism." *Proceedings of the Classical Association* 18 (1921) 67–84; P. Kyle McCarter, Jr. *Recovering the Text of the Hebrew Bible* (1986); Lee Martin McDonald. *The Biblical Canon: Its Origin, Transmission, and Authority* (2007); James Sanders. "The Task of Text Criticism." *Problems in Biblical Theology: Essays in Honor of Rolf Knierim.* Henry T. C. Sun and Keith L. Eades, eds. (1996) 315–27; Emanuel Tov. "The Original Shape of the Biblical Text." *Congress Volume Leuven, 1989.* J. A. Emerton, ed. (1991) 355–56; Eugene Ulrich. "Multiple Literary Editions: Reflections toward a Theory of the History of the Biblical Text." *Current Research and Technological Developments on the Dead Sea Scrolls.* D. W. Parry and S. D. Hicks, eds. *Studies on the Texts* *of the Desert of Judah* (1996) 79–105; Eugene Ulrich. "The Dead Sea Scrolls and the Hebrew Scriptural Texts." *The Bible and the Dead Sea Scrolls Vol. 1: The Hebrew Bible and Qumran.* James H. Charlesworth, ed. (2000) 105–133.

RUSSELL E. FULLER

TEXT, HEBREW, HISTORY OF. The text printed in our Bibles appears neat, uniform, and clear, similar to modern books composed by a single author. But behind that clarity is both a long and fascinating history of growth from innumerable sources into unified books, as well as an intriguing political-social-religious history of the selection of which books were eventually to be included or excluded. The apparent clarity of the final form is achieved through myriad decisions between alternatives by the scholarly and ecclesiastical teams responsible for producing each particular Bible.

Unfortunately, there is no manuscript evidence for tracing the history of the biblical text until ca. 250 BCE; up to that point it is necessary to rely on scholarly hypotheses: the cumulative results of centuries of intense international and interconfessional biblical scholarship.

A. Origins of the Components of the Biblical Texts
  1. Use of disparate sources
  2. Borrowing foreign literature
  3. Dynamics of oral composition and transmission
B. Growth of the Books
C. From Literature to Scripture
  1. Historical shifts
  2. The word of God
D. Early Translations into Aramaic and Greek
E. Manuscript Evidence
  1. The Qumran manuscripts
  2. Different levels of textual variation
  3. Two periods in the history of the text
F. From Collection of Scriptures to Canon
G. A Guide to the Witnesses to the Text
  1. The scrolls
  2. The Masoretic Text
  3. The Samaritan Pentateuch
  4. The Septuagint
Bibliography

A. Origins of the Components of the Biblical Texts

The origins of the many passages that eventually came to form the biblical text are quite diverse and require understanding of several factors: the weaving together of disparate sources, the borrowing and adaptation of foreign literature, and the dynamics of oral composition and transmission.

1. Use of disparate sources

With regard to the use of disparate sources, most of the narrative, legal, prophetic, and wisdom books betray a compilation of numerous originally separate sources.

Many of the episodes that now constitute, e.g., the book of Genesis originated as single stories about a certain patriarch or tribal leader. Each had a life in the preserved memory of the people and then was assembled by a creative author into a continuous narrative, attached to the names of Abraham, Isaac, and Jacob, and unified in a dramatic sequence. For prophetic books, many of the sayings gathered into them were isolated pronouncements of warning or encouragement as responses to specific situations often widely separated in time. Many of the psalms and proverbs began as individual simple prayers or pithy sayings uttered at different times and places in Israel's history.

For example, in Gen 18:2 Abraham "looked up and saw three men" who had come his way, and the story continues as a model hospitality story, originally unconnected with previous or following stories. But an author or editor, classically identified as the Yahwist (*see* J, YAHWIST), introduced the story with "The LORD appeared to Abraham ...," as he incorporated this free-floating story into his larger narrative framework of the Abraham–Isaac–Jacob story. It then served to function as the divine birth announcement of the son and heir promised in Gen 12 and 15. Similarly, Gen 22, the test of Abraham to sacrifice Isaac, had earlier been a separate story explaining why child sacrifice had been replaced by animal sacrifice (and possibly yet earlier a narrative encouraging child sacrifice). As that separate story was incorporated into the larger patriarchal narrative collection, it served to function as Abraham's passing a final test before the blessing was handed on to the divinely saved son.

Just as the Genesis stories had disparate origins, so were parts of prophetic and wisdom books also assembled from widely different settings. For example, Isaiah's prophetic rebuke of King Ahaz—"Look, the young woman is with child and shall bear a son, and shall name him Immanuel" (Isa 7:14)—was a warning aimed at making the correct decision in the Syro-Ephraimite War in the 8th cent. BCE. In contrast, the later promise in the same book—"The grass withers, the flower fades; but the word of our God will stand forever" (Isa 40:8)—was a statement of confidence by Second Isaiah concerning Judah's release from Babylonian captivity in the 6th cent. BCE. Finally, the likely setting for a psalm such as Ps 2 was the preexilic independent monarchy, whereas the postexilic experience of the Babylonian captivity produced Ps 137. These select examples illustrate the general process by which numerous sources from different periods were collected and gradually unified into the books as transmitted in the Jewish community.

2. Borrowing foreign literature

Some of those sources did not have their origins within Israel. Just as Israel emerged as a state within the matrix of more ancient and more magnificent kingdoms, so too did its literature borrow from the vast and impressive literature of Egypt, Mesopotamia, and Canaan.

Those long-established cultures had developed a variety of genres: legal materials, royal annals, treaties, hymns, prayers, letters, wisdom texts, and others. These genres in general and certain specific literary traditions and themes influenced Israel's developing literature, though Israel adapted them to its Yahwistic beliefs and cultural norms. For example, Ps 104 is acknowledged as reminiscent of the Egyptian hymn to the sun god Aten; Ps 29 shows influences of Canaanite hymnic patterns and praise of the storm god Baal; and Proverbs shows many similarities to the sayings of the Assyrian sage Ahikar.

3. Dynamics of oral composition and transmission

Moreover, Israelite culture, like most ancient cultures, was primarily an oral culture. Even when extended narratives, law codes, prophetic traditions, or wisdom collections were written down, they were nonetheless primarily recited and transmitted orally. Although oral transmission can preserve texts with great accuracy, it is quite likely that certain variations of synonymous words and phrases, as well as expansions by inclusion of related materials, characterized the handing down of the texts through the centuries. Thus, the origins of the components of the biblical books were from disparate historical settings, sometimes from foreign settings, and subject to variation due to their oral transmission. In addition, the wording of those original sources would often have been revised to fit into the larger literary and religious contexts into which they were incorporated. Thus, the core texts for many books were early, were dynamically growing, and were primarily oral in form.

B. Growth of the Books

As the process of gathering the originally oral stories, legal formulations, wisdom sayings, and songs into small collections continued, eventually those collections grew into major complexes that form the basis of individual biblical books and groups of books. This process occurred at different times for different books. For example, it is quite likely that toward the end of the 7th cent. BCE there were already two large complexes of historical literature, the early strata of the pentateuchal or hexateuchal narrative and the DEUTERONOMISTIC HISTORY (Deuteronomy–Kings, minus Ruth). There were probably also sizable collections of priestly ritual practices and of temple hymns and prayers, as well as growing collections of prophetic and wisdom materials.

In the century or two after the return from the Babylonian captivity, a rethinking of the old religious traditions was required. The unexpected destruction and exile, plus what some surely supposed was a sign of God's abandonment, necessitated a re-theologizing and brought about updated forms of a number of those collections that we would recognize as early forms of biblical books. Interwoven into the preexilic narrative traditions of Israel's origins (traditional JE) were the postexilic re-theologized passages (P) now found in the Pentateuch (compare Gen 2–3 with Gen 1, and Gen 15 with 17). Similarly, at some point Ezra's legal materials—"the law of your God, which is in your hand" (Ezra 7:14)—were incorporated into the framework of the pentateuchal narrative. The originally balanced but hopeful Deuteronomistic History was revised and updated in light of the unexpected destruction and exile. The earlier prophetic collections were expanded with salvation oracles, which then balanced the ominous oracles of judgment with consolation and hope. The growing collections of Psalms and Proverbs were also amplified with revised theological components.

The end product of all the stages and types of development described above was a collection of many books of the law and the prophets that were close to the textual forms transmitted in the modern Bible. But those processes of development show that the traditional goal of textual criticism, i.e., to establish "the original text," is a highly complicated notion and proves to be a frustratingly protean and elusive goal. Though an attempt to establish "the original text" at each of the stages described would be interesting for literary history, with respect to the biblical text many of those developing stages of the books are probably not sufficiently developed to be useful. The dynamics of this development, however, are important for understanding numerous aspects of the text: the Qumran biblical evidence, a newly illumined period in the history of the biblical text, and indeed proper interpretation of the message of the Bible.

C. From Literature to Scripture
1. Historical shifts

As the different books were developing literarily, each on its own trajectory, so too were they growing in sacralization along different time-lines. The Bible we receive is viewed as divinely inspired Scripture, a collection of complete books; it is the textual basis of the Jewish and Christian religions, the wording of which is fixed, and there are definitive contents bound into a book. Those features that characterize the final form of the Bible, however, had earlier histories that are useful to trace, even if the process is mostly clouded in history. First, as we have seen, many of the books contain earlier disparate, anonymous, oral sources incorporated into larger contexts. It is difficult to establish that the originators of such sources thought they were composing "Scripture." Thus, there was a shift, mostly imperceptible, from Israel's literature to its Scripture. Second, it is similarly unlikely that collectors of individual prophetic sayings that were understood as God's message thought that their own prose editorial framework for those sayings and their biographical accounts were "Scripture," though eventually the entire book was viewed as inspired. Thus, there was a shift of God's message from the prophetic words to a complete written book. Third, though the text has been viewed as fundamental and central since the destruction of the Temple in the First

Jewish Revolt and the geographic scattering of the Jewish population after the Second Revolt, prior to that destruction the Temple was the centripetal focus of the Jewish religion, and the texts were apparently secondary; thus, there was a shift from auxiliary status to primary focus and central importance for the texts. Fourth, we have seen that the text, viewed since about the 2nd cent. CE as unchangeable, was earlier characterized by dynamic growth; thus there was a shift from a pluriform to uniform text. Finally, as we will see below, the codex or bound set of pages with defined contents was not in use at the origins of rabbinic Judaism and Christianity; it did not become common until about the 3rd cent. CE. The Scriptures were rather an undefined, not-yet-finalized collection of "the law and the prophets," with some books clearly required, other books debated, and perhaps some not yet even under consideration. Thus, there was a fifth shift from a vague collection of "the law and the prophets" (as still seen in NT times) to a finally decided and physically delimited collection of books. These five shifts, and perhaps others, each moving on its own particular journey, transformed Israel's literature into the Hebrew Scriptures.

2. The word of God

Just as those diverse historical currents were contributing to the increasing sacralization of the books, so too was the religious experience of the communities. Those trajectories mostly began with what may aptly be called national literature and gradually grew, through the successive communities' life before God, to become experienced and recognized as sacred Scripture. The canonical process involved two important factors: repetition, the handing down of the traditions from generation to generation, and resignification, the adaptability of the tradition to speak meaningfully to new and diverse situations. As communities repeatedly found that they heard the voice of God guiding them through the older religious literature in their new situations, they recognized these writings as the word of God.

There were a number of features that contributed to this process. As was frequent in the ANE, Israel had numerous religious narratives with God as an actor and speaker, and thus, God's speaking to humans was not unusual. Both the liturgy and educational settings also instilled in the people the conviction that "this is what God says, what God wants." Editorial development of the text also contributed, with introductory statements added to frame traditional passages, such as "God said to Moses: Say to the people ...." Again, insertions were added to frame prophetic texts, such as "The word that came to Jeremiah from the LORD: ..." (Jer 7:1), which was not in the earlier edition of the book as witnessed in the LXX but is inserted into the later edition as witnessed in the MT. Note also the conclusion to one section of the continuing passage: "... says the LORD of hosts" (Jer 8:3bβ), which was not in the earlier LXX edition but is inserted into the later MT edition. Finally,

the more ancient a work had become, and the more it had proved itself valuable in Israel's life before God, the more likely it was to be accepted as divinely inspired. More recent works, such as *1 Enoch*, *Jubilees*, and apocryphal books, though accepted by certain communities, could be rejected by others.

Again, prior to the 3rd cent. BCE there is no direct evidence of the dynamics described thus far, though the literary evidence is quite persuasive. But several factors starting from that century indicate both that the individual books had attained a form sufficiently close to be recognized from our received forms, and that the law and perhaps some of the prophets had already achieved their status as the word of God. On the other hand, fixation of the text against further addition or loss—another indicator that later would become a sign of status as sacred Scripture—was not a perceptible feature prior to approximately the 1st or even the 2nd cent. CE.

In the past, when less knowledge and less evidence was available, the religious imagination envisioned the divine dictation of complete books to single individuals, who produced autographs that were handed down as exemplars of "the original text" (*Urtext*). Sustained literary and historical study of the biblical texts, however, confirmed now by the documentary evidence of the biblical scrolls, provides a revision of that picture. In the continuing attempt to understand the divine plan and will, countless contributors over the centuries pondered the divine-human relationship, heard the word in diverse forms, expressed it in human words, and helped develop the books dynamically over the centuries. They added minor or sometimes major components, producing individual supplements to their current edition or expanded new editions of their inherited texts. Through these processes for "the law and the prophets," what had earlier been regarded mainly as national literature, or the word of humans, increasingly became experienced and recognized as sacred Scripture or the word of God.

D. Early Translations into Aramaic and Greek

The first indication that the five books of the Torah and perhaps some of the prophetic books were virtually complete and considered as essential Scripture was that they were important enough to be translated into the languages spoken by the Jewish communities in Babylon and Alexandria. Such a literal translation of a major literary composition was unique in the ancient world. Though three different Sumerian compositions featuring the hero Gilgamesh find echoes in the later Akkadian epic, the latter cannot be considered a translation. Similarly, though the *Iliad* and the *Odyssey* remained essential texts when Rome adopted Greek culture, they were never translated into Latin (except for the *Ilias Latina*, a brief epitome of the *Iliad*, only 1,070 hexameters for the original 15,693).

Although there is no surviving evidence, it is probably safe to assume that the five books of the Torah and perhaps some of the prophetic books were translated into Aramaic for the Jewish community that remained in Babylon, where Aramaic was the lingua franca of the Persian Empire. The specifics of Neh 8:8 are not clear, but the incident portrays the necessity of proclaiming the Torah in a way that could be understood by the average people; increasing numbers of Jews were losing the Hebrew language and speaking Aramaic or Greek. Part of the lack of clarity entails whether the first Aramaic translations were oral or written, but presumably they were eventually written. All extant forms of the TARGUMS, however, show that they have later been revised to conform to the rabbinic version of the Torah. Thus, they are of little independent value for the ancient Hebrew text beyond the forms in the MT, and it is difficult to establish convincingly that any specific element predates the Christian period.

The Old Greek translation of the Torah enjoys stronger evidence to anchor it plausibly in the early 3rd cent. BCE. Though the *Letter of Aristeas* cannot be viewed as historical literature, its setting nonetheless coincides with other types of evidence. Quotations of the Greek surface already in the late 3rd cent., and fragmentary manuscripts of the Old Greek dated to the 2nd cent. BCE have been recovered in both Palestine and Egypt. Apparently only the five books of the law were translated into Greek in the first stage of the process. The conviction that these five were the only books of essential Scripture seems to have endured for some time in certain circles, since the Samaritans took only these when they separated from the Judeans, and since it is difficult to show that the Sadducees recognized more than these. In contrast to the lack of solid, plentiful witness by the Targums to the early text, the early Greek translations remain an important and faithful witness to ancient forms of the Hebrew text (*see* VERSIONS, ANCIENT).

E. Manuscript Evidence

Beginning in the latter half of the 3rd cent. BCE, abundant documentary evidence for the biblical text becomes available. It is not an exaggeration to claim that the more than 200 scrolls of the scriptural texts discovered at QUMRAN have revolutionized the understanding of the text of the Bible in antiquity. As the light shed by the documentary manuscript evidence illumines the developmental growth process of the Scriptures during the late Second Temple period, it shows, and thus confirms, the identical features that historical and literary-critical studies had reconstructed theoretically for earlier periods that provide no manuscript evidence.

Before examining this evidence in detail, it is important to be aware that it is the most ancient and authentic evidence in existence for the nature of the biblical text in antiquity. It illumines a period in the history of the biblical text otherwise lost in the darkness of history and thus requires a shift in paradigm from pre-Qumran views to a post-Qumran view. Prior to 1947, scholarly

understanding of the biblical text centered primarily on medieval Hebrew manuscripts and envisioned a uniform text for each book. The following discussion aims at presenting a path from the earlier views to a contemporary view.

1. The Qumran manuscripts

In 1947, the first two biblical scrolls were found: a beautiful and completely preserved scroll of the book of Isaiah (1QIsaᵃ) and many large fragments from a second, quite damaged scroll of Isaiah (1QIsaᵇ). 1QIsaᵇ proved to be very close to the MT and served to support scholarly confidence that the received texts had maintained great accuracy throughout the centuries of repeated hand copying until the invention of the printing press. That confidence is firmly based, but there was a counterbalancing major surprise. 1QIsaᵃ, in contrast, appeared to be a more favored and well-preserved scroll but, though basically similar to the traditional *textus receptus* of Isaiah, the orthography was noticeably different and it exhibited a large number and wide array of individual textual variants. Furthermore, comparison with the MT highlighted at least seven instances in which large, interpretive additions of up to three verses had been inserted into the MT text tradition (Isa 2:9b-10; 34:17bβ–35:2; 37:5-7; 38:20b-22; 40:7aβ-8a [= Old Greek], 14-16; 51:6aβ?; 63:aβ-bα). The first two biblical scrolls discovered thus displayed over fifty years ago the two basic learnings from the ancient manuscripts concerning the early biblical text: that our MT preserves very accurately one form of the ancient Hebrew texts for each book, but that the nature of the biblical text in antiquity was pluriform and still developing until into the Christian era. Thus, the MT, just like the SAMARITAN PENTATEUCH and the LXX, witnesses to only one of the several, presumably equally valued, forms of the text of each book. Due to the loss of ancient manuscripts and the passage of centuries, we had simply lost awareness of that crucial knowledge.

In addition to the three levels of differing approaches to orthography, frequent individual textual variants, and large interpretive insertions, a fourth level emerged: "new and expanded editions" of biblical books.

For the Torah, manuscripts of Exodus (4QpaleoExodᵐ [4Q22]) and Numbers (4QNumᵇ [4Q27]) exhibited revised, expanded editions of those two books. Their basis was a text close to the edition preserved in the MT, but some creative scribe had introduced frequent, intentional additions (e.g., harmonizations from parallel Deuteronomy material and explicit lengthy reports that God's commands to Moses had in fact been carried out) as well as transpositions of material, presumably for thematic connections. It did not take long to realize that these texts were nearly identical with the Samaritan Pentateuch, except that they did not have the specific Samaritan focus on Mount Gerizim. Then a yet earlier edition was recognized insofar as the Old Greek translation of Exod 35–40 shows a variant, and probably earlier, edition of the construction of the tabernacle; the Hebrew text behind the LXX was subsequently elaborated and rearranged in the MT tradition to fit more closely with the corresponding commands in Exod 25–31.

The prophetic texts also benefited from these insights. Once this developmental pattern of a series of successive editions became clear, once scholars realized that the Samaritan Pentateuch had been revalidated as an important witness to the common Jewish text, and once the 4QJeremiah fragments were analyzed, the LXX of Jeremiah could be appreciated and revalidated as well. 4QJer[b] (4Q71) and 4QJer[d] (4Q72a) proved to contain a short, early edition of the Hebrew text that the Old Greek had translated faithfully. On the other hand, 4QJer[a] (4Q70) and 4QJer[c] (4Q72) displayed the traditional longer text transmitted by the MT, which can be recognized as a revised and expanded edition beyond the 4Q71–4Q72s–Old Greek edition.

A number of other scrolls continued to shed helpful light on the development of various biblical passages and on the anomalies encountered in the Hebrew and Greek manuscript tradition. For example, 4QDeut[q] (4Q44) and 4QSam[a–b] (4Q51–52) similarly displayed Hebrew readings that are found faithfully translated in the LXX, although they are at variance with the MT. 4QJosh[a] (4Q47), 4QJudg[a] (4Q49), and 4Q51 all produced earlier versions of the corresponding texts in the MT. 4Q47 contained an earlier account of the building of the first altar in the newly entered land: at Gilgal immediately after crossing the Jordan, as opposed both to the Samaritan Pentateuch and Old Latin, which listed it at Mount Gerizim, and to the MT, which curiously changed the locus to the implausible Mount Ebal. 4Q49 shows that the MT tradition had secondarily added a deuteronomistic, theological insert at Judg 6:7-10, introducing a prophet who typically accuses Israel of disobedience. 4Q51 preserves an entire paragraph lost from all other biblical manuscripts for the past two millennia. Thus, the MT contains a sectarian variant in Joshua, adds a small theological paragraph in Judges, and lost a paragraph from Samuel, for each of which the Qumran manuscripts provide superior texts. Moreover, Josephus' narrative in his *Jewish Antiquities* shows that his scriptural manuscripts had texts similar to the early reading of 4Q47 (*Ant.* 5.20) and to the original long reading of 4Q51 (*Ant.* 6.68–69).

2. Different levels of textual variation

Accordingly, not only do the scrolls display all the types of textual variation traditionally described in the older text-critical manuals, they both display much wider variation in each category than previously envisioned and illumine a type of major variation previously underappreciated. First, at the level of orthography, the noticeably more "baroque" approach to orthography and morphology (unlikely to be confined only to a scribal school at Qumran) should have been imagined, just as

one should expect a wide variety of spelling practices in English to appear in a literary anthology, elements of which derive from sources spanning nearly a millennium.

Second, the level of individual textual variants operates independently from orthography. With a much expanded collection of textual witnesses, the richer assembly of individual textual variants includes a more abundant and wider variety of synonymous variants, inadvertent errors, intentional clarifications, and the like. The traditional text-critical manuals remain good guides to rules of thumb for adjudicating such variants.

Third, the larger isolated interpretive additions operate independently from both levels of orthography and individual textual variants. Such interpretive additions, noted, for example, in 1QIsa[a] above, offer rich exegetical promise for the depiction of Second Temple religious thought. The origin of such interpretive additions can easily be imagined as occurring in the scenes behind the *Rule of the Community*, the Gospels, the PESHARIM, and rabbinic oral torah (*see* ORAL LAW, ORAL TORAH). The *Rule of the Community* directs the members to study the law continually; they are to read, interpret, and pray together (1QS VI, 6–8). The interpretations, perhaps often repeated in subsequent readings of the text, might easily be copied into margins of manuscripts and eventually into the text itself. An illustration of the latter might be the Lord's Prayer in Luke 11 and Matt 6. It was presumably prayed in common worship, a doxology gradually became a fixed conclusion, and the doxology eventually came to be added into many manuscripts of Matt 6.

Fourth, successive literary editions of many of the biblical books are perhaps the most noteworthy discovery provided by the scrolls, and this level operates independently, as do all the other three levels of variation. The variant editions in the Samaritan Pentateuch and some of the LXX books, such as Jeremiah and Daniel, had long since been available, but their witness had been denigrated due to their deviance from the MT. The successive editions show that sometimes the MT exhibits the earlier edition (e.g., in Exodus, Numbers, Psalms, Daniel) but that sometimes it contains the later edition (e.g., in Joshua, Jeremiah, and perhaps Judges, Samuel, and Isaiah, though there is insufficient evidence surviving to prove that these last three constitute variant editions and not just variant passages). In light of all that has been presented above, the notion of an "original text" recedes further toward the distant horizon. It should be stressed, however, that the pattern of new and expanded editions of different books means that all the texts of a given book are in fact genetically related, and theoretically, if enough manuscript evidence were preserved, could be directly linked with all other manuscripts of that book.

3. Two periods in the history of the text

These newly discovered manuscripts from the late 3rd cent. BCE to the early 1st cent. CE each illustrate different examples of variation, but their cumulative evidence all points in the same inescapable direction: there were two quite different periods in the history of the biblical text. During the first period, from the shadowy origins of the components of the texts until near the beginning of the 2nd cent. CE, the texts were pluriform and dynamically developing in tandem with Israel's ongoing history and religion. Starting with the second period, when the texts became the central focus of Judaism, the development ceased abruptly, and only one form of the text of each book perdured in the rabbinic Bible. There appears to be no evidence that those specific textual forms were actively selected or chosen in preference to others, but they were simply the texts that the rabbis happened to have. The texts, therefore, did not so much achieve final form but rather were suddenly frozen in their natural development.

F. From Collection of Scriptures to Canon

Gradually, the individual books that had been circulating on separate scrolls were linked in large complexes, and eventually, by approximately the 3rd cent. CE, the collection was viewed as a single text, the Bible.

The chronologically and thematically linked pentateuchal narrative from the promise of land to the gaining of the land must have enjoyed at least a conceptual unity from monarchic times. At some point in the Second Temple period (4th cent. BCE?) the priestly legal sections were incorporated into the national origins narrative, and presumably later, the book of Deuteronomy was separated from the Deuteronomistic History and linked with "the Law of Moses." The basic form of the five books of Moses was thus established and began to be seen as a unity, "the Book of the Law" or "the Book of Moses" (see Josh 1:8; Neh 8:1-2; 4Q397 14-21 10). The translation of the LXX (early 3rd cent. BCE) presumes a clear unity; the *Letter of Aristeas* repeatedly speaks about "the Law" (e.g., 3, 5, 38), and even "the scrolls of the Law" (30). The conceptual unity took on physical form in the manuscripts that hold more than one book of the Torah (e.g., 4QGen-Exod^a [4Q1], 4QExod-Lev^f [4Q17], 4QLev-Num^a [4Q23], and indeed 4Q158, 4Q364–67). The authoritative status of *Jubilees* in certain circles raises the question whether the category of Torah was strictly confined to the five books. But it is clear that all religious parties within Judaism accorded supreme authoritative status to the books of Moses as divinely inspired. Thus the idea that would eventually blossom into the canon had begun to emerge before the middle of the Second Temple period.

The prophetic books also began to be seen as a collection, though the contents of the collection as well as their relative importance apparently varied from party to party and continued to develop until the 1st cent. CE. From the evidence, Psalms (viewed, like Daniel, as a prophetic book) and Isaiah were the most honored, followed by Daniel (relative to its size), the book of the Twelve, Ezekiel, and Jeremiah. Josephus enigmatically lists the number of prophetic histories as thirteen (*Ag. Ap.* 1.37–43). As with *Jubilees* in relation to the Torah, it is difficult to know how to position *1 Enoch* in relation to the prophetic collection (note its apparent authoritative role at Qumran, its quotation at Jude 14-15 in the NT, and its inclusion in the Ethiopian canon). The prophetic books were highly valued and emphasized by the Qumran community and the early Christian movement; but they were eventually subordinated to the Torah by the rabbis, not accepted as Scripture by the Samaritans, and apparently not viewed as Scripture by the Sadducees.

Books considered to have divine authority formed a special group distinct from other works. Already by the end of the 2nd cent. BCE, "the law and the prophets" or "Moses and the prophets" (see 1QS I, 3) was in use as the designation for the collection that functioned as authoritative for guiding conscience and practice. Whereas that core collection of writings was well established, other books now among the Writings or poetic and wisdom books, among the Apocrypha, or otherwise unknown, were still finding their place in the 1st cent. CE. For some their relative status was perhaps being considered; for others, perhaps not yet. Not until at least the 2nd cent. CE did Judaism, and not until the 4th cent. did Christianity, establish a canon properly so called: a definitive, inclusive, and exclusive list of the books retrospectively recognized as permanently authoritative for community identity and practice. Though the contents of the collection differed for each of the different communities, the process toward canon, the results of the process, and the general timeline were similar in the several communities.

G. A Guide to the Witnesses to the Text

1. The scrolls

The biblical scrolls found at Qumran constitute our oldest and most authentic contemporary witness to the state of the Scriptures at the end of the Second Temple period and the birth of Christianity and rabbinic Judaism. They display no "sectarian variants" but represent the Scriptures of Judaism in general and attest a rich pluriformity characteristic of the biblical text from the beginnings up to "the great divide," sometime between the First and the Second Jewish Revolts. And they now offer the possibility, together with the MT, the Samaritan Pentateuch, and LXX, and the versions, of constructing the first critically established edition of the OT (under preparation as *The Oxford Hebrew Bible*). An English translation of the biblical scrolls is provided in *The Dead Sea Scrolls Bible*.

2. The Masoretic Text

The MT is held in veneration as the central text for the Jewish religion and the basis of its history, thought, and practice. It is also important as the textual basis of western biblical scholarship from the Renaissance until the first half of the 20th cent. It remains the only complete collection in the original language of the traditional Jewish and Protestant OT canon, and thus retains its place as the standard text of the OT—not, however, as the authoritative standard, but as the practical standard, since there is no complete alternative text in the original language preserved. The Targums, the Peshitta, the Vulgate, and recensional Greek texts are all witnesses to the MT.

3. The Samaritan Pentateuch

The Samaritan Pentateuch should be more seriously studied for several reasons, including its illustrations of the ways biblical texts developed. The great majority of its variants from the traditional pentateuchal texts were not produced by the Samaritans but were produced and used within Jewish circles. The only specifically Samaritan change was its focus on Mount Gerizim: both the commandment to build an altar at Mount Gerizim added in Exod 20 and Deut 5 (its wording taken, however, from Deut 11 and 27, common to the MT, the Samaritan Pentateuch, and the LXX), and the recurrent formula claiming Mount Gerizim, not Jerusalem, as "the place that the LORD your God has chosen out of all your tribes as his habitation to put his name there" (Deut 12:5, etc.; NRSV, "will choose").

4. The Septuagint

The Old Greek translation of each book offers a double witness. For most books it should generally be considered a faithful, sometimes free but still faithful, witness to the ancient form of the Hebrew text from which it was translated; sometimes that form happens to be the same as the one inherited by the MT, sometimes it agrees with a Qumran manuscript, and sometimes it offers a Hebrew witness otherwise lost. It also provides a witness to the texts of the Scriptures used by Greek-speaking Jews in the late Second Temple period and the Diaspora, as well as the texts and canon of Christianity until the 4th or 5th cent. in the West, and until the present in the East. *See* CANON OF THE OLD TESTAMENT; DEAD SEA SCROLLS; SEPTUAGINT; TEXT CRITICISM, OT.

Bibliography: Martin Abegg Jr., Peter Flint, and Eugene Ulrich. *The Dead Sea Scrolls Bible: The Oldest Known Bible Translated for the First Time into English* (1999); Julio Trebolle Barrera. *The Jewish Bible and the Christian Bible: An Introduction to the History of the Bible* (1998); Frank Moore Cross and Shemaryahu Talmon, eds. *Qumran and the History of the Biblical Text* (1975); Peter W. Flint and James C. VanderKam, eds. *The Dead Sea Scrolls after Fifty Years: A Comprehensive Assessment* (1998); Peter W. Flint and James C. VanderKam. *The Meaning of the Dead Sea Scrolls: Their Significance for Understanding the Bible,* *Judaism, Jesus, and Christianity* (2002); Emanuel Tov. *The Greek and Hebrew Bible: Collected Essays on the Septuagint* (1999); Emanuel Tov. *Textual Criticism of the Hebrew Bible.* 2nd ed. (2001); Eugene Ulrich. *The Dead Sea Scrolls and the Origins of the Bible* (1999); Eugene Ulrich. "The Text of the Hebrew Scriptures at the Time of Hillel and Jesus." *Congress Volume Basel 2001.* André Lemaire, ed. (2002) 85–108.

EUGENE ULRICH

TEXT, NT. The text of the writings comprising the NT is attested by a very large number of witnesses both in the original Greek tongue and in several ancient versions. Research on this text includes the study of the material witnesses (the manuscripts), of the many variant readings these witnesses contain, of the transmission history of the text in general, and of the reconstruction, if not the original, at least of the most reliable form of the text that can still be reached on the basis if the material that has been preserved. All these various aspects are studied in the discipline of textual criticism. The following offers a brief survey of the different kinds of sources that are available, of the principles and rules that have been developed for practicing textual criticism, and of the history of the edition of the text of the NT.

A. The Witnesses
  1. Direct witnesses to the Greek text
    a. Papyri
    b. Uncials
    c. Minuscules
    d. Lectionaries
  2. Indirect witnesses
    a. Citations in the Greek Fathers
    b. Ancient versions
B. Textual Criticism at Work
  1. General hypotheses
  2. Rules and principles
    a. In general
    b. In practice
C. The History
  1. The Fathers
  2. From the early 16th to the early 19th centuries
  3. From the mid-19th to the mid-20th centuries
  4. The current situation
    a. Teamwork
    b. Technology
Bibliography

A. The Witnesses

Scholars generally distinguish two categories, direct (Greek biblical manuscripts) and indirect witnesses (ancient versions and citations in the Fathers).

1. Direct witnesses to the Greek text

The first category can be subdivided into four groups of varying importance.

a. Papyri. A number of witnesses are gathered into one group on the basis of the material they are written on (*see* PAPYRUS, PAPYRI). These are referred to with a capital P and raised number (e.g., P²). Currently 118 papyri containing fragments of the Greek text have been published, but the list is constantly being expanded. The first papyri were published already in the late 19th cent., but it took two decades and the publication of some important papyri in the 1930s (P⁴⁵⁻⁴⁷) before their value for establishing the text of the NT was really appreciated. A good number of these papyri were discovered at Oxyrhynchus in Egypt and are published in the series of the OXYRHYNCHUS PAPYRI. Some of the most important and best studied papyri belong to famous collections of ancient manuscripts, such as the Chester Beatty Collection in Dublin (P⁴⁵.⁴⁶), the John Rylands Library in Manchester (P⁵²), or the Bodmer Collection at Coligny near Geneva (P⁷² and esp. P⁶⁶.⁷⁵). No papyrus contains the full text of the NT, and few have portions of more than one book (P⁴⁵, 3rd cent.: fragments from all four Gospels and Acts; P⁴⁶, ca. 200: almost complete for Romans, 1–2 Corinthians, Galatians, Ephesians, Philippians, Colossians, and Hebrews, three fragments of 1 Thessalonians; P⁷⁴, 7th cent.: almost complete for Acts and James, large sections of 1 Peter and 1 John, fragments of all the other Catholic Epistles; P⁷⁵, 3rd cent.: important sections from Luke and John). The great majority, however, contain only a few lines of text. Yet the importance of the papyri can hardly be underestimated. Among them are the oldest extant witnesses of the Greek NT (P⁴⁶.⁵².⁶⁴.⁶⁶ are dated ca. 200; P⁵² and P⁹⁰ might be from the 2nd cent.). Papyri demonstrate that the major textual traditions that can be discovered in later manuscripts were already relatively well represented or established very early.

b. Uncials. The second and third group of direct witnesses are indicated, not by the material (mostly parchment), but by the format of the writing. One group is formed by the so-called UNCIAL manuscripts or majuscles, i.e., written in capital letters and without any division between the words (*scriptio continua*). Uncials are referred to by Arabic numbers preceded by a "0," but some of the more important ones are often also identified by a letter, or by the name of the location where they were produced or discovered or are currently preserved: 1) Codex Sinaiticus (‬ℵ 01, 4th cent.), discovered by C. Tischendorf in 1844 at St. Catherine's Monastery in the Sinai desert; acquired by the Tsar in 1859 but sold to England in 1933 and now in the British Library—an almost complete Bible, along with the letter of *Barnabas* and the *Shepherd of Hermas*; a major representative of the Alexandrian text-type. 2) Codex Alexandrinus (A 02, 5th cent.), originally preserved at the Patriarchal Library in Alexandria, but in 1628 presented to Charles I of England and now in the British Library—an almost complete Bible, with some lacunae for the NT, and also containing the text of *1 Clement* and the larger part of *2 Clement*; a mixed text-type, in part Byzantine. 3) Codex Vaticanus (B 03, 4th cent.), earliest history unknown, but first recorded in 1475 in a catalogue of the Vatican Library where it is still being preserved today—an almost complete Bible. 4) Codex Ephraemi Syri Rescriptus (C 04, 5th cent.), now in the Bibliothèque Nationale in Paris—originally a complete Bible but now with substantial lacunae for the NT. 5) Codex Bezae Cantabrigiensis (Dᵉ ᵃ 05, 5th cent.), once in the possession of the 16th cent. Calvinist scholar Theodore Beza, now in Cambridge University Library—contains the Greek text of the Gospels and Acts and the Catholic Epistles with a Latin translation; an important witness of the Western text-type. 6) Codex Claromontanus (Dᵖ 06, 6th cent.), also once acquired by Beza, now in the Bibliothèque Nationale in Paris—the Greek text of Paul's letters with Latin translation.

Many of these manuscripts testify not only to the respect for the biblical text but also to the high standards of quality some Christian scriptoria had reached as early as the 4th cent., both in copying texts and in applying the most expensive techniques and material for the production of manuscripts (e.g., gold ink on purple parchment). Quite often such works were commissioned by the highest authorities. Some of these manuscripts are somewhat peculiar because the text of the NT has later been erased and overwritten with another text (Codex 04 takes its name from the fact that the upper text consists of thirty-eight tractates of the 4th cent. Syriac Father Ephrem the Great), or because the Greek is accompanied with a (mostly Latin) translation written side by side or in between the lines (Codex 05 and 06 above). The former are called palimpsests, the latter diglots.

c. Minuscules. These are manuscripts written in a cursive hand, a method of writing and copying first attested in the 9th cent., which replaced the more laborious and expensive uncial writing. Minuscules are listed by Arabic numbers (without a "0"). Some of these manuscripts are fairly late (of the 14th or 15th cent.), but a number can be dated to the 9th cent., such as Codex 461, from 835, and probably our oldest known MINUSCULE, Codex 33, of the 9th or 10th cent., and generally regarded as "the Queen of the Cursives" because of the quality of its text, which is often close to that of Codex Vaticanus.

Minuscules have been used for reconstructing the text of the NT since the 16th cent. and constituted the most important or even the sole evidence until the discoveries of the great uncials in the 19th cent. However, since the larger part of them belongs to the Byzantine text-type, they contributed to the ongoing dominance of that text well into the 19th cent. Nevertheless, not a few minuscules are of singular importance because they have carried on one of the other text-types. Until very recently the sheer number of manuscripts made a closer analysis very difficult, but scholars have managed to discover strong links between sets of manuscripts, some of which have been gathered into "families" (e.g., the "Lake family" or f^1, established in 1902 by K. Lake, which includes Codices 1, 118, 131, 209, 1582, etc.; the "Ferrar family" or f^{13}, identified by W. Ferrar as early as 1868, including Codices 13, 69, 124, 174, 230, 346, 543, etc.).

d. Lectionaries. A fourth group of witnesses are the lectionary manuscripts, composed for use in the liturgy. They are listed by Arabic numbers preceded by an l ("lectionary"). This group currently counts 2,436 instances. Research of this corpus is still in its initial stages and is hampered by our limited knowledge of the origins and development of the lectionary system and its impact on the way the material was rearranged, copied, and often altered (esp. at the beginning and closing of a pericope) to serve its purpose in worship. Nestle-Aland, the leading critical edition, makes sparing use of these witnesses: only nine are listed, some of them dating back as early as the 9th cent.

2. Indirect witnesses

Two categories of indirect witnesses to the Greek text can be distinguished.

a. Citations in the Greek Fathers. As a rule this evidence can best be regarded as an indirect witness, unless it can be demonstrated that the author was directly copying from a biblical manuscript when entering a citation in his text—a most difficult exercise. There are tens of thousands of such citations. They have been culled from reading through patristic literature and from the critical apparatus of editions of the Fathers. The more important or interesting ones have been included in editions of the NT since the 17th cent. These citations are of obvious importance for studying the exegesis and interpretation of the text but can also be put to use in reconstructing the transmission history of the text and even for editing a critical text.

One obstacle to using this material in text criticism has to do with the evidence that can be gained from the oldest authors, up to the middle of the 2nd cent. It is often impossible to demonstrate that these authors had access to the written text. The often remarkable divergences in "citations" in the text of the critical editions have been variously explained as proof that these authors were basically relying on oral tradition, that the transmission of the text was still very flexible, that the text was not yet regarded as authoritative and consequently could be handled more freely than would later be the case, or that a different text was circulated from the one that would be sanctioned in 4th-cent. Alexandria. For authors of later generations who certainly had access to a written text of the NT, one has first to distinguish between passages that are presented as formal citations and those that seem to be more allusive or free citations, while also realizing that the latter are not always a priori less reliable; and second to find how accurately a particular author is in citing his sources and whether polemical or other reasons may have led him to edit the text.

b. Ancient versions. Important indirect comparative evidence for the Greek text can be found in the many ancient translations that have been preserved, and correspondingly, but to a lesser degree, in the citations of authors writing in that tongue. Of these ancient versions, the Latin (the Old Latin or Vetus Latina, and the VULGATE, the translation produced by Jerome towards the end of the 4th cent.) and the Syriac ones (the Diatessaron, the Old Syriac or Vetus Syra, the Peshitta, the Philoxeniana, the Harklensis, and the Palestinian-Syriac) stand out because of their date, influence, and the quality of some. Slightly less important are the several Coptic versions (there are witnesses in six dialects or subdialects: Akhmimic, Subakhmimic, Proto-Bohairic, Sahidic, Middle Egyptian, and Middle Egyptian Fayumic). The Armenian, Georgian, Ethiopic, Old-Slavonic, or Gothic translation (some of these again in several dialects), and other more fragmentary ones, are of less interest for reconstructing the text because they are more recent, less well documented, and in some cases not directly made on the Greek text (*see* VERSIONS, ANCIENT).

B. Textual Criticism at Work

Many theories and methods have been developed for studying the textual evidence in view of a critical edition. One can distinguish between, on the one hand, general principles and practical rules, and on the other, more general hypotheses that are considered to be helpful in surveying and assessing the material and in drawing an overall framework for reconstructing the transmission history of the text.

1. General hypotheses

Important examples of the latter are the concept of "the original text," text-type theories, or methods for classifying the manuscripts. It is commonly accepted among textual critics that it is impossible, not only to reconstruct the "original text" of the NT on the basis of the material that has been preserved (there is no autograph of any NT book), but also that there may well never have been such a thing. Text-type theories have been developed since the 19th cent. and are still very much called upon today, but scholars have become increasingly aware that a considerable number of manuscripts are of a mixed type—hence that the theory is to be used flexibly—and also that some types are more difficult to identify (e.g., the so-called Caesarean text), and that one should be careful not to rush into further subdividing the evidence in this respect (e.g., a "Proto-Caesarean text"). Probably the most influential classification is the one that was developed, on the basis of extensive soundings, at the Münster Institut für NT Textforschung. The material is divided into five categories according to the quality and purity of the text, beginning with manuscripts of "a very special quality" (I, "Alexandrian text"), and further those of "a special quality" but exhibiting "alien influences" (II) and of "a distinctive character with an independent text" (III), and finally manuscripts that belong to "the D text" (IV, the "Western text") and those "with a purely or predominantly Byzantine text" (V). Only the first three categories can be used for reconstructing "the standard text."

2. Rules and principles

a. In general. In trying to establish what may be the most plausible reading, the large majority of textual critics tries to balance the "external evidence" (assessing the number and above all the quality of the material witnesses, the manuscripts, the versions, and the patristic citations that attest to a particular reading) and the "internal evidence" (the characteristics of the author's style, as this can be defined from parallel uses of a certain word or phrase, but also scribal habits in general and as found throughout a particular manuscript). This approach is known as "reasoned eclecticism." There are also three other approaches, each of which is defended and practiced by only a small minority of textual critics. Two of these are characterized by the fact that they primarily (or exclusively) focus on only one of the two types of evidence, either the "internal" (this approach is called "radical" or "thoroughgoing eclecticism") or the external (which some have called the "documentary approach"). The former of these tends to give undue importance to an exceptional or singular reading because it is in line with an author's style, even if this reading is attested only very rarely or in very recent and secondary or problematic witnesses. The latter approach is in danger of giving too much credit to particular material witnesses, though no one manuscript can be said to be absolutely reliable or flawless. A fourth and perhaps even more debatable approach exclusively relies on the evidence of the Byzantine text. Here textual criticism is made subservient to a dogmatic-theological concept ("the revealed text").

b. In practice. In performing the actual exercise of comparing and assessing variant readings, critics can rely on a number of principles and rules that take into account the overall reconstruction of the textual tradition and its development (text-types) and a set of practical rules that are known to have played in copying a text. The more original reading is likely to be the one that best explains how the other variants came about, or that is (grammatically or stylistically) the more difficult one (on the hypothesis that scribes tend to do away with complicated readings), or the shorter one (scribes tend to "explain" a word or phrase), or still, that best fits the (larger) context or is attested elsewhere in the same document (authors have their own style and vocabulary). All these rules are amply attested in the manuscripts. Above all one should realize that practicing textual criticism is primarily a matter of balancing the evidence, hence that the rules just mentioned have to be used flexibly, and that there is not one rule that applies in each and every case.

C. The History

Only a few names from an impressive scholarly tradition can be mentioned. That history can be divided most conveniently into four periods.

1. The Fathers

Text-critical study of the text of the NT is attested from the 2nd cent. on. It is probably best not to include in this list Marcion or Tatian because there is little or no evidence that their daring enterprises were somehow driven by text-critical considerations. But an interest of this kind is documented slightly later by Irenaeus, who once argues for a reading in Rev 13:18 because of the quality of the manuscripts that attest it, and especially by Origen, who in his commentaries not infrequently takes care to comment on variant readings. Jerome's commentaries, and above all his translation of the Bible, constitute the climax of this first period.

2. From the early 16th to the early 19th centuries

A new era opened up when the West rediscovered its Greek heritage in the late 15th and early 16th cent., thanks in part to the influx of Byzantine scholars and the manuscripts they carried with them. This soon resulted in two major projects that competed for the honor of being the first to produce an edition of the Greek NT (one of them even of the whole Bible), the Complutensian Polyglot Bible published by the University of Alcala de Henares in Spain between 1514 (NT) and 1517 (complete, but officially recognized and promulgated by the Pope only in 1522) and Erasmus's *Novum Testamentum Omne* of 1516. Neither of these projects comes near to the standards that would be developed and used in the 19th cent. Erasmus' edition reproduces a corrected version of a few late manuscripts to which he happened to have access. The basic problem is not so much that the manuscript evidence was dealt with in a most irresponsible way, but rather that this edition sanctioned the dominance of the Byzantine text, for that was the type of text represented by the manuscripts Erasmus used.

3. From the mid-19th to the mid-20th centuries

It was an outsider, K. Lachmann, a classical philologist by training and profession, who formulated the basic principle that would guide the next century of research into the text ("Back to the text of the early fourth-century church!"), but also actively contributing to realize it by publishing an edition of the NT. The 19th cent., a golden age of NT textual criticism, saw the addition of a good number of the more important manuscripts and the publication of two of the most influential critical editions of the NT, C. Tischendorf's *Editio octava critica maior* of 1869–72, featuring the Codex Sinaiticus as its main star; and B. F. Westcott and F. J. A. Hort's *The New Testament in the Original Greek* of 1881, which gave the leading part to the Codex Vaticanus. Compared to these "giants," Eberhard Nestle's *Novum Testamentum*

Graece (*NTG*), first published in 1898, was a far more modest initiative, reconstructing the Greek text in an almost mechanical way by comparing the edition of Tischendorf with that of Westcott-Hort and using R.F. Weymouth's (1898) and B. Weiss's (1901) editions to reach a "majority reading" in those cases where the two major editions differed.

4. The current situation

Two features of recent and current research illustrate the importance of textual criticism in the last half-century.

a. Teamwork. Scholars have become increasingly aware that this is the key to success for any kind of project in this field, editorial or other. Three initiatives deserve to be mentioned. The most successful is that of the Institute for New Testament Textual Research at Münster (Germany) under the direction of its founder K. Aland and his successors, B. Aland and, currently, H. Strutwolf. Appointed associate editor of Erwin Nestle, who continued his father's work on the *NTG* in the early 1950s, K. Aland gradually turned the completely revised "Nestle" ([25]1963, [26]1979, [27]1993) into the most widely used critical edition (Nestle-Aland). The Münster team is also preparing a more complete edition, the *Novi Testamenti editio critica maior*, of which the Catholic Epistles have been published in several installments since 1997. The second project was initiated by the American Bible Society in 1955 and conducted by an international team of which Aland was a member, together with M. Black, B. M. Metzger, and A. P. Wikgren, to prepare a critical edition called *The Greek New Testament* (*GNT*) that first appeared in 1966 ([2]1968). Under the impetus of Aland, this project and the one at Münster gradually grew closer to each other, which finally resulted in *NTG*[27] and *GNT*[4] (1994) producing a completely identical text. The third project, The International Greek New Testament Apparatus Project, started in 1942 as a joint American-British initiative to cover the complete textual tradition, which was first to be published as an apparatus to the text of the TEXTUS RECEPTUS and then worked into a critical edition. Only the apparatus of Luke has been published (1984–87).

Besides editions of the Greek text and of some of the versions (the Vetus Latina Institute in Beuron, Germany, and the Peshitta Institute in Leiden, The Netherlands), other team projects are producing important contributions to the study of the text and its transmission. Thus the *Biblia Patristica* (Paris, 1975– ; 8 vols.) offers an exhaustive list of biblical citations and allusions from patristic literature. The *New Testament in the Greek Fathers* series publishes monographs on the NT text of particular authors. The Birmingham (UK) *Principio* project has published transcriptions of all papyri containing the text of John as well as a full documentation for the majuscules.

b. Technology. Progress in technology is continuously opening up unexpected and promising new approaches to the material. Textual criticism is a technical discipline in terms of methodology, but now also in a technological sense, introducing the use of complicated search and processing programs for comparing data and establishing stemmata and links among manuscripts. The Münster Institute has the leading part; in collaboration with colleagues of the Institute for Textual Scholarship and Electronic Editing at the University of Birmingham (UK), it is currently making available a digitalized copy of the editions and transcripts of the manuscripts. *See* TEXT CRITICISM, NT.

Bibliography: B. Aland and J. Delobel, eds. *New Testament Textual Criticism, Exegesis and Church History: A Discussion of Methods* (1994); K. Aland and B. Aland. *The Text of the New Testament: An Introduction to the Critical Editions and to the Theory and Practice of Modern Textual Criticism.* E. F. Rhodes, trans. (1995); C.-B. Amphoux and J. K. Elliott, eds. *The New Testament in Early Christianity* (2003); T. Baarda. *Early Transmission of Words of Jesus: Thomas, Tatian and the Text of the New Testament: A Collection of Studies.* J. Helderman and S. J. Noorda, eds. (1983); J. N. Birdsall. "The New Testament Text." *The Cambridge History of the Bible: Volume 1: From the Beginnings to Jerome.* P. R. Ackroyd and C. F. Evans, eds. (1970) 308–77; J. W. Childers and D. C. Parker, eds. *Transmission and Reception: New Testament Text-critical and Exegetical Studies* (2006); E. C. Colwell. *Studies in Methodology in Textual Criticism of the New Testament* (1969); P. W. Comfort. *Early Manuscripts & Modern Translations of the New Testament* (1990); B. D. Ehrman. *The Orthodox Corruption of Scripture: The Effect of Early Christological Controversies on the Text of the New Testament* (1993); B. D. Ehrman. *Studies in the Textual Criticism of the New Testament* (2006); B. D. Ehrman and M. W. Holmes, eds. *The Text of the New Testament in Contemporary Research: Essays on the Status Quaestionis* (1995); J. K. Elliott. *A Bibliography of Greek New Testament Manuscripts* (2000); J. K. Elliott. *A Survey of Manuscripts Used in Editions of the Greek New Testament* (1987); E. J. Epp. *Perspectives on New Testament Textual Criticism: Collected Essays, 1962-2004* (2005); E. J. Epp and G. D. Fee, eds. *New Testament Textual Criticism: Its Significance for Exegesis* (1981); E. J. Epp and G. D. Fee. *Studies in the Theory and Method of New Testament Textual Criticism* (1993); P. J. Hartin and J. H. Petzer, eds. *Text and Interpretation: New Approaches in the Criticism of the New Testament* (1991); L. W. Hurtado. *The Earliest Christian Artifacts: Manuscripts and Christian Origins* (2006); G. D. Kilpatrick. *The Principles and Practice of New Testament Textual Criticism.* J. K. Elliott, ed. (1990); T. J. Kraus and T. Nicklas, eds. *New Testament Manuscripts: Their Texts and Their World* (2006); B. M. Metzger. *Chapters in the History of New Testament Textual Criticism* (1963); B. M. Metzger. *The Early Versions of the New Testament: Their Origin, Transmission, and Limitations* (1977); B. M. Metzger. *Historical and Literary Studies: Pagan, Jewish, and Christian* (1968); B. M. Metzger. *Manuscripts of the Greek Bible: An Introduction to Greek Palaeography* (1981); B. M. Metzger. *New Testament Studies: Philological, Versional, and Patristic* (1980); B. M. Metzger. *The Text of the New Testament: Its Transmission, Corruption, and Restoration* (2005); B. M. Metzger, ed. *A Textual Commentary on the New Testament: A Companion Volume to the United Bible Societies' Greek New Testament* (1994); D. C. Parker. *The Living Text of the Gospels* (1997); D. C. Parker, et al. *The New Testament in Greek.* IV. *The Gospel according to St. John.* I. *The Papyri* (1995); II. *Majuscles* (2007); W. L. Petersen, ed. *Gospel Traditions in the Second Century: Origins, Recensions, Text, and Transmission* (1989); H. A. Sturz. *The Byzantine Text-Type and New Testament Textual Criticism* (1984); P. D. Wegner. *A Student's Guide to Textual Criticism of the Bible: Its History, Methods and Results* (2006).

JOSEPH VERHEYDEN

TEXTILES. Interwoven within the biblical narratives are depictions of clothing and the textiles and fabrics from which they are made. The most important of these textiles was WOOL. Since herding flocks of sheep and goats was a huge factor in the economy of ancient Syria-Palestine, numerous stories are centered on this activity and on the harvesting of the wool when the sheep are gathered for shearing (Gen 38:12-13; 1 Sam 25:2-4). Everyday garments were woven from the coarse strands combed from the fleece, spun into threads, and strung on looms in nearly every house. Yarn was made by drawing wool fibers out from a mass of wool and spinning them together on a hand-held spindle, a weighted stick suspended in the air and spun on the thigh. The spindle was weighted with a small stone or ceramic weight called a spindle whorl. The many loom weights from these warp-weighted looms that have been discovered by archaeologists dating from the early Bronze Age to the Iron Age attest to both the ubiquitous cottage industry as well as large-scale operations utilizing the skills of professional weavers (see the Egyptian guildsmen in Isa 19:9-10 and the women who are "weaving for Asherah" in the Jerusalem Temple precincts in 2 Kgs 23:7). The roughest weave, known as SACKCLOTH (1 Kgs 21:27; Luke 10:13), was worn as a sign of mourning or repentance. These garments were more likely made from the more resilient goat hair, which was also used for durable items like tenting and rope. Wool does not have a natural twisting tendency and it can be spun either clockwise or counterclockwise. Archaeologists have determined that there is a correlation between the direction of spin and place of origin of a woven garment. For example, ancient Egyptian wool and linen is tightly spun to the left, and if a woolen garment found in Egypt has been spun tightly to the right, it can be assumed that it was woven elsewhere and therefore, by comparative means, can be used to track trading patterns and cultural influences.

Specific textiles are significant social markers for individuals determining rank and elements of personal identity based on the style, shape, decoration, and quality of the various types of garments that are made from wool, linen, silk, and cotton (see Joseph's change of status with his change of robe in Gen 41:42). In the same fashion, the law banning the mixing of wool and linen within the weave of a single garment attests to the desire to separate the social significance of particular textiles (Deut 22:11).

The very familiar work of the weaver also contributes to many metaphorical references to their activities. For instance, King Hezekiah's despairing assessment following his illness in Isa 38:12 compares his approaching demise to the common task of a weaver who cuts a garment from the loom and rolls it up. Similarly, Job describes the brevity of a human life, noting that it goes "swifter than a weaver's shuttle" (Job 7:6), the device used by weavers to pass or shoot the thread of the woof (that run across) between the threads of the warp (that run lengthwise). Drawing on the well-known sturdy design of the weaver's loom is a stock phrase, "like a weaver's beam," associated with the massive spear carried by two giant warriors (Goliath in 1 Sam 17:7 and a five-cubit-tall Egyptian in 1 Chr 11:23). A secondary fabric, one more associated with the priesthood and the wealthy, is LINEN. Made from strands of plant fiber stripped from dried flax (Josh 2:6), linen could be woven into fine, white tunics (Exod 29:27; Mark 14:51). Like SILK (Rev 18:12), the finest quality linen, such as that imported from Egypt, was considered a luxury item (Ezek 27:7). Most often linen was reserved for priestly robes (Exod 28:39; 1 Sam 22:18), the clothing of the upper classes (Joseph's robes in Gen 41:42; Luke 16:19); and scribes (Ezek 9:11). In the NT period, linen also was used for burial shrouds (Luke 23:53). Even though not everyone could afford to wear linen garments, most women would have included the working of both wool and flax in their daily routine and as a part of their contribution to the economy of their household (Prov 31:13). In later periods, COTTON, which may have been introduced by traders from India, came into fashion for woven draperies (Esth 1:6) and for expensive garments (Esth 8:15). *See* CLOTH, CLOTHES.

VICTOR H. MATTHEWS

TEXTUAL VARIANT. A difference between manuscript witnesses to the same biblical passage, usually caused by an error in transmission or by an editorial gloss. Textual variants include differences in spelling, word order, and even content. The task of the textual critic is to determine which variant is more original and thus more "correct." *See* DITTOGRAPHY; HAPLOGRAPHY; HARMONIZATION; HOMOIOTELEUTON; ITACISM;

QERE-KETHIBH; TEXT CRITICISM, NT; TEXT CRITICISM, OT; TRANSPOSITION.

R. JUSTIN HARKINS

TEXTUS RECEPTUS teks´tuhs-ri-sep´tuhs. The term "Textus Receptus" ("received text") designates the Greek text found in virtually all printed editions of the Greek NT from its initial publication by Erasmus (1516) through the late 19th cent. It derives from a publisher's "blurb" (*textum … ab omnibus receptum*, "the text … received by all") attached to the Elzevirs' second (1633) edition, which, via its dependence on editions by Beza (1565) and Stephanus (1551), closely reflects Erasmus' work (4th ed., 1527). Erasmus had only a small number of medieval manuscripts with which to work—in some instances, only one, and in a few (e.g., the final verses of Revelation) none, in which case he back-translated from Latin to Greek, creating a Greek text found in no known manuscript. His text, generally representative of the Byzantine (or "Majority") textual tradition, nonetheless differs from it in over 1,800 places. The dominant form of Greek text in Western Europe for over three centuries, it underlies all principal Protestant translations of the NT into European languages prior to 1881. *See* TEXT CRITICISM, NT.

Bibliography: Bruce M. Metzger and Bart D. Ehrman. *The Text of the New Testament.* 4th ed. (2005).

MICHAEL W. HOLMES

THADDAEUS thad´ee-uhs [Θαδδαῖος Thaddaios]. One of the twelve disciples of Jesus according to Matt 10:3 and Mark 3:18. It is puzzling that some manuscripts of Matt 10:3 in the Western text family cite "Lebbaeus (Lebbaios Λεββαῖος)" (D) or "Lebbaeus who was called Thaddaeus" (C², L, W, D, Θ), while Luke lists "Judas son of James" in his place (Luke 6:16; Acts 1:13).

The name Thaddaios might be derived from Aramaic tadh (תַד, "breast, nipple"), suggesting warmth of personality, and Lebbaios from Hebrew lev (לֵב, "heart, bosom"), indicating endearment and intimacy. Both might be nicknames. If all three Synoptic Gospels refer to the same disciple, it is likely that his given name was Judas son of James, as attested in Luke, but that he became known by his nickname Thaddaeus in Matthew and Mark, and Lebbaeus in other traditions, in order to be differentiated from Judas Iscariot the traitor. He might then be the disciple "Judas, not Iscariot" who asked Jesus at the Last Supper how he would reveal himself to the disciples but not to the world (John 14:22).

Jerome believed that Thaddaeus was called both Lebbaeus and Judas son of James, and that he became a missionary to Abgar, king of Edessa (*Comm. Matt.* 1.10.2). Stories of his activities and miracles in Mesopotamia are found in the Greek and Syriac versions of the *Acts of Thaddaeus* (*see* THADDAEUS, ACTS OF). Eusebius also mentioned him as one of the

seventy whom Jesus sent out in pairs to preach the kingdom of God (Luke 10:1; *Hist. eccl.* 1.13.4, 11).

JOHN Y. H. YIEH

THADDAEUS, ACTS OF thad´ee-uhs. A 6th-cent. CE Greek elaboration of the interaction between Jesus and King Abgar of Edessa. When the king requests healing, Jesus sends Thaddaeus, one of the seventy, to Edessa, where he establishes Christianity. Earlier versions of the story can be found in Eusebius (*Hist. eccl.* 1.13.1–10, early 4th cent.) and the Syriac *Teaching of Addai* (early 5th cent.). *See* ABGARUS, EPISTLES OF CHRIST AND.

MARK DELCOGLIANO

THALLUS. Greek chronographer of the early imperial period. Several early Christian apologists mention Thallus as a pagan witness to the darkness at the death of Christ (compare Mark 15:33; Luke 23:44), though the Armenian translation of the *Chronicle* of Eusebius records that the history of Thallus terminated with the 167th Olympiad (112–109 BCE). Some identify him with either the Samaritan Thallus (Josephus, *Ant.* 18.167) or the secretary of Augustus (Suetonius, *Aug.* 67).

MARK DELCOGLIANO

THANK OFFERING. *See* SACRIFICES AND OFFERINGS.

THANKSGIVING [תּוֹדָה todhah; εὐχαριστία eucharistia]. The Hebrew noun **todhah** is derived from the common verb of praise **yadhah** (יָדָה), which means "to give thanks" or "to confess." Todhah is sometimes rendered as "thank offering." A thank offering was, as the name suggests, a sacrifice, perhaps of unleavened bread (Lev 7:12; Amos 4:5), made with the purpose of giving thanks. More commonly, both the verb and noun refer to the act of offering verbal praise to God, usually in a liturgical setting. This may have been a metaphorical extension of the concept of the thanksgiving sacrifice, e.g., Ps 50:23: "Those who bring thanksgiving as their sacrifice honor me" (compare Ps 54:6; Jonah 2:9).

Both verb and noun appear repeatedly in parallel with phrases that clarify their meaning, e.g., Ps 69:30: "I will praise the name of God with a song; I will magnify him with thanksgiving." This suggests that thanksgiving is a song of praise to God (compare Sir 51:11). (A todhah may have become a technical term for a psalm of praise; see Ps 100:1.) This understanding fits with the repeated summons in the psalms, "O give thanks to the LORD, for he is good; for his steadfast love endures forever" (Pss 107:1; 118:1; 136:1, 2, 3). To give thanks may also be to bear witness to others: "The living … they thank you, as I do this day; fathers make known to children your faithfulness" (Isa 38:19). Thanksgiving may be a corporate activity, e.g., Ps 100, or individual, e.g., Ps 26:6-7. Thanks may be offered either for God's attributes or repeated actions (Ps 107:1 and elsewhere), or for some specific act of blessing or deliverance (Pss 138).

In the NT the noun *thanksgiving* is eucharistia and the verb "to give thanks," eucharisteō (εὐχαριστέω). In secular Greek, eucharistia described the attitude of thankfulness. In the NT, however, thanksgiving is, as in the OT, primarily praise spoken or sung aloud. Others can say "Amen" to it (1 Cor 14:16).

Most notably, Jesus gives thanks over food, including at the Last Supper where "give thanks" is essentially synonymous with "bless." Eucharistia shortly became a technical term for the sacrament (*Did.* 9:1), but this use is not yet present in the NT. It is assumed Christians will imitate Jesus' example of thanksgiving when they eat (1 Tim 4:3-4). A thanksgiving prayer appears near the beginning of all Pauline or Deuteropauline letters except Galatians (e.g., 1 Cor 1:4). Here and elsewhere in the epistles Paul gives thanks for the work of God among his readers and urges them constantly to do likewise.

Giving thanks to humans is rare in the Bible. Eucharisteō is used in this way only in Rom 16:4 and 1 Macc 12:31. Other forms of thanks to humans appear in Luke 17:9; 17:16; and occasionally in the Apocrypha. Thanksgiving is in the strict sense a theological act. Both the Greek verb and noun have at their center the word charis (χάρις) or "grace." God grants grace; humans respond with thanksgiving. Perhaps thanksgiving may be best understood as the human response to the grace of God. *See* GRATITUDE; LETTER; PRAYER.

STEPHEN FARRIS

THANKSGIVING PSALMS. The Thanksgiving Psalms, or *Hodayot,* are a collection of poetic prayers found among the DEAD SEA SCROLLS. The name is derived from the opening line of many of the compositions, "I thank you, O Lord" ('wdk 'dwny אודך אדוני).

The most complete copy of the Thanksgiving Psalms (1QH^a) was among the original seven scrolls found by the Bedouin in 1947. An additional fragmentary copy (1Q35) was later found in Cave 1, as well as six very fragmentary manuscripts from Cave 4 (4Q427–432). Despite the damaged condition of the manuscripts, it is clear that the various copies differ from one another in length, organization, and contents, evidence that suggests that different collections of the Thanksgiving Psalms existed side by side in the community. 1QH^a, apparently the longest collection, originally consisted of at least seven sheets of leather, divided into twenty-eight columns of forty-one or forty-two lines each. The number of individual compositions in the collection is uncertain, with recent estimates ranging from twenty-eight to fifty.

Psalmic compositions are notoriously difficult to date, since they usually do not contain historical references. The handwriting of the earliest copies of the Thanksgiving Psalms is considered to date from 100–50 BCE, suggesting some time in the 2nd cent. BCE for the composition of the psalms. The questions of authorship and function have been deeply contested. Since almost all of the Thanksgiving Psalms are couched in the first person singular, one early suggestion was that they are all compositions of the founder of the sectarian community, the figure known as the TEACHER OF RIGHTEOUSNESS. Form critical work on the Thanksgiving Psalms, however, has led most scholars to differentiate between two types of psalms: the "psalms of the teacher" and the "psalms of the community." A certain group of the psalms (e.g., 1QH^a XII, 5–XIII, 4) do appear to represent the particular perspective of a leader of the community, and these psalms seem to have been placed together or even copied separately in certain of the manuscripts. There is no complete consensus, however, as to whether these psalms are actually compositions written by the Teacher of Righteousness and reflecting his spiritual experience, psalms written in the persona of the Teacher of Righteousness but not composed by him, or psalms composed by various leaders of the community. These psalms do, however, reflect a significant stylistic and thematic unity. The hymns of the community (e.g., 1QH^a VI, 8–22), by contrast, do not construct such a distinctive "I" and seem to reflect the religious experience of the ordinary sectarian.

No direct evidence exists to suggest how the Thanksgiving Psalms were used. Some scholars have suggested that they were recited as part of public worship, perhaps in connection with the annual covenant renewal ceremony, though the Thanksgiving Psalms lack the formal elements that characterize liturgical works. Others have suggested that the psalms were used in practices of individual piety, though no description of such practices exists. Philo's account of the common meals of the Therapeutae, an Egyptian community of contemplative Jews with strong similarities to the Qumran Essenes, may provide a clue as to how the Thanksgiving Psalms were used. According to Philo, after the meal and a discourse on a scriptural text, a member of the assembly would rise and sing a hymn, either a new one of his own composition or an old one (*Contempl. Life* 80). However the Thanksgiving Psalms were used, whether publically or privately, they have a noticeable didactic quality and certainly served to inculcate a set of desirable religious dispositions, attitudes, and beliefs.

The only formally structured part of the Qumran Thanksgiving Psalms is the opening, which begins with an expression of thanks or blessing ("I thank you O Lord," or "Blessed are you"), followed by a statement of the reasons for which the speaker thanks God. These reasons may include gifts of knowledge and spirits, forgiveness of sin, divine mercy, salvation and election, and in general for having acted wondrously with the speaker. In some of the compositions, especially those associated with the Teacher, there may be a vivid recollection of a time of persecution or oppression from which the speaker was rescued by God (e.g.,

1QHª XVII, 1–36). Although it is clear that the Qumran Thanksgiving Psalms evoke the tradition of biblical thanksgivings and utilize some of the same motifs, they are very different in their structure and content. The body of the Thanksgiving Psalms often includes hymnic passages, as well as meditations on God's acts of creation, predetermination of all things, and eschatological judgment. Often a sharp contrast is drawn between divine and human being, with humanity characterized in a negative fashion that is alien to the biblical psalms (e.g., 1QHª V, 19–24; XI, 23–25).

Poetically, too, the Qumran Thanksgiving Psalms differ sharply from biblical psalms. Although employing forms of poetic parallelism familiar from biblical poetry, the Thanksgiving Psalms often exhibit complex syntactical parallelisms, repetition of key terms, highly elaborated metaphors, and a variety of word plays. Most striking is the intensely allusive style. Many of the compositions are a dense pastiche of biblical citations and phraseology (e.g., 1QHª XI, 6–18). In some cases the allusions reflect exegetical interpretation of biblical texts, while in others the author simply uses a biblicizing style. Though early commentators often denigrated the poetic style of the Thanksgiving Psalms, they are increasingly recognized as highly sophisticated, literate, and theologically significant compositions of late Second Temple Judaism.

Bibliography: Svend Holm-Nielsen. *Hodayot: Psalms from Qumran* (1960); Julie A. Hughes. *Scriptural Allusions and Exegesis in the Hodayot* (2006); Bonnie Pedrotti Kittel. *The Hymns of Qumran: Translation and Commentary* (1981); Carol A. Newsom. *The Self as Symbolic Space: Constructing Identity and Community at Qumran* (2004); Bilhah Nitzan. *Qumran Prayer and Religious Poetry* (1994); Eileen Schuller. "Hodayot." *Qumran Cave 4.XX: Poetical and Liturgical Texts, Part 2.* E. Chazon et al., eds. (1999); Hartmut Stegemann with Eileen Schuller. *1QHodayotª* (2009); Eleazar L. Sukenik. *The Dead Sea Scrolls of the Hebrew University* (1955).

CAROL A. NEWSOM

THASSI thas´i [Θασσεί Thassei]. Another name of SIMON Maccabee, the son of Mattathias. The name appears in 1 Macc 2:3, where five sons of Mattathias are listed. Simon Thassi's name appears second in the list (behind John, ahead of Judas). The meaning of this name is uncertain. Some scholars have proposed that Thassi means "burning." Simon Thassi played an important role in the Hasmonean dynasty (1 Macc 9–14). *See* HASMONEANS.

SAMUEL BOYD

THAWWAB, JEBEL ABU. Abu Thawwab is a small, Late Neolithic 1 (Yarmoukian phase, ca. 6400–5900 BCE and Ghrubba phase, ca. 5900–5500 BCE) and Early Bronze I village located in the well-watered mountain-

ous country about 25 km north of Amman at an altitude of ca. 500 m above sea level. Poorly preserved Neolithic architecture included both curvilinear and rectilinear houses, and the Early Bronze Age structures were principally rectangular (Kafafi). The size of the settlements is difficult to determine, but they were probably about 1 ha. (ca. 2.48 ac.) or larger.

Domesticated plants included wheat, barley, chickpeas, lentils, peas, bitter vetch, and flax. Animal bones included domesticated sheep, goat, and cattle; pig was present, as was equid, but the wild/domestic status could not be determined. Dogs were present, possibly an aid in the hunting of gazelle. *See* PRE-HISTORY IN THE ANCIENT NEAR EAST.

Bibliography: Zeidan Abdel-Kafi Kafafi, Nizar Abu-Jaber, and Bo Dahl Hermansen. *Jebel Abu Thawwab (Er-Rumman), Central Jordan* (2001).

GARY O. ROLLEFSON

THEATER [θέατρον theatron]. From the late 1st cent. BCE to the early 3rd cent. CE, theaters were built in cities in and around the Roman province of Palestine. Theater construction was a significant part of city planning in the Roman period. Theaters were constructed in Antipatris (Aphek), Beth-Shan (Sythopolis), CAESAREA MARITIMA, Dor, Elusa (in the Negev), Jericho, Jerusalem, Legio (Kefar Otnay near Megiddo), Neapolis (Shechem), Samaria, SEPPHORIS, Shuni (north of Caesarea), and Tiberias. Many of these theaters continued to be used into the Byzantine period.

The first theaters were built under the authority of Herod the Great. The theater that Josephus reports was built in Jerusalem has not been located (Josephus, *Ant.* 15.268–74). He states that the theater in Jerusalem was built for athletic contests in honor of Caesar held every fifth year. These games imitated Rome's Actium Games, which celebrated Octavian's victory at Actium in 31 BCE. The construction of a theater, temples, marketplaces, and gymnasia, representing Roman culture, signaled that Herod's kingdom of Judea was part of the larger empire. A theater was a venue for introducing Roman culture as well as a place for mass entertainment. The theater in Jerusalem was either destroyed by fire or dismantled later in the Roman period. Herod also built theaters in Caesarea Maritima, Samaria, Jericho, and Sidon (in Phoenicia).

The theater at Caesarea is the earliest in Roman Palestine to be excavated and restored. It was built in the Roman style, which differs from a classical Greek theater in several respects. Roman theaters were enclosed; the front stage was raised and closed in with an imposing multi-story structure (a *scaenae frons* with columns and statues) that did not allow the audience to see beyond the stage. Roman theaters, like the one at Caesarea, were built from the ground up with stadium-style seating. They used vaults and arches to support massive tiered seating arrangements (*cavea*), which were accessed through passageways (*vomitoria*) within the structure.

Following the building projects of Herod the Great, a second period of theater construction occurred later in the 1st cent. and early 2nd cent. CE. Theaters served as settings for either religious rituals or mass entertainment. Interest in traditional Greek dramatic performance was minimal; rather, theaters were used for popular, circus-like entertainment such as mime plays, crude comedy, and shows featuring wild and exotic animals. One might see traveling troops of gladiators, athletes, acrobats, musicians, and jugglers in theater performances sponsored by local elite families. A typical theater would have room for approximately 5 percent of the city's population, with a special area of front-row seating for the elite, whose sponsorship of a performance was understood as part of the Roman patron-client relationship. Elite families gained political influence by sponsoring such entertainment.

In Acts 19:23-41, Demetrius the silversmith stirs up a group of Ephesians against the apostle Paul, who had been declaring that handmade gods were not gods. The crowd drags Paul's companions Gaius and Aristarchus into the theater, where they are quieted by the town clerk, who reminds them that they could be charged with rioting. *See* EPHESUS.

Roman cities in the Transjordan that had theaters include Abila, Adraa, Birketein, Bosra, Damascus, Gadara, Gerasa, Hammat-Gader, Kanawat, Pella, Petra, Philadelphia (Amman), Sahr, and Wadi Sabra. There is no evidence for theater construction in the Decapolis during the Hellenistic period. Most of the construction occurred in the 2nd cent. CE. As cities began to identify more closely with the Roman Empire, theater construction was a natural result of their civic pride and Romanization.

The theater at Sepphoris in central Galilee has gained a great deal of attention due to its proximity to the childhood home of Jesus in Nazareth. Parts of the theater were excavated by four teams of archaeologists, beginning with Leroy Watermanin 1931. There is no agreed-upon date for the construction of the theater. An early 1st cent. CE date (during the time of Herod Antipas and Jesus) is less likely than the early 2nd cent. There may, however, have been two phases its construction: an earlier structure that was carved from the bedrock on the city's northern hill, and a more elaborate later structure with vaults and *vomitoria*.

The presence of dozens of theaters in the region of Roman Palestine and the Transjordan demonstrates the process of Romanization that began with the rule of Herod the Great. Theaters were vehicles for the spread of culture, not through the performance of serious Greek plays, but through popular entertainment and the social system of Roman patronage.

Bibliography: E. K. Gazda and E. A. Friedland, eds. *The Scientific Test of the Spade: Leroy Waterman and the University of Michigan Excavations at Sepphoris, 1931* (1997); Arthur Segal. *Theaters in Roman Palestine and Provincia Arabia* (1994).

MILTON C. MORELAND

THEBES theebz [נֹא noʾ, נֹא אָמוֹן noʾ ʾamon]. Thebes (Thēbai Θῆβαι) is the Greek designation for the Egyptian city Waset. Thebes was located in Upper EGYPT about 350 mi. south of Memphis in the fourth nome, Waset, the name that also applied to the city. Thebes became the chief city of Upper Egypt during the First Intermediate Period and the capital of Egypt during the Eleventh Dynasty, unifying Upper and Lower Egypt. While the capital was moved from Thebes and relocated in Memphis during a major part of the Middle Kingdom, Thebes continued to attract the attention of Egypt's pharaohs and was the site at which they built temples and monuments of themselves. The city reached its height during the period of the New Kingdom, ushered in by the pharaohs of the Eighteenth Dynasty. It was regarded as the richest city in the ancient world (Homer, *Il.* 9.381–385), and the city of the world's greatest monuments and tombs. Nonetheless, it ended in 663 BCE with the arrival of the Assyrians, who took the city and toppled the empire.

Ancient Thebes, known today as Luxor, was a city of kings, gods, and the dead. Divided by the Nile, Thebes had two main parts: the eastern sector, the city of the living, and the western sector, the city of the dead. The city on the east bank had two large temple precincts, the temple of Luxor and the temple of Karnak, symbolizing and significantly advancing the city's status as a major administrative and religious center. The temple of Luxor, built by Amenhotep III, had major additions by RAMESSES II and others. The magnitude of this architecture is clearly demonstrated in the four colossal figures of Ramesses II, each over 75 ft. high, that stood at the entrance of the pylon. The temple of Karnak was a large complex comprising the massive temple dedicated to the god Amon to which the pharaohs added their own sanctuaries and statuaries. Amon-Re, the god of Thebes, was recognized as the head of the Egyptian pantheon and the god of all Egypt.

The western sector of Thebes was the great repository of the dead. Much larger than Thebes east of the Nile, the city on the west bank had an assortment of mortuary temples, including the temple of Amon, the temple of Ramesses III at Medinet Habu, and the temple of Queen Hatshepsut and THUTMOSE III at Deir el-Bahri. The greatest display of the pharaohs' loyalty to Thebes as the royal necropolis is demonstrated in the dozens of burials in the rock-cut tombs in the Valley of the Kings and Queens.

While Egypt appears prominently in the OT, starting with the Genesis stories about ancestors/patriarchs and the oppression in Egypt, references to the city of Thebes are few and appear only in the prophetic literature (Jer 46:25; Ezek 30:14-16; Nah 3:8). The theme of each prophetic utterance is the same: the doom or judgment of Thebes. Jeremiah and Ezekiel speak of the destruction of Thebes as a poignant event to happen in the future, at the hands of the king of Babylon. Nahum treats it as a past event that he uses to chide Nineveh.

Bibliography: Nigel C. Strudwick and Helen Strudwick. *Thebes in Egypt: A Guide to the Tombs and Temples of Ancient Luxor* (1999).

LAMOINE F. DEVRIES

THEBEZ thee´biz [תֵבֵץ tevets]. A fortified city, identified with the modern town of Tubas, located about 11 mi. northeast of Shechem in the fertile hill country of Ephraim. The city was located on one of the main roads leading to the Jordan Valley. GIDEON's son, ABIMELECH, seized and conquered the city because Thebez had joined Shechem in a revolt against him (Judg 9:50-57). The residents locked themselves on the roof of a tower in the center of town. When Abimelech ventured too close, a woman threw a millstone from the tower, hitting him and crushing his skull, whereupon his armor-bearer thrust him through with a sword and he died. Second Samuel 11:21 refers to the incident. *See* EPHRAIM, EPHRAIMITES; MILL, MILLSTONE; SHECHEM, TOWER OF.

TERRY W. EDDINGER

THECLA, ACTS OF PAUL AND thek´luh. The *Acts of Paul and Thecla* is one of three sections in the *Acts of Paul* (including the *Acts of Paul and Thecla*, the *Martyrdom of Paul*, and *3 Corinthians*) that circulated independently (*see* PAUL, ACTS OF). Recent discovery and reconstruction of the Coptic Papyrus Heidelburg confirms that the stories about Paul and Thecla and about his martyrdom belonged to the larger work before their eventual separation and independent circulation.

The *Acts of Paul and Thecla* features the CONVERSION of an elite Gentile woman to Christianity and has been the object of intense study in recent years, due in part to Thecla's striking prominence in the narrative. While it has been argued that the stories about women in this and other apocryphal acts originated orally among circles of women, the influence of the Hellenistic romance or adventure novel of ordeal is unmistakable in the story of Paul and Thecla. In a dramatic reversal of the erotic script of the novel, the virgin Thecla, upon hearing Paul preach "the word of God concerning continence and resurrection," dares to reject her betrothed in order to devote herself to "a new desire and fearful passion." That desire is sorely tested by the series of trials and ordeals that subsequently ensue: condemnation first to the pyre and later to the beasts. Consistent with the pattern of testing in Jewish and Christian traditions and in the ancient romance, Thecla is sorely afflicted but perseveres in the face of death, thereby gaining divine deliverance and approval. Her desires consummate not in marriage, as in the romances, but in baptism and

an apostolic commission by Paul to teach the word of God (*see* APOSTLE). The narrative sequence—from trials and ordeals endured to apostolic commission—reflects the Pauline standard for the apostolic life, which is endurance of suffering and hardship in imitation of the crucified Christ (2 Cor 11–12).

That this story of Paul's virgin convert circulated independently of the larger work and is extant in multiple ancient languages attests its popularity. For the ancient audience it was, however, far more than the story of a woman's conversion to Christianity by Paul's preaching. The Thecla story inspired a vibrant and widespread cult that lasted well into the 5th cent. and apparently also inspired some women's aspirations to ministry. In his treatise on baptism Tertullian criticizes women who cite the example of Thecla in claiming authority to teach and baptize (*Bapt.* 17). *See* APOCRYPHA, NT; VIRGIN.

Bibliography: J. Bremmer. *The Apocryphal Acts of Paul and Thecla* (1996); Virginia Burrus. *Chastity as Autonomy: Women in the Stories of the Apocryphal Acts* (1987); Susan A. Calef. "Thecla 'Tried and True' and the Inversion of Romance." *A Feminist Companion to the New Testament Apocrypha.* A.-J. Levine, ed. (2006) 163–85; W. Schneemelcher. "Acts of Paul." *New Testament Apocrypha,* Vol. 2. W. Schneemelcher, ed. (1992) 213–70; Gail P. C. Streete. "Buying the Stairway to Heaven: Perpetua and Thecla as Early Christian Heroines." *A Feminist Companion to the New Testament Apocrypha.* A.-J. Levine, ed. (2006) 186–205.

SUSAN A. CALEF

THEFT, THIEVES. *See* CRIMES AND PUNISHMENT, OT AND NT; LAND.

THEOCRACY thee-ok´ruh-see. *Theocracy* was probably coined by the 1st cent. CE Jewish historian, priest, and apologist Josephus, who uses it in *Against Apion* to contrast the Jewish manner of government to other forms, such as monarchies. He defines it there as "placing all sovereignty and authority in the hands of God" (*Ag. Ap.* 2.165). The exact meaning of the Greek term is debated, and Josephus suggests later that the priests represent Yahweh in the theocracy (*Ag. Ap.* 2.185). Often the term is used in its broader etymological sense of "divine government." Thus, theocracy in the Bible should be explored from at least two perspectives: Yahweh ruling directly and ruling through a human agent.

In pre-eschatological time, Yahweh cannot rule directly. Both Exod 20:18 and Deut 5:25-26 depict the Israelites as extremely frightened after their direct encounter with Yahweh as lawgiver on Sinai. This results in Moses being appointed as an intermediary.

Isaiah 2:2-4 and its parallel in Mic 4:1-3 envision Yahweh ruling directly in the eschatological period. There, "In days to come," Yahweh has many royal roles: God has a house (temple or palace) that is raised up at the center of the political world; the Lord is judge, and rather than being warrior, God makes sure that the nations will "beat their swords into plowshares, and their spears into pruning hooks" (Isa 2:4; Mic 4:3). Although many texts depict an ideal future king or messiah who acts on Yahweh's behalf in this period (*see* MESSIAH, JEWISH), other texts support this vision of Yahweh's unmediated control of the world in the future. Deutero-Isaiah (Isa 40–55) never depicts the return of a Davidic king and insists on Yahweh's direct control of the world—he alone is "king of Jacob" (Isa 41:21) and "the LORD, the King of Israel" (Isa 44:6). Several psalms describe Yahweh's kingship as direct and unmediated (Pss 95–99). Their interpretation is contested, but they are likely imagining the future ideal world as already having arrived, and are in that sense eschatological psalms.

More typically, a human agent represents Yahweh in the theocracy. Moses is the first such agent, and as prophet, judge, king, and priest he represents the main types of officials who will stand in for Yahweh. According to Deut 18:18, a line of prophets like Moses was established after the revelation at Horeb (Sinai) to transmit the divine will. Their mission is to fulfill the same role as Moses: "But you, stand here by me, and I will tell you all the commandments, the statutes and the ordinances, that you shall teach them" (Deut 5:31). Prophets played an especially important role in establishing the monarchy, identifying for the people the correct divinely chosen king (see, e.g., 1 Sam 9–10).

Judges had a similar role, according to the paradigm offered at the beginning of the book of Judges, "the LORD raised up judges, who delivered [the Israelites]" (2:16). Othniel son of Kenaz is the first whom "the LORD raised up [as] a deliverer for the Israelites" (Judg 3:9). The author of Judges understood these figures as acting on behalf of Yahweh in the premonarchic period. Even the impious Samson plays this role.

According to the Bible, kings followed judges. The Davidic kings in particular were chosen by Yahweh for an eternal dynasty. These kings represent Yahweh to the extent that some view them as God's son (2 Sam 7:14; Ps 2:7). Once, in this role, the king is even called "God" (Ps 45:6 [Heb. 45:7]). *See* KING, KINGSHIP.

It is extremely difficult to reconstruct the judicial system in ancient Israel, but judges may also be seen as participants in the theocracy as interpreters of the divine will. They share this role with priests in Deut 17:8-9 and 2 Chr 19:4-11. In Exod 18 and Deut 1, appointed judges (without any connection to the priests) have this role.

Priests were stand-ins for Yahweh in other ways as well: they organized the cult; they ate the sacrificial meat and the shewbread that was really Yahweh's (Lev 24:9); they cast sacred lots so the divine will could be known (e.g., 1 Sam 23:9); and they blessed the people in Yahweh's name (Num 6:23) so that "they shall put my name on the Israelites, and I will bless them" (Num 6:27). The history of the priesthood is extremely complicated, and it is unclear in what sense different groups at different times understood priests as divine surrogates. In the postexilic period, however, the priesthood gained tremendous power as the monarchy was not reestablished and as prophecy weakened. It is therefore not surprising that Josephus considered the priests as Yahweh's agents. More than two centuries earlier, Ben Sira had depicted the high priest Simon the Just in laudatory terms, at the climax to his poem praising the ancestors (Sir 50). This too indicates their crucial role as divine representatives in the Second Temple period.

Theocracy is thus a complex idea in the Bible. Josephus is insightful in coining the term, but it has been understood in a wide variety of ways, reflecting different understandings of Yahweh's kingship in different periods by different groups.

Bibliography: Marc Zvi Brettler. *God Is King: Understanding an Israelite Metaphor* (1989); H. St. J. Thackery, trans. *Josephus.* Vol. 1 (1926); Gershon Weiler. *Jewish Theocracy* (1989).

MARC ZVI BRETTLER

THEODICY thee-od´uh-see. The word *theodicy*, first used by Gottfried Wilhelm Leibniz in 1710, is a combination of two Greek words, theos (θεός, "god") and dikē (δίκη, "justice"). Since its introduction, it has come to be used in three different ways: 1) to indicate a philosophical discussion of the problem of evil; 2) to designate a defense of the justice of God in light of the existence of evil; and less often 3) to signify rational theology. A shift has taken place in modern treatments of theodicy from a problem within the Christian faith to a problem about the Christian faith. Another change has followed, from doubting the self to doubting God. For some theologians, theodicy has fallen out of favor because of its theoretical, as opposed to practical, nature, and because it occasionally embarks on the impossible task of vindicating Christianity rationally. Long before Leibniz coined the word, probably on the basis of Rom 3:4-5, ancient thinkers pondered the co-existence of an all-good and powerful deity with moral and natural evil. Biblical writers were particularly energetic in both protest theology and defending God despite apparent contradictions of divine oversight in rewarding virtue and punishing sin in exact accord with an individual's actions. In this essay, theodicy is understood in this latter sense.

    A. The Problem of Evil
      1. Ancient Near Eastern discussions
      2. Types of evil
    B. The Responses to Evil's Presence
      1. Retributive
      2. Educative
      3. Probative
      4. Eschatological
      5. Revelational

A. The Problem of Evil

1. Ancient Near Eastern discussions

Human beings have sought to understand the presence of evil from the beginning of recorded history. That struggle in the ANE antedates the biblical account by nearly two millennia. It presupposes a rational resemblance between the deities (or deity) and humans. An unknown god renders defense impossible, hence theodicy requires at least minimal revelation (either directly through an oracle or indirectly by means of divination) or reasoning by analogy from the material creation. The principle of similarity permits one to ascribe to deity human values elevated to the highest degree.

The earliest theodicies reveal uncertainty about the extent to which the gods could be known, as well as confidence that they should administer justice in society. The expression of ignorance in *Ludlul* (*I Will Praise the Lord of Wisdom*, ca. 1200 BCE) amounts to this: We cannot know what God desires; it may even be the opposite of what we think.

The Babylonian Theodicy shifts the emphasis to the gods' endowment of humans with a deceitful nature, a point made somewhat differently in the Sumerian *Man and his God*, to wit, that everyone is sinful. The Egyptian *Admonition of Ipu-Wer* complains that the gods have neglected their responsibility of shepherding the human "flock" and have permitted injustice to prevail. The resulting social turmoil makes suicide an intellectual option, both in Egypt and in Mesopotamia, as evidenced by *A Dispute Between a Man and his Ba* and *A Dialogue between a Master and his Slave*, respectively.

History's unexpected turns expose the disparity between belief in a just deity and daily experience, a point easily recognized in the literary contribution of the Canaanite Ilimalku, specifically, *Ba'al and Anat*, *Dan'el and Aqhat*, and *Keret*. In Israel, the emergence of monotheism exacerbated a long-standing problem, one intensified by the emphasis on a covenantal relationship between Yahweh and Abraham's descendants.

2. Types of evil

Modern scholars distinguish two types of evil, moral and natural (religious evil, especially idolatry, is usually treated under the first type, its primary offense lying outside the human arena). These two (or three) categories of evil cover conduct at odds with standards either ascribed to a divine legislator or attributed to moral thinkers from the ranks of prophets, sages, and priests; as well as disasters such as earthquakes, fire, disease, and the like.

The suffering and premature death that accompany the different manifestations of evil test the human spirit to the limit; in the process they evoke literary classics such as *The Gilgamesh Epic* and the book of Job. Within Israel and Judah, the emphasis on divine election and royal messianism created conditions for a crisis of faith when the destruction of Jerusalem precipitated the collapse of Davidic rule. To some degree the early death of Josiah refuted the claims of the Deuteronomistic historiographer and prefigured major cognitive dissonance.

B. The Responses to Evil's Presence

1. Retributive

The dominant response to evil's ubiquity is to view all suffering as punishment for sin, whether the transgression is intentional or unintentional. A psalmist states the matter in a nutshell when asserting that he has never seen the righteous forsaken or their progeny forced to beg for food (Ps 37:25), a view similar to that of the friend in *The Babylonian Theodicy*. Job's three friends argue from an axiomatic position that allows them to deduce horrendous wickedness on his part, just as historians of ancient Israel and Judah paint an unfavorable portrait of the two nations to explain unfolding catastrophic events.

The retributive understanding of evil derives from warfare, particularly vassal treaties, and from jurisprudence, with its basis in legal statutes and tradition. It also assumes free will, although various stories in the Bible indicate uncertainty in this respect. The acknowledgment that Yahweh sometimes overrode a pharaoh's will and compelled humans to act contrary to their inclination (Isa 6:9-10; compare Mark 4:10-12) reveals a desire to ease the burden placed on humans. Not everyone welcomed this relaxing of guilt; Ben Sira, for one, insists that individuals possess free will (e.g., Sir 15:15) and therefore cannot rightly blame God for their misconduct. In any event, the retributive view pervades the Bible from beginning to end.

2. Educative

The family setting gave rise to the educative response to evil. Just as parents discipline children to shape character, God sends adversity for the purpose of instilling virtue in loyal disciples. This approach to theodicy, succinctly articulated in Isa 30:20-21, occurs above all in prophetic texts such as Amos 4:6-11 and Hos 11:1-7, but also in sapiential texts like Sir 4:11-19 and Wis 11:15–12:27. Such soul-building implies a harsh demeanor on God's part or on that of the divine representative, hokhmah (חָכְמָה, personified wisdom). Although the goal of a heavy yoke was growth in obedience, the sting of "sacred chastisements" was real despite assurances that God was merciful even in such unpleasant circumstances. Divine discipline did not always succeed; natural disasters and warfare failed to generate genuine change, according to Amos, who viewed at least one series of disciplinary actions as wasted opportunity on Israel's part.

3. Probative

The testing of metal and probing for precious gems offered yet a third response to evil, one that inspired two texts with enormous evocative power. The first of these narratives records the harrowing tale of the near sacrifice of Isaac by his father Abraham (Gen 22:1-19), a story anticipated by his abandonment of another son, Ishmael, to the harsh wilderness. The second text tells about a test of the servant Job that robs him of children, prosperity, and health. Similarly, Jesus is said to have been subjected to temptation in the wilderness and to the ultimate sacrifice on Golgotha.

Underlying the idea of putting individuals to a test administered by the deity, or God's agent in the case of Job, is the belief that God lacks complete knowledge. The Bible freely concedes that Yahweh gains information from such tests, for not even the deity knows how an individual will respond to temptation until it is past. Hence the divine declaration, "For now I know ..." (Gen 22:12), and God's silent waiting to see how Job will react to a monstrous test (Job 1–2).

4. Eschatological

One way of dealing with apparent injustice is to defer compensation for good or bad behavior until some future time. This response to evil was not subject to confirmation, nor could it be invalidated. Although some prophets, especially Habakkuk, Joel, and Deutero-Isaiah, waited for God to set things right within history, the author of Dan 12:1-2 and possibly Isa 26:19 expected divine recompense outside history altogether. The hope of resurrection (or eternal punishment for sinners) was soon inserted into certain parts of the Septuagint and the Greek versions of Sirach (19:19). It eventually became the dominant explanation of Jesus' death and the pervasive expectation in the NT. Apocryphal and pseudepigraphic works such as Wisdom of Solomon (3:4), 2 Esdras (8:1), the *Psalms of Solomon* (3:12), and 4 Maccabees (18:23) express similar hope.

5. Revelational

For some, the intensity of a personal relationship with God produced a conviction that the resulting communion was more priceless than material goods. The author of Ps 73 experiences serious doubt about divine goodness when observing the prosperity of the wicked but undergoes a transformation in the house of God. The touch of the divine hand and felt presence convince him that God's nearness alone matters. The author of the closing hymn in the book of Habakkuk even sings God's praise despite signs that normally were thought to indicate divine abandonment (Hab 3:17-19). In all of these instances the cult functioned as a buttress against loss of faith when the principle of reward and retribution seemed inoperative.

The belief that suffering can bring one closer to God arose from wide experience, whether Zion's destruction or personal betrayal, as in the case of Jeremiah and Job. Close encounter with God did not necessarily result in communion; Jonah's response (chap. 2) is shrouded in mystery, and the same ambiguity surrounds Jeremiah as depicted in the "confessions" (12:1-6; 15:10-21; 17:14-18; 20:7-18) and Job's response in Job 42:6. If pathos characterizes the biblical God in the same way that justice and mercy do, according to Exod 34:6-7, then the person undergoing suffering participates in the divine nature. The NT presses that insight to the extreme with reference to Christ's passion.

6. Mysterious

The recognition that a self-disclosing deity such as Yahweh remains hidden even when acquiescing to a desire to be seen (Exod 33:18-23) means that God was always believed to be, in the language of later theologians, *Deus absconditus* ("the hidden God"; compare Isa 45:15). Theodicy therefore is by necessity deferred, for all theological knowledge is partial. The poem in Job 28 denies that any human can discover wisdom, let alone God. This limited knowledge will persist in the realm to which all are destined, for Abaddon and Sheol are said to have heard only a rumor of wisdom. In the same vein, the author of Ecclesiastes emphasizes wisdom's remoteness (7:23-24), while Jer 17:5-11 places theological dogma under a cloud of suspicion ("Most perverse—the mind, and twisted is it; who can grasp it?" v. 9). The Hellenistic author of Wisdom of Solomon considers sterility and an early death areas that defy comprehension (3:13; 4:1, 14), and the angel frequently reminds the author of 2 Esdras that the mind cannot comprehend the anomalies of earthly existence, much less divine mysteries (e.g., 4:1-2, 10-11).

7. Determinist

Occasionally, so much emphasis falls on divine control of humanity that it comes perilously close to determinism. That is true of Qoheleth, whose skepticism follows from belief that a distant deity holds everyone's fate and dispenses it without regard to merit (e.g., Eccl 3:16-22). A similar view finds expression in 2 Esdras and *2 Baruch* (e.g., 14:8-12), both of which stress the limits imposed on humans and their destiny as a condemned populace, with a few exceptions. The Reform theologian John Calvin believed that God micro-managed humans; a similar position, perhaps attested in the book of Ruth and the story of Joseph, was taken by Islamic theologians known as Ash'arites.

8. Substitutionary

The priestly realm of sacrifice became the source of another response to theodicy. According to the final poem about a suffering servant, the death of an innocent functioned as a vicarious offering, bringing pardon to guilty individuals (Isa 52:13–53:12). The familiar story involving Abraham's intercession for the doomed cities of Sodom and Gomorrah involves this idea of a few righteous persons preventing punishment of the guilty (Gen 18–19). This approach, rooted in the ritual of the scapegoat, was useful in coming to terms with the death of Jesus at the hands of Roman soldiers (e.g., Heb 10:10).

9. Trans-generational

In early Israel the importance of the extended family provided a plausible response to failed instances of reward and retribution. The well-being of the larger entity compensated for loss of individual felicity. The principle of trans-generational reward and punishment is attributed to Yahweh in Exod 34:6-7, but emerging individualism brought wide disillusionment to the notion. That dissent was expressed in a popular proverb ("The parents have eaten sour grapes and the children's teeth are sensitive," Ezek 18:2; Jer 31:29).

10. Denial

This response, present in Vedantic Buddhism and Christian Science, is not found in the ANE. The closest thing to it is practical atheism, in which "fools" are said to deny the existence of deity (Pss 10 and 14, the latter repeated almost exactly in Ps 53; perhaps Prov 30:1-14). As Ps 82 and Deut 32:8-9 demonstrate, polytheism retained a powerful attraction among ancient Israelites.

C. The Function of Theodicy
1. To remind God of the covenant

Within the Bible theodicy enables individuals to appeal to a divine promise that mercy will prevail in the relationship between God and human beings. When all evidence appears to indicate that the powerless have no protector in the heavens, belief in God's ultimate goodness empowers a psalmist to urge an inattentive One to rise from slumber and aid widows and orphans (Ps 82:8).

Human nature notwithstanding, traditionists wish to believe that their creator is no tyrant zealously guarding life's bounty for exclusive enjoyment. Thus they have Eve come to God's defense while also "building a fence around Torah," that is, adding to the prohibition about the special tree(s).

The inevitable calamities that strike individuals and nations raise questions about religious convictions forged in better times. Protest theology is an effective means of pressing toward new and imaginative formulations that shape world views. Laments permit the verbalization of honest doubt that otherwise would lie under the surface and fester (e.g., Ps 88). Failed promises do not go undetected, as the story about Gideon's sharp response to an angel illustrates (Judg 6:13). Sickness, death, and loneliness evoke cries in search of answers. "Why?" and "How long?" are questions that cannot be suppressed forever. Gravest of all is this one: "My God, my God, why have you abandoned me?" (Ps 22:1; NRSV, "forsaken").

Because religion and politics were tightly interwoven, signal events such as the fall of Samaria and Jerusalem required explanation. The Deuteronomistic History thus offered a monumental theodicy similar to the so-called primeval history in Gen 1–11, which gave a reason for the flood. The ethicization of Yahweh over time meant that dubious behavior attributed to God needed to be transferred to another figure. The emergence of Satan into prominence met this need (2 Sam 24:1 and 1 Chr 21:1). The tension between the prose and poetry in the book of Job reveals the difficulty of resolving the problem in this way. At least one prophet takes umbrage at the idea of a deity whose mercy knows no limits (Jonah 4). The desire to leave no cracks in divine justice actualized adjustments to historical records, at least in the case of king Manasseh whose long reign defied Deuteronomistic logic (2 Chr 33:10-13; the *Prayer of Manasseh*). Similar devotion underlies the story about Moses' willingness to be erased from the divine record rather than see fury unleashed (Exod 32:32).

2. To keep theologians honest

By its very nature, religious language tends toward dogmatism. Enthusiasts affirm their devotion even in the face of strong evidence of disconfirmation on particular points. They also resist winds of change, consequently threatening to transform churches into museums. The most effective answer to this transformation of vital faith is straight talk that takes the anomalies of existence seriously and places them in perspective within honest religious discourse. In this formidable task, biblical responses to the problem of evil serve as a helpful model.

Bibliography: Peter Berger. *The Sacred Canopy* (1967); James L. Crenshaw. *Defending God: Biblical Responses to the Problem of Evil* (2005); James L. Crenshaw. "Theodicy in the Book of the Twelve." *Thematic Threads in the Book of the Twelve.* Paul L. Redditt and Aaron Schart, eds. (2003) 175–91; James L. Crenshaw, ed. *Theodicy in the Old Testament* (1983); James L. Crenshaw. *Urgent Advice and Probing Questions* (1995) 141–221; David Nelson Duke. "Theodicy at the Turn of Another Century: An Introduction." *PRSt* 26 (1999) 241–48; Antti Laato and Johannes C. de Moor, eds. *Theodicy in the World of the Bible* (2003); Gottfried Wilhelm Leibniz. *Theodicy: Essays on the Goodness of God, the Freedom of Man, and the Origin of Evil* (1988); Jon D. Levenson. *Creation and the Persistence of Evil* (1988); David Penchansky and Paul L. Redditt, eds. *Shall Not the Judge of All the Earth Do What Is Right?* (2000); J. A. Sanders. *Suffering as Divine Discipline in the Old Testament and Post-Biblical Judaism* (1955); Harold M. Schulweis. *Evil and the Morality of God* (1984); Terrence W. Tilley.

The Evils of Theodicy (2000); David Tracy and Hermann Häring, eds. *The Fascination of Evil* (1998).

JAMES L. CRENSHAW

THEODIUS, DISCOURSE OF. *See* VIRGIN, ASSUMPTION OF THE.

THEODOTION thee´uh-doh´shuhn. Active in the 2nd cent. CE, Theodotion of Ephesus translated Hebrew biblical texts into Greek and revised existing Greek biblical texts. Theodotion's version of the book of Daniel replaced the older Greek text in almost all manuscripts of the SEPTUAGINT. Origen placed in the sixth column of his HEXAPLA the text he attributed to Theodotion. Origen often used this material (not all of which was in fact Theodotion's) to prepare the "corrected" Greek text in his fifth column.

Readings that display distinctive characteristics of Theodotion occur in the NT, antedating by at least a century the "historical" Theodotion. Scholars thus postulate an Ur- or Proto-Theodotion, active in the 1st cent. CE.

The surviving evidence indicates that Theodotion translated and/or revised with an eye toward the Hebrew text that ultimately became the MT. He sought to provide standard representations for many Hebrew and Aramaic terms and to remain reasonably faithful to the original Semitic texts; his version would have had considerable appeal to his target audience. Aquila made use of Theodotion's version, often carrying much further his practice of adhering to the Hebrew and Aramaic texts (*see* AQUILA'S VERSION).

LEONARD GREENSPOON

THEODOTUS thee-od´uh-tuhs [Θεόδοτος Theodotos]. Meaning "gift of God." 1. A man sent along with Posidonius and Mattathias by the general Nicanor to pledge friendship to Judas Maccabeus (2 Macc 14:19).

2. A man who attempted to assassinate Ptolemy IV Philopator in his sleep. His plan was disrupted by Dositheus, a man who had turned away from the Jewish religion (3 Macc 1:2; see also Polybius, *Hist.* 5.81).

KATY VALENTINE

THEOLOGICAL HERMENEUTICS thee´uh-loj´i-kuhl huhr´muh-nyoo´tik. *Hermeneutics* refers to a theory of interpretation, to reflection on and the practice of human understanding. *Theological hermeneutics* refers broadly to how doctrine impinges on the enterprise of human understanding, and narrowly to the potentially mutual influence of Scripture and doctrine in theological discourse and the theological role of Scripture in the formation of persons and ecclesial communities.

Impetus for theological interpretation is found already in the Scriptures—first, in the interpretation of biblical texts in other biblical texts within the OT, then in the interpretation of Israel's Scriptures within the writings of the NT. The translation of the OT into Greek

(LXX) and the growth of the targumic tradition served further to codify interpretive traditions (*see* TARGUMS). The Qumran scrolls evidence an enormous exegetical enterprise. The traditions of Midrashim that developed around the Scriptures similarly engaged in a dialogue with the biblical texts, extending their meaning from the past into the present (*see* MIDRASH). These forms of interpretation displayed twin commitments to the truth and authority of the Scriptures and to their legitimate interpretation and embodiment in the community of the faithful.

Proponents of theological hermeneutics find support among Christian interpreters of the premodern era. Early on, theology was an exegetical enterprise, and typical forms of interpretation included homilies, theological treatises, catechetical lectures, and pastoral letters. Following hermeneutical strategies found already in the OT, remembered as used by Jesus, and practiced among the writers of what would become the NT documents, interpreters recontextualized biblical texts, providing updated rereadings of these texts in the service of Scripture's messianic and ecclesial message of salvation.

Biblical study since the 1600s has been less hospitable to theological interpretation. When Protestant interpretation emphasized instead the "literal sense" of biblical texts, hermeneutics, broadly conceived, was loosed from the specifically religious concerns to which it had previously been tethered. This eventuated in a hermeneutical commitment to observer neutrality (as opposed to an interpreter guided by theological commitments). The historical rootedness of the text, the historicity of events to which the text bears witness, and the historical gap separating text and reader emerged as key coordinates in the work of interpretation. Increasingly, the interpretive project was to move forward apart from interests of contemporary significance, whether political or theological or some other.

Proponents of theological hermeneutics counter, first, that one cannot address the meaning of the biblical texts without attention to their manifest concern with speaking of and for the God of Israel and Jesus Christ. Theology is, therefore, a non-negotiable locus of biblical studies.

This prompts a second issue: the relation of the Bible's message to Christian theology. J. P. Gabler (1753–1826) led biblical scholarship to emphasize above all the task of describing what the biblical text meant, apart from a concern with the constructive and prescriptive work of theology and ethics. Hence, whereas critical exegesis has typically highlighted the historical chasm separating ancient text and contemporary readers, theological exegesis focuses on whether we share (or refuse) the theological vision of the biblical text and on our disposition toward "standing under" (or resisting) the Scriptures. This is because theological hermeneutics takes as its starting point and central axis the theological claim that the Bible is Scripture, a claim that draws attention to the origin, role, and aim of these texts in God's self-communication and locates those who read the Bible as Scripture on a particular textual map, a location possessing its own assumptions, values, and norms for guiding and animating particular beliefs, dispositions, and practices constitutive of that people. Because of its priority in the generation and sustenance of the world it envisions, Scripture holds the potential in theological hermeneutics for confirming or reconfiguring the beliefs and commitments that orient our lives.

Of course, theological hermeneutics is not apathetic toward historical questions, for it recognizes that these texts are present to us as cultural products that draw on, actualize, propagate, and/or undermine the contexts within which they were generated. Attention to historical questions serves to shield the text from domestication or objectification by the reader, since it allows the text its own voice from within its own sociocultural horizons.

We may characterize theological hermeneutics as follows. First, it assumes the theological claim of one church, and thus works with the hermeneutical motto that the community within which the biblical texts were generated, the community who came to regard these books as canonical, and the community that now interprets these texts as Scripture are the same community.

Second, the aim of interpretation is less to generate and organize faith claims and more to put into play (or facilitate the performance of) the witness of Scripture. We do not invite the text into a transformation of its original meaning in order to achieve a new application geared toward our thought forms; rather, the text invites us into a transformation of allegiances and commitments, which will manifest itself in behaviors appropriate to our social worlds.

Third, theological hermeneutics locates itself self-consciously within the particularity of an ecclesial community. This means that the measure of validity in interpretation cannot be taken apart from the church's understanding of its historic faith (e.g., the Rule of Faith and the ecumenical creeds) and the history of Christian interpretation and its embodiment in Christian lives and communities.

Fourth, the constraints of working with this historical text and the work of theological interpretation need not be mutually exclusive. Instead, the aim of historical work shifts from the discovery of meaning embedded in or behind the text to enabling the text its robust voice in theological discourse.

Fifth, no particular method can ensure theological interpretation, but some methods are more theologically friendly than others. In addition to approaches that situate the voice of Scripture sociohistorically, of special interest in theological interpretation would be modes of analysis that take seriously the generally narrative content of Scripture; the theological unity of Scripture, which takes its point of departure from the character

and purpose of the God of Israel and of Jesus Christ; and the final form and canonical location of the biblical texts. *See* CULTURAL HERMENEUTICS.

Bibliography: Stephen E. Fowl, ed. *The Theological Interpretation of Scripture: Classic and Contemporary Readings* (1997); Joel B. Green and Max Turner, eds. *Between Two Horizons: Spanning New Testament Studies and Systematic Theology* (2000); Richard B. Hays. "Reading the Bible with the Eyes of Faith: The Practice of Theological Exegesis." *JTI* 1 (2007) 5–21; Christopher R. Seitz. *Word without End: The Old Testament as Abiding Theological Witness* (1998); Daniel J. Treier. *Introducing Theological Interpretation of Scripture* (2008); Francis Watson. *Text and Truth: Redefining Biblical Theology* (1997).

JOEL B. GREEN

THEOLOGY, BIBLICAL. *See* BIBLICAL THEOLOGY.

THEOLOGY, NT. New Testament theology may be characterized as an exegetically executed, theologically sensitive endeavor to describe and to assess the NT's comprehensive interpretations of God's involvement with humanity and the world, especially as that relationship is revealed in Jesus Christ.

A. Short History of New Testament Theology
  1. From the Patristic Era through the Reformation
    a. The early and medieval church
    b. Luther and Reformation orthodoxy
  2. From the Enlightenment through the 20th century
    a. Gabler and his successors
    b. The nature of New Testament theology: Wrede and Schlatter
    c. Re-proclaiming the *Kerygma*: Barth and Bultmann
B. Recurring Questions for Continued Study
  1. How does one approach New Testament theology?
  2. Does the New Testament exhibit a unifying core?
  3. How is New Testament theology related to Old Testament theology?
  4. Is Jesus' proclamation intrinsic to New Testament theology?
  5. How does philosophy bear on New Testament theology?
  6. How does New Testament theology bear on dogmatics, witness, and practice?
C. Conclusion
Bibliography

A. Short History of New Testament Theology

1. From the Patristic Era through the Reformation

a. The early and medieval church. Explicit, coherent theologies of the Christian Bible are traceable as early as Irenaeus of Lyons (2nd cent.), whose *regula fidei* ("rule of faith") stipulated that the NT's message is properly interpreted as a development of the OT's chronicle of God's interaction with Israel (*Haer.* 1.10.1). For Augustine of Hippo (354–430) the NT's meaning lies hidden in the Old; that of the OT is revealed by the New (*Doctr. chr.* 2.1–14). Attention to Scripture's literal sense, amplified by various spiritual senses, characterized theological commentary produced in medieval monastic and cathedral schools, culminating in the *Summa Theologiae* of Thomas Aquinas (ca. 1225–1274). The quest for the NT's—indeed, the Bible's—theological coherence was eased by the assumption that Christ is Scripture's central point of reference.

b. Luther and Reformation orthodoxy. Martin Luther's (1483–1546) quarrel with the pope turned on the Holy Spirit's unique residence in a single interpreter (*Address to the German Nobility*, 1520). With the important caveat that the interpreter requires inspiration by the same Spirit operative among Scripture's various authors, Luther opened the possibility of a hermeneutical democratization that modern NT theology projects would presuppose. Perception of the NT's theological unity and diversity was sharpened by the Reformers' avowal that all Scripture, though inspired, was neither historically inerrant, nor theologically harmonious, nor equally profound.

2. From the Enlightenment through the 20th century

a. Gabler and his successors. Luther distinguished Israel's particular law-code from natural law, inscribed on the human heart and universally binding ("How Christians Should Regard Moses," 1525). By the 18th cent., rationalism accorded the primary basis of human authority to autonomous reason in its search for truth. Rooted in Renaissance humanism, the Enlightenment in Europe and North America produced critical studies of Scripture, questioning its historical and doctrinal reliability (*see* BIBLICAL CRITICISM). Thus was set the stage for Johann Philipp Gabler's (1753–1826) inaugural address at Altdorf University in 1787 (Sandys–Wunsch and Eldredge). For Gabler, truth resides in transhistorical "universal ideas" or "the unchanging idea of the doctrine of salvation," clothed in "some particular era or testament." The task of biblical theology is to peel away the contingent husk in which the NT witness has been "accommodated," in order to recover for the benefit of systematic theologians "the unchanging testament of Christian doctrine."

Gabler synthesized and clearly articulated the views of his Enlightenment precursors and in at least two ways anticipated subsequent research. First is the distinction between religion ("everyday, transparently clear knowledge") and theology ("subtle, learned knowledge"). Second is the procedure of differentiating historical recovery from systematic formulation.

Roughly a decade after Gabler's lecture, his colleague G. L. Bauer (1755–1806) published the first historical-critical OT theology (*see* THEOLOGY, OT), at once distinguishing that enterprise from NT theology and raising questions for their subsequent reintegration. Emphasizing unconditional obedience to God's law (*see* LAW IN THE OT), Bauer offered the first modern treatment of NT ethics (1804–05; *see* ETHICS IN THE NT), which sharpened Gabler's historical perspective by differentiating Jesus' religion from that of the Evangelists and discriminating the various NT witnesses. W. M. L. de Wette (1780–1849) extended Bauer's differentiation by grouping NT books in their presumed religious provenances: Jewish Christianity (the Synoptics, most of the CATHOLIC EPISTLES, Revelation), Alexandrian Hellenism (the Gospel of John, the letters of John, the Letter to the Hebrews), and Pauline Christianity (letters ascribed to Paul). Structuring their analyses of the NT in accordance with such topics as CHRISTOLOGY, theological anthropology, and SOTERIOLOGY, both Bauer and de Wette produced systematic theologies whose source and norm were biblical (*see* ANTHROPOLOGY, NT THEOLOGICAL).

b. The nature of New Testament theology: Wrede and Schlatter. During much of the 19th cent., NT theology suffered partial eclipse by historical preoccupations filtered through Hegelian idealism: F. C. Bauer's five-volume *History of the Christian Church* (1853–62) and D. F. Strauss's *Life of Jesus* (1835). In a theologically liberal era B. Weiss's (1827–1918) conservative essay in NT theology predicated careful examination of God's salvific self-revelation in history. More influential was H. J. Holtzmann's (1832–1920) liberal presentation of the HISTORICAL JESUS as a religious genius, Paul as christology's creator, and John as an Alexandrian consummation of Logos–mysticism.

Enter William Wrede (1859–1906), whose lectures for clergy at Breslau on "The Task and Methods of 'New Testament Theology'" (1897; Morgan 1973) rent asunder the conceptual marriage that Gabler had attempted to broker a century earlier. For Wrede grouping thoughts expressed by the NT in alignment with dogmatic topics betrays scientific criticism and provokes caricature of NT writers as systematicians in the modern sense. That method's acknowledgment of canonical documents is likewise misguided: a document's canonization makes no difference for either the Protestant theologian or historical investigator. New Testament theology is, or should be, the attempt to understand the development of primitive Christian religion in its historical situation. The clearest rebuttal of Wrede's position may be that of his contemporary Adolf Schlatter (1852–1938). Although Schlatter does not dismiss the necessity of historical research, for him the historian is no neutral observer but, rather, one whose own perception is molded by historically conditioned convictions. An objective, "merely historical purpose" is an illusory self-deception; indeed, religious criteria inevitably reenter through the door Wrede had shut. The historian's own consciousness is wedded to God. Moreover, faith is endemic to the historical task. Thus, NT theology should concern itself with the NT (and not other documents, apart from the OT), and the tasks of NT theology and dogmatics are inextricably reciprocal.

By somewhat unpredictable routes 20th cent. scholarship pursued the alternatives that Wrede and Schlatter posed. Concentrating on traditional genres within the Gospels, form critics such as M. Dibelius (*From Tradition to Gospel*, 1919) answered Wrede's challenge to reconstruct earliest Christian beliefs, values, and aspirations within their broader religious and cultural setting (*see* FORM CRITICISM, NT). Wrede's abjuration of canonical distinctions is maintained with illuminating results in G. Kittel and G. Friedrich's ten-volume *Theological Dictionary of the New Testament* (1933–74, dedicated to Schlatter). Lamenting that Wrede's vision remains unrealized, H. Räisänen (1941–) has sketched a program for doing so (1990).

Eschatology seems an abortive approach to NT theology after the dead end reached by the 19th cent. quest for the historical Jesus (Schweitzer 1906; *see* ESCHATOLOGY OF THE NT). Yet Schlatter's call for historians' engagement with the God who acts in history is manifest in his progeny, who led the variegated biblical theology movement in Britain and North America during the decades before and after World War II (Hoskyns and Davey; Piper; Wright and Fuller; Cullmann).

c. Re-proclaiming the *Kerygma*: Barth and Bultmann. Schlatter's truest successor may have been Karl Barth (1886–1968), who broke with Enlightenment epistemology by regarding all humans as living nowhere other than within a God-centered history, the sphere of God's self-communicative action. The monument to neo-orthodoxy's "theology of the word"—the Reformation's identification of divine revelation in the *kerygma*, the proclaimed word of God, instead of biblical history—is Barth's commentary on Romans (1919, 1921), in whose prefaces he expresses "feel[ing him]self most closely related" to Schlatter. The avowed aim of Barth's *Church Dogmatics* (1932–70) is *Nachdenken*: faithful listening to biblical narratives, "after-pondering" their God as "the One who loves in freedom," then thinking through all the implications of God's self-revelation for the church's faith and life.

Rudolf Bultmann's (1884–1976) *Theology of the New Testament* (1951–55) is universally recognized as the 20th cent.'s most important experiment in NT theology. It is also the most fascinating: an unstable hybrid of Wrede and Schlatter's equally stubborn, seemingly contradictory positions. For Bultmann, theology's "intent" is human self-understanding, whose character remains the same across time and this becomes the structuring

principle of his work. The backdrop for NT theology is Jesus' message—the call to human decision at the dawning of God's reign—and its reformulation in the earliest church's *kerygma*. Because "Paul's theology is at the same time anthropology," Bultmann can reconstruct from "the founder of Christian theology" a coherent position whose poles are humanity prior to faith's revelation and humanity under faith. Before faith loses its eschatological tension, deteriorating into "bourgeois piety" in the NT's sub-apostolic writings, John presents humanity confronted by the crisis of decision for or against Jesus, both the bringer of the Revelation and himself the revelation.

Both Bultmann and Barth systematize NT theology in ways the NT does not. Bultmann generates theology through historical criticism; Barth's theology of history challenges that method's assumptions. Reminiscent of Gabler, Bultmann's "demythologization" is a well-intentioned attempt to retrieve what NT writers meant from what they said; for Barth, just what the NT narratives say defines what they mean. Both Bultmann and Barth accord to NT study a potential for radical change in the interpreter's self-understanding. Since NT theology is for Bultmann anthropocentric, that change is of primary importance; for Barth it is secondary, because NT theology is christocentric.

B. Recurring Questions for Continued Study

1. How does one approach New Testament theology?

The discipline's historical dimension is uncontested, but the question of approach remains in parts. One concerns the interpreter's perspective. Is NT theology primarily confessional, even denominational (Bonsirven; Stylianopoulos)? Existentialist (Bultmann; Strecker)? Extra-ecclesial, for the sake of the global village (Räisänen)? Historically descriptive within the socially constructed framework of communion with the saints (Esler)? Structuring principles have tended to be historical-genetic (Strecker), systematic-conceptual (Vouga), or some conjunction of attitudes diachronic and synchronic (Hahn; Wilckens).

2. Does the New Testament exhibit a unifying core?

After historians disqualified dogmatic answers to this question, E. Käsemann (1906–1998) spoke for many when he wrote that the NT canon provides the basis for the multiplicity of the church's confessions. Some recent studies highlight the NT's theological diversity (Strecker; Gnilka). Marshall (2004) accents the NT's harmonious, essentially missionary theology. Käsemann regards the apocalyptic Lordship of the crucified Christ as the real clue amidst the NT's pluralism (1972–73). Similarly, J. D. G. Dunn's synchronic-diachronic inquiry (1977) concludes that the unity between the historical Jesus and the exalted Christ is the integrative center for earliest Christianity's diverse expressions. Lately one detects a more deliberately theocentric articulation of the NT's core (Dahl): the self–revelation of Israel's God in Jesus Christ (Hahn; Wilckens; Stuhlmacher), emerging from imaginary, roundtable debates among NT witnesses (Vouga; Caird and Hurst) or from renewed respect for the NT's narrative world (Matera). This development is reminiscent of the mid-20th cent. biblical theology movement, tweaked to take seriously the Bible's use of stories to communicate its vision of reality.

3. How is New Testament theology related to Old Testament theology?

This question is as old as the NT itself, whose constituent witnesses variously interact with Israel's Scripture. Hübner assesses the NT account of God's self-revelation as adequate in isolation. At the other extreme Stuhlmacher insists on the entire canon within NT theology's purview. Appreciation of OT citations and allusions in NT texts has long been assumed and refined (Dodd). The location of NT theology within the broader Christian canon has received fresh impetus by B. S. Childs (1923–2007) and other proponents of CANONICAL CRITICISM. Before proceeding to NT theology, N. T. Wright (1948–) devotes an entire volume to Israel's faith and other aspects of the church's milieu (1992). As NT theology evolves into BIBLICAL THEOLOGY, maintaining a dialectical balance between the Testaments remains a perennial challenge.

4. Is Jesus' proclamation intrinsic to New Testament theology?

During the second half of the 20th cent., recovering an implied theology from Jesus' own preaching was often reckoned a necessary first stage of NT theology (Kümmel; Jeremias; Goppelt). For many it remains so (Stuhlmacher; Caird and Hurst; Wright [1996]; Marshall). Other recent contributions tend to encompass, not the historically reconstructed Jesus, but rather the proclamation of Jesus as rendered by the NT evangelists (Räisänen; Gnilka; Wilckens; Matera). Different procedures follow in part from an investigator's prior decision whether NT theology is an essentially descriptive (historical) or normative (dogmatic) enterprise.

5. How does philosophy bear on New Testament theology?

The brief answer is heavily and often covertly. To articulate their views NT writers themselves drew, not only from the OT, but also from HELLENISM and GREEK RELIGION AND PHILOSOPHY. Likewise, every generation of NT interpreters partakes of its era's philosophical milieu. The Reformers were children of scholasticism and humanism; Wrede and Barth and Bultmann were partially informed by Kant and Hegel and Heidegger. As a self–reflective discipline, current NT theology is coming to terms with modernity's resources and limitations (Adam). Whereas a contemporary "hermeneutics of suspicion" drinks from the wells of L. Feuerbach (1804–1872), K. Marx (1818–1883), and F. Nietzsche (1844–1900), an ecclesially sympathetic "hermeneutics of conviction" (Vanhoozer) converses with such philosophers as H.-G. Gadamer (1900–2002), P. Ricoeur (1913–2005), and J. Derrida (1930–2004). Why NT theology itself has been to date a preponderantly European project, with occasional Anglo-American contributions, but few from Asia, Africa, or Latin America is an unresolved question whose answer may entail the history of philosophy and perhaps also cultural epistemology (see THEOLOGICAL HERMENEUTICS).

6. How does New Testament theology bear on dogmatics, witness, and practice?

Exponents of NT theology have typically engaged the church, whether devotedly or not. Renewed efforts to describe and to encourage reciprocity among NT theology and patristics, dogmatics, and praxis characterize late 20th-cent. scholarship (Young; Watson; Green and Turner). Important in this endeavor is R. Morgan's (1940–) clarification that NT theology does not argue for Christianity's truth but, rather, assists in clarifying its authentic identity (1996).

C. Conclusion

As the curtain rises on the 21st cent., NT theology appears alive, well, and vigorous. If history is a reliable guide, its health and fertility will depend on a continuously calibrated balance of its descriptive and normative aspects: exegetically understanding the NT's multifarious claim for God's salvation in Jesus Christ while standing under the liberating judgment of that conviction. *See* FOLKLORE IN BIBLICAL INTERPRETATION; HISTORY AND HISTORIOGRAPHY, NT; INTERTEXTUALITY; JESUS, METAPHORS FOR; NARRATIVE CRITICISM; POSTMODERN BIBLICAL INTERPRETATION; REDACTION CRITICISM, NT.

Bibliography: A. K. M. Adam. *Making Sense of New Testament Theology* (1995); K. Barth. *The Epistle to the Romans* (1919, 1921); K. Barth. *Church Dogmatics.* 14 vols. (1932–70); G. L. Bauer. *Biblical Theology of the New Testament.* 4 vols. (1800–02); G. L. Bauer. *Biblical Morality of the New Testament.* 2 vols. (1804–05); H. Boers. *What Is New Testament Theology?* (1979); J. Bonsirven. *Theology of the New Testament* (1951); R. Bultmann. *Theology of the New Testament.* 2 vols. (1951–55); G. D. Caird and L. D. Hurst. *New Testament Theology* (1994); B. S. Childs. *The New Testament as Canon* (1984); O. Cullmann. *Salvation in History* (1965); N. A. Dahl. "The Neglected Factor in New Testament Theology." *Reflections* 75 (1975) 5–8; C. H. Dodd. *According to the Scriptures* (1952); J. D. G. Dunn. *Unity and Diversity in the New Testament* (1977); P. S. Esler. *New Testament Theology* (2005); J. Gnilka. *Theology of the New Testament* (1994); L. Goppelt. *New Testament Theology.* 2 vols. (1975);

J. B. Green and M. Turner, eds. *Between Two Horizons* (2000); F. Hahn. *Theology of the New Testament.* 2 vols. (2002–05); H. J. Holtzmann. *Textbook of the New Testament* (1896–97); E. C. Hoskyns and F. N. Davey. *The Riddle of the New Testament* (1931); H. Hübner. *Biblical Theology of the New Testament.* 3 vols. (1990–93); J. Jeremias. *New Testament Theology* (1971); E. Käsemann. "The Problem of a New Testament Theology." *NTS* 19 (1972–73) 235–45; W. G. Kümmel. *The New Testament According to Its Major Witnesses: Jesus–Paul–John* (1969); I. H. Marshall. *New Testament Theology* (2004); F. J. Matera. *New Testament Theology* (2007); R. Morgan. *The Nature of New Testament Theology* (1973); R. Morgan. "Can the Critical Study of Scripture Provide a Doctrinal Norm?" *JR* 76 (1996) 206–32; O. A. Piper. *God in History* (1939); H. Räisänen. *Beyond New Testament Theology* (1990); C. K. Rowe. "New Testament Theology: The Revival of a Discipline." *JBL* 125 (2006) 393–410; J. Sandys-Wunsch and L. Eldredge. "J. P. Gabler and the Distinction between Biblical and Dogmatic Theology." *SJT* 33 (1980) 133–58; A. Schlatter. *New Testament Theology.* 2nd ed. (1921–22); A. Schweitzer. *The Quest of the Historical Jesus* (1906, 1912, 1950); G. Strecker. *Theology of the New Testament* (2000); P. Stuhlmacher. *Biblical Theology of the New Testament* (1991–99); T. G. Stylianopoulos. *The New Testament* (1997); K. J. Vanhoozer. *Is There a Meaning in This Text?* (1998); D. O. Via. *What Is New Testament Theology?* (2002); F. Vouga. *A Theology of the New Testament* (2001); F. Watson. *Text, Church and World* (1994); B. Weiss. *Biblical Theology of the New Testament* (1868); W. M. L. de Wette. *Biblical Dogmatics.* 3rd ed. (1831); U. Wilckens. *Theology of the New Testament.* 4 vols. (2002–05); G. E. Wright and R. H. Fuller. *The Book of the Acts of God* (1957); N. T. Wright. *The New Testament and the People of God* (1992); N. T. Wright. *Jesus and the Victory of God* (1996); F. M. Young. *The Art of Performance* (1990).

C. CLIFTON BLACK

THEOLOGY, OT. Old Testament theology is a critical and constructive inquiry into the OT focusing especially on the OT's portrayals of God and God's relationships. Old Testament theology has been defined and conducted as a sub-discipline within biblical theology, with a view to the OT's relation to the NT and to Christian (systematic or doctrinal) theology and ethics; as a part of historical theology; or as a strictly historical endeavor, joined to, or identical with, the history of Israel's religion. For these reasons, OT theology is also a field of debate about its history, nature, purpose, and even its possibility.

The issues that have occupied OT theology, and those that still confront it, can be grasped in consideration of its history.

A. Old Testament Theology's History
  1. Nineteenth century
  2. Twentieth century
    a. Walther Eichrodt and Gerhard von Rad
    b. Brevard Childs and Walter Brueggemann
B. Continuing Issues
  1. History, religion, and theology
  2. A "center" of Old Testament theology?
  3. Old Testament, New Testament, and Christian theology
C. Conclusion
Bibliography

A. Old Testament Theology's History

After J. P. Gabler proposed, in 1787, a distinction between biblical and dogmatic theology, his Altdorf University colleague G. L. Bauer produced the first OT theology (*Theologie des Alten Testaments*) in 1796. Bauer insisted that OT theology must be pursued in a rigorously historical manner. He shared Gabler's notions about the historical development of human reason, and saw especially a historical development from the particular to the universal. The Pentateuch, as he saw it, betrayed a primitive nationalism or particularism, focused exclusively on Israel. According to Bauer, the OT reached its highest level of development in Proverbs, which begins to transcend Israelite particularism in the direction of more properly universal ideas about God. Despite stressing historical-critical interpretation, Bauer's presentation of OT theology focused exclusively on ideas, which he arranged under doctrinal categories.

1. Nineteenth century

Biblical theology in the early 19th cent. worked under the competing philosophies of Kant and Hegel, while struggling to develop a consistently historical analysis of the OT. In OT theology, the quest was for criteria by which to assess the Bible's historically and theologically diverse contents and to define its coherence.

The theme of universal versus particular, and the denigration of the OT and Judaism, which characterized Bauer, continued with W. M. L. de Wette. In his 1813 *Biblische Dogmatik*, he combined a Kantian philosophical anthropology with historical interpretation to distinguish the OT's pure ideas from their historical expression. With this theory-rich method and a moral conception of God in place, de Wette drew a distinction between the OT and Judaism, which he regarded as a decline. The seeds of that decline lay within the OT itself, whose authors tended to confuse the particular for the universal, and to misunderstand the theocratic symbols—those associated with the tabernacle and Temple, for example. They tended, that is, to reify those symbols, mistaking the sign for the subject matter to which it pointed. That subject matter was, for de Wette, the "ideal universalism" of doctrine, especially the OT doctrines of God and humanity. For Wilhelm Vatke, in

1835 (*Die Religion des Alten Testaments*), Hegel provided the conceptual framework. Such a framework he regarded as necessary, because historical investigation itself is subjective and not scientific, so it cannot arrive at the truth. It can attain the status of science and a relative objectivity if taken up into a conceptual analysis—Hegel's—that comprehends history as a whole. The concept of a religion unfolds historically and dialectically, so that the subjectivity of the concept (notions or ideas) and the objectivity of its manifestations (institutions and events) are sublated in the religion's "Idea." Thus, only from the perspective of its completed history, in the postexilic period, can one understand Israel's religion.

Several theologians in the middle of the century produced works in OT theology that emphasized history apart from a philosophical framework. While their presentations of OT theology did not consistently take historical form, in their methods they held to an organic view of history. Constituting Israel's history as an organic whole was God's activity in it. While their predecessors had focused on the OT's ideas, these theologians stressed the facts of God's activity in historical events, which corresponded generally to the OT's own account. They insisted on faith and on participation in the spirit of revelation as conditions of understanding and viewed Israel's history as salvation history.

A different approach to Israel's history and to OT scholarship rapidly gained dominance. Julius Wellhausen became preeminent in the critical reconstruction of Israel's history, including the history of its religion. Wellhausen, though not a theologian, exercised a powerful effect on OT theology. By the end of the century, any distinction between OT theology and the history of Israel's religion had virtually collapsed. Books that included OT theology in their titles or in their earlier editions were content to reprise past precedent and trace the development of OT ideas through Judaism and into the NT, or to its threshold. By the century's end, OT theology itself, as previously conceived, lacked an intellectually justifiable rationale, strategy, or purpose.

2. Twentieth century

When the past century began, the history-of-religion school dominated biblical studies. Hermann Gunkel, its leading figure, described the school as interested in religion, not in (dogmatic) theology. He wanted to move, exegetically, behind the OT's concepts to discover the personalities and "inner life," the piety, of its authors. None of the inherited conceptions of OT theology served these purposes, and no one was certain how to proceed. The situation demanded fresh methodological reflection, which eventually produced the imposing theologies of Walther Eichrodt and Gerhard von Rad. They also helped set the agenda for debates and for the theologies that followed.

a. **Walther Eichrodt and Gerhard von Rad.** Eichrodt in his OT theology wanted to avoid both the static doctrinal categories of earlier theologies and the historicism that reduced OT theology to the history of religion. His alternative was to take a "cross-section" of OT thought, in order to determine what was essential within Israel's "faith world." This would permit the necessary systematic structure and expose its underlying principles, while at the same time conforming to the OT's dynamism. Pervading the OT's ideas is also a basic tendency and character, detectable throughout Israel's history and epitomized by the concept of covenant. Eichrodt's innovation was to propose covenant as the OT's unifying theological principle.

Eichrodt structured his presentation systematically, in two volumes. The first treated covenant in various dimensions of Israel's religious life, while the second treated God's relationships with humankind and the world. He was aware that neither the term nor the notion of covenant appears everywhere in the OT, and he was aware of differences among the particular covenant traditions. Eichrodt understood *covenant* to refer to God's initiative or "intervention" in, and as God's relationship with, Israel, and Israel's conviction of its unique relationship with God. Further, covenant referred to those "spiritual values" that come variously to expression in Israel's history, and also variously in all parts of the OT. These spiritual values were established at the very beginning of Israel's religion, in Moses' direct and unmediated converse with God, and they persisted through Israel's religious history and, thus, through the OT's "incessant growth." Finally, for Eichrodt, *covenant* refers to the in-breaking and establishment of God's kingship in the world. This also constituted the OT's fundamental continuity with the NT, giving Judaism the appearance of a mere "torso."

Eichrodt's achievement was substantial. His mediation, if not resolution, of historical and systematic approaches to OT theology marked an advance over his predecessors, even as he shared with them a disparaging view of Judaism. While Eichrodt gave OT theology new life in the 20th cent., his work could also count as the culminating effort of the 19th cent. It has that appearance in comparison with the OT theology, two decades later, of von Rad.

Gerhard von Rad's approach to OT theology grew out of his own form and tradition-historical studies. From these he had concluded that the HEXATEUCH developed out of brief creed-like statements such as Deut 26:5-9. Originating in the cult, these creedal recitals were later expanded and incorporated within the Hexateuch, which von Rad saw as a grand narrative. This narrative, from creation to the conquest of Canaan, was itself a creed summarizing the history of God's redemptive acts. Von Rad brought these conclusions into his OT theology. Specifically, he insisted that OT theology's subject matter must be Israel's own assertions about God, and those assertions have the form of narrating God's redemptive acts on Israel's behalf. For von Rad, then, neither history of religion nor Eichrodt's systematic approach was adequate to the task. The former had something other than Israel's own explicit assertions as its object, while the latter ignored the OT's historical and diverse character, imposing upon it extraneous systematic categories. For von Rad, the search for a theological center was futile, since the OT exhibits not one theology but several. Neither can OT theology satisfy itself with describing Israel's world of faith or the OT's ideas. In conforming to its object, OT theology will best be conducted as recital or "retelling."

Von Rad made the Hexateuch and the historical books foundational in his theology. But he did not proceed simply by "retelling" the often disjunctive narratives or harmonizing them. Rather, by way of his tradition-historical method, he showed how these narratives continually take up older traditions and "actualize" them in new ways. Israel found accounts of God's past actions to have the character of promise and to be revelatory in and of the present. In this way a kind of typological interpretation has taken place in the growth of the traditions themselves. Consequently, and also in virtue of their content, the historical narratives are kerygmatic; they are testimonies to the revelation of God in word and deed in history. Since they are kerygmatic, and because of the traditioning process that formed them, the events these testimonies narrate differ from the historical course of events that critical scholarship can reconstruct. Moreover, the OT's confessional traditions are continually open to the future, as the traditioning process itself demonstrates. That process reaches a conclusion with the NT. Von Rad maintained that OT theology had to show this tradition-historical connection between the two Testaments, or else it would be merely a history of OT religion.

Since von Rad gave priority to the historical books, which provided the content of the OT's foundational confessions and its "theology of history," other material required separate treatment. In his first volume, von Rad brought the psalms and wisdom literature under the category of "Israel's answer." He treated the prophets in a second volume, since they proclaimed an interruption in Israel's saving history and judged Israel's life in relation to it.

Neither Eichrodt nor von Rad found the other's theology acceptable. Von Rad wrote of Eichrodt that he had imposed "bloodless schemata" on the diverse and historically dynamic biblical texts. Eichrodt, in turn, accused von Rad of robbing OT theology of its factual nature and leaving us with religious philosophy. Neither charge seems justified.

b. Brevard Childs and Walter Brueggemann. Scholars writing in the wake of von Rad granted his insight into the dynamic and diverse character of the OT but sought to establish its theological coherence. Late in the century, when von Rad's challenge had been absorbed and other options in biblical studies had emerged, OT theologies of wide variety appeared in Europe and in North America. The most comprehen-

sive of these was that of H. D. Preuss, whose structured approach to the OT's "world of faith and witness" resembled Eichrodt. New voices and fresh developments in biblical studies also emerged. Gisela Kittel became the first woman to publish an OT theology, one that gave greater attention to social location. Several evangelical scholars published volumes, and Jewish scholars debated the desirability or possibility of biblical theology. Jon Levenson explained why Jews are not interested in biblical theology, while Moshe Goshen-Gottstein proposed a "Tanakh Theology." Meanwhile, different interpretive methods, strategies, and interests provided both challenges and opportunities. Among other things, the historical paradigm, regnant since Bauer and de Wette, came under scrutiny in the work of Brevard Childs and Walter Brueggemann.

Childs deployed his canonical approach in an OT theology. For Childs, historical criticism remained indispensable, but its contribution lay in providing a depth or "diachronic" dimension to the "final form" of the text, a stable text—the biblical (Hebrew) text we have—as the proper object of interpretation. The biblical texts' (or books') latest strands of tradition, or their editors, let stand earlier views in tension with their own. Thus, OT theology requires a multi-layered reading, but one that discerns within the history a trajectory and within the diversity a unity: a coherent witness. Childs employed the notion of intertextuality as a kind of synonym for *canonical.* Opposing a crass historical referential reading of the OT, which interpreted biblical texts according to their success in describing historical states of affairs—thus as sources, rather than as witnesses—Childs tended to refer specific texts to other biblical texts. Whether, or the degree to which, a particular complex of texts required a referential reading depended on the particularities of the texts or traditions, but also on how productive or problematic Childs himself found the prior historical-critical discussion about them. The intentionality of the text and the stability of the text's final form were essential ingredients in his approach. While he insisted that OT theology is part of Christian theology, his volume on the subject equally insists on granting the OT its own discrete voice. The inconsistency is only apparent.

Brueggemann appealed to postmodern insights, Jewish practice, and the diverse, polyphonic character of the OT itself to argue against "reductionistic" approaches that subject the text to categories outside it. Like Childs, he resisted both the hegemony of historical criticism and attempts to find within the OT a theological center, while insisting on the OT's character as normative witness. Brueggemann employed the notions of witness and testimony in their courtroom sense as a way of putting the disparate texts into "disputatious" dialogue. First he treated Israel's core testimony, primarily in the Torah, stressing God's acts of liberation and faithfulness on Israel's behalf. This core testimony was then cross-examined by Israel's counter-testimony, which brought to expression God's untamed and sometimes excessively violent side. Unsolicited testimony came from God's partners: Israel, "the human person," the nations, and creation. Finally, embodied testimony, e.g., the institutions of cult and kingship, embodied God's presence. To these courtroom metaphors, Brueggemann joined a grammatical one, that of the verbal sentence. Israel's core testimony moves from strong verbs narrating God's action to adjectives describing God's character, and then to noun metaphors (e. g., God as judge and king, artist and healer). Testimony and grammar finally give way to rhetoric. Brueggemann insisted that the elusive subject of the OT and of OT theology is God. While Childs referred to the OT's voice, Brueggemann wrote of its utterance. God's identity and reality depend on the utterance of the text.

The contributions of Childs and Brueggemann remain distinctive. However, the canonical approach of Childs influenced the OT theology of Rolf Rendtorff, which first, "retells" the OT material in canonical succession and then treats themes that arise out of the material. John Goldingay in his multi-volume work followed a similar canonical pattern, but restricted his retelling to the OT's narrative books, leaving thematic discussion of Israel's faith to consideration of the prophets. Neither Rendtorff nor Goldingay depended on a reconstructed history of Israel's traditions, and their use of historical criticism remained occasional and modest, focusing as they did on the "final form" of the text. Among the differences between them was their willingness or refusal to relate OT theology to the NT and to Christian theology. Rendtorff envisioned OT/biblical theology as a project in which Christians and Jews could collaborate, while Goldingay related his work to the NT and engaged Christian theologians. Bruce Waltke has followed Goldingay. His encyclopedic OT theology combines a thematic arrangement and canonical order under the rubric of *gift*. It mediates between evangelical theology (the OT's theological center includes Jesus Christ) and critical scholarship (ancient cosmogonies influenced the OT's authors).

B. Continuing Issues
1. History, religion, and theology
How, or whether, OT theology should relate itself to the history of Israel's religion remains contested. However, it is no longer possible to collapse the former into the latter. Research into the history of Israel and Judah, including their religions, proceeds by studying archaeological, epigraphic, and iconographic remains. It may also make critical use of the OT. But regardless of the extent to which the OT preserves historical records or memories, it does not document the history of Israel's religion. Indeed, the OT presents theological and social criticisms of and alternatives to it. Historical research can shed light on Israel's religion and its practices and on the theologies associated with or implied by them. Thereby, it can aid in understanding the OT's

own diverse expressions, genres, and traditions—both their history and the communities that formed them. Further, historical-critical inquiry may illumine how the OT or Tanakh became normative and canonical, in different respects and in different forms, for Christians and Jews. Yet historical research can neither justify that status, which OT theology has presupposed from the beginning, nor determine its particular character.

2. A "center" of Old Testament theology?
The OT's manifold diversity has challenged OT theology from its beginning. Responses to this challenge have varied widely. Early efforts tended to gather texts around doctrinal categories, which stood in tension with the avowedly historical character of biblical theology. Versions of this tension continue, even when doctrinal categories are avoided. Since OT theology cannot simply recite the texts it studies, some way of organizing its presentation and summarizing the material remains necessary. Having become relatively independent of both NT and dogmatic theology, and of the history of religion, OT theology struggled to find categories within the OT itself that would disclose its coherence or its dynamic essence. Thus emerged proposals for the theological center or centers of the OT. These included, among others: covenant, the Torah, Yahweh, righteousness, salvation and blessing, God's steadfast love, the first commandment, Deuteronomy, and the psalms. Others denied any such center but accounted for the OT's wholeness or tensive coherence in other ways. While disavowing a center, Rolf Knierim proposed a criterion—God's universal reign of justice and righteousness—for discerning priorities among the OT's diverse themes and traditions. No proposal has won, or will win, a consensus, but each has provided a fresh angle of vision on the texts in their inter-relationships and their diversity. Any theological account of the whole OT will be a critically constructive achievement and a provisional one, grounded in exegesis but not determined by it. The OT's dynamic subject, God in relation, cannot be finally defined. For that reason, the OT's coherence can be only an occasional, variable event and its diversity a gift.

3. Old Testament, New Testament, and Christian theology
At its inception, a reforming impulse motivated OT theology. One object of reform was dogmatic theology and with it, Christian preaching. The relative independence of OT theology from dogmatic (or systematic) theology was on behalf of this reforming purpose, which also entailed a close association with NT theology. Subsequently, and also currently, these relationships have been the subject of debate. Energizing this debate has been the emergence of interpretive approaches that, while not repudiating the variety of historical-critical methods, have made their use relative to larger interpretive purposes and interests.

Even operating within historical-critical parameters, some have argued that OT theology depends on the NT for its criteria of assessment. Others insist, similarly, that the OT is, by definition, part of Christian Scripture and prepares us to understand Jesus Christ who is its center. These arguments represent serious challenges to OT theology as an independent field. Its independence can remain only relative if it will be constituent in theological inquiry and exercise a theological responsibility. That responsibility, in turn, will be both critical and constructive. The church preserved and transmitted the OT as a book, as Scripture, open to and requiring continued interpretation. Old Testament theology responds to that requirement, even when it goes beyond the NT. For Christians the OT and the NT are necessarily related. But no global definition of that relationship (e. g., promise and fulfillment) suffices.

Some have conceived OT or biblical theology as providing the foundation or the material for dogmatic (Christian) theology. That foundational picture is an illusion and a distraction. Old Testament theology works within a long history of biblical interpretation, including—as it is variously represented in contemporary theologies—and embodied in communities of faith. Dogmatic or systematic theology—any robust account of Christian faith and conviction—does not depend on a theology of either or both Testaments. But it does depend on Scripture. The reforming and critical impulses that first gave rise to biblical theology may seem naïve in retrospect, but they have endured. Old Testament theology does not proceed by imposing doctrinal categories on biblical texts. Rather, it can contribute to Christian theology and faith by regarding doctrines as examples of biblical interpretation and "retextualizing" them: putting them in mutually critical conversation with the biblical texts.

C. Conclusion

New hermeneutical and ethical perspectives and new methodologies, as well as new voices from diverse social locations, have had an impact on OT theology not yet fully realized. Dialogue with efforts in Jewish biblical theology will bring new vitality and raise different questions from those that have dominated the field for two centuries. Gershom Ratheiser, rejecting OT theology in favor of Jewish ethics, proposes a mitzvoth-ethical model stressing the mitzvoth ("instructions for life") covenant, which is "the central biblical connection" between Israel and God. Its concerns focus on holiness and liberating justice, of which the Jewish Bible offers human examples; the "paradigm of examples" is Ratheiser's hermeneutical axis. His chosen example is Joshua: the "exemplary warrior" who represents the "ideal warrior" (God). Sweeney, with the Shoah (Holocaust) as his hermeneutical axis, raises and urges questions about God as the ideal warrior. Old Testament theology has been occupied with theodicy, with justifying God's power and righteousness even, especially,

when Israel/Judah was a victim. The Shoah compels a rereading of the entire Tanakh in its light, and thus with questions about God's fidelity.

The production of comprehensive OT theologies will continue, but just as valuable will be theological interpretation directed to specific texts or text complexes, and engagement with contemporary social and theological issues. Along these lines, OT theology, as a species of biblical theology, may participate with historical and dogmatic theology and with ethics and practical theology, in a shared theological task. Regardless, OT theologians will need to offer rationale, including theological rationale, for 1) the particular aims and purposes of their inquiry, 2) the model or theory of the text with which they are working, and 3) the strategy or methods by which they will conduct their inquiries. Many options are currently available in each of these interrelated areas, and none can be simply assumed. Methodology is also theology. Old Testament theology will remain a diverse and contested field. May it foster, in all its diversity, love of God and love of neighbor; on these hang all the law and the prophets (Matt 22:40). *See* BIBLICAL THEOLOGY; THEOLOGICAL HERMENEUTICS.

Bibliography: Walter Brueggemann. *Theology of the Old Testament: Testimony, Dispute, Advocacy* (1997); Brevard Childs. *Old Testament Theology in a Canonical Context* (1984); Walther Eichrodt. *Theology of the Old Testament.* 2 vols. (1961–67); John Goldingay. *Old Testament Theology.* 3 vols. (2003–); M. H. Goshen-Gottstein. "Tanakh Theology." *Ancient Israelite Religion* (1987) 617–44; J. H. Hayes and F. C. Prussner. *Old Testament Theology: Its History and Development* (1985); Gisela Kittel. *Der Name über alle Namen 1: Biblische Theologie/AT* (1989); Rolf Knierim. *The Task of Old Testament Theology* (1995); Reinhard G. Kratz. "Noch einmal: Theologie im Alten Testament." *Vergegenwärtigung des Alten Testaments* (2002) 310–26; Jon D. Levenson. *The Hebrew Bible, the Old Testament, and Historical Criticism* (1993); B. C. Ollenburger, ed. *Old Testament Theology: Flowering and Future* (2004); H. D. Preuss. *Theology of the Old Testament.* 2 vols. (1995–96); Gerhard von Rad. *Old Testament Theology.* 2 vols. (1962–65); G. H. M. Ratheiser. *Mitzvoth Ethics and the Jewish Bible* (2007); Rolf Rendtorff. *The Canonical Hebrew Bible: A Theology of the Old Testament* (2006); Marvin A. Sweeney. *Reading the Hebrew Bible After the Shoah* (2008); Bruce Waltke. *An Old Testament Theology* (2007).

BEN C. OLLENBURGER

THEON. Alexandrian rhetorician and author of a collection of "preliminary exercises" (*progymnasmata*) designed for training schoolchildren in rhetorical composition. Theon's compilation, which is the earliest extant representative of the genre, is typically dated to the 1st cent. CE and is therefore important for studying rhetorical features and forms in early Christian narratives and letters.

JAMES A. METZGER

THEOPHANY IN THE NT [θεοφάνια theophania] The word *theophany* does not occur in the Bible. Rather, it describes a category of narrative in which God appears to human beings. *Theophany* is derived from the Greek words for God, theos (θεός), and for "appearance" or "manifestation," phaneros (φανερός).

Biblical theophanies must be understood in light of a near paradox: that God is totally "other" so that humans are incapable of grasping the majesty and greatness of God and, on the other hand, that God can and does make the divine self and the divine will known, at least in part, to human beings. Both understandings must be maintained. A god who can be grasped is no God; a god who cannot be known might as well be no God. Another way of stating the paradox is that God draws near while simultaneously maintaining a distance. In a theophany both sides of the paradox are displayed simultaneously. The divine presence is made known but the stories are often replete with imagery of disruptions to nature that emphasizes the otherness of God. In a number of cases in the Pentateuch God appears to humans in the person of an ANGEL, clearly a representation of the divine self (Gen 16:7, Exod 3:2, Num 22:22). Employing an angel as the means of appearance to humans may also serve to preserve the otherness of God in a way parallel to the natural phenomena of the Sinai theophanies. This tension between nearness and distance, the unknowable and the known, is present also in the NT. The NT resolves the tension, however, in a manner that is of primary theological significance.

Theophanies, then, are stories in which a self revelation by God takes place. Many such stories appear in the OT and form the background for similar yet significantly different stories in the NT. The most significant of the many OT theophanies for the NT are the various appearances at Sinai (Exod 19:1-20:8, 24:1-18, 33.) The Sinai theophany tradition is then echoed in the narrative of Elijah at Horeb (1 Kgs 19:9-18.) The substance of this entry is the literary and theological use the NT makes of those narratives (*see* SINAI, MOUNT; THEOPHANY IN THE OT). From these narratives the NT takes over a stock of imagery. These images include location on a mountain, the mention of glory, especially glory pictured as a bright light and a heavenly voice. Those who behold the manifestation may react with fear, though theophanies are not always associated with fear. The NT uses the imagery of these OT narratives in two ways, as expressions of continuity and of contrast. That is to say they describe appearances of God in such a way as to assure the reader that the God at work in Jesus Christ is the God of Israel's scriptures. The imagery is also used, however, to demonstrate a contrast between the presence of God in the old and new covenants.

In the Synoptic Gospels the glory of God will be made known at the end of time (so, for example, in Mark 13:26). But that glory is already anticipated within the life of Jesus at key points. So, in the familiar words of Luke's Christmas story, "the glory of the Lord shone around [the shepherds], and they were terrified" (Luke 2:9). Theophanic motifs, such as the voice of God, the opening of the heavens, and a voice from heaven, also appear in the accounts of the baptism of Jesus. Those accounts, in turn, anticipate the TRANSFIGURATION of Jesus (Mark 9:1-8 and parallels) in which theophanic imagery occurs even more markedly. Those stories simultaneously employ and undercut that imagery. As in the OT, the story takes place on a mountain, there is a cloud and, eventually, a dazzling brightness. Moses and Elijah appear, representing the Law and the Prophets; they are also the two figures who most clearly represent the theophanic tradition. They do not, however, merit reverence equal to Jesus. The mode of divine self-revelation of the theophanies is superseded by the drawing near of the kingdom in the person of Jesus. Therefore "This is my Son, the Beloved; listen to him!" (Mark 9:7)

There are also certain echoes of theophanies in Acts. Stephen's account of salvation history is framed by manifestations of the glory of God, first in the recollection of the theophany to Abraham in Genesis (Acts 7:22) and then Stephen's own vision of Christ's heavenly glory with God (Acts 7:55). The appearance of the risen Christ to Paul on the Damascus Road (Acts 9:1-7, Acts 22:6-11, 26:12-18) includes two elements of a theophany, light and a heavenly voice. One might even add that the Ascension (Acts 1:6-11) makes use of theophany imagery to signify the absence of Jesus!

Theophanies are also related to two other categories of NT narrative. First, they are related to apocalyptic literature of both testaments in which a vision of God or of heavenly things is granted. In an apocalypse, however, the seer is lifted up to the heavenly places. In a theophany, God descends to earth and makes the divine self known within the natural realm. In contrast to visions and dreams, moreover, those to whom God appears in a theophany are represented as being in a normal state of consciousness. Imagery reminiscent of theophanies can, however, be found in apocalyptic literature. Most notably, the vision of Christ in Rev 1:9-20 is replete with such imagery, a voice (v. 10, 15), unearthly brightness (v. 14), and the command, "Do not be afraid" (v. 17). Similar imagery is repeated at various points in Revelation. The vision of the one seated on the throne, especially in Rev 4, also contains theophanic imagery, clearly echoing the vision of Isa 6.

The second category involves narratives of the appearance of angels. Some such narratives do bear a resemblance to the angelic theophanies in the Pentateuch. In the Pentateuch, however, it is clear that the angels indicate the presence of the Lord. By the time of the NT angels are seen not as direct manifestations of God but as a class of heavenly beings who serve as messengers from God. This difference is significant enough that angelic appearances should not be automatically classified as theophanies. Nevertheless, some of these accounts do display theophanic motifs. Chief among these is the angel announcing the resurrection in Matt 28:2-8 accompanied by the earthquake (compare Elijah at Horeb,) with appearance "like lightning," clothing of shining white, and fearful witnesses (compare Luke 24:4-5 and perhaps Mark 16:5).

The question then arises whether the appearances of the resurrected Christ ought also to be classified as theophanies. Except for the appearance of the risen Jesus to Paul on the Damascus road (Acts 9:3-6), these narratives lack the imagery associated with the OT theophanies. It is startling to note that theophanic imagery in the Gospels is employed only with respect to the appearance of the angels, who merely anticipate the presence of the risen Christ. The stories of the appearances of Jesus are told very simply, as if to minimize anything extraordinary in the tale, except, of course, the presence of the resurrected one. The only extraordinary thing about the resurrection is the resurrection itself (see RESURRECTION, NT).

The experience of the presence of God in the theophanies of the OT is sometimes directly named but transcended in the NT. So Paul uses the imagery of the Sinai theophany to describe the new freedom of access granted to Christian believers through the Spirit: the veil that obscured the glory reflected in Moses is now being removed, and believers are transformed from one degree of glory to another (2 Cor 3:7-18). In Heb 12:18-24 Sinai imagery is also used by way of contrast. Christians do not come to a mountain that must not be touched, and they need not be terrified by fearful natural phenomena. They come rather to a heavenly assembly and to Jesus, the mediator of a new covenant.

What the transfiguration stories make clear narratively, several key passages assert theologically, making use of Sinai imagery. What and who God is, is made manifest in Jesus of Nazareth. Jesus is the "reflection of God's glory" (Heb 1:3), but one must not suppose that he makes known this glory in a manner similar to that of the angelic appearances the OT, as the remainder of that chapter takes pains to make clear. He is no angel but rather the "exact imprint of God's very being." Similarly, the prologue to John's Gospel echoes the Sinai stories when it asserts that "the Word became flesh and lived among us, and we have seen his glory .... No one has ever seen God. It is God the only Son, who is close to the Father's heart, who has made him known" (John 1:14, 18). The distant God, who is totally other, is made known not amidst frightening phenomena but in the Word made flesh. Indeed, one might venture to offer a simple definition of theophany in the NT: the self-manifestation of God is Jesus.

Bibliography: Richard B. Hays. *Echoes of Scripture in the Letters of Paul* (1989) 125–53; Morna D. Hooker "The Johannine Prologue and the Messianic Secret," *NTS* 21 (1974) 40–58; L. D. Hurst and N. T. Wright, eds. *The Glory of Christ in the NT: Studies in Christology In Memory of George Bradford Caird* (1987); Dorothy Lee. *Transfiguration* (2004); George W. Savran. *Encountering the Divine: Theophany in Biblical Narrative* (2005).

STEPHEN FARRIS

THEOPHANY IN THE OT thee-of'uh-nee. The term *theophany* refers to an appearance of a god or gods. Some theophanies in ancient Greece involved festive presentations of a deity or several deities as statues of the gods were brought forth in procession. Such a meaning does not, of course, apply to uses of the term to the biblical world. The scholarly use of the term refers to both public (and often highly significant) appearances of the deity to Israel and/or one of its leaders. The second use of the term, more imprecise and open to many nuances of meaning, applies to the experience of the deity by individuals and groups, as described in the various biblical literatures.

A. Characteristics of Biblical Theophanies
B. Theophanic Places
C. Sacred Times
D. Modes of God's Appearance
  1. Dream visions
  2. Word
  3. Wisdom
  4. Spirit
  5. Personal experiences
Bibliography

A. Characteristics of Biblical Theophanies

Genesis 2–3 is the fullest and most intimate of the OT theophanies. The Lord God shares the garden with the first human pair, walking with them in the cool of the evening and sharing their lives and thoughts, it would seem. Disobedience to the divine command breaks this harmony and results in the entrance of human beings into the world as it is now known: a world in which, according to biblical texts, human beings live with stated responsibilities and assurances (see Gen 1), but with God now withdrawn from the intimate life shared with mortals before their disobedience. The cosmic flood further distances this intimacy with God, but does not, of course, bring it to an end (Gen 7–9).

The story of God's call of Abram (Gen 12:1-3) offers the characteristic theophany: God addresses the human being and invites obedience to the divine word. No reference is made to God's actual appearance to the named individual until Gen 12:7, where God is said to have "appeared" to Abram and promised the land of Canaan to him and his descendants. The verb used is the passive form of the verb ra'ah (רָאָה, "to see"): God "was seen" or "appeared." Various forms of the verb ra'ah are used, including the direct assertion, "I saw the Lord" (Isa 6:1). But the use of references to the divine word continues to dominate. Even in the Isa 6 passage, the prophet sees God's garments and the accompanying angelic beings, not God in the divine fullness. In one critical text in Deut 4:12, the point is underscored: even at the sacred mountain of Sinai, Moses only heard God's voice; he saw no form of God.

These special theophanies found in early biblical texts tend to avoid any too specific portrayal of the deity, holding fast to the second commandment of the Decalogue: "You shall make no idol" (Exod 20:4). Not even words of the poets and sages go so far as to describe the appearance of the deity. God may be referred to as divine warrior (Exod 15; Judg 5; Pss 68; 104), but no more is given than the portrayal of God as the warrior who leads Israel in victorious battle. Epithets such as judge or king or mother writhing in birth-pangs or grieving widow offer important aspects of the deity's relationship to humankind and to Israel, but they give no image of deity.

B. Theophanic Places

Chief among the major places associated with a critical appearance of Israel's God Yahweh are mountains. Mountains join the earthly world with the underworld and they reach out toward God's heavenly abode, thus uniting the three parts of the universe as known by ANE peoples. In West Semitic cultures, the primeval mountain, such as Zaphon in the culture of ancient Ugarit, discloses the literary assertion that the high god has a dwelling on earth that is the counterpart of the deity's primordial dwelling in the heavens (see, e.g., Ps 48; see ZAPHON, MOUNT). It is hardly surprising, therefore, that Moses should have been addressed by the deity from a burning bush on Mount Sinai (Exod 3). There the future deliverer of Israel from slavery in Egypt receives the enigmatic name of God, YHWH (see TETRAGRAMMATON), and also receives his commission to bring the freed slaves to this very mountain. Later, at the same mountain, the God of Israel appears before the people in the form of lightning, storm, earthquake, and perhaps volcano as well (Exod 19). The deity also is experienced by Moses, Aaron, and the elders as a kind of sapphire pavement, above which rests the heavenly warrior in glorious resplendence (Exod 24:10). Later, Moses will see the backside of this deity as Moses takes refuge in a hiding place in the rocks of Sinai (Exod 33:18-23). And then he will hear the deity pronounce the divine name, followed by epithets that characterize this deity as "merciful and gracious, slow to anger, and abounding in steadfast love and faithfulness, keeping steadfast love for the thousandth generation" (Exod 34:6-7).

Another mountain of special import is Mount Gerizim, with its counterpart Mount Ebal to its north (Deut 27; Josh 8; 24), where a special ceremony of ritual cursings and blessings took place. Mount Gerizim continues to this day to be the holy mountain site for the Samaritan community. See EBAL, MOUNT; GERIZIM, MOUNT.

God is identified for all time with Mount Sinai, also called Horeb, and perhaps to be identified with Mount PARAN. Sinai is the place where the deity reveals the Ten Commandments and the other moral and ritual laws that guide the community of Israel for the future (Exod 20). No site, not even Mount ZION, the locale captured by David from the Jebusites (2 Sam 5) and destined to become the site of Solomon's Temple, surpasses Mount Sinai in importance. See SINAI, MOUNT.

Even so, Mount Zion will become of critical importance as a place of God's regular appearance among the people. This ancient Jebusite town and shrine is first hallowed by becoming the site of the oracular tent of wilderness times (Exod 33), when David moves the tent to the threshing floor of Araunah (2 Sam 24). Mount Zion had its counterpart in the wilderness tabernacle, which enabled the Israelites on their way to Canaan to carry along with them a replica of God's self-disclosure and abiding presence known to all at the sacred mountain. No continuous story of the tabernacle completes the narrative of the march from Sinai to Canaan and finally to the Temple of Solomon, but in all likelihood the Israelite community had no difficulty in seeing this continuity.

While the shrine of the city of David did not immediately become the central place of God's regular appearance (see 1 Kgs 12), because of David's artistic and other gifts, it continued to grow in importance, it seems, as the guarantor of God's presence and protection of Israel and its land and people. Not even the invasion of Babylonia in 597 BCE and the city's destruction in 586 BCE could eliminate the recognition that at Zion God made special and regular appearance. Prophetic threats against the city and its worship practices were sobering realities (Jer 7; 26; Amos 9; Mic 3) but they could not lead the people to give up on God's choice of Zion as the central meeting place of the deity with the people of God's choice. The return of some exiles from Babylonia and Persia only strengthened this conviction that at Zion, God drew close to Israel. Although only the high priest, once a year, was allowed to enter the holy of holies, where the divine presence was experienced at its most intense, all other Israelites shared in the divine presence at Zion.

C. Sacred Times

Although God may appear at any time, the biblical record singles out particular times during which God seems regularly to be most near. The great festivals of Passover (connected with the barley harvest), Weeks or Pentecost (connected with the wheat harvest), and Ingathering or Booths (connected with the grape and olive harvests) are experienced as festivals in which the deity shares the joys of the community. As mentioned above, the Day of Atonement allows the high priest to enter God's presence in the holy of holies once a year. And all occasions of festive joy and special prayers of petition and intercession are experienced as times of closeness and shared life with the deity. *See* FEASTS AND FASTS.

D. Modes of God's Appearance

1. Dream visions

The biblical literature records many experiences of God in dreams. One of the early DREAM visions is recorded in Gen 15. In two distinct literary sections, this chapter first records a conversation with Abram and God (vv. 1-6) and then proceeds to present an eerie scene in which the deity is discerned passing between the dismembered pieces of sacrificed animals, assuring Abram that what has happened to these dismembered animals will happen to the deity, should God not fulfill the promise made to Abram (7-19). Many similar dream-scenes are narrated in the biblical literature, the most famous of which, perhaps, is that of Samuel, who as a young boy sleeps by the ark of the covenant, has a dream, and is confident that the priest Eli is calling him, only finally to discover that in the dream, Yahweh is disclosing through him a bitter message for Eli and his sons (1 Sam 3). Such dream visions continue in the prophetic literature, in the Psalms, and in apocalyptic texts (see, for example, the dream visions in the book of Daniel).

More important, however, are other forms in which the community of Israel experienced the presence of the deity. The list is long and can only be summarized here.

2. Word

The Bible opens with the unselfconscious presentation of the deity calling the entire universe into existence by means of divine speech, by the word (Gen 1). Word becomes immensely important as a conveyor of the divine presence. The entire universe is both equipped for and attuned to the hearing of God's word. Psalm 19 supports such a view. The heavenly bodies may not be able to speak and render praise to God, but they are equipped to hear God's summons to share in the orderly movements of the universe as God has directed. *See* WORD, THE.

3. Wisdom

Similarly, God's Wisdom, viewed as a female partner with the deity, came more and more to be a mode of theophanic presence for the people, or at least for some circles of the people. It is easy to trace the move toward a near identification of the deity with Wisdom, a female partner and co-creator with the deity (*see* WISDOM IN THE OT). In Prov 8, Wisdom is present with God the creator, assisting in the work of creation, or at the very least, sharing in the remarkable acts of divine creation.

According to Sir 24, hundreds of years later, Wisdom is a full partner in the creation, mysteriously working with the deity in the very structure of the universe (*see* SOPHIA). Wisdom, it seems, is perceived as the reality behind the teachings of the wise, who offer both practical counsel for the society and who stand in special and intimate relation with God. Then, not much later, some circles in the Jewish community portray Wisdom as a "pure emanation" from the divine reality, bringing God's active presence and power into the very interior of the lives of those who pursue and welcome Wisdom's presence (see Wis 6–8).

4. Spirit

The term *spirit* (ruakh רוּחַ) also has a growing movement in Israel as a mode of experiencing God's presence. The second verse of the Bible includes an enigmatic reference to God's breath or spirit at the time of creation (Gen 1:2). One may suspect that there is an analogy to the place of Wisdom in the act of creation. Here, spirit is present, but its (her) role is not clearly defined. In psalmody, this role is clarified (see, e.g., Ps 33:6: "By the word of the LORD the heavens were made, and all their host by the breath of his mouth").

Since, however, God's presence in the form of breath or spirit in human beings carried the perceived danger of misunderstanding God's presence, power, and purpose; Israel's prophets are slow to attribute their revelations to the Spirit. See, for instance, the challenge of the leader of some 400 prophets to the prophet Micaiah: "Which way did the spirit of the LORD pass from me to speak to you?" (1 Kgs 22:24). That is to say, I am as much in possession of the Spirit as you are! Jeremiah 23 seems also to have spirit-possession in mind when the prophet challenges those who say, "I have dreamed, I have dreamed!" (Jer 23:25) to hear and speak God's Word faithfully.

This reluctance of use of inspiration by the Spirit is laid aside by prophets who speak of the consummating Day of the Lord, when God's purposes find realization (see Isa 11; 61; Joel 2–3, and many similar passages). In the literature of the community that preserved the Dead Sea Scrolls, this reluctance to speak of God's presence and appearance by the spirit or the Holy Spirit (a term rarely found in the Hebrew Scriptures) disappears. The NT community also has to develop safeguards against excessive claims for spirit-possession (see 1 Cor 12–14). In later Jewish experience, God's presence and dwelling with the community are expressed through the use of the term SHEKINAH.

5. Personal experiences

It is, of course, not possible to know just how individuals and groups actually experienced God's presence. Biblical literature does, however, contain a few clues. The extended presence of Moses on the sacred mountain resulted, we read, in a countenance suffused with divine glory. Moses must wear a mask to prevent harm from those not so exposed (Exod 34:33-35). The prophet Isaiah is said to have cried out in alarm when the vision unfolds: "Woe is me!" he cries, "My eyes have seen the King, the Lord of hosts!" (Isa 6:5). The author of the book of Job records an experience of Job's friend Eliphaz (Job 4) that leaves the sage gasping and full of awe. And Job himself is overwhelmed by God, who terrifies him with dreams and fantasies (Job 7). He is also utterly shattered by the closing appearance and challenge of the deity (Job 37–42).

The personal piety of psalmists, sages, and prophets shines forth in their writings, especially in the praises and prayers recorded in their names. These personal responses to theophanies are among the special treasures of biblical literature.

Bibliography: James Barr. *The Concept of Biblical Theology: An Old Testament Perspective* (1999); Walter Brueggemann. *Theology of the Old Testament: Testimony, Dispute, Advocacy* (1997); Richard J. Clifford. *The Cosmic Mountain in Canaan and the Old Testament* (1972); Alberto R. W. Green. *The Storm-God in the Ancient Near East* (2003); Esther J. Hamori. *When Gods Were Men: The Embodied God in Biblical and Near Eastern Literature* (2008); Kenneth Kuntz. *The Self-revelation of God* (1967); H. W. F. Saggs. *The Encounter with the Divine in Mesopotamia and Israel* (1978).

WALTER J. HARRELSON

THEOPHILUS thee-of'uh-luhs [Θεόφιλος Theophilos]. The individual to whom the author of Luke–Acts addresses and presumably dedicates both volumes of his work (Luke 1:3; Acts 1:1). Since the time of Origen (*Hom. Luc.* 1.6), it has been popular to interpret the name allegorically according to its etymology as "lover of God" or perhaps "beloved of God," and to understand Luke–Acts to be written for all who love God. But there is little basis for this. The name *Theophilus* is attested in both pagan and Jewish circles from the 3rd cent. BCE, and the honorific "most excellent" (kratistos κράτιστος) was a widely used form of address for individuals of rank from imperial freedman to governors (e.g., Acts 23:26 [NRSV, "his Excellency"]; 26:25). Theophilus was therefore almost certainly a ranking Roman official. That he was also a Christian convert is implied in Luke 1:4: "that you may know the truth concerning the things about which you have been instructed." He may also have provided financial underwriting for the two volumes. That Luke–Acts was composed for a Roman official, albeit a Christian official, is prima facie warrant for attempting to read it as apologetic history. Apart from his mention in Luke–Acts, this Theophilus is otherwise unknown.

PAUL A. HOLLOWAY

THEOPHRASTUS. Meaning "divine expression," *Theophrastus* was the nickname of the peripatetic philosopher Tyrtamus (ca. 371–287 BCE) because of his elegant discourse. Born in Lesbos, he studied under Aristotle, whom he succeeded as leader of the Lyceum. He was tried for impiety and acquitted by the Athenian jury. Among his disciples were Demetrius of Phalerum and Menander. Theophrastus made modifications to Aristotle's thought that proved important for later Hellenic, Islamic, and Christian theology and philosophy. He also composed a large compendium of the doctrines of previous philosophers—now lost—which probably formed the basis for a much later doxography that is our main source of information on pre-Socratic philosophers.

A great popularizer of science, Theophrastus wrote on botany, mineralogy, philosophy, and religion. Diogenes Laertes and other authors attribute over 200 works to him, but only a few, mostly botanical, works have survived intact. As a botanist, Theophrastus far surpassed his predecessors, and his *On the History of Plants* and *On the Causes of Plants* became very influential in the Middle Ages. He was best known, however, for an attack on marriage preserved by Jerome. Of his shorter surviving works, *On Stones* was probably used by Jacob of Edessa in his Hexaemeron.

MARINA GREATREX

THERAS thee'ruhs [Θερά Thera]. Alternate name for the river AHAVA (1 Esd 8:41, 61).

THESSALONIANS, FIRST LETTER TO THE thes'uh-loh'nee-uhn [Πρός Θεσσαλονικείς A Pros Thessalonikeis A]. First Thessalonians appears in the NT as the eighth of the thirteen letters attributed to Paul. Its canonical position prior to the other letter ostensibly addressed to the same congregation (*see* THESSALONIANS, SECOND LETTER TO THE) is due to its longer length. With a few exceptions (e.g., Wanamaker), most scholars agree that the first letter has chronological priority, and there is little doubt about its authenticity, despite challenges put forth in the late 19th cent. It is generally judged to be the earliest of Paul's surviving letters, likely written from Corinth in the early 50s CE, at least a decade after Paul began proclaiming Jesus. Paul's primary purpose in writing 1 Thessalonians is to encourage the Jesus-believers to persevere and make progress in their faith. In so doing, Paul addresses a number of issues about which the Thessalonians have expressed concern, such as sexual morality (4:1-8), the nature of brotherly love (4:9-12), the fate of believers who have died before Jesus' return (4:13-18), and signs preceding Jesus' return (5:1-11).

A. Division of the Book
B. Detailed Analysis
   1. Letter opening (*prescript*)—1:1
   2. Thanksgiving (*exordium*)—1:2–2:12
   3. Interpolation?—2:13-16
   4. Apostolic parousia (*narratio*)—2:17–3:13

A. Division of the Book

The overall integrity of 1 Thessalonians is debated, although not to the same degree as other authentic letters of Paul (e.g., *see* CORINTHIANS, SECOND LETTER TO THE). Some commentators (e.g., Richard) note the atypical presence of two thanksgiving sections in the letter (1:2-10; 2:13-16; and perhaps even a third at 3:9-10) and suggest that the canonical form of 1 Thessalonians is a composite of an earlier, friendly letter (2:13–4:2) inserted into a later letter that is more didactic in tone (1:1–2:12 and 4:3–5:28). More contentious is the hypothesis that there are interpolations in the letter. A few commentators suggest that a writer from the Lukan school added 5:1-11 to correct possible false inferences about Jesus' return from 4:13-18. This argument has not won general acceptance, however.

More widely debated is the nature of the second thanksgiving in 2:13-16, which many commentators suggest is a later interpolation into the letter. Pointing to features such as the misfit of 2:13-16 within the context of the argument, the fit of v. 12 and v. 17 together if vv. 13-16 are removed, and the unusual language, commentators argue that Paul could not have written this section. The strongly anti-Jewish tone seems to run counter to Paul's rhetoric in other letters, in which he rarely refers to those involved in the death of Jesus. Furthermore, the claim that "God's wrath has overtaken them at last" (2:16) contradicts Paul's more conciliatory tone in Rom 9–11 (esp. Rom 11:25-32). The phrase may even be a reference to the destruction of the Temple in Jerusalem in 70 CE, which suggests that this particular passage was added after Paul's death and reflects developing tensions between non-Christian Jews and Jesus-believers after the Jewish war (66–70 CE).

Commentators arguing for the authenticity of 2:13-16 note that the circumstances of opposition in 2:14 fit with the suggestion of suffering elsewhere in the letter (1:6; 2:2) and that Paul is not condemning all Jews but limiting his comments to Judeans, that is, those who live in the Roman province of Judea. They further note that typical Pauline expressions such as "imitators" (2:14) and the liturgical or creedal language of 2:15 point to Pauline authorship. While they agree that the text is awkwardly placed, they suggest that v. 17 fits no better after v. 12 than after v. 16. For those who do not accept 2:13-16 as authentic, most troubling is the lack of any manuscript evidence to support its omission.

The debate over the inclusion of 2:13-16 continues, but even were it to be settled there is still little consensus on the structure of 1 Thessalonians. The letter contains the primary divisions of ancient epistolary convention: opening greeting, thanksgiving, body, closing, and there is general agreement concerning the identification of the opening (1:1). Considerable debate continues, however, over how best to divide the remainder of the letter, a problem complicated by the presence of the second thanksgiving section at 2:13-16. Modern commentators address this problem through the lens of Greco-Roman rhetoric (*see* RHETORICAL CRITICISM, NT), but even this leads them to divergent conclusions. The primary differences lie in the extent of the *exordium* (thanksgiving) and the *probatio* (argumentation or "proof"). Most commentators agree that the *probatio* includes 4:1-5:11, although some see it ending earlier in chap. 5, while others extend it to v. 22 or even to the end of the chapter.

Without rehearsing the arguments for and against the various ways of assessing the rhetoric of the letter, summaries of which can be found in many commentaries, we offer here our own division of the letter by epistolary conventions and theme, noting the overlap with the rhetorical categories:

First Letter to the Thessalonians		
Letter Opening	1:1	*Prescript*
Thanksgiving	1:2–2:12	*Exordium*
Body		
(Interpolation?	2:13-16)	
Apostolic *Parousia*	2:17–3:13	*Narratio*
Responses to Issues Raised	4:1–5:11	*Probatio*
Proper Sexual Conduct	4:1-8	
Brotherly love	4:9-112	
Jesus' *Parousia*	4:13-18	
Times and Seasons	5:1-11	
Local Leadership Issues	5:12-22	*Peroratio*
Letter Closing	5:23-28	*Postscript*

The central concern of the letter is found in 2:19-20, where Paul writes to reassure the Thessalonian believers of the soundness of their faith and of his continued concern for them: "For what is our hope or joy or crown of boasting before our Lord Jesus at his coming? Is it not you? Yes, you are our glory and joy!" Specific problems that have been raised by the Thessalonians are addressed in the letter (sexual morality, 4:1-8; brotherly love, 4:9-12; those who have died, 4:13-18; times and seasons, 5:1-11) but are framed within Paul's reaffirmation that the Thessalonians are fulfilling the obligations of their commitment to the living and true God (1:3; 4:1*b*, 9; 5:1-2, 11).

It is not unusual to find that Paul's letters have a structure similar to one another, as Paul tended to follow the general form of letter writing in antiquity. Deviation from this general form is more noteworthy and can be seen several times in 1 Thessalonians. The first deviation is the inclusion of a second thanksgiving section, granting that 2:13-16 is part of the original letter (see above). The second deviation from the standard epistolary form is a benediction placed at the end of the main body of the letter (3:11-13), which is then followed by the word "finally" and an extended discussion of various themes. Both these deviations have parallels in the other letter ostensibly written by Paul to the Thessalonians.

B. Detailed Analysis

According to the book of Acts, Paul's stay at THESSALONICA was no more than three weeks long (Acts 17:2, 10). However, the Philippians sent Paul money at least twice while he was at Thessalonica, indicating a longer stay (Phil 4:16). After his departure he remained in contact by sending Timothy from Athens to Thessalonica (1 Thess 3:1-2). Thus, it is possible that Paul was writing from Achaia, perhaps Athens itself, although more likely is the assumption of most commentators that he was writing from Corinth, where he was working when Timothy returned from Macedonia (Acts 18:5). In writing 1 Thessalonians, Paul seems to be responding to Timothy's report, which included specific questions and concerns of the Thessalonians themselves.

Recent attempts at categorizing Paul's letters according to the species of rhetoric have led commentators to two positions on the type of rhetoric Paul employs in 1 Thessalonians. Some argue that the letter falls into the category of deliberative rhetoric, the aim of which is to persuade the audience of the expediency or disadvantage of particular courses of action. In this case, Paul is understood, particularly in 2:1–3:10, to be defending his ministry among the Thessalonians and particularly his rather hasty departure and lengthy absence. More commentators, however, argue that the letter is composed in the epideictic style of rhetoric, which functions to praise particular actions and urge the imitation of such. Paul's praise for the Thessalonians throughout the letter and his inclusion of rather mild injunctions suggest that he finds their faith to be strong overall and understands their relationship with him to be solid.

1. Letter opening (*prescript*)—1:1

The epistolary opening (1:1) includes greetings from three co-workers—Paul, Silvanus, and Timothy—and attributes the writing of the letter to all three, a fact reiterated in the frequent use of the first person plural pronoun "we" throughout the letter. Nevertheless, there are times when Paul uses the first person singular (2:18; 3:5; 5:27), suggesting that he bears primary responsibility for the writing of the letter. Interestingly, 1 and 2 Thessalonians are the only Pauline letters in which Paul does not in the opening give himself a title such as "apostle" or "servant," or attribute any such titles to his coworkers.

2. Thanksgiving (*exordium*)—1:2–2:12

Following the opening, Paul's thanksgiving begins the extended *exordium* (1:2–2:12). Paul exploits the function of the *exordium* to its fullest, both to introduce a number of topics of the letter and to establish his own *ethos*. Paul begins with high praise for the Thessalonians; apart from living out the triad of faith, hope, and love (1:3), they are chosen by God (1:4) and have become an example to believers elsewhere (1:7-8). The issues of their communal faith and social relations (1:3) and the coming of Christ (1:10) are raised but not elaborated upon until later in the letter (4:1-12 and 4:13–5:11, respectively).

The emphasis of the *exordium* is placed upon the *ethos* of Paul and his companions as it is expressed in their relationship with the Thessalonians. He opens by reminding the Thessalonians that they already know "what kind of persons we proved to be" in bringing the gospel to them in word and power, with the Holy Spirit, and with conviction (1:5). It is noteworthy that the Thessalonians are the only ones already engaged in imitation of Paul and his coworkers (1:6), in contrast to other communities that required varying degrees of exhortation to imitate Paul (1 Cor 4:16; 11:1; Phil 3:17; Eph 5:1; 2 Thess 3:7, 9; 1 Tim 1:16). Other Jesus-groups are said to be imitating the Thessalonians and commenting on Paul's intimate relationship with the Thessalonians (1:9).

Although Acts 17:1-8 suggest that the Thessalonian Christian community was composed of Jews and Gentiles, the reference in 1 Thess 1:9 to the believers turning "to God from idols" when Paul and his coworkers arrived among them indicates that the community was primarily, if not exclusively, comprised of Gentiles. It is not likely that Paul would have referred to Jews, or even God-fearers, as having been oriented towards idols, since he understood the God of Jesus to be the same as that of the Jews.

Paul's *ethos* becomes the primary focus of the second half of the *exordium*, which begins in 2:1. Paul's somewhat defensive tone has been interpreted as his self-justification in the face of criticism that he and his coworkers only preached for financial gain, evidenced by their hasty departure and failure to return to Thessalonica, although it is better understood as taking the form of a self-recommendation. Paul and his companions brought the gospel to the Thessalonians with full approval from God (2:4). Their motives were not impure (2:5-6), nor did they act improperly (2:9-10), for they acted as caregivers to the Thessalonians (2:7, 11-12), "So deeply do we care for you that we are determined to share with you not only the gospel of God but also our own selves, because you have become very dear to us" (2:8). Paul's self-praise is an example of ancient paraenetic. Such paraenetic material could be used in two ways: either as a means to alter behavior (as in deliberative rhetoric) or as a means to affirm present behavior (its function in epideictic rhetoric). It is functioning in the latter sense in 1 Thess 2:1-12.

In this section Paul also gives some indication of his activity among the Thessalonians, thus providing material from which one can discern his recruitment strategy in this particular city. Paul recalls the "labor and toil" that he and his companions exerted among them by working "night and day," the impact of which was a lessening of the "burden" they were to the Jesus-group—that is, Paul and his companions worked in order to support themselves financially during their time in Thessalonica (although while in Thessalonica they did also receive financial contributions from the Philippian believers on at least two occasions; Phil 4:16). Such labor would have given little time for proclaiming Jesus outside of work, so many commentators understand Paul's claim to indicate that he talked about Jesus among his fellow workers, among which the core of the Jesus-group was formed. This seems to find some affirmation in the later injunction that the Thessalonians "work with [their] hands" (4:11), a directive that makes most sense if aimed at those who earn a living through manual labor, most likely artisans of some sort. Traditionally, Paul has been assumed to be a tentmaker (skēnopoios [σκηνοποιός]; Acts 18:3), or perhaps a leather-worker, an occupation that would lend itself to an itinerant lifestyle and the procuring of occasional work in local factories. Epigraphic and literary evidence do point to extensive leatherwork in Thessalonica in the Roman period, leading to suggestions that it was among the leatherworkers that Paul plied his trade.

3. Interpolation?—2:13-16

Although we noted above the arguments for and against the authenticity of 1 Thess 2:13-16, we should recognize that if it is considered authentic then it continues the *exordium* but represents a contrast to the praise that has predominated to this point. In 2:13-16, blame is placed on those who would attempt to hinder the Thessalonians' faith, just as others have hindered Jesus-believers elsewhere. This "blame" is the antithesis of praise and is appropriately placed within an epideictic argument.

4. Apostolic parousia (*narratio*)—2:17–3:13

The *narratio* begins at 2:17 and extends to 3:13. Paul opens in 2:17-20 with the central concern of the letter. He has dwelt at length on his own *ethos* and his relationship to the Thessalonians in order to prepare them for the full impact of his claim: his honor is intimately tied to their faith (2:19-20). Paul emphasizes here his concern for his honor before God at the PAROUSIA, the "arrival," of Christ (2:19), although he has already made it clear that the Thessalonians' faith also brings him honor within the human realm (1:7-9). He again affirms that the Thessalonians are his hope and his joy (2:19), words of high praise for the Thessalonians, and an important component of community building.

Having reviewed his past history with the Thessalonians in the *narratio*, he next elaborates on their present and future history together. He has noted

his desire to be with them again (2:17-18), so he now explains why Timothy was sent in his stead and praises the Thessalonians on the basis of the report he has received from Timothy (3:1-6). Although he was fearful that they might have given up their faith (thus dishonoring Paul), he is pleased to hear that their faith is growing stronger (3:5-6). He is praying night and day for a future reunion (3:10), and he even includes in the letter an example of the type of prayer offered (3:11-13). This prayer serves to recapitulate Paul's central concern: that the Thessalonians continue in the way they are living the Christian life. Throughout both the *exordium* and the *narratio* Paul affirms the good relationship he has with the Thessalonians. Nowhere in the letter does Paul rebuke the Thessalonians as a whole; he encourages them to continue the path upon which they have embarked (4:1, 10). There is no need to correct their faith, although from Paul's perspective it is not fully developed and thus remains to be completed. Timothy was sent to strengthen them (3:2) and Paul hopes to come that he might "restore whatever is lacking" in their faith (3:10), even praying that their faith increases (3:11-12).

5. Responses to issues raised (*probatio*)— 4:1–5:11

Verse 4:1 opens the next rhetorical unit, the *probatio*, in which reasons are offered as proofs to support Paul's claim that the Thessalonians are his glory and joy. In so doing, he directly addresses issues of which he has heard, either through Timothy, through emissaries, or through a letter from the Thessalonians themselves, as indicated through his use of introductory formulae such as peri de (περὶ δὲ, "now concerning"; 4:9, 5:1), ou thelomen hymas agnoein ... peri (οὐ θέλομεν ὑμᾶς ἀγνοεῖν ... περὶ, "we do not want you to be ignorant concerning"; 4:13), and perhaps even in the way he argues in 4:1-2. Although Paul offers some exhortation, it is provided in a context of encouragement and clarification. In all the situations discussed, Paul takes the opportunity to affirm the Thessalonians in what they are already doing (4:1, 10; 5:11).

Verses 4:1-8 open with an exhortation: "Finally, brothers and sisters, we ask and urge you in the Lord Jesus that, as you learned from us how you ought to live and to please God (as, in fact, you are doing), you should do so more and more." The urging is tempered somewhat by Paul's note that they are already fulfilling this obligation (4:1); he simply wants them to increase their commitment to it. Although it is generally agreed that the situation under discussion in this unit involves sexual ethics, since Paul makes reference to porneia (πορνεία, "sexual immorality"; 4:3) and epithymia (ἐπιθυμία, "lust"; 4:5), the exact nature of the issue hinges on how one interprets Paul's injunction in 4:4. His employment of the enigmatic metaphor skeuos (σκεῦος)—a word that literally indicates a "vessel," but could suggest one's "body," one's "male member," or one's "wife"—along with his use of the verb ktaomai (κτάομαι), which can be rendered "acquire" or "control," has led to a variety of renderings such as "control your own body" (NRSV), "master your (male) genitalia" (Richard; Wanamaker; Ascough), or "acquire your own wife" (Malherbe; Witherington). Whichever interpretation is taken here, however, it is clear that Paul's concern is as much about community relations as sexual ethics, as Paul links the actions not only to purity and holiness (4:4, 7) but to how one's actions impacts one's fellow believer (4:6).

This leads Paul to pursue further an issue of community interaction that has been brought to his attention by the Thessalonians themselves: the nature of philadelphia (φιλαδελφία, "brotherly love"; 4:9-12). Paul again affirms their current practices, pointing out the redundancy of his own words in light of their having been "taught by God" (theodidaktos [θεοδίδακτος]; 4:9). Rather than answer directly on the nature of brotherly love, Paul provides guidance for their interactions with one another. In contrast to the zeal for honor that marks so much of Greco-Roman life, the Thessalonians are to have zeal to "live quietly," minding their own business (that is, not becoming entangled in the public affairs typical of the culture), and working with their hands in order to be self-reliant, a recommendation that points not only to the Thessalonians' status as artisans but also to a counter-cultural position of eschewing patronage for their group. Although Paul is concerned about how they conduct themselves towards outsiders, there is little here to suggest they were actively engaged in recruiting new members, although again this issue is debated by commentators.

In 4:13-17 Paul turns his attention to an issue that seems to have given rise to considerable consternation among the Thessalonians, although the exact nature of the issue raised by them remains, like so much in the letter, a point of discussion among commentators. Paul opens his comments by addressing the issue of grieving and loss of hope sparked by the death of some believers at Thessalonica. Referring to them metaphorically as having "fallen asleep" (vv. 12, 14; NRSV, "have died"), Paul affirms their status as part of the Christian community, going so far as to suggest that they will be the first in the order of the resurrection of the faithful at Jesus' return. Paul uses the opportunity to note that "we who are alive" (4:15), including himself with the Thessalonians, will also meet Jesus at his Parousia, tying this section to his affirmation in 2:19-20. The events surrounding the Parousia—a summons, a cry, a trumpet blast (4:16)—evoke an imperial procession, as if the emperor is entering the city. While Paul's apocalyptic vision is developed further in later letters, particularly 1 Cor 15, Paul's key concern here is not to lay out systematically the timeframe, but to instigate hope among the Thessalonians (4:18).

It is just such a time frame about which the Thessalonians have also expressed some concern (compare 5:1), and Paul again reassures rather than corrects or chastises them. Employing diverse and oddly conceived metaphors of nocturnal house burglary and imminent childbirth, Paul suggests that while Jesus' return is assured, its timing remains unknown. The upshot is that the Thessalonians, along with all believers, need to apply constant vigilance in their preparation for Jesus' Parousia (5:8). Nevertheless, despite the didactic tone of this section, the central aim is again to stoke the continuing of hope and encouragement among the Thessalonians (5:11).

All four units in the *probatio* (4:1-8, 9-12, 13-18; 5:1-11) not only provide the Thessalonians with guidance for their life of faith but also serve as opportunities for Paul to prove what he states earlier, that their commitment to the life of faith will be the source of his honor at Jesus' Parousia. In doing so, he is able to affirm their current practices and exhort them to continue.

6. Local leadership issues and closing (*peroratio* and *postscript*)—5:12-28

The final rhetorical unit, the *peroratio* (5:12-28) forms the summation of the letter. In a rhetorical composition the *peroratio* often include an exhortation, and Paul follows this convention in exhorting respect for the community leaders and mutual exhortation and encouragement among the members of the community.

The benediction (5:23-24) begins the formal closing of the letter and recalls Paul's central concern by invoking God to sanctify the Thessalonians completely, keeping them complete and without blame until the Parousia of Jesus. The postscript includes a number of elements typical not only of Pauline letter closings but also of letter closings more generally: a request for prayers, a general greeting, and wishes for good health or safety, although the latter takes the form of a blessing in 1 Thessalonians (5:28). Paul also insists that the letter be read aloud to all of the Thessalonian believers and encourages the exchange among them of a "holy kiss" (5:26). The kiss could be a form of family greeting, although the adjective hagios (ἅγιος, "holy") might indicate it is to take part in a liturgical context. It is perhaps indicative of the Thessalonians' fictive familial relations and suggestive that their meetings took place in households, which would coincide with Paul's employment of familial images throughout the letter: brothers and sisters (adelphoi [ἀδελφοί]; 2:1; 3:7; 4:1; 5:12), fathers (2:11), nursing mothers (2:7), and orphans (2:17).

C. Theological and Religious Significance

Study of 1 Thessalonians has generated a number of fruitful avenues of exploration in areas beyond those engendered by exegesis of particular passages such as those noted in the above section. For example, various commentators have emphasized different aspects of the background of the Thessalonian Jesus-group, none of which are mutually exclusive, and all of which serve to fill out the picture of the context in which the group formed and grew. Hendrix utilizes inscriptions from Thessalonica to show how the city held Romans in high esteem and honored them for their civic involvement and their benefaction, although it stopped short of attributing to them divine status. Malherbe finds in 1 Thessalonians some parallels to ancient philosophers and their ethical teachings and self-presentation, looking particularly at the Cynics and the orations of Dio Chrysostom for understanding Paul's arguments in 2:1-12. He also draws upon the philosophic moralists and their paraenetic to understand Paul's argumentation throughout the letter. Donfried gives particular attention to the polytheistic cults in the area, noting particularly the cults of Dionysos and of Cabirus as background for Paul's discussion of sexual morality (4:1-8) and the return of Jesus (4:13-18). Ascough looks to evidence from the inscriptions of the voluntary associations at Thessalonica and elsewhere in order to illuminate the nature of the community structure and the types of interactions one finds throughout the letter in Paul's rhetoric.

Other commentators have been drawn to the theological language of 1 Thessalonians, particularly since Paul uses what seem to be creedal formulae in 1:9-10; 4:14; and 5:9-10. These formulae are as much eschatological as they are christological in nature, with an emphasis on what Jesus has and will provide for those who believe. At his return, Jesus will deliver the Thessalonians from a coming wrath (1:10), while the Thessalonians can look to Jesus' death and, more important, resurrection as a prefiguring of their own resurrection (4:14) and have confidence that Jesus' death provides assurance of their deliverance from future wrath (5:9-10). Such formulae fit with the overall emphasis in the *probatio* on Jesus' return and the fate of the Thessalonians (4:13–5:11). Less clear is whether these formulae, which appear here in the earliest of Paul's writings, are in wider use among the Jesus-believing communities, or whether they are already in use in Thessalonica and are simply reported to Paul subsequent to his visit, or whether Paul is using them here for the first time. If they reflect wider use across diverse Jesus-groups, then we get a glimpse into how the first generation of Jesus-believers reflected upon the significance of Jesus' death and resurrection.

The dual use of the triadic formula "faith, hope, and love" in 1:3 and 5:8 is the first instance of what, for Paul, will function as his climactic line at the end of his poetic explication on the nature of love in 1 Cor 13:13. In 1 Thessalonians the triad is used with different images; in the first instance with work-related images (work, labor, endurance) and in the second case with images taken from military armor (breastplate, helmet). Faith and love are mentioned together in 3:6 with reference to the Thessalonians (compare 3:10), and in 4:13 Paul seeks to address an issue that has the potential to cause them to lose hope: the death of loved ones. Elsewhere in the letter the words or their cognates are used frequently, suggesting that the three elements of faith,

hope, and love reflect the social and ethical standards to which the Thessalonian Jesus-believers aspire.

Bibliography: Richard S. Ascough. *Paul's Macedonian Associations: The Social Context of 1 Thessalonians and Philippians* (2003); Karl P. Donfried. *Paul, Thessalonica, and Early Christianity* (2002); Karl P. Donfried and Johannes Beutler, eds. *The Thessalonians Debate: Methodological Discord or Methodological Synthesis?* (2000); Holland L. Hendrix. "Thessalonians Honor Romans." Unpublished Ph.D. dissertation (1984); John C. Hurd. *The Earlier Letters of Paul–and Other Studies* (1998); Robert Jewett. *The Thessalonian Correspondence: Pauline Rhetoric and Millenarian Piety* (1986); Abraham J. Malherbe. *The Letters to the Thessalonians.* AB 32B (2000); Earl J. Richard. *First and Second Thessalonians.* SP 11 (1995); Charles A. Wanamaker. *The Epistles to the Thessalonians: A Commentary on the Greek Text.* NIGTC (1990); Ben Witherington III. *1 and 2 Thessalonians: A Socio-Rhetorical Commentary* (2006).

RICHARD S. ASCOUGH

THESSALONIANS, SECOND LETTER TO THE

thes'uh-loh'nee-uhn [Πρός Θεσσαλονικείς B Pros Thessalonikeis B]. Second Thessalonians appears in the NT as the ninth of the thirteen Pauline letters. Unlike 1 Thessalonians, there is considerable debate over Paul's authorship of the letter. Nevertheless, it contains numerous Pauline themes and thus must have originated in "Pauline" circles. Its primary purpose is to bring hope to those who are experiencing persecution, to alleviate their anxiety and confusion over the Parousia (the return) of Jesus, and to correct behavior that is disrupting the community. Clear emphasis lies on God's faithfulness to those who believe in Jesus and the need for believers to remain faithful to God in the face of persecution, anxiety, and community disruption.

- A. Division of the Book
- B. Detailed Analysis
- C. Theological and Religious Significance
- Bibliography

A. Division of the Book

Second Thessalonians is shorter than many of the other letters attributed to Paul, which makes it closer in length to typical letters from antiquity. It contains the primary divisions of ancient epistolary conventions: opening greeting, thanksgiving, body, and closing (*see* LETTER). Commentators are in general agreement concerning the extent of the opening (1:1-2), thanksgiving (1:3-12), and closing (3:16-18). However, there is some debate over how best to divide the body of the letter. Some suggest that the body discusses theological and community issues from 2:1 through 3:15. Others suggest that the body proper is best analyzed as spanning only 2:1–3:5, while 3:6-15 is a separate exhortation

Division of Second Thessalonians			
Divisions of the Book	Rhetorical Categories	Epistolary Conventions	Greco-Roman Conventions
Letter Opening	*Prescript*	1:1-2	1:1-2
Thanksgiving	*Exordium*	1:3-12	1:3-12

Body
  Body Opening
  Jesus' Parousia
  God's Faithfulness
	
	Partitio
	Probatio
	Peroratio
		
		2:1-2
		2:3-12
		2:13–3:5
			
			2:1-2
			2:3-15
			2:16-18

Exhortation concerning the ataktoi	*Exhortatio*	3:6-15	3:1-15
Letter Closing	*Postscript*	3:16-18	3:16-18

that leads into the letter closing, much like the paraenesis in other letters of Paul. The formal analysis is further complicated by the presence of a second thanksgiving section, 2:13-15.

Some attempts at discerning the structure of 2 Thessalonians have employed Greco-Roman rhetorical conventions (*see* RHETORIC AND ORATORY). Again, there is much similarity in terms of the major divisions, with differences in the realm of fine-tuning rather than substantive disagreement. The primary differences among commentators lie in the analysis of 2:1–3:15, although here there is general agreement that 3:1-15, or at least 6-15, constitutes an exhortation. I will suggest a division of the letter by epistolary conventions and theme, noting the overlap with the rhetorical categories:

Not surprisingly, given the conventions of letter writing in antiquity, 2 Thessalonians has a very similar structure to 1 Thessalonians. Both letters also depart from ordinary patterns in containing an unusually placed second "thanksgiving" (1 Thess 2:13; 2 Thess 2:13) and a benediction at the end of a main portion of the body of the letter, followed by the word "finally" (1 Thess 3:11-13; 2 Thess 2:16-17). This similarity, along with other factors, has led some commentators to suggest that 2 Thessalonians copied the structure of 1 Thessalonians, while its content is written by and for a later generation of Christians.

B. Detailed Analysis

There is little debate over the structural unity of 2 Thessalonians as a single letter composition. There is, however, considerable debate over whether Paul himself composed the letter or not and, therefore, whether it was addressed to the Christian community at Thessalonica. It is difficult to decide when and where 2 Thessalonians was written until one resolves the problem of its authenticity. Unlike 1 Thessalonians, there are no details about Paul's location, present situation, or his future plans.

The opening verse of 2 Thessalonians attributes authorship to Paul and his companions, Silvanus and Timothy. Much of the letter bears the style and theology found in the letters that were unquestionably written by Paul. The letter claims to have borne the signature of Paul himself; "I, Paul, write this greeting with my own hand. This is the mark in every letter of mine; it is the way I write" (3:17). Such a self-reference also marks three other letters of Paul: 1 Cor 16:21; Gal 5:11; and Phlm 19, although curiously none of the three employ the signature as validation of authenticity. This claim in 2 Thessalonians might be meant to reassure the readers that this letter is genuine, unlike the false letter mentioned in 2 Thess 2:2.

One issue concerning authorship that is difficult to adjudicate is the language and style of 2 Thessalonians. Pauline terms such as agapētos ($\mathring{\alpha}\gamma\alpha\pi\eta\tau\acute{o}\varsigma$, "love"), hamartia ($\mathring{\alpha}\mu\alpha\rho\tau\acute{\iota}\alpha$, "sin"), and apostolos ($\mathring{\alpha}\pi\acute{o}\sigma\tau o\lambda o\varsigma$, "apostle"), among others, are missing from 2 Thessalonians, and the long sentence structure of this letter contrasts with the shorter sentence structure found elsewhere in Paul. Nevertheless, more than three-quarters of the vocabulary in 2 Thessalonians is found in the genuine Pauline letters, and differences in vocabulary can be explained by the limited focus of the letter or the use of an amanuensis (a secretary). This is also the case for the observation that 2 Thessalonians lacks the "warmth" or personal tone of Paul's other letters. Ultimately, brevity does not allow for a large enough data set with which to undertake an adequate linguistic analysis of 2 Thessalonians, and thus the question of authorship cannot be solved on the basis of language and style alone.

Another consideration bearing on the authenticity of 2 Thessalonians concerns literary dependency on 1 Thessalonians. There are many places where 2 Thessalonians appears to copy its wording and structure from 1 Thessalonians, particularly in the opening and closing. Many commentators present the parallels in this fashion:

On the one hand, this is precisely where one might expect to find duplication of an earlier authentic Pauline letter. On the other hand, such similarity can also be explained by assuming that the same author was writing to the same community within a short space of time.

Structure of the Letters to the Thessalonians		
Section	2 Thess	1 Thess
A. Opening	1:1-12	1:1-10
1. Prescript	1:1-2	1:1
2. Thanksgiving	1:3-12	1:2-10
B. Closing	3:1-18	4:1–5:28
1. Paraenesis	3:1-15	4:1–5:22
2. Peace Wish	3:16	5:23-24
3. Greetings	3:17	5:26
4. Benediction	3:18	5:28

Thus, once again the evidence in and of itself is inconclusive, particularly since overlap in content and vocabulary in these sections is very general. For example, in 1 Thessalonians the greeting reads "Grace to you and peace" (1:1) while in 2 Thessalonians it reads "Grace to you and peace from God our Father and the Lord Jesus Christ" (1:2). One finds opening greetings similar to 2 Thessalonians in Rom 1:7; 1 Cor 1:3; 2 Cor 1:2; Gal 1:3-5; Phil 1:2; and Phlm 1:3, suggesting that such openings are typical of Paul himself.

The content of the closing of each of the Thessalonian letters is distinctive enough to obviate the need to posit literary dependency. The admonition against the idle is quite general in 1 Thess 5:14 and part of the wider sweep of the paraenetic section, whereas in 2 Thessalonians the admonition is more specific and detailed, likely directed to a particular situation (hence my placing of it as a separate exhortation). While both letters include a request for prayer, in 1 Thess 5:25 it is very general ("Beloved, pray for us") while in 2 Thess 3:1 not only does it occur earlier in the letter but it also includes very specific requests. The elements of each closing are different—1 Thessalonians contains an admonition to read the letter to the entire assembly (5:27) and the exchange of a holy kiss among them (5:26), while 2 Thessalonians carries a personal greeting from Paul's own hand (3:17).

All in all, one can see that the overall structural similarities of the openings and closings pale in significance when one looks at the contents in detail. This is not the case, however, when one looks at the structure of the body of each letter. Here one finds two striking similarities that are unusual not only for ancient letter structure in general but also for Paul's letters. Within the body section of both 1 and 2 Thessalonians there occurs a second thanksgiving section (2:13 in each letter) along with a benediction at the end of the body (3:11-13 and 2:16, respectively). Although different in content, their structural singularity raises questions about the literary dependence of one letter upon the other. In the case of the second thanksgiving section, this is compounded by the nature of the thanksgiving itself. The clearly anti-Jewish nature of 1 Thess 2:13-16 contrasts starkly with Rom 9–11, suggesting that the second thanksgiving of

1 Thessalonians is a later non-Pauline interpolation. If this is so, the inclusion of a second thanksgiving in 2 Thessalonians might suggest its dependence upon this later, edited version of 1 Thessalonians. One must keep in mind, however, that were 2 Thessalonians to be demonstrably authentic, then one could argue that the presence of a second thanksgiving (one that is Pauline in tone) provided the opportunity for a later scribe to add a second thanksgiving to 1 Thessalonians, albeit one that reflected his own predispositions and contexts rather than Paul's.

The most significant issue concerning the authenticity of 2 Thessalonians is the reconciliation of its eschatological schema with that of 1 Thessalonians. There are places where the overlap is significant and other places where the two letters seem to imagine differing scenarios with respect to the events around the return of Jesus.

The letters evidence disagreement as to whether the end will come suddenly (1 Thessalonians) or will be preceded by a series of apocalyptic events (2 Thessalonians). In 2 Thessalonians the writer claims that "the coming of our Lord Jesus Christ and our being gathered together to him ... will not come unless the rebellion comes first and the lawless one is revealed, the one destined for destruction" (2:1-3). This arrival of the lawless one will be accompanied by "power, signs, lying wonders" (2:9). All of this is aimed to assure the readers that they have not missed out on the return of Jesus—other events must precede Jesus' return and thus they will know when the time is near. In contrast, in 1 Thessalonians there will be no forewarning of the coming of Christ (1 Thess 4:13-17). The writer claims that "the day of the Lord will come like a thief in the night" and the destruction will be sudden (5:2-3). In 2 Thessalonians the writer presents an apocalyptic timetable that seems to postpone the end, while in 1 Thessalonians Paul indicates that he and some of his readers will be alive at the Parousia of Jesus (4:17).

There is a fair amount of similarity between the eschatological schema in 1 Thessalonians and that found in 1 Cor 15:51-58 (probably written a few years later than 1 Thessalonians) with perhaps some elaboration around the nature of the body in the latter ("we will all be changed," 1 Cor 15:51). Nevertheless, there are differences between 1 Thessalonians and 1 Corinthians. In 1 Corinthians there is no wrath, no archangel, no descent, and no meeting in the air, while 1 Thessalonians does not include the reference to the reign of Christ on earth until death is defeated (1 Cor 15:20-28). These differences can be explained as developments in Paul's thinking between the writing of 1 Thessalonians and the writing of 1 Corinthians, since the details are not mutually exclusive. This is not the case with the details found in comparing the eschatological schema of 1 Corinthians and 2 Thessalonians, where the order of resurrection seems to be different. In 1 Corinthians Christ returns and those who are "in Christ" are "made alive" (15:22-23) at which point the end comes when

Letters Compared	
2 Thessalonians	1 Thessalonians
Day of the Lord (2:2)	Day of the Lord (5:2)
The Parousia of the Lord (2:1, 8); the revelation of Jesus (1:7)	The Parousia of the Lord (2:19; 4:15)
A period of apostasy (2:3a) and a time of delusion (2:11)	The time will be marked as one of peace and safety (5:3)
The time is preceded by the revelation of "the lawless one," the "son of destruction," who claims himself a god, and demonstrates power, signs, and wonders (2:3b-4, 9-10a)	The events come unexpectedly (5:3a)—like a "thief in the night" (5:2, 4); like birth pains to a pregnant woman (5:3b)
The destruction of the "lawless one" (2:8)	
Jesus comes from heaven (1:7)	Jesus comes out of the heavens (1:10)
Jesus is accompanied by powerful angels and flaming fire (1:7)	Jesus is accompanied by the cry of an archangel, along with a summons and a trumpet blast (4:16)
	Believers who have died are to rise and believers still living are to be snatched up (4:16b-17a)
Believers gather together with Jesus (2:1)	Believers are to meet Jesus in the air, in the clouds (4:17)
	Believers are always to be with Jesus (4:17)
Vengeance is meted out upon those not knowing God (1:8)	Believers are delivered from the coming wrath (1:10; 5:9); destruction comes upon those not raised (5:3)

Christ will reign and destroy his enemies, as well as death. In 2 Thessalonians the "lawless one" is destroyed at the very time of Christ's coming (2:8).

How one understands the eschatology of 1 and 2 Thessalonians becomes decisive in determining the authenticity of 2 Thessalonians. If the letter is considered a post-Pauline, pseudonymous letter (deutero-Pauline) on the basis of the tensions in the eschatological schema, then it could be addressing a new situation in a new locality (in Macedonia or elsewhere) and there is no need to reconcile it with the schema in 1 Thessalonians. If, however, 2 Thessalonians is understood to be a genuine letter of Paul, it does seem to address a different situation than that of 1 Thessalonians, which needs to be explained. One solution is that the letters were both written by Paul but are separated by some years that would allow for development and change in Paul's thought. Nevertheless, the structural and linguistic similarities between 1 and 2 Thessalonians suggest that if they are written by Paul they were composed in temporal proximity to one another (so Jewett; Malherbe; Witherington).

A solution for Pauline authorship for 2 Thessalonians that addresses the eschatological tensions while maintaining temporal proximity is the inversion of the order of the letters. Given that 2 Thessalonians appears second in canonical order only because it is shorter than 1 Thessalonians, it is possible to posit that it was written before 1 Thessalonians (so Wanamaker; Hurd). Proponents of this position argue that the "present" trouble in 2 Thessalonians is presented as "past" in 1 Thessalonians. Paul's direct responses to questions in 1 Thess 4:9, 13; and 5:1, as indicated by his use of disclosure formulae, indicates that the Thessalonians themselves have communicated with Paul and raised questions, perhaps even based on what Paul has written in 2 Thessalonians. The autograph greeting (2 Thess 3:17-18) makes most sense in a first letter in order to authenticate epistolary exchange as a means of communication. More importantly, the Thessalonians do not need to be told of times and seasons surrounding the return of Jesus (1 Thess 5:1) because 2 Thess 2:3-15 is already known—that is, they have already been told what the signs will be.

Nevertheless, a number of scholars are persuaded by the distinct differences between the timetable of the events surrounding the Parousia of Jesus and the timetable surrounding those events. They therefore cautiously maintain that 2 Thessalonians is not a genuine letter of Paul (so Hughes; Donfried; Menken; Richard).

It is a deutero-Pauline letter written to address the eschatological enthusiasm of some Jesus-believers and others' concern that they have, in fact, missed the Parousia of Christ. Whatever position is maintained, it is important to recognize that the ambiguity and controversy surrounding 2 Thessalonians is such that when discussing Paul's theology or chronology, one must not base arguments primarily upon 2 Thessalonians itself. A much better approach is to draw one's primary arguments from letters considered to be genuinely Pauline (Romans, 1 and 2 Corinthians, Galatians, Philippians, 1 Thessalonians, and Philemon) and then to supplement such arguments with reference to 2 Thessalonians, if indeed it is possible. Doing so can also help one determine whether or not one will deem 2 Thessalonians to be an authentic letter of Paul.

C. Theological and Religious Significance

Paul's second letter to the Thessalonians employs strategies and argumentation that one finds within the broader realm of Greco-Roman rhetoric; the species of rhetoric into which the letter most obviously falls is that of deliberative rhetoric. As such, its primary aim is to persuade the audience of the expediency or disadvantage of particular courses of action. There are three areas of concern for Paul for which he advocates a particular course of action: standing firm in the face of ongoing persecutions, the reduction of eschatological anxiety, and the cessation of disruptive behavior within the community. All three of these concerns are grounded in his overall theological affirmation that as God is faithful to those who believe (3:3-5) so too must followers of Jesus remain steadfast and faithful to God (2:15).

Within the opening thanksgiving Paul notes that the assembly of Thessalonian believers has undergone persecutions and sufferings, which they patiently endure. Not only that, Paul and his companions are able to boast about them to other assemblies because the Thessalonians hold steadfast and maintain their faith (1:4). The nature of these sufferings is not made clear, but it does seem to involve both physical and psychological anguish, as indicated by the use of "persecution" (diōgmos διωγμός) and "distress" (thlipsis [θλῖψις]; 1:4). That it is ongoing rather than a one-time event is suggested by Paul's use of the present active form of "suffering" (paschō [πάσχω]; 1:5). While Paul holds out the hope of relief from such afflictions, it comes only with the "revelation" of Jesus in the final, apocalyptic events, and will carry with it vengeance upon the perpetrators (1:6-10). Paul's claim that the Thessalonians are cause for his own honor ("boasting"; 1:4) would encourage them to remain steadfast in the face of their afflictions. He returns to this theme again in the second thanksgiving section when he exhorts the Thessalonians to stand firm in their convictions (2:15) promising them God's comfort and strength (2:17) as well as protection from "the evil one" (3:3). As God is faithful to the

Thessalonians, so must they remain faithful to God even while undergoing persecution.

Another major concern for Paul is the anxiety and confusion among the Thessalonian believers concerning the Parousia of Jesus (2:1-12). From Paul's opening sentence it seems likely that he has received reports that the Thessalonians are distressed that Jesus' return has already taken place and, in effect, left them out of all the benefits that his return was expected to bring. Referencing sources of information such as "spirit," "word," or a "letter" falsely written in his name (2:2), Paul indicates that contradiction and misinformation seems to be extensive at Thessalonica. Paul attempts clarification by setting out a very general timetable of events that will precede the actual Parousia of Jesus: a period of apostasy and delusion in which people reject God (2:3a, 10-12), and the appearance and subsequent judgment of a "man of lawlessness" (2:3b-8), whose presence will be known through the manifestation of false signs and wonders (2:9). This "lawless one," Paul suggests, is currently being restrained and will only be revealed according to God's timing (2:6).

Paul's interest in presenting this information is to strengthen the Thessalonians' faithfulness not only during their physical persecutions but also during their periods of doubt and worry. Paul initiates the conversation about the Parousia of Jesus with no preamble, suggesting that the Thessalonians are already familiar with the basic concept of Jesus' return, either through Paul's preaching or through receiving 1 Thessalonians. The identity of the "man of lawlessness" (ho anthrōpos tēs anomias ὁ ἄνθρωπος τῆς ἀνομίας) is not clear. There has been a tendency in Christian tradition to conflate this figure with the antichrist figure mentioned in the Johannine epistles (1 John 2:18, 22; 4:3; 2 John 1:7), and sometimes also with the equally enigmatic figure of the beast mentioned in Revelation, associated with the number 666 (Rev 13:11-18). Given the paucity of context in 2 Thess 2:1-12, however, it is not clear whether such connections can be made. It is likely that the Thessalonians have some familiarity with this figure through earlier teachings or, just as likely, that Paul is content to leave the reference rather vague and generic—a human being who does not follow the rule of law—clearly an agent of Satan (2:9). The identity of "the restrainer" (to katechon [τὸ κατέχον]; 2:6) is equally enigmatic and scholars still have not contextualized this figure, although again it is presented as a figure with whom the Thessalonians are expected to be familiar. The overall thrust of the passage again affirms the faithfulness of God, who is in control of all aspects of the eschatological events. The Thessalonians can remain confident that God will be faithful and remember them at the Parousia of Jesus.

The third area of concern for Paul in 2 Thessalonians involves some members of the Thessalonian assembly who are not contributing to the overall good. Paul addresses first the faithful participants in the life of the assembly, commanding them to shun those who are acting against the community interests (3:6-10, 14-15). The nature of the offense is expressed by Paul as ataktōs peripatountos (ἀτάκτως περιπατοῦντος), which can be translated literally as "walking about disorderly" but might also indicate disruptive behavior, laziness, or idleness. In support of the latter understanding, one can note that Paul points to his own behavior among the Thessalonians, working night and day and reluctant to burden anyone by eating their food (3:8). The injunction that "anyone unwilling to work should not eat" (3:10) further suggests that laziness might be the root problem. In favor of understanding the text as referencing disorderly or disruptive behavior, however, is Paul's indication that in lieu of working these persons are acting as "busybodies" (3:11). Some commentators suggest that such people are involved in the false rumors surrounding the Parousia of Jesus, and may even have given up working in anticipation of Jesus' return (so Jewett). In addressing the problem such persons have created, Paul again emphasizes the reciprocal nature of faithfulness between God and the Thessalonians, although here the reciprocity extends to relations among the Thessalonians themselves—they are to behave toward one another in ways that are mutually supportive. Overall, by remaining faithful in persecution, reducing their eschatological anxiety, and minimizing their community disruption, the Thessalonians will experience God's peace "at all times in all ways" (3:16). See THESSALONIANS, FIRST LETTER TO THE; THESSALONICA.

Bibliography: Karl Paul Donfried. *Paul, Thessalonica, and Early Christianity* (2002); Karl Paul Donfried and I. Howard Marshall. *The Theology of the Shorter Pauline Epistles* (1993); Frank W. Hughes. *Early Christian Rhetoric and 2 Thessalonians* (1989); John C. Hurd. *The Earlier Letters of Paul—and Other Studies* (1998); Robert Jewett. *The Thessalonian Correspondence: Pauline Rhetoric and Millenarian Piety* (1986); Abraham J. Malherbe. *The Letters to the Thessalonians.* AB 32B (2000); Maarten J. J. Menken. *2 Thessalonians.* New Testament Readings (1994); Earl J. Richard. *First and Second Thessalonians.* SP 11 (1995); Charles A. Wanamaker. *The Epistles to the Thessalonians: A Commentary on the Greek Text.* NIGTC (1990); Ben Witherington III. *1 and 2 Thessalonians: A Socio-Rhetorical Commentary* (2006).

RICHARD S. ASCOUGH

THESSALONICA thes'uh-luh-nΐ'kuh [Θεσσαλονική Thessalonikē]. Thessalonica, modern Thessaloniki or Salonika, was founded by Cassander (one of Alexander the Great's generals) in 315 BCE. According to Strabo, the town had been called Therma, but Cassander named it after his wife, Alexander's sister (*Geogr.* 7. Frg. 24).

From its beginning (ca. 500 BCE), Thessalonica was strategically located on important trade routes, espe-

cially on the Roman *Via Egnatia*, where it was the most important port. Thessalonica became the capital of the second district of Macedonia and the seat of the Roman governor in 167 BCE. In 146 it became the capital of the reorganized province of Macedonia. Cicero described abuses by provincial governors during his exile there (58 BCE; *Att.* 3.15).

The mention of a synagogue in Acts 17:1 suggests that neither of the previous cities that Paul passed through—Philippi to Amphipolis, Amphipolis to Apollonia, Apollonia to Thessalonica—had a Jewish population. The distance between each of the cities is 30–35 mi. It would have taken approximately two days to travel from one to the next by foot. There is no indication that Paul and his companions stopped long enough to preach either at Amphipolis or Apollonia.

Once Paul reached Thessalonica he engaged in a brief ministry before being driven out by Jewish opposition (Acts 17:1-13; compare 1 Thess 1:8-9). The response to his message was the establishment of a strong church. After Timothy's report that the new congregation remained strong despite persecution, Paul wrote 1 Thessalonians (*see* THESSALONIANS, FIRST LETTER TO THE). The city is mentioned elsewhere in the NT in Acts 20:4; 27:2; Phil 4:16; and 2 Tim 4:10.

The archaeological museum in Thessalonica contains the burial remains of Philip II of Macedon. An archaic temple has been found on the west side of the city. Much of the old Roman forum (*agora*) dates from the 2nd cent., but the many shops and the main street uncovered by archaeologists date from the 1st cent. CE. Not far to the east of the forum is the Arch of Galerius, an early 4th-cent. CE gateway to the city depicting the tetrarchs Maximianus, Constantius, Diocletian, and Galerius and their Roman victories in the east. Portions of the Hellenistic and Roman walls remain, especially on the north side of the city.

Galerius executed the patron saint of the city, St. Demetrius, in 303 CE. A church was later built on the traditional site of his martyrdom beneath the present basilica of Hagios Demetrios. In 325 CE, a bishop of this city attended the Council of Nicea. In the 5th and 6th cent., a number of Galerian monuments were converted into churches and many new church buildings were constructed. The rotunda mausoleum built to contain the body of Galerius was itself converted into a church by the end of the 4th cent.

Bibliography: Karl P. Donfried. "The Cults of Thessalonica and the Thessalonians." *NTS* 31 (1985) 336–56.

LEE MARTIN MCDONALD

THETA [θ th, Θ Th]. The eighth letter of the Greek alphabet, based on the Phoenician *tet, an emphatic t, which was not needed in Greek, and so the sign was used to represent the aspirated t [th]. See ALPHABET.

THEUDAS thoo′duhs [Θευδᾶς Theudas]. A Judean who led an unsuccessful rebellion against the Romans, possibly ca. 6 CE (Acts 5:36), but more probably ca. 44 CE (Josephus, *Ant.* 20.97). Claiming to be a prophet, Theudas attracted a crowd to the Jordan, which he intended to separate as Elijah and Elisha (2 Kgs 2) and Joshua (Josh 3) had done. Perceiving him to be a threat, like other popular prophets and leaders (including Jesus), the Romans killed him and many of his followers. Theudas made a lasting impression, since both Luke and Josephus were familiar with him over fifty years later.

ADAM L. PORTER

THICKETS OF THE JORDAN. *See* JORDAN, THICKETS OF THE.

THIEF. *See* CRIMES AND PUNISHMENT, OT AND NT; LAND.

THIGH [יָרֵךְ yarekh; μηρός mēros]. The thigh is mention in the Bible in three contexts. First, it features in key patriarchal stories. Second, it is simply a body part referenced descriptively. And in the cult, it is offered to God and then shared by the priests.

Abraham and Jacob ask those making promises to place their hands under the thigh of the one asking a commitment and swear to their words. Scholars presume that the thigh is a euphemism for the male reproductive organs, suggesting that placing the hand there is a sign of trust. Abraham has his servant swear that he will not take Isaac off the land to find a wife, even should the servant fail to accomplish this task when he visits Abraham's kin (Gen 24:2). Jacob has Joseph promise that he will not bury his father in Egypt but in the ancestral land (Gen 47:29). And a thigh muscle is a place of injury sustained by Jacob while struggling with an angel on his way back to meet his brother, Esau, after a long estrangement. The narrator reports that, from that time on, Israelites do not eat that particular portion of an animal's haunch (Gen 32:32).

Some narratives simply name the thigh to explain a detail: the place where a warrior's sword rests (Judg 3:16; Ps 45:3 [Heb. 45:4]; Song 3:8); a place where one strikes oneself to express strong negative feeling (Jer 31:19; Ezek 21:12); a portion of an animal to be eaten (1 Sam 9:24; Ezek 24:4); and the place where God's Word has engraved the name "King of kings and Lord of lords" (Rev 19:16).

Cultic passages describe the ordination ceremony of Aaron and sons, where the thigh is their portion of the sacrifice (Exod 29:22; Lev 7:32-34; 8:25-26; 9:21; 10:14-15), or general circumstances where the thigh is their portion or serves as analogy for portions due them (Num 6:20; 18:18).

BARBARA GREEN, O.P.

THINK [חָשַׁב khashav; δοκέω dokeō, λογίζομαι logizomai, νομίζω nomizō]. The English word *think* renders various words and phrases in both Hebrew and Greek. For example, having a thought in one's mind is often depicted in the OT as internal speech: "Fools say in their hearts (i.e., think), 'There is no God'" (Ps 14:1). Thinking can be also be represented visually. The NRSV uses "think" to translate be῾ene (בְּעֵינֵי, lit., "in the eyes of"), as in "Fools think their own way is right" (Prov 12:15; lit., "the way of a fool is right in his eyes). Similarly, the word most commonly translated "think" in the NT is dokeō, which can also be translated "to seem" (Acts 15:28).

Derivatives of the Hebrew khashav can imply a more constructive form of thinking. Its meanings range from a simple impression (1 Sam 1:13, where Eli "thought" that Hannah was drunk) to laborious mental grappling (Ps 73:16, where the psalmist "thought how to understand" the prosperity of the wicked). Many uses of khashav involve planning, e.g., Ezek 38:10.

Sometimes khashav has arithmetic overtones. It can refer, e.g., to counting the years since a sale of land (Lev 25:27). Qoheleth describes his intellectual search as an exercise in calculation: "adding one thing to another to find the sum (kheshbon חֶשְׁבּוֹן)" (Eccl 7:27). **Khashav** can also convey choosing to regard someone or something in a particular way, e.g., "accounted as sheep for the slaughter" (Ps 44:22 [Heb. 44:23]) or "regarded as a strange thing" (Hos 8:12). The best-known use of this sense occurs where Abraham "believed the LORD; and the LORD reckoned it to him as righteousness" (Gen 15:6). When Paul quotes Gen 15:6 in Romans and Galatians, he uses the verb **logizomai** (Rom 4:3-5; Gal 3:6), which the LXX generally employs to translate **khashav**.

WILL SOLL

THIRD DAY [הַיּוֹם הַשְּׁלִישִׁי hayyom hashelishi; ἡ τρίτη ἡμέρα hē tritē hēmera]. In OT narrative, a stereotypical phrase marking the passage of a few days (e.g., Gen 22:4; 31:22; 34:25; Judg 20:30; 1 Kgs 3:18). In ritual contexts, it is more specific: meat from sacrifices must be consumed before the third day (Lev 7:17-18; 19:6-7), and certain purification rites must occur on the third day (Num 19:12, 19).

According to early Christian tradition, Jesus "was raised on the third day in accordance with the scriptures" (1 Cor 15:4; compare Matt 16:21; 17:23; 20:19; 27:64; Luke 9:22; 18:33; 24:7, 21, 46; Acts 10:40). According to the Markan passion predictions, Jesus will be raised "after three days" (8:31; 9:31; 10:34; compare Matt 27:63; note John 2:19-22: "Destroy this temple [i.e., Jesus' body], and in three days I will raise it up"). In the LXX and Josephus, "after three days" and "on the third day" are used synonymously. The early church may have preferred "on the third day" because it echoes Hos 6:2. *See* RESURRECTION, NT; SACRIFICES AND OFFERINGS.

JUDITH ANNE JONES

THIRST, THIRSTY [צָמֵא tsama², צָמֵא tsame²; διψάω dipsao, δίψος dipsos]. Biblical references to thirst appertain both to the physical need for WATER to sustain life and to the metaphorical spiritual thirst for God. Finding a sufficient amount of water was a perpetual problem for humans and animals because the climate of Palestine is regularly hot and dry, particularly away from the hill country and coast, and rainfall is unpredictable. Thirst could easily become life-threatening. Thus, the biblical references to WELLS and other sources of water in Palestine and the larger ANE signify places that genuinely provide life preservation for humans and animals, while water metaphors describe new spiritual life.

In the OT, when the Israelites are journeying through the wilderness, the Lord provides water from a rock (Exod 17:6; Num 20:11; compare Neh 9:15, 20; Wis 11:4; 2 Esd 1:20). In the Deuteronomic curses, divine judgment brings thirst to the people as punishment for their lack of adherence to Torah (Deut 28:48). Several references in the prophets indicate this same result of divine judgment (Isa 5:13; Ezek 19:13; Hos 2:3 [Heb. 2:5]; compare Amos 8:11, 13). The book of Isaiah provides hope that the exiles will overcome thirst when they return to their former homeland from Babylon (Isa 35:7; 41:17; 44:3; 48:21; 49:10). In several psalms, the psalmist describes his craving for the presence and transforming power of the Lord by using a thirst metaphor (Pss 42:2 [Heb. 42:3]; 63:1; 143:6).

Romans 12:20 quotes Prov 25:21 as a directive against vengeance: "No, 'if your enemies are hungry, feed them; if they are thirsty, give them something to drink ...'." Jesus' authentic disciples will offer a drink to the thirsty (Matt 25:35, 37, 42, 44). Several references to thirst in John's Gospel and the book of Revelation express that Jesus quenches the spiritual thirst of any person who comes to him for nourishment (John 4:13-15; 6:35; 7:37; Rev 7:16-17; 21:6; 22:17; compare Isa 49:10; 55:1). Thirst describes a desire for righteousness in the Sermon on the Mount: "Blessed are those who hunger and thirst for righteousness" (Matt 5:6). Finally, Paul twice refers to being thirsty and hungry as characteristic of the sufferings of an apostle (1 Cor 4:11; 2 Cor 11:27). *See* SAMARITAN WOMAN.

MICHAEL D. MATLOCK

THIRTEEN. *See* NUMBERS, NUMBERING.

THIRTY. *See* NUMBERS, NUMBERING.

THIRTY, THE. *See* DAVID'S CHAMPIONS.

THISBE this´bee [Θίσβη Thisbē]. A city of the Upper Galilee, captured by Shalmaneser and the Assyrian army (Tob 1:2). While the book of Tobit describes the location of the city in great detail, its actual site has not been determined. The inhabitants of Thisbe, including Tobit, were exiled to Nineveh following Shalmaneser's attack.

JESSICA TINKLENBERG DEVEGA

THISTLE, THORN [דַּרְדַּר dardar, חוֹחַ khoakh, קוֹץ quts; ἄκανθα akantha, ἀκάνθινος akanthinos, σκόλοψ skolops, τρίβολος tribolos]. One of the most obvious features of the diverse flora of the Middle East is the number of well-armed plants, a survival mechanism for grazing pressure. The Bible does not always distinguish among these. Three of the most prominent are the crown of thorns, thornbush, and a group of plants collectively known as thistles.

Despite its Latin name, the thornbush (*Ziziphus spinichristi*, literally, "spine of Christ") is probably not the plant used for the crown of thorns at Jesus' crucifixion (Matt 27:29; Mark 15:17; John 19:2). The low-growing, common shrub *Sarcopoterium spinosum* is more likely. This shrub is one of the most conspicuous plants in the degraded Mediterranean ecosystem in the mountains along the Rift Valley. *Ziziphus spinichristi* is more frequent in drier sites and at lower elevations than Jerusalem.

Spiny burnet, the "common" name for *S. spinosum*, forms mound-like growth among the rocks of the overgrazed vegetation in the Middle East. Leaves are divided and fall during the dry season. True thorns are produced; these can be up to 10 cm (4 in.) long. Though a member of the rose family, the flowers, which appear in March, are inconspicuous and unisexual. Small fleshy fruits develop in May; these are edible but not harvested.

This is a flexible plant. Farmers sometimes use the branches for cleaning animal stalls and other applications where a strong yet flexuous broom is needed. So it would be easy to weave a crown from it. There is a common houseplant called crown of thorns (*Euphorbia milii*), but this plant originates from South Africa and though well armed is not native to the Middle East and is unrelated to either the true crown of thorns or thornbush.

Thornbush is included in the first botanical discourse in the Bible, by Jotham on Mount Gerizim (modern-day Nablus) where five trees are mentioned: cedar of Lebanon, olive, fig, grape, and thornbush (sometimes translated as bramble) (Judg 9:7-15). The most likely plant for thornbush is *Z. spinichristi* because it is a common component of the steppe vegetation in a region where olives, figs, and grapes are also grown. Thus, it comports well both with the ecology of the region and with the literary image of a valueless tree.

This is a straggling shrub or small tree, which thrives in areas of low rainfall. The plants are viciously armed with specialized stipules (modified leaf bases) in a curious way. One of the spines is straight, the other is curved. Often the only tree in an arid region, the thornbush is sought out for its shade.

Unlike thorny burnet or thornbush, thistles are not woody plants. In much of the Middle East, thistles are the most conspicuous vegetation. At the edge of barley and wheat fields, a painful border of thistles guards the harvest.

The OT word for thistle, khoakh, is cognate with the modern Arabic shawk ("thorn"). This is sometimes translated as "thorn" or "thistle." In the first reference to armed plants in the Bible, Gen 3:18, "Thorns and thistles it [the cursed ground] shall bring forth for you; and you shall eat the plants of the field." The word translated "thorn" is qots. Thus, the two words (as well as several others) can be translated as "thistle" or "thorn."

LYTTON MUSSELMAN

THOMAS tom´uhs [אתֹּאמָא teʾomaʾ; Θωμᾶς Thōmas]. One of the twelve disciples of Jesus (Matt 10:2-4; Mark 3:16-19; Luke 6:14-16; Acts 1:13), often referred to as "doubting Thomas" because of his initial refusal to believe in Jesus' resurrection (John 20:25). The apocryphal Acts of Thomas reports that he was the first missionary taking the gospel to India with miracles and was martyred there.

"Thomas" is a Greek transliteration of the Aramaic teʾomaʾ and Hebrew toʾam (תֹּאוֹם), meaning "twin." It is not clear whether it is a proper name or a nickname. Some Syriac manuscripts (sy^s and sy^c) call him "Judas Thomas" in place of "Judas, not Iscariot" (John 14:22), who is listed as "Judas son of James" in Luke 6:16 and Acts 1:13. This may suggest that "Thomas" was understood as a nickname for Judas son of James in Syriac-speaking churches. In the Gospel of John, he is specified three times as "Thomas who was called Didymus (Didymos Δίδυμος)" meaning "Thomas the Twin" (John 11:16; 20:24; 21:2). This may suggest that he was better known as "Didymus" in Greek-speaking churches.

Thomas is mentioned in all four Gospels, but stories in which Thomas figures as a character appear only in the Gospel of John. When Jesus decides to go to Bethany in Judea, Thomas remarks, "Let us also go, that we may die with him" (John 11:16), because he is aware of the danger facing Jesus in Jerusalem (John 10:39). His words show his loyalty to and solidarity with Jesus. When Jesus speaks about his departure from the world to return to the "Father's house" (14:2), Thomas, reflecting the literary technique of obtuse questions used in Johannine dialogue, says to Jesus, "Lord, we do not know where you are going" (John 14:5). This prompts Jesus to declare that he is the way, the truth, and the life, and only through Jesus can one go to the Father. With an inquiring mind, Thomas does not hesitate to admit his ignorance and ask for explanation in order to understand Jesus. The same intellectual honesty leads him to say that he cannot believe in Jesus' resurrection without physical evidence (John 20:25) even though the other disciples have testified to it. The risen Jesus then appears to Thomas and invites him to see Jesus' hands and touch his side. Seeing Jesus, Thomas confesses with deep conviction and highest honor, calling Jesus, "My Lord and my God!" (John 20:28). Thomas might be slow to believe, but his searching mind is re-

warded with a spiritual insight to Jesus' divine identity; even as Jesus blesses those who believe without the benefit of seeing (John 20:29).

According to Eusebius, Thomas conducted missionary work in Parthia (Hist. eccl. 3.1). His apostolic status and influence are attested by the fact that he was identified as "the twin of our Lord" in the Acts of Thomas, and by the claim that he received secret revelations from the risen Lord in the Gospel of Thomas and the Apocalypse of Thomas.

JOHN Y. H. YIEH

THOMAS, ACTS OF tom´uhs. The early Christian novel known as the Acts of Thomas purports to tell the story of the travels of the apostle Thomas in the "land of the Indians," whence he journeyed to preach the gospel. The work is a product of Christianity, in several ways close to the Semitic roots of early Christianity. The Acts of Thomas contains a distinctive understanding of the Christian life, giving evidence of ascetic Christianity in which sexual renunciation is required of all believers. The work is also noted for its descriptions of liturgical rites, as well as its distinctive God language and its presentation of the apostle Thomas as the twin of Jesus.

A. Author, Language, Provenance, Dating
B. Organization and Content
C. Hymns and Prayers
D. Historical, Liturgical, and Theological Significance
Bibliography

A. Author, Language, Provenance, Dating

The Acts of Thomas is an anonymous work, but was, together with four other apocryphal acts of apostles, attributed to a single author, Leucius Charinus. The variety of styles evident within these early Christian novels makes attribution to a single author impossible, while discussion of an author of the Acts of Thomas itself is complicated by the composite nature of and variations in extant versions of the work. Although the Acts of Thomas was translated into several languages, the two earliest and most significant versions are in Greek and Syriac. The author apparently wrote in Syriac, the language of the city of Edessa and its environs, but the earliest surviving Syriac manuscripts represent a later revision. Indeed, the extant Greek version appears to be closer to the original than is the extant Syriac. Despite the internal claims that the novel is set in India, the notion that Thomas traveled to the Indian peninsula (and the later association of the apostle with the "Thomas Christians" of the Malabar coast) lacks historical credibility. Although the precise place of origin of the Acts of Thomas is unclear, the novel represents the type of Christianity found in northern Mesopotamia and has often been associated with Edessa, which boasted, at least by the late 4th cent., to be the resting place of the bones of the apostle Thomas. Although some sections may have circulated independently at an earlier date, the work reached a complete form around the middle of the 3rd cent.

B. Organization and Content

The *Acts of Thomas* can be divided into two distinct halves; the first half comprises discrete stories about the travels of the apostle, while the second half is a unified tale about the conversion of members of the royal court, notably women. In Act 1, Thomas (called Judas Thomas in the Syriac; this summary follows the Greek) is sold to a merchant and travels to a city in which there is celebration for the marriage of the king's daughter. After Thomas blesses the bride and groom, they are visited by Jesus (in the likeness of the apostle), who convinces them to renounce sexual activity in favor of marriage to the true spouse. Thomas continues to travel in Act 2, and arrives in the land of King Gundafar, who hires him as royal carpenter and commissions the building of a palace. The apostle distributes among the poor the construction funds provided by the king. When the king learns what has happened, he threatens Thomas with death, but his own brother dies before he can carry out the sentence. Gundafar's brother revives and tells of seeing the king's palace built in heaven, after which both the king and his brother decide to become Christian. Acts 3 and 4 tell, respectively, of a talking serpent and a talking ass, providing one of several areas of similarity (that of talking animals, together with travels and adventures) between this novel and the ancient Greek novel genre. The serpent had killed then raised a young man, while the ass, who addresses Thomas as "twin of Christ," carries the apostle to the next city. There (Act 5), Thomas meets a woman who was tormented by a demon; the woman requests "the seal" ("sign" in Syriac) to protect her from the demon, and a description of Christian initiation, including eucharist, follows. A young man approaches the eucharist (Act 6), but his hands shrivel up, convicting him of sin. He reveals that he had killed a woman and is encouraged by the apostle to raise her from the dead. She then tells a story of the torments she witnessed in her tour of hell. In Act 7, Thomas encounters a general who says that his wife and daughter have been repeatedly attacked by demons. Thomas leaves with the general, appointing a deacon to minister to the people in his absence. Wild asses appear in Act 8 to pull the carriage in which Thomas and the general are riding; when they arrive at the general's house, one of the asses speaks, calling forth the general's wife and daughter. The apostle, at the urging of the talking ass, exorcises the demons from the women.

With Act 8 begins a unified story that continues through Act 13, in which the principal character, Mygdonia, is the wife of Carish, a relative of Mizdai, the king. Mygdonia is attracted to the words of the apostle and shuns the advances of her husband, who enlists the king's help. The king questions his general (here called

Sifor and identified as the one who brought the apostle to the city, thus providing a link with the earlier tales). Sifor proclaims his newfound faith to the king, who arrests and threatens the apostle. While in prison, Thomas recites the beautiful "Hymn of the Pearl," and continues to be visited by Mygdonia. Mygdonia requests the "seal of Jesus Christ," is anointed by her nurse, and is baptized by Thomas. Mygdonia returns to her home and continues to resist her husband, claiming that Jesus is her true bridegroom. Carish appeals to the king, who frees Thomas after ordering him to tell Mygdonia to return to her husband; Thomas complies but Mygdonia refuses. The apostle goes to live with Sifor, who, together with his wife and daughter, vows to live in chastity. The scene ends with their anointing, baptism, and celebration of eucharist.

King Mizdai's anger with Thomas grows when his own wife is convinced by Thomas' preaching and converts to a life of sexual renunciation. Mizdai personally accosts Thomas and has him brought to the place of sentencing, only to find that his own son, who had attempted to free Thomas, was swayed by the apostle's words. Thomas and many of his followers are thrown in prison, where his aristocratic converts visit him. The doors of the prison are miraculously opened to them and all exit, proceeding to the house of Mizdai's son, Vizan. On the way, they meet Vizan's wife, formerly unable to walk, but now cured. Another initiation ceremony marks the conversion of many, including those in the king's family.

The martyrdom of Thomas that follows originally may have been composed separately; it was independently distributed, enjoying a life of its own. The martyrdom recounts the trial, sentencing, and death of Thomas, as well as the eventual conversion of the king, brought about when one of the bones of the apostle heals a son of the king. Thomas and his gospel prove victorious, even after his death.

C. Hymns and Prayers

Notable in the *Acts of Thomas* is the inclusion of numerous hymns, speeches, and prayers, some clearly composed independently of the rest of the work. Best known is the Hymn of the Pearl, the story of a prince sent to retrieve a pearl guarded by a serpent. The youth removes his own splendid robe and soon forgets his identity, falling into a deep sleep. Only when his royal parents send him a letter does he rouse, seize the pearl, and don his robe, which aids in his self-recognition, before returning to his true home. The origin of the poem has been debated, since it can be understood from a Manichaean viewpoint and applied to Mani (the Manichaeans read and used the *Acts of Thomas*) as well as from a gnostic or non-gnostic Christian perspective, as a tale describing a life of delusion or the journey of the soul.

Other speeches and prayers celebrate liturgical elements (water, oil, bread) or the identity of characters in the story (the serpent, the apostle), or offer praises addressed to God, to Jesus, or to chastity. Some prayers appear to have been composed in their present context, while others seem to reflect liturgical usage.

D. Historical, Liturgical, and Theological Significance

The *Acts of Thomas* provides some of the earliest evidence available for the Christianity that flourished among Syriac-speaking Christians. Many of the ideas presented in the novel were commonplace among Christians of northern Mesopotamia prior to influence from the Greek-speaking West. During and after the 4th cent., emphasis on a Western understanding of orthodoxy led to a loss of some of the colorful language and images that graced this region in earlier centuries.

Christian ascetics from northern Mesopotamia became famous for their enthusiasm, which they literally demonstrated with their bodies, whether bound by chains, exposed to the elements, or perched on pillars. The *Acts of Thomas* gives evidence of an early understanding of the requirement of single-minded devotion to Christ, including devotion of one's body in a commitment akin to marriage. All adherents to the Christian life in the *Acts of Thomas* know that a life of celibacy is required of them after hearing the apostle's preaching, and freely offer themselves and their bodies to Christ. The work also demonstrates that the practice of renouncing sexual activity was especially attractive to women.

An anointing with oil has long been a prominent fixture in initiation rites in Syriac-speaking Christianity. The *Acts of Thomas* provides evidence for early liturgical practice in this region. Five initiation scenes in the *Acts of Thomas* demonstrate the prominence of anointing in initiation; in two scenes, no water baptism is present. Traces of an ascetic eucharist of bread and water can still be found in the Greek text, as well as recognition of a heavenly reality that is present in the earthly elements, such as water or oil, used in initiation.

To the Western reader, a striking aspect of Syriac-speaking Christianity is the use of feminine imagery for God's spirit (a feminine term in Semitic languages). A direct development of the understanding of *spirit* in the Hebrew tradition, this feminine spirit is seen most clearly in the *Acts of Thomas* in the use of the term *Mother* in prayers that address the Holy Spirit, as well as in other words and phrases applied to the Spirit. The feminine Spirit is also a revealer of mysteries and is present especially in the oil of anointing.

The *Acts of Thomas* also represents an early attestation of the idea that Jesus and Thomas were twins, as the name *Thomas* (te'oma' [תְּאוֹמָא], Aramaic for "twin" and therefore parallel to the Greek **Didymos** [Δίδυμος]), suggests. Like Jesus (Phil 2:7), Thomas becomes a slave; also like Jesus, Thomas is a carpenter. Jesus and Thomas are sometimes mistaken for each other, and characters indicate that they have spoken with, or have been guided by, one who looked just like Thomas. Animals with otherworldly knowledge address Thomas as the "twin of Christ." Being the twin of Jesus helps to explain how Thomas has special knowledge of God's will.

The *Acts of Thomas* is the latest and most fully developed example of an early Christian novel. Among the apocryphal acts of the apostles, it survives in the most complete form, a testament to the popularity it enjoyed in its own day. Its use by Manichaeans, among others, led to questions regarding its value and the eventual rejection of the work in some circles. *See* APOCRYPHA, NT; THOMAS.

Bibliography: A. F. J. Klijn. *The Acts of Thomas: Introduction-Text-Commentary.* 2nd rev. ed. (2003).

SUSAN E. MYERS

THOMAS, APOCALYPSE OF. Written in the 4th cent. CE, the apocryphal *Apocalypse of Thomas* survives in both a longer version and a shorter, older version. It draws on the NT book of Revelation and postbiblical apocalypses for much of its imagery. "Thomas" receives from the Son of God the details about the end times. The end comes over a seven-day period; on the eighth day salvation will be complete. The text emphasizes the destruction of the wicked of this world and the transfer of the elect to heaven; despite its use of the eight-day sequence that is used in some early Christian documents to recapitulate creation, it includes no explicit statement that a new earth will replace this one. Thomas is a Christian document, but the important role played by cosmic light as well as other thematic features indicate Manichean and Priscillianist touches that entered after it was originally composed. *See* APOCALYPTICISM; APOCRYPHA, NT; THOMAS.

ROBERT E. VAN VOORST

THOMAS, GOSPEL OF tom'uhs. The *Gospel of Thomas* is one of fifty-two individual writings of the NAG HAMMADI TEXTS, discovered in Upper Egypt in 1945 near the modern city of Nag Hammadi. It survives complete in a 4th-cent. manuscript translated from Greek into the ancient Egyptian language of Coptic (a mixed form of Sahidic) and in three Greek fragments (P. Oxy. 1, 654, 655)—which are not identical to the Coptic—discovered at Oxyrhynchus in Egypt near the beginning of the 20th cent. On the basis of handwriting analysis, the editors of the Greek fragments dated them to the beginning of the 3rd cent. and their original composition as no later than 140 CE. They left open the possibility that the gospel may have originated within the 1st cent. Some modern scholars have argued that the *Gospel of Thomas* could have originated as early as 50 CE, around the time the sayings collection Q began to be compiled (*see* Q, QUELLE).

The *Gospel of Thomas* was known, quoted, and rejected as apocryphal at the beginning of the 3rd cent. by

Origen (*Hom. Luc.* 1 on Luke 2) and Hippolytus (*Haer.* 5.7.20). Later, in the 4th cent., the *Gospel of Thomas* appears in Eusebius' list of rejected heretical works (*Hist. eccl.* 3.25.6). Origen quotes with some misgivings saying 82 from the *Gospel of Thomas* as a genuine saying of Jesus (*Hom. Jer.* 20.3), although he likely knew the saying from a source other than the *Gospel of Thomas.*

In form, the *Gospel of Thomas* is not a narrative gospel like the four canonical Gospels, which tell a story about Jesus. Rather, it is a collection of 114 sayings attributed to Jesus. Hence scholars have dubbed it a "sayings gospel" like the hypothetical sayings gospel Q. The number of sayings in the *Gospel of Thomas* is based on the general convention of the collector(s) of the *Gospel of Thomas* to introduce most (ninety-one) of the sayings with "Jesus said." Three sayings lack this characteristic introduction (sayings 27; 93; 101), and the modern editors provide it because they assume another discrete saying begins at this point. There are also twenty pronouncement stories, usually beginning with a question put to Jesus (6; 12; 18; 20; 22; 24; 37; 43; 51; 52; 53; 60; 79; 91; 99; 100; 104; 113; 114). Thus the number of sayings in the collection (114) is a modern convention designed to serve as a reference tool for the modern reader, like chapter and verse divisions in the Bible. A difficulty with the convention is that the ancient collector frequently includes as a single saying in the *Gospel of Thomas* what appears in the canonical Gospels as multiple unrelated sayings. For example, saying 47 is counted as a single saying in the *Gospel of Thomas* but includes versions of Luke 16:13 and 5:36-39, which in the canonical tradition are two independent and completely unrelated sayings. This arrangement of sayings in the *Gospel of Thomas* raises the following question: Is this work faithfully recording a pre-synoptic arrangement of the material taken over from the oral tradition or does its arrangement reflect a Thomasine editing of the tradition? If the former option is the case, then Luke has broken up an original (oral) form of a saying for use in different literary contexts in Luke. Scholars do not agree on how this question should be answered.

A literary frame identifies the scribe as Didymus Judas Thomas (i.e., Judas Thomas, the twin). Both Didymus (Greek) and Thomas (Syriac) mean "twin." In the east, Judas Thomas was revered as the twin brother and true companion of the savior (*Thom. Cont.* 138:1-10). Early in the history of the Jesus tradition, churches appealed to authoritative figures in the tradition as the eponymous ideal leader who became patron and guarantor for their community traditions (compare 1 Cor 1:10-13). No concluding literary frame exists to the text.

In the early 20th cent., scholars discovered that the material in the Synoptic Gospels existed as oral tradition prior to writing. The literary types of sayings in the *Gospel of Thomas* are similar to those traditional types found in the canonical Gospels. Like the Synoptic Gospels, the *Gospel of Thomas* has parables, macarisms (blessings), curses, pronouncement stories, proverbs/aphorisms, dialogues, legal sayings, woes, prophetic sayings, and community rules. As to content, the sayings in the *Gospel of Thomas* have been described in terms of different traditions known in the ancient world: Christian, Jewish (e.g., 17), gnostic (e.g., 7; 15; 18), and Hellenistic wisdom (i.e., Aesop, *Fab.* 102, 8). Many sayings in the *Gospel of Thomas* are already known from the canonical Gospels (9; 14; 16; 20; 26; 31; 32; 45; 47), but other sayings, described as Christian (39a; 77b; 82), are not in the canonical Gospels. As yet no one has convincingly demonstrated the logic of the ordering for the sayings, other than the occasional "catchword" associations between sayings (e.g., the word *cast*, sayings 8–10), characteristic of the oral period. The catchwords would have served as an aide to memory in performing multiple sayings orally. Other groupings are obviously made on the basis of similar literary forms (e.g., parables, 64–65; 97–98; or macarisms, 49a and b), or similar motifs between sayings (e.g., the motifs of seeking, knowing, finding in sayings 1–6).

Since the Greek fragments are not identical to the same sayings in the Coptic version, the Coptic exemplar is thought to represent a different Greek version of the *Gospel of Thomas* before it was translated into Coptic. The Coptic version and the Greek fragments overlap in the following sayings: P. Oxy. 1 = sayings 26–30 (+77:2); 31–33; P. Oxy 654 = prologue, sayings 1–7; P. Oxy. 655 = sayings 24; 36–39.

These observations have led some to the suggestion that the *Gospel of Thomas* is a collection comprised of collections of sayings from different parts of the ancient world along with other individual sayings added as the text was reformulated and recopied. This theory is supported by the existence of "duplicates" of sayings in the collection (e.g., 3 and 113; 5 and 6; 6 and 14; 48 and 106; 55 and 101; 56, 80, and 111b; 87 and 112) and striking contradictions (95 and 109:3). These features are easier explained as oversights by the collectors rather than as deliberate incorporation of known variants for some reason, now completely unclear. It is a simple matter to emend a collection of sayings having no clear order of arrangement by dropping or adding every time the list is recopied. Compare, e.g., Matthew's expansion (Matt 13) of Mark's parables chapter (Mark 4). Under these conditions, each reproduction of the collection should be conceived as a new "composition."

Describing a consistent theological stance for the *Gospel of Thomas* is difficult, if not impossible, because of these diverse traditions. Undoubtedly the collectors were able to "read" the sayings from a particular slant, which enabled them to see a consistency to the whole. The principle is similar to the early Christian hermeneutic enabling Christian theologians to read Jewish books (i.e., the OT) from a Christian perspective. In general, however, the stance of the collection as a whole is "world denying" rather than "world affirming." They reflect a retreat from the world and its ways into an esoteric, mystic, and ascetic faith. In the *Gospel of Thomas* one finds no allusions to the dramatic events that characterized the public career of Jesus as known from the canonical Gospels: divine birth narratives, miraculous healings, nature miracles, exorcisms, temple cleansing, crucifixion, and resurrection. What brings eternal life in the *Gospel of Thomas* are the words of Jesus, provided one is able to discover the esoteric truth they contain. Thus, the *Gospel of Thomas* gives the appearance of a collection of sayings that were not influenced by early Christian orthodoxy. Thomas was able to explain the significance of Jesus for faith without recourse to a cross/resurrection gospel, which dominates the NT.

The image of Jesus that emerges from the *Gospel of Thomas* is quite different from portrayals in the Synoptic Gospels and John, although in many ways the "spirit" of the *Gospel of Thomas* and John are rather similar. Jesus is described as the "living Jesus," the son of the "Living One" (*Gos. Thom.* 37:3), who proclaims the "Living Father" (3:4). He announces the "present rule" of the Father (3:1-3; 113) and rejects future apocalyptic expectations (51). In his person he mediates the rule of the Father (82). He is not of this world but from beyond (28:1) and hence is "unknown" (43). What saves in the *Gospel of Thomas* are the esoteric words of Jesus, and whoever discovers their meaning will live forever (1). He speaks wisdom's message—in terms of community wisdom having hidden meanings (35), in vague aphorisms (7:1-2), in parables (97–98), in paradoxes (105)—but he never explains the secret meaning of his sayings. Although he calls (90) and people follow him as disciples (12), he rejects the title "teacher" (13:5). His "wisdom" cannot be taught; rather it must be intuited (2; 3:5). He seems to function as "leader" (12:1). The christological titles Messiah and Lord are not used in the *Gospel of Thomas*. Jesus directs his followers to become solitary wanderers (42; 49); he advocates the conditions of being poor, persecuted, and hungry (54; 68; 69). Thus his followers are to reject the world (110), the marketplace (64:12), and commercialism (95; but compare 109:3). He disavows traditional piety, i.e., fasting, prayer, almsgiving (6:1; 14:1-3), and normal community obligations (55). Because of this radical lifestyle his followers must expect the world to be full of conflict for them. In return he promises "disturbance and rest" (2; 90), "reigning with the Father" (2), and deathlessness/eternal life (18).

The sayings in the *Gospel of Thomas* shared by the canonical Gospels seem to be simpler and less developed along the lines of traditional Christian thought. For example, the parables the *Gospel of Thomas* share with the canonical Gospels (8–9; 20; 63–65) lack interpretations as well as the allegorical and theological shaping characteristic of the parables in the canonical Gospels (compare *Gos. Thom.* 65 to Mark 12:1-11). Many see in the *Gospel of Thomas* an independent source for new sayings originating with Jesus (82; 97; 98) and argue that Thomas acquired these sayings

from the same oral sources as the canonical Gospels. Currently, however, scholars are divided on whether the *Gospel of Thomas* used the canonical Gospels as sources for the material it shares with the canonical Gospels. If the collectors of the *Gospel of Thomas* did use the canonical Gospels for some of their material, they clearly did not use them as sources for all their material. The conclusion that the *Gospel of Thomas* used other sources as well, and the use of multiple sources increases the likelihood that it also drew material from the same oral sources as the canonical evangelists. For example, saying 82 in the *Gospel of Thomas* is not in the canonical Gospels but is known from four ancient and independent sources. No evidence exists that the *Gospel of Thomas* knew any of the documents containing this saying. Consequently it appears all drew the saying from oral tradition. If so, in principle the *Gospel of Thomas* could have drawn many sayings shared with the canonical Gospels from the same oral sources as the canonical evangelists. Thus, aside from potentially being a source for new sayings of Jesus, the *Gospel of Thomas* offers an unparalleled opportunity for critiquing sayings in the canonical Gospels with material uninfluenced by orthodox preaching.

Because of the nature of its contents, the *Gospel of Thomas* raises the issue of how to study the Jesus tradition. Does one study early Christian tradition from the perspective of a canonical bias and automatically exclude non-canonical texts like the *Gospel of Thomas* from consideration? Or does one adapt a broad history of religions stance, and study the canonical Gospels within the matrix of all early Jesus traditions in Greco-Roman antiquity? *See* APOCRYPHA, NT; HYMN OF THE PEARL; INFANCY NARRATIVES.

Bibliography: Stevan Davies. *The Gospel of Thomas: Annotated and Explained* (2002); April D. DeConick. *The Original Gospel of Thomas in Translation* (2007); John S. Kloppenborg et al. *Q Thomas Reader* (1993); Bentley Layton, ed. *Nag Hammadi Codex II, 2–7 together with XII, 2*, Brit. Lib. Or.4926 (1), and P. Oxy. 1, 654, 655.* Vol. 1: *Gospel According to Thomas, Gospel According to Philip, Hypostasis of the Archons, and Indexes* (1989); Uwe-Karsten Plisch. *The Gospel of Thomas: Original Text with Commentary* (2008).

CHARLES W. HEDRICK

THOMAS, INFANCY GOSPEL OF tom´uhs. The canonical Gospels say nothing about Jesus' childhood except for one story of the twelve-year-old Jesus conversing with the teachers in the Temple in Luke 2:41-52. The earliest source for other such tales of the young Jesus is the *Infancy Gospel of Thomas*.

The *Infancy Gospel of Thomas* traces the life of Jesus from the age of five to twelve. The childhood stories reflect many activities of the adult Jesus, including miracles, healings, resuscitations, and displays of wisdom and authority. What is most striking about the text is the young Jesus' behavior. He is as likely to curse as to bless. In one story he strikes a boy dead for bumping into him in the marketplace (chap. 4), then he blinds those who criticize him for it (chap. 5), and later kills a teacher who strikes him (chap. 14). Roused by these shocking stories, scholars have spared few invectives in describing the gospel; indeed, it is the most vilified of all non-canonical Christian literature. But, when looked at through ancient, not modern, eyes, the text is not quite as shocking. The problems attending the proper understanding of the *Infancy Gospel of Thomas* are intertwined with material evidence for this work. Scholars' first look at the gospel came in the 17th-cent. publication of two manuscripts. Their attribution to "Thomas the Israelite" led some to think the text was a *Gospel of Thomas* associated with MANICHAEISM by several church fathers (*see* THOMAS, GOSPEL OF). More manuscripts were published, but none of them seemed to match the ancient descriptions of the *Gospel of Thomas*. As a solution, a theory was proposed that later editors must have stripped the text of its gnostic contents. This theory should have been laid to rest with the discovery of the true *Gospel of Thomas* in 1956, but it continues to affect commentary on the text. Nevertheless, it now appears that the attribution to Thomas is a late development traceable to the 8th or 9th cent. Likely the *Infancy Gospel of Thomas* was originally anonymous and went by the title "The Childhood of the Lord." Irenaeus, writing ca. 180 CE, may have known this text, as he attributes one of its stories to the heretical Marcosians (*Haer.* 1.20.1). If this is the case, the *Infancy Gospel of Thomas* must have been composed around the early to mid-2nd cent., making it one of the earliest of the non-canonical gospels. As for where it was written, some have suggested Palestine, and others Egypt, Syria, or Asia Minor.

Over the centuries, the *Infancy Gospel of Thomas* underwent numerous transformations. The original form of the text is best represented by the early versions: Syriac, Old Latin, Ethiopic, and Georgian. These contain chaps. 2–9, 11–16, and 19 of the conventional numbering. Missing are the introduction with its attribution to Thomas and three episodes reminiscent of Synoptic-style miracle accounts. Around the 8th or 9th cent., chaps. 1 and 10 were added; this form of the text is found in an 11th-cent. manuscript assigned the designation "Greek S." By the 10th cent., chaps. 17 and 18 were added to form the well-known nineteen-chapter "Greek A" recension. At this time also the text was translated into Slavonic. By the 12th cent., a prologue was attached, featuring stories of the holy family in Egypt. This is reflected in the "Greek D" recension and a Late Latin version. Finally, sometime prior to the 15th cent., "Greek A" was shortened to form the eleven-chapter "Greek B" recension. The *Infancy Gospel of Thomas* reached additional audiences via its incorporation into three larger works: the Latin *Gospel of Pseudo-Matthew*, which, in some manuscripts, grafts

the Old Latin *Infancy Gospel of Thomas* on to the *Protevangelium of James* and other childhood stories, and two different compilations of Marian texts in Syriac, one of which later was transformed into the *Arabic Gospel of the Infancy* (*see* JAMES, PROTEVANGELIUM OF; PSEUDO-MATTHEW, GOSPEL OF).

The *Infancy Gospel of Thomas* is understood best in relation to ancient biographical literature. In antiquity, it was believed that one's character and personality were fixed at birth. Thus, when composing biographies, authors would fill in details of their subject's early lives with stories that foreshadowed their adult accomplishments. A great ruler, for example, would be chosen king in a game played with other children; a holy man would perform wonders in the cradle; a philosopher would amaze his schoolteacher with his superior knowledge. Criminals and tyrants likewise showed their colors at an early age. The praiseworthy figures do not display the typical qualities associated with children; instead they are portrayed as mature and wise beyond their years. Given the tendencies of ancient biography, the *Infancy Gospel of Thomas'* Jesus also must be based on a conception of the adult Jesus, an adult Jesus who was as likely to curse as to bless. Such an image is prevalent in Acts, where both God and the apostles perform punitive miracles (e.g., the curse on Ananias and Sapphira in 5:2-11, the blinding of Elymas in 13:4-12). Though Luke's Gospel does not feature cursing stories, the evangelist's portrayal of Jesus is said to be influenced heavily by the stories of Elijah and Elisha, two prophets who also cursed their opponents. Such continuity with Luke-Acts is appropriate given that the *Infancy Gospel of Thomas* in its earliest form shows contact with very few other early Christian texts—indeed, its final story is taken virtually verbatim from Luke 2, suggesting that it was composed as a supplement to this particular Gospel.

Though modern readers find the *Infancy Gospel of Thomas* a difficult text, likely the author and original audience would have seen nothing offensive in its depiction of Jesus. Much of the early commentary on the text, from the 2nd to the 9th cent., takes issue not with the behavior of Jesus but with the gospel's challenge to John 2:11, which states that Jesus' first miracle was performed in Cana as an adult. A cursing, arrogant young Jesus may seem extraordinary to us today, but such a portrayal was not out of place in antiquity. *See* APOCRYPHA, NT; BIOGRAPHY.

Bibliography: Tony Chartrand-Burke. "The Greek Manuscript Tradition of the *Infancy Gospel of Thomas*." *Apocrypha* 14 (2004) 129–51; Stephen Gero. "The Infancy Gospel of Thomas: A Study of the Textual and Literary Problems." *NovT* 13 (1971) 46–80; Ronald F. Hock. *The Infancy Gospels of James and Thomas* (1995); Christopher Pelling. "Childhood and Personality in Greek Literature." *Characterization and Individuality in Greek Literature*. Christopher Pelling, ed. (1990)

235–40; Thomas Rosén. *The Slavonic Translation of the Apocryphal Infancy Gospel of Thomas* (1997).

TONY BURKE

THONG, SANDAL [שְׂרוֹךְ־נַעַל serokh-naʿal; ἱμάς himas]. A strap that holds the sandal to the foot. Abram swears to accept not even so slight a reward as a sandal-thong in return for his efforts (Gen 14:23). Isaiah (5:27) describes returning exiles whose easy journey has not broken their sandal-thongs. John expresses his relationship to Jesus by saying he is not worthy to "untie the thong of his sandals" (Mark 1:7). *See* SANDALS AND SHOES.

VICTOR H. MATTHEWS

THORN. *See* BRAMBLE; BRIER; PLANTS OF THE BIBLE; THISTLE, THORN.

THORNS, CROWN OF. *See* CROWN OF THORNS.

THOUSAND. *See* NUMBERS, NUMBERING.

THRACIAN thray'shee-uhn [Θρᾷξ Thrax]. An inhabitant of Thrace, which is the southern part of the Balkan peninsula, east of Macedonia. Thracians were famous for their fierceness and became the prototypical "barbarians" in Greek imagination. Herodotus (*Hist.* 5.3–8; 7.75) says that they had a high regard for living by war and plunder, that they did not supervise women properly, and that they practiced polygamy. Given their reputation as fierce warriors, it is no surprise that Thracians served as mercenaries in many armies. According to 2 Macc 12:35, a Thracian soldier rescued the Seleucid Gorgias from Judas Maccabeus.

ADAM L. PORTER

THREAD. *See* CLOTH, CLOTHES.

THREE. *See* NUMBERS, NUMBERING.

THREE CHILDREN, SONG OF THE. *See* SONG OF THE THREE JEWS.

THREE DAYS. *See* THIRD DAY.

THREE TAVERNS [Τρεῖς Ταβέρναι Treis Tabernai]. Or "three shops," refers to a way station 30 mi. south of Rome, a frequent gathering place and stop for relays along the APPIAN WAY, located near the city of Cisterna. Similar to a modern-day rest stop, Three Taverns included a store, a hotel-like house, and the local blacksmith shop. Acts 28:15 records that believers from the Three Taverns came to meet Paul while he was traveling to Rome.

STEPHANIE BUCKHANON CROWDER

THREE YOUNG MEN, SONG OF THE. *See* SONG OF THE THREE JEWS.

THRESHING [דּוּשׁ dush, דַּיִשׁ dayish, חָבַט khavat; ἀλοάω aloaō]. Threshing is the process of beating GRAIN in order to release the individual seeds. Once the fields of grain were harvested, farmers brought their stalks of wheat and barley to a communal THRESHING FLOOR (Job 5:26; Matt 3:12). Laid upon this flat, open surface, the stalks were crushed under the hoofs of cattle (Hos 10:11) yoked to a wooden threshing sledge (moragh [מוֹרַג]; 2 Sam 24:22; *see* SLEDGE, THRESHING). Conventional wisdom based on long practice determined how long to thresh the grain with this wheeled cart (ʿaghalah [עֲגָלָה]) so as not to crush it into useless dust (Isa 28:28).

The process lent itself to prophetic metaphor, especially as an image of savage warfare. Amos (1:3) condemns Damascus for threshing Gilead with "sledges of iron." Micah speaks of Yahweh gathering nations like grain to the threshing floor for destruction (4:12), and Habakkuk (3:12) states that Yahweh has "trampled" (lit., "threshed") nations to destroy them. But threshing may also be an image of hope, since the process forces the ears of grain to release the individual seeds. Thus, Isaiah (27:12) promises that Yahweh will thresh the earth "from the channel of the Euphrates to the Wadi of Egypt" in order to release the exiles. Second Isaiah (Isa 41:15-16) evokes the activity on the threshing floor by comparing the progress of the released exiles to the crushing action of a sledge studded with spikes that will crush mountains and "make the hills like chaff." *See* AGRICULTURE.

VICTOR H. MATTHEWS

THRESHING FLOOR [גֹּרֶן goren; ἅλων halōn]. The threshing floor was an open space, often on or near the top of a hill, where grain would be threshed and winnowed. The open space allowed oxen or other draft animals to pull the threshing sledge over the grain and break up the stalks from the heads of grain. In the winnowing process, the higher ground permitted the wind to blow the lighter straw and chaff a distance away while the heavier heads of grain fell to be gathered from the ground. *See* SLEDGE, THRESHING; THRESHING.

The threshing floor of ARAUNAH the Jebusite (2 Sam 24:16-24; ORNAN in 1 Chr 21:15-28) marked the site where the plague brought on by David's census of Israel was halted. David then purchased that threshing floor to be the site of the Temple Solomon would later build. According to 2 Chr 3:1, the threshing floor was located on Mount MORIAH. The site is identified with the Temple Mount, which lay north of the Jebusite city of Jerusalem at a higher elevation than the Jebusite city.

In Samaria, the kings of Israel and Judah met at a threshing floor outside the entrance to the city gate (1 Kgs 22:10). The open space of a threshing floor would provide an ideal place for public assembly, leading some commentators to argue that "threshing floor" here refers merely to an open space for assembly, not an actual threshing floor. However, there is no need to understand the space as other than an actual threshing floor.

In a number of passages, the threshing floor is a symbol of blessing or judgment depending on whether the threshing floor yields plenty (Joel 2:24) or is empty (Hos 9:2). In the NT, John the Baptist uses winnowing as a metaphor for salvation and judgment (Matt 3:12; Luke 3:17). *See* WINNOW.

JOEL F. DRINKARD JR.

THRESHOLD [מִפְתָּן miftan, סַף saf]. A threshold is an architectural element, usually of stone, that lies at the entrance of a building or gate. The threshold often forms the base against which a door closes. The threshold marks the boundary between what is inside and what is outside the structure. Archaeological excavations frequently expose the thresholds of gates, usually built of a single stone or multiple stones set across the entranceway and serving as a stop for a door.

A threshold is part of the architecture of a house (Judg 19:27; 1 Kgs 14:17), as well as of larger structures such as a temple gate (Ezek 40:6-7; 46:2) or the Temple itself (Isa 6:4; Ezek 9:3; 10:4, 18; 41:16, with NRSV footnote; 47:1; Amos 9:1). Because Dagan's statue was destroyed on the threshold of his temple, those who enter the temple do not step on the threshold (1 Sam 5:4-5). Zephaniah promises punishment for people who "leap over the threshold" (Zeph 1:9), possibly a reference to a proscribed religious practice similar to that at Dagan's temple.

Among the important temple personnel were three "keepers (author's trans.; NRSV, "guardians") of the threshold" (2 Kgs 25:18, compare 12:9 [Heb. 12:10]), who guarded access to the Temple and received contributions to the Temple (2 Kgs 22:4). These high-ranking temple officials are listed third behind the chief priest and the second priest in the deportation of 587 BCE (2 Kgs 25:18; Jer 52:24). First Chronicles 9:19 refers to a larger group of Levitical "guardians of the thresholds," descendants of ones who had held that position at the tent of meeting or tabernacle. Although not specifically mentioned in reference to Israel or Judah, such keepers or guardians of the threshold served as bodyguards for the king of Persia (Esth 2:21; 6:2). These guards served at the threshold or entrance to the palace. *See* FOUNDATION; PASSOVER AND FEAST OF UNLEAVENED BREAD; TEMPLE, JERUSALEM.

JOEL F. DRINKARD JR.

THRONE [כִּסֵּא kisse'; θρόνος thronos]. A throne is the seat of a monarch. Usually the term *throne* is reserved for the ceremonial seat used for official, administrative, or diplomatic functions. *Throne* also refers to the sovereignty of the kingdom or empire. The Hebrew kisse' is also used for the seat of any important persons, royal or priestly, but English translations usually do not render these occurrences as "throne."

From ancient Egypt archaeologists have discovered actual thrones, e.g., the thrones of Tutankhamen and of Satamun. Tutankhamen's throne is of wood with gold overlay. The front of the arms and the legs depicts lions' heads and feet. The sides of the arms have winged uraei (sacred serpents) wearing the crowns of Upper and Lower Egypt. The back of the throne shows the king seated on a chair with a footstool, and the queen, standing, facing him and touching him with her hand.

Numerous Mesopotamian reliefs depicting thrones have been discovered. One panel of a relief from Persepolis depicts an Achaemenid king on a high-backed throne receiving tribute. He sits with his feet on a FOOTSTOOL, all others are standing. The throne has few decorative features. The sarcophagus of Ahiram of Phoenicia has a relief depicting the king sitting on his throne, the side of which depicts a winged sphinx/cherub. The king sits before an offering table, his feet on a footstool, a priestess and others standing before him. An ivory carving from Megiddo depicts a ruler sitting on a similar winged sphinx/cherub throne, his feet on a footstool, drinking from a bowl, and others standing before him. These examples help one understand what thrones in the ANE looked like. In all these examples, the king is shown sitting on an elevated throne and having a footstool. All other figures stand before the king.

The OT describes the throne of King Solomon as made of ivory overlaid with gold, having a calf's head at the back and two lions standing by the armrests. The throne had six steps, with two lions at each step (1 Kgs 10:18-20). It also had a gold footstool (2 Chr 9:18). This description indicates Solomon's throne had closest affinity to the Egyptian and Canaanite-Phoenician thrones.

Although not described in any detail, the thrones of Pharaoh in Egypt (Exod 11:5), Nebuchadnezzar of Babylon (Jer 43:10), the king of Nineveh (Jonah 3:6), and Ahasuerus of Persia (Esth 1:2) are mentioned.

The OT also mentions portable thrones a number of times. When kings traveled on diplomatic or military trips, they went with their thrones. Thus the kings of Israel and Judah sat on their thrones in the plaza at the gate of Samaria (1 Kgs 22:10). And Jeremiah speaks of a siege against Jerusalem at which kings from the north will set their thrones at the gates of Jerusalem (Jer 1:15). The Lachish reliefs show King Sennacherib of Assyria on his throne in the encampment during the siege of Lachish. One description of a new king's assumption of kingship is that he ascended to the throne, both a literal description of the fact that the throne was elevated, and a symbolic description of his sovereignty (2 Chr 21:4).

In the biblical usage, *throne* more often is used as a symbol of power, authority, kingship, kingdom, or dynasty rather than the physical throne. Thus the text speaks of the throne of David being established forever (2 Sam 7:13, 16 and frequently). When David officially appoints Solomon as his successor, David's attendants pray that God will make Solomon's throne greater than David's, clearly a reference to the kingdom (1 Kgs 1:37, 47).

Across the ANE, reliefs, seals, and paintings depict gods sitting on thrones much like the human kings. In the OT, Yahweh is depicted as sitting on a throne just like an earthly monarch (Ps 47:8; Isa 6:1). Heaven can be his throne, and earth his footstool (Isa 66:1). Ezekiel's vision of the chariot throne (Ezek 1), although attempting to describe the indescribable, does indicate some of the features of Yahweh's throne: it had winged creatures each having the heads and feet of different animals; it had wheels and it moved; and the likeness of the appearance of the glory of Yahweh was seated above the throne (Ezek 1:26-28). Ezekiel's description of the chariot throne is clearly related to the description of the ark of the covenant with the winged cherubim on each side. Yahweh is several times described as being enthroned (literally, seated) above the cherubim, once specifically related to the ark (1 Sam 4:4). Once the ark is called the footstool of God (1 Chr 28:2). One could say Yahweh is depicted on a throne like a human monarch or that the human king is depicted sitting on a throne like Yahweh (and other gods).

The NT references to throne parallel those of the OT. The NT has few references to human thrones (e.g., Luke 1:52), instead primarily referring to God's heavenly throne (Rev 4). Most occurrences are found in the book of Revelation (forty-seven of sixty-two times in the NT) and refer to the throne of God (Rev 7:15) or the throne of God and of the Lamb (Rev 22:1). Christologically, the risen Messiah/Christ is depicted as sitting on a throne along with God. There are also references to the thrones of the twenty-four elders (Rev 4:4), which surround the throne of God, and to the throne of Satan (Rev 2:13) and the throne of the beast (Rev 16:10). These references recognize that Satan and the beast have some power, but ultimate power resides in God and the risen Messiah whose throne alone is found in the new Jerusalem (Rev 22:3). See KING, KINGSHIP.

JOEL F. DRINKARD JR.

THRONE, HALL OF THE. See HALL.

THUCYDIDES. Thucydides (born ca. 455 BCE) was a member of an Athenian aristocratic family that had financial and probably political ties with Thrace, including interest in a silver mine. In 424 BCE, he was given the command of Athenian forces in Thrace. As a result of his failure to stop the Spartans, he was exiled from ATHENS and did not return until 404 BCE. He died a short time later (ca. 400 BCE). His most significant contribution, however, was his incomplete history of the Peloponnesian War, covering 431–411 BCE. Fourth-cent. successors completed the history of the remaining six years of the war. His extant work consists of an eight-book narrative that relied on eyewitness accounts, avoided supernatural causality, and used speeches as an analytical tool. The eighth book may be incomplete or indicate a change in method. His writing profoundly influenced subsequent histories, including early Christian historical monographs.

JEFFREY R. ASHER

THUMMIM. See URIM AND THUMMIM.

THUNDER AND LIGHTNING [אוֹר 'or, בָּרָק brq, קוֹל qol; ἀστραπή astrapē, βροντή brontē]. The two primary OT terms for thunder are the root r'm (רעם)—used fewer than twenty times—and qol; the latter term is used 505 times in the OT, often with the nuances of voice, sound, or noise. The parallel LXX terms generally follow the pattern of brontē for r'm and phōnē (φωνή) for qol, but not exclusively. Brontē is the typical NT word for thunder. Lightning is characteristically represented by two OT terms also: brq and 'or. Lightning is also described in some OT texts (e.g., "fire flashing," Exod 9:24; "sent out his arrows," 2 Sam 22:15//Ps 18:14; compare Ps 77:17). The LXX parallel terms are astrapē for brq and phōs (φῶς) for 'or. Astrapē is the usual NT term for lightning.

The two phenomena appear together in twelve texts: five in the OT (Exod 19:16; 20:18; 2 Sam 22:14-15//Pss 18:13-14; 77:18), three in the Apocrypha (Sir 32:10; 2 Esd 6:2; 7:40), and four in the NT (Rev 4:5; 8:5; 11:19; 16:18). Three different combinations of terms are used in the OT texts. Exodus 19:16, describing Israelite preparation for the receipt of the Decalogue, employs qol ("thunder") and brq ("lightning"). Exodus 20:18 reports the response of the nation to the giving of the Decalogue, and uses qol and lappidh (לַפִּיד, "lightning"). Second Samuel 22:14-15 (//Ps 18:14-15), which preserves the Davidic testimony regarding divine deliverance from his enemies, and Ps 77:18, in recalling Israel's passage of the Sea of Reeds (vv. 16-20), use the terms r'm ("thunder") and brq ("lightning"). The same pair of terms characterizes the four NT texts: astrapē and brontē. Of interest is the fact that in each of these apocalyptic texts brontē is accompanied by phōnē, the Greek counterpart of the OT qol in the LXX.

That people of the ANE believed thunder to be a manifestation of the deity's voice (qol) seems to be supported both by ANE lore and OT texts; perhaps the NT apocalyptic texts' use of phōnē, in addition to brontē, represents an intended verbal link to the OT concept. The majority of both the OT and NT texts associates thunder and lightning with deity, and certain texts specifically portray them as a medium of divine self-revelation (Exod 19:16; 20:18; Rev 4:5).

More specifically, lightning and thunder appear to serve as metaphorical portrayals of God's awe-inspiring majesty (Exod 19:16; 20:18; 2 Sam 22:14-15//Ps 18:13-14; Rev 4:5), expressions of divine displeasure with God's own people because of rebellion (1 Sam 12:17-18; Isa 29:6), and visitations of the deity against the enemies of the people (Exod 9:22-35; 1 Sam 2:10;

7:10). Immediately preceding the two divine discourses to Job (38–39; 40–41), Elihu eloquently draws his companions' attention to the majesty of "God's thundering voice" (Job 37:2-5). The approving heavenly voice of response to Jesus' request ("glorify thy name") was interpreted by some of those present as thunder, while others thought it to be the voice of an angel (John 12:29). *See* THEOPHANY IN THE NT; THEOPHANY IN THE OT.

JOHN I. LAWLOR

THUNDER, SONS OF. *See* BOANERGES.

THUTMOSE thy*oot´*mohs. The name of four kings from the Eighteenth Dynasty in EGYPT, none of whom are mentioned in the Bible. The best-known is Thutmose III (r. 1504–1452 BCE), who established the Egyptian Empire in Canaan during the Late Bronze period. Around 1483 BCE, Thutmose III led his forces into Canaan, where he encountered a large army at MEGIDDO. A surprise maneuver through a narrow pass allowed Thutmose to catch the Canaanite army unaware, which led to their quick defeat. Thutmose III's empire stretched all the way from Nubia in the south to the kingdom of MITANNI in Mesopotamia.

KEVIN A. WILSON

THYATIRA thi´uh-ti´ruh [Θυάτιρα Thyatira]. Thyatira (modern Akhisar), a city of ancient Lydia, was at the junction of the roads between PERGAMUM and SARDIS (*see* LYDIA, LYDIANS). It is approximately 50 mi. northeast of ancient SMYRNA (modern Izmir), 40 mi. east-northeast of Pergamum (modern Bergama), and approximately 40 mi. from the Aegean Sea. The city sits on a level plain bordered by hills. A watershed separates its basin from the Caicus River. A sandy plain lies to the south toward Sardis. Thyatira has provided little archaeological evidence because the modern town of Akhisar covers it. Thyatira's vulnerable position on an open plain made it an easy victim for repeated military conquests throughout its history. The city is mentioned in Acts 16:14 (compare 16:15, 39) and in Rev 1:11; 2:18-29.

SELEUCUS I Nicator is credited with establishing Thyatira as a Seleucid colony ca. 300 BCE. Since the name is Lydian, it is possible that an earlier settlement preceded Nicator's enclave. By 190 BCE, Pergamum ruled over Thyatira, to be replaced in 133 BCE by the Romans.

Thyatira had a large number of industrial and commercial trade guilds, and these groups had significant social influence. Inscriptions and writings point to wool, linen, leather, bronze, armor, dye, tanning, pottery, and baking guilds. The city was particularly well known for its PURPLE dyeing industry. The dye was made from the madder root. C. J. Hemer has suggested that the trade guilds even rivaled familial and tribal groups for loyalty. Furthermore, he argues that the coexistence of

trade and also village organizations attests to the Lydian origins and antiquity of these groups. While Hemer may be correct and such a development would be quite possible in this region, there is not enough solid evidence to support or refute it. The evidence does suggest that the guilds were well established over several generations. They were founded upon local religious traditions. Over time, their place in society would have been a given. Thus, uprooting them would have been very difficult, if possible at all. Apollo Tyrimnaeus was their patron-god, and the guilds held their feasts in Apollo's temple.

Thyatira was an ethnically mixed city, and its religions borrowed extensively from one another, a common phenomenon in Hellenistic culture that began during the reign of Alexander the Great. Alexander encouraged such cultural borrowing and integration as a means of providing cohesion to his multicultural empire. His Seleucid, Ptolemaic, and Roman successors continued the practice for similar reasons. The official name of the patron-god of Thyatira—Helios Pythius Tyrimnaeus Apollo—contained Lydian, Macedonian, and Greek names. The city also had shrines to Artemis Boreitene and Helius. Hemer also believed that Thyatira was originally an Anatolian settlement where Artemis Boreitene was worshiped. Apollo was also associated with the imperial cult in Thyatira. The city also had three GYMNASIUMs where exposure to religious traditions would have been ongoing. During the imperial period the diversity of the population probably reached its apex due to the ease and safety of travel by land and by sea.

Acts 16:14 mentions a native of Thyatira, "a dealer in purple cloth," named Lydia as the first Christian convert in Philippi. The reference to her as a seller of purple dyed cloth is consistent with what we know of that trade in Thyatira. The passage also describes her as a "worshiper of God." This description could mean that she was a Gentile who regularly attended synagogue, or it could merely be a reference to her piety made manifest in other ways. There is no solid evidence that either Philippi or Thyatira had a synagogue at the time.

Thyatira is mentioned in Rev 1:11 as one of the seven churches in Roman Asia to which John is to write; the letter itself, found in Rev 2:18-29, contains several interesting features. First, it is the longest of the seven missives. Second, its description of the son of God as one with "eyes like a flame of fire" and "feet ... like burnished bronze" connotes omniscience and omnipotence, respectively. The fiery eyes also provided a contrast with the sun-god Helios, who was worshiped in Thyatira. Hemer argued that the "burnished bronze" imagery, found only here in ancient literature, referred to a high-quality copper-zinc alloy that was a special product of the local smelting industry. Thus, the imagery within the letter made connections with local industrial and religious traditions to convey its message of the lordship of Christ. There is strong evidence supporting such connections in other letters in Rev 2–3.

A third outstanding feature of the letter to Thyatira is the reference to "Jezebel" (1 Kgs 16–21). Such a reference indicates a great deal of enmity between John and his adversary. Notably, the conservative John condemns her not for her gender but for her religious practices (similarly in Rev 2:14-15, where the protagonists appear to be male). What we have here, in all likelihood, are two competing prophetic movements. There are three possibilities. 1) The two provided strikingly different prophecies and understandings of the socioreligious context. If those prophecies were mutually exclusive as well, this would explain why John chose the name "Jezebel," a much hated figure in the OT. 2) John is more conservative and probably less accommodating to other religious traditions than his opponent, something John would have shared with many of his Jewish contemporaries. Within this Asian context, John would have been seen as an extremist and a nonconformist, while "Jezebel" would have been looked upon more favorably by the broader society. 3) The third possibility is that it was some combination of the two aforementioned possibilities.

Bibliography: C. J. Hemer. *The Letters to the Seven Churches of Asia in Their Local Setting* (1986); Thomas B. Slater. *Christ and Community: A Socio-historical Study of the Christology of Revelation* (1999).

THOMAS B. SLATER

TIAMAT tee-ah′maht. The Akkadian name, meaning "sea," of a female creature who personifies the primeval salt waters in the Babylonian creation epic ENUMA ELISH. Through the mingling of Tiamat's waters with those of her male counterpart Apsu, fresh water, the pair gave birth to a line of gods who eventually destroyed them. The god Marduk split Tiamat's carcass in half "like a dried fish" (4.137). He used one half to make heaven and the other to form earth; her breasts became mountains, her spittle formed clouds, and her eyes became the Euphrates and the Tigris.

A trace of the Babylonian figure of Tiamat may be present in the biblical creation story. According to Gen 1:2, a wind from Yahweh swept over the face of the **tehom** (תְּהוֹם, "deep"; author's trans.; NRSV, "waters"), which may be an allusion to Tiamat specifically or to primeval chaos generally.

Bibliography: Benjamin R. Foster. "Epic of Creation." *COS* 1.390–402; Alexander Heidel. *The Babylonian Genesis* (1951).

RALPH K. HAWKINS

TIBER RIVER. Arising in the Apennines, the Tiber is the third largest river in Italy and flows generally south, emptying into the Tyrrhenian Sea southwest of Rome. At the mouth of the Tiber, Ostia served as the port city of Rome, albeit with recurring siltation problems. The river is shallow and swift, carries a heavy silt load,

and was commonly labeled the "yellow Tiber" (*flavus Tiberis*). It was the primary water source for Rome and also the depository of its ample sewage. According to myth, the river was named after a legendary king, Tiberinus, who was commonly believed to be the personified deity of the river. Throughout Rome's history, the Tiber has served as a source of Roman civic identity. Juvenal used it to describe the influx of foreigners into Rome (*Sat.* 3.62–65), and it was associated with the legendary founders of the city, Romulus and Remus (Livy, *Hist.* 1.4).

JEFFREY R. ASHER

TIBERIAS ti-bihr′ee-uhs [Τιβεριάς *Tiberias*]. A city founded by HEROD ANTIPAS on the west coast of the Sea of Galilee. He established Tiberias as the new capital of the region of Galilee between 17 and 20 CE. The city was named for TIBERIUS CAESAR, the Roman emperor (14–37 CE). It remained the capital until 61 CE when it was annexed to the region of Herod Agrippa II, who ruled from Caesarea Philippi. The city is mentioned in passing in John 6:23 ("boats from Tiberias"). Twice the Fourth Gospel refers to the Sea of Galilee (Lake of Gennesareth) as the Sea of Tiberias (6:1; 21:1). No other reference to the city is made in the NT, but the early history of the city is well known from Josephus (see below) and the Talmud (e.g., *b. Ber.* 8a; *y. Shev.* 9:38d; *y. Pesah.* 4:2).

Like his father (Herod the Great), whose port city of Caesarea influenced trade patterns in the eastern Mediterranean, Antipas built Tiberias in order to control commerce in his region. The location of the city established Antipas' authority over the fishing industry around the lake. He also built Tiberias in a location that would have brought more travel and commerce to the west shore of the lake along the route of the ancient Via Maris, the road between Damascus and Egypt. Archaeologists have excavated Roman and Byzantine public buildings, a basilica, parts of the city wall with towers, sections of a theater, a cardo, a market, a major bathhouse, churches, and synagogues at the site. The royal palace in the city has not been discovered.

The city was established to the north of a popular area of therapeutic hot springs known as Hammath (just south of the modern city of Tiberias). In Josh 19:35, in the list of the fortified towns of Naphtali, Hammath and Rakkath are mentioned. While it is possible that these cities should be identified with the Hellenistic and Roman settlements of Hammath and Tiberias, the direct association is made difficult because archaeological excavations at the site have not revealed significant material remains that date earlier than the Hellenistic period.

Josephus states that Antipas' city was established on the site of an ancient cemetery (*Ant.* 18.38); thus some Jewish leaders originally considered it uninhabitable. After the Bar Kochba revolt in 135 CE, Tiberias was declared ritually purified, and the city became the center of the Jewish SANHEDRIN. Scholars at the Great Academy in Tiberias were responsible for writing much of the Jerusalem Talmud (see TALMUD, JERUSALEM). The earliest SYNAGOGUE that has been excavated at Tiberias dates to the 4th cent. and contains a beautiful zodiac mosaic.

During the early Byzantine period, the city was a popular pilgrimage stop for Christians who were visiting such sites as Tabgha and Capernaum approximately 10 mi. north of Tiberias. After this period of Christian dominance in the region (5th–6th cent.), the city regained its status as a major center of Jewish intellectual life. Following the Arab conquest in the 7th cent., Tiberias was the capital of Jund al-Urdunn (District of Jordan). During this time, the Yeshiva (Jewish Academy) in Tiberias grew to be a key center of the scribal and Masoretic tradition (see MASORETES). It remained a lively cultural and religious hub until it was destroyed by earthquakes in the 11th cent. By the early 12th cent., Crusaders had razed the remainder of ancient Tiberias and reestablished a new city of Tiberias north of the ruins.

Bibliography: Yizhar Hirschfeld and Katharina Galor. "New Excavations in Roman, Byzantine, and Early Islamic Tiberias." *Religion, Ethnicity, and Identity in Ancient Galilee: A Region in Transition.* Jürgen Zangenberg, Harold W. Attridge, and Dale B. Martin, eds. (2007) 207–29.

MILTON C. MORELAND

TIBERIAS, SEA OF. *See* GALILEE, SEA OF.

TIBERIUS CAESAR t*i*-bihr´ee-uhs see´zuhr. Emperor of Rome from 14–37 CE, Tiberius Claudius Nero's reign marks the consolidation of AUGUSTUS' imperial government and represents the larger historical context for the events of Jesus' adult life. Born on 16 November 42 BCE, Tiberius grew up during the civil wars of the late Republic. In 38 BCE, his father divorced Tiberius' mother Livia so she could marry the triumvir Octavian ("Augustus"). Some months later Livia gave birth to Drusus, the son of Tiberius' father. Livia and Augustus never produced any children. With the establishment of Augustus' principate in 31 BCE, such relationships between members of the imperial family, important for the stability of the empire, were fraught with intrigue.

After accompanying his stepfather on a military campaign in Spain, Tiberius began his public career in Rome as a quaestor in 23 BCE, and subsequently passed through the prescribed sequence of offices, arriving at the consulship in 13 BCE, an office he held three times. Tiberius spent most of his early career as a military officer, earning key victories as a commander in Pannonia and Germany. His domestic life was complicated by dynastic politics. Tiberius was, in 12 BCE, ordered to divorce Vipsania, daughter of the great general M. Vipsanius Agrippa, in favor of Augustus' only daughter Julia, the widow

of this same Agrippa. Julia's subsequent adulterous and political intrigues resulted in her exile in 2 BCE, not long after Tiberius' retirement from public life on the island of Rhodes, beginning in 6 BCE.

Tiberius extracted himself from retirement in 2 CE with the assistance of his mother. Augustus' adopted sons, Gaius (d. 4 CE) and Lucius Caesar (d. 2 CE), the sons of his disgraced daughter Julia, died in quick succession, leaving Augustus with few options for a successor from his own family, so the emperor adopted Tiberius in 4 CE. When Augustus died in 14 CE, Tiberius, now fifty-five years old, with a distinguished career as a general and senator, took command of the armies and obtained an oath of loyalty from magistrates, senators, soldiers, and citizens. The Senate soon confirmed his other rights and powers. Despite the dynastic turmoil within the imperial family, Tiberius was a firm and frugal administrator who left his successor Gaius CALIGULA vast sums in the treasury.

Tiberius allowed his prefect of the PRAETORIAN GUARD, Sejanus, to consolidate the hitherto scattered soldiers into a permanent camp just outside Rome, thus making it clear that the army was the source of imperial power. Sejanus served as Tiberius' confidant, amassing great personal power, after Tiberius retired to Campania in 26 CE. Tiberius ordered that Sejanus be executed for conspiracy in 31 CE, but the praetorian camp remained, and praetorians would play a critical role in the selection of subsequent EMPERORs. Tiberius also transferred elections from voting assemblies of the populace to the Senate, thus completing the destruction of the old Republican constitution. But the most tyrannical aspect of his reign was the rise of a class of political informers and accusers who prosecuted their victims on charges of treason. Records of over one hundred such trials, generally conducted before the Senate, survive. Under Tiberius, the provinces enjoyed freedom from war or invasion, justly administered taxation (he famously declared that provincials should be taxed, not fleeced), and stable government. Judea was, for example, governed by Valerius Gratus from 15–26 CE and Pontius Pilate from 26–36 CE (see PILATE, PONTIUS).

Although Tiberius discouraged worship of himself as a god, evidence abounds that he was much worshiped, especially outside Rome. In all events, Tiberius was himself deeply interested in astrology as well as traditional Roman religion, and he actively promoted the worship of his deified predecessor and father Augustus (this rendered him a *divi filius* or "son of god"), whose precepts formed in general the basis of his deeply conservative policies (see EMPEROR WORSHIP). *See* ROMAN EMPIRE.

Bibliography: Barbara Levick. *Tiberius the Politician.* Rev. ed. (1999); Hans-Friedrich Mueller. *Roman Religion in Valerius Maximus* (2002); Robin Seager. *Tiberius.* 2nd ed. (2005).

HANS-FRIEDRICH MUELLER

TIBHATH tib´hath [תִּבְחַת tivkhath]. City of HADADEZER, the Aramean king of Zobah (1 Chr 18:8); perhaps the same as BETAH (2 Sam 8:8). Bronze seized in Tibhath was used in the construction of the temple vessels.

TIBNI tib´ni [תִּבְנִי tivni]. According to 1 Kgs 16:15-22, Tibni, son of Ginath, lost a three- to five-year civil war against King OMRI of Israel after the death of the usurper ZIMRI, who assassinated ELAH. Josephus reports that Omri's supporters killed Tibni (*Ant.* 8.311–12). Tibni may mean "man of straw."

DAVID M. BATTLE

TIDAL ti´duhl [תִּדְעָל tidh'al]. In Gen 14:1, 9, Tidal is the "king of GOIIM," who, with King Amraphel of Shinar (Babylon), Arioch of Ellasar, and CHEDORLAOMER of Elam, goes to war against five other kings. The Sumerian equivalent for Tidal is "Tudhula," meaning "an evil offspring." In a series of Babylonian political assassinations, Tudhula, the son of Gazza, may be the ruler responsible for the murder of Durmah-ilani's son. Whether this is historically accurate is unknown.

Bibliography: Michael C. Astour. "Political and Cosmic Symbolism in Genesis 14 and in Its Babylonian Sources." *Biblical Motifs: Origins and Transformations.* Alexander Altmann, ed. (1966) 65–112; Othniel Margalith. "The Riddle of Genesis 14 and Melchizedek." *ZAW* 112 (2000) 501–508.

JOHN J. AHN

TIDINGS. *See* GOOD NEWS; GOSPEL, MESSAGE.

TIGLATH-PILESER III tig´lath-pi-lee´zuhr [פּוּל pul, תִּגְלַת פִּלְאֶסֶר tighlath pil'eser, תִּגְלַת פֶּלֶסֶר tighlath peleser, תִּלְגַת פִּלְנְאֶסֶר tilleghath pilne'eser]. Three Assyrian kings were named Tiglath-pileser: 1) Tiglath-pileser I (1114–1076 BCE), whose campaigns reached Lebanon; 2) Tiglath-pileser II (966–935 BCE), an insignificant king of whom little is known; and 3) Tiglath-pileser III (r. 745–727 BCE), the only one of the three mentioned in the Bible, who in 733–32 conquered and annexed most of the northern kingdom of Israel, deporting significant elements of its population (2 Kgs 15:19, 29; 16:7, 10; 1 Chr 5:6, 26; 2 Chr 28:20). The Akkadian form of his name, Tukulti-apil-Esharra, means "My trust is in the firstborn (the god Ninurta) of (the temple) Esharra." The shorter form of his name, Pulu, was originally thought to be a Babylonian throne name, since it occurs in the Babylonian King List, but the name is a well-attested Assyrian name, and it is probably either his original name or a quasi-hypocoristic for the second element of his name.

Tiglath-pileser III seized the throne of Assyria in 745 BCE after an extended period of Assyrian weakness. The central government had become so weak that a number of powerful provincial governors had set up monuments in their own names as if they were independent rulers. Assyria's control of its former vassals in north Syria and thus its western trade routes were threatened by the growing power of URARTU to the north, while unruly Arameans in Babylonia and rebellious tribes in Iran to the east threatened Assyria's eastern and southern trade routes. Tiglath-pileser III quickly addressed all these problems. He reorganized the Assyrian governmental structure, severely limiting the independent military power of the provincial governors. To limit future rebellions among conquered vassals, he also introduced the policy of massive two-way deportations of a defeated country's elite to other parts of the Assyrian Empire, replacing them with exiles from other areas, thus leaving conquered areas without a generally accepted native leadership and thus more dependent on Assyria. As a corollary to this policy, he also annexed the conquered territories of such rebellious vassals and turned them into Assyrian provinces under Assyrian governors.

After successful campaigns against the Arameans in Babylonia and the Medes in Iran, he was ready to deal with Urartu and its western allies. In 743 BCE, Tiglath-pileser defeated Sarduri of Urartu and his north Syrian allies, and put Arpad, the capital of Bit-Agusi, under siege. The siege lasted for three years, but Arpad fell in 740 and all its territory was annexed as an Assyrian province. With Arpad's fall many of its former Syrian allies, including Unqi (Pattina) with its capital Kullani/Kinalia/Kunalia (Calno, Isa 10:9; Calneh, Amos 6:2), submitted and accepted treaties with Assyria. In 739, while Tiglath-pileser was occupied in the north against Urartu, the anti-Assyrian sentiment in the west led to the formation of a south Syrian league led by a certain Azariah. Though the identification of this Azariah is still disputed, he may have been UZZIAH/Azariah of Judah (2 Kgs 14–15; 2 Chr 26). The coalition seems to have involved all the Palestinian and south Syrian states including Damascus and most of the area along the Mediterranean as far north as Unqi. Some nineteen provinces of Hamath joined the coalition, though Ḥamath itself may have stayed out. The strength of the coalition apparently convinced Unqi to break its recent treaty with Assyria, and the territory of Hatarikka (Hadrach) farther inland also joined the revolt. In 738, however, Tiglath-pileser captured Kullani, crushing the coalition, and most of the coalition members, with the notable exception of Judah, tripped over one another trying to be the first to pay tribute to the Assyrian king. In the aftermath of this victory, Tiglath-pileser annexed all of Unqi, Hatarikka, and much of the former territories of Hamath as Assyrian provinces, moving the Assyrian frontier south to the border with Damascus and Phoenicia. The fall of Kullani and Hatarikka in 738 and the earlier fall of Arpad in 740 apparently had a profound impact on the public psyche in Israel and Judah; several prophets cite these events as warnings to Israel and Judah (Isa 10:9; Amos 6:2; compare Zech 9:1).

For the next three years Tiglath-pileser was occupied in the east and the north against the Medes and Urartu, and by 735 BCE REZIN of Damascus was attempting to reconstitute the south Syrian league under his leadership. Phoenicia, Philistia, and Israel all joined, but Judah, under JOTHAM and AHAZ, who replaced Jotham that same year in the midst of the crisis, refused. Aram, under Rezin, and Israel, under PEKAH the son of Remaliah, responded to this refusal with a surprise attack on Jerusalem in an attempt to remove Ahaz and replace him with a more compliant ruler, perhaps a son of Ittobaal of Tyre (2 Kgs 16:5-9; Isa 7:1-6). Despite Isaiah's admonitions to trust Yahweh for deliverance (Isa 7:1–8:4), Ahaz sent tribute to Tiglath-pileser, asking for Assyrian help. In 734, the Assyrians marched down the Philistine coast taking Gaza and blocking Egyptian support for the revolt. The following year the Assyrians ravaged Israel, Aram, and Aram's Arab allies, putting Aram's capital, Damascus, under siege. Damascus fell in 732, and Assyria annexed the whole region, including the Galilee and Transjordan. At some point in this fiasco, HOSHEA replaced Pekah in a coup d'etat and was able to gain acceptance as an Assyrian vassal, though Hoshea's surviving Israel was limited to a small area in the Cisjordan around Samaria.

Having subdued the west, Tiglath-pileser successfully campaigned against the Chaldean chieftains of central and southern Babylonia in 731 BCE. He remained home in Assyria the following year, but in 729, after defeating Nabu-Mukin-zeri, the king of Babylonia, Tiglath-pileser ascended the throne of Babylonia, where he ruled as the legitimate Babylonian king until his death in 727. He participated in the Babylonian *akitu* festivals in 729 and 728, and the Babylonian scribes recorded his reign in the Babylonian King List. *See* ASSYRIA AND BABYLONIA.

Bibliography: Hayim Tadmor. *The Inscriptions of Tiglath-pileser III King of Assyria: Critical Edition, with Introductions, Translations and Commentary* (1994).

J. J. M. ROBERTS

TIGRIS RIVER ti′gris [חִדֶּקֶל khiddeqel, חִדָּקֶל khiddaqel; Τίγρης Tigrēs, Τίγρις Tigris]. The Tigris River, 1,150 mi. long, arises in the Taurus Mountains of eastern Turkey and flows in a southeasterly direction through northern Iraq, the heartland of ancient Assyria. Near Baghdad in central Iraq it takes up a roughly parallel course with the Euphrates River as it flows through the territory of ancient Babylon and then ancient Sumer. The two rivers join in the far south of Iraq at Al Qurna to form the Shatt al-Arab waterway, which empties into the Persian Gulf. The earliest name of the river, Sumerian idigna, means "the river that goes," alluding to the swiftness of the Tigris in contrast to the slower-moving Euphrates. The Akkadian rendering of idigna as idiqlat is the direct source of the Hebrew name and the ultimate source via Persian of the Greek.

The Tigris is mentioned six times in the OT and Apocrypha. According to Gen 2:14, the Tigris, which passed east of Assyria, was one of the four rivers flowing out of Eden. Sirach compares the flow of these rivers to the flow of wisdom from the Torah (24:25). Daniel is standing on the banks of the Tigris when he receives the final revelation of the book (Dan 10:4). Tobias follows the course of the Tigris when he travels from Nineveh to Rages (Tob 6:2-3), and he cures his father's blindness with the gall of the fish he takes from the river, on the advice of Raphael. In Jdt 1:6, the Tigris basin is part of the territory allied to or controlled by Nebuchadnezzar.

J. J. M. ROBERTS

TIKVAH tik′vuh [תִּקְוָה tiqwah; Θωκᾶνος Thōkanos]. Means "hope." 1. The father of Shallum, husband of the prophetess Hulda of Jerusalem, who authenticated the temple scroll found during the reign of Josiah (2 Kgs 22:14). He is called Tokhath in 2 Chr 34:22.

2. The father of Jahzeiah, who was one of the small minority that opposed Ezra's plan to dissolve the Judean marriages with foreign women (Ezra 10:15; 1 Esd 9:14).

F. RACHEL MAGDALENE

TILGATH-PILNESER. *See* PUL; TIGLATH-PILESER III.

TILON ti′luhn [תִּילוֹן tilon]. Head of a Judahite clan and the fourth of Shimon's four sons (1 Chr 4:20).

TIMAEUS ti-mee′uhs [Τιμαῖος Timaios]. Father of BARTIMAEUS, a blind beggar whom Jesus heals en route to Jerusalem (Mark 10:46).

TIMARCHUS. According to Appian (*Syrian Wars*, 45, 47), Antiochus IV Epiphanes (175–163 BCE) appointed Timarchus governor of Babylon (*see* ANTIOCHUS). When Antiochus IV died, several pretenders arose, including Lysias (the steward of Antiochus V) and Demetrius I, who killed Lysias in 162. Timarchus rebelled, presumably trying to usurp the throne, but Demetrius killed him in 160. Timarchus' brother, Heracleides, supported Alexander Balas, who claimed to be the son of Antiochus IV. Heracleides persuaded the Roman Senate to support Balas against Demetrius, who was killed in 150 BCE; thus, Heracleides avenged his brother.

ADAM L. PORTER

TIMBER. *See* WOOD.

TIMBREL. *See* MUSICAL INSTRUMENTS.

TIME. When using abstract language and categories such as "time" to describe the biblical texts, one must be careful not to impose modern foreign understandings onto these ancient texts. The authors of both the OT and the NT tend not to talk about things in the abstract.

Rather, they tend to think in concrete, material ways. The emphasis is not on ideas, but on actions, people, and things.

In the modern West, time is often conceived of as a dimension, along with that of space, that humans imagine, name, measure, and order to locate themselves in this world and in history. For much of the biblical world, people's thinking was not focused on such abstract categories, but on the content that makes up the categories. There are no words in biblical Hebrew and Greek that exactly match the English words *time* in the sense of a dimension or *history* as a singular totality encompassing the past, present, and future. Rather, in the biblical world, the focus was not on abstract concepts of time or history but on the people, the places, the things, the actions, and the events that occupy moments or periods of time. The biblical words indicate the ways that things change, people move, and events are associated with one another.

A. Terminology–Old Testament
B. Terminology–Septuagint and New Testament
C. Emphasis on Praxis
D. God over History
Bibliography

A. Terminology–Old Testament

The basic words for time reflect the changes in the world and the movement of celestial objects—day and night, month, and year. Many temporal words and phrases developed to coordinate different events, situating them in relationship to one another. Ultimately, the numbering or counting of these elements led to systems of recording time, both in terms of calendrical texts and historical literature (*see* CALENDAR; HISTORY AND HISTORIOGRAPHY, OT).

The most basic term in the OT is *day* (yom יוֹם), which originally referred to the period of daylight from dawn to dusk (*see* DAY, OT). While grounded in this specific image, *day* often functions in a more general way to designate a time when something occurs. The usage becomes so generic that the phrase "on the day" often may be translated as "when" (e.g., Gen 3:5; 5:1; Ps 20:9 [Heb. 20:10]; Lam 3:57). In both the OT and in the NT, the plural "days" is used in dating formulas often with a proper name and is synonymous with the English "times" (e.g., Ruth 1; compare Matt 24:37; Luke 17:28).

The coordination of temporal duration and space is represented in the technical terms DAY'S JOURNEY (e.g., Num 11:31; compare Luke 2:44), "three days' journey" (e.g., Gen 30:36), and SABBATH DAY'S JOURNEY. Note that in these examples, the emphasis is on the content of *day*, in these cases spatial distance. On a larger scale, the terms that are translated GENERATION (dor דּוֹר; toledhoth תּוֹלְדוֹת; genea γενεά, genesis γένεσις) serve to relate and coordinate the people and events of each period.

With an emphasis on actions, there is a concern for the "timing" of events. The early Israelite economy included agricultural production that was affected by the seasonal cycles. In the ANE, AGRICULTURE was intimately related to the cult; thus, many of the biblical festivals were agricultural in origin. Eventually there was concern to regularize the observance of these celebrations. Lists of these festivals as an annual cycle include Exod 23:14-17; 34:18-23; Deut 16:1-17; Num 28–29; and Lev 23:4-44. For the cycle of holy days through the year, *see* FEASTS AND FASTS and YEAR.

The noun moʿedh (מוֹעֵד) can have both spatial ("appointed place," "meeting place," and by extension, "assembly") and temporal referents ("appointed time"). The temporal instances may be general—the time designated or appointed for something (e.g., 1 Sam 9:24; 13:8; 20:35). Moʿedh also takes on the technical sense of "appointed festival" (Lev 23:2, 4, 37, 44; 1 Chr 23:31; Isa 1:14; 33:20; Hos 2:11; 9:5; 12:9)—that is, the time appointed by God to celebrate what God has done. In biblical creation traditions, the lights in the heavens (Gen 1:14) and the moon (Ps 104:19) mark the "seasons" (moʿadhim מוֹעֲדִים), although one could also imagine these passages playing a role in calendrical controversies. Eventually, moʿedh is used to designate the time when God will intervene: "For there is still a vision for the appointed time; it speaks of the end), and does not lie" (Hab 2:3; compare 1QpHab VII, 5–8). This temporal sense is often translated in the Septuagint by kairos (καιρός).

Authors in the OT develop a technical term, DAY OF THE LORD, to refer to a time when God or God's agent will intervene on earth, often in judgment. The earliest attestation is in Amos (5:18, 20) and is used frequently by other prophets (Isa 13:6, 9; 58:13; Jer 46:10; Ezek 13:5; 30:3; Joel 1:15; 2:1, 11, 31; 3:14; Obad 15; Zeph 1:7, 14; Mal 4:5). Associated with the day of the Lord is the "day of vengeance" (Isa 34:8; 61:2; 63:4) and "day of retribution" (Jer 46:10), which Luke echoes (21:22). While the exact phrase "day of judgment" does not appear in the OT, "day of wrath" does (Ezek 7:19; Zeph 1:15, 18; Prov 11:4; Job 21:30; Ps 110:5), as does "day of salvation" (Isa 49:8).

ʿEth (עֵת) is the most common Hebrew word typically translated as "time." Again, ʿeth does not refer to "time" as a dimension or even as a long period of time; rather, it refers to a definite moment or short period of time. This is indicated by its common use with prepositions such as *in, at, for, to, from,* "up to," and the adjectives *near* and *far*. Often, ʿeth is coupled with a demonstrative pronoun to refer to a particular moment in the past or sometimes in the future ("at that time"). ʿEth often refers to the time to do something (e.g., Gen 24:11; Hos 10:12; Eccl 3:1-8) or when something happens (e.g., Lev 15:25; Ruth 2:14; 1 Sam 4:20). It is sometimes coupled with a modifier to describe the moment or period, such as "the time of your distress" (Judg 10:14), "the time of their suffering" (Neh 9:27), "evil time" (Ps 37:19; Amos 5:13), or "a time of healing" (Jer 8:15; 14:19). In the prophetic literature, constructions with ʿeth often refer to God's intervention in "the time of their punishment" (Jer 10:15; 50:27; 51:18; compare Ezek 21:29) and "the time of the LORD's vengeance" (Jer 51:6). Many of these instances are synonymous with the day of the Lord (e.g., Ezek 30:3; compare Ezek 7:7, 12; 21:25, 29; 22:3; 35:5). Daniel describes this time as "the time of the end" (Dan 8:17; 11:40; 12:4, 9).

Qets (קֵץ) can have spatial sense of an "end, border" (e.g., Isa 37:24), but generally has temporal referents. It often indicates the "end of" a certain period of time (e.g., Gen 8:6; Exod 12:41). It is also used to represent the "end" in the sense of cessation or "limit" of things, such as "windy words" (Job 16:3), "iniquities" (Job 22:5), "peace" (Isa 9:7), and specifically of life—"let me know my end, and what is the measure of my days" (Ps 39:4; compare Jer 51:13; Lam 4:18). In Ezekiel, it is used to express the "time of final judgment" for Zedekiah, Judah's last king (21:25 [Heb. 21:30]), and, in turn, for the Babylonians (21:29 [Heb. 21:34]). In Daniel, the phrase "time of the end" is used to refer to the period when the visions would be fulfilled (8:17; 12:4, 9).

Another word with both spatial (e.g., Ps 139:9), but predominantly temporal connotations is ʾakharith (אַחֲרִית). It may simply refer to that which will come, which NRSV translates simply as "future" (e.g., Prov 19:20; 23:18; 24:14, 20; Jer 29:11; 31:17). It occurs in several places with "days" in the phrase often translated as the "days to come," which may refer to an unspecified time in the future, as it does in the introduction to Jacob's testament in Gen 49:1. In other prophetic and so-called apocalyptic texts, it refers to a time in the future when the predictions will be fulfilled: "In days to come the mountain of the LORD's house shall be established as the highest of the mountains" (Isa 2:2; Mic 4:1; compare "latter days" in Ezek 38:16 and "end of days" in Dan 10:14).

The emphasis on the content rather than abstract notions of time is also indicated by the use of *generation* (dor; genea), which refers both to a person's life span (variously considered roughly forty years or thirty-three and a third) to a group of people who live at the same time. Many of the commandments in the Pentateuch are enjoined upon the people "throughout your generations" (e.g., Exod 12:14). Expressions such as "all generations" are synonymous with "forever" (ʿolam עוֹלָם) as in Ps 89:1 (Heb. 89:2).

Even with the term ʿolam, variously translated in the NRSV as "forever," "eternal," "everlasting," and "perpetual," one must be careful not to impose a strict abstract or philosophical concept, i.e., an "eternity" that encompasses or transcends time. Rather, ʿolam typically refers to "long or most remote time," sometimes in the past, other times in the future, or both. It often occurs with the prepositions "from," "to" or "for," and "until." The basic meaning may be illustrated by Isa 42:14: "For a long time I have held my peace." When referring to the past, it may refer to a remote, distant past: "remember the former things of old; for I am God, and there is no other" (Isa 46:9; compare Gen 6:4); "Remember the days of old, consider the years long past" (Deut 32:7). Elsewhere, it has a more specific sense: "Long ago your ancestors—Terah and his sons Abraham and Nahor—lived beyond the Euphrates and served other gods" (Josh 24:2). In Isa 63:11, the "days of old" explicitly refers to the time of Moses. In Proverbs, it refers to the time of creation; Wisdom declares, "Ages ago I was set up, at the first, before the beginning of the earth" (8:23).

ʿOlam is often used with the prepositions "until" and "to" or "for" when it refers to the future. That future may be as short as a person's lifetime: "He shall be brought to the door or the doorpost; and his master shall pierce his ear with an awl; and he shall serve him for life" (Exod 21:6). While it is often translated by the English "forever" and its synonyms, its use is often hyperbolic. This is exemplified by the psalmists and other poetic writers, who assert that "we will bless the LORD from this time on and forevermore" (Ps 115:18; compare Pss 125:2; 131:3; Isa 59:21) and "I will rejoice forever" (Ps 75:9 [Heb. 75:10]).

ʿOlam also has the sense of "perpetuity." In Gen 6:3, for example, "the LORD said, 'My spirit shall not abide in mortals forever'" (compare Gen 3:22; Exod 3:15; 15:18, etc.). Many of God's promises are given in perpetuity. So, for example, the Lord promises Abram the land in Gen 13:15 "forever" (compare Josh 14:9). Similarly, the Lord promises David that God will establish a dynasty through his son Solomon "forever" (2 Sam 7:13). The construct berith ʿolam (בְּרִית עוֹלָם) becomes a technical term in the biblical texts, variously translated in the NRSV as "everlasting covenant" (e.g., Gen 17:7), "perpetual covenant" (e.g., Exod 31:16), and "covenant forever" (e.g., Lev 24:8). Commandments are also often enjoined in perpetuity; see, for example, the phrases "perpetual ordinance" (e.g., Exod 12:14), "perpetual statute" (e.g., Lev 3:17), or "statute forever" (e.g., Lev 23:14).

The most abstract meditation on time in the OT occurs in Eccl 3. In the introduction to the poem of Eccl 3:1-8, ʿeth ("time") is set in synonymous parallelism to zeman (זְמָן, "season"): "For everything there is a season, and a time for every matter under heaven" (Eccl 3:1). The poem itself consists of a litany of antithetical pairs of occurrences that make up human life, each with its own set moment or appropriate "time": "a time to be born, and a time to die; a time to plant, and a time to pluck up what has been planted," and so forth. The prose commentary on the poem (3:9-15) attributes this activity to God who "has made everything suitable for its time" (3:11). Despite the symmetrical structure of the poem, which portrays human life as very orderly, the commentary portrays human life as inscrutable: "moreover he has put a sense of past and future into their minds, yet they cannot find out what God has done from the beginning to the end" (Eccl 3:11). The commentary concludes, "That which is, already has been; that which is to be, already is; and God seeks out what has gone by" (Eccl 3:15). Rather than seeking to provide an explication of time itself, the point of the author's meditation in this section of Ecclesiastes expands the contention that "there is nothing new under the sun."

B. Terminology–Septuagint and New Testament

The translators of the OT into Greek had at their disposal words and conceptions of time that were more abstract. The most common word for "time" in Classical and Hellenistic Greek is chronos (χρόνος), which may refer to an abstract notion of "time in general" as well as a span or interval of time. Kairos (καιρός), on the other hand, is less common in Classical and Hellenistic Greek. When it is used, kairos often has connotations of the appropriate or decisive moment or period of time. Despite philosophical and linguistic developments, it is difficult to exaggerate the influence of the books of the OT—often mediated through the Septuagintal traditions—on the writers of the NT documents. Thus, we must again be careful of imposing our modern understanding of time as an abstract dimension on these texts. In contrast to Classical and Hellenistic usages, kairos is more common than is chronos in both the Septuagintal traditions and the NT. Chronos and kairos are often synonymous, as exemplified by 1 Thess 5:1: "Now concerning the times (tōn chronōn τῶν χρόνων) and the seasons (tōn kairōn τῶν καιρῶν), brothers and sisters, you do not need to have anything written to you" (compare Acts 1:7).

While in Classical Greek chronos may refer to a more abstract notion of "time" in general, in the Septuagintal traditions it typically refers to a span of time, and may be modified by adjectives that indicate a duration— "much" or "long," or "little," "short," or "brief." While in Hebrew a span of time typically is expressed by "day" or "days," chronos is occasionally used in the Greek translations (e.g., Job 10:20), although the literal translation hēmera (ἡμέρα, "day") is more common. Following Septuagintal usage, chronos generally refers to an "interval of time" in the Greek of the NT. This is indicated by the use of adjectives such as "little" (e.g., John 12:35), "long" (e.g., Matt 25:19; Luke 8:27) or "many" (e.g., Luke 8:29), or "as long as" (e.g., Mark 2:19). Chronos may also indicate when something happens; "now the time came for Elizabeth to give birth" (Luke 1:57). Chronos is sometimes coupled with a modifier to describe content of the period, such as "the times of human ignorance" (Acts 17:30) or "the time of your exile" (1 Pet 1:17). Chronos also appears in the plural, often indicating an expanse of time, which the NRSV appropriately translates as "ages" (e.g., Rom 16:25; 2 Tim 1:9; Titus 1:2; 1 Pet 1:20).

In contrast to Classical Greek, kairos is used more often than chronos in the Septuagint and the NT. Kairos most often translates ʿeth and shares with it the sense of a definite moment or short period of time. So, for example, it may be used to designate a general moment (e.g., "at that time" in Matt 11:25). In Classical and Hellenistic Greek, however, kairos often has connotations of the appropriate or decisive moment or period of time. Similarly, ʿeth may convey the notion of the appropriate or opportune time to do something or for something to happen (e.g., Num 23:23; Eccl 10:17). So, in the NT, kairos may refer to "the harvest time (ho kairos tōn kairōn ὁ καιρὸς τῶν καιρῶν)" (Matt 21:34) or "the proper time" when slaves received their food allowance (Luke 12:42). Kairos is also used to translate moʿedh, both to refer to fixed times such as "seasons" (e.g., Gen 1:14) as well as in the technical designation to indicate the decisive moment or period when God will intervene on earth (e.g., Hab 2:3).

Since the authors of the NT documents understood themselves as living in a decisive moment, when God either had already intervened or is about to intervene in human affairs, kairos often expresses these connotations. Thus, for example, in Matthew, the Gadarene demoniacs challenge Jesus saying, "Have you come here to torment us before the time?" (Matt 8:29), and in Luke, Jesus predicts the destruction of Jerusalem because "you did not recognize the time of your visitation from God" (Luke 19:44). In Luke 12:54-56, Jesus challenges the crowds, saying that they are able to discern the weather by observing the skies, but they do not "not know how to interpret the present time." For the early followers of Jesus, the time of God's intervention may refer to Jesus' death or resurrection (e.g., 1 Pet 1:10-11; Matt 26:18). In other passages, kairos refers to a moment in the near future, such as the "manifestation of our Lord Jesus Christ, which [God] will bring about at the right time" (1 Tim 6:14-15). The book of Revelation, for example is framed by the inclusio "the time is near" (1:3; 22:10), declaring that the events described in the body of the document are about to occur. That "the time" became a technical term for God's intervention is evident in a passage from Luke, which the author has crafted to account for the delay of the Parousia; Jesus responds to his disciples' questions when his predictions will happen by saying, "Beware that you are not led astray; for many will come in my name and say, 'I am he!' and, 'The time is near!' Do not go after them" (Luke 21:8). Finally, kairos may also refer to the time when people are challenged to decide how they are to prepare for God's imminent intervention; so Paul urges his readers, "you know what time it is, how it is now the moment for you to wake from sleep. For salvation is nearer to us now than when we became believers" (Rom 13:11).

The basic units of time in the NT include "day" (*see* DAY, NT), "month," and "year." The NT documents also employ a narrow unit, the HOUR. Following the OT, books in the NT often speak of the "day of the

Lord" (hē hēmera tou kyriou [ἡ ἡμέρα τοῦ κυρίου]; e.g., 2 Thess 2:2; 1 Thess 5:2; 1 Cor 5:5; 2 Pet 3:10). Paul also calls this the "day of our Lord Jesus Christ" (1 Cor 1:8 and, with variation, 2 Cor 1:14; Phil 1:6, 10; 2:16). Luke uses the plural to refer to the "days of the Son of Man" (Luke 17:22, 26). The NT documents also refer to the DAY OF JUDGMENT (e.g., Matt 10:15; 11:22, 24; 12:36; 2 Pet 2:9; 3:7; Jude 6; a notion also attested in Jdt 16:17; Wis 3:18; 2 Esd 7:38, 102, 104, 113; 12:34; *1 En.* 22:11, 13; 81:4; 84:4; 97:3; 100:4; *Jub.* 4:19; 9:15; 10:17, 22; 24:33; compare Tob 1:18). Also following the OT, Paul refers to the "day of wrath" (Rom 2:5) and "day of salvation" (2 Cor 6:2), while the author of Ephesians uses the term "day of redemption" (4:30).

The NT documents also use *hour* (hōra ὥρα) with specific referents. In the Gospels, "the hour" often refers to Jesus' passion (Mark 14:35, 41; Matt 26:45). In John's Gospel, "the hour" serves as a device to tie together important moments in the narrative (4:21, 23; 5:25, 28; 12:23; 16:2, 25, 32; 17:1). In Matthew and Luke, Jesus warns that the Son of Man will come at an "unexpected hour" (Matt 24:44, 50; Luke 12:39-40, 46). First John 2:18 warns that it is the "last hour." And in Revelation, God's judgment is referred as "the hour of trial" (3:10), "the hour of his judgment" (14:7). The judgment of Babylon is described as happening in "one hour" (18:10, 17, 19). In these examples, the use of *hour* emphasizes the imminence and, in some places, even the punctiliar nature of judgment (although note that in Rev 17:12 the ten kings receive authority for "one hour").

The basic sense of the Greek word aiōn (αἰών) is the relative time associated with something, such as a person's life or a generation in the sense of an "age" or an "era." In Col 1:26, aiōn ("age") is parallel to genea ("generation"): "the mystery that has been hidden throughout the ages and generations." It may refer to an indefinite past or future, often with prepositional constructions; e.g., "from of old" (Luke 1:70), "before the ages" (1 Cor 2:7), "forever" (Luke 1:55; 2 Cor 9:9). Thus, aiōn and the adjective aiōnios (αἰώνιος) resemble use of ʿolam in the OT. Similarly, they may also have the sense of "in perpetuity" and thus are translated "forever" or "eternal" (e.g., John 8:35); this especially case with the doxological affirmations that mirror the sentiments of the psalms (e.g., Gal 1:5; Phil 4:20; Jude 25). Aiōn as the time of the world elides with a notion of the "world" itself. In 1 Cor 1:20, Paul parallels aiōn ("age") with kosmos (κόσμος, "world"). Thus, in the NRSV, aiōn is also translated "world" (e.g., Mark 4:19; Rom 12:2; 2 Cor 4:4; contrast Eph 2:2).

While the early followers of Jesus anticipated the "close" or "end of the age" (Matt 13:39, 40, 49; 24:3; 28:20), this phrase does not necessarily signify an end of time. The author of Hebrews declares that Jesus "has appeared once for all at the end of the age to remove sin by the sacrifice of himself" (Heb 9:26), clearly referring

to his death, a past event from the perspective of the author. Rather, the early followers of Jesus envisioned an end of their era, to be followed by a glorious era. In the NT, "this age" is often contrasted with the "one to come" (Matt 12:32; Eph 1:21; compare Luke 20:34-35). Often implicit in the contrast is the understanding that the present age is evil, an understanding that Paul makes explicit in Gal 1:4. The most graphic description of the anticipated coming age is provided by the book of Revelation, especially in chaps. 20–21. Revelation 20 speaks of a thousand-year reign of Christ followed by the final destruction of "Death and Hades" (*see* IMMORTALITY). What is then envisioned is not a timeless, immaterial, spiritual existence, but rather "a new heaven and a new earth" along with a "new Jerusalem" in which "the Lord God the Almighty and the Lamb" reign on earth (Rev 21).

C. Emphasis on Praxis

The Priestly writer of the Pentateuch understands creation as the ordering of the world through separation and distinction: light from darkness, dry land from water, day from night (Gen 1). Within this order, some days are set apart as holy (*see* HOLY, HOLINESS, OT). The most basic of these is the SABBATH. In the Israelite as well as early Jewish contexts, observance of the Sabbath and the other holy days is understood within the covenantal relationship between God and the people. Fulfilling commandments of the covenant is understood as the people's response to God's gracious acts. Rather than focusing on abstract philosophical reflections for their own sake, the emphasis for the biblical writers is on the present, specifically on what people should do in the present. This concern about practice, how and when the people are to fulfill God's commandments, leads to the calendrical controversies that are attested in *1 Enoch, Jubilees*, and the Qumran community, as well as debates over the Sabbath reflected in the Gospels and the rabbinic literature.

D. God over History

Throughout the OT, starting with Genesis and Exodus, but especially in the prophets, one sees the developing affirmation that the Lord is the God over the political order of the world, what we might call "history." Once again, however, we must careful not to impose modern understandings of history as dimension. Rather, in the polytheistic context of the ANE, where gods are often understood as patrons of different peoples and nations, the prophets affirmed the Lord as an international God who controls and determines political powers and arrangements. This idea is developed in the traditions preserved in *1 Enoch* and other so-called apocalyptic texts. In Dan 7–12, the events of the political world from the Babylonian Empire through Antiochus IV are revealed to Daniel in a series of dreams. While modern scholars understand these "prophecies" as *ex eventu* (having been written after the fact), the portrayal in the book gives the impression that God has ordained and organized the progression of history. The Qumran community even affirmed that "From the God of knowledge (comes) all that is and (all) that shall be" (1QS III, 15; compare 4Q400 1 5 and 4Q180 1 1–2a). In the Matthean genealogy of Jesus, the schematic portrayal of fourteen generations between Abraham to David, fourteen between David and the exile, and then finally fourteen between the exile to Jesus sets the stage for the portrayal of Jesus' life in the Gospel as the fulfillment of what God has predicted through the prophets (Matt 1:17). The Lukan Paul in Acts declares that "From one ancestor he made all nations to inhabit the whole earth, and he allotted the times of their existence and the boundaries of the places where they would live" (Acts 17:26). Similarly, Paul understands God's sending of Jesus as occuring at a predetermined moment, "when the fullness of time had come" (Gal 4:4). *See* CHRONOLOGY OF THE ANCIENT NEAR EAST; CHRONOLOGY OF THE NT; CHRONOLOGY OF THE OT; DIAL; ESCHATOLOGY IN EARLY JUDAISM; ESCHATOLOGY OF THE NT; ESCHATOLOGY OF THE OT; FULLNESS OF TIME; JUBILEE, YEAR OF; MOON; NEW YEAR; PASSOVER AND FEAST OF UNLEAVENED BREAD; SUN; WEEK; WEEKS, FEAST OF; YEAR.

Bibliography: James Barr. *Biblical Words for Time* (1962); Gershon Brin. *The Concept of Time in the Bible and the Dead Sea Scrolls* (2001); Erik Eynikel and Katrin Hauspie. "The Use of Καιρός and Χρόνος in the Septuagint." *ETL* 73 (1997) 369–85; Denis Feeney. *Caesar's Calendar: Ancient Time and the Beginnings of History* (2007); Sacha Stern. *Time and Process in Ancient Judaism* (2003).

HENRY W. MORISADA RIETZ

TIMNA tim'nuh [תִּמְנָע timnaʿ]. 1. Sister of the Horite tribal leader Lotan (Gen 36:22; 1 Chr 1:39). She is listed as the concubine of Eliphaz, the son of Esau, who bore him Amalek (Gen 36:12). The parallel passage in 1 Chr 1:36 lists Timna as one of the sons of Eliphaz, but the LXX of 1 Chr 1:36, which reads "and from Timna, Amalek," agrees with Gen 36:12 in treating Timna as a woman and the mother of Amalek.

2. A tribal leader listed among the tribes descended from Esau (Gen 36:40). This listing might be a reference to the location of the tribal group rather than its ancestral designation. *See* ARAB, ARABIAN, ARABIA; EDOM, EDOMITES.

C. MARK MCCORMICK

TIMNAH, TIMNITE tim'nuh, tim'nit [תִּמְנָה timnah, תִּמְנִי timni]. 1. A town in Judah, identified with Tel Batash in the fertile Sorek Valley, between Beth-shemesh and Ekron (Josh 15:10-11). Timnah was ideally situated for agriculture and was a cultural and commercial link between the coastal plain and the hill country. It was

assigned to the tribe of Dan (Josh 19:43) but held for a time by the Philistines (Judg 14:1-5; compare 2 Chr 28:18). Judah had flocks at Timnah (Gen 38:12-14) and Samson married a Timnite woman (Judg 14:1-8; 15:6).

The site was occupied in the Middle and Late Bronze Ages and destroyed and rebuilt several times. The Iron Age I walled city (Str. V) yielded typical Philistine pottery, as well as Philistine seals and clay figurines. It was abandoned in the late 11th cent. During the Iron Age IIA (Str. IV, probably 10th cent. BCE), the town was partially rebuilt and finds reflect a new material culture, suggesting that it was now controlled by the Israelite united monarchy. After an occupation break, the city was rebuilt during the 8th cent. (Str. III) and fortified with a massive stone wall and city gate, probably as a border city of Judah. It was destroyed by Sennacherib in 701 BCE, as recorded in his annals. Typical Judean lmlk jars were found in the rubble.

During the 7th cent., the city was again rebuilt and it flourished until destroyed violently by the Babylonians in 604 BCE. Olive oil production and trade relations with Greece as well as with Judah are evidenced in the rich finds. Following the second destruction, the mound was abandoned.

2. A town in the hill country of Judah (Josh 15:57).

Bibliography: George L. Kelm and Amihai Mazar. *Timnah: A Biblical Town in the Sorek Valley* (1995); Amihai Mazar. *Timnah (Tel Batash) I: Stratigraphy and Architecture* (1997); Amihai Mazar and Nava Panitz-Cohen. *Timnah (Tel Batash) II: The Finds from the First Millennium BCE* (2001); Nava Panitz-Cohen and Amihai Mazar, eds. *Timnah (Tel Batash) II: The Finds from the Second Millennium BCE* (2005).

AMIHAI MAZAR

TIMNATH-HERES, TIMNATH-SERAH tim'nath-hee'riz, tim'nath-sihr'uh [תִּמְנַת־חֶרֶס timnath-kheres, תִּמְנַת־סֶרַח timnath-serakh]. A city of JOSHUA's inheritance and place of his burial (Josh 19:50; 24:30; Judg 2:9). Joshua 19:50 says the Israelites gave Joshua the city at the Lord's command and he built it up and lived there. Scholars believe Timnath-heres (Judg 2:9), meaning "portion of the sun," is the city's older name and suggest that it was a place dedicated to sun worship. The name was changed to Timnath-serah (Josh 19:50; 24:30), meaning "portion remaining." Some scholars suggest that the name change is due to scribal error, or was introduced to dissociate Joshua from sun worship. Rabbinic tradition offers a different perspective, associating the name "Timnath-heres" with Joshua's success in causing the sun to stand still (Josh 10:13) and claiming that his tomb had an image of the sun on it.

Judges 2:9 places the site in the hill country of Ephraim, north of Mount Gaash (compare 2 Sam 23:30), whose location is unknown. Tradition associates the city of Joshua's burial with Kefr Haris, a site about 9 mi. southwest of Nablus (biblical Shechem).

However, this is a late tradition and lacks archaeological support. The most likely location is Khirbet Tibneh, a site located approximately 17 mi. southwest of Nablus, which preserves part of the ancient name and has several ancient, rock-hewn tombs.

TERRY W. EDDINGER

TIMON tí′muhn [Τίμων Timōn]. One of seven men commissioned by the twelve apostles to attend to the daily distribution of food in the Jerusalem community (Acts 6:5). Because his name is Greek (as are the names of the other six), it is likely that Timon was selected from among the Hellenists. *See* HELLENISTS; SEVEN, THE.

J. TED BLAKLEY

TIMOTHY tim′oh-thee [Τιμόθεος Timotheos]. The Greek name **Timotheos** literally means "one who honors God," but alone indicates nothing about religious status. 1. Leader of an Ammonite army who fought against Judas Maccabeus and his army on several occasions around 164 BCE (1 Macc 5:6-8; 2 Macc 8:30-33; 9:3; 10:24-38; 12:2-9). The Maccabees found him hidden in a cistern at the fortress of Gazara and killed him.

TERRY W. EDDINGER

2. In the NT, Timothy is a close associate of the apostle Paul and the apparent recipient of two of the Pastoral Epistles. The traditions about Timothy's family are varied and illustrate the differences between the Lukan and Pauline witnesses. On the one hand, Luke reports that Timothy was from Lystra in the Lycaonian region of the province of Galatia, the son of a pious (pistēs πιστῆς) Jewish mother and a Greek father (Acts 16:1-3), thus perhaps Jewish by matrilineal descent, though that principle is not clearly attested until the 2nd cent. CE. On the other hand, 2 Tim 2:5 speaks of Timothy's grandmother Lois and his mother, Eunice, both Greek names and both Christian women, perhaps converts during Paul's first mission in Lystra (Acts 14:6-20). Perhaps the adjective "faithful" in Acts 16:1 designates her as a "Christian" rather than a "pious" Jew. According to Acts, Paul encountered Timothy in Lystra where his good reputation there and in Iconium 18 mi. away led Paul to circumcise and incorporate Timothy into the missionary team. Although Paul asserts circumcision is not, in itself, important (Gal 5:6; 6:15), it would have been necessary for Timothy's acceptance in Jewish circles and in the synagogues from which Paul launched new missions, especially if the son of a Jewish woman married to a Gentile was considered a Gentile in the Jewish communities of Asia Minor.

In the Acts of the Apostles, Timothy figures prominently in Paul's second and third missionary journeys. He remains with Silas in Beroea with a plan to go on to Athens to meet Paul (Acts 17:14-15). Acts 18:5 reports that he arrives in Corinth. Paul sends him to Macedonia

with Erastus (Acts 19:22), and he later travels with Paul through Macedonia and Greece and is with him in Corinth on the eve of his journey to Jerusalem (Acts 20:4; Rom 16:21). As related in Paul's epistles, Timothy serves as Paul's representative.

Timothy appears frequently in the Pauline epistles where he is referred to as Paul's "co-worker," a term frequently used for Paul's fellow missionaries (Rom 16:21; 1 Thess 3:2), as well as his "brother" (i.e., in the faith, 2 Cor 1:1; Col 1:1; 1 Thess 3:2; Phlm 1:1), "son" (Phil 2:22), and "loyal child" (1 Tim 1:2; 2 Tim 1:2). The language Paul uses about Timothy indicates that the relationship between them was close and familial as well as professional. Especially in Phil 3:19-24 one glimpses the warmth of feeling Paul had for his young friend and protégé who often served as his primary emissary and whom Paul described as a living example of the mind of Christ. Timothy appears as coauthor of six epistles (2 Corinthians, Philippians, Colossians, 1 and 2 Thessalonians, and Philemon). None of the prison epistles (Philippians, Colossians, or Philemon) mention Timothy sharing Paul's imprisonment, so apparently Timothy was free to serve Paul in these incarcerations. Timothy's position in these letters demonstrates his importance as an associate in ministry and as a friend upon whom the apostle depended. Of Timothy, Paul writes in Philippians "like a son with a father he has served with me in the work of the gospel" (Phil 2:22).

With Silvanus, Timothy had been part of the missionary team in Corinth. Later, Paul sent Timothy to Corinth to remind that church of Paul's message. The translation of **epempsa** (ἔπεμψα) in 1 Cor 4:17 is significant for Pauline chronology. If it is translated as a simple aorist, "I sent," it suggests Timothy had been there before the letter; if as an epistolary aorist, "I am sending," it suggests Timothy carried the letter (compare Acts 19:22). That Paul charges the Corinthians to treat Timothy well when he comes may indicate that he was nervous, or previously rejected, or perhaps left without support. The commands "let no one despise him" and "send him on his way in peace" suggest that his reception and mission in Corinth may not have been completely irenic or successful and are a subtle indication that he did not have the forceful personality of his master (1 Cor 16:10-11).

Timothy had been sent from Athens to Thessalonica (1 Thess 3:1-2) to encourage that persecuted church and returned from there to Paul with a good report on conditions there (1 Thess 3:6). Apparently, because of that success, Paul hoped to send him to Philippi on a similar mission (Phil 2:19-24). Wherever Paul was imprisoned at the time he wrote Philippians, Timothy was in attendance, but evidently not imprisoned with the apostle.

Although their authorship is far from certain, two of the Pastoral Epistles are addressed from Paul to Timothy. Many scholars think they are pseudonymous works of the late 1st to early 2nd cent. It is difficult to imagine that the seasoned associate of Paul's correspondence would require the instructions in church leadership found in 1 Timothy. Second Timothy might incorporate material from Paul's final imprisonment at Rome. In any case, presenting Timothy as recipient and guarantor of the Pauline tradition indicates how well known and highly regarded he was in the early church. First and Second Timothy are general exhortations and provide scant new biographical information about the younger man to whom they are addressed. They suggest that Paul's "loyal child in the faith" (1 Tim 1:2; 2 Tim 1:2; 2:1) is maintaining Paul's teaching (1 Tim 1:3) in Ephesus. Timothy is given instructions "in accordance with the prophecies made earlier about you" (1 Tim 1:18), which are largely about church order. He is charged to "guard what has been entrusted to you" (1 Tim 6:20), a change in vocabulary (from "pass on" in Paul's letters to "guard" in the Pastorals) that appears to point to a church living after the death of the apostles.

One must wonder whether the exhortations in 1 Tim 1:18-19a; 4:14-16; and 6:3-16 are general or suggest that Timothy is growing lax. Would Paul remind someone to do something already being done? Second Timothy 1:7 suggests Timothy is a bit timid, perhaps about suffering (2:3; compare 1 Cor 16:10-11). Whatever his disciple's behavior in Ephesus, in 2 Tim 4:6-12 Paul requests that Timothy gather various possessions and join Paul in Rome. If authentic, these instructions indicate the closeness of the two; Paul wants Timothy nearby as Paul faces death.

It is not known whether the Timothy that Heb 13:23 reports "has been set free" (from prison?) is the Timothy of the Pauline mission. Eusebius reports that a "Timothy" was the first bishop of Ephesus (*Hist. eccl.* 3.4). Such legendary evidence indicates Timothy's continuing influence in early church tradition. *See* PASTORAL LETTERS; PAUL, THE APOSTLE; TIMOTHY, FIRST AND SECOND LETTERS TO.

Bibliography: Frederick Fyvie Bruce. *The Pauline Circle* (1985); Shaye J. D. Cohen. "Was Timothy Jewish? (Acts 16:1-3)." *JBL* 105 (1986) 251–68; John D. Legg. "Our Brother Timothy." *EvQ* 40 (1968) 220–23.

BONNIE BOWMAN THURSTON

TIMOTHY, FIRST AND SECOND LETTERS TO [Πρός Τιμόθεον A, B Pros Timotheon A, B]. Two letters that present Paul as an elder and authoritative teacher instructing Timothy on the conduct of community life, probably written well after the death of Paul, and that may incorporate information from Titus (Marshall). Though the canonical order places Titus after 1 and 2 Timothy, many scholars think that Titus was composed before these two epistles (*see* TITUS, LETTER TO).

A. Structure of the Letters
  1. First Timothy
  2. Second Timothy
B. Detailed Analysis
  1. Author and date
  2. Genre
  3. Characterization
  4. Church structure
  5. Political context
C. Theological and Religious Significance
  1. Salvation as the savior's epiphany
  2. Genuine piety
  3. Authentic teaching
Bibliography

A. Structure of the Letters
1. First Timothy

The greeting identifies Paul as apostle "by the command of God our Savior and of Christ Jesus our hope"; Timothy is addressed as "my loyal child"; the greeting adds mercy to the conventional Pauline formula "grace and peace" (1 Tim 1:1-2). Paul recalls his request that Timothy stay in Ephesus to oppose those who claim to teach the law (1 Tim 1:3-11). A thanksgiving for Paul's conversion, offering the apostle as an example of God's mercy to sinners, closes with a doxology (1 Tim 1:12-17). Recalling the command given to Timothy by Paul's prophetic direction, the author employs a military metaphor to encourage resistance to false teachers (1 Tim 1:18-20).

The letter body opens with an entreaty to pray for all human beings, especially rulers (1 Tim 2:1-7). Counsel on the behavior of men at prayer (1 Tim 2:8) and of women in the assembly (1 Tim 2:9-15) is followed by moral requirements for "bishops" (or overseers; 1 Tim 3:1-7) and for "deacons" (or ministers), and women (1 Tim 3:8-13).

The purpose of the letter, that Timothy "may know how one ought to behave in the household of God," is warranted with a tradition proclaiming Christ's manifestation as "the mystery of our religion" (1 Tim 3:15-16). A prophecy denounces false teaching that undermines this purpose (1 Tim 4:1-5).

Advice to Timothy, urging him to nurture his gift and teach by example (1 Tim 4:6-16), introduces instruction for elders: on how to admonish elder men and women (1 Tim 5:1-2), on which widows to acknowledge and support (1 Tim 5:3-16), on support of (male) elders (1 Tim 5:17-20), on impartiality in judgment, and on Timothy's health (1 Tim 5:21-25). Instruction to slaves (1 Tim 6:1-2) inculcates submission to both unbelieving and believing owners. Those whose teaching differs from "sound words" are discredited as seeking to exploit godliness for material gain (1 Tim 6:3-10). Commands to Timothy are warranted with the reminder of Jesus' good confession before Pontius Pilate. Expectation of Jesus' future manifestation culminates in a doxology. Turning again to money, Paul counsels the rich to seek true riches (1 Tim 6:17-19). The letter closes with a final address to Timothy and a grace (1 Tim 6:20-21).

2. Second Timothy

The greeting in 2 Tim 1:1-2 has been modeled on 1 Tim 1:2, tracing Paul's apostleship back to the divine command in 1 Tim 1:1 (God's will in 2 Tim 1:1). Whereas 1 Timothy associated Christ with God in giving the command, 2 Timothy speaks of the "promise of life in Christ" as the purpose of God's activity.

The epistolary thanksgiving, a feature of Paul's own letters, takes up the motif of encouraging the recipient. It reports the apostle's conviction that Timothy's faith remains strong along with Paul's fervent prayer for his associate (2 Tim 1:3-5).

The letter body involves a series of reminders that are overshadowed by the circumstances: Paul's Roman imprisonment and impending death. The author encourages Timothy to rekindle his gift and be ready to follow Paul's example of suffering for the gospel (2 Tim 1:6-14). News of colleagues, another feature typical of personal letters, names individuals who have abandoned Paul, as well as his supporters (2 Tim 1:15-18).

Military metaphors return as the author counsels Timothy to convey sound teaching to others (2 Tim 2:1-26). Like a soldier enduring hardship, Timothy must "share in suffering" (2 Tim 2:3), remembering both Paul's chains and endurance and Christ's (2 Tim 2:9-13).

Earlier references to false teaching and desertion return in the second section of the letter body (2 Tim 3:1–4:8). A prophetic word points to a worsening situation (2 Tim 3:1-9) that will involve persecution (2 Tim 3:12) and rejection of the truth (4:3-4). Reminders of Paul's examples and suffering (2 Tim 3:10–4:5) should encourage believers to remain steadfast now that Paul's own life is ending (2 Tim 4:6-8).

Following epistolary conventions, the final section of the letter incorporates personal information and instructions to the addressees. Travel instructions (2 Tim 4:9-15) introduce a report on Paul's first defense (2 Tim 4:16-18). The letter closes with greetings and grace (2 Tim 4:19-22).

B. Detailed Analysis

1. Author and date

The authorship of 1 and 2 Timothy has been disputed since the early 19th cent. While many scholars now see them as pseudonymous, others strenuously defend their authenticity. Cited by Irenaeus (*Haer.* 2.14.7; 3.3.3; 3.14.1), Clement (*Strom.* 2.11), and Tertullian (*Ux.* 1.7; *Praescr.* 6; 7) as Pauline, they must predate 180 CE. Scholars who attribute them to Paul place them late in his career. Strong verbal resonance between 1 Timothy and Polycarp (compare 1 Tim 6:7, 10; Pol. *Phil.* 4:1) are best explained by shared genre and context and, like other indications, suggest a date in the first half of the 2nd cent.

2. Genre

Both 1 and 2 Timothy are sometimes classified as official rather than friendly letters. But Pseudo-Demetrius observes that official letters frequently use the conventions of friendly letters to persuade (*Epistolary Types* 1). Like most other early Christian letters, they use the language not merely of friendship but also of family. Scholars who read the letters as pseudonymous describe them as examples of personification (*prosopopoeia*), an ancient pedagogical technique that sought to emulate figures from the past. Pseudonymous letters were employed to extend the teachings of famous philosophers (e.g., Socrates, Plato, Diogenes) by later followers. Both 1 and 2 Timothy combine the genre of a letter that contains a famous teacher's instruction with other genres; in 1 Timothy, a letter of entreaty (1 Tim 1:3, 5, 18) incorporates ethical teaching using the conventions of the household code (*see* HOUSEHOLD CODES), transferred from proper conduct for those in an individual household to the "the household of God, which is the church of the living God" (1 Tim 3:15).

Second Timothy functions as a final testament of Paul, who entrusts his mission and sound teaching to God (2 Tim 1:12) and to Timothy (2 Tim 1:14; compare 1 Tim 1:18; 6:20), who must then entrust them to those who will be able to teach others (2 Tim 2:2-3). *Entrust* evokes, as metaphor, the ancient practice of depositing money with unimpeachably trustworthy persons. The letter "predicts" the tribulation and dissension that its author already detects in the churches of the Pauline mission (2 Tim 3:1-9; 4:3-5).

3. Characterization

The ancient critic Demetrius required that letters be full of character (*Eloc.* 4.227), and the two letters bearing Timothy's name—whether authentic or pseudonymous—take pains to characterize the writer and the recipients. In 1 Timothy, supposedly written from Macedonia to Ephesus, Paul is the example of sinners who receive mercy, and so of those who would believe (1 Tim 1:16). Calling himself "herald" and (as in the undisputed letters) "apostle," he is yet more "teacher of the Gentiles in faith and truth" (1 Tim 2:7). His "sound teaching" (1 Tim 1:10; 4:6; 6:3) is primarily moral; theological speculation and dispute are eschewed.

Timothy is apparently the companion of Paul who co-signs 2 Corinthians (1:1), 1 Thessalonians (1:1), and Philemon (1), and sends greetings in Rom 16:21. The address "loyal [or genuine] child in the faith" (1 Tim 1:2) probably draws on Philippians, where Paul says that Timothy served the imprisoned Paul as a son would a father (Phil 2:22) and was "genuinely concerned for [the Philippians'] welfare" (Phil 2:19-20). Youthful and zealous, Timothy is abstemious to the point of endangering his health (1 Tim 4:12; 5:23).

In 2 Timothy, ostensibly written from imprisonment in Rome, "Paul" virtually announces his death by proclaiming that he has "finished the race" (2 Tim 4:6-8).

Contrast Phil 3:12-14, where the imprisoned Paul insists on the incompleteness of his course. The impression of a voice from beyond the grave is strengthened by the reporting of his "first defense" (2 Tim 4:16). The exhortation to co-suffer along with Paul and Christ may draw upon early Christian memories of Timothy's martyrdom. Addressed as beloved child, Timothy becomes a model for second generation believers. He has inherited a faith from his mother and grandmother grounded in the scriptures (2 Tim 1:5-6; 3:15).

4. Church structure

The terms episkopos (ἐπίσκοπος; 1 Tim 3:2), diakonos (διάκονος; 1 Tim 3:8, 12), and presbyteros (πρεσβύτερος; 1 Tim 5:17, 19), often translated "bishop," "deacon," and "presbyter," respectively, are the source of those English words. But their functions and relations are undefined in 1 Timothy. The translations "overseer," "minister," and "elder" help to convey the ambiguity of these designations. Diakonos can refer to Timothy (1 Tim 4:6; NRSV, "servant"). Paul also uses diakonos for himself and Apollos (1 Cor 3:5) and Phoebe (Rom 16:1). The stipulations for "overseers" and "deacons" in 1 Tim 3:1-7, 8-13 reflect a conventional morality for the head of a household: good character, ability to discipline his family, civic respect. The letters do not explain what functions these individuals carried out within the church community. Perhaps their formal appointment was similar to Timothy's (1 Tim 4:14). The community may have assembled in the house of an overseer or deacon, as the "head of household" charged with hospitality, for its celebration of the Lord's Supper, worship, and instruction, but the letters provide no clues to such details. It appears that the "elders" responsible for teaching in 1 Tim 5:17-25 have the same responsibilities as "overseers" and "deacons." See BISHOP; DEACON; ELDER IN THE NT.

5. Political context

The exhortation to co-suffer (2 Tim 1:8; 2:3; 4:5), the many references to Paul's suffering, and the commemoration of Jesus who "before Pontius Pilate made the good confession" (1 Tim 6:13) reflect the risk of martyrdom. Though the martyr/apostle is idealized, the letters urge behavior that will secure the good opinion of outsiders. They seem to struggle with the contradictions of Roman policy on Christians as it was articulated in the exchange between Pliny, the Roman governor of Bithynia, and Emperor Trajan (Ep. Tra. 10.96–97, around 112 CE). Christians were not sought out, but if they were denounced or arrested for other crimes and refused to recant, they were executed. Throughout much of the 2nd and 3rd cent., Christians could live and worship with impunity unless they attracted the hostility of their neighbors.

C. Theological and Religious Significance

Both 1 and 2 Timothy incorporate a number of traditions that offer access to the theology and exhortation of the early Christian mission after—and perhaps even before—Paul. For instance, creedal hymns or proclamations lie behind passages like 1 Tim 2:5-6; 3:16; 2 Tim 1:9-10, 11-12.

1. Salvation as the savior's epiphany

Despite reservations about theological debates and speculation, the author integrates the traditional material into a developed theology, speaking of both God and Christ as savior, recalling and looking forward to Christ's "appearing" (epiphaneia [ἐπιφάνεια]; 1 Tim 6:14; 2 Tim 1:10; 4:1, 8), and celebrating God's grace or gift. God "our savior" (1 Tim 1:1; 2:3) also "desires everyone to be saved and to come to the knowledge of the truth" (1 Tim 2:4; compare 4:10). This salvation comes by grace "revealed through the appearing of our Savior Christ Jesus" (2 Tim 1:10) and is complete only with the future appearing of Christ (1 Tim 6:14; 2 Tim 4:1, 8). The terms savior and appearing derive from the OT through the LXX and were shaped by cults of Greek gods and Hellenistic rulers. By the 1st cent. CE, they had been transferred to the Roman emperors. In these letters, savior and appearing function in a theology that both absorbs imperial imagery and resists imperial claims. Recalling Jesus' death at the hands of the empire, when he "in his testimony before Pontius Pilate made the good confession," the author exhorts Timothy to endure "until the manifestation of our Lord Jesus Christ" (1 Tim 6:13-15). This EPIPHANY will be brought about by God, "the blessed and only Sovereign, the King of kings and Lord of lords" (1 Tim 6:15), who implicitly surpasses and negates the emperor's dominion. The need to resist an emperor's claim to divinity is underlined when Paul the martyr calls on Timothy to share Paul's suffering. Even though God is the only true king, the author urges prayer for "kings and all who are in high positions (that is, emperors and their administrators), so that we may lead a quiet and peaceable life in all godliness and dignity" (1 Tim 2:2).

2. Genuine piety

"Godliness" translates eusebeia (εὐσέβεια), the virtue of duty and devotion toward the deity, but also toward all to whom one is related: parents, children, spouses, siblings, one's country, the emperor, and even clients and slaves. As the Roman virtue pietas, it was central to imperial ideology. The letters frequently invoke this virtue (1 Tim 3:16; 4:7-8; 5:4; 6:3-6, 11; 2 Tim 3:5). In 1 Tim 3:16, the words "mystery of our religion," identified as Christ's manifestation and triumph, could also be translated "the secret of godliness." Godliness is the Christian message, ministry, and way of life, as well as religious duty toward one's relatives (1 Tim 5:4).

Godliness is thus reflected in the central image for the church in 1 Timothy: the household of God (1 Tim 3:5). The household code extends the metaphor into the life and structure of the community. Episkopos, diakonos, and presbyteros had both household and public referents, and the counsel to these figures—as well as the advice to men in general (1 Tim 2:8), to women (1 Tim 2:9-15), and to widows (1 Tim 5:3-16-)—is shaped by the highly gendered public and domestic virtues of the early empire. The instruction on women (1 Tim 2:9-15) requires unostentatious dress, forbidding a woman "to teach or have authority over a man," and demanding that she be silent. These strictures are explained with an exegesis of Gen 2:7–3:24 that not only insists on Adam's prior creation but also claims that "the woman" alone became a transgressor, because she, and not Adam, was deceived (Gen 3:13). For women, then, salvation comes not from learning and teaching but from childbearing, "provided they continue in faith and love and holiness, with modesty" (1 Tim 2:15; compare 5:14). The instruction on widows similarly demands that widows remarry until the age of sixty, thus accommodating and indeed exceeding the Julian law, which required widowed or divorced women to remarry until the age of fifty. For women, learning and teaching lead only to opportunities for gossip and sexual misbehavior. The vituperative belittling of women constantly studying but driven by sin and desire and unable to "arrive at a knowledge of the truth" (2 Tim 3:6-7) recalls the misogynist diatribes of Juvenal's *Sixth Satire*. The author seeks to both accommodate and exceed Roman ideals of familial virtue, particularly in the control of women's sexuality.

3. Authentic teaching

The question of Paul's opponents in these letters is an important one. The letters refer to "teach[ing] ... different doctrine" (heterodidaskalein [ἑτεροδιδασκαλειν]; 1 Tim 1:3, 6:3-10; compare 4:1-6; 2 Tim 2:14-18, 23; 3:1-9) and disparage "myths and endless genealogies" (1 Tim 1:4; compare 4:7; 2 Tim 4:4) and the "contradictions (antitheseis ἀντιθέσεις) of what is falsely called knowledge (gnōsis γνῶσις)" (1 Tim 6:20). First Timothy rejects sexual and food asceticism (1 Tim 4:1-5). Some are accused of saying that the resurrection has already happened (2 Tim 2:18). These features caused most 20th-cent. scholars to posit gnostic opponents, but recent study has underlined the diversity of ancient Christianities and raised questions about use of the category *gnostic*. The reference to those wishing to be "teachers of the law" (1 Tim 1:7) is elusive; the phrase may refer to Jewish teachers, to Judaizing Christian teachers, or to Christian opponents the author seeks to discredit by association with Judaism. It may target contemporary teachers or attempt to evoke the context of Paul. The author's rejection of food asceticism, women celibates, and women teaching may oppose Christians represented by the legends incorporated into the *Acts of Paul and Thecla,* which not only promotes sexual and food asceticism but also presents Paul as commanding Thecla to "go and teach" (*Acts Paul* 41; *see* THECLA, ACTS OF PAUL AND).

The misogyny of 1 and 2 Timothy, like the commands to slaves, presents a continuing problem to preaching and instruction. But these letters have contributed to the development of theology by preserving early Christian tradition. Their focus on the past and future appearings of Christ would inform the later theology of Advent, Christmas, and Epiphany. They combine the exemplary use of martyrs and an attempt to negotiate and theologize a way to live with empire. The rejection of women's leadership won longstanding allegiance, but celibacy for women received increasing and widespread approval. Thecla became and remained an enormously popular patron of women in a wide variety of Christian cultures. *See* PASTORAL LETTERS.

Bibliography: Jouette Bassler. *1 Timothy, 2 Timothy, and Titus.* ANTC (1996); Raymond F. Collins. *I & II Timothy and Titus.* NTL (2002); Mary Rose D'Angelo. "Εὐσέβεια: Roman Imperial Family Values and the Sexual Politics of 4 Maccabees and the Pastorals." *BibInt* 11 (2003) 139–65; Benjamin Fiore. *The Pastoral Epistles.* SP 12 (2007); Luke Timothy Johnson. *First and Second Letters to Timothy.* AB 35A (2001); Dennis Ronald MacDonald. *The Legend and the Apostle: The Battle for Paul in Story and Canon* (1983); I. Howard Marshall. *The Pastoral Epistles.* ICC (1999); Phillip Towner. *The Letters to Timothy and Titus.* NICNT (2006).

MARY ROSE D'ANGELO

TIN [בְּדִיל bedhil; κασσίτερος kassiteros]. A silvery-gray, easily fusible soft metal that melts at 232° C. Ancients found the metal too soft for most uses; however, around 3500 BCE, they began mixing it with copper to form BRONZE, a strong alloy with a plethora of uses (hence the Bronze Age). Midianite merchants traded tin in patriarchal times, perhaps transporting the metal from mines in the Caucusus (Num 31:22). The Phoenicians imported tin through Tyre (Ezek 27:12). Tin ore may also have been imported and smelted in Syria, since several smelting factories have been found there. The prophet Ezekiel's metaphor of Israel as the dross of various metals—including silver, tin, iron, and bronze—in a smelter's furnace suggests that the Israelites were familiar with the smelting process (Ezek 22:18, 20). Despite its utility, tin was not considered a precious metal; Sirach praises Solomon for having acquired gold as easily as if it were tin (Sir 47:18).

TERRY W. EDDINGER

TIPHSAH tif'suh [תִּפְסַח tifsah]. 1. A city mentioned in a phrase ("from Tiphsah to Gaza") that expresses the geographical extent of Solomon's empire (1 Kgs 4:24 [Heb. 5:4]). Accordingly, Tiphsah should lie at the extreme northeast of Solomon's domain. The name does not appear in cuneiform sources, however, and there is no scholarly consensus as to its location. Xenophon (*Anab.* 1.4, 11, 17) mentions a ford on the Euphrates called "Thapsacus."

2. A city in the Ephraimite hill country attacked by Menahem (2 Kgs 15:16).

STEVE COOK

TIQQUNE SOPHERIM. *See* EMENDATIONS OF THE SCRIBES; QERE-KETHIBH.

TIRAS *ti'*ruhs [תִּירָס *tiras*]. A son of Japheth, son of Noah (Gen 10:2; 1 Chr 1:5), who represents a people who probably dwelled in Asia Minor near the Caspian Sea. Scholars see the name reflected in the **trsh** or **tursha** mentioned on the MERNEPTAH Stele (ca. 1232 BCE)—probably the same group named in an inscription commemorating Ramesses III's victory over the "Sea Peoples." The name may also be related to Τyrsēnoi (Τυρσηνοί) and Τyrrēnoi (Τυρρηνοί), Greek names for the Etruscans.

Bibliography: Alan Henderson Gardiner. *Ancient Egyptian Onomastica* (1947).

JOHN J. AHN

TIRATHITES *ti'*ruh-th*it* [תִּרְעָתִים *tir'athim*]. The Tirathites were a Kenite clan living in JABEZ, a city in Judah. They were associated with scribal activity (1 Chr 2:55). *See* KENITES.

TIRHAKAH tuhr-hay'kuh [תִּרְהָקָה *tirhaqah*]. Tirhakah is an Egyptian ruler mentioned in the Bible, often identified as Taharqa, the fourth king of the Kushite Twenty-Fifth Dynasty, a dynasty whose earlier rulers united Egypt under Napatan rule. Taharqa led an aggressive twenty-six-year reign (690–664 BCE) marked by considerable building activity, war, and the end of his dynasty. In the Bible, "King Tirhakah of Ethiopia" is said to have fought against the Assyrian king SENNACHERIB during the reign of HEZEKIAH of Judah (2 Kgs 19:9; Isa 37:9). According to Egyptian records at Kawa temple, Taharqa defeated King ESARHADDON of the Assyrian Empire in year seventeen, but was driven out of Memphis in year twenty. A few years later, Assyria's next king, Assurbanipal (*see* ASHURBANIPAL, ASSURBANIPAL), was able to force Taharqa back to his native Kushite capital, Napata, where he died. He left Egypt to his nephew Tanutamani, who failed to restore the rule of the dynasty. With Taharqa in exile, the Assyrians left control of Egypt in the hands of the delta prince NECO of the Saite Twenty-Sixth Dynasty. Taharqa's best-known monuments are at the sacred sites of Karnak, Kawa, Gebel Barkal, Medinet Habu, and Sanam. He was buried in a tall pyramid at Nuri, a royal Kushite necropolis.

Bibliography: P. A. Clayton. *Chronicle of the Pharaohs* (1994); J. H. Taylor. "The Third Intermediate Period (1069–664 BC)." *The Oxford History of Ancient Egypt.* I. Shaw, ed. (2000) 330–68; L. Török. *The Birth of an Ancient African Kingdom: Kush and Her Myth of the State in the First Millennium BC* (1995).

KATHLYN MARY COONEY

TIRHANAH turh-hay'nuh [תִּרְחֲנָה *tirkhanah*]. One of several sons of Caleb and his concubine Maacah in the listing of Judah's descendants (1 Chr 2:48).

TIRIA tihr'ee-uh [תִּירְיָא *tireya'*]. Judahite head of a clan, the third of Jehallelel's four sons (1 Chr 4:16).

TIRZAH tihr'zuh [תִּרְצָה *tirtsah*]. 1. One of the five daughters of ZELOPHEHAD from the tribe of Manasseh (Num 26:33; Josh 17:3). Zelophehad had no male heirs; after his death, his daughters successfully petitioned Moses to pass the inheritance on to them (Num 27:1-5). Their claim set a precedent for inheritance among all the Israelites (Num 27:6-11; see also Num 36:5-11). *See* ZELOPHEHAD, DAUGHTERS OF.

JESSICA TINKLENBERG DEVEGA

2. A town in Canaan whose king the Israelites killed in the conquest (Josh 12:24) and which then was apparently allotted to the territory of Manasseh (Josh 17:3-13; *see* MANASSEH, MANASSITES). The name *Tirzah* means "pleasure," "beauty." In the Song of Songs, this plays into the poet's reference to the city as a site of beauty as he parallels his love's beauty to that of the towns of Tirzah and Jerusalem (Song 6:4).

After the conquest, Tirzah plays no role in the narratives until the kingdom of Israel divides upon the death of Solomon. JEROBOAM son of Nebat made Tirzah one of the capitals of his kingdom when it seceded from Judah (1 Kgs 14:17), and the site served as Israel's capital through the reigns of BAASHA (1 Kgs 15:21), ELAH (1 Kgs 16:8), and the abbreviated reign of ZIMRI (1 Kgs 16:15). OMRI besieged the city during Zimri's reign, and Zimri committed suicide through arson as he destroyed the palace (1 Kgs 16:17-18). Omri continued to rule from Tirzah for the first six years of his reign, and he then moved the capital to SAMARIA (1 Kgs 16:23-24). Tirzah was apparently the hometown of MENAHEM (2 Kgs 15:14), one of the last kings of Israel.

Most scholars identify Tell el-Farah (North) with Tirzah. The site is ca. 11 km northeast of Shechem and rests near the head of the Wadi Farah beside two springs that supply ample water for the region. The wadi valley serves as a main route westward from the Jordan Valley into the central mountain region. The site has ruins ranging intermittently from the Neolithic period to the Persian period.

As far as the Israelite period is concerned, the finds of the excavations dovetail well with the biblical account. Roland de Vaux identified Late Bronze Age ruins at the site (Period VI), which may date from the Israelites' campaign when they killed the king (Josh 12:24). The remains, however, are too poorly preserved to identify a town plan. With the Iron Age, several levels appear (Periods VIIa–e). Periods VIIa–b span the 12th–10th cent. BCE and coordinate with the periods of the Israelite monarchy and the advent of Jeroboam's reign. The destruction of Period VIIb may reflect Omri's capture of the site from Zimri (ca. 885 BCE). The subsequent level shows evidence of incomplete construction, which corresponds to Omri's transfer of the capital to Samaria (1 Kgs 16:23-24).

Level VIId (9th–8th cent. BCE) shows obvious social stratification with distinctly elegant structures in the northern part of the town and markedly poorer structures to the south. This kind of social stratification at Tirzah may reflect the object of the prophets' tirades (e.g., Amos) as they lambaste the people of Israel for their lack of concern for the poor.

Bibliography: Roland de Vaux. "The Excavations at Tell el-Farʿah and the Site of Ancient Tirzah." *PEQ* 88 (1956) 125–40.

DALE W. MANOR

TISHBE tish´bee [תִּשְׁבִּי tishbe]. A city of uncertain location associated with the prophet ELIJAH. Six times in the OT, Elijah is referred to as "the Tishbite" (hattishbi [הַתִּשְׁבִּי]; 1 Kgs 17:1; 21:17, 28; 2 Kgs 1:3, 8; 9:36), apparently a reference to his hometown. Other prophets are similarly identified by association with their hometowns, e.g., Ahijah the Shilonite (1 Kgs 11:29). In 1 Kgs 17:1, where Elijah is first introduced in the Bible, the designation "Elijah the Tishbite" is further specified by the phrase mittoshave ghilʿadh (מִתֹּשָׁבֵי גִלְעָד, "one of the sojourners of Gilead"). This expression is linguistically difficult, and scholars typically emend the Hebrew text. Suggested emendations include miyosheve (מִיּשְׁבֵי, "one of the inhabitants") and mittoshbe (מִתֹּשְׁבֵי, "one of the settlers"), but most modern translations follow the LXX and read mittishbe gilʿadh (מִתִּשְׁבֵי גִלְעָד, "from/of Tishbe of Gilead").

Tishbe of Gilead is mentioned nowhere else in biblical or extra-biblical sources prior to the Common Era. The apocryphal book of Tobit (1:2) refers to a Tishbe (NRSV, "Thisbe") in upper Galilee, but this is clearly a different place. Christian pilgrims beginning in the early Byzantine period located Gileadite Tishbe at el-Istib, a site in Transjordan a few miles west of Jabesh-gilead, atop Jebel Ajlun. This identification was based upon the similarity of the names Tishbe and el-Istib, the change in pronunciation presumably having arisen from the transposition of two letters. Further evidence for this identification is provided by a 14th-cent. CE rabbinic text that explicitly links Tishbe with el-Istib and by the presence in the vicinity of a chapel built in the 6th cent. CE dedicated to Mar Elias (Saint Elijah). The association of Elijah with the general area likely predates the chapel.

The equation of Tishbe and el-Istib is, nevertheless, far from certain. Archaeological survey work in the 1940s discovered no signs of Iron Age occupation at el-Istib; this conclusion was confirmed by further field work in 1986. El-Istib's first residents appear to have settled the site no earlier than the late Roman period. The lack of Iron Age material evidence at el-Istib has led some scholars to eliminate it from consideration. Since no other viable candidate has been suggested, one is left with little to say about Tishbe other than that it was located somewhere in Gilead, an expansive territory. Some scholars have noted, however, that sites with Iron Age remains are found in the vicinity of el-Istib; they propose that el-Istib may have migrated from one of these sites to its present location.

BRIAN C. JONES

TISHRI tish´ree [תִּשְׁרִי tishri]. In rabbinic literature, the name of the seventh month in the Hebrew CALENDAR, roughly September–October.

TITANS. *See* GIANTS.

TITHE [מַעֲשֵׂר maʿaser; δεκάτη dekatē]. The Hebrew word maʿaser, "tithe," derives from the verb ʿasar (עָשַׂר, "to take a tenth part"). The Greek equivalents in the LXX and in the NT are dekatē ("a tenth," "a tithe") and apodekatoō (ἀποδεκατόω, "to tithe").

The word occurs first in the OT in the story of Abram's encounter with MELCHIZEDEK, "king of Salem" and priest in that place "of God Most High" (Gen 14:18a). Having heard that the four kings had taken his nephew Lot captive, Abram defeated the kings and liberated Lot. Upon his return King Melchizedek came out to meet Abram in the Valley of Shaveh with bread and wine to offer a blessing to Abram and to the God Most High (Gen 14:18b-20a). Abram responded by tithing all that was his to Melchizedek (Gen 14:20). The date and purpose of this mysterious text make saying anything significant about its use of the tithe concept difficult.

The tithe occurs again in Gen 28:10-22. Fleeing from Beer-sheba and his brother's wrath to Haran, Jacob had a night vision in Luz of the heavenly angels descending upon him and reascending. In the vision, God's promise to make Jacob the father of a nation was confirmed, so when he awoke Jacob declared the place to be Bethel ("the house of God"), erected a standing stone in memorial of the event, and vowed to give to God a tenth part of all that was his (Gen 28:20-22). There is, however, no evidence in the OT that Jacob fulfilled his vow, an embarrassment remedied by early Jewish literature (see below). The passage is usually assigned to the J (or E) tradition, and depending on how one adjudicates the debate about its date and provenance the significance of addressing the tithe in this passage remains in question. If J is dated as early as the 10th cent. BCE, then the passage would provide our earliest evidence of tithing in ancient Israel. If one accepts instead an exilic-era date for J and reads the work as responding to the covenantal bilateralism of the Deuteronomic tradition with the unilateralism of God's promises to the ancestors, then Jacob's failure to fulfill his promised tithe could be read as another instance in which God acts on and confirms the promise for a faithless patriarch (compare Gen 12:10-20; 20:1-18; 26:1-11).

The Deuteronomic tradition offers a more fully articulated view of tithes and tithing. While Deut 12:6, 11 make clear that tithing is necessary, vv. 7 and 17 also certify that the person making the tithe consumes it, but must do so in the presence of the sanctuary. These measures reflect Deuteronomy's emphasis on centralizing cult practice and seeing to the well-being of all Israel. Other practices further evince these two interests of the Deuteronomic tradition. When Israelites live so far from the sanctuary that bringing tithes in their material form would be impracticable, Deut 14:22-27 permits them to convert the tithes into money to be carried more easily to the Temple; there they were to purchase with the money whatever foodstuffs they wished to consume in the presence of the sanctuary as their tithes. Deuteronomy 14:28-29 requires that Israelites also set aside a tithe every third year in their towns to feed the Levites, widows, orphans, and sojourners among them (compare Deut 26:12). It is in light of these principles of charity and centralization that the remaining tithing language in the Deuteronomic corpus should be judged. In 1 Sam 8:15, 17 Samuel uses ʿasar to warn the people seeking a king that he will take a tenth of their grain and their vineyards (v. 15) and of their flocks (v. 17). Whether this passage was a Deuteronomic composition or a source adapted by the Deuteronomists, the stark contrast between a human king who takes a tenth of Israelites' goods for his own use and a God who accepts tithes as offerings and then gives them back to the people of Israel for their own use coheres with the witness of Deuteronomy.

The Priestly tradition shifts the focus to the sanctity of tithes to the Temple and the devotion of their proceeds to the priestly class; it also uses the distribution of tithes to mark out its hierarchical view of the priesthood. Numbers 18:21-24 demands a yearly tithe for the Levites (but not for orphans, widows, and sojourners; compare Deut 14:28-29; 26:12) because it is their due since they have no allotment of land and they approach God in the sanctuary on behalf of all Israel. Numbers 18:25-29 decrees that the Levites must give from their tithe the best tenth to the altar priests, Aaron and his descendants. Numbers 18:30-32 allows the Levites to consume the tithe they receive wherever they wish, so long as they do not profane it. Though it is perhaps not a Priestly composition, Lev 27:30-33 coheres well with this concern to ensure sacerdotal and temple hegemony over the proceeds of the tithes: contrary to Deut 14:22-27, if a layperson wishes to redeem a tithe by offering cash instead of the grain or livestock, then a 20 percent surcharge attaches (Lev 27:30-31); and every tenth creature among one's livestock to "pass under the shepherd's staff" must be turned over as a tithe without substitution, and if a substitution is made, then both the substitute and the creature actually owed are counted as sacred to the Temple and its personnel without possibility of redemption.

Second Chronicles and Nehemiah emphasize provisioning the priests and Levites with tithes without distinguishing between them. Nehemiah 10:38 insists that the priests accompany the Levites when tithes are received from the countryside, and 10:39 indicates that the role of the two priestly classes is to ensure together the proper delivery and distribution of the tithe among the Levites in the Temple (e.g., gatekeepers, singers; compare Neh 12:44). Underscoring the focus on gathering tithes to support the temple personnel, Nehemiah responds to the discovery that the Levites were not receiving their due with a vigorous tithe-collection campaign (Neh 13:10-13). The Chronicler also equalizes the priests and Levites and emphasizes the importance of tithes for their sustenance: after Hezekiah appointed the divisions of the priests and Levites the Chronicler reports that the people's tithe response from the abundance of the land was so great as to produce a surplus for storage (2 Chr 31:2-12).

Tithe language also appears in two prophetic books from two different time periods with two different emphases. The prophet's taunt in Amos 4:4 proves that the tithe was known as early as the 8th cent. BCE and could be derided as meaningless to God in the absence of social justice (Amos 4:4). By contrast, Mal 3:8, 10 demonstrates that by the 5th cent. BCE a prophet could declare tithes so important to God as to determine—through their retention of offering—whether God causes the people of Israel to starve or prosper.

The NT Gospels mention tithing only a handful of times. In Matt 23:23 (par. Luke 11:42), Jesus echoes Amos 4:4, accusing the Pharisees of ensuring payment of tithes while disregarding mercy and justice. Luke redeploys this Jesus saying in the parable of the Pharisee and the tax collector (Luke 18:9-14). Hebrews 7:4-10 also takes up tithing. The author recalls the Melchizedek episode to argue that as a priest of the order of Melchizedek Jesus' priesthood is superior to that of the Levites: not only does Gen 14 indicate that priests of the order of Melchizedek are unbegotten and eternal; Melchizedek also received tithes from Levi inasmuch as the latter was "in the loins of his ancestor [Abraham] when Melchizedek met him" (Heb 7:9-10).

Discussions of tithing in early Jewish literature address two interests: elaborating the biblical traditions about tithing and refining the practice. A vignette that appears first in the *Aramaic Levi Document* and then in *Jub.* 32:1-3 and *T. Levi* 9:1-4 explains Jacob's failure to fulfill his vow to tithe his possessions (Gen 28:22): his omission was for lack of a priest to receive the tithe, but once Levi was appointed to the role Jacob quickly fulfilled his vow. Tobit 1:6-8 reports Tobit's special righteousness in adapting a mixture of the OT practices to pay multiple types of tithes to priests, Levites, and the widows, sojourners, and orphans; he even consumed some with his family in the holy city. Mishnah tractate *Maaserot* reflects the single largest body of evidence for early Jewish thought on the practice.

Early Christian thought on tithing develops predictably. As currency economies developed, money became explicitly subject to tithing (*Did.* 13:7). And reflecting both the early Christian habit of claiming greater seriousness about the practice than the Jewish community and often failing to do so in practice is the story in Acts 5:1-11 of Ananias and Sapphira and their fate for an ungenerous disposition of the proceeds of a rich land sale. *See* FIRST FRUITS; GOVERNMENT, NT; GOVERNMENT, OT; PRIESTS AND LEVITES; TEMPLE, JERUSALEM; WIDOW.

ROBERT KUGLER

TITIUS JUSTUS. *See* JUSTUS.

TITLE ON THE CROSS. *See* INSCRIPTION ON THE CROSS.

TITLES FOR JESUS. *See* CHIEF; HIGH PRIEST; CHRIST; HOLY ONE; LAMB; LORD; MASTER, TITLE OF JESUS; MESSIAH, JEWISH; RABBI, RABBONI; SERVANT; SON OF DAVID; SON OF GOD; SON OF MAN; TEACHER.

TITUS *ti'*tuhs [Τίτος *Titos*]. 1. Titus was a traveling companion of Paul by the time of the visit to Jerusalem recorded in Gal 2:1 (identified as either Acts 11:27-30; 12:25; or 15:1-29; *see* JERUSALEM, COUNCIL OF). From a Gentile background (Gal 2:3), possibly in Antioch, he may have come to faith in Christ through Paul (Titus 1:4). He accompanied Paul for some years on his travels. Paul speaks of him with great affection as "our brother" (2 Cor 2:13) and "my partner (koinōnos κοινωνός) and coworker (synergos συνεργός)" (2 Cor 8:23), terms that Paul rarely or never uses for others. Thus Paul asks Titus to take on the tough assignment of going to CORINTH after the apostle himself had suffered a humiliating visit to that church (2 Cor 7:14-15; on Paul's visit, 2 Cor 2:1-13). Paul regards Titus as sharing his concerns (2 Cor 7:7), notably in Titus' desire to return to Corinth (2 Cor 8:17).

It is debated whether Titus was circumcised. Some take "Titus ... was not compelled to be circumcised" (Gal 2:3) to mean that Titus voluntarily submitted to circumcision in Jerusalem. However, if Titus was circumcised, this fact would have undermined Paul's vehement argument against the necessity of circumcision for Gentile believers (e.g., Gal 5:2-6). Consequently, it is more likely that Titus remained uncircumcised.

Titus acted as Paul's envoy (on this role, see Mitchell) during a crucial period in his up and down relationship with the church in Corinth. Titus seems to have visited Corinth at least three times. First, he went after the sending of 1 Corinthians to begin arrangements for the collection on behalf of the Jerusalem church (1 Cor 16:1-4; 2 Cor 8:6a; *see* COLLECTION, THE). After Paul's "painful visit" to Corinth (2 Cor 2:1), Titus was the bearer of Paul's "severe letter" (2 Cor 7:8), which led to reconciliation between Paul and the Corinthian church (2 Cor 7:9-16). This visit may have been the occasion to revive interest in the collection, once it became clear that the "severe letter" was received well (2 Cor 8:6b[?]). Finally, Titus delivered 2 Corinthians and thus was part of the delegation charged with completing the collection (2 Cor 8:16-24). As a key person in this difficult period, Titus seems to have acted with great diplomacy, for Paul describes Titus' conduct toward the Corinthians as exemplary (2 Cor 12:18).

Titus is not mentioned in Acts. Assuming that Titus 1:4-5 preserves authentic memory of Titus, it locates him in Crete later in life as Paul's delegate overseeing the churches there. Tradition identifies his burial place as the Basilica of St. Titus in Gortyn, Crete. *See* MANIUS, TITUS; PASTORAL LETTERS; TITUS, LETTER TO.

Bibliography: C. K. Barrett. "Titus." *Essays on Paul* (1982); 118–31; F. F. Bruce. *The Pauline Circle* (1985); M. M. Mitchell. "New Testament Envoys in the Context of Greco-Roman Diplomatic and Epistolary Conventions: The Example of Timothy and Titus." *JBL* 111 (1992) 641–62.

STEVE WALTON

2. Titus Flavius Vespasianus (39–81 CE) became emperor as the elder son of his predecessor Vespasian, the founder of the Flavian Dynasty. He was a popular ruler whose reign lasted just over two years (79–81) until his death (almost certainly) from natural causes.

Titus benefited from his father's influence long before the latter became emperor: he was raised in the imperial court during the reigns of Claudius and Nero. Titus later served in the army with distinction as a junior officer in Britain and especially Germany. When Nero entrusted his father with the responsibility for repressing the Jewish revolt (*see* JEWISH WARS), the youthful Titus was given charge of a legion. After Vespasian withdrew to engage in a successful struggle for the imperial throne, Titus assumed command, conquering Jerusalem after a difficult siege in 70 CE. He was a competent general who inspired the loyalty of his troops, though on the strength of his association with his father he tended to receive greater credit than was his due.

After two brief marriages, Titus, while in Judea, began an affair with Queen Berenice. She later followed him to Rome, remaining there for some years until he, recognizing that their relationship was a political liability, reluctantly ended it soon after he became emperor.

Bibliography: Brian W. Jones. *The Emperor Titus* (1984).

THOMAS A. J. MCGINN

TITUS, APOCRYPHAL EPISTLE OF. The *Epistle of Titus disciple of Paul, Concerning the State of Holiness* is a Latin pseudepigraphon dated to the late 4th or early 5th cent CE, extant in only one late 8th-cent. manuscript. Written to both male and female ascetics, it promotes a form of asceticism the text calls *sanctimonium*. The men, called "eunuchs," should be unfettered by carnal love and live in solitude without any contact with women. The women, sometimes referred to as "brides of Christ" and other times as "virgins," should never associate with a man, since God is their master. Those who remain pure will receive heavenly rewards; those who do not will experience eternal torment. The text berates both sexes for associating with each other. Although the exact nature of the domestic situation is unknown, earlier scholars have described this relationship as a form of nonsexual cohabitation, because the text refers to it as a false marriage. However, the text actually faults the men for using unrelated women, presumably the female ascetics addressed in the text, as servants.

To support its agenda of *sanctimonium*, the *Apocryphal Epistle of Titus*—in language that vividly describes life in hell as well as heaven—uses more than 100 references from Christian and Jewish biblical and noncanonical sources. Traditionally placed within a Spanish Priscillianist milieu because of its use of extracanonical material, more recent scholarship has demonstrated similarities between the *Apocryphal Epistle of Titus* and a wide range of Christian late antique ascetic material. *See* APOCRYPHA, NT.

DEBRA J. BUCHER

TITUS, LETTER TO ti'tuhs [Πρός Τίτον Pros Titon]. A letter that presents Paul instructing his representative, Titus, on how to order the communal life of Pauline churches on Crete.

A. Structure of the Letter
B. Detailed Analysis
  1. Author and date
  2. Characterization
  3. Genre
  4. Church structure
C. Theological and Religious Significance
Bibliography

A. Structure of the Letter

The salutation expands the standard reference to sender, recipient, and greeting (1:1*a*, 4) with one of the longest descriptions in the Pauline corpus of the apostle's commission and the message of salvation (1:1*a*-3).

The letter body (1:5–3:11) comprises instructions to Titus as the ideal church leader. The first part (1:5-16) details the commission given him by Paul: to appoint

elders/overseers singled out by their virtuous lives and empowered to "preach with sound doctrine" and to refute those who oppose it as in the example provided. Citing the Cretan poet Epimenides as a prophet, the letter castigates opponents as liars, and warns especially against "those of the circumcision" and against teachers and commandments that see impurity everywhere (1:10-16).

The rest of the letter body is devoted to exhortation by sound teaching (2:1–3:11). The household code (2:1-10), introduced by a command to "teach what is consistent with sound doctrine," provides instruction on virtuous behavior for elder men (v. 2), elder women (v. 3), younger women (vv. 4-5), younger men (vv. 6-8), and slaves (vv. 9-10). This sound teaching is backed up with a formulaic proclamation that God's saving grace has appeared (vv. 11-14). Additional commands (2:15–3:1) incorporate instruction on how to behave toward "rulers and authorities" (3:1-2). Another formulaic proclamation of salvation explains "our" transformation through baptism (3:3-8*a*). The final instruction urges Titus to instruct believers in good works and to avoid both theological controversies and "anyone who causes divisions" (3:8*b*-11).

A conventional letter ending incorporates travel plans, requests, and the concluding greetings. Paul urges Titus to join him in Nicopolis and to supply Zenas the lawyer and Apollos for their journey (3:12-13), followed by a general instruction on good works (v. 14). The letter ends with greetings from those with Paul and to "those who love us (Paul) in the faith" and a farewell (3:15). The phrase "those who love us" may be crafted to exclude the false teachers.

B. Detailed Analysis

1. Author and date

Like 1 and 2 Timothy, Titus is widely regarded as pseudonymous, the product of a late 1st-cent. or early 2nd-cent. Paulinist seeking to borrow Paul's authority to address problems in the church after the apostle's death. Similar to 1 Timothy in form, content, and diction, Titus is usually attributed to the same author. Small but significant differences could be attributed to a different author, different traditions, or changes in style and thought of a single author. For example, Titus has no thanksgiving, never uses kyrios (κύριος) for either God or Christ, and never refers to a "church." Rather than forbidding women to teach men (1 Tim 2:12), the letter commands older women to teach younger women (2:4-5).

The first evidence for Titus comes from the end of the 2nd cent. and the beginning of the 3rd. Two portions of the letter appear on a leaf of papyrus from around 200 CE (Papyrus 32), and citations of the letter as Paul's appear in Irenaeus (*Haer.* 1.16.3; 3.3.4), Tertullian (*An.* 20.3), and Clement (*Protr.* 1.5, 7). Thus, Titus must be earlier than 180 CE. Scholars who attribute the letter to Paul place it late in his career, before his martyrdom under Nero (d. 68). With 1 and 2 Timothy, Titus formed part of a second grouping among the thirteen letters of Paul as letters to individuals along with Philemon.

2. Characterization

The Paul of this letter introduces himself as "a slave [NRSV, "servant"] of God and an apostle of Jesus Christ" (1:1). His apostleship is a divine commission to bring the elect to belief and to the knowledge of the truth as defined by godliness (eusebeia [εὐσέβεια], "piety"). "Slave of God" (not of Christ, as in Rom 1:1; 1 Cor 7:22; Gal 1:10; Eph 6:6; Phil 1:1) may reflect a prophetic status for this Paul (compare Jer 25:4; Amos 3:7).

Titus is addressed as Paul's "loyal child in the faith we share" (1:4), a description that implies that his teaching is inherited directly from Paul. Titus was the Gentile associate whom Paul refused to circumcise on his visit to "pillars" in Jerusalem (Gal 2:1, 3). In 2 Corinthians Paul calls him "brother" (2:13) and "partner and co-worker" (8:23); he traveled between Paul and the Corinthians for their mutual consolation (2:13; 7:6-7, 13-16), and at Paul's entreaty, undertook to supervise the collection in Corinth and accompany Paul to Jerusalem with it (8:6-7, 16-24; 12:17-18). Second Corinthians uses a single word (parakaleō [παρακαλέω]), which means both "console" (7:6-7, 13-14) and "entreat" (8:4, 6, 17; 12:18), in these passages. In Titus the word always means "entreat" or "appeal" (1:9).

3. Genre

Titus has been classified as an "official deliberative letter" reiterating the commission Paul bestowed on Titus. But the distinction between official and friendly letters is blurred; Pseudo-Demetrius observes that official letters frequently use the conventions of friendly letters to persuade (*Epistolary Types* 1). Like most other early Christian letters, Titus uses both the language of friendship and of family. A later epistolary theorist speaks of "mixed" letters, and includes three types that recall "Paul's" charge to Titus: the entreating, the didactic, and the refuting or accusatory (Pseudo-Libanius, *Epistolary Styles* 4.41, 3, 27, 28; 7.31, 32, 92). It seems likely that the author signals the genre of Titus in stipulating that an overseer must be able to "entreat (NRSV, "preach") by sound teaching (NRSV, "doctrine")" and "refute those who contradict it." The letter refutes and accuses the opponents explicitly in 1:10-16 and indirectly in 3:9-11, while entreating with the sound teaching of the household code (2:1–3:8) and exhorting Titus to do likewise (2:15; NRSV, "exhort and reprove").

4. Church structure

One problem is the apparently synonymous use of presbyter (NRSV, "elder") and "bishop" (or overseer) in 1:5-9. The criteria for appointing elders and the virtues of the overseer are very similar to those for the overseer/bishop of 1 Tim 3:1-7. Scholars who wish to distinguish the two roles offer various solutions: that overseers are drawn from among the elders; that 1:7-9 is a careless interpolation from 1 Timothy; that the author draws on an older source. The best solution seems to be to recognize that these terms overlap in Titus.

C. Theological and Religious Significance

Like 1 and 2 Timothy, Titus incorporates much traditional matter. The important role of the household code suggests that the virtue godliness (eusebeia) has much the same meaning as in 1 Timothy—appropriate devotion and duty toward the deity and all to whom one is related. The sound teaching of the household code reflects conventional Roman household duties, including Roman stereotypes of older women's vices (slander and the habit of drinking wine) and slaves (talking back, pilfering); the counsel on elder women, younger women, and slaves each closes with an explanation that the submission commanded here protects the reputation of the community in the outside world. The vituperative misogyny of 1 and 2 Timothy is lacking. There is no advice to masters; it is possible, though unlikely, that the communities on Crete are not envisioned as including slave owners.

As do 1 and 2 Timothy, Titus refers to God and Christ as savior, and uses the imagery "appear" or "manifest" of his coming. This language evokes biblical images of God, reinterpreted through the images and language used in cults of Greek savior gods and kings, as well as the Roman imperial cult. Two formulaic proclamations employ this terminology for the manifestation of God's saving deed: "There has appeared the saving grace of God to all human beings ..." (2:11; author's trans.; NRSV, "For the grace of God has appeared, bringing salvation to all") and "When the goodness and human-loving nature (philanthrōpia [φιλανθρωπία], NRSV, "loving kindness") of God our savior appeared ..." (3:4). Clement of Alexandria cites these passages as illustrative of the "new song" of Christ (*Protr.* 1); they may be fragments of early Christian hymns. While 1 and 2 Timothy look back to the first appearance of Christ and forward to his future appearance, Titus focuses on the present appearance of divine grace in the moral transformation of those who are being saved through baptism (3:5-6). This moral transformation produces lives that are "self-controlled, upright, and godly" (2:12), characterized by three of the empire's cardinal virtues: moderation, justice, and piety. Between the two proclamations of the appearance of God's grace, the author counsels subjection to "rulers and authorities" (3:1-2), strongly suggesting the relation of the savior and appearance imagery to the imperial order. At the same time, Titus 2:13, which celebrates the "manifestation of the glory of our great God and Savior Jesus Christ," also reminds the readers of a different order. Titus exhibits the same dialectic of resistance and accommodation as do the letters to

Timothy. Titus 2:13 appears to be one of the NT's very few explicit identifications of Jesus as God.

Bibliography: I. Howard Marshall. *The Pastoral Epistles.* ICC (1999); Jerome T. Quinn. *The Letter to Titus.* AB 35 (1990); William A. Richards. *Difference and Distance in Post-Pauline Christianity: An Epistolary Analysis of the Pastorals* (2002).

MARY ROSE D'ANGELO

TIZITE t*iz'*it [תִּיצִי titsi]. A designation given to JOHA, son of Shimri and brother of Jediael, one of the MIGHTY MEN of David's army. The term *Tizite* only occurs in 1 Chr 11:45. Nothing further is known of the village or family the name represents.

TOAH toh'uh [תּוֹחַ toakh]. An ancestor of Heman, a Kohathite musician (1 Chr 6:34). His name in a similar list is NAHATH (1 Chr 6:26), and in the ancestry of Samuel he is called TOHU (1 Sam 1:1). *See* KOHATH, KOHATHITE.

TOB tob [טוֹב tov; Τουβίας Toubias]. Biblical authors consistently locate Tob on the margins of Israel's settlement, but they may have used the toponym to refer to two different places in Transjordan. The story of Jephthah suggests a northern location in Hauran, east of the Sea of Galilee. Jephthah was originally from Gilead but fled to Tob and became a bandit leader (Judg 11:3, 5). Also, the Ammonites hired mercenaries from northern regions to fight David; Tob supplied 12,000 men (2 Sam 10:6, 8).

A southern location is suggested by references in the Zenon Papyrii (mid-3rd cent. BCE) to a "land of Toubias," probably near the Iraq el-Emir, about 10 mi. south by southwest of modern Amman. But according to 1 Macc 5:13, Judas Maccabeus led a rescue mission to the land of Tob, apparently in Hauran. Some have suggested that this may refer to a group of refugees from the "land of Toubias" who fled north.

ADAM L. PORTER

TOB-ADONIJAH tob'ad-uh-n*i'*juh [טוֹב אֲדוֹנִיָּה tov ʾadhoniyah]. One of several Levites sent by Jehoshaphat to teach in the cities of Judah (2 Chr 17:8). The Greek, Syriac, and Arabic witnesses omit the name, which is probably the result of a copying error. A scribe either wrote the preceding name in the list of Levites (Tobijah) twice (albeit in somewhat different forms), or combined the two preceding names, Adonijah and Tobijah, and included that name too.

STEVE COOK

TOBIAH toh-b*i'*uh [טוֹבִיָּה toviyah; Τουβαν Touban]. 1. The head of a family in Zerubbabel's group of returnees from exile, mentioned in par. lists in Ezra 2:60; Neh 7:62; and 1 Esd 5:37. They were among those who were unable to prove their Israelite descent using genealogical records.

2. An Ammonite by birth and/or the Persian governor over Ammon. Mentioned frequently in the book of Nehemiah, Tobiah was a prominent figure in the restoration period, who, along with SANBALLAT, opposed Nehemiah's efforts to rebuild Jerusalem's walls (Neh 2:10, 19; 4:3, 7 [Heb. 3:35; 4:1]; 6:1-19). He took up residence in the Temple while Nehemiah was away from Jerusalem, but Nehemiah evicted him upon his return (Neh 13:4-9).

DEREK E. WITTMAN

TOBIAS toh-b*i'*uhs [Τωβίας Tōbías]. Meaning "God is my good." 1. Tobias, the only son of Tobit and Anna. By following the instructions of the angel RAPHAEL Tobias brings about in the resolution of the two problems in the book of Tobit. Tobias burns a fish liver to drive out the demon afflicting his bride Sarah and leads her in prayer. Back in Nineveh he applies the fish gall to his father's eyes, thus curing his blindness. With Sarah he had seven sons. He died at the age of 117 in Ecbatana. *See* TOBIT, BOOK OF.

2. Tobias, ancestor of Hyrcanus (2 Macc 3:11), who deposited money in the Temple during the high priesthood of ONIAS II (mid-3rd cent. BCE). He was possibly the Tobias who, according to Josephus (*Ant.* 12.160), married the sister of Onias II and was the father of Joseph, the grandfather of Hyrcanus, and the eponymous ancestor of the Tobiads, tax collectors for the Ptolemies and later the Seleucids.

IRENE NOWELL, OSB

TOBIEL toh'bee-uhl [Τωβιήλ Tōbiēl]. Means "God is my good." Father of Tobit (Tob 1:1), who died while Tobit was still a child (Tob 1:8). *See* TOBIT, BOOK OF.

TOBIJAH toh-b*i'*juh [טוֹבִיָּה toviyah, טוֹבִיָּהוּ toviyahu]. 1. A Levite whom King Jehoshaphat sent along with other Levites, priests, and royal officials throughout Judah to teach the people the law (2 Chr 17:8).

2. One of the Babylonian returnees who donated some of the silver and gold used to make a crown (or "crowns," as the NRSV observes in a footnote) that symbolized the participation of the Jewish Diaspora in the rebuilding of the Temple (Zech 6:10-14).

LJUBICA JOVANOVIC

TOBIT, BOOK OF toh'bit [Τωβίτ Tōbit]. The name *Tobit* is a short form of either TOBIEL ("God is my good") or TOBIAS ("The Lord is my good"). The book of Tobit, which tells the story of two families united through marriage, is both an adventure story and a moral tale. Two faithful people pray to God out of deep distress: Tobit, who has been blinded, and Sarah, whose bridegrooms are killed by a demon. In answer to their prayers, God sends the angel RAPHAEL, who guides

Tobit's son Tobias on a dangerous quest and teaches him how to heal both sufferers.

A. Structure of the Book

The structure of the book of Tobit is shaped by three factors: the maladies, followed by their healings, and the journey between these two events. After a brief title (1:1-2) the story begins with a description of Tobit's past goodness (1:3-22), his affliction (2:1-14), and his prayer for death (3:1-6). Sarah's affliction and prayer are reported next (3:10-15). This opening section ends with the information that the angel Raphael has been sent to heal them both (3:16-17).

The second major section (4:1–6:18) portrays the journey. It begins with Tobit's decision to send his son, Tobias, on a journey to recover funds deposited with a friend, and his exhortation to follow Tobit's example in leading a good life (4:1-21). When Tobias goes to search for a guide, he meets Raphael immediately and brings him to meet Tobit (5:1-22). During the ensuing journey, Tobias catches a threatening fish and is instructed by Raphael on the use of the fish for healing both Tobit and Sarah, whom Raphael tells him to marry (6:1-18).

The third major section (7:1–11:18) tells the story of the healings. Sarah is given to Tobias in marriage (7:1-18) and follows Raphael's instructions to drive away the demon afflicting her (8:1-21). Raphael goes to RAGES to collect the funds that inspired the journey (9:1-6). As their son celebrates his wedding feast, Tobit's parents fret over the delay (10:1-13). Finally, Tobias returns home with his new bride and, following Raphael's instructions once more, heals his father's blindness; another wedding feast is celebrated (11:1-18).

The loose ends of the story are wrapped up in a three-part conclusion: the revelation of Raphael's identity (12:1-22); Tobit's prayer of praise and thanksgiving (13:1-17); and a final report on the lives and deaths of the main characters (14:1-14).

B. Detailed Analysis

1. Textual tradition and original language

The textual tradition of the book of Tobit is very complex. Until the discovery of the QUMRAN scrolls in the mid-20th cent., the major witnesses to the book were in Greek and Latin. Three distinct recensions are extant in Greek. The first, known as G^I, is found in the 4th-cent. manuscript known as Vaticanus (B) and the 5th-cent. manuscript Alexandrinus (A). The language of this recension is good idiomatic Greek. It is sometimes called the "Short Recension."

The second Greek witness, G^{II}, is represented in the manuscript Sinaiticus (S) from the 4th–5th cent. A gap in S (4:7-19b) can be filled in from an 11th-cent. minuscule, MS 319, which contains 3:6–6:16. To reconstruct a second gap in S (13:6-10), G^I and the Old Latin (VL; see below) must be used. This "Long Recension" has a strong Semitic flavor and is about 1,700 words longer than G^I.

The third Greek witness, G^{III}, is represented only in fragmentary minuscules, MSS 44, 106, 107. It contains only 6:9–12:22 and seems to be a composite of the previous two recensions.

The Old Latin translation of the book (VL) reflects but is not identical to G^{II}. It is much more useful for comparison with the Greek manuscripts and filling lacunae than the Vulgate (Vg), which Jerome claims he translated in one day from the Aramaic with the help of an interpreter. The Vulgate contains several passages that are not found in either the Greek recensions or the Qumran manuscripts. The book of Tobit is not found in the Syriac Peshitta; the Syriac witness is represented primarily by a Syro-Hexaplaric text (7th–8th cent.) and agrees generally with G^{III}.

The discovery in Qumran Cave 4 of some sixty-nine fragments of five manuscripts—four in Aramaic and one in Hebrew—clarified the origins of Tobit considerably. The Qumran witnesses, dating from the 1st cent. BCE to the early 1st cent. CE, represent and even expand the recension found in G^{II} and VL. The Qumran fragments, however, contain only about one-fifth of the total book.

Study of the Qumran manuscripts has led most scholars to conclude that G^{II} is primary and that the original language of the book of Tobit was Semitic, probably Aramaic. Most recent translations, including the NRSV, have opted to use G^{II}, with help from VL and the Qumran fragments, as their base text.

2. Author, date, and place

Situating the book of Tobit in a particular time and place has proved very difficult. Two elements indicate the point after which the book must have been written: 1) The phrase "Book of Moses" (Tob 6:13; 7:11-12) is found elsewhere only in Ezra–Nehemiah (Ezra 6:18; Neh 13:1) and Chronicles (2 Chr 25:4; 35:12), in the first half of the 4th cent. BCE. 2) The Prophetic Books are considered authoritative (see Tob 1:8; 6:13; 7:11-13; 14:4), as they are in Sir 48:23–49:10, dated around 180 BCE. The book must have been written before the mid-2nd cent. BCE. There is no evidence of the mid-2nd-cent. persecution under ANTIOCHUS IV Epiphanes, which inspired the Maccabean revolt (168–142 BCE), nor is there any indication of a belief in resurrection, which is found in 2 Maccabees (see 7:9, 11, 14, 22-23, 37; 12:41-45). Thus a likely date for composition is the early 2nd cent. BCE.

Three areas are commonly suggested as the place where the book of Tobit was written: Egypt, Mesopotamia, or Judea. The marriage formula in Tob 7:11 is similar to a formula found in a manuscript at Elephantine, Egypt, and a manuscript of *The Story of Ahiqar*, who is also a minor character in Tobit, was also found at Elephantine. But Egypt seems to be a faraway place when the demon ASMODEUS flees there (8:3). Since the story takes place in the Diaspora, Mesopotamia is also proposed as a likely site of origin. But the author of the book does not know the distance between the Mesopotamian cities of ECBATANA and Rages (Tob 5:6) or basic Assyrian history, including the succession of Assyrian kings (Tob 1:15-22). The third possible place is Judea. While it is true that the setting of the story is the Diaspora, there is great interest in the Jerusalem Temple and its ritual (Tob 1:4-8; 13:9-17; 14:5-7). Thus Judea is the most likely candidate for the origin of the book.

3. Canonicity

The book of Tobit is clearly a Jewish book. Its characters are Jewish; it promotes Jewish values and was found among the manuscripts at Qumran. But the book of Tobit was not included in the final listing of books in the Hebrew canon. It was, however, translated into Greek by Jewish scribes and became part of the LXX. Christians, who also did not agree on the book's canonicity, used the LXX version. Throughout the early centuries, Christian writers quoted from the book. In the 3rd cent. Origen relied on the book to describe the work of angels (*Princ.* 1.8.1; *Or.* 11.1; *Cels.* 1.25). Another 3rd-cent. writer, Cyprian of Carthage, praises Tobit's good works and his patience when he is blinded (*Eleem.* 5; *Pat.* 18). Augustine refers frequently to the book of Tobit (e.g., *Civ.* 1.13; 13.22; *Doctr. Chr.* 18.27; *Conf.* 34.52).

Not all Christian writers regarded the book as canonical, however. In his Easter letter, in which he outlines the canon, Athanasius identifies the book of Tobit as noncanonical but finds it useful for instruction and says it should be read by Christians (*Ep. fest.* 39.7). Jerome also did not consider it canonical and did not want to translate it, since it was not part of the Hebrew canon. He agreed only reluctantly as a favor to two bishops who were friends of his.

Because the book of Tobit is not included in the Jewish Scriptures, it did not become part of the Protestant canon of the OT. It is included in the Roman Catholic canon, however, because the 16th-cent. Council of Trent declared the whole Vulgate canonical. In the Catholic canon the book is placed in the midst of the historical books between Nehemiah and Job, along with Judith, Esther, and Maccabees. In translations made under Protestant auspices, such as the NRSV, the book of Tobit is either not included or is put in a section called "Apocrypha."

4. Literary qualities

The genre of the book of Tobit combines elements of romance, of miracle story, and of biography. In G^{II} the tale begins as an autobiography with Tobit telling his life story (1:1–3:7). A third-person narrator takes up the story in 3:7. The plot turns on two miracle stories, the healings worked by Tobias according to the instructions of the angel Raphael. Several characteristics of a romance appear in the story of Tobias. To accomplish the healings, Tobias sets out on a quest. He struggles with a dangerous animal, which, when it is conquered, provides the life-giving material for the healings. He wins a bride by freeing her from a demon. Everyone lives happily ever after.

A major literary characteristic of the book of Tobit is irony. Irony results from a situation in which the audience or reader knows more than the characters. The angel Raphael is an ironic character. The narrator persists in telling the reader that he is an angel (5:4; 6:1-2, 4-5, 7), but the characters do not understand his identity until the end (12:15). This irony is heightened by Tobit's comments to Tobias and to his wife, Anna, that "a good angel" will accompany their son on his journey (5:17, 22). He does not know how true his words are. RAGUEL's action of digging the grave for Tobias is both humorous and ironic. Even as Raguel prepares to bury Tobias, the reader already knows that he is safe and that the demon Asmodeus has been banished to Egypt.

The technique of simultaneity foreshadows the linking of the families of Tobit and Raguel. Tobit and Sarah are grieved and pray for relief on the same day (3:7). The prayers of both are heard at the same time and Raphael is sent to heal both (3:16-17). At the same time each of them returns from prayer to the family group (3:17).

5. Intertextuality

The author of Tobit has drawn upon many other biblical passages. The connections are most evident between Tobit and the pentateuchal books of Genesis and Deuteronomy. There are several direct allusions to Genesis. The conversation between Tobias and Raguel at the arrival in Ecbatana (Tob 7:3-5) is an almost exact repetition of the conversation between Jacob and the shepherds in Haran (Gen 29:4-6). Like the servant Abraham sent to find a wife for Isaac, Tobias will not eat until the matter of his marriage to Sarah is settled (Gen 24:33; Tob 7:11). In his prayer on the wedding night, Tobias recalls God's creation of Adam and Eve and quotes Gen 2:18 (Tob 8:6). This marriage, like the marriage of Isaac and Rebekah, has been decreed by God (Gen 24:50; Tob 7:11).

Other characters are modeled on the ancestors. Tobit, like Abraham, walks in righteousness before God (Tob 1:3; Gen 15:6; 17:1) and is tested by God

(Tob 12:14; Gen 22:1). Both Tobit and Abraham are convinced that an angel will act as guide on an important journey (Tobias' in Tob 5:17, 22; and the servant's in Gen 24:7, 40). Jacob gives a long farewell discourse to his sons in Gen 49, and Tobit gives two speeches of farewell to Tobias (Tob 4:1-19; 14:3-11). The hospitality of Raguel and EDNA (Tob 7:9; 8:19) is patterned after that of Abraham and Sarah (Gen 18:1-8). Tobit's wife Anna is accused of deceiving her blind husband with a goat in a scene reminiscent of Rebekah's deception of Isaac (Tob 2:12-14; Gen 27:9-13). Raguel's daughter Sarah, like the ancestral Sarah, is childless and suffers the scorn of her maids (Tob 3:7; Gen 16:4). Finally, burial is a significant issue in both books (see Gen 23:4-20; 47:29-31; 49:29–50:13; Tob 1:17-19; 2:3-8; 8:9-12; 14:10).

Deuteronomy is the other significant pentateuchal source. The plot of Tobit is a reflection on the theory of retribution outlined in Deut 28: doing good will bring blessing and doing evil will bring curses. Tobit, a good man, is struck blind while performing a good deed; his wife points out the challenge to the theory of retribution: "Where are your righteous deeds?" (Tob 2:14). Tobit's healing demonstrates both the truth of the theory and the ambiguity of its application. His second farewell discourse elaborates on retribution (14:3-11). On the national level, the fate of Assyria, symbol of great wickedness, which Tobit anticipates, confirms the other side of the theory (Tob 14:4-5, 15). The significance of tithing (Tob 1:6-7; see Lev 27:30-33; Num 18:21-32; Deut 14:22-29) and the uncleanness resulting from contact with a corpse (Tob 2:9; see Num 19:11-22) are pentateuchal issues.

Prophetic allusions also appear in the book. Tobit's vision of a glorious Jerusalem (Tob 13:11-17) suggests the prophetic words of Isaiah of the exile (Isa 54:11-12; 60:1-14; 66:10, 14). In his farewell discourse (Tob 14:4), Tobit refers to the oracle of the prophet Nahum concerning the fall of Nineveh (G^{II}). G^{I} reads Jonah here, but Tobit's words contradict the message of Jonah. There may be an allusion to Jonah, however, in the great fish that tries to swallow Tobias' foot but becomes instead a means of healing (Tob 6:3).

The story of Tobit parallels the story of Job, another good man whose story challenges the deuteronomic theory of retribution. Tobit's emphasis on almsgiving appears too in Sirach (see 3:30; 7:10; 12:3; 17:22; 29:12; 40:24), also a 2nd-cent. book. The language of the prayers in Tobit echoes the language of the psalms. The careful reader will find many more allusions, especially to Genesis.

Just as the book of Tobit draws on material from the rest of the OT, so also the NT authors echo themes found in Tobit. The description of the new Jerusalem in Rev 21 uses much of the same imagery as that found in Tob 13. The portrayal of Jesus' ascension in Luke 24 suggests Raphael's ascension in Tob 12. The three pillars of pharisaic Judaism—prayer, fasting, and almsgiving—are recommended in both Tob 12:8 and Matt 6:2-18. Tobit exhorts Tobias to keep the golden rule, formulated negatively in Tobit (4:15), whereas Jesus exhorts his followers to the same rule, formulated positively (Matt 7:12; Luke 6:31). Revelation describes seven angels who stand before God and mediate human prayer (Rev 8:2-4), echoing Raphael's description of himself in Tobit (Tob 12:12, 15). The encouragement in the letter to the Hebrews to show hospitality because some have unknowingly entertained angels (Heb 13:2) describes the experience of the households of both Tobit and Raguel.

C. Theological Contribution

1. Prayer

The book of Tobit has been called a primer of prayer. Almost 15 percent of the verses in this book are devoted to the prayers of several of the main characters: Tobit (Tob 3:2-6; 11:14-15; 13:1-17), Sarah (Tob 3:11-15), Tobias (Tob 8:5-8), and Raguel (Tob 8:15-17). Sarah also declares her "Amen" at the end of Tobias' prayer (Tob 8:8). (In 8:15, the NRSV indicates that Edna joins in Raguel's prayer.) Other descriptions of prayer occur frequently: Tobit prays for the success of his son's journey (5:17); Gabael blesses God when he sees Tobias (9:6); Tobias praises God for the success of his journey (10:13; see 14:15).

The response of both Tobit and Sarah to their afflictions is to pray. Both pray for relief. Tobit believes that only death will end his distress (3:6); Sarah ponders that solution also, but allows God more flexibility (3:15). At the same moment that their prayers are ended, God hears and answers them (3:16-17). Neither will experience God's answer, however, until much later (8:3-9; 11:13-14).

The actions of the characters suggest the proper way to pray. Both Tobit and Sarah go to a private place to pray: Tobit to the courtyard and Sarah to an upper room (3:17). Tobit weeps as he prays (3:1), and Sarah spreads her hands and faces the window, possibly looking in the direction of Jerusalem (3:11). Their prayers and the prayers of all the other characters begin with praise of God.

Another important teaching concerns the frequency of prayer. Tobit blesses God continually (14:2), exhorts his son to bless God at all times (4:19; 14:8[9]), and in his hymn of joy calls everyone to bless the Lord (13:6, 10). Raphael tells Tobias to pray as part of the exorcism of the demon afflicting Sarah (6:18). Later he instructs Tobit and Tobias to bless God every day (12:6, 17-18).

The communal aspect of prayer is evident. The characters consistently bless one another: Tobit blesses Raphael (5:17) as well as Tobias and Sarah and her parents (11:17); Raguel and Gabael both bless Tobias (7:7; 9:6); Tobias blesses Raguel and Edna (10:13).

2. Angels and divine providence

The book of Tobit has the most developed portrait of angels in Scripture. The angel Raphael is a major character in the story. Raphael, whose name means "God heals," is sent by God to bring about the healing of Sarah and Tobit (3:17). The word *angel* means "messenger," and Raphael's primary task is instruction. He instructs Tobias regarding the use of the fish to heal both Tobit and Sarah (6:4-9; 11:4); he also instructs Tobias and Tobit regarding prayer. He reminds Tobias of Tobit's instruction regarding marriage (6:16) and exhorts Tobias and Tobit to practice almsgiving, fasting, and prayer (12:8). He informs Gabael of Tobit's need to collect the deposited money and invites him to Tobias' wedding celebration (9:5). As part of his task as messenger, Raphael carries the prayers of Tobit and Sarah to God and brings God's testing and healing to Tobit (12:12-14). Finally, he reveals his own identity and mission to Tobit and Tobias (12:11-15).

Raphael also guides and protects Tobias on the journey. He leads Tobias straight to Raguel's house where he will find a bride, even though Tobias did not initially know this was the journey's purpose (7:1). He saves him from the fish and binds the demon Asmodeus in Egypt to protect Sarah from further affliction (8:3). He leads the happy couple back to Nineveh (11:1).

Raphael is characterized by speed and knowledge. He appears as soon as Tobias goes to look for a guide (5:4). He claims to know all the routes to Media and its geography (5:6, 11). He knows what to do with the fish and that Sarah is a near relative of Tobias (6:8-14). He does not know everything, however; he only presumes that Tobias and Sarah will have children (6:18).

The angel Raphael is a messenger of God's providing care, but he is not the primary agent of the healings. To heal both Tobit and Sarah, God works through the human character Tobias. Raphael teaches Tobias how to bring about the healings and then disappears from the scene. Tobias begins tentatively, expecting the angel to do the work of arranging the marriage and healing Sarah (7:9). But as soon as Raguel hesitates, Tobias takes over in the marriage negotiations and Raphael recedes from the action (7:10-13). Later in the bedroom Tobias remembers Raphael's instructions (8:2); it is he who burns the fish's organs and leads Sarah in prayer (8:3-8). Raphael's binding of the demon only secures the healing. Tobias is also the main actor in the healing of his father (11:10-14), urged on by Raphael's reminder (11:1-4, 7-8). God's providence works primarily through human beings.

3. Marriage and family

The story of Tobit revolves around marriage and family. Tobit instructs his son to follow his example and marry someone within the clan relationship as was the custom (Tob 1:9; 4:12-13). He knows from experience that a faithful wife will be a great support to her husband. His wife, Anna, stayed with him when he was exiled and stripped of his property (1:19-20). When he was blinded, she became a working mother, taking outside employment in order to support the family (2:11).

Theirs is a marriage of equals, with each party able to speak honestly and sometimes sharply (2:13-14; 5:18-20; 10:7). Even in disagreement, however, it is evident that they love each other and their son. Tobit's deepest grief comes not from his blindness but from his wife's challenge (3:1). When her worry about her son leads her to strike out at her husband, he comforts her (5:21-22; 10:6) although he worries too (10:1-3). She is eyes for her blind husband, watching for their son's return. Her words when he appears reveal her love for both men: "Look, your son is coming" (11:6).

Tobias and Sarah begin their marriage with prayer (8:4-8). Tobias recognizes the gift of marriage in the story of Adam and Eve and prays that he and Sarah may live together to a happy old age. Their marriage joins two families. When the newlyweds leave Ecbatana, Raguel declares that his daughter Sarah is now also the daughter of Tobit and Anna; Edna claims Tobias as her son (10:12). In his joyful welcome, Tobit names Sarah his daughter four times (11:17). The families have become one.

Women are respected in this book. Anna is the most independent. She works to support the family when Tobit is blinded. She receives a bonus for work well done (2:12). She speaks her mind without hesitation, but she is not unkind. Edna supports Raguel and does most of the talking when the strangers arrive. She prepares Sarah for the wedding and, at Raguel's request, sends the maid to discover whether Tobias is alive or not (8:11-12). Sarah is the least prominent of the women. She declares her sorrow to God in prayer and she answers the "Amen" to Tobias' prayer on the wedding night. Otherwise she does not speak. She is not asked if she wishes to marry Tobias or if she wishes to go to Nineveh. She is given away by her parents and welcomed warmly by her in-laws. She bears Tobias seven sons.

Tobias and Sarah welcome children (14:3); they also honor their aged parents. Tobit had exhorted Tobias to care for his mother, respecting her for the dangers she faced in bearing him, and asked Tobias to give him a proper burial and to bury Anna by his side (4:3-4; 14:10). Tobias honors his father's wishes (14:11-12). He treats Raguel and Edna with great respect also and sees to their burial (14:13). The example of family love and fidelity is richly shown in this book.

In the Roman Catholic Church the book of Tobit has been a traditional source for marriage instruction and the wedding ceremony. Readings at the ceremony may be chosen from the book of Tobit and the words of Raguel are often used for the blessing of the newlyweds (Tob 8:15-17).

4. Hospitality and almsgiving

Two virtues are characteristic of the relationship with those outside the immediate family: hospitality and almsgiving. Both families are hospitable. Tobit will not eat his festival dinner until a poor person is invited to share it with him (2:2). Presumably, Anna has fixed the special meal. Later when Tobias brings Raphael in, Tobit welcomes him warmly (5:14). Raguel and Edna welcome visitors also and prepare a feast for Tobias and Raphael at their arrival in Ecbatana (7:1-9). Both families hold lavish wedding celebrations for the new-lyweds with many invited guests (8:19-20; 9:2, 5-6; 11:17-18).

The Greek word for almsgiving, eleēmosynē (ἐλεημοσύνη), occurs more often in Tobit than in any other OT book. This book, along with Sirach, forms a bridge between the OT and NT understanding of alms-giving. Through most of the LXX this word is used to describe a characteristic of God or of righteous persons, such as justice, mercy, or loyalty (e.g., Pss 33:5; 103:6; Prov 3:3; 19:22). In the NT eleēmosynē has moved to action, connoting primarily a gift or other kind deed to support someone in need (e.g., Matt 6:2-4; Acts 3:2-3). All four meanings are found in Tobit: God is generous in mercy (Tob 3:2) and so is Tobit (Tob 7:7; 9:6). The primary use of the word has to do with Tobit's chari-table acts of feeding the hungry, clothing the naked, and especially burying the dead (Tob 1:3, 16-17; 14:2). He exhorts Tobias to follow his example (Tob 4:3-4, 7-11, 16-17; 14:8-9). Raphael declares almsgiving better than either prayer or fasting and promises that it saves from death and wipes away sin (Tob 12:8-9). Tobit reiterates Raphael's promise: injustice brings death but almsgiving brings life (Tob 14:10-11). *See* CANON OF THE OLD TESTAMENT.

Bibliography: Jeremy Corley and Vincent Skemp, eds. *Intertextual Studies in Ben Sira and Tobit: Essays in Honor of Alexander A. Di Lella, OFM* (2005); Joseph A. Fitzmyer. *Tobit.* Commentaries on Early Jewish Literature (2003); Carey A. Moore. *Tobit: A New Translation with Introduction and Commentary.* AB 40A (1996); Stuart Weeks, Simon J. Gathercole, and Loren T. Stuckenbruck, eds. *The Book of Tobit: Texts from the Principal Ancient and Medieval Traditions: With Synopsis, Concordances, and Annotated Texts in Aramaic, Hebrew Greek, Latin, and Syriac* (2004).

IRENE NOWELL, OSB

TOCHEN toh´kuhn [תֹּכֶן *tokhen*]. The fourth in a list of five towns inhabited by members of the tribe of Simeon prior to the reign of David (1 Chr 4:32). Its precise geo-graphical location is unknown. It does not appear in a similar list of Simeonite towns found in Josh 19:7.

TOGARMAH toh-gahr´muh [תֹּגַרְמָה *togharmah*]. The genealogy of Gen 10 presents Togarmah as the de-scendant of Gomer the son of Japheth the son of Noah (10:3). The parallel genealogy of 1 Chr 1 offers the same information. Ezekiel 38:6 describes the house of Togarmah (NRSV, "Beth-togarmah") as "from the remot-est parts of the north," and seems to be the basis for the view that the descendants of Togarmah populated and

gave their name to the region west of the headwaters of the Euphrates in central Turkey, and to a city in the region. In Ezekiel's oracle concerning Tyre, the house of Togarmah is described as Tyre's trading partner, trading in draft-horses, riding-horses, and mules (Ezek 27:14). The region was known for horse breeding. Included in an account of Suppiluliumas' destruction of the king-dom of Mitanni is a reference to *Tegarama*, biblical Togarmah (*ANET*, 318).

JOHN I. LAWLOR

TOHU toh´hyoo [תֹּחוּ *tokhu*]. The father of Elihu and the son of Zuph, an eponymous ancestor of the region (1 Sam 1:1) and a forebear of Samuel. The genealogy in 1 Sam 1:1 establishes Samuel's Ephraimite descent. In order to legitimate Samuel's Levitical lineage, however, the Chronicler makes his ancestors Kohathite Levites (*see* KOHATH, KOHATHITE). Tohu appears under slightly different names in these lists: "NAHATH" in 1 Chr 6:26 [Heb. 6:11] and "TOAH" in 1 Chr 6:34 [Heb. 6:19].

LJUBICA JOVANOVIC

TOI toi [תֹּעִי *to'i*, תֹּעוּ *to'u*]. Toi ruled the Neo-Hittite kingdom of Hamath, approximately 120 mi. north of Damascus, during the period of David's ascendancy in the 10th cent. BCE. After David crushed an Aramean co-alition that included Hamath's neighbor and perennial enemy Hadadezer of Zobah (2 Sam 8:3-7), Toi sent his son with gifts of gold, silver, and bronze to congratulate David and presumably to sue for peace (2 Sam 8:9-10). David accepted the gift and apparently did not invade Hamath, leaving it as a buffer between David's growing empire and the Mesopotamian kingdoms to the east. *See* HAMATH, HAMATHITE.

TONY W. CARTLEDGE

TOIL. *See* CRAFTS; ESCHATOLOGY OF THE NT; LA-BOR; OCCUPATIONS; SERVANT; SLAVERY; TOOLS.

TOKHATH. *See* TIKVAH.

TOLA toh´luh [תּוֹלָע *tol'a*]. As it is not certain whether this name is related to the identical Hebrew noun refer-ring to the color red (Lam 4:5, NRSV "purple"), which was extracted from a special worm, the meaning of the name is not clear. 1. The eldest of Issachar's four sons (Gen 46:13; 1 Chr 7:1) and ancestor of the Tolaites (Num 26:23; 1 Chr 7:2 lists the names of six sons).

2. A judge (Judg 10:1-2), the first in a list of five so-called minor judges (Judg 10:1-5; 12:8-15), as op-posed to major judges, charismatic leaders and deliver-ers such as Gideon. Information about Tola is scarce and given in a stereotyped pattern. His name, genealogy (embracing the tribe of Issachar, his father Puah and his grandfather Dodo), and location (Shamir in the hills of Ephraim, a place otherwise unknown) are given in Judg 10:1. Judges 10:2 mentions the duration of his activity

(twenty years) followed by a death-and-burial notice. As with all minor judges, the text does not tell us what exactly his function was. The Hebrew shafat (שָׁפַט) means either to judge or to govern. Tola fulfilled what was clearly an administrative function during a peaceful period. Some scholars think that the list of minor judges preserves old historical material. Others regard the passage as fiction because the stereotyped listing reminds them of the succession notices in 1 and 2 Kings, as if modeled on these. In addition, the striking similarity of the names mentioned in Judg 10:1 and Num 26:23-24 made scholars suppose that Judg 10:1-2 was a fiction shaped on the genealogy in Numbers. Even if the material is old, it was obviously integrated into the present context by assimilating the list to the language of the deliverer stories by using the verbs "to rise" and "to deliver" (Judg 10:1). In any case, the list including Tola fills in the space between the narratives on Abimelech and Jephthah. See JUDGE; JUDGES, BOOK OF.

Bibliography: Daniel I. Block. *Judges, Ruth.* NAC (1999) 336–339; Robert G. Boling. *Judges.* AB 6A (1975) 186–89; A. H. D. Mayes. *Judges.* OTG (1985) 30–31.

KARIN SCHÖPFLIN

TOLAD. *See* ELTOLAD.

TOLL. *See* TAX BOOTH; TAX COLLECTOR; TAXES, TAXATION.

TOMB [קֶבֶר qever, קְבוּרָה qevurah; μνῆμα mnēma, μνημεῖον mnēmeion, τάφος taphos]. A place of interment for human remains. All known human societies have a preferred treatment of human remains, a ritual process by which a deceased human body is transported to and deposited in its final resting place. In many cases, this ritual process concludes in a tomb, as the remains of the deceased are placed in a built structure, either above ground or underground.

When tombs are mentioned in the OT and the Gospels, they generally are presumed to be located underground, either in natural caves (see Gen 23:9, where Abraham asks for the "CAVE of MACHPELAH" as a burial place for Sarah) or in humanly constructed subterranean chambers (see Mark 15:46, where the body of Jesus is laid in a tomb "that had been hewn out of the rock"). Archaeological evidence shows that the typical characteristics of these underground tombs underwent specific changes over time.

A. Pre-biblical Burial Practices in the Ancient Near East
B. Burial Practices in the Old Testament Era
C. Burial Practices in the Hellenistic Period
D. Burial Practices of the Early Roman Period
  1. Ossuaries
  2. First-century changes in tomb architecture

E. Burial Practices in the Second Century
Bibliography

A. Pre-biblical Burial Practices in the Ancient Near East

Prior to the periods of history described in the Bible, an assortment of types of underground tombs had already become common in the ANE. In the Paleolithic and Neolithic Aages, e.g. (up to 4500 BCE), simple pit burials in the floors of houses were typical. Human remains were interred in shallow cavities dug into the dirt floors of human dwellings. By the Chalcolithic Period (4500–3300 BCE), pit burials in the floors of houses were still widely distributed, but burial places were increasingly located outside of—and often at some distance from—human dwelling places. In particular, caves began to be used as final resting places for the dead. By the time of the Bronze Age (3300–1200 BCE), burial in underground chambers was widespread, and several different types of rock-cut tombs had become common. Most frequent was the so-called "shaft" tomb, which customarily included most (or all) of the following features: a narrow passageway several feet long, but wide enough for only one person to pass through at a time (hence the term *shaft*), served as the means of entrance to a roughly hewn underground burial chamber. The burial chamber was normally about 8–12 ft. in diameter (if roughly circular) or about 8–10 ft. on a side (if roughly square or rectangular), with a ceiling of only about 4–5 ft. high. Shaft tombs frequently included more than one burial chamber, and these multi-chambered tombs could hold the remains of many people, usually several generations of an extended family group.

The patterns of burial practices evident in these Bronze Age shaft tombs cohere with the systems of kinship relations among the people who used them. In Tomb #10 in Field #1 at Gezer, from the Late Bronze Age, e.g., bodies were placed in a cleared space near the center of the burial chamber. Although there was no particular pattern to the orientation of the bodies, all were carefully arranged in an orderly manner, apparently by means of a ritual process. Notable in this tomb was the practice of secondary burial—i.e., the reburial of the bones after the flesh of the bodies had decayed. When decomposition of the flesh of a body was complete, the bones were moved to one side of the chamber, away from the primary burials in the center. Such practices suggest that the kinship connections between the living and dead continued to be recognized after death, as the living returned to the tomb to perform secondary burial for their deceased family members, and as successive generations of the extended family continued to use the same tomb over time. This pattern, i.e., secondary burial in underground tombs by groups of extended kin, would persist in the ANE throughout the periods of history described in the OT and NT. Other examples of Bronze Age shaft tombs with secondary burial have been found at MEGIDDO and BETH-SHAN; at these sites some of the tombs have as many as four or five burial chambers.

While rock-cut underground tombs—of which the shaft tomb was the most common—were widely used during the Bronze Age, they were by no means the only form of interment at that time. Three other types of burial places also appeared frequently: 1) pit burials, which were still frequent along the coastal plain throughout the Bronze Age; 2) dolmens: megalithic stone structures built above ground in the shape of a large table; these were most common along the Rift Valley in the Early Bronze Age (3300–2000 BCE); and 3) cist tombs: stone-lined trenches or graves, which also were common in the coastal plain.

B. Burial Practices in the Old Testament Era

By the Iron Age I (1200–1000 BCE), the era during which the biblical stories of early Israel are set, tombs in the lands of the Bible were beginning to conform to a more stable and well-defined typological pattern. Of particular interest for readers of the Bible is the emergence during the Iron II (1000–721 BCE) of the so-called "bench tomb," a type of tomb that was extremely frequent within the territory of the ancient kingdom of Judah. These rock-cut tombs reprise and update many features of Bronze Age shaft tombs. They are typically located, e.g., at some distance from human dwellings. Access is through a narrow door, which leads into an underground burial chamber, of which there may be more than one. In bench tombs, the burial chambers are typically square (or slightly rectangular), usually about 8–10 ft. on a side, with a low ceiling about 5 ft. high. Other features, however, are new. The term "bench tomb," e.g., comes from the fact that a bench, approximately waist high, runs around three sides of each burial chamber. The side in which the entrance or doorway was situated usually does not have a bench. Bodies were laid upon these benches in primary burial, and many benches include pillow-shaped head-rests for the corpses. In addition, the area under one of the benches—there is no standard pattern for which one it might be—is hollowed out so as to create a space under the bench that served as a repository for bones in secondary burial. An example of this type of tomb is the complex of tombs located today on the grounds of the École biblique in East Jerusalem (these tombs are also often referred to as the "St. Etienne tombs"). An interesting feature of the tombs at the École biblique—a characteristic that is not especially widespread in Iron Age bench tombs—is that the ceilings are higher than is typical, about 6 ft. The so-called "Garden Tomb," mistakenly identified as the tomb of Jesus, also belongs to the complex of Iron II tombs at the École biblique. It lies just outside the wall of the École, very close to the rest of the tombs in the complex. Although the "Garden Tomb" is revered by many Christian pilgrims as Jesus' tomb, it is instead a thoroughly typical example of an Iron II bench tomb. Tomb #106 at Lachish supplies yet another good example of this very common tomb type.

In Iron II bench tombs, the ritual process of burial unfolded in two stages: 1) primary burial: at the time of death, the body of the deceased was laid on one of the benches; and 2) secondary burial: several months later, when decomposition of the flesh of the corpse was complete (or nearly so), the bones were gathered into the repository hollowed out beneath one of the benches. It is striking to observe that a well-known and recurrent biblical idiom coheres remarkably well with the archaeology of these Israelite bench tombs. When referring to death and burial, the Bible often says that a person "slept and was gathered to their ancestors" (e.g., Gen 25:8; 35:29; Judg 2:10; 2 Kgs 22:20). In a typical Iron Age bench tomb, the bones of the dead would eventually all wind up beneath one of the benches in a bone repository. Over long periods of time, the repository would come to hold the bones of all the deceased members of the family or extended kin group who used the tomb. And when an individual's bones were placed into the repository at the time of secondary burial, that individual's identity would disappear into the collective ancestral heap. The biblical idiom "he/she slept and was gathered to the ancestors" vividly reflects the material culture of the practice of secondary burial in an Israelite bench tomb.

The biblical concept of SHEOL (she'ol שְׁאל) also has significant consonances with the typical Iron II bench tomb. When the Bible uses she'ol with reference to the afterlife, it generally denotes a gray and shadowy, filmy existence in which the dead persist without much joy or comfort. The resemblances between she'ol and Iron II bench tombs are so strong that in some biblical texts she'ol is a synonym for *tomb* (e.g., Pss 49:14; 141:7; Prov 1:12; Isa 38:18).

One further point of consonance between the Iron II bench tomb and daily life in ancient Israel is also of interest here. Archaeologists have noted that the plan of a typical bench tomb closely resembles the plan of a typical Israelite four-roomed house. The plan of these houses, which were extremely common in the villages, towns, and cities of ancient Israel, is organized into four rooms. Starting at the front of the house, three rooms run parallel to each other, while at the back of the house a fourth room runs perpendicular to the other three. The plan of an Iron II bench tomb is organized on the same pattern: starting at the entrance of the tomb, two benches and the central work area run parallel to each other, while at the back of the tomb, another bench runs perpendicular to the other two benches and the work area. The floor plan of the tomb, in other words, is a homology of the floor plan of the house. Such homologies between houses and tombs have been observed by anthropologists and archaeologists in many other cultures, places, and historical periods, and they suggest that in these cultures the tomb was regarded as a house or place of residence for the dead.

C. Burial Practices in the Hellenistic Period

Iron Age (and earlier) patterns of tomb architecture persisted through the Persian period (520–332 BCE), with bench tombs, cist tombs, and shaft tombs all appearing in the archaeological record. During the Hellenistic period (332–63 BCE), however, several significant new developments appeared, brought about by cultural and political pressures from the West. In Greece and Rome it was customary for wealthy and prominent families to construct large and richly ornamented tombs along the roads leading into and out of their city. In this way the families' prestige and social status was symbolically represented on a prominent scale. During the Hellenistic period, this type of monumental tomb construction began to appear in the lands of the Bible. The most famous examples are the large and richly ornamented tombs in the Kidron Valley directly east of the Old City of Jerusalem. Traditionally (but incorrectly) known as the tomb of Absalom, the tomb of Zechariah, and the tomb of the Bene Hezir, these tombs actually belonged to prominent Jerusalem families of the Hellenistic period. Their exterior architecture includes features that were generally typical of Hellenistic tomb construction. Each tomb, e.g., features a prominent marker (called a nefesh [נֶפֶשׁ]) in the shape of either a pyramid or a tholos.

An additional example of Hellenistic tomb architecture is "Jason's tomb," located today in a residential neighborhood in West Jerusalem. Like the tombs in the Kidron Valley, "Jason's tomb" (so-called because of an inscription found in its interior) is built on a monumen-

tal scale, and it also features a pyramid as well as two exterior courtyards.

Other new developments during the Hellenistic period included changes not only in the exterior architecture of tombs but in their interiors as well. A low shelf still ran around three sides of the burial chamber, although now the height of the shelf was significantly lower than the bench that had typified an Iron II tomb. During the Hellenistic period, the shelf was about knee-high rather than about waist-high. Also significant during this period is the emergence of two new types of burial niches that began to appear, carved into the walls above the shelf. The two types of niche are: 1) the arcosolium niche (pl. arcosolia), a wide, shallow, arch-shaped niche carved along the wall of the burial chamber, in which a body could be laid parallel to the wall; and 2) the loculus niche (pl. loculi), a long, narrow slot carved deep into the wall of the tomb, in which a body could be laid perpendicular to the wall of the tomb. These niches had already become popular elsewhere in the Mediterranean, and they made their first appearance in the lands of the Bible during the Hellenistic period at MARESHAH, in the famous painted tombs. Because an arcosolium niche covered considerably more wall space than a loculus niche, a burial chamber with arcosolia could typically contain only three or four such niches (i.e., one on each wall of the chamber). A loculus niche, by contrast, took up far less wall space than an arcosolium, so that a burial chamber with loculi might contain as many as twelve or more such niches (i.e., three or four on each wall). This difference accounts for the

Erich Lessing /Art Resource, NY

Figure 1: Rock-cut tombs of the Bene Hezir (left), and the so-called tomb of Zechariah (right). Kidron Valley, Jerusalem, Israel.

fact that, although both kinds of niche were widespread during the Hellenistic period, the loculus niche was by far the more common of the two.

In addition, the practice of secondary burial also changed during the Hellenistic period. During the Iron Age, bones had typically been gathered into a repository beneath a bench in the burial chamber. But since the typical shelf in a Hellenistic tomb was of lower height, secondary burial into repositories beneath such low shelves was no longer practical. Now bones were often gathered into an entirely separate chamber within the tomb. In "charnel houses," as these bone-gathering chambers are often called, bones were gathered into a collective heap, with individual identity disappearing into the pile. Yet the process of secondary burial could entail the relocation of bones from one chamber to another within the tomb. Jason's Tomb supplies an example of this practice: this tomb had two chambers, one with loculus niches for primary burial, and the other a charnel house with no niches. At primary burial, bodies were laid in loculus niches in the burial chamber, and at secondary burial the bones were carried into the charnel house and piled together there. No primary burials were found in the charnel house, and no secondary burials were found in the chamber with the loculus niches.

Yet even with these significant new developments, tombs from the Hellenistic period still preserved many of the important characteristics from earlier eras. Despite the significant increase in the scale of outward ornamentation, e.g., the actual entrance to the tomb itself was still typically quite small (ca. .50 × .80 m). Thus even though a tomb might be so large as to include a courtyard and an ornamented gateway, the entry through which one passed into the burial chambers was still (as it had been since the Bronze Age) small enough to accommodate only one person at a time. In the Hellenistic period, in other words, the opening through which one passed from outside into the burial chambers of a tomb was still small enough to be covered by a stone. Once inside the tomb, the burial chambers were also still of the same general dimensions as they had been for centuries, i.e., roughly square or slightly rectangular, approximately 8–10 ft. on a side. As in earlier periods, most burial chambers had low ceilings, except in larger and more ornate tombs.

D. Burial Practices of the Early Roman Period

In the Early Roman period (i.e., 63 BCE–132 CE), the closing phase of the archaeological chronology of tombs in the world of the Bible, long-standing characteristic features of tomb architecture and burial practices were once again preserved, while innovations also emerged. Secondary burial in underground chambers by extended kin groups continued to be the norm, with tombs located at some distance from human dwellings. Tomb entrances were, as before, small enough to be covered by a stone. Burial chambers were still roughly square or

rectangular, approximately 8–10 ft. on a side, with low ceilings. A low shelf, about knee-high, still ran along the walls of a burial chamber. Many tombs featured more than one burial chamber. Arcosolium and loculus niches continued to proliferate, with loculi appearing more frequently than arcosolia. A famous (and monumental) example of these features is located today in East Jerusalem on the Nablus Road. Mistakenly identified as "the tombs of the kings" mentioned in the books of Chronicles, this tomb is still popularly known by that name. With a broad forecourt (26 × 27 m square and 8.5 m deep) and a facade ornamented with reliefs in floral and geometric motifs, the neatly executed tomb features eight burial chambers, each with several arcosolia and/or loculi. The tomb is from the 1st cent. CE, having belonged to Queen Helene of Adiabene and her family, proselytes to Judaism. Another well-known (but much smaller) example of Early Roman tomb architecture comes from the Church of the Holy Sepulcher, where three rock-cut loculus niches in a small cave are preserved near the main rotunda of the church, indicating that an Early Roman tomb was once located on the site.

New developments during the Early Roman period included the rare use of round stones to block the entrance to a tomb. Virtually all tomb entrances in this period were blocked by square or rectangular stones, many of which were worked so as to fit tightly into the opening. But in two cases—the so-called "Tomb of the Kings" and the so-called "Herod's tomb"—round (or "rolling") stones were used to block the entrance. Both of these tombs are located in Jerusalem, and both are among the largest and most splendid tombs in the city. The resurrection narratives in the Gospels refer to "rolling" stones, a depiction that would probably have evoked the impression of a splendid upper-class tomb. It is likely that these references are part of the Gospels' well-established tendency to dignify the circumstances of Jesus' burial.

1. Ossuaries

Certainly the most important development during the Early Roman period, however, was the rise of the ossuary as a container for bones in secondary burial. Beginning early in the reign of Herod the Great, Jews in and around Jerusalem began to gather bones in ossuaries rather than in charnel rooms or other forms of secondary deposition. An ossuary is a chest or box, typically hollowed out from a single block of the limestone that is so common in the area around Jerusalem. In keeping with their function, ossuaries are proportional in size to the large and long bones of the body (skull and femur, e.g.). Thus an average ossuary for an adult measures about 24 in. × 14 in. × 12 in., with smaller measurements for the ossuaries of children. Most ossuaries are plain and undecorated, but many are ornamented with motifs typical of Jewish art during the Early Roman period (geometric and floral designs, e.g.), and some are inscribed with the names of the person whose bones are contained inside. With the use of an ossuary, the long-standing custom of secondary burial took on a new and slightly different form: at primary burial, the body was laid in a niche or on the shelf, and when decomposition was complete (or nearly so), family members returned to the tomb and collected the bones in an ossuary. The ossuary might then be placed virtually anywhere in the tomb, including in a niche, on the shelf, or on the floor. The use of an ossuary thus preserved the identity of the deceased individual long after their death. During the Iron Age, by contrast, when repositories in "bench" tombs were used, or during the Hellenistic period, when charnel houses were common, secondary burial had caused the identity of the individual to be dissolved into a collective ancestral heap of bones. An ossuary, however, especially one that was inscribed with the name of the deceased, protected the individuality of the deceased from dissolution. The reasons for this Early Roman change in the practice of secondary burial are currently a matter of scholarly uncertainty.

Most ossuaries have been found in Jewish tombs from the Early Roman period in the area of Jerusalem. Although they continued to be used sporadically into the Late Roman period (i.e., 250–324 CE), the frequency of their appearance in the archaeological record drops off substantially in the early 2nd cent. CE. It is likely that the violence of the Bar-Kochba Revolt, along with the exclusion of Jews from the city of Jerusalem after the revolt, effectively destroyed the stone-carving industry that had previously been producing ossuaries.

2. First-century changes in tomb architecture

To this point the discussion has covered tombs from the land of the OT and the Gospels. In the urban Roman world of Paul and his congregations, however, tomb architecture was significantly different from that which was typical in the land of Jesus. In cities of the Roman Empire during the 1st cent. CE, tombs were customarily built not underground but above ground, with construction materials and techniques that were commonly used in houses. Roman tombs thus included many of the principal architectural features of a Roman house, such as brick walls, a front door, a pediment over the door, windows, interior frescoes and wall paintings. Once again the well-known homology between tomb and house can be observed. Roman tombs were customarily located along the main roads leading into and out of a city.

In the Latin West, including the city of Rome, cremation was the most common form of burial, so that tombs were equipped with small niches in which cremation urns could be placed. A typical niche is approximately 2 ft. × 2 ft. × 1 ft. and is furnished with holders for two cremation urns. A tomb of this type (called a columbarium; pl. columbaria) could sometimes hold rather large numbers of cremation urns: at Ostia and Isola Sacra, e.g., several tombs were large enough to include dozens of niches. Many tombs belonged to individual families, but every city in the empire included residents whose social and economic circumstances could not support the construction of a family tomb. Such people usually joined a *collegium*, i.e., a voluntary association that provided burial services, including a tomb, for its members.

Many Roman tombs feature stone couches extending outward from the front of the tomb on either side of the main entrance. These couches were used in the Roman custom of feasting with the dead. On regularly scheduled festive occasions, including certain annual holidays as well as the anniversaries of deaths, Romans went to the cemetery to eat and drink with the dead. Because the dead were believed to participate, food and drink were provided for them as well. Romans called these meals *refrigeria,* because they were believed to be "refreshing" to both the living and the dead. The arrangement of couches on either side of the main entrance to some tombs symbolically recapitulates the customary arrangement of couches in a Roman dining room (or *triclinium*), placing the dead in the position of the host.

In the Greek East, by contrast, inhumation (not cremation) was the most common form of burial: bodies were typically placed in niches, usually of the arcosolium type.

E. Burial Practices in the Second Century

During the second half of the 2nd cent. CE, the dominant burial practice in the Latin West changed from cremation to inhumation. The reasons for this change are unclear, but when the aristocracy in the city of Rome made the change, the rest of the Western Empire rapidly followed. Since burial by inhumation requires considerably more space than cremation, overcrowding in and among tombs soon became a problem. By the late 2nd cent. CE, catacombs had emerged as a practical solution. Along the roads leading into and out of Rome, burial places were now built underground. Some families had private burial rooms in a catacomb, but most corpses were interred in rectangular niches carved into the walls of the long narrow passageways, which made up a catacomb. Each of these rectangular niches was large enough to contain an individual body (ca. 5 ft. × 1 ft. × 2 ft.). Once the body was placed inside, the niches were then sealed, often with roof tiles from houses. When needed, space for more burials could easily be created, either by lengthening the passageways or by lowering the floors of the passageways. As a result, the passageways in most catacombs extend for many miles in complicated labyrinthine networks, and in every passageway burial niches run from the bottom to the top of the walls, often as many as nine or ten high. The presence of Christians in the catacombs of Rome can be documented as early as the 3rd cent. CE, but despite many popular stories, Christians never sought refuge from persecution therein. *See* BIER; BURIAL;

DOLMENS; EMBALM, EMBALMING; IMMORTALITY; MONUMENT; MOURNING; OSSUARIES; PIT; TOMBS OF THE KINGS.

Bibliography: Elizabeth Bloch-Smith. *Judahite Burial Practices and Beliefs about the Dead* (1992); Rachel Hachlili. *Ancient Jewish Art and Archaeology in the Land of Israel* (1988); Byron R. McCane. *Roll Back the Stone: Death and Burial in the World of Jesus* (2003); Ian Morris. *Death Ritual and Social Structure in Classical Antiquity* (1992); Jocelyn M. C. Toynbee. *Death and Burial in the Roman World* (1971).
                                                    BYRON R. MCCANE

TOMB OF JESUS. *See* HOLY SEPULCHRE; RESURRECTION, NT.

TOMBS OF THE KINGS [קִבְרוֹת הַמְּלָכִים qivroth hammelakhim]. A phrase designating the burial places in Jerusalem reserved for the kings of Judah. The phrase appears three times in 2 Chr 24–32, each time in the context of a narrative about the reign of a king of Judah. In particular, each use of this phrase serves as the crowning touch in a negative evaluation of a king of Judah, as the narrative closes with the observation that a particular king was not buried in the tombs of the kings. In 2 Chr 21:20, e.g., a thoroughly critical account of the reign of Jehoram concludes with the comment that he was buried in the city of David, "but not in the tombs of the kings." The phrase appears again in 2 Chr 24:25, where a negative judgment of the reign of Joash ends with the statement that "they did not bury him in the tombs of the kings." Similarly, in 2 Chr 28:27 the Chronicler's criticism of Ahaz closes with the observation that he was buried in Jerusalem, "but they did not bring him into the tombs of the kings of Israel."

The rhetoric of these texts presupposes the existence of burial places in Jerusalem reserved for the kings of Judah. It also presumes that the kings of Judah were supposed to be buried in these "tombs of the kings." This presumption is also shared by three other texts in 2 Chronicles, even though these texts do not use the exact phrase "the tombs of the kings." The rhetoric of these passages, however, is consonant with the texts that do use that phrase. In each of these cases the Chronicler remarks that a king or priest was buried among the kings of Judah, and this remark serves as the crowning touch in a positive evaluation of the reign of that king or priest. In 2 Chr 24:16, e.g., the priest Jehoiada is said to have been buried "in the city of David among the kings." In 2 Chr 26:23, King Uzziah is laid to rest "near his ancestors in the burial field that belonged to the kings." And in 2 Chr 32:33, Hezekiah is buried "on the ascent to the tombs of the descendants of David."

Outside the book of 2 Chronicles, however, mention of burial places in Jerusalem reserved for the kings of Judah is rare, and the phrase "the tombs of the kings" does not appear. In 2 Kings, e.g., narratives about the reigns of Judahite kings typically end with the observation that a king was buried "with his ancestors in the city of David" (e.g., 12:21; 15:7, 38; 16:20). Occasionally, 2 Kings reports that a ruler of the Northern Kingdom was buried in Samaria "with the kings of Israel" (e.g., 2 Kgs 14:16, 29), but this expression is used only for the kings of Israel, never for the kings of Judah. Finally, Neh 3:16, from the same general time period as 2 Chronicles, refers to "the graves of David" (qivre dhawidh קִבְרֵי דָוִיד) and notes the locations of these graves in relation to the rebuilt wall of Jerusalem.

It thus appears that traditions in circulation at the time of the writing of 2 Chronicles included a general conception that some burial places in Jerusalem had been reserved for the kings of Judah, and that these burial places had been the preferred final resting places for the kings of Judah. Second Chronicles draws upon these impressions and employs the phrase "the tombs of the kings" as part of its program of theological evaluation of the kings of Judah.

Based on these biblical references, archaeologists have occasionally attempted to locate and identify "the tombs of the kings." To this point, however, no such effort has been successful. In 1863, e.g., F. de Saulcy mistakenly identified a large tomb located just north of the Old City of Jerusalem on the Nablus Road as "the tombs of the kings." The tomb, the largest and most magnificent ancient tomb yet found in Jerusalem, is still popularly known as "the tombs of the kings." With a broad forecourt (26 × 27 m square and 8.5 m deep) and a facade ornamented with reliefs in floral and geometric motifs, the neatly executed tomb features eight interior rooms, each with several arcosolia and/or loculi for the disposition of corpses. Several decorated sarcophagi were also found within. However, the tomb is not from the Iron Age (1200–586 BCE) but from the Early Roman period (63 BCE–132 CE). It was built during the 1st cent. CE, and it belonged to Queen Helene of Adiabene and her family, proselytes to Judaism. In 1920, R. Weill proposed that several barrel-vaulted tombs found in the City of David, just south of the Old City, were the "tombs of the kings." These tombs were badly disturbed by quarrying before excavation, and their archaeological features are unfortunately not entirely clear, but the architectural features that have been exposed are not consistent with a date any earlier than the Late Hellenistic period (200–63 BCE), and it is possible that the tombs may be as late as the Byzantine period (324–638 CE). *See* INSCRIPTIONS; TOMBS.

Bibliography: M. Kon. *The Tombs of the Kings* (1947); F. de Saulcy. *Voyage en Terre Sainte* (1865); R. Weill. *La Cité de David* (1947).
                                                    BYRON R. MCCANE

TONGS. *See* SNUFFERS.

TONGUE [לָשׁוֹן lashon; γλῶσσα glōssa]. The word *tongue* refers to the muscular organ in the mouth of the human body that extends from the throat to the teeth and lips, providing the facility to speak words. For example, Jesus heals a man with a speech impediment by "releasing" his tongue so that he can speak (Mark 7:33, 35; compare Luke 1:64). A few uses of *tongue* in the Bible are generic references to this physical part of human anatomy (Ps 22:15 [Heb. 22:16]; Lam 4:4; Luke16:24). However, *tongue* is most often used as a metonym for speech. This extends beyond speech capacity, however, to the differentiation of human speech into distinct languages (Deut 28:49) and the use of this for counting up the diversity of tribes and nations (Gen 10:5; Rev 5:9; 7:9; 10:11; 11:9; 13:7; 14:6; 17:15).

Two unique circumstances in the NT, both originating from the Holy Spirit, involve *tongue* as language. First, in Acts 2:3-4, tongues of fire rested on the heads of each apostle, signaling that the Holy Spirit enabled them to speak the gospel in a variety of human languages and dialects. Second, in 1 Cor 12–14, the Holy Spirit enables believers to speak regularly, both in the public assembly of believers and in the privacy of their own homes. Though interpreters are tempted to assume that these are also known, human languages, as at Pentecost, the fact that Paul assumes no one in the assembly can interpret what they are saying unless the Spirit has given them the gift of interpretation leans against this conclusion. Theologically and psychologically, one could say that the Spirit taps into the language capacity embedded into every human at a pre-cognitive level, something akin to the "sighs too deep for words" described in Rom 8:26. Paul encourages believers to speak in the acquired language of those gathered, engaging both mind and spirit (1 Cor 14:13-16). On this basis, he discourages uninterpreted tongues in the assembly, while encouraging prophetic teaching (*see* TONGUES, GIFT OF).

As the focal point for the utterance of words, moral instruction about human speech habits targets the tongue, usually depicting the tongue negatively and as personifying people who are dangerous, hateful, full of evil, and opposed to God. Thus, the tongue can be "wrong" (Job 6:30), "crafty" (Job 15:5), "mischievous" (Prov 17:4), "perverse" (Prov 17:20), "lying" (Prov 6:17; 21:6; 26:28), and "deceitful" (Job 27:4; Pss 50:19; 52:2 [Heb. 52:4]; 120:2; Zeph 3:13). It can hide "wickedness" (Job 20:12) and "iniquity" (Ps 10:7), speak "wickedness" (Isa 59:3), "make great boasts" (Ps 12:3 [Heb. 12:4]), "flatter" (Ps 5:9; Prov 28:23), "slander" (Ps 15:3), and be "backbiting" (Prov 25:3), "kill" (Job 20:16). The tongue is compared to a sword (Ps 57:4; 64:3), a razor (Ps 52:2 [Heb. 52:4]), a poisonous viper (Job 20:16), and an arrow (Jer 9:8).

Godly people use their tongues to extol God and sing God's praises (Pss 35:28; 51:14 [Heb. 51:16]; 66:17; 71:24; 126:2) and do not sin with their tongues (Ps 39:1 [Heb. 39:2]). The tongues of the wise are soft (Prov 25:15), dispense knowledge (Prov 15:2) and healing (Prov 12:18), and are compared to "silver" (Prov 10:20) and "a tree of life" (Prov 15:4).

A more comprehensive understanding of the tongue requires the study of its semantic context of lips, mouth, teeth, words, and speech. Poetic parallelism includes: tongue and lips (Pss 12:4; 34:13 [Heb. 34:14]; 140:3 [Heb. 140:4]), tongue and mouth (Pss 10:7; Luke 1:64), tongue and word (Ps 52:4 [Heb. 52:6]), and mouth and lips (Ps 141:3). The morality of the tongue is a sign of a mature individual in ANE Wisdom literature. Thus, the earliest Egyptian literature instructs that the wise will be aware of the power and destructive evil of the human tongue and will exert control over the tongue to tap its powers beneficially (e.g., *Amenemope* 9, 15, 18; *Ptahhotep* 25). Such concern is manifest in Jewish apocryphal and pseudepigraphal literature (e.g., *Sir* 23:7-15; Wis 1:6-11), as well as in rabbinic literature (*see* WISDOM IN THE OT).

Consistent with the views of Wisdom literature, Jesus observes (in Matt 12:33-37) that the words people speak capture the essence of their person. Their words reveal them to be good or bad. Not only that, but it matters deeply to God how people wield the power of words they have been given and that these will stand as evidence in their judgment. The continuing concern for speech-ethics can be seen in the NT vice lists that include "speech sins" such as gossip, slander, angry outbursts, shouting, disputes, dissensions, insults, deceit, perjury, boastfulness, lying, vulgarity, silly talk, and coarse jesting (Matt 15:19; Rom 1:29-31; 1 Cor 6:10; 2 Cor 12:20; Gal 5:19-21; Eph 4:31-32; 5:4; Col 3:8-9; 1 Tim 1:10; 2 Tim 3:2-4; 1 Pet 2:1). It also is asserted most directly in Eph 4:17-32, in which holiness is to be manifested in honest, beneficial speech void of gossip, slander, and lying. First Peter 3:10 says controlling the tongue's evil is necessary to receive the Lord's bounty. First John 3:18 extols integrity between words and deeds.

The most concentrated biblical consideration of the tongue is in James, where the concerns of Jesus and Wisdom literature come together. James understands control of speech to be the highest virtue, mandatory for every believer, and that it must be integrated with positive action that benefits others (Jas 1:19–2:25). James recognizes that the tongue's evil is too powerful, too in league with Satan, to be anything more than partially subdued (3:1-12). Yet control must be exerted to be counted a mature disciple of Christ, qualified to teach (Jas 3:1). Directly paralleling Jesus in Matt 5:33-35, Jas 5:12 warns disciples not to undercut the virtue of honest speech by offering oaths as substitutes for personal integrity. James also sees the human tongue at its moral height in praising God but at its depths in cursing people God has created (Jas 3:9-10). *See* IMPEDIMENT OF SPEECH; MOUTH; SAY, SPEAK.

Bibliography: William R. Baker. *Personal Speech-Ethics in the Epistle of James* (1995); William R. Baker. *Sticks & Stones: The Discipleship of Our Speech* (1996); William P. Brown. *Character in Crisis: A Fresh Approach to the Wisdom Literature of the Old Testament* (1996). M. Lichtheim. *Ancient Egyptian Literature*. 3 vols. (1977–80).

WILLIAM R. BAKER

TONGUES, CONFUSION OF. *See* BABEL.

TONGUES, GIFT OF [γλῶσσα glōssa]. Speaking in tongues (glossolalia) is a gift of the spirit (1 Cor 12:10) in which a person who is inspired or who is in an ecstatic state begins to utter words in another language (glōssa).

A. The Challenge of Interpretation
B. 1 Corinthians 12–14
C. The Acts of the Apostles
Bibliography

A. The Challenge of Interpretation

For several reasons, identifying experiences of the gift of tongues in the early church is difficult. First, in 1 Cor 12–14, where glossolalia is discussed in detail, Paul uses different expressions for phenomena that may be related but not identical. He refers to tongue(s) or language(s) (glōssa in 1 Cor 13:8; 14:22); speaking in a tongue/language (laleō glōssē [λαλέω γλώσσῃ] in 14:2, 4, 13, 27; see 14:19); speaking in tongues/languages (laleō glōssais [λαλέω γλώσσαις] in 13:1; 14:5-6, 18, 23, 39); praying in a tongue/language (proseuchomai glōssē [προσεύχομαι γλώσσῃ] in 14:14); speaking with the tongues/languages of angels (glōssais laleō tōn angelōn [γλώσσαις λαλέω τῶν ἀγγέλων] in 13:1); and to various sorts of tongues (genē glōssōn [γένη γλωσσῶν] in 12:10, 28). This variety raises several questions. Does the Greek word glōssa refer to incomprehensible sounds that originate in a psychological state in which the brain's linguistic centers revert to simple phonemes? Or does it refer to actual languages? In the latter case, are tongues an angelic language (1 Cor 13:1)? Or are tongues human languages? Does the word glōssa ordinarily refer to a language unknown to the speaker? Or do the various expressions indicate that Paul has more than one sort of speech act in view?

Second, the challenge expands when other NT books are considered. Paul and Luke do not present glossolalia in the same way. According to Paul, this experience can be incomprehensible; the spirit prays but not the mind, and interpretation by someone else is required. Luke blunts this dimension by consistently associating glossolalia with comprehensible speech. The longer ending of Mark's Gospel provides scant evidence. Jesus promises that certain signs will follow believers, who will cast out demons, speak in new tongues, pick up snakes, drink poison with impunity, and heal the sick by the laying on of hands (Mark 16:17-18). Whether the "new tongues" with which they will "speak" (glōssais lalēlousin kainais γλώσσαις λαλήλουσιν καιναῖς) are similar to the various tongues in Paul's letters and Acts is difficult to determine.

Third, insight from Greco-Roman accounts of inspiration, such as the Delphic priestess, whose prophetic utterances were interpreted by trained hearers, provide little help because the same uncertainties apply also to them. Did the Delphic priestess, e.g., speak incomprehensible syllables that were interpreted as Greek, or did she speak intelligible but obscure Greek phrases that demanded interpretation? A possible analogue to Luke's narrative of Pentecost in Acts 2 occurs in the Homeric Hymn to Delian Apollo. Toward the end of a festival held in honor of Apollo, the girls of Delos would sing about the glorious past by imitating the languages of all people. This resembles Luke's account, in which believers spoke the powerful acts of God in foreign languages. The Homeric spectacle, however, may not have been an act of inspiration; the girls may have recited foreign verses that they had memorized (in the same way that modern choirs might sing in Latin without understanding the words). Possible Greco-Roman parallels, therefore, are not ultimately an exact fit (Forbes).

Fourth, parallels in early Jewish texts, particularly with respect to the phrase "language (tongues) of angels," may not be applicable. In the *Apocalypse of Zephaniah*, a pseudonymous composition written prior to the 3rd cent. CE, Zephaniah claims, "I saw all of those angels praying. I, myself, prayed together with them, I knew their language, which they spoke with me" (8:2-4). A more detailed scene occurs in the *Testament of Job*, another pseudonymous text composed prior to the 3rd cent. CE, in which each of Job's daughters spoke in "the angelic dialect" (48:3), "the dialect of the archons" (49:2), "the dialect of those on high" (50:1), and "the dialect of the cherubim" (50:2). Just prior to Job's death, they "blessed and glorified God each one in her own distinctive dialect" (52:7). While these texts parallel "the tongues of mortals and of angels" in 1 Cor 13:1, they offer little to specify more precisely the speech act, the content of speech, or other questions associated with early Christian experiences of glossolalia.

Fifth, attempts to identify glossolalia with psychological states, such as trance or communal hysteria, are inadequate, in part because of ambiguities in 1 Cor 12–14. For instance, Paul writes, "For nobody understands them, since they are speaking mysteries in the Spirit" (1 Cor 14:2). Paul, somewhat oddly, sets incomprehensibility alongside mysteries that, elsewhere in 1 Corinthians, are comprehensible (1 Cor 15:51-52). Even Paul's limitation of glossolalia to two or three times in worship suggests a measure of control on the part of speakers, though how much is not indicated.

All questions about the content and character of glossolalia lead back to 1 Cor 12–14 and Acts 2, 10, and 19. It is necessary to ascertain the nature of glossolalia in early Christianity by assessing: 1) Paul's correction of a Corinthian overvaluation of glossolalia; and 2) Luke's effort to redirect this phenomenon away from the incomprehensible toward comprehensible speech.

B. 1 Corinthians 12–14

The Corinthian overvaluation of glossolalia compels Paul to offer several correctives. First, in a list of spiritual gifts, Paul refers first to wisdom and knowledge and last to glossolalia and their interpretation (1 Cor 12:4-11). This placement of glossolalia corrects the assumption that the communication of inspired wisdom or knowledge arises out of an experience in which the understanding is dormant. Glossolalia, this order implies, is not the principal source of inspired wisdom and knowledge. In another list, Paul again sets glossolalia and their interpretation in secondary positions, perhaps to imply that no worship experience, not even glossolalia, should be permitted to reverse the proper order of the church: first apostles, second prophets, third teachers, then powers, then gifts of healing, assistance, and leadership, and then various kinds of glossolalia (1 Cor 12:27-28). Apostles, prophets, and teachers are the anchors of the "greater gifts" (12:31). In other lists, in Rom 12:3-8 and Eph 4:11-12, Paul does not even mention glossolalia.

Second, set within this discussion of spiritual gifts is a poetically phrased paean on love that relativizes the value of all spiritual gifts (1 Cor 13:1-13). Without love, the inspired ability to speak "in the tongues of mortals or angels" is mere clanging and crashing noise. Similarly, "prophetic powers," the ability to "understand all mysteries and all knowledge," the gift of extraordinary faith, to the point of moving mountains, the exercise of inspired generosity, even self-sacrifice, are of no value without love. None of the gifts that appear to mesmerize the Corinthians is of any worth without an extraordinary exercise of love.

Third, Paul topples the Corinthians' priorities by advising them to pursue prophecy rather than tongues in order to build up the community: "for those who speak in a tongue do not speak to other people but to God; for nobody understands them, since they are speaking mysteries in the Spirit. On the other hand, those who prophesy speak to other people for their upbuilding and encouragement and consolation. Those who speak in a tongue build up themselves, but those who prophesy build up the church" (14:2-4).

Fourth, the clarity of the discussion in 1 Cor 14 dissipates as Paul shifts to the interpretation of glossolalia. He is now less troubled by glossolalia than by glossolalia left uninterpreted. Paul admits, "I would like all of you to speak in tongues, but even more to prophesy," though, he concedes, prophesying is greater than tongues "unless someone interprets, so that the church may be built up" (14:5). This caveat suggests that, despite Paul's preference for prophesying, interpreted glossolalia can be as edifying as prophecy. Paul advises the tongues-speaker to pray for the power to interpret, so that those around may say amen in agreement, may be built up, may be instructed (14:13-19). Later he implies that interpretation and glossolalia are not spontaneous acts when he advises tongues-speakers to keep it to themselves and to God if there is no interpreter present (14:27-28).

Fifth, among his corrections Paul cites (14:21) a solitary OT text to reinforce his preference for prophesying over uninterpreted tongues. The LXX Isa 28:11-12 is notoriously difficult to interpret. Although it has the catchwords "other tongues" (dia glōssēs heteras [διὰ γλώσσης ἑτέρας]; NRSV, "alien tongue"), this text is about the judgment of Israel at the hands of foreign nations. With a strained application of Isa 28, Paul suggests that uninterpreted glossolalia brings some form of judgment or sign to unbelievers. What may be concluded is this: if in 1 Cor 12 Paul demonstrated that uninterpreted glossolalia did not edify believers, this OT citation implies that uninterpreted glossolalia also have a devastating effect upon unbelievers, who will charge that the church is mad (1 Cor 14:22-23). Prophesying, in contrast, can open their hearts and lead them to faith (1 Cor 14:24-25).

Sixth, in order to remind the Corinthians that everything should be done "for building up" the community (14:26), Paul concludes with practical advice: every gift in worship should be exercised one at a time. Whether glossolalia or prophesying or hymns or revelations—these must take place in order, while all others remain silent (14:26-33).

Seventh, based upon his own experience, Paul suggests that the best arena for the exercise of glossolalia is private, personal prayer. In a thinly veiled boast, Paul thanks God that he speaks in tongues more than all of the Corinthians. Still, despite the vitality of his personal prayer life, Paul would prefer to speak five words in public with his mind intact "in order to instruct others also" (14:18-20). It is not clear what Paul would make of 10,000 words spoken in tongues were there an interpreter present to make them comprehensible. This, in a nutshell, is the ambiguous core of Paul's discussion. Is the gift of glossolalia inferior, especially to prophecy, or is it inferior only when an interpreter fails to be present?

Despite some confusion, three foci emerge from Paul's discussion. First, glossolalia is beneficial, perhaps even essential, to the private spiritual life of individuals, and Paul appeals to his own frequent experiences of glossolalia to support his conviction. It is even possible to associate his description, "my spirit prays but my mind is unproductive" (14:14) with his description of prayer, in which "the Spirit helps us in our weakness; for we do not know how to pray as we ought, but that very Spirit intercedes with sighs too deep for words" (Rom 8:26). Prayer in tongues, from this perspective, leads the believer to an intimate and intense experience of agonizing prayer. Second, no matter how much Paul squirms in discussing spiritual gifts, he never instructs the Corinthians to eschew this gift. His advice, in the end, is not to restrict the public exercise of glossolalia but to increase those who have the gift of interpretation. Third, practiced love, free of arrogance and impatience, alone will last.

C. The Acts of the Apostles

At three epochal junctures in the book of Acts—the beginning of the church (Acts 2:4), the inclusion of Gentiles (10:44-46), and the completion of John's promise of baptism with the Holy Spirit (19:6)—there occurs a lucid association between the gift of the Holy Spirit and some form of speaking in tongues. In none of these epochal situations is the phrase "speaking in tongues" left to stand alone.

In Acts 2, Luke conveys an experience in which the early believers, on the day of PENTECOST, "were filled with the Holy Spirit and began to speak in other languages (ērxanto laleō heterais glōssais ἤρξαντο λαλέω ἑτέραις γλώσσαις)" (2:4). With the word *other*, the miracle of Pentecost becomes one of comprehensibility; Jews who had gathered from around the world could understand the disciples' recitation of God's powerful acts in their own languages (2:5-7). Luke underscores this through narration, "each one heard them speaking in the native language of each" (2:6), and dialogue, "And how is it that we hear, each of us, in our own native language? ... In our own languages we hear them speaking about God's deeds of power" (2:8, 11).

When, in the second example, the Holy Spirit comes upon Cornelius and his Gentile friends, Peter and his coterie hear them "speaking in tongues and extolling God" (10:46). The association of speaking in tongues with praise draws the reader back to Acts 2, where the recitation of God's powerful acts in other languages is comprehensible; the verb megalynō (μεγαλύνω, "praise") in Acts 10:46 is even related to the plural noun, ta megaleia (τὰ μεγαλεῖα, "powerful acts")—perhaps "praiseworthy acts" would be a better translation—in Acts 2:11. This literary parallel suggests that this second instance also consists of intelligible praise in foreign languages.

A similar scenario characterizes the third instance of speaking in (other) tongues, a band of "disciples" who had not heard of the Holy Spirit; when Paul laid his hands upon them, "the Holy Spirit came upon them, and they spoke in tongues and prophesied" (elaloun te glōssais kai eprophēteuon [ἐλάλουν τε γλώσσαις καὶ ἐπροφήτευον]; 19:6). Prophesying in Acts, like praise, is comprehensible. Prophets punctuate the history of the early church with occasional but certain clarity about the future. For example, the prophet Agabus correctly predicts a famine (11:27-28). Judas and Silas, themselves prophets, are sent to Antioch with a letter to interpret the Jerusalem Council's decision "by word of mouth." When they arrive in Antioch, they encourage and strengthen the believers; this speech, of course, is comprehensible (15:22, 27, 32).

Luke's portrayal of speaking in (other) tongues is, then, dramatically different from the Corinthian examples of incomprehensible speech. In Acts 2 the believers speak in "other" tongues. In Acts 10, they speak in tongues and praise. In Acts 19, they speak in tongues and prophesy. All of these are comprehensible speech acts. In associating glossolalia with comprehensible speech, Luke differs from the Corinthians, with their penchant for the incomprehensible; in this respect, Luke allies himself with Paul, who prefers five comprehensible words in worship to any number of incomprehensible ones.

Bibliography: Mark Cartledge. *The Gift of Speaking in Tongues: The Holy Spirit, the Human Spirit and the Gift of Holy Speech* (2005); Mark J. Cartledge, ed. *Speaking in Tongues: Multi-disciplinary Perspectives* (2006); Gordon Fee. *God's Empowering Presence* (1994); Christopher Forbes. *Prophecy and Inspired Speech: In Early Christianity and Its Hellenistic Environment* (1995); Thomas Gillespie. *The First Theologians: A Study in Early Christian Prophecy* (1994); Felicitas Goodman. *Speaking in Tongues: A Cross-cultural Study of Glossolalia* (1972); Gerald Hovenden. *Speaking in Tongues: The New Testament Evidence in Context* (2002); Max Turner. *The Holy Spirit and Spiritual Gifts* (1996); Antoinette Clark Wire. *The Corinthian Women Prophets: A Reconstruction through Paul's Rhetoric* (1995).

JOHN R. LEVISON

TOOLS [בַּרְזֶל barzel, חֹרֶשׁ khoresh, כְּלִי keli]. Every craft has its sets of tools. As the Egyptian *Instruction of Dua-Khety* explains, every worker is marked physically and socially by his or her tools. The scribe is known by his pen and writing case (Ezek 9:2) and the barber by his razor (Ezek 5:1); the potter is recognized sitting astride his wheel (Jer 18:3), the warrior is dependent upon his weapons (1 Sam 17:5-7), and the dutiful wife is defined by her tasks: spinning, weaving, sowing, cooking, and filling the lamps (Prov 31:10-22).

Because the culture of ancient Israel was so dependent upon agriculture, many of the tools mentioned in the Bible relate to the various aspects of this year-round activity. Of course, there are also tools associated with construction, food processing, weaving and clothing manufacture, fishing and hunting, and the fabrication of pottery, jewelry, weapons, and sacred objects. The technology that produced and kept them in repair is an indicator of the development of new or improved skills in mining, metallurgy (Gen 4:22; Job 28:2), carpentry, sculpting, and ceramics.

Basic agricultural tools include the PLOW, MATTOCK, AX, and SICKLE (1 Sam 13:20). They allowed farmers to cut down trees and trim branches for firewood

(Deut 19:5; Judg 9:48-49), open furrows of earth (1 Kgs 19:19), break up clods of dirt, and harvest standing grain (Isa 17:5). Initially, they used wooden plows, but eventually and sometimes with the assistance of blacksmiths from neighboring cultures, a metal sheath was added to cut deeper into the soil (1 Sam 13:21). The threshing sled pulled by oxen and sometimes tipped with metal fragments facilitated the crushing of the stalks of grain (wheat and barley; 2 Sam 24:22). Winnowing FORKs (Jer 15:7; Matt 3:12) and SIEVEs (Amos 9:9) then completed the process of separating the kernels from the chaff and small stones for distribution to the field owners, to the Levites and the destitute, and as offerings to God (Num 15:20; 18:30; Deut 26:12). In order to transform the grain into flour, women labored daily over their saddle quern hand mills (Matt 24:41; see MILL, MILLSTONE). Loaves of bread were baked in beehive-shaped ovens or grilled on hot stones (1 Sam 28:24).

Since no farmer concentrated on a single crop, other tools, such as the PRUNING HOOK (Isa 18:5), were developed to cultivate, prune, and harvest olives, grapes, and other fruits. The hilly spine of central Palestine where most of the Israelite settlements were established also required the construction of terraces on the hillsides in order to provide additional cultivation space (Isa 5:1-2). As with the construction of fortifications (2 Sam 12:31), the tools to dig out stones and transport topsoil to fill terraces included the PICK, the SHOVEL, and strong backs. The importance of olive oil as a basic commodity of trade and an ingredient in food, cosmetics, and ointments, and as lamp oil, lead to the development of specialized tools to crush the fruit that had been beaten from the trees with staves (Deut 24:20; Isa 24:13) and extract the oil. Placed in baskets, the harvested olives were thoroughly flattened using a lever and weights press such as those found at Gezer and at Tel Miqne-Ekron. With a wooden beam anchored in a stone niche in the wall, stone weights were hung from the beam to add greater pressure on the baskets so that the fluid could be collected below in a basin.

Numerous episodes in the biblical text indicate that there was a thriving fishing industry that included fishermen casting their nets from the shore and from boats sailing on the Sea of Galilee (Matt 4:18-22; John 21:6-11). This work would have depended upon the ability to weave nets and construct sturdy boats that could withstand the waves and storms on the lake (Mark 4:37; see DRAGNET; NET). Hunters also developed tools to bring down their prey with TRAPS AND SNARES (Ps 91:3; Prov 7:23) and weapons such as bows and spears.

There was a constant need for builders to construct and repair private dwellings in villages as well as monumental structures in the larger cities, including wall systems, temples, and palaces. Their tools included the brick mold (Nah 3:14) and iron chisels to cut and shape the stones (although not on altars; Exod 20:25) or to carve inscriptions or decorations (Job 19:24; 2 Cor 3:7). The SAW was also used to cut stones as well as

lumber (1 Kgs 7:9), and PLANEs smoothed the wood (Isa 44:13). HAMMER and NAILs were reserved for fine work in attaching decoration to sacred structures (1 Chr 22:3) or in the adornment of idols (Jer 10:4). In household construction, augurs were used to drill holes in beams of wood that were then connected with wooden pegs pounded in with a MALLET (Judg 5:26). Standard construction methods also required the use of the PLUMB LINE, a string with a weight attached that helped to ensure that walls were straight and true (Amos 7:7-8).

For those involved in the manufacture of cloth and garments, the LOOM, spindle, and NEEDLE were their primary tools. Once the wool had been sheared from the sheep (Gen 38:12), the fibers were carded from the fleece (Isa 19:9) and then spun into thread that could be tied to the frame of the loom, affixed with pins (Judg 16:14), and, using a SHUTTLE (Job 7:6), woven into cloth (Isa 38:12). Needles not only stitched the pieces of cloth together but also embroidered garments with intricate designs using dyed threads (Exod 26:36). Leather workers also used needles to stitch together belts, purses, and sandals.

To augment worship practices, artisans used their skills in cutting stones, carving wood, and weaving fabric to fashion sacred objects for temples and priests. When their work included the creation of idols, the prophets ridiculed them. To do this work, they poured molten metal into molds (Exod 32:4) or worked, in combination with the ironsmith and the carpenter (using stylus, plane, and compass), to shape the figures from metal and wood (Isa 44:12-17). Priests employed incense shovels, forks, basins (Exod 38:3), and the sacrificial knife as sacred tools in their role as religious practitioners.

VICTOR H. MATTHEWS

TOOTH [שֵׁן shen; ὀδούς odous]. The Hebrew term shen means "tooth, ivory," and probably derives from the root shnn (שָׁנַן), which means "to whet, sharpen," although not all Hebraists agree on the etymology. Shen usually refers to the teeth of human beings (e.g., Gen 49:12; Exod 21:27; 4 Macc 7:6), and less frequently to animal teeth (e.g., Deut 32:24; Job 4:10; Joel 1:6). First Samuel 2:13 speaks of a "three-toothed" fork (author's trans.; NRSV, "three-pronged") used in tabernacle service.

Teeth are the subject of several recurring idiomatic and metaphorical expressions. "A tooth for a tooth" is the formula of the LEX TALIONIS (Exod 21:24; Lev 24:20; Deut 19:21; Matt 5:38). "Gnashing" of teeth frequently indicates the hostility of adversaries (Job 16:9; Pss 35:16; 37:12; 112:10; Lam 2:16; Sir 51:3; Acts 7:54) and occasionally individual suffering (Sir 30:10). In the NT, "weeping and gnashing of teeth" refers to those suffering in the netherworld (Matt 8:12; 13:42, 50; 22:13; 24:51; 25:30; Luke 13:28). Jeremiah and Ezekiel cite the same proverb about teeth in discussions of individual responsibility (Jer 31:29-30; Ezek 18:2). Other proverbs use teeth as a simile (Prov 10:26) or a metaphor (Prov 25:19).

Other noteworthy metaphors include "cleanness of teeth" (Amos 4:6), which refers to famine. Conversely, the idiom "have something to eat" (NRSV) literally means "have something to bite with their teeth" (Mic 3:5; author's trans.). Yahweh declares against Philistia, "I will take away ... its abominations from between its teeth" (Zech 9:7; compare Num 11:33). Job expresses the risk he is taking in challenging God by stating, "I will take my flesh in my teeth" (13:14). Job's description of his physical suffering includes the remark, "I have escaped by the skin of my teeth" (19:20), which may indicate that his teeth have fallen from his gums. Agur describes the wicked as those "whose teeth are swords" and "knives" (Prov 30:14; compare Ps 57:4 [Heb. 57:5]). In the Song of Songs, the praises of the woman's beauty include the statement that her "teeth are like a flock of shorn ewes" (4:2; 6:6).

JOHN I. LAWLOR

TOPARCHY top'ahr-kee [τοπαρχία toparchia, νομός nomos]. An administrative subdivision of a province in the Hellenistic and Roman periods. The three toparchies (author's trans.; NRSV, "districts") of Samaria are mentioned in 1 Macc 11:28. The same administrative units are also called nomes (nomoi νομοί; 1 Macc 11:34; author's trans.; NRSV, "districts"). Roman Judea consisted of ten (Pliny, *Nat.* 5.70) or eleven (Josephus, *J.W.* 3.54–56) toparchies. *See* PROVINCE.

LJUBICA JOVANOVIC

TOPAZ [τοπάζιον topazion]. The ninth stone in the foundation wall of the New Jerusalem (Rev 21:20). In antiquity, *topaz* was a general term for several different stones based solely on their yellow coloring. Current usage refers to a gem composed of fluosilicate of aluminum, which is generally colorless but may also range from blue to yellowish brown.

ELIZABETH E. PLATT

TOPHEL toh'fuhl [תֹּפֶל tofel]. Referenced in only one place in the OT, Tophel is cited in the opening lines of Deuteronomy, where the narrator describes Israel's location when Moses begins to address the nation prior to their crossing the Jordan into Canaan (Deut 1:1). To be noted is the absence of any reference to Tophel in the itinerary of Israel's sojourn recorded in Num 33. Precise identification of the location is elusive; the popular suggestion of et-Tafileh (Jordan)—a few kilometers south of the Wadi el-Hasa (Zered)—has difficulties.

Bibliography: Yohanan Aharoni, Michael Avi-Yonah, Anson F. Rainey, and Ze'ev Safrai. *The MacMillan Bible Atlas.* 3rd ed. (1993).

JOHN I. LAWLOR

TOPHETH toh'fith [תֹּפֶת tofeth]. Topheth's location, according to 2 Kgs 23:10 and Jer 7:31, is "in the valley of Ben-hinnom," which is well established to be located at the southwest corner of Jerusalem's old city, at the base of Mount Zion (*see* HINNOM, VALLEY OF). Referenced only nine times in the OT, Topheth was notorious because of its identification with child sacrifice to the god Molech (2 Kgs 23:10; Jer 7:31; *see* MOLECH, MOLOCH). Other than the Kings text, reference to Topheth is found only in Jer 7 (vv. 31-32) and Jer 19 (vv. 6, 11-14). The former text comes at the conclusion of the prophet's Temple Sermon (7:1–8:3) and, among other dynamics, points to the nation's violation of Deut 18:10. The latter text has Jeremiah confronting the activity in Topheth by first visiting the potter's house, buying a vessel, going to Topheth, and inveighing against the practice of the place; the vessel was then to be smashed—a symbol of what was to happen to Jerusalem because of its Topheth activity. The Kings (2 Kgs 23:10) text records Josiah's defiling Topheth subsequent to the summary of Manasseh's reign (2 Kgs 21:1-18)—a summary that includes reference to his participation in child sacrifice.

JOHN I. LAWLOR

TORAH toh'ruh [תּוֹרָה torah; νόμος nomos]. **Torah** is a Hebrew word meaning "instruction," "teaching," and "law." It is the OT's general term for God's commandments to Israel. It came to typify the literary corpus that contains those commandments (i.e., the first five books of the OT—Genesis, Exodus, Leviticus, Numbers, and Deuteronomy—otherwise known as the PENTATEUCH), as well as the divine will for Israel in general.

Many texts associate **torah** with instructions by priests. Priestly texts (P) of the Pentateuch use the word to label specific ritual instructions (e.g., "This is the **torah** [NRSV, 'ritual'] of the burnt offering"; Lev 6:9 [Heb. 6:2]; compare Lev 6:14, 25 [Heb. 6:7, 18]; 7:1, 11; 14:2), but also as a summary term for a set of instructions (Lev 7:37; 14:54; Num 5:29-30). Other texts relate the **torah** of Yahweh to Israel's commemoration of the exodus and covenant (Exod 13:9). **Torah** frequently appears as one in a list of nearly synonymous terms for the stipulations of God's covenant with Israel (Gen 26:5; Exod 16:8; 18:16, 20; 24:12; Lev 26:46; Ps 105:45; Jer 44:23; Neh 9:14). *See* P, PRIESTLY WRITERS.

A wide variety of sources use **torah** to describe priestly instruction in general (Deut 33:10; 22:26; Hos 4:6; Zeph 3: 4; Hag 2:11; Mal 2:6-9). The broader meaning informs the use of the cognate verb yarah (יָרָה, "to teach") in P's summary of the priest's teaching responsibilities (Lev 10:10-11; compare Ezek 22:26's summary of this verse as "my [God's] **torah** [NRSV, 'teaching']"). This widespread usage in texts from before and after the exile undermines the common assertion that, in one or the other period, priests did not perform teaching duties. It also supports the LXX translation of **torah** by nomos—a word that, throughout the history of the ancient Greek language, connoted correct performance of temple rituals as well as the more usual connotations of "law."

Jeremiah and Ezekiel distinguish priestly torah from the davar (דָּבָר, "word") or khazon (חָזוֹן, "vision") of prophets and the ʿetsah (עֵצָה, "counsel") of sages (Jer 18:18; Ezek 7:26). Isaiah, however, associates torah with prophets and the servant of God (Isa 8:16, 20; 42:4, 21; 51:4), and Proverbs uses the term for the teachings of the wise sage (Prov 1:8; 3:1; 4:2; 6:20, 23; 7:2; 13:14; 28:9; 31:26). The Psalms' celebration of the torah of Yahweh (Pss 1:2; 19:7-10; 119:1) probably melds priestly and wisdom ideas into a general conception of the divine will behind normative traditions.

Deuteronomy employs wisdom formulations and acknowledges the priests' special association with torah, but it applies the term, most often reflexively, to itself as the summation of the covenant (Deut 1:5; 4:44; 27:3, 26; 28:58), which is now explicitly a written book (Deut 28:61; 29:20; 30:10; 31:26; compare 2 Kgs 22:8, 11). Other books also specify this usage by connecting torah with Moses (Josh 8:31; 23:6; 1 Kgs 2:3; 2 Kgs 14:6; 23:25; 2 Chr 23:18; 25:4; 30:16; 34:14; Ezra 3:2; 7:6; Neh 8:8; Dan 9:13; Mal 3:22).

As a result, torah became indelibly associated with the five books Genesis through Deuteronomy in Second Temple and rabbinic Judaism, so much so that "the Torah" now refers to a divison of the Jewish canon. Yet the concept of torah never lost its wider connotations. If anything, they were strengthened by the Torah scroll's increasing prestige. The concept merged with the old tradition of hypostasized wisdom (Prov 8:22) to cast the Torah as a heavenly object that existed before the creation of the world (Sir 24:23; Bar 3:9-4:4). The word torah described, however, not just the delimited book but also the traditions of its interpretation and application, as in the "oral torah" of the Pharisees and rabbinic sages (see ORAL LAW, ORAL TORAH). Torah then came to designate not just a text and its interpretation but also the life of those devoted to its study and to following its precepts, i.e., a life of faithful piety.

Many scholars have challenged the traditional translation of torah with "law" as too restrictive. Ancient Mesopotamian "law" collections did not function as binding legislation; and Israel's torah originally did not have that function either. Its origins lay rather in priestly and wisdom teachings. As a result, the OT applies the term to a wide variety of literature and traditions. Even for the Pentateuch, the term is multivalent, describing part of its contents (the "laws" or "instructions") as well as the normative status of the Pentateuch itself. The Pentateuch's mixing of ritual and legal instructions with ethical exhortations, narratives, and even psalms becomes constitutive of the meaning of torah both within and beyond its own pages (Deut 1:5; Ps 78).

Law remains, however, the best English rendering for torah. The Pentateuch presents torah as legislation issued by a legitimate authority (Yahweh) that is binding on all those within its self-described jurisdiction (Israel). A distinctive feature of the Pentateuch is that its torah is explicitly addressed to all Israel, and it demands that they hear it and learn it (Deut 6:6-8; 31:10-13). Its normative force was at first probably restricted to ritual practices at temples. Much, however, of subsequent Jewish and Christian concern for the interpretation and application of all the contents of the Torah, and of the rest of scripture, arose from the extension of torah's instructional authority to other genres of literature. The Torah's unprecedented standing in Second Temple Judaism as a written authority for religious practice and belief decisively shaped the idea of scripture in Jewish, Christian, and Muslim traditions. It also strengthened the ideal of normative written law in political cultures influenced by those religion traditions. See LAW IN THE OT.

Bibliography: Frank Crüsemann. *The Torah: Theology and Social History of Old Testament Law* (1996); Anne Fitzpatrick-McKinley. *The Transformation of Torah from Scribal Advice to Law* (1999); Moshe Greenberg. "Three Conceptions of the Torah in Hebrew Scriptures." *Studies in the Bible and Jewish Thought* (1995) 11–24; Bernard S. Jackson. *Studies in the Semiotics of Biblical Law* (2000); Michael LeFebvre. *Collections, Codes, and Torah: The Re-characterization of Israel's Written Law.* LHB/OTS 451 (2006); James W. Watts. *Reading Law: The Rhetorical Shaping of the Pentateuch* (1999).

JAMES W. WATTS

TORAH READING. The cycle of public readings of the Torah and Prophets as part of the synagogue service, referred to in Jewish literature as "Torah Reading." The public reading of the Law of Deut 31:10-13 and Neh 8:1-8 were special, one-time covenant renewal ceremonies, but the SEPTUAGINT was prepared for use in public readings in synagogues. Many references to reading the Torah in the DEAD SEA SCROLLS refer simply to studying the texts. However, the Damascus Document, stating that a priest whose voice is inaudible or unintelligible cannot read, describes a public Torah reading (4Q266 5 II, 1-3=4Q267 5 III, 3-5=4Q273 2 1). Philo (*Dreams* 2, 127) and Josephus (*Ag. Ap.* 2.175) note the Sabbath reading of the Law in the house of prayer for instructional purposes. We do not actually know when the reading of Scripture for liturgical purposes began. The Talmud states (*y. Meg.* 4:1, 75a; *b. B. Qam.* 82a) that Moses instituted the Torah readings on Sabbaths (see also Acts 15:21) and festivals, and Ezra added Mondays, Thursdays, and Sabbath afternoons. From the Mishnah (2nd cent. CE) it is clear that just after the destruction of the Second Temple there was already a fixed, consecutive sequence of Sabbath portions. The Mishnah cites regular Torah readings (*m. Meg.* 3:4-6) but does not indicate how much was read. According to the Babylonian Talmud (*b. Meg.* 29b), the land of Israel completed reading the Torah in a little over three years. In Babylonia and other places outside the land of Israel, the Torah was divided into fifty-four portions (sedharim [סְדָרִים] or parashiyoth [פָּרָשִׁיוֹת]). One was read each week with a few double portions to complete the cycle annually. For a while the two cycles coexisted. As a result of the increasing influence of the Babylonian Jewish tradition, eventually the annual cycle superseded the triennial, ending and beginning anew on Simhat Torah (simkhath torah [שִׂמְחַת תּוֹרָה], "Rejoicing in the Law"), an extra festival day added to the fall Sukkot holiday.

A ritual quorum of ten men (minyan מִנְיָן) must be present in order to read the Torah (m. Meg. 4:1-3). Three men are called to the scroll to recite the blessings ('aliyoth עֲלִיוֹת) on Mondays, Thursdays, and Sabbath afternoons; four on minor festivals; five on major festival days; six on Yom Kippur; and seven on Sabbath mornings. The first 'aliyah (עֲלִיָּה) goes to the priest (kohen כֹּהֵן), the second to the Levite (lewi לֵוִי), and the third and on to anyone else (yisra'el יִשְׂרָאֵל; m. Git. 5:8). While originally each read his portion, many were not competent to do so, so that a reader was engaged, leaving those called to the 'aliyoth simply to recite the blessings. Many communities also translated into the vernacular each verse as it was read.

The mishnah also mentions the addition of a haftarah (הַפְטָרָה, "completion") from one of the prophets, linked to the theme of the Torah reading. Luke recounts that Jesus went to the synagogue on the Sabbath in Nazareth and read from the prophet Isaiah (Luke 4:16-21), and Paul preached in the synagogue of Antioch of Pisidia, Asia Minor, "after the reading of the law and the prophets" (Acts 13:15). A chapter of Psalms was also read every Sabbath.

The Torah was always a scroll, handwritten by a qualified scribe following ancient traditional techniques. The centrality of the Torah is in evidence in excavated synagogues from the Byzantine period in the land of Israel and the Greco-Roman world. These synagogues feature an ark or niche ('aron אָרוֹן) on the wall for storing a Torah scroll. See LECTIONARY.

LAWRENCE H. SCHIFFMAN

TORCH. See LAMP, NT; LAMPSTAND.

TORTURE [βασανίζω basanizō, τυμπανίζω tympanizō]. Painful physical ordeals imposed for coercion and intimidation. ANTIOCHUS IV Epiphanes tortured Jews to force them to renounce their religion and eat unclean food, most notably the aged ELEAZAR (2 Macc 6:18-31; 4 Macc 6–7) and a mother and her seven sons (2 Macc 7; 4 Macc 8–18; compare Heb 11:35). With poetic justice, Antiochus suffered divinely inflicted torture (2 Macc 9:5). In the NT, torture is the punishment of the unforgiving servant (Matt 18:34). Believers will endure torture in the present (Matt 24:9; Heb 13:3), but in the future it is reserved for those not

protected by God's seal (Rev 9:5). See CRIMES AND PUNISHMENT, OT AND NT; PERSECUTION.

LISA MICHELE WOLFE

TOSEPHTA, TOSEPTA, TOSEFTA toh-sef'tuh [תּוֹסֶפְתָּא tosefta']. Means "addition." The Tosefta, an early collection of Jewish law and lore, is a companion volume to the MISHNAH. It was produced by the Sages at the beginning of the 3rd cent. CE, in Hebrew, in the land of Israel. The Tosefta is arranged just like the Mishnah: it is subdivided into orders, tractates, chapters, and individual paragraphs called halakhot (rulings; see HALAKHAH). It is about three to four times the size of the Mishnah. The Tosefta is available today in two principal editions: the complete Tosefta (Zuckermandel), and the first four orders of the Tosefta (Lieberman) as well as a complete English translation (Neusner).

Like the Mishnah, the Tosefta comments on Jewish agricultural law, Jewish holidays, marital law, civil and criminal law, Temple offerings, and ritual purity. It contains more anecdotal material than the Mishnah and more haggadic exhortations (see HAGGADAH). The two versions of the TALMUD often cite passages from the Tosefta—in a somewhat modified version—in order to explain and augment the Mishnah. On occasion, the Talmud favors the Tosefta over the Mishnah and forces the Mishnah to align itself with the rulings of the Tosefta.

For many years, scholars have debated the nature of the Tosefta's relationship to the Mishnah. The regnant theory until the 1990s was that, as its name indicates, the Tosefta was a supplement to the Mishnah. This meant that it cited and commented on passages in the Mishnah, brought dissenting opinions that were not included in the Mishnah, and introduced independent materials only peripherally related to the Mishnah. Many thought that the Tosefta was a poorly edited collection of materials that was not selected by the redactor for inclusion in the Mishnah.

In the 1990s these theories unraveled, when some scholars showed that it made more sense to read the Tosefta as a source of the Mishnah (e.g., Hauptman). They demonstrated that viewing the Tosefta as the raw material of the Mishnah solved many problems. For instance, it no longer mattered that the order of paragraphs in the Tosefta did not match the order of the Mishnah because the Tosefta was either following the order of an earlier collection of Jewish law or creating its own order. In fact, when one views the Tosefta as preceding the Mishnah, it is possible, on occasion, to chart the evolution of Jewish law over time. Whereas the key elements of the Tosefta's Passover Seder are drinking four cups of wine, beginning Hallel (Pss 113–118), and after dinner finishing Hallel and studying the laws of Passover, the key elements of the Mishnah's Seder are drinking four cups of wine, asking questions, telling the story of the exodus, and beginning Hallel—all before dinner.

The importance of the Tosefta lies in the fact that it provides an alternate statement of early Jewish law. Since the Mishnah became, over time, the basis of Jewish practice, the Tosefta provides a glimpse of paths not taken even though available to the redactor of Mishnah. The Tosefta helps place the Mishnah onto an ideological and jurisprudential continuum. *See* GITTIN; MEGILLOTH.

Bibliography: Shamma Friedman. *Tosefta Atiqta* (2002); Judith Hauptman. *Rereading the Mishnah: A New Approach to Ancient Jewish Texts* (2005); Alberdina Houtman. *Mishnah and Tosefta* (1995); Saul Lieberman. *The Tosefta (Zera'im through Bava Batra)* (1955–88); Jacob Neusner. *The Tosefta: Translated from the Hebrew with a New Introduction* (2002); Moshe Shmuel Zuckermandel. *Tosefta* (1879–81).

JUDITH HAUPTMAN

TOTEMISM. A former feature of biblical scholarship derived from social anthropology, but rarely if ever mentioned today, totemism refers to the association of an individual or group with an animal, plant, or other figure from nature. The group may be named after the plant or animal with which it believes it has a special affinity. A totemic myth narrates this connection, and it may be actualized by ritualized behaviors and sometimes food avoidances. From a kinship perspective, totemism describes the notion that an affinity group considers itself to be descended from a nonhuman primary ancestor, termed a *totem*. Totemism was usually thought to be associated with matrilineal descent, exogamy with regard to the totem clan, and taboos against killing or eating the totem.

Based largely on evidence from Australian Aboriginal and Native American cultures, totemism developed into a universalized hypothetical framework for the study of religion in the 19th and early 20th cent. It fit into the conventional evolutionary mind-set of the period, which understood contemporary, so-called "primitive" societies as survivals of ancient, foundational systems of culture and thought. Well-known names associated with this approach include Émile Durkheim (who saw totemism as the universal basis for religion), James G. Frazer, and Sigmund Freud. In OT studies, totemism was pioneered and popularized by W. Robertson Smith, who argued that it was the foundation of what he termed Semitic religion. He saw totemic thinking as the basis for sacrifice, which he presumed to be the fundamental Semitic ritual action. Sacrifice, he believed, involved the killing and communal eating of one's totem as a scapegoat. Participants expected beneficial things from their ancestral totems and understood sacrifice as a way of renewing a blood alliance between the group and its totem.

Standard arguments were commonly advanced to support the existence of totemism in ancient Israel. Scholars pointed to various animal and plant names

borne by individuals: Jael (ibex, Judg 4:17-22), Jonah (dove), Shaphan (rock badger, e.g., 2 Kgs 22:3), Tola (worm, Gen 46:13), Zimri (supposedly chamois, see 1 Kgs 16:8-20). Clans also were named for animals (*see* CLAN; FAMILY). Examples include the Arelites of Gad (lion, Num 26:17), the Becherites of Ephraim (camel, Num 26:35), the Calebites (dog), Shual of Asher (jackal, 1 Chr 7:36), the Shuphamites of Benjamin (snake, Num 26:39), and the Zorathites (hornet, 1 Chr 2:53). The golden calf and the bronze serpent (Num 21:9) were seen as examples of animal worship, confirmed by Ezek 8:7-11. Lists of unclean animals forbidden as food (Lev 11; Deut 14) were taken as evidence of the avoidance of totem animals. Metaphors in the tribal blessings of Gen 49 and Deut 33 were understood as highlighting associations between tribes and certain animals: "Judah is a lion's whelp" (Gen 49:9); "Issachar is a strong donkey" (Gen 49:14); "Dan shall be a snake" (Gen 49:17; or a "lion's whelp", Deut 33:22; "Naphtali is a doe" (Gen 49:21); "Benjamin is a ravenous wolf" (Gen 49:27; Ephraim is like "a firstborn bull" (Deut 33:17); "Gad lives like a lion" (Deut 33:20).

Early in the 20th cent. the notion of totemism as a universal, evolutionary model for primitive religion was undermined by methodologically improved fieldwork. It gradually faded as a principal element in the study of the OT. *See* CLEAN AND UNCLEAN; KINSHIP; MARRIAGE, OT; PLANTS OF THE BIBLE.

Bibliography: Gilian M. Bediako. *Primal Religion and the Bible: William Robertson Smith and His Heritage* (1997); Émile Durkheim. *The Elementary Forms of Religious Life* (1915); James G. Frazer. *Totemism and Exogamy* (1910); Sigmund Freud. *Totemism and Taboo* (1918); Robert A. Jones. *The Secret of the Totem: Religion and Society from McLennan to Freud* (2005); Adam Kuper. *The Invention of Primitive Society* (1988); W. Robertson Smith. *Lectures on the Religion of the Semites* (1889).

RICHARD D. NELSON

TOU. *See* TOI.

TOUBIANI. *See* TOB.

TOUCH [נָגַע nagha', נָגַשׁ naghash, פָּגַע pagha'; ἅπτω haptō, ψαύω psauō, ψηλαφάω psēlaphaō]. The power of physical contact is a pervasive theme in the Bible. Old Testament codes stress that impurity can be communicated by touching unclean animals (Lev 5:2; 11:24-28), persons (Lev 15), or corpses (Num 19:11-20; compare Sir 34:30). Touching may be a component of rituals, as in Passover (Exod 12:22; compare Exod 4:24-26). A seraph touches the mouth of Isaiah (6:6-7) to purify him, and God touches the mouth of Jeremiah (1:9) to prepare him to prophesy.

In the Synoptic Gospels, Jesus often touches people to heal them (e.g., Matt 8:3; Luke 5:13; 22:51), and a woman who touches Jesus is herself healed (Mark 5:25-34; compare Matt 14:35-36). Strikingly, in the Gospel of John, Jesus touches no one and forbids Mary Magdalene to touch him (author's trans.; NRSV, "Do not hold on to me"). Paul's reference to touching a woman in 1 Cor 7:1 alludes, it seems, to sex. *See* CLEAN AND UNCLEAN; HEALING.

TERESA J. HORNSBY

TOWEL [λέντιον lention]. A linen cloth used, and perhaps worn, by servants in antiquity. During his last meal with his disciples, Jesus arises, undresses, wraps a towel around his waist, and washes his disciples' feet, drying them with the towel (John 13:4-5). *See* FOOT WASHING.

TOWER [מִגְדָּל mighdal, מְצָד metsadh, מִשְׂגָּב misgav; πύργος pyrgos]. A *tower* is a building constructed for agricultural purposes or as a fortress or stronghold, sometimes as part of a city wall. Stone towers of various shapes and sizes dot the landscape of the Levant and seem to have served a variety of purposes, but chief among them were defense and agriculture. It is against such background that the metaphorical use in reference to Yahweh occurs (Ps 61:3 [Heb. 61:4]).

The circular tower at Jericho is the earliest documented tower in the land of Canaan and has been dated to the Pre-Pottery Neolithic period (*see* ARCHAEOLOGY). It was architecturally associated with the city wall. It stood to a height of 8.25 m, and its outside diameter was 8 m. It was engineered with a staircase going up through the tower's interior; twelve skeletons were discovered in this staircase. Generally explained as a defensive tower, an alternative view proposes that the tower was used for ceremonial purposes.

Uzziah built towers in the wilderness (2 Chr 26:10). While "wilderness" (midbar מִדְבָּר) is usually associated with the Negev or the Wilderness of Judah, it is also used in reference to regions northeast of Jerusalem, perhaps down in the Jordan Valley or the easternmost escarpment of the Judean/Samarian hill country (Josh 16:1; 18:12). Three nearly identical circular towers, built during the Iron II period (10th–7th cent. BCE)—Khirbet es-Saqq, Khirbet el-Makhruq, and Rujm Mukheir—perhaps illustrate the tower-building project of Uzziah. That all three are strategically located in relationship to routes linking the eastern plateau with the western hill country via the Jordan Valley suggests that the function of the towers was defensive.

Jotham built towers on wooded hills (2 Chr 27:4). The construction of towers in an elevated, secluded setting also bespeaks a military, defensive, warning function for the tower. Numerous such towers have been archaeologically documented in the regions both east and west of the Jordan River.

The "song of the vineyard" (Isa 5:1-7) images the clearing of a field of stones and the building—presumably with the gathered stones—of a "watchtower" in its midst (Isa 5:2). This seems to illustrate an agricultural use of towers, as distinct from military. The tower most likely would have been used to protect the field against animals or thieves, perhaps even to store agricultural equipment used in cultivating the field (*see* WATCHTOWER).

A few towers identified with specific OT sites are narratively integrated into the textual landscape, but none are specifically described as to their purpose or use. Of particular interest are the three towers that appear in three successive narratives: tower of Penuel (Judg 8:9, 17), tower of Shechem (Judg 9:46-49), tower of Thebez (Judg 9:51-52). The Thebez tower is portrayed as a "strong tower within the city." Apparently there were grain-grinding implements on the tower's roof (Judg 9:51-53). This latter instance may suggest dual purposes of this tower: protection and grain-processing.

Towers architecturally integrated with the walls of Jerusalem are referenced generally (2 Chr 26:9, 15; 32:5; Neh 3:27; Ps 48:12 [Heb. 48:13]). More descriptively, Neh 3:25-26 speaks of "projecting towers" in the Jerusalem wall. Specific towers in Jerusalem's wall are identified in the Nehemiah description as well as a few other texts: Tower of the Hundred (Neh 3:1), Tower of the Ovens (Neh 3:11; 12:38), Tower of Hananel (Neh 12:39; see also Jer 31:38; Zech 14:10). Jesus speaks of the "tower of Siloam", a structure that evidently fell and crushed eighteen people (Luke 13:4).

The tower of BABEL is an etiological story in which the people of the earth united to build a brick tower "with its top in the heavens" to make a name for themselves, so God scattered them across the earth and confused their language (Gen 11:1-9). Metaphorical uses of tower, often translated "FORTRESS," refer to Yahweh and the divine name (Pss 18:2 [Heb. 18:3]//2 Sam 22:3; Pss 59:9, 17 [Heb. 59:10, 18]; 61:3 [Heb. 61:4]; 62:2, 7 [Heb. 62:3, 8]; 144:2; Prov 18:10). In Song of Songs, the lovers use the term in their playful anatomical descriptors (Song 4:4; 7:4 [Heb. 7:5]; 8:10). The "tower of the flock" is a place-name (Gen 35:21; *see* EDER, TOWER OF) and also may be a metaphorical reference to Jerusalem (Mic 4:8). Jesus teaches about the cost of discipleship with the example of how much planning goes into building a tower (Luke 14:28). *See* ANTONIA, FORTRESS; HERODIAN FORTRESSES; HERODIUM; JERUSALEM; WALLS.

JOHN I. LAWLOR

TOWER OF BABEL. *See* BABEL.

TOWER OF HANANEL. *See* HANANEL, TOWER OF.

TOWER OF SHECHEM. *See* SHECHEM, TOWER OF.

TOWER OF THE HUNDRED [מִגְדַּל הַמֵּאָה mighdal hamme'ah]. A tower purportedly located on the northern side of the city wall of JERUSALEM, apparently near the Sheep Gate and the Tower of Hananel. It is mentioned in Neh 3:1 as part of the portion of the wall rebuilt by the high priest Eliashib and his associates. In Neh 12:39, it is a location through which a thanksgiving procession passes as part of a dedication ceremony.

DEREK E. WITTMAN

TOWER OF THE OVENS. *See* OVENS, TOWER OF THE.

TOWN CLERK [γραμματεύς grammateus]. "Town clerk" has been the usual translation of grammateus (mentioned in Acts 19:35) in all major English versions of Acts. By the Persian period, Mediterranean societies witnessed a small number of persons who were literate (less than 1 percent). Some of these literate persons had the task of dealing with the composition, production, interpretation, and maintenance of written documents (such as Egyptian accountants in LXX Exod 5:6 and Israelite military registrars in LXX Deut 20:5, 8). The general Hellenistic name for the occupation of such persons was grammateus. From the Persian period on in Israel, these documents included Israel's sacred writings, the Torah. Grammateus in that cultural sphere meant a Torah expert (frequently mentioned in the Gospels [e.g., Matt 2:4; Mark 8:31] and Acts, translated "scribe"). In Egypt, the grammateus was a public official who kept census records, land holding titles, and "liturgy" lists of those obliged to public works for submission to the central authority. Thus the Egyptian grammateus was a town or "city" clerk or registrar, depending on the civic unit in question. The situation was similar in Asia Minor where the grammateus dealt with civic written documents: official correspondence to and from the civic unit in question: tax registers, land deeds, and the like.

In the Ephesus episode described in Acts 19, the person who steps forward to quiet the riotous crowd is the grammateus (v. 35). Since Ephesus was a polis (πόλις, "city"), it seems appropriate to translate the word as "city clerk." This city clerk was one of the highest local officials in Ephesus. He could exercise great influence in the affairs of the city. It is from the context of use in the Acts report that translators have rightly concluded that the clerk in question was a person of some consequence, hence a local city official in Ephesus. His full title would be grammateus tou dēmou (γραμματεὺς τοῦ δημοῦ), "clerk of the people," one of the varied clerks or secretaries who served in a number of Hellenistic civic institutions (e.g., "city" councils, collegial magistracies, and the like). He was elected from the citizenry by lot, usually for a term of one year. His task involved reading out important, official dispatches, registering and keeping city records, and drafting important documents for the city assembly, in which he often took a leadership role, alone or with the magistrates. As Acts 19:38-39 describes, the city clerk was also concerned that the proper civic procedure was followed, involving the courts, the proconsul, and the regular assembly. The city clerk frequently led city politics and spoke for the city assembly. Inscriptions were often dated by the clerk's year in office, and the clerk appears on Ephesian coinage from the time of Augustus, again indicating his importance. The city clerk also was responsible for many details of civic administration. He was thus an appropriate person to take leadership in the sort of situation Luke describes in the theater of Ephesus. *See* ASIARCH.

Bibliography: James Hope Moulton and George Milligan. *The Vocabulary of the Greek Testament* (1976); Paul Trebilco. "Asia." *The Book of Acts in Its Graeco-Roman Setting. Vol. 2: The Book of Acts in Its First Century Setting.* David W. J. Gill and Conrad Gempf, eds. (1994) 291–362.

BRUCE J. MALINA

TRACHONITIS trak'uh-ni'tis [Τραχωνῖτις Trachōnitis]. A region in northern Transjordan ruled by Herod Philip. It is mentioned in the Bible only in Luke 3:1, a passage that establishes the chronological setting of John the Baptist's ministry. The area of Trachonitis is known in the OT as BASHAN, corresponding to the modern area of southern Syria called the Hauran. Trachonitis' name is derived from the word trachys (τραχύς, "rough, rocky region"; Josephus, *Ant.* 15.344–47; Strabo, *Geogr.* 16.2.16, 20). The area consists of a large basalt flow of over 350 sq. mi. The basalt flow is rough and in many places is more than 50 ft. thick. This creates a wild terrain with caves that has been a haven for brigands and rebels down through the centuries. In fact, a portion of the area is still known as el-Leja, "the Refuge." Strabo mentions the roughness of the terrain (*Geogr.* 16.2.20), and Josephus describes the difficulty of ruling over the people of this region (*Ant.* 15.342–48; 17.23–28).

Roman control began in 64 BCE under Pompey the Great but mainly through client rulers like Zenodorus. In 23 BCE, Augustus placed the area under the control of Herod the Great, who had to suppress rebellion by force (*Ant.* 15.342–48; 16.130). Trachonitis was willed by Herod in 4 BCE to his son Philip as a part of his tetrarchy (Luke 3:1; *Ant.* 17.189; *J.W.* 2.93–94; *see* TETRARCH, TETRARCHY). Philip ruled the area well for almost forty years. Upon his death in 34 CE, it came under the control of the Roman governor of Syria. In 37 CE it was given to Herod Agrippa I by Caligula. Agrippa ruled Trachonitis until his death in 44 CE. The Roman governor controlled the area until Herod Agrippa II came of age, and then he ruled the territory from 53–98 CE. The Romans then made the area a part of the Roman province of Syria until it was added to the province of Arabia in 295 CE.

The area is rugged but the basalt flows can produce fertile soil in areas where enough water is available, which makes limited agriculture possible. The area produces some wheat and grapes, but it is especially well suited for grazing sheep and goats. The area is famous for its buildings constructed solely of basalt. Large communities developed in the early Christian era, and many churches were constructed from the basalt.

JOHN D. WINELAND

TRADE AND COMMERCE. Trade is moving things through a distance and exchanging them with other people; commerce is a system of cultural practices that facilitate trade.

A. Introduction

In the ANE people walked great distances, sometimes very great distances. They might hunt and gather things to eat as they went along, and they might carry things with them. They have done so for a very long time, and the archaeological evidence for their efforts is small but intriguing.

Scholars assume that these trips were a mechanism for diffusing new tools, techniques, and ideas. The motives for undertaking such journeys may have included a desire to see new lands and to escape old ones, to enlarge political boundaries and to avoid cultural limitations, to make profits and to fulfill obligations.

B. Early Trade

Light and shiny things were most likely to be carried: light because the traveler did not want to be overly burdened and shiny because they might appeal to people with whom one could not directly communicate. Silver worked, and gold, probably, but the first thing we see in archaeology is obsidian, a shiny black rock that is found around some volcanoes; it is brittle and breaks easily, but it makes a very sharp knife while it lasts, and it does not dull for a long time. In the Near East it comes only from extinct volcanoes in what is now Turkey, but its attractions led it to be carried south across the Taurus Mountains and into the Mesopotamian plain and down the Mediterranean coast.

Obsidian blades are found widely in sites in the period of the Neolithic ("New Stone") Age that saw the regularization of agriculture and the establishment of settled village life in a broad arc from the Iranian mountains over to Southern Jordan and Israel between 9000 and 6000 BCE. After the Neolithic, blades found did not diminish in number as distance from the sources increased, meaning probably that some kind of systematic trade was pursued, and deliveries could be expected where there was need for them.

Obsidian became increasingly important and then dropped off in importance everywhere, though for some functions it may still have been preferred. Some city sites, like Hamoukar in eastern Syria and Jericho in the Jordan Valley, do not seem to have had a viable agricultural base but may have been trading cities for obsidian or other minerals and for other goods that have not been preserved.

One way to see ancient trade is as a set of traditional relationships that did not change much on the basis of what was available and what was needed. Maybe the early obsidian traders passed their obsidian only from one village to the next and got in return a set amount of food or other material. Another way to see trade is as an exchange that was subject to negotiation between the parties and that might reflect the supply of obsidian and of whatever was traded for the obsidian and the need of the participants for both. Or there might be some combination of a traditional social relationship and of a supply and demand driven by price negotiation.

A key question in choosing models is whether the societies in which the trade was taking place were simple communal structures centered on extended families or whether they were edging toward more hierarchy and complexity. If we are very early in human social organization in the Neolithic, maybe trade flourished among traditional trade partners only and involved traditional goods in traditional amounts. If we are later, and if we imagine traders arriving not just with the obsidian but with other crops and products no one in the receiving village had ever seen before, perhaps speaking a language different from the village's, we edge into difficult but ultimately successful negotiations about prices.

Maybe at first villagers just beat up the stranger and took his goods, but other strangers came later, and the villagers figured out that being nice to them would encourage them to come back in another year with other neat things. This commitment to kindness to strangers as trading partners has been called "bourgeois virtue," and is a key value in societies around the world. We see it first in the ANE.

In some cases this virtue on the part of the recipients, coupled with the adventurousness of the travelers, led to the creation of settlements of foreigners that survived on trading, though they might do a little agriculture too. These have been called "trade diasporas," strewings of people away from their usual homes. The old Sumerian settlements up and down the Euphrates

River before 3500 BCE in Syria and in what is now Iran were such transplanted settlements as were the Old Assyrian enclaves in Anatolia, modern Turkey, in the early 2nd millennium.

Perhaps in the early contexts goods had to be paid for in full to sever any obligation to a foreign merchant. But bourgeois virtue dictates, and successful modern companies preach, that people are willing to pay slightly higher prices if they have a personal connection with the sellers. The logic of the market was probably always tempered by personal interactions.

The Sumerian tale of Enmerkar and the Lord of Aratta describes the interaction between an Early Dynastic ruler of Uruk and the lord of an Iranian city, probably in Kerman province. The text was copied around 1800 BCE, but the events depicted date back to 2800 BCE. The city of Uruk was to send grain to Aratta in nets on pack asses, not carts as was usual. Envoys went back and forth, instead. There was a translation problem between the rulers, which was overcome by the witty Mesopotamians' use of a clay tablet, though how the Lord of Aratta managed to make sense of it is unclear. The initial hostile posturing gave way to peaceful trade.

Elam, meaning apparently "the heights," to the east of Iraq in what is now Iran, was always a major trading partner. Productive relations with Elam were signs of the success of centralizing governments, and there is a treaty preserved with a Mesopotamian king around 2200 BCE.

C. Money and Prices

What was money? Some say that until coinage there was none, and people were constantly involved in bartering, exchanging whatever goods or services they had of any sort for other things or services they wanted or needed. This doubtless happened from time to time, as it still does in our economies. But the writing civilizations all seem to have been multi-money economies, where a small variety of things could be used to pay for particular goods or services.

This began perhaps with the use of grains, which lasted indefinitely if they did not get wet, especially for payments to people who lived nearby and could transform the grain into tasty bread or gruel. But the societies also had other goods that worked in other circumstances, particularly silver. In most of the Near East, silver had to come from elsewhere, Turkey or Africa, but it continued to be the money of choice for some things from very early times down to the middle of the 2nd millennium. Then, because perhaps of a constriction in the supply of silver, people turned to bronze as money, and gold, presumably from Egypt, was also used. In the 1st millennium some of these other moneys continued to be relied on, but silver reasserted its power, and that is mostly what we see in the uses of money in the OT.

Such moneys were weighed, not counted. Bits of silver have been found in hoards, and that is probably how most silver moved. The weights were usually locally established standards that could differ considerably. The Ulu Burun shipwreck from the late 2nd millennium off the coast of Turkey, for example, had seven different sets of weights to conform to the different standards around the Mediterranean. This seems very confusing, though the English-speaking world still labors between pounds and kilograms; a greater variety obtained in ancient communities.

Coinage was invented in Lydia, now central western Turkey, in the 600s BCE, apparently to store very expensive metals. Gradually over the next one hundred years coinage developed into a means of payment. In the Bible there are references to darics of gold, named after the image of the Persian king Darius (521–486 BCE) on the coins. The Chronicler assumed in 1 Chr 29:7 that the coins existed already in David's time; the Persians' subjects might well have had such coins by the periods of Ezra 2:69 and Neh 7:70-72.

Prices attested in the OT are listed here in roughly chronological order: 1) Land—Gen 23:15: 400 shekels silver for a field; Gen 33:19: 100 qesitah (קְשִׂיטָה, a weight of silver) for a field; 2 Sam 24:24: fifty shekels silver for a threshing floor; contrast 1 Chr 21:25 with 600 shekels gold for the same site (there clearly was inflation in the value of the site to the culture between the earlier and later story); 1 Kgs 16:24: two talents = 6,000 shekels silver for a hill; Jer 32:9: seventeen shekels for a field under siege conditions. 2) Slaves—Gen 37:28: twenty shekels silver for Joseph; Hos 3:2: fifteen shekels silver for an adulteress along with a measure of barley (a homer and a lethech, perhaps an ass-load and a half, quite a lot of barley). 3) Wages—Zech 11:12: thirty shekels silver for a herder for a month. *See* MONEY, COINS; WEIGHTS AND MEASURES.

D. Means of Transport

Water-borne trade in the ancient world always seems to have been cheaper and maybe safer than overland trade. Israel's coast in biblical times was usually in foreign hands, and the River Jordan was hardly a major thoroughfare, but Prov 31:14 used the ships of the merchant as a positive image. Israel sat on the major land route between Egypt and northern Mesopotamia, modern Syria, and so was likely the beneficiary of the traffic. Tolls collected from travelers may have been a major source of revenue when the state was powerful enough to impose them.

Roads in the ANE were unpaved and rutted, slow to travel on, and easily flooded out. So land travel was not fast, and it was fraught with delays, some imposed by local governments wanting customs duties and some by highwaymen. Pack animals were useful, and sometimes, as in Gen 45:19–46:5, so was the wheeled wagon, which was apparently invented in southern Iraq around 3500 BCE. While donkeys seem to have been able to go 25–30 km or 15–20 mi. a day, camels could go farther, 40–60 km or 25–40 mi. a day; ships might go 100–150 km or 60–95 mi. if they sailed all day and night, so they could be a bit faster than camels.

E. Third and Second Millennium BCE Trade
1. The Persian Gulf

The archaeological record reveals that there was movement up and down the Persian or Arab Gulf to southern Mesopotomia or Iraq in the 3rd millennium. It is not clear what the Mesopotamians were exporting, though as in later periods they may have been sending their textiles abroad, especially wool, perhaps as finished products from their work houses. But back was coming lapis lazuli, a highly prized blue stone that came from what is now northern Afghanistan.

In Shahr-i Sokhte ("Hardship City") in central Iran, archaeologists found a lapis lazuli working center, far from the source of the material and far also from the population of Mesopotamia that valued the stone. There was a source of tin nearby, which may have attracted traders first. Lapis was used to decorate walls and statues and for small ornaments and parts of ornaments. Since it was light and valuable, it might have come into southern Iraq overland, but in later periods the trade came by boat.

In Mesopotamian texts the sources of the Gulf trade were called Magan and Meluhha, perhaps meaning the Oman coast of Arabia and the Iranian coast, or perhaps they were extended to mean anything to the east. Copper from Oman was sent north, and the island of Bahrain got grain from Mesopotamia. In the 2nd millennium, there were seals found in Mesopotamia from as far away as the Indus Valley, and their bearers may have come, too, to buy wool and unload their minerals. The rulers of Mesopotamia under the Sargonic kings, who put together the first multi-city empire around 2300 BCE, were aware that one symbol of their success was the flourishing of the Gulf trade, and when it ended with their fall, elites were upset by the absence of goods they regarded as necessary luxuries.

2. The Old Assyrian trade

In the early 2nd millennium BCE, a two-month mule ride would bring an Assyrian from northern Iraq along with a cargo of textiles and of tin, probably ultimately from Iran, into the highlands of Turkey. Locals there would pay a pretty price in silver or gold for the tin so they could combine it with their local copper and make bronze. Bronze was the hardest and best metal for weapons known at the time. It took only a tenth of the amount of tin as copper to make it, so it made sense to bring the tin in.

The Assyrians sometimes came away with profits of as much as 100 percent on tin and 200 percent on textiles for their journeys through the lawless mountains. Many sold their donkeys and immediately set out to return to Assur, their home city, but many stayed.

The traveler might remain a year and go back to Assur, or he might settle in and marry an Anatolian wife, have children who would grow up bilingual and who might continue in the trade. This family with others derived from Assyria constituted a merchant association, termed a "quay" or "harbor," which negotiated with the locals and disciplined its members. Brigands on the road could stop the whole thing, or a war down the Euphrates might make it prohibitively dangerous to get the goods through.

These arrangements began around 1900 BCE and ended around 1700 BCE. Assyrian merchants also traveled from Assur in northern Iraq to Babylonia to the south to pick up wool and other textiles. Others headed out with these things to Anatolia, along with the all-important tin that probably had come from the east. Not a few young Assyrians succumbed to the lure of the trade in spite of the distance, the danger, and the possible social isolation when they got to Anatolia.

From five generations of those who stayed we learn of the details of their community and even get some insight into what was happening back at Assur; there are very few if any texts from Assur in this period. The majority of the texts from this trade are letters exchanged between Assur and the colonies, and a significant minority shows how caravans were organized and financed by merchants who went in together to outfit them.

One letter tells of a run-in with local authorities. A man sent his smuggled goods to someone named Pushu-ken, but Pushu-ken was caught and put in jail. The letter warns that the queen has sent messages all over the land concerning smuggling, and she has posted look-outs, so that it would be unwise to try to smuggle anything. But another contract spells out terms for one Puzar-Ishtar to smuggle Akkadian textiles, tin, and a donkey with a harness. The contract provides payment for the smuggler, so clearly there was money to be made in evading the taxes.

Trade diasporas like this were useful to the profit-making emigrants, but also to the elites of the towns in which they were set up. They existed at the pleasure of the local powers. In the period a new and later important group of Indo-Europeans, the Hittites, came into central Anatolia, and, although we cannot say for certain, they may not have appreciated the foreign merchants and so threw them out. In some sort of upheaval the caravans stopped coming, and the Assyrians either returned to Assur or died abroad, not to be replaced.

3. The Amarna age

Around 1350 BCE letters in Akkadian language and cuneiform script from Amarna in central Egypt reveal international relations among the kings of Western Asia as they addressed the king of Egypt. As with the Old Assyrian letters, these may give us a one-sided view, and yet the king of Egypt was on ostensibly good terms with rulers from across the ancient world, and some of the reason was trade. Values were given in gold, and the range of Egypt's trade ran from Babylonia into the Hittite area of Anatolia, Cyprus, and the coast of Syria and Palestine. The letters show that significant trade was in royal hands, and royal merchants were supposed to be protected by local rulers as the merchants moved about on their business. This was not an easy task, and kings sometimes had to compensate other sovereigns for merchants killed in their territories. The Hittites dominated the north of Syria politically, but traders tended to be Syrians familiar with the coastal trade. And the pesky Hapiru people lurked as brigands. One letter announces that the writer had to pay a large sum of money to the king to compensate for merchants who were struck down by the ʿApiru (*see* HABIRU, HAPIRU).

There is an irrational element in this trade, since sometimes goods were exchanged not for economic but for ceremonial purposes, as when a ruler on the island of Cyprus sent the king of Egypt gold, which Egypt had in abundance in the eastern mountains. There was a rough reciprocity in these exchanges, but kings sought advantages for themselves to get new and interesting things from abroad.

Most interesting is the flow of persons into and out of Egypt. The Egyptians saw this as a natural result of the superiority of their climate and their highly productive river. Foreigners may have come as temporary sojourners, as in the stories of the biblical patriarchs, or as more or less permanent settlers who started off as mercenary soldiers. All sorts of people came, including even physicians. A statue of a goddess came too from Upper Mesopotamia in today's Syria all the way to Egypt on a temporary visit.

4. Ugarit

Ugarit, near the modern Syrian coastal city of Latakia, in the late 2nd millennium was a transshipment point for goods from the Syrian interior, especially wool and other processed textiles, which were exchanged for metals and stones from elsewhere. Its cuneiform archives show that Ugarit had seafarers from across the Aegean and Egypt stopping in its port.

Merchants imported grain, wine, and oil from distant Crete to Ugarit. Pottery came from Cyprus and also from mainland Greece and the islands. Hurrians, Hittites, and Egyptians lived in Ugarit to take advantage of the trade. After the establishment of peace between the Egyptians and the Hittites in Ramesses II's reign (1279–1213 BCE), archaeology shows trade became even more important. But this city, like much of the ANE, was ravaged around 1200 by the ethnic movements that the Egyptians called the invasions of the Sea Peoples, presumably Aegeans fleeing unrest or famine at home, and Ugarit and the Hittite empire were never reconstituted.

From this time of uncertainty comes a unique Egyptian composition, the Journey of Wen-Amon (*see* WENAMUN, JOURNEY OF). The priest who wrote the report had been sent by sea in a Syrian ship to the Syro-Lebanese coast to buy wood for the sacred barge of the temple he worked for, but the coastal ruler he encountered felt no piety at all toward the Egyptian god. The priest had to pay cash and had to send for more when his money was stolen. Pirates threatened Wen-Amon's success, and the local rulers could or would do little about them. When Wen-Amon went to Cyprus, he begged for someone who spoke Egyptian and found one who could communicate with the ruling princess there. The end of the report is not preserved, but presumably we would not have it at all if the priest had been unable to return home. Though the story may be read as a lament for lost Egyptian influence, it may show a normal frustrating adventure of someone who wanted to conduct seaborne trade.

F. First Millennium BCE Trade

1. The Phoenicians

The Syrian and Lebanese coasts continued to be crossroads for trade and looked to the sea for goods and people. The Greeks called these areas "Phoenician," after a purple dye derived from a sea mussel that grew there. But the locals just referred to themselves as citizens of their particular cities. They were not politically unified, but they represented a continuation of Ugaritic culture in that they used a simplified writing system, no longer on clay but on papyrus and stone in the so-called Phoenician alphabet, the source of all subsequent alphabets in which we still read and write. This is probably the single most important result of trade in the ANE, but the Phoenicians were involved in moving other goods to where they were wanted.

Since we lack archival texts from Phoenician home ports, we do not know how the trade was organized, but the cities were each independent, and there probably was lots of room for private enterprise. That sometimes might look like piracy, as in the *Od.* 15.410–85, where the swineherd Eumaios explained how the Phoenicians had seduced his Phoenician nursemaid, enslaved him, and sold him to a Greek.

The Phoenicians sent out not just trading voyages but also permanent colonies, some of which developed into thriving cities on their own. The Marseilles tariff found in France in one of those cities shows an effort to regulate prices paid for religious sacrifices, though as always with such texts, a government's desire to regulate something shows there must have been a history of violations of fair pricing.

In the Bible, Ezek 27 and 28 paint a portrait of the complexity of the trade of the Phoenician cities of Tyre and Sidon in the middle of the 1st millennium. They moved goods from the ends of the Mediterranean but took only agricultural products from the relatively backward land of Judah. Silver, iron, tin, and lead came from Tarshish (the name maybe meaning topaz or some other semiprecious stone), perhaps the Spanish one or the one in Anatolia. The Greeks and Anatolians traded slaves and bronze for the Phoenicians' merchandise.

The Phoenician coast became part of the Assyrian Empire. The Assyrians' interest in minerals from the far west may have encouraged voyaging. Archaeology shows Phoenicians in Spain by 800 BCE, but they may have come earlier to trade for silver and tin. They got beyond Cádiz in Spain (the name may derive from the Phoenician word for "holy") and had outposts on the Atlantic coast of Morocco.

As seafarers, the Phoenicians may have kept mainly within sight of the coasts, but later North Africans thought they had gotten to the Canary Islands out in the Atlantic. Evidence from coins that they reached the Azores is doubtful since the coins are now lost.

Herodotus' sketch of Phoenicians sailing around Africa for the Egyptian king Necho II (610–595 BCE) in *Hist.* 4.42 seems fantastic, though some scholars have found it credible. While the Punic Wars against Carthage, the most successful Phoenician colony, were still raging in the 2nd cent. BCE, the Roman comedian Plautus underlined the cosmopolitan skill but also the sneakiness of the Phoenician enemy: they understand all languages but pretend they do not.

The Assyrian Empire as it stretched westward after 883 BCE forced a redistribution of goods from the tribute-paying states to the capital area in the form of war booty and taxes, and also encouraged state-sponsored commerce. But goods also flowed out from the center to the provinces in the form of pay for vassals and soldiers. The Empire also was a market for fine goods, notably ivory trinkets carved in Syria and found in the Assyrian capital.

2. Solomon

The stories about Solomon stress the thriving of his state and its connection with long-distance trade. Though the archaeological evidence for the reign is scant, the books of Kings and Chronicles assert that his legendary wealth derived from his bringing chariots and horses, the super-weapons of the age, from Egypt and Anatolia. Egypt is tough on horses, but they love it in Anatolia, so the Israelite prince may have been an intermediary in that exchange, which was an essential arms race for 1st millennium powers.

Less easy to understand are the assertions about Solomon's sea-borne trade, which included building boats on the Red Sea. Perhaps he was tapping into the trade in light and valuable edible and aromatic spices coming from India and beyond. The marvelous visit of the Queen of Sheba (Saba in south Arabia) was a reflection of this contact. Solomon is said to have used Phoenician experts to sail trading ships on the Red Sea. Later kings may have tried to repeat the feat (1 Kgs 22:48-49; 2 Kgs 14:22), though not always with success since the southern port of Elat fell to the neighboring state of Edom in the 730s BCE (2 Kgs 16:6). It has been argued that the wisdom of Solomon, reflected in attributions in the books of Proverbs, Ecclesiastes, Psalms, and even Song of Songs, as in 1 Kings, derived from the logic that to get rich one must be wise.

The relations with the Phoenicians, however, reflect deficit spending of a most unwise-sounding kind, resulting in Solomon's giving up twenty villages in Israel as payment to the ruler of Tyre. The biblical text says that the ruler was dissatisfied with the villages, but the donation must have reflected badly on Solomon among Israelites even if the Phoenicians had appreciated it. The Tyrian king had given 120 talents of gold, so each city was worth about 6 talents (1 Kgs 9:10-14).

Another corollary of the long-distance trade may have been the numerous marriage alliances the king made. Some scholars wonder about the historicity of the unprecedented marriage with a daughter of the king of Egypt; the Egyptians accepted foreign brides for their kings but never, except possibly for Solomon, sent their royal daughters abroad. But Egypt was weak in this period, and a princess may have seemed a small price to pay for a peaceful eastern border.

The foreign brides allegedly led to Solomon's building temples to foreign gods, though, and this assertion colors all other allusions to the king outside the wisdom literature. Egyptians really were concerned about Israel as we see archaeologically in the invasion of Sheshonk I around 925 BCE; that invasion may have ended Solomon's reign or merely underlined the weakness of his successors.

3. Crossing the deserts

The camel may have been domesticated in Arabia much earlier, but it is only in the 1st millennium that it became a standard beast of burden in attempts to cross the central deserts of the ANE with trade goods. Camels and Arabs were mentioned in 8th-cent. Assyrian royal inscriptions as a factor in warfare. The Aramaeans may have started the trade across the deserts, and later the Nabateans took it up, sophisticated desert-dwellers who wrote inscriptions in Aramaic but may have spoken Arabic, if we judge from their names. And the last independent king of Babylonia, Nabonidus, subdued the Arabs around the north central Arabian oasis of Teima when he moved his capital there for eleven years. People back home thought he was insane, but he said he was reacting to a famine in Babylonia. Modern speculation on his motives centers on his desire to control and tax the caravan trade in spices that led to Egypt. A brief mention of the cross-desert trade is the description of how Joseph's brothers got rid of him by selling him to camel-riding Midianites or Ishmaelites who were going down to Egypt (Gen 37:25-28).

G. Goods Traded

The list here is not exhaustive of the goods that moved over the course of 3,000 years of written history in the ANE, but it is representative of some of the more lucrative and perhaps luxurious things that appear in texts both in the Bible and outside it. The movement of most of these goods was a form of luxury consumption and may not have been available for ordinary people to enjoy.

Israel exported olive oil, wine, perhaps perfume, and grain. Occasional exports included honey, pistachios, almonds, and a glue-like substance used in crafts (Gen 37:25; 43:11).

Imports included, in English alphabetical order: 1) Chariots and horses from Egypt, 1 Kgs 10:28-29. 2) Copper from Asia Minor, Cyprus, and the Arabah, the mountains to the southeast of Israel. 3) Cotton probably from India (Esth 1:6). The book of Esther is set in the Persian Empire, when vistas to the east had opened up. The king Sennacherib had already tried to grow cotton in Assyria. 4) Fish (Neh 13:16). The foreign merchants Nehemiah tried to keep out of Jerusalem on the Sabbath brought fish, perhaps only from the sea of Galilee or from the Mediterranean. 5) Gold from southern Arabia (Gen 2:11; 1 Kgs 9:28; 10:10-11, 14-15; 2 Chr 8:18; 9:9). 6) Iron from Asia Minor and the Arabah. Early in Israel's existence the Philistine monopoly on weapons technology, not necessarily including iron (1 Sam 13:19-22), seems not to be clear archaeologically. 7) Linen from Egypt and Syria (Exod 9:31; Ezek 27:7, 16, reading Edom or Aram?), but Josh 2:6; Hos 2:5, 9; and the Gezer calendar show flax, the source of linen, was grown in Israel too. 8) Silver from Anatolia. 9) Slaves, especially under Hellenism (Joel 3:6), including women and children as war booty (1 Macc 3:41; 2 Macc 8:10-11), where traders bought slaves with silver and gold after battles. 10) Spices from southern Arabia, Ethiopia, and beyond. 11) Timber from Lebanon. Though pollen evidence indicates that by the 1st millennium there were many fewer trees in Lebanon than earlier, there may have been more than in Israel itself. 12) Tin, lead, and silver from Khurasan in eastern Iran. 13) Wool and sheep from Moab as tribute to the king of Israel (2 Kgs 3:4).

H. Attitudes toward Trade

Trade in the ANE always involved dislocation and making money by bringing things from a distance. As in later societies, the merchant was usually an outsider who was distrusted and thought capable of being a spy. After all, he mysteriously worked for cash, unlike most peasants.

This attitude of distrust may be seen in the terms for trader, including "Canaanite" (kena'ani [כְּנַעֲנִי]; NRSV, "merchant" or "trader") among Israelites in Isa 23:3, 8; Ezek 17:4; Hos 12:7 (Heb. 12:8); Prov 31:24; and also in the contempt for "unjust gain" (Prov 15:27). The question, then as now, is what gain is unjust. The sins of traders included using false and diverse balances and also hoarding (Amos 8:4-8; Hos 12:7; Prov 11:26).

Another Hebrew word for trader is sokher (סֹחֵר, "circulator") and contexts show such people could travel far (Gen 37:28), go overseas (Isa 23:2), form joint partnerships (Job 41:6), and even work for a temple (Zech 14:21). There were some influential ones (Isa

47:15), but not all were honest (Hos 12:7). Still, their disappearance boded ill for the civil peace of a country (Zeph 1:11; Judg 5:6). Other terms included "men of commerce" (1 Kgs 10:15 // 2 Chr 9:14) bearing gold, and "travelers," Ezek 27's favorite term.

The distrust of traders can be seen also in Egypt of the New Kingdom (1550–1069 BCE), when international trade seems to have been in Syrian hands. Though merchants were not necessarily foreigners, there were accusations against them of misappropriating goods, and they were involved in receiving goods stolen in tomb robberies, and those in authority would not have held them in high regard. In later periods, the city that the Greeks called Naucratis, Egyptian for "city of Crates," in Egypt's western delta may have been founded to try to restrict the movements of Greek merchants, but it did not work since Herodotus found them in many places (*Hist.* 2.39).

The later association of Jews with commerce arose in medieval times when Jews took advantage of their forced diaspora to trade with co-religionists living elsewhere. Later anti-Semitism may owe some of its features to the distrust of traders.

Bibliography: George F. Bass. "Sea and River Craft in the Ancient Near East." *Civilizations of the Ancient Near East.* Jack Sasson, ed. (1995) 1421–31; Carlos Cordova. "The Degradation of the Ancient Near Eastern Environment." *A Companion to the Ancient Near East.* Daniel C. Snell, ed. (2005); 109–25; Philip D. Curtin. *Cross-Cultural Trade in World History* (1984); Herbert H. Gowen. "Hebrew Trade and Trade Terms in Old Testament Times." *JSOR* 6 (1922) 1–16; Yutaka Ikeda. "Solomon's Trade in Horses and Chariots." *Studies in the Period of David and Solomon.* Tomoo Ishida, ed. (1982) 215–38; Thorkild Jacobsen. *The Harps That Once ...* (1987); Deidre McCloskey. *The Bourgeois Virtues* (2006); Christopher M. Monroe. "Money and Trade." *A Companion to the Ancient Near East.* Daniel C. Snell, ed. (2005) 154–68; William Moran. *The Amarna Letters* (1992); Franz Rosenthal. "Canaanite and Aramaic Inscriptions." *Ancient Near Eastern Texts.* James Pritchard, ed. (1969) 653–62; William K. Simpson et al. *The Literature of Ancient Egypt.* 3rd ed. (2003); Daniel C. Snell. *Life in the Ancient Near East* (1997); Klaus R. Veenhof. *Aspects of Old Assyrian Trade and Its Terminology* (1972).

DANIEL C. SNELL

I. Trade in Greek and Roman Society

Greek and Roman sources indicate that while commercial activities were potentially profitable, tradesmen did not enjoy high social status (Herodotus, *Hist.* 2.166-67; Athenaeus, *Deipn.* 12.526d-e; Cicero, *Off.* I.150–52). Rome's senatorial class traditionally viewed agriculture as the only honorable source of wealth for aristocrats and frowned upon direct involvement in commerce (Cicero, *Verr.* 5.45–46; Tacitus, *Ann.*

4.13.2). Indeed, the *lex claudia* of 219/218 BCE forbid members of the Roman Senate from engaging in commerce, although some members of the senate were profiting from trade (Livy, *Hist.* 21.63.3–4). The *lex claudia* appears to have continued in force until the 3rd cent. CE. Some contemporary Jewish and early Christian authors held similar attitudes towards commerce, as suggested in the NT accounts of Jesus' confrontation with the merchants and money-changers at the Jerusalem Temple (Matt 21:12-13; Mark 11:15-17; Luke 19:45-46; John 2:13-17). Similarly, Sirach decries the moral deficiencies of merchants (26:29–27:2), an attitude echoed by Ambrose of Milan (*Hel.* 70–71). In a reversal of these values, the Letter of James warns Christian traders against relying on their future plans (Jas 4:13-17) and decries the injustices of a wealthy, agricultural elite (5:1-6).

This prejudice against commercial activities did not mean that the elite failed to profit from trade. Cato the Elder (234–149 BCE), the paragon of Roman conservatism, profited from shipping investments and maritime loans (Plutarch, *Cat. Maj.* 21.506), and Pliny the Younger (61–112 CE) reports that he lent out money, presumably at a profit (*Ep.* 3.19). However, Roman elites did not typically engage directly in commercial transactions. Rather, senatorial and land-holding elites utilized their freedmen or slaves to handle commercial transactions (Plutarch, *Cat. Maj.* 21.506). Thus, freedmen and slaves moved the products and handled the commercial transactions, allowing their patron to profit while avoiding the stigma of direct participation in commerce. The apparent ability of such freedmen-agents to act independently permitted them to profit while serving their patrons. In some cases freedmen traders became wealthy enough to become patrons themselves. Although wealthy tradesmen were typically not part of the governing elite, there are some exceptions, as in the case of Lucius Erastus of Ephesus, who specialized in transporting dignitaries by ship, and whose entry to the Ephesus city council the emperor Hadrian sponsored (*SIG* 838). However, Roman attitudes towards commerce suggest that wealthy tradesmen were not readily accepted within the society of the governing class, as indicated in the fictional satire of the nouveau-riche freedman Trimalchio (Petronius, *Satyr.* 76).

Although typically excluded from the governing class, papyri and inscriptions suggest that Roman traders often secured their status in society by membership in trade associations (*collegia*). Such organizations advanced the interests of their members, provided common funds for religious festivals and celebrations, and sometimes secured and distributed monopolies among the members. Associations of ship-owners, *corpora naviculariorum*, came to play an important role in securing the grain supply of Rome and supplying necessities to the army. As a result, the ship-owners' associations were able to gain exemption from public services for those members who assisted in the transport of grain to Rome.

Most trade in the Greek and Roman world was local. Long-distance trade was primarily limited to luxury items, such as purple cloth and spices, and agricultural commodities, such as grain, olive oil, and wine. In general, the cities of the Greco-Roman world were centers of consumption rather than production and manufacture. Rome was the single greatest center of consumption in the Mediterranean region during the principate, as depicted in the prophetic lament of Rev 18. Imperial resources were devoted to ensuring the supply of grain to Rome. However, other cities of the empire were significant consumers as well, and they typically hosted markets at which agricultural products and various commodities and luxury items could be bought and sold. An anonymous 4th-cent. commentator on trade routes relates that Antioch, Tyre, Caesarea, Ascalon, and Gaza were thriving commercial centers that abounded in all kinds of goods (*Expositio Totius Mundi* 23–33). This account also singles out some cities for the export of certain goods. For example, Caesarea and Neapolis were known for exporting purple cloth; Byblos, Tyre, and Berytus were known for the production and export of linen. The same source reports that Ascalon and Gaza exported a "very fine wine" to Syria and Egypt. However, all of these cities are located on major trade routes. For smaller towns and villages, trade was typically local and occasionally regional. For this reason, yearly festivals such as the Passover at Jerusalem or the annual festival and market at Mamre (Sozomen, *Eccl. hist.* 2.4.1–3) were significant occasions for the sale and distribution of goods to those who lived further from urban centers.

Long-distance trade primarily concerned grain, wine, olive oil, slaves, wool and textiles, building materials such as lumber and marble, and luxury goods such as amber, spices, and silk. The major grain exporters of the Greco-Roman world were the Black Sea region and Egypt, although a number of smaller exporters existed. Cities that could not produce enough grain for local demand depended upon imports. The suitability of grain for long-distance trade by sea facilitated its export from major production regions to locations where grain was not produced in great quantity. Classical Athens, for example, which was an exporter of a well-regarded olive oil, imported much of its grain from the Black Sea region. Rome, which depended on grain from Campania and Sicily in the later Republic, became increasingly dependent on grain from further away as the population of the city grew. The most important single exporter of grain to Rome during the NT era was Egypt, with its port city of Alexandria. Egypt was so important to Rome's grain supply that it was considered the personal property of the emperor and those of the senatorial class required the emperor's permission to visit the province.

Wine had been traded over long distances in the Greek world since at least the Late Bronze Age. Homer's poems suggest that by the Archaic period the vintages of certain regions known for their quality were in high demand (*Il.* 7.465–475). Commercial production of wine and the long-distance trade in wine increased during the Hellenistic and Roman periods (Diodorus Siculus, *Bib. Hist.* 5.26.2–3). Much of the wine consumed in the Roman period was locally produced. However, the demand for wines from specific regions and the suitability of wine for long-distance trade by ship ensured that commerce in imported wines was a constant feature of the empire's major ports.

Olive oil was produced in many areas of the Mediterranean. However, increased urbanization, increased olive cultivation, the popularity of particular olive oils, and the suitability of olive oil for long-distance export by ship meant that trade in high-quality oils over long distances was profitable. Athens exported olive oil to various parts of the Greek world from at least the 6th cent. BCE (Plutarch, *Sol.* 24.1; SEG XV 108). During the Roman Republic, much of Rome's olive oil was supplied from Italy. However, Rome's demand for olive oil during the empire was such that oil was also imported from other areas. By the 2nd cent. CE, the importation of olive oil reached such proportions that the transport amphorae required a special dump, eventually forming an artificial mound in Rome's suburbs, Monte Testaccio.

Warfare and piracy supplied the slave trade in the Greek and Roman worlds, although slaves were also bred on larger estates. During the late 1st cent. BCE, the slave trade grew to staggering proportions, with the slave market at Delos reportedly able to process 10,000 slaves in one day (Strabo, *Geogr.* 14.5.2). Wool and textiles formed a portion of long-distance trade in the Greek and Roman worlds, in particular those judged to be superior to locally produced goods (Pliny, *Nat.* 8.190–93). Likewise, building materials such as wood and marble judged to be of high quality were traded over long distances (Xenophon, *Hell.* 6.1.11; Strabo, *Geogr.* 4.6.2; 12.8.4). Purple dyed stuffs from specific centers of production in the Mediterranean were of high value. Chinese silks came into the Roman world via India to Roman ports on the Red Sea, then overland to the Nile, and then to Alexandria; spices such as pepper and some gemstones followed a similar route from India (*Periplus Maris Erythraei* 39, 49; Pliny, *Nat.* 6.101–106; 12.84). Amber was imported to the Greek and Roman worlds from northern and eastern Europe through the Bosporus, as well as by more direct routes (Diodorus Siculus, *Bib. Hist.* 5.22–23).

In antiquity the movement of goods over land was expensive and slow. Most of the roads in the Greco-Roman world were narrow and sporadically maintained. In more rural areas, the roads were often little more than footpaths that could accommodate single-file pack animals. However, the Roman Empire maintained a number of highways that connected its various territories and major cities (Strabo, *Geogr.* 5.3.8; Pausanias, *Descr.* 8.54.5). These highways were built to facilitate the governance of the empire and the movement of the army. Nevertheless, travelers and traders used these roads as well, and such roads facilitated overland commerce. Rome's major roads typically connected the larger cities of the empire with commercial and military ports. For example, the Via Egnatia linked Thessalonica and Philippi with Byzantium on the Bosporus and Dyrrachium on the Adriatic. Some of these highways still survive in portions, most famously the Via Appia outside of Rome, a road that once connected Rome to Brundisium, a harbor used for travel to the eastern Mediterranean.

Although Rome's highways facilitated overland trade, in the Greco-Roman era the cheapest way to move products over long distances was by water. River transport was critical in Egypt, but also in Gaul, where movement by river was often preferable to land (Strabo, *Geogr.* 4.1.14). Seagoing vessels varied in size from small boats used by local fishermen, which could be used for local commerce, to the very large ships used to transport grain and building materials to Rome. Shipwreck remains reveal that larger trading ships were over 40 m long and could carry 400 metric tons. In the Roman imperial period, extraordinarily large ships used to transport grain and building materials to Rome could hold up to 1,000 metric tons. Such enormous ships could only dock in larger harbors such as Ostia, Alexandria, Antioch, Piraeus, and Marseille. Larger commercial ships also carried passengers. Josephus describes his experience shipwrecked while traveling on such a vessel, reporting that nearly 600 people were on board (*Life* 15). The author of Acts describes Paul's travel on board an Alexandrian merchant ship bound for Rome and the vessel's wreck on Malta (Acts 27). Such a ship would likely have been a larger commercial vessel.

Bibliography: J. Andreau. *Banking and Business in the Roman World* (1999); L. Casson. *Ancient Trade and Society* (1984); L. Casson. *The Periplus Maris Erythraei* (1989); J. H. D'Arms and E. C. Kopf, eds. *The Seaborne Commerce of Ancient Rome: Studies in Archaeology and History* (1980); R. Duncan-Jones. *Structure and Scale of the Roman Economy* (1990); P. Garnsey. *Famine and Food Supply in the Graeco-Roman World* (1988); P. Garnsey, K. Tompkins, and C. R. Whittaker. *Trade in the Ancient Economy* (1983); K. Greene. *The Archaeology of the Roman Economy* (1986); F. Meijer and O. van Niff, eds. *Trade, Transport, and Society in the Ancient World: A Sourcebook* (1992); N. Morley. *Trade in Classical Antiquity* (2007); D. P. S. Peacock and D. F. Williams. *Amphorae and the Roman Economy* (1986); W. Scheidel and S. von Redden. *The Ancient Economy* (2002).

RANGAR H. CLINE

TRADER [כְּנַעַן kenaʿan, סֹחֵר sokher; ἔμπορος emporos]. Traders were merchants who traveled with their wares (Gen 37:28). They traded locally and internationally (1 Kgs 10:15; 2 Chr 9:14), had royal commissions (1 Kgs 10:28; 2 Chr 1:16), and were important carriers of regional wealth (1 Kgs 10:15; Isa 23:8; Ezek 17:4; Zeph 1:11; Zech 14:21; 1 Macc 3:41). Canaanite commercial dominance in the biblical world led to that ethnonym becoming synonymous with "trader" and "foreigner" (Job 41:6 [Heb. 40:30]; Hos 12:7 [Heb. 12:8]; Zech 14:21). Paul lists slave traders as sinners (andrapodistēs [ἀνδραποδιστής], 1 Tim 1:10). *Trader* and MERCHANT are interchangeable terms (Gen 23:16; Prov 31:24; Isa 23:8; Ezek 27:36).

LJUBICA JOVANOVIC

TRADITION HISTORY, NT. In the academic study of biblical literature, there is a general consensus that the texts as we know them are quite often the culminating product of the transmission and creative adaptation of traditions that antedate their present written form. By *tradition* (in this context), scholars are normally referring to discrete units of material—sayings, stories, parables, instructions, songs, etc.—drawn upon in the composition of the text. (*Tradition* sometimes bears a second meaning, namely a body of materials similar in outlook, theological tendency, or sharing an originating context; e.g., the Johannine tradition, Petrine tradition, apocalyptic tradition.)

The study of tradition history (sometimes called tradition criticism) is concerned with tracing the trajectory of such traditions from their originating contexts through stages of oral and written transmission up to and including their employment in a final written text. Thus, one way of conceiving tradition history is as the aggregate of diachronic analysis (dia + chronos [διά + χρόνος] = "through time") with regard to a discrete tradition. At least four such modes of analysis, sometimes overlapping, are routinely practiced within NT studies: 1) Historical criticism seeks to account for the origin of a tradition, including the assessment of its probable authenticity; 2) Form criticism discerns the formal type of the materials and traces their development as remembered in Christian preaching, worship, and mission, especially in oral and communal contexts; 3) Source criticism considers the collation and preservation of traditions especially in written forms; 4) Redaction criticism seeks to understand the ideological motivations of authors by tracing their editorial activity upon the traditional material in the composition of the text. As a subdiscipline of NT studies, tradition history is most closely associated with the methods of form criticism, but, in fact, the evolution of tradition is by no means limited to the oral stage, so it is proper to consider tradition history as a broader enterprise, even if much attention naturally focuses on the oral stage. In principle, the ongoing transmission and reception of the "final" text (partially accessible by means of textual criticism and the history of interpretation) might be a further object of tradition history, although the expression is less often used in this way (*see* FORM CRITICISM, NT; SOURCE CRITICISM).

These modes of analysis are most obviously relevant to the traditions that ostensibly underlie the NT narratives, especially the Jesus traditions found in the Gospels. Working backward from the extant materials (both canonical and extra-canonical), scholars observe differences in the form and function of various stories, sayings, and parables and hypothesize concerning the trajectory of their development. A critical factor in that analysis is the positing of a plausible social setting (German *Sitz im Leben*, "setting in life"), which provides the context in which the traditions would have been used and by means of which they might have been adapted, transformed, or even created. For example, that the extant versions of the parable of the Lost Sheep are put to different uses—communal discipline in Matt 18:12-14 and as an apologetic for Jesus' open table fellowship in Luke 15:4-7—bears witness to the flexible adaptation of a Jesus tradition. At the same time, that the data available are limited to extant texts chastens an overconfident reconstruction of the history of any tradition.

It is a matter of enduring debate to what extent the traditioning process transforms the Jesus traditions and other putatively historical materials. Are the traditions radically altered or even freely created? Or does the traditioning process preserve the memory of the historical Jesus more or less intact? The issues are complex and the debate often carried out in extreme terms by those committed to either pole of the spectrum. Three observations urge moderation: 1) What was remembered about or attributed to Jesus was surely passed along because it proved to be relevant to the ongoing life and self-understanding of those primitive Christian communities. That the early Christians' interest in Jesus was not narrowly or disinterestedly historical is a fundamental tenet of form criticism that can scarcely be doubted. 2) On the other hand, the early communities' interest in the Jesus tradition was not simply a matter of existential or pragmatic utility. At least one of the motives must have been historical curiosity on the part of Jesus' followers, a genuine interest in the words and deeds of Jesus and a corresponding interest to conserve their memory for the sake of posterity. 3) While the evidence suggests that early Christians exercised freedom in adapting Jesus' traditions, the instability of the oral tradition has sometimes been exaggerated by scholars, who, working within textual paradigms, fail to take into account the constraining dynamics of memory and community characteristic of predominately oral cultures (*see* TRADITION, ORAL).

Although tradition history will most often have to do with the NT narratives, it is also relevant to other NT literature at those points where the use of traditional materials is demonstrable or probable. A broad consensus maintains that even the most occasional or spontaneous of NT letters include preexisting traditions, including hymns (e.g., Phil 2:6-11; Col 1:15-20), summaries of early Christian preaching (e.g., 1 Cor 15:3-5), creedal fragments (e.g., Rom 3:21-26; 1 Cor 8:4-6; 1 Tim 3:16), and various sayings (e.g., 1 Tim 1:15; 3:1; 4:9; 2 Tim 2:11; Titus 3:8), including even the occasional reminiscence of a Jesus tradition outside the Gospels (e.g., 1 Cor 7:10; 11:23-25; compare Acts 20:35). *See* BIBLICAL CRITICISM; BIBLICAL INTERPRETATION, HISTORY OF.

Bibliography: Kenneth E. Bailey. "Informal Controlled Oral Tradition and the Synoptic Gospels." *AJT* 5 (1991) 34–54; Richard J. Bauckham. *Jesus and the Eyewitnesses: The Gospels as Eyewitness Testimony* (2006); Rudolf Bultmann. *History of the Synoptic Tradition* (1963); Martin Dibelius. *From Tradition to Gospel* (1971); James D. G. Dunn. *A New Perspective on Jesus: What the Quest for the Historical Jesus Missed* (2005); Birger Gerhardsson. *The Gospel Tradition* (1986); Joachim Jeremias. *The Parables of Jesus.* Rev. ed. (1963); Werner Kelber. *The Oral and Written Gospel: The Hermeneutics of Speaking and Writing in the Synoptic Tradition, Mark, Paul, and Q* (1983); Helmut Koester. *Ancient Christian Gospels: Their History and Development* (1990); E. P. Sanders. *The Tendencies of the Synoptic Tradition* (1969).

GARWOOD P. ANDERSON

TRADITION HISTORY, OT. The "tradition historical method" seeks to recover and narrate the development of both the oral and written stages of biblical material. Traditional historical research grew out of, and continues to change in keeping with, folklore studies. Three overarching assumptions inform this approach. First, the social institutions of ancient Israel used traditions as a type of rhetorical shorthand that shapes poetic and narrative identity formation. Tradition as content is a recurring rhetorical device. Second, tradition historians assume that the geographical origin, social, and religious locations of a tradition provide important interpretive keys. At the same time tradition historians assume that tradition is also a social process. So, third, these rhetorical building blocks have their origin in oral performance; they are an oral tradition. Tradition history proposed a transmission history from oral performance to written text. Tradition-historical research, like SOURCE CRITICISM and form criticism, understands that the results of its research can help generate a history of the region during the biblical period. Tradition-historical research begins with the same premise as form criticism, namely, that the social institutions that gave rise to the Bible had a linguistic "vocabulary," the content of the traditions, and a "grammar," the tradition-historical process (*see* FORM CRITICISM, OT).

Tradition history as a method distills the traditions that structure the OT and the development of those traditions. A tradition is a recurring metaphor that varies in its linguistic structure but gives a consistent set of meaning for a listening or reading audience. The first step of tradition history is to define the tradition. The tradition

as a recurring metaphor may take multiple verbal expressions, which complicates this first step. The second step presents the reconstruction of the development of oral prehistory traditions to provide the background for a history of the political and religious history of Israel. The third step includes the collection of comparative practices; stories and poetry from the ANE are used to assign a date to the biblical traditions and further understand the functions of the tradition. In step four, the tradition historian proposes a reconstruction of how the oral tradition migrated from an oral expression or earlier written expression to its present written form. Through the years the first step has remained methodologically unaltered. The reconstruction of the development of traditions and the use of comparative ANE material has, on the other hand, been a matter of significant debate. For example, both Gerhard von Rad and Martin Noth attempted to locate the oral prehistory traditions in the period of early Israel. Von Rad argued that the traditions of the Hexateuch arose from short historical creed. He later developed his OT theology around the traditions. Noth proposed that the Pentateuch developed around five traditions (ancestors, exodus, wilderness, Sinai, and entrance into arable land). However, Noth's re-evaluation of the tradition history content and process resulted in a different reconstruction of the political and religious history of ancient Israel.

The third assumption of tradition historical research concerns the idea of oral tradition; the fourth step of the method considers the relation of oral to written tradition. The perception of oral tradition has been debated over the years. German scholars described a short period of time that separated the oral tradition from the literary activity posited through source criticism. Scandinavian scholars sometimes referred to as the Uppsala School, on the other hand, drew a picture of the development of traditions through a protracted oral tradition. John Van Seters and Thomas Thompson have questioned the earlier contention proposed by both German and Scandinavian scholarship that there was a substantial oral prehistory. Susan Niditch makes a more fundamental criticism, positing that the concept of orality and literacy require a new understanding that is in keeping with new developments in folklore studies today (*see* FOLKLORE IN BIBLICAL INTERPRETATION). Michael Fishbane has interpreted tradition historical criticism to include the transmission history that extended well into the literary period as well as any oral prehistory. The INTERTEXTUALITY that is the use of biblical texts embedded in later biblical text is also an expression of tradition history. The transmission history can take the form of oral expression to textual expression or it may reconstruct the movement of one textual expression to another.

Bibliography: Robert A. DiVito. "Tradition Historical Criticism." *To Each Its Own Meaning: An Introduction to Biblical Criticisms and Their Application* (1993)

53–67; Michael Fishbane. *Biblical Interpretation in Ancient Israel* (1985); R. Gnuse. "Tradition History." *Methods of Biblical Interpretation* (2004) 127–133; Douglas A. Knight. *Rediscovering the Traditions of Israel* (1975); Susan Niditch. *Oral World and Written Word: Ancient Israelite Literature* (1996); Martin Noth. *A History of Pentateuchal Traditions* (1948; ET 1972); Gerhard von Rad. "The Form Critical Problem of the Hexateuch." *The Problem of the Hexateuch and Other Essays* (1938; ET 1966); Gerhard von Rad. *Old Testament Theology.* 2 vols. (1957, 1960; ET 1962, 1965); Walter E. Rast. *Tradition History and the Old Testament* (1972); Thomas Thompson. *The Origin Tradition of Ancient Israel* (1987); John Van Seters. *Abraham in History and Tradition* (1975).

STEPHEN BRECK REID

TRADITION, ORAL. The stories, myths, poetry, folktales, legends, and songs of the Israelite people and the first followers of Jesus emerged out of cultures that were more accustomed to hearing than reading. Some traditions were passed along from group to group and from generation to generation by word of mouth before they were eventually written down, assembled, and edited into the written text that we have today. The general acknowledgment by scholars that an oral tradition underlies the formation and transmission of the Bible has led to a long-standing interest in orality in biblical scholarship.

    A. Old Testament
    Bibliography
    B. New Testament
    Bibliography

A. Old Testament

Hermann Gunkel, the father of form criticism (*see* FORM CRITICISM, OT), believed that Israelite literature originally began as an oral production, usually short, simple, poetic, and folksy, which was utilized, performed, and received in a particular life setting (*Sitz im Leben*) of the Israelites. Scandinavian scholars of the Uppsala School maintained that OT traditions had a long period of oral transmission. They argue that it was through this transmission that OT traditions crystallized into a fixed form that was finally put down in writing (Engell; Nielsen). Especially influential to the study of oral traditions in the OT has been Albert Bates Lord and Milman Parry's study of formulaic language in Homeric literature. Their work has been utilized by biblical scholars in their exploration of formulaic language in the OT and in their examination of the performative roots of biblical literature (Culley 1967; Gunn).

Recent scholarship on orality in the OT has added nuance to these previous understandings, especially by noting that oral traditions can occur in a myriad of varieties and styles. Likewise, it has been shown that orality and literacy interact with and influence each other, not exist in a strict, separate dichotomy. Orality does not disappear with writing. Even a work that from its very inception is written is still influenced by the primarily oral culture from which it emerged and, thus, can contain oral aspects and elements (Niditch).

The recognition of the "oral mind-set" behind the OT has led to a search for vestiges of orality. While language in the OT does not evidence a clear metric or prosodic pattern, the OT conveys other stylized traits that can be associated with orality. Scholars have suggested the following literary patterns as belonging within the "oral register" or as indicative of an oral style (most examples from Niditch): 1) formulaic phrases, such as epithets (e.g., "the Ancient of Days" or the "the God of Abraham, Isaac, and Jacob") or longer formulas (e.g., the use of the pattern "call to/sends for" + "chain of bureaucrats" when a character in court needs to solve a difficult problem); 2) intertextuality, including quotations in the OT from other parts of the Bible or other types of referentiality; 3) repetitions of particular phrases, key words, or even full sentences such as the recurrence of the phrase "It is good" in the creation tale in Gen 1; 4) literary forms, including larger recurring thematic patterns or tropes such as the trickster motif or the victory-enthronement pattern; and 5) fixed synonymous word pairs in biblical poetry whereby two words are juxtaposed in parallel lines (*see* PARALLELISM; POETRY, HEBREW); for example, *deliver* and *judge* form a word-pair in these lines:

> "God by your name *deliver* me/
>   and by your might *judge* me"
>   (Ps 54:1)

> "Let him *judge* the poor of the people/
>   *deliver* the needy and crush the oppressor"
>   (Ps 72:4)

Scholars have delineated and recorded these various oral patterns in the poetic books of the OT (Whallon; Yoder), for example, in the psalms (Culley 1967) and in Job (Urbock), and in prose materials, such as in Judges and Samuel (Gunn).

Due to this complex interplay between the oral and the written, however, even a part of the OT that contains oral elements cannot be definitively said to have originated orally. Rather, Niditch has suggested four models for how oral and literate elements of Israelite culture interacted to create the OT: 1) the oral performance is dictated to a writer, who writes it down in an archive and thereby preserves the event; 2) the traditions of Israel slowly become fixed through many performances over a long period of time to audiences with an a shared group identity before being finally written down; through the process, the pan-Israelite become increasingly distilled in the tales; 3) a composition is written imitating an oral style; and 4) at the most literate end of the oral-literate continuum, a written source is used by an author, who reshapes and edits it, to create another written document; however, in this instance, the newly created document and the written sources that were used for it have still been influenced by an oral mind-set.

In summary, a complex interplay between orality and literacy underlies the composition, formulation, and transmission of the OT. An awareness of the relationship between the written text of the OT and the oral world that lies behind this text is thus a crucial part of the study of the OT.

Bibliography: Robert Culley. *Oral Formulaic Language in the Biblical Psalms* (1967); Robert Culley. "Oral Tradition and Biblical Studies." *Oral Tradition* 1 (1986) 30–65; Ivan Engell. *A Rigid Scrutiny: Critical Essays on the Old Testament* (1969); John Miles Foley. *The Singer of Tales in Performance* (1995); Hermann Gunkel. *Genesis.* 3rd ed. (1910); David Gunn. "Narrative Patterns and Oral Tradition in Judges and Samuel." *VT* 24 (1974) 286–317; Burke Long. "Recent Field Studies in Oral Literature and Their Bearing on OT Criticism." *VT* 26 (1976) 187–98; Albert Bates Lord. *A Singer of Tales* (1968); Edward Nielsen. *Oral Tradition: A Modern Problem in Old Testament Introduction* (1954); Susan Niditch. *Oral Word and Written Word* (1996); William Urbock. "Oral Antecedents to Job: A Survey of Formulas and Formulaic Systems." *Semeia* 5 (1976) 111–37; William Whallon. *Formula, Character, and Context: Studies in Homeric, Old English, and Old Testament Poetry* (1969); Perry Bruce Yoder. "A-B Pairs and Oral Composition in Hebrew Poetry." *VT* 21 (1971) 470–89.

SONG SUZIE PARK

B. New Testament

Much like any other society that is familiar with both oral and written means of expressing and mediating culture, Greco-Roman society of the Classical, Hellenistic, and Roman periods made use of both these forms in characteristic fashion, and this obviously also had its effects on the way Christianity took shape and shaped its own world and tradition (Millard 2000). Education relied above all on hearing and memorizing a set of stories, most of them transmitted in a written form but intended to be heard by an audience and performed by (semi-)professionals. The Jews of the Second Temple period in turn heard the law and the prophets read aloud in the synagogue, while at the same time some of their teachers were developing a whole set of instructions that were not recorded in writing and came to be known in Pharisaic-rabbinic tradition as the "Oral Torah," a phenomenon that is also mentioned in a polemical setting (Mark 7:1-23//Matt 15:1-20; "the tradition of the elders"; *see* ORAL LAW, ORAL TORAH).

The Gospel of Luke says that Jesus read and commented upon Scripture in the synagogue (Luke 4:16-21), but he himself never put down in writing anything

of what he taught. His disciples continued in this way, learning from Scripture and instructing their audience in their gatherings (1 Tim 4:13; 1 Cor 14:26) and proclaiming and preaching the message to those outside (Acts 2:14-36). Soon, however, some also began to write letters and then gospels, but these too were meant to be read before an audience, as Paul indicates for his own letters (1 Thess 5:27; compare Col 4:16) and Justin Martyr testifies for the Gospels as early as the mid-2nd cent. (*1 Apol.* 67). These few examples show that oral tradition and orality were formative elements in the way Christianity expressed and spread its message, and they very much remained so throughout its further history, shaping the church's praying and its preaching.

In NT studies oral tradition is a given, and for that reason it has perhaps not always received due consideration. It played a crucial role in the late 18th cent. in the "Oral Gospel Hypothesis" of J. G. Herder, who argued that the written Gospels were (trustworthy) reproductions of the way the story of Jesus was originally told (1797). Throughout most of the 19th cent., interest in the oral stage of the transmission of tradition was greatly eclipsed by source criticism (*see* SOURCE CRITICISM). It surfaced again in the 1920s with the rise of form criticism (*see* FORM CRITICISM, NT), which made it the cornerstone in reconstructing how the earliest expressions of the message as these took shape in the life and preaching of the first Christian communities were gradually transformed into a body of texts (Dibelius 1919; Bultmann 1921). This reconstruction, in which oral tradition appeared to be nothing but the result of a dynamic but somewhat chaotic creativity on the part of the early church, was severely criticized by B. Gerhardsson (1961, 1964, 1986; see also Byrskog, 1994, 2000, 2004), who instead promoted the very opposite view that the Gospels basically reproduce a tradition that had been shaped in utmost fidelity to Jesus and his teaching and had already received its definite form from the earliest times on, a model Gerhardsson compared with the way later rabbinic tradition was shaped and transmitted. A middle way between the form critics' "informal uncontrolled" and Gerhardsson's "formal controlled" model for explaining how oral tradition functioned and was transmitted in early Christianity is offered by K. Bailey (1991), whose definition of oral tradition as an "informal controlled" entity combines elements from the two others.

W. Kelber (1983) pointed out the strengths and above all the weaknesses of both the form-critical and the rabbinic model. A major problem with the former is the fact that it is based on a linear view of how oral tradition gradually develops and is turned into a text with the correlating idea that the original form of a tradition can rather easily be rediscovered by peeling off the layers. The other suffers from lack of evidence and possible anachronism when comparing the origins of early Christian with rabbinic tradition, which post-dates early Christianity. But above all Kelber wanted to introduce a more systematic reflection on the concepts of oral tradition and of orality, which he saw as exponents of a completely different mind-set that was largely lost when that tradition was put to writing in the latter decades of the 1st cent. CE. There is no easy path from orality to literacy. Kelber has in turn been criticized for this conclusion, and he has nuanced it in later publications by taking into account the dynamics that exist between orality and literacy, but he has been most helpful in drawing attention to a whole set of questions and issues regarding the status and form of oral tradition, oral performance, and the characteristic features of oral culture in general.

In the past thirty years or so biblical scholars have gradually become more familiar with the work of anthropologists or linguists studying the oral transmission of tales and epics, such as M. Parry (1933) or A. B. Lord (1960, 1978), and of specialists of oral culture, such as J. Vansina (1965, 1985), R. Finnegan (1977), W. J. Ong (1982), E. A. Havelock (1986), and J. M. Foley (1988), which has resulted in a wide range of studies on oral tradition and orality and its place and function in understanding the broader context in which Christianity, its traditions, and its writings took shape. Scholars have been probing—with rather different results—the literacy rate of Roman Palestine (Hezser 2001) and even of the Roman Empire at large. They have paid attention to the way memory, and above all collective memory, functions in sanctioning tradition. They have been listing the many various factors that play a role in how orality functions (Anderson 1991). They have been studying the interaction of oral and written culture and tradition in early Christianity (Achtemeier 1990) and in rabbinic Judaism (Jaffee 1994), the social components and implications that are involved in this interaction (Horsley 2006), or the ways concerns for oral performance have helped to shape redactional composition and can still be traced in texts (Horsley and Draper 1999). Four insights in particular are to be singled out.

Christianity originated and developed in a mixed oral and literate culture. As a consequence, it is important to realize that studies emphasizing the limited rate of literacy in ancient societies should not be used to demonstrate that writing and literature were only secondary phenomena, or that these were totally different things. Orality and literacy live side by side, or perhaps more correctly, in interaction with each other.

Oral tradition is not synonymous with mechanical reproduction or with the more primitive version of a story. It allows for variability and lives by several techniques, including the use of mnemonic aids and a love for redundancy in style and expression. And this is even true when a well-known story is performed by a professional. Hence it is an illusion to think that one can distil the "authentic and original" form of a tradition from a written text. Oral tradition is by definition unique because it is "performed."

Both within the Greco-Roman and the Jewish culture in which Christianity took shape, orality and aurality (listening to the story being performed) are part of the written form of the story, because in these societies most texts were produced to be performed and heard. A speaker who became an author kept on "speaking" to his secretary, who was putting his words on paper. Thus, some scholars have debated whether or not part of the sayings material in the Gospels might stem from oral tradition rather than from the (hypothetical) source Q (Dunn 2000, 2003, 2004; Holmberg 2004; Mournet 2005; see Q, QUELLE). One of the major insights of orality studies, that in ancient literature orality/aurality and literacy are intrinsically linked to each other, militates against any attempt at demonstrating this hypothesis. Variability and redundancy may be important characteristics of orally transmitted tradition, but the evangelists made these same characteristics function in written tradition as well.

Oral tradition did not fade away after the Gospels were written but lives on alongside the texts. Oral transmission of traditions about Jesus' life and ministry may well have influenced the written versions and probably also have been influenced by it. Likewise "the oral mind-set" has proven to be most inventive in creating new stories and traditions about Jesus, some of which ultimately found a home in non-canonical writings.

It remains a very hazardous task to try and identify even traces of "authentic" oral tradition in the NT. A more reliable option is to attempt to demonstrate how oral performance of the written text has influenced its composition, both with regard to style and content. The core problem in dealing with oral tradition is that Jesus was remembered, and memory played a significant role in preserving traditions about his life and his ministry, but also in reshaping and even in shaping such traditions.

Bibliography: Paul J. Achtemeier. "Omne verbum sonat: The New Testament and the Oral Environment of Late Western Antiquity." *JBL* 109 (1990) 3–27; Oivind Andersen. "Oral Tradition." *Jesus and the Oral Gospel Tradition.* Henri Wansbrough, ed. (1991) 17–58; Kenneth Bailey. "Informal Controlled Oral Tradition and the Synoptic Gospels." *AJT* 5 (1991) 34–54; Rudolph Bultmann. *The History of the Synoptic Tradition.* John Marsh, trans. (1963); Samuel Byrskog. *Jesus the Only Teacher: Didactic Authority and Transmission in Ancient Israel, Ancient Judaism and the Matthean Community* (1994); Samuel Byrskog. *Story as History– History as Story: The Gospel Tradition in the Context of Ancient Oral History* (2000); Samuel Byrskog. "A New Perspective on the Jesus Tradition: Reflections on James D. G. Dunn's *Jesus Remembered.*" *JSNT* 26 (2004) 459–71; Martin Dibelius. *Die Formgeschichte des Evangeliums* (1919, 1959); James D. G. Dunn. "Jesus in Oral Memory: The Initial Stages of the Jesus Tradition." SBLSP 39 (2000) 287–326; James D. G. Dunn.

"Altering the Default Setting: Re-envisaging the Early Transmission of the Jesus Tradition." *NTS* 49 (2003) 139–75; James D. G. Dunn. *Jesus Remembered* (2003); James D. G. Dunn. "On History, Memory and Eyewitnesses: In Response to Bengt Holmberg and Samuel Byrskog." *JSNT* 26 (2004) 473–87; Ruth Finnegan. *Oral Poetry: Its Nature, Significance, and Social Context* (1977); John Miles Foley. *The Theory of Oral Composition: History and Methodology* (1988); Birger Gerhardsson. *Memory and Manuscript: Oral Tradition and Written Transmission in Rabbinic Judaism and Early Christianity* (1961, 1998); Birger Gerhardsson. *Tradition and Transmission in Early Christianity* (1964, 1998); Birger Gerhardsson. *The Gospel Tradition* (1986); Eric A. Havelock. *The Muse Learns to Write: Reflections on Orality and Literacy from Antiquity to the Present* (1986); Catherine Hezser. *Jewish Literacy in Roman Palestine* (2001); Bengt Holmberg. "Questions of Method in James Dunn's *Jesus Remembered*." *JSNT* 26 (2004) 445–57; Richard A. Horsley and Jonathan A. Draper. *Whoever Hears You Hears Me: Prophets, Performance and Tradition in Q* (1999); Richard A. Horsley, ed. *Oral Performance, Popular Tradition, and Hidden Transcript in Q* (2006); Martin S. Jaffee. "Writing and Rabbinic Oral Tradition: On Mishnaic Narrative Lists and Mnemonics." *Journal of Jewish Thought and Philosophy* 4 (1994) 123–46; Werner H. Kelber. *The Oral and the Written Gospel: The Hermeneutics of Speaking and Writing in the Synoptic Tradition, Mark, Paul, and Q* (1983, 1994); Albert B. Lord. *The Singer of Tales* (1960); Albert B. Lord. "The Gospels as Oral Traditional Literature." *The Relationships among the Gospels: An Interdisciplinary Dialogue.* William O. Walker Jr., ed. (1978) 33–91; Alan R. Millard. *Reading and Writing in the Time of Jesus* (2000); Terence C. Mournet. *Oral Tradition and Literary Dependency: Variability and Stability on the Synoptic Tradition and Q* (2005); Walter J. Ong. *Orality and Literacy: The Technologizing of the World* (1982); Milman Parry. "Whole Formulaic Verses in Greek and Southslavic Heroic Song." *TAPA* 64 (1933) 179–97; Jan Vansina. *Oral Tradition: A Study in Historical Methodology* (1965); Jan Vansina. *Oral Tradition as History* (1985).

JOSEPH VERHEYDEN

TRADITIONS OF MATTHIAS. *See* MATTHIAS, TRADITIONS OF.

TRADITIONS OF THE ELDERS [παράδοσις paradosis]. Following the return of Jews from the Babylonian exile, and particularly after the Maccabean Revolt (begun in 167 BCE), there was a movement within Judaism to find ways to apply the Mosaic Law to the details of life. The goal was to be holy and spiritually pure while under foreign rule in order to avoid further judgment or exile by God. The PHARISEES emerged as teachers who sought to determine how to live in a way that fully pleased God. In order to avoid breaking the TORAH in any way, the Pharisees developed a set of traditions. These traditions, which may well have been ancestral customs rather than explicit teachings, served as a "fence" around the Torah. If a person practiced the traditions passed down from the ancestors, traditions that were more detailed and strict, he or she would be in no danger of breaking the written Law. These traditions grew over time.

While we cannot tell how much of the "traditions of the elders" stands in continuity with the later Oral Torah, it does seem clear from references to the traditions of the elders in Josephus and the NT that such traditions were known in the 1st cent. CE (*see* ORAL LAW, ORAL TORAH). Because the NT and Josephus use the term paradosis, it was probably a technical term for the traditions passed on by the Pharisees. Josephus states that the Pharisees have traditions they have received from their fathers that are not written in the Law of Moses, but since they are not part of the written Law, the Sadducees reject these traditions (*Ant.* 13.297). After King Alexander died, his widow, Alexandra, required the people of Jerusalem to follow the traditions of the fathers that the Pharisees taught (*Ant.* 13.408). The Dead Sea Scrolls refer negatively to those who follow after "smooth things," which is probably a reference to the Pharisees, because they follow their own traditions; to the writers of the Dead Sea Scrolls, these traditions were not the same thing as following the Law (CD I, 18; 1QH X, 31–32). Ben Sirach may be referring to the traditions of the elders in his praise of ancestors who honored the covenant (see Sir 44:1, 12).

The Gospels present an example of one of these "traditions" in an encounter between Jesus and the Pharisees. Jesus' disciples have not observed the traditions of the elders with regard to washing their hands before eating (Matt 15:2; Mark 7:3, 5). When Jesus responds to the Pharisees, he refers to their "tradition" (paradosis, Matt 15:3, 6). In Mark 7:9 and 7:13, Jesus asserts that the Pharisees and scribes have elevated the traditions of the elders above the written Law and that some traditions conflict with parts of the Torah (Matt 15:3-10; Mark 7:8-13). Jesus supports his critique of the Pharisees by citing Isa 29:13, which condemns Isaiah's audience for saying the things they have learned as tradition, while their hearts remain far from God (Mark 7:6-7). Perhaps ironically, Jesus required his followers to be even more righteous than the scribes and Pharisees (Matt 5:20) and also taught a very strict interpretation of the Law (Matt 5:17-48).

Paul, who was himself a Pharisee, says that he was zealous for the traditions of the ancestors (paradosis) and that he considered himself more faithful to these traditions than his contemporaries (Gal 1:14). *See* LAW IN EARLY JUDAISM.

Bibliography: A. Baumgarten. "The Pharisaic Paradosis." *HTR* 80 (1987) 63–77; M. Goodman. "A Note on Josephus, the Pharisees, and Ancestral Tradition." *Journal of Jewish Studies* 50 (1999) 17–20.

KENNETH D. LITWAK

TRAGACANTH. *See* GUM.

TRAIN [ἔνδυσις endysis, ὄχλος ochlos]. Part of a skirt HEM that trails in the back (Add Esth 15:4). Metaphorically, *train* is used of captives following their captors (Dan 11:43 [mitsʿadh מִצְעָד]) and of supply trains following an army (Jdt 7:18).

TRAJAN tray´juhn. Born in Roman Spain around 53 CE, Trajan (Marcus Ulpius Traianus) was the first Roman emperor born outside Italy. His reign (January 28, 98 to August 7, 117) marked the high point of Roman territorial expansion, and his surviving correspondence with PLINY supplies important evidence for the early treatment of Christians.

NERVA had adopted this experienced and respected soldier in 97 to placate mutinous Praetorians. After Nerva died, Trajan's first task was to restore military discipline. Along with disciplinary measures, Trajan offered troops the donatives (cash payments) customary upon the accession of a new emperor, but he reduced the sums. Largesse was also bestowed on citizens more widely in the form of *congiaria* (cash payments), grain distributions, and funding for the *alimenta* system (state support of poor children). Trajan initiated many public works projects. These included repairs to infrastructure throughout the empire as well as new buildings and roads. Despite these outlays, Trajan remitted some taxes and reduced others.

Trajan's finances no doubt benefited from the two wars he waged against Decebalus (101–102 and 105–107). Not only was Dacia annexed as a province (the territory roughly corresponds with modern Romania) but the treasury also reputedly netted more than 5 million pounds of captured gold and more than 10 million pounds of silver. According to Pliny the Younger's hymn of praise (*Panegyricus*), the watchwords of Trajan's reign included *securitas* ("national security"), *felicitas* ("divine fortune"), *aequitas* ("fairness"), *iustitia* ("due process"), and *salus* ("general human welfare" [*Pan.* 8, 38, 54, 74]). In 113, Trajan began his Parthian campaign, capturing Armenia in 114 and the Parthian capital Ctesiphon (near the site of modern Baghdad) in 115. In that same year, Jews, who remained bitter after the destruction of the Temple, revolted in Cyrene, Egypt, Cyprus, and recently captured portions of Mesopotamia. Marcius Turbo and Lusius Quietus quelled these disruptions with great savagery over the space of the next few years. Trajan, in the meantime, grew sick, and died in 117 before he could consolidate his last conquests. His successor HADRIAN quickly relinquished Mesopotamia to the Parthians.

Trajan, who had received the title *Optimus* ("best") while alive, was consecrated as a state god (*Divus*) after his death. His memory was long cherished, and the Senate, according to Eutropius, acclaimed subsequent emperors with the wish that they be "more fortunate than Augustus and better than Trajan" (*Hist. rom. brev.* 8.5.3). Later legend even alleged that Pope Gregory I (590–604) obtained Trajan's transfer from hell to paradise. Trajan's famous policy toward Christians steered a middle course between toleration and persecution, and may be found in his surviving correspondence with Pliny, who wrote to the emperor for advice while serving as governor of Bithynia. According to their correspondence (Pliny *Ep.* 10.96–97), Christian identity (the *nomen Christianum*) incurred guilt that merited capital punishment, but magistrates were neither to search actively for Christians nor to accept anonymous accusations. Those accused of professing Christianity were also to be granted an opportunity to curse Christ and to sacrifice to ancestral gods in order either to prove their innocence or to repent, thereby, in either instance, escaping conviction. Only those who stubbornly persisted in their profession of faith were to be executed or remanded (if citizens) to Rome for trial. *See* CHRISTIANS, PERSECUTION OF.

Bibliography: Julian Bennett. *Trajan: Optimus Princeps* (2001).

HANS-FRIEDRICH MUELLER

TRANCE [נִרְדָּם nirdam; ἔκστασις ekstasis]. To be outside or beside oneself, implying dissociation. The Greek words used for *trance* are also translated "confused," "amazed," or "outside of oneself" (Mark 5:42; compare Gen 27:33 [LXX]; Ezek 26:16 [LXX]; 27:35 [LXX]; Mark 16:8; Luke 5:26; Acts 3:10). The trances of Peter and Paul (Acts 10:10; 11:5; 22:17) are described as ecstasies or receptive states for visions (compare 2 Cor 12:1-4).

Trance states (anything from frenzy to light hypnosis to meditative states to deep unconsciousness) are usually dictated by the cultural group promoting them and esoterically taught to novices. The adept—usually a prophet or seer in the Bible—valorizes a report by saying that he or she has entered a special, religiously interpreted state of consciousness. Therefore, the SONS OF PROPHETS refers to prophetic guilds that teach new apprentices how to achieve and use this religiously interpreted state of consciousness (1 Kgs 20:35; 2 Kgs 2:1-25; 4:1, 38; 5:22; 6:1; Amos 2:11).

Biblical prophecy, associated with the outpouring of the "spirit of the Lord," sometimes is trance-like. Joel refers to God pouring out the divine spirit so that both old and young will prophesy through "dreams" and "visions" (Joel 2:28 [Heb. 3:1]). The wilderness is a prime place to meet with the Lord in a trance (Exod 19–24; Num 14:22; 1 Kgs 19:12; compare Isa 40:3; Matt 3:3; Mark 1:3; Luke 3:4; John 1:23). Indeed the stillness and majesty of the desert may aid in the production of religious consciousness.

The story of Micaiah ben Imlah illustrates the political as well as ecstatic roles of the prophet (1 Kgs 22). The book of Daniel suggests that a vision could be received with appropriate preparation. Daniel had been mourning for three weeks (compare *4 Ezra* 5:20), possibly lamenting in appropriate ascetic states: he had eaten no rich food, no meat or wine. On the twenty-fourth day of his regimen, Daniel received a vision; he grew weak and pale, heard a voice, and fell to his face in a trance (Dan 10:2-11).

In the Second Temple period, dreams were considered prophetic; Philo and Josephus use many different instances in which religiously interpreted states of consciousness and trance were respected as sources of religious information. The authority of Paul's apostleship depends on his receiving a vision of the risen Jesus (Acts 9:1-19). *See* DREAM; ECSTASY; TONGUES, GIFT OF; VISION.

ALAN F. SEGAL

TRANSCENDENCE. *See* GOD, OT VIEW OF.

TRANSFIGURATION trans´fig´yuh-ray´-shuhn. The traditional name of an episode found at Matt 17:1-9; Mark 9:2-9; Luke 9:28-37; and summarized in 2 Pet 1:16-18. The label "transfiguration" derives from the KJV rendering of Matt 17:2 and Mark 9:2: "And he was transfigured (metemorphōthē μετεμορφώθη) before them." Each of the Synoptic Gospels relates essentially the same story: three disciples are taken to a mountain where Jesus' external appearance is changed, manifesting great brightness. Moses and Elijah appear and converse with Jesus. Peter suggests that three booths or tents be built. From a cloud a voice speaks, identifies Jesus as God's son, and demands obedience to him ("Listen to him!" borrowing language from Deut 18:15). The story ends with Jesus alone with the three disciples.

Small but striking differences distinguish the synoptic accounts. Sometimes scholars consider these differences evidence of non-Markan sources behind the accounts of Matthew and Luke. More often they consider differences as clues to the particular theological interests of the evangelists.

The question of historicity arises with respect to the transfiguration. Some maintain the historicity of the story or of a kernel within it, while acknowledging that it is couched in symbolic language deliberately echoing the OT (especially Exod 24; 34). Others argue that it is a purely symbolic narrative, picturing a psychological and spiritual apprehension of Jesus' true nature. One's answer to this question cannot be separated from one's estimation of the historicity of the Synoptic Gospels as a whole. Whatever its historicity, the symbolic and allusive nature of its language cannot be doubted. Many earlier scholars considered the transfiguration a misplaced resurrection story or an anticipation of the parousia. It is more fruitful, however, to consider the role of the scene in the narrative structure of each of the Gospels and as a theological testimony to the identity of Jesus as each evangelist understood that identity.

Though the site of the transfiguration has traditionally been identified with Mount Tabor, even more important than the scene's location is the mountain symbolism. A mountain generally represents the boundary and meeting place between earth and heaven. More significant, a mountain is the site of the theophany to Moses and the giving of the law. The mountain of transfiguration is thus the holy mountain of divine-human encounter, and much of the symbolism of the story (e.g., the shining brightness, the cloud, and the voice) is recognizable to a reader familiar with the stories of Sinai. Although some think that Moses and Elijah, two figures who encounter God on a mountain, appear representing the Law and the Prophets, we should not overlook the OT portrayal of Moses as himself the prototypical prophet (see Deut 18:15-18).

In Mark, the scene follows immediately upon the confession of Peter and the first prediction of the passion in which Jesus is identified as Messiah and Son of Man (Mark 8:29, 31). This pericope focuses on Jesus' suffering, but in the transfiguration he is named by a heavenly voice as "my Son, the Beloved" (Mark 9:7), thus emphasizing Jesus' glory. Mark's structure establishes Jesus' identity as Messiah, Son of Man, and Son of God. Indeed, Jesus' identity as Son of God is thematic for the whole of Mark (compare Mark 1:1, 11; 15:39.

Matthew and Luke take over much of what we find in Mark, including its relation to Peter's confession and the passion prediction. Matthew adds that Jesus' face "shone like the sun" (compare Moses, Exod 33:29), which may function to further emphasize the identity of Jesus as a new and greater Moses. Luke adds that the purpose of ascending the mountain was prayer (a powerful hint in Luke's Gospel that Jesus' identity is about to be revealed [compare, e.g., Luke 3:21-22]) and that the three disciples were sleepy (compare 22:39-46). Luke adds that Moses and Elijah speak with Jesus about his "departure" (exodos ἔξοδος) from Jerusalem (9:31), a probable reference to Jesus' death, resurrection, and ascension. Indeed, shortly thereafter, Jesus begins his journey to death and exaltation in Jerusalem (9:51). Like the exodus, this journey effects the people's salvation.

In all three Synoptic Gospels, Peter wishes to remain on the mountain and to build booths for Moses, Elijah, and Jesus. To do so would be to mistake Jesus' identity and the nature of his mission; he is greater than the OT figures. It is also to miss the fact that this quintessential "mountaintop experience" is incomplete without the rest of the gospel story, with its emphasis on the self-sacrificial mission of Jesus.

Bibliography: John Paul Heil. *The Transfiguration of Jesus: Narrative Meaning and Function of Mark 9:2-8, Matt 17:1-8 and Luke 9:28-36* (2000); Morna Hooker.

"'What Doest Thou Here, Elijah?' A Look at St. Mark's Account of the Transfiguration." *The Glory of Christ in the New Testament: Studies in Christology in Memory of George Bradford Caird.* Lincoln D. Hurst and Nicholas T. Wright, eds. (1987) 59–70; Dorothy Lee. *Transfiguration* (2004); John McGuckin. *The Transfiguration of Christ in Scripture and Tradition* (1986); A. D. A. Moses. *Matthew's Transfiguration Story and Jewish-Christian Controversy* (1996); Joseph Ratzinger, Pope Benedict XVI. *Jesus of Nazareth: From the Baptism in the Jordan to the Transfiguration* (2007); Allison Trites. "Transfiguration in the Theology of Luke: Some Redactional Links." *The Glory of Christ in the New Testament: Studies in Christology in Memory of George Bradford Caird.* L. D. Hurst and N. T. Wright, eds. (1987) 71–82; Andrew Wilson. *Transfigured: A Derridean Rereading of the Markan Transfiguration* (2007).

STEPHEN FARRIS

TRANSGRESSION. *See* CRIMES AND PUNISHMENT, OT AND NT; SIN, SINNERS.

TRANSJORDAN trans-jor´duhn. The Transjordan lies east of the Jordan River and extends from the modern border with Syria at the Yarmuk River to the Red Sea at Aqaba. Its eastern limits are lost in the Syrian Desert, while the Jordan Valley rift forms a clear boundary on the west. Within this territory, several small kingdoms and tribal areas contemporary with Israel and Judah flourished during the Iron Age (900–540 BCE). The territorial states of Ammon and Moab were located on the central plateau, with Edom to the south (*see* AMMON, AMMONITES; EDOM, EDOMITES; MOAB, MOABITES). Gilead in the north was an area alternately under the control of Israel or the Arameans of Damascus. The Jordan Valley was a distinct region, sometimes under Israelite control, but linked by its pottery and artifacts, and probably by its language (*see* DEIR ʿALLA, TEXTS), to Transjordanian religions and culture.

Sites with Ammonite-style pottery extend from north of Amman to the area of Madaba. Sites immediately to the south of Madaba have a different (Moabite) ceramic tradition. Israel's forays into the Jordan Valley and temporary occupation of the "land of Madaba" are reflected in 2 Kgs 3, as well as in the 9th-cent. Mesha Inscription, which is our main source concerning the upheavals in Moab during the Omride dynasty (*see* MOABITE STONE). North–south trade routes transected the region, bringing goods from Arabia and Edom to Damascus and beyond. In northern Moab, a wayside shrine on the Wadi ath-Thamad yielded good evidence of regional trade and cultural diversity in the form of statues, figurines, and hundreds of votive offerings. Archaeologists are uncovering many of the towns and cities of Ammon and Moab, but few of those named in Judges and Jeremiah can be located with certainty.

Edom in the south was linked by trade routes to the Negeb in southern Judah, where aspects of Edomite religion were revealed at the shrine sites of Horvat Qitmit and En Haseva. Late in the Iron Age (8th–7th cent.), the settlement of Edom developed under the influence of Assyrian imperialism, eager to facilitate trade from Arabia.

All of Transjordan was included in the Persian Empire (539–332 BCE). Following the conquest of Alexander, a network of Hellenized cities (DECAPOLIS) appeared in Transjordan, and Arab tribes dominated the region. The NABATEANS of northern Arabia had settled at PETRA and expanded north toward Damascus. In Moab, the Nabatean boundary was close to Machaerus, the mountaintop fortress of Herod southwest of Madaba. Like the Edomites before them, the Nabateans established settlements in southern Judea, linking Petra and Gaza.

The story of Lot's daughters posits a family connection among Israel, Ammon, and Moab (Gen 19:30-38), and Edom is portrayed as Jacob's unlucky brother Esau (Gen 25:30). Several stories in the books of Judges and Samuel (especially 2 Sam 10) report warfare among these small kingdoms, with occasional good relations (e.g., 2 Sam 17:24-29). The prophets (above all, Amos 1–2) cursed Israel's eastern neighbors, although features in the book of Job may have their setting in Edom.

In Mark, Jesus goes to Gadara, east of the Sea of Galilee, and may have stayed in Transjordan on his way to Jerusalem, crossing the river at Bethany of the Jordan. Christians and Jews sought refuge in the Decapolis during the Jewish wars with Rome (63–70 CE and 132–35 CE). Later on, numerous churches paved with colorful mosaics testify to a large and wealthy Christian population, with bishoprics at Petra and PHILADELPHIA (Amman).

P. M. MICHÈLE DAVIAU

TRANSLATIONS. *See* BIBLE TRANSLATION THEORY; VERSIONS, ANCIENT; VERSIONS, ENGLISH; VERSIONS, JEWISH; VERSIONS, MEDIEVAL; VERSIONS, MODERN (NON-ENGLISH).

TRANSPOSITION. Also known as metathesis. The reversal of the order of consonants in a word to facilitate pronunciation. While transposition or metathesis is a regular feature of the conjugation of some Hebrew verbs, the textual critic should be wary of such reversals: the transposition of letters, as well as words, may also be the result of transmission error. *See* TEXT CRITICISM, NT; TEXT CRITICISM, OT.

R. JUSTIN HARKINS

TRAPS AND SNARES [פַּח pakh, מוֹקֵשׁ moqesh; παγίς pagis]. Based on recent zooarchaeological examination of animal remains, it is clear that the vast majority of meat eaten by the ancient Israelites was taken from domesticated animals (principally sheep and goats). There is some archaeological evidence for HUNTING of large game animals such as deer and gazelle, but that generally involved driving the herd into a triangular-shaped corral or kite and trapping them (a method possibly referred to by madhkhefah [מַדְחֵפָה] "hunt down" in Ps 140:11 [Heb. 140:12]). It may be that trapping the hare and the coney, or hyrax, is not explicitly mentioned in the Bible because they are prohibited as unclean from the Israelite diet (Lev 11:6; Deut 14:7). However, there are quite a number of references to laying a snare on a path (Ps 142:3 [Heb. 142:4]; Prov 22:5; Hos 9:8) and that would be an appropriate location to trap small animals as they crossed game trails. This suggests that the practice was known and that supplementing the diet with a little fresh meat while sparing one's domesticated stock seemed to be a plausible strategy, especially in hard times.

The type of hunting most associated with traps or snares in the Bible is fowling. The fowling net or snare (pakh) as depicted in Egyptian tomb art consisted of a net spread over a wooden frame that was supported by a stick in such a way that it fell with the slightest touch (Ps 91:3; Amos 3:5). There were also draw nets that required the hunters to coordinate the pulling of drawstrings that would close the net around the birds' legs (see Job 18:8-9 for a similar technique that entraps the wicked).

The sense of the unexpected associated with a trap lends itself easily to the use of these utilitarian devices in metaphorical contexts (Luke 21:34-36). Thus, in Josh 23:13 the Israelite leader warns the people that the foreign nations of Canaan will become a "snare and a trap" for them if they intermarry or fail in their devotion to God. Similarly, the qualifications for a bishop include avoiding the "snare of the devil" (1 Tim 3:7). It is that sense of the unwary quarry that comes clear in the warning to avoid the seductress (Prov 7:23) lest the young man "[rush] into a snare" like a bird (see also Eccl 9:12). Perhaps it is the recognition that life is filled with potential pitfalls that encourages the psalmist to repeatedly bewail the fact that "the wicked have laid a snare for me" (Ps 119:110; compare Pss 140:5 [Heb. 140:6]; 141:9). Jeremiah utilizes this metaphor in his cursing of those who have "laid snares for my feet" and obstructed his ability to freely voice his message (Jer 18:22-23). This type of warning is also employed by the prophets, who speak of the impending judgment upon the peoples of the earth and the fact that even those who manage to clamor out of the pit "shall be caught in the snare" of God (Isa 24:17-18).

VICTOR H. MATTHEWS

TRAVEL AND COMMUNICATION IN THE NT.
Given that the NT details the growth and expansion of early Christianity from Palestine into the larger Mediterranean world, it contains many references to travel and communication. A survey of these references in the NT reveals that the early Christians largely relied on the travel structures and communication mediums that were already in place in the 1st cent. CE.

A. Travel in the New Testament World

Despite notions that travel was unusual or that it was reserved for a very slim minority of the population, it is becoming increasingly evident that people in NT times were more mobile and traveled more extensively than was once thought. The Mediterranean Sea and other bodies of water and rivers provided convenient mediums for travel by boat and ship, and by the 1st cent. CE Rome had constructed an extensive network of roads that stretched throughout its vast empire and connected its various cities. The rapid expansion of the early church therefore benefited greatly from the imperial structures that made travel and communication in the 1st cent. CE much easier than it had been previously.

1. Roads and highways

Long before Rome became master of the Mediterranean world it realized the necessity of a good road system for effective governance. Its roads were therefore well planned and strategically placed to best serve administrative, commercial, and military interests. In newly conquered territories roads were promptly constructed in order to effectively link them with the rest of the empire, although certain areas such as Asia Minor, which already had an efficient road system, remained largely intact with few innovations. Given that the primary purpose of roads was to facilitate governance and communication, roads were usually constructed with an orientation toward local centers. On a larger scale roads were orientated toward the city of Rome in order to effectively link the capital to other parts of the empire and create some degree of imperial cohesion. Consequently, the old proverb "all roads lead to Rome" is not a complete overstatement.

Most Roman roads were completely paved with a flat stone surface, something that was novel in antiquity and ranged anywhere from a little over 1 m to 7 m in width. Roads were usually named after the censor who ordered their construction, or reconstruction, with the most famous road being the Via Appia that ran south from Rome to Capua and was initiated by Appius Claudius in 312 BCE (see APPIAN WAY; likely traveled by Paul, see §B.2). Because roads were completely paved they could easily accommodate drawn vehicles, all sorts of pack animals, and considerable human traffic. In the summer months (June to September) travel volume on the roads was exceptionally high; however, during the winter months (November to March) many roads, especially those at higher elevations or through mountain passes, were mostly closed (Vegetius, *De Re Militari* 4.39).

A hallmark of the Roman road system was its directional straightness, despite elevation changes, as it sought to connect two locations by the shortest possible route. Regular markers, or mileposts, inscribed with the distances to and from various cities along the roadway helped to guide travelers toward their destinations, and many of the busier roads were dotted with way stations and hostels to accommodate travelers. At its peak in the early 2nd cent. CE the Roman road system spanned more than 50,000 mi. and its enduring remains serve not only as a testament to its workmanship but also to the importance of land travel in the Roman world.

2. Waterways

Though travel by sea or river was not as common as land travel, in most cases it tended to be much faster and was an easier form of transportation. During the sailing season (April to October) the Mediterranean was literally dotted with thousands of ships at any one time, most of which were either commercial transport ships or small fishing vessels. During the winter months (November to March) little sailing was done, especially on the open seas, because it was extremely dangerous due to bad weather and unpredictable winds (Pliny, *Nat.* 2.122; Vegetius, *De Re Militari* 4.39). Passenger ships were virtually unknown in NT times; if someone desired to travel by boat they had to book passage on a freighter and make the necessary arrangements with its captain.

Most ships sailed along the coastline and tended to anchor at night, either in a port or a little ways offshore. During the sailing season the prevailing northerly winds made it easier to sail southeast. Accordingly, ships usually sailed in a clockwise flow around the Mediterranean (Rome to Greece to Turkey to Palestine to Egypt and back to Rome). While most ships were sailing vessels they were almost always equipped with oars. The largest ships on the sea were grain transport ships, many of them moving back and forth from Egypt to Rome since Egypt supplied the capital with approximately one-third of its annual grain, and could range anywhere from 130–150 ft. in length (Tactitus, *Ann.* 2.59). Such large ships could host a number of passengers in addition to its crew. Josephus reports being on a ship with 600 passengers (*Life* 15.3) and one of Paul's ships reportedly carried 276 passengers (Acts 27:37). *See* SHIPS AND SAILING IN THE NT.

3. Reasons for travel

People in NT times traveled for all sorts of reasons: to find work, conduct business, transport merchandise, carry correspondence, visit loved ones, attend school, and to fulfill various government and religious obligations and duties. Leisure travel was extremely rare and was undertaken only by a very small minority of the population who had the necessary means.

Partly facilitated by the newly established Roman peace (*pax Romana*), which made travel safer and much easier than it had been previously, commerce flourished and afforded people opportunities all over the empire. Skilled artisans and laborers of all kinds traversed the Mediterranean as various projects required their special skills, and merchants traveled extensively importing and exporting goods. There is the notable example of the merchant Flavius Zeuxis from Hierapolis in Phrygia who traveled extensively and who is reported to have voyaged from Asia Minor to Rome some seventy-two times on business (*CIG* 3920).

While certain types of work might require that people travel great distances, with many occupations people might travel only locally but frequently. In the agricultural industry, which was by far the largest industry in antiquity, people would have to travel constantly in order to tend to crops, obtain supplies, or transport produce to markets. At tax time, which tended to coincide with the harvest, travel volume was especially high as produce was being moved about and tax collectors and landlords went about collecting dues.

In NT times religious motives also served as important reasons for travel, and this travel was not limited to either Jews or Christians. Worshipers of Greek and Roman deities might travel regularly to particular shrines or temples to venerate and invoke certain gods and goddesses. The cult of Asclepius, the Greek demigod of medicine and healing, frequently attracted a number of pilgrims to his various shrines because they were thought of as places of healing. The many inscriptions and votive offerings found at the shrines (most notably Epidaurus) show that his devotees often traveled great distances to seek his healing powers. People also traveled to attend various festivals and games for particular deities, since attendance was often seen as an act of devotion and offered entertainment typically in the form of games and contests.

For Jews in NT times religious travel was most often brought about by one of the three pilgrimage festivals: Passover, Pentecost, and Tabernacles. During such times Jews from all over the Mediterranean world were known to travel to Jerusalem to partake in the festivities. In Acts 2:5-13 it is reported that Jews from all over the Diaspora came to Jerusalem to celebrate Pentecost, and Josephus reports that so many Jews would travel to Jerusalem for Passover that the city was literally overflowing with visitors during the time of its celebration (*J.W.* 6.423–25).

4. Private and public correspondence

In the NT world the most common form of long-distance correspondence was epistolary, and individuals, both lay and professional, were frequently employed to transmit such correspondence. In many cases private letters were transmitted via a mutual friend or acquaintance to the receiving party. With the letters of Paul and Peter this seems to have been done by a close friend or associate who was a member of their inner missionary circle (Rom 16:1; 1 Pet 5:12). On occasion private correspondence might also be sent via a complete stranger who happened to be passing by in the direction in which the letter was traveling. Consequently, many personal letters did not always make it to their final destination. The wealthier in society who owned slaves would frequently employ them to transmit correspondence. Cicero frequently employed his slaves to transmit his letters and the wealthy Epicurean Papirus Paetus, who exchanged numerous letters with Cicero, reportedly had two slaves retained solely for such errands (Cicero, *Fam.* 9.15.1).

While the Roman Empire had an official postal system (*cursus publicus*), which was modeled on the earlier Greek and Persian systems that employed mounted horsemen operating between relay stations, it was used only for official government and military business. In NT times the courier assigned to convey a particular message transported it the whole distance to its final destination and received fresh horses at each relay station along the way (Suetonius, *Aug.* 49.3). Though this system was reserved for official business, on rare occasions prominent persons could use it for personal communications (Pliny the Younger, *Ep.* 10.120, 121).

5. Rates of travel and communication

By modern standards travel and communication in NT times was extremely slow. It has been estimated that the ordinary person going on foot could cover about 20 mi. per day, but this average could easily change depending on terrain, weather conditions, or a number of other factors (Sabbaths, stopovers, sickness, etc.). For shorter trips a 20 mi. per day average was certainly realistic; Peter's trip from Joppa to Caesarea (about 40 mi.) took two days (Acts 10:23-30) and Josephus reports that a journey from the southern edge of the Galilee to Jerusalem (about 65 mi.) took three days (*Life* 269). However, for longer trips it cannot always be assumed that such a rate was always maintained. Likewise, this rate could certainly be increased if necessity required.

For the most part, travel by donkey, mule, or even camel moved at about the same rate as walking. Wagons and chariots tended to move a little quicker provided one stayed on a paved road, and travel by horse was much quicker as one could average about 50 mi. per day. However, horses were rarely used by anyone except the military and *cursus publicus*. Since speed was one of the main purposes of the imperial post, on rare occasions when important correspondence had to be relayed a rider could cover a distance of 100 to 150 mi. in a single day, but this was very unusual. In 9 BCE the future emperor Tiberius was able to cover a distance of about 500 mi. in three days using horses and relays supplied by the imperial post when he learned that his brother Drusus was on the point of death (Valerius Maximus, *Facta et dicta memorabilia* 5.3).

In favorable conditions ships could average about 7 mi. an hour. In such conditions a boat leaving Rome could make it to Alexandria in about ten days (Philo, *Flaccus* 27). However, a return trip against the winds could easily take at least twice as long. Luke reports in Acts 16:11-12 that a voyage from Troas to Philippi with favorable winds took two days, while the return trip took five (Acts 20:6). While ships could move at a fairly swift speed, the frequent loading and unloading of cargo, unfavorable winds or storms, waiting for connecting ships, and unscheduled stops could substantially prolong a voyage.

6. Perils of travel

Despite the advent of the Roman peace, in NT times travel could still be quite perilous and had to be undertaken with forethought and care in order to ensure one's safety. Consequently, most people opted to travel in groups because it tended to afford more safety (Epictetus, *Diatr.* 4.1.91). Paul's summary of some of the many dangers he faced on his various missionary journeys is certainly indicative of the types of perils many travelers faced in NT times (2 Cor 11:26-27). Gangs of bandits frequently preyed along ancient highways looking for their next victim (Luke 10:30-36), and though Julius Caesar had done an effective job purging the Mediterranean of pirates, they continued to be a threat to those traveling by ship. Disturbances such as local fighting or war greatly added to the perils of travel by causing instability in certain regions (Suetonius, *Aug.* 32), and all sorts of troublemakers were known to frequently hang out on the roadways (Plutarch, *Mor.* 304e). Severe weather always posed a problem for travelers, by land (Seneca, *Ep.* 57.1–2; 96.3) and by sea (Acts 27), and roadside inns, which might seem like a place of relative safety, were often filthy and usually frequented by people of unscrupulous character (Pliny, *Nat.* 9.154; Cicero, *Div.* 1.27; *Inv.* 2.4.14–15).

B. Travel in the New Testament

1. Jesus

In the Gospels Jesus is depicted as traveling most frequently throughout the Galilee, and on occasion into parts of Phoenicia, Paneas, Samaria, the Decapolis, and Judea. While these regions were mostly connected via a number of footpaths (smaller roads and minor highways that primarily served local traffic), at least one major highway ran south from Damascus through Capernaum and Tiberias and then in a southwest direction through the plain of Esdraelon to Megiddo before it reached Caesarea and continued south along the coast to Egypt.

Consequently, a number of these smaller roads hooked up with this international trade route at various junctures.

Both Matthew and Luke give the impression that Jesus traveled quite extensively as a child. After his parents had gone from Nazareth to Bethlehem to register for the census (Luke 2:1-5) Matthew reports that as a small child Jesus' parents took him to Egypt to escape Herod (Matt 2:13-14). Sometime later, after Herod's death, they returned to settle in the village of Nazareth in the Galilee (Matt 2:19-23). On at least one occasion, it is reported that as a youth Jesus made the trek from Nazareth to Jerusalem for Passover (Luke 2:41-42).

While Jesus' formal ministry appears to have begun in Judea with the baptism by John, most of his subsequent ministry was spent traversing the Galilee. Among the notable villages he traveled among were Bethsaida (Mark 8:22; Luke 9:10), Cana (John 2:1-11; 4:46), Capernaum (Matt 4:13; 8:5; 17:24; Mark 1:21; 2:1; 9:33; Luke 4:31; 7:1; John 2:12; 6:59), Nain (Luke 7:11) and Nazareth (Matt 13:53-58; Luke 4:16). While Jesus' most common mode of transportation between these villages was by foot (Matt 10:10-14), he sometimes made these trips via boat across Lake Tiberias (Matt 9:1; 15:39). On the Sunday before his crucifixion he is reported to have entered Jerusalem riding a donkey (John 12:12-15), the only time that Jesus is ever presented traveling via a pack animal.

Occasionally Jesus' ministry took him outside of the Galilee. On at least three occasions Jesus passed through Samaria (Luke 5:51-45; 17:11-16; John 4:3-43), he went to Caesarea Philippi (Matt 16:13; Mark 8:27), twice into the region of the Decapolis (Mark 5:1-20; 7:31-37), and on one occasion he went as far north as the region of Tyre and Sidon (Matt 15:21-28; Mark 7:24-30). However, after the Galilee, Jesus spent most of his time in Judea, even if he sometimes avoided travel there because of hostility toward him (John 7:1). In the Gospels Jesus is depicted as going to Judea, and more specifically to Jerusalem, most often to attend one of the pilgrimage festivals (John 2:13; 7:2, 10). Besides Jerusalem, which was the center of Jesus' activities in Judea (Matt 16:21; Luke 5:1; 12:12; 13:22), he also spent time in Bethany (John 11:1-18), Bethpage (Matt 21:1), Ephraim (John 11:54), and Jericho (Mark 10:46).

2. Paul

While Paul's letters offer some clues to the extent of his travel itinerary, any picture of his travelogue has to be constructed primarily from Acts. Here Paul is depicted as an avid traveler, logging some 6,200 mi. on his various missions in order to carry the gospel "to the ends of the earth" (Acts 1:8). Acts gives the impression that as a youth Paul was already a seasoned traveler, as he was raised in Tarsus but was educated in Jerusalem (Acts 22:3); when he first emerges as a character in the book (other than a brief appearance in Acts 7:58) he

is on the road traveling from Jerusalem to Damascus (Acts 9:1-8).

Acts 13:1–14:28, which details the first formal missionary activities of Paul, shows how he carried the gospel to parts of Asia Minor, particularly to a number of cities in Pisidia. Starting out from Antioch and sailing from Seleucia he spent time in Cyprus and in the cities of Salamis and Paphos before sailing north to the port of Perga in Pamphylia. From there he went by land to Pisidian Antioch, which was a well-connected Roman colony with many major roads, and presumably took the military road leading east, which took him to Iconium, Lystra, and Derbe.

During the initial part of Paul's next missionary travels (Acts 15:40–18:23a) he returned to Pisidia. However, he opted to travel from Antioch by land through Syria and Cilicia (Acts 16:1). Making his way to Tarsus via the Cilician Gates that lead through the Taurus mountain range, he then went on to Derbe, Lystra, Iconium, and Pisidian Antioch. From there Acts reports that he headed in a northwesterly direction through Phrygia until he arrived at the port city of Troas on the Aegean (Acts 16:8). At Troas Luke may have accompanied Paul's party since it is at this point that the narrative begins to employ the "we" passages (Acts 16:10). From there Paul sailed across the Aegean to Neapolis in Macedonia and then took the Via Egnatia west to Philippi and Thessalonica. Owing to Thessalonian troubles Paul departed and went south, apparently via ship (Acts 17:14), to Athens. After spending a short time in Athens he moved on to Corinth, where he stayed eighteen months (Acts 18:11), and then set sail for Caesarea with a brief stopover in Ephesus.

In Paul's last missionary journey (Acts 18:23b–21:15) he departed from Antioch and presumably took the same inland route through Syria and Cilicia he had formerly taken to Pisidia. However, upon reaching Pisidian Antioch he continued east until he reached Ephesus (Acts 19:1). Following a three-year sojourn (Acts 20:31) he carried on to Macedonia and Greece. While this trip is hastily reported, making his travel itinerary here uncertain (Acts 20:1-2), the return trip to Miletus is given with considerable detail (Acts 20:3-16). Likewise, Paul's voyage from Miletus to Caesarea is equally detailed as it contains a number of particulars about his route, stopovers, and travel times (Acts 20:17–21:8).

Acts 27, which contains an in-depth travelogue of Paul's treacherous voyage from Caesarea to Rome, is recounted with considerable detail. So much information is relayed that it may be regarded as one of the best sources from antiquity detailing ancient seamanship. Acts reports that Paul's ship, leaving from Caesarea, sailed to Sidon and then onto Myra, a port city of Lycia, where Paul changed ships and boarded one bound for Italy. Passing by Cnidus the ship made its way to Crete, intending to harbor for the winter, but was caught in a severe storm and was driven into the open sea by a fierce northeast wind. After days of intense weather and unable to obtain an astronomical bearing all seemed lost for the crew and passengers. However, land was eventually spotted and the ship made a treacherous crash landing on what turned out to be the island of Malta. Following a three-month stay, Paul was boarded on another ship that eventually made it to Italy and landed at Puteoli. After disembarking Paul and his company took the Via Appia north (Acts 28:15) some 135 mi. to Rome where Acts concludes (Acts 28:30-31). In Rom 15:24, 28 Paul had expressed his intention to carry the gospel to Spain. While Acts says nothing of a trip to Spain and there is no conclusive evidence that Paul ever made it there, *1 Clem.* 5:5-7 may suggest otherwise.

Finally, it must be emphasized that Paul did not travel alone but that he had a number of associates who traveled with him and who helped him keep in touch with certain congregations. Paul employed Phoebe, a servant of the church in Cenchreae, to transport his letter to the Romans and a scribe by the name of Tertius to help him compose it (Rom 16:1, 22). If tradition can be trusted, then Luke, whom Paul identifies as a "fellow worker" (Phlm 24), may have accompanied Paul in his later missionary efforts and on his trip to Rome. Likewise, Sosthenes, Silvanus, Barnabas, John Mark, and a host of other named individuals are depicted both in Acts and the letters as vital figures of Paul's inner circle, whom he used to keep his mission going and to keep communication flowing. However, in his letters it appears that Timothy may have played the most important role in Paul's inner missionary circle. Paul employed him as a conduit of communication among certain communities and occasionally used him to transport letters. When Paul heard of the Corinthian trouble from those of the house of Chloe (1 Cor 1:11), he sent Timothy from Ephesus to investigate (1 Cor 4:17), and while in prison in Rome he sent Timothy to Philippi to carry word of Paul's condition (Phil 2:19).

3. Other early Christians

Given the nature of the works preserved in the NT, the travels and correspondences of Paul receive the most attention; nevertheless, there is evidence that a number of other early Christians played important roles in the expansion of the gospel to the larger Mediterranean world. Peter is frequently found alongside Jesus traversing the Galilee and Judea. In Acts Peter figures prominently in Jerusalem, Samaria, and the coastal cities of Lydda, Joppa, and Caesarea (Acts 8–10). If 1 Peter is authentically Peter's then it may also be supposed that Peter had either traveled to parts of Asia Minor or was in communication with the various Christian groups located there, and that he may have even spent time in Rome. As with Peter, John also appears to have played a significant role in the early church by traveling to various communities in order to evangelize and oversee certain activities. In Acts he appears by Peter's side in Jerusalem and also in Samaria. The John who authored

Revelation had established contacts in Asia Minor, especially the seven churches established in Ephesus, Smyrna, Pergamum, Thyatira, Sardis, Philadelphia, and Laodicea (Rev 2–3).

Bibliography: Colin Adams and Ray Laurence, eds. *Travel and Geography in the Roman Empire* (2001); Lionel Casson. *Travel in the Ancient World* (1994 [1974]); Raymond Chevallier. *Roman Roads* (1976); Eldon Jay Epp. "New Testament Papyrus Manuscripts and Letter Carrying in Greco-Roman Times." *The Future of Christianity: Essays in Honor of Helmut Koester.* Birger A. Pearson, ed. (1994) 35–56; David H. French. "Acts and the Roman Roads of Asia Minor." *The Book of Acts in Its Graeco-Roman Setting*, Vol. 2. David W. J. Gill and Conrad Gempf, eds. (1994) 49–58; Peregrine Horden and Nicholas Purcell. *The Corrupting Sea: A Study of Mediterranean History* (2000); Brian M. Rapske. "Acts, Travel and Shipwreck." *The Book of Acts in Its Graeco-Roman Setting*, Vol. 2. David W. J. Gill and Conrad Gempf, eds. (1994) 1–47.

LINCOLN H. BLUMELL

TRAVEL AND COMMUNICATION IN THE OT. The earliest stories of the OT reveal a world of travel and travail for humans on the move. Within the context of the ANE, peoples moved long distances along paths and roads discovered by trial and error, formed by the feet of countless travelers. Ancient travel was time-consuming and fraught with complications and danger. Yet large numbers of people traveled the fertile crescent of the ANE well before the call and movement of Abram from Ur to the small, narrow land of Canaan (Gen 12). For the purposes of reading the OT, one should also note that travel was not necessarily a voluntary act; much OT literature centers on the forced exile and dislocation of the Israelite people.

Travel begins with infrastructure and security. Finding the way somewhere was a matter of life and death in the ancient world. Various Hebrew terms are translated "road," "highway," or most commonly, "way." These include: nathiv (נָתִיב) and nethivah (נְתִיבָה; Prov 8:2, "crossroads"; Jer 6:16, "ancient paths"); ʾorakh (אֹרַח; "path," "way"); mesillah (מְסִלָּה; "highway," usually denoting an intentionally constructed "built-up" road; Isa 40:3-4; 57:14; 62:10; Jer 31:21); shevil (שְׁבִיל; Jer 18:15, "ancient roads"); and mishʿol (מִשְׁעוֹל; Num 22:24, "narrow path"). Only in Num 22:24 does a "narrow path" represent a beaten walkway. The most common term used is derekh (דֶּרֶךְ, "way," "road," "route," "highway"; Num 20:17, "king's highway"; Isa 9:1 [Heb. 8:23], "the way of the sea"; Ezek 21:21 [Heb. 21:26], "parting of the way").

Often the image of "the way" or a "highway in the desert" that is leveled, open, or straight metaphorically denotes a period of peace, usually a prophetic view of the future. "A voice cries out '... make straight in the desert a highway for our God'" (Isa 40:3). Road systems that were free, protected, and in good condition represented prosperity and peace for the people and nations of the ancient world.

Canaan/Israel/Palestine was a geographic thoroughfare between the major powers of Egypt and Mesopotamia. Vast deserts to the east of Canaan discouraged direct travel between the emerging empires in Mesopotamia and Egypt in North Africa. A circuitous route traveled northwest from the gulf region then south to pass through the land between the Mediterranean Sea and the Great Rift (Jordan Valley) on the way to Egypt. A section of the road became the major trade route along the coast of Israel known as the VIA MARIS or "way of the sea" (derekh hayyam [דֶּרֶךְ הַיָּם] ; Isa 9:1 [Heb. 8:23]).

From north to south, this portion of the trade route departed Damascus, traveling southwest to Hazor. Traversing the western shore of the Sea of Galilee, the road moved through the Jezreel Valley. Near Megiddo, the Aruna Pass provided access through the Carmel chain to the Plain of Sharon and on to Joppa. Then, "by way of the land of the Philistines" (Exod 13:17) through Ashdod and Gaza, the route reached Egypt.

A second trade route known as the KING'S HIGHWAY (derekh hammelekh [דֶּרֶךְ הַמֶּלֶךְ]; Num 20:17) traveled northeast between the eastern deserts and the Jordan Valley to the west. The route began at Elath on the modern-day Gulf of Aqabah and moved north through the arid wilderness of Edom. Passing north through Moab into Ammonite territory, the road crossed deep ravines, the biblical Wadi al-Hasa (*see* ZERED, WADI), and the Arnon River (*see* MUJIB, WADI EL). Ashtaroth in Bashan provided rest before the final leg to Damascus in Syria. With both major trade routes connecting at Damascus (Aram/Syria), the city became a hub of communication and commerce and played a major role in the region for centuries.

The Israelite march, from the wilderness wanderings to the Plains of Moab next to the Jordan River (Num 21:21-35), followed the King's Highway. Sweeping east of Edom through the desert to the Wadi Zered, the Israelites moved north, capturing numerous Amorite (Heshbon) and Moabite towns (Ar, Dibon, and Medeba) along the highway.

Trade caravans proceeded west from the eastern desert regions by using the "way of the plain" that connected with the King's Highway at Rabbath-Ammon (modern Amman). The journey west crossed the Jordan River at Adam. Passing Beth-shean, the road traversed the Ein Harrod gap near Mount Gilboa, through the Jezreel Valley, and eventually bisected the Via Maris near the town of Megiddo. This route joined a major road at Megiddo that continued northwest to the great Phoenician seaports of Tyre and Sidon.

Key to the success and expansion of the kingdoms of David and Solomon was control of the Jezreel Valley and the key routes leading to both Phoenicia and Damascus. During the divided kingdom period, the presence of these two major trade routes in northern Israel created not only financial opportunity but also the religious syncretism seen within the Ahab–Jezebel–Elijah stories (1 Kgs 16:29–22:40). Control of the trade led to great wealth, reflected in the oracles of Amos against the northern kingdom of Israel in the mid-8th cent. BCE.

The routes were more curse than blessing for Israel as the mighty armies of Egypt, Assyria, and Babylon traveled upon them, wreaking destruction along the way. The struggle between the major powers over control of the area played an intricate role in Israel's history. Megiddo faced destruction on numerous occasions by invading armies. Often, Egypt's shadow covered the routes of trade around Megiddo. Assyria's movement into the northern kingdom of Israel was fed by lucrative trade income. Judah's righteous king Josiah was killed at Megiddo trying to stop the Egyptians on the Via Maris (2 Kgs 23:29).

Throughout the ANE, goods, agricultural products, and people traveled by caravans or small groups across mountains and through valleys, rivers, and hostile, arid regions. Numerous roads developed off of the main trade routes and led to major cities such as Jebus/ Jerusalem. Abraham traveled extensively within the land of Canaan (Gen 12:6-9). Later, God commanded Abraham to journey to Moriah (traditionally the future site of Jerusalem) from Beer-sheba to sacrifice Isaac (Gen 22), a three-day journey through desert areas and along the central hill country ridges.

A few examples of roadways employed in the OT suffice to show the importance of the road system. Joseph was sold to Midianite/Ishmaelite traders in caravan from Gilead (east of the Jordan) headed for Egypt in the south (Gen 37). Joshua's defeat of the five kings at Gibeon reveals a chase southwest "by the way of the ascent of Beth-horon, and [Israel] struck them down as far as Azekah and Makkedah" (Josh 10:10).

Pack donkeys, oxen, sheep, and other commodities traveled with their owners. By the 12th cent. BCE, many caravans from the desert regions utilized camels for transport of goods. Most humans traveled by foot. The common verb halakh (הָלַךְ, "to walk," "to go") appears ca. 250 times in the OT (e.g., Gen 13:17; 24:65), and is used of both humans and animals. Depending on topography, weather conditions, and the conditions of the roads, 20 mi. per day was the norm. Abraham and Isaac's 50-mi. journey from Beer-sheba to Moriah in three days probably indicates the difficulty of the terrain.

The Israelites were not seafaring peoples. Solomon built a fleet and port at Ezion-geber on the Red Sea/Gulf of Aqabah, but required sailors from Tyre to train his servants about the sea (1 Kgs 9:26-28). The Phoenician Hiram of Tyre's fleet brought great quantities of gold and goods from North Africa (1 Kgs 10:11).

The Philistines of the southern plains of Palestine first invaded Egypt by sea (ca. 1188 BCE), during the reign of Ramesses III. After a brutal battle, the Philistines settled along the shores of Palestine north of Egypt. The OT notes that the Philistines originated in Caphtor (Crete) and moved east by sea (Deut 2:23; Jer 47:4; Amos 9:7).

Communication among towns, city-states, and nations traveled the road system by messengers with oral or written correspondence. Extra-biblical evidence of roadways and communication is abundant. Dangers awaited in desolate areas where famine and drought made sustenance imperative, where wild animals still roamed, and where bandits lurked waiting for caravans or individuals to rob. A mid-14th cent. BCE communication between King Burnaburiash II of Babylon and the Egyptian pharaoh Amenophis IV relates the hazards of travel through Canaan, noting the scarcity of water, the heat, and the area's history of banditry (EA 7.53-76).

Royal correspondence and trade necessitated proper road conditions and care. The 9th cent. BCE MOABITE STONE notes MESHA's creation of the road through the Arnon (line 26). Without safe and passable roads everyone suffered. Deborah and Barak note, "caravans ceased and travelers kept to the byways" (Judg 5:6). The annals of the 15th cent. BCE pharaoh Thutmose III described the main artery through Canaan as a dangerous place, so narrow in one area that only by single file could his troops pass (AEL 2:31). Conditions on the roadway are described by a late 13th-cent. BCE Egyptian official as overgrown with trees (ANET 477).

Messages took various forms. Simple notes written with black resin ink on broken potsherds (ostraca), official communiqués on tablets of clay in Mesopotamian cuneiform or papyri in Egyptian hieroglyphs or demotic script, and beaten/tanned pieces of leather written by the hand of a scribe are representative of written communications. Over the millennia the organic materials decomposed unless stored in antiquity in extremely arid places like the deserts of Egypt or the wilderness areas of southern Palestine (e.g., the Dead Sea Scrolls). The majority of ancient documents still extant are ostraca and cuneiform tablets from Mesopotamian empires.

Royal and business documents maintained confidentiality through the use of official seals. The document was rolled and bound with leather straps. The official or entrepreneur then pressed a personal seal into clay or wax set onto the knot of the tied document. These clay seals, known as bullae, are ubiquitous in excavations of major cities and commerce centers. Breaking the seal was a serious offense. The intriguing story of David, Bathsheba, and Uriah illuminates the use of messengers, written correspondence, and confidentiality. David sent Uriah back to battle carrying the written orders that would lead to Uriah's own death (2 Sam 11:14-15). See ROAD; SHIPS AND SAILING IN THE OT.

Bibliography: Yohanan Aharoni et al. *The Carta Bible Atlas.* 4th ed. (2002); Barry L. Beitzel. *Biblica: The Bible Atlas* (2007); Barry L. Beitzel. "The Via Maris in Literary and Cartographic Sources." *BA* 54:2 (1991) 64–75; J. Andrew Dearman. "Roads and Settlements in Moab." *BA* 60 (1997) 205–13; David A. Dorsey. *The Roads and Highways of Ancient Israel* (1991); R. Steven Notley and Anson Rainey. *The Sacred Bridge* (2006).

MICHAEL G. VANZANT

TRAVELERS, VALLEY OF THE. *See* VALLEY OF THE TRAVELERS.

TRAY [מַחְתָּה *makhtah*]. A utensil associated with the tabernacle's LAMPSTAND (Exod 25:38; 37:23; Num 4:9). Like the lampstand, the trays were made of pure gold. Mentioned with SNUFFERS and other appurtenances for the tabernacle service, the trays were probably bowls used as receptacles for burned wicks. *See* CENSER.

TREASURE CITIES. *See* STORE-CITIES, STOREHOUSES.

TREASURE, TREASURER, TREASURY [אוֹצָר *'otsar*, גִּזְבָּר *gizbar*, גְּנָזִים *genazim*, חֹסֶן *khosen*, מַטְמוֹן *matmon*, סְגֻלָּה *segullah*, צָפִין *tsafin*; γάζα *gaza*, γαζοφυλακεῖον *gazophylakeion*, κορβανᾶς *korbanas*, θησαυρός *thēsauros*]. In the OT treasure is either a form of wealth, often concealed, or something that is stored up or hoarded. The most common Hebrew word translated into English as "treasure" or "treasury" is *'otsar*, although there are several other terms that are also used in the OT. One of the most common meanings of *treasure* is hidden wealth. The concealed nature appears in the Hebrew noun **matmon**, which is found in Gen 43:23, where money is hidden, in Isa 45:3, where darkness is the hidden treasure, and in Prov 2:4, which commands that one look for wisdom and "search for it as for hidden treasure." Treasure does not have an overall negative meaning in the OT. It is considered worthy to be sought (Prov 2:4); the righteous possess it (Prov 15:6); and the foolish are without (Prov 21:20). Yet it can be gained improperly, as in the case of Prov 21:6, "The getting of treasures by a lying tongue is a fleeting vapor and a snare of death." Another Hebrew term that means hidden treasure is **tsafin**, which can have either positive or negative connotations. It can mean something that is stored up or reserved for the wicked (see Job 15:20; Hos 13:12).

Another common use for *treasure* is as a concept of personal identity. The Hebrew term **khosen**, which means "treasure" or "wealth," is from a verb meaning "to store up" or "to hoard." Several verses echo the idea of storing or hoarding in a positive sense. Isaiah 33:6 states, "the fear of the LORD is Zion's treasure." Also, Prov 15:6 maintains, "In the house of the righteous there is much treasure." In a negative sense, *treasure* is commonly mentioned in the context of items that can be removed or taken away. This is evident in Jer 20:5, where Yahweh will give "all the treasures of the kings of Judah into the hand of their enemies." Also, Ezek

22:25 records, "They have taken treasure and precious things." *Treasure* can also refer to one's personal possessions, as in the case of 1 Chr 29:3, where David states, "I have a treasure of my own of gold and silver, and because of my devotion to the house of my God I give it to the house of my God" (see 1 Chr 27:25-31; Eccl 2:8). Another usage of *treasure* is in Exod 19:5, where God promises to make Israel a "treasured possession" (segullah) in return for obedience.

In the OT, the word sometimes translated as "treasure" can also refer to the place where treasure is kept, i.e., a storehouse or even a collection box for tithes. The use of a storage area to house precious items was common throughout the ANE and was often connected to the palace and temple complexes (Josh 6:19, 24; 1 Kgs 7:51; 14:26; 15:18; 2 Kgs 14:14; 16:8; 18:15; 20:15; Neh 7:70-72; 10:38; Esth 3:9; 4:7; Isa 39:4).

A *treasurer* can besomeone who is responsible for wealth, taxation, or tithes. The Hebrew for treasurer is gizbar, a loanword from the Persian ganza-bara, which is a title for one in charge of the treasury. This position appears in postexilic literature like Ezra 1:8, when Cyrus, king of Persia, had the temple vessels "released into the charge of Mithredath the treasurer, who counted them out to Sheshbazzar the prince of Judah." Also, ʾotsar is used in Neh 13:13, when the temple personnel were "appointed as treasurers over the storehouses." It specifies the role of the treasurers, which was to distribute funds to their associates. First Chronicles 9:26-29 and 26:20 list the temple workers in charge of the treasury and specifies the types of jobs for which they were responsible. This included guarding the gates and counting the utensils daily, as well as responsibility over the furniture.

Apocryphal texts most commonly use the Greek word thesauros denoting treasure, granary, or hidden things. It is from the verb thēsaurizō (θησαυρίζω). One can store up or lay up treasure (Tob 4:9; Sir 3:4; 2 Esd 7:77). By extension, the idea of a treasure that is stored is found in several contexts (e.g., 1 Esd 1:54; 4 Macc 4:4). In 1 Macc 1:23, Antiochus looted the Temple in Jerusalem and "took the silver and the gold, and the costly vessels; he took also the hidden treasures that he found."

A treasury, a storehouse for precious items, is mentioned 1 Macc 3:29. Also, tamieion (ταμιεῖον), which means a storehouse or warehouse, is used to refer to a place to store riches in Sir 29:12. The term gazophylakeion also refers to a place to store valuable possessions in 2 Macc 3:6, 24, 28, 40; 1 Esd 5:45 [LXX 5:44]; 4 Macc 4:4, 6. The treasury could also serve as an archive where important documents were placed (see 1 Macc 14:49). The position of treasurer appears in 1 Esd 2:11 [LXX 2:8]; 4:49; 8:19-45, retaining the same meaning as in the postexilic references in the OT.

Unlike the OT, the NT uses only four terms for treasure and treasury. Thesauros means wealth or some-thing that is stored up either physically or spiritually. Unlike in the OT, treasure as earthly wealth tends to have a more negative connotation in the NT. Whereas the OT kings are often praised for storing up great earthly treasures and Proverbs commends prudent practices that bring great wealth, the NT contrasts earthly treasure with spiritual treasure, and so tends to cast the former into opposition with the latter. In the context of treasure as a horde of goods or deposit, Matt 6:19-21; Luke 12:21 clearly reflect the idea that they are negative possessions. But spiritual treasure is deemed a worthy possession (Matt 19:21; Mark 10:21; Luke 12:33; 18:22).

A treasury, a place where wealth is collected or stored up, is most often gazophylakeion, alternatively gaza in Acts 8:27 or korbanas in Matt 27:6. The gazophylakeion was a place or a collection box in the Temple (as an area, see John 8:20; for collection box, see Mark 12:41-42; Luke 21:1).

Another term that is translated "treasury" is korbanas, from the Hebrew qorban (קָרְבָּן). This particular term usually means gifts as sacrifices or offerings to God in the OT and NT, but can also mean gifts given to the temple treasury. In Matt 27:6, when Judas throws down the money he is given to betray Jesus, the chief priests comment that, "It is not lawful to put them [the money] into the treasury (korbanas)." Finally the term gaza only appears in Acts 8:27 in connection with the Ethiopian who was "a court official of the Candace, queen of the Ethiopians, in charge of her entire treasury," who had visited Jerusalem. This verse employs a generic Ptolemaic and Seleucid formula for recording a royal position: "Person X is in charge of (literally 'over') a specific position."

Bibliography: Gary N. Knoppers. "Treasures Won and Lost: Royal (Mis)appropriations in Kings and Chronicles." *The Chronicler as Author.* M. Patrick Graham and Steven L. McKenzie, ed. (1999) 181–208; E. T. Mullen. "Crime and Punishment: The Sins of the King and the Despoilation of the Treasuries." *CBQ* 54 (1992) 231–48; Joachim Schaper. "The Temple Treasury Committee in the Times of Nehemiah and Ezra." *VT* 47 (1997) 200–206.

DEIRDRE N. FULTON

TREATY. *See* ALLIANCE.

TREE OF KNOWLEDGE, TREE OF LIFE [עֵץ הַדַּעַת ʿets haddaʿath, עֵץ הַחַיִּים ʿets hakhayyim; ξύλον ζωῆς xylon zōēs]. The "Tree of Knowledge" (ʿets haddaʿath) and the "Tree of Life" (ʿets hakhayyim) both appear in Gen 2–3. The Tree of Knowledge appears only in Genesis and symbolizes a particular way of perceiving the world. The Tree of Knowledge is somewhat connected in the Genesis story with the Tree of Life, which is a much more pervasive image in the Bible and in ANE texts and art. "The Tree of Life" connotes life, longevity, fertility, and in certain occurrences, wisdom.

A. The Tree of Knowledge

The creation story in Gen 2:8-9 states that after God had formed the first human, God planted a garden in Eden and placed the human there (see ADAM; EDEN, GARDEN OF). God then caused various trees to grow, including the tree of life, which was located in the midst of the garden, and the tree of knowledge of GOOD and EVIL, literally, "the tree of the knowledge of good and bad" ('ets hadda'ath tov wara' עֵץ הַדַּעַת טוֹב וָרָע). Its location in the garden is not made explicit. In vv. 16-17, God commands the human, "You may freely eat of every tree of the garden; but of the tree of the knowledge, good and evil, you shall not eat, for in the day that you eat of it you shall die."

The narrative continues in chap. 3 with the exchange between the SERPENT and the woman (see EVE). The serpent asks, "Did God say, 'You shall not eat from any tree in the garden'?" (v. 1). The woman replies that she and the man may eat of any tree of the garden, but that God said, "You [plural] shall not eat of the fruit of the tree that is in the middle of the garden, nor shall you touch it, or you shall die" (v. 3). But the serpent convinces the woman that the only reason God does not want her and the man to eat of the tree is that their eyes will be opened and they will be like God (v. 5). The words of the serpent create enough doubt in the woman's mind that both she and the man end up eating the fruit of the tree (v. 6).

Two questions present themselves in an examination of this story. First, from which tree did the first human pair eat, "the tree of the knowledge of good and evil" or "the tree of life"? The woman tells the serpent that they are forbidden to eat from the tree "in the middle (bethokh בְּתוֹךְ) of the garden" (3:3). Genesis 2:9 indicates that the tree of life is located in the middle of the garden, while the location of the tree of the knowledge, good and evil is not specified in that verse. In Gen 3:11, however, God asks the human whether he has have eaten from the tree "of which I commanded you not to eat." That tree, according to Gen 2:17, is "the tree of the knowledge of good and evil"; thus one may infer that it also was located in the middle of the garden. Despite the ambiguity of the exchange between the serpent and the woman in Gen 3 and further missing indicators of the identity of the tree of which the first human pair ate, most scholars agree that the tree in question is the tree of the knowledge of good and evil. Such a conclusion is further corroborated by the conclusion of the story in Gen 3:22-24, in which cherubim and a flaming sword are stationed to guard the way to the tree of life, indicating that the human pair had not eaten from it and that God intended that they not eat from it in the future.

Thus, we may surmise that the first human pair ate from the tree of the knowledge of good and evil, and because of that, their lives and the shape of human life were forever changed. The precise scope of the knowledge of good and evil that eating from the tree imparts is a debated question. Some insight may be gained from the humans' reaction to their new-found knowledge: "Then the eyes of both were opened, and they knew that they were naked; and they sewed fig leaves together and made loincloths for themselves" (Gen 3:7); and from God's words in Gen 3:22: " 'See the human has become like one of us, knowing good and evil.' " Some scholars suggest that this knowledge had to do with sexual awareness: before eating of the tree, the first human pair lived blissfully in the garden, enjoying each other with no awareness of their physical and sexual difference; however, after eating, the recognition of their sexuality caused them to think and behave differently. The idea of sexual knowledge as the knowledge proffered by the tree is based on the meaning of the Hebrew verb yadha' (יָדַע), which encompasses every aspect of "to know," from mere acquaintance to sexual relations.

Others contend that the knowledge gained was more all-encompassing and pervasive, a full awareness of all of life's experiences—a knowledge gained without having actually lived through the experiences. With that first taste of the fruit, the first human pair is bombarded with a myriad of memories and emotions that they have not experienced firsthand. The knowledge is the sum total of the experiences of a life lived fully, and the humans were able to look back and forward and to bring those experiences to bear on their current human condition.

Many scholars maintain that the story in Gen 2 and 3 initially dealt with only one tree, the tree of the knowledge of good and evil; that later authors added a more familiar element, the tree of life. There are several reasons for this theory: the varied ways in which the Genesis creation story speaks of the tree of the knowledge of good and evil; "the tree of life" appears in the Genesis creation narrative only in its introduction (2:9) and conclusion (3:22-24); "the tree of life" is a common theme in the ANE (and in other biblical texts), while the tree of the knowledge of good and evil is unique to the Genesis creation story.

B. The Tree of Life

1. In biblical and early Jewish texts

The term "the tree of life" appears not only in Genesis but also in other parts of the OT, in the NT, and in non-biblical early Jewish literature. Wisdom texts refer frequently to the "tree of life" frequently. For example, in Prov 3:18, Woman Wisdom (khokhmah חָכְמָה)

is called "a tree of life to those who lay hold of her" (*see* SOPHIA). In 11:30, a tree of life is "the fruit of the righteous." "A desire fulfilled is a tree of life" in 13:12, while in 15:4 a tree of life is "a gentle tongue."

In Psalms, the righteous "flourish like the palm tree and grow like a cedar in Lebanon" (92:12 [Heb. 92:13]), and "in old age they still produce fruit; they are always green and full of sap" (92:14 [Heb 92:15]). Psalm 1 compares the righteous person to a tree planted by streams of water, which yields its fruit in its season and whose leaves do not wither (compare Prov 3:18). *First Enoch* discusses a tree that no human is permitted to touch until the great judgment when it will become food for "the righteous and the holy" (*1 En* 25:4-5).

Daniel 4:10-12 [Heb. 4:7-9] describes a tree at the center of the earth whose height was great and foliage was strong, whose fruit was abundant, "and it provided food for all."

The book of Ezekiel speaks of a life-giving tree: "On the mountain height of Israel I will plant it, in order that it may produce boughs and bear fruit, and become a noble cedar" (17:22-24). In Ezek 47:12, the prophet describes the trees that will grow in the restored city of Jerusalem: "there will grow all kinds of trees for food. Their leaves will not wither nor their fruit fail, but they will bear fresh fruit every month ... Their fruit will be for food, and their leaves for healing."

The book of Revelation uses OT imagery of the tree of life (xylon tēs zōēs) planted by streams of living water, to describe the New Jerusalem: "Then the angel showed me the river of the water of life, bright as crystal, flowing from the throne of God and of the Lamb through the middle of the street of the city. On either side of the river is the tree of life" (Rev 22:2; see also v. 14; compare Gen. 2:1-14). Revelation also borrows Ezekiel's distinctive imagery to describe the tree of life "with its twelve kinds of fruit, producing its fruit each month; and the leaves of the tree are for the healing of the nations" (Rev 22:2). As in Psalms and *1 Enoch*, Revelation reserves the tree of life for the righteous: those who "wash their robes" will have the right to the tree of life and may enter the city by the gates (Rev 22:14-15, 19).

2. In the Ancient Near East

As the biblical references suggest, the "tree of life" connotes life, longevity, and fertility. Likewise, the tree is a common metaphor for life and fertility in the literature and art of the ANE. In the "Epic of Gilgamesh," a lengthy Mesopotamian composition that dates to as early as the 3rd millennium BCE, the protagonist of the story, Gilgamesh, embarks on a journey to find the secret of immortality. On Tablet XI, lines 266–295, of the epic, Utnapishtim tells Gilgamesh about a plant that grows in deep waters that will give him new life. Gilgamesh ties stones to his feet, descends into the water, and finds the plant. Back on shore, he declares that this plant is

unique in that it gives back life's breath, and he calls it Man-Shall-Become-Young-in-Old-Age. Gilgamesh plans to eat it to regain a state of youth. But on his way back to Uruk, a serpent steals the plant and eats it instead (*ANET*, 96; compare the serpent in Gen 3:1-4). The serpent eating the plant is an etiological explanation for why snakes slough their skins and appear to have new life.

Trees as symbols of life-giving entities, depicted on monuments, stelae, tomb inscriptions, and cylinder seals, are common elements of the art of the ANE from as early as the Middle Bronze Age. The tree is often associated with Canaanite fertility goddesses, particularly ASHERAH. An ivory carving from 14th-cent. Ugarit depicts two ibexes on either side of the figure of a woman with large breasts and exaggerated hips, a common symbol of fertility. In her hands are what appear to be leafy branches of a tree. A drawing on a storage jar from Kuntillet ʿAjrud in northern Sinai from the early 8th cent. BCE depicts two ibexes nibbling on a tree. A Middle Bronze Age scarab from Tell el-Farah, located 16 mi. west of Beer-sheba, also depicts two ibexes feeding on a tree. Although the female figure is not explicit in these examples, the fertility and nourishment connection may be inferred, especially since the ibex is associated with steppe regions where forage is not readily available.

Of particular interest for its size and detail is an elaborate mural, most likely from the 18th-cent. BCE king of Mari named Zimri-Lim. On the wall of the vestibule leading to the throne room is a painting of a royal ceremony. In it, the royal family is in a garden with large trees, winged sphinxes, and other fantastic creatures. The members of the royal family are shown climbing and picking the fruit of the various trees, thus symbolizing the ongoing fertility of the royal line. *See* KNOWLEDGE; LIFE.

Bibliography: William P. Brown. "The Transplanted Tree: Psalm 1 and the Psalter's Threshold." *Seeing the Psalms: A Theology of Metaphor* (2002) 55–79; Wilfred J. Harrington. *Revelation.* SP 16 (1993); Othmar Keel. *Goddesses and Trees, New Moon and Yahweh: Ancient Near Eastern Art and the Hebrew Bible* (1998); Roland Murphy. *The Tree of Life: An Exploration of Biblical Wisdom Literature* (2002); Claus Westermann. *Genesis 1–11.* CC. John J. Scullion, trans. (1994).

NANCY DECLAISSÉ-WALFORD

TREES. *See* CEDAR; OAK; OLIVE, OLIVE TREE; PLANTS OF THE BIBLE; WOOD.

TRELLIS [שְׂבָךְ־עֵץ *sevok-ʿets*]. The NRSV understands this as a crisscrossing ornament on the capitals of the columns at the entrance to Solomon's Temple (i.e., JACHIN AND BOAZ; compare 1 Kgs 7:18-21, 41-42). Psalm 74:5 probably describes marauding Babylonian troops hewing this LATTICEWORK with their battle axes. *See* TEMPLE, JERUSALEM.

JOEL M. LEMON

TRESPASS OFFERING. *See* SACRIFICES AND OFFERINGS.

TRESSES [רהט rahat]. The word translated "tresses" in Song 7:5 literally means "troughs for watering cattle." A footnote in the NRSV indicates that "tresses" is a speculative translation, assuming a parallel with "flowing locks."

TRIAL. *See* TEMPT, TEMPTATION.

TRIAL BY ORDEAL. A physical test used to determine the veracity of an OATH in the absence of human witnesses or evidence. Presumably, the deity will indicate whether the oath is false by the outcome of the trial. Numbers 5:11-31 prescribes a trial by ordeal—drinking the WATER OF BITTERNESS—for a woman who is suspected of ADULTERY and/or who has a jealous husband. The ordeal itself contains the divinely determined verdict and sentence: guilt results in MISCARRIAGE, deformity, and/or sterility. Other passages associating DRINK with punishment include Exod 32:20; Ps 75:6-8 [Heb. 75:7-9]; Isa 51:17; Jer 49:12; Ezek 23:31-34; Hab 2:15-16; and 1 Cor 11:21-32. *See* ABORTION; CURSE; LAW IN THE OT; ORDEAL, JUDICIAL; TORTURE; WOMEN IN THE OT.

LISA MICHELE WOLFE

TRIAL OF JESUS. The trial (or "hearing") of Jesus refers to the appearance of Jesus before Jewish and Roman authorities who condemned him to death. Since the 19th cent. the topic has been hotly debated, often with reference to Christian ANTI-SEMITISM (*see* ANTI-JUDAISM). Some scholars have argued that the trial of Jesus was entirely a Roman affair, while others have asserted that it was mostly a Jewish affair. Today most scholars rightly recognize the involvement of both Jewish and Roman authorities.

A. The Trial of Jesus in the New Testament

1. Gospels

All four NT Gospels relate appearances of Jesus before Jewish and Roman authorities, who to one degree or another work in concert. Although there is considerable overlap in the four Gospels, there are some distinctive elements.

a. Mark. According to Mark, Jesus predicts his rejection at the hands of the "elders, chief priests, and the scribes," his death, and his resurrection (8:31; 9:31; 10:33-34). The events of Passion Week unfold roughly as predicted. The ruling priests, scribes, and elders challenge Jesus in the temple precincts, and, as may be inferred from the narrative, reject him (11:18, 27-33; 12:10-12). The ruling priests and scribes seek the means to affect a quiet arrest of Jesus (14:1-2). Judas Iscariot agrees to assist the ruling priests (14:10-11). During prayer in a place called GETHSEMANE (14:32) Jesus is arrested by people acting under the authority of the ruling priests, scribes, and elders (14:43-50). Jesus is taken to the high priest (14:53). Jewish authorities then gather at "the courtyard of the high priest," which may imply that the proceedings took place at the home of Caiaphas, though that is only an inference. The ruling priests and council seek testimony against Jesus (14:55-56). Various accusations are made, including Jesus' threat against the Temple (14:57-58; see 13:1-2). When Jesus confesses that he is indeed the Messiah, the Son of God, who will be seated at the right hand, he is accused of blasphemy and condemned as deserving death (14:61-64). The following morning the Jewish authorities deliver Jesus to Pilate, the Roman prefect of Judea and Samaria (15:1). Pilate questions Jesus ("Are you the King of the Jews?") and offers to release him, as part of the governor's traditional "Passover Pardon" (15:2-14). The crowd requests the release of Barabbas and calls for Jesus' death, whereupon Pilate gives Jesus up to be crucified (15:15).

b. Matthew. In narrating the trial before Pilate, Matthew follows Mark fairly closely. The noticeable difference is seen in the reference to the disturbing dream Pilate's wife has, warning the governor to "have nothing to do with that righteous (NRSV, "innocent") man" (27:19). The Matthean version of the trial before Pilate ends with the governor washing his hands and declaring that he is "innocent of this man's blood" (27:24), to which the crowd responds with the fateful words, "His blood be on us and on our children!" (27:25).

c. Luke. The Lukan evangelist abridges the narrative of Jesus before the chief priests and council (22:66-71). We hear nothing of false witnesses or the accusation that Jesus threatened to destroy the Temple. Moreover, Jesus' confession is recounted so that the coming of the son of man "with the clouds of heaven" is downplayed

(22:69-70; compare Mark 14:61-62). Luke's version of the trial before Pilate exhibits further differences. Jesus is accused of forbidding the payment of tribute to Caesar (23:2) and of stirring up the people (23:5). The evangelist also adds the interesting account of Herod Antipas meeting Jesus and of Pilate and Herod's new-found friendship (23:6-12) and emphasizes the innocence of Jesus (23:20-25). The innocent Jesus stands in stark contrast to the murderer Barabbas, whose release the crowd demands.

d. John. The narrative of the fourth evangelist offers many distinctive features. Judas and officers of the chief priests are accompanied by a Roman cohort (18:3, 12; NRSV, "soldiers"), as the word speira (σπεῖρα) implies (see Acts 10:1; 21:31; 27:1). Although it has been suggested, it is not probable that the evangelist mistakenly used a word that refers to Roman troops, when he had in mind Jewish soldiers or guards. The evangelist evidently thought that Roman soldiers were involved in the arrest of Jesus. This interesting detail should be taken very seriously. When arrested, Jesus is taken to Annas, a former high priest and father-in-law of Caiaphas, the current high priest (18:12-13). While being questioned, Jesus is struck (18:22-23). After this Jesus is sent to Caiaphas (18:24) and from there to the Roman Praetorium (18:28; NRSV, "headquarters"). Here the Fourth Gospel differs noticeably from the Synoptic tradition, in that nothing is said of any interrogation or exchange between Caiaphas and Jesus. But the most distinctive feature of the trial of Jesus in the Gospel of John is the dialogue between Pilate and Jesus (18:29-38), in which Jesus declares that his kingdom "is not from this world" (18:36) and Pilate asks, "What is truth?" (18:38). From a theological point of view, perhaps the most important feature is the emphasis on the legal point that the Jewish authorities were not allowed to execute anyone (18:31-32). Not only would this guarantee CRUCIFIXION (and, therefore, Jesus would be "lifted up"; see 12:32) but it may have served an apologetic purpose, mitigating the embarrassment of execution at the hands of the Roman authorities.

2. Acts and Epistles

The trial of Jesus is mentioned in passing elsewhere in NT writings. In the Pentecost sermon, Peter refers to Jesus as "a man attested to you by God with deeds of power, wonders, and signs that God did through among you ... handed over to you according to the definite plan and foreknowledge of God, you crucified and killed by the hands of those outside the law" (Acts 2:22-23). Peter's "you" refers to the Jewish people in Jerusalem (see Acts 2:14), while the "lawless men" doubtlessly refers to the Roman authorities. The point is made again in the temple sermon, where Peter this time accuses Jerusalemites: "God ... glorified his servant Jesus, whom you handed over and rejected in the presence of Pilate ... and you killed the Author of life" (Acts 3:13-15). Peter's accusations presuppose the collaboration

between Jewish and Roman authorities in examining and condemning Jesus. We hear this again as part of an interpretation of Ps 2, which asks why the nations plot against the Lord and God's anointed one (Acts 4:25-26). The apostles in prayer declare that "in this city, in fact, both Herod and Pontius Pilate, with the Gentiles and the peoples of Israel, gathered together against your holy servant Jesus, whom you anointed" (Acts 4:27). This theme is echoed in a sermon attributed to Paul (Acts 13:28; "Though they [i.e., the Jewish authorities] found no cause for a sentence of death, they asked Pilate to have him killed"). In 1 Tim 6:13, the author charges his readers "in the presence of God, who gives life to all things, and of Christ Jesus, who in his testimony before Pontius Pilate made the good confession."

B. The Trial of Jesus in Non-Christian Sources

1. Josephus

The 1st-cent. Jewish historian and apologist Josephus is our most important non-Christian source for information regarding the trial of Jesus. In his famous *Testimonium* (*Ant.* 18.63–64), Josephus draws the important link between the Jewish authorities and Pilate the Roman governor. He suggests that Jesus was accused by the ruling priests and their colleagues (compare *Ant.* 11.140–41), and was condemned to the cross by Pilate. In broad outline, this is precisely the juridical process we see narrated in the NT Gospels and elsewhere in Josephus himself, in reference to the prophet of doom Jesus ben Ananias, who foretold the coming destruction of the city of Jerusalem. The latter Jesus, like the former, was abused by the Jewish authorities and then was delivered to the Roman governor with calls for the man's death (*J.W.* 6.300–309). Admittedly we cannot be sure how much of Josephus' knowledge of the trial of Jesus of Nazareth was independent of the Christian tradition, if any. Nevertheless, the similar process described in the case of Jesus ben Ananias confirms the general accuracy of the testimony of early Christian literature, to the effect that the trial of Jesus was part of a process in which Jewish and Roman authorities were participants.

2. Greco-Roman writers

A few early Greco-Roman historians, politicians, and writers were in possession of basic information about the early Christian movement, including the trial and death of Jesus. In referring to the Christians, falsely blamed for the fire that destroyed part of Rome, Tacitus (ca. 110) explains that Christus had been executed during the reign of Tiberius by order of Pontius Pilate (*Ann.* 15.44). A half century later Lucian of Samosata refers to Jesus as a man crucified in Palestine (*Peregr.* §11). The statements of Tacitus and Lucian tell us very little about the trial of Jesus, apart from the bare fact that it resulted in his execution at the hands of the Romans.

3. Rabbinic literature and other sources

According to the Talmud Jesus was stoned and hanged on the eve of Passover (b. Sanh. 43a). This interesting version, which says nothing about Roman involvement, reflects a Jewish manner of execution (see Deut 21:21-23). The Talmudic tradition also says that the execution of Jesus was preceded by an invitation to the public to come forward and speak on his behalf, thus implying a trial of some sort. Although this material does not appear to be dependent on the NT Gospels, it is probably little more than a reflection of late anti-Christian polemic that circulated in the rabbinic academy.

In his letter to his son, Mara bar Serapion (2nd cent.?) refers to the death of a Jewish king in a way that apparently means Jesus. Nothing directly is said about a trial or even a manner of death, but the comparison with the death of Socrates at the hands of the Athenians is perhaps suggestive of some sort of trial and miscarriage of justice. In any event, bar Serapion's comparison of the death of Jesus with the deaths of Socrates and Pythagoras is remarkable, even if not especially informative.

C. The Trial of Jesus and History

1. Arrest

According to the Gospels Jesus was arrested at night, more or less in private, while in prayer at a place called Gethsemane on the Mount of Olives. Mark describes the arresting group as "a crowd with swords and clubs, from the chief priests, the scribes, and the elders" (14:43; see John 18:3; "a detachment of soldiers together with police"). This group knew where to find Jesus because of information received from Judas Iscariot, and because Judas led them to Jesus (Mark 14:10-11, 43-45). Both of these details—men sent by the chief priests armed with weapons and offering bribes—are in a general sense corroborated by Josephus, who tells of similar actions taken by the most powerful of the ruling priests in the 1st cent. (see Josephus, Ant. 20.205-207).

2. Nighttime hearing before Jewish authorities

Exactly where Jesus was taken the evening of his arrest is not clear. Mark says he was taken to the high priest (14:53; followed by Luke 22:54), but this priest is not named. Matthew identifies the priest as Caiaphas (26:57). The fourth evangelist complicates things by saying that "first they took him to Annas, who was the father-in-law of Caiaphas" (John 18:13a). Annas is called "high priest" (18:19), even though it was his son-in-law who was actually in office "that year," that is, the year of Jesus' execution (18:13b). According to the Fourth Gospel, Annas interrogates Jesus and then sends him to Caiaphas (18:24). The picture is complicated still further in the Gospel of Luke, wherein the evangelist situates the hearing before the Jewish authorities in the morning following the arrest of Jesus (Luke 22:66-71).

It is probable that the evangelist has done this because Mark says the ruling priests, elders, and scribes "held a consultation" in the morning and then delivered Jesus to Pilate (Mark 15:1; see Matt 27:1-2). It is probable that Jesus was interrogated the evening of his arrest and that the following morning; after a rehearsal of the charges and testimony, a decision was reached to deliver Jesus to Pilate with a capital recommendation.

3. Trial before Pilate

According to all four Gospels the focus of Pilate's examination of Jesus was on the allegation that Jesus had presented himself as the king of the Jews (Matt 27:11; Mark 15:2; Luke 23:3; John 18:33). This appears to be confirmed by Jesus' crucifixion as "King of the Jews" (Mark 15:18, 26). It has been persuasively argued that such an epithet was no Christian creation, confessional or otherwise, for Christians regarded Jesus as the Messiah (or Christ), Son of God, Lord, and Savior, not "King of the Jews," a title Rome granted to Herod the Great (see Josephus, J.W. 1.282–85).

4. Offer of a "Passover Pardon"

All four NT Gospels know of Pilate's so-called "Passover Pardon" (Matt 27:15-23; Mark 15:6-15; Luke 23:18-25; John 19:10-12). Although some critical scholars have cast doubts on the historicity of this tradition (e.g., Winter), it is improbable that inauthentic tradition, whose falsity could so readily be exposed, would be utilized by all four evangelists. There are accounts of Roman and other Jewish officials releasing prisoners on occasion of special days (see Ptolemy, Flor. 61.59–64; Livy, Hist. 5.13.8; Pliny the Younger, Ep. 10.31; Josephus, Ant. 17.204; 20.215; m. Pesah. 8:6).

5. Condemnation to the cross

The best attested historical datum pertaining to Jesus of Nazareth is his execution by crucifixion. That Jesus was executed and that he was executed by crucifixion—publicly and on the eve of the Passover holiday—testifies to the gravity with which his claims were met. Execution as "King of the Jews" lends support to the view that at issue in the trial of Jesus was the claim, either made by himself or by his followers, that he was Israel's Messiah. See DEATH OF CHRIST; PASSION NARRATIVES; SANHEDRIN.

Bibliography: Ernst Bammel, ed. *The Trial of Jesus: Cambridge Studies in Honour of C. F. D. Moule* (1970); Ernst Bammel and Charles Francis Digby Moule, eds. *Jesus and the Politics of His Day* (1984); Matthew Black. "The Arrest and Trial of Jesus and the Date of the Last Supper." *New Testament Essays: Studies in Memory of Thomas Walter Manson, 1893–1958.* Angus John Brockhurst Higgins, ed. (1959) 19–33; Lynne Courter Boughton. "The Priestly Perspective of the Johannine Trial Narratives." *RB* 110 (2003) 517–51; Raymond Edward Brown. *The Death of the Messiah: From*

Gethsemane to the Grave. A Commentary on the Passion Narratives in the Four Gospels. 2 vols. (1994); T. Alec Burkill. "The Competence of the Sanhedrin." *VC* 10 (1956) 80–96; William Sanger Campbell. "Engagement, Disengagement and Obstruction: Jesus' Defense Strategies in Mark's Trial and Execution Scenes (14.53–64; 15.1–39)." *JSNT* 26 (2004) 283–300; John T. Carrol and Joel B. Green. *The Death of Jesus in Early Christianity* (1995); David R. Catchpole. *The Trial of Jesus* (1971); Bruce Chilton. "The So-called Trial before the Sanhedrin. Mark 14:53–72." *Forum* 1 (1998) 163–80; Bruce Chilton. "The Trial of Jesus Reconsidered." *Jesus in Context: Temple, Purity, and Restoration.* Bruce Chilton and Craig A. Evans, eds. (1997) 481–500; John R. Donahue. *Are You the Christ? The Trial Narrative in the Gospel of Mark* (1973); Joel B. Green. *The Death of Jesus* (1988); John J. Kilgallen. "Jesus' First Trial: Messiah and Son of God (Luke 22, 66–71)." *Bib* 80 (1999) 401–14; Frank J. Matera. "Luke 22:66–71: Jesus before the ΠΡΕΣΒΥΤΕΡΙΟΝ." *ETL* 65 (1989) 43–59; Frank J. Matera. "The Trial of Jesus: Problems and Proposals." *Int* 45 (1991) 5–16; James S. McLaren. "Exploring the Execution of a Provincial: Adopting a Roman Perspective on the Death of Jesus." *Australian Biblical Review* 49 (2001) 5–18; Fergus Millar. "Reflections on the Trial of Jesus." *A Tribute to Geza Vermes: Essays on Jewish and Christian Literature and History.* Philip R. Davies and Richard T. White, eds. (1990) 355–81; Maurits Sabbe. "The Trial of Jesus before Pilate in John and Its Relation to the Synoptic Gospels." *John and the Synoptics.* Adelbert Denaux, ed. (1992) 341–85; Adrian Nicholas Sherwin-White. *The Trial of Christ: Historicity and Chronology in the Gospels* (1965); Alan Watson. *The Trial of Jesus* (1995); Paul Winter. *On the Trial of Jesus* (1974).

CRAIG A. EVANS

TRIBE [מַטֶּה matteh, שֵׁבֶט shevet; φυλή phylē]. In the social system of ancient Israel, about a dozen large groupings called "tribes" constructed and expressed affinity among clans (mishpakhah [מִשְׁפָּחָה]; *see* CLAN) and their constitutive families (beth ʾav [בֵּית אָב], "father's house"; *see* FAMILY). *Tribe* translates two Hebrew synonyms that occur as parallel terms in Num 18:2. The concrete meaning of both **matteh** and **shevet** is "stick," "rod," or "staff." Two theories suggest how words designating a physical object came to describe a social group. *Staff*, in the sense of "scepter of authority," could have been extended to signify a group under the command of the scepter holder (Amos 1:5, 8). Alternatively, this usage could rest on a biological metaphor of *branch* or *stem*, signifying those related by descent (compare Isa 11:1, in which a similar metaphor is used, although with different Hebrew words). Ezekiel 19:11-14 uses both words in a complex image involving *stem* and *scepter*.

A. Social Function
B. Names and Territory
C. Fluidity
D. Intertribal Relationships
E. Tribes and the State
F. Ideology
Bibliography

A. Social Function

The institution of the tribe preceded state formation in Israel but continued to function alongside the monarchy. From the perspective of anthropology, tribes organize and socially construct smaller associations of corporate descent groups (clans). Tribes can characterize pre-state arrangements, as among pre-Islamic Arabs, but can also serve as a mechanism for organizing a state, as in the case of ancient Athens and Rome. Anthropological parallels must be used with caution. Present-day tribes are not necessarily survivals of ancient social systems. Indeed many seem to have emerged to meet the needs of centralized states or to resist the demands of state authority. As a way of organizing affiliations and resources, tribes share functions with states but have few if any institutions and minimal hierarchy.

Almost everything we know about Israel's tribes comes from sources from the monarchic period or later. It is difficult to separate historically useful data from later idealism. Tribal affinities were expressed in terms of descent from a common eponymous ancestor, as well as by recognized spheres of territorial occupation. Tribal structure was egalitarian. Whether tribes were structured enough to have institutionalized leadership is doubtful. Deuteronomy 5:23 refers to heads of tribes and elders, but this probably refers to the leadership of individual clans and towns within tribes (*see* ELDER IN THE OT).

Israel's tribes seem to have been a social strategy to negotiate changing resources and defend territory. By encompassing larger areas and more diverse means of food production than individual families or clans, tribes could distribute resources efficiently and provide a cushion in times of scarcity. Sanctuaries with tribal status would have been mechanisms for distributing resources in the form of sacrifices. A tribe could also muster a substantial military force to fend off attack.

Individuals could be located socially by the three kinship levels of tribe, clan, and family/household (Josh 7:16-18; 1 Sam 10:20-21). Identifying one's clan and tribe (Deut 29:18 [Heb. 29:17]; Judg 6:15; 21:24) or tribe and family (1 Sam 9:21; 2 Sam 15:2) described personal identity. *See* HOUSEHOLD, HOUSEHOLDER; KINSHIP.

The effective unit of organization above the family level was not the tribe but the clan. Both legal and narrative texts indicate that clans functioned as independent, active entities. Clans were territorial, economic, and biological associations of families claiming descent from a common ancestor. Marriage was to be outside one's family and inside one's clan. Genealogies in Numbers and Chronicles preserve clan names. Town names and clan names often coincided. Thus, towns are incorporated into the Manasseh genealogy: Shechem, Tirzah, Hepher (Num 26:28-34; Josh 17:2-3). The SAMARIA OSTRACA bear witness to district names around Samaria that parallel clans of Manasseh preserved in Num 26:30-33 and Josh 17:2-3. The designations *clan* and *tribe* were used with some fluidity. The small tribe of Dan is sometimes called a clan (Judg 13:2 [NRSV, "tribe"]; 18:2, 11; contrast 18:1; in 18:19 both terms are used in parallel). Dan itself had only one subsidiary clan according to Gen 46:23 and Num 26:42 (note: "Hashum" and "Shuham" are the same name, with transposition of letters). The Levite of Judg 17:7 is said to have belonged to the clan of Judah. In contrast, Judg 21:8 seems to speak of Jabesh-gilead as a tribe. Further complication is introduced by the existence of what one might call "super clans" that encompassed several clans and towns: Machir (Josh 13:31; 1 Chr 2:21-23; 7:14-17; considered a tribe in Judg 5:14), Zelophehad (Num 26:33; 27:1; Josh 17:3; 1 Chr 7:15), and Jair (Josh 13:30; 1 Kgs 4:13; 1 Chr 2:22).

B. Names and Territory

Tribal names sometimes give clues to early realities. Egyptian texts mention Asher as an entity, with the determinative for a foreign land, present quite early in western Galilee. The name Issachar (perhaps "hired man") may relate to that group's sociopolitical or economic situation in an area dominated by Canaanite cities (compare Gen 49:15). Gad may derive from the name of a god of good fortune, perhaps referred to in Isa 65:11 (NRSV, "Fortune"). Certain tribal names were originally geographical designations, indicating that the tribe first emerged only when settled in that locality. Ephraim ("-aim" is a place name ending) was positioned in the south part of a larger hill country of Ephraim. Gilead, a tribe according to Judg 5:17, designates territory east of the Jordan. Judah may also be a territorial designation derived from the "hill country of Judah" (Josh 11:21). Benjamin—meaning "son of the south," "southerner"—reflects its location to the south of Ephraim and Manasseh. The practice of naming a group after its compass direction from another party is illustrated by the same name, "sons of the south," used to describe a tribal grouping at MARI.

Israel understood its tribal structure in terms of territory as well as kinship. Location is a feature of several tribal sayings and blessings in Gen 49 and Deut 33. Joshua 13–19 preserves territorial information in two forms, border descriptions and town lists, merged into a single picture that leaves no internal gaps. This system of tribal territories appears to be an artificial, scribal construction, although based on historically valuable data from a variety of sources. *See* TRIBES, TERRITORIES OF.

Regional sanctuaries played a role in generating intertribal solidarity. Tabor, as the unnamed sanctuary in Deut 33:18-19, was shared by Zebulun and Issachar, and also probably Naphtali, since the boundary lines of these three tribes converge near there (Josh 19:12, 22, 34). Dan had its own cultic center of regional importance (Judg 18:30-31; Amos 8:14). The important sanctuary of Bethel was situated just north of the common boundary of Ephraim and Benjamin. The enigmatic "between his shoulders" in Deut 33:12 may refer to Benjamin's favored situation between the sanctuaries of Bethel and Jerusalem. Gilgal lay within easy reach of Manasseh, Ephraim, Benjamin, and Judah. Shechem was close to the shared border of Ephraim and Manasseh. According to Josh 17:2, 7, it was in Manasseh but was the patrimony of both Joseph tribes according to the punning word play between Shechem and "shoulder" or "mountain ridge" in Gen 48:22 (NRSV, "portion").

The designation Levi expressed the affiliation of a professional group as a kinship association, not as a territorial entity. Thus, members of Levi could be found in Judah, Dan, and the hill country of Ephraim (Judg 17:7; 18:30; 19:1). Levi is presented as a conventional tribe in Gen 34:25-29, where it (in the shape of its eponym) joins Simeon in an assault on Shechem. The actual historical relationship between Levi and priestly groups associated with Aaron and Eli of Shiloh is unclear, but in the end Levites and all legitimate priests were coordinated into a unified genealogical system.

C. Fluidity

Disparities among the tribes mentioned in the Song of Deborah in Judg 5 and later lists indicate that the tribal roster remained in flux until the traditional twelve tribe system was completely established. Judah and Simeon are absent. Neither Manasseh nor Gad is mentioned; instead Machir and Gilead appear (Judg 5:14, 17). Since Machir and Gilead eventually became part of the clan structure of Manasseh (Num 32:39-40; Deut 3:15; Josh 17:1-6), the suggestion that they represent alternate names for Manasseh and Gad is not convincing. Genesis 50:23 hints at Machir's earlier independent status.

The fortunes of individual tribes changed over time, and there was some fluidity in tribal membership and territory. Reuben's firstborn position in patriarchal narratives and his positive role in the Elohist version of the kidnapping of Joseph (Gen 37:22, 29; eclipsed by Judah in the Yahwist version) suggest early importance, but the tribe was small and under pressure from Moab. The place name "Stone of Bohan, Reuben's son" (Josh 15:6; 18:17) suggests an early presence of Reuben west of the Jordan. Gad seems to have expanded at the expense of Reuben (Dibon is in Reuben according to Josh 13:17, but a city of Gad in Num 32:34). Reuben ultimately diminished size and power. The tribe is missing from the census itinerary of 2 Sam 24:5-6. Likewise, the MOABITE STONE mentions only Gad, not Reuben.

The story of Reuben having sex with his father's concubine Bilhah was recounted to provide an explanation for the tribe's decline (Gen 35:22; 49:4; Deut 33:6). In a similar way, the story of the defeat of Benjamin in Judg 20 accounted for Benjamin's relatively small size. Simeon and Levi are chastised for their violence against Shechem in Gen 49:5-7 (see Gen 34) to explain their respective situations. Simeon was under Judahite dominance, and Levi lacked consolidated territory. The story of Jacob's blessing of Ephraim and Manasseh not only provided a reason for their mutual association within the larger "house of Joseph" but also witnessed to Ephraim's eventual increase in importance over against its brother tribe (Gen 48:13-14). Manasseh's originally more significant role may be indicated by the fact that two of the major judges were associated with Manasseh (Gideon, Jephthah), but none with Ephraim.

The stories of Dan's difficult situation under Philistine pressure in the southwest and the move of some or all of the tribe north to the city of Dan are confirmed in several ways. The tribe's original geographical position is evidenced by two different locations in the southwest named Mahaneh-dan ("camp of Dan"; Judg 13:25; 18:12). The stories of Samson with their connection to Zorah and Eshtoal, the Valley of Sorek, and the Philistines also reflect Dan's southern location. That the city of Dan actually was once known as Laish is established by the EXECRATION Texts and other extra-biblical sources. This provides confirmation for the outcome (if not the details) of Judg 18–19.

Territory and tribe were not totally coterminous categories, and clans seem to have shifted from one tribe to another. For example, Carmi is a clan of Judah according to Josh 7:18, but part of Reuben in Gen 46:9 (compare Hezron in Num 26:6 and 26:21). Along the Wadi Kanah and around Tappuah, the boundary between Manasseh and Ephraim was flexible and fluid (Josh 16:9; 17:8-9). Bethel lay north of the border in Ephraim (Josh 16:2; 18:13), but appears in the Benjamin town list at Josh 18:22. There were enclaves of Manasseh in the territory of Issachar and Asher (Josh 17:11). Tola, an eponymous clan ancestor of Issachar had his home in the hill country of Ephraim (Gen 46:13; Num 26:23; Judg 10:1-2), and Shimron, another Issachar notable, seems to have been associated with Samaria in Manasseh (Gen 46:13; Num 26:24; 1 Kgs 16:24; Shimron and Samaria are equivalent in Hebrew). Asher seems to have some relation to an Ashurite group in the south central hill country of Ephraim (2 Sam 2:9; note the overlap in clan names between Asher and Benjamin in 1 Chr 7:30-31 and 8:13, 16-17). Hints of maritime associations for Zebulun (Gen 49:13) and Asher (Judg 5:17) may refer to trade links with the Mediterranean coast, but the reference to Dan's association with ships (Judg 5:17) is harder to explain. The suggestion of a connection between Dan and the Danaioi or Danuna, one of the so-called Sea Peoples, is unverifiable.

D. Intertribal Relationships

Some tribes seem to have had particularly close association with others. Common descent from Rachel expressed an association of Benjamin with Ephraim and Manasseh as the house of Joseph (1 Kgs 11:28; Amos 5:6) in a transtribal affiliation along the axis of Shechem, Shiloh, and Bethel. This connection is also evidenced by 2 Sam 19:20 [Heb. 19:21], where the Benjaminite Shimei is said to be of the house of Joseph, as well as by the order of tribal sayings in Gen 49:22-27 and Deut 33:12-17. Bonds between Ephraim and Benjamin are also suggested in the Song of Deborah (Judg 5:14). It is significant that Joshua the Ephraimite (Josh 19:50) is said to have led a conquest against territory that is predominantly Benjaminite. This transtribal Rachel affiliation represented the core of the Northern Kingdom, with its early Ephraimite leadership (1 Kgs 11:26) and its anti-Davidic ideology recalling the kingship of Saul the Benjaminite.

Judah may be understood as a "super tribe," an association of groups connected with the names Simeon, Caleb, Jerahmeel, Othniel, and Kenaz, along with the Kenites. Distinctions made between the Negeb of Judah and those of the Jerahmeelites, of the Kenites, and of Caleb (1 Sam 27:10; 30:14) provide confirmation of this state of affairs. It is also implied in the story of Achsah (Josh 15:13-19).

Judges 21:8-14 and incidents from the career of Saul (1 Sam 11:1-15; 31:11) give evidence of a special tie between Benjamin and Jabesh-gilead. Relationships between Naphtali and Zebulun are evident in Judg 4:6, 10, and Ps 68:27 [Heb. 68:28]. A particular association of Zebulun with Issachar is apparent in the mandrake incident of Gen 30:14-20, as well as Deut 33:18-19. Gad and Reuben often appear as a pair because of their common geographic situation (1 Sam 10:27). Simeon was naturally closely associated with Judah (Judg 1:1-17).

In contrast, intertribal hostility and stress is reported in Josh 22 and Judg 19–21. Episodes in the stories about Gideon and Jephthah recount Ephraim's sometimes antagonistic relations with Manasseh and Gilead (Judg 8:1-3; 12:1-6). According to Judg 12:5-6, Gilead and Ephraim were isolated from each other enough for there to be a difference in the way they spoke. The gulf dividing Judah and Simeon from the northern tribes appears in Song of Deborah and is also evidenced in absence from or special treatment of Judah in the Solomonic district roster of 1 Kgs 4:7-19. In pre-monarchic times, Simeon and Judah would have been separated from the central and northern core of Israel by a wedge of foreign territory running from Gezer to Jerusalem. Judah's marriage to Canaanite Shua may reflect a northern negative judgment of Judah's situation (Gen 38:2).

E. Tribes and the State

Tribal affiliation continued to be important in the monarchic period. For example, the stories about

Saul show recurrent stress between Benjamin and the Davidic monarchy of Judah. The rebel Sheba was a Benjaminite (2 Sam 20:1). Tribal identities are mentioned for Jeroboam I (Ephraim; 1 Kgs 11:26) and Baasha (Issachar; 1 Kgs 15:27). Tribal territory plays a role in the Solomonic district roster of 1 Kgs 4:7-19. Naphtali, Asher (apparently incorporating Zebulun), Issachar, and Benjamin are Districts VIII–XI (vv. 15-18). The Dan town list of Josh 19:40-46 essentially corresponds to District II (v. 9). The territory of Gad largely matches District XII (v. 19). However, tribal concerns play little or no role in the other six districts. The "hill country of Ephraim" district (v. 8) is geographic rather than tribal. Districts III–V (vv. 10-12) are organized on the basis of important cities rather than tribal territory. Two districts manage central and northern territory east of the Jordan (vv. 13-14). If authentic, this list may reflect attempts to co-opt tribal structures into the monarchic system, while also undermining divisive tribal loyalties in Ephraim and Manasseh.

The population of Yehud in the Persian period included those of Benjaminite background, some of whom lived in a particular territory (Neh 11:31-35). Claims to this special tribal identity continued into the Roman period (Rom 11:1; Phil 3:5).

F. Ideology

Tribes played an important role in literature and ideology. Several tribes are described as having special characteristics. The warlike nature of Benjamin is indicated in texts like Judg 20:16. A war cry connected to this tribe seems to be preserved in Hos 5:8 ("We follow you, Benjamin!" author's trans.; NRSV, "look behind you, Benjamin") and Judg 5:14. Genesis 49 and Deut 33 preserve two collections of sayings or blessings that describe tribal interactions, prosperity, temperament, assertiveness, and circumstances.

The number TWELVE and standardized tribal lists embodied an idealized unity of and common history for Israel as a whole. Tribal affinity, interaction, and status are expressed in the stories of Jacob's sons in Genesis. Some tribes are the children of concubines rather than wives, indicating their more marginal connection to Israel's core tribes: Asher and Gad are born to Zilpah; Dan and Naphtali are sons of Bilhah. Similarly, presumed common descent from Rachel (Manasseh, Ephraim, Benjamin) articulates political relationships in genealogical terms. In Deut 27:11-13, the twelve tribes ceremonially adopt covenant law. Twelve tribes or simply the number twelve itself repeatedly signify all Israel (e.g., Deut 1:23; Josh 3:12; 4:4; Judg 19:29; 1 Kgs 11:30; 18:31). *Twelve* as a pointer to the wholeness of Israel is reflected in those Jesus chose as his inner circle (Luke 22:30; Acts 1:21-26).

In Rev 7:5-8, a non-standard listing of the twelve tribes signifies a special group of God's servants who are protected from the coming tribulation. Dan is absent from this list, probably because of the negative judg-

ment of Gen 49:17. Luke 2:36 assigns Anna to Asher, probably as an idealized spokesperson for exiled Israel.

Bibliography: C. H. J. de Geus. *The Tribes of Israel* (1976); Norman K. Gottwald. *The Tribes of Yahweh* (1976, 1999); Zekharyah Kalai. *Historical Geography of the Bible: The Tribal Territories of Israel* (1986).

RICHARD D. NELSON

TRIBES, TERRITORIES OF. Israel's tradition of tribal territories represents a blend of practical reality involving actual terrain and administrative structures with an ideology of ethnic and national identity. Although tribal territories are often drawn onto reference maps with seeming assurance, our actual knowledge of borders and territories is sometimes much less exact, especially with regard to tribes east of the Jordan and in Galilee.

A. Maps and Identity
B. Tribal Territories in Joshua 13–19
   1. East Jordan tribes
      a. Reuben (13:15-23)
      b. Gad (13:24-28)
      c. East Jordan Manasseh (13:29-31)
   2. Judah
      a. Judah's south border (15:1-4)
      b. Judah's north border (15:5b-11)
      c. Judahite towns by districts (15:21-62)
   3. House of Joseph
      a. Ephraim (16:1-10)
      b. Manasseh (17:7-10)
   4. Division at Shiloh
      a. Benjamin (18:11-28)
      b. Simeon (19:1-9)
      c. Zebulun (19:10-16)
      d. Issachar (19:17-23)
      e. Asher (19:24-31)
      f. Naphtali (19:32-39)
      g. Dan (19:40-48)
C. Other Texts
   1. Solomon's districts (1 Kgs 4:7-19)
   2. Unconquered cities (Judg 1)
   3. Levitical cities (Josh 21)
D. Ezekiel's Vision
Bibliography

A. Maps and Identity

Israel described its identity and presence in the land in terms of at least three verbal maps. The first, namely, the concept of the land of Canaan, treats the Jordan as the eastern boundary (Num 34:1-12; compare Ezek 47:13–48:29) and derives from Egyptian imperial traditions. Crossing the Jordan is the equivalent of entering the land (Josh 1–4), and the legitimacy of settlement east of the Jordan is thus undermined (Josh 22). A second map, expressed in utopian texts that extend Israel's realm from the Mediterranean to the Euphrates, encompasses a much more expansive territory (Gen 15:18;

Exod 23:31; Deut 1:7; 11:24; Josh 1:4; 1 Kgs 4:21 [Heb. 5:1]). This "greater Israel" relates to the Mesopotamian and Persian notion of a province BEYOND THE RIVER incorporating Palestine and Syria (as in Ezra 4:10-20; compare 2 Kgs 24:7). The tribal boundaries and towns encompassed within them in Josh 13–19 represents a third approach, closer to actual political and geographic reality, but still influenced by ideological considerations. Joshua's verbal map of tribal territories fills every corner of the land and thus de-legitimizes all non-Israelite peoples living within it. The list of Solomon's twelve districts (1 Kgs 4:7-19) follows the same template (that is, incorporating territory east of the Jordan), but combines tribal designations with the interests of a multi-ethnic, centralized state.

The tribal makeup of Israel was established before the emergence of the monarchy and holds true for a general picture of tribal territories, although the final pattern of the twelve tribes differs somewhat. Israel's tribes may be understood as secondary associations of kinship-based endogamous "clans" into larger social organizations intended to meet challenges that transcended the purely local, such as the need to defend territory. Documents from Mari reveal groups in a social situation comparable to that of tribal Israel. The old poem preserved in Judg 5 suggests that the tribes were related to the muster for war of "the people of the LORD" (v. 13) and that each had an identifiable home territory (v. 17). Certain tribal names originated from their location: Ephraim from Mount Ephraim, Benjamin ("son of the south") from its location just south of the Joseph tribes Ephraim and Manasseh, and Issachar ("bond-servant, hireling") reflecting oppression caused by its precarious location in a non-Israelite valley. Geographic location is a feature in the tribal sayings and blessings in Gen 49 and Deut 33. Deuteronomy 33:12 implies that Benjamin is surrounded by the sanctuaries of Jerusalem and Bethel. According to Deut 33:18-19, Zebulun and Issachar are associated with the sanctuary at Mount Tabor (presumably) and have access through the Jezreel Valley to the riches of the coast (of the Mediterranean or of Chinnereth). Territorial expansion is the theme of Deut 33:20 (Gad) and 33:23 (Naphtali). Genesis 49:15 connects Issachar's subservient state to its geographic location. The reference in Gen 49:13 to Zebulun at (or toward) the shore with a connection to ships and a border at Sidon is puzzling, but may reflect that tribe's nearness to Phoenician territory in general and the sea trade connections described by Deut 33:19.

The tribal boundary around Jerusalem, which incorporates it into Benjamin and excludes it from Judah (Josh 15:8; 18:16), appears to be a pre-monarchic survival earlier than the integration of the city into Israel's territory. Dan's pre-monarchic southwestern location was remembered not only in literature (Judges), but by a surviving place name (Judg 13:25; 18:12). The administrative districts associated with Solomon in 1 Kgs 4:7-19 indicate that the continuing tribal self-consciousness and the identification of tribes with their territories had to be accommodated by the newly emerging monarchic nation state, but could be co-opted by the central government for taxation purposes. Another indication of the persistence of tribal territorial identity is the long survival of the Benjaminite homeland, not only in the face of its division into two by the rival kingdoms of Judah and Israel, but even after the interruption of Babylonian exile (except for the last six, most of the towns in Neh 11:31-35 are within Benjamin's traditional borders).

Identification of a tribe with its territory must have had important social purposes. A consciousness of shared geography, in concert with traditions of a supposedly shared genealogy, would strengthen the mutual connection of the clans that constituted a tribe. Mustering tribes seen as having concrete territorial interests would provide an effective response to geographically limited threats. Judges 5:14-15 suggests the largest organized military unit would be the tribe, and a sense of geographical solidarity would help bind warriors together as they fought. Easy access to a shared sanctuary would help strengthen tribal solidarity: the temple at Dan; Hebron for Judah; and Mount Tabor for Zebulun, and Naphtali, and perhaps Issachar. A shared sense of geography must have been all the more important in that there is no evidence for any sort of institutional structure on the tribal level.

The ability to assert frontiers and land claims would have been important in the face of foreign incursions, at first by Philistia, Moab or Ammon (compare Judg 11:26, 33), later by Syria and Assyria, and even later by Edom. Moreover, the continued capacity to visualize concrete boundaries and articulate tribal homelands must have been a powerful source of identity during repeated crises of defeat, exile, and imperial subjugation.

B. Tribal Territories in Joshua 13–19

The system of tribal territories in Joshua appears to be an artificial, scribal construction, although clearly based on inherited, historically valuable data from a variety of sources. The nature of these sources remains unclear, except for the administrative district system for the kingdom of Judah found in Josh 15:21-62; 18:21-28. The descriptions for the boundaries between Judah and Benjamin, Benjamin and Ephraim, and Ephraim and Manasseh are detailed and can be traced on a map with a good deal of confidence. In contrast, the boundaries for tribes in and north of the Jezreel Valley are less precise, tending to deal in generalities. The territories of Dan and Simeon are designated only by lists of included towns, without any boundary descriptions. The data for the east Jordan tribes combines town lists along with broadly generalized lines of extent describing wide swaths of territory in an indefinite way (Josh 13:9, 16, 26).

Irregularities and incidental observations indicate that Josh 13–19 is not simply a product of scribal imagination. Issachar's special, subjugated situation may be the reason it is represented only by a town list, with only a small fragment of border description. The idealized border between Ephraim and Manasseh down the Wadi Kanah does not represent the actual facts (16:9; 17:8-9), and Manasseh has towns in Issachar and Asher (17:11). The administrative districts for the kingdom of Judah include not only eleven in tribal Judah (15:21-63) and one in Benjamin (18:25-28), but add a thirteenth describing territory that had once been part of the kingdom of Israel (18:21-24).

This assortment of material has been fashioned into a system for ideological and theological purposes. That the land is a divine gift is repeatedly emphasized by mention of the "lot" indicating God's will (Josh 15:1; 17:14, 17; eleven times in chaps. 18–19). Israel's rightful possession is underscored by "this is the inheritance" (15:20; 18:20, 28; five times in chap. 19). The tribes fill the land entirely, with no legitimate space authorized for other peoples, even though their temporary survival is admitted (15:63; 16:10; 17:12-13). Territory east of Jordan belongs to Israel by right of conquest (13:10, 12, 21, 30-31). Running Judah's boundaries right down to the Mediterranean ignores the existence of the Philistines and reflects idealism rather than reality (15:4, 11; compare 15:45-47), while the Gibeonite coalition (9:17) is included in Benjamin without comment (18:25-26, 28; compare 2 Sam 4:2-3; Ezra 2:25).

It is unlikely that this idealized description of tribal territories, taken as a whole, reflects any single period in the history of Israel. Because it encompasses both Judah and Israel, one could assign its origin as a genuine administrative document only to the pre-state period or to the united monarchy. The latter period is improbable because tribes and tribal territories do not fit the needs and goals of a monarchic state, something clearly evidenced by the system of taxation zones attributed to the reign of Solomon (1 Kgs 4:7-19). At the same time, we know of no institutions from the pre-monarchy period that would have a need for a system based purely on geography (rather than real or fictive kinship), nor does there seem to be much likelihood of such a scheme being constructed or preserved without the agency of state-supported scribes. Moreover, the only arguably pre-monarchic portrayal of Israel's tribal structure (Judg 5) identifies tribal groupings different to some extent from those in the tribal territory descriptions. It is much more probable that the description of tribal territories in Joshua is an erudite scribal composition, perhaps transmitted as a pedagogical text.

Geographic data is presented in three forms: lines of extent, boundaries, and town lists. Lines of extent are used for the less defined east Jordan territory instead of boundaries (Josh 13:9, 16, 26; compare Num 21:24; Josh 13:3-5; 2 Sam 24:2). They draw a line from one reference point outward in some direction or to another locale giving a generalized indication of the tribe's range. Boundaries consist of landmarks or towns joined with verbs ("goes," "crosses," "goes up,"

"turns," "goes down") to create a line that runs across the ground. Comparisons between parallel boundary texts show that these verbs vary and are clearly secondary to the border points themselves (compare Josh 15:1-4 with Num 34:3-6, or Josh 15:5-10 with 18:15-20). Directional modifiers sometimes indicate the bearing of the borderline as it runs (e.g., "in a northward direction") but sometimes indicate instead the position of the line with respect to some locality (e.g., "to the north of"). It is not always clear which option is intended. Streambeds and ridges play a role in the course of the boundary line (Josh 15:8; 16:8; 18:18; 19:11). In tracing boundaries one must allow for territory around named towns to accommodate the fields, grazing, and outlying settlements (NRSV, "villages") regularly associated with towns (Josh 13:23; 15:32). Boundaries are detailed for the lines between Judah and Benjamin and between Ephraim and Manasseh but vague and general for the four Galilee tribes. No boundaries are given for Dan and Simeon. Town lists give the impression of being derived from administrative units of some sort, analogous to the Judah districts in Josh 15:21-62; 18:21-28. The boundary system and the town lists stem from originally independent sources of data, as evidenced by irregularities and contradictions between the two and the inconsistent way in which they have been used to depict different tribes. Thus, borders and town lists are kept completely separate for Judah and Benjamin, but partially integrated for the four Galilee tribes. Only town lists describe Dan and Simeon.

Narratives, poems, and genealogies present a picture of tribal territory that generally corresponds to the data in Joshua but also indicates that shifts took place over time. In Deut 34:1-2, Moses sees tribal territories in north to south order as Dan, Naphtali, Ephraim/Manasseh, and Judah. The neighborly association of Naphtali, Asher, and Manasseh is attested in Judg 7:23 and that of Reuben and Gad in Num 32:1, 29. Naphtali and Zebulun are linked together in Isa 9:1 [Heb. 8:23] and with the Mount Tabor sanctuary in Judg 4:6. The east Jordan situation of Reuben, Gad, and Manasseh is reflected in 2 Sam 24:5; 2 Kgs 10:33; and more broadly in the ancient songs preserved in Num 21:14-15, 27-30. Judah and Simeon work together in Judg 1, and Simeon's connection with Hormah (Josh 19:4) is reaffirmed in Judg 1:17. The extent of Benjaminite territory—revealed in Judg 1:21; 19:14; 1 Sam 10:2; 13:16; 2 Sam 4:2; 19:16; 21:14; Jer 1:1; and Hos 5:8—corresponds to the data in Joshua. Genesis 49:7 describes Simeon and Levi as divided and scattered. There are also puzzles and complications. Genesis 34:25 suggests the presence of Simeon and Levi at Shechem. The stone of Bohan son of Reuben, located in the west segment of Judah's boundary (Josh 15:6), hints at a (former?) west of Jordan setting for elements of that tribe. First Kings 9:10-13 reports the alienation of Cabul from Asher in contrast to Josh 19:27.

Uncertainty as to how to construe the text in places, textual corruptions, and problems with the identification of many landmarks and towns means that our understanding of tribal territories remains incomplete.

1. East Jordan tribes

Joshua 13:8-13 uses lines of extent and town lists to summarize the situation east of the Jordan and to introduce the territories of individual tribes. A line of extent is drawn from the Arnon northward around the Medeba plateau and then back south to Dibon (v. 9). Verse 10 supplements this by referencing Sihon's towns farther north to the Ammonite border. Verse 11 moves farther north again to include Gilead and Bashan, the former kingdom of Og, eastward to Salecah, but excluding the regions of Geshur and Maachath (v. 13). The fixed point "Aroer, which is on the edge of the Wadi Arnon, and the town that is in the middle of the valley" (v. 9) recurs in descriptions of east Jordan both in Joshua (12:2; 13:16) and elsewhere (Deut 2:36; 3:12; 4:48; 2 Sam 24:5; 2 Kgs 10:33). AROER was a critical marker because it was a stress point in attempts to hold the Arnon as the frontier with Moab (compare Judg 11:26, 33). The remainder of chap. 13 follows the format of vv. 8-13. The controlling concept is that the conquest of Sihon's kingdom establishes Israel's claims in the south (vv. 10, 21, 27) and that of Og's kingdom lays claim to the north (vv. 12, 30). The wide territorial sweeps of vv. 9-12 are repeated in vv. 15-23 for Reuben, in vv. 24-28 for Gad, and in vv. 29-31 for Manasseh. The formulaic "Aroer ... Arnon" (v. 9) serves as the starting point for Reuben (v. 16). The extension through Gilead (v. 11) describes Gad (v. 25) along with Bashan and Manasseh (vv. 30-31). The eastern edges of tribal control are left vague: the desert for Reuben, Ammon for Gad, and far-distant Salecah for Manasseh. The text emphasizes throughout that Moses gave these territories as an inheritance (vv. 8, 15, 24, 29, 32).

a. Reuben (13:15-23). The viability of Reuben as a tribe with defined territory declined over time from its appearance as one of the ten tribal groups in the Song of Deborah (Judg 5:15-16; compare Deut 33:6; see REUBEN, REUBENITES). The territory north of the Arnon was lost to Moab beginning in the mid-9th cent. (Isa 15:2, 4, 9; 16:8-9; Jer 48; Ezek 25:9), explaining the emphasis on the Arnon in Josh 13:16. Reuben's territory was also inhabited by Gad (MOABITE STONE, lines 10–11; compare the place name Dibon-gad in Num 33:45; Heshbon is in Gad according to Josh 21:39). Reuben itself is absent from David's census text (2 Sam 24:5-6, "from Aroer ... toward Gad ... Jazer") and the Moabite Stone. Thus one suspects that the neat division between Reuben and Gad in Josh 13 is an oversimplification.

A line of extent is drawn from Aroer northward to Heshbon (vv. 16-17). Appended to this is a list of twelve towns (vv. 17-20). Apparently these originally represented a "tableland" district with nine towns (vv.

17b-19) and a "hill of the valley" district with three towns (end of v. 19 and v. 20, taking NRSV, "slopes of Pisgah," as a town, Asdot-pisgah). Reuben's southern border is given as the Arnon, and its northern border runs somewhere north of the identifiable sites Beth-jeshimoth, Heshbon, and Mephaath. There is a relation of some sort between Reuben's territory and Solomon's District XII (1 Kgs 4:19).

b. Gad (13:24-28). Gad receives the rest of the kingdom of Sihon ("all the towns of Gilead," v. 25) north of that part ascribed to Reuben (see GAD, GADITES). Its territory is protected from potential Ammonite claims (compare "half of the land of the Ammonites," v. 25) by mention of Jazer and Aroer, the latter pressing "near" the Ammonite capital Rabbah (v. 25; not NRSV, "east of"; this Aroer is different from the one in vv. 9, 16). Two lines of extent describe the situation in general terms (v. 26). The first runs north from Heshbon to Ramath-mizpeh and Betonim. A second runs yet farther north of this from Mahanaim to Lidebir (Lodebar; NRSV, "Debir"), thus incorporating territory east of the Jordan up to the Sea of Galilee. A four-item town list follows in v. 27 in south to north order in the Jordan Valley: Beth-haram, Beth-nimrah, Succoth, and Zaphon. These would seem to make up a "valley" district (compare in Reuben the "tableland," vv. 17b-19, and the "hill of the valley," v. 20). Zaphon appears elsewhere as a clan of Gad (Gen 46:16; Num 26:15). Gad's territory relates to Solomon's District VII (1 Kgs 4:14).

Numbers 32 offers a different picture of the situation, with Gad settled both north and south throughout the area (Dibon, Ataroth, Aroer, Atroth-shophan, Jazer, Jogbehah, Beth-nimrah, Beth-haran = Beth-haram; vv. 34-36) and Reuben intermingled with Gad in the region around Heshbon (Heshbon, Elealeh, Kiriathaim, Nebo, Baal-meon = Beth-baal-meon, Sibmah; vv. 37-38).

c. East Jordan Manasseh (13:29-31). Some clans of Manasseh ("half of the Machirites," v. 31) inhabit territory east of the Jordan (see MANASSEH, MANASSITES). A general line of extent runs from Mahanaim (v. 30) north to encompass Bashan, the allied towns of Jair, and to the east the former capital cities of Og, Ashtaroth, and Edrei. The reference to "half of Gilead" (v. 31, contradicting v. 25) means the part north of the Jabbok. Manasseh's east Jordan territory correlates with Solomon's District VI (1 Kgs 4:13).

2. Judah

Not surprisingly, Judah receives more attention and space than any other tribe: a boundary description (Josh 15:1-12), stories about Caleb, Othniel, and Achsah (15:13-19), and an extensive list of towns divided into administrative districts (15:21-62; see JUDAH, JUDAHITES). Judah's borders do not always match information given in town lists. The boundaries exclude Eshtaol and Zorah (Dan), but these are found in Judah's town list (15:33). They include Benjaminite Beth-arabah (15:6) and perhaps Beth-hoglah (18:21), and Simeonite towns listed in 19:2-7 (compare 15:26, 28, 30-32, 42; in 15:31-32, Madmannah = Beth-marcaboth, Sansannah = Hazar-susah, Shilhim = Sharuhen). Inclusion of Philistine territory (15:4, 11; compare 15:45-47) is historically untenable.

The town lists for Judah (and Benjamin) are widely considered to derive from an authentic archival source. There are eleven districts of Judahite towns in 15:21-62; the one between vv. 59 and 60 was lost in MT but is preserved by LXX (absent from NRSV; see NAB, NJB). Judah's districts are part of the same administrative system reflected by the two districts of Benjamin (18:21-28). The period of Josiah is seen by many as the most likely setting for the system embracing all thirteen districts.

a. Judah's south border (15:1-4). Judah's east and west borders are the Dead Sea (v. 5a) and the Mediterranean (v. 12). Its southern border runs east to west and closely parallels the border description of the land of Canaan given in Num 34:3-6. The border points are almost identical, but the linking verbs are different. The bay of the Dead Sea "that faces southward" (Josh 15:2) is on the eastern shore (compare Num 34:3), so the boundary curves around from east to south before heading west through the Ascent of Akrabbim (Scorpion Pass) and then south of Kadesh-barnea, indicating that the Wadi of Egypt is the Wadi el-ʿArish. The other sites mentioned cannot be identified with any confidence.

b. Judah's north border (15:5b-11). Running from east to west, this line is described in meticulous detail because it divided Judah from Benjamin, disclosing a Judahite perspective. The same border is repeated in the opposite direction as Benjamin's south boundary in 18:15-19. Almost every marker can be identified. From somewhere near the mouth of the Jordan it runs from Beth-hoglah north to include Beth-arabah then trends back south via the ascent of Adummim to En-shemesh. The line around the south of Jerusalem is carefully detailed. It turns south to En-rogel (2 Sam 17:17; 1 Kgs 1:9; modern Bir Ayyub near the junction of the Hinnom and Kidron valleys), then up the Hinnom Valley, skirting the southern slope of Jerusalem to the top of the mountain between the Hinnom and Rephaim valleys. The Waters of Nephtoah appear as the Spring of Merneptah in an Egyptian source (*ANET*, 258). Through an area called Mount Ephron it bends a bit north to Baalah (identical to or neighboring Kiriath-jearim), circles west of Baalah and north of two mountainous areas (Mount Jearim and Mount Seir) to include Chesalon, drops southwest to Beth-shemesh, and then runs (via the Sorek Valley) by Timnah, north of Ekron, by Shikkeron and Mount Baalah, to Jabneel and the sea.

c. Judahite towns by districts (15:21-62). Eleven administrative districts of the kingdom of Judah follow the border descriptions, with Philistia as a historically implausible twelfth district (vv. 45-47). Two more districts of the same character appear in the material for Benjamin (18:21-28). The Judah districts are grouped

into four administrative regions: Negeb (NRSV, "in the extreme south," 15:21-32; one district), the lowland (vv. 33-47; three districts plus Philistia as an unlikely fourth), the hill country (vv. 48-60, six districts, one preserved only in LXX), and the wilderness (vv. 61-62; one district). These districts clearly refer to Judah as a nation state, not to the tribal entity presented in the border descriptions. Thus the Negeb district incorporates towns assigned to Simeon in 19:2-7. Eshtoal and Zorah in the first lowland district described in 15:33-36 are actually north of the border of Judah (compare Beth-shemesh in 15:10) and described as belonging to Dan in 19:41. The association of two Benjamin districts (18:21-28) provides further evidence of the origin of this district system in the monarchy period.

3. House of Joseph

a. Ephraim (16:1-10). The descriptions for Ephraim and Manasseh are difficult to understand and contain few assured identifications (*see* EPHRAIM, EPHRAIMITES). Apparently an older form of this description dealt with the house of Joseph as a unit (vv. 1, 4). This has caused a fragment of Joseph's south border to be restated as Ephraim's south border in v. 5. This south border (vv. 1-3) corresponds to 18:12-13 (Benjamin's north border). The border is drawn westward from the Jordan to the Mediterranean, excluding Jericho (in Benjamin) but skirting close to the nearby spring east of the city ("waters of Jericho"). It incorporates Bethel and both Upper and Lower Beth-horon, then goes via Gezer to the Mediterranean.

Ephraim's north border (16:6-8) corresponds to Manasseh's south border (17:7-9). It is drawn in two segments, first eastward and then westward from the center. The first segment (16:6-7) goes eastward from Michmethath running just south of Shechem (17:7b), then bends clockwise around Taanath-shiloh. It backtracks west slightly to Janoah, then southeast to Naarah to include the hill country and exclude the Jordan Valley, finally touching but not including Jericho, and running to the Jordan. Then the description goes back to Tappuah, near the point where the eastward segment began, and traces a second, westward section (v. 8) down to the Mediterranean along the Wadi Kanah. This boundary leaves Shechem in Manasseh (compare 17:2; 1 Chr 7:19; contrast Josh 21:20-21). Joshua 16:9 indicates that the Wadi Kanah boundary is an idealized simplification in that Ephraimite towns were situated within the border of Manasseh (compare 17:9).

b. Manasseh (17:7-10). Instead of a northern border, an imprecise line of extent is drawn from Asher to Michmethath (v. 7a), apparently indicating that certain Manassehite towns were situated in the territories of Asher (and Issachar; compare v. 11). Then the western portion only of the boundary with Ephraim is covered (17:7b-9; compare 16:8). "The inhabitants" (17:7b, NRSV) should be read with LXX as "Jashub" (Iassib). Manasseh possessed En-tappuah ("spring of Tappuah") and the territory around Tappuah, but the town itself was in Ephraim (compare 16:8). The intermixture of Ephraim and Manasseh along the Wadi Kanah is again noted (17:9). According to vv. 11-13, Manasseh possessed towns within a wedge of overlap in Issachar and Asher that remained for a time under Canaanite control. Beth-shean, Ibleam, Dor, En-dor, Taanach, and Megiddo. A similar list is repeated in Judg 1:27. Apparently Israelite control came late to the Jezreel Valley.

The story in Josh 17:1-6 about the daughters of Zelophehad, who represent five clans (towns) of Manasseh, taken together with clan districts mentioned in the SAMARIA OSTRACA (administrative records from the Jehu Dynasty), reveal additional data about Manasseh's geographical situation. One of these towns is Tirzah (v. 3). Verses 14-18 look forward to an expansion of settlement for Ephraim and Manasseh.

4. Division at Shiloh

Land distribution in chaps. 18–19 follows a different pattern from that utilized for the three principal tribes Judah, Ephraim, and Manasseh. A survey commission first determines seven areas, and then these are distributed by lot (18:1-10).

a. Benjamin (18:11-28). Benjamin's boundary is described counterclockwise (vv. 11-20; *see* BENJAMIN, BENJAMINITES). The north border runs from east to west (18:12-13 = 16:1-3*a*), stopping south of lower Beth-horon, presumably to give room for Dan's allotment. It includes Jericho (18:12) and moves west through the highlands to the wilderness of Beth-aven (either an alternate name for Bethel or a separate place located between Bethel and Jericho; 1 Sam 13:5; 14:23). It excludes Bethel and Beth-horon. The west termination as it turns south (18:14) is Kiriath-baal, definitely in Judah. Perhaps Kiriath-jearim in Benjamin (18:28; compare 9:17; 1 Sam 7:1-2) and Kiriath-baal in Judah (Josh 15:60; 18:14; called "Baalah" in 15:9 and "Baale-judah" in 2 Sam 6:2) were neighboring towns in close proximity. The southern border runs eastward (18:15-19 = 15:5*b*-9 in a reverse direction). Textual corruption causes confusion in 18:15 (NRSV, "Ephron"; NJB, "Gasin" following LXX; TNK, "westward" following MT). Joshua 18:17 has Geliloth in place of Gilgal (15:7). If one follows the MT of 18:18 ("to the slope over against the Arabah"; NRSV corrects to "Beth-arabah") the border tracks along the line of cliffs bordering the Jordan Valley and Dead Sea. A segment of the Jordan is Benjamin's east boundary (v. 20).

Benjaminite towns are listed in two districts in 18:21-28, part of the same administrative system as the eleven Judah districts in 15:21-62. A district of fourteen towns in 18:25-28 stretches north and west of Jerusalem within the territory of the kingdom of Judah, as evidenced by the incorporation of Mizpeh/Mizpah and Ramah (1 Kgs 15:22). This catalog includes the enclave of Gibeonite towns listed in Josh 9:17: Gibeon, Kiriath-

jearim, Beeroth, and Chephirah. Besides Jerusalem, the other identifiable site is Mozah and perhaps Gibeah (unless this is actually the same place as Geba in 18:24). An apparent overlap between Judah's small district in 15:60 and this Benjaminite district (Ramah, Kiriath-jearim or Kiriath-baal) can be eliminated by understanding Kiriath-jearim in Benjamin and Kiriath-baal/Baalah/Baale-judah in Judah as neighboring towns and postulating a second Ramah.

Another district comprising twelve towns in 18:21-24 lies east of the central ridge and in the plains of Jericho within what would have been the kingdom of Israel. Several sites are unidentifiable, but Jericho, Beth-hoglah, Beth-arabah, Bethel, Parah, Ophrah, and Geba give a clear picture of its extent. It is probable that this district represents territory added as a thirteenth district to Judah's original twelve by subsequent expansion, perhaps by Josiah (2 Kgs 23:8, 15). These district rosters are not completely in accord with the border description. Three towns are listed in Benjaminite districts but excluded by their boundaries: Beth-hoglah (Josh 18:19, 21), Beth-arabah (18:18, 22, compare 15:6, 61), and Bethel (18:13, 22).

b. Simeon (19:1-9). Simeon is surrounded by Judah and, like Dan, is depicted only by a town list set out in two districts of thirteen and four towns respectively (repeated in 1 Chr 4:28-33; *see* SIMEON, SIMEONITES). These are difficult to locate except for Beer-sheba and En-rimmon (NRSV, "Ain" and "Rimmon"), and probably Sharuhen and Hormah. Hazar-susah, [El]todah, Ezem, and Ramath-negeb appear on ostraca from the Negeb area. The towns in 19:2-6 along with En-rimmon are related to Judah's Negeb district (15:21-32). Perhaps Ether and Ashan (19:7) are not the same towns as those appearing in another of Judah's districts (15:42). Simeon is said to extend south to two towns in Negeb (19:8).

c. Zebulun (19:10-16). Both boundaries and town lists are given for Zebulun, Issachar, Asher, and Naphtali (*see* ZEBULUN, ZEBULUNITES). The boundaries consist of frontier towns to be included in the tribal territory along with their peripheral areas rather than precise border points. Perhaps this began as a roster of frontier towns and was later turned into a loose boundary description.

Zebulun has a detailed border description (vv. 10*b*-14) and town list (v. 15). The boundary is described in two segments run out from a common center ("goes in the other direction," v. 12). The southern border is described first, running west from Sadud (NRSV, "Sarid"), apparently along the Kishon River (v. 11), then going back to Sadud to run east and then north (v. 12) via Chisloth-tabor (identical with Chesulloth in v. 18) and Daberath, then turning back towards Japhia. Because Chesulloth and Daberath are also in Issachar's town list, the boundary is to be understood as excluding them from Zebulun ("to the boundary of," v. 12). Verse 13 depicts the eastern portion running northward by Gath-hepher, with a turning point at Rimmon bending toward Neah (site unknown). Verse 14 describes the northern border running to the west (Hannathon). Zebulun, Issachar, and Naphtali all meet at Mount Tabor: Chisloth-tabor, v. 12; Tabor, v. 22; and Aznoth-tabor, v. 34. Identifiable sites in the town list of v. 15 are Shimron and Bethlehem.

d. Issachar (19:17-23). Issachar's description consists of a town list (vv. 18-21) and a small piece of boundary (v. 22; *see* ISSACHAR, ISSACHARITES). Known or presumed locations in the town list are Jezreel, Chesulloth, Shunem, Daberath, Remeth (identical with Jarmuth in 21:29), En-gannim, and En-haddah. The border described in v. 22 is apparently Issachar's northern limit, touching Tabor, Shahazumah (perhaps a conflation of Shahaz and Yammah), including Beth-shemesh, and ending at the Jordan. There is a relationship between this territory and Solomon's district X (1 Kgs 4:17).

e. Asher (19:24-31). Boundary markers and town list material are mixed together (*see* ASHER, ASHERITES). After removing the town lists, the south boundary runs from Helkath west of Mount Carmel and down the Shihor-libnath (the lower reaches of the Kishon River) to the Mediterranean (vv. 25-26). Then the line of the border returns to its starting point ("turns eastward," v. 27) to Beth-dagon and heads north to run with Zebulun on the east and then with the Valley of Iphtah-el to the north. Then it goes northward past Beth-emek, Neiel, and Cabul, as far as (and thus not including) the territory of Sidon (v. 28). At this point it turns west (v. 29) to run south of Sidon's territory, bending south with Tyre's territory on the west until it reaches the Mediterranean Sea south of Tyre in the vicinity of Hosah (properly Usu). The north border of Asher is similar to the census itinerary reported in 2 Sam 24:6-7.

Data from a town list have been inserted at three places into the border description, causing the repetition of Rehob (Josh 19:28, 30). The first list is set into the westward segment of the southern border (vv. 25-26): Hali (near Carmel), Beten, Achshaph, Allammelech, Amad, and Mishal. A second list of north Asher towns is put into the east border as it runs past Cabul (v. 28): Ebron, Rehob, Hammon, and Kanah. A miscellaneous third group is appended to the end of the boundary description: Mahalab (just north of Tyre), Achzib, Acco (NRSV, "Ummah") in the middle portion of Asher on the coast, and Aphek and Rehob inland. First Kings 9:11-13 reports Solomon's loss of twenty towns in the district of Cabul.

f. Naphtali (19:32-39). This territory depiction consists of a border description (vv. 33-34) and a town list (vv. 35-38; *see* NAPHTALI, NAPHTALITES). The southern border is described in two segments. First, it runs eastward from Heleph and a landmark oak in Zaanannim, past Adami-nekeb, Jabneel, and Lakkum, and ends at the Jordan. At v. 34 it "turns," that is, returns to Heleph, so that a second segment of the border runs westward to Aznoth-tabor then moves

northwards towards Hukkok. This course touches first on Zebulun to the south and then on Asher to the west. The mention of Judah is mystifying. The Jordan forms the eastern border. Several sites in the town list can be identified: Ramah, Hazor, Kedesh, Iron, and Beth-anath. Beth-shemesh is apparently not the town of Issachar mentioned in v. 22.

g. Dan (19:40-48). The territory of Dan is described only with a town list (*see* DAN, DANITES). Those sites that can be identified lie west of Benjamin and Ephraim: Shaalabbin, Aijalon, Ekron, Eltekeh, Gibbethon, Baalath, Jehud, Bene-berak, and Gath-rimmon. Eshtaol and Zorah are in one of the Judah districts (15:33), and Ir-shemesh (as Beth-shemesh) and Timnah are part of the border between Judah and Benjamin (15:10). There is an overlap with Solomonic District II (1 Kgs 4:9). Verse 47 reports the tribe's transfer to the city of Dan in the north (compare Judg 18:11-31).

C. Other Texts

The list of King Solomon's twelve district officials (1 Kgs 4:7-19) provides further data on tribal territories and suggests that the material in Josh 13-19 is no merely utopian invention. The territorial descriptions of Judg 1 and the list of Levitical cities in Josh 21 do not appear to provide independent geographical data but are dependent on information derived from elsewhere in Joshua.

1. Solomon's districts (1 Kgs 4:7-19)

Both the origin and historicity of the list of Solomon's district officials are open to dispute, but many if not most scholars consider it to be authentic. If so, the list shows an effort to modify the traditional tribal territorial divisions to meet the needs of a centralized monarchy. It excludes Judah but includes (presumably all) tribal Benjamin. At least four districts are designated by tribal names: Naphtali (v. 15), Asher (v. 16), Issachar (v. 17), Benjamin (v. 18), and perhaps Gilead (v. 19). It may be significant that these represent five of the ten tribal groupings found in the Song of Deborah. Three districts correspond to the east Jordan tribal allotments described in Joshua: Ramoth-gilead (east Manasseh, v. 13), Mahanaim (Gad, v. 14), and apparently the problematic final district Gilead covering Reuben (v. 19, southern Gilead must be meant; LXX, "Gad"). The others have geographic ("hill country of Ephraim," v. 8) or town designations (vv. 9-12). The district in v. 9 overlaps to some extent with the town list for Simeon (Josh 19:41-46). A portion of the district in v. 12 relates to the wedge of towns not immediately controlled by Manasseh according to Josh 17:11-13. Even if it is not an actual record from the time of the united monarchy, this source document still provides an independent witness to the tradition of tribal territories as understood at the time of its composition.

2. Unconquered cities (Judg 1)

Judges 1 was previously thought to preserve an older source document that provided a more historically accurate version of an Israelite conquest than that of the book of Joshua (a "negative settlement list"). This view has largely been abandoned. Scholars now generally understand Judg 1 as a composite text constructed out of disparate materials, including data taken from the book of Joshua. Thus, Judg 1:18 seems to derive from Josh 15:45-47, Judg 1:21 from Josh 15:63, and Judg 1:27-28 from Josh 17:11-13. The direction of dependence may be reversed in regard to Judg 1:29 and Josh 16:10. The cities listed in Judg 1:30, 31, 33, 35 appear in Josh 19:15, 29-30, 38, 41-42. In Judg 1:30, Kitron is the equivalent of Kattath, and Nahalol equals Nahalal (Josh 19:15). Judges 1:31 has Ahlab and Helbah as a doublet for Mahalab (MT, "Mehebel") from Josh 19:29. Judges 1:35 picks up three towns from Dan's boundary list in Josh 19:41-42 (taking Har-heres, "hill of the sun," as equivalent to Ir-Shemesh, "city of the sun"). Moreover, Judg 1:16-17 has some sort of literary relationship to Num 21:1-3.

3. Levitical cities (Josh 21)

First Chronicles 6:54-81 [Heb. 6:39-66] preserves a parallel form of the list of Levitical cities in Josh 21. Although scholars often assume that Josh 21 represents some sort of historical reality, the list of Levitical cities is most likely a literary, scribal composition rather than a genuine archival source. It stresses the centrality of Levites, presses their contemporary claims on community resources, and asserts the superiority of the priestly Aaronic branch. It is best to see this chapter as a largely artificial construction that extracted its data from towns named in Josh 13–20. That the final product covers the territory of all twelve tribes is a function of its literary purpose, not evidence of early origin. The composition process has created some disparities. Shechem, properly a town of Manasseh (Josh 17:2, 7) is located in Ephraim (21:21). Heshbon is assigned to Gad (21:39) and not Reuben (13:17).

At the heart of this scribal composition, however, Josh 21:13-18 stands out as an archival source list of towns covering the kingdom of Judah (that is, Judah plus Simeon and Benjamin). Its status as an inherited source is evidenced by the non-idealized total in v. 19 (nine plus four equals thirteen). This awkward total required a deviation in the remaining idealized system (each tribe providing four towns) so that only three cities could be assigned in Naphtali (v. 32) in order to reach the ideal total of forty-eight (v. 41; twelve times four). The original core list is not entirely in harmony with other data in Joshua. Beth-shemesh (in Judah according to 21:16) is a town in Dan in 19:41 (as Ir-Shemesh). Two of the Benjaminite towns in 21:18—Anathoth and Almon—are not listed elsewhere in Joshua. Plotting the towns of this core list on a map describes an area around the heartland of Judah, south and west and then north:

Jattir, Eshtemoa, Debir, and Holon on the south; Ashan, Libnah, and Juttah on the west; Beth-shemesh farther north on the west; and four Benjaminite towns in border areas north of Jerusalem. A general resemblance to the list of Rehoboam's fortresses (2 Chr 11:5-12) suggests a similar origin for the core list as a description of a defensive ring around Jerusalem.

The rest of the chapter was generated artificially to match the core list inherited by the author. This was done by picking up the cities of refuge (along with their geographical situations) from Josh 20 and then culling cities from the tribal lists of Josh 13; 16–17; 19. The telltale b [ב, "in"] that begins Beeshterah (Josh 21:27) carries over the preposition from "in Ashtaroth" in 13:12. Kartah (21:34) is probably equivalent to Kattath (19:15).

Joshua 21:36-37 reproduces the three names of 13:18 in the same order. This also is true (with a gap) for 21:28-29 and 19:20-21 (Jarmuth = Remeth). Joshua 21:38-39 reproduces selected items from 13:25-26 in reverse order. Pairs recur in the same order between 21:32 and 19:35 (Kartan = Rakkath) and between 21:23 and 19:44. In fact, except for the enigmatic Kibzaim (21:22; Jokmeam in 1 Chr 6:68 [Heb. 6:53]), every town in Josh 21:20-40 may be found in Josh 13; 16–17; 19; and 20.

D. Ezekiel's Vision

As part of a vision of the nation's promised future (Ezek 47:13–48:29), Ezekiel redraws tribal boundaries on the old map of Canaan (compare Num 34:3-12) in a stylized and idealized way. Each of the tribes is allotted territory in strips running east and west in a configuration that has little to do with their traditional locations. For example, Benjamin is south of Judah along with Issachar and Zebulun. The east Jordan tribes Reuben and Gad are moved west of the Jordan, so that the Jordan serves as an east border (Ezek 47:18, compare Num 34:12; Josh 22:10-34). However, the north to south sequence Dan–Asher–Naphtali–Manasseh–Ephraim (Ezek 48:1-5) coordinates with the order of their historical arrangement. The northern limit is extended to the latitude of Damascus (47:15-17). All twelve tribes are present, including those exiled by the Assyrians. Each tribe receives an equal portion (47:14). Special grants in the neighborhood of Jerusalem are allotted to the priests (48:8-12), the Levites (48:13-14), and the "prince" (48:21-22). At this point, the tradition of tribal territory has lost its mooring in history and realistic geography to become a way of visualizing the eschatological future and the hope of a restoration of all tribes settled in all the land. Although identification by tribes continued to some degree after the exile (Luke 2:36; Rom 11:1), their association with distinct territory is last witnessed by Neh 11:31-35, which specifies fifteen Benjaminite settlement both within its traditional territory and in other towns farther north and west.

Bibliography: Yohanan Aharoni. *The Land of the Bible* (1979); Ehud Ben-Zvi. "The List of the Levitical Cities." *JSOT* 54 (1992) 77–106; Edward F. Campbell. "The Boundary Between Ephraim and Manasseh." *The Answers Lie Below.* H. O. Thompson, ed. (1984) 67–74; C. H. J. de Geus. *The Tribes of Israel* (1976); Zvi Gal. "Cabul, Jiphthah-El and the Boundary Between Asher and Zebulun in the Light of Archaeological Evidence." *ZDPV* 101 (1985) 114–27; R. S. Hess. "Asking Historical Questions of Joshua 13–19: Recent Discussion Concerning the Date of the Boundary Lists." *Faith, Tradition, History: Old Testament Historiography in Its Near Eastern Context.* A. Millard, J. Hoffmeier, and D. Baker, eds. (1994) 191–205; David Jobling. "The Jordan a Border: Transjordan in Israel's Ideological Geography." *The Sense of Biblical Narrative: Structural Analyses in the Hebrew Bible II* (1986) 88–134; Zechariah Kallai. *Historical Geography of the Bible: The Tribes of Ancient Israel* (1986); A. R. Millard. "Cartography in the Ancient Near East." *The History of Cartography: Cartography in Prehistoric, Ancient and Medieval Europe and the Mediterranean.* Vol. 1. J. B. Harley and D. Woodward, eds. (1987) 107–16; J. Maxwell Miller. "Rehoboam's Cities of Defense and the Levitical Cities." *Archaeology and Biblical Interpretation.* G. Johnson, L. Perdue, and L. Toombs, eds. (1987) 273–86; Nadav Na'aman. *Borders and Districts in Biblical Historiography* (1986); Nadav Na'aman. "The Inheritance of the Sons of Simeon." *ZDPV* 96 (1980) 136–52; Nadav Na'aman. "The Kingdom of Judah under Josiah." *TA* 18 (1991) 3–71; Jan J. Simons. *The Geographical and Topographical Texts of the Old Testament* (1959); Jan Svensson. *Towns and Toponyms in the Old Testament* (1994); Moshe Weinfeld. "The Extent of the Promised Land–The Status of Transjordan." *Das Land Israel in biblischer Zeit.* D. Strecker, ed. (1983) 59–75; K. Lawson Younger. "The Configuring of Judicial Preliminaries: Judges 1.1–2.5 and Its Dependence on the Book of Joshua." *JSOT* 68 (1995) 75–92.

RICHARD D. NELSON

TRIBULATION [צָרָה tsarah, תְּלָאָה tela'ah; θλῖψις thlipsis]. Persecution unto death (1 Sam 26:24) or the result of divine wrath (Lam 3:5). In the Apocrypha, thlipsis can be the chaos of war (Add Esth 11:8) or a terrible, divine eschatological punishment avoidable by God's elect (2 Esd 15:19; 16:19, 67, 74). Although the term *tribulation* is not used in the NRSV of the NT, thlipsis is variously translated as "affliction," "anguish," "DISTRESS," "hardship," "ordeal," "PERSECUTION," "suffering," "torture," and "trouble."

R. ANDREW COMPTON

TRIBULATION, GREAT. The phrase "the great tribulation" is used in the KJV to describe a period of turmoil and suffering prior to Christ's return. The NRSV translates "tribulation" with words such as "ordeal," "suffering," and "distress." The phrase comes from a scene in Revelation identifying "a great multitude" of the redeemed "standing before the throne" (Rev 7:9) as "they who have come out of the great ordeal [tribulation]; they have washed their robes and made them white in the blood of the Lamb" (7:14). The definite articles (lit., "the tribulation, the great one") suggest a concept familiar to the readers of Revelation. Jesus speaks in the Gospels of "great suffering [tribulation], such as has not been from the beginning of the world until now, no, and never will be" (Matt 24:21; Mark 13:19 lacks the word *great*, and substitutes "from the beginning of the creation that God created"). The unprecedented "tribulation" (thlipsis θλῖψις) goes back to Daniel, where it (NRSV, "anguish") is said to have "never occurred since nations first came into existence" (Dan 12:1; also 1 Macc 9:27, "great distress [tribulation] in Israel, such as had not been since the time that prophets ceased to appear among them"). Jesus' more sweeping horizons ("from the beginning of the world") are presupposed in Revelation, implying that "tribulation" has always been present for God's people (see John 16:33; Acts 14:22; Rev 1:9), but that at the end of the age it will be greatly intensified, both to test and to vindicate the people (see 2 Thess 1:5-7; Rev 2:22).

The tribulation in Judaism was often generalized as "messianic woes" or "birth pangs" (see John 16:21) preceding the messianic age, but in Revelation it becomes a specific three-and-a-half-year period (see 12:14, "a time, and [two] times, and half a time," as in Dan 7:25; 12:7; also "forty-two months," Rev 11:2; 13:5; "one thousand two hundred sixty days," 11:3; 12:6). A traditional "week" of seven years (see Dan 9:24-27) seems to have been "shortened" (cut in half) for the sake of God's elect, just as Jesus promised (Matt 24:22; Mark 13:20). Whether the period is literal, or whether it represents the whole era between Christ's first and second coming is debated. In the 2nd-cent. *Shepherd of Hermas*, where those who endure "the coming great tribulation" are pronounced blessed (Herm. *Vis.* 2.2.7, author's trans.), it is future, as Hermas sees "an enormous beast, like some sea monster ... about a hundred feet long, with a head like a pottery jar" (4.1.6, author's trans.), identified as a foreshadowing of "the coming great tribulation" (4.2.5, author's trans.). He faces it bravely, and is told, "You have escaped great tribulation because ... you were not of two minds when you saw such a great beast" (4.2.4; author's trans.). The faithful escape tribulation not by being taken to heaven before it begins (as in certain popular scenarios) but by facing it head-on, as they "cast their cares on the Lord" (Herm. *Vis.* 4.2.5, author's trans.; also 1 Pet 5:7-9). Whether as martyrs or survivors, theirs is the promise of "coming out of the great ordeal," to live with God forever (see Rev 7:14-17). *See* REVELATION, BOOK OF.

Bibliography: Leonard L. Thompson. *The Book of Revelation* (1990).

J. RAMSEY MICHAELS

TRIBUNAL tri-byoo'nuhl [βῆμα bēma]. A raised platform and magistrate's chair for judging (Acts 18:12, 16-17; 25:6, 10, 17). Elsewhere bēma is translated "JUDGMENT SEAT."

TRIBUNE trib'yoon [χιλίαρχος chiliarchos]. A high-ranking military officer (Acts 24:22; 25:23). The official whom Paul encounters while in Jerusalem (Acts 21:31-40; 22:22-30; 23:10-22) appears to be a *tribunus militum*, a Roman military commander in charge of a COHORT (approximately 600 soldiers).

TRIBUTE [בְּלוֹ belo, מִנְחָה minkhah, מַשָּׂא massaʾ, עֹנֶשׁ ʿonesh; φόρος phoros]. Payment by a ruler or people to a superior foreign king, indicating political submission or loyalty. Tribute is voluntary in that it is given, not forcibly seized. At the same time, however, it is compulsory, since the superior king usually expects the payment and regards the failure to give it as a punishable offense.

In the OT, tribute usually consists of gold and silver, but occasionally it includes other items, e.g., livestock, spices, grain, special garments, weapons, and cultic images (1 Kgs 10:25; 2 Kgs 3:4; 2 Chr 27:5; Hos 10:6). Tribute from foreign vassals serves to enrich the kings of Israel and Judah and to supply the needs of their courts.

According to the royal Zion theology, God gives to the Davidic king dominion over the nations of the world (see Ps 2:8), and consequently the Davidic king receives the tribute of foreign rulers (*see* ZION TRADITION). Psalm 72:10-11 thus prays: "May the kings of Tarshish and of the isles render him tribute.... May all kings fall down before him, all nations give him service." The biblical account of Solomon reflects the influence of the royal Zion theology. First Kings 4:21 [Heb. 5:1] asserts: "Solomon was sovereign over all the kingdoms from the Euphrates to the land of the Philistines, even to the border of Egypt; they brought tribute and served Solomon all the days of his life." In similar fashion, 1 Kgs 10:23-25 speaks of "all the kings of the earth" seeking Solomon's presence and annually bringing him tribute. Both passages likely are exaggerations by late editors, intent on depicting Solomon's reign as a golden age.

Similar but less grandiose claims are made about David in 2 Sam 8. While the historical accuracy of this account is debatable, this text reports the king's subjugation of Israel's several neighbors. Moab and Aram-Damascus, specifically, become "servants to David and brought tribute" (vv. 2, 6).

During the first half of the 9th cent. BCE, Omri and Ahab of Israel subjugated Moab (*see* MOABITE STONE). Second Kings 3:4 states that, prior to the death of Ahab (ca. 851 BCE), King MESHA of Moab "used to deliver to the king of Israel one hundred thousand lambs and the wool of one hundred thousand rams." Jehoshaphat of Judah was a contemporary of the Omrides, and according to 2 Chr 17:11 the Philistines and Arabs brought him tribute. The accuracy of this claim is hard to assess, since much of the Chronicler's picture of Jehoshaphat is idealized. To a lesser degree, the same difficulty pertains to the Chronicler's reports on Uzziah and Jotham, kings of Judah during the 8th cent. BCE. Second Chronicles 26:8 and 27:5 report that the Ammonites gave tribute to the two kings. The original reference in both texts was probably to the Meunites, a nomadic people in the Negev region.

For most of their history, the Israelites were subordinate to other states, and so they were more accustomed to paying tribute than to receiving it. Judges 3:15 states specifically that the Israelites sent tribute to King EGLON of Moab by the hand of the judge Ehud. The biblical writers present such domination as divine punishment for the sins of the people.

After the death of Solomon and the defection of the northern kingdom of Israel from Davidic rule, Pharaoh SHISHAK of Egypt invaded Palestine, advanced against Jerusalem, and took the treasures of the Temple and royal palace (1 Kgs 14:25-26). The episode is depicted here as an instance of plunder, but historically Rehoboam may have offered the treasures as a one-time payment of tribute. According to a fragmentary inscription of the Egyptian king at Karnak, his campaign was directed mainly against the Northern Kingdom and non-Judean parts of the Negev. Jerusalem is missing from the extant list of conquered towns.

From the late 840s BCE onward, Israel and Judah were subject to the kings of Assyria and Aram-Damascus. The inscriptions of SHALMANESER III of Assyria record the tribute of King Jehu of Israel in 841 BCE. Jehu had usurped the throne in Samaria (2 Kgs 9–10), and his payment to Shalmaneser probably bought Assyria's recognition of his kingship. With the decline of Assyrian influence in the west after 738 BCE, HAZAEL of Damascus moved to attack Jerusalem, and King Jehoash of Judah sent to Hazael "all the gold that was found in the treasuries of the house of the LORD and of the king's house" (2 Kgs 12:17-18). In the last decade of the 9th cent. BCE, Adad-nirari III reestablished Assyria's dominance in the region. According to his inscriptions, several western states and rulers, including Jehoash of Israel, paid tribute (ca. 803 BCE).

The kings of Israel continued as tributaries of Assyria during the 8th cent. BCE. According to 2 Kgs 15:19-20, the usurper Menahem (746–737 BCE) gave a thousand talents of silver to TIGLATH-PILESER III to confirm Menahem's hold on the royal power. Many scholars regard this payment as tribute, but it may have been for hiring Assyrian troops as mercenaries. Tiglath-pileser's own inscriptions (*ITP*, 55, 69, 107, 189) attest the reception of tribute from Menahem in 743–740 and 738 BCE, as well as the tribute of Hoshea (730–722 BCE), which he sent to Tiglath-pileser in southern Babylonia (ca. 730 BCE). According to 2 Kgs 17:3-4, Hoshea submitted annual tribute until his rebellion against Shalmaneser V (ca. 725 BCE).

The Judean kings Ahaz (743–728 BCE) and Hezekiah (727–699 BCE) also paid tribute to Assyria. Second Kings 16:7-8 claims that, when the rulers of Aram-Damascus and Israel attacked Ahaz in Jerusalem, Ahaz appealed to Tiglath-pileser for deliverance and sent him silver and gold as a "present." The inscriptions of the Assyrian king are silent about this special plea and "present," but they do record Ahaz's payment of normal tribute in 734–733 BCE (ANET, 282). At the end of the 8th cent. BCE, Hezekiah rebelled against Assyria, and consequently SENNACHERIB invaded Judah in 701 BCE. Second Kings 18:13-15 reports that Hezekiah sent his apology to the Assyrian king at Lachish, along with a large sum of tribute. According to Sennacherib's own account of the invasion (ANET, 287–88), the Assyrian king had returned to Nineveh when he received tribute from Hezekiah.

NECO of Egypt deposed Jehoahaz II (609 BCE), installed Jehoiakim as king of Judah, and imposed tribute on the land (2 Kgs 23:31-35). From the late 6th cent. onward, Jews were obliged to pay provincial tribute to the Persian king (Ezra 4:13; Neh 5:4; compare Ezra 6:8).

According to 1 and 2 Maccabees, Jews owed tribute and other taxes to the Seleucid kings during the 2nd cent. BCE. If Jason's payment to ANTIOCHUS IV in 175 BCE is any indication, annual tribute was approximately 350 talents of silver (2 Macc 4:8). The Seleucid rulers occasionally offered exemptions to the Jews in order to gain their political support against rival claimants to the Seleucid throne (see SELEUCID EMPIRE). Thus Demetrius I (162–150 BCE) promised to excuse the Jews from "the payment of tribute and salt tax and crown levies" and pledged not to collect "the third of the grain and half of the fruit of the trees that he should receive" (1 Macc 10:29-30; compare 11:28-37). Demetrius II (146–140 BCE) and Antiochus VII (139–129 BCE) made similar offers to the Hasmonean leader Simon (1 Macc 13:37 and 15:8).

Bibliography: J. M. Miller and J. H. Hayes. *A History of Ancient Israel and Judah.* 2nd ed. (2006); J. J. M. Roberts. "Solomon's Jerusalem and the Zion Tradition." *Jerusalem in Bible and Archaeology: The First Temple Period.* Andrew G. Vaughn and Ann E. Killebrew, eds. (2003) 163–70; H. Tadmor. *The Inscriptions of Tiglath-pileser III King of Assyria* (1994).

STUART IRVINE

TRIGON. *See* MUSICAL INSTRUMENTS.

TRINITY. The NT speaks about God as Father, Son, and Holy Spirit (Matt 28:19). By the 2nd cent. CE, this formulation was used in baptism, and the first summaries of Christian faith were baptismal creeds (*see* CREED). Because of its importance, the Trinity soon became a focus of controversy. To avoid "tritheism," some early thinkers emphasized God's unity, asserting that *Father, Son,* and *Spirit* are merely names for different modes of activity by one and the same God, first in creation, then in redemption, then in sanctification. Others, concerned to maintain the difference of persons, were puzzled by biblical passages that sometimes implied that the Son or Word was inferior to the Father, while other passages implied equality.

The Council of Nicea (325 CE) declared that the Son is of the same essence as the Father, and some decades later it was agreed (by theologians, not councils) that God is one essence in three equal persons, mutually related. A new dispute then emerged: Does the Spirit proceed from the Father alone (John 15:26) or also from the Son? The East held to the former view, the West to the latter. The controversy hinged on the Lat. word *filioque* ("and the Son"), which was later added to the Nicene Creed. This remains a major point of controversy between East and West even today.

The Protestant Reformers retained the doctrine of the Trinity, but other Protestants concluded that the doctrine was not scriptural. They became an organized movement chiefly among the Socinians on the Continent and the Unitarians in England and the United States. During the Enlightenment, with its emphasis on what can be known about God through reason, the doctrine of the Trinity was widely ignored. G. W. F. Hegel's speculative system revived the Christian doctrines of Trinity and incarnation, and this has influenced many theologians up to the present.

Bibliography: G. W. F. Hegel. *Lectures on the Philosophy of Religion: The Lectures of 1827* (1988); Peter C. Hodgson. *Hegel and Christian Theology: A Reading of the Lectures on the Philosophy of Religion* (2005).

EUGENE TESELLE

TRIPARTITE TRACTATE. The *Tripartite Tractate* is the modern title given to the unnamed text discovered at Nag Hammadi (NHC I, 5). Previously unattested in Christian literature, the *Tripartite Tractate* is a systematic exploration of the process of creation and the eventual return of this creation to its source, the preexistent Father. These dramatic events unfold in three distinct movements: the emergence of the pleromatic realm, the creation of humanity, and the role of the Savior in the restoration of humanity. The theology of the *Tripartite Tractate* most closely resembles the teachings of Heracleon and the western branch of Valentinianism, but the tractate displays a willingness to distinguish itself from these currents in important ways. It posits, e.g., an original monad rather than a dyad; identifies the logos (λόγος) as the aeon responsible for the pleromatic disturbance and the one who appoints a demiurge to organize the created realm; and displays a tendency to merge with emerging orthodox thought (e.g., the concept of the Trinity, the relatively positive evaluation of the demiurge, and the affirmation of a single baptism). This accommodation to orthodoxy represents a later development in Valentinianism, perhaps placing the text in the 3rd or early 4th cent. *See* GNOSTICISM; NAG HAMMADI TEXTS.

DAVID M. REIS

TRIPOLIS trip′uh-lis [Τρίπολις *Tripolis*]. The modern city of Tarabulus or Tripoli, located about 40 mi. north of Beirut along the coast of the Mediterranean Sea. Though the Phoenician name of the city is lost, the Greek name **Tripolis** literally means "three cities" and is derived from its origin. The three Phoenician cities of Tyre, Sidon, and Aradus founded the city on a prominent peninsula that extends into the Mediterranean Sea. Pliny the Elder (*Nat.* 5.17) and Strabo (*Geogr.* 16.2.15) record that these three cities later controlled a walled section of Tripolis. The strategic location of Tripolis provided it with an excellent harbor as well as a safe haven from land-based attacks. It was surrounded by water on three sides, and a deep trench dug along the peninsula cut it off from the mainland.

During the Persian period, Tripolis became the administrative hub of PHOENICIA. Tripolis did not resist Alexander the Great's advance through the region, and it later became an important Seleucid city. In 162 BCE, a rival for the Seleucid throne, Demetrius I, led his army to victory here over Antiochus V and General Lysias (1 Macc 7:1-4; 2 Macc 14:1; Josephus, *Ant.* 12.389–91). After the decline of the Seleucids, Tripolis became an independent city in 111 BCE. Pompey the Great brought the city under Roman control in 65 BCE, and later Herod the Great funded the construction of a gymnasium in the city. Reportedly, Peter established a Christian community in the city (*Ps.-Clem., Recognitions* 4.6; *Homilies* 11.36).

JOHN D. WINELAND

TRIREME [τριήρης *triērēs*]. A Greek warship characterized by three rows of oars on each side. When the quadrennial games were being held in Tyre, the usurper-high priest Jason sent 300 silver drachma for the sacrifice to Hercules in order to impress the king (2 Macc 4:20). Jason's couriers instead put the money toward the construction of triremes. Conventional English renders Greek *triērēs* according to the Latin *triremis*.

BENNIE H. REYNOLDS III

TRITO-ISAIAH. *See* ISAIAH, BOOK OF.

TRIUMPH [גָּאָה *ga'ah*, רוּעַ *rua'*; κατακαυχάομαι *katakauchaomai*, θριαμβεύω *thriambeuō*]. The joy or exultation of victory. Triumph is understood as God's to give or withhold. It may be achieved through attack or defense. In either case, it transforms a situation of danger, injustice, uncertainty, and fear into one of safety, justice, peace, and exultation for the triumphant.

The Bible speaks of God's triumph (Exod 15:1, 21; Ps 54:7 [Heb. 54:9]; 2 Cor 2:14; Col 2:15); of human triumph, usually through God (Pss 41:11 [Heb. 41:12]; 60:8 [Heb. 60:10]; 108:9 [Heb. 108:10]); and of the triumph of enemies (Lam 1:9). At times the enemy does triumph, causing consternation (Ps 94:3). Triumph is seen as the gift of God; when enemies fail to triumph, it is because God has prevented it (Ps 41:11 [Heb. 41:12]; Col 2:15). James encourages his readers to be merciful, because "mercy triumphs over judgment" (Jas 2:13).

CAROL GRIZZARD BROWNING

TRIUMPHAL ENTRY. Jesus' formal, ceremonial entrance into JERUSALEM and the Temple, which signaled the climax of his mission and anticipated his arrest, trial, and crucifixion. Reported in each of the NT Gospels (Matt 21:1-17; Mark 11:1-19; Luke 19:28-48; John 12:12-19), this scene has profound christological implications and helps to explain the hostility Jesus encountered among the Jerusalem leadership (*see* TEMPLE, JERUSALEM).

Two interpretive frames shape our understanding of the significance of Jesus' entry into the Holy City. First, even if the Gospels differ somewhat in what details they provide in their respective accounts, almost every one of those details has an OT precursor. The tying and untying of the colt brings to mind the role of an anticipated ruler in Gen 49:11. According to 1 Sam 8:10-18, kings have the right to requisition an animal. Zechariah 9:9 urges Jerusalem to rejoice for "your king comes to you; triumphant and victorious is he, humble and riding on a DONKEY, on a colt, the foal of a donkey." For example, Solomon, David's heir, rides a mule to his coronation (1 Kgs 1:32-40; compare 2 Sam 18:9 and 19:26, where contenders for the Davidic throne ride a mule or donkey). The spreading of garments on the pathway is a form of greeting appropriate to royalty (2 Kgs 9:13). Shouts of "Hosanna!" recall Ps 118—a psalm of royal enthronement (118:25, hoshi'ah na' [הוֹשִׁיעָה נָּא]; NRSV, "Save us ... !"); as does the exuberant acclamation, "Blessed is the one who comes in the name of the LORD" (Ps 118:26; see Matt 23:39; Luke 13:35). *See* HOSANNA.

Reference to the use of leafy branches (Mark 11:8), leafy tree branches (Matt 21:8), or palm branches (John 12:13; *see* PALM TREE) in the parade is reminiscent of the hero's welcome given Judas Maccabeus, whose reception in the city is, like Jesus', associated with his purification of the Temple (2 Macc 10:1-8). Moreover, according to *m. Sanh.* 2:5, no one may use an animal on which the king rides; this directive has its counterpart in the description shared by Mark and Luke of "a colt that has never been ridden" (Mark 11:2; Luke 19:30), itself evocative of Zechariah's reference in the LXX to a "new colt" (pōlon neon [πῶλον νέον]; 9:9). Second, biblical and extra-biblical literature evidences a relatively stable type scene with the following components (Catchpole): 1) the prior recognition of the status of the protagonist, who has already achieved a victory; 2) a ritual entry; 3) shouts of welcome and/or acclamation as well as prayers to God; 4) entry into the city's temple; and 5) some form of temple action, whether sacrificial offering or temple cleansing. These components are witnessed in the Synoptic Gospels, though in John the temple action is found earlier (2:13-22). This type scene is evidenced in at least a dozen cases, including Alexander's journey from Gaza to Jerusalem (Josephus, *Ant.* 11.325–30), Alexander's entry into Shechem (Josephus, *Ant.* 11.342–45), Judas Maccabeus' entry into Jerusalem (1 Macc 4:36-40), Judas' return from battle to Jerusalem (1 Macc 5:45-54; Josephus, *Ant.* 12.348–49), Simon Maccabeus' entry into Gaza (1 Macc 13:43-48), and Simon's entry into Jerusalem (1 Macc 13:49-51). In addition, it is easily correlated with the probable precedent in 1 Kgs 1:32-40 (compare Zech 9:9).

The use of these interpretive frames leads to four interpretive conclusions. First, Jesus' entrance into Jerusalem cannot be interpreted apart from the progress of his ministry. This is because a hero's welcome assumes victory has already been won, prayers are offered for the great things already accomplished, and acclamation is recognition of a status already achieved. In fact, the use of the type scene of the triumphal entry interprets Jesus' mission of teaching and healing both as a victory and as key to others' recognition of his status. This is explicit in the reference in Luke 19:37 to praising God "for all the deeds of power that they had seen," and in the collocation of triumphal entry and the resuscitation of Lazarus in John 12:10-11, 17-19. Second, the royal and, indeed, messianic connotations of Jesus' entry into Jerusalem are inescapable. Note the identification of "the one who comes in the name of the LORD" (Matt 21:9; compare Ps 118:26); as "the king" in Luke 19:38; the explicit citation of Zech 9:9, "your king comes to you" (Matt 21:5; John 12:13); and reference to Jesus as heir to David's kingdom (Matt 21:9; Mark 11:10). Third, the significance of Jesus' temple action is interwoven with that of his entrance into the city. It is as one with widely acclaimed authority that Jesus acts on God's behalf to cleanse the Temple. Interestingly, Jesus fulfills the anticipated messianic role of purging Jerusalem (*Pss. Sol.* 17:30), but not by ridding the city of Gentiles (*Pss. Sol.* 17:22). Rather, in the Gospel of Mark, he proclaims the Temple a house of prayer for the Gentiles (11:17; NRSV, "nations"). In all of our accounts, he cleanses the Temple and prophesies its destruction. Moreover, in Luke, Jesus indicts Jerusalem for its failure to recognize the time of God's redemptive visitation (19:41-44). Fourth, not surprisingly, then, the triumphal entry triggered hostility against Jesus from the Jerusalem leadership whose authority would have been challenged by popular acknowledgment of Jesus'

royal status. *See* KING OF THE JEWS; KINGDOM OF GOD, KINGDOM OF HEAVEN.

Bibliography: D. R. Catchpole. "The 'Triumphal' Entry." *Jesus and the Politics of His Day.* E. Bammel and C. F. D. Moule, eds. (1984) 319–34; J. A. Sanders. "A Hermeneutical Fabric: Psalm 118 in Luke's Entrance Narrative." *Luke and Scripture.* C. A. Evans and J. A. Sanders, eds. (1993) 140–53.

JOEL B. GREEN

TROAS troh´az [Τρῳάς Trōas]. The city of Troas was situated on a gently sloping coastal plain in northwestern Asia Minor, about 20 km (12 mi.) southwest of ancient Troy (Ilium). Founded in 310 BCE by Antigonus and named Antigonia, it was renamed Alexandria Troas by Lysimachus about a decade later. The city quickly became the main seaport in the area, as well as an important commercial and administrative center, and so functioned as the primary land and sea hub for travelers going in all directions. The artificial harbor, which provided shelter from the prevailing northwesterly winds, was protected by city walls that encompassed about 1,000 square ac.

In 133 BCE Troas came under the control of the Romans, who sought to capitalize on its strategic location. Julius Caesar was rumored to have considered moving his capital there (Suetonius, *Jul.* 79.3). Augustus made it a Roman colony, giving it the name *Colonia Augusta Troadensium*, and in the early 1st cent. Troas was considered an important city (Strabo, *Geogr.* 13.1.26). At its height there were perhaps as many as 100,000 residents from a number of different ethnic groups, since throughout its history Troas had been the site of numerous attempts to amalgamate villages and cities in the area.

According to Acts, Paul visited Troas twice. While passing through the city during his travels in Asia Minor, he experienced a night vision calling him to Macedonia (Acts 16:8-11). Later, Paul stopped for a week in Troas en route to Jerusalem (Acts 20:5-12). It was during this visit that EUTYCHUS, while listening to Paul speaking at length in an upper room, fell asleep and tumbled from a window to his death, only to be revived by Paul.

In 2 Cor 2:12, Paul notes that when he arrived at Troas to preach a door was opened "in the Lord." He did not remain there long, however, but continued on to Macedonia in search of Titus. If this text can be harmonized with Acts, then it seems that a Christian community was founded at Troas after Paul's first visit but prior to the visit mentioned in 2 Corinthians. By the time of the second visit in Acts, a Christian community was meeting regularly in Troas. The continuation of this community is suggested by the reference in 2 Tim 4:13 to Paul having left a cloak, books, and parchment with Carpus at Troas. Early in the 2nd cent., Ignatius of Antioch dispatched three letters from Troas while being escorted under guard to Rome, where he was eventually put to death (see Ign. *Phld.* 11:2; Ign. *Smyrn.* 12:1; Ign. *Pol.* 8:1).

Very little of ancient Troas remains today, although archaeological investigation continues. Visible remains include the harbor, bath-gymnasium complex, agora, stadium, theater, two temples, the east gate, and several kilometers of walls. Most of the remains reflect the extensive building work done in the early 2nd cent. CE.

Bibliography: John Manuel Cook. *The Troad: An Archaeological and Topographical Study* (1973).

RICHARD S. ASCOUGH

TROGYLLIUM troh-jil´ee-uhm [Τρωγύλλιον Trōgyllion]. A promontory on the western shore of Asia Minor between EPHESUS and MILETUS, and a possible point of anchorage on Paul's third missionary journey. Trogyllium projects westward from Mount Mycale toward the island of SAMOS. The waterway dividing Samos from Trogyllium is less than a mile wide and was part of a shipping lane commonly used to traverse the coast of Asia Minor. According to the shorter form of Acts attested in the Alexandrian text, Paul and his companions on the return trip to Jerusalem "touched at Samos" and on the next day "came to Miletus" (Acts 20:15), meaning that they sailed through this waterway, passing Trogyllium. The longer form of Acts attested in the Western text (*see* BEZAE, CODEX), however, claims that Paul and his companions arrived at Miletus only "after remaining at Trogyllium" (the NRSV offers this reading in a footnote to Acts 20:15). Because the Alexandrian text is generally preferred to the "wild" and "undisciplined" Western text, which is especially given to interpolation in Acts, the shorter reading is judged by most to be the original.

MICHAEL W. MARTIN

TROPHIMUS trof´uh-muhs [Τρόφιμος Trophimos]. Along with TYCHICUS, one of two "Asians" (Acts 20:4, author's trans.; NRSV, "from Asia") who accompanied Paul for at least part of the final journey to Jerusalem (Acts 19:21–21:17), probably as representatives of the Asian churches in the collection for the poor in Jerusalem (1 Cor 16:1-4). Upon arrival in the city, Trophimus became embroiled in the controversy that led to Paul's arrest. According to Acts 21:27-29, "the Jews from Asia" falsely accused Paul of taking "Greeks" into the Temple, their only evidence being that they had previously seen Paul with "Trophimus the Ephesian" in the city.

In the only other text that mentions Trophimus, an imprisoned Paul tells Timothy that he has left Trophimus in Miletus (2 Tim 4:20). Whether an authentic Pauline communication of Trophimus' whereabouts or a deuteropauline attempt at verisimilitude, the text agrees with Acts that Trophimus was a trusted companion of Paul.

MICHAEL W. MARTIN

TROUGH [רַהַט rahat, שֹׁקֶת shoqeth]. Stone boxes or hollowed-out stones were positioned near wells to accommodate animals. Rebekah and the daughters of Reuel pour water in troughs for their respective animals (Gen 24:20; Exod 2:16). Jacob uses the times when animals gather at the trough to trick his father-in-law, Laban (Gen 30:37-43).

VICTOR H. MATTHEWS

TRUMPET. *See* FEASTS AND FASTS; FESTIVALS, GRECO-ROMAN; MUSICAL INSTRUMENTS; REVELATION, BOOK OF.

TRUST [אֵימוּן ʾemon, בָּטַח batakh, כֶּסֶל kesel; πείθω peithō, πιστεύω pisteuō, πίστις pistis]. Trust is confidence or faith in God's promises. The psalms frequently exhort the reader to trust the Lord (e.g., 4:5; 9:10; 25:2; 31:6; 37:3; 40:3-4; 52:8; 56:3-4; 62:8; 115:8-11; 119:42). Paul says that a person who has trust or faith (pistis) is justified before God (Rom 5:1). *See* FAITH, FAITHFULNESS; JUSTIFICATION, JUSTIFY.

TRUSTEE [οἰκονόμος oikonomos]. A manager or administrator of an estate or household (Gal 4:2).

TRUTH [אֱמֶת ʾemeth; ἀλήθεια alētheia, ἀληθεύω alētheuō, ἀληθής alēthēs, ἀληθινός alēthinos, ἀληθῶς alēthōs]. In the OT, the word translated "truth" (ʾemeth) means "reliability." In the NT, the Greek word that is translated as "truth" (alētheia) can mean "reality," "accuracy," and "honesty." Its sense is sometimes influenced by OT usage, however, to become "faithfulness" or "reliability." Writers in both the OT and the NT value "truth" in the sense of correspondence between words and reality. Yet they also often use words metaphorically, sacrificing some descriptive correspondence in order to communicate realities difficult to grasp with "literal" language.

A. Truth in the Old Testament
  1. The sense of ʾemeth
    a. A pattern of action
    b. Help, responsibility, and reliability
    c. Ambiguous uses of ʾemeth
  2. Truth, correspondence, and metaphor in the Old Testament
    a. The idea of correspondence
    b. Metaphor, history, and prophecy
    c. Deception as judgment
B. Truth in the New Testament
  1. The sense of alētheia
    a. Alētheia in Hellenistic Greek
    b. Reality, correspondence, and honesty
    c. Reliability, faithfulness, and righteousness
    d. The gospel message as alētheia
    e. Alētheia in the Johannine literature

2. Truth, correspondence, and metaphor in the
New Testament
   a. The idea of correspondence
   b. Metaphor, history, and prophecy
   c. Parables as judgment and salvation
Bibliography

A. Truth in the Old Testament

1. The sense of 'emeth

a. A pattern of action. The Hebrew word 'emeth
can be translated "truth," "faithfulness," or "trustworthiness" (*see* FAITH, FAITHFULNESS; TRUST). 'Emeth
is primarily a characteristic of actions rather than words.
It is something one can do, as when Bethuel grants his
daughter as a wife for Isaac (Gen 24:49) or the Israelite
spies protect Rahab and her family (Josh 2:14; see also
Gen 47:29; 2 Sam 2:6). God practices 'emeth when
the deity delivers the people (Mic 7:20) or gives Jacob
success (Gen 32:10-11 [Heb. 32:11-12]). 'Emeth can
be "kept" (Ps 146:6), and various acts can be performed
"with 'emeth," i.e., following this pattern of behavior
(e.g., Josh 24:14; Judg 9:15; 1 Sam 12:24; 1 Kgs 2:4;
Prov 29:14; Isa 10:20).

b. Help, responsibility, and reliability. An action
is 'emeth if it is reliable. It may be helpful or beneficial behavior on which others can rely. In Ezek 18:9
the person who does 'emeth is one who does not
commit adultery, oppress the poor, steal, make unjust
judgments, etc. (18:6-8; compare Isa 59:14; Hos 4:1-
2). Hence, 'emeth is often paired with khesedh (חֶסֶד,
"lovingkindness"; see, e.g., Gen 24:27; Exod 34:6; Josh
2:12; 2 Sam 15:20; Ps 25:10). Yet some acts of 'emeth
are not immediately beneficial to anyone. One can practice 'emeth simply by keeping Israel's cultic or purity
requirements (Josh 24:14; 1 Sam 12:24; 2 Kgs 20:3;
2 Chr 31:20; Ezek 18:6-9; Zech 8:8), and God does
'emeth by punishing Israel (Neh 9:33; compare Exod
34:6-7). Such acts of 'emeth are "reliable" in that they
fulfill one's responsibilities. In Mic 7:20, God's act of
'emeth in rescuing Israel satisfies the deity's promises to
the patriarchs (compare Ps 89:14-18 [Heb. 89:15-19];
Isa 61:8). Joseph's burial of his father in Canaan fulfills
his oath (Gen 47:29-30), and the king who rules with
'emeth fulfils his duty as regent (Isa 16:5; compare Judg
9:15-19). All Israelites ought to demonstrate 'emeth by
living up to their obligation to treat others fairly and
kindly (Ps 25:10; 85:10-11 [Heb. 85:11-12]; Hos 4:1-2),
hence the association between 'emeth and justice (e.g.,
Ps 89:14 [Heb. 89:15]; Isa 59:14-15). Still, the active
reliability of 'emeth does not always involve fulfilling an
obligation either. Jacob emphasizes that he is not deserving of God's merciful blessings, God's acts of 'emeth
(Gen 32:10 [Heb. 32:11]; compare Ps 54:5 [Heb. 54:7];
Jer 32:41).

Thus the word 'emeth simply characterizes an act
as one on which one can depend, whether it is Rahab
trusting the Israelite spies to keep their promise (Josh
2:14), God depending on human beings to keep Torah

(2 Chr 31:20; Ezek 18:9), the psalmist relying on God
for deliverance (Pss 54:5 [Heb. 54:7]; 57:10 [Heb.
57:11]), or even Israel anticipating God's punishment
for their rebellion (Neh 9:33). A "person of 'emeth"
is one whose actions can be trusted (Exod 18:21; Neh
7:2; compare Zech 8:3), and the "God of 'emeth" is the
one on whom Israel can depend (2 Chr 15:3; Ps 31:5
[Heb. 31:6]; Jer 10:10).

c. Ambiguous uses of 'emeth. In light of this general use of 'emeth, we can clarify some ambiguous
cases. When acts of devotion toward God are performed "with 'emeth," the term is often understood to
mean "sincerely." More likely, though, this worship is
being characterized as an expression of reliable obedience (1 Sam 12:24; 2 Kgs 20:3; Pss 86:11; 145:18; Isa
10:20; Jer 4:2). Where Jeremiah talks about God having sent prophets "in 'emeth," this probably does not
mean that he really sent them, but rather that God's
commissioning of these messengers is an expression of
reliable help and/or faithfulness to the covenant (Jer
26:15; 28:9). On the other hand, when social peace is
called 'emeth, it is probably not just "lasting," but rather the state in which people "do 'emeth" toward one
another (Jer 14:13; compare 2 Kgs 20:19; Esth 9:30;
Jer 33:6). A "judgment of 'emeth" is probably one that
does not violate the judge's responsibilities to the community (Ezek 18:8; Zech 7:9). When the "little horn" of
Dan 8:12 throws 'emeth to the ground, the term probably does not mean "true religion," but rather Israel's
"reliable" observance of the temple rituals. Where inanimate objects are occasionally said to be 'emeth, this
likely means not that they are "genuine," but that they
can be relied on to do what they are supposed to (Prov
11:18; Jer 2:21).

Several scholars have argued in recent years that
when 'emeth characterizes acts of speaking it denotes
correspondence between words and the world (e.g.,
Barr). Yet these verses also make good sense if we understand 'emeth in the same sense it carries elsewhere. To
"speak 'emeth" is, then, to say words on which others
can depend (Ps 15:2; Prov 8:7; Jer 9:5 [Heb. 9:4]; Zech
8:16). A "witness of 'emeth" gives reliable testimony
(Prov 14:25; Jer 42:5), and testimony is 'emeth if it can
be trusted as a basis for judgment (Deut 13:14 [Heb.
13:15]; 17:4; 22:20; compare Isa 43:9). God's promises
to David are 'emeth in that the deity can be trusted to
fulfill them (2 Sam 7:28), and prophetic messages are
'emeth when their predictions can be trusted (1 Kgs
17:24; Dan 8:26; 10:1; 11:2; compare Dan 10:21). The
reference of 'emeth in these cases is often speech that
corresponds to reality (e.g., 1 Kgs 10:6; 2 Chr 9:5). Yet
the sense of the term 'emeth itself probably remains
"reliability."

Certainly God's law and teaching are called 'emeth
not merely because this speech corresponds to the reality of the divine will, but because these words can be
trusted as the basis for one's life (Neh 9:13; Ps 119:142;
Mal 2:6; compare Ps 119:43; Prov 8:7). Hence "God's

'emeth" can be depicted as a reliable path in which to walk, a lifestyle that mimics God's own reliability (Pss 26:3; 86:11; compare 25:5).

2. Truth, correspondence, and metaphor in the Old Testament

a. The idea of correspondence. The fact that Hebrew did not include a word for correspondence between speech and the world does not mean, though, that the idea was unfamiliar to ancient Israel. Testimony is considered reliable ('emeth) precisely because the words accord with the evidence of what actually took place (Deut 13:14 [Heb. 13:15]; 17:4; 22:20). Prophetic predictions were expected to correspond with the way events actually unfolded (Deut 18:21-22). Commands and instructions depict a virtual world with which the real world may be compared. So God tells Joshua to "be careful to act in accordance with (ke בְּ) all that is written in" the "book of the law" (Josh 1:8).

b. Metaphor, history, and prophecy. At the same time, the prominence of metaphorical language in the OT suggests that literal correspondence is not always the chief kind of truth that the texts were shaped to communicate. Biblical writers refer to God's "nostrils" (Ps 18:8, 15 [Heb. 18:9, 16]) or God's "arm" (Isa 30:30, 32). Wisdom is a "wife" (Prov 7:1–9:18). These metaphors involve a deliberate lack of correspondence between the words and the reality they describe. Yet this very lack of literal correspondence allows in each case for a clearer depiction of certain aspects of reality. The "inaccurate" image allows the writer to isolate and highlight a specific aspect of some reality that might otherwise be overlooked in the complexity or familiarity of a straightforward description. In many cases the metaphor does not merely illustrate a facet of reality that could be stated more clearly. Rather, the image itself suggests new and fruitful ways of talking about and interacting with that reality. One cannot get "behind" the metaphorical talk about God as a king (Num 23:21; 1 Sam 12:12; Pss 5:2 [Heb. 5:3]; 44:4 [Heb. 44:5]; 68:24 [Heb. 68:25]; 145:1; Isa 44:6; Jer 10:10; Ezek 20:33), as a parent (Jer 3:14, 19; 31:20; Hos 11:1-11), or as a husband (Jer 31:3-4, 32; Ezek 16:32, 45; Hos 2:1-20; Joel 1:8). Rather, the biblical writers often reason about God by extending the metaphors, asking how the deity will act and respond if God is like a husband, etc. Hence, although these metaphors do not correspond with the world in the usual way, they can communicate something about reality that would be difficult or impossible to communicate literally. Indeed, the emphasis in some texts on the partial nature of human knowledge (Deut 29:29; Job 38–41), implies that a completely literal and systematic description of the cosmos is impossible for human beings, so that metaphor will always be a necessary mode for communicating about reality.

This recognition helps make sense of how freely some authors can reshape past events. The Chronicler, for example, resolves the problem of wicked Manasseh's long and peaceful reign in 2 Kings, inexplicable in terms of covenant theology, by introducing the suspiciously tidy narrative of the king's repentance (2 Chr 33:10-12, 18-19). Such reshaping of the past operates metaphorically, surrendering some literal correspondence with past reality in order to communicate something about God's dealings with humanity, which would be obscured by the sheer complexity of what actually happened.

In some places God's own communication about the future seems to work in this metaphorical manner. We find in 2 Kgs 20:1-11 that God's announcement of Hezekiah's impending death goes unfulfilled. Hezekiah repents and is then told he will be healed after all (compare Exod 33:3, 12-17). Some would argue that God here simply does not know the future with precision. Alternately, we may understand God's initial message to Hezekiah as a metaphor for the future, an "inaccurate" statement that nevertheless reveals something real about Hezekiah's present relationship with God and facilitates the king's right response.

c. Deception as judgment. Elsewhere God is so focused on provoking a response through speech that correspondence of any kind is no longer a concern. God sends a lying spirit to Jehoshaphat, leading him to his death in battle (1 Kgs 22). Then in Ezek 20:24-26 we hear that God gave Israel false commands in order to "horrify" them. In both cases God's message is calculated not to correspond with the reality of the divine will. These messages are, in a sense, no longer acts of communication, but rather acts of judgment designed to provoke a self-destructive response. Such speech-acts are not "true" in the English sense, but they are "reliable" as instruments in God's hands.

B. Truth in the New Testament

1. The sense of alētheia

a. Alētheia in Hellenistic Greek. In Classical and Hellenistic Greek alētheia generally means "what is real" (Isocrates, *Evag.* 5). Speaking alētheia means using words to make some reality evident (Homer, *Il.* 24.407; *Od.* 11.507; Herodotus, *Hist.* 1.116–17). Hence alētheia can also mean "honesty" or "correspondence" between words and reality (Herodotus, *Hist.* 1.55; Aristotle, *Pol.* 3.1281a, 42).

Early Jewish writers often use alētheia and its cognates in their ordinary senses (e.g., 4 Macc 5:11, 18; Wis 6:22). Yet the LXX translators often use alētheia for 'emeth where the idea is clearly the "reliability" of personal actions (e.g., Gen 32:10 [Heb. and LXX 32:11]; Josh 2:14; 2 Sam 2:6; Neh 9:33; Ps 25:10 [LXX 24:10]; Hos 4:1), as well as for the cognate term 'emunah (אֱמוּנָה, "faithfulness"; 2 Chr 19:9; Ps 31:23 [Heb. 31:24; LXX 30:24]; Isa 11:5; compare 26:2). In other Jewish literature as well, alētheia often denotes a reliably righteous lifestyle (1 Esd 4:37; 3:2, 5; 1 Macc 7:18; Sir 7:20; Tob 1:3; Wis 5:6; *Pss. Sol.* 3:6), something one "does" (Sir 27:9; Tob 4:6; 13:6; *Odes Sol.* 5:10; *Pss. Sol.* 17:15).

b. Reality, correspondence, and honesty. The NT writers, too, sometimes use alētheia in its standard sense of "reality" (Mark 5:33). The phrase ep alētheias (ἐπ' ἀληθείας) is used to mean "really, actually" (Mark 12:32), "indeed, truly" (Luke 4:25; 22:59; Acts 4:27; 10:34), or "in keeping with truth" (Mark 12:14; Luke 20:21). In Rom 2:2, God's judgment is carried out "in accordance with truth," based on people's real behavior. Where "speaking alētheia" is opposed to lying, the OT use of 'emeth and Greek use of alētheia are so formally similar that the NT writers were likely not even aware of the subtle difference in sense (John 8:40; 16:7; Acts 26:25; Rom 9:1; compare alētheuō in Gal 4:16; Eph 4:15). The adjective alēthinos is often used in the sense "genuine, real" (Luke 16:11; John 1:8; 6:32; 15:1; Heb 8:2; 9:24; 1 John 2:8) or "accurate" (John 4:23; 19:35). Alēthēs (ἀληθής), too, can mean "real" (Acts 12:9); "genuine" (John 6:55), "accurate" (John 4:18; 10:41; 19:35; Titus 1:13; 2 Pet 2:22), and probably "sincere" (Matt 22:16; Mark 12:14).

c. Reliability, faithfulness, and righteousness. In other cases, however, the NT writers continued to use alētheia in ways influenced by 'emeth in the OT. One can "do alētheia" (John 3:21; 1 John 1:6), and the noun sometimes seems to denote "reliability" or consistent "righteousness" (1 Cor 5:8; 13:6; Eph 5:9; Phil 1:18; and perhaps 2 Cor 13:8 [compare 13:5, 7, 9]; Eph 4:24). "True" (alēthēs) can mean "morally upright" (Phil 4:8) or "faithful" (2 Cor 6:8; 1 Pet 5:12; compare John 21:24), and human hearts can be called alēthinos in the sense of "morally pure" (Heb 10:22; compare Ps 19:9 [LXX 18:10]). The "truth" embodied by torah in Rom 2:20 is the reliable moral teaching that guides human beings in making right ethical judgments (compare 2:18). Hence one can "obey alētheia" (Rom 2:8).

God's alētheia is reliability, demonstrated in fulfilling the promises to the patriarchs (Rom 3:7; 15:8; compare alēthes in Rom 3:4). In keeping with Jewish usage, God and God's judgments, works, and words are all alēthinos in the sense of "faithful, reliable" (John 7:28; 17:3; 1 Thess 1:9; 1 John 5:20; Rev 3:7, 14; 6:10; 15:3; compare the LXX of Exod 34:6; Num 14:18; Deut 32:4; 2 Chr 15:3; Ps 85:15 [Eng. and Heb. 86:15]; 1 Esd 8:86; 3 Macc 2:11; 6:18; Tob 3:2, 5; see also Rev 19:11). Similarly, John discusses whether Jesus' testimony is alēthēs, meaning "valid" or (better) "trustworthy" (John 5:31-32; 8:13-17; compare 8:26).

We also find in the NT distinctively Jewish phrases using alētheia that seem to be influenced by Hebrew expressions involving 'emeth. The expression "in/ with truth" (en alētheia ἐν αληθείᾳ) is the standard LXX rendering for "with 'emeth" (e.g., Ps 68:14 [Eng. 69:13; Heb. 69:14]; 2 Chr 19:9). So when Paul says in Col 1:6 that his audience accepted the gospel "in/ with alētheia," this probably means they responded "faithfully" (compare 2 Cor 7:14; Eph 6:14; 1 Tim 2:7; 1 John 3:18). Talk about alētheia being "in" someone reflects a Hebrew idiom meaning "to be reliable" (1 Esd

4:37; 1 Macc 7:18; compare Gen 42:16). So "there is no truth in" Satan in the sense that Satan is unreliable, treacherous, and wicked (John 8:44; see also 2 Cor 11:10; Eph 4:21; 1 John 1:8; 2:4).

The ideas of reality and moral faithfulness seem to be fused in Paul's statement that the wicked "suppress the truth" (Rom 1:18), since what humanity rejects in the following verses includes both the reality of God's identity as creator and the attitude of worship that forms the basis of human moral faithfulness (1:21-26, 28).

d. The gospel message as alētheia. In the NT letters the gospel message is often called "the truth of the gospel" (Gal 2:5, 14), "the word of truth" (Col 1:5; Eph 1:13; 2 Tim 2:15; Jas 1:18), or simply "the truth" (1 Tim 3:15; 4:3; Titus 1:1; Heb 10:26; 1 Pet 1:22; 2 Pet 1:12; 2 John 1:1). In the Pastorals, the gospel is primarily truth in the sense of accurate teaching about reality, to be contrasted with mere "myths" (2 Tim 4:4; Titus 1:14) or false doctrine (e.g., 1 Tim 2:4; 6:5; 2 Tim 2:15, 18). Elsewhere, the emphasis seems to fall on the reliability of this message as a guide for life (e.g., 2 Pet 1:12). This recalls the Jewish characterization of reliable teaching as "truth" (1QS I, 15; IV, 6; compare Rom 2:20) and the use of the expression "word(s) of truth" for Torah (Ps 119:43 [LXX 118:43]) or wisdom (Eccl 12:10; compare *Pss. Sol.* 16:10). This gospel "truth" too is a "path" (2 Pet 2:2; compare the LXX of Ps 119:30 [LXX 118:30]; Tob 1:3; Wis 5:6; 1QS IV, 17) in which one "walks" (Gal 2:14; 2 John 4; 3 John 3, 4; compare Jas 5:19). It is to be "obeyed" (Gal 5:7; 1 Pet 1:22) and involves a commitment not to sin (Heb 10:26). James in particular seems to view the Christian path as the organic extension of Israelite moral truth (Jas 3:14), though his reference to the new "birth" that this truth brings suggests that these older traditions have been taken up, for him, into the more complete "word" of the Christian message (Jas 1:18). So while knowledge of the truth in these writings includes an accurate understanding of God's acts and will, it also involves to a greater or lesser extent participation in the gospel way of life (Heb 10:26; 2 John 1). Even in the Pastorals, this knowledge is inseparable from repentance (2 Tim 2:25) and "godliness" (Titus 1:1).

e. Alētheia in the Johannine literature. The Johannine penchant for playing on the multiple meanings of words gives alētheia a distinctive, polyvalent quality in these writings. In John 1:14, 17 the Greek terms alētheia and charis (χάρις, often translated "grace" or "mercy") seem to stand for the Hebrew pair 'emeth and khesedh, describing God's faithful commitment to God's people (compare Exod 34:6; see §A.1.b). Yet by depicting Jesus here as the revelation of the invisible God (John 1:18), the author also suggests that the incarnate "Word" makes God's "truth" accessible in the sense that Jesus displays the reality of the divine person. Jesus is at once the manifestation of God's faithful character and the divine reality (compare the similar polyvalence in, e.g., John 3:33; 4:23-24; 8:44).

A further level of meaning is added to the Johannine use of alētheia when Jesus announces his identity as "the way, the truth, and the life" (John 14:6). Here again, Jesus likely embodies "the truth" both in the sense that he reveals God's being and that human beings can find their way reliably to eternal life in relationship with him. In retrospect, we can then detect this idea of Christ as the personification of truth behind many earlier uses of alētheia. When the disciples are told that "the truth will make you free," one can hear a reference both to the gospel message and to the liberating power of Christ's presence (John 8:32; compare, e.g., John 5:33).

Similarly, we hear in 1 John 5:6 that "the Spirit is the truth," emphasizing the Spirit's reliability as a witness to Christ's incarnation. More broadly, this identification depicts the Spirit as impelling us reliably toward eternal life, shielding us from the hostile "spirit of error" (1 John 4:6; compare John 14:17; 16:13; 1QS III, 17–IV, 26). At the same time, this identification with truth hints that the Spirit is a manifestation of God's reality and reveals that reality to the community. Once again this identification hovers behind other uses of alētheia in the Johannine letters (e.g., 3 John 12).

Hence, "the truth" often appears to be an active power in the lives of the Johannine believers. It consists at one level of the convictions transmitted by the community's teachers (1 John 4:6). Yet beneath and within this speech lies the reality of God's intervention in the world. The "truth that abides in us and will be with us forever" in 2 John 2 is the elder's teaching, but it is inseparable from the Spirit's salvific presence (compare John 14:16-17; see 1 John 4:6; 3 John 8). To "know" this truth is not merely to adopt certain beliefs and a righteous lifestyle, it is to encounter the living power of God (1 John 2:21). Hence the Johannine believers are people "of the truth," those who live and work within the sphere of God's redemptive presence (1 John 3:19; compare 1QpHab VII, 10–12; 1QS IV, 6).

2. Truth, correspondence, and metaphor in the New Testament

a. The idea of correspondence. As in the OT, we find in the NT a concern to understand reality and communicate that understanding in words. Most agree that the Gospels and Acts are interested (at least in part) in preserving the memory of what actually happened in the past (see, esp., Luke 1:1-4; John 21:24). A similar impulse is evident in the use of traditions claiming to originate in eyewitness testimony (1 Cor 15:1-11; compare 1 John 1:1). It is in light of these past realities, properly understood, that the NT writers claim we can anticipate the shape of the future and navigate the coming judgment. Paul, for one, is conscious that his sacrifices in service of Christ are reasonable only if past events like the resurrection actually took place (1 Cor 15:17-18, 32).

b. Metaphor, history, and prophecy. At the same time, we must recognize again in the NT the prominence of metaphors: God as "Father" (Matt 5:45; Mark 8:38; John 4:23), the believer as crucified along with Christ (Gal 2:20), etc. And once again, these metaphors are often presented not as mere illustrations but as irreducible paradigms on the basis of which fruitful thought can proceed. It is because, for example, believers' bodies are "temples" that they must not have relations with prostitutes (1 Cor 6:19). The lack of full correspondence between such metaphorical speech and reality is, once more, what allows any talk about God when human understanding is incomplete. Even the total knowledge that Paul anticipates in the resurrection is likely a matter of personal communion with God, rather than conceptual understanding (1 Cor 13:9, 12).

Here again the biblical writers' dependence on metaphors helps us to understand their reshaping of the past. When, for example, Matthew has Jesus enter Jerusalem while riding two animals simultaneously (Matt 21:1-3), this is to emphasize Jesus' fulfillment of Zech 9:9. Like the Chronicler, e.g., Matthew feels no need to flag the boundaries between these interpretive adaptations and more straightforward reporting of tradition. He does not anticipate any need to tease apart "what really happened" from his interpretive shaping. The concern is, rather, to preserve the past in a form whose meaning for present life is clear.

On the other hand, we find in the NT an even stronger sense that because prophetic talk about the future is metaphorical, one cannot necessarily anticipate exactly what the corresponding future events will look like (1 Cor 13:9-12). Indeed, the unexpected way in which Jesus fulfilled Israel's messianic expectation may be related to the reticence of NT authors to describe the future in any detail. Even the florid metaphorical visions of Revelation seem geared not to provide a detailed map of the future but to reinforce the immediate, pastoral message of the opening letters to the seven churches (Rev 2–3).

c. Parables as judgment and salvation. Finally, we find in Jesus' PARABLEs a counterpart to the use of deception in God's judgment in the OT. For here again, the highly metaphorical nature of Jesus' parables is explained as a deliberate strategy to prevent some from hearing the message of God's kingdom (Mark 4:10-12 and par.; compare John 12:37-41 regarding "signs"). For these hearers, Jesus' speech is again not a vehicle for communication but a means of making their condemnation manifest. Even for those with "ears to hear," Jesus' parables often seem intended to destabilize the hearers' understanding of the world, clearing the way for them to experience a grace that transcends and even transgresses their usual understanding (e.g., Matt 20:1-16). Jesus' parabolic speech is true for these hearers in the sense that it is a saving, restoring event.

Bibliography: J. Barr. *The Semantics of Biblical Language* (1961); R. E. Brown. *John.* AB 29 (1970); C. H. Dodd. *The Bible and the Greeks* (1935); C. S. Keener. *The Gospel of John* (2003); L. J. Kuyper. "Grace and Truth." *Int* 18 (1964) 3–19; J. Murphy-O'Connor. "Truth: Paul and Qumran." *Paul and Qumran* (1968) 179–230; R. R. Nicole. "The Biblical Concept of Truth." D. A. Carson and J. D. Woodbridge, eds. *Scripture and Truth* (1983) 287–302; A. G. Padgett, ed. *But Is It All True?* (2006); R. Schnackenburg. *The Gospel according to St. John* (1980); D. J. Theron. "Alētheia in the Pauline Corpus." *EQ* 26 (1954) 3–18.

IAN W. SCOTT

TRUTH, GOSPEL OF. The *Gospel of Truth* (NHC I, 3) is an early Christian sermon on the saving function of Jesus Christ. This 4th-cent. Coptic text is probably a translation of a Greek work known to Irenaeus (ca. 180 CE) as the Valentinian "Gospel of Truth" (*Haer.* 3.11.9). Sahidic fragments in NHC XII, 2 cannot be used to establish the text. Composed by a brilliant orator, the sermon describes how the Savior effects the transformation from ignorance to knowledge. Speaking in the first person at the conclusion of the sermon from a place of rest (*Gos. Truth* 43), the author enjoins listeners to be concerned about the Father of all and the true brothers. We learn little of the author or the implied audience. Through familiar Valentinian Christian topics—the Father, aeons, the Pleroma (fullness), deficiency, and rest—the sermon describes the role of Plane (Error) as a type of lower creator or Demiurge. The *Gospel of Truth* may have been directed to Christians inquiring about Valentinian teaching, comparable to the letter from a Valentinian teacher, Ptolemy, to Flora (Epiphanius, *Pan.* 33.3–7). It is difficult to determine whether the interests of the author or concerns of the listeners are reflected in the sermon's emphases. The author highlights truth as the spoken and written disclosure in which the Son is the name of the Father.

In the opening paragraph, the term *gospel* is explained as the result of a search for the Father: "The gospel of Truth is joy for those who have received from the Father of truth the grace of knowing him, through the power of the Word that came forth from the [Fullness] that was in the thought and mind of the Father and who is called the Savior, because that was the name of the work he was to perform for the redemption of those who were ignorant of the Father" (adapted from Attridge and MacRae). Those who embark on a search for the Father will rediscover their origins from the Father (Thomassen calls this a protological myth); their search is at one and the same time external and yet also contained within the Father. It is set in motion from the thought and mind of the Father through the naming implied in speech and word. Knowledge is dynamic, not static. Declaring the Son as the Father's name implies a movement of creation but not of separation.

The *Gospel of Truth* describes searching as both promise and ignorance. Ignorance generates agitation, fear, and its palpable effects. In such a climate, personified Error grows powerful, creating a material substance that shapes substitutes for the truth. Error's forms of forgetfulness and fear hold people captive and blind.

To overcome the fog of ignorance, forgetfulness must be annulled. Once knowledge of one's true origins in the heavenly realm is regained (such knowledge lies dormant in humanity), error ceases to exist as it has no root. As Savior, Jesus brings a way of truth and knowledge that awakens humanity's awareness of its identity as children of God. The Savior does this as speech, in that the Word teaches; as Light, in that he enlightens the way; as fruit of the Father's knowledge, in that he is eaten and the result is joy; as Book, in that he publishes the Father's edict on the cross in being nailed to a tree, thus overcoming fear and offering life for many.

When the Savior calls their names, the elect respond by turning to the one who calls. Now they know whence they come and where they are going. The analogy of the revealed book in which their names are written is not to a list of names read by someone but to names spoken aloud by each in recognition of true identity. Thus the elect are brought back "into the Father, the Mother, Jesus of the infinite gentleness" (*Gos. Truth* 24, 8), into the bosom that is the holy spirit. From a state of weary searching they attain a state of dynamic rest. The author plays with the external/internal dynamic of this search and muses out loud, "It is amazing that they were in the Father without knowing him, and that they were able to come forth by themselves, inasmuch as they were not able to perceive or recognize the one in whom they were" (*Gos. Truth* 22, 27-34). Such reflections should evoke gratitude from listeners.

It is the function of the Savior to transform the external search for knowledge into recognition by the saved that the Father contains the movement from ignorance to knowledge. This transformation eventually collapses any distinction between external and internal spheres. Because the Savior has become incarnate and has died on the cross in the external (cosmic) sphere, it ceases to exist. Thus, what happens at the end of the process becomes what exists implicitly in the Father at the beginning. The rest attained by enlightened ones at the end is what was in the Father's thought from the beginning.

Towards the end of the sermon, a paraenetic section exhorts listeners to follow the Savior's example as a way for the lost, knowledge for those who were ignorant, discovery for those who were searching, and support for those who were wavering. They are to speak of the truth with searchers, strengthen the feet of those who stumble, feed the hungry, give rest to the weary, and awaken those who sleep (*Gos. Truth* 31, 26-33, 32). Using imagery of an alluring fragrance, the children are drawn back to the Father. The sermon concludes with images of unity and rest.

Bibliography: Harold W. Attridge and George W. MacRae. "The Gospel of Truth (I,3 and XII,2)." *The Nag Hammadi Library in English.* James M. Robinson, ed. (1990); Bentley Layton. *The Gnostic Scriptures: A New Translation with Annotations and Introductions* (1987); Patricia Cox Miller. "'Words with an Alien Voice': Gnostics, Scripture and Canon." *JAAR* 57 (1989) 459–83; James M. Robinson. *The Nag Hammadi Library in English.* 4th ed. (1996); Einar Thomassen. *The Spiritual Seed: The Church of the Valentinians* (2006).

DEIRDRE GOOD

TRYPHAENA AND TRYPHOSA tri-fee´nuh, tri-foh´suh [Τρύφαινα Tryphaina, Τρυφῶσα Tryphōsa]. In Rom 16:12, Paul describes these women as "workers in the Lord." Elsewhere (e.g., 1 Cor 16:10) Paul uses similar language for Timothy's ministry, and his own. Evidently, Tryphaena and Tryphosa had prominent roles in the early church.

Both names are derived from a Greek root meaning "luxury," leading some to conclude that they were sisters. Both names occur in inscriptions, often as slave names. There were Ptolemaic queens named Tryphena, and the queen Tryphaena who befriended Thecla in the *Acts of Paul and Thecla* is attested by coins as a historical person.

JUDITH ANNE JONES

TRYPHO tri´foh [Τρύφων Tryphōn]. Nickname (meaning "luxurious") of Diodotus, a usurper who ruled the Seleucid kingdom from 142–138 BCE.

Trypho took advantage of the unpopularity of Demetrius II by bringing the child Antiochus VI forward as the "true" king. After capturing Antioch in 145 BCE, Trypho sought support from the Hasmoneans. They gave it, because Demetrius had previously betrayed them (1 Macc 11:52-59). Fearing Jonathan's growing power, Trypho captured and imprisoned him in Ptolemais (1 Macc 12:39-48; 13:12). Although Simon paid the ransom for Jonathan, Trypho killed him. At some point, Trypho also killed Antiochus VI and assumed the throne (1 Macc 13:19, 31).

The Parthians captured Demetrius II around 140 BCE, prompting his younger brother, Antiochus VII, to claim the throne. To gain Jewish support, he confirmed boons granted to the Hasmoneans earlier (1 Macc 15:1-9). Antiochus VII attacked Trypho. When Trypho's troops abandoned him, he committed suicide (Strabo, *Geogr.* 14.5.2).

ADAM L. PORTER

TRYPHOSA. *See* TRYPHAENA AND TRYPHOSA.

TSADE tsah´deh [צ ts, ץ ts]. The eighteenth letter of the Hebrew alphabet. *See* ALPHABET.

TSURRU. *See* TYRE.

TUBAL too´buhl [תֻּבָל tuval]. The fifth son of Japheth, son of Noah, listed in the Table of Nations (Gen 10:2; see also 1 Chr 1:5). His brothers include Gomer, MAGOG, Madai, JAVAN, MESHECH, and Tiras. The descendants of Japheth are located north of Israel, namely in Greece, Asia Minor, and Syria, but Tubal's exact location is unclear. Tubal is significant in the writings of Ezekiel as one of the nations that will be punished by God for threatening Israel. Specifically, Javan, Tubal, and Meshech are listed among the traders of slaves and vessels of bronze with Tyre, the city being lamented (Ezek 27:13). In an oracle against Egypt, the "uncircumcised" Tubal and Meshech are condemned because they spread terror (Ezek 32:26), and in an oracle against GOG of the land of Magog, Gog is described as the "chief prince of Meshech and Tubal," suggesting that Gog maintained the highest position among a regional group of leaders (Ezek 38:2-3; 39:1; *see* GOG AND MAGOG). In Isa 66:19, however, Tubal and Javan appear in a more positive context as distant places to which God will send messengers to declare God's grace and glory. Other nations mentioned here include Lud, "which draw[s] the bow." The LXX, in line with the texts in Ezekiel, revocalizes the epithet to read "Meshech."

MARK RONCACE

TUBAL-CAIN too´buhl-kayn´ [תּוּבַל קַיִן tuval qayin]. Son of LAMECH and ZILLAH, and the half-brother of JABAL, the ancestor of tent dwellers and herds, and JUBAL, the ancestor of lyre and pipe players. He also had a sister named NAAMAH. All three of them are mentioned in the genealogical notice concerning their father (Gen 4:19-22). Tubal-cain is associated with the origins of metalworking, specifically the manufacture of implements of bronze and iron. The verb translated as "made" in v. 22 (latash לָטַשׁ) commonly refers to the act of sharpening, leading many to suggest that Tubal-cain was crafting weapons.

The meaning of the name remains conjectural. Many associate the first part, *Tubal*, with a common Semitic root (ybl יבל) meaning "to bring," as with Jabal/Jubal in vv. 20-21; others regard it as the name of a territory, possibly Assyrian Tabal. *Cain* means "blacksmith."

The mention of Tubal-cain and his siblings in the genealogy of Lamech illustrates the origin of various aspects of human culture. The portrayal of the brothers as the individuals who introduced their crafts and trades to the world is reminiscent of the role attributed to the seven antediluvian sages (Akk. apkallū) of Mesopotamian mythology.

E. THEODORE MULLEN JR.

TUBAS. Modern name for the ancient fortified town of THEBEZ, located northeast of Shechem. Gideon's son Abimelech was killed there (Judg 9:50-57).

TUBEIQA, KHIRBET ET. A fortified ancient site, believed to be the biblical BETH-ZUR, about 20 mi.

south of Jerusalem and 3.5 mi. north of Hebron on the Jerusalem–Hebron road. Located on a conical hill at over 3,325 ft. above sea level, it is the highest city ruin in Palestine. Ideally situated to protect Jerusalem's southern approach, it was a prominent location for battles between the Ptolemies and Seleucids and later between the Maccabees and Seleucids. Although occupied in the Early and Middle Bronze and Iron ages, the site reached its zenith in the Second Temple period.

TERRY W. EDDINGER

TULEILAT EL-BATASHI. *See* BATASHI, TULEILAT EL.

TULEILAT EL-GHASSÛL. *See* GHASSÛL, TELEILÂT EL.

TUMORS [עֲפָלִים ʿofalim]. Swollen sores, inflicted by Yahweh on the Philistines after they captured the ark (1 Sam 5:6, 9, 12). To appease Yahweh, the Philistines offered gold tumors and mice (*see* MOUSE) as a sacrifice (6:4-5, 11, 17).

The QERE-KETHIBH tradition reads "hemorrhoids" (tekhorim טְחֹרִים) for "tumors," suggesting to some that the Philistines suffered dysentery. Others argue that the Philistines experienced the bubonic PLAGUE, which is carried by mice and produces swellings. Whatever their cause, in the biblical text the tumors are a sign of Yahweh's terrible power.

LISA MICHELE WOLFE

TUNIC [כֻּתֹּנֶת kuttoneth; χιτών chitōn]. An ankle-length linen garment worn next to the skin with a sash and a robe (Exod 28:39-40; Lev 8:7; Job 30:18). *See* CLOTH, CLOTHING.

TURBAN [מִצְנֶפֶת mitsnefeth]. A head covering for men made of cloth that was wrapped around the head. A turban was generally a sign of status and was worn by people of wealth or on special occasions, and could be a sign of office (Ezek 21:26 [Heb. 21:31]). Turbans are listed in Isa 3:23 as one of the pieces of finery that the Lord will remove from the people in the day of punishment.

Priests in ancient Israel were required to wear turbans made out of linen when they ministered before the Lord (Exod 28:4, 39). Wool garments were not allowed (Ezek 44:17). The turban, along with the other vestments, was placed on the priest at the time of his consecration (Lev 8:6-9). Priests were required to bathe before putting on the turban, TUNIC, and EPHOD (Lev 16:4). After serving in the Temple, the priests were to remove the vestments before going back out to the people, in order that the holiness of the garments would not be communicated to the people (Ezek 44:19). In Zech 3:1-5, when God takes away the sins of the high priest Joshua after the exile, Joshua is clothed in a new

turban to symbolize his cleansed status and his restoration to the priesthood.

KEVIN A. WILSON

TURQUOISE [נֹפֶךְ nofekh]. The fourth stone of the high priest's breastpiece (Exod 28:18; 39:11), an item of trade with Tyre (Ezek 27:16), and one of the gems of Eden adorning the king of Tyre (Ezek 28:13). Valued by the Egyptians but less so in Mesopotamia, turquoise was primarily used in jewelry. It is a semiprecious stone with a variety of tones ranging from green to blue.

ELIZABETH E. PLATT

TURTLEDOVE [יוֹנָה yonah, תּוֹר tor; τρυγών trygōn]. Any of several species of the genus *Streptopelia*, including *S. turtur*, a migratory dove (Jer 8:7) named for its purring call of "turrr turrr" (Song 2:12). Turtledoves (presumably domesticated, although wild birds are not explicitly prohibited) were among the animals used as burnt offerings (Lev 1:14) and were prescribed for various purification offerings (Lev 15:14, 29; Num 6:10). Those who could not afford more expensive animals could substitute a pair of turtledoves or pigeons as offerings for unintentional sins, for cleansing from leprosy, and for purification after childbirth (Lev 5:7; 12:6, 8; 14:21-32). Mary and Joseph's offering after Jesus' birth thus locates them among the poor (Luke 2:24). *See* BIRDS OF THE BIBLE; PIGEON.

JUDITH ANNE JONES

TWEIN, KHIRBET ABU EL. An Iron Age site located on the western slopes of the Hebron Hills. Excavations directed by Mazar revealed a large fortified building on a hilltop overlooking the Shephelah and coastal plain. The building had a central courtyard surrounded by large halls, some of them crossed by a row of monolithic pillars. A cistern was found nearby, and remains of a village comprising several scattered houses were located near the bottom of the hill. The pottery indicates that the building was founded during the 8th–7th cent. BCE and was probably abandoned after the fall of Judah in 586 BCE. A few pottery sherds dating to the Hellenistic period hint at a reuse during that period. The main building may be explained as a military stronghold or an administrative center. The excellent view to the west raises the possibility that this fortress was part of a chain of Iron Age fortresses and that one of their functions was to transfer fire signals through several points in the Judean mountains to Jerusalem.

Bibliography: Amihai Mazar. "Khirbet Abu et-Twein: An Israelite Fortress in the Hebron Hills." *PEQ* 114 (1982) 87–109.

AMIHAI MAZAR

TWELFTH BENEDICTION. The "twelfth berakhah" [בְּרָכָה, "blessing") in the Jewish *Shemoneh Esreh* (shemoneh ʿesreh שְׁמֹנֶה עֶשְׂרֵה; Eighteen [Benedictions]) is usually called *Birkat ha-minim* (birkhath hamminim בִּרְכַּת הַמִּינִים), "a blessing of the heretics," which is a euphemism for "a curse against the heretics." According to a possibly legendary rabbinic tradition, this curse was composed by Samuel ha-Qatan at the request of Rabban Gamaliel II in Yavneh (*see* JABNEH) by the end of the 1ˢᵗ cent. CE (*b. Ber.* 28b–29a). Unfortunately for those who would like to see it behind the reference to exclusion from the synagogue in John 9:22; 16:2, the text of this **berakhah** is never quoted in the early rabbinic sources. The earliest surviving versions of this text, in the prayer book of Rav Amram Gaon and in Genizah documents, do not pre-date the 9ᵗʰ cent. and also widely differ from each other. Hence, the original text is almost impossible to reconstruct. What seems certain, however, is that the following elements did occur in its earliest form: God is asked to see to it that there is no hope for the apostates, that the "heretics" (minim [מִינִין], from min [מִין], "sectarian," "apostate") will perish speedily, and that the arrogant (or the kingdom of the arrogant) will be humiliated. In most of the extant versions the curse is directed against the notsrim (נוֹצְרִים, "Christians") and minim ("heretics"), but it is improbable that the word **notsrim** was part of the original text, for in that case the curse would have become known as the *Birkat ha-notsrim* (birkhath hannotsrim [בִּרְכַּת הַנּוֹצְרִים], "blessing of the Christians"). The word **notsrim** was probably introduced into the text only during the 4ᵗʰ cent. CE, as is apparent from some Christian writings of the late 4ᵗʰ cent. (see Epiphanius, *Pan.* 29.9; Jerome, *Comm. Isa.* 5.18, *Epist.* 112.13). For that reason it is a matter of debate whether the introduction of the *Birkat ha-minim* should be related to the passages in the Gospel of John where Jesus' followers are said to be thrown out of the synagogue (John 9:22; 12:42; 16:2). Consequently, it is unlikely that such a curse played a major role in the schism between synagogue and church.

It seems highly probable that **minim** in Tannaitic times (the first two centuries CE) are always Jewish heretics. Even though it is improbable that the word **notsrim** (Christians) was part of the earliest version(s) of the twelfth benediction, it is certain that the development of the relations between Judaism and Christianity in the first two centuries (as far as we can trace them) was such that an increasing enmity created a climate in which mutual curses would have been a distinct possibility. That Jewish Christians were the primary target—or at least one of the targets—of this curse seems obvious. Further, it is probable that the curse had as its primary purpose to strengthen the unity within the Jewish people, since the lack of unity had proved so disastrous in the first war with the Romans. That the curse applied to Jewish Christians, aside from other "heretics" (the "apostates" and "arrogant"), is extremely likely also in view of other data about the relations between Christians and Jews in this period. The 2ⁿᵈ-cent. apologist Justin Martyr repeatedly states that Jews cursed the Christians in their synagogues (*Dial.* 16.4;

93.4; 95.4). Possibly Justin misunderstood a curse that was directed against Jewish Christians, among others, as referring to Christians in general. In the polemical situation in which Justin wrote, such a misunderstanding seems quite natural. For the situation at the end of the 4ᵗʰ cent., however, we can rely upon Jerome's testimony. That is to say that, probably not long before Jerome's time, notsrim, in the sense of Christians in general, was added to the twelfth benediction. The anti-Jewish measures taken by the Roman government, which was a Christian government by that time, made such a development well-nigh unavoidable. So in all likelihood it was only in the course of the 4ᵗʰ cent. (probably the second half) that the rapidly deteriorating relations between Christianity and the government on the one hand, and Judaism on the other, eventually led to the insertion of the curse against Christians in general into the Eighteen Benedictions. This curse is not the cause but the effect of the ever-growing estrangement between the two religions. The original *Birkat ha-minim*, however, was a curse that served to strengthen the bonds of unity within the Jewish nation in a time of catastrophe by deterring all those who threatened that unity. *See* BENEDICTION; BLESSINGS AND CURSINGS; CHRISTIAN-JEWISH RELATIONS; EXCOMMUNICATION.

Bibliography: Daniel Boyarin. *Border Lines: The Partition of Judaeo-Christianity* (2004); William Horbury. "The Benediction of the *Minim* and Early Jewish-Christian Controversy." *JTS* n.s. 33 (1982) 19–61. Pieter W. van der Horst. "The Birkat ha-minim in Recent Research." *Hellenism–Judaism–Christianity: Essays on Their Interaction* (1998) 113–24; Reuven Kimelman. "Birkat ha-minim and the Lack of Evidence for an Anti-Christian Jewish Prayer in Late Antiquity." *Jewish and Christian Self-Definition II: Aspects of Judaism in the Graeco-Roman World.* E. P. Sanders, ed. (1981) 226–44 and 391–403; Lawrence H. Schiffman. *Who Was a Jew? Rabbinic and Halakhic Perspectives on the Jewish-Christian Schism* (1985); Yaakov Y. Teppler. *Birkat haMinim: Jews and Christians in Conflict in the Ancient World* (2007).

PIETER W. VAN DER HORST

TWELVE [שְׁנֵים עָשָׂר shenem ʿasar; δώδεκα dōdeka]. Beginning with the progeny in Genesis, the number twelve is important throughout the Bible. In a parallel with the later Jacob, Ishmael is blessed as the father of twelve princes (Gen 17:20; 25:16). Shortly after Jacob's name is changed to Israel (Gen 35:9-15; compare Gen 32:22-32), his twelve sons are listed (Gen 35:22-29). These sons are first called "the twelve tribes of Israel" (Gen 49:28) when they receive their final blessing. Beyond the foundation stories in Genesis, biblical writers employ the number twelve in various ways to symbolize Israel as God's people. At the covenant's ratification, for instance, Moses sets up twelve stones to stand for the tribes (Exod 24:4; compare Josh 4:1-7). Similarly, the priestly breastplate must have twelve stones with a tribal name on each (Exod 28:21; 39:14). In a list that replaces Levi with Manasseh, twelve tribal representatives are chosen for the first census (Num 1:44; compare Deut 1:23).

This pattern of selecting twelve persons or things to represent the nation includes twelve loaves for the tabernacle (Lev 24:5) and several sets of twelve items offered for the tabernacle's dedication (Num 7:84-88; compare Num 17:1-13). Likewise, David creates twelve military divisions with 24,000 soldiers in each (1 Chr 27:1-15), and Solomon devises twelve districts overseen by twelve administrators (1 Kgs 4:7-19). Multiples of twelve also appear, such as forty-eight Levitical cities (Num 35:6-8) and the organization of priests and musicians into twenty-four divisions, respectively (1 Chr 24:1-19; 25:1-31). In addition, twelve and its multiples are used more broadly to symbolize divine presence. In Esther, e.g., Haman's plot develops when the lot is cast in the first month of the king's twelfth year. It sets a date for annihilation of Jews on the thirteenth day of the twelfth month (Esth 3:7). Accordingly, Purim is celebrated in that month (Esth 3:7, 13; 8:12-14; 9:16-19). Likewise, Ezekiel receives God's word on the month's twelfth day (29:1), in the twelfth year's twelfth month (32:1), and in the exile's twelfth year (32:17; 33:21).

This broader symbolic use continues in the NT. Luke depicts Jesus at age twelve challenging Torah scholars in Jerusalem after Passover (Luke 2:41-42). Jesus heals a woman who has suffered for twelve years (Matt 9:20; Mark 5:25; Luke 8:43) and restores life to a twelve-year-old girl (Mark 5:42). Similarly, after Jesus feeds the 5,000, twelve baskets of food are left over (Matt 14:20; Mark 6:43; Luke 9:17). The symbolism that links *twelve* with God's people is retained in the NT. Jesus selects twelve from among his followers to be his closest disciples (Matt 10:1-4; Mark 3:13-19; Luke 6:12-16; Acts 1:12-26). These twelve represent a transformative restoration for Israel; they will sit on twelve thrones judging the twelve tribes (Matt 19:28; Luke 22:30). Both types of symbolism are evident in Revelation. John sees twenty-four elders around God's throne (Rev 4:4; 5:8; 11:16; 19:4). God's people are also represented by the vision of 144,000, with 12,000 from each of Israel's tribes (Rev 7:4-8).

JOSEPH F. SCRIVNER

TWELVE, THE [οἱ δώδεκα hoi dōdeka]. The Gospels describe the Twelve as disciples whom Jesus chose to accompany him during his ministry and to whom he gave authority to preach, to heal, and to cast out demons (Matt 10:1-3; Mark 3:14-19; Luke 6:13-16; 9:1-2). In Mark and Luke they are selected from among a larger group and are usually identified simply as "the Twelve," without the addition of "disciples" or "apostles" (*see* APOSTLE; DISCIPLE, DISCIPLESHIP). The number represents

the twelve tribes of Israel (Matt 19:28; Luke 22:30). Acts recounts the selection of Judas' replacement, Matthias, who was qualified to join the eleven as a witness to the resurrection because he was among those who accompanied Jesus from the time of John the Baptist until the ascension (1:15-26). The Twelve play a less significant role in John than in the Synoptic Gospels, but the evangelist evidently assumes that readers already know about them, since he mentions them without introduction or explanation in John 6:67, 70-71; and 20:24. Paul says that the resurrected Jesus appeared to the Twelve (1 Cor 15:5). According to Revelation, their names are written on the twelve foundations of the new Jerusalem (21:14).

The precise identity of the Twelve is disputed. All the Synoptics list the Twelve in three groups, with the same names heading each group of four: Simon (Peter), Philip, and James son of Alphaeus. All the lists include Andrew, James and John, Bartholomew, Thomas, Matthew, and Judas. The lists disagree regarding the remaining two names. John identifies no one but Thomas as belonging to the Twelve, but he mentions all the above disciples except Bartholomew and Matthew. The question whether the Twelve existed as a group during the historical ministry of Jesus is a matter of some debate, with obvious significance for conclusions about Jesus' self-understanding and the eschatological character of his ministry. *See* MINISTRY, CHRISTIAN.

JUDITH ANNE JONES

TWENTY. *See* NUMBERS, NUMBERING.

TWILIGHT [בֵּין הָעַרְבָּיִם ben ha'arbayim, נֶשֶׁף neshef]. This is a term that probably refers to dusk, the time between the setting of the sun and darkness. Every instance in the Pentateuch represents a form of the two words bayin 'erev (בֵּין עֶרֶב), literally meaning "between evenings," while neshef is the Hebrew term for twilight in the rest of the OT. Twilight is often the prerequisite for performing a sacrifice at an appointed time, most notably the original Passover and its remembrance (Exod 12:6; Lev 23:5; Num 9:3, 5, 11). Twilight is also a favorable time to besiege an enemy due to the decrease in natural light (e.g., 1 Sam 30:17; 2 Kgs 7:5). In the same vein, it represents a time when evil and sin more frequently take place (e.g., Job 24:15; Prov 7:6-9) and represents an appropriate time for God's judgment (e.g., Jer 13:16). *See* DAY, NT; DAY, OT; LIGHT AND DARKNESS; NIGHT.

STEVEN D. MASON

TWINS [תְּאֹם ta'am, תּוֹאִם to'am; Δίδυμος Didymos, Θωμᾶς Thōmas]. Twin gods are pervasive in ancient pantheons. In ANE and Greco-Roman texts appear Uta and Inanna (Sumer), Aegyptus and Danaus (Egypt), Shahar and Shalim (Ugarit), Artemis and Apollo (Greece), and Romulus and Remus (Rome). The birth of twins to the gods demonstrates divine fertility, though each pair functions differently in the respective theogonies. The birth of human twins, however, was often viewed as abnormal, sometimes as a sign of adversity. This is especially evident in Mesopotamian birth omens (see OMEN).

The words translated "twin" or "twins" have relatively few appearances in the Bible. Perhaps the best-known occurrence is the story about the birth of Esau and Jacob to Isaac and Rebekah (Gen 25:24). These eponymous twins wrestle even before birth, foreshadowing longstanding conflict between Israel (Jacob) and Edom (Esau). Of course, beginning with his purchase of the birthright from his older brother, Jacob has the upper hand (see ESAU, ESAUITES; JACOB). A lesser-known birth of twins transpires when Judah impregnates Tamar (Gen 38:27). Just as Jacob usurps Esau's place, Tamar's younger twin, Perez, proves more significant in Israel's history, because King David's Judahite lineage proceeds through him (see Ruth 4:18-22; compare Matt 1:3). In both cases, twins are born at crucial points in the narrative, and one of the twins becomes an important progenitor.

DIDYMUS (Didymos) is an alternate name for THOMAS (from Hebrew to'am or Aramaic the'oma' [תְּאוֹמָא]), one of Jesus' twelve disciples. Though he is mentioned in the Synoptic Gospels (Matt 10:3; Mark 3:18; Luke 6:15), only John informs the reader that he is called "Twin" or "Didymus" (John 11:16; 20:24; 21:2). Since the evangelist does not identify a sibling for Thomas, later tradition fills the void with various speculations.

From the tradition that Judas was one of Jesus' brothers (Mark 6:3), a tradition arose in Syria that Judas was Jesus' twin, and thus he is called "Judas Thomas" or "Jude, the Twin" (e.g., Acts Thom. 15.31).

The term twin also occurs in Luke's description of Paul's journey to Rome. Luke portrays Paul sailing on "an Alexandrian ship with the Twin Brothers as its figurehead" (Acts 28:11). The phrase "Twin Brothers" translates a Greek title, Dioskouroi (Διόσκουροι), which is the name for Castor and Pollux—the twin sons of Zeus—protectors of sailors, who appear in mythology as bright stars of the Gemini constellation and are associated with the meteorological phenomenon known as "Saint Elmo's fire."

JOSEPH F. SCRIVNER

TWISTED LINEN [שֵׁשׁ מָשְׁזָר shesh moshar]. LINEN is a fiber obtained from the FLAX plant. In the manufacture of linen thread for weaving, the ends of flax fibers were twisted together prior to spinning several strands together. The technique was known in ancient Egypt, and the women who had been slaves in Egypt would have been proficient in the manufacture of linen. Twined linen is used for the material of the tabernacle and priestly vestments (Exod 26:1, 31, 36; 27:9-18; 28:6-8, 15; 36:8, 35-38; 38:16, 18; 39:22-29).

MARY PETRINA BOYD

TWO. See NUMBERS, NUMBERING.

TYCHICUS tik'uh-kuhs [Τυχικός Tychikos]. According to Acts 20:4, Tychicus was one of two "Asians" (the other was TROPHIMUS) who accompanied Paul for at least part of the final journey from Ephesus through Macedonia and Achaia and on to Jerusalem (Acts 19:21–21:17). It is likely that Tychicus and Trophimus undertook this journey as representatives of the Asian churches in the collection for the poor in Jerusalem (1 Cor 16:1-4).

The only other references to Tychicus are in the disputed letters of Paul. In Col 4:7-9, Paul commends Tychicus to the Colossians, sending him (together with Onesimus) with news of Paul and his companions, words of encouragement, and (probably) the letter itself. In Eph 6:21-22, verses in which extensive verbatim borrowing from Colossians is apparent, Tychicus is again commended as a bearer of encouragement, news, and (probably) the letter. In Titus 3:12, Paul informs Titus that he intends to send either Artemas or Tychicus to Crete where Titus is residing, and that upon the arrival of either, Titus is to come to Paul at Nicopolis. The implication is that Artemas or Tychicus will take Titus' place in the leadership of the churches in Crete. Similarly in 2 Timothy, Paul summons Timothy (4:9) and sends Tychicus to Ephesus (4:12), perhaps as his replacement. Hence all the letters that mention Tychicus, be they Pauline or deuteropauline, portray him as a trusted emissary of Paul and an important leader in Paul's churches, a portrait consistent with Acts.

MICHAEL W. MARTIN

TYCONIUS, RULES OF. The Donatist rhetor and exegete Tyconius (d. ca 390 CE) was arguably the most original biblical interpreter in the church of North Africa. Only his Book of Rules survives, together with extensive fragments of his full commentary on Revelation. In the Book of Rules, Tyconius sets out to provide keys or "lamps" for understanding the logic of the seven "mystical rules" with which the Holy Spirit has sealed the scriptures. If one follows the logic of the rules of the Spirit, what is hidden in the recesses of scripture will be revealed. The seven rules are: On the Lord and His Body; On the Lord's Bipartite Body; On the Promises and the Law; On Species and Genus; On Times; On Recapitulation; On the Devil and His Body.

Denounced by his fellow Donatists for his understanding of the Church as inclusive of both saints and sinners, Tyconius influenced AUGUSTINE, who agreed that there should be no separation of sinners until the judgment (Matt 13:24-30). The most fateful moment for the reception of Tyconius was Augustine's extensive summary and commentary on the Book of Rules in Doctr. chr. 3.

Bibliography: W. S. Babcock. *Tyconius: The Book of Rules* (1989); P. Bright. *The Book of Rules: Its Purpose* and *Inner Logic* (1988); C. Kannengiesser. *Handbook of Patristic Exegesis* (2004) 1139–48.

PAMELA BRIGHT

TYPOLOGY t*i*-pol´uh-jee [τύπος typos]. The word typos denotes a mark left by a blow (compare John 20:25, where typos refers to the mark of the nails in Jesus' hands) or the impression of a seal on wax. For Philo (*Ebr.* 31) typos is something that mediates between heavenly ideas and earthly copies. In theology, the term *typology* describes a study of continuity between the OT and the NT through *types* of events that are seen to foreshadow and give historical meaning to events in the NT. For example, the twelve tribes of Israel are types for the twelve disciples of Jesus. Jonah's experience of three days and nights in the belly of the great fish (Jon 1:17) is a type for Jesus in the tomb (compare Luke 11:29). The Jewish festivals are types for "the things to come" in Christ (Col 2:16-17). One could speak of typology as an "analogy of events," as opposed to ALLEGORY, which is about the analogy of words.

Typology is already found in the OT, e.g., where Isaiah uses imagery from the exodus event—God making a way through the sea, the destruction of the chariots, and the escape to the wilderness (Exod 14–15)—to capture the theme of a new exodus for the Jews who were in captivity in Babylon (Isa 43:14-21).

A NT use of the exodus imagery appears in 1 Cor 10:1-11. Paul uses the story of Moses hitting a rock to make water come out (Exod 17:6; Num 20:10-11) as a type for the spiritual rock, which is Christ. In this passage, typoi (τύποι) refers not only to Moses or the rock, but rather to "these things" (tauta ταῦτα)—the events that unfolded around the people's ongoing complaints and immorality as they wandered in the desert. "Now these things occurred as an example for us, so that we might not desire evil, as they did" (1 Cor 10:6). Thus the wilderness experience of Israel is interpreted for the church as dealing with discipline, not punishment.

New Testament authors also use fulfillment of prophecy to interpret OT events that prefigure the NT. The early church believed that Jesus fulfilled a role already set out in the history of the covenant people (e.g., Matt 1:23; 2:5-6, 17-18; 4:14-16; 11:10; 12:15-21; Luke 4:16-19).

A well-known typology is Christ as "second Adam." The first or original Adam who sinned and brought death (Gen 1–3) is the "type of the one ... to come" (Rom 5:14), who is Jesus Christ, the one without sin who brings life (*see* SECOND ADAM). The Adam–Christ typology involves antitype (antitypos [ἀντίτυπος], meaning a "copy" or "counterpart") that describes a relationship of opposition yet similarity between two things, the type and antitype. Irenaeus (*Haer.* 1.5.6; 1.24.3) defines antitypos as a copy of the real; thus the real (often spiritual or heavenly thing) is the type and the copy (often an earthly, material thing) is the antitype. *Second Clement* 14.3–4 provides this example:

the flesh is an antitype of the Spirit, and no one who corrupts the flesh (antitype) shall receive the Spirit (type). In 1 Pet 3:18-21, the antitypos is the ark of Noah that passes through the water and saves only a few people from the flood (Gen 7–8). Baptism is the heavenly type, as people pass through the waters of baptism to join in the resurrection of Christ. In Hebrews, the Temple is an antitype for the heavenly temple (Heb 9:24). Hebrews and Revelation use the city of Jerusalem as antitype for the heavenly Jerusalem (Heb 12:22-24; Rev 21:2, 9-27; compare Ezek 40–47; *see* NEW JERUSALEM). Through the Middle Ages the tabernacle was seen as a mystical presence in the church. To illustrate this concept, at the Bamberg Cathedral the carved apostles stand on the shoulders of prophets (Ohly).

For the purposes of application, Christ (as fulfillment of the OT) becomes a type for Christians. However, there is a loss of typology in modern times, when the NT text is interpreted as the experience of the self and loses its anchoring in the OT. By losing this anchoring to the OT as *type*, the NT loses some of it distinctive history of salvation. The beginning and the end of text is story, but it is story that draws us into historical reality. *See* RHETORICAL CRITICISM, NT; RHETORICAL CRITICISM, OT.

Bibliography: David Dawson. *Christian Figural Reading and the Fashioning of Identity* (2001); L. Goppelt. *Typos: The Typological Interpretation of the Old Testament in the New* (1981); G. W. H. Lampe and K. J. Woollcombe. *Essays on Typology* (1957); Julia Reinhard Lupton. *Afterlives of the Saints: Hagiography, Typology, and Renaissance Literature* (1996); E. Miner, ed. *Literary Uses of Typology from the Late Middle Ages to the Present* (1977); F. Ohly. "Synagoge und Ecclesia: Typologisches in Mittelalterlicger Dichtung." *Schriften zur mittelalterlichen Bedeutungsforschung* (1977) 312–37; John J. O'Keefe. "'A Letter that Killeth': Toward a Reassessment of Antiochene Exegesis, or Diodore, Theodore, and Theodoret on the Psalms." *JECS* 8 (2000) 83–104; Christopher Seitz. *Figured Out: Typology and Providence in Christian Scripture* (2001).

MARK W. ELLIOTT

TYRANNUS, HALL OF t*i*-ran´uhs [σχολὴ Τυράννου scholē Tyrannou]. Paul removed his students from the hostility of the Ephesian synagogue and began to lecture in the scholē ("lecture hall") of Tyrannus (Acts 19:8-9). Scholē usually means "leisure" or "something done during leisure" but can also refer to a "school" of teacher and students or a building for teaching (Plutarch, *Mor.* 42a). Many understand the text to mean that Paul leased the lecture hall from someone with the common name Tyrannus.

Western witnesses read at the end of Acts 19:9: "scholē of a certain Tyrannus from the seventh hour to the tenth" (author's trans.; NRSV offers the reading in a footnote: "lecture hall of a certain Tyrannus, from eleven o'clock in the morning to four in the afternoon"). Several interpreters prefer this text because it suggests that Paul used the hall during the normal time of midday rest in Ephesus. The textual evidence against this reading, however, is weighty.

Discovery of the Greek word meaning "auditorium" (audeitōrion αὐδειτώριον) in a pavement inscription near the Library of Celsus at Ephesus has no clear bearing on Acts 19:9. Despite speculation to the contrary, nothing connects the inscription to Paul or to the scholē of Tyrannus.

Bibliography: C. J. Hemer. "Audeitorion." *TynBul* 24 (1973) 128.

FRED L. HORTON

TYRE *tír* [צוֹר tsor; Τύρος Tyros]. An important Phoenician island city just off the coast of southern Lebanon, about 80 km (50 mi.) south of Beirut. Since the time of its siege by Alexander the Great in 332 BCE, the island site has been connected to the mainland as a peninsula (the result of a mole or causeway Alexander constructed using debris from the mainland in order to subjugate the city, with later sand deposits from sea currents widening the isthmus). Tyre's present Arabic name Tsur clearly attests Tyre's historic name (akin to the word tsur [צוֹר], "rock," in Hebrew). Nearly continuously occupied since the middle of the 3rd millennium BCE, Tyre and its wealth and beauty became proverbial in both classical and ANE literature. References to Tyre also appear some forty times in the OT, often in contexts of condemning materialism and pride. In any case, Tyre, "queen of the seas," represents one of the most significant historical sites in the entire Mediterranean littoral; as the prophet Ezekiel acknowledged, "your borders are in the heart of the seas; your builders made perfect your beauty" (Ezek 27:4).

The EBLA TEXTS of the 3rd millennium (ca. 2500–2300 BCE) already attest Tyre's existence, although the city of Byblos in northern Lebanon represented the principal Mediterranean trading port during this time. Archaeological soundings by Patricia Bikai in Tyre proper uncovered pottery sequences datable to ca. 2700 BCE, up through 700 BCE, with the only significant gap occurring at the end of the Early Bronze Age (ca. 2000 BCE) when the island city was apparently abandoned (this was also the case for Byblos).

By the Late Bronze Age (ca. 1550–1200 BCE), the cities of Ugarit, Byblos, and Tyre formed part of the great Mediterranean trading networks that linked Egypt, Asia Minor, Syria-Palestine, and Mesopotamia. The AMARNA LETTERS (ca. 1350 BCE) include correspondences from Abi-Milki, king of Tyre, addressed to Pharaoh Amenophis IV. We find the city of Tyre described as a monarchy, enjoying a measure of prestige and political influence, and with a "satellite city" on the mainland named Ushu (curiously referenced in the

classical Greek and Roman texts as "Palaeotyre," meaning "Old Tyre"). The location of Ushu is uncertain, but presumably lies close to the island-city. In any case, literary sources attest that Ushu provided water and food for the island city throughout much of its history, except during times of war. This was also the time when the so-called "purple industry" began to flourish, extracting a rich, reddish-purple pigment from marine snails found in the region. Indeed, many scholars suggest that the etymology of the name *Phoenician* ("purple-ites," possibly from phoinos [φοινός], "red") derives from this industry (the Semitic term *Canaanite* [kena'ani כְּנַעֲנִי] in turn, probably means "merchant" [kena'an כְּנַעַן] or the like, in reference to the trading proclivities of these Phoenicians).

The end of the Bronze Age in Canaan brought widespread examples of violence and sociopolitical upheaval throughout the region. Ugarit in northern Syria was completely abandoned at this time (ca. 1200 BCE), and Tyre suffered symptoms of decline and interruption of industrial activities (although indications of its outright destruction remain less than clear). The arrival of the so-called Sea Peoples from the Aegean region (including the biblical Philistines) probably contributed significantly to this, as well as the arrival of the "Israelites" into the hill-country of Canaan during the period of Joshua and the judges.

For the Iron Age, we have virtually no direct sources from Phoenicia; all inferences are from foreign, often hostile, textual traditions. Whether in Assyrian annals, biblical texts such as Samuel or Kings, or the later recollections of the classical Greek and Roman writers, the city of Tyre reappears in a big way. Probably as the result of King David's victories over the PHILISTINES as recorded in the books of Samuel, the Phoenician port cities were free once again to develop their trading economies, largely to the west. It is likely that as the result of inland Philistine, Israelite, and especially Aramean pressures from the east, the territory of "Canaan" proper was reduced to one-tenth of its original size, necessitating nautical expansion to the west. In any case, sources clearly attest remarkable Phoenician trading efforts throughout the entire Mediterranean region during the early centuries of the 1st millennium BCE, with Tyre once again playing the major role. Already in the 10th cent. BCE, trade between Tyre and its colony of Kition in Cyprus (near present-day Larnaka) was widespread, and the search for new sources of metal eventually led to Phoenician trading colonies in Asia Minor, as well as in North Africa, Sicily, and Sardinia, and even the silver mines of Spain. The city of Carthage (Canaanite "Qart-Khadasht" or "New Town") in present day Tunisia, North Africa, is undoubtedly the best known Tyrian colony in Greco-Roman times, and classical writers take pains to date its founding to either 814 or 825 BCE.

The Tyrian "golden age," however, must be dated back to the 10th cent. BCE, with the accession of HIRAM I to the throne (ca. 980 BCE). Friend to both kings David and Solomon of Israel (see below), this king apparently built no less than three lavish temples in Tyre. Two freestanding pillars next to the temple of Heracles, which also appear on an Assyrian relief, are reminiscent of the two pillars in front of Solomon's temple (1 Kgs 7:21). H. Jacob Katzenstein has suggested that the reign of ETHBAAL I (ca. 878–847 BCE) represented a second "golden age" in Tyre's history. By now, Tyre and SIDON had become a single political entity, and Ethbaal ("Baal is with him") had succeeded in re-establishing his dominion over the entire southern territory of Phoenicia (JEZEBEL, his daughter, was married to King Ahab of Israel). By this time, the city of Tyre had two harbors: the original northern harbor known as the "Sidonian port," as well as a later, artificial harbor to the south known as the "Egyptian port." Indeed, Tyrian influence was felt not only in the northern kingdom of Israel but even in the southern kingdom of Judah, e.g., with the marriage of ATHALIAH, daughter of Ahab and Jezebel, to Jehoram of Judah. It is not surprising, therefore, that Baal worship grew even more prevalent in both Israelite kingdoms, to the strong consternation of the biblical prophets.

Eventually, however, the rise of the Neo-Assyrian Empire to the east helped put an end to such strong Tyrian influence. By repeated payment of tribute, Tyre and the other Phoenician cities were largely spared direct conquest (they also served as an effective counterweight to Assyria's great rival, Egypt), but by the late 8th cent. BCE, Tyrian trade autonomy was mostly a thing of the past. And by the time of Nebuchadnezzar, the Neo-Babylonian ruler, Tyre's monarchy came to an abrupt end, as the prophet Ezekiel had predicted. During the 6th and 5th cent. BCE, Sidon took over prominence in international trade until Alexander the Great's conquest of Phoenicia (as well as most of the then-known world) in the 330s.

Often, biblical references to Tyre represent geographical markers, nothing more. This is the case in the repeated references to "Hiram king of Tyre" in 2 Samuel and 1 Kings (and their parallels in 1–2 Chronicles). Perhaps, however, one could argue that Hiram's influence over Solomon was seen as negative by the writers of Kings (compare 1 Kgs 11). Whatever the case, we are told that Hiram helped build David his palace (2 Sam 5:11), and he is ready to help Solomon build the temple, providing cedar and cypress timber, gold, metalworkers, and other materials (1 Kgs 5:1 [Heb. 5:15]; 7:13-14; 9:11). In 1 Kgs 9, Hiram receives twenty Galilean cities as payment for his services, but after inspecting them he expresses disappointment as to their worth (1 Kgs 9:12-13; the parallel in 2 Chr 8:1-2 is less critical of Solomon).

Jeremiah's three scattered references to Tyre and its kings (25:22; 27:3; 47:4) are parts of larger lists of foreign leaders, relatively neutral in scope, in sharp distinction to Jeremiah's younger counterpart, Ezekiel (see below). Passing references to Tyre in 1 and 2 Maccabees (1 Macc 5:15; 11:59; 2 Macc 4:18, 32, 44, 49), and in the NT Gospels and Acts also generally fit this category

(indeed, Jesus speaks somewhat positively of "Tyre and Sidon" in Matt 11:21-22; Luke 10:13-14).

Condemnatory references to Tyre are found in Joel 3:4 [Heb. 4:4]; in Amos 1:9-10; and in Zech 9:2-3. In Amos and Joel, Tyre is accused of social sin (enslaving peoples), and of ostentatious wealth in Zechariah. But it is in Isa 23, and especially in Ezek 26–28, where Tyre infamously symbolizes proud, willful opposition to the God of Israel, and where its inevitable doom is celebrated at length. In the complicated oracle in Isa 23, Tyre (along with Sidon, Cyprus, and other Phoenician locations) comes under condemnation because of pride and materialism. But in the end (23:17-18), it is Tyre specifically who will be restored to former glory, and though likened to a prostitute, Tyre's wages will soon be dedicated to Yahweh.

Once again, it is the prophet Ezekiel who most notably holds up Tyre to condemnation, and he goes to great rhetorical lengths to do so. In three lengthy sections (Ezek 26:1-21; 27:1-36; 28:1-19), along with a curious postscript at the end of an oracle against Egypt (29:17-21), this 6th-cent. prophet gives us the most colorful imagery of Tyre to be found anywhere in the Bible. With detailed maritime and commercial references (part of chap. 27 may have been taken from a cargo list; see CANNEH), Ezekiel relentlessly pictures Tyre as a doomed city in the hands of Nebuchadnezzar, just as Jerusalem had been (26:2, 7), richly deserving of (satirical) lamentation as if dead already (27:25*b*-36). Indeed, Tyre is already "cast down to the ground" from the Edenic mountain of God, just as the rebellious astral deities had been in times past (28:12*b*-19; compare Isa 14:12-15). Striking nautical images pervade Ezekiel's poetry: e.g., 27:3*b*-11 pictures Tyre in glorious detail as a great ocean-going vessel, "perfect in beauty." The postscript in chap. 29, however, is more prosaic. Nebuchadnezzar's siege of Tyre may have lasted some thirteen years; and Ezekiel's oracle suggests he and his army were disappointed with the meager results after all that effort (presumably the Tyrians had been able to carry off much of their wealth by sea). In any case, the "wealth of Egypt" would more than make up for all that Babylonian labor against Tyre—those who execute Yahweh's judgment may be sure that they will be properly paid one way or the other.

Bibliography: Maria Eugenia Aubet. *The Phoenicians and the West* (1987); William Hamilton Barnes. "The Tyrian King List." *Studies in the Chronology of the Divided Monarchy of Israel* (1991) 29–55; Patricia M. Bikai. *The Pottery of Tyre* (1978); H. Jacob Katzenstein. *The History of Tyre.* Rev ed. (1997).

WILLIAM HAMILTON BARNES

TYRE, LADDER OF tír [κλîμαξ Τύρου klimax Tyrou]. The location constituting the northern boundary of the territory over which the Seleucid king ANTIOCHUS VI is said to have appointed SIMON Maccabeus governor

(1 Macc 11:59). Josephus locates it 100 stadia to the north of Acre and states that it has the highest elevation in Galilee and Carmel (*J.W.* 2.188), although no location in the area rises to as high an elevation as that of Carmel. Some suggest that a series of ridges that rises from the Mediterranean Sea along the coastline between Acre and Tyre forms the Ladder of Tyre.

DEREK E. WITTMAN

TYROPOEON VALLEY ti-roh´pee-uhn [Τυροποιῶν φάραγξ Tyropoiōnpharanx]. Meaning "Cheesemakers' Valley." Josephus (*J.W.* 5.140) apparently named this central valley, which ran north–south through the old city of Jerusalem, for cheesemakers. Passing along the western side of the Temple Mount and Ophel, it ended at the pools of Siloam. At least one bridge, Wilson's Arch, the key route to the Temple, crossed over a Herodian street arrayed with shops and situated in the valley floor. Today the valley is called "el-Wad."

LJUBICA JOVANOVIC

TZADDI. *See* TSADE.

Uu

UBAID, AL. Tell al-Ubaid, approximately 4 mi. from Ur, exhibits the quintessence of Mesopotamian material culture prior to the advent of writing, lending its name to the period lasting from ca. 6200–3800 BCE. It also contains the remnants of an elaborately decorated temple complex unparalleled in Sumer during the mid-3rd millennium. *See* SUMER, SUMERIANS.

JASON R. TATLOCK

UCAL yoo´kuhl [אֻכָל ʾukhal]. One of the two designated recipients, along with Ithiel, of the teaching of Agur (Prov 30:1). It seems reasonable to assume that he was one of Agur's students. The meaning of the verse in the Hebrew text is unclear, and it is possible that Ithiel and Ucal are not proper names at all. The word translated "and Ucal" may actually be a verb. In that case, it would be rendered "and I cease" (from klh [כלה]), which corresponds to the reading in the LXX (pauomai παύομαι), or possibly "and I am consumed" (from ʾkl [אכל]).

DEREK E. WITTMAN

UDUM. A location in the Ugaritic legend of Keret. The god El appears to King Keret in a dream and instructs him to wage a military campaign against Udum and to claim as his bride Hurriya, the daughter of Udum's king, Pabel. *See* KIRTU, KERET, KIRTA, EPIC OF.

UEL yoo´uhl [אוּאֵל ʾuʾel]. One of the descendants of BANI who divorced his foreign wife as part of Ezra's postexilic reforms (Ezra 10:34). The name is peculiar and may be a corrupted or shortened form. The parallel text in 1 Esd 9:34 lists Joel instead. Bani can be assumed to be the BINNUI of Neh 7:15; thus Uel was part of a family who returned from exile under Zerubbabel.

MARK RONCACE

UGARIT, HISTORY AND ARCHAEOLOGY oo´guh-rit. The city-state of Ugarit, modern Tell Ras Shamra ("Fennel Mound"), is located along the Syrian coast of the Mediterranean Sea. The importance of Ugarit for understanding both the culture of ancient Israel and its language is substantial; in the ruins of the ancient city was discovered an abundance of clay cuneiform tablets written in a Semitic language related to Hebrew. These texts describe an earlier political, religious, and social West Semitic world of which ancient Israel was also part.

Ugarit's site and surrounding environs were inhabited nearly continuously for 5,000 years, lasting from the 7th millennium BCE in the Neolithic period until its ultimate and total destruction at the beginning of the 12th cent. BCE. Its longevity was not by chance; bounded by the Mediterranean Sea to the west and the Alouite Mountains to the east, the coastal plain encompassing Ugarit was ideal for agriculture in a region with relatively little arable land. Abundant rainfall (average annual rainfall of more than 800 mm), along with two streams that ran along the north and south of the tell, provided adequate water for both the city and its farmers, and behind the dense forests of the eastern mountain range the more arid steppe provided room for grazing and animal husbandry. The yield of this fertile plain included grains, olive oil, wine, precious wood, linen, and wool, much of which, as Ugarit gained prominence in international commerce, was used as exports. Particularly coveted by Ugarit's trading partners were the fine woolen clothes produced in the city and dyed with shades of purple colored by crushed MUREX shells found on Ugarit's shores. Ugarit's most significant natural resource, however, was not one located on land. Located 800 m from the city, a natural harbor—today called Minet el-Beida or "White Harbor" for its distinctive white cliffs—provided Ugarit with access to the sea so critical for its economy and prosperity. A short distance by boat to both Cyprus and the southern coast of modern-day Turkey, Ugarit was also a crucial maritime center for goods traveling between Mesopotamia and the Aegean world.

The city of Ugarit was discovered by chance when in 1928 a Syrian farmer inadvertently struck a large stone from the top of an elaborate tomb chamber a short distance from the tell. Subsequent archaeological investigations uncovered a sprawling city (22 ha.) that, with the decipherment of its language, was recognized as the ancient city of Ugarit referenced in texts throughout the ANE. Though Ugarit was already a large and thriving city by the early 2nd millennium, it is best known from the archaeological and written record during its height in the 14th and 13th cent. BCE. During this period the city-state of Ugarit controlled an area of about 2,000 sq. km with a population, including city and countryside, estimated between 25,000 and 35,000 people. Of the many fine structures preserved in the ruins of the city, the most stunning edifice was the palace complex; situated over nearly 2.5 ac. with twelve staircases, over ninety rooms, and a large walled garden, the royal palace was renowned throughout the eastern Mediterranean world. Walking east from the royal zone along the city's public streets, one encounters the highest point of the tell, on which stood two monumental structures with biblical resonance: the temples of BAAL and Dagan (see DAGON). Built according to identical plans, the two temples were separated by the "House of the High Priest," within which the famous mythological texts of Ugarit were recovered (see UGARIT, TEXTS AND LITERATURE).

Ugarit, as a hub of commerce in the Middle and Late Bronze periods, was a city with an international flavor. While the majority of its citizens bore West Semitic names, reference to a number of Egyptian, Akkadian, and, most abundantly, Hurrian individuals saturate documents and inscriptions within the city (see HURRIANS). Ugaritic society was divided into two sectors: those in service to and dependent upon the palace ("people of the king") and another class of free individuals ("sons of Ugarit"). Both groups, it seems, were hierarchical in structure, with an upper class reserved for those most closely attached to the palace. Among the "people of the king" a number of guilds are attested, including metallurgists, merchants, and a thriving scribal class. Large houses for wealthy citizens, some with at least thirty rooms and private libraries, have been discovered and attest to the city's affluence. The countryside consisted of primarily small towns and villages, whose duty was to provide food for the city and those connected to the palace.

Erich Lessing /Art Resource, NY

Figure 1: Two persons in a chariot, from Ugarit. Terracotta, Late Bronze, 14ᵗʰ–12ᵗʰ cent. BCE. Louvre, Paris, France.

The king's extensive property rights allowed him to offer land grants to his supporters. He engaged in diplomacy, led the military, and, importantly, performed various duties in worship leadership. Royal statues and reliefs depict both the common motif of a warrior on a hunt as well as the royal figure vested in priestly garments. The queen also was not without power; texts detail the queen's role in the mediation and intervention of diplomatic affairs as well as participation in religious duties alongside the king.

Due to its geographical position in northern SYRIA as a crossroads between both the east–west trade network of the Aegean and Mesopotamia worlds and the north–south route between EGYPT and the HITTITES, Ugarit's allegiance and resources were prized possessions of all the great empires during the Middle and Late Bronze periods. Possessing a comparatively weak military but much wealth, Ugarit's existence and welfare depended upon shrewd decisions within the sphere of international politics, shifting loyalties when prudent and acquiescing to a hegemonic state when necessary. Ugarit, it appears, was initially within Egypt's sphere of influence, but the extent of the relationship is difficult to ascertain as a fire (and perhaps earthquake) ca. 1360 BCE destroyed part of the royal palace and any archives it may have housed. Around the time of this misfortune, the balance of power tipped in northern Syria toward the Hittites' favor with the reign of Suppiluliuma I. Solicited to be part of an anti-Hittite coalition by the Mitannians, the Ugaritic king Niqmaddu II instead appealed to the ascending strength of the Hittites for protection. The Hittite king received the Ugaritic overtures gladly and granted Ugarit a considerable amount of territory for its loyalty. The dynastic turmoil occasioned by Suppiluliuma's death, combined with a devastating plague in the region, offered Hittite vassal kingdoms the opportunity for a revolt against their overlord. During this period, Egypt again attempted to exert its influence, and a renewed rapprochement was established between Egypt and Ugarit. The rebellion in northern Syria was short-lived, however, with Suppiluliuma's son, Mursili II, finally regaining control of the empire and placing a new, Hittite-controlled king on Ugarit's throne. The tribute sent to the Hittite kingdom during this time was considerable: along with the loss of nearly one-third of its territory, Ugarit was forced to pay great quantities of gold bullion, gold and silver vessels, and purple garments. Nevertheless, the Hittites refrained from delivering a debilitating military or economic blow to the city because of its vital economic importance to their kingdom, and Ugarit soon regained its position as a preeminent maritime center.

Ugarit's loyalty to the Hittites appears to have remained intact until the city's final destruction. At the famous battle of Qadesh (ca. 1275 BCE), Ugarit is numbered among those kingdoms fighting alongside the Hittites even while other north Syrian Hittite vassals, such as Amurru, are recorded as having taken up arms with the Egyptians. The Hittites' ability to retain control of the region after the battle, as witnessed in the Hittite–Egyptian treaty between Hattusilis III and Ramesses II, was a happy development for Ugarit, and for nearly a century the city-state lived in general peace and prosperity. At the beginning of the 12th cent., however, a new and formidable threat to the eastern Mediterranean world emerged, known from our sources as the "Sea Peoples." This marauding and destructive force, whose presence was felt from the Hittite Empire in the north down to Egypt in the south, wrought chaos along the Mediterranean coast. Having sent its naval fleet to aid the Hittites against the Sea Peoples and neglecting its own fortifications, Ugarit lay exposed and vulnerable. Although a number of factors can be linked to the downfall of the city alongside the presence of the Sea Peoples, including a weakened Hittite Empire and widespread famine in the region, the archaeological evidence—vestiges of ash discernible from widespread burning, unfinished clay documents beside the kiln waiting to be fired, and possessions hidden in walls and under floors—suggests a sudden and catastrophic end to the ancient and remarkable city.

Bibliography: Mark S. Smith. *Untold Stories: The Bible and Ugaritic Studies in the Twentieth Century* (2001); Wilfred van Soldt. "Ugarit: A Second-Millennium Kingdom on the Mediterranean Coast." *CANE* 2. Jack M. Sasson, ed. (1995) 1255–66; W. G. E. Watson and N. Wyatt, eds. *Handbook of Ugaritic Studies* (1999); Marguerite Yon. *The City of Ugarit at Tell Ras Shamra* (2006).

DANIEL PIOSKE

UGARIT, TEXTS AND LITERATURE *oo´*guh-rit. Ugaritic is a West Semitic language closely related to Phoenician and Hebrew. It was the local language of (and thus named after) Late Bronze Age Ugarit (ca. 1400–1180 BCE), a city located on the coast of Syria about 100 mi. north of modern-day Beirut (*see* UGARIT, HISTORY AND ARCHAEOLOGY). While the site of Ugarit yielded texts in many different languages due to its cosmopolitan character and its international trade, Ugaritic was the local language used for its own traditional literary texts and rituals, as well as a number of letters, legal texts, administrative texts, and other matters. The texts shed light on many aspects of the religious and general cultural milieu of which biblical Israel was a part, as illustrated by the many comparative OT references in this article.

    A. Texts
    B. Sites of the Texts and the Shorter Alphabet
    C. Literary Texts
       1. The Baal Cycle
       2. Kirta
       3. Aqhat
       4. The Rephaim texts

    D. Rituals and Related Texts
    E. Letters
    F. Legal Texts
    G. Economic Texts
    H. Scribal Exercises
    I. Inscriptions on Seals, Labels, Ivories, etc.
    Bibliography

A. Texts

    The standard edition of the Ugaritic texts (in German, KTU; in English, CTU, *The Cuneiform Alphabetic Texts from Ugarit*) uses the following categories: literary and religious texts (CTU 1); letters (CTU 2); legal texts (CTU 3); economic texts (CTU 4); scribal exercises (CTU 5); inscriptions on seal, labels, ivories, etc. (CTU 6); unclassified texts (CTU 7); illegible tablets and uninscribed fragments (CTU 8); unpublished texts (CTU 9); and one Ugaritic text in syllabic script (CTU 10). This listing includes many Hurrian texts, as well as two Akkadian religious texts in CUNEIFORM alphabetic writing, as well as another text that has seven lines of Akkadian followed by another ten lines in Ugaritic. The discussion below omits discussion of CTU 7–9, as they furnish little information.

    In addition to the texts in CTU, about another sixty Ugaritic texts (along with about 300 Akkadian texts) were discovered in the 1994 and 1996 excavations. About fifteen of these texts have received an initial publication by Pierre Bordreuil and Dennis Pardee or by Pardee by himself (some cited below according to their "RS" or RAS SHAMRA number); the majority awaits publication. These will also be incorporated in the next CTU edition of the Ugaritic texts (presently in preparation). In 2004 Bordreuil and Pardee, the team of scholars charged with the publication of the Ugaritic texts, tallied about fifty Ugaritic poetic texts and 1,500 Ugaritic prose texts.

B. Sites of the Texts and the Shorter Alphabet

    The Ugaritic texts are not confined to the site of Ugarit proper. Many were also discovered at nearby Ras ibn-Hani; one text remains unprovenanced. Like almost all Ugaritic texts found at Ugarit, these texts use a thirty-letter alphabet and read from left to right. Two texts from Ugarit are written in a shorter Ugaritic alphabet running from right to left (CTU 4.31 and 4.710), as are several others from Levantine and Cypriot sites outside of Ugarit. This shorter alphabet stands closer to the number of letters in the Hebrew and Aramaic alphabets. Whether of the longer or shorter variety, the writing of alphabetic signs in cuneiform suggests the influence of Mesopotamian cuneiform scribal traditions on the Levant in the Late Bronze Age.

C. Literary Texts

    The literary texts (CTU 1.1-1.25; 1.61-1.63 [?]; 1.83; 1.92; 1.93; 1.96; 1.101; 1.108; 1.114.1-28) are characterized by poetic parallelism consisting mostly of two- and three-line units, as found in biblical poetry. Four sets of multi-tablet collections dominate the literary texts: 1) stories centered around the warrior god of the storm, Baal (the Baal Cycle, 1.1-1.3 + 1.8; 1.4-1.6); 2) episodes in the life of King Kirta (1.14-1.16); 3) the short life of the hero, Aqhat (1.17-1.19); and 4) the ancient deceased heroes, the Rephaim (1.20-1.22; see REPHAIM).

Shorter mythic texts narrate Baal's fathering a bull (1.10); a birth involving several deities (1.11); Baal's conflict with monstrous foes called the "Eaters" (1.12); the exaltation of the warrior goddess, Anat, for her military prowess (1.13); the birth, banishment, and inclusion of the dangerous "Goodly Gods," sired by El and two unnamed females (1.23.30-76), following a series of ritual instructions (1.23.1-29); the wedding-song of Nikkal, the Mesopotamian moon-goddess, and Yarih, the Ugaritic moon-god (1.24); the binding of the monstrous tnn (1.83; compare biblical "dragons" in Ps 74:13 and "sea monsters" in Gen 1:21); the hunt of the goddess Astarte, marked by a roiling of the cosmic "deep" (1.92; compare "deep" in Gen 1:2), perhaps followed by Baal's (sexual?) encounter with the goddess; the cry of the cow on (or against) a mountain (1.93); the dangerous eye (or perhaps the goddess Anat) consuming "her brother's flesh without a knife" and drinking "his blood without a cup" (1.96); a hymnic description of Baal (1.101); a hymnic description of a feast for the god Rapiu (evidently the leader of the Rephaim; see below) and his companions (perhaps the Rephaim), as well as Anat (1.108), which is combined for a wish for blessing, perhaps for the king; El's drunken feast and the goddesses' hunt for ingredients for a cure (1.114.1-28), followed by a prescription for a hangover (1.114.29-31; see below, under medical prescriptions). One of the newer texts (RIH 98/02) is a hymn to Astarte as a leonine. The subject of some texts is unclear (e.g., 1.9; 1.25; 1.61-1.63; 1.75; 1.79; 1.81). At this point, we review the four longer literary cycles.

1. The Baal Cycle

The longest Ugaritic text, the Baal Cycle (CTU 1.1-1.6), relates Baal's attainment of divine kingship, represented by the construction of his royal palace (1.3 III–1.4 VII), flanked by his conflicts with the cosmic, personified Sea beforehand (1.1–1.3 II), and his struggle with Death personified (1.4 VIII–1.6).

The first tablet of the Baal Cycle (CTU 1.1) begins with El's naming Sea as divine champion (1.1 V-IV). El then summons Kothar from his home to build a palace, apparently for Yamm (1.1 III). El then summons Anat to desist from conflict (1.1 II). The second tablet is missing one column and most of a second. In the first clear column (1.2 I), Sea's messengers come to the divine council headed by the patriarchal god El to demand the surrender of Baal, who stands at attention while the other deities of the divine assembly are enjoying a meal. The sight of Sea's messengers inspires fear in the divine

assembly, and El decrees that Baal is to become Sea's servant. The scene breaks off with Baal's resisting this decision and the warrior goddesses Anat and Astarte rebuking him.

The classic setting of the divine council is represented in biblical literature in the vision of the prophet Micaiah ben Imlah (1 Kgs 22:19-23), who sees the host of heaven standing on either side of Yahweh. In Ps 82, God stands in the divine council and accuses the other gods (see also Dan 7). In divine council scenes, the god who heads the divine assembly typically commissions a member to carry out or announce the divine decree. In biblical prophetic scenes, the prophet may be commissioned (see Isa 6 and Ezek 1–3; compare the lying spirit in 1 Kgs 22:20-23). In the Baal Cycle, a member of the council, such as Baal, might be expected to serve as the divine council's champion against an enemy such as Sea. This is the situation with Marduk in the Akkadian Epic of Creation (ENUMA ELISH). Baal is instead handed over to Sea, showing his weak position at this point.

In the next clear column, CTU 1.2 IV, Baal resists the decision of the divine assembly by defeating Sea, thanks to the weapons made by Kothar, the craftsman-god. Powered by incantations pronounced over them by Kothar, the weapons fly like powerful birds attacking Sea. The theme of the divine battle against Sea is well known in Ps 74:13, where Sea is one of Yahweh's cosmic enemies (see also Ps 89:9-11 [Heb. 89:10-12]; Isa 51:9-11; see also Ps 29). After his victory, Baal celebrates with a private feast (1.3 I). It is attended initially only by his servant, who sings and serves him a superhuman-sized cup of alcohol that no woman, not even the goddess Asherah, can see. Only at the end of the feast does any female presence intrude. This feast of males generally excludes females, perhaps except from their part in sexual relations at the end.

Anat comes into this story first with the description of her savage battle against enemies (1.3 II). It may be that she is fighting on Baal's behalf on the terrestrial level, while Baal fights against cosmic Sea. In this scene, she attacks human warriors; she is knee-deep in blood and gore (compare the imagery of treading in wine presses in Lam 1:15; Joel 3:13 [Heb. 4:13]; Rev 14:14-20; 19:15). She has hands and heads affixed to her waist as trophies; still she is unsatisfied. She takes her human captives to her palace, where she sets up tables and chairs, evidently for a feast; then she is satisfied. Anat is evidently satisfied because the feast there includes her captives as the main course. The cannibalistic feast here is a divine counterpart to the biblical notion of "devoted things" in warfare (e.g., Josh 7:1); the corresponding Ugaritic term is applied to Anat's battling in 1.13.2-7 (see below). Vestiges of this bloody, divine warfare appear in Yahweh's martial march against enemies (see Isa 34:5-7; 49:25-26; 63:1-6; see also Deut 32:41-42; Pss 58:10 [Heb. 55:11]; 68:23 [Heb. 68:24]; Ezek 39:19).

In the second major part (1.3 III–1.4 VII), Baal seeks to have a palace built in his honor as the pantheon's new king. The process is stalled by his need to gain El's permission for the construction project. The text of 1.3 III-1.3 V centers on Baal's effort to gain this permission first by intercession attempted by his sister, Anat. The text of 1.3 III-V relates Baal's summons to Anat to his holy mountain (compare Exod 15:15-17), and her subsequent efforts to gain El's permission for Baal's palace. Baal then commissions Kothar to make a number of valuable furnishings (1.3 VI + 1.8–1.4 I) in order to induce Asherah to go to El on Baal's behalf (1.4 II-III). This she does with great success (1.4 IV-V). With El's permission granted, the building of the palace proceeds, culminating in its inauguration by a great feast celebrated by a multitudinous gathering of deities (1.4 VI). Baal then goes on a victory tour leading to the final addition to the palace, namely his window, which permits his theophanous, thunderous voice to ring forth (1.4 VII). Baal is now recognized as divine king in heaven and on earth.

The third major section of the Baal Cycle (1.4 VIII–1.6) begins when Baal wishes to extend his kingship to the underworld and its lord, Death. Baal's initial communication with Death results in Death's rebuke of Baal (1.4 VIII–1.5 I). In this speech, Death mentions Baal's evidently earlier defeat of enemies, known from the Bible as Leviathan and the seven-headed dragon (compare Job 3:8; 7:12; 41:1 [Heb. 40:25]; Ps 74:14; Isa 27:1). Baal's decision to assert his kingship over the underworld proves foolhardy as his efforts result instead in his descent to the underworld (1.5 II-VI). After learning the news of his death, Anat and El follow proper mourning and burial rituals (1.5 VI–1.6 I), after which two minor gods try unsuccessfully to display their physical qualifications for kingship (1.6 I). This signals the reason why Baal is king: no other god can measure up, anticipating his return. Thanks to Anat's destruction of Death (1.6 II), Baal returns to life (1.6 III-IV), though he remains unable to defeat Death (1.6 V). Thanks to El's intervention, Baal is able to retain his rule (1.6 VI). This conflict recalls biblical passages celebrating divine victory over death (see Isa 25:7-8, echoed in Rev 21:4, the context of which in vv. 1-4 offers a parallel to all three major episodes of the Baal Cycle). The Baal Cycle offers a view of divine kingship that offers prosperity and well-being on the divine, human, and natural levels despite destructive forces in the universe; this fragile kingship of Baal's stands under threat and needs help from a variety of deities. The Cycle offered a vision of kingship for a small though prosperous city-state, often standing in the shadow of great powers such as the Egyptians and the Hittites.

2. Kirta

Another Ugaritic text is the Kirta legend (CTU 1.14-1.16; *see* KIRTU, KERET, KIRTA, EPIC OF). At the outset, Kirta loses his wife and children (1.14 I), as suggested by his name (*krt, "to cut") and much like the figure of Job in Job 1–2. Kirta then laments to his patron-god El that he needs an heir (compare Absalom's lack of an heir in 2 Sam 18:18). In a dream vision (1.14 I), El asks him what he wants (compare Solomon's dream in 1 Kgs 3:5-15), and the god instructs him to go on a military march to besiege the city of Udm (1.14 II-III). Kirta follows El's directions virtually to the letter (1.14 III), apart from a stop at the sanctuary of Asherah of Tyre and Sidon, when the king offers a vow to the goddess in exchange for her help. After completing his march and siege (1.14 IV-V), Kirta gains the object of his quest, the daughter of the king of Udm. Thus, Kirta is able to reestablish his royal family, celebrated at a wedding feast attended by several deities and blessed by El (1.15 I-III).

After the feast, Asherah remembers Kirta's unpaid vow, evidently the cause of his sickly condition (1.15 IV-VI; compare the illness of Hezekiah in 2 Kgs 20// Isa 38). When his son and daughter learn of the serious illness, they come to him in lamentation (1.16 I-II). His dutiful daughter asks if the king is a son of El and can really die. Here the paradox of kingship captures both the ideal that the dynasty and its king ideally last forever and the reality that every king is ultimately mortal. The king's illness is not only a political problem; it also leads to agricultural infertility (1.16 III). The crisis evokes a meeting of the divine council (1.16 IV) in which El invites the gods to offer to expel the illness (1.16 V). When no deity responds, El takes up the challenge by creating an expeller who flies to Kirta's palace and dispels the illness.

The third challenge to Kirta's kingship involves his son's rebellion (1.16 VI; compare Absalom's rebellion against David in 2 Sam 15–20). Kirta's son claims that during his illness he has ignored his royal responsibility to adjudicate the case of the widow, the poor, and the orphan. In the story's closing lines, Kirta curses his son. In sum, the story of Kirta relates three paradigmatic challenges to kingship: the need for an heir, illness, and rebellion. Aided by the divine world, Kirta is able to overcome all three challenges.

3. Aqhat

The Aqhat story (CTU 1.17-1.19) opens with the patriarch Danil (compare Daniel in Ezek 14:14, 20 and 28:3, from whom Daniel of the book of Daniel takes his name). Danil laments that he has no son to perform the traditional filial duties (1.17 I). Moved to compassion, Baal takes Danil's case to El. Divine help arrives in the form of the Kotharat, goddesses who aid in conception. The illegible columns (1.17 III-IV) perhaps relate the birth and youth of the new son, for when the story resumes (1.17 V), Danil is hearing the cases of the widow and the orphan and receives the craftsman-god Kothar, who gives him a bow and arrows. Danil gives the weapons to his son, Aqhat, and commands him to give the first of his hunt to the temple. While Anat feasts, evidently at her temple (1.17 VI), she sees Aqhat and his bow. Perhaps expecting the weapons as a votive gift rather than the first of the hunt, she offers silver and gold in exchange; he suggests that she have Kothar make her own. She offers him eternal life; he refuses, claiming the offer is a lie—death is the fate of all mortals. He evidently oversteps in his response in suggesting that hunting is not for women, since Anat is a hunter (see CTU 1.114). Anat laughs at him and threatens him. She travels to El, whom she threatens with violence; El acquiesces to her request (1.18 I). After two lost columns (1.18 II-III), Anat tells her warrior, Ytpn, how the two of them will execute Aqhat (1.18 IV). Anat flies among a flock of vultures and releases Ytpn to strike Aqhat on the head. She then weeps for the dead Aqhat.

A drought ensues, and Danil notes the failing vegetation. Vultures circle above, and Pughat, Danil's daughter and Aqhat's sister, weeps as Danil laments. The father now expresses the lack of precipitation: "no dew, no rain, no upsurging of the deeps, no good voice of Baal." Together father and daughter go to the fields to see their desiccated vegetation, when the news of Aqhat's death arrives (1.19 II). On hearing the report, Danil expresses the wish that the bird that feasted on his son's corpse would give it up (1.19 III). Upon recovering the body, he buries it and proceeds to curse the place where the lethal attack took place. The patriarch returns home to lament his son with weepers (1.19 IV) for seven years. In the seventh year, he sends them off and offers a meal for the gods. At this point, Pughat presents herself to her father to ask for his blessing to avenge her brother's death. After cleaning herself, she puts "a hero's outfit" under her "woman's outfit." She goes to Ytpn's military camp, where he greets her and invites her to drink. The story then breaks off, leading to speculation that a fourth tablet would have described how Pughat succeeded and avenged her brother's death by killing Ytpn (compare Jael's attack on Sisera in Judg 4–5 and Judith's killing of the enemy general Holofernes in Jdt 13).

Rituals and interactions with deities predominate in Aqhat. The story's opening highlights the proper roles of the son, and the closing stresses the proper role of the daughter, as well as the rituals undertaken by the father. The story has no mother; its world focuses on the patriarch and his children. This older male has become a model elder in the society while the younger figure fails to complete his transition into adulthood. The two figures reflect the successful and unsuccessful sides of life for warriors; the daughter in her victory is the traditional exception in her warrior-role.

4. The Rephaim texts

Rephaim texts (CTU 1.20-1.22) are fragmentary texts that might be a sequel to the story of Aqhat, since they mention Danil and they concern the Rephaim, deceased warrior heroes of old (named also in the royal funerary text 1.161, discussed below; see also the Rephaim in Isa 14:9). They relate an invitation to the Rephaim to attend an elaborate feast. The Rephaim travel on chariots to reach the threshing floor, where they are to be fed. They are invited also to a temple or palace, apparently by the god El. There they enjoy a magnificent banquet.

D. Rituals and Related Texts

The sacrificial cult of Ugarit (see CTU 1.27-1.176) presents the king as the principal ritual actor, along with priests (khnm, the same term as in Hebrew) as well as "holy ones" (see also 4.752). The sacrificial cult is lunar in its overall calendrical reckoning. One ritual (1.41/1.87) includes offerings for the beginning of fall corresponding to the Israelite fall New Year and festival of Booths or Tabernacles. In one section, there are to be dwellings of branches where sacrifices are offered to a deity. A single-day royal offering (1.115) includes the instruction that "a woman/women may eat of it." This additional notation, otherwise unknown, would suggest that women did not generally partake in eating ritual offerings. Another ritual (1.162) includes an offering of a shield (compare the dedication of Saul's weapons in Astarte's temple in 1 Sam 31:10). Three texts focus on a royal ritual of seeing or contemplation (1.90; 1.164; 1.168), perhaps parallel to the biblical idea of "seeing" God in a sanctuary context (e.g., Pss 11:7; 17:15; 42:2 [Heb. 42:3]; 63:2 [Heb. 63:3]).

The rituals include one (1.40) concerned with uprightness, adjudication of sin, and national unity offered on behalf of the oppressed and the impoverished as well as foreigners. A number of Ugaritic terms correspond to biblical names for offerings: "peace offering" (the same term as the biblical sacrifice of "well-being," as in Lev 3:1), "burnt offering" (Lev 1:3), and "elevation offering" (Num 8:11-15, 21; 18:11, etc.); these texts also use the general term for "sacrifice" (zevakh זֶבַח) found in Hebrew. One ritual addresses the problem of sin (1.40), which is a regular concern in the biblical material (e.g., Exod 29:14, 36; Lev 4–9; 14–16; Num 6–7, 29; Ezek 43–45); unlike the biblical ritual texts, the Ugaritic rituals do not refer to expiation or cleansing (see, however, atonement mentioned along with sin in the Ugaritic letter 2.72). Unlike biblical ritual, the Ugaritic texts lack references to the blood and fat of sacrifices, as well as incense. As in the Bible, there is no sacrifice of wild animals, dogs, or pigs. There is no clear reference to child sacrifice at Ugarit. The requirements for bodily purity are similar in the biblical and Ugaritic rituals. There is no celebration of "fertility cult" as understood by earlier generations of scholars. One text (1.132) may possibly allude to "sacred marriage," but no sexual relations are actually mentioned. The Ugaritic rituals mention garments to be worn by priests or deities or both; priestly garments are well known in the Bible, but garments for deities less so (compare "weaving for Asherah" in 2 Kgs 23:7; and see also the listing of material for deities in CTU 4.182). Prayers are relatively rare in the ritual texts (see 1.119 and perhaps 1.127), as is also the case in ritual texts in the Bible. The deity lists (CTU 1.65; 1.74; 1.102; 1.148) are apparently tied to the sacrificial cult, as they order names of deities as found in ritual texts. Typically the number of deities listed comes to about thirty-three. These are evidently the main deities, as the total number of deities mentioned in rituals and related texts tallies to 234, with 178 specifically named as recipients of offerings.

A funerary ritual (CTU 1.161), set in poetic lines, summons two deceased kings of Ugarit as well as the ancient heroes of old, the Rephaim. One of the ancient heroes named in this text is consulted in another text for healing (1.124). A third text (1.113) lists the dead kings of Ugarit labeled as "divine" on one side, and on the other side describes music played, apparently for the kings.

Descriptive rituals include ritual slaughter of animals in a rural context outside the city of Ugarit (CTU 1.79; 1.80; compare Judg 6:19-24; 13:19).

Divination texts include practice texts, such as liver models (CTU 1.141-1.145; 1.155), a lung model report (1.127), a liver omen (1.155), dream omens (1.86), and an astrological report (1.78) and lunar omens (1.163), as well as manuals for omens derived from a reading of the physical features of malformed animal and human fetuses (1.103 + 1.145; 1.140).

Medical literature includes hippiatric texts (texts dealing with horse diseases; CTU 1.71; 1.72; 1.85; 1.97). CTU 1.82, 1.100, and 1.107 are incantations against snakebites (compare the healing from snakebites through the bronze serpent in Num 21:8-9; 2 Kgs 18:4). CTU 9.435 (= RS 92.2014) is to protect against snakes and scorpions and also to ward off verbal attacks from enemies and sorcerers (compare "sorcerer" in the list of proscribed specialists in Deut 18:10-11). CTU 1.169 is to relieve impotency. Another (1.114) provides a prescription for the effects of excessive intoxication, following a mythic narrative about the drunkenness of the god El. The mythic setting includes the god's MARZEAH ("feast"), known from other Ugaritic texts (e.g., a contract for this institution in 3.9) and two biblical texts (Jer 16:5; Amos 6:7) as an upper-class male social institution.

E. Letters

The eighty-three letters in CTU 2 record communication between a number of figures, most notably involving the royal family and other elite figures (such as "the chief of the priests" in 2.4; compare the biblical "chief priest"), as well as their servants. Occasionally, the communication is international in nature (2.20; 2.39; see also 2.72). Letters report a variety of domestic matters involving communication and shipping (2.37), as well as threats from enemies (2.33), battle (2.82), foreigners (2.30), the "sin" of an Amurrite princess married to the Ugaritic king (2.72), and perhaps plague (2.10). The letters contain some expressions familiar from the Bible, such as the ideas of a force (plague?) being "very strong like death" (2.10; compare Song 8:6) or the "face" of the king shining on the sender (2.13 and 2.16; compare the priestly blessing of Num 6:24-26).

The letters usually name the sender and the recipient. They regularly request blessing of deities upon the recipient (see the list of deities from various places in 2.42). If the sender is inferior in social status, the sender is said to bow down before the recipient. Many letters relate a further message from the sender, before closing with a request to the recipient to send information as to his or her situation.

F. Legal Texts

The ten texts labeled as legal texts (CTU 3) are broad in scope. They include: a record of disbursement of tribute from the Ugaritic king to his Hittite overlord (CTU 3.1); royal grants to individuals (CTU 3.2; 3.5; compare RS 94.2965); records of guarantee made on behalf of one or more individuals (CTU 3.3; 3.7; 3.8); a record of "ransom" (*pdy, CTU 3.4; compare the biblical redemption expressed by the verb *pdh, e.g., the Israelites' redemption from Egypt in Deut 7:8; 13:5 [Heb. 13:6]; compare the redemption of the Passover animal in Exod 13:13-15); a legal contract protecting the head of the marzeah (see above) from any potential legal claims made against him by any of its members (CTU 3.9); and a legal list of funds owed (CTU 3.10).

In the context of legal texts, the legal record (CTU 2.19) may be mentioned, as it records the manumission of a royal slave (compare Exod 21:2-6). CTU 4.172 and 4.266 record purchases of licenses to handle payments of customs duty, while 4.336 and 4.338 record the purchase of a trading concession (see also 2.36; compare the problem of transit recalled in Judg 5:6).

G. Economic Texts

The nearly 800 texts in the category economic texts (CTU 4) mostly list places, property and equipment, personnel and occupations, foodstuffs, metals, and other goods. These records show a network of economic relations largely revolving around the royal administration. Some of these include those who eat at the "table" (4.13); singers, ship-builders, and archers (4.35; see also 4.66); ship crews (4.40) and ships (4.81); ploughmen (4.65); weapons (4.169); wine sold to shrines and individuals (4.219); and silver given for "the cup of the gods" (4.280). Cultic matters play relatively little role in these texts (see 4.728, found in the House of the Hurrian Priest). Some lists (e.g., 4.102) show families consisting of fathers, their wives, and their children, as well as young men and women, probably retainers or servants. One (4.360) lists various family lineages as three heads of households, with their patriarchal lord called "Bull" (compare the title of the god El, "Bull El my Father," and Num 23:22; 24:8), along with his four daughters.

H. Scribal Exercises

Scribal exercise texts (CTU 5) include partial or complete abecedaries: 5.4; 5.5; 5.6; 5.8; 5.12; 5.13; 5.16; 5.17; 5.19-5.21; 5.24 = 8.1; 5.25; and RS 92.2440. One text (5.14) lists the Ugaritic letters, each followed by an Akkadian syllabic sign (possibly standing for the Ugaritic letter-name). Other scribal exercises show the writing out of consonants (5.2; 5.15), lists of words beginning with the same letter of the alphabet (5.1) or written with the same word (5.3), and personal names (5.7; 5.18; 5.22). Two texts show the scribal practice of correspondence (5.10; 5.11), while a third (5.9) combines a practice letter with an abecedary and a number of consonants. In addition to the texts in this section of CTU, other texts are thought by CTU's editors to be scribal exercises (e.g., 1.9; 1.13; 1.67; 1.69; 1.71; 1.73; 1.133).

I. Inscriptions on Seals, Labels, Ivories, etc.

The seventy-six texts placed in the category of inscriptions (CTU 6) are mostly very short inscriptions made on items, some indicating their ownership. Some axes (6.6-6.10) are inscribed with the title "chief of the priests" (see above). Two standing steles (CTU 6.13; 6.14) have inscriptions marking the steles as mortuary offerings on behalf of their donor (compare 2 Sam 18:18; for the sort of mortuary offering, compare Lev 26:30; Ezek 43:7). One inscription appears on the lion head on a rhyton (drinking vessel) dedicated to the god Resheph (6.62).

Bibliography: Kenneth T. Aitken. *The Aqhat Narrative: A Study in the Narrative Structure and Composition of an Ugaritic Tale* (1990); Pierre Bordreuil and Dennis Pardee. *Manuel d'ougaritique* (2004); David M. Clements. *Sources for Ugaritic Ritual and Sacrifice: Vol. I. Ugaritic and Ugarit Akkadian Texts* (2001); John Huehnergard. *Ugaritic Vocabulary in Syllabic Transcription* (2008); Theodore J. Lewis. *Cults of the Dead in Ancient Israel and Ugarit* (1989); Kevin M. McGeough. *Exchange Relationships at Ugarit* (2007); Michael Patrick O'Connor. "The Human Characters' Names in the Ugaritic Poems: Onomastic Eccentricity in Bronze-Age Semitic and the Name Daniel in Particular." *Biblical Hebrew in Its Northwest Semitic Setting: Typological and Historical Perspectives.* Steven E. Fassberg and Avi Hurvitz, eds. (2006) 269–83; Dennis Pardee. "Preliminary Presentation of a New Ugaritic Song to ʿAṯtartu (RIH 98/02)." *Ugarit at Seventy-Five.* K. Lawson Younger Jr., ed. (2007) 27–39; Dennis Pardee. *Ritual and Cult at Ugarit* (2002); Simon B. Parker, ed. *Ugaritic Narrative Poetry* (1997); J. David Schloen. *The House of the Father as Fact and Symbol: Patrimonialism in Ugarit and the Ancient Near East* (2001); Mark S. Smith. *The Sacrificial Rituals and Myths of the Goodly Gods, KTU/CAT 1.23: Royal Constructions of Opposition, Intersection, Integration and Domination* (2006); Mark S. Smith.

The Ugaritic Baal Cycle. Volume 1: Introduction with Text, Translation and Commentary of CTU 1.1–1.2 (1994); Mark S. Smith and Wayne T. Pitard. *The Ugaritic Baal Cycle: Volume 2. Introduction with Text, Translation and Commentary of KTU 1.3–1.4* (2008); Chloe Sun. *The Ethics of Violence in the Story of Aqhat* (2008); David P. Wright. *Ritual in Narrative: The Dynamics of Feasting, Mourning, and Retaliation Rites in the Ugaritic Tale of Aqhat* (2001); Marguerite Yon. *The City of Ugarit* (2006).

MARK S. SMITH

ULA, AL. The site of al-Khuraybah (biblical DEDAN) in the fertile al-Ula Valley of northwestern Arabia was an important political and economic center from at least the 6th to 1st cent. BCE.

ULAI yooʾli [אוּלָי ʾulay]. The river that Daniel stood beside in his vision of a conflict between a two-horned ram representing the kings of Media and Persia and a he-goat representing the king of Greece (Dan 8:2). A voice from the middle of the Ulai called out to the angel Gabriel with instructions to interpret the vision to Daniel (8:16). Scholars believe the Ulai to have been an artificial canal that flowed on the northern side of the ancient Elamite capital city of Susa, connecting the Choaspes (present-day Kerkha) and Coprates (present-day Abdizful) rivers. Some scholars believe, on the basis of an Akkadian cognate, that the term ʾuval (אוּבָל) translated "river" in Dan 8:2, 3, and 6, instead denotes a city gate. In that case, Daniel's vision would be set near the Ulai Gate in Susa, which probably would have been located on the northern side of the city.

DEREK E. WITTMAN

ULAM yooʾluhm [אוּלָם ʾulam]. 1. Father of Bedan and one of two sons of Sheresh, a descendant of Manasseh (1 Chr 7:16-17).

2. A warrior and archer, the firstborn son of Eshek, a Benjaminite (1 Chr 8:39-40). In both cases, the name can be understood as an eponym for a clan.

EMILY R. CHENEY

ULCER [עֹפֶל ʿofel]. Crater-like lesions on the skin or mucous membrane, ulcers are threatened as a divine punishment for violation of the covenant (Deut 28:27). The Hebrew word ʿofel comes from verb meaning "to swell" (ʿafal, עָפַל), and may perhaps be translated "bump" or "swelling" rather than "ulcer." It is rendered as "tumor" in 1 Sam 5–6. *See* DISEASE; TUMORS.

JOHN J. PILCH

ULLA uhlʾuh [עֻלָּא ʿullaʾ]. First Chronicles 7:39 lists Ulla, father of Arah, Hanniel, and Rizia, among the descendants of Asher. The name, which does not appear in the Syriac version, might be a corruption of another name in the genealogy; perhaps Shua (v. 32), Amal (v. 35), Shual (v. 36), or Ara (v. 38).

JOAN E. COOK, SC

ʿUMAYRI, TALL AL. This small but densely occupied multi-period site is located on a natural ridge 9 mi. south of Amman's Seventh Circle on the airport freeway next to Amman National Park. The presence of a spring at the northern foot of the site was the probable reason for settlement. Using an itinerary of THUTMOSE III, some identify it with ABEL-KERAMIM of Judg 11:33.

Large-scale excavations begun in 1984 by Andrews University have continued for eleven seasons, though the dig is now sponsored by La Sierra University in consortium with several other schools. The excavations show that the site was occupied by twenty-two separate settlements (strata) stretching from the Early Bronze to the Islamic Age, but the primary periods of occupation were the Bronze and Iron ages.

Chalcolithic (Str. 22) remains were found by a survey team at the eastern foot of the site under the modern freeway. A dolmen without its capstone is on the southeastern foot of the hill and dates to the Early Bronze I (Str. 21). The dolmen contained the remains of twenty secondary burials with beads, flint tools, mace heads, and twenty complete pottery vessels from the Early Bronze IB period (ca. 3000 BCE). This is the first time a dolmen from anywhere in the Mediterranean basin has produced so many finds and such solid dating and functional evidence.

Strata 20–19 (Early Bronze Age II–III, ca. 3000–2300 BCE) consist of a series of houses built on the southern and northern slopes of the site, one on top of the other, using the walls of the previous strata to found later walls. The last stratum (19) was well preserved by collapsed walls and ceilings, complete with plastered reeds and beams. There are no signs that the site was fortified.

Strata 18–17 (Early Bronze Age IV, ca. 2300–2100 BCE) are directly above the well-preserved houses of Early Bronze III. There were two much smaller houses made of single rooms, each with one pillar in the center. Above them and also dated to Early Bronze IV was a more ephemeral series of small stone walls, possibly used for animal pens.

Figure 1: Late Bronze Age five-room building at Tall al-ʿUmayri with shrine

After a hiatus during the early stages of the Middle Bronze Age, a major site was again established during the Middle Bronze Age IIC (Str. 16–15; ca. 1700–1550 BCE). On the western side, after the inhabitants had already constructed their houses over much of the site (Stratum 16), they fortified it by creating a hill out of the original ridge (Stratum 15). The site was also protected by a dry moat 16 ft. deep and a steep rampart 16 ft. high.

Stratum 14 (Late Bronze Age II, ca. 1400–1230 BCE) had a major building of five rooms built inside the Middle Bronze rampart. Some walls are preserved 5–8 ft. high.

A large shrine room containing a plastered cultic niche with five standing stones 3 ft. above the floor was recovered. The rooms of the building (palace and/or temple) were filled with 10 ft. of destruction debris.

Figure 2: Close-up view of the shrine in the Late Bronze Age building at Tall al-ʿUmayri with the small standing stones embedded in a thick plaster floor. Also visible are a few of the votive pottery vessels.

After the destruction of Stratum 14 the settlement was rebuilt (Str. 13–12; Late Bronze IIB/Early Iron I, ca. 1230–1200 BCE), but the palace/temple area was abandoned. This occupation (Str. 13) was destroyed by an earthquake but was immediately rebuilt by the inhabitants (Str. 12). A house from this period is the earliest and best-preserved four-room house in the southern Levant with walls reaching 7 ft. high.

Over eighty large, collar-rimmed jars were found in the back room of the house. In a neighboring house was a standing stone, suggesting a religious function for at least part of the house (*see* TEMPLES, SEMITIC; figure 1). The destruction of this stratum was caused by military attack, suggested by weapons in the debris near the perimeter wall. The finds represent a flourishing tribal society, possibly the beginnings of the Ammonites or Reubenites.

Only isolated rooms or parts of houses come from Str. 11–10 (Late Iron I, ca. 11th cent. BCE), which were separated by a destruction layer. What may have been a sanctuary was found south of the gate in a large open courtyard.

Madaba Plains Project

Figure 3: A cutaway painting of the "four-room house" found at Tall al-'Umayri. Everything in the drawing, except the blankets and the ladders, was found on the floors and in the destruction debris of the house. Painting by Rhonda Root.

The Iron II periods (Str. 9–8; Iron II, ca. late 10th to 7th cent. BCE) are poorly represented, attested mainly by potsherds and wall fragments.

The Late Iron II/Persian (6th cent. BCE) Str. 7–6 shows evidence of major building (Str. 7, beginning of the 6th cent.), probably under the royal patronage of the Ammonite king Baʿalyashaʿ (biblical BAALIS of Jer 40:14) to administer the production of wine at many regional farmsteads. Many small finds were recovered, including ceramic figurines and scores of seals and seal impressions, the most famous of which is the impression of Milkomʾur the Servant of Baʿalyashaʿ (see AMMON, AMMONITES; figure 2). A second stratum (6) constituted new walls and major repairs to the walls of the administrative complex, but there was no destruction. So far, five inscribed seal impressions in an Aramaic script dating to around 500 BCE mention Ammon, indicating the presence of an Ammonite province in the Persian Empire.

Remains from Str. 5–1 (Persian [5]; Hellenistic [4]; Early Roman [3]; Byzantine [2]; Islamic [1]) suggest the site was used primarily for agriculture activities. Little has been recovered in the way of coherent plans for the occupations. See AMMON, AMMONITES; ARCHAEOLOGY; FORTIFICATION; MILCOM; TRANSJORDAN.

Bibliography: L. T. Geraty, L. G. Herr, Ø. S. LaBianca, and R. W. Younker, eds. *Madaba Plains Project 1: The 1984 Season at Tell el-'Umeiri and Vicinity and Subsequent Studies* (1989); L. G. Herr, L. T. Geraty, Ø. S. LaBianca, and R. W. Younker, eds. *Madaba Plains Project 2: The 1987 Season at Tell el-'Umeiri and Vicinity and Subsequent Studies* (1991); L. G. Herr, L. T. Geraty, Ø. S. LaBianca, R. W. Younker, and D. R. Clark, eds. *Madaba Plains Project 3: The 1989 Season at Tell el-'Umeiri and Vicinity and Subsequent Studies* (1997); L. G. Herr, L. T. Geraty, Ø. S. LaBianca, R. W. Younker, and D. R. Clark, eds. *Madaba Plains Project 4: The 1992 Season at Tall al-'Umayri and Subsequent Studies* (2000); L. G. Herr, D. R. Clark, L. T. Geraty, R. W. Younker, and Ø. S. LaBianca, eds. *Madaba Plains Project 5: The 1994 Season at Tall al-'Umayri and Subsequent Studies* (2002).

LARRY G. HERR

UMEIRI, TELL EL. *See* 'UMAYRI, TALL AL.

UMM AL-BIYARA. An Iron Age domestic site situated on a 300 m plateau overlooking Petra, Jordan, which was once part of ancient Edom (*see* EDOM, EDOMITES). It consists of a network of dry-stone houses whose square and rectangular rooms vary in size. The site was occupied for one phase; subsequently, it appears, one area of the settlement was damaged by fire and then reused.

The site was excavated in the 1960s, primarily because it was believed to be biblical SELA. However, no evidence of occupation in the early 8th cent. BCE, during the reign of Amaziah (2 Chr 25:12), was found. All Edomite pottery and small finds point to an early 7th-cent. BCE date, during the Iron Age II C period. Among the finds is a royal seal impression naming "Qos-Gabr, king of Edom," who is mentioned in two Assyrian inscriptions dating to this period.

KATHERINE E. BAXTER

UMM EL-BIYARA. *See* UMM AL-BIYARA.

UMM EL-JIMAL. An archaeological site in northern Jordan. The ancient name of the city is unknown, although some plausible suggestions have been made. The nearby town of Al-Hirra was settled in the 1st cent. CE by the Romans, with Nabatean influence. During the Late Roman period, as Rome's influence in the area waned, Umm El-Jimal was settled. In its prime (5th and 6th cent. CE) the town consisted of 129 houses and 15 churches. The town shows no evidence of population after an earthquake destroyed it in 747 CE.

Bibliography: Bert de Vries. *Umm El-Jimal: A Frontier Town and Its Landscape in Northern Jordan* (1998).

NATHAN P. LAMONTAGNE

UMMAH uhm'uh [עֻמָּה 'ummah]. A town in the territory allotted to Asher (Josh 19:30). Several Greek manuscripts list it as Acco, a port city in northern Israel, which appears in the list of unconquered cities in Judg 1:31 but not in Joshua (*see* ACCO, AKKO).

UMPIRE [מוֹכִיחַ mokhiakh]. One who settles a dispute, arbitrates, or delivers a judgment. Job notes that there is no such intermediary who can step in to settle the dispute between himself and God about the injustice of his suffering (Job 9:33).

UNBELIEF [ἀπιστία apistia]. A lack of BELIEF. Parallel accounts of Jesus' Galilean ministry draw attention to the unbelief of those from his own region and his response to it (Matt 13:58; Mark 6:6). Mark seems to juxtapose the unbelief of the crowd approaching Jesus subsequent to his transfiguration ("faithless [apistia] generation"; Mark 9:19) with the appeal of one member of the crowd ("help my unbelief"; Mark 9:24). Paul links his own acts of persecution and blasphemy to his ignorance in unbelief (1 Tim 1:13) and teaches on the relationship between believers and unbelievers (e.g., 1 Cor 7:12-16; 14:22-25; 2 Cor 6:14-15).

Rhetorically, the OT expresses the concept of unbelief through the negation of the root ʾamen (אָמֵן) or the related noun ʾemunah (אֱמוּנָה). The divine response to Israel's conduct at Kadesh-barnea is noteworthy: "How long will they refuse to believe in me, in spite of all the signs that I have done among them?" (Num 14:11; see Deut 9:23; Heb 3:19). The Assyrian exile was explained by likening the people to their unbelieving ancestors (2 Kgs 17:14). Psalm 78, devoted to describing the Yahweh–Israel relationship, repeatedly stresses Israel's unbelief (Ps 78:8, 22, 32, 37; see also Rom 11:20, 23). *See* ACT FAITHLESSLY.

JOHN I. LAWLOR

UNCIAL un´shuhl. A formal style of handwriting and a category of biblical manuscripts. Uncial letters resembled and developed from the straight-lined, separated capitals used to inscribe texts in stone or metal, but uncials were a more rounded form appropriate for writing with ink on parchment or papyrus. Although some biblical papyri were written in uncial script, the biblical manuscripts called "uncials" are parchment codices written with uncial letters, as distinguished from codices written in the later MINUSCULE style. Some of the most important uncials are Codex Sinaiticus, Codex Vaticanus, and Codex Alexandrinus. *See* ALEXANDRINUS, CODEX; CODEX; SINAITICUS, CODEX; TEXT CRITICISM, NT; VATICANUS, CODEX.

JUDITH ANNE JONES

UNCIRCUMCISED. *See* CIRCUMCISION.

UNCLEAN, UNCLEANNESS. *See* CLEAN AND UNCLEAN.

UNCOVER [גָּלָה galah; ἀποκαλύπτω apokalyptō]. In the OT, to "uncover" most often refers to exposing NAKEDNESS. "You shall not uncover the nakedness of …" is a phrase used in a sequence of sexual prohibitions in Lev 18:6-19 (see also Deut 22:30; 27:20). One of the sons of Noah is cursed when he sees his father's nakedness as Noah lies drunk and "uncovered" in his tent (Gen 9:21-27; compare Gen 19:30-38; Ezek 22:10). Perhaps intentionally echoing Leviticus, Ezekiel describes Israel's humiliation at the hands of the Babylonians as uncovering the nakedness of the nation (Ezek 16:37; 23:10; compare Hos 2:10). Michal is scandalized by her husband David's dancing that uncovers him "before the eyes of maidservants, as any vulgar fellow would do" (2 Sam 6:20). Naomi suggests that Ruth obtain Levirate marriage from Boaz by uncovering his "feet" (probably a euphemism for genitalia) and lying with him (Ruth 3:4-9). Metaphorically, God uncovers or reveals sins (Lam 4:22; Ezek 16:57; 21:24).

In the NT, the term *uncover* (apokalyptō) refers most often to apocalyptic eschatological expectation. "Nothing is covered up that will not be uncovered" (Matt 10:26//Luke 12:2). The book of Revelation (apokalypsis ἀποκάλυψις) literally means "revealing, uncovering," when signs of the end-times are revealed. *See* APOCALYPTICISM.

JOHN I. LAWLOR

UNDERSTAND [בִּין bin, בִּינָה binah, תְּבוּנָה tevunah, יָדַע yadhaʿ, נָכַר nakhar, שָׂכַל sakhal; γνωρίζω gnōrizō, διαλογίζομαι dialogizomai, ἐκζητέω ekzēteō, ἐπιγινώσκω epiginōskō, νοέω noeō, οἶδα oida, συνίημι syniēmi]. A popular concept in wisdom teachings and prophetic warnings, the biblical idea of understanding refers to more than simple acquisition of knowledge, although it certainly carries that aspect as well. First, the expressions used range from bin, "to understand," to yadhaʿ, "to know." God, Woman Wisdom, the Hebrew prophets, and the Evangelists all passionately want to "cause" their hearers to understand what divine reality is attempting to teach. Various idioms that convey intellectual activity make clear that this cerebral behavior is clearly lodged within the body: Solomon asks for a "listening heart" in order to understand and judge his people (1 Kgs 3:9, 11; compare Job 8:10; 11:12 for similar uses). When God confuses human language, the people of Babel "do not hear"—that is, no longer understand—the speech of their neighbors (Gen 11), and prophets warn that an unrepentant nation will be given to foreigners whom they "cannot hear" (Jer 5:15; Ezek 3:6). The people wandering in the wilderness do not "have the heart to know" the nature of God's providential miracles: people do not live by bread alone, but by understanding the nourishing word (Deut 8:3). In most of these cases, it should be remembered that the ancient concept of "heart" refers to what moderns would call "mind."

The intellectual activity of understanding includes various aspects: things are recognized properly or distinguished from one another (nakhar, Deut 32:27); some knowers have insight and perceive deeper meanings (sakhal, Deut 32:29; Dan 9:25). In the NT, diverse ideas are also reflected: "bringing together" facts, one understands (syniēmi; Matt 13:14, 23; Mark 8:21; 12:33; Acts 7:25; Eph 5:7; Col 1:9, 22; 2 Tim 2:7, etc.); other terms highlight an assiduous search (dialogizomai, Mark 8:17; ekzēteo, Rom 3:11).

Binah and its poetic variant, tevunah, are often found in poetic parallelism with "wisdom," whether understood as an abstract concept or a female personification (Job 12:12-13; Prov 2:2; 3:13). God alone knows the way to wisdom and understanding (Job 28:12, 23, 28), but through the application of rational thought—understanding properly oriented toward God—one can discern a provisional wisdom at work in the natural world and human life (Job 42:3). This is the attitude toward life that the biblical sages wish to instill in their students.

In the Hebrew prophets, we find that the concept of knowing or understanding goes well beyond simple reasoning skills. This becomes critical as the people continually misinterpret or disregard what is going on all around them. Isaiah's famous oracles make use of the contradiction between simply registering a fact (yadha^c, "know") and knowing its implications (bin, "understand") in Isa 1:3. Isaiah's mission is characterized by this unnatural situation:

> And he said to me, "Go, and say to this people:
> "Hear and hear, but do not perceive (bin),
>   See and see but do not understand (yadha^c)."
> Dull the mind of this people, stop their ears,
>   And blind their eyes
> Lest they look with their eyes,
>   And hear with their ears,
> And understand (bin) with their minds,
>   And turn and be healed.
> (Isa 6:1-9, author's trans.)

Normally, prophets are called to enlighten the people with respect to the meaning of events and their own deeds. Here, God warns ironically that the prophet's speech will so harden Judah against repentance that it will be as if the prophet had deliberately set out to rob them of knowledge!

This disruptive idea becomes key in the NT with respect to the people's mixed responses to the activity of Jesus. Directly quoting Isaiah in Matt 13:10-13 (//Mark 4:10-12; Luke 8:10), Jesus explains that he teaches people in parables so they won't understand and repent, making use of the prophet's now traditional explanation. Something "greater than Solomon" (Matt 12:42) is present in Jesus' proclamation about life in the Spirit, but the people simply cannot see or understand it. The wisdom of the philosophers is no longer the measure of life-giving knowledge (1 Cor 1:17-29). Dramatic reversals in the worldly view of life herald the radical inbreaking of the reign of God; they announce a profound cosmic inversion. See WISDOM IN THE ANCIENT NEAR EAST; WISDOM IN THE NT; WISDOM IN THE OT.

CAROLE R. FONTAINE

UNDERWORLD. See DEAD, ABODE OF THE; DEITIES, UNDERWORLD; SHEOL; UNDERWORLD, DESCENT INTO THE.

UNDERWORLD, DESCENT INTO THE. Mythic journeys to and from the realm of the dead are widespread in Near Eastern and classical antiquity, and are found also in early Jewish and Christian literature. They bear witness to some degree of cultural connection, yet their frequency should be attributed not to a mythic archetype but instead to basic factors of the human experience such as the universal problem of death, the common belief in a partition between the living and the dead, and curiosity regarding the fate of the dead. These factors explain the extraordinary nature of an underworld descent and allow for a definition that distinguishes it from the general belief in a postmortem journey. The underworld descent often involves a deity rather than a dead person, and it necessarily includes a return from the realm of the dead. Regardless of whether the central character descends to the underworld because of death or for other reasons, the central character transgresses the conventional divide between the living and the dead. Despite the popularity of the myth throughout the cultural world of the Bible, the underworld descent trope is ambiguous and problematic in the Bible (both OT and NT).

A. Ancient Near Eastern and Classical Sources
B. Old Testament and Ancient Israel
C. New Testament
D. Early Jewish and Christian Literature
Bibliography

A. Ancient Near Eastern and Classical Sources

The earliest and most unambiguous examples of descent into the underworld are found in Sumerian texts from the late 3rd through the mid-2nd millennium BCE. Although there are several Sumerian tales of the descent of the dead into the netherworld with no return, most prominently the *Death of Ur-Nammu*, the most important of the myths that include a character's return from the underworld are *Gilgamesh, Enkidu, and the Netherworld* and *Inanna's Descent into the Netherworld*. In these stories, the underworld descents are undertaken for a variety of reasons, underscoring the complexity of the human response to death.

In *Gilgamesh, Enkidu, and the Netherworld*, Enkidu returns to his grieving friend Gilgamesh after having been seized by the underworld where he had tried to retrieve lost belongings. The ghostly Enkidu describes the underworld and explains the correlation between the status of the dead in the afterlife and the care they receive from their surviving family members. The Sumerian myth of Inanna's netherworld journey, translated into Akkadian as *Ishtar's Descent*, describes the goddess' attempt to usurp the throne of her sister Ereshkigal, the queen of the underworld. Inanna's descent emulates death as she enters the underworld through a series of seven gates, eventually arriving at her destination naked and lifeless. Ereshkigal's power is too potent for Inanna, and the "death" of the goddess creates concern among the other gods who devise a way to allow Inanna to return to the living. Erishkigal is eventually placated through the substitution of Inanna's lover Dumuzi in the underworld, allowing her return to the living. The compromise with death is extended further when Dumuzi's sister Geshtinanna offers herself as a substitute for her brother and the two alternate their time in the underworld every six months. The significance of the underworld descent remains a problem. *Inanna's Descent* serves (in part) as an etiology for the ritual mourning of Dumuzi (i.e., Tammuz) as seen in Ezek 8:14. This aspect is evident also in the Greek myth of Adonis, originating in the cult of Tammuz (from the West Semitic word ʾadhoni), where the god is ritually lamented after being killed by a boar. These myths probably do not relate to fertility rites or seasonal patterns because the focus of the stories is placed on the god's death and not necessarily on their return.

The Babylonian "Epic of Gilgamesh" does not include any underworld descent, outside of Tablet XII (which is a partial Akkadian translation of *Gilgamesh, Enkidu, and the Netherworld*). Yet Gilgamesh's journey to the ends of the earth is modeled upon the underworld descent in several ways, not the least of which is the fact that the Sumerian netherworld is located in the distant mountains. The purpose of the search is to discover the secret of immortality by reaching the flood hero Utnapishtim. Accordingly, Gilgamesh must make a journey that no mortal has ever made before, and at the journey's end is ferried across an ominous body of water by a chthonic-type boatman, Urshanabi (compare Charon and the river Styx). Ultimately, what Gilgamesh receives is wisdom and not immortality (as stated in the epic's introduction), which also relates to an important element in mythic descents: the acquisition of secret knowledge. The knowledge of the afterlife is a privilege reserved only for those who are able to make the exceptional journey to the underworld. This theme is extended further in an 8th-cent. BCE Assyrian text concerning a prince who is taken to the underworld in a dream where he receives knowledge regarding the policies of the king (*ANET* 109–10).

A common concern expressed through tales of mythic descents is the power and propriety of death, as is evident in Inanna's helplessness before Ereshkigal. In Greek mythology, Persephone is seized by Hades and brought to the underworld, only to return for two-thirds of the year through the intervention of Zeus. An early (and possibly alternate) myth of Adonis associates him with Persephone in the underworld, and has him return to the living for only part of the year (again through the intervention of Zeus). The Egyptian god Osiris may be the exception, as he dies and is patched back together by Isis (after his body is sundered into fourteen pieces), which results in his rule over the underworld. Even so, the revitalization of Osiris still occurs within the strict confines of death and the underworld, where he sits as judge. The power of death and its realm is also expressed in its separate and inescapable nature, as is stated when Inanna enters the gates of the underworld: "Why have you traveled to the place of no return?" As a result, underworld descents could be presented as heroic feats, as is found in Greek mythology. Hercules' twelfth labor involves his journey to the underworld in order to steal Cerberus, the monstrous guard dog of Hades. Orpheus descends into the underworld in order to follow his wife, Eurydice, and rescue her from the power of death.

B. Old Testament and Ancient Israel

Descriptions of death in the OT often incorporated images reflective of burial that involved the verb of descending, yaradh (יָרַד, "go down"; e.g., Gen 37:35; 42:38; Ps 22:30; Isa 38:18). This image is consistent with the portrayal of the place of the dead, Sheol, using terms reminiscent of the tomb. Yet the OT does not contain any accounts of a return from an underworld descent, aside from the story of Samuel at Endor (1 Sam 28), which is an example of necromancy. Furthermore, verbal descriptions of descents into the underworld are always incidental to the main theme of the respective text, such as the plight of the psalmist in Ps 88, and thus are not intended to serve a larger motif of an extraordinary journey.

At best, the literature of the OT preserves only faint echoes of the underworld descent myth and even in the few instances its interpretation remains problematic. For instance, Ps 24:7-10 probably does not describe a descent where the divine warrior Yahweh triumphantly enters the underworld, although some scholars have read this myth into the text. The interpretation would conform to later Christian readings of the psalm involving Christ's victory over death (see below); yet it is speculative and has no direct parallel in ANE mythology, where neither Inanna/Ishtar nor Baal descend victoriously into the underworld. An interesting allusion to mythic descents is found in Jonah, where the prophet's plight is described in his prayer as confinement within (and salvation from) Sheol (Jonah 2:6). Jonah's three days inside the fish is identical to the time it took Inanna to descend into the underworld. Yet the mythic trope in Jonah is used not as a metaphor for death but instead represents the prophet's isolation. The oracle in Isa 14:3-23 provides one of the few biblical reflexes of the underworld descent myth. The passage describes the ignominious death of the "King of Babylon," and mocks his inability to ascend to the heavens (Isa 14:12-15). Instead, the king lies unburied, and descends to Sheol where the Rephaim rise up to greet him (vv. 9-10). As is typical in the literature of the OT, the biblical writer subverts a mythic theme for polemical purposes.

C. New Testament

Like the OT, the full representation of an underworld descent in the NT is lacking, and its vestige in this corpus of literature is a matter of debate. The figure of Jesus Christ, who died and subsequently rose from the dead before ascending to heaven, embodies the underworld descent-myth. While early Christian writers recognized this aspect in the doctrine of the descent into hell (e.g., Origen, *Cels.* 2.43), NT writers did not emphasize it. For instance, in Acts 2:23-31 the ascent of Jesus from death is understood in light of the OT psalmist's plea not to be forsaken in Sheol (compare Ps 16). Yet the journey to the realm of the dead and the return are only implied and not described. The implication of an underworld descent is evident in the reference to Jonah's three-day sojourn in the belly of the fish as an analogue for the three-day period between the crucifixion and the resurrection (Matt 12:40). This reference in the NT to what is only an allusion (in Jonah) and not an actual underworld descent highlights the interpretive problems involved in identifying this type of mythology in the NT.

The resurrection and ascension of Jesus that is described in 1 Pet 3:18-20 alludes to an underworld descent; however, it is referenced only in brief and left unexplained. The passage states that Jesus "made a proclamation to the spirits in prison" (v. 19) after "he was put to death in the flesh, but made alive in the spirit" (v. 18). It is unclear if Jesus' proclamation was made during his descent to Hades (the underworld) or ascent to heaven, although the verb of motion is not "descend" but poreutheis (πορευθείς, "he went"). Furthermore, the identity of the imprisoned spirits is uncertain, as they could be the dead in Hades, or fallen angels and their offspring (based on the reference to the antediluvian age in v. 20 and parallels in Enochic traditions). The descent of Christ is commented on in Eph 4:7-11, yet it is not explicated in detail. As a result, the passage has long remained a source of debate regarding what this descent means (from the grave or from the underworld) along with its implications for christology.

D. Early Jewish and Christian Literature

In *1 Enoch* (17–36, the Book of the Watchers), which dates to the last quarter of the 1st millennium BCE, the biblical character of Enoch is given several cosmic tours that include the heavens as well as the underworld (compare also *2 En.* 7–10). Enoch is guided on his journey by angels, and is shown the places where the fallen angels and their offspring, the Nephilim (compare Gen 6:1-4), are bound captive until the day of judgment. The journey is portrayed not as a descent but rather as a voyage to the extreme ends of the earth, and the purpose is to enlighten the antediluvian hero regarding matters of eschatology. These two prevalent themes, journeys to the far reaches of the cosmos and the subsequent acquisition of secret knowledge, both correspond to the "Epic of Gilgamesh" (Tablets IX–XI). Indeed, the eschatological knowledge in *1 Enoch* impacted later Jewish and Christian literature that explained the fate of the dead through the trope of an underworld descent, such as the *Apocalypse of Peter* (the earliest dating to the 2nd

cent. CE) and the *Apocalypse of Paul*. An important development in the eschatological theme of cosmic tours is the transformation of the underworld from a holding place for the dead awaiting final judgment such as in the Enochic traditions (*1 En.* 22; 4Q2051 I, 1–3), to the location of immediate and ongoing punishment such as in the apocalypses mentioned above. This development, which originated in prophetic visions of the final judgment (such as *2 Bar.* 59:11), culminated in a later literary tradition made most famous in Dante Alighieri's *Divine Comedy. See* AFTERLIFE; DEAD, ABODE OF THE; DEATH, NT; DEATH, OT; IMMORTALITY; IMMORTALITY IN EARLY JUDAISM; SHEOL.

Bibliography: R. Bauckham. *The Fate of the Dead* (1998); A. M. Cooper. "Ps 24:7-10: Mythology and Exegesis." *JBL* 102 (1983) 37–60; W. J. Dalton. *Christ's Proclamation to the Spirits: A Study of 1 Peter 3:18–4:6* (1965); W. H. Harris. *The Descent of Christ: Ephesians 4:7-11 and Traditional Hebrew Imagery* (1996); M. Himmelfarb. *Tours of Hell* (1985); G. M. Landes. "The 'Three Days and Three Nights' Motif in Jonah 2:1." *JBL* 86 (1967) 446–50; R. M. Shipp. *Of Dead Kings and Dirges* (2002).

MATTHEW J. SURIANO

UNFAITHFUL. *See* FAITH, FAITHFULNESS.

UNFORGIVABLE SIN. At three points in the NT, reference is made to an unforgivable sin: in the Synoptic Gospels, Jesus speaks of unforgivable sin against the Holy Spirit (Matt 12:32; Mark 3:29; Luke 12:10); Hebrews denies a second repentance to apostates (Heb 6:4-6); and 1 John distinguishes between sins that are "mortal" and sins that are not (5:16-17). In each case, attention to context is essential for interpretation.

Jesus refers to unforgivable sin when religious authorities attribute his exorcising ministry to demonic power at work within him (Matt 12:22-32; Mark 3:19b-30; Luke 11:14-26; 12:1-12). Jesus is possessed, but not by Beelzebul, the ruler of demons, as they suppose; God's own Spirit descended upon him at his baptism (Mark 1:10), empowering him for messianic ministry that liberates people from Satan's control (e.g., Mark 1:21-39). To deny that the Spirit at work within Jesus is God's own saving power is to blaspheme and to cut oneself off from the very source of forgiveness. Thus, Jesus warns his accusers that it is an "eternal sin" (Mark 3:29). God's power to forgive is by no means limited (see Mark 3:28), but some prove unable to receive it, biting the very hand that seeks to feed them.

Hebrews stresses the impossibility of restoring apostates again to repentance (Heb 6:4-6; see also 10:26-31; 12:15-17) as it addresses a serious pastoral crisis: believers have grown weary in the Christian way and are in danger of abandoning their Christian vocation (see 2:1-3; 3:12; 6:11-12; 10:23-25; 12:12). The severe words of warning, denying the possibility of a second repentance, aim to dissuade them. Sin in general is not in view, but rather the specific and extreme sin of apostasy, that is, the continuing, public, and defiant repudiation of Christian faith by baptized believers who have experienced the grace of God in Jesus Christ. Apostates exclude themselves from the possibility of repentance because there is no other means of salvation available than that which they have rejected. By denying Jesus Christ, they cut themselves off from the one who is the very "foundation" of repentance and faith (6:1).

In its concluding verses, 1 John refers, obscurely and parenthetically, to sin that is "mortal" (literally, "sin to death") and sin that is not ("sin not to death"; 5:16-17). Believers are discouraged from praying for persons who commit the former, but are assured of the life-giving power of prayers of intercession on behalf of fellow Christians who commit the latter. The nature of the sin that leads to death is not specified, but 1 John is addressed to a community that has been racked by schism (see 2:18-25) and the sin of those who left the community is probably in view: their failure to confess that Jesus Christ has come in the flesh and to embody the love of God revealed therein (see 4:1-6, 7-12, 19-21). In 1 John's view, inadequate christological confession that does not do justice to the humanity of Jesus, along with lack of love, leads to spiritual death in the present and lasting death beyond the grave: "Whoever has the Son has life; whoever does not have the Son of God does not have life" (5:12); moreover, those who love one another "have passed from death to life" and "whoever does not love abides in death" (3:14).

FRANCES TAYLOR GENCH

UNGODLY. See GODLY.

UNITY [יַחַד yakhadh; ἑνότης henotēs, ἑνόω henoō]. Unity is an important, though often elusive, concept in the biblical corpus. Two prominent OT examples are the oneness of God and the unity of the Israelites. Monotheism, the cornerstone of rabbinic Judaism, emerges only gradually in the OT. Indeed, the principal declarations of the God of Israel, the Shema (Deut 6:4-9) and the first commandment of the Decalogue (Exod 20:2-6; Deut 5:6-10), tacitly acknowledge the existence of other gods. Whether the Israelites for a time worshiped multiple gods, including Yahweh, as some texts may suggest (e.g., 2 Kgs 21:1-9; 23:4-20; Jer 8:1-2; 19:13; Zeph 1:5), or instead turned to foreign gods at various intervals at the expense of Yahweh worship is unclear, but the OT chronicles the Israelites' uneven progress toward the concept of one God. This monotheizing process comes to its fullest expression in Deutero-Isaiah, written during the Babylonian exile in the 6th cent. BCE (Isa 43:10-13; 44:6-20; 45:5-25; 46:8-11; see also Deut 4:35-39; 1 Sam 2:1-10; 2 Sam 7:22; 2 Kgs 19:15-19; Isa 37:15-20).

Although Israel's nationhood is announced at Sinai (Exod 19:6), Israelite political unity develops only grad-

ually in the OT and is a short-lived achievement. After migrating to Canaan, the Israelite tribes form a loose confederation (e.g., Judg 1:1-34; 2:6; 20:1-2). The rise of Saul (ca. 1020 BCE) brings unity to the tribes (1 Sam 10:1a, 17-24; 11:14-15; 13:1; 14:47-48). Following Saul, DAVID (ca. 1000 BCE) completes Israel's transition to a united monarchy, centralizing power (2 Sam 5:1-5; 8:15-18) and making Jerusalem the nation's capital (2 Sam 5:5b-12; 6:12-19). The United Kingdom reaches its zenith under SOLOMON (ca. 961 BCE): powerful (e.g., 1 Kgs 4:21), wealthy (e.g., 1 Kgs 4:20-28; 10:14-22, 26-29), and admired (e.g., 1 Kgs 4:34; 9:26-28; 10:1-13, 23-25). After his death, however, the unified state collapses, dividing into northern (Israel) and southern (Judah) kingdoms (1 Kgs 12:16-20).

In the NT, Paul is a forceful proponent of unity, though his understanding is often presented in response to disunity (e.g., 1 Cor 1:10-17; 11:19-22; Gal 2:11-14). For Paul, one of the key effects of the fulfillment of God's reign will be the eschatological unity of humanity. During the end-time period inaugurated with Christ's crucifixion and resurrection, however, Paul insists that his communities model this unity: unity in Christ and, therefore, unity with and for one another (e.g., Rom 12:15-16; 15:5-6; 1 Cor 3:21-23; 6:1-11; Gal 5:25-26; Phil 1:27–2:11; 4:2-3). The baptized are united in Christ's death and will share in his resurrection when he returns (e.g., Rom 6:1-11). Having been "clothed in Christ," differences that formerly divided community members are eliminated (Gal 3:27-28; see also Rom 10:12; 1 Cor 12:13). Paul uses the image of the body, with many parts that form a unified whole, to symbolize the unity he is urging (Rom 12:3-8; 1 Cor 10:16-17; 12:12-26). Unity carries with it responsibility for community members (e.g., Rom 12:9-21; 13:8-11; 14:1-4, 13-21; 15:1-6; 1 Cor 13:1-13; Gal 5:13-14; 16:1-9) as well as for the wider church (Rom 15:25-27; 1 Cor 16:1-4; 2 Cor 8-9; Gal 2:10). See ASHERAH; ASTARTE; AUTHORITY; BAAL; CHURCH, IDEA OF THE; CHURCH, LIFE AND ORGANIZATION OF; ESCHATOLOGY OF THE NT; GOD, OT VIEW OF; ISRAEL, HISTORY OF; PAUL, THE APOSTLE; SAUL, SON OF KISH; SHEMA, THE; TEN COMMANDMENTS; TRIBES, TERRITORIES OF; TRINITY.

WILLIAM SANGER CAMPBELL

UNIVERSALISM. The theological doctrine that all humans will eventually be saved (see SALVATION). The unique situation of Israel and the church, as specially CHOSEN by God, seems to be in tension with the belief that God is creator of all things and ruler of all nations. How can the ideas of a divinely chosen people and universal salvation be reconciled?

Israel is often understood to be specially chosen for the sake of all the nations; it is hoped that in the last time they will all come to God in pilgrimage through Israel and Mount Zion (Isa 2:2-4; Mic 4:1-3). Similarly, the church, which begins in Israel with apparent exclusiveness (Matt 10:5-6; 15:24), is told to go to all the nations (Matt 28:19; compare Rev 14:6; 15:4). Even more broadly, some books in the OT (e.g., Amos, Deutero-Isaiah, Jonah) emphasize God's direct concern and care for all nations. Some important figures in biblical history, furthermore, were known or assumed to be non-Israelites (Job, Ruth, Naaman the Syrian).

Especially since the age of exploration, when the vast extent of the human race became known, there has been concern about the statement that salvation comes only through the name of Jesus (Acts 4:12). Some have suggested that the grace of Christ is made inwardly available to all human beings, enabling them to be Christians in fact though not in name. Universalism in the sense of the belief that all humans receive salvation has been asserted in modern times by the Universalist Church. Even those who do not affirm the actual salvation of all persons frequently affirm the universality of God's offer of grace, which calls for and stimulates a positive response but may be refused.

EUGENE TESELLE

UNIVERSE [κόσμος kosmos, τὸ πᾶν to pan]. God's creation in its entirety (Sir 18:1; 23:20; 42:17; Wis 16:17; Col 2:8, 20), over which God reigns (2 Macc 7:9).

UNKNOWN GOD, ALTAR TO AN [Ἀγνώστῳ Θεῷ Agnōstō Theō]. In his speech before the AREOPAGUS in ATHENS, the Lukan Paul refers to having observed an altar in the city bearing the inscription Agnōstō Theō, "to an unknown god" (Acts 17:23a). Paul proceeds to make the proclamation of this unknown god the theme of his speech (v. 23b). Historical and literary issues concerning this verse—and the speech as a whole—have generated an enormous amount of scholarly debate because archaeologists have not yet found an altar dedicated "to an unknown god," nor is there any mention of such an inscription in surviving Greco-Roman literature. While some scholars have categorically denied that such inscriptions could exist, others have offered plausible scenarios for their creation. Passages in Pausanias, Diogenes Laertius, and Philostratus (Horst; Witherington) perhaps establish the probability that there were altars dedicated to unknown gods, although caution is warranted because these references can be interpreted in various ways. Furthermore, while an extant altar from the temple of Demeter in Pergamum is often cited as evidence for the existence of such altars, the inscription is damaged precisely at the crucial point (the brackets indicate which letters are missing): THEOIS AG[NOSTOIS] (ΘΕΟΙΣ ΑΓ[ΝΩΣΤΟΙΣ]) and could be restored with letters that spell other words.

Interestingly, the church father Jerome suggested that Paul was paraphrasing an inscription that actually read, "To the gods of Asia, Europe, and Africa, to the unknown and foreign gods." This clue may provide the most valuable insight for interpretation. Jerome, Luke,

and Paul belonged to an age that was more concerned with rhetorical skill than factual exactitude. One should compare how often Paul, Luke, and other NT writers make quite significant changes to Scripture quotations to make their points. If Paul invented a singular form of a similar plural inscription to introduce his speech, this might well have impressed rather than scandalized his rhetorically sophisticated audience. See ACTS OF THE APOSTLES; GREEK RELIGION AND PHILOSOPHY.

Bibliography: P. W. van der Horst. "The Altar of the 'Unknown God' in Athens (Acts 17.23) and the Cults of 'Unknown Gods' in the Graeco-Roman World." *Hellenism–Judaism–Christianity: Essays on Their Interaction* (1994) 165–202; Ben Witherington III. *The Acts of the Apostles: A Socio-Rhetorical Commentary* (1998).

MARK D. GIVEN

UNLEAVENED BREAD uhn-lev´uhnd-bred´ [מַצָּה matsah; ἄζυμος azymos]. Unleavened bread figures in several contexts in the OT. Since bread of this type lacked a leavening agent and therefore did not require a time for the dough to rise, it was convenient to prepare for a visitor, especially an unexpected one. Scriptural examples are Lot, who served the two angels who came to Sodom (Gen 19:3), Gideon, who presented it to his angelic guest (Judg 6:19-22), and the medium of Endor, who baked it for Saul (1 Sam 28:24).

The most familiar references to unleavened bread occur in the context of the exodus from Egypt. Exodus 12 provides the legislation for both the Passover meal, which included unleavened bread (12:8), and the Festival of Unleavened Bread when, for the seven days after Passover, unleavened bread was to be eaten and no leaven was to be found among the Israelites (12:15, 17-20; 13:1-6; see also Exod 23:15; 34:18; Lev 23:6; Num 28:17; Deut 16:3-4, 8, 16; Ezek 45:21; *see* PASSOVER AND FEAST OF UNLEAVENED BREAD). As a result there were eight consecutive days in the first month of the year (1/14–21) when the only bread that could be consumed lacked yeast. An explanation for this law is offered later in the chapter, when the Egyptians were urging the Israelites to leave their land after the tenth plague: "the people took their dough before it was leavened, with their kneading bowls wrapped in their cloaks on their shoulders" (12:34). The element of haste is underscored in 12:39: "it was not leavened, because they were driven out of Egypt and could not wait, nor had they prepared any provisions for themselves" (see also Deut 16:3). Eating unleavened bread was also the rule at the second Passover (Num 9:11; 2 Chr 30:13, 21).

The other context in which unleavened bread plays a role is the priestly legislation regarding the grain offering. Leviticus 2 provides the rules covering the different forms these sacrifices could take. If the offering is prepared in an oven, there are to be "unleavened cakes mixed with oil, or unleavened wafers spread with oil" (2:4); there was also to be unleavened bread if it is heated on a griddle (vv. 5-6). The legislator announces a general principle on this matter in 2:11: "No grain offering that you bring to the LORD shall be made with leaven, for you must not turn any leaven or honey into smoke as an offering by fire to the LORD" (see also 1 Chr 23:29). The implication appears to be that there is something objectionable about leaven (and honey) with its fermenting properties in a sacrificial context; exactly what is objectionable about it is not explained here (compare Matt 16:6-12, where Jesus warns the disciples against "the yeast of the Pharisees and Sadducees"). Once a portion of the grain offering has been burned for the deity, the priests eat the remainder as unleavened cakes (Lev 6:16-17 [Heb. 6:9-10]; see also 10:12 and contrast 2 Kgs 23:9). In addition, when the sacrifice of well-being serves as a thanksgiving offering it includes unleavened cakes and wafers (Lev 7:11-12, but see v. 13). For the ordination ceremony for Aaron and his sons, the deity commands Moses to take, among other items, a basket of unleavened bread (Lev 8:2). In the course of the ritual he places a cake of unleavened bread in the priests' palms; they are presented as an elevation offering. These rites effect the commands given in Exod 29:2-3, 23-25; similar actions are part of the ceremony at the completion of a Nazirite's term (Num 6:15, 17, 19).

In 1 Cor 5:8, the apostle Paul contrasts "the unleavened bread of sincerity and truth" with "the yeast of malice and evil" in admonishing the Corinthians to "clean out the old yeast" (v. 7). *See* LEAVEN.

JAMES C. VANDERKAM

UNNI, UNNO uhn´*i*, uhn´oh [עֻנִּי 'unni, עֻנּוֹ 'unno].
1. A Levite of secondary rank mentioned in 1 Chr 15:18, 20. The name appears in a list of Levites who were charged with providing musical accompaniment during David's second attempt to transport the ark of the covenant from the house of Obed-edom to Jerusalem.

2. A Levite listed among those who returned from exile with Zerubbabel and Jeshua in Neh 12:9. The Kethibh reading of the name in this verse is "Unno," but the Qere supports the alternative reading "Unni."

DEREK E. WITTMAN

UNPARDONABLE SIN. *See* UNFORGIVABLE SIN.

UNWRITTEN SAYINGS. *See* AGRAPHA.

UPHAZ yoo´faz [אוּפָז 'ufaz]. Esteemed for its GOLD (Jer 10:9; Dan 10:5), Uphaz may be a variant spelling for OPHIR, a site more frequently referenced for its production of this precious metal. This view, going back to the 18th cent., is supported by the Syriac version of Jer 10:9.

UPPER BETH-HORON. *See* BETH-HORON.

UPPER GATE [שַׁעַר הָעֶלְיוֹן sha'ar ha'elyon]. A gate of the preexilic temple precincts. Biblical passages make its location unclear (2 Chr 23:20, south?; Ezek 9:2, north?). Jotham (re)built this gate as part of his building project (2 Kgs 15:35; 2 Chr 27:3); hence, it may also be identified as the NEW GATE of Jeremiah's court hearing (Jer 26:10; 36:10). *See* TEMPLE, JERUSALEM.

JAMES RILEY STRANGE

UPPER ROOM [ἀνάγαιον anagaion, ὑπερῷον hyperōon]. A room in an upper story of a private house or multi-unit housing. In Mark 14:12-16 (compare Matt 26:17-25; Luke 22:7-13), two disciples enter Jerusalem to prepare a Passover meal in an upstairs room (anagaion; Mark 14:15; Luke 22:12) where Jesus and the Twelve will eat what becomes their final meal together. The room is described as large and furnished, possibly indicating couches spread out for guests to recline at a banquet. Also referred to as a guest room (Mark 14:14), this type of room was made available for pilgrims to commemorate Passover in overcrowded Jerusalem (compare Luke 2:7). The house was probably a two-story private urban home, where second-floor rooms were often used as living areas or dining rooms while first-floor rooms might be work spaces, living areas, or shops.

This upper room served as a temporary refuge during Jesus' final turbulent days. Sharing the meal solidified social bonds before these ties were again challenged. Yet the room may not have provided much privacy or security. Most houses were not closed off from neighbors but included fluid spaces between rooms, floors, and other houses. This lack of protected space, along with the precautions Jesus takes to secure the room (Mark 14:13-15), highlight the narrative's danger and suspense.

Acts uses a different Greek word for an upper-story room (hyperōon). After the eleven male apostles witness Jesus' ascension, they return to Jerusalem and gather in an upper room with certain women followers (compare Luke 8:1-3; 23:49, 54-56; 24:1-12) and Jesus' mother and brothers (Acts 1:12-14). Shown to be united and in prayer (v. 14), Jesus' followers regroup during this transition stage as they await the Holy Spirit (1:5, 8; compare 1:21-26). The women's presence correlates with recent archaeological studies arguing that household space was dynamic and not clearly divided by gender. The diverse group assembled suggests the inclusiveness of the early church and its leaders. This may be the same upper room where the disciples ate the Passover meal (see also Acts 2:1; 12:12).

In Acts 9:36-43, Tabitha, a disciple and benefactor, is laid in a room upstairs after her death where Peter then prays for her and shows "her to be alive." Later in Acts, Eutychus falls out of a window from the third story of an apartment house where Paul is meeting with others to break bread and preach. The young man is found dead but Paul holds him and finds that "his life is in him" (Acts 20:7-12). These two stories echo the healing miracles of Elijah (1 Kgs 17:17-24) and Elisha (2 Kgs 4:8-37), who both bring back to life, in an upper chamber on the roof, those who have died. The theme of death and new life is curiously associated with the upper room.

The use of an upper-story room for regular gatherings to break bread and worship, for healings and prayer, for eating and celebrating festivals, and for refuge underscore the critical role of these rooms, houses, and hospitality for the early followers of Jesus. *See* ARCHITECTURE, NT; ARCHITECTURE, OT; BANQUET; CHAMBER; HOSPITALITY; HOUSE CHURCH; ROOF.

JAMES P. GRIMSHAW

UPPER ROOM OF THE CORNER [עֲלִיַּת הַפִּנָּה ʿaliyath happinnah]. A site located at the northeast corner of Jerusalem's city wall between the Muster and Sheep Gates. It served as a marker for responsibilities in the repair of Jerusalem's walls (Neh 3:31-32). Given its strategic position in the northern wall, it doubtless served a significant defensive function.

TIMOTHY G. CRAWFORD

UPRIGHT. *See* RIGHTEOUSNESS IN EARLY JEWISH LITERATURE; RIGHTEOUSNESS IN THE NT; RIGHTEOUSNESS IN THE OT.

UPSILON [υ y Υ y]. The twenty-first letter of the Greek alphabet, based on the Phoenician *waw [<*waww], which was the prototype not only of the consonant fau (v) but also the vowel u, later upsilon ("simple u," to distinguish it from oi, which had come to have the same pronunciation). *See* ALPHABET.

P. KYLE MCCARTER JR.

UR oor [אוּר ʾur]. 1. Ur was a very ancient and important city of lower Mesopotamia, located at modern Tell el-Muqayyar, a few kilometers southwest of the modern city of Nasiriyah, Iraq. Though Tell el-Muqayyar lies in the desert at some distance from the Euphrates and quite removed from the head of the Persian Gulf, this is due to changes in the course of the Euphrates and to a receding coastline. An ancient bed of the Euphrates runs along the western and northern walls of Ur, and in its heyday Ur was served by both a western and northern harbor on the right bank of the river. It is generally believed that the Persian Gulf extended farther north in antiquity, and thus access to the Persian Gulf via the Euphrates through the marshes would have been far easier in the periods of Ur's greatest prosperity. Its location was ideal for trade by both sea and land, and this advantageous location as a transit point between the whole Persian Gulf region and upper Mesopotamia contributed to the great prosperity of Ur in the 3rd and early 2nd millennium BCE.

A. Archaeology
B. History
C. Biblical References
Bibliography

A. Archaeology

The ruins at Tell el-Muqayyar concealed a roughly oval-shaped walled city, measuring about 1,000 m long from north to south, and over 600 m at its widest point from east to west. The most impressive feature of the site was the still distinctive shape of the well-preserved ziggurat, measuring some 62.5 m by 43 m at its base, in the northwestern part of the ruins. Pietra della Valle was the first European to "discover" the site in 1625, and Sir William Loftus did some excavation there in 1849, but it was not until J. E. Taylor's recovery of an inscribed brick there in 1855 that Sir H. C. Rawlinson was able to identify the site with biblical Ur. Campbell Thompson did some soundings there in 1918, and H. R. Hall did some further excavations at Ur, Eridu, and Ubaid in 1918–19, but it was not until 1922 that a major expedition could be mounted. Sir C. L. Woolley directed this expedition from 1922–34 under the joint sponsorship of the British Museum and the University of Pennsylvania, and this expedition yielded some of the richest results of any excavation in ancient Mesopotamia.

Figure 1: Alabaster statuette of a woman from Ur (2450 BCE). Iraq Museum, Baghdad, Iraq.

The most famous of these discoveries involved two groups of royal tombs, one group from the ED III period (ca. 2600–2350) and the other from the Ur III period (ca. 2111–2003). Some of the tombs from the ED III period were discovered intact or relatively intact, and their contents were both rich and surprising. The royal tombs were of stone with corbeled ceilings accessible by a sloping ramp, and along the foot of these ramps the excavators found a large number of bodies of soldiers, female attendants, wagon drivers, and musicians in elaborate regalia along with the bodies of teams of equids, wagons, funerary chariots, expensive weapons, and musical instruments. The humans had obviously been sacrificed to accompany their king or queen into the afterlife along with the tools of their trade, but the positioning of the bodies gave no indication of resistance or of violent death. Within the burial chambers themselves the body of the royal personage lay on a wooden bier surrounded by a great wealth of very expensive personal possessions—jewelry, ornamental weapons, musical instruments, game boards, ornamental furniture, and precious vases. Many of these objects are well known to the general public, having long been on display in the British Museum or the Museum of the University of Pennsylvania, and even more widely circulated in photographs published in numerous books and pamphlets. The amazing quality of the workmanship and artistry of these luxury items still impresses a modern audience, and that together with the sheer volume of the gold, silver, lapis lazuli, and other precious stones or metals found in the tombs gives eloquent testimony to the wealth of Ur at this period.

The royal tombs were found at the southeastern end of the great temenos or sacred enclosure that had been expanded southward over the earlier tombs by Nebuchadnezzar II in the 6th cent. BCE. The ziggurat rises in the northwestern corner of this temenos, but it is blocked off from the rest of the temenos by another large double-walled enclosure more than 100 m in length. It was originally constructed by Ur-Nammu of the Third Dynasty of Ur (2111–2094 BCE) for the moon god Nanna (Akkadian sin), the patron deity of Ur. It was built of unbaked bricks with a protective outside layer of baked bricks, and it originally stood three stories high, with a sanctuary for Nanna at the top. There were three stairways to the first stage, two to the second, and one to the chapel at the top. The ziggurat, which has been partially restored, is still an impressive sight, and though recent history has discouraged general tourism in Iraq, the site is a favorite tourist spot for American military personnel in the region. South of the ziggurat enclosure was a temple dedicated to Ningal, the spouse of Nanna. It consisted of two large sanctuaries, a chapel, private apartments, workshops, stores, and kitchens, and gave scholars important insights into the workings of ancient Sumerian temples. There was another major building to the east of the ziggurat enclosure, and farther to the southeast, near the tombs, was the palace of Ur-Nammu

and Shulgi. Woolley's excavation focused on the tombs and the large public buildings, and because there have been no major archaeological excavations at the site since Woolley's excavation ended, little is known about the private dwellings of ordinary citizens of Ur. There is still much to be learned from future excavations at the site.

B. History

Ur was already inhabited in the Ubaid period in the middle of the 5th millennium BCE in the earliest stages of village settlement in lower Mesopotamia. It may have been abandoned for a period, but if so, it was resettled in the 4th millennium, and by the end of the 4th millennium it began to emerge as one of those urban centers resulting from the consolidation of the scattered farming villages of the earlier period. This process of consolidation may have taken place in order to facilitate large-scale centralized irrigation works made necessary by a drying climate. By the middle of the 3rd millennium, in the ED III period, during the reigns of such kings as Mesanepada and Aanepada of the Ur I dynasty (ca. 2600–2500 BCE), Ur was a wealthy and flourishing city, enriched by both successful agriculture and foreign trade. The tombs of Puabi and Meskalamdug, who was probably a slightly earlier member of this dynasty, testifys to the wealth and importance of Ur during this period.

Ur then went through a period of decline as other Sumerian city-states struggled with Ur for supremacy in the south only to see the Akkadian ruler Sargon the Great defeat them all. Sargon's conquest of Sumer shifted the wealth of the Persian Gulf trade upstream, north to Akkad, and Ur could not regain its former prominence as long as the Akkad dynasty held sway (ca. 2350–2150 BCE).

With the collapse of the Akkad dynasty, however, Ur recovered quickly. After serving briefly as a governor of Utu-hegal of Uruk, Ur-Nammu, the founder of the Third Dynasty of Ur (2111–2094 BCE), and his capable successor, Shulgi (2093–2046 BCE), created an empire that almost rivaled that of the earlier rulers of Akkad. Ur-Nammu, or perhaps Shulgi, was responsible for the publication of the earliest known Mesopotamian law code, and both Ur-Nammu and Shulgi were deified in their lifetimes. Their successors, however, were threatened by the constant and increasing volume of the infiltration of semi-nomadic tribes known as the Amorites into the territory controlled by Ur. They tried to block this disruptive immigration by building a defensive wall against the Amorites, but the strategy failed, and faced with drought, crop shortages, and a loss of central control over other cities supposedly subject to Ur, Ur eventually fell (ca. 2003 BCE) to an attack of resurgent Elam.

Ur never recovered the prominence it had during the Ur I and Ur III dynasties. It remained an important southern city and a religious center for the worship of the moon god, but the political center of power in

Mesopotamia had moved much farther north. The Neo-Babylonian kings, beginning with Nebuchadnezzar II (605–562 BCE), did some major construction work in Ur, and during the reign of Nabonidus (556–539 BCE), the last king of the Neo-Babylonian dynasty, the city gained renewed prominence as a religious center.

Nabonidus gave special attention to the two main centers for the worship of the moon god, Harran (biblical Haran), in far northern Mesopotamia, where his mother had been a devotee of the moon god, and Ur in the south. Whatever the reason for this devotion to the cult of the moon god, it provoked serious conflict between Nabonidus and the priests of Marduk in Babylon, and they appear to have welcomed Cyrus as a liberator when Babylon fell to the Persians in 539 BCE. With the Persian conquest and the loss of royal support from its former Neo-Babylonian patrons, Ur fell into a steady decline and eventually into total oblivion.

C. Biblical References

The Bible mentions Ur four times as the original home of Abraham, always in the expression "Ur of the Chaldeans" (Gen 11:28, 31; 15:7; Neh 9:7), and the book of *Jubilees*, obviously dependent on these biblical passages, also mentions Ur (*Jub.* 11:7). The LXX never translates Ur as a proper name, always rendering the expression as "the region of the Chaldeans" (hē chōra tōn Xaldaiōn ἡ χώρα τῶν Χαλδαίων), but the other ancient translations all correctly identify Ur as a proper name. The further designation of Ur as "of the Chaldeans" identifies the biblical Ur with the Ur of southern Mesopotamia, because that is the homeland of the Chaldean tribes; however, the expression appears to be anachronistic, since the Chaldeans first appear in cuneiform sources in the 9th cent. BCE, while Abraham, if historical, must clearly be a figure of the 2nd millennium. According to the biblical tradition, Abraham first emigrated from Ur to Haran (Harran in cuneiform sources) in upper Mesopotamia and eventually from there to Canaan. Many of the names of Abraham's family members are attested as place names in upper Mesopotamia and that, together with the long distance between the southern Mesopotamian Ur and Haran, has led some scholars to suggest that Abraham's original home was actually a different Ur or Ura in upper Mesopotamia or northern Syria far closer to Haran. There is a religious connection between Haran and the southern Ur, however, in that both were cities dedicated to the worship of the moon god. Moreover, the semi-nomadic Amorites moved throughout this whole region, from upper Mesopotamia to the far south, and as semi-nomads they did not always settle down permanently in the regions into which they infiltrated. If the movements of Israel's ancestral clans are to be associated with the Amorite movement, as many scholars assume because of the similarity between ancestral names and Amorite names, then the ancestral migration from southern Mesopotamian Ur to upper Mesopotamian Haran, and

from there to Canaan, is not a problem. In any case, there is no compelling reason to reject the biblical tradition's identification of Abraham's original homeland as the southern Ur, even if the biblical tradition anachronistically associates that Ur with the later Chaldeans. *See* AMORITES; ASSYRIA AND BABYLONIA; CHALDEA, CHALDEANS; ELAM, ELAMITES; ERECH; ERIDU; HARAN; NEBUCHADNEZZAR, NEBUCHADREZZAR; SUMER, SUMERIANS.

Bibliography: H. R. Hall. *A Season's Work at Ur, al-'Ubaid, Abu Shahrain (Eridu) and Elsewhere; Being an Unofficial Account of the British Museum Archaeological Mission to Babylonia, 1919* (1930); Thorkild Jacobsen. *The Sumerian King List* (1939); Amélie Kuhrt. *The Ancient Near East c. 3000–330 BC, Volume One* (1995); Seton Lloyd. *The Archaeology of Mesopotamia: From the Old Stone Age to the Persian Conquest* (1978); William Kennett Loftus. *Travels and Researches in Chaldea and Susiana; With an Account of Excavations at Warka, the "Erech" of Nimrod, Shush, "Shushan the Palace" of Esther, in 1849–52* (1857); P. R. S. Moorey, ed. *Ur 'of the Chaldees': A Revised and Updated Edition of Sir Leonard Woolley's Excavations at Ur*, by Sir Leonard Woolley (1982).

J. J. M. ROBERTS

2. The father of ELIPHAL (1 Chr 11:35). Eliphal's name appears in a list of warriors in the service of David. In a parallel list in 2 Sam 23:34, a person named AHASBAI appears as the father of the warrior ELIPHELET, presumably a variant form of the name Eliphal.

DEREK E. WITTMAN

URARTU. Ancient kingdom in the area of present Armenia. Assyrian sources refer to the area as *Urartu*, but it was known to the biblical writers as ARARAT. According to 2 Kgs 19:37; Isa 37:38; Jer 51:27; and Tob 1:21, the sons of Sennacherib, king of Assyria, fled there after killing their father.

JOAN E. COOK, SC

URBANUS uhr-bay′nuhs [Οὐρβανός *Ourbanos*]. One of many individuals greeted by Paul at the end of Romans (16:9), but only one of four mentioned in the letter who are explicitly identified as being a "co-worker" (synergos συνεργός) of Paul, the others being Prisca and Aquila (16:3) and Timothy (16:21). Urbanus was most likely a Gentile Christian, although there is still some debate as to whether his name indicates that he was freeborn or slaveborn.

J. TED BLAKLEY

URI yoor′*i* [אוּרִי *'uri*]. **1.** A Judahite, father of Bezalel, one of the tabernacle builders (Exod 31:2; 35:30; 38:22; 2 Chr 1:5). He is a grandson of Caleb according to the genealogy of Judah in 1 Chr 2:20.

2. Father of Geber, the district officer in Gilead under Solomon (1 Kgs 4:19).

3. A gatekeeper who was compelled to divorce his foreign wife in the days of Ezra (Ezra 10:24).

JOAN E. COOK, SC

URIAH yoo-rí´uh [אוּרִיָּה ʾuriyah, אוּרִיָּהוּ ʾuriyahu; Οὐρίου Ouriou]. Means "Yahweh is light (or fire)." 1. A Hittite and an officer of DAVID's army who died because of David's BETRAYAL. He was named in a list of an elite group of officers in the Israelite army (2 Sam 23:24-39), and the fact that his house was near the king's house may indicate that he was from a prominent member of the royal-military circles that antedated David's conquest of Jerusalem. The name *Uriah* is a Yahwistic name although some have suggested that the name is foreign. But the fact that four other persons by this name in the Bible are either a prophet or a priest of Yahweh indicates that the name itself does not indicate a foreign ancestry. It was the term *Hittite* that marked him as non-Israelite. He was on the battlefield against the Ammonites at Rabbah when David took advantage of his wife BATHSHEBA in his absence and, as a result, she became pregnant (2 Sam 11:1-5). David's first attempt to cover up his sin failed when Uriah refused to go down to his house and sleep with his wife (2 Sam 11:6-13). Then David ordered Joab to put Uriah in the frontline of the battle and then withdraw so that his death would be inevitable (2 Sam 11:14-15). For this murderous act, David was censured by the Lord through the prophet Nathan (2 Sam 12:1-13). This episode is remembered as "the matter of Uriah the Hittite" (1 Kgs 15:5). The Chronicler omits this embarrassing episode, but the genealogy of Jesus in Matthew notes Solomon's mother as "the wife of Uriah" (Matt 1:6).

2. A priest in the reign of Ahaz of Judah and a contemporary of the prophet Isaiah. While in Damascus to meet Tiglath-pileser, king of Assyria, Ahaz sent him detailed descriptions of the altar in Damascus (2 Kgs 16:10). He built the altar before Ahaz returned from Damascus. When Ahaz arrived in Jerusalem, the king gave the priest instructions for the use of the altar (2 Kgs 16:15), and the priest "did everything that King Ahaz commanded" (2 Kgs 16:16). Apparently, this Uriah was one of the two "reliable witnesses" whom Isaiah called upon to attest to an oracle against Damascus and Samaria (Isa 8:1-2).

3. A prophet from Kiriath-jearim, son of Shemaiah. He prophesied against Jerusalem in words similar to Jeremiah's temple sermon (Jer 26:20). Jeremiah's life was spared by the intervention of Ahikam son of Shaphan (Jer 26:24), but no one intervened on behalf of Uriah. He fled to Egypt, but Jehoiakim sent an envoy to bring him back, struck him down with the sword, and threw his body into the common graveyard (Jer 26:23).

4. The father of the priest Meremoth who returned to Jerusalem with Ezra (8:33; compare 1 Esd 8:62) and

partook in the rebuilding of the Jerusalem wall under Nehemiah's leadership (Neh 3:4, 21). He was remembered in his son's good deeds.

5. One of the leaders who was given the honor of standing at the right hand of Ezra on a wooden platform made for the occasion of the public reading of "the book of the law of Moses" (Neh 8:4; 1 Esd 9:43).

Bibliography: Daniel Bodi. "Outraging the Resident-Alien: King David, Uriah the Hittite, and an El-Amarna Parallel." *UF* 35 (2003) 29–56; Uriah Y. Kim. "Uriah the Hittite: A Con(text) of Struggle for Identity." *Semeia* 90/91 (2002) 69–85.

URIAH Y. KIM

URIEL yoor´ee-uhl [אוּרִיאֵל ʾuriʾel]. 1. A Levite whose name appears in a list of the descendants of Kohath in 1 Chr 6:24 (Heb. 6:9). He appears again in 1 Chr 15:5 and 1 Chr 15:11 as the head of the Kohathite clan during the reign of David, and he is listed among those Levites who participated in the transportation of the ark of the covenant to Jerusalem from the house of Obed-edom.

2. A man from Gibeah who is mentioned in 2 Chr 13:2 as the maternal grandfather of the Judahite king Abijah and whose mother was Micaiah. Elsewhere in the Hebrew and the LXX of 2 Chr 13:2, Micaiah's name appears as "Maacah." Uriel's paternity is somewhat unclear, because Micaiah appears as the daughter of Absalom in 1 Kgs 15:2 and 2 Chr 11:20. She is generally believed to be Uriel's daughter and Absalom's granddaughter.

DEREK E. WITTMAN

3. An angel ("God's flame") who appears to Ezra and instructs him about the end of the age (2 Esd 4:1; 5:20; 10:28). In *1 Enoch*, he is Enoch's guide and reveals astrological knowledge, whereas in the SIBYLLINE ORACLES he leads souls from Hades to judgment, which is also his role in the *Apocalypse of Peter*. For the rabbis, Uriel was one of the four angels around God's throne (*Num. Rab.* 2:10) and one of the four wise (angelic) teachers who laid Moses to his final rest (*Tg. Ps.-J.* Deut 34:6). *See* ENOCH, FIRST BOOK OF; GABRIEL; MICHAEL; PETER, APOCALYPSE OF; RAPHAEL.

FRED L. HORTON

URIM AND THUMMIM yoor´im, thum´im [אוּרִים ʾurim, תֻּמִּים tummim]. Urim (ʾurim) and Thummim (tummim) are words of uncertain etymology. Some suspect that the terms come from the words for light (ʾor אוֹר) and truth (tom תֹּם) and in that way signal their obviously divinatory character. Others argue that they are formed from the roots for curse (ʾrr ארר) and faultlessness (tmm תמם) and thus signal two possible outcomes of using the Urim and Thummim to judge a person. Still others suggest that they form a merism, denoting the first and last letters of the alphabet, ALEF

(ʾ **א**) and TAV (t **ת**), and therefore the instruments referred to with the name "Urim and Thummim" would actually be the letters of the Hebrew alphabet, from which the user would derive oracular meaning. None of these etymologies—nor any of those that rely on weak linguistic echoes in related languages (e.g., **urm, ttrp ipd** from Ugarit)—have found sufficient following to obtain the status of anything approaching a consensus.

Though few in number, occurrences of the pair of terms (or of one of them singly) do provide some useful information (but still less than one might hope). From the occurrences in the Priestly source in the Pentateuch we learn where the Urim and Thummim are kept (in the breastpiece attached to the high priest's ephod; Exod 28:30; Lev 8:8), that they can serve as a means of judgment exercised by the high priest (Exod 28:30), and that the judgment might be more expansive than merely providing a yes or no answer to a question (Num 27:21; Urim only). One might also argue that the Priestly source limits the locus of the use of the Urim and Thummim by the high priest to the holy of holies ("before the LORD" in Exod 28:30; Num 27:21). Jacob Milgrom speculates that the reason for this was the Priestly writers' desire to avoid the use of the Urim and Thummim in the wider public, lest such a practice encourage the laity's use of unsanctioned media for divinatory actions (see, e.g., Hos 4:12; Zech 10:2). Indeed, the remaining occurrences of the term imply that it took place outside the Temple, inasmuch as the users are to a person not the high priest. From Moses' testamentary poem addressing each of the tribes of Israel, we learn that, contrary to the Priestly work's assignment of the objects to the high priest, the Thummim and Urim (in that order) are to be given to Levi and to "your loyal one," respectively (Deut 33:8). Likewise, the report in 1 Sam 28:6 that Saul consulted the Urim (alone) contradicts the Priestly work's restrictive allotment of the Urim (and Thummim) to the high priest. That Saul does so to determine how to proceed against the Philistine army suggests, like Num 27:21, that the Urim, at least, could provide more substantive information than a simple yes or no response when consulted. Lastly, Ezra 2:63 (// Neh 7:65) indicates that in the postexilic period the Urim and Thummim continued to function as divinatory devices, but that they could be used, apparently, by any priest, and, again, quite apart from the Temple and holy of holies (and only if a priest could be found to use them; see below).

Unsatisfied with the limited scope of the evidence, some scholars have argued for including as implicit accounts of the use of the devices texts that employ (roughly) the same circumlocution for consulting the Urim that appears in Num 27:21, shaʾal le (**לְ שָׁאַל**), "inquire of," with reference to God or the Lord. Candidates for this pool of texts include Judg 1:1; 20:18, 23, 27; 1 Sam 10:22; 14:37; 22:10; 23:2, 4; 30:8; 2 Sam 2:1; 5:19, 23-24 (Milgrom; Van Dam). The chief result of expanding the data pool in this way is to uncover a fair number of uses that are, once again, not accomplished by the high priest and that occur apart from the Temple.

Even with this enlarged body of evidence, though, none of these passages tell us what the Urim and Thummim were, nor do they indicate how their users consulted them. Not surprisingly, then, a good deal of the attention paid to them has been devoted to dispelling these mysteries. The endeavor has not achieved any measurable success, even if it has produced some imaginative possibilities.

As for what shape the Urim and Thummim took, multiple suggestions have been made, none of them having any greater or lesser weight by the measure of the evidence. If any of the suggestions can claim some degree of textual support, it is the one that holds, by analogy with Hos 4:12 ("My people consult a piece of wood, and their divining rod gives them oracles"), that the Urim and Thummim were sticks, perhaps arrows (compare Ezek 21:28-29; see also the Arab practice of **istiqsam**, divining by sticks). The difficulty with this, of course, is that the divination remarked upon in Hosea is declared idolatrous, and in both Hosea and Ezekiel non-priests carry out the act. The other most frequently mentioned objects to play the role of the Urim and Thummim are a pair of dice that aided divinatory or oracular judgment. Just how dice would accomplish that goal determines in part how one might expect them to appear and what markings they might bear. They may have carried some markings (letters of the alphabet, symbols unknown to us, etc.) or they may have been multicolored. In the latter case, they may have been like the stones in Assyrian psephomancy, which were white and black in color and deemed the desired and undesired stones. In the case of the former, it is conceivable that the stones or dice bore the letters of the alphabet and in combination could form any number of tri-consonantal roots. Some believe that the objects were luminous stones that provided insight through a sort of refraction of light. Lastly, some argue that the terms *Urim* and *Thummim* are plurals only in name and that they, in fact, refer to a single, unknown divinatory device.

With so little clarity on the physical nature of the Urim and Thummim it is hardly surprising that there is even more uncertainty—and speculation—as to how they were used. To even begin to answer this question scholarship has relied on the LXX's expanded reading of 1 Sam 14:41 that adds another text in which the actual terms, or at least near equivalents, appear. In determining why God had not answered an unrelated query, the additional material in the LXX (which presumably fell out of the MT) says of Saul that he consulted "clear ones" (= Urim?) and "holiness" (= Thummim?) to see who was at fault for God's reticence. From this, many assume that the Urim and Thummim were some form of lots cast to get a basic positive or negative answer to the query put to them. However, the passages noted above that lack the terms *Urim* and *Thummim,* but contain the language for a query to God (and so are considered as further evidence for the use of the device[s]), require that the divination accomplished could provide more information than a simple yes or no. In Judg 1:1-2; 20:18 the Lord reveals who among the tribes should go first in battle against foes; in 1 Sam 10:22 they reveal Saul's presence among the baggage; and in 2 Sam 2:1 and 5:23-24 David learns from God (again, presumably through the Urim and Thummim) that he is to go up to Hebron at one point, and at another to advance on the Philistines when he hears the sound of marching in the treetops. These oracles concern far more than simple yes and no answers. By further contrast still, Josephus, *Ant.* 3.216–18, may be read to suggest that the Urim and Thummim were the twelve stones on or in the breastpiece of the high priest, and that they simply shone to give a favorable response from God regarding a decision to march against enemies. It is not merely the lack of certainty regarding the nature of the Urim and Thummim that prohibits clarity on their use; it is the diversity of testimony as well.

When did the Urim and Thummim cease to serve their purpose? The evidence of Ezra 2:63 (//Neh 7:65) implies that already in the Second Temple period they had gone out of use (or there was no priest to use them effectively): there simply was no priest to give Urim and Thummim to settle the priestly status of claimants to the office. By contrast, the description of the contemporary high priest in Sir 45:7-13 (early 2nd cent. BCE) insists that he still possessed the "oracle of judgment," and Josephus says that the stones of the breastpiece (really the Urim and Thummim?) still shone until nearly the end of the 2nd cent. BCE (*Ant.* 3.218).

Bibliography: Jacob Milgrom. *Leviticus 1–16: A New Translation and Introduction with Commentary.* AB 3 (1991); Cornelis Van Dam. *The Urim and Thummim: A Means of Revelation in Ancient Israel* (1997).

ROBERT KUGLER

URN [στάμνος stamnos]. A jar. An urn holds the manna of the exodus inside the ark of the covenant within the earthly tabernacle, according to the author of Hebrews (9:4; compare Exod 16:33-34).

USHTANI ['Υοτανης Hystanēs]. A satrap of the Persian satrapy of Babylon and BEYOND THE RIVER appointed by DARIUS I. He was also the priest of the Ebabbarra temple in Sippar. He was likely the superior of the governor Tattenai (Ezra 5:3, 6; 6:6, 13). *See* BABYLON, OT; SATRAP, SATRAPY.

DEREK E. WITTMAN

UTENSILS [כֵּלִים kelim; σκεῦος skeuos]. A generic term primarily referring to the vessels and tools used in cultic services. Vessels for the table of the BREAD OF PRESENCE and the LAMPSTAND were made of pure gold and included plates, dishes for incense, flagons and bowls for drink offerings, cups, snuffers, and trays (Exod 25:23-40). Bronze implements for the altar of burnt offering included pots for the ashes, shovels, basins, forks, and firepans (Exod 27:3). The tabernacle utensils were consecrated with special anointing oil (Exod 30:26-29), and unauthorized persons who touched them would incur death (Num 18:3). The valuable implements were sometimes royal votive gifts (1 Kgs 15:15). In 2 Tim 2:20-21, those who serve in the church are compared to household utensils.

SUSAN E. HADDOX

UTHAI yoo'th*i* [עוּתַי 'uthay]. 1. The son of Ammihud, of the Judaite clan of Perez (1 Chr 9:4). Uthai was the head of his ancestral house (v. 9) and settled in Jerusalem with other exiles returning from Babylon (vv. 2-3). The meaning of his name is highly disputed. The alternatives include: 1) "Yahweh has shown himself surpassing" or "Yahweh has surpassed himself"; 2) a variant of ATHAIAH, "pride of Yahweh" or "Yahweh is my pride"; 3) a shorted form of ATHALIAH, "Yahweh has shown himself preeminent"; and 4) "Yahweh succors."

2. One of the descendants of Bigvai, who, with seventy males, accompanied Ezra from Babylon under Artaxerxes (Ezra 8:14; 1 Esd 8:40).

3. One whose descendants returned from Babylon under Zerubbabel as temple servants (1 Esd 5:30).

F. RACHEL MAGDALENE

UTTERANCE [אֵמֶר 'emer; λόγος logos]. The product of an act of speech, sometimes the product of divine influence (1 Cor 12:8).

UTTERLY DESTROY. *See* DESTROY, UTTERLY.

UZ uhz [עוּץ 'uts]. 1. Son of Aram (Gen 10:23).

2. Son of Nahor, Abraham's brother (Gen 22:21).

3. Son of the Horite chief Dishan (Gen 36:21, 28).

4. The homeland of Job, east of Israel but of an uncertain location (Job 1:1). One tradition places Uz in Edom. Lamentations 4:21 parallels Uz and Edom. Uz is listed in the Edomite genealogy (Gen 36:28) and several personal names in the book of Job are Edomite. Furthermore, the LXX appendix to the book of Job places the city between Idumea and Arabia, which supports an Edomite location. Another less probable tradition places Uz in northern Mesopotamia. *See* EDOM, EDOMITES.

TERRY W. EDDINGER

'UZA, HORVAT. The royal fortress of Horvat 'Uza stood on the eastern border of Judah, ca. 10 km south of Arad. Measuring 51 m × 42 m, it was erected during the 7th cent. BCE to guard against incursions by Arabic and Edomite tribes. Its defenses included a thick (1.5 m) wall and ten towers along its perimeter. Excavations uncovered a gate house, soldiers' quarters, streets, and an altar, as well as thirty Hebrew inscriptions (administrative documents and a literary text) and one Edomite inscription. The fortress was destroyed at the end of the Iron Age by the Edomites who invaded the Arad valley or by the Babylonians in 585 BCE. *See* EDOM, EDOMITES.

ITZHAQ BEIT-ARIEH

UZAI yoo´zi [עוּזַי ʾuzay]. Uzai is the father of PALAL, an individual who helped rebuild the walls and towers of Jerusalem ca. 447 BCE (Neh 3:25). The name may be a shortened form of a name meaning "Yahu has heard."

UZAL yoo´zuhl [אוּזָל ʾuzal]. The son of Joktan, a descendant of Shem, and the eponymous ancestor of a tribe in south Arabia (Gen 10:27; 1 Chr 1:21). The site is traditionally associated with ʿAzal, which is Sanaa, the modern capital of Yemen. Other scholars connect Uzal with a site near Medina named Azalla, based upon the similarity of these names, as well as the similarity of the names of nearby villages (Yarki and Hurarina) to those of Uzal's brothers, Jerah and Hadoram. Ezekiel 27:19 also apparently mentions Uzal in a list of nations and towns that were trading partners of Tyre, but the meaning of the Hebrew text is uncertain.

Bibliography: Walther Eichrodt. *Ezekiel: A Commentary.* OTL (1970).

TERRY W. EDDINGER

UZZA. *See* UZZAH.

UZZAH uhz´uh [עֻזָּא ʿuzzaʾ, עֻזָּה ʿuzzah]. 1. The son of Abinadab, involved with his brother Ahio in the transport of the ark of the covenant under the aegis of David. As the new cart on which the ark was being transported began to falter on uneven terrain—thereby jeopardizing the ark—Uzzah reached out to steady the sacred chest. Upon touching it, he was struck dead by God (2 Sam 6; 1 Chr 13). The disastrous ark scenario apparently provides the etiological background for the name given to the location: PEREZ-UZZAH.

2. The garden of Uzzah is identified as the burial place both for Manasseh and his son Amon (2 Kgs 21:18, 26, respectively); the parallel Chronicles account does not record this detail (2 Chr 33:20, 24).

3. A Levite, of the sons of Merari, specifically, the son of Shimei (1 Chr 6:29 [Heb. 6:14]).

4. A Benjaminite of Geba, descendant of Ehud and Gera (1 Chr 8:6-7; NRSV, "Uzza").

5. Descendants of Uzza, listed among the temple servants that were among the returnees under the leadership of Zerubbabel (Ezra 2:49; Neh 7:51; 1 Esd 5:31).

JOHN I. LAWLOR

UZZEN-SHEERAH uhz´uhn-shee´uh-ruh [אֻזֵּן שֶׁאֱרָה ʾuzzen sheʾerah]. A town named Uzzen-sheerah (per-

haps meaning "ear of Sheerah") is mentioned in 1 Chr 7:24; its location is unknown. SHEERAH was the daughter of either Ephraim or his son Beriah (1 Chr 7:23). She is the only woman credited in the Bible with building a city, and she is said to have built three: Uzzen-sheerah itself, as well as Lower BETH-HORON and Upper Beth-horon.

Bibliography: Sara Japhet. *I & II Chronicles.* OTL (1993).

TIMOTHY G. CRAWFORD

UZZI uhz´i [עֻזִּי ʿuzzi; Ὀζιού Oziou]. A shortened form of UZZIAH or UZZIEL, meaning "the Lord/God is my strength." 1. Son of Bukki and a descendant of Eleazar in the line of Aaron (1 Chr 6:5-6, 51 [Heb. 5:31-32; 6:36]; Ezra 7:4; 1 Esd 8:2).

2. Grandson of Issachar and son of Tola (1 Chr 7:2-3).

3. Grandson of Benjamin and son of Bela (1 Chr 7:7).

4. Son of Michri and father of Elah who was a member of a family of Benjamin (1 Chr 9:8).

5. Son of Bani who was an overseer of the Levites after the return from exile (Neh 11:22).

6. The head of the priestly family of Jedaiah during the time of the high priest Joiakim (Neh 12:19).

7. A priest, perhaps a musician, who participated in the dedication of the walls of Jerusalem (Neh 12:42).

MARK RONCACE

UZZIA uh-zi´uh [עֻזִּיָּא ʿuziyaʾ]. Meaning "My strength is Yahweh." An ASHTERATHITE named among the sixteen Reubenites from Transjordan added by the Chronicler to the list of David's thirty mighty men (1 Chr 11:44).

UZZIAH uh-zi´uh [עֻזִּיָּהוּ ʿuzziyahu, עֻזִּיָּה ʿuzziyah; Ὀζίας Ozias]. Means "Yahweh is my strength." Five individuals in the OT bear this name. 1. An early 8th-cent. king of Judah. Uzziah (twenty-five times) is also called Azariah ("Yahweh is my help") nine times in the OT. The two names differ by a single consonant in Hebrew and are therefore much more similar than they appear in English. The roots on which the names are based (ʿzr עזר, ʿzz עזז) are also very close semantically, sharing nuances of help, strength, valor, and victory. However, it has been suggested "Uzziah" was the king's throne name and "Azariah" his personal name, to which he reverted when disease forced him off the throne. This suggestion is based on the fact that the prophets use "Uzziah" exclusively (Isa 1:1; 6:1; 7:1; Hos 1:1; Amos 1:1; Zech 14:5). Nevertheless, the suggestion is speculative, and the reason for the variation of names remains unknown. Chronicles levels through the name "Uzziah" except for 1 Chr 3:12, perhaps to avoid confusion with Azariah the priest (2 Chr 26:17, 20).

The brief description of Azariah's reign in 2 Kgs 15:1-7 portrays him as a basically righteous king except for his failure to take away the "high places," but whom Yahweh also struck with a skin disease (probably not what is known today as leprosy, i.e., Hansen's disease) that forced him to vacate the palace ("the house") for a "house of freedom," perhaps a euphemism for a sanatorium (2 Kgs 15:5; NRSV, "separate house"). The very different version of Uzziah's reign in 2 Chr 26 is the result primarily of theological considerations. The Chronicler was compelled to account theologically for both Uzziah's longevity and his disease, which indicated opposite divine judgments according to his worldview. This he accomplished through the technique—common for him—of "periodization," by which a king's reign was divided into distinctly positive and negative parts. In effect, 2 Chr 26:5-20 represents an addition to the Kings account of Uzziah's reign. Verse 5 spells out the doctrine of reward/retribution that drove the Chronicler's periodization. As long as Uzziah sought Yahweh, he prospered. Hence, for the first part of his reign, while he followed the instruction of Zechariah (an otherwise unknown prophet), he experienced success in military endeavors and building projects—both typical signs of blessing in Chronicles. But then his success made him excessively proud and led him to try to make an incense offering in the Temple—a task that properly belonged only to the priests (26:16-18). His angry response at the priests' rebuke caused God to strike him with "leprosy" (26:19-20). The repeated use of the verbs "help" ('azar עָזַר) and "be strong" (khazaq חָזַק) plays on the meanings of Azariah/Uzziah, the latter verb being a synonym for the root 'zz (עזז) that makes up the first part of the name Uzziah. While it is not impossible that some extra-biblical source lay behind the Chronicles version, it seems unlikely that this was the case. Some have implied that the "Meunites" mentioned in Chronicles preserves a genuine element from the 8th cent., since the annals of Tiglath-pileser III refer to the same group—apparently an Arab tribe in the frontier between Egypt and Palestine. But in the Bible "Meunites" occurs only in the late books of Chronicles and Ezra–Nehemiah, and it may refer to a region in southern Edom or to a distinct Arabian city-state associated with the Mineans, who are known from the 4th-cent. incense trade. Chronicles' reference to Uzziah's burial in a field near but not identical with the royal tombs (26:23) is also different from Kings and is probably another exhibit of judgment against Uzziah. However, a burial marker discovered in 1931 and written in Aramaic in the late Hasmonean/early Roman period (ca. 150 BCE–50 CE) has been taken as confirmation of Uzziah's distinct burial due to his skin disease. The inscription on the marker reads, "The bones of Azariah king of Judah were brought here. Not to be opened."

The accounts of Uzziah's reign in Kings and Chronicles agree in attributing to him a fifty-two-year reign, beginning at age sixteen (2 Kgs 15:1; 2 Chr 26:3). In part because of the longevity ascribed to him, the information about his reign is rife with chronological difficulties. For instance, the statement that Uzziah/Azariah began his reign in the twenty-seventh year of King Jeroboam of Israel (2 Kgs 15:1) contradicts the figures in 2 Kgs 14:2, 23, which indicate that Jeroboam II began his forty-one-year reign in the fifteenth year of Azariah's predecessor, Amaziah, who reigned twenty-nine years. According to chap. 14, then, Azariah succeeded Amaziah in Jeroboam's fourteenth or fifteenth year, not in his twenty-seventh year. In 2 Kgs 15 the reigns of kings Zechariah, Shallum, Menahem, Pekahiah, and Pekah of Israel are all synchronized with Uzziah/Azariah of Judah. Not counting Pekah's reign, which began in Uzziah's last year (2 Kgs 15:27), the maximum total of the reigns of the kings of Israel that coincided with Uzziah is forty-one years according to the figures in this chapter (Jeroboam—twenty-seven, Zechariah—one, Shallum—one, Menahem—ten, Pekahiah—two), and the total may be as low as twenty-six years (Jeroboam—14, Zechariah—0, Shallum—0, Menahem—10, Pekahiah—2). Both totals are well short of Uzziah's purported fifty-two-year reign. The explanations for this discrepancy include assuming a simple error in transmission or calculation (e.g., forty-two for fifty-two) and positing one or more co-regencies. The reference in 2 Kgs 15:5 to Uzziah dwelling in a "separate house" (literally, "house of freedom") because of his disease while his son Jotham took charge of the palace and government is typically taken as a description of a co-regency. Yet, this is far from certain. The verse actually states that Jotham was "over the house, judging/ruling the people of the land." The exact meaning of these statements is unclear, but the fact that Jotham's reign does not begin until after his father's death (15:32) indicates that Uzziah was considered king as long as he lived and that whatever administrative duties he may have shared with his son, his time in the "house of freedom" was not reckoned as a co-regency. A co-regency has also been posited between Azariah/Uzziah and his predecessor, Amaziah, based on the references to popular dissatisfaction with the latter at his defeat by Jehoash of Israel and the conspiracy against him that led to his replacement (2 Kgs 14:19-21; 2 Chr 25:27–26:1). The evidence for a co-regency at the beginning of Uzziah's reign, then, is even weaker than the evidence for one at its end, and the chronological problems remain.

The reign of Uzziah appears to have been a relatively peaceful and prosperous time for Judah. This is largely because it overlapped with Jeroboam II of Israel, with whom Uzziah was at peace and by whom Judah was probably overshadowed if not dominated. An indication of Uzziah's success is the note in 2 Kgs 14:22 that he rebuilt and restored Elat to Judah. It is reasonable to assume that this success came with the help of Jeroboam, who subsequently profited from the trade benefits afforded by Elat's port. Both Amos (1:1) and Zechariah (14:5) mention an earthquake during Uzziah's reign that must have been devastating to be so remembered. Again, it is not unreasonable to suggest that Judah recovered from the devastation with Jeroboam's and Israel's help. A principal reason for Israel's and Judah's general prosperity during this time was the lull before the rise of the Assyrian Empire under Tiglath-pileser III (745–727 BCE), whose annals indicate that he defeated and received tribute from a coalition of Syro-Palestinian kings including Menahem of Israel apparently ca. 738 BCE.

The mention of Azriyau of Iaudi in the annals of Tiglath-pileser III has often been taken as a reference to Azariah of Judah. It has been shown, though, that this reference, which was at the juncture of two fragments, actually comes from two different inscriptions, the second, containing the country name, from the later Assyrian king Sennacherib. Hence, this Azriyau's country is unknown, and he is probably not to be identified with the king of Judah but, judging from the inscription's context, appears rather to have been a ruler in northern Syria. Uzziah's name appears on two seals with the identical formula: "Belonging to Abijah servant of Uzziah" and "Belonging to Shebnaiah servant of Uzziah." While the Uzziah in both cases is likely the king of Judah, neither of the servants named is mentioned in the Bible, and the seals alone give no additional information about King Uzziah.

2. Father of Jonathan, an official over David's outlying treasuries (1 Chr 27:25).

3. A Levite of the Kohathite branch (1 Chr 6:24 [Heb. 6:9]).

4. One of the priests commanded by Ezra to divorce his foreign wife (Ezra 10:21).

5. Father of Athaiah, a postexilic Judahite resident of Jerusalem (Neh 11:4).

Bibliography: W. H. Barnes. *Studies in the Chronology of the Divided Monarchy of Israel* (1991); M. Cogan and H. Tadmor. *2 Kings.* AB 11 (1988); G. N. Knoppers. *1 Chronicles 1–9.* AB 12 (2004); J. M. Miller and J. H. Hayes. *A History of Ancient Israel and Judah.* 2nd ed. (2006); E. L. Sukenik. "Funerary Tablet of Uzziah, King of Judah." *PEQ* 63 (1931) 217–21; H. Tadmor. *The Inscriptions of Tiglath-Pileser III King of Assyria* (1994); M. C. Tetley. *The Reconstructed Chronology of the Divided Kingdom* (2005).

                                              STEVEN L. MCKENZIE

UZZIAH, DEEDS OF. *See* BOOKS REFERRED TO IN THE BIBLE.

UZZIEL uhz′ee-uhl [עֻזִּיאֵל ʿuzziʾel]. Meaning "God is my strength." 1. The son of Kohath and grandson of Levi, who had three sons (Mishael, Elzaphan, and Sithri) and whose nephews were Aaron and Moses (Exod 6:18-22; Lev 10:4; Num 3:19; 1 Chr 6:2 [Heb. 5:28]; 23:12, 20). The Kohathites were charged with the care of the ark, the table, lampstands, altars, sanctuary vessels, and the screen (Num 3:27-31). When King David reorganized the cultic personnel, Amminadab led 112 of Uzziel's descendants (1 Chr 15:10), and as David's death drew near, the king's reorganization of the Levites found Micah, as the chief of Uzziel's clan and Isshiah, as his lieutenant (1 Chr 23:10; 24:24-25).

2. One of the sons of Ishi, a Simeonite, who led 500 of their tribesmen to destroy the survivors of the Amalekites at Mount Seir and then settled there (1 Chr 4:42).

3. The son of Bela, a Benjaminite who was a warrior. With his four brothers (Ezbon, Uzzi, Jerimoth, and Iri), he led 22,034 men of the tribe (1 Chr 7:7).

4. A Levite, who served with his thirteen brothers as temple musicians under the direction of their father, Heman, who was King David's seer (1 Chr 25:4). Uzziel's name is given as Azarel in 1 Chr 25:18, perhaps a scribal error due to misreading the YOD (y י) in Uzziel's name for a RESH (r ר).

5. A Levite, son of Jeduthun and brother of Shemaiah (2 Chr 29:14), who joined others of the tribe in obedience to King Hezekiah's command that they sanctify themselves, cleanse the Temple, and reinstitute the faithful service of God there (2 Chr 29:3-19).

6. A goldsmith, who was the son of Harhaiah and who participated in the rebuilding of Jerusalem's walls under Nehemiah's leadership (Neh 3:8).

                                              M. PATRICK GRAHAM

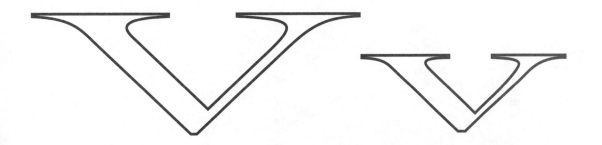

VAIN [ריק riq, שָׁוְא shawe', שֶׁקֶר sheqer; κενός kenos, μάτην matēn]. The modern use of *vain* to describe an attitude toward one's personal appearance is not found in the Bible. Rather, *vain* is typically used to translate a cluster of words that carry the sense of being useless, ineffectual, or empty. It is frequently employed in the adverbial expression "in vain," as when God complains of having punished Israel "in vain" (shawe'; Jer 2:30) or when Paul assures the church at Corinth that God's grace was not given to him "in vain" (kenos; 1 Cor 15:10). The root meanings of shawe' and kenos involve falsehood and emptiness, respectively, but these and similar verses refer primarily to ineffectuality (e.g., 1 Sam 25:21; Job 9:29; Gal 2:2; 1 Thess 2:1). This meaning of *vain* also applies to worship that is directed toward the wrong object (e.g., idols; Jonah 2:8) or does not come from the heart (Matt 15:8-9; Mark 7:7).

Vain is often used to describe false hope: "the war horse is a vain hope (sheqer, "lie") for victory" (Ps 33:17); the nations conspire against God's anointed "in vain" (riq, "emptiness"; Ps 2:1). The phrase can be used to express religious doubt, as when the psalmist wonders whether he has cleansed his heart "in vain" (riq; Ps 73:13).

Perhaps the best-known biblical use of "vain" is the prohibition against taking God's name "in vain" in the TEN COMMANDMENTS (Exod 20:7; Deut 5:11; NRSV, "make wrongful use of"). The commandment could prohibit invoking God as a guarantor of fraud, using the name in a way that belies its efficacy, or linking the name to "vain idols." *See* VANITY.

WILL SOLL

VAIZATHA vi'zuh-thuh [וַיְזָתָא wayzatha']. One of Haman's ten sons, killed by the Jews in Susa and later impaled on a stake (Esth 9:9, 14). He is called Zabutheus (Zabouthaios Ζαβουθαῖος) in the LXX. The Jews also struck down 500 men in addition to Haman's sons as retribution for Haman's plan of annihilation.

TRISHA GAMBAIANA WHEELOCK

VALENTINUS. *See* GNOSTICISM.

VALIANT MAN, SOLDIER. *See* MIGHTY MEN.

VALLEY [בִּקְעָה biq'ah, גַּיְא gay', נַחַל nakhal, עֵמֶק 'emeq; πεδίον pedion, φάραγξ pharanx, χειμάρρους cheimarrous]. Because they are more conducive to agriculture and urban life than the surrounding arid hills, valleys are the center of much material and metaphorical action in the biblical text. Used most commonly in the physical sense to refer to a low place between mountains or other geographical depression, the term also appears symbolically to indicate situations of divine judgment and human difficulty. The topography of Israel contains innumerable valleys, so they occur frequently as place references in the text. Valleys represent agricultural abundance, described as places of grain (Isa 17:5), orchards (Song 6:11), and cattle (Isa 63:14). Many battles are fought in valleys, both human (Gen 14:8; 2 Sam 5:22; 2 Kgs 14:7; 2 Chr 14:10) and divine (Isa 22:5; Ezek 39:11, 15; Hos 1:5; Zech 14:4-5). The transformation of valleys is a sign of the coming of the Lord (Isa 40:4; Mic 1:4). Valleys serve as a place for divine visions (Isa 22:1; Ezek 3:22; 37:1-2), while the "darkest valley" (Ps 23:4) represents the low places of human existence. Several Hebrew and Greek words are translated as "valley," some of which are alternatively translated "plain," "vale," "wadi," or "ravine."

'Emeq is used most frequently as a geographic designation. This term indicates a broad valley, often identified with or used as a genitive of an adjacent city or region, including ACHOR (Isa 65:10; Hos 2:15), AIJALON (Josh 10:12), Jezreel (Josh 17:16; Judg 6:33; Hos 1:5; *see* JEZREEL, JEZREELITE), Hebron (Gen 37:14; *see* HEBRON, HEBRONITES), or a person or group, including JEHOSHAPHAT (Joel 3:2; *see* JEHOSHAPHAT, VALLEY OF), REPHAIM (Josh 15:8; 2 Sam 5:18; *see* REPHAIM, VALLEY OF), and the king (Gen 14:17; 2 Sam 18:18). It is also used metaphorically to refer to the valley of decision (Joel 3:14), representing God's judgment.

Biq'ah is a term that refers to a broad geographical lowland, and is used either with a specific place of reference, such as Aven (Amos 1:5; *see* AVEN VALLEY) or Mizpeh (Josh 11:8), or as a generic reference to a low place, as opposed to mountains (Deut 8:7; Ps 104:8).

Gay' indicates a steeper geographical feature, such as a gorge or ravine. This term is also frequently used in metaphorical contexts of God's judgment. The valley of the son of Hinnom is associated with sacrifices to Molech in Jeremiah (Jer 19:6; 32:35), though it is used strictly as a geographical reference in Joshua (Josh 15:8; 18:16; *see* HINNOM, VALLEY OF). The Valley of HAMON-GOG (Ezek 39:11, 15) indicates the burial place of God's enemies on the day of divine judgment.

Nakhal is more frequently translated as "wadi," a term indicating a seasonal river valley (*see* WADI). It is often used generically (1 Sam 15:5; Ps 104:10; Song 6:11), but is also associated with place names like GERAR (Gen 26:17), Eshcol (Deut 1:24; *see* ESHCOL, WADI), and Sorek (Judg 16:4; *see* SOREK, VALLEY OF).

Pharanx is the most common Greek term for *valley* in the LXX. It also appears in the quotation from Isaiah (40:4) in Luke 3:5.

Cheimarrous generally refers to a wadi in the LXX. It occurs as the KIDRON VALLEY in John 18:1, one of only two NT uses of *valley*.

SUSAN E. HADDOX

VALLEY GATE [שַׁעַר הַגַּיְא sha'ar haggay']. A city GATE of JERUSALEM. Uzziah built towers for it (2 Chr 26:9), and Nehemiah began his inspection tour from it (Neh 2:13, 15). It was rebuilt under Nehemiah's supervision (Neh 3:13). It may correspond to the "Western Gate" uncovered in the western wall of the City of David, which provided access to the city from the TYROPOEON VALLEY, approximately 500 m north of the DUNG GATE. *See* DAVID, CITY OF.

JAMES RILEY STRANGE

VALLEY OF DECISION [עֵמֶק הֶחָרוּץ 'emeq hekharuts]. The Hebrew expression appears only twice in the OT, both in a single verse (Joel 3:14 [Heb. 4:14]) in Yahweh's call to the nations to assemble for war in the Valley of Jehoshaphat. Then at this "Valley of Decision," Yahweh will face and judge them on a tumultuous "day of the LORD" that involves cosmic events. Due to multiple possible meanings of kharuts (חָרוּץ), the expression may denote "the valley of decision," but it at least connotes a sense of "the valley of the sharp threshing sledge" (Isa 41:15; Amos 1:3), and thus the name implies that this is both a valley of decision and of threshing (i.e., massive destruction). In addition, the consonants of the word kharuts carry a pun on the verb qatsar (קָצַר), conveying a sense of harvesting, thus reinforcing the agrarian images of destruction raised by the text in Joel 3:13 [Heb. 4:13].

EHUD BEN ZVI

VALLEY OF DRY BONES. In Ezek 37:1-14 the prophet records a vision of a valley full of dry bones that represents the "whole house of Israel" in exile (v. 11). God instructs Ezekiel to announce to the bones that God will bring them back to life by giving them BREATH, providing sinews, and covering the bones with flesh. As Ezekiel speaks, he witnesses the animation of the bones. The imagery shifts a bit in the final part of the vision as Ezekiel prophesies that God will resurrect Israel from their graves. The vision is meant to convey the power of God and to bring hope to the exilic community. *See* EZEKIEL, BOOK OF.

MARK RONCACE

VALLEY OF GEHINNON. *See* HINNOM, VALLEY OF.

VALLEY OF HAMON-GOG. *See* HAMON-GOG.

VALLEY OF HINNOM. *See* HINNOM, VALLEY OF.

VALLEY OF JEHOSHAPHAT. *See* JEHOSHAPHAT, VALLEY OF.

VALLEY OF REPHAIM. *See* REPHAIM, VALLEY OF.

VALLEY OF SALT [גֵּיא הַמֶּלַח ge' hammelakh, גֵּיא מֶלַח ge' melakh]. The Valley of Salt plays a significant role in Israel's history at two different points. During the Davidic monarchy a major battle was waged against the Edomites in the Valley of Salt under Abishai (2 Sam 8:13; 1 Chr 18:12), David's capable lieutenant (see also Ps 60, superscription [Heb. 60:2]). The second battle occurred under King Amaziah around 200 years later, when it is said that Amaziah put to death 10,000 Edomites in the Valley of Salt (2 Kgs 14:7; 2 Chr 25:11). The only times the OT mentions the Valley of Salt are during Israel's geopolitical expansion. Two sites—the Wadi el-Milch and es-Sebkah—have been identified as possible locations for the Valley of Salt. Currently the consensus regards the Wadi el-Milch as the best possible location.

JOSEPH R. CATHEY

VALLEY OF SHITTIM. *See* SHITTIM, WADI.

VALLEY OF SIDDIM. *See* SIDDIM, VALLEY OF.

VALLEY OF THE SHADOW, DARK VALLEY [צַלְמָוֶת tsalmaweth]. Perhaps a compound formed from tsel (צֵל, "shadow") and maweth (מָוֶת, "death"). The term is familiar from its use in Ps 23:4, where the NRSV translates it as "darkest valley." Elsewhere it is translated "deep darkness" (e.g., Ps 44:19 [Heb. 44:20]; Amos 5:8) or "gloom" (e.g., Ps 107:10, 14).

God's creative powers are described in terms of his control over deep darkness (Job 12:22; 34:22; 38:17; Jer 13:16; Amos 5:8). The term often appears in contexts expressing hope (e.g., Isa 9:2 [Heb. 9:1], which promises that light will shine on those who live in "a land of deep darkness") or comfort (e.g., Ps 107:10, 14, where prisoners are brought out of darkness into the light; Jer 2:6, where Yawheh guided Israel through darkness in the wilderness). The term may also express despair, however, and thus is a favorite of Job (16:16; 24:17; 28:3), who wishes that the day of his birth would be turned into deep darkness (3:4) and hopes for the darkness of death (10:21-22).

Bibliography: D. Winton Thomas. "צַלְמָוֶת in the Old Testament." *JSS* 7 (1962) 191–200.

JOHN I. LAWLOR

VALLEY OF THE TRAVELERS [גֵּי הָעֹבְרִים gey ha'ovrim]. An unidentified valley where, in latter times, GOG and his followers will be slain and buried (Ezek 39:11). Afterward, the place will be called the Valley of HAMON-GOG. Scholars disagree on the location due to wording of the text. Some take "east of the sea" to refer to the Dead Sea and place the valley in the Transjordan, perhaps in the ABARIM MOUNTAINS (Num 27:12; 33:47-48; Deut 32:49; Jer 22:20). Others say the site must be somewhere west of the Jordan River, in Israel proper, since the text says the valley is "in Israel."

TERRY W. EDDINGER

VALLEY OF VISION [גֵּיא חִזָּיוֹן gey' khizzayon]. The "oracle concerning the valley of vision" occurs near the end of Isaiah's collection of oracles against nations (Isa 22:1-14). Although the oracle itself does not equate the "valley of vision" (vv. 1, 5) with Jerusalem, references to the "city of David" (v. 9) and "houses of Jerusalem" (v. 10) suggest that the valley is near the city. The LXX interprets both occurrences of the phrase as "valley of Zion" (pharangos Ziōn φάραγγος Σιών).

Jerusalem was located on a hill, but valleys on three sides surround the city. Some have attempted to identify the "valley of vision" with a specific valley (e.g., the Valley of Hinnom; see HINNOM, VALLEY OF). An alternative suggestion is that the appellation refers to the frequency with which prophetic vision was given and received in Jerusalem.

JOHN I. LAWLOR

VALOR, MAN OF. See MIGHTY MEN.

VANIAH vuh-ni'uh [וַנְיָה wanyah; Ἄνως Anōs]. A descendant of Bani and returnee from exile, who is listed among Israelites who had to divorce their foreign wives (Ezra 10:36). He appears in a parallel list in 1 Esd 9:34. Variations in the spelling of the name raise questions about whether Vaniah is a proper name.

DEREK E. WITTMAN

VANITY [הֶבֶל hevel; μάταιοτης mataiotēs]. The word hevel occurs in verbal and noun forms in the OT seventy-six times, thirty-eight times in the book of Ecclesiastes, where it is translated consistently in most English versions as "vanity." The word opens and closes the book in 1:2 and 12:8: "Vanity of vanities, says the Teacher, vanity of vanities! All is vanity." The phrases "all is vanity" (hakkol hevel הַכֹּל הֶבֶל) and "this is (also) vanity" ([gam-]zeh hevel [גַּם־]זֶה הֶבֶל) form a refrain throughout the book (1:14; 2:11, 17, 23, 26; 4:4, 16; 5:10; 6:2, 9; 7:6; 8:14; 9:2).

In Jerome's 425 CE Vulgate, he translated hevel as vanitas, a word that means in Latin "unsubstantial," "empty," or "illusory." The KJV translated the word as "vanitie." Modern English translations (e.g., ASV, RSV, NASB, NKJV, NRSV) render the Hebrew word as "vanity."

While "vanity" was an apt translation for hevel in the English of King James' day, the word has undergone a transformation of meaning that obscures its original intent in the biblical text (see KING JAMES VERSION, ARCHAIC TERMS). In the 21st cent., vanity is associated with pride in self-appearance and self-worth and is more concretely associated with the dressing tables at which women sit and apply their makeup and style their hair.

The meaning of the Hebrew word hevel, however, is "breath," "vapor," or "puff of air." It connotes a transitory nature and an inability to grasp. The first occurrence of the word hevel in the OT is the name of Adam and Eve's second child, ABEL, whose name in Hebrew is hevel. Abel is killed by his brother, Cain, after God "looked upon" Abel's sacrifice rather than Cain's (Gen 4:4; NRSV, "had regard for"). Abel's life was a fleeting moment, a breath or a puff of air.

In Prov 21:6, treasures obtained by a "lying tongue" are called hevel (NRSV, "fleeting vapor"). In Isa 57:13, the prophet says of the idols of the people, "The wind will carry them off, / a breath (hevel) will take them away." The psalmist muses over the transitory nature of human existence in Ps 144:3-4: "O LORD, what are human beings that you regard them, / or mortals that you think of them? They are like a breath (hevel); / their days are like a passing shadow."

Thus, the word hevel might be translated better for 21st-cent. readers of the biblical text as "breath," "fleeting," or "ungraspable." Life, according to the author of Ecclesiastes, is not useless or meaningless, but rather is beyond comprehension, beyond humanity's capability to grasp—it is fleeting, as fleeting as the breath that escapes from us as we inhale and exhale.

In certain places in Ecclesiastes, hevel seems to have a negative connotation (e.g., 2:21; 4:8; 6:2), but in each of these instances hevel describes human activity rather than life itself. Such undertakings are "beyond comprehension" and are viewed by the teacher as "a great evil" (2:21); "an unhappy business" (4:8); and "a grievous ill" (6:2). The LXX translates hevel as mataiotēs, which means "nothingness" or "emptiness," perpetuating the notion that the Hebrew word conveyed a sense of negative meaninglessness.

NANCY DECLAISSÉ-WALFORD

VAPHRES [Οὐάφρης Houaphrēs]. Eusebius cites from the Jewish historian Eupolemus transcripts of letters allegedly exchanged between King Vaphres of Egypt and King Solomon (Praep. ev. 9.30–34). The letters indicate that Solomon married Vaphres' daughter (compare 1 Kgs 3:1). Vaphres is also the Greek form of HOPHRA (Jer 44:30, LXX), the pharaoh who reigned during the Babylonian destruction of Jerusalem.

LJUBICA JOVANOVIC

VASHNI vash'ni [וַשְׁנִי washni]. The KJV translates the Hebrew washni as the name of one of Samuel's sons;

however, following the Lucianic Greek text most understand washni to mean "and the second," referring to Abijah, with Joel's name missing from the Hebrew (1 Chr 6:28 [Heb. 6:13]).

VASHTI vash´ti [וַשְׁתִּי washti]. Esther's predecessor as queen (Esth 1:9–2:4). Vashti holds a banquet for the women, which echoes the king's lavish banquet for the men. King Ahasuerus commands her to leave the women's space for the men's, to show off her beauty. Her refusal, for reasons unstated, sets up Esther's entrance into the court and the story and emphasizes that the boundary between women's and men's space is a treacherous one. Ironically, Vashti's punishment for refusing to enter the king's court is banishment from it, as well as loss of her position as queen. The king's advisors are not satisfied with punishing her, however, and convince the king that since her act threatens patriarchy itself, it must be countered by law. Together with Mordecai's refusal (to bow before Haman), Vashti's establishes the dangers of noncooperation, dangers that Esther avoids, since she is notable for her compliance. *See* ESTHER, BOOK OF.

NICOLE WILKINSON DURAN

VASSAL [מַס mas, עֶבֶד ʿevedh]. A subordinate or dependent ruling under a suzerain. Vassals gave homage and allegiance to their suzerains, and in return they received protection. The term appears twice in the NRSV. When SHALMANESER V "came up against him," HOSHEA "became his vassal, and paid him TRIBUTE" (2 Kgs 17:3). The NRSV translates ʿevedh, the usual word for "servant," as "vassal" to connote Hoshea's ongoing subservience. Lamentations 1:1 bewails the fact that Jerusalem "has become a vassal" following the desolation of 586 BCE. Here, the underlying word is mas, a term typically used for a body of forced laborers.

RALPH K. HAWKINS

VAT [יֶקֶב yeqev]. A hollow space created within or cut into rock (Isa 5:2), often square or circular in shape, in which grapes and olives were pressed into oil and wine (Prov 3:10; Hos 9:2; Joel 2:24; 3:13). *See* OIL; WINE.

VATICANUS, CODEX vat´i-kan´uhs, koh´deks. A mid-4th cent. CE Greek manuscript generally considered the oldest UNCIAL of the Bible. With some lacunae, it contains the OT, NT, and much of the Apocrypha. Referred to as B, II, or Vatican Greek 1209, it has resided in the Vatican Library since at least the late 15th cent. (except when Napoleon transported it to Paris in the late 18th cent.). The manuscript is tri-columnar (except in poetical passages), with forty lines to each page. It exhibits a number of corrections by the original scribe and later hands, along with the addition of accents and breathing marks as well as decorative elements. There is no consensus as to the place of origin for Vaticanus; Egypt vies with Rome, southern Italy, and Caesarea in recent discussions. Some have argued that it was once in the same library as Codex Sinaiticus (*see* SINAITICUS, CODEX).

For the OT, Vaticanus varies considerably in its text-critical value, sometimes reflecting well the LXX (e.g., Pentateuch), at other times presenting a version that is inferior (e.g., Isaiah), unusual (e.g., Judges), or later (e.g., Daniel). In spite of this unevenness, Vaticanus has been frequently collated and used as the basis for editions of the LXX. For the NT, it represents a "neutral" or Alexandrian text-type. *See* VERSIONS, ANCIENT.

LEONARD GREENSPOON

VAULT [אֲגֻדָּה ʾaghuddah; γῦρος gyros, στερέωμα stereōma]. Meaning a band fitting something together, in the context of Amos 9:6 ʾaghuddah represents the FIRMAMENT within which Yahweh created the divine dwelling place (see Sir 24:5). The ancients believed the sky to be a solid firmament that rested on the ends of the earth. Stereōma, translated "vault" in Sir 43:1, 8, is the same LXX term translated "firmament" in other places and "dome" in Gen 1:6. *See* ARCHITECTURE, NT; ARCHITECTURE, OT; CHAMBER.

STEVEN D. MASON

VAV. *See* ALPHABET; WAW.

VEGETABLE. *See* PLANTS OF THE BIBLE.

VEIL [מַסְוֶה masweh, צַמָּה tsammah, צָעִיף tsaʿif; κάλυμμα kalymma, κατακαλύπτομαι katakalyptomai]. Since the earliest church, it has been a common practice for Christian women to cover their heads in worship, and many continue to do so, largely citing 1 Cor 11:5-15. This passage is the subject of debate since Paul on the one hand affirms the interdependence of the genders and on the other hand the hierarchy that places the man (or husband) as the head of the woman (or wife). In ancient Mediterranean culture most married women covered their heads to indicate that a husband protected them. Paul thus seems to reassert the Corinthian women's marital and social status, even while assuming that these same women lead worship.

In OT narratives, the practice of covering face and body is often associated with mistaken identity and unlikely sexual union (Gen 38:14-19; compare 29:23-25). Removing a veil can indicate humiliation or mourning instead of luxury or wedding celebration (Isa 3:23; 47:2; see also Sus 32; 3 Macc 4:6). The facial veil can highlight the outlines of what it covers as though it enhances, rather than conceals, the beauty beneath (Song 4:1, 3; 6:7). Similarly, Moses' unusual use of the veil in Exod 34:33-35 seems to emphasize the divine glow of his face after speaking with the Lord, while it also shields the Israelites from the apparent danger. The veil as protection from divine power echoes a general fear of seeing the face or glory of God, like the veil that shields the ark of the covenant and the holiest area of the Temple (see CURTAINS; VEIL OF THE TEMPLE). Paul, on the other hand, portrays Moses' veiling as the latter's attempt to hide the fading of the divine presence and uses the veil as a metaphor for the blindness of non-Christian Jews in reading the Jewish Scriptures (2 Cor 3:13-16). See CLOTH, CLOTHES; HEAD COVERING.

NICOLE WILKINSON DURAN

VEIL OF THE TEMPLE [τὸ καταπέτασμα τοῦ ναοῦ to katapetasma tou naou]. In Zerubbabel's and Herod's Temple, a curtain or veil blocked the entrance into the shrine from the central nave (Josephus, *J.W.* 5.219). Another elaborately decorated curtain hung inside the massive doors that led from the open vestibule into the central nave (*J.W.* 5.212–14; Sir 50:5). These curtains have a precedent in the curtain (**parokheth** פָּרֹכֶת) and screen of the TABERNACLE (Exod 26:31-37).

Solomon's Temple had wooden doors between the shrine and the nave (1 Kgs 6:31) and between the nave and the vestibule (1 Kgs 6:33-34), but no curtains are mentioned. Second Chronicles 3:14 mentions a curtain, not a door, before the shrine, but this may reflect the layout of the Second Temple. Nonetheless, many scholars think that a curtain hung behind the doors into the shrine to veil the shrine when the doors were open (see 1 Kgs 8:8, which suggests that a curtain blocked a direct view of the ark from the open doorway but the gap between the doorway and the ends of the curtain permitted a view of the ends of the long poles).

The NT claims that the curtain between the nave and the shrine was mysteriously torn from top to bottom at the time of Jesus' crucifixion (Matt 27:51; Mark 15:38; Luke 23:45), indicating that access into the presence of God had been provided for all the followers of Jesus by his self-sacrifice (Heb 6:19; 10:20). See TEMPLE, JERUSALEM.

J. J. M. ROBERTS

VENGEANCE [נָקָם naqam, נְקָמָה neqamah; ἐκδίκησις ekdikēsis, ἔκδικος, ekdikos]. While the word *vengeance* and its verbal form AVENGE have a pejorative connotation in English (that of excessive, indiscriminate force driven by a desire to restore someone's honor and humiliate the other), Hebrew does not have that connotation. Most occurrences of *vengeance* are ascribed to God in the OT (thirteen of seventeen occurrences of naqam; sixteen of twenty of neqamah), and in most cases, the noun has the nuance of RETRIBUTION.

Sometimes Israel is the recipient of God's vengeance (naqam). Naqam is used in the table of curses in Lev 26 and the poetic prophecy delivered by Moses just before his death (Deut 32). God imposes troubles on Israel for violating weighty provisions of God's covenant, "I will bring the sword against you, executing vengeance for the covenant" (Lev 26:25a). The warning, "Vengeance is mine, and recompense, for the time when their [Israel's] foot shall slip ..." (Deut 32:35) threatens divine retribu-

tion on the people under Yahweh's sovereign authority, although the very next verse offers "vindication" for Israel. Vengeance is correlated with recompense in Isa 34:8 and 35:4.

Yahweh also threatens Israel's "adversaries" with vengeance, singling out foreign nations (Deut 32:41-43). The God who judges Israel for violating the covenant inflicts retribution on foreign nations when they assault Israel (even though the nations are portrayed as serving Yahweh's purpose). For example, in Isa 47:3 vengeance is directed to Babylon, Yahweh's instrument in the punishment of Judah.

Yahweh takes vengeance on other nations through Israel, as when Israel assaults the Midianites during the conquest of Transjordan (Num 31:3); although vengeance (neqamah) is carried out by Israel, it is the Lord's vengeance: God has authorized it as Israel's "patron," their protector. In Ps 149:7, the people of Israel are to take up arms to act as the Lord's agent of revenge. God answers Jephthah's vow and intervenes to save Israel from a violent, aggressive neighbor, as Jephthah's daughter informs him: "the LORD has given you vengeance (neqamah) against your enemies, the Ammonites" (Judg 11:36). Ezekiel condemns the Edomites and Philistines for vengeful action against Judah, using naqam for a violent, aggressive human action and neqamah for reciprocating divine vengeance (Ezek 25:12-17).

Individuals also seek vengeance and sometimes receive it through Yahweh. In Judg 16:28, Samson prays vindictively for revenge (naqam). Jeremiah twice seeks divine vengeance (neqamah) against those persecuting him (11:20; 20:12). While this may seem an appeal for favoritism, it is actually a reasonable expectation for a prophet suffering for the unpopular message he is told to deliver. Psalm 79:10 requests divine retaliation for the killing of Israelites as a demonstration before the nations of Yahweh's reality. The other occurrences are in prophecies against foreign nations (46:10; 50:15, 28; 51:11, 36); one is characterized as vengeance for Israel (51:36).

Vengeance (naqam) sometimes refers to human retaliation, such as that of a husband against the lover of his unfaithful wife (Prov 6:34). New Testament examples of human vengeance (ekdikēsis, ekdikos) include the punishment of wrongdoers by governmental authorities (Rom 13:4 1; Pet 2:14) and self-inflicted punishment (2 Cor 7:11).

Vengeance also is part of eschatological judgment. Isaiah 61:2 and 63:4 use the expression "day of vengeance" in parallel to "year of the LORD's favor" (61:2) and "year for my redeeming" (63:4). The final judgment is the day the righteous and holy will be saved, while their oppressors and adversaries are brought low. Micah 5:15 also announces vengeance on all rebellious nations "in that day" (5:10). Psalm 94 calls upon the Lord to intervene to destroy the wicked and oppressive. Although the psalm doesn't refer to a final judgment, it is open to that interpretation: God will intervene in the future to set things right, an intervention that includes "vengeance." *Vengeance* is used for the "troubles" preceding the last judgment in Luke 21:22 and in 2 Thess 1:8 for punishments imposed on those who do not know God or Christ.

Romans 12:19 and Heb 10:30 cite Deut 32:35 for the principle that "vengeance" belongs to God alone, not believers, and supports exhortations not to be vengeful (also 1 Thess 4:6), an understanding that fairly accurately characterizes the whole biblical tradition, with varying degrees of vindictiveness from passage to passage. The importance of vengeance is never disputed, but the determination of who deserves retribution and what it will be is up to God. *See* AVENGE; AVENGER OF BLOOD; REDEEM, REDEEMER.

Bibliography: Mark E. Biddle. *Missing the Mark: Sin and Its Consequences in Biblical Theology* (2005); Erich Zengler. *A God of Vengeance: Understanding the Psalms of Divine Wrath* (1996).

DALE PATRICK

VERMILION [שָׁשֵׁר shasher]. Vermilion designates a shade of RED. Paint was given this color by adding a pigment obtained from iron-bearing ocher or from cinnabar, a naturally occurring compound of mercury and sulfur. Biblical examples suggest that vermilion paint was used in homes of wealth and prestige. Jeremiah judges Jehoiakim for building himself a luxurious house while living unjustly. This house is painted with vermilion (Jer 22:14). Ezekiel describes the faithlessness of Oholibah, who lusted after the carved figures of Babylonian men, figures that were painted vermilion (Ezek 23:14). *See* COLORS.

Bibliography: Athalya Brenner. *Colour Terms in the Old Testament* (1982).

MARY PETRINA BOYD

VERSION, BASHMURIC bash-moor´ik. Coptic fragments of Scriptures (ca. 2nd cent. CE) published as Codices Basmyrici, but now referred to as the Fayumic Version. *See* VERSIONS, ANCIENT.

VERSION, BOHAIRIC. *See* COPTIC LANGUAGE; VERSIONS, ANCIENT; VERSIONS, COPTIC.

VERSION, DOUAY doo´ay. The original Douay Version, also called the Rheims-Douay Version, was the basis for nearly all English Catholic versions of the Bible and was produced in reaction to 16th-cent. Protestant versions. The work began in 1568 at the English College at Douay, in Flanders, then moved to Rheims (1578), and back to Douay (1593). The principal translator, former Oxford scholar Gregory Martin, published the NT at Rheims (1582), then the OT at Douay (1609/10). Although not ignoring Gk. and Hebrew texts, the translators took the Latin Vulgate as the original text in ac-

cordance with the Council of Trent's decision (1546). *See* VERSIONS, ENGLISH.

PETER ARZT-GRABNER

VERSION, ETHIOPIC ee´thee-op´ik. An ancient version of the Bible that was translated from Greek (and possibly Syriac) between the 4th and 7th cent. CE and represents a mixture of Byzantine and Western text traditions. The oldest surviving manuscripts date to the 13th cent. *See* VERSIONS, ANCIENT.

VERSION, GEORGIAN. Translation of the Bible into Georgian, undertaken after the early 4th cent. CE. Probably based on the Armenian version, it is considered a witness to the Old Syriac text. *See* VERSIONS, ANCIENT.

VERSION, GOTHIC. A literal translation of the Bible from Greek into Gothic dating to the middle of the 4th cent. CE. *See* VERSIONS, ANCIENT.

VERSION, MEMPHITIC. *See* VERSIONS, COPTIC.

VERSION, SAHIDIC. *See* VERSIONS, COPTIC.

VERSION, TYNDALE'S tin´duhl. Convinced of the authority of Scripture, William Tyndale struggled to provide English-speaking people a Bible in their own language. He translated the complete NT by 1526 (rev. 1534) and half the OT before his execution in 1536, codifying regional dialects into a common national tongue. A groundbreaking effort and monumental literary achievement, Tyndale's Version was stylistically pleasing, true to the original languages, and made good sense; it reflected his facility with English and the ancient languages and set the standard for subsequent translations. The Authorized Version (KJV) follows Tyndale 90 percent of the time. *See* VERSIONS, ENGLISH.

MILES S. MULLIN II

VERSION, WYCLIFFE'S wik´lif. The first complete English translation of the Bible, produced under the direction of John Wycliffe (d. 1384) in the late 14th cent. This translation was undertaken to make the Bible widely accessible to the public and was based primarily on the Latin Vulgate. It proved popular but controversial and was censored by the Roman Catholic Church and the nation of England. *See* VERSIONS, ENGLISH.

MICHAEL K. TURNER

VERSIONS, ANCIENT. The term "ancient versions" is used for a wide range of early translations of OT and NT writings and also, sometimes, for the SAMARITAN PENTATEUCH, which is not a translation. There is considerable diversity in the way each version has been studied by scholars, reflecting factors such as the number and date of manuscripts available, the significance of the version for reconstruction of the original from which it was translated, the linguistic interest of the version as well as the interest of the translation as an interpretation, and the nature of the translation technique it reflects. Additional cultural factors determine the extent of academic interest in a particular version such as its place within the literature of its language and the religious authority commanded by that translation. The approach taken here is to categorize versions primarily on the basis of the community to which they belonged and, where appropriate, to analyze the translations of OT and NT together. The following generalizations may be made about ancient Bible translation: in the earliest phase of Bible translation, when the OT was first being rendered into Greek, a system of fully analytical translation had not been developed, so that it was not possible to achieve the literal, word for word translations that later translators sought to achieve. The earliest phase of translation of the Bible into other languages—including Latin, Syriac, and Coptic—is generally not characterized by consistent, regular equivalence between the original source and the target language. In several cases (Armenian, Coptic, Georgian, Gothic, Syriac) the translation of the Bible was one of the first literary activities within that language and may even have been the motivation in the development of their alphabets (Armenian, Georgian, Gothic). Within Bible translation projects undertaken by Christians, the Gospels tend to be translated earlier or more frequently than other parts of the NT and to have been transmitted in more copies.

Versions that are the subject of major articles elsewhere in the dictionary receive only brief treatment here.

A. Greek Old Testament
B. Samaritan Scriptures
C. Aramaic Versions
   1. Jewish Aramaic translations of the
      Old Testament
   2. Syriac
   3. Christian Palestinian Aramaic
D. Latin
E. Coptic
F. Gothic
G. Armenian
H. Georgian
I. Ethiopic
J. Other Versions
Bibliography

A. Greek Old Testament

Jewish translation of the OT into Greek probably began in the early 3rd cent. BCE. Texts that suggest the existence of earlier translations (*Let. Aris.* 314 [*see* ARISTEAS, LETTER OF] and Aristobulus in Eusebius, *Praep. ev.* 13.12) are in all probability anachronistic. The *Letter of Aristeas* gives a legendary account of the translation of the Pentateuch into Greek, placing it dur-

ing the reign of Ptolemy Philadelphus (285–247 BCE). According to the *Letter of Aristeas* the Pentateuch was the first part of the OT to be translated, and it is to this alone that the term *Septuagint* was originally applied, after the seventy(-two) translators who were alleged to have translated it. From the Prologue to Sirach we may conclude that the bulk of the OT had been translated by the second half of the 2nd cent. BCE. By the 2nd cent. CE the work of the seventy translators was understood to have covered other books of the OT and thereafter the term *Septuagint* eventually came to be applied to books, e.g., Wisdom of Solomon, that were not translations at all.

The earliest form of the Greek OT, known as the Old Greek, is the stage that differs most from the MT (*see* MT, MASORETIC TEXT), though scholars disagree about the extent to which one should appeal to the possibility of a non-Masoretic Hebrew text behind the Old Greek or attribute differences to the technique of the translators. Moreover, this stage of the text is only imperfectly known since our earliest extensive LXX manuscripts come from the 4th cent. CE. In pre-Christian manuscripts of the Greek OT, the Tetragrammaton was generally written in the Aram. or Paleo-Hebrew script, or transliterated into Gk. Over time the Old Greek appears to have been found unsatisfactory on grounds of both its text and its method of translation. Efforts to revise the Old Greek were underway in pre-Christian times. Post-Christian revision of the Greek OT is found in the translations of Aquila (*see* AQUILA'S VERSION) and SYMMACHUS. Aquila offers a slavishly literal translation of the OT, which uses regular and transparent etymological equivalence between Hebrew and Greek texts; Symmachus produced a more idiomatic Greek rendering. Translations of certain biblical books (e.g., Samuel–Kings and Daniel), showing considerable affinity to the version attributed to the 2nd-cent. CE THEODOTION of Ephesus, are found in the 1st cent. BCE or 1st cent. CE, leading some scholars to speak of "Proto-Theodotion." Analogous to "Proto-Theodotion" is what some scholars call "Proto-Lucian" or the early appearance of texts with traits associated with Lucian of Antioch (d. 312 CE). Agreements between later Greek manuscripts, the Old Latin, and Josephus have led to the identification of a "Proto-Lucianic" or "Antiochene" text of Samuel, Kings, Chronicles, the Prophets, 1–2 Ezra, and 1–3 Maccabees. Under the hypotheses of a "Proto-Theodotion" and a "Proto-Lucian" both Theodotion and Lucian used prior translations on which to build their revised translations.

The Hexapla ("sixfold") is the name of the massive six-column edition of the OT produced by Origen (ca. 185–254 CE). The contents of the six columns appear to have been the Hebrew text in Hebrew script (1st column); the Hebrew in Gk. transliteration (2nd column); Aquila (3rd column); Symmachus (4th column); the LXX with editorial changes and critical signs introduced by Origen (5th column); Theodotion (6th column). In the

Psalms it also had up to three more columns, known now as Quinta, Sexta, and Septima. The Hexapla was too bulky to have been copied in its entirety and the original is lost. However, the materials from the Hexapla survive in various forms including: 1) fragmentary manuscripts containing extracts from the Hexapla; 2) marginal notes in Gk. manuscripts; often these give the renderings of one of "the three" (Aquila, Symmachus, or Theodotion), though sometimes the name of the translator to whom the rendering is due is not retained; 3) the Syrohexapla (see VERSIONS, SYRIAC), which more often preserves the critical signs of the Hexapla and the notes of attribution; 4) patristic citations; 5) catena manuscripts.

B. Samaritan Scriptures

The Samaritans have their own version of the Pentateuch written in an alphabet visually similar to the Paleo-Hebrew script and found in manuscripts dating from the 12th cent., the earliest most likely being Cambridge University Library Add. 1846. The manuscripts have few vowel markings, though there is greater use of vowel letters than in the MT, and the current oral tradition of vocalization of the text among Samaritans has roots in antiquity. The Samaritan Pentateuch may be characterized by more than one stage of differentiation between it and other early strands of pentateuchal transmission (especially those leading to the MT and the LXX). Agreements between Dead Sea Scrolls (e.g., 4Q22 and 2Q7) and the Samaritan manuscripts are demonstrably early, and the differing chronology of the Samaritan Pentateuch (e.g., over the ages in Gen 5 and 11) most likely so. Later differences appear to come from a time when sectarian division between Samaritans and Jews was fully entrenched and particularly pertain to Samaritan theological claims. Thus, twenty-one times in Deuteronomy the Samaritan Pentateuch has altered yivkhar (יִבְחַר, "will choose") to bakhar (בָּחַר, "chose") in relation to the place where God elects to place God's name, reflecting the Samaritan claim that Gerizim (see GERIZIM, MOUNT), not Jerusalem, is God's chosen place. Similarly, there are expansions to the Decalogue in Exod 20:17 and Deut 5:21 so that the tenth commandment enjoins the construction of an altar on Mount Gerizim. The Samaritans translated their Pentateuch into Aram., producing what is known as the Samaritan Targum. This is available in dozens of manuscripts, which show considerable linguistic variation among themselves, the earliest coming from the 14th cent.

C. Aramaic Versions

Aramaic (see ARAMAIC, ARAMAISM) has a wider variety of extant ancient translations of the Bible than any other language. Aside from the Samaritan Targum (see §B), 11Q10 (a pre-Christian translation of Job sometimes misnamed a "Targum"), and the Christian Palestinian Aramaic version, these translations are either Targums or Syriac versions.

1. Jewish Aramaic translations of the Old Testament

The earliest Aramaic version of part of the biblical text is of Job (11Q10). The manuscript is from around the middle of the 1st cent. BCE, though the translation itself may be somewhat earlier. It is moderately close to the MT, though it apparently ends at Job 42:11. Other 1st-millennium Jewish Aramaic translations are Targums, which must be dated largely by internal criteria and are represented only in medieval manuscripts. The Targums are characterized by certain common periphrases in relation to designation of the divine person and actions carried out by or to the divine person and also by a tendency to give explanatory expansions on the text. The Pentateuch is well provided with Targums: the earliest and least expansive is *Onqelos*, which was the official Targum in Babylonia. The Palestinian Targums display both common traditions and significant variation from one another. Representatives of the tradition are: 1) *Targum Neofiti I*, a manuscript from 1504 CE, which was discovered in the Vatican Library in 1956. 2) *Targum Pseudo-Jonathan*, so named because its initial scholarly edition mistakenly took the abbreviation *Y* to indicate Jonathan ben Uzziel rather Jerusalem; it is attested in two late 16th-cent. witnesses, one printed, which contains references to Mohammed's wives that could not have arisen before the 7th cent. Due to expansions it is about double the length of the Hebrew. 3) Incomplete or fragmentary manuscripts from the Cairo Genizah, the earliest of which dates from the 8th or 9th cent. 4) The *Fragmentary Targum*, which covers only extracts from the Pentateuch and is represented by several recensions. The official Targum of the Prophets is *Targum Jonathan*, which like *Onqelos* stems from Babylonia, though it is more expansive in poetic sections than *Onqelos*. With the exception of books with Aramaic portions (Ezra–Nehemiah and Daniel), the Writings are served by various Targums: the Targum to Proverbs has some genetic relationship with the Peshitta of Proverbs; the MEGILLOTH either have at least two Targums each or one Targum in textually diverse forms. *See* VERSIONS, JEWISH.

2. Syriac

Syriac, the native Aram. dialect of Edessa and its surrounding region, was the recipient of numerous Bible translation projects. The OT was translated into Syr. in the 1st or 2nd cent. CE from a Hebrew source. Its earliest manuscripts date from the 5th cent., and the earliest complete manuscript comes from around the 7th cent. In 615–17 CE Paul of Tella produced the Syrohexapla, a Syr. translation based on the Gk. Hexapla. Toward the end of his life Jacob of Edessa (ca. 640–708 CE) produced his own scholarly revision of the OT Peshitta on the basis of Gk. texts, aiming to include material from both Syr. and Gk. traditions. The earliest Syriac version of part of the NT is probably the DIATESSARON produced by Tatian ca. 167–175 CE. The Old Syriac Gospels, a relatively free translation that originated some time between the 2nd and 4th cent., are represented by two manuscripts: Codex Curetonianus (5th cent.) and Codex Sinaiticus (a palimpsest of the late 4th or early 5th cent.). The Peshitta NT, which lacked 2 Peter, 2 and 3 John, Jude, and Revelation, originated at the end of the 4th or the beginning of the 5th cent. and became the ecclesiastically accepted NT text. The five NT books not represented in the Peshitta appear in a later translation, probably the Philoxenian version, produced in 507/8 CE. In 616 CE, in conjunction with the creation of the Syrohexapla, Thomas of Harkel produced the Harclean version, a literalistic scholarly translation covering the whole NT and including a critical apparatus. The tendency from the 5th through the early 8th cent. was to revise previous translations in order to follow authoritative sources more literally, even if this meant abandoning native Syriac idiom.

3. Christian Palestinian Aramaic

Christian Palestinian Aramaic (CPA), formerly known as Syro-Palestinian or Palestinian Syriac, is the form of Aramaic used by Melkites in Palestine, the Transjordan, and Egypt. In contrast to Syriac it is a form of western Aramaic, though it has a script adapted from the Syriac Estrangela script, with one additional letter. The CPA alphabet distinguishes between two forms of *p*, with one form predominantly used to represent the Gk. letter PI (ⲡ π). The remnants of CPA literature were translated from Gk. and the translation of the Bible into CPA is probably to be dated to the 5th cent. The translation is preserved in manuscripts dating from the 6th to 13th cent. Manuscripts from the 11th to 13th cent. indicate a lack of knowledge of the language on the part of the scribes and it appears that by then the language had been replaced in daily use by Arabic. Unfortunately, most manuscripts are palimpsests and the biblical material is found in lectionary or liturgical texts or in fragmentary manuscripts, and therefore extended passages of the Bible are not preserved, though a few passages are preserved in multiple witnesses. The CPA OT was translated from a Gk. original that had been influenced by the Hexapla. Only about 10 percent of this translation has survived, representing the following: Genesis–Joshua, 1–4 Kingdoms, Job, Psalms, Proverbs, Ecclesiastes, Isaiah, Jeremiah, Lamentations, Epistle of Jeremiah, Ezekiel, the Song of the Three Children, Hosea, Joel, Micah, Wisdom of Solomon, Sirach. The coverage suggests that all or nearly all of the OT along with parts of the Apocrypha were translated. Parts of all books of the NT survive with the exception of 1 Timothy, 1 Peter, James, 2 John, 3 John, Jude, and Revelation. While it is not certain whether all parts of the NT were translated into CPA, the existence of 2 Peter suggests that the CPA canon was wider than that

of the Syriac Peshitta. The textual basis for the NT has been variously claimed to show affinity with Western, Caesarean, and Byzantine Gk. texts as well as with the Old Syriac. However, it is likely that no simple classification is adequate to express its textual affinity. The translation style is moderately literal.

D. Latin

Until the second half of the 2nd cent. the Roman church was predominantly Greek speaking, and it is probably in Africa that the need for Lat. versions of biblical books first arose (*see* VERSIONS, LATIN). It is debated whether Tertullian's biblical citations attest such versions, though the citations of Cyprian (d. 258 CE) agree with the text of later manuscripts and thereby provide conclusive evidence for the existence of written translations by the time he wrote. Latin versions prior to Jerome are generally known as Old Latin, or *Vetus Latina*. A revised Latin translation initiated by Jerome, known as the Vulgate, is preserved in the majority of manuscripts. Old Latin texts survive in a smaller number of manuscripts or in parts of manuscripts that otherwise have Vulg. text, as well as in glosses, citations, and some liturgical works. The precursor of the Old Latin for both Testaments was Gk., parts of the OT showing Lucianic influence and occasional evidence of other contact with the Hebrew. Prior to Jerome multiple translations of some biblical books as well as the poor quality of much Latin translation led to considerable confusion, even disdain for the biblical text (see Augustine, *Doctr. chr.* 2.15; 3.4). Jerome, who resorted to study of the Hebrew text in order to correct both the LXX and its Latin translators (*Quaestionum hebraicarum liber in Genesim*), was the principal person behind the revised translation of individual books and is credited with the Latin Bible that would gradually become dominant in the West. The translation of the NT at least was commissioned by Pope Damasus and the revision of the Gospels was published in 383 CE. For other parts of the NT the revision, whether by Jerome or someone else, was lighter. Subsequent to his work on the Gospels, Jerome moved to the more controversial project of using the Hebrew to revise translations that had been based on the Greek OT, a project completed by ca. 405 CE. Wisdom, Sirach, and Maccabees were not revised with the result that their Old Latin text was incorporated into what became the Vulgate. Because Christians considered the LXX translators to be inspired, unlike those responsible for the Old Latin versions (Augustine, *Doctr. chr.* 2.11–12), reception of the OT revision of Jerome was slower than that of the NT. In the case of Psalms Jerome's revision on the basis of the Gk. continued to be preferred over his later revision on the basis of the Hebrew.

E. Coptic

The language of the earliest Christian documents in Egypt was Greek, since Greek was the language of government and trade. However, as Christianity spread, parts of the OT and NT began to be translated from Gk. into Coptic, the indigenous language of Egypt, which ultimately descended from the language of the hieroglyphs. Coptic was written in a form of the Gk. script with six or seven additional letters used to represent native Egyptian sounds. The number of Gk. loan words in Coptic is rather high, sometimes estimated to be 15 percent, though it is not always possible to conclude that a particular Gk. word was in the Gk. original on the basis of its occurrence in the Coptic text. Manuscripts of parts of the Coptic Bible may be as early as the 3rd or 4th cent. (*see* VERSIONS, COPTIC). However, whereas Gk. provides abundant examples of dated documents from Egypt, Coptic provides very few since it was not generally the language for commerce. The dating of early Coptic documents is therefore open to dispute, with latitude of some centuries in dating sometimes being necessary.

The dialectology of Coptic is complex, but within recent textual criticism the Coptic versions have been examined as representative of the six main dialects identified by linguists: Sahidic, Bohairic, Middle Egyptian (also called the dialect of Oxyrhynchus), Fayumic, Akhmimic, and Subakhmimic. The history of transmission may broadly be divided into four phases. During the first phase, beginning probably in the 3rd cent., various dialects received translations of individual biblical books. Translation of the Bible as a whole does not appear to have been systematically carried out: two independent translations of one book appear in the same dialect; many books are unrepresented and codices often contain miscellaneous collections of canonical and noncanonical writings. Sahidic began to emerge as the standard literary dialect. From this phase come some of the most textually significant codices, including manuscripts of the Gospel of John in different dialects. The second phase, from the 6th to 9th cent., is marked by the dominance of Sahidic and the decline of other dialects. The third phase saw the dominance of Bohairic and the discontinuation of the use of Sahidic, and the fourth phase witnessed the final death of Bohairic as a living language during the 16th cent. and its restriction to entirely ecclesiastical functions. The quantity of patristic material in Coptic is considerably less than that in Gk., Lat., or Syr. We will deal with witnesses by dialect: Sahidic manuscripts survive covering nearly the whole NT. One of the earliest Sahidic manuscripts is the Crosby-Schøyen ms 193 from the 3rd cent., whose contents include 2 Maccabees (part), 1 Peter, and Jonah. Akhmimic is represented primarily by a 4th-cent. manuscript containing parts of John and James. Subakhmimic is the dialect of a number of the Nag Hammadi texts and also of a 4th-cent. codex of John's Gospel, which preserves the Gospel from 2:12 to 20:27. Middle Egyptian and Fayumic are two distinct dialects. However, there are some documents that have been ascribed by different scholars to each dialect while others show traits of both

dialects. A Greek–Middle Egyptian glossary on Hosea and Amos from the late 3rd cent. may have served to assist oral translation and thus indicate that these books had not yet been translated. From the 4th or 5th cent. there are two Middle Egyptian manuscripts of Matthew (Codex Scheide and Codex Schøyen, representing two different versions) and one of Acts (Codex Glazier, G67). Manuscripts of the Bohairic version generally begin in the 9th cent., though there are some remains of Bohairic texts (known as Proto-Bohairic) from earlier, the most important of which is Papyrus Bodmer III containing John and Gen 1:1–4:2 and dating, probably, to the 4th cent. The reason for the nonpreservation of Bohairic texts before the 9th cent. may be this dialect's general restriction to the region of the Nile delta where conditions were not dry enough to support the preservation of texts. Around the 11th cent., Bohairic superseded Sahidic and was used more widely, and thus texts were preserved. Many of the Bohairic biblical manuscripts are bilingual Coptic–Arabic texts. Early Coptic biblical manuscripts are not generally complete, and in many instances leaves of manuscripts were separated and dispersed between their discovery and their acquisition by collectors or museums. Consequently it is rare for a biblical manuscript of a whole book to be extant in any dialect other than Bohairic. There remains much to be done to identify and reassemble manuscripts, and study of the Coptic versions of the NT is far more advanced than that of the OT, which lacks any general edition. The *Biblia Coptica* project at the University of Salzburg is aiming to identify and produce a catalog of all the early Coptic biblical manuscripts.

F. Gothic

In the mid-4th cent., the West-Gothic bishop Ulfilas, or Wulfila, developed an alphabet for the Gothic language, based mainly on the Gk. alphabet, but also using Lat. and runic characters, and translated much of the Bible into Gothic. Gothic manuscripts date almost entirely from the 5th to early 6th cent., the period when Gothic power was at its height. Thereafter the use of Gothic declined and all but two of the biblical manuscripts became used as palimpsests. The chief Gothic manuscript is the Codex Argenteus, a codex of purple vellum with silver (and occasional gold) writing, dating from around 520 CE and now held in the University Library of Uppsala. This deluxe manuscript, of which 188 leaves survive, contains the Gospels in the order Matthew, John, Luke, Mark, and is equipped with the Eusebian canon list. A further important collection of manuscripts is in the Ambrosian Library in Milan. There are also two Gothic–Latin bilingual manuscripts. Of the NT only parts of the Gospels and Pauline Epistles survive. Hebrews was probably not included in the Pauline Epistles. Philostorgius, *Eccl. hist.* 2.5, alleges that Wulfila translated all but the books of Samuel and Kings. Jerome, *Epist.* 106, confirms the existence in antiquity of the psalter in Gothic. However, the Gothic

OT is now extant only for Neh 5:13-18; 6:14–7:45 and some numbers from Gen 5. In the NT it is extant for Matt 5:15–6:32; 7:12–10:1; 10:23–11:25; 25:38–26:3; 26:65–27:19; 27:42-66; Mark 1:1–12:38; 13:16-29; 14:4-16; 14:41–16:20; Luke 1:1–10:30; 14:9–16:24; 17:3–20:46; 23:11-14; 24:13-17; John 5:45–11:47; 12:1-49; 13:11–19:13; Rom 6:23–8:10; 8:34–11:1; 11:11–14:5; 14:9-20; 15:3-13; 16:21-24; 1 Cor 1:12-25; 4:2-12; 5:3–6:1; 7:5-28; 8:9–9:9; 9:19–10:4; 10:15–11:6; 11:21-31; 12:10-22; 13:1-12; 14:20-27; 15:1-35; 15:46–16:24; 2 Cor 1:1–13:13; Gal 1:1-7; 1:20–3:6; 3:27–6:18; Eph 1:1–5:29; 6:8-24; Phil 1:14–2:8; 2:22–4:17; Col 1:6-29; 2:11–4:18; 1 Thess 2:10–5:28; 2 Thess 1:1–2:4; 2:15–3:18; 1 Tim 1:1–6:16; 2 Tim 1:1–4:16; Titus 1:1–2:1; Phlm 11-23. A few further texts are cited in the four leaves preserved of a Gothic commentary on John known as *Skeireins*. The sections of Nehemiah preserved appear to be based on the Lucianic recension of the LXX. The Gothic NT is often based on a text close to the Byzantine text, though there are many exceptions to this (e.g., "Isaiah the prophet" in Mark 1:2; "of our God" in Mark 1:3). John lacks the Pericope Adulterae (7:53–8:11) and Romans ends at 16:24 (with 16:25-27 probably in an earlier lacuna). One of the open questions in research is the extent to which agreements between the Gothic and Old Latin (or "Western") witnesses result from the original source of the Gothic or from the history of transmission of the Gothic in an environment where Lat. was in wide use.

G. Armenian

Armenia adopted Christianity as its official religion in 301 CE and thereby became the first Christian kingdom (Sozomen, *Eccl. hist.* 2.8). However, it was not until the last decade of the 4th cent. or the first decade of the 5th that Mashtoc' (ca. 361–439 CE), known also as Mesrob or Mesrop, created the alphabet of thirty-six letters, thereby enabling translation of the Bible into Armenian to begin. The first book to be translated was Proverbs, and thereafter the NT and the rest of the OT followed, bringing the translation of the entire Bible to completion within the early 5th cent. The Armenian Bible is represented by a large number of manuscripts, many richly illuminated and provided with colophons. Of these the tetraevangelia, manuscripts containing the four Gospels, are the oldest and most numerous, the earliest dated tetraevangelium being from 887 CE. The earliest OT manuscript is Venice, St. Lazare 1651 (from the 10th or 11th cent.). The Armenian OT is based predominantly on a Gk. source influenced by Origen. In at least 1,461 locations in the OT, Hexaplaric signs (*see* HEXAPLA) are preserved in many Armenian manuscripts. For many parts of the Bible it is possible to identify earlier and later forms of books, and in the Armenian NT scholars distinguish the earlier arm[1], a version postulated partly on the basis of early patristic citations, from arm[2], which is represented by the major-

ity of manuscripts. Scholars often identify internal evidence that a Syriac basis was used at the earliest stage of translation (arm[1]) and that some of the readings of arm[1] survived the revision process whereby arm[2] was produced. The importance or influence of the Syriac version for the Armenian may be supported by the possibility that 3 Corinthians was included in the earliest version of the Armenian Pauline corpus along with additional examples of Semitic style. The earliest version of the Armenian NT did not include Mark 16:9-20. A critical edition of the Armenian Bible is an urgent need for scholarship if its value to the critical study of the Bible is to be realized. For the OT and much of the NT we must still rely on the 1805 edition of Zohrab, based on a single manuscript with references to up to fifty-eight unspecified manuscripts.

H. Georgian

Christianity was introduced into Georgia (ancient Iberia) from Armenia during the 4th cent. According to Armenian tradition Mashtoc', who created the Armenian alphabet (§G), was also responsible for the Georgian alphabet, which was followed by the translation of Scripture into Georgian. Scholars identify several stages in the translation of the Bible into Georgian. The earliest stage, known as geo[1], began in the 5th cent. and, though the extent of Syr. and Gk. influence on the translation is uncertain, it seems probable that it was largely based on a form of the Armenian Bible no longer extant. Geo[1] is partly represented by the Adysh tetraevangelium dated to 897 CE. The second stage, known as geo[2], represented a revision toward the Gk. It is chiefly represented by the Opiza tetraevangelium of 913 (geoA) and the Tbet' tetraevangelium of 995 (geoB). The Adysh and Opiza manuscripts lack Mark 16:9-20, while these verses are contained in the Tbet' manuscript. Both geo[1] and geo[2] show textual affinity in the Gospels to Codex Koridethianus, fam[1], and fam[13]. The earliest Georgian texts are undated, but may be assigned dates using the linguistic criterion of the verbal prefix *khan*, which developed into *hae*, and which was later omitted. The earliest manuscripts are known as *khanmeti* and those of the immediately following phase as *haemeti*. Some *khanmeti* palimpsest fragments of the Gospels are thought to date to the 5th or 6th cent. A further stage of revision of the Bible was undertaken by the Georgian monks at the Iveron monastery on Mount Athos in Greece. Saint Euthymius the Athonite (d. 1028 CE) revised the Georgian NT toward the Byzantine text and first translated into Georgian the book of Revelation along with the commentary by Andreas (the earliest copy of Revelation is from 978 CE). His successor Saint George the Hagiorite (d. 1065 CE) continued this revision, including the Pericope Adulterae (John 7:53–8:11) in the Georgian NT for the first time. It was George's version that became the standard ecclesiastical text thereafter. An early and important manuscript of the Georgian OT is the Athos Iveron Georg. 1 written in 978 CE (originally lacking Psalms, Chronicles, and Maccabees). The Georgian OT was probably based on Armenian. It shows significant Lucianic elements and in addition preserves some Hexaplaric material.

I. Ethiopic

The Aksumite kingdom adopted Christianity in the 4th cent. and inscriptional evidence indicates the existence of biblical translation by the early 6th cent. However, the bulk of biblical manuscripts comes from the 16th cent. onward, and the dates of some of the earliest biblical manuscripts are agreed to only within several centuries. Two tetraevangelia, Abba Garima I and III, appear to be among the oldest biblical manuscripts, written before 1270 CE, perhaps as early as the 10th cent. Translations of both Testaments were from Gk.: the OT often displays a pre-Hexaplaric text, and many books of both Testaments were subject to revision from the 14th cent. onward on the basis of Syriac-influenced Arabic manuscripts. Research on biblical texts is hampered by a lack of critical editions: although recent editions produced by individual scholars now cover more than half of the NT, the majority of the OT is without such treatment. The Ethiopic OT is distinguished by its wide canon, and its unique preservation of some early pseudepigrapha shows that it is capable of retaining much from earlier tradition.

J. Other Versions

Other versions are often included among the ancient versions, including Arabic, which received a number of independent translation projects including translations from Bohairic and Syr. as well as Gk.; manuscripts date from the 9th cent., and a Middle Persian version of some books of the Bible was translated from Syr. A psalter is preserved from the 6th cent. Fragments of the NT and psalter of a 5th or 6th cent. Sogdian version survive. See also VERSIONS, MEDIEVAL.

Bibliography: Sebastian P. Brock. *The Bible in the Syriac Tradition* (2006); Philip Burton. *The Old Latin Gospels: A Study of Their Texts and Language* (2000); Bart D. Ehrman and Michael W. Holmes, eds. *The Text of the New Testament in Contemporary Research: Essays on the Status Quaestionis* (1995); Anthony Grafton and Megan Hale Williams. *Christianity and the Transformation of the Book* (2006); Karen H. Jobes and Moises Silva. *Invitation to the Septuagint* (2000); Michael A. Knibb. *Translating the Bible: The Ethiopic Version of the Old Testament* (1999); Bruce M. Metzger. *The Early Versions of the New Testament: Their Origin, Transmission, and Limitations* (1977); Martin Jan Mulder, ed. *Mikra* (1988); Christ Müller-Kessler and Michael Sokoloff, eds. *A Corpus of Christian Palestinian Aramaic* (1996–99); Aliston Salvesen, ed. *Origen's Hexapla and Fragments: Papers Presented at the Rich Seminar on the Hexapla, Oxford Centre for Hebrew and Jewish Studies, 25th July–3rd August*

1994 (1998); Abraham Tal. *The Samaritan Targum of the Pentateuch* (1980); Megan Hale Williams. *The Monk and the Book: Jerome and the Making of Christian Scholarship* (2006).

P. J. WILLIAMS

VERSIONS, ARABIC. The advent of Islam in 622 CE catalyzed the spread of Arabic and hence the need for Arabic versions of the Christian Scriptures. Arabic Christian texts are largely based on the LXX and the Peshitta. There is, however, no standardized Arabic version of the OT.

Saadia ha Gaon translated the first Arabic version of the Bible (10th cent. CE), while the Samaritan version is attributed to Abu Sa'id (13th cent. CE). In 1671, a Catholic Arabic Bible was published under the authority of the archbishop of Damascus. The Bible Society issued a reprint of this version in London in 1822.

ALICE MANDELL

VERSIONS, ARAMAIC. *See* VERSIONS, ANCIENT.

VERSIONS, ARMENIAN ahr-mee′nee-uhn. In the early 5th cent. CE, Mesrob Mashtoc' (ca. 361–439 CE) created the Armenian alphabet and initiated translation of the Bible into Armenian. The earliest dated edition of the four Gospels is from 887 CE. Armenian Bible versions are more numerous than those of other Eastern manuscript traditions. They are often richly illustrated and illuminated. *See* VERSIONS, ANCIENT.

P. J. WILLIAMS

VERSIONS, AUTHORIZED. *See* AUTHORIZED VERSIONS.

VERSIONS, BIBLE. Many religious communities define the core of their faith and identity through their holy scriptures. Language is a key part in the formation of identity. When language becomes outdated and is no longer understood by the vast majority of community members, the community may decide to commission a new translation of sacred texts. Sometimes a new translation or interpretation of an older version may include other changes in content. For example, the sequence of books could be rearranged, the collection might include enlarged or shortened versions of some books, or it might even include new books or exclude original books. Different interpretations of the earlier language by various communities may lead to different revisions of the earlier text. *See* BIBLE TRANSLATION THEORY; CANON OF THE NEW TESTAMENT; CANON OF THE OLD TESTAMENT; VERSIONS, ANCIENT; VERSIONS, ENGLISH; VERSIONS, MODERN (NON-ENGLISH).

Bibliography: Peter R. Ackroyd and Christopher F. Evans, eds. *The Cambridge History of the Bible.* 3 vols. (1975–76); Julio Trebolle Barrera. *The Jewish Bible and the Christian Bible: An Introduction to the History of the Bible* (1998); Frederick F. Bruce. *The English Bible: A History of Translations from the Earliest English Versions to the New English Bible* (1970); David Norton. *A History of the Bible as Literature, Vol. I: From Antiquity to 1700* (1993); David Norton. *A History of the Bible as Literature, Vol. II: From 1700 to the Present Day* (2005).

PETER ARZT-GRABNER

VERSIONS, CATHOLIC kath´uh-lik. Though *catholic* can refer to the Western half of the church that was divided from Eastern Christianity at the end of the 1st millennium, in this article it refers primarily to the part of the Western church that remained in communion with the bishop of Rome (the pope) after the 16th cent. The Catholic Church (in both senses) inherited the Latin language from the Roman Empire, and Latin united the diverse peoples of the church and provided the language for official approaches to God (Bible translations, liturgy, and theology). After the 4th cent., Jerome's Latin VULGATE ("common version") came to be the Bible of Western Christianity, and it remained so until the 16th cent. Without an appreciation of this Latin tradition and its insistence on linking Scripture and tradition, one cannot appreciate Roman Catholic approaches to Bible translation.

Beginning in the 16th cent., publication of biblical texts in the original languages (e.g., successive editions of Erasmus' Gk. NT) and vernacular translations (especially Luther's in 1522 and Tyndale's in 1523) diminished the Vulgate's authority and called into question some of its renderings. Translations abounded—the Coverdale Bible (1535), Great Bible (1539–41), the Geneva Bible (1560) and, most famously, the Authorized Version (King James, 1611). Roman Catholic authorities tended to be suspicious of laity reading vernacular Bibles, linked as they sometimes were to the reformers' ideas.

In response to what they considered tendentious renderings and explanatory notes, exiled Catholics at the English college in Douay, France, produced a literal translation of the Vulgate: the NT in 1582 and the OT in 1609–10. (Because the college temporarily relocated to Rheims from 1578 to 1593, it was called the Douay/Rheims.) The translation was not intended for the laity, but as an aid to clergy in disputations with Protestants. Bishop Richard Challoner made revisions in 1749–50, and that version served English-speaking Catholics up to the mid-20th cent. Scholarly Catholics' dissatisfaction with Vulgate-based translations was redressed in the 1943 encyclical *Divino afflante spiritu*. Reversing the Council of Trent's insistence, made at the height of the Reformation, that official Catholic translations be from the Vulgate, Pope Pius XII directed translators to consider the original biblical languages. *Dei Verbum* of Vatican II affirmed and expanded this policy (§22).

Two Catholic translations appeared in England about that time: 1) the Westminster Version of Holy Scriptures by Cuthbert Lattey and Joseph Keating (NT, 1935; OT, incomplete) from the original languages with an eye on the Vulgate, and 2) a version by Ronald Knox (NT, 1944; OT, 1948–50) from the Clementine Vulgate with an eye on the Gk. for the NT. Both were eventually displaced by The Jerusalem Bible in 1966, a translation of the renowned La Bible de Jérusalem (1956). Though its introductions and notes were from the French original, its biblical text was translated afresh from the original languages. The revised edition of the French in 1973 resulted in The New Jerusalem Bible in 1985, a substantial improvement over the first edition.

In the United States, the Confraternity of Christian Doctrine (CCD) had already translated a third of the OT from the Vulgate, but in 1943 abandoned that effort to work from the original languages. The New American Bible appeared in 1970, with a revised NT in 1986 and revised Psalms in 1991. (The NAB-revised Psalms were not approved for liturgical use by a 2001 Roman instruction, *Liturgiam authenticam*.) In addition to the NAB, Roman Catholic authorities in Great Britain and North America also approved "Catholic versions" of well-known Protestant and ecumenical translations—The Revised Standard Version, The New Revised Standard Version, and The Good News Bible. Cardinal Richard Cushing of Boston gave an imprimatur to the unaltered form of the RSV as it appeared in the 1966 Oxford Annotated Bible. In contrast, the British Catholic RSV version made a few changes, e.g., "brethren" of Jesus for "brothers" in order to favor the perpetual virginity of Mary (though nothing was said about his "sisters") and "full of grace" for "favored one" in the angel's greeting to Mary (Luke 1:28). The American Catholic bishops approved the RSV for lectionary use and the Canadian bishops have also approved the NRSV for their lectionary.

Other countries followed suit. In 1956, French Dominicans at the École Biblique in Jerusalem and other distinguished scholars published La Bible de Jérusalem from the original languages with extensive notes. Immediately hailed as a great work of interpretation and popularization, it was translated into English, and its notes became a model for annotated Bibles in other languages. In 1979, the German-speaking Catholic bishops of Europe sponsored a single translation for all their regions, aptly naming it *Die Einheitsübersetzung* (the "unified" or "unity translation"). An ecumenical dimension was added when the German Protestant bishops approved its Psalms and NT for church use, though Protestant cooperation has since ended because of disagreement with the principles stated in *Liturgiam authenticam*.

RICHARD J. CLIFFORD

VERSIONS, COPTIC kop´tik. Translations of the Gk. Bible into the COPTIC LANGUAGE. Fragmentary versions exist in every Coptic dialect, but the most complete are in Sahidic (the dialect of southern [Upper] Egypt) and Bohairic (of northern [Lower] Egypt).

Sahidic and Bohairic versions are attested from the 4th cent. CE, but most Bohairic manuscripts are considerably later. Bohairic became the Coptic Church's liturgical language. Coptic versions occasionally yield notable textual variants; e.g., Matt 6:13 (Sahidic) includes "for yours is the power and the glory forever" (compare *Did.* 8.2). *See* VERSIONS, ANCIENT.

Bibliography: Bruce M. Metzger. *The Early Versions of the New Testament* (1977) 99–152.

JAMES W. BARKER

VERSIONS, EGYPTIAN. *See* VERSIONS, ANCIENT.

VERSIONS, ENGLISH. The term "English versions" refers to the resulting work of a translation from ancient languages to English. Complete English versions of the Bible began with the Wycliffe Bible in 1382. From Wycliffe the history of English versions provides the basis for analysis of some of the modern English versions that have used various translation theories and a variety of stated purposes.

God's communication with humanity is a testimony of the struggle to produce the Scriptures in a language form understood by the masses. Resistance, persecution, Bible burning, and martyrdom have bloodied the path along which history has passed. The history of Bible translation bears witness to how God's Word passed from being exclusively for those in the pulpit to a text read, understood, and acted upon by those in the pew.

A. Setting the Stage for English Versions
  1. The beginning
  2. The origin of the English language
  3. Early portions of pre-English Scriptures
B. From the Quill to the Press: 1382–1455
  1. John Wycliffe and his times
  2. The Wycliffe Bible
    a. The Early Wycliffe Version 1380–84
    b. The Later Wycliffe Version 1388–95
  3. The printing press advances Bible versions
C. The Bible in the Reign of Henry VIII 1509–47
  1. The Golden Legend 1483–1527
  2. Tyndale's version
    a. The life and work of William Tyndale 1494–1536
    b. The Tyndale New Testament
    c. Typical readings of Tyndale New Testament
  3. The Coverdale Bible
  4. The Matthew's Bible
  5. The Taverner Bible
  6. The Great Bible
D. The Bible of the Exiles: Queen Mary 1553–58
  1. The Geneva Bible
  2. The impact of the Geneva Bible
E. The Elizabethan Bible 1558–1603

  1. The Bishops' Bible 1568
  2. The Roman Catholic Rheims/Douay Version 1582/1610
F. The King James Version 1603–25
  1. The birth of a new version
  2. Translation begins
  3. The early struggle for acceptance
G. The Bible Stabilized 1625–1881
  1. The revisions of the King James Version
  2. The 1881–85 revision
  3. The legacy of the King James Version
H. The Modern Translation Debate 1885–Present
  1. The need for modern versions
  2. The theories of translation
  3. Translation theories in practice
  4. The original language texts in modern versions
I. Analysis of Modern Versions
  1. Criteria for judging a translation
  2. Modern versions compared
  3. Modern translation texts compared: 2 Peter 1:5-7
  4. Statistical comparison of modern versions
Bibliography

A. Setting the Stage for English Versions

1. The beginning

The OT Bible books were written in Hebrew with limited portions in Aramaic and the NT books in Greek. In the West, Latin—the language of scholars—provided an antidote to the decline of the ancient biblical languages.

A devoted priest and language scholar, St. Jerome recognized the need to translate the decaying original languages into the contemporary, vernacular Latin. Tradition places him sequestered in an underground cave in the holy city of Jesus' birth, Bethlehem, dedicating himself from 386 CE to his death in 420 to scholarly pursuits. His greatest triumph was his translation of the Latin Vulgate from the original languages into the language of the literate masses. The struggle for religious power had begun.

2. The origin of the English language

The history of the Celtic island of Britain gives us a background for the origin of the English language. There were a succession of invasions, from Julius Caesar in 55 BCE to the withdrawal of the Roman legions in 410 CE and the subsequent collapse of the Roman Empire. The Germanic people—the Anglos, Saxons, and Jutes—all invaded the island. The native Britons withdrew to the western areas of the island and adopted the term *wedlas* from which the word *Welsh* came.

The closely related language of the invaders formed the basis of English and is known today as Old English or Anglo-Saxon English. The love of the Anglo-Saxon for its ambiguity, innuendo, and word play was shared with English in every age and characterizes its written literature.

3. Early portions of pre-English Scriptures

The earliest portions of Scripture in Anglo-Saxon were songs set to verse by a layman named Caedmon. The only known verses are preserved in a hymn of creation. Bishop Aldhelm of Sherborne, in the 8th cent. CE, translated the first known biblical text when he selected portions of the psalms.

Interlinear glossing of manuscripts, a practice of placing English word equivalents directly below the Latin words, characterized the Old English period. This pedagogical method introduced students to the Latin text as they became literate.

The most important pre-English influence was the work of Aelfric. His work in translating Scripture led eventually to the 10th cent. anonymous Wessex Gospels, the first true translation of Scripture.

The French invasion brought to a close the Anglo-Saxon period of English and introduced Middle English (1100–1500). The invaders declared Norman French as the official language of England. This strong French influence delayed the progress of an English-language Bible. During the next two hundred years, the Anglo-Saxon language gradually assimilated the French into the Anglo-Norman language. (It was not until the period of Shakespeare in the 16th cent. that a modern English language emerged.)

In the following decades, the faithful had to rely on liturgy, songs, poems, medieval dramas, and oral transmissions of Scripture stories. Latin and French Bibles of the aristocracy and the teachings of the priesthood were substitutes for an English Bible prior to the 14th cent.

Even for the modestly educated clergy, the Bible was accessible only in the Latin language. Medieval Latin Bibles were large folio copies, bound in two or three volumes. The exorbitant price and the scarcity of copies made reading and studying nearly impossible. The clergy could hope to put their hands on only portions of Scripture and, for the most part, relied heavily upon prayer books. Service manuals, used by the clergy, contained only select portions of Scripture, making it impossible to understand the flow, context, and meaning of the Scriptures as the original authors intended. This, undoubtedly, attributed to the poor methods of Bible interpretation and the faulty worship of words and phrases taken out of context.

Without the availability of the Scriptures, and with an often-illiterate clergy, one can easily imagine a church corrupted by false doctrine. The passing centuries awaited the reforms of John Wycliffe. Even with the many controversies of the pre-Reformation period, the greatest threat must rest with the medieval problems of the relationship between the church and the clergy, caused, in part, by inaccessibility to the Bible in English.

This period produced a veneration of the words of the Bible that extended beyond the meaning of those words. Biblical words had an innate mystery and power, so much so that the manuscripts themselves held a divine authority and the words of the text a special meaning in spiritual life. The translation of the Bible into the vernacular upset the culture and worldview of medieval Christianity.

B. From the Quill to the Press: 1382–1455

1. John Wycliffe and his times

During the political and religious unrest of the 12th and 13th cent., John Wycliffe (ca. 1330–84), the "Morning Star of the Reformation," introduced reforms that led to the Reformation in England and Europe. His analysis of the religious climate convinced him of the need to turn to the Scriptures as the rule of life. No longer were the Scriptures to be worshiped as oracles; Scripture was to be obeyed. Wycliffe's deep opposition to the church's views of the eucharist, its selling of indulgences, its authority, prayers for the saints, and pilgrimages set him at odds with the established church and its teachings. This inevitability led to the conclusion that everyone must have a copy of the Bible in his/her own language. Wycliffe believed the laity should be taught the faith in whatever language was most easily understood.

John Wycliffe was born in the early 1330s in the small village of Wycliffe-on-Tees in Yorkshire. He attended Balliol College in Oxford and in 1356 completed a Bachelor of Arts at Merton College. He received his Doctor of Theology in 1372/1373. By the time Wycliffe left Oxford, he had advanced to Master of Balliol College and Warden of Canterbury Hall. His studies were rooted in Latin, the language of a medieval scholar.

The opposition to the Bible in the vernacular came primarily from the belief that the Bible could be understood only by scholars by virtue of their education, and priests by virtue of the authority of their office. Until Wycliffe's Bible, opposition to Scripture in plays, songs, poems, or in oral recitations posed no threat to the church authority structure. After the years of the success of the Wycliffe Bible and the work of his loyal followers, known as Lollards, the Bible in the English language became the "forbidden book." Just twenty years after the first production of the complete Bible in the English language, the statute *De heretic comburendo* (1401) promised death by public burning to heretics. The definition of *heretic* was soon expanded to include the reading, owning, or memorizing of Scriptures in any language other than Latin.

In 1409, Archbishop Arundel called a provincial council and adopted the *Constitutions* that forbade the translation of the sacred Latin Vulgate Bible into a common tongue without express supervision of the church.

The growing intolerance of laypeople for the abuse of the absolute authority of the church awaited John

Wycliffe in the 14th cent. He fueled the fires of reform by translating the first complete Bible into the English language using the Latin Vulgate. Greek and Hebrew scholarship was not yet established in many of the educational institutions in England.

2. The Wycliffe Bible

Tradition assigns the translation of the Wycliffe Bible to John Wycliffe in 1382. Modern scholarship challenges this concept. Many believe it was translated by the Lollards (Wycliffe's faithful followers) who were the evangelists spreading the reforms of Wycliffe. They emphasized authority of Scripture, need for a personal relationship with Christ, and they attacked the church on such issues as celibacy, transubstantiation, and indulgences. Nevertheless, Wycliffe is still the most likely choice for some of the translation.

About 250 copies of the manuscripts of the Wycliffe NT and Bible exist today, a large number for a forbidden book. These hand-copied manuscript Bibles were produced about seventy years before the printing press presented itself to Europe (ca. 1450). These copies do not agree with one another. There are at least two major distinct texts known as the Early Version (EV) and the Later Version (LV).

a. The Early Wycliffe Version 1380–1384. Readings in the copies of the EV are inconsistent among themselves. It is not as if one man translated the entire Bible and everyone copied it. Persecutions, difficulty in obtaining leather sheets, time, and secrecy led to hurried scribes copying portions from any manuscript available. It is not hard to imagine scribes copying small portions and, on other safe occasions, copying the rest from different copies. In spite of these perilous times, many of the extant copies are beautifully illuminated. Ironically, most copies were written after 1408 when it was forbidden to have an English translation. Many Wycliffe Bibles were used for public liturgy with OT and NT readings accompanied by readings from prayer books.

The EV was probably completed in 1382 and the LV not before 1388, perhaps later. The EV was very literal and closely followed the Latin word order while the LV attempted to use idiomatic language and English word order. To read the EV, the assistance of a Latin dictionary and grammar are helpful.

There are three early manuscripts of the EV that provide evidence for possible translators of the EV. MS Bodley 959 at the Bodleian Library in Oxford is a large manuscript with many corrections and alterations, formerly believed to be the original autograph of the Wycliffe OT. The manuscript followed the order of books that included the apocryphal book of Baruch among the prophets. The manuscript ends in the middle of 3:20, *"ye place hem /risen /ye (the) yunge"* at the bottom of the leaf. Then it reads, "Here ends the translation of Nicholas."

MS Douce 369, EV, also in the Bodleian Library, ends abruptly at the very same place in the text but only one quarter down the second column of the page. Then added to the abrupt ending is *"Explicit translacom Nicholay de herford"* ("Here ends the translation of Nicholas of Hereford"). It is possible that the EV began as a glossed text, then went through various revisions and was copied with alterations by at least five scribes. The obvious implication is that Nicholas Hereford translated this portion of the OT and that the five other unidentifiable handwritings were Lollard translators.

Another manuscript in the Cambridge University Library, MS Ee.10., ends at exactly the same place in Baruch and records, *"Here endith the translacioun of N and now bigynneth the translacioun of J & of othere men."* It is obvious "N" refers to Nicholas Hereford but the "J" is in question. Several suggestions have surfaced: John Wycliffe, John Trevisa, or John Purvey. No one can say for sure to whom the initials belong.

Despite the controversy surrounding the translators of the OT, Wycliffe's name became synonymous with the work of translation. The earliest mention of Wycliffe's association with the Bible translation is Henry Knighton's reference in his *Chronicon.* Writing in the 1390s, he refers back to 1382 as the time John Wycliffe translated the Gospels.

It is interesting that even though the OT in the EV is very literal and difficult to understand, the NT in the EV is much more idiomatic. It is quite possible Knighton's reference is testimony to the greater possibility of Wycliffe's translation of the NT.

b. The Later Wycliffe Version 1388–95. Among Wycliffe's followers was a scholar named John Purvey (ca.1353–1428). John Purvey was a quiet, highly esteemed scholar who was Wycliffe's secretary at Lutterworth. The LV translation of the Wycliffe Bible is judged by many scholars to be the work of John Purvey.

Shortly after Wycliffe died in 1384, Purvey sought refuge in Bristol where, it is thought, he began a thorough revision of the complete Bible. His emphasis on English idiom and word order improved the revision by making it more readable.

A general prologue introduced the LV of the Wycliffe Bible. While it has been understood for many years that John Purvey wrote the prologue, scholars today are uncertain as to its authorship. It contains fifteen chaps.: 12–14 discuss general rules for interpretation, and chap. 15 records the method used in his revision.

The first principle suggested use of the most accurate text. Because all Bibles were in handwritten form, variants were inevitable. A careful comparison of the variants, including the use of commentaries, would enable one to determine the correct Latin text.

Second, the writer believed a translator must be a competent interpreter of the biblical text. Understanding the passage is dependent on the translator's ability to interpret.

The third principle called for the consultation of grammars, dictionaries, and other reference works that gave the translator insight for difficult words. He described his approach to translation as centered on meaning, rather than a literal, word-for-word translation. Finally, it had to be carefully reviewed by holy and scholarly men.

3. The printing press advances Bible versions

Johann Gutenberg did not invent the printing press. Prior to Gutenberg, printing consisted of carving the outlines of pictures and limited texts from a solid block of wood, inking them, and then pressing the block to the paper or vellum with the use of a press similar to the wine press. This kind of printing was limited by the slow tedious work, crude images, and short-lived woodcuts. The earliest form of block printing of books in Europe surfaced at the beginning of the 14th cent. in the form of the *Biblia Pauperum* (*Bible of the Poor*). These "picture Bibles" enabled the uneducated laity to learn the biblical stories by viewing the stories in pictures. Each *Biblia Pauperum* contained thirty-four to forty-eight scenes of NT events sandwiched between OT pre-figuring of these NT events.

Johann Gutenberg (1396–1468) is credited with the invention of movable type. Movable type was made of individual lead composite letters placed into lines and rows until a page was complete. This printing was faster, cheaper, clearer, and worn letters were easily replaced. The Gutenberg Bible, long recognized as the first printed Bible (1455–1456), was printed in Mainz, Germany using movable type.

Gutenberg, poor and forgotten, died February 3, 1468, in his native Mainz. Certainly the Gutenberg contribution to the centuries of Bible production did not end the day he was laid in the grave. By the year 1500 (a mere thirty-two years after his death), Bibles from printing presses were found in seventeen European countries and 260 printing towns with 1,120 established printing offices. Approximately 40,000 different works in multiple editions totaling more than ten million copies had been produced from Gutenberg's invention. In spite of this progress, there was still no printed Bible in English. The English-speaking world was confined to the handwritten manuscripts of the translation of John Wycliffe.

C. The Bible in the Reign of Henry VIII 1509–47
1. The Golden Legend 1483–1527

The Golden Legend (1483) was the first printing of any part of the Bible in English. William Caxton imported printing into England in 1475. Caxton could have printed the Wycliffe Version, but because of the possible heretical association with the Wycliffe Bible among the clergy and the Constitutions of 1408 prohibiting a Bible in English, he avoided the possible consequences. Caxton chose the safe route, printing a surrogate of the biblical text by publishing Jacobus de Voragine's *Golden Legend*. This popular work consisted of the stories of the lives of saints from both the OT and NT. The Golden Legend was the primary source of printed biblical teaching for the English-speaking world for more than forty years. The Tyndale NT in 1526 finally replaced it as the primary NT.

2. Tyndale's version

The 15th-cent. church in Europe was groaning with the birth of the Renaissance, about to bring forth the modern world. The church was still in turmoil from the Great Schism. Monarchs challenged the church's power, the Lollards defied her doctrines, and the faithful questioned her ability to reform. The medieval church was unwilling to accept the reforms of John Wycliffe and John Huss (reformer in Bohemia) and resisted the emergence of a middle class. With the failure of land reform, a 16th-cent. reformation was inevitable.

The Reformation accentuated the authority of Scripture, personal piety, and the study of Scripture in the original languages (a principle of the Renaissance). Reformers firmly believed that without knowledge of the Bible, it was impossible to live a pious life. The academic atmosphere that created Martin Luther (1483–1546, Germany), John Calvin (1509-64, France), and Ulrich Zwingli (1484–1531, Switzerland) contributed to the passion of the precocious translator, William Tyndale.

More than fifty years following the printing of the Gutenberg Bible in Latin, there was no printed Greek NT or English Bible. This is more easily understood if one remembers that Greek did not occupy the interest of many scholars in Europe prior to the fall of Constantinople (1453). The Turk invasion forced Greek scholars from the Eastern church to Europe and the resurgence of interest in the Greek language.

The emphasis upon the interpretation of Scriptures from the original languages and the rebirth of Greek learning paved the way for a printed Greek NT and were the basis for an English NT from the original Greek. In 1515, Erasmus began searching for manuscripts for editing and typesetting. Since the project required the utmost haste in order to produce the first published text, Erasmus settled for manuscripts that were faulty. The original manuscripts had been handwritten centuries before and copied over and over again. By the 16th cent. they were quite rare. Using five late manuscripts, he began the task of editing. When parts of the text were indecipherable or missing, Erasmus used the Latin text and translated it back into Greek.

a. The life and work of William Tyndale 1494–1536. William Tyndale (family name also known as Hytchins) was born in Gloucestershire ca. 1494. He entered Oxford University in 1510 and completed his MA in 1515. He is thought to have spent the next six years studying at Cambridge University under the continuing influence of Erasmus' Greek NT. He became an authority in the original biblical languages. Such study, however, came in the midst of a period when theological and biblical studies had fallen on hard times. Luther, the Augustinian monk, had begun to expound on the Epistle to the Romans at the University of Wittenberg in 1515. The Reformation was underway.

By the time of Luther's bold declaration of justification by faith, Tyndale had rejected most biblical and theological studies taught at the universities and even called some of the teachers "apostles of ignorance." The revival of Hebrew and Greek stirred the English clergy into a new appreciation for the study of Scripture. But the "sacred" Latin Bible continued as the primary source for biblical study.

Tyndale journeyed to Little Sodbury in 1522 where he tutored the children of John Walsh. At Little Sodbury, while continuing to study Scripture and translating Erasmus' *Enchiridion Militis Christiani*, Tyndale became convinced that the root cause of theological confusion was the ignorance of Scripture, which could be corrected if even the plough boy had the Bible in his own language.

Tyndale, still under the prohibitions of the Constitutions, decided to approach the recently appointed bishop of London, Cuthbert Tunstall, to gain authority for translating the NT into English. Tyndale expected to gain not only approval for his work but also a "living" as chaplain. Tyndale was denied both.

In May 1524, Tyndale left his beloved England for the continent, spending time in Wittenberg, Hamburg, and finally Cologne. Just after he completed a portion of the Gospel of Matthew, the city authorities forbade the printer Peter Quentel to continue printing the work. With just eighty quarto pages completed, Tyndale fled to Worms where in 1526 the first complete NT in the English language was printed. Only three copies of this edition of the NT exist today: two complete copies (one lacking the title leaf) and one imperfect copy.

A popular story states that Bishop Tunstall began using merchants to purchase copies of Tyndale's translation on the continent to prevent their entrance into England where English versions were forbidden. Tyndale NTs were nearly always printed in small, inexpensive pocket-sized volumes for easy transport. The London merchant Augustine Packington, a supporter of Tyndale's work, met with Tyndale to inform him of Tunstall's strategy. To his surprise, Tyndale welcomed the news with enthusiasm. Tyndale believed that when the NTs got to England and people witnessed the burning of "God's Word," the populace would react with condemnation. In addition the profits from the sale could provide for a future revision—which he did.

Tyndale attempted to live in anonymity; therefore it is difficult historically to authenticate his residences for these years. It is fairly certain that the last years of his life were in Antwerp with Thomas Poyntz. His old English enemies were denied access to him while he was living outside of England. However, England's political influence had long arms. Antwerp was under the jurisdiction of Charles V, a staunch Roman Catholic. An accusation of heresy would be more acceptable than any other charge to Catholic Charles. Tyndale's future was uncertain.

Tyndale found safe haven while staying in Antwerp. The Poyntz family was related to the Walsh family, Tyndale's patrons in Little Sodbury. On May 21, 1535, betrayed by Henry Phillips, Tyndale was kidnapped by the king's officers and imprisoned in Vilvorde near Brussels. By now Thomas Cromwell, and even Henry VIII, held some sympathy for an English translation and had made token attempts earlier to intervene on his behalf. Charles V, the nephew of Henry's recently divorced wife, Catharine of Argon, was in no mood to accommodate an intervention.

Tyndale's enemies finally captured their archenemy. They charged him with heresy and when he was found guilty, he was led to the stake where he was strangled and burned on October 6, 1536.

Tyndale's final words at the stake were, "Lord, open the king of England's eyes." Unfortunately he did not live long enough to see his prayer answered. England's eyes were opened, but the challenges of a Bible in English were to face another, greater threat as kings and queens entered the fray.

b. The Tyndale New Testament. The Cologne printing had marginal notes and an extensive prologue. It also had a list of the books of the NT following Luther's 1522 NT with Hebrews, James, Jude, and Revelation separated from the rest of the books. Even though Luther questioned the canonical authority of these books, there is no evidence to suggest Tyndale held to the same canonical view. Undoubtedly, Tyndale had a copy of Luther's German translation before him. The Great Bible (1539) of Coverdale changed the order of Tyndale's books and standardized the order of books as we have them today.

Peter Schoeffer, the Worms printer, published the Tyndale NT in 1526. Unlike the Cologne fragment, it was printed in octavo (pocket size) without the prologue or notes. This enabled the books to be smuggled into England in bales of cloth. It was immediately forbidden entry into England and in 1526 Tunstall ordered a Bible burning that took place at St. Paul's Church. After Henry VIII's arrest of Cardinal Wolsey, Thomas Bilney launched an intense persecution of those possessing the NT. The Bible—locked up for centuries in monasteries and in a language unknown by many—was now available to all who dared challenge the consequences.

Scholars and clergy prior to the 16th cent. believed Latin was so holy that no vulgar words could reach the lofty stature and beauty of the Latin. Tyndale's NT changed that for many. Using the simplicity of Saxon sentences, short, direct prose lines, and diversity of vocabulary, Tyndale demonstrated English could be a beautiful, harmonic expression of God's communication. And yet, Tyndale remained close to the meaning of the Greek NT. It has been estimated that eighty percent of the King James Version reflects the work of William Tyndale.

In January 1530, the Pentateuch appeared with a general preface headed "WT to the Reader." He also translated the historical books, which can be found in the Matthew's Bible, and the book of Jonah. His martyrdom in 1536 prevented his completion of the whole Bible.

Tyndale revised his NT in 1534. In his introduction he stated he was always willing to revise or amend any of his translation that was not correct. It was a small octavo edition of about 400 pages with Tyndale's name appearing on it for the first time. Attached to it were two large prefaces. The first is a typical introduction, but the second is a scathing rebuke of George Joye for making unauthorized revisions to the Tyndale NT. Tyndale was upset with Joye for distributing Tyndale's version and attaching his own name to it. The revision also contained prefaces to the various books of the NT, many of which followed Luther's version.

c. Typical readings of Tyndale New Testament. While some have suggested Tyndale relied upon Luther's German translation and the Latin Vulgate, it is more likely that he did not stray far from the Greek and Hebrew texts. Rather than depending on Luther or the Latin, the text first passed through his scholarly judgment. His revision in 1534 was his finest work. It shows improvements in his understanding of Greek terms and constructions.

Some notable readings that have survived almost word-for-word in the King James Version from Tyndale are as follows (verse numbers were not used in Tyndale's): 1) Matt 11:27: "Come unto me all ye that labor and are laden and I will ease you"; 2) Matt 7:7: "Ask, and it shall be given you; seek, and ye shall find; knock, and it shall be opened unto you"; 3) Acts 17:11: "The noblest ... searched the scriptures daily whether those things were even so"; 4) Heb 12:2: "Looking unto Jesus, the author and finisher of our faith ..."; 5) Rev 3:20: "Behold I stand at the door and knock. If any man hear my voice and open the door, I will come in unto him and will sup with him, and he with me"; 6) Rev 7:17: "and God shall wipe away all tears from their eyes."

3. The Coverdale Bible

William Tyndale's martyrdom in 1536 prevented his translation of the entire Bible. Our greatest loss may be the disappointment of not having the psalms in the words of Tyndale. Tyndale paved the way for a complete English Bible, but it was left to his associate, Miles Coverdale, to finally break the barrier of the 1408 Constitutions and pave the way for every church in England to have the complete Bible in English.

Miles Coverdale, born ca. 1488, was educated as an Augustinian monk at Cambridge and admitted to the priesthood in 1514. However, by 1528 Coverdale fell under the influence of the reformation and abandoned his Catholic priesthood, left the Augustinian order, and fully embraced Lutheranism.

Coverdale attracted some powerful protectors that eventually enabled his translation to become one of the first Bibles authorized in the British Empire. Coverdale, rather than seeking church approval for his Bible, sought support from the royal family. His Bible contained an elaborate dedication to King Henry VIII. This overt attempt to please Henry has caused many to believe Henry, through Thomas Cromwell and Thomas More, actually encouraged Coverdale to translate the Bible. Henry's open opposition to an earlier English translation compelled him to avoid approval of the work of Tyndale.

More and Cromwell's support of Coverdale explains his successful, long life as a translator. The dedication introducing the Bible made reference to Henry's wife, Anne. However, after Henry's divorce some surviving copies show a correction of "Anne" (Boleyn) with "Jane" (Seymour). Anne, while in Henry's favor, had supported Coverdale's work on the Bible and no doubt assisted him through her court influence. The success of the Coverdale Bible followed the queen's destiny. Her arrest and execution in May 1536 prevented the king from authorizing the Bible she supported.

Coverdale primarily incorporated Tyndale's work from all the books Tyndale translated. Coverdale personally translated the books not prepared by Tyndale. Coverdale's lack of intimate knowledge of the original languages forced him to rely on German and Latin translations. His choice of English expressions had more to do with aesthetic judgment than linguistic accuracy. Coverdale's work resulted in a fairly smooth and stylistic translation. Tyndale's version intentionally sought linguistic faithfulness to the original language's intended meaning—and he did it with unintended literary style.

In 1535 Jacob van Meteren published the Coverdale Bible, the first complete English Bible. By now the Bible was in great demand in England. In 1533 a new act was passed compelling foreigners to sell their printed pages to London binderies. This was a blatant attempt at protectionism on the part of the bindery industry. Jacob van Meteren sold the sheets from the Coverdale Bible to James Nicholson of Southwark. Although printed in Antwerp, all extant copies of the Coverdale Bible have English bindings.

Coverdale wisely omitted the offensive notes and preliminaries that troubled church authorities and had been a part of Tyndale's earlier editions. Coverdale's margins contained alternate readings, interpretations, and parallel passages. About 150 small, scattered woodcuts adorned the black letter text of his 1535 first edition.

Coverdale was the first to separate the apocryphal books from within the text and place them together in a separate grouping between the Testaments. He made it clear that they were not to be viewed with the same authority as the other books of the Bible. All Protestant

English Bibles from that time have followed Coverdale's example.

Coverdale's unique contribution to the translation of the Bible can be seen in the books not translated by Tyndale. The psalms and prophetic books were his handiwork: 1) Ps 1:1: "O Blessed is the man, that goeth not in the councell of the ungodly: that abydeth not in the waye off synners, or sytteth not in the seate of the scornefull"; 2) Ps 22:1-3 (23 in KJV and NRSV): "The Lorde is my shepherd, I can want nothing. He feedeth me in a green pasture, and leadeth me to a fresh water. He quickeneth my soul, and bringeth me forth in the way of rightness for his name sake"; 3) Isa 53:6: "As for us, we go all astraye (like shepe), every one turneth his owne waye"; 4) Jer 22:1: "Graven upon the edge of your altars with a pen of iron and with an adamant claw."

4. The Matthew's Bible

The marriage saga of Henry VIII, Catherine of Aragon, Anne Boleyn, and the church's inability to accept it influenced the Bible and its ultimate success as much as any other event of the 16th cent. The Roman Catholic church's refusal to accept Henry's divorce from Catherine and marriage to Anne forced Henry to break with Rome. This weakened the papacy in England and opened the door for a Church of England with a Bible in English.

Most modern readers believe that the King James Bible was the first "Authorized Bible." Interestingly, it was never officially authorized. Its worldwide influence and its common name, "The Authorized Version," implied James' authorization. Actually it was the Bible under the reign of Henry VIII that became the first genuinely authorized Bible. In a letter dated August 4, 1537, Archbishop Cranmer wrote to Thomas Cromwell (the most powerful ecclesiastical figure appointed by Henry) commending a new Bible translation for his approval. This was the first step toward an authorized Bible.

After receiving the letter, Cromwell presented the idea of a new Bible translation to Henry for his royal approval. Henry, after some consideration, granted the request. The first "authorized" Bible was soon to flood the English countryside. The next decision was to appoint a printer to receive the royal license for publishing the first "authorized Bible."

Two English printers competed for the prize of the "authorized Bible" market. Richard Grafton received the license to print the Matthew's Bible and Nicolson the Coverdale Bible. For many years the only Bibles an English citizen could buy were the Latin Vulgate, outdated Wycliffe Bibles, or black-market Tyndale NTs. Grafton begged Cromwell to permit him to be the sole publisher of all "authorized" Bibles. Although Cromwell did not grant his petition, he restricted Nicolson's publication to the Coverdale Bible.

John Rogers, the translator of the Matthew's Bible, was born near Birmingham at the turn of the 16th cent.

He received his BA in 1525 from Cambridge University. Under duress in 1534, he fled from England to Antwerp where he worked in the printing business with Jacob Van Meteren. Returning to England in 1548, he lectured at St. Paul's Cathedral while continuing his association with another printer, Edward Whitchurch. He was placed under house arrest for seditious preaching in 1553 and burned at the stake in 1555—the first martyr under the reign of "Bloody Mary."

While living in Antwerp, Rogers took the pseudonym Thomas Matthew to conceal his association with the "outlaw" William Tyndale. Rogers' translation work was primarily one of editing previous translations. He viewed Tyndale's as superior to Coverdale's. When the two disagreed, he used Tyndale or edited it himself. In many cases, he simply reprinted entire chapters from previous Bibles without alterations. At the end of the book of Malachi, Rogers printed in large letters the initials "WT." Most believe he was acknowledging William Tyndale's contribution as the primary translator of his revision.

The Matthew's Bible clearly reflects a style of English that surpasses Coverdale's. It is viewed as more faithful in its interpretation of Hebrew parallelism and accuracy in the translation of the text. Its superiority to Coverdale's 1535 Bible is recognized by Coverdale himself, who used the Matthew's Bible in his translation of the Great Bible rather than using his own.

The Matthew's Bible restored the use of notes. They were inserted to give added explanations in difficult passages. Not all of the notes were original. Some were taken from existing published commentaries. Rogers' notes were intended to reduce the inflammatory comments relating to church doctrine. He did, however, attack certain customs and beliefs of the Roman Catholic Church.

Matthew's Bible became known as the "primary version" of the English Bible upon which all later versions relied. The words clearly reflect its authority as the bottom of the title page reads, "Set forth with the kinges most gracyous lycence."

5. The Taverner Bible

Richard Taverner (1505–1575) received his MA at Cambridge University and was a scholar in Greek, but lacked a legitimate knowledge of Hebrew. He sought official license for his revision of Matthew's Bible. Taverner had been in the employment of Cromwell, as a clerk, and may have learned of the king's desire to seek an authorized Bible.

Whether Taverner learned of it from Cromwell or by other means, he began a revision of the Tyndale and Matthew's versions. His Bible appeared in 1539 shortly before the Great Bible. While Taverner is not given much credit for influencing later English translations, Heb 1:3 may be an original translation that has survived today. The Son of God is called the "express image" of God's person. Taverner introduced a few new words like "parable" for Tyndale's "similitude." Most differences, however, from Matthew's version were almost entirely limited to style and idiomatic renderings. For example, 1 John 2:5 in Matthew's reads, "We have an advocate with the Father." Taverner reads, "We have a spokesman with the Father." While both are acceptable translations, "spokesman" reflects an attempt at a more idiomatic rendering.

6. The Great Bible

Henry's attitude toward the Bible ran full circle. From forbidding it to authorizing it, Henry succeeded in keeping England independent of Rome. He had authorized two Bibles: Matthew's and Coverdale's. Just three years after the death of Tyndale, Henry and Cromwell encouraged the reading of the Bible. The notes of the Matthew's Bible still offended many of the clergy. The division and complaining among the clergy forced Cromwell to support the idea of a standard Bible that would be approved by the state and placed in every church in England.

Cromwell supported a standardized Bible and convinced Henry to commission a new translation to meet the growing needs of the royal throne and the bishops. Cromwell chose Miles Coverdale, a friend of the court, to undertake the new translation. In 1539 Richard Grafton and Edward Whitchurch published the famous "Great Bible" (so designated because of its size, 14x9 inches).

Coverdale's new translation depended heavily on Tyndale's NT, Sebastian Munster's, and Erasmus' Latin texts (and probably Pagninus'). Coverdale actually revised the Matthew's Bible rather than using his own 1535 edition. Pressure from Cromwell to get the edition completed resulted in a hurriedly produced translation that soon needed revision. The printing of a carefully revised text along with a prologue by Thomas Cranmer appeared in April 1540.

An edition dated November 1540 in the colophon and 1541 on the title page removed Cromwell's coat-of-arms. Cromwell's fall from Henry's favor in July 1540 meant his downfall and disgrace. It was a statement that Cromwell had no part in Henry's administration. This same edition claims Bishop Cuthbert of Duresme as a faithful supporter of this Bible. This is the same Bishop Tunstall, formerly bishop of London, who so relentlessly fought Tyndale's NT entrance into England. Yet the Great Bible is nothing more than a minor revision of Tyndale's NT.

The production of the Great Bible made it possible for churches to conform to Henry VIII's 1538 decree that the Bible should be placed in every church. The Great Bible was officially standardized so that all religious authorities could support its use.

D. The Bible of the Exiles: Queen Mary 1553–58

1. The Geneva Bible

Henry VIII's death on January 28, 1547 brought Edward VI to the throne of England. Edward approved the reading of the English Bible in services. During his reign, more than fifty editions of the Scriptures rolled off English printing presses. Printers anxious to take advantage of the new market rushed to print any edition possible. This often meant printing editions without adequate editing procedures.

Edward's reign abounded with complaints of the diversity of biblical teachings connected with the vast number of Bibles printed. Both Protestants and Catholics were concerned that these diversities would be contrary to official teachings. As might be anticipated, Bibles with theological notes to direct the Bible readers to the correct meanings of the text would soon follow. Organized doctrinal persuasions could be taught from the Bible itself by means of well-placed and carefully explained authorized notes. It also provided the established church with the opportunity to challenge anyone not holding to the truth of the text and notes.

Catholic Mary ascended to the throne in 1553. Her attacks were not on the reading of Bibles, but on the teachings of the Protestant Bible. The notorious Act of 1543, "For the Advancement of True Religion," blamed the reading and preaching from the Bible for the corruption of established doctrine. The church felt that people could absorb faith through the liturgy and the sacraments rather than through reading the Bible. This led to the forbidding of the reading of Scripture in private or in public.

Mary's opposition to the Bible and persecution in England signaled the flight of Protestants to Geneva. Geneva offered a sanctuary for the exiles. Many of Protestantism's finest scholars including, William Whittingham, Anthony Gilby, John Knox, John Foxe, and John Calvin took up residence in Geneva. The outpouring of scholarly writings from these scholars soon demanded a new translation.

A new translation in an easy-to-read format and an affordable size provided the laity with a Bible of their own. The Geneva Bible was the first to be printed in a quarto size in its first edition. With the Latin script, rather than the thick black letters, and verse divisions for ease in finding texts, the Geneva Bible set the standard for the next seventy years. Printed in 140 editions from 1560 to 1644, the Geneva Bible remained the most popular edition for many years.

The Geneva NT of 1557 and the complete Bible of 1560 were the products of theologians. While the Tyndale, Coverdale, and Matthew's Bibles primarily emphasized linguistic accuracy, the Geneva Bible's focus included theological notes.

The English Bibles fared well when Elizabeth ascended the throne in 1558. The Geneva exiles could now complete the task of translation. For the first time the 1550 Stephanus Greek NT was available as an up-to-date Greek text from which the new translation could draw. The translators dedicated the Geneva Bible to Queen Elizabeth. Her support guaranteed the survival of the translation.

2. The impact of the Geneva Bible

The Geneva's notes, small size, and easy-to-read Latin letter script guaranteed its popularity among the faithful. Ironically the popularity of the notes among the Puritans ultimately signaled its final doom as the King James Version abandoned marginal notes some fifty years later. The Geneva notes helped strengthen Puritan theology in America and Britain, and the translation was a major source for Shakespeare's quotes.

The Geneva Bible was an excellent translation and perhaps more accurate than many of its predecessors. Its idiomatic English and superb scholarship rendered it a great intermediate step between Tyndale and the ultimate triumph of the King James Version.

The Geneva translators leaned heavily upon Tyndale for the NT and from Genesis through 2 Chronicles for the OT. The rest of the OT was a direct translation from the Hebrew. This was the first time this portion of the Bible had been translated directly from the Hebrew.

The Geneva has a number of distinguishable readings: 1) Gen 3:7: "Breeches" for "aprons" (KJV) or "loincloths" (NRSV); 2) Luke 2:7: "cratch" for "manger"; 3) Luke 4:8: "Hence from me, Satan" for "Get thee behind me, Satan" (KJV); 4) John 16:2: "They shall excommunicate you" for "They will put you out of the synagogues" (KJV & NRSV).

E. The Elizabethan Bible 1558–1603

1. The Bishops' Bible 1568

Protestant Elizabeth I's ascension to the throne of England in 1558 brought reform to the church. Only five of the bishops appointed by Edward survived Mary's bloody reign of terror. The Bible had been banned for five years. Now men and women everywhere could start reading again.

The popularity accorded the Geneva Bible after 1560 did not include the majority of the clergy in England. Although they recognized the superior quality of the translation, the Calvinistic notes were offensive. The need for a new version emerged among the Anglican bishops.

Matthew Parker, born in Norwich in 1504, received his education at Corpus Christi College in Cambridge. He became Dean of Lincoln and a chaplain to Queen Anne Boleyn. This scholarly, mild-mannered theologian filled the ecclesiastical seat at Canterbury and thus was chief editor of the new Bible.

In 1563 the massive Bishops' Bible project was launched. The translators relied on the Stephanus Greek NT (1550), Pagninus' Latin (1528), and Munster's Hebrew (1539). They omitted any marginal notes that might cause offense. In 1571 the Convocation of Canterbury ordered every bishop to have a copy of the

new translation at his house for use by servants and strangers.

The Bishops' Bible was never officially licensed as the authorized Bible. Nevertheless the church and state enthusiastically received it. Its translation fell short of the quality and simplicity of the Geneva Bible and never gained popular support.

Published by Richard Jugge, many consider the Bishops' Bible the most beautifully illustrated and finely printed edition of the 16th cent. The peace in the empire allowed the printers to concentrate on producing an exquisitely printed Bible with many excellent illustrations. Parker included an extensive preface that became a defining element of the Bishops' Bible. The lasting legacy of the Bishop's Bible was that the 1602 edition influenced the King James Version.

2. The Roman Catholic Rheims/Douay Version 1582/1610

The Roman Catholics resented the publication of the vast number of English versions. First, through persecution when in power, and then, when out of power, they met the challenge of printed Bibles with silence. The success of the Geneva Bible among the laity troubled the papacy. The Bible in a language and size that could be owned and read by the masses forced the church to respond. The official Roman Catholic Bible was the Latin Vulgate translated by Jerome (completed in the early 5th cent.). The Louvain Latin Bible (1547) received official approval at the Council of Trent. In 1592 under Pope Sixtus, a new edition, called the Sixtine-Clementine Bible, received official sanction. The many English Catholics, however, had no access to an authorized Catholic Bible in their language.

The first English translation of the Roman Catholic NT was published in 1582 in Rheims, France. Because of financial difficulties, the printers delayed publication of the OT until 1609/10 at Douay, France.

The new Roman Catholic official English translation included notes similar in style to the Geneva Bible but with Roman Catholic theology. While the church authorities were not happy with laity access to private interpretation, they supported a translation that retarded the use of the Protestant Geneva Bible by Catholics.

The Rheims NT translation team, headed by Gregory Martin and assisted by William Allen, Richard Bristow, and William Reynolds, began their work at the College of Douay, France in 1578. The translators consulted the Latin Bible (not the Greek), but they also drew from the English Geneva Bible and Coverdale's NT (Regnault, France) edition of the diglot of 1538. Some of Coverdale's readings were adopted, e.g., "the Son of man hath not where to lay his head" (Matt 8:20) and "I see men as it were trees, walking" (Mark 8:24). From the Geneva Bible, the Rheims adopted the phrase "the wicked generation" (Matt 12:45) and "whited tombs" (Matt 23:27).

The OT was completed in 1610 after the college was moved to Douay, France. It is generally agreed that the end product of both the OT and NT, known as the Rheims/Douay Bible, achieved success. Its weaknesses were primarily in its lack of vernacular expressions and normal English word order.

F. The King James Version 1603–25

1. The birth of a new version

With the news of Elizabeth's death on March 22, 1603, the Privy Council was summoned to clarify the succession to the throne. Their decision followed the wishes of the queen, even though her illness had left the kingdom in financial difficulty and a state of turmoil. They approved King James VI of Scotland as King James I of England, France, Scotland, and Ireland. When James of Scotland was proclaimed King of England, the throne of England passed from the House of Tudor to the House of Stuart. From Henry VII (the first of the Tudors) through the "Virgin" Queen Elizabeth I (the last Tudor) the House of Tudor maintained a very powerful monarchy.

James' classical education in the Scottish reformed faith brought a reign that would confuse the relationship between the church and state. Declared sovereign head of the Scottish church and of state in 1584, James' reign was a history of interference. His enthusiastic claim of divine right to rule over both civil and spiritual matters ultimately brought his reign into conflict.

The motive for a new translation came as a result of conflict in church polity rather than a felt need for a new translation. The Puritans, complaining about issues they perceived Elizabeth ignored, presented James with a petition signed by 1,000 petitioners. The petition found an immediate connection with James who had a critical attitude toward the Roman church and the Geneva Bible as they expressed the authority of kingship, even though the Bassadyne Bible, a Geneva translation, was dedicated to James while he was king in Scotland. In 1604 James I convened a conference at Hampton Court to discuss church practices and to consider the complaints of the Puritans.

The anti-Puritan tenor of the conference was immediately apparent. John Rainolds, a Puritan representative, made a bold move by proposing a new translation. His suggestion may have arisen out of a motive to encourage ratification of the Geneva Bible over the Bishops' Bible. James pounced on the idea and gave the order to appoint translators for the task. He intended that his version would eliminate the objectionable notes and support the divine right of the monarchy.

2. Translation begins

Previous 16th-cent. translations were primarily the work of one person or several unorganized individuals. James decided to use the finest scholars in England to ensure the success of the new version. He appointed fifty-four highly qualified translators and organized them into six groups: two from Westminster (Genesis–2 Kings and Romans–Jude), two from Cambridge (1 Chronicles–Song of Songs and the Apocrypha), and two from Oxford (Isaiah–Malachi, Matthew–Acts, and Revelation). Upon completion of the initial translation, they met in an equally represented committee of twelve to review the final product. Miles Smith contributed the introduction and Thomas Bilson added the headings to chapters.

Unlike previous versions—other than Purvey's very broad translation principles—Richard Bancroft, bishop of London, constructed fifteen translation principles to govern the work. The first of these stated that the Bishops' version was the foundation to act as the guideline and would be altered only when the Greek or Hebrew demanded it. Rule fifteen listed the other English versions to be used when they agreed and represented the original text: Tyndale, Matthew, Coverdale, the Great Bible, and the Geneva. Another important rule eliminated the offensive exegetical and theological notes.

The license for printing the King James Version went to Robert Barker, the king's printer. The printing monopoly remained in the hands of the Barkers for many years. The original manuscript may have been delivered to the Barkers as an annotated Bishops' Bible or an actual manuscript. There is one theory associated with the London circulation in 1660 of a pamphlet complaining that certain printers possessed the manuscript copy of the Holy Bible in English. It is speculated that this was the manuscript of the King James Bible. The great fire of 1666 may be the culprit that destroyed the manuscript. Whatever form the completed translation took as delivered to the printers has disappeared.

The most popular printing controversy of the early King James Version involves the two editions claiming to be printed in 1611. They are known as the "He" Bible and the "She" Bible for their readings in Ruth 3:15: "And he/she went into the citie." Although both readings have their support in later versions, most scholars today maintain the "he" reading belongs to the first edition. Regardless of which is original to the Hebrew text, the question is which reading represented the first edition of the King James Version. Other differences also exist between these two editions. In the "She" Bible, Matt 26:36 substitutes "Judas" for "Jesus": "Then commeth Judas with them unto a place called Gethsemane."

The 1611 edition was a large folio about 16×10.5 inches printed on a linen and rag paper in large black letter type with the chapter titles, summaries, parallel passages, and marginal references in a Latin letter. The title page, signed by Cornelius Boel, an Antwerp artist, was engraved with Moses and Aaron standing in ornate niches with the apostles seated below the Tetragrammaton. The title clearly stated: "Appointed to be read in Churches." While no official license was ever given to the new version, James I watched over it very carefully. In England, the popular title "Authorized

Bible" gained wide acceptance. The woodcut NT title page, depicting the twelve tribes and twelve apostles, was taken from the title page of the 1602 Bishops' Bible whose title page read, "Authorized and appointed to be read in Churches."

There were a total of five folio editions, all with nearly interchangeable leaves printed word for word: 1611, 1613, 1617, 1634, and 1639/40. A smaller folio edition printed in 1613 had seventy-two lines per page instead of the fifty-nine lines of the other folio editions. The smaller edition reduced the total pages from 738 to 508. The printing of each page of the fifty-nine-line editions used the same number of lines, word-for-word and line-for-line, enabling the printer to substitute reprinted pages when errors surfaced. In the event additional copies were needed, some leaves left over from a previous printing could be used in the new printing. However, careful examination reveals many variants in the printing of the leaves.

3. The early struggle for acceptance

Immediate acceptance as the standard version eluded the expectant translators. Hugh Broughton, respected by many scholars but ignored by the translation assignment committee, criticized the translation as having hundreds of words that he confidently condemned as totally erroneous. He predicted the translators would answer for their corrupt work on the "Day of Judgment."

For several more years, the Geneva Bible continued to be the popular Bible of the masses. Curiously, Miles Smith, in his introduction to the King James Version, quoted from the Geneva and continued to quote from it in sermons. George Abbot and the poet John Donne, however, made frequent use of the new version almost immediately.

By the end of its second decade of printing, the King James Version had established itself as the version of nearly every household. It took about thirty years to displace the popular Geneva Bible completely. Scotland began printing the King James Version in 1629 and officially recognized it by 1634. The Geneva continued to be popular among the Puritans and the pilgrims in America. By 1644 the Geneva Bible was no longer printed.

G. The Bible Stabilized 1625–1881

1. The revisions of the King James Version

During the next 270 years, a number of revisions of the King James Version took place. Sometimes the revision included correcting spelling mistakes, adjusting notes, and modernizing phrases. The first thorough revision was done in 1629 by the original translators, Samuel Ward and John Bois. Joined by Thomas Goad and Joseph Mead, Ward and Bois continued in 1638 revising their 1629 edition.

The printed text between 1638 and 1762—apart from printers' errors, and there were many—remained

fairly stable. The revision of 1638 formed the text that most printers followed. It is possible to find many variants and errors in the editions between the publications of these two major revisions.

In 1762 Thomas Paris edited the text for Joseph Bentham at Cambridge. It had been more than 100 years since there had been a serious attempt to revise the text. Some editions had revised certain aspects of the text, but none that took a careful look at the text itself.

Thomas Paris introduced a rather interesting marginal note in Acts 7:45. The text reads, "Which also our fathers *that came after*, brought in with Jesus." The note comments "or *having received.*" No notice is made of the alternate rendering of the Greek phrase in the 1881 Revised Version or the 1901 American Standard Version. However, the 1979 New King James Bible published by Thomas Nelson picked up the same rendering when it placed in the text itself, not in the margin, "which our fathers, having received it in succession . . . ."

Benjamin Blayney edited the King James Version in 1769. His expansion of Paris' work became the standard version for the next 100 years. Blayney contributed new spellings, italics, and marginal notes. Paris' edition incorporated Bishop William Lloyd's chronology and continued it in the text of Blayney. The two editions of 1762 and 1769 changed the diction and set the stage for future work in the 19th cent. With a few exceptions, the notes, and especially the italics, remained the same in subsequent editions.

2. The 1881–85 revision

In February 1870, both houses of the Convocation of Canterbury unanimously passed a resolution to appoint a committee of scholars to begin the task of a new translation. Its stated purpose was to revise the King James Version and make as few alterations as possible; however, it became more than a simple revision. For the first time, modern discoveries of Greek manuscripts and textual criticism came into play. Completed in 1885, the English Revised Version with the American variations in 1901 became the first genuine text revision. Scholars delighted in the new translation, but the general public remained loyal to the King James Version. As a King James Version revision, it followed the rules of a word-for-word translation.

3. The legacy of the King James Version

The King James Version appeared in England's history during its golden age of literature. The period produced its greatest English writer, William Shakespeare. If it is true that language marks an educated man, his use of the language displayed his intelligence and enabled him to mold the thoughts and dreams of others. The jewel that is the King James Version crowned English literature. It should be revered, but not worshiped, enjoyed but not glorified, and loved but not deified.

H. The Modern Translation Debate 1885–Present

1. The need for modern versions

The original languages of the OT and NT are no longer spoken today. The question remains: should the Bible appear in modern, everyday language? Should it retain the archaic style of *thees* and *thous*? Is its "holiness" of character too sacred for ordinary people? Are the clergy alone capable of understanding and delivering the real hidden meaning of the "jots and tittles"? People, from the inception of Bible translation, have asked and debated these same questions. Their answers have shaped Christianity—some for good and some for bad.

The use of archaic and formal language as evidence of religious authority and spiritual awareness entrenched the Latin Vulgate as the standard Bible of the medieval church. The Vulgate also brought the greatest opposition to the acceptance of the first English translation in the 14th cent. The clergies' discouragement of the laity reading the Bible led to a "forbidden book." An understanding of Scriptures by laity would reduce the authority of the clergy—or so they reasoned. If the principles for life came from personal Bible reading, then an authoritative church was in danger of losing its relevance.

God surely intended that everyone understand the Bible. There would be little need to transmit Scripture if this were not true. However, can the laity understand the intended meaning of the Bible on their own or must they have an official interpreter? If, as most believe today, everyone can understand the Scripture without the aid and authority of educated clergy, then what translation is the best? Should the guiding principle be accuracy to the original language text or simple comprehension of God's words?

A superficial reading of the KJV, the standard version for many years, reveals the need for an updated translation to accommodate modern readers. Expressions like "superfluity of naughtiness" (Jas 1:21) and words like *fetched*, *ye*, *thou*, and *behooved* are replaced in modern versions with expressions and words of modern English usage.

Translators have struggled throughout history with the difficulty of transferring the meaning of a text from one language to another. The process of translation brings immediate challenges and problems. Debate surfaced with the first attempt and continues today.

Success in translation depends upon not only a thorough understanding of the original languages but also upon an acceptable knowledge of the receptor language. A new translation means new words. New words often challenge old, established doctrines. When a new translation of an old, accepted word is substituted, it can bring a challenge to a doctrine. The safety of an established translation can be a lure to the acceptance of a traditional version. Then, one need only refine the meaning of an established term rather than struggle over a new word. Theological pressures often decide the ultimate success of a translation and not the linguistic accuracy or vernacular acceptability.

The nature of Bible translations changed with the turn of the 20th cent. From the Wycliffe Bible (1384) to the English Revised Version (1885) translators emphasized the accuracy of each new translation. They tried to answer the question: Does the translation accurately reflect the original languages? In the fifteen rules for translation, the King James translators did not have a single rule for style, nor did they consider the educated readers versus the less educated. In the 20th cent. a plethora of modern versions placed the emphasis on the receptor language. Style, reading audience, vocabulary, and syntax play a greater role than a simple, accurate translation from the original (source language). This is the heart of the modern translation debate.

It has been the practice in recent years to produce translations by committees using either a "word-for-word" or a "thought-for-thought" translation and then offer frequent revisions. There is a call to the public for input and evaluation, which is then incorporated in the revisions. New Testaments are usually published first and then the OT. This new system of publication has caused modern Christians considerable confusion as to what translation should be used.

2. The theories of translation

God revealed himself in the Scriptures out of a desire to communicate a message to God's people, to have them respond, and to motivate them to action. The Bible, in the hands of the populace, may be a deterrent to professional religious leaders asserting their authority beyond the Bible's intention. If history guides us, and our lessons drawn from the medieval clergy and early American Puritans serve us, then the Bible must be read and understood by the laity.

Which translation best reflects that message of the Bible as the church's Scripture? Should a universal translation be adopted by the whole church? Why continue to multiply translations? How much of a translation is interpretation? If a translation contains elements of interpretation by the translator, then who is qualified to translate the Bible? Should translations incorporate footnotes and study aids? These questions shape one's spiritual pilgrimage and selection of a translation.

The goal of translation is the transfer of the meaning of a passage from the original language (source language) to modern English vernacular (receptor language). *Meaning* includes lexical definitions, affective engagement, and motivational impact. The ultimate goal is equivalence of meaning and not just a strict literal word-for-word or grammatical equivalence.

The message of the NT reached the audience first in oral language form. It was customary among early civilizations for literary works and stories to be read or spoken aloud in public and in private. The NT implies Paul's messages were intended to be read orally to other churches (Col 4:16).

Most 1st-cent. people could not read and needed the Scriptures read to them. Common belief suggests that only about five to ten percent, at most perhaps fifteen percent, of the population in Greek and Roman societies could read. The percentage of Christians may have been slightly less. This shows up in the scriptural use of memory devices such as summary statements, repeated phrases, common words, and mnemonic devices.

The authors of the Scriptures wrote, not only as an aid in understanding for its initial recipients, but also for preservation and transmission. The Scripture was handed down from generation to generation by written transmission rather than depending on an oral message.

3. Translation theories in practice

Modern linguists face a large barrier when studying biblical languages. Two millennia have passed from Greek language usage and more than three millennia from Hebrew. Some aspects of biblical culture have been lost over this vast period of time. This makes the recovery of the culture for a study of the Greek and Hebrew languages challenging.

Since the goal of translation is the transfer of meaning from one language to another, there are two basic approaches that attempt to bring focus to the goal. One advocates literal, word-for-word translation while another prefers meaning based on thought-for-thought translation.

Thought-for-thought translation is favored by modern linguistic theory. It recognizes that no two languages can have a direct transfer of meaning in a word-for-word translation. It also recognizes that no English translation is sacrosanct and that the evolution of language demands new translations to accommodate the change. This approach recognizes that translators as interpreters must make decisions concerning meaning as they translate. The emphasis is on the receptor language and a clear meaning for the English reader. The goal is to translate the biblical materials as effectively as possible in the language of the reader. Style, readability, and meaning will be its judge.

Thought-for-thought translation theory ("functional" or "dynamic equivalence") places importance on the equivalence of response to the message by the modern and original readers. Passages in the psalms and emotive language are handled with particular care, but they must avoid the cultural extremes expressed in versions such as the Cotton Patch Version.

Word-for-word translation ("formal equivalence") emphasizes the seriousness of the source language as the base for meaning. It must be remembered that no translation is really a word-for-word equivalence. All languages have linguistic features that simply cannot be translated literally from one language to another. It does attempt to consider biblical metaphors and idioms, sees the original text as God's Word, and typically emphasizes the importance of theology. It realizes the importance of culture in language, the necessity of style for meaning, and the exegetical potential of the original text. Fidelity of the original words and the confidence of accuracy of the transfer of meaning is its hallmark. It refuses to let a translation become a commentary.

Few scholars seeking sound exegesis, cultural clarity, and theological accuracy will ever be satisfied with an English translation. No English word study, no diagramming of a sentence or comparing of verses can substitute for a study of the original languages. The scholar must study the Scriptures in their original languages, cultural setting, theological worldview, and biblical contexts.

In recent years some new versions have attempted to combine the strengths of each theory as a base for their translations. This third theory has emerged called "optimal equivalence." It relies on seeking the nearest English semantic and linguistic equivalents used to convey the intended meaning of the original text.

4. The original language texts in modern versions

Translators must decide which Hebrew and Greek texts will be the base of their work. Most OT versions use the standard Hebrew text. The science of NT textual criticism has grown to maturity over the past 100 years and generally demands more attention than the text of the OT.

The various revisions of The King James Version have used the Byzantine (*textus receptus*) text, while most modern translations use the Nestle-Aland text (critical text). One's philosophy of textual criticism will be an important factor. Textual criticism is a science that classifies and evaluates readings in extant manuscripts. For our purpose, only the three major text families will be used: Byzantine, Western, and Alexandrian. It must be noted, however, that some manuscripts do not fit in one of these three families and quite a number have mixed readings. The following chart classifying modern versions, their use of the NT Greek families, and their corresponding Greek NTs will be limited to some of the most popular translations from the beginning of the 20th cent.

I. Analysis of Modern Versions

1. Criteria for judging a translation

Translations from the Tyndale NT (1526) to the English Revised Version (1885) were primarily concerned with the accuracy of the text from Greek and Hebrew to English. Beginning with the turn of the 20th cent., many, but not all, translators became more concerned with the readability and understandability to the common reader. The text played the role normally occupied by notes and explanations from commentaries.

The answer to the following questions will assist the reader in choosing a translation: 1) Is it comprehensive enough to avoid expanding the text with redundant explanations? 2) Does it reveal the original intent of the author insofar as this can be understood from the text? 3) Is the reader response equivalent to the original hearer response? 4) Does it provide readers with a good style for public reading? 5) Does it allow for interpretive ambiguities?

Greek Texts Used in Modern Versions			
Greek Families	Alexandrian Family	Byzantine Family	Western Family
Representative manuscripts	Codex Sinaiticus Codex Vaticanus	Codex Alexandrinus Codex Ephraemi (mixed)	Codex Beza Codex Claromontanus
Popular names	Critical text (Eclectic Text)	*Textus Receptus* (represents majority manuscripts)	Latin text (Catholic Text)
Early printed texts	Westcott/Hort 1881	Stephanus 1550 Beza 1565	Latin Vulgate 16th cent.
Modern printed representatives	Nestle/Aland Metzger	Majority text: Hodges Robinson/Pierpont	Latin Vulgate
	English translations	English translations	English translations
	English Revised Version (ERV) 1881–85	King James Version (KJV) 1611	Challoner NT 1749
	American Standard Version 1901 (ASV)	King James Version (Paragraph Bible) 1873	Knox Version 1955
	Revised Standard Version (RSV) 1946–52	New King James Version (NKJV) 1982	Jerusalem Bible 1966
	Amplified Bible (AB) 1965	21st Cent. King James Version 1994	New American Bible (NAB) 1970 (NEB occasionally)
	New English Bible (NEB) 1970	New Cambridge Paragraph Bible (NCPB) 2005	New Jerusalem Bible (NJB) 1985
	Living Bible (LB) 1971		
	New American Standard Bible (NASB) 1971		
	J.B.Phillip's NT (JBPNT) 1972		
	Today's English Version (TEV) (Good News Bible) 1976		
	New International Version (NIV) 1978		
	Revised English Bible (REB) 1989		
	New Revised Standard Version (NRSV) 1990		
	God's Word Translation (GWT) 1995		
	Contemporary English Version (CEV) 1995		
	English Standard Version (ESV) 2001		
	Today's New International Version (TNIV) 2001		
	The Net Bible (NET) 2001		
	The Message (TM) 2002		
	Holman Christian Standard Bible (HCSB) 2003		
	New Living Translation Revised (NLTR) 2004		
	The Voice NT (VNT) 2008		

Table 1: Greek Texts Used in Modern Versions

Why are so many translations needed? It may seem as if book publishers are proliferating versions in order to generate profits. After all, only in English are versions being so multiplied. While it is a lucrative business, a better reason comes to mind. Modern translations have personalized the selection of a Bible. The pastor, theological student, and scholar often want a word-for-word translation and choose to use commentaries and study aids for fuller explanations. The layperson may want a version that expands the translation to include brief explanations. Seniors, teenagers, athletes, golfers, women, and social groups may want Bibles that reflect their interests. Hence, more than 350 versions have been published since 1900.

The modern translator must have a multitude of skills: have a thorough knowledge of the original languages, be a competent biblical interpreter, and have an ability to express thoughts and concepts in writing. The requirements are so demanding that no individual possesses the skills to meet all the qualifications to the degree needed. This accounts for the modern practice of soliciting many qualified scholars from various backgrounds, with necessary talents, and from many denominations. While individual, sectarian, and denominational versions may be popular among a limited audience, they may not have the staying power of co-operative works.

2. Modern versions compared

It is a mistake to think that the plethora of translations means none of them are correct. This raises skepticism and doubts about the reliability of translations. While no translation is perfect, they all have a distinct purpose and may fit certain needs. The introduction to the version will give the reader a clear description of its purpose and scholarly reviews of the versions will help buyers decide which best suits their needs.

Constant changes in language over an expanded number of years, new discoveries of manuscripts, developing knowledge of the original languages, and linguistic awareness have all made new translations inevitable.

An attempt has been made to categorize various versions; however, many versions incorporate principles from various classifications.

Comparisons and Comments—Modern Versions 1901–2008					
Translation Date	"Formal Equivalent" Word-for-word	"Dynamic Equivalent" Thought-for-thought	"Optimal Equivalent" Intended meaning	"Paraphrase" Expanded meaning	Comments/primary uses
ASV 1901	Primarily				Very literal (The American version of ERV 1885) For study; outdated
RSV 1946-1952	Primarily				Contains some archaic forms Intended to be ecumenical but offended some evangelicals For study; outdated
Knox 1955	From Latin Vulgate	Primarily			Roman Catholic Version For comparisons; outdated
AB 1965				Primarily	The text is greatly expanded Assumes a word carried multiple meanings in each context For range of meanings
JB 1966		Primarily		Occasionally	By Roman Catholic committee Claims to be from Greek and Hebrew For comparisons; outdated
NEB 1970	Primarily			Occasionally	Considered a new, freer translation than RSV; uses "Thee/thou" when addressing God Prepared by British scholars For public reading & comparison
NAB 1970		Primarily			Widely used by Roman Catholics From Greek and Hebrew Omits "thees/thous" Replaces JB For comparison and reading
LB 1971				Primarily	A free translation originally written by Ken Taylor for his children For reading and comprehension

Table 2: Comparisons and Comments—Modern Versions 1901–2008

Table 2: Comparisons and Comments—Modern Versions 1901–2008 *(continued)*

NASB 1971	Primarily				Often very wooden, not an English anyone uses (omits "thees/thous") For study
JBPNT 1972				Primarily	Still readable today Conservative For comparisons; outdated
TEV (GNB) 1976		Primarily		Often	Designed for those having difficulty with reading skills For comprehension
NIV 1978	Often	Primarily	Intended		Extremely popular version New translation by evangelical scholars For study and public reading
NKJV 1982	Primarily				Archaic words updated; "thees/thous" omitted Revision of KJV For study and public reading
NJB 1985	Occasionally	Primarily			Roman Catholic from Greek and Hebrew For reading and comprehension
REB 1989	Primarily		Intended		Revision of NEB (1970) Omits "thees/thous" for God For study and public reading
NRSV 1990	Primarily		Intended		Revised RSV Omits "thees/thous" Improved style for public reading Inclusive language For study and comprehension
21st KJV 1994	Primarily				Minimal update of KJV Improved archaic vocabulary For traditional KJV readers
GWT 1995			Primarily	Occasionally	Lutheran, seeks "closest natural equivalent" Simplistic language For casual reading
CEV 1995		Primarily		Often	Often removes difficult terms to help readers with deficiencies For casual reading
ESV 2001	Primarily	Occasionally			Slight revision of RSV (1952) Omits "thees/thous" Some inclusive language For study and comparisons
TNIV 2001	Occasionally		Primarily		Gender-inclusive language Denounced by some conservatives For study and reading
NET 2001	Primarily		Often		Contains massive marginal notes: Linguistic, exegetical, textual, and background notes Available on Internet For study; notes very helpful
Message 2002				Primarily	May lack precision For casual reading
HCSB 2003			Primarily		Southern Baptist version Often includes Byzantine readings in margins For study and reading
NLT-R 2004			Primarily	Occasionally	Complete revision of LB (1971) For reading and comprehension
Voice NT 2008				Primarily Storytelling emphasis	Attempts to give a human writer's voice to each of the Gospels Appeals to postmodern audience For casual reading

Modern Translation Texts Compared: 2 Peter 1:5-7

ASV 1901	"Yea, and for this very cause adding on your part all diligence, in your faith supply virtue; and in *your* virtue knowledge; and in *your* knowledge self-control; and in *your* self-control patience; and in *your* patience godliness; and in *your* godliness brotherly kindness; and in *your* brotherly kindness love."
RSV 1952	"For this very reason make every effort to supplement your faith with virtue, and virtue with knowledge, and knowledge with self-control, and self-control with steadfastness, and steadfastness with godliness, and godliness with brotherly affection, and brotherly affection with love."
Knox 1955	"And you too have to contribute every effort on your own part, crowning your faith with virtue, and virtue, with enlightenment, and enlightenment with continence, and continence with endurance and endurance with holiness and holiness with brotherly love, and brotherly love charity."
AB 1965	"For this very reason, adding your diligence [to the divine promises], employ every effort in exercising your faith to develop virtue (excellence, resolution, Christian energy), and in [exercising] virtue [develop] knowledge (intelligence), And in [exercising] knowledge [develop] self-control, and in [exercising] self-control [develop] steadfastness (patience, endurance), and in [exercising] steadfastness [develop] godliness (piety), and in [exercising] godliness [develop] brotherly affection, and in [exercising] brotherly affection [develop] Christian love."
JB 1966	"With this in view, do your utmost to support your faith with goodness, goodness with understanding, understanding with self-control, self-control with perseverance, perseverance with devotion, devotion with kindness to the brothers, and kindness to the brothers with love."
NEB 1970	"With all this in view, you should try your hardest to supplement your faith with virtue, virtue with knowledge, knowledge with self-control, self-control with fortitude, fortitude with piety, piety with brotherly kindness, and brotherly kindness with love."
NAB 1970	"For this very reason, make every effort to supplement your faith with virtue, virtue with knowledge, knowledge with self-control, self-control with endurance, endurance with devotion, devotion with mutual affection, mutual affection with love."
LB 1971	"In view of all this, make every effort to respond to God's promises. Supplement your faith with a generous provision of moral excellence, and moral excellence with knowledge, and knowledge with self-control, and self-control with patient endurance, and patient endurance with godliness, and godliness with brotherly affection, and brotherly affection with love for everyone."
NASB 1971	"Now for this very reason also, applying all diligence, in your faith supply moral excellence, and in *your* moral excellence, knowledge; and in *your* knowledge, self-control, and in *your* self-control, perseverance, and in *your* perseverance, godliness; and in *your* godliness, brotherly kindness, and in *your* brotherly kindness, love."
JBP NT 1972	"For this very reason you must do your utmost from your side, and see that your faith carries with it real goodness of life. Your goodness must be accompanied by knowledge, your knowledge by self-control, your self-control by the ability to endure. Your endurance too must always be accompanied by a real trust in God; that in turn must have in it the quality of brotherliness, and your brotherliness must lead on to Christian love."
TEV (GNB) 1976	"For this very reason, do your best to add goodness to your faith; and to your faith goodness add knowledge; to our knowledge add self-control; to our self-control add endurance; to your endurance add godliness; to your godliness add brotherly love; and to your brotherly love add love."
NIV 1978	"For this very reason, make every effort to add to your faith goodness; and to goodness, knowledge; and to knowledge, self-control; and to self-control, perseverance; and to perseverance, godliness; and to godliness, brotherly kindness; and to brotherly kindness, love."
NKJV 1982	"But also for this very reason, giving all diligence, add to your faith virtue, to virtue knowledge, to knowledge self-control, to self-control perseverance, to perseverance godliness, to godliness brotherly kindness, and to brotherly kindness love."
NJB 1985	"With this in view, do your utmost to support your faith with goodness, goodness with understanding, understanding with self-control, self-control with perseverance, perseverance with devotion, devotion with kindness to the brothers, and kindness to the brothers with love."
REB 1989	"For this very reason, you must make every effort to support your faith with goodness, and goodness with knowledge, and knowledge with self-control, and self-control with endurance, and endurance with godliness, and godliness with mutual affection, and mutual affection with love."
NRSV 1990	"For this very reason, you must make every effort to support your faith with goodness, and goodness with knowledge, and knowledge with self-control, and self-control with endurance, and endurance with godliness, and godliness with mutual affection, and mutual affection with love."
21st KJV 1994	"And besides this, using all diligence, add to your faith virtue, and to virtue knowledge, and to knowledge temperance, and to temperance patience, and to patience godliness, and to godliness brotherly kindness, and to brotherly kindness charity."

Table 3: Modern Translation Texts Compared: 2 Peter 1:5-7

Table 3: Modern Translation Texts Compared: 2 Peter 1:5-7 *(continued)*

GWT 1995	"Because of this, make every effort to add integrity to your faith; and to integrity add knowledge; to knowledge add self-control; to self-control add endurance; to endurance add godliness; to godliness add Christian affection; and to Christian affection add love."
CEV 1995	"Do your best to improve your faith. You can do this by adding goodness, understanding, self-control, patience, devotion to God, concern for others, and love."
ESV 2001	"For this very reason, make every effort to supplement your faith with virtue, and virtue with knowledge, and knowledge with self-control, and self-control with steadfastness, and steadfastness with godliness, and godliness with brotherly affection, and brotherly affection with love."
TNIV 2001	"For this very reason, make every effort to add to your faith goodness; and to goodness, knowledge; and to knowledge, self-control; and to self-control, perseverance; and to perseverance, godliness; and to godliness, mutual affection; and to mutual affection, love."
NET 2001	"For this very reason, make every effort to add to your faith excellence, to excellence, knowledge; to knowledge, self-control; to self-control, perseverance; to perseverance, godliness; to godliness, brotherly affection; to brotherly affection, unselfish love."
Message 2002	"So don't lose a minute in building on what you've been given, complementing your basic faith with good character, spiritual understanding, alert discipline, passionate patience, reverent wonder, warm friendliness, and generous love, each dimension fitting into and developing the others."
HCSB 2003	"For this very reason, make every effort to supplement your faith with goodness, goodness with knowledge, knowledge with self-control, self-control with endurance, endurance with godliness, godliness with brotherly affection, and brotherly affection with love."
NLTR 2004	"So make every effort to apply the benefits of these promises to your life. Then your faith will produce a life of moral excellence. A life of moral excellence leads to knowing God better. Knowing God leads to self-control. Self control leads to patient endurance and patient endurance leads to godliness. Godliness leads to love for other Christians, and finally you will grow to have genuine love for everyone."
Voice NT 2008	"To achieve this, you will need to add virtue to your faith, and then knowledge to your virtue; to knowledge, add discipline; to discipline, add endurance; to endurance, add godliness; to godliness, add affection for others as sisters and brothers; and to affection, *at last*, add love."

The growing number of new translations flooding the market offers multiple choices to the Bible customer. But with the choices comes confusion. The responsibility rests on buyers to compare the purposes of each translation to see if it meets their needs.

John 1:6-8 in Modern Versions

Greek Text of John 1:6-8

[1]Ἐγένετο [2]ἄνθρωπος, [3]ἀπεσταλμένος [4]παρὰ [5]θεοῦ, [6]ὄνομα [7]αὐτῷ [8]Ἰωάννης [9]οὗτος [10]ἦλθεν [11]εἰς [12]μαρτυρίαν [13]ἵνα [14]μαρτυρήσῃ [15]περὶ [16]τοῦ [17]φωτός [18]ἵνα [19]πάντες [20]πιστεύσωσιν [21]δι' [22]αὐτοῦ [23]οὐκ [24]ἦν [25]ἐκεῖνος [26]τὸ [27]φῶς [28]ἀλλ' [29]ἵνα [30]μαρτυρήσῃ [31]περὶ [32]τοῦ [33]φωτός.

Transliteration of John 1:6-8

[1]Egeneto [2]anthrōpos, [3]apestalmenos [4]para [5]theou, [6]onoma [7]autō [8]Iōannēs [9]houtos [10]ēlthen [11]eis [12]martyrian [13]hina [14]martyrēsē [15]peri [16]tou [17]phōtos [18]hina [19]pantes [20]pisteusōsin [21]di [22]autou [23]ouk [24]ēn [25]ekeinos [26]to [27]phōs [28]all [29]hina [30]martyrēsē [31]peri [32]tou [33]phōtos.

Literal transfer—lexical equivalents word-for-word (interlinear text)

[1]Became [2]man [3]sent [4]from [5]god [6]name [7]to-him [8]John; [9]this [10]came-he [11]into/for [12]testimony, [13]that [14]testify [15]concerning/to [16]the [17]light, [18]that [19]all [20]believe-might-they [21]through [22]him, [23]not [24]was [25]he/that-one [26]the [27]light, [28]but [29]that [30]witness-might-he [31]concerning/to [32]the [33]light.

Italics = added to text
CAPITALS = structural alterations
* = Omissions
[124635] = Word order

Table 4: John 1:6-8 in Modern Versions

Table 4: John 1:6-8 in Modern Versions *(continued)*

Minimal transfer—basic meaning (word-for-word)

There [1]was *a* [2]man [3]sent [4]from [5]God, [7]WHOSE [6]name *was* [8]John; [9]This *one* [10]came [11]for *a* [12]testimony, *so* [13]that *he might* [14]testify [15]about [16]the [17]light, *so* [18]that [19]all *might* [20]believe [21]through [22]him. [25]He [24]was [23]not [26]the [27]light, [28]but *was sent so* [29]that *he might* [30]testify [31]concerning [32]the [33]light.

Minimal literary transfer—literal versions (primarily "formal equivalent" translation)

American Standard Version (ASV) 1901

There [1]CAME *a* [2]man, [3]sent [4]from [5]God, [7]WHOSE [6]name *was* [8]John. [9]The same [10]came [11]for [12]witness, [13]that *he might* BEAR [14]witness [15]of [16]the [17]light, [18]that [19]all *might* [21]believe [21]through [22]him. [25]He [24]was [23]not [26]the [27]light, [28]but *came* [29]that *he might* BEAR [30]witness [31]of [32]the [33]light.

New American Standard Version (NASV) 1971

There [1]came *a* [2]man [3]sent [4]from [5]God, [7]WHOSE [6]name *was* [8]John. [9]He [10]came [11]AS A [12]witness, [13]to [14]testify [15]about [16]the [17]Light, *so* [18]that [19]all *might* [20]believe [21]through [22]him. [25]He [24]was [23]not [26]the [27]Light, [28]but *he came* [29]to [30]testify [31]ABOUT [32]the [33]Light.

The King James Version 1611

There [1]was *a* [2]man [3]sent [4]from [5]God, [7]WHOSE [6]name *was* [8]John. [9]The same [10]came [11]for *a* [12]witnesse, [13]to BEARE [14]witness [15]of [16]the [17]light, [18]that [19]all *men* [21]through [22]him *might* [20]beleeve. [25]Hee [24]was [23]not [26]THAT [27]light, [28]but *was sent* [29]to BEARE [30]witness [31]of [32]THAT [33]light.

New King James Version (NKJV) 1982

There [1]was *a* [2]man [3]sent [4]from [5]God, [7]WHOSE [6]name *was* [8]John. [9]This man [10]came [11]for *a* [12]witness, [13]to BEAR [14]witness [15]of [16]the [17]Light, [18]that [19]all [21]through [22]him *might* [20]believe. [25]He [24]was [23]not [26]THAT [27]Light, [28]but *was sent* [29]to BEAR [30]witness [31]of [32]THAT [33]Light.

New Revised Standard Version (NRSV) 1990

There [1]was *a* [2]man [3]sent [4]from [5]God, [7]WHOSE [6]name *was* [8]John. [9] He [10]came [11]AS A [12]witness [13]TO [14]testify [15]to [16]the [17]light, *so* [18]that [19]all *might* [20]believe [21]through [22]him. [25]He *himself* was [23]not [26]the [27]light, [28]but *he came* [29]to [30]testify [31]to [32]the [33]light.

The Holman Christian Standard Bible (HCSB) 2000

There [1]was *a* [2]man [6]named [8]John *who was* [3]sent [4]from [5]God; [7*] [9]He [10]came [11]AS A [12]witness [13]to [14]testify [15]ABOUT [16]the [17]light, *so* [18]that [19]all *might* [20]believe [21]through [22]him. [25]He [24]was [23]not [26]the [27]light, [28]but *he came* [29]to [30]testify [31]about [32]the [33]light.

Moderate to extreme literary transfer—dynamic equivalent versions (primarily "functional equivalent").
The following are somewhat mixed between dynamic transfer and expanded transfers.

The New International Version (NIV) 1978

There [1]came *a* [2]man *who was* [3]sent [4]from [5]God; [7] his [6]name *was* [8]John. [9]He [10]came [11]AS A [12]witness [13]to [14]testify [15]concerning [16]that [17]light, *so* [18]that [21]through [22]him [19]all *men might* [20]believe. [25]He *himself* [24]was [23]not [26]the [27]Light, [28]; *he came only* [29]as *a* [30]witness [31]to [32]the [33]Light.

Today's New International Version (TNIV) 2001

There [1]was *a* [2]man [3]sent [4]from [5]God; [7] WHOSE [6]name *was* [8]John. [9]He [10]came [11]AS A [12]witness [13]TO [14]testify [15]CONCERNING [16]that [17]light, *so* [18]that [21]through [22]him [19]all *might* [20]believe. [25]He *himself* [24]was [23]not [26]the [27]Light, [28]; *he came only* [29]as *a* [30]witness [31]to [32]the [33]Light.

Table 4: John 1:6-8 in Modern Versions *(continued)*

The New Living Translation (NLT) 1996

[1*][2*][5]God [6*][3*][4]sent [7*][8]John *the Baptist* [9*][10*][11*][12*][13]to [14]tell *everyone* [15]ABOUT [16]the [17]light *so* [18]that [19]EVERY-ONE *might* [20]believe because of his testimony. [25]JOHN *himself* [24]was [23]not [26]the [27]light [28]; *he was only a* [30]witness [31]to [32]the [33]light.

New English Translation (NET) 1996

A [2]man [1]came, [3]sent [4]from [5]God, [7]WHOSE [6]name *was* [8]John. [9]He [10]came [11]AS A [12]witness, [13]to [14]testify [15]about [16]the [17]light, *so* [18]that [19]EVERYONE *may* [20]believe [21]through [22]him. [25]He *himself* [24]was [23]not [26]the [27]light, [28]but *he came* [29]to [30]testify [31]ABOUT [32]the [33]light.

Today's English Version (TEV) 1966

[1*][4*][5]God [3]sent *his* [2]MESSENGER, *a* [7]MAN [6]named [8]John, [9]WHO [10]came [11]TO [12]TELL [13*][14*]*people* [15]ABOUT [16]the [17]light. *He came to tell them, so* [18]that [19]all *should hear the message and* [20]believe. [25]He *himself* [24]was [23]not [26]the [27]light [28]; *he came* to tell [31]ABOUT [32]the [33]light.

God's Word Translation (GWT) 1995

[1*][5]God [3]sent [4][*][2]a [2]man [6]named [7*][8]John [9*] *to be his MESSENGER.* JOHN [10]came [11*] *to* [12]DECLARE [13*][14*] *THE truth* about [16]the [17]light so [18]that [19]*EVERYONE would become* [20]BELIEVERS [21]through *his MESSAGE.* JOHN [24]was [22*][23]not [25*][26]the [27]light, [28]but *he came* [29]to [30]DECLARE THE TRUTH [31]*about* [32]the [33]light.

4. Statistical comparison of modern versions

The analysis below describes the differences among translations by comparing literal word-for-word meaning transfers, literary transfers, and expanded transfers. These comparisons will include changes in word order, omissions, structural alterations, and additions. This sample from John 1:6-8 will demonstrate the basic differences in the versions and perhaps give the reader a better base for selecting a translation. I have used the template of Eugene Nida and expanded it to include new versions.

From this limited analysis, it appears that the versions with the lowest number totals are more literal ("formal equivalence") and the highest numbers are less literal ("functional equivalent" or "paraphrase"). Comparative scores of individual versions could vary with a larger sample.

Summary of Analysis				
Version	Changes in Word Order	Omissions	Structural Alterations	Additions	Total
ASV	3	0	4	9	16
NASV	3	0	5	7	15
KJV	3	0	4	8	15
NKJV	3	0	5	7	15
HCSB	7	1	3	8	19
NRSV	5	0	4	8	17
NIV	6	0	12	11	29
TNIV	6	0	6	9	21
NLT	8	9	4	9	30
NET	5	0	5	7	17
TEV	8	4	8	16	36
GWT	8	9	8	21	46

Table 5: Summary of Analysis

Bibliography: Donald L. Brake. *A Visual History of the English Bible* (2008); David Daniel. *The Bible in English* (2003); David Dewey. *A User's Guide to Bible Translations* (2004); Sakae Kubo and Walter F. Specht. *So Many Versions?* (1983); Alister McGrath. *In the Beginning* (2001); Eugene A. Nida. *Toward a Science of Translation* (1964); Glen G. Scrogie, Mark L. Strauss and Steven M. Voth Gen. eds. *The Challenge of Bible Translation* (2003).

DONALD L. BRAKE, SR.

VERSIONS, GREEK. Translations of the OT into Greek began as early as the 3ʳᵈ cent. BCE in Alexandria, Egypt. Almost certainly the Pentateuch or Torah was first translated and named the SEPTUAGINT. Even as other books were translated, Jewish revisers worked to bring the Greek more closely into line with the Hebrew current in their communities, preparing new versions and revision*s* (*see* AQUILA'S VERSION; SYMMACHUS; THEODOTION). With Christian adoption of the LXX as their OT, Jewish interest lessened but did not end for some time. The LXX also formed the basis for many later translations, such as Armenian, Coptic, and Ethiopic. *See* HEXAPLA; VERSIONS, ANCIENT.

LEONARD GREENSPOON

VERSIONS, JEWISH. It is recorded in the Talmud: "If one translates a verse literally, he is a liar; if he adds to it, he is a blasphemer and a libeler" (*Qidd.* 49a). Early in his work, Josephus promises that he will describe the contents of Scripture without adding or omitting any details (*Ant.*, Preface). When Ben Sirach's grandson translated his grandfather's Hebrew book into Greek, he wrote: "For what was originally expressed in Hebrew does not have exactly the same sense when translated into another language. Not only this book, but even the Law itself, the Prophecies, and the rest of the books differ not a little when read in the original" (Sirach, Prologue).

These statements share with each other, as with almost all pronouncements about translation, recognition of the difficulties inherent in any rendering from one language to another. At the same time, they are linked together by what we might term a distinctly Jewish concern: the primacy of the Hebrew text. No matter what its origins, a Jewish version of the Scripture is not intended to replace the original, but rather to take a place alongside it or to serve as a guide to its proper understanding. This is often observable by the placement of the foreign-language version and the Hebrew text on facing pages. Even when this is not the case, the Jewish version reflects, through its wording and annotation, interpretations that developed within the exegetical and liturgical traditions of the Jewish community. Moreover, the format and layout of a Jewish version are shaped by practices initially associated with the practices of scribes who transmitted the Hebrew text. These are among the elements that we can trace from the earliest to the most recent of Jewish renderings of Scripture.

A. The Septuagint
B. Targumim and Other Ancient Versions
C. Arabic Versions
D. German and Yiddish Versions
E. Spanish and Italian Versions
F. Anglo-Jewish Versions
G. American Versions
H. Conclusion
Bibliography

A. The Septuagint

The earliest translation of Scripture, the Septuagint (LXX), dates to approximately 275 BCE. According to tradition, largely confirmed by generations of scholars, it was prepared in Alexandria, the Egyptian capital city, during the reign of the second ruler of Hellenistic Egypt, Ptolemy II Philadelphus. A narrative account of this event, penned at least a century after its occurrence, is contained in the *Letter of Aristeas.* According to this source, the Egyptian monarch persuaded the high priest in Jerusalem to dispatch to Alexandria seventy-two Jewish elders, each of whom exhibited impeccable linguistic skills as well as unblemished moral rectitude. Working in subcommittees and frequently consulting with each, they produced a Greek rendering of the five books of Moses (the TORAH or PENTATEUCH) in seventy-two days.

In its final verses, the *Letter of Aristeas* describes a formal ceremony in which the Greek Torah was acclaimed by the Jewish community, as well as its royal patron. For the former, this acclamation, which would have immediately struck ancient readers as consciously modeled on the Israelites' reception of the Law (as described in the book of Exodus), served to ratify the Greek text as sacred writ. To protect this status, an anathema was pronounced against anyone who would make even the slightest change in the wording of this Greek version.

Such an attitude toward the Greek surely reflected the conditions and circumstances at the time when the *Letter of Aristeas* was composed, sometime during the first half of the 2ⁿᵈ cent. BCE. We can well imagine that, by this date, the Greek text of the Pentateuch, and presumably of much of the remainder of the Hebrew Scripture, circulated as an independent document, functioning as what we might call the Bible for various Hellenistic Jewish communities. The *Letter of Aristeas* would affirm the unique status of this Greek text against those who would revise or revile it. Against all such critics, the *Letter of Aristeas* argued that this rendering accurately and faithfully preserved the Hebrew original for those no longer able to consult it directly.

A number of scholars have recently proposed an interlinear Hebrew-Greek model for understanding the origins of much of the LXX, which ultimately encompassed all of the Hebrew and Aramaic writings of ancient Jewish Scripture. Locating such activity within an educational (rather than, e.g., a liturgical) context, these scholars picture the activity of the earliest translators as part of a process that can be described as bringing the reader (or, in this case, hearer) to the text. As such, whether or not the Hebrew and Greek were actually written next to each other is less important than the observation that much of the Greek would not have been comprehensible without access to the Hebrew.

In any case, as we noted earlier, at some point, perhaps within only a generation of two after its inception, the LXX began an independent existence among people who did not and could not have recourse to the Hebrew. One such individual was the 1st-cent. CE Jewish philosopher Philo, himself an Alexandrian, who accorded to the translators the status of prophets, thus equating their Greek words with the inspired utterances of the authors of the Hebrew Scripture. Although Philo apparently did not know Hebrew, others, both within the Jewish community of Palestine and in the Diaspora, maintained their familiarity with the Semitic languages. Some of these individuals would surely have noticed that the Greek text in use in their community did not, in fact, reflect the developing Hebrew text that was gaining prominence (and eventually dominance) in Jerusalem and elsewhere. Such concerns led to revisions of the older Greek version; battling against this activity may well have been on the mind of the author of the *Letter of Aristeas*, which would mean that the revisers were at work perhaps within decades after various portions of the LXX appeared.

The initial translators of the Torah into Greek generally followed a reasonably literal approach to their Hebrew text. Those responsible for the LXX of other books, about whom we know very little if anything, were probably familiar with this earliest Greek rendering of the Pentateuch. Some of these later translators (see, e.g., the LXX book of Joshua) consciously followed this generally literal model, while other translators (see, e.g., LXX Proverbs, among others) produced freer renderings. Although we cannot know all of the factors that would have motivated such an approach, such translators were undoubtedly influenced by what they perceived as the needs of their respective communities.

As we noted above, revision of the Old Greek, with an eye toward the evolving Hebrew text, may well have been under way as early as the mid-2nd cent. BCE. However, the earliest reviser or retranslator that we know by name dates to the late 1st cent. BCE, namely, THEODOTION. Chronologically, he was followed by Aquila and SYMMACHUS, who may have been active as late as the beginning of the 3rd cent. CE (*see* AQUILA'S VERSION). Although considerable uncertainty remains about the actual identity of the individuals whose names are associated with these texts, we believe that they all operated within a Jewish environ-

ment. Their motivations were theological as well as stylistic; in fact, it would have been difficult, if not impossible, to distinguish between these concerns in antiquity. For example, by being hyper-literal, Aquila was making as much of a theological point as any other translator or commentator from the ancient world.

Although it is often claimed that Jews abandoned the LXX when it was adopted (or co-opted) by the early Christians, the examples especially of Theodotion and Aquila, both of whom were demonstrably dependent on the older Greek even as they revised it, call for caution in making any sweeping judgments. While it is true that Jewish scholars did not concentrate on LXX studies again until the early 19th cent., Greek-speaking Jews were using forms of the LXX and of Aquila into the Byzantine period.

Rabbinic sources, as transmitted in the Talmud and other documents of the period, contain both condemnations (e.g., *Sof.* 1:7) and positive statements (*b. Meg.* 9a) about biblical versions in languages other than Hebrew; such statements were often specifically directed to the Greek text. Although certainty is not possible, it is probable that these divergent opinions reflect differences in ideology, geography, and chronology.

B. Targumim and Other Ancient Versions

The LXX is the earliest recorded written version of Scripture in a language other than Hebrew. But the Hebrew Scripture itself contains evidence of its translation or interpretation several centuries earlier than 275 BCE. As described in Neh 8 (dated to the mid-5th cent. BCE), Ezra the scribe read in Hebrew from the Book of the Law to an assembly of the people at Jerusalem's Water Gate. The residents of Jerusalem, no longer able to easily understand Hebrew, were provided with interpretation in Aramaic, by then the lingua franca of the Near East. Within this context (oral rather than written), Aramaic served to supplement, but not supplant, the Hebrew.

The precise time when, or circumstances under which, scribes began to write down Aramaic renderings of the Hebrew Scripture is not known. The term *Targum* (pl. Targumim or Targums) came to designate these texts. Among the DEAD SEA SCROLLS, the longest Targum found is for the book of Job.

The most important and well-preserved Targumim date from a somewhat later period, although they may well incorporate much earlier material. The most influential Targumim were composed in Babylonia. There are several important Targumim for the Torah, the Former Prophets, the Latter Prophets, and the Writings. At least initially, these Targumim functioned as supplements to the Hebrew in liturgical settings (bringing to mind the narrative of Neh 8).

Study of the Targumim has often focused on large blocks of "nonbiblical" material that were inserted into narrative and (less often) into legal sections. Those responsible for these renderings into Aramaic also adopted circumlocutions for the name and certain characteristics of God and could, on occasion, modify the Hebrew in accordance with the Oral Tradition and other factors. Nonetheless, it would be erroneous to describe the Targumim overall as periphrastic.

C. Arabic Versions

The rapid expansion of Islam in the mid-7th cent. CE pushed the Arabic language to prominence throughout the Middle East and in North Africa. Jews living in these lands adopted it for most purposes, but did not immediately produce a major version of the Hebrew Scripture in Arabic. Early in the 10th cent., Saadia ben Joseph, a Gaon (head of a Babylonian rabbinic academy), undertook this task. His Arabic translation may have first appeared written in Hebrew characters; some later Jewish translators, such as Moses Mendelssohn, adopted a similar strategy for the first editions of their versions. Saadia's version, often referred to as the *Tafsir*, was enormously popular, rapidly becoming the standard text for Arabic-speaking Jews—a position that it retains to this day. Saadia's version, however, did not go unchallenged. As a staunch supporter of rabbinic Judaism, he often interpreted the Hebrew text in a way that his Karaite (non-rabbinic Jews) opponents challenged. This led to the subsequent production of several Karaite Arabic versions of the Tanakh.

Saadia's project was also challenged on what might be termed literary grounds. The Arabic of his rendering was clear and uncluttered, representing his primary goal of bringing (his understanding of) the biblical text to his contemporary readers. In the process, he regularly simplified complicated Hebrew expressions or even omitted them entirely.

D. German and Yiddish Versions

Jews were in German-speaking lands for almost a millennium before the appearance, in the 1200s, of a translation of the Hebrew Scripture into any of the German dialects. These earliest texts were literal, even wooden, renderings of the Hebrew, intended primarily for the home and primary school (or cheder), which were the two domains that women directed. Implicit in such editions was the supposition that adult males would not need a Bible in any version other than the Hebrew original. Such an understanding, which was carried forth for a considerable amount of time, was explicit in the *Teutsch Humash* of Jacob ben Isaac of Yarnow, who lived in the mid-1600s. This edition, which incorporated into its text numerous moral sayings and haggadic material, came to be widely known as the *Tsena Urena* or "Women's Bible."

It was not until the late 1700s that a Jewish leader, Moses Mendelssohn, sought to elevate the language of German versions available to members of his community. As an intellectual and Enlightenment figure, he asked: How could members of his Jewish community gain entry into the elite cultural and social circles then opening to them, if they remained unacquainted with the High German style spoken and written by the Christian leadership of his day? Mendelssohn's version, produced by him and others whom he inspired, served as his response to this situation. He accepted some of the language of the by-then classic formulations of Martin Luther, from the 1500s, while at the same time he excluded all of the specifically Christian renderings Luther had formulated. In support of his Jewish renderings, Mendelssohn marshaled an array of Jewish commentators. Like Saadia's work, the first editions of Mendelssohn's version, called the *Biur*, were printed in Hebrew characters.

Mendelssohn's work was controversial from its inception. Many Jewish leaders feared that their students, once introduced to High German through Mendelssohn's rendering, would abandon the texts that they traditionally studied. Although Mendelssohn (who, like Saadia, sought the plain meaning of the text) remained true to his understanding of Judaism, as did his followers, it is the case that almost all of his direct descendants became Christian within two generations.

Mendelssohn's version, now printed in German characters, sold well in the 19th cent. At the same time, the beginnings and growth of Reform Judaism and neo-Orthodoxy led to the production of German-language versions aimed at these segments of the market. For neo-Orthodox Jews, the editions of Samuel Raphael Hirsch and his son Mendel were especially popular. For the Reform community, versions such as those published by Leopold Zunz and Ludwig Philippson incorporated much of the critical scholarship then in vogue among liberal Protestant researchers.

In addition to German versions, Jews had also been preparing Yiddish (also known as Judeo-German) translations of the Hebrew Bible for their fellow Jews. In the late 19th cent., a new development took place in connection with Yiddish Bibles: Christians (typically recent converts from Judaism) also became active in this area. For the most part, such individuals were in the employ of organizations like the British and Foreign Bible Society. The goal was to produce a Yiddish Bible (OT and NT) that Christian missionaries could use when traveling to the Yiddish-speaking Jewish communities of Eastern Europe.

Slightly later, in the first decades of the 20th cent., Yehoash (the pen name of Solomon Bloomgarden) undertook what is probably the best-known Jewish translation of the Bible into Yiddish. For almost two decades before his death in 1927, Yehoash published and revised in serial format his popular translation. Another decade passed before his work was gathered together and appeared in a single volume. Alas, by then (on the eve of World War II), large numbers of Yiddish speakers were already on the road to destruction.

One German version was the result of a collaboration between the Jewish philosophers Martin Buber and Franz Rosenzweig. They began work on their text prior to World War I; it was left to Buber to complete it (Rosenzweig died in 1929) after World II and the Holocaust. Their goal was to transport their readers back to a time, place, and society far different from 20th-cent. Europe. Only in this way, Buber and Rosenzweig believed, would such readers experience the Hebrew Scripture in an authentic way. In order to accomplish this goal, they created something unique in German literature, to the point where those unfamiliar with Hebrew (precisely the audience for a Bible translation) would have to labor to comprehend the meaning of what they were reading. For them, and for at least some of their readers, the struggle was worth it, as they came face to face with many literary and theological features of the Hebrew text that up until then were available only to those who could encounter it in the original. As we shall see, Buber-Rosenzweig is the inspiration for at least one modern English-language version.

E. Spanish and Italian Versions

Before turning to an extended treatment of Jewish translations of the Bible into English, we should note that there are a vast number of Jewish versions in languages spoken (or at least once spoken) throughout the world. In Spanish, e.g., there are the Alba Bible, prepared by Rabbi Moses Arragel in the early 1400s, and the Ferrara Bible of 1553. Those responsible for the influential Ferrara Bible were considerably influenced by Arragel's earlier version. Jewish translations into Italian go back to at least the 16th cent.; however, what are widely judged the most distinguished versions in this language are the work of the Samuel David Luzzatto (also known as Shadal), who lived in the 19th cent. Successive editions of his work covered the Torah, the Prophets, and the book of Job.

F. Anglo-Jewish Versions

For almost three centuries, the King James Version (KJV) of 1611 was the standard for English speakers, as Martin Luther's version had been for those who spoke German. Even though there were no Jewish members on the translation committees for the KJV, a number of these Christian translators had deep knowledge both of the Hebrew language and the interpretive traditions of Judaism. This helps to account for the many KJV readings directly indebted to the exegetical insights of David KIMCHI (late 12th–early 13th cent.). Moreover, the KJV translators powerfully evoked the cadence and eloquence of the Hebrew original through word choice and overall structure, even as they introduced traditionally Christian readings into many OT passages. This overall evocation of the original undoubtedly played a large role in the Anglo-Jewish community's use of the KJV for more than a century.

In the 1780s and early 1790s, distinctly Jewish versions of the Bible in English emerged, at first limited in extent to the Torah. Rather than constituting new translations, these earliest versions consisted of alternating pages of the KJV and the corresponding Hebrew text, with exegetical notes drawn from RASHI and other traditional Jewish sources.

These early steps, and the even larger strides that came later, were the result of concerns both external to and within the Anglo-Jewish community. For example, the earliest editions, as described in the previous paragraph, might have served as a Jewish response to Hebrew-English texts being published under Protestant auspices. More broadly, English-speaking Jews, among others, were increasingly the target of missionary societies, notably the London Jews Society. Although Christian proselytizing was not without precedent, by the early 1800s such groups were benefiting from the rapid growth in the printing trade that allowed for the mass production of Bibles that could be widely distributed at little or no cost. Some of these versions (see also the Yiddish Bibles mentioned above) were produced so as to specifically appeal to newly arrived members of the expanding Jewish communities in London and elsewhere in Great Britain. "Jewish" versions, incorporating traditional rabbinic exegesis and excluding typically Christian interpretation, could be seen as a valuable and effective way to counter such efforts.

Within the Jewish community itself, there were also trends at work that would lead ultimately to the acceptance of English-language versions. The Anglo-Jewish community consisted of Jews from both German/Yiddish-speaking lands and Sephardic backgrounds. By the beginning of the 19th cent., increasing numbers of Jews were becoming comfortable with English, leading, e.g., to the inclusion of this language in prayer books and rabbinic sermons. It is in tandem with these internal developments that we can view the appearance of biblical texts in English.

It is very interesting to observe that the earliest Jewish versions in English did not emanate from those with leadership positions in the community, but rather from those on the periphery. By the mid-1800s, individuals closely associated with the Jewish establishment were preparing and promoting such versions, two of which were sanctioned by the Chief Rabbi of the British Empire for use in schools and homes. Although the translators varied considerably in terms of their openness to critical scholarship, the English texts they published rarely produced major linguistic or stylistic variations from the KJV.

G. American Versions

The first Jewish translation into English in the United States was the work of one man, Isaac Leeser. As has frequently been the case with Jewish versions, he first introduced a translation of the Torah, which appeared in the 1840s; his rendering of the entire Tanakh followed a decade later. Critics varied widely in their assessment of Leeser's version; nonetheless, it very quickly found its way into almost all American Jewish homes—and it remained there until early in the 20th cent.

In the latter part of the 19ᵗʰ cent., the aristocracy of American Jewry established the Jewish Publication Society (JPS). After several false starts at producing a successor to Leeser's version, they finally succeeded, in the first part of the 20ᵗʰ cent., in constituting a translation committee, headed by the eminent scholar Max L. Margolis.

Institutionally, JPS wanted a version that would fill the same spot in Jewish homes that the KJV occupied in Christian residences. The resultant version—first published in 1917 and reissued in many editions for the next half-century—looked and sounded very much like the KJV. This was no accident, for Margolis felt that a "Judaized" KJV would best serve the vast number of new immigrants to America, for which the "King's English" was the best model as they sought to accommodate themselves to the New World.

By the mid-1950s, when the JPS set out to produce a successor to Margolis' work, new trends had entered into the world of Bible translating, namely, what eventually became known as functional (earlier, dynamic) equivalence. A (probably the) leading exponent of these approaches within the Jewish community was biblical scholar Harry M. Orlinsky, and it was to Orlinsky that JPS turned for leadership in their new effort.

Orlinsky, as was (and continues to be) the case with other practitioners of functional equivalence, placed primary emphasis on the ease with which contemporary readers could understand a given translation of the Bible. A guiding question in his work could be posed as: What did the original authors intend to say to their audience and how can we convey that meaning to today's audience? Unlike many, perhaps most, earlier Jewish versions, the new JPS translation was to take the text to the reader, rather than the reader to the text. Among his Jewish predecessors, Orlinsky closely identified with Saadia Gaon. More broadly, Orlinsky allied himself with Protestant scholars associated with the American Bible Society, who promoted this functional equivalence approach to Bible translation in the Good News Bible and other publications.

The Torah translation of the NJPS first appeared in the mid-1960s. A group of scholars from North America and Israel oversaw the translation of the Writings. The entire Tanakh appeared in 1985, and JPS published its first Hebrew-English language edition in 1999.

Although first Leeser and then the JPS version of 1917 had little if any competition within the English-speaking Jewish world, contemporary consumers have several choices in addition to the NJPS. This parallels the ever more crowded market that has developed, especially among Protestants, in recent decades.

On the right, as it were, is the ArtScroll's Tanach (like Tanakh, Tanach is an acronym reflecting the traditional tripartite Jewish division of the Hebrew Scripture). It has been widely marketed, primarily among more traditional or Orthodox segments of the Jewish community. Especially for the Torah, its translators often incorporate into the text the classic interpretations of the influential medieval exegete Rashi.

The Living Torah is another version intended primarily for Orthodox and other traditional Jews. It is the work of Rabbi Aryeh Kaplan. Kaplan, who wrote voluminously on a wide variety of Jewish topics, frequently emphasized mystical or spiritual elements in Jewish thought and practice—an emphasis that he incorporated into his text as well as in his notes. For legal interpretation, Kaplan and his followers were especially indebted to the philosopher MAIMONIDES.

The Jewish scholar Everett Fox had adopted an approach reminiscent of Buber-Rosenzweig. As they sought to accomplish for the German reader, so Fox draws the contemporary English reader into the world of antiquity through a modern-language version that incorporates distinctive aspects of the ancient Hebrew text absent in other renderings. As a result, his *Schocken Bible: The Five Books of Moses* has attracted considerable interest, as have his later renderings of portions of the Prophets.

Two other individual efforts merit mention as well: Richard Elliott Friedman, *Commentary on the Torah with a New English Translation*, and Robert Alter, *The Five Books of Moses: A Translation with Commentary.* Most recently, JPS introduced *The Contemporary Torah: A Gender-Sensitive Adaptation of the JPS Translation.* In keeping with its subtitle, this version strives for gender-neutral language for references to God, in addition to numerous changes with respect to humans.

H. Conclusion

Other English-language translations have also appeared or are in the offing, either as new versions or as revisions of existing texts. As with similar trends in the larger, Christian world, a number of concerns play a role in this phenomenon: theological, literary, cultural, and even fiscal. For Jews, the questions that arise are ancient and perennial, modern and immediate: What is it that makes a translation of the Hebrew Scripture Jewish? Should a Jewish translation ever supplant, rather than supplement, the Hebrew original? Who, if anyone, should determine which mode of translation, or presentation, or annotation is best? Do differing versions serve to divide Jews, and, if so, should there be one version to unite? There is every reason to hope that future generations will build on the foundations constructed for them by earlier Jewish translators. But it is impossible to know all of the directions that they will take. *See* BIBLE TRANSLATION THEORY.

Bibliography: Leonard Greenspoon. "Jewish Translations of the Bible." *The Jewish Study Bible.* Adele Berlin and Marc Zvi Brettler, eds. (2003) 2005–20; Leonard Greenspoon. "The King James Bible and Jewish Bible Translations." *The Translation That Openeth the Window: Reflections on the History and Legacy of the King James Version.* David G. Burke, ed. (2007) 123–38; Frederick W. Knobloch, ed. *Biblical Translation in Context* (2002); Harry M. Orlinsky and Roger G. Bratcher. *A History of Bible Translation and the North American Contribution* (1991).

LEONARD GREENSPOON

VERSIONS, LATIN. The Latin versions of the Bible witness to the ever-changing place of Latin in Christian life and worship. From early, informal translations to modern critical editions of the Vulgate, Latin Bibles transmit not only particular Latin versions but also the approach to sacred scriptures adopted by the communities that produced and employed them. As such, they offer valuable insight into the circumstances and priorities of Christians over time, attesting to the living character of biblical traditions.

A. From Greek to Latin
   1. Early translations
   2. The rise of Latin
   3. The first systematic translations
B. Transmission of Latin Texts
   1. Matters of origin and provenance
   2. Arrangement and order of Latin biblical books
C. Characteristic Features of Latin Bibles
   1. The continuing importance of Greek and Old Latin
   2. Early attempts to stabilize text and content
D. The Latin Bible Today
Bibliography

A. From Greek to Latin

The principal language of the earliest Christians was Greek, in the city of Rome as elsewhere, and this remained true well into the late 2nd cent. Clement of Rome (ca. 96 CE) wrote in Greek, as did Hermas (ca. 140), and Justin Martyr (d. ca. 165). Irenaeus of Lyons (ca. 130–200), a leader of the church in Gaul, also wrote in Greek. Catacomb inscriptions in Rome are regularly rendered in Greek, the bishops of that city possessed Greek names well into the 3rd cent., and the *Apostolic Tradition*, a 3rd-cent. church order, was written in Greek, providing evidence of the central place of Greek in Roman worship. Toward the end of the 3rd cent., Roman bishops with Latin names do begin to appear, yet, with one exception, the epitaphs of these popes were written in Greek, not Latin. Still, as the Roman church grew, Latin became more prevalent. According to Jerome, Pope Victor (ca. 189–99) was the first to write treatises in the city's vernacular (*Vir. ill.* 34; 53). Victor's example was followed by Novatian (d. ca. 258), a Roman theologian later deemed a heretic for his rigorist views. Latin was more common in North Africa, though Greek was important in this context as well. The principal language of Tertullian (ca. 160–225), a prolific North African theologian and exegete, was Latin, but he occasionally wrote in Greek and he assumed the primacy of that language, whether citing Jewish Scriptures, the Gospels, or the letters of Paul.

1. Early translations

Greek Scriptures held the greater authority, but Latin versions of LXX books and Christian writings were undoubtedly circulating by the mid-2nd cent., in North Africa and probably elsewhere. The author of the *Acts of the Scillitan Martyrs* (ca. 180), a dramatic account of the execution of nine North African Christians by the governor of Carthage, reports that the martyrs carried "books and letters of Paul" (*libri et epistulae Pauli*) with them at the time of their arrest. Specific allusions to Pauline letters imply that Latin translations were known by the author, if not carried by the martyrs themselves; the books (*libri*) they held might well have been Latin Gospels. Tertullian knew and employed previous Latin translations, as he occasionally indicates. For example, in his treatise *Against Marcion* he signals an awareness of an existing Latin version by expressing dissatisfaction with the translation *spiritus* for the Greek pnoē (πνοή, "breath") in Gen 2:7 ("then the LORD God formed man from the dust of the ground, and breathed into his nostrils the breath of life"). He preferred *afflatus* (*Marc.* 2.9.1–2). Extant Old Latin copies of Genesis corroborate Tertullian's observation, vacillating between *spiritus* and *flatus*, as well as other terms, when translating this verse. Cyprian of Carthage (ca. 200–58) depended heavily upon Latin translations made by others, citing nearly every book of the LXX in Latin, including books now regarded as apocryphal (Wisdom, Sirach, and Tobit), as well as the Gospels, Acts, most of the Pauline letters (Philemon and Hebrews are omitted), 1 Peter, 1 John, and the Apocalypse (Fahey). His preference for such terms as *lumen* for the Greek phōs (φῶς; e.g., citing John 1:9-10 in *Test.* 1.7) and *clarificare* for the Greek doxazō (δοξάζω; e.g., citing Matt 5:16 in *Test.* 3.26) links him to Old Latin versions of the Gospels identified with North Africa. Both Tertullian and Cyprian also relied upon a Latin collection of *testimonia*, verses from the Jewish Scriptures designed to prove that Jesus fulfills the Law and the Prophets, traces of which are found in the mistaken attribution of prophetic sayings and in the quotation of statements found in no extant copy of the Jewish Scriptures, in any language.

2. The rise of Latin

The sense that Greek was the language of the apostolic books and of the Jewish Scriptures—Christians read and defended the LXX translation as sacred text, not the Hebrew—meant that Latin versions were simply that, versions, and therefore without the same weight as the originals. Nevertheless, as the Latin church grew, so did the demand for Latin translations. By the 4th cent., literally hundreds of copies were circulating, probably in a number of different versions. The North African martyr Felix, a victim of the Great Persecution (d. 303), reportedly refused to hand over the numerous books of the Carthaginian church, despite an imperial decree demanding that he do so, and was therefore beheaded (*Acts of Saint Felix*). The church of Cirta was less successful, losing most of its library when, in May of 303, thirty-four biblical manuscripts of varying sizes were seized by the proconsul, including one very large manuscript, five large, two small, twenty-five of unspecified size, and one of unbound quinions (McGurk). These early Latin translations, known to Tertullian and Cyprian, possessed by the churches of Carthage and Cirta and employed by the Roman authors such as Victor and Novatian, were informal, however precious they may have been to the churches that held them. As Augustine famously put it, anyone who obtained a Greek manuscript and thought that he had some ability in Greek and Latin went ahead and translated it (*Doctr. chr.* 2.11.16), a neat explanation for the diversity of the versions known to him at the turn of the 4th cent. Latin-speaking Christians were defining and delimiting their sacred books, and their relationships to them, at the very same time that they were translating them, locally, anonymously, and without a discernible scheme.

During the 4th cent., Latin became a focus not only of the Roman imperial administration but of Latin-speaking Christians as well. The emperor Diocletian (r. 284–305) promulgated imperial law solely in Latin, though his capital was in Greek-speaking Asia Minor. Constantine continued this practice, writing speeches in Latin and leaving it to others to translate (Eusebius, *Vit. Const.* 3.13.1; 4.8). A bilingual law school was founded in Berytus, Syria (modern Beirut), Latin appears with increasing frequency in surviving papyri from Roman Egypt, and significant pagan authors living in Antioch and Alexandria adopted Latin as their literary language of choice (Lafferty). Christians followed suit: Latin was adopted as the principal liturgical language in Rome and Milan, revisions of existing Latin translations were undertaken in earnest, and there was a proliferation of theological writings in Latin by such authors as Hilary of Poitiers (d. ca. 367) and Ambrose of Milan (ca. 339–97). The writings of Origen (ca. 185–254) and other Greek Christian authors began to be carefully translated into Latin by scholars such as Rufinus (ca. 345–411) and Jerome (ca. 345–420). It was in this context that Damasus, bishop of Rome from 366 to 384, likely commissioned Jerome to compose a new translation of the Gospels based on the best Greek manuscripts and yet mindful of ancient Latin Christian traditions. This translation, completed in 383, was designed to produce a version free of the errors of inaccurate translators and copyists (Jerome, *Letter to Damasus*). Twenty years later, Augustine complimented Jerome for the success of his version, thanking him for producing such a careful translation; he was significantly less enthusiastic about Jerome's approach to the LXX (see Jerome's *Epist.* 71).

3. The first systematic translations

Early Christians regarded the LXX as sacred, yet there was an awareness of the occasionally significant differences among Hebrew versions, the LXX, and other Greek translations in circulation. The accomplished Alexandrian theologian Origen sought to address these differences by producing a massive six-column edition of the OT containing a Hebrew text, a Greek transliteration of the Hebrew, the LXX, and three other Greek translations, all on a single page (Grafton and Williams). Though only fragments of this Bible, the "Hexapla," survive, Jerome indicates that he knew and admired it (*Comm. Tit.* 3.9). After translating the Gospels, he relied heavily upon the Hexapla when producing the first of two translations of the psalms and it was this translation that became the received version of the psalms in the Latin West during the reforms of the 9th cent., though his translation from the Hebrew was also known. Working on a second edition, Jerome adopted the practice of marking passages that, while present in the Greek, did not appear in the Hebrew (*Preface to the Psalms*), a procedure he continued to pursue when translating Job (*Preface to Job*). Jerome immersed himself in the study of Hebrew, concluding that the Hebrew text should often be preferred over the Greek, a principle he followed when translating the remainder of the OT books. This decision met with serious criticism, however, leaving Jerome susceptible to the charge of "Judaizing." He responded by justifying his translation procedures with biblical prefaces and in letters, intricate commentaries on Scripture, and a set of reference works designed to accompany his editions (*Hebrew Names*, the *Book of Places*, and *Hebrew Questions*). Still, his OT translations remained controversial during his own lifetime, however elegant their Latin and scholarly their approach. Augustine consulted Jerome's translations, particularly of the Gospels, but he also relied upon older Latin versions. Cassiodorus (ca. 485–580) and Gregory the Great (ca. 560–604) followed Augustine's example, praising Jerome's accomplishments and yet referring to older translations as well. The Vulgate, the now famous version attributed to Jerome, gained full recognition only gradually, a situation that is confirmed by the transmission of Latin biblical texts.

B. Transmission of Latin Texts

1. Matters of origin and provenance

Latin Bibles available today are the result of a long process of transmission, revision, and emendation, beginning with the pioneering work of Jerome and continuing even now as scholars revisit, revise, and reconsider what Jerome's text might have been. Yet Jerome's translation is only part of the story. He translated all of the OT from the Hebrew, along with Tobit and Judith from the Greek, the Gospels, and two versions of Psalms, but other, older versions of these books continued to circulate, sometimes on their own and sometimes as portions of Bibles with mixed Vulgate and Old

Latin texts. Since it is likely that older translations were produced locally, in response to the needs of particular communities, an attempt has been made to categorize surviving translations by geographical region, with some Old Latin texts identified as "African," others as "European," and still others as "eccentric" or "mixed." For example, the Latin text of Codex Bobiensis, a late 4th- or early 5th-cent. copy of the Gospels from which only Mark and Matthew survive, has been identified as African in origin on the basis of its correspondence to the Gospel citations of Cyprian and Optatus, a North African bishop who wrote a detailed condemnation of the Donatists (ca. 367), though this conclusion has been challenged (Burton). Other manuscripts are said to preserve a text of European origin; e.g., the editor of Codex Corbeiensis concludes that characteristic orthography and grammatical errors associate the manuscript with Gaul (Buchanan). Still, a lack of available external evidence makes firm conclusions about provenance difficult. Vulgate texts present similar problems, with lines of transmission concealed both by the relative paucity of early manuscripts and by the confusing distribution of those that do survive (Marsden).

2. Arrangement and order of Latin biblical books

Latin Scriptures commonly circulated not as entire Bibles but as a library of books, accompanied by diverse prefatory material. The earliest complete Bible, or "pandect," to survive is Codex Amiatinus, an elaborate, large manuscript produced before 716 CE and given as a gift by Ceolfrith, Abbot of the Wearmouth-Jarrow double monastery, to Pope Gregory II (715–31). Copied in Britain from a 6th-cent. Roman original, brought to Rome by Ceolfrith sometime later, updated on the basis of a Vulgate translation, and made up of elements reproduced from earlier exemplars but with a series of emendations designed to bring both its text and its textual apparatus up to date, this codex provides just one example of the complexity of Latin biblical texts. Amiatinus' prefatory material is particularly striking: an image of the tabernacle, a dedicatory poem to Pope Gregory, three separate diagrams indicating the divisions of the OT and NT books attributed to Jerome, Augustine, and Pope Hilary (461–68), a prologue that may have been authored by Cassiodorus, a poem about Jerome, and a listing of the contents of the codex all appear before the commencement of the OT books. Here Amiatinus likely reproduces a number of images originally included in a 6th-cent. pandect created under the direction of Cassiodorus, the now lost Codex Grandior. Cassiodorus had also listed three canonical arrangements, but those preferred by Jerome, Augustine, and in the LXX (*Institutions* 1.12–14). He further recommended that the Bible be approached in nine "sections" (*codices*), referring to separate books held by his monastery, to an idealized scheme of scriptural study or, perhaps, to both (*Institutions* 1.1–9; Vessey). This nine-volume arrangement included the Octateuch (the

Pentateuch, Joshua, Judges, and Ruth), Kings (1–4 Kings, 1–2 Chronicles), the Histories (Job, Tobit, Esther, Judith, 1–2 Esdras, and 1–2 Maccabees), Psalms, the books of Solomon (Proverbs, Ecclesiastes, Song of Songs, Wisdom, Sirach), the Prophets (Isaiah, Jeremiah, Daniel, Ezekiel, and the twelve Minor Prophets), the Four Gospels, the Apostolic Letters, and the Acts of the Apostles together with the Apocalypse, a detail that was reproduced in one of Amiatinus' prefatory images. An illustration identified as Ezra seated before a library of books reproduces an image of Cassiodorus seated before his nine-codex Bible, reinterpreted in this manuscript as Ceolfrith's hero Ezra. Thus, the 6th-cent. images of Codex Grandior were both imitated and freely updated to suit current tastes. The text of this Bible met a similar fate; according to the Venerable Bede (ca. 673–735), the scribes of Wearmouth-Jarrow replaced the "old translation" (*vetus translatio*), available in their exemplar, with a "new translation" (*nova translatio*), that is, with a Vulgate text, when producing three pandects, including one that was taken as a gift to Rome: Codex Amiatinus (*Lives of the Holy Abbots of Wearmouth and Jarrow*).

The production of a magnificent one-volume Bible on the order of Amiatinus was a tremendous undertaking, as Bede recognized when he praised Ceolfrith's three pandects as an example of the abbot's deep dedication to religion. More often, biblical books were published in multiple volumes of varying order and content, sometimes with the Vulgate text and sometimes in an Old Latin translation. Most popular were Gospel collections, though the survival of so many Gospel codices may attest to their importance in local churches and monasteries rather than to the number of copies actually made. Other biblical books survive as well, but in fewer numbers. A review of manuscripts dated before 600 CE notes that there are ten surviving manuscripts with content from the Octateuch, eight with all or portions of Kings–Job, two with historical books, five with copies of Psalms, five of the books of Solomon, eight of one or more of the Prophets, forty-one of the Gospels, twelve of various apostolic letters in diverse collections, and six of Acts and the Apocalypse (Petitmengin). This survey on the basis of Cassiodorus' nine-codex scheme is somewhat misleading, however, since there is little indication that manuscripts were produced with his particular order in mind. Indeed, a closer look at these same manuscripts shows a varied arrangement, not a shared understanding of canonical order, an impression confirmed by a comparison of OT arrangements employed over time (Marsden). As Samuel Berger has noted, prior to the 13th cent., the Latin Bible was not a book per se, it was an anthology of traditions that could be grouped in almost any order (Berger).

C. Characteristic Features of Latin Bibles

1. The continuing importance of Greek and Old Latin

Latin manuscripts display a remarkable variety of form and content, but a few general observations are possible: Greek continued to serve as an important backdrop to the Latin, as evidenced by the number of Greco-Latin copies of the Gospels, Psalms, the letters of Paul, and Acts. For example, one late 6th-cent. bilingual copy of Psalms was divided into separate quires in the 9th cent., perhaps as an aid to monks studying Greek (Verona, Biblioteca capitolare I [I]; Lowe IV, 472). Codex Bezae (ca. 400), an important bilingual manuscript of the Gospels and Acts copied in Syria, made its way to Lyons at some point in the mid-9th cent., perhaps as part of a transfer of books from the libraries of Berytus to the law libraries of Lyons, and was then employed by Ado, a Benedictine monk who composed a martyrology in the 850s (Parker). Codex Claromontanus, Codex Augiensis, and Codex Boernerianus preserve the Pauline Epistles in both Greek and Latin, showing evidence of repeated use over time in the form of corrections and liturgical markings. Also, despite a gradual ascendancy of the Vulgate, Old Latin versions continued to be read and copied as legitimate translations for centuries. The 12th-cent. Codex Colbertinus offers a remarkable example, retaining the Old Latin of the Gospels long after the Vulgate Gospels had become the norm (Vogels). Moreover, once copied, Latin biblical books were revered, studied, used, and reused by successive generations of Latin-speaking Christians, who left their own traces behind in the form of corrections, marginal notes, supplements, and liturgical markings. Very ancient copies were occasionally recycled, serving as palimpsests for other books of more contemporary interest or taken apart and employed as a binding for another manuscript. Folia from a 5th-cent. copy of Judges and Ruth survive in this way, having been reused in the 8th cent. to copy two different works by Isidore, bishop of Seville (ca. 560–636). Other very old biblical books were admired as sacred objects, guaranteeing both their survival and their continuing importance to local church communities. For example, a 6th-cent. Irish psalter known as the Cathach of St. Columba was placed in a shrine and carried into battle as a talisman designed to guarantee victory, and a small 5th- or 6th-cent. copy of the Gospel of John survived when it was sewn into a reliquary of the Virgin's shirt at Chartres.

2. Early attempts to stabilize text and content

Standardization of text and content may not have been a principal goal of most ancient and medieval scriptoria, but certain features did become increasingly widespread as scribes carefully copied the traditions that had come down to them. Thus, Gospel collections were regularly accompanied by canon tables, a device invented by Eusebius of Caesarea (ca. 260–340) to indicate parallels between Gospel passages; many manuscripts appear *per cola et commata*, that is, in sense lines designed to ease both reading and comprehension (Jerome, *Preface to Isaiah*, *Preface to Ezekiel*; Cassiodorus, *Institutions* 1.9), and early copies of Vulgate texts are often accompanied by Jerome's prefaces. Eighth-cent. victories of the Franks over the Lombards, culminating in the crowning of Charlemagne in Rome by Pope Leo III in 800, led to a new emphasis on the production of full Bibles, accompanied by an attempt to correct and normalize the biblical text. In a series of public letters, Charlemagne called for the correction of the OT and NT, the furnishing of lectionaries to the churches, and the revision of psalters, calendars, catholic books, and grammars available in monasteries. Though the impact of Charlemagne's edicts should not be overestimated, Bibles produced in Corbie under the direction of Maudramnus (772–81), in Fleury under Theodulf of Orléans (ca. 798–818), and, most important, under Alcuin of York (ca. 740–804) and his successors Fridigus (807–34), Adalhard (834–43), and Vivian (844–51) at Tours, influenced the form and appearance of biblical texts across the Latin West, as evidenced by the sheer number of surviving manuscripts from this period. Thanks to the Carolingian reform, the order of the biblical books was stabilized, at least to some degree, a preference for Vulgate translations became fixed, and Jerome's hexaplic translation of Psalms, the Gallican Psalter, was chosen as the church's liturgical standard. Nevertheless, innovations in the production and presentation of the Bible continued, with the glorious 11th-cent. Italian illuminated Bibles, the 12th-cent. *Glossa ordinaria*, multi-volume Bibles with marginal and interlinear annotation drawn from patristic and other sources, and the 13th-cent. "Paris Bible," a set of Bibles with an order and chapter divisions resembling what is printed in most Bibles today, worthy of special notice.

The advent of movable type, accompanied in the Renaissance by a "return to the sources," led to yet another phase of revision and correction, exemplified by the Complutensian Polyglot (1514–17). This five-volume Bible, published under the direction of Cardinal Ximénes de Cisneros (1436–1517), included a newly edited version of the Vulgate accompanied by the LXX, Hebrew Bible, and the Greek NT, printed in parallel columns. Designed to defend the Vulgate by means of comparison with the Greek and Hebrew, the Complutensian Polyglot can fruitfully be compared to the more widely known fresh Latin translation of Erasmus (ca. 1469–1536) from the Greek, the *Novum instrumentum omne*, a version that significantly revised some traditional Vulgate readings and paved the way for a wider challenge to the Latin text launched in the context of the Protestant Reformation (de Hamel; Pelikan). A succession of newly edited Vulgate texts appeared in print following Erasmus' translation, beginning with the version of Robert Estienne (1503–59) and culminating in the Clementine edition of 1592–93. This version, begun by Pope Sixtus V in 1586 in response to the affirmation of the Vulgate as the sacred text of the Catholic Church by the Council of Trent (third session, 1546), remained the sanctioned edition of the Roman Catholic Church until 1943, when Pope Pius XII (1939–58) called for new translations from the original languages.

D. The Latin Bible Today

Interest in the Latin versions of the Bible continues unabated, as scholars seek to recover and better understand Old Latin and Vulgate Bibles, both in their own contexts and as witnesses to church tradition. Critical modern editions of the books of the Vulgate OT have now been issued in full by the Benedictine Fathers in Rome. The Vetus Latina Institut in Beuron, Germany, has been diligently compiling all known sources of Old Latin versions, as well as information on Vulgate manuscripts, making available a series of comprehensive reference works and an online, searchable data bank of Old Latin citations. These resources are of particular interest to scholars seeking to understand the Greek source of Latin OT and NT books. As H. F. D. Sparks explains, the word-for-word literalness of Old Latin translations resulted in an awkward and occasionally ungrammatical Latin, but their faithfulness to the Greek offers valuable evidence to very early Greek texts. Other scholars are less optimistic about their potential for reconstructing Greek forms, noting the unpredictable freedom that translators could exhibit as well as important differences between Greek and Latin syntax (Fischer). Yet Latin versions of the Bible remain precious, not only to those who regard them as sacred text but also to historians, text critics, philologists, codicologists, paleographers, and others. To offer just one example, the Latin Codex Fuldensis (ca. 546), a Gospel harmony and early witness to Jerome's translation, provides crucial evidence to the Diatessaron of Tatian, a 2nd-cent. harmony of the four Gospels, written in Greek but surviving almost entirely in patristic citations and versional witnesses (Petersen). As Codex Fuldensis and the many other manuscripts mentioned in this essay demonstrate, understanding even one Latin version provides a window not only into the history of the Bible but also into Christian life and practice writ large, from antiquity until today. *See* DIATESSARON; VULGATE.

Bibliography: Kurt and Barbara Aland. *The Text of the New Testament: An Introduction to the Critical Editions and to the Theory and Practice of Modern Textual Criticism.* Erroll F. Rhodes, trans. 2nd ed. (1989); Samuel Berger. *Histoire de la Vulgate pendant les premiers siècles du moyen age* (1893); Walter Berschin. *Greek Letters and the Latin Middle Ages: From Jerome to Nicholas of Cusa.* Jerold C. Frakes, trans. Rev. and expanded ed. (1988); Bernhard Bischoff. *Manuscripts and Libraries in the Age of Charlemagne.* Michael Gorman, trans. (1994); Pamela Bright, ed. and trans. *Augustine and the Bible* (1999); E. S. Buchanan. *The Four Gospels from the Codex Corbeiensis together with Fragments of the Catholic Epistles, of the Acts and of the Apocalypse from the Fleury Palimpsest* (1907); Philip Burton. *The Old Latin Gospels: A Study of Their Texts and Language* (2000); Michael Andrew Fahey. *Cyprian and the Bible: A Study in Third-Century Exegesis* (1971); B. Fischer. "Das Neue Testament in Lateinischer Sprache." *Die alten Übersetzungen des Neuen Testaments, die Kirchenväterzitate und Lektionare.* Kurt Aland, ed. (1972) 1–92; Harry Y. Gamble. *Books and Readers in the Early Church: A History of Early Christian Texts* (1995); Margaret Gibson. *The Bible in the Latin West* (1993); Anthony Grafton and Megan Williams. *Christianity and the Transformation of the Book: Origen, Eusebius, and the Library of Caesarea* (2006); Christopher de Hamel. *The Book: A History of the Bible* (2001); Maura K. Lafferty. "Translating Faith from Greek to Latin: Romanitas and Christianitas in Late Fourth-Century Rome and Milan." *JECS* 11 (2003) 21–62; Richard Marsden. *The Text of the Old Testament in Anglo-Saxon England* (1995); Patrick McGurk. "The Oldest Manuscripts of the Latin Bible." *The Early Medieval Bible: Its Production, Decoration and Use.* Richard Gameson, ed. (1995) 1–23; Rosamond McKitterick. "Carolingian Bible Production: The Tours Anomaly." *The Early Medieval Bible: Its Production, Decoration and Use.* Richard Gameson, ed. (1994) 63–77; Rosamond McKitterick. *The Carolingians and the Written Word* (1989); Bruce M. Metzger. *The Early Versions of the New Testament: Their Origin, Transmission and Limitations* (1977); James J. O'Donnell. *Cassiodorus* (1979); David C. Parker. *Codex Bezae: An Early Christian Manuscript and Its Text* (1992); Jaroslav Pelikan. *The Reformation of the Bible/The Bible of the Reformation* (1996); William L. Petersen. *Tatian's Diatessaron: Its Creation, Dissemination, Significance, and History in Scholarship* (1994); Pierre Petitmengin. "Les plus anciens manuscrits de la Bible latine." *Le monde latin antique et la Bible.* Jacques Fontaine and Charles Pietri, eds. (1985) 89–128; Joseph M. Petzer. "The Latin Version of the New Testament." *The Text of the New Testament in Contemporary Research: Essays on the Status Quaestionis.* Bart D. Ehrman and Michael W. Holmes, eds. (2001) 113–30; H. F. D. Sparks. "The Latin Bible." *The Bible in Its Ancient and English Versions.* H. Wheeler Robinson, ed. (1940) 100–27; Mark Vessey. *Introduction to Cassiodorus: Institutions of Divine and Secular Learning on the Soul.* James W. Halporn, trans. (2004); Heinrich Josef Vogels. *Evangelium Colbertinum. Codex Latin 254 der Bibliothèque nationale zu Paris* (1953).

JENNIFER WRIGHT KNUST

VERSIONS, MEDIEVAL. Historians of ancient Christianity usually conclude with either the death of the emperor Justinian (565 CE) or that of Gregory the Great, who was Bishop of Rome from 590–604 CE. Efforts at reorganizing the Roman Empire, at reconciling

East and West, and at promoting a Catholic orthodoxy among the numerous regional forms of Christian faith and practice did not succeed. By the end of Gregory's pontificate the churches associated with Latin-speaking Rome and those allied with Greek-speaking Byzantium were permanently separated.

One can speak of three main periods between the end of the 6th cent. CE and the Reformation in the 16th cent. with its new editions of the Hebrew and Greek Testaments and widely disseminated vernacular translations. Between the 7th and 11th cent. the Latin VULGATE served as the Bible within the former Roman Empire. New editions, primarily of liturgical portions of the Bible, were produced among Christians on the periphery or well beyond the former imperial territories. During the High Middle Ages, from the 12th to early 14th cent., the return of vernacular preaching in continental Europe fueled the demand for vernacular biblical material. This lay renewal coincided with renewed scholarly activity, as universities developed and produced new commentaries on the Latin Bible. For this period, the definition of "Bible version" needs to be expanded, to include paraphrases and nonliterary presentations of biblical content. Finally, the 14th- to 15th-cent. Renaissance, with a new influx of ancient Greek manuscripts from the Greek-speaking East and a move toward literary use of vernacular languages, sought to reclaim the West's classical roots. These developments combined with a growing sense of nationalism and new printing technology to propel the creation of national-language Bibles. In each era, the cases examined are representative, not exhaustive.

A. Geographical Diversification: Missionary Translations at the Empire's Fringes

1. Period overview

In the early medieval period, translation work within the Roman Empire halted. The Vulgate, a translation commissioned to normalize the Latin text, had become the standard Bible. This magnum opus that initially ensured that Scripture would be accessible to all believers mutated into the preserve of the learned for the next millennium as Latin was no longer a language of the streets by the early 7th cent. The emerging vernaculars (which would become French, Italian, Castilian, Catalan, Occitan, Portuguese, and Galician, among others) were considered too rough and barbarous to serve as vehicles of divine truth. In this sense, postimperial Christianity resembled Islam, which does not recognize translations of the Qur'an as authoritative, hallowing even the very sounds in which the original text was delivered, not merely its content.

New translations in this era emerged on the edges and outside of the former empire's boundaries. In these areas, neither Greek nor Latin was common, so vernacular translations were the norm, but not universal. Although Ireland, e.g., had never been part of the Roman Empire, Latin was adopted as a liturgical language in order to make a theological point about unity with the rising papacy. Just as Latin transformed from a "people's tongue" to an elite language, so some of these new translations (Old Church Slavonic, Jacobite Syriac, and Ge'ez) would also fossilize into liturgical verbiage unintelligible to common people.

2. Northeastern Africa: Ge'ez

Egypt was one of the earliest areas in which Christianity developed. Many key thinkers and movements arose within Roman Egypt. As a result, most translations in the region predate the Middle Ages. As one moves southerly, however, to peoples living on the edge of this ancient Christian heartland, one encounters the Ge'ez (or Gecez) language. Translation of the Bible unfolded between the 5th and 7th cent. Ge'ez remains the liturgical language of the Ethiopian Orthodox Tewahedo Church. The church is "Non-Chalcedonian"; "tewahedo" means "unified" or "being one."

3. Persia: Jacobite Syriac

A Syrian church emerged in the region outside of the Roman Empire, to the east of Egypt. A Jacobite Syriac translation of the entire Bible was complete by 508 CE, although only isolated portions are extant today. The Jacobite Syrian church expanded eastward from Persia and Mesopotamia as Syrian expatriates formed churches in India. A tiny minority for centuries, the Syrians in India avoided religious assimilation only by divorcing their liturgical language from everyday life. Syriac became a calcified relic, a technical language with no existence apart from worship. Some texts had been inscribed on copper plates. These were destroyed in the 15th cent. by Portuguese missionaries who mistook their nature, thinking them to be idolatrous.

4. China: Paraphrastic "Jesus Sutras"

Alopen (mid-600s), a Nestorian bishop, arrived in China in 635. Over the following decades, the "Jesus Sutras" appeared. These works were not translations, strictly speaking, but a rendering of key biblical stories into Chinese language and thought. The documents, which make extensive use of Taoist concepts and imagery, have been described as weak paraphrases that abandon a distinctly Christian identity. On the other hand, the assertion of corporality in the Gospel stories, particularly of Jesus' resurrection, was a potentially offensive concept that maintained a distinctively Christian tone. It is not clear whether the Sutras were translated from Syrian or Sogdian (a widely used Central Asian trade language). The Sutras were not in use when Christian missionaries arrived in the late 16th cent. and were rediscovered in the early 20th cent.

5. Central Europe: Old Church Slavonic

Continuing counterclockwise around the periphery of the former Roman Empire, one encounters the late 9th-cent. mission work sponsored by the Byzantine court. Two Macedonian brothers, Cyril (ca. 826–69) and Methodius (ca. 815–85), answered an invitation to preach among the Slavic-speaking folk of Great Moravia. The notation they devised, the Glagolitic alphabet, was derived predominantly from Greek, but included a few modified Hebrew characters (to accommodate Slavic phonemes unrepresented by the Greek alphabet). These missionaries created a translation that would remain in use for almost a millennium. Although Roman missionaries from what is now Germany displaced this mission in 885, the language continued in use. Around 900 CE, a disciple of Methodius developed the Cyrillic alphabet. As elsewhere, an erstwhile vernacular tongue petrified into a formal shell of itself, used unaltered for centuries throughout Orthodox churches in Eastern Europe, even though the people using it spoke a variety of newer Slavic dialects derived from Old Church Slavonic. The language followed missionaries into Russia and Ukraine when the region converted to Christianity in 988. The translation remained in use until the 19th cent., despite the 1499 Russian Gennadievskaia Bible, translated under the patronage of Archbishop Gennady of Novgorod (late 1400s).

6. England: Anglo-Saxon

On the northwestern frontier, the evangelization of England got underway in the late 6th cent. Celtic Britons, many of whom had converted under Roman rule, were forced into marginal lands to the west and north. Fearing missionary work would encourage the invading Anglo-Saxons to stay, Celts left mission work to Roman-oriented priests. Efforts were very successful. Newly converted from paganism, this group of related Germanic dialects produced a wealth of Christian material. The early 8th-cent. *Ecclesiastical History* by Bede (672/3–735) provides evidence of a strong vernacular preaching tradition, in addition to the translation of liturgical portions. Sermon collections from the 10th and 11th cent. display creativity, as well as testimony to the fact that England was unified religiously before it was politically. Translation remained sporadic, with no one stating an intention to translate the entire corpus. Although a Germanic translation had been undertaken by Ulfilas (ca. 310–88), an Arian, this was deemed unacceptable to the trinitarian English evangelists sent to what is now northern Germany to proselytize among their distant relatives. Several German words, such as "Heiland" (meaning "savior"), which developed into technical terms, are loanwords from Anglo-Saxon.

B. Class Diversification: The High Medieval Turn from the Clergy

1. Period overview

The High Middle Ages were a time of great spiritual ferment. Vernacular preaching was revived, at the same time that formal learning moved out of the monasteries and cathedral chapters to the new universities, which promoted a scientific approach to study of the Latin Bible. Biblical paraphrases were commonly used in preaching with most translation based on the Latin Vulgate. These developments can all be associated with the emergence of large urban centers in Europe. They also indicate a shift from Scripture's being the preserve of an elite.

2. Urbanization and the rise of the mendicant preaching Orders

From the middle of the 11th cent., physical and social conditions in Europe altered sufficiently that it became possible, even necessary, to reestablish significant urban populations. Small by 21st-cent. standards, the cities that grew up a millennium ago marked a shift from subsistence agriculture to a society with sufficient food and other resources to support higher forms of culture. A salient feature of this new culture was the increased use of the vernacular for social and religious purposes.

Optimism arose concerning the possibility that someone outside a monastery might be preserved from God's wrath. Urbanites' spiritual needs were increasingly met by a new kind of monk who appeared in the 12th cent. Freed from cloister walls, these new Franciscan and Dominican friars preached and prayed in exchange for alms. The laity were not an accidental audience, but the intentional target group.

Biblical material circulated in many forms. Poetic versifications were especially popular in France, ranging from a 7,000-line blending of OT and NT stories, through a 20,800-line setting of Genesis, to a 43,000-

line text and commentary that appeared around 1300. Moderns may be skeptical of poetic expressions of revealed truth, but medieval folk valued poetry's power to engage memory and thus ensure retention. The 1271 Dutch Rijmbijbel was a poetic translation; a prose version followed in the next century.

Prose translations tended to be more modest, intended for liturgical needs. The Psalter was frequently among the first to be translated, as was the Revelation. The aims of the Spiritual Franciscans ensured that several chapters of John's Gospel were translated in French, Occitan, Catalan, and Italian; it also ensured that these translations were quashed when the movement was. The Roman hierarchy also took a dim view of Peter Waldo's 1170 rendering of several portions of the Bible, which were suppressed. There is an oblique reference in 1233 to a Spanish vernacular version, banned by the monarch. Later, the royal ban was lifted, and patronage extended to a new edition. Several Jewish scholars also translated portions of the OT into Castilian and Ladino (a Judeo-Spanish idiom). Icelanders, having converted to Christianity around 1000, translated from Genesis to 2 Kings around the middle of the 13th cent. Italian translators produced Gospel harmonies in the 13th and 14th cent.

3. Rationalization of education: the universities and Scripture

For centuries, Western knowledge had been preserved almost by accident, in the extremities of Christendom, Ireland and Spain. With a shift of territorial momentum from Islam to Christianity in the 11th cent., and growing Christian exposure to otherwise "lost" ancient teaching through contact with Islamic scholarship, learning began to take a new shape in Europe. Professional schools for training lawyers and physicians began in Italy and France; their methods were adapted by clerics, giving rise to the movement known as Scholasticism and the institution known as the university. Theological masters were expected to preach publicly and to comment methodically on books of the Bible as well as the theological compendium, the "Sentences of Peter Lombard." With the rise of the new analytic approaches to theology, the methodology underlying their study of Scripture shifted. With the influx of scientific treatises and philosophical works, some masters spent their careers in the arts faculty, never moving on to theology. The roots of modern "secular learning" could be said to appear in the 13th cent.

A group of scholars at the University of Paris managed to translate most of the Bible into French in the second quarter of the 13th cent. Another group attempted, about the same time, to normalize the Vulgate's text. New to the science of textual criticism, they encountered many difficulties. By the time they were done, the state of the text was even more confused than when they started. It is crucial to note, however, that the process of textual criticism, then in its infancy, would be

refined with time. The university context also changed the Bible as artifact. For centuries, the copying of biblical texts occurred in monasteries, as a spiritual exercise. Strong regional traditions of decorative artwork emerged. The 13th cent. saw the production of some of the most elaborate and costly illuminated Bibles. Yet, at the same time, the Bible was in transition. Even before the invention of movable type, a "book trade" in cheap copies for university students emerged. Narrower margins, smaller script, no illumination, and less substantial binding all contributed to the transformation of the Bible from a work of art into a commodity, a tool of the "learned guild."

This era is also significant for the emergence of a new presentation of the biblical text, the concordance. Accurate citation of biblical quotations could be difficult before the division of the text into smaller portions, especially of a passage buried in some of the larger canonical books. The 12th cent. saw "chapters" become the standard subdivisions of canonical books; versification began in the 13th cent., but standardization of these minute divisions took centuries. The concordance, developed ca. 1250, constitutes a radical reordering of the biblical text, a version without the "usual" flow from Genesis to Revelation. This new order allows for nonlinear access to the text, encouraging the exploration of broader themes, in addition to sequential study.

4. Nonliteral "popular" Bibles: cathedrals, plays, devotional artwork

Since the vast majority of medieval folk were illiterate, one wonders how they received biblical instruction, especially before the 12th-cent. return of vernacular preaching. Study of "versions" of the Bible in the Middle Ages should embrace nontextual forms of biblical representation. Principally these involve artwork, from the grand scale of the Gothic cathedral to the personal scale of an item capable of being carried in one's pocket, as well as street theater and popular plays on biblical themes that were performed in churches.

The High Middle Ages witnessed a transformation in technology and theology that resulted in a new liturgical building style, later termed *Gothic*. A key innovation was a load-bearing framework that allowed for a radical increase in the percentage of glass in the walls. Stained-glass windows portrayed wagonloads of biblical figures and saints, providing a substitute "Bible" for illiterate medieval persons. With as many as a dozen figures in a single window, and 200 windows in larger Gothic cathedrals, one could not escape the flood of spiritual imagery. Friezes over entrances depicted cycles of stories meant to circumvent the viewers' inability to read the text.

A verbal, yet largely unwritten form of late medieval biblical presentation was the morality play cycle. Many of these street dramas were presented for years (even centuries) before the text was written down. The cycle performed in the English city of York, perhaps the most famous, was the capstone of the city's annual Corpus Christi celebration. Each of the city's craft guilds presented one of forty-seven plays, each a vernacular rendition of a key biblical story from Creation to the Last Judgment.

Didactic devotional art also served to reinforce biblical stories for an illiterate laity. Fairly common among financially secure 11th- and 12th-cent. urbanites were small carved ivory diptychs. A common design involved two panels, hinged to close for safe transport, then opened when in private as an aid to contemplation. Images depicted series of biblical events, such as groupings focused on Jesus' birth or death. Illiteracy was less of a barrier to devotion with this personalized visualization of the text.

C. National Diversification: The Renaissance and the Rise of the Nation-State

1. Period overview

Nationalism emerged in the 14th through 16th cent. as a powerful organizing force in European society. France was perhaps the first nation in which political and ethno-linguistic lines became roughly coterminous. England and Spain followed suit. Language played a political role. Henry IV spoke in English at his 1399 coronation, the first king to do since 1066. Henry V, conveying news of his victory at Agincourt, wrote home in English, not diplomatic Latin. State bureaucracies, crude by our standards, nonetheless created settings in which dialects were unwelcome and normalized administrative languages the goal. In the 15th cent., England's Chancery began to enforce standardized spelling in legal documents. At the same time, Renaissance scholars restored classical learning, focusing on languages ancient and modern.

2. John Wycliffe and the English Bible

This towering figure in the English language has inspired much hagiography in the six centuries since his work of organizing the translation of the entire Bible into English. In trying to answer the question of the extent to which he was directly involved in the English Bible's creation, it is easy to forget that the titles "diplomat" and "bureaucrat" apply as readily to John Wycliffe (ca. 1320–84) as "academic" and "cleric." The overlap of administrative and scholarly roles is significant, especially in light of the impending dismissal of French as the language of government. Parallel to the return of English to national prominence was the growing belief that vernacular tongues were indeed capable of transmitting both the subtle and magnificent aspects of biblical truth. Wycliffe appears not have had complete confidence in English's power of precise expression, as the translation's syntax more closely resembled that of the Latin Vulgate from which it was translated, than common English. Nevertheless, a robust translation, including phrases that have entered the general

English word-hoard, came into being. *See* VERSION, WYCLIFFE'S.

3. Movable type printing press as change facilitator

The rising power of normalized national languages was reinforced by the invention of the movable type printing press. The press, however, created thorny issues for the upper clergy. A heretic's preaching could be silenced readily enough, and a relatively small number of manuscript documents could be hunted down and destroyed. Once a heretical document was printed, it would be near impossible to retract and suppress it, giving the error a greater impression of substance.

The (relative) mass production of Bibles led to further changes in the artifact. Early printed editions retained the "pen-flourished initials," hand-done lettering that resembled the somber illustration of the cheap, "tool"-type Bibles created by the university publishers. Wood-block illustrations became popular; Albrecht Dürer (1471–1528) is perhaps the most famous artist of this new genre.

4. Salient Renaissance translations

While the Czech proto-reformer Jan Hus (1369–1415) was burned at the Council of Konstanz, his followers still had access to a 14th-cent. Psalter. The English Bible fought to regain legal status, but local language translations were common in late 15th-cent. Europe. While the first printed book was a Latin Bible (no less than ninety-two editions of the Vulgate appeared before 1500), its presence stimulated demand for non-Latin versions. The first of those was a 1466 German Bible, also derived from the Vulgate. At least twenty-two whole text German Bibles appeared by 1522. Versions appeared rapidly thereafter in Italian (1471), French (NT in 1477, OT in 1487), Dutch (OT in 1477, minus the psalms, which appeared in 1480; the NT was delayed until 1522), and Czech (separate versions in 1488 and 1489). A 1478 Spanish translation may have been banned and burned, but it did not set a precedent against the vernacular, as an approved version arrived in 1492. Liturgical portions were translated into Serbo-Croat in 1495, a fascinating development in light of papal approval of an Old Church Slavonic liturgy for Croatian churches.

One must avoid the misconception that the rise of normalized national translations of the entire Bible meant ready access for the entire population. Not only were literacy rates low by modern standards but also the cost of a Bible remained beyond the reach of anyone but the reasonably wealthy. What is important is that increasingly accurate and eloquent translations of the Bible were now available in vernacular tongues. Those who could not afford their own copy could listen to the reading of someone else's copy, whether in private or in church.

5. Suppression of regional languages

Another side of the emergence of national languages is the suppression of regional dialects. Nationalism actually narrowed the range of languages that were acceptable candidates for Bible translation. Many minority languages never received a Bible translation before the 19th or 20th cent.; the Channel Island dialects never have. The reason is straightforward. The political integrity of the new nations could easily be undermined by the potency of a mixture of religion and language, two of the strongest markers of self-identity. Occitan began to suffer under the extension of French hegemony in the 14th cent. In that case, the regional language was associated with heresy (both the Spiritual Franciscans and the Cathars), thus attracting government force against its use.

In the case of Catalan, the process of downplaying the dialect was prolonged, reaching its peak after the period covered in this article and lasting into the 20th cent. Although several Catalan translations were created in the latter Middle Ages, none were made as the rise of "national" self-consciousness crested in the region, in the wake of Spain's unification after the success of the reconquista. The 1469 marriage of Ferdinand of Aragon and Isabella of Castille and the 1492 fall of Muslim-held Granada set the new nation's agenda. If vernacular translations were, among other things, assertions of national hegemony and pride by emerging central monarchies, then the separatist implications of regional dialects could not be ignored.

6. Preservation and transmission of texts

Brief consideration needs to be given to a change in those having care for the biblical texts. The life and work of Renaissance textual scholar Desiderius Erasmus (1469–1536) illustrates this basic shift. He was raised among the "Brethren of the Common Life," a key manifestation of the so-called "Modern Devotion," a movement that increased pressure for good vernacular translations. Whereas preservation and transmission of biblical texts had been the realm of monks, with the Renaissance, this task was increasingly engaged by humanist scholars. To the core task, the academics added redaction. Erasmus' 1516 publication of a critical Greek NT set the stage for a new round of Bible translations, this time from the original language. The 1522 German NT by Martin Luther (1483–1546) used this edition. Luther's Bible exerted perhaps the strongest influence of any translation in establishing what would be normative speech for its host language, making it the high water mark of early modern national language translations.

Bibliography: Lynne Long. *Translating the Bible: From the Seventh to the Seventeenth Century* (2002); James H. Morey. "Peter Comestor, Biblical Paraphrase, and the Medieval Popular Bible." *Spec* 68 (1993) 6–35;

John Rogerson, ed. *The Oxford Illustrated History of the Bible* (2001).

C. MARK STEINACHER

VERSIONS, MODERN (NON-ENGLISH). Although English has the greatest number of versions of the Bible available, English is not the only language or even the original language of the Christian Scriptures. The original biblical languages of Greek, Hebrew, and Aramaic have been translated into over 2,000 languages and dialects. The Christian church believes that it has a mandate to take the Scriptures, as God's Word, to people of every land and language (Matt 28:19-20). Individual translators or translation organizations appeal to a number of scriptural references as the basis of their mandate.

First, translation is rooted in the incarnation, the notion that the Word became a human being in the person of Jesus and lived as a fully human being, both linguistically and culturally (John 1:14; Phil 2:7). In his incarnation, Jesus the living Word of God offers a prime example that the gospel of salvation was communicated in human language that people easily understood.

Second, on the first Pentecost, the coming of the Spirit of God manifested itself in the miracle of the communication of the gospel in many languages (Acts 2:1-13). The comprehensive list of languages represented at that time encompassed the whole of the ancient Mediterranean and Middle Eastern world.

Third, Scripture itself is linked to the biblical hope that one day God will be praised by everyone in every language (Rom 14:11; Rev 5:9).

Rowan Williams, the archbishop of Canterbury (2002–), highlighted the obvious and pervasive investment that Christianity has in translation during his address at the service of the bicentenary of the British and Foreign Bible Society in 2004 (Batalden et al.). He stated that Christianity does not have a sacred language, but that Christians are convinced that every human language can bear scriptural revelation. He described translation as an act of faith that God's word and the narrative of Jesus' life can be told in every human language, past or future.

Just as the Word of God became a human being and lived with the people he served, the written Bible has been translated for the peoples in a fully human context, both linguistically and culturally. Hence, Bible translation into indigenous languages is always the re-enactment of the incarnation. It is a manifestation of the mission of the church. Not only do diverse peoples read, listen, understand, and respond to the biblical communication from their cultural perspectives but also God's living Word engages, judges, and transforms the cultures, lives, and destiny of the readers and listeners.

There are numerous organizations with involvement in translation of the Bible into languages other than English, including Evangel Bible Translators, Institute for Bible Translation, International Bible Society, Lutheran Bible Translators, Pioneer Bible Translators, United Bible

Societies and the 146 national Bible Societies globally, Wycliffe Bible Translators International and Summer Institute of Linguistics, Bibles International, Word for the World, and World Bible Translation Center.

    A. Scriptures in Languages other than English
    B. Revision of Existing Non-English Translations
    C. Multiple Versions for Different Audiences
    D. Technology and Translation
    E. Interconfessional Translation
    F. Translating Divine Names
    Bibliography

A. Scriptures in Languages other than English

By the time Johannes Gutenberg printed the Latin VULGATE version (1456), the Bible had been translated, either partly or entirely, into a total of thirty-three languages: twenty-two European languages, seven Asian languages, and four African languages. One of these was English, with the first meaningful English Bible translated by John Wycliffe in ca. 1382 (see VERSION, WYCLIFFE'S). Two hundred years later, the Bible had been translated into a total of seventy languages: forty-eight European languages, thirteen Asian languages, four African languages, three North American languages, and two Latin American languages. In the first quarter of the 19th cent., all or part of the Bible had been translated into approximately 125 languages. By the second quarter of the 19th cent., the Bible had been translated into a total of 205 languages, and by the turn of the 21st cent., the number had reached 2,261.

As of the end of 2008 part of the Bible or the entire Bible have been translated into a total of 2,479 different languages and dialects. The OT and NT of the Bible have been translated into 451 languages, of which 128 languages also have the deuterocanonical books. In addition, one of the Testaments (usually the NT) has been translated into another 1,185 languages, and at least one complete book of the Bible has been translated into an additional 843 languages. These languages represent about 97 percent of the population of the world. At the beginning of 2009, there were 209 first translations being prepared for about 3 percent of the world's population that have had no written form of the Bible.

B. Revision of Existing Non-English Translations

As well as original translations, existing translations need to be revised. There are several reasons for this. First, today's Bible translators have access to better Hebrew, Aramaic, and Greek texts from which to translate. For instance, in 1947–56 a series of most important discoveries of ancient Scriptures, the DEAD SEA SCROLLS, were found in Khirbet QUMRAN and the areas near Masada, Nahal Hever, Wadi Murabbaat, Nahel Se'elim, Khirbet Mird, and Nahal Mishmar. These contain the complete manuscripts of the OT (except the book of Esther) from the 3rd cent. BCE to the 1st cent. CE. Due to these discoveries, philologists have been able

to study more ancient manuscripts, and modern translations have been based on their work. For example, in the formal Indonesian Bible translation, *Terjemahan Baru* ("New Translation"), sections that were integral parts of the texts in the first edition (1974) but not found in the best and most ancient manuscripts are now enclosed in square brackets in the second edition (1997), e.g., the doxology of the Lord's Prayer (Matt 6:13b), and the longer ending of Mark (16:9-20).

Second, developments and findings in the studies of biblical languages and interpretation have given exegetes greater knowledge of the meaning of the original texts, which enable translators to produce a better-quality translation that is faithful to the meaning of the source texts. Increased use of lexicons, Bible dictionaries, and exegetical commentaries has influenced the translation process. For example, understanding of the meaning of the original text based on exegetical interpretation made the second edition of the Indonesian Bible more accurate. In Mark 9:5, e.g., the Indonesian words *kami ... kami* ("we [exclusive] ... we [exclusive]") have been changed to *kita ... kami* ("we [inclusive] ... we [exclusive]"). The translators' decision between exclusive and inclusive forms of this pronoun was made on the basis of sound exegesis of the biblical texts in the original languages.

Third, since the beginning of the 19th cent., the era of the modern missionary movement, many missionaries have translated the Bible. However, in recent times, more use has been made of translation theory (see BIBLE TRANSLATION THEORY). Findings in the fields of linguistics and communication have given us a better understanding of the translator's task. For example, translators are able to be guided by understanding the strengths and weaknesses of the dynamic functional-equivalence translation method, compared to the strengths and weaknesses of the traditional method (formal equivalence). The dynamic functional-equivalence translation method has given us translations that are both faithful to the original meaning and probable intent of the source texts, presented in the most natural and fluent forms of the target languages. These translations are used for mission, evangelism, and private devotion. The traditional method (formal equivalence) serves the needs of churches in public worship, liturgical use, and Christian nurture. Another recent feature is the use of native speakers as translators.

The history of Bible translation in the Malagasy language of Madagascar illustrates the change in translation practices over the generations. Malagasy is a living synthesis of Indonesian, African, and Arabic elements, and is the only Polynesian-African culture in the world. The original Malagasy Bibles, in Catholic and Protestant versions, are very literal. The first Protestant OT portion was published in 1828, the NT was published in 1830, and the full Protestant Bible was first published in 1835 and revised in 1887. The Roman Catholic version of the NT was published in 1884, and the OT followed in

1924. These outdated translations had become difficult for modern readers to understand.

In order to better serve the Malagasy people, the Malagasy Common Language Bible translation project was established, under the auspices of the Malagasy Bible Society. Three full-time translators, a Catholic priest trained in Rome and two representatives from other churches, were involved in translating the Bible into modern Malagasy beginning in 1984. Their work was checked by eight reviewers, two from each of the four largest churches in Madagascar: the Roman Catholic, Lutheran, Reformed, and Episcopal churches. Another thirty reviewers were drawn from the smaller churches, so that all church leaders had the opportunity to see the new translation as it was being prepared and to make their comments. The priest-translator explained that this translation is especially for young people; it is much clearer and easier to understand.

Fourth, revisions help keep up with the changes in the target language. All living languages change. Some words become obsolete, new ones enter the language, and other words change meaning. Time and usage determine which new terms are accepted and which are not. Unless our translations reflect current usage, there is a good chance of communicating incorrect and unintended meanings to the readers.

For example, the Chinese phrase *xi-xiao* ("happy-laugh") from Luke 6:21*b* ("Blessed are you who weep now, for you will laugh") in the Chinese Union version (1919) was replaced by a more modern Chinese phrase, *huan-xiao* ("joy-laugh"), in the Revised Chinese Union Version (2006). Similarly in Vietnamese, the translation of the phrase "precious things" (NRSV, "treasure chests") of Matt 2:11 had to be revised because the original phrase had acquired a profane meaning.

Ideally, the source texts for all Bible translations are the original languages—the *Biblia Hebraica Stuttgartensia* for Hebrew and the latest edition of the Nestle-Aland *Novum Testamentum Graece* or *The Greek New Testament* (UBS)—especially if the translations are meant for serious study or training and for Christian nurture. However, there may be local limitations, such as in a minority language situation, where the mother-tongue translation team will not have knowledge of the source languages and may also have limited access to other translations. In these cases, it is highly recommended that each team member have at least two versions with which to work, preferably a formal equivalent translation either in the national language or in an international language (or both) as the base text(s), and a functional equivalent translation in the national or international language (or both) as the model text(s). These two types of translations will serve as windows into the form and meaning of the source texts. In this situation, the team would also need references such as Bible dictionaries, translators' handbooks, and audio-visual resources that give translators an appreciation of the landscape, plants, animals, and artifacts referred to in Scripture. In addition, the translation consultant will have to check the translation drafts more carefully on the basis of the original biblical languages.

C. Multiple Versions for Different Audiences

Previously, only one Bible translation for an individual language was prepared to cater to all kinds of audiences. It is now understood that in Bible translation there is no "one size that fits all." It is unrealistic to think that one translation will meet the needs of everyone from all walks of life. For each subculture and segment of the society, translations should be adjusted to its style of communication, its level of understanding, and its mastery of language in order to facilitate reasonably good communication and to grasp the meaning of the Bible.

A literal translation is a formal correspondence translation that attempts as much as possible to retain the forms of the original languages, though often at the expense of naturalness. It was taken for granted for centuries that only literal translations could be considered to be serious translations (e.g., the King James Version), and numerous Bible translations were prepared according to this translation philosophy.

A functional equivalent translation attempts to provide a meaning-based translation on the literary level or on the common language level (e.g., Good News Translation). There are more than 200 languages from around the globe that have Bible versions prepared after this model.

For some languages and cultures, a cultural reinterpretation translation is appropriate. This transfers meaning from the biblical language-culture context to a modern local language-culture. For example, long before the modern transcription of selected biblical passages into Australian language and culture (in 1989), an Indonesian pastor from North Sulawesi reinterpreted "I am the true vine" (John 15:1) as "*Akulah Cengkeh, Pala dan Kopra yang Benar*" (literally, "I am the true clove, nutmeg, and copra"), referring to the three main agricultural products of that island.

There are still thousands of language groups that have no written language. Hence, a first step will be, among other things, to start by putting the oral language into a written system. One example is the Lunga language of Ranonga in the Solomon Islands, where a native speaker spent six years writing down Lunga and then, along with his team, translated the Lunga NT. This was published by the Bible Society of the South Pacific in 2004.

In addition, other formats are possible. Depending on their needs, the target audience may also require liturgical translations, study Bibles, diglots, triglots, polyglots, interlinear Bibles, Bible software, interactive Bibles, translations for new readers or new literates, Bible comics, translations for teenagers, children's Bibles, Braille Bibles, and so forth.

Non-print Bibles are also useful in contexts where there is widespread illiteracy or an oral culture. Even in societies where literacy is widespread, there can be a generation that, due the pervasive dominance of television and other electronic media, prefers to watch and listen rather than read. In order to reach out to people who have not received the biblical message through conventional means, a number of agencies and publishers have made Bibles available using the latest advancements in audio technology. For example, the MegaVoice project has developed a self-contained device that can hold a recorded audio message. It can fit into a small pocket, cannot be taped over, does not need electricity to run, and does not need a player. The Talk Bible, developed by the Japan Bible Society, is aimed at people with hearing impairment and is also useful for people who travel. The whole Bible can be loaded into it, and listeners can select the passage to which they want to listen.

D. Technology and Translation

Many translation projects around the world these days are utilizing computers for their work, as this increases the efficiency and effectiveness of the process. Although there are a few exceptions, it is inevitable that Bible translation projects will be computerized. In places where there is no electricity, solar panels with a deep cycle battery and inverter can be used to run a computer.

Specialist software can be used to assist the Bible translator. There are now half a dozen commercial Bible software programs available. One of these, Paratext, allows translators to upload their own translation drafts to scroll along with the Hebrew, Aramaic, and Greek counterparts, and a number of well-known translations in a number of international languages.

However, it should be noted that machine translation is still not capable of dealing with compound and complex sentence constructions, and the multifaceted contents and multilayered teaching in the Bible, without close checking by an experienced translator and extensive testing with speakers of the language.

E. Interconfessional Translation

The old tradition was to have separate Bible translations for Protestants, Roman Catholics, and the Orthodox. Interconfessional cooperation in Bible translation work between the Protestant and the Roman Catholic churches increased significantly after the joint statement "Guiding Principles for Interconfessional Cooperation in Translating the Bible" was issued by United Bible Society and the Vatican Secretariat for Christian Unity in 1968 (later revised in 1987). An example is the Indonesian Bible Society's interconfessional Indonesian Bible published in 1974, with the deuterocanonical books following in 1975 and a second edition of the NT in 1997. Revision of the OT and deuterocanonical books is currently underway. The Japan Bible

Society first published the Japanese Interconfessional Bible in 1987. The Bible Society of Malaysia published its first interconfessional Malay Bible and deuterocanonical books in 1996. There is also an interconfessional translation in each of the eight major languages of the Philippines published by the Philippines Bible Society: Tagalog, Cebuano, Hiligaynon, Ilocano, Bikol, Pangasinan, Kapampangan, and Samarenyo. The Pakistan Bible Society has just started the Urdu Bible interconfessional translation project.

The Orthodox tradition has a larger deuterocanon than the Roman Catholic. The LXX is the base text for the OT, and the base text for the Orthodox NT is the Byzantine or ecclesiastical text. Although at the moment we do not have guidelines for interconfessional translation with the Orthodox, there are many ongoing translation projects with Orthodox involvement, primarily in European and Middle Eastern languages including Arabic, Armenian, Finnish, Modern Greek, Latvian, Russian, and Syriac.

F. Translating Divine Names

In English, the majority of translations has agreed upon "God" as the equivalent for 'elohim (אֱלֹהִים). However, in many areas of the world, the acceptable translation of divine names is an area of debate in Bible translation. In Chinese, there are two major terms—*shen* and *shangdi*—used for the Christian God. This conflict also has the appearance of an international struggle, because the lines were drawn between British and German missionaries (pro-*shangdi*) and American missionaries (pro-*shen*). The British decided in November 1848 against the use of *shen*, whereas the American Bible Society (ABS) in November 1850 formed a subcommittee that finally decided on *shen*. Chinese Bibles are still published in separate *shen* and *shangdi* editions.

Korean Bible translation has faced a similar challenge. John Ross of Scotland translated 'elohim by using the traditional Korean term *Hananim*, "Lord of Heaven" (1911). The Catholic Church, which came to Korea a hundred years earlier than the Protestant Church, used the term *Chonju*, "Heavenly Lord." From 1804 to 1904, Korean Scriptures were published in two versions, the *Chonju* version and the *Hananim* version. When the Korean NT was published in 1904, *Hananim* was finally settled on as the term for God.

A similar challenge is presently facing Mongolian Bible translation. There has been significant disagreement within the Mongolian Christian community regarding the correct terms to use for the name of God and other key theological terms. The first meaning-based Mongolian NT, published in 1990, uses a composite name for God, *Yertentsin Ezen*, which translates literally as "Master of the Universe." Their conviction was that new Christians should not be confused into equating the biblical God with the Buddha, through use of the local term for "Buddha," *burhan* (*bur* means *burhesen* or "covered, everything, the whole universe"; *han* means "king, ruler"). However, another group that prepared a formal-equivalence Bible in Mongolian, first published in 2000, insisted that the local term *burhan* is suitable to refer to the biblical God.

The Indonesian and Malay Bible translators also face challenges relating to divine names. These countries have a Muslim majority, and there are differing positions regarding the use of divine names in this context. One position held by one evangelistic organization and its followers is that Christians cannot use *Allah* (the name of God in Islam). One such organization systematically changed the divine names in the Indonesian formal translation published by the Indonesian Bible Society so that Jesus is written as *Yesua* ("Joshua") instead of the widely accepted form *Yesus*, and Jesus Christ is rendered *Yesua Hamasiah* instead of *Yesus Kristus*. The Tetragrammaton (YHWH) is transliterated as *YAHWE* instead of *TUHAN* (LORD), and God is transliterated as *Eloim* (not *Elohim*) instead of *Allah*. These changes have created problems and confusion among Christians. Other organizations and Bible scholars argue that *Allah* is an Arabic loanword, the cognate of the Hebrew names of God ʾel (אֵל), ʾelohim, and ʾeloah (אֱלוֹהַּ) in the OT. It can be argued that Arab Christians have been using *Allah* from before the dawn of Islam, that *Allah* was used by Christian theologians writing in Arabic, and that the Christian usage of *Allah* predates Islam, so it is appropriate for Christians to use. *Allah* has been in use continuously since the very first Malay translation of Matthew's Gospel (1629).

One of the reasons for the controversy about divine names is that some missionaries and Christian workers think that adopting local divine names can lead to confusion and syncretism. However, Lamin Sanneh, a West African theologian and professor of Missions and World Christianity at Yale University, has noted that there are important differences between Christianized African societies in which indigenous names for God have been retained and those in which it was thought necessary to borrow a foreign word. Sanneh argues that the former show greater levels of church growth, of Christian stability, and of social vigor and engagement within the churches.

Bibliography: Stephen Batalden, Kathleen Cann, and John Dean, eds. *Sowing the Word: The Cultural Impact of the British and Foreign Bible Society* (2004); Liana Lupas and Erroll F. Rhodes, eds. *Scriptures of the World* (1996); Eugene A. Nida, ed. *The Book of a Thousand Tongues*. 2nd ed. (1972); Lamin Sanneh. *Translating the Message: The Missionary Impact on Culture* (2008); Philip C. Stine, ed. *Bible Translation and the Spread of the Church: The Last 200 Years* (1992); Jan de Waard and Eugene A. Nida. *Functional Equivalence in Bible Translating: From One Language to Another* (1986).

DAUD SOESILO

VERSIONS, SLAVONIC sluh-von´ik. Cyril and Methodius, the apostles to the Slavs, invented the Cyrillic alphabet in the mid-9th cent. CE in order to translate the Sunday lectionary into Old Church Slavonic. By the 12th cent., this translation had been expanded into a "short lectionary" and a "long lectionary." The four Gospels were translated into Old Slavonic in the 10th cent. The oldest manuscripts of Acts, the Catholic Epistles, and Revelation date from the 12th cent., though these books may have been translated earlier. *See* VERSIONS, MEDIEVAL.

MARK DELCOGLIANO

VERSIONS, SYRIAC sihr´ee-ak. During the 1st millennium CE, Syriac—the native Aramaic dialect of EDESSA and its surrounding region—became widely used across Christianized areas of Asia and was the focus of Bible translation projects. The tendency from the 5th to the early 8th cent. was to revise previous translations in order to follow authoritative sources more literally, even if this meant abandoning native Syriac idiom (for the Christian Palestinian Aramaic version, formerly known as the Palestinian Syriac version, *see* VERSIONS, ANCIENT).

The earliest Syriac Bible translation is probably the OT PESHITTA, a translation based mainly on a Hebrew original close to the MT, with occasional influence from the LXX. The books of Chronicles, whose status was questioned in the Syriac church, show the greatest textual divergence from the MT. The OT Peshitta was preserved by Christians, but without any tradition of when and by whom it was translated. A date in the 1st or 2nd cent. is likely. The fact that the translation was made from Hebrew, combined with various indications of Jewish exegesis, points to a Jewish or Jewish-Christian origin. The Peshitta OT boasts the two earliest dated biblical manuscripts: British Library Add. 14512 (a palimpsest of Isaiah from 459/60 CE) and British Library Add. 14425 (a pentateuchal manuscript from 463/4 CE). The earliest manuscript of the entire Syriac OT, B21 Inferiore of the Ambrosian Library, Milan, comes from the 7th cent. and lacks 1 Esdras, Tobit, and the Prayer of Manasseh, but includes *4 Ezra*, the *Apocalypse of Baruch*, and Book 6 of Josephus' *Jewish War*. An authoritative edition of the Peshitta OT has been produced under the auspices of the Peshitta Institute, Leiden, which is also producing a concordance and an English translation.

In 615–17 CE, Paul of Tella produced the Syrohexapla, a Syriac translation based on the Greek HEXAPLA. The Syrohexapla is useful for scholars since it is a nearly literal rendering of Origen's revised LXX text, preserves readings of the later Jewish Greek revisers (*see* AQUILA'S VERSION; SYMMACHUS; THEODOTION), and retains some of the critical signs that were lost in Greek manuscripts of the Hexapla.

Toward the end of his life, Jacob of Edessa (ca. 640–708 CE) produced his own revision of the OT Peshitta on the basis of Greek texts, aiming to include material from both Syriac and Greek traditions. Two notable manuscripts, both dated to 705 CE, are Bibliothèque Nationale Paris 26 (Pentateuch) and British Library Add. 14429 (Samuel).

Although scholars in the past have debated the relative order of the origin of the DIATESSARON and Old Syriac Gospels, the priority of the Diatessaron is now widely accepted. The Diatessaron was produced by Tatian ca. 170–75 CE, most probably in Syriac rather than Greek. Evidence of its circulation includes its use by Ephrem in the 4th cent. and Theodoret of Cyrrhus' claim in the 5th cent. to have found more than 200 copies in his diocese. The Diatessaron is now only accessible through indirect sources, by far the most important of which is the commentary by Ephrem.

The Old Syriac Gospels, a relatively free translation that originated some time between the 2nd and 4th cent., are represented by two manuscripts: Codex Curetonianus (British Library Add. 14451, 5th cent., preserving significant parts of Matt 1–8; 10–23; Luke 2–3; 7–24; John 1; 3–8; 14; as well as Mark 16:17-20) and Codex Sinaiticus (Sin. Syr. 30, late 4th or early 5th cent., palimpsest, preserving parts of every chap. of the Gospels except Matt 7). There are significant differences between these two manuscripts, most notably that Sinaiticus ends Mark at 16:8. In general, Sinaiticus preserves readings that are typologically earlier than those of Curetonianus. Many scholars hold that Armenian texts provide evidence for Old Syriac versions of Acts and the Pauline corpus. The Old Syriac Gospels show some significant textual agreements with Codex Bezae and the Old Latin Gospels.

The Peshitta NT originated at the end of the 4th or the beginning of the 5th cent. It became the ecclesiastically accepted NT text, and its earliest manuscripts come from the end of the 5th cent. It represents an attempt to conform the Syriac translation more closely to the Greek and shows some affinity to the Byzantine Greek text. The original Peshitta NT did not include the Pericope Adulterae (John 7:53–8:11), 2 Peter, 2 and 3 John, Jude, and Revelation. The five NT books not represented in the Peshitta appear in a later translation, which may be the Philoxenian version, produced in 507/8 CE under the sponsorship of Philoxenus, bishop of Mabbog. Apart from these five books, the Philoxenian version of the NT is not extant as a continuous text, though some of its renderings may be gleaned from Philoxenus' own biblical citations. In 616 CE, in conjunction with the creation of the Syrohexapla, Thomas of Harkel produced the Harclean version, a literalistic scholarly translation covering the whole NT and including a critical apparatus. The marginal readings of the Harclean version are particularly important in Acts where they often agree with the "Western" text.

Bibliography: P. B. Dirksen. "The Old Testament Peshitta." *Mikra.* Martin Jan Mulder, ed. (1988) 255–97; Peter B. Dirksen. *An Annotated Bibliography of the Peshitta of the Old Testament* (1989); Michael P. Weitzman. *The Syriac Version of the Old Testament: An Introduction* (1999).

P. J. WILLIAMS

VESPASIAN ves-pay′zhuhn. Titus Flavius Vespasianus (9–79 CE; r. 69–79) became EMPEROR of the ROMAN EMPIRE as the last of a series of rulers during a year of civil war. He founded the Flavian Dynasty, which embraced the reigns of his sons, Titus and Domitian. Vespasian was less well-born than his predecessors, including both the Julio-Claudians and the three unsuccessful claimants in 69 CE. His appointment late in Nero's reign as the commander tasked with the suppression of a revolt in Judea placed him in a position to launch his bid for the supreme power.

Earlier in his career, Vespasian prospered through the patronage of Claudius, only to be checked by the rise of Agrippina, wife of Claudius and mother of Nero. After her death, Vespasian was able to return to favor. His competence as a general (especially in Britain) and administrator (above all, in financial matters) made him useful, while his low birth rendered him less threatening to those in power.

Embarking upon his reign without the advantage of high birth, Vespasian shrewdly publicized divine omens proclaiming his ascendancy and procured a bloc grant of powers as diverse means of validating his claims and solidifying his authority. He made a virtue of his low origins, projecting an air of competence and civility while emphasizing traditional values like simplicity in his mode of life, setting an example that others were to follow. Vespasian's political message was advertised through his extensive building program, including the Colosseum, erected on land taken from Nero's palace complex. Nero's extravagance and the ravages of civil war played havoc with public finances, a situation Vespasian worked hard to amend. Fiscal considerations inform much of his provincial policy, though he also seems to have built on the inclusive inclinations of his predecessor Claudius.

Vespasian's shrewd self-confidence is manifested in his policy of succession. Having already helped his elder son, Titus, achieve success as a general, he appointed him to the powerful post of praetorian prefect. By contrast, he kept his younger son, Domitian, well away from the military. His success in reconciling the contradictions inherent in his position emerges, paradoxically, in the sensitivity felt over the question of his post-mortem deification. He was eventually proclaimed a god, but the initial hesitation is in part explained by the power of the image Vespasian created for himself as a modest, unassuming, civil emperor. *See* JEWISH WARS.

Bibliography: Barbara Levick. *Vespasian* (1999).

THOMAS A. J. MCGINN

VESSELS [כְּלִי keli; σκεῦος skeuos]. *Vessel* is represented by a very broad range of categories, concepts, and images, and is reflected in the biblical text by a rather extensive vocabulary across the range of both Testaments. There are nearly as many biblical terms translated "vessel" by the NRSV, and others not so translated, as there are vessel forms known from antiquity. No fewer than forty-eight Hebrew and Greek terms contribute to the subject: at least thirty-three in the OT and fifteen in the LXX and NT. While translations of the terms and the uses to which the various vessels were put vary, all are legitimately subsumed under the category "vessel."

Perhaps the most common single term, basic to the discussion, is keli, a term that appears in the OT 325 times and reflects a rather broad range of nuances, including "vessel," "utensil," "implement," and "weapon." The use of ceramic vessels was integral to the everyday life of the people of the Bible, and that is reflected both in the biblical material and in the vast amounts of pottery that archaeological excavations in those regions have uncovered; the majority of these would be classified as receptacles. But vessels made from other materials—such as stone, wood, leather, bronze, silver, and gold—and vessels used for purposes other than the normal domestic use are also known through those same sources. Keli is used with a variety of qualifiers that express materials from which or by whom they were made.

In a number of OT texts the term keli is used generally to refer to the "vessels of the Temple" (NRSV, "of the LORD's house") (e.g., Jer 27:16, 18-19, 21; 28:3, 6), many of which were made of gold, silver, bronze, or wood overlaid with precious metal. As there was a variety of materials from which vessels were made, so there was a wide variety of vessel forms and functions. Generally, those of the OT were used for either domestic or liturgical purpose. In the former category, liquid and food storage are examples (1 Kgs 17:12, 14; 2 Kgs 4:2-6). The latter category would include the sacred furnishings of the tabernacle and Temple, as well as the variety of utensils used in the exercise of the cult (Exod 25–30; 1 Sam 2:14; 1 Kgs 7:45; Ezra 1:7-11; Jer 52:18). Gideon is recorded as having used "jars" (kadh כַּד) containing torches in his defeat of the Midianites; but this might also be considered liturgical since it seems to be understood as holy war (Judg 6–7; especially 7:15-20). Jeremiah was instructed to store his property deed in "an earthenware vessel (keli-kharesh כְּלִי־חָרֶשׂ) in order that they may last for a long time" (Jer 32:14; compare the storage of Dead Sea Scrolls). Figurative use of vessel terminology is to be noted: Job 38:37; Ps 31:12 [Heb. 31:13]; Eccl 12:6; Jer 25:15; Lam 4:2; Ezek 12:7; Hos 8:8; Zech 12:2.

The LXX uses skeuos generally as the counterpart to keli, and the NT employs the term twenty-two times, more than any other single term in the semantic field. Skeuos can refer to a container of some sort ("jar"; John 19:29), but like its OT complement, it seems to be used more broadly, in reference to "belongings" and "property" (Matt 12:29; Luke 17:31). It is also used figuratively of human beings in several texts: Rom 9:21-22, "objects of wrath that are made for destruction"; 2 Tim 2:20-21, with the metaphorical modifiers "gold and silver," "wood and clay," "special," "dedicated and useful"; 1 Thess 4:4, "control your own body"; 1 Pet 3:7, "paying honor to the woman as the weaker sex." As in the case of the OT, a variety of more specific terms referencing different kinds of containment vessels—different in form and function—is encountered in the NT.

JOHN I. LAWLOR

VESTIBULE [אוּלָם 'ulam]. One entered the nave or central hall of the TEMPLE OF SOLOMON through a vestibule or portico that measured 20 cubits wide, 10 cubits deep, and 30 cubits high (1 Kgs 6:2-3). In front of the vestibule were two freestanding bronze pillars, each topped by a bronze capital. Supporting the roof of the vestibule were two other columns with capitals of lily work (1 Kgs 7:19-22; *see* JACHIN AND BOAZ). Between the vestibule and the nave, a massive double door opened inward and perhaps had smaller double doors that also opened inward. Ezekiel's vision of the vestibule to the Temple has roughly the same dimensions as that of Solomon's Temple (Ezek 40:48-49), but Ezekiel also mentions vestibules associated with gates into the outer and inner courts of the Temple (Ezek 40:7-39; 46:2, 8). The altar for burnt sacrifices was located in the courtyard outside the Temple (2 Kgs 16:14), and when the priests led in public lamentations, they apparently stood outside between the vestibule and the altar (Joel 2:17).

While the vestibule in Zerubbabel's Temple may have been taller than in Solomon's (2 Chr 3:4), the vestibule in Herod's Temple, to which one ascended by twelve steps from the courtyard, was clearly wider, higher, and deeper. In the front it was 100 cubits wide and 100 cubits high, but on the inside, stairways at the two wings reduced the open area to 60 cubits wide by 20 cubits deep. Massive gates opened into a much smaller nave, only 20 cubits wide and 30 cubits high. A curtain also separated the vestibule from the nave (Josephus, *J.W.* 5.207–14). *See* TEMPLE, JERUSALEM; TEMPLES, HEROD'S; VEIL OF THE TEMPLE.

Misderon (מִסְדְּרוֹן) translated "vestibule" in the NRSV of Judg 3:23 is a different word and of very uncertain meaning (see NRSV footnote).

J. J. M. ROBERTS

VIA MARIS. The customary name for the major international highway that ran along the coast of the land of Canaan and connected Syria and Mesopotamia with Egypt. The southwestern section of the highway, between Egypt and Canaan, was called the "way of Horus" in Egyptian literature and the "way of the land of the Philistines" in the Bible (Exod 13:17). The name

"Via Maris" comes from the Vulgate translation of "the way of the sea" (Isa 9:1 [Heb 8:23]), which in fact refers to a local route between Dan and Tyre.

The highway began at Memphis, passed through the Egyptian towns of Raamses and Sile, and continued northward through Gaza and Aphek. After passing between the Sharon Plain and the hills of Samaria, it turned east to Megiddo, where two branches led to Acco and Beth-shean while the main route continued north through Hazor to Damascus, joining roads to Mesopotamia and northern Syria.

Bibliography: Barry J. Beitzel. "The *Via Maris* in Literary and Cartographic Sources." *BA* 54 (1991) 64–75; David A. Dorsey. *The Roads and Highways of Ancient Israel* (1991).

GREGORY L. LINTON

VIAL [פַּךְ pakh]. Small ceramic jar for the storage of oil-based perfumes. Samuel carried the oil used to anoint Saul as king of Israel in a vial (1 Sam 10:1; compare the anointing of Jehu in 2 Kgs 9:1-3). *See* FLASK; POTTERY.

VICES. *See* LISTS, ETHICAL.

VICTORINUS. Bishop of Pettau (Styria, Austria), Victorinus lived in the second half of the 3rd cent. CE and died around 303, during the Diocletian persecutions. According to Jerome (*Vir. ill.* 74), Victorinus was a prolific exegete, having composed numerous commentaries on OT books (e.g., Genesis, Exodus, Leviticus, Isaiah, Ezekiel, Habakkuk, Ecclesiastes, and Song of Songs) and a commentary on Matthew. His sole extant work is his commentary on Revelation, preserved in a 15th-cent. manuscript (*Ottobonianus Lat.* 3288 A). This text weaves together literalist and allegorical readings of the apocalypse. Following writers such as Papias and Irenaeus, Victorinus advances a literal interpretation of the millennium (Rev 20–21), but elsewhere in the same text he displays an affinity for allegorical exegesis typical of Origen, one of his primary influences. The ideas found in this commentary have led scholars to credit Victorinus with authorship of *De fabrica mundi*, a fragment that argues that the seven days of creation signify the 7,000 years of world history (see Ps 90:4), with the last day representing the millennium reign of Christ. Jerome also mentions that Victorinus wrote *Against All Heresies* (*Vir. ill.* 74). Earlier scholarship that equated this work with the Pseudo-Tertullian treatise has not found universal acceptance.

DAVID M. REIS

VICTORY [יְשׁוּעָה yeshu'ah, נֶצַח netsakh, תְּשׁוּעָה teshu'ah; νίκη nikē]. In the OT, the word *victory* usually translates some form of the root ysh' (יֹשַׁע). It is used far more frequently in modern translations (e.g., NRSV) than in older translations (e.g., KJV), which tend to prefer some variant of the word SALVATION, implying a more specifically religious context. The word netsakh is also used with the sense of "victory," though it generally means "forever." With the meaning "victory," it occurs in 1 Chr 29:11a, which has been employed in Jewish and Christian doxologies: "Yours, O LORD, are the greatness, the power, the glory, the victory, and the majesty."

Most biblical texts ascribe victory to God, often in the context of a battle fought by humans (Deut 20:4; 1 Sam 14:23; Pss 20:6, 9 [Heb. 20:7, 10]; 60:5 [Heb. 60:7]; 144:10; Zeph 3:17; 1 Esd 4:58). Several extended passages are songs celebrating God's victories (Exod 15:1-18; Judg 5:3-5). Some texts also speak of Yahweh's victory in battles against primeval and/or destructive forces (Ps 98:1-3), while other texts echo language of such mythic battles in describing Yahweh's defeat of earthly enemies. *See* WARRIOR, DIVINE.

In the NT, Paul speaks of death as having been "swallowed up in victory" (1 Cor 15:54b). He quotes Isa 25:8, which reads, "He has swallowed up death forever (lenetsakh לָנֶצַח)," but he uses the Greek, which interprets netsakh as "victory" (nikos [νῖκος], Aquila; Theodotian) instead of "forever." First John speaks of faith bringing victory over the world (1 John 5:4).

WILL SOLL

VILLAGE [חָצֵר khatser, כָּפָר kafar; κώμη kōmē]. Historically, the largest percentage of the population of ancient Israel lived in small, unwalled agricultural villages (1 Sam 6:18, kofer happerazi כֹּפֶר הַפְּרָזִי; Ezek 38:11, perazoth פְּרָזוֹת). The average size of these settlements in the hill country of Judah and Samaria during the Iron Age was no more than 5 ac. with a population of between 75 and 100 persons. Their inhabitants, like the prophet Amos, engaged in a mixed economy of herding and farming that provided them a basic subsistence level and perhaps a small surplus for trade or to pay their taxes (Amos 7:14). Both narrative and administrative accounts regularly describe these small, rural communities as tied politically and socially to nearby towns and cities. For example, the enumeration of the twenty-nine towns and cities ('arim [עָרִים]; *see* CITY) in Josh 15:32 also encompasses "their villages." Scribal choice or style in the Hebrew sometimes identifies *towns* as the "daughters of ..." larger population centers as distinct from nearby villages (Josh 15:47; 2 Chr 28:18, benotheha [בְּנוֹתֶיהָ]). However, this convention is not reflected in the translation. Context is sometimes necessary to distinguish relative settlement size when 'ir (עִיר) is used for both cities and towns/villages (Josh 10:37). Given the large number of villages scattered throughout the country, an effort is sometimes made to orient the reader geographically. Therefore when an otherwise unfamiliar site is mentioned, specific geographic information is provided on a village's general location (Luke 24:13: Emmaus is "about seven miles from Jerusalem").

Because inheritance patterns are so important in ancient Israel, tribal members are tied to the specific territory ceded to them "according to their clans, with their towns and villages" (Josh 13:28). In later periods, this information is augmented for administrative purposes to include "villages, with their fields" (that is, with their economic assets) while being identified with a neighboring population center, probably for taxation purposes (Neh 11:25-30). Legal differentiation is also made between walled and unwalled settlements. For example, unwalled villages are classified as "open country" with respect to the law of the Jubilee (Lev 25:31).

One way the biblical text is able to create a euphemistic sense of geographic and demographic totality is through the use of the phrase "all the cities ... both fortified cities and unwalled villages" (1 Sam 6:18). In a similar manner in the NT period, the Gospel writer provides an impression of the inclusiveness of Jesus' mission by noting that his itinerary included "all the cities and villages" of a particular area (Matt 9:35). Similarly, the widespread interest among the Pharisees in Jesus' message is conveyed by a narrative aside in Luke 5:17 saying, "they had come from every village of Galilee and Judea and from Jerusalem." The collective form also appears in cases in which the prophets wish to link a city's fate to that of its surrounding, smaller settlements (Jer 19:15; 'ir is used for both city and town here).

At the level of the individual, each person's identity is linked to both a lineage and to a local village. For instance, Jeroboam is described as the "son of Nebat, an Ephramite of Zeredah" (1 Kgs 11:26). In some cases the village, home district, and a tribal territory are also included for greater clarity (see 1 Sam 1:1). These details assist the reader by establishing kinship ties, tribal membership, and a specific link to the promised land that is the heritage of the covenant community.

VICTOR H. MATTHEWS

VINDICATE [דִּין din, רִיב riv, שָׁפַט shafat; δικαιόω dikaioō, κρίνω krinō]. Vindication is the process whereby God establishes one's cause as just (1 Sam 24:15; compare Matt 11:19; Luke 7:35). Job and the psalmists frequently look forward to vindication (Job 6:29; 13:18; Pss 17:2; 24:5; 135:14). *See* JUDGMENT; JUSTIFICATION, JUSTIFY; REDEEM, REDEEMER.

JOAN E. COOK

VINE OF SODOM. *See* SODOM, VINE OF.

VINE, VINEYARD [גֶּפֶן gefen, כֶּרֶם kerem, שֹׂרֵק soreq; ἄμπελος ampelos]. From earliest memory, vineyards were essential to the well-being of the people of the Levant; according to tradition, Noah planted a vineyard after the flood subsided (Gen 9:20). Grapevines thrived in arid climates and provided much of the community's subsistence. The fruit was dried and stored for later consumption, used as a source of sugar, or pressed to make WINE. Vineyards also provided food for the poor,

widows, orphans, and sojourners, who were allowed to pick behind the harvesters (Lev 19:10; Deut 24:21; see 4 Macc 2:9). Extended family and friends helped pick and tread grapes during the short time between the fruit's ripening and rotting on the vine. Jesus' parable about an owner who goes out to hire more laborers up to the last moment may reflect such harvest-time pressures (Matt 20:1-9).

The vineyard's importance in the community was evidenced by the mandate to choose vine tending over military service (Deut 20:6). It was traumatic for a family to lose its vineyard, its inheritance, as illustrated by Naboth's refusal to part with his to Ahab and Naboth's subsequent murder by Ahab and/or Jezebel (1 Kgs 21; 2 Kgs 9:25-26). Vineyards were tended by generations of family members. The centrality of the vineyard to the families of Israel made the vineyard a likely symbol for the nation of Israel and its people: "Israel is a luxuriant vine that yields its fruit" (Hos 10:1; see also Ps 80:8-11; Isa 5:1-7; Jer 2:21; 2 Esd 5:23). Christians adapted the vine imagery for their new community united with Jesus, as Jesus becomes the vine and his followers the branches that bear fruit (John 15:1-6).

The vine was a metaphor for peace (Mic 4:4; Zech 3:10; compare 2 Kgs 18:31; Isa 36:16) and prosperity (Ps 128:1-6). Prophets often turned to the image of the fruitless vine to illustrate religious and economic disorder (Isa 32:10-15; 34:4; Jer 8:13; Joel 1:11-12; 2 Esd 16:26, 30). Isaiah's "song of the vineyard" (Isa 5:1-7; 27:1-6) refers to unjust and unfaithful Israel as a vineyard bearing "wild grapes" (Isa 5:2). Jesus adapts Isaiah's language for a parable of unfaithful vineyard workers who try to gain the vineyard for themselves (Matt 21:33-46; Mark 12:1-9; Luke 20:9-19). Burning or uprooting the vines is a metaphor for divine judgment (Ezek 15:1-7; 17:1-10). Harvesting and pressing the grapes serve as imagery for eschatological judgment, when an angel gathers "the clusters of the vine" and throws them into the "great wine press of the wrath of God" (Rev 14:18-20).

The fertility of the vine and imagery of luscious, juicy grapes might have inspired the poet(s) of the Song of Songs to apply the vineyard and vine metaphorically to represent the woman's sexuality: "they made me keeper of the vineyards, but my own vineyard I have not kept" (Song 1:6*b*; see also 2:13; 6:11; 7:8, 12; 8:11-12). Likewise, personified "Wisdom" praises herself, saying, "Like the vine I bud forth delights .... Come to me, you who desire me, and eat your fill of my fruits" (Sir 24:17-19).

Bibliography: Michal Dayagi-Mendels. *Drink and Be Merry: Wine and Beer in Ancient Times* (1999); J. S. Kloppenborg. *The Tenants in the Vineyard: Ideology, Economics and Agrarian Conflict in Jewish Palestine* (2006); V. Matthews. "Treading the Winepress: Actual and Metaphorical Viticulture in the Ancient Near East." *Semeia* 86 (1999) 19–32; J. M. Sasson. "The Blood of

Grapes." *Drinking in Ancient Societies: History and Culture of Drinks in the Ancient Near East/Studies VI.* Lucio Milano, ed. (1994) 411–19; C. Walsh. *The Fruit of the Vine: Viticulture in Ancient Israel* (2000).

DEBORAH A. APPLER

VINEDRESSERS [כֹּרֵם korem]. Vinedressers planted and tended vines for the production of wine (Joel 1:11). Vineyards required great care if they were to remain fruitful, and the Babylonian conquerors of Judah appointed "some of the poorest people of the land" to remain as vinedressers (2 Kgs 25:12; 2 Chr 26:10; Jer 52:16).

Isaiah's "Song of the Vineyard" (5:1-7) describes the duties of vinedressers: preparing the ground by digging and hoeing and removing stones (v. 2), planting shoots, and, over the first few years, pruning the branches and leaf growth to strengthen the trunk of the vine. For protection, the vinedresser surrounded the vineyard with a FENCE and built a BOOTH in the midst of its grove from which its security could be monitored (compare Isa 1:8).

The "Song of the Vineyard" allegorically presents Yahweh as a vinedresser who takes special care of the vineyard that represents Judah, selecting rare or "choice vines" and building a "watchtower," rather than a booth, in its midst (v. 2). *See* FARMER.

RALPH K. HAWKINS

VINEGAR [חֹמֶץ khomets; ὄξος oxos]. When wine is exposed to air, it turns to vinegar, or "sour wine," as the NRSV often translates this term (compare Num 6:3, "wine vinegar"). In Ruth 2:14, during the time of the barley harvest, Boaz invited Ruth to dip her bread in "vinegar" (author's trans.; NRSV, "sour wine"). It is not clear in this instance whether vinegar was being used as a condiment, or whether it served as a sign of Boaz's generosity to Ruth, for the vinegar or sour wine may have constituted the last of Boaz's wine supply. Since the barley harvest typically occurred in the spring, Boaz's supply of wine from the previous year may have been exhausted, not to be replenished until the fall harvest.

According to other biblical texts, vinegar does not seem to be a particularly enjoyable beverage. In Ps 69:21 [Heb. 69:22], the psalmist receives vinegar as a thirst quencher, along with "poison for food." In Prov 25:20, forcing a grieving person to listen to songs is compared to pouring vinegar on a wound; compare Prov 10:26, which likens the effect of vinegar on the teeth to that of smoke on the eyes.

In all four Gospels (Matt 27:48; Mark 15:36; Luke 23:36; John 19:29), just before his death, Jesus is offered a sponge filled with vinegar (NRSV, "sour wine"). In John, Jesus drinks and then says "It is finished" (v. 30); his action seems to be portrayed as a fulfillment of Ps 69:21 [Heb. 69:22]. *See* DRINK; WINE.

Bibliography: Carey Ellen Walsh. *The Fruit of the Vine: Viticulture in Ancient Israel* (2000).

L. JULIANA CLAASSENS

VIOLENCE [חָמָס khamas, שֹׁד shodh; βία bia, ὅρμημα hormēma]. Violence may take the form of explicit physical force resulting in bodily harm, or it may be systemic and structural, as in a racist or ethnocentric social order, the institution of slavery, a patriarchal society, or an unjust economic system.

Some violence in the Bible is recognized as EVIL, though some is viewed as God's will or is attributed directly to God. Yet paradoxically, the Bible's vision of God's intent for human life ultimately dissents from violence. While there are multiple perspectives on violence within Scripture, the overarching biblical story yields a canonical framework for interpreting—and indeed judging—the violence it recounts.

Creation is the first important canonical marker of the Bible's normative perspective on violence. Genesis portrays creation as good (Gen 1:4, 10, 12, 18, 21, 25, 31), a gift from a generous creator. Humans are made in the image of this generous creator with the mandate to rule the earth and its animals (Gen 1:26-28). Human life is thus meant to be characterized by a nonviolent, generous, and creative use of power vis-à-vis the non-human world. Furthermore, no human being is given dominion over another human being at creation. This provides a normative basis to critique inter-human injustice, the misuse of power over others, and the inequities of patriarchy and sexism that arise in history, including the history of God's people recorded in Scripture. And since the creation of humanity in God's image with the mandate to rule is prior to any ethnic, racial, or national divisions, this provides a normative basis to critique ethnocentrism, racism, or any form of national superiority. God's intent from the beginning is thus a cooperative world of shalom and blessing, where violence has no place.

The Bible portrays violence as rooted in the primal transgression of humans (symbolized by the prohibition to eat from the tree of the knowledge of good and evil; Gen 2:17; 3:6). The initial consequences of the primal violation include examples of inter-human violence, such as the domination of women by men (Gen 3:16*b*), fratricide (Gen 4:8), and revenge killing (Gen 4:23-24). This inter-human violence spirals so out of control that the earth is filled with violence and becomes corrupted or ruined (Gen 6:11), resulting in the flood, which is intended to remove the violence and allow a new beginning. God even institutes a law to limit killing (Gen 9:6). But the flood does not change the human heart (compare Gen 6:5-6 with 8:21).

With the human race still embroiled in violence, God calls Abram (later named Abraham) out from the nations of the earth. Intending to create from Abram's descendants a great nation (Israel) that will exhibit righteousness and justice (Gen 18:19), God specifies that through this nation all the families or nations of the world will find blessing (Gen 12:3; 18:18; 22:18; 26:4; 28:14). In the context of the story of increasing human violence recounted in Genesis and in the early chapters of Exodus, we are warranted to take Israel's vocation as intended to address (and perhaps reverse) the violence that has humanity in thrall.

Yet Israel's vocation is contradicted by what seems to be an intractable ethnocentrism. While the covenant God makes with Israel at Sinai enjoins the newly constituted people to enact justice within their own community, there is no explicit mandate for Israel to enact this justice toward other nations, except in the case of sojourners or aliens living within Israel (Exod 22:21; 23:9; Lev 19:33-34; Deut 10:17-19; 24:17-22). In fact, Israel is commanded to exterminate the inhabitants of Canaan in order to receive their land as a gift from God (Deut 7:1-6). This tension between the divine call to bring blessing to the nations and the divine injunction to destroy the Canaanites constitutes one of the primary ethical tensions in Scripture. Without denying any of the violence that Scripture portrays Israel (or God) committing toward the non-elect, we may discern that this violence is called into question by the canonical trajectory that understands Israel's vocation as contributing to the blessing of the nations. Indeed, in the time of the Babylonian exile, the Abrahamic calling of bringing blessing to the nations is explicitly rearticulated for God's servant people (Isa 42:1-7; 49:5-6) with a new, distinctive emphasis on the servant's suffering at the hands of the violent on behalf of the world (Isa 52:13–53:12).

In the NT, the life, death, and resurrection of Jesus are understood as the fulfillment of this trajectory of mediating blessing to others. Jesus takes up Israel's vocation for the sake of both Israel and the world. Jesus is understood in the NT as the turning point of the entire biblical narrative, the decisive plot twist that begins to unravel the twin problems of rebellion toward God and violence toward neighbor. He accomplishes this by the willing acceptance of violence against his own person on the cross as an alternative to returning violence with violence. In this, Jesus models what it means to be human in a world of violence. At the same time, the cross is also in fundamental continuity with God's early decision not to eradicate sinful humanity but to work toward their redemption; God suffers in Christ as the culmination of a long story of God's participation in human history.

It is precisely God's embrace of suffering that will ultimately purge violence from the world. This needs to be taken into consideration in any account of the divine violence recounted in the Bible, including eschatological violence, the final judgment meant to purge violence from creation and reestablish a world of shalom. Without claiming to explain fully the violence attributed to God in Scripture, we could say minimally that divine violence is always a response to human vio-

lence. Violence, even if it is justifiable in some way, is not God's original intent. *See* CROSS; SIN, SINNERS; WAR, IDEAS OF.

Bibliography: Hans Boersma. *Violence, Hospitality, and the Cross: Reappropriating the Atonement Tradition* (2006); John J. Collins. "The Zeal of Phinehas: The Bible and the Legitimation of Violence." *JBL* 122 (2003) 3–21; Terence E. Fretheim. "God and Violence in the OT." *WW* 24 (2004) 18–28; J. Richard Middleton. "Created in the Image of a Violent God? The Ethical Problem of the Conquest of Chaos in Biblical Creation Texts." *Int* 58 (2004) 341–55; Phyllis Trible. *Texts of Terror: Literary-Feminist Readings of Biblical Narratives* (1984).

J. RICHARD MIDDLETON

VIOLET [ὑάκινθος hyakinthos]. A shade of PURPLE mentioned in a description of embroidery on priestly vestments (Sir 45:10). The dye is likely derived from MUREX.

VIPER [אֶפְעֶה ʾefʿeh, עַכְשׁוּב ʿakhshuv, שְׁפִיפֹן shefifon; ἔχιδνα echidna]. A viper is a type of snake, usually venomous. The NRSV uses the term to translate several words. In the OT, ʾefʿeh refers to the *Echis colata*, a poisonous snake (Job 20:16; Isa 30:6; 59:5). shefifon, which occurs only in Gen 49:17, is probably a horned viper, *Vipera cerastes*. This species has the habit of hiding itself in the sand, as suggested in Gen 49. ʿAkhshuv refers to a horned viper or ADDER (Ps 140:3). *See* SERPENT.

In the NT, echidna does not point to a definite species of snake, but probably refers to a poisonous snake such as *Vipera ammodytes*, the sandviper. This is used literally in Acts 28:3 for a snake that bites Paul, those around him expect him to die from the bite. It is used figuratively of religious leaders whom Jesus saw as hypocrites (Matt 12:34; 23:33) and those John the Baptist warned of their need to repent (Matt 3:7; Luke 3:7). *Viper* and the more general word *serpent*, used metaphorically, symbolize evil or danger (e.g., Rom 3:13). Most species of snakes in Israel are not poisonous.

KENNETH D. LITWAK

VIRGIL. Publius Vergilius Marol (70–19 BCE), Rome's greatest poet, lived through the conclusion of Rome's civil wars, when AUGUSTUS replaced the Republic with monarchy. Society looked to Rome's origins to justify the new order, to inspire a return to Rome's (imagined) original moral and religious values, and to understand what had gone so terribly wrong. Virgil's *Eclogues* and *Georgics* mix idealized rural themes with myth, religion, and allusions to contemporary politics. *Eclogue* 4, prophesying the birth of a divine child who would usher in a golden age, later excited the interest—and sometimes the hostility—of early Christians. The *Aeneid* traces the path of the refugee Aeneas from

Troy to Italy. Aeneas' descendants included Romulus, Julius Caesar, and his adopted son, Octavian, who became Augustus. This epic "prequel" to Roman history encapsulates the cultural, religious, and moral spirit of the Augustan Age.

Bibliography: Nicholas Horsfall. *A Companion to the Study of Virgil* (2000); Charles Martindale, ed. *The Cambridge Companion to Virgil* (1997).

HANS-FRIEDRICH MUELLER

VIRGIN [בְּתוּלָה bethulah; παρθένος parthenos]. The term bethulah ("young woman" or *virgin*), or its related abstract noun, bethulim (בְּתוּלִים), occurs fifty times in the OT; the Greek parthenos, or its plural, parthenoi (παρθένοι), appears in the NT.

In the OT the term bethulah refers generally to a nubile young woman. As suggested by its frequent pairing with bakhur (בָּחוּר, "young man," Deut 32:25; 2 Chr 36:17; Pss 78:63; 148:12; Isa 23:4; 62:5; Jer 51:22; Lam 1:18; 2:21; Ezek 9:6), the primary meaning of the noun is not focused on virginity. When the text wants to emphasize the virginal state of a girl, it adds the phrase, "had never slept with a man" (Gen 24:16; Judg 11:39; 21:12). Thus bethulah most often refers to a young, unmarried woman. Nevertheless, multiple occurrences of the term speak to additional valences associated with bethulah. As has long been observed, the meaning of bethulah in Joel 1:8 ("like a bethulah dressed in sackcloth for the husband of her youth") suggests a young, married woman rather than a young unmarried woman or an unwed virgin. Therefore readers must depend upon the specific literary context in which bethulah occurs to determine its meaning.

The abstract noun bethulim (technically a plural form in Hebrew, but without a plural meaning) can imply sexual inexperience on the part of the nubile female with whom it is associated, yet like bethulah, the term is not without ambiguity. For example, scholars examining the law of the slandered bride in Deut 22:13-21 have read bethulim in two different ways. Whereas bethulim has traditionally been rendered as "virginity," some scholars hold to Gordon Wenham's argument that the husband of Deut 22:13-21 accuses his wife, not primarily of having lost her virginity prior to the wedding night, but of having entered into the marriage already pregnant from a union with another man. According to this interpretation, the lack of a garment stained by menstrual blood serves as evidence of the woman's pregnancy and previous sexual transgression (the garment produced by her parents is intended to show that she was menstruating immediately prior to the wedding). Other scholars remain persuaded by the longer held view that the charge against the woman is simply a reference to the absence of a proof of the bride's virginity, namely, a blood-stained sheet from the couple's wedding night, as is used for evidence of virginity in other cultures. Tikva Frymer-Kensky contends that the

scenario suggested by Wenham would be unique in a cultural context where inspection of a bloody sheet was used to enforce the virginity of daughters. Regardless of the translation, either interpretation implies the expectation of the woman's sexual purity.

Again, in Lev 21:13 and Judg 11:37, bethulim is often understood to indicate virginity. In reading the Levitical teaching that stipulates that a High Priest can marry only a young woman in her bethulim (Lev 21:13) and a bethulah from his people (v. 14), Jacob Milgrom argues that the basic meaning is a woman in her adolescence, but that her virginity is simply assumed. Rather than thinking of "virgin" and "young nubile woman" as distinct choices, it may be more useful, as Frymer-Kensky suggests, to consider how each sometimes implicates the other, since biblical culture held to the norm that young women entering marriage should be virgins. Although bethulah fails to correlate precisely with the modern understanding of *virgin* or the construct of the *virgo intacta*, it does sometimes connote female sexual inexperience. Seen in this light, the tradition of the bride-price may underscore the degree to which virginity before marriage was valued (Exod 22:16-17; Deut 22:28-29).

As is the case with bethulah in the OT, the term parthenos in the NT has been the subject of debate. Classicists, like biblical scholars investigating the meaning of bethulah, have pondered whether parthenos refers only to age and marital status (in other words, to a nubile young woman) or to sexual inexperience as well. Just as classical literature expresses more than the loss of a bride's youth when her parthenia (παρθενία, "virginity") is taken, parthenos often connotes more than age or marital status (Sissa). As it occurs in the NT, parthenos can signal virginity.

The most well-known NT occurrences of parthenos refer to Mary, the mother of Jesus. The infancy narratives of both Matthew and Luke portray Mary as parthenos. In each case, including Matthew's citation of Isa 7:14 in the LXX (which translates the Hebrew ʿalmah [עַלְמָה, "young woman"] as parthenos), emphasis on Mary's virginity underscores Jesus' extraordinary conception (*see* VIRGIN BIRTH). Whereas the Matthean parable of the "ten virgins" (Matt 25:1-13) emphasizes the marital, not the sexual, status of the young women in the story, Rev 14:4 uses parthenoi to emphasize the cultic purity of the faithful 144,000. Its misogynistic imagery of parthenoi "who have not defiled themselves with women" so emphasizes the notion of virginity as purity that it extends the typical meaning of parthenos to include men.

In the NT Epistles, Paul uses parthenos twice, the first time in 1 Cor 7:36-38 and the second time in 2 Cor 11:2. In the former example, parthenos appears repeatedly in reference to either a man's daughter or his betrothed. The discussion centers on the question of whether the man whom Paul is addressing should marry the parthenos, either to another or to himself, depending on the translation. While Paul approaches the matter primarily from the perspective of eschatological concerns, the passage reveals much about what parthenos connotes. Here Paul suggests that the parthenos is reason for concern because, in Dale Martin's assessment, Paul believes that celibacy may be especially difficult for young women and therefore should not be forced upon them lest it lead them to excessive and dangerous desire.

Biblical constructions of the virgin underscore its multivalence. Virginity carries with it the threat of loss of control as well as the need for external control. Lest they become "out of control," virgins are considered cause for concern and protection. Virginity provides the rationale for the family's exercise of control over the bethulah or parthenos (Frymer-Kensky). Thus when referring to the cities of Israel—such as Samaria (Jer 31:4, 21; Amos 5:2) and Jerusalem (Jer 18:13)—the prophets sometimes draw upon the trope of the "virgin of Israel" as a means of illustrating the relationship between the city and the God of Israel.

In the OT, bethulah can convey youth, nubility, virginity, or threat. Similarly, NT uses of parthenos connote multiple meanings and images. Such multivalence mirrors what can be said of ancient, especially Greco-Roman, understandings of the parthenos (Foskett). As a figure moving from childhood toward adulthood that will presumably involve marriage and motherhood, the virgin is construed in terms of social, moral, and physical liminality. In ancient discourse, she is the topic of medical, moral, religious, legal, and historical discussion, as well as the focus of several ancient narratives. She is viewed in alternating light as a moral agent (one who does or does not remain chaste), an object of exchange (marriage), the site of health or disease, even as a sacred space or site of sacred encounter (prophecy). Thus the virgin is cause for both celebration and concern, signaling ripeness on the one hand and incompleteness on the other. It is not so much how bethulah or parthenos ought to be defined, but rather what each connotes that is most informative for readers seeking to understand the meaning of the terms as they appear in the Bible. See CELIBACY; MARRIAGE, NT; MARRIAGE, OT.

Bibliography: Mary F. Foskett. A Virgin Conceived: Mary and Classical Representations of Virginity (2002); Tikva Frymer-Kensky. "Virginity in the Bible." Gender and Law in the Hebrew Bible and the Ancient Near East. Victor H. Matthews, Bernard M. Levinson, and Tikva Frymer-Kensky, eds. (1998); Dale B. Martin. The Corinthian Body (1995); Jacob Milgrom. Leviticus 17–22: A New Translation with Introduction and Commentary. AB 3A (2000); Giulia Sissa. Greek Virginity. Arthur Goldhammer, trans. (1990); Bruce Wells. "Sex, Lies, and Virginal Rape: The Slandered Bride and False Accusation in Deuteronomy." JBL 124 (2005) 41–72; Gordon J. Wenham. "Betulah 'A Girl of Marriageable Age'" VT 22 (1972) 326–48.

MARY F. FOSKETT

VIRGIN BIRTH. "Virgin birth" is an imprecise reference to the manner of Jesus' conception, who is regarded in both the Gospels of Matthew and Luke and in the creedal tradition as having been conceived without the biological contribution of a human father and born of a human mother who had not had sexual relations with a man. A more accurate designation, therefore, would be "virginal conception."

Early veneration of MARY resulted in the further affirmation of her "virgin birth"—that is, her virginity before, in, and after birth (e.g., Jerome, Homily 87). This tradition has roots in the Protevangelium of James (2nd cent.; see JAMES, PROTEVANGELIUM OF). "Virgin birth," in this more narrow sense, is mariological in focus and encourages the view that virginity is a correlate of religious purity. Virginal conception, on the other hand, is christological in emphasis, and is concerned with how Jesus, Son of God, became human.

According to the Apostles' Creed, Jesus Christ "was conceived by the Holy Spirit, born of the virgin Mary" (7th cent.); the Nicene-Constantinopolitan Creed has it similarly that "the Lord Jesus Christ ... was incarnate by the Holy Spirit and the Virgin Mary, and became human" (4th cent.). The beliefs represented by these formal, ecumenical statements already appear in Ignatius of Antioch (early 2nd cent.), whose affirmation of the virginal conception appears in creed-like statements, employed against persons who denied of Jesus a human birth or who claimed that his conception was that of any human: "For our God, Jesus the Christ, was conceived (ekyophorethē ἐκυοφορήθη) by Mary according to God's plan, both from the seed of David and of the Holy Spirit" (Ign. Eph. 18:1; see 19:1: "the virginity of Mary"; Ign. Smyrn. 1:1–2: "our Lord ... is ... Son of God with respect to the divine will and power, truly born of a virgin") (Holmes). Clearly, Ignatius and the Christian tradition he represents understood the NT writings as teaching the miraculous conception of Jesus, by means of the intervention of the Holy Spirit and without sexual intercourse.

A. The New Testament and Beyond
  1. Gospel of Matthew
  2. Gospel of Luke
  3. Other New Testament texts?
  4. Protevangelium of James
B. Historical Issues and Scientific Questions
C. Theological Significance
Bibliography

A. The New Testament and Beyond
  1. Gospel of Matthew
Matthew's birth narrative draws on multiple traditions, especially the OT type scene of the birth an-

nouncement and traditions about Moses. Matthew's witness to the virginal conception of Jesus comes into focus in 1:16, 18-20, 22-23.

Jesus' genealogy reaches its conclusion by departing from the typical pattern "X the father of Y" (gennaō [γεννάω]; literally, X "fathered" or "beget" Y) in Matt 1:16: "Joseph the husband of Mary, of whom Jesus was born, who is called the Messiah." Rather than identify Joseph as the male parent of Jesus, Matthew identifies Joseph as Mary's husband while naming Mary as the one to whom Jesus was born. The language Matthew uses is reminiscent of similar phrases used earlier in the genealogy where women are mentioned (X ek tēs [ἐκ τῆς] Y): "Zerah by Tamar" (1:3), "Boaz by Rahab" (1:5), "Obed by Ruth" (1:5), and "Solomon by the wife of Uriah" (1:6). In the case of Mary and Jesus, however, the phrase is X ex hēs egennēthē (ἐξ ἧς ἐγεννήθη) Y: "Mary, of whom Jesus was born." In itself, this shift to the mother does not prove the unique nature of Jesus' birth but, by circumventing the normal position of a father in the genealogy, it may presuppose Jesus' virgin birth.

In 1st-cent. Judaism, marriage ordinarily followed the completion of a marriage agreement, including the payment of a bride price and a period of betrothal during which a woman continued to live in her father's household, but was legally bound to her husband-to-be. This period of betrothal is signified in Matt 1:18: "before they lived together" (prin ē synelthein autous πρὶν ἢ συνελθεῖν αὐτούς). Further significance is urged by two observations. First, synerchomai (συνέρχομαι) has the general sense of "to come together," but can also be used with reference to the intimacy of sexual relations (see, e.g., Wis 7:2; 1 Cor 7:5 [P46 Ψ M]; Josephus, Ant. 7.168, 213). Accordingly, Matthew's text would read that Mary was found to be with child "before their engaging in sexual intercourse." Having ruled out the biological contribution of Joseph, the Evangelist goes on to assert that Mary's pregnancy was the consequence of divine agency. This is "from the Holy Spirit" (ek pneumatos hagiou ἐκ πνεύματος ἁγίου)—not a reference to the Spirit's taking the role of a male in a sexual encounter but to the inexplicable exercise of creative power by God. Second, Matthew has Joseph demonstrate his lack of involvement in the conception of Mary's baby by assuming that he is required to divorce her for infidelity (1:19). Moreover, using terminology employed in 1:16 and 18, an angel reports to Joseph that Mary's pregnancy has occurred apart from a father and is a result of divine intervention.

Matthew's commentary on these matters is provided in the citation of Isa 7:14 in Matt 1:23: "'Look, the virgin shall conceive and bear a son, and they shall name him Emmanuel,' which means, 'God is with us.'" This is the second time at the outset of Matthew's account that the Evangelist has introduced a name for the child, followed immediately by Matthew's interpretation of the significance of that name for the identity and role of the child. The first is in 1:21: "Jesus, for he will save his people from their sins"—an interpretation that depends on the common view that the name "Jesus" derives from the root of the verb "to save" in Hebrew: yshʿ (ישׁע). That is, in both verses, Matthew's emphasis falls on the significance of the name given the child. The Evangelist's real interest in Isa 7:14 lies less in finding a proof text to support the virginal conception of Jesus and more in Isaiah's warning regarding the need for faithfulness appropriate to the time of God's own presence (see Watts). Nevertheless, citing the Isaianic text in its Greek form, Matthew's use of the term parthenos (παρθένος) contributes to the portrait of Mary and her pregnancy thus far painted. This is because parthenos refers not only to a girl of marriageable age (as in the MT: ʿalmah [עַלְמָה]) but typically, more narrowly, to one who has never engaged in sexual intercourse.

It is worth inquiring into the potentially generative role Isa 7:14 might have played in Matthew's affirmation of the virginal conception. Has Matthew created his emphasis on the virginal conception in order to show how the Isaianic prophecy was actualized? Two considerations support a negative response to this question. First, Matthew's reason for citing Isa 7:14 is christological. He is affirming the role of Mary's child as "God with us." Although his citation of the Isaianic text is congruent with the virginal conception, then, this is more assumed on account of other aspects of the text and not at all developed in Matthew's exegesis of Isa 7:14 in his account of the birth announcement. Second, although ʿalmah in Isa 7:14 typically refers to a "young woman," it may refer more narrowly to a "virgin," as it seems to do in Gen 24:43; Exod 2:8; Ps 68:25. This means that virginal conception is a possible reading of Isa 7:14; however, we have no evidence that it was read in this way in the 1st cent. CE or, more particularly, that it was employed as a text for messianic speculation. That is, not only does Matthew minimize a reading of Isa 7:14 as foretelling the virginal conception of Jesus but also there is no evidence that Isa 7:14 was being read as a predictive prophecy needing thus to be fulfilled.

2. Gospel of Luke

Luke 1:26-38 comprises the Lukan account of the announcement of Jesus' birth and provides the most direct witness to the virginal conception of Jesus in the Third Gospel. From the beginning, Luke emphasizes Mary's status as a "virgin" (parthenos), identifying her in this way twice in 1:27 and observing further that she was "betrothed" to Joseph. This would identify Mary as a young woman having just achieved puberty, perhaps twelve or thirteen years old. Luke does not cite Isa 7:14, but his account parallels Isa 7:10-17 in a number of telling ways: "house of David" (1:27; Isa 7:13), "the Lord" (1:28; Isa 7:10), "virgin" (1:27; Isa 7:14), "will conceive" (1:31; Isa 7:14), "will ... bear a son" (1:31; Isa 7:14), "you will name him" (1:31; Isa 7:14), and "over the house" (1:33; Isa 7:17); we may also hear an echo of the child's name in Isaiah, "Immanuel" (Isa 7:14)—that is, "God is with us"—in Gabriel's words of greeting, "The Lord is with you" (1:28). Luke is not recounting the "fulfillment" of the Isaianic text, but rather underscoring the significance of God's intervention in history to actualize his saving purpose.

That **parthenos** must be read as a reference not simply to Mary's relative youth but also to her lack of prior sexual activity becomes obvious in 1:34. Having been informed by Gabriel, the angel of the Lord, that she would conceive in her womb and bear a son (1:31), Mary responds, "How can this be, since I am a virgin [literally, "since I do not have a sexual relationship with a man]?" The first two phrases of Gabriel's response parallel each other, preparing for a single conclusion: "The Holy Spirit will come upon you, and the power of the Most High will overshadow you; therefore the child to be born will be holy; he will be called Son of God" (1:35).

Both phrases—"to come upon" and "to overshadow"—have a prehistory in Israel's narrative, and neither suggests sexual activity (see, e.g., Exod 40:35; Isa 32:15; also Luke 9:34; Acts 1:8), as though God (or God by means of the Spirit) might take the male role in a conjugal liaison. Luke does not portray God as fathering Jesus. Rather, the text demonstrates that but not how, in this case, God's creative power substitutes for the biological contribution of a man.

Luke's genealogy of Jesus comports well with this emphasis. The Evangelist initiates the genealogy with an aside to his audience: "He was the son (as was thought) of Joseph" (3:23). Other occurrences in Luke's narrative of the verb nomizō (νομίζω, "to think," "to assume"; e.g., 2:44; Acts 7:25) suggest an assumption wrongly held, and this is likely the case in this instance. Although Luke might want to emphasize Jesus' legal heritage as son of David by means of tracing his lineage through Joseph, Luke has informed his audience that, in fact, Jesus is son of God (see, e.g., 1:32-35; 2:49; 3:21-22).

3. Other New Testament texts?

Outside of the birth narratives of the Gospels of Matthew and Luke we find in the NT no explicit references to the virginal conception of Jesus. This means, first, that the virginal conception plays no particular role in the subsequent narratives of Matthew and Luke; and, second, that the Gospels of Mark and John, the NT letters, and Revelation provide no clear reference to the virginal conception or any theological interest in considering his birth in this way. For example, it is never mentioned in the sermons and kerygmatic summaries in Acts nor in the creedal traditions found in the Pauline letters (e.g., 1 Cor 15:3-5). Accordingly, it is easy to conclude that the virginal conception of Jesus did not figure in 1st-cent. forms of Christian catechesis or missionary preaching.

However, a few texts refer to the birth of Jesus in ways that might be regarded as implying knowledge of the virginal conception. For example, there is a peculiar reference to Jesus as "the son of Mary" (Mark 6:3), peculiar since a reference to Jesus as his father's son would have been expected (compare, e.g., Matt 13:55; Luke 4:22). This is true even when the father is dead (as in Doeg son of Joseph in *b. Yoma* 38b). Accordingly, Mark 6:3 might be a clue that questions had been raised about the circumstances of Jesus' birth: Who was his father? Later Jewish tradition, perhaps reflected in John 8:41, characterizes Jesus as illegitimate (e.g., Origen *Cels.* 128–32; *b. Sanh.* 67a), whereas the developing Christian tradition asserted his virginal conception. Apparently, the circumstances surrounding Jesus' birth were the subject of controversy from a very early period. However, this speculation does not require that Mark implicitly recognizes the virginal conception of Jesus, though Mark 6:3 is congruent with such an affirmation.

Some have found in Gal 4:4 ("But when the fullness of time had come, God sent his Son, born of a woman") further reference to the virginal conception of Jesus. The phrase in question is "born of a woman," but nothing can be garnered from it with respect to Mary's virginity. Similar phraseology is found, e.g., in Matt 11:11 and Luke 7:28, where it functions idiomatically to refer to a human being. Paul thus speaks to Jesus' humanity, not about the nature of his conception and birth.

4. *Protevangelium of James*

The *Protevangelium of James* circulated under myriad titles; the earliest manuscript evidence has "Birth of Mary, Revelation of James" (Papyrus Bodmer V). This title describes the content of the work: a book attributed to James, brother of Jesus, recounting events from the birth and childhood of Mary to the birth of her son, Jesus. Since 1) it depends on the Gospels of Matthew and Luke, 2) the earliest manuscript evidence dates from the early 4th cent., and 3) it is likely to have been known from at least the time of Origen, the work is usually dated within the middle or second half of the 2nd cent.

The *Protevangelium of James* focuses primarily on the purity of Mary, mother of Jesus. This emphasis serves a christological purpose, underscoring the perfect holiness of God's son, but also lauding Mary for her unqualified purity. Not only Jesus' but also Mary's was a miraculous conception. Mary was raised in a constant state of religious purity: she spent her childhood years in the Temple, she was fed by angels, and she did not engage in sexual relations with Joseph—in fact, she was a virgin before and after the birth of Jesus. For this gospel, Jesus' siblings are actually Joseph's children by a former marriage.

The importance of the *Protevangelium of James* is difficult to exaggerate, especially with regard to mariology and to Christian art and liturgy. Subsequent veneration of Mary as well as artistic renditions of "the Christmas story" are often more indebted to this apocryphal gospel than to the NT writings.

B. Historical Issues and Scientific Questions

The relevant historical evidence admits of either conclusion, for or against historicity of the virginal conception of Jesus. For example, that Matthew and Luke independently bear witness to the virginal conception can be taken as an argument (on the basis of the tradition-critical criterion of multiple attestations) in favor of the historicity of the event to which they testify. At the same time, that we have such scant evidence supporting this event renders problematic a decision favoring its historicity.

Also the numerous reports of the virginal conceptions of mythological figures, such as Heracles or Perseus, or of such historical figures as Alexander the Great, Apollonius, or even Plato could have motivated Jesus' followers to have him recognized as the offspring of a god. Some scholars argue that early Christians sought to counter the divinizing of the Roman emperor by creating a similar legend of Jesus having been fathered by a God. It is easy enough to dismiss these parallels since none of them provide a real analogy to what we find in the Gospels of Matthew and Luke (see already Dibelius). On the one hand, the Gospel reports actually exclude the view found in some allegedly parallel reports of a god taking on human form in order to impregnate a woman. On the other hand, one might argue that the presence of so many analogues provides a literary and conceptual environment that rendered such birth legends in the case of Jesus credible.

Though Isa 7:14 LXX ("Look, the virgin shall be with child and bear a son, and you shall call him Emmanuel"; author's trans.) could have played a formative role in the early tradition about Jesus' birth by demonstrating how Jesus fulfilled OT prophecy, the only citation of Isa 7:14 by NT writers is found in the Gospel of Matthew, where it does not play this role. Moreover, there is no evidence from Jewish sources of the period that Isa 7:14 was read so as to predict the birth of a messianic child to a virgin. The reverse is easier to imagine: those who had come already to believe in the virginal conception of Jesus would have found in Isa 7:14 LXX a ready confirmation of their belief.

Early Christians regarded Jesus as Messiah and of Davidic descent (Rom 1:3); yet reference to Jesus as Mary's but not Joseph's son complicates Jesus' identification as son of David. This difficulty makes it possible to argue against the virginal conception of Jesus as a mere invention by his early followers.

The chief reason to reject the historicity of the virginal conception of Jesus is its scientific implausibility. Matthew and Luke provide nothing by way of an explanation, biological or otherwise, of how Mary became pregnant. This led already in the 2nd cent. CE to debates regarding the nature of Jesus' birth (see, e.g., Justin

Martyr, *Dial.* 43–127). Indeed, with terms like *conceived* and *born*, we seem to have entered the world of gynecology—an observation not lost on Mary herself, according to the Gospel of Luke: "How can this be, since I am a virgin?"

Appeals to scientific reasoning that such a conception would be biologically impossible are not as secure as they might seem. Against an incredulity grounded in scientific reasoning, geneticist R. J. Berry urges that our developing knowledge of the biological process of parthenogenesis (i.e., procreation apart from the immediate contribution of a male) ought to mitigate the significance of this apparent assault on modern sensibilities. Nevertheless, while sketching the biological mechanisms by which such a birth might be possible, Berry himself rejects the view that Jesus was the offspring of parthenogenesis, preferring instead to view the conception of Jesus as a miracle. In this regard, his view is at home in the Gospels of Matthew and Luke, which affirm divine agency without recourse to normal biological processes. In fact, neither the Gospels nor the early tradition regarding Jesus' birth to a virgin invite biological explanation, preferring instead a pneumatological explanation. As Matthew has it, this is "from the Holy Spirit" (1:20; compare Luke 1:35).

Of course, in a naturalist view of the cosmos, a virginal conception is ruled nonhistorical, as are all other MIRACLEs in the biblical tradition. Alternatively, those who allow for the presence and activity of God might explain the miraculous as God's setting into motion a cascade of quantum events leading to the virginal conception of Jesus—a view that would picture the miracle of Jesus' birth less as God intruding in the normal workings of the world and more in terms of God's working within the world he has made.

Whether one affirms the historicity of the virginal conception of Jesus, then, is not simply a question of weighing the evidence pro and con. Philosophical and theological assumptions about the possibility of a God who intervenes in human affairs to accomplish his saving purpose will weigh heavily. Nor is one's decision regarding the virginal conception of Jesus merely a question of deciding for or against eliminative naturalism—that is, whether one acknowledges the ability of God to interact with the cosmos. That God is capable of creating a human being apart from the biological contribution of a human father does not imply that God has done so. In the end, a great deal will depend on the weight one gives to the witness of the Gospels of Matthew and Luke and, then, to the developing tradition of the early church.

C. Theological Significance

The significance of the virginal conception of Jesus for early Christian theology, from the 2nd cent. on, is underscored by its early and widespread entry into early versions of the Rule of Faith (or Rule of Truth). Although mentioned explicitly only twice in the NT and in spite of its absence from all creedal formulations found in the NT itself, the virginal conception found its way centrally into these proto-confessional statements of the early church. By way of contrast, we should note that other aspects of Jesus' life and ministry—such as his broadly attested ministry of healing, his baptism, or his practices of table fellowship—did not find their way into the developing creedal tradition. How, then, might we account for the theological importance allocated the nature of Jesus' birth?

That the contours of the affirmation of the virginal conception of Jesus were worked out early on in contentious settings suggests its theological significance in the face of two counterclaims: 1) against those denying that Jesus was a human being and 2) against those contending that Jesus was nothing but a human being. As Karl Barth explained, the claims, that Jesus was conceived by the Holy Spirit and born of a virgin named Mary, speak to the uniqueness of Jesus' birth in two ways: as the profound expression of the divine grace and sovereignty by means of which the Word of God comes into human existence and as the profound self-limitation of God in that Jesus was real as his mother was real. Accordingly, Jesus is truly human and truly God.

As such, the enigma of the virginal conception of Jesus does not prove the incarnation, but serves as its sign. What is more, it speaks to the character of salvation. God's redemptive purpose is not the product of business as usual in a world whose systems too often oppose life with and before God, but comes to fruition instead through a fundamental alteration in the patterns of this world. For this reason and in this ultimate sense, biological questions and answers regarding the virginal conception of Jesus are unsatisfying, for they are simply incapable of recognizing that, in the remarkable and enigmatic birth of Jesus, God has acted graciously and creatively to reconcile the world to himself. *See* INFANCY NARRATIVES.

Bibliography: Roger David Aus. *Matthew 1–2 and the Virginal Conception: In Light of Palestinian and Hellenistic Judaic Traditions on the Birth of Israel's First Redeemer, Moses* (2004); Karl Barth. *Church Dogmatics,* I/2:172–202, IV/1:207–10 (1956); R. J. Berry. "The Virgin Birth of Christ." *Science and Christian Belief* 8 (1996) 101–10; George J. Brooke, ed. *The Birth of Jesus: Biblical and Theological Reflections* (2000); Raymond E. Brown. *The Birth of the Messiah: A Commentary on the Infancy Narratives in the Gospels of Matthew and Luke.* Rev. ed. (1993); Charles E. B. Cranfield. "Some Reflections on the Subject of the Virgin Birth." *SJT* 41 (1988) 177–89; Oliver D. Crisp. "On the 'Fittingness' of the Virgin Birth." *HeyJ* 49 (2008) 197–221; David S. Cunningham. "Explicating Those 'Troublesome' Texts of the Creeds: The Promise of Realistic Fiction." *Di* 42 (2003) 111–19; J. Duncan and M. Derrett. "Shared Themes: The Virgin Birth (Matt 1:18–2:12)." *Journal of Higher Criticism* 4 (1997) 57–67; Martin Dibelius. *Jungfrauensohn und Krippenkind: Untersuchungen zur Geburtsgeschichte Jesu im Lukas-Evangelium* (1932); Mary F. Foskett. *A Virgin Conceived: Mary and Classical Representations of Virginity* (2002); Michael W. Holmes. *The Apostolic Fathers: Greek Texts and English Translations.* 3rd ed. (2007); Tal Ilan. "'Man Born of Woman ...' (Job 14:1): The Phenomenon of Men Bearing Metronyms at the Time of Jesus." *NovT* 34 (1992) 23–45; A. Robert and C. Leaney. "The Virgin Birth in Lucan Theology and in the Classical Creeds." *Scripture, Tradition and Reason: A Study in the Criteria of Christian Doctrine: Essays in Honour of Richard P. C. Hanson.* Richard Bauckham and Benjamin Drewery, eds. (1988) 65–100; Andrew T. Lincoln. "'Born of the Virgin Mary': Creedal Affirmation and Critical Reading." *Christology and Scripture: Interdisciplinary Perspectives.* Andrew T. Lincoln and Angus Paddison, eds. (2007) 84–103; Gerd Lüdemann. *Virgin Birth? The Real Story of Mary and Her Son Jesus* (1998); J. Gresham Machen. *The Virgin Birth of Christ* (1930); John P. Meier. *A Marginal Jew: Rethinking the Historical Jesus.* Vol. 1: *The Roots of the Problem and the Person* (1991); Robert J. Miller. *Born Divine: The Births of Jesus and Other Sons of God* (2003); Jane Schaberg. *The Illegitimacy of Jesus: A Feminist Theological Interpretation of the Infancy Narratives* (1987); Thomas F. Torrance. *The Incarnation: The Person and Life of Christ.* Robert T. Walker, ed. (2008); Hoek Van Holland. "The Historicity of the Virginal Conception: A Study in Argumentation." *EuroJTh* 13 (2004) 91–101; Rikk E. Watts. "Immanuel: Virgin Birth Proof Text or Programmatic Warning of Things to Come (Isa 7:14 in Matt 1:23)?" *From Prophecy to Testament: The Function of the Old Testament in the New.* Craig A. Evans, ed. (2004) 92–113.

JOEL B. GREEN

VIRGIN, APOCALYPSES OF THE. The earliest *Apocalypses of the Virgin* are preserved within the oldest apocrypha related to the Dormition (i.e., the death or "sleep") of Mary, which themselves date to the 4th cent. CE (if not even earlier). After Mary's resurrection in paradise, these Dormition narratives conclude with a cosmic tour in which Mary (accompanied sometimes by the apostles) visits the storehouses of the wind and rain, the heavenly Jerusalem, and the future abode of the righteous, and beholds the present torments of the wicked, successfully interceding on their behalf. Two very different accounts of Mary's heavenly journey survive in the earliest Dormition apocrypha from the Palm and Bethlehem traditions, the Ethiopic *Liber Requiei* and the "Six Books" apocryphon respectively. It is likely that these apocalypses of the Virgin circulated independently prior to their incorporation into the Dormition narratives. The apocalypse from the *Liber Requiei* is closely related to the *Apocalypse of Paul*, it appears that the latter used this early *Apocalypse of the Virgin* as one of its primary sources. There is also a Greek *Apocalypse* *of the Virgin*, probably from the 9th cent., whose relation to the *Apocalypse of Paul*, the *Apocalypse of Peter*, and the ancient *Apocalypses of the Virgin* is not well established. The Slavonic translation of this text was especially influential in medieval Russia. Finally, there is another *Apocalypse of the Virgin* preserved uniquely in Ethiopic, estimated to be a 7th-cent. adaptation of the *Apocalypse of Paul*, although this document has not been well studied.

Bibliography: Richard Bauckham. *The Fate of the Dead: Studies on Jewish and Christian Apocalypses* (1998); Stephen J. Shoemaker. *Ancient Traditions of the Virgin Mary's Dormition and Assumption* (2002).

STEPHEN J. SHOEMAKER

VIRGIN, ASSUMPTION OF THE. In modern Roman Catholic theology, the Assumption of the Virgin refers to Mary's ascension in body and soul to heaven at the end of her life. During the first few centuries of Christianity, there is little apparent concern with the end of Mary's life, but in the later 5th cent., several surprisingly diverse traditions suddenly come into view. These narrative and liturgical traditions commemorate the Virgin's Dormition, that is, the separation of her body and soul, and sometimes (but not always) her Assumption. Approximately forty different narratives of Mary's Dormition survive from the early church, preserved in nine ancient and medieval languages. The oldest narrative, probably written during the 3rd cent., is the *Liber Requiei* or *Obsequies of the Virgin*. This apocryphon survives intact only in an Ethiopic translation, but there are significant fragments extant in Syriac and Georgian. Another important early narrative is the so-called "Six Books" apocryphon, a 4th-cent. work preserved in several 5th- and 6th-cent. Syriac manuscripts. This narrative is particularly striking for its witness to a cult of the Virgin already organized by the 4th cent.

Bibliography: Stephen J. Shoemaker. *Ancient Traditions of the Virgin Mary's Dormition and Assumption* (2002).

STEPHEN J. SHOEMAKER

VIRTUES. *See* LISTS, ETHICAL; PATIENCE.

VISION [חָזוֹן khazon; ὅραμα *horama*, ὅρασις *horasis*]. A mystical revelatory experience involving a visual dimension. The OT narrates both waking visions and night visions. Visions often include auditory components and are usually, but not always, associated with prophetic activity or apocalyptic revelation. Visions occur throughout the OT, though in the NT most are clustered in Acts and Revelation.

Various Hebrew and Greek words translated *vision* encompass a range of meanings and literary forms. God establishes the covenant with Abraham through a vision that includes both a conversation and a dream

(Gen 15:1-21). In a night vision Daniel receives the interpretation of Nebuchadnezzar's dream (2:17-45). The Hebrew word **khazon** can serve as a generic introduction to prophetic books (Isa 1:1; Obad 1:1; Nah 1:1) or units (2 Sam 7:17; 1 Chr 17:15; Ezek 7:13; Hab 2:2-3), even as it applies to visions generally (e.g., 1 Sam 3:1; Ps 89:19; Lam 2:9; Hos 12:10). Visions may convey messages from God, introduce the seer to mysteries such as heavenly and eschatological beings and places (1 Kgs 22:19-23; Isa 6; Ezek 40–48; Amos 9:1-10; Revelation includes visions of the risen Jesus, the heavenly court, and the New Jerusalem), provide images that require interpretation (Ezek 1; Amos 7–8), or even require participation on the part of the visionary (Ezek 8:1-18; Rev 10:8-10). Some visions rely upon word plays (Jer 1:11-12; Amos 8:1-3).

Visions play an especially important role in Acts, particularly legitimating the inclusion of the Gentiles. Peter's Pentecost sermon alludes to Joel's prophecy concerning visions and dreams in the last days (Joel 2:28-32 [Heb. 3:1-5]; Acts 2:17-21). Through a visionary encounter with the risen Jesus, Saul turns from a persecutor of the church into its most prominent missionary to the Gentiles (Acts 9:1-9; 22:1-21; 26:2-23). A vision also convinces Peter to evangelize the Gentile Cornelius (10:9-16; 11:1-18). The effectiveness of these visions depends upon complementary visions received by Ananias (9:10-19) and Cornelius (10:1-8). Paul appeals to his visionary and apocalyptic experiences in defending his authority (2 Cor 12:1-10; Gal 1:11-17).

Among the Synoptic Gospels, Matthew alone describes the transfiguration as a vision (17:9). Both biblical apocalypses, Daniel and Revelation, narrate sequences of visions. Visions constitute an essential component for the definition of classical literary apocalypses such as *1 Enoch*, 2 Esd 3–14 (*4 Ezra*), *2* and *3 Baruch*, and the Shepherd of Hermas (*Vision*). *See* APOCALYPTICISM; DREAM; PROPHET, PROPHECY.

GREG CAREY

VISIONS OF IDDO THE SEER. *See* BOOKS REFERRED TO IN THE BIBLE.

VISIT, VISITOR [פָּקַד *paqadh*, רָאָה *ra'ah*; ἐπισκέπτομαι *episkeptomai*, ἔρχομαι *erchomai*, ἐφοδεύω *ephodeuō*, ἱστορέω *historeō*]. A visit entails travel in an effort to make contact with another person or group, while a visitor is the one traveling. **Paqadh** most often refers simply to divine or human movement with the intent to see a person (Judg 15:1; Ps 17:3; Isa 23:17). In the OT, rules of conduct stipulated the GUEST's relationship to the host. Visitors could expect sustenance and certain legal protections while among the Israelites (Gen 18:2-8; Lev 19:10, 33-34; *see* HOSPITALITY; STRANGER). **Paqadh** sometimes had the sense of an unfriendly or menacing visit. Job laments that the Lord visits humans "every morning" to test them (Job 7:18). In Isa 23:17, the Lord visits Tyre for punishment, claiming the wages and merchandise that the city had gained (compare Isa 29:6). But a visit from God could also bring the fulfillment of a promise (Gen 18:14; Jer 29:10).

In the NT, *visit* can again carry the simple meaning of going to see someone (Acts 10:28; 1 Cor 16:5, 12; 2 Cor 1:16; Gal 1:18). Perhaps the most theologically significant NT use of visitation occurs in Matt 25:34-46. At the judgment, the "sheep" are lauded and welcomed because they visited those who were sick (compare Sir 7:35) or imprisoned and welcomed the stranger. Clearly mirroring OT standards of hospitality, the author of the Gospel indicates that acceptance into the kingdom in some way hinges on proper visitation to those in need.

JESSICA TINKLENBERG DEVEGA

VOCATION, NT. Although in non-religious usage the term concerns remunerated employment or profession, a biblical understanding of *vocation* emphasizes the etymological sense of being "called" by God to live out a specific identity, as well as to undertake particular responsibilities and a particular way of life (*see* CALL, CALLING, CALL STORIES). Yet the term *vocation* is to be distinguished from *work* (*see* OCCUPATIONS) in that its primary focus is on context and purpose, rather than activities or accomplishments. A biblical vision of vocation thus implies a divine-human relationship according to which human life is not self-directed or self-sustaining, but contingent upon the gifts and grace of God. From a NT perspective, human identity and vocation are perfectly expressed in the person of Jesus of Nazareth, whose fulfillment of the vocation of humanity enables a similar fulfillment on the part of those who are "in Christ" (Rom 8:1). Thus the foundational human vocation is our call to be restored to the image and likeness of God (Gen 1:26) by becoming "conformed to the image of his Son" (Rom 8:29). In concrete terms, vocation in NT perspective is above all a summons both from Christ and to Christ that is at once radically imperative (Mark 1:16-20; 2:14; 3:13; etc.) and countercultural (1 Cor 1:26-29), yet allows respondents freedom to choose (Mark 10:22-23; Luke 9:59-62; e.g., Judas, Matt 26:14-16; Mark 14:10-11; Luke 22:3-6; John 18:2-5). It is a call for disciples to be both Christ's (Rom 1:6; 1 Cor 1:9) and Christ-like (Rom 13:14), seeking to become all that Christ makes them (Eph 4:1; 2 Thess 1:11), before it is a call to carry out specific tasks or travel to particular places (compare Mark 3:14: "he appointed twelve ... to be with him, and to be sent out"). In particular, Christian vocation is marked by its conscious imitation of Jesus' death and resurrection (Gal 2:20; Phil 2:1-11), which entails a yielding of moral (2 Tim 1:9) and social prerogatives (Mark 10:42-45) in favor of divine vindication and "new creation" (2 Cor 5:17). For followers of Jesus, then, vocation is wholly christocentric, for it consists of obeying, emulating, and cooperating with Christ, yet it is also of universal import, for it concerns the essence of true human identity.

In union with Christ, this universal human vocation is expressed socially in reconciliation and community, as believers reflect in interpersonal relations and the life of the church the same peace and harmony that God has established with and for humanity as a whole (1 Cor 7:15; Col 3:15; Heb 12:14). And insofar as, through Christ, God calls into existence a community marked by holiness (Rom 1:7; 1 Cor 1:2; 2 Pet 1:3-10), so the life of the church is to be characterized by its ethical conduct, its embodiment of social justice, and its stewardship of creation (compare Gen 1:28; 2:15), rather than by monastic withdrawal from the conditions of the world.

Individual vocations—whether or not in direct service to the church—may be understood within the broader salvific goals of fostering human well-being and mutual fidelity under God. Such vocations (however apparently "secular") focus first on serving God (Eph 6:7-8) and may, no less than his calling of the Twelve, be initiated by Christ, to the extent that they reflect and cooperate with his saving purpose. Notwithstanding its radical character, God's call in Christ accommodates and incorporates personal gifts and circumstances, rather than obviating or opposing them (1 Cor 7:17-24). Yet it also relativizes such circumstances by directing our attention beyond them to the things of God (Phil 3:14-15; Col 3:1-3) and the hope of an eschatological future (Eph 1:18; 4:4) in which both human and divine-human relationships will be complete (1 Cor 13:12; Phil 3:20; Rev 21:3).

Vocations within the Christian community are distinguished by their specific focus and function. While charisms bestowed by the Holy Spirit (*see* SPIRITUAL GIFTS) may directly or indirectly benefit humanity in general, cooperating with God in the transformation of creation, their immediate purpose is "to equip the saints for the work of ministry, for building up the body of Christ until, all of us come ... to the measure of the full stature of Christ" (Eph 4:12-13). The gifts of the Spirit thus enable the church to be the church: to model the personal, social, and public identities to which all humanity is called, and to facilitate the particular vocations of individual members whereby they, in turn, articulate and embody God's call in the public arena. In this sense, Christian vocation is bi-directional, exercising particular gifts in response to God, but for the benefit of others (so 1 Pet 4:10: "Like good stewards of the manifold grace of God, serve one another with whatever gift each of you has received"; compare Matt 25:40: "Just as you did it to one of the least of these ... you did it to me").

Accordingly, a NT definition of vocation includes past, present, and future dimensions: having been called into God's kingdom through Christ (salvation), we are presently called to live out the conditions of God's reign (sanctification and service), yet with a view to future fulfillment (eschatological hope). Vocation is also fully trinitarian, fulfilling the will of the Father, imitating Jesus and sharing in his mission as enabled by the Spirit. Disciples of Jesus are thus called by God, in Christ, to the service of humanity, empowered by the Spirit in anticipation of "new heavens and a new earth" (2 Pet 3:13).

Bibliography: Marva J. Dawn. *The Sense of the Call: A Sabbath Way of Life for Those Who Serve God, the Church, and the World* (2006); A. Katherine Grieb. "'The One Who Called You ...': Vocation and Leadership in the Pauline Literature." *Int* 59 (2005) 154–65; Douglas J. Schuurman. *Vocation: Discerning Our Callings in Life* (2004); F. Scott Spencer. "'Follow Me': The Imperious Call of Jesus in the Synoptic Gospels." *Int* 59 (2005) 142–53; R. Paul Stevens. *The Other Six Days: Vocation, Work, and Ministry in Biblical Perspective* (1999).

MICHAEL P. KNOWLES

VOID [וָבֹהוּ תֹהוּ tohu wavohu; ἀκυράω akyraō, καταργέω katergeō]. The emptiness and lack of structure of the universe in an uncreated state. According to Gen 1:2, the universe prior to God's act of creation was chaotic, "a formless void," out of whose watery depths God separated the features of the world. The concept of *void* conveys a sense of formlessness rather than of nonexistence. Hebrew cosmology thus shows a similarity to other ANE descriptions of creation from chaos, in which the forces of disorder are overcome, rather than to the Greek notion of creation *ex nihilo*. The void is contrasted with the created order of things in Job 26:7. *Void* appears in Jer 4:23 to describe the state of the world after a catastrophic judgment, which reverses creation, returning it to unstructured chaos.

In other contexts, *void* may mean "lacking" (Deut 32:28, "a nation void of sense"), "useless" (Jer 19:7; 2 Esd 2:1), or "without (legal) force" (Num 6:12; Matt 15:6; Mark 7:13; Rom 4:14).

SUSAN E. HADDOX

VOPHSI vof'si [וָפְסִי wofsi]. According to Num 13:14, he was the father of Nahbi, the Naphtalite leader sent with other tribal leaders by Moses to spy out Canaan. His name appears in the LXX as Iabi (Ἰαβί), which casts doubt on the MT form of the name.

VOTIVE OFFERING. *See* VOW.

VOW [נֶדֶר nedher; εὐχή euchē, εὔχομαι euchomai]. A speech act similar to PROMISE and OATH. The Hebrew root ndr (נדר, both noun and verb), the Greek noun euchē, and the Greek verb euchomai more specifically refer to a person's explicit commitment to perform a favor for a deity if the deity will respond to his or her request for a favor. Often the noun is used as the object of the verb, as in "to vow a vow."

Vow making was typically motivated by a desire for divine help in daily life, particularly in distress. Vows undertaken at a sanctuary in a complaint ritual in connection with a PRAYER for deliverance would be fulfilled with the complementary ritual of thanksgiving, including public praise of God as well as sacrifice (Pss 22:22-25 [Heb. 22:23-26]; 50:14-15; 116:12-19; *see* SACRIFICES AND OFFERINGS). Vows undertaken in a noncultic context, as acts of personal or communal devotion, might likewise be fulfilled by sacrifices or other offerings, but also by noncultic means (Gen 28:20; Num 21:1-3; 2 Sam 15:7-8). No one was obliged to make a vow, but once spoken, a vow was irrevocably in force, and failure to fulfill it could have negative consequences (Deut 23:21-23; Eccl 5:4-5).

In a cultic context vow making intersected with the regulations maintained by priests. Thus, sacrificial animals offered in fulfillment of vows must be males without blemish (Lev 22:18, 21; compare Mal 1:14) whose flesh must be eaten within two days (Lev 7:16). And when one person's vow entailed the encumbrance of another person (perhaps in service to the sanctuary; compare 1 Sam 1:22), the vow maker could redeem the other person by paying a fee to the priests. The amount depended upon the age and sex of the person redeemed, as well as the vow maker's economic capability (Lev 27:1-8). When a woman's vow was unacceptable to her father or husband, he had a right to nullify it if he acted promptly; otherwise it remained in force (Num 30). Women wanting to fulfill vows despite their husbands' opposition might resort to prostitution as a way of getting funds that they themselves could control and use for this purpose (a practice alluded to in Prov 7:10-20). Such behavior was common enough to provoke a priestly proscription against vows being paid with a prostitute's wages (Deut 23:18).

Vow making also intersected with setting apart certain persons as special devotees of Yahweh, e.g., the Nazirites (*see* NAZIR, NAZIRITE). Their consecration was marked by not consuming wine, not cutting their hair, and not incurring impurity by contact with a corpse (Num 6:3-6). Nazirite status could be maintained under extenuating circumstances or terminated at the appointed time with appropriate sacrifices (Num 6:9-20). Narratives describe persons being obligated to become Nazirites before they were born, on the basis of commitments made by their parents. Samuel's mother, Hannah, vows that if Yahweh will enable her to bear a son, she will give him to serve in a sanctuary and be raised as a perpetual Nazirite (1 Sam 1:9-28, LXX, 4Q51; the term *Nazirite* is lacking in the MT). A similar vow is implied in Samson's parents' acceptance of the angel's promise that God will grant them a son if they observe certain Nazirite practices—but here the mother is to avoid wine and impurity, and the son is to avoid cutting his hair (Judg 13:2-14). In these cases Nazirite status is the consequence of a vow but does not entail taking vows. In contrast, the rules in Num 6 apply vow terminology to the commitments made by Nazirites themselves. This is the only instance of vows being defined negatively in terms of abstinence. These differences could mean that one became a Nazirite in various ways, either perpetually or temporarily, because of vows made by others or vows undertaken on one's own, and by taking on some or all of the characteristic abstentions.

In two stories of tribal leaders, tension between a vow and another obligation produces the central conflict of the narrative. Jephthah promises that if Yahweh gives him victory, he will sacrifice whatever he first meets when he returns. When it is his daughter, he finds himself caught between his vow and Yahweh's ban of child sacrifice (Judg 11:30-40; compare Lev 18:21; 20:2-5; Deut 18:9-14; *see* JEPHTHAH'S DAUGHTER). When Delilah begs Samson to tell her the secret of his strength, he finds himself caught between ensuring the maintenance of his mother's vow that his hair will never be cut and being intimately truthful with his wife (Judg 13–16). In Jephthah's case, the vow is maintained, and in Samson's case it is betrayed; but in both cases misplaced loyalties have tragic consequences. The DtrH thus shows that as the zeal and heroism of the judges increases, the effectiveness of the tribal league ironically decreases.

As a form of "bargaining with God," vow making is embarrassing to some modern sensibilities. Some scholars have attempted to explain it away as a primitive practice beyond which biblical religion gradually progressed. The theory and practice of vows may have changed over time, particularly in connection with postexilic cultic centralization (Deut 12:5-6, 11, 17, 26), but such changes cannot be precisely described because the relevant texts are hard to date and give only scattered impressions. In any case, it is unlikely that vow making evolved to the point of not entailing a quid pro quo. Late references are sparse (Sir 18:22-23; Acts 18:18; 21:23), but they suggest continuity with earlier customs.

The continued prominence of vows in contemporary popular religion reflects the biblical view that a God who cannot be somehow bargained with is no god at all. Theological attempts to reckon with this should note two things. First, what is promised in fulfillment of a vow is never a payment in the sense that it has a value equivalent to the favor bestowed by God—just as what I might do to thank someone for saving my life could never be truly equivalent. And second, the vow maker does not necessarily assume that God's response can only be what is asked for.

Bibliography: T. W. Cartledge. *Vows in the Hebrew Bible and the Ancient Near East* (1992).

MICHAEL H. FLOYD

VULGATE vuhl´gayt. From Latin *vulgatus*, "common," the standardized Latin version of the Bible ascribed to JEROME (342–420 CE) and used by the Christian church as an authoritative translation for over 1,000 years. *See* VERSIONS, LATIN.

VULTURE [נֶשֶׁר nesher, פֶּרֶס peres, רָחָם rakham; ἀετός aetos]. Since vultures are notorious carrion eaters, several species are mentioned in the lists of unclean birds. It is generally assumed that peres (Lev 11:13; Deut 14:12) denotes the magnificent bearded vulture (*Gypaëtus barbatus*), while rakham (Lev 11:18; Deut 14:16) designates the Egyptian vulture (*Neophron percnopterus*). Unfortunately, the English word *vulture* denotes both the latter species, a scavenger feeding on offal, and the majestic Griffon vulture (*Gyps fulvus*), still a common sight in the 19th cent. (Tristram). Despite scholarly consensus that nesher in most cases designates the Griffon vulture (e.g., in Mic 1:16 where this bird is described as being "bald"), modern Bible versions tend to retain the traditional translation "EAGLE" (e.g., Mic 1:16 NRSV, although NIV renders "vulture").

The negative associations evoked by *vulture* often influence the translation "eagle" in cases when nesher is used as a metaphor for divine agency (e.g., Exod 19:4; Deut 32:11). Thus "vulture" is often the translation in passages that highlight the negative (Prov 30:17; Hos 8:1; Matt 24:28//Luke 17:37). Various passages indicate the Griffon's ("eagle's") swiftness (Deut 28:49; Hab 1:8), its aeries found in inaccessible cliffs (Jer 49:16), its powerful wings (Isa 40:31), its exceptional sight (Job 39:29), or its care for its young (Deut 32:11). *See* BIRDS OF THE BIBLE.

Bibliography: J. Feliks. *The Animal World of the Bible* (1962); Henry B. Tristram. *The Fauna and Flora of Palestine* (1884).

GÖRAN EIDEVALL

WADI wah´dee [נַחַל nakhal; χειμάρρους cheimarrous]. A valley or canyon carved by running water. Wadis usually contain rivers created by runoff during the rainy season but are dry during other parts of the year (1 Kgs 17:7). Flash flooding can occur rapidly in wadis, turning them into dangerous torrents. The term can also refer to the dry riverbed at the bottom of a valley.

KEVIN A. WILSON

WADI BESOR. *See* BESOR, WADI.

WADI ED-DALIYEH. *See* DALIYEH, WADI ED.

WADI EL-ARISH. *See* EGYPT, WADI OF.

WADI EL-HESA. *See* HESA, WADI EL.

WADI EL-MUJIB. *See* MUJIB, WADI EL.

WADI ESHCOL. *See* ESHCOL, WADI.

WADI ES-SANT. *See* SANT, WADI ES.

WADI KIDRON. *See* KIDRON VALLEY.

WADI MURABBAAT. *See* MURABBAAT, WADI.

WADI MUSA. *See* MUSA, WADI.

WADI OF EGYPT. *See* EGYPT, WADI OF.

WADI OF THE WILLOWS [נַחַל הָעֲרָבִים nakhal ha'aravim]. Willows are a genus of trees that thrive near waterways; thus Isa 44:4 refers to "willows by flowing streams." The Wadi of the Willows is thought to be on the ancient frontier of Moab, part of the modern Wadi el-Hesa. Isaiah 15:7 describes the Moabites fleeing over the Wadi of the Willows, carrying their belongings. *See* HESA, WADI EL; WILLOW.

JOAN E. COOK, SC

WADI SHITTIM. *See* SHITTIM, WADI.

WADI ZERED. *See* ZERED, WADI.

WAFERS [צַפִּיחִת tsappikhith, רָקִיק raqiq]. Pieces of thin, unleavened bread that served as offerings in the Israelite cult. The Levites were responsible for assisting in the preparation of "wafers of unleavened bread" for the Temple (1 Chr 23:29). The regulations for baked grain offerings prescribed unleavened wafers made of choice flour and spread with oil (Lev 2:4). Unleavened wafers were among the cereal gifts offered during the consecration of Aaron and his sons as priests (Exod 29:2, 23; Lev 8:26). Wafers were prescribed for typical thanksgiving offerings (Lev 7:12) as well as for the offerings required of persons completing a Nazirite vow (Num 6:15, 19). Manna is said to have tasted "like wafers made with honey" (Exod 16:31). *See* NAZIR, NAZIRITE; SACRIFICES AND OFFERINGS.

TONY W. CARTLEDGE

WAGES [מַשְׂכֹּרֶת maskoreth, פְּעֻלָּה pe'ullah, שָׂכָר sakhar; μισθός misthos, ὀψώνιον opsōnion]. In English, the word *wages* refers to payment for work performed or services rendered for another on the basis of an explicit or implicit agreement. The word refers to the outcome of a reciprocal interaction (quid pro quo) between some person performing some service or task on behalf of another and the other requiting the agent for services rendered.

In the OT, words translated as "wages" include maskkoreth, pe'ullah, and sakhar. The LXX uses misthos for all of these. However, as the English versions indicate, these words cover a far broader area than "wages." They include any reciprocation for services rendered, whether contracted for or not, such as a benefaction, reward, or retribution, depending on context. As benefaction or retribution, the words refer to a form of generalized reciprocity not based on obligation ("I give with no expectation of specific repayment"). Thus as contracted obligation, misthos (and its Hebrew equivalents) means wages, payment, and (expected) recompense; but as benefaction, it refers to unexpected recompense, to reward.

In Mediterranean antiquity when people were of either high (2 percent) or low (98 percent) social status, people who worked for and accepted wages were of low social status. A frequent lament among biblical writers, aimed at elites, is that daily wage earners were deprived of the pay owed to them (Lev 19:13; Deut 24:14-15; Jer 22:23; Mal 3:5; see also Jas 5:4). Sirach considers depriving an employee of wages to be tantamount to murder (Sir 34:22). As a rule, the services such wage earners rendered involved physical, manual labor. Elites and elite professionals (lawyers, physicians, politicians, prophets, and priests) believed it was beneath their dignity to accept recompense for services rendered, while to work with one's hands was totally demeaning. The prohibition of (manual) work on the Sabbath in Israel enabled Israelites to act like elites for one day in the week (Exod 20:8-11).

Later, another word for wages, opsōnion, emerged among Greek speakers. This word originally referred to soldier's pay (for food) in the Hellenistic period (see 1 Esd 4:56; 1 Macc 3:28; 14:32; Luke 3:14; 1 Cor 9:7). It eventually was used to refer to any pay or wages for a contracted job. Opsōnion was the outcome of an interaction of balanced reciprocity based on mutual obligation (see 2 Cor 11:8). Paul's well-known statement in Rom 6:23 that "the wages (opsōnion) of sin is death," presumes the reader understands that sin here is a personified entity. Romans personified Victory, War, Health, and the like, and even built temples in their honor. Paul understood Sin as such an entity. Personified Sin functioned as a cultural value of willingness to challenge God's honor. Sin was like a person who claimed worth for dishonoring God, for claiming superiority to God. The quality here is enveloped in an attitude of feeling superior to God and God's honor, a willingness to shame God and anybody else, a willingness to stand up to God, a willingness to put oneself over and opposite God. To serve and honor Sin was a task deserving of recompense, in this case death. On the other hand, endless life in Christ Jesus is the outcome of generalized reciprocity, the unearned, free gift of God (Rom 6:23).

The NT writers continue to use misthos as in the OT in both senses: contracted wages and noncontracted payment or reward. In the LXX, misthos as the outcome of balanced reciprocity (wages or pay) is found in the well-known haggling between Laban and Jacob (Gen 30–31) and frequently in the OT (Exod 2:9; 22:19; Lev 19:13; Num 18:31; Deut 15:18; 24:14-15; 2 Chr 15:7; Job 7:2; Jer 22:13; 38:16; Ezek 29:18-19; Mic 3:11; Hag 1:6; Zech 8:10; Mal 3:5). In the NT, the word in this sense is found in Matt 20:8; Luke 10:7; John 4:36; Rom 4:4; 1 Cor 3:8-14; 1 Tim 5:18; Jas 5:4; Rev 22:12.

Misthos as the outcome of generalized reciprocity is found in the LXX Gen 15:1; Ruth 2:12; Prov 11:18-21; Isa 23:18; 40:10; 62:11; Ezek 27:16, 27, 33 and in the NT: Matt 6:2, 5, 16; Mark 9:41; Luke 6:23, 35; 1 Cor 9:17-18; 2 John 1:18; Jude 1:11; Rev 11:18. "Wages of wickedness" in Acts 1:18 and 2 Pet 2:13-15 refers to unjust gain, bribery, extortion, and the like. See LABOR; OCCUPATIONS; TRADE AND COMMERCE.

Bibliography: Bruce J. Malina. *Christian Origins and Cultural Anthropology* (1986).

BRUCE J. MALINA

WAGON. *See* CART.

WAHEB way'heb [וָהֵב wahev]. Place listed in a fragment of epic poetry cited from the "Book of the Wars of the LORD" (Num 21:14-15). The citation seems to locate Waheb near the Arnon River, a boundary of Moab and one of the stops on the wilderness itinerary. Another poetic fragment appears in Num 21:17-18, supporting the theory that the citations are meant to corroborate details of the journey.

JOAN E. COOK, SC

WAILING. *See* MOURNING.

WAISTCLOTH [אֵזוֹר 'ezor]. An undergarment worn by men around the loins (*see* LOINCLOTH). Describing God's ability to humble the mighty, Job states that God will strip a king of his sash and replace it with waistcloth. *See* CLOTH, CLOTHES.

WAIT, WAITING ON THE LORD, GOD [יָחַל yakhal, קָוָה qawah, תִּקְוָה tiqwah; διαλείπω dialeipō, ἐλπίζω elpizō, ἐλπίς elpis, ἐπέχω epechō, προσδέχομαι prosdechomai, προσδοκάω prosdokaō, προσέχω prosechō, ὑπομένω hypomenō]. In English, this word is represented by two overlapping concepts, "to wait for" and "to hope in" someone or something. Waiting can be quite literal as in waiting for something or someone. In Gen 8:12, Noah waits for the flood to abate. Saul waits seven days for Samuel in 1 Sam 13:8. There is also a sense of waiting for a battle or in ambush against enemies as "lay in wait against Shechem in four companies" (Judg 9:34). Waiting in these cases is in a literal sense. In the Psalms and the Prophets, the word can have that same meaning of waiting for someone or "lying in wait." Enemies often "lie in wait" to ambush the one praying, giving a sinister meaning (Pss 59:3; 119:95; Prov 1:11; 24:15; Hos 6:9; Mic 7:2).

However, another important and indeed the central focus in the Psalms and much of the Prophets is "to wait for the Lord" (Ps 25:5 and seventeen more times; Isa 25:9; 40:31; Mic 7:7). Waiting for the Lord is an act of faith that God will hear the individual's or the people's prayers and act on their behalf. *Waiting* is also a term in complaint sections where the one praying is waiting and God seems to be distant (Ps 69:3; Isa 8:17). Just as in the modern world, waiting for results is a challenge and one that both the individual and the community needs to be reminded of in times when God seems absent.

In the NT, *wait* has the same meanings as in the OT such as to wait for someone or something (Luke 8:40; Acts 17:16). Yet, as above, "waiting" can also have a theological and spiritual meaning. In Matt 11:3, the disciples of John the Baptist come to Jesus and ask, "Are you the one who is to come, or are we to wait for another?" referring, of course, to the wait for the Lord's Messiah that is the center of much of the Gospels' theology. In the Epistles, there is a theological dimension to the waiting as well. In Rom 8:19 and 8:23, the creation and the first fruits of the Spirit wait for the coming of God. In 1 Cor 1:7, Christians wait for "the revealing of our Lord Jesus Christ." Just as in the OT, this waiting is a faith stance that is closely related to hope (also compare, e.g., Sir 2:7). Waiting on the Lord and the coming again of God is clearly a spiritual endeavor that requires patience and growth. *See* HOPE.

BETH L. TANNER

WALLS [חוֹמָה khomah, קִיר qir; φραγμός phragmos, τεῖχος teichos]. A vertical structure enclosing or dividing an area. One thinks immediately of the walls of buildings, but cities and fortresses were also distinguished by their defensive walls.

The primary materials for walls in the ANE were stone and mud brick. Frequently, the two would be combined, with the foundation and lower courses of a structure being of stone and the upper courses being mud brick. Mud brick walls in particular would regularly be plastered to prevent rainwater from causing the wall to deteriorate. Simple walls in a house could be constructed of field stone; more impressive structures would be made using hewn stone. These shaped stones gave the wall a nearly vertical face and created level horizontal courses. Quite frequently, even simple house walls would have two rows of larger stones providing relatively smooth inner and outer faces and smaller chink stones filling the gaps. Other houses used a "pier and rubble" construction with piers constructed of large, rough-hewn stone at intervals and field stones filling the space between the piers. Such piers provided better support for ceiling or roof beams.

Monumental structures such as palaces and temples often had walls constructed of ashlar masonry, very finely hewn stones that fit so well they required no mortar. These walls frequently utilized a header-stretcher construction (the longer axis of the stone running perpendicular [header] or parallel [stretcher] to the face of the wall).

City walls were often quite massive. Some cities also had a sloping glacis protecting the base of the outer face of the wall. In the Middle Bronze Age, earthen ramparts were sometimes constructed, with the wall built on top of the rampart. Typical city wall types were the casemate wall (parallel inner and outer walls with perpendicular walls linking them at intervals), the filled casemate, and the solid wall. Some city walls were constructed with offsets and insets rather than having a straight face, which both strengthened the wall and provided better defense against attack.

In figurative usage, the parted waters of the Red Sea are called "walls" (Exod 14:22, 29). God makes the prophet Jeremiah "a fortified city, an iron pillar, and a bronze wall" against the attacks of all the people (Jer 1:18; 15:20). In Zechariah's vision, the restored Jerusalem is "like villages without walls" (Zech 2:4), with God as a wall of fire to protect the city (Zech 2:5).

JOEL F. DRINKARD JR.

WANDER [נָדַד nadhadh, נוּד nudh, נוּעַ nua‘, שָׁגָה shaghah, תָּעָה ta‘ah; ἀποπλανάω apoplanaō, διέρχομαι dierchomai, ἐκτρέπω ektrepō, πλανάω planaō]. The term *wander* is often used in the OT to refer to those who are not settled and therefore move about constantly, sometimes aimlessly. Cain is forced to wander after killing Abel (Gen 4:12-14), and Hagar wanders after being expelled by Sarah (Gen 21:14). Abraham and Jacob are said to wander, sometimes at God's command (Gen 20:13; Deut 26:50; Ps 105:12-13). As punishment, Israel must wander in the wilderness for forty years before entering Canaan (Num 32:12), and the prophets foresaw a time when Israel would be made to wander again (Hos 9:17; Amos 8:12). Wandering can also serve as a metaphor for those who turn from God (Jer 14:10) or lack leadership (Zech 10:2).

In the NT, *wander* is used negatively of those who turn from truth (1 Tim 6:10; 2 Tim 4:2; Jas 5:19-20) and more positively of the saints of the past who wandered to escape persecution (Heb 11:38). A demon who is cast out is said to wander until it decides to return to the person from whom it was cast out (Matt 12:43; Luke 11:24).

JOHN I. LAWLOR

WANT [אָוָה ’awah, חָסֵר khaser, חֶסֶר kheser, חָפֵץ khafets, חָשַׁק khashaq, מַחְסוֹר makhsor; חָסִר khassir; βούλομαι boulomai, ἐπιθυμέω epithymeō, ζητέω zēteō, θέλω thelō]. The term *want* is frequently used periphrastically in the NRSV with no directly corresponding word in the text (e.g., Judg 19:24; 2 Cor 8:1). In those instances where there is a corresponding term, *want* translates a variety of words that convey different senses of wishing or desiring. In the OT, *want* is used to express ideas as diverse as a longing for the "day of the LORD" (Amos 5:18, ’awah), David's desire to conduct a census (2 Sam 24:3, khafets), and a man's feeling of sexual attachment to a woman (Deut 21:11, khashaq). A number of Greek terms are similarly translated as "want" in the NT (e.g., Matt 12:46, zēteō; John 18:39, boulomai; Heb 6:11, epithymeō), though thelō is the underlying term in the overwhelming number of cases.

The word *want* is also used for a quite different semantic field in the OT, rendering the root khsr (חסר), which is otherwise frequently translated "lack" (e.g., Deut 2:7; Neh 9:21). "Wanting" in this sense of khsr takes on a theological significance in the OT. The Deuteronomic covenant promises Israel a land of great prosperity, where they "will lack nothing" (Deut 8:9). A similar assumption underlies Ps 34:9-10 ([Heb. 34:10-11]; "those who fear him have no want.... those who seek the LORD lack no good thing") and, more famously, Ps 23:1: "The LORD is my shepherd, I shall not want."

MATT JACKSON-MCCABE

WAR CLUB. *See* CLUB.

WAR HORSE. *See* HORSE.

WAR OF THE SONS OF LIGHT AND THE SONS OF DARKNESS. *See* WAR SCROLL.

WAR SCROLL. A manuscript from Qumran Cave 1 that depicts the preparation for, and the various phases of, the eschatological battle (1QM). The "Sons of Light," the faithful remnant of Israel, are to be opposed to the "Sons of Darkness," a coalition including Edom, Moab, Ammon, Philistia, the Kittim of Asshur, and "the violators of the covenant," under the rule of Belial. Helped by Michael and the heavenly hosts, the Sons of Light are to be an instrument of God to bring an end to wickedness and to establish Israel's domination forever.

After an introductory apocalyptic overview derived from Dan 11–12 (1QM 1), the scroll provides instructions to prepare for the war and to direct the troops (1QM I–IX), a collection of prayers and hymns (1QM IX–XIV), and a description of the ultimate military engagements after speeches of encouragement (1QM XIV–XX?). The bottom lines of all the columns and the end of the manuscript after 1QM XIX are lost (a small fragment recovered from cave 1, 1Q33, may preserve a few letters from 1QM XX). The *War Scroll* was copied during the second half of the 1st cent. BCE.

Several other manuscripts about war were discovered in Qumran Caves 4 and 11. All were copied during the 1st cent. BCE or the beginning of the 1st cent. CE. Some come from the same recension as 1QM (4Q492, 4Q494, 4Q495, 4Q496): belonging to all parts of the text, they preserve a few of its missing elements and significant variants (e.g., the mention of the "prince" in the Rule for the standards, 4Q496 10, which is not found in 1QM III, 13). Others preserve different recensions (4Q471, 4Q491, 4Q493, 4Q497): they contain a few parallels to the text of 1QM, illuminate its redactional history, offer hints of what might have stood in its lacunae, or add new details (e.g., particular types of trumpets or war machines, reference to the collection of booty, and the triumphal gathering in Jerusalem).

Two copies of a related "Book of the War" (4Q285, 11Q14) describe the final victory over the Kittim, including the capture, trial, and execution of their king by the Prince of the Congregation, and the blessing of the eschatological community in the purified land. An independent "Self-Glorification Hymn" (4Q491c) reports the exceptional claim of a speaker to have been exalted among divine beings, eventually sitting on a throne in judgment (three copies of a similar text have been identified in manuscripts of Hymns: 1QH^a XXVI, 6–17, 4Q427 7, and 4Q431 = 4Q471b).

The *War Scroll* achieved its form through literary growth, as confirmed by: 1) the tensions and duplications among the main parts of the document; and 2) the fact that different recensions from Cave 4 provide a shorter and probably earlier text in almost every case where a comparison is possible. Its older elements date from the Hellenistic period (parts of col. 3–9 are close to the Maccabean art of warfare), whereas the final composition probably took place soon after the Roman takeover of Palestine (63 BCE).

The scroll is an eschatological rule that imitates, in a religious and utopian way, a Greco-Roman tactical treatise. Its authors have adapted and shaped collections of rules, prayers, and speeches of biblical inspiration into a sort of guidebook for the priests and Levites in charge of leading the eschatological war so that they can properly perform their future duties. This powerful vision certainly contributed to legitimate the separation of the Qumran sectarians from a corrupted environment and to support their claim as the true remnant of Israel committed to the Mosaic Law. It may also have motivated part of the congregation to join the Great Revolt against Rome (66–70 CE).

Bibliography: Philip R. Davies. *1QM, the War Scroll from Qumran: Its Structure and History* (1977); Jean Duhaime. "War Scroll." *The Dead Sea Scrolls, 2. Text, Translation, Notes.* James H. Charlesworth, ed. (1995); Jean Duhaime. *The War Texts* (2004); Yigael Yadin. *The Scroll of the War of the Sons of Light against the Sons of Darkness* (1962, Heb. 1955).

JEAN DUHAIME

WAR, HOLY. *See* COVENANT, OT AND NT; HOLY WAR; WAR, IDEAS OF.

WAR, IDEAS OF. Despite the diverse ideas of war in the Bible, much of past biblical scholarship has been unduly focused on only one of these ideas, namely "holy war" or "Yahweh-war." In contrast, the present article examines the various ideologies and theologies of war in the OT canonically, progressing from Genesis to the Prophets and Writings. A final section treats war in the NT.

A. Accounts of Israel's Origins
   1. Genesis
   2. Exodus–Joshua
   3. Judges
   4. 1–2 Samuel and 1–2 Kings
B. The Latter Prophets
C. The Writings
D. The New Testament
Bibliography

A. Accounts of Israel's Origins

In the narrative extending from Genesis to 2 Kings, one can distinguish three accounts of Israel's origins that correspond to what may have been three, formerly independent, literary works: Genesis, Exodus–Joshua, and 1–2 Samuel (and 1–2 Kings). According to this view, the book of Judges serves as a literary bridge connecting the latter two works. Each of these accounts sets forth a distinct idea of war.

1. Genesis

The political ideal of the book of Genesis is not world unity but rather a plurality of peoples. After recounting how Yahweh disrupted the building project at Babel and scattered nations over the face of the earth, the authors continue in the patriarchal narratives to unfold their concept of harmonious and peaceful coexistence. Isaac, e.g., in order to avoid conflict over access to water sources (a typical case for war), opted simply to move on and build other wells (26:15-22).

The patriarchs are, however, not pacifists. Abram goes to war in order to defend his southern Canaanite neighbors against external aggression (chap. 14). Nevertheless, he does not engage in "holy war," and the book makes clear that the patriarchs did not employ military methods to establish territorial rights or increase their wealth (for Abram, see 14:21-24; an exception is Jacob's peculiar statement in 48:22). Overall, the book of Genesis contradicts view of ancient Israel as a militant people.

2. Exodus–Joshua

Whereas Genesis portrays Israel's origins as within the land (Jacob/Israel is born in the land), the narrative beginning in Exodus and extending to Joshua presents Israel coming to Canaan, a new land (e.g., see Exod 3:8) from far away (Egypt). The redactional connection of the two works alters the interpretation of what were originally alternative concepts: the first (patriarchal) tenure in the land is peaceful, while the second follows liberation and military conquest. The war ideology in Exodus–Joshua could not be more different from that of Genesis: whereas Abraham fought in solidarity with his neighbors, the Israelites now wage war in order to wipe out the land's former inhabitants. Moreover, this work attributes military success to divine rather than human heroic action.

Israel's most formative war is also her first war. What directly occasions the exodus is ironically the pharaoh's strategy to oppress the Israelites so that the latter would not pose a threat in the event of war or "escape from the land" (Exod 1:9-10). The climax of the exodus itself is presented as a battle between the pharaoh and his select armies against Yahweh, the divine warrior (15:3) who fights for Israel (14:13-14). As Israel's first war hero, Yahweh is also Israel's first and rightful king, and is accordingly celebrated as such (compare 15:21-22 with 1 Sam 18:6-7). Before divine kingship is replaced by that of a human war hero (see §A4, 1–2 Samuel), the Israelites fight against a series of kings, and the descriptions of these battles have a pronounced antimonarchic tendency (Num 21–24; 31:8; Deut 2:26–3:11; 4:47; 7:24; 29:7-8 [Heb. 29:6-7]; Josh 2–13; see also Judg 3–5, 11). In Exodus–Deuteronomy, the role of the human warrior-king is assumed by the prophet Moses and his successor Joshua, who act as mediators and representatives of divine power to Israel. Moses' authority and the power of "the staff of God" are confirmed in the

victories over the Egyptians and later the Amalekites (Exod 14:31; 17:8-16).

Throughout Exodus–Joshua, war is not the special responsibility of a king, stratified military personnel, or a standing army. Instead, all Israel is expected to fight (see especially Num 1–3), and insofar as they wage many wars in their journey through the wilderness and entrance into the land, Israel may be described as a nation of warriors (see "the generation of warriors" in Deut 2:14-16) in this formative period of her history.

In keeping with this identity, Israelite society is conceived as a war camp, which is organized around the tabernacle housing the ark of the covenant. The ark leads Israel on its journey through the desert, which is conceived as a battle (Num 10:35-36). Any military action without the ark is doomed to failure (Num 14:39-45; compare Deut 1:42). Later Moses presents the Torah he declared in the plains of Moab to the Levites who carry the ark (Deut 31:9, 25-26). The ark then plays a central role in the representative victory after crossing the Jordan (Josh 6). What seems originally to have served as means of transporting a cultic figurine into battle (e.g., compare "ark of God/Yahweh" in 1 Sam 4–7) symbolizes here the covenant as the guarantee of Israel's military success and political prosperity. One may compare this idea to the promise that Joshua would succeed in conquering the land as long as he remained steadfast in meditating upon the Torah (Josh 1:8).

A prominent theme in the war accounts of Exodus–Joshua is faith in Yahweh. At the Red Sea, Israel is commanded to be still and to allow Yahweh to fight for them (Exod 14:13-14). In the end, the people "trust" Yahweh and Moses his prophet (14:31; compare 2 Chr 20:20; Isa 7:9). On the next stage of their journey, the spies return with conflicting reports, and the people express their desire to return to Egypt. Yahweh then asks how long the Israelites will persist in their disbelief (Num 14:11; compare Deut 1:32; 9:23). The threatened punishment is complete abandonment, which Moses succeeds in reducing to a sentence of death in the desert for the unbelieving generation (Num 14:13-38).

After "the generation of warriors" has finally passed away (Deut 2:14-16), Moses addresses Israel in the plains of Moab in preparation for the impending wars of conquest. His speeches, which take up the better part of Deuteronomy, review past battles (chaps. 1–3; 7:18-19; 8:14-15; 29:1-7 [Heb. 28:69–29:6]) and emphasize that it is Yahweh who fights Israel's wars (7:17-24; 9:1-7; 31:1-8, 23). However, Israel's God will not dislodge the inhabitants of the land all at once lest wild animals rise up in unoccupied regions (7:22; see Exod 23:29-30). Other passages reflect upon the reason for Yahweh's military assistance: in addition to the covenant with the patriarchs and Yahweh's own honor, it is the indigenous nations' wickedness (e.g., 7:7-8; 9:4-7, 27-29). Here war is understood as divine punishment and judgment, which differs from its character hitherto (liberation, defense, and conquest of land).

Moses' discourses in Deuteronomy frame a law code that aims to regulate life once the land is conquered. Within this code, rules pertaining to war and the military, which are in themselves relatively unique for the ANE, occupy a considerable amount of space (20:1-20; 21:10-14; 23:10-14 [Heb. 23:11-15]; 25:17-19) and reflect a range of perspectives. The rules of engagement in chap. 20 anticipate principles of just war theory insofar as they require Israelite armies to demonstrate restraint. An important aspect of the Torah's war ideology is found in Lev 26 and Deut 28, which delineate the blessings/curses for obedience/disobedience. Among the various blessings, Israel is promised military success and political strength. Failure to keep the commandments will be punished with defeat on the battlefield and exile, which are described at greater length. These curse-texts introduce the idea that it is Israel's God who afflicts her with war. In Gen 6–9 the whole earth is wiped out by a flood, which often symbolizes war elsewhere (Isa 8:7-8; Dan 11:10, 40). The divine "bow" that Yahweh places in the clouds serves as a sign of the promise never again to cause this kind of devastation (Gen 9:13-17). Here, however, Yahweh threatens to wage war against not the earth as a whole but rather Israel in particular. This notion, which likely originated in the Prophets, is the presupposition for all that follows in the biblical narrative. Joshua and Judges split the double role played by war in Deut 28, the former portraying compliance and military conquest, and the latter transgression and the loss of the land.

With respect to the BAN, the conception in Deuteronomy and Joshua is unique. Most often this practice functions as a form of severe punishment and retribution (e.g., Isa 34:2), which resembles ban notions elsewhere in the ANE (see, e.g., the Mesha Stele or MOABITE STONE). Other texts link the ban with special gratitude for divine assistance inasmuch as the victor forgoes any material gain (see, e.g., Num 21:1-3). In Deuteronomy and Joshua, however, the idea is not only more prevalent (compare, e.g., Deut 2:34; 3:6; and Josh 2:10 with the accounts in Numbers) but also the Israelites are required to wipe out the prior inhabitants of the land (the "seven nations") in order to avoid their cultic influence (Deut 7:2-5; 20:15-18). The ban in these two books is therefore not elicited by anger or desire for retribution, although such vengeance is required for other peoples (see, e.g., Deut 25:17-19). In contrast to Deut 7:2-5, which treats the ban together with prohibitions of intermarriage and alliances, the passages 2:34; 3:6; and 20:15-18 make it clear that all men, women, and children were to be annihilated. Many scholars treat the passages 2:34 and 3:6, along with all of chaps. 1–3, as part of a late Deuteronomistic redactional framework. Similarly, 20:15-18 is widely considered to be an addition, which confines the application of the forgoing lenient regulations solely to "very distant" cities. The transmitted shape of the book of Joshua presupposes these advanced compositional stages of Deuteronomy

insofar as it portrays how Joshua executes the ban on all the cities he conquers. The only group not wiped out is the Hivites/Gibeonites, who pretend to come from a distant country (chap. 9). An instance of conscious noncompliance with the ban requirement jeopardized Israel's military success (chap. 7). That Joshua did not leave a soul alive in all the cities he conquered is underscored in 11:10-22. However, the second half of the book affirms that many of the land's prior inhabitants survived (e.g., 16:10; 17:12-18).

3. Judges

In order to explain how the hegemony established by Joshua had been largely forfeited by the time of Samuel, the book of Judges creates an intermediate era initiated by a generation "who did not know the LORD" (2:10; compare "who did not know Joseph" [Exod 1:8] in the redactional bridge between Genesis and Exodus–Joshua). National unity dissolves as Israel abandons her own God in a favor of a plurality of other Gods (e.g., 2:12). This, in turn, leads to suffering in war: Yahweh withdraws protection so that Israel is both assaulted by her enemies and no longer witnesses success on her military campaigns (2:15-16). The "rest" from wars enjoyed by the land at the climax of the book of Joshua (11:23) is replaced by perennial fighting interrupted by intermediate periods of "rest" (Judg 3:11, 30; 5:31; 8:28). In the most desperate moments, "champions" or "judges" are divinely raised up to deliver Israel from her enemies. However, these engagements never lead to Israel's political centralization and consolidation. Indeed, victories often arouse intertribal jealousy and conflicts that evolve into protracted internecine fighting (e.g., 5:15-18; 8:1-3; 9:23-57; 12:1-6; chaps. 17–21). The generation that conquered the land avoided such conflict (see Josh 22:10-34).

The stories of the judges themselves seem to consist in large part of older regional legends of war heroes. The reconstructed forms of these legends reflect a type of warfare that is comparable to that in the portrayals of Saul and David as well as the later kings of Israel and Judah. Characteristic of these texts is the nexus between military victory and rule of kingship. Thus, Jephthah is promised to be made the "head" of Gileadite society if he returns victorious from battle (11:4-10). The same ideology of monarchic rule is found in the stories of Gideon (8:22-23), Saul (1 Sam 11:14-15), and David (inter alia 2 Sam 5:1-3). One could catalog other features of these texts, such as pre-battle oracles, valor, chivalric code of conduct, dueling, taunts, kinship, sharing the booty, capturing divine images and symbols, tricksterism, etc. According to this literature, war is not explained theologically but is regarded basically as a positive and natural activity through which both rulers and groups consolidate their power.

In drawing upon these legends to write a history from a pan-Israelite perspective, the authors of Judges portray Yahweh exploiting the military prowess and personal agendas of individual warriors (Othniel, Ehud, Barak, Gideon, Jephthah, and Samson) for the welfare of the people as a whole. As elsewhere in the ANE, military success and glory is attributed ultimately to the national God. However, here Yahweh grants victory for the sake of Israel rather than a dynasty or ruler (see however 11:9-11). This characteristic feature is accompanied by a shift of attention from the human heroes to divine involvement. For example, in the story of Deborah and Barak, a prophetess of Yahweh directs each moment of a battle (4:4-16), delivers the enemy general into the hand of a woman rather than Israel's commander (4:9), throws the enemy into a panic (4:15), and finally is celebrated as a war hero after the battle (chap. 5). Indeed, the book often casts shadows on individual warriors, emphasizing their hubris and tragic deaths (8:24-27; 9:53-55; 11:30-40; 16:4-31). The most important message of Judges is that the generations after Joshua must fight wars because they have sinned. It thus presents a punitive conception of war rather than identifying it as an unavoidable condition of the nation's existence.

4. 1–2 Samuel and 1–2 Kings

While the book of Judges presents war as the means through which Israel forfeits the unity enjoyed in the age of Joshua, the book of Samuel portrays war as the path to Israel's political consolidation. Although one can isolate a "Judges redaction" in the book of Samuel, especially in the first eight chapters, war is not linked to Israel's prior failure as it always is in Judges. Inasmuch as war is fought for self-defense, political autonomy, and territorial conquest, Samuel resembles the conquest account in Exodus–Joshua, which also emphasizes the positive role of war. Similarly, the book of Judges may be compared to Kings, which begins by portraying a period of peace (the reign of Solomon) and moves on to recount the division of the kingdom, the battles fought between Israel and Judah, and the wars that finally brought an end to their political autonomy. The primary difference between Judges and Kings is that the former depicts a cycle of war and peace, whereas the latter presents a gradual demise (see, however, Judg 17–21).

In recounting the emergence of the monarchy, 1–2 Samuel emphasizes the changes this institution would bring to Israelite society—not least in the areas of warfare and the military. Samuel describes in his address to the Israelites the chariot-warfare and the weapons industry that will accompany the establishment of a kingdom (1 Sam 8:11-12). When pleading for a monarchy, the people refer to the king's role in battle (8:20), and beginning with Saul's first battle against the Ammonites (chap. 11), it is this role that dominates the account of the monarchy in the rest of Samuel and Kings. Both Judges and Samuel are critical of Israel's natural impulse to crown human military heroes: Yahweh is responsible for all victory and is therefore Israel's king. Though the book of Samuel ultimately embraces the monarchy, it sets the anointing of Saul and David before their first battles. Rather than the places where kings are made, battlefields serve as divine testing grounds: failure to fight according to divine commandment results in forfeiture of office (1 Sam 15). In David's first programmatic battle, which sets the interpretive framework for all that follows, he eschews the weaponry of the monarchy so that "all this assembly may know that the LORD does not save by sword and spear" (1 Sam 17:47).

The descriptions of war in the book of Kings have many themes in common with Samuel (even though Kings presents war for the most part as a divine punitive measure). Thus, the most problematic wars for both are the civil wars. In Samuel these internal battles are fought between father and son (2 Sam 15–19) as well as political opponents (2 Sam 2–4, 20). Kings refers often to the wars between Israel and Judah (see, e.g., 1 Kgs 14:30), and recounts how Israel or Judah even entered into alliances with other nations to fight against each other (e.g., 1 Kgs 15:16-22; 2 Kgs 16:5-9). One of the overarching emphases of both books is adherence to the prophetic word, not least in wartime situations (1 Sam 15; 28; 30:8; 2 Sam 2:1; 5:19, 23; 1 Kgs 20; 22; 2 Kgs 3; 6–7; 9–10; 14:25; 18–20). Because the Northern Kingdom does not heed the prophets and turn from the sins of Jeroboam, it is exiled from the land (2 Kgs 17). Enemy armies later devastate the land of Judah. Because Hezekiah seeks Isaiah's assistance and repents (chaps. 18–19), Jerusalem is saved. Yet Manasseh's sins (21:10-15; 23:26-27; 24:3-4) eventually bring about the conquest of the Southern Kingdom as well.

B. The Latter Prophets

War looms large in the Latter Prophets. Although they mirror a variety of perspectives on war, they have much in common—not least a will to perceive divine judgment in the destruction and to pinpoint exactly what elicited the judgment. By identifying the ills in the society that is threatened to be wiped out in war, they already lay the groundwork for its restoration after war.

A recurring notion in these books is that Israel's God inflicts war upon Israel because she has strayed from divine teachings. Accordingly, war is not caused merely by international political dynamics but also and primarily by internal socioeconomic injustices and religious violations. In addition to drawing attention to various social injustices and cultic impurities that have elicited the punishment in the first place, the prophets also criticize what they deem to be quick military fixes that avoid an honest confrontation with the problem (e.g., Isa 22:8-11). Most of the prophets repudiate the political game of alliance formation. Military alliances supported by those who wish to maintain their positions of power jeopardize the welfare of the people as a whole. Because of these alliances, the prophets refer to Israel and Judah under the female metaphors of harlot and adulterer. Enchanted by what others have to offer, she abandons Yahweh. She is thus punished in war, and the descriptions of these scenes are graphic in their sexual metaphors (see, e.g., Ezek 23; Hos 2).

Yahweh's warring against Israel and Judah at times contravenes the very restrictions Yahweh places on Israel's military conduct in pentateuchal law. For example, many passages in the Latter Prophets refer to the devastation of Israel's and Judah's lands: "I will lay waste her vines and her fig trees ... I will make them a forest, and the wild animals shall devour them" (Hos 2:12 [Heb. 2:14]). Israel is, however, forbidden to treat her enemies this way (Deut 20:19-20). The same applies to Yahweh's indiscriminate slaughter of women and children (e.g., Nah 3; compare Deut 20:10-14; 21:10-14).

Finally, many books of the Latter Prophets include oracles against the surrounding nations that consist in large part of descriptions of wars. These texts make the claim of divine sovereignty over the international sphere and an expectation of fair "rules of engagement" in the international sphere. Amos attributes divine punishment to the ruthless way contemporary nations waged war (chaps. 1–2). A more common reason for the divine wrath is the hubris of these nations (e.g., Isa 16). Although the nations were once used as instruments of judgment, they fail to recognize the source of their strength and thus are punished (Isa 10:5-15). The hope expressed in Isa 2:4; Hos 2:18-23 [Heb. 2:20-25]; Mic 4:3; and Zech 9:10 is that the instruments of war used by these nations, and indeed war itself, will be abolished as the nations allow Israel's God to adjudicate their disputes.

C. The Writings

Within the book of Psalms, war represents a central theme. In the older layers of many psalms, the king prays for deliverance from his enemies, who threaten not only him but also his people (Ps 3). At other moments he also laments defeat or gives thanks for victory (e.g., Pss 18; 54). In appropriating and reworking these older traditions, the book both individualizes and collectivizes the prayers, emphasizing justice and piety as the conditions for deliverance. This process of expansion, juxtaposition, and adaptation transforms the identity of the enemy, who is now no longer solely a military aggressor but also those opposed to particular groups (e.g., the righteous, the poor, and the lowly). Many of the communal laments devote special attention to war, reflecting upon its causes and pleading for salvation. While most recognize sin as the cause (e.g., Pss 74; 79; 80; 83; 85), others affirm innocence despite punishment (e.g., Ps 44).

Reflecting upon the destruction wrought by war, the book of Lamentations cries out in anger against Israel's God for wiping out Jacob and Zion without mercy. In verbalizing their rage and posing questions, the voices of the book discover solidarity, form a community of mourners, and eventually find answers and healing. They begin with the most rudimentary form

of language—the alphabet—and, by means of acrostic poetry, undertake the daunting task of reordering the fundamental components of life that were torn apart as Yahweh acted the part of Israel's enemy (2:4-5). Although culpability is confessed, it does not obviate the need to draw attention to the suffering (e.g., 1:18-20) and to pose the accusative question whether the punishment fit the crime (2:20; 3:42-54; 4:1-20; 5:20-22).

Daniel espouses a unique historical perspective in the OT. According to its apocalyptic outlook, world history and political turmoil should not cause despair. The war waged against the Jews will eventually come to an end. All transpires according to the divine plan written in the "book of truth" (10:21), and the community of the faithful are made privy to this plan thanks to the writings of a key figure, whose righteous deeds had been rewarded with visions (chaps. 9; 10). According to the interpretation of these visions by the angel, there is a struggle in heaven between "the chief princes" representing various peoples, and this struggle directly affects the political events on earth. All empires ultimately perish and in the end are replaced by an everlasting kingdom established by the God of heaven and governed by the holy ones. In the meantime, one is to engage in textual study, pious behavior, prayer, and confession for the sins that occasioned Israel's exile (see especially chaps. 6; 9; 10).

The book of 1–2 Chronicles presents unique and complex notions of war when recounting Israel's and Judah's monarchic history. The book, written long after the catastrophe of 586 BCE, connects the peace ("rest from war") to the behavior of each generation, rather than depicting a gradual demise of Israel and Judah as in 1–2 Kings. It identifies pious kings as aggressive military leaders and ambitious builders, whose construction projects often include fortifications and other military installations in Judah and Jerusalem (e.g., 2 Chr 8:1-6). In the face of invasions, humility and repentance are rewarded with divine mercy (e.g., 2 Chr 12:1-12). The book depicts a return to the military ideals of the conquest traditions: Yahweh actively fights for Yahweh's people, and cultic officials, musicians, and cultic objects play a central role (e.g., 2 Chr 13:3-19; 20:1-30). In its battle accounts, the surrounding nations are unified in their animosity for Judah. They threaten the existence of the people as a whole rather than solely the political autonomy of their rulers. Significantly, the divinely wrought victory brings with it an abundance of material rewards (e.g., 2 Chr 14:12-14 [Heb. 14:11-13]; 20:24-26).

D. The New Testament

Compared to the OT, the topic of war plays a relatively minor role in the NT. This fact is closely tied to its origins in nonterritorial, multiethnic communities living with the context of the Pax Romana. But war is nevertheless an important subject within the NT.

Although the Gospel of Luke presents Jesus as the successor to warriors from the OT such as Gideon, Samson, and David (see especially chap. 1), it regards his kingdom as spiritual in nature (e.g., 17:20-21) and thus eschews the use of the sword (Luke 22:49-51; see however 22:36-38). Elsewhere Jesus teaches non-retaliation (Matt 5:39; Luke 6:29) and love for one's enemy (Matt 5:43-48). Similarly, Paul distinguishes between "governing authorities" who bear the sword, on the one hand, and the community to which he writes (Rom 13:1-10), on the other. The spiritual nature of the kingdom does not preclude the possibility of Christians serving as soldiers (Acts 10). Without an army of its own, however, the church did not develop a doctrine of war until much later. In general, war is considered to be a common feature of the former, passing world; it is thus taken for granted just as much as other social and natural phenomena, such as famine and earthquakes (Mark 13:7-8).

Most warfare in the NT is not physical. Paul tells the Corinthians that they "do not wage war according to human standards; for the weapons of our warfare are not merely human, but they have divine power to destroy strongholds" (2 Cor 10:3-4). These strongholds are identified with "arguments and every proud obstacle raised up against the knowledge of God" (2 Cor 10:4-5). The author of Ephesians develops this Pauline idea into the notion of "the whole armor of God" (6:10-17). Furthermore, Timothy is exhorted to "fight the good fight" (1 Tim 1:18), and Peter urges his readers "as aliens and exiles to abstain from the desires of the flesh that wage war against the soul" (1 Pet 2:11). The wide acceptance of this spiritual-warrior identity is indicated by the popular use of "soldier" for the ideal Christian (Phil 2:25; 2 Tim 2:3; Phlm 2). This notion of spiritual warfare is closely related to the war fought within the individual Christian: James refers to a war of inner cravings (4:1-3); and describing the body of death, Paul speaks of another law warring with the law of his mind and making him captive to the law of sin (Rom 7:21-24).

Physical warfare nevertheless does occupy a place in the descriptions of the eschaton. In the so-called Olivet discourse, Jesus refers to the apocalyptic wars that will be fought between nations and kingdoms as signs of the end of the age (Matt 24:9-28; Mark 13:7-13; Luke 21:12-24). At this point, the Son of Man will come in a cloud with power and great glory, sending out his angels to gather the elect from the four winds.

Finally, as in earlier apocalyptic works such as Daniel and the *War Scroll* from Qumran (1QM and 4Q491–96), spiritual and physical warfare coalesce in the Revelation to John. Here, a series of battles is depicted: Michael and his angels fight a war in heaven against the dragon and his angels (12:7-12); a demonic spirit performs signs and assembles the kings of the world at Armageddon for battle (16:12-17); the beast and the kings of the earth

battle against the rider on the horse and his heavenly army; Satan gathers all the nations from Gog and Magog (see Ezek 39) to do battle against the camp of the saints; and fire comes down from heaven and consumes the army, and Satan is thrown into the lake of fire and sulfur (Rev 20:7-10). The final scenes of the book draw on imagery from the first chapters of Genesis, depicting a future free of chaos and struggle (21:1).

Bibliography: Adela Y. Collins. "The Political Perspective of the Revelation of John." *JBL* 96 (1977) 241–56; John J. Collins. "The Mythology of Holy War in Daniel and the Qumran War Scroll." *VT* 25 (1975) 596–612; Adolf von Harnack. *Militia Christi: The Christian Religion and the Military in the First Three Centuries.* David McInnes Gracie, trans. (1981); William Klassen. "Vengeance in the Apocalypse." *CBQ* 28 (1966) 300–11; Gary N. Knoppers. "'Battling against Yahweh': Israel's War against Judah in 2 Chr. 13:2-20." *RB* 100 (1993) 511–32; Gary N. Knoppers. "Jerusalem at War in Chronicles." *Zion, City of Our God.* Richard S. Hess and Gordon J. Wenham, eds. (1999) 55–76; Reinhard G. Kratz. *The Composition of the Narrative Books of the Old Testament.* John Bowden, trans. (2005); Susan Niditch. *War in the Hebrew Bible: A Study in the Ethics of Violence* (1993); David L. Petersen. "Genesis and Family Values." *JBL* 124 (2005) 5–23; Gerhard von Rad. *Holy War in Ancient Israel.* Marva J. Dawn, ed. and trans. (1991); Jacob L. Wright. "Military Valor and Kingship: A Book-Oriented Approach to the Study of a Major War Theme." *Writing and Reading War: Rhetoric, Gender, and Ethics in Biblical and Modern Contexts.* Brad E. Kelle and Frank Ritchel Ames, eds. (2008) 33–56; Jacob L. Wright. "Warfare and Wanton Destruction: A Reexamination of Deuteronomy 20:19-20 in Relation to Ancient Siegecraft." *JBL* 127 (2008) 423–58.

JACOB WRIGHT

WAR, IMPLEMENTS OF. *See* WAR, METHODS, TACTICS, WEAPONS OF (BRONZE AGE THROUGH PERSIAN PERIOD); WAR, METHODS, TACTICS, WEAPONS OF (HELLENISTIC THROUGH ROMAN PERIODS).

WAR, JUST. *See* WAR, IDEAS OF.

WAR, METHODS, TACTICS, WEAPONS OF (BRONZE AGE THROUGH PERSIAN PERIOD). War is a state of open and declared armed hostile conflict between cities, states, or nations for the purposes of conquest and exploitation, retaliation to a foreign aggressor, or in defense of certain ideals. The methods and tactics, weaponry, and movements of warfare in the OT are not isolated from the ANE environment. Biblical accounts can be prescriptive, proscriptive, and descriptive in providing information about the methods, tactics, and weapons of war. These accounts are vividly illuminated by the textual, pictographic, and archaeological data found throughout the ANE.

A. Early Developments
B. Weapons and Armor
   1. Short-range weapons
   2. Long-range weapons
   3. Armor
C. Methods and Tactics
   1. Egyptian
   2. Hittite
   3. Canaanite
   4. Assyrian
   5. Babylonian
   6. Persian
Bibliography

A. Early Developments

Scenes and texts reflecting domination and conquest are among the earliest records known in the ANE and Egypt. In Mesopotamia the Royal Standard of Ur (ca. 2600 BCE) depicts Sumerian war-carts charging across a battlefield strewn with enemy corpses. The warriors in the carts are armed with either a javelin or an ax. In the central scene soldiers wearing leather caps/helmets and armed with short swords advance in line while others collect prisoners. In the upper scene these prisoners are presented before the king. The three scenes may be interpreted as the aftermath of a victorious battle. Later battles between early city-states are attested from Lagash, Umma, and Uruk. In the Early Dynastic period cities are surrounded by massive fortifications and such extravagant use of manpower suggests the need for protection from invaders. The Royal Cemetery and common cemetery at Ur produced some of the earliest weapons, including daggers, javelins, broad-headed spears, and the first attested copper helmet.

In Egypt the Narmer Palette is the earliest depiction of domination where the Egyptian king is shown smiting an enemy with a mace. In the lower register, below his feet, two overthrown enemies are depicted with legs sprawling and heads turned back in fear and subjugation. On the other side of the palette the king strides forth carrying a mace and a flail. Before him four men carry standards before ten slain enemies. Although the interpretation of these scenes is debated, both in Mesopotamia and Egypt the earliest objects of art provide evidence for domination and warfare.

B. Weapons and Armor

Weapons of war can be defined as tools employed as extensions of the human body designed to destroy or disable an enemy. The development of weapons continued to be refined during the centuries and included innovations in technology, the introduction of stronger metals and alloys, and design. They can be classified into two broad categories: 1) close-combat weapons designed for short-range and hand-to-hand combat; 2) long-range weapons used as missiles.

1. Short-range weapons

The mace or club consisted of a short handle with heavy metal or stone head, oval-shaped like a pear, apple, or saucer. These were wielded in order to beat, crush, or smash the enemy, usually in the head. The mace is one of the earliest attested weapons and can be found in the 3rd millennium Egyptian and Mesopotamian depictions of war. The mace has been found in the archaeological record from earliest times throughout the ANE. It ceased to be an effective weapon when armor and particularly helmets were introduced, but continued to serve as a ceremonial weapon for the Egyptian kings in smiting their enemies.

The ax and adze were similar in design. Instead of a blunt oval shape attached to the end of the handle, they had a sharp, pointed head made of stone, and, later, metal. They were used not only as tools to cut down trees but also as weapons. The development of this weapon changed over time as it was adapted to meet new defenses, particularly armor. The flat, socketless cutting ax was most effective before the development of armor. In the Middle Bronze Age the duck-bill ax was developed as an effective piercing instrument by lengthening the blade. Other piercing blade styles were developed in Egypt and Mesopotamia.

The sword was the primary short-range weapon. Two basic types of swords existed, those used for thrusting or stabbing and those employed for striking. Swords consisted of a handle, hilt, and metal blade. The first known swords were short and resembled daggers. Later they developed into longer two-edged thrusting swords. In the Late Bronze Age the widely used **khopesh** or sickle-sword may be referred to in the battles of the conquest where the often-repeated phrase "to strike with the edge of the sword" is employed (Josh 8:24; 10:30-39; 11:11-14). This was a cutting weapon of bronze with a single edge.

2. Long-range weapons

The bow and arrow were used as long-range weapons from earliest times by hunters. The bow is made up of the body and the string. In the earliest bows the shape of the wood body was a single convex arc. The maximum tension came from pulling the string back as far as possible and releasing the arrow. Later it was discovered that by placing the fist area of the bow further back one could achieve maximum tension. This was called the double-convex bow. The breakthrough in range and accuracy came with the development of the composite bow made of several natural materials: wood, animal bones, animal sinews and tendons, and glue. This bow could have an accurate range of up to 400 m and a total range twice that far. Arrows fitted into the bow were first made of stone or flint, later of bronze, and finally of iron. The stronger the metal, the more effectively the weapon penetrated armor. Various types of bows can be seen in the Egyptian and Assyrian reliefs. A collection of intact bows was discovered in the tomb of Tutankhamen.

The sling and sling stone were effective weapons used by the infantry. Lines of slingers can be seen in the reliefs of Sennacherib in his attack against Lachish and dozens of sling stones were found in the excavations around the siege ramp (see LACHISH; SENNACHERIB). Sling stones could be thrown by hand a distance in excess of 300 m and could penetrate the body if a soldier was not protected by armor. Judges 20:16 describes the accuracy that slingers could achieve at great distances.

The javelin and spear were made of a long wooden shaft with a stone or metal tip affixed at the end. It was hurled by hand. The weight and form of the metal tip aided in the aim and propulsion of the weapon. The spear was a heavier weapon used as a thrusting weapon. It was used in a phalanx formation with infantry. In the OT the spear is mentioned forty-eight times and is found in a variety of contexts. David faces Goliath with a sling, while the latter carries a spear (1 Sam 17:7). David is targeted by Saul on several occasions with a spear (1 Sam 18:11).

Erich Lessing/Art Resource, NY

Figure 1: Archers. Fragment of a bronze sheet, cover of a wooden door (858–824 BCE; from Yeni-Assur [Tell Balawat], Iraq). Museum of Oriental Antiquities, Istanbul, Turkey.

3. Armor

Personal body armor became necessary for charioteers and archers who required the use of both hands and therefore could not carry a shield. Hittite warriors, as depicted in New Kingdom reliefs of RAMESSES II, overcame this weakness by manning their chariots with three men: the driver, the archer, and the shield bearer. But earlier reliefs of battles against Canaanites indicate that the Egyptians and other Asiatics generally had only one or two soldiers in a chariot. These would then have required armor. After Thutmose III's campaign against MEGIDDO, he recounts taking over 200 coats of mail

as spoils of war. On Thutmose IV's chariot several of these Asiatic charioteers are depicted wearing coats of scaled armor. He is pierced by an arrow in one of the weakest points, his armpit (compare 1 Kgs 22:34-35; 2 Chr 18:33). Tutankhamen's tomb contained a box with a complete leather cuirass made up of scales of thick leather.

The Philistine champion GOLIATH is described as having body armor (1 Sam 17:5-6), but when Saul offers DAVID his coat of mail (1 Sam 17:38), he refuses and goes armed only with a sling. After the death of Saul, the Philistines take off his armor and place it in their temple (1 Chr 10:10). Body armor is also described in the preparations AMAZIAH (Uzziah) makes for war in addition to shields, spears, helmets, bows, and sling stones (2 Chr 26:14).

Assyrian slingers and archers in the Lachish reliefs of Sennacherib are shown wearing scaled armor wrapped around their shoulders and torsos. Individual scales of Assyrian armor as well as a helmet identical to those depicted were found during the archaeological excavations at Lachish.

C. Methods and Tactics

Methods and tactics of warfare involve the goal, focus, means, and extent of military activity. Non-specialists often infer that when a particular city or other entity is mentioned in a campaign account, that entity was captured, burned, and destroyed. But this assumption cannot be applied universally without understanding the motives and historical context of individual campaigns together with the wider practices of those societies over time. In other words, the focus, means, and extent of Assyrian military practices may have been entirely different from Egyptian methods. Even within the Assyrian Empire there was variation in the tactics employed, depending on circumstances. A working paradigm of military methods and tactics within each culture and individual reign could be established with these guiding questions: 1) What was the goal for military activity (retaliation, expulsion, genocide, subjugation, economic gain)? 2) What was the focus of destruction (enemies and inhabitants; cities and villages; fields, orchards, and crops)? 3) What was the means of destruction (open terrain warfare [infantry, cavalry, or chariotry]; siege warfare [battering ram, scaling, sapper operation, siege wall]; conflagration)? 4) What was the extent of destruction (gates and defensive systems; administrative and cultic centers; domestic buildings, fields, orchards, and crops)? The final step would be to compare these tactics as described within each period and civilization with the reality of that activity in the archaeological record.

1. Egyptian

The earliest biblical descriptions of conflict with EGYPT relate to the exodus, generally assigned in the

Late Bronze Age (1550–1200 BCE). The arrival of the Asiatic Hyksos rulers in the Second Intermediate period and the ensuing wars of expulsion by Kamose and Ahmose at the beginning of the Eighteenth Dynasty mark a major transition in Egyptian warfare. The Hyksos introduce the Egyptians to widespread use of chariots and the horse. Both the textual and iconographic sources indicate that siege warfare was well developed in the Egyptian New Kingdom.

The annals of Thutmose III at Karnak relate the siege of Megiddo, where Egyptian forces surrounded the wall with a ditch and placed a siege wall built of felled fruit trees. The description of this siege wall is illuminated in another text from a stela found in the Ptah temple at Karnak. This tactic of destroying fruit trees for the building of siege works is reminiscent of the polemic found in Deut 20:19-20 where Israel's laws of warfare prohibit this kind of action. The context suggests that the intent was to keep the inhabitants from having access to their fields and sources of subsistence.

The Egyptian use of siege equipment is found in Ramesses II's siege of Dapur. Here four mantelets are shown at the base of the city. Beneath the mantelets, battering rams are used against the fortification system. On the relief of Ashkelon at Karnak, two siege ladders rest on the city walls in the battle led by Merneptah in 1209 BCE, a campaign also documented in the Merneptah stela where the people of Israel are mentioned for the first time (see MERNEPTAH). The battle of Ramesses III against Tunip likewise has two ladders on either side of the city. During the siege of Irqata on the Amara West temple of Ramesses II, another scene demonstrates the use of rams in sapping the walls of the city.

Overall, it should be noted that the Egyptian scribes of the New Kingdom were stereotypical and general in their references to specific military actions. There is rarely an indication of what parts of cities were destroyed. The texts communicate a sense of totality and conquest, as all is plundered or carried away. In the Nineteenth and Twentieth dynasties there is very little evidence to suggest that the Egyptians systematically burned down the cities that they conquered. The language and iconography suggest that if destruction occurred it was localized. The Egyptians were more interested in subjugating and dominating western Asia for economic exploitation and using it as a buffer against the Hittite Empire to the north.

2. Hittite

The Hittite military engaged in siege warfare when the enemy retreated to fortified cities and refused to surrender. The annals of Hattushili I mention at least two sieges, often with attacks commencing under the protection of darkness, but no direct mention is made of siege equipment or machinery.

The Siege of Urshu text mentions the battering ram, which the soldiers broke, and of commands to build a new one. A siege tower is also discussed in connection with the battering ram. A siege mound referred to literally as a "mountain" was to be built under the command of the king. Currently, little iconography sheds light on these Hittite military activities.

Hittite military action against a city frequently included its destruction. When a city surrendered, tribute or spoils would be taken and the city would be left intact. A detailed investigation of the terminology for destructive activity when a city did resist suggests that at times cities were first burned and then destroyed while others were first destroyed and then burned. Overall, most of the cities were burned to the ground, indicating an important tactic of the Hittite military.

It is significant that a recent analysis of Hittite military terminology led to the conclusion that the desolation of the land follows the primary destructive activity of a campaign. This activity takes place after these events have been accomplished. This suggests that an intentional military tactic was used to destroy the life-subsistence systems of the enemy and that no attempt was made to avoid its destruction. See HITTITES.

3. Canaanite

The AMARNA LETTERS provide a glimpse of the political organization and military practices in Canaan during the Late Bronze Age. Specific reconstruction of these tactics cannot be complete from the corpus of Amarna texts themselves, but several accounts employ language that illuminates siege practices. Most of the internecine warfare takes place between rival cities and their leaders.

In EA 88, Rib-Hadda, ruler of Gubla (Byblos), laments that there is an attempt to capture Byblos and that the inhabitants, besieged within the city walls, seek chariot and troop reinforcements from Egypt. In EA 244 Biridiya cites a war against his city of Megiddo. Because the inhabitants are not allowed to leave the city gate, the produce remains unharvested. Archaeologists have affirmed the existence of a gate at Megiddo during this period and both the Amarna letters and Egyptian accounts seem to indicate that Megiddo was well fortified in order to withstand a siege first by Egyptian forces led by Thutmose III and later by Canaanite forces.

The Amarna letters often describe the destruction of cities by fire. One reference is EA 185–86 where one finds a repeated pattern: first the city is captured, then it is plundered, and finally the city is burned. The tactic of burning cities, then, was not restricted to later Assyrian and Babylonian military policies. Instead, we find that already in the 2nd millennium BCE, the Hittites, the Apiru, and other leaders from Amurru engaged in this ultimately devastating tactic.

4. Assyrian

The Assyrians were known for sophisticated military tactics, use of siege equipment, and psychological warfare as they expanded and maintained their empire. Beginning in the 9th and 8th cent. BCE, Assyrian pressure was increasingly placed on Israel and Judah. The Black Obelisk of SHALMENESER III (859–824 BCE) depicts Jehu, king of Israel, bowing before him in submission toward the conclusion of his 841 BCE campaign (2 Kgs 9–10; see OBELISK, BLACK). Later Assyrian records recount that TIGLATH-PILESER III (745–727 BCE) campaigned against Amaziah (Uzziah), king of Judah (2 Chr 26) and eventually reached Philistia and Israel by 732 BCE, exacting 1,000 talents of silver tribute from Menahem of Israel (2 Kgs 15:19) and subsequently defeating Pekah (2 Kgs 15:29). His campaign records recount the use of battering rams and siege ramps against cities.

Shalmaneser V (727–722 BCE) besieged Israel's capital Samaria for over three years (2 Kgs 17:1-4; 19:9-11)—an event recorded in the Babylonian Chronicles—and carried off captives to Assyria. The annals of SARGON II (722–705 BCE) also claim responsibility for the fall of the city, but most scholars, based on Hayim Tadmor's study, have discounted this claim. Sargon recounts his use of battering rams in smashing fortified walls and leveling them to the ground. The campaign against Ashdod, cited in Isa 20:1-3, has been seen as an authentic campaign dated to 713–711 BCE.

Later that same century, Sennacherib (704–681 BCE) boasts in the Oriental Institute Prism that he besieged and captured forty-six of Hezekiah's cities through the use of battering rams, siege engines, and tunnels. This complements the OT record of the same campaign in 701 BCE (2 Kgs 18–19; 2 Chr 32; Isa 36–37), giving more detail about the territory of Judah and its devastation compared to the biblical focus on Jerusalem.

The task of battering rams was to destroy the city wall by forcing a way through the stone or brick or by undermining the wall. The early siege machines during the reign of Ashurnasirpal II had rams shaped with a flat surface, while later models during the reigns of Tiglath-pileser III, Sargon II, and Sennacherib had shafts of wood and a strong metal head with a sharp, spear-like shape. The early, 9th-cent. rams were heavy, six-wheeled vehicles built of wood and covered in metal, probably copper. Later battering rams were lighter and more mobile, covered by stretched leather. This is noticeable in the reliefs of Sennacherib's attack against Lachish in Judah where the leather skins and prefabricated parts are attached by securing pins.

The use of such massive machines required the construction of siege ramps to bring the machines to appropriate places along the wall. These ramps are depicted in Assyrian reliefs and suggest several methods of construction. In some cases the ramps were made out of mud brick. The depiction in Sennacherib's reliefs at Nineveh shows ramps built against Lachish (compare Isa 36:1-2). The renewed archaeological excavations conducted at Tell ed-Duweir (Lachish) produced important insights concerning the construction of ancient Assyrian siege works. The siege ramp represents the oldest ramp ever excavated and the only one known from the Assyrian period.

Another tactic was undermining the wall through sapping procedures or tunneling. In the palace of Tiglath-pileser III, a soldier uses a rod to pry apart the city wall. On the wall of Sargon II's palace at Khorsabad, an Assyrian soldier just above the battering ram on the left works against the city wall with his sword. Both sapping and tunneling were thus effective ways of gaining access to an enemy city.

Scaling ladders brought against the wall was another effective tactic. Tiglath-pileser III employs this method against a city in Babylonia, and Shalmaneser III's bronze gates likewise attest to the use of scaling ladders in several attacks against enemy cities. Assyrian texts vividly portray the city's inhabitants taken captive and its goods removed as plunder. The Assyrians boast and depict that they had utterly destroyed the city by razing it to the ground. Numerous Assyrian reliefs confirm the utter destruction of cities as demonstrated archaeologically at numerous sites throughout Israel after attacks by Tiglath-pileser III, Sennacherib, and Sargon II.

5. Babylonian

The Babylonian Chronicles are the most accessible sources for the study of Babylonian military tactics in comparison with the OT accounts of the sieges of Jerusalem, Judah, and Philistia. The Babylonian references to siege tactics against fortified cities are not as detailed as the Assyrian sources. Constructed siege works are only mentioned three times and very few iconographic records have survived.

The campaign in 605 BCE against Carchemish ensured Nebuchadnezzar victory against the Egyptian king NECO II (see NEBUCHADNEZZAR, NEBUCHADREZZAR). According to the Babylonian Chronicles, Nebuchadnezzar conquered the territory of Israel and Judah once held by Egypt. This is the campaign related in Dan 1:1 and Jer 46.

The Babylonian Chronicles describe the 597 BCE campaign when Nebuchadnezzar besieged Jerusalem, captured its king, and appointed a king of his own choice. The biblical reference to this campaign in 2 Kgs 24:10-16 states that King Jehoiachin and 10,000 others were taken as prisoners into Babylon with spoils from the palace and Temple.

The final campaign by Nebuchadnezzar in 586 BCE is found in 2 Kgs 25 and Jer 52; the Babylonian Chronicle covering these years of the king has not been recovered. The specific date of the beginning of the siege is provided: the ninth year of Zedekiah's reign; the tenth day of the tenth month. The text goes on to describe the construction of a siege wall around the city. After a prolonged siege, the city was finally destroyed on the seventh day of the fifth month of Nebuchadnezzar's nineteenth year. The description of the destruction includes the Temple, the palace, and all the houses of Jerusalem.

It is apparent that after a city was conquered it could also be systematically destroyed and burned to the ground. Such tactics are preserved in the Babylonian Chronicles in relation to other cities including Ashkelon in 603 BCE. Here Nebuchadnezzar reduced the city to ruins and marched back to Babylon. The archaeological evidence at the site reflects in a graphic portrayal the devastation that the Babylonian military forces could inflict on ancient cities.

6. Persian

The military campaigns of Cyrus the Great (559–530 BCE)—who first conquered Media followed by Lydia and Babylon—are documented in several ancient sources. The Nabonidus Chronicle confirms that the armies of Cyrus entered the city of Babylon on October 12, 539 BCE without a battle. Herodotus (*Hist.* 1.191), writing in the 5th cent. BCE, claims that the Persians entered the city by diverting the Euphrates River and entering through a water channel. In Dan 5 Belshazzar celebrates a festival by using vessels from the Temple in Jerusalem that Nebuchadnezzar had taken as spoils on the night of capitulation. Herodotus (*Hist.* 1.191) confirms that the Babylonians were celebrating as at a festival. Xenophon (*Cyr.* 7.5.15) records that the Persians chose to attack at a moment when the Babylonians were used to reveling through the night. The Cyrus Cylinder describes Cyrus as entering Babylon "without fighting or battle." Such were not the tactics used throughout his campaigns. In the Lydo-Persian War, which commenced in 547 BCE, Sardis is taken and archaeological excavations conducted at the site have found burned levels and arrowheads from the attack. It is an edict of Cyrus that allows the Jews to return to Jerusalem after their captivity in Babylon (2 Chr 36:22-23; Ezra 1:1-4; 6:3-5).

The Greco-Persian Wars by Darius (522–486 BCE) and his son Xerxes (485–465 BCE) swept through Greece, devastating temples and cities and leaving a bitter memory. The result of the campaigns was the revenge exacted by the young Macedonian king Alexander, who would expand the Greek Empire far beyond the reaches of previous kings, ushering in a universal Greek language and the lasting influences of Hellenistic culture.

Bibliography: Richard H. Beal. *The Organisation of the Hittite Military* (1992); Gary Beckman. "The Siege of Uršu Text (CTH 7) and Hittite Historiography." *JCS* 47 (1995) 23–34; Robert Drews. *The End of the Bronze Age: Changes in Warfare and the Catastrophe, ca. 1200 BC* (1993); A. K. Grayson. *Assyrian and Babylonian Chronicles* (1975); William J. Hamblin. *Warfare in the Ancient Near East to 1600 BC* (2006); Michael G. Hasel. *Domination and Resistance: Egyptian Military Activity in the Southern Levant, 1300–1185 BC* (1998); Michael G. Hasel. *Military Practice and Polemic: Israel's Laws of Warfare in Near Eastern Perspective* (2005); Chaim Herzog and Mordechai Gichon. *Battles of the Bible* (1997); Paul Bentley Kern. *Ancient Siege Warfare* (1999); Daniel David Luckenbill. *The Annals of Sennacherib* (1924); William L. Moran. *The Amarna Letters* (1992); Donald B. Redford. *The Wars in Syria and Palestine of Thutmosis III* (2003); Nick V. Sekunda and Simon Chew. *The Persian Army 560–330 BC* (1992); Ian Shaw. *Egyptian Warfare and Weapons* (1991); Anthony J. Spalinger. *War in Ancient Egypt* (2005); Hayim Tadmor. "The Campaign of Sargon II of Assur: A Chronological-Historical Study." *JCS* 12 (1958) 22–42, 77–100; Hayim Tadmor. *The Inscriptions of Tiglath-pileser III, King of Assyria* (1994); David Ussishkin. *The Conquest of Lachish by Sennacherib* (1982); D. J. Wiseman. *Chronicles of the Chaldean Kings* (1956); Yigael Yadin. *The Art of Warfare in Biblical Lands.* 2 vols. (1963); Edwin M. Yamauchi. *Persia and the Bible* (1989).

MICHAEL G. HASEL

WAR, METHODS, TACTICS, WEAPONS OF (HELLENISTIC THROUGH ROMAN PERIODS).

The ideology of empire was the natural order in antiquity. War was woven into the cultural fabric of society. Revenge and security were accepted justifications for war, and alliances allowed stronger powers to intervene in the conflicts of others. Civil wars and revolts were matters of imperial security. Rules of war protected heralds and temples and decried excessive cruelty. The rules of war were consistently broken.

A. Hellenistic and Roman Wars
B. Weapons and Armor
C. Armies and Soldiers
D. Preparation
E. Warfare
  1. Open warfare
  2. Naval warfare
  3. Siege warfare
F. Aftermath of War
Bibliography

A. Hellenistic and Roman Wars

Wars of the Hellenistic period (334–63 BCE) were principally of conquest. Alexander of Macedon's swift and savage subjection of the Persian Empire was followed by the wars of his successors, the Diadochi, who divided the territory into three kingdoms: the Seleucids, based in Syria, controlled much of Asia Minor and Persia; the Ptolemies ruled Egypt and Palestine; and greater Macedonia, which partially reverted to leagues of Greek city-states. At this time the Latin city-state of Rome extended its domination of the Greek and Latin city-states in southern Italy, and over the Etruscans and Gauls (Celts to the Greeks) in the north. The rise to power threatened Carthage and led to the three Punic Wars. A second phase of Roman conquest was facilitated by Macedonian involvement in the Second Punic War, and by 146 BCE Rome controlled the Mediterranean. In a third phase, Rome extended its control across Asia Minor to the Euphrates, including Palestine.

Wars of the Roman period (63 BCE–324 CE) continued the conquest of Gaul to the Rhine, a foothold in Britain, Ptolemaic Egypt, and central Europe south of the Danube. After Augustus, most of Rome's wars were defensive against uprisings in Europe and Asia Minor, and to consolidate its empire against Parthians and Sasanians in Mesopotamia west of the Euphrates. Jews initiated three of Rome's most difficult wars: the revolt of Judea (66–70 CE), the Diaspora revolt (115–17 CE), and the Bar Kochba revolt (132–36 CE). During the "age of crisis" (235–384 CE), the empire was plagued by wars between aspiring and short-lived emperors until Diocletian restored order and Constantine brought the empire back under a single ruler.

B. Weapons and Armor

Josephus describes the Roman soldier of his day equipped with a cuirass and helmet, a sword (*gladius*) on his left, dagger (*pugio*) on the right, some carrying a lance (*hasta*) and round shield (*parma*), others a javelin (*pilum*) and oblong shield (*scutum*), and, on the march, a saw, basket, pick and an ax, strap, bill-hook, and chain (*J.W.* 3.94–95).

Swords varied according to the task of the soldier: straight or curved, single- or double-edged, long or short. The Macedonian hoplite carried the kopis (κοπίς), a single-edged slashing sword with a scythe-like curved blade, approximately 70 cm (28 in.) long. The Roman soldier of the republic carried a similar weapon, the *falcata*. During the imperial era, the common issue was the solid, straight, double-edged sword, 42–50 cm (17–20 in.), designed for thrust and slash in close-quarter combat. Cavalry used the *spatha*, a long sword of Celtic origin, 76 cm (30 in.), for slashing foot soldiers. By the 3rd cent. CE the long sword replaced the short sword for all troops. Daggers seem to have disappeared from the rank and file by the time of Trajan (1st cent. CE).

Spears and lances were designed for stabbing at close quarters or to be thrown from a short distance. Spearheads varied in length and width, and shafts usually bore a pointed counterweight on the end. The Macedonian phalangite (infantryman) carried the long pike (sarisa σάρισα), between 5–6 m (17–20 ft.) long, weighted at the butt for balance. With a shield strapped to his left forearm, he grasped the shaft with his left hand 6 ft. and right hand 3 ft. from the back.

The javelin was a long iron shank—like an arrow—attached to a shaft either by riveted tang or a socket, designed for close-distance armor piercing. The slender shank, often weighted at the shaft for greater thrust, tended to bend upon impact, rendering it useless to the enemy. The barbed head might remain in a shield and hamper the soldier's mobility.

Bows and slings were used to harass the enemy from a distance. Among Greeks and Romans the single wood longbow had been replaced by the composite bow, which consisted of strips of horn glued to the inner wood facing the archer, sinew on the outside, and horn nocks to reinforce the ends. The stretched sinew and compressed horn increased the tension and thrust. Arrowheads were iron, usually two- or three-edged, barbed or smooth. The effective range of the bow was 150–200 m. Slingers could launch missiles in excess of 300 m. Sling shot was made of baked clay or lead, plum shaped, and often inscribed with slogans or insults. The standard weight was between 20–50 g. Balearic slingers reportedly used stones up to a mina, about 1 lb., in weight, nearly the size of a tennis ball.

The need for launching missiles faster and farther, which had spawned the composite bow, led to the invention of new missile "machines" (mēchanē μηχανή), now called artillery. The earliest artillery was a species of large crossbow called the "belly-bow" (gastraphetēs γαστραφέτης) because the archer leaned with his belly on the slide mechanism, using body weight to set the bow string in a ratchet. Developed at Syracuse around 400 BCE, it became the basic model for larger machines that could send heavier darts and stones. A revolution in propulsion was invented—possibly by the artificers of Philip I (ca. 340 BCE)—in torsion springs. The springs consisted of woven strands of stretched sinew, horsehair, or human hair, looped and held in tension by a metal-plated wood frame. The lever base twisted the spring (like a pencil in rubber bands) and two lever arms served like the old bow, connected by a bowstring. Both types of torsion, bow and spring, continued in use through the Hellenistic and Roman periods in a progression of machines generally known as the catapult from Greek katapaltēs (καταπάλτης), "thrown against"(Lat. *catapulta*). The missiles were darts or iron bolts, and stones. Spring torsion stone throwers (*ballistae*) were built with the same double torsion arms, but a large single spring and lever machine—called the Onager (wild ass) because of its kick—launched stones weighing up to 75 kg (165 lbs.) in the vertical position of a now traditional catapult.

The basic helmet was a semispherical bronze or iron bowl with a neck guard of varying length, and cheek guards, secured by a strap behind the ears, through the cheek guard, and fastened under the chin. Styles varied greatly over time and geography. Cavalry helmets were often covered in copper alloy, embossed to look like hair. During the Dominate (the latter phases of the government of Rome from the 3rd cent. CE until the fall of the Roman Empire in 476 CE), a cheap helmet was mass produced as a two-piece bowl with a ridge crest for joining the halves, and the neck and ear guards attached to a leather lining. Crests and plumes were reserved for parade and battle.

Republican-era legionaries wore body armor according to wealth and status. Officers sometimes wore the

Vanni/Art Resource, NY

Figure 1: Modern reconstruction of the body armor of an infantry soldier of Trajan's army (early 2nd cent. CE). Museo della Civilta Romana, Rome, Italy.

muscled cuirass of classical Greece. The early cuirass was a linen or leather vest with breastplates and back plate. Later, body armor was made of metal scales fastened by wire, sown or worn over a padded shirt of leather or stiffened linen. Ring mail—developed by Celts—was made of stamped rings interlaced by riveted rings. The typical mail tunic weighed 12–15 kg (26–33 lbs.), and belts worn over the armor transferred some shoulder weight to the hips. During the late 1st cent. CE, the legions adopted a new Celtic body armor, the *lorica segmentata*, made of articulated metal bands and plates fastened by leather straps and rivets. By the 3rd cent., soldiers had returned to mail and scale armor.

Greaves (shin armor) were used intermittently, more often by officers and cavalry, and less so by infantry. The military sandals, *caligae*, made famous by the emperor Gaius (37–41 CE)—nicknamed Caligula for the "little booties" he wore as a child—are known only from the imperial era onward. The upper insole was made of multiple straps cut from a single piece of leather that were laced to conform to the individual foot and offered good ventilation. The insole was stitched to a heavy leather sole hobnailed in patterns designed for traction, similar to modern sport training shoes, but was dangerous on a hard surface. Josephus tells of a Roman officer during the siege of Jerusalem who slipped on the stone pavement of the Temple Mount and fell flat on his back, which cost him his life (*J.W.* 6.85–87).

Shields varied in shape from round and oblong to rectangular, flat, or curved. Wicker shields were common for some auxiliaries, but the standard Roman shield was made of wood, faced with leather, and often strengthened with metal bars. Wood strips were glued cross grained in two or three ply, in which the outer strips ran horizontal for better resistance to vertical sword strokes. The wood was covered with linen and leather, painted and rimmed with metal or rawhide. The center was covered by an iron or bronze boss to deflect missiles.

C. Armies and Soldiers

A full army combined infantry, cavalry, and auxiliary units of specialized forces. The ancient infantry formation was the phalanx, a block of foot soldiers standing shield to shield in ranks (abreast) and files (deep). This formation was designed for maximum shock power, but sacrificed mobility and was vulnerable on its flanks. By the time of Alexander, Greeks had articulated the phalanx into smaller and highly trained segments able to wheel, defend the flanks, and enter different formations. A standard phalanx of 256 men was arranged 16 by 16. Romans of the early republic adapted the unwieldy phalanx to the hilly terrain of central Italy by reducing it into smaller units (maniples) of 120 men, 10 ranks and 12 files, supplemented by 20 to 40 light infantry javelin throwers. Three maniples made a cohort and 10 cohorts a legion. By the Principate (the first period of the Roman Empire, from Augustus [63 BCE–19 CE] until the rise of the Dominate in the 3rd cent.), the basic units became centuries of about 80 men. A legion consisted of 10 cohorts of 6 centuries and 120 scouts and dispatchers on horse.

Chariots were still used by Persians but Greeks had abandoned them for war well before Alexander. The Seleucids employed scythed chariots with long rotating blades projecting from the axle-trees to cut down infantrymen. The Celts drove chariots into battle but often jumped out for combat, and Romans never used them in battle. Cavalry had greater mobility, especially on rough terrain. The Roman saddle and bridle was probably borrowed from the Celts. Stirrups came centuries later from the East but the four corner pommels on the saddle secured the rider for an impressive array of maneuvers. Gallic and German cavalry were renowned. Heavy cavalry, known as the cataphract, were well armored and carried pikes, lances, and long swords. Horses were protected by a blanket of scale mail and face guard. Light cavalry were highly mobile, and some, like Numidian archers, rode bareback and without armor. Arab auxiliaries rode camels.

Elephants entered Hellenistic warfare after Seleucus I bargained his eastern territories to Chandragupta for an elephant brigade numbering some 400 (or fewer), and used them effectively in the battle of Ipsus. Ptolemy I captured and trained elephants found in the Red Sea hinterland. These were the smaller African forest elephant (*Loxodonta cyclotis*)—also used later by Hannibal—not the savanna elephant (*Loxodonta africana*), apparently unknown to the Mediterranean world. Pikemen and archers fought from a tower box chained to the elephant's back and a driver in front on the elephant's neck also carried javelins. When interspersed between infantry units, elephants strengthened the front lines and could frighten horses, but overall they were of dubious strategic value. When frightened or wounded themselves, they could wreak havoc among their own army.

Troops were drawn ideally from the citizens, but as needs arose, mercenaries were hired. Alexander supplemented his Macedonian troops with mercenaries and confronted Greek mercenaries in all his major battles. The Diadochi had no choice but to raise their phalanxes with mercenaries. Jews had a long history of mercenary service—such as the fortress at Elephantine on the Nile—and joined Alexander's army. Ptolemy I armed 30,000 Jews as occupation troops of fortresses in Egypt and Libya (*Let. Aris.* 12–13; *Ag. Ap.* 1.192–200). Ptolemaic armies were commanded by Jewish generals and some units were fully Jewish.

The early Roman Republic conscripted only landowners for the military, of which the poorest went to the navy, the better off to the infantry, and the wealthiest to the cavalry. As Roman expansion demanded more legions, the property requirement was waived. Poor men joined for twenty years (later twenty-five) and

the basis of a professional army was laid. When that proved insufficient, citizenship was granted to any soldier, along with his offspring, who enlisted. Specialized units of noncitizen militia (*auxilia*) played an important role in the Roman civil wars, and thereafter they were essential to the Roman army, typically as javelin throwers, slingers and archers, and especially cavalry. Under the empire, client kingdoms provided allied armies or auxiliaries, who usually fought as units under their own officers. Herod sent auxiliaries in support of Julius Caesar, Antony, and Octavian. Jews also served in the Roman military. Caesar exempted Jewish Roman citizens from military conscription on grounds of Sabbath and diet (*Ant.* 14.228–30), but Jews enlisted, most famously Tiberius Alexander, a nephew of Philo, who rose through the military ranks to become procurator of Judea and later prefect of Egypt. The Theodosian law in 418 CE that banned Jews from the army admits to many Jewish soldiers (Cod. theod. 16.8.24). Some church fathers frowned on a military career, but soldiers who became Christian continued to serve, while other Christians likely joined. The Twelfth Fulminata ("Thundering") Legion was known for its Christian soldiers and some credited their prayers for a rainstorm that saved the army of Marcus Aurelius (Eusebius, *Hist. eccl.* 5.5).

D. Preparation

Monarchs sometimes declared war and the Senate of the Roman Republic almost always did, but preparation for war long preceded its declaration. The Macedonian prime directive was speed to the point of battle, rapid and decisive engagement. Philip had hardened his men by thirty-five-mile-a-day marches without a supply train. The Romans followed with a daily exercise regimen augmented by regular double-time marches in full gear. Soldiers trained relentlessly for conditioning and combat maneuvers. The only difference between Roman training and real war, says Josephus, is the amount of blood spilled (*J.W.* 3.75).

Baggage trains were kept to a minimum. Whenever possible, local officials cached provisions in advance, allowing the army to march swiftly from one depot to the next. Alexander's army required daily 250 tons of grain and forage and 70,000 gallons of water. Roman soldiers carried at least three days' rations.

Knowledge about the enemy began with spies and bribes for defectors. Secrecy and feeding the enemy disinformation were common tactics. Coded messages and primitive cryptography were used, as well as the torture of spies. On the march, scouts determined the safety of a route and the best terrain for battle.

All armies sought the assurance of divine favor. Alexander thought it necessary to visit the oracles of Delphi and of Ammon in the Libyan desert before his Persian campaign. Diviners for the Roman legions read the activities of birds or inspected the entrails of sacrificial victims prior to war. Commanders often vowed to dedicate a shrine to a god if victorious. Roman religion sought to secure the peace of the gods (*pax deorum*) to help them master their foes, both human and divine. Romans were convinced their victory in war was due to the precision of their religious rituals. The Roman state religion and the imperial cult were designed to foster religious patriotism. The Jewish alternative was to offer up sacrifices for the empire and prayers in the synagogues. Christians took up the same cause and early apologists assured the emperors that Christians formed a spiritual army in their support.

E. Warfare

The tactics of battle—like boxing or chess—depend on power and guile. Each side seeks weaknesses in the defense of the other and exploits them as best they can. In battles between roughly equal armies, the victory is usually granted to the decisions and timing of the commander.

1. Open warfare

The battle array of the Macedonians centered on the phalanxes—tight columns of heavy infantry whose long pikes penetrated beyond the front line in four or five rows—and cavalry, both heavy and light. The cavalry swept the sides of a battle seeking to penetrate infantry lines, or more often exploit any gaps that formed, and went in pursuit of fleeing soldiers when the enemy had been routed. Alexander's Companions cavalry (the elite cavalry of the Macedonian army created by Philip II, the father of Alexander) carried lances of cornel wood and won the victory in his major battles. The Roman legions used similar tactics but preferred javelin and sword to the pike. Legionaries weakened the enemy with a volley of light, and then heavy javelins, and with greater mobility they were able to force gaps in the phalanx. Once the legionaries attained close quarter, they were powerful in slash and thrust combat with the sword. Field armies became progressively articulated with greater reliance on auxiliaries. Units of archers, slingers, and field artillery tactically weakened the enemy, and reserve units stood by in case of need.

By the time the Hellenistic phalanx met the Roman legion, the flexibility pioneered by Philip and Alexander had been lost to the Macedonians and adopted by the Romans. In the decisive battle of Magnesia-by-Sipylos (189 BCE) between Hellenistic and Roman forces, Antiochus III led an army of phalanxes interspersed by elephants, scythed chariots, heavy Persian cavalry, and auxiliaries of Arab swordsmen on swift camels. The Roman legionaries, archers, and slingers, supported by Pergamum cavalry, nevertheless annihilated the Hellenistic army by superior tactics of feint and mobility.

A novel tactic of Alexander was to exterminate the enemy on the grounds that dead men cannot return to fight. The Romans imitated Alexander and the death toll in war increased dramatically. Hellenistic wars killed 30 to 40 percent of soldiers, while Roman battles killed 50 to 80 percent.

Wars to protect the empire were more difficult than conquering it. Rebels fought by guerilla tactics, appearing suddenly in ambush, fighting furiously, and disappearing. Augustus garrisoned legions and auxiliaries at the frontiers, and the proportion of cavalry increased to a quarter of the troops in order to deal with the barbarian raids and rough terrain. The Roman general Varus put down a minor insurrection of the Jews in 6 CE when Rome began direct rule of Judea, but three years later he was given false information by Arminius and lured into the Teutoburg forest where his three legions were destroyed by the Germans.

2. Naval warfare

Naval power was key in controlling a Mediterranean empire. Ships transported invasion troops and secured the shipping routes by which the grain supplies fed the great cities, or disrupted the supplies of the enemy. Piracy was both a plague to coastal cities, and a trade war often used by one power against another. Mithridates used pirates as auxiliaries until Rome gave Pompey the resources and authority to wipe them out.

Ships of war were designed either for ramming or boarding. The trireme—so named for its three banks of oars—was the basic warship of antiquity. Larger ships used two or more rowers per oar but probably never more than three banks. A bronze ram protruded from the prow at the water line. Masts and sails were often used for long voyages but were removed before battle. The trireme traveled at 9 knots, and modern testing has shown a trireme could briefly reach 15–18 knots for ramming or shearing off the oars of the enemy ship. Early Roman warships developed for the Punic Wars were equipped with the *corvus*, a boarding bridge with an iron spike at the end, which was raised up to a mast and let fall into the deck of the enemy ship. Marines then streamed over and occupied the vessel. The *corvus*, however, made ships top heavy, and, by the battle of Actium, catapult grapnel hooks were used to secure the enemy ship and reel it in.

3. Siege warfare

Walled cities were the treasuries and defense centers of kingdoms. Siege warfare attempted to take the city by going over, under, or through the walls, while the defenders tried to stop them. Siege equipment included mobile towers, catapults, mobile sheds to protect ditch fillers, sappers, battering rams, drawbridges, and ladders. Besides penetrating the walls, a siege aimed to starve the city into submission or gain entrance by deception and treachery.

Ancient siege-craft was revolutionized by the Greek torsion catapults and new feats of engineering. The island city of Tyre that had repulsed Nebuchadnezzar for thirteen years succumbed to the floating siege towers and catapults of Alexander. Demetrius I of Macedonia, in his siege of Rhodes (305 BCE), constructed a siege tower, the Helepolis ("city destroyer"), about 43 m (140 ft.) high with nine stories for catapults and archers. It was protected on three sides by iron plates and built on iron-rimmed castor wheels, movable in any direction by a squadron of men.

Romans favored the blockade by circumvallation, a complete trench and rampart around the city that would ultimately starve the defenders. Fortified camps protected soldiers and laborers from sorties of the defenders. Siege ramps were built along the walls by a lacework of logs usually cut from the surrounding area and filled in by earth. Sappers—protected by the "tortoise," a portable shed, or a contingent of soldiers holding locked shields above them—dug at the base of the walls and removed stone blocks with crowbars. Others dug tunnels supported by wood beams near the walls and gates, and when the supports were fired, the earth collapsed, and walls sagged or fell. Rams, protected by leather-covered sheds, battered the walls and gates. From siege towers catapults weakened the upper wall and lighter artillery attacked the defenders. Torsion-powered bolts could rip through a row of men.

Defenders of a city employed many of the same techniques. They tunneled under the siege machines and towers, causing collapse. They used artillery against the attackers, and at opportune moments they sallied forth to attack workers or torch siege engines. Defenders poured boiling oil on soldiers below and lowered chaff-filled sacks to blunt the impact of the rams, or deflect them with chains and grapnel. Secondary walls were built behind the place of imminent breach. Siege defense was the one war in which women played vital roles, usually of support, but also manning the battlements. Even when the city was breached, fighting carried on street by street at great cost, and women pelted the soldiers with stones or tiles from the roofs. After a long and bloody siege, soldiers often engaged in frenzied rape and slaughter, and, in the end, many women and children committed suicide rather than fall into the hands of their enemies.

F. Aftermath of War

Wars of all ages were marked by loss of life and transfer of wealth. The laws of war granted the victor the right to kill his enemy and confiscate all wealth. The conqueror might exercise *clementia* and forgo the rights. This most often occurred when clemency was of strategic value to the conquerors and the tribute of a defeated people would provide more wealth. Pompey solved the piracy plague by settling pirates on underused lands. However, generals could not always control the army after a battle, and a soldier's pay often included pillage.

A conservative estimate of Alexander's conquest numbers 200,000 slain in battle and a quarter of a million civilians slaughtered or enslaved. The human devastation from war is incalculable, but war was the primary source for the slave economy of antiquity. Slave traders followed an army to war and purchased wholesale the men not slain, along with women and children. The number of slaves in Italy during the empire is reckoned at 2,000,000 or a quarter of the population. The Jewish community of 50,000 in Rome under Augustus came largely from emancipated slaves, and slavery was a significant cause of the Jewish Diaspora.

The tons of gold that poured out of Persia increased the disparity of wealth in the new Hellenistic kingdoms and helped end the Greek experiment with democracy. The Roman conquest had a similar effect on its society and the demise of the Republic. The building of Rome came largely from booty. The Flavian amphitheater (Colosseum), e.g., was begun by Vespasian with the booty from the Jerusalem war, and the arch of Titus depicts the Jerusalem temple vessels confiscated.

Bibliography: M. C. Bishop and J. C. N. Coulston. *Roman Military Equipment: From the Punic Wars to the Fall of Rome* (2006); Peter Connolly. *Greece and Rome at War* (2006); J. E. Lendon. *Soldiers and Ghosts: A History of Battle in Classical Antiquity* (2005).
LEO D. SANDGREN

WARDROBE. *See* CLOTH, CLOTHES.

WARDROBE, KEEPER OF THE [שֹׁמֵר הַבְּגָדִים shomer habbeghadhim]. The profession of Shallum, the prophetess Huldah's husband (2 Kgs 22:14; 2 Chr 34:22). Prophetesses held advisory roles in surrounding royal courts of the time, so "keeper of the wardrobe" may have been another temple or court position adopted from neighboring cultures (Egypt, Mari, Assyria, Greece). The "keeper of the wardrobe" at the temple of Baal in Samaria was literally in charge of the priestly vestments (2 Kgs 10:22).

LJUBICA JOVANOVIC

WARES, MERCHANDISE. *See* TRADE AND COMMERCE.

WARRIOR, DIVINE. Throughout the religions of the world, both male and female deities are depicted as warriors. Ancient Near Eastern and Greco-Roman religions provide many examples of this usage, as do biblical traditions.

On a mythological level, the warrior deity can be depicted as battling other gods or goddesses. The centerpiece of *Enuma Elish*, a hymn in praise of the Mesopotamian storm god MARDUK, is Marduk's victorious battle against TIAMAT, the goddess who personifies the primeval SEA; after his victory he establishes the cosmos and orders the creation of humans. Similarly, in Ugaritic myth, the storm god BAAL defeats Prince Sea and then is proclaimed king of the gods. Reflexes of these myths occur frequently in the Bible. It is Yahweh who defeats the primeval waters of chaos and then creates the world (Pss 74:12-17; 89:8-12 [Heb. 89:9-13]; 104:5-9). In apocalyptic literature, the final defeat of the sea monster will occur in the end time (Isa 27:1; Rev 12:7-9; 21:1; *see* APOCALYPSE; APOCALYPTICISM).

On a historical level, the divine warrior is the deity who—either alone or with human armies—marches into battle against the enemies of his city or his people. In the account of his campaign in 701 BCE, the Assyrian king SENNACHERIB boasts that the god Ashur fought alongside his own army in defeating the city of Sidon. Likewise, Yahweh marches with his people from the south, with the accoutrements of a storm god (Judg 5:4-5; Hab 3:3). Like a drunken warrior roused from sleep, Yahweh attacks his enemies (Ps 78:65-66) and returns victorious from battle with his robes stained with blood (Isa 63:1-6). In some of the Prophets, Yahweh the warrior fights against Israel itself, accompanying foreign armies that are the agents he uses to punish Israel for failing to live up to its covenant obligations (e.g., Isa 9:8–10:11 [Heb. 9:7–10:11]; Mic 1).

The title of the God of Israel, yhwh tsevaʾoth (יְהוָה צְבָאוֹת, traditionally translated "Lord of hosts"), also refers to the divine warrior. The "hosts" are Yahweh's heavenly army, numbering in the tens of thousands (Deut 33:2-3) or even uncountable, like the stars, the "host of heaven" (Deut 4:19; Jer 33:22). As the army of the divine warrior, the stars fight for Yahweh's people (Judg 5:20). In later biblical tradition, the divine army has commanders, preeminent among whom is the angel MICHAEL (Dan 12:1; Rev 12:7; see also Josh 5:14).

The paradigmatic example of Yahweh as divine warrior is the defeat of Pharaoh and the Egyptian army at the Red Sea. In an ancient poetic version of the event, Yahweh the warrior (Exod 15:3) is described as a storm god who blows with his wind and causes the Egyptians to sink in the "mighty waters" (Exod 15:10), and then is acclaimed as the preeminent deity (Exod 15:11). This is an Israelite historicization of the primeval combat between the storm god and the sea. The battle with Pharaoh is also characterized as one between Yahweh and the gods of Egypt (Exod 12:12).

MICHAEL D. COOGAN

WARRIORS [גִּבֹּר gibbor]. In the ancient and classical world, male character was often defined on the field of battle. Desired of an ideal leader were physical and moral courage. Ancient Near Eastern battle reports lauded the exploits of warrior-kings. Thucydides praised leaders who are obligated to preserve security, honor, and self-interest (*War* 1.76).

Within the Bible, the first of such characters so depicted is Joshua, who is presented as the ideal warrior, conqueror, and liberator; he is brave, just, and pious.

Joshua's army organization and their careful, ordered conquest of the land all suggest a strong centralized social control that can pull together the resources to execute such a successful strategy. Within the book of Judges, with Israel on the defensive, there are still elements of the character and mission of Joshua. Physical courage and divine selection are prominent among the admired traits.

In the stories of the kings of Israel and Judah, the main characters are examined not only for their piety but also for their battle success or lack thereof (2 Kgs 12; 13:7-19). David's reputation is built on his battle prowess (1 Sam 18:7), and, as with many ancient warrior-leaders, he surrounds himself with like-minded characters, such as the "MIGHTY MEN" (2 Sam 23:8-12). The ordered strategy and organization seen in the Joshua story and the faithfulness (piety) of the main protagonist become the characteristics sought for in the stories of later heroes.

Exodus 15:3 claims that Yahweh is a Warrior, and in the hymn that follows—together with numerous psalms and prophetic poems—the character of a savior God (Isa 43:3), liberator God (2 Sam 22:2), a conqueror of enemies (Ps 18:48), and a compassionate (Ps 86:15), faithful God emerges. This God bears all the marks of a victor in battle (Isa 42:13; Pss 18:46-48; 83; 89:10), who teaches his servants the arts of war (Ps 18:34-42).

Messianic hopes also portray some of the characteristics of the warrior. Defeat of surrounding enemies (Ps 108:13), expansion of the influence of the Torah and "justice" (Isa 42:4), dominion over a conquered or submissive population (Ps 72:11), commitment to uprightness and the rule of law (Isa 42:1-4), and care for the people (Isa 46:3-4) are all characteristics of the classical warrior. Demonstrations of "virtue," are seen par excellence in the messiah.

In the NT the characteristics of the warrior are desired of the church leader. By placing the struggles of the church's life within the context of "spiritual warfare" (2 Cor 10:1-5), Paul invites the comparison of leaders with warriors. In 1 Tim 1:18 and 2 Tim 2:3-4 the comparison is explicit. Members of faith communities are identified as "fellow soldiers" (Phil 2:25; Phlm 2), and the scars from following Christ are now battle wounds (2 Tim 2:3). The writer of Eph 6 encourages the Warrior-Believer to be armed for conflict, changing the foundational metaphor of the Christian life from the transformed family to the army. *See* MIGHTY ONE.

T. R. HOBBS

WARS OF THE LORD, BOOK OF [סֵפֶר מִלְחֲמֹת יְהוָה sefer milkhamoth yhwh]. A poem mentioned in Num 21:14-15, reciting the wars of Israel in the conquest of the Transjordan. *See* NUMBERS, BOOK OF.

WASH, WASHING. *See* BATHING; CLEAN AND UNCLEAN; FOOT WASHING.

WASHINGTONIANUS, CODEX. A late 4th-/early 5th-cent. Greek UNCIAL, designated by the sigla W, containing the Gospels in the "Western" order: Matthew, John, Luke, Mark. Also called the Washington Gospels and the Freer Manuscript of the Gospels, W is part of the Freer Gallery of Art at Washington D.C.'s Smithsonian Institution. The "Freer logion" is W's interpolation within Mark's Longer Ending (16:9-20) where Jesus declares the end of Satan's authority and explains the significance of his death as leading sinners to stop sinning and inherit righteousness in heaven.

Bibliography: Bruce M. Metzger. *The Text of the New Testament* (1992).

JAMES W. BARKER

WASM. A firebrand used by bedouin (pastoral) and hadar (agricultural or urban) clans to mark an animal with a symbol indicating ownership. Brands were usually placed on a camel's thigh, shoulder, neck, or cheek. A sub-clan could further distinguish its property by branding a particular location on the camel, by employing a variant wasm, or by employing an auxiliary wasm called a shahid. Wasms were not used on horses or on smaller herd animals such as sheep and goats. The wasm symbol could be used as a marker on rocks around and inside wells, on boulders around property, and on gravestones.

TERRY W. EDDINGER

WASP [σφήξ sphēx]. A flying insect belonging to the families of *Vespoidea* or *Sphecoidea* that is often known for its painful sting. The word occurs only once in the Apocrypha (Wis 12:8), where it refers to the gradual ("little by little") judgment on the Canaanites. This reference could be an extrapolation from Exod 23:28 and Deut 7:20 in regard to the term *pestilence* (tsir'ah צִרְעָה; LXX sphēkia [σφηκία], "HORNET") that plagued the Canaanites before the Israelites entered their land. The NRSV translates tsir'ah as "hornet" in Josh 24:12. *See* BEE.

BRUCE W. GENTRY

WASTE [חָרֵב kharev, חָרְבָּה khorbah, עָשֵׁשׁ 'ashesh, שָׁדַד shadhadh, שַׁמָּה shammah, שָׁמֵם shamem, שְׁמָמָה shemamah, תֹהוּ tohu; ἀπώλεια apōleia, ἐρημόω erēmoō, ἐξερημόω exerēmoō]. The term *waste* has a variety of meanings in the OT and the NT ranging from divine and human devastation of people or land to the weakening of a human's physical condition (Job 33:21; Pss 6:7; 31:9-10; 32:3; 102:4).

One of the most prevalent themes related to *waste* in the Bible is that of laying something to waste—i.e., the devastation that Israel and other nations would experience as a result of divine judgment (e.g., Lev 26:31; Isa 15:1; Jer 4:20, 23; 25:11; Ezek 12:20; 29:9-12; 30:7; 36:35; Zeph 3:6; Sir 10:16; Rev 18:17-19) or the destruction of other nations or people by Israel (e.g.,

Num 21:30). Jesus uses the devastation of kingdoms as a metaphor (Matt 12:25), and *waste* also refers to the unwise use of resources (Matt 26:8). *Waste* also describes land that is difficult to inhabit such as the desert of wilderness (Deut 32:10; Job 6:18; 12:24).

JOHN I. LAWLOR

WATCH. *See* HOUR; NIGHT; TIME.

WATCHER [שֹׁמֵר shomer; עִיר 'ir]. A guard or sentry (Isa 21:8, according to a Qumran manuscript, as the NRSV notes; Jer 4:17). Job addresses God as the "watcher of humanity" (7:20). Daniel 4 uses *watcher* ('ir) to refer to heavenly beings whose name is apparently derived from the root 'wr (עוּר), "to be awake." Nebuchadnezzar dreams that a watcher comes down from heaven (Dan 4:13, 23) and speaks of a sentence by the decree of the watchers (v. 17). In each verse *watcher* is defined further as "holy one" (qaddish קַדִּישׁ). Hence, the watchers seem to be angels who communicate with humans and pass decrees on God's behalf. This understanding of the watchers is reflected in *Jub.* 4:15 and the *Apocalypse of Weeks* (*1 En.* 91:15-16).

According to an elaborate retelling of the cryptic verse Gen 6:4 in the *Book of the Watchers* (*1 En.* 1–36, especially 6–16), the watchers came down to the daughters of men and fathered giants by them and led them astray in other ways, only to be bound in chains and thrown into darkness to await the great day of judgment. This understanding of the watchers became widespread and is attested in the NT (1 Pet 3:19-20; 2 Pet 2:4-5; Jude 6). *See* ANGEL; ARCHANGEL; DANIEL, BOOK OF; ENOCH, FIRST BOOK OF.

JOSEPH L. TRAFTON

WATCHERS, BOOK OF THE. *See* ENOCH, FIRST BOOK OF; NEPHILIM.

WATCHTOWER [בַּחַן bakhan, מִגְדָּל mighdal, מִצְפֶּה mitspeh; πύργος pyrgos, σκοπή skopē]. A tall stone or brick structure built as a lookout post and fortification. Farmers built watchtowers in their fields so that the owners or workmen could guard their crops from looters or animals (Isa 5:2; Matt 21:33; Mark 12:1). Often watchtowers had a lower room that would serve as the workers' living quarters during harvest season.

Watchtowers were also part of the fortification system. Some stood alone on hills as observation posts such as those Jotham built in Judah (2 Chr 27:4, author's trans.; NRSV, "towers"; compare 2 Kgs 17:9; Isa 21:8; 32:14). Others were built into city walls as a part of city defenses. These served as strongholds and observation posts for defenders. Often they jutted out from the city walls, thus allowing the defenders to observe the base of the outside walls (Neh 3:25-27, author's trans.; NRSV, "towers"). The human mind is compared to a watchtower in Sir 37:14. *See* TOWER.

TERRY W. EDDINGER

WATEN, KHIRBET EL. A collection of ruins, known in modern Hebrew as Hurvat Yittan, located about 12 km east of Beer-sheba. Khirbet el-Waten is one of several eastern Negev sites that flourished in the 7ᵗʰ cent. BCE. It has been associated with MOLADAH (Josh 15:26; 19:2; 1 Chr 4:28; Neh 11:26) but no definitive identification has been made.

TERRY W. EDDINGER

WATER [מַיִם mayim; ὕδωρ hydōr]. Water is essential for human, animal, and plant life, and securing a sufficient supply represented a major part of life activities in the time of the OT and the NT. Water was often limited and costly, thus a close link between divine blessings and an ample supply of water (and thus food) existed in the minds of the authors of the Bible. Drought, and in consequence, hunger, was understood to be the result of idolatry—the illegitimate relationship of the people (or an individual) with other gods—and could be remedied by God (2 Chr 6:26-31), if there was a change of relationship. Water was also essential in ritual and religious activities in both the OT and the NT and thus carried important theological connotations.

A. The Semantics of Water in the Bible
   1. Hebrew
   2. Greek
B. Water and Daily Life
C. Water and Creation (and De-creation)
D. Water in Ritual
E. Water and Theology
Bibliography

A. The Semantics of Water in the Bible
1. Hebrew

Since water played such an important role in the daily life of someone living in the ANE, it is not surprising to note the vast semantic domain of nouns associated with water. Even without including verbal forms involving water manipulation, the list is extensive. The most frequently used term for water is mayim, which appears nearly 600 times in the OT. It can indicate a literal body of water, as in Exod 2:10 where it refers to the Nile River from which Moses had been saved. It is also used as a metaphor for Yahweh in the phrase meqor mayim khayyim (מְקוֹר מַיִם חַיִּים), "the fountain of living water," which is put in contrast to a cistern whose inside plaster is broken and thus cannot hold water (Jer 2:13). The force of Yahweh's judgment is compared to the force of water rushing down a steep mountain (Mic 1:4).

A water source determines the type of water one enjoys. Spring water is fresh and sweet, and there are a number of Hebrew terms denoting *spring*. Mabbakh (מַבָּךְ) occurs only once in Job 28:11, and based on the use of the root in Ugarit, has been translated as "sources of the rivers." Another word for a spring that occurs once is nevekh (נֶבֶךְ), where God challenges Job:

"Have you entered into the springs of the sea?" (Job 38:16). A more common word for *spring* is ma'yan (מַעְיָן), which indicates a source of fresh water that is desperately searched for in times of drought (1 Kgs 18:5). Springs can receive names and may function as boundary markers of territory (Josh 15:9; 18:5). In wartime springs of fresh water can be stopped up as part of a comprehensive war effort (2 Kgs 3:19, 25; 2 Chr 32:4). Related to ma'yan is 'ayin (עַיִן), "fountain, source, spring," a term generally indicating an eye, but which is used in several instances as a reference to a source of water (Gen 16:7; Num 33:9), most likely due to the fact that phenomenologically the eye is the source of tears. Other terms referring to a spring include maqor (מָקוֹר; Jer 51:36; Hos 13:15) and mabbua' (מַבּוּעַ; Isa 35:7; 49:10).

Cisterns and wells played an important role in the human strategy to secure water access during times of drought or seasonal variations. The terms be'er (בְּאֵר), "well, pit" (Gen 26:18, 22; Num 20:17), bor (בּוֹר), "cistern" (Gen 37:20; 1 Sam 13:6), gev (גֵּב), "cistern" (2 Kgs 3:16; Jer 14:3), geve' (גֶּבֶא), "cistern, pool" (Isa 30:14), berekhah (בְּרֵכָה), "pool, pond" (2 Kgs 20:20; Neh 3:16), mikhal (מִיכָל), "reservoir" (2 Sam 17:20), and miqwah (מִקְוֶה), "reservoir" (Isa 22:11) all seem to refer to man-made constructions that served the sole purpose of securing a constant supply of water and were part of the larger process of sedentarization of people as opposed to a nomadic lifestyle with seasonal movements, that were mostly determined by water access.

Hebrew references to sea water include yam (יָם), "sea," which is used generically as a reference to the accumulation of large bodies of water (Gen 1:10; Deut 33:19) or in conjunction with other nouns or adjectives as a reference to the Mediterranean Sea (Josh 1:4) or the Dead Sea (Gen 14:3; 2 Kgs 14:25). Other terms describe the depth of water, including metsulah (מְצוּלָה), "deep, depth" (Exod 15:5), tsulah (צוּלָה), "abyss" (only in Isa 44:27), and the important tehom (תְּהוֹם), "primeval ocean, deeps of the sea, subterranean water" (Gen 1:2).

Hebrew terms referring to rivers or streams include nahar (נָהָר), "river, stream" (Num 24:6), which represents a major permanent watercourse, and, in combination with other nouns or adjectives, refers to the Euphrates (Gen 15:18), Tigris (Dan 10:4), or Nile (Gen 15:18). On the other hand, nakhal (נַחַל), "stream, small river, wadi, tunnel" can refer to a perennial body of water (1 Kgs 17:7), which will only carry water during specific seasons. Other relevant terminology involving water included different forms of precipitation, including rain, snow, ice, and hail.

2. Greek

The NT terminology referring to water is also varied, including thalassa (θάλασσα), "sea, lake, large body of water" (Mark 9:42), limnē (λίμνη), "lake, pool, harbor" (Luke 5:1; Acts 27:12), pelagos (πέλαγος), "open sea, ocean, deep" (Acts 27:5; 2 Cor 11:25), kolpos (κόλπος), "bay, gulf" (Acts 27:39), potamos (ποταμός), "river, stream" (Matt 3:6), referring to a permanent watercourse, cheimarros (χείμαρρος), "brook, perennial river" (John 18:1), pēgē (πηγή), "spring, well" (John 4:6; Rev 8:10), and kolymbēthra (κολυμβήθρα), "pool" (John 5:2). Generic references to water as a liquid include hydōr, "water" (Matt 3:11), ikmas (ἰκμάς), "moisture" (Luke 8:6), hyetos (ὑετός), "rain, rain water" (Acts 14:17), krystallos (κρύσταλλος), "ice" (Rev 4:6), chiōn (χιών), "snow" (Matt 28:3, only used as a symbol of complete whiteness), and chalaza (χάλαζα), "hail" (Rev 8:7). Besides these nouns there are numerous verbs (both in Hebrew and Greek) that indicate manipulation and movement of fluids, including water.

B. Water and Daily Life

Geography, topography, climate, and other ecological factors determine many cultural and also religious traits of a particular place or region. In consequence, the scarcity of water sources in Palestine and its effects on daily life are highly noticeable in the texts of the Bible. Since perennial water sources were limited, dependency on rain and dew was very high and, as a result, human responses to this situation included the digging of wells (Gen 26:19-25), the construction of cisterns and pools that collected runoff water during the rainy season, as well as other constructions (such as small dams or shafts and tunnels) that helped in the preservation of this essential ingredient of life. Other responses to the scarcity of water included the adoption of a mixed economy, often involving a mix of nomadic and sedentary lifestyles (compare the patriarchs in Genesis), also known as subsistence pastoralism, which interacted with the larger urban centers and small villages. Above and beyond all these pragmatic responses, however, water served as an important link between the deity and humanity. Water was considered more than a measurable chemical formula (H_2O), and its presence and effect on the land was associated with divine blessings, while lack of water and rain was understood as an expression of divine wrath (1 Kgs 18), which often was due to idolatrous behavior of (at least) some of the members of the people of Yahweh and thus required repentance and a changed attitude (2 Chr 6:26-31; 20:9). The control of access to dependable water supplies also played a role in war strategies, including destruction and pollution of existing water supplies (2 Kgs 3:25; 2 Chr 32:3-4), which often was more devastating than a frontal attack of the enemy. The lack of water also affected ideals of cleanliness and hygiene. Priests were required to wash their hands and feet before performing their duties (Exod 30:18-19, 21; 40:30-31; Deut 21:6), and during their ordination ritual they had to completely undress and were washed before changing into their newly made priestly garments (Exod 29:4; Lev 8:6), marking a clear rite of passage, involving rites of separation, transition, and incorporation. Over time, a "clean hand" became a metaphor for a clean conscience (Deut 21:6-7; 2 Sam 22:21; Ps 18:20-21) and the washing of feet was integrated in hospitality rituals (Gen 18:4; 19:2; 24:32; Judg 19:21), which later became part of the communion ritual initiated by Jesus (John 13:4-17; compare 1 Tim 5:10). The washing of the entire body was more common for people living close to a source of running water and sometimes had religious connotations, as, e,g,, can be seen in the purification rites of women after menstruation (Lev 15:19-24; compare 2 Sam 11:4).

C. Water and Creation (and De-creation)

Water plays an important role in creation, and, due to the use of the term tehom ("primeval ocean, deeps of the sea, subterranean water"; Gen 1:2), some have suggested a close link between the Hebrew concept of the tehom and the Akkadian word TIAMAT, which refers to the goddess of primeval ocean in the Babylonian epic *Enuma Elish*. However, more careful lexical research has demonstrated that it is almost impossible to conclude that Akkadian tiamat was borrowed by Hebrew as tehom with an intervocalic /h/, which tends to disappear in Hebrew. Worthy of notice is also the fact that tehom does not appear in the Hebrew texts from the Dead Sea Scrolls in a mythological sense, suggesting that (at least at that time) this semantic aspect was insignificant. Others have posited a close Canaanite background of Gen 1:2, linking the Ugaritic myth of the Baal Cycle with Gen 1:2 and the common motif of a *Chaoskampf* ("chaos fight"). It is interesting to note that in the OT tehom is never used as an indication for yam ("sea") in a tripartite description of the world, i.e., heaven–earth–sea (Exod 20:11; Neh 9:6; Ps 146:6; Hag 2:6), even though there are references where yam and tehom appear in parallelism (Job 28:14; 38:16; Isa 51:10). In Isa 51:10, the parallelism seems to point to the miraculous drying up of the Red Sea in Exod 14:21-22. Different from other ANE creation myths, water does not play an active role in the creation account of the OT. It is God's spirit that hovers over the waters (and it should be noted that there is no reference to the Canaanite deity yam in Gen 1:2) and it is God's speech act that produces life and the separation of the created elements. In Gen 1:6-8 the waters of the heavens (= rain) are separated from the waters of the sea (Gen 1:9-10), which in turn are filled with creatures on the fifth day. Interestingly, the complementary creation account of Gen 2 begins with a description of the dry and desolate state of the earth, prior to God causing rain to fall on the land (and thus producing plants). The term ʾedh (אֵד, "high water"), used in Gen 2:6, appears only twice in the OT (Gen 2:6; Job 36:27) and most likely was a Sumerian loanword indicating "water flooding out of the subterranean ocean," which is in contrast to most English translations (e.g., "mist" [NKJV, RSV, ESV], "stream" [NIV], "springs" [NET]). If understood in this sense it may be linked to the tehom described in Gen 1:2.

Water is also a significant element of judgment or de-creation. When the increasing wickedness of humanity becomes obvious, Yahweh decides to destroy the inhab-itants of the earth (including animals) by means of a flood (Gen 6:7, 17), saving only Noah's family and some animals (Gen 6:8, 18). The divine diagnostic laments the khamas (חָמָס), "violence" of humanity (Gen 6:11), a theme that also plays a significant role in the writings of the prophets (Isa 59:6; Jer 6:7; 20:8; Ezek 7:11; Amos 3:10; etc.) and thus links the flood judgment with the judgment of the exile. The flood narrative transforms water into a means of judgment; the agent of blessing (i.e., there is no life without water) becomes an agent of curse. This primordial judgment by water reappears repeatedly in other texts of the OT (Pss 18:16; 29:10; 65:5-8; 89:9; 93:3; Isa 24:1-5; 43:2). References to the wicked times of Noah prior to the flood appear also in the NT where they are linked to the time just prior to the second coming (Matt 24:37-39; Luke 17:26-27), even though there is no specific reference to the ele-ment of water. As already noted, the lack of water (i.e., rain) is also closely associated with divine judgment, as the Elijah narrative in 1 Kgs 18 demonstrates. In har-mony with widespread thinking in the ANE, the provi-sion of rain is considered a divine attribute. On Mount Carmel it is Yahweh against Baal, the creator god versus the weather god.

D. Water in Ritual

Water plays many different roles in biblical ritual, thus underlining the multivalent nature of biblical ritual and ritual per se. It is used to wash parts of sacrificial animals that are later burned on the altar (Lev 1:9, 13; 8:21). During the ordination ritual, Aaron and his sons have to undergo a comprehensive washing rite before they can be clothed in their new garments, indicating their changed status in society (Exod 29:4; Lev 8:6) and their importance for the cult. Similarly, the Levites are also to be sprinkled with "water of purification" (me khatta᾽t מֵי חַטָּאת), which is accompanied by a shaving of the whole body and the washing of their clothing (Num 8:7). The purifying function of water can also be noted in the nonpriestly ritual use of water that could have affected any Israelite. Skin diseases and mildew (Lev 13:6, 34, 54; 14:8, 9, 47) and bodily discharge (Lev 15:5-8, 10, 11, 13, 21, 22, 27) all required wash-ing rites as an important element of the larger purifica-tion ritual. While reference is not made specifically to the use of water in all cases, the verbal action involving washing rites would presuppose that. It is interesting to note that the OT is in some instances more specific and uses the Semiticism mayim khayyim (מַיִם חַיִּים), "liv-ing water" (Lev 14:5, 50; 15:13; Num 19:17; NRSV, "fresh" or "running" water), indicating the preference of running water for a particular ritual. A similar Greek expression appears also in the early Christian Didache

(late 1st/early 2nd cent. CE) regarding the Christian bap-tism rite (Did. 7:1-4), which may provide an interesting window into the Jewish background of this particular ritual and its purification aspect in some quarters of early Christianity.

Another relevant ritual use of water in some type of judicial context can be found in Exod 32:20 and Num 5:17. To be sure, both rituals are not dealing with the same issues. While Exod 32 involves a specific rite that seems to be part of a larger ritual response to the dis-ruption of the covenant by the Israelites, the enigmatic ritual of the "test for an unfaithful wife" (Num 5:11-31) concerns the resolution of a highly emotive issue in the context of a marriage, i.e., suspected adultery. In both instances water is mixed with another substance that is then given to some of the participants for consumption. In Exod 32:20 the remains of the golden calf image are burned, ground to powder, mixed with water, and the resulting concoction is given to the Israelites to drink. However, this does not completely resolve the problem, and on Moses' command the Levites execute about 3,000 men (Exod 32:28), thus threatening the com-munity even further. While the ritual action in Num 5:11-31 does not concern the entire community, the threat to the smallest unit of society, i.e., the marriage covenant, requires external arbitration (marked by the prominence of the priestly officiant) and involves water as part of a surprising cocktail (involving me hammarim [מֵי הַמָּרִים], "the WATER OF BITTERNESS" [Num 5:18]), whose consumption is required, together with a public declaration by the suspected woman (Num 5:22) and other ritual acts.

One of the most significant uses of water in ritual, already prefigured in the purification rites of the OT and further developed during the Second Temple pe-riod in the various ritual washings prevalent in Judaism, involves the NT baptism ritual. It is interesting to note that the NT itself makes a clear distinction between the "baptism of John," which denoted repentance (Acts 18:25; 19:1-4) and the "baptism of Jesus" (Acts 19:5), involving the ministry of the Holy Spirit, which apparently included an element of service. Both rituals seemed to have involved the complete immersion of the person to be baptized into water (Acts 8:36, 38). The NT authors provide complementing rationales for bap-tism, often linking it to events mentioned in the OT, and thus highlighting the innovative power of ritual and the polyvalence of ritual elements such as water. Romans 6:3-4 (compare also Col 2:12) links going into the wa-ter and coming out of it to the substitutionary death and resurrection of Jesus: in the same sense that Jesus died and was raised, baptism marks the death and res-urrection experience of every Christian—a notion that clearly goes beyond the predominant purification motif associated with water in the OT. However, remainders of this usage can also be found in the NT as can be seen in Eph 5:26, which links purification and cleansing by the washing of water with the sanctifying work of the

Word of God. Baptism also creates unity and functions as a leveling agent (1 Cor 12:13; Gal 3:27-28; Eph 4:5), but is the result of an individual recognizing personal sinfulness and seeking to repent (Acts 2:37-38), even though it could also involve larger groups (Acts 2:41; 8:12; 10:24-48; 16:33).

E. Water and Theology

The close link between the creator and the sustainer God that existed in the minds of authors and readers of the OT often finds its expression in water metaphors. Rain showers were often considered a special symbol of God's blessings (Ezek 34:26), and the lack of rain was clearly understood by the prophets of the OT as the result of a covenant breach (Jer 3:1-3; 14:22). The description of the eschatological restoration of Israel was often linked to idyllic descriptions of easily accessible water sources and dependable rain patterns (Isa 35:7; 41:18; 49:10; Zech 10:1) and echoes the pentateuchal descriptions of a good and fertile land with ample water supplies (Deut 8:7) and the experience of divine leadership during the wanderings through the wilderness. The water in the wilderness motif (Exod 15:25; 17:1-6; Num 20:8-11) reflects to a certain degree the creation link of water. This link between the provision of water and creation can again be found in the NT, where Jesus describes himself as the divine water giver (John 4:10, 13-14) and thus provides a link between the OT and the NT. This living water transforms the one partaking of it from within and becomes a "spring of water gushing up to eternal life" (John 4:14). Later, Jesus links this claim with another theological motif of the OT, i.e., the manna, when he refers to himself as the "bread of life" (John 6:35), which will result in no more hunger and thirst for those partaking of this bread. Another reinterpreted theological motif of the OT associated with water can be found in Paul's discussion of the lessons of Israelite history for the early church in 1 Cor 10:1-5. While all were "baptized into Moses in the cloud and in the sea" and also ate the same "spiritual food" and drank the same "spiritual drink" from the rock, they were still scattered by God. Paul's point is straightforward: membership, even shared experiences, does not guarantee salvation.

Finally, the NT ends with an important echo of Genesis and creation. John describes the river of the water of life (Rev 22:1), which seems to echo the stream that went out of Eden (Gen 2:10). This river of the water of life emanates from the throne of God and the Lamb located in the city of God, again highlighting that God is not only the creator but also the sustainer of life, even eternal life. In a further echo of Jesus' dialogue with the Samaritan woman in John 4, the final invitation of the last book of the NT concerns access for those thirsty for the water of life to come and receive this water for free (Rev 22:17). This theological motif has already been introduced in Rev 21:6 and again points to the Alpha and Omega, the beginning and the end, creator and sustainer, who is truly the giver of the water of life. *See* BAAL; BAPTISM; COMMUNION; CREATION; FLOOD; RITUAL.

Bibliography: Oded Borowski. *Daily Life in Biblical Times* (2003); David S. Dockery. "Baptism in the New Testament." *SwJT* 43 (2001) 4–16; Gerald A. Klingbeil. *Bridging the Gap: Ritual and Ritual Texts in the Bible* (2007); Jonathan David Lawrence. *Washing in Water: Trajectories of Ritual Bathing in the Hebrew Bible and Second Temple Literature* (2006); Jerome H. Neyrey. "The Footwashing in John 13:6-11: Transformation Ritual or Ceremony?" *The Social World of the First Christians: Essays in Honor of Wayne A. Meeks.* L. Michael White and O. Larry Yarbrough, eds. (1995) 198–213; William Henry Propp. *Water in the Wilderness: A Biblical Motif and Its Mythological Background* (1987); David Toshio Tsumura. *Creation and Destruction: A Reappraisal of the Chaoskampf Theory of the Old Testament* (2005).
GERALD A. KLINGBEIL

WATER FOR IMPURITY [מֵי הַנִּדָּה me hanniddah]. The water for impurity is a special water/ash mixture used for purification after corpse contamination. The ashes were produced by sacrificing an unblemished, untamed red heifer outside the camp in the presence of a priest. The priest sprinkled the heifer's blood seven times toward the front of the tent of meeting, and its entire body, including the skin, flesh, blood, and internal organs, was burned. While the flesh of the heifer was burning several other items were cast into the fire, including cedar, hyssop, and crimson string (Num 19:1-6). The exact function of these objects is uncertain, though possibly the red color of the cedar and string (as well as the heifer) symbolized blood, which is representative of life. The ashes were gathered and kept outside of the camp in a clean place until needed (Num 19:9). For cleansing ceremonies, the ashes were mixed with running water to create the purificatory solution (Num 19:17).

Persons who touched a corpse, a bone, or a grave or those who entered a tent where a person died required purification (Num 19:11, 13, 14, 16; 31:19). Such persons were unclean for seven days, and the purification ritual required two sprinklings with the water for impurity, one on the third day and one on the seventh (Num 19:19). A clean layperson (not a priest) performed the ceremonies by dipping hyssop in the water and sprinkling the contaminated persons (Num 19:18). Corpse-contaminated objects, such as the spoils of war or a tent where death occurred, also required purification (Num 19:15, 18; 31:20-23).

The water for impurity created a passageway from death (corpse contamination) back into life. *See* CLEAN AND UNCLEAN.

Bibliography: Jacob Milgrom. *Leviticus 1–16.* AB 3 (1991).

SUSAN M. PIGOTT

WATER GATE [מַיִם שַׁעַר shaʿar hammayim]. Nehemiah mentions that the Water Gate lay in the eastern part of Jerusalem near a "projecting tower" (Neh 3:26; 12:37) and a gathering place where Ezra read from the Torah (Neh 8:1, 3). Parallel accounts in 1 Esdras associate this gate ("the east gate") with the Temple precincts (1 Esd 9:38, 41; compare *m. Mid.* 1:4; *m. Sheq.* 6:3). *See* GATE; NEHEMIAH; TEMPLE, JERUSALEM.

JAMES RILEY STRANGE

WATER HEN [תִּנְשֶׁמֶת tinshemeth; πορφυρίων porphyriōn]. A bird such as the coot or rail (family *Rallidae*) that inhabits marshlands. The animal is listed among the abhorrent or unclean animals forbidden as food for the Israelites (Lev 11:18; Deut 14:16). The NRSV translates the same Hebrew consonantal term as "chameleon" in a list of swarming land animals (Lev 11:30). The meaning of this word, as with many terms in biblical lists of animals, is speculative. *See* BIRDS OF THE BIBLE.

BRUCE W. GENTRY

WATER OF BITTERNESS [הַמָּרִים מֵי me hammarim]. A potion created by a priest out of water, dust from the floor of the sanctuary, and the washed-off ink that spelled out adulterous accusations against a wife (Num 5:18, 19, 23, 24). According to the casuistic law of Num 5:11-31, a woman who drank this and suffered miscarriage, sterility, or deformity of her reproductive organs was considered guilty; a woman who had no physical consequences was deemed innocent. In 5:24 the potion is called the "water of bitterness that brings the curse." Thus "bitterness" referred to the outcome of the ritual for one who was judged guilty and perhaps to the taste of the brew as well. The bitter water ordeal began with a jealousy offering from the accusing husband (Num 5:15-16). The priest disheveled the wife's hair, had her hold the offering, and made her take an oath that the curse would betray her guilt or innocence. The priest then washed the ink of the written oath into the potion, and, having burned the offering, made her imbibe the concoction to determine the verdict and sentence at once.

The grounds for such a trial are unclear. Perhaps the woman was pregnant, in which case the punishment apparently indicates abortion. Yet the text allows for the possibility that any jealous husband could impose this ordeal on his wife, pregnant or not. This law relied on theological beliefs about divine justice and ancient assumptions about fertility and childbirth. Nonetheless, it would have brought immediate and unjust condemnation for any woman who was married to an infertile man, who was herself infertile, or who had deformed

reproductive organs. Furthermore, the threat of this trial may have procured an easy divorce for the husband. While this "trial" may sound like torture in order to ease a jealous husband's suspicions of his wife, the context suggests it was a way to protect the cultic community from uncleanness (Num 5:1-3). The bitter water ordeal was discontinued by the 3rd cent. BCE, but the use of this ordeal for a "sotah," or "errant woman," was still a matter for discussion in postbiblical times (*m. Sotah*). *See* TRIAL BY ORDEAL.

Bibliography: Thomas B. Dozeman. "The Book of Numbers." *NIB* 2 (1998) 1–268; Tikva Frymer-Kensky. "The Strange Case of the Suspected Sotah (Numbers v 11-31)." *VT* 34 (1984) 11–26; Baruch Levine. *Numbers 1–20.* AB 4A (1993) 200–12.

LISA MICHELE WOLFE

WATER SHAFT [צִנּוֹר tsinnor]. Place where David instructed his troops to attack the Jebusites (2 Sam 5:8). As a system to convey water from an external spring to the interior of Jerusalem, the water shaft would have been a weakness in the city wall. The LXX, however, translates batsinnor (בַּצִּנּוֹר) as "with a dagger" (en paraxiphidi ἐν παραξιφίδι), suggesting that tsinnor was a type of weapon David expected his troops to use. *See* WELLS.

T. DELAYNE VAUGHN

WATER WORKS [מַיִם mayim]. Water is crucial for survival for all living creatures, especially so in arid lands such as in the biblical world. Earliest habitation focused on a consistent supply of water in settlement choices. Springs, rivers, and lakes attracted settlers with prospects of irrigation and water for herds and flocks. In biblical lands, however, consistent supply was a constant problem. The nomadic lifestyle reflected in the patriarchal narratives (Gen 12–35) depicts the movement of peoples and herds from one source of water/food to another. Technological development allowed collection and irrigation from seasonal water sources. Human and animal preservation rather than irrigation is prevalent in the biblical texts.

Three key aspects of water systems include a source, transfer, and collection. Israel/Judah lacked the numerous rivers and lakes necessary for expansion. Springs did exist in the land. The Gihon Spring provided water to Jerusalem (1 Kgs 1:33-45; 2 Chr 32:30; 33:14). The springs of En-Gedi, near the Dead Sea, provided David with protection from Saul (1 Sam 23:29).

The wells existed from patriarchal times. Beer-sheba (seven wells) delineated the southern scope of Israel's territory (Gen 21:14-33; 46:1, 5; 2 Sam 3:20; 24:2-15; and others). Underground aquifers supplied water through human construction and excavation of wells.

Growing villages and towns required increased water storage. Seasonal rains were collected and stored in cisterns or pools. Due to the porous nature of the indigenous limestone, lime was processed to plaster cisterns. Israel's short rainy season supplied the needs of the population when water was stored and managed. Roof runoff collection into storage pits/cisterns was common (2 Kgs 18:31). Archaeological investigation uncovered small cisterns that honeycombed entire villages for personal use. The Moabite king Mesha required cisterns in every home of Qarhoh (*see* MOABITE STONE). Community cisterns provided a supply of water in times of siege or emergencies (Jer 41:9).

Movement of water from these stationary supplies was necessary to fill community cisterns and pools, especially during times of siege. Conduits, trenches, and ditches served as means for water transfer from springs, wells, and smaller cisterns. Water was necessary in Israelite faith for ritual cleansing in pools before entering the Temple precinct or for cleansing after contact with a corpse (Lev 16:4, 24).

When a water source was located outside the city walls, water works were designed to bring the water into a central storage containment system within the city complex. In Megiddo, construction of a water system (ca. 9th cent. BCE) included a shaft lined with steps reaching down 115 ft. to the level of the spring outside of the city walls, and a tunnel that ran horizontally 200 ft. to the spring. In Jerusalem, preparation for a siege by the Assyrian king Sennacherib led Hezekiah to tunnel under the city from the Gihon Spring to the Pool of Siloam in the 8th cent. BCE (2 Kgs 18:13–19:37; 20:20; 2 Chr 32:30). An inscription discovered in the tunnel describes two teams working from opposite directions to complete the 1,749 ft.-long tunnel. *See* WATER; WELLS.

MICHAEL G. VANZANT

WATERCOURSE [אָפִיק 'afiq]. A dry stream bed, or wadi (e.g., Joel 1:20). A symbol of prosperity when filled with water (Ps 126:4) and of destruction when filled with blood (Ezek 32:6).

WATERS OF MEGIDDO. *See* MEGIDDO, WATERS OF.

WATERS OF MEROM. *See* MEROM, WATERS OF.

WATERS OF NEPHTOAH. *See* NEPHTOAH, WATERS OF.

WATERS OF NIMRIM. *See* NIMRIM, THE WATERS OF.

WATERS OF SHILOAH. *See* SHILOAH, WATERS OF.

WATERS, MANY [מַיִם רַבִּים mayim rabbim; ὕδατα πολλά hudata polla]. An allusion to the primeval watery chaos in Song 8:7 and Isa 17:13, as well as in Rev 17:1. In Rev 1:15; 14:2; 19:6 it describes a power-

ful voice with connotations of goodness, echoing the "mighty waters" heard in the vision of Ezekiel (1:24).

JOAN E. COOK, SC

WATERSKINS [נֵבֶל nevel]. The Hebrew word translated "waterskins" in Job 38:37 usually refers to containers used for storing wine (e.g., 1 Sam 1:24; 10:3; *see* WINESKIN). The term is used in Job as a metaphor for clouds, the "waterskins of the heavens," whose contents only God can heft and pour down as rain. Though animal skins were often used as containers for storing and transporting liquids, such containers seem to have been more commonly made of clay (e.g., Isa 30:14, "potter's vessel"; Lam 4:2, "earthen pots"). Thus "vessel" might be a more accurate translation than "waterskins."

T. DELAYNE VAUGHN

WAW wou [ו w]. The sixth letter of the Hebrew alphabet, which derives from the Semitic pictograph *waww-, "hook." *See* ALPHABET.

WAX [דּוֹנַג donagh; κηρός kēros]. Wax (beeswax) was used to seal documents (Isa 8:16; Jer 32:10; Rev 5:1). Wax appears figuratively in comparisons drawing on the image of change from solid to easily flowing liquid, highlighting the power of the cause of change or the weakness of the one changed: mountains flow before God (Ps 97:5; Mic 1:4; Jdt 16:15) as do enemies (Ps 68:2 [Heb. 68:3]), and the psalmist melts in a crisis (Ps 22:14 [Heb. 22:15]). Wooden writing boards once covered in wax have been discovered in the Middle East. *See* WRITING BOARDS.

PETER TRUDINGER

WAY [אֹרַח 'orakh, דֶּרֶךְ derekh; ὁδός hodos]. In both the OT and NT, *way* has both literal and figurative meanings. It indicates a road or path (e.g., Gen 38:21; 2 Sam 18:23; Matt 2:12; Luke 10:31) or denotes direction toward something (i.e., Ezek 21:2: "set your face toward Jerusalem"; compare Matt 4:15). In the OT, *way* also commonly refers to God's deliverance of Israel: God "makes a way in the sea" (Isa 43:16; compare Ps 77:19; Isa 51:10).

Way also has a number of metaphorical uses. The ancient figurative uses are similar to those of modern English. The "way" of a person or animal refers to its customary or habitual behavior: "Go to the ant, you lazybones; / consider its ways, and be wise" (Prov 6:6; compare Josh 23:14; Acts 14:16). This is also extended to the moral actions of individuals or groups, both positive (e.g., Prov 11:20; Matt 21:32) and negative (e.g., Jer 3:21; Rom 3:16). Because life is often conceived as a journey, the way or path may refer generally to the course of one's life (e.g., 2 Sam 22:33; Ps 10:5).

God's customary actions or habits are also referred to as "God's ways" (e.g., Exod 33:13; Ps 25:10; Heb 3:10; Rev 15:3). God's ways are beyond human understanding (e.g., Job 26:14; Rom 11:33) and contrast with human ways (i.e., "my ways" vs. "your ways"; Isa 55:8-9). However, God's ways are also made available to humans by following the law. God's commandments are known as "the way in which the LORD your God commanded you to walk" (Deut 13:5; compare Exod 32:8). Wisdom is likewise described as the "way" (e.g., Prov 8:32; 23:19). Following the logic of the metaphor, those who do not live according to God's law or wisdom "turn from the way" (Deut 9:12; compare Deut 11:28; Job 31:7) or "stumble" (Jer 18:15).

New Testament interpreters have often understood Jesus' "way" as replacing the OT way to God. A better alternative may be to read the NT uses as extensions of the OT imagery. *Way* often appears in a direct quotation of the OT. John the Baptist is described as "the voice of one crying out in the wilderness: 'Prepare the way of the Lord'" (Matt 3:3//Isa 40:3; compare Matt 11:10// Mal 3:1; Acts 2:28//Ps 16:11). The OT quotation communicates that the "way of the Lord" that has been known to Israel before is present in the person of Jesus. In other instances, "the way" takes on new meaning when understood as an allusion to the law or wisdom as providing access to God. Matthew's statement, "the gate is narrow and the way (NRSV, "road") is hard that leads to life" (Matt 7:14), implies that the way to life is following God's commands. Throughout Matthew, Jesus teaches people to find the same life offered by the law. John's Gospel makes the connection between Jesus and the way more explicit by offering that Jesus is "the way, and the truth, and the life" (John 14:6; *see* also JESUS CHRIST). In using this language John describes Jesus in terms that also describe God's law or wisdom. Jesus takes on a function similar to the law, providing followers access to his "Father's house" (14:2), to which Jesus is about to depart. Acts uses "the way" as a description or name for the early Christian church (Acts 9:2; 18:25-26; 19:9, 23; 22:4; 24:14, 22). Because it is also called "the way of God" (Acts 18:26), it seems that Acts also claims that "the way" God showed people in the Jewish Scriptures is now embodied in those who follow Jesus.

SUSAN E. HYLEN

WAYFARER [אֹרֵחַ 'oreakh]. A person who travels by road, usually on foot, and who is journeying through a region (Judg 19:17; 2 Sam 12:4). Such travelers might be merchants, exiles, or sojourners. Ancient Near Eastern custom required hosts to provide food, water, shelter, and protection for the traveler (Gen 18:1-8); otherwise, travelers could not survive (Gen 19:1-11; Judg 19:16-26). Traveling was dangerous in times of war or enemy occupation (Judg 5:6; Isa 33:8; Jer 6:25). In areas without villages, the wayfarer faced the dangers of the climate, wild animals, and bandits (2 Kgs 2:24; Luke 10:30-37). *See* SOJOURNER; TRADER; TRAVEL AND COMMUNICATION IN THE NT; TRAVEL AND COMMUNICATION IN THE OT.

TERRY W. EDDINGER

WAYSIDE [עַל־הַדָּרֶךְ 'al-haddarekh]. A place frequently associated with encounter and often occupied by marginalized characters intentionally waiting to meet someone (Gen 38:21; Jer 3:2). The Hebrew phrase is often translated "along the ROAD," or "by the road."

WEAK. *See* STRONG AND WEAK; WEAKNESS.

WEAKNESS [רָפָה rafah, רָפֶה rafeh, חָלָה khalah; ἀσθένημα asthenēma, ἀσθενεία astheneia]. In the OT, the conception of being "weak" is a translation of four different Hebrew word families. Being "weak/slack (rafah, rafeh) in hand" is an idiom referring to one's lack of mental resolve for action (e.g., 2 Chr 15:7; Job 4:3; Isa 35:3; Zeph 3:16; compare Isa 17:10). Reference to physical weakness and human frailty (khalah) occurs several times (Judg 16:7, 11, 13, 17; Isa 14:10; compare Judg 16:19 ('anah [עָנָה], "to be humbled"), and sometimes being weak (khalah and dal [דַּל]) has social dimensions as a consequence of oppression that the Lord will rectify (Pss 72:12; 83:3; Ezek 34:4, 16, 21; compare 2 Sam 3:1).

Most NT occurrences of *weakness* are found in Paul's letters. Weakness due to moral failing or sinfulness characterizes the human condition; precisely in this circumstance God sent Christ to die for all (Rom 5:6). Salvation in Christ is necessary because the law of God "was weakened by the flesh" (8:3; compare Gal 4:9; Heb 7:18); the weakness associated with sin makes it impossible to fulfill its requirements (see Rom 7:5, 7-25; 8:4). However, even believers remain weak in certain respects and thus need the Spirit's intercession (Rom 8:26; compare Matt 26:41). Likewise, Paul offers admonitions to "welcome those who are weak in faith" (Rom 14:1) and "to put up with the failings of the weak" (Rom 15:1); such weak people include those unable to eat meat sacrificed to idols in clear conscience (Rom 14:2; 1 Cor 8:7, 10). The strong believers should guard against despising the weak (Rom 14:3) or causing them to stumble (Rom 14:15, 20; 1 Cor 8:9-12). *See* STRONG AND WEAK.

In 1 Corinthians, Paul argues against using cultural standards of power, wisdom, and influence to evaluate apostles, especially himself, which makes the apostle appear "weak." God's standards differ: "God's weakness is stronger than human strength" (1:25) and that "God chose what is weak in the world to shame the strong" (1:27). Christians should not evaluate others in terms of social influence or weakness. Indeed, "the members of the body that seem to be weaker are indispensable" (12:22). Therefore, Paul is not afraid to be weak among the Corinthians (2:3; 4:10), nor especially to associate with the weak in order to win them for Christ (9:22).

Paul's fuller defense of his adjudged "weakness" is found in 2 Corinthians. This formal *apologia* is given in response to an evaluation of his persona as "weak" and his speech as "contemptible" (10:10). Paul boasts of his weaknesses repeatedly (11:21, 29; 12:5), and by Christ's grace God has transformed his weaknesses into strength (12:9), apostolic authority to confront the Corinthians' immorality and urge their moral perfection (13:1-9). Acts 20:35 records Paul's ministerial ethos: working to "support the weak" (see 1 Thess 5:14). *See* STRENGTH.

FREDERICK J. LONG

WEALTH [הוֹן hon, חַיִל khayil, כָּבוֹד kavodh, עֹשֶׁר 'osher; πλοῦτος ploutos]. Biblical attitudes to wealth cannot be understood except in the framework of economic, social, cultural, and political systems within which people lived. The system assumed in most of the OT was not based on individual wealth, whereas the Roman system assumed in the NT was. The OT, because of Israel's egalitarian beginnings, most often shows suspicion or negativity toward wealth, but sometimes views it neutrally or positively (as a gift from God or a legitimate reward for effort). The NT rejects the ambient economic system and offers an alternative to it. It extends God's invitation to rich along with poor, but wealth is a barrier to accepting the invitation unless one makes it wholly available as a community resource.

    A. Attitudes toward Wealth in the Bible
      1. Old Testament
      2. New Testament
    B. Social and Political Issues
      1. Old Testament
      2. New Testament
    Bibliography

A. Attitudes toward Wealth in the Bible
1. Old Testament
Wealth is often national rather than individual: God is the giver of Israel's wealth (Deut 8:17-18), Assyria will acquire the wealth of nations as booty (Isa 8:4), etc. The wealth often ascribed to kings should be understood as national rather than individual wealth, the king embodying the nation. The wealth of Israel's kings appears particularly frequently in Chronicles (1 Chr 29:28; 2 Chr 9:22; 17:5); examples of the wealth of foreign kings are found in Esth 1:4 and Dan 11.

Sometimes no particular implication is attached to personal wealth. Communities have their "big men" (e.g., 2 Sam 19:32; author's trans.; NRSV, "wealthy man"), or, in one case, a "big woman" (2 Kgs 4:8; author's trans.; NRSV, "wealthy woman"). To remote figures like Israel's first ancestors (Gen 13:2; 26:13) or Job are ascribed the legendary riches characteristic of folktales. Divine blessing is often the reason for wealth (Gen 24:35; Ps 112:1-3); 1 Sam 2:7 suggests divine causation for all wealth or poverty. Divine blessing does not rule out the employment of human cunning (Gen 30:41-43). Zechariah 11:5 parodies the idea that wealth is evidence of God's blessing.

Though the poor are very often referred to as a specific segment of Israelite society, the rich (outside of Wisdom literature) rarely are. Many psalms complain of the oppression of the poor, but their oppressors are "the wicked" (e.g., 10:2) rather than the wealthy as such, even if a few passages link wealth with wickedness (Pss 49:5-6; 73:12). A similar picture, on a larger scale, is presented by the prophets. They relate wealth to wickedness (Isa 53:9; Jer 5:27) or violence (Mic 6:12) and see it as sometimes unjustly gotten (Jer 17:11), but they do not usually equate the oppressive class with the wealthy. The oppressors, rather, are people in positions of power within the social, political, and religious systems. Actually, most prophetic references to wealth are to the wealth of nations. The oracles against foreign nations are full of announcements that these nations will forfeit their wealth (e.g., Ezek 26–28). In different phases of their oracles, the prophets predict either that Israel's wealth will be lost (Jer 15:13; 20:5; Ezek 7:11) or that Israel will acquire the wealth of the nations (particularly Third Isaiah, e.g., 60:5; 61:6; 66:12).

The OT's only lengthy reflection on individual wealth and poverty is in the Wisdom literature, particularly Proverbs. Wealth in Proverbs is, on the one hand, a positive value within a secure system. It is a blessing from God (10:22) or personified Wisdom (8:18, 21). It brings social power (22:7) and popularity (14:20). Hard work brings wealth (10:4), but so also does a correct attitude toward God (22:4; 28:25). Generosity increases wealth (11:24-25). Many passages express the reverse side: people who lack these virtues dissipate their wealth (13:22; 21:17; 22:16; 28:8). However, the passages in Proverbs that undermine this view are almost as numerous as those that establish it. To trust in wealth is both wrong in itself (11:28) and foolish, for wealth doesn't last forever (27:24), and offers no security in extremity (11:4). So there should be no straining after wealth (23:4; 28:20). A good name is more valuable (22:1); it is better to be poor and righteous (28:6). Different passages of Proverbs seem systematically to offer opposed points of view: hustling brings wealth (11:16), but steady accumulation is the recipe (13:11); there is safety in wealth (10:15), but this is wishful thinking (18:11). One voice expresses a desire to be neither rich nor poor (30:8).

The book of Job depicts a living disproof of the equation of wealth and virtue: Job's wealth is lost despite his godliness, though it is eventually restored and increased. Ecclesiastes questions the equation by discerning tragic dimensions in wealth. It is a blessing from God only if one has power to enjoy it (5:19; 6:2). Someone may have wealth but nobody to leave it to (4:8). Fools are as likely to be in charge as the wise and wealthy (10:6). But Job and Ecclesiastes only explore more fully territory that Proverbs has staked out.

As in English ("wealth of options," "rich variety"), the OT language of wealth has metaphorical meanings: food (Judg 9:9), fabric (Ezek 16:10), land and its yield

(Isa 30:23), etc., may be "rich." Such usage is, however, linked to the economic: the people who eat rich food and wear rich clothes tend to be rich.

2. New Testament

The Synoptic Gospels occasionally mention wealthy individuals without particular comment (Matt 27:57; Luke 16:1). It is suggested that some members of the early church were wealthy (Cornelius in Acts 10 or associates of Paul, like Prisca and Aquila who could sponsor a house church, Rom 16:3-5), and that such wealth was a community resource.

However, positive or even neutral references to personal wealth are few; it almost always carries some negative implication. Many sayings of Jesus denigrate wealth. It is prohibitively hard for a rich person to enter the kingdom (Mark 10:23, 25 and parallels). One cannot serve God and Mammon (Matt 6:24, Q). The quest for wealth chokes God's Word (Mark 4:19 and parallels). Don't favor the rich when showing hospitality (Luke 14:12). A poor widow is more generous than rich people (Mark 12:41-44; Luke 21:1-4). Parables have the same tendency: the rich man building a barn (Luke 12:16-21), Dives and Lazarus (Luke 16:19-31). In summary: "woe to you who are rich" (Luke 6:24).

Elsewhere in the NT, 1 Tim 6:17-19 accepts rich congregation members, provided they are generous and not haughty; but this is in some tension with the statement earlier in the chapter that "the love of money" is "a root of all kinds of evil" (6:9-10). The letter of James is harsher. The rich and their goods are withering away (1:10-11; 5:1-2). Partiality toward rich members of the congregation over poor ones is sharply rebuked, with the comment that the rich are typically oppressors (2:1-6). Revelation decries pride in wealth (3:17-18), and in its visions the rich and powerful must hide from the wrath of the Lamb (6:15-16). Chapter 18 is a long dirge over the coming destruction of those who have won wealth by serving the whore Babylon (figuring Rome).

The NT often uses the language of wealth in a spiritual sense. Christians experience "the riches of [God's] grace" (Eph 2:7), the riches of Christ dwelling in them (Col 1:27), etc. This kind of wealth is preferable to economic wealth. The rich man who builds new barns exemplifies those not "rich toward God" (Luke 12:21). Macedonian Christians, though very poor, exhibit a "wealth of generosity" (2 Cor 8:2). In Hebrews, Moses despises "the treasures of Egypt," preferring the "wealth" of suffering abuse for the Messiah (11:26). God has chosen the poor to be "rich in faith" (Jas 2:5). In Rev 3:17-18 the rich do not realize that really they are poor. These passages, drawn from diverse parts of the NT, share an impulse not only to denigrate wealth but also to subvert the very rhetoric of wealth.

B. Social and Political Issues

In the ancient Mediterranean world, the central place that money has for us was held by honor, whose opposite term is *shame*. This has a profound effect on how we understand wealth in the Bible. Honor came from upholding one's particular role in a class-divided society; shame came from departing from that role. This system was controlled by the powerful, whose power came partly from wealth but at least equally from birth and placement in political hierarchy. For the powerful, life was a competition with their peers for maximum social prestige. Accumulating wealth for its own sake was dishonorable; honor lay in using wealth to benefit one's society, and particularly to acquire clients to whom one was patron. A powerful man made others dependent on him, by economic and other means, and could then demand their support as he sought to increase his honor. The domination of persons was more important than the domination of goods. The patron-client system was at its most pervasive in Roman times, but it goes back much earlier: the Job of chaps. 29–31 is best understood as patron of many clients.

For those in the client role—and for women generally—honor was a passive matter of conforming to rules imposed from above. Honor was the avoidance of shame; stepping out of line would impugn the honor of the client, on whose support one depended. Those in the lower echelons were resentful if one of their number tried to advance beyond his station.

Within traditional constraints of this sort, the total workings of a society might take any of a number of different forms. The term "mode of production" is applied to the comprehensive network of relationships among the different structures and activities of a given society (what we loosely call "the system").

1. Old Testament

Pre-monarchical Israel had a communitarian mode. Early Israelites were probably peasant farmers who freed themselves from the influence of Canaanite city-states and formed relatively egalitarian communities in the less productive hill country. Local communities were economically self-sufficient, but bound themselves into larger units with others with whom they shared fundamental needs and religious ideology. Communitarian ideals began to weaken even before the appearance of monarchy, as local grandees (Nabal in 1 Sam 25 may be an example) and probably chieftains established themselves. Nonetheless, these ideals were deeply stamped in the consciousness of village peasants, who would always form the vast majority of the population, and who continued to be powerful throughout the biblical period.

Israel's monarchy was a version of the tributary (or "Asiatic") mode of production that characterized the empires of Egypt and Mesopotamia. It worked through a highly centralized and bureaucratized government that gathered tribute from innumerable villages. This system is personified in a Great King and serviced by a civil servant class occupying the rungs of a ladder of power and influence under the king. It is necessary to understand that under this system, individuals cannot, in principle, accumulate personal wealth. Bureaucrats can use their power to get goods for their use, but they do not legally own such goods, since all ownership is vested in the state; the state may confiscate anyone's goods without legal recourse. Among the goods bureaucrats might be granted was land; hence the phenomenon of powerful people (starting with the king himself) building up estates by taking over the land of free peasants (by getting them into debt, by controlling legal process, etc.).

This system was relatively undeveloped in Israel due to the country's small size and the persistence of communitarian assumptions. But it explains why the Hebrew vocabulary translated by NRSV as "wealth" or "riches" is so varied, most of the words having meanings beyond the narrowly economic. **Khayil**, e.g., basically means power—what the bureaucrats had—while **kavodh** means honor or reputation. An exception is the root ῾shr, which has only the economic meaning.

The prophets are conservatives who judge the society of their time by the communitarian ideals of Israel's beginnings. They castigate the bureaucratic class for its impositions on the free peasantry, particularly the accumulation of land and reduction of some peasants to serfdom. But they tend not to equate oppression with wealth as such. The similar championing, in the psalms, of the poor against the "wicked" suggests that the Temple, though in theory part of the tributary system, may at least sometimes have been the most effective counterweight to the oppression of the individual.

In the Wisdom literature we find a debate about wealth and poverty whose participants are all "wealthy" in the sense just defined. The wisdom scholars were part of the bureaucracy. Their linking of wealth to diligence, e.g., is born of their experience that if you don't work to capacity there are plenty of young men waiting to take your job. They debate in general terms whether wealth is good, but this debate has nothing to do with the economic condition of the vast majority of the population.

The Wisdom literature comes mainly from the postexilic period when the tributary mode of production had its greatest hold on Israel. Even before the exile, Israel's independence was limited by incursions of the tributary empires of Assyria and Babylon; after the exile, it was simply incorporated into the Persian Empire, the most developed tributary state in Near Eastern history. The system in Israel was now two-tiered: a native Judean bureaucracy (controlled from the Temple in the absence of a king) continued to extract taxes from the native population, but must itself supply massive tribute to the Persian overlord. In theory, no Israelite was wealthy during this time, since all goods were held under Persian sufferance.

2. New Testament
The NT came into being under the "classical" mode of production of Greece and Rome, which was founded on individual wealth and legal ownership. This mode is better termed "slave-based": while any free person might own goods, significant wealth began with ownership of persons and their labor. The productive unit under this mode was not the village but the estate, owned by a wealthy, often aristocratic person, and worked by slaves. Slaves, though they might on rare occasions acquire some wealth and even buy their freedom, were entirely outside the more fundamental honor system. Even being freed hardly improved a slave's status, since "freedmen" usually became weak clients of their former masters.

Jesus invited everyone, regardless of wealth or honor, into the kingdom of God. For the powerful, the invitation came at an obvious cost—undermining of the social arrangements that made them powerful, and acceptance of equality before God. But even for the powerless there could be a cost: giving up the security of a patronage relationship. As often in social revolution, early leadership came mostly neither from the very poor nor the rich. Such leadership comes typically from groups with real freedom of action but relatively little to lose. Particularly important seems to have been the artisan class, to which Jesus himself probably belonged.

The Jesus movement, especially in its initial stages, expanded by a reciprocal arrangement of itinerancy and hospitality. Apostles traveled from place to place preaching, and were sustained by developing local communities. These two groups differed in respect to wealth. Itinerancy entailed renouncing wealth (it has been suggested that one of Jesus' reasons for choosing itinerancy was to avoid any patron-like role). It should therefore have attracted the very poor, but there is little evidence that many early itinerants came from this stratum. Givers of hospitality were settled people whose wealth, if they had it, was a community resource; their vocation was to share wealth, not abandon it. Serious tension could develop between the two groups (see especially the early Christian work called the *Didache*).

Christianity was not, in the forms represented by NT writings, a movement of the very poor (though some groups, like the one that produced the apocryphal but early *Gospel of Thomas*, probably did represent the very poor). The frequent exhortations to prefer spiritual to economic wealth suggests an audience with some access to the latter. But Christianity certainly appealed to the poor, who could find material relief in local churches and might aspire to status there that they could never have had outside. The appeal to the rich was much more complicated. Developing Christianity made practical use of the patronage system (Paul, e.g., calls upon rich patrons) while demolishing it theoretically. The system already laid an expectation upon the rich to use their wealth for the benefit of others; this expectation was laid even more heavily on wealthy Christians. But the patronage system assumed that such benevolence could earn increased power and prestige. The NT writings allow no such possibility. In practice, no doubt, socially powerful congregation members sometimes expected to be deferred to (1 Tim 6:17; Jas 2:2-3) and sometimes were, but no NT writing approves such partiality. The rich had to make do with personal salvation, a pure and meaningful life on earth, and eternal life. An increasing number accepted this, but Christianity still expanded its appeal to the wealthy only gradually. It is very doubtful that it made real inroads into the Roman aristocratic class during the NT period.

Early Christianity entailed a radical critique of the Roman system. For the most part it exercised this critique not overtly, still less violently, but while submitting to the system's claims in nonessentials by living a counter-system. In Revelation, however, the absoluteness of the critique comes rhetorically to the fore. A system that makes the few wealthy through the enslavement or impoverishment of the many stands under the imminent judgment of God. The Christian mode of production is—via Jesus and the prophets—a return to and radicalization of the communitarian mode of earliest Israel. *See* DIVES; POOR; POVERTY.

Bibliography: Norman K. Gottwald. *The Hebrew Bible in Its Social World and Ours* (1993); Reggie M. Kidd. *Wealth and Beneficence in the Pastoral Epistles* (1990); Bruce J. Malina. *The New Testament World: Insights from Cultural Anthropology* (1981); Umberto Melotti. *Marx and the Third World* (1977).

DAVID JOBLING

WEAPONS OF WAR. *See* WAR, METHODS, TACTICS, WEAPONS OF (BRONZE AGE THROUGH PERSIAN PERIOD); WAR, METHODS, TACTICS, WEAPONS OF (HELLENISTIC THROUGH ROMAN PERIODS).

WEASEL [חֹלֶד *kholedh*; γαλῆ *galē*]. Small, carnivorous mammal belonging to the cat family. In instructions that Moses and Aaron provided to the Israelites, it is the first animal listed among the swarming creatures considered unclean when touched or when an object with which the animal has come into contact has been touched (Lev 11:29). Although the Hebrew word and its cognates can be translated as "mole," "field rat," and "mole-rat," its use in manuscripts, including the LXX, the Vulgate, the Targums, and the Peshitta, suggests this animal is most likely the weasel. *See* ANIMALS OF THE BIBLE.

EMILY R. CHENEY

WEATHER. Although the NRSV translates eudia (εὐδία; Matt 6:2; Sir 3:15) as "fair weather" and cheimōn (χειμών; 1 Esd 9:6) as "bad weather," there are no Hebrew or Greek terms that precisely mean "weather." There are abundant references to weather patterns (Prov 16:15) and weather phenomena (1 Kgs 17:1; Acts 27:13-14), and God is frequently associated with storm imagery (Ps 77:17-18 [Heb. 77:18-19]). In narratives, weather may supply an important element

for the plot (Jonah 1:4; Mark 4:37). It is used didactically (Prov 25:23; 26:1) and figuratively (Ps 51:7 [Heb. 51:9]). Biblical cosmology explains the sources of the weather (Mal 3:10; Rev 7:1), which is always under God's control (Job 37:6-11; Amos 4:7; Matt 8:27). *See* ISRAEL, CLIMATE OF.

PETER TRUDINGER

WEAVING. *See* CLOTH, CLOTHES; LOOM; SHUTTLE.

WEDDING. *See* BANQUET; BRIDE; BRIDEGROOM; CANA; MARRIAGE, NT; MARRIAGE, OT.

WEEDS [בָּאְשָׁה *bo'shah*, רֹאשׁ *ro'sh*; ζιζάνιον *zizanion*]. The proliferation of numerous species of weeds in cultivated fields was a continual problem for farmers in ancient Israel. Part of the problem was the inability of these farmers to plow furrows deep enough to turn up the bulbs to allow the sun to dry them out and thus destroy the next generation of useless weeds. As a result, these noxious plants intermingled with the grain, stealing its moisture and sometimes overwhelming the edible plants. At harvest time, it was often difficult (despite the instructions in Matt 13:25-40) to separate the stalks of wheat or barley from the weeds. As a result, their seeds, which often look quite similar to the wheat, were mixed together, and when the sowing occurred in the next growing season both good seeds and bad seeds were cast into the newly turned furrows. The prophet Hosea provides an apt comparison between lawsuits and "poisonous weeds (ro'sh) in the furrows of the field" (Hos 10:4).

Among the plants that fit the category of weeds is the veined henbane (*Hyoscyamus reticulates*), which may grow to a height of 2 ft. and has viscid, hairy foliage and a yellow flower, and the prickly rest-harrow (*Ononis antiquorum*) that gets its name from the way its long, thickly matted root defeats the work of the harrow. Another candidate, perhaps the basis for Job's reference to the growth of "foul weeds" in his barley fields as a punishment for immoral behavior (31:40), may be the Syrian scabious (*Cephalaria syriaca*), which can grow to as much as 3 ft. and has a purple flower. Although the mixture of this weed's seed with wheat can add flavor and a bluish color, its high oil content can cause the bread to become rancid quickly. *See* NETTLE; THISTLE, THORN.

VICTOR H. MATTHEWS

WEEK [שָׁבוּעַ *shavua'*; σάββατον *sabbaton*]. A period lasting seven days. It does not seem possible to determine when the notion of a week arose in Israel, but a number of passages treat a seven-day span as a meaningful unit of time. For example, Isa 66:23 supplies "from sabbath to sabbath" as a poetic parallel to "from new moon to new moon." In the flood accounts, there are a few references to waiting for seven days (Gen 7:4, 10;

8:10, 12), while Daniel is said to have mourned and fasted for three weeks (Dan 10:2-3). But the priestly legislation offers a larger number of cases in which a seven-day period is required for the handling of certain problems. There are many references to a seven-day waiting period in connection with skin diseases (e.g., Lev 13:5-6, 21, 26-27, 31-34, 50-51, 54; 14:8, 38; see also Num 12:14-15) or bodily discharges (Lev 15:13, 19, 24, 28). The priestly ordination took seven days (Lev 8:33, 35). The law regarding the new mother uses both the expression "seven days" and the term "week": if she gives birth to a boy she is unclean for seven days; if she bears a girl the time of uncleanness last two weeks (Lev 12:2, 5).

In other priestly passages, the concept of the week figures prominently. The story of creation in Gen 1:1–2:3, which does not use the word *week*, says that God worked for six days and rested on the seventh. That pattern of six + one was rendered normative for Israel in the fourth commandment, which in its formulation in Exod 20:8-11 grounds the commandment in the divine model at creation. Two of the pilgrimage holidays, the Festivals of Unleavened Bread and of Tabernacles, last for seven days and take place exactly one-half year apart: Unleavened Bread on month one, days 15–21 (1/15–21; Exod 12:14-20; 13:3-10; Lev 23:6-8; Num 28:17-25; *see* PASSOVER AND FEAST OF UNLEAVENED BREAD) and Tabernacles on 7/15–21 (Lev 23:33-36, 39-43; Num 29:12-34; *see* BOOTHS, FEAST OR FESTIVAL OF). And the third of the pilgrimage holidays, which lasts only one day, is named the Festival of Weeks (Exod 34:22; Deut 16:16; 2 Chr 8:13; 2 Macc 12:31; Tob 2:1) because of the way in which its date was calculated (*see* WEEKS, FEAST OF). Starting from a point a short time after Passover, one was to count off seven full weeks. The next or fiftieth day was the time for the Festival of Weeks (Lev 23:15-16; Deut 16:9-10). This pattern of 49 + 1 is repeated to define the interval between four consecutive harvest festivals in the *Temple Scroll* from Qumran (11Q19 XVIII, 10–XXIII, 2).

In later texts the seven-day week continues to be mentioned. According to some of the calendar texts from Qumran, the twenty-four priestly groups that rotated service in the Temple were on duty for one week each before being relieved by the next group in the list of 1 Chr 24:7-18. This fact allowed the group using these texts to designate each week by the name of the priestly course then on duty (4Q319–25; 4Q328–30). In the NT, the word *week* figures in the statements in all four Gospels regarding when Jesus' resurrection occurred: it was early on the first day of the week (Matt 28:1; Mark 16:1-2, 9; Luke 24:1; John 20:1, 19). The day of the week on which the resurrection took place served as a time when the Christians in Corinth put aside money for the Pauline collection on behalf of believers in Jerusalem (1 Cor 16:1-2), and those in Troas met to break bread on the same day (Acts 20:7). In the

story about the tax collector and the Pharisee, the latter says he fasted twice per week (Luke 18:12).

Beginning already in the OT, there is attested a practice of designating a seven-year period as a week or a week of years. In Gen 29:27-28, Laban refers to the time that Jacob worked for his two wives as weeks, but the text makes clear that periods of seven years are meant (29:18, 20, 27; 31:41). The institution of the SABBATICAL YEAR is modeled on the pattern for the seven-day week: after six years of planting crops, one was to allow a field to lie fallow in the seventh year. The close connection between Sabbath and sabbatical year is expressed by the fact that the two are paired in Exod 23:10-12. In Lev 25:8, the sabbatical period is termed a "week of years"; seven of these units total forty-nine years, after which comes the year of Jubilee (as in the pattern for the date of the Festival of Weeks; *see* JUBILEE, YEAR OF). A span of seven years understood as a week of years figures prominently in Dan 9:24-27, where Gabriel explains to Daniel the meaning of Jeremiah's prophecy (Jer 25:11-12; 29:10) that Jerusalem would lie desolate for seventy years. The angel—in keeping with the teaching in Lev 26:18, 21, 24, 28 that the divine punishment of sinful Israel would be multiplied seven times—tells Daniel that the seventy years are to be understood as seventy weeks or 490 years. He then subdivides that unit into parts consisting of seven and sixty-two weeks, after which comes the last week; he also relates these divisions to significant events.

The concept of a week of years is used in some surveys of history, whether past or future. The book of *Jubilees* makes the week of years a basic building block of its chronology: seven of these weeks constitute a Jubilee period of forty-nine years. The author dates many events, as he retells the stories in Genesis and the first half of Exodus, by noting the year, the week of years, and the Jubilee period in which each occurred (see also *4 Ezra* 7:43). A similar practice is attested in several texts uncovered at Qumran. Examples are 4Q390 (see 2 I, 4) and 11Q13 (II, 7). The Apocalypse of Weeks (*1 En.* 91:11-17; 93:1-10) divides all of history into ten units it calls weeks. They cover far more than just seven years (e.g., the period before the flood), but the seventh of these longer units is the period for the decisive turning points in history with the judgment following after it.

Bibliography: James C. VanderKam. *Calendars in the Dead Sea Scrolls: Measuring Time* (1998).

JAMES C. VANDERKAM

WEEKS, FEAST OF [חַג שָׁבֻעוֹת *khagh shavu'oth*; ἑβδομάδων ἑορτή *hedomodōn heortē*]. The Feast of Weeks is one of the three scripturally mandated pilgrimage festivals in the OT.

Exodus 23:16, part of the Covenant Code, mentions a harvest festival "of the first fruits of your labor, of what you sow in the field," while the parallel in Exod 34:22 (J) provides its name and identifies the crop: "the festival of weeks, the first fruits of wheat harvest." Neither of these texts specifies a date for the festival; only in Deut 16:9-12 and Lev 23:15-16 (H; see H, HOLINESS CODE) are there instructions for determining when it was to be celebrated. According to Deuteronomy, one should count seven weeks, beginning from the time the sickle is set to the standing grain, and then celebrate the festival of weeks with a freewill offering and rejoicing by all of the population, free or slave, native or sojourner. Leviticus 23 also mentions the seven weeks but adds other details: "from the day after the sabbath, from the day on which you bring the sheaf of the elevation offering, you shall count off seven weeks; they shall be complete. You shall count until the day after the seventh sabbath, fifty days; then you shall present an offering of new grain to the LORD" (vv. 15-16). The same chapter records that bringing the sheaf of the elevation offering occurred at a point shortly after Passover (23:9-11, 15); as a result, the Festival of Weeks would take place at some time in the third month of the year (May-June). However, since no fixed date is given for the ceremony involving the elevation offering, the chapter also does not yield an exact date for the festival fifty days later. Additional details about offerings, such as the two loaves of bread made with leaven (they and perhaps other items are presented as an elevation offering in Lev 23:17, 20), are found in Lev 23:17-20 and Num 28:26-31, although the two passages do not agree fully about the numbers of animals that constitute the whole burnt sacrifice of the day. Leviticus 23:21 and Num 28:26 require an assembly on this day on which work was prohibited. Elsewhere in the OT the festival is mentioned only in 2 Chr 8:13, although 2 Chr 15:10-15 refers to a gathering in the third month when King Asa and the people made a covenant with an oath. This is of some interest, because later the Festival of Weeks became associated with covenant and oath (shevuʿah [שְׁבוּעָה] = "oath" allowed an association with the name of the holiday shavuʿoth = "weeks"; shavuaʿ [שָׁבוּעַ] is the word for "week"). In fact, the Targum of the passage places the event on the Festival of Weeks. Ezekiel makes no reference to the day in his calendar of holidays (Ezek 45:18-25).

While the festival is mentioned only a few times in the OT—exclusively in lists of holidays—there is evidence that it served an important function in later Jewish history, as indicated in both Hebrew and Greek literature. The book of *Jubilees* mentions the Festival of Weeks in connection with the covenant that God made with Noah in the third month and later associates it with other scriptural covenants. In *Jub.* 6:17-18, an angel of the presence explains that Israel is to celebrate the holiday in the third month every year to renew the covenant—a law so important it is inscribed on the heavenly tablets. He adds that the festival was celebrat-

ed in heaven from the time of creation, while Noah and his family were the first to observe it on the earth. The writer places the covenants of Gen 15 (*Jub.* 14:1, 10, 20) and Gen 17 (*Jub.* 15:1) in the same month—more precisely, in the middle of the month (i.e., 3/15)—and, following the scriptural example, calls it the first fruits festival of the wheat harvest (*Jub.* 15:1). He also draws a connection between the time of the holiday and the date of the covenant at Mount Sinai (according to Exod 19:1, the Israelites entered the Wilderness of Sinai on the first day of the third month). Moses was ordered to ascend the mountain to obtain the two stone tablets on 3/16, the date after the festival of weeks (*Jub.* 1:1). This means that the covenant of Exod 19–24 was made on 3/15, the festal date. *Jubilees* refers to it as a festival of both weeks and first fruits (6:21).

The Festival of Weeks occurs in several contexts in the Qumran texts. For one, it is mentioned in some calendar texts from which one can calculate the date when the writers of the texts celebrated it. 4Q320 correlates the priestly watches (see 1 Chr 24:7-19, where the twenty-four watches are listed in their fixed order) with the holidays in the 364-day calendar shared with *Jubilees*. Since the priestly watches or courses served one week at a time, it is possible to determine the number of days between the holidays that are mentioned. So, in one year (4Q320 4 III, 1–3) Passover (1/14) falls in the third day of the week when the course of Maaziah (the twenty-fourth in the list) was on duty, and the waving of the elevation offering on the first day in Jedaiah's shift (he is the second in the list). One priestly watch occurs between these two; therefore, the elevation offering took place twelve days after Passover (i.e., on 1/26). The Festival of Weeks, whose date depends on that of the elevation offering, falls on the fiftieth day (day one of Jeshua's duty [the ninth in the list]), i.e., on 3/15 as it does in *Jubilees* (see also 4Q320 4 IV, 1, 10; 4 V, 4, 13; 4 VI, 8). From these data it follows that in this tradition the phrase "the day after the sabbath" in Lev 23:11, 15-16 was understood to mean the day after the seventh day of the week, that is, a Sunday. The Sunday for the elevation offering was assumed to be the first one after the completion of the Festival of Unleavened Bread (1/15–1/21), not the one during that weeklong holiday.

The TEMPLE SCROLL illustrates another context in which the Festival of Weeks plays a role. In 11Q19 XVIII, 10–15, the *Temple Scroll* reproduces legislation from Lev 23, although it rearranges the text. The calendar in the Temple Scroll shows that for the author the festival was observed on 3/15. However, 11Q19 XLIII, 5–7 prescribes, as it deals with tithes, that the new harvest of grain may be eaten, beginning from the time of the first fruits feast of wheat (= the Festival of Weeks) until that date the next year (the same rules apply for the other first fruits holidays, all of which are separated from one another by fifty days). *Jubilees* makes a related point in connection with the second tithe (32:10-15).

4Q251 5 1–6 also directs that grain, wine, and oil are not to be consumed before their respective first fruits holidays.

The Festival of Weeks probably functioned in a third context—as the time for a covenantal ceremony every year—just as in *Jubilees*. The *Rule of the Community* describes an annual ritual at which candidates for admission entered the group and continuing members apparently renewed their commitment (1QS I, 16–III, 12). The text does not say when the ceremony occurred, but according to two of the Cave 4 copies of the *Damascus Document*—4Q266 11 17–18 = 4Q270 7 II, 11–12—at a meeting in the third month involving Levites and other members, those who departed from the law were cursed. Since the Levites utter the curses as a part of the annual covenantal ceremony in the *Rule of the Community*, this may be the same occasion. If so, the Qumran community renewed the covenant while observing the holiday on which *Jubilees* dates the great biblical covenants. It is possible that 4Q286–90 contains blessings recited during the ritual.

The tradition represented in *Jubilees* and the Qumran scrolls read the scriptural legislation in such a way that it dated the elevation offering to 1/26 and the Festival of Weeks to 3/15, but others calculated their dates differently. Josephus, who uses the Greek name PENTECOST (meaning "fiftieth") for the holiday, first documents the view that the fifty-day count began on the sixteenth day of the first month (*Ant.* 3.250–52). This is the approach found later in rabbinic literature (see below); according to it, the phrase "the day after the sabbath" in Lev 23 referred to the day after a holiday (an attested meaning of *Sabbath*), with the holiday understood to be the first day of the Festival of Unleavened Bread (1/15; see Josh 5:11: "On the day after the passover, on that very day, they ate the produce of the land, unleavened cakes and parched grain"). In *Ant.* 13.251–52 Josephus wrote that warfare is not permitted on Pentecost, while in 14.337 (compare *J.W.* 1.253) he noted that large crowds of people went to Jerusalem for the holiday (see also *Ant.* 17.254; compare *J.W.* 2.42; 2 Macc 12:31-32). According to *J.W.* 6.299–300, the priests entered the inner court of the Temple during the previous night, apparently in preparation for the large number of sacrifices that would have to be offered the next day (see also Tob 2:1; Philo, *Decalogue* 160; *Spec. Laws* 2.176–87). In the NT, the outpouring of the Holy Spirit on the first followers of Jesus is dated to Pentecost, when a large crowd of Jewish people from many countries gathered at the Temple (Acts 2).

The MISHNAH shows that the date for the Festival of Weeks continued to be debated in later times. Without naming them, it refers to people, possibly SADDUCEES or Boethusians, who say that the holiday is celebrated on the day after the Sabbath (*m. Hag.* 2.4; compare *m. Menah.* 10.3), as it is in the Qumran/*Jubilees* calendar. Naturally, the festival, along with others tied to the harvest cycle, served as the point before which the ap-

propriate first fruits could not be brought to the Temple (*m. Hal.* 4.10). Mishnah tractate *Megillah* 3:5 says that Deut 16:8-12 was the pentateuchal passage read during this festival. Because it occurred in the third month of the year, the very month when Israel reached Sinai, the Festival of Weeks was eventually associated with the giving of the Torah at Mount Sinai. *See* BOOTHS, FEAST OR FESTIVAL OF; FEASTS AND FASTS; PASSOVER AND FEAST OF UNLEAVENED BREAD.

Bibliography: Jacob Milgrom. *Leviticus 23–27.* AB 3B (2001); James C. VanderKam. "The Festival of Weeks and the Story of Pentecost in Acts 2." *From Prophecy to Testament: The Function of the Old Testament in the New.* C. Evans, ed. (2004) 185–205.

JAMES C. VANDERKAM

WEEPING. *See* MOURNING.

WEIGHTS AND MEASURES. Weights and measures are an important key for understanding the economy of ancient societies. Economy before the invention of coins (ca. 600 BCE) was different from ours. We must be aware of, e.g., the extent to which our thoughts are shaped by coinage and by monetary economy. We speak about two sides of a coin, face value (from faces of rulers on coins), and small change—none of these existed prior to coinage. Another example comes from biblical Hebrew, which recognizes silver only as metal, never as "money." This is because biblical Hebrew predated the invention of coins (*see* MONEY, COINS).

A. Ancient Economy
  1. Measuring value
  2. Hacksilber hoards
B. Weights
  1. Ancient Near Eastern weight systems
    a. Egypt
    b. Mesopotamia
    c. Syria, Ugarit, and Canaan
    d. Phoenicia and Philistia
  2. Biblical weight systems
    a. Shekel
    b. Common units of the shekel
    c. Shekel of the sanctuary
  3. Archaeological data from Iron Age Judah
    and Israel
  4. Weights in later periods and in the
    New Testament
C. Measures of Capacity
  1. Egypt
  2. Mesopotamia
  3. Biblical measures of capacity
    a. Dry measures
    b. Liquid measures
  4. Reconstruction of the biblical systems
    of capacity
  5. Later measures of capacity

A. Ancient Economy

Ancient economies were not the same as modern notions of economy and capitalism, although there are some similarities. The concept of a free market did not exist before the industrial revolution in the 17th cent. CE; however, there were markets where prices were influenced by the laws of supply and demand. Just as in the modern world, monetary profit was desirable. However, labor and land were not considered to be commodities in the same way they are in modern times. Production was for subsistence, or for the wealthy, as a means to achieve higher social status. As in modern times, the ancient world was capable of complex economic systems and of flourishing, long-distance trade (*see* ISRAEL, SOCIAL AND ECONOMIC DEVELOPMENT OF).

1. Measuring value

In a world without coins, value was measured by quantity. Since prehistoric periods, rare metals (mainly silver) were used as means of evaluation. SILVER appears in this role already in the first written records of the 3rd millennium BCE. The value of silver itself had to be measured by weight. Weighing was a complicated process, so it was performed only when absolutely necessary. Most commodities, such as wine, oil, and grains, were measured by volume. Thus, the basic and most common form of economy in the ancient world was barter. Objects were exchanged from hand to hand, without weighing or exchange of metal. Taxes to authorities were usually given in kind, not in silver; work was not paid by monetary salaries, but by (mainly agricultural) products. Today we might go to a bakery each time we need bread and buy a loaf, giving a few small coins and receiving change. This was impossible before the spread of bronze coins of small denominations around the 5th cent. BCE. In the ancient world (and in many rural places even until the 20th cent. CE), one would take flour to the baker perhaps once a week. The baker's "salary" consisted of a portion of the bread that he baked. One could also exchange other products with the baker in return for the bread. Thus, for daily life people did not need to carry, weigh, or exchange silver.

Silver (more rarely, gold) was used as storage of wealth, for those rich enough to hold it. It also served as a unit of evaluation, as it determined prices of objects, defined by weight. Kings often took great pains to set stable prices. For example, Hittite laws stipulated that a bull was worth twelve silver shekels, a cow five

shekels, and a calf three shekels. Thus, one could easily trade four calves for one bull. We also know that prices fluctuated according to supply and demand. Prices of wheat could vary according to seasons of the year, being lower after a plentiful harvest and higher when farmers required seeds for planting. In besieged cities, prices became inflated, soaring many times higher than usual (2 Kgs 6:25; though many times the stories can be exaggerations). It is crucial to understand that even when sources mention payment in metal, it was often made in kind. For example, in his laws King Hammurabi declared that the wage of hired agriculture laborers should be six unit weights of silver per day. In fact, hired laborers almost always received the equivalent value in agricultural products, instead of in silver.

Jeremiah 32:9-10 is the closest picture of a commercial weighing described in the OT. Jeremiah bought a field for seventeen silver shekels. The author stressed the weighing, mentioning it twice, because weighing was part of the buying process. In this case, payment was probably made in silver and not in kind. The author wanted to assure us that Jeremiah paid, so that the field was legally bought. Similarly, in the story about Abraham and the cave of Machpelah (Gen 23), the author wanted to stress that Abraham bought the property for a full price, and as a result, he owned it legitimately.

Interesting data appear in the story about the fixing of the Temple in 2 Kgs 12. Donations of silver were collected, apparently in varied forms: from whole vessels and jewels to irregular pieces. Donations were placed in a chest ('aron [אֲרוֹן]; 2 Kgs 12:9 [Heb. 12:10]). Similar procedures from Mesopotamia mention the arannu. When the 'aron became full, the royal scribe and the high priest performed what was often translated as "[they] counted the money ... and tied up in bags" (2 Kgs 12:10 [Heb. 12:11]). If we accept the reading "they tied" (some scholars prefer the readings "they emptied" or "they cast"), the process described is probably that of tying the silver pieces in linen wrappings or bundles that were later counted. The story does not mention weighing the pieces, but this step can be assumed, as it would have been necessary. The weighing could have been done before the bundles were distributed, or at the point when payment was delivered to the workmen (such bundles are known from Iron Age hoards; see below). Prices in the ancient world were not exact. Weighing was made by BALANCES and was inaccurate, with about a 3 percent margin of error. Gain or loss of a few percents was not considered problematical. The archive of Mari on the Euphrates (18th cent. BCE) demonstrates weighing in a royal context. Smiths received certain amounts of metal from the palace in order to produce finished products. The metal was weighed when given, and the finished product was reweighed. The palace acknowledged the fact that a minute quantity of metal is lost during working, but wanted to make sure that artists did not steal extra amounts. In the ancient world, price was determined mainly by weight, and a finished silver product was not much more expensive than a raw ingot of silver of the same weight.

There is little point in speaking about exact standards in the ancient world. Our standards imply the notion of an original unit, like the famous gold meter kept in the Louvre, to which all other meters are compared. Later rabbinical sources assumed that a standard cubit was kept in the Temple. This claim is based solely on 1 Chr 23:29, where the Levites have responsibility over things brought to the Temple, hardly implying an official, "original unit." Even if there was something of the sort in the ancient world, we do not know what the original units were. When we speak about an ancient standard, we actually mean an average calculated from written sources and archaeological finds. Such averages include normal deviations from any assumed standard, for many reasons. Measuring was inaccurate in ancient times. Moreover, archaeological finds have been subjected to years of wear and tear that preclude exact calculation of the measurements. In addition, one must factor in that there were errors of production as well as deliberate fraud. Written sources are also not free of such factors. For example, they may reflect fluctuations due to changing demands or temporal changes. Fraud was a recognized problem, as many OT verses acknowledge. Merchants used different sets of measures, one for selling, another for buying, such as the "dishonest weights" mentioned by Micah (6:11, compare Prov 20:10, 23). Others chipped or rubbed the weights, hence the demand for "just"—meaning whole—measures (Prov 11:1).

2. *Hacksilber* hoards

An important source about economy in the ancient world comes from the discovery of hoards. During the 3rd millennium BCE in Israel/Palestine, we find hoarding of intact bronze tools (e.g., at Kfar Monash). Starting with the 2nd millennium BCE in Israel/Palestine, we find hoards of broken, irregular pieces of silver (German *Hacksilber*, literally "cut" or "hacked" silver). Often, these hoards include other items of value, such as broken or intact jewelry, beads, and semiprecious stones. This shows that these hoards served mainly as storage of valuables; they are, in fact, someone's "capital," and not the property of metal smiths (as was often thought earlier). *Hacksilber* hoards appear throughout the Late Bronze and Iron ages. Some twenty-five hoards have been discovered to date from Israel/Palestine of the Bronze and Iron ages. The most famous and largest hoard was found at Eshtemoa, dated by the excavators to the 10th cent. BCE (but perhaps from the 8–7th cent. BCE). Other hoards are known from Dor, En-Gedi, Ekron, Beth Shan, Megiddo, and Arad. The OT refers to cut pieces of silver under the term betsaʿ kesef (בֶּצַע כֶּסֶף; Judg 5:19), a term that comports with the nature of *Hacksilber* hoards found in ancient Judah. Most of these hoards were buried underground in pits, usually in simple, undecorated pottery vessels. Some luck and very careful excavation is required to retrieve not just the hoards, but also their stratigraphic context. Thus, the exact date of many hoards remains uncertain.

Some scholars believe that *Hacksilber* hoards are monetary hoards that reflect some prehistoric form of coinage, but this is not likely to be the case. Unlike coinage, *Hacksilber* pieces are random in weight, they carry no mark, and they have no guarantee of an authority. For use as a medium of exchange, they had to be weighed for each transaction. The silver pieces were sometimes bundled together by textile and rarely sealed by bullae (round seals that identify value or ownership). However, such bundles do not conform to specific weight units. The bullae used on such bundles do not carry names or inscriptions. One hoard from Dor used Middle Bronze Age bullae that were hundreds of years older than the hoard. Only those who knew the owners personally could identify them from such bullae. Hence, seals used on such bundles functioned not as guarantee of value but as personal indication of ownership, the most common function of seals in the Bronze and Iron ages (*see* SEALS AND SCARABS). Coins, on the other hand, carry marks (drawings and inscriptions) that announce an issuing authority that guarantees the value of the coin. The trust of a society in the guarantee of the issuing authority, which is expressed by the marks, is the most important feature of coinage and monetary economy. This trust did not exist before the invention of coins, and only with it coins could became such a hugely successful means of exchange.

Bundles in hoards might reflect the biblical tseror (צְרוֹר). The tseror was not a coin, but a means of safely carrying small *Hacksilber* pieces, wrapped in textile to prevent their loss. The OT mentions that both silver and scale-weights were carried in the purse or bag (Deut 25:13; Isa 46:6). Scale-weights were required for weighing bundles (more likely, a few pieces at each time and not entire bundles). The bundles are similar to our purses, which are also used to carry money. We do not normally weigh our purses (weighing of merchant's purses in medieval times is a rare exception, not the norm). Mesopotamian sources about transfer of sealed silver bundles prove that they were not compatible to coinage or to money. Even when bundles were sealed by kings, the recipient had to verify the value by weighing each bundle.

Hoards do not reflect exactly the daily economic conditions. Many were hidden in circumstances of insecurity. Thus, there are many hoards from the 604 BCE destruction of Ekron, but few earlier hoards from the same city. At present we have about one hoard per century for any of the Iron Age kingdoms in Israel/Palestine. This is hardly enough for detailed economic reconstruction.

The invention of coins (ca. 600 BCE) was only the starting point in a gradual change from *Hacksilber* or bullion economy to coins and monetary economy. In this process, *Hacksilber* hoards were replaced by hoards of coins. The first coins were made of electrum, and they lacked explicit guarantee of authority (such as names of rulers). They were accurate in that their value still depended on weight. We do not know the exact circumstances, but perhaps the earliest coins were personalized gifts and not real coins. Monetary economy developed at a later stage. Silver coins appeared ca. 550 BCE, and only then did types (marks) that define authority and guarantee the value become regular. At that time, large numbers of small denominations—the feature that enabled retail trade—appeared. Units of value were marked on coins since the early 5th cent. BCE. By 500 BCE, about 100 mints existed just in Greece. The separation of coins/money from weight became clearer with bronze coins, used since the second half of the 5th cent. BCE. Monetary economy did not replace completely earlier modes of economy; barter remained common in many periods and places because of its simplicity.

B. Weights

1. Ancient Near Eastern weight systems

Because it is impossible to review all the ANE systems in detail, only the major weight systems will be discussed here. Since the Late Bronze Age at the latest, the major weight systems of the ANE could be tied by fixed units that served as points of contact. However, the relation between the Mesopotamian shekel of about 8.1–8.4 g and the other major weight-systems remains an unsolved problem. There were many forms of weights in the ANE: domes, cubes, cylinders, grains, zoomorphic, and even anthropomorphic. Such weights required a flat base; otherwise they would roll on the pans of the scales.

a. Egypt. Thousands of weights have been found in Egypt, but unfortunately, most of them were discovered out of context. Relatively few weight-systems were used in Egypt. A "gold standard" of about 12–13 g was perhaps used in the Middle Kingdom period. The main weight system was decimal, with a unit called deben (ca. 90 g) subdivided into ten qedet units (each about 9 g). Common weight-units included 1, 2, 5 qedet; smaller units were 1/2, 1/3, and 1/4 qedet. Some Egyptian weights were inscribed, and there were also inscribed royal weights. The Egyptians also recognized a unit called sniw, roughly 7.5 g silver; a similar or derivative unit appears in the 1st millennium BCE in Syria.

b. Mesopotamia. Mesopotamia was an extensive area with several major cultures, so various weight systems were used. The best-known one employed a sexigecimal system with a shekel of about 8.3 g; heavier units were the mina (60 shekel) and the talent (60 mina). The common mina was about 500 g, and the talent was about 30 kg. However, there were many fluctuations and changes in these units. Typical forms

of Mesopotamian weights were grains (sphenodoids) and ducks, often made of hematite. The shekel was divided into 24 parts (1/24 = **giru**, later called the carat). The Neo-Assyrian system was quite similar, but it had a "light" and a "heavy" or double mina (ca. 504 and 1000 g, respectively). Assyrian weights made of bronze and shaped as crouching lions were the first to be identified as weights in Mesopotamia. In the Persian Empire, the mina was also about 500 g, based on a darik of 8.3–8.4 g.

c. Syria, Ugarit, and Canaan. It is clear that Ugarit used a basic shekel unit of ca. 9.3 g that was the equivalent of the Egyptian qedet. Ugarit of the Late Bronze Age is often taken for granted as a representation of Canaanite society; however, it was outside Canaan. Removing Ugarit from the perceived notion of Canaan means there are no written sources about its weight systems. Late Bronze Canaanite and Phoenician weights appear also in other regions, a fact that fits the international character of this period. Common forms include "grain-shaped" hematite weights and animal-shaped bronze weights. However, these weights do not conform to one system. The systems found in major cities of the Late Bronze Age varied, but were interrelated in a way that facilitated trade:

Ugarit: shekel (9.4 g) × 50 = mina (470 g) × 60 = talent (ca. 28.2 kg)

Hittite: shekel (11.75 g) × 40 = mina (470 g) × 60 = talent

Karkemish: shekel (7.83 g) × 60 = mina (470 g) × 60 = talent

d. Phoenicia and Philistia. Though small groups of weights have been found in Phoenician Iron Age sites, such as Byblos, Sarepta, and Tell Sukas, the lack of many inscribed weights and the scarcity of written sources makes it hard to reconstruct a Phoenician weight-system. Perhaps each city used a different system. It seems that weights in Phoenicia were adjusted with the Egyptian system; the basic unit was probably a shekel of ca. 7.6 g. In later times, the famous Tyrian shekel (known from coins) was double this value. In both Phoenicia and in Philistia were found cubical metal weights, often marked with letters. Such weights appear already in the Iron Age II period and continue into the Persian period, but they seem to conform to various standards.

2. Biblical weight systems

The OT calls scale weights "stones." Indeed, most ancient weights were made of stone. Most OT references on weighing of gold, silver, or copper involve huge sums, related to the royal court and to big events such as taxes on, or booty from, entire kingdoms; some scholars consider these sums as exaggerations. In any case, daily weighing and private trade are rarely mentioned.

a. Shekel. As in other Semitic cultures, the biblical systems were based upon the shekel (sheqel שֶׁקֶל) as the basic unit of weight. The shekel is not only the most frequently mentioned unit of weight but also holds a central position in the systems, while larger units are multiples of it. The shekel was so common that the OT often drops out the word, speaking about "x [NRSV, pieces of] silver" instead of "x silver shekels" (Gen 37:28; Judg 9:4; Isa 7:23). Numbers 7:85 proves that the missing word in such formulas is the word *shekel.* The same phenomenon appears in Hebrew Iron Age OSTRACA, e.g., in Ostraca 29 and 48 from Arad, where one finds the formula: "x silver for [someone]," meaning "x shekels of silver for [someone]." We find traces of three weight systems for the shekel in the OT: the royal system, the shekel of the sanctuary, and common units of measure.

The royal system was based on "the king's weight" in 2 Sam 14:26. This verse does not reveal the nature of the unit. The internal logic of the story is that Absalom, a king's son, who used to weigh his cut hair, naturally used royal weights. Yet, it cannot be assumed that weighing hair was a regular act. Archaeological finds about this royal system exist in the shape of one bronze weight from Gezer inscribed "II lmlk" (למלך, "2 to the King"), that is, two royal units. Just like the famous lmlk jars (*see* LMLK SEALS), this label indicates that these weights belonged to the royal court. However, the unit of weight of this specimen is equal to the regular shekel. Thus, it could be that the royal system differed from the regular system only in the shapes or in the inscriptions of the weights, and not in their standards.

b. Common units of the shekel. The second OT weight system can be called common or daily, and this was the system used commonly in Iron Age Judah. It appears in many OT genres, but we do not know the exact relations between the various weight-units. We learn that the shekel was the main unit, with sub-units.

The shekel was divided in a different way, most likely having a different number of gerahs (gerah גֵּרָה). Some gerahs are 1/20 of a shekel (Exod 30:13), and some are 1/24 of a shekel (see "Shekel of the sanctuary," §B.2.c).

A BEKA (beqaʿ בֶּקַע) probably means "half" (= 10 gerahs, where a gerah is worth 1/20 of a shekel); it is mentioned only twice (Gen 24:22; Exod 38:26). A pim (pim פִּים) is 2/3 of a shekel or about 7.8 g (= 16 gerahs, where the gerah is 1/24 of a shekel), mentioned only in the difficult verse of 1 Sam 13:21 (see NRSV note). The best reading of the Hebrew, as in the NRSV, renders this verse as "two-thirds of a shekel ... and one-third (of a shekel)" as payment given to the Philistines.

The letters ntsp (נצף) appear on weight units of about 9.66 g, or 5/6 shekel. This weight does not appear in the OT, and the vowels are not known. The maneh

(מָנֶה; derivation of mina; see §B.1.b) is mentioned only five times, all rather late in date (1 Kgs 10:17; Ezra 2:69; Neh 7:70-71; Ezek 45:12). Scholars debate if it was original to Judah, or a later, postexilic unit. Ezekiel 45:12 is crucial for understanding the maneh, but the verse in Hebrew is very difficult. A notable reading harmonizes the difficulties, suggesting that they indicate an earlier maneh of 50 shekels, reformed by Ezekiel into a maneh of 60 shekels (influenced by the Mesopotamian system). None of the many suggestions for understanding this term is completely satisfactory.

The heaviest unit in this system was the kikkar (כִּכָּר), but the numbers of shekels it included is not known. The name finds comparison in Ugaritic as kikarum. Kikkar is translated into Greek as talanton (τάλαντον, "talent"; literally "loaf," perhaps related to its shape). The qeshitah (קְשִׂיטָה), mentioned in Gen 33:19; Josh 24:32; Job 42:11 ("qesitah" in NRSV notes), was perhaps not an official, established weight unit. The ʾaghora (אֲגוֹרָה) is cited in 1 Sam 2:36 as "a piece of silver," but its weight is uncertain. Parsin (פַּרְסִין), peres (פְּרֵס), and phares are measures that come from the Persian period (Dan 5:25), and their meanings are obscure.

c. Shekel of the sanctuary. A third system for measuring is the shekel of the sanctuary (sheqel haqqodesh [שֶׁקֶל הַקֹּדֶשׁ], literally "holy shekel"). The value is not known, but the text says that this shekel had twenty sub-units (gerahs), and also a half shekel (beka = 10 gerahs), while larger units included a kikkar of 3,000 shekels (Exod 38:25-26). In Ezek 45 this shekel is connected not with kikkar but with a maneh (a mina) of sixty shekels. This system is mentioned only in relation to religious contexts, such as taxes, vows, and gifts to God (Exod 30:13-16; Num 3:44-51). It is never mentioned in relation to daily activities, private commerce, or acts between kings. The "shekel of the sanctuary" appears only in the Priestly code of the Pentateuch and in Ezekiel. It is completely lacking from the Deuteronomic literature. It seems likely that the shekel of the sanctuary did not exist in Iron Age Judah, but was a later, ideal creation (not much later, since it still reflects a time before coins). There are no archaeological finds from the Iron Age that show such a system existed. Reliable OT sources also indicate that the Jerusalem Temple was not a freestanding economic entity, but part of the royal house. It was built by a king, and at first, the kings' sons were priests (2 Sam 8:18). The kings of Judah decided about the property of the Temple in times of emergency (2 Kgs 12:11; 22:4) and supervised its maintenance (2 Kgs 11).

3. Archaeological data from Iron Age Judah and Israel

Almost 500 inscribed Judean scale weights from the Iron Age are known so far, and they create a very homogeneous weight-system. This system finds close comparison with the evidence of Hebrew Iron Age ostraca from places such as Lachish, Arad, Mezad Hashavyahu, and Samaria. This system undoubtedly represents the one common in Iron Age Judah. Almost all these weights are made of limestone, local to Judah, shaped as domes with flat bases. Very few weights are an exception; some are made of bronze, often shaped as cubes. The inscriptions are also very homogeneous: Hebrew names of the units with hieratic numerals on the smaller weights, and hieratic numerals plus a unique sign on the heavier weights, such as the shekel multiples. The weights appear mainly in strata of the 7th cent. BCE, but a few appear in the late 8th cent. BCE (at Arad level VIII, Beer-sheba level II, Lachish level III, etc.).

A weight-system functions as a whole, like a living organism, so even the appearance of a few weights indicates that the entire system already existed by that time. While archaeological knowledge of the Babylonian period is still scanty, it seems that the Judean weights went out of use at 586 BCE or perhaps slightly later. They did not function by the time of the Persian period. The geographical distribution of the weights is limited to Judah, with few scattered weights reaching (probably by trade) sites outside Judah. Some Judean weights were found in Philistine cities (Ekron, Ashdod), indicating perhaps closer economic relations or conquest of such cities by Judah. Within Judah, Jerusalem was the center of economic activity, as is reflected in the large numbers of weights found there in almost every excavation since 1882. Many weights were also found at Lachish (25), Arad (15), and Gezer (11). Regarding regions, the Jerusalem mountain area and the area associated with the tribe of Benjamin are dominant, followed by the Shephelah and the Negev. The Hebron area and the Judean desert are almost negligible on the map of distribution of inscribed weights; but this picture is partially related to factors such as the scope and nature of excavations.

The inscribed Judean weights belonged to one system only. First, their homogeneous material shapes and inscriptions prove this. Second, one often finds in Judean sites weights of different units in the same rooms or houses. This indicates that they were used together at the same time and place, that is, as part of one system. Third, only the shekel has multiples. For example, there are no inscribed weights of two beka or three pim. Fourth, the relatively short period of use and the limited area of distribution favor one system, because we need not assume various systems for different periods or regions (as was perhaps the case in Egypt or Mesopotamia). The system was based on one shekel standard, which was also the regular shekel of the OT and the Hebrew ostraca. This fits the evidence much better than earlier theories, which tried to find several standards (including foreign ones) among the inscribed Judean weights, but without success. Furthermore, there were foreign standards of weight in Iron Age Judah and Israel, in the shape of (not very common)

foreign weights. A notable example is an Assyrian type of weight in the form of a crouching lion, weighing 10 Mesopotamian shekels (ca. 82 g), found at Arad. Such weights could be used for measuring foreign standards. If so, there was no need to include foreign standards in the local Judean weights.

The inscribed Judean weights were found in various archaeological contexts. Many contexts imply secondary use or dumping places, such as pits, cisterns, caves, and tombs, rather than original places of use. Some weights were found in what may be termed public contexts (storage buildings or gates). Very few weights can be related to sacred contexts (because very few sacred buildings have been discovered in Judah so far). Many weights were found in domestic contexts, such as rooms and courtyards of houses. It thus seems that these weights were used by the population as a whole (of course, mainly by merchants and richer people). They were not part of a royal or a sacred system.

The Judean weight system was centered on a central unit of ca. 11.33 g, which can be safely equated with the OT regular shekel (corroboration for this conclusion comes from ostraca, especially from Kuntilet ʿAjrud). In addition to inscribed weights, uninscribed weights of similar shape and material were also used. Occasionally, uninscribed weights supplemented the inscribed system with decimal units, such as 5 and 10 shekels. The appearance of inscribed weights in the late 8th cent. BCE does not necessarily mean a weight reform. It seems that uninscribed weights existed earlier, and only now, in accordance with the growing use of script, they were marked, but the same units remained. The existence of an inscribed weight system is unique to Judah among all its neighbors. Israel lacked such a system, perhaps because it was conquered by the Assyrians before being able to develop such a system. We do not know why Edom, Moab, Ammon, and Philistia failed to develop similar inscribed systems. Archaeological evidence for these kingdoms, however, is more limited, yet they all employed weights. In Ekron, weights were adjusted to the Egyptian system (as in Judah), while the local standards are not well understood.

There are inscribed Judean weights of 1, 2, 4, 8, 16, 24, and 40 shekels. Heavy weights were rare; the common units were 4 and 8 shekels. These multiples are not a coincidence but an adjustment made on purpose with the Egyptian deben weight system. Four Judean shekels equaled a half-deben, while 8 Judean shekels equaled 1 deben. The Judeans chose units of 4 and 8 so that weights would be useful for trade with Egypt. This explains why 4 and 8 shekels were common, while 1-shekel weights were less common because they were useful only for inner-Judean transactions. Numerals inscribed on the Judean weights were adjusted to numbers of Egyptian qedet units (5, 10, 20, etc.) and written in hieratic script, because there were no special Hebrew numerals. This is true also for the Hebrew ostraca.

The Judean shekel was subdivided into 24 gerahs. This is proved by col. 4 in Ostracon 6 from Kadesh-barnea, which gives a sequence of weights that reaches 20 gerahs and, after one missing item, the value of 2 shekels. The missing item must be one shekel, thus it included more than the former item of 20 gerahs. There were inscribed weights of 3–10 gerahs, but not of 12 gerahs, since this place was occupied by inscribed beka weights (= half shekel = 12 gerahs). Other units in the system were the ntsp (5/6 shekel, ca. 9.6 g) and the pim (2/3 shekel, ca. 7.8 g). The small units are heavier than their expected norms. For example, beka weights weigh on average 6 g, while the expected half-shekel norm is ca. 5.66 g. The gerah weights are the least accurate, and many are much heavier than their expected standards. This fact caused a lot of headaches for scholars, who saw many different standards behind the deviating examples. Yet, the explanation is simpler: smaller weights are less accurate and more difficult to manufacture. The tendency toward the heavy side is consistent, and is most likely related to the production of such weights. Producers of small weights, trying not to err, preferred to stay on the heavy side of the scales (manufacture was probably made by placing new weights on the scales against an earlier specimen; chipping slowly until equilibrium was reached).

Inscribed talent (kikkar) and mina weights are found in Mesopotamia but not in Judah/Israel; we do not know why. A few heavy, uninscribed weights from Judah and Israel exist, but they can be interpreted in several ways. The number of shekels per mina is unknown; so is the number of mina per kikkar. One uninscribed weight from Malhata favors a mina of 50 shekels, but this has not been proved.

We know very little about manufacture of weights and their allocation in Judah. Were they made at one center, such as Jerusalem, or in royal workshops? Evidence for manufacture of weights was found in Gezer, but many questions remain. Possibly, the artists who manufactured inscribed seals were also those who could engrave letters on the small and rounded weights. This finds some corroboration in a weight of 2 shekels from Nebi-Rubin, which carries the name brky, written left to right, like names on seals, which were meant to be impressed or stamped. Weights with private names, as signs for ownership, are also known from Mesopotamia and Egypt.

The OT does not mention the ntsp (though a weight of the same name existed in Ugarit). This is not surprising; other units were mentioned only once. It is another indication that the ntsp was a secondary unit in the Judean shekel system, not a major unit that functioned as the basis of another, independent weight-system, as was commonly believed in the past.

4. Weights in later periods and in the New Testament

Coins are mentioned only in postexilic books and the NT. The Apocrypha mentions shekels, minas, and talents (1 Macc 10:40; 1 Esd 1:36; 5:45). By the time of the NT, weighing lost its special role in favor of a monetary economy. The DARIC (ʾadharkon אֲדַרְכֹּן) was made of gold and weighed 8.3–8.4 g (1 Chr 29:7; Ezra 8:27). The term DRACHMA (drachmē δραχμή) may be a confusion of the word *daric* (Ezra 2:69; Neh 7:69-72). The talent was used for large sums of money or weight (Matt 18:24; 25:15-22; Rev 16:21). Talanton sometimes translated the Hebrew kikkar. The mina (mna μνᾶ) appears in Luke 19:13-25, translated as POUND. Various Roman and Byzantine weight units existed, but a detailed review is impossible here. The litra (λίτρα), a Roman pound (12 oz.), appears in John 12:3 and 19:39 in relation to expensive ointment.

C. Measures of Capacity

1. Egypt

Egypt developed sophisticated and complex systems of measures of capacity from an early period. Evidence from Egypt includes many measuring vessels, some inscribed with numbers and names of units. The HIN was a small unit, used since the New Kingdom period mainly for oil. It was 0.473 L at first, then became 0.458 and 0.539 L. Grain was measured by several major capacity units (hekat, oipe, and khar); they could denote a volume as well as vessels or baskets that held this volume. The Bible does not mention specifically these Egyptian units of measure; however, there is an allusion to the measuring of grain in the story of Joseph, who, as a governor in Egypt, filled his brothers' bags with grain that they had come to purchase from the Egyptians (Gen 42:25).

The oipe was at first a wooden container, shaped like a barrel, which equaled normally 40 hin. Such vessels appear in wall drawings and were also found in excavations. In the New Kingdom oipe became a fixed measure of 19.22 L. The khar was a larger unit, normally containing 4 oipe (76.8 L). The hekat, ca. 4.8 L, was a quarter of an oipe, equaling 10 hin. Various subdivisions developed, as each unit could include different numbers of subunits.

2. Mesopotamia

The Mesopotamian measures of capacity are a very difficult subject. The capacity system was perhaps the oldest of all the measuring systems, probably originating from containers that had customary sizes. By the 3rd millennium BCE the system is well established and standardized. In texts from Fara we find the following system: 1 gur = 4 bariga = 24 ban = 240 sila (ca. 240 L). In the Akkadian period, a gur of 300 L replaced that of 240 L. Later, other gur were created, having various numbers of sila between 120 and 360. In the Neo and Late Babylonian periods, the standard system was: 1 gur = 5 bariga = 30 ban = 180 sila (ca. 180 L). The imeru ("ass load") was a common large measure, which originated perhaps in western Asia. It appears in Mesopotamia in the early 2nd millennium BCE in a decimal system: 1 imeru = 10 sutu = 100 qu (ca. 100 L). Later, variations developed with different numbers of qu per sutu: 8 or 10 in Nuzi and 8, 9, or 10 in Middle Assyrian texts. In the Neo-Assyrian period, we hear about a big sutu of 9 Assyrian qu, perhaps indicating a larger qu of 1.777 L. There were also sutu of 8 qu (ca. 14.22 L) and a "qu of the King" whose size is unknown. Few containers were studied, and they seem to strengthen the identification of sila/qu as the equivalent of about 1 L. Such vessels also seem to indicate two variations of the ban/sutu—one of 10 sila and another of 6 sila. An inscribed jar from Tell al-Rimakh seems to indicate a different, smaller qu of ca. 0.8 L in northern Mesopotamia.

3. Biblical measures of capacity

Names of OT measures of capacity usually originate from Mesopotamia, but a few units carry Egyptian names. The OT follows a common Near Eastern differentiation between "dry" and "liquid" measures. The benefits of such differentiation are not clear. Presumably, the OT inherited it from an earlier culture, but in the exilic and postexilic periods there was an effort to merge the "dry" and "liquid" measures, perhaps under Babylonian influence. Our understanding of this is very limited. The OT hardly gives details about daily use of capacity measures or about the relations between various units. It is also extremely hard to translate their values into our terms. Often, commodities were measured by commonly used, but not fixed, "official" units. These included the nevel (נֵבֶל), a leather flask of wine, which appears in 1 Sam 1:24, as well as in the SAMARIA OSTRACA. Another such measure was the "handful" mentioned for ash, barley, flour, oil, a meal, or figuratively for quietness (Exod 9:8; Lev 2:2; 5:12; Num 5:26; 1 Kgs 17:12; Eccl 4:6; Ezek 13:19). Sometimes, the number of the units appears without the unit's name (1 Sam 25:18; 2 Sam 16:1). The following capacity units were part of the formal system/s.

a. Dry measures. The HOMER (khomer חֹמֶר) was the largest dry measure, mentioned for barley and wheat (Lev 27:16; Num 11:32; Isa 5:10; Hos 3:2). The name "homer," which shares the same root as the word for donkey (khamor חֲמוֹר), is comparable to the Akkadian imeru, meaning an "ass load." A lethech (lethekh לֶתֶךְ) is mentioned only in Hos 3:2 (see NRSV note). The order of the sentence shows that it is probably smaller than the homer.

The EPHAH (ʾephah אֵיפָה) was the most common unit of capacity, mentioned in Exod 16:36 as a unit of 10 omer (ʿomer עֹמֶר). One-tenth of an ephah was a measure used for offerings (Lev 5:11; 6:20; Num 28:5), elsewhere mentioned under the name ʿissaron (עִשָּׂרוֹן), presumably another name for omer (Num 28). The

ephah is mentioned in early sources (Judg 6:19; 1 Sam 1:24). David as a boy could carry ten loaves of bread and 1 ephah of roasted corn (1 Sam 17:17). Ezekiel 45–46 identifies explicitly the ephah and the bath as the same measure (but this difficult passage is open to other interpretations). Ruth (2:17) collected about 1 ephah of barley in a day. Zechariah (5:6-10) provides a vision of a woman seated in an ephah measure; this does not prove that ephah was larger than a person, for visions do not necessarily present normal proportions.

A quantity of 3 SEAHs (seʾah סְאָה) is mentioned in Gen 18:6 (see NRSV note); but other references, which are early in date, use it for small quantities of flour and cereals: 5 seahs of roasted corn (1 Sam 25:18; NRSV, "five measures of parched grain"), or a trench with an extent of 2 seahs by Elijah's altar (1 Kgs 18:32, using the method of measuring area by quantity of seed). Elisha's promise about prices after the end of the Samaria siege is interesting: 1 seah of wheat or 2 seahs of barley per one [silver] shekel (2 Kgs 7:1, 16, 18; NRSV, "measures"). This reflects a quite common relation between wheat and barley. However, if a seah was ca. 7 L, the price was still very high in relation to normal conditions (assuming a shekel of 11.3 g silver). It does not prove the historicity of this story, but its inner logic is fine.

The word OMER means "sheaf"; this unit is mentioned only in Exod 16 (in relation to the manna) and in Lev 23:10-15 (in relation to offering of harvests). According to a gloss in Exod 16:36, the omer was 1/10 of an ephah. In Mesopotamia, we find the comparable imeru (see §C.2 above).

The ʿissaron appears only in liturgical texts (as "measure" in NRSV) in Exod 29:40; Lev 14–23; and Num 15; 28–29. We hear about 1, 2, or 3 units of this measure; the name suggests that it was "one-tenth" of a larger unit, which was not explicitly mentioned. The verb is used for taking 1/10 as tax in early sources (e.g., 1 Sam 8:15, 17 and Hebrew Ostraca).

A KAB (qav קַב) is mentioned only in 2 Kgs 6:25, in the context of the Samaria siege. It relates to an unusual commodity (probably dove's dung). We do not know the nature of this unit, but some scholars relate it to the Mesopotamian qu of roughly 1 L.

b. Liquid measures. The COR (kor כֹּר) was a large measure of capacity, but Deuteronomistic sources (e.g., 1 Kgs 4:22; 5:11) relate it to cereals, not liquids. The term is missing from the Pentateuch, but appears in Ezek 45:14 as equal to a homer.

That the BATH (bath בַּת) was an ancient unit is clear from 1 Kgs 7:26, 38 (compare 2 Chr 2:10; 4:5). Scholars have tried to calculate the bath from the capacity of the Temple's bronze sea (see SEA, MOLTEN). One problem is the conflicting measurements in Kings and Chronicles: the measurement is 2,000 baths in Kings and 3,000 baths in Chronicles. A second problem is that the exact shape of the bronze sea is unknown; also unknown is how close to the rim it was filled. Using a calculation based on the information in Kings, the capacity of the bronze sea is half a bath. Further assuming a royal cubit of ca. 52 cm, the bath would have measured about 16.7 L. As for the bronze basin of the Temple, its shape is unknown, so it does not help us to decide the measurement indicated by the bath. Significantly, these sources do not use the large measure homer, but calculate large volumes in numbers of baths. Only Ezek 45:10, 11, 14 indicates that the homer contained 10 baths, but this could have been a later equation.

The hin measure is mentioned in Exodus, Leviticus, Numbers, and Ezekiel, in relation to oil and wine. The name hin (hin הִין) is Egyptian, but in Egypt it was ca. 0.5 L. In relation to offerings, we hear about 1/4, 1/3, and 1/2 hin. Ezekiel 45:24 specifies the offering for 1 ephah as 1 hin of oil. In Ezek 4:11, the prophet is told to consume water very sparingly, at the rate of 1/6 hin per day. If this hin is equivalent to the Egyptian measure of 0.5 L, it results in ca. 90 cc per day, hardly sufficient in a hot climate. This may hint that the biblical hin was larger than the Egyptian counterpart. The LOG (logh לֹג) is mentioned only in Lev 14, in relation to oil used to purify lepers.

4. Reconstruction of the biblical systems of capacity

It is very difficult to reconstruct a system out of the available data. A decimal system of measures may be deduced as follows (quite comparable to the Mesopotamian imeru system): 1 homer = 10 ephah (= bath) = 100 omer (= ʿissaron). If we assume that the measures were similar in structure and volume to those in Babylon at roughly the same period, we may reach a second, sexagecimal system: 1 cor (gur) = 30 seah (sutu) = 180 kab (qu).

Interrelating these two systems depends upon the equation of homer and cor in Ezekiel, and upon Greek versions of Exod 16:36 and Isa 5:10, which render the ephah in terms ordinarily denoting the seah, perhaps indicating that the two were equal. For the log and the hin we have to rely on even later sources, such as Josephus (*Ant.* 3.139–43) and the Talmud, which may indicate that log = 4 kab and bath = hin. This would result in the following system: homer = cor = 2 lethech = 10 ephah (bath) = 30 seah = 60 hin = 100 omer (ʿissaron) = 180 kab = 720 log.

It results in a homer of about 180 L. However, it does not fit well the Mesopotamian relations between the units; e.g., the imeru was different from the gur and the sutu (seah) was 1/10 of an imeru. These reconstructions must take into account the difficulty of reconstructing the Iron Age system in Israel/Judah.

Archaeological data supply one solid piece of evidence: the volume of the bath, according to the inscriptions ("bt lmlk" בת למלך) found on jars from Lachish. Taking into account that some volume was perhaps left empty for stoppers, and that the jars perhaps were not filled up completely, the inscribed jars have a maximum capacity of about 21–22 L. Therefore, the bath could

not excede 21–22 L. The fact that other jars, marked only by the word lmlk, had various different capacities is not a problem. The lmlk jars were not a standard "official" measure, but served as an approximated unit. On the other hand, the bath was a fixed measure. A bath of about 18–19 L fits well with texts and inscribed vessels from Mesopotamia, which indicate a kor of 180–187 L (since bath was 1/10 of a cor; if this cor was equal to the Mesopotamian gur of 180–187 L, the bath was about 18–19 L). Furthermore, the common Egyptian oire measured 19.22 L, and if it was equal to the biblical ephah, than the bath was, indeed, equal to the ephah.

Understanding of the biblical system/s of capacity requires deciphering the Hebrew Ostraca. The unit bath appears in these ostraca in a shortened form, the letter "b" (ב). Similar shortened forms perhaps appear in the Persian period: "s" (ס) could stand for seah and "q" (ק) for kab in the Arad Ostraca. Unfortunately, other units do not appear in full or in short writing (except some approximated measures like the nevel).

5. Later measures of capacity

In the Persian period, the measures artabē (ἀρτάβη) and metrētēs (μετρητής) were used (Bel 3; compare John 2:6). The artabē enjoyed a wide distribution reaching Egypt and Greece, with a variety of measures between approximately 20 and 50 L. Choinix (χοῖνιξ; NRSV, "quart") in the famine prices of Rev 6:6 equaled a day's ration roughly similar to 1 L (or 2 log). The modios (μόδιος; Matt 5:15; Mark 4:21), translated as "bushel," is presumably ca. 8 L (16 log), but it appears as a vessel and not a unit of measure. John 12:3 mentions the Roman litra (λίτρα; pound) of 12 ounces.

D. Measures of Length and Area

1. Ancient Near Eastern measures of length and area

In the larger Near Eastern cultures the capacity, length, and weight systems were all interconnected.

a. Egypt. In Egypt, it is commonly believed that the major unit of length was a CUBIT of approximately 52.5 cm. There were rods with marks of units, though rods with a cubit of 52.5 cm appear only since the New Kingdom period, when this cubit is defined as "royal cubit." Studies of sizes of buildings seem to indicate that this unit existed much earlier. There is also evidence of vessels with signs of height and diameter that fit this cubit. The cubit was divided into 7 HANDBREADTHs of 7.5 cm and 28 "fingers" of 1.875 cm. These units appear on votive rods, which survived in the archaeological record. The rods show also the existence of a "small cubit" of 6 handbreadths (ca. 45 cm) and various other derivative units. The cubit was subdivided into 28 or 7 particles. The finger was divided into 16 particles. The cubit was related to the hekat by the formula: 1 hekat[1] (4.8 L) = 1/30 cubit[3]. This hints of a development from a cubit of 52.5 cm in the Pharaonic period (with corresponding heket of about 4.8 L), to a cubit of 53.2 in the Greek-Roman times (with heket of 0.502 L).

b. Mesopotamia. In Mesopotamia, most of the major units existed since the 3rd millennium BCE at the latest. The basic unit was the cubit ("forearm," about 50 cm) that included 30 fingers (about 1.666 cm) = 180 barleycorns. There were also a half-cubit (15 fingers) and a third cubit (10 fingers). Graduated rules on the statues of Gudea seem to indicate a cubit of 49.5 cm. There was also a "big cubit" (75 cm). Larger units were the reed (qanu◻= 6 cubits), the ROD or pole (nindan◻= 2 reeds = 12 cubits), the rope (10 nindan = 120 cubits), and the ush (= 6 ropes = 720 cubits). In the Neo- and Late Babylonian periods, the cubit was of the same length, but divided into 24 and not 30 fingers (the finger was now about 2.0833 cm). The reed was 7 cubits (3.5 m) and the rod 14 cubits (approximately 7 m). In Assyria, royal inscriptions use several terms, including a "large cubit," but these could be synonyms; there is no corresponding "small cubit." The Assyrian cubit was perhaps slightly larger than the Babylonian one, ca. 53–54 cm (composed of 32 "regular" fingers). A "royal cubit" is attested only in the Persian period, but its size is not certain. Herodotus suggested that it included 3 more fingers, but buildings from Persepolis seem to imply the cubit of 52 cm.

2. Biblical measures of length and area

Simple measures of length used organs of the human body as approximate units, which later developed into more formal measures. Hence, many measures of length were named after human limbs. In the OT, distances are sometimes given by approximations, such as the distance of the flight of an arrow (Gen 21:16) or a day's walking (Gen 30:36; 31:23). Distances were often measured with a rope, rod, or a flaxen cord (1 Kgs 7:15; Ezek 40:3; Zech 1:16; Rev 11:1; 21:15-16). The gomedh (גֹּמֶד; NRSV, "cubit") mentioned as the length of Ehud's sword (Judg 3:16) is otherwise unknown.

Unlike Mesopotamia and Egypt, which saw sophisticated systems for measuring area, the OT lacks units for measuring areas. Rather, the length and breadth of a square/rectangle are given, or the diameter and circumference of a circular area, usually in cubits (1 Kgs 6:2; 7:23; Ezek 40:47-49). Sometimes, an area was measured by approximated terms, such as the acre (tsemedh צֶמֶד)—the extent of a field worked during one day by a pair of oxen (1 Sam 14:14; Isa 5:10). Another method defined an area by the amount of seed required for planting it (1 Kgs 18:32). Comparable methods are known from Mesopotamia, where usually 33.5 qu of grain (approx. 33.5 L) were identified as the quantity that defines an area of 100 x 100 cubits (2,500 m^2).

More "formal units" of length are mentioned in the OT, such as a rod (qaneh [קָנֶה]; or "reed"). It is mentioned only in Ezek 40 and 42, more as an instrument for measuring than a measure. In Ezekiel it contained 6

"great cubits" similar to the Mesopotamian qanu, from where the name derives.

The cubit ('ammah אַמָּה; pēchys πῆχυς) was the basic unit of length. It was the distance between the tip of the middle finger and the point of the elbow. The cubit continued to be used in later periods, but the exact length is uncertain (Matt 6:27; Rev 21:17). During the Sabbath, Jews could travel to a limited distance (Acts 1:12), usually 2,000 cubits (about 1 km).

The span (zereth זֶרֶת) was the distance between the tip of the thumb to the tip of the little finger, when the fingers are set wide apart. The Vulgate translated it as *palmus*. A handbreadth (tefakh טֶפַח, tofakh טֹפַח) was the width of the hand at the base of the fingers; translated often as "palm," it should not be confused with the span. A fingerbreadth ('etsba' אֶצְבַּע) was the length of the finger or the thumb. It is mentioned only in Jer 52:21, but is common in the Talmud. The OT does not give the relation among these units. Because similar units based on body parts existed in Mesopotamia and in Egypt, perhaps the relations were similar, namely: 1 rod = 6 cubits = 12 spans = 36 handbreadths = 144 fingers.

In both Mesopotamia and Egypt there were probably also royal cubits, larger than the common ones: 27 fingers in Mesopotamia (if Herodotus is right) and 28 fingers in Egypt. Second Chronicles 3:3 informs us that the measures of Solomon's Temple were taken in "cubits of the old measure," so perhaps there was a royal cubit in Israel and Judah as well. Ezekiel (40–42) mentions a rod of 6 cubits "of a cubit and a palm." This can be interpreted as evidence for two units: an earlier, shorter cubit of 24 fingers = 6 handbreadths and a later, longer cubit of 7 handbreadths. The last was used to describe the future Temple and was perhaps a royal cubit.

In order to understand the OT units in our terms, we have to assume that units with similar names in Egypt and Mesopotamia had similar lengths; however, these units vary. The most likely identification for the biblical cubit is the royal Egyptian cubit of 52.5 cm. Another method is to measure ancient buildings and architectural complexes, trying to see if they fit a certain unit. This method is fraught with problems, since buildings sometimes have been altered or do not survive to their full extent, or are not entirely excavated. A good example is the famous "Hezekiah tunnel" in Jerusalem. The inscription in this tunnel proclaims that it is 1,200 cubits long, resulting in a cubit of 41 or 44 cm. Yet, perhaps the number 1,200 was rounded or exaggerated; also, we are not certain about the exact endpoints for measuring this tunnel.

3. Greek and Roman measures of length in biblical texts

The fathom (orguia ὀργυιά) appears in Acts 27:28. It measures 4 cubits or roughly 2 m. A mile (milion μίλιον) appears in Matt 5:41; a Roman unit from *mille passus* meaning a "thousand paces." A pace was about

29.6 cm, so the Roman mile was approximately 1,480 m.

Often translated as "miles" or "furlongs," a stadion (στάδιον, pl. stadia [στάδια]) was 600 ft. (e.g., 2 Macc 12:9-10; Luke 24:13). Usually one Roman mile included 8 1/3 stadia, but Jewish sources reckoned 7.5 stadia per mile. A group of 5 stadia was called a schoinos (σχοῖνος; 2 Macc 11:5). This unit was used to measure various multiples of stadia (e.g., 30, 40, 48, 60). It was perhaps similar to the Persian parasang of about 5.4 km.

Bibliography: Miram S. Balmuth, ed. *Hacksilber to Coinage: New Insights into the Monetary History of the Near East and Greece* (2001) 77–91; Seymour Gitin and Amir Golani. "A Silver-Based Monetary Economy in the 7th Century BCE." *Levant* 36 (2004) 203–5; Asher S. Kaufman. "Determining the Length of the Medium Cubit." *PEQ* 116 (1984) 120–32; Raz Kletter. *Economic Keystones: The Weight System of the Kingdom of Judah* (1998); Raz Kletter. "Iron Age Hoards of Precious Metals in Palestine—an 'Underground Economy'?" *Levant* 35 (2003) 139–52; Marc van de Mieroop. "Economic Theories and the Ancient Near East." *Commerce and Monetary Systems in the Ancient World: Means of Transmission and Cultural Interaction.* Robert Rollinger and Christoph Ulf, eds. (2004) 54–64; Ofra Rimon, ed. *Measuring and Weighing in Ancient Times* (2000); Walter Scheidel and Sitta von Reden, eds. *The Ancient Economy* (2002); Joe D. Seger. "Stone Scale Weights of the Judean Standard from Tell Halif." *Hesed ve-Emet: Studies in Honor of Ernest S. Frerichs.* Jodi Magness and Seymour Gitin, eds. (1998) 357–71.

RAZ KLETTER

WELL BEING [שֶׁלֶם shelem; σωτήριος sōtērios]. The phrase "well being" occurs most often in relation to sacrifices and offerings, specifically, sacrifices of well being (e.g., Exod 20:24; 24:5; Lev 3:3; Num 7:65; 1 Macc 4:56; Sir 35:2; 47:2). The general sense of the phrase, however, is communicated through the use of the words *well* and *welfare*. In this regard, "well being" can connote concern for the preservation of one's life as in the case where Abram asks Sarah to tell Pharaoh that she is his sister so that it will go well with him, and so that his life would be spared on her account (Gen 12:13). In Deut 22:7, Moses instructs the Israelites concerning a nest where the mother bird is sitting on eggs or fledglings. They are to take only the eggs or young, and to set the mother bird free so that it may go well for the Israelites and that they may live long.

"Well being" also connotes a general state of physical and material health, and a concern for the general common good of people (e.g., Jacob asks if things are well with his uncle Laban [Gen 29:4-6]). Jacob sends Joseph to his brothers to see if it is well with them and the flock (Gen 37:14). Joseph inquires about his brothers' welfare in relation to their father's health (Gen 43:27-28);

Moses meets his father-in-law Jethro, and they each ask about each other's welfare (Exod 18:7). The Israelites are to keep God's commands "for your own well being and that of your descendants after you" (Deut 4:40). In an exchange with Jonathan, David tells Jonathan that if Jonathan's father, Saul, responds favorably to hearing that he, David, has gone up to Bethlehem for the yearly sacrifice, then Jonathan is to know that it will be well with David; if the father responds angrily, then Jonathan is to know that evil has been determined by his father (1 Sam 20:7-8). When Nehemiah goes to the governors to seek the welfare of the people of Israel, the governors are displeased that someone would come to them on behalf of the Israelites (Neh 2:10). In contrast, a group of King Zedekiah's officials accuse Jeremiah of not seeking the welfare of his people (Jer 38:4). Elsewhere, God commands Jeremiah not to pray for the general welfare of the people (Jer 14:11). In the NT, Paul tells the Philippians that he has no one like Timothy "who will be genuinely concerned for your welfare" (Phil 2:20).

Understood as "prosperity," well being is the reward for following God and God's ways. Moses instructs the Israelites to hear and obey all God's decrees and commands and to "observe them diligently so that it may go well with you, and so that you may multiply greatly in a land flowing with milk and honey" (Deut 6:3; compare Deut 6:18; 12:25-28; 19:13). In Ps 128:1-2, the psalmist proclaims that it shall go well for those who fear the Lord; they shall "eat of the fruit of the labor of your hands" and "be happy" (compare Prov 3:1-2). God deals well with those who follow God's ways (Exod 1:20; Ps 119:65).

Finally, well being pertains to cities. God commands the exiled Judahites to "seek the welfare" of the city of Babylon, and to "pray to the LORD on its behalf, for in its welfare you will find your welfare (Jer 29:7). *See* SHALOM.

CAROL J. DEMPSEY, OP

WELL OR FOUNTAIN OF LIVING WATER, LIFE. *See* NEW LIFE; WATER; WELLS.

WELL-BEING, OFFERING OF. *See* OFFERING OF WELL-BEING.

WELLS [בְּאֵר be'er, בּוֹר bor; πηγή pēgē, φρέαρ phrear]. Access to underground water required extensive human labor to produce and to draw the precious resource from the ground. Therefore, wells were highly valued and coveted throughout the ancient world. While spring water was preferred, often well water was necessary to supplement the water resources of towns and villages (1 Sam 19:22; 2 Sam 23:15; John 4:6). Due to the intensive labor, wells were dug to deliver water for human and animal sustenance (Gen 29:2) rather than irrigation.

Wells in the biblical world were dug in cities (Gen 24:11; 2 Sam 17:18) and in various topographical locations such as valleys (Gen 26:17) and fields (Gen 29:2). In the nomad's world of the wilderness, possession of wells was literally a life-and-death issue. Conflict over wells among nomadic peoples (Gen 26:20-21) has continued throughout time.

Moses' request for the Israelites to pass through Edom on their way to the promised land included a promise not to drink from any well in Edom (Num 20:17), and then he added that any water the people or animals did consume would be purchased (Num 20:19; Deut 2:27-28). The enormous value of water in the arid biblical lands comes into view in the request and in the denial by Edom.

In the biblical texts women usually performed the difficult task of drawing water from a well. Biblical writers display the qualities of individuals in stories involving wells. Eliezer arrived in Nahor seeking a wife for Isaac, son of Abraham. Willingness to draw water for Eliezer and his camels was the sign of the right woman. Rebekah's actions revealed character. She was to be Isaac's wife (Gen 24:10-50). Moses drew water for the flocks of the priest of Midian after defending his daughters from shepherds. Moses' marriage to Zipporah resulted (Exod 2:15-22). The account of Jesus and the Samaritan woman at the well (John 4:6-15) reveals the woman's desire for water she does not draw. The tedious and difficult task of drawing water is implied along with the revelation of her questionable character.

The word *well* can depict a cistern (2 Sam 17:18) or a pit. Oxen can fall into a pit (Luke 14:5). Often a pit was thought to reach the underworld (Pss 55:23 [Heb. 55:24]; 69:15 [Heb. 69:16]). In the ancient world wells were sometimes thought to be the home of spirits (see, e.g., Gen 16:14). In frightening imagery, the term is defined as a bottomless pit with smoke pouring from the underworld (Rev 9:1-6) teeming with locusts rising to plague the earth.

Names of many places were based upon an event at a well. At Beer-sheba ("seven wells" or "well of seven") Abraham requested King Abimelech to make an oath over seven lambs proclaiming Abraham's ownership of the well (Gen 21:30-31). Other sites include Beer-lahai-roi (Gen 16:14); Beer in Moab (Num 21:16); Beeroth in Sinai (Deut 10:6); Beer in Israel (Judg 9:21); Beeroth in Benjamin (Josh 9:17); and Beer-elim (Isa 15:8). *See* CISTERN; FOUNTAIN; PIT; RACHEL; RESERVOIR; WATER; WATER WORKS.

MICHAEL G. VANZANT

WENAMUN, JOURNEY OF. The Journey of Wenamun is a late 11th-cent. BCE Egyptian literary text recounting the journey of a temple servant to Byblos to acquire cedar for a new bark (ritual boat) for the god Amun. The story asserts the imperial ideology of the Egyptian Third Intermediate Period. Combining features of an administrative report and autobiography, the text reflects Egyptian understanding of cultural and political conditions along the Phoenician coast, including an ap-

parent reference to ecstatic prophecy with parallels to biblical prophecy (1 Sam 10:1-13; 19:20-24). Although some key words are otherwise unattested in Egyptian, the text seemingly indicates that a god seized a servant or priest of the ruler of Byblos and put the servant/priest into a trance in which the servant/priest directs the ruler of Byblos to send for Wenamun, whom Amun has sent. *See* EGYPT; PROPHET, PROPHECY.

Bibliography: Miriam Lichtheim. *AEL 2* (1976) 224–30.

CAROLYN R. HIGGINBOTHAM

WEST. *See* ORIENTATION.

WESTERN SEA [הַיָּם הָאַחֲרוֹן hayyam ha'akharon]. The Mediterranean Sea, which forms the western boundary of the promised land (Deut 11:24; 34:2). It is sometimes named in conjunction with the "eastern sea," that is, the Dead Sea (Joel 2:20; Zech 14:8). *See* SEA, GREAT.

WHALE [דָּג dagh; κῆτος kētos]. Often translated "whale" in Jonah, the word dagh means "fish" (as in the NRSV). Though called a "large fish" (Jonah 1:17 [Heb. 2:1]; LXX kētos), dagh is used elsewhere to refer to fish generically. In Sg Three 57, the NRSV uses *whale* to translate kētos, but kētos refers to a sea monster or a large fish, not a whale.

MEGAN M. MCMURTRY

WHEAT [בַּר bar, חִטָּה khittah, חִנְטִין khintin; σῖτος sitos]. There are a number of distinct species (based on chromosomal patterns and characteristics) of wheat cultivated in the ANE: emmer (*Triticum dicoccum*; kussemeth [כֻּסֶּמֶת]; *see* SPELT), bread wheat (*Triticum aestivum*), and hard wheat (*Triticum durum*; most common in the Roman period throughout the Mediterranean area). Susceptible to saline soils, it grows best in clay-loam at moderate temperatures, and requires between 500–700 mm of rain per year (a rainfall amount common in the Jezreel and Upper Jordan valleys). Based on the discovery of carbonized remains, it is clear that emmer was more common in Egypt, while bread wheat was the principal variety cultivated in Canaan/Israel during the Iron Age. The 10th-cent. BCE GEZER CALENDAR as well as numerous references in the biblical text (Ruth 2:23; 1 Sam 6:13) provide evidence of the planting and harvesting seasons for the major cereal crops. Winter wheat was sown from the end of October to mid-December, taking advantage of seasonal rains (Deut 11:14), and then harvested with hand sickles (Deut 16:9) between the end of April and the end of May (Gen 30:14; 1 Sam 12:17). The celebration of this event included the covenantal requirement of setting aside a portion of the threshed and winnowed GRAIN as part of the offering of the first fruits (Deut 18:4) and the Feast of Booths (Deut 16:13-15), rejoicing in the bounty provided by God. The mounds of grain piled on the threshing floor represented life to the community (Ruth 3:7) and an apt metaphor for beauty (Song 7:2).

Solomon's payment of 20,000 cors of wheat to Hiram of Tyre for materials obtained to construct the Temple demonstrates that quantities of processed wheat also served as a medium of exchange (1 Kgs 5:11). It could also be part of a daily ration for priests (Ezra 6:9) and workers (Rev 6:6). As a staple of the diet, wheat was ground into FLOUR using hand mills and in later periods a circular millstone (Num 11:8; Matt 24:41; see MILL, MILLSTONE) and then baked in the beehive shaped oven found in nearly every household's compound. Surplus was gathered and placed into storage areas of the house (2 Sam 4:6) or into granaries (Matt 3:12). Because it was so much a part of everyday life, wheat and its processing fit well into metaphorical usage: Satan "sifting" each person's soul like wheat to test them (Luke 22:31) or in the parable of the weeds sown among the wheat (Matt 13:24-30). Even the name for an "ear of grain" (shibboleth [שִׁבֹּלֶת]; see SHIBBOLETH) becomes the basis for a dialectic test in Jephthah's conflict with the Ephraimites (Judg 12:1-6). Wheat also played a role in the prophets' injunctions on social justice and honest behavior. Amos, for instance, chides grain merchants for complaining that the Sabbath restrictions hurt their business, and condemns those who cheat their customers by "selling the sweepings of the wheat" (Amos 8:5-6). See BREAD; SACRIFICES AND OFFERINGS.

VICTOR H. MATTHEWS

WHEEL [אָבְנַיִם ʾovnayim, אוֹפַן ʾofan, גַּלְגַּל galgal; τροχός trochos]. The wheel's invention represents a pivotal point in cultural advancement. It was known and used in the ANE as early as the 4th millennium BCE. The Hebrew word ʾofan (pl. ʾofannim אוֹפַנִּים) is the primary term of interest in the OT, although two other words translated "wheel" by the NRSV are to be noted: galgal and ʾovnayim. The LXX uses trochos to render both ʾofan and galgal. An early view of ʾofannim understood them as a personified order of angelic beings—called "ophannim"—along with the cherubim and seraphim (1 En. 61:10; 71:7). The suggestion was apparently based on a view of Ezek 10:12 that proposed the transformation of the wheels in the preceding verses into angelic beings.

Twenty-five of the thirty-five uses of ʾofan appear in Ezekiel. Twenty-three of those twenty-five uses are found in two concentrated visionary settings: Ezek 1 and 10. The other two uses in Ezekiel (3:13; 11:22) are also related to the respective visions. Although ambiguity in the description and uncertainty regarding the function of the wheels in the Ezekiel visions call for caution on the part of the interpreter, current consensus seems to understand Ezekiel's "wheels" as depicting the wheels of a sacred chariot or cart. In an Ezekiel-

like vision alluded to in Enoch, a "wheeled-throne" is described (1 En. 14:18).

Texts other than Ezekiel that clearly refer to chariot wheels include Exod 14:25, which references the Egyptian chariot wheels, and Nah 3:2. Ten bronze stands, each with four wheels, were constructed as basin bases for the Solomonic Temple (1 Kgs 7:30-33); the wheels apparently facilitated the moving of the bases/basins. It has been suggested, however, that the description contained in these verses is of the basins, which were wheel-shaped. The proverb of Prov 20:26 associates a wheel with the threshing process, perhaps the wheel of a threshing cart (see also Isa 28:27).

The NRSV translates the term galgal as "wheel"/"wheelwork" (Eccl 12:6; Isa 5:28; 28:28; Jer 47:3; Ezek 10:2, 6, 13; 26:10; Dan 7:9). Most of these texts seem to refer to chariot wheels. Exceptions are Isa 28:28 (wheel of a threshing cart; compare Isa 28:27, where ʾofan is used), Eccl 12:6 (a wheel that facilitated water-drawing from a well), and Dan 7:9 (throne wheels). Ezekiel 10:13 is noteworthy for its use of both ʾofannim and galgal in Ezekiel's explanation of his visionary wheels: "As for the wheels (ʾofannim), they were called in my hearing 'the wheelwork (galgal)'."

Jeremiah 18:3 employs the term ʾovnayim, a dual form in Hebrew (LXX, lithōs [λίθως]; "stone") in reference to the potter's wheel. The dual form of the Hebrew in this text is picturesque inasmuch as early examples of the POTTER'S WHEEL are known to have consisted of two integrated, lubricated stones.

The LXX speaks dramatically about the use of torture wheels (trochos) against Jewish martyrs in the Maccabean period (4 Macc 5:3, 32; 8:13; 9:12-20; 10:8; 11:10, 17; 15:22; compare 2 Macc 7). Trochos is used in Jas 3:6 to refer to "the cycle of nature."

JOHN I. LAWLOR

WHEEL, POTTER'S. See POTTER'S WHEEL.

WHELP [בֵּן ben, גּוֹר gor, גּוּר gur]. The CUB of a lion or jackal that is still suckling, as opposed to a kefir (כְּפִיר), a cub that has been weaned and is seeking prey by itself. Lamentations 4:3 (compare Job 4:11) expresses the dependent status of whelps: "Even the jackals offer the breast and nurse their whelps" (gurehen [גּוּרֵיהֶן], author's trans.; NRSV, "their young").

Judah (Gen 49:9) and Dan (Deut 33:22) are each described as a "lion's whelp" in the blessings of Jacob and Moses, respectively. The term is used in judgment oracles against Nineveh (Nah 2:12 [Heb. 2:13]) and Babylon (Jer 51:38), in each case perhaps alluding to the place of the lion in Assyrian and Babylonian culture. See DEN OF LIONS; ELIPHAZ; JUDAH, JUDAHITES; LION.

JOHN I. LAWLOR

WHET [לָטַשׁ latash, קִלְקַל qilqal, שָׁנַן shanan]. To sharpen tools or weapons (1 Sam 13:20; Pss 45:5 [Heb.

45:6]; 120:4; Isa 5:28; Jer 51:11) and used figuratively to characterize a process of readying for action, usually hostile (Job 16:9; Eccl 10:10). A "sharpened TONGUE" carries out slanderous verbal assaults (52:2 [Heb. 52:4]; Pss 64:3 [Heb. 64:4]; 140:3 [Heb. 140:4]; Prov 25:18). God sharpens supernatural weapons for judgment (Deut 32:41; Ps 7:12 [Heb. 7:13]).

PETER TRUDINGER

WHIP [שׁוֹט shot; μάστιξ mastix, φραγέλλιον fragellion]. Instrument of punishment made of pieces of leather attached to a handle, used on people (1 Kgs 12:11, 14; 2 Macc 7:1; Sir 28:17; 30:1) and animals (Prov 26:3; Nah 3:2). Deuteronomy 25:1-3 regulates its use as a legal punishment. In John 2:15 Jesus uses a whip to cleanse the Temple of money changers, sellers, and animals. The whip is a metaphor for divine punishment (Isa 10:26) as well as for mental discipline (Sir 23:2). *See* CRIMES AND PUNISHMENT, OT AND NT; SCOURGE.

JOAN E. COOK, SC

WHIRLWIND [גַּלְגַּל galgal, סוּפָה sufah, סְעָרָה se'arah; λαῖλαψ lailaps, συστροφὴ πνεῦμα systrophē pneuma]. The word *whirlwind* designates the furious and potentially destructive wind (sufah), tempest, or windstorm (se'arah) associated either with the northwest sea-gales (mezarim מְזָרִים) common in the rainy winter season, but only rarely cyclonic, or with the less destructive, scorching-hot southeastern sirocco (zal'afah זַלְעָפָה]; Ps 11:6), winds that are commonly associated with cyclonic dust devils (galgal; Ps 77:18 [Heb. 77:19]; Isa 17:13) or sand/palm-columns (timarah תִּימָרָה]; Song 3:6) that come from the Syro-Arabian desert (Isa 21:1) during the spring harvest season (compare Luke 12:55). The noun forms find their antonym in "silence" (demamah דְּמָמָה]; Ps 107:29) and the verbal forms in "become quiet/still" (shathaq שָׁתַק]; Jonah 1:11).

The whirlwind is frequently associated with theophany. As such it symbolizes the sovereign wisdom and power (Job 38:1; Ps 77:18 [Heb. 77:19]; Nah 1:3; Hab 3:14; Sir 43:17) by which God rides and yokes the four winds (compare Pss 18:10 [Heb. 18:11]; 104:3; Isa 19:1; Ezek 1:4) to serve him (compare Mark 4:35-41). God may use this whirlwind to assume people into heaven (2 Kgs 2:1, 11-12) or chastise them on earth or sea (Jonah 1:4, 12). Alternatively, the whirlwind functions as the symbolic instrument of (or a metaphor for) the divine judgment or holy war by which God's enemies are routed (Ps 83:15 [Heb. 83:16]; Prov 1:27; Isa 21:1; Jer 23:19; 49:32; Ezek 12:14; 17:21; Hos 8:7; Amos 1:14; Hab 3:14; Zech 9:14). When this fate is experienced by God's covenanted people (Isa 5:28; Jer 4:13; Zech 7:14), they pray for shelter, envisioning its location under God's wings (or) in the Temple (Pss 55:8 [Heb. 55:9]; 61:4 [Heb. 61:5]; 91:1), whose four "sides"

may be denoted by the term for wind (ruakh רוּחַ]; 1 Chr 9:24; Ezek 42:16-20). *See* JOB, BOOK OF.

GREG GLAZOV

WHITE [לָבָן lavan; λευκός leukos]. *White* is a term indicating lightness or opaqueness, often denoting the absence of color. Because of its bright, clean appearance, the color white frequently symbolizes purity.

The term *white* is used to describe the hair of animals, including goats (Gen 30:35, 37), donkeys (Judg 5:10), and horses (Zech 1:8; 6:3, 6). It refers to the color of human hair (Matt 5:36; Rev 1:14), and the wake of the leviathan in the water is described as being like white hair (Job 41:32). White describes the color of various objects, such as manna (Exod 16:31), a stone (Rev 2:17), a cloud (Rev 14:14), a throne (Rev 20:11), teeth (Gen 49:12), tree branches (Joel 1:7), and a film on the eyes (Tob 2:10; 3:17; 6:9; 11:8, 13).

White refers to the color of leprous skin or hair growing in leprous skin (Lev 13). Moses is able to make his skin leprous in order to impress Pharaoh (Exod 4:6), and both Miriam (Num 12:10) and Gehazi (2 Kgs 5:27) exhibit the white skin of leprosy.

The most frequent use of *white* refers to the color of textiles, most often garments. In his instructions on the good life, the Teacher commands: "Let your garments always be white" (Eccl 9:8*a*). White garments can connote royalty (Esth 8:15), glory (Dan 7:9), and faithfulness (2 Esd 2:40). Through a process of bleaching, all stains are removed, and hence the garment is a sign of moral purity (Rev 3:4-5). The color white is implicit in Isaiah's promise of a cleansing of sin: "though your sins are like scarlet, they shall be like snow ... [and] become like wool" (Isa 1:18). Whiteness indicates purity of character, as when the penitent pleads, "Purge me with hyssop and I shall be clean; wash me, and I shall be whiter than snow" (Ps 51:7 [Heb. 51:9]). Snow is often used as a simile to describe whiteness (Exod 4:6; Num 12:10; 2 Kgs 5:27; Ps 51:7 [Heb. 51:9]; Lam 4:7; Dan 7:9; Matt 28:3; Rev 1:14), and milk is used as a simile for white in Gen 49:12 and Lam 4:7.

In the NT white garments often connote glory. At the transfiguration, Jesus' garments are dazzling white (Matt 17:2; Mark 9:3; Luke 9:29). White garments appear in the resurrection accounts. In Matthew the angel at the tomb wears white (Matt 28:3), in Mark a young man inside the tomb is clothed in white (Mark 16:5), and in John two angels wear white (John 20:12). In Revelation, white robes indicate those who are worthy (Rev 3:4-5). The martyrs are given white robes (Rev 6:11), the great multitude wears white (Rev 7:9, 13-14), and the armies of heaven wear white (Rev 19:14). The color white thus encompasses both negative connotations as a sign of a leprous infection and positive meanings of glory and moral purity. *See* COLORS.

Bibliography: Athalya Brenner. *Colour Terms in the Old Testament* (1982).

MARY PETRINA BOYD

WHITE HORSE [סוּס לָבָן sus lavan; ἵππος λευκός hippos leukos]. In Rev 6:1-8, the white horse is the first in the series of four horses and their riders, which loosely echoes the four teams of horses in Zech 1:7-11 (in Zech 6:1-8 God sends these chariots to punish Israel's enemies). Revelation focuses upon the white horse's rider, carrying a bow and receiving a crown, who goes out "conquering and to conquer" (6:2). Some interpreters view this image as largely symbolic: the white horse represents imperial conquest, while the other horses depict war, famine, and death. These conditions either mark the end-time tribulation or the general state of human affairs until the end. Others locate the white horse within the specific context of Revelation and generally evoke the threat of a Parthian invasion of the eastern Roman Empire, as Parthian armies notoriously featured skilled archers. A few interpreters have identified this rider with Christ, based on Rev 19. In 19:11-16, Christ (the Word of God) rides a white horse to judge and make war. Crowned with diadems and clothed in a robe dipped in blood, he leads the armies of heaven, who are dressed in white and ride white horses, to defeat the enemy. *See* HORSE; REVELATION, BOOK OF.

GREG CAREY

WHITE THRONE [λευκός θρόνος leukos thronos]. Found only in Rev 20:11, "a great WHITE throne" is associated with God's final judgment. *Throne* in Revelation represents God's sovereign rule and authority. A white throne contributes not only to the spectacle of Rev 20:11-15 but also speaks to the purity and righteousness of the judgment proceeding from it.

GARY COLLEDGE

WHORE. *See* PROSTITUTION.

WHORE OF BABYLON [πόρνη pornē]. Among the many fantastic apocalyptic images in the book of Revelation is the vision of a woman clothed in purple and scarlet, adorned with gold, jewels, and pearls, who is seated on a scarlet beast with seven heads and ten horns (Rev 17:1-4). On her forehead is written "Babylon the great, mother of whores and of earth's abominations" (17:5). This symbolic woman is commonly known as the "Whore of Babylon." An angel explains that the seven heads of the beast that the Whore rides represent seven mountains, and its horns are ten kings (17:9-12). The 1st-cent. reader would recognize that the "seven mountains" are the seven hills of Rome, and the ten kings the emperors of the Roman Empire. Thus, "Babylon" is a code word for Rome, known for its wealth and power as well as its cruelty and oppression (*see* BABYLON, NT; REVELATION, BOOK OF; ROME,

EARLY CHRISTIAN ATTITUDES TOWARD; compare 1 Pet 5:13).

The depiction of a city or a people as a prostitute or adulteress (*see* PROSTITUTION §B) is a well-known theme in prophetic literature (e.g., Isa 23:16-17; Ezek 23; Hos 1–3; Nah 3:4). John, the author of Revelation, particularly has in mind (as he does throughout much of chap. 17) imagery from Jer 51 (especially 51:12-13). The OT prophet proclaims judgment against the powerful city of Babylon, which has been destructive of God's people and has imperiously and idolatrously set itself up as an entity deserving the kind of worship due only God (Jer 50–51). John will specifically identify the Whore with the name Babylon (Rev 17:5). As John certainly knows, Jeremiah describes Babylon in the same way that he now envisions Rome, as a city sitting (i.e., enthroned) on many waters (Jer 51:13). Babylon literally sat on the Euphrates River. The Whore is seated on "waters" that are described as peoples, multitudes, nations, and languages (Rev 17:15). Through this image, John's hearers and readers recognize that the great Whore's/city's allure comes from her intimate and illicit relationships, her commercial and political alliances with the nations and peoples of the world, alliances that create the great wealth and power that even now seduce them. Even the apostle Paul enlisted the striking image of the illicit and destructive prostitute (1 Cor 6:15-16). In fact, the Corinthian text has much in common with John's warning here in chap. 17. John fears that his people will destroy their relationship with Christ by accommodating themselves, through either social fear or economic lust, to a prostituting relationship with Rome (chaps. 2–3). John images this destruction of God's people as the Whore's drinking of believers' blood. So successful is the Whore at destroying believers' relationships with God that she is pictured as drunk on the blood of those she destroys. She either slaughters believers because of their profession of Christ's Lordship, or destroys them by luring them into a prostituting relationship with her (Blount 2009).

John continues to draw on OT imagery to describe the demise of the Whore. Like the "daughter of Babylon" (Isa 47:1-15), the Whore of Babylon (Rev 17:16) is stripped naked and punished (compare Ezek 16:39; 23:10; Nah 3:5). Like the much-reviled Jezebel, whose flesh is eaten (2 Kgs 9:36-37), the Whore of Babylon's flesh is devoured (Rev 17:16; compare Rev 2:20-23). Even though the Whore's downfall is a cathartic victory over evil, some interpreters have expressed concern that the graphically violent description of the Whore's destruction—"they will make her desolate and naked; they will devour her flesh and burn her up with fire" (Rev 17:16)—is potentially dangerous to real women. Even though the Whore is a symbol, readers will see her as a woman, because that is the power of metaphor. In addition, like Jezebel, who is presented elsewhere as a real flesh-and-blood woman (1 Kgs 18–21; 2 Kgs 9; Rev 2:20), the Whore is reviled and eaten.

To some feminist interpreters, the fact that the narrative always portrays the "fornication" (porneia πορνεία) as the woman's is problematic. For example, even though the kings and nations participate in porneia with the Whore, John says the Whore "made" them do it (Rev 14:8), and the abomination is always described specifically as "her" fornication (porneia autēs [πορνεία αὐτῆς], 17:2; 18:3; 19:2 [Vander Stichele]). This description of the Whore of Babylon reinforces the idea that women are responsible for sexual sin (even for sin in general; compare Gen 3:1-19), and that they deserve to be violently abused. *See* APOCALYPTICISM.

Bibliography: David L. Barr. *Tales of the End: A Narrative Commentary on the Book of Revelation* (1998); Brian K. Blount. *Can I Get a Witness? Reading Revelation through African American Culture* (2005); Brian K. Blount. *Revelation.* NTL (2009); Allan A. Boesak. *Comfort and Protest: The Apocalypse from a South African Perspective* (1987); Tina Pippin. *Death and Desire: The Rhetoric of Gender in the Apocalypse of John* (1992); Gail Corrington Streete. *Strange Woman: Power and Sex in the Bible* (1997); Caroline Vander Stichele. "Re-membering the Whore: The Fate of Babylon according to Revelation 17:16." *A Feminist Companion to the Apocalypse of John.* Amy-Jill Levine and Maria Mayo Robbins, eds. (2009) 106–20.

BRIAN BLOUNT AND MARIANNE BLICKENSTAFF

WICK [פִּשְׁתָּה pishtah; λίνον linon]. FLAX or LINEN threads lit in oil lamps; metaphorically the Egyptians' sudden death (Isa 43:17) and the servant's task (Isa 42:3; Matt 12:20). *See* LAMP, NT; LAMP, OT.

WICKED PRIEST. *See* HABAKKUK COMMENTARY, PESHER; PRIEST, WICKED.

WIDOW [אַלְמָנָה ʾalmanah; χήρα chēra]. *Widow* in Hebrew is ʾalmanah, from the root ʾalam (אָלַם), "one unable to speak." The widow is also in a sense unspoken for, that is, she has no husband, and is therefore without legal status. The Greek chēra is from the Indo-European root ghe, "forsaken" or "left without" (i.e., a husband). The NT uses chēra both for a woman without a husband and for a single, celibate woman. In the 1st cent. CE monandros (μονάνδρος, "having one husband") described a woman married only once, and the Latin *univira* was used for widows who did not remarry. Paul's advice in 1 Cor 7:39-40 ("she is more blessed if she remains as she is") describes the *univira* and retains the positive connotations it has in Roman funerary inscriptions.

A childless widow could be returned to her father's house (Gen 38:11; Lev 22:13) or to her mother's house (Ruth 1:8) until such time as she could remarry (Ruth 1:9). Alternatively, a childless widow could be subject to Levirate marriage (Deut 25:5-10) in order to procure children to carry on her husband's name (*see*

LEVIRATE LAW). Evidently, a widow could bring her deceased husband's estate into a Levirate marriage (e.g., Ruth 4:10). Conditions for remarriage are mentioned only a few times in the OT. In addition to Ruth 4:5-10, discussed above, a priest may not marry a widow or divorced woman (Lev 21:14; Ezek 44:22).

The OT portrays Israel's God as the special helper and refuge of widows, along with strangers, orphans, and the poor (e.g., Exod 22:21-24; Deut 10:18; 27:19; Pss 68:5; 146:9; Jer 49:11). Job included his treatment of widows as evidence for his righteousness (Job 29:13; 31:16). Widows were allowed to glean in the fields (Deut 24:19-22; Ruth 2:1-23) and to share in the tithe (Deut 14:28-29; 26:12) and meals at public festivals (Deut 16:11, 14). In spite of these protections, the widow's plight was sometimes serious, as Elijah's encounter with the starving WIDOW OF ZAREPHATH (1 Kgs 17:8-24) and Elisha's encounter with the prophet's widow whose children were to be sold into slavery to pay a creditor (2 Kgs 4:1-7) indicate. The cause of the widow was a particular example of the poor and powerless (Isa 1:17; Jer 7:6; 22:3; 49:11; Zech 7:10; Mal 3:5). Isaiah and Jeremiah used the widow as a metaphor for Israel's lost and powerless state without God (Isa 47:9; Lam 1:1; 5:3; compare Rev 18:7). As such, the widow was an image of "the remnant," the desolate few destined to receive God's promises (*see* REMNANT). The Gospel of Luke portrays a widow's spiritual task as waiting and praying for the fulfillment of God's promises, as did the prophet Anna, a widow who never left the Temple, "fasting and [praying] night and day," who spoke about Jesus as the expected redeemer (Luke 2:36-37).

Widows are prominent in the ministry of Jesus. As a pious Jew, Jesus was concerned for those for whom God was concerned. Jesus felt compassion for a widow in Nain whose only son had died, and like Elijah and Elisha, he restored the young man to life (Luke 7:11-15; compare 1 Kgs 17:8-24; 2 Kgs 4:1-7). Jesus uses a widow as a positive example of the constancy of prayer (Luke 18:1-8), an activity with which widows are associated in the NT (see also Luke 2:36-37; 1 Tim 5:3-16). Jesus also highlights a widow's generosity (Mark 12:41-44; Luke 21:1-4), and he attacks those who "devour widows' houses" (Luke 20:46-47).

Some scholars suggest that, in the NT, when a woman appears with no father or husband named, she is probably a widow (chēra). If any woman without a husband could be a widow, it is possible that some of the Galilean women who accompanied Jesus and the disciples, "who provided for them out of their resources" (Mark 15:40-41; Luke 8:1-3), were widows. These women subsequently were present at the death, burial, and resurrection of Jesus (Luke 23:49, 55; 24:1-9) and remained in Jerusalem with the eleven apostles (Acts 1:14).

In the Acts of the Apostles, widows are a recognized group within the Christian community. Care of Hebrew widows who became Christians precipitated the "division of labor" in 6:1-7, so that "there was not a needy person among" the Christians (4:34). The care for widows in Acts serves to illustrate that "religion that is pure and undefiled before God ... is ... to care for orphans and widows in their distress" (Jas 1:27). The Pastoral Epistles confirm that widows not only had a claim to benevolence from the early church but also that they had status and privilege; they were a category of leader with prescribed duties, an office with special responsibility for prayer (1 Tim 5:3-16; *see* ORDER OF WIDOWS). These widows are mentioned in Ignatius (*Smyrn.* 13:1), and Polycarp (*Phil.* 4:3), writings that some scholars take to be contemporaneous with 1 Timothy.

The incident at Joppa in which Peter raises Tabitha from the dead (Acts 9:36-43) indicates that she was apparently a woman of independent means who had gathered around her a community of widows. Under Roman law, widows were independent, legal parties who could inherit from their husbands and manage their own property. Augustan laws, such as the *Lex iulia de maritandis ordinibus*, encouraged single women to marry and widows to remarry, with penalties for those who did not (Dio Cassius, *Rom.* 54.16.1–2). However, funerary inscriptions show that despite the legislation to encourage widows to remarry, the usual pattern of second marriages was discouraged and that the **monandros** or *univira* was especially honored. Paul mentions "the unmarried and the widows" among whom he numbers himself as a celibate person (1 Cor 7:8; *see* CELIBACY). Paul suggests the widow should remain single, although as a concession (as indeed, is marriage in general for Paul), and to avoid being "aflame with passion," he allows remarriage (1 Cor 7:8-9, 39-40; compare Rom 7:1-3). *See* FAMILY; INHERITANCE IN THE NT; INHERITANCE IN THE OT; MARRIAGE, NT; MARRIAGE, OT; WOMEN IN THE ANCIENT NEAR EAST; WOMEN IN THE APOCRYPHA; WOMEN IN THE NT; WOMEN IN THE OT.

Bibliography: A.-J. Levine and M. Blickenstaff, eds. *A Feminist Companion to the Deutero-Pauline Epistles* (2003); Robert H. Price. *The Widow Traditions in Luke–Acts* (1997); Bonnie Bowman Thurston. *The Widows: A Women's Ministry in the Early Church* (1989).
BONNIE BOWMAN THURSTON

WIDOW OF ZAREPHATH zair'uh-fath. An unnamed woman who fed and sheltered the fugitive Elijah during the drought he predicted (1 Kgs 17:8-24). She was a Phoenician who lived in Zarephath (possibly modern Sarafand), near Tyre and Sidon. Her desperate economic situation (v. 12) mirrors that of other widows in the Bible (*see* WIDOW), but her hospitality to the Israelite prophet is miraculously rewarded with an abundance of grain and oil (vv. 15-16) and the reviving of her dead son (vv. 17-24). Jesus alludes to the incident (Luke 4:24-27) when arguing that "no prophet is accepted in the prophet's hometown." *See* ZAREPHATH.

JESSICA TINKLENBERG DEVEGA

WIFE. *See* MARRIAGE, NT; MARRIAGE, OT.

WILD ASS [פֶּרֶא *pere*'; ὄνος ἄγριος *onos agrios*]. The wild ass, progenitor of the domesticated donkey (*Equus asinus*), was well known in the Bible (Job 6:5; 11:12; 39:5). Yahweh's angel tells Hagar that her unborn son Ishmael will be a "wild ass of a man" (Gen 16:12), one of several places where human behavior is compared to that of a wild ass (Jer 2:23-24; 48:6; Hos 8:9), suggesting that people were well aware of the animal.

The *pere*' may refer to the Asiatic (Syrian) wild ass (*Equus hemionus*), known also as Syrian onager. Captured onagers were bred with domestic donkeys and horses to produce mules, but were never domesticated. A second Asiatic wild ass known as the kiang inhabits the Tibetan uplands. *See* ANIMALS OF THE BIBLE; ASS; DONKEY.

Bibliography: Oded Borowski. *Every Living Thing: Daily Use of Animals in Ancient Israel* (1998).
ODED BOROWSKI

WILD BEAST [חַיָּה *khayyah*; θήρ *thēr*, θηρίον *thērion*]. The term *wild* does not occur separately in Hebrew or Greek when referring to animals, although sometimes *khayyah* is qualified by words such as ha'arets (הָאָרֶץ, "of the earth"; Gen 1:24-25; Job 5:22; Ps 79:2; compare *tēs gēs* [τῆς γῆς], "of the earth"; Rev 6:8), hassadheh (הַשָּׂדֶה, "of the field"; Jer 27:6), or even ra'ah (רָעָה, "bad"; Ezek 34:25, NRSV "wild").

The exact phrase "wild beast(s)" is used only three times in the NRSV (Gen 31:39; 2 Macc 4:25; Mark 1:13). In the first of these, Jacob defends himself against his uncle and father-in-law, Laban, by including the observation "that which was torn by wild beasts I did not bring to you." The entire English clause is conveyed by a single Hebrew word, terefah (טְרֵפָה, "torn meat"; see Exod 22:13), food that makes the one who eats it ritually unclean (Lev 17:15; 22:8; in modern Hebrew the word comes to mean simply nonkosher food). The Hebrew *khayyah* is not involved at all. The phrase "wild beast" is used metaphorically in 2 Macc 4:25 to describe the rage and savagery of Menelaus, a usurper of the high priesthood in the days of Antiochus IV Epiphanes (175–163 BCE). That leaves only the wistful account of Jesus' forty days in the wilderness, wherein, after the temptations by Satan, it is said that "he was with the wild beasts" (Mark 1:13).

An animal (i.e., beast) is wild when it is contrasted with cattle and other domestic animals (behemoth בְּהֵמוֹת), as is explicitly the case in such narratives as the creation of the animals (Gen 1:24-26) and the list of the animal passengers on Noah's ark (Gen 7:14, 21; 8:1). Ancient Israel was, of course, familiar with a variety of wild animals, including the undomesticated species of wild ass, wild goat, and wild ox. They also spoke of the gazelle, ibex, stag, bear, fox, wolf, hyena, jackal, panther, and lion, not to mention numerous small rodents, bats, snakes, scorpions, and insects. They encountered birds of prey such as the vulture or eagle, hawk, and owl, as well as the crow, the stork, the hoopoe, and the foolish but speedy ostrich (Job 39:13-18).

Wild animals and the WILDERNESS itself were viewed with ambivalence by ancient Israel. In the past, the garden of Genesis (chap. 2) was a wild but "peaceable kingdom" in which the childlike man and woman mingled freely with the animals. Though Israel's wilderness wandering was remembered as a time of danger, privation, and complaint (e.g., Exod 16:1-3), those forty years also constituted a kind of golden age in which the people relied utterly on God's providential care, eating the manna with which God sustained them (e.g., Exod 16:4-36) and looking to the bronze serpent that God provided as a cure for snakebite (Num 21:4-9).

In the present, God exhibits affection for the wild animals (see Ps 50:10-11) and they reciprocate by crying to the Lord their maker when they face privation (Joel 1:20). The Yahweh speeches near the end of the book of Job (chaps. 38–41) are a loving inventory of God's work of creation, including the wild animals and the monsters BEHEMOTH and LEVIATHAN. But the animals play darker roles as well. One of those is the manifestation of the divine disfavor set forth by Moses in his farewell song: "The teeth of beasts I will send against them, with venom of things crawling in the dust" (Deut 32:24).

When the prophets contemplate the eschatological age of the future, again they exhibit the same ambivalence. Their scenes of the desolation of the nations include ruins inhabited by wild animals (e.g., Isa 34:8-17). Ezekiel's famous vision of the idyllic new age begins with the promise "I will make with them a covenant of peace and banish wild animals from the land" (Ezek 34:25, see also Isa 35:9). But other promise oracles imagine a peaceable kingdom, where "the wolf shall live with the lamb, the leopard shall lie down with the kid" (Isa 11:6; see also 65:17-25).

The peaceable kingdom motif of the prophets, which is itself a recapitulation of the creation story, is part of the deep background of the brief account of the temptation of Jesus in Mark 1:13: "He was in the wilderness forty days, tempted by Satan; and he was with the wild beasts; and the angels waited on him." This tender scene suggests that Jesus, the new Adam, returned through the wilderness and through the alienation and hostility among creatures introduced in Gen 3 by the serpent (often seen by early interpreters as a satanic figure) to the peace that existed between wild beast and human being in the garden of Eden. *See* ANIMALS OF THE BIBLE; BEAST.

W. SIBLEY TOWNER

WILD BOAR [חֲזִיר khazir; ὗς hys, ὑός hyos]. The domesticated pig (*Sus scrofa*) is a descendant of the wild boar, although Hebrew and Greek terms do not distin-

guish between wild and domestic. The boar is characteristicly aggressive and dangerous (2 Esd 15:30), and it "ravages" the ground for food (Ps 80:13 [Heb. 80:14]). *See* ANIMALS OF THE BIBLE; SWINE.

WILD GOAT [אַקּוֹ ʾaqqo, יָעֵל yaʿel]. The wild goat (*Capra aegargus*) is a member of the Caprid family. The NRSV translates the term ʾaqqo (Deut 14:5) and the term yaʿel (1 Sam 24:2; Ps 104:18) as "wild goat." *See* ANIMALS OF THE BIBLE; IBEX.

WILD GOURDS. *See* GOURDS; PLANTS OF THE BIBLE.

WILD GRAPES. *See* GRAPES.

WILD OLIVE. *See* OLIVE, OLIVE TREE; PLANTS OF THE BIBLE.

WILD OX [רְאֵם reʾem; μονόκερως monokerōs]. The various spellings of the Hebrew reʾem are translated "wild ox" by the ASV and NRSV, while the KJV follows the LXX's "one horn" to render "unicorn." The horns of the wild ox often symbolized power (Num 23:22; 24:8; Deut 33:17; Pss 29:6; 92:10) or unruliness (Job 39:9). The domesticated cow evolved from one of two species of wild ox. *See* ANIMALS OF THE BIBLE; OX, OXEN.

Bibliography: Oded Borowski. *Every Living Thing: Daily Use of Animals in Ancient Israel* (1998).

ODED BOROWSKI

WILDERNESS [חָרְבָּה khorbah, יְשִׁימוֹן yeshimon, מִדְבָּר midhbar, עֲרָבָה ʾaravah, צִיָּה tsiyah, שָׂדֶה sadheh, שְׁמָמָה shemamah, תֹהוּ tohu; ἔρημος erēmos]. *Wilderness* denotes a range of landscapes, from open plains and rugged mountains offering seasonal pasturage, to scrub or nearly barren desert, to scorched, toxic land incapable of supporting vegetation. The term typically refers to unsettled and uncultivated land, the natural habitation of wild animals but not of humans, a place through which shepherds and Bedouin pass following pasturage and travelers hasten to safer havens.

A. Wilderness Terminology
B. Wilderness as Place and as Symbol
  1. In the Old Testament
    a. The wilderness sojourn
    b. *Wilderness* used without reference to the wilderness sojourn
      i. Negative associations
      ii. Ambiguous and positive associations
  2. In the New Testament
Bibliography

A. Wilderness Terminology

The OT uses a number of Hebrew words to designate wilderness, of which midhbar is the most common.

It is used most frequently to refer to the wilderness through which the Israelites wandered on their journey to Canaan or to some other definite, but unnamed, wilderness. It occurs in a genitival relationship with a proper name: "the wilderness of X," e.g., "the wilderness of Sin" (Exod 16:1) or "the wilderness of Sinai" (Exod 19:1). Midhbar can refer to semi-arid, unsettled and uncultivated land with pasturage sufficient to support migratory flocks and herds (e.g., Gen 36:24; Ps 65:12 [Heb. 65:13]). ʿAravah designates an arid, infertile plain. When referring to the rift valley north and (rarely) south of the Dead Sea, the word is almost always transliterated as a proper noun, ARABAH. In genitival relationships it designates "the sea of the Arabah" (the DEAD SEA; e.g., Deut 3:17), "the way of the Arabah" (2 Sam 4:7), and "the Wadi Arabah" (Amos 6:14). When treated as a common noun, it is sometimes translated "plain" (Deut 1:1; Zech 14:10). Sadheh, while almost always translated "field," is also used to designate wilderness about 10 percent of the time. This is clearest when it is synonymous with midhbar (Josh 8:24; Isa 43:20; Ezek 29:5; Joel 1:19).

Shemamah and yeshimon designate a wasteland or a desolation, usually a destroyed land or city (e.g., 2 Kgs 22:19; Jer 12:10). Yeshimon also occurs as a synonym for "the wilderness" of the sojourn (Deut 32:10; Pss 68:7 [Heb. 68:8]; 78:40; 106:14) and of the second exodus (Isa 43:19, 20) as well as the proper name of a place in the Arabah at the northwest end of the Dead Sea (e.g., 1 Sam 23:19, 24; see JESHIMON). Khorbah refers to land naturally dry and desolate (Ps 102:6 [Heb. 102:7]) or, most frequently, to land or cities destroyed by war. Tsiyah describes either land plagued by drought or a permanent desert and is often used in conjunction with midhbar, ʿaravah, or shemamah (Ps 107:33-35; Isa 35:1; Jer 50:12-13; Hos 2:3 [Heb. 2:5]; Zeph 2:13). Tohu denotes a trackless wilderness (Job 6:18; 12:24; Ps 107:40).

The SEPTUAGINT uses erēmos primarily to translate midhbar as well as many of the other Hebrew terms. The NT uses erēmos as an adjective modifying topos (τόπος), "a lonely/abandoned/desolate place."

B. Wilderness as Place and as Symbol

Wilderness usually designates a place, but it is also an evocative symbol with layers of meaning. There is a tensive relationship among these layers, especially in the OT where the ambivalence of the symbolism is most apparent. The ambivalence probably arises from varied sociological realities and historical experiences, as well as from fundamental archetypes (Leal). Broadly, *wilderness* connotes unstructured space and time; its opposites are garden, city, the seasons, and the feasts and fasts. The biblical story moves from primal chaos and wilderness (Gen 1:2; 2:5) to a physically and temporally organized cosmos (Gen 1) and a garden (Gen 2–3). Human sin leads to exile from the garden into a wilderness where humans must labor to create order.

Eschatological salvation is pictured as a return either to a garden land (Jer 31:12; Hos 14:4-7 [Heb. 14:5-8]) or to an idealized city at the center of a restored earth (Isa 24–27; Jer 31; Ezek 40–47; Rev 21:1–22:5). The mythic polarity of chaos versus cosmos and of wilderness versus garden/city informs the depictions of judgment and salvation throughout the Bible and defines the shape of human purpose and hope.

The Bible never romanticizes the wilderness (as is typical of some Christian monastic traditions and modern environmentalist thought). Except when using it for pasturage or travel, biblical characters seek out the wilderness primarily as a refuge from persecution or as a place to prepare for the advent of God's kingdom. Although the wilderness has mainly negative associations (Talmon), it is sometimes represented positively, especially as a place of new beginnings. As such, *wilderness* denotes both a place and an existential condition. It is a zone of liminality where individuals or groups encounter existential limits and where they are tested and transformed through numinous encounter (Oropeza). For humans, wilderness is a passageway, not a destination.

1. In the Old Testament

a. The wilderness sojourn. The wilderness is preeminently the place of the forty-year sojourn, and the most frequent and significant references to wilderness in the OT pertain to Israel's experiences there. Israel was decisively formed in the wilderness. There God's name, Yahweh, was revealed to Moses. There God saved Israel at the Red Sea in a paradigmatic act of deliverance. There Israel tested—and was tested by—God. There God chose Israel and made with it the covenant that would define the shape of its existence. There Israel received God's law and almost all the elements of its cultic life: the ark of the covenant, the tabernacle (archetype of the later Temple), its most important holy days, and the orders, rituals, and privileges of its priests. The bulk of the Pentateuch—almost all of Exodus through Deuteronomy—is devoted to retelling these events.

The wilderness sojourn has many negative associations, of course. Deuteronomy characterizes the wilderness itself as a "great and terrible wilderness, an arid wasteland with poisonous snakes and scorpions" (8:15) and a "howling wilderness waste" (32:10; see also 1:19; 2:7). The main source of negative associations, however, is Israel's rebellion and its consequences. In the wilderness Israel lacked food and water, complained against Moses and the Lord, threatened to return to Egypt, failed to act in obedient trust and enter Canaan, and suffered various punishments meted out by God. The wilderness story, contrasting God's gracious provision and protection with Israel's faithlessness, apostasy, and rebellion, decisively shaped Israel's identity, and summary retellings of the wilderness sojourn served as a lens through which the nation's later experiences were interpreted (Neh 9:9-21; Pss 78:12-41; 106;

2 Esd 1:12-22). Occasionally, only the positive aspects of the wilderness sojourn are summarized (Pss 68:7-10 [Heb. 68:8-11]; 105:26-45).

Prophetic rhetoric also appeals to the wilderness sojourn. In language reminiscent of Deuteronomy, Jeremiah characterizes the wilderness as a terrible place, "a land of deserts and pits ... a land of drought and deep darkness" (2:6). The prophets admonish Israel for its past and present faithlessness by contrasting God's gracious provision in the wilderness with Israel's faithlessness and disobedience. Sometimes the wilderness represents a good start that went bad (Isa 63:7-14; Jer 2:2-3; Hos 13:5-6; Amos 2:10) and sometimes a bad start that never improved (Jer 7:23-25; Ezek 20:1-38). Since the wilderness represents the crucial starting point, the place God "found" Israel (Ezek 16:5-8; Hos 9:10; compare Deut 32:10), nurtured her, and formed a covenant with her, it also represents a fitting place to start over. Back in the wilderness, God will purify Israel (Ezek 20:33-38) or woo her a second time as a bride (Hos 2:14-20 [Heb. 2:16-22]; 12:9).

In the exilic period the idea of a new beginning blossoms into an extravagant vision of a second exodus through a wilderness made lush as a garden and safe from wild animals (Isa 35; 40–55; Jer 23:7-8; 31:7-12). A new covenant will be made (Jer 31:31-34; 32:36-41), and Judah and Jerusalem will be transformed from a wilderness to an edenic garden land (Ezek 36:8-12, 33-36).

b. *Wilderness* used without reference to the wilderness sojourn. Apart from contexts in which the wilderness sojourn is thematic, wilderness has associations boding both good and ill for humans. Occasionally, the positive and negative associations blend in an ambiguous rendering of the wilderness.

i. Negative associations. The wilderness is a dangerous and disorienting place, avoided by humans, and it is the source of destructive winds. Humans do not normally live in the wilderness (Job 38:26), except as brigands who survive by robbing, raiding, and kidnapping (Job 24:2-9). Jeremiah characterizes the wilderness as "a land in which no one lives, and through which no mortal passes" (51:43), and "a land of thick darkness" (2:31). The wilderness can bewilder; disoriented travelers "wander in trackless wastes" until they perish (Ps 107:40; see also Job 6:18; 12:24). When Israel reverses its course, the Lord predicts Pharaoh will conclude, "They are wandering aimlessly in the land; the wilderness has closed in on them" (Exod 14:3). From the wilderness come scorching, destructive winds (Isa 21:1; Jer 4:11-12; Hos 13:15). Such winds occasionally symbolize the judgment of God scattering the people into exile (Isa 27:8; Jer 13:24; 18:17).

The wilderness is the haunt of wild animals and demons. Predatory animals such as jackals, lions, vipers, ostriches, hawks, hedgehogs, owls, and ravens prowl there (Exod 23:29; Isa 30:6; 34:9-15; 35:9; 43:20; Lam 4:3; Mal 1:3). Demonic creatures are there, too,

especially in ruined cities. AZAZEL is perhaps the best-known representative of this clan (Lev 16:8, 10; *1 En.* 10:4), but Isaiah mentions others: goat-demons, fiery flying serpents, and LILITH (13:21-22; 30:6; 34:8-15; compare 4 Macc 18:8). The listing of demonic beings alongside wild animals suggests that the two classes were not entirely separate in the ancient mind; both are associated in the Bible and ANE texts with forces inimical to the created order (*see* DEMON). The association of demonic beings with the wilderness appears also in the NT (Matt 12:43; Mark 5:1-20; Luke 8:26-33). The Lord's assault upon Moses in the wilderness and Jacob's struggle with an angel at the Jabbok reinforce the association between the wilderness and numinous dangers (Gen 32:22-32 [Heb. 32:23-33]; Exod 4:24-26).

Under God's judgment, the ordered world returns to wilderness. Wilderness can be described as tohu ("waste"), a place whose disorder is inimical to humans (Deut 32:10; Job 6:18; 12:24; Ps 107:40). In response to sin, God allows the cosmos to dissolve into chaos, returning it to its primal state (tohu wavohu [תֹהוּ וָבֹהוּ], "waste and void"; Jer 4:23-28; compare Gen 1:2; Isa 24; see also the contrasting of wilderness and Eden, Isa 51:3; Joel 2:3). Divine judgment makes a wilderness of cities (Isa 13:19-22; 14:17; 27:10; 64:10 [Heb. 64:9]; Jer 9:11 [Heb. 9:10]; 22:6) and of whole nations (Jer 50:12; Zeph 2:9). Depopulated land becomes a desolation for purely natural reasons as well (Exod 23:29).

ii. Ambiguous and positive associations. The wilderness is a place of testing, revelation, and promise. The wilderness—especially a wilderness mountain—is often associated with theophanies. Abraham passes God's test on a mountain in the land of Moriah and there receives God's promise of blessing (Gen 22). The frightened and despondent Elijah journeys to Horeb, where God reassures and instructs him (1 Kgs 19; compare Mark 9:2-13). Wilderness theophanies not involving a mountain include Jacob's vision/audition at Bethel (Gen 28:10-22) and at the Jabbok (Gen 32:22-32 [Heb. 32:23-33]; see also 32:2), and the exiled slave Hagar's two encounters (Gen 16:7-14; 20:15-19). The Jacob and Hagar stories share common themes: flight from troubled clan relationships, a journey through the wilderness, life-threatening dangers, a promise of blessing and descendants, and etiology. These themes appear with a puzzling twist in the story of the Lord's attempt on Moses' (his son's?) life (Exod 4:24-26).

The wilderness is Yahweh's original home. Several texts imply that the Lord is uniquely present in, or originates from, the wilderness south of Palestine. The Lord first appears to Moses in the wilderness of Sinai and there reveals the divine name (*see* GOD, NAMES OF). Moses demands that Pharaoh allow Israel to go into the wilderness to offer sacrifices to the Lord (Exod 5:1-3; 8:25-28). Several poetic texts, including Judg 5, a text of great antiquity, describe the Lord as "the One of Sinai," who "went out from Seir ... from the region of Edom" (Judg 5:4-5) or "from Teman ... from Mount

Paran" (Hab 3:3; see also Deut 33:2), all places in or near the wilderness of Sinai. The Lord is "the God of Sinai" who leads Israel through the wilderness to where he is enthroned on Mount Zion, a march reenacted in a processional liturgy (Ps 68:7-8, 17-18 [Heb. 68:8-9, 18-19]). Elijah's journey to Horeb, "the mountain of God," suggests that the Lord could be considered to inhabit the desert mountain in the time of the monarchy (1 Kgs 19:4-18). Quite possibly certain semi-nomadic groups loosely associated with Israel maintained the worship of the Lord as a wilderness deity (see KENITES; RECHAB, RECHABITES).

The wilderness will be transformed. The negative aspects of wilderness will be overcome on the day of salvation (Isa 32:15-16). A prominent sign of God's restoration of the earth will involve the removal or rendering benign of wild animals (Isa 11:6-9; 43:20; 65:25; Ezek 34:25-26, 28; Hos 2:18-19 [Heb. 2:20-21]) or chaos beasts (Isa 27:1; Dan 7; 1 En. 60:7-8). With the return from exile in view, the prophets promise that rough wilderness terrain will be made smooth, infertile soil will yield food, and arid places will be well watered (Isa 35:1; 40:3-4; 41:18-20; 55:12-13; Jer 31:9).

In Job, the wilderness is the object of God's delight and care. Although terms for wilderness appear infrequently in Job, the symbolism associated with wilderness plays a prominent role in the divine speeches. Job accuses God of having created a physically and morally disordered world (9:4-7, 22-24), and God answers by showcasing creatures of the wilderness and showing delight in the ways of all wild creatures, be they fierce, violent, perverse, cruel, or majestically terrifying (38:39–39:30; compare Ps 104:14-30). Surprisingly, the primordial beasts BEHEMOTH and LEVIATHAN, the mighty chaos monsters, are portrayed as God's greatest achievements and great delight, rather than as enemies of God and cosmic order (40:15–41:34, especially 40:19 and 41:33-34; similarly "the sea" in 38:8-11 symbolizes chaos; see COSMOGONY, COSMOLOGY; CREATION). Wilderness, wild creatures, and chaos beasts are presented not as inimical to the ordered world but as a divinely ordained part of it and the object of God's special care (38:8-9, 26; 39:6). God offers Job a perspective from which God's power, wisdom, and blessing are expressed in the domain of wilderness just as much as they are in the world ordered for human benefit and purposes.

The wilderness also serves as a home or a refuge for some. Ishmael makes his home in the wilderness of PARAN, presumably a place with game since his expertise with a bow is noted (Gen 21:20-21). Life in the wilderness, although a blighted existence (Jer 17:6), is preferable to one full of domestic strife (Prov 21:19). The wilderness is a place of retreat or exile for those who are persecuted by enemies or disenfranchised by the current regime (Ps 55:6-8 [Heb. 55:7-9]; Jer 9:2 [Heb. 9:1]). David, e.g., gathered a small army of mal-

contents in the wilderness (1 Sam 22:1-2), as did Judas Maccabeus (1 Macc 2:27-38; 2 Macc 5:27).

2. In the New Testament

In the Greco-Roman period, Palestinian Jews sometimes retreated to the wilderness for ascetic purification, often conceived as preparation for the messianic age. Josephus became an ascetic for a time (Life 11), and the separatist community at QUMRAN lived as ascetics "preparing the way in the wilderness" through repentance (4Q171 II, 11; III, 1), studying Torah (1QS VIII, 13–15; IV, 19–20), and preparing for battles that are to precede the messianic age (1QM I, 2–3; see Talmon). Many Jews cherished messianic expectations similar to those of the Qumran sectarians. Popular eschatology held that deliverance would begin in the wilderness where the Messiah would first appear (Matt 24:26; Acts 21:38; Ant. 20.167; J.W. 2.259–63; 7.437–38). This is the context for understanding John the Baptist, whom the Gospels cast as a latter-day Elijah crying in the wilderness, "Prepare the way of the Lord" (Mark 1:3). John was considered the forerunner of the Messiah, calling Israel to repentance (Matt 11:14; 17:12; Mark 1:2-8; 9:12-13; Luke 1:13-17; see Isa 40:3; Mal 3:1; 4:5 [Heb. 3:23]). Luke adds that John even grew up in the wilderness (1:80). The Revelation of John also plays on the connection between the wilderness and eschatology. The revelator sees "a woman clothed with the sun" (12:1; the mother of the Messiah and the saints), who flees to the wilderness to escape the persecution of the red dragon (i.e., Satan; 12:6, 14). Later, he is shown "the whore of Babylon" (Rome) astride a seven-headed beast in the wilderness (17:1-6, 15).

Where the NT refers explicitly to the Pentateuch's wilderness narratives, an apologetic (John 3:14; 6:25-59; Acts 7:17-50; 13:18) or hortatory (1 Cor 10:1-11; Heb 2:1-4; 3:7–4:13; 12:18-29) concern is apparent. Stephen's apologetic rendering of Israel's history in Acts 7 makes an implicit comparison between the Jews' rejection of Jesus and Israel's rebellion against Moses in the wilderness. First Corinthians and Hebrews both use Israel's wilderness rebellion and punishment to exhort Christians against unbelief and idolatry, and to present Christian discipleship as a recapitulation of Israel's testing in the wilderness with all of its dangers and promises. As part of his midrash on Deut 32, Paul claims that Christ was "the spiritual rock" that followed Israel in the wilderness (1 Cor 10:4).

The Synoptics implicitly associate Jesus' wilderness experiences with those of Israel and Elijah. Jesus' quotations of Scripture during the wilderness temptation compare his obedience with Israel's failure (Matt 4:4, 7, 10 draw on Deut 8:3; 6:16; and 6:13, respectively; // Luke 4:1-13). In the wilderness, Jesus—like Israel—hears God speak to him from heaven (Mark 1:9-11; see Exod 20:22). Like Elijah, Jesus was in the wilderness forty days, attended by angels (Mark 1:13; 1 Kgs 19:5-8; for manna as "bread of angels" see Ps 78:25; Wis

16:20). In the wilderness Jesus miraculously provided bread and meat for thousands (Matt 14:13-21; 15:32-39), and he taught his disciples to pray "Give us this day our daily bread," an apparent allusion to the manna tradition (Matt 6:11//Luke 11:3).

The Gospel of John connects Jesus to the wilderness traditions more explicitly than does the synoptic tradition. Just as Moses lifted up the serpent in the wilderness (Num 21:8-9), so too must the Son of Man be lifted up on the cross (John 3:14-15). Jesus not only supplies but is himself manna and water, providing eternal rather than transitory sustenance (John 4:7-15; 6:35). The water Jesus offers symbolizes the eschatological bestowal of the Spirit (John 7:37-39, drawing on Isa 44:3; 55:1).

Elsewhere in the Gospels, with no obvious typology intended, the writers record that Jesus withdraws to the wilderness to teach ever-growing crowds (Mark 1:45), to rest alone (Matt 14:13; Luke 4:42; John 6:15) or with his disciples (Mark 6:31-32), or to pray (Mark 1:35//Luke 5:16; on "the mountain," Matt 14:23; Mark 6:46; Luke 6:12). *See* BEER-SHEBA; BETH-AVEN; DAMASCUS; DESERT; EDOM, EDOMITES; ETHAM; ISRAEL, GEOGRAPHY OF; JERUEL; JUDAH, WILDERNESS OF; KADESH, KADESH-BARNEA; KEDEMOTH; MAON; MOAB, MOABITES; SHUR, WILDERNESS OF; SINAI, MOUNT; TEKOA; ZIN, WILDERNESS OF; ZIPH, ZIPHITES.

Bibliography: Susan Power Bratton. *Christianity, Wilderness, and Wildlife* (1993); Robert Funk. "The Wilderness." *JBL* 78 (1959) 205–14; Robert Barry Leal. *Wilderness in the Bible: Toward a Theology of Wilderness* (2004); Ulrich Mauser. *Christ in the Wilderness: The Wilderness Theme in the Second Gospel and Its Basis in the Biblical Tradition* (1963); Ranen Omer-Sherman. *Israel in Exile: Jewish Writing and the Desert* (2006); B. J. Oropeza. "Apostasy in the Wilderness: Paul's Message to the Corinthians in a State of Eschatological Liminality." *JSNT* 22 (2000) 69–86; R. S. Sugirtharajah, ed. *Wilderness: Essays in Honour of Frances Young* (2005); Shemaryahu Talmon. "The Desert Motif in the Bible and Qumran Literature." *Biblical Motifs: Origins and Transformations.* A. Altmann, ed. (1966) 31–63; John Wright. "Spirit and Wilderness: The Interplay of Two Motifs within the Hebrew Bible as a Background to Mark 1:2-13." *Perspectives on Language & Text.* Edgar Conrad and Edward Newing, eds. (1987) 269–98.

BRIAN C. JONES

WILDERNESS OF PARAN. *See* PARAN.

WILDERNESS OF SHUR. *See* SHUR, WILDERNESS OF.

WILDERNESS OF SIN. *See* SIN, WILDERNESS OF.

WILDERNESS OF SINAI. *See* SINAI PENINSULA.

WILDERNESS OF ZIN. *See* ZIN, WILDERNESS OF.

WILDERNESS OF ZIPH. *See* ZIPH, ZIPHITES.

WILL [חֵפֶץ khefets, חָפֵץ khafets; αἱρετίζω hairetizō, βούλομαι boulomai, ἐκλεκτός eklektos, θέλημα thelēma, θέλω thelō, πρᾶγμα pragma]. The desire or inclination to bring about something (e.g., 1 Kgs 10:9; 2 Chr 9:8; Ps 40:8; Mal 1:10; Matt 8:3; Mark 1:41; Rom 1:13). *Will*, in both the OT and NT, can be defined as "desire," "delight," or "pleasure." In the OT, God makes known the divine desire, or will, to Israel (Ps 103:7); it is up to the righteous in Israel to do God's will (Ps 103:21). The righteous person asks God continually to teach him or her how to do God's will (Ps 143:10; 2 Macc 1:3). For those who fulfill God's desire there is great reward (4 Macc 18:16). The OT makes it clear that God does not force the divine will on people. Isaiah 58:3 suggests that humans have a selfish will and are prone to do evil (Isa 58:3; Jer 23:17; Sir 32:17).

The NT use refers to the "will of God" for humanity, especially in the life of Christ (Matt 7:21; John 4:34; 5:30; Heb 10:7). Old Testament themes also appear in the NT: God's will for humans is to be holy (1 Thess 4:3); to do right (1 Pet 2:15); to give thanks in all things (1 Thess 5:18); to know the will of God (Eph 5:17). The NT declares that there is a "will" of Satan ("devil" in 2 Tim 2:26), in which unbelievers can become ensnared. Those who follow God's will are promised reward (1 John 2:17; Heb 10:36); at the same time, they also may suffer (1 Pet 4:19; Heb 10:7, 9). *See* DESIRE; WILL OF GOD.

ARCHIE T. WRIGHT

WILL OF GOD. The concept of the will of God stands at the confluence of numerous biblical references to God's words, actions, and thoughts, as well as such feelings as pleasure and displeasure. That God is purposeful, that God's will stands behind the existence of the cosmos and progression of history, and that God's will makes possible and invites, even demands, human response in conformity with the divine purpose—these convictions are axiomatic in the Scriptures. This is true even if these convictions are not developed as explicitly as we who are temporally removed from the writing of the OT and NT books might wish.

The importance of discerning and performing God's will was assumed in the OT, and this conviction was both assumed for Jewish readers of the NT materials and cultivated among Gentile readers. Indeed, according to the Gospel of Matthew, Jesus taught his disciples to pray, "Your will be done, on earth as it is in heaven" (Matt 6:10), and the synoptic Gospels portray Jesus himself as exemplifying this central disposition in his anguished prayer on the eve of his crucifixion (Matt 26:36-46; Mark 14:32-42; Luke 22:39-46).

It is not too much to say that the biblical materials are bent on articulating and bearing witness to God's will wherever they speak of God's character, performative word, and responses to God's creation. God's ways are often understood in contrast to human ways (e.g., Isa 55:8-9; Mark 8:31-33); this includes those texts wherein God's will is said to be at work even through the contrary ways of human beings (e.g., Gen 50:20; Acts 3:13-18). That is, God's will is marked by such power and flexibility that both the faithfulness and faithlessness of humans contribute to its actualization (see Caird and Hurst). More pervasively, God's will surfaces as the aim or telos (goal) of creation and, thus, serves as the canon by which human faithfulness is measured. For the OT and NT, then, God's will is not portrayed as a detailed road map that must be followed meticulously, but rather as a call to a way of life marked by loving mercy, doing justice, and walking humbly with God (Mic 6:8; see Hos 12:6)—or, in other central formulations, by loving God and neighbor (e.g., Deut 6:4-5; Lev 19:18; Mark 12:29-33) and by the words of the Sermon on the Mount, "In everything do to others as you would have them do to you; for this is the law and the prophets" (Matt 7:12; compare Luke 6:31).

A. Will of God in the Old Testament
    1. Terminology and related motifs
    2. Discerning and performing the will of God
B. Will of God in the New Testament
    1. Terminology and related motifs
    2. Discerning and performing the will of God
Bibliography

A. Will of God in the Old Testament
1. Terminology and related motifs

The language connoting the divine will is extensive and it is possible here only to examine briefly some of the more obvious terms of relevance. No "theology of God's will" could be limited to these terms, since God's people refer to God's will both explicitly and implicitly in many and varied ways. On the other hand, examination of these terms evidences both the variety of motifs inextricably tied to the OT witness to the divine will and the degree to which Israel has represented God's planning and volition with anthropomorphic images.

Old Testament writers use a variety of terms to connote God's purposefulness, intent, or planning (e.g., zamam זָמַם, khashav חָשַׁב, mezimmah מְזִמָּה, makhashavah מַחֲשָׁבָה, ʿatsar עָצַר, yaʿats יָעַץ, ʿetsah עֵצָה). References to God's plans are typically tied to specific situations (e.g., with reference to Babylon [Jer 51:12]) and cannot be generalized. What can be generalized, however, is that God's plans cannot be thwarted; they will surely be actualized. In the accomplishment of God's purpose, God can even make use of the counterplanning of humans, as in Joseph's words to his brothers, which provide an epitome of his own story: "Even though you intended to do harm to me, God intended it for good, in order to preserve a numerous people, as he is doing today" (Gen 50:20). Elsewhere, human

plans may be just (Prov 12:5), but even the best human plans depend for their success on God's agenda. "The human mind may devise many plans, but it is the purpose of the LORD that will be established" (Prov 19:21; compare Prov 16:9). At the same time, God's plans can undermine or counter human plans that run against God's will (e.g., Ps 33:10-11; Mic 2:1-5). When God calls the people to repentance, God does so by calling them to acknowledge the utter distinction between human planning and God's own and to recognize that the divine purpose will be realized (Isa 55:6-11).

Old Testament writers use a variety of terms to connote God's "taking pleasure" or "having favor" (e.g., ratsah רָצָה, ratson רָצוֹן, khafets חָפֵץ, khefets חֵפֶץ, yaʾal יָאַל, ʾawah אָוָה, ʾawah אַוָּה). Attributing the freedom of choice assumed to be characteristic of humans to God, some texts ground God's choices in desire, as in Ps 132:13-14: "For the LORD has chosen Zion; he has desired it for his habitation: 'This is my resting place forever; here I will reside, for I have desired it'" (compare Job 23:13-14). God's freedom is unlimited, except by God's own character: "he does whatever he pleases" (Ps 115:3; compare Ps 135:6). (This is not true of idols [Ps 115:4-7], whose impotence is thus contrasted with God's freedom and power.) This is the God who delights in loving-kindness (e.g., Mic 7:18), and who calls on God's people to desire the same.

To speak of God's good pleasure is to attribute to God a human-like "inner life." This is a useful anthropomorphism that weaves together the content of God's will with God's care and concern for God's people. God thus takes delight in David (1 Chr 28:4) and in God's servant (Isa 42:1), as well as in those who fear God (Ps 147:10-11), in uprightness (1 Chr 29:17), and so on.

Old Testament materials sometimes refer to God's will in relation to individuals or a people by speaking of God's pleasure or delight in them. "If the LORD is pleased with us [that is, if it is God's will], he will bring us into this land and give it to us, a land that flows with milk and honey" (Num 14:8). As an expression of God's righteousness, God wills the welfare of his oppressed servant (Ps 35:27-28).

In Isa 40–55, God's desire or pleasure is expressed in God's will, which is articulated both in terms of exile and suffering and in terms of subsequent liberation and restoration (see especially Isa 42; 49). God's purpose can be brought about by means of God's chosen shepherd, Cyrus; "he shall carry out all my purpose" (Isa 44:28), specifically vis-à-vis God's purpose with Babylon (Isa 48:14). At the same time, it is through the Lord's suffering servant that "the will of the LORD shall prosper" (Isa 53:10). The prophetic word will not fail, says the Lord, "but it shall accomplish that which I purpose, and succeed in the thing for which I sent it" (Isa 55:11). With respect to the coming deliverance and salvation, the judgment against eunuchs (Deut 23:1) will be overturned, provided that they are those who "keep my sabbaths, who choose the things that please me and hold fast my covenant ..." (Isa 56:4). These texts exemplify how God partners with human beings, including persons outside the covenant, to accomplish the divine will; how God calls upon persons to make God's will their own; and how suffering in relation to God's purpose can serve as a means by which God's will comes to fruition.

The Lord's unwillingness to destroy Israel in the wilderness (Deut 10:10) or to pardon the obdurate among God's people (29:20; compare 2 Kgs 24:4) is expressed by ʾavah (אָבָה), with the sense "to be willing."

More significant for understanding the OT concept of the will of God is the use of the term lev (לֵב), often translated "heart," connoting the center of volition and motivation, and the locus of conceiving and planning activity. When the OT makes reference to Yahweh's HEART, it indicates again the tendency to think of God in anthropomorphic terms. God's "heart" is the seat of decision making when God determines "never again [to] curse the ground because of humankind" (Gen 8:21), just as, earlier, God's grieving in his heart on account of human wickedness had led to God's declaration, "I will blot out from the earth the human beings I have created—people together with animals and creeping things and birds of the air, for I am sorry that I have made them" (Gen 6:5-7). From his heart, the Lord reveals and accomplishes the divine plan (e.g., 2 Sam 7:21; 1 Chr 17:19). God's determination to restore and covenant with the people has its grounding in God's "heart and ... soul" (Jer 32:41). Given the collocation of God's heart and God's will (e.g., Ps 33:11), it is no surprise that idolatry stands in opposition to God's heart (Jer 7:31; 19:5 [NRSV "mind"]). God's heart becomes the norm by which to gauge human faithfulness—that is, a person after God's own heart is one who does God's will (e.g., 1 Sam 13:14; Jer 3:15; compare 1 Sam 2:35; 2 Kgs 10:30).

2. Discerning and performing the will of God

If following in the ways of God is the *sine qua non* for covenant faithfulness among God's people, then knowledge of the divine will is crucial. Certain avenues for accessing God's will are forbidden, however, including the practice of sorcery, augury, and soothsaying; and seeking help from mediums and wizards, as well as from false interpreters of dreams and pseudo-prophets. These practices signify disloyalty to Yahweh (compare Deut 10:11-13; 13; 1 Sam 28; 2 Kgs 21:6; 2 Chr 33:6). God's people are to be set apart from the peoples around them. Thus, in a programmatic statement that would have significant repercussions for understanding the later significance of Jesus, we read, "Although these nations that you are about to dispossess do give heed to soothsayers and diviners, as for you, the LORD your God does not permit you to do so. The LORD your God will raise up for you a prophet like me from among your own people; you shall heed such a prophet" (Deut 18:14-15; compare Mark 9:7; Luke 7:16; Acts 3:22-26).

Of course, this means that God would make his ways known by means of prophets, just as God also communicated at times by means of dreams and their interpretation (e.g., Gen 41). This required the development of criteria by which to adjudicate between true and false prophecy (e.g., Deut 13; 18:19-22; Jer 28:9). True prophets, according to Jeremiah, stand in the council of God and proclaim God's words to God's people; accordingly, the Lord can ask, "Am I a God near by ... and not a God far off?" (23:23). As a whole, the prophets defined the will of God in terms of a mutually reinforcing relationship among justice, mercy, and the knowledge of God (*see* PROPHET, PROPHECY). We find a telling précis of this prophetic ethos in Mic 6:8: "He has told you, O mortal, what is good; and what does the LORD require of you but to do justice, and to love kindness, and to walk humbly with your God?"

One can also speak of knowing God's purpose through Israel's story (How does the narrator represent God's dispositions and responses to human activity? What view of reality does the OT narrative underwrite and promulgate?); through TORAH—that is, the teaching attributed to Moses, woven together as it is with the account of God's saving acts on behalf of Israel and, thus, deeply rooted in and indicative of the covenantal relations of God and God's people (see, e.g., Exod 19–24; Pss 1; 19:7-14; 119; *see* COVENANT, OT AND NT); and by reflection on the world that bears witness to the nature of the God who created it (see, e.g., Prov 3:19-20). The profundity of Torah rests to a large degree on the way that legal materials are embedded within the story of God's self-revelation. Thus, e.g., the enumeration of the TEN COMMANDMENTS in Exod 20:1-17 is prefaced with God's self-disclosure: "I am the LORD your God, who brought you out of the land of Egypt, out of the house of slavery" (Exod 20:2), which is itself set within the covenant narrative of Exod 19–24. God thus reveals the divine nature at the same time that God imparts to Israel the law. *Torah* itself refers to teaching or instruction—a way of life drawn from the divine nature and will, and that puts on display the divine nature and will.

According to the OT's Wisdom literature, the natural and the social realms are ordered such that certain acts yield predictable consequences. Thus, e.g., "The wage of the righteous leads to life, the gain of the wicked to sin" (Prov 10:16). This is the world that God has made, so it is an expression of God's will, which to recognize and to follow is nothing less than the "fear of the LORD." That God's will is anchored in the cosmos itself permeates Wisdom literature (*see* WISDOM IN THE OT). However, whereas Proverbs is typically happy to associate righteous behavior with happiness and hard work with wealth, both Job and Ecclesiastes recognize that the patterns of cause-and-effect are not so straightforward; these latter books thus press the question of how to make sense of suffering and evil among the righteous.

Many readers of the OT today face particular obstacles when turning to these Scriptures to understand the will of God. They might wrongly imagine that the OT teaches that everything that happens is God's will, e.g., that God has a set plan for humanity or for individuals, that God's plans are detailed blueprints, or, in the case of Torah, that God's will takes the form of a legalistic code of behavior. If these are inappropriate ways of thinking about the divine will in the OT, what better represents its witness to the will of God? The OT speaks irreducibly to purposefulness in God's creative and redeeming activity so that the very existence of the cosmos and of a people called to serve God must be understood in terms of their *telos* (goal). If this *telos* is known, however, this is not to say that each step along the way has been predetermined. The particular character of God's will is shaped in relation to unfolding circumstances, with God's activity in the context of flood and temple-building and exile, to name only three examples, not so much preplanned agenda but context-specific outworking of the original aim God has set for God's CREATION and God's people. This means that God is neither the god of Deism who watches comfortably and untouched from a rocking chair the machinations of humans in the world, nor a frantic micromanager barking prearranged orders so as to orchestrate every human move. It also means that God's will is at once both constant and changing in relation to the actions, needs, and concerns of human beings, and that not everything (e.g., oppression and suffering) is an outworking of God's will. For the OT, the ways of God are expressions of God's own character and, therefore, are oriented toward the flourishing of human life and human communities within the context of the world God has made (*see* GOD, OT VIEW OF).

B. Will of God in the New Testament
1. Terminology and related motifs

Direct references to the will of God in the NT make use of only a couple of terms –thelō/thelēma (θέλω/θέλημα, "to want" or "to desire" / "that which is desired") and boulomai/boulēma/boulē (βούλομαι/βούλημα/βουλή, "to want" or "to purpose" / "desire" or "intention" / "purpose" or "plan"). For example, in the Gospel of Matthew, Jesus teaches his followers to pray, "Your will be done, on earth as it is in heaven" (6:10), then himself prays, "[Y]our will be done" (26:42; see v. 39); later in the NT, James will urge those who make future plans to say, "If the Lord wishes, we will live and do this or that" (Jas 4:15). In each case, a form of thelō or thelēma is used. An especially interesting reference to God's will is found in Acts 20:27, where in his farewell address to the Ephesian elders Paul claims that he "did not shrink from declaring to you the whole purpose [boulē] of God." This statement is consistent with the pivotal role God plays in the narrative of Luke–Acts—the one whose will is being actualized in the narrative of Jesus and his witnesses and whose aims

drive the narrative forward. God's will is actualized in the movement of the gospel across ethnic and sociopolitical lines, and is the rough equivalent of the message of salvation to Jew and Gentile. Indeed, in this context, "declaring . . . the whole purpose of God" is set in parallel with "proclaiming the kingdom" (20:25).

Typically, the divine will serves as an invitation for and measure of human response, even a badge of discipleship. Jesus' "family," we learn, consists of those who do the will of God (Matt 12:50; compare 7:21). In 1 Pet 4:1-2, believers are called upon "to live for the rest of your earthly life no longer by human desires (epithymia ἐπιθυμία) but by the will of God." The contrast is between the epithymia of humans and the thelēma of God. Both terms can refer to "desire," but epithymia in ethical discourse typically carries such negative connotations as "insatiable cravings" or "lust" (Wis 4:12; 4 Macc 1:22; Rom 1:24; Jas 1:14-15; Plato *Phaedr.* 83b; Epictetus, *Discourses* 2.16.45; 2.18.8-9). (Note that 1 Pet 4:3 picks up on the motif of "human desires" by referring to "what the Gentiles like to do" [literally, "the will of the Gentiles," using the term boulēma] and then listing a series of immoral behaviors, another way of contrasting the will of God with the will of humans.) A similar distinction appears in Jas 4:13-17, where acknowledging that one's future rests on God's will is contrasted with prideful independence.

Numerous additional terms and motifs contribute to the NT portrait of the will of God. In Luke–Acts, e.g., the term dei (δεῖ, "it is necessary") can often, though not always, be read as "it is necessary according to God's will." The itinerant nature of Jesus' ministry is grounded in divine necessity; e.g., "I must (dei) proclaim the good news of the kingdom of God to the other cities also; for I was sent for this purpose" (Luke 4:43). Indeed, in the Gospel of Luke, Jesus' self-understanding is tied to the Scriptures (e.g., Luke 4:16-30) with the result that he portrays his messianic activity as the fulfillment of a series of divine "musts." However, this does not turn Jesus into a marionette whose movements are simply orchestrated by divine fiat. Instead, Jesus is himself an agent in the divine drama, whose willingness to embrace and embody God's will is central to the narrative; this is true throughout the narrative as Jesus lives out his mission as the obedient Son of God but is nowhere more transparent than in his prayer on the Mount of Olives: "Father, if you are willing, remove this cup from me; yet, not my will but yours be done" (Luke 22:42). Similarly, Saul/Paul is chosen as the instrument of the Lord, who "will show him how much he must suffer for the sake of my name" (Acts 9:16), but the ensuing narrative shows Paul actively discerning and following the missionary path set before him. By means of his will, then, God initiates, provokes, directs, and empowers, but the fulfillment of this divine necessity is tethered to faithful response (Cosgrove).

This emphasis on synergism (the interrelation of divine and human agency in the fulfillment of God's plan) does not mean that the divine will can be held hostage by those who oppose God's agenda, however. When announcing his betrayal, Jesus observes, "For the Son of Man is going as it has been determined (horizō ὁρίζω), but woe to that one by whom he is betrayed!" (Luke 22:22). Evidently, the betrayer acts on his own volition and is responsible for his treachery, but even this cannot detract from the ability of God to inscribe this element of the passion story into the narrative of the divine will. Indeed, the Markan parallel has it that "the Son of Man goes as it is written of him" (Mark 14:21; presumably an allusion to Ps 41:9; compare John 13:18), giving a scriptural background for the infidelity of one of Jesus' closest associates. God was not surprised by this betrayal, nor would it frustrate God's will. Indeed, in Peter's Pentecost address, the apostle declares that the passion of Jesus took place "according to the definite plan (horizo + boulē) and foreknowledge of God" (Acts 2:23; compare 4:27-28: proorizō [προορίζω], "to determine beforehand"). Elsewhere, in the wider Pauline corpus, the language of "determining beforehand" is used to mark God's past choice of believers "for adoption as his children through Jesus Christ, according to the good pleasure of his will" (Eph 1:5; compare 1:11).

God's will is also communicated through VISION, DREAM, and angelic visitation (*see* ANGEL); once in the NT through the casting of LOTS; and by means of prophets and the prophetic word (e.g., Acts 11:27-30; 21:10-11; 1 Cor 14; Rev 2–3). To cite a few examples, Joseph is directed by an angel of the Lord in a dream not to divorce Mary, his betrothed, but to marry her and to name her son Jesus (Matt 1:20-25), then receives further warnings and directives in dreams (Matt 2:12, 13, 19, 22). In Acts 10, the Gentile centurion Cornelius receives assurance and direction from an angel (vv. 3-6), and Peter receives puzzling instructions through a vision (vv. 9-16). In a classic case of divine-human partnership, God initiates and directs, but the outcome both for Cornelius (and his household) and for Peter rests on their obedience to the directives they receive from God. In Acts 1:15-26, a replacement for Judas is chosen through a process involving the articulation of required qualifications, the nomination of two candidates, prayer, and the casting of lots. Although God had forbidden practices of magic among his people (see above), the casting of lots was used to ascertain God's choice (e.g., Lev 16:18; Neh 11:1; compare the use of URIM AND THUMMIM, e.g., Exod 28:30; Num 27:21). Through the casting of lots, the intrusion of human desires could be bypassed in favor of ascertaining the divine will. Interestingly, when new leadership is selected again in Acts, the process moves from articulating the required qualifications to the choice of leaders to prayer and laying on of hands (6:1-7), and the practice of the casting of lots appears nowhere else in the NT. Why this is so is never explained, though we might imagine that the coming of the HOLY SPIRIT to empower and guide God's people (Acts 2) rendered re-

course to lot-casting unnecessary. Apparently, at times, the will of God is communicated directly by means of the Spirit—or, more likely, people regard the Spirit as standing behind or authorizing the communication of God's will, whether by a prophet (as is perhaps the case with the setting apart of Barnabas and Paul within a community that included prophets and teachers—Acts 13:1-2; compare vv. 3-4, where the pair are sent off by the church and by the Spirit) or by circumstances (e.g., Acts 16:6-7?).

More prominent is the voice of the Spirit heard through the Scriptures (e.g., Acts 1:16; 4:25; 28:25), or the work of the Spirit as the enabler of scriptural interpretation (e.g., Acts 2; the role of the Spirit in inspired exegesis is well known in the Second Temple period [e.g., Ezra 9:20; Josephus, *J.W.* 3.351–53; 1QS V, 9; 1QH IX, 11-13; see Levison). More pervasive, still, is the role of Israel's Scriptures, the OT, as witness to God's will. Simply put, Israel's Scriptures structured the NT witness to God so that God's will could be accessed above all through engagement with the OT (*see* AUTHORITY OF SCRIPTURE). Of course, for NT writers, these Scriptures did not stand alone but had to be read in relation to revelation of God in Jesus Christ. As a result, the OT Scriptures provide both context and content for making sense of Jesus, but Jesus' followers also needed to read these Scriptures in light of the advent, mission, death, and resurrection of Jesus. Thus, Jesus helps one makes sense of Israel's Scriptures. A passage near the end of Luke's Gospel clarifies: "Then he said to them, 'Oh, how foolish you are, and how slow of heart to believe all that the prophets have declared! Was it not necessary that the Messiah should suffer these things and then enter into his glory?' Then beginning with Moses and all the prophets, he interpreted to them the things about himself in all the scriptures" (Luke 24:25-27).

The dilemma Jesus' followers faced was not their lack of knowledge of Moses and the prophets, but their inability to correlate their knowledge of the Scriptures with the events surrounding Jesus. After his resurrection, then, Jesus does not provide them with new scriptures but with new understanding of their Scriptures. The end result is a two-way dialectic between Jesus and Israel's Scriptures, with both necessary for grasping the scriptural witness to the purpose of the God of Abraham and Sarah, the God who raised Jesus from the dead.

2. Discerning and performing the will of God

It will be clear from the data already sketched that the divine will is especially thematic for Luke–Acts. These two volumes, the Gospel of Luke and the Acts of the Apostles, provide the most explicit and full witness to this motif (see Caird and Hurst; Squires). Luke narrates the long-anticipated coming of God to bring to fruition the divine promise to Abraham, that Abraham would "be the ancestor of a multitude of nations" (Gen 17:4). It is of special interest that Luke works out the actualization of God's purpose in narrative form, since narrative has the effect of aligning its characters within the story (and inviting the readers of the story to align themselves) in relation to its central aim. This is because God's aim will not be achieved without resistance. If God's plan (for Luke–Acts) is to bring SALVATION in all of its fullness to all people, then persons align themselves either as helpers (or servants) of this aim or its opponents. Expressions of God's will for persons throughout the narrative, then, are set within the larger purpose of God to achieve this salvation, as the achievement of God's purpose necessarily for Luke involves the collusion of human agents. With the opening of the Gospel of Luke (chaps. 1–2), we discover that God's purpose invites and receives positive responses by such persons as Mary, Elizabeth, Simeon, and Anna, who readily participate in the choreography by which God accomplishes the divine plan. Others, though, such as Zechariah, are more reticent, and still others partner with evil and so set themselves over against God's aims (e.g., Luke 22:52-53). However ironically, though, even hostility to Jesus—and, by extension, to God's purpose—can be admitted into the service of God's plan, as God advances God's plan through opposition to Jesus and his witnesses.

For the Gospel of Matthew, the divine will is understood with reference to Jesus as teacher and interpreter of the law. The final verses of the SERMON ON THE MOUNT, with their emphasis on "the one who does the will of my Father in heaven" (7:21), show that the whole Sermon (Matt 5–7) expresses God's will. This is accomplished for Matthew by linking the notion of God's will to God's coming kingdom, and this provides the basis for Jesus' affirmations and interpretations of Torah. The LORD'S PRAYER appears as the centerpiece of the Sermon, and it underscores the divine will again: "Your kingdom come. Your will be done, on earth as it is in heaven" (Matt 6:10). Heaven is thus the sphere in which God's dynamic rule is already actualized, and Jesus' followers are to pray that God's will might extend and become powerful in this world as well (compare Eph 1:9-11).

Moreover, the logic of the prayer weaves together the hallowing of God's name with the behavior of God's people (Matt 6:9-10), a perspective that surfaces instructively in a text like Ezek 36:16-32. There God asserts, "I will sanctify my great name, which has been profaned among the nations, and which you have profaned among them; and the nations shall know that I am the LORD, says the Lord GOD, when through you I display my holiness before their eyes" (v. 23). That is, Jesus' followers hallow the name of God by embracing God's will for their lives. A similar perspective is found in 1 Pet 3, where the directive, "in your hearts sanctify Christ as Lord" (v. 15) is tied to two further expectations: to keep one's "conscience clear" and to practice "good conduct" (v. 16). Here are intertwined a person's center of innermost feelings and loyalties ("heart"), moral awareness ("conscience"), and behavior ("way of life" or "conduct"). Other NT texts use the language of God's will to ground behavioral directives (e.g., Eph 5:17-20; 1 Thess 4:3; Heb 10:32-36; 13:21; 1 Pet 2:15). See GOD, NT VIEW OF.

Bibliography: G. B. Caird with L. D. Hurst. *New Testament Theology* (1994); Charles H. Cosgrove. "The Divine ΔΕΙ in Luke–Acts." *NovT* 26 (1984) 168–90; John Goldingay. *Old Testament Theology, Vol. 1: Israel's Gospel* (2003); John R. Levison. *The Spirit in First-Century Judaism* (1997); Charles H. H. Scobie. *The Ways of Our God: An Approach to Biblical Theology* (2003); John T. Squires. *The Plan of God in Luke–Acts* (1993).

JOEL B. GREEN

WILLOW [עֲרָבָה 'aravah]. Two species of willow, *Salix acmophylla* and the white willow (*S. alba*) grow in Israel. Both species are small trees with numerous stems and branches that easily root in moist soil; they are found in wet places that are not salty. Willows (with Euphrates poplars and tamarisks in saline parts) form thickets along the Jordan River, which in biblical times were inhabited by wild beasts, including lions (Jer 12:5; 49:19).

There has been confusion between willows and poplars (*see* POPLAR), due in part to their similar habitat and to the narrow willow-like young leaves of the Euphrates poplar (*Populus euphratica*). The writer of Isa 44:3-4 was apparently familiar with the stream habitat of willows (compare Ezek 17:5). However, it is generally agreed that "willows" ('aravim עֲרָבִים) in Ps 137:1-3 refers to the Euphrates poplar (*Populus euphratica*), not to a willow. The "willows of the brook" collected for the Festival of Booths (Lev 23:40) may be either *S. acmophylla* or oleander (*Nerium oleander*). *See* ARABAH; PLANTS OF THE BIBLE; WADI OF THE WILLOWS.

F. NIGEL HEPPER

WIND [דָּרוֹם darom, קָדִים qadhim, רוּחַ ruakh; ἄνεμος anemos, νότος notos, πνεῦμα pneuma, πνοή pnoē]. The OT identifies wind primarily with the term ruakh ("wind, breath, spirit"). The LXX equivalent is pneuma. Old Testament authors imply that the wind is a creation of God and is subject to God's command (2 Kgs 3:17; Prov 30:4; Jer 4:12; 10:13; 51:16; Ezek 13:13; Hos 13:15; Amos 4:13; Jonah 1:4; 4:8; it is implied in Job 1:19 and Ps 148:8). Some winds hold particular characteristics in the OT. The north wind (ruakh tsafon רוּחַ צָפוֹן) is responsible for bringing rain to the land (Prov 25:23), while the east wind (qadhim) is seen to be of a particularly destructive nature (Ezek 17:10; 27:26; Hos 12:1; 13:15; Jonah 4:8). Interestingly, Ps 78:39 (also 103:16) compares the human spirit to the wind. This comparison may reflect the use of ruakh and pneuma for "spirit" as well as "wind." These two terms are used to identify various spiritual entities, including the spirit of God (created human spirit, Job 33:4; within a human, Exod 31:3; 35:31; the Spirit of God comes upon a human, Judg 3:10; 14:6; 1 Sam 11:6; 16:13, 14; 19:20, 23; Isa 61:1; 63:14; see also Isa 59:19; Dan 4:8, 18 [Aram. 4:5, 15]), God's holy spirit (Num 27:18; Isa 63:10, 11), the human spirit (1 Sam 1:15; Ezra 1:1; Job 32:8, 18; Isa 54:6; 65:14; 66:2), an evil spirit (from God, Judg 9:23; 1 Sam 16:14-15, 23; 19:9), a spirit of jealousy (Num 5:14), a spirit of wisdom (Deut 34:9), a deceiving spirit (1 Kgs 22:22-23; 2 Chr 18:22), and a destroying spirit (Jer 51:1). **Ruakh** and **pneuma** are also used to describe the "breath of life" (Gen 6:17; 7:15, 22) or the "breath of God" (Job 4:9; 39:10).

Wind is designated in the NT by three terms that carry various meanings. The first term, **anemos**, most often refers to strong winds on the sea (e.g., Matt 14:24, 32; Mark 4:37; Luke 8:23; John 6:18; Jas 3:4; Jude 1:12). Similar to the wind in the OT, the wind in the NT is under the control of God (Matt 14:32; Mark 4:39, 41; 6:51; Rev 7:1). The term **anemos** is used in a negative sense in Eph 4:14 in a warning to believers not to chase after every "wind" of doctrine. The second Greek term that refers to wind in the NT is **pnoē**. This word is used only twice: once in Acts 2:2, where it identifies the wind of Pentecost, and a second instance in Acts 17:25, where it describes the breath from God that gives life to humans. The third Greek term used to identify "wind" in the NT is **pneuma**. In reference to a natural wind it is used only once (John 3:8). This use may offer a similar connection between wind and spirit that is reflected in the OT mentioned above. All other uses of the Greek term **pneuma** and its forms refer to a spiritual entity (e.g., spirit of God, Matt 3:16; the Holy Spirit, Luke 11:13; spirit of Christ, 1 Pet 1:11; spirit of Jesus, Matt 27:50; spirit of the Lord, Acts 8:39; unclean spirit, Mark 7:25; demonic spirit, Luke 9:39; spirit of prophecy, Rev 19:10; deceitful spirit, 1 Tim 4:1). *See* EAST WIND; ISRAEL, CLIMATE OF; SPIRIT; STORM; WHIRLWIND.

ARCHIE T. WRIGHT

WINDOW [אֲרֻבָּה ʾarubbah, חַלּוֹן khallon; θυρίς thyris]. The most common Hebrew word for "window," khallon, refers to the openings in the wall of a structure or building, such as a house (Josh 2:15), a palace (1 Kgs 7:4-5), or Noah's ark (Gen 8:6). It is also used of the Solomonic Temple (1 Kgs 6:4), as well as the restored Temple (Ezek 41:16) and the temple gates of Ezekiel's vision (Ezek 40:16-36). Some windows could be opened (Gen 8:6; 2 Kgs 13:17), so they were not just openings in a structure (although the root meaning of khallon does refer to boring or piercing through an object). **Khallon** is thus used of a window with a LATTICE (Judg 5:28; Song 2:9). One well-known type of ANE relief is the so-called woman in the window (compare 2 Kgs 9:30-32).

The other Hebrew word for window, ʾarubbah, is used of the small openings of a dovecote (Isa 60:8), and of an opening through which smoke escapes (Hos 13:3). Metaphorically, it refers to the windows of heaven. When opened, they released the rains that caused the flood, and their closure marked the end of the rainfall (Gen 7:11; 8:2). God also could open the windows of heaven to pour down great blessing on his people (Mal 3:10).

The only NT references to a window relate how Eutychus fell asleep during Paul's sermon and fell out a window (Acts 20:9), and how Paul escaped from Damascus in a basket let down through a window (2 Cor 11:33; compare Josh 2; 1 Sam 19:12). *See* ARCHITECTURE, NT; ARCHITECTURE, OT.

JOEL F. DRINKARD JR.

WINE [יַיִן yayin; οἶνος oinos]. In ancient Israel, where water was frequently scarce or contaminated, wine was the most commonly consumed beverage. The Mediterranean climate of the land of Israel with its winter rains and summer drought offered favorable conditions for producing wine (similar to contemporary wine-producing regions such as Italy, France, and California). Moreover, archaeological remains such as storage jars, jugs, as well as wine vats and presses indicate that by Iron Age II, the production and consumption of wine was an integral part of Israelite culture (compare Walsh; also the multiple references to wine vats/presses in, e.g., Num 18:27; Deut 16:13). It is thus no surprise that wine offers a rich resource for biblical imagery in both the OT and NT. However, in scholarship and in many church traditions, wine is often viewed in a negative light, regularly attracting the moral and cultural biases of the interpreter. Even though the biblical text refers to the dangers of drinking wine in excess, this is not the predominant biblical perspective with regard to wine. Rather, the production and consumption of wine in the biblical tradition had an important social function.

A. Biblical Languages
B. The Production of Wine
C. The Consumption of Wine
   1. Wine as basic fare
   2. Wine and celebration
   3. Misuse of wine
D. The Theological Significance of Wine
   1. Wine as judgment and joy
   2. Wine and the cult
   3. Wine and the Lord's Supper
Bibliography

A. Biblical Languages

Several terms are used in the biblical text to denote *wine*. The word yayin is the most commonly used term in the OT (141 times) and is typically translated in the LXX with oinos, which also is the general term for *wine* in the NT. The "new wine" that is associated with the treading of grapes is tirosh (תִּירוֹשׁ; Prov 3:10; Mic 6:15). Due to the speed of fermentation, thirosh probably was not unfermented juice (see discussion below). The exilic/postexilic term is ʿasis (עָסִיס), usually translated "sweet wine." New wine (oinos neos οἶνος νέος) also occurs in the synoptic saying of Jesus regarding the common wisdom of putting new wine into fresh WINESKINs that were more pliable than old fragile skins that could burst due to the built-up pressure of carbon dioxide (Matt 9:17; Mark 2:22; Luke 5:37-38). The typical word for wine in Aramaic is khamar (חֲמַר, Dan 5:1-2, 4, 23; Ezra 6:9; 7:22)—in Hebrew used only in Deut 32:14 (khemer חֶמֶר). Shekhar (שֵׁכָר) is typically translated as "strong" or "intoxicating drink," and often used in parallel with wine. Probably made from dates, this DRINK had a very high alcoholic content (20 to 60 percent). Compare also the verb shakhar (שָׁכַר, "to become intoxicated").

B. The Production of Wine

The Gezer CALENDAR, which lists major agriculture activities, indicates that by the 10th cent. BCE, grape cultivation, including the actions of pruning grape vines and gathering grapes and olives, was a well-established part of the yearly agricultural cycle (see AGRICULTURE).

The cultivation of vineyards served as a way to diversify crops. For instance, in Deut 8:8 vines are being cultivated alongside grain, olive trees, fruit trees, and honey. Wine soon became a desired agricultural product. This liquid resource was easily stored, could be exchanged for other products, and contributed to the economic stability of the farmers. But even more significant, the production of wine indicates a significant shift in the human control of food, moving beyond food as mere sustenance, to food that exists to be enjoyed. In the parable of the Trees Who Wanted to Have a King, the vine's refusal to be king refers to this latter aspect when it says: "Shall I stop producing my wine that cheers gods and mortals?" (Judg 9:13).

The production of wine required only two elements: grapes and yeast. The grapes were harvested in the fall at the height of ripening, at which time the water/sugar ratio (70 to 80 percent water, 10 to 25 percent sugar) would be optimal for producing the most wine. If harvested too early, the grapes would be smaller and sour (compare the image of the sour grapes in Ezek 18:2).

A natural amount of yeast on the grape skins began to work as soon as the grapes were crushed—typically by being trodden in WINE VATs or presses (see Jesus' parable of the Wicked Tenants [Matt 21:33; compare Rev 14:18-20; 19:15]). Considering the warm climate and this natural fermentation process, unfermented grape juice was most likely rare in ancient Israel. The fermentation process reached its peak about six to twelve hours after the treading of the grapes and then proceeded at a slower rate for another two to five days. The wine was transferred into jars for storage where the fermentation process would be completed. At this point, it was important to allow the carbon dioxide to escape, but at the same time prevent exposure to air.

There was a definite social aspect to the grape harvest and the ensuing production of wine. The event of picking and treading grapes constituted a celebratory occasion to which friends and family were invited to share in the labor, as well as to enjoy the forthcoming wine. Despite wine producers' best efforts to prevent prolonged contact with air (which converted wine into VINEGAR), toward the end of the agricultural year, wine may either have become scarce or turned sour. The grape harvest and new wine that it yielded was thus greatly anticipated. This joyous expectation is evident in the numerous references to shouts of joy, song, and dancing women (Judg 21:21; compare also texts like Isa 16:10 and Jer 48:33 that refer to the absence of joy, gladness, and song when the grape harvest, due to enemy attacks, did not take place).

The cultivation of a vineyard was a work of love that implied a long-term commitment (see VINE, VINEYARD). The laborious work was well rewarded when the harvest came and the whole town could enjoy the fruit of the vine. This passion involved with the cultivation and production of wine found its way into the images Israel used for God. In Isa 5:1-7, God's love for Israel is expressed in terms of a vintner's love and continuing care for a vineyard (note the threefold use of the term beloved). The image of God as the divine vintner extends into the NT when God is portrayed as the vinegrower, Jesus the true vine, and Jesus' followers the branches that bear fruit (John 15:1-17).

In terms of gender, in Prov 31:16 the woman of substance is praised for her role in wine production when she buys a field to plant a vineyard. In Song 8:12, the woman owns her own vineyard—the vineyard in this book functions as a metaphor for her sexual power. Throughout, wine imagery intersects with female sexuality (e.g., Song 7:8 where the woman's breasts are likened to clusters of grapes, her kisses to sweet wine [vv. 9-10], and her navel to a bowl of wine [v. 3]).

C. The Consumption of Wine
1. Wine as basic fare

Wine formed a basic part of daily meals in the biblical tradition. Grain and wine were considered to be the essential foods for Israel (Judg 19:19; Prov 9:5; Eccl 9:7; Hos 9:2). Moreover, wine is listed as part of the daily provisions while traveling (Josh 9:13; 1 Sam 16:20).

The everyday drinking of wine is often colored in terms of enjoyment. So in Ps 104:15, wine's function is described as gladdening the heart. And in Eccl 9:7, the call to enjoy life is expressed in terms of eating your bread with joy and drinking wine with a merry heart. An ode to wine in Sir 31:27 says: "Wine is very life to human beings if taken in moderation. What is life to one who is without wine? It has been created to make people happy." Wine had a distinctive social function.

Sharing meals and drinking wine together was a natural extension of sharing work. In addition, the act of eating and drinking together contributed to the establishment of a group identity, marking boundaries of inclusion and exclusion among the participants. The act of drinking wine thus contributed to a sense of social cohesion, easing tension, and aiding in communication (Walsh).

Finally, wine was considered to be an all-purpose cure. In 1 Tim 5:23, Timothy, Paul's missionary helper, is advised to drink a little wine for the sake of his stomach. And in the story of the Good Samaritan, wine is used to dress wounds (Luke 10:34). Wine furthermore was offered to prisoners to reduce the anguish of capital punishment. Jesus was offered wine at his crucifixion ("sour wine" in Matt 27:48; Mark 15:36; Luke 23:36; compare the references to "wine mixed with myrrh" in Mark 15:23 and "wine mixed with gall" in Matt 27:34).

2. Wine and celebration

Wine is associated especially with celebrations. Festivals with sumptuous food and plenty of wine resembled the daily meals with the basic elements of bread, wine, and oil, but on a grander scale and with greater quantities. So one would find on the festival menu wine mixed with spices (Prov 9:2; 23:30) that would be served alongside a luxury item such as meat.

Festivals constituted ritualized celebrations that offered a break from the regular routines that marked daily life. Commemorating special occasions such as the weaning of a child (Gen 21:8-9), a marriage festival (Gen 29:22-25), or the celebration of the vintage (Judg 9:27), these festivals offered a common outlet of the anxieties and tensions associated with the arduous agricultural labor that was necessary for subsistence living. Wine served as a social lubricant, providing for a sense of social cohesion among its participants. So the effects of wine at a festival are described as a "merry heart" (Judg 19:6; Esth 1:10; Eccl 9:7) denoting a general state of enjoyment. In John 2:1-11, it is significant that Jesus' first sign occurred at a wedding feast at CANA, where he supplied an abundance of good wine by changing 120 gallons of water into wine.

Two types of banquets are referenced in the biblical tradition. The mishteh (מִשְׁתֶּה) festival (derived from the verb shathah [שָׁתָה], "to drink") illustrates that it is increased drinking that turns an ordinary meal into a feast. The marzeakh (מַרְזֵחַ) festival is mentioned only twice but seems to have a different social function than the mishteh festival. In Amos 6:7 the marzeakh festival is surrounded by references of utter opulence, denoting a lavish banquet, which includes drinking, singing, and lounging on ivory beds. In Jer 16:5-7, this festival is used in conjunction with mourning rituals. It seems that death may have been an occasion for drinking as was a marriage; the act of drinking together offering a group shaken by the loss of one of its members the opportunity to be consoled and to regroup.

3. Misuse of wine

Even though wine formed a central part of Israel's culture, the biblical tradition also notes the misuse of wine. Sirach 31:28-29 best summarizes the biblical traditions' balanced attitude toward wine: "Wine drunk at the proper time and in moderation is rejoicing of heart and gladness of soul. Wine drunk to excess leads to bitterness of spirit, to quarrels and stumbling." The biblical text consistently critiques overindulgence with regard to wine (Prov 23:29-35; Isa 28:7-8; compare also Jdt 12:19–13:9; Tob 4:15; Eph 5:18; 1 Tim 3:2, 8; Titus 1:7). In Gal 5:21 and 1 Cor 6:9-10, drunkards are grouped together with other categories of evildoers (compare also Paul's advice in Rom 14:19-21 to abstain from wine if it may cause a brother or sister to fall away).

DRUNKENNESS manifested itself in confusion (Prov 23:30-35; Isa 28:7), foolishness (Prov 20:1), staggering (Isa 28:7; 29:9), aggression (Prov 4:17), exposure (Gen 9:21), nausea (Prov 23:34), vomiting (Jer 25:27), and comatose sleep (Gen 9:21; 1 Sam 25:37; Jdt 13:2). In Isa 5:11, the metaphor of being intoxicated by wine and STRONG DRINK is used to accuse those who fail to heed God's commandments (compare also Hos 4:11). The impact of alcohol abuse on family relations is evident in the ensuing family strife in response to Noah's drunkenness (Gen 9:22-27), Hagar and Ishmael being expelled at the occasion of the weaning festival (Gen 21:14), Jacob getting the wrong wife (Gen 29:23, 25), and Amnon being killed by order of Absalom (2 Sam 13:28). Deuteronomy 21:18-21 deals harshly with a son who is constantly drunk and gluttonous. More than a social embarrassment, this individual threatens the family's livelihood by ingesting too much of the farm's produce. However, note that Jesus says he came "eating and drinking"; he neither preached nor practiced abstinence, and some of his contemporaries accused him of being a glutton and a drunkard (Matt 11:19; Luke 7:34).

D. The Theological Significance of Wine
1. Wine as judgment and joy

The theological significance of wine is depicted in terms of the dual images of judgment and joy. Wine, as part of the bounty of land, is foremost a sign of God's blessing (Gen 27:28; Deut 7:13; 11:14; 32:14). In Num 13:23, the fruit of the vine is viewed as a symbol of the fertility of land, describing in hyperbolic terms how it took two people to lift one cluster of grapes. Moreover, the vine serves as a symbol of peace and prosperity. In 1 Kgs 4:25 [Heb. 5:5] and Mic 4:4 the peaceful ideal is that everyone may sit under his/her own vine and fig tree.

Wine is also used as a symbol of God's judgment. In a number of texts, Israel's disobedience is said to affect their vineyards and accordingly their wine supply. The ultimate symbol of misfortune would be to go through all the hard work of cultivating a vineyard and treading its grapes and then not to get to drink the wine (Deut 28:39; Job 24:11; Amos 5:11; Zeph 1:13). Several prophetic texts continue this link between disaster and disobedience, with vivid depictions of wine shortages (compare Isa 24:7, 11; Hos 2:12; 9:2; Joel 1:7, 10, 12). Lamentations 2:12 furthermore contains the harrowing laments of the children of Jerusalem calling in vain for grain and wine. God's disappointment at finding inedible grapes causes God to wreck his own vineyard (Isa 5:1-7). A particularly gruesome image of judgment is God treading the wine press, the people being trodden like grapes, and their "juice" spattered on God's garments (Isa 63:3, 6; compare Rev 14:18-20).

Wine as an image of judgment is used to climactic effect in the book of Revelation. Because Babylon has made all the nations drink of "the wine of the wrath of her fornication" (Rev 14: 8), God's judgment will be "the wine of God's wrath, poured unmixed into the cup of his anger" (v. 10; compare also Rev 17:2; 18:3). Drawing on the Isaianic imagery of God treading the wine press, an angel will gather the grapes of the earth, throwing them into "the great wine press of the wrath of God" (Rev 14:18-20; compare also Rev 19:15).

However, wine is also used as an image of God's restoration when in prophetic texts like Joel 2:24-26 and Jer 31:11-14 a return of joy accompanies the replenished grain, wine, and oil supplies. This link between wine and joy is even more evident in texts of an eschatological nature. In Amos 9:13, the superabundance of God's provision of food naturally leads into a euphoric statement of there being so many grapes that the mountains shall drip with the newly pressed wine (compare also Joel 3:18). And in Isa 25, the "golden age" is imaged in terms of a banquet, an ongoing meal where God is the host who presents a feast of rich food and well-aged wines (v. 6). The emphasis on the "well-aged" quality of the wines conveys that these wines have time to be preserved and will not run out or turn sour (*see* MESSIANIC BANQUET).

2. Wine and the cult

Wine fulfills a central role in the religious expression of Israel. From Mount Sinai where God and humans ate and drank together in order to seal the covenant (Exod 24:9-11), to the act of eating and drinking at the sanctuaries (1 Sam 1:9, 18; Jer 35:2; Amos 2:8), wine is clothed with religious significance. Wine is offered together with grain and meat as sacrifice (Exod 29:40; Lev 23:13; Num 15:5, 7, 10; 28:14; Deut 32:38). In Deut 14:23, Israel is commanded to eat the tithe of their grain, wine, oil, and livestock in the presence of God so that they may learn to revere or fear God. The wine points beyond itself to the giver of the wine (*see* SACRIFICES AND OFFERINGS).

On the other hand, abstaining from wine also held religious significance. One of the most important characteristics associated with the Nazirites is their abstention from wine; they are to drink nothing from the vine

including grape juice, fresh or dried grapes, vinegar, and even grape skins (Num 6:1-5; compare also the instructions to Samson's mother in Judg 13:4-7). *See* NAZIR, NAZIRITE.

The act of drinking wine became a preferred means of describing the act of making a message or words or wisdom one's own. In Isa 55:1-2, the exilic community is invited to "come," "buy," and "eat" from the wine and milk that the prophet offers. Just as food and drink become part of the body, so the word and the prophet's message should be fully internalized. A similar dynamic is at work in Woman Wisdom's invitation in Prov 9:1-5 to a lavish banquet with the luxury items of meat and wine mixed with spices (*see* SOPHIA). Once again the act of eating and drinking serves as a means to participate in the gifts offered by the Giver.

3. Wine and the Lord's Supper

This invitation to participate in the feast is continued in the NT portrayal of Jesus. The theological significance of wine is no more evident than in the EUCHARIST. During Jesus' final Passover meal (called the Last Supper; *see* LAST SUPPER, THE), Jesus took a CUP of wine and said, "This is my blood of the covenant, which is poured out for many" (Mark 14:23-25; compare the slightly different wording in Matt 26:27-29; Luke 22:20). The wine poured out serves as a symbol of Jesus' imminent suffering—a reality from which his followers are not precluded. The wine moreover is a sign of the new covenant—the new community coming together in remembering and celebrating the death of Jesus Christ until he comes again (1 Cor 11:23-26). The wine finally serves as a hopeful reminder of the end of time when the faithful will eat and drink together with Christ at the heavenly banquet in the kingdom of God (Mark 14:25).

Bibliography: Andrea Bieler and Luise Schottroff. *The Eucharist: Bodies, Bread and Resurrection* (2007); Oded Borowski. *Agriculture in Iron Age Israel* (2002); L. Juliana M. Claassens. *The God Who Provides: Biblical Images of Divine Nourishment* (2004); Philip J. King and Lawrence E. Stager. *Life in Biblical Israel* (2001); Carey Ellen Walsh. *The Fruit of the Vine: Viticulture in Ancient Israel* (2000).

L. JULIANA CLAASSENS

WINE PRESS. *See* WINE.

WINE VAT [יֶקֶב yeqev]. A pit hewn out of rock (Isa 5:2; compare Matt 21:33; Mark 12:1) used for the collection and treading of grapes. The juice flowed through a channel into a deeper, neighboring vat. Even when mechanical wine presses were available, treading grapes by foot in wine vats was customary. After the newly pressed wine was collected in wine vats (Hos 9:2; Hag 2:16), the wine was transferred into large jars for storage. Wine vats that overflow are a sign of God's blessing

(Prov 3:10; Joel 2:24). Yeqev is also translated "wine press" (e.g., Num 18:27; Isa 63:2); *see* WINE.

L. JULIANA CLAASSENS

WINESKIN [נֹאד no'dh, נֵבֶל nevel; ἀσκός askos]. A container made from the hide of a goat or sheep, used to carry wine or other liquids while traveling (Josh 9:4, 13; 1 Sam 16:20). Wineskins were easier to handle than pitchers or jars. The pressure of carbon dioxide released by the fermentation of new wine could rupture old, fragile wineskins (compare Ps 119:83) or stress new ones (Job 32:19). Jesus alludes to the fragility of old wineskins in Mark 2:22 (compare Matt 9:17; Luke 5:37-38), observing that putting new wine into old skins would result in the loss of both. *See* WINE.

L. JULIANA CLAASSENS

WING [כָּנָף kanaf; πτέρυξ pteryx]. The appendage of a creature that enables flight. The OT mentions a number of "winged birds" (Gen 1:21; Deut 4:17; Ps 78:27; compare "winged creature" in Eccl 10:20): the eagle (Exod 19:4; Deut 32:11; Prov 23:5; Jer 48:40; 49:22; Ezek 17:3, 7), stork (Zech 5:9), dove (Lev 1:14-17; Ps 68:13), ostrich (Job 39:13), and hawk (Job 39:26). In each case, the identification of the species is rhetorically followed by kanaf. The NT refers to the wing of a hen (Matt 23:37; Luke 13:34). *See* BIRDS OF THE BIBLE.

Other winged creatures include the cherubim (Exod 25:20; 37:9; 1 Kgs 6:24, 27; Ezek 10:5) and seraphim (Isa 6:2), and winged insects (Lev 11:20-23; Deut 14:19-20). Metaphorically, the sun of righteousness is winged (Mal 4:2 [Heb. 3:20]), as well as the dawn (Ps 139:9) and the wind (2 Sam 22:11; Pss 18:10; 104:3; Hos 4:19). Perhaps best seen as "apocalyptic winged creatures" are the two women in Zech 5:9, the four living creatures in Rev 4:8 (compare Ezek 1; 10), the locusts in Rev 9:9, and the woman in Rev 12:14. Several psalms allude to the "shadow" or "refuge" offered by Yahweh's wings (Pss 17:8; 36:7; 57:1; 61:4; 63:7; 91:4; see also Ruth 2:12).

The term kanaf is also used of an extremity or edge, including the corners of the earth (Job 37:3; Isa 11:12; 24:16; Ezek 7:2) and the edges of a garment (1 Sam 24:12; Hag 2:12; compare the metaphor for marriage in Ruth 3:9; Ezek 16:8; and euphemistic use in Deut 22:30; 27:20).

JOHN I. LAWLOR

WINNOW [זָרָה zarah]. Winnowing is an activity designed to separate the grain from the CHAFF after THRESHING takes place. Winnowing is done at the THRESHING FLOOR, usually located outside the settlement where the wind can be utilized in the process (Jer 4:11). Sometimes it can be done at night when the proper wind is available (Ruth 3:2). The mixture of grain and chaff is thrown in the air with a special fork, usually made of wood. The wind separates the mixture according to the weight of the components and various piles

are formed, first the grain, which is heaviest, then the straw, and lastly the chaff. Further cleaning of the grain by throwing it up with a wooden shovel and letting the wind continue to separate follows this. The final activity utilizes sieves of different sizes. Winnowing is often used metaphorically (Prov 20:8; Luke 3:17).

Bibliography: Oded Borowski. *Agriculture in Iron Age Israel* (2002).

ODED BOROWSKI

WINTER. *See* ISRAEL, CLIMATE OF; SUMMER AND WINTER.

WISDOM IN THE ANCIENT NEAR EAST. Wisdom is a concept that finds expression in nearly every culture, in every time and place. Persons with particular insights into human motivations and interactions, those with exceptional abilities at artisanship and the crafting of words, and those with encyclopedic knowledge are called "wise."

    A. Biblical Context
    B. Ancient Near Eastern Context
    C. Wisdom Literature
      1. Mesopotamia
      2. Egypt
      3. "The Words of Ahiqar"
    D. Summary
    Bibliography

A. Biblical Context

The OT tells us that in the early days of Israel, certain people, particularly women, were sought out for their advice and counsel on the interworkings of human relationships. In 2 Sam 14:2, e.g., Joab sends "a wise woman" from Tekoa to David to try to persuade him to reconcile with Absalom (*see* WISE WOMAN OF TEKOA). Later in the narrative, Joab is confronted by "a wise woman" from the city of Abel (2 Sam 20:16). The skilled artisans who crafted the gold, silver, and bronze vessels and the intricate cloth works for the tabernacle are described as being filled with "wisdom" (hokhmah חָכְמָה; NSRV, "skill"), "intelligence, and knowledge in every kind of craft" (Exod 35:31, 35). Joseph is described as "wise" after he successfully interprets Pharaoh's dream in Gen 41:39; and 1 Kgs 10 celebrates the great wisdom of Solomon. In addition, the book of Proverbs outlines the attributes and actions of any person who wishes to be considered as wise.

The OT also speaks of wise persons outside of Israel. In the Joseph and Moses stories, Pharaoh summons his magicians, sorcerers, and wise men to interpret dreams and perform miracles (Gen 41:8; Exod 7:11); the writer of 1 Kgs 4:30 (Heb. 5:10) states that Solomon's wisdom surpassed the wisdom of all the people of the east and all of the wisdom of Egypt. And in the book of Daniel, Belshazzar summons the wise men of his kingdom to interpret the mysterious writing that appeared on the wall during a royal banquet (Dan 5:15).

B. Ancient Near Eastern Context

In the ANE context, *wisdom* is an umbrella term that encompasses humanity's quest to understand and organize reality, to find answers to basic existential questions, and to pass that information along from one generation to another. Wisdom's roots were located in the family unit, where each generation shared insights into a life lived well with the next generation, and generation after generation passed the insights along. As societies became more established and institutionalized, wisdom percolated up through families to the administrative and religious systems of city-states and empires. Thus the accumulation and transmission of wisdom transferred from the family to the national setting.

Regardless of the venue (family or nation), in the process of taking notice of nature, of human relationships, and of the larger world, humanity throughout the millennia observed myriad patterns of cause and effect. One natural event almost always preceded another; a particular consequence regularly followed an action in human relationships; the stars and moon and sun moved in set ways that affected the earth. Such observations engendered a belief that the gods had established a basic order in the world by which all were bound. In ancient Egypt, this belief was called ma'at, variously translated as "truth," "order," or "justice." The major creation stories from the ANE depict the gods (or God) forming order out of chaos as part of the creative process. In Gen 1, the earth begins as tohu (תֹהוּ)and bohu (בֹהוּ) and the ruakh (רוּחַ, "wind, spirit") of God hovers over the chaotic dark waters of tehom (תְהוֹם, the deep; v. 2). The first creative act of God is to divide the darkness from the light (v. 3). In the Mesopotamian epic *Enuma Elish* MARDUK defeats TIAMAT, the goddess of the stormy sea and forms the earth out of her dead carcass. In the Egyptian pantheon, Ma'at is the daughter of Re, the sun god. Many scholars maintain that Ma'at is the model or prototype of the biblical Woman Wisdom, who is portrayed in Prov 8:22-31 as an active presence at the creation of the world.

The gods created order, and the events in and the fortunes of people's lives were direct consequences of the gods' actions. When the order was disrupted (by earthquake, flood, an eclipse of the sun or moon, infidelity in human relationships, or war), chaos ensued, indicating that humanity had in some way violated the basic order of the world. The only way to end the chaos was to restore the order that had been established by the gods.

Wise persons in the ANE were those who understood the basic order of the created world and lived in fidelity with it. This fidelity took on many forms: an accomplished artisan was considered to be wise (Exod 35:31); one who cataloged flora, fauna, and language

was wise (1 Kgs 4:33); one who offered insights into life was wise (2 Sam 14:2); a skilled scribe was wise.

C. Wisdom Literature

Texts categorized by scholars as "Wisdom literature" appeared in Mesopotamia and Egypt beginning in the early 3rd millennium BCE. A number of scholars maintain, however, that were it not for the wisdom books of the OT, the various texts from Egypt and Mesopotamia now designated as "wisdom" would not be considered a distinct collection, since their subject matters and forms are far from uniform and univocal. Indeed, the so-called wisdom texts of the ANE include a great variety of forms and subject matters. A major issue in wisdom studies today is whether a text should be categorized as "wisdom" based on its content or on its literary form: 1) What are the topics addressed by the wisdom writers? 2) What literary forms are used by the wisdom writers to convey their messages?

In terms of content, wisdom has been defined as a way of thinking about and ordering reality that reflects a shared ethos regarding assumptions and expectations about life. Thus wisdom writers attempted to categorize the world, measure human actions, evaluate the relative status of events and movements of life, and prescribe paths of life. Their writings thereby created a mythos, a particular view of reality around which human society organized.

The literary forms of wisdom compositions are varied and include, among others, catalogs and lexical lists, instructions handed on from parents to children (or teachers to students), introspective musings, dialogues, and didactic stories. Thus, the most we are permitted to say is that wisdom compositions come in a variety of shapes and sizes, and that they address basic existential questions of being. Whatever precise definition of "Wisdom literature" one accepts, however, the texts now designated as "wisdom" are among the most ancient pieces of literature.

1. Mesopotamia

In ancient Mesopotamia, writing and scribal schools (the Sumerian **edubba** and later the Akkadian **bit tuppi**) were well established by the 3rd millennium BCE. The schools drew students from the elite of society, children of well-to-do families. The educational process in the scribal schools was lengthy and grueling. Only those who excelled in their studies advanced beyond a basic education in recording business transactions and administrative records to more advanced work in science, literature, and religion. These advanced scribes were the keepers and transmitters of the wisdom tradition in ancient Mesopotamia, and in some cases they were the authors. From their hands came the various works known today by the name "wisdom." Such works were numerous and varied, and included lexical lists— words arranged either by theme, such as professions or geographical names, or by the shape of cuneiform signs—that appeared as early as the beginning of the 3rd millennium and continued to be compiled as long as cuneiform writing was in use. Later, lexicons of Sumerian-Akkadian equivalents were developed.

Other early wisdom compositions include the "Instructions of Shuruppak" (*ANET*, 594–96). In this document, copies of which date from 2600 to 1100 and include both Sumerian and Akkadian versions, a father named Shuruppak (perhaps a personification of the city of Shuruppak) gives advice to his son Ziusudra, the hero of the great flood in its Sumerian version (in the Akkadian version of the text, Ziusudra is replaced by Utnapishtim, the Akkadian flood hero). In the "Instructions," Shuruppak conveys his advice in the form of admonitions to Ziusudra, followed by reasons for the admonitions. A related early form of wisdom composition in Mesopotamia was the proverb, which is much like the form "proverb" in the biblical book of Proverbs. At least twenty-four collections of Sumerian and Akkadian proverbs have been discovered and identified (*ANET*, 425–27; 593–94).

Common themes of ANE Wisdom literature included understanding the misfortune that befell a person who appeared to live a life of justice and kindness as well as the good that seemed to come to a person who was unjust and self-centered, and musings over the concept of immortality. The Sumerian composition "A Man and His God," also known as "The Sumerian Job," dates to 2000 BCE. The protagonist in the text maintains that he is a victim of undeserved misfortune and calls his personal god to account for not heeding his continual pleas for mercy and justice. The rationale for his lament is that the world is ordered and he has not violated that order.

Ludlul Bel Nemeqi (I Will Praise the Lord of Wisdom), a composition from the mid- to late 1st millennium, contains a similar theme. In it, one Shubshi-meshre-Shakkan claims to have been abandoned by humans and his personal god, but he continues to praise Marduk, the "lord of wisdom." Eventually, he receives a promise that the gods will restore his good fortune. "The Babylonian Theodicy," composed around 1000 BCE, is an acrostic poem in the form of a dialogue between a righteous sufferer and his friend. The sufferer laments his lot in life and his friend defends the conventional wisdom of the day that maintains that suffering is a consequence of one's own actions.

Other compositions from Mesopotamia, while not categorized as "wisdom," incorporate wisdom motifs. The "Epic of Gilgamesh" is arguably the most popular epic story from the ANE (*see* GILGAMESH, EPIC OF). The story was in circulation as early as 2100, but the twelve-tablet version known to most students of the ANE dates to about 1200 BCE. In the epic, Gilgamesh, king of Uruk, forges a strong friendship with Enkidu, a creature who is half man and half beast. When Enkidu dies, Gilgamesh embarks on a journey to find the secret of immortality. The epic begins and ends with speeches of Gilgamesh that recount the knowledge and insight he has gained through his sufferings. The remainder of the epic chronicles Gilgamesh's journey of discovery. During the journey, he encounters an ale-wife who says to him, in what might be understood as a summary statement of the message of the epic, "You will not find the eternal life you seek .... Go eat your bread with enjoyment .... Enjoy life with the wife whom you love."

2. Egypt

In Egypt, as in Mesopotamia, wisdom texts appear at an early date and fall into much the same categories as do the Mesopotamian texts. The Egyptian texts originated in what is known as "The House of Life," a center of scribal activity usually tied to a particular temple. A number of texts from the "Houses of Life" are categorized as "instruction," in which parents or teachers give very specific and concrete (rather than abstract) instructions to their charges. Such instructions may be compared to those found in the biblical book of Proverbs, particularly those that contrast the wise and the foolish person.

One of the earliest instructional texts from Egypt is "The Instruction of Ptahhotep," which dates to 2500–2000 BCE. In it, an aging father, an important official in the court of Pharaoh, instructs his son, who is in line to take over his office, about proper conduct at court. Another text, the "Instruction of Merikare" (1500 BCE), recounts a father's instruction to his son about what to do and not to do in order to be a successful ruler. The mid-2nd-millennium "Instruction of Any" is, like Ptahhotep and Merikare, the advice of a father to a son. But Any is a lower official in Pharaoh's court and thus his instructions are less court-oriented and more appropriate to common human relationship—i.e., how to avoid suffering, conflicts, and disappointments in life. Another unique feature of this text is the son's hesitancy to accept his father's counsel, which is recorded in the work's epilogue.

The "Instruction of Amenemope" is perhaps the best known of Egyptian wisdom texts because of its connections with Prov 22:17–24:22 (*see* AMENEMOPE, INSTRUCTION OF). A lengthy document, the "Instruction" dates to 1100 BCE and contains the admonitions of a teacher to his student concerning proper conduct in Pharaoh's court. It differs significantly from the previously discussed instructional documents in its view of success and goodness. Wealth and power are less esteemed than care for others and inward contemplation.

As with the biblical and Mesopotamian texts, Egyptian wisdom compositions also grapple with questions of unjust suffering. A popular story from the late 3rd millennium is "The Eloquent Peasant," about a peasant who is arrested because, while driving his animals to pasture, one of them strayed and ate some grain belonging to a noble. The peasant is taken to prison and subsequently allowed to plead his case before the pharaoh. The pharaoh is so taken with the man's ability to speak and persuade that he keeps him in prison just so that he can listen to the man's arguments. The arguments are recorded in the story as a series of nine speeches between the peasant and an official of Pharaoh.

Among a collection of Egyptian tomb inscriptions known as the "Songs of the Harper," "The Song from the Tomb of King Intef" (end of 3rd millennium) is unique. The "Songs of the Harper" were originally composed as funerary texts in praise of life after death; "The Song from the Tomb of King Intef," however, reflects a movement in the Songs away from confidence in the afterlife toward enjoyment of this life and all it has to offer. Another 3rd-millennium Egyptian tale called "The DISPUTE BETWEEN A MAN AND HIS BA" is the story of a man who, because of his suffering, longs for death and the blissful life that will follow. His **ba** (his life force) threatens to leave him if he insists on wishing for death, thereby annulling all hope for a blissful afterlife. The man pleads with his **ba** to remain with him (*ANET*, 405–7).

3. "The Words of Ahiqar"

"The Words of Ahiqar" is an Aramaic composition that dates to the 6th or 5th cent. BCE (*see* AHIKAR, AHIQAR). Discovered at the Jewish colony of Elephantine, located near the first cataract of the Nile River in Egypt, it tells the story of an official in the Assyrian court of Sennacherib, Ahiqar, who is falsely accused by his nephew of treason. An executioner spares Ahiqar's life and Ahiqar speaks words of wisdom to anyone who will listen. "The Words of Ahiqar" is often compared to the biblical court tales of Joseph and Daniel.

D. Summary

The wide variety of wisdom texts in the Mesopotamia and Egypt literary corpora is characteristic of the wisdom texts in the OT, in which the books of Proverbs, Job, and Ecclesiastes are categorized as "wisdom." Proverbs presents a traditional view of the path of wisdom, the path to a good life: live in harmony with others, obey the commandments of God, and be sensitive to and caring for those less fortunate than yourself. Job tells the story of a person who has walked in the traditional paths of wisdom but whose life is turned upside down by misfortune after misfortune. Job calls God to account for what has happened and arrives at a deeper understanding of the God he worships. In the book of Ecclesiastes, the teacher, Qoheleth, muses over the intent and purpose of life and finally draws the conclusion that, in the end, humanity is called to enjoy the life that it has been given and to fear God and keep the commandments.

The Wisdom literature of the ANE gives the reader a glimpse into the struggling of humanity with the age-old questions of life: What is the place of each of us within the greater scheme of life? How do we negotiate the myriad relationships that present themselves to us in the course of our lives? How do we understand what

appears to us to be unjust suffering? Wisdom texts begin with the basic premise that the gods (or God) created the world with some measure of order. It is the duty of humanity to understand that order and to maintain it. When the order is disturbed, the world returns to its pre-created state and chaos ensues. Wisdom is the ability to calm the chaos and return the world to its rightful order. Thus the wisdom movement in the ANE was an attempt to define the good created order, to explore those instances in life when humanity's actions or mere circumstances conflicted with that order, and to prescribe the means by which humanity could maintain or restore the good created order. The varied forms and content of the Wisdom literature that occur in the ANE are each a valuable element in humankind's ongoing quest for finding order out of chaos. *See* WISDOM IN THE NT; WISDOM IN THE OT.

Bibliography: James Crenshaw. *Old Testament Wisdom: An Introduction* (1998); John G. Gammie and Leo Purdue, eds. *The Sage in Israel and the Ancient Near East* (1990); Kathleen O'Connor. *The Wisdom Literature* (1988); Jack M. Sasson, ed. *Civilizations of the Ancient Near East.* Vols. 1–4 (1995).

NANCY DECLAISSÉ-WALFORD

WISDOM IN THE NT [σοφία sophia]. To his contemporaries Jesus would have looked like both a sage and a prophet. He often used the literary forms of wisdom teachers to proclaim the coming kingdom of God and to provide guidance on how to prepare for and enter it. In some early Christian circles Jesus was celebrated not only as a wisdom teacher but also as Wisdom incarnate and personified. John identified Jesus as the Word of God, while Paul insisted that Christians must take account of the cross as the wisdom of God. The "letter" of James is best interpreted as a wisdom instruction with many parallels to the Synoptic Gospels. Some theological issues raised in the OT wisdom books—the law of retribution, innocent suffering, and theodicy—find a distinctive resolution in the NT.

    A. Jesus the Wisdom Teacher
        1. Old Testament sources
        2. Jesus in the Synoptic Gospels
        3. The Sermon on the Mount
    B. Jesus the Wisdom of God
        1. Backgrounds
        2. Wisdom christology
    C. Other Perspectives
        1. John
        2. Paul
        3. James
    D. Theological Problems
        1. Theodicy and retribution
        2. The apocalyptic solution
        3. The Christian solution
    Bibliography

A. Jesus the Wisdom Teacher

1. Old Testament sources

The most important OT and apocryphal books for understanding wisdom in the NT are Proverbs, Sirach, and the Wisdom of Solomon. Ecclesiastes has little impact (perhaps due to its skepticism). But the book of Job is very significant theologically for challenging the law of retribution and raising questions about innocent suffering and God's justice. Jewish apocalyptic writings such as Daniel and *1 Enoch*, as well as the wisdom texts from Qumran (especially 4Q418), illustrate how in NT times the sapiential and prophetic/apocalyptic strands of thought were joined. Of special significance for wisdom christology are those passages that portray Wisdom as a female figure (Prov 8:22-36; Sir 24:1-22; Wis 7:22-26).

2. Jesus in the Synoptic Gospels

As he appears in the Synoptic Gospels, Jesus looks like (at least in part) a Jewish wisdom teacher. He gathers around himself a circle of disciples (mathētai μαθηταί), that is, persons eager to learn wisdom from him. Both his followers and outsiders regard him as a teacher. Many of the topics found in his teachings are treated by other wisdom teachers: money matters, social relations, speech, family issues, and so on. The literary forms he often uses—aphorisms, maxims, prohibitions, admonitions, beatitudes, and parables—were those typically employed by wisdom teachers. His joining of wisdom and apocalyptic traditions (especially "kingdom of God") was in line with similar efforts at their integration in Daniel, *1 Enoch*, and 4Q418. So it should come as no surprise when in Matt 11:28-30 Jesus uses the language that an earlier Jewish wisdom teacher, Jesus Ben Sira of Jerusalem, used to invite prospective students to his wisdom school: "Put your neck under her [wisdom's] yoke ... I have labored but little and found for myself much serenity" (Sir 51:26-27).

Throughout Matthew's Gospel Jesus offers relatively long instructions (chaps. 5–7, 10, 13, 18, and 24–25) consisting of short sayings, many of them cast in typical wisdom forms. Mark presents Jesus as teaching about God's kingdom by means of parables (e.g., 4:26-31) and shows how, through his extraordinary wisdom, Jesus manages to elude the traps set for him by rival teachers (e.g., 12:13-34). Luke makes effective use of the Markan journey narrative as a vehicle for Jesus' most memorable parables (the Good Samaritan [10:25-37], the Prodigal Son [15:11-32]). And, of course, the Sayings Source Q used independently by Matthew and Luke for so much of Jesus' teaching seems to have been a collection of Jesus' wise teachings (e.g., Matt 6:24// Luke 16:13; Matt 5:13//Luke 14:34-35), much like the books of Proverbs and Sirach.

3. The Sermon on the Mount

Jesus' initial discourse in Matt 5–7 provides a good illustration of Jesus' dual identity as both sage and prophet of God's kingdom. Matthew constructed this sermon out of sayings found in the Sayings Source Q, Mark, and his other source(s). Whether or not he provides the exact words of Jesus, most scholars agree that at least he allows us to hear the voice of Jesus.

Some of the best parallels in both form and content to the Sermon on the Mount appear in Prov 1–9 and 22–24, Sirach, and 4Q418. In them the sage hands on, to those willing and eager to learn, the fruit of human experience captured in the wisdom tradition. Using a variety of literary forms, the sage moves from topic to topic, without offering detailed developments. The students were presumably expected to commit these sayings to memory, meditate on them and make them their own, and be prepared to apply them when the right situation might arise.

Jesus' sermon is introduced in Matt 5:3-12 with a series of beatitudes ("blessed are the poor in spirit ..."), a typical literary form used by Jewish wisdom teachers. A beatitude declares someone "happy" or "fortunate" because of certain character traits, attitudes, or possessions. In the Matthean beatitudes (compare Luke 6:20-23) there is, beside the declaration of good fortune, a promise of perfect happiness when the fullness of God's kingdom comes ("for theirs is the kingdom of heaven").

In 5:17-48 Jesus the sage offers interpretations of biblical commandments, and challenges his hearers to go to their roots ("not to abolish but to fulfill"). For example, if you wish to avoid breaking the biblical commandment against murder (Exod 20:13//Deut 5:17), avoid the anger that leads to murder (Matt 5:21-26). Long before Jesus of Nazareth, Ben Sira brought biblical interpretation into the curriculum of his wisdom school (e.g., 3:3-5, 14-15). Then in 6:1-18 Jesus comments on three acts of Jewish piety (almsgiving, prayer, and fasting) and in each case he contrasts how the "hypocrites" act (ostentatiously) and their reward (a good public reputation) with how "you" should act (in secret) and "your" reward (from God). Again, Ben Sira frequently advised his pupils to pray for wisdom and infuse their studies with religious practices and humility before God (e.g., 1:26; 3:17-20).

Even more typical of Jewish wisdom instructions is Matt 6:19–7:12 where Jesus moves through several different topics: treasures in heaven, sound eyes, serving two masters, anxiety, judgment, dogs and pigs, prayers of petition, and the golden rule. Likewise, the concluding exhortation to put these teachings into practice (7:13-27) fits well with the Jewish wisdom tradition's emphasis on application in daily life. The images of gates and ways, trees and their fruits, and houses and their foundations all bring home the practical implications of Jesus' wisdom teachings.

B. Jesus the Wisdom of God

1. Backgrounds

In some early Christian circles Jesus was celebrated as the Wisdom of God, that is, the incarnation and personification of divine wisdom. The roots of this transition from Jesus the wisdom teacher to Jesus the Wisdom of God can be discerned in the Synoptic tradition when Jesus declares that "wisdom is vindicated by her deeds" (Matt 11:19) and "something greater than Solomon is here" (Matt 12:42).

The even deeper roots of wisdom christology are to be found in the OT texts in which Wisdom appears as a female figure. In Prov 8:22-36 personified Wisdom claims to have been created at the beginning of God's work and to have been present at God's creating heaven and earth, and is now "rejoicing in his inhabited world and delighting in the human race" (8:31). In Sir 24:1-22 Wisdom sings her own praises as the firstborn of creation and as having been present at the creation of everything else. She then describes her search for a home on earth and finding her dwelling place in the Jerusalem Temple and among the people of Israel. In his initial comment on Wisdom's discourse, Ben Sira identifies her with the Torah: "All this is the book of the covenant of the Most High God, the law that Moses commanded us" (Sir 24:23).

In the Wisdom of Solomon, the figure of Wisdom takes the form of the Stoic world soul: "the spirit of the Lord has filled the world, and that which holds all things together knows what is said" (Wis 1:7). In Wis 7:22-26 Wisdom is first described with a list of twenty-one attributes of the world soul ("intelligent, holy, unique, manifold, subtle ..."), and then she is called "a breath of the power of God, and a pure emanation of the glory of the Almighty ... a reflection of eternal light, a spotless mirror of the working of God, and an image of his goodness." In short, Wisdom is everywhere and holds all creation together.

These visions of Wisdom and creation in Sirach and Wisdom contrast with that of *1 En.* 42, where Wisdom fails to find a home on earth and returns to heaven. There she is accessible only in dreams and visions or through the mediation of those like Enoch who take heavenly journeys and report on what they see.

2. Wisdom christology

These Jewish traditions about personified Wisdom raise two questions: Who (or what) is Wisdom? Where is Wisdom to be found? Early Christians found their answers in the risen Jesus. In what is generally regarded as an early Christian hymn preserved in Col 1:15-20, Jesus Christ is celebrated as first in the order of creation (1:15-18a) and first in the order of redemption (1:18b-20).

Echoing words and images found in Prov 8:22-36 and Wis 7:22-26, the first part of the hymn describes Jesus as "the image of the invisible God, the firstborn of all creation," places him as present at the creation, and claims that "all things have been created through him

and for him." It calls him "the head of the body," which the text identifies as the church. The second part of the hymn celebrates Jesus as "the firstborn from the dead" (in his resurrection) and asserts that "in him all the fullness of God was pleased to dwell." Through Jesus as the incarnation of divine wisdom, God has been able to bring about a cosmic reconciliation. The ending of the hymn specifies "the blood of his cross" as the means of this reconciliation.

In the letter to the Colossians this hymn serves as the key text on which Paul (or the Pauline author) develops his case for the absolute sufficiency of Jesus' death and resurrection to bring Jews and Gentiles into right relationship with God (justification). Some scholars regard "the church" and "through the blood of his cross" as Pauline editorial touches added to the hymn. At any rate, the Colossians hymn reflects an early christology in which Jesus is described in terms of the Wisdom of God dwelling in the body of Christ (whether this is understood on the cosmic or the ecclesial level).

A similar wisdom christology echoing Wis 7:22-26 appears in the prologue to the letter to the Hebrews: "He [Christ] is the reflection of God's glory and the exact imprint of God's very being, and he sustains all things by his powerful word" (1:3). Here also Jesus is the Wisdom of God, and as such sustains all creation.

C. Other Perspectives

1. John

In John's Gospel Jesus is not so much the wisdom teacher that he is in the Synoptic Gospels as he is the Wisdom or Word of God. This identity is expressed most clearly in the Gospel's prologue (John 1:1-18), which has often been described as an early Christian hymn celebrating Jesus as the Wisdom of God. John used the hymn to introduce the central conviction of his narrative: Jesus is both the revealer and the revelation of God: "In the beginning was the Word" (1:1). While the "Word" can be interpreted in the light of God's prophetic word or the Logos of Hellenistic and Philonic philosophy, its most obvious background is the figure of personified Wisdom in the tradition of Prov 8:22-36; Sir 24:1-22; Wis 7:22-26; Col 1:15-20.

In John 1:1-5, Jesus as the Word of God is said to have been with God "in the beginning" and to have been God's agent in bringing the cosmos into existence. This hymn goes further and makes the claim that "the Word was God" (1:1). In 1:10-13 there is a description of the mixed reception granted to Jesus the Word of God when he came into the world in search of his home. Even though "his own people did not accept him," he has enabled those who believe in him to become "children of God." The most important affirmation of all in John's prologue comes in 1:14: "And the Word became flesh and lived among us." Whereas in the other Jewish wisdom texts it is difficult to discern whether Wisdom is an attribute of God, a hypostasis, or even a goddess figure, in John 1:14 the Wisdom (or

Word) of God is Jesus of Nazareth. As such he is the manifestation of the glory of God and the authoritative interpreter or "exegete" of God, the one who makes God known (1:18).

The placing of this Wisdom text at the beginning of John's Gospel as a prologue or overture makes the "signs" performed by Jesus and the long discourses given by him into revelations of God's own wisdom. It also provides a theological context for John's interpretation of Jesus' passion, death, and resurrection as an exaltation ("lifting up") and a manifestation of God's glory.

2. Paul

In 1 Cor 1–4, Paul seeks to relate God's wisdom to the cross of Jesus Christ. The occasion seems to have been a dispute among Corinthian Christians about their wisdom and spiritual gifts. The disputants appeal to the apostles (Paul, Apollos, and Cephas) who had baptized them and to the superior wisdom granted to them.

In 1 Cor 1:18–2:16 Paul reminds the Corinthians that the wisdom into which they have been baptized is the wisdom of the cross. He first asserts in 1:18-25 that through the cross of Christ God has turned human perceptions of wisdom upside down, and notes that Christ crucified is a "stumbling block to Jews and foolishness to Gentiles." Nevertheless, Christ is "the power of God and the wisdom of God," precisely because only Jesus' suffering and death could bring about right relationship with God. That means that "God's foolishness is wiser than human wisdom, and God's weakness is stronger than human strength" (1:25).

Next in 1:26-31 Paul challenges the Corinthians to look carefully at themselves ("not many of you were wise by human standards") and to recognize from the case of Jesus that God's wisdom works through what is foolish, weak, lowly, and despised in the world. Then he reminds them that the new life they have received and the gifts of righteousness, sanctification, and redemption have come through the cross of Christ "who became for us wisdom from God" (1:30).

In 2:1-5 Paul appeals to his own example. He denies that he preached the mystery of God "in lofty words or wisdom" or "with plausible words of wisdom" (see 2 Cor 10–13). Rather, he came in weakness and fear, knowing only "Jesus Christ, and him crucified." He goes on in 2:6-13 to draw a contrast between "the wisdom of this age" and the wisdom that is "taught by the Spirit." He concludes in 2:14-16 by reminding the Corinthian disputants that those who fail to discern the gifts of God's Spirit and the wisdom of the cross have no right to boast over their wisdom and spiritual possessions.

3. James

Only the epistolary salutation in Jas 1:1 establishes this document as a letter. Otherwise, it looks much more like a wisdom instruction, like parts of Proverbs, Sirach, and the Sermon on the Mount. It mentions Jesus

only twice and even then in a formulaic manner ("Lord Jesus Christ"). If the author was James "the brother of the Lord," it is a very early document (from the 50s CE), representing a primitive form of Jewish Christianity based in Jerusalem. If (as most scholars today contend) it was written in the name of James and therefore is pseudonymous, it would be from the late 1st cent. but would still represent an unusual (sapiential) form of Christianity.

As is the case with most wisdom instructions, it is difficult to discern the literary structure of James. In 1:2-11 it introduces three themes—the trials of life, wisdom, and rich and poor—that are prominent in the body of the instruction. Other common wisdom themes treated by James include hearing and doing, partiality in social relations, correct speech, contentiousness and conflicts, and greed. There are many parallels with Jesus' sayings in the Synoptic Gospels and in Matthew's Gospel and the Sermon on the Mount in particular. The most obvious example is the prohibition against swearing oaths in Matt 5:33-37 and Jas 5:12. As in the Sermon on the Mount, the various wisdom teachings are set in an eschatological context: "Strengthen your hearts, for the coming of the Lord is near" (5:8).

In the history of theology the most famous part of James' wisdom instruction is the section devoted to the relationship between faith and works in 2:14-26. Here James takes issue with a teaching that claims that faith alone (apart from works) is sufficient for justification and salvation. Whether this teaching was understood as coming directly from Paul is not clear. It was more likely a popular misconstrual of Paul's doctrine of justification by faith developed most completely in his letters to the Galatians and the Romans. Paul's own ideal of Christian life was "faith working through love" (Gal 5:6). James' response to claims about faith without works is the typical Jewish emphasis on wisdom as something to be acted upon or put into practice (see Matt 7:13-27). Thus he contends that "faith apart from works is barren" (2:20) and that "faith without works is also dead" (2:26).

D. Theological Problems

1. Theodicy and retribution

One theme that runs through OT wisdom writings is the law of retribution: Wise and righteous persons prosper, and foolish and wicked persons suffer and die. In the various parts of the book of Proverbs this principle is upheld with confidence: For example, "the LORD does not let the righteous go hungry, but he thwarts the craving of the wicked" (Prov 10:3). However, the sage known as Ecclesiastes/Qoheleth questions its validity in the light of his own experience and notes that "the same fate" (death) comes to us all (Eccl 9:2). Moreover, the book of Job is a relentless examination of this principle as applied to someone who was "blameless and upright, one who feared God and turned away from evil" (1:1). The debate between Job and his friends revolves around three theological propositions: God is omnipotent, God is just, and an innocent person (Job) is suffering. Job's friends insist that he must have sinned; otherwise he would not be suffering. Job defends his integrity and in turn raises questions about God's justice and omnipotence. God's speeches from the whirlwind end the conversation, without really answering Job's questions.

2. The apocalyptic solution

The apocalyptic solution to the problem of theodicy (justifying God) is to defer the definitive manifestation of God's justice to life after death and the full coming of God's kingdom. So in Daniel, Revelation, and other apocalypses (see also 2 Macc 7) there appear beliefs in the resurrection of the dead, divine judgment according to one's deeds, and appropriate rewards and punishments. Likewise, in the book of Wisdom, eternal life with God is the ultimate reward for righteous and wise living, whereas the wicked can expect punishments after death.

3. The Christian solution

As Mark 12:18-27 indicates, Jesus shared with the Pharisees beliefs in the resurrection of the dead, final judgment, and postmortem rewards and punishments. Early Christian convictions about Jesus' own resurrection and his vindication at Easter after suffering "for us" and "for our sins" put the whole debate about theodicy and retribution on a new basis, as least for Christians. According to the NT, Jesus' sacrificial death made possible a new and better relationship with God (justification). When the fullness of God's kingdom comes, the righteous will be rewarded and the wicked will be punished, with the risen Christ serving as the judge in some scenarios (Matt 25:31-46). In the meantime, Christians (following Paul) are advised to regard their present sufferings as sharing in the sufferings of Christ and as "not worth comparing with the glory about to be revealed" (Rom 8:18). *See* CHRISTOLOGY; GOSPELS; JAMES, LETTER OF; PAUL, THE APOSTLE; TEACHING OF JESUS.

Bibliography: John J. Collins. *Jewish Wisdom in the Hellenistic Age* (1997); Celia M. Deutsch. *Lady Wisdom, Jesus and the Sages: Metaphor and Social Context in Matthew's Gospel* (1997); Matthew Goff. *Discerning Wisdom: The Sapiential Literature of the Dead Sea Scrolls* (2007); Daniel J. Harrington. *Jesus Ben Sira of Jerusalem* (2005); Ben Witherington. *Jesus the Sage: The Pilgrimage of Wisdom* (2000).

DANIEL J. HARRINGTON, SJ

WISDOM IN THE OT [חָכְמָה khokhmah; σοφία sophia, φρόνησις phronēsis]. Wisdom is a quality of being wise, i.e., having the ability to make the right use of knowledge, being learned, discreet, skillful, perceptive, and judging rightly. It is the quality that transcends the human sphere to become a spiritual perception,

linked to God. In the OT there is a distinct set of books known as Wisdom literature, notably Proverbs, Job, and Ecclesiastes. In the Apocrypha the wisdom books are Ben Sira/Ecclesiasticus and the Wisdom of Solomon. However, wisdom influence—defined by formal similarities, links in subject matter, and contextual concerns—is found in other literature in the OT. The question is raised how far the definition of Wisdom literature should be extended. At the center of the wisdom worldview stands the figure of Wisdom, a personification of the attribute who mediates among human beings, the wider world, and the divine realm.

I shall divide the discussion into three major areas that are of principal concern in the scholarship: social context, an overview of what constitutes Wisdom literature, and theological context.

  A. Social Context
    1. Wisdom of the people
    2. The sages at court and school
    3. The wise as a class
    4. The royal link
    5. Egyptian and Mesopotamian wisdom
    6. Mantic wisdom
  B. Wisdom Literature
    1. Proverbs
    2. Job
    3. Ecclesiastes
    4. Song of Songs
    5. Wisdom psalms
    6. Wisdom narratives
    7. Daniel
    8. Ben Sira/Ecclesiasticus
    9. The Wisdom of Solomon
  C. Theological Context
    1. Humanity and the natural world
    2. God and Wisdom
  Bibliography

A. Social Context

Wisdom in the OT cannot be fully understood without an appreciation of the diverse social contexts that gave rise to it and perpetuated it over many centuries.

1. Wisdom of the people

It is likely that the activity of coining proverbs goes far back into time and was a common practice of people of all types and social strata. The coining of pithy sayings in order to express a truth within one or two lines is common to most cultures in the world (Vikings, Chinese, African, European), and the largely domestic nature of the subject matter of many proverbs indicates this. Oral tradition is the most likely milieu for the transmission of proverbs within families and tribes over many centuries. The question then arises how orally transmitted proverbs became a part of the book of Proverbs and an important literary tradition. It had to be the educated and those who could write who eventually fixed the proverbs in writing, even if their origin was broader. It is notable that many proverbs concern wealth and poverty, the one coming to the righteous, the other to the wicked (e.g., Prov 11:18). This may indicate a special concern with the danger of falling into poverty—often through laziness (e.g., Prov 20:13)—and may indicate a social group for whom wealth was not to be taken for granted and for whom poverty was a real danger. Many proverbs have an agricultural concern and use natural imagery to illuminate human behavior, which may indicate a farming background (e.g., Prov 12:11). However, some also advise on table manners in the presence of the king and those would hardly belong outside a court context (Prov 23:1-3). Thus the original sociohistorical context of the proverbs is likely to have been more than one context, possibly with pockets of oral and written tradition on a continuum and with an important distinction being needed between broader origins and a narrower "writing-down" context.

2. The sages at court and school

As the literature of the educated, wisdom has its natural home in two main environments: the court and the school. While the court context may have been overplayed in the past, it is clear that the king needed an educated circle around him to act as advisors, administrators, and recorders of events. Second Chronicles 25:16-17 uses the expression "royal counselor." Such a group of sages would have needed education, and a court school based in Jerusalem seems the most likely possibility. We know from Sumerian and Egyptian contexts that wisdom was used in a school context; the copying of sayings on a tablet was a means of learning to read and write.

The Egyptian "Instruction of Amenemope" was used as such a text for schoolboys, and numerous copies of it have been found (*see* AMENEMOPE, INSTRUCTION OF). Interestingly, it is strongly echoed (with intimations of literary dependence) in Prov 22:17–24:22. Other parts of Proverbs strongly suggest an educational context, notably chaps. 1–9 with its exhortations from father and mother to "listen ... to a father's instruction" (Prov 4:1) or "be attentive to my wisdom" (Prov 5:1). This indicates a family context for education; the mother's teaching refers to that given to the young child, and yet this does not preclude the teacher/pupil relationship also being the referent here. Education probably started and continued in the home, although there may have been families of scribes with more educational roles, such as the ability to teach and write. The book of Ecclesiastes indicates a teaching situation with the author in Solomonic persona instructing his listeners in what he has learned of life. Later evidence from Ben Sira/Ecclesiasticus indicates a teaching context, made clear in the prologue to the book: that "those who love learning might make even greater progress in living according to the law." Whether there was a widespread system of schooling in Israel has been debated at length

but suffers from lack of any evidence, archaeological or otherwise. Given the size and resources of the state, it is perhaps unlikely that any sophisticated school network existed. Any kind of higher education beyond family or local scribal circles is likely to have been at the court.

In Sumerian culture the archival function is an important one and this may well have featured at the Israelite court. There may also have been sages at court who were dissatisfied with the status quo and sought to express that in their writing. The book of Job may have arisen in a situation in which a sage wished to challenge the dominant worldview of the proverbial material and ask difficult questions about the real nature of relationship with God given the reality of suffering. Thus the sages' roles included theological reflection as well as political and social advice and education. Whether there were any female sages remains an open question. Some biblical books might indicate female authorship (e.g., Ruth, Song of Songs) but that is by no means definite. There may have been some female sages in the ANE (notably in Mesopotamian culture), and the references to "mother" in Prov 1–9 (also in Prov 31:1, the mother of King Lemuel) may indicate a prominent role for women in education.

3. The wise as a class

The main evidence that "the wise" were a recognized group or class of people in ancient Israel comes from the prophets—Isaiah, Jeremiah, and Ezekiel—who generally castigate them. The wise probably represented the status quo in their association with the court. They were the powerful, having the ear of the king. Isaiah 29:14-15 speaks of the wise who gave advice ("The wisdom of their wise") to resist, with the expectation of aid from Egypt; although God's advice was different. Jeremiah 18:18 famously speaks of "counsel from the wise" as does Ezek 7:26, "counsel from the elders." The function of this group was clearly to provide counsel ('etsah עֵצָה). One should be careful, however, not to split groups too firmly, acknowledging important overlap between different groups, e.g., prophetic influence on the portrayal of Wisdom in Prov 1–9, cultic hints such as Prov 3:9-10, and wisdom influence in other material (see below). Many skilled people are called wise in the sense of "skilled" or "able," e.g., those who fashion the tabernacle (Exod 28:3) or Jerusalem Temple (1 Kgs 7:14). A distinction should probably be made between "sage" and "scribe." The category of "the wise" probably includes both. However, the scribes had more of a writing role, in preservation and redaction of sayings and books, while the sages were probably more active in advising the king and in political and social roles. Scribe (sofer סֹפֵר) is hence a broader category than sage (khakham חָכָם).

4. The royal link

King Solomon is reputed to have been a great wise king (1 Kgs 4:29-34) and is likely to have established such an entourage at his court, perhaps modeled on Egyptian parallels. We have evidence in Prov 25:1 that King Hezekiah had scribes who "copied" "other proverbs of Solomon," thus indicating a court context in the later monarchic period for the wisdom enterprise. There is also the evidence provided by the Joseph story in Gen 37–50, which tells of a young Israelite who rose to prominence at the court of Pharaoh. In many ways he is the ideal of the successful wise man: someone who rises to a position of such prominence that he is right-hand man to the king himself. It is interesting that the later author of Ecclesiastes takes on the persona of Solomon in an autobiographical section about the quest for happiness (Eccl 1:16–2:12). It is also significant that the Song of Songs (traditionally attributed to Solomon in his youth by rabbinic tradition) also contains references to Solomon and his wedding festivities (Song 3:11). This suggests that the Solomonic link lives on in the wisdom tradition well beyond his original role in relation to wisdom. In 1 Kgs 10 he is described as having international connections and he riddles with the Queen of Sheba who comes from a far country to meet him. This suggests international connections and an opening up of the state. It is likely that influences from abroad came into Israel at this point, and the adoption of an Egyptian-style model of wise men becomes more plausible in this light.

5. Egyptian and Mesopotamian wisdom

The Egyptian context is clearly the primary background for the wisdom enterprise. The Wisdom literature was sometimes regarded by older scholars as a "foreign element" in Israelite thought, largely due to its closer connections with the wider ANE context. From Egypt we have instruction texts, thought to be paralleled in Prov 1–9. There is also a figure of Ma'at who has certain descriptive resemblances with the figure of Woman Wisdom in Prov 8. We know that Egyptian wisdom had a court context and an important educational role, and so our contextual conclusions regarding Israelite wisdom tend to be based on these models. Whether there were direct parallels between types of administrators and vizier remains unproved. From Mesopotamia we find a very different tradition of protest and complaint that seems to have influenced Israelite Wisdom literature at the point of the book of Job, with its critique of the status quo as represented by Proverbs. We find close parallels to Job, such as the Babylonian Job and Babylonian Theodicy. We also find parallels to Ecclesiastes in the Dialogue of Pessimism.

6. Mantic wisdom

Another development out of the original wisdom worldview was that of mantic wisdom: the interpretation of dreams and secrets. Ironically, the earlier wisdom enterprise is available to all and universal in its scope (unlike so much of the OT, which is specifically addressed to the Israelite people within a covenant context). However, in later times, wisdom became aligned with the knowledge that is available only to a small group of the righteous. This is partly due to its identification with Torah in the apocryphal wisdom tradition (see below), but it has biblical roots in mantic wisdom, as evidenced in a small way in the book of Job (in Eliphaz's vision in Job 4:13-17) and in the book of Daniel, in which Daniel is the wise man who interprets the dreams of Pharaoh. In Dan 2:12-14 the term "wise men" (Aram.: khakkimayya> חַכִּימַיָּא) includes "the magicians, the enchanters, the sorcerers and the Chaldeans" (Dan 2:2) as well as astrologers. This suggests a much broader remit for "the wise" by this late postexilic time, certainly for those working in Persian circles.

B. Wisdom Literature

1. Proverbs

The book of Proverbs is the starting point of the Wisdom literature, with the proverb as its distinguishing genre. The book should be divided into sections since each has a different provenance and character. Proverbs 1–9 is often thought to be the latest section of the book, added as a kind of preface to the rest of the book. Its main genres are instruction and wisdom poem; there are also small groupings of proverbial sayings and pieces of autobiographical narrative. It is the most theological of the sections, with the figures of Woman Wisdom and Woman Folly providing a theological counterpoint between righteous and wicked paths, but then with Wisdom revealing herself as present with God at the creative act itself (Prov 8:22-31). The main body of sayings is contained in Prov 10:1–22:16 and consists of proverbs, one after another. A debate has taken place in the scholarship over whether there are any patterns in the ordering of the sayings. Some chapters seem to have thematic clusters (e.g., Prov 16 on God and the king), but many proverbs seem to be randomly placed. There are some repetitions, often with subtle variations (e.g., Prov 20:10, 23). Another distinct section is contained in Prov 22:17–24:22, the section parallel with the "Instruction of Amenemope" from Egypt (see §A.2). This also contains proverbial sayings material on various familiar topics (e.g., the poor, avoiding angry people, or giving pledges). Proverbs 24:23-34 is a very small section of ethical sayings. The next main section is in Prov 25–29, which is very like Prov 10:1–22:16 in character, but is attributed to the "men of Hezekiah." There are strings of proverbs, some of them repetitions from the previous section (e.g., Prov 25:5, compare 16:12). Finally, there are smaller sections in Prov 30:1-14; 30:15-33; 31:1-9; and 31:10-31. Each of these chapters is differently attributed: Prov 30 to Agur and Prov 31 to Lemuel. Proverbs 30 begins with a questioning piece that sounds as if it belongs more closely to the Job tradition. This may represent the beginnings of dissatisfaction with the rather black-and-white proverbial worldview that the righteous are always rewarded and the wicked punished. Proverbs 30:16-33 contains nature wisdom used in numerical sayings for comparison with human attributes. Proverbs 31:1-9 contains admonitions to a young king about his juridical duties, indicating a court background here. Proverbs 31:10-31 contains the poem on the capable wife that praises her from a male perspective. With the emphasis on Woman Wisdom in Prov 1–9 there is the feeling of inclusion between the beginning and end of Proverbs in relation to female characters, the work of final redactors perhaps. It is clear then that the book of Proverbs was not written at one sitting, but represents a mass of material, probably much of it originally oral, brought together over a period of time. The main proverbial section may have come together as early as the 8th cent. BCE with 25–29 attributable to the 7th cent. BCE. The other collections are largely impossible to date, but Prov 1–9 with its more theological reflection and nature as a prologue could be as late as the postexilic period, although some scholars would place it earlier. The book of Proverbs is a compendium for life, containing proverbs on a huge range of topics from money, work, and power to relationships between parents, children, brothers, friends, neighbors, and effective communication. It has a clear message of guidance for young men seeking to gain wisdom and to start their path of life. Wisdom assists in this process, as do parents (through the instruction texts), and ultimately God, who stands at the beginning and end of the wisdom quest. Every act has its consequence, and through education the young man can learn appropriate modes of behavior that lead to desired consequences. There is a prescientific interest in ordering the world, including the natural world, according to principles of order. God is portrayed in Proverbs as essentially the creator and sustainer of that order. Human society with the king at its head also fits into that order, as does the natural world.

2. Job

The book of Job takes its starting point from the doctrine of retribution so familiar from the proverbial literature, but it takes the issue further in the example story of Job, a man who was fully righteous but who suffered undeservedly. It is composed of a prologue and epilogue in narrative form that outlines the simple tale of Job who was blameless and upright and did all God instructed him to do, including good works on behalf of others. He tragically loses his wealth and family and then his health, and at first his reaction seems to be uncomplaining and accepting (Job 1:21; 2:10). There are scenes in the prologue set in heaven with God and Satan engaging in a wager, which is given as the reason for Job's trial. The issue here is disinterested righteousness: does Job serve God simply because of the rewards or does he serve God for nothing? However, Job does not know about this. In the epilogue, Job is restored twice over with goods and a new family. It is the debate in between that is really theologically interesting (Job

3:1–42:6). It may be that the author of the so-called "dialogue" knew the early folktale about Job and decided to use it as a vehicle to say something more theologically profound. The character of Job seems to be known to Ezekiel (14:14, 20). In chap. 3 we are introduced to the lamenting Job who blames God for his suffering and wishes that he had never been born, nor even conceived. Then comes a dialogue in which Job converses with three friends who have ostensibly come to comfort him (Job 4–27). This is where the debate over the doctrine of retribution takes place. Job maintains his innocence throughout while the friends believe that Job must have sinned, otherwise he would not be punished. The friends maintain the traditional wisdom view that righteousness must be rewarded and wickedness punished. Job's experience tells him that this is not the case and that God can act in an arbitrary way. The debate moves on—at least for Job—to a discussion of the relationship between God and humanity: can there be any real relationship given the limitations of just action on God's part? At the book's climax (after the arrival of a fourth friend, Elihu [32–37], to add to the debate) God appears in a whirlwind ostensibly to answer Job's questions, although he does not address them directly (Job 38–41). Rather, we find a rehearsal of God's creative acts and continuing nurturing of creation on a daily basis. We find strange descriptions of wild animals and mythological ones, beyond human comprehension. It seems that Job is decidedly put in his place as he lays his hand on his mouth (Job 40:4) and is quieted. The restoration of Job then follows (42:7-17), according to the original narrative tale. The genres of Job—narrative tale, dialogue, lament, and theophany—are very different from anything found in Proverbs. In fact, there is hardly any similarity between genres in the two books. Rather, Job can be seen to reflect other genres from OT tradition, notably psalmic laments and legal genres. In his quest for justice, Job makes use of formal legal genres to plead his case. Moreover, the author of Job enjoys ironically parodying existing genres to show his undermining of traditional sentiments. Thus Job is a radical questioning of not just the wisdom worldview but also the traditions of lament and justice in the wider OT. Its author may well have been a renegade sage on the edges of the wisdom tradition. The work has sometimes been compared to a Greek tragedy, such as Aeschylus' *Prometheus Bound*, but with its probable date between the 6th and 4th cent., dependence on such works is unlikely. Rather, the closer parallels are with Mesopotamian tradition (see §A.5).

3. Ecclesiastes

The questioning tradition continues in the book of Ecclesiastes, which also undermines the simple certainties of the book of Proverbs. The author often cites proverbs in order to refute them and provide his own analysis, peppered with repeated key words that express his view on life, such as "vanity of vanities! All is vanity!"

(Eccl 1:2*b*), "toil" (Eccl 1:3), "under the sun" (Eccl 1:3), and "eat and drink, and find enjoyment" (Eccl 2:24). This author is preoccupied with the quest for happiness and the certainty of death. He seeks meaning in life and has difficulty finding it. He sees death as the great leveler, making a mockery of social hierarchy and grandeur. The author takes on a Solomonic persona early on (Eccl 1:1; 1:12; 1:16–2:12) in which he tests pleasure in relation to material wealth and social opportunity. Later on he seems to drop that persona, and there arises an interesting tension in his thought between affirmation of enjoyment in life and a deep despair about the pointlessness of it. The epilogue section (Eccl 12:9-14)—often thought to have been added later, possibly even by the author himself—commends fearing God, which is a rather more pious conclusion than is found in the main body of the work, aligning more with Proverbs itself where the fear of the Lord is the beginning of wisdom (see Prov 1:7). Ecclesiastes is thought to belong to the postexilic period and may have come under the influence of Greek thought. It has been likened to the work of Stoics and Epicureans, but no one conclusion as to its provenance has been definitively adopted. It is steeped in the Israelite wisdom tradition and so is unlikely to have any direct dependence upon Greek works, although it was probably written in the 3rd cent. BCE (some scholars argue for the 5th cent.), so some contact with Hellenistic culture would be likely.

4. Song of Songs

The Song of Songs is not generally regarded as mainstream Wisdom literature, its primary genre being that of "love song." However, there are indications of wisdom influence that may indicate a closer relationship than previously thought. The link with Solomon is interesting: there are seven references (1:1, 5; 3:7, 9, 11; 8:11, 12) and a number more to a king figure that is likely to be him. The luxuriant description of a wedding seems to belong to a royal context (Song 3:11). Then there are a few abstract wisdom sayings in the book (e.g., Song 3:5*b*; 8:4*b*, 6*b*-7). Finally, there are close similarities in the portrayal of the characters in the Song, and the figures of Woman Wisdom and Woman Folly in Prov 1–9. This adds up to a picture at least of influence from the wisdom tradition, if not an origin there, and a deliberate connection made with Solomon, the figurehead of the wisdom enterprise.

5. Wisdom psalms

The Psalter is not without the influence of wisdom. There are certain psalms that have similarities to mainstream wisdom books and so are described as "wisdom psalms." There are also parts of other psalms that might come under this heading. The problem is deciding the criteria regarding what is to be included under this heading, and various scholars seem to have their own lists. My long list is as follows: Pss 1; 14; 19; 25; 32; 33; 34; 36; 37; 39; 49; 51; 53; 62; 73; 78; 90;

92; 94; 104; 105; 106; 111; 112; 119; 127; 128. A shorter list might simply include 1; 34; 37; 39; 49; and 73. There is a further question whether wisdom was a formative influence on the Psalter—wisdom sentiments came into psalms at an early stage as it was a part of the thought-world of the time—or predominantly a redactional influence, with scribes possibly responsible for bringing the whole Psalter together into a cohesive whole. There is probably truth in both possibilities; it is hard to believe that the wisdom worldview was absent from early expressions of worship. God the creator is a regular theme in psalms, and unless they are all late (as was once maintained) it is likely to be an early motif. The world of education and ethics is represented in these wisdom psalms, as are the complaints of Job and Ecclesiastes.

6. Wisdom narratives

It is thought that some narrative texts have come under the influence of the wisdom worldview, notably the Joseph story in Gen 37–50 and the Succession Narrative in 2 Sam 20–1 Kgs 2. As mentioned above, Joseph is the epitome of the successful wise man who has reached high position in the court of Pharaoh (Gen 41:33-44). He also interprets dreams, like Daniel: an indication perhaps of a mantic wisdom link. "All the magicians of Egypt and all its wise men" (Gen 41:8) are unable to compete with Joseph, who successfully finds the meaning of the dreams (Gen 41:9-32). The Succession Narrative is linked with wisdom largely on the grounds that God is behind the scenes in the narrative, much more than his more direct role in other OT narratives. The concern is who is to succeed King David, and interest is in human intrigue and politics. If the wise men were at court, then this would be just the kind of narrative they would have enjoyed. At the end of the process it is none other than their hero King Solomon who becomes king of the united kingdom. There may be other contenders for the wisdom category among narratives but they are outside the scope of this article.

7. Daniel

Daniel is another biblical book not normally classified as Wisdom literature but as apocalyptic, yet there are aspects within it that hint at the wisdom tradition, particularly the mantic wisdom tradition. Like Joseph, Daniel finds himself at the court of the king: this time of the Persian king Nebuchadnezzar. He too interprets dreams and reaches high position in court. He is a faithful, wise man who receives God's protection and praises God's wisdom (Dan 2:20-23). The existence of Persian "wise men" is indicated here: they fail to interpret the king's dream and are ordered to be put to death; meanwhile, with God's help Daniel explains the dream, saving his own life and those of his companions.

8. Ben Sira/Ecclesiasticus

Ben Sira, or Ecclesiasticus, from the 2nd cent. BCE, is in the Apocrypha, yet it is an important wisdom book. It contains many proverbs and maxims along the lines of the book of Proverbs, although it is not ascribed to Solomon. These are often clustered according to subject in a more obvious way than in Proverbs, and there are longer discourses. The book also contains prayers (Sir 36:1-17), poems about great personalities of the OT (Sir 44–49), and wider genres from other parts of Israelite life, including an interest in Temple, cult, and priesthood. The author's major theological step is the identification of the figure of Wisdom with the Torah, which then enables a reconciliation of Wisdom with Israelite identity and history. Thus, just as Wisdom was alongside God at the creative act (Prov 8), so was the Torah (Sir 24).

9. The Wisdom of Solomon

The Wisdom of Solomon, a 1st-cent. BCE document written in Greek, is also in the Apocrypha. Although attributed to Solomon, its eschatological nature is a far cry from the kind of wisdom Solomon excelled in (see 1 Kgs 4:29-32). It praises Wisdom and elevates her to an attribute or hypostasis of the divine and so makes the theological leap from seeing Wisdom as a mediator but strictly created, to a hypostasis of God, hence preexistent and coexistent with God (Wis 7:2–8:1). Again there is more interaction with other genres of Israelite life including cultic and priestly genres. The righteous are now to be rewarded in an afterlife, rather than strictly upon earth—thus circumventing the problem of unrighteous suffering in this life—and the wicked are to be condemned to eternal punishment. This leads the author—using Greek categories—to describe the soul as a separate entity. The NT idea of Logos (John 1) may have its origins in the hypostasis of Wisdom as presented in the Wisdom of Solomon.

C. Theological Context
1. Humanity and the natural world

An important interrelationship is established in the Wisdom literature between humanity and the natural world. God is the creator of the world, of humans, animals, plants, the elements, and of the order that holds the fabric of life together. The world to which the wisdom writers look is the natural one; proverbs often draw comparisons between unlike phenomena: one human, one nonhuman: e.g., "The north wind produces rain, and a backbiting tongue, angry looks" (Prov 25:23). Animal imagery is frequently used: e.g., "Better to meet a she-bear robbed of its cubs than to confront a fool immersed in folly" (Prov 17:12). There are also chapters, such as Prov 30, that seek to understand the way of the world in reference to the behavior of animals in comparison with human beings. The book of Job epitomizes this interaction with nature in the God speeches that identify God closely with the world that God has made. The descriptions of animals in Job 38–41, especially wild ones, and the pleasure that God has taken in creating them puts Job—a mere human—in his place as he tries to understand the workings of God's justice. In abandoning her young, the ostrich is an example of an animal that behaves totally contrary to how humans would behave (Job 39:13-18), and yet God has created the animals as they are, in all their wild, proud freedom. Also in Job 28 there is a rich description of the gems found in the earth and of the birds and animals that find their home there. Ecclesiastes contains little nature imagery but the Song of Songs achieves some of its rich language in the description of lushness, fine perfumes, and so on (e.g., Song 1:3). Humanity is chiefly engaged in the wisdom quest, although there are occasional hints that the animals could sometimes teach humans (e.g., Job 2:7-10). Attaining wisdom means acquiring knowledge and combining that with native intelligence, but also learning from the experience of others and listening to the word of God.

2. God and Wisdom

Humanity and nature are two parts of a triangle that has God at its head. God is the creator and imparter of all life. God also orders and sustains the world. God is at the head of the social order for human beings, the king being God's representative on earth. However, the figure of Wisdom is also a part of this triangle. She holds for the biblical wisdom books a mediating role, imparting wisdom to human beings, acting for the divine, primeval yet herself created. However, by the later wisdom book of Wisdom of Solomon she joins God at the top of the triangle as one of the key attributes that God makes available to human beings. Wisdom is therefore a gift from God to the whole creation, attainable to all who seek to follow its ways. *See* DANIEL, BOOK OF; ECCLESIASTES, BOOK OF; JOB, BOOK OF; PROVERB; PROVERBS, BOOK OF; PSALMS, BOOK OF; SIRACH; SOLOMON, WISDOM OF; WISDOM IN THE ANCIENT NEAR EAST; WORD, THE.

Bibliography: James L. Crenshaw. *Old Testament Wisdom: An Introduction.* Rev. and enl. ed (1998); Katharine J. Dell. *The Book of Proverbs in Social and Theological Context* (2006); Katharine J. Dell. "Does the Song of Songs Have Any Connections to Wisdom?" *Perspectives on the Song of Songs.* Anselm C. Hagedorn, ed. (2005) 8–26; J. Kenneth Kuntz. "The Canonical Wisdom Psalms of Ancient Israel, Their Rhetorical, Thematic and Formal Dimensions." *Rhetorical Criticism: Essays in Honour of James Muilenberg.* Jared Judd Jackson and Martin Kessler, eds. (1974) 186–222; Roland E. Murphy. *The Tree of Life: An Exploration of Biblical Wisdom Literature.* Rev. and enl. ed. (2002); Leo G. Perdue. *Wisdom and Creation* (1994); Leo G. Perdue. *Wisdom Literature: A Theological History* (2007); Gerhard von Rad. "The Joseph Narrative and Ancient Wisdom." *The Problem* of the Hexateuch and Other Essays (1984) 292–300; R. N. Whybray. *The Succession Narrative* (1968); R. N. Whybray. *Wealth and Poverty in the Book of Proverbs* (1990).

KATHARINE J. DELL

WISDOM OF JESUS BEN SIRA. *See* SIRACH.

WISDOM OF JESUS SON OF SIRACH. *See* SIRACH.

WISDOM OF SIRACH. *See* SIRACH.

WISDOM OF SOLOMON. *See* SOLOMON, WISDOM OF.

WISDOM, BOOK OF. *See* SOLOMON, WISDOM OF.

WISDOM, PERSONIFIED. *See* SOPHIA; WISDOM IN THE NT; WISDOM IN THE OT.

WISE. *See* WISDOM IN THE ANCIENT NEAR EAST; WISDOM IN THE NT; WISDOM IN THE OT.

WISE MAN. *See* SAGE; SOLOMON; WISDOM IN THE ANCIENT NEAR EAST; WISDOM IN THE NT; WISDOM IN THE OT.

WISE MEN. *See* MAGI.

WISE WOMAN OF TEKOA tuh-koh′uh [הָאִשָּׁה הַתְּקוֹעִית ha’ishah hatteqo‘ith]. The unnamed woman of TEKOA collaborated with Joab, convincing David to bring Absalom home (2 Sam 14:1-20). Playing a mourner, the woman told David a fictional story paralleling her situation with his own, manipulating the king into declaring a solution with implications for his relationship with Absalom. Subsequently, David agreed to bring Absalom home, which culminated in Absalom's rebellion and demise.

On the one hand, the woman may be truly "wise," a positive character who reunited David with Absalom. On the other hand, she may be seen as "shrewd," in a negative sense or merely as a pawn in the bloody feud over David's successor (compare Jonadab in 2 Sam 13:3).

SUSAN M. PIGOTT

WITCH, WITCHCRAFT. *See* DIVINATION; ENDOR, MEDIUM OF; MAGIC, MAGICIAN; NECROMANCY.

WITHER [יָבֵשׁ yavesh; ξηραίνω xērainō]. Usually refers to a state of dryness, such as bodies of water that are dried up (i.e., Nah 1:4). In the Bible, it most commonly refers to plants that are not productive or the future state of currently productive plants (Joel 1:12; Jonah 4:7). It is also used metaphorically: the prophets refer to the withering of Israel or Judah (Isa 1:30); the rich wither away (Prov 11:28; Jas 1:11); people wither

like grass (Ps 102:11). The term can refer to parts of the human body as well, most commonly hands (1 Kgs 13:4; Mark 3:1-3).

ERIC C. STEWART

WITHERED FIG TREE [ἡ συκῆ ἐξηραμμένη hē sykē exērammenē]. Jesus curses the fig tree and it withers. The story is related in variant versions (Matt 21:18-20; Mark 11:12-14, 20-21). In Mark the story is divided into two parts, sandwiching the "cleansing" of the Temple. In Matthew the story is told in one textual unit immediately following the temple incident. In both cases the motive for Jesus' cursing the fig tree is the lack of fruit available to him when he is hungry. In Mark it is not until the next morning that the disciples notice that the tree has withered, while in Matthew it occurs immediately before their eyes, but in both contexts Jesus uses it as an object lesson about the power of faith. The story may be related to Jer 8:13, where the Lord seeks to gather figs where there are none and the leaves are "withered."

ERIC C. STEWART

WITHERED HAND [ἡ ξηρὰ χείρ hē xēra cheir]. Jesus' healing of a withered hand in a synagogue occurs in Mark 3:1-6 and the other Synoptics (Matt 12:9-14; Luke 6:6-11, stating it was the right hand). The hand is described as dried up, or "withered" (xēra), but specific diagnosis is not given. Indeed, the focus of the intense scene is not on the hand, but whether Jesus will heal on the Sabbath. The healing possibly echoes 1 Kgs 13:4-6, when a defiant Jeroboam is inflicted with a withered hand (compare Zech 11:17) and then healed of the same through the intercession of the "man of God." The Greek word is used not only of certain bodily conditions (Mark 9:18; compare John 5:3) but also of withered vegetation, such as the cursed fig tree (Matt 21:19-20; Mark 11:20-21) and the seed cast on rocky ground (Matt 13:6; Mark 4:6; Luke 8:6).

BRETT S. PROVANCE

WITNESS [עֵד ‘edh; μάρτυς martys]. *Witness*, a juridical term, originally signified a person who had personal knowledge about something and could speak about it before a court of law. Witnesses appear in the Bible in a number of ways. They function to attest contracts and confirm proceedings (Ruth 4:9-11; Jer 32:10, 12). Sometimes inanimate objects act as witnesses of an agreement (Gen 31:44-54; Josh 22:27; 24:27). The tables of the law were called the "tablets of testimony" (Exod 32:15; 34:29; NRSV, "tablets of the covenant"), as they were engraved with God's commandments (Exod 31:18); sometimes the ark itself was described as the "ark of the testimony" (Exod 25:16, 21; Num 17:4, 10; NRSV, "the ark of the covenant").

False or malicious witness was forbidden (Exod 20:16; 23:1-3) but was common (Prov 6:19; 12:17) and punishable (Deut 19:15-19; Prov 19:5, 9). In the

NT false witnesses are noted in the trials of Jesus and Stephen (Matt 26:60; Acts 6:13; 7:58). In Israelite tradition, the TESTIMONY of two or three witnesses was required to secure the conviction of a person on a capital offense (Num 35:30; Deut 17:6-7; 19:15; see Heb 10:28). This legal principle of multiple witness is evident in the NT (John 8:13-18; 1 John 5:7-8), where it is applied in cases of church discipline (Matt 18:16; 2 Cor 13:1; 1 Tim 5:19).

Witness terminology is applied metaphorically to the role of Israel and later to Jesus and his followers. "You are my witnesses," God says to Israel, referring to its task to bear witness to God as God's chosen servant (Isa 43:10, 12; 44:8). Israel was to take Yahweh's side and serve as a witness to the only true God, the Lord of history, and Israel's savior and redeemer. This is an innovative use of lawsuit or controversy language.

In the NT the witness theme surfaces again, especially in the Gospel of John, the Acts of the Apostles, and the book of Revelation. John's Gospel presents a cosmic lawsuit—God in Christ has a controversy with a hostile world (John 5:31-47). Each side offers its evidence and argues its case. The apostles act as witnesses (John 15:27; 1 John 1:1-3; compare Luke 24:48). Jesus himself is a witness to the truth (John 3:31-33; 18:37), and the Holy Spirit serves as the "Advocate" (15:26; 16:8; compare 1 John 2:1).

In Acts, emphasis is placed on the witness of the apostles (1:8, 21-22; 4:33; 10:38-43) and Paul (22:14-15; 26:16). The key point of their testimony is the resurrection of Jesus (2:32; 3:15; 5:30-32; 13:30-31; compare 1 Cor 15:3-11).

John's Apocalypse depicts witness against the background of persecution. Jesus is "the faithful and true witness" (Rev 1:5; 3:14), who sets the pattern for believers (1:9). They offer testimony as they follow Christ (6:9; 12:11, 17). Faithfulness to Jesus may entail martyrdom, as it did for ANTIPAS (2:13; compare Acts 7:54-60). In this way the path is cleared for the Greek word martys ("witness") to develop into the later sense of "martyr."

Bibliography: Allison A. Trites. *The New Testament Concept of Witness* (1977).

ALLISON A. TRITES

WITNESS, ALTAR OF [לְמִזְבֵּחַ כִּי עֵד lammizbeakh ki 'edh; Μαρτύριον Martyrion]. An ALTAR built by the tribes of Reuben, Gad, and Manasseh at the end of the period of conquest (Josh 22:10-34). The name *witness* does not appear in the Hebrew text but appears in the LXX. The altar was built on the Jordan, which marked the boundary between these three tribes east of the Jordan and the rest of the tribes on the west. When the other nine tribes heard of the altar, they gathered for war against Reuben, Gad, and Manasseh, because offerings were supposed to be made only at the tabernacle. War was averted when the three tribes assured the rest of the Israelites that the altar was set up merely

as a witness and that they had no intention of making sacrifices on this altar.

KEVIN A. WILSON

WIZARD. *See* MAGIC, MAGICIAN.

WOE [אוֹי 'oy; οὐαί ouai]. An interjection or exclamation of lament (the similar hoy [הוֹי] is often translated "alas"). *Woe* can express authentic grief when calamity or pain befalls an individual or a community (1 Sam 4:7-8; Jer 10:19; 15:10), as well as regret for sinful or offensive behavior (Job 10:15; Isa 6:5; Lam 5:16). *Woe* can also pronounce divine judgment or rebuke an individual or group (Num 21:29; Hos 7:13). Especially prominent in Isaiah (3:9, 11), Ezekiel (24:6, 9), and Jeremiah (13:27; 48:46), the exclamation, "Woe to ..." often prefaces an oracle of judgment. This pattern is attributed to Jesus in the Gospels of Matthew (11:21; 23:13-29) and Luke (10:13; 11:42-52) as well. In Luke (6:24-26), the Beatitudes are counterbalanced with a set of woes. *Woe* can also function as a substantive to indicate specific instances of distress, or sorrow, as in Prov 23:29 and the three "woes" of Rev 9:12; 11:14.

GREG CAREY

WOLF [זְאֵב ze'ev; λύκος lykos]. The wolf (*Canis lupus*), ancestor of the domestic DOG, is a fierce animal of prey (Gen 49:27; Jer 5:6; Ezek 22:27; John 10:12) still prevalent in the Middle East and known to attack domestic animals as big as cattle. Depicting peaceful coexistence as when "the wolf will live with the lamb" (Isa 11:6; 65:25) is a striking metaphor for the end of days. Zeeb (ze'ev) is also the name of a Midianite captain and a place name (Judg 7:25). *See* ANIMALS OF THE BIBLE; OREB AND ZEEB.

Bibliography: Oded Borowski. *Every Living Thing: Daily Use of Animals in Ancient Israel* (1998).

ODED BOROWSKI

WOMAN CAUGHT IN ADULTERY [γυνὴ κατείληπται ἐπὶ μοιχείᾳ gynē kateilēptai epi moicheia]. The traditional canonical placement of the adulterous woman's story at John 7:53–8:11 is not supported by most ancient witnesses (hence the bracketing of this unit in the NIV and NRSV). Moreover, the text ill fits the style of John's Gospel and interrupts the flow between 7:52 and 8:12. It works no better after 7:36; 7:44; 21:25; or Luke 21:8, attested by a few manuscripts, often with a scribal symbol flagging the text's uncertain history. Despite its homeless literary status, however, the story has a strong ring of authenticity resonant with the earliest traditions of Jesus' life and ministry.

While Jesus teaches a large audience in the temple compound, certain Jewish legal experts intrude on the scene, making a woman "caught in the very act of committing adultery" stand before the assembly's critical gaze. Addressing Jesus as "Teacher," these "scribes and Pharisees" ask Jesus' opinion on the Mosaic law's death penalty (by stoning) for "such women" (John 8:3-5). Their main concern, however, from the narrator's viewpoint, is not with proper interpretation of the law, still less with just treatment of the woman, but rather with entrapment of Jesus in a legal blunder (8:6a). Ironically, their tactics reveal their own utter disregard for due process in two key respects: they present neither corroborating witnesses nor the collaborating male adulterer (also subject to capital punishment)—both mandated by biblical law (see Lev 20:10; Num 35:30; Deut 17:2-7; 22:22-24). Under the guise of jurisprudence, the lawyers illicitly exploit the woman for their own interests.

Jesus strategically disarms the woman's accusers with pointed physical and verbal responses. Physically he rebuffs the prosecutors by twice bending down and writing in the dirt with his finger (John 8:6-8)—deliberately distancing himself from them (and the exposed woman). This "scribal" gesture (whatever its content, which is never disclosed) may represent an act of protest against the scribes and Pharisees' use of Scripture (see Exod 24:12; Deut 9:10 for the image of the law written by God's "finger").

Each time he stoops and scribbles on the ground, he straightens up to make a pronouncement. First, he rises and challenges any "sinless" accuser to hurl the first punitive stone (and then promptly bends down again). Put back on their heels by this dare, the legal officials leave "one by one" after their leaders (John 8:7-9). Then, "left alone" with the adulterous woman—with him stooped and her still standing—Jesus straightens up and addresses her on her level. In this story, only Jesus speaks with the woman and treats her with respect, mercy, and seriousness. Observing the absence of accusers, Jesus assures the woman he does not condemn her; but neither does he condone her behavior. He dispatches her with not only a clean slate but also a clear mandate that she "not sin again" (8:10-11). *See* ADULTERY; CRIMES AND PUNISHMENT, OT AND NT; FORGIVENESS; STONING.

Bibliography: Larry J. Kreitzer and Deborah W. Rooke. *Ciphers in the Sand: Interpretations of the Woman Taken in Adultery (John 7.53–8.11)* (2000); Bruce M. Metzger. *A Textual Commentary on the Greek New Testament.* 2nd ed. (1994); Gail R. O'Day. "John 7:53–8:11: A Study in Misreading." *JBL* 111 (1992) 631–40; Holly J. Toensing. "Divine Intervention or Divine Intrusion: Jesus and the Adulteress in John's Gospel." Amy-Jill Levine with Marianne Blickenstaff, eds. *A Feminist Companion to John.* Vol. 1 (2003) 159–72.

F. SCOTT SPENCER

WOMAN WHO ANOINTED JESUS. A woman featured in multiple Gospel stories who ANOINTs Jesus with expensive perfume. Matthew and Mark describe an anonymous woman who lavishly anoints Jesus' head with an alabaster jarful of "very costly OINTMENT" (worth 300 denarii in Mark 14:5), while he reclines at table during Passover week in the Bethany home of Simon the leper (Matt 26:6-13; Mark 14:3-9). Although pouring fragrant oil on the head could signify the inauguration of priests and kings (see Exod 29:7; Lev 8:12; 1 Sam 10:1; 16:1, 13; 1 Kgs 1:39; Ps 133:2), it also functioned as a standard act of hospitality (see Luke 7:46).

Guests ("disciples" in Matt 26:8) object to the woman's frivolous "waste" of a valuable commodity that could have been sold to aid the poor. However, Jesus affirms the timeliness of her "good service" (Matt 26:10). While the poor can be helped later, Jesus faces imminent execution. Although he repeatedly predicted his violent end (see Matt 16:21; 17:22-23; 20:17-19; 26:1-2; Mark 8:31; 9:31; 10:32-34), this woman is the only follower who grasps the reality of his death and pre-anoints his body "for burial" (Matt 26:12; Mark 14:8). She will be Jesus' only anointer, as the women who come to his tomb (bearing spices in Mark 16:1) find no body. Her unique act thus merits special remembrance "wherever the good news is proclaimed in the whole world" (Matt 26:13; Mark 14:9).

According to John 12:1-8, Mary of Bethany anoints Jesus' feet. Several elements distinguish this scene. First, it takes place at a dinner party in the Bethany home of Lazarus (12:1)—whom Jesus recently raised from the dead—and sisters Martha and Mary. Second, Mary anoints Jesus' feet and wipes them with her hair (12:3). Along with oil for their heads, honored guests expected to receive water for foot washing (see Luke 7:44-46; John 13:5). Going beyond the call of duty, Mary's slathering Jesus' feet with "a pound of costly perfume," and substituting her hair for a towel represents an unusually extravagant and intimate gesture. Third, Judas now emerges as the main objector to Mary's prodigal act, but not (in the narrator's view) because he cares about the poor (12:4-6). Finally, the sweet fragrance that anticipates Jesus' burial deodorizes, so to speak, the stench of death so palpable after Lazarus' four-day entombment (John 11:39). Although sharing some elements with the other anointing stories, Luke's narrative stands out as more distinctive than derivative (Luke 7:36-50). A woman pours "an alabaster jar of ointment" on Jesus' feet and dries them with her hair at a meal hosted by a Pharisee (not leper; compare Matt 26:6//Mark 14:3) named Simon. The anointing woman, a "sinner" of "many" sins (she is never identified as a prostitute; Luke 7:37, 39, 47), douses Jesus' feet with oil, but also with profuse tears and kisses as an expression of grateful love for his forgiveness (Luke 7:47).

Bibliography: F. Scott Spencer. *Dancing Girls, "Loose" Ladies and Women of "the Cloth": Women in Jesus' Life* (2004).

F. SCOTT SPENCER

WOMAN WITH FLOW OF BLOOD [γυνὴ ἐν ῥύσει αἵματος gynē en rhysei haimatos]. A woman in the Synoptic Gospels healed from a chronic bleeding condition (Matt 9:20-22; Mark 5:24b-34; Luke 8:42b-48).

Each Synoptic Gospel splices the bleeding woman's story into a narrative about a dying daughter: a synagogue leader named Jairus (Mark 5:22-23a; Luke 8:41-42; anonymous in Matt 9:18-19) begs Jesus to come help his gravely ill daughter (already deceased, in Matt 9:18). Just then, a hemorrhaging woman breaks through a crowd, touches Jesus' cloak (FRINGE; Matt 9:20; Luke 8:44), and is cured. When Jesus reaches the leader's house, he raises the daughter to new life.

In these intertwined incidents, Jesus powerfully restores two women to health; his addressing the bleeding woman as "daughter" provides a linguistic link with the ruler's "daughter" (see Matt 12:46-50; Mark 3:31-35; Luke 8:19-21; 11:27-28); Mark's and Luke's versions establish twelve years as the length of the woman's suffering and the age of the leader's daughter.

Mark and Luke describe the woman's ailment as a chronic FLOW OF BLOOD (rhysis tou haimotos [ῥύσις τοῦ αἵματος]; Mark 5:25; Luke 8:43-44). Mark includes "fountain of blood" (pēgē tou haimotos [πηγὴ τοῦ αἵματος]; 5:29) and a "plague" (mastix [μάστιξ], literally "whip" or "scourge" in 5:29). Matthew simply mentions she had been "hemorrhaging" (haimorrousa αἱμαρροῦσα) for twelve years (9:20). That she suffered from some type of menstrual or vaginal bleeding disorder is possible, but not certain. The Greek Leviticus uses rhysis broadly to describe various genital discharges, both regular and irregular, of men as well as women, involving blood, semen, or other fluids (Lev 15); it restricts pēge, however, to a woman's "flow" (12:7 [after birth]; 20:18). All such discharges render one ritually "unclean," as well as anyone having sex with him or her or touching their beds, couches, chairs, saddles, and such. None of these circumstances apply to the bleeding woman's contact with Jesus (her touching his clothing does not transgress Levitical case law), and the Gospel story suggests nothing about ritual purity. If the Gospels do allude to genital bleeding, the woman's impurity (easily remediable by prescribed washings) would be negligible compared to her discomfort and debilitation and the trauma of barrenness.

Unique among Jesus' healing stories, the hemorrhaging woman's cure follows her touching his garment. Matthew mitigates the bleeding woman's audacious initiative by reporting her healing after Jesus turns and pronounces her well (9:22). Mark and Luke, however, declare her hemorrhaging immediately stopped (dried up): her touch triggers a flow of Jesus' power that stanches her flow of blood (Mark 5:29; Luke 8:44, 47). Moreover, Jesus responds with a measure of surprise, if not agitation: "Who touched me?" (Mark 5:31//Luke 8:45). When Jesus calls her "daughter," he affirms that her "faith has made [her] well (Mark 5:34//Luke 8:48).

Ultimately, the woman stands as a model of bold, persevering faith in action.

Bibliography: F. T. Gench. *Back to the Well: Women's Encounters with Jesus in the Gospels* (2004) 28–55; A.-J. Levine. "Discharging Responsibility: Matthean Jesus, Biblical Law, and Hemorrhaging Woman." *A Feminist Companion to Matthew.* A.-J. Levine, ed. with M. Blickenstaff (2001) 70–87.

F. SCOTT SPENCER

WOMAN WITH SICK DAUGHTER. *See* SYRO-PHOENICIAN WOMAN.

WOMAN, SAMARITAN. *See* SAMARITAN WOMAN.

WOMAN, SYROPHOENICIAN. *See* SYROPHOE-NICIAN WOMAN.

WOMANIST INTERPRETATION. How we interpret the Bible often depends on the communities from which we come and how much we identify with them. These interpretive communities give us authoritative reading strategies that guide how we read Scripture and the meanings we often draw from it. Womanist interpretation emerges from the interpretive community of African American religious people and, more specifically, from the lives of Black women and their spiritual journeys. It takes seriously the interaction between Scripture as authority and the motivations of readers from marginalized communities who continue to regard the Bible as a meaningful resource and guide for life. It examines the values of Black readers and the relationship between authority and truth claims—at times questioning a monolithic Western understanding of truth by arguing that truths can be discerned from a range of cultural traditions.

The Bible is one of the highest sources of authority for Black Christian women. However, part of the history of the use of the Bible in the Americas includes using Scripture as an authoritative text to sanction enslavement and to instigate insurrection and protest. With such a wide range of interpretative strategies at work, womanist interpretation consciously chooses to mine biblical sources that help to refute dehumanization and oppression. This focus on the prophetic tradition of the Bible serves many functions. First, it provides a firm foundation for religious values that inspire faithful living. Second, it empowers Black women and men to develop a set of virtues that assert the full humanity of Black people. Third, it provides biblical guideposts for eradicating negative stereotypes and radical distortions about Black people that are often imposed by the larger society and culture. Finally, womanist interpretation recovers the voice of the oppressed within biblical texts, such as HAGAR and ONESIMUS.

In preaching, womanist interpretation relies on portions of the Bible to provide insight and guidance for living for the various social and spiritual issues Black women face such as discipleship, evangelism, health care, mission work, poverty, public education, racism, reproductive choice, sexism in the church and society, sexuality, and welfare reform. Here, attention is given to the emotional, spiritual, ethical, theological, and sociopolitical implications of the social setting and the sermon. This necessitates a deeply integrative approach to explore Scripture and its relationship to people's lives. This integrative approach provides a rich tension among life, the Bible, the preacher, the hearer, and God. The individual is placed within this dynamic tension through the interpretative community that seeks a liberating word and strategies for faithful survival.

Ultimately, womanist interpretation gives us yet another way to become sensitive interpreters of Scripture and its impact in human lives. By looking at the Bible and the world through the eyes of those who are often at the margins in our world, we can develop homiletical strategies that expand the possibilities for those who can hear the good news and work to bring about a world of peace and justice founded on God's love for creation.

EMILIE M. TOWNES

WOMEN IN THE ANCIENT NEAR EAST. Public and private texts, artifacts and images, skeletal remains, and grave goods attest to the range and diversity of women's lives in the ANE. From Mesopotamia to Anatolia, through the Levant and Egypt, competing cultures thrived in the three millennia of recorded history before the Common Era. Pioneering studies since the 1960s have brought data on women to light from these records. Early studies followed a supplementary approach, providing information on women's lives in relation to the patriarchal family and male religious and political elites. These frequently took the form of synthetic descriptions of women as a group, organized along the continuum of marriage, childbirth, divorce, and widowhood. Recent studies have pushed scholarly work forward by investigating how our conception of gender shapes both the manner in which we access the past and the social world our efforts reconstruct. The data on women, like all textual and archaeological data for the ANE, are partial at best. Extant records cannot convey the full range of the social world that produced them. Therefore, the methodological lens through which we view our sources is crucial. While relations between elite men have been the traditional focus of scholarship, accurate and nuanced analysis of male relationships, and the rest of the ancient world, depends upon our grasp of the relations among women and between women and men across social strata. Rather than asserting a set of normative statements concerning women in the ANE, this article presents material selected to convey the diversity of data on women.

A. Gender and Social Status in the Tombs of Ur (2600–2450 BCE)
B. Royal Women and Laborers in Lagash (2400–2350 BCE)
C. Enheduanna, Priestess of Nanna (ca. 2300 BCE)
D. Royal Women of the Ur III Dynasty (2112–2004 BCE)
E. Women Partners in Trade from Assur to Kanesh (1910–1830 BCE)
F. Naditu Women (1894–1595 BCE)
G. Daughters of Zimri-Lim (1800–1762 BCE)
H. Women Owning Women at Nuzi (1500–1350 BCE)
I. Queens of Ugarit (1350–1215 BCE)
J. Neo-Assyrian Royal Women and Imperial Politics (883–627 BCE)
Bibliography

A. Gender and Social Status in the Tombs of Ur (2600–2450 BCE)

The "Royal Tombs" of Ur offer a dramatic view of Early Dynastic society. Modes of adornment and grave goods indicate that gender affiliation and differentiation were vital to the social hierarchies represented in these tombs. In the majority of the 2,000 burials at Ur, the dead were wrapped in reed mats and interred individually in earthen pits. Sixteen tombs, however, consist of built chambers in which numerous individuals, many of whom appear to have been sacrificed, were simultaneously interred with one primary adult. Whether or not these adults were royalty or temple elites, their lavish personal adornments and the cylinder seals, vessels, musical instruments, furniture, and even wagons and cattle buried alongside them communicate a political power enhanced by indications that the accompanying dead were their attendants. Markers of high social status cut across gender lines. One of the most richly furnished burials is of a woman, Puabi. Gender distinctions are evident in the adornments on the primary adults and on their attendants. Women wore distinctive jewelry such as gold vegetal wreath diadems, while weapons and other types of headdresses accompanied men. Recurrent sets of adornment types indicate subgroupings within gendered categories. Rare individuals were buried with items associated with both genders.

B. Royal Women and Laborers in Lagash (2400–2350 BCE)

The distribution of wealth evident in the tombs of Ur is echoed in administrative texts from another southern Mesopotamian city, Girsu in the city-state of Lagash. The primary textual source for Early Dynastic Lagash is the archive of the temple of the goddess Bau, wife of the city-god Ningirsu, which was administrated by Shasha, wife of the ruler of Lagash. The temple, understood as the "household" of Bau, was a self-sustaining center of economic production, consumption, and redistribution. Ration lists signed with Shasha's name indicate the enormous number of dependent laborers and agricultural holdings that supplied the temple complex. One list indicates a distribution of 2,935 liters of barley to 192 people, 162 of whom were women. Female laborers worked primarily as millers and weavers. While skeletal and architectural remains are not documented from Girsu, skeletons excavated from a Neolithic site of women who performed comparable levels of manual labor show the damage to knees, wrists, lower backs, and the deformation of toes tucked repeatedly under foot caused by the sustained physical strain of milling and weaving. The resources distributed in the name of one royal woman were the product of multiple nameless women's labor.

C. Enheduanna, Priestess of Nanna (ca. 2300 BCE)

When Sargon of Akkad seized power over Sumer, thereby uniting southern Mesopotamia, he installed his daughter as high priestess of the moon god Nanna at Ur. She was given the Sumerian name Enheduanna. An Akkadian princess assuming the highest office of a central institution in Sumer was politically and ideologically strategic. The authorship of major Sumerian literary compositions, including *The Exaltation of Inanna*, has been attributed to Enheduanna. Among these compositions are hymns honoring temples in thirty-five cities of Sumer and Akkad. The regional cohesion Sargon effected militarily was thus embodied in the scope of the texts attributed to her. The significance of Enheduanna's status is also evident in her visual depiction on an alabaster disk found at Ur. Enheduanna's headdress, flounced robes, long hair, and her position relative to the other figures on the disk connect her with similar depictions of Sumerian priestesses of the Early Dynastic period. This visual continuity communicates Enheduanna's role in legitimizing the new Akkadian dynasty. Successive high priestesses of Nanna were also royal women who, by running their god's estate, helped to maintain the power of their families.

D. Royal Women of the Ur III Dynasty (2112–2004 BCE)

After the Sargonic dynasty fell, a new dynasty arose in Ur. Over five generations, this dynasty produced an immense number of cuneiform tablets, estimated at 100,000, the majority of which are administrative texts. Some 500 tablets from a period of less than twenty years are associated with Shulgi-simti, one of the wives of Shulgi, ruler of Ur. This archive consists of records of livestock presented by named women and men as deliveries to Shulgi-simti, received by named officials. The animals were used to provision the temples of female deities and Shulgi-simti's household, which, like households of other royal women, was independent of the king's. Although the data are abundant, interpretation

is problematic. Records of transactions in the name of a royal woman cannot determine the extent to which she managed the institution that kept the archives or tell us much about her private life. Nonetheless, the small amount and lower quality of the livestock Shulgi-simti received and dispatched for sacrifices, in comparison with other royal archives, confirm her status as a secondary wife.

E. Women Partners in Trade from Assur to Kanesh (1910–1830 BCE)

Private letters exchanged between women and men concerning family business ventures in long-range trade between northern Mesopotamia and Anatolia offer a rare glimpse of life between the extremes of royal wealth and servitude. More than 20,000 tablets from Kanesh in central Anatolia record the dealings between women who managed the production of textiles in Assur and their husbands, fathers, or brothers who made the 1,000 km journey to trade these textiles, along with tin from Iran, for gold and silver in Kanesh. The words exchanged in their letters are lively. In one of many letters she wrote to her prosperous husband, Lamassi defends the quality of her textiles against his complaints and points out that her hard labor is what earns him his silver. Taram-Kubi berates her husband for enjoying extravagance while she is in an empty house, left without a shekel of silver or a liter of barley. She demands that he send her the full value of her textiles. In another lengthy letter, she informs him that a deal he has negotiated is off and demands he send silver by the next courier.

F. Naditu Women (1894–1595 BCE)

The **naditu** are a relatively well-documented group of women in the Old Babylonian period whose financial and social autonomy are much debated. **Naditu** were dedicated for life to a particular god. They normally did not marry and never bore children. They lived together in compounds in major cities, such as Sippar, Nippur, and Kish, residing in private homes within the compound. **Naditu** were from wealthy families and would receive a share of the patrimonial estate upon entering the service of the god. They bought and sold property and slaves and, in some cases, adopted other **naditu** as heirs. These adoptees were generally patrilineal relations, as multiple generations of women in a family frequently became **naditu**. In most cases, however, the property of **naditu** reverted immediately back to their families at their death. One analysis of the institution is that it allowed wealthy families to consolidate and even expand their wealth over several generations rather than divide it among successive male heirs. Whether **naditu** brokered their transactions as free agents or were representatives for male kinsmen cannot be definitely discerned. Nonetheless, some **naditu** received "ring money" from their fathers at their initiation to invest as they wished, and many had the power to disinherit male heirs who did not pay them their share of the patrimony.

G. Daughters of Zimri-Lim (1800–1762 BCE)

The letters that Inib-sharri, Kiru, and their sisters sent to their father Zimri-Lim, king of MARI, afford an inside view of the diplomatic marriages that were crucial to the balance of power in the ANE, particularly in the 2nd millennium. The breadth of the diplomatic correspondence in the Mari archives reflects Mari's strategic location between southern Mesopotamia and Syria, as well as the ambitions of its ruler. Although the archives predate him, the majority of the texts comes from the reign of Zimri-Lim. Along with letters from governors, vassals, and officials, the letters of Zimri-Lim's daughters informed him about the foreign courts in which they resided and the rulers to whom they were married. Even their colorful complaints about their treatment in court or their loss of status in relation to other wives convey more than personal unhappiness. The loyalty of their husbands to Zimri-Lim could be gauged by their fate after marriage. Kiru was not only married to one of her father's vassals, she appears to have been appointed by her father as mayor of the city-state. She gave her father diplomatic advice, and when he suffered by ignoring it, she did not hesitate to point this out.

H. Women Owning Women at Nuzi (1500–1350 BCE)

Four texts from NUZI concerning Tulpanaya, Kisaya, and Kisaya's mother, Arimmatka, dramatize relations between women across social strata. Like other elite women, Tulpanaya owned slaves as well as property. Arimmatka, an impoverished woman, sold her daughter to Tulpanaya. While their agreement was written in the form of an adoption, the stipulations indicate that Kisaya was to be Tulpanaya's slave. Tulpanaya had the power to give Kisaya as a wife to any of her slaves and to choose Kisaya's second husband if she was widowed. Kisaya was forbidden to leave Tulpanaya's house for life. An impossible penalty in silver and gold was assigned if she were to leave. Nonetheless, Kisaya resisted Tulpanaya's choice for her husband and gave herself in marriage to another man. Kisaya gave her son by this marriage to Tulpanaya, but this was apparently not enough. Tulpanaya brought a lawsuit against Kisaya and prevailed. The arc of power and resistance across these four documents does not bend toward justice of a kind modern readers would recognize. These records remind us that the correlation between gender and power is not simple, nor is human agency always limited by law.

I. Queens of Ugarit (1350–1215 BCE)

The correspondence of the queens of Ugarit indicates the breadth of their involvement in the internal and external affairs of the city-state. Their political power continued beyond the reign of their husbands into the reigns of their sons and even grandsons. During the reigns of her son Niqmaddu III and grandson Ammurapi, Queen Sharelli corresponded with rulers in Egypt, Assyria, Amurru, Hatti, and Carchemish. The Carchemish letters are particularly revealing. In a double letter, the sender addresses her before he addresses the king. In another letter, addressed to Sharelli alone, the king of Carchemish responds to a list of her concerns, ranging from negotiations over the distance Ugarit's ships may sail, to payment of compensation due from a successful lawsuit on behalf of the king of Ugarit. Royal women from other courts also sent Sharelli diplomatic letters, and she received reports from the king of Ugarit during his visits to Hatti. The integral role of royal women in the political life of Ugarit and the duration of their influence over the reigns of several male rulers may require us to rethink our conception of Ugarit's political structure beyond simply a kingdom in which queens had active roles. *See* UGARIT, HISTORY AND ARCHAEOLOGY; UGARIT, TEXTS AND LITERATURE.

J. Neo-Assyrian Royal Women and Imperial Politics (883–627 BCE)

Although rarely mentioned in surveys of the male rulers who devastated Israel and Judah (*see* ASSYRIA AND BABYLONIA), Neo-Assyrian royal women were influential in the politics of the empire. The best known of these women is Naqia/Zakutu, wife of SENNACHERIB and mother of ESARHADDON. Naqia's promotion of her son as crown prince led to Sennacherib's murder by his demoted heir-apparent, an elder son by another wife. Naqia's origins are unknown, but her West Semitic

Erich Lessing/Art Resource, NY

Figure 1: Statue of a woman from Ur (1900–1800 BCE) originally set up in a temple to pray, symbolically, on behalf of the donor. Traces of red and black paint show that the statue was originally painted. The eyes are separately made out of a whiter stone; the eyeballs are lost. British Museum, London, Great Britain.

name suggests non-Assyrian ethnicity. Her receipt of tribute and booty, her estates, her donations to temples, her gifts to courtiers, and the address of reports on military and cultic matters to her are well documented. The depiction of Naqia on a bronze plaque is one of the rare representations of a Neo-Assyrian royal woman on a public monument. Not even the powerful queen mother Sammu-ramat, wife of Shamshi-Adad V, is depicted on her own stele, which she installed at Assur. Naqia is identified by name in the inscription on the plaque, but whether the male ruler with her is Sennacherib or Esarhaddon is debated. Naqia stands behind the king, holding ritual objects that indicate a religious ceremony. Along with the elaborate depiction of Libbali-sharrat with her husband Ashurbanipal on a wall relief, this image of Naqia stands in stark contrast to the more common depiction of women amid throngs of conquered enemies. *See* FAMILY; LEVIRATE LAW; MARRIAGE, OT; SEX, SEXUALITY; WOMEN IN THE APOCRYPHA; WOMEN IN THE NT; WOMEN IN THE OT.

Bibliography: Julia Asher-Greve and Mary Francis Wogec. "Women and Gender in Ancient Near Eastern Cultures: Bibliography 1885 to 2001 AD." Nin 3 (2002) 33–114; Jack Cheng and Marian H. Feldman, eds. *Ancient Near East in Context: Studies in Honor of Irene J. Winter by Her Students* (2007); Amy Rebecca Gansell. "Identity and Adornment in the Third-millennium BCE Mesopotamian 'Royal Cemetery' at Ur." *Cambridge Archaeological Journal* 17 (2007) 29–46; Barbara Lesko, ed. *Women's Earliest Records: From Ancient Egypt and Western Asia* (1989); Joan Oates and David Oates. *Nimrud: An Assyrian Imperial City Revealed* (2001); Tallay Ornan. "The Queen in Public: Royal Women in Neo-Assyrian Art." *Sex and Gender in the Ancient Near East.* Simo Parpola and R. M. Whiting, eds. (2002) 461–77; Susan Pollock. *Ancient Mesopotamia: The Eden That Never Was* (1999); Itamar Singer. "A Political History of Ugarit." *Handbook of Ugaritic Studies.* Wilfred G. E. Watson and Nicholas Wyatt, eds. (1999) 601–733; Elna Solvang. *A Woman's Place Is in the House: Royal Women of Judah and Their Involvement in the House of David* (2003); Elisabeth Meier Tetlow. *Women, Crime and Punishment in Ancient Law and Society: Volume I, The Ancient Near East* (2004); Marc Van de Mieroop. *A History of the Ancient Near East* (2007); Irene J. Winter. "Women in Public: The Disk of Enheduanna, the Beginning of the Office of the En-Priestess, and the Weight of the Visual Evidence." *La Femme dans le Proche-Orient Antique.* Jean-Marie Durand, ed. (1987) 356–93.

CHRISTINE NEAL THOMAS

WOMEN IN THE APOCRYPHA. Female figures appear frequently in the Jewish literature comprising the Apocrypha, the Protestant term for scriptural books and expansions of earlier works that were written between the 4th cent. BCE and the 1st cent. CE and largely preserved in Greek (*see* APOCRYPHA, DEUTEROCANONICAL).

There is no uniform depiction of women in the literature of the Apocrypha. In addition to their customary familiar roles as wives, mothers, and daughters, women are independently mentioned as prostitutes (Sir 26:22; 41:20; 2 Esd 15:55) or slaves (Jdt 8:10, 33; Tob 3:8; 8:13-14; NRSV, "maid"). Some of the authors "think with women," that is to say, females are epitomized, idealized, metaphorized, and stereotyped in order to express larger cultural values or ideals. The depictions of women in this literature of the Greco-Roman era allow us only to gain a remote understanding of the daily life of everyday women. We cannot hope to construct a social history of women during this period from the literature alone.

A. Women in Narrative Roles
B. Women Objectified
C. Figured Women
Bibliography

A. Women in Narrative Roles

Women characters play central roles in a number of the narratives: Greek Esther, Judith, Tobit, and Susanna, an expansion of the book of Daniel. The book of Judith is more like the book of Esther than any of its companion literature in the Apocrypha in that both tell the tale of a vulnerable yet brave Jewish woman who saves her people when they are threatened by foreign enemies (*see* ESTHER; ESTHER, BOOK OF; JUDITH; JUDITH, BOOK OF). Both are described as beautiful women who adorn and clothe themselves to erotic effect in order to seduce the male enemy (King Ahasuerus, Holofernes). While both transcend the traditional domestic role of Israelite women in order to accomplish their tasks, they do not remain in the public sphere once they have accomplished their missions. Judith returns to her life as a pious and quiet widow, rather than being elevated to public leadership of her people. There are some significant differences. Esther is set in the Persian diaspora during the reign of the fictive king Ahasuerus (normally identified with Xerxes I, who ruled from 486–465 BCE). The book of Judith, written in the first quarter of the 2nd cent. BCE, is set in Palestine some 350 years prior, soon after the Jews had returned from the Babylonian exile. Esther serves as an etiological tale for the beginning of the Jewish festival of Purim. Judith simply ends with a victory procession to the Temple in Jerusalem with a hymn hearkening to Miriam and Moses' hymn in Exod 15. While the Hebrew version of Esther does not mention God overtly and Esther shows no signs of obeying Jewish dietary laws or observing such traditions as the Sabbath, in the expanded account of Esther's story in the Greek version the heroine is very much engaged in observant Jewish life. God is not mentioned once in Hebrew Esther, but is mentioned over fifty times in the Greek version. In both Judith and Greek Esther, the heroines offer prayers and praise to the God of Israel (Add Esth 13:15-17; 14:3-19; Jdt 9:2-14; 13:4-5; 16:1-17) as the real and righteous king of the Jews, in contradistinction to the foreign human kings threatening the people.

The book of Tobit, anachronistically set in Assyria after the fall of the Northern Kingdom in the 8th cent. BCE, also includes two prominent women, Tobit's wife, Anna, and Sarah, a woman beset by a jealous demon who kills off seven successive bridegrooms (see TOBIT, BOOK OF). Sarah's tale parallels Tobit's: both offer a prayer of praise, refer to almsgiving, and interact with angels. Yet in spite of the central role of women in the plot, the book depicts a patriarchal society in which males dominate. Sarah is introduced as "daughter of Raguel," and is described as wanting to preserve her father from disgrace (3:15). Illustrative is the fact that once Tobias enters the narrative with Sarah, Sarah no longer speaks until she affirms his prayer with an "Amen, Amen" (8:8). Tobit provides instruction about motherhood and marriage to his son Tobias (4:1-14).

The tale of SUSANNA, one of the Greek additions to Daniel, offers another chaste, beautiful, and pious female lead character (v. 2). Two lecherous old judges spy her in the garden while bathing and conspire to seduce her. When they approach her, she cries out with a loud voice, the correct legal action in such an instance. Yet her voice goes unheard. Wrongly accused of adultery by them, Susanna affirms her commitment to living according to the law (v. 23). Although she is not believed by those around her and is condemned to die, Daniel overhears her prayer of vindication and intervenes to expertly cross-examine the accusers, trapping them in their lies and forestalling her execution. As in other tales, the woman is defined by her subordinate relationships in patriarchal households: Susannah is "daughter of Hilkiah, the wife of Joakim" (v. 29). The story ends not with a statement of praise for Susanna's courage and faithfulness, but with the recognition that Daniel gained in stature and reputation as a result of his involvement.

The book of 1 Maccabees, which recounts the rise of the Hasmonean dynasty, contains virtually no mention of women, a fact that itself bespeaks something of their negligible importance in the public sphere from the perspective of its author (see MACCABEES, FIRST BOOK OF). They are mentioned only as mourners for the Temple (1:26-27) and as victims of persecution (1:60-61). It is interesting that Shelamzion (see ALEXANDRA SALOME), the only Jewish queen during the Greco-Roman era, who assumed the Hasmonean throne in 76 BCE, goes unmentioned in all of the literature under consideration. Josephus refers to her (Ant. 13.430–32) and she is seemingly mentioned twice in the DEAD SEA SCROLLS (4Q324b 1 II, 7; 4Q322 2 4). No female relative of the Hasmonean brothers is ever mentioned by name, although Simon builds an elaborate tomb for his father, mother, and brothers (1 Macc 13:28). Jonathan and Simon both are said to have children (1

Macc 13:16-20; 16:16), so wives can be inferred, but they are not mentioned.

By contrast, 2 Maccabees, a book that interprets the religious significance of the events of the persecution during the time of the Hasmonean revolt, develops a theology of martyrdom (see MACCABEES, SECOND BOOK OF). Both men and women figure as martyrs. Most striking are the parallel accounts of the ninety-year-old elite scribe Eleazar (2 Macc 6:18-31) and the unnamed mother of seven anonymous sons (2 Macc 7:1-42). Eleazar refuses to eat swine's flesh, and thus is tortured and killed for his beliefs. Even more potent is the story of the mother who must witness her sons each be tortured and killed in turn because they would not forsake the Mosaic ancestral law. A significant feature of the tale is that the mother herself utters theological teaching to one of her sons in their mother tongue of Hebrew in order to bolster him in the face of torment, presenting what has been understood as the first articulation of creatio ex nihilo in the tradition as well as a belief in resurrection:

> I beg you, my child, to look at the heaven and the earth and see everything that is in them, and recognize that God did not make them out of things that existed. And in the same way the human race came into being. Do not fear this butcher, but prove worthy of your brothers. Accept death, so that in God's mercy I may get you back again along with your brothers. (2 Macc 7:28-29)

Each of their deaths was to serve as "an example of nobility and a memorial of courage" (2 Macc 6:31). The same tradition of martyrdom appears in 4 Macc 8:1–14:10, a book that extols the power of human reason over emotion, although the reward of the martyrs is there understood as immortality of the soul rather than bodily resurrection (9:22; 14:5).

B. Women Objectified

In addition to including women as actors in the narrative, several apocryphal books offer descriptions, or perhaps more accurately, prescriptions, of women's roles. The book of SIRACH (Ben Sira in Hebrew) is unique among Jewish books in that we know the name of its author and the circumstances of its composition, written in the early 2nd cent. BCE and translated into Greek by his grandson in 132 BCE for the Jewish population of Egypt. The book also contains the most negative characterization of women in the Apocrypha. Women are blamed as the origin of sin (25:24) and from his perspective have a propensity for wickedness (25:16-19). He offers androcentric advice on a good marriage, in which a wife's role is modestly, chastely, and silently to keep a well-ordered home in order to enhance her husband's reputation (26:13-18; 36:26-31). Sirach 42:9-14 offers a particularly toxic view of women generally, and female sexuality and the threat of female independence in particular:

> A daughter is a secret anxiety to her father, and worry over her robs him of sleep; when she is young, for fear she may not marry, or if married, for fear she may be disliked; while a virgin, for fear she may be seduced and become pregnant in her father's house; or having a husband, for fear she may go astray, or, though married, for fear she may be barren. Keep strict watch over a headstrong daughter, or she may make you a laughingstock to your enemies, a byword in the city and the assembly of the people, and put you to shame in public gatherings.... for from garments comes the moth, and from a woman comes woman's wickedness. Better is the wickedness of a man than a woman who does good; it is woman who brings shame and disgrace.

This passage follows a section of Ben Sira (41:14–42:8) that describes two kinds of shame. Women are a potential threat to male "honor," an ancient Mediterranean virtue whose opposite was shame. The pungently negative characterization of women precedes the final seven chapters of the book that are in praise of famous men and men only.

Although much of 1 Esdras reduplicates material in Chronicles and Ezra–Nehemiah, the book also uniquely includes a tale of the three bodyguards in the court of Persian king Darius (*see* ESDRAS, FIRST BOOK OF). They propose a debating challenge to name the strongest thing in the world. Each bodyguard gives his answer in turn: wine, kings, and women. The bodyguard Zerubbabel offers a long speech (1 Esd 4:13-32) as entertainment to a male audience that wins the contest. From an androcentric perspective he argues that women give birth to kings, receive the hard-won spoils of war and other treasures that men bestow upon them, and in other ways entrap men who are depicted as having no will to resist them. For answering the challenge correctly, the king sponsors Zerubbabel's return to Jerusalem to rebuild the Temple. Thus this essential "truth" about women that is recounted in the story becomes the narrative catalyst by which the exiles are permitted to return to their homeland.

C. Figured Women

Another way in which women appear in this literature is as personified figures, instantiating inanimate objects, such as Wisdom, the Temple, and the city of Jerusalem, but also Earth. The most prominent of these is the female Wisdom figure known from the OT by the feminine Hebrew noun khokhmah (חָכְמָה) and the Greek word sophia (σοφία). Described already in Prov 1, 8–9, and Job 28, Woman Wisdom is contrasted as an antidote to the sexual temptress/prostitute figures; the idealized Wisdom is meant to protect young heterosex-

ual males from her predatory temptations. The female Wisdom figure in Sirach reflects a development of the earlier Israelite wisdom tradition in which the universal ideas are intertwined with particularistic Israelite traditions of covenant and Torah. In Sir 24, Wisdom is understood as akin to the ruakh (רוּחַ; spirit or wind) of God, the spirit of God that hovers over creation in Gen 1:1: "I came forth from the mouth of the Most High, and covered the earth like a mist" (Sir 24:3). She was not only present at creation but appeared in the pillar of cloud guiding the Israelites in the wilderness, eventually coming to settle in the Temple of Jerusalem, effectively the kavodh (כָּבוֹד, "glory") of God. She is also described in erotic terms that evoke male desire: "Come to me, you who desire me, and eat your fill of my fruits" (Sir 24:19). At the end of her speech, she identifies her wisdom as equated with Scripture, "the book of the covenant of the Most High God" (v. 23). Wisdom of Solomon (*see* SOLOMON, WISDOM OF) also takes up the female Wisdom figure in the central part of the book, with the pseudonymous author tracing Wisdom's influence since creation (6:22). "Solomon" lists her twenty-one attributes in a passage likely influenced by conceptions of the Greek goddess Isis (7:22-23), and describes his desire to take Wisdom as his bride and guide (Wis 8–9). Baruch 3:9–4:4 (*see* BARUCH, BOOK OF) contains a hymn in praise of Wisdom personified as well. In a passage that weaves together language from Deuteronomy, Jeremiah, and Job, the answer to the question "Where can wisdom be found?" is the same as in Ben Sira: Wisdom is identified as Scripture, "The book of the commandments of God, the law that endures forever" (Bar 4:1). Both Jewish and Christian thought were influenced by the female cast of wisdom in the Greco-Roman era.

Female figurations of the city of Jerusalem or Zion as mother or daughter, sometimes indistinguishable from references to the Temple, occur in the OT (Isa 51:17–52:10; 54; 60–62; Lamentations). The female city lament tradition has ancient roots in Mesopotamian literature. The tradition continues in Bar 4:5–5:9, in which "mother Zion" mourns the loss of her Israelite "children" in the destruction and exile of Babylon and addresses her offspring to comfort and encourage them. The passage pushes beyond lament to joy and hopeful expectation of restoration in the future, in language drawn from Second Isaiah.

The figuration of women can be subtly complex. In the book of Judith, e.g., Judith in her long prayer (Jdt 9:2-14) calls on God to give her a strong hand and wily words like her ancestor Simeon to prevent harm to the Temple and Zion. The language used for the rape of the unnamed victim, alluding to the story of Dinah (Gen 34), is understood as analogous to the threatened "rape" or desecration of the Temple by the foreign enemy. The holy of holies of the Temple must be kept as pure as the womb of an unmarried Israelite woman. Another complexly woven figuration occurs in the symbolic language of 2 Esdras (*see* ESDRAS, SECOND BOOK OF). The imaginative author of 2 Esdras depicts Ezra engaged in a conversation with Earth, depicted as a female (2 Esd 7:62-69). Perhaps most surreal of all, in the central vision of the seven visions, as a response to his prayer, Ezra sees a lamenting woman. As she recounts her story of the loss of her son, she is suddenly transformed into a brilliant city being built with enormous foundations laid. The mediating angel Uriel must reveal to Ezra the meaning of this vision: the city of Zion being restored after its destruction (2 Esd 9–10). The Apocrypha thus includes "women" from the seductive to the sublime, depictions that must be evaluated on their own terms within their narrative contexts. *See* FEMINIST INTERPRETATION; SEPTUAGINT; WISDOM IN THE OT.

Bibliography: Claudia Camp. "Understanding a Patriarchy: Women in Second Century Jerusalem Through the Eyes of *Ben Sira.*" *"Women Like This": New Perspectives on Jewish Women in the Greco-Roman World.* A.-J. Levine, ed. (1991) 1–40; Tal Ilan. *Integrating Women into Second Temple History* (1999); Carol A. Newsom and Sharon H. Ringe, eds. *Women's Bible Commentary: Expanded Edition with Apocrypha* (1998); Lawrence M. Wills. *The Jewish Novel in the Ancient World* (1995).

JUDITH H. NEWMAN

WOMEN IN THE NT. The image of a pyramid illustrates the structure of households and economic and political systems in which NT women lived. At the top of the household pyramid was the *pater familias*, the male head, and beneath him the extended family, then, if the family were wealthy, slaves and retainers (*see* FAMILY; HOUSEHOLD, HOUSEHOLDER). Wealthy families were a minority at the top of the economic pyramid, and below them a class of relatively prosperous merchants and landowners; the large "base" population lived at subsistence level. Caesar's household was at the top of the imperial pyramid, along with wealthy landed aristocrats, and below them estate owners, members of a local city's aristocracy and merchants, and finally the masses of the population, free persons who barely scraped out a living and slaves, formed the base of the socioeconomic pyramid. The majority of NT women belonged to the masses as village peasants or the destitute poor.

The greatest differences among women were not cultural or religious but economic. Whether or not she belonged to a wealthy family or was a Roman citizen determined a woman's day-to-day circumstances more profoundly than her religious or ethnic ties. Because wealthier women had more choices and opportunities, we know more about them. On the other hand, poorer rural women and those involved in a family trade or shop in towns and cities had more freedom of movement than women who belonged to the more comfortable groups in the middle of the pyramid.

A. Jewish Women
B. Greek and Roman Women
C. Approaches to Texts on Women
D. Women in the Pauline Letters
E. Women in the Gospels
   1. Women in Mark
   2. Women in John
F. Women in Luke–Acts
G. Conclusions
Bibliography

A. Jewish Women

Understanding women in the Second Temple period is complicated by variant pictures in rabbinic sources and archaeological remains. There were many ways of being Jewish; there were Pharisaic, Sadducean, Essene, and Christian Jews. The situation of Jewish women was influenced by Hellenistic culture and by the political and economic systems of the Roman Empire. Rabbinic sources depict woman's "place" as domestic, her value chiefly her fertility, her duty to her husband and their children. Religiously she was subject to Torah prohibitions, three of which were binding: lighting the Sabbath candles, burning a small piece of dough prior to baking bread, and observing laws of menstrual purity.

Most NT women lived in villages in Roman Palestine where families survived by farming, fishing, and running small businesses. Female labor was essential to the family's survival, although the dangers of pregnancy made women's lives brief. Women had an important role in domestic religious practice, local festivals, and funerary rites. Evidence from inscriptions shows that wealthy women supported synagogues financially and sometimes held leadership positions.

B. Greek and Roman Women

The position of Greek women was much less restricted than it had been in the classical period as rights of married women expanded. As they could inherit and manage wealth, their social influence increased. Education was available to wealthier women, and decrees honoring women, some of whom were citizens with political rights, have been found in cities during the Roman period.

Elite women were deeply involved in the economic, political, and religious life of republican and imperial Rome, even though Roman legal theory regarded women as *infirmitas sexus* (the "weaker sex"). The *pater familias* controlled the lives of "his" females. Marriage and motherhood were expected civic duties, although divorce was as readily available to women as men. The Roman matron was responsible for managing the household, which functioned like a small business. In a household with slaves, she was free to supervise her children's education, visit, shop, attend religious ceremonies, and participate in civic life. Lives of noncitizen, poor women or female slaves were quite different. Slaves were "property" and not only did the household work but also were sexually available to their owners. Children born to slaves were the owner's property. While slaves could be manumitted at thirty years of age or buy their freedom, their lives were unenviable.

Both Greek and Roman women had many religious options; the concept of belonging to only one religion was unusual. As a means of unifying a vast, diverse empire, Roman state religious festivals were the mainstay of religious life along with the cults of a city's patron deities. The eastern cults (including Christianity?) introduced into the cities of the Roman Empire by sailors, soldiers, merchants, and travelers were also popular.

C. Approaches to Texts on Women

New Testament books are 1st-cent. documents subject to the limitations of their culture. The NT authors do not set out to describe women's lives. Examining NT texts to learn about women involves first discerning the author's intentions. Why is the evangelist telling this bit of the Jesus story, or what is Paul's purpose in writing to this particular church or individual? Who benefits and who is disadvantaged from the telling or teaching? What is not said and why? Second, one attends to literary issues like genre and where in the text a passage occurs and the social, cultural, and theological context.

Some passages are descriptive, some prescriptive. Material on women in the Gospels is largely narrative and descriptive. Women occur as characters in Jesus' story, normally as "foils" to Jesus, who only rarely teaches about women. Paul's letters say nothing about the daily lives of women in the cities to which he writes; the information they offer on that topic is found in theological or ethical consideration of something else. Paul's epistles may be read to discover information about women in a particular church (descriptively) or instructions Paul gives regarding women (prescriptively). If a text is prescriptive the further question is whether what is prescribed is to limit an existing behavior or initiate a new one. The book of Revelation describes, not "real" women, but women as symbols (e.g., the Whore of Babylon [Rev 17–18] and Bride of Christ [19:7-8; 21:1-2]) or as defilers of men (Rev 14:3-4). After reading the text in its contexts and determining what sort of material it is, one must decide whether the text is normative, for "all time," or culturally conditioned, applying only to a situation in the NT period, or even only to the problems of a single Christian community as in the case of women prophesying in Corinth (1 Cor 11:2-16). When examining the NT witness about a particular issue, passages dealing systematically with it should be used to clarify incidental references. It is crucial to examine how our own presuppositions influence the interpretation of issues and texts.

D. Women in the Pauline Letters

Paul's letters represent our earliest information on women in the NT. Paul's basic theological insight is that "if anyone is in Christ, there is a new creation: everything old has passed away; see, everything has become new" (2 Cor 5:17); "there is no longer Jew or Greek, there is no longer slave or free, there is no longer male and female; for all of you are one in Christ Jesus" (Gal 3:28). Being "in Christ" supersedes ethnic, economic, and gender divisions. Paul's principle is clear; his application is less so.

Corinth had a house church led by the woman Chloe (1 Cor 1:11). In 1 Cor 7 Paul grants husbands and wives equal conjugal rights, but considers it wiser if virgins and widows remain unmarried. Much of Paul's prescriptive material on women concerns marriage, which, for him, is concessionary (Rom 7:2-3; 1 Cor 7; 2 Cor 6:14–7:1; and perhaps Eph 5:21-33; Col 3:18-19). The complicated discussion of women's head covering in 1 Cor 11:2-16 sometimes obscures Paul's assumption that women pray and prophesy in church, supporting the text-critical evaluation that silencing women in 14:33b-36 is a later interpolation to bring the text in line with later church practice.

Paul greets many women in his churches. Exhorting them to "be of the same mind," Paul calls Euodia and Syntyche in Philippi "co-workers" who "struggled beside me in the work of the gospel" (Phil 4:2-4). In Rom 16 Paul calls women deacon, patron, fellow worker, hard worker, and apostle; only three of the women named have no role mentioned. Prisca (the female half of a missionary couple, 1 Cor 16:19) is a fellow worker (Rom 16:3) as apparently are Mary (Rom 16:6) and Tryphaena and Tryphosa (Rom 16:12). Paul greets Phoebe, a deacon who may be carrying the letter to Rome (Rom 16:1-2), and Junia, who is "prominent among the apostles" (Rom 16:7). Paul employs metaphors from "women's work" (especially baking), features Hagar and Sarah in the important allegory in Gal 4:21–5:1, and refers to himself as a wet nurse (1 Cor 3:2), a nurse (1 Thess 2:7), and in labor with the Galatians (4:19).

All this belies a common misconception of Paul's misogyny. The most damaging passages in the Pauline corpus appear in the Pastoral Epistles (1 Tim 2:11-15; 2 Tim 3:6, e.g.), probably written later by leaders in Pauline churches concerned with the church's reputation in society. Paul does not advocate for women, but neither does he censor women he knew in leadership; he praised many of them. The epistles show Paul living the tension between what was and what was to be, a tension often apparent in differences between prescriptive and descriptive passages. Paul struggles with cultural customs, teaching a theology of equality that he had not quite integrated into his overall theological or ethical program (*see* PASTORAL LETTERS).

E. Women in the Gospels

Study of women in light of an evangelist's purposes highlights a Gospel's characteristics. Women in Matthew reveal its Jewishness, Mark's concern with discipleship and the Gentile mission, Luke's universalism, and the prescience of John's Jesus. Generally, Jesus behaves toward women as an observant, pious male Jew of the Second Temple period, one who occasionally "breaks the rules" and does not allow cultural presupposition to proscribe his activities. His disciples and peripatetic ministry included men and women (Mark 15:40-41; Luke 8:1-3) who were not only the recipients of his benevolence and healing power but also positive examples in teaching about the kingdom of God. The following examples illustrate these generalizations.

1. Women in Mark

Mark's Gospel was written ca. 70 CE for a primarily Gentile community. It reflects the Palestinian Jewish culture of the characters in the story and the concerns of the evangelist's church. About one-quarter of Mark's characters are women, but only five are named: Mary, Jesus' mother; Herodias; Mary Magdalene; Mary the mother of James and Joses; and Salome. However, women were present in the Markan "crowds" who approved of Jesus and were among his disciples. Initially, women disciples are portrayed more positively than males who misunderstand and disobey Jesus. Simon's mother-in-law "serves," the prototypical act of discipleship (1:31; 9:35; 10:43-45). The woman with a flow of blood has faith to approach Jesus (5:24-34). An anonymous widow and an anointing woman are models of self-giving (12:41-44; 14:3-9). But finally, women charged to proclaim resurrection "fear" (16:8), making the evangelist's point, that, for everyone, discipleship is partial and continually learned "on the way."

The account of the Syrophoenician woman (7:24-30) is instructive. With the wrong sex, wrong ethnic status, and wrong religious background, this single mother of a demon-possessed daughter elicits a christologically troubling response from Jesus (7:27), but her quick-witted reply unravels the distinction between Jew and Gentile, leading to her daughter's deliverance (7:29). Mark contrasts her to the legalistic religious authorities in 7:1-23 and implies that Jesus learned from a Gentile woman. The account was important for understanding the church's Gentile mission. Women in Mark are vivid examples, positive and negative, of discipleship, engaging in its paradigmatic work; they follow, serve, suffer, and are charged to "go and tell."

2. Women in John

As the last canonical Gospel, written ca. 90 CE and edited ca. 100, John tells Jesus' story differently from the Synoptics, suggesting he had different sources. The Gospel is structured around the great Jewish feasts (2:23; 6:4; 7:2; 10:22; 11:55). Its author's knowledge of Judaism is extensive. John often introduces unnamed "types" like a Samaritan woman, a paralytic, and a blind man, making their stories paradigmatic. Several important texts feature women (2:1-12; 4:1-42; 7:53–8:11; 11:1-44), although the named women include only Jesus' mother, Mary and Martha of Bethany, and the women at the cross (19:25-27).

The Samaritan woman in John 4:4-42 argues like a theologian, defending her Samaritan traditions. This exchange characterizes John's method. Jesus stops at a well in Samaria (enemy territory) associated with Jacob where, at noon, he meets an unnamed woman. He breaks several taboos by asking her for a drink and initiating a theological discussion in which she is treated with the same seriousness as Nicodemus in the previous chapter. Recent scholarship has established that the woman is probably not sexually profligate, but is highly theologically informed (see vv. 9, 12, 19-20, 25). Jesus leads her from her five lords/husbands to the "truth" so important in John's Gospel (8:32). Chapters 2–4 illustrate John's pattern of movement through disbelief to partial belief to full belief in Jesus. (Compare the progress toward faith of the blind man in John 9:1-38.)

John places his most fully developed christological confession on the lips of Martha (11:27). Her sister Mary's act of foot washing (12:1-8) both predicts Jesus' death and incorrupt resurrection and gives him a dramatic image to illustrate the meaning of discipleship (13:1-11). Although John's Jesus does not directly address "women's issues," his relationships with women illustrate the principle of Christian mutuality. Women are depicted as strong, independent followers of Jesus who sometimes play unconventional roles. The Gospel opens and closes with Mary the mother of Jesus as model disciple.

F. Women in Luke–Acts

A two-part work, Luke–Acts contains an extraordinary amount of material on women, apparently from Luke's special source. Written ca. 85 CE by a Gentile Christian for Gentiles, the Gospel has thirty passages dealing with women, eleven of whom are named. Lukan infancy material focuses on women (chaps. 1–2). Five healing miracles are done for women. Luke's Jesus pairs kingdom parables treating women's and men's activities (13:18-21; 15:4-10; 18:1-14). Although exemplary women tend to be silent (Anna, 2:36-38; Mary, 10:38-42), a crucial text (8:1-3) indicates women traveled with Jesus and financed his ministry.

Although not history in the modern sense, the Acts of the Apostles is a primary source of information about the early church. Twelve women are mentioned by name; they are married, single, professional, homemakers, Jews, Greeks, Romans, goddesses, sisters, mothers, mothers-in-law, queens, slaves, martyrs, and of questionable reputation. In Acts both men and women become Christians and assume leadership. Women are missionaries, prophets, disciples, and leaders of house churches. Passages on Tabitha/Dorcas (9:36-42) and Lydia (16:11-15) especially reveal women's importance in Petrine and Pauline missions. Although some feminist scholarship questions whether Luke is woman's champion, his writing multiplies the number of texts that feature them, highlighting their prominence in early Christianity.

G. Conclusions

The volume of material on women in the NT is extraordinary for a time and cultures that did not ordinarily take them very seriously. Some passages disdain women and seek to limit their activity and command their subordination. Issues of authority are issues of power, and the powerful write history. One wonders how the NT might have looked had it been written by Jesus' mother, Mary of Magdala, Tabitha, Lydia, Priscilla, Phoebe, or Junia. Nevertheless, their stories are told. Finally, NT women are women of their time and cultures, subject to those limitations, but in the process of liberation and leadership in the kingdom of God. To paraphrase Paul, "for freedom Christ set them free" (Gal 5:1). Like everything Christian, that freedom was, and continues to be, partial. But its perfection is promised. *See* AQUILA AND PRISCILLA; ETHICS IN THE NT; FEMINIST INTERPRETATION; HOUSEHOLD CODES; MARRIAGE, NT; ORDER OF WIDOWS; PROSTITUTION; SEX, SEXUALITY; WIDOW.

Bibliography: David Balch and Carolyn Osiek, eds. *Families in the New Testament World* (1997); Shaye J. D. Cohen. *The Jewish Family in Antiquity* (1993); Joan Connelly. *Portrait of a Priestess* (2007); Eve D'Ambra. *Roman Women* (2007); Elisabeth Schüssler Fiorenza. *In Memory of Her* (1983); Tal Ilan. *Integrating Women into Second Temple History* (2001); Tal Ilan. *Jewish Women in Greco-Roman Palestine: An Inquiry into Image and Status* (1996); Ross Shepard Kraemer and Mary Rose D'Angelo, eds. *Women and Christian Origins* (1999); Carol A. Newsom and Sharon H. Ringe, eds. *The Women's Bible Commentary* (1992); Carolyn Osiek, Margaret Y. MacDonald, and Janet H. Tulloch, eds. *A Woman's Place: House Churches in Earliest Christianity* (2005); Bonnie Bowman Thurston. *Women in the New Testament* (2004).

BONNIE BOWMAN THURSTON

WOMEN IN THE OT [אִשָּׁה ʾishah, אִשֹּׁת ʾishoth, נָשִׁים nashim]. Women appear throughout the OT as supporting and sometimes major characters in narratives, as generic females in legal and other texts, and as part of the imagery in biblical poetry and some prose. Their varied depictions serve their scriptural contexts and also provide information about Israelite women.

A. Women in Old Testament Texts
  1. Named women
  2. Unnamed women
    a. Individuals and groups
    b. Gender pairs and common-gender terms
  3. Personified female figures
B. Israelite Women
  1. Household roles
  2. Community roles
Bibliography

A. Women in Old Testament Texts

The androcentric nature of the OT is evident in the disproportionately few women mentioned by name. The 135 named women represent less than 10 percent of the total number of named individuals, and they are less likely than their male counterparts to have significant roles in the narratives and other passages in which they are found. Unnamed women are more common, and their presence contributes to the agendas of the passages in which they appear.

Two concentrations of female figures are notable in the distribution of women across the OT canon. With thirty-two named and forty-six unnamed women, the greatest concentration is in Genesis. This reflects the fact that family stories dominate the first book of the Bible and also that its genealogies occasionally mention daughters, necessary for the demographic increase that the lists convey, as well as sons. Another large group of women, forty-six named and fifteen unnamed, appears in 1 Chronicles, mainly in the extensive genealogies of chaps. 1–9. Those tribal lists sometimes include a man's wife or daughter, usually to a mark a significant member of a family group; this is especially evident for the tribe of Judah, which contains the ancestral line of the Davidic monarchy.

Otherwise, women appear somewhat sporadically. For example, the corporate national focus of biblical prophecy means that individuals appear relatively rarely in those fifteen books. Specific women appear in only five prophetic books: Isa 51:2 (SARAH), Jeremiah (HAMUTAL; Jer 52:1; NEHUSHTA, though unnamed here, she appears in Jer 13:18; 22:26; 29:2 as mother of Jehoiacin/Jeconiah/Coniah; and RACHEL; Jer 31:15), Ezek 19:1-14 (HAMUTAL, unnamed mother of Jehoahaz, also appears in Jer 52:1), Hos 1:3 (GOMER and LO-RUHAMAH = Ruhamah; Hos 1:6, 8), and Mic 6:4 (MIRIAM). Generic women and men are occasionally part of prophetic imagery; but five prophets (Obadiah, Jonah, Habakkuk, Zephaniah, and Haggai) never mention women. Similarly, the poetic language of much of wisdom and psalmic literature employs some female figures but no named ones except for BATHSHEBA in Ps 51 (superscription [Heb. 51:2]) and the hero's three daughters in Job (42:14). In the historical books, most women are mentioned because of their relationship to a king, although Joshua and especially Judges portray named and unnamed women with national roles in their own right, probably reflecting realities of early Israel. The two books bearing a woman's name (RUTH and ESTHER) have significant female figures (*see* ESTHER, BOOK OF; RUTH, BOOK OF).

1. Named women

Miriam is perhaps the most prominent OT woman (Exod 14; Num 12; Deut 24:9; 1 Chr 6:3; Mic 6:4), in that she is the only one to appear in five different books (Exodus, Numbers, Deuteronomy, 1 Chronicles, and Micah). Only two women, Bathsheba (2 Sam 11:3; 12:24; 1 Kgs 1:11-31; the introduction to Ps 51; and as "Bath-shua" in 1 Chr 3:5) and ZERUIAH (a sister of David, e.g., 1 Sam 26:6; 2 Sam 2:13; 1 Kgs 1:7; 1 Chr 2:16) are mentioned in four different books (1 Samuel, 1 Kings, 1 Chronicles, and Psalms). Eight are found in three books; and twenty-six are mentioned twice, mainly because they appear in the monarchic narratives in the books of Samuel and Kings and also in the parallel account in the books of Chronicles.

Named women are almost always identified relationally as someone's wife, secondary wife, or concubine—in contrast to the way men are identified by their patrilineage. Women also achieve an identity as mothers, with mothers named for virtually every Judean king and several Israelite ones. In several instances, a named woman is introduced as someone's daughter, usually to serve narrative purposes. For example, DINAH figures in a tragic episode of her father Jacob's story (Gen 34); and Caleb's daughter ACHSAH acquires property (Josh 15:16-19; Judg 1:12-15), as do the five daughters (Hoglah, Mahlah, Milcah, Noah, and Tirzah) of Zelophehad (Num 26:33; 27:1; 36:11; Josh 17:3), indicating the possibility of occasional female land holding (*see* ZELOPHEHAD, DAUGHTERS OF). Daughters of prominent monarchs also have narrative roles: Saul's daughters MERAB (1 Sam 14:49; 18:17, 19; 2 Sam 21:8) and MICHAL (1 Sam 14:49; 18:20, 27, 28; 19:11-13, 17; 25:44; 2 Sam 3:13, 14; 6:16, 20, 21, 23; 1 Chr 15:29), David's daughter TAMAR (2 Sam 13:1-32), Solomon's daughters Basemath (1 Kgs 4:15) and Taphath (1 Kgs 4:11), Joram's (Jehoram's) daughter Jehosheba (2 Kgs 11:2; 2 Chr 22:31), and Ahab's (or Omri's) daughter ATHALIAH (2 Kgs 11; 2 Chr 22–23). Otherwise, women are generally clustered around important monarchs and have little narrative function other than to contribute to the prominence of their famous relative. Almost half of the named royal women, who comprise 36 percent of all named women, are relatives of the preeminent monarch David, who is also the only king for whom a niece (Abihail, 2 Chr 11:28) and a granddaughter (another Tamar, 2 Sam 14:27) are mentioned.

Only four named women appear without reference to a male relative: the matriarch REBEKAH's nurse DEBORAH (Gen 35:8); the two midwives, SHIPHRAH and PUAH (Exod 1:15), in the exodus story; and the heroic harlot RAHAB of Jericho (Josh 2; 6:17, 23, 25). A

fifth woman, the judge and prophet Deborah, is linked with "Lappidoth" (Judg 4:4), which may be the name of her spouse but just as likely denotes her hometown.

The majority (107) of the named women are presented as Hebrew, Israelite, or Jewish. About one-third of them, all in biblical prose—including Gomer, who appears in the largely prose chapters of Hosea (1–3)—have significant narrative roles. In accord with the clustering of women in Genesis, the ancestor stories feature six matriarchs and handmaids—Sarah (Gen 17–25), Rebekah (Gen 22; 24–28), Rachel (Gen 29–31), LEAH (Gen 29–31; 33–35), BILHAH (Gen 30:3-7; 35:22-25), and ZILPAH (Gen 30:9-12)—as well as Jacob's daughter Dinah (Gen 30:21; 34:1-26) and Judah's daughter-in-law Tamar (Gen 38). Several more women, namely Miriam (Exod 15; Num 12), Deborah (Judg 4–5), DELILAH (Judg 16), and HANNAH (1 Sam 1–2), appear in extended passages depicting the pre-monarchic era, a period in which women may have had prominent supra-household roles. The accounts of the monarchy provide a glimpse of women in elite contexts and include several women with sustained or cameo roles, mostly in the David narratives: his wives ABIGAIL (1 Sam 25), Bathsheba, and Michal, and his daughter Tamar. The only other Israelite queen with a significant role is Athaliah; and the only named, non-royal woman who stands out in the accounts of the monarchy is the prophet HULDAH (2 Kgs 22; 2 Chr 34). Finally, NAOMI and Esther are heroic figures in the novellas Ruth and Esther.

The rest of the named women (about 22 percent) are pre-Hebrew or foreign. Most appear briefly in genealogies or lists; but eight have significant narrative roles, most notably EVE (Gen 2–3) as "mother of all the living" (Gen 3:20). Strong female figures account for the other seven: the Egyptian slave-wife HAGAR, who is the mother of Abraham's first son (Gen 16; 21:9-21; 25:12); the Midianite woman ZIPPORAH, who saves the life of her husband, Moses (Exod 2:21-22; 4:20-26; 18:2-6); the Canaanite prostitute Rahab, who provides refuge to Israelite spies (Josh 2; 6:17-25); the Kenite woman JAEL, who slays the Canaanite general Sisera (Judg 4:17-22; 5:24-27); the infamous Phoenician princess JEZEBEL, who becomes Ahab's wife and perhaps co-regent (1 Kgs 16:31; 18; 19:1-3; 21; 2 Kgs 9); the Moabite Ruth, ancestor of David, in the book bearing her name; and the Persian queen VASHTI in Esth 1–2.

Only ten named OT women recur in the NT or Apocryphal/Deuterocanonical books. Esther and Vashti are mentioned only in the Apocrypha (ESTHER, ADDITIONS TO), while Eve (Tob 8:6; 2 Cor 11:3; 1 Tim 2:13) and Hagar (Bar 3:23; Gal 4:24-25) appear in both the Apocryphal/Deuterocanonical books and the NT. The other six are found only in the NT: three—Tamar, Ruth, and Rahab (along with an allusion to Bathsheba)—are in Matthew's genealogy (Matt 1:3, 5, 6); and the other three are the matriarchs, with Sarah referred to three times (Rom 4:19; 9:9; Heb 11:11) and Rachel (Matt 2:18) and Rebekah (Rom 9:10) each named once.

2. Unnamed women

a. Individuals and groups. Unnamed women are mentioned individually or in groups about 600 times in the OT. They are usually designated by their family roles, thus reflecting the kinship orientation of ancient Israel. Marital relationships (wife, concubine, widow, divorcée) are most common, followed by offspring (daughter, daughter-in-law, granddaughter), parents (mother, stepmother, and mother-in-law), and other female relatives (aunt, sister, and sister-in-law). Generic figures—designated "young women," "maidens," or simply "women"—also appear, as do miscellaneous others including "foreign women" and those labeled "female slaves" or "maidservants." These figures are almost always denoted by plural or collective terms and represent groups of indeterminable size.

Many of the unnamed women are representatives of the female gender in biblical poetry, where they appear in a variety of positive (e.g., Ps 113:9; Prov 18:22) and negative (Prov 21:9; Amos 4:1) images. They convey a range of emotions, including both joy (Song 6:9) and despair (e.g., Isa 24:1-2; Lam 2:20; Hos 10:14). Often the tropes invoke women's reproductive functions (e.g., Ps 22:9-10 [Heb. 22:10-11]; Isa 54:1; Jer 6:24), especially in female images for God (e.g., Job 38:29; Isa 42:14; 45:10-11).

Legal texts also mention generic women, especially in matters relating to patrilineality and paternity: adultery (Lev 20:10; Num 5:11-31; Deut 22:22), prostitution (Lev 19:29), widows in levirate marriage (Deut 25:5-10), virginity (Exod 22:16-17 [Heb. 22:15-16]; Deut 22:13-21, 23-29), and probably incest (Lev 18 and 20). Other family matters, such as parental relationships with offspring—probably adult children—also appear (Exod 21:15, 17; Lev 20:9). Purity issues relating to bodily emissions and blemishes (Lev 13:29, 38; 15:18-33; 18:19; 20:18; Num 5:2-4) and childbirth (Lev 12:1-8) are another focus of laws mentioning women.

Otherwise, unnamed women appear as generic types or narrative figures in OT prose, although relatively few have noteworthy narrative roles. Only fifteen are featured as individuals in extended narratives. Of these, two—Potiphar's wife (Gen 39) and Pharaoh's daughter (Exod 2:5-10)—appear in the Pentateuch. The other thirteen appear in the historical books: JEPHTHAH'S DAUGHTER (Judg 11:34-40); Samson's mother (Judg 13:22-25; 14:2-9, 16; 16:17); Samson's wife (Judg 14:1–15:8); Micah's mother (Judg 17:1-4); the LEVITE'S CONCUBINE (Judg 19–20); the medium of Endor (1 Sam 28:7-25); the wise woman of Tekoa (2 Sam 14:1-20); the wise woman of Abel of Beth-maacah (2 Sam 20:14-22); the Queen of Sheba (1 Kgs 10:1-13 // 2 Chr 9:1-12); Jeroboam's wife (1 Kgs 14); the widow of Zarephath (1 Kgs 17:8-24); the prophet's widow (2 Kgs 4:1-7); and the Shunammite (2 Kgs 4:8-

37; 8:1-6). Others—e.g., the woman of Thebez (Judg 9:53-54; 2 Sam 11:21) and JOB'S WIFE (Job 2:9-10)—have brief but no less important narrative roles. In addition, several women—the sensuous SHULAMMITE of the Song of Songs (6:13); Lemuel's wise mother; and the adroit household manager, both in Prov 31—figure prominently in poetic passages.

Women also appear briefly in pairs or small groups in many other texts. Among the more prominent are LOT'S WIFE and LOT'S DAUGHTERS (Gen 19); Zipporah's six sisters (Exod 2:16-20); the women of Jabesh-gilead and Shiloh (Judg 21); two prostitutes who are mothers (1 Kgs 3:16-28); two mothers of Samaria (2 Kgs 6:26-33); the daughters of Jerusalem or Zion who are dramatic foils to the Shulammite in Song of Songs; women who worship the Queen of Heaven (Jer 7:18; 44:15-19, 25); women who went to Egypt (Jer 43:6-7; 44); and prophesying women (Ezek 13:17-23).

b. Gender pairs and common-gender terms. In these two kinds of references unnamed women are linked with unnamed men as equivalent persons. Family relationships predominate in approximately 200 gender pairs, which couple females with their male counterparts, usually in the plural, to indicate a general category: son/DAUGHTER is used in seventy-nine instances (e.g., Deut 12:12), father/MOTHER is found in thirty-one texts (e.g., 1 Kgs 19:20), groom/BRIDE appears five times (e.g., Jer 7:34), and the brother/SISTER unit is in three passages (e.g., Josh 2:13). Otherwise, male and female servants are coupled in twenty-eight passages (e.g., Gen 12:16); and opposite genders in age groups are paired in fourteen texts: old women with old men (e.g., Zech 8:4), and young men with young women (e.g., Ezek 9:6). In the rest, the pair is simply man-woman or male-female (e.g., Esth 4:11), with family groups indicated in six passages by the addition of "children" to the male-female pair (e.g., Ezra 10:1). These gender pairs are especially prominent in OT poetry, where they intensify the meaning of parallel lines, and in the family narratives and genealogies of Genesis.

In addition, women are often understood to be present when common-gender or gender-inclusive terms are used. Terms for community—such as "children (banim [בָּנִים]; literally "sons") of Israel," "all the people ('am עַם)," "the whole congregation ('edhah עֵדָה)," and "the assembly (qahal קָהָל)"—can denote both women and men collectively. Similarly, some terms for individuals—such as humankind ('adham אָדָם) and person (nefesh נֶפֶשׁ)—are often used collectively for both genders. Designations of groups using geographical terms (e.g., Canaanites) also are usually gender inclusive.

3. Personified female figures

Women appear as personifications of places or peoples, most frequently in prophetic images. Family terms dominate in these personifications. Most common is *daughter*, which is found some eighty-four times to represent eight different countries or peoples and five different cities. The most frequently personified place is Jerusalem, appearing not only as a daughter but also as a bride, maid, mother, princess, queen, sister, whore, or woman. Sometimes the imagery is used positively, especially in Third Isaiah, where Jerusalem appears as a loving mother or bride of God (e.g., Isa 62:4-5; 66:7-12). Prominent among the negative personifications are the depictions of Jerusalem and Samaria in the troubling oracles of Ezek 16 and 23, where they are named, respectively, OHOLAH AND OHOLIBAH.

Abstract qualities, especially wisdom and folly, are personified as women in Prov 8–9; wickedness is depicted as a woman in Zech 5:8.

B. Israelite Women

Because of their overriding interest in national matters, in patrilineages, and in the monarchy, and also because most of their authors were elite males, biblical texts provide little direct information about, and perhaps even a distorted view of, the daily lives of most Israelite women. Thus archaeological data and ethnographic evidence supplement OT references in considering Israelite women.

1. Household roles

Most Israelite women and men of the OT period lived in agricultural settlements. The work place for everyone, with the exception of a few specialists and those with government, priestly, or military positions, was the family household. Virtually all the basic commodities necessary for a family's survival were produced by the combined labor of women, men, and children. For women, this entailed expertise in transforming the family's crops and animals into edible form and also in producing clothing and other textiles (*see* AGRICULTURE; CLOTH, CLOTHES). Women also had auxiliary responsibilities in other aspects of the household economy. Senior women in every family had a managerial role, supervising the labor of children and perhaps other family members; if their husbands were well-to-do landowners or were part of bureaucratic elites, they also supervised servants or slaves. Men may have controlled female sexuality, but otherwise considerable power accrued to women because of their essential roles in the economic functions of their households (*see* HOUSEHOLD, HOUSEHOLDER).

The social fabric of Israelite communities was structured along male kinship lines but functioned through the relationships formed by both women and men across the various units comprising local and clan groups. Because women from several households often performed tedious and time-consuming chores together, women became linked more than men in informal networks that facilitated mutual aid among families in times of crisis, such as when illness or death interrupted essential subsistence tasks. Moreover, because marriage involved women moving to their husband's households, women had connections with two family groups, their natal and their marital ones; this also positioned them to facilitate inter-group relationships (*see* MARRIAGE, OT).

Religious activities considered essential for the well-being of the household and its members were integral to family life; and women in particular performed rituals attempting to ensure their reproductive success. The all-too-common problems of infertility, maternal death, and infant mortality—which are dealt with by medicine in the modern world—were addressed by the use of a variety of substances and objects meant to secure healthy pregnancies and safe BIRTHs (*see* BARREN, BARRENNESS). Such practices are inherently religious, for they invoke beneficent divine action and aim to dispel supernatural malevolent forces.

2. Community roles

Women's community roles included many that can be considered "professional." The one mentioned most frequently in the OT is PROSTITUTION, which is discouraged but never absolutely forbidden; one prostitute (Rahab, Josh 2, 6) and one woman (Tamar, Gen 38) disguising herself as a prostitute are regarded positively. Women also practice trades or crafts that develop from their household work; e.g., women produce sumptuous fabrics for the tabernacle (Exod 35:25-26), and the woman of Prov 31 markets garments she produces (vv. 13, 24). The discovery of seals inscribed with women's names and presumably used in commercial transactions likewise suggests the existence of Israelite businesswomen (*see* SEALS AND SCARABS). State industries or palace workshops conscripted female perfumers, cooks, and bakers (1 Sam 8:13). Women were also midwives (Gen 35:17; 38:28; Exod 1:15-21); and two "nurses," probably wet-nurses, are mentioned (Gen 24:59; 35:8; 2 Kgs 11:2-3). Most couriers were men carrying dispatches to other men, but a servant girl bears messages between Jonathan and David (2 Sam 17:17). Women usually sent female messengers (Prov 9:3-4), and the metaphor of female heralds ("Those who bear tidings" [f. pl.]) making announcements to a wider audience in Ps 68:11 (Heb. 68:12) suggests the existence of female heralds in ancient Israel.

Community leadership roles are notable. Deborah is a prominent military leader who also adjudicated and is called a prophet (see Judg 4:4-5). Unnamed but no less significant are the two wise women, whose psychological acumen and sagacity play a national role (2 Sam 14:1-20; 20:14-22). Royal women, by virtue of their class, exercised political power; notable in this regard are Jezebel and Athaliah. Several royal women (e.g., Maacah, 1 Kgs 15:13) bear the title gevirah (גְּבִירָה, "queen mother") that may designate a court functionary, and at least some elite women were literate (1 Kgs 21:8-9; Esth 9:29).

Women contributed to the cultural realm. Poems with significant religious themes are attributed to

Miriam, Deborah, and Hannah; and one or more anonymous women may have composed some or all of the love poetry in Song of Songs. Women performed with musical instruments, especially the frame-drum (NRSV "tambourine," perhaps a woman's instrument; *see* MUSICAL INSTRUMENTS), which accompanied female dancing and singing at victory celebrations (Exod 15:20-21; 1 Sam 18:6-7; Jer 31:4). Women were also vocalists in secular (e.g., 2 Sam 19:35 [Heb. 19:36]; Eccl 2:8) and perhaps religious (1 Chr 25:5-6) contexts, and they were experts in the performance of funerary laments (e.g., Jer 9:17-20 [Heb. 9:16-19]). Although not attested in the OT, it is likely that female artisans produced many of the artifacts—pottery, terra-cotta figurines, amulets, baskets, textile tools, and even grinding tools—recovered from Iron Age sites.

Several community religious roles for women are mentioned in the OT. Menial cultic tasks were likely performed by the enigmatic women at the entrance to the tent of meeting (Exod 38:8; 1 Sam 2:22). More prominent are prophets like Miriam, Deborah, Huldah, and NOADIAH, and unnamed women (Isa 8:3; Ezek 13:17-23; Joel 2:28 [Heb. 3:1]). Some women provided divinatory services and are viewed negatively by the OT (Exod 22:18 [Heb. 22:17]; Lev 20:27), but the medium of Endor (1 Sam 28:7-14) seems to escape censure (*see* ENDOR, MEDIUM OF).

Many women with supra-household roles would have earned a measure of prestige for their contributions and would have experienced the general satisfaction of serving a constituency beyond their families. Also, those professions requiring technical expertise or group performance provided skilled women with mentoring roles and concomitant status as well as the positive regard of those whom they served. *See* FAMILY; GENDER; ISRAEL, DAUGHTERS OF; JOCHEBED; MATRIARCHS; PHARAOH'S DAUGHTER; SEX, SEXUALITY; ZION, DAUGHTER OF.

Bibliography: A. Brenner. *The Israelite Woman: Social Role and Literary Type in Biblical Narrative* (1985); Carol Meyers. "Guilds and Gatherings: Women's Groups in Ancient Israel." *Realia Dei: Essays in Archaeology and Biblical Interpretation in Honor of Edward F. Campbell, Jr. at His Retirement.* Prescott H. Williams Jr. and Theodore Hiebert, eds. (1999) 154–84; Carol Meyers. *Households and Holiness: The Religious Culture of Israelite Women* (2005); Carol Meyers. "Material Remains and Social Relations: Women's Culture in Agrarian Households of the Iron Age." *Symbiosis, Symbolism, and the Power of the Past: Canaan, Ancient Israel, and Their Neighbors from the Late Bronze Age through Roman Palestina.* William G. Dever and Seymor Gitin, eds. (2002) 425–44; Carol Meyers, Toni Craven, and Ross S. Kraemer, eds. *Women in Scripture: A Dictionary of Named and Unnamed Women in the Hebrew Bible, the Apocryphal/Deuterocanonical Books, and the New Testament* (2000); Carol A. Newsom and Sharon Ringe, eds. *Women's Bible Commentary*, expanded ed. (1998).

CAROL MEYERS

WONDERS AND SIGNS. *See* SIGNS AND WONDERS.

WONDROUS [פָּלָא pala², פֶּלֶא pele²; ἔνδοξος endoxos, θαυμάσιας thaumasias]. The NRSV employs the term *wondrous* or *wonderful* and related words to refer to things that are incredible or beyond the power of most people. Descriptions of the deity and celebrations of what God does constitute the majority of contexts in which *wonderous* or *wonderful* appear, including in the Psalms, which contains frequent references to *wondrous*, "wonderful deeds," and "wonderful works" of the Lord (9:1 [Heb. 9:2]; 26:7; 75:1 [Heb. 75:2]; 105:2, 5; 106:7, 22; 107:8, 15, 21, 24, 31).

In the LXX, Sir 48:4 extols the "wondrous deeds" of Elijah, while 2 Esd 6:48 speaks of God's "wondrous works" in creation. The single NRSV use of "wonderful" in the NT appears in Luke 13:17, where Jesus releases a woman from a crippling spirit. As in the Sirach text recalling Elijah's deeds, Luke reports that the "crowd was rejoicing at all the wonderful things that he was doing." *See* SIGNS AND WONDERS.

JOHN I. LAWLOR

WOOD [עֵץ ʿets; ξύλον xylon]. Wood was one of the primary materials for construction in the ANE, along with stone and mud brick. The Hebrew word for *wood* (ʿets) is also the word for *tree*. In general, when describing standing timber, the word is translated as "tree"; when describing the material from timber that has been cut, sawn, or carved for specific uses, the word is translated as "wood." The same Hebrew word is also translated as "timber" in a number of instances, timber being the more general term to refer to either a tree or its wood. The Greek word xylov in the LXX and NT has the same connotations.

Wood was a major fuel for fire, so wood is often mentioned in the context of burnt offerings (Gen 22:3-9; Lev 1:7-17; 1 Kgs 18:23-38). The particular phrase "hewers of wood and drawers of water" is used for the menial work given to the Gibeonites; it designated them as the lowest social class, as virtual slaves (Josh 9:16-27). However, hewers of wood were also among the specialty workers Solomon requested and Hiram provided to cut the timber for the Temple and palace (2 Chr 2:8-16).

Wood as rough-cut timber was used vertically as pillars or columns to support the roof or second story of a house; it was used horizontally as beams and to hold the ceiling, the floor above, or the roof.

Sawn and squared wood beams were used for monumental structures such as palaces and temples. Monumental structures often had a course of wooden beams placed after several courses of hewn stone (Ezra 6:4). The course of wooden beams actually strengthened the building against collapse in the event of an earthquake. Wood was also sawn into planks that were used as paneling in monumental buildings (1 Kgs 6:15). Carved or worked wood was used for furniture such as the tabernacle (Exod 31:5). Also, idols were often carved of wood or stone (Isa 37:19; 40:20; 44:19).

References to specific varieties of wood include CYPRESS wood for Noah's ark (Gen 6:14), ACACIA wood for the ark of the covenant, its poles, and the furnishings and frame for the tabernacle (Exod 25–26, 35–37). One word usually translated as cypress (berosh [בְּרוֹשׁ]; 1 Kgs 6:15, 34) was more likely a variety of juniper or other fir. The ALGUM tree and its variant ALMUG was a prized wood from Ophir and Lebanon. It was used for steps and supports for the Temple, as well as musical instruments such as lyres and harps (1 Kgs 10:11-12; 2 Chr 2:8; 9:10-11). It is often identified as sandalwood, box, or a variety of fir. Cedar of Lebanon was used for beams as well as paneling (1 Kgs 6:9, 15) and flooring in palaces and the Solomonic Temple. This wood was especially prized throughout the ANE, as there are numerous references to Egyptian, Assyrian, and Babylonian kings bringing back cedar wood from the mountainous regions of Lebanon and Syria.

JOEL F. DRINKARD JR.

WOOL [גֵּז gez, עֲמַר ʿamar, צֶמֶר tsemer; ἔριον erion]. Sheep herding and the attendant shearing of the sheep for their wool was an industry common in the ANE (Gen 31:19; 2 Kgs 3:4; Isa 53:7). Wool was the substance of most of the everyday garments fashioned by the women of the household (Prov 31:13; Ezek 34:3; Hos 2:9). Once the fleece was cleaned and dried (Judg 6:37), the wool was carded. Strands of yarn were spun into fabric on looms and sown together using elaborate running stitches. Some woolen strands were dyed and used as embroidery thread (Exod 28:39); however, the mixing of wool and LINEN was prohibited except for the priestly class (Deut 22:11). The white color of wool is used metaphorically to equate with purity (Isa 1:18), snow (Ps 147:16), and the shining white hair of the deity (Dan 7:9; Rev 1:14). *See* CLOTH, CLOTHES; TEXTILES.

VICTOR H. MATTHEWS

WORD, THE [אֹמֶר ʾomer, אִמְרָה ʾimrah, דָּבָר davar; λόγος logos, ῥῆμα rhēma]. *Word* in the Bible denotes the means of communication between subjects, and it also connotes that activity. Between persons, words are associated with actions, impacting reality: one's word conveys integrity and promise; the word of the authentic prophet comes true; the sharing of words implies receptivity and responsiveness between parties; one's word communicates oneself. Between God and humanity, God's word is the source of creation; God's revealing word guides discerning individuals; God's written

word, Scripture, is inspired and sustaining; God's incarnate Word, Jesus Christ, is the agent of both creation and redemption; the fulfilled word of Jesus shows that he is authentically sent by the Father; the word of the gospel is the message preached by the apostles. Indeed, the only hope for humanity is a believing response to the divine initiative—the word of God received by faith and expressed in faithfulness. As communication is central to relationship, the ways words are expressed and received are significant.

In the OT, the word (davar) Yahweh is the explicit, commissioning mantle of nearly two-thirds of the prophetic books. As the lion-voice of the Lord roars from Zion (Amos 1:2), Israel is exhorted to "hear this word that the LORD has spoken" (Amos 3:1) in repentance and restored faithfulness. Logos in the NT is often packed with theological meaning. Normally translated "word," it also connotes "idea," "principle," "thought," "study," and "communication." Especially important are its associations with the creative action of the deity, the preexistent Son of God, and the incarnation. While Hellenistic parallels are found in Heraclitus and Philo, the Jewish background of the term is also clear. Historically, the Johannine Prologue (John 1:1-18) has been the focus of the most intense theological debates, from the early church to the present. As an early Christian hymn about Jesus Christ as the Word of God made flesh, this passage reflects the convictions of early believers and contributes to important literary, historical, and theological discussions ever since.

A. Terminology and Uses in the Old Testament and New Testament
B. Apocryphal Uses of the Term
C. The "Word" as Christological Reference
D. The Background and Form of the Johannine Prologue
E. Words, Discourse, and Revelation
Bibliography

A. Terminology and Uses in the Old Testament and New Testament

The words for *word* in Hebrew and Greek are impossible to translate in narrow ways. On the one hand, several Hebrew and Greek words are rendered "word" in English translations; on the other, those same words are also translated into dozens of different English words in most translations. In the OT, by one estimate, the Hebrew davar is rendered over eighty-five different ways in the KJV alone. The NASV translates the verb form in 48 different ways, and the noun form in 125. Interplays are also rife between the verb and the noun forms of the terms in most languages, including Hebrew and Greek. A far more common term in Hebrew for the act of speaking (occurring over 5,200 times in the OT), ʾamar (אָמַר, "say, speak"), most commonly refers to discourse between persons, but it also is used as a noun (*see* SAY, SPEAK). In the garden of Eden,

God's discourse with humans is referred to thusly by the tempter, the woman, the man, and the narrator (Gen 3). Occurring fifty-six times in the OT is the most common noun form, 'omer ("saying, word"), and the psalmist prays, "Let the words of my mouth and the meditation of my heart be acceptable to you, O LORD, my rock and my redeemer" (Ps 19:14). Occurring thirty-seven times in the OT is 'imrah ("word, utterance"), and it is especially associated with the ordinances of the Lord. Over half of the uses of this term are in Ps 119 alone: "I treasure your word in my heart, so that I may not sin against you" (Ps 119:11), although these are matched in number by the largely interchangeable use of davar in the same psalm.

The most common term rendered "word" in the OT is davar, which occurs as a verb over 1,140 times (speak, say), and as a noun over 1,400 times (act/s, chronicle/s, thing/s, word/s), with only around half of the translations of davar being "word/s" in English. For instance, of the approximately sixty times davar occurs in Genesis, it is rendered "thing/s" just over two dozen times in the KJV and as "word/s" just under two dozen times. Two distinct uses involve discourse between humans and between humans and God.

Between humans, associations include: 1) dialogue among persons (Abner and the elders, 2 Sam 3:17); 2) a promise or a vow (a man "shall not break his word," Num 30:2); 3) advice or counsel (the counsel of Balaam, Num 31:16); 4) a message or a report (word of Joseph's brothers, Gen 37:14); 5) a command or royal edict (Esth 1:19); 6) a charge or a complaint (compare a false charge against a woman, Deut 22:14); 7) a judgment or a sentence (the judgment of the priests, Deut 17:9); 8) a historical record (the words of the discovered book, 2 Chr 34:21); 9) words of a song ("A Psalm of David," Ps 18:1 [Hebrew; English superscription]); 10) a timely utterance ("a word in season," Prov 15:23); 11) vain words of humans ("windy words," Job 16:3); 12) a particular "matter" (with Uriah, 1 Kgs 15:5); 13) a case against someone (to be settled before Aaron and Hur, Exod 24:14); 14) business dealings ("no dealings with Aram"; Judg 18:7); 15) acts and deeds (of Rehoboam, 1 Kgs 14:29); 16) events (Abraham's travels, Gen 22:20); 17) a manner or posture (Jacob and Esau, Gen 32:20); 18) a general thing (whatever passes through the fire; Num 31:23); 19) an explanatory reason (why Joshua circumcises the Israelites again, Josh 5:4); and 20) the words of blessing (Isaac pronounces upon Jacob, Gen 27:34). These examples give a broad sample of the multiple ways davar is used in the OT.

Between humans and God, the term davar refers in the OT to God's discourse with humanity: God's word comes to humanity, and humans express their words to God. God's action is often described as davar, yielding multiple associations. "The Word of the Lord" occurs some 240 times and forms the legitimizing fanfare of 10 of the 16 prophetic books (Jeremiah, Ezekiel, Hosea, Joel, Jonah, Micah, Zephaniah, Haggai, Zechariah, and

Malachi). The word of the Lord: 1) comes to Abram in a vision (promising blessing, Gen 15:1-6); 2) is feared by some discerning Egyptians (thus escaping the hail, Exod 9:20-21); 3) instructs Moses to enroll the Levites by clans (Num 3:14-16); 4) forms the content parameters of the authentic prophet's words (Num 24:11-14); 5) is rare at times (1 Sam 3:1); 6) is rejected by Saul, which leads to his own rejection by the Lord (1 Sam 15:23); 7) guides Nathan in his confrontation of David (2 Sam 7:4); 8) leads Solomon to build the Temple (1 Kgs 6:11); 9) leads the man of God to prophesy against Bethel (1 Kgs 13:1-2); 10) informs the message of Elijah (1 Kgs 17); 11) guides Jeremiah and Ezekiel (over fifty and nearly sixty references); and 12) will bring the dry bones to life by its hearing (Ezek 37:4). Similarly, the word of God 1) confirms Saul's kingship (1 Sam 9:27); 2) is confirmed by Solomon's building of the Temple (1 Kgs 8:26); 3) comes to Shemiah, leading him to challenge Rehoboam against going to war against Israel (1 Kgs 12:22); 4) stands true (Prov 30:5); and 5) endures eternally: "The grass withers, the flower fades; but the word of our God will stand forever" (Isa 40:8). Somewhat distinctively, the word of the Lord God brings judgment and predicts disaster (to Judah, Jer 19:3; to the Ammonites, Ezek 25:3-4), and yet it also brings comfort and hope (to the remnant of Israel, Jer 42:11-16; to Israel, Ezek 36:1-5). Similar to descriptions of human means and agencies of communication, the word of the Lord and of God refers to God's action and disclosure in the world. In addition, the word of the Lord refers to God's upright character and righteous ways, as the divine communication bespeaks the ways and being of the communicator (Ps 33:4-5). Alluding to Gen 1, the psalmist continues, linking the word of God with the activity of creation:

> By the word of the LORD the heavens were made,
>   and all their host by the breath of his mouth.
> He gathered the waters of the sea as in a bottle;
>   he put the deeps in storehouses.
> Let all the earth fear the LORD;
>   let all the inhabitants of the world stand in awe
>   of him.
> For he spoke, and it came to be;
>   he commanded, and it stood firm.
>
> (Ps 33:6-9)

The word of the Lord also connects with the agency and commandments of Moses (Josh 1:13), providing the basis for Jewish legal and prophetic traditions. Foundational to all prophetic action and expectation is God's promise to Moses (Deut 18:18) that "I will raise up for them a prophet like you from among their own people; I will put my words in the mouth of the prophet, who shall speak to them everything that I command." The authenticity of the prophet is confirmed by his speaking not his own words but only God's, confirmed by the prophet's word coming true. The fulfilled word is thus the marker of the authentic prophet, in contrast to those who convey their own agendas or perform for audience approval (compare Micaiah ben Imlah, 1 Kgs 22). The king can also be a messenger of the Lord (2 Sam 14:16-19), but a special emphasis is made upon the prophet as the agent of God (2 Kgs 5:6-15), whose word functions in ways similar to the word of God. The "ten words" (commandments) also show the framework of God's will for humanity (Exod 34:28), and the words of Moses and the law eventually become associated with the word of Scripture (Deut 8:3). Implicitly or explicitly, half of the commandments involve persons' words. Yahweh's promise is remembered as his holy word (Ps 105:42), and his promises are fulfilled (Deut 9:5). The book of Deuteronomy is from beginning to end a presentation of the word of God for Israel as spoken through the words of Moses (Deut 1:1).

Prayer, supplication, thanksgiving, and praise are also rendered as words of persons directed to God. While the essence of prayerful communication is authenticity and heartfelt expression before the Lord, this is rendered literally and metaphorically as "words." Whether God hears the words of the people depends on God's sovereign designs and plans, but it also is portrayed as contingent upon the people's having "heard" the word of the Lord by obeying the commandments of the covenant. For humans, to hear the word of the Lord is to obey it, which is interpreted as having a bearing on God's hearing the words of God's people. Despite reciprocity, God's word in the OT is often one of grace and mercy, as well as reward.

Within the wisdom traditions, wisdom is associated ontologically with the word of the Lord. Proverbs 8:22-31 describe wisdom's creation by the Lord at the beginning of his work—the first of God's creative acts. Preexistent Lady Wisdom was brought forth before water abounded and before the mountains were shaped. Established in the heavens, Wisdom was present when the Lord marked the foundations of the earth and confined the sea to its bounds by command. Cocreating with God, Wisdom declares: "I was beside him, like a master worker; and I was daily his delight, rejoicing before him always, rejoicing in his inhabited world and delighting in the human race" (Prov 8:30-31). God's creative working through Word and Wisdom is developed further within the wisdom tradition, especially in the books Wisdom of Solomon and Sirach.

In the NT, rhēma refers primarily to speaking and discourse, while logos has a far richer constellation of meanings, including understanding, reason, thought, and basis. Matthew and Luke follow the LXX in rendering the word that proceeds from mouth of the Lord in Deut 8:3 as rhēma. The words of Jesus are rhēmata (ῥήματα) in all four Gospels, and for Paul "the sword of the Spirit ... is the word of God" (rhēma; Eph 6:17)—a connotation with Scripture, but possibly simply a more general reference to divine disclosure. The word preached, according to Paul, is essential for a response to the gospel (Rom 10:8-18). In Heb 1:3 all things are created and sustained by the rhēma of the Son's power, and yet the rhēma of God is the means by which the worlds were framed.

In many ways rhēma and logos are interchangeable, but logos yields a far broader spectrum of meaning. Like the Hebrew davar, logos refers to content, a saying, a message, and understanding. In the Synoptics, Jesus comes bringing the logos of the kingdom. Luke/Acts refers to the proclamation of the gospel as "preaching the word." One's word should be "'Yes, Yes' or 'No, No'" (Matt 5:37; Jas 5:12), bolstered by integrity, not by swearing. For Paul, the logos of the cross (1 Cor 1:18) is the hope of the world, and yet "the kingdom of God depends not on talk but on power" (1 Cor 4:20). Spiritual gifts include a "word of wisdom" for some and a "word of knowledge" for others (1 Cor 12:8); "the word of truth" refers to the gospel (Col 1:5). Logos denotes the "trustworthy saying" motif of the Pastoral Epistles (1 Tim 1:15), and sound words are worth embracing (2 Tim 1:13). Hebrews notes that the logos of God is spoken by angels (Heb 2:2), and James exhorts us to be "doers of the word," not hearers only (Jas 1:22). In 1 John 1:1, the gospel is referred to as "the word of life," and the "word of God" indwells believers (1 John 2:14). In the Gospel of John, Jesus is referred to as "the Word of God" (John 1:1) who is one with the Father, full of grace and truth (John 1:14, 17-18). In Revelation, the angel delivers "true words of God" (19:9), the name of the rider of the white horse is named "The Word of God" (19:13), and martyrs have borne "testimony to Jesus and for the word of God" (20:4). Theologically, it is the references to Jesus as the Word of God, being one with the Father in agency and being, that have created the most intensive and extensive debates throughout the history of Christianity.

B. Apocryphal Uses of the Term

In the LXX, the word of the Lord or God is frequently added as an anthropomorphic reference to divine activity, and this metaphorical move carries over into apocryphal and NT writings. In the Apocrypha, characteristic OT uses of "word" are embellished: 1) the predictive word of the prophet describes Nahum's prediction of Nineveh's destruction (Tob 14:4); 2) by the word and wisdom of God are all things created and humans formed (Wis 9:1); 3) God's word is powerful enough to destroy foes (Wis 12:9); 4) the word of the Lord heals the sick (Wis 16:12); 5) the word of the Lord sustains those who trust in the Lord (Wis 16:26); 6) the word of the Lord leaps from the heavens as an avenging sword (Wis 18:15, 22); 7) the created order heeds the Lord's ordering word (Sir 16:28); 8) the word of the Lord commands the waters (Sir 39:17); 9) by the Lord's word are his works effected and creatures do his bidding (Sir 42:15); 10) the "word of the Holy One" gathers Jerusalem's children from east and west (Bar 5:5);

11) the word of the Lord is accomplished by the word of Jeremiah (1 Esd 1:57); and 12) by it Elijah's miracles are performed (Sir 48:1-5).

While these presentations of the word fall short of its personification in the Gospel of John, the personification of wisdom as the cosmic divine agency is clearer. In Wis 7:22, the term monogenēs (μονογενής) is used as a means of denoting the unique character of Wisdom, similar to the presentation of the "only begotten Son of God" in John 1:1-18. While later texts modify the language, the earliest manuscripts render John 1:18 "the only begotten God, who is at the Father's side." The sojourn of "the word" in Jewish/Christian Scripture has thus traversed the most mundane valleys to the most elevated of celestial heights.

C. The "Word" as Christological Reference

By far the most hotly debated issue related to *word* in the Bible is how Jesus as the Logos of God is both God and with God, from the beginning, through whom the created world came into being (John 1:1-3). While the Fourth Evangelist did not think in terms of 4th-cent. CE Greek categories of being—as those developing doctrines of the Trinity and the dual nature of the Son did—the biblical seeds of the major patristic, theological debates are clearly evident within the Fourth Gospel. On the one hand, the divinity, preexistence, and cocreative work of Jesus as the Son of God are apparent in the Johannine Prologue's rendering of logos:

> In the beginning was the Word,
> And the word was with God, and the word was
>   God;
> This one (NRSV "He") was in the beginning with
>   God.
> All things came into being through him,
> And nothing that has come into being
> has come into being without him (NRSV, "and
>   without him not one thing came into
>   being").
>
> (John 1:1-3)

On the other hand, Jesus' humanity is also asserted centrally in the Johannine Christ-hymn, as the flesh-becoming Word is encountered and worshiped by believers.

> And the Word became flesh
> and lived among us,
> and we have seen his glory,
> the glory as of a father's only son,
> full of grace and truth.
>
> (John 1:14)

The Fourth Gospel asserts the Son's oneness with the Father (10:30) while at the same time emphasizing the Son can do nothing except what he sees the Father doing (5:19), as his faithful agent. Debates have raged on whether the pivot of the Prologue emphasizes the hu-manity of Jesus (the flesh becoming Word—Bultmann) or his divinity (we have beheld his glory—Käsemann). Discerning the center of the Prologue might provide a lens for inferring the heart of the Gospel's message, and thereby the Father-Son relationship debated within Christian theology. However, John 1:14 emphasizes both the Son's humanity and divinity, and keeping dialectical poles in tension is essential for rightly interpreting most of John's theological motifs.

An alternative pivot of the Prologue (Culpepper) is v. 12, which declares the "power to become children of God" received by all who believe in his name. In that sense, the communicative role of "the Word of God" is fulfilled within loving relationship, restored by faithful human response to the eschatological divine initiative in the incarnation. The initial response of faith (John 20:31) leads to receiving life in the name of the Son, but it continues in faithful responsiveness to the living Word of Christ conveyed by the Holy Spirit (14:26; 16:13). The work of Jesus Christ as the divine Logos thus effects creation, conveys revelation, and offers salvation (Pollard). Like Plato's allegory of the cave (*Respecially* 7.514a–17), those confined to darkness would be liberated from their chains if they but look to the light and believe, but the darkness has neither comprehended nor overcome it (1:4-5), reflecting this community's history. While all may have access to the light (1:9) responding to it in faith involves the willingness to leave one's darkness and to respond receptively to the revelation (John 3:16-21). Parallel to the christological hymns in Paul's writings (Phil 2:5-11; Col 1:15-20) and in Hebrews (1:1-4), connecting Jesus as the Christ with the firstborn of creation, the final word of God, and the appointed heir of all things, the Johannine Prologue celebrates God's cosmic redemptive work through the agency of the divine Word, connecting believers with the same.

D. The Background and Form of the Johannine Prologue

While the Hebrew antecedents to davar and 'amar are unclear, the background and form of the Johannine Prologue are clearer but disputed. Heraclitus, the synthesizing philosopher of Ephesus (d. 475 BCE), saw the Logos as the divine agency and principle by which order is wrought out of chaos and unity is created within flux. How could the corruptible material world continue to move from disintegration to the orderly cycles and harmonies of the cosmos? It is the Logos of God that integrates and reconciles all opposites. Referred to also as "fire" and "God," Logos for Heraclitus is also the source of human reason. While it is universally accessible, humans are not its origin but its recipients—providing they attend its liberating work.

Plato drew on the work of Heraclitus, but even more so did the Stoics. Their work in turn provided the context in which Philo of Alexandria applied the concept of the divine Logos to God's creation and ordering of the world. Making use of logos as many as 1,300 times, Philo applied the Logos concept to: 1) the glue and chain that holds all things together (*Heir.* 188); 2) the agency by which God created the world (*Alleg. Interp.* 3:95); 3) the receiving of light from light (*Rewards* 46); 4) human reason's origin (*Creation* 146); 5) God's angelic communication of the divine image (*Dreams* 1:239); 6) as the firstborn among the created beings—a peacemaking mediator between worlds created and uncreated (*Heir.* 205–208); 7) references to God in Scripture when theos (θεός) is used without the article ho (ὁ), although Logos should not be referred to as God (*Dreams* 1:229–30); and 8) only through the divinely imparted Logos is humanity drawn to God (*Alleg. Interp.* 1.38). On account of these parallels some interpreters have located the Johannine situation in Alexandria, but this is unwarranted. Concourse between Asia Minor and Egypt was prolific, and if Apollos of Alexandria preached in Ephesus (Acts 18:24), the Philonic Logos doctrine could certainly have been in play in the hometown of Heraclitus before the Johannine leadership relocated in the area after 70 CE.

The gnostic redeemer-myth has also been posed as the source of the Johannine Logos christology, and Rudolf Bultmann argued that later Mandaean connections with John the Baptist suggest the religious origins of the Johannine Christ-hymn and "I am" sayings. Parallels in the *Odes of Solomon* include the worlds being created by the Lord's word (*Odes Sol.* 16:19); the messiah imparts life, shines the glory of the Lord, conveys the presence of God's word, is the savior of the world, and radiates the light that dawned before time itself (*Odes Sol.* 41). Most likely, however, the gnostic redeemer-myth presupposes the Gospel of John rather than inspiring it. Parallels are much closer in the 2nd-cent. CE *Gospel of Truth*, although such parallels evidence expansions upon the Johannine Prologue instead of influences upon it.

The Johannine agency motif is more centrally rooted in the prophet-like-Moses agency schema rooted in Deut 18:15-22, whereby the Son is equated with the Father precisely because his words are not his own, but identically ambassadorial of the word of God. The proleptic word of Jesus in John, whereby his word comes true (12:23; 14:29; 18:9, 32), attests explicitly that he is to be received as the prophet predicted by Moses, who would speak not his own words but only the words of God. This feature best accounts for the tension within the Father-Son relationship in John—the Son is equal to the Father precisely because he does/says nothing except what the Father commands. Jesus may have understood his mission in terms of the prophet-like-Moses, so Johannine expansions upon "the word" likely rooted in connections with the Jesus of history as well as the Christ of faith.

In addition to the vast treatment of *word* in the OT as a backdrop for the Johannine Prologue, contemporary Jewish preaching reflected Palestinian Targumic traditions. Within these Aramaic expansions on Hebrew Scripture, the word of God becomes a euphemistic way of denoting God's supportive and guiding presence among his people. Therein lie the closest parallels with the hypostatic union doctrine developed later within Christian theology. Despite the fact that the Johannine personification of the Logos is not identical to earlier or contemporary corollaries, such targumic homiletical renderings would have been familiar to both Palestinian and later Hellenistic Jewish audiences within the larger Johannine situation. Therefore, one can understand how the term came to be applied to the creating/revealing/saving work of Jesus as the Christ within late 1st-cent. contexts involving Jewish and Greek audiences. With Augustine, however, while all the other features of the Johannine Logos may be found in contemporary religions, the one feature that is unique is John 1:14—that "the Word was made flesh, and dwelt among us" (*Conf.* 6.9.14). That contribution is unique.

The form and development of the Prologue also contribute to understanding the meaning of *Logos*. The presentation of Jesus as the divine Logos in John 1:1-18 is somewhat out of step with the language and much of the mundane Johannine narrative that follows, but parallels with the Prologue of the first Epistle (1 John 1:1-4) are many. What has been seen and heard "from the beginning" (the Gospel narrative) is witnessed to corporately, and the mission of Jesus as the Word is transposed to "the beginning" in the form of a worship hymn. As the Johannine Prologue also testifies to the experience of Johannine Christians (some have received the Word/Light, but others not) the corporate confession connects community and cosmic histories together. As a captivating introduction to the completed Johannine evangel, the hymn to Jesus as the Logos of God reflects the corporate confession of those who have heard the message of the gospel and have "beheld his glory" (John 1:14). It draws upon motifs in Jewish and Hellenistic environs, connecting the agency of the cosmic Logos with the worldly work of the historic Jesus, encountered in the flesh and remembered accordingly. The Johannine presentation of Jesus as the Logos of God is thus not just like anything. It reflects a distinctive presentation of a unique subject—God's self-communication to humanity—inviting humanity's response.

E. Words, Discourse, and Revelation

As with all communication, what is being said relates centrally to how it is said. So it is with the biblical word *word*. While words are central to communication between humans, they also exercise power precisely because of their powerlessness. On the one hand, the word of the patriarch cannot be withdrawn after the blessing of Jacob because it has effected reality, thus affecting reality. The word of blessing moves across the land, creating a new relationship as an action. On the other hand, defying the Babylonian creation myth wherein order is created by violence (Marduk slew the goddess Tiamat, creating dry land from her corpse), the ordered world created by the Hebrew God is effected merely by the pronouncement of his word (Gen 1:1–2:4). The source of cosmic (and political) order is thus neither violence nor force, but truth, conveyed by a feeble word. God's same word orders the lives of humanity in the Decalogue and the Torah, and confronting kings and the powerful, authentic representatives speak God's word with prophetic clarity and penetrating relevance.

Within discourse, the impact of an utterance is not the conveyance of sound but the transmission of meaning. Between humans, words pose the means by which understandings are expressed and received. Between God and humans, communication happens neither by sound nor audition, but by listening, discerning, and responding. As communication happens most directly within relationship, the place where the human-divine dialogue transpires most powerfully is within communion. As discourse implies exchange, so words and actions imply reception and response—resulting in dialogue and mutual engagement. Uses and meanings of words, therefore, are more dialogical than monological, as utterance centrally implies encounter.

Throughout the Bible, the meaning of *word* is ever expanded with multiple associations and metaphors, but these are only descriptors of the revelatory process itself. Indeed, God's revelatory word comes to the world at many times and in many ways—through creation, prophecy, the law, the Scriptures, and in spiritual openings—yet in the fullness of time God has spoken in his son Jesus Christ, the source and heir of all things (Heb 1:1-4). The meaning of Christ as the eternal Logos of God pivots finally not upon whether Jesus is like God but upon God's being like Jesus. In that sense, the Son conveys the character and will of the Father who sent him, and in the world's response to the divine initiative, the Word of God is fulfilled. *See* CHRISTOLOGY; CREATION; INSPIRATION AND REVELATION; JOHN, GOSPEL OF; LIGHT AND DARKNESS; MOSES; PROPHET, PROPHECY; SALVATION; TEN COMMANDMENTS; TORAH; WISDOM IN THE NT.

Bibliography: Paul N. Anderson. *The Christology of the Fourth Gospel* (1996); Peder Borgen. *Logos Was the True Light and Other Essays on the Gospel of John* (1983); Raymond E. Brown. "Appendix II: The 'Word'." *The Gospel according to John (i–xii).* AB 29 (1966) 519–24; Rudolf Bultmann. "The History of Religions Background of the Prologue to the Gospel of John." *Eucharisterion: Festschrift für H. Gunkel* (1923) 3–26; Oscar Cullmann. *The Christology of the New Testament* (1959); R. Alan Culpepper. "The Pivot of John's Prologue." *NTS* 27 (1980) 1–31; Charles Harold Dodd. *The Interpretation of the Fourth Gospel* (1953); Craig A. Evans. *Word and Glory* (1993); Ernst Käsemann. "The Structure and Purpose of the Prologue to John's Gospel." *New Testament Questions*

of Today (1969) 138–67; Craig Keener. *The Gospel of John: A Commentary, Vol. 1* (2003); T. Evan Pollard. "Cosmology and the Prologue of the Fourth Gospel." *VC* 12 (1958) 147–53; John A. T. Robinson. "The Relation of the Prologue to the Gospel of John." *NTS* 9 (1963) 120–29; Rudolf Schnackenburg. "The Origin and Nature of the Johannine Concept of the Logos." *The Gospel according to St John, Vol. 1* (1980) 481–93; Harry A. Wolfson. *Philo* (1947).

PAUL N. ANDERSON

WORDPLAY IN THE OT. Wordplay involves two (or more) words with different meanings, but almost coinciding in sound, that occur in the same context. This is known as paronomasia in classical rhetoric. Wordplay can also involve one and the same word used in the same context with different meanings. Wordplay creates a special effect: it intensifies the message and draws attention to a certain point. It may add a touch of irony to what is otherwise a serious context (*see* IRONY AND SATIRE). Such wordplay does not depend on the written word. It is the repetition of sound between the words involved that reinforces the sense of the passage.

A. Oral Wordplay
  1. Words with different meanings but similar in sound
  2. Homonymy
  3. Polysemy
  4. Words similar in meaning as well as sound
B. Oral Wordplay on Names
  1. A proper name and a word similar in meaning and sound
  2. A name and an antonym (a word with the opposite meaning)
C. Visual Wordplay
D. Wordplay in Translation
Bibliography

A. Oral Wordplay

1. Words with different meanings but similar in sound

Wordplay in the Bible often operates with words that are very close in sound. The first well-known wordplay in the OT occurs in Gen 2:23: "this one shall be called Woman (ʾishah אִשָּׁה), / for out of Man (ʾish אִישׁ) this one was taken." Isaiah 5:7 ends with an accusation "he expected justice (mishpat מִשְׁפָּט), / but saw bloodshed (mispakh מִשְׂפָּח); / righteousness (tsedhaqah צְדָקָה), / but heard a cry (tseʿaqah צְעָקָה)." What makes this accusation sharply ironic is that the strong, unexpected contrast in each pair of lines is expressed with words that are very close in pronunciation.

In examples like the following, the change of meaning depends on vowel mutation. Wordplay features in prophetic visions—when the word that refers to what the prophet sees, on the one hand, and a word in the explanation, on the other—are connected through similarity in sound. Examples include: "a branch of an almond tree (shaqedh שָׁקֵד) ... I am watching (shoqedh שֹׁקֵד) over my word to perform it" (Jer 1:11-12); "a basket of summer fruit (qayits קָיִץ) ... the end (qets קֵץ) has come" (Amos 8:1-2). Such vowel mutation often involves a change of stem of the verbal root: "If you are willing ... you shall eat (to'khelu תֹּאכֵלוּ).... If you refuse ... / you will be eaten (te'ukkelu תְּאֻכְּלוּ; NRSV, devoured) by the sword" (Isa 1:19-20).

Wordplay may consist in repeating consonants of one word in another word but in a differing order, a technique known as metathesis: "how fleeting (khadhel חָדֵל) my life is / ... my lifetime (kheledh חֶלֶד) is as nothing in your sight" (Ps 39:4-5 [Heb. 39:5-6]), in which kheledh repeats the same consonants in a differing order. Compare also pe'er (פְּאֵר) and 'efer (אֵפֶר) in Isa 61:3 (a "garland" instead of "ashes"). An example beyond the confines of one paragraph is Esau's consistent use of bekhor (בְּכוֹר, "firstborn") and barakh (בָּרַךְ, "to bless") in Gen 27:19 and bekhorah (בְּכֹרָה, "birthright") and berakhah (בְּרָכָה, "blessing") in 27:36. Wordplay further intensifies the message. Compare also Jacob (ya'aqov יַעֲקֹב) who struggles (ye'aveq יֵאָבֵק) at the Jabbok (yabboq יַבֹּק) in Gen 32:22-24 [Heb. 32:23-25], where the metathesis of the consonants adds to the sense of fate.

2. Homonymy

Homonymy, words with different meanings but identical in sound, involves complete sound repetition and is also known as antanaclasis. Genesis 3:1 is linked to 2:25 through homonymy: 'arum (עָרוּם, the serpent was most "crafty") plays against the word 'arummim (עֲרוּמִּים, the man and the woman were "naked"), which is different in meaning but sounds the same. In Judg 5:6 'orakhoth (אֳרָחוֹת, "caravans") is repeated in the next phrase with the meaning "byways." Jacob's blessing of Joseph with a "mountain slope" (shekhem [שְׁכֶם; NRSV, "portion") in Gen 48:22 implicitly plays on the city of Shechem in Joseph's territorial inheritance. In Exodus, the question "What (man מָן) is it?" in 16:15 is a play on the food called man ("manna") in 16:31.

3. Polysemy

Polysemy (the same word with a shift in meaning) is used in 2 Sam 7, which plays on the literal and metaphorical meanings of bayith (בַּיִת): after David has finished building his own bayith ("house"; vv. 1-2), and Yahweh asks rhetorically whether David can build him a bayith ("house, temple"; vv. 5-7), Yahweh promises that he will make David a bayith (but with the meaning "dynasty"; v. 11). Thus bayith is a leading word in this chapter. Lamentations 2:6 plays on two meanings of mo'edh (מוֹעֵד, "assembly"): "tabernacle" (place for assembly) and "festival" (appointed time for assembly).

In Dan 5, mene' mene' teqel ufarsin (מְנֵא מְנֵא תְּקֵל וּפַרְסִין; 5:25) refers to three weights: a mina, a shekel, and two halves (see WEIGHTS AND MEASURES). But because of the roots involved the same Aramaic forms mene', teqel, and peres (פְּרַס, the singular of parsin) are also taken to mean "numbered," "weighed," and "divided." Hence the interpretation in vv. 26-28: "God has numbered (menah מְנָה)"; "you have been weighed (teqiltah תְּקִילְתָּה)"; "your kingdom is divided (perisath פְּרִיסַת)." Another wordplay in v. 28 links perisath ("divided") to paras (פָּרַס, "Persia").

4. Words similar in meaning as well as sound

The wordplay in Isa 30:16 involves words of the same root and has an ironic effect. Israel expects to flee: "We will ride on swift ones (qal קָל)" (author's trans.; NRSV, "We will flee upon horses."). But contrary to expectation, it is their pursuers who will overtake them: they "shall be swift (yiqqallu יֵקַלּוּ)"!

Near-synonyms in one line that sound similar are primarily examples of assonance (the use of the same vowel sounds with different consonants) or alliteration (the same consonants with different vowels). Examples of the former are tohu wavohu (תֹהוּ וָבֹהוּ, "wild and waste" [author's trans.; NRSV, "a formless void"]; Gen 1:2); and pakhadh wafakhath wafakh (פַּחַד וָפַחַת וָפָח, "terror, and the pit, and the snare"; Isa 24:17). An example of the latter is the two lines in Isa 27:7: hakkemakkath makkehu hikkahu (הַכְּמַכַּת מַכֵּהוּ הִכָּהוּ, "Has he struck them down as he struck down those who struck them?" Such examples are often regarded as wordplay as well.

B. Oral Wordplay on Names

1. A proper name and a word similar in meaning and sound

Not infrequently, biblical characters apply wordplay to proper names. It is in such cases that wordplay is the most explicit. When in Gen 29:31–30:24 Jacob's sons are born, Leah or Rachel makes a statement, explaining the meaning of the name. The name is similar in sound to the corresponding key word in the statement made. For example, Leah's statement in 29:35—"I will praise" ('odeh אוֹדֶה)—introduces the name Judah (yehudhah יְהוּדָה). In Gen 30:6-24, the names given to the sons are related to the circumstances of their respective births.

Similarly, in Exod 2:10 Pharaoh's daughter explains the name Moses: "I drew him (meshithihu מְשִׁיתִהוּ) out of the water." The form mosheh (מֹשֶׁה, "one who draws out") points to his destiny at the same time: Moses will lead Israel out of Egypt through the sea.

Genesis 49 also plays on the names of Jacob's sons, this time referring to their destinies: "Judah, your brothers shall praise you (yodhukha יוֹדוּךָ)" (v. 8); "Dan shall judge (yadhin יָדִין) his people" (v. 16). Compare also Noah (noakh נֹחַ), whose destiny is connected with the key word yenakhamenu (יְנַחֲמֵנוּ, "[he] shall bring us relief") in Gen 5:29. Making this a motif, Gen 6–8 continues to play on the consonants of Noah's name: Yahweh "was sorry" (wayyinnakhem וַיִּנָּחֶם) in 6:6; "the ark came to rest" (wattanakh וַתָּנַח) in 8:4; "[resting] place" (manoakh מָנוֹחַ) in 8:9; "pleasing odor" (nikhoakh נִיחֹחַ) in 8:21.

The text usually does not point out explicitly that there is similarity in (meaning and) sound. An exception to this is 1 Sam 25:25: "for as his name is, so is he; Nabal (naval [נָבָל], "fool") is his name, and folly (nevalah נְבָלָה) is with him."

In Mic 1:10-16 the message concerning each town is highlighted by a wordplay based on its name. In 1:10a —"Tell it not in Gath"—the name of Gath (gath גַּת) is similar in sound to "tell" (taggidhu תַּגִּידוּ). In 1:10b— "in Beth-leaphrah roll yourselves in the dust"—the place-name is similar in meaning ("house of dust") as well as sound to the word *dust* (ʿafar עָפָר).

2. A name and an antonym (a word with the opposite meaning)

In Mic 1:11a, the town name *Shaphir* means "pleasant," but its fate is the opposite: "nakedness and shame." In 1:12, "good" is the opposite of the meaning of *Maroth*, mar (מַר, "bitter"), while "disaster" stands in contrast to Jerusalem (shalem [שָׁלֵם], "to be peaceful, unharmed").

At the end of Amos 5:5, "nothing" is the opposite of the meaning of the town name Bethel ("house of God"). Compare also "Gilgal shall surely go into exile (haggilgal galoh yighleh הַגִּלְגָּל גָּלֹה יִגְלֶה)" in the same verse, which relates gilgal (גִּלְגָּל, "rolling," from the root gll [גלל]; Josh 5:9) to the root glh (גלה) with a very different meaning: "to go into exile." Gilgal is similar in sound to the two words that follow. This is also an example of alliteration of consonants, since the words involved occur together in the same line.

C. Visual Wordplay

Forms of visual wordplay depend on the written word and alphabet. An ACROSTIC is a poetic form in which the initial letters of lines form an alphabet. Examples are Ps 119 and Lam 1–4. The OT also contains a few examples of visual wordplay on names. In an ATHBASH, the first letter of the alphabet is used as a substitute for the last, the second for the penultimate, etc. Thus sh-sh-k (שׁ-שׁ-ך, "Sheshach"; Jer 25:26; 51:41) and l-b-q-m-y (ל-ב-ק-מ-י, "Leb-qamai"; Jer 51:1) are athbash for b-b-l (ב-ב-ל, "Babylon") and k-s-d-y-m (כ-שׂ-ד-י-ם, "Chaldea"; Chaldaios [Χαλδαῖος] in the LXX), respectively. It has been suggested that this was to protect the prophet, since Babylon was a major power. In Hebrew, a numerical equivalent (gematria) existed for every consonant. Thus Gad, whose gematria is 3 + 4 = 7, is reckoned seventh not only in the listing of tribes in Gen 46 (where he is also ascribed seven sons) but also in Gen

29:31–30:24 in what is otherwise a different ordering of the sons. *See* NUMBERS, NUMBERING.

D. Wordplay in Translation

A literal translation can rarely convey wordplay into the target language. In dynamic translation, however, the connection between the words involved in the wordplay can sometimes be expressed by other means: "ripe fruit.... The time is ripe" (Amos 8:1-2 [NIV; NRSV, "summer fruit.... The end has come"]); "a branch of almonds that ripen early.... I always rise early to keep a promise" (Jer 1:11-12 [CEV; NRSV, "a branch of an almond tree.... I am watching over my word to perform it"]). The NJPS of Isa 5:7 improves on the translation given above (§A.1) as follows: "He hoped for justice, / but behold, injustice; / for equity, / but behold, iniquity!" In Josh 7:26, ʿemeq ʿakhor (עֵמֶק עָכוֹר, "Valley of Achor") can be rendered "Trouble Valley," thus showing the connection with the first part of v. 25 ("The LORD is bringing trouble on you [yaʿkorekha יַעְכָּרְךָ] today."). Thus, although in many instances only a footnote can convey wordplay in the translation, on occasion it is possible to convey them in a creative manner with a similar effect. *See* BIBLE TRANSLATION THEORY; HUMOR.

Bibliography: Robert Alter. *Genesis: Translation and Commentary* (1996); John Ellington. "Wit and Humor in Bible Translation." *The Bible Translator* 42 (1991) 301–13; Scott B. Noegel, ed. *Puns and Pundits: Word Play in the Hebrew Bible and Ancient Near Eastern Literature* (2000); Lynell Zogbo and Ernst R. Wendland. *Hebrew Poetry in the Bible* (2000).

L. J. DE REGT

WORDS OF GAD THE SEER. *See* BOOKS REFERRED TO IN THE BIBLE.

WORDS OF NATHAN THE PROPHET. *See* BOOKS REFERRED TO IN THE BIBLE.

WORDS OF SAMUEL THE SEER. *See* BOOKS REFERRED TO IN THE BIBLE.

WORDS OF SHEMAIAH THE PROPHET. *See* BOOKS REFERRED TO IN THE BIBLE.

WORDS OF THE KINGS OF ISRAEL. *See* BOOKS REFERRED TO IN THE BIBLE.

WORDS OF THE LUMINARIES, HEAVENLY LIGHTS [דִּבְרֵי הַמְּאֹרוֹת divre hammeʾoroth]. A collection of prayer texts found at Qumran that exhibits an inscribed title on the back of the first column of the scroll. The most plausible explanation for the title relates to the liturgical function of the prayers, with divre referring to the words of the prayers and hammeʾoroth indicating the luminaries, i.e., days used as units of time for which these prayers are designated (compare Gen 1:14). The item numbers of the Qumran texts are 4Q504 and 4Q506; the oldest and most intact exemplar is 4Q504. Considering the current evidence presented by scholarship, a date of composition seems most probably in the early or mid-2nd cent. BCE with no compelling evidence to indicate sectarian provenance.

Words of the Luminaries provides the earliest examples of daily recitation of petitions for deliverance. The prayers correlate to the days of the week, concluding with the Sabbath. One or two prayers are recited each day, and there are notations that give directions for using the prayers in public worship. All six weekday prayers open with a historical review and combine a concern for spiritual and physical assistance in varying degrees. The Tuesday, Wednesday, and Friday prayers focus more on physical deliverance, while the Sunday and Thursday prayers concentrate more on spiritual steadfastness. The Monday petitionary prayer is missing from the collection. The prayers have the following common structure: 1) title with date formula; 2) introduction; 3) historical summary of Israel's relationship with God incorporating chronological progression of these historical summaries from the first to the sixth day; 4) either a petition for physical deliverance or spiritual fortitude; 5) concluding benediction; and 6) a brief response of "Amen, Amen." Unlike the weekday prayers, the Sabbath prayer contains doxological hymns and does not contain the chronological progression of historical summaries.

Because of the petitionary nature of the *Words of the Luminaries*, scholars have made comparison to certain prayers in the later Jewish synagogue liturgy such as the *Takhanunim* and the *Amidah*. Within the Qumran corpus, *Words of the Luminaries* is comparatively studied with other prayer collections such as the *Daily Prayers* and the *Festival Prayers*. See DEAD SEA SCROLLS.

Bibliography: Esther Chazon. "4QDibHam: Liturgy or Literature?" *RevQ* 15 (1992) 447–55; Daniel Falk. "Words of the Luminaries." *Daily, Sabbath, and Festival Prayers in the Dead Sea Scrolls* (1998) 59–94.

         MICHAEL D. MATLOCK

WORKS AND RIGHTEOUSNESS [δικαιοσύνη dikaiosynē, ἔργον ergon]. In Romans and Galatians, Paul argues that works do not bring about righteousness (Rom 3:9-10, 21, 28; Gal 2:16, 21; 3:11); rather, justification comes from God on the basis of faith (Rom 3:30; 4:1-5). Although works are ineffective to procure righteousness, once a person has received faith, works are the necessary corollary (Gal 5:6; Eph 2:10; 1 Thess 1:3; 2 Thess 1:11). In James, works are likewise seen as living evidence of righteousness, in opposition to those who claim to be saved by faith apart from works (Jas 2:14-26). See RIGHTEOUSNESS IN THE NT.

         CATHERINE JONES

WORKS OF GOD [מַעֲלְלֵי־אֵל ma'alle-'el, מַעֲשֵׂה אֱלֹהִים ma'aseh 'elohim, מַעֲשֵׂה יְהוָה ma'aseh yhwh; ἔργον τοῦ θεοῦ ergon tou theou]. The primary work of God is CREATION. Genesis 2:2-3 summarizes the content of God's creative acts as "the work (mela'khah מְלָאכָה) that [God] had done." This work of creation is ongoing. God exhorts the people not to do work (mela'khah) on the seventh day (e.g., Exod 20:9-10; 31:15; 35:2), because God rested from his work (mela'khah) the seventh day (Gen 2:2-3; *see* SABBATH). The term mela'khah primarily means "sending," and often it implies physical labor. The same nuance of hard, even physical, labor accompanies mela'khah in Jer 50:25, where "the Lord GOD of hosts has a task to do"—here, in war.

The second and equally dominant reference for the "work(s) of God" in the OT is Israel's deliverance from Egypt and establishment as God's people through the Sinai covenant (*see* COVENANT, OT AND NT). Israel's election, in turn, is an ongoing event; just as the deliverance is recalled annually at Passover, so it is repeated in the continuing process of Israel's becoming a holy people. The formative effect of the initial events is reflected in passages like Josh 24:31: "Israel served the LORD ... all the days of the elders who ... had known all the work that the LORD (ma'aseh yhwh) did for Israel" (compare Judg 2:7, 10). Psalm 78:7 urges that future generations not "forget the works of God (ma'alle-'el)" as their ancestors did. The prophets speak of renewed deliverance from slavery and exile as "his work" (*see* Isa 10:12; 28:21; Jer 51:10). The very tablets of the Ten Commandments "were the work of God (ma'aseh 'elohim)" (Exod 32:16). Especially in the psalms and Wisdom literature there is repeated reference to the "works" or "deeds" of God/the LORD in the lives of individuals and groups: not only "great are the works of the LORD (ma'aseh yhwh), studied by all who delight in them" (Ps 111:2), but "I shall live, and recount the deeds of the LORD (ma'aseh yhwh)" (Ps 118:17) and "I will meditate on all your work, and muse on your mighty deeds" in Ps 77:12. Qoheleth stresses the mysterious nature of God's working (ma'aseh 'elohim) in Eccl 3:11; 7:13; 11:5. A special form of thanksgiving for the working of God in individual lives was the song of THANKSGIVING (todhah תּוֹדָה). Psalm 26 is a classic example, describing how the person giving thanks in the Temple will tell "all your wondrous deeds (nifla'oth [נִפְלָאֹת], "marvels")."

Sometimes the text does not say exactly what God's action is—God simply "does" something—e.g., Ps 109:27, "you, O LORD, have done it" ('asah עָשָׂה). References to an "act of God" or to God "acting" may also be included in the category of "works of God," and such acts are usually expressed verbally, with 'asah, rather than with a substantive. In one exceptional instance at Exod 21:13, the text speaks of an "act of God" with the verb 'anah (אָנָה, "cause to occur") and with the "hand" of God (yadh יָד) as the agent (compare the

LXX: ho theos paredōken eis tas cheiras autou [ὁ θεὸς παρέδωκεν εἰς τὰς χεῖρας αὐτοῦ], "God gave [him] into his hand"). "The act of God who rules over all things" is expressed by hē energeia theou (ἡ ἐνέργεια θεοῦ, "action/work of God") in 3 Macc 5:28.

The phrase "works of God" (ta erga tou theou τὰ ἔργα τοῦ θεοῦ) is relatively common in the Apocrypha. The book of Sirach says, "God's works will never be finished" (38:8), and 1 Esdras proclaims that "all God's works quake and tremble" (4:36). An interesting parallel exists between the apocryphal book of Tobit and the Gospel of John: among the works of God (ta erga tou theou) that should be acknowledged and revealed (Tob 12:7, 11) is the healing of a blind man (Tob 11:7-15). Similarly, before giving sight to a man born blind, Jesus says that the works of God (to ergon tou theou) would be revealed in his healing (John 9:1-7).

Most of the NT references to God working are, in fact, in the Fourth Gospel. For example, the crowd asks Jesus, "What must we do (poieō) to perform (ergazomai ἐργάζομαι) the works (erga) of God?" Jesus answers, "This is the work of God (to ergon tou theou), that you believe in him whom he has sent." Then they ask him to perform (poieō) a work (literally, "sign") to prove himself (John 6:28-30). Here the emphasis has clearly shifted from God's sovereign work to the work humans must do with and for God. Jesus, as the incarnate Logos (*see* WORD, THE), plays a co-creative role similar to that of Wisdom (see Prov 8), and as the light of the world makes God's works manifest (and also the disciples with him).

In the Acts of the Apostles, Luke is especially concerned to illustrate that God is intensively at work in the spread of the gospel throughout the known world, but the phrase "works of God" is replaced by such expressions as "God's deeds of power" (ta megaleia tou theou τὰ μεγαλεῖα τοῦ θεοῦ) in Acts 2:11, or "all that God had done (hosa epoiēsen ho theos [ὅσα ἐποίησεν ὁ θεός], from poieō [ποιέω], "make/do/cause/accomplish") with them" in Acts 14:27; 15:4. Romans 14:20 refers to "the work of God" (to ergon tou theou) in the same sense intended in Acts: the building up of the church. *See* MIRACLE; SALVATION; SIGNS AND WONDERS.

Bibliography: Gerhard Lohfink. *The Work of God Goes On* (1987); Linda M. Maloney. *"All That God Had Done with Them": The Narration of the Works of God in the Early Christian Community as Described in the Acts of the Apostles* (1991).

LINDA M. MALONEY

WORKS, GOOD [ἔργον ἀγαθόν ergon agathon, ἔργον καλόν ergon kalon]. In the NT, the good works of believers give glory to God (e.g., Matt 5:16). For John, Jesus' good works reveal the Father (John 10:32). Paul states that all persons will be judged by God on the basis of their works (Rom 2:6-7); thus, good works

must be plentiful (2 Cor 9:8; Col 1:10; 2 Thess 2:17). The Pastoral Letters place an emphasis on good works as a characteristic of believers (1 Tim 2:10; 5:10, 25; 6:18; 2 Tim 2:21; 3:17; Titus 2:7; 3:1, 8, 14). *See* RIGHTOUSNESS IN THE NT.

CATHERINE JONES

WORM [סס sas, רִמָּה rimmah, תּוֹלָע tolaʿ, תּוֹלָעָה toleʿah, תּוֹלַעַת tolaʿath; σκώληξ skōlēx]. The worm plays various roles in the Bible. Sometimes the worm is portrayed as an instrument of God; most explicit in this regard is the divinely appointed worm of Jonah 4:7. Here, though small in comparison to the "great fish" (Jonah 1), the worm achieves the divine intention of causing the demise of Jonah's provision, the vine. Somewhat similar is the earlier curse text of Deut 28, which anticipates the results of disobedience to the covenant. In a series of "divine causation statements" the worm is depicted as eating the grapes (v. 39). While not precisely the same situation, the description of Israelite manna gathering on regular days (tolaʿath; Exod 16:20) versus the sixth day (rimmah; Exod 16:24) appears as a divine use of the worm to "enforce" compliance.

The worm as symbolic of death and decay is certainly present in texts such as Job 21:26, but in the context Job's point is that the worm is the destiny of both the prosperous (21:23) and the less fortunate (21:25). Where human flesh once existed, the worm will prevail. Physical corruption seems to be the sense of the vivid expression of Job 17:14: "If I say to the Pit, 'You are my father,' and to the worm, 'My mother,' or 'my sister' ...." A variation of this theme is found in texts that suggest that the worm provides a particularly appropriate end for the wicked and rebellious, including those who rebel against the light (Job 24:20), the king of Babylon (Isa 14:11), reproachers of the godly (Isa 51:8), and those who rebel against God (Isa 66:24; compare Jesus' statement about the eye that causes one to stumble in Mark 9:48). Acts 12:23 describes Herod Agrippa as being eaten by worms because he did not give glory to God. Apocryphal books also predict this same fate for the ungodly and rebellious (see Jdt 16:17; 1 Macc 2:62; 2 Macc 9:9; Sir 7:17; 10:11; 19:3).

In Job 25:6, Bildad uses worm imagery to express the degradation of humanity, and the psalmist, expressing himself in the tradition of lament, describes himself as less than human, i.e., as a worm (Ps 22:6 [Heb. 22:7]). The portrayal of Jacob as a worm (Isa 41:14) seems intended to acknowledge the diminished role and status of Israel among the nations but also anticipates a reversal. *See* JONAH, BOOK OF; MOTH.

JOHN I. LAWLOR

WORMWOOD [לַעֲנָה laʿanah; ἄψινθος apsinthos]. Plants of the genus *Artemisia*, especially lowly *A. herba-alba* in stony gray desert, the taller *A. judaica* in sandy desert, and the bushier *A. monosperma* in coastal sands. They belong to the daisy family, having small heads of inconspicuous compound flowers. Their whitish hairy leaves yield a bitter infusion traditionally used in medicine. In Rev 8:10-11 when the star Wormwood fell: "A third of the waters became wormwood, and many died from the water, because it was made bitter." The wormwood of Amos 5:7 and 6:12 (in the latter verse, in parallel with "poison" [rosh רֹאשׁ]), however, was probably hemlock, *Conium maculatum.*

Wormwood in the Bible is linked with gall (Lam 3:19). It may symbolize personal bitterness (Lam 3:15, 19). The speech of a "loose woman" may seem attractive, like honey, but prove "bitter as wormwood" in the end (Prov 5:4). One who desires to commit idolatry is compared to "a root sprouting poison and wormwood" (Deut 29:18 [Heb. 29:17], author's trans.; NRSV, "a root sprouting poisonous and bitter growth"). Yahweh threatens to punish Israel and the prophets of Jerusalem by giving them wormwood to eat and poisonous water to drink (Jer 9:15 [Heb. 9:14]; 23:15). *See* PLANTS OF THE BIBLE; POISON.

F. NIGEL HEPPER

WORSHIP, EARLY JEWISH. Early Jewish worship, in its variety of formats, may be traced from the periods before and after the Babylonian exile, through the Second Temple era and into the 1st–2nd cent. CE. It relates to the liturgies of the Jerusalem Temple, to the earliest forms of the synagogue, to the functionaries associated with these institutions, and to the rituals and prayers that developed in and around them, as well as among the people at large. The evidence is to be found in the later books of the OT, the literature of the Apocrypha and Pseudepigrapha, the texts discovered in the caves by the Dead Sea, and the writings of Hellenistic Jews, as well as in the earliest NT and rabbinic traditions. It reflects the theological notions that were inherited, expanded, and adjusted, as well as being given liturgical expression, by a medley of Jewish groups at different times and in various locations. Israel's national history, seasonal calendar, and educational ideology all played roles in shaping developments. Precisely how Christianity and rabbinic Judaism fed on such a liturgical background is broadly obvious but more obscure in the detail. Important Hebrew terms are miqdash (מִקְדָּשׁ; "sanctuary"), 'avodhah (עֲבוֹדָה; "cult," "liturgy"), tefillah (תְּפִלָּה; "prayer"), berakhah (בְּרָכָה; "benediction") and torah (תּוֹרָה; "religious teaching").

A. Simple Prayers
B. Psalms
C. Individual Prayers
D. Temple Ritual
E. Penitential Prayers
F. Apocrypha and Pseudepigrapha
G. Synagogue
H. Qumran
I. The Shema and Decalogue
J. Benedictions
K. 'Amidah
L. Rabbinic Innovation
Bibliography

A. Simple Prayers

Those who returned from Babylonian exile to the state of Judah, reestablished under Persian hegemony at the end of the 6th cent. BCE, were reconstructing a Jewish religious faith and practice that was built not only on what they had experienced and contemplated in Mesopotamia but also on the older traditions that they had taken with them from the homeland. Some have described such traditions as the "pre-historic roots" of the people. Their approach to worship was therefore, like so much else, a conglomerate of notions and inspirations. One of these was undoubtedly the simple human appeal to God for the removal of a troublesome situation or enemy, or for the granting of some other personal request. Some examples include or reflect what appear to be established Israelite concepts of simple prayer. The word **tefillah** is rarely used, the context is not normally that of a shrine, and the style of the appeal is more reminiscent of negotiation or debate rather than of liturgy in any formal sense. Ancestral merit and personal behavior are often brought into the debate almost as a bargaining counter. Abraham's appeal on behalf of the wicked of Sodom (Gen 18:22-33) includes elements of theological challenge as well as judicial debate while Jacob strikes a bargain with God at Bethel, offering loyalty and tithes in return for sustenance and security (Gen 28:16-22), and requests protection from Esau because of the special relationship already established with God (Gen 32:11-12).

One of the simplest and most powerful prayers ever expressed (Num 12:13) was offered by Moses in his appeal to God on behalf of his sister Miriam ("O God, please heal her") but the debating style is again invoked in the report of his entreaty on behalf of Israel after the golden calf incident. There (Exod 32:11-14) he calls into question God's right to be angry, points out that Israel's destruction will be bad for the divine reputation, and refers to previous promises to the patriarchs about how Israel will flourish. Joshua makes a similar comment (Josh 7:6-9) about a threat to God's reputation when the people face defeat and destruction at the hands of the Amalekites. A prayer by Samson (Judg 15:18) points out the heavenly inconsistency of granting him victory over the Philistines and then allowing him to die of thirst, while his final entreaty (Judg 16:30) constitutes a simple appeal for the revenge of his deprived eyesight. Hannah is distraught about her lack of offspring and addresses God (1 Sam 1:10-16) in tears, promising him a special devotee if he grants her request for a male child. Her intense, quiet, and lengthy prayer is the epitome of sincere, personal invocation of God. Equally personal and dialectical (though with some more formal elements included or added) are the prayers of David for his dynasty (2 Sam 7:18-29) and

Solomon for wisdom (1 Kgs 3:5-15) and the simple request of Hezekiah (2 Kgs 20:1-3) for a restoration of his health. The context of all such prayers (as indeed such older poetic texts as Gen 49 and Deut 33) is more akin to that of oaths and blessings than institutional rituals or literary formulations.

B. Psalms

While it was once fashionable among scholars to regard the whole of the book of Psalms as the hymn-book for Israelite and Jewish worship in biblical times, there is now an admission that the evidence for this is not wholly convincing and a preference for seeing each chapter as a literary unit in its own right. In that case, the book has a great variety of dates and contexts and instead of being defined as an attachment to formal temple liturgy it should be viewed as a rich collection of poems, each of which is connected with some aspect of ancient worship. Some psalms relate to the Temple, pilgrimage, and formal liturgy, perhaps for festivals and during the annual calendar, while others are more closely representative of personal prayer, whether expressive of great joy or of deep sadness. Among topics that occupy the composers of psalms are the praise of God for a variety of different powers, the glories of the royal house and of Zion, and the importance of wisdom or torah. Since there are psalms (e.g., 29; 104) that resemble Canaanite or Egyptian hymns, there is every reason to suppose that some go back to preexilic times. Given the wide variety of psalmic themes and contents, it is not, however, an easy or productive task to separate the preexilic from the exilic. Whatever the origins and early development of this genre of literature, it undoubtedly developed into a formal collection or collections and grew in importance in the Second Temple period. For that reason it became increasingly significant for Jewish liturgical history. Its contents, language, and style became the prototypes for the composition of Jewish prayers and its constituent parts, as individual chapters or sets of psalms were gradually absorbed into the forerunners of what later became rabbinic and Christian liturgy.

C. Individual Prayers

The individual prayers offered by leading biblical figures (and perhaps also at least some of the more personal hymns just mentioned) amount to independent expressions of religiosity. They are not necessarily linked with a cultic shrine, although such a use may at times have been made of them. They rather represent a democratic and egalitarian way of approaching God. They depend on specific circumstances and are more likely to have been created by inspired worshipers in the broader context of life than by any elitist group within a formal system of liturgy. If this interpretation is valid, it would indicate that proto-forms of Jewish worship may in some ways have been unique. The literatures of the surrounding peoples, such as those from Mesopotamia

and Egypt, testify to the existence of hymns and prayers within the formal cults. These are found on the lips of rulers, priests, and other officials, are recited in palaces and shrines, and deal with the powers of the gods in the natural world and their championing of various groups in society. The suppliant expresses humility, repentance, and a conviction that all rituals have been correctly completed, and requests are made for blessings on the homeland and an end to unpleasant life experiences, so that the established reputations of the god or gods may be maintained.

D. Temple Ritual

If we are to credit the traditions emanating from the period of the Israelite monarchies with any degree of historicity, there was a Jerusalem Temple that functioned until the Babylonian exile. There is no specific archaeological evidence for it, nor can it be proved that it was Solomon who built it, but the notion of Jerusalem's special religious significance is certainly common in some of the oldest material and there are physical remnants of the Davidic city. In addition, great detail is recorded about the first Temple's structure and utensils, which, although included in books that were edited at a later time, indicates some basis in reality, as well as a deep nostalgia for a lost national treasure. What is more, the total absence of such an institution would make it difficult to understand many of the arguments about the sacrificial system that occur so frequently in the prophetic texts and to make sense of the campaign for centralization that became so much a part of the Israelite religious scene perhaps from as early as the 8th cent. BCE. If such shrines as Shechem, Bethel, Gilgal, Shiloh, and Carmel were to be replaced by one liturgical center, and if tribal heads, kings, and prophets were to be replaced by the exclusive services of priests, the Jerusalem locus must have offered an impressive, and highly competitive, cultic institution. If ceremonies to do with festivals and the calendar were to be held in the city of Jerusalem rather than in the Judahite countryside, an appropriate building, with attendant officiants and adequate utensils, would seem to have been desirable.

But were there not also poems and prayers in such a center and some form of verbalization for the rituals? A strict reading of the evidence does not testify to the existence of such phenomena. There are ancient formulas such as the priestly benediction (Num 6:22-27) and the declaration to be made by the farmer who brings his first fruit to the Temple (Deut 26:3-10). Evidence that the former was in use in the preexilic period as a popular liturgical text is to be found in the existence of a silver amulet containing a version of the text and dated to the 7th cent. BCE (*see* INSCRIPTIONS). The explanations of the Passover sacrifice (Exod 12:25-27; 13:8, 14) and the reading of the torah to the assembled people on Tabernacles at the end of the sabbatical year and during the pilgrimage to the Temple (Deut 6:20 and

31:9-13) may also claim a respectable pedigree. Isaiah's famous threefold proclamation of God's holiness (6:1-7) also smacks of a well-rehearsed formula, but there is no clear indication that it was part of a liturgical repertoire recited by the priests. Indeed, none of these formulas appear to have been linked directly to the sacrificial cult. In that area, the only words to be recited were perhaps a brief statement of guilt admission by the priest or the layperson before the completion of a sacrificial ritual (Lev 5:5; 16:21). Other than that, the Jerusalem Temple in the period leading up to the Babylonian exile hosted a ritual of verbal silence.

The returning community built its Temple in a form much more modest (according to Hag 2:3) than that of its predecessor but did restore the sacrificial services. The Jerusalem priesthood grew in strength and established what was in many respects a theocracy, at least until the time of the Hasmoneans when broader political and military considerations led to changes in the power structure. Although there is evidence of the existence of Jewish shrines at various times in Iraq el-Emir (see EMIR, IRAQ EL) in the Transjordan, as well as in Elephantine and Leontopolis in Egypt, these appear to have been of marginal importance in the total Jewish situation. The Temple and the priesthood stood at the center of Jewish worship and the leadership ensured that sacrifices and tithes (Neh 13) were again fully operational. The more exclusive approach of the priesthood ensured that the Samaritans were kept out of the new arrangements and that the Levites operated as secondary functionaries in matters of administration and security. In addition, the author of 1 Chr 15 puts into the mouth of David an instruction to appoint men and women of Levite families as singers and players to make joyous music in the sanctuary, no doubt reflecting the actual practice of the author's own day.

Two festivals that came to involve large numbers of pilgrims in the temple service and considerable excitement were Passover and the DAY OF ATONEMENT. The first of these occasions required large retinues of priests and Levites to cope with the numerous paschal offerings and was perhaps accompanied by the singing of psalms within the temple precincts. The second involved various rituals being carried out by the high priest, some of which are pentateuchal, such as the confession, the sacrifice, and the scapegoat, while others, such as his spiritual preparation, the text of his confessions, and his pronunciation of the TETRAGRAMMATON are given in detail only in Sir 50 and in the Mishnah (Yoma). Here too the role of the Levites and the people appears to have expanded during the Second Temple period. The festival of Hanukkah, whatever its earliest origins, was associated with the restoration of the temple service after the Hasmonean victory over Antiochus IV of Syria in the 2nd cent., but its earliest celebration consisted of lighting torches, marching in procession, and using psalms and music to praise God, no formal liturgy developing until talmudic times.

E. Penitential Prayers

What can be clearly traced during the Second Temple period is a gradual coming together of these two originally disparate elements of temple cult and personal prayer. There appears to have been a number of factors that inspired the early beginnings of such a novel development. There had been an exposure to the ideas and practice of other nations and there was a growing need to stress and strengthen the communal and the formal at the expense of individuality and improvisation, and to maintain a more exclusive religious and ethnic identity than had once been the case. The powerful ideologies associated with the priestly and prophetic circles, as exemplified in the pentateuchal books of Leviticus and Deuteronomy, had taken even greater hold during the exile and were seeking ways of expressing themselves in liturgical contexts and restoring religious system and order. Religious leaders were eager to provide answers to theological questions that were more spiritually acceptable to them than the complaints or challenges of the individual (however pious) and to incorporate them into more standard liturgical formulations. When prayers were composed on the specific occasions that demanded it, they should mention both sides of the covenant arrangement with God, confess the people's guilt, and offer repentance. It was not Jewish formal and communal liturgies that first exemplified such tendencies—these would take some additional time to evolve—but rather the penitential prayers to be found in the postexilic books of the OT.

Such prayers have fresh characteristics and may best be understood against the ideological background just described. The text recorded in Ezra 9:5-15 is lengthy and formal and follows acts of mourning and contrition. It begins at the onset of evening and is accompanied by physical manifestations of penitence, humiliation, and entreaty. It includes an admission of communal guilt, an acknowledgment of God's just punishment, and regret that in spite of the return from exile the people have still not mended their ways, as evidenced by their tendency to intermarry with Gentiles. The conclusion challenges the people to do better and to assuage God's deserved anger so that the small remnant of the nation can rebuild its relationship with God. In addition to mournful weeping and fasting, Nehemiah's prayer in Neh 1:4-11 formally recites the divine attributes and intricately seeks God's favorable response. There is an admission of guilt and a reminder (as it were) that God had exiled the people for their misdeeds and restored them after their repentance. God's blessing is sought for his activities. Daniel (Dan 9:3-19) gets on his knees three times a day and prays. Mourning and confession are again central to the appeal and the historical punishment of Israel for its backsliding is rehearsed. Forgiveness is sought for the sake of God's reputation, not because Israel is a deserving case. An apocalyptic element is introduced with the appearance of the angel Gabriel with prophecy and instructions.

There are a number of other passages that shed light on liturgical developments within the postexilic Jewish community. According to Neh 8:1-8, Ezra, surrounded by other leaders, blessed God from a special platform and the participating people raised their hands, prostrated themselves, and twice exclaimed AMEN. Ezra read from the Pentateuch and the Levites explained the text. Praise of God is here accompanied by physical demonstrations of allegiance and the exposition of torah. Didactic and historical elements are found in Neh 9:5-37, which opens with the blessing of God and goes on to contrast the spiritual benefits granted to the Israelites in Egypt, at the Red Sea, and on Mount Sinai with their subsequent recalcitrance, and the praiseworthy attributes of God and his generosity after the entry into Canaan with the unworthy behavior of the people in response, both in the past and in the present, which has led to their enslavement by foreign powers. The confession here has taken on a historical guise. When, according to 1 Chr 29:10-22, David designates his son Solomon as his successor, he blesses God with the use of a formula reminiscent of later Jewish liturgy, declaring, "Blessed are you, O LORD, the God of our ancestor Israel, forever and ever." He stresses the wonderful characteristics of God and how everything is under divine, and not human, control. Alluding to the patriarchs, he entreats God to encourage appropriate religious behavior on the part of the people and their new king, Solomon. At his invitation the people bless God and prostrate themselves before him. Next day, sacrifice follows prayer and a feast is held to celebrate Solomon's appointment as ruler-designate. It should be emphasized that all these prayers bear the hallmarks of literary productions. They testify to a move toward the merger of individual prayer with institutional worship but there is still no evidence of fixed liturgy outside the Temple on the part of the Judahite community.

F. Apocrypha and Pseudepigrapha

The books of the Apocrypha and Pseudepigrapha testify to additional liturgical developments. Personal prayers for God's intervention in times of individual and national hardship are fairly common (1 Macc 4:30-33; Jdt 13:4-7; 8:30-32, T. Sim. 2:13; T. Jud. 19:2) and there are also requests for the divine blessing before journeys or at mealtime (Tob 4:19; Let. Aris., 183–85). Broader cosmological, angelological, eschatological, and mystical themes occur in the prayers of righteous individuals (2 Macc 10:25-30; Jub. 10:5-6; 12:22-24; Tob 3:16-17). As far as specific liturgical themes are concerned, Baruch's prayer (1:13–3:8) includes confession, divine attributes and pardon, and Israel's recalcitrance, much as they appear in the prayers of Ezra, Nehemiah, and Daniel cited above. The didactic element is, however, also present in prayers that call for wisdom, understanding, and torah (Let. Aris. 256; Wis 9:1-18; 15:3). Obviously, the Temple was still of central liturgical significance but there seem to have devel-

oped during the latter part of the Second Temple period closer associations between that institution and other aspects of religious expression. In Jdt 4:9-15 the people of Jerusalem, including women and children, are said to have fasted, supplicated, and prayed before the Temple and put sackcloth on the altar, while 2 Macc 1:21-30 reports that the restoration of the sacred fire on the altar achieved by Nehemiah was accompanied by prayer and hymns. According to 2 Macc 3:15, the priests responded to the attack made by Heliodorus on Jerusalem by flinging themselves before the altar and entreating God to save the Temple from the enemy. In Wis 18:21 Aaron is said to have responded to the episode of the golden calf by offering prayer and incense.

Although these passages indicate some changes in liturgical outlook, there is little to indicate formal and communal prayers adopted by any Jewish community. A close examination of *Psalms of Solomon* (e.g., 17:23-24) reveals some texts that resemble common motifs in early rabbinic liturgy, and a more detailed analysis of Sirach is important for the same reason. In that book (36:1-17) use is made of a number of phrases that later became part of the standard rabbinic prayers, and the text seems to be more nationally and publicly oriented than many other prayers of the period. From chaps. 7; 32; 34; 39; 47–48; and 50–51, a clearer picture emerges. Ben Sira was convinced of the centrality of the Temple and the priesthood. He testifies to a greater public involvement in and around the Temple Mount and perhaps of a development of the musical aspect of liturgy. He makes a close association among torah, ritual, social precepts, wisdom, prayer, and charity, all of them by necessity requiring high degrees of sincerity. He makes use of the hymn of praise as well as of the benediction. He formulates personal supplications and appeals to God with language and vocabulary that mimic and borrow those of the OT but moves in the direction of Qumranic and rabbinic formulation. He does not, however, provide evidence of any fixed set of texts that represents formal prayer regularly recited on specific occasions.

G. Synagogue

Although it is tempting to associate such prototypes of later Jewish and Christian prayer with the early development of the SYNAGOGUE, latest research on the subject militates against such an assumption. The earliest documented synagogue in the Levant apparently had more to do with Scripture, ritual practice, and hospitality than with prayers and benedictions. It was not a mini-temple and its leadership had little, if anything, to do with rabbinic prayer forms. An inscription found in such a communal center in Jerusalem dating from the 1st (2nd?) cent. BCE testifies to this. It records the generosity of Theodotos in building, and evidently also leading, a synagogue the purpose of which was to read the torah, observe the religious precepts, and provide hospitality for visitors. No mention whatsoever is made of prayer. Some of the synagogue's basic characteristics may have been imported into the homeland from Diaspora communities where such functions were doubly useful in protecting religious identity as well as centralizing its practical expression. It has even been suggested that the prototype in the homeland had been a national and official institution that evolved into a local and informal assembly under the influence of its equivalent in the Greco-Roman world. There are Tannaitic traditions about the existence of another communal activity known as the ma'amadh (מַעֲמָד). Those who could not accompany the priests and Levites from their area when it was their turn to function in the Jerusalem Temple would gather in the hometown to fast, recite scriptural passages, and perhaps also to pray. Since such an activity is not one that is in any way central to the rabbinic tradition, it seems reasonable to ascribe at least a degree of historical reality to such traditions. What therefore may be said is that the synagogue existed as a parallel to the Temple and provided the kind of communal context in which prayer could develop but not until the Jews were reconsidering their liturgical priorities and expressions after the Herodian Temple's destruction. The grandeur of that temple—comprising a virtual third temple given its major redevelopment and expansion—may also have played a part in encouraging a more extensive use of the temple precincts for prayer, not just for activities directly linked with the sacrificial cult.

H. Qumran

It should never be forgotten that prayer in the DEAD SEA SCROLLS is not a uniform phenomenon but has a variety of forms, functions, and socio-liturgical settings that are perhaps being welded together at Qumran. Given the breadth of the liturgical material found at Qumran, there was clearly more than one provenance for the development of hymns and prayers during the Second Temple period. It is therefore likely that borrowings were being made from various contexts, among them the Jerusalem Temple, the priesthood, Levitical groups, communal gatherings such as the ma'amadhoth (מַעֲמָדוֹת), pietistic and mystical circles, and popular practice. What is beyond doubt is that the groups represented at Qumran were committed to the practice of reciting regular prayers at specific times even if there is no obvious consistency of text and context for these. It also seems clear that many of the hymns and prayers found there represent the religious activities of the "common Judaism" of the Second Temple period. Whatever the extent of these liturgical texts, the possibility should not be ruled out that oral liturgical traditions also existed during that period.

The liturgical texts from Qumran have biblical precedents but the composers are utilizing them in their own ways, in order to take account of their own predilections and theological motivations. The notions of Israel, the city of Jerusalem, and the Jerusalem Temple

that lie behind the various textual constructions are common to various Jewish groups but have their own interpretation within each. Divine attributes such as tuv (טוב; goodness), khesedh (חֶסֶד; kindness; steadfast love), and rakhamim (רְחָמִים; compassion) are regarded at Qumran as the models for human piety and idealistic behavior while the stress in later Jewish writings is more on the blessings they confer on Israel. Formulations and concepts known in tannaitic Judaism and early Christianity are already foreshadowed in such psalms as that found in 4Q372 1, as well as in the texts to be found in 4Q408 and 4Q503, and the Qumranic scrolls are of major importance for tracing the origins of the Jewish liturgical benediction, with regard to both its use and its formulation. What emerges from all this data is that the liturgical developments at Qumran should be plotted at a point between the biblical beginning and the rabbinic progression that is close to the position occupied by the apocryphal and pseudepigraphical literature. The prayers found at Qumran belong to a reservoir of prayer traditions from which later Jewish groups also drew. Rabbinic, and indeed Christian, institutionalized prayer did not have its origins exclusively in the Qumranic context but also arose out of a fondness for the temple cult, rather than a desire to replace it. Just as the Qumran writings record views that reflect distress about the politicization and corruption of the Jerusalem cult and apply its best aspects to their own liturgical practice, so later Christian and Jewish prayer take close account of what they regard as the Temple at its best in order to construct something that will be as spiritually moving and significant within their own developing traditions.

I. The Shema and Decalogue

Before describing the Jewish liturgical innovations and developments championed by the rabbis of the early part of the 2nd cent. CE, it is necessary to identify those items that were already in existence when they set about their task. The two most important texts in this connection are the Decalogue and the Shema (Deut 6:4-9; Deut 11:13-21; Num 15:37-41), both of them biblical texts but with a special significance that encouraged their use in the liturgical sphere (see SHEMA, THE; TEN COMMANDMENTS). This is clear from a number of sources, the best known of which is probably the Nash Papyrus. This text, dated ca. 200 BCE and housed at Cambridge University Library, was discovered in Egypt early in the 20th cent. It consists of twenty-four lines of square Hebrew script containing a text of the Decalogue that is sometimes in agreement with Exodus and sometimes with Deuteronomy, and occasionally supports the text presupposed by the LXX. Appended to the Decalogue is the first verse of the Shema prefaced by a verse not found in the MT but similar to that which occurs in the LXX. Given the joint use of these passages, it seems that this papyrus is to be defined as a piece of popular liturgy in the form of a charm, amulet, or phylactery. Among the literary treasures of the Dead Sea Scrolls are to be found texts that also contain the Decalogue and the Shema within tefillin (תְּפִלִּין; usually translated "phylacteries") and mezuzoth (מְזוּזוֹת; for attachment to doorposts). It is also possible that the texts in 1QS X, 10–14 that refer to blessing God's name early and late each day may allude to the recitation of the Decalogue and the Shema.

If we move on to the period of the Gospels, we find passages in Matt 22:34-40; and Mark 12:28-34; 10:17-19 that deal with definitions of the OT's most important commandments. Here too it is clear that the Decalogue and Shema are among the candidates for texts that best summarize the Jewish religious message. There are mishnaic passages (*m. Tamid* 5:1; 7:2-3; *m. Yoma* 7:1) that list the prayers and benedictions recited in the Jerusalem Temple. They may reflect some late 2nd-cent. editing but it is likely that in their earliest formats they made reference at least to the Decalogue, the Shema, and the public blessing of God's name in various formulations, as well, of course, as to the priestly benediction. With the exception of the last mentioned, the other items were not intrinsically of temple origin. Their recitation at the Temple represents part of the tendency, already noted, to merge broader liturgical practice with what was more closely associated with the sacrificial cult and the activities of the priests.

Also of relevance for this reconstruction of what constituted early Jewish liturgy is the fact that these two biblical texts already had special significance for the authors of some of the books of the OT. Regarding the Decalogue, reference may be made to Ps 50:7; Jer 7:9; Hos 4:2; and, perhaps the clearest example, Ps 81:10-11, in which texts mention is made of lying, murdering, stealing, and adultery, as well as of the demand for strict monotheism. Recent research has also found allusions to the first paragraph of the Shema in texts as varied as 2 Kgs 23:25; Prov 3:1-12; Jer 32:39-41; and Zech 14:9. There one can detect intensification and clarification of various parts of the message of the Shema, as well as a stress on God's uniqueness. The reason why such passages should have acquired a special liturgical function relates to the theological messages contained in them. The Decalogue, which in any case has a central role in the Sinaitic theophany, emphasizes the need to reject belief in, and worship of, all alternative divinities, and to be loyal and respectful to God who brought the people of Israel out of Egypt. It demands parental respect and observance of the Sabbath, as well as the avoidance of murder, adultery, theft, lying, and covetous behavior. The religious message of the Shema has undoubted similarities. It also presents itself as direct instruction from God, declares God's uniqueness, and warns against idolatry. It takes account of the special adult/child relationship, mentions the exodus, and promises longevity as a reward. Both passages amount to summaries of the Jewish theological essentials and are therefore self-evidently suitable for a form of catechismal use. The style

of the Decalogue, unlike the Shema, is, however, apodictic and less concerned with ritual detail, and there is little of personal devotion to God, of the didactic element, and of environmental circumstances. It should also be noted that the earliest references to the Shema do not make it clear whether the text consists of one verse, or one, two, or three paragraphs.

J. Benedictions

The other expressions of Jewish liturgy that were most likely in existence before the destruction of the Second Temple were those that related to daily activities rather than to theological statements. Opportunities were taken to thank God for using his power to assist humanity in circumstances relating to the natural world, concerning events of a joyous or sad kind, and in the matter of food provision. In their simplest form, such benedictions stated simply "You are praised, Lord God" (barukh ʾattah ʾadhonay בָּרוּךְ אַתָּה אֲדֹנָי) with an appended phrase that related to the particular divine activity that had inspired the praise. One of them was probably used to celebrate the arrival of Sabbath at dusk on Friday evening, later spawning the qiddush (קִדּוּשׁ; blessing) formulas of rabbinic practice, while another was recited to mark its termination on Saturday evening, an obvious predecessor of the havdalah (הַבְדָּלָה) ritual. The consumption of the paschal lamb was accompanied at home by a formal praise of God, presumably through the use of chapters from Psalms, and also by a liturgy that was developed later by the rabbis but may have had a simpler benedictory format in its earliest manifestation. In periods of drought, a fast would be declared and the people would gather in the central areas of their settlements to perform acts of mourning and contrition, and to recite special biblical verses and benedictions, as well as prayers for God to answer them as he had all the famous ancestors of the Jewish people during their times of trouble. The instruction to bless God after eating (Deut 8:10) was observed by way of another such benediction which began as praise of God for feeding the world and later attached to itself additional benedictions about the special relationship of God and Israel as exemplified in the gifts of the land of Israel, the covenant, the torah, life, and sustenance, and, later, about his promise to restore Jerusalem, the Temple, and the Davidic dynasty. If a group context is to be sought for these rituals, it might well have been that of the pharisaic khavuroth (חֲבוּרוֹת; "collegialities") and ritual purity may have been required by them for at least some of them, since the later talmudic sources argue the point and then opt to abandon such a stringency within the standard prayer context.

K. ʿAmidah

Undoubtedly, the most important innovation made by the 2nd-cent. rabbis, led by Rabban Gamaliel, was the creation of a collection of benedictions, perhaps some of them originally with their own independent contexts (popular rather than elitist), and the requirement that they be recited morning and afternoon. The very fact that they go out of their way to link the ʿamidhah (עֲמִדָה) with earlier biblical personalities and Jewish institutions itself testifies to an anxiety about having it accepted as authoritative. Known as the **tefillah** ("the prayer," par excellence), it once consisted of eighteen benedictions (hence its secondary title of **shemoneh ʿesreh** [שְׁמֹנֶה עֶשְׂרֵה]) and later expanded to nineteen. There was controversy as to whether the return of the Davidic dynasty was to be included in the prayer for the restoration of Jerusalem or recited as an independent benediction, and also as to whether there should be a third, evening ʿamidhah. The language and style of the benedictions have evidently at some stage been standardized to a degree but there are indications that this was not the case in their earliest formats. Some of the themes and the phraseology already occur in Sir 36; 51; and the Dead Sea Scrolls but there is no evidence in any pre-rabbinic Jewish literature of any composition that might be designated as a proto-ʿamidhah. The mishnaic rulings about when and how the Shema and the ʿamidhah are to be recited acknowledge that they are not to be treated identically, but demands were subsequently made that the ʿamidhah should follow immediately on the Shema in order to create an indivisible framework for the daily prayers.

Some Jewish liturgical historians have suggested that the ʿamidhah for Sabbaths and festivals, which contains the same first three and last three benedictions but does not list the mundane daily requirements that Jews request from God (concentrating rather on the exclusive theme or themes of the special day), may belong to an earlier period. The topics of these six common benedictions are the biblical patriarchs, life after death, and divine sanctity at the beginning, and cultic restoration, thanksgiving, and peace (including the priestly benediction) at the end. The others that make up the remainder of the daily ʿamidhah deal with requests for knowledge, repentance, pardon, redemption, healing, plentiful produce, an end to exile and persecution, restoration of autonomy, removal of apostasy, blessing of the righteous and of converts, the reestablishment of Jerusalem and the Davidic dynasty, and the success of prayer. The subjects chosen for inclusion testify to the theological concerns of the rabbinic leadership. The loss of the national institutions was obviously of major concern and there was clearly a polemical need to stress the link between rabbinic Judaism and the patriarchs, the end of time and the next world, the importance of becoming and remaining Jewish, the inclusion of knowledge, holiness and goodness in God's attributes, and the divine control of reward and punishment.

L. Rabbinic Innovation

The early rabbinic sources also testify to adjustments being made in the liturgical use of the Shema. Doubts about the extent of its contents gave way to a convic-

tion that all three paragraphs should be used. It also became a central plank of rabbinic theology to define the Shema as the "acceptance of the yoke of the heavenly kingdom," so much so that a formulation was introduced between the first two verses of the opening paragraph that blessed God's glorious kingdom to eternity. It was agreed that this act of loyalty might in certain circumstances even require martyrdom, as in the case of Rabbi Akiva after the Bar Kosiba revolt of 132–35 CE. This, together with the stress placed on freedom in the domestic liturgy for the first Passover eve, amounted to supreme, theological confidence in the face of an utterly depressing political situation. The rabbinic need to argue that all parts of the pentateuchal legislation were equally important and should not be subject to theological "cherry-picking" forced them into the radical argument that the Shema was superior in religious content to the Decalogue, which should no longer have a central place in Jewish worship. The Shema was therefore surrounded by benedictions concerning the natural world, the role of Israel, and the redemption from Egypt, the whole office being introduced by a call to the formal prayer session and followed by the ʿamidhah. A unique system of recitation by the prayer leader and the congregation, possibly antiphonal in nature, was also introduced but somehow lost to subsequent generations.

The role of worship in Jewish religious life was a controversial issue in early rabbinic Judaism. For some, prayer replaced the sacrifices and took on their formal and central role (ʿavodhah). It counted with devotional study (torah) and correct ethical behavior (**gemiluth khesedh** [גְּמִלוּת חֶסֶד]) as one of the pillars of the faith. For others, prayer could never replace the Temple and amounted to no more than one of the 613 religious requirements. Another question was whether the mystic was central to Jewish prayer. Was the efficacy of prayer not dependent on the remarkable piety and well-prepared spirituality of special individuals, and dependent on a mysterious and even magical aspect that only the most saintly possessed? A more pragmatic view admitted the frailties of humanity and the inability of ordinary individuals to become ascetics at will. The early rabbinic works also debated the language, length, location, and direction of prayer. The discussions centered on whether Greek and Aramaic could match Hebrew, whether prayers should be recited antiphonally, and whether brevity or prolixity was the preferred option. Another question was whether the synagogue was inevitably a better place for prayer than the home and there was doubt about whether it was always necessary to face Jerusalem during worship. The synagogue had not yet attracted to itself all the liturgical rituals but was of central importance to many (but not all) of the teachers. The academy and the home were still alternative locations. Some preferred not to move out of the study context for any purpose, including individual or communal prayer. Some prayers and benedictions had their origin in the academic setting, particularly those centering on **torah** study, although their incorporation into the daily liturgy was not completed until later.

Among examples of an early interest in scriptural reading and study were Greek and Aramaic translations of the OT (*see* SEPTUAGINT; TARGUMS); the pesher system of biblical exegesis that permeates the Qumranic writings (*see* PESHARIM); the allegorical teachings of the Jewish philosophers of the Hellenistic world; the use of the **tefillin** and the **mezuzoth** as ritual objects with scriptural content; and the biblical exposition championed by both early Christianity and rabbinic Judaism. The early rabbis transformed such an interest into a more formal liturgical exercise. Use was made of pentateuchal, prophetical, and hagiographical readings but the precise details of the lectionaries—if they were already established as such—are known only from later. The triennial cycle that was used in the land of Israel in the post-talmudic period may consistently have been the rite used in the homeland or it may earlier have shared its liturgical role with the annual cycle that became standard in Iraq.

In spite of reservations about the study of Greek wisdom, the rabbis were sufficiently impressed by the universal importance of Greek to permit its use for major parts of the Jewish liturgy. This must have applied even more in such Hellenistic centers as Egypt. Aramaic was also widely employed by the Jews but, interestingly enough, it seems to have been Hebrew, perhaps because of the link with the OT, that predominated in the local liturgy. Once Hebrew was established as the main liturgical language there could later be a more relaxed approach and Aramaic could also find a respected place in the prayers. There are indeed Jewish prayers in Greek, sometimes with contents that parallel the ʿamidhah, that were undoubtedly in circulation in the 3rd and 4th cent. and may also have been used earlier. Among Greek-speaking communities there is evidence of a more central role for women in the synagogue. What is already known from early rabbinic literature is that it was only because of the fear of inappropriate behavior that women and men were separated at one of the temple ceremonies (*m. Sukkah* 5:2; *m. Mid.* 2:5). There is also no categorical evidence from archaeological discoveries that there were women's sections or galleries in the earliest synagogues. It is also clear that the talmudic position about the role of women in Jewish liturgy is somewhat more lax than the approach taken by later Jewish authorities. What emerges from epigraphic evidence obtained from some Diaspora synagogues is that complimentary titles referring to women as leaders of the synagogue are attached to their names, and such titles might betray functional and not merely honorific status.

During the 1st cent. CE, Jewish mystics, possibly influenced by the gnostic teachings then being disseminated among Christian and pagan intellectuals, pursued mystical themes as well as detailed speculation about the divine palaces (hekhaloth הֵיכָלוֹת) and the nature of the Godhead. It was among such groups that **hekhaloth** hymns were composed. Most of the leading rabbinic

teachers were originally, at best, ambivalent and maybe even somewhat skeptical about the religious value and theological safety of such material (and of the use of magic in amulets) so that it is no surprise to find it absent among the prayer forms that were regarded as central in the first two cent. CE. The liturgy of the talmudic period, like much of its practice and ideology, had little serious interest in, or mastery of, historical and chronological matters. A limited interest may already have existed in the land of Israel rather than in the Iraqi centers but it did not manifest itself to any significant degree in rabbinic circles until the post-talmudic era. The biblical patriarchs receive cursory note in the daily ʿamidhah, Moses hardly appears at all in the Passover HAGGADAH, and the mention of David in the Babylonian if not the Palestinian ʿamidhah has more to do with eschatology than history. Similarly, historical events such as the exodus from Egypt are included only as theological ciphers. *See* BLESSINGS AND CURSINGS; FEAST OF DEDICATION; LEVI, LEVITES; PASSOVER AND FEAST OF UNLEAVENED BREAD; PRIESTS AND LEVITES; PSALMS, BOOK OF; QUMRAN; RABBI, RABBONI; SABBATH; SACRIFICES AND OFFERINGS; TEMPLE, JERUSALEM.

Bibliography: Mark J. Boda, Daniel K. Falk, and Rodney A. Werline, eds. *Seeking the Favor of God Volume 1: The Origins of Penitential Prayer in Second Temple Judaism* (2006); Mark J. Boda, Daniel K. Falk, and Rodney A. Werline, eds. *Seeking the Favor of God Volume 2: The Development of Penitential Prayer in Second Temple Judaism* (2007); Renate Egger-Wenzel and Jeremy Corley, eds. *Prayer from Tobit to Qumran: Deuterocanonical and Cognate Literature, Yearbook 2004* (2004); Daniel K. Falk. *Daily, Sabbath and Festival Prayers in the Dead Sea Scrolls* (1998); Moshe Greenberg. *Biblical Prose Prayer as a Window to the Popular Religion of Ancient Israel* (1983); Joseph Heinemann. *Prayer in the Talmud: Forms and Patterns.* Richard S. Sarason, trans. (1977); Lee I. Levine. *The Ancient Synagogue: The First Thousand Years* (2000); Stefan C. Reif. *Judaism and Hebrew Prayer: New Perspectives on Jewish Liturgical History* (1993); Stefan C. Reif. *Problems with Prayers: Studies in the Textual History of Early Rabbinic Liturgy* (2006); Moshe Weinfeld. *Early Jewish Liturgy: From Psalms to the Prayers in Qumran and Rabbinic Literature* (2004).

STEFAN C. REIF

WORSHIP, NT CHRISTIAN. Worship comprises those actions by which people express and reaffirm their devotional stance toward, and relationship to, a deity. These actions can be done by individuals, privately or in a public place such as a temple/shrine, or by groups of devotees gathered for corporate worship. Worship characteristically involves ritualized actions, but not all religious rituals really function as acts of worship. For example, some ritual actions can be apotropaic (i.e., to ward off evil from spirits) or intended to coerce a spirit/

deity to obey the will of the person who performs the ritual (e.g., as in magical charms/spells). By contrast, worship more typically involves expressions of praise and adoration and also appeals directed to a deity, the devotee(s) usually expressing subordination to and/or dependence on the intended recipient of worship while also affirming a positive relationship with the recipient. In the NT—and in Christian tradition generally—although prayer and praise can be offered by individuals privately, Christian worship is more characteristically set in the gathered ekklēsia (ἐκκλησία), the church, and that is the focus here.

From the earliest references onward, two of the key identifying features of Christian worship are 1) the programmatic inclusion of Jesus as the central subject of praise and thanksgiving, and the one through whom and with whom God is worshiped, and 2) the particular importance of the "first day of the week" for corporate worship by the ekklēsia. In other ways as well, early Christian worship is distinguishable from the more typical religious phenomena of the Roman context. In particular, blood-sacrifice (which in that setting was generally regarded as perhaps the most overtly religious action) did not feature in Christian worship, and likewise it did not involve temples/shrines, altars, or images. But Christian worship was also supposed to be exclusivist. That is, the NT advocates a refusal to participate in the worship of any deity other than the God of biblical tradition. Many in the Roman world may have had their favorite deities, but this would not have involved the refusal or rejection of other deities and the due observances of them. Christians, however, were expected to regard other deities as illusions or even demonic beings, and certainly unworthy of worship.

Of course, ancient Jewish synagogue gatherings did not involve sacrifices or images either; until its destruction in 70 CE, the Jerusalem Temple and its sacrificial rites were—probably for most devout Jews wherever they lived—of central significance in affirming and maintaining the relationship of the people of Israel with their God. According to Acts, the Jerusalem Temple (so long as it stood) appears to have been regarded as a holy site also by Jewish Christians for pilgrimage, prayer, and other religious activities (including at least some sacrificial offerings, e.g., Acts 3:1; 20:16; 21:20-26; 22:17-18). But early Christian worship was in general not conducted in or oriented toward shrines or other sacred sites/spaces. Apart from the regard for the Jerusalem Temple among Jewish Christians, the whole idea of a "sacred space" such as a shrine as especially fit for worship seems not to feature in earliest Christianity. Likewise, the exclusivist stance of earliest Christianity was inherited from the Jewish tradition. The crucial difference between early Christian worship and the Jewish tradition was the programmatic place of Jesus in the religious rhetoric and devotional practice of believers.

In distinction from the larger religious environment of the Roman era, early Christian worship was heavily verbal, typically comprising invocations, prayers, psalms and odes/hymns, prophecy, teaching, faith-confessions, and (though perhaps not always in the earliest decades) readings from Scripture (the OT) and other edifying texts (e.g., letters of Paul), as well as other liturgical expressions, such as benedictions. Furthermore, earliest Christian worship gatherings did not apparently include use of musical instruments or other phenomena familiar in the religious environment of the time, such as incense, officiating priests, or elaborate ceremonies. Thus for many "pagans" of the Roman period, the Christian worship gathering may have seemed curious as a genuinely religious event and more akin to a meeting of a philosophical circle.

Although early Christian worship lacked many of the features characterizing worship in the larger religious setting of the time and was conducted in mundane settings such as the home, the evidence suggests that earliest Christians ascribed a high meaning to their worship gatherings. They appear to have seen their worship as responding to, reflecting, and attesting heavenly realities (especially the exaltation of Jesus to God's "right hand"), and also as prefiguring eschatological realities (particularly the universal acclamation of Jesus as "Lord"). Moreover, in the worship gathering God's Spirit might speak through Christian prophets, giving revelations and divine words of direction. In short, NT texts urge that the worship gathering was not simply a human/earthly transaction but partook in transcendent realities, and was energized and enabled by God's Spirit.

A. Limitations of New Testament Evidence
  1. No liturgical order
  2. More allusive than descriptive
  3. Key New Testament evidence
B. Approach and Presuppositions
C. General Characteristics
  1. Setting
  2. Leadership
  3. Holy Spirit
  4. Eschatology
  5. Content and focus
D. "Binitarian Shape"
  1. Worship of Jesus
  2. Forces and factors
E. Major Phenomena of Early Christian Worship
  1. The "Lord's Day"
  2. Invocation and confession of Jesus
  3. Prayers
  4. Psalms and hymns
  5. Prophecy and related phenomena
  6. Teaching
  7. Readings
  8. The sacred meal
  9. Other liturgical formulas
F. Conclusion
Bibliography

A. Limitations of New Testament Evidence

Unquestionably, the NT texts give us evidence about earliest Christian worship; but we must also respect the limits of that evidence and its circumstantial nature. For example, except for 1 Cor 11–14, we have hardly any extended description of or teaching about corporate worship, and were it not for apparent problems with corporate worship in the Corinthian church, we would likely not have this particularly valuable but very limited body of material.

1. No liturgical order

In particular, it is not possible to determine whether any order of worship was followed in the churches reflected in the NT. Indeed, the earliest Christian description of a basic order of Christian worship is by Justin Martyr (*1 Apol.* 67; ca. 160 CE), who portrays a sequence of readings from "the memoirs of the apostles or the writings of the prophets," followed by instruction and exhortation by a presiding figure, corporate prayers, and then the eucharist. From various NT texts, we can surmise that actions such as acclamation, prayers, hymns/odes, teaching, and a sacred meal were common; but we cannot infer any commonly preferred sequence in these and other actions. For example, when there was a meal, did it come first, followed then by other phenomena, or did these other actions come first (a so-called "service of the Word"), followed by the meal? Some scholars (e.g., Smith) have proposed that phenomena such as odes, prophecies, and teaching would have come after the meal if the typical structure of the Roman-era symposium was appropriated (a group meal, which might be followed by discussion or other entertainments, the precise nature of which depended on the nature of the group, and might even include drunken and orgiastic behavior). Although it is reasonable to suppose that early Christians might have followed this basic structure of the symposium, we do not have confirming evidence that they did so. Moreover, why should we assume that the sacred meal and such other components such as prophecy, teaching, or even the singing of hymns/odes had to form two distinguishable stages of the worship gathering? It is also perfectly plausible to suppose that the latter actions could have been performed during the meal. It is perhaps worth noting that in the earliest Christian text giving specific instructions about the eucharist, the *Didache* (in its present form variously dated ca. 70–140 CE), prophets appear to be expected to exercise their verbal gifts in prayers that form part of the eucharist itself (*Did.* 10:7).

In any case, we cannot find any clear ordering of worship actions in any of the NT texts. Thus the NT will prove disappointing for those conventional inquiries about liturgical history that have been concerned with tracing orders of worship.

2. More allusive than descriptive

Yet we certainly do have references to worship in the NT and we can draw some observations about it. The NT more presupposes early Christian worship than describes or prescribes it. Thus, it is necessary to gather up what are often short, even passing, references to and reflections of worship attitudes and practices, and attempt some synthesizing discussion.

Moreover, the identification of allusions to early Christian worship in the NT often requires some care and informed judgment. For example, if (as is widely surmised among scholars) the Gospel accounts of Jesus feeding the multitudes and of meals with the risen Jesus were not simply intended as stories about Jesus but also were written to reflect and inspire early Christian sacred meal practice, then these accounts give some hints relevant to our understanding of early Christian eucharistic traditions.

Similarly, although it is clear that the singing (or chanting) of hymns was a feature of early Christian worship (e.g., 1 Cor 14:26; Eph 5:18-20; Col 3:16), we do not have any text explicitly identified by a NT author as a Christian hymn. But scholars commonly judge that some NT passages are quotations from or adaptations of hymns (e.g., Eph 5:14; Phil 2:6-11; Col 1:15-20). This judgment is largely based on the poetic qualities of these passages, e.g., their psalm-like phrasing and compacted expressions. The only passages explicitly identified as hymnic are the chants that the author of Revelation sets in heavenly scenes, e.g., the ceaseless refrain of the four living creatures in 4:8, and the exuberant adoration voiced by the twenty-four elders in 4:11 and 5:9-10, and by all creation in 5:12-14. It is reasonable to suppose that in these passages the author may reflect, or may have intended to inspire, the worshipful chanting of the churches of Asia to which he wrote. These passages may give us indirect indication of aspects of the worship of some early circles.

In short, one can find evidence of earliest Christian worship, but this requires a sensitive sifting of the NT and judicious inferences ventured with appropriate regard for the circumstantial and varied body of texts involved.

3. Key New Testament evidence

Among the NT evidence to be considered, certain texts are particularly important to note. Some include overt references to early Christian worship, among which 1 Cor 11–14 forms the most extended body of such material, especially valuable because of the early date of 1 Corinthians (ca. 53–56 CE). In 1 Cor 11, Paul first deals with some sort of question about women's head/hair appearance, quite possibly arising from (certain) women thinking that their new spiritual status in Christ (evidenced by charismatic phenomena) meant that gender differences should be obscured. However, the precise question about women's appearance, which occupies the bulk of 11:1-16, seems to have been specific to this church, as we find no such instructions in his other letters. The more relevant matter for this article is that Paul presupposes that Christian women contribute overtly to corporate worship, e.g., in prayer and/or prophecy (11:5). (Thus, if the now notorious statements in 1 Cor 14:34-35 exhorting women to silence in the church are authentically Paul's, they cannot be taken as forbidding such contributions by women. There are good reasons to think that these statements originated as marginal glosses that made their way into the text of 1 Corinthians in the process of copying it.)

Following this discussion of women's head attire, in 1 Cor 11:17-34 we have the most extended discussion of the early Christian sacred meal in the NT, a passage often drawn upon in Christian eucharistic traditions. The passage implies that a shared meal is a central feature of and reason for the gathering of the church (especially v. 33). Paul's concern here is to underscore the theological meaning and associations of the meal, and to exhort behavior appropriate for this setting. He also claims a certain continuity between the tradition that he taught to the Corinthians and that which he had received (v. 23). We shall return to these matters later (§E.6 below).

In 1 Cor 12–14, Paul gives further exhortations about right attitudes and behavior in Christian worship, especially concerning phenomena such as prophecy and tongues-speaking. It must be recognized that the extended treatment of the variety of gifts as components of the church-body in 12:4-31 has the gathered church as the implicit setting where these gifts are typically exercised. The lyrical extolling of Christian love (for fellow believers) in chap. 13 functions as Paul's "still more excellent way" to assess these charismatic phenomena (12:31), in preference to any misguided attempt to rank them as to importance or prestige (compare 12:14-26). Then, in chap. 14 Paul gives an extended illustration of how this loving concern for others can be exhibited in the exercise of charismatic gifts in corporate worship, arguing that in this setting prophecy is to be preferred. Paul claims to practice and even commends tongues-speaking (14:2-4, 18) as a feature of Christian devotional life; however, he urges that the inability to understand what is said in tongues-speaking means that this gift cannot edify others (especially 14:5-6, 18-19, 23-25) unless someone interprets (vv. 13, 27). By contrast, prophecy, in virtue of being uttered in the vernacular language, can have a powerful effect of edifying and/or convicting the hearers (especially vv. 14-25).

For our purposes, the most important observation is that in 1 Cor 12–14 Paul refers to the components of corporate worship as richly varied (e.g., "a hymn, a lesson, a revelation, a tongue, or an interpretation"), and contributed (at least in principle) by various participants (14:26). Indeed, he seems to assume multiple prophets present, each prophetic utterance to be weighed (diakrinō διακρίνω) apparently by the other prophets (14:29). There is no hint of a fixed order of worship,

but Paul does urge believers to conduct themselves in keeping with the exalted significance of the gathered ekklēsia, and in due regard for one another as fellow members of "the body of Christ" (12:27).

In Acts we have no such extended treatment of Christian worship, but there are several likely scenes of believers gathered in a worship occasion from which we can sift relevant evidence about settings and phenomena probably typical in this author's experience. There is, e.g., the scene of corporate worship in Acts 13:1-3 where Paul and Barnabas are identified through a prophetic oracle for an itinerant mission. It is also possible (but not certain) that the events in Acts 20:7-12 are set in an evening worship gathering, which included a meal and Paul's rather extended speaking (v. 7). In the narratives about the Jerusalem church, the reference to believers meeting daily in the Temple and sharing food in their homes (2:46-47) may allude to both venues for corporate worship, and the scene of believers gathered for prayer in the house of Mary (mother of John Mark), to which Peter goes after his miraculous release from jail (12:12), may be another reflection of Christians meeting for worship in the homes of those able to provide such accommodation.

B. Approach and Presuppositions

In addition to the demands of careful identification and analysis of relevant evidence, it is also important to approach the question of worship in the NT properly. A good deal of earlier scholarship on the subject can be criticized for dubious assumptions and inappropriate questions.

For instance, contrary to some earlier scholarship, we do not actually know enough about any liturgical sequence(s) observed in Jewish synagogue gatherings to assert direct influence upon earliest Christian orders of worship (especially Bradshaw 2002). Various evidence (e.g., Acts 13:15; 15:21; Josephus, *Ag. Ap.* 2.175; *Ant.* 16.43) indicates that synagogue worship typically included Scripture reading and also prayer (much of the Eighteen Benedictions that became part of synagogue worship in later centuries probably derives from 1st-cent. synagogue prayers), and perhaps also recitation of the Shema (Deut 6:4, plus Deut 11:13-21 and Num 15:37-41 in later usage), but we know little beyond this. For the same reason, occasional confident claims that early Christian worship can be sharply contrasted with Jewish synagogue practice (e.g., in the Christian use of hymns) are equally dubious. It is likely that early Christian worship was influenced in some respects by Jewish synagogue practice, but we do not have bases for any grand theory.

It is also dubious to treat the somewhat limited evidence of Christian worship in the NT as reflections of some early common order of worship from which later liturgical sequences derived. That developed orders of worship are attested later (e.g., the *Trad. ap.*, ca. 215 CE) does not require that these orders derive from 1st-cent. Christian practices. The 150 years between the churches of Paul's day and the evidence of orders of worship provide plenty of time for them to develop. Paul Bradshaw has also rightly criticized a tendency toward "panliturgism" in some previous scholarship, in which, without any confirmatory evidence, various NT texts were portrayed as reflecting liturgical settings (e.g., claims that the Gospels reflect supposed 1st-cent. Christian lectionaries, or that 1 Peter reflects an early baptismal liturgy).

It is yet another mistake to assume too much standardization in Christian worship sequence or practices in the 1st cent. To be sure, there are indications that Paul strove to promote a serious sense among his churches of being co-religionists with one another and also with their predecessor Jewish believers in Judea (e.g., Rom 15:25-27; 2 Cor 9:13-15; 1 Thess 2:14-16), and in particular that he claimed a continuity in faith between Judean and Gentile circles (especially 1 Cor 15:1-11). Thus, it is reasonable also to assume some general similarity in the actions that composed corporate worship, e.g., prophecy, prayer, reading Scriptures, and a sacred common meal; yet we must also take account of the diversity of 1st-cent. Christianity in geography, languages, cultures, background influences, and social makeup.

Although we have to synthesize to some degree the somewhat fragmentary evidence of Christian worship in the NT, we also must recognize that the NT texts reflect different situations and settings requiring some caution in how widely representative we may make the evidence that we are given.

C. General Characteristics

1. Setting

From various references in the NT, we can judge that the typical (though perhaps not the sole) setting of earliest Christian worship was in the homes of those able to accommodate such a gathering. In Rom 16:3-16 Paul greets the church that meets in the home of Prisca and Aquila (vv. 3-5) as well as other groups of believers who appear to be based in the households of other leading Christians (those linked with Aristobulus, v. 10; Narcissus, v. 11; Asyncritus and others, v. 14; Philologus and others, v. 15); the epistle to Philemon is also addressed to the church that meets in his home (Phlm 1). In L. Michael White's analysis, over the first few centuries the settings of Christian worship shifted from these ordinary domestic settings to redesigned rooms and buildings dedicated as church meeting spaces, and then to purpose-built structures.

The typical domestic settings of early Christian worship were likely significant in reflecting and promoting greater intimacy and the familial-like ties of believers advocated in the NT. Because domestic space was regarded as particularly pertaining to women in the Roman era, this setting was likely more conducive to women participating actively in corporate worship, including presiding (as urged by Osiek et al.), whereas the later shift to nondomestic worship settings (regarded as public space) probably contributed to fewer opportunities for women to play such roles in worship.

It is likely, however, that the specific domestic spaces in which Christians initially met varied, depending on the economic status of believers. The homes of wealthier Christians might well have accommodated groups as large as forty or so, whereas poorer believers might have lived in simple quarters in multi-occupant buildings (*insulae*), accommodating only very small groups. We cannot be sure what size a group would have met in any particular house church.

2. Leadership

Just as it is difficult to find any common liturgical order in the NT, it is also difficult to perceive any set leadership roles in corporate worship. Indeed, it is noteworthy that in Paul's various and extended instructions about behavior and order in corporate worship in 1 Cor 11–14 there is no reference to any leaders or presiding figures. Instead, he appeals to the church as a whole to participate in worship with a keen regard for one another and for the high significance of the church and its worship.

In other Pauline letters, however, there is a reference to "BISHOPs and deacons" (Phil 1:1) and exhortation to respect "those who labor among you and are over you (proïstamenous [προϊσταμένους]; NRSV, "have charge of you") in the Lord" (1 Thess 5:12-13), and in Rom 12:6-8 we have a short list of several types of roles that may have corporate worship as the typical setting: prophecy, teaching, exhortation, and "leading" (proïstamenos προϊστάμενος). In the so-called deuteropauline letters, we have more extended description of the desired attributes of the "bishop" and the "deacon" (e.g., 1 Tim 3:1-14), and in various NT texts "elders" are mentioned as leading figures in churches (e.g., 1 Tim 5:17; Jas 5:14-15; 1 Pet 5:1-5). But it is not clear that any of these roles did or did not include responsibility for leadership in the worship service. Even in the *Didache*, which gives directions about celebration of eucharist (chaps. 9–10) and also urges the appointment of bishops and deacons (15:1-2), there is no explicit statement about liturgical leadership.

To be sure, across the 2nd cent. CE those charged with oversight of churches also came more regularly to take on liturgical leadership. First-century churches may have had someone (or a delegated group) to act as convener, but perhaps not always. In small and more intimately connected circles, formal leadership may have been less necessary and may even have been deemed inappropriate, but as larger congregations formed, designated leadership in worship quite likely seemed a good thing.

3. Holy Spirit

The NT rather consistently links Christian worship with the Holy Spirit. We have noted already Paul's references to various phenomena set within the corporate worship setting as "gifts" (*see* SPIRITUAL GIFTS) of the Spirit (1 Cor 12:4-11), but Paul also refers to corporate Christian prayer and the confession/acclamation of Jesus as Lord as prompted by the Spirit (e.g., Rom 8:15-16; 1 Cor 12:3; Gal 4:4-6). In other NT texts as well, the Spirit is presented as the empowerment behind such phenomena as prophecy in Christian worship (e.g., Acts 13:2); in Rev 1:10 the author refers to being "in the Spirit on the Lord's day," which likely describes a worship setting.

This is, of course, consistent with the wider sense promoted in the NT that believers were recipients of God's Spirit, the gift of the Spirit reflecting the exaltation of Jesus (Acts 2:33-36) and the consequent inauguration of eschatological blessings. Indeed, the bestowal of the Spirit constitutes the foretaste of the full eschatological redemption (e.g., Rom 8:23; Eph 1:13-14; Heb 6:4-6). In the NT, the whole of Christian existence is characterized and empowered by the Spirit (e.g., Rom 8:9-11), but the gathered Christian ekklēsia is particularly an occasion for the manifestations of the Spirit and for celebration of God's present and anticipated eschatological redemption. So, the NT references to Christian worship suggest that it was to be characterized by energy and vitality, and a joy and enthusiasm that reflect the experience of God's enlivening Spirit and the consequent sense of eschatological and heavenly realities.

We get a vivid, even unsettling, reflection of the sense of the gathered church as being a locus of spiritual power in Paul's directions to the Corinthians about how to deal with the believer who was having a sexual relationship with "his father's wife" (1 Cor 5:1-13). When the believers have gathered in Jesus' name and "with the power of our Lord Jesus," they are to hand the offending man over to Satan "for the destruction of his flesh, so that his spirit may be saved in the day of the Lord" (1 Cor 5:4-5). There is a more positive reflection of the Christian worship assembly as an occasion for powerful Spirit-phenomena in 1 Cor 14:24-25, where Paul envisions a scene in which an "outsider or unbeliever" enters and, through the effects of prophetic oracles that reveal his/her inner thoughts, bows down and declares, "God is really among you."

4. Eschatology

The NT evidence also indicates that Christian worship should be seen as predicated upon and anticipating eschatological redemption. Jesus' resurrection is the initial stage of the resurrection of all the redeemed and inaugurates his heavenly reign that is to culminate in the subjection of all things to him and to God (1 Cor 15:20-28). Christians now live in the eschatologically charged period between Jesus' resurrection and his parousia (παρουσία), having been given life in the Spirit but awaiting the consummation of redemption, which is to include a full bodily transformation (e.g., Rom 8:9-11, 23-25; Phil 3:20-21; 1 John 3:2-3).

Consequently, in this situation Christian worship includes the declaration and prefiguring of these eschatological hopes. One of its principal distinguishing marks, the acclamation of Jesus as the one Lord, alluded to in several texts (e.g., Rom 10:9-13; 1 Cor 1:2; 12:3), is an emphatic anticipation of the future universal acclamation of Jesus that has been ordained by God (Phil 2:9-11). Likewise, the inclusion of various kinds of people in the ekklēsia and its corporate worship (e.g., male/female, Jew/Gentile, slave/free, Gal 3:28), i.e., the very social composition and character of worship, is to be seen as reflecting the new humanity that is to be formed through the gospel and fashioned after the risen Christ, transcending the divisions as well as the mortality and moral frailty of humankind in Adam (e.g., Rom 8:12-21; 1 Cor 15:45-58).

Together with the collective experiences of God's Spirit, especially in prophecy and other such phenomena, this strong eschatological tone both reflects and seems intended to promote an atmosphere of worship marked by joy (e.g., Rom 14:17; 15:13) and confidence in God's present and future intentions. The NT texts suggest that, though insignificant in size and outward and immediate social impact, each little ekklēsia is to see itself in its life and worship as a witness to and vanguards of final redemption. As David Aune (1972) showed, in early Christianity (as also in the Qumran community) it is especially in collective worship that heavenly and eschatological realities seem to have been more vividly in focus and experienced, and the worship setting is seen as taking on a vertical dimension for participants. This outlook that earthly corporate worship is somehow connected with heavenly realities is likely reflected in Paul's frustratingly fleeting reference to the presence of angels in the worship setting of the ekklēsia (1 Cor 11:10; see also Heb 12:22-24).

5. Content and focus

The content and focus of worship in the NT are God's actions, especially God's redemptive actions in and through Jesus. As a key illustration of this, the NT passages that have been identified by scholars as hymns/odes and confessional formulas concentrate heavily on celebrating the actions of God and/or Jesus. For example, Phil 2:6-11 declares Jesus' self-humbling, sacrificial obedience, and consequent exaltation to unique glory, and Col 1:5-20 heralds his divine status and unique agency in creation and redemption. Likewise, in Rom 10:9-13 where we apparently have a reference to a practice of corporate confession of faith, the focus is on Jesus' resurrection and its redemptive consequences for believers.

Another passage widely regarded as preserving an early confessional form (Rom 4:24-25) recounts Jesus' redemptive death and resurrection, and declares them as also acts of God. As yet a further illustration, the content of the heavenly worship portrayed in Rev 4–5 consists in praising God as almighty (4:8) and creator of all (4:11), and in praise to Jesus for his self-sacrifice and its marvelous redemptive consequences (5:9-12). It is certain that for the author this scene of heavenly worship is to inform and shape worship in the earthly churches to which he directs his text.

In 1 Cor 11:23-26, Paul makes the shared ecclesial meal a recurring reference to Jesus' redemptive death, and an anticipation of his future appearance. By contrast, the eucharistic prayers in *Did.* 9–10 make no explicit reference to Jesus' death and resurrection; nevertheless they express thanks for God for life, spiritual knowledge, and other blessings given through Jesus, reflecting thereby the sort of focus that we find typical in the NT and other texts of what became mainstream Christian tradition.

In addition to praise and thanksgiving for creation and redemption, we have references to "teaching," "prophecy," and other phenomena (including petitionary prayer) that appear to be set in the context of corporate worship (e.g., the list of "gifts" in 1 Cor 12:4-11), and it is likely that these had a certain breadth of content and emphases (see §E). Nevertheless, it is clear that the NT presents worship as fundamentally a proper response to God's creative and redemptive actions. That is, in this view worship is a grateful reaction to God's prior acts, the declaration and celebration of them the core content and aim in worship. But perhaps the most obvious demonstration that early Christian worship was intended as a response to God's actions is the choice of the "first day of the week" as the key day for gathered worship, Sunday worship thus a continuing commemoration of the day of Jesus' resurrection.

D. "Binitarian Shape"

As noted earlier, the key distinguishing characteristic of the nature of Christian worship in the NT is that it is directed to Jesus as well as God (the Father). Indeed, such is the place of Jesus in early Christian devotion that Paul can refer to Christians simply as "all those who in every place call on the name of our Lord Jesus Christ" (1 Cor 1:2), "to call upon" (epikaleō ἐπικαλέω) used in the LXX to indicate worship of God (e.g., 1 Sam 12:18), and strikingly appropriated here and elsewhere in the NT to designate the ritual invocation of Jesus (e.g., Acts 9:14; 22:16).

1. Worship of Jesus

In a number of other ways as well, the NT attests a remarkable programmatic incorporation of Jesus with God as recipients of Christian devotion, amounting to what may be termed a "binitarian" devotional pattern (Hurtado 1988). The identifiable hymns/odes in the NT are essentially concerned with Jesus, and these seem to have been both central and characteristic in early Christian worship (§E.4 below). As a particularly vivid illustration that likely reflects the devotional practice favored by the Jewish Christian author and his fellow believers in Asia, note again the scene of heavenly

(ideal) worship in Rev 5:9-14, which includes praise given to Jesus ("the Lamb") and culminates in a universal joint acclamation of God ("seated on the throne") and Jesus (5:13-14). In John 16:23-24 believers are told to pray to God in Jesus' name, a practice that appears to have been established long before John was written. Indeed, in 1 Thess 3:11-13, we have what appears to be a prayer of Paul addressed jointly to God and Jesus.

Paul's references to the Christian sacred meal as "the Lord's supper" (1 Cor 11:20), "the cup of the Lord," and "table of the Lord" (1 Cor 10:21; 11:27) clearly indicate the focus on Jesus in this central feature of early Christian corporate worship (§E.8). We may also note that in the NT, Christian baptism seems to involve the ritual invocation of Jesus' name over (or by) the candidate (e.g., Acts 2:38; 22:16).

Indeed, in the NT the inclusion of Jesus as a rightful recipient of Christian worship is presented not only as characteristic in Christian churches but even as mandatory. John 5:23 seems to reflect this stance, insisting that it is God's will that all should "honor the Son just as they honor the Father," and that "anyone who does not honor the Son does not honor the Father who sent him." Clearly the distinctive inclusion of Jesus with God as the content and recipients of worship urged and reflected in the NT was not an experiment or an unconscious appropriation of pagan reverence of deified kings or heroes (apotheosis). Instead, it was intended as an obedient response to what early Christians perceived to be the will of God, and a failure to reverence Jesus in worship would be disobedience to God.

Moreover, the NT advocacy of reverence for Jesus does not reflect any diminution of the place of God (the Father) in Christian devotion. Jesus is not worshiped at the expense of God, so to speak, and certainly does not replace God or become the new de facto Christian God in some simplistic manner (as, however, does appear to have happened in some forms of popular Christian piety reflected in some apocryphal texts and in some forms of popular Christianity down to the present time). The NT reflects a firm allegiance to the exclusive worship of the one God, a powerful scruple obviously inherited from the Jewish matrix of the Christian movement (e.g., Mark 12:28-31; Rom 1:18-32; Rev 19:10). This is another reason to doubt that reverence for Jesus reflected the pagan outlook of the time in which new deities could be added to the pantheon. Unlike pagan practice with the various deities and divinized humans, in the NT Jesus does not get his own rituals or shrine or his own times to receive worship. Instead, in the NT, worship of God (the Father) is to be offered through Jesus and is to include Jesus as both subject/occasion and corecipient, for he is the "image" (eikōn εἰκών) of God and the one who shares in God's glory and has been installed by God as the unique ruling "Son" to whom such reverence is now due.

In other words, in the NT we do not simply have two divine recipients of devotion, but rather a linked or "shaped" duality, so to speak, in which Jesus' place in worship is consistently defined with reference to God. The reverence and devotion directed to Jesus is presented as according to God's will and intended "to the glory of God the Father" (Phil 2:11). The NT does not reflect a simple "di-theism" of two divine beings, but instead what we might term a "binitarian" stance in theology and worship, in which Jesus' exalted position and place in Christian devotion are both defined and justified with reference to actions and will of the one God, and God is defined with reference to Jesus. So, Paul refers to the deity to whom prayer and praise is directed as "the God and Father of our Lord Jesus Christ" (Rom 15:6; 2 Cor 1:3; 11:31; and Eph 1:3). In short, in NT perspective, Jesus can be given worship only with reference to the one God (e.g., as God's "image" and unique "Son"), and God can be identified and worshiped adequately only as the Father who sent forth Jesus and ordains that he be now reverenced. In this distinctive devotional pattern we nevertheless see the continuing strong influence of ancient Jewish emphasis on "one God."

However, this "binitarian" devotional pattern represents a remarkable and apparently novel development, which had no real precedent or analogy in the Roman religious environment, either in pagan or in Jewish worship practices (see Hurtado 2000). It represents neither the addition of a second god by apotheosis (as in pagan practice) nor the sort of honorific rhetoric given to angels, patriarchs, or royal and messianic figures (as in Jewish texts). Moreover, the worship of Jesus is not only the most distinguishing feature of early Christianity; it is also probably the most notable development characterizing the circles of Jesus' followers in the post-Easter period. Although the NT bears witness to a broadly shared triadic-shaped religious outlook in which God, Jesus, and the Holy Spirit all feature (this triad obviously forming a basis of the later doctrine of the Trinity), the Spirit never is referred to in the NT as a recipient of worship in the ways that God and Jesus are. So, the religious rhetoric of the NT is triadic, but in the pattern of devotion there is a duality, a "binitarian" pattern.

2. Forces and factors

Such a notable and unparalleled historical development presents a problem for historical explanation. It is understandable that some scholars prefer to reduce the problem, either by downplaying the evidence (proposing that the reverence for Jesus reflected in earliest NT texts did not really amount to worship of him, e.g., Casey), or by contending that the Jesus-devotion in the NT is only a particularly intense example of the sorts of reverence that were given in ancient Jewish tradition to martyrs and royal/messianic figures (e.g., Horbury). Still others contend that though early Christians were opposed to the idea of deified kings and heroes, early Christians nevertheless were influenced by pagan notions of apotheosis (e.g., Collins). But all such arguments are subject to criticism for not really doing justice to all the evidence, and/or for invoking putative explanations that themselves require explanation. For example, how would early Jewish Christians of the first few years (among whom this intense Jesus-devotion first appeared) supposedly appropriate ideas of royal-apotheosis and emperor-reverence that devout Jews typically regarded as foolish blasphemy?

Thus, the worship of Jesus reflected in the NT is not so easily brushed aside as is thought by some scholars, and historical analysis requires an effort to account for it. Several factors can be invoked. Jesus' own impact upon his contemporaries (both followers and opponents) is surely an obvious reason that he remained central in the religious outlook of his followers. Furthermore, shortly after his execution followers became convinced that God had raised him from death and exalted him to heavenly glory, and this conviction revalidated him and further assured Jesus' continuing centrality for them. It is also likely that Jewish traditions about God having a principal agent (e.g., a high angel or revered patriarch) provided early believers a basic conceptual category for accommodating Jesus as uniquely exalted "at God's right hand."

But this Jewish principal-agent category did not allow for the figure to receive worship, and so the extent and intensity of early Christian Jesus-devotion requires some further factor(s). A comparison of other major religious innovations in history indicates that they frequently arose from powerful religious experiences that generated a significant reconfiguring of the beliefs and/or practices of recipients (see Hurtado 2005). There is good evidence that earliest Christianity was characterized by such phenomena (e.g., visions of the risen/glorified Jesus, and heavenly scenes that include the exalted Jesus) and it seems fully plausible that such experiences contributed to the novel conviction that God now ordained that Jesus should receive worship. Thereby, a new "mutation" in Jewish devotional practice appeared, generating a devotional pattern that quickly became characteristic of early Christianity and that demanded and shaped subsequent doctrinal reflection as well.

E. Major Phenomena of Early Christian Worship

We have noted earlier that we cannot find in the NT clear evidence of any regularized liturgical sequence, but we do have indication of major features and characteristic components of early Christian worship.

1. The "Lord's Day"

All four canonical Gospels set Jesus' resurrection on "the first day of the week" (Matt 28:1; Mark 16:2; Luke 24:1; John 20:1) and it is commonly accepted that at a very early point Sunday became the particularly significant day for corporate Christian worship, and Sunday worship thus a weekly commemoration of Jesus' resurrection (Rordorf). Already in the letters of Paul (ca. 50–65 CE) we have a reference to this day, suggesting that it bears a special significance (1 Cor 16:2) as is reflected also in Acts 20:7. In Rev 1:10, the phrase "the Lord's day" (kyriakē hēmera κυριακῇ ἡμέρᾳ) designates Sunday, this distinctive way of referring to the day reflecting its established status in the early Christian outlook. This way of referring to Sunday is reflected in other early Christian texts as well (e.g., *Did.* 14:1, which has the curious phrasing kyriakēn de kyriou [κυριακὴν δὲ κυρίου], "the royal day of the Lord" or "the Lord's own day").

Jewish Christians, who also identified themselves as members of the Jewish people, participated in synagogue worship on the Sabbath day, at least until after the Jewish revolt of 66–72 CE when Jewish believers came under much stronger pressure to renounce faith in Jesus or suffer expulsion from synagogues. Even thereafter, it is likely that Sabbath observance continued among many Jewish Christians. But it also seems that at a very early point both Jewish and Gentile Christian circles met particularly on Sundays as Christians. Then, as Jewish Christians progressively became a smaller portion of the Christian constituency, Sabbath observance declined, but Sunday remained central and became still more emphatically the day of gathered Christian worship (e.g., *1 Apol.* 67).

2. Invocation and confession of Jesus

We have noted that early Christians can be described simply as those who "call on the name of the Lord Jesus" (1 Cor 1:2) and that this likely refers more broadly to the worship of Jesus. But, more specifically, it probably refers to the particular liturgical practice of invoking the exalted Jesus, especially in the context of gathered Christian worship. It is not clear whether this (probably collective) ritual action functioned to inaugurate the worship service or was done at some particular point within it. In any case, this calling upon (the name of) Jesus seems to have been a characteristic and crucially distinguishing feature of earliest Christian worship, marking off and identifying believers in their devotional practice.

Moreover, there is good evidence that the practice of invoking Jesus originated in the earliest circles of believers and was certainly not unique to Greek-speaking Gentile churches such as those founded by Paul. It is now widely granted by scholars that the Aramaic expression included by Paul in 1 Cor 16:22, marana tha (μαράνα θά), derives from the liturgical practice of circles of Aramaic-speaking Jewish believers (probably in Roman Judea), and that the expression is likely best translated "O Lord, come!" It remains debated among scholars whether this appeal was for the return of Christ in eschatological glory or for his presence in the gathered worship setting. We may well have the same expression rendered in Greek in Rev 22:20, "Come, Lord Jesus!" where it clearly is used in a strongly eschatological context. But it might well be that the expression was an appeal both for Jesus' immediate presence in the worship setting and also for his eschatological return.

Whatever the case, it is very significant that the appeal functioned as a component in early worship services, further confirming the programmatic importance of Jesus in the devotional practice of 1st-cent. Christian circles. That Paul includes the expression untranslated here suggests that he expects the Corinthian church to know it, likely because it was one of the Semitic liturgical expressions that he taught his converts to use, reflecting Paul's desire to promote a strong sense of religious solidarity among them with their religious predecessors and coreligionists in Judea. The liturgical provenance of the expression is corroborated by its inclusion in the prescribed eucharist prayer in *Did.* 10:6, which also has a strong eschatological flavor and is widely assumed to derive from Jewish-Christian circles (or circles influenced by Jewish Christians).

Moreover, this liturgical appeal to the risen/glorified Jesus simply has no analogy or precedent in what we know of Jewish devotional practices of the time. This is not to be compared with the secretive appeals to angels found in some Jewish magical texts. The appeal to Jesus that we see reflected in the NT is an open, corporate, and apparently quite regular component in Christian worship, both in Jewish-Christian and Gentile-Christian circles, and represents a notable innovation.

It is also rather clear that NT worship involved a ritual (collective) "confession" (homologeōs ὁμολόγεως) of Jesus as Lord. Several NT passages are taken as indicative of this practice. The reference in Rom 10:9-13 to confessing "Jesus is Lord" (kyrios Iēsous κύριος Ἰησοῦς) is one such, and the same confessional formula appears in another passage likewise reflecting a liturgical setting, 1 Cor 12:3. The acclamation in Phil 2:11, kyrios Iēsous Christos (κύριος Ἰησοῦς Χριστὸς), is simply a slightly extended form of the same confession, which in all these cases emphasizes Jesus' divinely exalted status as the "Lord" of the gathered ekklēsia, and, indeed, of the whole creation.

3. Prayers

We can be certain that prayers formed part of early Christian worship, but it is far less certain exactly what these prayers comprised. Given the lack of trans-local ecclesiastical structures, it is likely that prayer practice varied from one location to another. There are indications, however, that forms of the "Lord's Prayer" were used in some (perhaps many) Christian circles by the late 1st cent. and perhaps even earlier. This custom probably lies behind the inclusion of the varying forms of the prayer in Matthew (6:9-13) and Luke (11:2-4), and a form nearly identical to the Matthean prayer also in *Did.* 8:2, although there it is prescribed for usage three times daily, which suggests a setting in personal/private prayer rather than corporate worship. But this does not mean that the prayer was used purely in private settings.

It is worth noting also that in letters sent to some of his own churches (Galatians) and also to Rome, a church that he did not establish, Paul refers to believers being prompted by the Holy Spirit to address God as "Abba! Father!" (Gal 4:6; Rom 8:15-16). It is not absolutely clear whether he alludes to individual or corporate actions, but we should probably not exclude either setting. If, as is sometimes suggested, Paul here reflects the use of the Lord's Prayer, that would take the practice back at least to the first few decades, and these two references would also reflect an impressively wide trans-local prayer practice in Christian groups.

In 2 Cor 9:11-14, Paul envisions the delivery of the collection for Jerusalem from his churches producing thanksgiving and prayers for them from the Judean recipients. This may reflect more generally the practice of prayers of thanksgiving and intercession in corporate worship. It is not certain, but entirely likely, that Paul's exhortations for "prayer and supplication with thanksgiving" in Phil 4:6 may apply to prayer in the congregational setting. This is still more likely in the case of the exhortation in 1 Tim 2:1-2, which includes the direction that prayers be offered for "kings and all who are in high positions." In sum, we can conclude that corporate prayers of thanksgiving and intercession were typical features of worship.

The prayers reflected in the NT are generally directed to God (the Father), especially, it appears, those offered in corporate worship; but this seems also true for private prayers. For example, Paul's descriptions of his own prayers of petition and thanksgiving for the various churches to whom he wrote portray them as directed to God (e.g., Rom 1:8; 1 Cor 1:4; 2 Cor 1:3-4; Phil 1:3; 1 Thess 1:2-3). Indeed, in the NT and other early Christian texts representative of emergent "proto-orthodox" Christianity in the first few centuries, liturgical prayers are overwhelmingly addressed to God. It is interesting that in Christian apocryphal texts, however, we find a much higher percentage of prayers directed to Jesus, perhaps reflecting the more populist ethos of some of these texts, or simply one expression of their divergence from the emerging mainstream Christian tradition.

Yet liturgical prayer in the NT is typically marked by the place of Jesus in early Christian faith. So, prayers and thanksgiving are offered to God "through Jesus Christ" (Rom 1:8), or "because of the grace of God that has been given you in Christ Jesus" (1 Cor 1:4-5), or God is identified as "the God and Father of our Lord Jesus Christ" (e.g., 2 Cor 1:3). As another expression of this, John 16:24-27 encourages believers to ask/pray to God in Jesus' name, which may have involved the actual invoking of his name in prayers, but likely also reflects a view of believers as having a standing before God "the Father" because of their belief in "the Son." Jesus' salvific work involved the redemption of believers so that they can be "a kingdom, priests serving his God and Father" (Rev 1:5-6), and so the prayers of the redeemed in the NT typically reflect this orientation. The lengthy and elegantly written prayer in *1 Clem.*

59–61 (ca. 95 CE) is a notable example of this "binitarian" shape of early Christian liturgical prayer practice, the petitions and the praise directed to God through and because of Jesus (especially 59:2; 61:3).

4. Psalms and hymns

The exhortations to believers to address one another in "psalms, hymns, and spiritual songs" in Eph 5:19 and Col 3:16 reflect another feature of worship in the NT. Given the domestic setting, however, and the absence of any mention of musical instruments, we should probably think of something closer to a simple chanting, rather than more elaborate melodic compositions of modern hymnody. The "psalms" in these two references are most likely biblical psalms. We know that the psalms were favorite proof texts for earliest Christians (e.g., Pss 2; 8; 110) from the frequency of the citation and allusion to them in the NT and as reflected in the catena of citations in Heb 1:5-13. It is also noteworthy that Psalms is the single most frequently attested text in Christian manuscripts of the first three centuries. It appears that the biblical psalms were broadly seen as expressive and predictive of Jesus and so Christians chanted them as scriptural anticipations and celebrations of him. The structural features of the individual Hebrew psalms were preserved in the LXX: the balancing lines and without the typical features of Greek poetry (e.g., rhythm, meter). These features lent them to chanting (as has remained the practice in more liturgical forms of Christian worship). But, unlike modern churches, early Christian congregations did not have multiple copies of texts, and so we must imagine either that the chanting was done or led by a reader (lines then echoed by the group), or that certain psalms became sufficiently familiar that a goodly number of the congregation could chant them collectively.

It is more difficult to say confidently whether the "psalms, hymns, and spiritual songs" (hymnois kai odais pneumatikais ὕμνοις καὶ ᾠδαῖς πνευματικαῖς) in Eph 5:19 and Col 3:16 represent two distinguishable types of melodic praise or whether the two terms designate the same phenomenon. In either case, we likely are dealing with new compositions that arose within circles of believers and were prompted by what they took to be the inspiration of the Holy Spirit. The reference to spiritual hymns/odes thus designates their charismatic character. In 1 Cor 14:15 Paul refers to singing "with the spirit" (tō pneumati τῷ πνεύματι) and "with the mind" (tō noi τῷ νοΐ), which appears to designate, respectively, singing in tongues and singing in one's own language, in both cases the songs seen as prompted by the Holy Spirit; corporate worship is the implied setting. Just a few verses later (14:26), Paul includes "a hymn" among the list of Spirit-prompted contributions that he presents as characterizing the Christian assembly. These spiritual songs may often have been uttered initially in a mode somewhat akin to prophetic oracles, impromptu and experienced as inspirations from God's

Spirit. For earliest Christians, they were one of the signs of the Spirit's presence among them, manifestations of which were particularly sought and expected in corporate worship.

In those NT passages widely thought to be (or derive from) early Christian "hymns," we likely have examples of these Spirit-odes. The earliest example is usually thought to be in Phil 2:6-11, a passage that consequently has received considerable scholarly attention (see Hurtado 2005). The contents are a recitation of Jesus' actions of self-humbling and obedience to God, even to the point of crucifixion in vv. 6-8, and in vv. 9-11 God's answering actions of exaltation and the bestowal of "the name that is above every name," with the intention that Jesus should be given universal acclamation as "Lord" (kyrios) "to the glory of God the Father." If indeed the passage preserves an early Christian hymn, believers would have intended their own acclamation of Jesus as Lord in gathered worship as demonstrating their obedience to God's intention and an anticipation of the future universal obeisance portrayed in the concluding statement.

Colossians 1:15-20 is another passage widely thought to preserve an early hymn, and in these verses, again, the focus is on Jesus' significance. But here he is lauded as having primacy in/over all creation (vv. 15-17) as well as in the church and redemption (vv. 18-20). Nevertheless, his divine status is expressed with reference to God, e.g., as God's "image" (v. 15) and the one in whom "all the fullness of God was pleased to dwell" in order to effect reconciliation of all things to God (vv. 19-20).

In the scenes of heavenly worship in Revelation noted earlier, the prophet John includes hymnic praise directed to God (Rev 4:11), to Jesus (5:9-12), and to them jointly (5:13-14). At other points John recounts praise that appears to be expressed in poetic/hymnic mode (e.g., 19:1-8). We have noted that these texts may reflect the sorts of enthusiastic praise with which John was familiar in the churches of Asia, and that he also intended the heavenly praise to inspire and shape the worship of these churches.

Martin Hengel has drawn attention to the probable importance of early spiritual songs as perhaps the crucial mode in which earliest christological claims about Jesus' messiahship and heavenly exaltation were developed further. In the setting of gathered worship, and in an atmosphere of profound religious devotion and intense feelings of the presence of God's Spirit, we can imagine that such Spirit-odes were voiced and then taken up by the group as part of their worship. If it is correct that a few of these songs are preserved in passages in the NT, this may indicate that some of them became used repeatedly and perhaps were shared trans-locally among churches. In any case, the singing/chanting of hymns/odes of praise, particularly reciting the acts of God in Jesus, appears quickly to have become a regular feature of Christian worship.

5. Prophecy and related phenomena

These Spirit-odes can also be thought of as one form of the prophetic-like phenomena that are linked with Christian worship in the NT. Various NT texts indicate that prophecies and prophets were common features in various early Christian circles (see Aune 1983) and they are typically set in the context of the gathered ekklēsia. We can note again Paul's references to prophecy in his extended treatment of various issues that arose in the Corinthian church in connection with corporate worship in 1 Cor 11–14. Prophecy is certainly referred to there as one of the Spirit's gifts (12:4-11), as one that can be exercised by women as well as men (11:4-5; and also Acts 21:9), and a gift that is particularly preferable to tongues-speaking in corporate worship because it can readily be understood by, and so edify, fellow believers present (1 Cor 14:4-12). It is important to note that Paul's purely pragmatic and functional preference of prophecy over tongues-speaking in this passage is based entirely on the importance of mutual edification as the controlling principle of corporate Christian worship. It is his extended example of making agapē (ἀγάπη, lyrically portrayed in 1 Cor 13) the "more excellent way" to regard the various charismata.

We note, also, his further instructions in 1 Cor 14:29-33 that prophecies should be limited to two or three, that "others" (others with prophetic gifts?) should assess what is said (v. 29), and that prophets should defer to one another (v. 30-31), the aim being "that all may learn and all be encouraged" (v. 31). Paul insists, thus, that charismatic phenomena in gathered worship should not involve chaotic excitement but that the Spirit's manifestations, which those gifted are responsible to exercise in an orderly manner, are to be deployed with a view to promoting "peace" in the ekklēsia (vv. 32-33).

In 1 Thess 5:19-22, Paul's exhortations "Do not quench the Spirit. Do not despise the words of prophets, but test everything ..." may address concerns in the Thessalonian church about certain prophetic oracles that generated anxieties such as those that Paul deals with earlier in this letter (e.g., the fate of deceased believers, 4:13-18, and the timing of Jesus' return in glory, 5:1-11). Paul urges against any reactionary prohibition of Spirit-charisms such as prophecy, but also advises that all manifestations be tested (dokimazō δοκιμάζω), with a view to holding on to "the good" (kalon καλόν) (vv. 19-21).

In several NT texts we have depictions of or allusions to the exercise of prophecy in gathered worship. In addition to the scene in Acts 13:1-3, noted already, where a prophetic oracle in the context of worship orders Paul and Barnabas to be set apart for a divine mission, in other passages of Acts we have references to oracles ascribed to a prophet named Agabus (11:27-30; 21:10-11). In all these cases, the oracles are directions and/or warnings with quite specific contents and intended force. This also seems to be reflected in the oracles that the seer John is told to communicate via letters to the seven churches addressed in Rev 2–3. In each case, the individual church is given specific commendations and/or warnings, and it seems certain that each oracle was to be delivered (in this case, read out) in the setting of the gathered church.

It is not entirely clear whether some of the other charismata listed in 1 Cor 12:4-11, specifically "the utterance of wisdom" and "the utterance of knowledge" (v. 8), are to be understood as fully distinguishable phenomena or as varying expressions of prophecy. In any case, it appears that in gathered worship, believers might convey what were presented as revelations given by the Spirit that perhaps composed guidance or other information.

6. Teaching

Likewise, it is not entirely clear how to take Paul's reference to "a teaching" (didachē [διδαχή]; 1 Cor 14:26; NRSV, "a lesson") as one of the phenomena of corporate worship, and whether it too was seen as a prophecy-like utterance, i.e., inspired by the Spirit, and perhaps impromptu. In Eph 4:11, we have "pastor-teachers" (author's trans.; tous de poimenas kai didaskalous [τοὺς δὲ ποιμένας καὶ διδασκάλους]) listed among the gifts of the exalted Christ to his churches, along with apostles, prophets, and evangelists. In this particular text, it appears that teaching and prophecy are distinguished.

Moreover, in other NT texts, teaching is presented, not so much as a charism, but more as a responsibility for which people with the right abilities are to be chosen. For example, an aptitude for teaching is one of the essential attributes of those who aspire to be an episkopos (ἐπίσκοπος) in 1 Tim 3:2 and Titus 1:9, and in 2 Tim 2:2 the author urges that reliable individuals be chosen who can teach others faithfully in accordance with the tradition. Such individuals are probably "the elders who rule well" and "labor in preaching and teaching" (1 Tim 5:17), and are thereby "worthy of double honor" (which probably means some financial remuneration; compare the reference to individuals teaching wrong doctrine "for base gain" in Titus 1:11 [NRSV, "sordid gain"], and the exhortation to "elders" to perform their roles freely and not for "shameful gain" in 1 Pet 5:2 [NRSV, "sordid gain"]).

So it appears that teaching is presented in the NT as one feature of gathered worship, and that, although the individuals who faithfully perform the tasks of tending and teaching can be regarded as Christ's gifts to churches, the activity of teaching was probably distinguished from charisms such as prophecy. The thrust of NT references to teaching is that it should exhibit faithfulness to the gospel and the traditions, which are often ascribed to apostolic figures.

7. Readings

By the 1st cent. CE, readings from the Torah and the Prophets seem to have been a regular part of Sabbath synagogue gatherings (as reflected, e.g., in synagogue scenes in Luke 4:16-20; Acts 13:15, 27; 15:21), and readings of OT and also Christian writings seem to have also become a part of Christian worship at a very early point. By the mid-2nd cent. CE, Justin (1 Apol. 67) includes readings from "the memoirs of the apostles or the writings of the prophets" as a regular feature of the worship gatherings of believers, followed then by instructions and exhortations from "the president" of the gathering. However, we have earlier reflections of the reading of texts as a part of Christian worship.

First Timothy 4:13 urges maintenance of the practice of public reading (anagnōsis ἀνάγνωσις) in worship, along with exhortation and teaching, and it is usually thought that the readings in view here were OT Scriptures. A number of other NT texts refer to the reading of Christian texts as well in the gathered ekklēsia. In the earliest of these references, 1 Thess 5:27, Paul orders that his letter be read out to all gathered, and, indeed, it is commonly accepted that all his letters (at least those whose authorship is not contested by scholars) were intended to be read in a gathering of the particular church addressed. This seems to be reflected in his references to the intended and unintended responses of churches to his letters (e.g., 1 Cor 5:9-13; 2 Cor 1:13; 10:9-10). In Col 4:16 we have a reference to a further developing practice of copying and sharing Paul's letters among churches. Whatever its authorship, Colossians is certainly evidence that this practice was underway at some point in the 1st cent. Indeed, 2 Pet 3:15-16 seems to reflect a collection of Pauline letters, and, strikingly, also refers to the use of Pauline letters as Scripture (v. 16). Whatever the authorship and date of 2 Peter (e.g., ca. 70–120 CE), it is an important early witness to an authoritative role of Pauline epistles in Christian circles, a Pauline letter collection being the likely embryo of the subsequent NT canon.

The fleeting exhortation in Mark 13:14, "let the reader (ho anaginōskōn ὁ ἀναγινώσκων) understand," is probably also to be taken as reflecting an intended reading of the Gospel of Mark publicly among gathered believers. This would suggest also that the other Evangelists primarily intended their accounts of Jesus to be read out in corporate worship. Thus, Justin's reference to the liturgical reading of the apostolic "memoirs … which are called Gospels" (1 Apol. 66) would reflect only the later regularization of a practice that had its beginnings at least several decades earlier than when he wrote.

Indeed, at least in the first two centuries CE, the reading of texts in corporate worship is probably the clearest indication of those texts functioning as Scripture. This means that corporate Christian worship is one of the factors to be taken into account in understanding the historical process that led to texts forming a Christian canon.

8. The sacred meal

A shared meal formed a key part of numerous religious occasions and gatherings in Roman antiquity (Smith). This is reflected in Paul's response to questions about Christian participation in the meals that formed part of what he terms "the worship of idols" (eidōlolatria εἰδωλολατρία) in 1 Cor 10:14-22. Here, Paul makes a direct comparison/contrast between meals held in the name of this or that deity and the church meal as "a participation (koinōnia [κοινωνία]; NRSV, "sharing") in the blood/body of Christ" (v. 16), and as "the cup/table of the Lord" (v. 21). The "Lord" in these statements is obviously the exalted Jesus. Given the typical place of a shared meal in religious gatherings in that time, it is not unusual at all for a meal to figure centrally also in Christian gatherings, and probably from the earliest years. There may well be additional influences, but the early Christian sacred meal also reflects the wider cultural environment of the time.

From these church meals derived the later forms of eucharist familiar in Christian traditions. But the NT rather consistently refers to a full meal, and the domestic setting typical of earliest Christian corporate worship obviously facilitated this sort of event. For example, Acts refers to the Jerusalem church's "breaking of bread" in their homes (2:42, 46), probably meaning a practice of group meals held as part of Christian gatherings, and Acts 20:7 pictures such an occasion. Moreover, the sorts of behavior that Paul criticizes in 1 Cor 11:17-34 reflect a full meal in which one can be drunk from excessive wine or left hungry by other inconsiderate participants (vv. 21-22, 33). Similarly, the stern condemnation of certain people as "blemishes (spilades σπιλάδες) on your love-feasts (agapais ἀγάπαις)" in Jude 12 reflects shared meals in Christian assemblies.

The different terms used in the NT to designate Christian sacred meals—"Lord's supper" (1 Cor 11:20), "love-feasts" (Jude 12), or simply "breaking of bread" (Acts 2:46)—suggest various meanings or emphases ascribed to the meals. An earlier scholarly view that there were two distinct types of meals, an original "breaking of bread" (focusing more on believers' solidarity and eschatological expectations), succeeded by a more recognizably eucharistic meal (focusing more on Jesus' redemptive death and resurrection), however, is now rightly viewed as an oversimplification. Instead, we should probably allow for varying emphases exhibited in different Christian circles synchronically and from the earliest moments of the Christian movement. Moreover, although interpretation and emphases may well have varied from one circle to another, it is also likely that in any given circle multiple meanings were associated with the Christian sacred meal. Note for example, Did. 14:1-3, which directs Christians gathered on "the Lord's own day" to "break bread and give thanks (eucharisteō εὐχαριστέω)," and goes on to refer to the same meal as a shared sacrifice-meal (thysia θυσία).

As another illustration, Paul's statement that in the church-meal believers "proclaim the Lord's death until he comes" (1 Cor 11:26) rather clearly links an emphasis on Jesus' death with an equally strong eschatological orientation and emphasis. This combination of emphases on Jesus' redemptive work and on eschatological expectation is reflected also in the Gospels' accounts of the Last Supper, which are commonly understood by scholars as intended to be read as prefiguring and authorizing the Christian sacred meals of the original readers (Matt 26:26-29; Mark 14:22-25; Luke 22:14-20).

However, an explicit reference to Jesus' redemptive death seems not always a feature of Christian sacred meals, as is demonstrated especially in the eucharistic prayers in Did. 9–10. This extra-canonical text is widely regarded as preserving liturgical material from a very early time, quite possibly from Jewish-Christian circles, or at least from Christian circles with a strong Jewish-Christian influence. The prayers' roots in very early tradition are reflected in the reference to Jesus as God's "servant" (pais παῖς), a Davidic-messianic title (e.g., Acts 4:25; Did. 9:2) applied elsewhere to Jesus only in several early prayers (Acts 3:13; 4:27; 1 Clem. 59:2-3), all of which likely derive from Jewish-Christian practice. The eucharistic prayers in Didache give thanks to God for Jesus as the unique agent of messianic fulfillment (9:2), and for the life, knowledge (of God), faith, and immortality bestowed through him (9:3; 10:2-3), and they look forward to the eschatological consummation of God's purposes (9:4; 10:5-6), but make no direct reference to his death.

Although Jesus' redemptive death and resurrection are not directly mentioned in these prayers in Didache, he is obviously central, the focus and continuing basis of the thanksgiving given to God. Moreover, there is no reason to read into these prayers some supposed reluctance to see Jesus' death as redemptive or to posit some radically different form of Christianity from which the prayers derive. For there are numerous other indications that Didache has historical connections with the beliefs and practices reflected also in the texts that became part of the NT (e.g., the regular use of the "Lord's prayer," Did. 8). Moreover, the explicit references to Jesus' death, and the familiar "words of institution" setting the bread and cup within the context of Jesus' last supper, when they were used in 1st-cent. circles, may have formed part of an introduction to the eucharist-meal and not part of the prayers recited as part of the eucharist.

In sum, the Christian sacred meals reflected in the NT and other very early Christian texts likely were varied in what was done and in what they meant for participants. But in all cases, Jesus was the central figure for whom and with whom thanks were offered to God, and the meal itself was a central feature of Christian corporate worship across various circles of the Christian movement. Further, as a group-meal, there was an emphasis on the solidarity of those who partook; it was a corporate action and not that of individuals in some private act of devotion. Finally, the meal seems typically to have been interpreted as an anticipation of eschatological redemption, which could be portrayed as a great banquet (e.g., Rev 19:9).

9. Other liturgical formulas

In addition to the invocation and ritual confession of Jesus, we have indication of other formulas used in worship in the NT. The numerous occurrences of "Amen" in the NT likely reflect its usage in Christian corporate worship (especially 1 Cor 14:16; 2 Cor 1:20; compare Rom 1:25; 9:5; 15:33; Gal 1:5; 6:18). Likewise, Paul's characteristic use of "Grace to you and peace" as a salutation in his letters (e.g., 1 Thess 1:1; and with variations as in Phil 1:2), and his use of "grace-benedictions" to conclude them (e.g., Gal 6:18; Phil 4:23; 1 Thess 5:28), are commonly seen by scholars as Paul's adaptation of formulas that have their provenance in the worship setting. His appropriation of these formulas, apparently intended to fit out his letters for reading in worship, provides us with allusions to their usage.

F. Conclusion

As illustrated in this discussion, several extra-canonical texts give valuable further evidence about early Christian worship and its initial developments. Among these, *Didache* preserves our earliest set of directions for baptism and eucharist, and Justin (especially *1 Apol.*) gives the earliest description of a basic order of worship. As is the case in dealing with NT texts, we should not presume a trans-local uniformity of worship practice or a unilinear development. Also, we cannot claim direct derivation of any liturgical order from worship practices reflected in the NT or these other early texts. Indeed, it is difficult to find evidence of any clear order of worship in any references to worship in the NT. But we do have indications of the sorts of actions that formed typical parts of Christian worship in 1st-cent. circles, and of what these actions likely meant. Moreover, we can sense something of the atmosphere of worship: the intimacy and sense of being personally known to the other participants facilitated by the typical domestic setting, the experience of Spirit-phenomena such as prophecy, and a sense of being participants in actions of transcendent and eschatological significance in which heavenly realities were reflected and ultimate ones were prefigured. Also, as we have noted, whatever the variations, collective worship seems always to have had Jesus as the explicit focus and occasion. Believers worshiped God in response to God's great acts of revelation and redemption in Jesus. *See* AGAPE; BAPTISM; BURIAL; CONFIRMATION; EXCOMMUNICATION; FAST, FASTING; GIFTS OF HEALING; HYMNS, NT; LAYING ON OF HANDS; LITURGY; LORD'S PRAYER; LORD'S SUPPER; MARRIAGE, NT; MINISTRY, CHRISTIAN; MUSIC; ORDINATION, ORDAIN; PASSOVER AND FEAST OF UNLEAVENED BREAD; PREACHING; VOW.

Bibliography: David E. Aune. *The Cultic Setting of Realized Eschatology in Early Christianity* (1972); David E. Aune. *Prophecy in Early Christianity and the Ancient Mediterranean World* (1983); David L. Balch. "Rich Pompeiian Houses, Shops for Rent, and the Huge Apartment Building in Herculaneum as Typical Spaces for Pauline House Churches." *JSNT* 27 (2004) 27–46; Richard J. Bauckham. "The Worship of Jesus." *The Climax of Prophecy: Studies on the Book of Revelation* (1993) 118–49; Paul F. Bradshaw. *Eucharistic Origins* (2004); Paul F. Bradshaw. *The Search for the Origins of Christian Worship: Sources and Methods for the Study of the Early Liturgy.* 2nd ed. (2002); P. M. Casey. "Monotheism, Worship and Christological Developments in the Pauline Churches." *The Jewish Roots of Christological Monotheism: Papers from the St. Andrews Conference on the Historical Origins of the Worship of Jesus.* Carey C. Newman, James R. Davila, and Gladys S. Lewis, eds. (1999) 214–33; Adela Yarbro Collins. "The Worship of Jesus and the Imperial Cult." *The Jewish Roots of Christological Monotheism: Papers from the St. Andrews Conference on the Historical Origins of the Worship of Jesus.* Carey C. Newman, James R. Davila, and Gladys S. Lewis, eds. (1999) 234–57; Oscar Cullmann. *Early Christian Worship* (1953); Ferdinand Hahn. *The Worship of the Early Church* (1973); Martin Hengel. "The Song about Christ in Earliest Worship." *Studies in Early Christology* (1995) 227–91; William Horbury. *Jewish Messianism and the Cult of Christ* (1998); Larry W. Hurtado. *At the Origins of Christian Worship: The Context and Character of Earliest Christian Devotion* (2000); Larry W. Hurtado. *How on Earth Did Jesus Become a God? Historical Questions about Earliest Devotion to Jesus* (2005); Larry W. Hurtado. *Lord Jesus Christ: Devotion to Jesus in Earliest Christianity* (2003); Larry W. Hurtado. *One God, One Lord: Early Christian Devotion and Ancient Jewish Monotheism* (1988); Joseph Jungmann. *The Place of Christ in Liturgical Prayer.* 2nd rev. ed. A. Peeler, trans. (1965); Ralph P. Martin. *Worship in the Early Church* (1974); Charles F. D. Moule. *Worship in the New Testament* (1978); Hughes Oliphant Old. "The Psalms of Praise in the Worship of the New Testament Church." *Int* 39 (1985) 20–33; Carolyn Osiek, Margaret Y. MacDonald, and Janet H. Tulloch. *A Woman's Place: House Churches in Earliest Christianity* (2005); Willy Rordorf. *Sunday* (1968); Dennis E. Smith. *From Symposium to Eucharist: The Banquet in the Early Christian World* (2003); L. Michael White. *Building God's House in the Roman World* (1990).

LARRY W. HURTADO

WORSHIP, OT. Worship may be defined as devotion, praise, and adoration offered to a deity or deities, evoked by a sense of numinous transcendence. It reflects the desire to be in a healthy, positive relationship with divine power and to share in the benefits such a relationship can offer. Worship may be understood as one aspect of the broader category of ritual, a culturally defined system of words and symbolic acts. Worship is ritual that expresses and negotiates constructive relationships with transcendent powers conceived of as personalized and sentient (such as gods or ancestors). Thus, this discussion excludes rituals such as ablutions, anointing, initiations, and rites of passage, as well as apotropaic rites and exorcisms.

A. Terminology and Settings
B. Sacrifice
   1. Types of sacrifice
   2. Procedures for sacrifice
   3. The meaning of sacrifice
      a. Food
      b. Gift
      c. Social balance
      d. Table fellowship
      e. Socioeconomic benefits
      f. Numinous power
      g. Blood
      h. Drama
      i. Purification and atonement
C. Festivals
   1. Passover
   2. Weeks
   3. Booths
   4. Other observances
D. Other Worship Practices
   1. Prayer
   2. Music
   3. Pilgrimage
E. Exclusion and Inclusion
F. Unorthodox Worship
G. The Cult of the Dead
H. Synagogue
I. Theologies of Worship
Bibliography

A. Terminology and Settings

The most common words for worship are "to serve" ('avadh עָבַד) and "to bow down" (shakhah [שָׁחָה], although most scholars now consider the root to be khawah [חָוָה]). Outside the framework of religion, slaves or political vassals "serve" social superiors. Thus, this word emphasizes what is done on behalf of a deity in ritual action, such as the offering of gifts or sacrifices (e.g., Isa 19:21). Especially in Deuteronomy and in the DtrH, "to serve" is frequently used more generally to indicate religious loyalty expressed through worship. "To bow down" to high-status humans is a sign of respect or submission. Used in the context of prayer or sacrifice, the verb describes the physical gesture of prostration. However, because the gesture reflects an inner attitude,

"to bow down" also signifies worship in a broader sense. It is also sometimes appropriate to translate the verb "to fear" (yare' יָרֵא) as "to worship" in the sense of "to pay reverence" as one element in the obedience that grows out of respectful loyalty (e.g., 2 Kgs 17:7-41).

Mountains (Exod 3:12; Josh 8:30-31), groves (Gen 13:18; Hos 4:13) or individual trees (Gen 21:33; Josh 24:26), and springs or wells (Gen 16:7; 26:24-25) were considered holy places and were customary settings for worship. The tradition of a theophany could sanction a place as an especially effective site for worship (Gen 18:1; 28:12-22; 2 Sam 24:16-25). Archaeology reveals more intimate settings for worship in the shape of domestic shrines with cult figurines (e.g., of women or horses with riders) and equipment for libations and incense offerings. Judges 17 describes a household temple (17:5, "shrine" [Heb. "house of God"]) for the use of an extended family. Worship at the family level is evidenced by Elkanah's annual sacrifice at Shiloh (1 Sam 1:3-4, 21), Hannah's weaning sacrifice for Samuel (1 Sam 1:24-28), and David's family sacrifice (1 Sam 20:6, 28-29). Some shrines apparently served individual clans, such as OPHRAH (for Abiezer; Judg 6:11, 24; 8:27) and the high place at RAMAH (1 Sam 9:12-14, 22-25; compare 8:4). Other worship sites were regional, such as the non-urban, open-air cult place known as the Bull Site discovered in the Samaria hill country. Worship sites could also be of intertribal (Mount Tabor, presumably the referent of Deut 33:18-19; compare Hos 5:1) or of national importance (Bethel, Gilgal, Mizpah, Shiloh, Jerusalem; *see* TEMPLE, JERUSALEM).

The precise nature of a shrine for sacrifice designated as a HIGH PLACE (bamah בָּמָה) is unclear. The descriptions in 1 Sam 9:11-25; 10:5 are tantalizing but provide little actual information. Influenced by some archaeological data, many scholars think in terms of an artificial platform. Verbs connected with high places ("to build," "to make," "to tear down") indicate that they involved architectural features of some sort, although the description given in Ezek 20:28-29 suggests locations of a more informal and unstructured nature. "Houses" (presumably temples) are sometimes associated with high places (1 Kgs 12:31; 13:32; 2 Kgs 23:19). The high place presided over by Samuel had a banquet hall (lishkah לִשְׁכָּה) for eating sacrifices associated with it (1 Sam 9:22). The term is sometimes used in connection with major worship sites (Gibeon, 1 Kgs 3:4; Bethel, 2 Kgs 23:15; Jerusalem, Mic 1:5), at times in a polemical sense. High places were used for the worship of both Yahweh and other gods (1 Kgs 11:7; Isa 16:12; Jer 7:31; 19:5; 48:35).

B. Sacrifice

Sacrifice was the most important component of Israelite worship. Attempts to understand sacrifice have been the focus of intense debate, and no single explanatory model has gained complete acceptance. Sacrifice involves offering something animate or inanimate in a ritual procedure to a transcendent power conceived of in personal terms in order to bring about or activate a relationship of mutuality. It entails the transformation of the entity offered (if an animal, the victim) from its usual mundane state into a more potent state appropriate for its sacrificial role; in OT terms the offering is sanctified or made holy (Lev 2:3; 6:17; 7:1). Sacrifice implies using dramatic action and perhaps words to indicate the transfer of the victim from the realm of human possession and control into the sphere of the divine. The general term in the priestly writings for such as offering is qorban (קָרְבָּן, from the verbal root meaning "to bring near"). In the OT this transfer could be achieved by turning the offering into smoke through burning (Gen 8:20-21; Lev 1:9; Ezek 20:28), "waving" or "elevating" it in a gesture of conveyance (Lev 7:30; *see* ELEVATION OFFERING; WAVE OFFERING), setting it out "before" God (Lev 24:5-6; Deut 26:4, 10), or pouring it out (Num 28:7). The altar fire served as a pipeline into the world above, vaporizing a burnt offering, the fat of a communion sacrifice, some grain, or even wine (Num 15:7, 10) up into God's domain. To use biblical language, they were converted into a "pleasing odor" for God (Gen 8:21; Lev 1:9; Ezek 20:28, 41). God could "inhale" the offering (1 Sam 26:19, literally "smell an offering" [NRSV, "accept an offering"]). Much OT sacrifice also involved eating portions of the sacrificial victim as a way of establishing shared table fellowship with God and among the participants (commensality; Gen 31:54; Deut 12:7, 18, 27; 14:22-26; 1 Sam 9:22). The slaughter of a sacrificed animal was a necessary first step in its being burned or eaten and in obtaining its blood for ritual purposes. However, death also decisively transferred the living animal out of the realm of the ordinary and mundane (compare Lev 17:11) into a state of holiness (Exod 29:34). It was slaughtered (sacrificed) "to the LORD" (Exod 13:15; 1 Sam 1:3; 2 Chr 11:16). *See* SACRIFICES AND OFFERINGS.

1. Types of sacrifice

Old Testament vocabulary distinguishes different kinds of sacrifice, although the specific procedures, significance, and purpose of each type likely changed over time and cannot be rationalized by us into a coherent system. Incidental references to sacrifice in nonpriestly texts do not always match up with the professionally oriented data presented in ritual laws. Therefore, actual historical practice and the rationalized theory of priestly specialists cannot simply be collapsed into each other. Another problem is that we have little knowledge about the explanatory words or formulas that presumably accompanied sacrificial rituals. Moreover, the viewpoints of the dominant priestly and Deuteronomic traditions were frequently at odds.

The first chapters of Leviticus set forth the conceptual order of the primary sacrificial types as the ʿolah (עֹלָה, "burnt offering," literally "ascending offering"; Lev 1), minkhah (מִנְחָה, "grain offering," literally "gift offering"; Lev 2), and zevakh (זֶבַח, literally "slaughtered offering") or zevakh shelamim (זֶבַח שְׁלָמִים, "sacrifice of well-being," "communion sacrifice," "peace offering"; Lev 3). This same sequence is found in other texts (1 Kgs 8:64; Amos 5:22). The burnt offering transferred the entire slaughtered animal to the divine realm by burning its carcass on an altar. Some of a grain offering—unprocessed grain, flour bread, or cakes—was burned and some was given over for the priests to eat. Zevakh seems to have been the generic term for an animal sacrifice that resulted in a meal eaten by the human participants after designated fatty portions were burned. The expression zevakh shelamim indicates that the purpose of certain of these "slaughter sacrifices" was to generate amity and solidarity, both among the worshipers and between the worshipers and God, as the victim was shared out in a communal meal (Lev 7:15-21; Deut 27:7). According to priestly guidelines, the potent blood from sacrificed animals (compare Lev 17:11-14) was to be treated with great care, sprinkled on or poured out around the altar, or utilized for a ritual purpose (Exod 29:20-21; Lev 4; 16; compare Deut 12:27).

Offering a TITHE, agricultural FIRST FRUITS, and firstlings of domestic animals recognized God's rights as sovereign and giver of the land. Tithes were a sort of taxation (compare the royal tithe in 1 Sam 8:15, 17), generally on agricultural products (Num 18:26-27; Deut 14:22-23), for the support of the cultic system (Num 18:21-32; Deut 14:27; Neh 10:37-38; 13:10-12). In Deuteronomy's distinctive vision, tithes were also an occasion for public celebration, and a special tithe of the third year was to be reserved for the poor (Deut 14:28-29; 26:12). The first (or the best) products of harvest were offered in thankfulness as "first fruits," notably during the Feast of Weeks (Exod 23:16; 34:22; Num 28:26; *see* WEEKS, FEAST OF). These too supported the priests and the sanctuary (Num 18:12-13; Deut 18:4; 26:1-4, 10). Any firstborn male domestic animal was to be offered as a "firstling" (Lev 27:26; Num 18:17; Deut 15:19). Linked with Israel's exemption from the death of Egypt's firstborn recounted at Passover, firstborn sons were to be redeemed by a cash payment (Exod 13:2, 12-13).

In addition to domestic animals and grain, offerings also involved incense burned on special altars and in censers (Exod 30:1; Lev 16:12), and libations of wine poured out (Exod 29:40-41; Lev 23:13; compare Ps 116:13). Loaves of the BREAD OF PRESENCE were set out periodically on a table in the sanctuary as a display offering (Exod 25:30; Lev 24:5-9; 1 Sam 21:6).

The nedher (נֶדֶר, "votive offering"), todhah (תּוֹדָה, "thanksgiving"), and nedhavah (נְדָבָה, "freewill offering") may be grouped together as appreciative responses to God's benevolence (Lev 7:12-16; 22:18-23). In contrast to the regularized tithes that were expected from all as a matter of course, these offerings were individual and situational. Their setting in life is nicely illustrated by 1 Sam 1:11, 21-28 and in the Psalms (50:14, 23; 54:6 [Heb. 54:8]; 66:13-15; 107:22; 116:12-19). A promised votive offering had to be carried out (Eccl 5:4-5 [Heb. 5:3-4]), but an unmarried woman's father or a wife's husband had the right to cancel her vow (Num 30:3-9).

In the Second Temple period, two sorts of sacrifices intended to perform expiation grew in importance, doubtless a response to the experience of defeat and exile interpreted as divine punishment for national transgression. The distinction between the khatta'th (חַטָּאת, "sin offering") and 'asham (אָשָׁם, "guilt offering") is not always clear. The sin offering (Lev 4:1–5:13) seems to have been thought to negate the negative effects of impurity resulting from sin on both the involved individual and the sanctuary (including its appurtenances). Sin offerings were central to the procedures of the DAY OF ATONEMENT (Lev 16; 23:26-32; Num 29:7-11). The guilt offering appears in situations involving fraud and misappropriation (Lev 5:14–6:7 [Heb. 5:14-26]; 7:1-6), lepers and Nazirites (Lev 14:12-28; Num 6:10-12), and reparation or compensation concerning the object of one's guilt (Lev 19:20-22). It was linked to monetary fines or the payment of equivalent values (Lev 5:15, 18; 6:6 [Heb. 5:25]). A nonpriestly example of a guilt offering is the reparation gift of gold mice and tumors offered by the Philistines (1 Sam 6:1-18).

2. Procedures for sacrifice

The word for ALTAR (mizbeakh מִזְבֵּחַ) implies a structure functioning in the act of sacrifice. Narratives reveal that altars were constructed at places thought to be specially connected to the divine realm (Gen 26:24-25; 28:12-18; 35:1; 2 Sam 24:16-25). Although a few narratives refer to sacrifices on unworked natural rock (Judg 13:15-20; compare 1 Sam 6:14-15; 14:33-34), most references are to altars erected from earth or stone (Exod 20:24-25). Although altars were primarily a platform for burning offerings, they were also places to apply or dispose of blood, to set out offerings as presentations to God (Deut 26:4; compare Ezek 41:22), to circumambulate (Ps 26:6), and to seek sanctuary (Exod 21:14; 1 Kgs 1:50; 2:28). Some operated in connection with temples; others did not (e.g., the altar Elijah restores on Mount Carmel; 1 Kgs 18:30). Altars could be associated with stone PILLARs and wooden ASHERAH poles (Exod 24:4; 34:13; Deut 7:5; 12:3; Judg 6:28; Hos 10:2). Multiple altars were sometimes linked together (Num 23; 2 Kgs 11:18; 23:12; Amos 3:14). The plural "altars" in Num 3:31 and Ps 84:3 [Heb. 84:4] refers to the Temple's interior incense altar and exterior burnt offering altar. Altars of sacrifice were sited in a temple's forecourt (1 Kgs 8:22, compare 8:64; Ezek 40:47) or erected on a roof (Judg 6:26; 2 Kgs 23:12). Interior incense altars functioned as part of a domestic ritual that treated a temple as an analogue to a royal palace, along with lighting and trimming lamps (Exod 30:7; 1 Kgs 7:49) and setting out the bread of the presence (Lev 24:8).

The animal victim would be killed in the near vicinity of the altar (Lev 1:11; 3:2) "before the LORD" (Exod 29:11; Lev 1:5; 4:4, 24; see DIVINE PRESENCE), although Gen 22:9-10 describes offering a human sacrifice directly on the unlit wood. Even in the Priestly Code, the lay offerand retained some responsibility for killing the animal (Lev 1:5; 3:2, 8; 4:24), as well as skinning and washing it (Lev 1:6, 9), although this fact is sometimes obscured in translations. The portions for human consumption were boiled in a pot (Deut 16:7; 1 Sam 2:14; Ezek 24:3-6; Zech 14:20-21) or roasted (Exod 12:8-9; 1 Sam 2:15).

3. The meaning of sacrifice

Sacrifice had a range of purposes and meanings, some explicitly understood and stated, others unacknowledged and unspoken. No single conceptual model can encompass the entire phenomenon of OT sacrifice.

a. Food. Among these interpretive models is the notion of sacrifice as food for God. The altar could be called Yahweh's table (Ezek 44:16; Mal 1:7) and the offerings God's food (Lev 3:11; 21:6, 17, 22; Num 28:2). God might be said to enjoy the sacrifice as a pleasing odor (Lev 1:9, 13; 2:2, 9; 3:5, 16; 26:31; Num 28:13, 24; in 1 Sam 26:19 the verb translated "accept" is literally "to smell a fragrance"). Yet voices even from within the religious establishment objected to any crass interpretation of the idea of sacrifice as food for God (Ps 50:9-13).

b. Gift. Gifts given to God are not necessarily any more mercenary than gifts given on the human level. Gifts establish or maintain an affinity between giver and recipient as tokens of gratitude or obligation. Some sacrifices fulfilled vows but were performed only after God had graciously acted (Gen 28:20-22; Judg 11:30-31; 2 Sam 15:7-9). Payment of tithes and gifts of first fruits fulfilled Israel's obligations as God's vassals, showed God proper loyalty and devotion, and thus maintained a cordial relationship with Israel's divine overlord. Sacrifice can be seen as the human side of an ongoing reciprocal exchange of gifts (Lev 23:38; Deut 16:17; 26:10-11; the classic Latin phrase is *do ut des*, "I give so that you might give"). Thus, a generic designation for sacrifice was mattanah (מַתָּנָה, "gift"; Exod 28:38; Deut 16:17; Ezek 20:26, 31, 39; compare Lev 23:38).

c. Social balance. Sacrifice may be understood as a social mechanism that renews the bonds of society and mends relationships that have been ruptured or are out of balance. Violated societal norms and broken human relationships upset the balance of society. Transgression and guilt damage the community and throw society out of balance. Societies turn to sacrifice in order to repair the damage by reestablishing equilibrium and social stability. Sacrifices leading to reconciliation or forgiveness have a much lower social cost than retribution or violence. They provide a cost-effective aid to the human reconciliation process. The regular burnt offering (tamidh תָּמִיד) presented every morning and evening (Exod 29:38-42; Num 28:3-8; 1 Chr 16:40) seems to have been intended to ensure cosmic balance and stability (Dan 8:10-12).

d. Table fellowship. Sacrifice may also be understood in terms of table fellowship with God, for whom a portion of the meal was set aside by burning. The company of diners would consist of family (Deut 12:18; 1 Sam 1:3-5) and a circle of invited guests (1 Sam 9:12-13; 16:3-5). Sacrificial meals strengthened family and group associations but also provided a means for making personal contact with God. The word generally used to describe the vertical and horizontal communion generated by sacrifice is *commensality*. Commensality builds a relational bridge over which benefits can cross from the realm of divine power into the communicants' lives.

e. Socioeconomic benefits. In the period before the centralization of sacrifice in Jerusalem, the distribution of animal protein to the general populace would have been facilitated and regulated by sacrificial practice (2 Sam 6:17-19; 2 Chr 35:7-8, 12-13). Festive sacrificial meals served as social support for the disadvantaged (Deut 12:11-12; 16:10-14; Ps 22:25-26 [Heb. 22:26-27]). First Samuel 1:4-5 and 9:23-24 (compare Gen 43:34) reveal the social status implications involved in the size of one's portion at a sacrificial meal. Sacrifice may have also had positive ecological benefits by encouraging slaughter of flocks and herds and thus reducing overgrazing. Over time the center of gravity shifted from sacrifices performed in local and family settings to those carried out in the service of the state cult in sanctuaries located at the frontiers of Israel (Dan) and Judah (Arad, Beer-sheba, Geba, Mizpah) and under royal patronage and control (Jerusalem and Bethel). Economic and political factors certainly lay behind the establishment of royal sanctuaries (by David and Jeroboam) and the centralization of sacrifice into the capital city (by Hezekiah and Josiah). Finally, cultural analogies from the ancient world suggest that sacrifice may have been a way of tempering feelings of guilt induced by killing animals for food.

f. Numinous power. Sacrifice can also be seen as generating and utilizing impersonal ritual power, serving as a sort of transmission line between the potent sphere of the holy and the human world. Sacrifice thus generated the requisite power upon which ritual could operate. The power produced by sacrifice could then be utilized to protect (so-called status maintenance rituals), cleanse (status reversal rituals), or move people into different social roles (status elevation rituals). The daily sacrifices and annual cycle of offerings described in Lev 23 and Num 28–29 were status maintenance rituals, intended to keep the world in equilibrium and to prevent cosmic disorder. Cleansing the cured leper (Lev 14) or the Day of Atonement liturgy (Lev 16) may be understood as status reversal rituals, intended to reverse impurity into purity and guilt into innocence. The

priestly installation ceremony in Lev 8–9 was a status elevation ritual that transferred a person into priestly office.

g. Blood. Perhaps behind sacrificial slaughter was an understanding that the death of the victim generated ritual power. Death can be seen as releasing a powerful vitality, concretized in the life blood (Gen 9:4; Deut 12:23). This blood, highly charged with power, could be used to cleanse people or the sanctuary. Equating blood and life, Lev 17:10-14 connects the taboo against eating blood with its powerful ritual use at the altar. Released by the victim's death, blood could then be smeared on the horns of the altar (Lev 8:15; Ezek 43:20) or thrown against its side, sprinkled before the sanctuary curtain (Lev 4:6), or applied to the earlobes, thumbs, and toes of priests and lepers (Lev 8:23; 14:14). Moses sprinkles sacrificial blood on both altar and people to bring about a covenant between God and Israel (Exod 24:4-8). Disposing of unused blood against the sides of the altar allowed it to drain harmlessly into the earth (compare Lev 17:13; Deut 12:24).

h. Drama. Sacrifice can be understood as a drama intended to have some effect on the participants and their society. It involved dramatic symbolic actions: lifting the offering, sprinkling blood, putting down the basket, and laying on hands. The theatrical production rehearsed for us in Lev 5 is especially colorful, complete with props, disheveled hair, dialogue, symbolic action, and suspense. Sacrificial drama uses action as a nonverbal language to communicate a reality: she is innocent; he is clean now; we are a community; God is our overlord. Sacrifice was a dramatic "performance" in two senses of the word, both acting out a communication event and bringing into being the reality being communicated. A treaty sacrifice, e.g., could simultaneously bring the desired covenantal relationship into being while at the same time communicating the threatening message: "Keep faith or you will split apart like this animal and be eaten by scavengers" (see Gen 15:9-11, 17; Jer 34:18-20). The drama of sacrificial slaughter may be presumed to have had a cathartic effect on participants, channeling and managing powerful emotions such as fear, guilt, and alienation.

i. Purification and atonement. Much of the sacrificial system can be understood as a way to "decontaminate" persons and objects from impurity. Bathing and washing one's clothes were routine procedures for removing everyday impurity. The "water for impurity" prepared from the ashes of a red heifer was used to cleanse those who had become unclean through corpse pollution (Num 19). People also needed to be purged from sin (khatta'th) and guilt ('awon עָוֹן). Leviticus 4–5 outlines sacrificial procedures for removing sin and guilt acquired by unintentional violations. Deliberate misdeeds are dealt with in Lev 6:1-7 and Num 5:5-8. Apparently, sin committed defiantly and without repentance ("high-handedly") could not be removed by these rituals at all (Num 15:30-31).

The verb *atone* (root kpr כפר) implies the removal of sin or guilt by wiping it off or covering it over. To atone means to remove a barrier or an obstacle to a relationship (Gen 32:20 by Jacob; Deut 21:8 by God; 2 Sam 21:3 by David; compare Prov 16:14). ATONEMENT could be accomplished by paying money (Exod 30:16) or burning incense (Num 16:47), but most often through the mechanism of sacrificial death and blood used to erase any impurity and sin that obstructed the relationship between Israel and God. Blood was sprinkled or daubed onto the altar and the sanctuary in order to eliminate whatever impurity had become attached to those sacred things (Exod 29:12; Lev 4:5-7, 17-18, 25, 30, 34; 5:9; 9:9). The action of laying both hands on an animal's head may imply a transfer of guilt to the sacrificial victim (Lev 16:21); however, in other contexts putting one's hand on the victim signifies that the person bringing the sacrifice owns the animal or identifies with it (Lev 1:4; 3:2; 4:4). The dramatic action of releasing one of the birds brought by the healed leper (Lev 14:7, 53) seems intended to send impurity and sin away in a spatial sense. Sin offerings were apparently thought to absorb impurity in some way, given that they possessed a defiling quality under certain circumstances (Lev 6:28; 16:28). Priests who ate sin offerings were thought to ingest this guilt (Lev 10:17).

C. Festivals

Interrelated liturgical calendars (Exod 23:14-17; 34:18-26*a*; Lev 23; Num 28:16–29:39; Deut 16:1-17; compare Ezek 45:18-25) affirm the primary importance of three major festivals: Passover with Unleavened Bread, Weeks, and Booths. All three have roots in the agricultural year. The basis of Passover connects to the springtime move of flocks to pasture. Unleavened Bread is linked to the start of the barley harvest at about the same time. The harvest festival of Weeks synchronizes with the conclusion of the wheat harvest seven weeks later (Exod 34:22). Finally, the autumn festival of Booths marks the harvest of grapes, olives, and nuts. Eventually all three of these celebrations were regarded as pilgrimage festivals during which all males were required to appear "before the LORD" at a sanctuary, ultimately Jerusalem (Exod 23:17; 34:23; Deut 16:16; *see* FEASTS AND FASTS).

1. Passover

The sacrificial ritual of Passover (pesakh פֶּסַח) and the seven-day avoidance of leavened dough in the Unleavened Bread festival (matsoth מַצּוֹת) are usually assumed to have had different origins and only subsequently became coordinated with each other into a single springtime observance (*see* PASSOVER AND FEAST OF UNLEAVENED BREAD). Scholars generally understand Passover to have started as a family-based pastoral ritual originally marking the transfer of flocks to springtime pasturage and intended to protect newly

born lambs and kids. Passover names both the spring festival and the sacrificial victim, initially slaughtered by the head of the household (Exod 12:21) and eaten by a family-oriented gathering of participants (12:4) at night (12:8, 10). Unleavened Bread is thought to have started as the observance of a taboo intended to establish a sharp break between the grain of the new harvest (compare Lev 23:10-11) and what remained from the previous year. Nevertheless, Unleavened Bread is already linked to the exodus in the earliest calendar texts (Exod 23:15; 34:18), and Deut 16:1, 6 makes the same connection for Passover. There is little question, however, that what began as a localized, family celebration (Exod 12:3, 21-24) developed into a national and centralized festival under priestly supervision (Deut 16:1-8; 2 Kgs 23:23).

In the narrative of Exod 12–13, Passover and Unleavened Bread have been united into a single celebration and associated fully with the night of the exodus and the death of Egypt's firstborn. The two celebrations are coordinated by the eating of unleavened bread as part of the sacrificial meal (12:8) and by a narrative device (12:33-34, 39). Deuteronomy 16:1-8 witnesses the transformation of Passover into a national pilgrimage festival and sacrifice at the central sanctuary. This radical shift is generally associated with the religious policies of Josiah (2 Kgs 23:21-23) and remained the pattern throughout the Second Temple period (Ezra 6:19-22; compare the perspective of 2 Chr 30; 35).

2. Weeks

The name of this festival (shavu'oth שָׁבֻעֹת; pentēkostē πεντηκοστή) is taken from its celebration seven weeks "from the time the sickle is first put to the standing grain" (Deut 16:9). A more exact dating is given by Lev 23:15-16. Its foundational agricultural connection was to the harvest of the wheat crop (Exod 23:16; 34:22) and the offering of first fruits (Exod 23:16; Num 28:26). *See* WEEKS, FEAST OF.

3. Booths

The great autumn celebration (sukkoth סֻכּוֹת, "tabernacles, booths") is often referred to simply as "the festival" (Lev 23:39; Ezek 45:25) and was the primary pilgrimage celebration in the monarchy period (1 Kgs 8:2, 65-66 in Jerusalem; 12:32-33 at Bethel; *see* BOOTHS, FEAST OR FESTIVAL OF). As the autumn festival, it was associated closely with the day of rest and trumpet blowing mentioned in Lev 23:24-25 and Num 29:1-6 (in postbiblical times designated as New Year's Day) and the Day of Atonement (Yom Kippur). Scholars often theorize a connection to an annual Jerusalem enthronement festival, the primary evidence for which comes from extra-biblical parallels and the book of Psalms (7:7 [Heb. 7:8]; 82; 132; in particular the enthronement psalms 47; 93; 96–99). The name *Booths* refers to the shelters in which harvesters lived out in the fields to stay near their worksites and protect the harvested crop.

Building and living in booths was the characteristic activity during the festival, described in a lively fashion by Neh 8:14-17. Numbers 29 also prescribes a substantial program of sacrifices. Deuteronomy 31:10-11 stipulates Booths as the celebration during which the law was to be read every seven years, and Solomon dedicated the Temple at this festival (1 Kgs 8:2). Eventually, Booths became associated with the memory of the wilderness wandering (Lev 23:39-43). Zechariah 14:16-21 envisions the eschatological sacrificial banquet in terms of Booths. A festival of seven days, Booths began on the fifteenth day of the seventh month, TISHRI. It is preceded in the liturgical calendar by the Day of Atonement on the tenth day of that month. Leviticus 16 gives a full account of the rituals intended to atone for the impurity attached to the sanctuary itself through the sin of the whole people, to "make atonement for the sanctuary, because of the uncleannesses of the people of Israel, and because of their transgressions, all their sins" (v. 16). These complex rites included the scapegoat (vv. 10, 21-22), which was thought to bear away the iniquities of the people as it moved from the sanctuary out into the chaotic desert where it would belong to AZAZEL, the desert demon.

4. Other observances

The new moon that began each month was celebrated (Num 29:6; 1 Sam 20; 2 Kgs 4:23; Ps 81:3 [Heb. 81:4]). Zechariah 7:3, 5 and 8:19 specify four annual fast days observed in the exilic period in the fourth, fifth, seventh, and tenth months. Three of these were evidently connected with the siege and fall of Jerusalem and the destruction of its Temple (Jer 52:4, 6-7, 12-13), and with the fast in the seventh remembering the assassination of GEDALIAH (2 Kgs 25:25). Other annual observances eventually included PURIM, commemorating the salvation brought about by Esther and Mordecai in the Persian period (Esth 9), and HANUKKAH, memorializing the rededication of the Jerusalem Temple in the Hellenistic period (1 Macc 4:59; 2 Macc 2:16; 10:6).

D. Other Worship Practices

1. Prayer

PRAYER is mentioned many times in the OT. Personal prayer included laments of an individual in family and shrine settings (1 Sam 1:10-15). Communal prayer was offered in times of national crisis (Judg 20:18, 23, 26-28; 21:1-4) in the context of other ritual actions (Joel 2:15-17). Literary reflections of the sort of prayers uttered in times of national significance or crisis are set forth in 1 Kgs 8; Ezra 9; Neh 9; Jdt 9; and several times in Chronicles (1 Chr 17:16-27; 29:10-19; 2 Chr 20:6-12).

The book of Psalms preserves examples of both individual and communal prayer originally used in settings that ranged from formal temple worship to personal piety. Individual laments (such as Pss 7; 22; 51) and community laments (Pss 79; 80) petitioned God for help in times of sickness, trouble, and danger. THANKSGIVING PSALMS (Pss 30; 32; 116; 124) were used after prayer had been answered and accompanied a thanksgiving sacrifice (Ps 116:17) or the payment of a vow made while in distress (Ps 116:14). Songs of trust expressed personal confidence in and closeness to God (Pss 23; 62; 131). Hymns offered praise for God's greatness as creator and as savior of Israel (Pss 100; 104; 105; see HYMNS, OT). Subcategories of the hymn genre engaged particular topics in distinctive liturgical settings. Enthronement psalms commemorated God's universal kingship and may have been used at an annual Jerusalem enthronement celebration to begin the new year (Pss 47; 93; 96–99). Zion songs celebrated in mythic terms God's presence in and protection of Jerusalem and its Temple (Pss 46; 48; 76). Royal psalms centered on the king, his quasi-divine eminence and way of life (Pss 2; 45; 72; 110). Other psalms paid tribute to wisdom and law (Pss 1; 19; 119).

2. Music

Lists of instruments in psalms (Pss 149; 150; compare 1 Sam 10:5) and descriptions of public worship in Chronicles (1 Chr 15:16-28; 25:1, 6; 2 Chr 29:25-30) show that music played an important role in worship. Dance was also part of worship (Exod 15:20; 2 Sam 6:14; Pss 87:7; 149:3; 150:4). Worshipers engaged in processions around the altar and perhaps around the city fortifications (Pss 26:6; 42:4 [Heb. 42:5]; 48:12 [Heb. 48:13]; 68:24 [Heb. 68:25]). Since 1 Kgs 8:8 reports that its carrying poles remained in place in the First Temple, perhaps the portable ARK OF THE COVENANT played a role in these processions.

3. Pilgrimage

Indirect evidence suggests pilgrimages to sacred places and ancestral tombs. Careful attention to the location of important tombs (Josh 24:30, 33; compare 2 Kgs 13:21; contrast Deut 34:6) and conspicuous installations there may indicate that they served as focal points for pilgrimages (Gen 35:20; 2 Sam 18:17; 2 Kgs 23:17). Elijah's trek to Sinai to encounter God (1 Kgs 19:4-18) and the preservation of the names of the camping stages between Sinai and the edge of Israelite territory (Num 33:16-49) suggest that pilgrimages to Sinai may have taken place.

E. Exclusion and Inclusion

Only priests could approach the altar and holy areas (Num 3:10; 16:40 [Heb. 17:5]; 18:3-4; Ezek 44:15-16); therefore, any worship involving the altar was exclusively the priest's responsibility. Only a priest could approach the altar to elevate offerings before God, bring the sacrificial victim or pieces of it into the holy space of the altar for burning, care for the altar fire and ashes, or pour libation sacrifices at its base. Only priests could slaughter sacrificial birds because they had to be killed directly over the altar to capture the small amount of blood involved (Lev 1:14-15). Priests who had bodily imperfections (Lev 21:16-23), who had contact with the unclean dead (21:1-5, 12), or who were married to women with inappropriate backgrounds (21:7) were excluded from active altar service. There were also limits on lay participation in public worship, sometimes defined as membership in the assembly (qahal קָהָל), the gathering of Israel for war and worship.

Behavioral standards for admittance are listed in the genre of "entrance torah" ("Who shall ascend the hill of the LORD?"; Ps 24:3; see also Ps 15:1-5) and in prophetic imitations of them (Isa 33:14-16; Mic 6:6-8). Ritual impurity excluded one from participation. Such impurity was usually temporary (e.g., one day for sexual intercourse, Lev 15:16-18; seven days for menstruation, 15:19-24) and could be removed by relatively ordinary means such as bathing and changing clothes. Other impurities required more rigorous ritual intervention (e.g., motherhood, Lev 12:1-8; abnormal bodily discharges, 15:2-15, 25-30; corpse pollution, Num 19:1-22). Some sorts of impurity were long-term or permanent conditions. The so-called leper (Lev 13–14) or a maimed person (Deut 23:1; compare 2 Sam 5:8) was barred from worship. The excluded "bastard" of Deut 23:2 seems to have been offspring of a forbidden degree of incest or perhaps a child of an interethnic relationship (Zech 9:6). Foreigners were excluded from Passover according to Exod 12:43. Deuteronomy 23:3-8 excludes Ammonites, Moabites, and first- and second-generation Edomites from the worship assembly, and Ezek 44:5-9 bars foreigners from the Temple. However, a more inclusive attitude is evidenced by 1 Kgs 8:41-43 and Isa 56:3-8. Moreover, a sojourner (NRSV, "alien") as a foreigner with legal status was permitted to join in Passover (Exod 12:48-49; Num 9:14) and the sacrificial cult (Lev 22:18; Num 15:14-16).

Women assisted with public worship in support roles (Exod 35:25-26; 38:8). although It is doubtful that the position of qedheshah (קְדֵשָׁה, "consecrated women," whose function remains unresolved) referred to temple prostitutes even though the position is condemned by Deuteronomistic sources (as NRSV; Gen 38:21-22; Deut 23:17-18; Hos 4:14). Women performed as singers and dancers (Ps 68:24-25 [Heb. 68:25-26]; perhaps Ezra 2:65). They attended pilgrimage festivals (Deut 12:12, 18; 16:11, 14) and public worship gatherings (Deut 29:10-11; 31:12; Ezra 10:1; Neh 12:43). Hannah not only shared in the family sacrificial meal (1 Sam 1:4-5) but is paired with her husband in offering sacrifice (1 Sam 1:24-25; 2:19-20). Women could also sponsor and present sacrifices on their own (Lev 12:6-7; 15:19-33). The carefully chosen language of Lev 1:2; 2:1; 4:2, 27; 5:1-4, 15, 17; 7:20; 20:6; and Num 15:27, 30-31 allows for either a man or a woman to be the actor.

F. Unorthodox Worship

Of course, Israel worshiped other gods. Most often mentioned is BAAL (and the associated female divinity or sacral pole called Asherah). Also popular were the Mesopotamian god TAMMUZ (Ezek 8:14-15) and the QUEEN OF HEAVEN (apparently Astarte or Ishtar), who was worshiped in family-centered practices of offering and libation (Jer 7:18-20; 44:15-25). Veneration was offered on rooftops to astral deities (Jer 19:13; 32:29; Zeph 1:5).

Many popular practices were eventually considered to be heterodox by later authorities and editors who fell under the influence of the dominant priestly and Deuteronomic movements and the judgments of the prophets. Isaiah 65:3-4; 66:3, 17; and Ezek 8:5-17 not only catalog reprehensible worship practices but suggest they were not particularly uncommon. It seems that worship performed in the domestic sphere of the family, particularly by women, tended to be judged unorthodox more often than not. Women's natural concerns for fertility, birthing, and lactation seem to be reflected in the archaeological evidence of figurines and domestic shrines. Perhaps this is why Deut 17:2, 5 and 29:18 carefully include "man or woman" when condemning improper worship.

Divination and necromancy were clearly practiced and stringently censured in legal and prophetic texts (Lev 19:31; 20:6, 27; Deut 18:10-11; 1 Sam 28:6-19; Isa 8:19; Mic 5:12 [Heb. 5:11]). Child sacrifice is described unambiguously in Judg 11:31, 34-39; Isa 57:5; Jer 7:31; 19:5; Ezek 16:20-21; 20:26, 31; 23:37-39. However, the contexts of Deut 18:10 and 2 Kgs 17:17; 21:6 suggest that to "pass" a child "through fire" was not a sacrifice but intended as a nonlethal divinatory practice or perhaps a dedication ritual. Stone pillars were part of Israel's patriarchal heritage (Gen 28:18; 35:14) but condemned in legal texts (Lev 26:1; Deut 16:22).

Similarly, the bronze serpent of Moses (Num 21:9; 2 Kgs 18:4), the silver image of Yahweh at Dan (Judg 17:3-4; 18:30), and the gold bull (NRSV, "calf") images at Dan and Bethel (1 Kgs 12:28-30) seem to have been formerly acceptable religious objects, later denounced by proponents of the imageless worship stipulated by early laws (Exod 20:4-5, 23; 34:17). The utilization of images in worship certainly continued throughout the time of the monarchy (2 Kgs 21:7), and the denunciation of images remained a standard feature of legal and prophetic texts in the exilic and Second Temple periods (Lev 19:4; 26:1; Deut 4:15-19, 25; Isa 42:17; Jer 10:3-5, 14-15; Ezek 20:7-8; Hab 2:18-19). In the era of Assyrian domination, perceptions of Yahweh were influenced by solar concepts (Ps 84:11 [Heb. 84:12]; Ezek 8:16; Mal 4:2; compare 2 Kgs 23:11).

G. The Cult of the Dead

Venerating and consulting dead ancestors were features of Israelite worship life, something clear from the number and intensity of texts critical of such practices (Lev 19:27-28; 21:5; Deut 26:14). Sacrifices to the dead are condemned by Deut 26:14 and Ps 106:28. Sirach

30:18 also speaks of food offered to the dead. The archaeological evidence of certain tomb features confirms that offerings of food and drink were made to the dead and consumed by gatherings of relatives and friends.

We know very little about a type of religious meal practiced in Israel, the marzeah (מַרְזֵחַ), mentioned in Jer 16:5-8 (NRSV, "mourning") and Amos 6:7 (NRSV, "revelry"; properly translated by TNK). If non-Israelite sources can be used to explain an Israelite institution, this would have been a banquet of food and wine held in the context of mourning the dead. Even though orthodox leaders sought to keep the whole realm of the dead outside the horizon of Yahwist worship (e.g., Pss 6:5 [Heb. 6:6]; 30:9 [Heb. 30:10]; 88:3-12 [Heb. 88:4-13]; 115:17), such practices obviously persisted into the Second Temple period (Isa 57:6-9; 65:4; Tob 4:17).

H. Synagogue

The SYNAGOGUE as a place of prayer and Scripture reading appears in a decidedly developed form in witnesses from the 1st cent. CE (Luke 4:16-22; Acts 13:13-16; Philo, *Hypothetica* 7.10–14; *Spec. Laws* 2.61–63; Josephus, *Ag. Ap.* 2.175). Consequently, most scholars assume that synagogues originated somewhat earlier in the Second Temple period, but there is really little or no evidence as to when, how, and where they developed. The earliest mention of a synagogue (as a proseuchē [προσευχή], "place of prayer") is a Greek dedicatory inscription from 3rd-cent. BCE Egypt, perhaps from the time of Ptolemy III Euergetes I (r. 246–221 BCE).

I. Theologies of Worship

Four theological perspectives on worship stand out. Deuteronomy envisions sacrificial worship gatherings at the central sanctuary both as occasions for public, collective celebration and joy, and as opportunities to provide sustenance and support for marginalized social groups (Deut 12:5-27; 14:22-27; 16:9-17). For Deuteronomy, proper worship was a demonstration of Israel's faith in the face of apostasy (Deut 7:1-5, 25-26; 12:2-4, 29-31; 13:1-18 [Heb. 13:2-19]; 17:2-7; 18:9-14).

The Priestly Writing (and the Holiness Code incorporated into it as Lev 17–26) looks at worship from a professional perspective, reflecting concern about the ritual categories clean and unclean in interaction with the categories holy and common (Lev 10:10-11). Instructions about the proper timing and performance of sacrificial ritual dominate. However, the issue is not simply professional competence in worship but the conviction that unless Israel made proper and faithful use of the worship procedures graciously provided by God, God might be forced to abandon the people on account of sin and impurity contaminating the sanctuary (compare Lev 16:16-17, 33) and the land (Lev 18:24-29; Num 35:33-34). The result would be total destruction (Lev 26). The Priestly Writing also evidences social concern in providing alternate, cheaper sacrificial procedures for those unable to afford the standard victim (Lev 5:6-13; 12:8; 14:21).

First and Second Chronicles emphasizes the joyful worship of the community gathered around the Temple in song, prayer, and praise. Worship follows the patterns of leadership laid down by Moses (1 Chr 6:49; 15:15; 2 Chr 8:13) and David (1 Chr 6:31-48; 15:16-24), which carefully distinguish the status and roles of priests (1 Chr 23:13; 24:19) and Levites (1 Chr 9:22; 2 Chr 8:14). Joyful national celebrations mark the turning points of Israel's history (1 Chr 12:38-40; 15:1-28; 29:10-22; 2 Chr 7:1-10; 20:27-28; 30:23-27). Psalms are used repeatedly and sung with joy (1 Chr 16:7-36; 2 Chr 5:13; 6:41-42; 20:21). True worship is a sign of the community's authenticity as God's people (2 Chr 13:4-12).

A fourth theological perspective on worship puts the others in perspective. It is found in the critique of the prophets, who warned that worship—vital as it is—can never be a substitute for true repentance, loyalty, and obedience (1 Sam 15:22-23; Isa 1:11-15; Hos 6:6; Amos 5:22; Mic 6:6-8; compare Ps 51:16-17 [Heb. 51:18-19]).

Bibliography: Susan Ackerman. *Under Every Green Tree: Popular Religion in Sixth-Century Judah* (1992); Rainer Albertz. *A History of Israelite Religion in the Old Testament Period.* 2 vols. (1994); Gary Anderson. *Sacrifices and Offerings in Ancient Israel: Studies in Their Social and Political Importance* (1987); Samuel E. Balentine. *Prayer in the Hebrew Bible: The Drama of Divine–Human Dialogue* (1993); Samuel E. Balentine. *The Torah's Vision of Worship* (1999); W. Boyd Barrick. "What Do We Really Know about 'High-Places'?" *SEÅ* 45 (1980) 50–57; Donald D. Binder. *Into the Temple Courts: The Place of the Synagogues in the Second Temple Period* (1999); Phyllis Bird. "The Place of Women in the Israelite Cultus." *Ancient Israelite Religion.* Patrick D. Miller Jr., Paul D. Hanson, and S. Dean McBride, eds. (1987) 397–419; Judith Bloch-Smith. *Judahite Burial Practices and Beliefs about the Dead* (1992); Walter Brueggemann. *Worship in Ancient Israel: An Essential Guide* (2005); J. Andrew Dearman. *Religion and Culture in Ancient Israel* (1992); John A. Emerton. "The Biblical High Place in the Light of Recent Study." *PEQ* 129 (1997) 116–32; Bernard R. Goldstein and Alla Cooper. "The Festivals of Israel and Judah and the Literary History of the Pentateuch." *JAOS* 110 (1990) 19–31; Matt P. Graham, Rick R. Marrs, Steven L. McKenzie, eds. *Worship and the Hebrew Bible: Essays in Honour of John T. Willis* (1999); John S. Holladay. "Religion in Israel and Judah under the Monarchy." *Ancient Israelite Religion.* Patrick D. Miller Jr., Paul D. Hanson, and S. Dean McBride, eds. (1987) 249–99; Othmar Keel. *Goddesses and Trees, New Moon and Yahweh: Ancient Near Eastern Art and the Hebrew Bible* (1998); Othmar Keel and Christoph Uehlinger. *Gods, Goddesses, and Images of God in*

Ancient Israel (1998); Hans-Joachim Kraus. *Worship in Israel* (1966); Lee I. Levine. "The Nature and Origin of the Palestinian Synagogue Reconsidered." *JBL* 115 (1996) 425–48; Theodore J. Lewis. *Cults of the Dead in Ancient Israel and Judah* (1989); Jacob Milgrom. *Leviticus: A Book of Ritual and Ethics* (2004); Jacob Milgrom. *Studies in Cultic Theology and Terminology* (1983); Patrick D. Miller. "The Absence of the Goddess in Israelite Religion." *HAR* 10 (1986); Patrick D. Miller. "Israelite Religion." *The Hebrew Bible and Its Modern Interpreters.* Douglas A. Knight and Gene M. Tucker, eds. (1985) 201–37; Patrick D. Miller. *The Religion of Ancient Israel* (2000); Patrick D. Miller. *They Cried to the Lord: The Form and Theology of Biblical Prayer* (1994); Richard D. Nelson. *Raising Up a Faithful Priest* (1993); Susan Niditch. *Ancient Israelite Religion* (1997); Harold H. Rowley. *Worship in Ancient Israel* (1967); Mark S. Smith. *The Early History of God: Yahweh and Other Deities in Ancient Israel* (1990); J. Alberto Soggin. *Israel in the Biblical Period: Institutions, Festivals, Ceremonies, Rituals* (2001); Glen J. Taylor. *Yahweh and the Sun: Biblical and Archaeological Evidence for Sun Worship in Ancient Israel* (1993); Karel van der Toorn. *From Her Cradle to Her Grave: The Role of Religion in the Life of the Israelite and Babylonian Woman* (1994); Roland de Vaux. *Studies in Old Testament Sacrifice* (1964); Clarence J. Vos. *Woman in Old Testament Worship* (1968).

RICHARD D. NELSON

WRATH [אַף 'af, עֶבְרָה 'evrah, קֶצֶף qetsef; ὀργή orgē]. The personal disposition of ANGER, often expressed by means of violence. Wrath may be expressed by mortals, by governing authorities, by God, and by other supernatural beings, such as Satan. Wrath often indicates the impulsive acting out of anger, though some biblical authors describe wrath as something God stores up for the last days (e.g., Zeph 1:15, 18; Rom 2:5; 1 Thess 1:10). One of the Hebrew words often translated wrath, 'af, derives from the verb "to snort" (see Ps 18:7-8 [Heb. 18:8-9]), indicating wrath's primal nature. Another word, 'evrah, is often translated "wrath" but has a related meaning of "overflow" or "outburst." Greek thinkers often described orgē as a natural force that wells up and breaks forth.

Greco-Roman authors debated the moral value of wrath. Some proposed that "righteous wrath" motivated persons to great deeds, while others regarded wrath as a personal weakness (Jas 1:20). Hence, some ancient persons attributed wrath to the gods, while others did not. Biblical authors typically regard wrath as a failing for mortals but an appropriate disposition for the deity. In the Bible, God is the subject of the great majority of occurrences of the term *wrath*. God demonstrates wrath particularly in response to idolatry, wickedness, and injustice. God also visits wrath against the enemies of God's people. Metaphorically, God's wrath is most

often expressed in terms of pouring out and burning up, consuming all that stands in its path. *See* WRATH OF GOD.

GREG CAREY

WRATH OF GOD [אַף 'af, זַעַם za'am, זַעַף za'af, חֵמָה khemah, חָרָה kharah, חָרוֹן kharon, כַּעַס ka'as, עֶבְרָה 'evrah, קֶצֶף qetsef; θυμός thymos, ὀργή orgē]. The wrath of God is an anthropomorphism (in which human characteristics are attributed to God). Anthropomorphic language simultaneously highlights God's differences from and likenesses to sentient beings. Accordingly, biblical descriptions of divine wrath align with the biblical paradigm of human wrath and also possess characteristics that are distinctly divine. The wrath of God is typically destructive and functions in the OT and NT as a rhetorical device to persuade people to acknowledge God as rightful authority.

A. Wrath in the Old Testament
  1. Terms for wrath
  2. Human and divine wrath
  3. Reasons for the wrath of God
    a. Spurned husband
    b. Rejected leader
    c. Rejected covenant partner
  4. Aim and consequences of the wrath of God
    a. Divine wrath at foreign nations
    b. Divine wrath at Israel
  5. The wrath of God and war
    a. Calamities of war
    b. The cup of God's wrath
B. Wrath in the New Testament
Bibliography

A. Wrath in the Old Testament
1. Terms for wrath

The two most frequent OT terms for divine and human wrath are 'af (Exod 32:19; Num 12:9; Deut 29:26-27; 2 Sam 12:5; Jer 4:8) and kharah (Num 22:27; Hab 3:9-13). The noun form, kharon, always refers to divine wrath (Exod 15:7; Jer 25:30-38). The roots of 'af and kharah are frequently paired. The term 'af literally means "nose," and kharah literally means "to burn" (e.g., Ezek 24:11). Thus, the idiom kharah 'af literally means "his nose burned." This description of anger may derive from the perceived physical locus of anger. Anger increases blood flow to the nose and face, so that anger is perceived as a "burning nose." God's "burning"/"burning nose" is also a concrete instrument of fiery destruction. Indeed, kharah describes the burning of the targets of God's wrath. "You sent out your fury (kharon), it consumed them like stubble" (Exod 15:7; compare Isa 30:27).

Khemah, which refers to the wrath of God (e.g., Num 25:11; 2 Kgs 22:13; Ezek 25:14) and human beings (e.g., Gen 27:44; 2 Kgs 5:12; Esth 5:9), may derive from a root meaning "to be hot." **Khemah** is frequently a tangible instrument of fiery destruction (2 Kgs 22:13; Ps 89:46; Jer 4:4). "My wrath will go forth like fire, and burn, with no one to quench it" (Jer 21:12; compare Isa 42:25; 2 Kgs 22:17). In addition, some scholars suggest that the cluster of images frequently associated with divine wrath, such as heat (Nah 1:6), withering vegetation, and wind (Isa 42:25; Ezek 19:12), indicates that the term may sometimes represent God's devastating presence in a sirocco storm.

The term ka‘as has been connected to Arabic kasa‘a, which means "fear." Human kasa‘a conveys the sadness that underlies human anger (1 Sam 1:6-7; Ps 6:8). It is felt in the heart (1 Sam 1:8; Ezek 32:9), body, and stomach (Ps 31:10), and is accompanied by anxiety (1 Sam 1:18), sorrow (Ps 6:8 [Heb. 6:7], sighing (Ps 6:7 [Heb. 6:6]), and bitterness (Hos 12:14). However, divine ka‘as is almost always accompanied by punishment. "The LORD will strike Israel, as a reed is shaken in the water; he will root up Israel out of this good land that he gave to their ancestors, and scatter them beyond the Euphrates, because they have made their sacred poles, provoking the LORD to anger" (1 Kgs 14:15). See GOD, OT VIEW OF.

2. Human and divine wrath

According to modern psychological theory, wrath (or anger) is a natural human response to a perceived offense or injustice. However, biblical wrath appears to be narrower in scope. Not all types of offenses elicit wrath, and wrath is not ascribed to all types of people. Biblical wrath typically arises within the context of struggles for authority and is expressed by figures in positions of authority.

As such, twenty-one out of the twenty-six named individuals to whom wrath is ascribed in the OT are kings, leaders, masters, or higher-ranking family members. Examples include Esau's anger at his younger brother, Isaac, for stealing his birthright (Gen 27:45), Potiphar's anger at his servant Joseph for allegedly violating his wife (Gen 39:19), Moses' anger at Korah, Dathan, and Abiram for rebelling against him (Num 16:15), Haman's anger at Mordecai for refusing to bow to him (Esth 3:5), and Nebuchadnezzar's anger at the Jews for refusing to bow to his statue (Dan 3:13, 19).

In these passages and in a myriad of other examples, individuals exhibit wrath when they perceive that someone has violated their authority over family (Gen 34:7; 39:19; Judg 14:19), property (Gen 27:45; 44:18), or a political group (Num 16:15; 1 Sam 18:8; Esth 3:5). In several passages, political leaders direct wrath at those who abuse power and commit social injustices (1 Sam 11:6; 2 Sam 12:5; Neh 5:6).Perhaps this is because leaders perceive that social injustice undermines their responsibility to maintain order. Notably, in two passages where a subordinate does appear to get angry at his superior—Jonathan's anger when he discovers Saul's intent to kill David (1 Sam 20:34) and David's anger over God's execution of Uzzah (2 Sam 6:8)—the

Bible avoids directly describing the subordinate as angry at his superior and, instead, describes him as angry at the outcome of the situation (see also Exod 11:8).

Typically, wrath compels individuals to annul any threats to their authority. Consequently, authority figures attempt to kill or banish foreign provokers and/or the provokers' kith or kin. When angered, Dinah's brothers kill Shechem and all the males of his town (Gen 34:25-26), Potiphar imprisons Joseph (Gen 39:19-20), Haman attempts to kill Mordecai and his nation (Esth 3:5-6), and Nebuchadnezzar attempts to kill Shadrach, Meshach, and Abednego (Dan 3:13-23).

In stark contrast to the consequences of anger at foreigners and other non-kin, anger at family members is almost never lethal (Gen 27:45; 1 Sam 20:30-34 [Saul throws a spear in Jonathan's direction, and yet Jonathan leaves Saul's presence unharmed]; 2 Sam 13:21; Esth 1:12-21). In fact, anger at family members often yields no punishment at all. Inaction prevails, possibly because safety, wealth, and well-being are defined by the familial group, and lethal anger at kin would be self-destructive. Nevertheless, the extent of force exerted in response to a family member's provocation appears to depend on the nature of the familial bond. Paternal anger is almost always benign (1 Sam 20:30-34; 2 Sam 13:21). David gets angry at Amnon for raping Tamar but he does nothing to his son (2 Sam 13:21). Spousal anger generally is not lethal (Gen 30:2), but a wife may be punished if her provocative behavior threatens her husband's broader political authority (Judg 14:19-20; Esth 1:12-21) or if she is suspected of adultery (Num 5). The bonds of brotherhood are not as steadfast as other family attachments (e.g., Cain kills Abel, Gen 4:5-8). However, when Esau wishes to kill Jacob, his anger wanes, and he does not commit fratricide (Gen 27:45). On the contrary, when time passes, Esau kisses and embraces Jacob (Gen 33:4).

Like human anger, the wrath of God is triggered by human disregard for God's authority. Expressions of divine wrath serve to reassert God's authority. However, the wrath of God differs from its human counterpart in its rhetorical nature and mechanism of action. While expressions of human anger function to annul a threat, expressions of divine wrath function rhetorically to persuade Israel to acknowledge that God is Lord. Additionally, whereas human wrath is an emotion that can compel action, God's wrath is also a concrete instrument of destruction.

3. Reasons for the wrath of God

Divine wrath is directed at the nation of Israel (Exod 32:10), individuals or groups among Israel (Lev 10:2; Josh 7:1-16), foreign nations (Ezek 25:14), or on all people (Rom 1:18). The most frequent cause of divine wrath at Israel is the worship of idols and foreign methods of worship (Exod 32:10; Lev 26:28; Num 25:3; Deut 4:25; Josh 23:16; 1 Kgs 11:9; 2 Kgs 13:3; Jer 7:18-20; Ezek 6:12; Hos 8:5). Perhaps the most famous example of God's wrath at Israel is the account of Israel's fashioning a golden calf. God instructs Moses, "Now let me alone, so that my wrath may burn hot against them and I may consume them" (Exod 32:10; compare Deut 9:8-14 and Ezek 20:11-17).

Social injustice, such as oppression of the weak, is another frequent cause of God's wrath at Israel (Exod 22:22-24; Ezek 22:27-31; Jer 21:12; Zech 7:9-12), and the most prominent reason for divine wrath in Isaiah (Isa 5:22-25; 10:1-6; 13:1-21). Other reasons for divine wrath at Israel include breaking the Sabbath (Ezek 20:13), migrating to Egypt (Jer 42:17-18), and cult purity infractions (Lev 1:6-16; 10:2; Num 18:5; Josh 7:1-16; 2 Sam 6:7; Jer 32:30-34).

Notably, while divine wrath at Israel is triggered by a variety of offenses, God gets angry at foreign nations primarily when they assault and/or oppress Israel (Exod 15:7-8; Jer 50:13; Ezek 25:14; Ps 2:11-12; an exception is Jonah 3:9). See ZEAL, ZEALOUS.

The Bible draws on human metaphors to convey the implications of sin. Biblical authors compare God's wrath to the wrath of a disregarded husband or father (Judg 2:17; Jer 2:2-35; Ezek 6:9-12; 16:7-63; Hos 11:1-9; 13:2-13), robbed property owner (Josh 7:1-26), defied political leader (Num 11:10-20, 33; Ezek 20:8-38; Zeph 3:7-15), and spurned covenant partner (Deut 4).

a. Spurned husband. Biblical authors, most explicitly the prophets and DtrH (Deuteronomy–2 Kings), adopt the metaphor of sexual infidelity to describe God's response to Israel's foreign worship. In the Prophets, Israel is portrayed as God's "wife" who incites God's wrath with her adultery (Jer 2:2, 35; Ezek 6:1-14; 16:8-42). "I will judge you as women who commit adultery and shed blood are judged, and bring blood upon you in wrath and jealousy" (Ezek 16:38). Deuteronomistic Historians describe Israel's foreign apostasy as "lustfulness" that provokes God's wrath, "for they lusted after other gods and bowed down to them.... So the anger of the LORD was kindled against Israel" (Judg 2:17-20).

b. Rejected leader. God becomes angry when Israel rejects God's authority as the supreme political leader who governs and protects Israel. For example, God interprets Israel's complaint against the manna as a rejection of God's governance in preference for Egyptian rule (Num 11:1, 20).

In the Pentateuch, God's wrath is a function of God's royal duty to avenge social injustice against the powerless. "You shall not wrong or oppress a resident alien, for you were aliens in the land of Egypt. You shall not abuse any widow or orphan. If you do abuse them, when they cry out to me, I will surely heed their cry; my wrath will burn, and I will kill you with the sword, and your wives shall become widows and your children orphans" (Exod 22:21-24).

God asserts God's kingship over Israel by avenging and protecting the nation with his wrath. He unleashes wrath at Egypt when the Egyptians pursue Israel at the sea (Exod 15:7). God proves that he is "the living God

and the everlasting King" with his wrath at nations (Jer 10:10). He assaults his petitioner's enemies in order to be known as the God who "rules over Jacob" (Ps 59:12-14).

According to Judahite prophets, God gets angry when Israel defies God's laws and ordinances, such as those that command Sabbath observance, social justice, and exclusive worship (Ezek 20:21-33; Zeph 3:4-15). "But the children rebelled against me; they did not follow my statutes, and were not careful to observe my ordinances, by whose observance everyone shall live; they profaned my sabbaths. Then I thought I would pour out my wrath upon them and spend my anger against them in the wilderness" (Ezek 20:21). Through his anger, God establishes his authority as king over Israel: "As I live, says the Lord GOD, surely with a mighty hand and an outstretched arm, and with wrath poured out, I will be king over you" (Ezek 20:33).

c. Rejected covenant partner. A treaty similar to ANE sovereign-vassal treaties is laid out in Deuteronomy and the DtrH, according to which God blesses Israel with security and well-being on the land if she fulfills her obligation to serve God exclusively. However, if Israel fails to adhere to her covenantal obligation and engages in foreign worship, she triggers divine wrath and endangers her well-being on the land (Deut 6:15; Judg 2:14-20; 1 Kgs 11:9; 2 Kgs 13:3-19).

When Israel refuses to adhere to her covenant obligation and engages in image worship (Deut 4:13-16), God responds with wrath and temporarily ceases to fulfill God's own covenantal responsibility to provide sustenance on safe land (4:21-27).

4. Aim and consequences of the wrath of God

The typical aim of divine wrath is to persuade Israel that God is the nation's rightful authority. This aim applies whether God's wrath is directed at Israel or at foreign nations. However, the consequences of divine wrath vary considerably depending upon whether it is directed at Israel or at foreign nations. Just as human wrath at foreigners is typically lethal and permanent, so too God's wrath at the foreign nations is wholly destructive. Just as human wrath at kin is tempered, so too God's wrath at the people of Israel is either temporary and then withdrawn, or restrained entirely.

a. Divine wrath at foreign nations. The imagery of wholesale slaughter and irreparable destruction describes the effects of divine wrath upon Israel's enemies. God's anger burns the Egyptian army like stubble (Exod 15:7) so that the chariots and horsemen of Pharaoh's entire army are drowned (Exod 14:28; 15:19). In the Prophets, God's anger totally annihilates the foreign NATIONS (Isa 34:2). Divine wrath turns Babylon into an utter desolation (Jer 50:11-13) that is never again inhabited (Jer 50:39), and it turns Edom into a wasteland (Ezek 25:12-14; 35:11-15). In the psalms, God destroys the foreign rulers who are enemies of God and the king of Zion (Ps 2).

God unleashes his devastating wrath at foreign nations in order to display his power before Israel and to persuade Israel to acknowledge that God is the nation's only reliable redeemer. As Ezekiel predicts to the foreign nations, "I will deal with you according to the anger and envy that you showed because of your hatred against them; and I will make myself known among you.... As you rejoiced over the inheritance of the house of Israel, because it was desolate, so I will deal with you; you shall be desolate, Mount Seir, and all Edom, all of it. Then they [Israel] shall know that I am the LORD" (Ezek 35:11-15).

b. Divine wrath at Israel. Divine wrath at Israel can be destructive as well. In addition to depicting the damaging impact of divine wrath upon Israel, the Bible also often emphasizes God's restraint of his anger and/or the turning away of his anger from Israel. The four main reasons God turns back his anger at Israel are: 1) God's affection for Israel; 2) the covenant between God and Israel; 3) Israel's repentance; and/or 4) God's reputation among the nations.

Sometimes, God restrains or turns back his anger because of his innate affection for Israel, regardless of whether Israel repents. Some passages imply that God's restraint stems from familial affection. Hosea explains that God cannot destroy his son Ephraim (Hos 11) in anger because of the compassion that stirs within him: "My heart recoils within me; my compassion grows warm and tender. I will not execute my fierce anger; I will not again destroy Ephraim" (Hos 11:8b-9a, compare 14:1-9). God also turns back his anger from Israel because of the affection that defines the covenantal relationship (Isa 54:8-11; Ezek 16:5-8, 42, 60-62). As we see in Isaiah, "In overflowing wrath for a moment I hid my face from you, but with everlasting love I will have compassion on you, says the LORD, your Redeemer ... so I have sworn that I will not be angry with you and will not rebuke you ... my steadfast love shall not depart from you, and my covenant of peace shall not be removed, says the LORD, who has compassion on you" (Isa 54:8-10).

Throughout the DtrH, God turns back his anger in response to Israel's repentance (Deut 4:23b-31; Judg 3:7-9; compare Judg 10:7-11; 1 Kgs 8:46-47). The covenant between God and Israel demands that God protect Israel when she remains faithful. Therefore, when Israel does evil and provokes God to anger, God threatens to utterly destroy the nation. However, when Israel repents God also promises to be merciful and "neither abandon you nor destroy you; he will not forget the covenant with your ancestors that he swore to them" (Deut 4:23b-31). Ironically, then, breach of covenant is both a source of God's wrath and also a reason God turns away his wrath.

Preserving his reputation in the eyes of the nations is another reason God restrains his wrath at Israel. Moses successfully convinces God to turn back his anger from Israel for the sake of his reputation (Exod 32:11-12).

God's restraint is reiterated in the prophetic recollection of Israel's desert sinning (Ezek 20:21b-22). Perhaps the biblical authors assume that Israel will acknowledge God's authority when the powerful foreign nations acknowledge God's power.

Many biblical passages describe God restraining or turning back his anger without offering a precise explanation for God's temperance (Exod 4:14; Pss 74:1-11; 79:5-12; Isa 10:25; 12:1; Jer 32–33; Ezek 14:21-23; Zeph 3:1-11). In Isaiah, God actually warns the nation to hide from his wrath: "Come, my people, enter your chambers, and shut your doors behind you; hide yourselves for a little while until the wrath is past" (Isa 26:20).

The only instance in which God gets angry but does not punish his provoker, threaten to do so, or demand repentance is when God gets angry at Moses for refusing to confront Pharaoh. Here, God accommodates Moses by offering Aaron as Moses' mouthpiece before Pharaoh (Exod 4:14). Perhaps such tempered wrath stems from the restraint that defines the uniquely intimate relationship between God and Moses, and by which God speaks to Moses "face to face" (Exod 33:11). *See* DAY OF ATONEMENT; FORGIVENESS.

5. The wrath of God and war

War is the primary expression of divine wrath throughout the OT. Some of the earliest biblical texts depict divine wrath as God's weapon of war by which God assaults offenders (Exod 15:7-8; Ps 18:8-16; Hab 3:3-13). In Exod 15:3-7, God is a warrior (15:3) who smashes enemies at the sea. God crushes the enemy when he forcefully hurls his anger with his mighty right arm (Exod 15:6-7).

The connection between divine anger and war is preserved in the Prophets and DtrH, which describe God's intervention in Israel's wars. The Prophets retain the preexilic portrait of divine wrath as a weapon of war. However, they describe God guiding human battle or realizing his anger through human battle (Isa 10:5-6; Jer 50:25-27).

The DtrH tends to depict God's wrath as an affective quality, similar to other emotions and not a concretized weapon of war: "the LORD your God, who is present with you, is a jealous God. The anger of the LORD your God would be kindled against you and he would destroy you from the face of the earth" (Deut 6:15). As an emotion (like human emotions) God's wrath can be swayed by his mercy (Judg 2:14-18; 3:8-10).

Notably, the motif of divine anger in war is evident also in a wide range of biblical texts that do not otherwise depict a military context (Exod 22:22-24; Job 20:19-20, 23-28; Ps 38:6-11). The pervasiveness of this motif points to its significance in biblical theology.

a. Calamities of war. The dominance of the link between divine wrath and war throughout the OT should be considered when analyzing the consequences of divine wrath. Passages from Israel's early poetic texts, Judahite prophetic texts, Job, and Psalms all identify God's divine wrath with human weapons of war, such as the sword, rod, bow, and smiting human arm (Ps 38:2-5; Isa 9:11-13; 10:4-6; Ezek 20:33-34). The Prophets also depict God's anger as manifested in fire, famine, and pestilence (Jer 21:4-9; 42:15-18; Ezek 7:8), tragedies that they also blame on the devastations of war (2 Kgs 25:9).

Divine wrath is most frequently manifested as burning fire (Exod 15:6-8; Ps 18:7-16; Hab 3:3-12). In addition to the perceived physiological process of increased heat when angry, images of the fire of divine wrath may also stem from storm-theophany mythologies in which warrior deities radiate dangerous lightning (compare Isa 30:27-33; Hab 3:4-9). Additionally, the context of God's fiery wrath in the Prophets may be found in the harsh reality of war, and particularly in the Babylonian invasion. Biblical authors ascribe the Babylonian invasion to God's wrath, and they also lament the calamitous fires that burn down towns during the siege and invasion (2 Kgs 25:9; Jer 21:5-10; Ezek 21:31-32).

b. The cup of God's wrath. The link between divine wrath and war is vividly expressed in the images of the cup of God's wrath (Isa 51:17-21; Jer 25:15-33) and God's poured wrath (Ezek 21:31-32 [Heb. 21:36-37]). In both contexts divine wrath is portrayed as a liquid that resembles blood. By describing divine wrath as blood, the Prophets may be trying to convey that Israel is responsible for unleashing God's wrath and incurring foreign invasion. Through their provocative sins the people have "poured" their own blood. By drinking from God's cup of wrath and swallowing the consequence of their own iniquity—that is, the blood of those slain by the sword—the people assume responsibility for their own destruction.

B. Wrath in the New Testament

In the NT, *wrath* is used almost exclusively of God. References to divine wrath occur mostly in the Pauline epistles and Revelation. In the NT, the words orgē (Matt 3:7; Mark 3:5; Rom 2:5; 1 Thess 1:10; Rev 6:16) and thymos (Rom 2:8; Rev 15:1) represent the variety of Hebrew words for wrath.

Nowhere in the NT is orgē or thymos rendered as an adjective or verb to describe an attribute of God or God's state of being. Instead, the wrath of God is a finite punishment that will be delivered in the future on the "day of wrath" (hēmera orgēs [ἡμέρα ὀργῆς], Rom 2:5; Rev 6:16-17), or was already expressed in the fall of Jerusalem to Babylon (Luke 21:23). The book of Revelation recalls the Hebrew prophets' "cup of wrath" (Isa 51:17-23; Jer 25:15-29) when it describes Babylon drinking from the cup of wrath, literally "wine of the wrath of God" (oinos tou thēmou tou theou [οἶνος τοῦ θημοῦ τοῦ θεοῦ], Rev 14:10; 16:19; compare Mark 14:36).

Paul and the book of Revelation echo the OT's emphasis on the dissipation and turning back of divine wrath by describing God's wrath as finite. Human beings are not destined for wrath, but for salvation through Jesus Christ (1 Thess 5:9). However, whereas the OT attributes the end of divine wrath to the covenant, affection, or repentance, Revelation states that God's wrath is finite because whatever opposes God's wrath disappears (Rev 20:14-15).

Paul reflects the view expressed in biblical poetry and in the Prophets that depicts God's wrath as a divine punishment for sin, more than an internal emotion (Rom 5:9; Eph 5:6). In Paul's understanding, Christ saves those who trust in God's love from the wrath of God through his crucifixion and resurrection (Rom 5:9; 1 Thess 1:10). However, those who are wicked, disobedient, stubborn, and unrepentant of their sins are not saved from God's wrath (Rom 1:18; 2:4-5; compare Eph 5:5-6). *See* ANGER; ATONEMENT; BLESSINGS AND CURSINGS; COVENANT, OT AND NT; DAY OF JUDGMENT; DAY OF THE LORD; ELECTION; ESCHATOLOGY IN EARLY JUDAISM; ESCHATOLOGY OF THE NT; ESCHATOLOGY OF THE OT; FEAR; HOLY, HOLINESS, NT; HOLY, HOLINESS, OT; JEALOUSY; JUDGMENT; JUDGMENT, ESCHATOLOGICAL; LOVE IN THE NT; LOVE IN THE OT; SALVATION; WAR, IDEAS OF.

Bibliography: Samuel E. Balentine. *The Hidden God: The Hiding of the Face of God in the Old Testament* (1983); Bruce Edward Baloian. *Anger in the Old Testament* (1992); Hans J. Bochen. *Justice in the Old Testament* (1980); Marc Zvi Brettler. *God Is King: Understanding an Israelite Metaphor* (1989); Aloysius Fitzgerald. *The Lord of the East Wind* (2002); Terence E. Fretheim. "Theological Reflections on the Wrath of God in the Old Testament." *HBT* 24 (2002) 1–26; Julie Galambush. *Jerusalem in the Book of Ezekiel: The City as Yahweh's Wife* (1991); Samantha Joo. *Provocation and Punishment: The Anger of God in the Book of Jeremiah and Deuteronomistic Theology* (2006); Sa-Moon Kang. *Divine War in the Old Testament and in the Ancient Near East* (1989); Kari Latvus. *God, Anger, and Ideology: The Anger of God in Joshua and Judges in Relation to Deuteronomy and the Priestly Writings* (1998); Patrick Miller. *The Divine Warrior in Early Israel* (1973); Patrick Miller. *Sin and Judgment in the Prophets: A Stylistic and Theological Analysis* (1982); Katrina Poetker. "The Anger of Yahweh." *Direction* 16 (1987) 55–59; Marius Reiser. *Jesus and Judgment: The Eschatological Proclamation in Its Jewish Context* (1997); M. R. Schlimm. "Different Perspectives on Divine Pathos: An Examination of Hermeneutics in Biblical Theology." *CBQ* 69 (2007) 673–94; Mark Smith. "The Heart and Innards in Israelite Emotional Expressions: Notes from Anthropology and Psychobiology." *JBL* 117 (1998) 427–36; Stephen H. Travis. *Christ and the Judgement of God: The Limits of Divine Retribution in New Testament Thought.* Rev. ed. (2009); Chris

VanLandingham. *Judgment and Justification in Early Judaism and the Apostle Paul* (2006).

DEENA GRANT

WREATH [גְּדִלִים gedhilim, לִיוֹת loyoth; στέφανος stephanos]. Wreaths include decorations and headwear wound from plants, such as olive or ivy. In 1 Kings, two different words are translated as "wreath" to describe accoutrements of Solomon's Temple. In 1 Kgs 7:17, gedhilim denotes chain-work wreaths on the capitals of pillars. In 1 Kgs 7:29, 30, 36, loyoth refers to wreaths that adorn temple courtyard laver stands.

In the Apocrypha, the heroine Judith and her confreres adorn themselves with victors' olive wreaths (Jdt 15:13). Second Maccabees 6:7 reports that Jews were compelled to participate in the Dionysiac festival and wear the trademark wreaths of ivy (kissos κισσός) as they marched in procession. Sirach 32:2 instructs the host of a feast to act humbly and receive "a wreath for your excellent leadership." The only NT reference is in 1 Cor 9:25, where Paul exalts the imperishable crown self-control brings to believers over the perishable crown won by athletes.

ROBERT A. KUGLER

WRESTLING [אָבַק ʾavaq, פָּתַל pathal; ἀγωνίζομαι agōnizomai]. A struggle or contest, either physical or spiritual. The encounter between Jacob and God at Peniel (Gen 32), as Jacob was returning from Mesopotamia with his clan, is the chief story of wrestling in a literal, physical way in the OT. The term ʾavaq (32:24, 25) carries the sense of "to embrace one another," hence, "to struggle, to wrestle." The use of this rare term is curious and perhaps to be explained as a wordplay with yabboq (יַבֹּק), the name of the river that Jacob crosses in the narrative (32:22).

Of similar interest is the earlier, and related, narrative of Rachel's agonizing over her barrenness. When her handmaid, Bilhah, bore a second son to Jacob, Rachel said, "With mighty wrestlings (naftule נַפְתּוּלֵי) I have wrestled (niftalti נִפְתַּלְתִּי) with my sister" (Gen 30:8). Twice the root ptl (פָּתַל) is used metaphorically in a narrative setting in which Rachel names the son "Naphtali" (naftali נַפְתָּלִי).

The NT uses a variety of terms to refer to spiritual struggling or wrestling in different life settings. Paul refers to Epaphras "wrestling" in his prayers (Col 4:12) and speaks of a "struggle" against the powers of darkness (Eph 6:12). The writer of Hebrews recognizes their "struggle" against sin (Heb 12:4; see also Col 1:29; 1 Tim 4:10) and with the reality of suffering and public ridicule (Heb 10:32).

JOHN I. LAWLOR

WRITING AND WRITING MATERIALS. Ancient writing systems can be divided into two basic categories: non-alphabetic (the earliest systems) and alphabetic. Writing began in Mesopotamia, ca. 3200 BCE in the non-Semitic, Sumerian language. The Sumerian writing system was pictographic not alphabetic. However, it soon became stylized, and much of its pictographic basis was lost. The wedge-shaped signs used to write Sumerian, called CUNEIFORM, represented consonants and vowels. Semitic Akkadian texts, first attested in Mesopotamia ca. 2350 BCE, employed a modified form of Sumerian cuneiform. Texts written in Egyptian, first attested ca. 3100 BCE, were in a non-alphabetic script referred to as Egyptian hieroglyphics. Hieroglyphics were used for monumental texts, but the cursive hieratic script derived from hieroglyphs was used for writing other texts (e.g., letters, receipts). Egyptian signs could be logographic (representing an entire word), uniconsonantal, biconsonantal, triconsonantal, or could function as determinatives. Unlike Sumerian and Akkadian, vowels were not indicated in either Egyptian script. Significantly, a number of INSCRIPTIONS written in these (and other) languages have direct relevance for the study of the OT and NT.

Alphabetic writing systems use a single grapheme to designate a single phoneme (*see* ALPHABET). Alphabetic writing is first attested in the early 2nd millennium BCE (e.g., Middle Bronze Age inscriptions from Wadi el-Hol, Serabit el-Khadem). The basis for the system is the acrophonic principle. That is, pictorial signs represented the initial sound of the objects depicted. Thus, the pictorial sign for bayith (בַּיִת, "house") represented the phoneme "B," and the pictorial sign for yadh (יָד, "hand") represented the phoneme "Y." The writing system for the Ugaritic language is alphabetic, but rather than using "standard" alphabetic letters, a unique "cuneiform alphabet" was developed at Bronze Age Ugarit. Iron Age languages such as Phoenician, Aramaic, Hebrew, Ammonite, and Moabite are Semitic languages that employ alphabetic writing systems. Significantly, these first alphabetic writing systems could represent consonants but not vowels (but note the gradual development of a system where consonants marked vowels). The Greek alphabet was derived from the Phoenician alphabet, but the Greeks modified it so as to be able to represent both vowels and consonants. The Latin alphabet derived in large part from the Greek alphabet with some Etruscan influence. Rigorous education was necessary for mastering writing (Rollston; van der Toorn).

Various writing implements are attested in the biblical and epigraphic record. The Hebrew word ʿet (עֵט) referred to a scribal writing implement (e.g., ʿet soferim [עֵט סֹפְרִים] "pen of the scribes"; Jer 8:8). The fact that the LXX translators could render ʿet with kalamos (κάλαμος, "reed"; Ps 45:1 [Heb. 45:2; LXX 44:2]) confirms that the term ʿet referred, at least sometimes, to a reed pen. Reed pens necessitated the use of INK (Jer 36:18; compare 3 Macc 4:20; 2 John 12; 3 John 13). Although damp ink could be washed off (compare Num 5:23), it became durable after drying. The color of the ink was normally black, but red ink is also attested in the Northwest Semitic epigraphic record (*see* DEIR ʿALLA, TEXTS). The scribe using a reed pen often had (and sometimes wore at the waist) a qeseth hassofer (קֶסֶת הַסֹּפֵר, "scribal palette" or "scribal pen case"; Ezek 9:2, 3, 11; *see* WRITING CASE). The term taʿar hassofer (תַּעַר הַסֹּפֵר, "scribal knife") refers to the PENKNIFE used to cut parchment and papyrus (e.g., for sizing; Jer 36:23). This implement could also have been used for erasures. It was probably also the instrument used to trim the end of a reed at a desired angle.

Another writing implement, the chisel, was used along with a hammer to cut Iron Age Hebrew inscriptions into stone (e.g., Ahiram Sarcophagus Inscription, Tel Dan Inscription, Siloam Tunnel Inscription). Similarly, many Iron Age Hebrew inscriptions were incised with some type of metal stylus. For clay vessels, incising with a stylus was sometimes done before firing, but more frequently after firing. Possible Hebrew terms for stylus and chisel include ʿet barzel (בַּרְזֶל עֵט, "iron pen"), a metal stylus that may have also referred to a chisel (Job 19:24; Jer 17:1), a type of writing implement of uncertain nature called a kheret (חֶרֶט; Isa 8:1), and very small specialized incising tools used for making of seals (compare Sir 38:24–39:11). A reed stylus shaped to make the wedge-shaped signs in moist clay was used on clay tablets in Mesopotamia.

Various types of media were used for writing linear alphabetic letters (e.g., Phoenician, Aramaic, Hebrew, Ammonite). Stone was used for writings intended to be more permanent (compare Exod 24:12; Josh 8:32; 1 Kgs 8:9; Job 19:24). Stone STELEs were sometimes commissioned by powerful elites (*see* INSCRIPTION, TELL DAN; MOABITE STONE). Stone surfaces could be used for religious and royal inscriptions of significant feats. Tombs could be inscribed as well as sarcophagi.

Papyrus was perishable, but some papyri have survived (*see* NASH PAPYRUS; PAPYRUS, PAPYRI). The extensive use of papyri for important documents is demonstrated by the recovery of bullae used to seal important documents (compare Jer 32:9-15). A few manuscripts from Qumran are papyrus, but most Qumran manuscripts are parchment ("leather"). The use of leather is also mentioned for documents from earlier periods. Although sefer (סֵפֶר) can have a variety of meanings, references to meghillath sefer (מְגִלַּת סֵפֶר; e.g., Jer 36:2, 4) must refer to papyrus or leather documents. OSTRACA, potsherds used as a writing surface, were not used for items intended to be permanent, but for utilitarian purposes (e.g., letters, fiscal records, and school practice texts). Complete pots were written on also (e.g., the pithoi from Kuntillet ʿAjrud, the "Gibeon"-inscribed jar handles, and the lmlk jar handle impressions all over Judah; *see* LMLK SEALS).

Writing on plaster walls is also well attested (e.g., Deir ʿAlla, Kuntillet ʿAjrud, and biblical references to the practice [Deut 27:2-4; Dan 5:5]). Although rare, metal was sometimes used as a writing surface (ax heads from Ugarit, Late Bronze Age arrowheads, Tell Siran bronze bottle, silver amulets from Jerusalem, and the COPPER SCROLL), but coins are common in later periods. Bone and ivory were used (e.g., Nimrud Inscription, Hazael Booty Inscriptions, the Samaria Ivories). Clay, wooden, and wax tablets were used for writing cuneiform and alphabetic inscriptions in Northwest Semitic (*see* TABLET; WRITING BOARDS). There are some examples of clay tablets with cuneiform inscriptions with accompanying linear alphabetic inscriptions, either in ink or incised (e.g., Aramaic inscriptions from Persepolis). John 7:53–8:11 refers to Jesus writing words in the sand.

Bibliography: Christopher A. Rollston. "Scribal Education in Ancient Israel: The Old Hebrew Epigraphic Evidence." *BASOR* 344 (2006) 47–74; Karel van der Toorn. *Scribal Culture and the Making of the Hebrew Bible* (2007).

CHRISTOPHER A. ROLLSTON

WRITING BOARDS. Boards of wood or ivory (though there are some references to boards of silver and gold), sometimes bound together with hinges, that were coated to provide a writing surface. Mesopotamian writing boards were coated with wax and used to write cuneiform. They could be erased and recoated, making them useful for composing the first draft of a document (i.e., before writing the final draft in clay or stone), and also for educational contexts. In Egypt, wooden writing boards were often coated with gesso and then used as a medium for writing with ink. *See* WRITING AND WRITING MATERIALS.

CHRISTOPHER A. ROLLSTON

WRITING CASE [קֶסֶת הַסֹּפֵר qeseth hassofer]. A case holding the basic equipment used by a scribe; such cases have been excavated in Mesopotamia and Egypt. Scribal tools are mentioned in ANE texts, including the Bible: a "scribal pen" (Jer 8:8, author's trans.; NRSV, "pen of the scribes") or "iron pen" (Jer 17:1; Job 19:24), "ink" (Jer 36:18; 2 John 12), and even a "scribal knife" (Jer 36:23, author's trans.; NRSV, "penknife"). Some have proposed that the "writing case" mentioned in Ezek 9:2, 3, 11 is, in fact, a scribal palette, used to hold ink. *See* WRITING AND WRITING MATERIALS.

CHRISTOPHER A. ROLLSTON

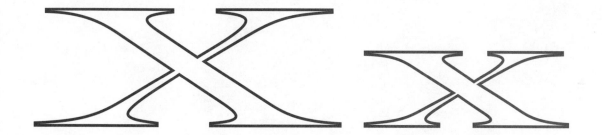

XANTHICUS zan'thi-kuhs [Ξανθικός Xanthikos]. The name of the month appearing in the letters sent from ANTIOCHUS V and the Romans to the Jews, allowing the Jews to return home (2 Macc 11:27-38). This month in the Seleucid or Macedonian CALENDAR is equivalent to the Jewish month of NISAN.

XERXES zuhrk'seez [Ξέρξης Xerxes]. 1. Xerxes I (Persian Xshayarshan) was the fourth Achaemenid king in the Persian Empire. He is reflected in the biblical tradition as AHASUERUS at Ezra 4:6 and in the book of Esther. The son of Darius I and his most powerful wife, Atossa, Xerxes was born in 518 BCE. Though he was not the eldest son, Darius named Xerxes as crown prince and appointed him as satrap over Babylonia, the second-highest position in the empire, in 498 BCE. With his father's death in 486 BCE, Xerxes ascended to the throne.

Like his father, Xerxes permitted a high degree of religious autonomy among the peoples in the empire. Yet he discontinued official funding for the construction and maintenance of local temples (including the new temple in Jerusalem, one would assume), and, in actions more political than religious, destroyed temples in areas where revolt broke out. His reign saw a period of increasing centralization of government, increasing legal and economic privileges given to ethnic Persians, and increasing economic difficulties especially in local economies.

Military exploits marked Xerxes' reign. He suppressed, but only after heavy fighting, a revolt by Egypt (486–483 BCE). In 484 and 482 BCE he squelched uprisings in the Babylonian territories, in part through the actions of his general Megabyzus' toppling and smelting an 18-ft.-tall statue of Marduk. It is his action against Greece, however, for which Xerxes is best remembered. In an attempt to increase Persian territories to the west, Xerxes moved his massive, skilled military forces against mainland Greece in 480–479 BCE. This campaign first met with success as Xerxes won a significant battle at Thermopylae. But as the Greeks became more aggressive, Persia subsequently suffered a naval defeat at Salamis, an army defeat and the slaying of their general Mardonis at Plataea, and a final naval defeat at Mycale.

Domestic concerns occupied Xerxes' later years. He oversaw grand construction projects at Persepolis, including a palace, monuments, and other official build-

ings; and instigated numerous harem intrigues at home, including the seduction of his niece Artayante. His courtier Artabanus killed Xerxes in an assassination plot in late 465 BCE.

2. Xerxes II, son of Artaxerxes and grandson of Xerxes I, reigned a mere forty-five days in 423 BCE before being assassinated by his half-brother Secydianus.

LINDA DAY

XI [ξ x, Ξ X]. The fourteenth letter of the Greek alphabet, based on the Phoenician *samk, which gave its form to Greek xi but not its sound; evidently it was a voiceless alveolar sibilant. *See* ALPHABET.

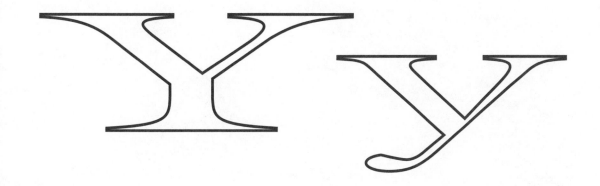

YAH. *See* JAH, YAH.

YAHWEH yah´weh [יהוה yhwh]. The distinctive name of Israel's God, originally consisting of only four consonants, yhwh, and consistently translated "(the) LORD." The pronunciation is a scholarly reconstruction based on Greek transcriptions of the name. *See* GOD, NAMES OF; LORD.

YAHWEH OF HOSTS. *See* GOD, NAMES OF; LORD OF HOSTS; YAHWEH.

YAHWIST. *See* J, YAHWIST.

YARKON RIVER. A river, also known as the Wadi ʿAuja, that starts near APHEK and runs west into the Mediterranean Sea at Tel Aviv. Tel Qasile lies along the river (*see* QASILE, TEL), and the VIA MARIS runs nearby. The Yarkon River is not mentioned in the Bible.

YARMULKE. *See* HEAD COVERING.

YARN. *See* CLOTH, CLOTHES; DISTAFF; TEXTILES.

YAʾUDI yaw´di. Some of the linear Northwest Semitic inscriptions found at Zincirli (ancient Samʾal) are written in a distinctive dialect of Aramaic that seems to reflect the national dialect of the kingdom of Yaʾudi. Primary exemplars of this dialect are the 8th-cent. BCE inscriptions dedicated to Hadad and King Panammu II. To be sure, some have argued that the Yaʾudi dialect actually preserves 2nd-millennium features that antedate the division of Northwest Semitic into Canaanite and Aramaic, but the consensus continues to be that Yaʾudi is indeed derived from a branch of Aramaic that became independent of the "standard dialect" of Aramaic (arguably around 1000 BCE) and subsequently developed certain distinctive features (isoglosses) that can be viewed as innovations. *See* INSCRIPTIONS.

Bibliography: Paul Dion. "The Language Spoken in Ancient Samʾal." *JNES* 37 (1978) 115–18; W. Randall Garr. *Dialect Geography of Syria-Palestine: 1000–586 B.C.E.* (1985).

CHRISTOPHER A. ROLLSTON

YAVNEH. *See* JABNEH; JAMNIA, COUNCIL OF.

YEAR [שָׁנָה shanah; ἐνιαυτός eniautos, ἔτος etos]. The biblical text does not specify the number of days in the year or a single CALENDAR system. There are three systems used in the biblical texts to refer to the months of the year. One uses Canaanite names, a second uses ordinal numbers, and a third uses Babylonian names. In all three systems, the year begins in what modern readers would call the spring, our March or April (the Canaanite month of ABIB ["ripe ears of barley"] and the Babylonian Nisan). The OT, however, has references that indicate yet another system, one that begins the NEW YEAR in the fall, our September or October.

In the modern world, a year is the time it takes for the earth to revolve around the sun. Of course, in a pre-Copernican world, where the celestial objects were thought to revolve around the earth, the year would measure other perceptions, such as the annual cycles of crops and plants, changing of the seasons, the cyclical movement of the points on the horizon where the sun rises and sets, and the cycle of stars and constellations visible at night.

The GEZER CALENDAR, a 10th-cent. BCE inscription, provides an early attestation of the year organized into twelve months around agricultural seasons, here beginning in our September or October:

Two months of ingathering.
Two months of sowing (cereals).
Two months of late planting (of legumes and vegetables).
A month of hoeing.
A month of harvesting barley.
A month of harvesting (wheat) and measuring (grain).
Two months of (summer) pruning.
A month of (ingathering) summer fruit.
    (trans. adapted from Dobbs-Allsopp et al.)

For the early Israelites and their neighbors, AGRICULTURE was intimately related to the cult. So many of the biblical festivals were agricultural in origin, including the three pilgrimage festivals, PASSOVER AND FEAST OF UNLEAVENED BREAD, the Feast of Weeks, and the Festival of Booths (*see* BOOTHS, FEAST OR FESTIVAL OF; WEEKS, FEAST OF). Exodus 23:14-17; 34:18-23; and Deut 16:1-17 list these festivals as an annual cycle, beginning with the Feast of Unleavened Bread in Abib. Similar lists also occur in the priestly sources Num 28–29 and Lev 23:4-44, which also begin with Passover, beginning "on the fourteenth day of the first month."

Although the festival lists begin with Passover in the spring, there are also indications of the system that began the year in the fall, in the seventh month (our September or October). Exodus 23:16 and 34:22 place the festival of ingathering (Festival of Booths) "at the end of the year" and "at the turn of the year," respectively. Both Lev 23:24 and Num 29:1 designate a "holy convocation" "on the first day of the seventh month," although it is not identified as the new year. According to Leviticus, the year of Jubilee begins on the DAY OF ATONEMENT, "the tenth day of the seventh month" (25:8-10). *See* FEASTS AND FASTS.

Located in the subtropical zone, the people of Israel experience two seasons, a dry summer season and a rainy winter season. Thus, the biblical books typically talk about two seasons, a "summer" (qayits קַיִץ; theros θέρος) and "winter" (khoref חֹרֶף, sethaw סְתָו; cheimōn χειμών). Psalm 74:17 affirms that God "made summer and winter." Zechariah anticipates a day when living waters shall flow out from Jerusalem, and "it shall continue in summer as in winter" (Zech 14:8). Using verbal forms of these roots, Isaiah, announcing judgment on the world, declares, "And the birds of prey will summer (qats קָץ) on them, and all the animals of the earth will winter (tekheraf תֶּחֱרָף) on them" (Isa 18:6). In these passages, summer typically precedes winter (although note Amos 3:15), roughly corresponding to the beginning of the year in what we would call spring and a "turn of the year" in the seventh month.

With two seasons, agricultural activities of planting (sowing, plowing) were associated with the rainy winter season, and harvesting associated with the dry summers. This is demonstrated by the poetic synonymous parallelism in God's oath after the flood in Gen 8:22 (J): "As long as the earth endures, seedtime and harvest, cold and heat, summer and winter, day and night, shall not cease." Rather than describing four seasons, in this poetic passage "seedtime" and "cold" are synonymous with "winter" and "night," while "harvest" and "heat" are synonymous with "summer" and "day." Harvest is the synonymous parallel with the dry season of summer in several proverbs; "it prepares its food in summer, and gathers its sustenance in harvest" (Prov 6:8) and "a child who gathers in summer is prudent, but a child who sleeps in harvest brings shame" (Prov 10:5). Proverbs 26:1 uses the inappropriateness of precipitation during the dry season, expressed in the synonymous parallelism of "like snow in summer or rain in harvest" to assert "so honor is not fitting for a fool" (compare the form of Prov 26:2, which also uses a synonymous parallel as a simile). Of course, the association of harvest throughout the warm season makes sense in the context of a diversified agriculture, in which different crops would be ready for harvest at different times throughout the warm season (compare the Gezer Calendar above).

Winter, on the other hand, was known as an especially difficult time to travel. Voyages across the Mediterranean Sea were particularly hazardous. Several words derived from the root of "winter" (cheimōn χειμών) are used to describe spending the winter in a place (paracheimazo [παραχειμάζω]; Acts 27:12; 28:11; 1 Cor 16:6; Titus 3:12; paracheimasia [παραχειμασία]; Acts 27:12). Even travel by land was to be avoided during that time; "Pray that your flight may not be in winter or on a sabbath" (Matt 24:20// Mark 13:18).

There are a few phrases used to describe the transitional periods between winter and summer; e.g., "the early and the late rain" (e.g., Jer 5:24, NRSV, "the autumn rain and the spring rain"; for "the spring rain" compare Prov 16:15; Hos 6:3; Zech 10:1). A periphrastic construction that the NRSV translates as "the spring of the year" or just "the spring" is literally "the turn of the year" (teshuvath hashanah תְּשׁוּבַת הַשָּׁנָה), as in the phrase "in the spring of the year, the time when kings go out to battle" (2 Sam 11:1//1 Chr 20:1; see also 1 Kgs 20:22, 26; 2 Chr 36:10). In many of Jesus' parables, the ability to discern the changing of the seasons is compared to the ability to anticipate God's intervention: "From the fig tree learn its lesson: as soon as its branch becomes tender and puts forth its leaves, you know that summer is near" (Mark 13:28//Matt 24:32; Luke 21:30); "Let both of them grow together until the harvest; and at harvest time I will tell the reapers" (Matt 13:30).

Within the traditions of the Pentateuch, seven-year cycles took on special significance. According to Exod 23:10-11 and Lev 25:1-7, fields, vineyards, and orchards are to lie fallow every seven years. Deuteronomy 15:1-11 prescribes the release of debts every seven years as a "year of remission." Exodus 21:1-6 (//Deut 15:12-18) enjoins the release of Hebrew slaves in their seventh year of service. Deuteronomy 31:10-13 instructs that "this law" be read every seven years "in the scheduled year of remission." Leviticus 25:8-55 counts seven sets of sabbatical years and institutes that year (vv. 8-9) or the next (v. 10) as the Jubilee. Traditions of the Jubilee are picked up in Third Isaiah (Isa 61:1-11), where the prophet is called "to proclaim the year of the LORD's favor" (Isa 61:2). Jesus, in Luke's Gospel, quotes Isa 61:1-2 at the beginning of his ministry (Luke 4:16-21). This postexilic Isaianic tradition is then cited in Luke to characterize Jesus' ministry. *See* CHRISTIAN YEAR, THE; ISRAEL, CLIMATE OF; JUBILEE, YEAR OF; MOON; SABBATICAL YEAR; SUN; TIME.

Bibliography: James Barr. *Biblical Words for Time* (1962); Gershon Brin. *The Concept of Time in the Bible and the Dead Sea Scrolls* (2001); F. W. Dobbs-Allsopp, J. J. M. Roberts, C. L. Seow, and R. E. Whitaker.

Hebrew Inscriptions: Texts from the Biblical Period of the Monarchy with Concordance (2005).

HENRY W. MORISADA RIETZ

YEAR OF RELEASE [שְׁנַת הַדְּרוֹר shenath hadderor]. The "year of release" is no doubt an idiom related to the SABBATICAL YEAR. Texts such as Lev 25:10 and Ezek 46:17 owe their understanding of this legislation to Deut 15:1-3. Scholarship generally has understood the year of release to be the Sabbatical Year or the Jubilee Year, an understanding involving the semantic relationship between deror and shamat (שָׁמַט), both meaning "release." Shamat is used to refer to allowing the land to lie fallow during the Sabbatical Year (Exod 23:11) and to the release of debt in the Jubilee Year (Deut 15:1-3; 31:10). *See* JUBILEE, YEAR OF.

JOSEPH R. CATHEY

YEAST [ζύμη zymē]. A raising or leavening agent kneaded into flour to create leavened bread (*see* LEAVEN). The leavening power of a small amount of yeast is used in the NT to theological effect. The effect of yeast on a batch of dough serves as a metaphor for the expansion of the kingdom of heaven from its humble beginnings (Matt 13:33; Luke 13:21). On the other hand, the action of yeast is compared to the negative effects of immorality (1 Cor 5:6-8) or harmful teaching (Gal 5:9). Jesus warns his disciples against the "yeast" or teaching of the Pharisees and Sadducees (Matt 16:6-12//Mark 8:15//Luke 12:1-3). *See* DIETARY LAWS; FOOD.

L. JULIANA CLAASSENS

YEHUD. *See* JUDEA, JUDEANS.

YELLOW [צָהֹב tsahov]. Tsahov refers to a pale to golden yellow that is gleaming or shiny. *Yellow* is used to describe the color of hair growing in skin that might be leprous. The presence of yellow hair is a diagnostic tool that allows the priest to declare an individual unclean (Lev 13:30, 32, 36). It is contrasted with black hair (Lev 13:31, 37). Yellow hair means the person is unclean, while black hair indicates that the person is clean. *See* COLORS.

Bibliography: Athalya Brenner. *Colour Terms in the Old Testament* (1982).

MARY P. BOYD

YERUSALMI, TARGUM. *See* TARGUMS.

YHWH. *See* GOD, NAMES OF; YAHWEH.

YOD yohd [י y]. The tenth letter of the Hebrew alphabet, which derives from the original Semitic word *yad-, "(fore)arm." *See* ALPHABET.

YOHANAN BEN ZAKKAI. A Tanna (*see* TANNA, TANNAIM), Yohanan ben Zakkai was a leader of Judaism following the Roman destruction of Jerusalem in 70 CE. According to rabbinic reports, he led their movement and transmitted teachings of the schools of both Hillel and Shammai (*see* HILLEL THE ELDER, HOUSE OF HILLEL; SHAMMAI THE ELDER). In a recurrent rabbinic legend, he escaped besieged Jerusalem by pretending to be dead and then made his way to the Roman general Vespasian to prophesy his elevation to emperor. As a reward, Vespasian granted Yohanan the right to establish an academy (or circle of disciples) at Yavneh (*see* JABNEH), preserving Torah-based Judaism. Yohanan and his students often stand in opposition to the Gamalielite patriarchal dynasty. *See* AKIVA, RABBI; GAMALIEL; RABBI, RABBONI; SAGE.

Bibliography: Jacob Neusner. *Development of a Legend: Studies on the Traditions Concerning Yohanan ben Zakkai* (1970); H. L. Strack and Günter Stemberger. *Introduction to the Talmud and Midrash* (1992).

BURTON L. VISOTZKY

YOKE [עֹל 'ol, צֶמֶד tsemedh; ζυγός zygos]. The term *yoke* has a wide range of uses, both literal and metaphorical, and is much more common in the OT. A literal yoke comprised a device that bound animals together and controlled them, enabling them to perform productive work. Animals are yoked (1 Kgs 19:19-21; Job 1:3; 42:12) or unyoked (Num 19:2; Deut 21:3).

This literal sense of control develops metaphorically to denote various agents of control, as well as notions of ownership and service. So *yoke* refers to the control, ownership, and service involved in slavery (Sir 33:26-27; 1 Tim 6:1). The image also applies to the uncontrolled tongue (Sir 28:18b-20) and to control by wisdom (Sir 51:26, only once). The yoke or the control that the Torah might exert is rejected by the rich (Jer 5:5), by those in Christ (Gal 5:1), and by Peter as unnecessary for Gentile disciples (Acts 15:10).

The majority of references, though, involve the sociopolitical realm. Israel's relationship to God is prominent, both the refusal to serve God (Jer 2:20) and the willingness to do so (*Pss. Sol.* 7:9). Beyond Israel, God's control extends to the nations who rebel against it or yield to it (*Pss. Sol.* 17:30).

Most frequent are uses of *yoke* to denote harsh rule. Solomon and Rehoboam's harsh rule/yoke over Israel involved forced labor, taxation, and violence (1 Kgs 12:4, 9-11, 14; 2 Chr 10:4, 9-11, 14). The imperial rule of nation over nation is a yoke. Edom will revolt against Israel's rule/yoke (Gen 27:40). God broke Egypt's rule/yoke over the Israelites (Lev 26:13). Israel's submission to imperial powers is viewed as judgment and punishment (Deut 28:48). God allows Assyrian and Babylonian rule/yoke over Israel as punishment but will bring it to an end (Isa 9:4; 10:27; 14:25). God authorizes submission to Babylon's rule/yoke, which Jeremiah is to symbolize by making a "yoke of straps and bars, and put them on your neck" (Jer 27:2, 8, 11). Though Babylon rules over Israel (Isa 47:6; Lam 3:27), God will break its yoke (Jer 28:2, 4, 10-14). God will free the people from Babylonian rule/yoke and establish God's fertile and just reign (Ezek 34:27). The heavy yoke of the Greeks enslaves Israel (1 Macc 8:18, 31) but the reign of Simon lifts the rule/yoke of the Gentiles (1 Macc 13:41).

That is, the term commonly designates the dominant imperial powers of the biblical tradition: Egypt, Assyria, Babylon, the Greeks. The contexts of these passages show that their rule was often exploitative and oppressive. The biblical texts put their rule/yoke into theological perspective, accomplishing God's will of punishing the people before God frees people from it.

In this context, Jesus' invitation in Matt 11:29-30 to "take my yoke" is best read as offering people a way of life that is an alternative to Rome's rule. The weary and burdened in 11:28 designate people living under burdensome and taxing Roman power. The promised "rest" echoes and anticipates the eschatological (re-)establishment of God's just and life-giving creation order (Gen 1; Isa 25:10) with freedom from imperial power (Deut 12:10; 2 Chr 20:29-30; 32:22).

Bibliography: Warren Carter. "Take My Yoke Not Rome's: Matt 11:28-30." *Matthew and Empire: Initial Explorations* (2001) 108–29.

WARREN CARTER

YOM KIPPUR. *See* DAY OF ATONEMENT.

YOSHUA BEN LEVI. A sage (ca. 180–260 CE) portrayed as a great authority, who presided over the academy in Lydda in Israel. He was a devoted grandfather. Rabbi Yoshua ben Levi is frequently described as having had conversations with Elijah, and he claimed to have found the Messiah among the lepers outside the city gates (*b. Sanh.* 98a). Physically disabled by a pronounced limp, he devoted himself to those who were shunned because they suffered from communicable diseases. He is ultimately described as having passed into the world to come without going through death (*b. Ketub.* 77b). *See* RABBI, RABBONI.

JUDITH ABRAMS

YOUTH [נַעַר na'ar; νεανίας neanias, νεανίσκος neaniskos]. A youth is a person whose age is somewhere between infancy and relative adulthood. Throughout the Bible, youth is a period of vigor, opportunity, and prophetic receptiveness to God's call, although sometimes marked by evil desires (e.g., 2 Tim 2:22).

In Hebrew na'ar means "youngster" or "servant" and implies high birth or great responsibility. Esau, Jacob, Joseph, and Samson are ne'arim (נְעָרִים, "youths," Gen 25:27; 37:2; Judg 13:5-7; NRSV, "boys"). Rebekah, Ruth, Esther, an unnamed concubine, and a slave are called na'arah (נַעֲרָה, "girl" or "young woman," Gen 24:16; Judg 19:3; Ruth 2:5-6; 2 Kgs 5:2; Esth 2:7). A young man in military service may be a bekhor (בְּכוֹר, literally, "firstborn," e.g., Samson in Judg 14:10; NRSV, "young man"), or neanias or neaniskos (e.g., Paul, at the stoning of Stephen [Acts 7:58]; the Vulgate term is *adulescentis*).

The numerical ages associated with biblical youth are unclear. Moses grows from infancy to adulthood in the space of three verses (Exod 2:9-11), and we know nothing about Jesus between ages twelve and thirty except that he grew (Luke 2:52). Indeed, *youth* or *young* refers to a broad spectrum of ages: the nursing infant Samuel (1 Sam 1:22; NRSV, "child"), the eight-year-old King Josiah (2 Chr 34:3; NRSV, "boy"), the thirty-year-old Joseph (Gen 41:12; NRSV, "young Hebrew"), and the forty-one-year-old King Rehoboam (2 Chr 13:7, though some scholars call this a transcription error, with the more accurate age being about twenty-one). In Exodus, census-takers only counted those over age nineteen (30:14), but Moses allowed a twenty-five-year-old na'ar to participate in the meeting tent (Num 8:24). Perhaps the most that we can say is that the majority of "youths" in the Bible are in their second or third decade of life and usually have not yet married or entered military service—with significant exceptions.

Yahweh repeatedly enlists young people in the salvation of Israel. Samuel, Jeremiah, and Timothy serve as God's envoys in spite of their apparent immaturity. The boy (na'ar) Samuel hears God's voice calling him (1 Sam 3:1-21) but is initially afraid to tell Eli what God said (3:15). Jeremiah protests against his calling: "I do not know how to speak, for I am only a boy" (na'ar, Jer 1:6). The Pauline writer admonishes Timothy, the young leader of the contentious Christian community in Ephesus, "Let no one despise your youth, but set the believers an example in speech and conduct, in love, in faith, in purity" (1 Tim 4:12). A young woman named Mary is chosen to be the mother of Jesus (Luke 1:26-38). As the angel Gabriel makes clear, low social status, inexperience, and economic or physical vulnerability do not deter God from employing her for this role. Even unnamed youth, like the Israelite girl who says Elisha can cure Naaman's leprosy (2 Kgs 5:2-3), and the slave girl who announces Paul and Silas in Philippi (Acts 16:16-17), set in motion a chain of events that proclaim God's salvation. *See* AGING.

Bibliography: Ron Becker. "Beyond a Godless Understanding of Youth." *The Journal of Youth and Theology* 5 (2006) 10–30; John MacDonald. "The Status and Role of the Na'ar in Israelite Society." *JNES* 35 (1976) 147–70.

KENDA CREASY DEAN

ZAANAN zay´uh-nan [צַאֲנָן tsa'anan]. An unidentified village in western Judah (Mic 1:11). Often identified with ZENAN, one of the villages in the lowland of Judah mentioned in Josh 15:37.

ZAANANNIM zay´uh-na´nim [צַעֲנַנִּים tsa'anannim]. May mean "travelers." "The oak in Zaanannim" is a point on the southern boundary of Naphtali (Josh 19:33), near Kedesh (Judg 4:11); its location is uncertain. Some scholars identify the site with Khan et-Tujjar, a caravan stop on the road from Beth-shan to Damascus, approximately 4 mi. southeast of Adam (Khirbet Damiyeh). Others associate the site with Lejjun, a site approximately 2 mi. north of Taanach, between Megiddo and Tell Abu Qedeis. Another possible location is Khirbet Bessum, approximately 3 mi. northeast of Mount Tabor.

This same site is mentioned in Judg 4:11 under the name ELON-BEZAANANNIM, which literally means "the oak in Zaanannim." Heber the Kenite camped here, and here his wife JAEL killed Sisera (Judg 4:17-22). Scholars debate whether "oak" ('elon אֵלוֹן) is the first word of a compound name or a reference to an actual (sacred?) tree located at Zaanannim.

TERRY W. EDDINGER

ZAAVAN zay´uh-vuhn [זַעֲוָן za'awan]. A grandson of SEIR the Horite and the second-listed son of the clan chief EZER (Gen 36:27; 1 Chr 1:42). As a clan name, Zaavan represents part of the indigenous Horite population disrupted by immigrating Esauite clans (Deut 2:12) and eventually absorbed into historical Edom (see EDOM, EDOMITES).

JASON C. DYKEHOUSE

ZABAD zay´bad [זָבָד zavadh; Σάβαθος Sabathos, Σαβανναιούς Sabannaious, Ζαβαδαίας Zabadaias]. 1. Nathan's son and Ephlal's father in a genealogy that traces Elishama back to Jerahmeel in the tribe of Judah (1 Chr 2:36-37).

2. Tahath's son in a genealogy that traces Joshua back to Ephraim (1 Chr 7:21).

3. Ahlai's son and one of the warriors in David's armies (1 Chr 11:41).

4. Son of Shimeath the Ammonite and one of King Joash's servants. With JEHOZABAD, he killed King Joash in his bed because King Joash had demanded that Zechariah, son of the priest Jehoida, be stoned to death (2 Chr 24:20-26). In 2 Kgs 12:21, his name is

JOZACAR, although some manuscripts and later editions have the name as Jozabad. The Chronicler, however, has abbreviated Jozabad to Zabad.

5. Descendant of Zattu. He dismissed his foreign wife and their children in accordance with the covenant God made with Ezra (Ezra 10:1-5, 27). In 1 Esd 9:28, he is a descendant of Zamoth.

6. Descendant of Hashum. He dismissed his foreign wife and their children in accordance with the covenant God made with Ezra (Ezra 10:1-5, 33; 1 Esd 9:33).

7. Descendant of Nebo. He dismissed his foreign wife and their children in accordance with the covenant God made with Ezra (Ezra 10:1-5, 43). In 1 Esd 9:35, he is a descendant of Nooma.

EMILY R. CHENEY

ZABADEANS zab´uh-dee´uhn [Ζαβαδαῖοι Zabadaioi]. A tribe of Arabs that was crushed and plundered by Jonathan during his battle with the generals of Demetrius (1 Macc 12:31). They were located approximately 30 mi. northwest of Damascus near the Eleutherus River, which separated Phoenicia and Syria. The name of this group may be preserved by place names along the road from Damascus to Beirut in the names of the region Zebadani and the town Zabed. The group could be linked to ZABDIEL (1 Macc 11:17).

Jonathan and his forces marched from Jerusalem intending to engage the commanders of Demetrius before they could move south. They camped near Demetrius' army by the town of Hamah in the Orontes Valley of southern Syria. Even though they had superior numbers, Demetrius' forces made campfires but then slipped away during the night. Jonathan and his men discovered the deception in the morning but not in time to catch them, so Jonathan decided to attack the Zabadeans and then marched to Damascus (1 Macc 12:24-31).

JOHN D. WINELAND

ZABBAI zab´i [זַבָּי zabbay; Ζάβδος Zabdos]. Possibly means "gift." 1. A descendant of Bebai listed among the Israelites who had married foreign wives upon their return from exile in Babylon. Following Ezra's decree condemning intermarriage with the people of the land, he joined the others named in sending away their foreign wives and children (Ezra 10:28; 1 Esd 9:29).

2. Father of Baruch, who helped to repair a section of the wall around Jerusalem from the Angle, near the

armory, to the door of the high priest Eliashib's house (Neh 3:20).

SUSAN E. HADDOX

ZABDI zab´di [זַבְדִּי zavdi]. 1. A Zerahite of Judah, whose grandson Achan was stoned for violating the ban at Jericho (Josh 7:1, 17-26).

2. A Benjaminite, the third son of Shimei (1 Chr 8:19; or Shema, v. 13).

3. A Shiphmite, one of twelve stewards appointed by King David, who supervised the produce of the vineyards (1 Chr 27:27).

4. A Levite, son of Asaph, listed in Neh 11:17 in the genealogy of Mattaniah, who lived in Jerusalem in the time of Nehemiah. First Chronicles 9:15 reads "Zichri" (zikhri [זִכְרִי]) instead of "Zabdi," suggesting that either Nehemiah or 1 Chronicles has miscopied the name.

M. PATRICK GRAHAM

ZABDIEL zab´dee-uhl [זַבְדִּיאֵל zavdi'el; Ζαβδιήλ Zabdiēl]. Means "My gift is God." 1. The father of Jashobeam, one of David's military leaders (1 Chr 27:2), descended from Perez, a Judahite tribe (Gen 38:29).

2. The overseer of a group of priests residing in Jerusalem (Neh 11:14) after the exile. He is called the son of "Haggedolim," which means "the great ones." It is unclear if this is a personal name or a title.

3. The Arab leader who decapitated the Seleucid king Alexander Balas when he sought refuge from the Egyptian king Ptolemy VI Philometer. Zabdiel sent Alexander's head to Ptolemy (1 Macc 11:16-17). Zabdiel may have operated in the Palmyra desert area or in Lebanon.

ADAM L. PORTER

ZABUD zay´buhd [זָבוּד zavudh]. A son of Nathan, and a priest and king's friend (i.e., counselor) in Solomon's time (1 Kgs 4:5).

ZACCAI zak´i [זַכָּי zakkay]. Head of one of the lay families who returned to Jerusalem with Zerubbabel from Babylon. According to Ezra 2:9 and Neh 7:14 the family had 760 members. This large number, like the others in the lists, suggests a political or theological purpose to the lists.

ZACCHAEUS za-kee´uhs [Ζακχαῖος Zakchaios]. Meaning "pure, righteous." 1. An officer in the Maccabean army (2 Macc 10:19).

2. In Luke 19:1-10, Zacchaeus was the wealthy, paradigmatic "chief tax collector" resident in Jericho near the Jordan fords used by traders. A hostile crowd prevented the undersized Zacchaeus from seeing Jesus passing through. He sacrificed his dignity (albeit limited due to his collaboration with oppressors) by climbing a tree to see Jesus. Jesus called him by name, saying he "must stay at [his] house today" (v. 5; key Lukan words). All

who saw grumbled at Jesus requiring hospitality from a sinful man, but Zacchaeus stood to confront his critics. The verbs in 19:8b-c are not a self-defense; Zacchaeus has been changed by Jesus' gracious outreach and now assures the Lord he will share his resources with a disciple's generosity. This conversion echoes the meal in Levi's house (Luke 5:27-32). It explains both how the Good Shepherd of Ezek 34 saves the lost sheep (Luke 19:10), and how "today salvation has come to this house, because he too is a son of Abraham" (v. 9; compare 13:16). There is intertextuality with the wealthy but righteous Abraham of Gen 18:1-19, who "ran" to meet his "lord" passing by, "hastened" to extend hospitality, "stood" under the "tree," and was known and blessed in all his "house." The Zacchaeus episode has elements of calling, controversy, conversion, and salvation fulfilling the divine promises to Abraham (a motif that helps to structure Luke–Acts). Jesus initiates the evangelization of households involving shared meals (also prominent in Luke–Acts). The converted, joyful Zacchaeus (contrast the rich but sad ruler of 18:18-30) is a model for generous patrons of house assemblies, damping down disputes about the rich retaining some of their wealth (compare 8:3).

BRIAN M. NOLAN

ZACCUR zak´uhr [זַכּוּר zakkur]. Means "remembered" or "is mindful"; perhaps "(God) has remembered." 1. A Reubenite whose son Shammua was among the spies Moses sent into Canaan (Num 13:4).

2. A Simeonite, son of Hammuel and father of Shimei (1 Chr 4:26).

3. A Levite, son of Jaaziah and grandson of Merari (1 Chr 24:27).

4. Son of Asaph and head of a group of twelve kinsmen who were singers in the Temple (1 Chr 25:2, 10; Neh 12:35).

5. Son of Bigvai and brother of Uthai, who followed Ezra back to Judah from Babylon (Ezra 8:14).

6. Son of Imri, who led his kinsmen in rebuilding a section of Jerusalem's wall (Neh 3:2).

7. A Levite, one of those signing a covenant to obey the law of God and separate themselves from Gentiles (Neh 10:12 [Heb. 10:13]).

8. Father of Hanan, appointed by Nehemiah to assist in the distribution of provisions to the Levites and priests (Neh 13:13).

9. A temple singer who divorced his foreign wife (1 Esd 9:24; Bakchouros [Βάκχουρος]).

M. PATRICK GRAHAM

ZADOK, ZADOKITES zay´dok, zay´duh-kit [צָדוֹק tsadhoq, בְּנֵי צָדוֹק bene tsadhoq; Σαδώκ Sadōk]. The name *Zadok* is mentioned fifty-three times in the Bible. The "sons of Zadok" (bene tsadhoq), or "Zadokites," are mentioned four times. 1. Zadok, along with ABIATHAR, was a priest for David (2 Sam 15–19; 1 Kgs 1), and he was Solomon's highest-ranking priest

(1 Kgs 2). Scholars have raised numerous theories about Zadok's origins and lineage. Some find Zadok's origin in a pre-Israelite, Jebusite priesthood of Jerusalem that later was legitimized by David. Some extend this argument to link Zadok and MELCHIZEDEK by noting the common tsdq (צדק) root.

Zadok and Abiathar remained loyal to David during Absalom's rebellion (2 Sam 15). David ordered Zadok and Abiathar to carry the ark of God into the city of Jerusalem (2 Sam 15:24-29). Zadok and Abiathar conspired with Hushai the Archite against Absalom (2 Sam 17:15-16), and after Absalom's death, David sent Zadok and Abiathar a message about his return to Jerusalem (2 Sam 19:11-12).

First Kings 1:8 mentions "the priest Zadok" who remained loyal to David during the struggle for the succession to David's throne (1 Kgs 1:26-45). David ordered Zadok and the prophet Nathan to anoint Solomon as king (1 Kgs 1:26-45). When Solomon took the throne, he set Zadok "in the place of" Abiathar (1 Kgs 2:28-35; however, compare 1 Kgs 4:4, where both Zadok and Abiathar are priests).

All other Samuel–Kings references to the priest Zadok include him in a list or name his children. Zadok is listed as son of Ahitub (2 Sam 8:17) and father of Ahimaaz (2 Sam 15:27, 36; 18:19, 27). Another list of David's officials names Zadok, Abiathar, and Ira as David's priests (2 Sam 20:23-26). A list of Solomon's officials includes Zadok's name twice (1 Kgs 4:1-6). First Kings 4:2 lists Azariah as son of Zadok, somewhat surprisingly, given the evidence from 2 Samuel (above).

Zadok appears in several genealogies in 1 Chronicles. The genealogies in 1 Chr 5:24–6:15 place Zadok among the sons of Levi in the line of Aaron (6:8). In 1 Chr 18:16, Zadok, son of Ahitub, is a priest alongside Abiathar. First Chronicles 24:1-6 presents the divisions of the sons of Aaron; Zadok is one of the "sons of Eleazar." Of the remaining occurrences of the name Zadok, some may be the same as this Zadok, or the same as one another.

2. Zadok was the father of Jerusha, the mother of King Jotham of Judah (2 Kgs 15:33; 2 Chr 27:1).

3. First Chronicles 9:11 lists Zadok as son of Meraioth and father of Meshullam. The six priestly houses in Neh 11 include Zadok as grandson of Ahitub, son of Meraioth, and father of Meshullam (v. 11).

4. Zadok, "a young warrior," brought twenty-two men from his father's house to David at Hebron (1 Chr 12:28).

5. Zadok is chief officer for Aaron in 1 Chr 27:17.

6. Ezra's Aaronite genealogy lists Zadok as son of Ahitub and father of Shallum (Ezra 7:2).

7. Zadok, son of Baana worked on the walls of Jerusalem (Neh 3:4).

8. Zadok, son of Immer helped build Jerusalem's walls (Neh 3:29).

9. Zadok is among the officials, Levites, and priests who signed a covenant (Neh 10:21).

10. A scribe named Zadok is one of four treasurers over the storehouses (Neh 13:4-14).

11. Zadok appears several times in the Dead Sea Scrolls. The *Damascus Document* tells of a book of the Torah that was sealed, unopened even by David and remaining unopened until Zadok (CD-A V, 2–5). This reference to Zadok may reveal the importance of Zadok to the writer(s) of the *Damascus Document* or could have an obscure meaning.

12. The *Copper Scroll* speaks of Zadok's tomb and Zadok's garden but gives no indication about his identity (3Q15 XI, 2–6).

13. Zadok is listed in Matthew's genealogical list for Jesus (Matt 1:14). This text names Azor as the father of Zadok and Zadok as the father of Achim.

14. References to Zadokites are more obscure. The historian Josephus mentions Zadok the priest (*Ant.* 7.56, 110, 222, 245, 293, 346; 8.12; 10.152) but does not mention Zadokites (sons of Zadok). The final eight chapters of Ezekiel provide four references to the "sons of Zadok" (Ezek 40:45-46; 43:18-19; 44:6-16; 48:9-11), the only biblical references. Unfortunately, Ezek 40–48, known as the Temple Vision, is one of the most difficult sections to place in historical context. Ironically, these chapters also have provided a linchpin in reconstructions of the religion and history of priesthood of ancient Israel. The four texts refer to a diminished status for Levitical priests as a result of their going away from Yahweh, and an elevation for the sons of Zadok, who remained true to Yahweh. Traditionally, these texts are assumed to be in reference to Josiah's reform (*see* JOSIAH §B).

Though many scholars claim that the Zadokites were the dominant priestly institution from the time of David through most of the Second Temple period, there is relatively little biblical or historical evidence to support this position, and the provenance of each of these references is unclear. While 2 Chr 31:10 refers to the "seed (NRSV, "house") of Zadok," Sara Japhet suggests this is a literary reference to Azariah of Solomon's reign (1 Kgs 4:2) and was likely added when there was an interest in increasing the prominence of a Zadokite priesthood. The sons of Zadok are mentioned once in one Hebrew copy of Sir 51:12.

Some scholars consider the Zadokites to be the founders of the QUMRAN community, associated with the DEAD SEA SCROLLS. The Zadokites, or "sons of Zadok," are found in several texts: the *Damascus Document* (CD IV, 1–3), *Rule of the Community* (1QS V, 2, 9; IX, 14), *Rule of the Congregation* (1Q28a I, 2, 24; II, 3), *Rule of the Blessings* (1Q28b III, 22), *Florilegium* (4Q174 1 I, 17), and perhaps *Isaiah Pesher*[c] (4Q163 22 3). Alternatively, the Qumran community included some priests who considered themselves Zadokites and who helped produce and/or subscribed to the community guidelines found in the *Damascus Document* and the *Rule of the Community*. The Dead Sea Scrolls, taken as a collection, give some, but not sole, prominence to Zadokites.

In the *Damascus Document*, which delineates internal and hierarchical structure of a community (where one would expect to see evidence of a dominant priesthood), the Zadokites are mentioned only twice, both in a midrash on Ezek 44:15. Of the three groups found in this text, the priests, the Levites, and the Zadokites, Philip Davies suggests three categories—the converts of Israel who left the land of Judah, the Levites who joined them, and the sons of Zadok who are the chosen of Israel (CD IV, 1–3)—that might describe the history of the Scrolls community in stages. Textual analysis of the references leads to the conclusion that while the Zadokites were not the only members of the Scrolls community, the founding members of the community, or the sole authority within the community, they likely had significant connection with the community.

Bibliography: Rainer Albertz. *A History of Israelite Religion in the Old Testament Period, Volume I: From the Beginnings to the End of the Monarchy* (1992); Philip R. Davies. *Behind the Essenes: History and Ideology in the Dead Sea Scrolls* (1987); Philip R. Davies. "The Prehistory of the Qumran Community." *The Dead Sea Scrolls: Forty Years of Research.* Devorah Dimant and Uriel Rappaport, eds. (1992) 116–25; Philip R. Davies. "Redaction and Sectarianism in the Qumran Scrolls." *The Scriptures and the Scrolls: Studies in Honour of A. S. Van Der Woude on the Occasion of His 65th Birthday.* F. García Martínez, A. Hilhorst, and C. J. Labuschagne, eds. (1992) 152–63; Christian E. Hauer Jr. "Who Was Zadok?" *JBL* 82 (1963) 89–94; Alice Wells Hunt. *Missing Priests: The Zadokites in Tradition and History* (2006); Sara Japhet. *I and II Chronicles: A Commentary.* OTL (1993); Walther Zimmerli. *Ezekiel 2: A Commentary on the Book of the Prophet Ezekiel Chapters 25–48.* James D. Martin, trans. Hermeneia (1983).

ALICE W. HUNT

ZADOKITE DOCUMENT. *See* DAMASCUS DOCUMENT; DEAD SEA SCROLLS.

ZAHAM zay´ham [זַהַם zaham]. One of Rehoboam's three sons by his wife Mahalath (2 Chr 11:18-19).

ZAIN. *See* ALPHABET; ZAYIN.

ZAIR zay´uhr [צָעִיר tsaʿir]. The location of an unsuccessful attack by King Joram of Judah and his chariotry against the Edomites, who had recently revolted against Judah's rule (2 Kgs 8:21). The parallel account in 2 Chr 21:9 replaces "Zair" with the expression "with his commanders." That Joram and his chariotry "crossed over to Zair" suggests that Zair lay somewhere in Edomite territory, but its location is uncertain. Some have proposed identifying Zair with the ZIOR (tsiʿor צִיעֹר)

of Josh 15:54, near Hebron, but placing Zair in Judah raises the question of what Joram and his army "crossed over" to reach the place. A perhaps more plausible solution is identifying Zair with ZOAR (tsoʿar צֹעַר]; Gen 13:10; 14:2, 8; 19:22-23, 30), at the southeastern tip of the Dead Sea. All three names—Zair, Zior, and Zoar—are related to a Hebrew word meaning "small, young" (tsaʿir).

JOHN I. LAWLOR

ZAKKAI, YOHANAN BEN. *See* YOHANAN BEN ZAKKAI.

ZALAPH zay´laf [צָלָף tsalaf]. Father of Hanun, who helped repair the walls of Jerusalem after the return from exile (Neh 3:30). Hanun was one of two workers assigned to the detail, thought to be along the eastern wall of the city, overlooking the Kidron Valley.

ZALMON zal´muhn [צַלְמוֹן tsalmon]. 1. Mount Zalmon appears in Judg 9:48 as a mountain near Shechem, in the northern extreme of Israel's central hill country, near the peaks of Mount Gerizim and Mount Ebal. The book of Judges asserts that Abimelech, the son of Gideon (Jerubaal) by a concubine who lived in Shechem, killed seventy of his brothers after Gideon's death, and had himself proclaimed king. When relations with city leaders in Shechem soured, he led his troops to cut bundles of brushwood on Mount Zalmon, then pile them against "the Tower of Shechem" (v. 49). The brushwood was set on fire, killing all who sought refuge inside. *See* SHECHEM, TOWER OF.

2. Psalm 68:14 [Heb. 68:15] speaks of a Mount Zalmon that may have been one of the peaks of the Bashan range in what is now northern Jordan. "When the Almighty scattered kings there, snow fell on Zalmon," possibly describes the fleeing kings as swirling about like snowflakes.

3. Zalmon the Ahohite appears in 2 Sam 23:28 as one of David's inner circle of warriors known as "the Thirty" (v. 24), but is not mentioned in the Chronicler's parallel list (1 Chr 11:26-47), and is otherwise unknown.

TONY W. CARTLEDGE

ZALMONAH zal-moh´nuh [צַלְמֹנָה tsalmonah]. An encampment on the Israelites' wilderness journey from Kadesh to the plains of Moab (Num 33:41-42), between Mount Hor and Punon. Though its exact location is unknown, Zalmonah was probably in the Arabah, 20–30 mi. south of the Dead Sea. Many scholars consider Num 33 to be the master list from which the other wilderness itineraries in the Pentateuch were drafted.

JOAN E. COOK, SC

ZALMUNNA. *See* ZEBAH AND ZALMUNNA.

ZAMZUMMIM zam-zuh´mim [זַמְזֻמִּים *zamzummim*]. According to Deut 2:20-23, this was the name given to the REPHAIM by the Ammonites, perhaps because of their muttering or indiscernible speech. Yahweh destroyed the Zamzummim so that the Ammonites could inhabit their territory. Many commentators equate the Zamzummim with the similarly named ZUZIM of Gen 14:5, but this is not certain.

The Zamzummim are described as "strong and numerous" and "as tall as the Anakim" (Deut 2:21; compare Num 13:28; Deut 9:2). The Anakim (*see* ANAK, ANAKIM, ANAKITES) inhabited Canaan before the Israelites arrived. When the Israelites learned that Canaan was populated by the towering Anakim, they refused to invade the land (Deut 1:26-28). The statement that the Ammonites were able to dispossess the Zamzummim because "the LORD destroyed them from before the Ammonites" (2:21) probably alludes to the Israelites' fear of the Anakites and their refusal to trust in Yahweh.

JOHN I. LAWLOR

ZANOAH zuh-noh´uh [זָנוֹחַ *zanoakh*]. 1. A Judean city in the northeastern Shephelah (Josh 15:34), perhaps to be identified with Khirbet Zanu (about 2 mi. southeast of Beth-shemesh). The founder of this city (or less likely, another city by the same name in the Judean hill country) is identified in Chronicles as JEKUTHIEL (1 Chr 4:18). The city was resettled by Jews returning from exile (Neh 11:30), and its inhabitants worked with Hanun to reconstruct Jerusalem's city wall, rebuilding the Valley Gate and about 500 yards ("a thousand cubits") of the wall, as far as the Dung Gate (Neh 3:13).

2. A city in the Judean hill country near Maon (Josh 15:56), perhaps to be identified with Khirbet Beit Amra (about 1 mi. east of Juttah).

M. PATRICK GRAHAM

ZAPHENATH-PANEAH zaf´uh-nath-puh-nee´uh [צָפְנַת פַּעְנֵחַ *tsafenath pa'neakh*]. According to Gen 41:45, the pharaoh of the Joseph account presents the former slave with an Egyptian name to correspond to his new position: Zaphenath-paneah. This appellation, which is of uncertain etymology, has served as a factor in dating the biblical narratives and in establishing their historical veracity.

While there is widespread agreement that the name derives from Egyptian, a consensus does not currently exist as to its meaning. A 19th-cent. proposal, "God speaks and he lives (ḏd-p3-ntr-iw.f-ʿnḫ)," has received significant attention. This style of name is characteristic of Egyptian personal names from the first two-thirds of the 1st millennium BCE, thereby influencing scholars to posit a late date for the narratives. Recent attempts to promote the viability of the biblical traditions have advanced an alternative reading, "Joseph who is called Ip-ankh (ḏd.n.f ʾip-ʿnḫ)" (Kitchen), which corresponds to name formulas of the first half of the 2nd millennium.

The latter would adhere more closely to biblical chronology.

Bibliography: William F. Albright. "Historical and Mythical Elements in the Story of Joseph." *JBL* 37 3/4 (1918) 111–43; Kenneth A. Kitchen. *On the Reliability of the Old Testament* (2003); Yoshiyuki Muchiki. *Egyptian Proper Names and Loanwords in North-West Semitic* (1999) 224–26.

JASON R. TATLOCK

ZAPHON zay´fon [צָפוֹן *tsafon*]. A city east of the Jordan River that was part of the kingdom of HESHBON, ruled by King SIHON (Josh 13:27). Along with several other cities in the Jordan Valley, Zaphon was included in the land given to the tribe of Gad (Josh 13:24-28). The men of Ephraim met JEPHTHAH there to challenge his campaign against the Ammonites (Judg 12:1). The toponym *Zaphon* in Job 26:7 and Isa 14:13 may not refer to a specific locality but could simply mean "north." Scholars have identified Zaphon with several sites north of the Jabbok River in modern-day Jordan, including Tell es-Saidiyeh, Tell el-Qos, and Tell el-Mazar. *See* GAD, GADITES; MAZAR, TELL EL; SAIDIYEH, TELL ES; ZAPHON, MOUNT.

HUMPHREY H. HARDY II

ZAPHON, MOUNT zay´fon [צָפוֹן *tsafon*]. Zaphon has several, possibly related meanings: 1) "north"; 2) the place names Zaphon on the eastern side of the Jordan River (Josh 13:27; Judg 12:1) and BAAL-ZEPHON in the eastern delta of Egypt (Exod 14:2, 9; Num 33:7); 3) a mountain residence of God (yarkethe tsafon [יַרְכְּתֵי צָפוֹן]; Ps 48:2 [Heb. 48:3]; Isa 14:13). A few scholars find a reference to Mount Zaphon in Ps 89:12 [Heb. 89:13], rendering "Zaphon and Amanus" (e.g., NAB) instead of "the north and the south" (NRSV). The etymology of tsafon is uncertain, though "look out (point)" (compare tsafah [צָפָה]) is frequently suggested.

Zaphon as a sacred mountain in the Bible has attracted much attention because in Ugaritic texts the storm god BAAL lives on tspn (= Hebrew tsafon), an imposing mountain 40 km (25 mi.) north of Ugarit known today as Jebel el-Aqraʿ (1,770 m [5,807 ft.]). Revered in Hurrian and Hittite sources as Hazzi and sometimes divinized, its Greek and Roman name was Casius (a Hellenized form of Hazzi), and Zeus Casius was worshiped there. The Hebrew tsafon, "north," may derive from the northern location of Mount Zaphon, just as yam (יָם), "west," derives from the (Mediterranean) sea.

Zaphon's sacred motifs could evidently be transferred to other sites. According to Herodotus (*Hist.* 2.6; 3.5), a site in the Nile delta on Lake Sirbon was named Casius, and Zeus was worshiped there. Some have suggested that Baal-zephon in Exod 14:2, 9 refers to this place. A similar transference of motifs appears in Ps 48:2 [Heb.

48:3|: "Mount Zion, the Heights of Zaphon, the city of the Great King" (author's trans.; NRSV, "Mount Zion, in the far north, the city of the great King"). Zaphon and ZION and their resident deities—Baal and Yahweh—have striking similarities: each god built his palace on the mountain to commemorate a cosmic victory (*CTU* 1.4.vi; Ps 93); each is a storm god who proclaims his rule in thunder and lightning (*CTU* 1.4.vii.25-39; Ps 29); a great battle took place near or at the mountain (*CTU* 1.6.vi.12-34; Pss 48; 76); and the mountains are a source of fertilizing rains or streams (*CTU* 1.6.iii.1-9; Ps 46:4 [Heb. 46:5]; Ezek 47:1-12). As Yahweh became the dominant deity in southern Canaan, motifs of Baal and his mountain were applied to Yahweh and his mountain. This is not of course to say that Israel's Lord, Yahweh, is simply one in a sequence of deities, but rather that Israelite poets used traditional religious language of their God.

"Heights of Zaphon" also occurs in Isa 14:13 in the Babylonian king's arrogant attempt to seize the throne of the Most High: "I will raise my throne above the stars of God; I will sit on the mount of assembly (moʿedh מוֹעֵד) on the heights of Zaphon." In extant Ugaritic mythology, the head of the divine assembly (phr mʿd) is El, and his mountain dwelling is not Zaphon. In one Ugaritic text, however, a lesser god attempts (unsuccessfully) to unseat Baal. It is possible that the Bible conflates traditions about El and Baal as it does elsewhere.

RICHARD J. CLIFFORD

ZARA, ʿAIN EZ. ʿAin ez-Zara, also called Callirhoe, is a set of hot springs located on the east coast of the Dead Sea, south of the mouth of the Wadi Zarqa Maʿin. Herod the Great, whose palace at Machaerus was located nearby, sought healing at the springs (Josephus, *Ant.* 17.171). Two OT locations have been identified with the site. First, Jerome located Lasha (Gen 10:19) there, but no archaeological evidence supports his identification. Second, the site has been identified as ZERETH-SHAHAR because of the similarity of the names. However, the description of Zereth-shahar as standing "on the hill of the valley" (Josh 13:19) does not suggest a site located on the coast of the Dead Sea. Furthermore, excavations that began in 1985 discovered only Early Roman and Byzantine settlements at ʿAin ez-Zara. Excavations at Boz al-Mushelle have led scholars to identify it with Zereth-shahar.

GREGORY L. LINTON

ZARATHUSTRA zair´uh-thoos´truh. Zarathustra, also called ZOROASTER, is the prophet of ZOROASTRIANISM. In the Zoroastrian scriptures, the AVESTA, Zarathustra is depicted as the mediator between god (AHURA MAZDÂ) and humans and the prototype of the human sacrificer. His installation by Ahura Mazdâ is described in the GÂTHÂS (Yasna 29), and the Young Avesta contains further details. He was born as the reward for his father's sacrifice to Haoma, the god of the

ritual drink *haoma* (Yasna 9). He is described as the first priest, warrior, and husbandman, as well as the first to think good thoughts, utter good speech, perform good actions, praise Ahura Mazdâ's Order (*asha*), and scorn the old gods (*daeuuas*). At his birth, the waters and plants grew, and all creatures rejoiced that they would now receive sacrifices (Yasht 13). The old gods were, at that time, still on earth in the shape of mortals and took wives among them, but Zarathustra deprived them of worship, sending them underground (Yasht 17). He fought the Dark Spirit (*angra manyu*) with sacred words and sent him back to hell (Videvdad 19).

In later tradition written down in the Islamic period, further details about Zarathustra's parents and birth are given. After Ohrmazd (late form of Ahura Mazdâ) sent Zarathustra's "pre-existing soul" (*fravashi*) down to the world of the living, it entered into the milk of a cow, which his father and mother drank after mixing it with the *haoma*. He laughed at birth, but enemies tried to kill him. At the age of thirty, he was visited by Wahman (Good Thought) and brought into Ohrmazd's presence. What he learned he brought to King Wishtâsp, who fought a great battle in support of Zarathustra's new religion. He was killed at the age of seventy-seven. Also according to the late tradition, he was active in western Iran.

Most 19th–20th-cent. Western scholars have assumed that the legendary Zarathustra vita is reliable as history, once miracles and obvious late features are subtracted, and have reconstructed his life, inspired by vitae of Moses and later prophets. Thus, they have ascribed to him a monotheistic reform and an ethical teaching anticipating those of modern religions, but there is no independent evidence to back up such claims.

Some have placed him in northeastern Iran ca. 1500 BCE (Boyce). Others have followed the chronology of the late tradition, which dated him 258 years before Alexander, a number cited by Muslim historians (Gnoli). Others have dated him to about 1000 BCE.

In early Christian (Armenian) and Islamic historiography, Zarathustra was synchronized with early biblical figures, often with Nimrod, but sometimes with Ham or Abraham. *See* PERSIA, HISTORY AND RELIGION OF; ZOROASTER, ZOROASTRIANISM.

Bibliography: M. Boyce. *A History of Zoroastrianism.* Vol. 1 (1975); G. Gnoli. *Zoroaster's Time and Homeland* (1980); P. O. Skjaervø. "Zarathustra: First Poet-Sacrificer." *Paitimana: Essays in Iranian, Indian, and Indo-European Studies in Honor of Hanns-Peter Schmidt.* S. Adhami, ed. (2003) 157–94.

P. OKTOR SKJAERVØ

ZAREPHATH zair´uh-fath [צָרְפַת tsarefath; Σάρεπτα Sarepta]. A town on the Phoenician coast approximately 14 mi. north of TYRE and 8 mi. south of SIDON. Most biblical references to the site occur in connection with the prophet Elijah who found refuge there after the brook of Cherith dried up in the land of Gilead (1 Kgs 17:9-10). A widow of Zarephath gave him sanctuary and sustained him while he was a refugee in Phoenicia. In return for her kindness, the Lord sustained her and when her son died, Elijah was instrumental in his restoration (1 Kgs 17:11-24).

When the people of Nazareth taunted Jesus about his work in Capernaum and elsewhere, Jesus addressed the tendency of people not to accept the greatness of their native sons. He cited Elijah's departure from Israel to go to a widow in Zarephath where the word of the Lord was more readily received (Luke 4:22-30). The reference to Zarephath of Sidon reflects the relative proximity of the town to its larger city.

The only other reference to Zarephath is in a visionary declaration by Obadiah (v. 20) noting the eventual spread of those who fear God to accommodate the area of Zarephath.

The site appears to have developed a commercial reputation early; it is cited during the Ramesside period in the Papyrus Anastasi I as a notable port along the coast (*COS* 3:12 [3.2]). Sennacherib's 701 BCE campaign to quell rebellion in the west lists Zarephath as one of the towns in his wake (appearing as Sariptu in *COS* 2:302 [2.119B]).

Archaeologists have identified Zarephath with Sarepta (modern Sarafand) in Lebanon. The site was excavated under the direction of James B. Pritchard (1969–74, 1978) and has yielded finds ranging from the 16th cent. BCE into the Roman era as late as the 6th cent. CE. The town's name derives from a Semitic root meaning "to refine" or "to color red," and its significance is confirmed by the prevalence of pottery kilns and evidence of commercial purple dye production as early as the Late Bronze Age. In addition, excavations have yielded many oil presses and evidence of metallurgy to mold jewelry. Allusions to the wealth of the region of Tyre appear in indictments in Ezek 27:12-25 where the area is known for its extensive trade including metals and jewels. Surely, situated between Tyre and Sidon, and known as a port from early times, Zarephath would have basked in the glow of this wealth.

Excavations have also uncovered a series of shrines beginning in the 8th cent. BCE. Among the finds are a symbol and inscription from the 8th and 7th cent. indicating that the shrine was dedicated to Tannit-Ashtart. Based upon extensive evidence from Carthage, there is reason to associate child sacrifice with the Tannit cult, and, hence, some have sought connections with the OT's indictments of the sacrificial practice in Judah and Israel (2 Kgs 23:10; Jer 7:31; 19:4-5; Ezek 23:37-39).

Bibliography: William P. Anderson. *Sarepta I* (1988); Issam A. Khalifeh. *Sarepta II* (1988); Robert B. Koehl. *Sarepta III* (1985); James B. Pritchard. "Sarepta in History and Tradition." *Understanding the Sacred Text.* J. Reumann, ed. (1972) 99–114; James B. Pritchard. *Sarepta* (1975); James B. Pritchard. *Sarepta IV* (1988); Jopie Siebert-Hommes. "The Widow of Zarephath and the Great Woman of Shunem: A Comparative Analysis of Two Stories." *On Reading Prophetic Texts.* Bob Becking and Meindert Dijkstra, eds. (1996) 231–50.

DALE W. MANOR

ZARETHAN zair′uh-than [צָרְתָן tsarethan]. A city or region near the Jordan River, between Adam and Succoth. When the Israelites crossed the Jordan, "the waters flowing from above stood still, rising up in a single heap far off at Adam, the city that is beside Zarethan, while those flowing toward the sea of the Arabah, the Dead Sea, were wholly cut off" (Josh 3:16). Zarethan later became a part of the fifth Solomonic district, which included territory on both sides of the Jordan (1 Kgs 4:12). Hiram cast the bronze vessels for the Temple between Succoth and Zarethan (1 Kgs 7:46).

The traditional identification of Zarethan with Tell ed-Damiyeh makes sense in light of its location near the Jisr el-Damiyeh, a well-known ford of the middle Jordan, where stoppages of the river have been recorded in modern times on at least three occasions: in 1266, 1906, and, most recently, in 1927, when the stoppage lasted for 21.5 hours. Another possibility is Tell es-Sa'idiyeh, which is 18 km (11 mi.) north of Tell ed-Damiyeh.

The stretch of river from Zarethan to Adam includes the juncture with the Jabbok from the east and the Wadi Far'ah from the west, the latter of which serves as the natural point of entry into the north-central hill country. It has been suggested that the Israelites entered Canaan not only by way of Jericho but also along the whole length of the Jordan from Adam to Jericho. The text stresses, however, that the Israelites crossed "opposite Jericho" while the waters backed up "far off at Adam" (Josh 3:16). That is, Zarethan and Adam are mentioned to emphasize the distance at which the waters backed up in order to create a ford for the Israelites. *See* ZERERAH.

RALPH K. HAWKINS

ZARIUS zair′ee-uhs [Ζάριος Zarios]. Zarius was Jehoiakim's brother, freed from Egyptian exile when JEHOIAKIM was placed on the throne by Egypt's king (1 Esd 1:38 [LXX 1:36]). But this account conflicts with 2 Kgs 23–24 and 2 Chr 36, and the name Zarius occurs only in 1 Esd 1:38.

ZATTU zat′oo [זַתּוּא zattu'; Ζαθοής Zathoēs, Ζατόν Zaton]. Ancestor of a non-priestly family whose members returned from the exile in two groups: 945 with Zerubbabel (Ezra 2:8; 1 Esd 5:12; Neh 7:13 gives the number of returnees as 845) and 300 with Ezra (Ezra 8:5; the Hebrew text lacks "of Zattu" and is corrected according to 1 Esd 8:32 as a footnote in the NRSV remarks). Six sons of Zattu divorced their foreign wives with their children when Ezra urged the people to do so

(Ezra 10:27; compare 1 Esd 9:28, "Zamoth"), and the family subscribed to the covenant to obey God that Ezra initiated (Neh 10:14 [Heb. 10:15]).

M. PATRICK GRAHAM

ZAYIN zah´yin [ז z]. The seventh letter of the Hebrew alphabet, which is derived from the Semitic word *zayn-, though the original meaning is unknown, and the shape may derive from DELTA (d δ), after d merged with *z. *See* ALPHABET.

ZAYIT, TELL. The approximately 30,000 sq. m site of Tell Zayit lies in the strategic Beth Guvrin valley in the Shephelah region of Judah, roughly halfway between Lachish and Tell es-Safi (Philistine Gath), and approximately 27 km east of Ashkelon. The borderland site belonged to Judah's lowland district four (Josh 15:42-44), centered around the principal site of Libnah; the site is probably to be identified with one of the cities in that list, perhaps even Libnah itself. In any event, the ancient town of Tell Zayit lay at the center of a communication and trade network that connected the highland culture(s) of Judah to the Canaanite and Philistine city-states in the hilly western flanks, along the Mediterranean seaboard, and toward the principal gateways into Egypt. The position of the town at this strategic interface is a key factor in the history of the overall region.

Excavations have revealed remains from the Middle Bronze Age through the late Ottoman Period, with an especially significant occupation in the Late Bronze Age and Iron Age II A–B periods. In the early Iron Age II A period, the town maintained its principal affiliations with the highland culture to the east, in the direction of Jerusalem.

In July 2005, excavators recovered a large stone bearing an incised, two-line inscription. The importance of the stone derives not only from its archaic alphabetic text (a twenty-two-letter abecedary) but also from its well-defined archaeological context in a structure dating securely to the 10th cent. BCE. The Tell Zayit Abecedary represents the linear alphabetic script of central and southern Canaan at the beginning of the 1st millennium BCE, a transitional script that developed from the Phoenician tradition of the early Iron Age and anticipated the distinctive features of the mature Hebrew national script. The early appearance of literacy at Tell Zayit makes a valuable contribution to the scholarly debate concerning the archaeology and history of Judah in the 10th cent. BCE.

RON E. TAPPY

ZAZA zay´zuh [זָזָא zaza']. A Jerahmeelite, son of Jonathan and brother of Peleth (1 Chr 2:33). He is mentioned only in the genealogy of Jerahmeel (1 Chr 2:25-33), of the tribe of Judah. The Jerahmeelites apparently lived in the south of Judah (1 Sam 27:10; 30:29). The

name Zaza may have arisen from a child's practice of doubling the initial syllable of a fond name.

M. PATRICK GRAHAM

ZEAL, ZEALOUS [קִנְאָה qin'ah; ζῆλος zēlos]. *Zeal* describes God's fervor (Isa 9:7; 26:11; 37:32; Wis 5:17) or human passion for God's righteousness (Ps 119:139; Jdt 9:4). By zealously killing a brazen offender, Phinehas turned back God's wrath from Israel (Num 25:11-13). Elijah was "zealous for the Lord" when he executed the prophets of Baal, then fled for his life (1 Kgs 18:40; 19:10; see Sir 48:2). Mattathias felt "righteous anger" and "burned with zeal" when he killed a fellow Jew for pagan sacrifice (1 Macc 2:24-58). Jesus cleansed the Temple with zeal (John 2:17; see Ps 69:9). Paul describes himself as once having been so zealous that he persecuted the church (Acts 22:3-4; Gal 1:13-14; Phil 3:6) and rejoices in the zeal expressed by the repentant Corinthians (2 Cor 7:7-12). *See* JEALOUSY; ZEALOT.

MARIANNE BLICKENSTAFF

ZEALOT zel´uht [ζηλωτής zēlōtēs]. The Zealots were Jewish revolutionaries in the 1st cent. CE. The study of the Zealots needs careful discussion, because there have been conclusions that have not been completely accurate, namely, that the Zealot movement began with a particular "Judas, the Galilean" in 6 CE (Josephus says that Judas the Galilean was a leader of the "fourth philosophy," a revolutionary faction that most likely refers to the Zealots [*Ant.* 18.23]).

A disciple of Jesus named "Simon the Zealot" was a recruit of this movement; and the Zealots were the ones responsible for inciting the First Jewish War (66–74 CE). The conclusion here is that the Zealots—a patchwork of Jewish insurgents, disaffected priests, and itinerant bandits—had precursors to be sure, but only became a strong political force near the beginning of the First Jewish War. It was only after Israel had de facto declared its independence from Rome that the Zealots overthrew the provisional Jewish government and attempted to take charge of the war. Furthermore, the Zealots had issues with the Jewish aristocracy and cannot be explained apart from the class struggle that existed during that time (*see* PHARISEES; SADDUCEES). Rome was just one of the grievances that the Zealots wanted to address. Sadly, by the end of the war, Israel was humiliated, most of the Zealot soldiers were dead or disbursed, and the Temple had been burned to the ground. Jewish resistance had been defeated, and the Zealots ceased to exist as a political party (*see* JEWISH WARS).

A. The Zealot Paradigm within Judaism
  1. Phinehas, the archetype
  2. The development of the Zealot paradigm
  3. Summary
B. The Rise of the Zealots as a Political Party
  1. The Jews declare their independence
    from Rome

A. The Zealot Paradigm within Judaism

1. Phinehas, the archetype

The Jewish notion of "zeal" has as its archetype PHINEHAS (Num 25:1-15). After God had caused a plague to fall upon Israel for its idolatrous compromises with the Moabites, Zimri, an Israelite man, was caught in his tent with a Moabite woman. Upon this discovery, Phinehas, the grandson of Moses' brother, Aaron, secured a spear and impaled them both simultaneously because he was "zealous for his God" (Num 25:13). God rewarded the righteous zeal of Phinehas by removing the plague from Israel and by making him and his descendants priests in perpetuity. Jewish interpreters saw in Phinehas' act of courage a spontaneous, righteous deed—inspired apart from official institutional sanction—that resulted in the appeasement of God's wrath, atonement for the nation, and the return of God's blessing and peace.

2. The development of the Zealot paradigm

This pentateuchal pericope would come to function paradigmatically in future generations when Israel was faced with foreign persecution and was in need of deliverance. Sirach notes those courageous ones whose lives showed zeal for God, listing Moses, Aaron, and Phinehas as the top three (Sir 45:1, 6, 23-24). In the Maccabean era, Phinehas is "our ancestor [who] was deeply zealous" (1 Macc 2:54), while 4 Macc 18:12 notes "the zeal of Phinehas." Mattathias, the Jewish warrior, is honored for demonstrating zeal "just as Phinehas did" (1 Macc 2:26). During this Maccabean period, not only was religious zeal required when one was faced with idolatry, but it was also expected when one was faced with almost any flagrant violation of the Mosaic law. In the name of "zeal for the law," pious Jews would not only embrace persecution rather than violate the law; they might even persecute their fellow countrymen for not keeping it. This zeal was seen as justified because Jewish violations of the law put the country at the risk of divine punishment. Thus, pious Jews, when stirred by zeal, might confiscate property, inflict physical suffering, or even enforce capital punishment when confronted with those who flagrantly violated the law. These were always acts of vigilantism carried out independently without official sanction and, most importantly, motivated by zeal.

Some of the transgressions that these "zealots" redressed included idolatry, stealing temple treasures, a Gentile's presence in the Temple's sacred court, an uncircumcised heathen resident in the land, the use of icons and images, taking God's name in vain, and sexual relations with foreign women. It is because of "zeal" that Jesus forcefully drove the merchandisers from the Temple (John 2:17). One of Jesus' recruits, SIMON the Zealot, no doubt earned his title by threatening or punishing lawbreakers (Luke 6:15). The apostle Paul is said to have been motivated by "zeal" to have persecuted Christians (Gal 1:14; Phil 3:6); moreover, after Paul's conversion, certain Jews "zealous for the law" returned the favor (Acts 21:20-22). Philo summarizes this aspect of the ethos of 1st-cent. Palestine when he says that there were thousands of watchful zealots, strict guardians of the laws and institutions of the fathers, who were merciless to anyone who subverted them (*Spec. Laws* 2.253).

3. Summary

In light of the above evidence it seems best to go no further than to conclude that there was a "zealot paradigm," modeled after Phinehas' zealous act, which inspired many Jews not to compromise but to remain faithful to the Torah in the face of persecution and even death. Zeal also inspired others to attempt piously and at times violently to uphold the law by punishing its transgressors. This "zeal" would ensure God's favor and precipitate prosperity and peace for the nation. Thus there would be in 1st-cent. Judaism a "zealot" paradigm that could be referenced (e.g., Simon the Zealot), but would fall short of being a movement and certainly not have any political implications. Some recent scholarship agrees with this view (Rhoads, Horsley, Smith), but there has not been unanimity among all interpreters.

Some scholars assert that when the terms *zeal* or *zealot* appear in a 1st-cent. Palestinian text that these often are quasi-technical terms that refer to a political movement dating to at least as early as Judas the Galilean (6 CE). Thus some scholars (e.g., Farmer, Hengel, Brandon) conclude that the revolutionary party described by Josephus (*J.W.* 4.161–62; 4.208–14; 4.283–389) as "zealots" was in existence perhaps as early as the beginning of the 1st cent. CE and is useful background to help inform our understanding of Jesus, some of his disciples, and perhaps even his betrayal, as well as other biblical texts and events. However, as the following discussion will demonstrate, it is difficult to make this equation. The Zealot revolutionary party has its origin in the social milieu and the events immediately preceding the war, not in the "zealot tradition" outlined above. The Jewish and Christian writings from the period surveyed earlier reflect more of a type of piety than they do a revolutionary political party.

B. The Rise of the Zealots as a Political Party

1. The Jews declare their independence from Rome

The formalizing of the "Zealots" as a Jewish revolutionary party committed to the defeat of Rome probably occurred in the near vicinity of winter 67–68 CE. The party's origin grew out of a clash between the Roman procurator Florus (64–66 CE) and the citizens of Jerusalem. While Florus was in office, he had brazenly stolen money from the temple treasury, allowed his army to loot the city, and attempted to capture and control the Temple. With these and other abuses unrequited, the city was understandably in a rebellious mood; the people felt that they had little to lose. Within the priestly hierarchy, the ones nearest the bottom were the first to begin to agitate for war. A certain Eleazar, son of the high priest Ananias and temple captain, gave ear to these priests and soon was persuaded to commit acts of treason against Rome. These priests, fueled by the encouragement of revolutionary lay leaders in Jerusalem, decided to terminate the twice-daily sacrifices offered on behalf of Rome and the Roman emperor. This sacrifice was important because it had previously been negotiated as an acceptable substitute for the worship of the emperor and was therefore a tangible sign of Jewish loyalty to Rome. Thus, this cessation of sacrifice was no less than a declaration of war; it flagrantly violated their peace treaty, and the Jews were now an enemy of the Roman state. Following this treasonous act, the Temple was cleansed from its Gentile contamination, rededicated to God, and in the "zealot" tradition the Jews now expected God's favor in exchange for their fidelity.

The chief priests and the prominent Pharisees who valued their social position did not want to anger the Romans and perhaps lose their favored status, so they actively resisted this new aggressive approach to Rome, and soon civil war erupted. The SICARII, a revolutionary faction that had long used guerilla tactics to oppose Rome, joined forces with Eleazar, and they quickly subdued their opposition. Unfortunately, the alliance between Eleazar's faction and the Sicarii was short-lived because they disagreed about military strategy against Rome. Fighting then broke out between the Sicarii and Eleazar; Eleazar's side was victorious, so the Sicarii fled and took refuge in the fortress at MASADA. Eleazar was now the de facto leader of Jerusalem.

2. Rome's military response

Rome needed to quell this rebellion in Jerusalem, and the governor of Syria, Cestius, was interested in expanding his power and control of the region. The two of them, therefore, joined forces and attacked Eleazar's militia in Jerusalem. Although the military might brought about by the alliance of Rome with Cestius was superior, Jerusalem achieved an improbable victory. Believing that God had wrought this military miracle because of Israel's faithfulness, Jerusalem's spirits soared. The surrounding Judean regions united under the high priest Ananias who became the nation's political head. Under Ananias, the high priests returned to their positions, and Eleazar remained part of the military structure as a general. The Romans, meanwhile, regrouped and

committed considerably more military resources to the reconquest of Palestine. The summer and fall of 67 CE saw Galilee fall; the Roman troops were now on the march through Judea to Jerusalem. Mainly through guerilla warfare, brigands and other revolutionary forces offered resistance, but they had to keep retreating under Rome's heavy military boot. As these revolutionary forces retreated, collapsing back toward Jerusalem, they finally took refuge in the holy city.

3. The Zealot party coalesces

While taking refuge in Jerusalem and engaging in dialogue with other dissenting factions, these retreating revolutionary forces discovered a resonance with the military perspectives of the priests who originally ceased making sacrifices for Rome and catalyzed the city's earlier rebellion. These rebel groups then joined forces, and this new coalition (disaffected priests, itinerant bandits, and other Jewish insurgents) seems to be the political and military entity for which Josephus uses the label "Zealots." This is now a new and distinct revolutionary party. United, this variegated band of revolutionaries, by lot, elected their own people, with questionable pedigree, to priestly offices. These revolutionaries also elected an uneducated layperson to be their high priest. The actions of these insurgents threatened the ruling aristocracy in Jerusalem; it was interpreted as an attempt to form a rival government. To add to the growing sense of threat, this newly formed revolutionary party attacked some Herodian nobles whom they accused of treason and against whom they still had some "ancient quarrels." The exact nature of these "ancient quarrels" is not exactly explained, but it almost certainly involved wealthy landowners who mistreated indebted peasant farmers. It is clear that this "Zealot" revolutionary party not only had issues with Rome, but they also resented the Jewish aristocracy because the privileged upper class possessed most of the wealth, neglected (or oppressed) their own people, and cooperated with Rome. They viewed Rome and the Jewish aristocracy as cut from the same cloth.

4. The Zealot party's rise to power

Since the wealthy Jewish leaders understood these aggressive actions as attempts to usurp control of the city and therefore control of the revolt against Rome, the Jewish aristocracy responded by viciously attacking the Zealots and trapping them in the inner court of the Temple. These Zealots appealed for help outside of Jerusalem. The Idumeans responded by storming Jerusalem, freeing the Zealots, and slaughtering many in the ruling class. Most of the Idumeans eventually withdrew; they left the city of Jerusalem in the control of the Zealots. The Zealots continued to consolidate their power and carried out additional purges of questionable members of the nobility and others in political power. The Zealots now had effective control of Jerusalem and the revolt against Rome.

C. The Demise of the Zealots as a Political Party

1. Internal conflicts and constant instability within the party

Because the Zealots comprised disparate groups, they could never establish a respected hierarchy and exist in unity unless faced with an outside threat. A Zealot leader, John of Gischala, attempted to gain control of the revolutionary party, but was unsuccessful, so he broke away from them and formed his own rival group. Another charismatic leader, Simon bar Giora, was gaining popularity in the countryside of Judea and was popularly acclaimed to be Messiah. Simon's charisma paired with his personal popularity attracted many of the men who had aligned themselves with John of Gischala. Eventually, significant numbers of John's men deserted him in favor of Simon. When this mass exodus occurred, John went back to the Zealot leadership and reconciled with them, and they hammered out an alliance. The Jewish aristocracy, still smarting from the loss of political control to the Zealots, conspired with the remaining Idumeans to invite Simon bar Giora into the city to wrest control back from the Zealots. Simon agreed and entered the city on a wave of popularity and was acclaimed as "savior and protector." Simon's army backed the Zealots up into the Temple where the faction-prone Zealots fractured once again. Unhappy with the leadership style of John of Gischala, Eleazar son of Simon and other Zealot leaders took control of the Temple's inner court, leaving John and his militia in the Temple's courtyard with Simon bar Giora's army at the Temple's gate. Although Simon was never able to wrest control of the Temple from John or the Zealots, Josephus called him "the master of Jerusalem," because he controlled the better part of the city (*J.W.* 4.577).

2. Final battle with the Romans

Until the Romans were at Jerusalem's gate, the fighting within the Zealot party and between rival revolutionary groups was always a problem. The imminent threat of the Roman army under Titus did finally galvanize all the rival factions together. Josephus' report is probably trustworthy: Simon son of Giora commanded 10,000 of his own troops and 5,000 Idumeans; John of Gischala led an additional 6,000 men; and the Zealots numbered 2,400 (*J.W.* 5.248–51). However, these combined militias were no match for the Romans. The Zealots did fight courageously until the end along with their Jewish compatriots, but the military might of the Roman army was just too much for the Jewish forces to handle. Near the end Simon donned white robes and surrendered, perhaps enacting some messianic notion or perhaps to influence the Romans to have mercy on his troops. Simon was paraded in Rome and then publicly executed. The city of Jerusalem was in ruins and the Temple was burned to the ground. Most of the aristocracy and the soldiers were dead and their families enslaved. Although Israel's religious zeal could never be quenched, the nation and the Zealots formally ceased as political entities.

Bibliography: S. G. F. Brandon. *Jesus and the Zealots* (1965); T. L. Donaldson. "Rural Bandits, City Mobs, and the Zealots." *JSJ* 21 (1990) 19–40; W. R. Farmer. *Maccabees, Zealots, and Josephus* (1956); M. Hengel. *The Zealots: Investigations into the Jewish Freedom Movement in the Period from Herod I until A.D. 70.* David W. Smith, trans. (1989); R. Horsley. "Menahem in Jerusalem: A Brief Messianic Episode among the Sicarii—Not 'Zealotic Messianism.'" *NovT* 27 (1985) 334–48; R. Horsley. "The Zealots: Their Origin, Relationships and Importance in the Jewish Revolt." *NovT* 28 (1986) 159–82; R. Horsley and J. Hanson. *Bandits, Prophets and Messiahs* (1985); K. P. Jackson. "Revolutionaries in the First Century." *BYU Studies* 36 (1996) 129–40; Flavius Josephus. *The Jewish War Book 4.* H. St. J. Thackery, trans. (1997); P. Kingdon. "Who Were the Zealots and Their Leaders in A.D. 66?" *NTS* 17 (1970) 68–72; U. Rappaport. "John of Gischala: From Galilee to Jerusalem." *JJS* 33 (1982) 477–93; D. Rhoads. *Israel in Revolution: 6–74 C.E.* (1976); M. Smith. "Zealots and Sicarii." *HTR* 64 (1971) 1–19; M. Stern. "Sicarii and Zealots." WHJP 8 (1977) 263–301; E. M. Yamauchi. "Christians and the Jewish Revolts against Rome." *Fides et Historia* 23 (1991) 11–30.

WARREN HEARD

ZEBADIAH zeb´uh-d*i*´uh [זְבַדְיָה zevadhyah, זְבַדְיָהוּ zevadhyahu; Ζαβδαῖος Zabdaios]. Meaning "Yah[weh] has given." 1. Son of Beriah, a Benjaminite leader who dwelled in Jerusalem (1 Chr 8:15).

2. Son of Elpaal, a Benjaminite leader who dwelled in Jerusalem (1 Chr 8:17).

3. Son of Jeroham of Gedor, a Benjaminite archer who defected to David at Ziklag and supported him, rather than following King Saul and his Benjaminite kinsmen (1 Chr 12:1-7).

4. A Levite gatekeeper of the Korahite clan, the third son of Meshelemiah (1 Chr 26:1-2).

5. One of King David's commanders, who served in the fourth month of the twelve monthly rotations. He was the son of Asahel, Joab's brother, and his contingent included 24,000 men (1 Chr 27:7).

6. A Levite whom King Jehoshaphat sent throughout Judah with other Levites, princes, and priests to teach the law of God to the people (2 Chr 17:7-9).

7. Son of Ishmael and governor of Judah who presided over Levitical judges in royal matters during the reign of King Jehoshaphat. His counterpart was the priest Amariah, who presided over the judges in matters related to God (2 Chr 19:8-11).

8. Son of Michael of the clan of Shephatiah, who, along with eighty of his kinsmen, followed Ezra back to Jerusalem from Babylonian exile (Ezra 8:8). First Esdras

8:34 misspells his name as Zeraiah (Zaraias Ζαραίας) and numbers his kinsmen at seventy.

9. Son of Immer, who was a priest and at the command of Ezra divorced his foreign wife (Ezra 10:20; 1 Esd 9:21).

M. PATRICK GRAHAM

ZEBAH AND ZALMUNNA zee´buh, zal-muhn´uh [זֶבַח zevakh, צַלְמֻנָּע tsalmunna‘]. The Midianite kings Zebah and Zalmunna are mentioned in the books of Judges (8:4-21) and Psalms (83:11 [Heb. 83:12]). *Zebah* may be translated "sacrifice," "victim," or "slain one." *Zalmunna* means "protection refused." These names are symbolic of the kings' fate; it is possible that they have been altered from original names that were honorable.

As Midianite leaders, Zebah and Zalmunna represent some of the worst foreign kings who oppress Israel in the days of the judges. Linked with the Amalekites, the Midianites are presented as marauders, murderers, and idolaters who encamp with their allies in order to wipe out the fledgling community of Israel (Num 22:1-7; 25:1-9; Judg 6–8). As a youth, GIDEON experienced their raids on his people (Judg 6:1-6); in response, Israel cried out to God, prompting the divine selection of Gideon as deliverer (Judg 6:11-16). *See* MIDIAN, MIDIANITES.

The presence of Zebah and Zalmunna in the book of Judges not only highlights the threat that the Midianites posed against Israel but also underscores the complexities in the book's presentation of Gideon. This heroic idol destroyer, although chosen by God to deliver Israel, repeatedly encounters resistance from his own people, who appear reluctant to follow his commands while preparing to battle the Midianites. Calling upon the Ephraimites and the soldiers of SUCCOTH and PENUEL to assist him, Gideon finds only their rebuff (Judg 8:1-9). Nevertheless, God leads him to victory against the Midianite nemesis (Judg 7:9, 15; 8:12). Gideon's battle against the Midianites is presented as an opportunity for God to deliver the covenantal people in a manner reminiscent of the exodus, of Joshua's battle of Jericho, and of the victories God grants throughout the days of the judges. God commands Gideon to reduce his army, so that only 300 go to battle (Judg 7:2-7). Gideon does not actually have to fight in the initial battle; the Midianites are routed by God. Examples of psychological warfare point to divine providence; hearing a Midianite's account of a dream wherein Israel is victorious, Gideon tells his men to use torches, shouting, and clashing sounds to effect victory (Judg 7:7-23; 8:12).

Although rebuffed by the citizens of Succoth and Penuel when he requested assistance before Zebah and Zalmunna were captured (Judg 8:6-9), Gideon successfully defeats the Midianite army, subduing these leaders. His compatriots' initial derision and the Midianites' apparent slaughter of Gideon's brothers (Judg 8:18-19) goad Gideon to make a particular example of the two kings. He attempts to have them killed in a most humiliating manner—by the sword of JETHER, his young son; this plan is quashed by the lad's fear, and Gideon carries out the death sentence himself. This encounter with the Midianites provides the backdrop for understanding the Israelite crisis of leadership. The tribes neglect, disobey, or are hostile to Gideon. With the death of Zebah and Zalmunna, however, they are ready not only to accept Gideon as their head but also to accept him as king (with dynastic succession). This is true even though Gideon goes beyond God's specific directives; in the absence of divine instruction, Gideon summarily executes Zebah and Zalmunna, taking their camels' crescents as spoil.

The tension surrounding Israel's view of kingship comes to the fore with the portrayal of the execution of Zebah and Zalmunna. Although Gideon resolves, "I will not rule over you, and my son will not rule over you; the LORD will rule over you" (Judg 8:23), his initial insistence that his son slay the Midianite rulers may have been Gideon's attempt to position his progeny to succeed him (Judg 8:20).

In Ps 83, Zebah and Zalmunna are presented as the archetypal enemies of God who baselessly attempt to annihilate Israel. Analogous to Philistia, Edom, Assyria, and other classic enemies, they defy God, saying, "Let us take the pastures of God for our own possession" (83:12 [Heb. 83:13]). Found in parallel with OREB AND ZEEB, commanders of the Midianite army, the psalmist anticipates that Israel's current enemies will be subdued as were Zebah and Zalmunna in the past (see Isa 10:26). The psalmist expresses the hope that all nations will acknowledge God's sovereignty: "Let them know that you alone, whose name is the Lord, are the Most High over all the earth" (Ps 83:18 [Heb. 83:19]).

SHARON PACE

ZEBEDEE zeb´uh-dee [Ζεβεδαῖος Zebedaios]. The name means "Gift of Yahweh" (compare 1 Chr 27:7; Ezra 8:8; Josephus, *Ant.* 5.33). Zebedee was the father of two core members of the Twelve, JAMES and JOHN. He is mentioned solely in the Gospels and in relation to these two sons (Matt 4:21; 10:2; 26:37; Mark 1:19-20; 3:17; 10:35; Luke 5:10; John 21:2). He was a fisherman from the Capernaum area (Matt 4:12-22) with a boat (owned or leased) and hired hands (Mark 1:20). His sons were partners of Simon Peter, perhaps in a fishing cooperative (Luke 5:10). This does not imply even moderate wealth. Yet he can dispense with the assistance of his wife and sons for perhaps several years, and is hardly toward the bottom of the socioeconomic scale. He continues fishing in Galilee and is able to contribute to the support of his sons and their unnamed mother traveling with Jesus. His wife (Matt 20:20; 27:56) is probably not the Salome of Mark 15:40, but is present at the cross (Matt 27:56).

BRIAN M. NOLAN

ZEBIDAH zuh-bi′duh [זְבוּדָּה zevudah]. Zebidah (qere: zevidhah זְבִידָה) was the mother of Judah's King JEHOIAKIM (2 Kgs 23:36) and daughter of Pedaiah. Her name is absent from the 2 Chr 36:5 parallel announcement of Jehoiakim's kingship.

ZEBINA zuh-bi′nuh [זְבִינָא zevina᾿]. From the Aram. root zbn (זבן), meaning "to buy." The fourth in a list of seven sons of Nebo found in Ezra 10:43. The name occurs in a broader list of returnees from the exile, married to foreign women whom Ezra mandated that they divorce. Zebina is one of two sons of Nebo (Nooma) absent from a parallel list in 1 Esd 9:35.

DEREK E. WITTMAN

ZEBOIIM zuh-boi′im [צְבֹעִים tsevo‘im]. Means "hyenas." One of the "cities of the Plain" (Gen 13:12; 19:25, 29) destroyed with Sodom, Gomorrah, and Admah (Deut 29:23 [Heb 29:22]). The so-called Table of Nations (Gen 10) places Zeboiim along with Sodom, Gomorrah, and Admah at the southern end of Canaan (v. 19), and Gen 14:3 locates them near the Dead Sea. Five Early Bronze Age cities found near the southeastern shore of the Dead Sea are often associated with the cities of the plain, though no direct links to the biblical cities have been discovered.

The Elamite king Chedorlaomer led a coalition of kings from the east in an invasion of Zeboiim and its neighbors (Gen 14:1-2); Shemeber is named as the king of Zeboiim. Zeboiim is not explicitly mentioned in the account of the destruction of Sodom in Gen 19, but like Sodom and Gomorrah, Zeboiim and Admah are bywords for Yahweh's wrath (Deut 29:23 [Heb. 29:22]). In Hos 11:8, Yahweh shows compassion toward Israel and refuses to destroy it as he did Zeboiim and Admah. *See* GOMORRAH; SODOM, SODOMITE.

Bibliography: James Penrose Harland. "Sodom and Gomorrah." *BARead.* G. Ernest Wright and David Noel Freedman, eds. (1961) 41–58.

RALPH K. HAWKINS

ZEBOIM zuh-boh′im [צְבֹעִים tsevo‘im]. 1. A valley near Michmash in the territory of Benjamin, approximately 7 mi. northeast of Jerusalem (1 Sam 13:18). During Saul's rule, Philistine troops took over the area around Michmash and sent out raiding parties in three directions, including an area that overlooked the valley of Zeboim, which stretched southeastward, toward the Jordan.

2. A village in the territory of Benjamin where Jews who had returned from the Babylonian exile with Zerubbabel were known to live (Neh 11:34). Nehemiah called for 10 percent of the families in each town to help repopulate Jerusalem (11:1).

TONY W. CARTLEDGE

ZEBUL zee′buhl [זְבֻל zevul]. The governor of Shechem, appointed by Abimelech son of Gideon. Zebul warned Abimelech about Gaal's plans to lead an insurrection and urged him to bring an army to lie in wait outside of Shechem (Judg 9:30-33). The next morning, when Gaal saw Abimelech's armies in the distance, Zebul disregarded it as shadows (9:36). When Gaal reasserted his observation, Zebul mockingly urged him to go fight Abimelech's troops (9:38). Once Gaal had been defeated, Zebul refused him access to the city again (9:40-41).

Zebul is described as Abimelech's "officer" (paqidh [פָּקִיד]; 9:28), a subordinate in a position of oversight over others. He is also referred to as the "ruler" (sar שַׂר) of the city, which can be translated as "chieftain" or "governor." The name *Zebul* ("exalted one") is probably the remnant of a sentence name exalting a deity, such as Baal or Yam (as in the Ugaritic texts).

RALPH K. HAWKINS

ZEBULUN, ZEBULUNITE zeb′yuh-luhn, zeb′yuh-luh-nit [זְבֻלוּן zevulun, זְבוּלֹנִי zevuloni; Ζαβουλών Zaboulōn]. 1. Zebulun is the personal name given to the sixth son of LEAH and JACOB (Gen 30:20; 35:23), the eponymous ancestor of one of the twelve tribes of Israel. Throughout the OT, Zebulun most frequently refers to the people or territory of the tribe bearing this name.

The birth of Zebulun is part of a larger patriarchal narrative that describes the birth and naming of Jacob's twelve sons (Gen 29:31–30:24). After already giving birth to four sons (Reuben, Simeon, Levi, and Judah), Leah becomes barren. She later conspires to sell Reuben's MANDRAKEs (an aphrodisiac) to RACHEL in exchange for the opportunity to lie with Jacob. Subsequently, Leah gives birth to Issachar and Zebulun. Upon Zebulun's birth Leah announces, "God has endowed me with a good dowry; now my husband will honor me, because I have borne him six sons" (Gen 30:20). Leah's declaration suggests two potential folk etymologies for the name Zebulun. Her first phrase suggests an association with the Hebrew word *dowry* (zevedh זֶבֶד), although this word has only the first two consonants in common; her second phrase connects the name Zebulun with the verb meaning "to honor, exalt" (zaval זָבַל).

2. Zebulun is listed among the names of the tribes of Israel (e.g., Exod 1:3; 1 Chr 2:1), typically after Issachar (Num 1:8-9; 2:5-8; but compare Deut 33:18-25, where Zebulun is before Issachar). In most lists, the six Leah tribes appear first, leading some scholars to suggest that this grouping might be evidence of a six-tribe confederacy that predated the formation of the well-known twelve-tribe system of the monarchic period. The Zebulun tribe is further divided into three clans, descendants of Zebulun's three sons: SERED, ELON, and JAHLEEL (Gen 46:14; Num 26:26).

Joshua 18:1-10 reports that Joshua allocated land to Zebulun and six other Israelite tribes who had not yet been assigned territory in Canaan (*see* TRIBES,

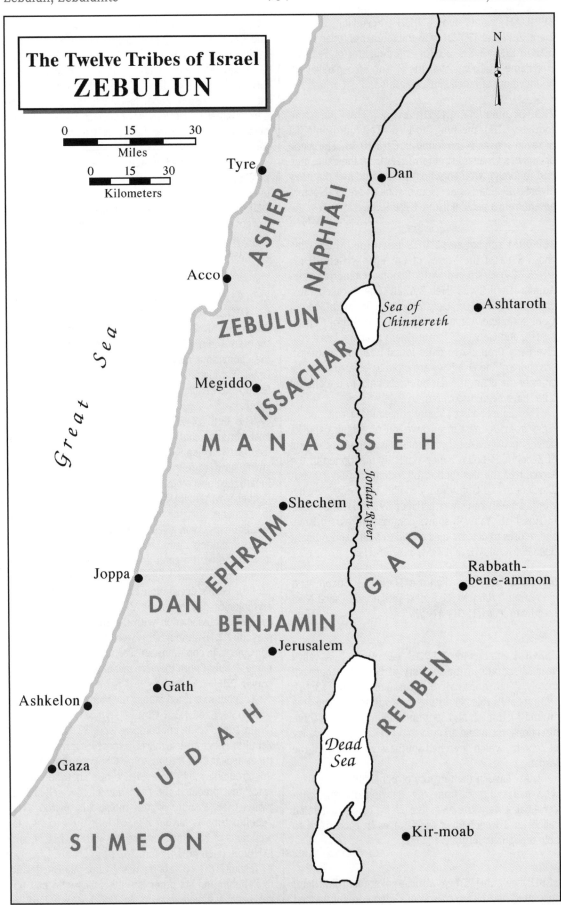

The Twelve Tribes of Israel
ZEBULUN

TERRITORIES OF). The description of Zebulun's boundaries (Josh 19:10-16) provides the most detailed report of the geographical territory of Zebulun, which is situated in the hill country of the upper Galilee, due west of the Sea of Galilee. Zebulun is landlocked, surrounded by Asher to the northwest, Naphtali to the northeast, Issachar to the southeast, and Manasseh to the southwest. A more general—and somewhat conflicting—geographical description is found in Gen 49:13, where Jacob promises Zebulun a land "at the shore of the sea" with borders "at Sidon." If SIDON is the Phoenician coastal city located west of Mount Lebanon, then it might appear that this territory was intended to include or at one time did include a northern coastal outlet to the Mediterranean Sea. In either case, it appears likely that Israelite tribes were less concerned with specific territorial borders than they were with maintaining rights of possession within extended social groups.

According to the census in Numbers, Zebulun was the fourth largest tribe both at the beginning of the wilderness journey (Num 1:31) and at the end (Num 26:27). Once settled in Canaan, the Zebulunites did not drive out all the indigenous Canaanite inhabitants within their territory (Judg 1:30). Military forces from Zebulun courageously joined with Barak against Sisera (Judg 4:6, 10; 5:14, 18) and with Gideon against the Midianites (Judg 6:35). Later, the Chronicler reports that Zebulun sent a contingent of armed troops and supplies to aid David in securing the kingdom from Saul (1 Chr 12:33, 40 [Heb. 12:34, 41]). During the reign of Hezekiah, some Zebulunites were among the few who responded to the king's invitation to return to Jerusalem to celebrate the Passover (2 Chr 30:1, 10-11). Zebulun, along with the rest of the northern kingdom of Israel, fell to the Assyrians in 722 BCE.

In the NT, much of Jesus' life and ministry is situated in Galilee, a region that includes, but is not limited to, the territory of Zebulun (Matt 4:13). Drawing upon the words of Isaiah (9:1-2 [Heb. 8:23–9:1]), the Gospel of Matthew speaks of Zebulun (and neighboring Naphtali) as "the people who sat in darkness [who] have seen a great light" in reference to the advent of Jesus' ministry in Galilee (Matt 4:14-16). In Rev 7:8, 12,000 people from the tribe of Zebulun—along with 12,000 from each of the other eleven tribes—are sealed as God's servants. The seal apparently serves to protect them from the punishments to come.

Bibliography: Norman K. Gottwald. *The Tribes of Yahweh* (1979); J. Maxwell Miller and John H. Hayes. *A History of Ancient Israel and Judah.* 2nd ed. (2006).

RYAN BONFIGLIO

ZECHARIAH zek´uh-ri´uh [זְכַרְיָה zekharyah, זְכַרְיָהוּ zekharyahu; Ζαχαρίας Zacharias]. A common name in biblical texts, spelled in Hebrew usually as zekharyah or zekharyahu, but also with the alternate short form zekher (זֶכֶר; 1 Chr 8:31; compare 9:37) and possi-

bly also zikhri (זִכְרִי; *see* ZICHRI), and in Greek as Zacharias. The long form of the Hebrew name means "Yahweh has remembered." This name is used for possibly as many as thirty people in the OT and NT. It is especially common in the books of Chronicles and Ezra–Nehemiah. 1. A monarch in the northern kingdom of Israel (2 Kgs 14:29; 15:8-12), the fifth and final member of the longest reigning northern dynasty (2 Kgs 10:30; 15:12), established by JEHU (2 Kgs 9:1-13). Zechariah would follow his father Jeroboam II, whose kingdom, together with that of his royal counterpart in the Southern Kingdom (Azariah/Uzziah), would not only endure for many decades but also even rival the extent of Solomon's ideal kingdom (2 Kgs 14:21–15:7). This Israelite expansion can be attributed to the weakness of the Assyrians in the first half of the 8th cent. BCE due to internal tensions and external pressures from its northern rival URARTU. However, the rise of Tiglath-pileser III in the mid-8th cent. BCE would signal the beginning of Assyria's greatest yet final phase of glory and power in the ANE. This resurgence of Assyrian power coincided with Zechariah's ascension to the throne after his father's death. Zechariah ruled for only six months at the capital in Samaria before being assassinated by SHALLUM (2 Kgs 15:10), who in turn would be assassinated within a month (2 Kgs 15:13) by Menahem (2 Kgs 15:14). The death of Zechariah and the demise of the dynasty of Jehu marked the beginning of the end for the Northern Kingdom, which would become a province of the Assyrian Empire by 722 BCE. The Deuteronomistic historian evaluates Zechariah negatively, linking him, as he does most of the kings of the Northern Kingdom, to the "sins of Jeroboam" (2 Kgs 15:7), who established two worship centers at Bethel and Dan to rival the Temple at Jerusalem.

2. A Reubenite (1 Chr 5:7).

3. A Levitical gatekeeper and son of Meshelemiah/Shelemiah/Shallum (1 Chr 9:17-22; see 26:14).

4. A Gibeonite (1 Chr 9:37).

5. A Levitical musician commissioned by David (1 Chr 15:18, 20; 16:5).

6. A priestly trumpeter commissioned by David (1 Chr 15:24).

7. A Levite and son of Isshiah who cast the lot during David's time (1 Chr 24:25).

8. A Levitical gatekeeper and son of Hosah from the clan of Merari during David's reign (1 Chr 26:11, 16).

9. The father of Iddo from the tribe of Manasseh (1 Chr 27:21).

10. A Judean official in Jehoshaphat's court who taught Torah among the towns of Judah (2 Chr 17:7-9).

11. A Levitical prophet and father of Jahaziel who announced victory for Jehoshaphat (2 Chr 20:14).

12. A son of the Judean king Jehoshaphat who was assassinated by his brother Jehoram (2 Chr 21:2).

13. The son of Jehoiada and a prophet through whom the spirit of the Lord spoke a message of condemnation against Joash and his people (2 Chr 24:17-22). Zechariah's father, JEHOIADA, was the high priest who had rescued the Judean king Joash from the lethal hands of Queen Athaliah (2 Chr 22–23). But when Jehoiada died, Joash reversed the reforms of his priestly mentor and in a tragic irony allowed the killing of his rescuer's son, Zechariah, through whom God warned the nation. The motif of Yahweh raising up prophets from the ranks of sacred personnel is common in the Chronicler's history (1 Chr 25:1; 2 Chr 20:13-17). While such figures elsewhere in Chronicles emerge from the Levitical orders, Zechariah is drawn from the priestly caste. There is irony in this death, first in the fact that Joash kills the son of the one who rescued him from sure death, but also in the fact that Zechariah's death defiles the holy precincts protected so carefully by Jehoiada in his purge of Athaliah. The death of Zechariah is mentioned in Matt 23:35 and Luke 11:51, even though his lineage in Matthew is traced through an individual named Berechiah (see #27).

14. A Levite from the clan of Asaph who assisted Hezekiah with his reforms (2 Chr 29:13).

15. A Levitical musician from the clan of Kohath who assisted Josiah with his temple restoration (2 Chr 34:12-13).

16. An administrator of the Temple during Josiah's reign (2 Chr 35:8; see 1 Esd 1:8).

17. A leader of the clan of Parosh (Ezra 8:3).

18. A leader of the clan of Bebai (Ezra 8:11).

19. One of the leaders sent by Ezra to Iddo to ask him to send ministers for the Temple (Ezra 8:16).

20. A layperson from the clan of Elam who agreed to divorce his Gentile wife (Ezra 10:26).

21. A layperson standing beside Ezra as he read the Torah to the assembly in Jerusalem (Neh 8:4).

22. An ancestor of Athaiah, a Judahite who volunteered to live in Jerusalem in the early Persian period (Neh 11:4).

23. An ancestor of Maaseiah, another Judahite who volunteered to live in Jerusalem (Neh 11:5).

24. An ancestor of Adaiah, a priest who volunteered to live in Jerusalem (Neh 11:12).

25. A priestly trumpeter and son of Jonathan who was commissioned by Nehemiah for the dedication of the wall (Neh 12:35, 41).

26. A Judean man who, together with Uriah the priest, served as a witness to Isaiah's prophecy of the birth of a son named Maher-shalal-hash-baz (Isa 8:2). Uriah is identified by his social role (priest), but Zechariah is identified by his lineage, suggesting that he was a layperson (son of Jeberechiah). It is possible—though not certain—that this Zechariah is the maternal grandfather of King Hezekiah (see 2 Kgs 18:2; 2 Chr 29:1) and possibly also the godly prophetic mentor of Uzziah (2 Chr 26:5).

27. The son of Berechiah son of IDDO (Zech 1:1, 7; see Ezra 5:1; 6:14). This prophetic figure traces his lineage to a priestly clan. His ancestor Iddo returned to the land with Zerubbabel and Jeshua around 520 BCE. While Iddo led one of the priestly clans during the generation of Jeshua's son Joiakim (Neh 12:4), Zechariah assumed leadership of this clan at a later point (Neh 12:16). Both the books of Ezra and Zechariah identify Zechariah as a figure who prophesied near the beginning of the reign of the Persian king DARIUS (Zech 1:1, 7 [520 BCE]; 7:1 [516 BCE]). Zechariah is depicted in the book of Ezra as a prophetic figure who along with Haggai was instrumental in the recommencement of the temple restoration project after a hiatus (Ezra 5:1-2; 6:14). The prophetic book that bears his name is witness to a prophet and prophetic community that was instrumental not only in the rebuilding of the Temple (Zech 1:16; 4:6-10a; 6:12-15) but also in the penitential renewal among the people (1:1-6), restoration of Jerusalem and Judah (1:7-17), announcement of the return of Yahweh (1:16; 2:5, 10, 13; 8:1-8), declaration of the punishment of foreign enemies (1:18-21 [Heb. 2:1-4]), and reinstatement of the priestly office (3:1-7; 6:13). The linear development of the book of Zechariah suggests a prophetic movement that became increasingly distanced from the early Persian period Jerusalemite leadership. While the early part of the book affirms the Temple and its services, Zechariah's confrontation of the community in chaps. 7–8 is linked to the priests, while the attacks on the shepherds through chaps. 9–14 are associated with temple personnel (see 11:13). It may be instructive that while the priestly Zadokite line associated with Levi's son Kohath (1 Chr 6:1-15) is affirmed in the early chapters of Zechariah (3; 6), in Zech 12:12-13 renewal is connected with the priestly line of Shimei associated with Levi's son GERSHOM (1 Chr 6:17; see Exod 6:16-17; Num 3:17-18). According to 1 Chr 6:20-21, the clan of Iddo, to which Zechariah belonged, was also in the line of Gershom. It may be that ultimately Zechariah or his prophetic disciples rejected Zadokite excesses and looked to a renewal from Zechariah's line (see ZECHARIAH, BOOK OF).

28. The father of John the Baptist and priest from the clan of Abijah during the reign of Herod the Great and Caesar Augustus (Luke 1:5; 3:2; see 1 Chr 24:10). Zechariah's wife was Elizabeth, the elderly barren woman whose womb God miraculously opened in order to bear the prophet John the Baptist, forerunner of Jesus Christ (Luke 1:5-7). Zechariah is depicted as an active priest whose division cared for the Temple for part of the year (Luke 1:8-10). Chosen by lot to burn incense in the Temple, Zechariah is confronted by the angel of the Lord who presages the birth and ministry of John (Luke 1:11-17). Because of his unbelief, the angel strikes Zechariah mute until the child is born and named John (Luke 1:18-25, 39-45, 57-66). Immediately upon naming his son, Zechariah is filled with Holy Spirit and his mouth opens to prophesy a song of praise to the Lord

for raising up John as a prophet of the Most High (Luke 1:64, 67-79).

MARK J. BODA

ZECHARIAH, BOOK OF zek′uh-ri′uh [זְכַרְיָה zekharyah; Ζαχαρίας Zacharias]. The eleventh book of the Minor Prophets (BOOK OF THE TWELVE) in the OT. The book of Zechariah addresses issues related to the Jewish community in the early Persian period (520–400 BCE) in the province of Yehud. The book begins with a description of a penitent community seeking to avoid the mistakes of past generations (1:1-6). Such penitence is rewarded through prophetic promises delivered through a series of night visions with accompanying oracles (1:7–6:15). These promises focus on a range of renewals including physical reconstruction, demographic revival, economic prosperity, and leadership renewal. Among these promises, however, there are indications of enduring problems in the province (see Zech 5). This comes to the fore in chaps. 7–8 in a pericope that puts restoration on hold because of insincere repentance, but retains hope for the future. These chapters provide a segue to chaps. 9–14, which trace the demise of initial hopes for Davidic leadership with the emergence of inappropriate leadership. The darker universal tone of chaps. 12–14 reveals that the answer lies in the direct action of Yahweh as divine warrior and king.

- A. Form and History
- B. Detailed Analysis
  - 1. God's call and prophetic visions (Zechariah 1–6)
  - 2. From fasts to feasts (Zechariah 7–8)
  - 3. Return, restoration, and cleansing (Zechariah 9–11)
  - 4. Future victory (Zechariah 12–14)
- C. Theological and Religious Significance
- Bibliography

A. Form and History

The prophecies found in Zech 1–8 are delivered against the backdrop of the construction of the Second Temple (Zech 1:12, 16-17; 4:6b-10a; 8:9-13) and the return of the Jewish community from exile (2:6-13 [Heb. 2:10-17]; 3:2; 6:10, 15) in the early Persian period. The book of Ezra offers evidence that Cyrus had given permission for reconstruction of the Temple and return of the exiles at the outset of his reign (Ezra 1:1-4; 6:12-15; 8:3-5), an action consistent with his treatment of other subjects in this early period (e.g., ANET 315–16). However, the book of Ezra shows that little was accomplished during the reigns of Cyrus and Cambyses, so that at the outset of Darius' reign there was a need for a renewed effort. In the wake of the unsettled transition of power from Cambyses to Darius (522–519 BCE), such a project on the western frontier of the Persian Empire

by individuals from the heart of the empire may have been seen as advantageous to the new regime.

Some scholars have focused on temple reconstruction as the key impetus for the creation of Zech 1–8, arguing that it was united with Haggai as a building deposit for the dedication of the Temple in 516 BCE (see Ezra 6:15). While the book of Haggai clearly reflects and may also be structured according to the pattern of rituals used for the reconstruction of temples throughout the ANE (see HAGGAI, BOOK OF), only a few scattered pericopae within Zech 1:7–6:15 reflect themes and rituals related to temple building. Instead, Zech 1–8 reflects a much broader agenda that includes repentance from social injustice, eradication of idolatry, restoration of sociological functionaries (royal, priestly, prophetic), institution of legal norms, return of the exiles, and punishment of past imperial abuses.

Past scholarship has usually driven a wedge between Zech 1–8 and Zech 9–14, arguing that because the latter reflects a different genre and worldview and that it mentions the Greeks in chap. 9, it must come from a much later era after the fall of the Persian Empire to Alexander the Great. This analysis was accentuated by many working on the sociological roots of apocalyptic literature, who suggested that Zech 9–14 reflects a community of revolutionaries who opposed the hierocrats responsible for Zech 1–8 (Plöger, Hanson). This view has been questioned over the past few decades, first by establishing tradition-historical connections between Zech 1–8 and 9–14 (e.g., Mason), then by highlighting the priestly (hierocratic) character of Zech 9–14 (e.g., Cook), then by noting literary connections between the first-person voice in both corpora (e.g., Sweeney), and finally by showing how prophetic groups can shift between center and periphery of society within one generation (e.g., Curtis).

In light of this evidence it is possible to once again interpret Zech 1–14 as a book arising from a single stream of prophetic tradition in the Persian period. Its original nucleus appears to have been a series of night visions that offered comfort and hope to a community recovering from the pain of exile, discouraged at the dismal results of their initial restoration efforts, and concerned over enduring unfaithfulness among some in the community (chap. 5). This nucleus was refined as the initial section took form with secondary levels emphasizing that hope lay with the return of the exilic community who will assume positions of leadership (2:6-13 [Heb. 2:10-17]; 3:1-10; 6:9-15). In the process of revising this nucleus, two sections (Zech 1:1-6; 7:1–8:23) have been placed around the night visions. These two sections are closely related in terms of style, structure, vocabulary, and theme, and focus attention on repentance. Introducing the book, the first (Zech 1:1-6) depicts an initial penitential response that prompts the positive response of Yahweh in the night visions (1:7–6:15). However, Zech 7:1–8:23 reveals that either this penitence was insincere or was limited to a smaller group whose example was not followed elsewhere in the province. Chapters 7–8 call for repentance while offering hope of a bright future when fasting rituals will turn to feasting celebrations. These two chapters play a rhetorical role, transitioning the reader from the high expectations of Zech 1–6 to the tempered optimism of the second half of the book (Boda).

Zechariah 9–14 is structured around a series of shepherd units that occur at 10:1-3; 11:1-3, 4-16, 17; 13:7-9 and trace increasing tension between the Zecharian prophetic group and leadership in the Persian period. One can discern a progressively hostile tone in these shepherd units as one reads through this series of texts that depict Yahweh's anger (10:1-3*a*), a prophecy of destruction (11:1-3), a curse (11:17), and finally the execution of judgment (13:7-9). One can also discern a clear shift in tone between the positive oracles that express hope for Judah and Israel in chaps. 9 and 10, and the darker oracles that focus on Judah and Jerusalem alone in chaps. 12–14 and envision a purging of Jerusalem and a great battle against the nations. Lying between these two sections (each of which is introduced by the superscription "oracle," 9:1*a*; 12:1*a*) is the enacted prophetic sign in 11:4-16. Playing off of two key prophetic sections in Ezekiel (chaps. 34; 37), this passage traces the demise of a Davidic leadership figure (vv. 4-14) who is replaced by a foolish shepherd (vv. 15-16). The shepherd's demise results in ruptures in two relationships: the relationship between the shepherd and the nations and the relationship between Judah and Israel. These ruptures explain the emphasis on the judgment of the nations and the absence of references to Israel in chaps. 12–14. The use of autobiography along with the enacted sign form in this central prophetic pericope (11:4-16) forge a strong link to the earlier section of Zechariah (see this form in 6:9-15; compare chap. 3). In light of the allusions to Ezekiel, it is possible that this pericope depicts the demise of Davidic leadership in the early Persian period after the heightened expectations created by Hag 2:20-23; Zech 3; 4:6*b*-10*a*; 6:9-15 (Boda). In the early Persian period there are only two leadership figures who are firmly linked to the Davidic house: Zerubbabel who was governor from around 520 until 510 BCE, and his daughter Shelomith whose husband, Elnathan, ruled after Zerubbabel until around 490 BCE (Meyers). After Shelomith there is no evidence of a Davidic figure involved in leadership in Yehud, suggesting that Zech 9–14 traces and reflects on this loss in the late 6th and early 5th cent. BCE. Zechariah 9–14 thus begins with great hope for the Davidic line (see Zech 9:9-10), but chaps. 12–14 speak only of Yahweh's kingship (14:9) even if they express muted hope for the Davidides (12:7-8, 10, 12; 13:1).

B. Detailed Analysis

1. God's call and prophetic visions (Zechariah 1–6)

The book of Zechariah begins with a presentation of the prophet's sermon (1:1-6) to the people in the eighth month of the second year of Darius' reign (520 BCE). The sermon recycles vocabulary from the earlier prophets (especially Jeremiah) to call the early Persian period community to the repentance that would have prevented the exile in 587 BCE. At the heart of this call is renewal of covenant relationship: as the people return to Yahweh, Yahweh will return to them (1:3). This return also has ethical implications (1:4). The section ends with a report of the positive response of the people through a declaration that Yahweh's discipline was justified.

Zechariah 1:7 represents the second superscription in the book, linking the material that follows (Zech 1:7–6:15) to the twenty-fourth day of the eleventh month of the second year of Darius' reign (520 BCE), thus about three months after the initial sermon. References to God's anger (1:2, 15) and return (1:3, 4, 6, 16) in both the initial sermon (1:1-6) and the first night vision (1:7-17) suggest that the night visions represent God's response to the people's repentance at the outset of the book. In the initial vision the prophet sees angels and variously colored horses, fresh from a reconnaissance mission throughout the earth, who report that all is peaceful. This prompts the angel of Yahweh to intercede for Israel, and God's answer promises comfort and mercy through rescuing God's people, punishing the nations (Babylon), returning to the Temple, reconstructing the city, and providing prosperity.

The second vision (Zech 1:18-21 [Heb. 2:1-4]) offers further insight into one aspect of the first vision, that is, the punishment of the nations. The prophet sees four horns (representing two animals), which are driven off by four blacksmiths; the former representative of former abusive empires of Assyria and Babylon and the latter representative of Persia, which has replaced them. It is during Darius' reign that Babylon is finally punished severely, having escaped serious discipline during Cyrus' takeover of Babylon in 539 BCE.

The third vision (Zech 2:1-5 [Heb. 2:5-9]) develops further another aspect of the first vision, in this case the promises articulated in 1:16-17: the return of Yahweh, the reconstruction of the city, and the restoration of prosperity. The scene reflects an ancient construction site and focuses on a figure who is about to measure the extent of Jerusalem, apparently to build a wall. The positive aspect of building a wall in the ancient world was that it provided security from opposing forces. The negative aspect was that it limited the growth of the city. Such a wall need not be built because of Yahweh's vision for its substantial growth and because of Yahweh's promise to provide protection. The reference to Yahweh's presence as a "wall of fire" may be an allusion to the exodus community (Exod 13:21-22;

24:17) as well as to the fire altars that surrounded the Persian royal city of Pasargadae. The latter suggests that Jerusalem is being identified as an imperial center.

Following the initial three visions, the oracle of 2:6-13 (Heb. 2:10-17) brings the message of the visions "down to earth," that is, in light of the divine promises articulated in these visions, the people are to respond by fleeing from exile in Babylon (2:6-9) and rejoicing in God's renewed presence (2:10-13). The section spells doom for the nations through promised punishment of Babylon (2:8-9), but also hope for the nations through promised covenant relationship with Yahweh (2:11).

The command to "be still" before Yahweh's approaching presence at the end of chap. 2 serves as segue to chap. 3, which provides a scene of court proceedings in the divine council. At issue is the sorry state of the Zadokite Joshua, accused by the heavenly prosecutor of being unworthy of his priestly office. In a scene reminiscent of the priestly investiture in the Torah (Exod 28–29), Yahweh commands that Joshua be reclothed, signifying the removal of his guilt, before commissioning him to take charge of the Temple. This commissioning introduces the oracle in 3:8-10, which, alluding to the close association between priestly and royal figures in Jer 33:15-16, shows that the commissioning of Joshua is a sign of the approaching arrival of a Davidic royal figure ("the Branch") who will inaugurate a new era of cleansing and prosperity.

The vision in Zech 3 takes place in the divine council, access to which is provided through the rebuilt Temple. It is not then surprising that Zech 4 contains an allusion to the sacred utensils found in the Temple proper. The prophet sees a gold lampstand topped by a bowl with seven flames around its circumference. This bowl is fed by an inexhaustible supply of oil through two pipes attached to two olive trees. The seven flames are identified as the eyes of God on earth (God's presence) and the two olive trees are two human figures called "sons of fresh oil." Since these figures are supplying (not receiving) oil they are most likely prophetic figures. This explains why two prophetic oracles have been inserted into this vision report (mid-sentence!) in 3:6b-10a. Most likely these figures are Haggai and Zechariah, whose prophetic words empowered the rebuilding of the Temple, that place of Yahweh's manifest presence on earth.

Having focused in the vision in chaps. 3–4 on the reconstitution and function of leadership figures in the restoration, chap. 5 widens the focus to address key problems in the community as a whole. The prophet sees a gargantuan scroll (vv. 1-4) that represents the curse that falls upon those who breach the covenant (Lev 5:1; Num 5:16-28). The two infractions written on this scroll probably represent the successive acts of one who first stole and then swore falsely regarding the theft (Lev 19:9-18).

While the first vision in chap. 5 deals with an infraction against the second half of the Decalogue (love your neighbor as yourself), the second vision (vv. 5-11) deals with an infraction against the first half, which promotes loving the Lord God with one's heart, soul, and strength. The prophet sees a miniature woman trapped inside a measuring basket and transported by two stork-winged women to a sacred platform in Babylon. This vision suggests that the people had brought idolatry with them from exile and the land needed to be cleansed of this wickedness.

The final night vision (6:1-8) takes place at the doorway to heaven, here depicted in ways strikingly similar to Mesopotamian iconography of the sun god, whose entrance doors are often drawn between two bronze mountains, a picture inspired by the sun rising to the east of the Mesopotamian plain. This vision brings closure to the series by once again presenting a scene involving variously colored horses. The use of chariots, however, shows that these horses are not for reconnaissance but rather for battle. Two groups are sent to the north, one group to the south, while one group (presumably) remains at the entranceway to protect the divine council. The purpose of the northern-bound group is "to set [Yahweh's] Spirit at rest," a phrase most likely drawn from Ezekiel (16:42) and referring to the full expression of God's wrath aimed, here in Zech 6, against the "north country," that is, Babylon.

As at the end of the first phase of the night visions (2:6-13), so at the end of the entire series of night visions one finds a prophetic sign-act that brings the visions "down to earth" (6:9-15). Having depicted the punishment of Babylon in the final night vision, this sign-act depicts a group of exilic returnees with contributions for the temple project. The significance of this passage is that, like Zech 3, it seeks to shape the relationship between priestly and royal figures in the early Persian period. Crowns are to be created for both Joshua (priest, see Zech 3) and the "Branch" figure, who is identified in Jer 23 and 33 as a royal figure from David's line. The priest will play a key role in the royal court, but it is the royal Branch figure who will build the Temple. This sign-act stresses the importance of a partnership between royal and priestly groups to realize the hopes set in motion by the night visions.

2. From fasts to feasts (Zechariah 7–8)

Although beginning as an oral message to a group inquiring about the validity of exilic fasting rituals, these two chapters now function to transition the reader from the optimism of the first six chapters of Zechariah to the realities of Zech 9–14. This section is closely related to the initial penitential sermon in Zech 1:1-6 in terms of style, vocabulary, and structure, but the message reveals that there is enduring need for repentance among the people. The disobedience of the people means that fasting will not be replaced by feasting until there is a change in behavior. The end of this chapter reveals the potential impact a penitential community can have on the surrounding nations who will be drawn to Jerusalem because they have heard of God's presence (8:23).

3. Return, restoration, and cleansing (Zechariah 9–11)

The word *oracle* at the outset of chap. 9 signals a literary transition into a new section of the book. The chapter begins by tracing the triumphant return of Yahweh as divine warrior marching from north to south in the Levant to God's residence in Zion (9:1b-8). This return opens the way for Yahweh to reestablish as vice-regent on earth the Davidic king presented to Zion in 9:9-10. Yahweh's return also involves the restoration of imprisoned exiles who are used as God's military weapons against God's enemies (9:11-13, 14-17). This chapter expresses the great optimism of the early Persian period, especially surrounding the renewal of Davidic hope through the appointment of Zerubbabel as governor in Yehud (Persian period Judah).

The first signs of trouble in chaps. 9–14 come at the outset of chap. 10 (10:1-3a), a section that challenges leaders who have led the people into idolatry. Nevertheless, most of the chapter continues the optimism expressed in chap. 9, highlighting how God will care for and transform the community in Yehud. In the latter part of the chapter emphasis is placed on the role returned Yehud will play in rescuing the northern tribes from exile (10:6-12).

With chap. 11 all optimism is extinguished. Drawing on various images depicting the destruction of plant life, the first section (11:1-3) announces judgment. The second section (11:4-16) is a description of the enacted prophetic sign mentioned above, in which the good shepherd becomes frustrated with the flock, owners, and fellow shepherds and quits his post. This action has implications both for the relationship between the community and the empire (nations) and for the relationship between the Yehudite community and their northern compatriots. The chapter ends with a woe oracle addressed to a worthless shepherd, and this oracle describes severe injury to his arm and right eye (11:17).

4. Future victory (Zechariah 12–14)

Zechariah 12 opens with the second mention of the word *oracle* (12:1a), a term that signals a new section in the book. The distinct character of the material that follows is immediately evident: first, in the regular use of "on that day"; second, in the focus on Judah, Jerusalem, and David with no mention of the northern tribes; and third, in the depiction of a great battle at Jerusalem against the nations. Zechariah 12:1–13:6 begins by describing how Yahweh will make Jerusalem impregnable to the nations and use Judah, Jerusalem, and David as a mighty army against the nations. This great victory (12:9) will be followed by a new era of penitence and cleansing as Yahweh removes idolatry and false prophecy from the land.

Zechariah 13:7-9 represents the final installment in the series of shepherd units that appear regularly throughout chaps. 9–14. In this one the shepherd is finally killed, which has serious implications for the people against whom Yahweh will turn. In the end this results in the refinement of the community, who emerge from this testing declaring that covenant formulary so common in the OT: "The LORD is our God" (13:9).

Reminiscent of chap. 12, Zech 14 looks to Yahweh's defeat of the nations and ascension as king. The chapter begins by depicting God's discipline of Jerusalem by the nations (14:1-2), but this action then reverses and Yahweh disciplines the nations in 14:3-15. This victory over the nations leads to their submission to Yahweh, which is evident in their pilgrimage to God's imperial capital at Jerusalem for the festival of booths (14:16-19). In this new imperial context not just Yahweh's palace (temple) but all of Jerusalem and Judah is considered holy (14:20-21). This status suggests the role that Yehud can still play among the nations.

C. Theological and Religious Significance

Zechariah is witness to the challenges that the early Persian period community faced in the wake of the Babylonian exile and the theological response from a prophetic community. The book opens with great hope, depicting a penitent community to which Yahweh responds with promise of renewal of the Temple, city, province, and the leadership necessary to sustain the community (king, priest, prophet). And yet there are signs even in the night visions that there are enduring problems within the community. The bright tones of chaps. 1–6 soon give way to the gray tones of chaps. 7–8 and 9–11 with the final chapters (12–14) portraying a world in which Yahweh must act in severe ways to establish God's kingdom on earth.

Bibliography: Mark J. Boda. "From Dystopia to Myopia: Utopian (Re)Visions in Haggai and Zechariah 1–8." *Utopia and Dystopia in Prophetic Texts.* Ehud Ben Zvi and Michael Floyd, eds. (2006) 211–49; Mark J. Boda. "From Fasts to Feasts: The Literary Function of Zechariah 7–8." *CBQ* 65 (2003) 390–407; Mark J. Boda. "Oil, Crowns and Thrones: Prophet, Priest and King in Zechariah 1:7–6:15." *Perspectives on Hebrew Scriptures.* Ehud ben Zvi, ed. (2006) 379–404; Mark J. Boda and Michael H. Floyd, eds. *Bringing Out the Treasure: Inner Biblical Allusion and Zechariah 9–14* (2003); Stephen L. Cook. *Prophecy & Apocalypticism: The Postexilic Social Setting* (1995); Byron G. Curtis. *Up the Steep and Stony Road: The Book of Zechariah in Social Location Trajectory Analysis* (2006); Baruch Halpern. "The Ritual Background of Zechariah's Temple Song." *CBQ* 40 (1978) 167–90; Paul D. Hanson. *The Dawn of Apocalyptic: The Historical and Sociological Roots of Jewish Apocalyptic Eschatology.* Rev. ed. (1979); Rex A. Mason. "The Relation of Zech 9–14 to proto-Zechariah." *ZAW* 88 (1976) 227–39; Carol

L. Meyers and Eric M. Meyers. *Haggai, Zechariah 1–8.* AB 25B (1987); Carol L. Meyers and Eric M. Meyers. *Zechariah 9–14: A New Translation with Introduction and Commentary.* AB 25C (1993); Eric M. Meyers. "The Shelomith Seal and Aspects of the Judean Restoration: Some Additional Reconsiderations." *EI* 18 (1985) 33*–38*; David L. Petersen. *Haggai and Zechariah 1–8: A Commentary.* OTL (1984); David L. Petersen. *Zechariah 9–14 and Malachi: A Commentary.* OTL (1995); Otto Plöger. *Theocracy and Eschatology.* S. Rudman, trans. (1968); Paul L. Redditt. *Haggai, Zechariah and Malachi.* NCB (1995); Walter H. Rose. *Zemah and Zerubbabel: Messianic Expectations in the Early Postexilic Period* (2000); Marvin A. Sweeney. *The Twelve Prophets.* 2 vols. Berit Olam. David W. Cotter, ed. (2000).

MARK J. BODA

ZECHARIAH, TARGUM. *See* TARGUMS.

ZECHER. *See* ZECHARIAH.

ZEDAD zee´dad [צְדָד *tsedhadh*]. According to Num 34:8-9 Zedad, the Great Sea, Mount Hor, Lebo-hamath, Ziphron, and Hazar-enan are among the northern boundary markers of Israel. Ezekiel 47:15 provides another description of the northern boundary, including Zedad, the Great Sea, Hethlon, Lebo-hamath, Berothah, Sibraim, Hazer-hatticon, and Hauran as markers. The precise location of Zedad, the proper construal of the northern boundary, and the time periods that Numbers and Ezekiel reflect are points of debate. *See* EZEKIEL, BOOK OF; NUMBERS, BOOK OF.

STEVEN D. MASON

ZEDEKIAH zed´uh-ki´uh [צִדְקִיָה *tsidhqiyah*, צִדְקִיָהוּ *tsidhqiyahu*; Σεδεκίας *Sedekias*]. 1. The son of Chenaanah. Zedekiah was a false prophet in Samaria who lived in the days of Ahab, king of Israel (1 Kgs 22:11, 24; 2 Chr 18:10, 23). When Ahaz prepared to recapture Ramoth-gilead from the Arameans, he asked Jehoshaphat, king of Judah, to join him in battle. Before going to battle, Jehoshaphat desired to consult the divine will concerning the outcome of the battle. Ahaz summoned his prophets who, with a unanimous voice, declared that he would be victorious in battle. Zedekiah, acting on behalf of the group of prophets, used prophetic symbolism to demonstrate to Ahab how he would defeat the Aramean army. He made horns of iron, placed them on his head, and told Ahab that he would be victorious against the Arameans at Ramoth-gilead, thus reinforcing the message that the 400 prophets had proclaimed (1 Kgs 22:6). Zedekiah's symbolic act used animal horns to represent might and power and to reinforce the validity of the prophet's message. When MICAIAH son of Imlah came, he contradicted Zedekiah's prophecy of victory. Micaiah had been summoned at the request of Jehoshaphat, who was unwilling

to accept the prophets' oracle. Micaiah declared that God had put a lying spirit in Zedekiah's mouth and in the mouth of all Ahab's prophets. Micaiah also prophesied that Ahab would die in battle. Zedekiah reacted to Micaiah's words by slapping Micaiah on the cheek. This act was a gesture of humiliation and represents Zedekiah's public challenge of the veracity of Micaiah's words, implying that Micaiah had spoken lies in God's name. Micaiah answered Zedekiah's challenge with an oracle announcing that Zedekiah would hide in fear in a shelter on the DAY OF JUDGMENT.

2. The twentieth and final king of Judah (r. 597–587 BCE). Zedekiah was placed on the throne after Nebuchadnezzar deported JEHOIACHIN, Zedekiah's nephew, to Babylon in 597 BCE. In 2 Chr 36:9-10, Zedekiah appears as the brother of Jehoiachin, but the word *brother* is used here with the meaning of "relative." Zedekiah was the third son of Josiah and the full brother of Jehoahaz (2 Kgs 23:31; 24:17-18); their mother's name was Hamutal, the daughter of Jeremiah of Libnah. His original name was MATTANIAH, but when the king of Babylon placed him on the throne after the deportation of the people who lived in Jerusalem, Nebuchadnezzar changed his name to Zedekiah as an act of sovereignty. Zedekiah was twenty-one years old when he ascended the throne of Judah and reigned eleven years (2 Kgs 24:18). According to the judgment of the writers of the book of Kings, Zedekiah "did what was evil in the sight of the LORD" (2 Kgs 24:19-20; see also Jer 52:2-3).

Zedekiah became king of Judah after Nebuchadnezzar had deported the palace officials who served under Jehoiachin, together with the leading citizens of Judah, the professional people, and thousands of skilled workers. When Zedekiah ascended the throne, Judah became a tributary to Babylon. As a vassal of Nebuchadnezzar, Zedekiah was compelled to pay an annual tribute and take an oath of allegiance to the king of Babylon (Ezek 17:13-14). However, incited by the prophets who were taken to Babylon (Jer 29:8-9) and by the nobles who formed part of the anti-Babylonian forces in Judah, Zedekiah eventually violated his oath of allegiance and rebelled against Babylon.

Zedekiah's reign was marked by extremism, primarily by those who favored insurrection against Babylon. Zedekiah was a weak king who was afraid of popular opinion (Jer 38:19) and almost powerless before a group of palace officials who were against any alliance with Babylon (Jer 38:5). These officials looked to Egypt for support in their rebellion against Babylonian domination. In addition, many people in Judah still regarded Jehoiachin as the legitimate king and considered Zedekiah a puppet of Babylon. Throughout the reign of Zedekiah, Jeremiah exhorted the leaders and the people of Judah to refrain from any act of rebellion against the Babylonians. However, Jeremiah was opposed by the leaders of Judah and by prophetic groups who proclaimed a message of hope and deliverance instead of a message of judgment. In 594 BCE, the fourth year of Zedekiah's reign, a conference was held in Jerusalem, and ambassadors from Tyre, Sidon, Edom, and Moab came to Jerusalem to plan a possible revolt against Babylon (Jer 27:1-22). Those who favored a revolt against Babylon also favored an alliance with Psammetichus II (r. 594–589 BCE), who had recently ascended the throne of Egypt and wanted to extend Egyptian control into Asia.

At that time the Lord commanded Jeremiah to make a wooden yoke and put it upon his neck to persuade Zedekiah not to rebel against the king of Babylon (Jer 27:1-7). The yoke symbolized submission to Babylon as the only hope for Judah's survival. Jeremiah was opposed by HANANIAH, a prophet from Gibeon, who proclaimed the end of Babylonian domination and the return of Jehoiachin from exile (Jer 28:1-17). Hananiah broke the yoke on Jeremiah's neck and declared that the Lord had broken the yoke of Babylon. He prophesied that within two years the sacred vessels taken to Babylon by Nebuchadnezzar would be returned to the Temple. Jeremiah pronounced an oracle of judgment against Hananiah and predicted his death. Hananiah died two months after Jeremiah's oracle (Jer 28:17). Hananiah's death convinced Zedekiah not to join with the neighboring states in their rebellion against Babylon. Zedekiah went to Babylon (Jer 51:59) with a delegation that included Seraiah, the brother of Baruch (Jer 32:12), probably to explain his role in the conspiracy against Babylon (Jer 27:1-22), to reaffirm his loyalty to Nebuchadnezzar, and to pay his annual tribute. Several times Zedekiah asked the prophet Jeremiah for advice (Jer 21:1-7; 37:3-10, 17; 38:14-23). Zedekiah was undecided as to whether to follow the advice of Jeremiah or go along with the fierce patriotism of some of the leaders of Judah. Notwithstanding the strong admonition of Jeremiah not to rebel and unable to resist the pressure of those who desired independence from Babylon, Zedekiah rebelled against Babylon in 589 BCE. Zedekiah abandoned his covenant with Nebuchadnezzar and entered into an alliance with the king of Egypt, requesting horses and a large army (Ezek 17:15).

Zedekiah's rebellion caused Nebuchadnezzar to invade Judah. The Babylonian army conquered all Judean cities except Lachish and Azekah, two fortified cities in the western plains (Jer 34:7). In addition, the Babylonians besieged Jerusalem. The siege of the city began on the tenth day of the tenth month in the ninth year of Zedekiah's reign and lasted eighteen months. During the time the Babylonians were fighting against Jerusalem, at the beginning of the siege, Zedekiah and some of the rich people of Jerusalem made a covenant to emancipate their Israelite slaves. But when the siege was temporarily lifted because of the advance of the Egyptian army, the people re-enslaved them (Jer 34:8-11). It is possible that the purpose of the manumission was to increase the number of people available to fight against the Babylonians. The siege of Jerusalem was lifted when the Egyptian army came to help Zedekiah and the people of Judah. Nebuchadnezzar withdrew his army to confront HOPHRA (Apries), the king of Egypt (Jer 34:21; 37:5). During the period of the siege, there was a severe famine in the city (2 Kgs 25:3); children begged for food and women boiled and ate the flesh of their own children (Lam 4:4, 10).

During the siege, Zedekiah sent a delegation to Jeremiah asking the prophet to pray for Jerusalem (Jer 37:3). Jeremiah responded with an oracle declaring that the Babylonians would return and destroy the city (Jer 37:6-10). In his last meeting with Jeremiah, Zedekiah again sought the prophet's advice. Jeremiah advised Zedekiah to surrender and said that submission to Babylon was the only way for the king to save his life and the life of the nation. However, if Zedekiah refused to surrender to Nebuchadnezzar, then Jerusalem would be captured and burned, and his life would not be spared. Zedekiah was willing to surrender, but he was afraid of the pro-Egyptian (Jer 37:5; Ezek 17:15) and the pro-Babylonian groups within his government (Jer 38:14-28).

In the eleventh year of Zedekiah's reign, on the ninth day of the fourth month, the Babylonian army entered Jerusalem, and Babylonian army officers sat in the middle gate of the city (Jer 39:1-3). Zedekiah, members of his family, and a few of his military officers who had survived the invasion of Jerusalem fled the city by night (2 Kgs 25:4; Jer 39:4) in order to seek refuge on the eastern side of the Jordan River. The Babylonian army pursued the king and his entourage and captured them on the road to Jericho. Zedekiah was taken to Nebuchadnezzar, who had established his camp at Riblah, the former Assyrian administrative province on the Orontes River.

There, Nebuchadnezzar passed judgment on Zedekiah. Zedekiah's sons were killed before him and his own eyes were put out. Zedekiah was bound in chains and taken captive to Babylon (2 Kgs 25:1-7; Jer 32:4-5; 34:2-3; 39:1-7; 52:4-11). The fate of Zedekiah while in Babylon is unknown, but he remained a prisoner until the day of his death (Jer 52:11). Zedekiah's exile and death in Babylon fulfilled Ezekiel's prediction that Zedekiah would come to Babylon and yet not see the land (Ezek 12:13). A month after Zedekiah's capture, Nebuzaradan, the commander of Nebuchadnezzar's army, entered Jerusalem. He plundered the Temple, burned the king's palace and all the houses of Jerusalem, and tore down the walls of Jerusalem (2 Kgs 25:8-10; Jer 39:8).

3. A son of Jehoiakim, king of Judah (1 Chr 3:16). This information does not appear in 2 Kgs 24:17, where Zedekiah appears as a son of Josiah and the uncle of Jehoiachin, also known as Jeconiah (Jer 24:1). In 2 Chr 36:9-10, Zedekiah appears as the brother of Jehoiachin. Since Zedekiah, the king of Judah, and Jehoahaz had the same mother, Hamutal, the daughter of Jeremiah of Libnah, this Zedekiah must be different from the one

who became the last king of Judah. The word *brother* in 2 Chr 36:10 should be understood as indicating a relative of Jehoiachin.

4. One of the officials in the postexilic community who added his name to the binding agreement between the civil and religious leaders and all the people that they would obey the law of Moses (Neh 10:1 [Heb. 10:2]).

5. The son of Maaseiah. Zedekiah was a false prophet who was taken into exile in Babylon at the time of the deportation of Jehoiachin, king of Judah in 597 BCE. Jeremiah denounced Zedekiah in a letter sent to the exiles because he and Ahab son of Kolaiah were inciting rebellion among the exiles by predicting an early return of Jehoiachin and the people of Judah from Babylon (Jer 29:21-22). Jeremiah denounced the claims of Zedekiah and Ahab by saying that they were prophesying lies in Yahweh's name. He also pronounced an oracle of judgment against Zedekiah and against Ahab. According to Jeremiah, their names would become a byword and their death a warning to others like them. Their terrible fate would become proverbial and their names would be used in cursing by the people who were in exile in Babylon. The name of Zedekiah son of Maaseiah appears on a Dead Sea Scroll fragment (4Q339) as one of the many false prophets that arose in Israel.

6. A son of Hananiah and a royal officer of Judah in the days of Jehoiakim, king of Judah (Jer 36:12). Zedekiah and several officers of the king were together in Elishama's chamber in the king's palace. Elishama was the king's secretary. During this meeting of Zedekiah and the royal officers, Micaiah son of Gemariah came in and told the royal officers that Baruch, Jeremiah's scribe, had read Jeremiah's words to the people who were gathered in the Temple (Jer 36:13).

7. The great-grandfather of BARUCH, Jeremiah's scribe and friend (Bar 1:1).

Bibliography: Shimon Bakon. "Zedekiah: Last King of Judah." *JBQ* 36 (2008) 93–101; Paul-Eugène Dion. "The Horned Prophet (1 Kings xxii 11)." *VT* 49 (1999) 259–61; Niels Peter Lemche. "What if Zedekiah Had Remained Loyal to His Master." *BibInt* 8 (2000) 115–28; Juha Pakkala. "Zedekiah's Fate and the Dynastic Succession." *JBL* 125 (2006) 443–52; Mark Roncace. *Jeremiah, Zedekiah, and the Fall of Jerusalem* (2005); Nahum M. Sarna. "Zedekiah's Emancipation of Slaves and the Sabbatical Year." *Orient and Occident*. H. A. Hoffner, ed. (1973) 143–49.

CLAUDE MARIOTTINI

ZEEB. *See* OREB AND ZEEB.

ZELA zee′luh [צֵלַע *tsela*ʿ]. Means "rib" or "side." One of fourteen cities allotted to Benjamin, located northwest of Jerusalem (Josh 18:28). Some scholars suggest that "Zela, Haeleph" should be read as a compound name ("Zela ha-eleph"), but Zela and Haeleph must be

counted separately in order for the list to have fourteen names. The location of the site is uncertain; however, some scholars identify it with Khirbet Salah, a site between Jerusalem and Gibeon.

Zela is the site of the family tomb of Kish, Saul's father. According to 2 Sam 21:14, David and his men buried the bones of Saul and his son Jonathan here after they died in battle against the Philistines at Gilboa. The Philistines hung their bodies on the city walls of Bethshan, until Israelites from Jabesh-gilead stole them. Zela may have been Saul's birthplace, since his family tomb was located here.

TERRY W. EDDINGER

ZELEK zee′lik [צֶלֶק *tseleq*]. Zelek the Ammonite is listed among "The Thirty," DAVID'S CHAMPIONS (2 Sam 23:37; 1 Chr 11:39). In these lists, names of warriors are given formulaically with their places of origin, clear evidence that David's most skilled fighters were mercenaries. *See* AMMON, AMMONITES.

ZELOPHEHAD zuh-loh′fuh-had [צְלָפְחָד *tselafekhadh*]. Zelophehad is listed among the descendants of Manasseh through Makir, Gilead, and finally Hepher (Num 27:1; 1 Chr 7:15). When he died in the wilderness without a male heir, his five daughters—Mahlah, Noah, Hoglah, Milcah, and Tirzah—appealed to Moses for an inheritance of property so that their father's name might not perish. When Moses brought the matter before God, Yahweh affirmed their request and decreed that the five receive their father's inheritance and that this become the rule for other such circumstances in Israel (Num 27:1-11).

Leaders of the Manassite clan of Gilead later approached Moses with their fear that Zelophehad's daughters would marry into other tribes and so take tribal land with them. Since this would void the original tribal allotments, God decreed that the daughters of Zelophehad (as well as other women in such circumstances) must marry within their clan in order to avoid the alienation of tribal lands. Such endogamous practice would ensure that land would not move from one tribe to another (Num 36:1-12). *See* ZELOPHEHAD, DAUGHTERS OF.

M. PATRICK GRAHAM

ZELOPHEHAD, DAUGHTERS OF zuh-loh′fuh-had [בְּנוֹת צְלָפְחָד *benoth tselafekhadh*]. ZELOPHEHAD, son of Hepher and a member of the tribe of Manasseh, had five daughters: MAHLAH, NOAH, HOGLAH, MILCAH, and TIRZAH (Num 26:33). At Zelophehad's death, the daughters petitioned Moses for their father's share of the inheritance of the land (Num 27:1-4). Moses brought the case before the Lord, who declared the daughters' right to the property in cases where no sons were available or living (Num 27:5-9). The five daughters later married cousins from their father's tribe, in order that "no inheritance of the Israelites shall be transferred from one tribe to another" (Num 36:5-9).

The bold actions of the women to defy the conventions of inheritance practice and seek their father's property for themselves is significant in that it not only changed their fortunes but also created new law for all of Israel (Num 27:8-9). As with the petition of the unclean men in Num 9:7-14, the inclusion of this story suggests that the Priestly writer understood the law as surprisingly malleable when human need was great.

JESSICA TINKLENBERG DEVEGA

ZELZAH zel´zuh [צֶלְצַח tseltsakh]. A site of uncertain location, near RACHEL'S TOMB on the border of the territory of Benjamin (1 Sam 10:2). According to Jer 31:15, Rachel's tomb is near Ramah, while Gen 35:19 places it near Bethlehem. Tradition locates the tomb along the modern road between Jerusalem and Bethlehem.

After anointing him as king, Samuel predicted that Saul would meet two men at Zelzah who would be looking for him to tell him that his father's donkeys had been found. This was the first of three signs reassuring Saul that God had appointed him king of Israel. The LXX interprets *Zelzah* as "by leaping greatly (halamenous megala ἁλαμένους μεγάλα)," i.e., as an action of the two men rather than as a place name.

TERRY W. EDDINGER

ZEMARAIM zem´uh-ray´im [צְמָרַיִם tsimarayim]. 1. Zemaraim appears in Josh 18:22 as the name of a city that was included in the lands allotted to the tribe of Benjamin when Joshua cast lots at Shiloh. The city is also mentioned in Pharaoh SHISHAK's list of cities when he campaigned against Judah and Israel. Since the 19th cent., it has been associated with Ras ez-Zeimara (5 mi. northeast of Bethel), but more recently it has been identified with Ras et-Tahuneh (2 mi. southwest of Bethel).

2. The name of a mountain in Ephraim where King Abijah of Judah stood with his army and addressed King Jeroboam I of Israel (2 Chr 13:4). It is unclear whether it was named for the city nearby or vice versa.

M. PATRICK GRAHAM

ZEMARITES zem´uh-rīt [צְמָרִי tsemari]. Descendants of Canaan, the son of Ham, in the Table of Nations given in Gen 10:18 (//1 Chr 1:16). The Zemarites are listed with other Canaanite ethnic groups that occur more frequently (Jebusites, Amorites, Hivites) in statements detailing Yahweh's plan to drive out the indigenous Canaanite tribes in order to give the land to Israel. No exact location is known for Zemar or the dwelling of the Zemarites, but Akkadian and Egyptian sources mention a city called tsimir/tsumur somewhere in Syria. The correlation between the two is possible but unverifiable.

JARED WOLFE

ZEMER zee´muhr [צֶמֶר tsemer]. Mentioned in the AMARNA LETTERS and in Assyrian texts, Zemer was an important Phoenician city; its modern name is Sumra, and it lies on the Mediterranean coast between Ruad and Tripoli. Ezekiel lists "skilled men of Zemer," along with people from the Phoenician cities of Sidon and Arvad, among the inhabitants of Tyre (Ezek 27:8). The Hebrew text reads "your skilled men, O Tyre" (khakhamayikh tsor צֹר חֲכָמַיִךְ), as the NRSV observes in a footnote, but has been emended to "skilled men of Zemer" (khakhme-tsemer חַכְמֵי־צֶמֶר), because ZEMARITES are listed among the descendants of Canaan in Gen 10:18.

MARK RONCACE

ZEMIRAH zuh-mi´ruh [זְמִירָה zemirah]. A Benjaminite, the son of Becher and grandson of Benjamin (1 Chr 7:8). The list of Benjaminites in 1 Chr 7:6-12 follows a list of Issacharites in 7:1-5 and is supplemented by the list of Benjaminites in 1 Chr 8. Consequently, some have suggested that 1 Chr 7:6-12 may contain a list of the descendants of Zebulun (or may have supplanted a Zebulunite genealogy), because Zebulun appears after Issachar in 1 Chr 2:1 but has no genealogy in 1 Chr 1–9.

Some scholars propose emending *Zemirah* to *Zemariah* (zemariyah זְמַרְיָה) on the basis of the LXX (Zamarias Ζαμαρίας), thus eliminating the feminine ending (-*ah*) on a male's name and supplying a theophoric element in the name (-*iah* for Yah or Yahweh).

M. PATRICK GRAHAM

ZENAN zee´nuhn [צְנָן tsenan; Σεννά Senna]. A town located in the southern lowlands of the territory allotted to the tribe of Judah following the conquest of Canaan (Josh 15:37). Zenan is sometimes identified with ZAANAN (tsa'anan צַאֲנָן) in Mic 1:11, possibly due to the similar spelling of each in the LXX: Senna and Sennaan (Σενναάν), respectively. Etymologically, the root tsnn (צנן) could mean "to be cold" (as in Jewish Aramaic) or "to protect, defend" (as in Arabic).

JAMIE A. BANISTER

ZENAS zee´nuhs [Ζηνᾶς Zēnas]. Zenas is mentioned only in Titus 3:13. The instruction to send him and Apollos on their journey well provisioned suggests that they are the bearers of the letter to Titus. Zenas is described as a LAWYER, perhaps to distinguish him from others by the same name. Whether *lawyer* denotes an expert in Jewish law or a Roman jurist is debatable, although the negative attitude in Titus 3:9 toward speculation about Jewish law leads most commentators to conclude that Zenas was a Roman jurist. According to several lists of the seventy apostles, Zenas was the first bishop of Lyyda in Palestine (Pseudo-Dorotheus, PG 92:1061–65; Pseudo-Hippolytus, PG 10:951–54; Chronicon Paschale, PG 92:521–24, 543–45). Some commentators suggest a connection with the Zeno, son of Onesiphorus, mentioned in *Acts Paul* 3:2.

JUDITH ANNE JONES

ZENO. The founder of Stoic philosophy, Zeno (ca. 330–260 BCE) came to Athens as a young man from Citium on Cypress. After attending the lectures of others, Zeno began to offer his own. Because he was not an Athenian citizen, Zeno could not own property, and so taught in a public hall known as the "Painted Porch" or *Stoa Poikile* (hence the term *Stoic*). His many writings on logic, physics, and ethics do not survive, but his philosophy strove to incorporate pragmatically what worked from a variety of schools rather than to create something entirely original. Opposed to Plato's conception of an authoritarian state ruled by a philosophical elite, Zeno substituted love, friendship, and freedom. His anarchic approach to government included opposition to coinage, police, and marriage, as well as opposition to popular religion and convention. His successors, however, shifted Stoic philosophy's focus from Zeno's emphasis on the individual's autonomous freedom to an inner freedom cultivated through the exercise of ethical behavior. They combined this emphasis on virtue with an outward respect for traditional religion and convention, thus winning for later Stoicism many adherents, especially among Roman statesmen and the upper classes. *See* PLATO, PLATONISM; STOICS, STOICISM.

HANS-FRIEDRICH MUELLER

ZEPHANIAH ze´fuh-ni´uh [צְפַנְיָה tsefanyah, צְפַנְיָהוּ tsefanyahu]. 1. Son of Maaseiah, a priest during the reign of Zedekiah, who sent Zephaniah to inquire of the prophet Jeremiah concerning the Babylonian crisis (Jer 21:1; 29:25, 29; 37:3). After the destruction of Jerusalem, Zephaniah was put to death by the Babylonians (2 Kgs 25:18-21//Jer 52:24-27).

2. A Kohathite (1 Chr 6:36 [Heb. 6:21]).

3. A prophet in Jerusalem during the reign of Josiah, king of Judah (Zeph 1:1; 2 Esd 1:40), and a contemporary of Jeremiah. *See* ZEPHANIAH, BOOK OF.

4. Father of Josiah, a priest who returned from the Babylonian exile (Zech 6:10, 14).

MARK RONCACE

ZEPHANIAH, APOCALYPSE OF zef´uh-ni´uh, uh-pok´uh-lip´s. Ancient and medieval lists of writings mention a prophecy or apocalypse of Sophonias (the Greek form of Zephaniah). But the only fragment (= A in *OTP*) known was a short passage describing a heavenly journey, attributed to a work of the prophet Sophonias in a quote in Clement of Alexandria (*Strom.* 5.11.77). At the end of the 19th cent., two manuscripts in Sahidic and Akhmimic Coptic were published, parts of which represented an *Apocalypse of Elijah*. But on one leaf of the Sahidic it reads "I, Sophonias, saw these things in my vision." So, this folio (= B in *OTP*) and nine Akhmimic folios (= chaps. 1–12 in *OTP*) were

attributed to the work. Since the prophet Zephaniah was not a prominent figure in later times, there might not have been too many works ascribed to him. So, A, B, and the Akhmimic folios could belong to the same work, but there are only a few parallels between B and the Akhmimic folios, and details in A both parallel and contradict B and the Akhmimic texts. Therefore, the fragments at least represent different recensions of a fluid textual tradition. Despite the fact that most scholars supported the common attribution in the past, it cannot be ascertained.

All fragments are accounts of a visionary reporting of cosmic journeys and represent the genre *apocalypse* or the subgenre of "accounts of cosmic journeys" (compare *1 En.* 21–25; *2 En.* 1–68; *3 Baruch*). In A, the seer (Sophonias?) is brought by a spirit to the fifth heaven where he sees angels sitting on brilliant thrones and singing hymns to the ineffable God. In B, Sophonias reports the vision of a soul in torment. In the Akhmimic folios the seer (without name) is carried around by the angel of the Lord. He is shown his city (Jerusalem?) from above; the angels recording all deeds on Mount Seir; the angels carrying off the souls of the ungodly (with parallels to B); the heavenly city; the sulfuric sea; the accuser and the angel over Hades; the book recording sins and good deeds; and—after a lacuna—the praise of angels; the triumph of the righteous; the souls in torment awaiting judgment; Abraham, Isaac, Jacob, and all saints praying for them; and finally the announcement of God's wrath. The end of the text is missing.

The original language of the work is Greek. The Akhmimic folios refer to SUSANNA and to the three men in the furnace, therefore presupposing the Greek *Additions to Daniel* (1st cent. BCE; *see* DANIEL, ADDITIONS TO). The quote in Clement suggests a date before 175 CE, but if A and B/the Akhmimic folios represent different stages, the Greek original of B/the Akhmimic folios could also be later. The work lacks clear signs of Christian thought, but the Akhmimic texts (2:3) suggest an influence of Matt 24:41-42 and Luke 17:24. The work is a call for repentance that provides vivid imagery of angels, judgment, and anthropology.

Bibliography: O. S. Wintermute. "Apocalypse of Zephaniah." *OTP* 1 (1983) 497–515.

JÖRG FREY

ZEPHANIAH, BOOK OF zef´uh-ni´uh [צְפַנְיָה tsefanyah; Σοφονίας Sophonias]. A collection of speeches attributed to ZEPHANIAH, an otherwise unknown prophet, addressing the city of Jerusalem during the reign of JOSIAH of Judah (640–609 BCE). It is the ninth book in the collection of Minor Prophets known as the BOOK OF THE TWELVE. Its major theme is the DAY OF THE LORD, an event that portends calamitous judgment for Judah's religious and moral corruption and promises renewal for a chastened and obedient remnant.

A. Structure

Zephaniah begins with an announcement of judgment against Jerusalem that encompasses all creation (1:2-6). It ends with the rejoicing of a restored Jerusalem celebrating Yahweh's reign over a remnant of gathered exiles (3:14-20). This movement from judgment to joy frames three exhortations to respond appropriately to Yahweh's announcement concerning Judah and its rival nations, as shown in the following outline:

I. Superscription (1:1)
II. Announcement of judgment on all creation centered in Jerusalem (1:2-6)
III. Exhortation to silence at the day of Yahweh's wrath against Jerusalem (1:7-18)
IV. Exhortation to seek Yahweh to escape the coming wrath against nations and Jerusalem (2:1–3:7)
V. Exhortation to wait for Yahweh to purify the nations and Jerusalem (3:8-13)
VI. Exhortation to Jerusalem to rejoice at Yahweh's triumphal reign over a renewed people (3:14-20)

B. Detailed Analysis

1. Historical setting

The book of Zephaniah is centered on Jerusalem, even to the point of mentioning specific neighborhoods (1:10-11). Judah had been under the rule of Assyria for over a century. Zephaniah denounced religious and cultural accommodation to Assyrian domination among Jerusalem's ruling classes. These included priests who worshiped the Assyrian astral deities, "the host of the heavens" (1:4-5), and royal officials who dressed in foreign clothes (1:8), possibly a reference to Assyrian dress or clothing associated with idolatrous practices. He further decried syncretistic worship of Yahweh, BAAL, and MILCOM of the Ammonites. The general description fits the depiction in 2 Kgs 21–23 of the time preceding Josiah's religious reforms.

Like many prophetic books, Zephaniah contains a series of oracles against surrounding nations (2:4-15). These include the Philistine city-states to the west (2:4-7), Moab and Ammon to the east (2:8-11), and Ethiopia to the south (2:12), nations experiencing upheaval during the waning years of Neo-Assyrian dominance. Assyria, with its capital in NINEVEH, "the exultant city," was still in power, although Zephaniah prophesied its destruction (2:13-15). Zephaniah addressed issues of apostasy, corruption, and international foment during the final years of the Assyrian Empire and appears to have provided support for Josiah's religious and political reforms.

2. Religious background

Zephaniah addressed his historical setting by drawing upon a religious tradition that emerged in Israel's history and was embodied in the liturgy and symbolism of the Jerusalem Temple. In this tradition, the Temple functioned as a microcosm of creation in which the cosmic drama of Yahweh's establishment and maintenance of the created order was celebrated and reenacted. In temple worship, the people of Judah proclaimed and participated in the drama of Yahweh's ongoing creation through sacrifices, observation of the sacred calendar, and a distinctive social ethic. Zephaniah transposed the themes of this liturgical drama onto the events of his day, interpreting history in light of the Temple's narration of Yahweh's purification and restoration of creation.

Zephaniah's creation theology is clear in the opening unit of 1:2-6. In language that echoes and reverses the Genesis creation account, Zephaniah announced divine judgment against the entire created order (1:2-3). The epicenter of this cosmic judgment was the idolatrous practices of Jerusalem's inhabitants. By their religious and moral corruption, Jerusalem's leaders had neglected their supporting role in Yahweh's maintenance of creation and had instead aided the powers opposing that order.

The Day of the Lord theme likewise reflects the theology of the Temple. The ritual calendar celebrated and supported Yahweh's renewal of creation in daily, weekly, and annual observances. The sacrifices of the Day of the Lord marked the sacred time when Yahweh acted to purify creation from the pollution of sin and to restore it to a state of life-sustaining order. Zephaniah 1:7 describes the Day of the Lord as such a day of appointed sacrifice. In irony reminiscent of the use of the Day of the Lord theme in Amos 5:18-20, Zephaniah announces that the leaders gathered to observe the sacrifice would themselves be "sacrificed" as punishment for their apostasy, corruption, and injustice. The ritual day of the Lord would be a historical day of wrath in which Jerusalem's religious and political elite would be swept away in a sacrifice of purification and renewal that would encompass "all the inhabitants of the earth" (1:18).

The Temple represented not only the cosmic center of Yahweh's reign but the political center as well. In Zeph 2:4-15, the theme of Yahweh's combat against the forces of chaos is expressed in oracles of judgment against surrounding nations, concluding with Assyria (2:13-15). An echo of the theme of divine combat can be heard in Yahweh's threat to "shrivel all the gods of the earth" (2:11). Again, in irony similar to that of Amos, Zephaniah numbered Jerusalem, a rebellious city, among the enemies that are subject to Yahweh's punishment (3:1-7).

Just as purification leads to renewal in temple liturgy, so Zeph 3:8-13 extends the theme of purification and renewal to the nations. In language that echoes and reverses Genesis, a transformation among the peoples will reverse the confusion and dispersion of the Tower of BABEL and lead to a conversion of the nations and a renewal of the covenant people, "the remnant of Israel" (3:9-13). This renewal will culminate in joyful restoration for Jerusalem (3:14-20). Yahweh, victorious in combat and enthroned on Mount Zion, will personally lead the festival celebrating his renewed people and creation.

The drama of temple worship provided an underlying narrative that united and informed the diverse speeches of Zephaniah. Zephaniah transformed the ritual narrative of the Temple into a prophetic critique of Jerusalem's leadership and announcement about its imminent future. The narrative of temple worship also provided a structure for later supplementation of Zephaniah's speeches such as in 3:19-20, which mentions the return of exiles and most likely originated after the time of Zephaniah. Although historically out of place within the timeframe of Zephaniah, it nevertheless fit into the narrative structure provided by the temple liturgy.

3. Rhetorical analysis

The speeches of Zephaniah addressed an intended audience and sought an intended response. The prophet described his desired audience as the "humble of the land, who do [Yahweh's] commands" (2:3). They formed the core of an envisioned community, "the remnant of the house of Judah" (2:7; compare 2:9; 3:12-13). The prophet exhorted this group to acknowledge with silent awe the movement of Yahweh in their midst (1:7), to "seek the LORD" in penitent worship (2:3), and to wait in faith for the day when Yahweh arises to act (3:8). The humble remnant is offered the possibility of escaping the day of wrath (2:3), receiving the spoils of punished nations (2:7, 9), finding refuge and security under Yahweh's protection (3:12-13), and rejoicing in a restored Jerusalem (3:14-20).

The prophet likewise described his desired audience by contrast with those identified for judgment. They dismiss Yahweh's sovereignty and "say in their hearts, 'The LORD will not do good, nor will he do harm'" (1:12). They neither trust in the Lord nor draw near to him in worship (3:2). They are the proud and haughty, who abuse their power and have no place in a purified Jerusalem (3:11).

An additional rhetorical strategy is Zephaniah's use of religious traditions known to his audience and reflected in texts such as Genesis, Deuteronomy, Isaiah, and Amos. Along with traditional language, Zephaniah also employed a number of unique expressions. The picture of Yahweh searching for the guilty of Jerusalem

with lamps (1:12) is one such image. He described Jerusalem's leaders as "rest[ing] complacently on their dregs" (1:12), an image of wine that has sat for too long, becoming thick and rotten. These and other phrases, such as the evocative description of the "day of wrath" (1:15-16) and Yahweh as a warrior king singing in celebration over a restored Jerusalem (3:17), make Zephaniah a brief exemplar of prophetic rhetoric.

4. Canonical setting

The book of Zephaniah represents the original speeches of the prophet in a written text contained within a collection of sacred Scriptures. This canonical setting places the prophet within the context of the broader OT narrative and gives the speeches an authoritative and historically transcendent dimension. The superscription in Zeph 1:1 facilitates this function by locating the prophet historically within the narrative told in 2 Kings. The unusually long genealogy in 1:1 perhaps served a similar function. It lists four generations of Zephaniah's ancestors, the fourth having the same name as the 8th-cent. king Hezekiah. The most likely reason for the long genealogy was to draw a connection between the time of Zephaniah and the account of Hezekiah's reforms in 2 Kings, similar to the way 2 Kings connects Hezekiah and Josiah in its assessment of their respective reigns.

Within the wider canonical narrative, the fall of Judah subsequent to the time of Josiah validates Zephaniah's announcement of judgment and his claim to speak the word of the Lord. The portrayal of future restoration also extends the message of the book beyond its historical setting, addressing readers living after Judah's destruction and exile. Later audiences hearing the book within the bounds of the canonical narrative are confronted with the same contrast between the proud, corrupt, and idolatrous elite of Jerusalem and the humble, obedient remnant, with the added knowledge of the historical fate of ancient Judah as a partial vindication of the prophet's message. Zephaniah urges later readers to identify with the humble remnant and to wait for God's purpose to unfold with faith, hope, and anticipation of future joy.

C. Religious and Theological Significance

Zephaniah is characteristically a "word of the Lord" in that it points beyond visible reality to the invisible but perceptible reality of God's direction of creation in spite of obstructions and opposition. It portrays an understanding of worship not as a diversion from the reality of daily life, but rather as a description of reality as it truly is and a model of life as it truly should be. It further takes seriously the idea of election and urges a covenant people to live out the responsibilities of its worship, identity, and commitments.

Bibliography: Adele Berlin. *Zephaniah: A New Translation with Introduction and Commentary.*

AB 25A (1994); Marvin Sweeney. *Zephaniah: A Commentary.* Hermeneia (2003).

BARRY A. JONES

ZEPHATH zee´fath [צְפַת tsefath]. A Canaanite city conquered by the Israelite tribes of Simeon and Judah (Judg 1:17), after which the city was renamed HORMAH (a wordplay with kharam (חָרַם), "to devote to destruction"). Zephath was included among the territory allotted to the tribe of Simeon. Its precise location in the northern Negev is uncertain; some suggestions include Khirbet el-Meshash (Tel Masos), Tel el-Milh (Malhata), Tel ʿIra (Khirbet el-Ghara), Sabeita (or Sebeita), and the pass of es-Sufah. Etymologically, *Zephath* might be related to mitspeh (מִצְפֶּה, "watchtower"). It is possibly the same word used as the place name ḏft in the Egyptian annals of the first campaign of Thutmose III when discussing possible routes from the Plain of Sharon to the Jezreel Valley.

JAMIE A. BANISTER

ZEPHATHAH zef´uh-thuh [צְפָתָה tsefathah]. Name of a valley near MARESHAH where King Asa of Judah and his army defeated a much larger army under the command of an Ethiopian named Zerah (2 Chr 14:9-13 [Heb. 14:8-12]). The location of this valley is uncertain, but the proximity of Mareshah would place it in the western plains of Judah. The LXX does not treat tsefathah in 2 Chr 14:8 [Heb. and LXX 14:9] as a proper noun but as indicating the location of the valley "to the north (kata borran κατὰ βορρᾶν) of Mareshah." The Wadi el-Afranj and the Wadi el-Safieh are two possible locations of this valley.

JAMIE A. BANISTER

ZEPHI. *See* ZEPHO.

ZEPHO zee´foh [צְפוֹ tsefo]. Third-listed son of ELIPHAZ and grandson of Esau and Adah, Zepho is also a clan chief of Esau (Gen 36:11, 15). A parallels passage (1 Chr 1:36) reads Zephi (tsefi צְפִי). The LXX renders both as Zophar (Sōphar Σωφάρ), perhaps influenced by the proximity of Zepho/Zephi to Eliphaz, a name shared by the high-status Temanite companion of ZOPHAR (tsofar צוֹפַר; LXX Sōphar) in the book of Job (e.g., 2:11).

JASON C. DYKEHOUSE

ZEPHON, ZEPHONITES zee´fon, zee´fuh-n*i*t [צְפוֹן tsefon, צְפוֹנִי tsifoni]. The firstborn son of Gad (Num 26:15), elsewhere spelled ZIPHION (tsifyon צִפְיוֹן; Gen 46:16). He was the progenitor of the clan of the Zephonites. A pseudepigraphic text, the book of Jubilees (44:20), witnesses a similar ancestry.

ZER zuhr [צֵר tser]. A fortified town mentioned in Josh 19:35. The town was located in the territory of the tribe of Naphtali. It is listed among nineteen fortified towns

in that territory. However, Josh 19:35 may be textually corrupt, resulting from the repetition of words in Josh 19:28-29 describing the allotment of territories to the tribe of Asher. If such a corruption is in the text, then the consonantal representation of TYRE (tsr צר) in Josh 19:29 is misspelled as tser in Josh 19:35 and misapplied to the tribe of Naphtali.

SAMUEL BOYD

ZERAH, ZERAHITES zihr´uh, zihr´uh-h*i*t [זֶרַח zerakh, בְּנֵי זֶרַח bene zerakh, זַרְחִי zarkhi]. The name *Zerah* (from zarakh זָרַח, "to rise") appears twenty-one times in the OT and once in the NT, as well as on a 6th-cent. clay seal (bulla). The name may be a shortened form of ZERAHIAH (zerakhyah זְרַחְיָה], "The LORD has risen [like the sun]"). The longer form is found in Levitical genealogies in 1 Chr 6:6 [Heb. 5:32], 51 [Heb. 6:36]; Ezra 7:4; 8:4; and 1 Esd 8:31. An alternate form, Yehozerah (yhwzrkh יהוזרח), appears on a 6th-cent. bulla. The Bible mentions seven individuals by this name. 1. A son of Reuel and grandson of Esau (Gen 36:13, 17; 1 Chr 1:37).

2. The father of JOBAB, a king of Edom (Gen 36:33; 1 Chr 1:44).

3. A son of Simeon. His descendants are called "Zerahites" (Num 26:13; 1 Chr 4:24). In Gen 46:10 and Exod 6:15, Simeon's son is called "Zohar" (tsokhar צֹחַר), which is probably a scribal error for Zerah.

4. A son of Judah by his daughter-in-law Tamar (Gen 46:12; 1 Chr 2:4) and the ancestor of the Judahite clan of the Zerahites (Num 26:20; Josh 7:17; 1 Chr 27:11, 13) or "son(s) of Zerah" (Josh 7:24; 22:20; 1 Chr 2:6; 9:6; Neh 11:24). He was the twin brother of PEREZ, the ancestor of David (and so is mentioned in Matt 1:3). According to a folk etymology in Gen 38:27-30, Zerah's name comes from the scarlet thread tied around his wrist by the midwife to mark him as firstborn before his hand was pulled back into the womb and his brother forced himself out first.

According to 1 Chr 2:6, Zerah had five sons. The name of the first son comes from Josh 7:1, 18 (though Chronicles has "ZIMRI" instead of "ZABDI," reflecting a scribal error in one of these sources). The names Chronicles gives for the other four sons of Zerah come from 1 Kgs 4:31 [Heb. 5:11], reading "Ezrahite" as "Zerahite," and ignoring the historical context of the passage in Solomon's reign, as well as the phrase "children of Mahol."

5. A Levite in the Gershomite line (1 Chr 6:21 [Heb. 6:6]).

6. A second Levite in the Gershomite line who is the ancestor of ASAPH (1 Chr 6:41 [Heb. 6:26]).

7. A Cushite [NRSV, "Ethiopian"] who attacked Judah during the reign of ASA (911–870 BCE; 2 Chr 14:9-15 [Heb. 14:8-14]). The account in Chronicles is exaggerated (Zerah's 1,000,000 troops are met by Asa's 580,000), but the conflict itself is probably historical. If Cush here refers to Ethiopia, Zerah may be a merce-

nary for Pharaoh SHISHAK, left behind with a contingent of Ethiopian troops (see 2 Chr 12:3 for Ethiopians in Shishak's army) to defend Egypt's northern frontier. But if Cush refers to CUSHAN in northern Arabia (Hab 3:7), Zerah may simply be an Arab raider, a possibility supported by the mention of tents and camels in the description of Asa's victory (2 Chr 14:15 [Heb. 14:14]).

STEVEN TUELL

ZERAHIAH zer'uh-hi'uh [זְרַחְיָה zerakhyah; Ζαραίας Zaraias]. Meaning "Yahweh has arisen/shined forth." 1. A Levite descendant of Aaron, he is the son of Uzzi and the father of Meraioth (1 Chr 6:6 [Heb. 5:32], 51 [Heb. 5:36]), and an ancestor of Ezra (Ezra 7:1-4).

2. A member of the family of Pahath-moab, whose son Eliehoenai led 200 of his kinsmen to return to Palestine with Ezra (Ezra 8:1-4; 1 Esd 8:31).

M. PATRICK GRAHAM

ZERED, WADI zihr'id, wah'dee [נַחַל זֶרֶד nakhal zeredh]. Numbers 21:12 identifies Wadi Zered as the place where the Israelites camped after leaving Iye-ibarim. From there, they traveled to "the other side of the Arnon" (Num 21:13). According to Deut 2:13-14, the Israelites' crossing of Wadi Zered was the event that marked the end of thirty-eight years of wandering in the wilderness. The wadi served as the northern boundary of Edom and the southern boundary of Moab.

The MADEBA MAP identified the Wadi Zered with Wadi el-Hesa, which is generally accepted today (see HESA, WADI EL). Some have questioned this identification because Num 21:11 locates Iye-ibarim "in the wilderness bordering Moab toward the sunrise." Wadi Zered is located between this point and "the other side of the Arnon." Consequently, some have identified it with locations farther north than Wadi el-Hesa, including various tributaries of either Wadi al-Karak or Wadi al-Mujib, such as Wadi al-Sultani or Wadi Tarfawiya.

Three other wadis in the OT have been identified with Wadi Zered: the wadi that was miraculously filled with water in 2 Kgs 3:16-20; "the Wadi of the Willows" in Isa 15:7; and the "Wadi Arabah" in Amos 6:14.

GREGORY L. LINTON

ZEREDAH zer'uh-duh [צְרֵדָה tseredhah, צְרֵדָתָה tseredhathah; Σαρειρά Sareira]. 1. In 1 Kgs 11:26, Zeredah is referenced as the hometown of the first king of the Northern Kingdom: Jeroboam, from the half-tribe of Ephraim. Although it was permissible for an Ephraimite to live within the territory of a different tribe, the LXX of 1 Kgs 11:43 and 12:24 explicitly situates the site within the hills of Ephraim, thereby disallowing any association between it and the Zeredah of 2 Chr 4:17. Ein-Sarida in the vicinity of Deir Ghassaneh south of Shechem could preserve the ancient toponym, making the Iron Age site of Khirbet Banat-Bar a tenable candidate.

2. According to 2 Chr 4:17, Solomon had the bronze objects for the Jerusalem Temple cast in the Jordan Valley at an unspecified location between Zeredah and Succoth. The verse is paralleled by 1 Kgs 7:46, where ZARETHAN (compare Josh 3:16) appears instead.

JASON R. TATLOCK

ZERERAH zer'uh-ruh [צְרֵרָה tsererah]. A place name in the Jordan Valley, called Gargatha (Garagatha Γαραγάθα) in the LXX. It was 25 km southwest of Nablus in the hill country of Samaria near Beth-Shittah and Abel-Meholah. The locale is mentioned in Judg 7:22. In the narrative setting of this verse, Zererah was along the route from the valley of Jezreel to Succoth. The toponym is likely a variant spelling of ZEREDAH, which appears in 1 Kgs 11:26 and 2 Chr 4:17. Another location, ZARETHAN, appears to be an alternate name of the same place (Josh 3:16; 1 Kgs 4:12; 7:46).

SAMUEL BOYD

ZERESH zihr'ish [זֶרֶשׁ zeresh]. Wife of HAMAN, MORDECAI's antagonist (see ESTHER, BOOK OF). Zeresh encourages Haman to destroy Mordecai (5:10-14) but later predicts her husband's downfall before Mordecai, because Mordecai "is of the Jewish people" (6:13). Thus, Zeresh echoes the story's main reversal: Mordecai, once doomed, will rise, while Haman, once in power, will hang.

NICOLE WILKINSON DURAN

ZERETH zihr'ith [צֶרֶת tsereth]. A descendant of Judah, and the first of three sons of Ashur by one of his wives, HELAH (1 Chr 4:7).

ZERETH-SHAHAR zihr'ith-shay'hahr [צֶרֶת הַשַּׁחַר tsereth hashakhar]. A town in Transjordan allotted to Reuben (Josh 13:19). Its ancient location is unknown, but the hot springs of ez-Zara (Callirrhoe) at the foot of Mount 'Attarus on the east side of the Dead Sea may preserve the first element of the name (see ZARA, 'AIN EZ). The situation of the town "on the hill of the valley" (Josh 13:19) suggests that it lay between the valley floor and the highlands.

KENT V. BRAMLETT

ZERI zihr'i [צְרִי tseri]. One of the six sons of JEDUTHUN whom David appointed to prophesy with the lyre under direction of their father (1 Chr 25:3). The name IZRI, possibly a variant of Zeri, appears later when the musicians cast lots for their duties (1 Chr 25:11). See MUSIC.

ZEROR zihr'or [צְרוֹר tseror]. A Benjaminite, the father of Abiel and the son of Becorath. He is the grandfather of Kish and thus the great-grandfather of King Saul (1 Sam 9:1).

ZERUAH zuh-*roo*´uh [צְרוּעָה *tseru'ah*]. Mother of JEROBOAM and widow of Nebat (1 Kgs 11:26). The LXX (1 Kgs 12:24) names Sarira (Sarira Σαριρά), a harlot, as Jeroboam's mother.

ZERUBBABEL zuh-ruhb´uh-buhl [זְרֻבָּבֶל *zerubbavel*; Ζοροβαβέλ *Zorobabel*]. Zerubbabel was a Jewish governor of Judah in the early postexilic period under Persian rule (beginning no later than 520 BCE) and a major leader in the reconstruction of Jewish life after exile. His name, meaning "seed of Babylon," is derived from **zeru-bibli** in East Semitic. This name (common in Babylonia) implies that Zerubbabel was born in Babylon.

The OT presents a credible (albeit limited) account of his importance in the postexilic era, crediting Zerubbabel with rebuilding the Temple. Each source, however, presents a distinct portrait of this role and its impact. Haggai 1:1 refers to Zerubbabel as "governor of Judah," a position consistent with the Persian policy of appointing a descendant of a local dynasty to govern a province in order to secure the people's good will.

According to 1 Chr 3:17-19, Zerubbabel is a Davidic descendant and grandson of Judah's last king JEHOIACHIN. This makes him the last Davidic heir to hold a leading position in Judah. Haggai and Ezra–Nehemiah list his father's name as SHEALTIEL (Ezra 3:2, 8; 5:2; Neh 12:1; Hag 1:1), whereas 1 Chr 3:19 has PEDAIAH, brother of Shealtiel. Attempts to harmonize the two lineages (such as assuming adoption when Zerubbabel lost his biological father) are unconvincing. It is better to accept different traditions, with Shealtiel the more firmly established.

The prophet Haggai repeatedly refers to Zerubbabel as the "governor of Judah." In messages dated to 520 BCE, during King DARIUS I's reign, Haggai urges both Zerubbabel and the high priest Joshua to rebuild the Temple (see, e.g., Hag 1:1-11); he indicates that Zerubbabel (whom he always names first), Joshua, and the people in fact did so (Hag 1:12). Haggai's last words announce Zerubbabel's unique role in God's plan, linking Zerubbabel with eschatological promises: Zerubbabel is God's "servant" and "signet ring," destined to be part of the great revolution that is at hand in which empires will be destroyed (Hag 2:20-23). Haggai's words imply hope in the restoration of the Davidic monarchy, freed from Persian control. In 520 BCE and shortly thereafter, the prophet Zechariah refers to Zerubbabel without a title or patronymic but likewise identify him as the restorer of the Temple's foundation (Zech 4:4-7); moreover, Zechariah claims that Zerubbabel will also complete the task (Zech 4:8-10). Additionally, Zechariah mentions an anointed branch that will be enthroned alongside the high priest Joshua, a possible allusion to a Davidic heir, either Zerubbabel or perhaps his descendant. The ambiguous language in Zechariah 6:12-15 reflects tension between the high priest and the "branch" (a term that elsewhere carries royal associations), probably indicat-

ing a conflict over leadership in the postexilic era under Persian rule.

Zerubbabel's death is not recorded. The royal expectations in Haggai and Zechariah, coupled with Zerubbabel's disappearance from accounts of the Temple's completion, have led some scholars to conclude that Zerubbabel was forcibly removed by Persian authorities in order to squelch monarchic or revolutionary hopes of independence. But it is as likely that he left office peacefully, either due to old age or death from natural causes. No other Davidic male descendant appears to have followed him in a leadership position, although some scholars believe that SHELOMITH, identified in 1 Chr 3:19 as his daughter, may have been prominent, as suggested by a Persian period seal bearing this name.

Ezra 1–6 places Zerubbabel at the head of the return from exile (Ezra 2:1-2; Neh 7:6-7) and regards him, along with the priest Jeshua (variant of *Joshua*) as the major leaders during the first stages of Judean reconstruction. He led the building of the altar (Ezra 3:1-7), the laying of the Temple's foundations (Ezra 3:8-13), and the renewed building efforts after a delay caused by opponents (Ezra 5:2). Ezra 1–6 highlights the imperial authorization that undergirds Zerubbabel's work. In fact, Zerubbabel refers to Cyrus' edict when rejecting the neighboring peoples' offer to join the returnees in rebuilding the Temple (Ezra 4:3). Ezra 1–6, however, complicates a straightforward interpretation of Zerubbabel's role in the restoration of the Temple. First, Ezra–Nehemiah never refers to Zerubbabel as "governor" or suggests a connection with David. Second, a letter in Ezra 5:14 refers to SHESHBAZZAR as governor and claims he laid the Temple's foundation (5:16). Third, the report about the completion of the Temple in Ezra 6:13-18 does not mention Zerubbabel, a picture that challenges Zechariah's prophecy in Zech 4:8-10 but may be consonant with the more ambiguous messages of Zech 6:12-15. Attempts to equate Sheshbazzar (a mysterious figure first identified as Judah's nasi' [נָשִׂיא, "prince, ruler"] in Ezra 1:8, to whom Cyrus entrusts the Temple's vessels) and Zerubbabel as two names of a single person are unconvincing and do not resolve the discrepancy. Most likely, Ezra–Nehemiah compresses events in the early stages of return and reconstruction to fit its thematic exposition. The probable historical picture is that Sheshbazzar figured in an early stage, during Cyrus' time after 538 BCE, but accomplished little. Zerubbabel (and Joshua/Jeshua) followed with the more successful reconstruction under Darius I beginning in 520 BCE.

The pairing of Zerubbabel with Joshua/Jeshua in the biblical sources implies that Zerubbabel was the administrative or civic ruler (presumably directly accountable to the king, as was NEHEMIAH; see Neh 1–6), while Joshua as high priest officiated in the Temple and supervised the cult. The loan word **pekhah** (פֶּחָה, "governor") applies to rulers of Persian satrapies (positions typically held by Persians from well-positioned families) as well as to officials in lower positions, usually heading provinces (*see* SATRAP, SATRAPY). It was not uncommon for the Persian imperial authorities to place indigenous rulers as governors of provinces in order to secure the loyalty of the population. Although the title does not define uniform, clearly delineated responsibilities, a governor's responsibilities would have included keeping the province loyal to the king and ensuring the flow of taxes to the royal coffers. Scholars used to debate whether Judah was even a province at the time of Darius (and thus to what extent Zerubbabel could be a genuine governor). But recent archaeological studies incline most to concur that the province remained distinct after the destruction of the Temple in 586 BCE and that Zerubbabel's governorship signals a social, economic, and religious revitalization of Jewish life.

Nehemiah 12:1 reiterates Zerubbabel's leading role in the return and restoration by beginning its genealogy of priests from the time of Zerubbabel, who is listed first for the earliest period of the return (see also Neh 7:6-7). It thus corroborates the memory of Zerubbabel's role at the beginning of Judah's reconstruction after exile.

First Esdras magnifies Zerubbabel's role beyond any of the other sources, making him the unquestioned hero who single-handedly convinces King Darius to permit the rebuilding of the Temple and who then persuades other Jews to go up, leading them to successfully complete the task. The book reflects a later, Hellenistic revision rather than an independent historical source for Zerubbabel's activities. It introduces Zerubbabel with what scholars consider an insertion of a preexisting tale about three bodyguards (1 Esd 3:1–5:6). In this story, Zerubbabel wins a contest of wits and gains King Darius' favor, which Zerubbabel uses for the benefit of his people. The rest of 1 Esdras' account of Zerubbabel largely follows Ezra 1–6 but includes Zerubbabel in places where he is absent in Ezra, making his role more persistent. Thus, 1 Esd 6:18 smoothes over ambiguities in Ezra 1–6 by specifying that Cyrus gave the vessels also to Zerubbabel (not only to Sheshbazzar as in Ezra 1) and that Zerubbabel was the governor specifically appointed by Darius to be in charge of the building (1 Esd 6:27) and to whom other governors must give provisions for the Temple (1 Esd 6:29). Nothing suggests that Zerubbabel did not complete the rebuilding project. In another apocryphal reference, Sir 49:11 refers to Zerubbabel as God's signet ring, echoing Haggai.

Zerubbabel appears in Jesus' genealogies. Both Matthew (1:12-13) and Luke (3:27) record him as Shealtiel's son (albeit with a transliterated version of the name) but with different grandfathers (Jechoniah in Matthew; Neri in Luke).

TAMARA COHN ESKENAZI

ZERUIAH zuh-roo′yuh [צְרוּיָה *tseruyah*]. From *tsori* (צֳרִי), "mastic balsam," and *yah* (יָה), an abbreviated

form of "Yahweh." First Chronicles 2:16 states that Zeruiah and Abigail were sisters of the sons of Jesse, and that Zeruiah had three sons: ABISHAI, JOAB, and ASAHEL. In twenty-four of twenty-six OT references, Zeruiah is identified in relation to one or more of her sons (e.g., "Joab son of Zeruiah," fourteen times); thus, her reputation was as the mother of sons who, in the Samuel narrative, were constant problems to David (e.g., 2 Sam 3:39). In the remaining two texts, she is identified as someone's sister: 1 Chr 2:16 calls her sister of the sons of Jesse; and 2 Sam 17:25 states that Abigail was "the sister of Zeruiah." This latter text identifies Amasa as the son of Abigail; Amasa, according to 2 Sam 20:10, was murdered by his cousin Joab, Zeruiah's son, in the context of Sheba's revolt against David.

JOHN I. LAWLOR

ZETA [ζ z, Ζ Z]. The sixth letter of the Greek alphabet. The exact name of the Phoenician prototype is unknown, but the name of the Greek letter probably arose from pattern leveling with ETA and THETA. The sound of the Phoenician letter is thought to have been a simple z, but it was adapted in Greek for the zd (or dz) of zeta. *See* ALPHABET.

P. KYLE McCARTER JR.

ZETHAM zee′thuhm [זֵתָם *zetham*]. Jehieli (*see* JEHIEL), Zetham, and Joel were sons of the Levite LADAN (1 Chr 23:8). However, 1 Chr 26:21-22 lists Zetham and Joel as sons of Jehieli and grandsons of Ladan.

ZETHAN zee′thuhn [זֵיתָן *zethan*]. The fifth of seven sons of BILHAN and grandsons of JEDIAEL, descendants of Benjamin (1 Chr 7:10). After a list of Issachar's descendants (1 Chr 7:1-5), a Zebulunite list normally follows, thus Jediael and his offspring may be descendants of Zebulun instead.

ZETHAR zee′thahr [זֵתַר *zethar*]. One of the seven eunuchs who served King Ahasuerus and were charged with bringing Queen Vashti before the king (Esth 1:10-11). He is not listed among Ahasuerus' closest advisors in Esth 1:14.

ZEUS zoos [Ζεύς *Zeus*]. In Greek mythology, Zeus is the primary member of the Greek pantheon, for he possesses more power than any other immortal, gives order to the universe, and assigns dominions to other gods. Early Greek writings extolled Zeus as "king of the gods" (e.g., Hesiod, *Theog.* 886; Pindar, *Ol.* 7.34), "omnipotent" (e.g., Aeschylus, *Sept.* 255; *Suppl.* 816), "savior" (e.g., Aeschylus, *Suppl.* 26; *Sept.* 520), and the "father" of humanity and other deities (e.g., Homer *Il.* 1.544; 11.182). According to the poet Hesiod, Zeus overthrew his father, Cronus, and established his supremacy by leading the battles that defeated the Titans, rulers of the cosmos prior to the Olympian gods (*Theog.* 453–720).

Although he did not create the universe, he established the world's current governance and allotted its regions to various deities. In partnership with numerous goddesses and mortal women he fathered scores of powerful offspring, both divine and human.

The name and core characteristics of Zeus find their origins in an Indo-European god of the sky. Zeus is master of the heavens, controlling the weather, sending rain and awesome thunderbolts. His typical abode is on a mountaintop, and he was most commonly associated with Mount Olympus, the Greek peninsula's tallest peak. Visual representations of Zeus regularly depict him brandishing thunderbolts or enthroned as a king. His administration of the world order and his record of dominance over those beings that sought to supplant or deceive him correspond to the multiple functions connected to him in his myths and cults. Zeus deals out both positive and negative destinies, ordains universal laws, rightly receives credit for victories in war and athletic contests, sustains social order, decrees hospitality, protects strangers and beggars, prescribes justice, and guards property and families. The influence and worship of this god was far-reaching in antiquity. Many peoples equated Zeus with their chief deity, just as the Romans identified him with their JUPITER. The 2nd-cent. Roman emperor Hadrian built and rebuilt a number of temples dedicated to Zeus.

The Bible reflects resistance to attempts to associate Zeus and the God of Israel. In the middle of the 2nd cent. BCE, the Seleucid king ANTIOCHUS IV (Epiphanes) tried to have the Jerusalem Temple renamed in honor of "Olympian Zeus" and the Samaritan temple on Mount Gerizim renamed in honor of "Zeus-the-Friend-of-Strangers." According to 2 Macc 6:2, this act contributed to the defilement of these sites, even though the verse may also scornfully allege that the Samaritans were amenable to this name.

In Acts 14:11-13, some residents of Lystra respond to the healing of a man who could not walk by identifying Barnabas as Zeus and Paul as Hermes. The poet Ovid preserves the legend of a simple, elderly couple in nearby Phrygia who unknowingly entertained Jupiter and Mercury (Zeus and Hermes' Roman equivalents) in human form (*Metam.* 8.618–724). The gods responded by sheltering the couple from a flood that destroyed their inhospitable neighbors. Ovid's account, along with the temple mentioned in Acts 14:13 and other inscriptions from the area indicating a cult devoted to both of these gods, sheds light on the deities' importance in Phrygia and Lycaonia and on the kind of piety commonly associated with the local populace. *See* DIOSCURI; GREEK RELIGION AND PHILOSOPHY.

MATTHEW L. SKINNER

ZIA zi′uh [זִיעַ zia‘]. A Gadite clan/clan leader among the sons of ABIHAIL (1 Chr 5:13), names that are absent from other Gadite lists (Gen 46:16; Num 26:15-17).

ZIBA zi′buh [צִיבָא tsiva’]. A servant or retainer of the house of Saul, Ziba plays a somewhat duplicitous role. When David inquired after survivors of the house of Saul, Ziba revealed the existence of Jonathan's lame son Mephibosheth (Meribbaal), who was brought to Jerusalem to be under David's watchful eye. Ziba was subsequently put in charge of Mephibosheth's holdings (2 Sam 9).

Ziba next appears during Absalom's revolt. While David was fleeing Jerusalem, he encountered Ziba and inquired after his master. Ziba replied that Mephibosheth was using Absalom's revolt to further his own anti-Davidic agenda. In return for Ziba's loyalty, David rewarded him with all of Mephibosheth's holdings (2 Sam 16:1-4).

When David returned to Jerusalem following Absalom's defeat, Ziba rushed to greet David (2 Sam 19:17b-18a). Shortly thereafter Mephibosheth also came out to greet David, protesting his innocence of any treachery (2 Sam 19:24-30). Although David divided the holdings evenly between Mephibosheth and Ziba, the narrator's sympathies appear to lie with the former, since he is presented as being in mourning as of the moment that David fled Jerusalem (v. 24). Ziba is thus revealed to be an opportunist; nonetheless, his success is indicated by the holdings he retains in the end.

CARL S. EHRLICH

ZIBEON zib′ee-uhn [צִבְעוֹן tsive‘on]. Father of Aiah and Anah (Gen 36:24; 1 Chr 1:40), son of Seir (Gen 36:20; 1 Chr 1:38), and grandfather of Esau's wife Oholibamah (Gen 36:2, 14). As a Horite (khori חֹרִי) clan name (Gen 36:29), Zibeon represents part of the indigenous population disrupted by immigrating Esauite clans (Deut 2:12). Zibeon is once called a Hivite (khiwwi חִוִּי; Gen 36:2), which might reflect scribal error, muddled traditions, or a now-obscure social history.

JASON C. DYKEHOUSE

ZIBIA zib′ee-uh [צִבְיָא tsivya’]. The second of seven sons of SHAHARAIM, a Benjaminite, by one of his wives, Hodesh (1 Chr 8:8-10). According to this report, Shaharaim and his clan lived in Moab, which was unusual for Benjaminites, and Shaharaim's clan is not found elsewhere among Benjaminite lists.

ZIBIAH zib′ee-uh [צִבְיָה tsivyah]. Zibiah of Beer-sheba was the mother of King JOASH (Jehoash) of Judah (2 Kgs 12:1 [Heb. 12:2]; 2 Chr 24:1). The name means "gazelle."

ZICHRI zik′ri [זִכְרִי zikhri]. Perhaps meaning "remembrance" or an abbreviated form of the name Zechariah. Twelve men in the OT bear this name. 1. The son of Izhar, a Kohathite (Exod 6:21).

2. A Benjaminite whose father was Shimei (1 Chr 8:19-21).

3. A Benjaminite whose father was Shashak (1 Chr 8:23-25).

4. One of the six sons of Jeroham, a Benjaminite (1 Chr 8:27).

5. A Levite, the son of Asaph and father of Mica (1 Chr 9:15). The name may be a corruption of ZABDI (compare Neh 11:17).

6. A Levite whose family cared for the treasuries under King David (1 Chr 26:25).

7. The father of Eliezer, chief officer of the Reubenites under King David (1 Chr 27:16).

8. A Judahite whose son, Amasiah, commanded 200,000 troops under King Jehoshaphat (2 Chr 17:16).

9. The father of Elishaphat, one of five military commanders who entered into a plot to overthrow Queen Athaliah (2 Chr 23:1).

10. The Ephraimite hero who slew Maaseiah, the son of King Ahaz, as well as Azrikam and Elkanah, two of Ahaz's officials (2 Chr 28:7).

11. The father of Joel, who oversaw the Benjaminites in Jerusalem after the return from exile (Neh 11:9).

12. A priest who led his clan in the postexilic period (Neh 12:17).

M. PATRICK GRAHAM

ZIDDIM zid'im [צִדִּים tsiddim]. A fortified city apportioned to the tribe of Naphtali (Josh 19:35). However, the MT version of Josh 19:35 seems to be corrupt; the first two names may not have been intended to be towns. The LXX version reads "and the fortified cities of the Tyrians, Tyre" (kai ai poleis teichēreis tōn Tyriōn Tyros καὶ αἱ πόλεις τειχήρεις τῶν Τυρίων Τύρος). "Tyrians" (tsorim צוֹרִים) rather than "Ziddim" (tsiddim) may have been the original reading, in which case there would have been no site known as "Ziddim." If it was an actual city, its location remains unknown.

RALPH K. HAWKINS

ZIGGURAT zig′oo-rat. A staged tower found in Mesopotamia, architecturally similar to the stepped pyramid of Egypt. On the summit a temple was normally situated. Two explanations are commonly offered regarding the ziggurat's purpose; the first, and perhaps the preferable view, suggests that they were artificial mountains. Since it was seen as appropriate to situate temples on natural elevations, the ziggurat provided an artificial elevation in the relatively flat terrain of Mesopotamia. A second proposal explains the purpose as that of a "ladder to heaven." With the shrine on the summit, the priests were able to carry on the cult in greater proximity to the deity. The description of the construction of the Tower of BABEL (Gen 11:1-9) seems somewhat similar to the manner in which the ziggurats were built. The remains of numerous ziggurats have been uncovered throughout the Mesopotamian Valley; the best preserved structure is in southern Mesopotamia at UR.

JOHN I. LAWLOR

Figure 1: High-angle view of a ziggurat, Agargouf, Iraq.

ZIHA zi´huh [צָחָא tsikha², צִיחָא tsikha²]. The descendants of Ziha are mentioned in Ezra 2:43 and Neh 7:46 among several groups of people that returned from exile and functioned as the temple servants (*see* NETHINIM). Nehemiah 11:21, however, says Ziha and GISHPA were in charge of the temple servants. It is possible, therefore, that Ziha is an eponym of a family of temple servants.

STEVEN D. MASON

ZIKLAG zik´lag [צִקְלַג tsiqlagh]. A town on the southern edge of the Shephelah originally allotted to the tribe of Simeon (Josh 19:5) and later assimilated into the territory of Judah (Josh 15:31). The Chronicler notes that descendants of Simeon still lived in Ziklag (1 Chr 4:30).

By the time of Saul, Ziklag was occupied by the Philistines. Achish, king of Gath, gave the city to David in return for his supposed loyalty (1 Sam 27:6). David, however, used Ziklag as a staging ground for campaigns against settlements that posed a threat to Judah's southern border (1 Sam 27:8). A number of Benjaminites, "Saul's kindred," joined David's ranks at Ziklag (1 Chr 12:1-7). David went to Aphek for the Philistine muster for the battle that would claim the life of King Saul but his participation was disallowed (1 Sam 29). Upon his return, David discovered that the Amalekites had attacked Ziklag, burned it down, and taken captives (1 Sam 30:1-3). David and his men pursued the Amalekites, rescued the captives, and returned to Ziklag (1 Sam 30:26). There they received report of the Israelites' defeat and the death of King Saul (2 Sam 1:1-4). The city continued as a Judean settlement through the end of the monarchy and, following the Babylonian exile, was resettled by the Judahites (Neh 11:28).

The identification of Ziklag is uncertain. Some scholars identify it with Tell Khuweilifeh, 16 km (10 mi.) northeast of Beer-sheba, where excavations have shown Philistine influence from ca. 1000 BCE onward. Tell Khuweilifeh, however, is located in Judahite, rather than Philistine, territory. A more likely candidate is Tell esh-Sharia (Tel Sera'), between Beer-sheba and Gaza, which evidences a significant Philistine presence in the 12th–11th cent. and Israelite stratum in the 10th–9th cent. BCE, with no destruction or gap in occupation.

RALPH K. HAWKINS

ZILLAH zil´uh [צִלָּה tsillah]. Zillah and ADAH were the two wives of LAMECH (Gen 4:19) in the lineage of Cain. Zillah bore TUBAL-CAIN and his sister NAAMAH (Gen 4:22). Both wives are addressed by name in a remnant of archaic poetry wherein Lamech brags about a revenge slaying (Gen 4:23-24).

A. HEATH JONES III

ZILLETHAI zil´uh-thi [צִלְּתַי tsillethay]. 1. In 1 Chr 8:20 Zillethai is one of the heads of a family within the tribe of Benjamin living in Jerusalem.

2. In 1 Chr 12:20, Zillethai is one of seven chiefs of the tribe of Manasseh who deserted Saul and became warriors and commanders in David's army at Ziklag.

STEVEN D. MASON

ZILPAH zil´puh [זִלְפָּה zilpah]. One of the servant women whom Laban gave as a handmaiden to Leah when she married Jacob (Gen 29:24). Later, Leah gave Zilpah, whose name means "trickling," to Jacob as a surrogate mother; she bore two sons, Gad and Asher (Gen 30:9-13; 35:26; 46:18), who tended Jacob's flocks with Rachel's son Joseph (37:2). *See* ASHER, ASHERITES; GAD, GADITES; TRIBES, TERRITORIES OF.

JESSICA TINKLENBERG DEVEGA

ZIMMAH zim´uh [זִמָּה zimmah]. A Levite musician descended from Gershom. The details are not clear, as he is the son of Jahath and the father of Joah according to 1 Chr 6:20 [Heb. 6:5] and 2 Chr 29:12, but the grandson of Jahath in 1 Chr 6:42-43 [Heb. 6:27-28].

ZIMRAN zim´ran [זִמְרָן zimran]. The first of six sons born to Abraham and Keturah (Gen 25:2; 1 Chr 1:32); the sons' names correspond to tribes or regions in Arabia. The location of Zimran is uncertain, though a connection with Zabram (compare **Zembran** [Ζεμβράν]; LXX 1 Chr 1:32), a tribe that Ptolemy (*Geog.* 6.7.5) locates west of Mecca, is probably correct. On the biblical evidence alone (Gen 25:2-4), Zimran could be placed anywhere between the Negev (Midian) and South Arabia (Sheba).

KENT V. BRAMLETT

ZIMRI zim´ri [זִמְרִי zimri; Ζαμβρεί Zambrei]. The name of four persons and one location in the OT. 1. Zimri son of Salu, a head of a Simeonite lineage, whom the priest PHINEHAS slew along with a Midianite woman for participating in the worship of Baal Peor (Num 25:14). The names of the slain couple may be a late addition to the story or a way of connecting the story to other tales now lost. This Zimri is also mentioned in 1 Macc 2:24-26, in the comparison of Mattathias' zeal for the law to that of Phinehas.

2. The fifth king of Israel (ca. 880 BCE). According to 1 Kgs 16:9-20, Zimri was a courtier and general of chariotry under King Elah. He revolted against his master and murdered the males of the royal family and their supporters in accordance with a prophecy of Jehu son of Hanani (1 Kgs 16:1-4) and hence with the support of the same circles that later opposed the Omrides. He reigned only a week because the army supported its commander OMRI, who besieged the capital, Tirzah, and took the throne after Zimri had set fire to the royal palace compound after the city fell.

The Deuteronomistic editor frames Zimri's reign with characteristic dating formulas and a negative assessment of his reign, connecting it to the typical "idolatry" of the Israelite kings. Second Kings 9:31

reports a taunt from Jezebel, calling Jehu "Zimri" as a synonym for "traitor," indicating that the name Zimri had become a byword for treachery, at least among the supporters of the Omride Dynasty. His reign typifies the periodic instability of the Northern Kingdom, which was prone to coups d'état.

3. Zimri the son of Zerah and grandson of Judah and thus the nominal ancestor of a Judahite clan (1 Chr 2:6). The LXX spells the name **Zambri**, while a parallel tradition in Josh 7:1 has it as zavdi (זַבְדִּי). The Greek spelling can be explained as the dissimilation of sounds for easier pronunciation. The Hebrew variations are easy to explain as well because the letters DALET and RESH were very similar at many time periods. It is unclear which was original.

4. The great-great-great-great-grandson of King Saul (1 Chr 8:36; 9:42), who would have lived in the mid- to late-9th cent. BCE. Although the two Saulide genealogies in 1 Chronicles exhibit slight discrepancies, they seem to date to the end of the 7th cent. (the time of the last names in them) and probably reflect the living tradition of the family of Saul from just before the end of the Judahite monarchy.

5. An otherwise unknown kingdom listed alongside Elam and Media (Jer 25:25; absent in LXX) and thus probably located in western Iran. Jeremiah's oracle anticipates upheaval throughout the Near East, leading to the destruction of many nations, including Judah.

Bibliography: Saul M. Olyan. "2 Kings 9:31—Jehu as Zimri." *HTR* 78 (1985) 203–7; Max Sicherman. "The Political Side of the Zimri–Cozbi Affair." *JBQ* 36 (2008) 22–24.

MARK WADE HAMILTON

ZIN, WILDERNESS OF zin [מִדְבַּר־צִן midhbar-tsin; ἔρημος Σίν erēmos Sin]. The "Wilderness of Zin" is a term used in the OT to refer to some portion of the desert wasteland that lies south of the Negev on the Sinai Peninsula (*see* NEGEB, NEGEV). It is described as lying west of Edom and north of the Wilderness of PARAN. The Wilderness of Zin appears in the OT in two distinct contexts: as a location in the narrative of the wanderings of the Israelites between the exodus and the entry into Canaan; and as a point of reference in boundary descriptions written subsequent to the emergence of Israel and Judah in Canaan.

The first mention of the Wilderness of Zin in the narrative is in the account of the scouts sent by Moses to assess Canaan and the Canaanites. With the Israelites encamped farther south, in the Wilderness of Paran, the scouts survey the land "from the wilderness of Zin to Rehob, near Lebo-hamath" (Num 13:21), probably a reference meant to signify the whole of the land from southernmost to northernmost borders. As a part of the wilderness itinerary of the Israelites, the Wilderness of Zin is most frequently associated with the oasis of Kadesh-Barnea, which was located within it (Num 20:1; 27:14; 33:36; Deut 32:51) and which served as one of the most important stopping places for the Israelites (*see* KADESH, KADESH-BARNEA). In this context, the Wilderness of Zin is particularly noted as the location of the death and burial of MIRIAM (Num 20:1). In association with the toponym MERIBAH, it is also the location of one version of the story of the Israelites' grumbling over the lack of water and Moses' subsequent disobedience (Num 20:2-13; compare Exod 17:1-7). In Yahweh's explanation to Moses of why he cannot enter the promised land (Num 27:14; Deut 32:51), Moses is reminded that the incident in question took place in the Wilderness of Zin.

The Wilderness of Zin also appears in two parallel descriptions of the ideal borders of the territory claimed by Israel and/or Judah. God's description to Moses in Num 34 of the extent of the land the Israelites were to inherit and the description of Judah's tribal allotment in Josh 15 both designate the Wilderness of Zin as part of the southern boundary of Israelite or Judahite territory (Num 34:3; Josh 15:1). Each of these references is followed by a detailed border description that includes reference to a place called simply "Zin," from which the wilderness may have taken its name (Num 34:4; Josh 15:3).

Despite the LXX's use of erēmos Sin to translate both terms, there should be no confusion between the Wilderness of Zin and the Wilderness of Sin (midhbar sin מִדְבַּר סִין), which is located on an earlier stage of the Israelites' journey (Num 33:11-12) and probably lay south and west of the Wilderness of Zin (*see* SIN, WILDERNESS OF).

D. MATTHEW STITH

ZINA. *See* ZIZAH.

ZION zi´uhn [צִיּוֹן tsiyon; Σιών Siōn]. In both the OT and the NT, the term *Zion* is used in various ways: as a name for the city of JERUSALEM or occasionally Judah, as a name for a particular part of Jerusalem, as a name for the inhabitants of the city, and as the name of the entire people of God.

The etymology of the word remains unclear. Various derivations have been proposed; two options are frequently discussed. The first is the Hebrew root tsyh (צִיה), "to be dry," which in the case of Zion would contain a suffix creating a place name that describes the characteristic of that place. Thus, Zion is named such because it was a dry place. Some scholars believe that a place would not be named after such a negative quality. The second option is the Arabic tsahweh that contains a range of meanings from "hilltop" or "mountain ridge" to "fortress," which comes to have the connotation of protection. This option fits with the function of the place as a fortress at the time of David's capture of the city.

Most often in the Bible, the term *Zion* refers to the city of Jerusalem and its environs or part of the city or to the country of which it is capital. A careful evaluation of usage provides helpful insight into the connotations of the name in various contexts. In both the OT and NT, Zion is always used as a proper name. In the OT, Zion is used over 150 times, often with an addition or parallel (Daughter of Zion, Mount Zion, Zion = Jerusalem). Over half of its occurrences can be found in the books of Isaiah and Psalms. The first occurrence of the word is 2 Sam 5:7 (1 Chr 11:5) in the narrative of David's capture of the Jebusite city, the "fortress of Zion." In this case Zion refers to a geographical area on the southeastern hill of Jerusalem, also known as the "City of David" (see DAVID, CITY OF). In expansion of its geographical usage, Zion often refers to the entire city of Jerusalem.

Zion is frequently used as a description of the place of Yahweh's seat or throne, thus suggesting a cultic center. As the dwelling of the deity, perfection and beauty underscore its nature. The Temple itself is referred to as Zion, and that is where Yahweh dwells and is enthroned (Ps 9; see TEMPLE, JERUSALEM). Indeed, within the Second Temple literature, Mount Zion occurs several times as a reference for the Temple itself, specifically in 1 Maccabees (4:37, 60; 6:48, 62; 7:33; 10:11). Yahweh has established this throne through battle (Ps 76:2 [Heb. 76:3]). Yahweh chose Zion because of a desire to dwell there (Ps 132:13-14). Yahweh's dwelling on Mount Zion is in line with the common ANE mythical idea that gods lived on cosmic hills. The choice of Zion as the abode of Israel's God gives the area special status; as such, the word *Zion* comes to take on a theological quality in some usage. Much scholarship has examined this Zion tradition and its development in biblical texts. For example, the prophet Isaiah highlights the special status of the city (e.g., 30:19), a result of its chosenness, while the prophet Jeremiah questions it (e.g., 30:17).

As the cultic center, Zion is the place where Israel goes to worship Yahweh. Praise and declarations rise from Zion to Yahweh who dwells there (Pss 9:11 [Heb. 9:12]; 102:21 [Heb. 102:22]). In Jeremiah the declarations are not concerning the praise of Yahweh, but the hope that Yahweh will bring vengeance upon the enemies who destroyed Zion (50:28; 51:10). Just as the people bring praise to Yahweh from Zion, Yahweh addresses the people from Zion. Zion is the place from which Yahweh both blesses (Pss 128:5; 134:3) and judges Israel and Israel's enemies (Joel 3:21 [Heb. 4:21]; Amos 1:2). It is also the place from which Yahweh's law goes forth (Isa 2:3; Mic 4:2). The rule of the earthly king is understood as an extension of the deity's rule. Zion is thus used in reference to the place where the earthly king of Israel/Judah rules with the help and blessing of Yahweh (Pss 2:6; 110:2). Jerusalem is used in reference to the earthly king's rule more often than Zion.

In addition to the geographic and cultic aspects, Zion is often used in reference to the people. "Daughter Zion" refers to the people twenty-two times in the OT and two times in the NT (see ZION, DAUGHTER OF). In Jer 4:31 and Mic 4:10, "daughter Zion" is suffering

as a woman in labor suffers. "Virgin daughter Zion" is used three times in the OT (2 Kgs 19:21; Isa 37:22; Lam 2:13). In addition, "daughters of," "women of," "sons of," and "people of Zion" are used for the inhabitants of Zion, Jerusalem, Judah, and even the whole land. Often the references to the inhabitants of Zion are used as a literary tool to personify the city. Zion hears (Ps 97:8), wails (Jer 9:19), is in labor (Isa 66:8; daughters of Zion—Jer 4:31; Mic 4:10), and needs to wake up (Isa 52:1).

Though the city functions as the dwelling of the deity, Zion is not free from sin nor is it able to escape judgment. Many of the uses of the term in prophetic literature are in the context of the coming judgment of its inhabitants. Lamentations 2:1 also expresses Yahweh's anger toward "daughter Zion." The reason for judgment is rooted in the ethical, social, and cultic sins of the inhabitants. The presence of Yahweh does not exclude the people from judgment; on the contrary, their behavior is in stark contrast to the expectations of Yahweh, and thus they are judged as a sinful city.

Zion is not left in a state of despair; it becomes a city of eschatological hope and the place from which salvation will come. Yahweh will restore Zion (Jer 30:17-18), and the city's inhabitants will return (Isa 51:11; Jer 3:14; Zech 2:7). Additionally, Yahweh will return to Zion (Zeph 3:14-17; Zech 8:3) and upon return, Yahweh will judge the enemies of Zion (Jer 51:24, 35). What Zion will become is what Zion was originally intended to be—the beautiful city of God. The restoration was not immediate; thus these hopes were projected onto a future, glorified Zion.

In the NT, Zion is used seven times—five times in relation to texts from the OT. Matthew 21:5 (Isa 62:11; Zech 9:9) and John 12:15 (Isa 62:11) refer to the daughter of Zion. Romans 9:33 (Isa 8:14-15; 28:16) and 1 Pet 2:6 (Isa 28:16) refer to a stone in Zion. Romans 11:26 (Ps 14:7; Isa 59:20) refers to salvation coming from Zion. The two remaining occurrences are found in Heb 12:22, which refers to Mount Zion, the city of the living God, and Rev 14:1, which depicts the Lamb standing on Mount Zion. In Revelation Mount Zion becomes the place of eschatological preservation.

By the 4th cent. CE, in early Christian usage, the term *Zion* was transferred to the southwestern hill of Jerusalem, thus creating confusion between Davidic Zion (southeastern hill) and Christian Zion (southwestern hill). Research in the 20th cent. determined the location of Davidic Zion to be on the southeastern hill, but today the southwestern hill is still referred to by Christians as Mount Zion. In that area, there are a number of preserved sites revered by Christians.

Bibliography: Bernard F. Batto and Kathryn L. Roberts, eds. *David and Zion: Biblical Studies in Honor of J. J. M. Roberts* (2004); Jon D. Levenson. *Sinai and Zion: An Entry into the Jewish Bible* (1985).

W. H. BELLINGER JR.

ZION TRADITION z i´uhn. The phrase "Zion Tradition," derived from ZION, an old name for Jerusalem, designates a complex set of interrelated religious and political beliefs that served to justify the new Davidic and Solomonic imperial state. The tradition continued to serve as legitimation and as the ideal for the Judean state and its Davidic dynasty down to Judah's collapse under the Babylonian onslaught. Even before Judah's fall but with increasing frequency afterward, the different elements of this tradition—now understood as envisioning future realities rather than the present—became the basis for a significant portion of Israel's messianic and eschatological expectations.

There were three main points to this tradition: 1) Yahweh, the God of Israel, is the imperial deity, ruler over the whole world, divine and human alike; 2) Yahweh has chosen David and his dynasty to serve as God's regent on earth; and 3) Yahweh has chosen Zion as his earthly dwelling place and imperial capital. The parallel between this structure and the analogous claim in the prologue to the Code of Hammurabi that the gods had chosen 1) Marduk, god of Babylon, to be the supreme ruler, 2) Hammurabi to be his human representative, and 3) Babylon to be his imperial capital is self-evident. Each point can be elaborated.

First, as the universal suzerain, Yahweh was identified as ʿelyon (עֶלְיוֹן, "the Most High") and as the "great king" (melekh gadhol מֶלֶךְ גָּדוֹל; Pss 47:2 [Heb. 47:3]; 95:3; melekh rav מֶלֶךְ רָב; Ps 48:2 [Heb. 48:3]), an earlier form of the later imperial title "King of kings" (e.g., 1 Tim 6:15; Rev 17:14; 19:16). The two expressions, "the Most High" and "great king" were basically synonymous and meant "suzerain" or "supreme ruler," since both expressions could be completed by such a phrase as "over all the earth" (Pss 47:2 [Heb. 47:3]; 83:18 [Heb. 83:19]; 97:9; compare "a great King above all gods"; Ps 95:3). Other peoples were viewed as Yahweh's vassals, and they were warned against any attempt to throw off Yahweh and David's rule, since such a rebellion was hopeless and would be suppressed with extreme violence (see Ps 2). Moreover, if the national deities of these vassal states did not uphold Yahweh's just rule among their own assigned peoples (see Deut 32:8-9), Yahweh as the imperial deity was justified in putting these gods on trial as if they were mere humans and imposing direct imperial rule over their states (Ps 82). Psalm 82 serves as theological justification for David's imposition of direct Israelite rule over the surrounding states of Edom, Moab, Ammon, and the Aramean territories. In short, Israel's vassals were better off under the just rule of Yahweh, administered by David, than they were under the corrupt rule of their own national gods and native regents. Nonetheless, despite the imperialistic thrust of this theology, one should not discount the importance of the characterization of Yahweh as "lover of justice" (Ps 99:4), whose throne is founded on righteousness and justice (Pss 89:14 [Heb. 89:15]; 97:2), who judges the world with righteousness and the peoples with equity (Ps 98:9). This emphasis on the universal justice of Yahweh's rule provides a basis within the Zion Tradition itself for a critique of the potential nationalistic abuses of this tradition.

Second, Yahweh chose David and his dynastic line to be his human king (Pss 78:67-72; 89:19-20 [Heb. 89:20-21]). As Yahweh's representative, the Davidic king had an elevated status. He was considered the son of Yahweh and heir of God's imperial possessions (Ps 2:7-8), God's firstborn and Elyon (the most high) over all the kings of the earth (Ps 89:27 [Heb. 89:28]). Moreover, this commitment to David was sealed by an eternal covenant between God and David (2 Sam 7:12-16; 23:1-5; Pss 89:3-4, 19-37 [Heb. 89:4-5, 20-38]; 132:11-12). This covenant apparently reassured David that his dynastic line was secure, that one of his descendants would always sit on the Judean throne, even though God was free to punish or even remove particular Davidic kings if they rebelled against him. But the elevation of the Davidic king was not just to a privileged status; it was first and foremost to a task. The Davidic king shared in Yahweh's work of establishing stability and justice. Psalm 89:25 [Heb. 89:26] gives mythological expression to this when it describes Yahweh as placing David's left hand on the sea and his right hand on the rivers. Just as God brought stability and order to the world by his conquest of the primeval chaos of sea and river (Ps 24:2), so David in the exercise of his rule shares in Yahweh's ongoing victory over chaos and disorder. Psalm 72:1 expresses this royal ideal of justice less mythologically in its prayer for the king that God might give him God's justice and righteousness, and in its repeated call for royal justice, particularly for the poor and powerless (72:2-4, 7, 12-14). The same ideal is found in the oath taken by a new king to cleanse his administration of corrupt and venal officials, and to "cut off evildoers from the city of the LORD" (Ps 101:8). Once again, the Zion Tradition's articulation of this royal ideal of justice provided prophets with the ammunition to critique any misuse of royal privilege.

Third, Yahweh also chose Zion/Jerusalem to be his earthly abode (Pss 2:6; 68:15-16, 29 [Heb. 68:16-17, 30]; 78:68-69; 132:13-14). Because Zion is the earthly dwelling place of the imperial God, Zion is glorified with the appropriate mythological topography. Despite the modest height of Zion relative to other hills in the vicinity—such as the higher Mount of Olives—Mount Zion is portrayed as a high mountain, praised as "beautiful in elevation" and even identified with Mount Zaphon (Ps 48:2 [Heb. 48:3]), the sacred mountain of Baal in Canaanite mythology and the mountain where the assembly of the gods met (Isa 14:13). The NRSV's translation of the relevant line in Ps 48:2 (Heb. 48:3) should be corrected from "Mount Zion, in the far north" to "Mount Zion is the heights of Zaphon," on analogy with the similar passage in Isa 14:13. God's city is also described as watered by a river whose streams make it glad (Ps 46:4 [Heb. 46:5]), though the closest thing to a river in Jerusalem is the modest water channel fed by the Gihon Spring on its eastern slope (*see* GIHON, SPRING). Interestingly, the spring bears the same name as one of the rivers of Eden (Gen 2:13). There is some indication that Solomon built a complex of irrigated royal parks with exotic plants and trees along this slope (see the tradition reflected in Eccl 2:4-6), and he may have kept a large collection of wild and exotic animals (see 1 Kgs 4:23; 10:22) in the same area. Solomon's building activity there may have intended to underscore the resemblance between the primeval abode of God in Eden and Solomon's Jerusalem.

The presence of God in Zion, however, has implications for the city. First, the city is richly provisioned (Ps 132:15-16) and safe from its enemies, for God is its refuge and strength (Pss 46:1 [Heb. 46:2]; 48:3 [Heb. 48:4]). Whether portrayed as the primeval waters of chaos (Ps 46:2-3 [Heb. 46:3-4]) or as rebellious nations and their kings who march against the city (Pss 46:6 [Heb. 46:7]; 48:4-5 [Heb. 48:5-6]; 76:3-6 [Heb. 76:4-7]), these enemies are subdued by Yahweh. On the other hand, Zion's human inhabitants must be righteous to live in God's presence (Pss 15:1-5; 24:3-6; Isa 33:14-16). There is the implicit threat that God will maintain residence in the city only as long as it is filled with the justice and righteousness appropriate to God's presence. Thus this motif provides a basis for critiquing the real Jerusalem on the basis of the ideal. Finally, the nations must go up to Zion to pay homage and tribute to the imperial God (Ps 68:29 [Heb. 68:30]) and to have their disputes arbitrated at the imperial court (see Isa 2:2-4).

This tripartite structure of the Zion Tradition was created in the Davidic–Solomonic period, when the imperial claims for Yahweh, the Davidic monarch, and Jerusalem made sense given the political balance of power at the time. Some scholars have argued that it would take centuries for Israel to create such an ideology, but this view does not conform to ANE practice. When a state rose to imperial prominence in the ANE, it did not take generations to articulate an imperial ideology. The imperial ideologies of Sargon of Akkad and of Hammurabi of Babylon were created in their lifetimes. Nor does one see such an ideology created for a state in periods of abject weakness. Once such an ideology is created, however, it can survive the collapse of the imperial power that gave rise to the ideology. The ideology remains as the ideal, with the hope for its fulfillment projected into the future. In Israel this process eventually gave rise to the hope for the coming kingdom of God, for the ideal Davidic Messiah of the future, and for the heavenly Jerusalem as the true abode of God and his people.

Bibliography: J. J. M. Roberts. "Solomon's Jerusalem and the Zion Tradition." *Jerusalem in Bible and Archaeology: The First Temple Period.* Andrew G. Vaughn and Ann E. Killebrew, eds. (2003) 163–70; L. E. Stager. "Jerusalem as Eden." *BAR* 26 (2000) 36–47.

J. J. M. ROBERTS

ZION, DAUGHTER OF [בַּת־צִיּוֹן] bath-tsiyon; θυγάτηρ Σιών thygatēr Siōn]. "Daughter of Zion," more accurately translated "daughter Zion," serves to personify Zion and, by extension, Jerusalem, in a particularly personal, tender, and—at times—vulnerable way (*see* ZION). This term of endearment appears twenty-six times in the OT and on seven occasions appears in parallel with its synonym "daughter Jerusalem" (bath yerushalam [בַּת יְרוּשָׁלַ͏ִם], 2 Kgs 19:21; Isa 37:22; Lam 2:13; Mic 4:8; Zeph 3:14; Zech 9:9). "Daughter Zion" appears most frequently in one of two formulations: either in reference to circumstances of real or impending distress or to redemption and a promising future. *See* ISRAEL, DAUGHTERS OF.

In the book of Lamentations, "daughter Zion" is humiliated (2:1) and has suffered destruction and desolation (2:4, 8, 10, 13, 15, 18). Lamentations 1:10 implies that Zion and her sanctuary have been raped. The use of "daughter Zion" in Lamentations is consistent with its use elsewhere in the OT (compare Isa 10:32; Jer 4:31). It stresses her vulnerability to invasion and subsequent defilement by foreigners. While the personification of Zion and Jerusalem remains an abstraction, the use of the term "daughter Zion" likely has some connection with the historical realities of ancient warfare, when women were most vulnerable to rape and defilement. Furthermore, we know that Zion, as the Temple Mount, was often a synonym for the sanctuary (see Lam 1:10), and that the sanctuary often was understood as God's feminine counterpart (Ezek 24:15-23). All of this suggests that the term "daughter Zion" could be understood to refer to God's vulnerability and loss as much as Zion's or that of her people. Finally, Israel itself sometimes was understood to be God's female counterpart and wife (Hos 2). In "daughter Zion," we hear resonance with the suffering of all of ancient Israel.

The more positive use of the term "daughter Zion" comes in responses to the type of distress outlined above, generally in terms of redemption from current suffering. Many of these instances are responses to the Babylonian destruction of Jerusalem and Zion. Typical of this use is "Sing aloud, O daughter Zion; shout, O Israel!" (Zeph 3:14). Zephaniah is speaking of a future restoration and the joy that will accompany it. Perhaps more well known to Christians is the appearance of the term in Zech 9:9 where the prophet articulates his vision of the full restoration of all of Israel: "Rejoice greatly, O daughter Zion! Shout aloud, O daughter Jerusalem! Lo, your king comes to you; triumphant and victorious is he, humble and riding on a donkey, on a colt, the foal of a donkey." This represents a total reversal of Zion's tragic past. Clearly, the NT authors who cite this verse (Matt 21:5; John 12:15) understood the profound nature of the hope for Zion's future.

In a rebuke of Sennacherib of Assyria (Isa 37:22-29; compare 2 Kgs 19:21-28), Isaiah says of Zion,

"She despises you, she scorns you—virgin daughter Zion; she tosses her head—behind your back, daughter Jerusalem" (v. 22). In this promise of a surviving remnant of Israel, Isaiah depicts a wonderfully spirited Zion. In a simple gesture, the author captures the defiant attitude of Israel toward her enemies.

LARRY L. LYKE

ZIOR *zi'or* [צִיעֹר *tsiʿor*]. A border town in the southern (sixth) district of Judah's tribal territory (Josh 15:52-54); its name comes from a root meaning "small, lowly." Its location has not been determined with any certainty. Based on similarity of names and approximate location, one proposal identifies Zior with the modern village of Siʿir, approximately 8 km east by northeast of Hebron. But this is not without its difficulties: Siʿir seems too far north to be associated with the sixth district; its location seems more aligned with district eight.

JOHN I. LAWLOR

ZIPH, ZIPHITES *zif, zif'it* [זִיף *zif*, זִיפִי *zifi*]. 1. A town in the extreme south of Israel near the boundary of Edom (Josh 15:24). In the LXX versions, the name of this town is either absent or garbled, leading some to question whether it existed at all.

2. Another town in the extreme south near the boundary of Edom, belonging to Judah (Josh 15:55). During David's flight from Saul, he and his men spent time in the Wilderness of Ziph (1 Sam 23:14). The Ziphites, however, were loyal to the king, to whom they reported David's whereabouts (23:19), which led to Saul's pursuit of him there (26:2). It was in Ziph that David snuck into Saul's camp and absconded with the king's spear and water jar to prove that he meant the king no harm (1 Sam 26:6-12). The superscription of Ps 54 is based on the Ziphites' betrayal of David. The town of Ziph was fortified during the time of Rehoboam (2 Chr 11:8). Tell Zif, located southeast of Hebron, has been generally accepted as the biblical site.

3. The father of Mesha, a Calebite (1 Chr 2:42).

4. A family or clan of the tribe of Judah (1 Chr 4:16).

RALPH K. HAWKINS

ZIPHAH *zi'fuh* [זִיפָה *zifah*]. Second of four sons of the Judahite Jehallelel (1 Chr 4:16). *Ziphah* is a feminine form of Ziph, the first son; perhaps Ziphah is a daughter or a scribal error.

ZIPHION *zif'ee-uhn* [צִפְיוֹן *tsifyon*]. The first of seven children of Gad, who are grandchildren of Jacob (Gen 46:16). He is named ZEPHON in Num 26:15.

ZIPHRON *zif'ron* [זִפְרֹן *zifron*]. A place, location unknown, that serves as one of the northern boundary markers for the conquered territory of Canaan (Num 34:9).

ZIPPOR *zip'or* [צִפּוֹר *tsippor*]. Father of Balak, king of Moab; Zippor presumably reigned at the time of the exodus (Num 22:2, 4, 10, 16; 23:18; Josh 24:9; Judg 11:25, always "son of Zippor," identifying Balak). Because his name means "little bird," or "sparrow," it carries totemistic implications. *See* NAME, NAMING; TOTEMISM.

DAEGYU J. JANG

ZIPPORAH *zi-por'uh* [צִפֹּרָה *tsipporah*]. Zipporah was the daughter of the Midianite priest REUEL (Exod 2:18-21; compare Exod 4:18; 18:2, daughter of Jethro), the wife of Moses, the mother of GERSHOM (Exod 2:22), and the mother of at least one additional son (Exod 4:20; two total in 18:3).

Zipporah saved either Moses or Gershom through the act of CIRCUMCISION when the Lord tried to kill one of them along the way to Egypt (Exod 4:24-26). In Hebrew, the pronouns in the account make determining the roles of the individuals in the story difficult. If the attack was against Moses, then by circumcising Gershom Zipporah might have been saving Moses from the sin of not having their son circumcised. If the attack was against Gershom, then the story could be echoing the Lord's words about Pharaoh's firstborn son (4:23) and foreshadowing the death of the firstborn of all the Egyptians (12:29-30). In one story Zipporah touches the feet (a euphemism for genitals in Hebrew) with the foreskin to prevent death; in the other narrative the Israelites touch blood to the door lintels to save their firstborn sons (12:22, 28). In addition to the lack of clarity regarding whom the Lord is attacking, whose feet Zipporah touches with the circumcised foreskin is also unclear. *See* MOSES §B.1.

Moses' relationship with Zipporah in the biblical narratives is complicated due in part to the different sources present in the Pentateuch (*see* SOURCE CRITICISM). In the final form of the narrative, Moses had at some point sent Zipporah and their children back to her father (Jethro), and she is only mentioned again when she returns to the Israelites' camp with her father. An additional wife is mentioned in Num 12 (*see* CUSHITE WIFE, MOSES'; for interpretations that equate Zipporah with the Cushite wife see Ezek. Trag. 60; Dem. frag. 4).

Bibliography: Brevard S. Childs. *The Book of Exodus.* OTL (1974).

HEATHER R. MCMURRAY

ZIV *ziv* [זִו *ziw*]. The second month in the Israelite calendar. It occurred during April and May. Construction on the Temple began in the month of Ziv (1 Kgs 6:1, 37). As a month name, the word *ziw* has not been identified in any other biblical or extrabiblical texts.

ZIZ, ASCENT OF *ziz* [מַעֲלֵה הַצִּיץ *maʿaleh hatsits*]. Meaning "ascent of the flower." A steep mountain pass used by the coalition of Ammonites, Moabites, and

Meunites in their attempt to invade Judah in the days of King Jehoshaphat (2 Chr 20:16). Place names in the narrative ("the wilderness of Jeruel," 20:16; "the wilderness of Tekoa," 20:20; "the Valley of Beracah," 20:26) suggest that the ascent was located along the escarpment on the west side of the Dead Sea, somewhere between En-gedi (20:2) and the upper reaches of Nahal ʿArugot, the wadi that drains the region of Tekoa. Divine intervention aborted the invasion attempt. The event is not recorded in Kings.

JOHN I. LAWLOR

ZIZA ziʹzuh [זִיזָא zizaʾ]. The name of two men in the OT. The name means "shining." 1. A son of Shiphi, a man in the tribe of Simeon (1 Chr 4:37). He was a leader in his family during the time of King Hezekiah.

2. The third son of Rehoboam through Maacah, his favorite wife (2 Chr 11:20). Ziza's brother Abijah became king of Judah after his father's death (2 Chr 12:16). According to 2 Chr 11:23, Rehoboam distributed his sons throughout the southern kingdom of Judah, presumably as governing officials.

KEVIN A. WILSON

ZIZAH ziʹzuh [זִיזָה zizah]. The second son of Shimei, a Gershonite (1 Chr 23:11). Zizah is among the Levites whom David registers for temple service. The Heb. also names Zina (zinaʾ זִינָא) as one of Shimei's sons (1 Chr 23:10), but this may be a variant of *Zizah* or an error.

ZOAN zohʹuhn [צֹעַן tsoʿan]. Biblical name of the Egyptian capital of the Twenty-first and Twenty-second Egyptian dynasties. The city is located ca. 47 km south of the Mediterranean in the eastern delta. In the 11th cent. BCE (1070–1044 BCE), Smendes, a resident of Zoan who had been governor of Lower Egypt under Ramesses XI, established the Twenty-first Dynasty following the death of the pharaoh and made Zoan the administrative center of Lower Egypt.

The account of the Israelite spies' survey of Canaan contains a parenthetical note that "Hebron was built seven years before Zoan in Egypt" (Num 13:22). The rabbis suggest that this statement was made to enhance the status of Hebron, David's first capital (2 Sam 2:11; 5:4-5), by noting that it was even older than the administrative center of Lower Egypt (*Tanh. Shelah* 1:8).

In the Psalms, the "fields of Zoan" are referred to as the location of some of the Egyptian plagues (Ps 78:12, 43). The city is named in oracles against Egypt delivered by Isaiah (Isa 19:11, 13; 30:4) and Ezekiel (Ezek 30:14). *See* HYKSOS.

Bibliography: K. A. Kitchen. *The Third Intermediate Period in Egypt (1100–650 B.C.)* (1973); Nadav Naaman. "Hebron Was Built Seven Years before Zoan in Egypt." *VT* 31 (1981) 488–92.

RALPH K. HAWKINS

ZOAR zohʹahr [צוֹעַר tsoʿar]. A city lying in the plain of the Jordan near the Dead Sea, best known for its association with Sodom, Gomorrah, Admah, and Zeboiim, the so-called "cities of the Plain" or "Five Cities" (Gen 13:12; Wis 10:6; *see* SODOM, SODOMITE). In Genesis, Zoar appears in stories related to the fate of LOT. When Abraham offered his nephew Lot a choice of where to pasture his flocks, Lot's eyes fell upon the well-watered "plain of the Jordan," which was "like the garden of the LORD, like the land of Egypt, in the direction of Zoar" (Gen 13:10). Genesis 14 tells of a battle between a coalition of four kings from the north and the five kings who ruled the Five Cities, including the king of "Bela (that is, Zoar)." BELA was apparently an earlier name for Zoar (Gen 14:2, 8).

In the well-known story of the destruction of Sodom and Gomorrah (Gen 18–19), Lot begged the angels to let him flee to nearby Zoar, a "little city." The narrator explains that Zoar derived its name from its size (tsoʿar means "little"; Gen 19:20-22). Because Lot took refuge in Zoar, it was spared the fate of the other cities. Very soon, however, Lot decided Zoar was unsafe and retreated with his daughters to a cave in the nearby hills (*see* LOT'S DAUGHTERS).

Zoar is mentioned in only three places outside of Genesis. In the description of Moses' survey of the promised land from Mount Pisgah, Zoar serves to mark the limit of "the Plain—that is, the valley of Jericho" (Deut 34:3). The other two instances occur in oracles against the Moabites found in Isa 15–16 and in Jer 48. In both texts Zoar is the destination to which the Moabites flee from an unnamed enemy (Isa 15:5; Jer 48:34).

The location of Zoar has been the subject of much debate. Most biblical texts suggest that the Five Cities, including Zoar, lay on a plain north of the Dead Sea. Writers in the Roman, Byzantine, and Medieval periods, however, located Zoar (variously referred to as Zoara, Zughar, Segor, Sukar) south of the sea. Since the sites of Sodom and its neighbors are unknown, Zoar's approximate location cannot be established with certainty. The location of the Valley of Siddim mentioned in Gen 14 is also unknown (*see* SIDDIM, VALLEY OF). The majority of scholars locates Zoar near Tell es-Safi (*see* SAFI, TELL ES), which lies south of the Dead Sea where the Wadi el-Hesa empties into the Ghor es-Safi. However, the manner of the cities' destruction and the scorched desolation described by biblical (Deut 29:23 [Heb. 29:22]; Zeph 2:9 and later writers offer little encouragement to those seeking actual ruins. Biblical texts cited in support of a southern location for the Five Cities include the oracle against Moab in Isa 15–16, Jer 48, and an oracle castigating Jerusalem in Ezek 16.

The most persuasive evidence for the southern location is the testimony of some writers from the 1st cent. CE and later. Josephus knew of a city named Zoar that flourished south of the Dead Sea in his day (*J.W.* 4.482). A number of Roman, Byzantine, and Medieval writers support Josephus' identification. A 6th-cent. CE mosaic map discovered at Madaba in Jordan depicts "Zoora" as a walled city south of the Dead Sea (*see* MADABA MAP). The existence and location of this well-known Zoora/Zoar is beyond dispute, but its connection to the destroyed city mentioned in the Bible is unknown.

Nevertheless, some scholars have maintained that biblical Zoar was located north of the Dead Sea (Simons). While admitting that Josephus and later writers locate Zoar in the south, these scholars point to other ancient authorities who place Sodom—Zoar's presumed neighbor—north of the Dead Sea. Conflicting traditions indicate that confusion about the location of the Five Cities existed from at least as early as the 1st cent. CE. Those who argue for the northern location have the majority of the biblical evidence on their side. Zoar lies on the border of "the plain (kikkar כִּכָּר) of the Jordan" (Gen 13:10; see 19:20-29; Deut 34:3). Presumably, as its name suggests, this region is located north of the Dead Sea. Lot presumably surveys the plain of the Jordan from Bethel, a prospect excluding the southern end of the Dead Sea. We are told that Lot journeyed east from Bethel to the plain of the Jordan, not south (Gen 13:2-12). Likewise, Moses' view from Pisgah as he surveyed "the Plain ... as far as Zoar" could not have included the area south of the Dead Sea (Deut 34:1-4). Finally, Moab and Ammon's origin in a cave near Zoar (Gen 19:30-38) makes better sense if Zoar lies near the border of both Moab and Ammon than if it lies far south in Edomite territory. Those who argue for a northern location suggest Tell es-Saghur (Byzantine Segor) and Tell Iktanu, both of which lie about 6 mi. northeast of the Dead Sea, as possible candidates for Zoar.

Bibliography: David Neev and Kenneth O. Emery. *The Destruction of Sodom, Gomorrah, and Jericho* (1995); J. Simons. *The Geographical and Topographical Texts of the Old Testament* (1959).

BRIAN C. JONES

ZOBAH zoh'buh [צוֹבָה tsovah]. A powerful Aramean kingdom of southern Syria during the 11th cent. BCE, also called Aram-Zobah. Zobah was located in the north Beqaʿ Valley of modern Lebanon. The OT is the only extant source of any considerable information about Zobah. The biblical accounts suggest that, during the late 11th cent., Zobah was the leading state in central and southern Syria and the center of a minor empire that encompassed most of the lesser states within its proximity and possibly portions of Transjordan, including Ammon. It also had a wide influence in northern Syria (e.g., 2 Sam 8:3; 10:16), though the extent of its reach is unclear.

The summary of Saul's military campaigns in 1 Sam 14:47-48 claims that he fought against and routed "the kings of Zobah." Further hostilities between Israel and Zobah resulted from a clash between Israel and Ammon (2 Sam 10:1-19). When the Ammonites realized that a military conflict with Israel was imminent, they "hired"

several armies, including that of Zobah, to make war against Israel (v. 6). (The battle described in 2 Sam 8:3-8 may be either the same conflict or a separate one.) Ultimately, David secured a decisive victory within the territory of King Hadadezer of Zobah and established garrisons there (2 Sam 8:4-8; 1 Chr 18:3-8). Afterward, several of Hadadezer's vassals transferred their allegiance to David (2 Sam 10:19; see also 1 Kgs 11:23), and the political influence of Zobah waned.

Bibliography: P. Kyle McCarter Jr. *II Samuel.* AB 9 (1984).

RALPH K. HAWKINS

ZOBEBAH zoh-bee'buh [צֹבֵבָה tsovevah]. One of the sons of Koz appearing in a nonlinear and thus confusing list of descendants of Judah (1 Chr 4:8).

ZODIAC zoh'dee-ak [ὁ κύκλος ζῳδιακός ho kyklos zodiakos]. *Zodiac* derives from the Greek ho kyklos zodiakos, "a circle of figures." To ancient observers, the sky was a circle marked by an imaginary line that passed through star constellations, through which the SUN and planets traveled. It was commonly believed that planets and stars were living entities, or that they were the residence of deities and angelic beings (see Gen 32:1-2 [Heb. 32:2-3]; 2 Kgs 23:5; Ps 19:1 [Heb. 19:2]; Dan 12:3). The Bible frequently mentions the "hosts of heaven," God's army (e.g., Deut 4:19; 2 Kgs 21:3-5; Pss 24:10; 84:1; Isa 6:3; Luke 2:13; Rev 19:14; *see* HOSTS, HOST OF HEAVEN).

Ancient observers noted how the movement of planets and stars correlated with events affecting human experience: calendars, feasts and seasons, climate changes, agricultural and animal reproduction, wars and other events (Gen 1:14; Job 38:31-33; Isa 13:10; Amos 5:8 [but heavenly readings are condemned in Isa 47:13; Jer 10:2; see also *Jub.* 12:16-18; *Sib. Or.* 5:688–711; *1 En* 8:3]). Temple personnel, as a rule, provided calendric determinations (*see* CALENDAR). Astrological readings were taken at the birth of kings and nobles (e.g., the MAGI observe a rising star that heralds the birth of a king in Matt 2:1-2; *see* STAR OF BETHLEHEM). Elite people consulted celestial movements to decide on beneficial times to begin travel or business and to determine the future course of events (there were no star readings for ordinary people). Josephus notes how misinterpretation of the signs was partially responsible for the outbreak and length of the revolt against Rome (*J.W.* 6.288–97). The Middle Eastern zodiac originated with the Babylonians and their Sumerian-Assyrian constellations. Babylonian arithmetic employed a sexagesimal system of numbers to mark off the circle of the sky. A sexagesimal system is based on sixty (e.g., sixty minutes in an hour, sixty seconds in a minute, and 360 degrees in a circle). Phoenicians and Israelites adapted this system, as did the Greeks, who plotted the sky with geometry. Following the Greeks, the Egyptians further subdivided each sign into three equal parts called "de-cans," each representing approximately ten days (or ten degrees). These thirty-six constellations "co-rise" with the twelve constellations of the zodiac. In the Hellenistic period, the zodiac signs marked years and months, while the planets marked days of the week, and decans marked hours.

For the most part, ancient Israel shared the zodiac signs of the Phoenicians: Teleh (Lamb), Aleph (Bull), Thomim (Twins), Sertan (Crab), Layish (Lion), Erek-hayim (Staff of Life?), Perosuth (Claws), Aqrab (Scorpion), Qesheth (Arrow), Gedi (Goat), Dely (Water Bucket), Dagim (Fish). In the Hellenistic period, they were personified (e.g., the Arrow became Sagittarius; the Water Bucket became Aquarius). *See* ASTRONOMY, ASTROLOGY.

Bibliography: Roger Beck. *A Brief History of Ancient Astrology* (2007); Robert Brown Jr. *Researches into the Origin of the Primitive Constellations of the Greeks, Phoenicians and Babylonians.* 2 vols. (1899–1900); Rupert Gleadow. *The Origin of the Zodiac* (1968); Bruce J. Malina. *On the Genre and Message of Revelation* (1995).

BRUCE J. MALINA

ZOHAR zoh´hahr [צֹחַר tsokhar]. 1. Father of Ephron the Hittite, who sold the cave of MACHPELAH to Abraham for Sarah's burial (Gen 23:8). Abraham was buried there later (Gen 25:9).

2. The fifth of the six sons of Simeon (Gen 46:10; Exod 6:15). Elsewhere the name is Zerah (Num 26:12-13; 1 Chr 4:24). *See* ZERAH, ZERAHITES.

A. HEATH JONES III

ZOHELETH zoh´huh-lith [אֶבֶן הַזֹּחֶלֶת 'even hazzokheleth]. The stone Zoheleth (literally "the stone of creeping things"; RSV, "serpent's stone") is mentioned in connection with Adonijah's sacrifices to commemorate his coronation (1 Kgs 1:9). The name is a Hebrew toponymic reference, most likely representing the place of a serpent deity. It is not uncommon in the ANE for the serpent to be associated with selected deities. The stone could also reference local fauna. It was not uncommon for place names to be associated with specific animals in a type of totemistic relationship.

JOSEPH R. CATHEY

ZOHETH zoh´heth [זוֹחֵת zokheth]. Son of Ishi, along with the puzzling BEN-ZOHETH, among the descendants of Judah (1 Chr 4:20).

ZOLDERA. *See* LYSTRA.

ZOPHAH zoh´fuh [צוֹפָח tsofakh]. Son of Helem and father of eleven sons, listed among the descendants of Asher (1 Chr 7:35-36). Zophah does not appear in other lists of Asherites.

ZOPHAI. *See* ZUPH.

ZOPHAR zoh´fahr [צוֹפַר tsofar, צֹפַר tsofar]. The name *Zophar* may come from a root meaning "to turn away." Zophar the Naamathite was one of Job's three friends who, after hearing of the disaster that had befallen him, traveled to Uz to console him (Job 2:11). Zophar is the third speaker in the three cycles of speeches offered by Job's friends (chaps. 11; 20—he offers no words in the third cycle). Zophar's speech presents a clear call for Job to repent, suggesting that he understands the cause of Job's affliction to be some form of iniquity in Job's life (11:4). In Job 11:13-14, Zophar attempts to convince Job to turn away from his iniquity ("if iniquity is in your hand, put it far away") and direct his heart to God. The speech of Zophar in chap. 20 judges Job more harshly. Interestingly, Zophar's words in 11:7-10 perhaps reflect some of the upcoming rebuke by God in chap. 38; it is likely these words reflect Zophar's reliance upon wisdom sayings. The conclusion of Job (42:7-9) suggests that it was Zophar (as well as Eliphaz and Bildad) who had turned Job's heart from God (speaking of him wrongly) and who needed to repent. *See* JOB, BOOK OF.

ARCHIE T. WRIGHT

ZOPHIM zoh´fim [צֹפִים tsofim]. Means "watchers." The second place to which Balak took Balaam when he hired him to curse Israel (Num 23:14). The text locates "the field of Zophim" at or near the top of Mount Pisgah. Both places were selected so that Balaam could see only a portion of the encamped Israelites (Num 22:41; 23:13). It has been suggested that the text should be interpreted as "field of watchers" (sedheh tsofim שְׂדֵה צֹפִים), rather than take tsofim as a proper noun. Zophim has been identified with the similarly named Talʿat es-Safa.

JOHN I. LAWLOR

ZORAH, ZORATHITES zor´uh, zor´uh-thit [צָרְעָה tsorʿah, צָרְעָתִי tsorʿathi]. A village located in the Sorek Valley, 21 km west of Jerusalem and 3 km north of Beth Shemesh. It is usually identified with Sarʿa (Tel Zorʿa), which is situated on a hilltop on the north side of the Wadi es-Sarar.

In the Amarna Period, the town of Zorah was one of the towns in the kingdom of Gezer besieged by ʿApiru (EA 273). During the Israelite settlement, it was allotted to the tribe of Dan (Josh 19:41) and, along with ESHTAOL, became the center of Danite settlement. Samson's father, Manoah, was from Zorah (Judg 13:2). The spirit of the Lord first stirred Samson between Zorah and Eshtaol (Judg 13:25), the vicinity of his father's tomb, in which Samson was ultimately buried (Judg 16:31). Finally, after having had little success in conquering its allotment (Judg 1:34), the tribe of Dan set out from Zorah and Eshtaol "seeking for itself a territory to live in" (Judg 18:1), and Zorah was assimilated into the territory of Judah (Josh 15:33).

In later periods, Zorah came to be inhabited by the families of KIRIATH-JEARIM, descended from Judah (1 Chr 2:53). The Chronicler reports that Zorah was one of the cities in Judah and Benjamin that Rehoboam fortified for defense (2 Chr 11:5-12). The city was also one the villages outside Jerusalem where Judeans settled after returning from the exile (Neh 11:29).

RALPH K. HAWKINS

ZORITES zor'it [צֹרְעִי *tsori*ʿ]. A clan or family in Judah, descended from Salma (1 Chr 2:54). Although the name is similar to that of the "Zorathites" (*tsor*ʿ*athi* צָרְעָתִי) of 1 Chr 2:53, also from Judah, it is not clear whether the two are related. *See* ZORAH, ZORATHITES.

ZOROASTER, ZOROASTRIANISM zoh'roh-as'tuhr, zoh'roh-as'tree-uhn-iz'uhm. Until authentic Zoroastrian texts became known in Europe, ZARATHUSTRA—known as Zoroaster, the Greek form of his name—remained a figure of legend and speculation in the West. Classical sources preserve bits of Zoroastrian tradition: Diogenes Laertius (3rd cent. CE) cites 5th-cent. BCE sources who believed Zoroaster lived 5,000 years before the Trojan War or 6,000 years before Xerxes' crossing of the Hellespont (*Vit. Phil.* 1.2). These numbers seem to reflect a form of the Zoroastrian millennia count known from PAHLAVI texts, according to which Zarathustra appeared 6,000 years after the creation of the world. But Zoroaster is not mentioned by Ctesias of Cnidus, Herodotus, or Xenophon, three 5th-cent. BCE writers who had detailed knowledge of Persian traditions. Pliny the Elder (1st cent. CE; *Nat.* 30.3.4) first mentions the story, corroborated by Zoroastrian texts, that Zarathustra laughed on the day he was born. AUGUSTINE (*Civ.* 21.14) repeats the tale, adding, however, a tradition that Zoroaster was a Bactrian king and contemporary of Queen Semiramis of Babylon.

Zoroaster developed a reputation as a teacher of esoteric knowledge, as he and his followers came to be associated with the MAGI described by Herodotus (*Hist.* 1.101; 132). Clement of Alexandria (late 2nd–early 3rd cent. CE) identified Zoroaster with Er, a legendary figure in Plato's *Republic* (10.614–21), and claimed that he had written an account of what he learned from the gods on a trip to Hades (*Strom.* 5). In the late medieval period, Zoroaster was seen as a Chaldean astrologer-magician and credited with writing the 2nd-cent. CE *Chaldean Oracles*. By the Renaissance, Zoroaster was transformed into an enlightened lawgiver and philosopher who lived in the time of Abraham and founded the seven liberal arts. Zoroaster subsequently became a reformer and theologian, the founder of the Persian religion, and ultimately a prophet, a view that persists despite little textual support.

When inexact translations of the AVESTA and several Pahlavi texts were finally published in Europe in the late 18th cent., scholars doubted their authenticity, since they seemed to contain platitudes and sheer nonsense that could not possibly be ascribed to the exalted Zoroaster of Western tradition and imagination. As more Zoroastrian texts emerged, it became clear that they contradicted the Western image of Zoroaster, but some scholars continued to interpret the texts of Zarathustra in light of the Zoroaster of Western imagination. Thus, the medieval image of Zoroaster survived into the 19th and 20th cent., despite advances in philology, historiography, and the understanding of oral literature and its transmission. *See* PERSIA, HISTORY AND RELIGION OF.

Bibliography: Gherardo Gnoli. *Zoroaster in History* (2000).

P. OKTOR SKJAERVØ

ZOSTRIANOS, APOCALYPSE OF zohs'tree-ah'nohs. A fragmentary Coptic text from the late 2nd or early 3rd cent. CE (*see* NAG HAMMADI TEXTS). It relates the heavenly journey of a certain Zostrianos, who is reported to be a kinsman of Zoroaster (*see* ZOROASTER, ZOROASTRIANISM). The main interest of the *Apocalypse of Zostrianos*, a nonhistorical apocalypse, lies in the afterlife and the knowledge of the heavenly world. The narrative of the mystical ascent of Zostrianos reflects a non-Christian Sethian variety of Gnosticism that shows the influence of Middle Platonism. Some identify this text with the revelation of Zostrianos mentioned by Porphyry (*Vit. Plot.* 16.3). *See* APOCRYPHA, NT.

MARK DELCOGLIANO

ZUAR zoo'uhr [צוּעָר *tsu*ʿ*ar*]. The father of NETHANEL, a leader in the tribe of Issachar (Num 1:8; 2:5; 7:18, 23; 10:15). The Hebrew word tsuʿar means "little" or "insignificant," an ironic name for the father of a tribal chief.

ZUPH zuhf [צוּף *tsuf*]. Means "honeycomb." 1. An Ephraimite ancestor of Elkanah, Samuel's father (1 Sam 1:1). The Chronicler makes him—and by extension Samuel—a Kohathite from the tribe of Levi, the line from which David appointed men for the musical ministry in the Temple (1 Chr 6:35 [Heb. 6:20]). He is called Zophai (tsofay צוֹפַי) in 1 Chr 6:26 [Heb. 6:11]. *See* PRIESTS AND LEVITES.

2. A district in Israel where Saul and his servant searched for his father's donkeys (1 Sam 9:5). Its location is uncertain, but it probably lay within the hill country of Ephraim, perhaps near Ramah (compare 1 Sam 1:19). Many scholars associate this region with the name of Samuel's ancestor (1 Sam 1:1).

Bibliography: P. Kyle McCarter Jr. *I Samuel*. AB 8 (1980).

TERRY W. EDDINGER

ZUR zuhr [צוּר tsur]. 1. A Midianite ruler, variously identified as the "head of a clan" in Num 25:15, as a "king" in Num 31:8, and as a "leader" and a "prince" in Josh 13:21. He is named among the five Midianite kings (Num 31:8) or leaders/princes (Josh 13:21) slain by the Israelites prior to their entrance into the land allotted to the Reubenites. Zur was the father of Cozbi (Num 25:15), one of the two individuals pierced through with a spear by Phinehas during the Israelites' stay at Shittim, when the Israelites "yoked themselves to the Baal of Peor" (Num 25:1-8, 15). *See* MIDIAN, MIDIANITES.

2. Second son of the Benjaminite Jeiel, who lived in Gibeon (1 Chr 8:30; 9:36).

JOHN I. LAWLOR

ZURIEL zoor′ee-uhl [צוּרִיאֵל tsuri′el]. Means "my rock is God." Zuriel son of Abihail (Num 3:35) was the chief or prince of the Levitical clans of Merari (the Mahlites and the Mushites). These clans camped on the north side of the tabernacle and were responsible for the framework of the portable sanctuary in the wilderness journeys; once the Temple was built their duties changed (see 1 Chr 6:31-48).

TIMOTHY G. CRAWFORD

ZURISHADDAI zoor′i-shad′i [צוּרִישַׁדָּי tsurishadday; Σαρασαδαί Sarasadai]. Means "Shaddai is my rock." The father of SHELUMIEL, who was the leader of the ancestral tribe of Simeon at the time of the exodus. He is referenced in conjunction with his son in the first census of the Israelites in the wilderness of Sinai (Num 1:6), in the encampment order (Num 2:12), at the completion of the tabernacle (Num 7:36, 41), and at the departure of the tribe of Simeon from Sinai (Num 10:19). He is also mentioned as a progenitor of the ancestral lineage of Judith (Jdt 8:1).

HUMPHREY H. HARDY II

ZUZIM zoo′zim [זוּזִים zuzim]. A Transjordanian people who lived in HAM and were subdued by CHEDORLAOMER and his coalition (Gen 14:5). The people are otherwise unknown. They are presumably the same as the ZAMZUMMIM of Deut 2:20, both of whom are listed alongside the Emim and the Rephaim, races of giants like the Anakim (Num 13:32-33). If the Zuzim and Zamzummim are to be equated, it is not clear which is the original wording.

The etymology of the name is unclear. One possibility is that the name is an epithet by which the Ammonites called this people, in imitation of their speech. In this case, *Zuzim* would be understood as an onomatopoeic form, a word with two near identical syllables commonly used to designate speakers of foreign languages (e.g., barbaros βάρβαρος), meaning something like "the Buzz-buzzers" or "the people whose talk sounds like buzzing."

RALPH K. HAWKINS

ABBREVIATIONS

GENERAL ABBREVIATIONS

*	reconstructed prototype of hypothetical letter or word form
Akkad.	Akkadian
AM	Anno Mundi (creation of the world)
ANE	Ancient Near East
Aram.	Aramaic
b.	born
BCE	Before the Common Era (replaces B.C.)
C	centigrade
c.	common
ca.	circa
CE	Common Era (replaces A.D.)
cent.	century
chap(s).	chapter(s)
Chr	Chronicler
cm	centimeter(s)
Cod. Theod.	Codex Theodosianus
col/s.	column/s
d.	died
D	Deuteronomist source (of the Pentateuch)
Dtr	Deuteronomistic
DtrH	Deuteronomistic History/Historian
E	Elohist source (of the Pentateuch)
ed(s).	editor(s), edited by
e.g.	*exempli gratia,* for example
esp.	especially
et al.	*et alii,* and others
etc.	*et cetera,* and the rest
f. or fem.	feminine
fig.	figure
frag.	fragment
ft.	feet (measurement)
FS	Festschrift
g	grams
Gk.	Greek
ha.	Hectare(s)
Heb.	Hebrew manuscripts
i.e.	*id est,* that is
in.	inch(es)
J	Jahwist or Yahwist source (of the Pentateuch)
km	kilometers
L	liters

LB	Late Bronze
lb(s)	pound(s)
lit.	literally
LXX	Septuagint (the Greek Old Testament)
m	meters
m. or masc.	masculine
MB	Middle Bronze
mi.	miles
mm	millimeters
MS(S)	manuscript(s)
MT	Masoretic Text (of the Hebrew Bible)
n(n).	note(s)
n.d.	no date
no(s).	number(s)
n.p.	no place; no publisher; no page
NHC	Nag Hammadi Codex
NS	new series
NT	New Testament
OT	Old Testament
P	Priestly source (of the Pentateuch)
P. Oxy.	Oxyrhyncus Papyri
p(p).	page(s)
par. or //	parallel
Q	Qumran (or Quelle)
r.	ruled
repr.	reprinted
rev.	revised (by)
ser.	series
sq. km	square kilometer(s)
sq. mi.	square mile(s)
suppl.	supplement
T	Tomb (Nag Hammadi)
Tg(s).	Targum(s); Targumic
trans.	translator, translated by
v(v).	verse(s)
vol(s).	volume(s)
yd(s).	yard(s)

BIBLE TRANSLATIONS

ASV	American Standard Version
CEV	Contemporary English Version
CSB	Catholic Study Bible
GNB	Good News Bible
JB	Jerusalem Bible
KJV	King James Version
LB	The Living Bible
NAB	New American Bible
NCB	New Century Bible
NEB	New English Bible
NIV	New International Version
NJB	New Jerusalem Bible
NJPS	New Jewish Publication Society Tanakh
NKJV	New King James Version
NLB	New Living Bible

NOAB	New Oxford Annotated Bible
NRSV	New Revised Standard Version
REB	Revised English Bible
RSV	Revised Standard Version
TEV	Today's English Version
TNK	Tanakh

OLD TESTAMENT

Gen	Genesis
Exod	Exodus
Lev	Leviticus
Num	Numbers
Deut	Deuteronomy
Josh	Joshua
Judg	Judges
Ruth	Ruth
1–2 Sam	1–2 Samuel
1–2 Kgs	1–2 Kings
1–2–3–4 Kgdms	1–2–3–4 Kingdoms (LXX)
1–2 Chr	1–2 Chronicles
Ezra	Ezra
Neh	Nehemiah
Esth	Esther
Job	Job
Ps(s)	Psalm(s)
Prov	Proverbs
Eccl	Ecclesiastes
Song	Song of Songs (Song of Solomon, or Canticles)
Isa	Isaiah
Jer	Jeremiah
Lam	Lamentations
Ezek	Ezekiel
Dan	Daniel
Hos	Hosea
Joel	Joel
Amos	Amos
Obad	Obadiah
Jonah	Jonah
Mic	Micah
Nah	Nahum
Hab	Habakkuk
Zeph	Zephaniah
Hag	Haggai
Zech	Zechariah
Mal	Malachi

NEW TESTAMENT

Matt	Matthew
Mark	Mark
Luke	Luke
John	John

Acts	Acts
Rom	Romans
1–2 Cor	1–2 Corinthians
Gal	Galatians
Eph	Ephesians
Phil	Philippians
Col	Colossians
1–2 Thess	1–2 Thessalonians
1–2 Tim	1–2 Timothy
Titus	Titus
Phlm	Philemon
Heb	Hebrews
Jas	James
1–2 Pet	1–2 Peter
1–2–3 John	1–2–3 John
Jude	Jude
Rev	Revelation

Apocrypha and Septuagint

Bar	Baruch
Add Dan	Additions to Daniel
Pr Azar	Prayer of Azariah
Bel	Bel and the Dragon
Sg Three	Song of the Three Jews
Sus	Susanna
1–2 Esd	1–2 Esdras
Add Esth	Additions to Esther
Ep Jer	Epistle of Jeremiah
Jdt	Judith
1–2–3–4 Macc	1–2–3–4 Maccabees
Pr Man	Prayer of Manasseh
Ps 151	Psalm 151
Sir	Sirach (Ecclesiasticus)
Tob	Tobit
Wis	Wisdom of Solomon

Pseudepigraphical and Early Patristic Books

Ahiqar	*Ahiqar*
Apoc. Ab.	*Apocalypse of Abraham*
Apoc. Adam	*Apocalypse of Adam*
Apoc. Dan.	*Apocalypse of Daniel*
Apoc. El. (C)	Coptic *Apocalypse of Elijah*
Apoc. El. (H)	Hebrew *Apocalypse of Elijah*
Apoc. Mos.	*Apocalypse of Moses*
Apoc. Sedr.	*Apocalypse of Sedrach*
Apoc. Zeph.	*Apocalypse of Zephaniah*
Apocr. Ezek.	*Apocrypon of Ezekiel*
Aris. Ex.	Aristeas the Exegete
Aristob.	Aristobulus
Artap.	Artapanus
Ascen. Isa.	*Mart. Ascen. Isa.* 6–11

As. Mos.	*Assumption of Moses*
2 Bar.	*2 Baruch (Syriac Apocalypse)*
3 Bar.	*3 Baruch (Greek Apocalypse)*
4 Bar.	*4 Baruch (Paraleipomena Jeremiou)*
Bk. Noah	*Book of Noah*
Cav. Tr.	*Cave of Treasures*
Cl. Mal.	Cleodemus Malchus
Dem.	Demetrius (the Chronographer)
El. Mod.	*Eldad and Modad*
1 En.	*1 Enoch (Ethiopic Apocalypse)*
2 En.	*2 Enoch (Slavonic Apocalypse)*
3 En.	*3 Enoch (Hebrew Apocalypse)*
Eup.	Eupolemus
Ezek. Trag.	Ezekiel the Tragedian
4 Ezra	*4 Ezra*
5 Apoc. Syr. Pss.	*Five Apocryphal Syriac Psalms*
Gk. Apoc. Ezra	*Greek Apocalypse of Ezra*
Hec. Ab.	Hecataeus of Abdera
Hel. Syn. Pr.	*Hellenistic Synagogal Prayers*
Hist. Jos.	*History of Joseph*
Hist. Rech.	*History of the Rechabites*
Jan. Jam.	*Jannes and Jambres*
Jos. Asen.	*Joseph and Aseneth*
Jub.	*Jubilees*
L.A.B.	*Liber antiquitatum biblicarum* (Pseudo-Philo)
L.A.E.	*Life of Adam and Eve*
Lad. Jac.	*Ladder of Jacob*
Let. Aris.	*Letter of Aristeas*
Liv. Pro.	*Lives of the Prophets*
Lost Tr.	*The Lost Tribes*
3 Macc.	*3 Maccabees*
4 Macc.	*4 Maccabees*
5 Macc.	*5 Maccabees* (Arabic)
Mart. Ascen. Isa.	*Martyrdom and Ascension of Isaiah*
Mart. Isa.	*Mart. Ascen. Isa.* 1–5
Odes Sol.	*Odes of Solomon*
Ph. E. Poet	Philo the Epic Poet
Pr. Jac.	*Prayer of Jacob*
Pr. Jos.	*Prayer of Joseph*
Pr. Man.	*Prayer of Manasseh*
Pr. Mos.	*Prayer of Moses*
Ps.-Eup.	Pseudo-Eupolemus
Ps.-Hec.	Pseudo-Hecataeus
Ps.-Orph.	Pseudo-Orpheus
Ps.-Phoc.	Pseudo-Phocylides
Pss. Sol.	*Psalms of Solomon*
Ques. Ezra	*Questions of Ezra*
Rev. Ezra	*Revelation of Ezra*
Sib. Or.	*Sibylline Oracles*
Syr. Men.	*Sentences of the Syriac Menander*
T. 12 Patr.	*Testaments of the Twelve Patriarchs*
T. Ash.	*Testament of Asher*
T. Benj.	*Testament of Benjamin*
T. Dan	*Testament of Dan*

T. Gad	Testament of Gad
T. Iss.	Testament of Issachar
T. Jos.	Testament of Joseph
T. Jud.	Testament of Judah
T. Levi	Testament of Levi
T. Naph.	Testament of Naphtali
T. Reu.	Testament of Reuben
T. Sim.	Testament of Simeon
T. Zeb.	Testament of Zebulun
T. 3 Patr.	Testaments of the Three Patriarchs
T. Ab.	Testament of Abraham
T. Isaac	Testament of Isaac
T. Jac.	Testament of Jacob
T. Adam	Testament of Adam
T. Hez.	Testament of Hezekiah (Mart. Ascen. Isa. 3:13–4:22)
T. Job	Testament of Job
T. Mos.	Testament of Moses
T. Sol.	Testament of Solomon
Theod.	Theodotus, On the Jews
Treat. Shem	Treatise of Shem
Vis. Ezra	Vision of Ezra

PHILO OF ALEXANDRIA

Latin		**English**	
Abr.	De Abrahamo	Abraham	On the Life of Abraham
Aet.	De aeternitate mundi	Eternity	On the Eternity of the World
Agr.	De agricultura	Agriculture	On Agriculture
Anim.	De animalibus	Animals	Whether Animals Have Reason (= Alexander)
Cher.	De cherubim	Cherubim	On the Cherubim
Conf.	De confusione linguarum	Confusion	On the Confusion of Tongues
Congr.	De congressueru ditionis gratia	Prelim. Studies	On the Preliminary Studies
Contempl.	De vita contemplativa	Contempl. Life	On the Contemplative Life
Decal.	De decalogo	Decalogue	On the Decalogue
Deo	De Deo	God	On God
Det.	Quod deterius potiori insidari soleat	Worse	That the Worse Attacks the Better
Deus	Quod Deus sit immutabilis	Unchangeable	That God Is Unchangeable
Ebr.	De ebrietate	Drunkenness	On Drunkenness
Exsecr.	De exsecrationibus	Curses	On Curses (= Rewards 127–72)
Flacc.	In Flaccum	Flaccus	Against Flaccus
Fug.	De fuga et inventione	Flight	On Flight and Finding
Gig.	De gigantibus	Giants	On Giants
Her.	Quis rerum divinarum heres sit	Heir	Who Is the Heir?
Hypoth.	Hypothetica	Hypothetica	Hypothetica
Ios.	De Iosepho	Joseph	On the Life of Joseph
Leg. 1, 2, 3	Legum allegoriae I, II, III	Alleg. Interp. 1, 2, 3	Allegorical Interpretation 1, 2, 3
Legat.	Legatio ad Gaium	Embassy	On the Embassy to Gaius
Migr.	De migratione Abrahami	Migration	On the Migration of Abraham
Mos. 1, 2	De vita Mosis I, II	Moses 1, 2	On the Life of Moses 1, 2
Mut.	De mutatione nominum	Names	On the Change of Names
Opif.	De opificio mundi	Creation	On the Creation of the World
Plant.	De plantatione	Planting	On Planting
Post.	De posteritate Caini	Posterity	On the Posterity of Cain
Praem.	De praemiis et poenis	Rewards	On Rewards and Punishments

Prob.	*Quod omnis probus liber sit*	*Good Person*	*That Every Good Person Is Free*
Prov. 1, 2	*De providentia* I, II	*Providence* 1, 2	*On Providence* 1, 2
QE 1, 2	*Quaestiones et solutiones in Exodum* I, II	*QE* 1, 2	*Questions and Answers on Exodus* 1, 2
QG 1, 2, 3, 4	*Quaestiones et solutiones in Genesin* I, II, III, IV	*QG* 1, 2, 3, 4	*Questions and Answers on Genesis 1, 2, 3, 4*
Sacr.	*De sacrificiis Abelis et Caini*	*Sacrifices*	*On the Sacrifices of Cain and Abel*
Sobr.	*De sobrietate*	*Sobriety*	*On Sobriety*
Somn. 1, 2,	*De somniis* I, II	*Dreams* 1, 2	*On Dreams* 1, 2
Spec. 1, 2, 3, 4	*De specialibus legibus* I, II, III, IV	*Spec. Laws*	*On the Special Laws* 1, 2, 3, 4
Virt.	*De virtutibus*	*Virtues*	*On the Virtues*

JOSEPHUS

Latin		**English**	
A.J.	*Antiquitates judaicae*	*Ant.*	*Jewish Antiquities*
B.J.	*Bellum judaicum*	*J. W.*	*Jewish War*
C. Ap.	*Contra Apionem*	*Ag. Ap.*	*Against Apion*
Vita	*Vita*	*Life*	*The Life*

DEAD SEA SCROLLS AND RELATED TEXTS

Number	**Abbreviation**	**Name**
	CD	Cairo Genizah copy of the *Damascus Document*
	1Qap Gen ar	*Genesis Apocryphon*
	1QH[a]	*Hodayot[a] or Thanksgiving Hymns[a]*
	1QpHab	*Pesher Habakkuk*
	1QM	*Milhamah or War Scroll*
	1QS	*Serek Hayahad or Rule of the Community*
	1QIsa[a]	Isaiah[a]
	1QIsa[b]	Isaiah[b]
1Q20	1Qap Gen ar	*Genesis Apocryphon*
1Q21	1QTLevi ar	*Testament of Levi*
1Q26	1QInstruction	*1QInstruction, formerly Wisdom Apocryphon*
1Q28a	1QSa	*Rule of the Congregation* (Appendix a to 1QS)
1Q28b	1QSb	*Rule of the Blessings* (Appendix b to 1QS)
3Q15		*Copper Scroll*
4Q17	4QExod-Lev[f]	
4Q22	4QpaleoExod[m]	
4Q58	4QIsa[d]	*4QIsaiah[d]*
4Q82	4QXII[g]	
4Q120	4QpapLXXLev[b]	
4Q127	4QpapParaExod gr	*ParaExodus*
4Q163	4Qpap pIsa[c]	*Isaiah Pesher[c]*
4Q171	4QpPsa	*Psalms Pesher[a]*
4Q174	4QFlor (MidrEschat[a])	*Florilegium,* also *Midrash on Eschatology[a]*
4Q175	4QTest	*Testimonia*
4Q177	4QCatena[a] (MidrEschat[b])	*Catena[a],* also *Midrash on Eschatology[b]*
4Q180	4QAgesCreat	*Ages of Creation*
4Q182	4QCatena[b] (MidrEschat[c])	*Catena[b],* also *Midrash on Eschatology[c]*
4Q213-14	4QLevi ar	*Aramaic Levi*
4Q242	4QPrNab ar	*Prayer of Nabonidus*
4Q246	4QapocrDan ar	*Apocryphon of Daniel*
4Q251	4QHalakhah A	Halakhah A

4Q252	4QCommGen A	*Commentary on Genesis A,* formerly *Patriarchal Blessings* or *Pesher Genesis*
4Q265	4QSD	*Miscellaneous*
4Q266	4QD^a	*Damascus Document^a*
4Q270	4QD^e	*Damascus Document^e*
4Q271	4QD^f	*Damascus Document^f,* formerly Damascus Document^c
4Q274	4QTohorot A	*Tohorot A*
4Q285		*Sefer Hamilhamah*
4Q286-90	4QBer^{a-e}	*Berakhot^{a-e}*
4Q299	4QMyst^a	*Mysteries^a*
4Q319-330	4QCalDoc A-I	*Calendrical Document A-I,* also *Mishmarot*
4Q320	4QCalDoc A	*Calendrical Document A,* formerly *Mishmarot A*
4Q325	4QCalDoc D	*Calendrical Document,* formerly *Mishmarot E^b*
4Q334	4Qord	*Order of Divine Office*
4Q337	4QCalDoc F	*Fragment of Calendar*
4Q365	4QRP^c	*Reworked Pentateuch^c*
4Q378	4QapocrJosh^a	*Apocryphon of Joshua^a* formerly *Psalms of Joshua^a*
4Q383	4QapocrJer A	*Apocryphon of Jeremiah A*
4Q384	4QpapApocrjer B?	*Apocryphon of Jeremiah B?*
4Q385a	4QapocrJer C^a	*Apocryphon of Jeremiah C,* formerly *Pseudo-Moses^a*
4Q387	4QJer C^b	*Apocryphon of Jeremiah C,* formerly *Pseudo-Moses^b*
4Q387b	4QapocrJer D	*Apocryphon of Jeremiah D*
4Q388a	4QJer C^c	*Apocryphon of Jeremiah C,* formerly *Pseudo-Moses^c*
4Q389	4QJer C^d	*Apocryphon of Jeremiah D,* formerly *Pseudo-Moses^d*
4Q390	4QapocrJerE (psMos^e)	*Apocryphon of Jeremiah E*
4Q394	4QMMT^a	*Miqsat Maase ha-Torah^a*
4Q395	4QMMT^b	*Halakhic Letter^b*
4Q396	4QMMT^c	*Halakhic Letter^c*
4Q397	4QMMT^d	*Halakhic Letter^d*
4Q398	4QMMT^e	*Halakhic Letter^e*
4Q399	4QMMT^f	*Halakhic Letter^f*
4Q400	4QShirShabb^a	*Songs of the Sabbath Sacrifice^a*
4Q414	4QRitPur A	*Ritual Purity A,* formerly *Baptismal Liturgy*
4Q415	4QInstruction^a	*Instruction^a,* formerly *Sapiental Work A^d*
4Q416	4QInstruction^b	*Instruction^b,* formerly *Sapiental Work A^b*
4Q417	4QInstruction^c	*Instruction^c,* formerly *Sapiental Work A^c*
4Q418	4QInstruction^d	*Instruction^d,* formerly *Sapiental Work A^a*
4Q418a	4QInstruction^e	*Instruction^e*
4Q418c	4QInstruction^e	*Instruction^f*
4Q423	4QInstruction^g	*Instruction^g,* formerly *Sapiental Work A^e* also *Tree of Knowledge*
4Q434	4QBarki Nafshi^a	*BarkhiNafshi^a*
4Q502	4QpapRitMar	*Ritual of Marriage*
4Q503	4QpapPrQuot	*Prières quotidiennes* or *Daily Prayers*
4Q504	4QDibHam^a	*Dibre Hame'orota* or *Words of the Luminaries^a*
4Q507	4QPrFêtes^a	*Prières pour les fêtesa* or *Festival Prayersa*
4Q510	4QShir^a	*Shirot^a* or *Songs of the Sage^a*
4Q512	4QpapRitPur B	*Ritual Purity B*
4Q521	4QMessAp	*Messianic Apocalypse*
4Q524	4QT^b	*4QTemple Scroll,* formerly *Halakhic Text*
4Q525	4QBeat	*Beatitudes*
7Q2		*Epistle of Jeremiah*
11Q5	11QPsa	*Psalms Scroll^a*

11Q10	11QtgJob	*Targum of Job*
11Q11	11QApPs	*Apocryphal Psalms*
11Q13	11QMelch	*Melchizedek*
11Q18	11QNJ ar	*New Jerusalem*
11Q19	11QTᵃ	*Temple Scrollᵃ*

MISHNAH, TALMUD, AND RELATED LITERATURE

Abbreviations distinguish the versions of the Talmudic tractates: *y.* for Jerusalem and *b.* for Babylonian. A prefixed *t.* denotes the tractates of the Tosefta and an *m.* those of the Mishnah. A prefixed *bar.* denotes a baraita (an authoritative Tannaitic rule external to the Mishnah).

Avod. Zar.	*Avodah Zarah*
Avot	*Avot*
Arak.	*Arakhin*
B. Bat.	*Bava Batra*
B. Metz.	*Bava Metzia*
B. Qam.	*Bava Qamma*
Bek.	*Bekhorot*
Ber.	*Berakhot*
Betzah	*Betzah (= Yom Tov)*
Bik.	*Bikkurim*
Demai	*Demai*
Eruv.	*Eruvin*
Ed.	*Eduyyot*
Git.	*Gittin*
Hag.	*Hagigah*
Hal.	*Hallah*
Hor.	*Horayot*
Hul.	*Hullin*
Kelim	*Kelim*
Ker.	*Keritot*
Ketub.	*Ketubbot*
Kil.	*Kilayim*
Maas. S.	*Maaser Sheni*
Maas.	*Maaserot*
Mak.	*Makkot*
Makh.	*Makhshirin*
Meg.	*Megillah*
Meil.	*Meilah*
Menah.	*Menahot*
Mid.	*Middot*
Mikw.	*Mikwaot*
Moed	*Moed*
Moed Qat.	*Moed Qatan*
Nash.	*Nashim*
Naz.	*Nazir*
Ned.	*Nedarim*
Neg.	*Negaim*
Nez.	*Neziqin*
Nid.	*Niddah*
Ohal.	*Ohalot*
Or.	*Orlah*
Parah	*Parah*

Peah	Peah
Pesah.	Pesahim
Qinnim	Qinnim
Qidd.	Qiddushin
Qod.	Qodashim
Rosh. Hash.	Rosh HaShanah
Sanh.	Sanhedrin
Shabb.	Shabbat
Shev.	Sheviit
Shevu.	Shevuot
Seder	Seder
Sheq.	Sheqalim
Sotah	Sotah
Sukkah	Sukkah
Taan.	Taanit
Tamid	Tamid
Tehar.	Teharot
Tem.	Temurah
Ter.	Terumot
T. Yom	Tevul Yom
Uq.	Uqtzin
Yad.	Yadayin
Yev.	Yevamot
Yoma	Yoma (= Kippurim)
Zabim	Zabim
Zevah.	Zevahim
Zera.	Zeraim

TARGUMIC TEXTS

Tg. Onq.	Targum Onqelos
Tg. Neb.	Targum of the Prophets
Tg. Ket.	Targum of the Writings
Frg. Tg.	Fragmentary Targum
Sam. Tg.	Samaritan Targum
Tg. Isa.	Targum Isaiah
Tg. Neof.	Targum Neofiti
Tg. Ps.-J.	Targum Pseudo-Jonathan
Tg. Yer. I, II	Targum Yerushalmi I, II
Yem. Tg.	Yemenite Targum
Tg. Esth. I, II	First or Second Targum of Esther

OTHER RABBINIC WORKS

Avad.	Avadim
Avot. R. Nat.	Avot of Rabbi Nathan
Ag. Ber.	Aggadat Bereshit
Bab.	Babylonian
Der. Er. Rab.	Derekh Eretz Rabbah
Der. Er. Zut.	Derekh Eretz Zuta
Gem.	Gemara
Gerim	Gerim
Kallah	Kallah

Kallah Rab.	*Kallah Rabbati*
Kutim	*Kutim*
Mas. Qet.	*Massekhtot Qetannot*
Mek.	*Mekilta*
Mez.	*Mezuzah*
Midr.	*Midrash*
Midr. Tann.	*Midrash Tannaim*
Pal.	*Palestinian*
Pesiq. Rab.	*Pesiqta Rabbati*
Pesiq. Rab Kah.	*Pesiqta of Rab Kahana*
Pirqe R. El.	*Pirqe Rabbi Eliezer*
Rab.	*Rabbah*
S. Eli. Rab.	*Seder Eliyahu Rabbah*
S. Eli. Zut.	*Seder Eliyahu Zuta*
Sem.	*Semahot*
Sef. Torah	*Sefer Torah*
Sifra	*Sifra*
Sifre	*Sifre*
Tzitz.	*Tzitzit*
Sof.	*Soferim*
S. Olam. Rab	*Seder Olam Rabbah*
Tanh.	*Tanhuma*
Tef.	*Tefillin*
Yal.	*Yalqut*

APOSTOLIC FATHERS

Barn.	*Barnabas*
1–2 Clem.	*1–2 Clement*
Did.	*Didache*
Diogn.	*Diognetus*
Herm. *Mand.*	Shepherd of Hermas, *Mandate*
Herm. *Sim.*	Shepherd of Hermas, *Similitude*
Herm. *Vis.*	Shepherd Hermas, *Vision*
Ign. *Eph.*	Ignatius, *To the Ephesians*
Ign. *Magn.*	Ignatius, *To the Magnesians*
Ign. *Phld.*	Ignatius, *To the Philadelphians*
Ign. *Pol.*	Ignatius, *To Polycarp*
Ign. *Rom.*	Ignatius, *To the Romans*
Ign. *Smyrn.*	Ignatius, *To the Smyrnaeans*
Ign. *Trall.*	Ignatius, *To the Trallians*
Mart. *Pol.*	*Martyrdom of Polycarp*
Pol. *Phil*	Polycarp, *To the Philippians*

NAG HAMMADI CODICES

Act Pet.	*Act of Peter*
Acts Pet. 12 Apos.	*Acts of Peter and the Twelve Apostles*
Allogenes	*Allogenes*
Ap. Jas.	*Apocryphon of James*
Ap. John	*Apocryphon of John*
Apoc. Adam	*Apocalypse of Adam*
1 Apoc. Jas.	*(First) Apocalypse of James*

2 Apoc. Jas.	(Second) Apocalypse of James
Apoc. Paul	Apocalypse of Paul
Apoc. Pet.	Apocalypse of Peter
Asclepius	Asclepius 21–29
Auth. Teach.	Authoritative Teaching
Dial. Sav.	Dialogue of the Savior
Disc. 8–9	Discourse on the Eighth and Ninth
Eugnostos	Eugnostos the Blessed (III, 3), (V, 1)
Exeg. Soul	Exegesis of the Soul
Frm.	Fragments
Gos. Eg.	Gospel of the Egyptians
Gos. Mary	Gospel of Mary
Gos. Phil.	Gospel of Philip
Gos. Thom.	Gospel of Thomas
Gos. Truth	Gospel of Truth
Great Pow.	Concept of our Great Power
Hyp. Arch.	Hypostasis of the Archons
Hypsiph.	Hypsiphrone
Interp. Know.	Interpretation of Knowledge
Marsanes	Marsanes
Melch.	Melchizedek
Norea	Thought of Norea
On Anointing	On the Anointing
On Bap. A	On Baptism A
On Bap. B	On Baptism B
On Euch. A	On the Eucharist A
On Euch. B	On the Eucharist B
Orig. World	On the Origin of the World
Paraph. Shem	Paraphrase of Shem
Plato Rep.	Plato, Republic 588b-589b
Pr. Paul	Prayer of the Apostle Paul
Pr. Thanks.	Prayer of Thanksgiving
Sent. Sextus	Sentences of Sextus
Soph. Jes. Chr.	Sophia of Jesus Christ
Steles Seth	Three Steles of Seth
Teach. Silv.	Teachings of Silvanus
Testim. Truth	Testimony of Truth
Thom. Cont.	Book of Thomas the Contender
Thund.	Thunder: Perfect Mind
Treat. Res.	Treatise on the Resurrection
Treat. Seth	Second Treatise of the Great Seth
Tri. Trac.	Tripartite Tractate
Trim. Prot.	Trimorphic Protennoia
Val. Exp.	Valentinian Exposition
Zost.	Zostrianos

NEW TESTAMENT APOCRYPHA AND PSEUDEPIGRAPHA

Acts Andr.	Acts of Andrew
Acts Andr. Mth.	Acts of Andrew and Matthias
Acts Andr. Paul	Acts of Andrew and Paul
Acts Barn.	Acts of Barnabas
Acts Jas.	Acts of James the Great
Acts John	Acts of John

Acts John Pro.	*Acts of John (by Prochorus)*
Acts Paul	*Acts of Paul (or Acts of Paul and Thecla)*
Acts Pet.	*Acts of Peter*
Acts Pet. (Slav.)	*Acts of Peter (Slavonic)*
Acts Pet. Andr.	*Acts of Peter and Andrew*
Acts Pet. Paul	*Acts of Peter and Paul*
Acts Phil.	*Acts of Philip*
Acts Phil. (Syr.)	*Acts of Philip (Syriac)*
Acts Pil.	*Acts of Pilate*
Acts Thad.	*Acts of Thaddaeus*
Acts Thom.	*Acts of Thomas*
Apoc. Pet.	*Apocalypse of Peter*
Ap. John	*Apocryphon of John*
Apoc. Dosith.	*Apocalypse of Dositheus*
Apoc. Messos	*Apocalypse of Messos*
Apoc. Thom.	*Apocalypse of Thomas*
Apoc. Vir.	*Apocalypse of the Virgin*
(Apocr.) Ep. Tit.	*Apocryphal Epistle of Titus*
(Apocr.) Gos. John	*Apocryphal Gospel of John*
Apos. Con.	*Apostolic Constitutions and Canons*
Ps.-Abd.	*Apostolic History of Pseudo-Abdias*
(Arab.) Gos. Inf.	*Arabic Gospel of the Infancy*
(Arm.) Gos. Inf.	*Armenian Gospel of the Infancy*
Asc. Jas.	*Ascents of James*
Assum. Vir.	*Assumption of the Virgin*
Bk. Barn.	*Book of the Resurrection of Christ by Barnabas the Apostle*
Bk. Elch.	*Book Elchasai*
Cerinthus	*Cerinthus*
3 Cor.	*3 Corinthians*
Ep. Alex.	*Epistle to the Alexandrians*
Ep. Apos.	*Epistle to the Apostles*
Ep. Chr. Abg.	*Epistle of Christ and Abgar*
Ep. Chr. Heav.	*Epistle of Christ from Heaven*
Ep. Lao.	*Epistle to the Laodiceans*
Ep. Lent.	*Epistle of Lentulus*
Ep. Paul Sen.	*Epistles of Paul and Seneca*
Gos. Barn.	*Gospel of Barnabas*
Gos. Bart.	*Gospel of Bartholomew*
Gos. Bas.	*Gospel of Basilides*
Gos. Bir. Mary	*Gospel of the Birth of Mary*
Gos. Eb.	*Gospel of the Ebionites*
Gos. Eg.	*Gospel of the Egyptians*
Gos. Eve	*Gospel of Eve*
Gos. Gam.	*Gospel of Gamaliel*
Gos. Heb.	*Gospel of the Hebrews*
Gos. Marcion	*Gospel of Marcion*
Gos. Mary	*Gospel of Mary*
Gos. Naass.	*Gospel of the Naassenes*
Gos. Naz.	*Gospel of the Nazarenes (Nazoreans)*
Gos. Nic.	*Gospel of Nicodemus*
Gos. Pet.	*Gospel of Peter*
Ps.-Mt.	*Gospel of Pseudo-Matthew*
Gos. Thom.	*Gospel of Thomas*
Gos. Trad. Mth.	*Gospel and Traditions of Matthias*
Hist. Jos. Carp.	*History of Joseph the Carpenter*
Hymn Dance	*Hymn of the Dance*
Hymn Pearl	*Hymn of the Pearl*

Inf. Gos. Thom.	*Infancy Gospel of Thomas*
Inf. Gos.	*Infancy Gospels*
Mart. Bart.	*Martyrdom of Bartholomew*
Mart. Mt.	*Martyrdom of Matthew*
Mart. On.	*Martyrdom of Onesimus*
Mart. Paul	*Martyrdom of Paul*
Mart. Pet.	*Martyrdom of Peter*
Mart. Pet. Paul	*Paul Martyrdom of Peter and Paul*
Mart. Phil.	*Martyrdom of Philip*
Melkon	*Melkon*
Mem. Apos.	*Memoria of Apostles*
Pre. Pet.	*Preaching of Peter*
Prot. Jas.	*Protevangelium of James*
Ps.-Clem.	*Pseudo-Clementines*
Rev. Steph.	*Revelation of Stephen*
Sec. Gos. Mk.	*Secret Gospel of Mark*
Vis. Paul	*Vision of Paul*

WORKS IN GREEK AND LATIN, SOME WITH ENGLISH TRANSLATIONS

ACHILLES TATIUS

Leuc. Clit.	*Leucippe et Clitophon*	*The Adventures of Leucippe and Clitophon*

AELIAN

Nat. an.	*De natura animalium*	*Nature of Animals*
Var. hist.	*Varia historia*	

AESCHINES

Ctes.	*In Ctesiphonem*	*Against Ctesiphon*
Fals. leg.	*De falsa legatione*	*False Embassy*
Tim.	*In Timarchum*	*Against Timarchus*

AESCHYLUS

Ag.	*Agamemnon*	*Agamemnon*
Cho.	*Choephori*	*Libation-Bearers*
Eum.	*Eumenides*	*Eumenides*
Pers.	*Persae*	*Persians*
Prom.	*Prometheus vinctus*	*Prometheus Bound*
Sept.	*Septem contra Thebas*	*Seven against Thebes*
Suppl.	*Supplices*	*Suppliant Women*

AESOP

Fab.	*Fabulae*	*Fables*

ALBINUS

Epit.	*Epitome doctrinae platonicae*	*Handbook of Platonism*
Intr.	*Introductio in Platonem*	*Introduction to Plato*

ALEXANDER OF APHRODISIAS

De an.	*De anima*
Comm. An. post.	*In Analytica posteriora commentariorum fragmenta*
Comm. An. pr.	*In Aristotelis Analyticorum priorum librum i commentarium*
Comm. Metaph.	*In Aristotelis Metaphysica commentaria*
Comm. Mete.	*In Aristotelis Meteorologicorum libros commentaria*
Comm. Sens.	*In librum De sensu commentarium*
Comm. Top.	*In Aristotelis Topicorum libros octo commentaria*
Fat.	*De fato*
Mixt.	*De mixtione*
Probl.	*Problemata*

AMBROSE

Abr.	*De Abraham*	
Apol. Dav.	*Apologia prophetae David*	
Aux.	*Sermo contra Auxentium de basilicis tradendis*	
Bon. mort.	*De bono mortis*	Death as a Good
Cain	*De Cain et Abel*	
Enarrat. Ps.	*Enarrationes in XII Psalmos davidicos*	
Exc.	*De excessufratris sui Satyri*	
Exh. virginit.	*Exhortatio virginitatis*	
Fid.	*De fide*	
Exp. Isa.	*Expositio Isaiae prophetae*	
Exp. Luc.	*Expositio Evangelii secundum Lucam*	
Exp. Ps. 118	*Expositio Psalmi CXVIII*	
Expl. symb.	*Explanatio symboli ad initiandos*	
Fid. Grat.	*De fide ad Gratianum*	
Fug.	*De fuga saeculi*	Flight from the World
Hel.	*De Helia et Jejunio*	
Hex.	*Hexaemeron libri sex*	Six Days of Creation
Hymn.	*Hymni*	
Incarn.	*De incarnationis dominicae sacramento*	Sacrament of the Incarnation of the Lord
Instit.	*De institutione virginis*	
Isaac	*De Isaac vel anima*	Isaac, or the Soul
Jac.	*De Jacob et vita beata*	Jacob and the Happy Life
Job	*De interpellatione Job et David*	Prayer of Job and David
Jos.	*De Joseph patriarcha*	
Myst.	*De mysteriis*	The Mysteries
Nab.	*De Nabuthae historia*	
Noe	*De Noe et arca*	
Ob. Theo.	*De obitu Theodosii*	
Ob. Val.	*De obitu Valentiniani consolatio*	
Off.	*De officiis ministrorum*	
Paen.	*De paenitentia*	
Parad.	*De paradiso*	Paradise
Patr.	*De benedictionibus patriarcharum*	The Patriarchs
Sacr.	*De sacramentis*	The Sacraments
Sacr. regen.	*De sacramento regenerationis sive de philosophia*	
Spir.	*De Spiritu Sancto*	The Holy Spirit
Symb.	*Explanatio symboli*	
Tob.	*De Tobia*	

Vid.	*De viduis*	
Virg.	*De virginibus*	
Virginit.	*De virginitate*	

ANAXIMENES OF LAMPSACUS

Rhet. Alex.	*Rhetorica ad Alexandrum (Ars rhetorica)*

ANDRONICUS

[Pass.]	*De passionibus*	*The Passions*

ANTH. PAL.	*Anthologia palatina*	*Palatine Anthology*

ANTH. PLAN.	*Anthologia planudea*	*Planudean Anthology*

ANTONINUS LIBERALIS

Metam.	*Metamorphôseôn synagôgē*

APOLLODORUS

Library	*The Library*

APOLLONIUS OF RHODES

Argon.	*Argonautica*	*Argonautica*

APOLLONIUS SOPHISTA

Lex. hom.	*Lexicon homericum*	*Homeric Lexicon*

APPIAN

Bell. civ.	*Bella civilia*	*Civil Wars*
Hist. rom.	*Historia romana*	*Roman History*

APULEIUS

Apol.	*Apologia (Pro se de magia)*	*Apology*
De deo Socr.	*De deo Socratico*	
Dogm. Plat.	*De dogma Platonis*	
Flor.	*Florida*	
Metam.	*Metamorphoses*	*The Golden Ass*

AQUINAS, THOMAS

ST	*Summa Theologiae*

ARATUS

Phaen.	*Phaenomena*

ARCHIMEDES

Aequil.	*De planorum aequilibriis*	Equilibriums of Planes
Aren.	*Arenarius*	The Sand-reckoner
Assumpt.	*Liber assumptorum*	
Bov.	*Problema bovinum*	
Circ.	*Dimensio circuli*	Measurement of a Circle
Con. sph.	*De conoidibus et sphaeroidibus*	On Conoids and Spheroids
Eratosth.	*Ad Eratosthenem methodus*	To Eratosthenes on the Mechanical Method Theorems
Fluit.	*De corporibus fluitantibus*	On Floating Bodies
Quadr.	*Quadratura parabolae*	Quadrature of the Parabola
Sph. cyl.	*De sphaera et cylindro*	On the Sphere and Cylinder
Spir.	*De lineis spiralibus*	On Spirals
Stom.	*Stomachion*	

ARETAEUS

Cur. acut.	*De curatione acutorum morborum*
Cur. diut.	*De curatione diuturnorum morborum*
Sign. acut.	*De causis et signis acutorum morborum*
Sign. diut.	*De causis et signis diuturnorum morborum*

ARISTOPHANES

Ach.	*Acharnenses*	Acharnians
Av.	*Aves*	Birds
Eccl.	*Ecclesiazusae*	Women of the Assembly
Eq.	*Equites*	Knights
Lys.	*Lysistrata*	Lysistrata
Nub.	*Nubes*	Clouds
Pax	*Pax*	Peace
Plut.	*Plutus*	The Rich Man
Ran.	*Ranae*	Frogs
Thesm.	*Thesmophoriazusae*	
Vesp.	*Vespae*	Wasps

ARISTOTLE

De an.	*De anima*	Soul
An. post.	*Analytica posteriora*	Posterior Analytics
An. pr.	*Analytica priora*	Prior Analytics
Ath. pol.	*Athēnaīn politeia*	Constitution of Athens
[Aud.]	*De audibilibus*	Sounds
Cael.	*De caelo*	Heavens
Cat.	*Categoriae*	Categories
Col.	*De coloribus*	Colors
Div. somn.	*De divinatio per somnum*	Prophesying by Dreams
Ep.	*Epistulae*	Letters
Eth. eud.	*Ethica eudemia*	Eudemian Ethics

Eth. nic.	Ethica nichomachea	Nichomachean Ethics
Gen. an.	De generatione anamalium	Generation of Animals
Gen. corr.	De generatione et corruptione	Generaion of Corruption
Hist. an.	Historia animalium	History of Animals
Inc. an.	De incessu animalium	Gait of Animals
Insomn.	De insomniis	
Int.	De interpretatione	Interpretation
Juv. sen.	De juventute et senectute	Youth and Old Age
[Lin. ins.]	De lineis insecabilibus	Indivisible Lines
Long. brev.	De longitudine et brevitate vitae	Longevity and Shortness of Life
[Mag. mor.]	Magna moralia	
[Mech.]	Mechanica	Mechanics
Mem. rem.	De memoria et reminiscentia	Memory and Reminiscence
Metaph.	Metaphysica	Metaphysics
Mete.	Meteorologica	Meteorology
[Mir. ausc.]	De mirabilibus auscultationibus	On Marvelous Things Heard
Mot. an.	De motu animalium	Movement of Animals
[Mund.]	De mundo	World
[Oec.]	Oeconomica	Economics
Part. an.	De partibus animalium	Parts of Animals
Phys.	Physica	Physics
[Physiogn.]	Physiognomonica	Physiognomonics
[Plant.]	De plantis	Plants
Poet.	Poetica	Poetics
Pol.	Politica	Politics
[Probl.]	Problemata	Problems
Protr.	Protrepticus	
Resp.	De respiratione	Respiration
Rhet.	Rhetorica	Rhetoric
[Rhet. Alex.]	Rhetorica ad Alexandrum	Rhetoric to Alexander
Sens.	De sensuet sensibilibus	Sense and Sensibilia
Somn.	De somniis	Dreams
Somn. vig.	De somno et vigilia	Sleep and Waking
Soph. elench.	Sophistici elenchi	Sophistical Refutations
[Spir.]	De spiritu	Spirit
Top.	Topica	Topics
[Vent.]	De ventorum situ et nominibus	Situations and Names of Winds
[Virt. vit.]	De virtutibus et vitiis	Virtues and Vices
Vit. mort.	De vita et morte	Life and Death
[Gorg.]	De Gorgia	
[Xen.]	De Xenophane	
[Zen.]	De Zenone	

ARRIAN

Anab.	Anabasis
Epict. diss.	Epicteti dissertationes
Peripl. M. Eux.	Periplus Maris Euxini
Tact.	Tactica

ARTEMIDORUS DALDIANUS

Onir.	Onirocritica

ATHANASIUS

Apol. Const.	*Apologia ad Constantium*	*Defense before Constantius*
Apol. sec.	*Apologia secunda (= Apologia contra Arianos)*	*Defense against the Arians*
[Apoll.]	*De incarnatione contra Apollinarium*	*On the Incarnation against Apollinarius*
C. Ar.	*Orationes contra Arianos*	*Orations against the Arians*
C. Gent.	*Contra gentes*	*Against Pagans*
Decr.	*De decretis*	*Defense of the Nicene Definition*
Dion.	*De sententia Dionysii*	*On the Opinion of Dionysius*
Ep. Adelph.	*Epistula ad Adelphium*	*Letter to Adelphius*
Ep. Aeg. Lib.	*Epistula ad episcopos Aegypti et Libyae*	*Letter to the Bishops of Egypt and Libya*
Ep. Afr.	*Epistula ad Afros episcopos*	*Letter to the Bishops of Africa*
Ep. Amun	*Epistula ad Amun*	*Letter to Ammoun*
Ep. cler. Alex.	*Epistula ad clerum Alexandriae*	*Letter to the Clergy of Alexandria*
Ep. cler. Mareot.	*Epistula ad clerum Mareotae*	*Letter to the Clergy of Mareotis*
Ep. Drac.	*Epistula ad Dracontium*	*Letter to Dracontius*
Ep. encycl.	*Epistula encyclica*	*Circular Letter*
Ep. Epict.	*Epistula ad Epictetum*	*Letter to Epictetus*
Ep. fest.	*Epistulae festales*	*Festal Letters*
Ep. Jo. Ant.	*Epistula ad Joannem et Antiochum presbyteros*	*Letter to John and Antiochus*
Ep. Jov.	*Epistula ad Jovianum*	*Letter to Jovian*
Ep. Marcell.	*Epistula ad Marcellinum de interpretatione Psalmorum*	*Letter to Marcellinus on the Interpretation of the Psalms*
Ep. Max.	*Epistula ad Maximum*	*Letter to Maximus*
Ep. mon. 1	*Epistula ad monachos i*	*First Letter to Monks*
Ep. mon. 2	*Epistula ad monachos ii*	*Second Letter to Monks*
Ep. mort. Ar.	*Epistula ad Serapionem de more Arii*	*Letter to Seapion Concerning Death of Arius*
Ep. Ors. 1	*Epistula ad Orsisium i*	*First Letter to Orsisius*
Ep. Ors. 2	*Epistula ad Orsisium ii*	*Second Letter to Orsisius*
Ep. Pall.	*Epistula ad Palladium*	*Letter to Palladius*
Ep. Rufin.	*Epistula ad Rufinianum*	*Letter to Rufinianus*
Ep. Serap.	*Epistulae ad Serapionem*	*Letters to serapion concerning the Holy Spirit*
Ep. virg. (Copt.)	*Epistula ad virgines (Coptice)*	*First (Coptic) Letter to Virgins*
Ep. virg. (Syr.)	*Epistula ad virgines (Syriace)*	*Second (Syriac) Letter to Virgins*
Ep. virg. (Syr./Arm.)	*Epistula ad virgines (Syriace et Armeniace)*	*Letter to Virgins*
Ep. virg. (Theod.)	*Epistula exhortatora ad virgines apud Theodoretum*	*Letter to Virgins*
Fug.	*Apologia de fuga sua*	*Defense of His Flight*
H. Ar.	*Historia Arianorum*	*History of the Arians*
Hen. sōm.	*Henos sōmatos*	*Encyclical Letter of Alexander concerning the Deposition of Arius*
Hom. Jo. 12:27	*In illud Nunc anima mea turbata est*	*Homily on John 12:27*
Hom. Luc. 12:10	*In illud Qui dixerit verbum in filium*	*Homily on Luke 12:10*
Hom. Matt. 11:27	*In illud Omnia mihi tradita sunt*	*Homily on Matt 11:27*
Inc.	*De incarnatione*	*On the Incarnation*
Mor. et val.	*De morbo et valitudine*	*On Sickness and Health*
Narr. fug.	*Narratio ad Ammonium episcopum de fuga sua*	*Report of Athanasius concerning Theodorus*
Syn.	*De synodis*	*On the Councils of Arimimum and Seleucia*
Tom.	*Tomus ad Antiochenos*	*Tome to the People of Antioch*
Vit. Ant.	*Vita Antonii*	*Life of Antony*

ATHENAEUS

    Deipn.   *Deipnosophistae*

ATHENAGORAS

    Leg.   *Legatio pro Christianis*
    Res.   *De resurrectione*

AUGUSTINE

Acad.	*Contra Academicos*	*Against the Academics*
Adim.	*Contra Adimantum*	*Agaiinst Adimantus*
Adnot. Job	*Adnotationum in Job liber I*	*Annotations on Job*
Adv. Jud.	*Tractatus adversus Judaeos*	*In Answer to the Jews*
Agon.	*De agone christiano*	*Christian Combat*
An. orig.	*De anima et eius origine*	*The Soul and Its Origin*
Arian.	*Contra sermonem Arianorum*	
Bapt.	*De baptismo contra Donatistas*	
Beat.	*De vita beata*	*Baptism*
Bon. conj.	*De bono conjugali*	*The Good Marriage*
Brev. coll.	*Breviculus collationis cum Donatistas*	
C. du. ep. Pelag.	*Contra duas epistulas Pelagianorum ad Bonifatium*	*Against the Two Letters of the Pelagians*
C. Jul.	*Contra Julianum*	*Against Julian*
C. Jul. op. imp.	*Contra secundam Juliani responsionem imperfectum opus*	*Against Julian: Opus Imperfectum*
C. litt. Petil.	*Contra litteras Petiliani*	
C. mend.	*Contra mendacium*	*Against Lying (to Consentius)*
Catech.	*De catechizandis rudibus*	*Catechizing the Uninstructed*
Civ.	*De civitate Dei*	*The City of God*
Coll. Max.	*Collatio cum Maximino Arianorum episcopo*	
Conf.	*Confessionum libri XIII*	*Confessions*
Cons.	*De consensu evangelistarum*	*Harmony of the Gospels*
Contin.	*De continentia*	*Continence*
Corrept.	*De correptione et gratia*	*Admonition and Grace*
Cresc.	*Contra Cresconium Donatistam*	
Cur.	*De cura pro mortuis gerenda*	*The Care to Be Taken for the Dead*
Dial.	*Principia dialecticae*	
Disc.	*De disciplina christiana*	
Div.	*De divinitate daemonum*	*The Divination of Demons*
Div. quaest. LXXXIII	*De diversis quaestionibus LXXXIII*	*Eighty-three Different Questions*
Div. quaest. Simpl.	*De diversis quaestionibus ad Simplicianum*	
Doctr. chr.	*De doctrina christiana*	*Christian Instruction*
Don.	*Post collationem adversus Donatistas*	
Duab.	*De duabus animabus*	*Two Souls*
Dulc.	*De octo Dulcitii quaestionibus*	*The Eight Questions of Dulcitius*
Emer.	*De gestis cum Emerino*	
Enarrat. Ps.	*Enarrationes in Psalmos*	*Enarrations on the Psalms*
Enchir.	*Enchiridion de fide, spe, et caritate*	*Enchiridion on Faith, Hope, and Love*
Exp. Gal.	*Expositio in epistulam ad Galatas*	
Exp. quaest. Rom.	*Expositio quarumdam quaestionum in epistula ad Romanos*	

Faust.	*Contra Faustum Manichaeum*	*Against Faustus the Manichaean*
Fel.	*Contra Felicem*	*Against Felix*
Fid.	*De fide rerum quae non videntur*	*Faith in Thiings Unseen*
Fid. op.	*De fide et operibus*	*Faith and Works*
Fid. symb.	*De fide et symbolo*	*Faith and the Creed*
Fort.	*Contra Fortunatum*	*Against Fortunatus*
Fund.	*Contra epistulam Manichaei quam vocant Fundamenti*	*Against the Letter of the Manichaeans That They Call "The Basics"*
Gaud.	*Contra Gaudentium Donatistarum episcopum*	*Against Gaudentius the Donatist Bishop*
Gen. imp.	*De Genesi ad litteram imperfectus liber*	*On the Literal Interpretation of Genesis: An Unfinished Book*
Gen. litt.	*De Genesi ad litteram*	*On Genesis Litarally Interpreted*
Gen. Man.	*De Genesi contra Manichaeos*	*On Genesis Against the Manicheans*
Gest. Pelag.	*De gestis Pelagii*	*Proceedings of Pelagius*
Gramm.	*De grammatica*	
Grat.	*De gratia et libero arbitrio*	*Grace and Free Will*
Grat. Chr.	*De gratia Christi, et de peccato originali*	*The Grace of Christ and Original Sin*
Haer.	*De haeresibus*	*Heresies*
Immort. an.	*De immortalitate animae*	*The Immortality of the Soul*
Incomp. nupt.	*De incompetentibus nuptiis*	*Adulterous Marriages*
Leg.	*Contra adversarium legis et prophetarum*	
Lib.	*De libero arbitrio*	*Free Will*
Locut. Hept.	*Locutionum in Heptateuchum libri septem*	
Mag.	*De magistro*	
Man.	*De moribus Manichaeorum*	*The Morals of the Manichaeans*
Maxim.	*Contra Maximinum Arianum*	*Against Maximimus the Arian*
De mend.	*De mendacio*	*On Lying*
Mor. eccl.	*De moribus ecclesiae catholicae*	*The Way of Life of the Catholic Church*
Mor. Manich.	*De moribus Manichaeorum*	*The Way of the Life of the Manichaeans*
Mus.	*De musica*	*Music*
Nat. bon.	*De natura boni contra Manichaeos*	*The Nature of the Good*
Nat. grat.	*De natura et gratia*	*Nature and Grace*
Nat. orig.	*De natura et origine animae*	*The Nature and Origin of the Soul*
Nupt.	*De nuptiis et concupiscentia ad Valerium comitem*	*Marriage and Concupiscence*
Oct. quaest. Vet. Test.	*De octo quaestionibus ex Veteri Testamento*	*Eight Questions from the Old Testament*
Op. mon.	*De opere monachorum*	*The Work of Monks*
Ord.	*De ordine*	
Parm.	*Contra epistulam Parmeniani*	
Pat.	*De patientia*	*Patience*
Pecc. merit.	*De peccatorum meritis et remissione*	*Guilt and Remission of Sins*
Pecc. orig.	*De peccato originali*	*Original sin*
Perf.	*De perfectione justitiae hominis*	*Perfection in Human Righteousness*
Persev.	*De dono perseverantiae*	*The Gift of Perseverance*
Praed.	*De praedestinatione sanctorum*	*The Predestination of the Saints*
Priscill.	*Ad Orosium contra Priscillianistas et Origenistas*	*To Orosius against the Priscillianists and the Origenists*
Psal. Don.	*Psalmus contra partem Donati*	
Quaest. ev.	*Quaestionum evangelicarum libri II*	

Quaest. Hept.	Quaestiones in Heptateuchum	
Quaest. Matt.	Quaestiones in evangelium Matthaei	
Quant. an.	De quantitate animae	The Magnitude of the Soul
Reg.	Regula ad servos Dei	
Retract.	Retractationum libri II	Retractions
Rhet.	De rhetorica, Rhetores Latini	
Secund.	Contra Secundinum Manichaeum	
Serm.	Sermones	
Serm. Dom.	De sermone Domini in monte	Sermon on the Mount
Solil.	Soliloquiorum libri II	Soliloquies
Spec.	De scriptura sancta speculum	
Spir. et litt.	De spiritu et littera	The Spirit and the Letter
Symb.	De symbolo ad catechumenos	The Creed: For Catechumens
Tract. ep. Jo.	In epistulam Johannis ad Parthos tractatus	Tractates on the First Epistle of John
Tract. Ev. Jo.	In Evangelium Johannis tractatus	Tractates on the Gospel of John
Trin.	De Trinitate	The Trinity
Unic. bapt.	De unico baptismo	
Unit. eccl.	De unitate ecclesiae	The Unity of the Church
Util. cred.	De utilitate credendi	The Usefulness of Believing
Util. jej.	De utilitate jejunii	The Usefulness of Fasting
Ver. rel.	De vera religione	True Religion
Vid.	De bono viduitatis	The Excellence of Widowhood
Virginit.	De sancta virginitate	Holy virginity
Vit. Christ.	De vita christiana	The Christian Life

Aulus Gellius

Bell. afr.	Bellum africum	African War
Bell. alex.	Bellum alexandrinum	Alexandrian War
Noct. att.	Noctes atticae	Attic Nights

Bede

Eccl. Hist.	Ecclesiastical History of the English People

Berossus

Hist.	History of Babylon

Bion

Epitaph. Adon.	Epitaphius Adonis	Lament for Adonis
[Epith. Achil.]	Epithalamium Achillis et Deidameiae	To Achilles and Deidamea

Caesar

Bell. civ.	Bellum civile	Civil War
Bell. gall.	Bellum gallicum	Gallic War

Callimachus

Aet.	Aetia (in P.Oxy. 2079)	Causes

Epigr.	Epigrammata	Epigrams
Hec.	Hecala	Hecale
Hymn.	Hymni	Hymns
Hymn. Apoll.	Hymnus in Apollinem	Hymn to Apollo
Hymn. Cer.	Hymnus in Cererem	Hymn to Ceres or Demeter
Hymn. Del.	Hymnus in Delum	Hymn to Delos
Hymn. Dian.	Hymnus in Dianam	Hymn to Diana or Artemis
Hymn. Jov.	Hymnus in Jovem	Hymn to Jove or Zeus
Hymn. lav. Pall.	Hymnus in lavacrum Palladis	Hymn to the Baths of Pallas

CAN. AP. Canones apostolicae Apostolic Canons

CATO

Agr.	De agricultura (De re rustica)	Agriculture
Orig.	Origines	Origins

CEB. TAB. Cebetis Tabula

CHARITON

Chaer.	De Chaerea et Callirhoe	Chaereas and Callirhoe

CHRYSOSTOM (See John Chrysostom)

CICERO

Acad.	Academicae quaestiones
Acad. post.	Academica posteriora (Lucullus)
Acad. pr.	Academica priora
Agr.	De Lege agraria
Amic.	De amicitia
Arch.	Pro Archia
Att.	Epistulae ad Atticum
Aug.	De auguriis
Balb.	Pro Balbo
Brut.	Brutus or De claris oratoribus
Caecin.	Pro Caecina
Cael.	Pro Caelio
Cat.	In Catalinam
Clu.	Pro Cluentio
Corn.	Pro Cornelio de maiestate
Deiot.	Pro rege Deiotaro
Div.	De divinatione
Div. Caec.	Divinatio in Caecilium
Dom.	De domo suo
Ep. Brut.	Epistulae ad Brutum
Epigr.	Epigrammata
Fam.	Epistulae ad familiares
Fat.	De fato
Fin.	De finibus
Flac.	Pro Flacco
Font.	Pro Fonteio

Har. resp.	De haruspicum responso
Inv.	De inventione rhetorica
Leg.	De legibus
Leg. man.	Pro Lege manilia (De imperio Cn. Pompeii)
Lig.	Pro Ligario
Lim.	Limon
Mar.	Marius
Marcell.	Pro Marcello
Mil.	Pro Milone
Mur.	Pro Murena
Nat. d.	De natura deorum
Off.	De officiis
Opt. gen.	De optimo genere oratorum
De or.	De oratore
Or. Brut.	Orator ad M. Brutum
Parad.	Paradoxa Stoicorum
Part. or.	Partitiones oratoriae
Phil.	Orationes philippicae
Pis.	In Pisonem
Planc.	Pro Plancio
Prov. cons.	De provinciis consularibus
Quinct.	Pro Quinctio
Quint. fratr.	Epistulae ad Quintum fratrem
Rab. Perd.	Pro Rabirio Perduellionis Reo
Rab. Post.	Pro Rabirio Postumo
Red. pop.	Post reditum ad populum
Red. sen.	Post reditum in senatu
Rep.	De republica
Rosc. Amer.	Pro Sexto Roscio Amerino
Rosc. com.	Pro Roscio comoedo
Scaur.	Pro Scauro
Sen.	De senectute
Sest.	Pro Sestio
Sull.	Pro Sulla
Tim.	Timaeus
Tog. cand.	Oratio in senatu in toga candida
Top.	Topica
Tull.	Pro Tullio
Tusc.	Tusculanae disputationes
Vat.	In Vatinium
Verr.	In Verrem

CLEMENT OF ALEXANDRIA

Ecl.	Eclogae propheticae	Extracts from the Prophets
Exc.	Excerpta ex Theodoto	Excerpts from Theodotus
Paed.	Paedagogus	Christ the Educator
Protr.	Protrepticus	Exhortation to the Greeks
Quis div.	Quis dives salvetur	Salvation of the Rich
Strom.	Stromata	Miscellanies

COD. JUSTIN.	Codex justinianus

COD. THEOD.	*Codex theodosianus*	

COLUMELLA

Arb.	*De arboribus*	
Rust.	*De re rustica*	

CONST. AP.	*Constitutiones apostolicae*	*Apostolic Constitutions*

CORNUTUS

Nat. d.	*De natura deorum (Epidrōme tō n kata tēn Hellēniken theologian paradedomenōn)*	*Summary of the Traditions concerning Greek Mythology*

CORP. HERM.	*Corpus hermeticum*	

COSMAS INDICOPLEUSTES

Top.	*Topographia christiana*	*Christian Topography*

CYPRIAN

Demetr.	*Ad Demetrianum*	*To Demetrian*
Dom. or.	*De dominica oratione*	*The Lord's Supper*
Don.	*Ad Donatum*	*To Donatus*
Eleem.	*De opere et eleemosynis*	*Works and Almsgiving*
Fort.	*Ad Fortunatum*	*To Fortunatus: Exhortation to Martyrdom*
Hab. virg.	*De habitu virginum*	*The Dress of Virgins*
[Idol.]	*Quod idola dii non sint*	*That Idols Are Not Gods*
Laps.	*De lapsis*	*The Lapsed*
Mort.	*De mortalitate*	*Mortality*
Pat.	*De bono patientiae*	*The Advantage of Patience*
Sent.	*Sententiae episcoporum de haereticis baptizandis*	
Test.	*Ad Quirinum testimonia adversus Judaeos*	*To Quirinius: Testimonies against the Jews*
Unit. eccl.	*De catholicae ecclesiae unitate*	*The Unity of the Catholic Church*
Zel. liv.	*De zelo et livore*	*Jealousy and Envy*

DEMETRIUS

Eloc.	*De elocutione (Peri hermeneias)*	*Style*

DEMOSTHENES

Andr.	*Adversus Androtionem*	*Against Androtion*
[Apat.]	*Contra Apatourium*	*Against Apaturius*
1–3 Aphob.	*In Aphobum*	*1–3 Against Aphobus*
Aristocr.	*In Aristocratem*	*Against Aristocrates*

1–2 Aristog.	In Aristogitonem	1–2 Against Aristogeiton
1 [2] Boeot.	Contra Boeotum i–ii	1–2 Against Boeotos
C. Phorm.	Contra Phormionem	Against Phormio
Call.	Contra Calliclem	Against Callicles
[Callip.]	Contra Callipum	Against Callipus
Chers.	De Chersoneso	On the Chersonese
Con.	In Cononem	Against Canon
Cor.	De corona	On the Crown
Cor. trier.	De corona trierarchiae	On the Trierarchic Crown
[Dionys.]	Contra Dionysodorum	Against Dionysodorus
Epitaph.	Epitaphius	Funeral Oration
[Erot.]	Eroticus	Eroticus
Eub.	Contra Eubulidem	Against Eubulides
[Everg.]	In Evergum et Mnesibulum	Against Evergus and Mnesibulus
Exord.	Exordia (Prooemia)	
Fals. leg.	De falsa legatione	False Embassy
Halon.	De Halonneso	On the Halonnesus
[Lacr.]	Contra Lacritum	Against Lacritus
[Leoch.]	Contra Leocharem	Against Leochares
Lept.	Adversus Leptinem	Against Leptines
[Macart.]	Contra Macartatum	Against Macartatus
Meg.	Pro Megalopolitanis	For the Megalopolitans
Mid.	In Midiam	Against Meidias
Naus.	Contra Nausimachum et Xenopeithea	Against Nausimachus
[Neaer.]	In Neaeram	Against Neaera
Nicostr.	Contra Nicostratum	Against Nicostratus
[Olymp.]	In Olympiodorum	Agaiinst Olympiodorus
1–3 Olynth.	Olynthiaca i–iii	1–3 Olynthiac
1–2 Onet.	Contra Onetorem	1–2 Against Onetor
De pace	De pace	On the Peace
Pant.	Contra Pantaenetum	Against Pantaenetus
1–3 [4] Philip.	Philippica i–iv	1–4 Philippic
Pro Phorm.	Pro Phormione	For Phormio
[Poly.]	Contra Polyclem	Against Polycles
Rhod. lib.	De Rhodiorum libertate	On the Liberty of the Rhodians
Spud.	Contra Spudiam	Against Spudia
1 [2] Steph.	In Stephanum i–ii	1–2 Against Stephanus
Symm.	De symmoriis	On the Symmories
[Syntax.]	Peri syntaxeôs	On Organization
[Theocr.]	In Theocrinem	Against Theocrines
[Tim.]	Contra Timotheum	Against Timotheus
Timocr.	In Timocratem	Against Timocrates
Zenoth.	Contra Zenothemin	Against Zenothemis

DIDYMUS

Comm. Eccl.	Commentarii in Ecclesiasten
Comm. Job	Commentarii in Job
Comm. Oct. Reg.	Commentarii in Octateuchum et Reges
Comm. Ps.	Commentarii in Psalmos
Comm. Zach.	Commentarii in Zachariam
Dial. haer.	Dialogus Didymi Caeci cum haeretico
Enarrat. Ep. Cath.	In Epistulas Catholicas brevis enarratio
Fr. Cant.	Fragmentum in Canticum canticorum

Fr. 1 Cor.	*Fragmenta in Epistulam i ad Corinthios*	
Fr. 2 Cor.	*Fragmenta in Epistulam ii ad Corinthios*	
Fr. Heb.	*Fragmentum in Epistulam ad Hebraeos*	
Fr. Jer.	*Fragmenta in Jeremiam*	
Fr. Jo.	*Fragmenta in Joannem*	
Fr. Prov.	*Fragmenta in Proverbia*	
Fr. Ps.	*Fragmenta in Psalmos*	
Fr. Rom.	*Fragmenta in Epistulam ad Romanos*	
In Gen.	*In Genesim*	
Incorp.	*De incorporeo*	
Man.	*Contra Manichaeos*	
Philos.	*Ad philosophum*	
Trin.	*De Trinitate*	

Dig.

Dig.	*Digesta*

Dinarchus

Aristog.	*In Aristogitonem*	*Against Aristogiton*
Demosth.	*In Demosthenem*	*Against Demosthenes*
Phil.	*In Philoclem*	*Against Philocles*

Dio (Cassius Dio)

Rom.	*Romaika*

Dio Chrysostom

Achill.	*Achilles (Or. 58)*	*Achilles and Cheiron*
Admin.	*De administratione (Or. 50)*	*His Past Record*
Aegr.	*De aegritudine (Or. 16)*	*Pain and Distress of Spirit*
Alex.	*Ad Alexandrinos (Or. 32)*	*To the People of Alexandria*
Apam.	*Ad Apamenses (Or. 41)*	*To the Apameians*
Aud. aff.	*De audiendi affectione (Or. 19)*	*Fondness for Listening*
Avar.	*De avaritia (Or. 17)*	*Covetousness*
Borysth.	*Borysthenitica (Or. 36)*	*Borysthenic Discourse*
Cel. Phryg.	*Celaenis Phrygiae (Or. 35)*	*At Celaenae in Phrygia*
Charid.	*Charidemus (Or. 30)*	
Chrys.	*Chryseis (Or. 61)*	
Compot.	*De compotatione (Or. 27)*	*Symposia*
Conc. Apam.	*De concordia cum Apamensibus (Or. 40)*	*On Concord with Apamea*
Consuet.	*De consuetudine (Or. 76)*	*Custom*
Consult.	*De consultatione (Or. 26)*	*Deliberation*
Cont.	*Contio (Or. 47)*	*In the Public Assembly at Prusa*
In cont.	*In contione (Or. 48)*	*Political Address in the Assembly*
[Cor.]	*Corinthiaca (Or. 37)*	*Corinthian Discourse*
Def.	*Defensio (Or. 45)*	*Defense*
Dei cogn.	*De dei cognitione (Or. 12)*	*Olympic Discourse*
Dial.	*Dialexis (Or. 42)*	*In His Native City*
Dic. exercit.	*De dicendi exercitatione (Or. 18)*	*Training for Public Speaking*

Diffid.	De diffidentia (Or. 74)	Distrust
Diod.	Ad Diodorum (Or. 51)	To Diodorus
Divit.	De divitiis (Or. 79)	Wealth
Exil.	De exilio (Or. 13)	Banishment
Fel.	De felicitate (Or. 24)	Happiness
Fel. sap.	De quod felix sit sapiens (Or. 23)	The Wise Man is Happy
Fid.	De fide (Or. 73)	Trust
1 Fort.	De fortuna i (Or. 63)	Fortune 1
2 Fort.	De fortuna ii (Or. 64)	Fortune 2
3 Fort.	De fortuna iii (Or. 65)	Fortune 3
Gen.	De genio (Or. 25)	The Guiding Spirit
1 Glor.	De gloria i (Or. 66)	Reputation
2 Glor.	De gloria ii (Or. 67)	Popular Opinion
3 Glor.	De gloria iii (Or. 68)	Opinion
Grat.	Gratitudo (Or. 44)	Friendship for Native Land
Hab.	De habitu (Or. 72)	Personal Appearance
Hom.	De Homero (Or. 53)	Homer
Hom. Socr.	De Homero et Socrate (Or. 55)	Homer and Socrates
Invid.	De invidia (Or. 77/78)	Envy
Isthm.	Isthmiaca (Or. 9)	Isthmian Discourse
De lege	De lege (Or. 75)	Law
Lib.	De libertate (Or. 80)	Freedom
Lib. myth.	Libycus mythos (Or. 5)	A Libyan Myth
1 Melanc.	Melancomas i (Or. 29)	Melancomas 1
2 Melanc.	Melancomas ii (Or. 28)	Melancomas 2
Ness.	Nessus (Or. 60)	Nessus, or Deianeira
Nest.	Nestor (Or. 57)	Homer's Portrayal of Nestor
Nicaeen.	Ad Nicaeenses (Or. 39)	To the Nicaeans
Nicom.	Ad Nicomedienses (Or. 38)	To the Nicomedians
De pace	De pace et bello (Or. 22)	Peace and War
Philoct. arc.	De Philoctetae arcu (Or. 52)	Appraisal of the Tragic Triad
Philoct.	Philoctetes (Or. 59)	
De philosophia	De philosophia (Or. 70)	Philosophy
De philosopho	De philosopho (Or. 71)	The Philosopher
Pol.	Politica (Or. 43)	Political Address
Pulchr.	De pulchritudine (Or. 21)	Beauty
Rec. mag.	Recusatio magistratus (Or. 49)	Refusal of the Office of Archon
Regn.	De regno (Or. 56)	Kingship
1 Regn.	De regno i (Or. 1)	Kingship 1
2 Regn.	De regno ii (Or. 2)	Kingship 2
3 Regn.	De regno iii (Or. 3)	Kingship 3
4 Regn.	De regno iv (Or. 4)	Kingship 4
Regn. tyr.	De regno et tyrannide (Or. 62)	Kingship and Tyranny
Rhod.	Rhodiaca (Or. 31)	To the People of Rhodes
Sec.	De secessu (Or. 20)	Retirement
Serv.	De servis (Or. 10)	Servants
1 Serv. lib.	De servitute et libertate i (Or. 14)	Slavery and Freedom 1
2 Serv. lib.	De servitute et libertate ii (Or. 15)	Slavery and Freedom 2
Socr.	De Socrate (Or. 54)	Socrates
1 Tars.	Tarsica prior (Or. 33)	First Tarsic Discourse
2 Tars.	Tarsica altera (Or. 34)	Second Tarsic Discourse
Troj.	Trojana (Or. 11)	Trojan Discourse
Tumult.	De tumultu (Or. 46)	Protest against Mistreatment
Tyr.	De tyrannide (Or. 6)	On Tyranny, or Diogenes
Ven.	Venator (Or. 7)	The Hunter
Virt. (Or. 8)	De virtute (Or. 8)	Virtue

Virt. (Or. 69)	*De virtute (Or. 69)*	*Virtue*

DIO OF PRUSA

Dis.	*Discourse*

DIODORUS SICULUS

Bib. Hist.	*Biblioteca Historica*

DIOGENES LAERTIUS

Vit. Phil.	*Vitae philosophorum*	*Lives of the Philosophers*

DIONYSIUS OF HALICARNASSUS

1–2 Amm.	*Epistula ad Ammaeum i–ii*
Ant. or.	*De antiquis oratoribus*
Ant. rom.	*Antiquitates romanae*
Comp.	*De compositione verborum*
Dem.	*De Demosthene*
Din.	*De Dinarcho*
Is.	*De Isaeo*
Isocr.	*De Isocrate*
Lys.	*De Lysia*
Pomp.	*Epistula ad Pompeium Geminum*
[Rhet.]	*Ars rhetorica*
Thuc.	*De Thucydide*
Thuc. id.	*De Thucydidis idiomatibus*

DIOSCORIDES PEDANIUS

[Alex.]	*Alexipharmaca*
Mat. med.	*De materia medica*

EPICTETUS

Diatr.	*Diatribai (Dissertationes)*
Ench.	*Enchiridion*
Gnom.	*Gnomologium*

EPIPHANIUS

Pan.	*Panarion (Adversus haereses)*	*Refutation of All Heresies*

EURIPIDES

Alc.	*Alcestis*	
Andr.	*Andromache*	
Bacch.	*Bacchae*	*Bacchanals*

Cycl.	*Cyclops*	
Dict.	*Dictys*	
El.	*Electra*	
Hec.	*Hecuba*	
Hel.	*Helena*	*Helen*
Heracl.	*Heraclidae*	*Children of Hercules*
Herc. fur.	*Hercules furens*	*Madness of Hercules*
Hipp.	*Hippolytus*	
Hyps.	*Hypsipyle*	
Iph. aul.	*Iphigenia aulidensis*	*Iphigenia at Aulis*
Iph. taur.	*Iphigenia taurica*	*Iphigenia at Tauris*
Med.	*Medea*	*Medea*
Orest.	*Orestes*	*Phoenician Maidens*
Phoen.	*Phoenissae*	
Rhes.	*Rhesus*	
Suppl.	*Supplices*	
Tro.	*Troades*	*Daughters of Troy*

EUSEBIUS

Chron.	*Chronicon*	*Chronicle*
Coet. sanct.	*Ad coetum sanctorum*	*To the Assembly of Saints*
Comm. Isa.	*Commentarius in Isaiam*	*Commentary on Isaiah*
Comm. Ps.	*Commentarius in Psalmos*	*Commentary on Psalms*
Dem. ev.	*Demonstratio evangelica*	*Demonstration of the Gospel*
Eccl. theol.	*De ecclesiastica theologia*	*Ecclesiastical Theology*
Ecl. proph.	*Eclogae propheticae*	*Extracts from the Prophets*
Hier.	*Contra Hieroclem*	*Against Hierocles*
Hist. eccl.	*Historia ecclesiastica*	*Church History*
Laud. Const.	*De laudibus Constantini*	*Praise of Constantine*
Marc.	*Contra Marcellum*	*Against Marcellus*
Mart. Pal.	*De martyribus Palaestinae*	*The Martyrs of Palestine*
Onom.	*Onomasticon*	*List of Names*
Praep. ev.	*Praeparatio evangelica*	*Preparations for the Gospel*
Theoph.	*Theophania*	*Divine Manifestation*
Vit. Const.	*Vita Constantini*	*Life of Constantine*

FIRMICUS MATERNUS

Err. prof. rel.	*De errore profanarum religionum*
Math.	*Mathesis*

FLORUS

Epit.	*Epitome of Roman History*

GAIUS

Inst.	*Institutiones*

GALEN

Simp. Med.	*De simplicium medicamentorum temperamentis ac facultatibus*

GORGIAS

Hel.	*Helena*
Pal.	*Palamedes*

GREGORY OF NAZIANZUS

Ep.	*Epistulae*
Or. Bas.	*Oratio in laudem Basilii*

GREGORY OF NYSSA
Deit.	*De deitate Filii et Spiritus Sancti*

GREGORY THE GREAT

Moral.	*Expositio in Librum Job, sive*	*Moralia*
	Moralium libri xxv	

HELIODORUS

Aeth.	*Aethiopica*

HERACLITUS

All.	*Allegoriae (Quaestiones homericae)*

HERODOTUS

Hist.	*Historiae*	*Histories*

HESIOD

Op.	*Opera et dies*	*Works and Days*
[Scut.]	*Scutum*	*Shield*
Theog.	*Theogonia*	*Theogony*

HIERONYMUS (See Jerome)

HIPPOCRATES

Acut.	*De ratione victus in morbis acutis*	*Regimen in Acute Diseases*
Aff.	*De affectionibus*	*Affections*
Alim.	*De alimento*	*Nutriment*
Aph.	*Aphorismata*	*Aphorisms*
Arte	*De arte*	*The Art*
Artic.	*De articulis reponendis*	*Joints*
Carn.	*De carne*	*Fleshes*
Coac.	*Praenotiones coacae*	
Decent.	*De habitu decenti*	*Decorum*
Dent.	*De dentitione*	*Dentition*
Epid.	*Epidemiae*	*Epidemics*

Fist.	Fistulae	Fistulas
Fract.	De fracturis	Fractures
Genit.	Genitalia	Genitals
Int.	De affectionibus internis	Internal Affections
Jusj.	Jus jurandum	The Oath
Lex	Lex	Law
Liq.	De liquidorum usu	Use of Liquids
Loc. hom.	De locis in homine	Places in Man
Med.	De medico	The Physician
Mochl.	Mochlichon	Instruments of Reduction
Morb.	De morbis	Diseases
Morb. sacr.	De morbo sacro	The Sacred Disease
Mul.	De morbis mulierum	Female Diseases
Nat. hom.	De natura hominis	Nature of Man
Nat. mul.	De natura muliebri	Nature of Woman
Nat. puer.	De natura pueri	Nature of the Chile
Oct.	De octimestri partu	
Off.	De officina medici	In the Surgery
Praec.	Praeceptiones	Precepts
Progn.	Prognostica	Prognostic
Prorrh.	Prorrhetica	Prorrhetic
Septim.	De septimestri partu	
Steril.	De sterilitate	Sterility
Vet. med.	De vetere medicina	Ancient Medicine
Vict.	De victu	Regimen
Vict. salubr.	De ratione victus salubris	Regimen in Health

HIPPOLYTUS

Antichr.	De antichristo	
Ben. Is. Jac.	De benedictionibus Isaaci et Jacobi	
Can. pasch.	Canon paschalis	
In Cant.	In Canticum canticorum	
Cant. Mos.	In canticum Mosis	
Chron.	Chronicon	
Comm. Dan.	Commentarium in Danielem	
Fr. Prov.	Fragmenta in Proverbia	
Fr. Ps.	Fragmenta in Psalmos	
Haer.	Refutatio omnium haeresium (Philosophoumena)	Refutation of All Heresies
Helc. Ann.	In Helcanam et Annam	
Noet.	Contra haeresin Noeti	
Trad. ap.	Traditio apostolica	The Apostolic Tradition
Univ.	De universo	

HOMER

Il.	Ilias	Iliad
Od.	Odyssea	Odyssey

HORACE

Ars	Ars poetica	
Carm.	Carmina	Odes
Ep.	Epistulae	Epistles
Epod.	Epodi	Epodes

Saec.	*Carmen saeculare*	
Sat.	*Satirae*	*Satires*

Iamblichus

Vit. Pyth.	*Vita Pythagorae*

Inscrip. Lat. Sel.

Inscriptiones Latinae Selectae (H. Dessau, ed.)

Irenaeus

Epid.	*Epideixis tou apostolikou kerygmatos*	*Demonstration of the Apostolic Preaching*
Haer.	*Adversus haereses*	*Against Heresies*

Isocrates

Aeginet.	*Aegineticus (Or. 19)*	
Antid.	*Antidosis (Or. 15)*	
Archid.	*Archidamus (Or. 6)*	
Areop.	*Areopagiticus (Or. 7)*	
Big.	*De bigis (Or. 16)*	*On the Team of Horses*
Bus.	*Busiris (Or. 11)*	
Callim.	*In Callimachum (Or. 18)*	*Agaiinst Callimachus*
De pace	*De pace (Or. 8)*	
Demon.	*Ad Demonicum (Or. 1)*	
Ep.	*Epistulae*	
Euth.	*In Euthynum (Or. 21)*	
Evag.	*Evagoras (Or. 9)*	
Hel. enc.	*Helenae encomium (Or. 10)*	
Loch.	*In Lochitum (Or. 20)*	
Nic.	*Nicocles (Or. 3)*	
Ad Nic.	*Ad Nicoclem (Or. 2)*	
Panath.	*Panathenaicus (Or. 12)*	
Paneg.	*Panegyricus (Or. 4)*	
Phil.	*Philippus (Or. 5)*	
Plat.	*Plataicus (Or. 14)*	
Soph.	*In sophistas (Or. 13)*	
Trapez.	*Trapeziticus (Or. 17)*	*On the Banker*

Jerome

Chron.	*Chronicon Eusebii a Graeco Latine redditum et continuatum*
Comm. Abd.	*Commentariorum in Abdiam liber*
Comm. Agg.	*Commentariorum in Aggaeum liber*
Comm. Am.	*Commentariorum in Amos libri III*
Comm. Eccl.	*Commentarii in Ecclesiasten*
Comm. Eph.	*Commentariorum in Epistulam ad Ephesios libri III*
Comm. Ezech.	*Commentariorum in Ezechielem libri XVI*
Comm. Gal.	*Commentariorum in Epistulam ad Galatas libri III*
Comm. Habac.	*Commentariorum in Habacuc libri II*
Comm. Isa.	*Commentariorum in Isaiam libri XVIII*
Comm. Jer.	*Commentariorum in Jeremiam libri VI*

Comm. Joel.	*Commentariorum in Joelem liber*
Comm. Jon.	*Commentariorum in Jonam liber*
Comm. Mal.	*Commentariorum in Malachiam liber*
Comm. Matt.	*Commentariorum in Matthaeum libri IV*
Comm. Mich.	*Commentariorum in Michaeum libri II*
Comm. Nah.	*Commentariorum in Nahum liber*
Comm. Os.	*Commentariorum in Osee libri III*
Comm. Phlm.	*Commentariorum in Epistulam ad Philemonem liber*
Comm. Ps.	*Commentarioli in Psalmos*
Comm. Soph.	*Commentariorum in Sophoniam libri III*
Comm. Tit.	*Commentariorum in Epistulam ad Titum liber*
Comm. Zach.	*Commentariorum in Zachariam libri III*
Did. Spir.	*Liber Didymi de Spiritu Sancto*
Epist.	*Epistulae*
Expl. Dan.	*Explanatio in Danielem*
Helv.	*Adversus Helvidium de Mariae virginitate perpetua*
Hom. Matth.	*Homilia in Evangelium secundum Matthaeum*
Interp. Job	*Libri Job versio, textus hexaplorum*
Jo. Hier.	*Adversus Joannem Hierosolymitanum liber*
Jov.	*Adversus Jovinianum libri II*
Lucif.	*Altercatio Luciferiani et orthodoxi seu dialogus contra Luciferianos*
Mon. Pachom.	*Monitorum Pachomii versio latina*
Monogr.	*Tractatus de monogrammate*
Nom. hebr.	*De nominibus hebraicis (Liber nominum)*
Orig. Hom. Cant.	*Homiliae II Origenis in Canticum canticorum Latine redditae*
Orig. Hom. Luc.	*In Lucam homiliae XXXIX ex Graeco Origenis Latine conversae*
Orig. Jer. Ezech.	*Homiliae XXVIII in Jeremiam et Ezechielem Graeco Origenis Latine redditae*
Orig. Princ.	*De principiis*
Pelag.	*Adversus Pelagianos dialogi III*
Psalt. Hebr.	*Psalterium secundum Hebraeos*
Qu. hebr. Gen.	*Quaestionum hebraicarum liber in Genesim*
Reg. Pachom.	*Regula S. Pachomii, e Graeco*
Ruf.	*Adversus Rufinum libri III*
Sit.	*De situ et nominibus locorum Hebraicorum (Liber locorum)*
Tract. Isa.	*Tractatus in Isaiam*
Tract. Marc.	*Tractatus in Evangelium Marci*
Tract. Ps.	*Tractatus in Psalmos*
Tract. var.	*Tractatus varii*
Vigil.	*Adversus Vigilantium*
Vir. ill.	*De viris illustribus*
Vit. Hil.	*Vita S. Hilarionis eremitae*
Vit. Malch.	*Vita Malchi monachi*
Vit. Paul.	*Vita S. Pauli, primi eremitae*

JOHN CHRYSOSTOM

Adfu.	*Adversus eos qui non adfuerant*	
Aeg.	*In martyres Aegyptios*	
Anna	*De Anna*	
Anom.	*Contra Anomoeos*	
Ant. exsil.	*Sermo antequam iret in exsilium*	
Ascens.	*In ascensionem domini nostri Jesu Christi*	
Bab.	*De sancto hieromartyre*	*Babyla Babylas the Martyr*

Bab. Jul.	*De Babyla contra Julianum et gentiles*
Bapt.	*De baptismo Christi*
Barl.	*In sanctum Barlaam martyrem*
Bern.	*De sanctis Bernice et Prosdoce*
Catech. illum.	*Catecheses ad illuminandos*
Catech. jur.	*Catechesis de juramento*
Catech. ult.	*Catechesis ultima ad baptizandos*
Cath.	*Adversus Catharos*
Coemet.	*De coemeterio et de cruce*
Comm. Isa.	*Commentarius in Isaiam*
Comm. Job	*Commentarius in Job*
Comp. reg. mon.	*Comparatio regis et monachi*
Compunct. Dem.	*Ad Demetrium de compunctione*
Compunct. Stel.	*Ad Stelechium de compunctione*
Cruc.	*De cruce et latrone homiliae II*
Cum exsil.	*Sermo cum iret in exsilium*
Dav.	*De Davide et Saule*
Delic.	*De futurae vitae deliciis*
Diab.	*De diabolo tentatore*
Diod.	*Laus Diodori episcopi*
Dros.	*De sancta Droside martyre*
Educ. lib.	*De educandis liberis*
El. vid.	*In Eliam et viduam*
Eleaz. puer.	*De Eleazaro et septem pueris*
Eleem.	*De eleemosyna*
Ep. carc.	*Epistula ad episcopos, presbyteros et diaconos in carcere*
Ep. Cyr.	*Epistula ad Cyriacum*
1 Ep. Innoc.	*Ad Innocentium papam epistula I*
2 Ep. Innoc.	*Ad Innocentium papam epistula II*
Ep. Olymp.	*Epistulae ad Olympiadem*
Ep. Theod.	*Letter to Theodore*
Eust.	*In sanctum Eustathium Antiochenum*
Eutrop.	*In Eutropium*
Exp. Ps.	*Expositiones in Psalmos*
Fat. prov.	*De fato et providentia*
Fem. reg.	*Quod regulares feminae viris cohabitare non debeant*
Fr. Ep. Cath.	*Fragmenta in Epistulas Catholicas*
Freq. conv.	*Quod frequenter conveniendum sit*
Goth. concin.	*Homilia habita postquam presbyter Gothus concionatus fuerat*
Grat.	*Non esse ad gratiam concionandum*
Hom. Act.	*Homiliae in Acta apostolorum*
Hom. Act. 9:1	*De mutatione nominum*
Hom. Col.	*Homiliae in epistulam ad Colossenses*
Hom. 1 Cor.	*Homiliae in epistulam i ad Corinthios*
Hom. 1 Cor. 7:2	*In illud: Propter fornicationes autem unusquisque suam uxorem habeat*
Hom. 1 Cor. 10:1	*In dictum Pauli: Nolo vos ignorare*
Hom. 1 Cor. 11:19	*In dictum Pauli: Oportet haereses esse*
Hom. 2 Cor.	*Homiliae in epistulam ii ad Corinthios*
Hom. 2 Cor. 4:13	*In illud: Habentes eundem spiritum*
Hom. 2 Cor. 11:1	*In illud: Utinam sustineretis modicum*
Hom. Eph.	*Homiliae in epistulam ad Ephesios*
Hom. Gal.	*Homiliae in epistulam ad Galatas commentarius*
Hom. Gal. 2:11	*In illud: In faciem ei restiti*
Hom. Gen.	*Homiliae in Genesim*

Hom. Heb.	Homiliae in epistulam ad Hebraeos	
Hom. Isa. 6:1	In illud: Vidi Dominum	
Hom. Isa. 45:7	In illud Isaiae: Ego Dominus Deus feci lumen	
Hom. Jer. 10:23	In illud: Domine, non est in homine	
Hom. Jo.	Homiliae in Joannem	
Hom. Jo. 5:17	In illud: Pater meus usque modo operatur	
Hom. Jo. 5:19	In illud: Filius ex se nihil facit	
Hom. Matt.	Homiliae in Matthaeum	
Hom. Matt. 9:37	In illud: Messis quidem multa	
Hom. Matt. 18:23	De decem millium talentorum debitore	
Hom. Matt. 26:39	In illud: Pater, si possibile est, transeat	
Hom. Phil.	Homiliae in epistulam ad Philippenses	
Hom. Phlm.	Homiliae in epistulam ad Philemonem	
Hom. princ. Act.	In principium Actorum	
Hom. Ps. 48:17	In illud: Ne timueris cum dives factus fuerit homo	
Hom. Rom.	Homiliae in epistulam ad Romanos	
Hom. Rom. 5:3	De gloria in tribulationibus	
Hom. Rom. 8:28	In illud: Diligentibus deum omnia cooperantur in bonum	
Hom. Rom. 12:20	In illud: Si esurierit inimicus	
Hom. Rom. 16:3	In illud: Salutate Priscillam et Aquilam	
Hom 1 Thess.	Homiliae in epistulam i ad Thessalonicenses	
Hom. 2 Thess.	Homiliae in epistulam ii ad Thessalonicenses	
Hom. 1 Tim.	Homiliae in epistulam i ad Timotheum	
Hom. 1 Tim. 5:9	In illud: Vidua eligatur	
Hom. 2 Tim.	Homiliae in epistulam ii ad Timotheum	
Hom. 2 Tim. 3:1	In illud: Hoc scitote quod in novissimis diebus	
Hom. Tit.	Homiliae in epistulam ad Titum	
Hom. Tit. 2:11	In illud: Apparuit gratia dei omnibus hominibus	
Ign.	In sanctum Ignatium martyrem	
Inan. glor.	De inani gloria	
Iter. conj.	De non iterando conjugio	
Adv. Jud.	Adversus Judaeos	Discourses against Judaizing Christians
Jud. gent.	Contra Judaeos et gentiles quod Christus sit deus	
Jul.	In sanctum Julianum martyrem	
Juv.	In Juventinum et Maximum martyres	
Kal.	In Kalendas	
Laed.	Quod nemo laeditur nisi a se ipso	No One Can Harm the Man Who Does Not Injure Himself
Laud. Max.	Quales ducendae sint uxores (=De laude Maximi)	
Laud. Paul.	De laudibus sancti Pauli apostoli	
Laz.	De Lazaro	
Lib. repud.	De libello repudii	
Liturg.	Liturgia	
Lucian.	In sanctum Lucianum martyrem	
Macc.	De Maccabeis	
Mart.	De sanctis martyribus; Homilia in martyres	
Melet.	De sancto Meletio Antiocheno	
Natal.	In diem natalem Christi	
Non desp.	Non esse desperandum	
Oppugn.	Adversus oppugnatores vitae monasticae	
Ordin.	Sermo cum presbyter fuit ordinatus	

Paenit.	*De paenitentia*	
Paralyt.	*In paralyticum demissum per tectum*	
Pasch.	*In sanctum pascha*	
Pecc.	*Peccata fratrum non evulganda*	*Against Publicly Exposing the Sins of the Brethren*
Pelag.	*De sancta Pelagia virgine et martyre*	
Pent.	*De sancta pentecoste*	
Phoc.	*De sancto hieromartyre Phoca*	
Praes. imp.	*Homilia dicta praesente imperatore*	
Prod. Jud.	*De proditione Judae*	
Prof. evang.	*De profectu evangelii*	*Lowliness of Mind*
Proph. obscurit.	*De prophetarum obscuritate*	
Quatr. Laz.	*In quatriduanum Lazarum*	
1 Redit.	*Post reditum a priore exsilio sermo I*	
2 Redit.	*Post reditum a priore exsilio sermo II*	
Regr.	*De regressu*	
Reliq. mart.	*Homilia dicta postquam reliquiae martyrum*	
Res. Chr.	*Adversus ebriosos et de resurrectione domini nostri JesuChristi*	
Res. mort.	*De resurrectione mortuorum*	
Rom. mart.	*In sanctum Romanum martyrem*	
Sac.	*De sacerdotio*	*Priesthood*
Sanct. Anast.	*Homilia dicta in templo sanctae Anastasiae*	
Saturn.	*Cum Saturninus et Aurelianus acti essent in exsilium*	
Scand.	*Ad eos qui scandalizati sunt*	
Serm. Gen.	*Sermones in Genesim*	
Stag.	*Ad Stagirium a daemone vexatum*	
Stat.	*Ad populum Antiochenum de statuis*	
Stud. praes.	*De studio praesentium*	
Subintr.	*Contra eos qui subintroductas habent virgines*	
Terr. mot.	*De terrae motu*	
Theatr.	*Contra ludos et theatra*	
Theod. laps.	*Ad Theodorum lapsum*	*Exhortation to Theodore after His Fall*
Vid.	*Ad viduam juniorem*	*To the Young Widow*
Virginit.	*De virginitate*	

JOHN MALALAS

Chron.	*Chronographia*

JOHN PHILOPONUS

Comm. De an.	*In Aristotelis De anima libros commentaria*

JOSEPHUS (See p. 875)

JUSTIN

1 Apol.	*Apologia i*	*First Apology*
2 Apol.	*Apologia ii*	*Second Apology*

Dial.	*Dialogus cum Tryphone*	*Dialogue with Trypho*

JUSTINIAN

Edict.	*Edicta*	
Nov.	*Novellae*	

JUVENAL

Sat.	*Satirae*	*Satires*

LACTANTIUS

Epit.	*Epitome divinarum institutionum*	*Epitome of the Divine Institutes*
Inst.	*Divinarum institutionum libri VII*	*The Divine Institutes*
Ir.	*De ira Dei*	*The Wrath of God*
Mort.	*De morte persecutorum*	*The Deaths of the Persecutors*
Opif.	*De opificio Dei*	*The Workmanship of God*

LIVY

Hist.	*The History of Rome*	

LONGINUS

[Subl.]	*De sublimitate*	*On the Sublime*

LONGUS

Daphn.	*Daphnis et Chloe*	*Daphnis and Chloe*

LUCIAN

Abdic.	*Abdicatus Disowned*	*Disowned*
Alex.	*Alexander (Pseudomantis)*	*Alexander the False Prophet*
[Am.]	*Amores*	*Affairs of the Heart*
Anach.	*Anacharsis*	
[Asin.]	*Asinus (Lucius)*	*Lucius, or The Ass*
Astr.	*Astrologia*	*Astrology*
Bis acc.	*Bis accusatus*	*The Double Indictment*
Cal.	*Calumniae non temere credendum*	*Slander*
Cat.	*Cataplus*	*The Downward Journey, or The Tyrant*
Char.	*Charon*	
Demon.	*Demonax*	
Deor. conc.	*Deorm concilium*	*Parliament of the Gods*
Dial. d.	*Dialogi deorum*	*Dialogues of the Gods*
Dial. meretr.	*Dialogi meretricii*	*Dialogues of the Courtesans*
Dial. mort.	*Diologi mortuorum*	*Dialogues of the Dead*
Dom.	*De domo*	*The Hall*
Electr.	*De electro*	*Amber, or The Swans*
[Encom. Demosth.]	*Demosthenous encomium*	*Praise of Demosthenes*
Eunuch.	*Eunuchus*	*The Eunuch*

Fug.	*Fugitivi*	The Runaways
Gall.	*Gallus*	The Dream, or The Cock
Hermot.	*Hermotimus (De sectis)*	Hermotimus, or Sects
Icar.	*Icaromenippus*	
Imag.	*Imagines*	Essays in Portraiture
Pro imag.	*Pro imaginibus*	Essays in Portraiture Defended
Ind.	*Adversus indoctum*	The Ignorant Book-Collector
Jud. voc.	*Judicium vocalium*	The Consonants at Law
Jupp. conf.	*Juppiter confutatus*	Zeus Catechized
Jupp. trag.	*Juppiter tragoedus*	Zeus Rants
Laps.	*Pro lapsu inter salutandum*	A Slip of the Tongue in Greeting
Lex.	*Lexiphanes*	
Luct.	*De luctu*	Funerals
Men.	*Menippus (Necyomantia)*	Menippus, or Descent into Hades
Merc. cond.	*De mercede conductis*	Salaried Posts in Great Houses
Musc. laud.	*Muscae laudatio*	The Fly
Nav.	*Navigium*	The Ship, or The Wishes
Nigr.	*Nigrinus*	
Par.	*De parasito*	The Parasite
Peregr.	*De morte Peregrini*	The Passing of Peregrinus
Phal.	*Phalaris*	
[Philopatr.]	*Philopatris*	The Patriot
Philops.	*Philopseudes*	The Lover of Lies
Pisc.	*Piscator*	The Dead Come to Life, or The Fisherman
Pseudol.	*Pseudologista*	The Mistaken Critic
Rhet. praec.	*Rhetorum praeceptor*	A Professor of Public Speaking
Sacr.	*De sacrificiis*	Sacrifices
Salt.	*De saltatione*	The Dance
Sat.		Saturnalia Conversation with Cronius
Scyth.	*Scytha*	The Scythian, or The Consul
Somn.	*Somnium (Vita Luciani)*	The Dream, or Lucians Career
Symp.	*Symposium*	The Carousal
Lapiths		
Syr. d.	*De syria dea*	The Goddess of Syria
Tim.	*Timon*	
Tox.	*Toxaris*	
Tyr.	*Tyrannicida*	The Tyrannicide
Ver. hist.	*Vera historia*	A True Story
Vit. auct.	*Vitarum auctio*	Philosophies for Sale

MARTIAL

Epi.	*Epigramma*	

MENANDER

Dysk.	*Dyskolos*
Epitr.	*Epitrepontes*
Georg.	*Georgos*
Mis.	*Misoumenos*
Mon.	*Monostichoi*
Perik.	*Perikeiromenē*
Phasm.	*Phasma*

Sam.	*Samia*
Sik.	*Sikyonios*
Thras.	*Thrasonidis*

METHODIUS OF OLYMPUS

Lib. arb.	*De libero arbitrio*
Res.	*De resurrectione*
Symp.	*Symposium (Convivium decem virginum)*

MINUCIUS FELIX

Oct.	*Octavius*

NEPOS

Ag.	*Agesilaus*
Alc.	*Alciabiades*
Arist.	*Aristides*
Att.	*Atticus*
Cat.	*Cato*
Chabr.	*Chabrias*
Cim.	*Cimon*
Con.	*Conon*
Dat.	*Datames*
Di.	*Dion*
Epam.	*Epaminondas*
Eum.	*Eumenes*
Ham.	*Hamilcar*
Han.	*Hannibal*
Iph.	*Iphicrates*
Lys.	*Lysander*
Milt.	*Miltiades*
Paus.	*Pausanias*
Pel.	*Pelopidas*
Phoc.	*Phocion*
Reg.	*De regibus*
Them.	*Themistocles*
Thras.	*Thrasybulus*
Timol.	*Timoleon*
Timoth.	*Timotheus*

NICANDER

Alex.	*Alexipharmaca*
Ther.	*Theriaca*

NICOLAUS OF DAMASCUS

Hist. univ.	*Historia universalis*	*Universal History (in Athanaeus)*
Vit. Caes.	*Vita Caesaris*	

NONNUS

Dion.	*Dionysiaca*
Paraphr. Jo.	*Paraphrasis sancti evangelii Joannei*

ORAC. CHALD.

	De oraculis chaldaicis	*Chaldean Oracles*

ORIGEN

Adnot. Deut.	*Adnotationes in Deuteronomium*	
Adnot. Exod.	*Adnotationes in Exodum*	
Adnot. Gen.	*Adnotationes in Genesim*	
Adnot. Jes. Nav.	*Adnotationes in Jesum filium Nave*	
Adnot. Judic.	*Adnotationes in Judices*	
Adnot. Lev.	*Adnotationes in Leviticum*	
Adnot. Num.	*Adnotationes in Numeros*	
Cant. (Adulesc.)	*In Canticum canticorum (libri duo quos scripsit in adulescentia)*	
Cels.	*Contra Celsum*	*Against Celsus*
Comm. Cant.	*Commentarius in Canticum*	
Comm. Gen.	*Commentarii in Genesim*	
Comm. Jo.	*Commentarii in evangelium Joannis*	
Comm. Matt.	*Commentarium in evangelium Matthaei*	
Comm. Rom.	*Commentarii in Romanos*	
Comm. ser. Matt.	*Commentarium series in evangelium Matthaei*	
Dial.	*Diologus cum Heraclide*	*Dialogue with Heraclides*
Enarrat. Job	*Enarrationes in Job*	
Engastr.	*De engastrimytho*	*Witch of Endor*
Ep. Afr.	*Epistula ad Africanum*	
Ep. Greg.	*Epistula ad Gregorium Thaumaturgum*	
Ep. ign.	*Epistula ad ignotum (Fabianum Romanum)*	
Exc. Ps.	*Excerpta in Psalmos*	
Exp. Prov.	*Expositio in Proverbia*	
Fr. Act.	*Fragmentum ex homiliis in Acta apostolorum*	
Fr. Cant.	*Libri x in Canticum canticorum*	
Fr. 1 Cor.	*Fragmenta ex commentariis in epistulam i ad Corinthios*	
Fr. Eph.	*Fragmenta ex commentariis in epistulam ad Ephesios*	
Fr. Exod.	*Fragmenta ex commentariis in Exodum*	
Fr. Ezech.	*Fragmenta ex commentariis in Ezechielem*	
Fr. Heb.	*Fragmenta ex homiliis in epistulam ad Hebraeos*	
Fr. Jer.	*Fragmenta in Jeremiam*	
Fr. Jo.	*Fragmenta in evangelium Joannis*	
Fr. Lam.	*Fragmenta in Lamentationes*	
Fr. Luc.	*Fragmenta in Lucam*	
Fr. Matt.	*Fragmenta ex commentariis in evangelium Matthaei*	
Fr. Os.	*Fragmentum ex commentariis in Osee*	
Fr. Prin.	*Fragmenta de principiis*	
Fr. Prov.	*Fragmenta ex commentariis in Proverbia*	
Fr. Ps.	*Fragmenta in Psalmos 1–150*	
Fr. 1 Reg.	*Fragmenta in librum primum Regnorum*	
Fr. Ruth	*Fragmentum in Ruth*	
Hex.	*Hexapla*	

Hom. Cant.	*Homiliae in Canticum*	
Hom. Exod.	*Homiliae in Exodum*	
Hom. Ezech.	*Homiliae in Ezechielem*	
Hom. Gen.	*Homiliae in Genesim*	
Hom. Isa.	*Homiliae in Isaiam*	
Hom. Jer.	*Homiliae in Jeremiam*	
Hom. Jes. Nav.	*In Jesu Nave homiliae xxvi*	
Hom. Job	*Homiliae in Job*	
Hom. Judic.	*Homiliae in Judices*	
Hom. Lev.	*Homiliae in Leviticum*	
Hom. Luc.	*Homiliae in Lucam*	
Hom. Num.	*Homiliae in Numeros*	
Hom. Ps.	*Homiliae in Psalmos*	
Hom. 1 Reg.	*Homiliae in I Reges*	
Mart.	*Exhortatio ad martyrium*	*Exhortation to Martyrdom*
Or.	*De oratione (Peri proseuchēs)*	*Prayer*
Pasch.	*De pascha*	*The Pascha*
Philoc.	*Philocalia*	
Princ.	*De principiis (Peri archōn)*	*First Principles*
Res.	*De resurrectione libri ii*	
Schol. Apoc.	*Scholia in Apocalypsem*	
Schol. Cant.	*Scholia in Canticum canticorum*	
Schol. Luc.	*Scholia in Lucam*	
Schol. Matt.	*Scholia in Matthaeum*	
Sel. Deut.	*Selecta in Deuteronomium*	
Sel. Exod.	*Selecta in Exodum*	
Sel. Ezech.	*Selecta in Ezechielem*	
Sel. Gen.	*Selecta in Genesim*	
Sel. Jes. Nav.	*Selecta in Jesum Nave*	
Sel. Job	*Selecta in Job*	
Sel. Judic.	*Selecta in Judices*	
Sel. Lev.	*Selecta in Leviticum*	
Sel. Num.	*Selecta in Numeros*	
Sel. Ps.	*Selecta in Psalmos*	

OROSIUS

Hist.	*Historiarum Adversum Paganos Libri VII* ("Seven Books of History Against the Pagans")

OVID

Am.	*Amores*
Ars	*Ars amatoria*
Fast.	*Fasti*
Hal.	*Halieutica*
Her.	*Heroides*
Ib.	*Ibis*
Med.	*Medicamina faciei femineae*
Metam.	*Metamorphoses*

PAUSANIAS

Descr.	*Graeciae description*	*Description of Greece*

PERIPL. M. RUBR.	Periplus Maris Rubri	The Periplus of the Erythraean Sea

PERSIUS

Sat.	*Satirae*

PETRONIUS

Satyr.	*Satyricon*

PHILO OF ALEXANDRIA (See pp. 874–75)

PHILODEMUS OF GADARA

Adv. Soph.	*Adversus sophistas*
D.	*De Diis*
Hom.	*De bono rege secundum Homerum*
Ir.	*De ira*
Lib.	*De libertate dicendi*
Mort.	*De morte*
Mus.	*De musica*
Piet.	*De pietate*
Rhet.	*Volumina rhetorica*
Sign.	*De signis*
Vit.	*De vitiis X*

PHILOSTORGIUS

Eccl. hist.	*Ecclesiastical History*

PHILOSTRATUS

Ep.	*Epistulae*
Gymn.	*De gymnastica*
Imag.	*Imagines*
Vit. Apoll.	*Vita Apollonii*
Vit. soph.	*Vitae sophistarum*

PHOTIUS

Lex.	*Lexicon*

PINDAR

Isthm.	*Isthmionikai*	*Isthmian Odes*
Nem.	*Nemeonikai*	*Nemean Odes*
Ol.	*Olympionikai*	*Olympian Odes*
Paean.	*Paeanes*	*Hymns*
Pyth.	*Pythionikai*	*Pythian Odes*
Thren.	*Threnoi*	*Dirges*

PLATO

[Alc. maj.]	*Alcibiades major*	*Greater Alcibiades*

Apol.	*Apologia*	*Apology of Socrates*
[Ax.]	*Axiochus*	
Charm.	*Charmides*	
Crat.	*Cratylus*	
[Def.]	*Definitiones*	*Definitions*
Ep.	*Epistulae*	*Letters*
[Epin.]	*Epinomis*	
Euthyd.	*Euthydemus*	
Euthyphr.	*Euthyphro*	
Gorg.	*Gorgias*	
Hipparch.	*Hipparchus*	
Hipp. maj.	*Hippias major*	*Greater Hippias*
Hipp. min.	*Hippias minor*	*Lesser Hippias*
Lach.	*Laches*	
Leg.	*Leges*	*Laws*
Menex.	*Menexenus*	
[Min.]	*Minos*	
Parm.	*Parmenides*	
Phaed.	*Phaedo*	
Phaedr.	*Phaedrus*	
Phileb.	*Philebus*	
Pol.	*Politicus*	*Statesman*
Prot.	*Protagoras*	
Resp.	*Respublica*	*Republic*
Soph.	*Sophista*	*Sophist*
Symp.	*Symposium*	
Theaet.	*Theaetetus*	
Tim.	*Timaeus*	

PLAUTUS

Amph.	*Amphitruo*
Asin.	*Asinaria*
Aul.	*Aulularia*
Bacch.	*Bacchides*
Capt.	*Captivi*
Cas.	*Casina*
Cist.	*Cistellaria*
Curc.	*Curculio*
Epid.	*Epidicus*
Men.	*Menaechmi*
Mil. glor.	*Miles gloriosus*
Most.	*Mostellaria*
Pers.	*Persae*
Poen.	*Poenulus*
Pseud.	*Pseudolus*
Rud.	*Rudens*
Stic.	*Sticus*
Trin.	*Trinummus*
Truc.	*Truculentus*
Vid.	*Vidularia*

Pliny the Elder

Nat.	*Naturalis historia*	*Natural History*

Pliny the Younger

Ep.	*Epistulae*
Ep. Tra.	*Epistulae ad Trajanum*
Pan.	*Panegyricus*

Plotinus

Enn.	*Enneades*

Plutarch

Adol. poet. aud.	*Quomodo adolescens poetas audire debeat*	
Adul. am.	*De adulatore et amico*	
Adul. amic.	*Quomodo adulator ab amico internoscatur*	
Aem.	*Aemilius Paullus*	
Ag. Cleom.	*Agis et Cleomenes*	
Ages.	*Agesilaus*	
Alc.	*Alcibiades*	
Alex.	*Alexander*	
Alex. fort.	*De Alexandri magni fortuna aut virtute*	
Am. prol.	*De amore prolis*	
Amat.	*Amatorius*	
[Amat. narr.]	*Amatoriae narrationes*	
Amic. mult.	*De amicorum multitudine*	
An. corp.	*Animine an corporis affectiones sint peiores*	
[An ignis]	*Aquane an ignis utilior*	
An. procr.	*De animae procreatione in Timaeo*	
An. procr. epit.	*Epitome libri de procreatione in Timaeo*	
An seni	*An seni respublica gerenda sit*	
An virt. doc.	*An virtus doceri possit*	
An vit.	*An vitiositas ad infelicitatem sufficiat*	
Ant.	*Antonius*	
[Apoph. lac.]	*Apophthegmata laconica*	
Arat.	*Aratus*	
Arist.	*Aristides*	
Art.	*Artaxerxes*	
Brut.	*Brutus*	
Brut. an.	*Bruta animalia ratione uti*	
Caes.	*Caesar*	
Cam.	*Camillus*	
Cat. Maj.	*Cato Major*	*Cato the Elder*
Cat. Min.	*Cato Minor*	*Cato the Younger*
Cic.	*Cicero*	
Cim.	*Cimon*	
Cleom.	*Cleomenes*	
Cohib. ira	*De cohibenda ira*	
Adv. Col.	*Adversus Colotem*	
Comm. not.	*De communibus notitiis contra stoicos*	

Comp. Aem. Tim.	*Comparatio Aemilii Paulli et Timoleontis*
Comp. Ag. Cleom. cum Ti. Gracch.	*Comparatio Agidis et Cleomenis cum Tiberio et Gaio Graccho*
Comp. Ages. Pomp.	*Comparatio Agesilai et Pompeii*
Comp. Alc. Cor.	*Comparatio Alcibiadis et Marcii Coriolani*
Comp. Arist. Cat.	*Comparatio Aristidis et Catonis*
Comp. Arist. Men. compend.	*Comparationis Aristophanis et Menandri compendium*
Comp. Cim. Luc.	*Comparatio Cimonis et Luculli*
Comp. Dem. Cic.	*Comparatio Demosthenis et Ciceronis*
Comp. Demetr. Ant.	*Comparatio Demetrii et Antonii*
Comp. Dion. Brut.	*Comparatio Dionis et Bruti*
Comp. Eum. Sert.	*Comparatio Eumenis et Sertorii*
Comp. Lyc. Num.	*Comparatio Lycurgi et Numae*
Comp. Lys. Sull.	*Comparatio Lysandri et Sullae*
Comp. Nic. Crass.	*Comparatio Nicae et Crassi*
Comp. Pel. Marc.	*Comparatio Pelopidae et Marcelli*
Comp. Per. Fab.	*Comparatio Periclis et Fabii Maximi*
Comp. Phil. Flam.	*Comparatio Philopoemenis et Titi Flaminini*
Comp. Sol. Publ.	*Comparatio Solonis et Publicolae*
Comp. Thes. Rom.	*Comparatio Thesei et Romuli*
Conj. praec.	*Conjugalia Praecepta*
[Cons. Apoll.]	*Consolatio ad Apollonium*
Cons. ux.	*Consolatio ad uxorem*
Cor.	*Marcius Coriolanus*
Crass.	*Crassus*
Cupid. divit.	*De cupiditate divitiarum*
Curios.	*De curiositate*
De esu	*De esu carnium*
De laude	*De laude ipsius*
Def. orac.	*De defectu oraculorum*
Dem.	*Demosthenes*
Demetr.	*Demetrius*
Dion	*Dion*
E Delph.	*De E apud Delphos*
Eum.	*Eumenes*
Exil.	*De exilio*
Fab.	*Fabius Maximus*
Fac.	*De facie in orbe lunae*
Flam.	*Titus Flamininus*
Fort.	*De fortuna*
Fort. Rom.	*De fortuna Romanorum*
Frat. amor.	*De fraterno amore*
Galb.	*Galba*
Garr.	*De garrulitate*
Gen. Socr.	*De genio Socratis*
Glor. Ath.	*De gloria Atheniensium*
Her. mal.	*De Herodoti malignitate*
Inim. util.	*De capienda ex inimicis utilitate*
Inv. od.	*De invidia et odio*
Is. Os.	*De Iside et Osiride*
Lat. viv.	*De latenter vivendo*
Lib. aegr.	*De libidine et aegritudine*
[Lib. ed.]	*De liberis educandis*

Luc.	Lucullus
Lyc.	Lycurgus
Lys.	Lysander
Mar.	Marius
Marc.	Marcellus
Max. princ.	Maxime cum principibus philosophiam esse disserendum
Mor.	Moralia
Mulier. virt.	Mulierum virtutes
[Mus.]	De musica
Nic.	Nicias
Num.	Numa
Oth.	Otho
Parsne an fac.	Parsne an facultas animi sit vita passiva
Pel.	Pelopidas
Per.	Pericles
Phil.	Philopoemen
Phoc.	Phocion
[Plac. philos.]	De placita philosophorum
Pomp.	Pompeius
Praec. ger. rei publ.	Praecepta gerendae rei publicae
Prim. frig.	De primo frigido
Princ. iner.	Ad principem ineruditum
Publ.	Publicola
Pyrrh.	Pyrrhus
Pyth. orac.	De Pythiae oraculis
Quaest. conv.	Quaestionum convivialum libri IX
Quaest. nat.	Quaestiones naturales (Aetia physica)
Quaest. plat.	Quaestiones platonicae
Quaest. rom.	Quaestiones romanae et graecae (Aetia romana et graeca)
Rect. rat. aud.	De recta ratione audiendi
[Reg. imp. apophth.]	Regum et imperatorum apophthegmata
Rom.	Romulus
Sept. sap. conv.	Septem sapientium convivium
Sera	De sera numinis vindicta
Sert.	Sertorius
Sol.	Solon
Soll. an.	De sollertia animalium
Stoic. abs.	Stoicos absurdiora poetis dicere
Stoic. rep.	De Stoicorum repugnantiis
Suav. viv.	Non posse suaviter vivi secundum Epicurum
Sull.	Sulla
Superst.	De superstitione
Them.	Themistocles
Thes.	Theseus
Ti. C. Gracch.	Tiberius et Caius Gracchus
Tim.	Timoleon
Tranq. an.	De tranquillitate animi
Trib. r. p. gen.	De tribus rei publicae generibus
Tu. san.	De tuenda sanitate praecepta
Un. rep. dom.	De unius in republica dominatione
Virt. mor.	De virtute morali
Virt. prof.	Quomodo quis suos in virtute sentiat profectus
Virt. vit.	De virtute et vitio
Vit. aere al.	De vitando aere alieno

[Vit. poes. Hom.]	De vita et poesi Homeri	
Vit. pud.	De vitioso pudore	
[Vit. X orat.]	Vitae decem oratorum	

POLLUX

Onom.	Onomasticon

POLYBIUS

Hist.	Historical

POMPONIUS MELA

De Chorog.	De Chorographia

PORPHYRY

Abst.	De abstinentia
Agalm.	Peri agalmatōn
Aneb.	Epistula ad Anebonem
Antr. nymph.	De antro nympharum
Christ.	Contra Christianos
Chron.	Chronica
Comm. harm.	Eis ta harmonika Ptolemaiou hypomnēma
Comm. Tim.	In Platonis Timaeum commentaria
Exp. Cat.	In Aristotelis Categorias expositio per interrogationem et responsionem
Isag.	Isagoge sive quinque voces
Marc.	Ad Marcellam
Philos. orac.	De philosophia ex oraculis
Quaest. hom.	Quaestiones homericae
Quaest. hom. Odd.	Quaestionum homericarum ad Odysseam pertinentium reliquiae
Sent.	Sententiae ad intelligibilia ducentes
Vit. Plot.	Vita Plotini
Vit. Pyth.	Vita Pythagorae

PTOLEMY

Geog.	Geography

PTOLEMY (THE GNOSTIC)

Flor.	Epistula ad Floram	Letter to Flora

QUINTILIAN

Decl.	Declamationes
Inst.	Institutio oratoria

Res gest. divi Aug. Res gestae divi Augusti

Rhet. Her. Rhetorica ad Herennium

Rufinus

Adam. Haer.	Adamantii libri Contra haereticos
Anast.	Apologia ad Anastasium papam
Apol. Hier.	Apologia adversus Hieronymum
Apol. Orig.	Eusebii et Pamphyli Apologia Origenis
Basil. hom.	Homiliae S. Basilii
Ben. patr.	De benedictionibus patriarcharum
Clem. Recogn.	Clementis quae feruntur Recognitiones
Greg. Orat.	Gregorii Orationes
Hist.	Eusebii Historia ecclesiastica a Rufino translata et continuata
Hist. mon.	Historia monachorum in Aegypto
Orig. Comm. Cant.	Origenis Commentarius in Canticum
Orig. Comm. Rom.	Origenis Commentarius in epistulam ad Romanos
Orig. Hom. Exod.	Origenis in Exodum homiliae
Orig. Hom. Gen.	Origenis in Genesism homiliae
Orig. Hom. Jos.	Origenis Homiliae in librum Josua
Orig. Hom. Judic.	Origenis in librum Judicum homiliae
Orig. Hom. Lev.	Origenis Homiliae in Leviticum
Orig. Hom. Num.	Origenis in Numeros homiliae
Orig. Hom. Ps.	Origenis Homiliae in Psalmos
Orig. Princ.	Origenis Libri Peri archōn seu De principiis libri IV
Sent. Sext.	Sexti philosophi Sententiae a Rufino translatae
Symb.	Commentarius in symbolum apostolorum

Sallust

Bell. Cat.	Bellum catilinae
Bell. Jug.	Bellum jugurthinum
Hist.	Historiae
Rep.	Epistulae ad Caesarem senem de re publica

Seneca

Ag.	Agamemnon
Apol.	Apolocyntosis
Ben.	De beneficiis
Clem.	De clementia
Dial.	Dialogi
Ep.	Epistulae morales
Helv.	Ad Helviam
Herc. fur.	Hercules furens
Herc. Ot.	Hercules Otaeus
Ira	De ira
Lucil.	Ad Lucilium

Marc.	Ad Marciam de consolatione
Med.	Medea
Nat.	Naturales quaestiones
Phaed.	Phaedra
Phoen.	Phoenissae
Polyb.	Ad Polybium de consolatione
Thy.	Thyestes
Tranq.	De tranquillitate animi
Tro.	Troades
Vit. beat.	De vita beata

SEXTUS EMPIRICUS

Math.	Adversus mathematicos	Against the Mathematicians
Pyr.	Pyrrhoniae hypotyposes	Outlines of Pyrrhonism

SOPHOCLES

Aj.	Ajax
Ant.	Antigone
El.	Elektra
Ichn.	Ichneutae
Oed. col.	Oedipus coloneus
Oed. tyr.	Oedipus tyrannus
Phil.	Philoctetes
Trach.	Trachiniae

SOZOMEN

Eccl. hist.	Ecclesiastical History

STOBAEUS

Ecl.	Eclogae
Flor.	Florilegium

STRABO

Geogr.	Geographica

SUETONIUS

Aug.	Divus Augustus
Cal.	Gaius Caligula
Claud.	Divus Claudius
Dom.	Domitianus
Galb.	Galba
Gramm.	De grammaticis
Jul.	Divus Julius
Nero	Nero
Otho	Otho
Poet.	De poetis
Rhet.	De rhetoribus
Tib.	Tiberius

Tit.	*Divus Titus*	
Vesp.	*Vespasianus*	
Vit.	*Vitellius*	

TACITUS

Agr.	*Agricola*
Ann.	*Annales*
Dial.	*Dialogus de oratoribus*
Germ.	*Germania*
Hist.	*Historiae*

TERENCE

Ad.	*Adelphi*
Andr.	*Andria*
Eun.	*Eunuchus*
Haut.	*Hauton timorumenos*
Hec.	*Hecyra*
Phorm.	*Phormio*

TERTULLIAN

An.	*De anima*	*The Soul*
Apol.	*Apologeticus*	*Apology*
Bapt.	*De baptismo*	*Baptism*
Carn. Chr.	*De carne Christi*	*The Flesh of Christ*
Cor.	*De corona militis*	*The Crown*
Cult. fem.	*De cultu feminarum*	*The Apparel of Women*
Exh. cast.	*De exhortatione castitatis*	*Exhortation to Chastity*
Fug.	*De fuga in persecutione*	*Flight in Persecution*
Herm.	*Adversus Hermogenem*	*Against Hermogenes*
Idol.	*De idololatria*	*Idolatry*
Jejun.	*De jejunio adversus psychicos*	*On Fasting, against the Psychics*
Adv. Jud.	*Adversus Judaeos*	*Against the Jews*
Marc.	*Adversus Marcionem*	*Against Marcion*
Mart.	*Ad martyras*	*To the Martyrs*
Mon.	*De monogamia*	*Monogamy*
Nat.	*Ad nationes*	*To the Heathen*
Or.	*De oratione*	*Prayer*
Paen.	*De paenitentia*	*Repentance*
Pall.	*De pallio*	*The Pallium*
Pat.	*De patientia*	*Patience*
Praescr.	*De praescriptione haereticorum*	*Prescription against Heretics*
Prax.	*Adversus Praxean*	*Against Praxeas*
Pud.	*De pudicitia*	*Modesty*
Res.	*De resurrectione carnis*	*The Resurrection of the Flesh*
Scap.	*Ad Scapulam*	*To Scapula*
Scorp.	*Scorpiace*	*Antidote for Scorpian's Sting*
Spect.	*De spectaculis*	*The Shows*
Test.	*De testimonio animae*	*The Soul's Testimony*
Ux.	*Ad uxorem*	*To His Wife*
Val.	*Adversus Valentinianos*	*Against the Valentinians*
Virg.	*De virginibus velandis*	*The Veiling of Virgins*

THEOCRITUS

   Id.   *Idylls*

THEOD.   THEODOTIAN

   Vg.   *Vulgate*

THEODORET

   Car.   *De caritate*
   Hist. eccl.   *Historia ecclesiastica*   *Ecclesiastical History*
   Phil. hist.   *Philotheos historia*   *History of Monks of Syria*

THEON OF ALEXANDRIA

   Comm. Alm.   *Commentarium in Almagestum*   *Commentary on the Almagest*

THEOPHILUS

   Autol.   *Ad Autolycum*   *To Autolycus*

THEOPHRASTUS

   Caus. plant.   *De causis plantarum*
   Char.   *Characteres*
   Hist. plant.   *Historia plantarum*
   Sens.   *De sensu*

THUCYDIDES

   War   *History of the Peloponnesian War*

TYCONIUS

   Reg.   *Liber regularum*

VARRO

   Rust.   *De re rustica*

VIRGIL

   Aen.   *Aeneid*
   Ecl.   *Eclogae*
   Georg.   *Georgica*

XENOPHON

   Ages.   *Agesilaus*
   Anab.   *Anabasis*
   Apol.   *Apologia Socratis*
   [Ath.]   *Respublica atheniensium*
   Cyn.   *Cynegeticus*
   Cyr.   *Cyropaedia*

Eq.	*De equitande ratione*
Eq. mag.	*De equitum magistro*
Hell.	*Hellenica*
Hier.	*Hiero*
Lac.	*Respublica Lacedaemoniorum*
Mem.	*Memorabilia*
Oec.	*Oeconomicus*
Symp.	*Symposium*

Periodicals, Reference Works, and Serials

AA	*Archäologischer Anzeiger*
AAA	Annals of Archaeology and Anthropology
AAeg	*Analecta aegyptiaca*
AAHG	*Anzeiger für die Altertumswissenschaft*
AARDS	American Academy of Religion Dissertation Series
AAS	*Acta apostolicae sedis*
AASF	Annales Academiae scientiarum fennicae
AASOR	Annual of the American Schools of Oriental Research
AASS	*Acta sanctorum quotquot toto orbe coluntur.* Antwerp, 1643–
AB	Anchor Bible
AB	*Assyriologische Bibliothek*
ABAT2	*Altorientalische Bilder zum Alten Testament.* Edited by H. Gressmann. 2d ed. Berlin, 1927
ABAW	Abhandlungen der Bayrischen Akademie der Wissenschaften
AbB	*Altbabylonische Briefe in Umschrift und Übersetzung.* Edited by F. R. Kraus. Leiden, 1964–
ABC	*Assyrian and Babylonian Chronicles.* A. K. Grayson. TCS 5. Locust Valley, New York, 1975
ABD	*Anchor Bible Dictionary.* Edited by D. N. Freedman. 6 vols. New York, 1992
ABL	*Assyrian and Babylonian Letters Belonging to the Kouyunjik Collections of the British Museum.* Edited by R. F. Harper. 14 vols. Chicago, 1892–1914
ABQ	*American Baptist Quarterly*
ABR	*Australian Biblical Review*
ABRL	Anchor Bible Reference Library
AbrN	*Abr-Nahrain*
AbrNSup	Abr-Nahrain: Supplement Series
ABW	*Archaeology in the Biblical World*
ABZ	*Assyrisch-babylonische Zeichenliste.* Rykle Borger. 3d ed. AOAT 33/33A. Neukirchen-Vluyn, 1986
ACCS	Ancient Christian Commentary on Scripture
ACEBT	*Amsterdamse Cahiers voor Exegese en bijbelse Theologie*
ACNT	Augsburg Commentaries on the New Testament
ACO	*Acta conciliorum oecumenicorum.* Edited by E. Schwartz. Berlin, 1914–
AcOr	*Acta orientalia*
ACR	*Australasian Catholic Record*
AcT	*Acta theologica*
ACW	Ancient Christian Writers. 1946–
ADAJ	*Annual of the Department of Antiquities of Jordan*
ADD	*Assyrian Deeds and Documents.* C. H. W. Johns. 4 vols. Cambridge, 1898–1923
ADOG	Abhandlungen der deutschen Orientgesellschaft
AE	*Année épigraphique*
AEB	*Annual Egyptological Bibliography*
Aeg	*Aegyptus*
AEL	*Ancient Egyptian Literature.* M. Lichtheim. 3 vols. Berkeley, 1971–1980
AEO	*Ancient Egyptian Onomastica.* A. H. Gardiner. 3 vols. London, 1947

AER	*American Ecclesiastical Review*
Aev	*Aevum: Rassegna de scienze, storiche, linguistiche, e filologiche*
ÄF	Ägyptologische Forschungen
AfK	*Archiv für Keilschriftforschung*
AfO	*Archiv für Orientforschung*
AfOB	Archiv für Orientforschung: Beiheft
ÄgAbh	Ägyptologische Abhandlungen
AGLB	*Aus der Geschichte der lateinischen Bibel (= Vetus Latina: Die Reste der altlateinischen Bibel: Aus der Geschichte der lateinischen Bibel).* Freiburg: Herder, 1957–
AGJU	Arbeiten zur Geschichte des antiken Judentums und des Urchristentums
AGSU	Arbeiten zur Geschichte des Spätjudentums und Urchristentums
AHAW	Abhandlungen der Heidelberger Akademie der Wissenschaften
AHR	*American Historical Review*
AHw	*Akkadisches Handwörterbuch.* W. von Soden. 3 vols. Wiesbaden, 1965–1981
AION	*Annali dell'Istituto Orientale di Napoli*
AIPHOS	*Annuaire de l'Institut de philologie et d'histoire orientales et slaves*
AJA	*American Journal of Archaeology*
AJAS	*American Journal of Arabic Studies*
AJBA	*Australian Journal of Biblical Archaeology*
AJBI	*Annual of the Japanese Biblical Institute*
AJBS	*African Journal of Biblical Studies*
AJP	*American Journal of Philology*
AJSL	*American Journal of Semitic Languages and Literature*
AJSR	*Association for Jewish Studies Review*
AJSUFS	Arbeiten aus dem Juristischen Seminar der Universität Freiburg, Schweiz
AJT	*American Journal of Theology*
AJT	*Asia Journal of Theology*
ALASP	Abhandlungen zur Literatur Alt-Syren-Palästinas und Mesopotamiens
ALBO	Analecta lovaniensia biblica et orientalia
ALGHJ	Arbeiten zur Literatur und Geschichte des hellenistischen Judentums
Altaner	Altaner, B. *Patrologie.* 8th ed. Freiburg, 1978
ALUOS	*Annual of Leeds University Oriental Society*
AMS	*Acta martyrum et sanctorum Syriace.* Edited by P. Bedjan. 7 vols. Paris, 1890–1897
AMWNE	*Apocalypticism in the Mediterranean World and the Near East. Proceedings of the International Colloquium on Apocalypticism.* Edited by D. Hellholm. Uppsala, 1979
Anám	*Anámnesis*
AnBib	Analecta biblica
AnBoll	Analecta Bollandiana
ANEP	*The Ancient Near East in Pictures Relating to the Old Testament.* Edited by J. B. Pritchard. Princeton, 1954
ANESTP	*The Ancient Near East: Supplementary Texts and Pictures Relating to the Old Testament.* Edited by J. B. Pritchard. Princeton, 1969.
ANET	*Ancient Near Eastern Texts Relating to the Old Testament.* Edited by J. B. Pritchard. 3d ed. Princeton, 1969
ANF	*Ante-Nicene Fathers*
Ang	*Angelicum*
AnL	*Anthropological Linguistics*
AnOr	Analecta orientalia
AnPhil	*L'année philologique*
ANQ	*Andover Newton Quarterly*
ANRW	*Aufstieg und Niedergang der römischen Welt: Geschichte und Kultur Roms im Spiegel der neueren Forschung.* Edited by H. Temporini and W. Haase. Berlin, 1972–
AnSt	*Anatolian Studies*
ANTC	Abingdon New Testament Commentaries

ANTF	Arbeiten zur neutestamentlichen Textforschung
AnthLyrGraec	*Anthologia lyrica graeca.* Edited by E. Diehl. Leipzig, 1954–
ANTJ	Arbeiten zum Neuen Testament und Judentum
Anton	*Antonianum*
Anuari	*Anuari de filología*
ANZSTR	Australian and New Zealand Studies in Theology and Religion
AO	*Der Alte Orient*
AOAT	Alter Orient und Altes Testament
AÖAW	Anzeiger der Österreichischen Akademie der Wissenschaften
AOBib	Altorientalische Bibliothek
AoF	Altorientalische Forschungen
AOS	American Oriental Series
AOSTS	American Oriental Society Translation Series
AOT	*The Apocryphal Old Testament.* Edited by H. F. D. Sparks. Oxford, 1984
AOTAT	*Altorientalische Texte zum Alten Testament.* Edited by H. Gressmann. 2d ed. Berlin, 1926
AOTC	Abingdon Old Testament Commentaries
APAT	*Die Apokryphen und Pseudepigraphen des Alten Testaments.* Translated and edited by E. Kautzsch. 2 vols. Tübingen, 1900
APF	*Archiv für Papyrusforschung*
APHM	Grohmann, A. *Arabic Papyri from Hirbet el-Mird.* Bibliothèque du Muséon 52. Louvain: Publications Universitaires, 1963.
APOT	*The Apocrypha and Pseudepigrapha of the Old Testament.* Edited by R. H. Charles. 2 vols. Oxford, 1913
APSP	*American Philosophical Society Proceedings*
AR	*Archiv für Religionswissenschaft*
ARAB	*Ancient Records of Assyria and Babylonia.* Daniel David Luckenbill. 2 vols. Chicago, 1926–1927
ArBib	The Aramaic Bible
Arch	*Archaeology*
ARE	*Ancient Records of Egypt.* Edited by J. H. Breasted. 5 vols. Chicago, 1905–1907. Reprint, New York, 1962
ARG	*Archiv für Reformationsgeschichte*
ARI	*Assyrian Royal Inscriptions.* A. K. Grayson. 2 vols. RANE. Wiesbaden, 1972–1976
ARM	Archives royales de Mari
ARMT	Archives royales de Mari, transcrite et traduite
ArOr	*Archiv Orientální*
ArSt	Arabian Studies
AS	Assyriological Studies
ASAE	*Annales duservice des antiquités de l'Egypte*
ASAW	Abhandlungen der Sächsischen Akademie der Wissenschaften
ASNU	Acta seminarii neotestamentici upsaliensis
ASOR	American Schools of Oriental Research
ASP	*American Studies in Papyrology*
Asp	*Asprenas: Rivista di scienze teologiche*
ASS	*Acta sanctae sedis*
AsSeign	*Assemblées du Seigneur*
ASSR	*Archives de sciences sociales des religions*
ASTI	*Annual of the Swedish Theological Institute*
AsTJ	*Asbury Theological Journal*
AT	*Annales theologici*
ATA	Alttestamentliche Abhandlungen
ATANT	Abhandlungen zur Theologie des Alten und Neuen Testaments
ATD	Das Alte Testament Deutsch
ATDan	Acta theologica danica

ATG	*Archivo teológico granadino*
AThR	*Anglican Theological Review*
Atiqot	ʿ*Atiqot*
ATJ	*Ashland Theological Journal*
ATLA	American Theological Library Association
ATR	*Australasian Theological Review*
Aug	*Augustinianum*
AugStud	*Augustinian Studies*
AuOr	*Aula orientalis*
AUSS	*Andrews University Seminary Studies*
AVTRW	Aufsätze und Vorträge zur Theologie und Religionswissenschaft
AzTh	Arbeiten zur Theologie
B&R	*Books and Religion*
BA	*Biblical Archaeologist*
Bab	*Babyloniaca*
BAC	Biblioteca de autores cristianos
BAG	Bauer, W., W. F. Arndt, and F. W. Gingrich. *Greek-English Lexicon of the New Testament and Other Early Christian Literature.* Chicago, 1957
BAGB	*Bulletin de l'Association G. Budé*
BAGD	Bauer, W., W. F. Arndt, F. W. Gingrich, and F. W. Danker. *Greek-English Lexicon of the New Testament and Other Early Christian Literature.* 2d ed. Chicago, 1979
BaghM	*Baghdader Mitteilungen*
BAIAS	*Bulletin of the Anglo-Israel Archeological Society*
BAP	*Beiträge zum altbabylonischen Privatrecht.* Bruno Meissner. Leipzig, 1893
BAR	*Biblical Archaeology Review*
BARead	*Biblical Archaeologist Reader*
Bar-Ilan	*Annual of Bar-Ilan University*
BASOR	*Bulletin of the American Schools of Oriental Research*
BASORSup	Bulletin of the American Schools of Oriental Research: Supplement Series
BASP	*Bulletin of the American Society of Papyrologists*
BASPSup	Bulletin of the American Society of Papyrologists: Supplement
BAT	Die Botschaft des Alten Testaments
BBB	Bonner biblische Beiträge
BBB	*Bulletin de bibliographie biblique*
BBET	Beiträge zur biblischen Exegese und Theologie
BBMS	Baker Biblical Monograph Series
BBR	*Bulletin for Biblical Research*
BBS	*Bulletin of Biblical Studies*
BCH	*Bulletin de correspondance hellénique*
BCPE	*Bulletin du Centre protestant d'études*
BCR	Biblioteca di cultura religiosa
BCSR	*Bulletin of the Council on the Study of Religion*
BDAG	Bauer, W., F. W. Danker, W. F. Arndt, and F. W. Gingrich. *Greek-English Lexicon of the New Testament and Other Early Christian Literature.* 3d ed. Chicago, 1999
BDB	Brown, F., S. R. Driver, and C. A. Briggs. *A Hebrew and English Lexicon of the Old Testament.* Oxford, 1907
BDF	Blass, F., A. Debrunner, and R. W. Funk. *A Greek Grammar of the New Testament and Other Early Christian Literature.* Chicago, 1961
BE	Milik, J. T. *The Books of Enoch.* Oxford: Clarendon, 1976.
BEATAJ	Beiträge zur Erforschung des Alten Testaments und des antiken Judentum
BEB	*Baker Encyclopedia of the Bible.* Edited by W. A. Elwell. 2 vols. Grand Rapids, 1988
BeO	*Bibbia e oriente*
Ber	*Berytus*
BerMatÖAI	Berichte und Materialien des Österreichischen archäologischen Instituts

BETL	Bibliotheca ephemeridum theologicarum lovaniensium
BEvT	Beiträge zur evangelischen Theologie
BFCT	Beiträge zur Förderung christlicher Theologie
BFT	Biblical Foundations in Theology
BGBE	Beiträge zur Geschichte der biblischen Exegese
BGU	*Aegyptische Urkunden aus den Königlichen Staatlichen Museen zu Berlin, Griechische Urkunden.* 15 vols. Berlin, 1895–1983.
BHEAT	*Bulletin d'histoire et d'exégèse de l'Ancien Testament*
BHG	*Bibliotheca hagiographica Graece.* Brussels, 1977
BHH	*Biblisch-historisches Handwörterbuch: Landeskunde, Geschichte, Religion, Kultur.* Edited by B. Reicke and L. Rost. 4 vols. Göttingen, 1962–1966
BHK	*Biblia Hebraica.* Edited by R. Kittel. Stuttgart, 1905–1906, 1925², 1937³, 1951⁴, 1973¹⁶
BHL	*Bibliotheca hagiographica latina antiquae et mediae aetatis.* 2 vols. Brussels, 1898–1901
BHLen	*Biblia Hebraica Leninradensia.* Edited by A. Dotan. Peabody, Mass., 2001.
BHO	*Bibliotheca hagiographica orientalis.* Brussels, 1910
BHS	*Biblia Hebraica Stuttgartensia.* Edited by K. Elliger and W. Rudolph. Stuttgart, 1983
BHT	Beiträge zur historischen Theologie
BI	*Biblical Illustrator*
Bib	*Biblica*
BibB	Biblische Beiträge
BiBh	*Bible Bhashyam*
BibInt	*Biblical Interpretation*
BibLeb	*Bibel und Leben*
BibOr	Biblica et orientalia
BibS(F)	Biblische Studien (Freiburg, 1895–)
BibS(N)	Biblische Studien (Neukirchen, 1951–)
BIES	*Bulletin of the Israel Exploration Society* (= *Yediot*)
BIFAO	*Bulletin de l'Institut français d'archéologie orientale*
Bijdr	*Bijdragen: Tijdschrift voor filosofie en theologie*
BIN	*Babylonian Inscriptions in the Collection of James B. Nies*
BIOSCS	*Bulletin of the International Organization for Septuagint and Cognate Studies*
BiPa	Biblia Patristica: Index des citations et allusions bibliques dans la littérature. Paris, 1975–
BJ	*Bonner Jahrbücher*
BJPES	*Bulletin of the Jewish Palestine Exploration Society*
BJRL	*Bulletin of the John Rylands University Library of Manchester*
BJS	Brown Judaic Studies
BJVF	*Berliner Jahrbuch für Vor- und Frühgeschichte*
BK	*Bibel und Kirche*
BKAT	Biblischer Kommentar, Altes Testament. Edited by M. Noth and H. W. Wolff
BL	*Bibel und Liturgie*
BLE	*Bulletin de littérature ecclésiastique*
BLit	*Bibliothèque liturgique*
BMes	Bibliotheca mesopotamica
BN	*Biblische Notizen*
BNTC	Black's New Testament Commentaries
BO	*Bibliotheca orientalis*
Böhl	Böhl, F. M. Th. de Liagre. *Opera minora: Studies en bijdragen op Assyriologisch en Oudtestamentisch terrein.* Groningen, 1953
BOR	*Babylonian and Oriental Record*
Bousset-Gressmann	Bousset, W., and H. Gressmann, *Die Religion des Judentums im späthellenistischen Zeitalter.* 3d ed. Tübingen, 1926

BR	*Biblical Research*
BRev	*Bible Review*
BRL2	*Biblisches Reallexikon.* 2d ed. Edited by K. Galling. HAT 1/1. Tübingen, 1977
BSAA	*Bulletin de la Société archéologique d'Alexandrie*
BSac	*Bibliotheca sacra*
BSAC	*Bulletin de la Société d'archéologie copte*
BSC	Bible Student's Commentary
BSGW	Berichte der Sächsischen Gesellschaft der Wissenschaften
BSOAS	*Bulletin of the School of Oriental and African Studies*
BT	*The Bible Translator*
BTB	*Biblical Theology Bulletin*
BThAM	*Bulletin de théologie ancienne et médiévale*
BTS	*Bible et terre sainte*
BTZ	*Berliner Theologische Zeitschrift*
Budé	Collection des universités de France, publiée sous le patronage de l'Association Guillaume Budé
Burg	*Burgense*
BurH	*Buried History*
BV	*Biblical Viewpoint*
BVC	*Bible et vie chrétienne*
BW	*The Biblical World: A Dictionary of Biblical Archaeology.* Edited by C. F. Pfeiffer. Grand Rapids, 1966
BWA(N)T	Beiträge zur Wissenschaft vom Alten (und Neuen) Testament
BWL	*Babylonian Wisdom Literature.* W. G. Lambert. Oxford, 1960
ByF	*Biblia y fe*
Byzantion	*Byzantion*
ByzF	*Byzantinische Forschungen*
ByzZ	*Byzantinische Zeitschrift*
BZ	*Biblische Zeitschrift*
BzA	Beiträge zur Assyriologie
BZAW	Beihefte zur Zeitschrift für die alttestamentliche Wissenschaft
BZNW	Beihefte zur Zeitschrift für die neutestamentliche Wissenschaft
BZRGG	Beihefte zur Zeitschrift für Religions und Geistesgeschichte
CA	*Convivium assisiense*
CAD	*The Assyrian Dictionary of the Oriental Institute of the University of Chicago.* Chicago, 1956–
CaE	*Cahiers évangile*
CAGN	*Collected Ancient Greek Novels.* Edited by B. P. Reardon. Berkeley, 1989
CAH	Cambridge Ancient History
CahRB	Cahiers de la Revue biblique
CahT	Cahiers Théologiques
CANE	*Civilizations of the Ancient Near East.* Edited by J. Sasson. 4 vols. New York, 1995
CAP	Cowley, A. E. *Aramaic Papyri of the Fifth Century B.C.* Oxford, 1923
Car	*Carthagiensia*
CAT	Commentaire de l'Ancien Testament
CB	*Cultura bíblica*
CBC	Cambridge Bible Commentary
CBET	Contributions to Biblical Exegesis and Theology
CBM	Chester Beatty Monographs
CBQ	*Catholic Biblical Quarterly*
CBQMS	Catholic Biblical Quarterly Monograph Series
CBTJ	*Calvary Baptist Theological Journal*
CC	Continental Commentaries
CCath	Corpus Catholicorum
CCCM	Corpus Christianorum: Continuatio mediaevalis. Turnhout, 1969–
CClCr	*Civiltà classica e cristiana*

CCSG	Corpus Christianorum: Series graeca. Turnhout, 1977–
CCSL	Corpus Christianorum: Series latina. Turnhout, 1953–
CCT	*Cuneiform Texts from Cappadocian Tablets in the British Museum*
CDME	*A Concise Dictionary of Middle Egyptian*. Edited by R. O. Faulkner. Oxford, 1962
CF	*Classical Folia*
CGTC	Cambridge Greek Testament Commentary
CGTSC	Cambridge Greek Testament for Schools and Colleges
CH	*Church History*
CHJ	*Cambridge History of Judaism*. Ed. W. D. Davies and Louis Finkelstein. Cambridge, 1984–
Chm	*Churchman*
CHR	*Catholic Historical Review*
ChrCent	*Christian Century*
ChrEg	*Chronique d'Egypte*
ChrLit	*Christianity and Literature*
CIC	*Corpus inscriptionum chaldicarum*
CIG	*Corpus inscriptionum graecarum*. Edited by A. Boeckh. 4 vols. Berlin, 1828–1877
CII	*Corpus inscriptionum iudaicarum*. Edited by J. B. Frey. 2 vols. Rome, 1936–1952
CIJ	*Corpus inscriptionum judaicarum*
CIL	*Corpus inscriptionum latinarum*
CIS	*Corpus inscriptionum semiticarum*
CJ	*Classical Journal*
CJT	*Canadian Journal of Theology*
Cmio	*Communio: Commentarii internationales de ecclesia et theología*
CML	*Canaanite Myths and Legends*. Edited by G. R. Driver. Edinburgh, 1956. Edited by J. C. L. Gibson, 1978²
CNS	*Cristianesimo nella storia*
CNT	Commentaire du Nouveau Testament
Coll	*Collationes*
Colloq	*Colloquium*
ColT	*Collectanea theologica*
Comm	*Communio*
Comp	*Compostellanum*
ConBNT	Coniectanea neotestamentica or Coniectanea biblica: New Testament Series
ConBOT	Coniectanea biblica: Old Testament Series
Cont	*Continuum*
COS	William W. Hallo, ed., *The Context of Scripture*. (3 vols.; Leiden: E. J. Brill, 1997–)
COut	Commentaar op het Oude Testament
CP	*Classical Philology*
CPG	*Clavis patrum graecorum*. Edited by M. Geerard. 5 vols. Turnhout, 1974–1987
CPJ	*Corpus papyrorum judaicorum*. Edited by V. Tcherikover. 3 vols. Cambridge, 1957–1964.
CPL	*Clavis patrum latinorum*. Edited by E. Dekkers. 2d ed. Steenbrugis, 1961
CQ	*Church Quarterly*
CQ	*Classical Quarterly*
CQR	*Church Quarterly Review*
CRAI	Comptes rendus de l'Académie des inscriptions et belleslettres
CRBR	*Critical Review of Books in Religion*
CRINT	Compendia rerum iudaicarum ad Novum Testamentum
CRTL	Cahiers de la Revue théologique de Louvain
Crux	*Crux*
CSCO	Corpus scriptorum christianorum orientalium. Edited by I. B. Chabot et al. Paris, 1903–
CSEL	Corpus scriptorum ecclesiasticorum latinorum
CSHB	Corpus scriptorum historiae byzantinae

CSJH	Chicago Studies in the History of Judaism
CSR	*Christian Scholar's Review*
CSRB	*Council on the Study of Religion: Bulletin*
CT	*Cuneiform Texts from Babylonian Tablets in the British Museum*
CTA	*Corpus des tablettes en cunéiformes alphabétiques découvertes à Ras Shamra-Ugarit de 1929 à 1939.* Edited by A. Herdner. Mission de Ras Shamra 10. Paris, 1963
CTAED	*Canaanite Toponyms in Ancient Egyptian Documents.* S. Ahituv. Jerusalem, 1984
CTJ	*Calvin Theological Journal*
CTM	*Concordia Theological Monthly*
CTQ	*Concordia Theological Quarterly*
CTR	*Criswell Theological Review*
CTU	*The Cuneiform Alphabetic Texts from Ugarit, Ras Ibn Hani, and Other Places.* Edited by M. Dietrich, O. Loretz, and J. Sanmartín. Münster, 1995.
CUL	*A Concordance of the Ugaritic Literature.* R. E. Whitaker. Cambridge, Mass., 1972
CurBS	*Currents in Research: Biblical Studies*
CurTM	*Currents in Theology and Mission*
CV	*Communio viatorum*
CW	*Classical World*
CWS	Classics of Western Spirituality. New York, 1978–
DACL	*Dictionnaire d'archéologie chrétienne et de liturgie.* Edited by F. Cabrol. 15 vols. Paris, 1907–1953
DB	*Dictionnaire de la Bible.* Edited by F. Vigouroux. 5 vols. 1895–1912
DBAT	*Dielheimer Blätter zum Alten Testament und seiner Rezeption in der Alten Kirche*
DBSup	*Dictionnaire de la Bible: Supplément.* Edited by L. Pirot and A. Robert. Paris, 1928–
DBT	*Dictionary of Biblical Theology.* Edited by X. Léon-Dufour. 2d ed. 1972
DCB	*Dictionary of Christian Biography.* Edited by W. Smith and H. Wace. 4 vols. London, 1877–1887
DCG	*Dictionary of Christ and the Gospels.* Edited by J. Hastings. 2 vols. Edinburgh, 1908
DCH	*Dictionary of Classical Hebrew.* Edited by D. J. A. Clines. Sheffield, 1993–
DDD	*Dictionary of Deities and Demons in the Bible.* Edited by K. van der Toorn, B. Becking, and P. W. van der Horst. Leiden, 1995
DHA	*Dialogues d'histoire ancienne*
Di	*Dialog*
Did	*Didaskalia*
DISO	*Dictionnaire des inscriptions sémitiques de l'ouest.* Edited by Ch. F. Jean and J. Hoftijzer. Leiden, 1965
DissAb	Dissertation Abstracts
DivThom	*Divus Thomas*
DJD	Discoveries in the Judaean Desert (of Jordan)
DJG	*Dictionary of Jesus and the Gospels.* Edited by J. B. Green and S. McKnight. Downers Grove, 1992
DLE	*Dictionary of Late Egyptian.* Edited by L. H. Lesko and B. S. Lesko. 4 vols. Berkeley, 1982–1989
DLNT	*Dictionary of the Later New Testament and Its Developments.* Edited by R. P. Martin and P. H. Davids. Downers Grove, 1997
DNP	*Der neue Pauly: Enzyklopädie der Antike.* Edited by H. Cancik and H. Schneider. Stuttgart, 1996–
DNWSI	*Dictionary of the North-West Semitic Inscriptions.* J. Hoftijzer and K. Jongeling. 2 vols. Leiden, 1995
DOP	*Dumbarton Oaks Papers*
DOTT	*Documents from Old Testament Times.* Edited by D. W. Thomas, London, 1958
DPAC	*Dizionario patristico e di antichità cristiane.* Edited by A. di Berardino. 3 vols. Casale Monferrato, 1983–1988

DPL	*Dictionary of Paul and His Letters.* Edited by G. F. Hawthorne and R. P. Martin. Downers Grove, 1993
DRev	*Downside Review*
DrewG	*Drew Gateway*
DSD	*Dead Sea Discoveries*
DSSSE	*Dead Sea Scrolls: Study Edition.* Edited by F. H. Martínez and E. J. C. Tigchelaar. New York, 1997–1998.
DTC	*Dictionnaire de théologie catholique.* Edited by A. Vacant et al. 15 vols. Paris, 1903–1950
DTT	*Dansk teologisk tidsskrift*
Duchesne	Duchesne, L., ed. *Le Liber pontificalis.* 2 vols. Paris, 1886, 1892. Reprinted with 3d vol. by C. Vogel. Paris, 1955–1957
DunRev	*Dunwoodie Review*
EA	El-Amarna tablets. According to the edition of J. A. Knudtzon. *Die el-Amarna-Tafeln.* Leipzig, 1908–1915. Reprint, Aalen, 1964. Continued in A. F. Rainey, *El-Amarna Tablets, 359–379.* 2d revised ed. Kevelaer, 1978
EAEHL	*Encyclopedia of Archaeological Excavations in the Holy Land.* Edited by M. Avi-Yonah. 4 vols. Jerusalem, 1975
EB	Echter Bibel
EBib	*Etudes bibliques*
ECR	*Eastern Churches Review*
ECT	*Egyptian Coffin Texts.* Edited by A. de Buck and A. H. Gardiner. Chicago, 1935–1947
EdF	Erträge der Forschung
EDNT	*Exegetical Dictionary of the New Testament.* Edited by H. Balz, G. Schneider. ET. Grand Rapids, 1990–1993
EEA	*L'epigrafia ebraica antica.* S. Moscati. Rome, 1951
EEC	*Encyclopedia of Early Christianity.* Edited by E. Ferguson. 2d ed. New York, 1990
EECh	*Encyclopedia of the Early Church.* Edited by A. di Berardino. Translated by A. Walford. New York, 1992
EfMex	*Efemerides mexicana*
EFN	Estudios de filología neotestamentaria. Cordova, Spain, 1988–
EgT	*Eglise et théologie*
EHAT	Exegetisches Handbuch zum Alten Testament
EKKNT	Evangelisch-katholischer Kommentar zum Neuen Testament
EKL	*Evangelisches Kirchenlexikon.* Edited by Erwin Fahlbusch et al. 4 vols. 3d ed. Göttingen, 1985–1996
Elenchus	*Elenchus bibliographicus biblicus* of *Biblica,* Rome, 1985–
ELKZ	*Evangelisch-Lutherische Kirchenzeitung*
EMC	*Echos dumonde classique/Classical Views*
Enc	*Encounter*
EnchBib	*Enchiridion biblicum*
EncJud	*Encyclopaedia Judaica.* 16 vols. Jerusalem, 1972
EPap	*Etudes de papyrologie*
Epiph	*Epiphany*
EPRO	Etudes préliminaires auxreligions orientales dans l'empire romain
ER	*The Encyclopedia of Religion.* Edited by M. Eliade. 16 vols. New York, 1987
ERAS	*Epithètes royales akkadiennes et sumériennes.* M.-J. Seux. Paris, 1967
ERE	*Encyclopedia of Religion and Ethics.* Edited by J. Hastings. 13 vols. New York, 1908–1927. Reprint, 7 vols., 1951
ErIsr	*Eretz-Israel*
ErJb	*Eranos-Jahrbuch*
EstAg	*Estudio Agustiniano*
EstBib	*Estudios bíblicos*
EstEcl	*Estudios eclesiásticos*
EstMin	*Estudios mindonienses*
EstTeo	*Estudios teológicos*

ETL	*Ephemerides theologicae lovanienses*
ETR	*Etudes théologiques et religieuses*
ETS	Erfurter theologische Studien
EuroJTh	*European Journal of Theology*
Even-Shoshan	Even-Shoshan, A., ed. *A New Concordance of the Bible.* Jerusalem, 1977, 1983
EvJ	*Evangelical Journal*
EvK	Evangelische Kommentare
EvQ	*Evangelical Quarterly*
EvT	*Evangelische Theologie*
ExAud	*Ex auditu*
Exeg	*Exegetica* [Japanese]
ExpTim	*Expository Times*
FAT	Forschungen zum Alten Testament
FB	Forschung zur Bibel
FBBS	Facet Books, Biblical Series
FBE	Forum for Bibelsk Eksegese
FC	Fathers of the Church. Washington, D.C., 1947–
FCB	Feminist Companion to the Bible
FF	*Forschungen und Fortschritte*
FF	Foundations and Facets
FGH	*Die Fragmente der griechischen Historiker.* Edited by F. Jacoby. Leiden, 1954–1964
FHG	Fragmenta historicorum graecorum. Paris, 1841–1870
FiE	*Forschungen in Ephesos*
FMSt	Frühmittelalterliche Studien
FO	*Folia orientalia*
FoiVie	*Foi et vie*
ForFasc	*Forum Fascicles*
Foster, *Muses*	Foster, Benjamin R. *Before the Muses: An Anthology of Akkadian Literature.* 2 vols. Bethesda, 1993
FOTL	Forms of the Old Testament Literature
Fran	*Franciscanum*
FRLANT	Forschungen zur Religion und Literatur des Alten und Neuen Testaments
FT	*Folia theologica*
Fund	*Fundamentum*
FZPhTh	*Freiburger Zeitschrift für Philosophie und Theologie*
GAG	*Grundriss der akkadischen Grammatik.* W. von Soden. 2d ed. Rome, 1969
GAT	Grundrisse zum Alten Testament
GBS	Guides to Biblical Scholarship
GCDS	*Graphic Concordance to the Dead Sea Scrolls.* Edited by J. H. Charlesworth et al. Tübingen, 1991
GCS	Die griechische christliche Schriftsteller der ersten [drei] Jahrhunderte Gesenius
Gesenius, *Thesaurus*	Gesenius, W. *Thesaurus philologicus criticus linquae hebraeae et chaldaeae Veteris Testamentia* Vols. 1-3. Leipzig, 1829–1842.
GKC	*Gesenius' Hebrew Grammar.* Edited by E. Kautzsch. Translated by A. E. Cowley. 2d. ed. Oxford, 1910
Gn	*Gnomon*
GNS	*Good News Studies*
GNT	Grundrisse zum Neuen Testament
GOTR	*Greek Orthodox Theological Review*
GP	*Géographie de la Palestine.* F. M. Abel. 2 vols. Paris, 1933
GR	*Greece and Rome*
GRBS	*Greek, Roman, and Byzantine Studies*
Greg	*Gregorianum*

GS	*Gesammelte Studien*
GTA	Göttinger theologischer Arbeiten
GTT	*Gereformeerd theologisch tijdschrift*
GTTOT	*The Geographical and Topographical Texts of the Old Testament.* Edited by J. J.Simons. Studia Francisci Scholten memoriae dicata 2. Leiden, 1959
GVG	*Grundriss der vergleichenden Grammatik der semitischen Sprachen.* C. Brockelmann, 2 vols. Berlin, 1908–1913. Reprint, Hildesheim, 1961
HAL	Koehler, L., W. Baumgartner, and J. J. Stamm. *Hebräisches und aramäisches Lexikon zum Alten Testament.* Fascicles 1–5, 1967–1995 (KBL3). ET: *HALOT*
HALOT	Koehler, L., W. Baumgartner, and J. J. Stamm, *The Hebrew and Aramaic Lexicon of the Old Testament.* Translated and edited under the supervision of M. E. J. Richardson. 4 vols. Leiden, 1994–1999
HAR	*Hebrew Annual Review*
Harris	Harris, Z. S. *A Grammar of the Phoenician Language.* AOS 8. New Haven, 1936. Reprint, 1990
HAT	Handbuch zum Alten Testament
HBC	*Harper's Bible Commentary.* Edited by J. L. Mays et al. San Francisco, 1988.
HBD	*HarperCollins Bible Dictionary.* Edited by P. J. Achtemeier et al. 2d ed. San Francisco, 1996
HBT	*Horizons in Biblical Theology*
HDR	Harvard Dissertations in Religion
Hell	*Hellenica: Recueil d'épigraphie, de numismatique et d'antiquités grecques*
Hen	*Henoch*
Herm	*Hermanthena*
Hesperia	*Hesperia: Journal of the American School of Classical Studies at Athens*
HeyJ	*Heythrop Journal*
HibJ	*Hibbert Journal*
HKAT	Handkommentar zum Alten Testament
HKL	*Handbuch der Keilschriftliteratur.* R. Borger. 3 vols. Berlin, 1967–1975
HKNT	Handkommentar zum Neuen Testament
HNT	Handbuch zum Neuen Testament
HNTC	Harper's New Testament Commentaries
HO	Handbuch der Orientalistik
Hok	*Hokhma*
HolBD	*Holman Bible Dictionary.* Edited by T. C. Butler. Nashville, 1991
Hor	*Horizons*
HR	*History of Religions*
HRCS	Hatch, E. and H. A. Redpath. *Concordance to the Septuagint and Other Greek Versions of the Old Testament.* 2 vols. Oxford, 1897. Suppl., 1906. Reprint, 3 vols. in 2, Grand Rapids, 1983
HS	*Hebrew Studies*
HSAT	*Die Heilige Schrift des Alten Testaments.* Edited by E. Kautzsch and A. Bertholet. 4th ed. Tübingen, 1922–1923
HSCP	*Harvard Studies in Classical Philology*
HSem	Horae semiticae. 9 vols. London, 1908–1912
HSM	Harvard Semitic Monographs
HSS	Harvard Semitic Studies
HT	*History Today*
HTB	Histoire du texte biblique. Lausanne, 1996–
HTh	*Ho Theológos*
HTKNT	Herders theologischer Kommentar zum Neuen Testament
HTR	*Harvard Theological Review*
HTS	Harvard Theological Studies
HUCA	*Hebrew Union College Annual*
HUCM	Monographs of the Hebrew Union College

HumTeo	Biblioteca humanística e teológica
HUT	Hermeneutische Untersuchungen zur Theologie
HvTSt	*Hervormde teologiese studies*
IAR	Iraq Archaeological Reports
IATG[2]	Schwertner, Siegfried M. *Internationales Abkürzungsverzeichnis für Theologie und Grenzgebeite.* 2d ed. Berlin, 1992
IB	*Interpreter's Bible.* Edited by G. A. Buttrick et al. 12 vols. New York, 1951–1957
IBC	Interpretation: A Bible Commentary for Teaching and Preaching.
IBHS	*An Introduction to Biblical Hebrew Syntax.* B. K. Waltke and M. O'Connor. Winona Lake, Indiana, 1990
IBS	*Irish Biblical Studies*
ICC	International Critical Commentary
ICUR	*Inscriptiones christianae urbis Romae.* Edited by J. B. de Rossi. Rome, 1857–1888
IDB	*The Interpreter's Dictionary of the Bible.* Edited by G. A. Buttrick. 4 vols. Nashville, 1962
IDBSup	*Interpreter's Dictionary of the Bible: Supplementary Volume.* Edited by K. Crim. Nashville, 1976
IDS	*In die Skriflig*
IEJ	*Israel Exploration Journal*
IESS	*International Encyclopedia of the Social Sciences.* Edited by D. L. Sills. New York, 1968–
IG	*Inscriptiones graecae.* Editio minor. Berlin, 1924–
IJT	*Indian Journal of Theology*
IKaZ	*Internationale katholische Zeitschrift*
IKZ	*Internationale kirchliche Zeitschrift*
ILCV	*Inscriptiones latinae christianae veteres.* Edited by E. Diehl. 2d ed. Berlin, 1961
Imm	*Immanuel*
Int	*Interpretation*
IOS	*Israel Oriental Society*
IPN	*Die israelitischen Personennamen.* M. Noth. BWANT 3/10. Stuttgart, 1928. Reprint, Hildesheim, 1980
Iran	*Iran*
Iraq	*Iraq*
Irén	*Irénikon*
IRT	Issues in Religion and Theology
ISBE	*International Standard Bible Encyclopedia.* Edited by G. W. Bromiley. 4 vols. Grand Rapids, 1979–1988
Isd	*Isidorianum*
Istina	*Istina*
IstMitt	*Istanbuler Mitteilungen*
Itala	*Itala: Das Neue Testament in altlateinischer Überlieferung.* 4 vols. Berlin, 1938–1963
ITC	International Theological Commentary
Iter	*Iter*
Itin (Italy)	*Itinerarium* (Italy)
Itin (Portugal)	*Itinerarium* (Portugal)
ITP	Tadmor, Hayim. *The Inscriptions of Tiglath-Pileser III, King of Assyria.* 2n ed. Jerusalem, 1994
ITQ	*Irish Theological Quarterly*
IZBG	*Internationale Zeitschriftenschaufür Bibelwissenschaft und Grenzgebiete*
JA	*Journal asiatique*
JAAL	*Journal of Afroasiatic Languages*
JAAR	*Journal of the American Academy of Religion*
JAARSup	Journal of the American Academy of Religious Supplement Series
JAC	Jahrbuch für Antike und Christentum
JACiv	*Journal of Ancient Civilizations*

Jahnow	Jahnow, J. *Das hebräische Leichenlied im Rahmen der Völkerdichtung.* Giessen, 1923
JAL	Jewish Apocryphal Literature Series
JANESCU	*Journal of the Ancient Near Eastern Society of Columbia University*
JAOS	*Journal of the American Oriental Society*
JAS	*Journal of Asian Studies*
Jastrow	Jastrow, M. *A Dictionary of the Targumim, the Talmud Babli and Yerushalmi, and the Midrashic Literature.* 2d ed. New York, 1903
JB	Jerusalem Bible
JBC	*Jerome Biblical Commentary.* Edited by R. E. Brown et al. Englewood Cliffs, 1968
JBL	*Journal of Biblical Literature*
JBQ	*Jewish Bible Quarterly*
JBR	*Journal of Bible and Religion*
JCS	*Journal of Cuneiform Studies*
JdI	*Jahrbuch des deutschen archäologischen Instituts*
JDS	Jewish Desert Studies
JDS	Judean Desert Studies
JDT	*Jahrbuch für deutsche Theologie*
JE	*The Jewish Encyclopedia.* Edited by I. Singer. 12 vols. New York, 1925
JEA	*Journal of Egyptian Archaeology*
JECS	*Journal of Early Christian Studies*
Jeev	*Jeevadhara*
JEH	*Journal of Ecclesiastical History*
JEOL	*Jaarbericht van het Vooraziatisch-Egyptisch Gezelschap (Genootschap) Ex oriente lux*
JES	*Journal of Ecumenical Studies*
JESHO	*Journal of the Economic and Social History of the Orient*
JET	*Jahrbuch für Evangelische Theologie*
JETS	*Journal of the Evangelical Theological Society*
JFSR	*Journal of Feminist Studies in Religion*
JHI	*Journal of the History of Ideas*
JHNES	Johns Hopkins Near Eastern Studies
JHS	*Journal of Hellenic Studies*
Jian Dao	*Jian Dao*
JJA	*Journal of Jewish Art*
JJP	*Journal of Juristic Papyrology*
JJS	*Journal of Jewish Studies*
JJT	*Josephinum Journal of Theology*
JLA	*Jewish Law Annual*
JLCRS	Jordan Lectures in Comparative Religion Series
JMedHist	*Journal of Medieval History*
JMES	*Journal of Middle Eastern Studies*
JMS	*Journal of Mithraic Studies*
JNES	*Journal of Near Eastern Studies*
JNSL	*Journal of Northwest Semitic Languages*
JÖAI	*Jahreshefte des Österreichischen archäologischen Instituts*
JOTT	*Journal of Translation and Textlinguistics*
Joüon	Joüon, P. *A Grammar of Biblical Hebrew.* Translated and revised by T. Muraoka. 2 vols. Subsidia biblica 14/1–2. Rome, 1991
JPJ	*Journal of Progressive Judaism*
JPOS	*Journal of the Palestine Oriental Society*
JPS	Jewish Publication Society
JQR	*Jewish Quarterly Review*
JQRMS	Jewish Quarterly Review Monograph Series
JR	*Journal of Religion*
JRAS	*Journal of the Royal Asiatic Society*

JRE	*Journal of Religious Ethics*
JRelS	*Journal of Religious Studies*
JRH	*Journal of Religious History*
JRitSt	*Journal of Ritual Studies*
JRS	*Journal of Roman Studies*
JRT	*Journal of Religious Thought*
JSem	*Journal of Semitics*
JSHRZ	*Jüdische Schriften aus hellenistisch-römischer Zeit*
JSJ	*Journal for the Study of Judaism in the Persian, Hellenistic, and Roman Periods*
JSNT	*Journal for the Study of the New Testament*
JSNTSup	Journal for the Study of the New Testament: Supplement Series
JSOR	*Journal of the Society of Oriental Research*
JSOT	*Journal for the Study of the Old Testament*
JSOTSup	Journal for the Study of the Old Testament: Supplement Series
JSP	*Journal for the Study of the Pseudepigrapha*
JSPSup	Journal for the Study of the Pseudepigrapha: Supplement Series
JSQ	*Jewish Studies Quarterly*
JSS	*Journal of Semitic Studies*
JSSEA	*Journal of the Society for the Study of Egyptian Antiquities*
JSSR	*Journal for the Scientific Study of Religion*
JTC	*Journal for Theology and the Church*
JTI	*Journal of Theological Interpretation*
JTS	*Journal of Theological Studies*
JTSA	*Journal of Theology for Southern Africa*
Jud	*Judaica*
Judaica	*Judaica: Beiträge zum Verständnis des jüdischen Schicksals in Vergangenheit und Gegenwart*
Judaism	*Judaism*
JWSTP	*Jewish Writings of the Second Temple Period: Apocrypha, Pseudepigrapha, Qumran Sectarian Writings, Philo, Josephus.* Edited by M. E. Stone. CRINT 2.2. Assen/Philadelphia, 1984
K&D	Keil, C. F., and F. Delitzsch, *Biblical Commentary on the Old Testament.* Translated by J. Martin et al. 25 vols. Edinburgh, 1857–1878. Reprint, 10 vols., Peabody, Mass., 1996
KAH 1	*Keilschrifttexte aus Assur historischen Inhalts.* L. Messerschmidt. Vol. 1. WVDOG 16. Leipzig, 1911
KAH 2	*Keilschrifttexte aus Assur historischen Inhalts.* O. Schroeder. Vol. 2. WVDOG 37. Leipzig, 1922
KAI	*Kanaanäische und aramäische Inschriften.* H. Donner and W. Röllig. 2d ed. Wiesbaden, 1966–1969
Kairós	*Kairós*
KAR	*Keilschrifttexte aus Assur religiösen Inhalts.* Edited by E. Ebeling. Leipzig, 1919–1923
KAT	Kommentar zum Alten Testament
KB	*Keilinschriftliche Bibliothek.* Edited by E. Schrader. 6 vols. Berlin, 1889–1915
KBANT	Kommentare und Beiträge zum Alten und Neuen Testament
KBL	Koehler, L., and W. Baumgartner, *Lexicon in Veteris Testamenti libros.* 2d ed. Leiden, 1958
KBo	*Keilschrifttexte aus Boghazköi.* WVDOG 30, 36, 68–70, 72–73, 77–80, 82–86, 89–90. Leipzig, 1916–
KD	*Kerygma und Dogma*
KEK	Kritisch-exegetischer Kommentar über das Neue Testament (Meyer-Kommentar)
Kerux	*Kerux*
KHC	Kurzer Hand-Commentar zum Alten Testament
KI	*Kanaanäische Inschriften (Moabitisch, Althebraisch, Phonizisch, Punisch).* Edited by M. Lidzbarski. Giessen, 1907
KK	*Katorikku Kenkyu*

KlPauly	*Der kleine Pauly*
KlT	Kleine Texte
KS	*Kirjath-Sepher*
KTU	*Die keilalphabetischen Texte aus Ugarit.* Edited by M. Dietrich, O. Loretz, and J. Sanmartín. AOAT 24/1. Neukirchen-Vluyn, 1976. 2d enlarged ed. of *KTU: The Cuneiform Alphabetic Texts from Ugarit, Ras Ibn Hani, and Other Places.* Edited by M. Dietrich, O. Loretz, and J. Sanmartín. Münster, 1995 (= *CTU*)
KUB	*Keilschrifturkunden aus Boghazköi*
Kuhn	Kuhn, K. G. *Konkordanz zuden Qumrantexten.* Göttingen, 1960
KVRG	Kölner Veroffentlichungen zur Religionsgeschichte
L&N	Louw and Nida. *Greek-English Lexicon of the New Testament: Based on Semantic Domains.* Edited by J. P. Louw and E. A. Nida. 2d ed. New York, 1989
LAE	*Literature of Ancient Egypt.* W. K. Simpson. New Haven, 1972
LAE[3]	*Literature of Ancient Egypt.* W. K. Simpson. 3d rev. ed. New Haven, 2003
Lane	Lane, E. W. *An Arabic-English Lexicon.* 8 vols. London. Reprint, 1968
LAPO	Littératures anciennes du Proche-Orient
LASBF	*Liber annuus Studii biblici franciscani*
Laur	*Laurentianum*
LÄ	*Lexikon der Ägyptologie.* Edited by W. Helck, E. Otto, and W. Westendorf. Wiesbaden, 1972
LB	*Linguistica Biblica*
LCC	Library of Christian Classics. Philadelphia, 1953–
LCL	Loeb Classical Library
LD	Lectio divina
LEC	Library of Early Christianity
Leš	*Lešonénu*
Levant	*Levant*
LexSyr	*Lexicon syriacum.* C. Brockelmann. 2d ed. Halle, 1928
LIMC	*Lexicon iconographicum mythologiae classicae.* Edited by H. C. Ackerman and J.-R. Gisler. 8 vols. Zurich, 1981–1997
List	*Listening: Journal of Religion and Culture*
LJPSTT	Literature of the Jewish People in the Period of the Second Temple and the Talmud
LQ	*Lutheran Quarterly*
LR	*Lutherische Rundschau*
LS	*Louvain Studies*
LSJ	Liddell, H. G., R. Scott, H. S. Jones, *A Greek-English Lexicon.* 9th ed. with revised supplement. Oxford, 1996
LSS	*Leipziger semitische Studien*
LTK	*Lexicon für Theologie und Kirche*
LTP	*Laval théologique et philosophique*
LTQ	*Lexington Theological Quarterly*
LUÅ	Lunds universitets årsskrift
Lum	*Lumen*
LumVie	*Lumière et vie*
LW	*Living Word*
MAAR	Memoirs of the American Academy in Rome
Maarav	*Maarav*
MAMA	*Monumenta Asiae Minoris Antiqua.* Manchester and London, 1928–1993
Mandl	Mandelkern, S. *Veteris Testamenti concordantiae hebraicae atque chaldaicae, etc.* Reprint, 1925. 2d ed. Jerusalem, 1967
MAOG	Mitteilungen der Altorientalischen Gesellschaft
MARI	*Mari: Annales de recherches interdisciplinaires*
MBPF	Münchener Beiträge zur Papyrusforschung und antiken Rechtsgeschichte
MBS	Message of Biblical Spirituality
McCQ	*McCormick Quarterly*

MCom	*Miscelánea Comillas*
MCuS	*Manchester Cuneiform Studies*
MDAI	*Mitteilungen des Deutschen archäologischen Instituts*
MDB	*Mercer Dictionary of the Bible.* Edited by W. E. Mills. Macon, 1990
MdB	*Le Monde de la Bible*
MDOG	Mitteilungen der Deutschen Orient-Gesellschaft
MEAH	*Miscelánea de estudios arabes y hebraicos*
Med	*Medellin*
MEFR	*Mélanges d'archéologie et d'histoire de l'école français de Rome*
MelT	*Melita theologica*
MGWJ	*Monatschrift für Geschichte und Wissenschaft des Judentums*
MH	*Museum helveticum*
Mid-Stream	*Mid-Stream*
Mils	*Milltown Studies*
MIO	*Mitteilungen des Instituts für Orientforschung*
MM	Moulton, J. H., and G. Milligan. *The Vocabulary of the Greek Testament.* London, 1930. Reprint, Peabody, Mass., 1997
MNTC	Moffatt New Testament Commentary
MPAIBL	Mémoires présentés à l'Academie des inscriptions et belleslettres
MS	*Mediaeval Studies*
MScRel	*Mélanges de science religieuse*
MSJ	*The Master's Seminary Journal*
MSL	*Materialien zum sumerischen Lexikon.* Benno Landsberger, ed.
MSU	Mitteilungen des Septuaginta-Unternehmens
MTSR	*Method and Theory in the Study of Religion*
MTZ	*Münchener theologische Zeitschrift*
Mursurillo	Mursurillo, H., ed. and trans. *The Acts of the Christian Martyrs.* Oxford, 1972
Mus	*Muséon: Revue d'études orientales*
MUSJ	*Mélanges de l'Université Saint-Joseph*
MVAG	Mitteilungen der Vorderasiatisch-ägyptischen Gesellschaft. Vols. 1–44. 1896–1939
NABU	*Nouvelles assyriologiques breves et utilitaires*
NAC	New American Commentary
NAWG	*Nachrichten (von) der Akademie der Wissenschaften in Göttingen*
NBD²	*New Bible Dictionary.* Edited by J. D. Douglas and N. Hillyer. 2d ed. Downers Grove, 1982
NBf	*New Blackfrairs*
NCB	New Century Bible
NCE	*New Catholic Encyclopedia.* Edited by W. J. McDonald et al. 15 vols. New York, 1967
NE	*Handbuch der nordsemitischen Epigraphik.* Edited by M. Lidzbarski. Weimar, 1898. Reprint, Hildesheim, 1962
NEA	*Near Eastern Archaeology*
NEAEHL	*The New Encyclopedia of Archaeological Excavations in the Holy Land.* Edited by E. Stern. 4 vols. Jerusalem, 1993
NEchtB	Neue Echter Bibel
NedTT	*Nederlands theologisch tijdschrift*
Nem	*Nemalah*
Neot	*Neotestamentica*
NETR	*Near East School of Theology Theological Review*
NewDocs	*New Documents Illustrating Early Christianity.* Edited by G. H. R. Horsley and S. Llewelyn. North Ryde, N.S.W., 1981–
NFT	New Frontiers in Theology
NGTT	*Nederduitse gereformeerde teologiese tydskrif*
NHC	Nag Hammadi Codices
NHL	*Nag Hammadi Library in English.* Edited by J. M. Robinson. 4th rev. ed. Leiden, 1996

NHS	Nag Hammadi Studies
NIB	*The New Interpreter's Bible*
NIBCNT	New International Biblical Commentary on the New Testament
NIBCOT	New International Biblical Commentary on the Old Testament
NICNT	New International Commentary on the New Testament
NICOT	New International Commentary on the Old Testament
NIDB	*New International Dictionary of the Bible.* Edited by J. D. Douglas and M. C. Tenney. Grand Rapids, 1987
NIDBA	*New International Dictionary of Biblical Archaeology.* Edited by E. M. Blaiklock and R. K. Harrison. Grand Rapids, 1983
NIDNTT	*New International Dictionary of New Testament Theology.* Edited by C. Brown. 4 vols. Grand Rapids, 1975–1985
NIDOTTE	*New International Dictionary of Old Testament Theology and Exegesis.* Edited by W. A. VanGemeren. 5 vols. Grand Rapids, 1997
NIGTC	New International Greek Testament Commentary
NJahrb	*Neue Jahrbücher für das klassische Altertum (1898–1925); Neue Jahrbücher für Wissenschaft und Jugendbildung (1925–1936)*
NJBC	*The New Jerome Biblical Commentary.* Edited by R. E. Brown et al. Englewood Cliffs, 1990
NKZ	*Neue kirchliche Zeitschrift*
Notes	*Notes on Translation*
NovT	*Novum Testamentum*
NovTSup	Supplements to Novum Testamentum
NPEPP	*New Princeton Encyclopedia of Poetry and Poetics*
NPNF[1]	*Nicene and Post-Nicene Fathers, Series 1*
NPNF[2]	*Nicene and Post-Nicene Fathers, Series 2*
NRTh	*La nouvelle revue théologique*
NTA	*New Testament Abstracts*
NTAbh	Neutestamentliche Abhandlungen
NTD	Das Neue Testament Deutsch
NTF	Neutestamentliche Forschungen
NTG	New Testament Guides
NTGF	New Testament in the Greek Fathers
NTL	New Testament Library
NTOA	Novum Testamentum et Orbis Antiquus
NTS	*New Testament Studies*
NTT	*Norsk Teologisk Tidsskrift*
NTTS	New Testament Tools and Studies
NumC	*Numismatic Chronicle*
Numen	*Numen: International Review for the History of Religions*
NuMu	*Nuevo mundo*
NV	*Nova et vetera*
OBO	Orbis biblicus et orientalis
ÖBS	Österreichische biblische Studien
OBT	Overtures to Biblical Theology
OCD	*Oxford Classical Dictionary.* Edited by S. Hornblower and A. Spawforth. 3d ed. Oxford, 1996
OCP	*Orientalia christiana periodica*
OCT	Oxford Classical Texts/Scriptorum classicorum bibliotheca oxoniensis
OCuT	Oxford Editions of Cuneiform Texts
ODCC	*The Oxford Dictionary of the Christian Church.* Edited by F. L. Cross and E. A. Livingstone. 2d ed. Oxford, 1983
OEANE	*The Oxford Encyclopedia of Archaeology in the Near East.* Edited by E. M. Meyers. New York, 1997
OECT	Oxford Early Christian Texts. Edited by H. Chadwick. Oxford, 1970–

OGIS	*Orientis graeci inscriptiones selectae.* Edited by W. Dittenberger. 2 vols. Leipzig, 1903–1905
OiC	*One in Christ*
OIC	*Oriental Institute Communications*
OIP	Oriental Institute Publications
OLA	Orientalia lovaniensia analecta
OLP	Orientalia lovaniensia periodica
OLZ	*Orientalistische Literaturzeitung*
Or	*Orientalia* (NS)
OrAnt	*Oriens antiquus*
OrChr	*Oriens christianus*
OrChrAn	Orientalia christiana analecta
Orita	*Orita*
OrSyr	*L'orient syrien*
OTA	*Old Testament Abstracts*
OTE	*Old Testament Essays*
OTG	Old Testament Guides
ÖTK	Ökumenischer Taschenbuch-Kommentar
OTL	Old Testament Library
OTM	Old Testament Message
OTP	*Old Testament Pseudepigrapha.* Edited by J. H. Charlesworth. 2 vols. New York, 1983
OTS	Old Testament Studies
OtSt	Oudtestamentische Studiën
PAAJR	*Proceedings of the American Academy of Jewish Research*
Pacifica	*Pacifica*
PapyCast	Papyrologica Castroctaviana, Studia et textus. Barcelona, 1967–
Parab	*Parabola*
ParOr	*Parole de l'orient*
PaVi	*Parole di vita*
Payne Smith	*Thesaurus syriacus.* Edited by R. Payne Smith. Oxford, 1879–1901
PDM	*Papyri demoticae magicae.* Demotic texts in *PGM* corpus as collated in H. D. Betz, ed. *The Greek Magical Papyri in Translation, including the Demotic Spells.* Chicago, 1996
PEFQS	Palestine Exploration Fund Quarterly Statement
PEQ	*Palestine Exploration Quarterly*
Per	*Perspectives*
PerTeol	*Perspectiva teológica*
PG	Patrologia graeca [= Patrologiae cursus completus: Series graeca]. Edited by J.-P. Migne. 162 vols. Paris, 1857–1886
PGL	*Patristic Greek Lexicon.* Edited by G. W. H. Lampe. Oxford, 1968
PGM	*Papyri graecae magicae: Die griechischen Zauberpapyri.* Edited by K. Preisendanz. Berlin, 1928
Phil	*Philologus*
Phon	*Phonetica*
PIASH	Proceedings of the Israel Academy of Sciences and Humanities
PIBA	Proceedings of the Irish Biblical Association
PJ	*Palästina-Jahrbuch*
PL	Patrologia latina [= Patrologiae cursus completus: Series latina]. Edited by J.-P. Migne. 217 vols. Paris, 1844–1864
Pneuma	*Pneuma: Journal for the Society of Pentecostal Studies*
PNTC	Pelican New Testament Commentaries
PO	Patrologia orientalis
POut	De Prediking van het Oude Testament
Presb	*Presbyterion*
ProEccl	*Pro ecclesia*

Proof	*Prooftexts: A Journal of Jewish Literary History*
Protest	*Protestantesimo*
Proy	*Proyección*
PRSt	*Perspectives in Religious Studies*
PRU	*Le palais royal d'Ugarit*
PS	Patrologia syriaca. Rev. ed. I. Ortiz de Urbina. Rome, 1965
PSB	*Princeton Seminary Bulletin*
PSTJ	*Perkins (School of Theology) Journal*
PTMS	Pittsburgh Theological Monograph Series
PTS	Patristische Texte und Studien
PVTG	Pseudepigrapha Veteris Testamenti Graece
PW	Pauly, A. F. *Paulys Realencyclopädie der classischen Altertumswissenschaft.* New edition G. Wissowa. 49 vols. Munich, 1980
PWSup	Supplement to PW
PzB	*Protokolle zur Bibel*
Qad	*Qadmoniot*
QC	*Qumran Chronicle*
QD	Quaestiones disputatae
QDAP	*Quarterly of the Department of Antiquities in Palestine*
QR	*Quarterly Review*
Quasten	Quasten, J. *Patrology.* 4 vols. Westminster, 1953–1986
R&T	*Religion and Theology*
RA	*Revue d'assyriologie et d'archéologie orientale*
RAC	*Reallexikon für Antike und Christentum.* Edited by T. Kluser et al. Stuttgart, 1950–
RANE	Records of the Ancient Near East
RAr	*Revue archéologique*
RÄR	*Reallexikon der ägyptischen Religionsgeschichte.* H. Bonnet. Berlin, 1952
RawlCu	*The Cuneiform Inscriptions of Western Asia.* Edited by H. C. Rawlinson. London, 1891
RB	*Revue biblique*
RBB	*Revista biblica brasileira*
RBén	*Revue bénédictine*
RBL	*Ruch biblijny i liturgiczny*
RBPH	*Revue belge de philologie et d'histoire*
RCB	*Revista de cultura bíblica*
RCT	*Revista catalana de teología*
RdT	*Rassegna di teologia*
RE	*Realencyklopädie für protestantische Theologie und Kirche*
REA	*Revue des études anciennes*
REAug	*Revue des études augustiniennes*
REB	*Revista eclesiástica brasileira*
RechBib	Recherches bibliques
RechPap	*Recherches de papyrologie*
RefLitM	*Reformed Liturgy and Music*
RefR	*Reformed Review*
REg	*Revue d'égyptologie*
REG	*Revue des études grecques*
REJ	*Revue des études juives*
RelArts	Religion and the Arts
RelEd	*Religious Education*
RelS	*Religious Studies*
RelSoc	*Religion and Society*
RelSRev	*Religious Studies Review*
RelStTh	*Religious Studies and Theology*
RES	*Répertoire d'épigraphie sémitique*

RES	*Revue des études sémitiques*
ResQ	*Restoration Quarterly*
RET	*Revista española de teología*
RevExp	*Review and Expositor*
RevistB	*Revista bíblica*
RevPhil	*Revue de philologie*
RevQ	*Revue de Qumran*
RevScRel	*Revue des sciences religieuses*
RGG	*Religion in Geschichte und Gegenwart.* Edited by K. Galling. 7 vols. 3d ed. Tübingen, 1957–1965
RHA	*Revue hittite et asianique*
RHE	*Revue d'histoire ecclésiastique*
RHPR	*Revue d'histoire et de philosophie religieuses*
RHR	*Revue de l'histoire des religions*
RIBLA	*Revista de interpretación bíblica latino-americana*
RIDA	*Revue internationale des droits de l'antiquité*
RIM	The Royal Inscriptions of Mesopotamia Project. Toronto
RIMA	The Royal Inscriptions of Mesopotamia, Assyrian Periods
RIMB	The Royal Inscriptions of Mesopotamia, Babylonian Periods
RIME	The Royal Inscriptions of Mesopotamia, Early Periods
RIMS	The Royal Inscriptions of Mesopotamia, Supplements
RISA	*Royal Inscriptions of Sumer and Akkad.* Edited by G. A. Barton. New Haven, 1929
RivB	*Rivista biblica italiana*
RivSR	*Rivista di scienze religiose*
RlA	*Reallexikon der Assyriologie.* Edited by Erich Ebeling et al. Berlin, 1928–
RLV	*Reallexikon der Vorgeschichte.* Edited by M. Ebert. Berlin, 1924–1932
RNT	Regensburger Neues Testament
RocT	*Roczniki teologiczne*
RomBarb	*Romanobarbarica*
RoMo	Rowohlts Monographien
RQ	*Römische Quartalschrift für christliche Altertumskunde und Kirchengeschichte*
RR	*Review of Religion*
RRef	*La revue réformée*
RRelRes	*Review of Religious Research*
RS	Ras Shamra
RSC	*Rivista di studi classici*
RSém	*Revue de sémitique*
RSF	*Rivista di studi fenici*
RSO	*Rivista degli studi orientali*
RSP	*Ras Shamra Parallels*
RSPT	*Revue des sciences philosophiques et théologiques*
RSR	*Recherches de science religieuse*
RST	Regensburger Studien zur Theologie
RStB	*Ricerche storico bibliche*
RTAM	*Recherches de théologie ancienne et médiévale*
RThom	*Revue thomiste*
RTL	*Revue théologique de Louvain*
RTP	*Revue de théologie et de philosophie*
RTR	*Reformed Theological Review*
RuBL	*Ruch biblijnu i liturgiczny*
RUO	*Revue de l'université d'Ottawa*
SA	Studia anselmiana
SAA	State Archives of Assyria
SAAB	*State Archives of Assyria Bulletin*

SAAS	State Archives of Assyria Studies
SAC	Studies in Antiquity and Christianity
SacEr	*Sacris erudiri: Jaarboek voor Godsdienstwetenschappen*
Salm	*Salmanticensis*
SANT	Studien zum Alten und Neuen Testaments
SAOC	Studies in Ancient Oriental Civilizations
Sap	*Sapienza*
SAQ	Sammlung ausgewählter Kirchen- und dogmengeschichtlicher Quellenschriften
SB	*Sammelbuch griechischer Urkunden aus Aegypten.* Edited by F. Preisigke et al. Vols. 1– , 1915–
SB	Sources bibliques
SBA	Studies in Biblical Archaeology
SBAB	Stuttgarter biblische Aufsatzbände
SBAW	Sitzungsberichte der bayerischen Akademie der Wissenschaften
SBB	Stuttgarter biblische Beiträge
SBFLA	*Studii biblici Franciscani liber annus*
SBL	Society of Biblical Literature
SBLABib	Society of Biblical Literature Academia Biblica
SBLABS	Society of Biblical Literature Archaeology and Biblical Studies
SBLBAC	Society of Biblical Literature The Bible and American Culture
SBLBMI	Society of Biblical Literature The Bible and Its Modern Interpreters
SBLBSNA	Society of Biblical Literature Biblical Scholarship in North America
SBLCP	Society of Biblical Literature Centennial Publications
SBLDS	Society of Biblical Literature Dissertation Series
SBLEJL	Society of Biblical Literature Early Judaism and Its Literature
SBLGPBS	Society of Biblical Literature Global Perspectives on Biblical Scholarship
SBLHS	*The SBL Handbook of Style,* Edited by P. Alexander et al. Peabody, Mass., 1999
SBLMasS	Society of Biblical Literature Masoretic Studies
SBLMS	Society of Biblical Literature Monograph Series
SBLNTGF	Society of Biblical Literature The New Testament in the Greek Fathers
SBLRBS	Society of Biblical Literature Resources for Biblical Study
SBLSBS	Society of Biblical Literature Sources for Biblical Study
SBLSC	Society of Biblical Literature Septuagint and Cognate Studies
SBLSP	Society of Biblical Literature Seminar Papers
SBLStBL	Society of Biblical Literature Studies in Biblical Literature
SBLSymS	Society of Biblical Literature Symposium Series
SBLTCS	Society of Biblical Literature Text-Critical Studies
SBLTT	Society of Biblical Literature Texts and Translations
SBLWAW	Society of Biblical Literature Writings from the Ancient World
SBLWGRW	Society of Biblical Literature Writings from the Greco-Roman World
SBM	Stuttgarter biblische Monographien
SBS	Stuttgarter Bibelstudien
SBT	Studies in Biblical Theology
SC	Sources chrétiennes. Paris: Cerf, 1943–
ScC	*La scuola cattolica*
ScEccl	*Sciences ecclésiastiques*
ScEs	*Science et esprit*
SCH	Studies in Church History
SCHNT	Studia ad corpus hellenisticum Novi Testamenti
Schol	*Scholastik*
Scr	*Scripture*
SCR	*Studies in Comparative Religion*
ScrB	*Scripture Bulletin*
ScrC	*Scripture in Church*

ScrHier	Scripta hierosolymitana
ScrTh	*Scripta theologica*
ScrVict	*Scriptorium victoriense*
SD	Studies and Documents
SDAW	Sitzungen der deutschen Akademie der Wissenschaften zu Berlin
SE	*Studia evangelica I, II, III* (= TU 73 [1959], 87 [1964], 88 [1964]. etc.)
SEÅ	*Svensk exegetisk årsbok*
SEAug	Studia ephemeridis Augustinianum
SecCent	*Second Century*
Sef	*Sefarad*
SEG	Supplementum epigraphicum graecum
SEL	*Studi epigrafici e linguistici*
Sem	*Semitica*
Semeia	*Semeia*
SemeiaSt	Semeia Studies
SFulg	*Scripta fulgentina*
SHANE	Studies in the History of the Ancient Near East
SHAW	Sitzungen der heidelberger Akademie der Wissenschaften
Shofar	*Shofar*
SHR	Studies in the History of Religions (supplement to *Numen*)
SHT	Studies in Historical Theology
SIDIC	*SIDIC* (Journal of the Service internationale de documentation judeo-chrétienne)
SIG	*Sylloge inscriptionum graecarum.* Edited by W. Dittenberger. 4 vols. 3d ed. Leipzig, 1915–1924
SJ	Studia judaica
SJLA	Studies in Judaism in Late Antiquity
SJOT	*Scandinavian Journal of the Old Testament*
SJT	*Scottish Journal of Theology*
SK	*Skrif en kerk*
SKKNT	Stuttgarter kleiner Kommentar, Neues Testament
SL	*Sumerisches Lexikon.* Edited by A. Deimel. 8 vols. Rome, 1928–1950
SLJT	*St. Luke's Journal of Theology*
SMBen	Série monographique de Benedictina: Section paulinienne *SMSR Studi e materiali di storia delle religioni*
SMSR	*Studi e materiali di storia delle religioni*
SMT	*Studii Montis Regii*
SNT	Studien zum Neuen Testament
SNTA	Studiorum Novi Testamenti Auxilia
SNTSMS	Society for New Testament Studies Monograph Series
SNTSU	Studien zum Neuen Testament und seiner Umwelt
SO	*Symbolae osloenses*
SÖAW	*Sitzungen der österreichischen Akademie der Wissenschaften in Wien*
Sobornost	*Sobornost*
SOTSMS	Society for Old Testament Studies Monograph Series
Sound	*Soundings*
SP	Sacra pagina
SPap	*Studia papyrologica*
SPAW	Sitzungsberichte der preussischen Akademie der Wissenschaften
Spec	*Speculum*
SPhilo	*Studia philonica*
SQAW	Schriften und Quellen der alten Welt
SR	*Studies in Religion*
SSEJC	Studies in Early Judaism and Christianity
SSN	Studia semitica neerlandica

SSS	Semitic Study Series
ST	*Studia theologica*
St	*Studium*
StABH	Studies in American Biblical Hermeneutics
StC	Studia catholica
STDJ	Studies on the Texts of the Desert of Judah
SThU	*Schweizerische theologische Umschau*
SThZ	*Schweizerische theologische Zeitschrift*
STJ	*Stulos Theological Journal*
STK	*Svensk teologisk kvartalskrift*
StOR	Studies in Oriental Religions
StPat	*Studia patavina*
StPatr	Studia patristica
StPB	Studia post-biblica
Str	*Stromata*
Str-B	Strack, H. L., and P. Billerbeck. *Kommentar zum Neuen Testament aus Talmud und Midrasch.* 6 vols. Munich, 1922–1961
STRev	*Sewanee Theological Review*
StSin	Studia Sinaitica
StudBib	Studia Biblica
StudMon	Studia monastica
StudNeot	Studia neotestamentica
StudOr	Studia orientalia
StZ	Stimmen der Zeit
Su	*Studia theological varsaviensia*
SubBi	*Subsidia biblica*
Sumer	*Sumer: A Journal of Archaeology and History in Iraq*
SUNT	Studien zur Umwelt des Neuen Testaments
SVF	*Stoicorum veterum fragmenta.* H. von Arnim. 4 vols. Leipzig, 1903–1924
SVTP	Studia in Veteris Testamenti pseudepigraphica
SVTQ	*St. Vladimir's Theological Quarterly*
SWBA	Social World of Biblical Antiquity
SwJT	*Southwestern Journal of Theology*
SymBU	Symbolae biblicae upsalienses
T&K	*Texte & Kontexte*
TA	*Tel Aviv*
TAD	*Textbook of Aramaic Documents from Ancient Egypt. Newly Copied, Edited and Translated into Hebrew and English.* Edited by Bazalel Porten and Ada Yardeni. Winona Lake, IN *(1986–1993)*
TAPA	*Transactions of the American Philological Association*
Tarbiz	*Tarbiz*
TB	Theologische Bücherei: Neudrucke und Berichte aus dem 20. Jahrhundert
TBC	Torch Bible Commentaries
TBei	*Theologische Beiträge*
TBl	*Theologische Blätter*
TBT	*The Bible Today*
TCL	Textes cunéiformes. Musée du Louvre
TCS	Texts from Cuneiform Sources
TCW	*Tydskrif vir Christelike Wetenskap*
TD	*Theology Digest*
TDNT	*Theological Dictionary of the New Testament.* Edited by G. Kittel and G. Friedrich. Translated by G. W. Bromiley. 10 vols. Grand Rapids, 1964–1976

TDOT	*Theological Dictionary of the Old Testament.* Edited by G. J. Botterweck and H. Ringgren. Translated by J. T. Willis, G. W. Bromiley, and D. E. Green. 8 vols. Grand Rapids, 1974–
TdT	Themen der Theologie
Teol	*Teología*
Teubner	Bibliotheca scriptorum graecorum et romanorum teubneriana
Text	*Textus*
TF	*Theologische Forschung*
TGI	*Textbuch zur Geschichte Israels.* Edited by K. Galling. 2d ed. Tübingen, 1968
TGl	*Theologie und Glaube*
TGUOS	Transactions of the Glasgow University Oriental Society
THAT	*Theologisches Handwörterbuch zum Alten Testament.* Edited by E. Jenni, with assistance from C. Westermann. 2 vols., Stuttgart, 1971–1976
Them	*Themelios*
Theo	*Theologika*
Theof	*Theoforum*
Theol	*Theologica*
ThH	Théologie historique
THKNT	Theologischer Handkommentar zum Neuen Testament
ThPQ	*Theologisch-praktische Quartalschrift*
ThSt	Theologische Studiën
ThT	*Theologisch tijdschrift*
ThTo	*Theology Today*
ThViat	*Theologia viatorum*
ThWAT	*Theologisches Wörterbuch zum Alten Testament.* Edited by G. J. Botterweck and H. Ringgren. Stuttgart, 1970–
TI	*Teologia iusi*
TimesLitSupp	*Times Literary Supplement*
TJ	*Trinity Journal*
TJT	*Toronto Journal of Theology*
TLG	*Thesaurus linguae graecae: Canon of Greek Authors and Works.* Edited by L. Berkowitz and K. A. Squitier. 3d ed. Oxford, 1990
TLL	*Thesaurus linguae latinae*
TLNT	*Theological Lexicon of the New Testament.* C. Spicq. Translated and edited by J. D. Ernest. 3 vols. Peabody, Mass., 1994
TLOT	*Theological Lexicon of the Old Testament.* Edited by E. Jenni, with assistance from C. Westermann. Translated by M. E. Biddle. 3 vols. Peabody, Mass., 1997
TLZ	*Theologische Literaturzeitung*
TNTC	Tyndale New Testament Commentaries
TOTC	Tyndale Old Testament Commentaries
TP	*Theologie und Philosophie*
TPINTC	TPI New Testament Commentaries
TPQ	*Theologisch-praktische Quartalschrift*
TQ	*Theologische Quartalschrift*
Transeu	*Transeuphratène*
TRE	*Theologische Realenzyklopädie.* Edited by G. Krause and G. Müller. Berlin, 1977–
TRev	*Theologische Revue*
TRSR	Testi e ricerche di scienze religiose
TRu	*Theologische Rundschau*
Trumah	*Trumah*
TS	Texts and Studies
TS	*Theological Studies*
TSAJ	Texte und Studien zum antiken Judentum
TSK	*Theologische Studien und Kritiken*

TTE	*The Theological Educator*
TThSt	Trierer theologische Studien
TTJ	*Trinity Theological Journal*
TTKi	*Tidsskrift for Teologi og Kirke*
TTZ	*Trierer theologische Zeitschrift*
TU	Texte und Untersuchungen
TUAT	*Texte aus der Umwelt des Alten Testaments.* Edited by Otto Kaiser. Gütersloh, 1984–
TUGAL	Texte und Untersuchungen zur Geschichte der altchristlichen Literatur
TUMSR	Trinity University Monograph Series in Religion
TV	*Teología y vida*
TVM	Theologische Verlagsgemeinschaft: Monographien
TvT	*Tijdschrift voor theologie*
TWNT	*Theologische Wörterbuch zum Neuen Testament.* Edited by G. Kittel and G. Friedrich. Stuttgart, 1932–1979
TWOT	*Theological Wordbook of the Old Testament.* Edited by R. L. Harris, G. L. Archer Jr. 2 vols. Chicago, 1980
TynBul	*Tyndale Bulletin*
TZ	*Theologische Zeitschrift*
UBL	Ugaritisch-biblische Literatur
UF	*Ugarit-Forschungen*
UHP	*Ugaritic-Hebrew Philology.* M. Dahood. 2d ed. Rome, 1989
UJEnc	*The Universal Jewish Encyclopedia.* Edited by I. Landman. 10 vols. New York, 1939–1943
UNP	*Ugaritic Narrative Poetry.* Edited by Simon B. Parker. SBLWAW 9. Atlanta, 1997
UNT	Untersuchungen zum Neuen Testament
UrE	Ur Excavations
UrET	Ur Excavations: Texts
USQR	*Union Seminary Quarterly Review*
UT	*Ugaritic Textbook.* C. H. Gordon. AnOr 38. Rome, 1965
UUA	Uppsala Universitets arskrift
VAB	Vorderasiatische Bibliothek
VAT	Vorderasiatische Abteilung Tontafel. Vorderasiatisches Museum, Berlin
VC	*Vigiliae christianae*
VCaro	*Verbum caro*
VD	*Verbum domini*
VE	*Vox evangelica*
VF	*Verkündigung und Forschung*
VH	*Vivens homo*
Vid	*Vidyajyoti*
VL	*Vetus Latina: Die Reste der altlateinischen Bibel.* Edited by E. Beuron, 1949–
VR	*Vox reformata*
VS	*Verbum Salutie*
VS	*Vox scripturae*
VSpir	*Vie spirituelle*
VT	*Vetus Testamentum*
VTSup	Supplements to Vetus Testamentum
WÄS	*Wörterbuch der ägyptischen Sprache.* A. Erman and H. Grapow. 5 vols. Berlin, 1926–1931. Reprint, 1963
WBC	Word Biblical Commentary
WC	Westminster Commentaries
WD	*Wort und Dienst*
WDB	*Westminster Dictionary of the Bible*
Wehr	Wehr, H. *A Dictionary of Modern Written Arabic.* Edited by J. M. Cowan. Ithaca, 1961, 1976[3]

WHAB	*Westminster Historical Atlas of the Bible*
WHJP	World History of the Jewish People
WKAS	*Das Wörterbuch der klassischen arabischen Sprache.* Edited by M. Ullmann. 1957– .
WMANT	Wissenschaftliche Monographien zum Alten und Neuen Testament
WO	*Die Welt des Orients*
WTJ	*Westminster Theological Journal*
WTM	*Das Wörterbuch über die Talmudim und Midraschim.* J. Levy. 2d ed. 1924
WUANT	Wissenschaftliche Untersuchungen zum Alten und Neuen Testament
WUNT	Wissenschaftliche Untersuchungen zum Neuen Testament
WUS	*Das Wörterbuch der ugaritischen Sprache.* J. Aistleitner. Edited by O. Eissfeldt. 3d ed. Berlin, 1967
WVDOG	Wissenschaftliche Veröffentlichungen der deutschen Orientgesellschaft
WW	*Word and World*
WZ	*Wissenschaftliche Zeitschrift*
WZKM	*Wiener Zeitschrift für die Kunde des Morgenlandes*
WZKSO	*Wiener Zeitschrift für die Kunde Süd- und Ostasiens*
YCS	Yale Classical Studies
YOS	Yale Oriental Series, Texts
YOSR	Yale Oriental Series, Researches
ZA	*Zeitschrift für Assyriologie*
ZABeih	Zeitschrift für Assyriologie: Beihefte
ZABR	*Zeitschrift für altorientalische und biblische Rechtgeschichte*
ZAC	*Zeitschrift für Antikes Christentum/Journal of Ancient Christianity*
ZAH	*Zeitschrift für Althebräistik*
ZÄS	*Zeitschrift für ägyptische Sprache und Altertumskunde*
ZAW	*Zeitschrift für die alttestamentliche Wissenschaft*
ZB	Zürcher Bibel
ZBK	Zürcher Bibelkommentare
ZDMG	*Zeitschrift der deutschen morgenländischen Gesellschaft*
ZDMGSup	Zeitschrift der deutschen morgenländischen Gesellschaft: Supplementbände
ZDPV	*Zeitschrift des deutschen Palästina-Vereins*
ZEE	*Zeitschrift für evangelische Ethik*
ZHT	*Zeitschrift für historische Theologie*
Zion	*Zion*
ZKG	*Zeitschrift für Kirchengeschichte*
ZKT	*Zeitschrift für katholische Theologie*
ZKunstG	*Zeitschrift für Kunstgeschichte*
ZNW	*Zeitschrift für die neutestamentliche Wissenschaft und die Kunde der älteren Kirche*
Zorell	Zorell, F. *Lexicon hebraicum et aramaicum Veteris Testamenti.* Rome, 1968
ZPE	*Zeitschrift für Papyrologie und Epigraphik*
ZPEB	*Zondervan Pictorial Encyclopedia of the Bible.* Edited by M. C. Tenney. 5 vols. Grand Rapids, 1975
ZRGG	*Zeitschrift für Religions- und Geistesgeschichte*
ZS	*Zeitschrift für Semitistik und verwandte Gebiete*
ZST	*Zeitschrift für systematische Theologie*
ZTK	*Zeitschrift für Theologie und Kirche*
ZWKL	*Zeitschrift für Wissenschaft und kirchliches Leben*
ZWT	*Zeitschrift für wissenschaftliche Theologie*

CHARTS, ILLUSTRATIONS, AND MAPS